LONDON

A-Z®

Geographers' A-Z Map Company Ltd.

A-Z Ǟz AtoZ

registered trade marks of
Geographers' A-Z Map Company Ltd

EDITION 12 2017

Copyright © Geographers' A-Z Map Company Limited

Telephone : 01732 781000 (Enquiries & Trade Sales)
01732 783422 (Retail Sales)

No reproduction by any method whatsoever of any part of this publication is
permitted without the prior consent of the copyright owners.

Every possible care has been taken to ensure that, to the best of our
knowledge, the information contained in this atlas is accurate at the date of
publication. However, we cannot warrant that our work is entirely error free and
whilst we would be grateful to learn of any inaccuracies, we do not accept
responsibility for loss or damage resulting from reliance on information
contained within this publication.

The representation on the maps of a road, track or footpath is no evidence of
the existence of a right of way.

© Crown Copyright and database rights 2016 OS 100017302.

Safety camera information supplied by www.PocketGPSWorld.com
Speed Camera Location Database Copyright 2016 © PocketGPSWorld.com

PocketGPSWorld.com's CamerAlert is a self-contained speed and
red light camera warning system for SatNavs and Android or Apple iOS
smartphones/tablets. Visit www.cameralert.com to download.

Safety camera locations are publicised by the Safer Roads Partnership
who operate them in order to encourage drivers to comply with speed limits
at these sites. It is the drivers absolute responsibility to be aware of and to
adhere to speed limits at all times.

By showing this safety camera information it is the intention of
Geographers' A-Z Map Company Ltd., to encourage safe driving and
greater awareness of speed limits and vehicle speed.
Data accurate at time of printing.

The publishers are deeply grateful for the ready co-operation and valuable help
given to them in the production of this atlas. They would like to record their
obligation to: The Engineers and Surveyors Departments and Planning Offices
of all the Local Authorities covered in this atlas, The Department for Transport,
Highways Agency, Transport for London, The Post Office, Police Authorities,
Fire Brigades, Taxi Drivers, members of the public.

www./az.co.uk

FSC
www.fsc.org

MIX
From responsible
sources
FSC® C015185

Congestion Charging Overview Map and Information	Inside Front Cover
Key to Map Pages	2-3
Super Scale Map Pages @ 5¾" to 1 mile	4-19
Map Pages @ approx. 3" to 1 mile	20-174
Index to Streets, Places, Areas and selected Places of Interest	175-448
Index to Hospitals etc.	449-454
Index to Stations	455-457
Railway Connections Map	458-459
Underground Railway Map	460-461
West End Theatres Map	462

REFERENCE

Motorway	**M1**	Airport	✈
A Road	**A2**	Car Park (selected)	**P**
B Road	**B408**	Church or Chapel	†
Dual Carriageway		Fire Station	■
One-way Street Traffic flow on A Roads is also indicated by a heavy line on the driver's left.		Hospital	**H**
Road Under Construction Opening dates are correct at the time of publication.		House Numbers (A & B Roads only)	51 19 22 48
Proposed Road		Information Centre	**i**
Junction Name	MARBLE ARCH	National Grid Reference	⁵30
Restricted Access		Police Station	▲
Pedestrianized Road		Post Office	★
Track / Footpath		River Bus Stop	**R**
Residential Walkway		Safety Camera with Speed Limit Fixed and long term road works cameras only. Symbols do not indicate camera direction.	③⓿ ⓥ
Congestion Charging Zone			
Low Emission Zone For information contact Transport for London (www.tfl.gov.uk/modes/driving/low-emission-zone)		Toilet: without facilities for the Disabled with facilities for the Disabled Disabled use only	▽ ▼ ▼
Railway Level Crossing Tunnel Super Scale Map Pages			
Stations:			
National Rail Network	⇌ ⇌	Educational Establishment	▢
Crossrail	⊠ ⊖	Hospital or Healthcare Building	▢
Docklands Light Railway	DLR DLR	Industrial Building	▢
Overground	⊖ ⊖	Leisure or Recreational Facility	▢
Underground	● ⊖	Place of Interest	▢
London Tramlink The boarding of Tramlink trams at stops may be limited to a single direction, indicated by the arrow. Tunnel Stop		Public Building	▢
Built-up Area BANK STREET		Shopping Centre or Market	▢
Postcode Boundary		Other Selected Buildings	▢
Map Continuation 62 Super Scale Map Pages 12			

SCALE

Map Pages 4-19   1:11,000

0   ⅛   ¼ Mile

0   100   200   300   400   500 Metres

5.75 inches (14.63cm) to 1 mile   9.1cm to 1 km

Map Pages 20-174   1:22,000

0   ¼   ½ Mile

0   250   500   750 Metres 1 Kilometre

2.88 inches (7.31cm) to 1 mile   4.55cm to 1 km

2

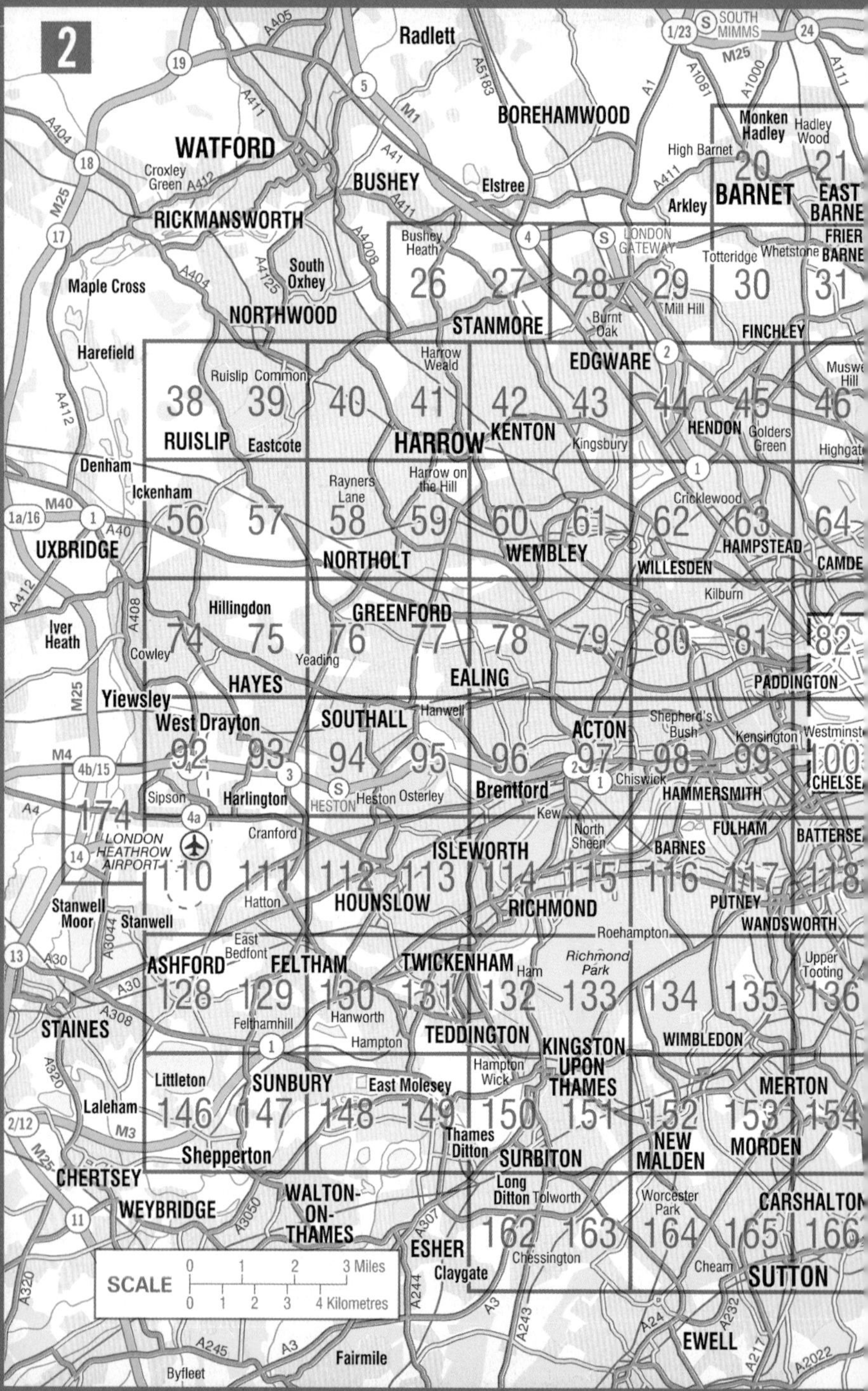

Radlett

BOREHAMWOOD

Monken Hadley — Hadley Wood

SOUTH MIMMS — S — 1/23 — 24

High Barnet

20 **BARNET** **21** **EAST BARNE**

Arkley

Totteridge — Whetstone — **FRIER BARNE**

WATFORD

Croxley Green — A412

BUSHEY

Elstree

RICKMANSWORTH

LONDON GATEWAY

Maple Cross

Bushey Heath

26 **27** **28** **29** **30** **31**

South Oxhey

NORTHWOOD

STANMORE

Burnt Oak

Mill Hill

FINCHLEY

Harefield

Harrow Weald

EDGWARE

Musw Hill

38 **39** **40** **41** **42** **43** **44** **45** **46**

Ruislip Common

RUISLIP Eastcote

HARROW **KENTON** Kingsbury

HENDON Golders Green

Highgat

Denham

Ickenham

Rayners Lane

Harrow on the Hill

Cricklewood

HAMPSTEAD

UXBRIDGE

56 **57** **58** **59** **60** **61** **62** **63** **64**

NORTHOLT **WEMBLEY** **WILLESDEN** **CAMDE**

Iver Heath

Cowley

Hillingdon

GREENFORD

Kilburn

Yeading

74 **75** **76** **77** **78** **79** **80** **81** **82**

HAYES **EALING** **PADDINGTON**

Yiewsley

Hanwell

Shepherd's Bush

Kensington Westminst

West Drayton **SOUTHALL** **ACTON**

92 **93** **94** **95** **96** **97** **98** **99** **100**

Chiswick

CHELSE

Sipson

Harlington

HESTON Heston Osterley

Brentford

HAMMERSMITH

174

Cranford

Kew

North Sheen

FULHAM **BATTERSE**

LONDON HEATHROW AIRPORT

110 **111** **112** **113** **114** **115** **116** **117** **118**

Hatton

ISLEWORTH **BARNES** **PUTNEY**

Stanwell Moor Stanwell

HOUNSLOW **RICHMOND** **WANDSWORTH**

East Bedfont

Roehampton

Upper Tooting

STAINES

128 **129** **130** **131** **132** **133** **134** **135** **136**

ASHFORD **FELTHAM** **TWICKENHAM** Ham

Richmond Park

Felthamhill

Hanworth

TEDDINGTON **WIMBLEDON**

Hampton

KINGSTON UPON THAMES

Littleton

Hampton Wick

146 **147** **148** **149** **150** **151** **152** **153** **154**

Laleham

SUNBURY East Molesey

MERTON

Shepperton

Thames Ditton

NEW MALDEN **MORDEN**

CHERTSEY

SURBITON

WEYBRIDGE **WALTON-ON-THAMES**

Long Ditton Tolworth

Worcester Park

CARSHALTON

162 **163** **164** **165** **166**

ESHER Claygate

Chessington

Cheam

SUTTON

Byfleet

Fairmile

EWELL

SCALE

0 — 1 — 2 — 3 Miles

0 — 1 — 2 — 3 — 4 Kilometres

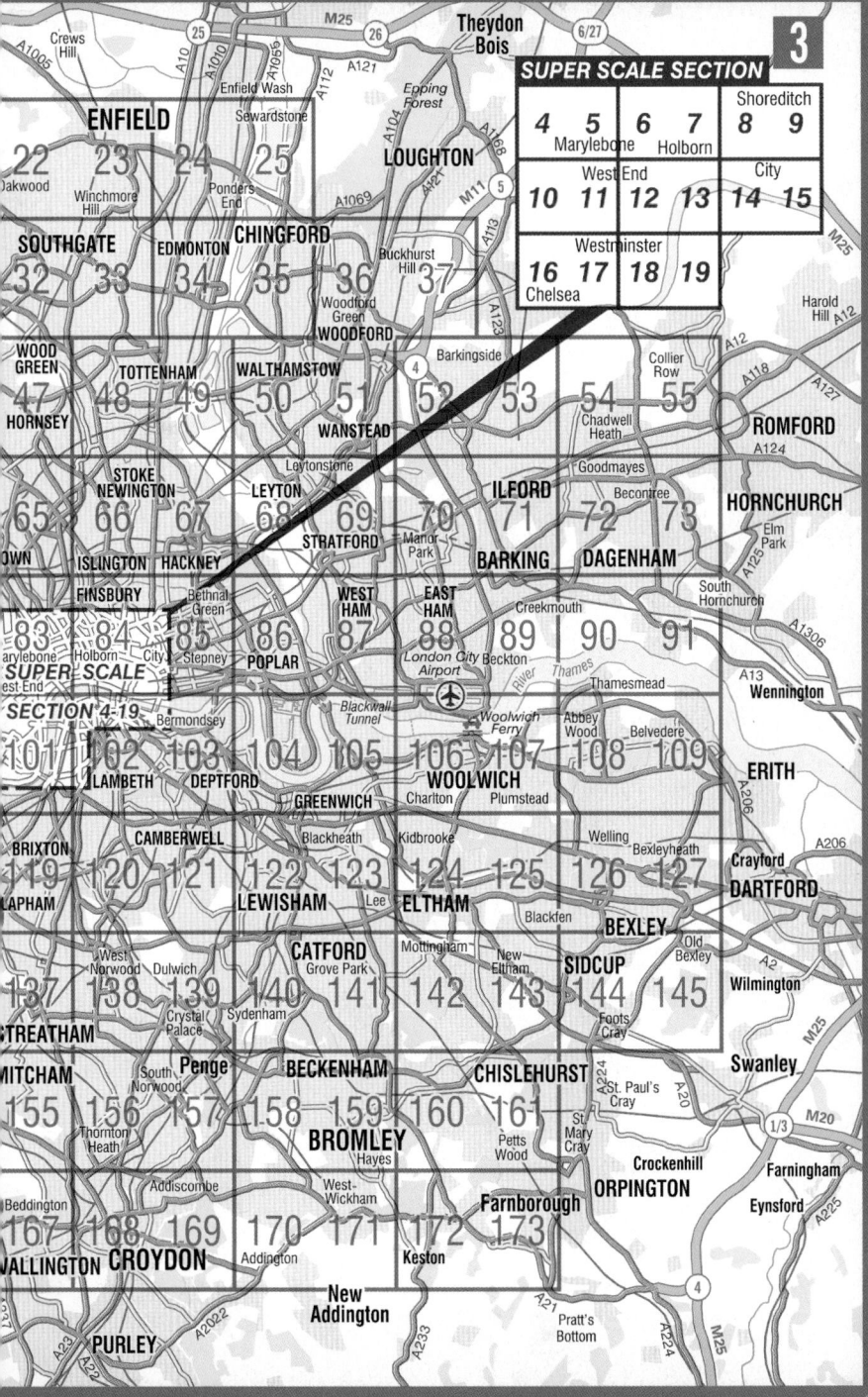
SUPER SCALE SECTION
4 5 Marylebone
6 7 Holborn
Shoreditch 8 9
West End 10 11 12 13
City 14 15
Westminster 16 17 18 19 Chelsea
ENFIELD
LOUGHTON
SOUTHGATE
EDMONTON
CHINGFORD
WOODFORD
TOTTENHAM
WALTHAMSTOW
WANSTEAD
ROMFORD
ILFORD
HORNCHURCH
STRATFORD
BARKING
DAGENHAM
POPLAR
WOOLWICH
ERITH
LEWISHAM
ELTHAM
DARTFORD
BEXLEY
SIDCUP
BECKENHAM
CHISLEHURST
BROMLEY
ORPINGTON
CROYDON
PURLEY
SUPER SCALE SECTION 4-19

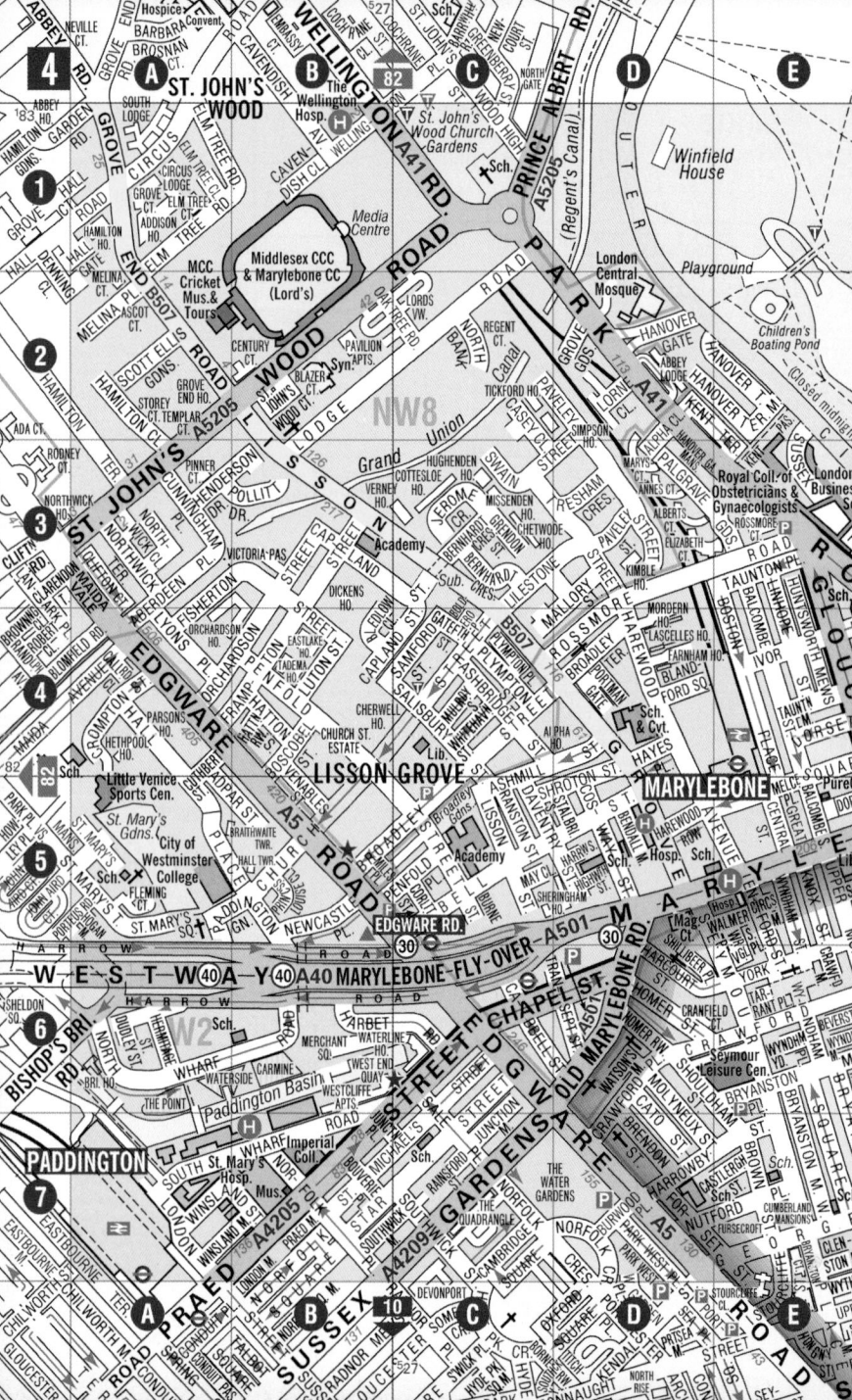
4
A
B
C
D
E
1
2
3
4
5
6
7
82
10
ST. JOHN'S WOOD
The Wellington Hosp.
St. John's Wood Church Gardens
Winfield House
Media Centre
Middlesex CCC & Marylebone CC (Lord's)
MCC Cricket Mus.& Tours
London Central Mosque
Playground
Children's Boating Pond
(Closed midnight
NW8
Grand Union Canal
(Regent's Canal)
Academy
Royal Coll. of Obstetricians & Gynaecologists
London Business Sch.
LISSON GROVE
Little Venice Sports Cen.
St. Mary's Gdns.
City of Westminster College
MARYLEBONE
EDGWARE RD.
PureGym
Seymour Leisure Cen.
W2
Paddington Basin
Imperial Coll.
St. Mary's Hosp.
Mus.
PADDINGTON
THE WATER GARDENS
THE QUADRANGLE
WELLINGTON A41 RD.
PRINCE ALBERT RD.
A5205
PARK ROAD
A41
ST. JOHN'S WOOD ROAD
A5205
LISSON GROVE
EDGWARE ROAD
A5
GROVE END ROAD
B507
MAIDA VALE
MAIDA AVENUE
HARROW ROAD
WESTWAY
A40 MARYLEBONE-FLY-OVER
A501
MARYLEBONE ROAD
CHAPEL ST.
OLD MARYLEBONE RD.
EDGWARE ROAD
SUSSEX GARDENS
A4209
PRAED STREET
A4205
EDGWARE RD
A5
GLOUCESTER PLACE
ROSSMORE ROAD
BISHOP'S BRI. RD
ABBEY RD.
CIRCUS ROAD
HAMILTON TER.

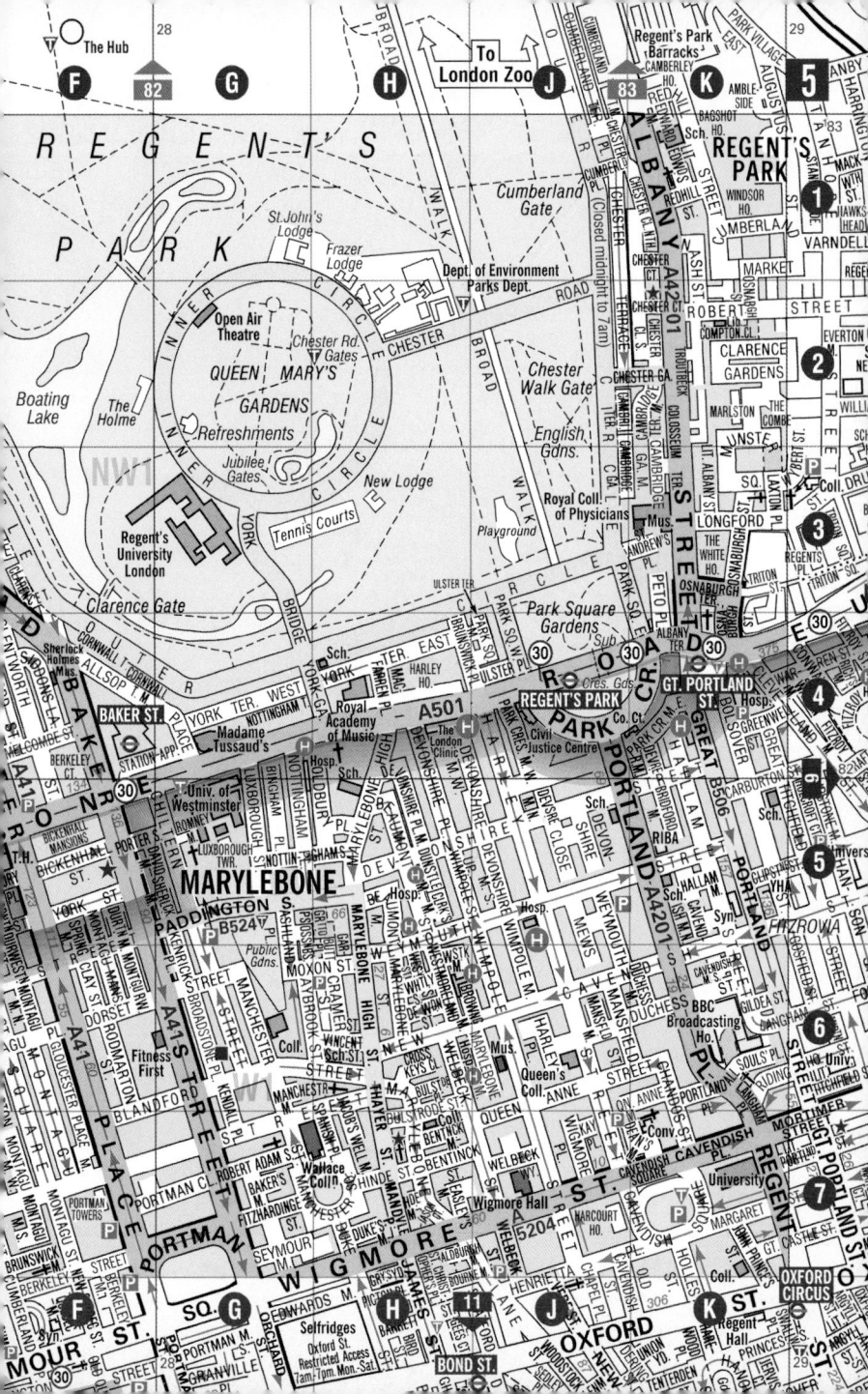

The Hub
28
82
F
G
H
To London Zoo
J
83
K
5
29
REGENT'S PARK
PARK
Regent's Park Barracks
CAMBERLEY HO.
PARK VILLAGE EAST
AUGUSTUS ST.
AMBLESIDE
BAGSHOT HO.
WINDSOR HO.
CUMBERLAND MARKET
VARNDELL
REDHILL ST.
NASH ST.
ALBANY STREET
A4201
Cumberland Gate
(Closed midnight to 7am)
CHESTER TERRACE
St.John's Lodge
Frazer Lodge
Dept. of Environment Parks Dept.
CHESTER ROAD
INNER CIRCLE
Open Air Theatre
Chester Rd. Gates
QUEEN MARY'S GARDENS
Refreshments
Jubilee Gates
Boating Lake
The Holme
NW1
Regent's University London
York Bridge
Tennis Courts
New Lodge
BROAD WALK
Chester Walk Gate
English Gdns.
Royal Coll. of Physicians
Playground
ROBERT STREET
CLARENCE GARDENS
MUNSTER SQ.
LONGFORD
OSNABURGH ST.
TRITON SQ.
1
2
3
4
Clarence Gate
OUTER CIRCLE
Park Square Gardens
PARK SQ. EAST
PARK SQ. W.
ULSTER TER.
YORK TER. EAST
YORK TER. WEST
Sherlock Holmes Mus.
BAKER ST.
Madame Tussaud's
Royal Academy of Music
The London Clinic
REGENT'S PARK
GT. PORTLAND ST.
PARK CR.
Civil Justice Centre
MARYLEBONE ROAD
A501
A41
A4201
30
Univ. of Westminster
BICKENHALL MANSIONS
BICKENHALL ST.
MARYLEBONE
PADDINGTON ST.
B524
Public Gdns.
MOXON ST.
MARYLEBONE HIGH ST.
DEVONSHIRE PL.
DEVONSHIRE ST.
WIMPOLE ST.
WEYMOUTH ST.
NEW CAVENDISH STREET
RIBA
GREAT PORTLAND STREET
FITZROVIA
5
6
7
BBC Broadcasting Ho.
DORSET ST.
GLOUCESTER PLACE
BAKER STREET
A41
Fitness First
W1
BLANDFORD ST.
MANCHESTER SQ.
Wallace Colln.
Coll.
QUEEN ANNE STREET
Queen's Coll.
HARLEY ST.
WELBECK ST.
WIGMORE STREET
Wigmore Hall
CAVENDISH SQUARE
University
REGENT STREET
MARGARET ST.
PORTMAN SQ.
PORTMAN TOWERS
MONTAGU SQUARE
SEYMOUR ST.
Selfridges
Oxford St. Restricted Access 7am-7pm Mon.-Sat.
BOND ST.
11
OXFORD ST.
Regent Hall
OXFORD CIRCUS
A5204
HENRIETTA PL.
VERE ST.
JAMES ST.
DUKE ST.
ORCHARD ST.
PORTMAN ST.
GRANVILLE PL.
F
G
H
J
K

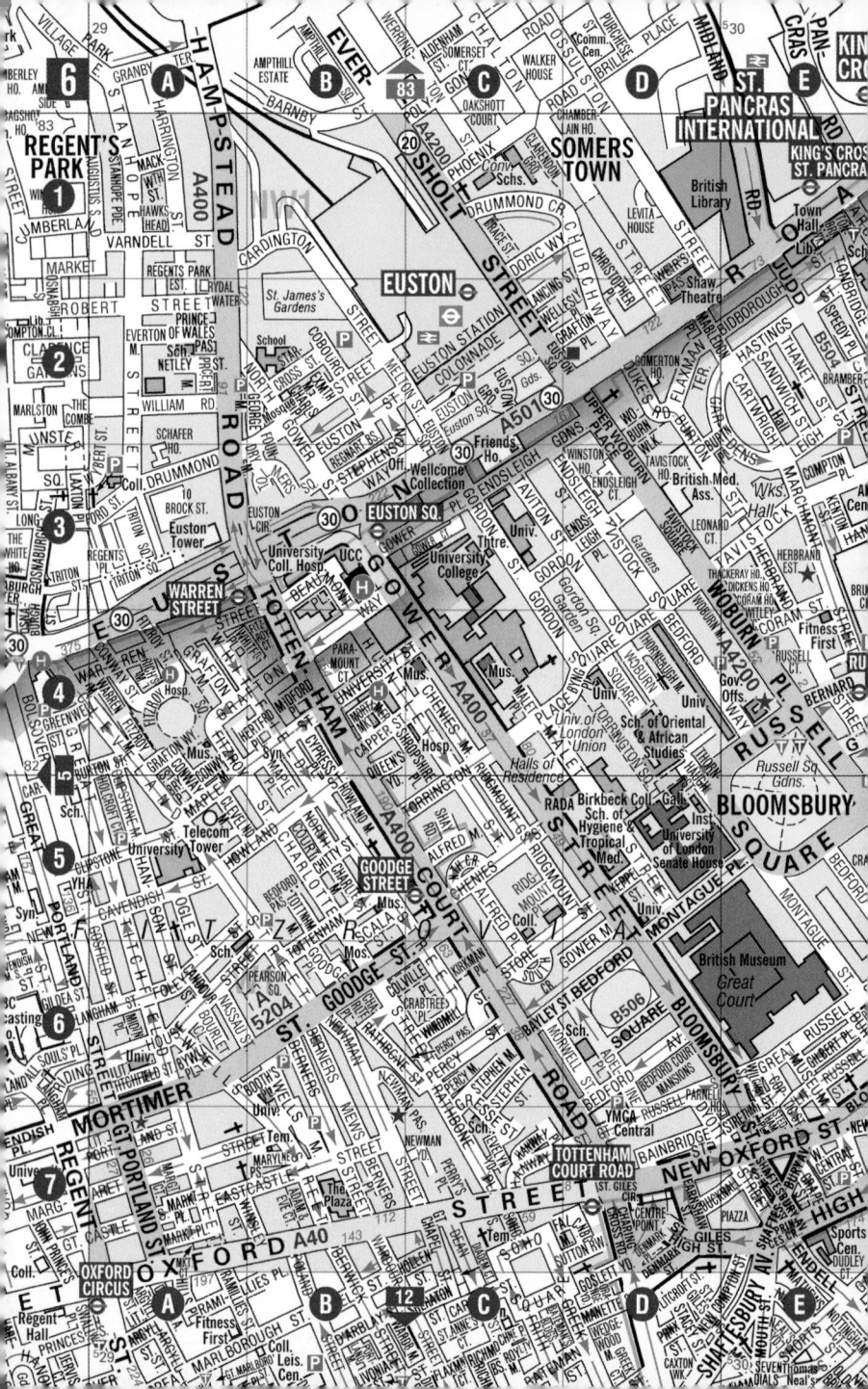

6
A
B
C
D
E
83
REGENT'S PARK
SOMERS TOWN
ST. PANCRAS INTERNATIONAL
KING'S CROSS ST. PANCRAS
British Library
NW1
EUSTON
St. James's Gardens
School
EUSTON SQ.
WARREN STREET
GOODGE STREET
TOTTENHAM COURT ROAD
OXFORD CIRCUS
BLOOMSBURY
British Museum
Great Court
Russell Sq. Gdns.
Gordon Sq. Garden
Tavistock Square Gardens
University College
University Coll. Hosp.
UCC
Wellcome Collection
Friends Ho.
Euston Tower
Telecom Tower
Birkbeck Coll.
Sch. of Hygiene & Tropical Med.
University of London Senate House
Sch. of Oriental & African Studies
Univ. of London Union
Halls of Residence
RADA
Shaw Theatre
British Med. Ass.
HAMPSTEAD ROAD
A400
EVERSHOLT STREET
A4200
EUSTON ROAD
A501
GOWER STREET
TOTTENHAM COURT ROAD
GT. PORTLAND ST.
PORTLAND PL.
REGENT ST.
MORTIMER ST.
OXFORD ST. A40
NEW OXFORD ST.
GOODGE ST.
WOBURN PL.
RUSSELL SQUARE
MONTAGUE PL.
MALET STREET
BLOOMSBURY ST.
BEDFORD SQUARE
FITZROVIA
SOHO SQUARE
CHARING CROSS RD.
SHAFTESBURY AV.
HIGH HOLBORN
ST. GILES CIR.
CENTRE POINT
The Plaza
YMCA Central
Fitness First
12
1
2
3
4
5
6
7
5

PENTONVILLE ROAD
A501
83
84
F
G
H
J
K
7
CITY ROAD
GOSWELL
KING'S CROSS ROAD
A201
GRAY'S INN ROAD
A5200
ST. PANCRAS
SWINTON ST.
ACTON ST.
ARGYLE SQUARE
HARRISON ST.
REGENT SQUARE
MECKLENBURGH SQUARE
St. George's Gdns.
The Foundling Museum
The Wolfson Assessment Cen.
Coram's Fields
Mecklenburgh Sq. Gds.
BRUNSWICK SQ.
GUILFORD ST.
Great Ormond Street Hosp. for Children
The National Hosp.
Westminster Kingsway Coll.
Eastman Dental Hosp. & Institute
St. Andrew's Gds.
The Charles Dickens Mus.
DOUGHTY STREET
The British Postal Mus. (2017)
Mount Pleasant Sorting Office
FARRINGDON ROAD
ROSEBERY AVENUE
CLERKENWELL
London Metropolitan Archives
Dania Sch.
Sadler's Wells
NEW RIVER HEAD
THE HYDRA BUILDING
MYDDELTON SQUARE
AMWELL STREET
SKINNER ST.
B502
ST. JOHN ST.
CLERKENWELL ROAD
A5201
A401
THEOBALD'S ROAD
Gray's Inn Gdns.
Gray's Inn
Budd. Cen.
Liby.
ITN
BOURNE ESTATE
Islamic Cen.
LEATHER LANE
HATTON GARDEN
SAFFRON HILL
B521
FARRINGDON ST.
HOLBORN VIADUCT
HOLBORN CIR.
CHANCERY LA.
HOLBORN
HIGH HOLBORN
A40
SOUTHAMPTON ROW
KINGSWAY
A4200
HOLBORN
Lincoln's Inn Fields
Lincoln's Inn Liby.
Lincoln's Inn Hall
Royal Coll. of Surgeons
Grand Connaught Rooms
Freemasons Hall
UAL
CHANCERY LANE
B400
FETTER LA.
NEW FETTER LA.
A4
Law Ct's.
King's Coll. Maughan Library
13
Royal Courts of Justice
FLEET ST.
LSE
Temple
GT. QUEEN ST.
B402
LONG ACRE
1
2
3
4
5
6
7
8

8
A
B
C
D
E
84
14
7
1
2
3
4
5
6
7
CITY ROAD
GOSWELL RD.
GOSWELL ROAD
ANGEL BUILDING
Fitness First
City Road Basin
Wenlock Basin
WHARF
Sadler's Wells
ROSEBERY AV.
ST. JOHN STREET
City University
Lib. & Mus.
SKINNER
Dania Sch.
FINSBURY
EC1
Baths
Leisure Cen.
Moreland Prim. Sch.
Spts. Cen.
Schs.
Colleges
OLD STREET
ST. LUKE'S
BUNHILL ROW
Bunhill Flds. Burial Grd.
Virgin Active
Moorfields Eye Hosp.
College
CLERKENWELL
CLERKENWELL ROAD
A5201
A501
A1
A40
A201
A1211
B144
B501
B502
B100
Queen Mary University of London
Charterhouse
St. John's Gardens
FARRINGDON
FARRINGDON RD.
FARRINGDON ST.
COWCROSS
BARBICAN
ALDERSGATE
BEECH STREET
CHISWELL
SILK ST.
GOLDEN LANE ESTATE
Lib. Arts Cen.
Museum
Ironmongers Hall
LONDON WALL
MOORGATE
Central Markets
SMITHFIELD
St. Bartholomew's Hospital
HOLBORN
HOLBORN CIR.
CITY THAMESLINK
V'DUCT
NEWGATE ST.
KING EDWARD ST.
Old Bailey
Cen. Crim. Ct.
British Telecom Cen.
ST. MARTIN'S LE GRAND
ST. PAUL'S
St. Paul's Cathedral
One New Change
CHEAPSIDE
POULTRY
GRESHAM ST.
Guildhall
Offs.
LUDGATE
The College of Law
HAC Ground
THE BREWERY
CITYPOINT
WHITE HORSE YD.

9
F
G
H
J
K
84
85
1
2
3
4
5
6
7
SHOREDITCH
N1
E2
E1
EC2
CITY
SPITALFIELDS
SHOREDITCH HIGH STREET
LIVERPOOL STREET
ALDGATE EAST
ALDGATE
HACKNEY ROAD
KINGSLAND RD.
A10
OLD STREET
A5201
GREAT EASTERN STREET
SHOREDITCH HIGH STREET
A1202
COMMERCIAL STREET
BETHNAL GREEN ROAD
A1209
COLUMBIA ROAD
B118
CITY ROAD
A501
NEW NORTH RD.
B101
PITFIELD ST.
HOXTON ST.
CURTAIN RD.
BISHOPSGATE
HOUNDSDITCH
BEVIS MARKS
LONDON WALL
FINSBURY CIRCUS
FINSBURY SQ.
WHITECHAPEL HIGH ST.
LEMAN STREET
MANSELL ST.
BRICK LANE
B134
B135
Hackney Comm. Coll.
Town Hall
Bethnal Green Academy
Old Spitalfields Market
Dennis Severs' Ho.
Broadgate Ice Rink
Broadgate Circle
Tower 42
"The Gherkin"
"The Cheesegrater"
"The Scalpel"
Lloyd's Bldg.
Heron Twr.
Toynbee Hall
Mosque
Royal Exch.
15

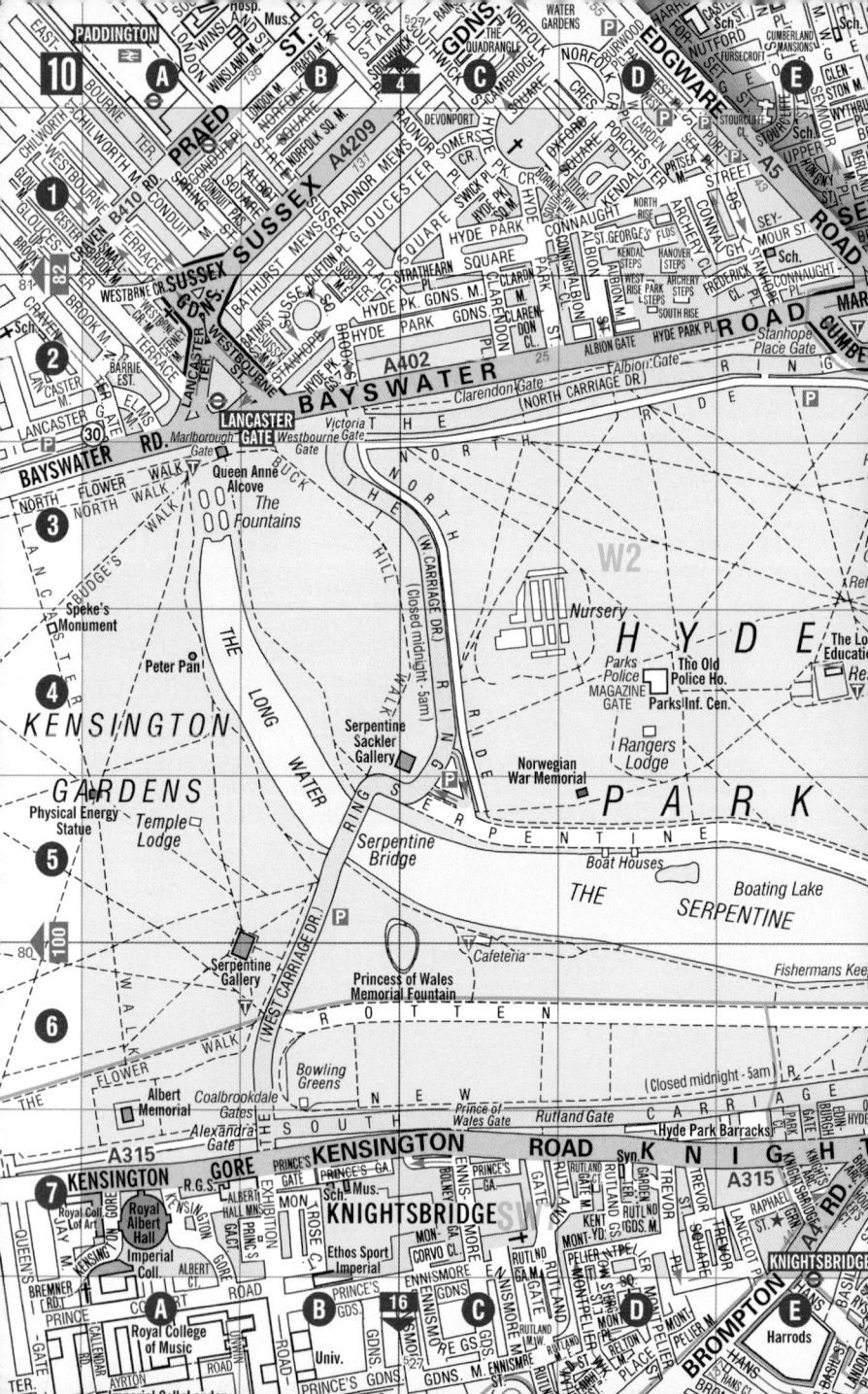

10
PADDINGTON
A
B
C
D
E
1
2
3
4
5
6
7
82
100
16
4
PRAED
SUSSEX
A4209
B410
EDGWARE ROAD
A5
BAYSWATER ROAD
A402
LANCASTER GATE
Marlborough Gate
Westbourne Gate
Victoria Gate
Clarendon Gate
Albion Gate
Stanhope Place Gate
Queen Anne Alcove
The Fountains
Speke's Monument
Peter Pan
KENSINGTON GARDENS
Physical Energy Statue
Temple Lodge
THE LONG WATER
Serpentine Sackler Gallery
W2
Nursery
HYDE PARK
Parks Police
The Old Police Ho.
MAGAZINE GATE
Parks Inf. Cen.
Rangers Lodge
Norwegian War Memorial
Serpentine Bridge
Boat Houses
THE SERPENTINE
Boating Lake
Cafeteria
Serpentine Gallery
Princess of Wales Memorial Fountain
ROTTEN ROW
Bowling Greens
Albert Memorial
Coalbrookdale Gates
Alexandra Gate
Prince of Wales Gate
Rutland Gate
Hyde Park Barracks
A315
KENSINGTON GORE
KENSINGTON ROAD
KNIGHTSBRIDGE
Royal Albert Hall
Royal Coll. of Art
Imperial Coll.
Royal College of Music
Ethos Sport Imperial
Univ.
BROMPTON
Harrods

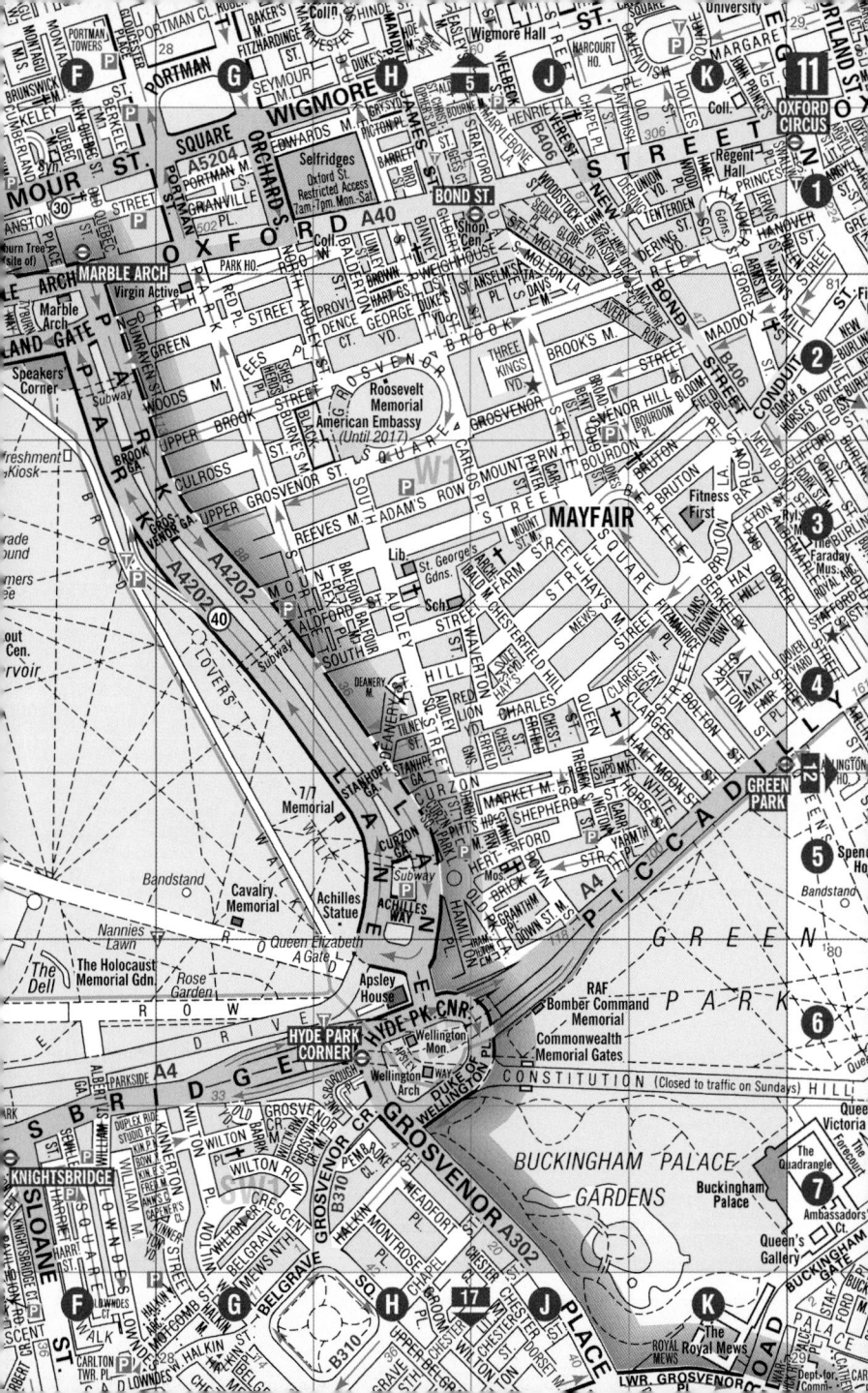

Portman Towers
Portman Cl.
Baker's M.
Wigmore Hall
Harcourt Ho.
University
11
Oxford Circus
Portman
Square
Seymour M.
Wigmore
Manchester Sq.
Duke's M.
Welbeck St.
Henrietta Pl.
Cavendish Sq.
Holles St.
Margaret St.
Coll.
5
A5204
Portman M.
Granville Pl.
Orchard St.
Edwards M.
Selfridges
Oxford St. Restricted Access 7am-7pm. Mon.-Sat.
James St.
Barrett St.
Bird St.
Marylebone La.
Stratford Pl.
Vere St.
B406
Regent Hall
Princes St.
Bond St.
Seymour St.
Marble Arch
Virgin Active
Tyburn Tree (site of)
Oxford Street
A40
Shopg. Cen.
Davies St.
South Molton St.
Woodstock St.
New Bond St.
Tenterden St.
Dering St.
Hanover Sq.
Hanover St.
St. George St.
North Row
Park St.
North Audley St.
Balderton St.
Brown Hart Gdns.
Weighhouse St.
Duke's Yd.
St. Anselm's Pl.
Davies M.
Lancashire Ct.
Avery Row
Maddox St.
Mill St.
Conduit St.
Park Ho.
Red Pl.
Providence Ct.
George Yd.
Brook St.
Brook's M.
Three Kings Yd.
Grosvenor Square
Roosevelt Memorial
American Embassy (Until 2017)
Grosvenor St.
Grosvenor Hill
Bourdon St.
Bourdon Pl.
Bloomfield Pl.
Coach & Horses Yd.
Boyle St.
Old Burlington St.
Clifford St.
Cork St.
Park Lane
Speakers' Corner
Cumberland Gate
Dunraven St.
Green St.
Woods M.
Lees Pl.
Shepherds Pl.
Upper Brook St.
Blacks Burnes M.
Upper Grosvenor St.
Culross St.
Brook Ga.
Grosvenor Ga.
Reeves M.
South St.
Adam's Row
Carlos Pl.
Mount Row
Mount St.
Carpenter St.
Mayfair
W1
Bruton St.
Bruton La.
Bruton Pl.
Berkeley Sq.
Fitness First
Barlow Pl.
Royal Arc.
Albemarle St.
The Faraday Mus.
Stafford St.
Dover St.
Hay Hill
Berkeley St.
Lansdowne Row
Fitzmaurice Pl.
Farm St.
Hay's M.
Chesterfield Hill
St. George's Gdns.
Lib.
Sch.
Audley St.
Waverton St.
Aldford St.
Rex Pl.
Balfour Pl.
Balfour M.
South St.
Deanery M.
Deanery St.
Tilney St.
Stanhope Ga.
Red Lion Yd.
Charles St.
Chesterfield Gdns.
Queen St.
Clarges M.
Clarges St.
Bolton St.
Stratton St.
Mayfair Pl.
Half Moon St.
White Horse St.
Curzon St.
Curzon Sq.
Market M.
Shepherd St.
Trebeck St.
Shepherd Mkt.
Hertford St.
Down St.
Down St. M.
Brick St.
Pitt's Head M.
Stanhope Row
Carrington St.
Yarmouth Pl.
Green Park
12
Arlington Ho.
Piccadilly
A4
A4202
40
Subway
Refreshment Kiosk
Broad Walk
Lovers' Walk
7/7 Memorial
Curzon Ga.
Achilles Statue
Achilles Way
Bandstand
Cavalry Memorial
Nannies Lawn
Queen Elizabeth Gate
The Dell
The Holocaust Memorial Gdn.
Rose Garden
Apsley House
Hamilton Pl.
Old Park La.
Grantham Pl.
Green Park
RAF Bomber Command Memorial
Commonwealth Memorial Gates
Rotten Row
South Carriage Drive
Hyde Park Corner
Hyde Pk. Cnr.
Wellington Mon.
Wellington Arch
Apsley Way
Duke of Wellington Pl.
Constitution Hill (Closed to traffic on Sundays)
Knightsbridge
A4
Parkside
Albert Ga.
William St.
Duplex Ride
Studio Pl.
Kinnerton St.
Wilton Pl.
Old Barrack Yd.
Wilton Row
Grosvenor Cr. M.
Grosvenor Cres.
Grosvenor Pl.
A302
Headfort Pl.
Pembroke Cl.
B310
Halkin Pl.
Montrose Pl.
Belgrave Mews Nth.
Wilton Cres.
SW1
Buckingham Palace Gardens
Queen Victoria Memorial
The Quadrangle
The Forecourt
Buckingham Palace
Ambassadors' Ct.
Queen's Gallery
Buckingham Gate
Sloane St.
Lowndes Sq.
Harriet St.
William M.
Capener's Cl.
Motcomb St.
Halkin Arc.
Belgrave Sq.
Chapel St.
Groom Pl.
Chester St.
Chester M.
Wilton M.
Upper Belgrave St.
17
The Royal Mews
Royal Mews
Lwr. Grosvenor Pl.
Buckingham Palace Road
Palace Pl.
Stafford Pl.
Dept. for Comm-
Carlton Twr. Pl.
Lowndes St.
W. Halkin St.
F
G
H
J
K
1
2
3
4
5
6
7

12
OXFORD CIRCUS
OXFORD ST.
REGENT STREET
Regent Hall
HANOVER SQ.
CONDUIT ST.
MADDOX ST.
NEW BURLINGTON ST.
SAVILE ROW
GREAT MARLBOROUGH ST.
Fitness First
Coll. Leis. Cen.
CARNABY ST.
BROADWICK ST.
WARDOUR ST.
DEAN ST.
GREEK ST.
SOHO SQUARE
SOHO
OLD COMPTON ST.
CHARING CROSS ROAD
CAMBRIDGE CIRCUS
SHAFTESBURY AVENUE
SEVEN DIALS
Thomas Neal's
EARLHAM ST.
COVENT GARDEN
LONG ACRE
ST. MARTIN'S LA.
GARRICK ST.
LEICESTER SQ.
China Town
GERRARD ST.
LISLE ST.
London Trocadero
PICCADILLY CIRCUS
Eros
COVENTRY ST.
GLASSHOUSE ST.
DENMAN ST.
VIGO ST.
BURLINGTON GS.
Ryl. Inst. Mus.
The Faraday Mus.
Royal Academy of Arts
ALBANY
SACKVILLE ST.
OLD BOND ST.
DOVER ST.
ALBEMARLE ST.
BERKELEY ST.
HAY HILL
BRUTON ST.
PICCADILLY
A4
JERMYN ST.
DUKE ST.
ST. JAMES'S SQUARE
ST. JAMES'S
London Lib.
HAYMARKET
REGENT ST.
PALL MALL
PALL MALL EAST
CHARLES II ST.
WATERLOO PL.
National Portrait Gallery
National Gallery
WILLIAM IV ST.
TRAFALGAR SQ.
Nelson's Column
Canada Ho.
COCKSPUR ST.
CHARING CROSS
NORTHUMBERLAND AV.
King Charles I Island
B308
DUNCANNON ST.
ADELAIDE ST.
Shop. Cen.
Cent. Lending Lib.
STRAND
CHANDOS PL.
Admiralty Arch
Mall Galls.
Inst. of Contemp. Arts
Duke of York Mem.
CARLTON HOUSE TER.
RAC
SW1
Marlborough Ho. (Commonwealth Secretariat)
King George VI & Qn. Mother Mems.
THE MALL
St. James's Palace
Clarence Ho.
Lancaster Ho.
Spencer Ho.
ARLINGTON ST.
GREEN PARK
11
QUEEN'S WALK
Bandstand
GREEN PARK
Stable Yard Gate
(Closed to traffic on Sundays)
HORSE GUARDS RD.
Guards Memorial
Old Admiralty Offices
Horse Guards
The Household Cavalry Mus.
Horse Guards Parade
Banqueting Ho.
Scotland Off.
Old War Office
WHITEHALL
A3212
DOWNING ST.
Cenotaph
Foreign Office
Government Offices
KING CHARLES ST.
Churchill War Rooms
PARLIAMENT ST.
PARLIAMENT SQ.
ST. JAMES'S PARK
Duck Island
Lake
Clive Steps
Parks Police
BIRDCAGE WALK
CONSTITUTION HILL
Queen Victoria Mem.
Buckingham Palace
The Quadrangle
The Forecourt
Ambassadors' Ct.
Queen's Gallery
Buckingham Gate
Queen Anne's Gate
COCKPIT STEPS
OLD QUEEN ST.
The Guards' Museum
Wellington Barracks
QEII Conf. Cen.
Guildhall
GREAT GEORGE ST.
STOREY'S GATE
TOTHILL ST.
BROADWAY
ST. JAMES'S PARK
CAXTON ST.
Caxton Hall
PETTY FRANCE
BUCKINGHAM GATE
PALACE ST.
18
VICTORIA ST.
Dept. for Bus.
BROAD SANCTUARY
Westminster Abbey
The Cloisters
The Close
Abbey Garden
ST. MARGARET ST.
OLD PALACE YD.
GREAT SMITH ST.
DEAN'S YARD
A B C D E
1 2 3 4 5 6 7

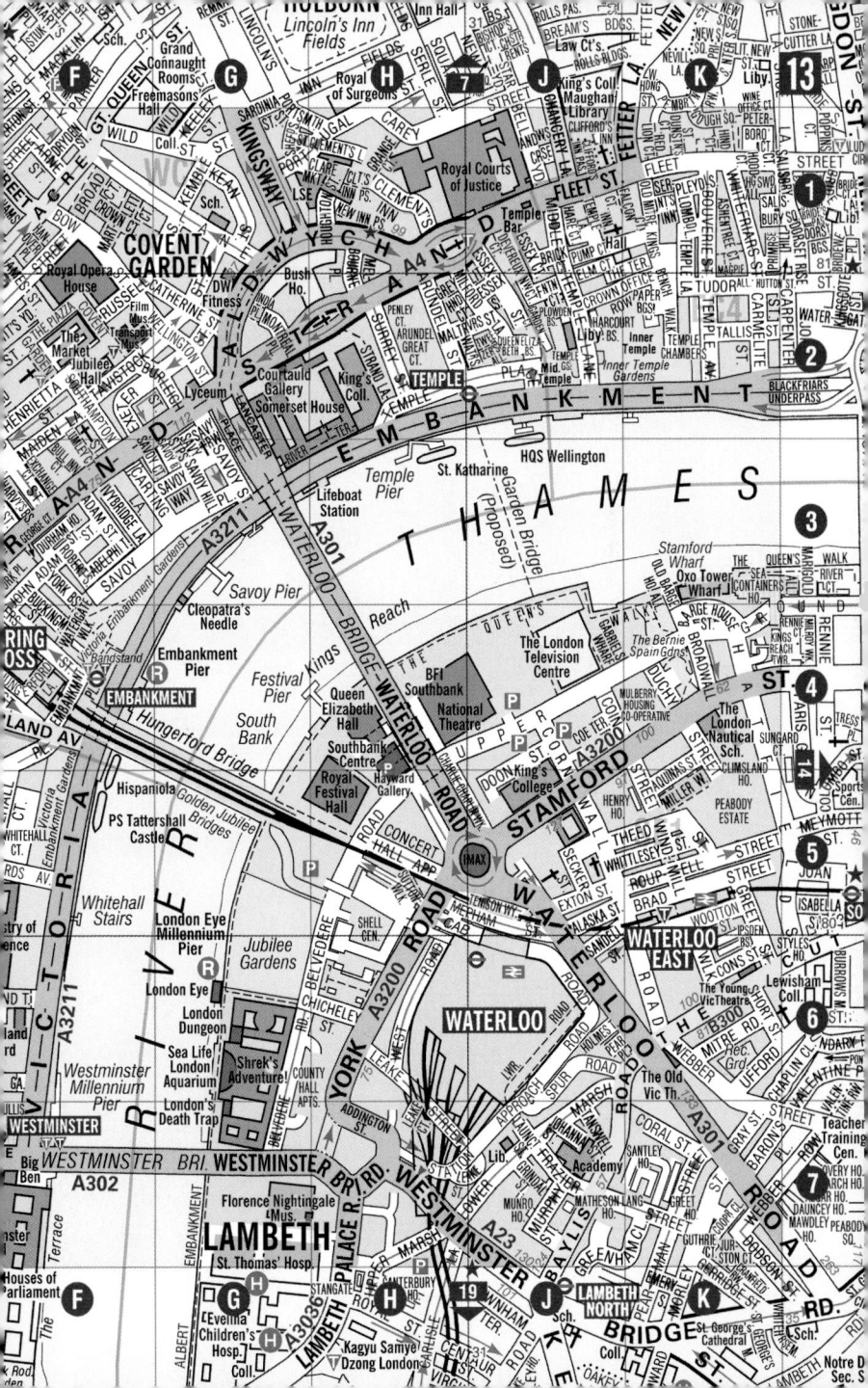

HOLBORN
Lincoln's Inn Fields
Royal Coll. of Surgeons
Grand Connaught Rooms
Freemasons' Hall
Law Ct's.
King's Coll. Maughan Library
Royal Courts of Justice
FLEET ST.
Temple Bar
LSE
COVENT GARDEN
Royal Opera House
The Market
Jubilee Hall
Film Mus.
Transport Mus.
DW Fitness
Bush Ho.
ALDWYCH
STRAND
A4
Courtauld Gallery
Somerset House
King's Coll.
Lyceum
TEMPLE
EMBANKMENT
Inner Temple
Inner Temple Gardens
Mid. Temple
TEMPLE CHAMBERS
BLACKFRIARS UNDERPASS
HQS Wellington
St. Katharine
Temple Pier
Lifeboat Station
Garden Bridge (Proposed)
THAMES
WATERLOO BRIDGE
A301
A3211
Savoy Pier
Cleopatra's Needle
Victoria Embankment Gardens
Embankment Pier
EMBANKMENT
Hungerford Bridge
Festival Pier
Kings Reach
South Bank
Queen Elizabeth Hall
BFI Southbank
National Theatre
Southbank Centre
Royal Festival Hall
Hayward Gallery
The London Television Centre
The Bernie Spain Gdns.
Oxo Tower Wharf
Stamford Wharf
STAMFORD ST.
A3200
King's College
The London Nautical Sch.
PEABODY ESTATE
IMAX
Hispaniola
PS Tattershall Castle
Golden Jubilee Bridges
Whitehall Stairs
London Eye Millennium Pier
Jubilee Gardens
London Eye
London Dungeon
Sea Life London Aquarium
Shrek's Adventure!
London's Death Trap
COUNTY HALL APTS.
Westminster Millennium Pier
WESTMINSTER
RIVER
VICTORIA
WATERLOO
WATERLOO EAST
YORK ROAD
WATERLOO ROAD
The Young Vic Theatre
Lewisham Coll.
The Old Vic Th.
Academy
Teacher Training Cen.
Big Ben
Houses of Parliament
WESTMINSTER BRI.
WESTMINSTER BRI. RD.
A302
A23
Florence Nightingale Mus.
LAMBETH
St. Thomas' Hosp.
Evelina Children's Hosp.
Kagyu Samye Dzong London
LAMBETH NORTH
St. George's Cathedral
Notre Dame Sec. Sch.
F
G
H
J
K
1
2
3
4
5
6
7
7
13
14
19

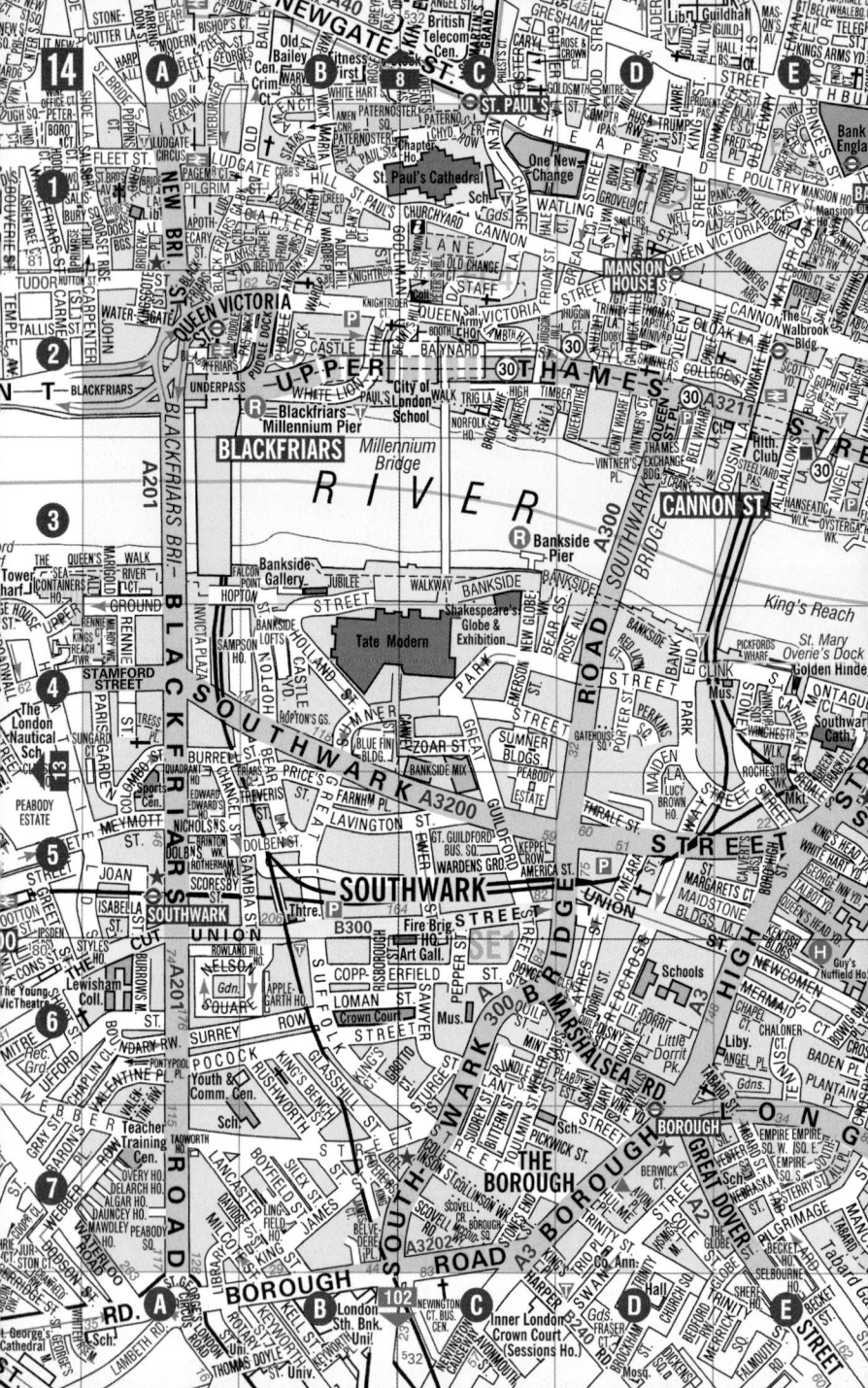

14
A
B
C
D
E
1
2
3
4
5
6
7
13
8
102
NEWGATE ST.
Old Bailey
Cen. Crim. Ct.
British Telecom Cen.
ST. PAUL'S
St. Paul's Cathedral
Chapter Ho.
One New Change
CHEAPSIDE
POULTRY
Bank
MANSION HOUSE
QUEEN VICTORIA ST.
CANNON ST.
WATLING ST.
FLEET ST.
LUDGATE CIRCUS
LUDGATE HILL
NEW BRI. ST.
BLACKFRIARS
BLACKFRIARS BRI.
BLACKFRIARS RD.
UNDERPASS
Blackfriars Millennium Pier
City of London School
UPPER THAMES ST.
Millennium Bridge
RIVER
Bankside Pier
A300
SOUTHWARK BRIDGE
CANNON ST.
King's Reach
St. Mary Overie's Dock
Golden Hinde
Southwark Cath.
Tate Modern
Shakespeare's Globe & Exhibition
Bankside Gallery
HOPTON ST.
SOUTHWARK ST.
A3200
STAMFORD STREET
The London Nautical Sch.
PEABODY ESTATE
MEYMOTT ST.
SOUTHWARK
UNION ST.
THE CUT
Lewisham Coll.
The Young VicTheatre
A201
Fire Brig. HQ.
Art Gall.
SE1
Crown Court
Schools
Little Dorrit Pk.
MARSHALSEA RD.
BOROUGH
BOROUGH HIGH ST.
A3
LONG LA.
GREAT DOVER ST.
A2
THE BOROUGH
BOROUGH RD.
A3202
Teacher Training Cen.
Youth & Comm. Cen.
London Sth. Bnk. Uni.
Inner London Crown Court (Sessions Ho.)
St. George's Cathedral
ST. GEORGE'S CIRCUS
LAMBETH RD.
NEWINGTON CAUSEWAY
Guy's Nuffield Ho.

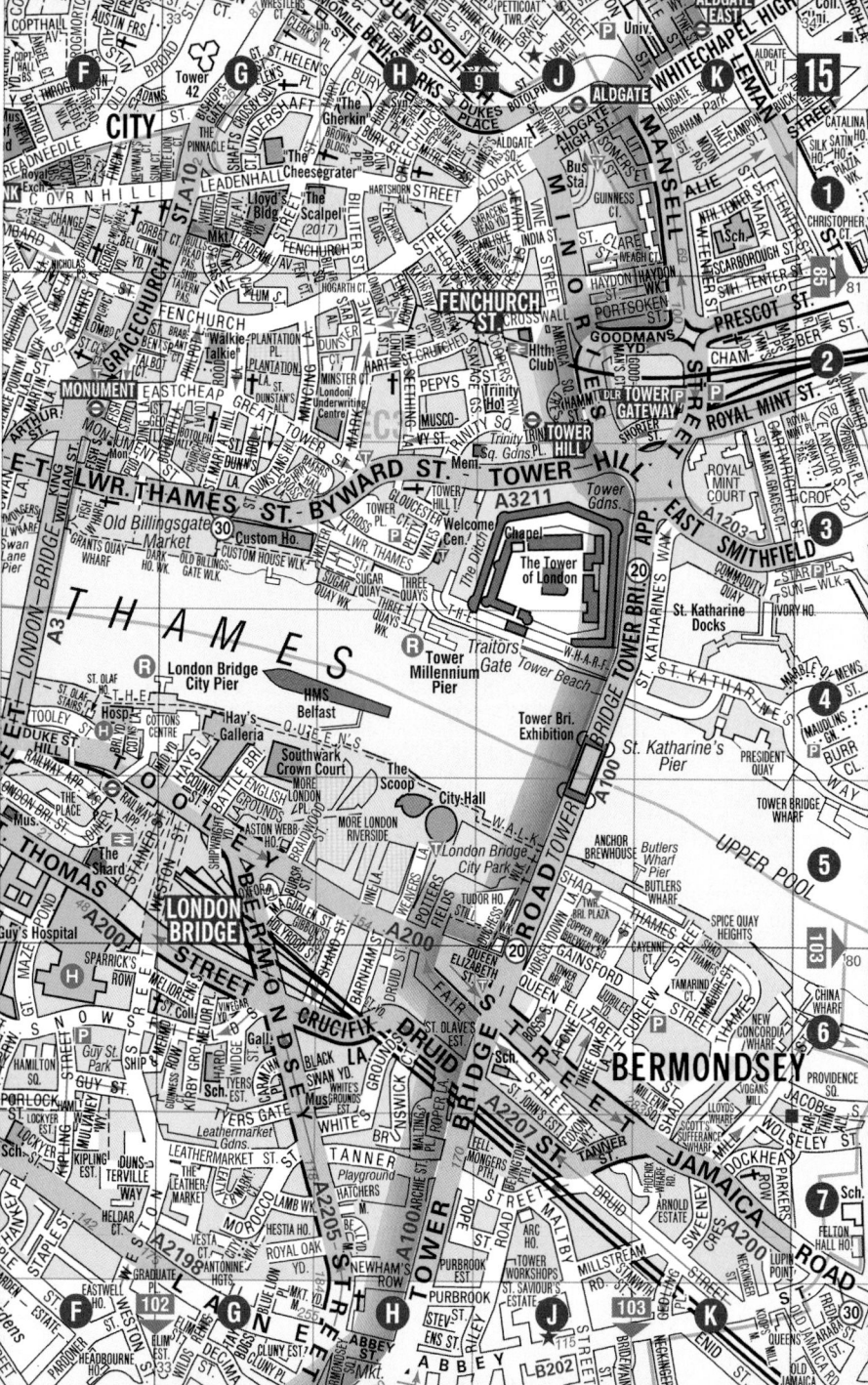

15
F
G
H
J
K
1
2
3
4
5
6
7
81
80
85
103
102
9
20
30
CITY
Tower 42
"The Gherkin"
"The Cheesegrater"
"The Scalpel" (2017)
Lloyd's Bldg
"Walkie-Talkie"
London Underwriting Centre
ALDGATE
ALDGATE EAST
WHITECHAPEL HIGH
LEMAN STREET
MANSELL
MINORIES
FENCHURCH ST.
MONUMENT
TOWER HILL
TOWER GATEWAY
ROYAL MINT ST.
ROYAL MINT COURT
EAST SMITHFIELD
PRESCOT ST.
LEADENHALL
CORNHILL
THREADNEEDLE
GRACECHURCH
EASTCHEAP
GREAT TOWER ST.
LWR. THAMES ST.
BYWARD ST.
TOWER HILL
A3211
The Tower of London
Chapel
The Ditch
Traitors Gate
Tower Beach
Tower Gdns.
Welcome Cen.
Custom Ho.
Old Billingsgate Market
THAMES
Tower Millennium Pier
London Bridge City Pier
HMS Belfast
St. Katharine Docks
St. Katharine's Pier
Tower Bri. Exhibition
TOWER BRI. APP.
TOWER BRIDGE ROAD
A100
LONDON BRIDGE
A3
TOOLEY ST.
Hay's Galleria
Southwark Crown Court
The Scoop
City Hall
More London Riverside
London Bridge City Park
The Shard
LONDON BRIDGE
Guy's Hospital
ST. THOMAS ST.
A200
BERMONDSEY STREET
CRUCIFIX LA.
DRUID ST.
TOWER BRIDGE ROAD
A2207
BERMONDSEY
JAMAICA ROAD
UPPER POOL
Butlers Wharf Pier
BUTLERS WHARF
SHAD THAMES
Leathermarket Gdns.
THE LEATHER MARKET
Guy St. Park
A2198
A2205
LONG LANE
WESTON ST.
TANNER ST.
ABBEY ST.
B202
St. Saviour's Estate

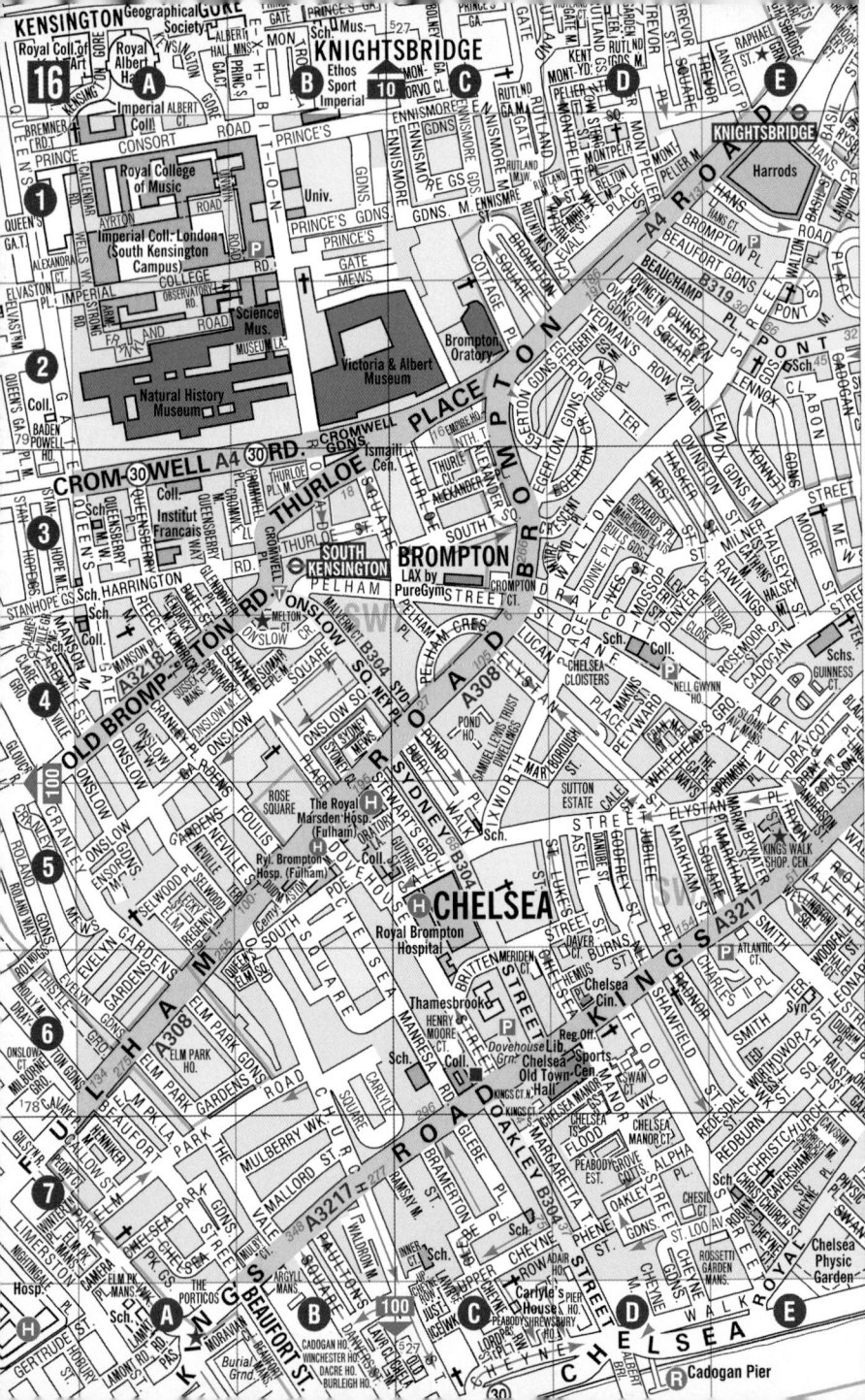

KENSINGTON
16
Geographical Society
GORE
Royal Coll. of Art
Royal Albert Hall
A
B
C
D
E
KNIGHTSBRIDGE
Ethos Sport Imperial
10
KNIGHTSBRIDGE
Harrods
Imperial Coll.
CONSORT ROAD
PRINCE'S GDNS.
Royal College of Music
Imperial Coll. London (South Kensington Campus)
Univ.
1
2
3
4
5
6
7
Science Mus.
Natural History Museum
Victoria & Albert Museum
Brompton Oratory
CROMWELL A4 RD.
CROMWELL PLACE
BROMPTON ROAD
A4 ROAD
BEAUCHAMP PL.
B319
Coll.
Institut Français
THURLOE
SOUTH KENSINGTON
BROMPTON
LAX by PureGym
PELHAM STREET
HARRINGTON
OLD BROMPTON RD.
A3218
A308
B304
ONSLOW SQ.
SYDNEY ST.
FULHAM ROAD
The Royal Marsden Hosp. (Fulham)
Ryl. Brompton Hosp. (Fulham)
CHELSEA
Royal Brompton Hospital
Thamesbrook
Chelsea Old Town Hall
Sports Cen.
KING'S ROAD
A3217
100
Chelsea Physic Garden
Carlyle's House
CHEYNE WALK
CHELSEA
Cadogan Pier
ROYAL
Burial Grnd.
BEAUFORT ST.
KINGS WALK SHOP. CEN.
SLOANE AVENUE
Chelsea Cin.

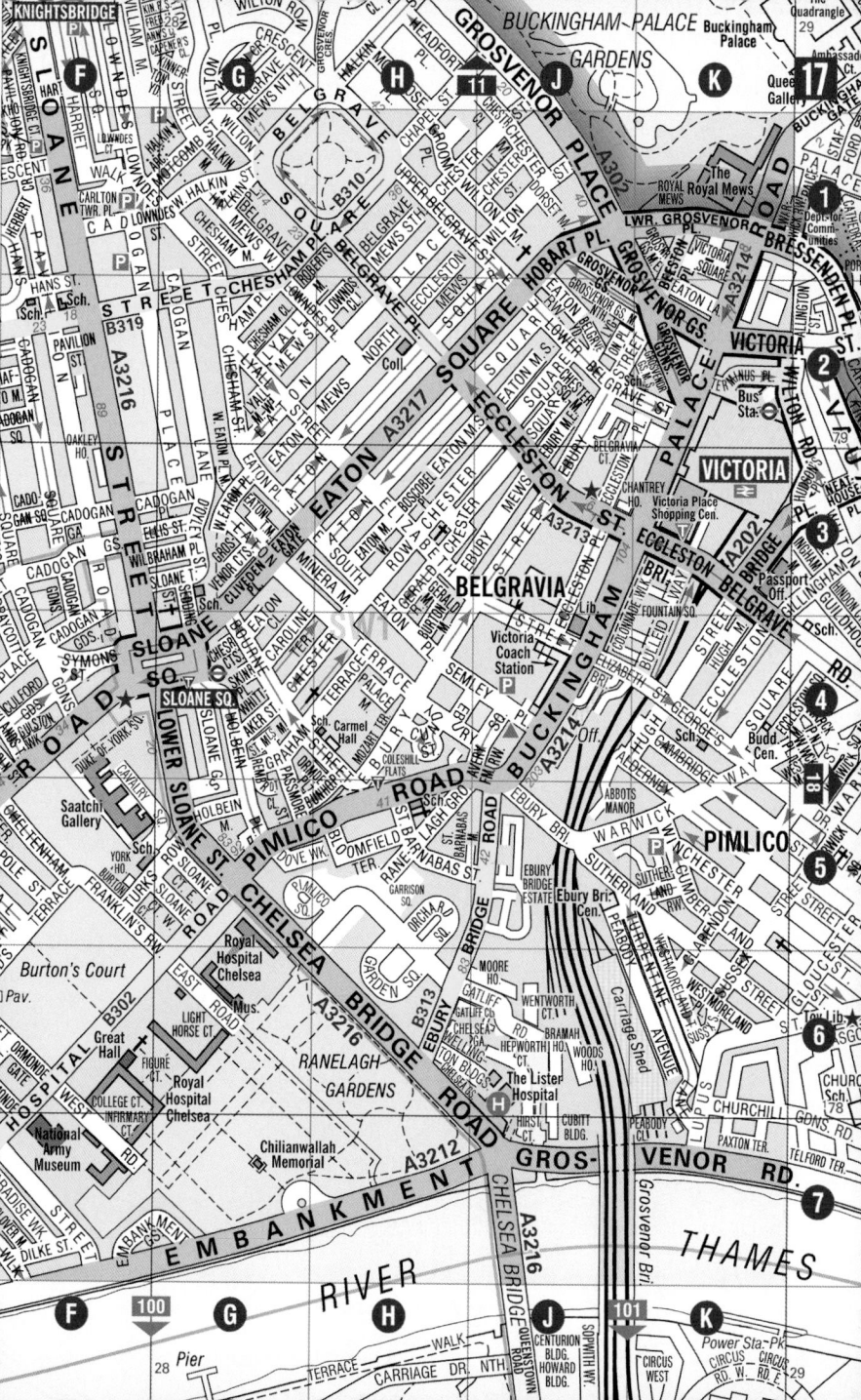

KNIGHTSBRIDGE
BUCKINGHAM PALACE GARDENS
Buckingham Palace
The Quadrangle
Queen's Gallery
17
11
GROSVENOR PLACE
BELGRAVE SQUARE
The Royal Mews
ROYAL MEWS
LWR. GROSVENOR PL.
BRESSENDEN PL.
Dept. for Communities
VICTORIA
VICTORIA ST.
Bus Sta.
Victoria Place Shopping Cen.
Passport Off.
BELGRAVIA
Victoria Coach Station
EATON SQUARE
ECCLESTON ST.
BUCKINGHAM PALACE ROAD
SLOANE STREET
SLOANE SQ.
LOWER SLOANE ST.
PIMLICO ROAD
PIMLICO
Saatchi Gallery
Burton's Court
Royal Hospital Chelsea
Great Hall
National Army Museum
RANELAGH GARDENS
Chilianwallah Memorial
The Lister Hospital
CHELSEA BRIDGE ROAD
GROSVENOR RD.
EMBANKMENT
CHELSEA BRIDGE
RIVER THAMES
Grosvenor Bri.
Carriage Shed
Power Sta. Pk.
CIRCUS WEST
Pier
CARRIAGE DR. NTH.
QUEENSTOWN ROAD
A3216
A3217
A3214
A3213
A302
A202
A3212
B302
B313
B319
B310
F
G
H
J
K
1
2
3
4
5
6
7
18
100
101
28
29

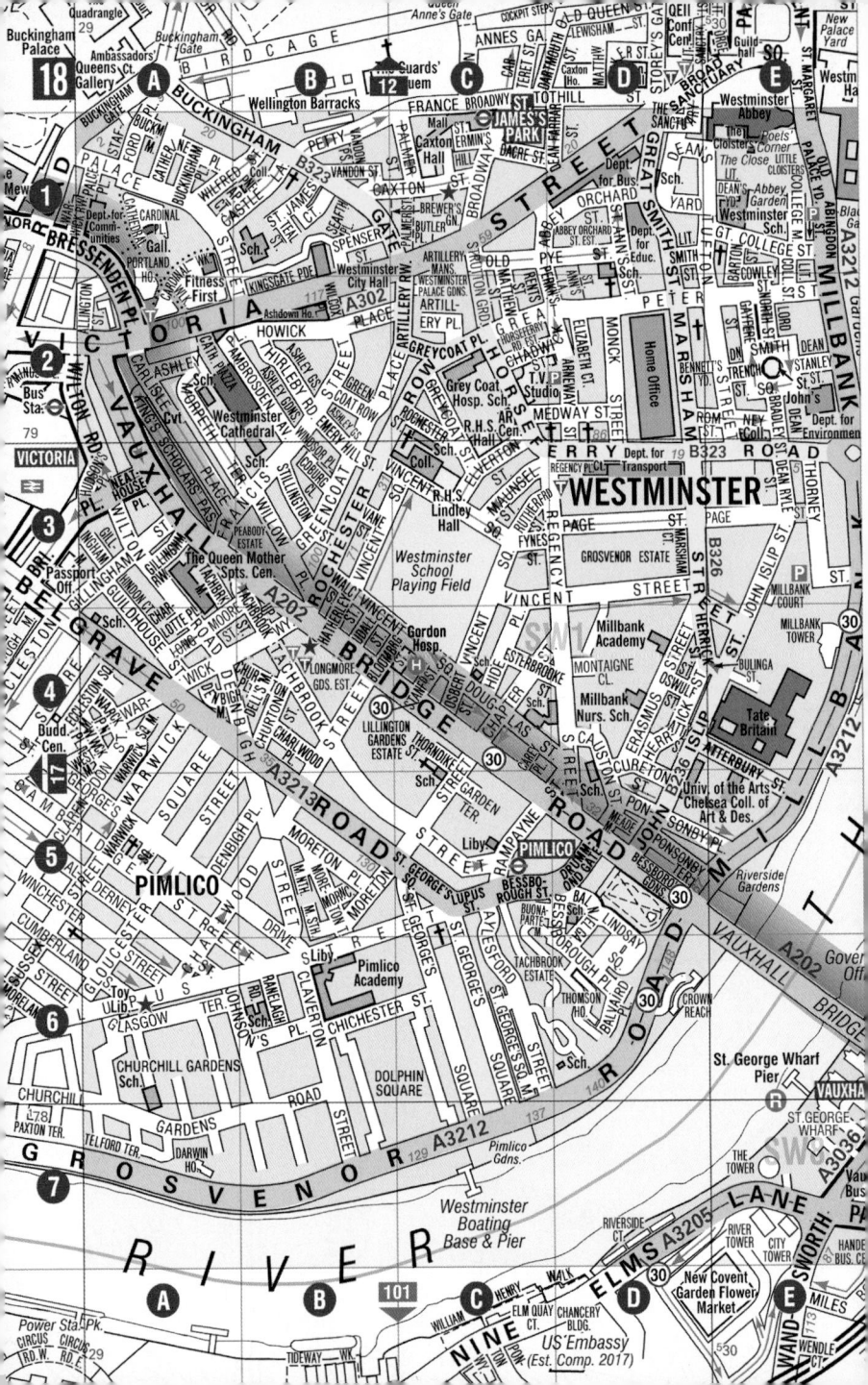

18
17
12
101
Buckingham Palace
Queens Gallery
Wellington Barracks
Guards' Museum
BIRDCAGE WALK
BUCKINGHAM GATE
Caxton Hall
ST. JAMES'S PARK
TOTHILL ST.
BROADWAY
Westminster Abbey
The Cloisters
Poets' Corner
Westminster Sch.
Dept. for Communities
Westminster City Hall
Fitness First
VICTORIA STREET
A302
B323
VICTORIA
Bus Sta.
Westminster Cathedral
VAUXHALL BRIDGE ROAD
A202
Grey Coat Hosp. Sch.
Home Office
Dept. for Educ.
Dept. for Bus.
Dept. for Environment
Dept. for Transport
HORSEFERRY ROAD
MARSHAM STREET
GREAT SMITH ST.
MILLBANK
A3212
WESTMINSTER
R.H.S. Lindley Hall
Westminster School Playing Field
GROSVENOR ESTATE
Millbank Academy
Millbank Nurs. Sch.
MILLBANK TOWER
Tate Britain
Univ. of the Arts Chelsea Coll. of Art & Des.
The Queen Mother Spts. Cen.
Gordon Hosp.
LILLINGTON GARDENS ESTATE
BELGRAVE ROAD
A3213
PIMLICO
Pimlico Academy
DOLPHIN SQUARE
CHURCHILL GARDENS
TACHBROOK ESTATE
GROSVENOR ROAD
A3212
Riverside Gardens
St. George Wharf Pier
ST. GEORGE WHARF
Westminster Boating Base & Pier
RIVER
NINE ELMS LANE
A3205
New Covent Garden Flower Market
US Embassy (Est. Comp. 2017)
SW1
SW8
A B C D E
1 2 3 4 5 6 7

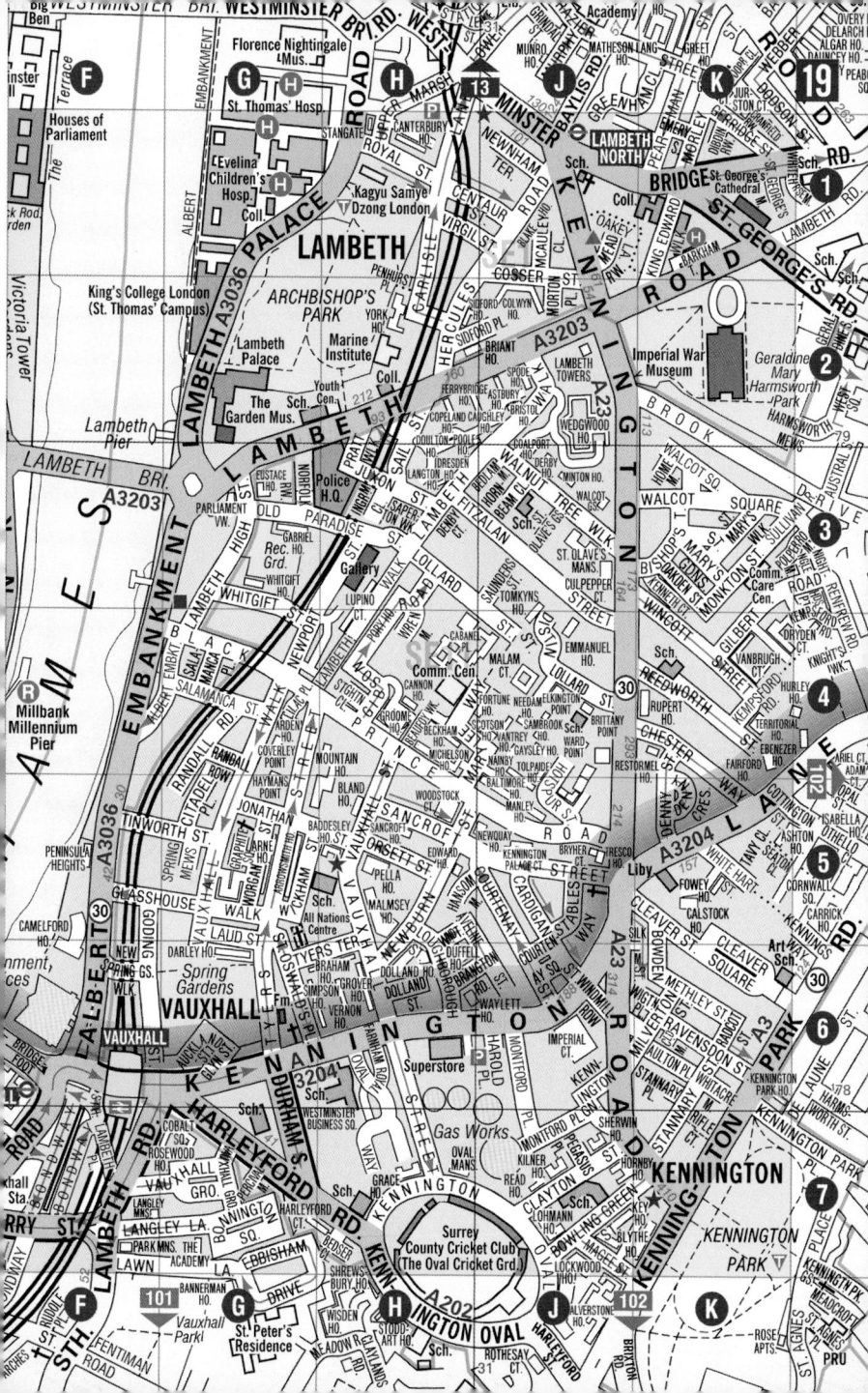

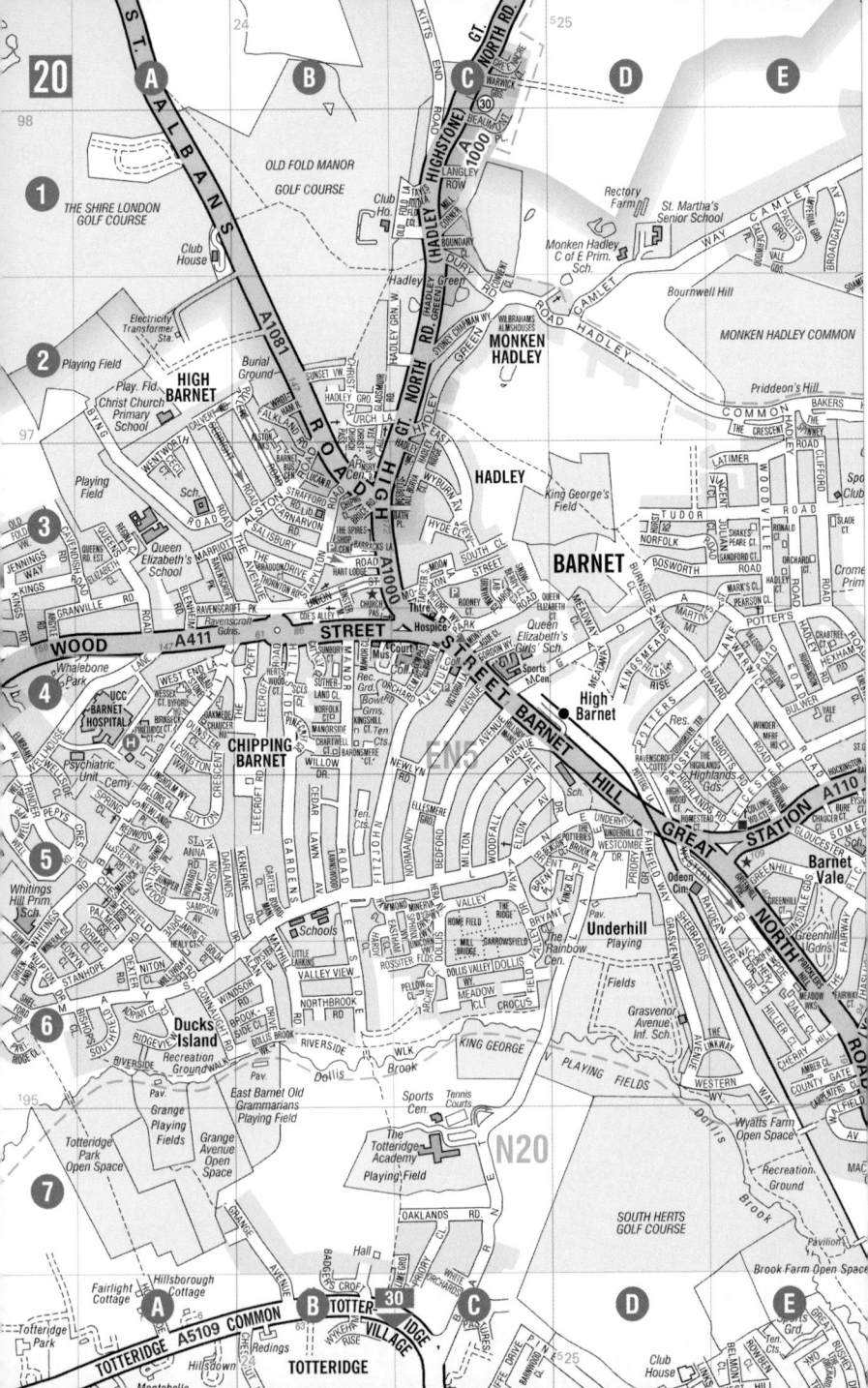
20
A
B
C
D
E
1
2
3
4
5
6
7
98
97
195
24
525
ST. ALBANS ROAD
A1081
GT. NORTH RD.
A1000
HIGHSTONE
OLD FOLD MANOR
GOLF COURSE
THE SHIRE LONDON
GOLF COURSE
Club House
Club Ho.
KITTS END ROAD
LANGLEY ROW
Rectory Farm
St. Martha's
Senior School
Monken Hadley
C of E Prim.
Sch.
CAMLET WAY
Bournwell Hill
MONKEN HADLEY COMMON
HADLEY ROAD
Electricity
Transformer
Sta.
Playing Field
Burial
Ground
HIGH
BARNET
Play. Fld.
Christ Church
Primary
School
MONKEN
HADLEY
Hadley Green
Priddeon's Hill
COMMON
HADLEY
Playing
Field
King George's
Field
BARNET
TUDOR
Queen
Elizabeth's
School
WOOD
A411
STREET
Hospice
Thtre.
Queen
Elizabeth's
Girls' Sch.
Whalebone
Park
BARNET
HOSPITAL
Psychiatric
Unit
Cemy.
CHIPPING
BARNET
EN5
High
Barnet
BARNET HILL
GREAT NORTH ROAD
STATION
A110
Barnet
Vale
Whitings
Hill Prim.
Sch.
Schools
Underhill
Playing
Fields
Odeon
Cin.
Ducks
Island
Recreation
Ground
KING GEORGE
PLAYING FIELDS
Dollis Brook
Grasvenor
Avenue
Inf. Sch.
Grange
Playing
Fields
East Barnet Old
Grammarians
Playing Field
Grange
Avenue
Open
Space
Totteridge
Park
Open Space
Sports
Cen.
Tennis
Courts
The
Totteridge
Academy
Playing Field
N20
Wyatts Farm
Open Space
Recreation
Ground
SOUTH HERTS
GOLF COURSE
Brook Farm Open Space
Pavilion
OAKLANDS RD.
Hall
Fairlight
Cottage
Hillsborough
Cottage
TOTTERIDGE A5109 COMMON
TOTTERIDGE VILLAGE
30
Redings
Totteridge
Park
Hillsdown
TOTTERIDGE
Club
House
Sports
Grd.

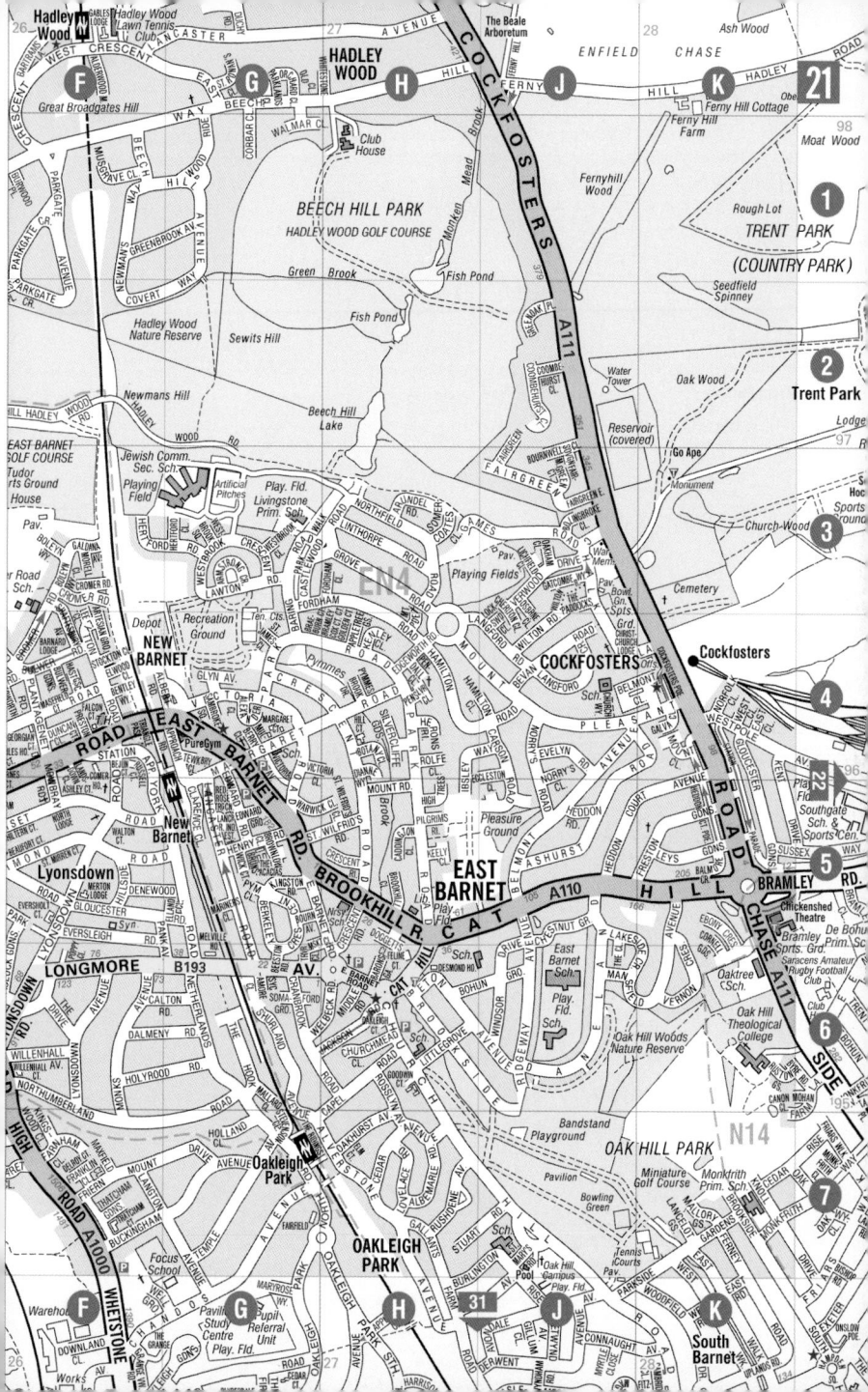

21
22
31
26
27
28
98
97
96
95
F
G
H
J
K
1
2
3
4
5
6
7
Hadley Wood
Hadley Wood Lawn Tennis Club
HADLEY WOOD
The Beale Arboretum
ENFIELD CHASE
Ash Wood
Ferny Hill Cottage
Ferny Hill Farm
Moat Wood
Great Broadgates Hill
Club House
BEECH HILL PARK
HADLEY WOOD GOLF COURSE
Fernyhill Wood
Rough Lot
TRENT PARK
(COUNTRY PARK)
Seedfield Spinney
Green Brook
Fish Pond
Hadley Wood Nature Reserve
Sewits Hill
Newmans Hill
Beech Hill Lake
Water Tower
Oak Wood
Trent Park
Reservoir (covered)
Go Ape
Monument
EAST BARNET GOLF COURSE
Jewish Comm. Sec. Sch.
Playing Field
Artificial Pitches
Play. Fld.
Livingstone Prim. Sch.
Church Wood
Cemetery
EN4
Playing Fields
Depot
Recreation Ground
NEW BARNET
Pymmes Brook
COCKFOSTERS
Cockfosters
PureGym
New Barnet
Lyonsdown
Pleasure Ground
EAST BARNET
Southgate Sch. & Sports Cen.
BRAMLEY RD.
Chickenshed Theatre
Bramley Sprts. Grd.
Saracens Amateur Rugby Football Club
Oaktree Sch.
Oak Hill Theological College
East Barnet Sch.
Oak Hill Woods Nature Reserve
LONGMORE AV.
B193
A110
A111
A1000
COCKFOSTERS
CAT HILL
BROOKHILL R.
EAST BARNET RD.
STATION ROAD
HIGH ROAD
WHETSTONE
Bandstand Playground
OAK HILL PARK
N14
Miniature Golf Course
Monkfrith Prim. Sch.
Pavilion
Bowling Green
Tennis Courts
Oakleigh Park
OAKLEIGH PARK
Focus School
Pavilion Study Centre
Pupil Referral Unit
Oak Hill Campus
Pool
South Barnet
CHASE SIDE

22
HADLEY ROAD
Camlet Moat
Park Farm
Park Farm Cottages
Reservoir
ENFIELD CHASE
Parkside Farm
Pumping Station
Obelisk
Moat Wood
Picnic Area
Camlet Hill
Ride Wood
Vicarage Farm
Wolverton
RIDGE ROAD
Kingfisher Ct.
TRENT PARK (COUNTRY PARK)
Leeging Beech Gutter
Salmon's Brook
Fish Pond
Icehouse Wood
Williams Wood
Hog Hill
Fish Pond
Noddins Well
Hall
College Ho.
Shaws Wood Cottages
Shaws Wood
Trent Park
Lodge
The Rookery
Rookery Cotts.
Miniature Rifle Range
Brook
Merryhills
Southgate Hockey Centre
Sports Ground
Hockey Pitches
TRENT PARK GOLF COURSE
Merryhills Brook
Church Wood
Snakes Lane
EN4
Triangular Wood
Trent Park Stables
ENFIELD ROAD A110
Driving Range
East Pole Cottages
Club Ho.
Lodge
Depot
Westpole Avenue
Play Fld.
Southgate Sch. & Sports Cen.
Oakwood
Bramley Road
Sussex Way
Chickenshed Theatre
Bramley Sprts. Grd.
De Bohun Prim. Sch.
Saracens Amateur Rugby Football Club
Club Ho.
Addison Ho. (PRU)
Masefield Avenue
Merrivale
Fairway
Cowper Gardens
Chase Side
Green Road
Merryhills Drive
Lonsdale Drive
Brayton Gdns.
Highlands Village
Nursing Home
Superstore
Chaseville Park Rd.
Prim. Sch.
Boxer's Lake
North Drive
Glenbrook S.
Silverdale
Roundhill Dr.
Rushey Hill
Trent Gdns
Oakwood Park
OAKWOOD
Yacht Pond
Ten. Cts.
N14
Oakwood Park Road
Oakwood Crescent
Prim. Sch.
Syn.
Orchard Av.
Osidge Lane
B1453
A111
Superstore
Leisure Cen.
Osidge Prim. Sch.
Waggon Mews
32
Southgate
Southgate Circus
The Bourne
Winchmore Hill Road
Grovelands Park
Bowling Green
Pav.
Tennis Courts
Boating Lake
North London Priory Hosp.
Queen Elizabeth's Dr.
Manor Dr.
Cecil Road
Woodlands
Shamrock Way
Burleigh Gardens
Monkfrith Way
Brookside
Friars Walk
Oak Hill
Mayfair Ter.
Ivy Road
Park Road
Hounsden Road
Eversley Park Road
Stangate Lodge
The Birches
Holly Hill
Willow Wlk.
A

23
FORTY HILL
CHASE FARM HOSPITAL
CEMETERY
Gordon Hill
Chase Side
A1005
RIDGEWAY
SLADES HILL
WINDMILL A110 HILL
World's End
Highlands School
ENFIELD GOLF COURSE
Club House
Moat
Enfield Chase
CHURCH ST.
SOUTHBURY ROAD
A110
Enfield Town
ENFIELD TOWN
Enfield Grammar School (Lower)
Chase Green
Town Park
New River (old course)
Chace Com. Sch. & Spts. Cen.
St. Michael's Hosp.
ENFIELD
EN1
EN2
LONDON ROAD A105
GRANGE PARK
Grange Park
Grange Park Prim. Sch.
BUSH HILL PARK GOLF COURSE
Bush Hill
BUSH HILL PARK
Bush Hill Park
N21
WINCHMORE HILL
Winchmore Hill
RIDGE A105 AV.
VILLAGE RD.
GREEN LANES
CHURCH ST. B154
N9
Hazelwood Sports Club
Aspire Sport & Fitness Cen.
The Paulin Ground
GT. CAMBRIDGE RD. A10
24
33
1
2
3
4
5
6
7
F
G
H
J
K

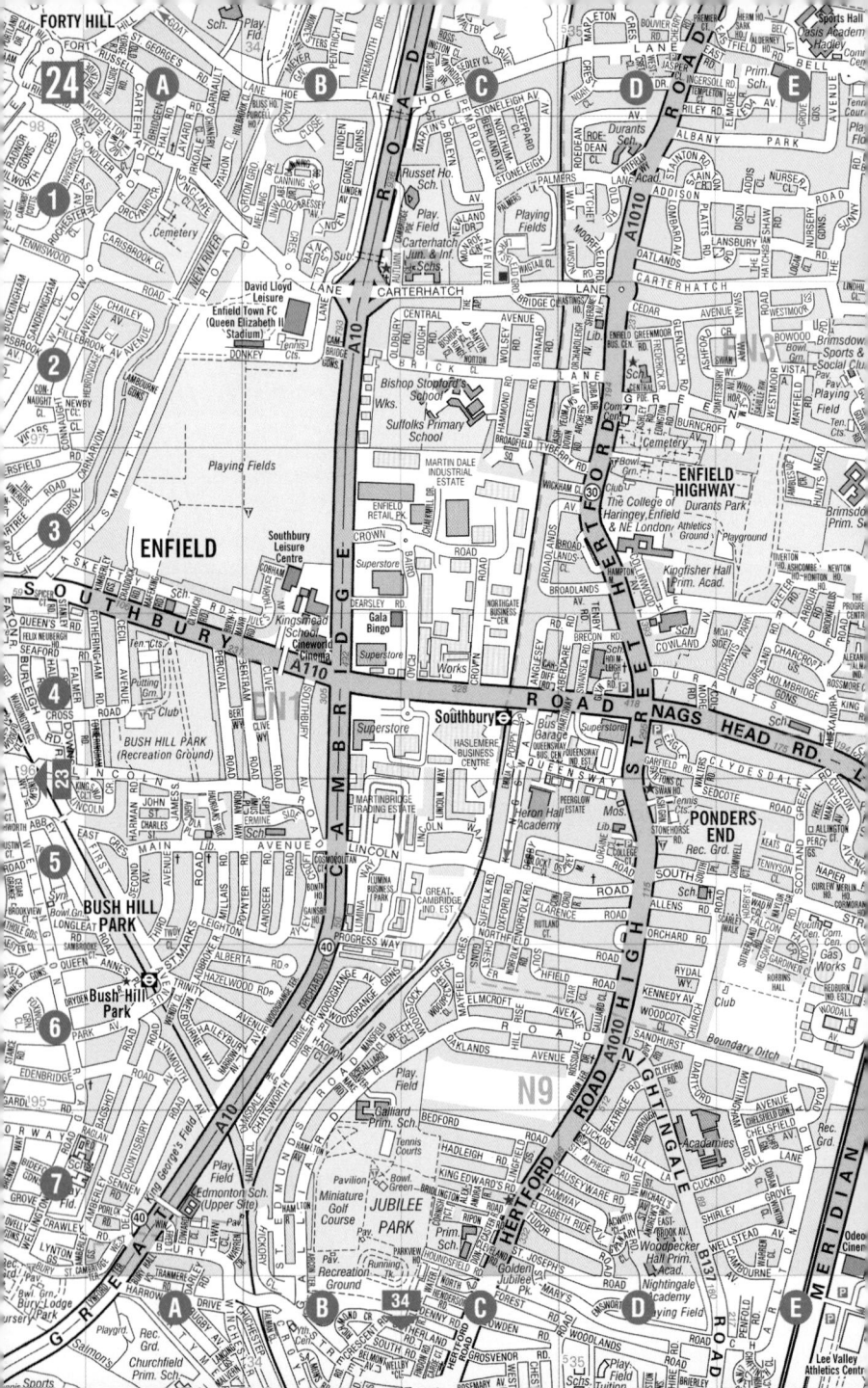

24
FORTY HILL
A
B
C
D
E
1
2
3
4
5
6
7
98
97
96
195
59
Oasis Academy Hadley
Sports Hall
Cemetery
CARTERHATCH LANE
David Lloyd Leisure
Enfield Town FC (Queen Elizabeth II Stadium)
Playing Fields
Russet Ho. Sch.
Carterhatch Jun. & Inf. Schs.
Durants Sch.
Bishop Stopford's School
Suffolks Primary School
MARTIN DALE INDUSTRIAL ESTATE
ENFIELD RETAIL PK.
Superstore
Gala Bingo
Cineworld Cinema
Kingsmead School
Southbury Leisure Centre
ENFIELD
SOUTHBURY ROAD
A110
A10
A1010
GREAT CAMBRIDGE ROAD
HERTFORD ROAD
HIGH STREET
NAGS HEAD RD.
Southbury
HASLEMERE BUSINESS CENTRE
MARTINBRIDGE TRADING ESTATE
LUMINA BUSINESS PARK
GREAT CAMBRIDGE IND. EST.
Heron Hall Academy
PEERGLOW ESTATE
ENFIELD HIGHWAY
The College of Haringey, Enfield & NE London
Durants Park
Athletics Ground
Kingfisher Hall Prim. Acad.
Brimsdown Sports & Social Club
EN3
EN1
N9
PONDERS END
Rec. Grd.
BUSH HILL PARK
(Recreation Ground)
Bush Hill Park
Putting Grn.
PROGRESS WAY
Galliard Prim. Sch.
JUBILEE PARK
Miniature Golf Course
Recreation Ground
Edmonton Sch. (Upper Site)
King George's Field
Bury Lodge Park
Churchfield Prim. Sch.
Golden Jubilee Pk.
Woodpecker Hall Prim. Acad.
Nightingale Academy
Academies
Boundary Ditch
Gas Works
MERIDIAN
Odeon Cinema
Lee Valley Athletics Centre
B137
23
34
40
30

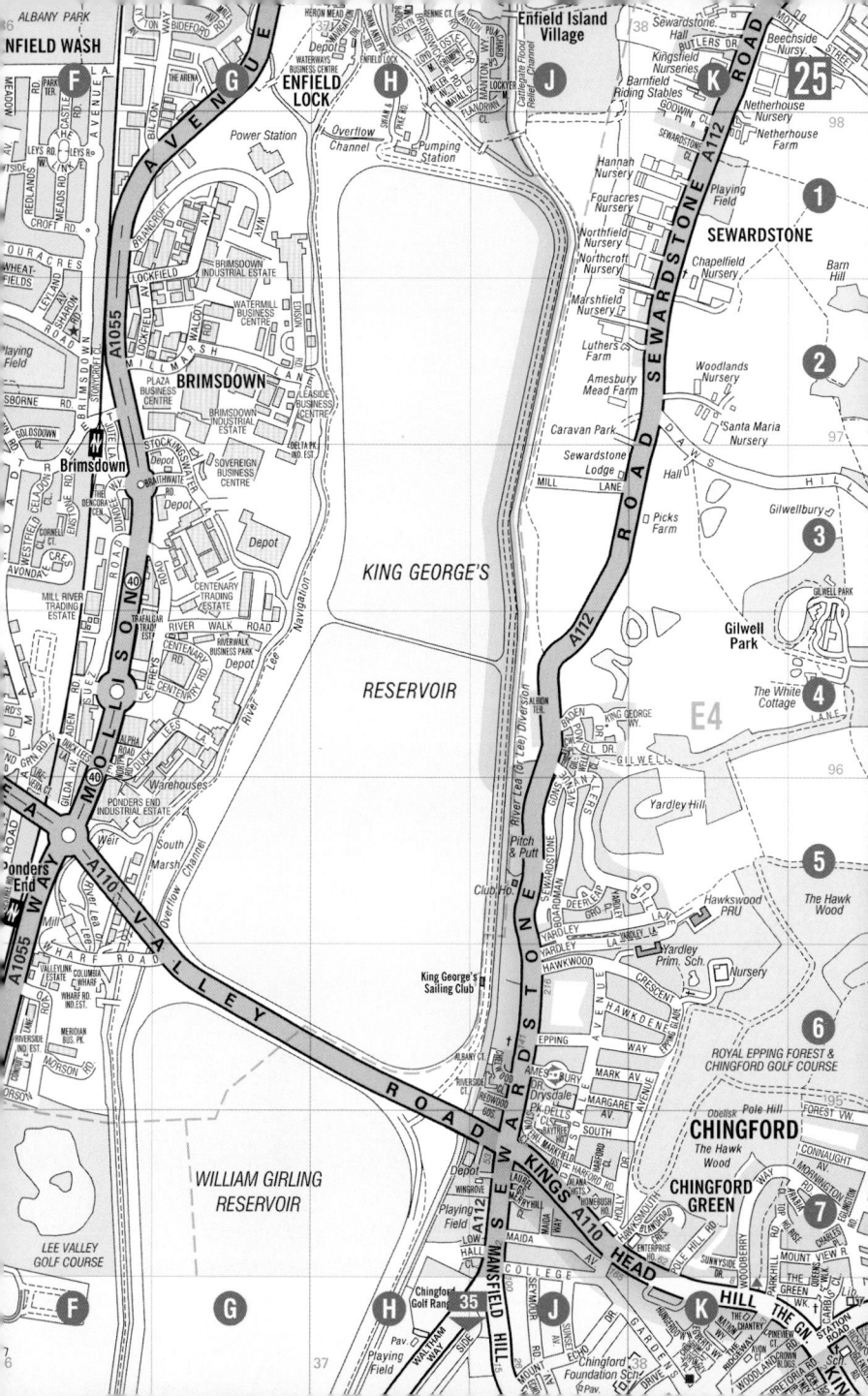

25
ENFIELD WASH
ALBANY PARK
ENFIELD LOCK
Enfield Island Village
Power Station
BRIMSDOWN
Brimsdown
SEWARDSTONE
KING GEORGE'S RESERVOIR
WILLIAM GIRLING RESERVOIR
LEE VALLEY GOLF COURSE
Ponders End
Gilwell Park
E4
CHINGFORD
CHINGFORD GREEN
ROYAL EPPING FOREST & CHINGFORD GOLF COURSE
SEWARDSTONE ROAD
MOLLISON AVENUE
LEA VALLEY ROAD
KINGS HEAD HILL
MANSFIELD HILL
A1055
A112
A110
35

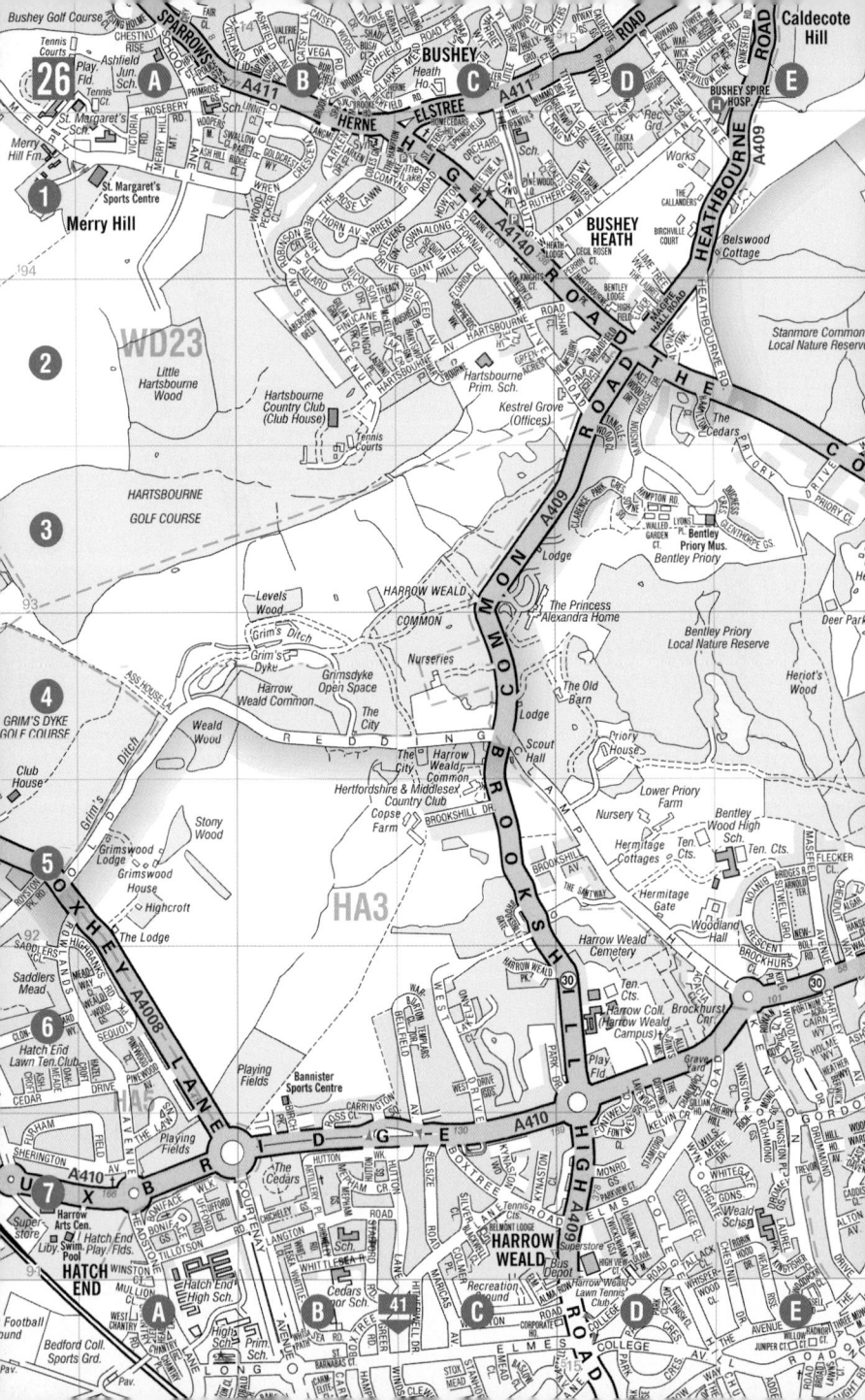
26
Bushey Golf Course
Merry Hill
BUSHEY
Caldecote Hill
BUSHEY HEATH
Bushey Spire Hosp.
WD23
Little Hartsbourne Wood
Hartsbourne Country Club (Club House)
Hartsbourne Prim. Sch.
HARTSBOURNE GOLF COURSE
Stanmore Common Local Nature Reserve
Bentley Priory Mus.
Bentley Priory
HARROW WEALD COMMON
The Princess Alexandra Home
Bentley Priory Local Nature Reserve
Grimsdyke Open Space
GRIM'S DYKE GOLF COURSE
Hertfordshire & Middlesex Country Club
HA3
Harrow Weald Cemetery
Harrow Coll. (Harrow Weald Campus)
Bannister Sports Centre
HA5
HATCH END
HARROW WEALD
Hatch End High Sch.
Cedars Manor Sch.
Bedford Coll. Sports Grd.
41

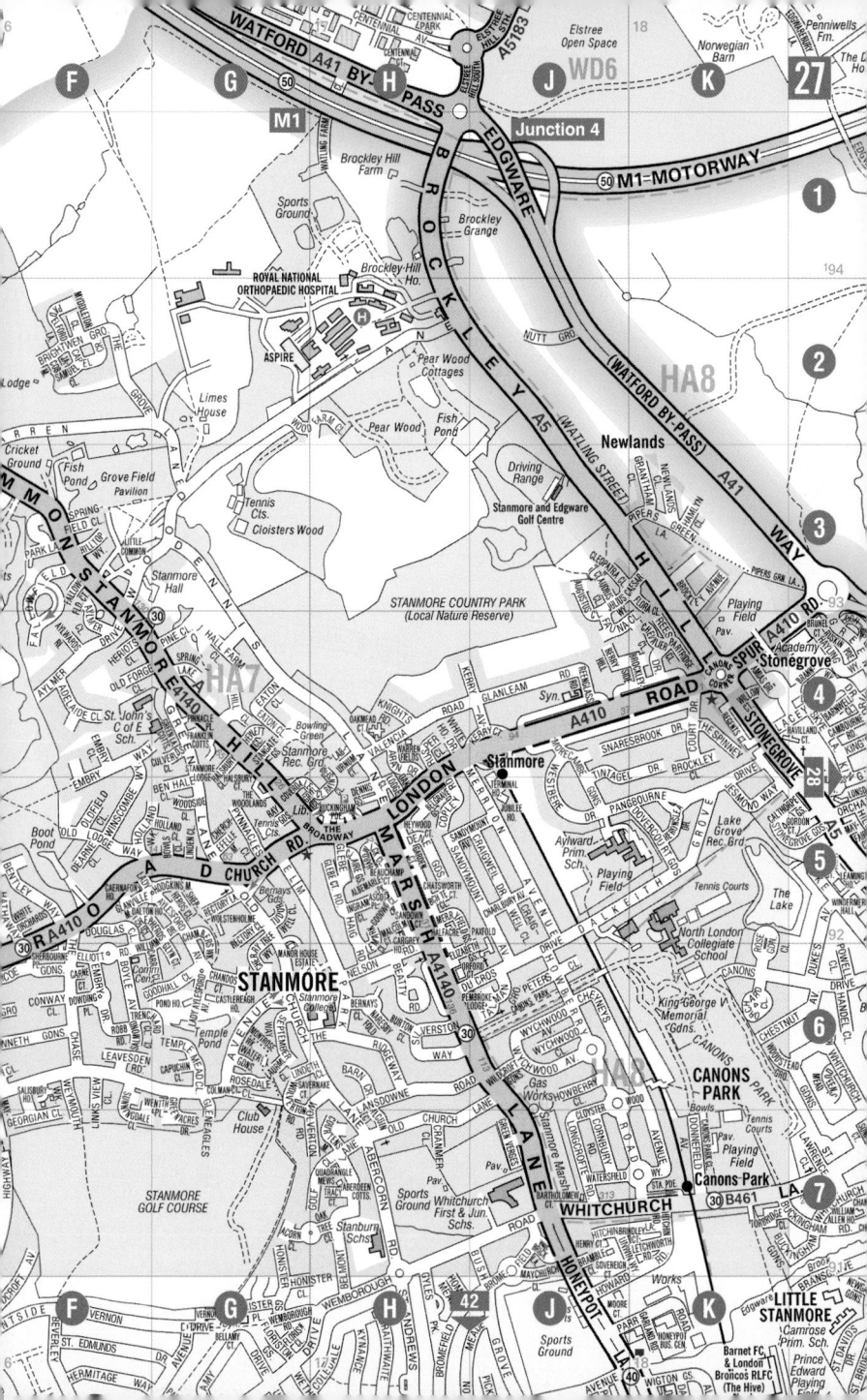

27
WATFORD A41 BY-PASS
M1
Junction 4
M1-MOTORWAY
EDGWARE
BROCKLEY HILL
Brockley Hill Farm
Brockley Grange
Sports Ground
ROYAL NATIONAL ORTHOPAEDIC HOSPITAL
Brockley Hill Ho.
ASPIRE
Pear Wood Cottages
Pear Wood
Fish Pond
Limes House
Cricket Ground
Grove Field Pavilion
Tennis Cts.
Cloisters Wood
Driving Range
Stanmore and Edgware Golf Centre
Newlands
(WATFORD BY-PASS)
A41
HA8
WD6
Elstree Open Space
Norwegian Barn
Penniwells Fm.
STANMORE COUNTRY PARK
(Local Nature Reserve)
Stanmore Hall
HA7
A5 (WATLING STREET)
A410 RD.
Playing Field
Stonegrove
Academy
A410 ROAD
LONDON RD.
Stanmore
STONEGROVE
28
A5
Bowling Green
Stanmore Rec. Grd.
St. John's C of E Sch.
STANMORE HILL A4140
THE BROADWAY
CHURCH RD.
Lake Grove Rec. Grd
The Lake
Aylward Prim. Sch.
Playing Field
Tennis Courts
North London Collegiate School
King George V Memorial Gdns.
MARSH LANE A4140
STANMORE
Stanmore College
Temple Pond
Gas Works
Stanmore Marsh
CANONS PARK
Canons Park
Club House
STANMORE GOLF COURSE
Sports Ground
Whitchurch First & Jun. Schs.
Stanburn Schs
WHITCHURCH LA.
B461
HONEYPOT LANE
Sports Ground
42
Works
HONEYPOT BUS. CEN.
LITTLE STANMORE
Camrose Prim. Sch.
Barnet FC & London Broncos RLFC (The Hive)
Prince Edward Playing
F
G
H
J
K
1
2
3
4
5
6
7

WD6
M1 MOTORWAY
M1
Penniwells Farm
The Dower Ho.
Boys Hill Wood
Thistle Wood
Scratchwood Open Space
Depot
Bury Farm
Edgware Bury
Gate Cottages
Nursery Cottage
London Gateway Service Area
Clump of Trees Wood
MILL HILL GOLF COURSE
Edgwarebury Cemetery
Playing Field
Sports Grd.
Tennis Courts
Broadfields Prim. Sch.
Hemmings Wood
Stoney Wood Lake
Stoney Wood
Fairway Prim. Sch.
Northway Sch.
EDGWAREBURY PARK
Tennis Courts
Pav.
Playground
A41
A410
EDGWARE WAY (WATFORD BY-PASS)
London Academy
Stonegrove
St. Mary's Convent
HA8
A5100
SELVAGE LANE
A5109
HALE LANE
The Hale
Lake Grove Rec. Grd.
The Lake
Stonegrove Park
Tennis Courts
STONEGROVE
HIGH STREET
STATION RD.
Lib.
Edgware
Edgware Bus Sta.
PureGym
Bus Depot
BROADWALK SHOPPING CENTRE
EDGWARE
The Basin
CANONS PARK
Tennis Courts
Playing Field
WHITCHURCH B461
Mill Hill Old Railway Nature Reserve
Schools
DEANS LANE
DEANSBROOK RD.
BURNT OAK
EDGWARE COMM. HOSP.
NHS Walk-in
Watling
WATLING PARK
Sports Ground
Chandos Recreation Grd.
Woodlands Sch.
Camrose Prim. Sch.
LITTLE STANMORE
Prince Edward Playing Field
Barnet FC & London Broncos RLFC (The Hive)
BROADWAY
Burnt Oak
Prim. Sch.
Sports
27
43

29
Totteridge Park Open Space
Hendon Wood Lane Open Space
Moat Mount Open Space
Totteridge Fields Local Nature Reserve
TOTTERIDGE COMMON
HIGHWOOD HILL
Highwood Hill
THE RIDGEWAY
MILL HILL
Mill Hill Broadway
MILL HILL CIRCUS
APEX CORNER
Arrandene Open Space
Featherstone Hill
National Centre for Medical Research
Mill Hill School
Mill Hill Cemetery
Copthall Leisure Centre
Saracens RFC (Allianz Park)
BARNET COPTHALL SPORTS CENTRE
HENDON GOLF COURSE
FIVEWAYS CORNER
Junc. 2
44
30
M1-MOTORWAY
WATFORD WAY
Grahame Park

30
A
B
C
D
E
1
2
3
4
5
6
7
20
29
45
Playing Field
Recreation Ground
Oaklands Rd.
Pavilion
Brook Farm Open Space
Hall
South Herts Golf Course
Fairlight Cottage
Hillsborough Cottage
Totteridge Common
Totteridge
A5109
Redings
Hillsdown
Montebello
Burnhams
Chestnut Cottages
The Warren
Wykeham Rise
Grange Avenue
Horseshoe La.
Chestnut La.
Lime Gro.
Priory Cl.
White Orchards
Barnet La.
The Pastures
Pine Grove
Barnwood Cl.
Northcliffe Drive
Harmsworth Way
Club House
Sports Grd.
Ten. Cts.
Links Dr.
Belmont Cl.
Rowben Cl.
West Hill Way
Great Bushey Dr.
Oak Tree Dr.
Totteridge Village
Crescent
N20
Greenway
The Close
Prim. Sch.
Waverley
Windyridge
Dell House
The Croft
Totteridge Green
Willow End
Cricket Ground
Green Way
Coppice Wlk.
South Way
Lynton
Ventnor
Mead
Longland Drive
Dollis Brook
Riverside
Folly Brook & Darland's Lake Nature Reserve
Laurel Farmhouse
Laurel Way
Woodridge Prim. Sch.
Chiddingfold
Northiam
Folly Farm
Burtonhole Lane Farm Estate
Sports Ground
Cricket Club
Pav.
Nursery
Burtonhole Farm
Burtonhole Lane
Hillview Rd.
Eleanor Cres.
Arlington
Framfield Cl.
Southover
Shortgate
Michleham Down
Woodside Park Club
Tennis Courts
Club Ho.
Sports Ground
Tillingham Way
Folly Brook
Chanctonbury Way
Woodside Park
Pyecombe Corner
Cissbury Ring North
Singleton Scarp
Mill Hill Sub. Sta.
London Equestrian Centre
Frith Manor Ho.
Lullington Garth
Oakfield House
NW7
Wentworth Hall
The Ridgeway
Partingdale Manor
Partingdale Lane
Works
Watch Tower House
Frith Manor Prim. Sch.
Offham Slope
Wolstonbury
Sussex Ring
Argyle Rd.
Saddlescombe Way
Poynings Way
Folkington Corner
Steynings Way
Frith Br.
Alexandra
Bittacy Park Av.
Bittacy Hill
Bittacy Rise
Maurice
Browne Av.
Darlot Dr.
Thirleby
Inglis Barracks
Curry Rd.
Finchley Golf Course
Lovers Walk
Linkside
Brookside
Westbury
Courthouse Gdns.
Nether St.
Hillcourt Av.
Rushden Gdns.
Woodcote
Avenue
Engel Park
Bittacy Hill Park
Ten. Cts.
Playgrd.
B552
Prim. Sch.
Royal Engineers Way
Mill Hill East
Bittacy Business Centre
Virgin Active Superstore
Nether Court Club House
Dollis Brook
West Finchley
Jun. & Inf. Schs.
Sanders La.
Tavistock
Devonshire Rd.
Club House
Aberdare Gdns.
Oakhampton Rd.
Ashley Walk
Lee Rd.
Vineyard Av.
Holders Hill Circus
Abercorn Rd.
Dollis Road
B1462
Sikh Cen.
Prim. Sch.
Lansdowne Rd.
Grosvenor Rd.
Eversleigh Rd.
Elm Park Rd.
Gordon Rd.
Hendon Crematorium
Hendon Cemetery
Hendon Golf Course
Shaftesbury Barnet Harriers
Holders Hill Rd.
Playing Fields
Poolside Manor
Finchley Manor Club
Tennis Courts
Nether St.
Ballards La.
A598
Finchley
N3
Bowling Green
Tennis Courts
Putting Green
Victoria Park
The Ridgeway
Seymour
Redbourne Av.
Dukes Av.
Church Crescent
Clifton Av.
Finchley

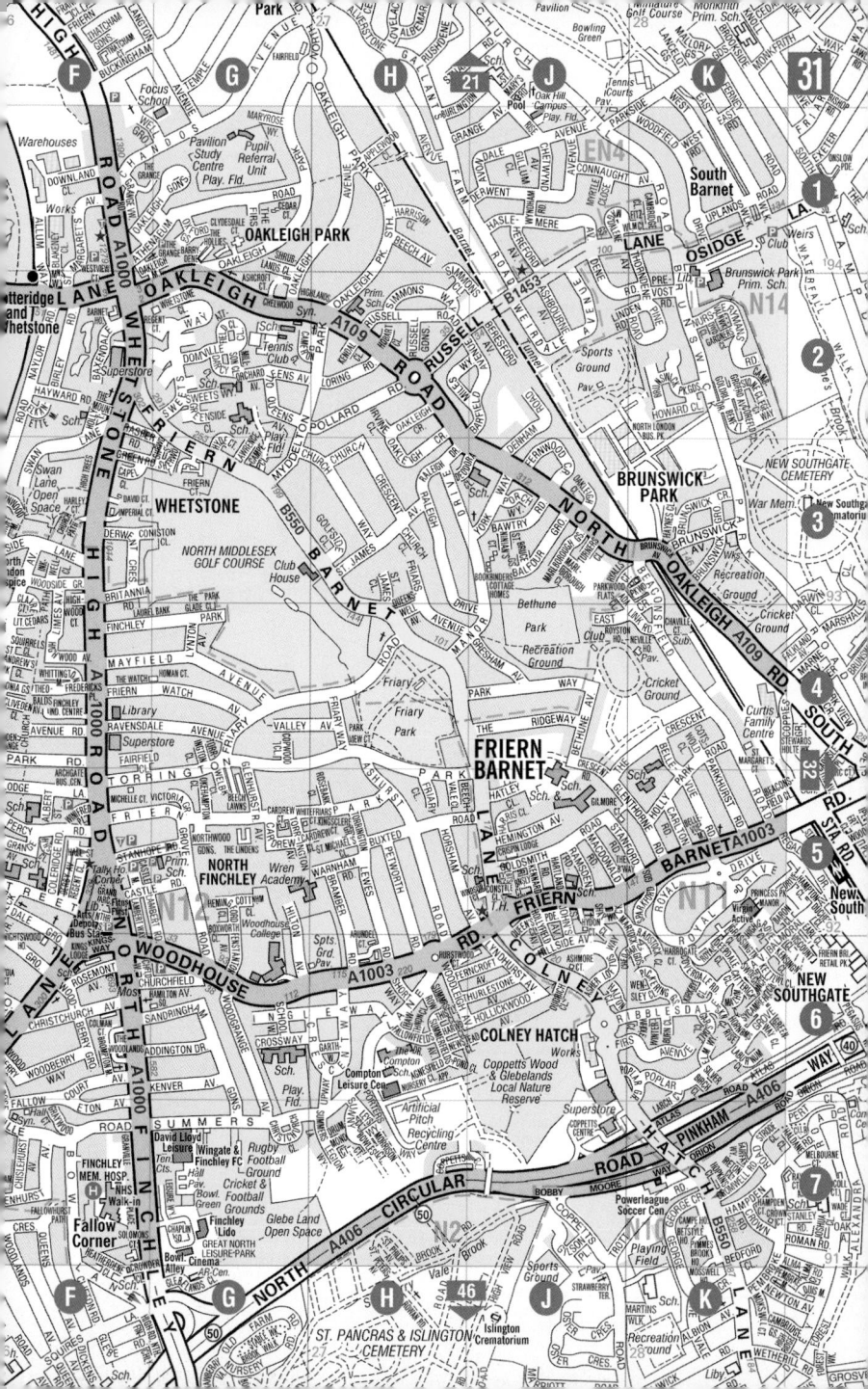
31
OAKLEIGH PARK
WHETSTONE
SOUTH BARNET
BRUNSWICK PARK
FRIERN BARNET
NORTH FINCHLEY
COLNEY HATCH
NEW SOUTHGATE
NORTH MIDDLESEX GOLF COURSE
Friary Park
Bethune Park
Coppetts Wood & Glebelands Local Nature Reserve
Glebe Land Open Space
ST. PANCRAS & ISLINGTON CEMETERY
Islington Crematorium
NEW SOUTHGATE CEMETERY
Fallow Corner
FINCHLEY MEM. HOSP.
21
32
46

32
22
31
47
SOUTHGATE
OSIDGE
NEW SOUTHGATE
N14
N11
N22
GROVELANDS PARK
ARNOS PARK
NEW SOUTHGATE CEMETERY
MUSWELL HILL GOLF COURSE
NORTH LONDON PRIORY HOSPITAL
Southgate
Arnos Grove
Bounds Green
Bowes Park
Palmers Green
New Southgate
CHASE SIDE
HIGH STREET
BOURNE
ALDERMANS HILL
BOWES RD.
BOUNDS GREEN RD.
NORTH CIRCULAR ROAD
WATERFALL RD.
CANNON HILL
TELFORD RD.
Southgate Cricket Club Ground
Broomfield Park
Pymme's Brook
Hollickwood Park
Alexandra Park School
Albert Road Rec. Grd.
CLOCKHOUSE JUNCTION

33
WINCHMORE HILL
Winchmore Hill
PALMERS GREEN
N21
N9
N13
N18
N22
N17
TOTTENHAM
White Hart Lane
23
34
48
A105
A10
A111
A406
A1080
B154
40
50
GREEN LANES
RIDGE AV.
HEDGE LANE
GREAT CAMBRIDGE ROAD
NORTH CIRCULAR ROAD
STERLING WAY
HERTFORD ROAD
WHITE HART LANE
THE ROUNDWAY
FIRS LANE
CHURCH ST.
SILVER STREET
WILBURY WAY
BRIDPORT
PASTEUR GARDENS
PRINCES AVENUE
TOTTENHALL ROAD
DEVONSHIRE HILL LANE
CREIGHTON RD.
LANSBURY AV.
HOLLYWOOD GARDENS
Edmonton Cemetery
Firs Farm Playing Fields
Firs Farm Prim. Sch.
Recreation Ground
The Latymer School
Aylward Academy
West Lea Sch.
Hazelbury Jun. & Inf. Schs.
North Middlesex University Hospital
Great Cambridge Junction
The Paulin Ground
Highfield Sch.
Winchmore Sch.
Sports Cen.
City Amenity Site
Clowes Sports Grd.
Nth. London Hospice
Tatem Rec. Grd.
Pymme's Sports Grd.
Wilbury Prim. Sch.
The Selby Cen.
Tottenham Cemetery
Garden of Peace
White Hart Lane Community Sports Centre
Woodside High Sch. & Riverside Sch.
Bruce Castle Park
Bruce Castle & Haringey Mus.
Aspire Sport & Fitness Cen.
Bury Lodge Park
Salmon's Brook
Starks Field Prim. Sch.
Superstore
Sports Ground
Playing Fields
Football Ground
New River
Pymme's Brook
F
G
H
J
K
1
2
3
4
5
6
7

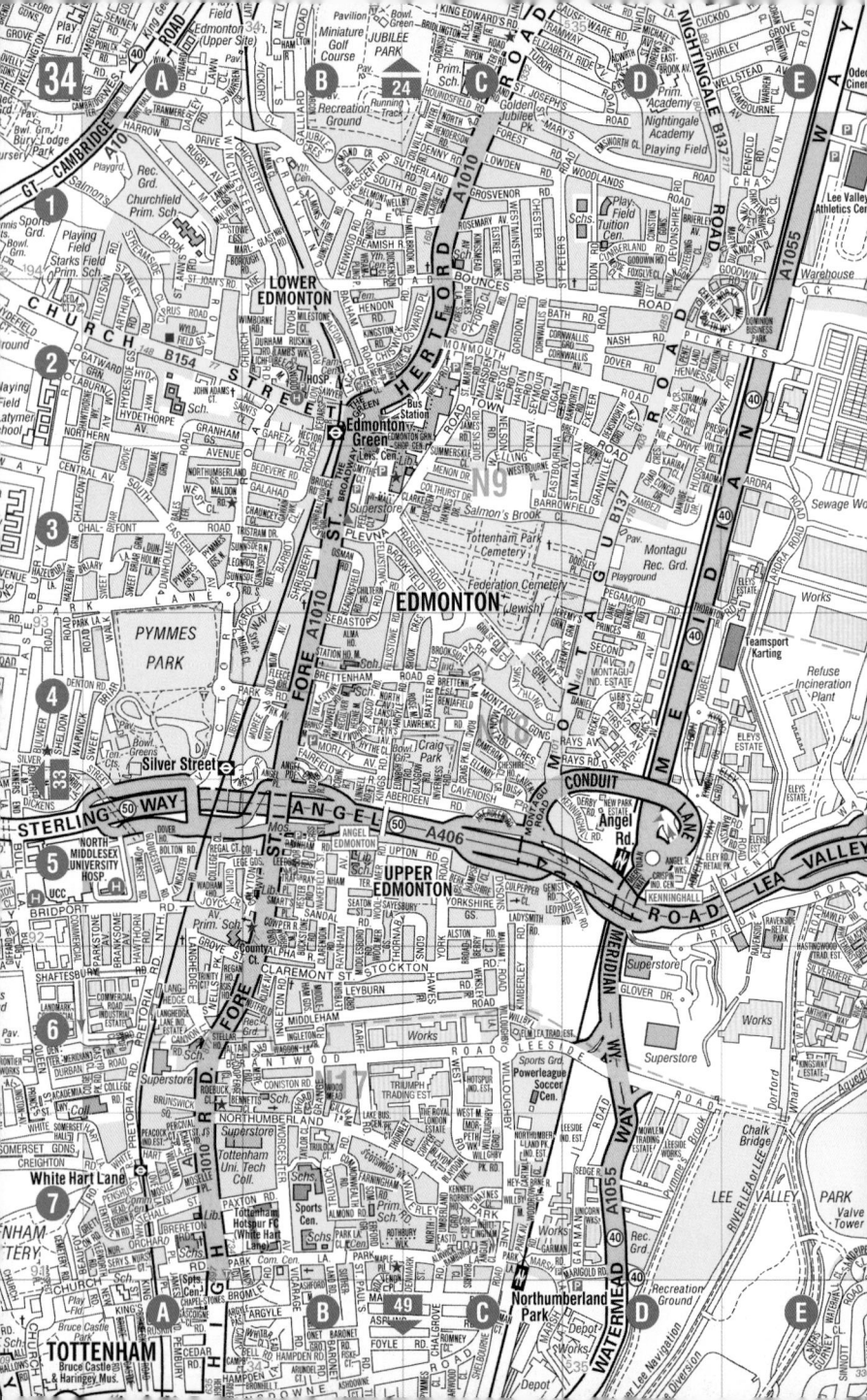

34
A
B
C
D
E
1
2
3
4
5
6
7
24
49
33
JUBILEE PARK
Miniature Golf Course
Recreation Ground
Running Track
Edmonton (Upper Site)
Bury Lodge Park
GT. CAMBRIDGE ROAD
A10
Churchfield Prim. Sch.
Playing Field
Starks Field Prim. Sch.
Prim. Academy
Nightingale Academy Playing Field
NIGHTINGALE B137
Golden Jubilee Pk.
Lee Valley Athletics Cen.
A1055
A1010
HERTFORD ROAD
LOWER EDMONTON
CHURCH STREET
B154
Edmonton Green
Bus Station
Leis. Cen.
Superstore
Salmon's Brook
Tottenham Park Cemetery
Federation Cemetery (Jewish)
EDMONTON
N9
N18
N17
Montagu Rec. Grd.
Playground
MONTAGU ROAD
B137
MERIDIAN WAY
Sewage Works
ARDRA ROAD
Teamsport Karting
Refuse Incineration Plant
ELEYS ESTATE
PYMMES PARK
Silver Street
Craig Park
STERLING WAY
ANGEL ROAD
A406
CONDUIT LANE
Angel Rd.
LEA VALLEY ROAD
NORTH MIDDLESEX UNIVERSITY HOSP.
UCC
UPPER EDMONTON
FORE ST.
Superstore
Works
LEESIDE ROAD
Sports Grd.
Powerleague Soccer Cen.
TRIUMPH TRADING EST.
Tottenham Uni. Tech Coll.
Tottenham Hotspur FC (White Hart Lane)
White Hart Lane
HIGH RD.
WATERMEAD WAY
Northumberland Park
Recreation Ground
LEE VALLEY PARK
Valve Tower
Chalk Bridge
RIVER LEA or LEE
Pymme's Brook
TOTTENHAM
Bruce Castle & Haringey Mus.
Bruce Castle Park
Depot

36
35
51
A
B
C
D
E
1
2
3
4
5
6
7
Queen Elizabeth's Hunting Lodge
RANGER'S RD.
The Warren
The Connaught Club
Tennis Courts
Bowl. Grn.
Warren Pond
Barn Hoppet
Albany Ho.
Oak Hall
Chingford
CHINGFORD
STATION ROAD
A1069
THE GN.
KINGS HEAD HILL
KINGS RD.
CHINGFORD GREEN
Cricket Ground
Club
Whitehall Plain
St. John's C of E Prim. School
WHITEHALL RD.
A110
Pimp Hall Nature Reserve
Pimp Hall Park
Friday Hill
Friday Hill Ho.
FRIDAY HILL
B146
Bluehouse Grove
Playing Field
Hatch Forest
Hatch Grove
River Ching
HOLLY HOUSE HOSP.
Reed's Forest
Bancroft's Sch. & Prep. Sch.
Knighton Wood
WOODFORD WELLS
EPPING NEW RD.
A104
HIGH RD.
A121
E4
IG8
LARKSHALL RD.
B160
NEW RD.
HATCH LA.
Football Ground
WOODFORD GOLF COURSE
The Lops
Suffield Hatch
CHINGFORD HATCH
CHINGFORD LANE
A1009
Woodford Side
Woodford Green Prim. Sch.
Club Ho.
Highams Park
The Highams Park
Boating Lake
Sports Ground
HIGHAMS PARK
Highams Pk.
HALE END
Schools
Football Ground
Rugby Football Grd.
Sports Grd.
Woodford High Sch. for Girls
Haven Ho. Hospice
WOODFORD GREEN
Sports Grd.
Club & Pav.
BROADMEAD RD.
Woodford
Woodbridge High Sch.
River Ching
EPPING FOREST
Hotel
St. Aubyn's Sch.
Sports Grd.
WOODFORD NEW RD.
HIGH ROAD WOODFORD GREEN
A1199
SOUTHEND-A406-RD.
Subway
Day Cen.
DERBY ROAD
CHELMSFORD ROAD
CHURCHFIELDS
Rec. Grd.
Junior Sch.
Inf. Sch.
39
40
540

37
F
G
H
J
K
1
2
3
4
5
6
7
Hill Fm.
Linder's Field Local Nature Reserve
Recreation Ground
Playing Field
Roding Valley Meadows Nature Reserve
David Lloyd Leisure
M11
Play. Flds.
Tennis Courts
Sports Ground
Wakes Hall
Club Ho.
The Rodings
RODING LANE
CHIGWELL LANE
LOUGHTON WAY
RODING RD.
B170
IG9
IG10
IG7
Buckhurst Hill
Buckhurst Hill Prim. Sch.
Playing Field
River Roding
Rec. Grd.
Sports Grd.
College
PRINCES WAY
Playground
BUCKHURST HILL
LORD'S BUSHES
M11 MOTORWAY
New Barns Farm
Old Loughtonians Hockey Club
CHIGWELL
Chigwell
LEE GROVE
RISE
BROOK WAY
GREAT OWL RD.
Roding Valley
LUXBOROUGH LANE
Rugby Football Ground
Luxborough
Playing Fields
Club
Chigwell Sewage Works
Playing Fields
West Hatch High School
A113
Club House
CHIGWELL GOLF COURSE
HIGH ROAD
Hill House
Lodge
Convent
St. John's RC Sch.
Sports Grd.
Tennis Courts
Ashton Playing Fields
RODING VALLEY PARK
Sports Ground
Sports Pitch
James Leal Cen.
Ray Park
Woodford Green Athletic Cen.
(Running Track)
Ray Lodge Prim. Sch.
Gas Works
MANOR ROAD
B173
TOMSWOOD ROAD
Kennels
Redbridge Av. Ho.
Sports Ground
Health Club
WOODFORD
Football Grd.
Roding Prim. Sch.
WOODFORD BRIDGE
Repton Park
Hospital Hill Wood
Hospital Hill
Cocked Hat Plantation
Egg Clump
Dartnalls Playing Field
Playing Field
Factory
CHIGWELL ROAD
Sports Ground
Daisy Lake
Cemetery
Cuthbert Lake
Ash Plantation
52
Wynn Bridge
RODING VALLEY PARK
Works
AVENSBOURNE

38
HAREFIELD
UB9
Shepherds Hill Farm
Shepherds Hill House
Battlers Wells Wood
Furzefield
Deadman's Grove
Ashain Spring
Scarlet Spring
Kiln Pond
Claypits
Knightscote Farm
Dell
Raveners Spring
Badminton Shooting Ground
Bourne Farm
Middle Lodge
Warren Farm
BAYHURST WOOD COUNTRY PARK
Willow Tree Farm
Willow Tree Centre
NORTH RIDING WOOD
MAD BESS WOOD
YOUNG WOOD
Mad Bess Wood Cottage
RUISLIP COMMON
Breakspear Crematorium (Ruislip)
Football Ground
Playing Field
Duck's Hill Farm
Ducks Hill Grange
Duck's Hill
Ashby Cottages
Ashby Farm
Youngwood Farm
COPSE WOOD
RUISLIP WOOD (National Nature
DUCK'S HILL ROAD A4180
Lower Lodge
The Bungalow
Dews Fm. Sand Pits Nature Reserve
Highway Farm
Dewes Farm Cottages
Newyears Green Covert
Newyears Green
Pylon Farm
Elm Tree Farm
High View Farm
St. Leonard's Farm
Oak Cottage
Braemar Farm
Crows Nest Farm
Old Clack Farm
The Corner
Tile Kiln
Grays Cottages
Dunster Cottage
Gatemead Farm
Brackenbury Barn
Works
Depot
RUISLIP GOLF COURSE
Playground
Whiteheath Jun. & Inf. Schs.
The Harefield Academy
NEW YEARS GREEN LANE
BREAKSPEAR ROAD
BREAKSPEAR ROAD NORTH
BREAKSPEAR ROAD SOUTH
HAREFIELD ROAD
NORTHWOOD ROAD
FINE BUSH LA.
SKIP LANE
56

39
NORTHWOOD
NORTHWOOD GOLF COURSE
HA6
NORTHWOOD HILLS
The Northwood Club
Club House
Miniature Rifle Range
Northwood FC
Cemetery
HASTE HILL GOLF COURSE
Haste Hill
Poor's Field
Ruislip Lido Railway
Waters Edge
RUISLIP LIDO
Ruislip Lido Woodlands Centre
Woody Bay
PARK WOOD
Grangewood School
Coteford Junior Sch.
RUISLIP WOODS
(National Nature Reserve)
Cannons Bridge Farm
Hillingdon Athletic Club
HA4
Kings College Playing Fields
Eastcote Hockey & Badminton Club
King's Coll. Play. Flds. Track
River Pinn
Winston Churchill Hall
Manor Farm
Church Field Gdns.
Warrender Prim. Sch.
Highgrove Swim. Pool
Bishop Ramsey C of E Sch.
Warrender Park
Ruislip Manor
EASTCOTE
EASTCOTE VILLAGE
Eastcote Ho. Gs.
HA5
Haydon School
Playing Field
Joel Street Farm
White Cottage
Harlyn Primary Sch.
Haydon Hall Pk.
Cricket Grd.
Cuckoo Hill
Northwood Hills
Northwood Sch.
Pinner Wood Sch.
Pinnerwood Park
Nurseries
A404 PINNER ROAD
RICKMANSWORTH ROAD
RICKMANSWORTH RD.
HIGH ST. A4125
JOEL STREET
B472
B466 ROAD
HIGH ROAD
EASTCOTE B466
A4180 HIGH STREET
40
57

40
PINNER HILL GOLF COURSE
Pinnerwood Park
PINNER GREEN
Montesole Play. Flds.
UXBRIDGE ROAD
A404
ST. THOMAS' DR.
GEORGE V AVENUE
HATCH END
Hatch End
A410
Rugby Football Ground
PINNER PARK
Pinner Park Farm
Pinner Lawn Tennis Club
Little Common
Paine's Br.
Cemetery
East End Farm
NHS Walk-in
Hlth. Club
Pinner Village Hall
Pinner Memorial Park
Pinner
PINNER
Reddiford Sch.
West Lodge Prim. Sch.
Nower Hill
Pinner New Cemetery
Nower Hill High Sch.
Woodlands Open Space
Pinner Village Gardens
HA5
HA4
Cuckoo Hill
B466
CUCKOO HILL
RICKMANSWORTH ROAD
HIGH RD.
EASTCOTE
Eastcote
North Harrow
Yeading Brook Open Space
The Croft
Cannon Lane Prim. Sch.
Heathfield Sch. for Girls
Streamside Rec. Grd.
Longfield Prim. Sch.
Roxborough Rough
Roxbourne Park
Rayners Lane
RAYNERS LANE
Sports Ground
Cavendish Recreation Ground
IMPERIAL
ALEXANDRA AV.
A4090
58
39

42
27
41
60
STANMORE GOLF COURSE
WHITCHURCH
Canons Park
BELMONT
HA7
WEALDSTONE
Byron Recreation Ground
Harrow Leisure Centre
Harrow Driving, Cycling and Road Safety Centre
Cemetery
Priestmead Rec. Grd.
Centenary Park
Park High Sch.
Sports Ground
Barnet FC & London Broncos RLFC (The Hive)
The Hive Football Fitness Centre
HA3
KENTON
Kenton Recreation Ground
Elmgrove Prim. Sch.
Glebe Prim. Sch.
St. Luke's Hospice
WOODCOCK PARK
Mt. Stewart Jun. & Inf. Sch.
HA1
Kenton
Northwick Park
University of Westminster (Harrow Campus)
Harrow Sports Hall
NORTHWICK PARK HOSPITAL
ST. MARK'S HOSP.
UCC
HARROW
Harrow School Playing Fields
NORTHWICK PARK
HA9
John Billam Playing Fields
PRESTON
Preston Road
KENTON ROAD
A4006
A4140
HONEYPOT LANE
WATFORD ROAD
A404
STREATFIELD AVENUE
KENTON LANE
WOODCOCK HILL
CHRISTCHURCH AVENUE
KENMORE AVENUE
Driving Range

43
BURNT OAK
EDGWARE COMM. HOSP.
28
NHS Walk-in
Watling
WATLING PARK
LITTLE STANMORE
Chandos Recreation Grd.
Burnt Oak
HA8
Sports Ground
Prim. Sch.
Schools
Canons High Sch.
Prince Edward Playing Field
MOLLISON
QUEENSBURY
Queensbury
Warehouse
Superstore
A4140
Queensbury Park
Rec. Grd.
Kingswood Centre
Eton Grove Open Space
BROADWAY
EDGWARE
A5
Silk Stream Park
Montrose Recreation Ground
Elysian House
National Blood Service
COLINDALE
European Business Centre
Colindale Business Park
Superstore
Mecca Burnt Oak
Sikh Tem.
Roe Green
NW9
COLINDEEP LA.
Colindale Ret. Pk.
Kingsbury High Sch.
Roe Grn. Jun. & Inf. Sch.
Play. Fld.
Kingsbury Manor
Roe Green Park
Kingsbury Manor Studio
Pupil Referral Unit
Comm. Cen.
44
Playground
Buddhist Cen.
KINGSBURY
Kingsbury
KINGSBURY CIRCLE
Fitness First
AR Centre
ROAD
A4006
Recreation Ground
Kingsbury Grn. Prim. Sch.
St. Robert Southwell RC Prim. Sch.
Sports Ground
JFS School
Sch.
Spts. Grd.
Kingsbury Green
B454
CHURCH
Silver Jubilee Park
Kingsbury Town FC Grd.
KINGSBURY
FRYENT COUNTRY PARK (Local Nature Reserve)
Barn Hill Open Space
Barn Hill
HA9
61
Field Study Centre
Woodfield Sch.
Nursery
F
G
H
J
K
1
2
3
4
5
6
7
19
20
21
88
89
90
91

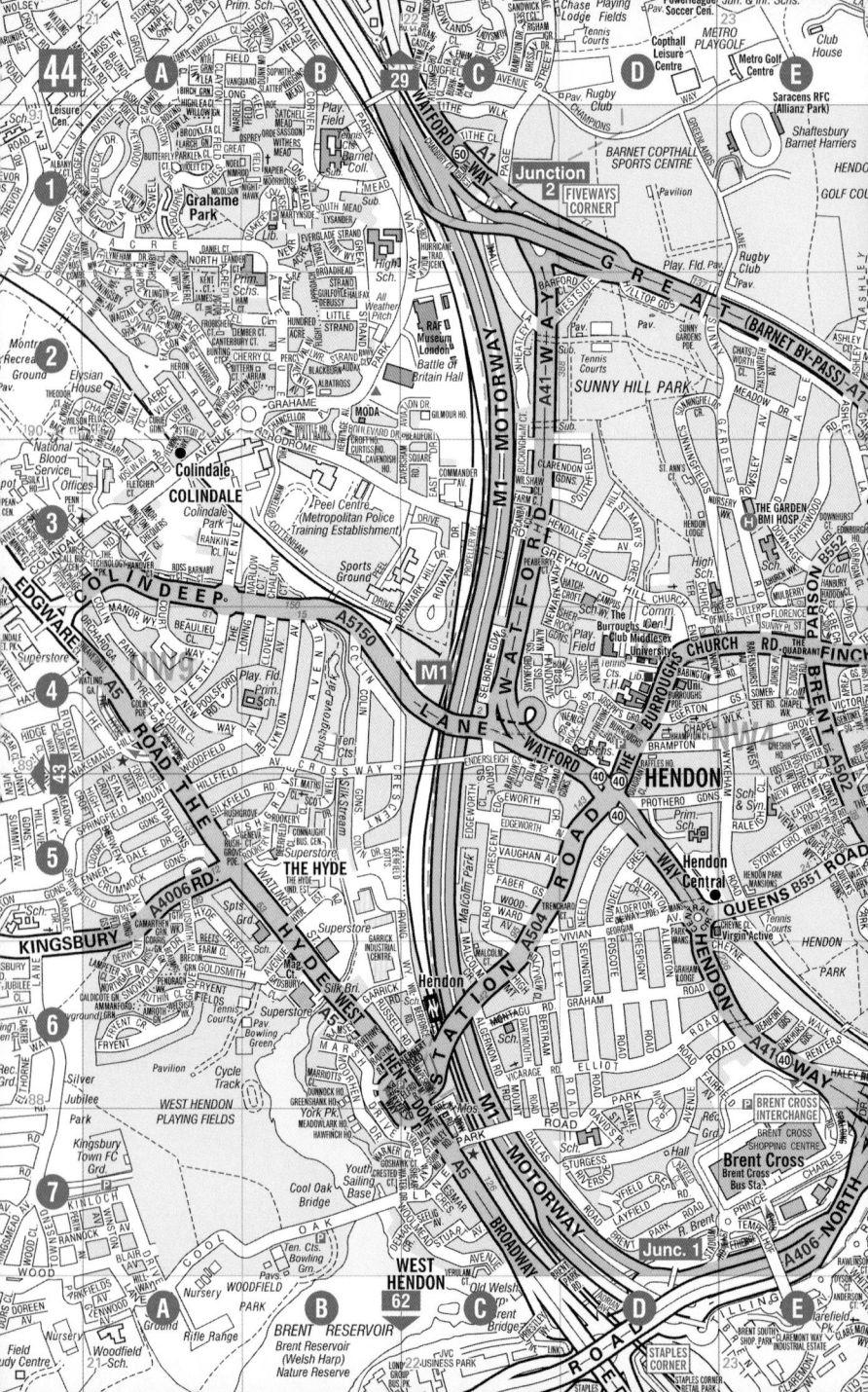

44
A
B
C
D
E
1
2
3
4
5
6
7
29
Junction 2
FIVEWAYS CORNER
Chase Lodge Playing Fields
Powerleague Soccer Cen.
Copthall Leisure Centre
METRO PLAYGOLF
Metro Golf Centre
Club House
Saracens RFC (Allianz Park)
Shaftesbury Barnet Harriers
BARNET COPTHALL SPORTS CENTRE
Rugby Club
Pavilion
HENDON GOLF CLUB
GREAT (BARNET BY-PASS) A1
WATFORD WAY A1
Grahame Park
Leisure Cen.
Barnet Coll.
High Sch.
All Weather Pitch
RAF Museum London
Battle of Britain Hall
SUNNY HILL PARK
Tennis Courts
MODA
GRAHAME PARK WAY
AERODROME
Colindale
COLINDALE
Colindale Park
National Blood Service Offices
Peel Centre (Metropolitan Police Training Establishment)
Sports Ground
COLINDEEP LANE
A5150
M1
M1 MOTORWAY
A41 WATFORD WAY
EDGWARE ROAD
A5
THE HYDE
NW9
Rushgrove Park
Silk Stream
Superstore
GARRICK INDUSTRIAL CENTRE
Hendon
KINGSBURY RD. A4006
WEST HENDON PLAYING FIELDS
Silver Jubilee Park
Kingsbury Town FC Grd.
Cycle Track
Pavilion
Cool Oak Bridge
Youth Sailing Base
WEST HENDON
62
BRENT RESERVOIR
Brent Reservoir (Welsh Harp) Nature Reserve
Woodfield Park
Rifle Range
Woodfield Sch.
STATION ROAD A504
HENDON
NW4
Hendon Central
QUEENS ROAD B551
The Burroughs
Middlesex University
THE GARDEN BMI HOSP
PARSON STREET B552
BRENT STREET A502
HENDON PARK
Virgin Active
HENDON WAY A41
BRENT CROSS INTERCHANGE
Brent Cross
BRENT CROSS SHOPPING CENTRE
Brent Cross Bus Sta.
Junc. 1
NORTH CIRCULAR ROAD A406
BROADWAY
STAPLES CORNER
Claremont Way Industrial Estate
Brent South Shop. Park

45
F
G
H
J
K
30
63
46
1
2
3
4
5
6
7
FINCHLEY
Finchley Central
Hendon Crematorium
HENDON CEMETERY
Holders Hill
CHURCH END
Poolside Manor
Finchley Manor Club
Windsor Open Space
Playing Fields
Avenue House Grounds
Sports Ground
The Sternberg Centre
The Academy
PureGym
St. Marylebone Crematorium
EAST FINCHLEY CEMETERY
Christ's College Finchley
Pentland Centre
Victoria Park
HENLYS CORNER
College Farm
Temple Fortune
Little Wood
Big Wood
Willifred Green
Princes Park
Jewish Cemetery
Golders Green Crematorium
GOLDERS GREEN
Golders Green
Brent Cross
HAMPSTEAD
HEATH
Bunkers Hill
Superstores
Leisure Cen.
Curtis & Staub
NW11
NW2
N3
N2
DOLLIS ROAD
HENDON LANE
REGENTS PARK ROAD
BALLARDS LANE
EAST END ROAD
NORTH CIRCULAR ROAD
HENDON WAY
FINCHLEY ROAD
FALLODEN WAY
A1 WAY
GOLDERS GREEN ROAD
NORTH END ROAD
HOLDERS HILL ROAD
A598
A504
A406
A502
A41
A1
B552
B1462

46
A
B
C
D
E
1
2
3
4
5
6
7
31
64
45
26
27
28
Fallow Corner
FINCHLEY MEM. HOSP.
Cricket & Football Grounds
Finchley Lido
Glebe Open Space
GT. NORTH LEISURE PARK
Bowl. Alley
Cinema
N12
N3
N2
N6
NW11
NORTH CIRCULAR ROAD
A406
HIGH RD. NTH. FINCHLEY-A1000
HIGH ROAD
EAST END ROAD
A504
EAST FINCHLEY
ST. PANCRAS & ISLINGTON CEM.
Islington Crematorium
Muswell Hill Spts. Grd.
COLDFALL WOOD
Coldfall Prim. Sch.
Martin Prim. Sch.
Eden Prim. Sch.
Fortismere Sch. (North Wing)
Fortismere Sch. (South Wing)
FORTIS GREEN
Powerleague Soccer Cen.
BOBBY MOORE WAY
Recreation Ground
Playing Field
Sports Ground
EAST FINCHLEY CEMETERY
St. Marylebone Crem.
Oak Lodge Sch.
LYTTELTON ROAD
A1
AYLMER ROAD
GREAT NORTH RD.
A1000
Cherry Tree Wood
Rec. Grd.
East Finchley
HAMPSTEAD GARDEN SUBURB
Playing Fields
HIGHGATE WOOD
Stormont Lawn Tennis & Squash Club
ARCHWAY ROAD
HIGHGATE GOLF COURSE
Club House
HIGHGATE
HIGHGATE HOSPITAL
Mallinson Sports Centre
Highgate School Playing Field
HAMPSTEAD GOLF COURSE
Bunkers Hill
HAMPSTEAD HEATH
Turners Wood
HAMPSTEAD LANE
B519
North Wood
Kenwood House
Athlone House
The Spaniards
Yth. Hostel
St. James C of E Prim. Sch.
Reservoir
B550
SOUTHWOOD LANE
HIGHGATE

29
30
31
32
47
48
65
F
G
H
J
K
1
2
3
4
5
6
7
MUSWELL HILL GOLF COURSE
Alexandra Park School
Albert Road Rec. Grd.
Club House
DURNSFORD RD.
ALBERT RD.
BOUNDS GREEN RD.
GREEN A109
A105
HIGH ROAD
WOOD GREEN
Wood Green
Alexandra Palace
The Lake
Ice Rink
Pitch & Putt Course
ALEXANDRA PARK
Cricket Ground
Playing Field
Filter Beds
Reservoir
Heartlands High Sch.
Wood-Gn. Common
STATION RD.
MAYES RD.
Gas Works
Depot
Nightingale Gdns.
N22
N10
N8
ALEXANDRA PARK RD.
B106
B550
MUSWELL HILL
Muswell Hill Prim. Sch.
The Grove
A504
PRIORY RD.
HIGH STREET A504
TURNPIKE LA.
Hornsey
HORNSEY
Parkland Walk
Cranley Gardens
QUEEN'S WOOD
PARK RD.
A1201
Park Road Leisure Centre
Hornsey Cricket Club
PRIORY PARK
TOTTENHAM LA.
CHURCH LA.
A103
HORNSEY VALE
Stationers Park
THE BROADWAY
CROUCH END
CROUCH END HILL
CROUCH HILL
Crouch Hill
St. Aloysius College Sports Ground
Coolhurst Club
Reservoirs (covered)
Nature Res.
STROUD GREEN
STROUD GRN. RD.
HORNSEY LANE
HORNSEY RISE
Highgate
HIGHGATE HILL
HIGH ST.
Lauderdale House
HORNSEY ROAD
A1
B540
B138
B151

48
TOTTENHAM
Tottenham Cemetery
Bruce Castle
Bruce Castle & Haringey Mus.
Woodside Pk.
Wood Gn. Cemy.
Woodside Hill & Riverside
Playing Field
Community Sports Centre
Garden of Peace
33
ROUNDWAY
A10
LORDSHIP LANE
A109
THE AVENUE
TOWER GARDENS
WHITE HART LANE
Wood Green
WOOD GREEN
N22
NOEL PARK
A1080
WESTBURY AVENUE
LORDSHIP RECREATION GROUND
Open Air Theatre
Comm. Cen.
The Moselle
Playing Field
BROADWATER FARM ESTATE
Belmont Rec. Grd.
DOWNHILLS WAY
DOWNHILLS PARK
B155
N17
Turnpike La.
A504
TURNPIKE LA.
WIGHTMAN ROAD
GREEN LANES
WEST GREEN
WEST GREEN ROAD
PHILIP LA.
Park View Academy Spts. Cen.
European Coll.
Hornsey
HORNSEY
47
HARRINGAY
Chestnuts Rec. Ground
ST. ANN'S ROAD
B152
ST. ANN'S HOSPITAL
SOUTH TOTTENHAM
N15
Harringay Green Lanes
Railway Fields Local Nature Reserve
GRAND PARADE
A105
B138
Harringay
HERMITAGE ROAD
N4
STROUD GREEN
Stationers Park
Cricket Ground
American Gds.
FINSBURY PARK
Track & Gym
MANOR HO.
Manor House
66
SEVEN SISTERS RD.
A503
AMHURST PARK
A107
Stamford Hill
EAST RESERVOIR
WEST RESERVOIR
Reservoir (covered)
Sir Thomas Abney Prim. Sch.
N16
STROUD GRN. RD.
ENDYMION ROAD
B150
31
32

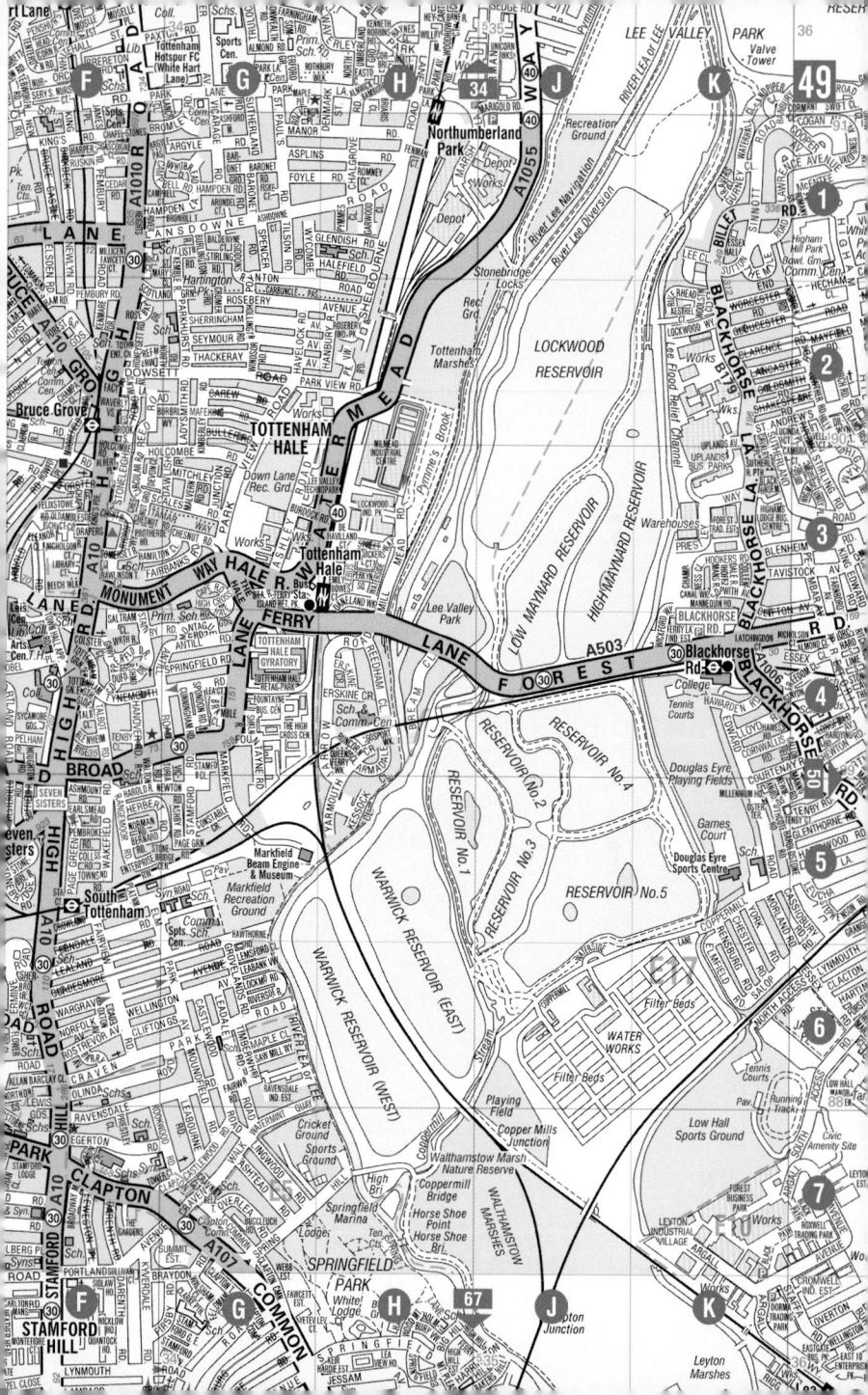

49
50
34
67
F
G
H
J
K
1
2
3
4
5
6
7
LEE VALLEY PARK
Valve Tower
Tottenham Hotspur FC (White Hart Lane)
Northumberland Park
Recreation Ground
River Lee Navigation
River Lee Diversion
Stonebridge Locks
Tottenham Marshes
LOCKWOOD RESERVOIR
LOW MAYNARD RESERVOIR
HIGH MAYNARD RESERVOIR
Lee Flood Relief Channel
Higham Hill Park
TOTTENHAM HALE
Tottenham Hale
Bruce Grove
A1010
A1055
A10
A503
A1006
A107
B179
WATERMEAD WAY
MONUMENT WAY
HALE R.
FERRY LANE
FOREST RD.
BLACKHORSE LA.
BLACKHORSE RD.
Blackhorse Rd.
TOTTENHAM HALE GYRATORY
Lee Valley Park
RESERVOIR No.1
RESERVOIR No.2
RESERVOIR No.3
RESERVOIR No.4
RESERVOIR No.5
WARWICK RESERVOIR (EAST)
WARWICK RESERVOIR (WEST)
Douglas Eyre Playing Fields
Douglas Eyre Sports Centre
Markfield Beam Engine & Museum
Markfield Recreation Ground
South Tottenham
SEVEN SISTERS
Filter Beds
WATER WORKS
E17
E5
E10
Low Hall Sports Ground
Civic Amenity Site
Playing Field
Copper Mills Junction
Walthamstow Marsh Nature Reserve
WALTHAMSTOW MARSHES
Coppermill Bridge
Horse Shoe Point
Springfield Marina
SPRINGFIELD PARK
Clapton Junction
LEYTON INDUSTRIAL VILLAGE
Leyton Marshes
STAMFORD HILL
HIGH ROAD
BROAD LANE
CLAPTON COMMON
STAMFORD HILL

50
BANBURY RESERVOIR
Valve Tower
36
37
38
Driving Range
Playing Field
Sports Ground
Britannia Sports Ground
35
SOUTHEND
A406
Peter May Sports Cen.
A
B
C
D
E
1
2
3
4
5
6
7
BILLET ROAD
B179
CROOKED BILLET
Walthamstow Academy
City Learning Cen.
SOUTHEND
A406
Sports Grd.
CHINGFORD ROAD
A112
FULBOURNE
Waltham Forest FC Ground
Chapel End
Higham Hill Park
Whittingham Prim. Acad.
William Morris Sch.
HIGHAM HILL
LLOYD PARK
Hillyfield Prim. Sch.
Waltham Forest Pool & Track
Chestnuts Sports Ground
WALTHAMSTOW
Town Hall
Civic Cen.
College
THE BELL
FOREST
ROAD
A503
30
THORPE COOMBE HOSP.
HOE ST.
BLACKHORSE
BLACKHORSE RD.
49
ST. JAMES'S ST.
St. James St.
MARKHOUSE
Walthamstow Central
Walthamstow Queens Rd.
Bus Sta.
Queens Road Cemetery
E17
A112
HIGH STREET
A104
ST. JAMES'S PARK
Tennis Courts
Running Track
Hall Ground
Civic Amenity Site
LEYTON LINK ESTATE
Walthamstow Leisure Cen.
A1006
ROAD
LEA BRIDGE ROAD
A104
Playground
Works
ROXWELL TRADING PARK
BOUNDARY
Brooks Farm
Superstore
Lei. Pool
Bus Depot
E10
Leyton Midland Rd.
LEYTON
Leyton Stadium
68
CHURCH RD.
Bingo
Bowls
Tennis Courts
Sports Grd.

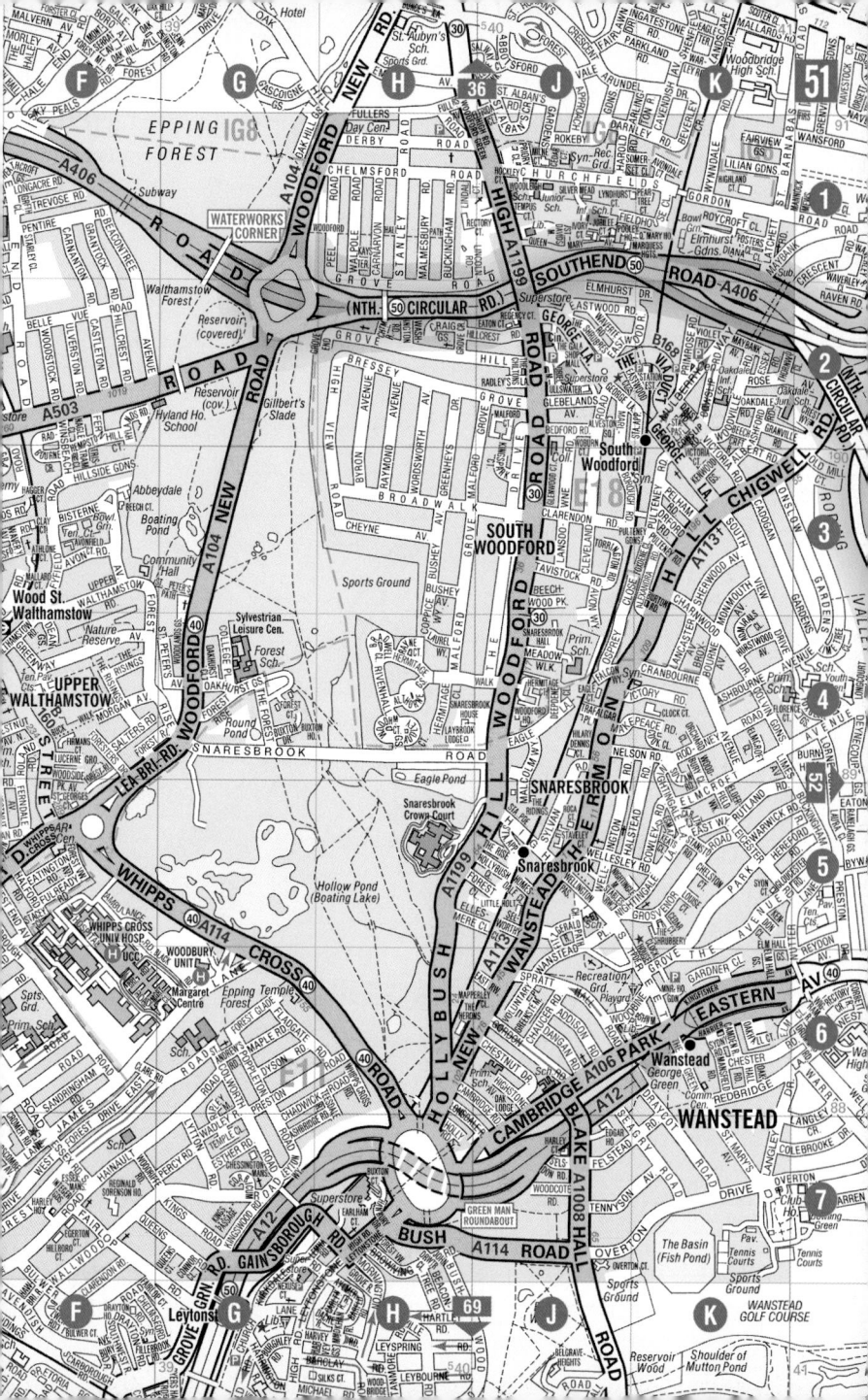
51
52
69
36
F
G
H
J
K
1
2
3
4
5
6
7
EPPING FOREST
IG8
A406
ROAD
WATERWORKS CORNER
A104 WOODFORD NEW RD.
SOUTHEND ROAD A406
(NTH. CIRCULAR RD.)
Walthamstow Forest
Reservoir (covered)
Reservoir (cov.)
A503 ROAD
Hyland Ho. School
Gilbert's Slade
Abbeydale
Boating Pond
Community Hall
Wood St. Walthamstow
Nature Reserve
UPPER WALTHAMSTOW
Sylvestrian Leisure Cen.
Forest Sch.
Round Pond
SNARESBROOK ROAD
Eagle Pond
Snaresbrook Crown Court
Hollow Pond (Boating Lake)
Sports Ground
SOUTH WOODFORD
South Woodford
E18
HIGH ROAD A1199
WOODFORD ROAD
HERMON HILL
SNARESBROOK
Snaresbrook
HOLLYBUSH HILL
NEW WANSTEAD A113
CHIGWELL ROAD A113
WHIPPS CROSS ROAD A114
WHIPPS CROSS UNIV. HOSP.
WOODBURY UNIT
Margaret Centre
Epping Forest
E11
CAMBRIDGE PARK A106
EASTERN AV.
Wanstead
George Green
WANSTEAD
BLAKE HALL ROAD A1008
A12
GREEN MAN ROUNDABOUT
BUSH ROAD A114
GAINSBOROUGH RD.
Leytonstone
The Basin (Fish Pond)
Tennis Courts
Sports Ground
WANSTEAD GOLF COURSE
Reservoir Wood
Shoulder of Mutton Pond
Recreation Grd.
Woodbridge High Sch.
Superstore

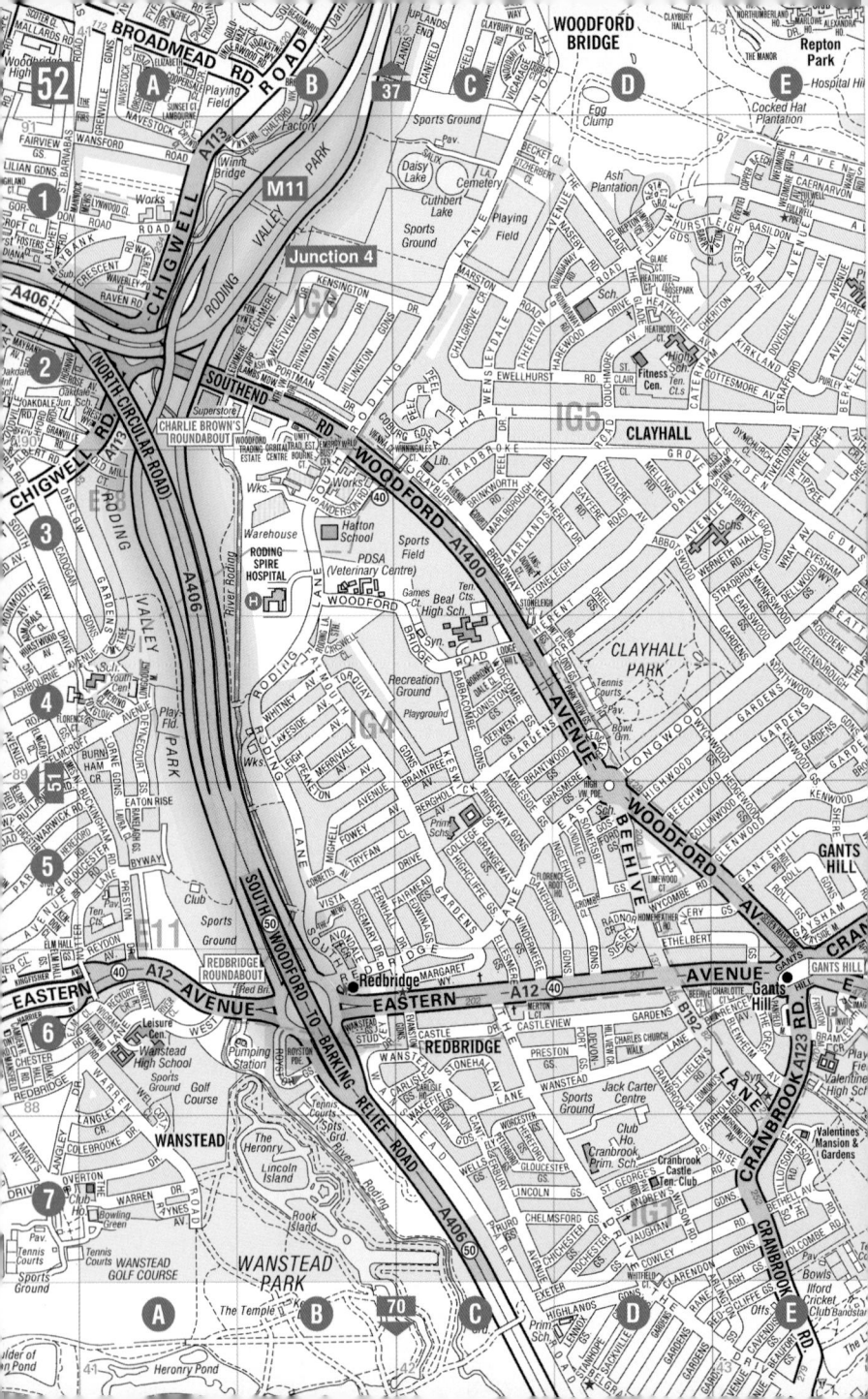

52
37
51
70
WOODFORD BRIDGE
Repton Park
BROADMEAD RD.
M11
Junction 4
CHIGWELL
A406
SOUTHEND RD
WOODFORD A1400
CHARLIE BROWN'S ROUNDABOUT
RODING SPIRE HOSPITAL
Hatton School
Beal High Sch.
CLAYHALL
CLAYHALL PARK
WOODFORD AV.
GANTS HILL
Gants Hill
EASTERN AVENUE
A12
REDBRIDGE ROUNDABOUT
Redbridge
REDBRIDGE
SOUTH WOODFORD TO BARKING RELIEF ROAD
CRANBROOK RD.
A123
Valentines Mansion & Gardens
WANSTEAD
WANSTEAD GOLF COURSE
WANSTEAD PARK
The Heronry
Lincoln Island
Rook Island
Heronry Pond
IG6
IG5
IG4
IG1
E18
E11

53
54
71
F
G
H
J
K
1
2
3
4
5
6
7
44
45
46
91
190
89
88
FAIRLOP
Fairlop
Fairlop Oak Recreation Ground
Hainault Recreation Grd.
NORTH VIEW CARAVAN SITE
Sports Grd.
Tennis Courts
Club House
Playing Field
Powerleague Soccer Cen.
Fairlop Sailing Centre
Fairlop Lake
Slipways
Fairlop Lodge
Forest Farm
Forest Farm Cottages
The Jean Brown Indoor Arena
Ilford & Redbridge Hockey Club
Old Parkonians
Redbridge Sports & Leisure Cen.
Oakfield Playing Field
Golf Driving Range
FAIRLOP WATERS COUNTRY PARK
FAIRLOP WATERS GOLF COURSE
Lagoon
Aldborough Hall Equestrian Centre
PAINTERS ROAD
NORTH ROAD
Aldborough Hall Farm
ALDBOROUGH HATCH
Aldborough Ho. Farm
Aldborough House
FULLWELL CROSS
FENCEPIECE A123
ROAD HIGH
FOREST ROAD
Ilford Jewish Prim. Sch.
King Solomon High Sch.
Fairlop Prim. Sch.
Ilford High Sch.
Avanti Court Primary School
BARKINGSIDE
Barkingside
Redbridge FC (Oakside Stadium)
Barkingside Rec. Grd.
Garden of Rest
Cemetery
Fullwood Prim. Sch.
Superstore
A123
A12
EASTERN AVENUE
NEWBURY PARK
Newbury Park
Oaks Park High Sch.
William Torbitt Prim. Sch.
Bowling Green
Sports Ground
SEVEN KINGS PARK
Skate Park
Farnham Green Prim.
SEVEN KINGS
IG1
IG2
IG3
VALENTINES PARK
Council Depot
High Sch.
Playing Field
HIGH RD.
Cran Brook
CRANBROOK
Hospital Hill

54
53
72
A
B
C
D
E
1
2
3
4
5
6
7
Fairlop Sailing Centre
FAIRLOP WATERS COUNTRY PARK
IG6
IG2
IG3
RM6
RM8
Hainault Works
Farm Cottages
Hainault Farm
Aldborough Hall Farm
ALDBOROUGH HATCH
PAINTERS ROAD
Red House Farm
Hainault House
Willow Farm
Playing Field
Little Heath Sch.
Sports Ground
Marks Gate
Furze Cottage
Furze House Farm
Chadwell Heath Cemetery
EASTERN AVENUE
A12
A118
A1112
WHALEBONE LANE NORTH
KING GEORGE HOSPITAL
GOODMAYES HOSPITAL
North Residence
South Residence
Redbridge College
LITTLE HEATH
ST. CHAD'S PARK
Chadwell Millennium Green
CHADWELL HEATH
HIGH ROAD
BARLEY LANE
Chadwell Heath
Goodmayes
Superstore
GOODMAYES RETAIL PARK
GROVE FARM RETAIL PK.
Mecca Bingo
MIRRAVALE TRADING EST.
Warehouse
Works
Farnham Green Prim. Sch.
Brookside
Skate Park
Games Court
Tennis Courts
Mayfield Sch.

55
Collier Row
Rise Park
Mawney
Romford
Crowlands
Rush Green
Beacontree Heath
RM5
RM1
RM7
Collier Row Lane
Eastern Avenue
London Road
Whalebone Lane
Crow Lane
Rush Green Road
Mawney Road
Havering Road
North Street
Waterloo Rd.
Golf Course
Westlands Playing Field
Romford Cemetery
Crowlands Sports Ground
Crowlands Heath Golf Course
Romford Stadium (Greyhound)
Queen's Hospital
Oldchurch Park
Gas Works
King Georges Field
Cottons Park
Moby Golf
Golf Kingdom
Warren Sports Centre
West Ham FC Training Grd.
St. Edward's C of E Sch.
Crownfield Jun. & Inf. Schs.
The City Pavilion
Football Grd.
Crown Farm
Crown Cottages
Whites Farm
Mill Farm
Warren Farm
Gobions Farm
Cold Blow Farm
Fords Sports Ground
Robert Clack Leisure Cen.
73

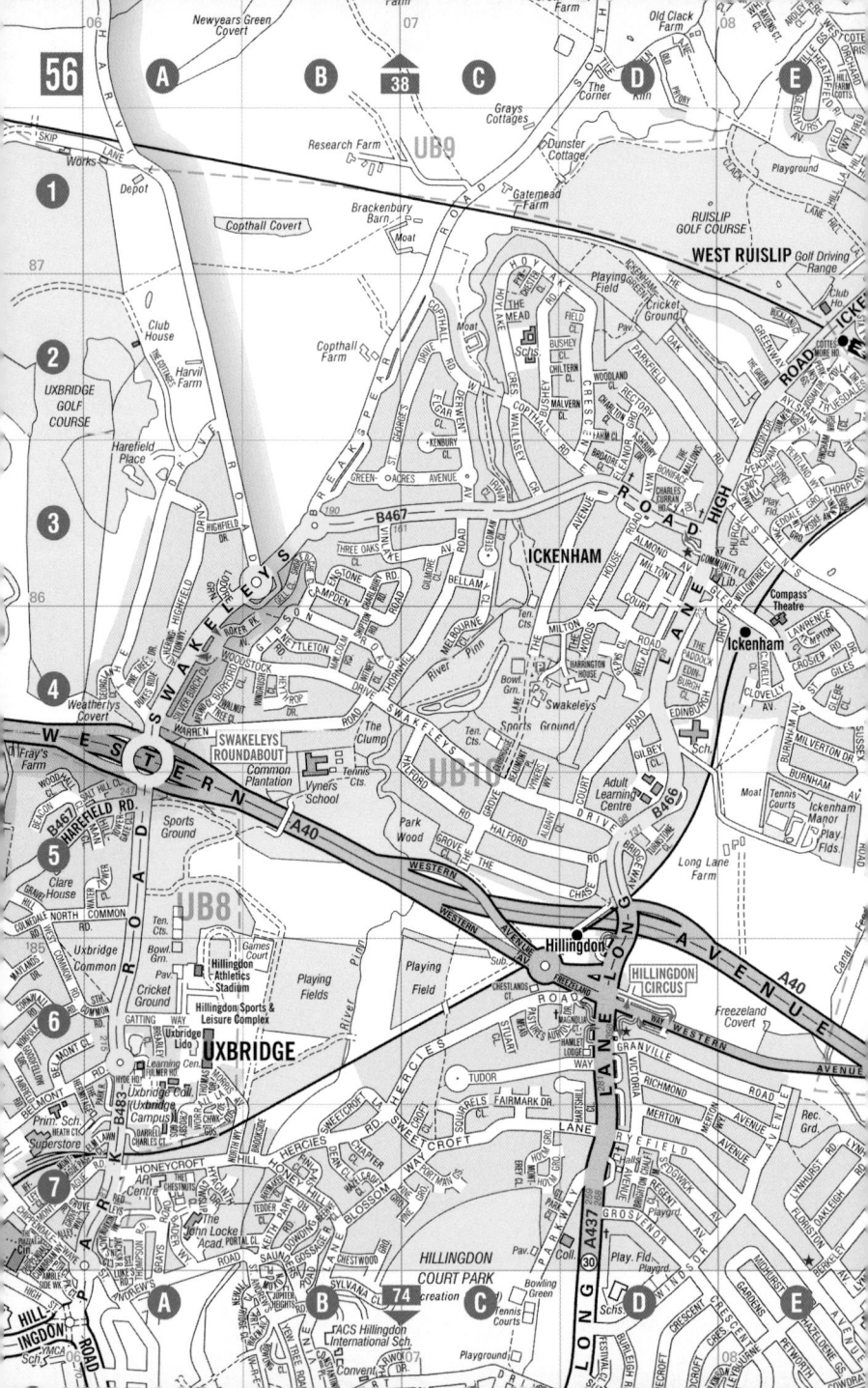

56
A
B
C
D
E
38
74
1
2
3
4
5
6
7
06
07
08
87
86
85
Newyears Green Covert
Old Clack Farm
The Corner
Kiln
Grays Cottages
Research Farm
UB9
Dunster Cottage
Gatemead Farm
Skip Lane
Works
Depot
Copthall Covert
Brackenbury Barn
Moat
Ruislip Golf Course
West Ruislip
Golf Driving Range
Playground
Club Ho.
Club House
The Cottages
Harvil Farm
Harvil Road
Copthall Farm
Uxbridge Golf Course
Harefield Place
Playing Field
Cricket Ground
Pav.
Schs.
The Mead
Hoylake Cres.
Copthall Rd. W.
Copthall Rd. E.
Breakspear Road
B467
Swakeleys Road
Swakeleys Drive
Greenacres Avenue
St. George's Dr.
Derwent Av.
Elgar Cl.
Kenbury Cl.
Wallasey Cr.
Bushey Cl.
Chiltern Cl.
Malvern Cl.
Woodland Cl.
Rectory Way
Oak Av.
Parkfield Av.
The Greenway
High Road
Ickenham Road
Ickenham
Community Lib.
Compass Theatre
Glebe Av.
Long Lane
Milton Court
Almond Av.
Vinlake Av.
Three Oaks Cl.
Stedman Cl.
Bellamy Cl.
Melbourne Cl.
River Pinn
Swakeleys Roundabout
Common Plantation
Vyners School
Tennis Cts.
The Clump
Ten. Cts.
Bowl. Grn.
Harrington House
Swakeleys
Sports Ground
Edinburgh Dr.
Gilbey Cl.
Adult Learning Centre
B466
Court Drive
Halford Rd.
Grove Cl.
The Chase
Park Wood
UB10
Milverton Dr.
Burnham Av.
Moat
Tennis Courts
Ickenham Manor
Play. Flds.
Long Lane Farm
Weatherlys Covert
Fray's Farm
Western Avenue
A40
Harefield Rd.
Clare House
North Common Rd.
UB8
Ten. Cts.
Bowl. Grn.
Games Court
Hillingdon Athletics Stadium
Hillingdon Sports & Leisure Complex
Cricket Ground
Uxbridge Common
Playing Fields
Playing Field
Hillingdon
Hillingdon Circus
Freezeland Way
Freezeland Covert
Uxbridge Lido
UXBRIDGE
Learning Cen.
Uxbridge Coll. (Uxbridge Campus)
Prim. Sch.
Superstore
B483
Park Road
Honeycroft Hill
AR Centre
The John Locke Acad.
Hercies Rd.
Sweetcroft La.
Tudor Way
Fairmark Dr.
Granville Rd.
Victoria Rd.
Richmond Road
Merton Avenue
Ryefield Avenue
Rec. Grd.
Lynhurst Rd.
Oakleigh Rd.
Floriston Av.
Grosvenor Av.
A437
Parkway
Coll.
Play. Fld.
Playgrd.
Hillingdon Court Park
Bowling Green
Tennis Courts
Playground
ACS Hillingdon International Sch.
Convent
Schs.
Hillingdon Hill
YMCA
Sch.
Windsor Av.
Crescent
Midhurst Gardens
Hazeldene Gs.
Petworth

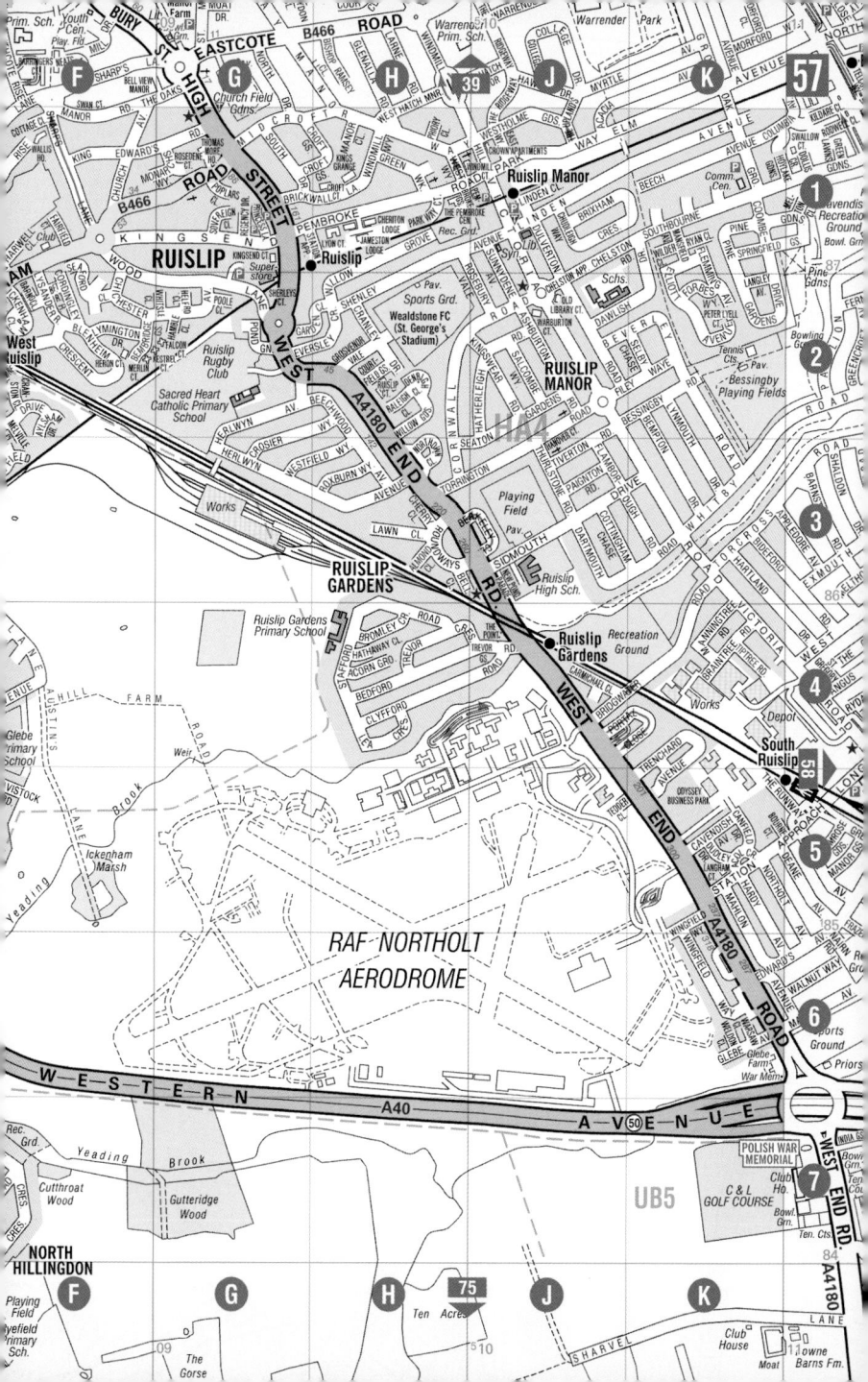
57
RUISLIP
Ruislip
Ruislip Manor
RUISLIP MANOR
RUISLIP GARDENS
Ruislip Gardens
South Ruislip
West Ruislip
HA4
RAF NORTHOLT AERODROME
WESTERN AVENUE
A40
A4180
WEST END RD.
HIGH STREET
UB5
C & L GOLF COURSE
POLISH WAR MEMORIAL
NORTH HILLINGDON
Wealdstone FC (St. George's Stadium)
Ruislip Rugby Club
Sacred Heart Catholic Primary School
Ruislip Gardens Primary School
Ruislip High Sch.
Recreation Ground
Playing Field
Ickenham Marsh
Cutthroat Wood
Gutteridge Wood
Ten Acres
The Gorse
Bessingby Playing Fields
ODYSSEY BUSINESS PARK
39
58
75
F G H J K
1 2 3 4 5 6 7

Eastcote
Rayners Lane
RAYNERS LANE
HA5
HA4
UB5
SOUTH RUISLIP
South Ruislip
NORTHOLT
Northolt
Cavendish Recreation Ground
Pine Gdns
Bessingby Playing Fields
Roxbourne Park
Roxbourne Prim. Sch.
Miniature Railway
Recreation Ground
Field End Jun. & Inf. Schs.
Newton Farm Jun. & Inf. Schs.
Newton Park West
Newton Ecology Park
NHS Walk-in Cen.
Alexandra Sch.
Heathland Sch.
Rooks Heath Coll.
Hendon FC, Harrow Borough FC (Earlsmead Stadium)
Deanesfield Prim. Sch.
Queensmead Sch.
Queensmead Sports Cen.
Goals Soccer Centre
Lib. & Adult Educ. Cen.
Playing Fields
Doane Park
Superstore
Depot
Warehouse
Victoria Retail Park
Chancerygate Bus. Cen.
Solid Waste Transfer Station
Bourne Prim. School
Sports Ground
Polish War Memorial
Priors Fm.
Glebe Farm
War Mem.
Lord Halsbury Memorial Playing Flds.
Willow Tree Prim. Sch.
Northolt High Sch.
Northolt Park
Play Centre
Leisure Cen.
Islip Manor Park
Comm. Cen.
Lime Trees Park Golf Course
C & L Golf Course
John Chilton Sch.
Alec Reed Academy
Target Roundabout
Belvue Park
PureGym (Northolt)
Towne Barns Fm.
Club House
Moat
WESTERN AVENUE
A40
A4180
A4090
A312
ALEXANDRA AVENUE
MANDEVILLE ROAD
CHURCH ROAD
WEST END ROAD
LONG DRIVE
EASTCOTE LANE
FIELD END ROAD
VICTORIA ROAD
WHITBY ROAD
40
57
76
A B C D E
A B C D E
1 2 3 4 5 6 7

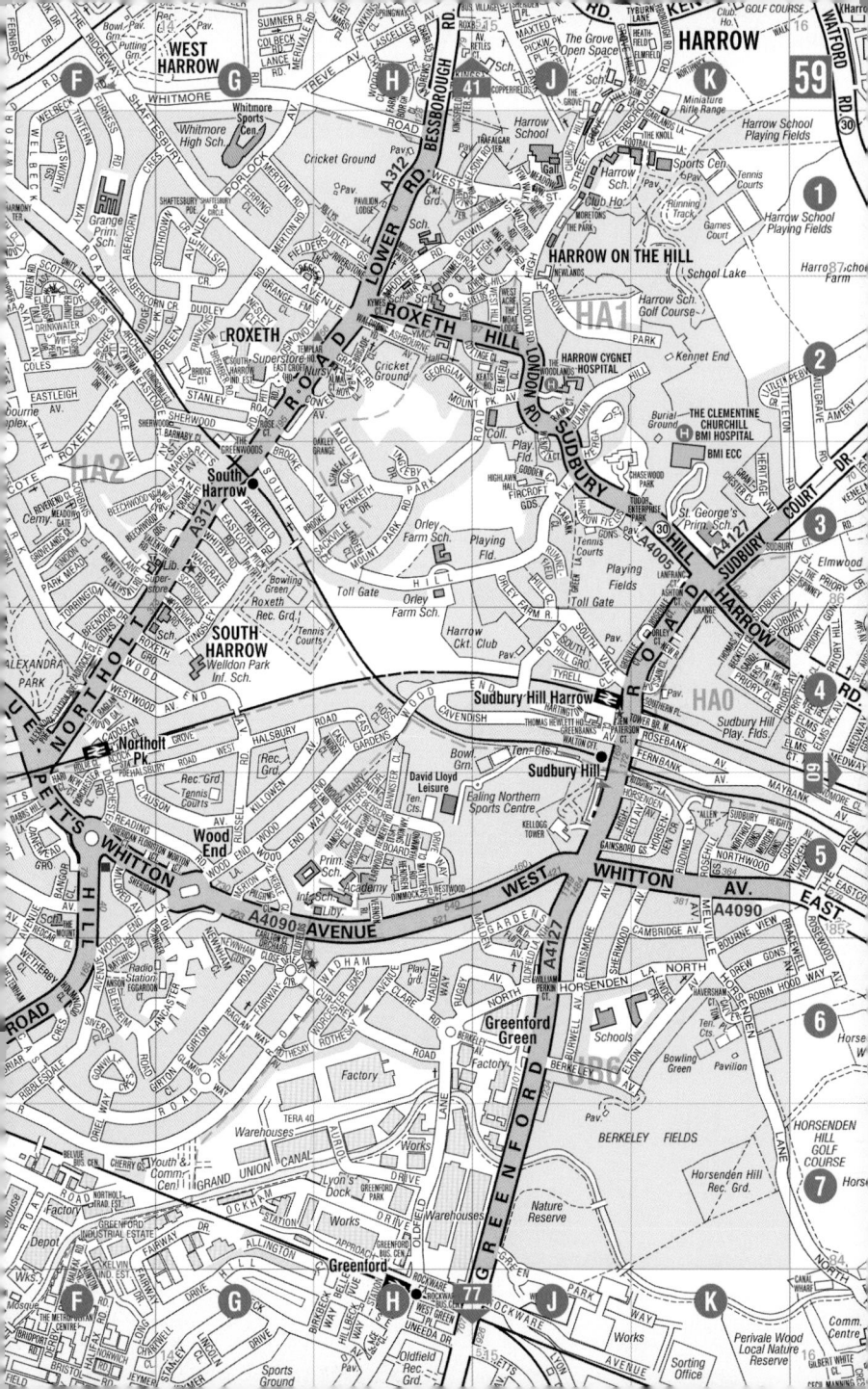

59
WEST HARROW
HARROW
HARROW ON THE HILL
ROXETH
SOUTH HARROW
South Harrow
Northolt Pk.
Sudbury Hill Harrow
Sudbury Hill
Wood End
Greenford Green
Greenford
HA1
HA2
HA0
UB6
HARROW CYGNET HOSPITAL
THE CLEMENTINE CHURCHILL BMI HOSPITAL
BMI ECC
Harrow School Playing Fields
Harrow Sch. Golf Course
David Lloyd Leisure
Ealing Northern Sports Centre
HORSENDEN HILL GOLF COURSE
Horsenden Hill Rec. Grd.
BERKELEY FIELDS
Perivale Wood Local Nature Reserve
GRAND UNION CANAL
A312
A4090
A4127
A4005
41
60
77

HARROW
60
42
59
78
HA1
HA3
HA0
UB6
NORTH WEMBLEY
SUDBURY
PERIVALE
Northwick Park Hospital
St. Mark's Hosp.
Harrow School Playing Fields
Harrow School Farm
Northwick Park
Driving Range
Club Ho.
Northwick Park Playgolf
Byron Ct. Prim. Sch.
South Kenton
Preston Road
Preston Park Recreation Ground
John Billam Playing Fields
North Wembley
East Lane Pavilion
Rugby Football Grd.
Vale Farm Sports Ground
Vale Farm Sports Centre
Wembley FC
East La. Theatre Club
Elmwood Pk.
Sudbury Hill Play. Flds.
Maybank Open Space
Sudbury & Harrow Road
Barham Park
Sudbury Town
NHS Walk-in Centre
Wembley Central
King Edward VII Park
Horsenden Wood
Horsenden Hill Golf Course
Horsenden Hill
Horsenden Farm
Sudbury Golf Course
Club House
Alperton Cemetery
One Tree Hill Rec. Grd.
Alperton
Perivale Wood Local Nature Reserve
Grand Union Canal (Paddington Branch)
Watford Road
A404
A4127
A4088
A4005
A4090
A4089
East Lane
Harrow Road
Whitton Avenue
Sudbury Court Drive
Bridgewater Rd.
High Road
Ealing Road
Horsenden Lane
1
2
3
4
5
6
7
A
B
C
D
E

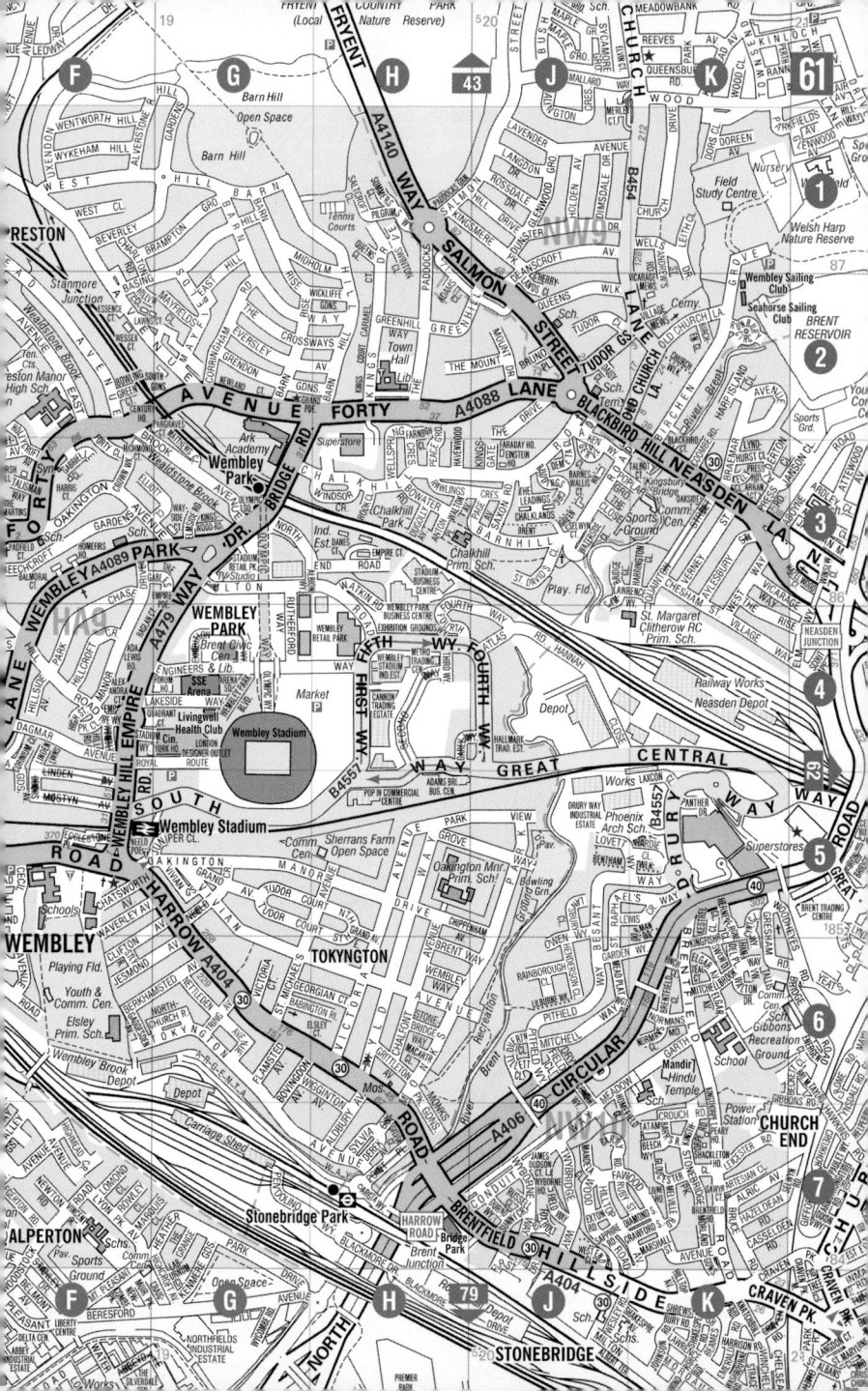

61
43
62
79
Barn Hill Open Space
Fryent Country Park (Local Nature Reserve)
PRESTON
NW9
HA9
WEMBLEY PARK
Wembley Stadium
SSE Arena
TOKYNGTON
WEMBLEY
ALPERTON
STONEBRIDGE
CHURCH END
NW10
Stonebridge Park
Wembley Park
Welsh Harp Nature Reserve
BRENT RESERVOIR
Wembley Sailing Club
Seahorse Sailing Club
Field Study Centre
Chalkhill Park
Chalkhill Prim. Sch.
St. Margaret Clitherow RC Prim. Sch.
Railway Works
Neasden Depot
NEASDEN JUNCTION
Oakington Mnr. Prim. Sch.
Sherrans Farm Open Space
Phoenix Arch Sch.
Mandir Hindu Temple
Gibbons Recreation Ground
Elsley Prim. Sch.
Wembley Brook Depot
Carriage Shed
Brent Junction
Bridge Park
Stanmore Junction
Preston Manor High Sch.
Ark Academy
Brent Civic Cen. & Lib.
Livingwell Health Club
London Designer Outlet
Market
Town Hall
Kingsbury Bridge
A4140 FRYENT WAY
SALMON STREET
FORTY AVENUE
A4088 FORTY LANE
BLACKBIRD HILL
NEASDEN LA.
A4089 PARK
WEMBLEY
A479 WAY
BRIDGE RD.
EMPIRE WAY
WEMBLEY HILL RD.
SOUTH WAY
GREAT CENTRAL WAY
B4557 DRURY WAY
HARROW ROAD A404
A406 CIRCULAR
BRENTFIELD
HILLSIDE
A404
B454 CHURCH LANE
NORTH

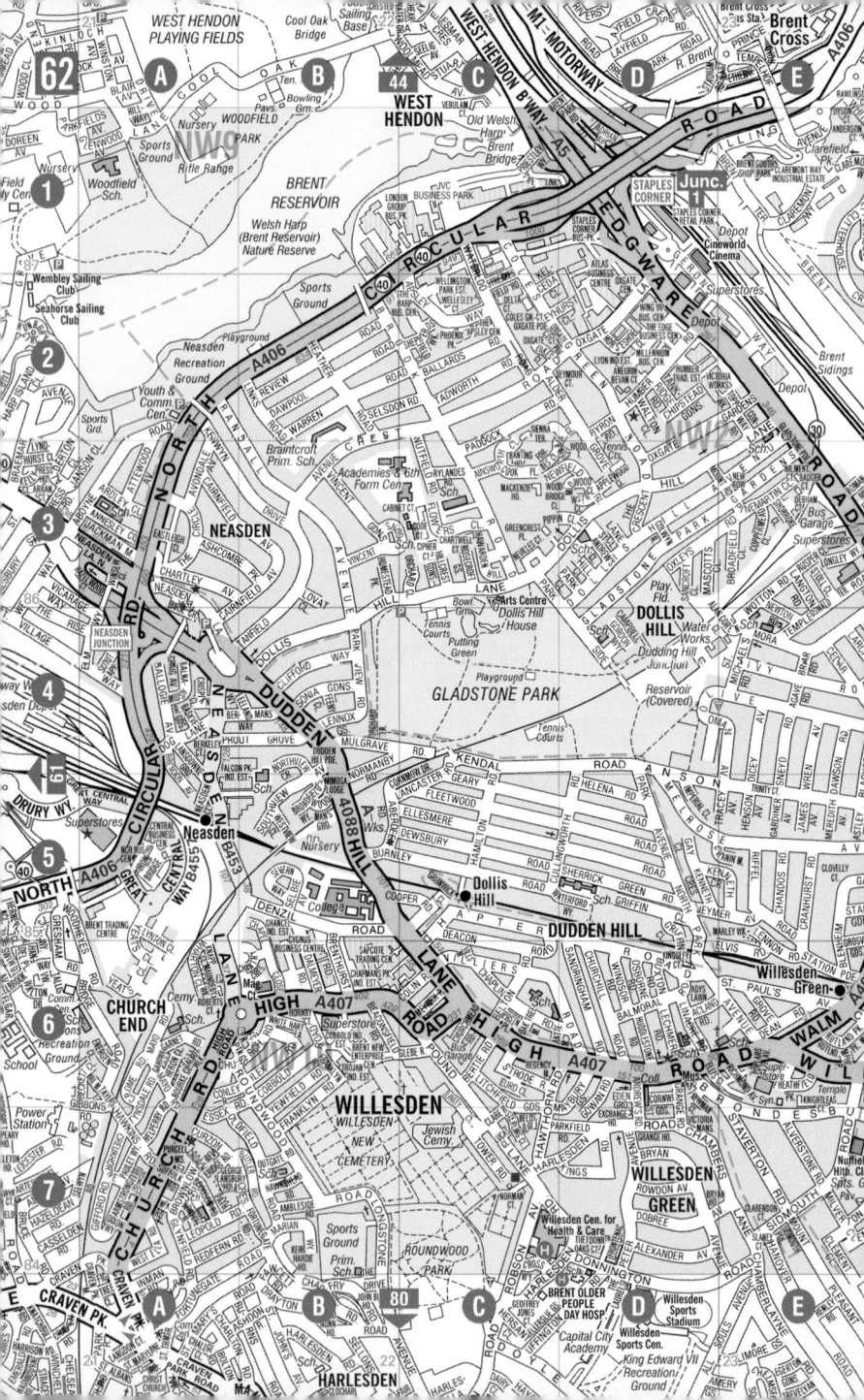
62
WEST HENDON PLAYING FIELDS
Cool Oak Bridge
Sailing Base
44
WEST HENDON
M1 MOTORWAY
Brent Cross
A406
WOODFIELD PARK
NW9
Sports Ground
Rifle Range
Nursery
Woodfield Sch.
Old Welsh Harp
Brent Bridge
BRENT RESERVOIR
Welsh Harp (Brent Reservoir) Nature Reserve
STAPLES CORNER
Junc. 1
Cineworld Cinema
Superstores
Depot
Brent Sidings
NORTH CIRCULAR ROAD
EDGWARE ROAD
A5
Wembley Sailing Club
Seahorse Sailing Club
Neasden Recreation Ground
Youth & Comm. Cen.
Playground
Sports Grd.
NW2
Braintcroft Prim. Sch.
Academies & 6th Form Cen.
NEASDEN
NEASDEN JUNCTION
DOLLIS HILL
Arts Centre
Dollis Hill House
Tennis Courts
Putting Green
Playground
GLADSTONE PARK
Water Works
Dudding Hill Junction
Reservoir (Covered)
Bus Garage
Superstores
DUDDEN HILL
61
DRURY WY.
Superstores
Neasden
B453
B455
4088
College
Dollis Hill
DUDDEN HILL
Willesden Green
CHURCH END
Recreation Ground
School
Power Station
A407
HIGH ROAD
Superstore
NW10
WILLESDEN
WILLESDEN NEW CEMETERY
Jewish Cemy.
WILLESDEN GREEN
Willesden Cen. for Health & Care
Sports Ground
Prim. Sch.
ROUNDWOOD PARK
80
BRENT OLDER PEOPLE DAY HOSP
Capital City Academy
Willesden Sports Stadium
Willesden Sports Cen.
King Edward VII Recreation Ground
HARLESDEN
CRAVEN PK.
A
B
C
D
E
1
2
3
4
5
6
7

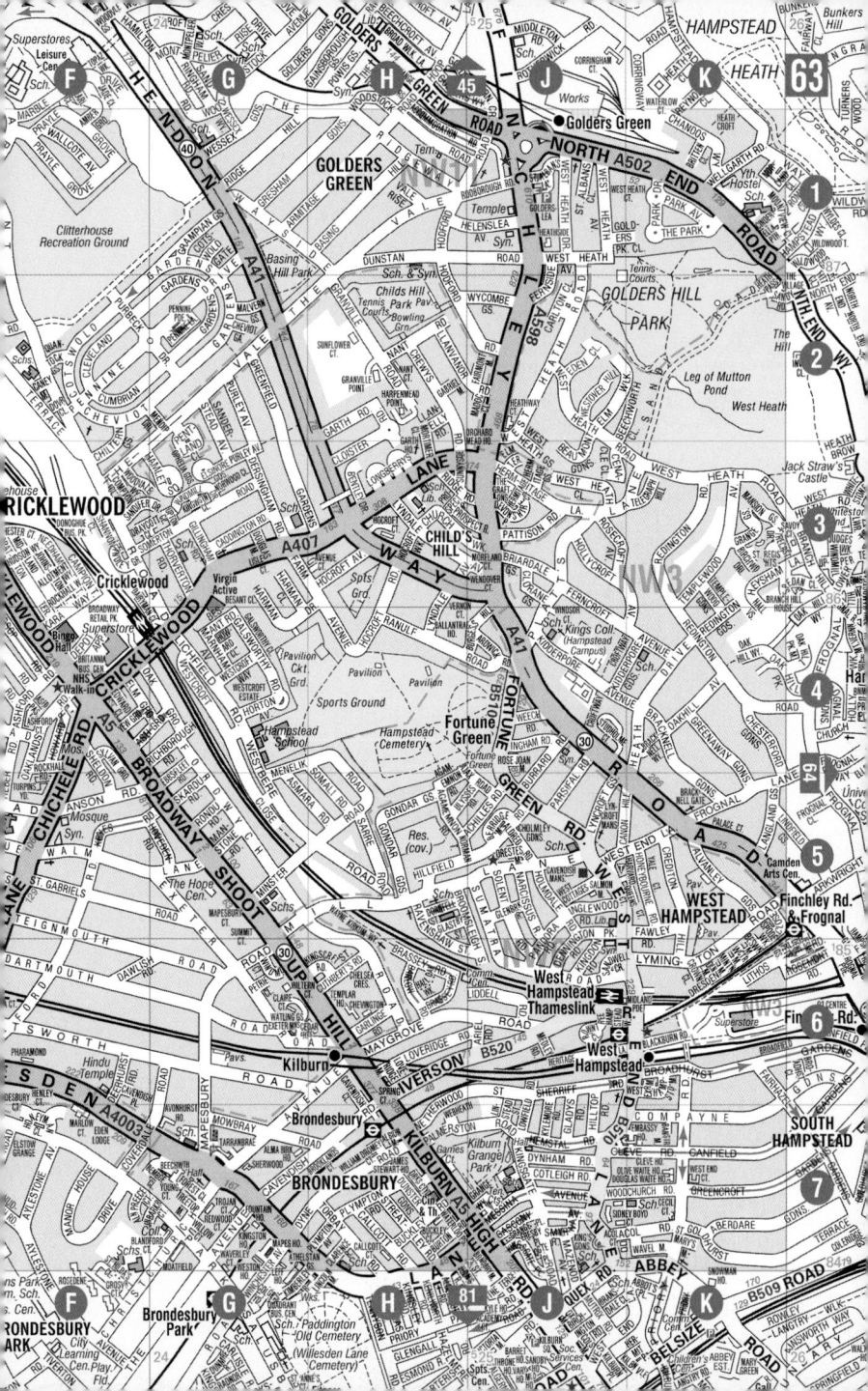

63
45
64
81
F
G
H
J
K
1
2
3
4
5
6
7
HAMPSTEAD
HEATH
Bunkers Hill
GOLDERS GREEN
Golders Green
NW11
HENDON
A41
NORTH END ROAD
A502
FINCHLEY ROAD
A598
Clitterhouse Recreation Ground
Basing Hill Park
Childs Hill Park
Tennis Courts
Bowling Grn.
GOLDERS HILL PARK
Leg of Mutton Pond
West Heath
The Hill
Jack Straw's Castle
WEST HEATH ROAD
CRICKLEWOOD
Cricklewood
CRICKLEWOOD BROADWAY
A407
A5
CRICKLEWOOD LANE
CHILD'S HILL
HOCROFT AV.
NW3
Virgin Active
Superstore
Bingo Hall
Pavilion Ckt. Grd.
Sports Ground
Fortune Green
Hampstead Cemetery
Hampstead School
FORTUNE GREEN RD.
B510
Kings Coll. (Hampstead Campus)
WEST END LANE
WEST HAMPSTEAD
Finchley Rd. & Frognal
Camden Arts Cen.
West Hampstead Thameslink
West Hampstead
Kilburn
Brondesbury
BRONDESBURY
Brondesbury Park
SHOOT UP HILL
KILBURN HIGH RD.
IVERSON
B520
CHICHELE RD.
BROADWAY
WILLESDEN LANE
A4003
Hindu Temple
Mosque
The Hope Cen.
Kilburn Grange Park
Paddington Old Cemetery (Willesden Lane Cemetery)
SOUTH HAMPSTEAD
ABBEY RD.
BELSIZE RD.
B509 ROAD
Superstore
MAYGROVE
WALM LANE
DARTMOUTH ROAD
TEIGNMOUTH ROAD
MAPESBURY RD.
MANOR HOUSE DRIVE
AYLESTONE AV.

64
46
63
82
A
B
C
D
E
1
2
3
4
5
6
7
HAMPSTEAD HEATH
HAMPSTEAD
HIGHGATE
GOSPEL OAK
VALE OF HEALTH
North End
PARLIAMENT HILL
SOUTH HAMPSTEAD
PRIMROSE HILL
NW11
NW3
NW6
N6
Kenwood House
Caen Wood
KEN WOOD
Open Air Stage
North Wood
Mount Tyndal
Sandy Heath
The Spaniards
Turners Wood
Club House
Athlone House
Highgate School
Highgate Ponds
Men's Bathing Pond
Ladies' Bathing Pond
Bowling Green
East Heath
West Heath
The Hill
Sports Ground
Bathing Pond
Hampstead Ponds
Jack Straw's Castle
Whitestone Pond
Burgh Ho.
Keats Ho.
Hampstead
Hampstead Heath
Belsize Pk.
Chalk Farm
Swiss Cottage
Finchley Rd. & Frognal
Finchley Rd.
South Hampstead
University College School
Camden Arts Cen.
Freud Mus.
Sigmund Freud Statue
ROYAL FREE HOSPITAL
Hospice
Parliament Hill Fields Athletics Track
Parliament Hill School
William Ellis Sch.
Hampstead Heath Educ. Centre
Parliament Hill Fields
Tennis Courts
Lido
Gospel Oak
Reservoir (covered)
NORTH END RD.
NORTH END
A502
SPANIARDS RD.
B519
HAMPSTEAD LANE
HEATH ST
FITZJOHN'S AV.
ROSSLYN HILL
HAVERSTOCK HILL
POND ST.
FLEET RD.
AGINCOURT RD.
MANSFIELD RD.
B518
MALDEN RD.
GORDON HO. RD.
B511
FINCHLEY RD.
A41
ADELAIDE RD.
B509
BELSIZE RD.
B525
CHALK FARM RD.
PRINCE OF WALES RD.
B517
WILLOW RD.
MILLFIELD LA.
WEST HEATH RD.
ETON RD.
BELSIZE AVENUE
BELSIZE PARK
ELSWORTHY RD.

65
47
83
66
F
G
H
J
K
1
2
3
4
5
6
7
ARCHWAY
HORNSEY
LANE
CROUCH HILL
Crouch Hill
STROUD GREEN ROAD
A1201
HIGHGATE HILL
HORNSEY RISE
A103
Elthorne Park
Lauderdale House
WATERLOW PARK
Waterlow Park Cen.
Highgate Mental Health Centre
WHITTINGTON HOSPITAL
HIGHGATE CEMETERY
Archway
ARCHWAY ROAD
A1
HOLLOWAY
Upper Holloway
UPPER HOLLOWAY
Whittington Park
DARTMOUTH PARK
JUNCTION ROAD
A400
HOLLOWAY ROAD
SEVEN SISTERS
A503
Sobell Leisure Cen.
TOLLINGTON
HOLLOWAY
Odeon Cinema
NAG'S HEAD
PARKHURST
CAMDEN ROAD
TUFNELL PARK
Tufnell Pk.
BRECKNOCK ROAD
A5200
HILLMARTON RD.
CALEDONIAN RD.
Holloway Rd.
LOWER HOLLOWAY
Arsenal (Emirates Stadium)
HIGHGATE RD.
FORTESS ROAD
KENTISH TOWN
Kentish Town
KENTISH TOWN ROAD
02 Forum Kentish Town
Caledonian Rd.
CALEDONIAN
A5203
Caledonian Park
Islington Ten. Cen.
HMP PENTONVILLE
YORK WAY
BARNSBURY
Caledonian Rd. & Barnsbury
City Farm
Camden Rd.
CAMDEN TOWN
Camden Town
ST. PANCRAS WAY
ROYAL COLLEGE ST.
A5202
High Speed 1
Lewis Cubitt Pk.
COPENHAGEN ST.
B514
BRITANNIA JUNC.
PARKWAY

66
A
B
C
D
E
48
65
84
1
2
3
4
5
6
7
FINSBURY PARK
Manor House
MANOR HO.
EAST RESERVOIR
WEST RESERVOIR
Reservoir (covered)
Sir Thomas Abney Prim. Sch.
West Reservoir Centre
The Castle Climbing Cen.
Abney Park Cemetery (Local Nature Reserve)
STOKE NEWINGTON
STOKE NEWINGTON CHURCH
CLISSOLD PARK
Clissold Leisure Cen.
Tennis Courts
Paddling Pool
FINSBURY PARK
Finsbury Park
Park Theatre
Rowans Complex
Interchange
BROWNSWOOD PARK
BROWNSWOOD
LORDSHIP
PARK
MANOR
SEVEN SISTERS RD.
SEVEN
SISTERS
GREEN
LANES
STROUD
GREEN RD.
BLACKSTOCK RD.
HIGHBURY PARK
HIGHBURY GROVE
HIGHBURY
Isledon Village
Gillespie Park Local Nature Res.
Arsenal
Ecology Cen.
Ashburton Grove
Arsenal FC (Emirates Stadium)
Drayton Pk.
HORNSEY RD.
TOLLINGTON
HOLLOWAY RD.
Holloway Rd.
University
LIVERPOOL RD.
Highbury & Islington
HIGHBURY CNR.
Highbury Pool
City Farm
Paradise Park
Canonbury
CANONBURY
CANONBURY RD.
UPPER ST.
ST. PAUL'S RD.
A1199 ROAD
BALLS POND A104 RD.
NEWINGTON GRN.
Dalston Kingsland
KINGSLAND
ESSEX RD.
Essex Rd.
NEW NORTH RD.
SOUTHGATE RD.
DE BEAUVOIR TOWN
Kingsland Basin
BARNSBURY
ISLINGTON
DOWNHAM
A1
A1201
A105
A503
A103
A104
B105
B104
B102
B150
B515
A10
N1
N5
N16
N7
30
20

67
F
G
H
J
K
49
85
68
1
2
3
4
5
6
7
CLAPTON
STAMFORD HILL
Stoke Newington
UPPER CLAPTON
SPRINGFIELD PARK
Springfield Marina
Coppermill Bridge
Horse Shoe Point
WALTHAMSTOW
Clapton Junction
MARSHES
E17
E10
E5
E8
E9
Leyton Marshes
Lea Valley Riding Centre
Playing Field
Lee Valley Ice Centre
LEYTON INDUSTRIAL VILLAGE
FOREST BUSINESS PARK
Lea Bridge
RIVER LEA or LEE
North Millfields Recreation Ground
Middlesex Filter Beds Nature Reserve
LEA BRIDGE
SOUTH MILL FIELDS
South Millfields Rec. Grd.
Clapton
NORTHWOLD RD.
Rectory Road
STOKE NEWINGTON HIGH ST.
LOWER CLAPTON
HACKNEY DOWNS
Stormont House Sch.
Mossbourne Community Academy
SHACKLEWELL
HOMERTON
HOMERTON UNIVERSITY HOSP.
CITY & HACKNEY
UCC
Homerton
HOMERTON HIGH ST.
Hackney Downs
Hackney Cen.
DALSTON
GRAHAM RD. A1207
DALSTON LA.
MORNING LA.
WICK RD.
CASSLAND RD.
WELL ST.
SOUTH HACKNEY
HACKNEY
London Fields Lido
London Fields
LONDON FIELDS
Haggerston
Dalston Junc.
QUEENSBRIDGE RD.
MARE ST.
VICTORIA PARK RD.
Victoria Fountain
Bandstand Pav.
Royal Gate East
Anton's Lock
Hospice
LEA BRIDGE ROAD A104
LOWER CLAPTON ROAD
UPPER CLAPTON RD. A107
A10
A102
A106
B108
B111
B113
SPRING HILL
MOUNT PLEASANT LA.
HOMERTON RD.
Superstore

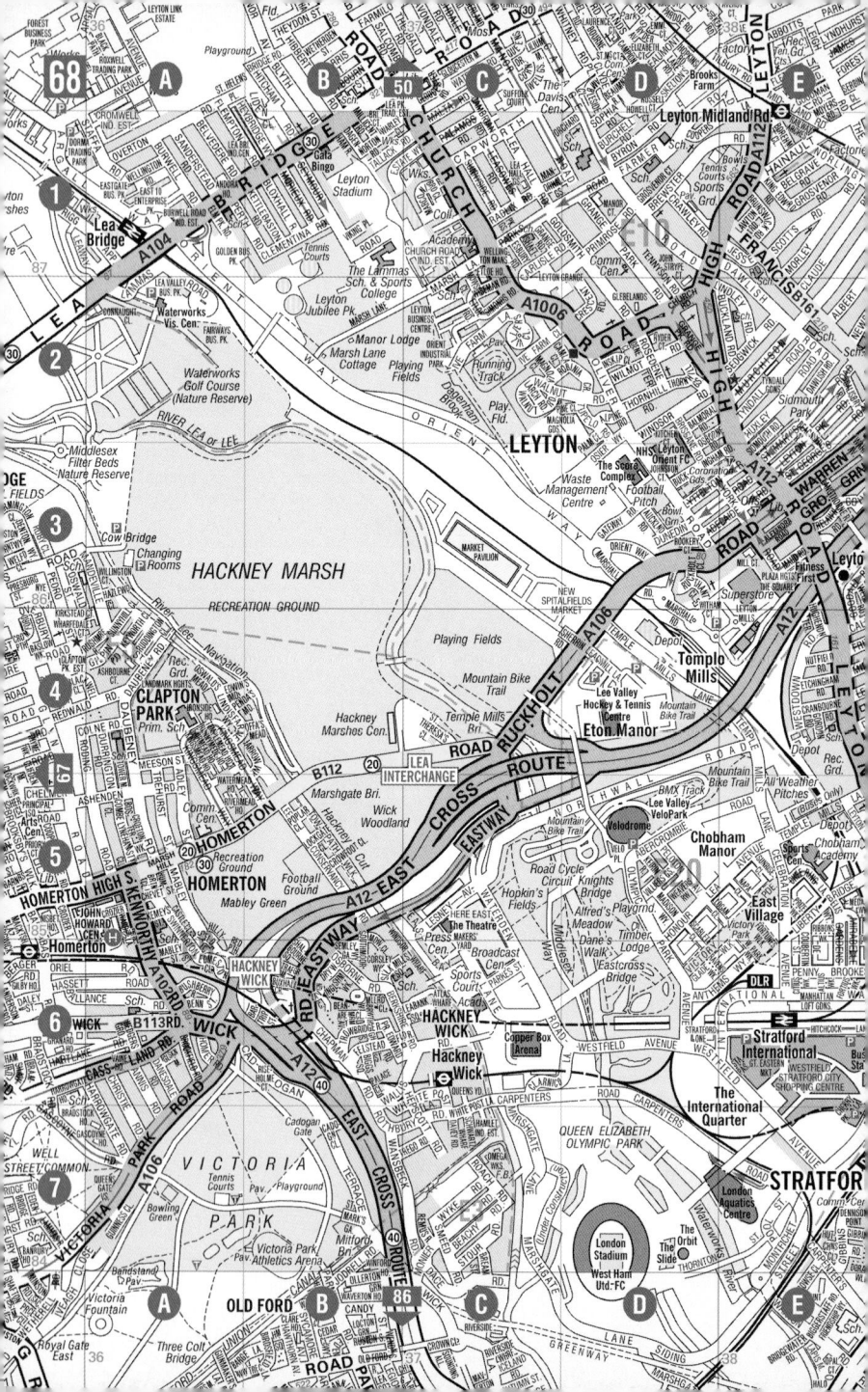

68
50
67
86
A
B
C
D
E
1
2
3
4
5
6
7
LEYTON
E10
HACKNEY MARSH
RECREATION GROUND
CLAPTON PARK
HOMERTON
HACKNEY WICK
OLD FORD
VICTORIA PARK
QUEEN ELIZABETH OLYMPIC PARK
STRATFOR
Leyton Midland Rd.
Lea Bridge
Homerton
Hackney Wick
Stratford International
Temple Mills
Leyton Stadium
Leyton Jubilee Pk.
Waterworks Golf Course (Nature Reserve)
Middlesex Filter Beds Nature Reserve
RIVER LEA or LEE
Lee Navigation
Marsh Lane Playing Fields
Manor Lodge
Marsh Lane Cottage
Running Track
NEW SPITALFIELDS MARKET
MARKET PAVILION
Playing Fields
Mountain Bike Trail
Hackney Marshes Cen.
Temple Mills Bri.
Eton Manor
Lee Valley Hockey & Tennis Centre
Lee Valley VeloPark
Velodrome
Chobham Manor
Chobham Academy
East Village
The International Quarter
Westfield Stratford City Shopping Centre
London Aquatics Centre
London Stadium West Ham Utd. FC
The Orbit
The Slide
Copper Box Arena
Here East
LEA INTERCHANGE
Wick Woodland
Marshgate Bri.
Mabley Green
Recreation Ground
Football Ground
Victoria Park Athletics Arena
Victoria Fountain
Bandstand
Royal Gate East
Three Colt Bridge
Leyton Orient FC
Waste Management Centre
Sidmouth Park
Superstore
Depot
A104
A106
A1006
A112
A12
A102
B112
B113
B161
LEA BRIDGE ROAD
CHURCH ROAD
HIGH ROAD
RUCKHOLT ROAD
EAST CROSS ROUTE
EASTWAY
HOMERTON ROAD
VICTORIA PARK ROAD
WICK ROAD
ORIENT WAY

69
70
51
87
GREEN MAN ROUNDABOUT
BUSH RD.
BLAKE HALL ROAD A114
OVERTON DRIVE
TENNYSON AV.
The Basin (Fish Pond)
Tennis Courts
Sports Ground
Bowling Green
WANSTEAD GOLF COURSE
Bush Wood
Reservoir Wood
Shoulder of Mutton Pond
WOODLANDS AVENUE
NORTHUMBERLAND AV.
ALDERSBROOK ROAD
A116
E12
E11
E7
E15
WANSTEAD FLATS
Playing Field
Horse Ride
LAKE HOUSE ROAD
CENTRE ROAD A114
WOODFORD ROAD
WOODGRANGE RD.
DAMES ROAD B161
HARROW ROAD
GAINSBOROUGH RD.
Leytonstone
LEYTONSTONE
Leytonstone High Rd.
GREEN
A12
GROVE A106
CATHALL
HOLLYDOWN WY.
St. Patrick's RC Cemetery
Langthorne Park
CANN HALL RD.
Cann Hall
West Ham Cemetery
Cemetery
Wanstead Pk.
CAPEL ROAD
SEBERT ROAD
HAMPTON RD.
OSBORNE RD.
CLAREMONT RD.
Forest Gate
FOREST GATE
FOREST LANE
Forest La. Pk.
EARLHAM GROVE
SPROWSTON RD.
ROMFORD ROAD A118
A118
Maryland
Stratford New Town
Stratford
LEYTON RD. A112
ANGEL LA.
GREAT EASTERN RD
BROADWAY
THE GROVE
WEST HAM LA. A112
VICARAGE LANE B164
WEST HAM PARK
Playground
Netball Court
Football Pitch
Tennis Courts
Football Ground
UPTON LANE A114
UPTON
PLASHET ROAD
B165
PORTWAY
UPTON PARK ROAD
GREEN STREET
Upton Park
Stratford High St.
HIGH ST. A118
WEST HAM
NEW PLAISTOW
Public Gdns.
F
G
H
J
K
1
2
3
4
5
6
7

70
52
69
88
A
B
C
D
E
1
2
3
4
5
6
7
WANSTEAD PARK
WANSTEAD GOLF COURSE
The Temple
Keepers Lodge
Heronry Pond
Perch Pond
Riding Sch.
Rook Island
E11
Aldersbrook Prim. Sch.
NORTHUMBERLAND AVENUE
ALDERSBROOK
A116
WANSTEAD FLATS
ALDERSBROOK
CITY OF LONDON CEMETERY
City of London Crematorium
ILFORD GOLF COURSE
River Roding
SOUTH WOODFORD TO BARKING RELIEF ROAD
A406
CRANBROOK
A123
Ilford Cricket Club
Cranbrook Coll.
Ilford
FOREST DRIVE
A116 ROAD
A118
ROMFORD ROAD
MANOR PARK
THE MANOR PARK CEMETERY
Manor Park Crem.
Manor Park
E12
LITTLE ILFORD LA.
LITTLE ILFORD
Little Ilford Park
CHURCH RD.
E7
Woodgrange Park
Woodgrange Park Cemetery
HIGH STREET NORTH
A117
PLASHET Jewish Cemetery
PLASHET PARK
Tennis Courts
Bowling Green
The Shrewsbury Cen.
GROVE
EAST AV.
East Ham
E6
B165
B167
B109
PLASHET RD.
GREEN ST.
KATHERINE RD.
BROWNING
Sports Ground
Gasholder
Running Track
Playing Field
Depot
SOUTH WOODFORD
Wallend
BARKING
Upton Park
UPTON PARK
RON LEIGHTON WY.

VALENTINES PARK
F
G
H
J
SEVEN KINGS
K
71
53
IG2
Seven Kings
HIGH ROAD
A118
1
LANE
2
GREEN
A1083
ILFORD
WINSTON WY.
SOUTH PARK
The Lake
IG3
IG1
3
4
72
5
LOXFORD
LOXFORD PARK
Loxford Sch. of Science & Technology
Barking Abbey Sch. (Lwr. Sch.)
FAIR CROSS
A124
BARKING PARK
Indoor Bowls Centre
Miniature Railway
LONGBRIDGE RD.
FANSHAWE AV.
A123
IG11
Eastbury Comp. Sch.
6
Barking Abbey Sch.
Leisure Centre
Manor Jun. & Inf. Schs.
BARKING NORTHERN RELIEF RD.
Barking
BARKING
BARKING HOSPITAL
Upney
7
A123
RIPPLE ROAD
89
F
G
H
J
K
Eastbury Manor Ho.
The Curfew Tower
Barking Abbey
ABBEY RD.
LONDON RD.
RODING TRADING ESTATE
HIGHBRIDGE RD.
BARKING RELIEF RD.
Langdon
ST. PAUL'S

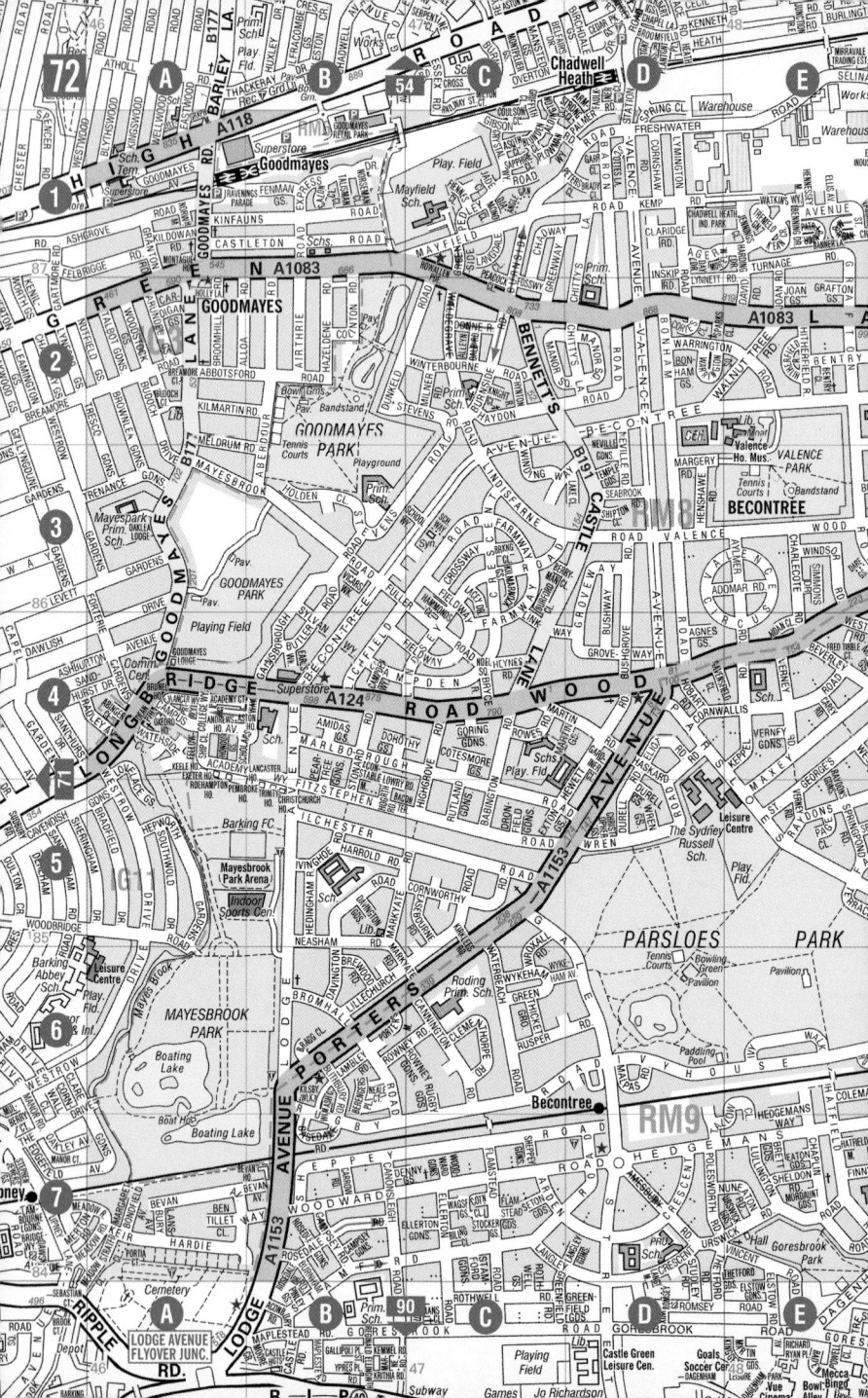

55
73
91
THE LEYS
QUEEN'S HOSPITAL
Romford Cemetery
RUSH GREEN
CROW LANE
Crowlands Sports Ground
CROWLANDS HEATH GOLF COURSE
BEACONTREE HEATH
Robert Clack Leisure Cen.
Robert Clack Sch. (Upper Site)
All Saints Cath. Sch. & Tech. Coll.
Aqua Driving Range
Club House
Football Ground
Fords Sports Ground
RUSH GREEN A124 ROAD
WOOD LANE A124
RUSH
Miniature Golf Course
Tennis Courts
Dagenham Civic Centre
CENTRAL PARK
RAINHAM A1112 ROAD
NORTH RAINHAM
WHALEBONE LA. A1112 STH.
HEATHWAY A1240
Superstore
Leisure Cen.
Barking & Dagenham Coll.
Nursing Home
Fels Farm
Eastbrookend Ho.
EASTBROOKEND COUNTRY PARK
White Hart Lakes
The Millennium Centre
Eastbrook Grove
Eastbrookend Country Park
Playing Field
Eastbrook Comp. Sch.
Sports Ground
Pavilions
Works
Dagenham & Redbridge FC (Victoria Road)
Pondfield Park
Dagenham East
Trinity Sch.
DAGENHAM
Dagenham Heathway
Goresbrook Park
William Ford C of E Prim. Sch.
Village Inf. Sch.
BMX Track
OLD DAGENHAM PARK
Dagenham Park Leisure Cen.
BALLARDS B178 ROAD
Wantz Stream
Leys Prim. Sch.
SOUTH A1112 DAGENHAM RD.
Dagenham Beam Bri.
Beam River
Newtons Corner
RM7
RM10
RM13

74
56
92
A
B
C
D
E
1
2
3
4
5
6
7
UXBRIDGE
HILLINGDON
HILLINGDON HEATH
COLHAM GREEN
COWLEY
PIELD HEATH
COWLEY PEACHEY
YIEWSLEY
WEST DRAYTON
Goulds Green
Stockley Park
UB10
UB8
UB7
UB11
HILLINGDON COURT PARK (Recreation Ground)
HILLINGDON GOLF COURSE
STOCKLEY COUNTRY PARK
STOCKLEY PARK GOLF COURSE
The John Locke Acad.
ACS Hillingdon International Sch.
RAF Uxbridge, Battle of Britain Bunker
Swakeleys School for Girls
Abbotsfield School
Uxbridge High Sch.
Brunel University (Uxbridge Campus)
Halls of Residence
Athletics Centre
Brunel Uni. Sports Park
The Grove Nature Reserve
Bishopshalt School
Hillingdon Cem.
Uxbridge Cem.
Pield Heath House RC Sch.
HILLINGDON HOSPITAL
Meadow High Sch.
Colham Manor Prim. Sch.
Moorcroft Sch.
Stockley Academy
Hillingdon Manor Sch.
Rabbsfarm Prim. Sch.
Uxbridge FC
Recreation Ground
Airport Parking
Virgin Active
The Arena
Club House
Mellow Lane Farm
Moorcroft Fm.
Philpot's Bri.
HILLINGDON ROAD
HILLINGDON HILL
UXBRIDGE ROAD
LONG LANE
HARLINGTON ROAD
FALLING LANE
STOCKLEY ROAD
WEST DRAYTON ROAD
PIELD HEATH ROAD
ROYAL LANE
COLHAM GREEN ROAD
DRAYTON ROAD
A4020
A437
A408
B465
B483

57
75
76
93
NORTH HILLINGDON
HAYES END
WOOD END GREEN
WOOD END
HAYES
YEADING
UB5
UB4
UB3
Ten Acres
The Gorse
Recreation Ground
Westways Fm.
Lane Covert
West London Shooting Grounds
Grosvenor Playing Field
Hayes Shrub
Hayes Park
Home Farm
Yeading Brook Meadows Nature Reserve
Belmore Playing Fields
Grange Park Jun. & Inf. Schs.
Charville Prim. Sch.
Hedgewood School
Belmore Prim. Sch.
Barnhill High Sch. Playing Fields
Rosedale College
Town Hall Park
Barra Hall
Uxbridge Coll. (Hayes Comm. Campus)
Lombardy Retail Park
Hillingdon Cycling Circuit
Lake Farm Country Park
BMX Track
Minet Jun. & Inf. Schs.
Mecca Bingo
County Court
UXBRIDGE ROAD
A4020
A312
A437
THE PARKWAY
OSSIE GARVIN ROUNDABOUT
SHARVEL LANE
WEST END RD.
RUISLIP
C & L GOLF COURSE

LIME TREES PARK GOLF COURSE
Alec Reed Academy
TARGET ROUNDABOUT
Lime Tree Park
West End
NORTHALA FIELDS
NORTHOLT GOLF COURSE
Gifford Primary Sch.
RECTORY PARK
(Recreation Ground)
RUISLIP ROAD
CHURCH ROAD
WESTERN AVENUE
PARK WAY
UXBRIDGE ROAD
Barnhill High Sch.
Belmore Prim. Sch.
YEADING
Yeading Schs.
Warren Park
Public Open Space
King George's Field
Durdans Park Primary Sch.
Willowtree Marina
GRAND UNION CANAL
Greenford High Sch.
Greenford Sports Cen.
Jubilee Park
Reservoir
Belvue Park
PureGym (Northolt)
Spikes Bridge Track
Hillingdon Cycling Circuit
Lombardy Retail Park
Hayes Bridge Retail Park
SOUTHALL
BROADWAY
HIGH ST.
Blair Peach Prim. Sch.
Goals Soccer Centre (Hayes)
Houston Business Park
Brook Industrial Estate

58
75
94

77
78
59
95
F
G
H
J
K
1
2
3
4
5
6
7
GREENFORD
DORMER'S WELLS
HANWELL
Elthorne Heights
Greenford
South Greenford
Castle Bar Pk.
Drayton Green
Hanwell
GREENFORD ROUNDABOUT
GRAND UNION
Lyon's Dock
GREENFORD PARK
NORTHOLT TRAD. EST.
GREENFORD INDUSTRIAL EST.
KELVIN IND. EST.
THE METROPOLITAN CENTRE
Factory
Depot
Wks.
Mosque
Works
Warehouses
Nature Reserve
Horsenden Hill Rec. Grd.
Perivale Wood Local Nature Reserve
Comm. Centre
Sorting Office
Sports Ground
Football Ground
Oldfield Rec. Grd.
Cayton Road Sports Ground
Selborne Prim. Sch.
Ealing Prim. Cen.
High Sch.
Prim. Sch.
RAVENOR PARK
London Motorcycle Museum (Ravenor Farm)
Hindu Tem.
Litten Nat. Res.
PERIVALE PARK
PERIVALE PARK GOLF COURSE
Perivale Park Athletics Track
Club Ho.
Sports Grd.
Playing Fields
Gurnell Leisure Cen.
Lib.
Bowling Green
Sports Grd.
Tennis Courts
Castlebar Sch.
Greenford Bridge
Playing Field
RC Prim. Sch.
Cardinal Wiseman RC Sch.
Stanhope Prim. Sch.
Rec. Grd.
Day Cen.
GREENFORD PARK CEMETERY
Recreation Ground
Depot
Mayfield Prim. Sch.
River Brent
BRENT VALLEY GOLF COURSE
Cricket Ground
Brent Lodge Park
Millennium Maze
Weir
Churchfields Rec. Grd.
Club House
Hanwell Community Centre
Rec. Grd.
Hobbayne Prim. Sch.
High Sch.
Dormers Wells Leisure Cen.
Dormers Wells Jun. Sch.
Dormers Wells Inf. Sch.
WEST MIDDLESEX GOLF COURSE
Kensington Cemetery
Running Track
Iron Bridge
A40
A4127
A4020
B452
B455
UB6
W7
W13
RUISLIP ROAD
GREENFORD ROAD
ARGYLE ROAD
WESTERN AVENUE
BROADWAY UXBRIDGE RD.
THE BROADWAY
EAST ROAD

78
A
B
C
D
E
1
2
3
4
5
6
7
60
96
77
Horsenden Hill Rec. Grd.
HORSENDEN HILL GOLF COURSE
Horsenden Hill
Horsenden Farm
SUDBURY GOLF COURSE
Moat
(PADDINGTON BRANCH)
GRAND UNION CANAL
Alperton Cemetery
BRIDGEWATER A4005 ROAD
One Tree Hill Rec. Grd.
Hindu Tem.
Alperton Sch. (Lower)
Alperton
EALING ROAD
A4089
BOWRONS AV.
BRAEMAR AV.
ST. JAMES GDS.
STANLEY AV.
KATHLEEN AV.
DOROTHY AV.
MOUNT PLEASANT
ALPERTON
Perivale Wood Local Nature Reserve
Comm. Centre
PERIVALE
Lib.
BILTON
BUCKINGHAM AV.
HORSENDEN LANE NTH.
JUBILEE RD.
WOODROW CL.
GEORGE V WAY
EMPIRE WAY
JORDAN RD.
LYNMOUTH RD.
LAUNCESTON RD.
TORRINGTON RD.
LEE RD.
DEVON CL.
BRINDLEY CL.
PHOENIX TRAD. EST.
ABERCORN COMMERCIAL CEN.
BURNSIDE CRES.
Bus Garage
THE BILTON CENTRE
WALMGATE RD.
FRASER RD.
FEDERAL RD.
FAIRFIELD DR.
BROOKLANDS
EDEN CL.
GRAND UNION HGTS.
Superstore
ATHLON INDUSTRIAL ESTATE
GLACIER WY
CAPITAL BUSINESS CENTRE
NORTHWICK RD.
BRAUNSTON HO.
CARLYON RD.
PERIVALE PARK
SARSFIELD RD.
Schools
PERIMEADE RD.
ATHLON RD.
BETHLEHEM CL.
PLEASANT WAY
MANOR FARM RD.
Metropolitan Police Traffic Unit
Alperton Sports Grd.
Bowls
Ten. Cts.
Perivale
SUNLEY GDNS.
SELBORNE GDNS.
WOODHOUSE AV.
RHYL RD.
BLEASDALE AV.
SCORTON AV.
Sports Ground Comm. Cen.
CHILHAM CL.
COLWYN AV.
Tennis Courts
AINTREE RD.
WADSWORTH RD.
IMPACT BUS. PK.
PERIVALE NEW BUSINESS CENTRE
WADSWORTH BUSINESS CENTRE
FLEETWAY WEST
SHERATON BUSINESS CENTRE
SILICON BUSINESS CENTRE
PRIMROSE WAY
LILY GARDENS
Vicar's Green Prim. Sch.
UB6
TAVISTOCK RD.
ROCKFORD AV.
BIDEFORD AV.
DAWLISH AV.
Superstore
B452
TEIGNMOUTH GDNS.
TEIGNMOUTH PDE.
RYDAL CRES.
CONISTON AV.
THIRLMERE AV.
MAY GS.
CRESCENT
ALPERTON B456 LANE
WEST LINKS
MARSH RD.
River Brent
Superstore
Vicar's Bri.
A4005
HANGER LA.
MANHATTAN BUSINESS PARK
WESTGATE
HANGER LANE
Hanger La.
WESTERN AV.
A40
CENTRAL PDE.
LANGDALE GARDENS
Depot
Subway
AVENUE
GREYSTOKE
PK. TER.
GORDON HO.
WELLINGTON HO.
PERIVALE LA.
PERIVALE GRANGE
LIT. GRANGE
Club House
EALING GOLF COURSE
Tennis Courts
Perivale Bri. Playing Fields
ARGYLE RD.
B452
Gurnell Leisure Cen.
Lib.
RUISLIP RD. EAST
Pitshanger Park
Football Ground
Bowl Grn.
Brentham Club
Ten. Cts.
Pav.
River Brent
Tennis Courts
Bowl. Pav. Grns.
MEADVALE ROAD
BRUNSWICK ROAD
MULGRAVE RD.
CLARENDON RD.
SANDALL RD.
Sports Grd.
B455
ROAD
GURNELL GRO.
CROSSWAY
AVALON RD.
Bowling Green
Sports Grd.
DOWNSIDE CR.
ROYLE CR.
AVALON CL.
Tennis Courts
Pitshanger Park
PERIVALE GS.
BRENTCOT CL.
BELLEVUE RD.
SUMMERFIELD RD.
CURZON RD.
HARROW VIEW
SELBY RD.
BARNFIELD RD.
LINDFIELD RD.
NORTH VIEW
HOLYOAKE WLK.
DENISON RD.
LUDLOW RD.
BRUNNER RD.
BRENTHAM WAY
FOWLERS WLK.
KINGFIELD RD.
ANNABELS M.
Pitch & Putt Course
Hanger Hill Park
Fox Wood Nature Reserve
FOX LANE
MARCOURT LAWNS
PITSHANGER LANE
Sch.
QUEEN'S WLK.
PRINCES GDNS.
MOUNT PLEASANT RD.
WOODFIELD RD.
FAIRLEA PL.
RC Prim. Sch.
WINSCOMBE WAY
MOUNT VIEW
DAVER CT.
BIRKDALE RD.
KENT GDS.
SCOTCH COMMON
CASTLEBAR RD.
VALLIS WAY
FOSSE WAY
Prim. Sch.
Castle Bar Pk.
Castlebar Sch.
CLAREMONT RD.
Cleveland Park
CLIVEDON CT.
MIDDLEFIELDE
THE MEAD
HARDWICK GN.
TEMPLEWOOD
VICTORIA RD.
QUEEN'S GDS.
BUCKINGHAM RD.
PENDLEWOOD
STANLEY CT.
PARK GATE
WESTMORLD PL.
HILLCREST RD.
Resr. (covered)
EALING CYGNET HOSP.
AVENUE
MOUNT AV.
MONTPELIER RD.
Prim. Sch.
NICHOLS GN.
HATHAWAY GDNS.
BRUTON WAY
CLEVELAND RD.
CAVENDISH AV.
COPLEY CL.
SOVEREIGN CL.
CASTLEBAR HILL
CASTLEBAR
THE FIRS
W5
HILLCROFT CRES.
THE CROFT
WESTERGATE
CORFTON LODGE
Barclays Sports
HIGHVIEW
KINGSLEY AV.
CHARLES RD.
ROSEMOUNT RD.
BRIAR RD.
ROSEBERY GDNS.
HOLLINGBOURNE GDNS.
RAVENSBOURNE GDNS.
NORTH AV.
WIMBORNE GS.
SHERBORNE GDNS.
High Sch.
THE GRANGE
THE CEDARS
THE KNOLL
Ealing Abbey
Jun. Sch.
MARCHWOOD CRES.
ELMCROFT CL.
PARK
Aston Ho. Sch.
Cricket Ground
ST. STEPHEN'S RD.
COLEBROOKE AV.
EGERTON GS.
MONTAGUE RD.
DELL WK.
HERONSFORDE
WHITELEDGES
BLAKESLEY AV.
WESTPARK
MOUNT PK. CR.
ASTON RD.
Drayton Green
BRIDGE
LYNTON AV.
COMPTON RD.
B452
BRADLEY GDNS.
MORTIMER RD.
AMHERST RD.
HURLEY CT.
W13
Pav. Play Fld.
Schs.
HAVEN GREEN CT.
ROAD
HAVEN GRN.
MADELEY RD.
EALING
WOODVILLE RD.
REGENCY CL.
DRAYTON PARK
GRAFTON CL.
COURTFIELD GS.
SUTHERLAND RD.
COLLEGE RD.
WALDECK RD.
ARLINGTON RD.
ALBANY RD.
Sch.
Running Track
Drayton Green
DRAYTON GRO.
DRAYTON GDS.
DRAYTON RD.
GORDON RD.
WEST EALING
DENBIGH RD.
CARLTON GDNS.
LONGFIELD RD.
Ealing Squash & Fitness Club
Ealing Broadway
HAMILTON RD.
West Ealing
Super-market
HASTINGS RD.
CRAVEN RD.
EALING
BROADWAY
THE MALL
NEW BROADWAY
BOND ST.
PERCEVAL HO.
T.H.
Sch.
A4020 ROAD
UXBRIDGE
The Questors Theatre
Uni. Coll. Sch.
HIGH B455 ST.
EALING BROADWAY CEN.
Lib.
NORTH COMMON RD.
Kensington Cemetery
FELIX RD.
ALEXANDRIA RD.
BRUNSWICK RD.
BROADWAY
DRAYTON GN.
PM Gallery & House
Ealing & West London Coll.
WALPOLE PARK
Ealing Studios
EALING GRN.
GROVE
GRANGE
WEBSTER GDNS.
BRIDGE RD.
NORTHFIELD AV.
ST. MARK'S R.

79
Stonebridge Park
STONEBRIDGE PARK
61
Brent Junction
Royal Mail Depot
Stonebridge Rec. Grd.
HILLSIDE
CRAVEN PK.
STONEBRIDGE
Sports Ground
Open Space
NORTHFIELDS INDUSTRIAL ESTATE
PREMIER PARK
PARK ROYAL JUNCTION
NORTH CIRCULAR
A406
Works
NW10
TOWNSEND INDUSTRIAL ESTATE
Harlesden
WAXLOW
Lower Place
GRAND UNION CANAL (Paddington Branch)
Power Station
Twyford Abbey
ORIGIN BUSINESS PARK
PARK ROYAL
CENTRAL MIDDLESEX HOSPITAL
Playing Field
FIRST CENTRAL BUSINESS PARK
CUMBERLAND AVENUE
ACTON
FROGMORE INDUSTRIAL ESTATE
PARK ROYAL
WESTERN
CORONATION
London Shootfighters Gym
Park Royal
Tenpin
Cinema
A40
NORTH ACTON
Cemetery
North Acton
VICTORIA A4000
80
82
Hanger Hill
GYPSY CORNER
NORTH ACTON PLAYING FIELDS
West Acton
WALES FARM RD.
Sports Ground
Nth. Ealing
West Acton
Acton Main Line
School
Play. Fld.
W3
Japanese Sch. London
Sports Ground
ACTON
Twyford Spts. Cen.
97
Ealing Common
GUNNERSBURY
HIGH
Acton Central
ACTON PARK
EAST ACTON
The Park Club
Football Pitch
F
G
H
J
K
1
2
3
4
5
6
7
19
20
21

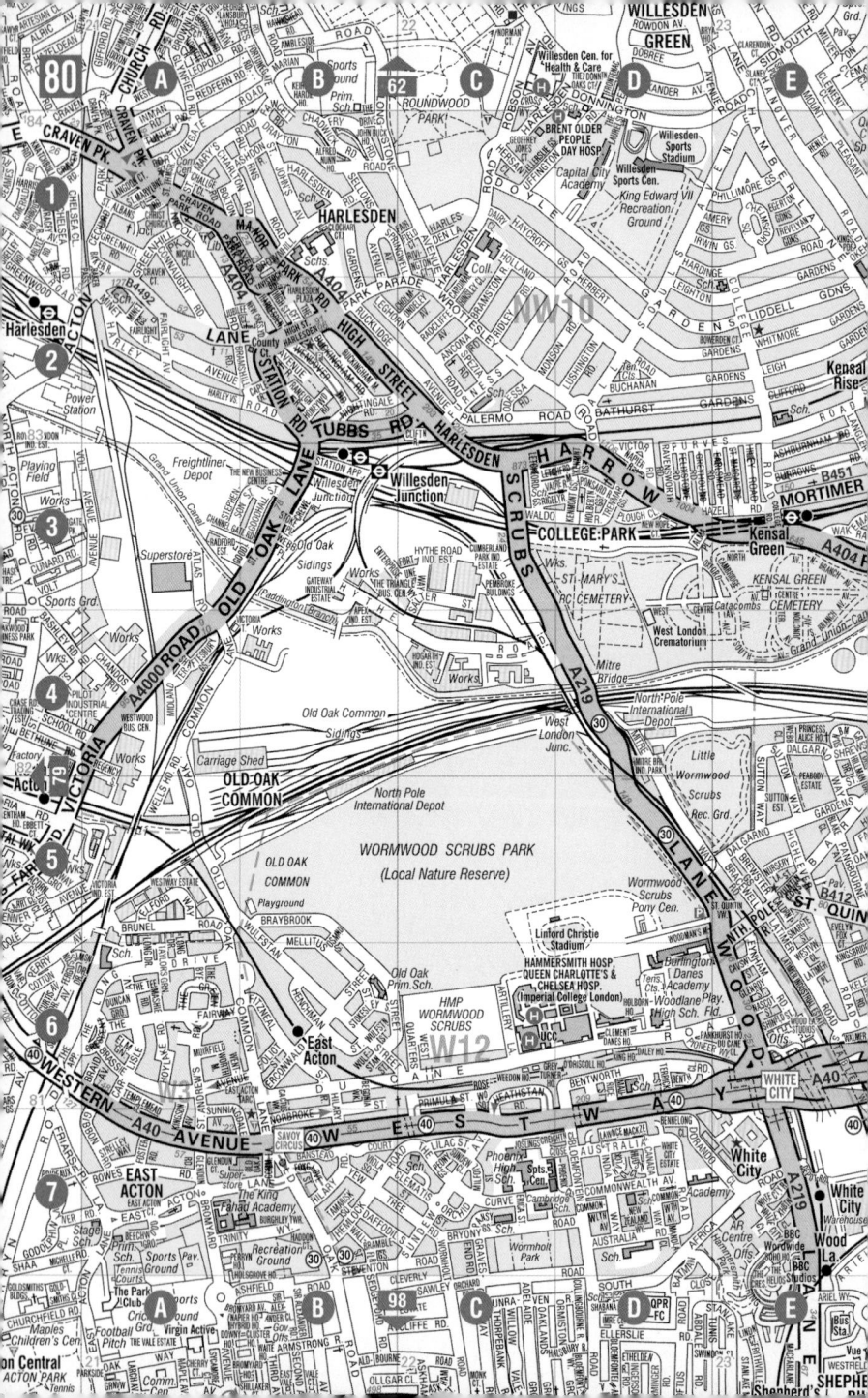
80
62
98
79
WILLESDEN GREEN
HARLESDEN
NW10
Harlesden
Power Station
Playing Field
Freightliner Depot
Grand Union Canal
Willesden Junction
Superstore
Old Oak Sidings
Paddington Branch
Old Oak Common Sidings
Carriage Shed
OLD OAK COMMON
North Pole International Depot
WORMWOOD SCRUBS PARK
(Local Nature Reserve)
HMP WORMWOOD SCRUBS
W12
W3
EAST ACTON
East Acton
Acton
Kensal Green
Kensal Rise
KENSAL GREEN CEMETERY
ST. MARY'S RC CEMETERY
West London Crematorium
Little Wormwood Scrubs Rec. Grd.
Wormwood Scrubs Pony Cen.
Linford Christie Stadium
HAMMERSMITH HOSP, QUEEN CHARLOTTE'S & CHELSEA HOSP. (Imperial College London)
Burlington Danes Academy
Woodlane High Sch.
White City
Wood La.
BBC Studios
Willesden Sports Stadium
Willesden Sports Cen.
King Edward VII Recreation Ground
Capital City Academy
BRENT OLDER PEOPLE DAY HOSP.
Willesden Cen. for Health & Care
ROUNDWOOD PARK
COLLEGE PARK
MORTIMER
Wormholt Park
Phoenix High Sch.
The King Fahad Academy
Recreation Ground
QPR FC
WESTERN AVENUE
WESTWAY
A40
A219
A404
A4000
B451
B412
B4492
VICTORIA ROAD
OLD OAK LANE
OLD OAK COMMON LANE
SCRUBS LANE
HARROW ROAD
HIGH STREET
WOOD LANE
SAVOY CIRCUS
WHITE CITY
On Central
ACTON PARK

81
F
G
H
J
K
1
2
3
4
5
6
7
63
99
82
BRONDESBURY
BRONDESBURY PARK
Brondesbury Park
WILLESDEN LA.
KILBURN HIGH ROAD
Paddington Old Cemetery
(Willesden Lane Cemetery)
Fitness First
QUEENS PARK
Queens Park
Bandstand
Tennis Courts
KENSAL RISE
KENSAL GREEN
City Learning Cen.
Play. Fld.
Comm. Cen.
CHEVENING ROAD
WRENTHAM AV.
SALUSBURY ROAD
BRONDESBURY ROAD
BRONDESBURY VILLAS
KILBURN
Kilburn High Road
Kilburn Park
BELSIZE ROAD
ABBEY ROAD
QUEX RD.
WEST END LA.
B509
B507
B451 ROAD
A5 ROAD
A4003
MAIDA VALE
Maida Vale
A5
BOUNDARY ROAD
CARLTON VALE
B413
HARVIST ROAD
KILBURN LANE
WEST KILBURN
Paddington Rec. Grd.
Cricket Ground
Tennis Cts.
Pav.
KILBURN PARK ROAD
B414
SHIRLAND ROAD
ELGIN AV.
Paddington Sports Club
BBC Studios
W9
LAUDERDALE ROAD
WARWICK AVENUE
CLIFTON GDNS.
HARROW ROAD
KENSAL TOWN
MAIDA HILL
A404
LADBROKE GROVE
B450
Gas Works
Superstore
(Paddington Branch)
CANAL
WESTBOURNE GREEN
Westbourne Park
WESTWAY
A40
GREAT WESTERN RD.
A4207
ST. CHARLES HOSPITAL
NORTH KENSINGTON
Carmelite Monastery
ST. MARK'S RD.
CAMBRIDGE GS.
Ladbroke Gro.
Isaac Newton Cen.
Health Club
WESTBOURNE PARK ROAD
WESTBOURNE PK. VS.
Royal Oak
PORCHESTER RD.
BISHOP'S BRI. RD.
BAYSWATER
WESTBOURNE GRO.
CHEPSTOW RD.
A4206
PEMBRIDGE VS.
W2
W11
W10
Latimer Rd.
WEST CROSS ROUTE
A3220
NOTTING HILL
NOTTING HILL GATE
Notting Hill Gate
KENSINGTON PARK RD.
B415
LADBROKE GROVE
Ladbroke Square Gardens
HOLLAND PARK AVENUE
Holland Park
QUEENSWAY
Queensway
Bayswater
BAYSWATER RD.
A402
Inverness Terrace Gate
Porchester Ter. Gate
Orme Sq. Gate
Black Lion Gate
Elfin Oak
The Orangery
KENSINGTON GARDENS
THE BROAD WALK
Kensington

82
A
B
C
D
E
1
2
3
4
5
6
7
64
4
5
81
10
100
South Hampstead
Swiss Cottage
Chalk Farm
Primrose Hill
PRIMROSE HILL
NW3
NW8
NW1
W9
W2
BELSIZE B509 RD.
ABBEY ROAD
FINCHLEY RD.
AVENUE
ADELAIDE
ALBERT A5205 RD.
PRINCE ALBERT RD.
Reservoir (covered)
Barrow Hill
Running Track
London Zoo
Gloucester Gate
REGENT'S PARK
The Hub
Winfield House
London Central Mosque
St. John's Lodge
Open Air Theatre
QUEEN MARY'S GARDENS
Boating Lake
The Holme
Regent's Univ. London
Clarence Gate
MARYLEBONE
Baker St.
Madame Tussaud's
St. John's Wood
WELLINGTON RD.
THE WELLINGTON HOSP
Middlesex CCC (Lord's)
ST. JOHN'S WOOD
ST. JOHN'S WOOD RD.
GROVE END RD.
LISSON GROVE
Lisson Green
Maida Vale
MAIDA VALE
MAIDA VALE
EDGWARE ROAD
Warwick Av.
Little Venice
Edgware Road
MARYLEBONE RD.
MARYLEBONE FLYOVER
WESTWAY A40
HARROW ROAD
A404
Royal Oak
PADDINGTON
Paddington
Paddington Basin
PRAED ST.
BISHOP'S BRIDGE RD.
ST. MARY'S HOSP
SUSSEX GDNS.
BAYSWATER
Bayswater
Queensway
BAYSWATER RD.
Lancaster Gate
A402
St. George's Field
Marble Arch
MARBLE ARCH
Speakers' Corner
HYDE PARK
PARK LANE
A4202
OXFORD ST.
WIGMORE ST.
BAKER ST.
PORTMAN SQUARE
Wallace Collection
MARYLEBONE HIGH ST.
MAYFAIR
Roosevelt Mem.
The Long Water
The Fountains
Victoria Gate
Speke's Monument
Peter Pan Statue
Serpentine Sackler Gallery
KENSINGTON GARDENS
Elfin Oak
The Orangery
Physical Energy Statue
Temple Lodge
Norwegian War Mem.
Parks Police
Parks Inf. Cen.
The Lookout
Joy of Life Fountain
Reformers Tree
Parade Ground
Refreshment Kiosk

83
84
65
101
6
7
F
G
H
J
K
1
2
3
4
5
6
7
CAMDEN TOWN
Camden Town
Camden Rd.
BRITANNIA JUNC.
KENTISH TOWN
& Barnsbury
REGENT'S PARK
Mornington Cres.
SOMERS TOWN
EUSTON
Euston
Euston Sq.
EUSTON UNDERPASS
ST. PANCRAS INTERNATIONAL
KING'S CROSS
King's Cross
British Library
Francis Crick Institute
PENTONVILLE
PENTONVILLE ROAD
COPENHAGEN ST.
CALEDONIAN RD.
YORK WAY
PANCRAS WAY
PANCRAS RD.
ST. PANCRAS
Coram's Fields
CLERKENWELL
FARRINGDON RD.
KING'S CROSS RD.
GRAY'S INN RD.
THEOBALDS RD.
HIGH HOLBORN
Holborn
HOLBORN
KINGSWAY
Chancery La.
Royal Courts of Justice
FLEET
Temple
EMBANKMENT
ALDWYCH
STRAND
Covent Gdn.
Opera Ho.
Leicester Sq.
Charing Cross
CHARING CROSS
Embankment
Embankment Pier
Cleopatra's Needle
Festival Pier
Royal Festival Hall
Southbank Cen.
National Theatre
BFI
The London Television Centre
SOUTH BANK
RIVER THAMES
VICTORIA
Courtauld Gall.
Somerset Ho.
Savoy Pier
Nelson's Col.
National Gallery
Admiralty Arch
NORTHUMBERLAND AV.
WHITEHALL
PALL MALL
PICCADILLY
Piccadilly Circus
Green Park
SHAFTESBURY
SOHO
Oxford Circus
Tottenham Ct. R.
NEW OXFORD
Goodge St.
Warren St.
Gt. Portland St.
Regent's Pk.
PARK CRES.
PORTLAND PL.
REGENT ST.
NEW BOND ST.
CONDUIT ST.
MORTIMER
GOODGE ST.
TOTTENHAM COURT RD.
GOWER ST.
University College London
Petrie Mus.
BLOOMSBURY
Russell Sq.
RUSSELL SQ.
British Museum
Univ. of London
Brunei Gall.
SOUTHAMPTON ROW
WOBURN PL.
GUILFORD ST.
BERNARD S.
EUSTON RD.
HAMPSTEAD RD.
EVERSHOLT
CROWNDALE RD.
CAMDEN ST.
COLLEGE ST.
PARKWAY
DELANCEY ST.
ALBANY ST.
Lewis Cubitt Pk.
Gasholder Pk.
WHARFDALE R.
Ryl. Veterinary Coll.
ST. PANCRAS HOSPITAL
Barracks
Avenue Gardens
English Gardens
Theatre
Sch.
Mus.
Hosp.

84
A
B
C
D
E
66
Essex Rd.
ISLINGTON
DE BEAUVOIR TOWN
DOWNHAM ROAD
NEW NORTH RD.
LIVERPOOL RD.
UPPER ST.
Barnard Park
Angel
PENTONVILLE A501 RD.
CITY ROAD
HOXTON
SHOREDITCH
FINSBURY
KING'S CROSS RD.
CLERKENWELL
GOSWELL RD.
ST. JOHN ST.
FARRINGDON RD.
Farringdon
Barbican
ST. LUKE'S
Old Street
OLD ST.
GREAT EASTERN ST.
Moorgate
LIVERPOOL ST.
LONDON WALL A1211
HOLBORN
HOLBORN VIADUCT
City Thameslink
St. Paul's
CHEAPSIDE
Bank
CITY
Mansion Ho.
FLEET ST.
STRAND
Royal Courts of Justice
Temple
VICTORIA EMB.
QUEEN VICTORIA ST.
UP. THAMES ST.
LOWER THAMES ST.
Monument
FENCHURCH ST.
CANNON STREET
BLACKFRIARS
SOUTHWARK
Blackfriars Millennium Pier
RIVER THAMES
Bankside Pier
Tate Modern
LONDON BR.
London Bridge City Pier
SOUTHWARK ST.
STAMFORD ST.
National Theatre
7
8
9
83
102
1
2
3
4
5
6
7

DALSTON
London Fields
SOUTH HACKNEY
F
G
H
J
K
67
85
Haggerston
QUEENSBRIDGE
Victoria Fountain
Royal Gate East
1
VICTORIA
PARK
GROVE
A1205
HAGGERSTON
Regent's Canal
Anton's Lock
Cambridge Heath
BISHOP'S
SEWARDSTONE RD.
B127
OLD FORD RD.
B118
2
Hoxton
HACKNEY RD.
A1208
Hackney City Farm
York Hall
OLD FORD RD.
GLOBE TOWN
MILE END
3
COLUMBIA RD.
GOSSET
BETHNAL GREEN RD.
A1209
Bethnal Grn.
BETHNAL GREEN
VALLANCE
ROMAN RD.
B135
THREE COLTS LA.
Bethnal Grn
CHESHIRE
DUN-BRIDGE
Shoreditch High St.
SPITALFIELDS
CAMBRIDGE HEATH RD.
A107
Stepney Green
MILE END RD.
A11
4
MILE END HOSPITAL
Queen Mary University of London
86
Whitechapel
The Royal London Hosp
STEPNEY GREEN
B140
5
WHITECHAPEL RD.
A11
Aldgate East
COMMERCIAL RD.
STEPNEY
RATCLIFF
Aldgate
WHITECHAPEL
A1202
CANNON ST. RD.
A13
6
MINORIES
MANSELL
Tower Gateway
Tower Hill
15
CABLE ST.
B126
Shadwell
DLR
THE HIGHWAY
A1203
Limehouse Link
7
TOWER HILL
The Tower of London
EAST SMITHFIELD
St. Katharine Docks
SHADWELL
Shadwell Basin
King Edward Mem. Park
A101
ROTHERHITHE TUNNEL
THAMES
RIVER
103
Wapping
TOWER BRI.
A100
St. Katharine's Pier
Butlers Wharf

86
68
85
104
A
B
C
D
E
1
2
3
4
5
6
7
SOUTH HACKNEY
STRATFORD
QUEEN ELIZABETH OLYMPIC PARK
London Stadium
West Ham Utd. FC
The Orbit
The Slide
London Aquatics Centre
VICTORIA PARK
Victoria Park Athletics Arena
Victoria Fountain
Bowling Green
Bandstand Pav.
Tennis Courts
Playground
Three Colt Bridge
Skew Bridge
Crown Gate East
Crown Gate West
E9
E20
OLD FORD
GROVE ROAD
OLD FORD ROAD
ROMAN ROAD
PARNELL RD
FAIRFIELD RD
EAST CROSS ROUTE
A12 BLACKWALL
Pudding Mill Lane
BOW INTERCHANGE
GREENWAY
BOW ROAD
Bow Church
Bow Rd.
HIGH ST
Three Mills Green
The House Mill
THREE MILL LA.
Bow Creek
Superstore
Bromley-by-Bow
BROMLEY
DEVAS ST.
Devons Rd.
DEVONS ROAD
BOW COMMON
DEVONS WAY
NORTHERN APPROACH
A12
MILE END
Mile End
MILE END HOSPITAL
TOWER HAMLETS CEN.
Queen Mary University of London
MILE END PARK
Mile End Park Leisure Centre
Mile End Stadium
MILE END ROAD
A11
BURDETT RD.
A1205
TOWER HAMLETS CEMETERY PARK
BEN JONSON RD.
ST. PAUL'S WAY
B140
RATCLIFF
LIMEHOUSE
Limehouse
COMMERCIAL RD.
LIMEHOUSE LINK
Limehouse Basin
Ratcliff Cross Stairs
RIVER THAMES
LIMEHOUSE REACH
Westferry
WESTFERRY RD.
EAST INDIA DOCK RD.
A13
POPLAR
Poplar
POPLAR HIGH ST.
Langdon Pk.
All Saints
ASPEN WAY
A1261
West India Quay
Canary Wharf
Billingsgate Market
WEST INDIA DOCKS
BLACKWALL BASIN
Canary Wharf Pier
Westferry Circus
Hilton Docklands Pier
ROTHERHITHE
SALTER RD.
B205
Globe Stairs
Pageant Stairs
Columbia Wharf
Ordnance Wharf
PRESTON'S RD.
COTTON ST.
Depot
PROLOGIS PARK
ACME STUDIOS
THREE MILLS STUDIOS
BOW LOCKS
Bartlett Park
Furze Grn.
Go-Kart Track
PureGym
Museum
South Dock

87
69
88
105
F
G
H
J
K
1
2
3
4
5
6
7
WEST HAM
PARK
UPTON
Upton Park
Stratford High St.
Abbey Road
PORTWAY
PLASHET
WEST HAM
NEW PLAISTOW RD.
PLAISTOW RD.
HIGH ST.
A112
Plaistow
MANOR RD.
A1011
Mill Meads
Prescott Channel
West Ham
East London Crematorium
EAST LONDON CEMETERY
Memorial Recreation Ground
PLAISTOW
GREENGATE ST.
BALAAM ST.
PRINCE REGENT LA.
A124
BARKING RD.
Recreation Ground
Newham College
Star Park
Star La.
STEPHENSON ST.
NEWHAM WAY
A13
Bow Creek
Creek Wharf
Canning Town
CANNING TOWN
SILVERTOWN WAY
LOWER LEA CROSSING
A1020
Bow Creek Ecology Park
East India
LEAMOUTH
Royal Victoria
Prince Regent
Custom House for ExCeL
ExCeL
ROYAL VICTORIA DOCK
Emirates Royal Docks
Royal Victoria Docks Watersports Cen.
RIVER THAMES
Blackwall
Blackwall Point
Virginia Quay
Blackwall Pier
SILVERTOWN VIADUCT
Millennium Mill
Pontoon Dock
SS Robin

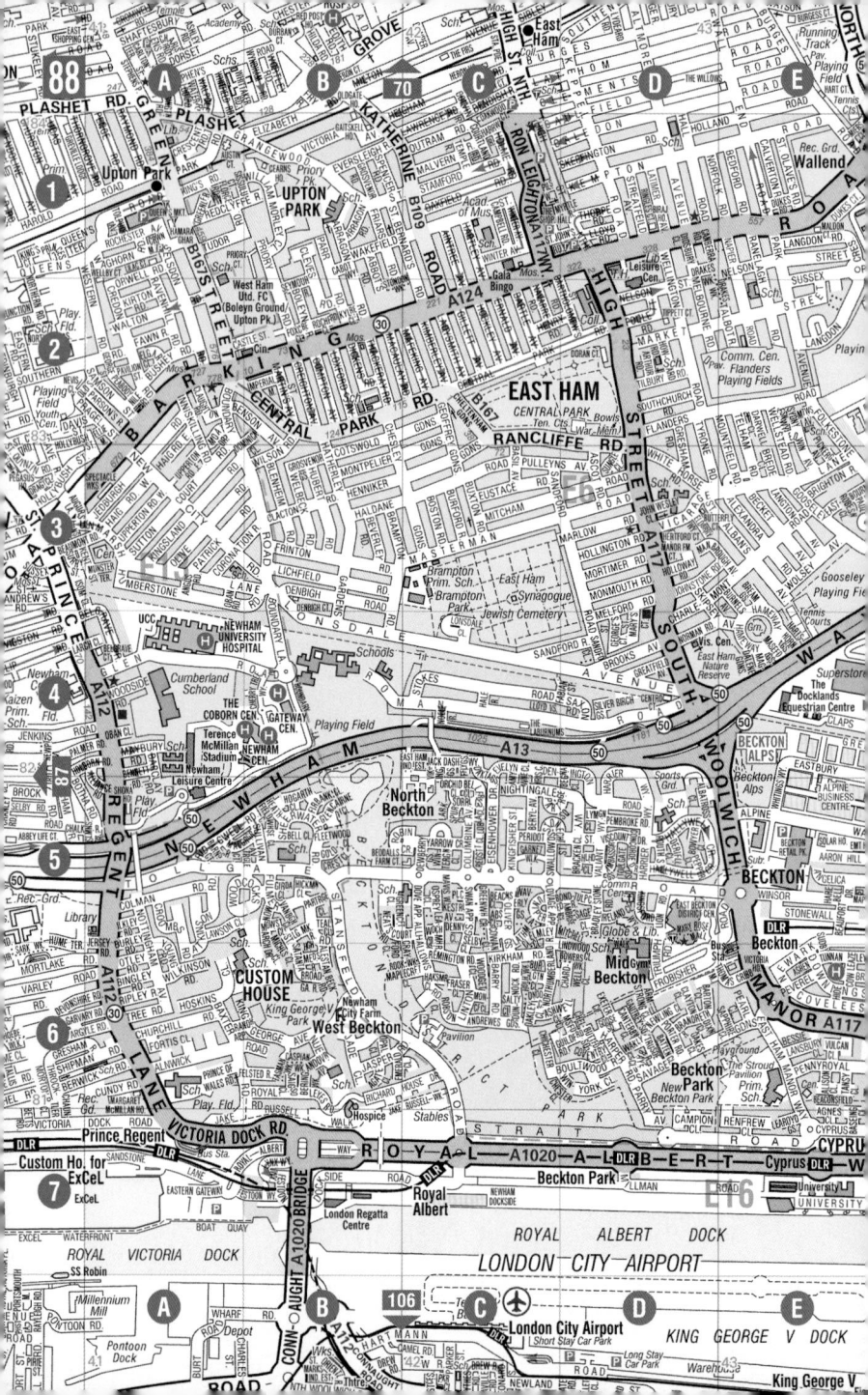

88
A
B
70
C
D
E
1
2
3
4
5
6
7
87
106
PLASHET RD.
GREEN
PLASHET
GROVE
HIGH ST. NTH.
East Ham
Upton Park
UPTON PARK
KATHERINE
B109
ROAD
RON LEIGHTON A117 WY.
Wallend
West Ham Utd. FC (Boleyn Ground/ Upton Pk.)
Gala Bingo
A124
BARKING
B167 STREET
CENTRAL
PARK
RD.
EAST HAM
CENTRAL PARK
RANCLIFFE RD.
HIGH STREET
SOUTH
A117
E6
E13
Comm. Cen.
Flanders Playing Fields
Gooseley Playing Fields
Brampton Prim. Sch.
Brampton Park
East Ham Jewish Cemetery
Synagogue
LONSDALE
Schools
UCC
NEWHAM UNIVERSITY HOSPITAL
Cumberland School
THE COBORN CEN.
GATEWAY CEN.
Terence McMillan Stadium
NEWHAM CEN.
Newham Leisure Centre
Playing Field
NEWHAM WAY
A13
East Ham Nature Reserve
The Docklands Equestrian Centre
BECKTON ALPS
Beckton Alps
ALPINE BUSINESS CENTRE
BECKTON RETAIL PK
WOOLWICH
MANOR A117
BECKTON
Beckton
North Beckton
PRINCE REGENT
A112
REGENT
LANE
TOLLGATE
CUSTOM HOUSE
King George V Park
Newham City Farm
West Beckton
Mid Beckton
Globe & Lib.
EAST BECKTON DISTRICT CEN.
Beckton Park
New Beckton Park
The Stroud Pavilion
EAST HAM MANOR WAY
DISTRICT PARK
Hospice
Stables
VICTORIA DOCK RD.
Prince Regent
Custom Ho. for ExCeL
ExCeL
EASTERN GATEWAY
ROYAL ALBERT A1020 WAY
Beckton Park
Royal Albert
London Regatta Centre
NEWHAM DOCKSIDE
Cyprus
University
UNIVERSITY
E16
CONNAUGHT BRIDGE A1020
ROYAL ALBERT DOCK
LONDON CITY AIRPORT
ROYAL VICTORIA DOCK
SS Robin
Millennium Mill
Pontoon Dock
Depot
London City Airport
Short Stay Car Park
Long Stay Car Park
KING GEORGE V DOCK
King George V
HARTMANN
CONNAUGHT
WHARF RD.
PONTOON RD.

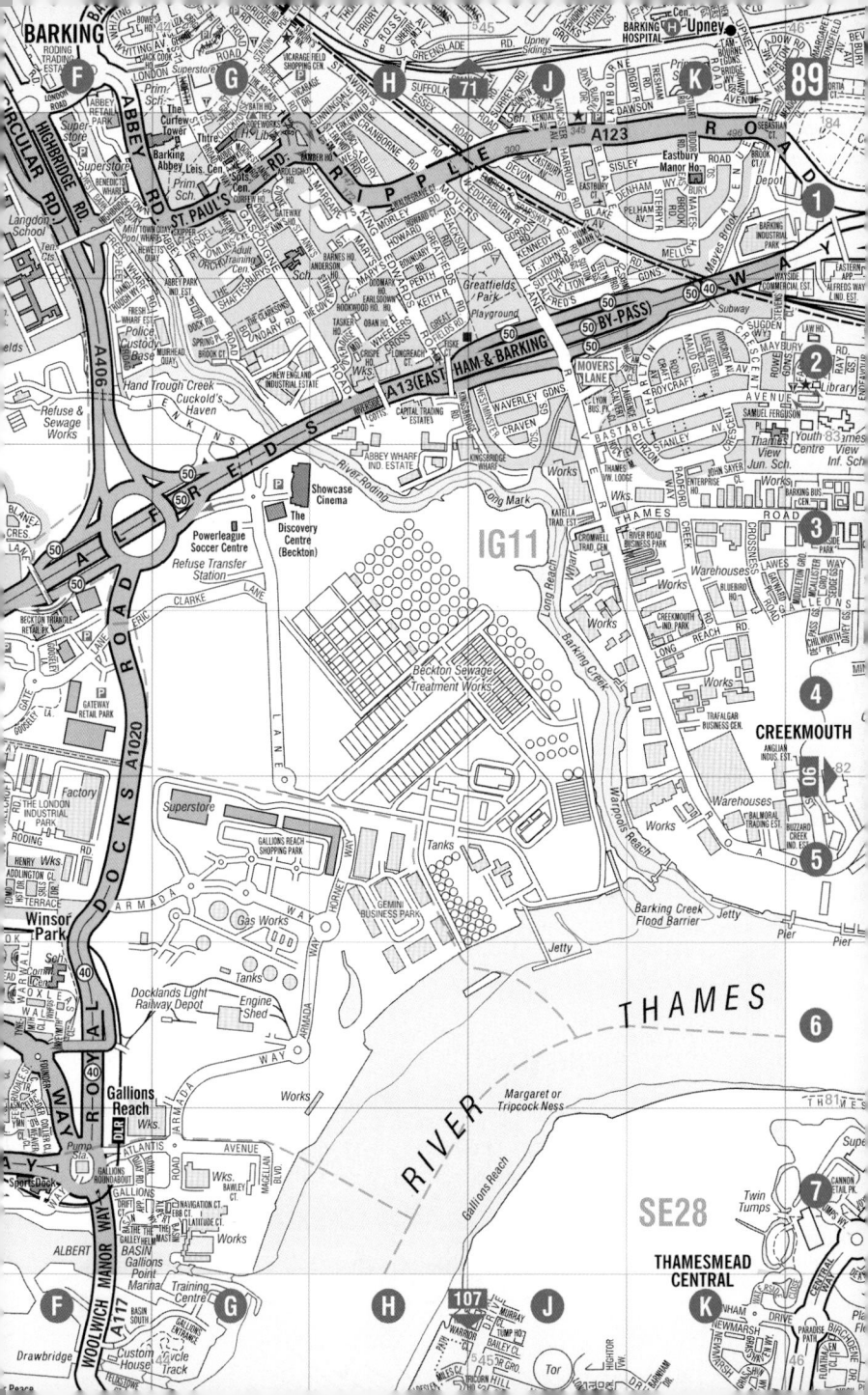
BARKING
RODING TRADING ESTATE
F
G
H
J
K
71
BARKING HOSPITAL
Upney
Upney Sidings
GREENSLADE RD.
VICARAGE FIELD SHOPPING CEN.
SUFFOLK RD.
ESSEX RD.
LAMBOURNE RD.
DIGBY RD.
DAWSON AV.
HIGHBRIDGE RD.
CIRCULAR RD.
ABBEY RD.
The Curfew Tower
Barking Abbey
Leis. Cen.
Superstore
ABBEY RETAIL PARK
RIPPLE RD.
A123
RIPPLE ROAD
Eastbury Manor Ho.
EASTBURY AV.
SISLEY RD.
DENHAM WY.
PELHAM AV.
BLAKE AV.
MELLIS AV.
Mayes Brook
Depot
BARKING INDUSTRIAL PARK
1
ST. PAUL'S RD.
Langdon School
Town Quay
Adult Training Cen.
ABBEY PARK IND. EST.
FRESH WHARF EST.
Police Custody Base
MUIRHEAD QUAY
DOCK RD.
SPRING PL.
BROOK CT.
THE SHAFTESBURYS
GASCOIGNE RD.
ST. MARY'S
KING EDWARDS RD.
MORLEY RD.
HOWARD RD.
PERTH RD.
KEITH R.
GREATFIELDS RD.
JACKSON RD.
MOVERS LANE
Greatfields Park
Playground
WHEELERS CROSS
LONGREACH CT.
NEW ENGLAND INDUSTRIAL ESTATE
A13 (EAST HAM & BARKING BY-PASS)
50
40
ALFREDS WAY
WAYSIDE COMMERCIAL EST.
EASTERN APP.
ALFREDS WAY IND. EST.
Subway
MAYBURY RD.
ROYCRAFT AV.
Library
2
SAMUEL FERGUSON PL.
Youth Centre
Thames View Jun. Sch.
Thames View Inf. Sch.
83
A406
Hand Trough Creek
Cuckold's Haven
Refuse & Sewage Works
JENKINS LANE
CAPITAL TRADING ESTATE
WAVERLEY GDNS.
CRAVEN GDNS.
KINGSBRIDGE WHARF
ABBEY WHARF IND. ESTATE
River Roding
Showcase Cinema
The Discovery Centre (Beckton)
Powerleague Soccer Centre
Refuse Transfer Station
Long Mark
Works
Wks.
THAMES VW. LODGE
BASTABLE AV.
STANLEY AV.
CURZON CRESCENT
RADFORD WAY
JOHN SAYER CL.
ENTERPRISE HO.
BARKING BUS CEN.
THAMES ROAD
3
KATELLA TRAD. EST.
CROMWELL TRAD. CEN.
RIVER ROAD BUSINESS PARK
IG11
CREEK RD.
CROSSNESS RD.
Warehouses
LAWES WAY
GALLEONS DR.
CHILWORTH PL.
CREEKMOUTH IND. PARK
LONG REACH RD.
Long Reach
Wharf
Barking Creek
BLANEY CRES.
CLARKE LANE
ERIC CLARKE LANE
BECKTON TRIANGLE RETAIL PK.
GOOSELEY LA.
GATEWAY RETAIL PARK
Beckton Sewage Treatment Works
Works
TRAFALGAR BUSINESS CEN.
4
CREEKMOUTH
ANGLIAN INDUS. EST.
90
82
DOCKS ROAD
A1020
Factory
THE LONDON INDUSTRIAL PARK
RODING RD.
HENRY RD.
ADDLINGTON CL.
Superstore
GALLIONS REACH SHOPPING PARK
HORNET WAY
Tanks
GEMINI BUSINESS PARK
Warpools Reach
Warehouses
BALMORAL TRADING EST.
BUZZARD CREEK IND. EST.
RIVER ROAD
5
ARMADA WAY
Gas Works
Winsor Park
Barking Creek Flood Barrier
Jetty
Pier
Jetty
Tanks
Docklands Light Railway Depot
Engine Shed
THAMES
6
ROYAL DOCKS RD.
WOOLWICH MANOR WAY
Gallions Reach
DLR
Wks.
Works
Margaret or Tripcock Ness
81
RIVER
Gallions Reach
ATLANTIS AVENUE
MAGELLAN BLVD.
Pump Sta.
GALLIONS ROUNDABOUT
SportsDock
NAVIGATION CT.
LATITUDE CT.
Works
ALBERT BASIN
Gallions Point Marina
Training Centre
SE28
Twin Tumps
7
CANNON RETAIL PK.
THAMESMEAD CENTRAL
CENTRAL WAY
A117
BASIN SOUTH
GALLIONS ENTRANCE
Drawbridge
Custom House
Cycle Track
F
G
H
107
J
K
MURRAY CL.
TUMP HO.
BAILEY CL.
WARRIOR CL.
MILES CL.
TRICORN HILL
Tor
HIGHTOR VW.
NEWMARSH
DRIVE
PARADISE PATH
BIRCHDENE DR.
44
45
46

90
72
108
68
A
B
C
D
E
1
2
3
4
5
6
7
IG11
RIPPLE ROAD
A123
LODGE AV.
A1153
LODGE AVENUE FLYOVER JUNC.
Cemetery
WOODWARD RD.
GORESBROOK ROAD
CASTLE GREEN
Playing Field
Castle Grn. Leis. Cen.
Jo Richardson Comm. Sch.
Games Cts.
Subway
A13
RIPPLE ROAD
ALFREDS WY.
Barking Industrial Park
Rippleside
Warehouse
Depot
Ripple Lane Sidings
WIVENHOE RD.
Newlands Park
Library
Youth Centre
Thames View Jun. Sch.
Thames View Inf. Sch.
High Speed 1
Scrattons Farm Eco-Park
Vue Cinema
Bowl. Alley
Mecca Bingo
Goals Soccer Cen.
THAMES ROAD
The Ripple Nature Reserve
Barking Riverside
Power Station (disused)
George Carey C of E Prim. Sch.
CREEKMOUTH
Barking Riverside Resource Centre
Barking Riverside Recycling Park
Dagenham Sunday Market
RENWICK ROAD
RIVER ROAD
Works
Warehouses
Jetty
Pier
Barking or False Point
Horse Shoe Corner
Depot
RIVER
BARKING REACH
Cross Ness
Abbey Sluice
THAMESMEAD
Thamesmead North
Driving Range
THAMESVIEW GOLF COURSE
Thamesmere Leisure Cen.
Superstore
Twin Tumps
THAMESMEAD CENTRAL
A2041
CARLYLE WAY
Bishop John Robinson Prim. Sch.
Ecumenical Cen.
Youth Club
Butts Wood
Woolwich Polytechnic School
Football Ground
Playing Field
Prim. Sch.
A2016
EASTERN WAY
BAZALGETTE WAY
Lakeside
THAMESIDE
Pumping Station
CENTRAL WAY

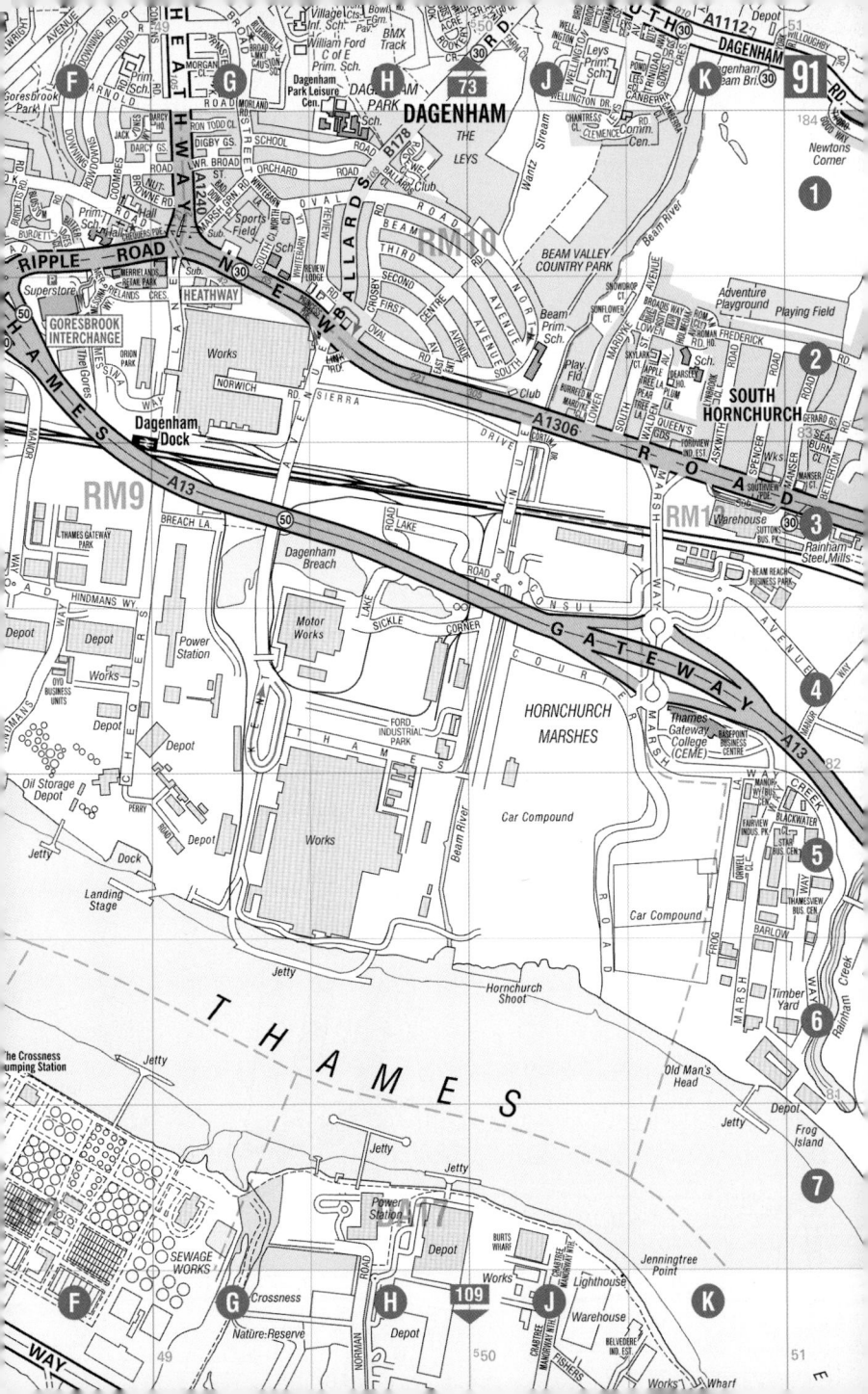

91
73
DAGENHAM
THE LEYS
RM10
RM9
RM13
SOUTH HORNCHURCH
BEAM VALLEY COUNTRY PARK
HORNCHURCH MARSHES
THAMES
RIPPLE ROAD
NEW ROAD
A13
A1306
GATEWAY
GORESBROOK INTERCHANGE
Dagenham Dock
Dagenham Breach
Power Station
Motor Works
Works
Car Compound
Hornchurch Shoot
Old Man's Head
Frog Island
Rainham Creek
Thames Gateway College (CEME)
Rainham Steel Mills
Newtons Corner
Adventure Playground
Playing Field
Oil Storage Depot
The Crossness Pumping Station
SEWAGE WORKS
Crossness Nature Reserve
Jenningtree Point
Lighthouse
109

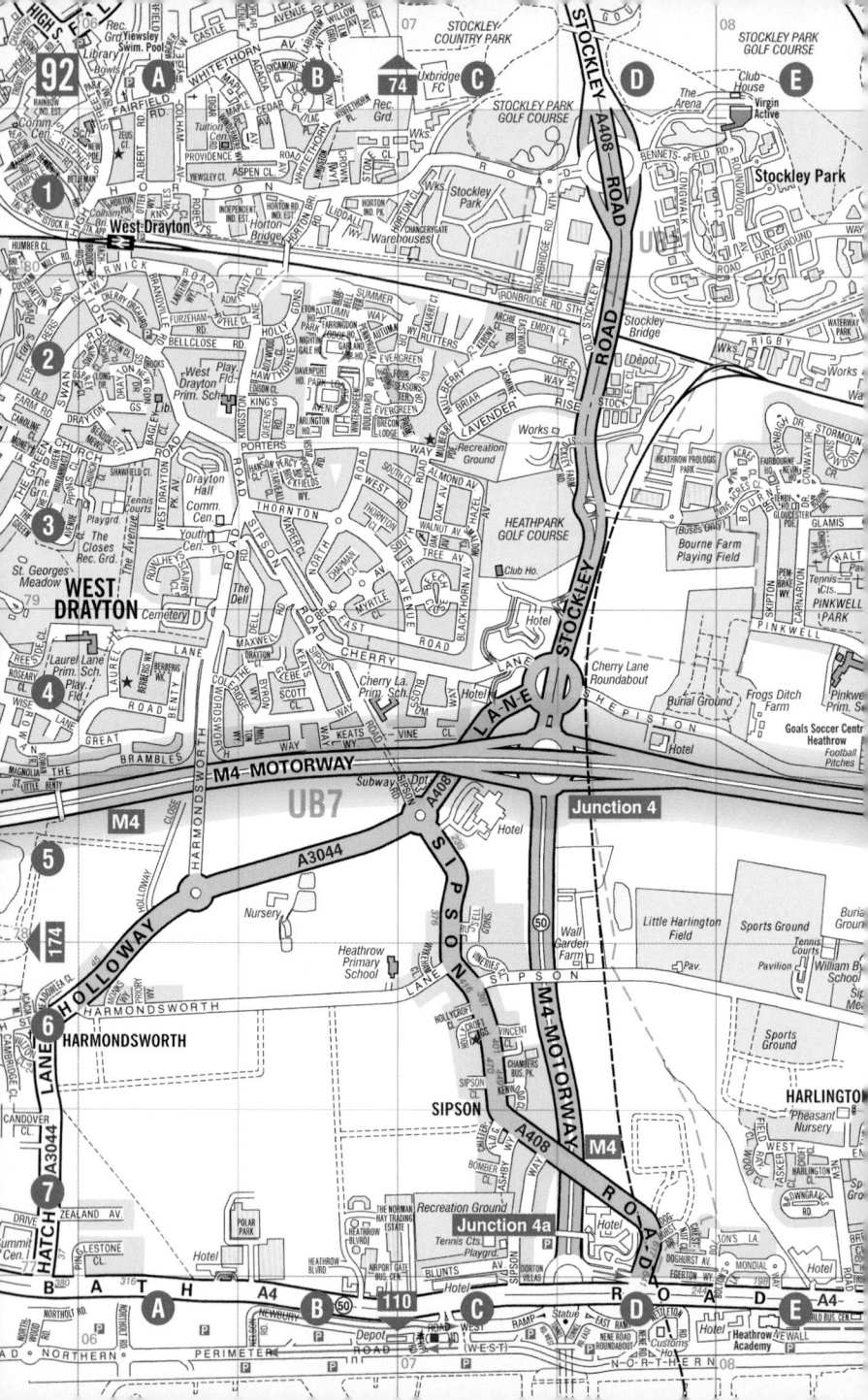

92
74
174
110
STOCKLEY COUNTRY PARK
STOCKLEY PARK GOLF COURSE
Stockley Park
Club House
The Arena
Virgin Active
Uxbridge FC
Rec. Grd.
Yiewsley Swim. Pool
Library
Bowls
West Drayton
WEST DRAYTON
HORTON ROAD
Horton Bridge
Warehouses
UB11
UB7
STOCKLEY ROAD
A408
Stockley Bridge
IRONBRIDGE RD. STH.
HEATHROW PROLOGIS PARK
Bourne Farm Playing Field
HEATHPARK GOLF COURSE
Club Ho.
Recreation Ground
West Drayton Prim. Sch.
Play. Fld.
Drayton Hall
Comm. Cen.
Youth Cen.
The Closes Rec. Grd.
St. Georges Meadow
Cemetery
The Dell
Laurel Lane Prim. Sch.
Cherry La. Prim. Sch.
Cherry Lane Roundabout
Burial Ground
Frogs Ditch Farm
Goals Soccer Centre Heathrow
Football Pitches
PINKWELL PARK
M4 MOTORWAY
M4
Junction 4
Junction 4a
A3044
HOLLOWAY
HARMONDSWORTH
Nursery
Heathrow Primary School
Little Harlington Field
Sports Ground
Pavilion
Wall Garden Farm
SIPSON
SIPSON ROAD
HARLINGTON
Pheasant Nursery
POLAR PARK
THE NORMAN HAY TRADING ESTATE
AIRPORT GATE BUS. CEN.
Recreation Ground
Tennis Cts.
Playgrd.
Hotel
BATH ROAD
A4
NORTHERN PERIMETER ROAD
Depot
Statue
NENE ROAD ROUNDABOUT
Customs Ho.
Heathrow Academy
HATCH LANE
Summit Cen.

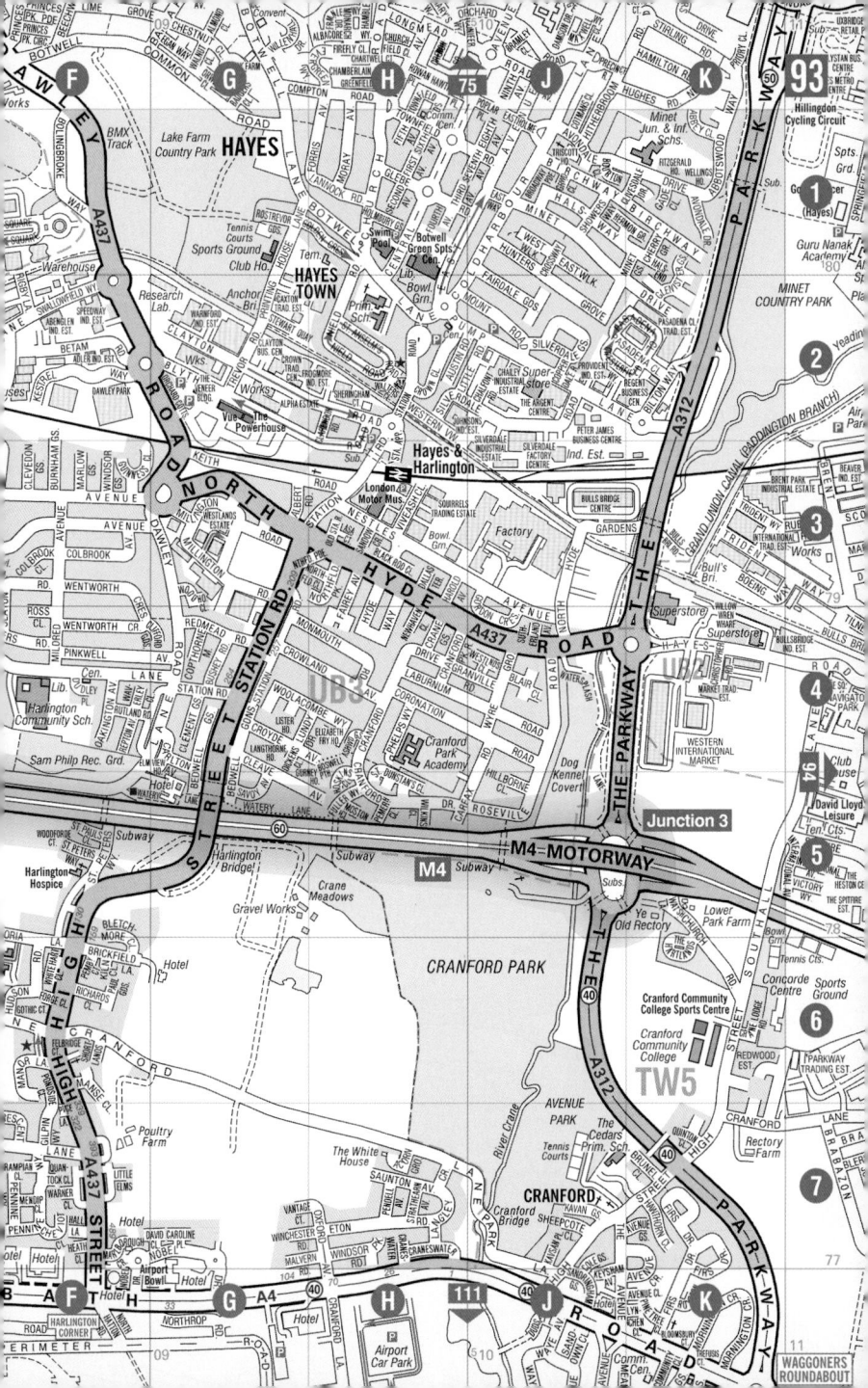

93
75
94
111
F
G
H
J
K
1
2
3
4
5
6
7
HAYES
HAYES TOWN
Lake Farm Country Park
BMX Track
Hillingdon Cycling Circuit
MINET COUNTRY PARK
Minet Jun. & Inf. Schs.
Guru Nanak Academy
Botwell Green Spts. Cen.
Swim. Pool
Hayes & Harlington
London Motor Mus.
Sports Ground
Research Lab.
Anchor Bri.
Vue
The Powerhouse
Bulls Bridge Centre
Factory
Superstore
Western International Market
Grand Union Canal (Paddington Branch)
Harlington Community Sch.
Sam Philp Rec. Grd.
Cranford Park Academy
Dog Kennel Covert
Junction 3
M4 MOTORWAY
M4
Harlington Bridge
Harlington Hospice
Crane Meadows
Gravel Works
CRANFORD PARK
Ye Old Rectory
Lower Park Farm
Cranford Community College Sports Centre
Cranford Community College
Concorde Centre
Sports Ground
Parkway Trading Est.
TW5
UB3
UB2
AVENUE PARK
The Cedars Prim. Sch.
River Crane
CRANFORD
Cranford Bridge
Rectory Farm
Poultry Farm
The White House
Airport Bowl
Airport Car Park
David Lloyd Leisure
Waggoners Roundabout
Harlington Corner
THE PARKWAY
DAWLEY ROAD
NORTH HYDE ROAD
STATION RD.
HIGH STREET
BATH ROAD
A437
A312
A4

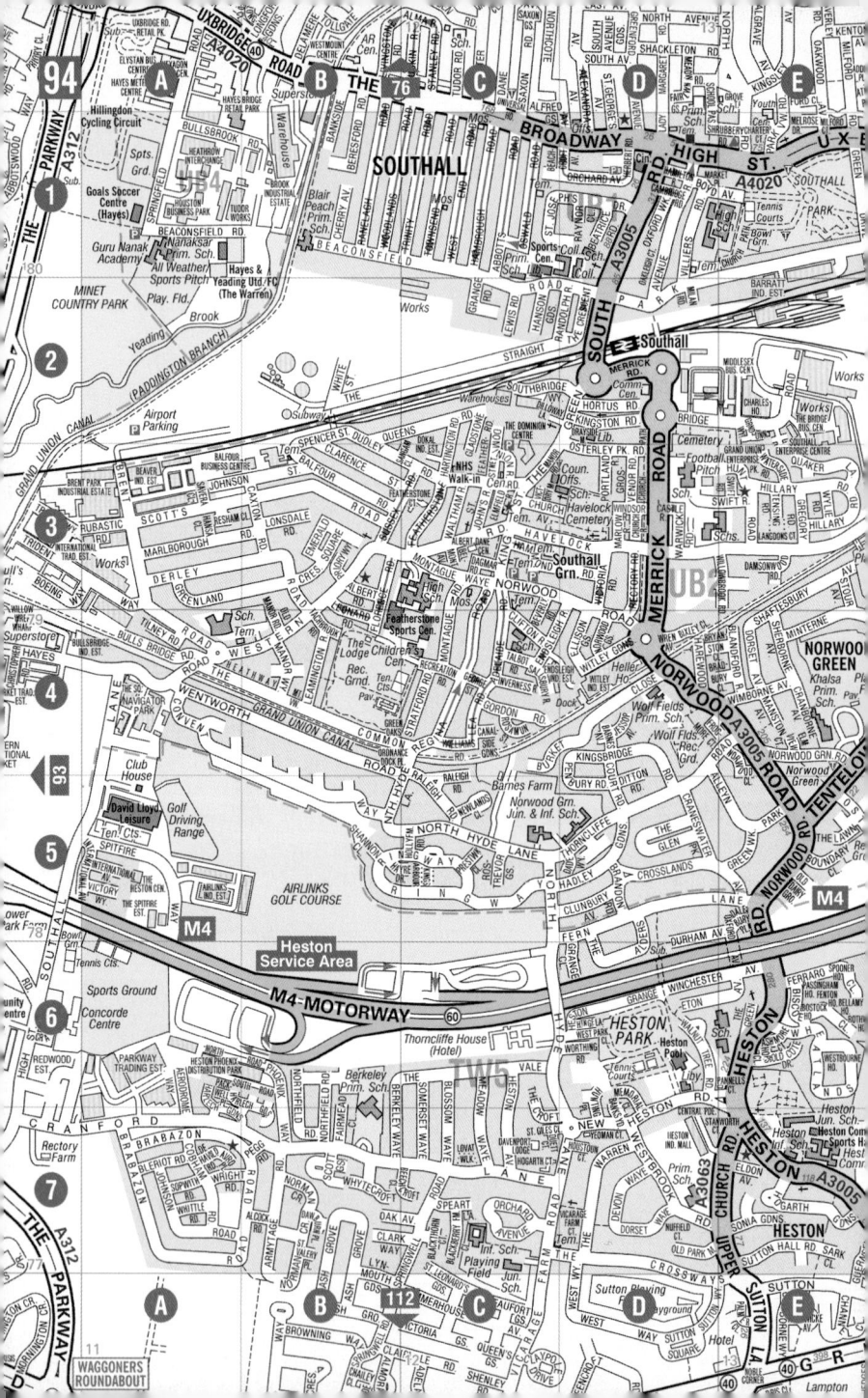

94
76
93
112
A
B
C
D
E
1
2
3
4
5
6
7
UXBRIDGE ROAD
A4020
THE BROADWAY
HIGH ST.
SOUTHALL
SOUTHALL PARK
THE PARKWAY
A312
SOUTH RD.
A3005
MERRICK ROAD
NORWOOD ROAD
NORWOOD GREEN
TENTELOW
M4
M4-MOTORWAY
Heston Service Area
HESTON
HESTON PARK
HESTON RD.
A3063
CHURCH RD.
UPPER SUTTON LA.
Hillingdon Cycling Circuit
Goals Soccer Centre (Hayes)
Guru Nanak Academy
All Weather Sports Pitch
Hayes & Yeading Utd FC (The Warren)
MINET COUNTRY PARK
Play. Fld.
Yeading Brook
GRAND UNION CANAL
(PADDINGTON BRANCH)
Airport Parking
Southall
Works
Warehouse
Warehouses
Blair Peach Prim. Sch.
BEACONSFIELD RD.
BULLSBROOK RD.
HEATHROW INTERCHANGE
BROOK INDUSTRIAL ESTATE
HOUSTON BUSINESS PARK
TUDOR WORKS
Nanaksar Prim. Sch.
HAYES BRIDGE RETAIL PARK
UXBRIDGE RD. RETAIL PK.
ELYSTAN BUS. CENTRE
HAYES METRO CENTRE
WESTMOUNT CENTRE
Superstore
UB4
UB1
UB2
TW5
BALFOUR BUSINESS CENTRE
BRENT PARK INDUSTRIAL ESTATE
INTERNATIONAL TRAD. EST.
BULLSBRIDGE IND. EST.
WESTERN ROAD
THE HEATHWAY
WENTWORTH
CONVENT WAY
COMMON ROAD
GRAND UNION CANAL
NHS Walk-in Cen.
Featherstone Sports Cen.
The Lodge Children's Cen.
Rec. Grnd.
Havelock Cemetery
Southall Grn.
Coun. Offs.
Lib.
Comm. Cen.
Cemetery
Football Pitch
Heller Ho.
Wolf Fields Prim. Sch.
Wolf Flds. Rec. Grd.
Barnes Farm
Norwood Grn. Jun. & Inf. Sch.
Norwood Green
Khalsa Prim. Sch.
NORTH HYDE LANE
RINGWAY
AIRLINKS GOLF COURSE
Club House
David Lloyd Leisure
Golf Driving Range
Tennis Cts.
Sports Ground
Concorde Centre
PARKWAY TRADING EST.
HESTON PHOENIX DISTRIBUTION PARK
Thorncliffe House (Hotel)
Berkeley Prim. Sch.
Heston Pool
Tennis Courts
Liby.
HESTON IND. MALL
Heston Jun. Sch.
Heston Inf. Sch.
Playing Field
Inf. Sch.
Jun. Sch.
Sutton Playing Fields
CRANFORD LANE
Rectory Farm
WAGGONERS ROUNDABOUT
THE CROSSWAYS
WEST WAY
Hotel
Lampton

DORMER'S WELLS
Dormers Wells Jun. Sch.
Dormers Wells Inf. Sch.
WEST MIDDLESEX GOLF COURSE
Club House
GREENFORD RD.
A4127
Brent Lodge Park
Millennium Maze
River Brent
Weir
Churchfields Rec. Grd.
Tennis
77
95
Hanwell
Kensington Cemetery
Iron Bridge
A4020 BROADWAY UXBRIDGE ROAD
Hanwell Bri.
City of Westminster Cemetery
HANWELL
EALING HOSP.
EALING UCC
ST. BERNARD'S HOSPITAL
Meadow Ho. Hospice
Prim. Sch.
Oaklands Primary Sch.
BOSTON RD.
A3002
GREAT WESTERN INDUSTRIAL PARK
ARMSTRONG WAY
Hanwell Locks
Windmill Bridge
THREE BRIDGES BUS. CEN.
Glade Lane Canalside Park
GRAND UNION CANAL
WINDMILL LANE
B454
Games Courts
Warren Farm Sports Centre
Sports Ground
Osterley Sports Club
WATERSIDE TRADING CENTRE
BOSTON BUSINESS PARK
RIVER BRENT BUSINESS PARK
Elthorne Park
Elthorne Park High Sch.
Elthorne Sports Cen.
Playing Field
The Aviary Farm
The Aviary
Weir
Wincott Farm
Osterley Lock
Evershed Spts. Grnd.
OSTERLEY
M4 MOTORWAY
M4
Long Wood
Trumpers Wood
96
Avenue Lodge
Devon Lodge
Osterley Park Farm
OSTERLEY LANE
WYKE GREEN GOLF COURSE
Garden Cen.
Lodges
Wyke Green
Warehouse
Lodge
Bothy Cottage
Osterley Park House
PARK
TW7
Club House
Tennis Courts
SYON LANE
Goals Soccer Centre
CENTAURS BUSINESS PARK
Superstore
Sports Ground
OSTERLEY
JERSEY ROAD
Playing Field
Pavilion
Jersey Gdns.
Lib.
A4 GREAT WEST ROAD
Osterley Sports & Athletics Centre
Osterley
Indian Gym Club
Spts. Grd.
113
Isleworth Crown Court
Education Service
SPRING GROVE
F G H J K
1 2 3 4 5 6 7

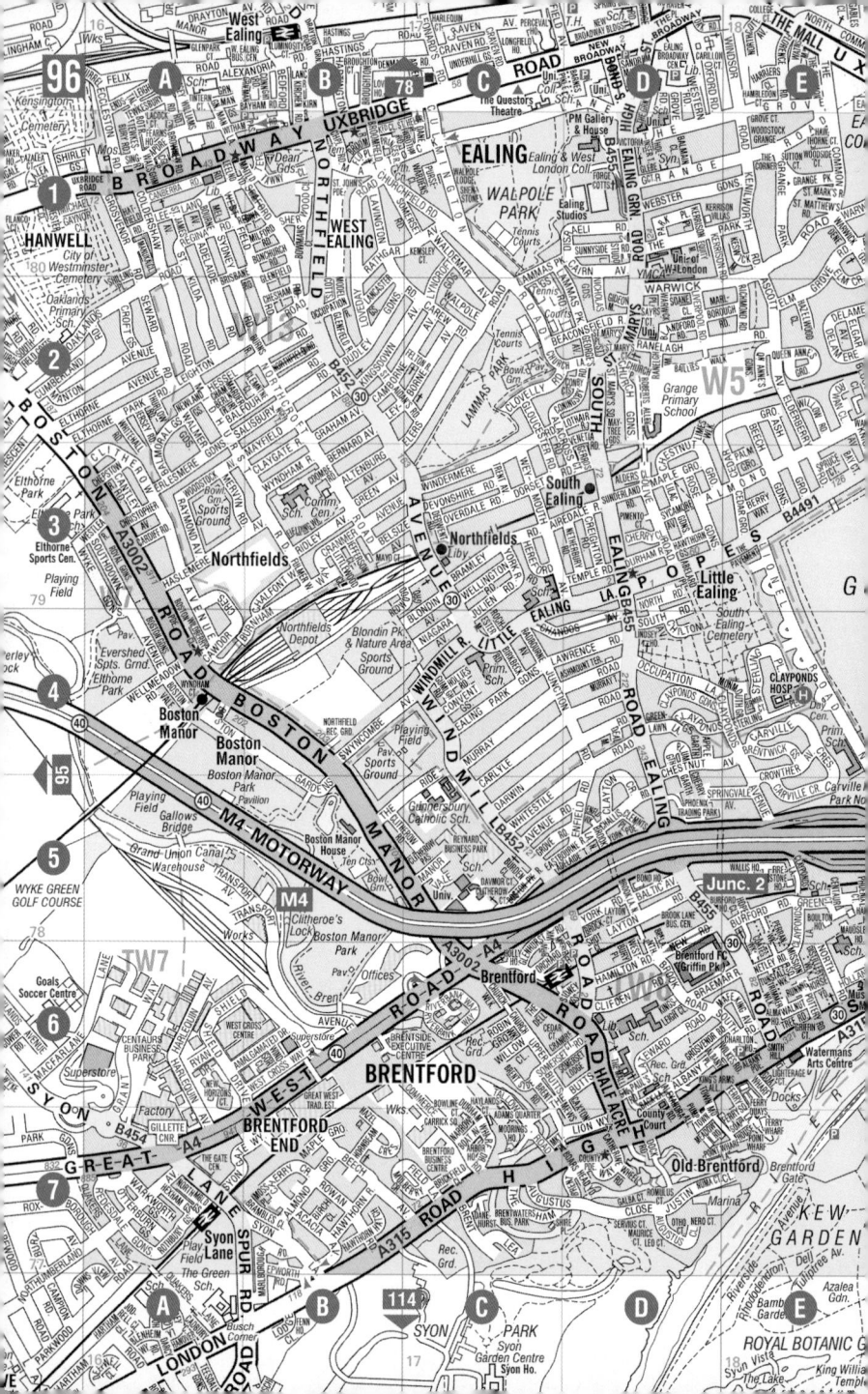
96
78
95
114
A
B
C
D
E
1
2
3
4
5
6
7
West Ealing
EALING
WEST EALING
HANWELL
Kensington Cemetery
City of Westminster Cemetery
Oaklands Primary Sch.
W13
W5
W7
TW7
TW8
UXBRIDGE ROAD
BROADWAY
NORTHFIELD
The Questors Theatre
PM Gallery & House
Ealing & West London Coll.
WALPOLE PARK
Ealing Studios
Uni. of W. London
YMCA
HIGH ST.
NEW BROADWAY
BOND ST.
THE MALL
Lammas Park
Grange Primary School
South Ealing
SOUTH EALING ROAD
Little Ealing
POPES LA.
South Ealing Cemetery
CLAYPONDS HOSP.
Northfields
Northfields Depot
Blondin Pk. & Nature Area
Sports Ground
Elthorne Park
Elthorne Sports Cen.
Playing Field
Evershed Spts. Grnd.
Boston Manor
Boston Manor Park
Boston Manor House
BOSTON ROAD
BOSTON MANOR ROAD
A3002
B452
B455
B4491
M4 MOTORWAY
M4
Junc. 2
Gallows Bridge
Grand Union Canal Warehouse
WYKE GREEN GOLF COURSE
Clitheroe's Lock
River Brent
Gunnersbury Catholic Sch.
Brentford
Brentford FC (Griffin Pk.)
BRENTFORD
BRENTFORD END
GREAT WEST ROAD
A4
A315
HIGH ROAD
Goals Soccer Centre
Centaurs Business Park
GILLETTE CNR.
SYON LANE
Syon Lane
Busch Corner
LONDON ROAD
Old Brentford
Watermans Arts Centre
County Court
Brentford Gate
KEW GARDENS
ROYAL BOTANIC G
SYON PARK
Syon Garden Centre
Syon Ho.
Syon Vista
The Lake

EAST ACTON
97
79
98
115
ACTON
Ealing Common
Acton Central
ACTON PARK
SOUTH ACTON
Acton Town
South Acton
ACTON GREEN
BEDFORD PARK
SOUTHFIELD
Southfields Rec. Grd.
GUNNERSBURY
Gunnersbury
Chiswick Pk.
GUNNERSBURY PARK
Gunnersbury Park Mus.
Boating Lake
Miniature Golf Course
International Sch. of London
Kensington Cemetery
Kew East Junc.
Virgin Active Health Club
Nature Res. Gunnersby Junc.
TURNHAM GREEN
CHISWICK
Chiswick House & Gardens
Chiswick Cemetery
Chiswick Common
Chiswick
GROVE PARK
Strand on the Green
Oliver's Island
The National Archives
KEW
Kew Bridge
Kew Green
Kew Gds.
Kew Pier
Mus. of Water & Steam
Brentford Fountain Leis. Cen.
Brentford FC Comm. Stadium (Open 2017)
Botanical Library
Kew Gardens Gallery
Davies Alpine House
Princess of Wales Conservatory
Plants & People Exhibition
Palm House
The Pond
Orangery
Main Gate
Visitor Centre
Temple of Bellona
London Transport Mus. Depot
Reynolds Sports Cen.
West London Coll.
Twyford Spts. Cen.
Sports Ground
Popefield Playing Flds.
Junc. 1
M4 MOTORWAY
GUNNERSBURY AV.
GUNNERSBURY LANE
UXBRIDGE RD.
A4020 THE VALE
HIGH ST.
ACTON LANE
CHISWICK HIGH RD. A315
A3000
GT. WEST RD.
CEDARS RD.
ELLESMERE RD.
A4
A406
A205
A307
A316
HEATHFIELD TER.
SOUTH PARADE
B491
B490
B409
KEW BRIDGE
KEW RD.
MORTLAKE RD.
GT. CHERTSEY RD.
BURLINGTON LANE
W3
W4
W9
F
G
H
J
K
1
2
3
4
5
6
7

98
80
97
116
EAST ACTON
The King Fahad Academy
Recreation Ground
Wormholt Park
Commonwealth Av.
White City
Wood La.
BBC Studios
QPR FC (Loftus Rd.)
Hammersmith Park
The Park Club
Sports Cricket Ground
Football Pitch
Virgin Active
THE VALE ESTATE
ACTON PARK
THE VALE
A4020
UXBRIDGE ROAD
Shepherd's Bush Mkt.
ACTON PARK ESTATE
Southfield Rd.
Wendell Park
Cathnor Park
Askew Rd.
B408
A402
Goldhawk Rd.
BEDFORD PARK
Bath Rd.
B409
The Avenue
B491
Adventure Playground
Ravenscourt Park
Paddenswick Rd.
Goldhawk Rd.
Stamford Brook
Turnham Green
Ravenscourt Park
Glenthorne Road
Hammersmith
Lyric Theatre
Chiswick Common
CHISWICK HIGH RD.
A315
KING ST.
Town Hall
A316
Homefield Recreation Ground
GREAT WEST ROAD
A4
HAMMERSMITH ROAD
Furnival Gdns.
Hammersmith Pier
Riverside Studios
TURNHAM GREEN
Hogarth La.
Hogarth Rbt.
Chiswick Lodge
Brewery
Chiswick Eyot
St. Pauls School
Playing Field
Play. Flds.
Tennis Courts
RIVER THAMES
SW13
Castelnau
A306
Hammersmith Bri. Rd.
CHISWICK
Chiswick House & Gardens
Temple
Burlington La.
Church Wharf
Corney Reach
Chiswick Pier
Lifeboat Sta.
Leg O'Mutton Local Nature Reserve
The Harrodian Sch.
Lonsdale Rd.
B350
Barnes
Rec. Grd.
Alexandra Av.
Pool
Riverside Recreation Ground
Sports Ground
Pavilion
Bandstand
LONDON WETLAND CENTRE
Visitor Centre
Blakes Wharves
Eternit Wharf
Barn Elms
A B C D E
1 2 3 4 5 6 7
21 22 23

NOTTING HILL
Notting Hill Gate
KENSINGTON GARDENS
The Orangery
Kensington Palace
Round Pond
Queen Victoria Statue
Elfin Oak
Holland Park
HOLLAND PARK
KENSINGTON
King George VI Memorial Youth Hostel
Holland Ho.
Cricket Field
Design Mus.
Leighton Ho. Mus.
Theatre
Town Hall
High St. Kensington
Shepherd's Bush
Kensington Olympia
Olympia
Brook Green
WEST KENSINGTON
West Kensington
Barons Court
Hammersmith Cemetery
The Queen's Club
Earl's Court
EARL'S COURT
Earls Court (Proposed)
EMPRESS STATE BUILDING
West Brompton
WEST BROMPTON
Brompton Cemetery
Lost River Park
Brompton Park
Chelsea FC (Stamford Bridge)
Fulham Broadway
The London Oratory Sch.
Fulham Pools
Fulham Cemetery
Fulham Cross Girls' Sch. & Coll.
FULHAM
WALHAM GREEN
Eel Brook Common
SANDS END
Imperial Wharf
Gloucester Rd.
SOUTH KENSINGTON
Superstore
Queensmill Sch.
Depot
HOLLAND PARK AVENUE
A402
KENSINGTON HIGH STREET
A315
CROMWELL ROAD
A4
WEST CROMWELL ROAD
TALGARTH RD.
FLYOVER
NORTH END ROAD
WARWICK RD.
EARL'S COURT ROAD
OLD BROMPTON ROAD
LILLIE ROAD
A3218
DAWES ROAD
A3219
FULHAM ROAD
A304
FULHAM PALACE ROAD
A219
KING'S RD.
REDCLIFFE
FINBOROUGH
A3220
WEST CROSS ROUTE
HOLLAND ROAD
BAYSWATER RD.
KENSINGTON RD.
F
G
H
J
K
1
2
3
4
5
6
7
81
100
117

100
A
B
C
D
E
1
2
3
4
5
6
7
82
10
16
17
99
118
BAYSWATER RD
Lancaster Gate
Marlborough Gate
Lancaster Gate
The Fountains
Victoria Gate
Clarendon Gate
Albion Gate
Speakers Corner
Refreshment Kiosk
Porchester Ter. Gate
Black Lion Gate
Elfin Oak
The Orangery
Kensington Palace
Queen Victoria Statue
Speke's Monument
Peter Pan Statue
The Long Water
Serpentine Sackler Gallery
Nursery
Parks Police
Parks Inf. Cen.
Reformers Tree
The Lookout Educ. Cen.
Joy of Life Fountain
Entrance to Underground Car Park
KENSINGTON
GARDENS
HYDE PARK
Round Pond
Physical Energy Statue
Temple Lodge
W2
Norwegian War Mem.
THE SERPENTINE
Fishermans Keep
Bandstand
Serpentine Gallery
Princess of Wales Memorial Fountain
Cafeteria
ROTTEN ROW
Holocaust Mem. Gdn
Rose Garden
Nannies Lawn
Queen Elizabeth Gate
7/7 Memorial
Albert Memorial
Alexandra Gate
Queen's Gate
Palace Gate
Prince of Wales Gate
SCOTCH HOUSE
Hyde Park Corner
KENSINGTON ROAD
KENSINGTON GORE
KNIGHTSBRIDGE
Knightsbridge
Royal Albert Hall
Sikorski Mus.
Ethos
KNIGHTSBRIDGE
Imperial Coll
IMPERIAL COLLEGE
Science Museum
Natural History Mus.
Victoria & Albert Museum
Brompton Oratory
Harrods
BROMPTON
BELGRAVE
GLOUCESTER RD.
CROMWELL RD
Gloucester Rd.
THURLOE PL.
Sth. Kensington
SOUTH KENSINGTON
BROMPTON ROAD
SLOANE ST
PONT ST.
CADOGAN
Sloane Square
EATON
PIMLICO
The Royal Marsden Hosp
Royal Brompton Hosp
SYDNEY ST.
Saatchi Gallery
Burton's Court
KING'S ROAD
CHELSEA
HOSPITAL RD
Royal Hospital Chelsea
Ranelagh Gardens
Chilianwallah Meml.
CHELSEA BRIDGE RD
OAKLEY ST
OLD BROMPTON ROAD
REDCLIFFE
BOROUGH
WEST BROMPTON
FULHAM RD
CHELSEA & WESTMINSTER HOSP
BEAUFORT ST.
CHEYNE WALK
CHELSEA EMBANKMENT
THAMES
RIVER
CHELSEA REACH
Cadogan Pier
Peace Pagoda
Children's Zoo
British Genius Site
SW11
BATTERSEA PARK
Pump House Gallery
Boating Lake
ALBERT BRIDGE ROAD
ALBERT BRI.
BATTERSEA BRI.
BATTERSEA BRI. RD
Cremorne Riverside Centre
Cremorne Gardens
Chelsea Wharf
Cremorne Wharf
Chelsea Creek
SANDS END
Gas Works
Imperial Wharf
WESTBRIDGE
BATTERSEA
Sun Gate
PRINCE OF WALES DR.

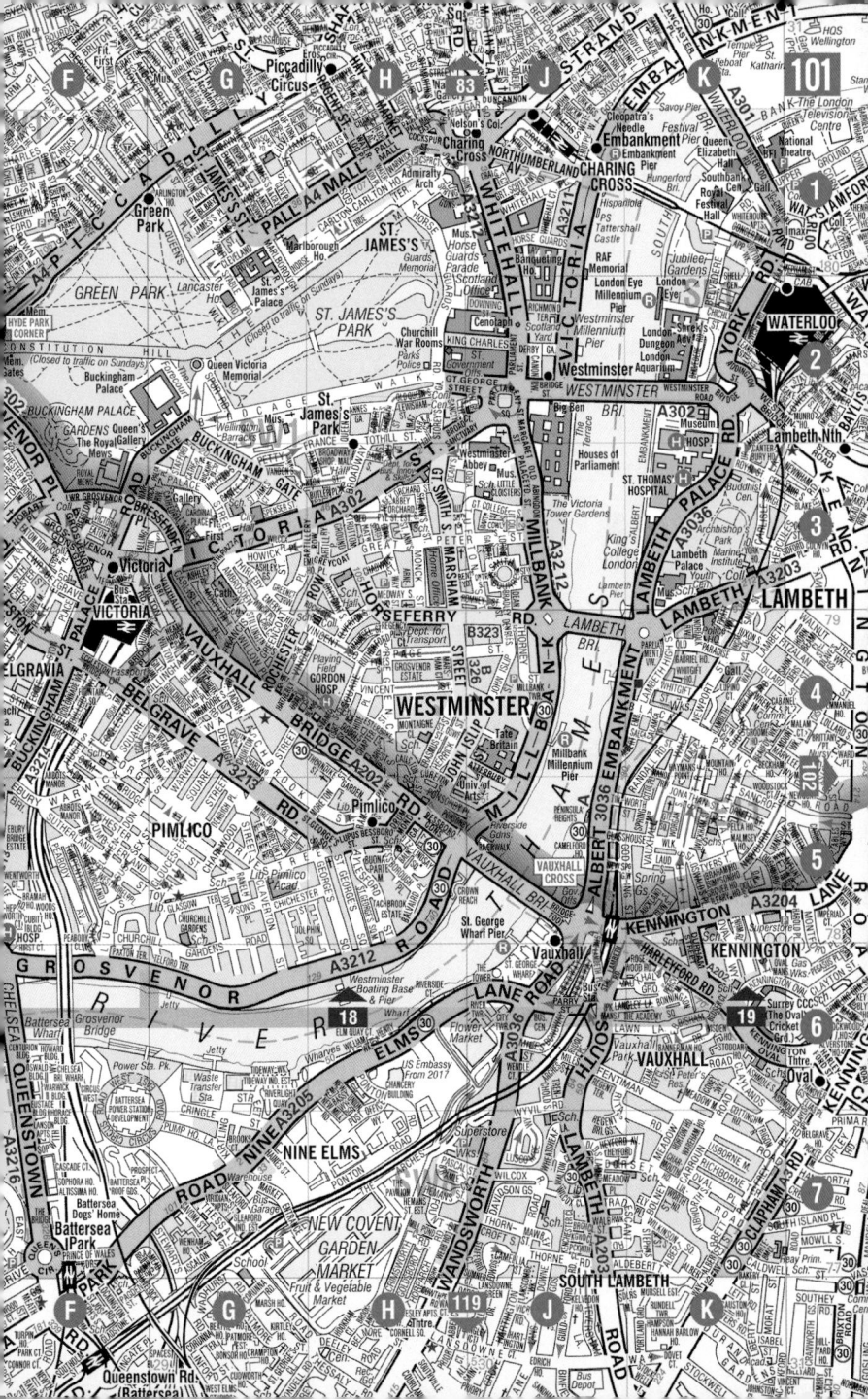
101
Piccadilly Circus
Green Park
GREEN PARK
HYDE PARK CORNER
CONSTITUTION HILL
(Closed to traffic on Sundays)
Buckingham Palace
BUCKINGHAM PALACE GARDENS
Queen's Gallery
The Royal Mews
Queen Victoria Memorial
St. James's Palace
Marlborough Ho.
Lancaster Ho.
ST. JAMES'S PARK
(Closed to traffic on Sundays)
ST. JAMES'S
Guards Memorial
PALL MALL
PICCADILLY
A4
Charing Cross
Nelson's Col.
Admiralty Arch
Churchill War Rooms
Horse Guards Parade
Scotland Office
Cenotaph
WHITEHALL
A3212
NORTHUMBERLAND AV.
STRAND
EMBANKMENT
Cleopatra's Needle
Embankment
Embankment Pier
CHARING CROSS
Hungerford Bri.
Hispaniola
PS Tattershall Castle
RAF Memorial
Banqueting Ho.
Festival Pier
Savoy Pier
Queen Elizabeth Hall
Southbank Cen.
Royal Festival Hall
National Theatre
BFI
The London Television Centre
WATERLOO
Imax
Jubilee Gardens
London Eye
London Eye Millennium Pier
Westminster Millennium Pier
Scotland Yard
London Dungeon
London Aquarium
Shrek's Adv.
Westminster
WESTMINSTER BRI.
WESTMINSTER BRIDGE ROAD
Big Ben
Houses of Parliament
Museum
HOSP.
ST. THOMAS' HOSPITAL
Lambeth Nth.
Westminster Abbey
St. James's Park
Wellington Barracks
BUCKINGHAM GATE
VICTORIA ST.
A302
Victoria
VICTORIA
BELGRAVIA
Cath.
HORSEFERRY RD.
Dept. for Transport
Home Office
MARSHAM ST.
MILLBANK
The Victoria Tower Gardens
King's College London
Lambeth Pier
LAMBETH PALACE RD.
A3036
Archbishop's Park
Lambeth Palace
Marine Institute
LAMBETH
LAMBETH BRI.
LAMBETH RD.
A3203
KENNINGTON RD.
WESTMINSTER
GORDON HOSP.
Playing Field
Tate Britain
Univ. of Arts
Millbank Millennium Pier
Riverside Gdns.
VAUXHALL BRIDGE RD.
A202
BELGRAVE RD.
A3213
PIMLICO
Pimlico
Lib.
Pimlico Acad.
BUCKINGHAM PALACE RD.
A3214
Ebury Bridge Estate
Churchill Gardens
GROSVENOR ROAD
A3212
RIVER THAMES
Grosvenor Bridge
Battersea Wharf
Westminster Boating Base & Pier
VAUXHALL BRI.
VAUXHALL CROSS
ALBERT EMBANKMENT
A3036
St. George Wharf Pier
Vauxhall
KENNINGTON LA.
A3204
KENNINGTON
HARLEYFORD RD.
VAUXHALL
Vauxhall Park
Surrey CCC The Oval Cricket Grd.
Oval
KENNINGTON OVAL
NINE ELMS LANE
A3205
NINE ELMS
US Embassy From 2017
Flower Market
Battersea Power Station Development
Power Sta. Pk.
Waste Transfer Sta.
NEW COVENT GARDEN MARKET
Fruit & Vegetable Market
Superstore
WANDSWORTH ROAD
A3036
SOUTH LAMBETH RD.
A203
SOUTH LAMBETH
CLAPHAM RD.
A3
QUEENSTOWN RD.
A3216
Battersea Dogs' Home
Battersea Park
Queenstown Rd. (Battersea)
CHELSEA BRIDGE
Bus Depot
18
19
83
102
119
F G H J K
1 2 3 4 5 6 7

RIVER THAMES
BLACKFRIARS
Blackfriars Millennium Pier
Bankside Pier
CANNON STREET
84
Tate Modern
SOUTHWARK
National Theatre
Royal Festival Hall
Golden Hinde
London Bridge City Pier
HMS Belfast
LONDON BRIDGE HOSP.
LONDON BRI.
THE BOROUGH
The Shard
GUY'S HOSP.
Waterloo East
WATERLOO
Southwark
UNION
SOUTHWARK ST.
STAMFORD ST.
BLACKFRIARS RD.
SOUTHWARK BRIDGE RD.
BOROUGH HIGH ST.
TOOLEY ST.
BERMONDSEY ST.
LONG LA.
GREAT DOVER ST.
Borough
14
15
Lambeth Nth.
BOROUGH RD
WESTMINSTER BRI. R.
ST. GEORGE'S CIRCUS
ST. GEORGE'S RD
LONDON RD
NEWINGTON CAUSEWAY
HARPER
NEWINGTON
Imperial War Mus.
Geraldine Mary Harmsworth Park
LAMBETH
LAMBETH RD
Elephant & Castle
ELEPHANT & CASTLE
NEW KENT RD.
BRICKLAYER'S ARMS
WALWORTH RD
WALWORTH
A215
TOWER BRIDGE RD
19
101
Kennington
KENNINGTON LANE
KENNINGTON ROAD
KENNINGTON PARK ROAD
KENNINGTON
Surrey CCC (The Oval) Cricket Grd.
Oval
Kennington Park
CAMBERWELL NEW ROAD
CAMBERWELL ROAD
ALBANY ROAD
Burgess Pk. Kart Track
Burgess Park
Playing Fields
SOUTHAMPTON WAY
BRIXTON RD.
120
CAMBERWELL GREEN
PECKHAM
A
B
C
D
E
1
2
3
4
5
6
7

103
85
15
104
121
F
G
H
J
K
1
2
3
4
5
6
7
SHADWELL
WAPPING
BERMONDSEY
ROTHERHITHE
THAMES
RIVER
UPPER POOL
LOWER POOL
The Tower of London
Tower Hill
St. Katharine Docks
Tower Bridge
Wapping
Rotherhithe
Canada Water
Bermondsey
Surrey Quays
South Bermondsey
New Cross Gate
Queens Rd. (Peckham)
JAMAICA RD.
SOUTHWARK PARK RD.
LOWER RD.
REDRIFF RD.
ROTHERHITHE NEW RD.
OLD KENT ROAD
NEW CROSS RD.
QUEEN'S RD.
PECKHAM HILL ST.
PECKHAM PARK RD.
ROLLS ROAD
TRAFALGAR AV.
RAYMOUTH RD.
PLOUGH WY.
BRUNEL RD.
TOWER BRI. RD.
SALTER RD.
ROTHERHITHE TUNNEL
SOUTHWARK PARK
Greenland Dock
Surrey Canal (Proposed)
Millwall FC (The Den)
Stave Hill Ecological Park
Russia Dock Woodland
South Eastern Gas Wks.
Waste Processing Facility
SE14
SE15
SE16
A100
A101
A200
A202
A2
A2206
A2208
B202
B203
B204
B205
B206
B207
B215
B216

A
B
C
D
E
86
LIMEHOUSE REACH
POPLAR
Poplar
West India Quay
Canary Wharf
WEST INDIA
DOCKS
Billingsgate Market
A1261
Canary Wharf Pier
Westferry Circus
Hilton Docklands Pier
South Dock Entrance
Heron Quays
Blackwall Basin
ISLE OF DOGS
South Quay
Crossharbour
Mudchute
Island Gds.
Cubitt Town
Mudchute Park
Mudchute Farm
Millwall Park
Millwall
Millwall Outer Dock
Docklands Sailing Cen.
Printing Works
Leisure Cen.
Sir John McDougall Gdns.
WESTFERRY RD.
A1206
PRESTON'S ROAD
MANCHESTER ROAD
Masthouse Terrace Pier
Britannia & St. Andrews Wharves
Machonochies Wharf
Locke's Wharf
GREENWICH REACH
Greenwich Pier
Greenwich Foot Tunnel
Cutty Sark for Maritime Greenwich
DEPTFORD
Deptford Bri.
Greenwich
RIVER THAMES
ROTHERHITHE
SALTER ROAD
Pageant Stairs
Sports Grd.
Ordnance Wharf
Columbia Wharf
Durand's Wharf
Surrey Docks Farm
Barnards Wharf
Sports Cen.
Academy
Stave Hill Ecological Park
Redriff Prim. Sch.
B205
REDRIFF ROAD
Russia Dock Woodland
Printing Works
Bowl. Alley & Gala Bingo
Odeon Cinema
GREENLAND DOCK
Greenland Pier
South Lock
Watersports Cen.
SOUTH DOCK
PLOUGH WAY
GROVE
St. George's Wharf
St. George's Stairs
EVELYN ST.
A200
Silwood Triangle
DEPTFORD PARK
Pepys Park
SE8
CONVOY'S WHARF
Landing Stage
Palmer's Wharf
Playground
B206
103
DEPTFORD HIGH ST.
Deptford
CREEK RD.
DEPTFORD CHURCH ST.
GREENWICH HIGH RD.
A206
NORMAN RD.
B208
Creekside Disc. Cen.
New Cross
New Cross Gate
NEW CROSS RD.
A2
SANFORD ST.
Goldsmiths' College
Fordham Pk.
Margaret McMillan Pk.
NEW CROSS
NEW CROSS GATE
Bus Garage
122
BLACKHEATH RD.
BLACKHEATH HILL
ROYAL HILL
The Point
1
2
3
4
5
6
7

105
87
106
123
East India
LEAMOUTH
Virginia Quay
Blackwall Pier
Wharves
Jetty
Works
ROYAL VICTORIA DOCK
ExCeL
for ExCeL
Emirates Royal Docks
Watersports Cen.
SS Robin
Millennium Mill
PONTOON RD.
SILVERTOWN WY.
NORTH WOOLWICH RD.
A1020
DLR
E16
West Silvertown
SILVERTOWN
Blackwall
BLACKWALL REACH
Blackwall Point
BLACKWALL TUNNEL
A102
The O2
Up at The O2
IndigO
Hotel
North Greenwich Pier
Emirates Air Line Cable Car
RIVER
THAMES
North Greenwich
Emirates Greenwich Peninsula
Thames Wharf
Brewery
Plaistow Wharf
Deanston Wharf
Crescent Wharf
Lyle Park
Kierbeck Business Complex
Manhattan Wharf
Wharf
Thames Barrier Yacht Club Marina
Delta Wharf
Greenwich Penninsula Golf Driving Range
Victoria Deep Water Terminal
Central Park
Gas Works
Lorry Park
Prim. Sch.
ORDNANCE CR.
TUNNEL APPROACH
MILLENNIUM WAY
WEST PARKSIDE
Greenwich Yacht Club
Greenwich Peninsula Ecology Park
Southern Park
Christie's Wharf
Jetty
Anchorage Point Ind. Est.
Meridian Trading Estate
Depot
SE7
Greenwich Millennium Village
Superstore
Nature Res.
Cinema
Superstores
Warehouses
Charlton Riverside Place
Warehouse
New Ch
Works
Primrose Wharf
Morden Wharf
Enderby's Wharf
Pipers Wharf
Granite Wharf
Cubitt Town Wharf
Newcastle Drawdock
Lovell's Wharf
Pier
BLACKWALL TUNNEL SOUTHERN APPROACH
A2203
DREADNOUGHT ST.
BUGSBY'S WAY
WOOLWICH RD.
A206 ROAD
Charlton
TRAFALGAR RD.
A206
Westcombe Park
Maze Hill
Trident Hall
Trinity Hospital
National Maritime Museum
GREENWICH
GREENWICH PARK
St. Mary's Gate
Circus Gate
Prime Meridian Line
Peter Harrison Planetarium
Royal Observatory Greenwich
Bandstand
Reservoir (covered)
The Gardens
The Wilderness (Deer Park)
Tennis Courts
Parks Police
Ranger's House
Playground
SE3
Woodland Dell
Blackheath RUFC (Rectory Fld.)
CHARLTON RD.
B210
B211
OLD DOVER ROAD
A207 ROAD
A102
VANBRUGH PARK
CHARLTON WY.
SHOOTERS HILL
A2
KIDBROOKE PK. RD.
ROCHESTER
Blackheath Nursy. & Prep. Sch.
Bowls
Sports Ground
F
G
H
J
K
1
2
3
4
5
6
7

106
88
124
105
A
B
C
D
E
1
2
3
4
5
6
7
E16
SE7
LONDON CITY AIRPORT
ROYAL ALBERT DOCK
ROYAL VICTORIA DOCK
KING GEORGE V DOCK
RIVER
WOOLWICH REACH
THAMES BARRIER
SILVERTOWN
NORTH WOOLWICH
NEW CHARLTON
WOOLWICH
CHARLTON
Royal Albert
Beckton Park
Pontoon Dock
King George V
Woolwich Dockyard
Charlton
London City Airport
Charlton Athletic FC (The Valley)
MARYON WILSON PARK
Maryon Park
CHARLTON PARK
CHARLTON CEMETERY
QUEEN ELIZABETH HOSPITAL
WOOLWICH COMMON
Hornfair Park
Royal Artillery Barracks
WOOLWICH FREE FERRY
NORTH WOOLWICH RD.
ALBERT RD.
WOOLWICH ROAD
WOOLWICH CHURCH ST.
SHOOTERS HILL ROAD
CHARLTON PARK RD.
LITTLE HEATH
HILL REACH
ARTILLERY PL.
GRAND DEPOT RD
WOOLWICH COMMON
A1020
A112
A117
A206
A205
A207
B210

THAMESMEAD
THAMESMEAD CENTRAL
THAMESMEAD WEST
Thamesmead South West
SE28
SE18
PLUMSTEAD
Plumstead Common
SHOOTERS HILL
SHREWSBURY PARK
SHOOTERS HILL GOLF COURSE
Royal Arsenal West
Woolwich Arsenal
THAMES
HMP BELMARSH
HMP THAMESIDE
HMP ISIS
WINN'S COMMON
East Wickham Open Space
107
108
89
125

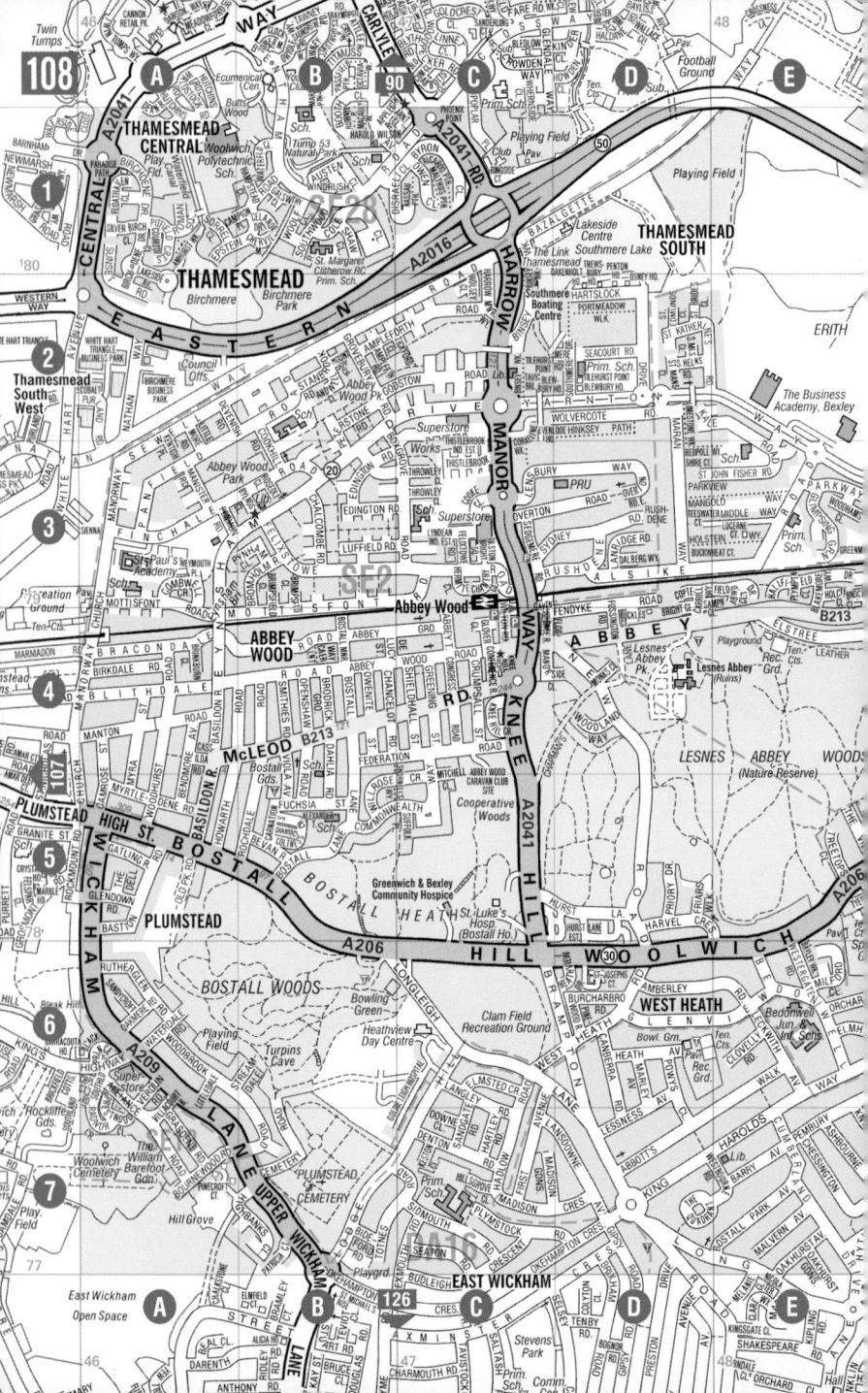

108
107
90
126
A
B
C
D
E
1
2
3
4
5
6
7
46
47
48
180
79
78
77
Twin Tumps
THAMESMEAD CENTRAL
Ecumenical Cen.
Butts Wood
Woolwich Polytechnic Sch.
Play Fld.
Tump 53 Natural Park
SE28
THAMESMEAD
Birchmere
Birchmere Park
St. Margaret Clitherow RC Prim. Sch.
Prim. Sch.
Playing Field
Football Ground
Playing Field
Lakeside Centre
Southmere Lake
THAMESMEAD SOUTH
The Link Thamesmead
Southmere Boating Centre
ERITH
The Business Academy, Bexley
EASTERN WAY
A2016
A2041
CENTRAL WAY
HARROW MANOR WAY
CARLYLE RD.
WESTERN WAY
Thamesmead South West
Council Offs.
Abbey Wood Pk.
Abbey Wood Park
Superstore
Works
SE2
Abbey Wood
ABBEY WOOD
St. Paul's Academy
Recreation Ground
Lesnes Abbey Pk.
Lesnes Abbey (Ruins)
LESNES ABBEY WOODS (Nature Reserve)
Playground
Rec. Grd.
McLEOD RD.
B213
Cooperative Woods
Abbey Wood Caravan Club Site
KNEE HILL
PLUMSTEAD HIGH ST.
BOSTALL HILL
A206
WOOLWICH
BOSTALL HEATH
Greenwich & Bexley Community Hospice
St. Luke's Hosp. (Bostall Ho.)
PLUMSTEAD
BOSTALL WOODS
Bowling Green
Clam Field Recreation Ground
WEST HEATH
Heathview Day Centre
Turpins Cave
Playing Field
WICKHAM LANE
A209
UPPER WICKHAM LANE
Woolwich Cemetery
The William Barefoot Gdn.
PLUMSTEAD CEMETERY
Hill Grove
Play. Field
Bedonwell Jun. & Inf. Schs.
DA16
EAST WICKHAM
East Wickham Open Space
Stevens Park
Playgrd.

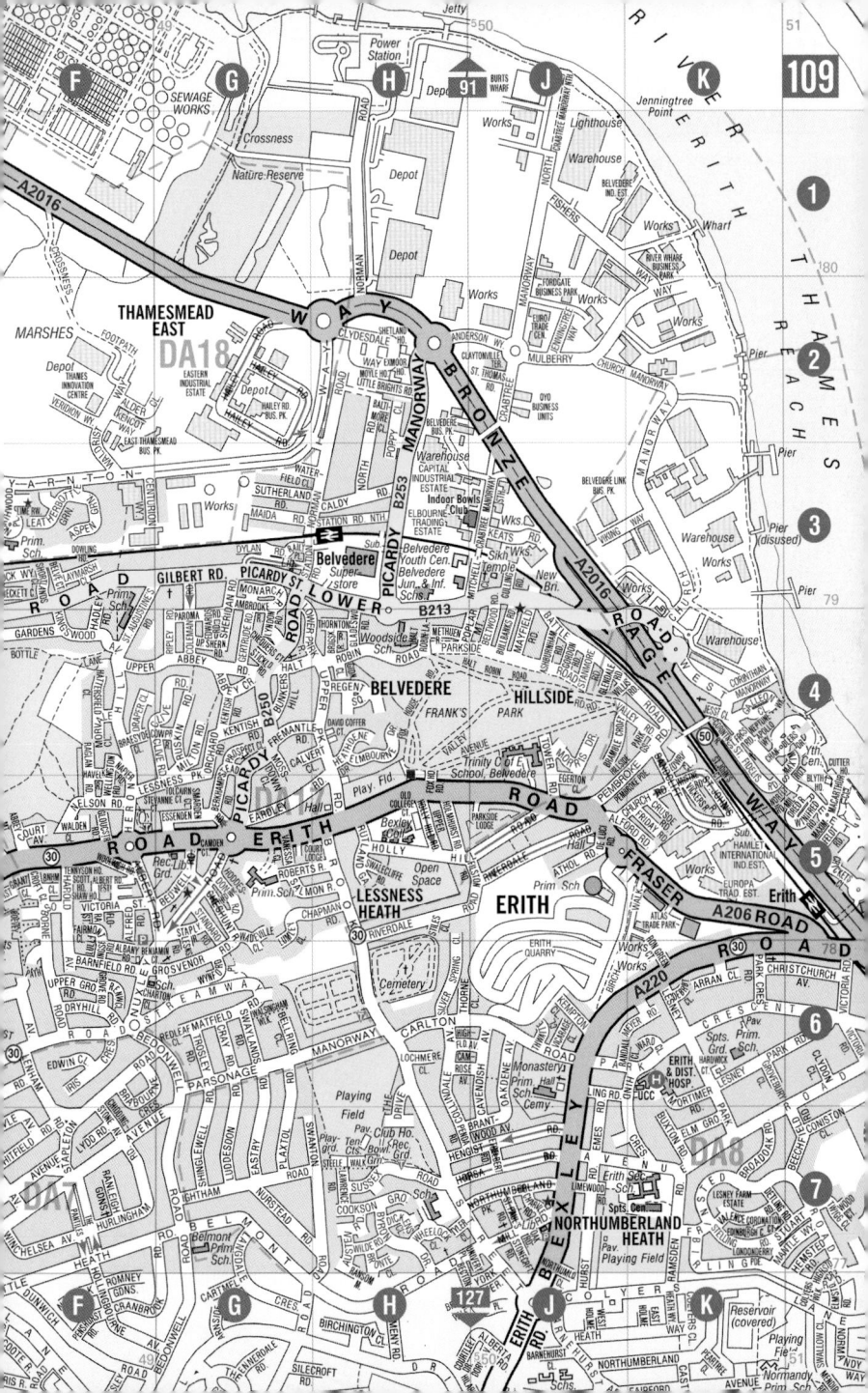

109
RIVER THAMES
ERITH REACH
Jetty
Power Station
SEWAGE WORKS
Crossness Nature Reserve
Depot
Depot
Depot
Works
Lighthouse
Warehouse
Jenningtree Point
BURTS WHARF
91
127
BELVEDERE IND. EST.
Wharf
Pier
Pier (disused)
RIVER WHARF BUSINESS PARK
FORDGATE BUSINESS PARK
EURO TRADE CEN.
BELVEDERE LINK BUS. PK.
A2016
WAY
BRONZE WAY
THAMESMEAD EAST
MARSHES
DA18
DA17
DA8
DA7
THAMES INNOVATION CENTRE
EASTERN INDUSTRIAL ESTATE
HAILEY RD. BUS. PK.
EAST THAMESMEAD BUS. PK.
CAPITAL INDUSTRIAL ESTATE
ELBOURNE TRADING ESTATE
Indoor Bowls Club
Belvedere
Super-store
Belvedere Youth Cen.
Belvedere Jun. & Inf. Schs.
Sikh Temple
New Bri.
PICARDY MANORWAY
B253
LOWER ROAD
B213
GILBERT RD.
BELVEDERE
HILLSIDE
FRANK'S PARK
Trinity C of E School, Belvedere
Play. Fld.
ERITH ROAD
PICARDY ROAD
B250
A206
FRASER ROAD
ROAD
A220
BEXLEY ROAD
LESSNESS HEATH
ERITH
ERITH QUARRY
Cemetery
Open Space
Bexley Coll.
HAMLET INTERNATIONAL IND. EST.
EUROPA TRAD. EST.
ATLAS TRADE PARK
Erith
ERITH & DIST. HOSP.
Monastery Prim. Sch.
Playing Field
NORTHUMBERLAND HEATH
Erith Sec. Sch.
Playing Field
LESNEY FARM ESTATE
Belmont Prim. Sch.
Reservoir (covered)
30
F
G
H
J
K
1
2
3
4
5
6
7
49
50
51
180
79
78
77

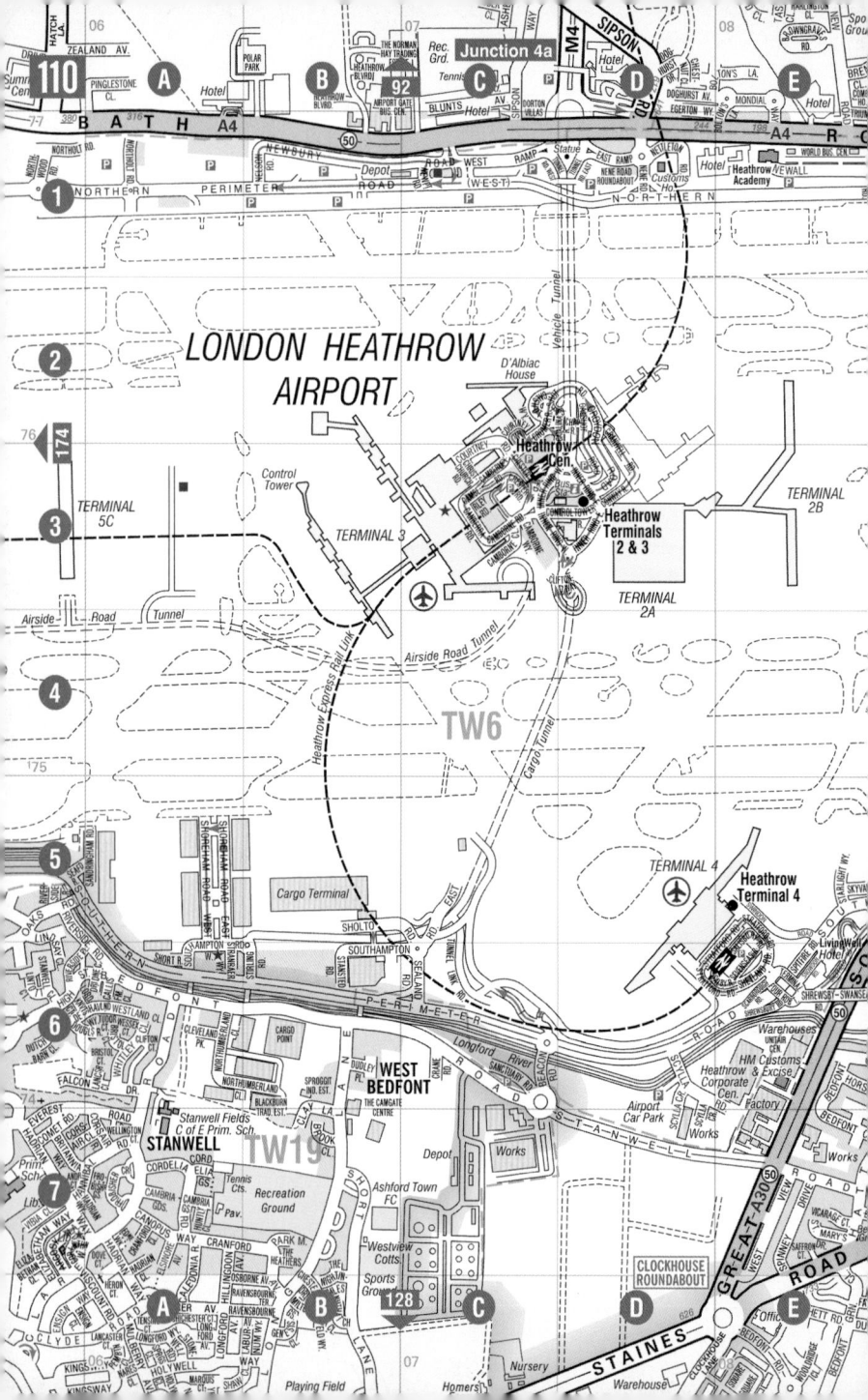

110
92
Junction 4a
174
128
LONDON HEATHROW AIRPORT
TERMINAL 5C
TERMINAL 3
TERMINAL 2B
TERMINAL 2A
TERMINAL 4
Heathrow Cen.
Heathrow Terminals 2 & 3
Heathrow Terminal 4
Control Tower
D'Albiac House
Cargo Terminal
Vehicle Tunnel
Cargo Tunnel
Airside Road Tunnel
Heathrow Express Rail Link
TW6
TW19
WEST BEDFONT
STANWELL
Stanwell Fields C of E Prim. Sch.
Recreation Ground
Ashford Town FC
Sports Ground
CLOCKHOUSE ROUNDABOUT
Heathrow Academy
HM Customs & Excise
Heathrow Corporate Cen.
Airport Car Park
BATH RD.
NORTHERN PERIMETER RD.
SOUTHERN PERIMETER RD.
STANWELL RD.
STAINES ROAD
GREAT SOUTH WEST RD.

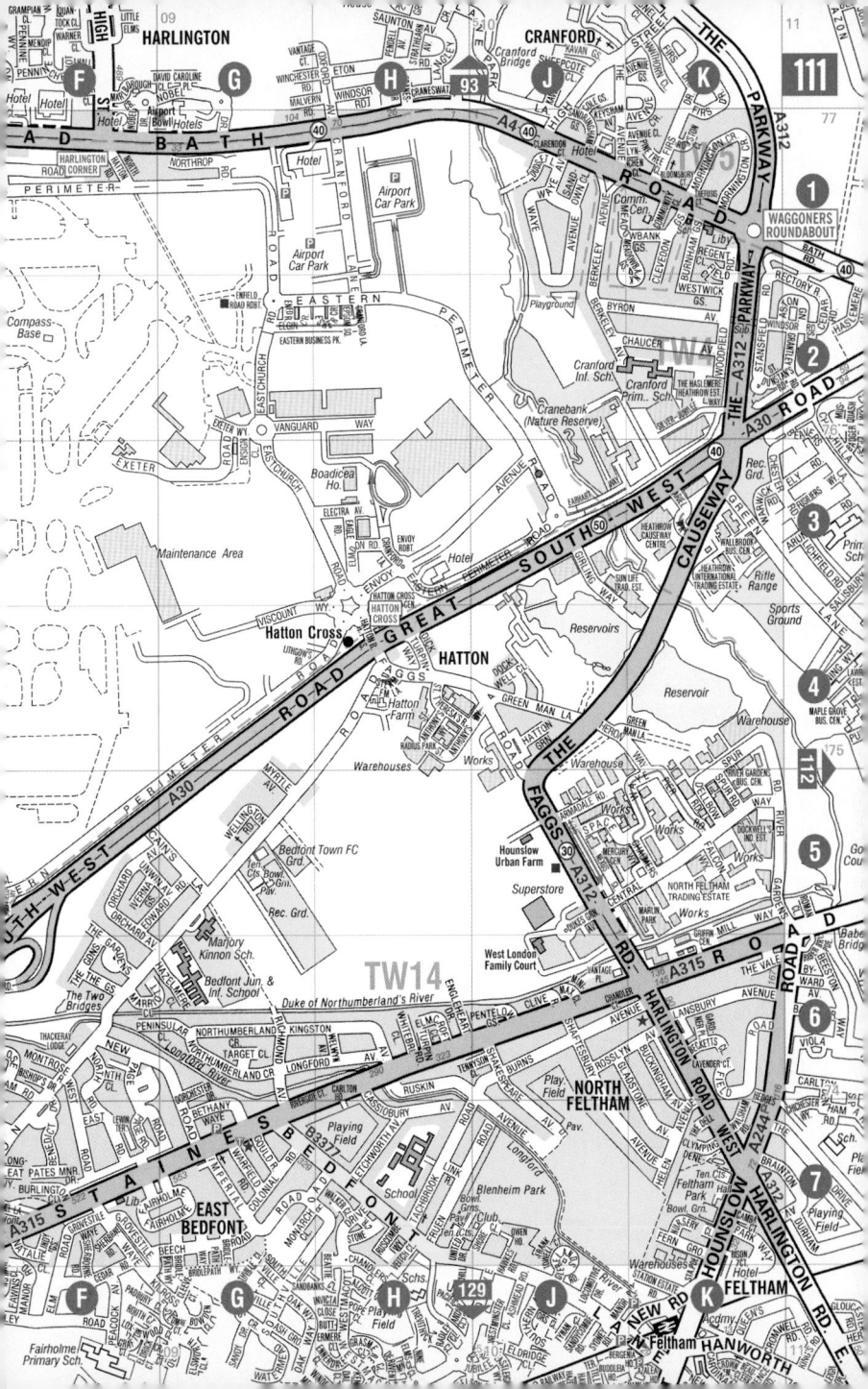

111
HARLINGTON
CRANFORD
Cranford Bridge
BATH ROAD
A4
HARLINGTON CORNER
NORTHROP
PERIMETER
Airport Bowl
Hotels
Hotel
Airport Car Park
CRANFORD LANE
THE PARKWAY
A312
WAGGONERS ROUNDABOUT
Comm. Cen.
TW5
TW4
Cranford Inf. Sch.
Cranford Prim.. Sch.
Cranebank (Nature Reserve)
Playground
BERKELEY AVENUE
BYRON AV.
CHAUCER AV.
EASTERN PERIMETER
EASTERN BUSINESS PK.
EASTCHURCH RD.
VANGUARD WAY
Compass Base
EXETER
Boadicea Ho.
Maintenance Area
ENVOY RDBT.
HATTON CROSS
Hatton Cross
A30 ROAD
GREAT SOUTH WEST ROAD
HATTON
Hatton Farm
GREEN MAN LA.
Reservoirs
Reservoir
HEATHROW CAUSEWAY CENTRE
THE CAUSEWAY
SUN LIFE TRAD. EST.
HEATHROW INTERNATIONAL TRADING ESTATE
Rifle Range
Sports Ground
Rec. Grd.
MAPLE GROVE BUS. CEN.
Warehouse
Warehouses
Works
112
175
THE FAGGS RD.
Hounslow Urban Farm
Superstore
West London Family Court
NORTH FELTHAM TRADING ESTATE
MILL WAY
Bedfont Town FC Grd.
Rec. Grd.
Marjory Kinnon Sch.
Bedfont Jun. & Inf. School
The Two Bridges
TW14
Duke of Northumberland's River
Longford River
HARLINGTON ROAD WEST
A315
NORTH FELTHAM
Play Field
STAINES ROAD
B3377
BEDFONT ROAD
Playing Field
School
Blenheim Park
Feltham Park
EAST BEDFONT
HOUNSLOW ROAD
HARLINGTON RD. E.
A244
Playing Field
FELTHAM
Feltham
HANWORTH
Fairholme Primary Sch.
129
93
F G H J K
1 2 3 4 5 6 7

112
94
111
130
A
B
C
D
E
1
2
3
4
5
6
7
THE PARKWAY
A312
WAGGONERS ROUNDABOUT
HENLYS ROUNDABOUT
BATH RD.
A4
GREAT WEST RD.
GT. SOUTH WEST RD.
A30
TW5
TW4
TW14
TW13
HESTON
Sutton Playing Field
Playground
Hotel
Lampton Academy
Lampton Sports Cen.
Playing Field
Civic Centre
LAMPTON PARK
Tennis Cts.
Bowling Green
Hounslow West
Bowls Club
Sports Grd.
Cemetery
A3063
A3006
SUTTON LANE
WELLINGTON RD. NTH.
WELLINGTON ROAD SOUTH
BULSTRODE AVENUE
Beaversfield Park
HOUNSLOW WEST
Playing Field
Cavalry Barracks
Prim. Sch.
Wks.
Lib.
Rifle Range
Sports Ground
PROLOGIS PARK
BEAVERS LANE
Warehouse
St. Mark's Cath. Sch.
Gala Bingo
A315
STAINES ROAD
Heath Nurseries
Golf Course
Club House
Baber Bridge
Weir
HOUNSLOW HEATH GOLF COURSE
HOUNSLOW HEATH
Hounslow Heath Nature Reserve
NORTH FELTHAM
A244
HOUNSLOW RD.
HARLINGTON ROAD EAST
River Crane
Play. Field
Jun. Sch.
Playing Field
Mosque
The Heathland School
Rec. Grd.
A314
HANWORTH ROAD
NELSON ROAD
Comm. Cen.
Hounslow Cemy.
HEATHROW GATEWAY
MILL FARM BUS. PK.
Bridge Farm Nursery
Cemetery
Recreation Grd.
Heathfield Jun. & Inf. Schs.
South West Middlesex Crematorium
De Brome Building
Hotel

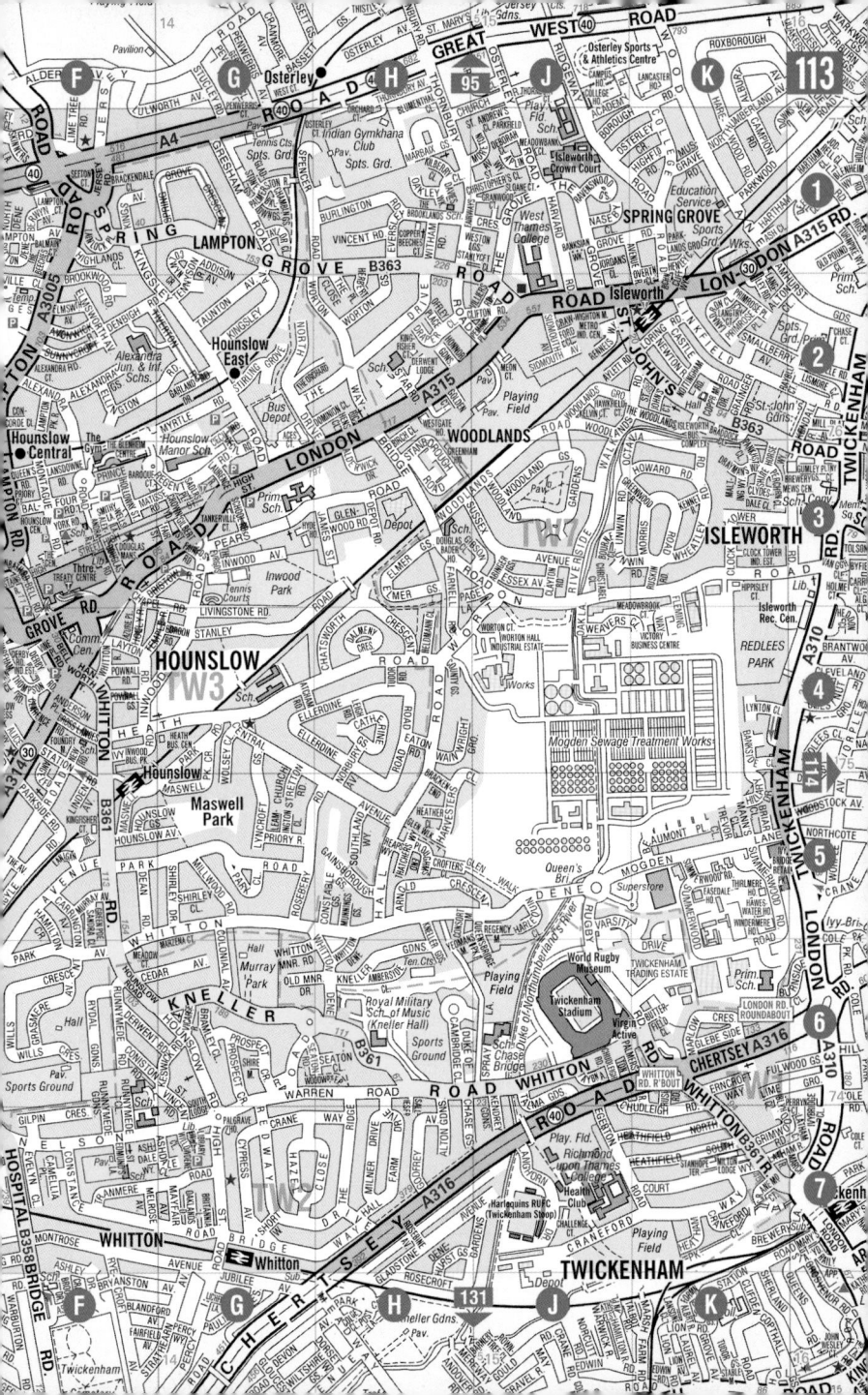

113
F
G
H
J
K
95
131
114
1
2
3
4
5
6
7
GREAT WEST ROAD
Osterley
Osterley Sports & Athletics Centre
Indian Gymkhana Club Spts. Grd.
Isleworth Crown Court
West Thames College
SPRING GROVE
Education Service
LAMPTON
SPRING GROVE ROAD
GROVE B363
LONDON ROAD
Isleworth
ST. JOHN'S ROAD
Hounslow East
Hounslow Central
Hounslow Manor Sch.
Alexandra Jun. & Inf. Schs.
Bus Depot
Playing Field
WOODLANDS
Depot
Inwood Park
Tennis Courts
Treaty Centre
Thtre.
HOUNSLOW
TW3
TW7
ISLEWORTH
Isleworth Rec. Cen.
REDLEES PARK
Worton Hall Industrial Estate
Victory Business Centre
Works
Mogden Sewage Treatment Works
Hounslow
Maswell Park
HEATH ROAD
Queen's Bri.
Superstore
World Rugby Museum
Twickenham Trading Estate
Twickenham Stadium
Virgin Active
Royal Military Sch. of Music (Kneller Hall)
Sports Ground
Murray Park
KNELLER ROAD
WHITTON ROAD
Harlequins RUFC (Twickenham Stoop)
Richmond upon Thames College
Health Club
Playing Field
CHERTSEY ROAD A316
TW2
TW1
WHITTON
Whitton
TWICKENHAM
LONDON ROAD A310
TWICKENHAM ROAD
HOSPITAL BRIDGE ROAD B358
Sports Ground
Twickenham
Kneller Gdns.
London Rd. Roundabout
Whitton Rd. R'bout

Syon Lane
SYON LA.
SPUR RD.
LONDON ROAD
A315
Busch Corner
96
SYON PARK
Syon Garden Centre
Syon House
TW8
DUKE OF NORTHUMBERLAND ESTATE
RIVER THAMES
Syon Reach
ROYAL BOTANIC GARDENS
Syon Vista
The Lake
Arboretum
King William's Temple
Rhododendron Dell
Bamboo Garden
Azalea Gdn.
Isleworth Ferry Gate (Closed)
Waterlily Pond
Evolution House
Temperate House
Cedar Vista
Conservation Area
Queen Charlotte's Cottage
Japanese Gateway & Landscape
Pagoda
OLD DEER PARK
ROYAL MID-SURREY GOLF COURSE
London Welsh RFC (Old Deer Park)
King's Observatory
Richmond Cricket Grnd.
Richmond Athletic Ground
Richmond and London Scottish RUFC
Cannons Health Club
Club House
Tennis Courts
Pools on the Park
Obelisk
Old Deer Park Recreation Ground
A316
TWICKENHAM ROAD
RICHMOND CIRCUS
LOWER
Richmond
RICHMOND
Richmond Green
SHEEN ROAD
PARADISE RD.
GEORGE ST.
HILL ST.
KEW RD.
THE QUADRANT
Asgill Ho.
Corporation Island
Visitor Cen.
RICHMOND ROAD
PETERSHAM ROAD
RICHMOND HILL
A307
B321
Terrace Gardens
Terrace Fld.
FRIARS STILE
The American Int. Uni. in London
Royal Star & Garter Home
Petersham Common
STAR & GARTER HILL
Buccleugh Gdns.
Glover's Island
Petersham Meadows
Petersham Farm
PETERSHAM
PETERSHAM ROAD
Petersham Gate
Sports Grd.
The German Sch. London
MARBLE HILL PARK
Marble Hill House
Tennis Courts
A305
ORLEANS RD.
Orleans Ho. Gallery
132
Orleans Gdns.
Foot Ferry
RIVER THAMES
WARREN
TWICKENHAM
KING ST.
Theatre
Twickenham
ARRAGON RD.
LONDON RD.
Sports Cen.
Playing Field
St. Margarets
ST. MARGARETS ROAD
CROWN RD.
ST. MARGARETS
THE AVENUE
ST. MARGARETS R'BOUT
A316 ROAD
Cole Park
Moor Mead Gd.
Moor Mead Bridge
LONDON RD. ROUNDABOUT
CHERTSEY
A310
TWICKENHAM ROAD
LONDON ROAD
Ivy Bri.
WHITTON RD.
113
ISLEWORTH
REDLEES PARK
Isleworth Rec. Cen.
WORTON
CLOCK TOWER IND. EST.
ST. JOHN'S RD.
B363
SOUTH ST.
RICHMOND RD.
A3004
Nazareth Ho.
Isleworth Ait Nature Reserve
Old Isleworth
Richmond Lock
Pleasure Gdns.
RANELAGH DRIVE
WEST MIDDLESEX UNIVERSITY HOSP
UCC
Cemetery
PARK ROAD
MILL PLAT
TWICKENHAM RD.
Wks.
The Green Sch.
Play Field
B454
ROXBOROUGH
A B C D E
1 2 3 4 5 6 7

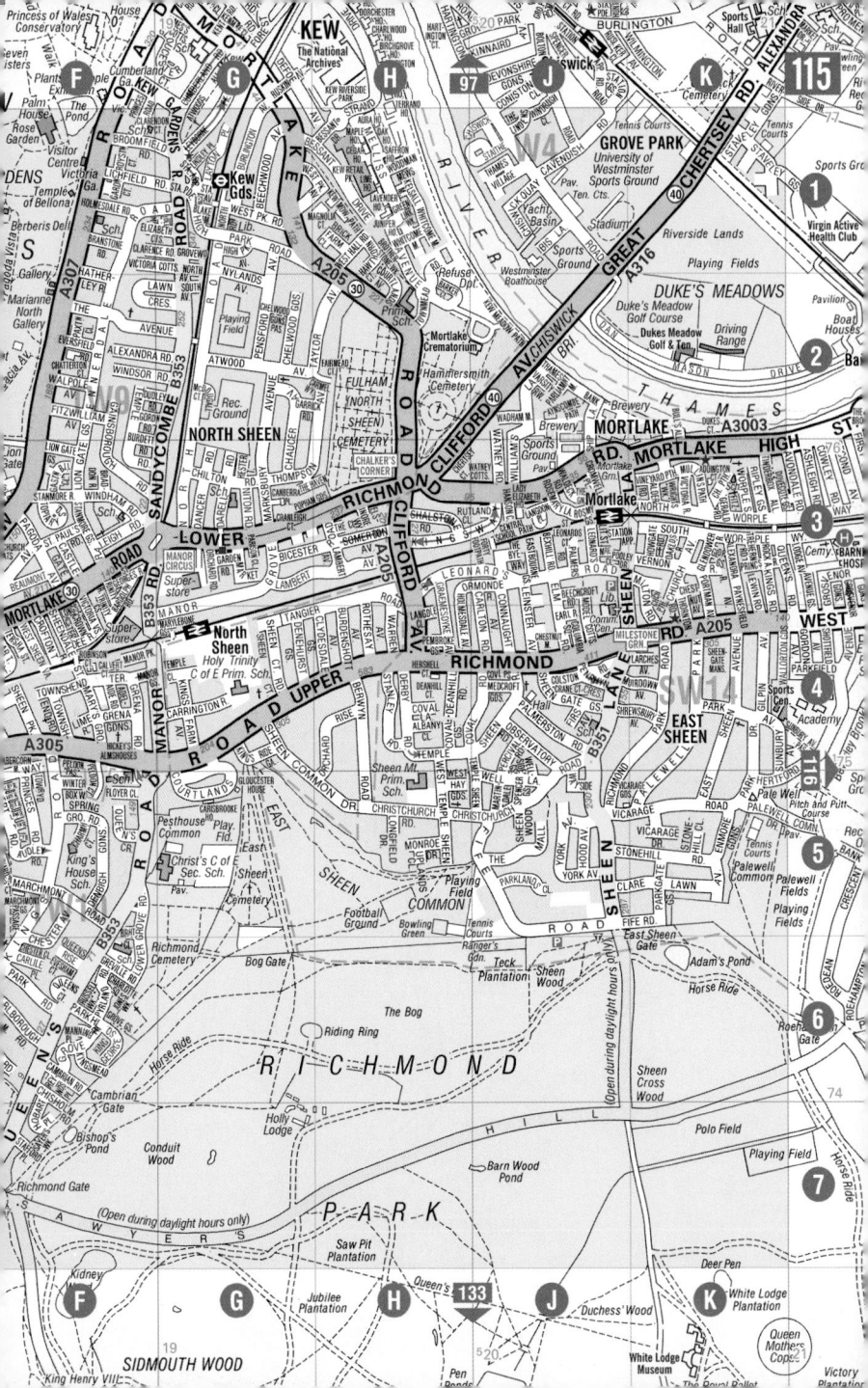

115
KEW
The National Archives
GROVE PARK
University of Westminster Sports Ground
DUKE'S MEADOWS
Duke's Meadow Golf Course
Playing Fields
Riverside Lands
RIVER THAMES
MORTLAKE
Mortlake Crematorium
Hammersmith Cemetery
NORTH SHEEN
FULHAM (NORTH SHEEN) CEMETERY
CHALKER'S CORNER
LOWER RICHMOND ROAD
UPPER RICHMOND ROAD
MORTLAKE HIGH ST.
GREAT CHISWICK AV.
SHEEN LANE
EAST SHEEN
WEST
North Sheen
Mortlake
Kew Gds.
Chiswick
SHEEN COMMON
Palewell Fields
Palewell Common
Adam's Pond
East Sheen Gate
Sheen Cross Wood
The Bog
Riding Ring
RICHMOND PARK
Holly Lodge
Conduit Wood
Bishop's Pond
Richmond Gate
Cambrian Gate
Barn Wood Pond
Polo Field
Playing Field
Saw Pit Plantation
Jubilee Plantation
Duchess' Wood
White Lodge Plantation
White Lodge Museum
Deer Pen
SIDMOUTH WOOD
Richmond Cemetery
East Sheen Cemetery
Pesthouse Common
King's House Sch.
Christ's C of E Sec. Sch.
Sheen Mt. Prim. Sch.
Holy Trinity C of E Prim. Sch.
Virgin Active Health Club
Roehampton Gate
97
116
133
A205
A316
A3003
A305
A307
B353
B351
W4
SW14
TW9
TW10
F
G
H
J
K
1
2
3
4
5
6
7

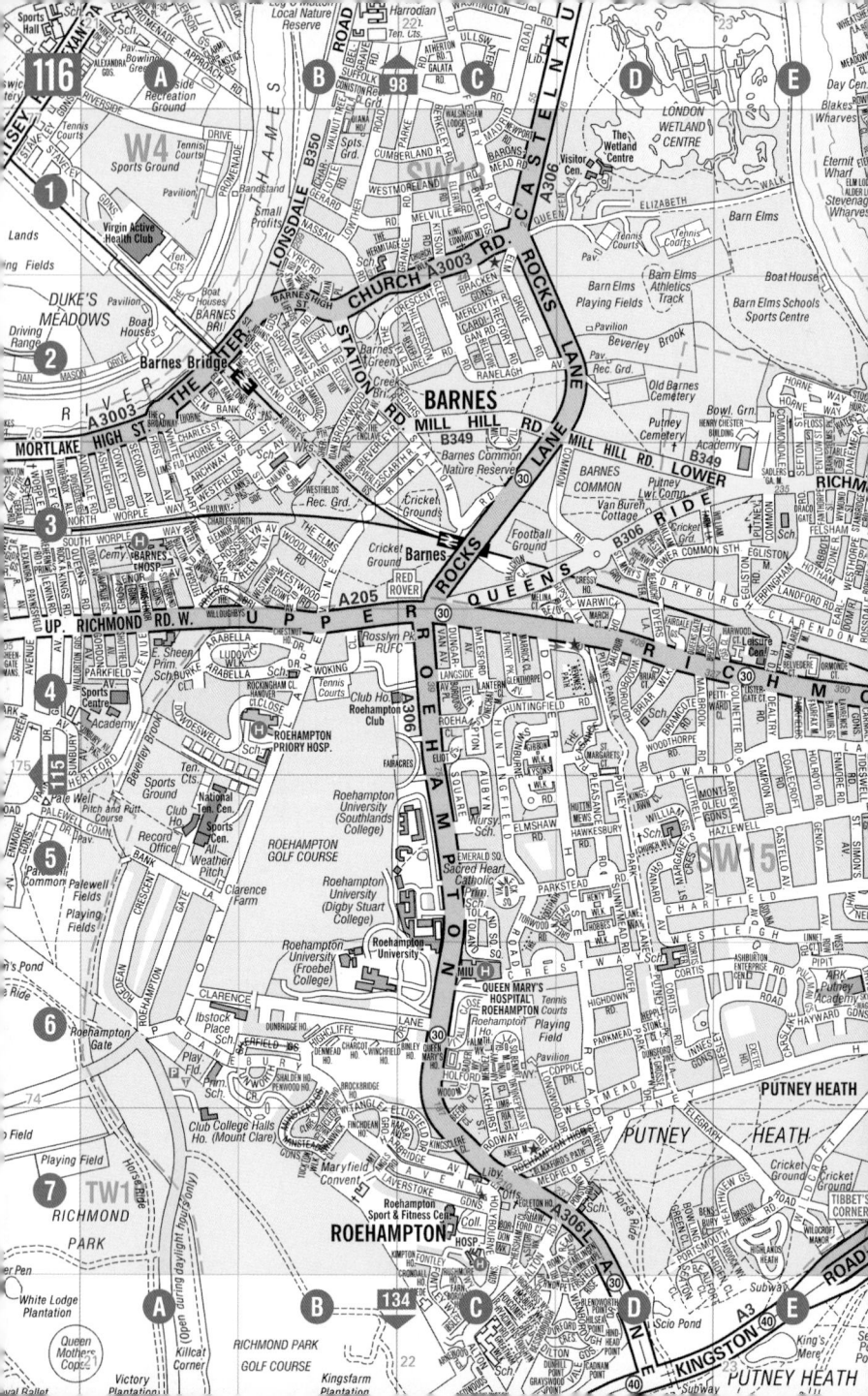
116
98
115
134
BARNES
ROEHAMPTON
PUTNEY HEATH
LONDON WETLAND CENTRE
RICHMOND PARK
ROEHAMPTON GOLF COURSE
BARNES COMMON
SW13
SW15
W4
TW1

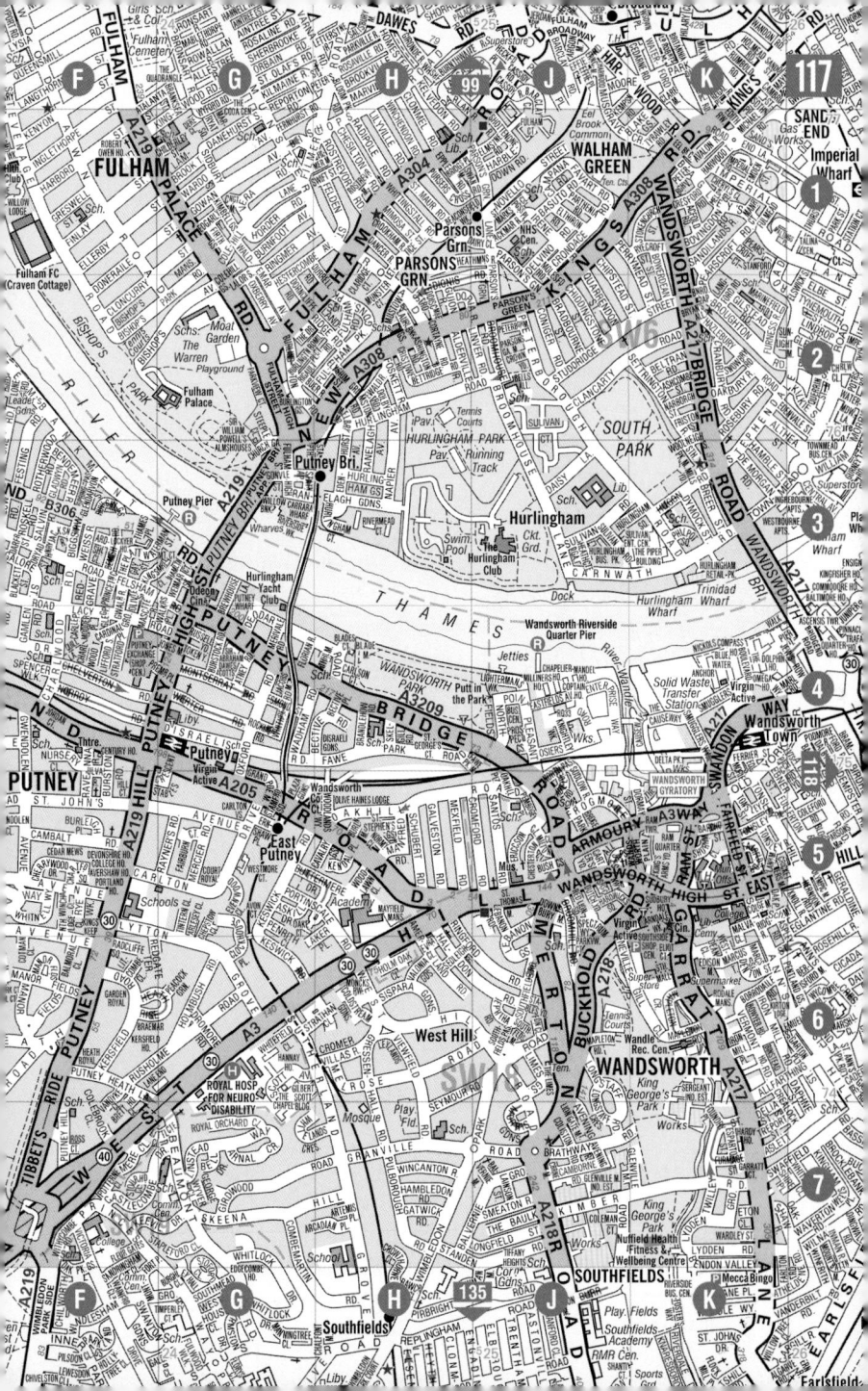

117
99
118
135
F
G
H
J
K
1
2
3
4
5
6
7
FULHAM
Fulham Cemetery
Fulham FC (Craven Cottage)
FULHAM PALACE RD.
Bishop's Park
Moat Garden
The Warren
Playground
Fulham Palace
Sir William Powell's Almshouses
FULHAM HIGH STREET
FULHAM RD.
A219
A304
A308
A3209
A205
A217
A218
A3
B306
PARSONS GRN.
Parsons Grn.
WALHAM GREEN
Eel Brook Common
KING'S RD.
WANDSWORTH BRIDGE RD.
SOUTH PARK
SW6
Sands End
Imperial Wharf
Gas Works
HURLINGHAM PARK
Running Track
Tennis Courts
Hurlingham
The Hurlingham Club
Swim. Pool
Ckt. Grd.
CARNWATH RD.
Hurlingham Wharf
Trinidad
Dock
Putney Bri.
Putney Pier
NEW KING'S RD.
THAMES
RIVER
Hurlingham Yacht Club
Wandsworth Riverside Quarter Pier
Wharves
Jetties
WANDSWORTH PARK
Putt in the Park
River Wandle
Solid Waste Transfer Station
Virgin Active
Wandsworth Town
SWANDON WAY
WANDSWORTH GYRATORY
PUTNEY BRIDGE RD.
PUTNEY HIGH ST.
PUTNEY HILL
PUTNEY
Putney
Odeon Cine.
Putney Exchange (Shop. Cen.)
Wandsworth Co. Ct.
East Putney
OAKHILL RD.
ARMOURY WAY
RAM ST.
WANDSWORTH HIGH ST.
EAST HILL
GARRATT LANE
BUCKHOLD RD.
MERTON RD.
WEST HILL
West Hill
SW18
Academy
Schools
Mus.
Cin.
Tennis Courts
Wandle Rec. Cen.
WANDSWORTH
King George's Park
Works
ROYAL HOSP FOR NEURO DISABILITY
Mosque
Play. Fld.
PUTNEY HEATH
TIBBET'S RIDE
WEST HILL
SW19
WIMBLEDON PARK SIDE
Southfields
SOUTHFIELDS
Nuffield Health Fitness & Wellbeing Centre
Mecca Bingo
Play. Fields
Southfields Academy
RMR Cen.
Earlsfield
College
School

118
A
B
C
D
E
1
2
3
4
5
6
7
100
117
136
BATTERSEA PARK
Pump House Gallery
Boating Lake
General Games Ground
Cremorne Riverside Centre
Cremorne Gardens
Chelsea Creek
Cremorne Wharf
SANDS END
Gas Works
Imperial Wharf
RIVER THAMES
Bascule Bri.
Chelsea Harbour Pier
Lensbury Wharf
Shell Wharf
THE LONDON HELIPORT
Plantation Wharf Pier
Fulham Wharf
Superstore
Leisure Cen.
WESTBRIDGE
SOMERSET ESTATE
College
VICARAGE CR.
LOMBARD RD.
BATTERSEA BRIDGE
ALBERT BRIDGE RD.
A3031
A3220
BATTERSEA PARK RD.
BATTERSEA
LATCHMERE RD.
SW11
Falcon Park
FALCON RD.
A3207
A3205
YORK RD.
PLOUGH RD.
York Gdns.
CLAPHAM JUNCTION
NHS Walk-in
Superstore
LAVENDER HILL
ST. JOHN'S HILL
A3036
ELSPETH R.
CLAPHAM COMMON NORTH SIDE
CLAPHAM COMN. W. SIDE
Playground
THE CHASE
A205
Rec. Grd.
A3
A217
WANDSWORTH BRI. ROAD
SWANDON WY.
Wandsworth Town
TRINITY RD.
EAST HILL
HUGUENOT PL.
NORTH SIDE WANDSWORTH COMMON
BATTERSEA RISE
NORTHCOTE ROAD
B229
St. Mary's Cemy.
Spencer Park
SPENCER PARK
B234
Emanuel School
Tennis Courts
Academy
WANDSWORTH COMMON
WINDMILL RD.
A214
HMP WANDSWORTH
Tennis Courts
Bowling Green
Cricket Ground
Wandsworth Common
THE AVENUE
Wandsworth Common
BOLINGBROKE GRO.
NIGHTINGALE LANE
B231
EARLSFIELD RD.
GARRATT LANE
The Chelsea Group of Children
WANDSWORTH CEMETERY
EARLSFIELD
Earlsfield
Beatrix Potter Prim. Sch.
BELLEVUE RD.
ST. JAMES'S DR.
BALHAM
Balham
Pavilion

119
101
120
137
NEW COVENT GARDEN MARKET
Fruit & Vegetable Market
Battersea Dogs' Home
Battersea Pk.
Queenstown Rd. (Battersea)
SOUTH LAMBETH
Stockwell
STOCKWELL
Angell Town
Larkhall Park
Heathbrook Park
Wandsworth Rd.
Clapham High St.
Clapham North
LAMBETH HOSPITAL
CLAPHAM
Trinity Hospice
Clapham Comm.
CLAPHAM COMMON
BRIXTON
Lambeth Academy
SW4
SW2
SW8
SW9
CLAPHAM PARK
HMP BRIXTON
Sports Ground
Windmill Gdns.
Clapham Sth.
Mount Pond
Eagle Pond
Long Pond
Basketball Courts
Bandstand
Platanos College
COMMON LONG RD.
CLAPHAM PARK RD.
ACRE LANE
CLAPHAM HIGH ST.
CLAPHAM RD.
STOCKWELL RD.
SOUTH LAMBETH RD.
WANDSWORTH RD.
QUEENSTOWN RD.
BRIXTON RD.
BRIXTON HILL
BEDFORD RD.
POYNDERS RD.
CAVENDISH RD.
CLAPHAM COMMON SOUTH SIDE
CLAPHAM COMMON NORTH SIDE
BALHAM HIGH RD.
KINGS AVENUE
STREATHAM PL.
CHRISTCHURCH RD.
TULSE HILL
ATKINS RD.
NEW PARK RD.
A3
A24
A23
A3036
A205
A2217
A204
B221
B224
B303
A3216
A3205
A203

120
102
138
119
A
B
C
D
E
1
2
3
4
5
6
7
CAMBERWELL
CAMBERWELL GREEN
SOUTHAMPTON
PECKHAM
Angell Town
STOCKWELL
Loughborough Junc.
CAMBERWELL Sports Cen.
Denmark Hill
THE MAUDSLEY HOSP.
KINGS COLLEGE HOSPITAL
RUSKIN PARK
Brixton
BRIXTON
COLDHARBOUR LANE A2217
DENMARK HILL A215
DULWICH ROAD A2214
HALF MOON LA.
VILLAGE WAY A2214
NORWOOD ROAD A215
CROXTED ROAD A2199
MILKWOOD ROAD
RAILTON ROAD
EFFRA RD.
TULSE HILL A204
Herne Hill
HERNE HILL
North Dulwich
East Dulwich
EAST DULWICH GROVE
DOG KENNEL HILL
GROVE LA.
CHAMPION PK. A2216
Dulwich Hamlet FC (Champion Hill Stadium)
The Charter School
James Allen's Girls' Sch.
Herne Hill Stadium
Brockwell Park Lido
BROCKWELL PARK
The Mansion
DULWICH VILLAGE
Dulwich Old College
Dulwich Picture Gallery
Belair Park
TURNEY ROAD
Sports Ground
Knight's Hill
TULSE
MYATTS FIELDS
St. Gabriel's Manor
Loughborough Park
LOUGHBOROUGH ESTATE
Max Roach Pk.
William Booth Coll.
Dental Institute
Lucas Gds.
Leisure Cen.
Brunswick Park
The Crypt
Bus Depot
Dog Kennel Hill Open Space
Superstore

121
122
103
139
F
G
H
J
K
1
2
3
4
5
6
7
PECKHAM
Peckham Rye
PECKHAM HIGH ST.
PECKHAM HILL ST.
A202
ROAD
QUEEN'S
Queens Rd. (Peckham)
NEW POMEROY ST.
NEW CROSS RD.
NEW CROSS ROAD
NEW CROSS GATE
Bus Garage
SE14
SE15
SE22
SE23
SE4
LAUSANNE RD.
CLAYTON RD.
CONSORT RD.
COPELAND RD.
HEATON RD.
RYE LANE
PECKHAM RYE
Warwick Gardens
Nunhead
EVELINA RD.
A2214
NUNHEAD LA.
GELLATLY RD.
DRAKEFELL ROAD
B2142
Telegraph Hill Park
College
NUNHEAD CEMETERY
Nunhead Cemetery Nature Reserve
NUNHEAD
BROCKLEY
Playing Field
Reservoirs (covered)
EAST DULWICH ROAD
EAST DULWICH
Leisure Cen.
PECKHAM RYE COMMON
PECKHAM RYE PARK
PECKHAM ROAD
B219
B238
Academy
Harris Sports Cen.
AQUARIUS GOLF COURSE
Water Works
Newlands
Honor Oak Crematorium
Camberwell New Cemetery
One Tree Hill Local Nature Reserve
HONOR OAK
Honor Oak Park
HONOR OAK ROAD
HONOR OAK PARK
FOREST HILL
FOREST HILL
Camberwell Old Cemetery
LORDSHIP LANE
A2216
GROVE VALE
DULWICH PARK
DULWICH COMMON
THE GROVE
Horniman Gardens
Visitor Centre
Nature Reserves
STANSTEAD RD.
BROCKLEY RI.
B218

122
A
B
C
D
E
104
New Cross Gate
New Cross
NEW CROSS ROAD
A2
Goldsmiths College
NEW CROSS
NEW CROSS GATE
Deptford Bri.
DEPTFORD BROADWAY
BROOKMILL ROAD
A2210
GREENWICH HIGH RD.
BLACKHEATH RD.
GREENWICH SOUTH ST.
BLACKHEATH HILL
LEWISHAM WAY
LEWISHAM RD.
A2211
1
2
3
4
5
6
7
Telegraph Hill
Vesta College
Crossways Sixth Form
DRAKEFELL B2142 RD.
MALPAS RD.
B218
ST. JOHNS
St. Johns
Elverson Rd
A20 WAY
LOAMPIT HILL
LOAMPIT VALE
THURSTON RD.
Lewisham
LeSoCo
Brockley
BROCKLEY RD.
BROCKLEY
HILLY FIELDS
Cricket Ground
Bowling Green
Prendergast Hilly Fields Coll.
LEWISHAM
MOLESWORTH ST.
LEWISHAM HIGH STREET
A21
ADELAIDE AV.
Brockley Cemetery
Ladywell Cemetery
Crofton Park
LADYWELL RD.
Ladywell
LADYWELL
UNIVERSITY HOSPITAL LEWISHAM
Lewisham Park
121
Crofton Pk.
Honor Oak Crematorium
Honor Oak Park
HONOR OAK PARK
HONOR OAK PK.
B238
STONDON PARK
Guy's Hosp. Athletic Grd.
Ladywell Arena (Running Track)
Ladywell Fields
Blythe Hill Fields
Blythe Hill
RUSHEY GRN.
BROWNHILL RD.
Catford Bridge
Catford
CATFORD A205 RD.
St. Dunstan's Coll.
St. Dunstan's Enterprises
St. Dunstan's College Jubilee Ground
STANSTEAD A205 ROAD
140
BROMLEY RD.
CATFORD
36
37
38

123
F
G
H
J
K
1
2
3
4
5
6
7
105
124
141
Peter Harrison Planetarium
Royal Observatory Greenwich
GREENWICH PARK
Reservoir (covered)
The Wilderness
The Gardens (Deer Park)
Parks Police
Ranger's House
Bandstand
Tennis Cts.
VANBRUGH PARK
OLD DOVER ROAD
SUN-IN-THE-SANDS
SHOOTERS HILL ROAD
A2
B210
B212
BLACK HEATH
Blackheath Vale
Hollyhedge Ho.
PRINCE OF WALES RD.
PRINCE CHARLES ROAD
KIDBROOKE PARK ROAD
A2213
ROCHESTER WAY RELIEF ROAD
Blackheath Nursy. & Prep. Sch.
Morden College (Almshouses)
SE3
Thomas Tallis Sch.
Thomas Tallis Sports Cen.
Kidbrooke Nature Reserve
Warehouse
OLD POST OFFICE LA.
Kidbrooke
BLACKHEATH
Blackheath
College
Academy
Concert Halls
LEE TERRACE
LEE PARK
BLACKHEATH PARK
The Priory
Bowl. Grn.
Sports Ground
Sports Grounds
David Lloyd Leis.
Cator Pk.
Roan School Playing Fields
SUTCLIFFE PARK
Sutcliffe Pk. Athletics Track
LEE HIGH ROAD
A20
Manor House Gdns.
Manor Park
Liby.
Euro Cen.
LEE GRN.
ELTHAM ROAD
BURNT ASH ROAD
A2212
SIDCUP ROAD
Horn Park
Brindishe Lee Sch.
LEE
Hither Green
HITHER GREEN
Depot
CHILTONIAN IND. EST.
Wks.
Lee
Colfes Prep. Sch.
Colfes Senior Sch.
Colfes Leisure Cen.
SE12
WESTHORNE AV.
A205
ST. MILDREDS ROAD
BARING ROAD
Rehab. Cen.
THE WOODLANDS
Warehouse
Hither Green Sidings
Northbrook Park
Grove Park Nature Reserve
Horn Park Prim. Sch.
Comm. Cen.
Hadlow Coll. (Mottingham Campus)
MOTTINGHAM ROAD

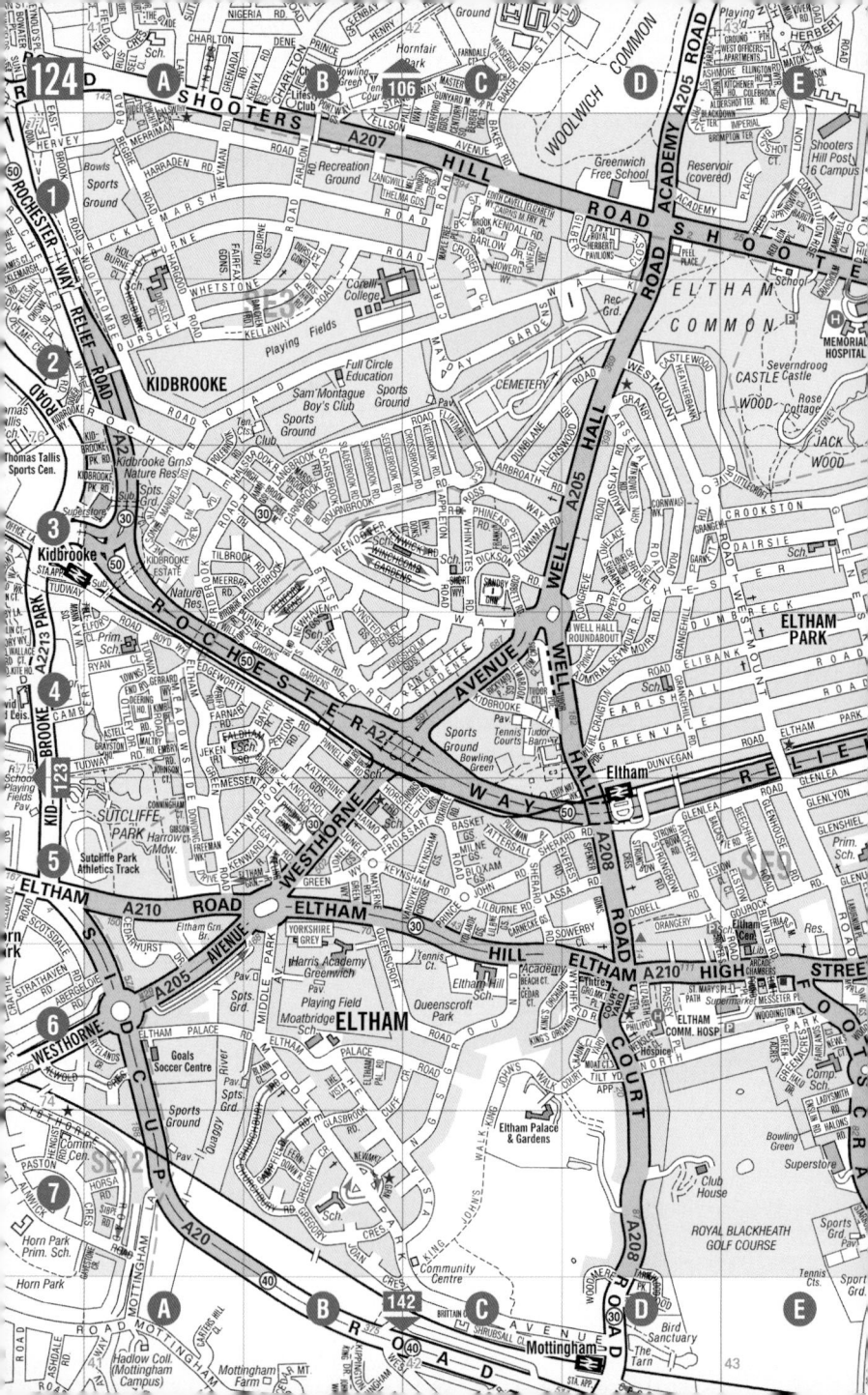

124
106
142
123
A
B
C
D
E
1
2
3
4
5
6
7
SHOOTERS HILL ROAD
A207
WOOLWICH COMMON
ACADEMY ROAD
A205
Greenwich Free School
Reservoir (covered)
Shooters Hill Post 16 Campus
ELTHAM COMMON
MEMORIAL HOSPITAL
Severndroog Castle
CASTLE WOOD
Rose Cottage
JACK WOOD
Bowls
Sports Ground
Recreation Ground
Corelli College
Playing Fields
KIDBROOKE
Full Circle Education
Sam Montague Boy's Club
Sports Ground
CEMETERY
WELL HALL ROAD
ROCHESTER WAY RELIEF ROAD
ROCHESTER WAY
A2
Kidbrooke Grn. Nature Res.
Thomas Tallis Sports Cen.
Kidbrooke
KIDBROOKE ESTATE
Nature Res.
KIDBROOKE PARK ROAD
A2213
SUTCLIFFE PARK
Sutcliffe Park Athletics Track
Harrow Mdw.
WELL HALL ROUNDABOUT
ELTHAM PARK
Eltham
ELTHAM ROAD
A210
ELTHAM HILL
WESTHORNE AVENUE
Eltham Grn. Br.
YORKSHIRE GREY
Harris Academy Greenwich
Playing Field
Moatbridge Sch.
ELTHAM
Queenscroft Park
Eltham Hill Sch.
ELTHAM HIGH STREET
ELTHAM COMM. HOSP
Hospice
Eltham Palace & Gardens
COURT ROAD
A208
Club House
ROYAL BLACKHEATH GOLF COURSE
Bowling Green
Superstore
SIDCUP ROAD
A20
Goals Soccer Centre
Sports Ground
Quaggy River
Horn Park Prim. Sch.
Horn Park
Community Centre
Mottingham
MOTTINGHAM ROAD
Hadlow Coll. (Mottingham Campus)
Mottingham Farm
Bird Sanctuary
The Tarn
SE3
SE9
SE12

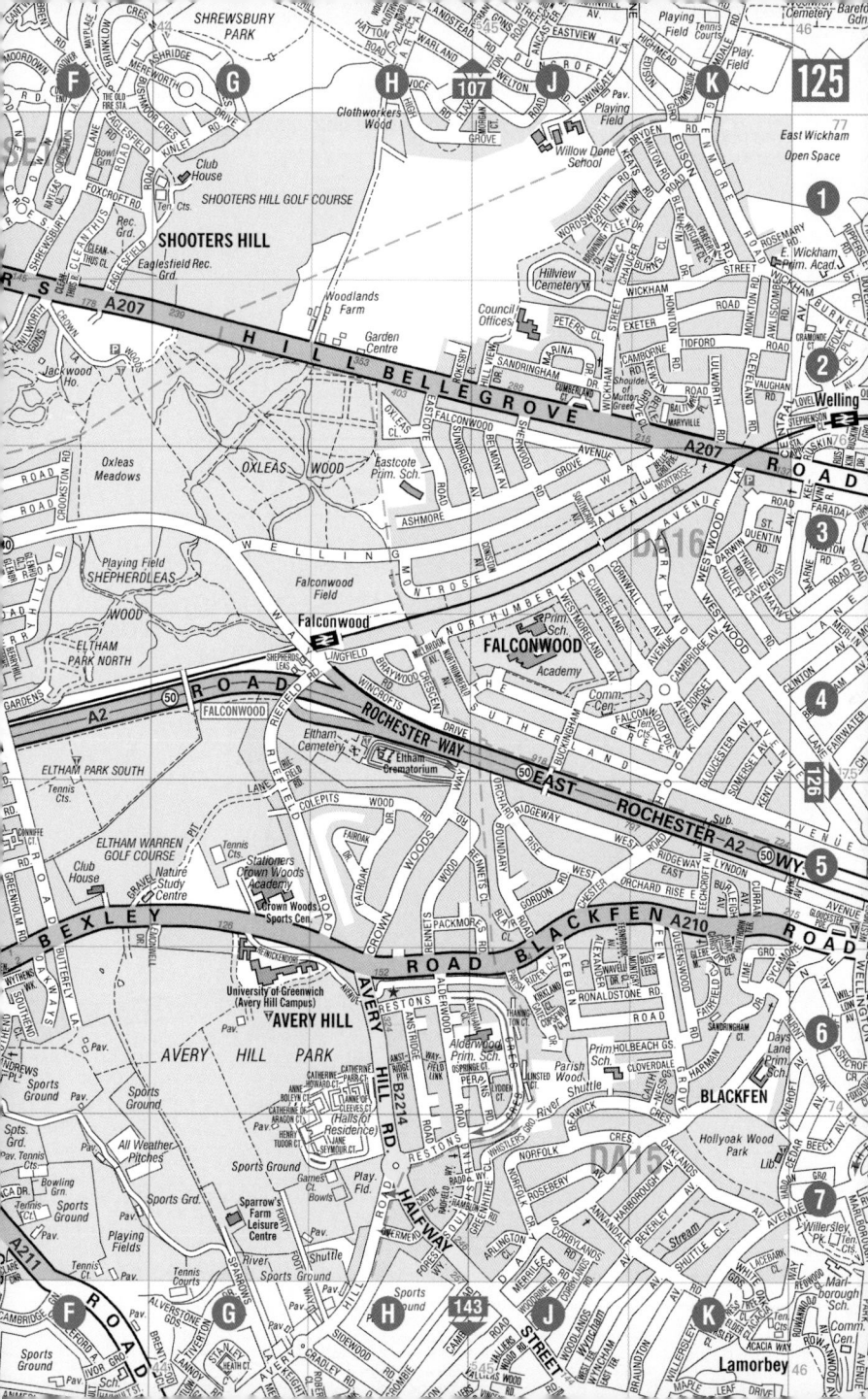
SHREWSBURY PARK
Clothworkers Wood
Willow Dene School
Playing Field
East Wickham Open Space
E. Wickham Prim. Acad.
Club House
SHOOTERS HILL GOLF COURSE
SHOOTERS HILL
Eaglesfield Rec. Grd.
Hillview Cemetery
Woodlands Farm
Council Offices
Garden Centre
Jackwood Ho.
SHOOTERS HILL
BELLEGROVE
A207
ROAD
Welling
Oxleas Meadows
OXLEAS WOOD
Eastcote Prim. Sch.
WELLING WAY
Falconwood Field
Playing Field
SHEPHERDLEAS WOOD
ELTHAM PARK NORTH
Falconwood
FALCONWOOD
Prim. Sch.
Academy
DA16
A2
ROAD
ROCHESTER WAY
EAST ROCHESTER WAY
Eltham Cemetery
Eltham Crematorium
ELTHAM PARK SOUTH
ELTHAM WARREN GOLF COURSE
Club House
Nature Study Centre
Stationers Crown Woods Academy
Crown Woods Sports Cen.
BEXLEY ROAD
BLACKFEN ROAD
A210
University of Greenwich (Avery Hill Campus)
AVERY HILL
AVERY HILL PARK
AVERY HILL RD.
B2214
Alderwood Prim. Sch.
(Halls of Residence)
Parish Wood
River Shuttle
BLACKFEN
Days Lane Prim. Sch.
Hollyoak Wood Park
DA15
Sports Ground
All Weather Pitches
Sparrow's Farm Leisure Centre
Playing Fields
A211
HALFWAY STREET
Willersley Pk.
Marlborough Sch.
Lamorbey
107
126
143
F
G
H
J
K
1
2
3
4
5
6
7

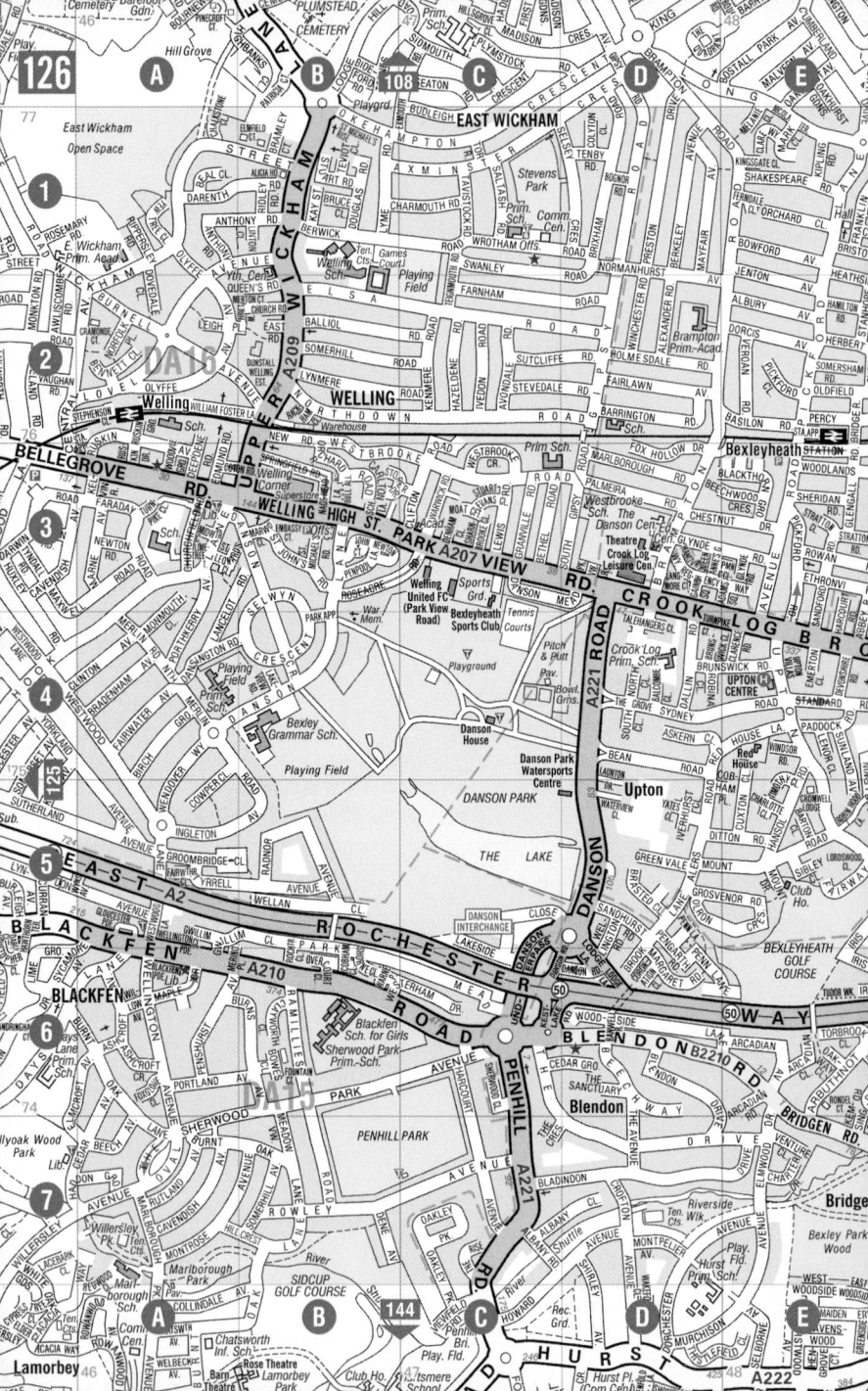

108
125
144
A
B
C
D
E
1
2
3
4
5
6
7
77
76
75
74
46
47
48
Plumstead Cemetery
Hill Grove
East Wickham Open Space
EAST WICKHAM
E. Wickham Prim. Acad.
Stevens Park
Welling Sch.
Playing Field
Games Court
DA16
WELLING
Welling
Warehouse
BELLEGROVE RD.
WELLING HIGH ST.
PARK VIEW RD.
A207
A209
UPPER WICKHAM LANE
Welling Corner
Superstore
Welling United FC (Park View Road)
Sports Grd.
Bexleyheath Sports Club
Tennis Courts
Pitch & Putt
Playground
War Mem.
Bexleyheath
STATION
Brampton Prim. Acad.
Westbrooke Sch.
The Danson Cen.
Crook Log Leisure Cen.
CROOK LOG
BROADWAY
Crook Log Prim. Sch.
UPTON CENTRE
A221
DANSON ROAD
Danson House
Danson Park Watersports Centre
Upton
DANSON PARK
THE LAKE
Red House
Bexley Grammar Sch.
Playing Field
SELWYN CRESCENT
Club Ho.
BEXLEYHEATH GOLF COURSE
EAST ROCHESTER WAY
A2
DANSON INTERCHANGE
DANSON UNDERPASS
BLACKFEN ROAD
A210
BLACKFEN
Blackfen Sch. for Girls
Sherwood Park Prim. Sch.
BLENDON ROAD
B2210
Blendon
THE SANCTUARY
BRIDGEN RD.
DA15
PENHILL ROAD
PENHILL PARK
Days Lane Prim. Sch.
Willersley Pk.
Marlborough Park
Marlborough Sch.
SIDCUP GOLF COURSE
River
Riverside Wlk.
Hurst Prim. Sch.
Play. Fld.
Rec. Grd.
Bexley Park Wood
Bridge
HURST ROAD
A222
Chatsworth Inf. Sch.
Rose Theatre
Lamorbey Park
Lamorbey
Rose Bruford
Barn Theatre
Hurst Pl. Com. Cen.
Lib.
Sch.
Prim. Sch.

127
F
G
H
J
K
109
145
1
2
3
4
5
6
7
49
50
51
74
75
76
77
DA1
DA5
DA6
DA7
DA8
NORTHUMBERLAND HEATH
BEXLEYHEATH
BARNEHURST
CRAYFORD
BEXLEY
OLD BEXLEY
Barnehurst
Bexley
A220
A221
A207
A223
A222
A2
A2000
B2210
50
30
ROCHESTER
WATLING
LONDON (WATLING ST.)
BROADWAY
ALBION
ROAD
BOURNE
GRAVEL HILL
DARTFORD-BY-PASS
BLACK PRINCE INTERCHANGE
Bexleyheath Academy
Goals Soccer Cen.
Cemetery
Tenpin
Cin.
Gala Bingo
Civic Offices
THE BROADWAY SHOP. CEN.
Bus Depot
Russell Park
Bowling Grn.
Tennis Cts.
Playing Field
Primary Sch.
Bursted Wood Prim. Sch.
Bursted Wood
Offices
Barnehurst Golf Course
Club House
Mayplace
Crayford Manor House
Rose Cott.
War. Mem.
Spts. Grd.
Youth Cen.
Mayplace Prim. Sch.
Martens Grove
Martens Grove Park
VCD Athletic FC Ground
Gravel Hill Prim. Sch.
St. Catherine's Catholic School for Girls
St. Columba's Catholic Boys Sch.
Bigs Hill Wood
Gas Works
SHENSTONE PARK
Grammar Sch.
Tennis Courts
Riverside Walk
Shuttle River
Hall Place & Gardens
Hall Place Sports Pav.
Hall Place Gardens
Mus.
SPORTS FIELD
Pumping Station
The Old Orchard
Recycling Cen.
Subway
Churchfield Wood
Works
Weir
Manor Ho.
Cem.
Sports Ground
Rec. Grd.
Bexley Lawn Tennis Club
Old Bexley C of E Prim. Sch.
Cricket Ground
Normandy Prim. Sch.
Res. (covered)
Playing Field
Erith Sec. Sch.
Spts. Cen.
Rec. Grd.
Ten. Courts
Pav.

128
110
146
STANWELL
ASHFORD
CHATTERN HILL
CLOCKHOUSE ROUNDABOUT
FORDBRIDGE ROUNDABOUT
SCHOOL ROAD JUNCTION
LONDON ROAD
STAINES ROAD
KINGSTON ROAD
STAINES-BY-PASS
CHURCH ROAD
FELTHAM ROAD
CLOCKHOUSE LANE
GT. SOUTH-WEST RD.
STAINES RESERVOIRS
QUEEN MARY RESERVOIR
ASHFORD MANOR GOLF COURSE
BEDFONT LAKES COUNTRY PARK
Staines Reservoirs Aqueduct
TW15
TW17
TW18
A30
A308
A315
B377
B378
B3003

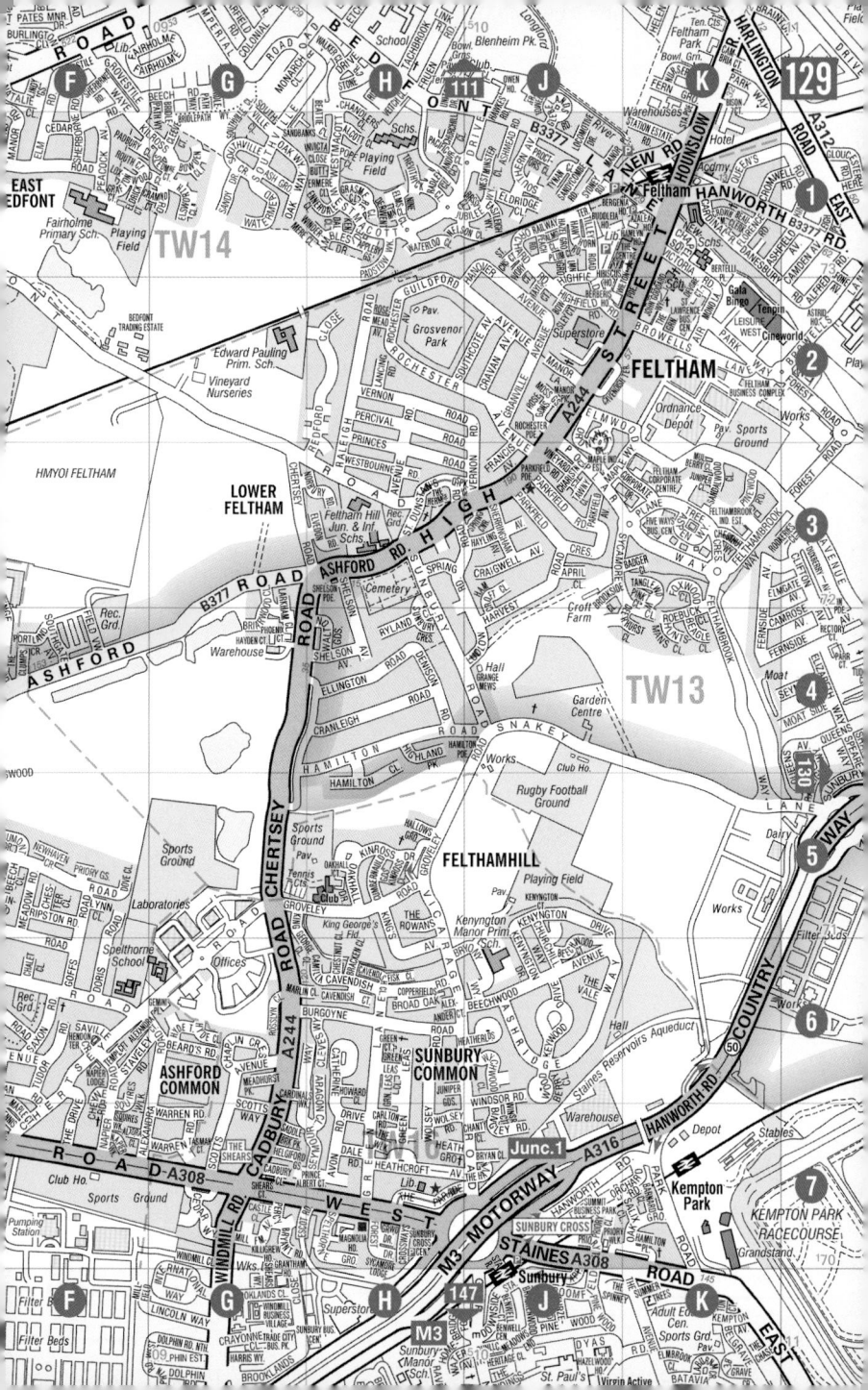

129
130
111
147
F
G
H
J
K
1
2
3
4
5
6
7
EAST BEDFONT
Fairholme Primary Sch.
Playing Field
TW14
Blenheim Pk.
Longford
Feltham Park
HARLINGTON ROAD EAST
A312
HANWORTH B3377 RD.
HOUNSLOW
Feltham
NEW RD
B3377
Superstore
Gala Bingo
Tenpin
Cineworld
LEISURE WEST
FELTHAM
FELTHAM BUSINESS COMPLEX
Ordnance Depot
Sports Ground
Grosvenor Park
BEDFONT TRADING ESTATE
Edward Pauling Prim. Sch.
Vineyard Nurseries
HMYOI FELTHAM
LOWER FELTHAM
Feltham Hill Jun. & Inf. Schs.
Cemetery
HIGH STREET
A244
ASHFORD RD.
B377 ROAD
ASHFORD
Rec. Grd.
Warehouse
TW13
Croft Farm
Garden Centre
Hall
GRANGE MEWS
Works
Club Ho.
SNAKEY LANE
Rugby Football Ground
FELTHAMHILL
Playing Field
Sports Ground
Laboratories
Spelthorne School
Offices
King George's Fld.
Kenyngton Manor Prim. Sch.
Dairy
Works
Filter Beds
Staines Reservoirs Aqueduct
CHERTSEY ROAD
A244
CADBURY ROAD
ASHFORD COMMON
SUNBURY COMMON
COUNTRY WAY
HANWORTH RD.
Junc.1
A316
M3 MOTORWAY
A308
STAINES ROAD WEST
Club Ho.
Sports Ground
Pumping Station
Filter Beds
SUNBURY CROSS
Sunbury
STAINES A308 ROAD
Kempton Park
KEMPTON PARK RACECOURSE
Grandstand
Stables
Depot
Warehouse
Superstore
Sunbury Manor Sch.
Adult Ed. Cen.
Sports Grd.
St. Paul's
Virgin Active
WINDMILL RD
LINCOLN WAY
M3

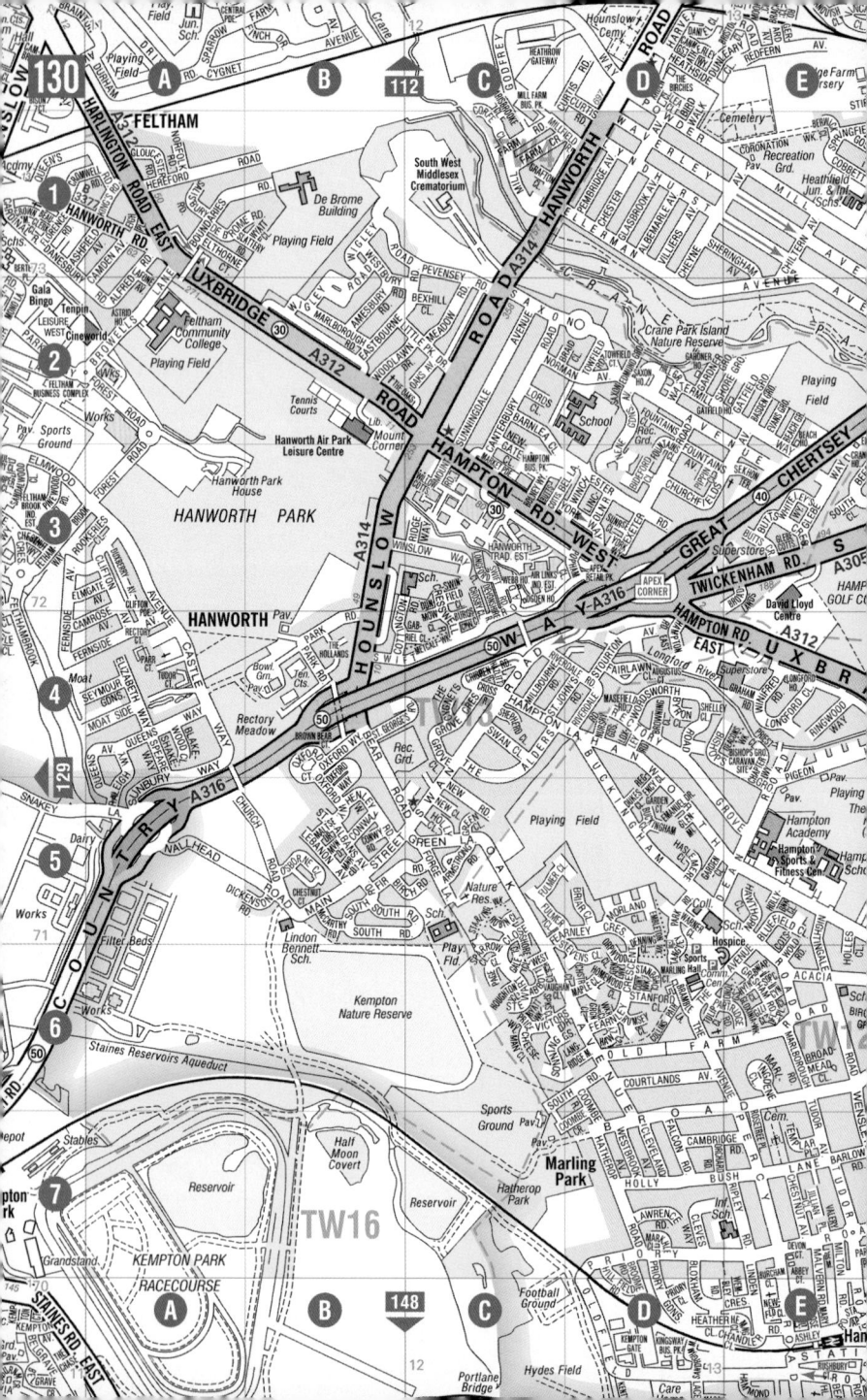

130
FELTHAM
HANWORTH
HANWORTH PARK
Hanworth Park House
South West Middlesex Crematorium
De Brome Building
Feltham Community College
Hanworth Air Park Leisure Centre
Crane Park Island Nature Reserve
Kempton Nature Reserve
Staines Reservoirs Aqueduct
KEMPTON PARK RACECOURSE
Marling Park
Hatherop Park
Half Moon Covert
Rectory Meadow
Hampton Academy
David Lloyd Centre
APEX CORNER
TW13
TW16
TW12
112
129
148

131
113
132
149
F
G
H
J
K
1
2
3
4
5
6
7
WHITTON
Whitton
TWICKENHAM
STRAWBERRY HILL
Strawberry Hill
TEDDINGTON
Teddington
HAMPTON HILL
HAMPTON
Fulwell
TW2
TW1
TW11
Harlequins RUFC (Twickenham Stoop)
Health Club
Playing Field
Depot
Kneller Gdns.
Twickenham Cemetery
Comm. Acad.
Spts. Cen.
Sports Ground
HOSPITAL BRIDGE ROUNDABOUT
Hospital Bridge
River Crane
Fulwell Park
FULWELL GOLF COURSE
STRAWBERRY HILL GOLF COURSE
St. James's Catholic Primary School
Waldegrave Sch. for Girls
Twickenham Green
Radnor Gardens
St. Mary's University College
Sports Cen.
Newland Ho. Sch.
Cemetery
Stanley Prim. Sch.
Bus Garage
Club House
National Phy. Lab.
HOSP.
Walk-In Cen.
Canal Plantation
Upper Lodge
Pantile Bridge
The Brew House
Bartons Cottage
Cricket Ground
Bushy House
Tennis Courts
Bowling Green
Sports Ground
Teddington Lodge
Round Plantation
Hampton Open Air Pool
Clarendon Sch.
Carlisle Park
Willow Plantation
Broom Clumps
The Pheasantry Welcome Centre
River Lodge
Deer Pen
Hampton & Richmond Borough FC (Beveree Stadium)
B U S H Y
P A R K
CHERTSEY ROAD
A316
STAINES ROAD
A305
HEATH ROAD
THE GREEN
HAMPTON ROAD
A311
SIXTH CROSS ROAD
B358
WELLINGTON RD.
STANLEY ROAD
HAMPTON ROAD
A313
PARK ROAD
A312
STREET HIGH
WALDEGRAVE ROAD
A309
CHURCH ROAD
B360
BROAD ST.
HIGH ST.
PARK RD.
CROSS DEEP
A310
STRAWBERRY VALE
WALDEGRAVE PARK

132
114
131
150
A
B
C
D
E
1
2
3
4
5
6
7
16
17
18
TWICKENHAM
TEDDINGTON
STRAWBERRY HILL
HAM
PETERSHAM
HAMPTON WICK
KINGSTON UPON THAMES
TW1
TW10
TW11
RIVER THAMES
MARBLE HILL PARK
Marble Hill House
Orleans Ho. Gallery
Orleans Gdns.
Glover's Island
Petersham Meadows
Petersham Farm
Royal Star & Garter Home
Petersham Common
Petersham Gate
Ham House & Garden
Polo Ground
The German Sch. London
The Russell Prim. Sch.
Strathmore Sch.
The Copse
Ham Lands Nature Reserve
Ham Riverside Lands
Radnor Gardens
Miniature Rifle Range
Playing Field
Grey Court School
Ham Green
Ham Fields
Thames Young Mariners Base
St. Mary's University College
SUDBROOK PARK
Sudbrook Park Club House
The Wilderness
RICHMOND GOLF COURSE
Convent
Cassel Hosp.
Teddington Lock
Teddington Studios
Teddington Weir
Lensbury Club
Sports Ground
Athletic Ground
Collis Prim. Sch.
Teddington Sch.
Recreation Ground
The Avenue Centre
Steven's Eyot
Canbury Gds.
St. George's Industrial Estate
YMCA Sports Grd.
The Tiffin Girls' Sch.
Tiffin Girls Comm. Spts. Cen.
Fern Hill Prim. Sch.
Ham Meadlands Prim. Sch.
Teddington Lodge
BUSHY PARK
Warren Plantation
Hawthorn Lodge
Half Moon Plantation
Deer Pen
Leg-of-Mutton Pond
Thatched Cottage
Virgin Active Superstore
A310
A305
A307
A313
B352
B358
RICHMOND RD.
LONDON RD.
KING ST.
HEATH RD.
CROSS DEEP
STRAWBERRY VALE
TWICKENHAM RD.
MANOR R.
KINGSTON ROAD
UP. TEDDINGTON RD.
HIGH STREET
STATION ROAD
PARK ROAD
SANDY LANE
PARK RD.
PETERSHAM ROAD
UPPER HAM RD.
RICHMOND ROAD
HAM COMMON
HAM GATE AV.
RIVERSIDE DRIVE
DUKES AVENUE
LOCK ROAD
SANDY LANE
BROOM ROAD
LOWER HAM ROAD
TUDOR AVENUE
CHURCH ROAD
PARKLEYS
BARNFIELD AVENUE
CARDINAL ROAD
WOLSEY DRIVE
LATCHMERE ROAD
CAMBRIDGE PARK
WALDEGRAVE PARK
FAIRFAX RD.
HARROWDENE GARDENS
(Open 7.30am - 7.00pm)

133
115
151
134
RICHMOND PARK
SIDMOUTH WOOD
Richmond Gate
Barn Wood Pond
Saw Pit Plantation
Kidney Wood
Jubilee Plantation
Queen's Ride
Duchess' Wood
Deer Pen
White Lodge Plantation
Queen Mothers Copse
White Lodge Museum
The Royal Ballet Lower School
Victory Plantation
King Henry VIII Mound
Pen Ponds
Leg of Mutton Pond
Queen Elizabeth's Plantation
Lawn Plantation
Treebox Wood
SPANKERS HILL WOOD
Oak Lodge
DEER PARK
King George V Jubilee Plantation
Playing Fields
Pond Plantation
White Ash Lodge
Tercentenary Plantation
Pond Slade
(National Nature Reserve)
Prince Charles's Spinney
Ham Cross Plantation
Isabella Plantation Garden
Gibbet Wood
Ham Bottom
Peg's Pond
Thomson's Pond
Broomfield Hill
Broomfield Hill Wood
Ham Cross
ISABELLA PLANTATION
Ham Gate
AVENUE
High Wood
Still Pond
Deer Fold
Ham Dip
Coronation Plantation
The Flat
Dann's Pond
Gallows Pond
King's Clump
Ladderstile Gate
Robin Hood Gate
Walkden Hall
Robin Hood Prim. Sch.
Kingston University (Kingston Hill Campus)
Warren House
COOMBE HILL GOLF COURSE
COOMBE WOOD GOLF COURSE
COOMBE
Kingston Gate
KINGSTON HILL A308
KINGSTON ROAD
QUEENS RD. B351
Holy Cross Preparatory RC Sch.
Rokeby Sch.
Marymount International School
Club House
KINGSTON HOSPITAL
Coombe Hill Jun. & Inf. Schools
COOMBE LANE WEST A238
TRAPS LA.
Latchmere Sch.
RC Prim. Sch.
Sports Ground
Park Hill Sch.
Canbury Sch.
Tennis Cts.
SW15
KT2

ROEHAMPTON
116
RICHMOND PARK GOLF COURSE
Kingsfarm Plantation
RICHMOND PARK
SW15
Victory Plantation
Killcat Corner
Queen Mothers Copse
White Lodge Plantation
Deer Pen
Royal Ballet Lower School
Treebox Wood
Playing Fields
Beverley Brook
Horse Ride
(Open during daylight hours only)
Robin Hood Gate
Beverley Bridge
Silver Hill
STAG LANE
Chohole Gate
Hyde Park Nursery
PUTNEY HEATH
Scio Pond
King's Mere
Subway
ROEHAMPTON LANE
Jerry's Hill
Stag Ride
Inner Park Ride
Ladies Mile
Putney Vale Crematorium
PUTNEY VALE CEMETERY
Superstore
Newlands Hall
PUTNEY VALE
Kingston University (Roehampton Vale Centre)
Memorial Gardens
War Memorial
Playing Fields
ROBIN HOOD
KINGSTON VALE
Queen's Mere
Wimbledon Windmill Museum
Club House
Manor Cottage
LONDON SCOTTISH GOLF COURSE
Silent Pools
Stag Bog
WIMBLEDON COMMON
Gravelly Ride
Horse Exercise Ring
Gravelly Hill
Horse Exercise Area
WIMBLEDON COMMON GOLF COURSE
White Cottage
Thatched Cottage
Horse Ride
ROBIN HOOD ROAD
Farm Bog
Farm Ravine
Caesar's Camp
Warren Farm
ROYAL WIMBLEDON GOLF COURSE
Fishpond Wood
Mill Corner
Beverley Meads & Fishpond Woods Nature Reserve
Shadwell Wood
The Warren
Cannizaro House
Cannizaro Park
Lady Jane's Wood
Southside Ho.
COOMBE HILL GOLF COURSE
ROBIN HOOD WAY (KINGSTON BY-PASS)
A3
KINGSTON VALE
ROEHAMPTON VALE
Robin Hood Prim. Sch.
133
KT2
SW20
Playing Field
Tennis Courts
Nature Res.
The Rowans Sch.
Wolfson Neurorehab. Centre
COPSE HILL
Sports Grd.
Tennis Club
COOMBE LANE WEST
COOMBE LANE
152
NEW VICTORIA HOSPITAL
Cottenham Park
DURHAM RD.
Holland Gdns.
School
Club Ho.
A B C D E
1 2 3 4 5 6 7

135
117
136
153
SOUTHFIELDS
Southfields
Earlsfield
SW18
SW19
SW17
WIMBLEDON PARK
Wimbledon Park
WIMBLEDON PARK GOLF COURSE
Golf Course
Wimbledon Park Athletics Track
Wimbledon Park Watersports Centre
Wimbledon All England Lawn Tennis & Croquet Club
Museum
Aorangi Park
Cricket Ground
Ricards Lodge High Sch.
Bishop Gilpin C of E Prim. Sch.
SUMMERSTOWN
Wimbledon Cemetery
Superstore
Carriage Cleaning Shed
King George's Park
Nuffield Health Fitness & Wellbeing Centre
Southfields Academy
RMR Cen.
Sports Grd.
Recreation Ground
Garratt Park
Buddhist Temple
PARKSIDE HOSP.
WIMBLEDON
Wimbledon
Wimbledon High Sch.
Wimbledon Coll.
Wimbledon Mag. Ct.
SOUTH WIMBLEDON
South Wimbledon
MERTON
Merton Park
Dundonald Rd.
Dundonald Prim. Sch.
South Park Gardens
The Priory C of E Sch.
Face Youth Sch.
Haydons Road
Hicks Gall.
THE BROADWAY
WIMBLEDON HILL A219
HIGH ST.
PARKSIDE A219
MERTON HIGH ST.
MERTON A218
DURNSFORD RD. A218
GARRATT LANE A217
HAYDONS ROAD A218
PLOUGH LANE
GAP ROAD B235
HARTFIELD RD. B285
KINGSTON ROAD
MERANTUN WAY A24
A238 RD.
WORPLE RD.
ALEXANDRA RD.
ARTHUR RD.
HOME PARK ROAD
WIMBLEDON PARK ROAD
VICTORIA DRIVE
AUGUSTUS RD.
QUEENSMERE ROAD
SOMERSET RD.
CHURCH RD.
F G H J K
1 2 3 4 5 6 7

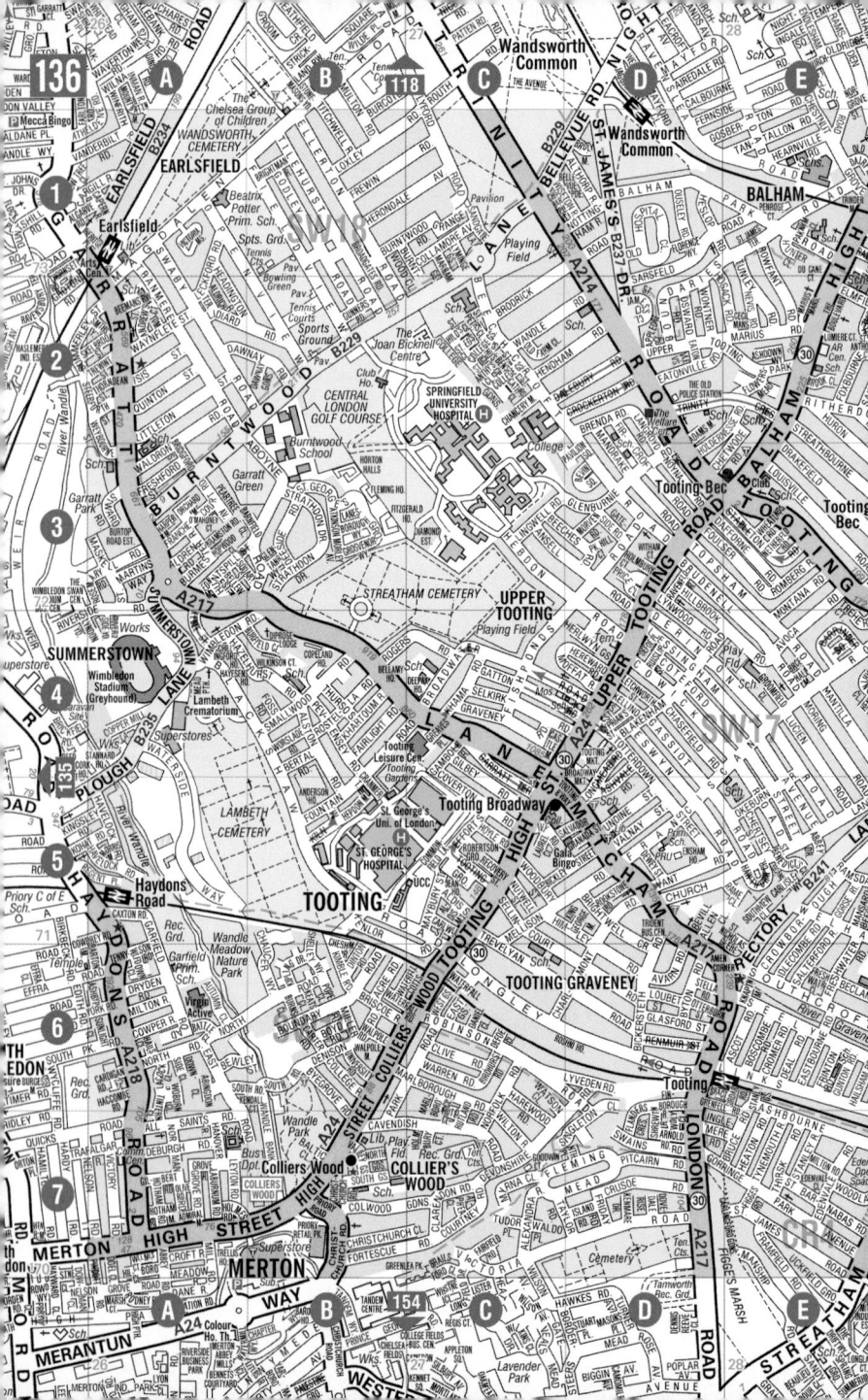

136
A
B
C
D
E
118
Wandsworth Common
Wandsworth Common
EARLSFIELD
Earlsfield
SW18
The Chelsea Group of Children
WANDSWORTH CEMETERY
Beatrix Potter Prim. Sch.
BALHAM
Playing Field
Sports Ground
The Joan Bicknell Centre
CENTRAL LONDON GOLF COURSE
SPRINGFIELD UNIVERSITY HOSPITAL
Burntwood School
Garratt Green
Garratt Park
River Wandle
Tooting Bec
Tooting Bec
STREATHAM CEMETERY
UPPER TOOTING
Playing Field
SUMMERSTOWN
Wimbledon Stadium (Greyhound)
Lambeth Crematorium
Superstores
LAMBETH CEMETERY
Tooting Leisure Cen.
Tooting Gardens
Tooting Broadway
St. George's Uni. of London
ST. GEORGE'S HOSPITAL
Gala Bingo
SW17
TOOTING
Haydons Road
Wandle Meadow Nature Park
Garfield Prim. Sch.
Virgin Active
TOOTING GRAVENEY
Tooting
Colliers Wood
COLLIER'S WOOD
Wandle Park
Cemetery
Tamworth Rec. Grd.
MERTON
Lavender Park
135
154
1
2
3
4
5
6
7
EARLSFIELD ROAD
GARRATT LANE
BURNTWOOD LANE
TRINITY ROAD
UPPER TOOTING ROAD
TOOTING HIGH ST.
MITCHAM ROAD
BALHAM HIGH ROAD
TOOTING BEC ROAD
COLLIERS WOOD
HAYDONS ROAD
MERTON HIGH STREET
PLOUGH LANE
SUMMERSTOWN
LONDON ROAD
STREATHAM
RECTORY LANE
MERANTUN WAY
A24
A217
A214
A218
B229
B234
B235
B237
B241

137
F
G
H
J
K
119
1
2
3
4
5
6
7
138
155
STREATHAM HILL
STREATHAM
STREATHAM PARK
STREATHAM VALE
FURZEDOWN
NORBURY
SW12
SW2
SW16
Balham
Streatham Hill
Streatham
Streatham Common
Norbury
Lonesome
TOOTING BEC COMMON
Tooting Graveney Common
Tooting Bec Lido
Tooting Bec Athletic Track
STREATHAM COMMON
NORBURY PARK
CHRISTCHURCH ROAD
A205
A23
A214
A216
B221
B242
B272
B273
BEC ROAD
STREATHAM HIGH ROAD
STREATHAM COMMON NORTH
MITCHAM ROAD
BEDFORD HILL
BRIXTON HILL
STREATHAM HILL
KINGS AV.
THORNTON AV.
GARRAD'S RD.
GREYHOUND LA.
GREEN LANE
CHURCH LANE
STREATHAM VALE
Football Pitch
Tennis Courts
Leisure Cen.
Beacon Bingo
Streatham Hub
Superstore
Paddling Pool
The Rookery
Bishop Thomas Grant Sch.
Hitherfield Prim. Sch.
Norwood Grove Recreation Gd.
Beecholme Prim. Sch.
Streatham Vale Park
School Playing Fields
Sports Ground
The Waldorf Sch.

138
BROCKWELL PARK
TULSE HILL
CHRISTCHURCH RD.
NORWOOD RD.
THURLOW PARK RD.
Knight's Hill
WEST DULWICH
West Dulwich
DULWICH ROAD
Dulwich Old College
Dulwich Picture Gallery
Sports Ground
Belair Park
Playing Fields
Dulwich College
Kingsdale Foundation Sch.
CROXTED RD.
West Norwood Crematorium
Cemetery
West Norwood
WEST NORWOOD
SE27
KNIGHTS HILL
NORWOOD HIGH ST.
GIPSY RD.
Gipsy Hill
NORWOOD PARK
Rec. Grd.
STREATHAM COMN. NTH.
CROWN LA.
CROWN DALE
CENTRAL HILL
STREATHAM COMMON
The Rookery
Norwood Grove Recreation Ground
Playing Fields
NORWOOD NEW TOWN
Rockmount Prim. Sch.
BEULAH HILL
Recreation Ground
SW16
Biggin Wood
Downsview Prim. Sch.
Harris Academy (Upper Norwood)
NORWOOD
Westow Park
SE19
UPPER NORWOOD
The Lawns
NORBURY PARK
NORBURY
Norbury Manor Business & Enterprise Coll. for Girls
GREEN LANE
CHURCH RD.
120
137
156

139
121
157
140
F
G
H
J
K
1
2
3
4
5
6
7
DULWICH PARK
Aviary
Court La. Gate
Horse Ride
Bowling Grn.
Tennis Cts.
Queen Mary's Gate
Sports Ground
Rosebery Lodge Ga.
COMMON
LORDSHIP
LA.
A205
30
THE GROVE
Horniman Gardens
Horniman Museum
LONDON
ROAD
Forest Hill
FOREST HILL
WALDRAM PK.
STANSTEAD RD.
SE23
Visitor Centre
Nature Reserves
DULWICH & SYDENHAM HILL GOLF COURSE
The Grange
Club House
DULWICH
Sydenham Hill Local Nature Reserve
Dulwich Wood
PECKARMANS WOOD
LOW CROSS WOOD LA.
Sydenham Hill
UPPER SYDENHAM
Sydenham Wells Park
DARTMOUTH
KIRKDALE
A2216
PERRY
VALE
B227
Forest Hill Sch. Sports Cen.
DACRES ESTATE
Mayow Park
LOWER SYDENHAM
SE26
A212
HILL
SYDENHAM
ROAD
PureGym
Sydenham
WESTWOOD HILL
CRYSTAL PALACE PARK
A234
Rockhills Entrance
Camping Site
TV Transmitter
Fisherman's Gate
Intermediate Lake
The Maze
Crystal Palace National Sports Centre
Sydenham Entrance
Playing Field
Hostel
Site of Crystal Palace
Bus Terminal
CRYSTAL PALACE
Crystal Palace Museum
Crystal Palace Athletics Stadium
Crystal Palace
Crystal Palace Pk. Farm
Crystal Palace Dinosaurs
Lower Lake
Penge Entrance
Anerley Entrance
SYDENHAM
St. Christopher's Hospice
The Haven
Penge East
NEWLANDS
PARK
A213
Alexandra Rec. Grd.
Alexandra Jun. Sch.
Playing Field
PARISH LANE
HIGH ST.
Penge West
Superstore
SE20
PENGE
ANERLEY
ANERLEY HILL
Anerley
Civic Halls
T.H. & Lib.
Harris City Academy
Leis. Cen.
Orchard Lodge (Remand Centre)
James Dixon Prim. Sch.
CROYDON RD.
Kent House
The Kentwood Cen.
Superstore
Play Fld

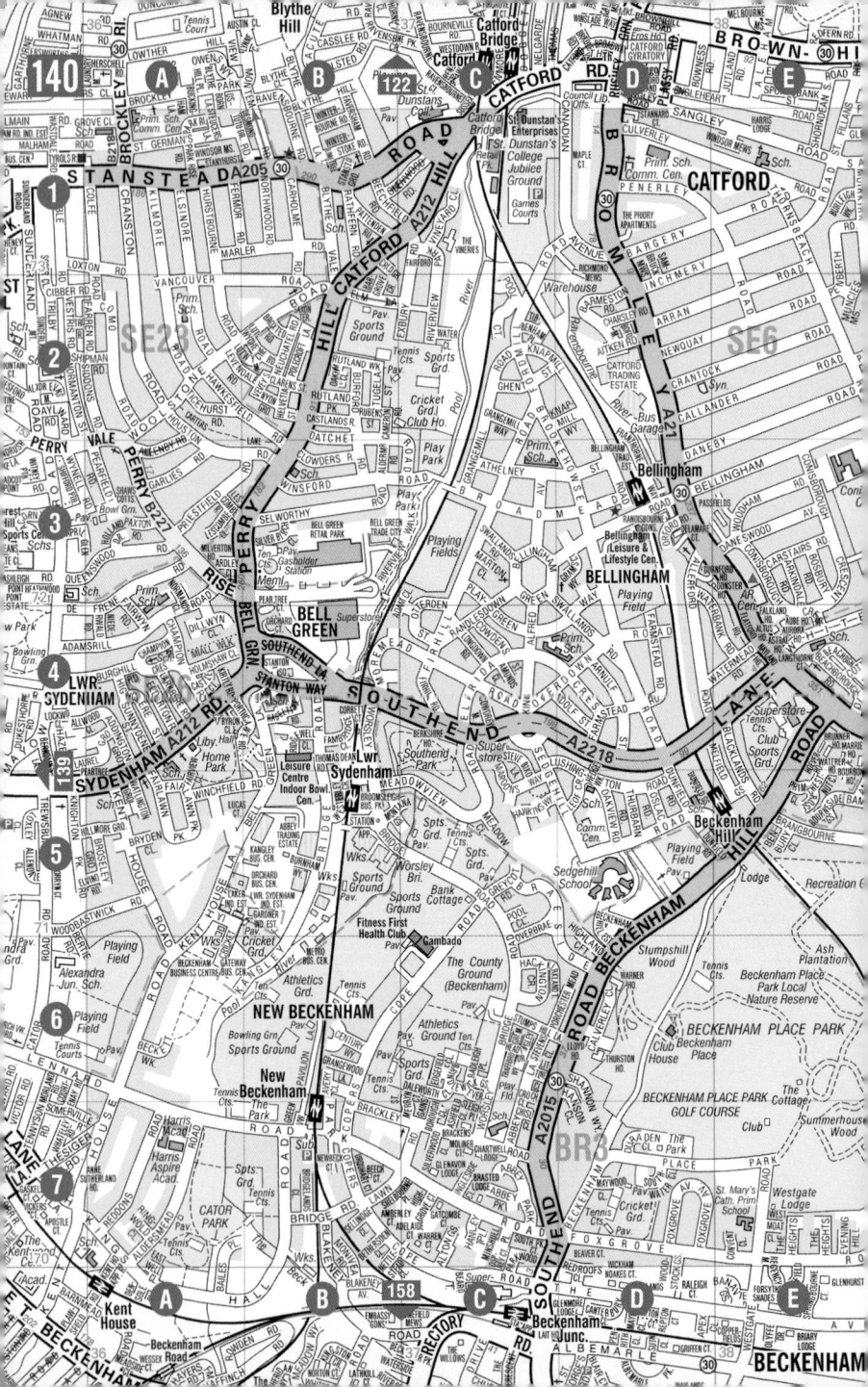

140
139
122
158
A
B
C
D
E
1
2
3
4
5
6
7
36
37
38
Blythe Hill
Catford Bridge
Catford
CATFORD
STANSTEAD A205 ROAD
CATFORD ROAD
CATFORD HILL A212
BROMLEY A21 ROAD
BROWNHILL
SE23
SE6
BR3
PERRY VALE
PERRY RISE B227
PERRY HILL
BELL GREEN
BELL GRN.
Superstore
BELL GREEN RETAIL PARK
BELL GREEN TRADE CITY
Gasholder Station
SOUTHEND LANE A2218
SOUTHEND ROAD A2015
SYDENHAM A212 RD.
LWR. SYDENHAM
Lwr. Sydenham
Bellingham
BELLINGHAM
Bellingham Leisure & Lifestyle Cen.
BROADMEAD
Playing Fields
Playing Field
Beckenham Hill
BECKENHAM HILL ROAD
Sedgehill School
Stumpshill Wood
Ash Plantation
Beckenham Place Park Local Nature Reserve
BECKENHAM PLACE PARK
BECKENHAM PLACE PARK GOLF COURSE
Summerhouse Wood
Club House
Beckenham Place
NEW BECKENHAM
New Beckenham
The County Ground (Beckenham)
Athletics Grd.
Athletics Ground
Fitness First Health Club
Gambado
Leisure Centre Indoor Bowl. Cen.
Home Park
Southend Park
Worsley Bri.
CATOR PARK
Harris Aspire Acad.
Kent House
Beckenham Road
Beckenham Junc.
BECKENHAM
Alexandra Jun. Sch.
St. Mary's Cath. Prim. School
Westgate Lodge
St. Dunstan's College Jubilee Ground
Games Courts
Catford Trading Estate
Bus Garage
Sports Ground
Cricket Grd.
Play Park
Recreation G
Tennis Courts

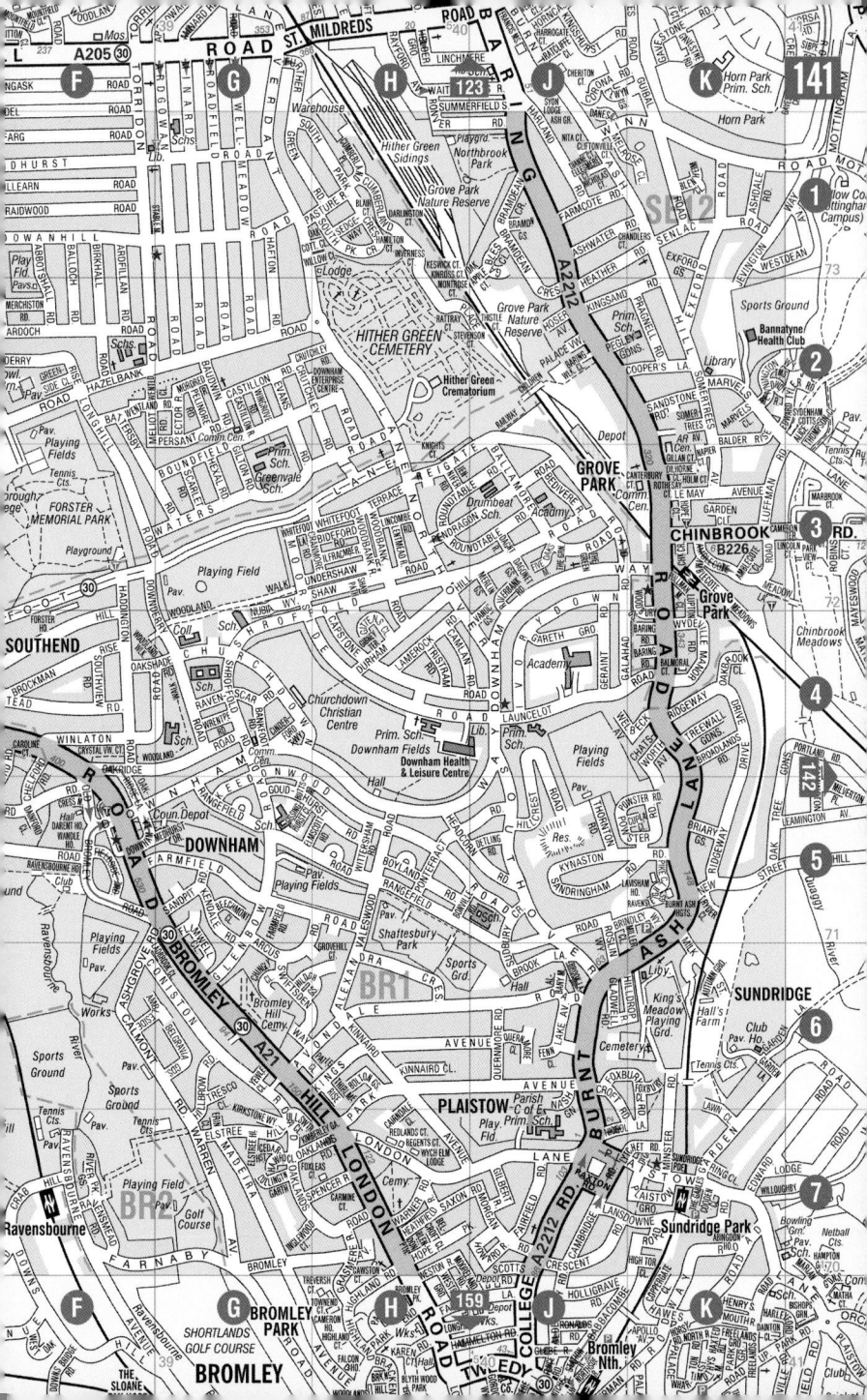
141
123
142
159
F
G
H
J
K
1
2
3
4
5
6
7
A205
A21
A2212
B226
ST. MILDREDS ROAD
BARING ROAD
Horn Park
Horn Park Prim. Sch.
SE12
Hither Green Sidings
Northbrook Park
Grove Park Nature Reserve
HITHER GREEN CEMETERY
Hither Green Crematorium
Sports Ground
Bannatyne Health Club
Library
Depot
GROVE PARK
Grove Park
CHINBROOK RD.
Chinbrook Meadows
FORSTER MEMORIAL PARK
Playing Field
SOUTHEND
Churchdown Christian Centre
Downham Fields
Downham Health & Leisure Centre
DOWNHAM
Academy
Playing Fields
Shaftesbury Park
BR1
BURNT ASH LANE
BURNT ASH HILL
King's Meadow Playing Grd.
Cemetery
SUNDRIDGE
Hall's Farm
BROMLEY ROAD
Bromley Hill Cemy.
LONDON ROAD
PLAISTOW
Sundridge Park
Ravensbourne
BR2
Golf Course
BROMLEY PARK
SHORTLANDS GOLF COURSE
BROMLEY
Bromley Nth.
COLLEGE RD.

142
124
141
160
A
B
C
D
E
1
2
3
4
5
6
7
SIDCUP ROAD
A20
40
A208
30
B226
Mottingham
MOTTINGHAM
MOTTINGHAM ROAD
COURT ROAD
GROVE PARK ROAD
WHITE HORSE HILL
Horn Park
Hadlow Coll. (Mottingham Campus)
Mottingham Farm
Eltham College Jun. Sch.
Eltham Coll.
Eric Liddell Spts. Cen.
Playing Fields
Sports Ground
Bannatyne Health Club
Library
Running Track
Community Centre
ROYAL BLACKHEATH GOLF COURSE
Bird Sanctuary
The Tarn
Fairy Hill
Coldharbour Leisure Centre
Netball Courts
SE9
SE12
CHINBROOK RD.
Chinbrook Meadows
Grove Park
Lower Marvels Wood
Marvels Wood
Grove Park Cemetery
Castlecombe Prim. Sch.
Youth Cen.
ELMSTEAD WOOD
ELMSTEAD
Elmstead Woods
SUNDRIDGE
SUNDRIDGE PARK GOLF COURSE
Garden Wood
Sundridge Park Manor
Botany Bay
Rockpit Wood
Kyd Brook
Quaggy River
Sundridge Park
BR1
CHISLEHURST WEST
Whyte's Woodland
Rec. Grd.
CAMDEN
Bullers Wood Sch.
St. Cecilia's
Scotts Park Prim. Sch.
Convent

143
125
144
161
Lamorbey
New Eltham
NEW ELTHAM
LONGLANDS
SIDCUP
CHISLEHURST
DA15
DA14
BR7
A20
A211
A222
A208
B263
B264
B2214
SIDCUP BY-PASS
MAIN ROAD
FIVEWAYS
FROGNAL CORNER
World of Golf at Sidcup
Flamingo Park Sports Grd.
Kemnal Park Cemetery
Old Farm Park
King George's Rec. Grd.
Virgin Active Health Club
Chislehurst Cemetery
Old Elthamians Sports Club
Chislehurst Sch. for Girls
Darul Uloom London
Farringtons School
SCADBURY PARK (Nature Reserve)
Edgebury Prim. Sch.
Dulverton Sch.
St. Olave's Prep. School
Sparrow's Farm Leisure Centre
Christ The King (St Mary's) Sixth Form College
Midfield Prim. Sch.
Camden Place Club House
Chislehurst Common
PARK WOOD

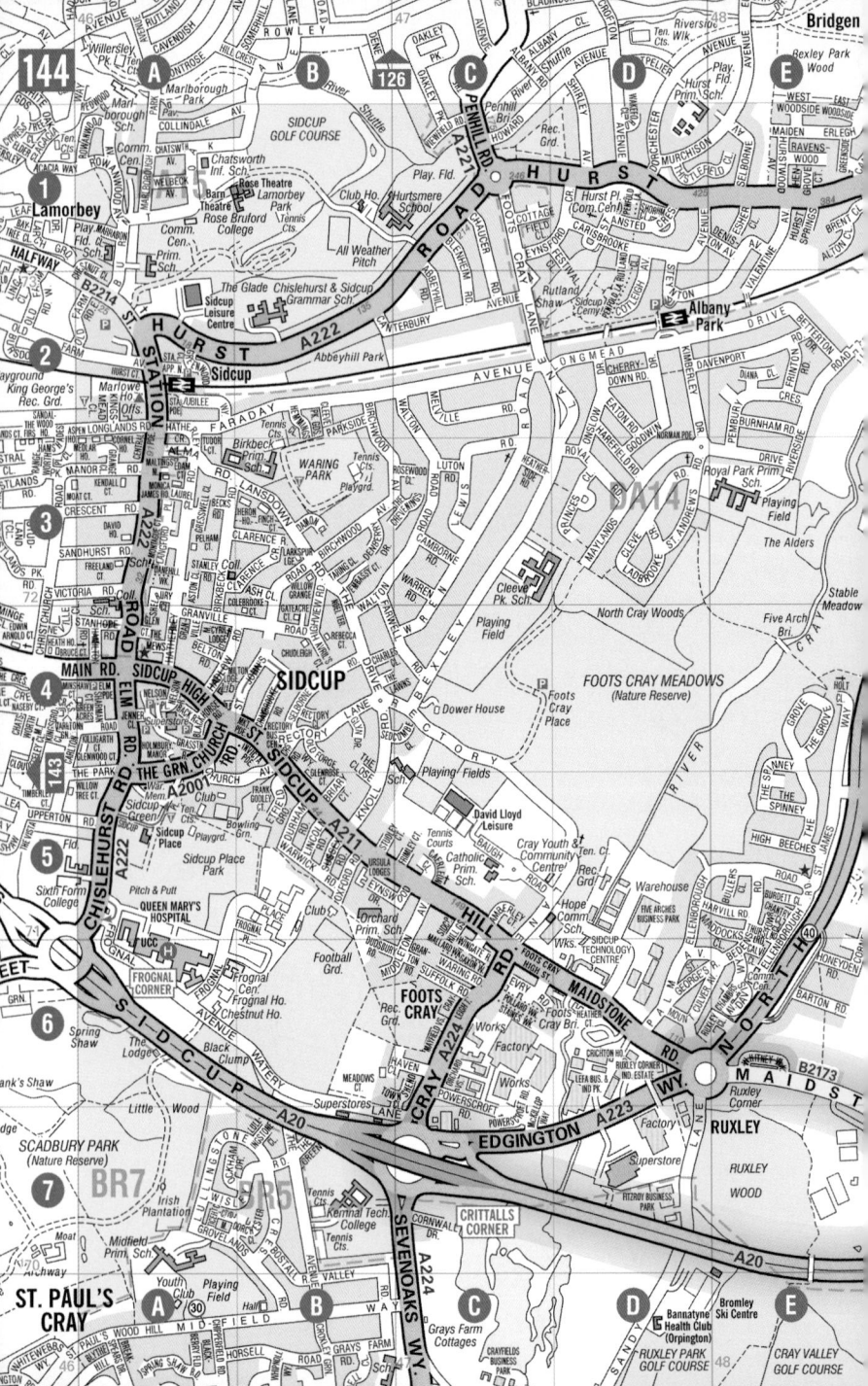

144
126
143
Bridgen
Bexley Park Wood
Lamorbey
HALFWAY
Willersley Pk.
Marlborough Park
Marlborough Sch.
SIDCUP GOLF COURSE
River Shuttle
Chatsworth Inf. Sch.
Rose Theatre
Lamorbey Park
Barn Theatre
Rose Bruford College
Play. Fld.
Club Ho.
Hurtsmere School
All Weather Pitch
Penhill Bri.
Rec. Grd.
Hurst Pl. (Com. Cen.)
Hurst Prim. Sch.
HURST ROAD
A221
PENHILL RD.
A222
B2214
The Glade
Chislehurst & Sidcup Grammar Sch.
Sidcup Leisure Centre
Abbeyhill Park
Rutland Shaw
Sidcup Cemy.
Albany Park
Sidcup
King George's Rec. Grd.
Marlowe Ho.
Offs.
Birkbeck Prim. Sch.
WARING PARK
Tennis Cts.
Playgrd.
Royal Park Prim. Sch.
Playing Field
The Alders
DA14
DA15
Cleeve Pk. Sch.
North Cray Woods
Stable Meadow
Five Arch Bri.
FOOTS CRAY MEADOWS
(Nature Reserve)
Foots Cray Place
Dower House
SIDCUP
Playing Fields
David Lloyd Leisure
Cray Youth & Community Centre
Catholic Prim. Sch.
Rec. Grd.
Warehouse
FIVE ARCHES BUSINESS PARK
Hope Comm. Sch.
SIDCUP TECHNOLOGY CENTRE
Sidcup Green
Sidcup Place
Sidcup Place Park
Bowling Grn.
War. Mem.
Pitch & Putt
Sixth Form College
QUEEN MARY'S HOSPITAL
UCC
FROGNAL CORNER
Frognal Cen.
Frognal Ho.
Chestnut Ho.
Orchard Prim. Sch.
Football Grd.
FOOTS CRAY
Foots Cray Bri.
Works
Factory
A2001
A211
A224
A223
A20
B2173
SIDCUP HIGH ST.
SIDCUP HILL
MAIDSTONE RD.
NORTH CRAY RD.
EDGINGTON WY.
SIDCUP BY-PASS
Spring Shaw
The Lodge
Black Clump
Little Wood
Superstores
SCADBURY PARK
(Nature Reserve)
BR7
BR5
Irish Plantation
Moat
Archway
Midfield Prim. Sch.
Youth Club
Playing Field
Kemnal Tech. College
CRITTALLS CORNER
Grays Farm Cottages
CRAYFIELDS BUSINESS PARK
ST. PAUL'S CRAY
RUXLEY
Ruxley Corner
Superstore
FITZROY BUSINESS PARK
RUXLEY WOOD
Bannatyne Health Club (Orpington)
Bromley Ski Centre
RUXLEY PARK GOLF COURSE
CRAY VALLEY GOLF COURSE
SEVENOAKS WY.

145
127
OLD BEXLEY
Bexley
Old Bexley C of E Prim. Sch.
Cricket Ground
Upper College Farm
Works
Weir
Bowl. Grn.
Churchfield Wood
Cemy.
Maypole
Coldblow
DARTFORD RD.
OLD BEXLEY LA.
VICARAGE RD.
A2018
A222
A223
A2
DARTFORD BY-PASS
CRAY ROAD
BEXLEY HIGH ST.
Pinewood Cottage
The Grove
Sands Spinney
Mount Mascal Stables
Mount Mascal Farm
Home Close Farm
Cavey's Spring
DA5
DA2
BR8
Woollett Hall Farm
Crayzee Barn
Sports Ground
Loring Hall
Nursery
Club
Playing Fields
Bowling Green
Maypole Prim. Sch.
Recycling Centre
Keeper's Cottage
Little Mascal Farm
Bunkers Hill
BUNKERS HILL
Pond Farm
COCKSURE LANE
Home Wood
Gattons Plantation
Gattons Wood
Nursy.
Nurseries
NORTH CRAY
Manor Cotts.
Manor Farm
PARSONAGE LA.
North Cray Poultry Farm
JOYDENS WOOD (Woodland Trust)
JOYDENS WOOD
CHALK WOOD
STONEHILL WOODS PARK
BIRCHWOOD PARK GOLF COURSE
Driving Range
Club House
Stonehill Green
Stonehill
Stanhill Farm
STANHILL COTTS.
Lambersland
Ruxley Manor Garden Centre
Caravan Site
MAIDSTONE RD.
Upper Ruxley
OLD LONDON ROAD
B2173
A20
BY-PASS
BIRCHWOOD ROAD
LEYDENHATCH LANE
PEMBROKE BUSINESS CENTRE
Nurseries
COLLEGE RD.
Spts. Grd.
NEW BARN RD.
TILE KILN LANE
BALDWYNS PARK
DYKEWOOD CL.
JOYDENS WOOD RD.
SUMMERHOUSE DR.
WOODLANDS PK
SQUIRES
NORFIELD RD.

128
QUEEN MARY RESERVOIR
LITTLETON
SHEPPERTON GREEN
TW18
TW17
KT16
KT13
CHARLTON
SHEPPERTON
Shepperton
Shepperton Film Studios
Pool End
M3 MOTORWAY
M3
LALEHAM ROAD
B376
SHEPPERTON RD
CHERTSEY ROAD
RENFREE WAY
RUSSELL
B375
RIVER THAMES
River Ash
Pumping Station
Round Copse
Laleham Nurseries
Nurseries
Squire's Bridge
Gravel Pit
Sheepwalk Lake
Works
Funky Footprints Nature Reserve
Halliford Mere Lake
Cemetery
Lords Bri.
War Close
Cricket Ground
Las Palmas Estate
Desborough Sailing Club
DESBOROUGH
ISLAND
Chertsey Meads Local Nature Reserve
Chertsey Meads
Riversleigh Farm
Mead Farm
The Range
Staines Road Farm
Manor Farm
Driving Range
SUNBURY GOLF
Rec. Grd.
Play. Fld.
Saxon Prim. Sch.
Littleton Fm.
The Green
Old Manor Ho. M.
Halliford Sch.
DUMSEY EYOT

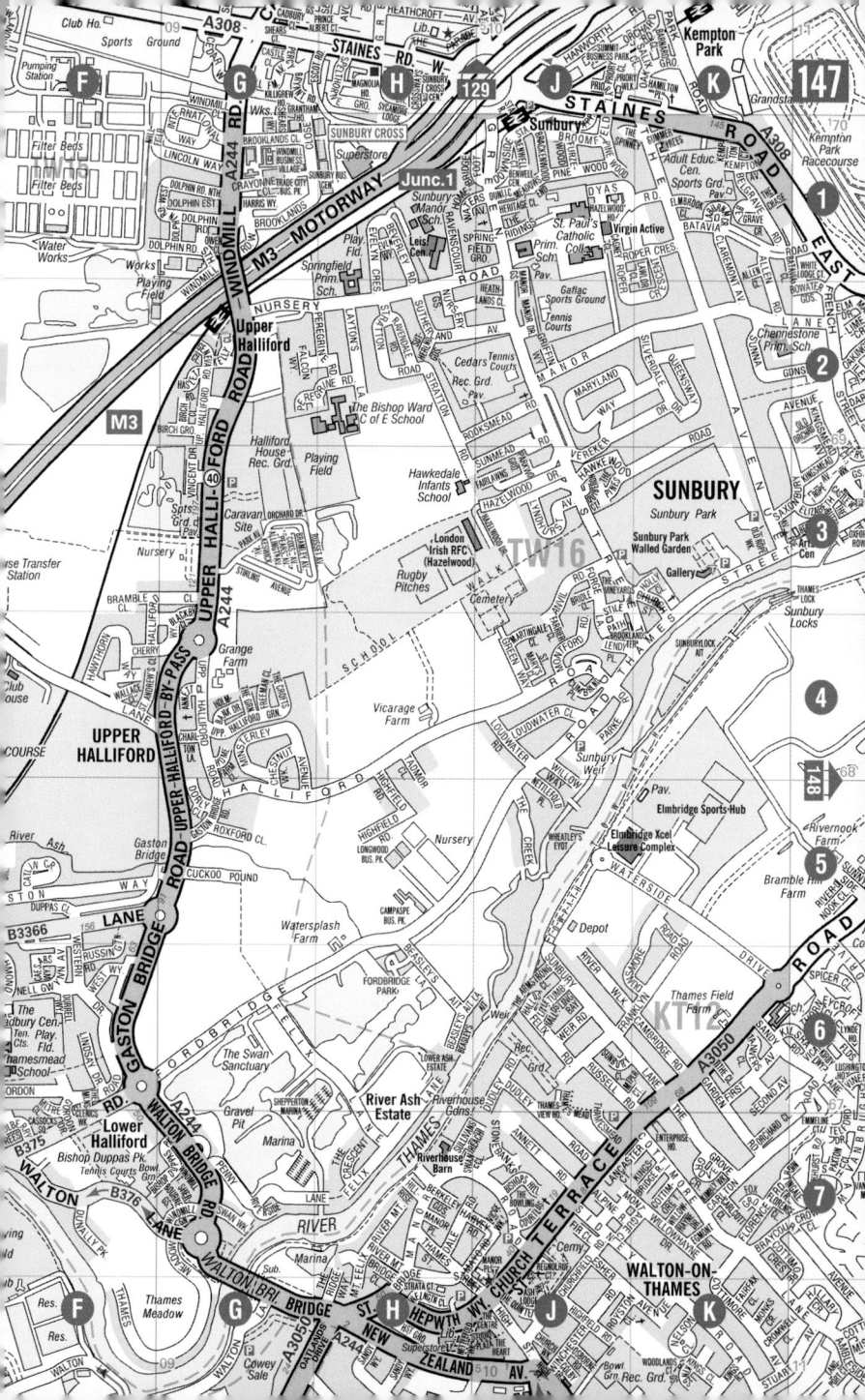

147
Kempton Park
Kempton Park Racecourse
STAINES ROAD
A308
STAINES RD. W.
Sunbury Cross
SUNBURY CROSS
Superstore
129
Junc.1
M3 MOTORWAY
M3
WINDMILL RD.
A244
Upper Halliford
UPPER HALLIFORD ROAD
UPPER HALLIFORD BY-PASS
UPPER HALLIFORD
Sports Ground
Club Ho.
Pumping Station
Filter Beds
Water Works
Works
Playing Field
Sunbury Manor Sch.
Springfield Prim. Sch.
Leis. Cen.
St. Paul's Catholic Coll.
Virgin Active
Gaflac Sports Ground
Tennis Courts
Adult Educ. Cen.
Sports Grd.
Chennestone Prim. Sch.
Cedars Rec. Grd.
The Bishop Ward C of E School
Halliford House Rec. Grd.
Hawkedale Infants School
London Irish RFC (Hazelwood)
Rugby Pitches
Cemetery
TW16
SUNBURY
Sunbury Park
Sunbury Park Walled Garden
Gallery
Arts Cen
Thames Lock
Sunbury Locks
Caravan Site
Nursery
Grange Farm
Vicarage Farm
Sunbury Weir
Elmbridge Sports Hub
Elmbridge Xcel Leisure Complex
Riverhouse Farm
Bramble Hill Farm
Depot
Thames Field Farm
KT12
148
Watersplash Farm
Fordbridge Park
The Swan Sanctuary
River Ash Estate
Riverhouse Gdns.
Riverhouse Barn
Gravel Pit
Marina
Shepperton Marina
Lower Halliford
Bishop Duppas Pk.
Thames Meadow
WALTON BRIDGE RD.
GASTON BRIDGE RD.
CUCKOO POUND
HALLIFORD RD.
FORDBRIDGE RD.
NEW ZEALAND AV.
CHURCH ST.
TERRACE RD.
A3050
WALTON-ON-THAMES
Cowey Sale
Rec. Grd.
B3366
B375
B376
F G H J K
1 2 3 4 5 6 7

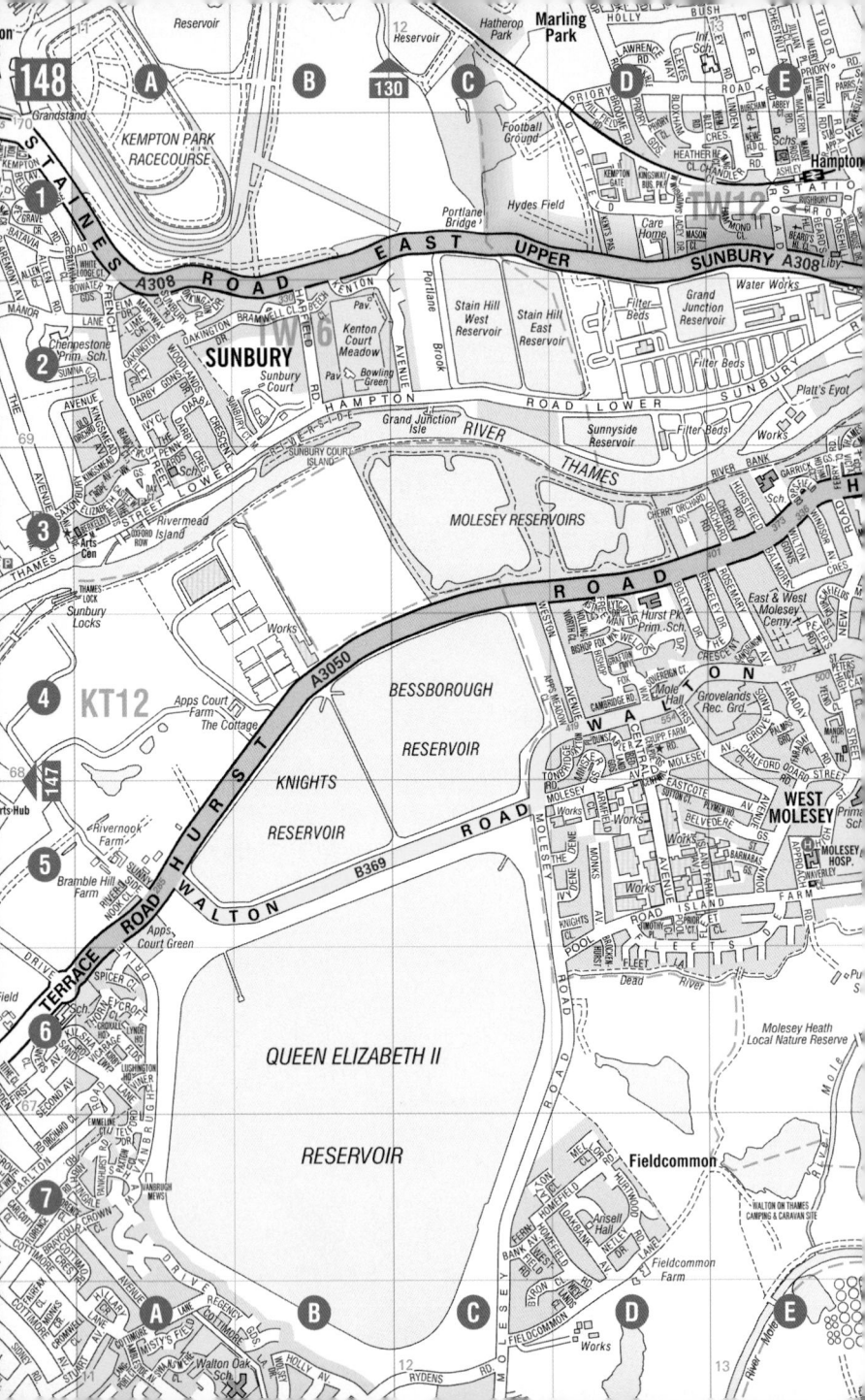

KEMPTON PARK RACECOURSE
Reservoir
Marling Park
Hatherop Park
Football Ground
Hydes Field
Portlane Bridge
130
Grandstand
STAINES ROAD
A308
EAST UPPER SUNBURY A308
Hampton
TW12
SUNBURY
TW16
Stain Hill West Reservoir
Stain Hill East Reservoir
Grand Junction Reservoir
Water Works
Filter Beds
Kenton Court Meadow
Sunbury Court
Chennestone Prim. Sch.
HAMPTON ROAD LOWER SUNBURY
Platt's Eyot
Grand Junction Isle
RIVER THAMES
Sunnyside Reservoir
Sunbury Court Island
MOLESEY RESERVOIRS
Rivermead Island
Arts Cen
Thames Lock
Sunbury Locks
KT12
Apps Court Farm
The Cottage
Works
A3050
HURST ROAD
BESSBOROUGH RESERVOIR
KNIGHTS RESERVOIR
Hurst Pk. Prim. Sch.
East & West Molesey Cemy.
Grovelands Rec. Grd.
WALTON
Mole Hall
WEST MOLESEY
Molesey Hosp.
Rivernook Farm
Bramble Hill Farm
B369
WALTON ROAD
Apps Court Green
TERRACE ROAD
QUEEN ELIZABETH II RESERVOIR
Dead River
Molesey Heath Local Nature Reserve
MOLESEY ROAD
Fieldcommon
Walton on Thames Camping & Caravan Site
Ansell Hall
Fieldcommon Farm
River Mole
Walton Oak Sch.
147

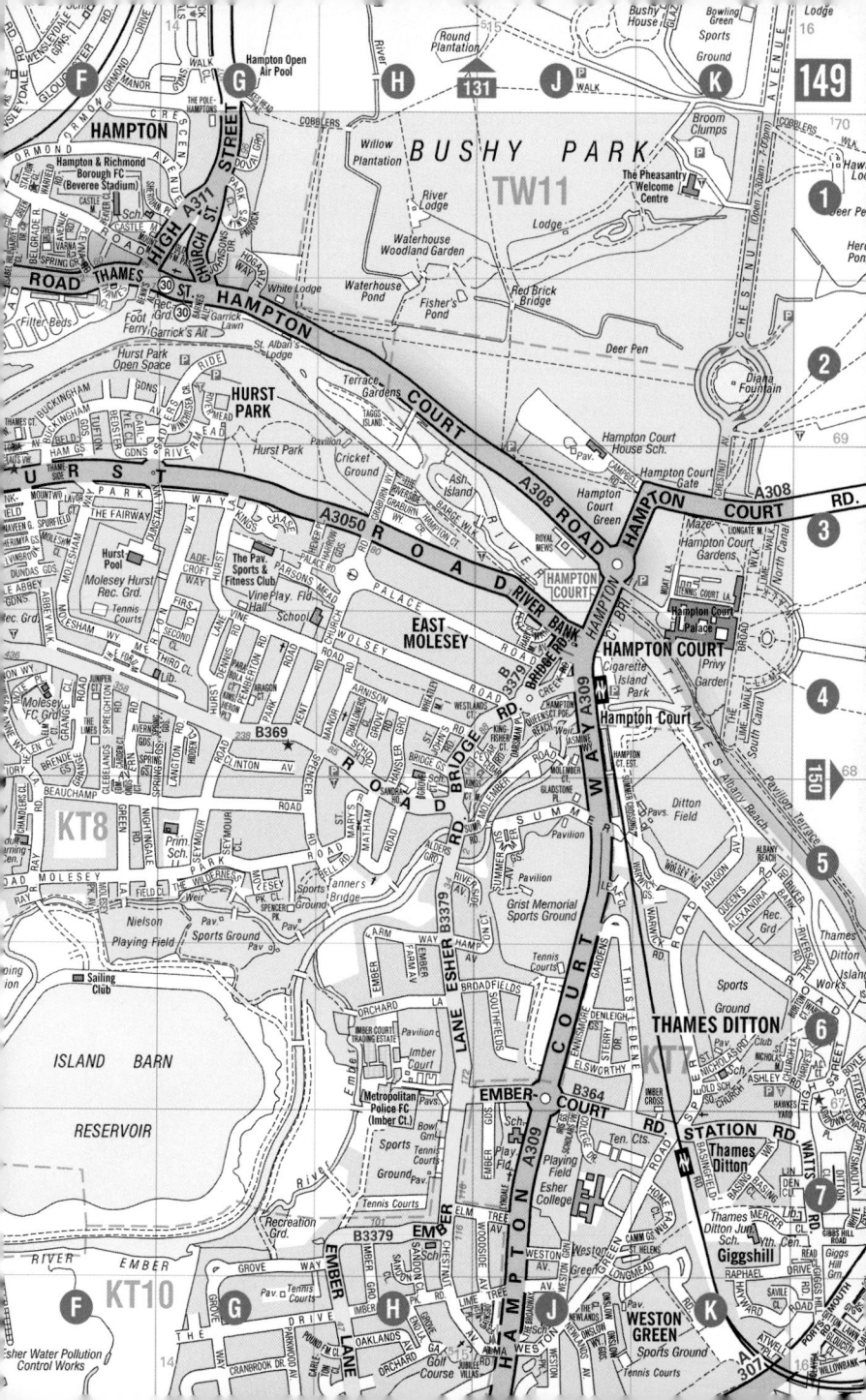
149
BUSHY PARK
HAMPTON
HURST PARK
EAST MOLESEY
HAMPTON COURT
THAMES DITTON
ISLAND BARN
RESERVOIR
WESTON GREEN
Giggshill
TW11
KT8
KT7
KT10
131
150

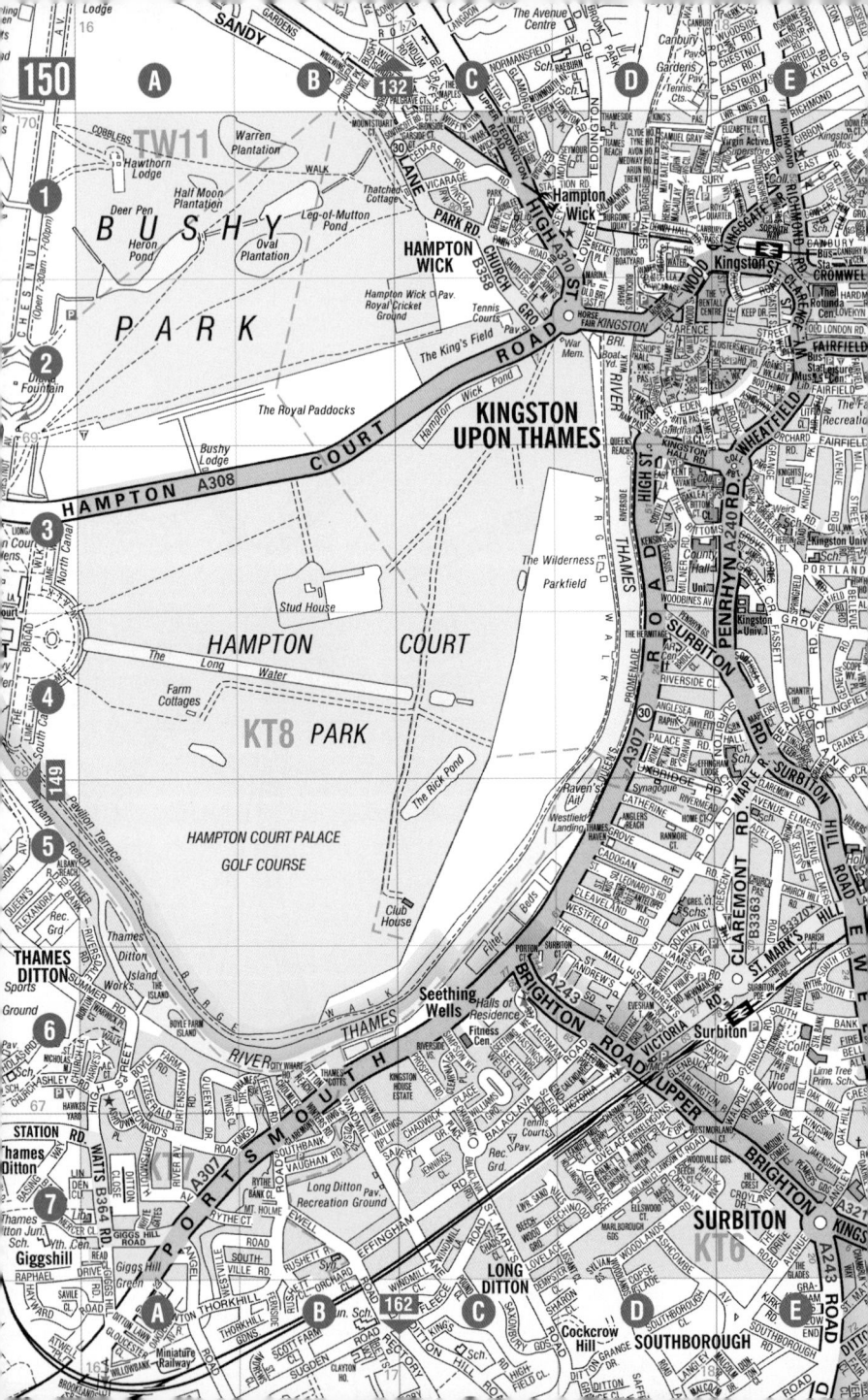
A
B
C
D
E
132
TW11
Warren Plantation
Hawthorn Lodge
Half Moon Plantation
Deer Pen
Heron Pond
Leg-of-Mutton Pond
Oval Plantation
Thatched Cottage
BUSHY
PARK
Diana Fountain
HAMPTON WICK
Hampton Wick Royal Cricket Ground
Tennis Courts
The King's Field
The Royal Paddocks
Hampton Wick Pond
Bushy Lodge
HAMPTON COURT ROAD A308
KINGSTON UPON THAMES
Hampton Wick
Kingston
The Bentall Centre
War Mem.
Boat Yd.
RIVER THAMES
Stud House
The Wilderness
Parkfield
HAMPTON COURT PARK
KT8
The Long Water
Farm Cottages
The Rick Pond
HAMPTON COURT PALACE GOLF COURSE
Club House
149
Pavilion Terrace
Albany Reach
Queen's Promenade
Raven's Ait
Westfield Landing
Filter Beds
Thames Ditton Island
Works
THAMES DITTON
Sports Ground
Seething Wells
Halls of Residence
Fitness Cen.
Kingston House Estate
Long Ditton Recreation Ground
PORTSMOUTH ROAD A307
BRIGHTON ROAD A243
SURBITON
KT6
Surbiton
KT7
Giggshill
Giggs Hill Green
Thames Ditton
Miniature Railway
162
LONG DITTON
Cockcrow Hill
SOUTHBOROUGH
County Hall
Kingston Univ.
Synagogue
PENRHYN RD. A240
CLAREMONT RD.
SURBITON HILL ROAD
HIGH ST.
UPPER BRIGHTON ROAD
VICTORIA RD.
STATION RD.
WATTS B364 RD.
1
2
3
4
5
6
7

151
133
152
163
F
G
H
J
K
1
2
3
4
5
6
7
KT2
KT3
KT5
COOMBE WOOD GOLF COURSE
Holy Cross Preparatory RC Sch.
Rokeby Sch.
Marymount International School
KINGSTON HOSPITAL
Park Hill Sch.
Coombe Hill Jun. & Inf. Schools
Coombe Girls' Sch.
COOMBE LANE WEST
A238
COOMBE ROAD
KINGSTON HILL
QUEENS RD. B351
LONDON RD. A308
CAMBRIDGE RD.
KINGSTON RD.
A2043
Norbiton
NORBITON
Super-store
Tiffin Sch.
Spts. Cen.
Norbiton Hall
Offices
Islamic Cen.
Rec. Grd.
Retail Park
Corpus Christi Catholic Prim. School
Kingston Cemetery
Kingston Crematorium
Athletics Centre
Indoor Bowls Club
AFC Wimbledon & Kingstonian FC (Kingsmeadow)
Recreation Ground
Comm. Cen.
Sludge Beds
Hogsmill River
Waste Disposal Centre
Sewage Works
Surbiton Cemetery
Berrylands
Recreation Ground
Pavilion
Tennis Courts
Sports Grounds
Bowling Green
Club House
BERRYLANDS
Sch.
Grand Avenue Prim. Sch.
Alexandra Millennium Green
Recreation Ground
Richard Challoner School
Sports Centre
Malden Manor Prim. Sch.
MALDEN WAY
A3
KINGSTON BY-PASS
SURBITON HILL
ELMBRIDGE AVENUE
HOGSMILL LANE
A240
TOLWORTH RISE NORTH
WARREN DRIVE NORTH
Prim. Sch.
Lib.

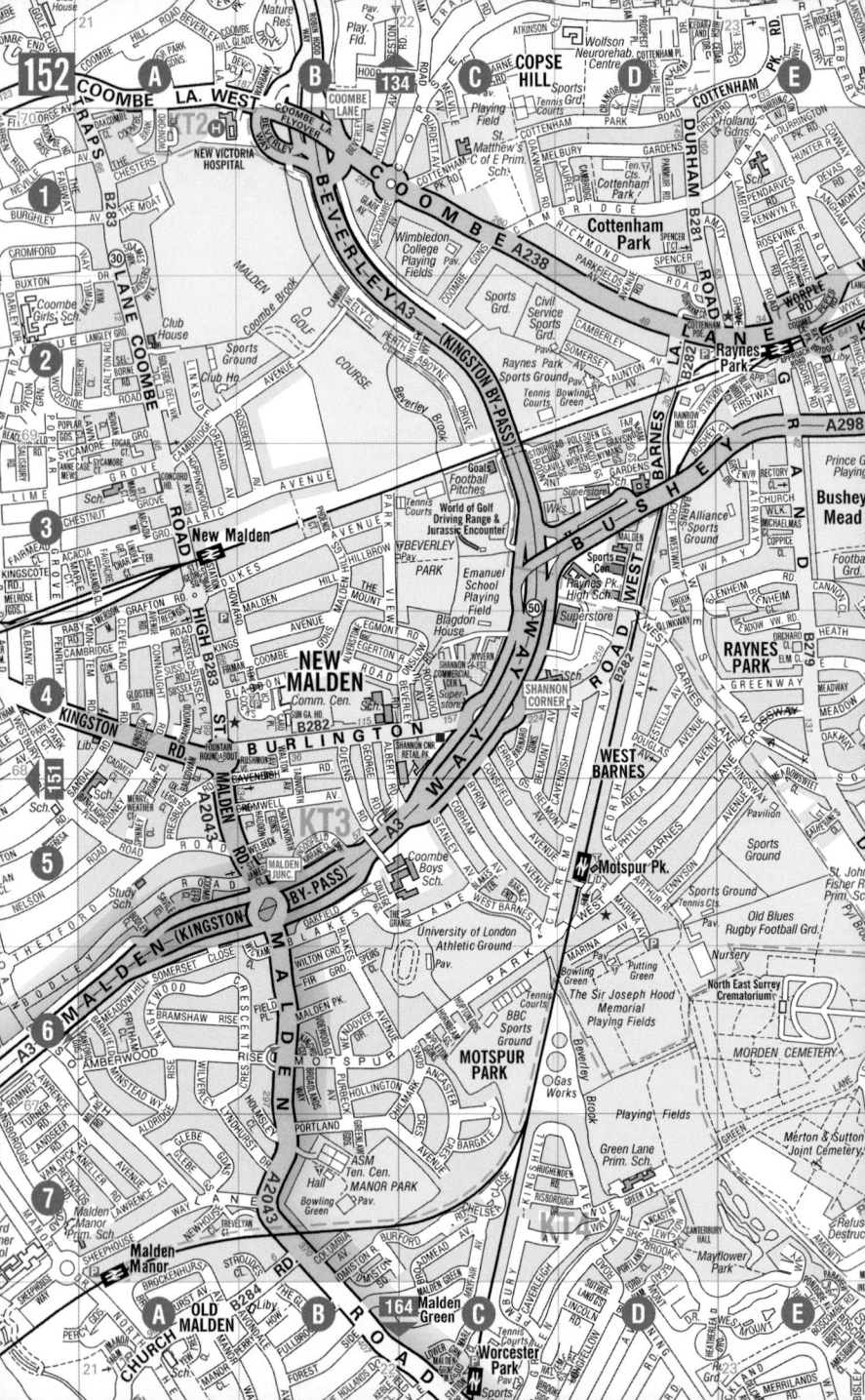

152
A
B
C
D
E
1
2
3
4
5
6
7
COOMBE LA. WEST
COOMBE LANE
134
COPSE HILL
Wolfson Neurorehab. Centre
COTTENHAM PK. RD.
COTTENHAM PARK ROAD
COTTENHAM PL.
NEW VICTORIA HOSPITAL
KT2
THE CHESTERS
THE MOAT
COOMBE FLYOVER
BEVERLEY WAY
COOMBE LANE A238
BEVERLEY A3
(KINGSTON BY-PASS)
Wimbledon College Playing Fields
Playing Field
St. Matthew's C of E Prim. Sch.
Cottenham Park
DURHAM ROAD B281
Sports Grd.
Civil Service Sports Grd.
RICHMOND AV.
CAMBRIDGE RD.
WORPLE RD.
Raynes Park
Raynes Park Sports Ground
Tennis Courts
Bowling Green
A298
BUSHEY ROAD
Prince Georges Playing Fields
Bushey Mead
Football Grd.
RAYNES PARK
West Barnes Lane B282
WEST BARNES
Alliance Sports Ground
Sports Cen.
Raynes Pk. High Sch.
Superstore
Goals Football Pitches
World of Golf Driving Range & Jurassic Encounter
BEVERLEY PARK
Emanuel School Playing Field
Blagdon House
SHANNON CORNER
Shannon Commercial Cen.
NEW MALDEN
Comm. Cen.
New Malden
HIGH ST. B283
COOMBE ROAD
COOMBE LANE
Coombe Girls Sch.
Club House
Sports Ground
Club Ho.
MALDEN GOLF COURSE
Coombe Brook
Beverley Brook
KINGSTON RD.
BURLINGTON RD. B282
MALDEN RD. A2043
KT3
MALDEN JUNC.
FOUNTAIN ROUNDABOUT
151
A3 MALDEN (KINGSTON BY-PASS)
Coombe Boys Sch.
Study Sch.
University of London Athletic Ground
WEST BARNES LA.
Motspur Pk.
MOTSPUR PARK
BBC Sports Ground
Sports Ground
Tennis Cts.
Old Blues Rugby Football Grd.
St. John Fisher R.C. Prim. Sch.
Nursery
North East Surrey Crematorium
The Sir Joseph Hood Memorial Playing Fields
MORDEN CEMETERY
Merton & Sutton Joint Cemetery
Gas Works
Playing Fields
Green Lane Prim. Sch.
KT4
Mayflower Park
Refuse Destruct.
ASM Ten. Cen.
MANOR PARK
Hall
Bowling Green
Malden Manor Prim. Sch.
Malden Manor
OLD MALDEN
CHURCH RD.
164
Malden Green
Worcester Park
Sports

153
135
154
165
F
G
H
J
K
1
2
3
4
5
6
7
MERTON
MERTON PARK
MORDEN
MORDEN PARK
SW20
SW19
Wimbledon Chase
South Merton
Morden
Morden South
St. Helier
Sth. Wimbledon
Merton Park
Morden Rd.
KINGSTON ROAD
A238
MARTIN WAY
B286
LONDON ROAD
A24
CENTRAL ROAD
A239
EPSOM ROAD
STONECOT HILL
SUTTON COMMON ROAD
B279
TUDOR DRIVE
LOWER MORDEN LANE
HILLCROSS AVENUE
CANNON HILL LANE
MORDEN ROAD
MORDEN HALL ROAD
A297
ST. HELIER AVENUE
ROSE HILL
ROSEHILL
ROSE HILL ROUNDABOUT
B278
B285
DORSET ROAD
MERANTUN WY.
NELSON HOSP.
John Innes Park
Rutlish Sch.
Dundonald Prim. Sch.
Recreation Ground
Face Youth Sch.
David Lloyd Leisure & Lloyds Lanes Raynes Park
Messines Playing Field
Joseph Hood Recreation Ground
CANNON HILL COMMON (Recreation Ground)
Cannon Hill
Raynes Park Playing Fields
Cherry Wood
Morden Park School Sports Centre
School Playing Fields
South Thames College (Merton College)
Morden Park Pools
Hatfeild Prim. Sch.
Aragon Prim. Sch.
King George's Field
Mostyn Gardens
Poplar Prim. Sch.
Kendor Gardens
Morden Hall
River Wandle
Civic Cen.
Mosque
Risley Sports Grd.
Recreation Ground
Abbey Prim. Sch.
Glenthorne High Sch.
Recreation Grounds
THE WOODSTOCK
Playing Field
Playing Fields
Scout Hall
Lombard Business Park
WORKS
Merton Ind. Park

154
MERTON
HIGH ST.
A238
MERANTUN WAY
A24
Superstore
136
Cemetery
LONDON RD.
A217
STREATHAM RD.
A216
WESTERN ROAD
A236
Lavender Park
Tandem Centre
MERTON
MORDEN RD.
Deen City Farm
CR4
MORDEN HALL PARK
Morden Hall
The London Acorn Sch. (Morden Cottage)
Phipps Bridge
River Wandle
MORDEN HALL RD.
A297
Morden Lodge
MORDEN ROAD
A239
Belgrave Wlk.
Ravensbury Park
Melrose Sch.
Playing Field
CRICKET GRN.
Cricket Green
Canons Leisure Centre
MITCHAM
COMMONSIDE WEST
Beehive Bridge
Blue Houses Bridge
MADEIRA RD.
CRANMER RD.
Mitcham
Wilson Hospital NHS Walk-In
CARSHALTON RD.
MITCHAM GOLF COURSE
Willow Lane Bri.
Mitcham Junction
A237
ST. HELIER AVENUE
153
CENTRAL RD.
SM4
Tooting & Mitcham United FC (Imperial Fields)
Watermeads
Harris Academy Morden
Poulter Park
Bennett's Hole
Willow Lane Industrial Estate
Moreton Green
BISHOPSFORD ROAD
Open Space
Playing Fields
Mill Green
ST. HELIER
Hill Ho. Comm. Cen.
Mecca Bingo
SM5
Running Track
Sutton Arena Leisure Centre
Nature Reserves
BEDDINGTON CORNER
ROSE HILL ROUNDABOUT
REIGATE AV.
ROSEHILL
St. Helier Open Space
166
B278
ST. HELIER HOSPITAL

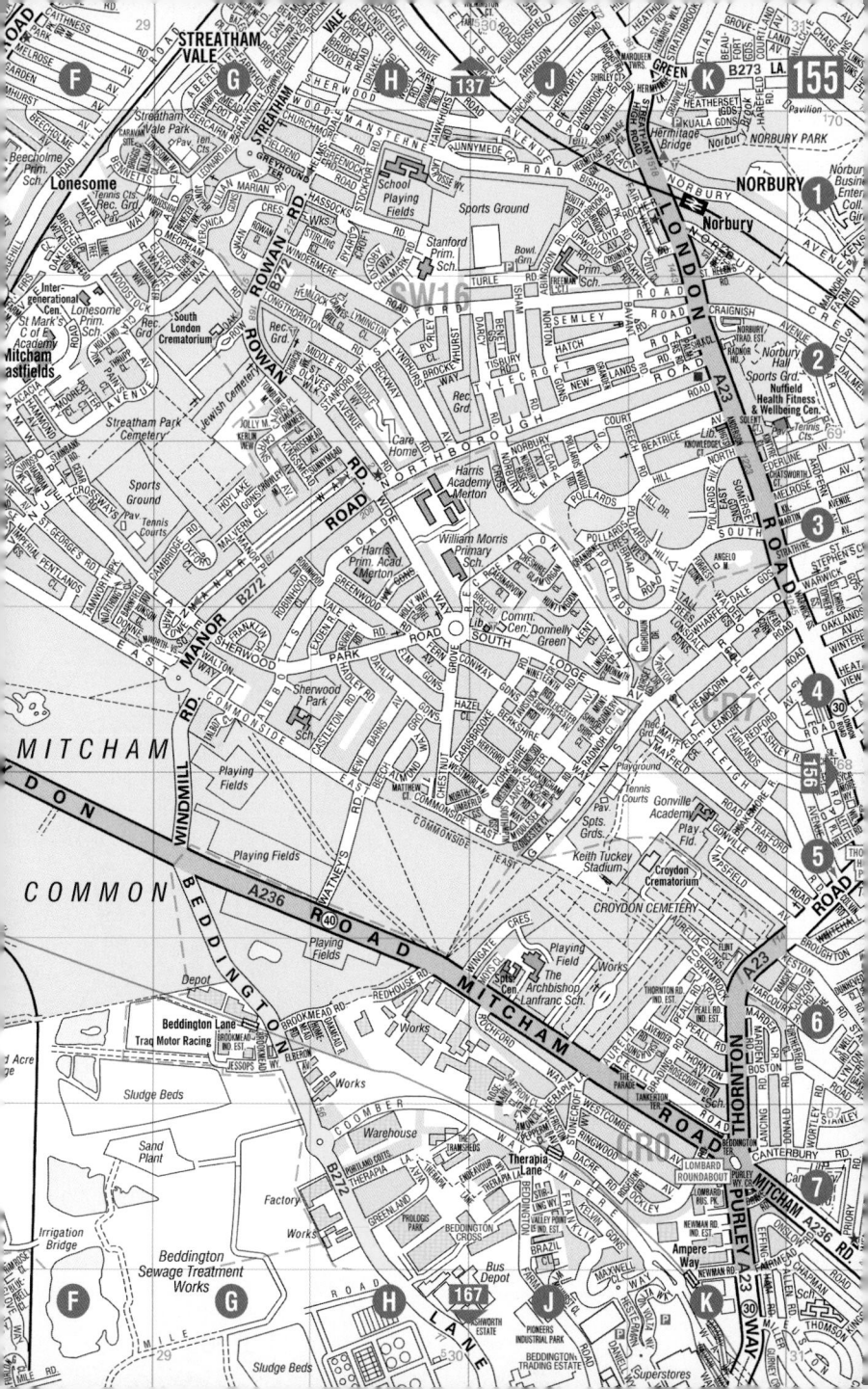

155
137
156
167
STREATHAM VALE
Streatham Vale Park
Lonesome
Beecholme Prim. Sch.
Lonesome Prim. Sch.
Inter-generational Cen.
St Mark's C of E Academy
Mitcham Eastfields
South London Crematorium
Jewish Cemetery
Streatham Park Cemetery
Sports Ground
Tennis Courts
School Playing Fields
Sports Ground
Stanford Prim. Sch.
SW16
NORBURY
Norbury
NORBURY PARK
Norbury Hall Sports Grd.
Nuffield Health Fitness & Wellbeing Cen.
Norbury Manor Business & Enterprise Coll. for Girls
Harris Academy Merton
Harris Prim. Acad. Merton
William Morris Primary Sch.
Care Home
Comm. Cen.
Donnelly Green
Sherwood Park Sch.
Playing Fields
Gonville Academy
Keith Tuckey Stadium
Croydon Crematorium
CROYDON CEMETERY
The Archbishop Lanfranc Sch.
CR7
CR0
MITCHAM COMMON
Beddington Lane
Traq Motor Racing
Sludge Beds
Sand Plant
Irrigation Bridge
Beddington Sewage Treatment Works
Warehouse
Works
Factory
Therapia Lane
Ampere Way
Bus Depot
PIONEERS INDUSTRIAL PARK
BEDDINGTON TRADING ESTATE
Superstores
LOMBARD ROUNDABOUT
LONDON ROAD
A23
A236
MITCHAM ROAD
ROWAN ROAD
B272
MANOR ROAD
WINDMILL RD.
BEDDINGTON LANE
NORTHBOROUGH ROAD
PURLEY WAY
THORNTON ROAD
GALPINS ROAD
STREATHAM HIGH ROAD
B273
F
G
H
J
K
1
2
3
4
5
6
7
29
530
31

156
A
B
C
D
E
1
2
3
4
5
6
7
138
155
168
NORBURY
NORBURY PARK
Norbury Manor Business & Enterprise Coll. for Girls
Kensington Avenue Prim. School
Sports Ground
Comm. Cen.
Nuffield Health Fitness & Wellbeing Cen.
SW16
UPPER NORWOOD
The Lawns
David Livingstone Prim. Acad.
Harris Academy (Upper Norwood)
Downsview Prim. Sch.
Biggin Wood
Spurgeon's College
Grangewood Park
Cypress Prim. Sch.
Beaulieu Heights
Rec. Ground
THORNTON HEATH
Thornton Heath
THORNTON HEATH POND
CR7
Crystal Palace FC (Selhurst Park)
Selhurst
SELHURST
Ecclesbourne Prim. Sch.
Queen's Rd. Cemy.
CROYDON UNIVERSITY HOSPITAL
Broad Green
West Croydon
CROYDON
St. Chad's Cath. Prim. Sch.
Heavers Resource Centre
Canterbury Rec. Grd.
Gloucester Rd. Junc.
Cottage Junc.
Lupin Bri.
LONDON ROAD A23
BRIGSTOCK ROAD
MELFORT AVENUE
PARCHMORE
B273
B266
A212
A213
A235
A236
A222
A215
HIGH STREET
WHITEHORSE ROAD
WINDMILL RD.
ST. JAMES'S
NORTHCOTE RD.
SELHURST
GRANGE ROAD
SOUTH HILL
CHURCH ROAD
BEULAH HILL
MITCHAM ROAD
PURLEY WAY
WELLESLEY RD.
LOWER ADDISCOMBE ROAD
SUMNER A213
QUEEN'S ROAD

157
F
G
H
J
K
1
2
3
4
5
6
7
139
158
169
PENGE
ANERLEY
Anerley
SE20
SE19
SE25
BR3
CRO
SOUTH NORWOOD
Norwood Junc.
WOODSIDE
ELMERS END
Elmers End
Birkbeck
Beckenham Crematorium
Kent House
Avenue Road
Harrington Rd.
Blind Corner
Pitch & Putt Course
SOUTH NORWOOD COUNTRY PARK
Visitor Centre
Croydon Sports Arena
Croydon FC Grd.
Oasis Academy Arena
Arena
World of Golf Centre
Woodside
Blackhorse La.
Addiscombe
Ashburton Park
Ashburton Playing Fields
SHIRLEY OAKS BMI HOSPITAL
Shirley Oaks
Oasis Academy Shirley Park (Seniors)
Harris City Academy
Phil Edwards PRU
Orchard Lodge (Remand Centre)
James Dixon Prim. Sch.
Orchard School Sports Centre
Nursing Home
Playing Field
Bowling Green
Tennis Courts
South Norwood Lake
Croydon Sailing Club
Bromley Junction
Harris Academy
Recreation Ground
Priory Sch.
Betts Pk.
Brickfields Mdw
Davidson Prim. Sch.
Chaffinch Brook Sch.
Monks Orchard Prim. Sch.
Bird Sanctuary
Long Lane Wood
Glade Wood
The Kentwood Cen.
Superstore
Recyling Cen.
Chaffinch Business Park
Primary School
A214
A213
A234
A215
A222
B243
CROYDON RD.
PENGE RD.
ELMERS END ROAD
PORTLAND RD.
LONG LANE
SPRING LA.
WOODSIDE GREEN
WOODSIDE ROAD
ADDISCOMBE RD.
SHIRLEY ROAD
LOWER ADDISCOMBE RD.
HIGH ST.
BECKENHAM RD.
CLOCK HOUSE RD.

158
A
B
C
D
E
1
2
3
4
5
6
7
140
157
170
36
37
38
Aspire Acad.
Spts. Grd.
CATOR PARK
Kent House
Beckenham Road
Clock Ho.
The Spa
Beckenham Junc.
BECKENHAM
A234 ROAD
RECTORY A2015
HIGH A222
MANOR RD.
BROMLEY
SOUTHEND
STREET
BROMLEY RD.
Theatre Cen.
CROYDON
A222
ROAD
BECKENHAM BEACON
Recreation Ground
Bandstand
BR3
KELSEY PARK
Kelsey Way
Elgood Play. Fld.
Harris Acad. Beckenham
Harris Prim. Acad. Beckenham
Crease Park
Putting Green
HAYES
PARK LANGLEY
The Parklangley Club
ELMERS END
UPPER ELMERS END
David Lloyd Leisure
EDEN PARK
Langley Court (Research Labs)
Eden Park
Unicorn Prim. Sch.
Langley Park School for Boys
Langley Park School for Girls
Langley Park Sports Centre
Crouch Oak Wood
MONKS ORCHARD
Cold Shaw
High Broom Wood
Bethlem & Maudsley Hospital Sch.
BETHLEM ROYAL HOSPITAL
Whitley House
Denis Hill Unit
Chelsham House
River House
Edenham High Sch.
CR0
Glade Wood
Monks Orchard Prim. Sch.
Primary School
Parkfields Recreation Ground
Playing Field
Caravan Park
LINKS WAY
SOUTH EDEN PARK RD.
A214
BECKENHAM RD.
ELMERS END A214 ROAD
Oak Lodge Prim. Sch.
Blake Recreation Ground
West Wickham
WEST WICKHAM
West Wickham Leisure C
The Rookery
LANGLEY
LANGLEY PARK GOLF COURSE
Sports Ground

159
141
160
171
F
G
H
J
K
1
2
3
4
5
6
7
Ravensbourne
Sundridge Park
Bromley Nth.
Bromley South
Shortlands
SHORTLANDS GOLF COURSE
Golf Course
Playing Field
BROMLEY PARK
THE SLOANE BMI HOSP.
Bishop Challoner Sch.
BROMLEY
SHORTLANDS
Churchill Theatre
Leisure Cen.
INTU BROMLEY (THE GLADES)
Queens Gdn.
Bromley Civic Centre
Moat
Church Ho. Gdns.
Tennis Courts
Martin's Hill
War Meml.
Rec. Grd. Queen's Mead
Playground
Harris Prim. Acad.
Highfield Inf. Sch.
Highfield Jun. Sch.
South Hill Wood Rec. Grd.
The Ravensbourne Sch.
Bromley Trust Academy
Hayesford
Nuffield Health Fitness & Wellbeing Centre
Bowling Green
Cricket Ground
Bromley FC & Cray Wanderers FC (Courage Stadium)
Fishers Wood
NORMAN PARK
Norman Park Athletics Track
Pavilion
Brook Wood
HAYES
Hayes Street Farm
Hayes Prim. Sch.
Hayes
Cupola Wood
Recreation Ground
Pickhurst Jun. & Inf. Schs.
Pickhurst Green
Club House
PARK
Sports Ground
Sports Grounds
Tennis Courts
BR1
BR2
BR4
A222
A21
A2212
B228
B2212
B265
B251
WIDMORE RD.
TWEEDY RD.
LONDON RD.
COLLEGE
BECKENHAM LANE
HIGH ST.
KENTISH WAY
MASONS HILL
HAYES ROAD
HAYES LANE
WESTMORELAND ROAD
PICKHURST LANE
ROCHESTER AVENUE
MEADOW WAY
BROMLEY ROAD
ROAD
FARNABY

160
142
172
159
A
B
C
D
E
1
2
3
4
5
6
7
41
42
43
67
68
69
170
Sundridge Park
Netball Cts.
Bowling Grn.
Pav.
Sch.
HAMPTON GRANGE
Convent
Scotts Park Prim. Sch.
ROMNEY
EDGEBOROUGH
SERVIDEN DR.
WOOD LODGE GDS.
HOLMBURY PK
AVENUE
LOGS
YESTER
CAMDEN
LUBBOCK
CHISLEHURST
ROAD
ORCHARD
PLAISTOW
ROSEWOOD
SUNDRIDGE
MAVELSTONE
Bullers Wood Sch.
HIGHGROVE
ST. NICOLAS LA.
St. Cecilia's
WESTBURY RD.
HILL
FARM
Widmore Green
Cricket Grd.
Club
HOMEFIELD RD.
FREELANDS
HENVILLE RD.
WIDMORE
A222
30
CHISLEHURST
ROAD
BICKLEY RD.
B264
ST. GEORGE'S RD. W.
BEECH COPSE
SPINNEYS
WYTHES CL.
WELLS RD.
DENBRIDGE
BOSCOBEL CL.
Chislehurst
OLD
ROAD
SUMMER
STATION APP.
Caves
Chalkpit Wood
CAMDEN WOOD
Brook
Kyd
PORRINGTON CL.
RAGGLESWOOD
OAKHURST
MERLEWOOD DR.
PRIORY CL.
ROAD
TUDOR CL.
CAVERLEIGH PL.
WANSTEAD CL.
BEECHFIELD RD.
CEDAR RD.
Rec. Grd.
SHAWFIELD PK.
Tennis Cts.
Pav.
Play. Fld.
PINES RD.
WOODLANDS
Hadlow
EASTMEAD CL.
INGLEWOOD COPSE
WOODLANDS RD.
HARTLEY
WOODLANDS CL.
COATES HILL
HEVER GDNS.
WELLSMOOR GS.
ROCHESTER AV.
NIGHTINGALE
School
The Widmore Cen.
Bickley Prim. Sch.
Ten. Cts.
Moat
Bromley Civic Centre
CHASE
MURRAY
SOUTH
FORDE AVENUE
BISHOPS AVENUE
CANON
LIDDON
FARRIER CL.
WIDMORE
Playing Field
Gas Works
Superstore
PALACE VW.
LANE
BIRD IN HAND LA.
WESTWOOD CL.
PARK
BICKLEY
Ckt. Gd.
Pav.
BICKLEY A222 PARK
ROAD
BR1
PAGE HEATH LA.
Sch.
CHARLOTTE PARK AV.
Bickley
SYLVAN WK.
ST. MATTHEW'S DR.
NEWNHAMS CL.
SYCAMORE PL.
OTFORD CL.
Bickley Junc.
REYNARD CL.
ROAD
LIBERTY CT.
ELLEN CL.
SIWARD
ROAD
GODWIN RD.
WALDO IND. EST.
WALDO
HAWTHORNE
ROAD
BEACONSFIELD RD.
AVENUE
SOUTHLANDS
GROVE
GLANVILLE
ROAD
GUNDULPH RD.
Tennis Cts.
Hall
Depot
MORNINGTON AV.
B265
Recreation Ground
Depot
LINDSEY CL.
Virgin Active Health Club
BATHS RD.
RUSHMORE CL.
FALCON AV.
CLARENCE AV.
LIME CL.
OLDFIELD ROAD
WYNCROFT CL.
SOUTHWARK PL.
ROSEMOUNT DR.
HURSTWOOD DR.
MEADOW-CROFT
THORNET WOOD RD.
BARFIELD
GOLF RD.
Play. Flds.
HOMESDALE
HAVELOCK
HAYWOOD RD.
BOURNE ROAD
FASHODA RD.
ELLIOTT RD.
JAFFRAY
TREDWELL
DRAPER CT.
TANGLEBERRY CL.
PARK HILL
HIGHFIELD
SPRINGFIELD RD.
OLDFIELD CL.
SPRINGFIELD GDNS.
Bromley High School
HAYES LA.
Tennis Courts
BROMLEY
Bromley Trust Academy
Playing Field
Whitehall Pleasure Ground
Bowl. Grn.
COWPER
CHATTERTON
WHITEHALL RD.
BLENHEIM RD.
CLAREMONT RD.
BURFORD RD.
WALDEGRAVE RD.
MAYFIELD RD.
FAIRMEAD
FAIRWAY
AVENUE
ROAD
BLACKBROOK LANE
SOUTHBOROUGH
BROOKLYN RD.
HERBERT RD.
SALISBURY
WOODSIDE RD.
SUNNINGDALE RD.
RINGMER WY.
CLOISTERS AV.
BROOKMEAD
HOMEMEAD
Health Wellbeing Centre
Pav.
Cricket Ground
Pavilion
P
BALFOUR RD.
ALBERT ROAD
VICTORIA ROAD
JOHNSON RD.
MOSSLEA
WAVERLEY CL.
POPE
WALPOLE
BIRDHAM CL.
SOUTHBOROUGH
AUSTIN AV.
WILLOW CL.
HOLMCROFT WY.
HOLBROOK WAY
FONTWELL DR.
30
Southborough Prim. Sch.
Playing Field
Fishers Wood
Ravens Bourne
Pavilion
NORMAN PARK
CROWN LA.
CROWN LANE
GREEN
LANE
SUNRAY AVENUE
RUSKIN WK.
WAY LANE
BR2
MONS WAY
Cemetery
Parkfield Recreation Ground
AVENUE
LOVELACE
ROW
HAZEL WK.
THE OAKS
Pavilion
Scrogginhall Wood
Playground
ROOKERY LA.
Bromley College of Further & Higher Education
A21
Bridgeways
NARROW WY.
BROOM CL.
SHELL CL.
MOSUL WAY
HALL
Rookery Lake
COMMON
BROMLEY COMMON
BROMLEY GOLF COURSE
HORNBEAM WY.
ASH
BIRCH
LARCH WAY
WHITEBEAM
ALMOND WY.
ALMOND CL.
FARRINGDON
TURPINGTON
Hall
MAGPIE
Club Ho.
Driving Range
BROMLEY COMMON
Bishop Justus C of E School
Playing Field
Princes Plain Prim. Sch.
Play. Fld.
Lord's Wood
Brook Wood
Oakley House
Mazzards Wood
Woodcock Grove
Ravens Bourne
GEORGE LA.
Hayes Prim. Sch.
Playing
Bolds
Pav. Play. Fld
CHURCH LA.
Prince's Plain
COTTAGE AV.
HASTINGS ROAD
BREWERY RD
CAPEL CT.
A233
OAKLEY RD.
Oakley Farm
PLAIN
PRINCES
LWR. GRAVEL RD.
LENNARD
ARAGON
Playing Field
Pav.
Scrubs Farm
Clay Wood

161
143
173
CHISLEHURST COMMON
BROMLEY LA.
ROYAL PDE.
BROMLEY RD.
PRINCE IMPERIAL RD.
B263
WATTS LA.
MANOR PARK RD.
B264
CHISLEHURST
Cricket Grd.
Coopers Sch.
Marjorie McClure School
Playing Field
Hawkwood Nursery
Rifle Range
Birch Wood
Pond Wood
BR7
Hawkwood Estate
Hawkwood Farm
Tongs Farm
Walk Wood
Chislehurst Junction
Great Thrift
SCADBURY PARK
(Nature Reserve)
PARK WOOD
Hadresham
The Fantails
Holbrook Wood Lodge
The Larches
St. Peter & St. Paul RC Prim. Sch.
The Gorse Children's Home
ST. PAUL'S CRAY
A208
ORPINGTON ROAD
Hoblingwell Wood
Brackenwood
ST. PAUL'S CRAY
Playing Field
St. Paul's Cray Common
PETTS WOOD
Edlmann Memorial Wood
Willett Memorial Wood
St. Mary Cray Junction
ORPINGTON RD.
CHISLEHURST RD.
BR5
Blackbrook Wood
JUBILEE COUNTRY PARK
Petts Wood Junction
Sydney Shaw
PETTS WOOD
POVEREST
Petts Wood
Lakeswood Hall
St. James' RC Prim. Sch.
Covet Wood
Recreation Ground
Perry Hall Prim. Sch.
PERRY HALL RD.
Petts Wood Recreation Ground
Crofton Jun. Sch.
Crofton Inf. Sch.
Sparrow Wood
Sparrow Common
Roundabout Wood
BR6
Broom Hill
Knoll Lawn Tennis Club
ORPINGTON
Heath

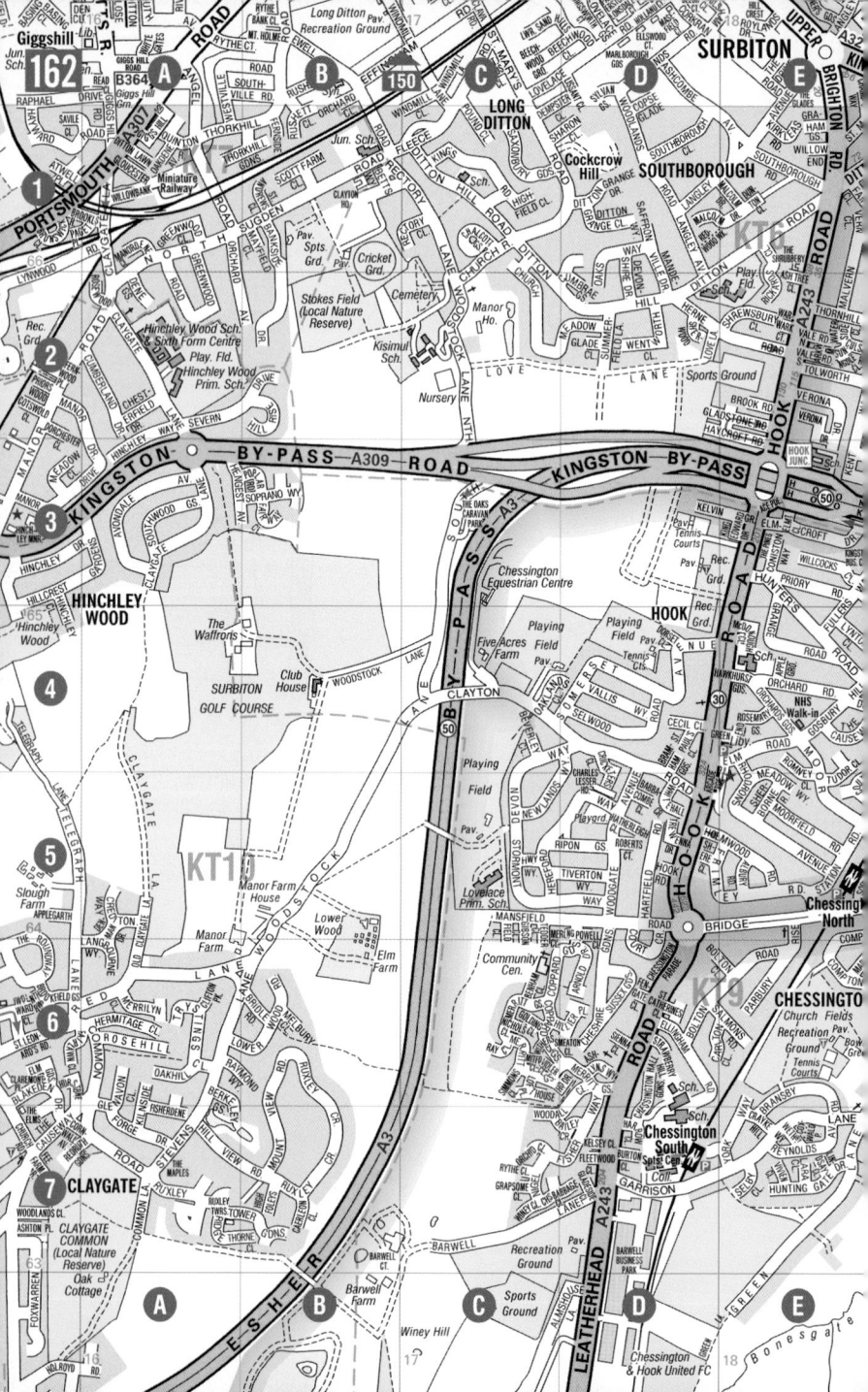
162
150
Giggshill
SURBITON
LONG DITTON
Cockcrow Hill
SOUTHBOROUGH
KT7
KT6
KT10
KT9
HINCHLEY WOOD
Hinchley Wood
HOOK
CHESSINGTON
Chessington North
Chessington South
CLAYGATE
Long Ditton Recreation Ground
PORTSMOUTH ROAD
A307
B364
Miniature Railway
KINGSTON BY-PASS A309 ROAD
KINGSTON BY-PASS
A3
ESHER BY-PASS
A243
HOOK ROAD
LEATHERHEAD ROAD
BRIGHTON RD.
UPPER
Stokes Field (Local Nature Reserve)
Cricket Grd.
Cemetery
Kisimul Sch.
Manor Ho.
Nursery
Hinchley Wood Sch. & Sixth Form Centre
Play. Fld.
Hinchley Wood Prim. Sch.
Rec. Grd.
The Waffrons
Club House
SURBITON GOLF COURSE
Chessington Equestrian Centre
Five Acres Farm
Playing Field
Sports Ground
Manor Farm House
Manor Farm
Lower Wood
Elm Farm
Lovelace Prim. Sch.
Community Cen.
Slough Farm
CLAYGATE COMMON (Local Nature Reserve)
Oak Cottage
Barwell Farm
Winey Hill
Recreation Ground
BARWELL BUSINESS PARK
Chessington & Hook United FC
Church Fields Recreation Ground
Tennis Courts
NHS Walk-in
HOOK JUNC.
Bonesgate
1
2
3
4
5
6
7
A
B
C
D
E
16
17
18
63
64
65
66

163
164
151
F
G
H
J
K
1
2
3
4
5
6
7
19
20
21
A240 ROAD
A3
KINGSTON-BY-PASS
KT5
KT4
TOLWORTH
Tolworth
TOLWORTH JUNCTION
Hollywood Bowl
Jubilee Way Training Track
Alexandra Millennium Green
Recreation Ground
Malden Manor
Sports Centre
Playing Field
Tennis Courts
Community Centre
Nursery
Maori Sports Ground
Knollmead Prim. Sch.
Sports Ground Goals Soccer Cen.
Football Pitches
Sports Ground
Riverhill
Sports Grd.
Crkt. Grd.
Surbiton Raceway
Linden Bridge School
RIVERHILL MOBILE HOME PARK
King George's Field Playing Field
Corinthian Casuals FC Grd.
Club
King George's Field
Tolworth Court Bridge
TOLWORTH HOSP.
Arts Cen.
Play. Fld.
Tolworth Rec. Cen.
Playing Field
CHANCERY GATE BUS. PK.
RED LION BUS. PARK
HOOK RISE SOUTH IND. PARK
KING GEORGE'S TRADING EST.
DAVIS ROAD INDUSTRIAL PARK
CHESSINGTON TRADE PK.
Works
Depot
Castle Hill Prim. Sch.
Hogsmill Local Nature Reserve
Bonesgate Stream
Youth Cen.
Comm. Cen.
Riverview C of E Prim. Sch.
Play. Fld.
Sports Direct Fitness
Sports Ground
West Ewell Inf. Sch.
Epsom & Ewell High Sch.
Playing Field
Weir
Hogsmill Local Nature Reserve
Pack Horse Bri.
King George's Field
The Harriers Cen.
Running Track
Bonesgate Open Space Local Nature Reserve
Butcher's Grove
Castle Hill Local Nature Reserve
HORTON COUNTRY PARK
HORTON PARK GOLF COURSE
Club Ho.
Driving Range
Hook Road Arena
Gt. Wood
St. Ebba's Farm Cottage
Cemetery
ST. EBBA'S
Horton Country Park Local Nature Reserve
Tennis Cts.
Playing Field
Jun. Sch.
WEST EWELL
Ewell Ct. Park
Rec. Grd.
CHESSINGTON ROAD
B284
B2200
HOOK ROAD
RUXLEY LANE
CHANTRY ROAD
MOOR LANE
WORCESTER PARK RD.
KINGSTON ROAD
JUBILEE WAY
MALDEN LANE
CHURCH RD.
KNOLLMEAD
WARREN DRIVE NORTH
WARREN DRIVE SOUTH
TOLWORTH BROADWAY
ALEXANDRA
HAMILTON AVENUE
TOLWORTH PARK ROAD
DAVIS ROAD
CHESSINGTON

164
152
163
A
B
C
D
E
1
2
3
4
5
6
7
Malden Manor
OLD MALDEN
Malden Green
Worcester Park
WORCESTER PARK
KT4
Mayflower Park
Dorchester Prim. Sch.
Linden Bridge School
Wandgas Athletics Ground
Dancer 'Dick Wood
Cuddington Prim. Sch.
Shadbolt Park
King George's Field
Auriol Park
Cuddington Recreation Ground
Beverley Brook
Meadow Prim. Sch.
STONELEIGH
Stoneleigh
KT17
KT19
BEGGAR'S HILL
Oak Plantation
London Road Plantation
NONSUCH PARK
Mansion House
WEST EWELL
Hogsmill River
Chamber Mead
Playing Fields
ORGAN CROSSROADS
Ewell West
Bourne Hall Mus.
Ewell Castle Jun. Sch.
Ewell Castle Senior Sch.
EWELL
OLD MALDEN LANE
MALDEN ROAD
CENTRAL ROAD
A2043
CHEAM COMMON ROAD
KINGSTON ROAD
A240
LONDON ROAD
A24
EWELL BY-PASS
SALISBURY ROAD
B284
B2200

165
153
166
F
G
H
J
K
1
2
3
4
5
6
7
ROSEHILL
Rosehill Recreation Ground
The Sports Village
Sutton Tennis Academy
ROSE HILL ROUNDABOUT
BENHILTON
NORTH CHEAM
SM4
SM3
SM1
SM2
SUTTON
CHEAM
CHEAM PARK
BELMONT
STONECOT HILL
LONDON ROAD
A24
A217
A232
A2043
B279
B230
B283
ST. DUNSTAN'S HILL
OLDFIELDS ROAD
COMMON ROAD
REIGATE AVENUE
SUTTON COMMON ROAD
ANGEL HILL
ROSE HILL
HIGH ST.
ST. NICHOLAS WAY
THROWLEY WAY
CARSHALTON ROAD
BRIGHTON ROAD
CHEAM ROAD
EWELL RD.
BELMONT RISE
BURDON LANE
MALDEN ROAD
GANDER GREEN LANE
Sutton Cemetery
Glenthorne High Sch.
Recreation Grounds
Collingwood Road Recreation Ground
Sutton United FC (Borough Sports Grd.)
West Sutton
Sutton Common
Westbourne Prim. Sch.
Cheam High Sch.
Cheam Leisure Cen.
Cheam Recreation Ground
Perrett's Field
Seears Park
Water Wks.
Sutton Ckt. Grd.
Fitness4Less (Sutton)
Secombe Thtre.
Civic Cen.
Cheam
CHEAM VILLAGE
Nonsuch High Sch.
Harefield Bri. Playing Field
Overton Grange Sch.
Overton Park
Sports Grd.
St. Anthony's Hosp.
St. Raphael's Hospice
Goals Soccer Cen. (Sutton)
Fairlands Pk.
Superstore
QUEEN VICTORIA
King George's Field
Recreation Ground
Playing Fields
Mecca Bingo
Rosehill Park East
Greenshaw Wood
Sutton

166
154
165
A
B
C
D
E
1
2
3
4
5
6
7
26
27
28
64
63
66
165
ROSEHILL
BENHILTON
THE WRYTHE
CARSHALTON
SUTTON
CARSHALTON BEECHES
CARSHALTON ON THE HILL
HACKBRID
SM1
SM2
SM5
CR4
Rosehill Park East
Greenshaw Wood
St. Helier Open Space
Sutton Arena Leisure Centre
Running Track
ST. HELIER HOSPITAL
QUEEN MARY'S HOSPITAL FOR CHILDREN
UCC
Mecca Bingo
Playing Fields
Rosehill Recreation Ground
Sports Village
Sutton Tennis Academy
Tennis Courts
Bowling Green
Royston Park
Benhill Rec. Grd.
Sports Cen.
Muschamp Prim. Sch.
Rushy Meadow Prim. Sch.
Limes Grn.
Wrythe Rec. Grd.
Carshalton Athletic FC (War Memorial Sports Ground)
Playing Field
Carshalton Coll.
Carshalton
Westcroft Leisure Cen.
The Grove
Council Offices
Studio Thtre.
St. Philomena's School
Coun. Offs.
Eco Cen.
Mus.
The Frying Pan
CARSHALTON PARK
Wilderness Island
Wandle Bri.
Hack Bri.
Comm Hall
Nature Reserves
Rec. Grd.
Super-store
Sutton
Manor Park
Carshalton Beeches
Stanley Pk. Rec. Grd.
Lit. Holland Ho.
Ten. Cts.
Tennis Cts.
Resrs (covered)
Sutton Heights
Coll.
Prim. Sch.
A217
A232
A22
B2230
B278
B277
B271
30
REIGATE AV.
WRYTHE LANE
ST. HELIER AVENUE
ROSE HILL
ANGEL HILL
HIGH ST.
THROWLEY WAY
BRIGHTON ROAD
CARSHALTON ROAD
WEST ST.
NORTH ST.
NIGHTINGALE RD.
HACKBRIDGE RD.
POUND ST.
HIGH ST.
ACRE LANE
RUSKIN RD.
PARK LANE
BEECHES AV.
WESTMEAD RD.
ERSKINE ROAD
BENHILL ROAD
PAGET AVENUE
SHIRLEY AVENUE
WALES AV.
GROSVENOR AVENUE
STANLEY PARK ROAD
BANSTEAD RD.
UPLAND RD.
THE CROSSWAYS
DOWNS WAY
GREENHILL WAY
WOODGREEN HILL
CAVENDISH RD.
CHRISTCHURCH PARK
EGMONT RD.
DEVONSHIRE AV.
CHALGROVE RD.
HARROW RD.
OXFORD RD.
CAMBRIDGE RD.
STAPLEHURST RD.
FARMDALE RD.
GORDON RD.
SUSSEX RD.
BUCKHURST AV.
WINCHCOMBE RD.
WOBURN RD.
MUSCHAMP RD.
CULVERS AV.
STRAWBERRY LANE
MILL LANE
BRAMBLEWOOD
DINGWALL RD.
BRAMBLEDOWN RD.

167
155
168
F
G
H
J
K
1
2
3
4
5
6
7
Beddington Sewage Treatment Works
Factory Works
Prologis Park
Beddington Cross
Bus Depot
Ashworth Estate
Pioneers Industrial Park
Beddington Trading Estate
Valley Leisure Park
Vue Cinema
Tenpin
Superstores
Ampere Way
Waddon Marsh
Mile Road Bridge
Hackbridge
Sludge Beds
Tennis Courts
Sports Ground
Pavilion
Beddington Park
River Wandle
Carew Manor & Dovecote
Carew Academy
The Grange
Boating Lake
Manor Gdn.
Grammar Sch.
Superstore
Warehouse
CR0
The Orion Centre
Electricity Switching Station
Beddington
Waddon
Mill Lane Trading Est.
Waddon Ponds
Church Paddock
The Warren
Croydon Road
A232
Road
London Road
A237
B272
A23
Waddon
Fiveways Corner
Retail Park
Playing Field
Bandon Hill Cemetery
SM6
Bandonhill
Mellows Park
Wallington
Woodcote Road
Manor Road
Stafford Road
B271
South Beddington
Sandy La.
Foresters Drive
Foresters Prim. Sch.
Wilson's Sch.
Powerleague Soccer Centre (Croydon)
Croydon Airport Ind. Est.
Virgin Active The Surrey Health & Racquets Club
Visitor Cen.
Roundshaw
Phoenix Cen.
Amy Johnson Prim. Sch.
Roundshaw Park (Playing Fields)
Roundshaw Downs Local Nature Reserve
Roundshaw Park
Stanley Park Rd.
Wallington Cen.
Plough Lane
Purley Way
Queensway
Sports Ground

CROYDON
West Croydon
East Croydon
South Croydon
SOUTH CROYDON
WADDON
Waddon
Waddon Marsh
Sanderstead
WANDLE PARK
Wandle Park
Duppas Hill
Recreation Ground
Sports Ground
FIVEWAYS CORNER
Whitgift Sch.
HALING PARK
Purley Way Playing Fields
Roundshaw Park (Playing Fields)
Roundshaw Downs Local Nature Reserve
Harris Academy Purley
St. Giles' School
The Colonnades Leisure Park
Kidspace
Health Club
Virgin Active Surrey Health Racquets Club
Sports Direct Fitness (Croydon)
Fairfield Halls
Croydon Coll.
Crown & County Cts.
Park Hill
Lunar Ho.
Centrale
Bingo
Queen's Gdn.
Cambridge Tutors Coll.
Russell Hill Resr. (covered)
S. Croydon Rec. Grd.
Cumnor House Sch.
Canterbury Rec. Grd.
MITCHAM
ST. JAMES'S
ROMAN WAY
OLD TOWN
THE CROYDON FLYOVER
DUPPAS HILL RD.
PURLEY WAY
BRIGHTON RD.
SOUTH END
COOMBE RD.
PARK LANE
WELLESLEY ROAD
LOWER ADDISCOMBE ROAD
CHERRY ORCHARD ROAD
FAIRFIELD RD.
BARCLAY R.
WARHAM AV.
DENNING AV.
CROHAM ROAD
SELSDON RD.
SOUTH PARK HILL RD.
PARK AVENUE
A23
A212
A213
A222
A232
A235
A236
B243
B269
B271
B274
B275
CR0
CR2
156
167
1
2
3
4
5
6
7
A
B
C
D
E

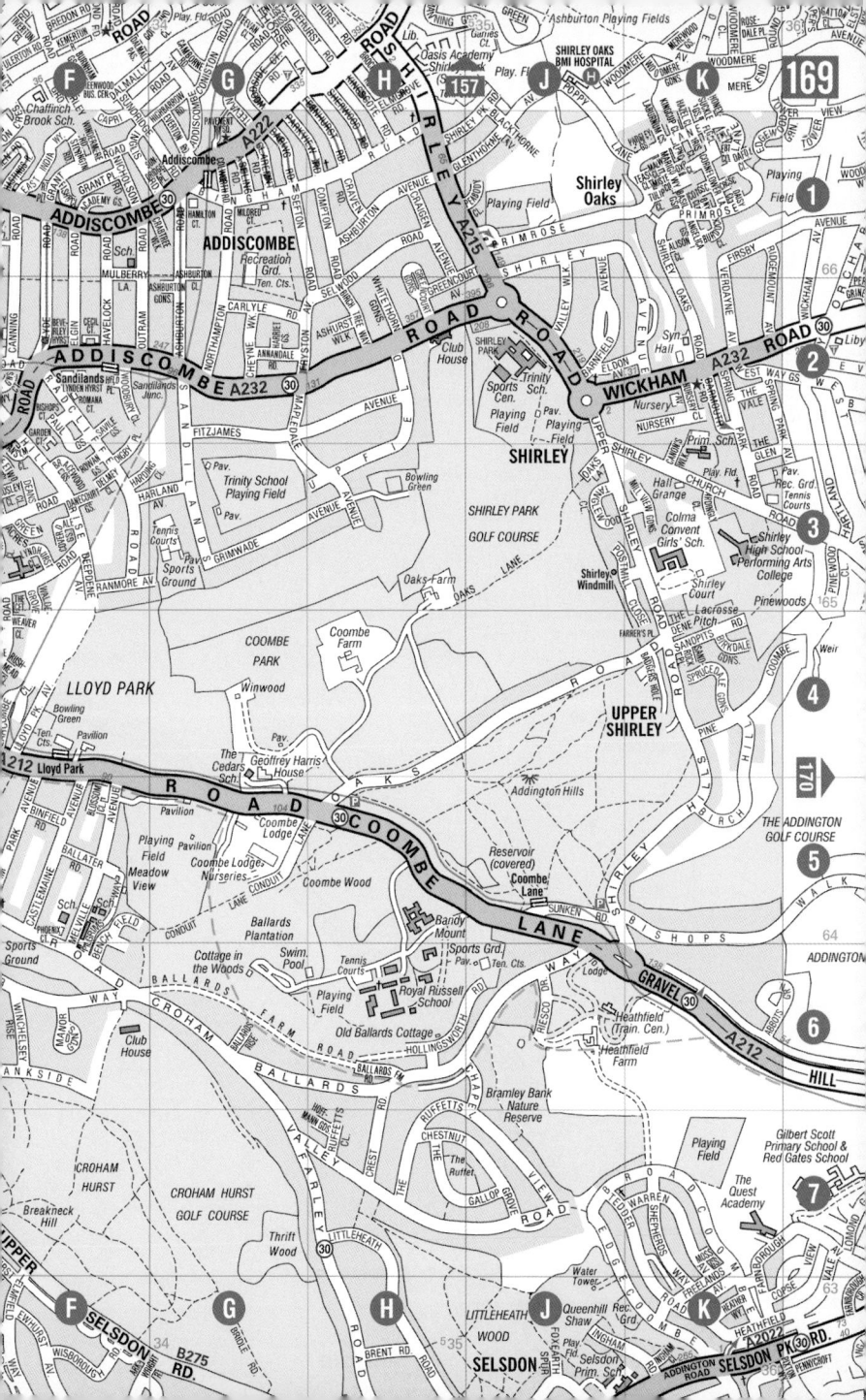
169
157
170
F
G
H
J
K
1
2
3
4
5
6
7
ADDISCOMBE
Addiscombe
ADDISCOMBE ROAD A222
ADDISCOMBE A232
Recreation Grd.
Oasis Academy Shirley Park
SHIRLEY OAKS BMI HOSPITAL
Ashburton Playing Fields
Shirley Oaks
Playing Field
SHIRLEY ROAD A215
WICKHAM ROAD A232
PRIMROSE
Club House
SHIRLEY PARK
Trinity Sch.
Sports Cen.
SHIRLEY
Sandilands
Sandilands Junc.
Trinity School Playing Field
SHIRLEY PARK GOLF COURSE
Colma Convent Girls' Sch.
Shirley High School Performing Arts College
Shirley Windmill
Oaks Farm
OAKS LANE
COOMBE PARK
Coombe Farm
Winwood
LLOYD PARK
Lloyd Park
A212
UPPER SHIRLEY
Addington Hills
THE ADDINGTON GOLF COURSE
The Cedars Sch.
Geoffrey Harris House
COOMBE ROAD
Coombe Lodge
Coombe Lodge Nurseries
Coombe Wood
Reservoir (covered)
Coombe Lane
COOMBE LANE
Bandy Mount
Ballards Plantation
Cottage in the Woods
Royal Russell School
Old Ballards Cottage
GRAVEL HILL A212
Heathfield (Train. Cen.)
Heathfield Farm
Bramley Bank Nature Reserve
BISHOPS WALK
ADDINGTON
CROHAM HURST
CROHAM HURST GOLF COURSE
Breakneck Hill
Thrift Wood
Playing Field
Gilbert Scott Primary School & Red Gates School
The Quest Academy
Water Tower
Queenhill Shaw
LITTLEHEATH WOOD
SELSDON
Selsdon Prim. Sch.
SELSDON PK. RD. A2022
ADDINGTON ROAD
SELSDON RD. B275
UPPER

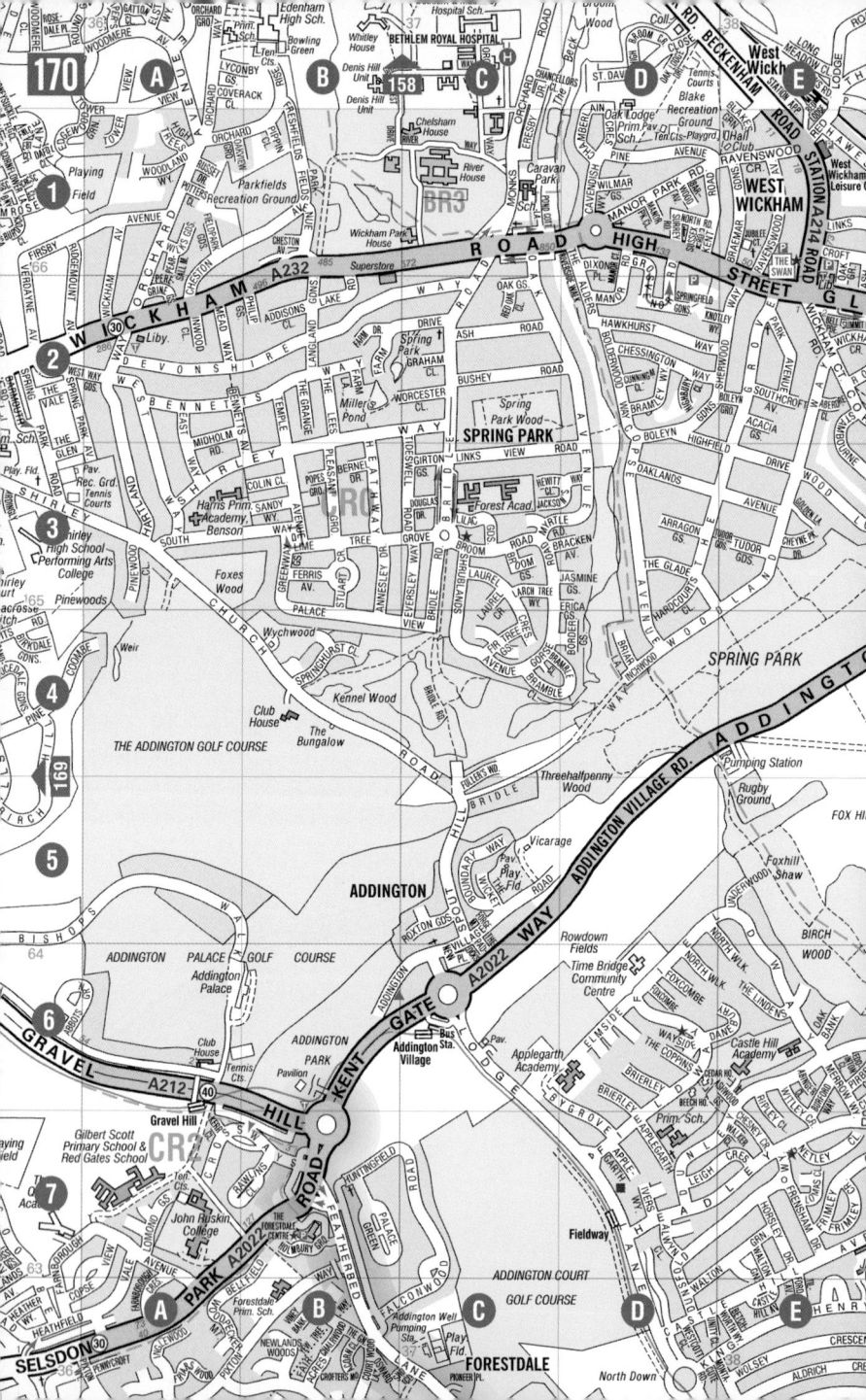

170
A
B
C
D
E
1
2
3
4
5
6
7
158
169
Edenham High Sch.
Bowling Green
Whitley House
Hospital Sch.
BETHLEM ROYAL HOSPITAL
Denis Hill Unit
Chelsham House
River House
BR3
Wickham Park House
Superstore
WICKHAM ROAD A232
HIGH STREET
WEST WICKHAM
West Wickham
West Wickham Leisure Centre
STATION ROAD A214
RD. BECKENHAM
Oak Lodge Prim. Sch.
Blake Recreation Ground
Tennis Courts
Caravan Park
Playing Field
Parkfields Recreation Ground
Liby.
Spring Park
Miller's Pond
Spring Park Wood
SPRING PARK
Forest Acad.
Harris Prim. Academy, Benson
Shirley High School Performing Arts College
Rec. Grd.
Tennis Courts
Play. Fld.
Foxes Wood
Pinewoods
Wychwood
Kennel Wood
Club House
The Bungalow
THE ADDINGTON GOLF COURSE
Threehalfpenny Wood
Pumping Station
Rugby Ground
Foxhill Shaw
BIRCH WOOD
ADDINGTON VILLAGE RD.
ADDINGTON
Vicarage
Pav.
Play. Fld.
Rowdown Fields
Time Bridge Community Centre
ADDINGTON PALACE GOLF COURSE
Addington Palace
Club House
Tennis Cts.
ADDINGTON PARK
Pavilion
Addington Village
Bus Sta.
Applegarth Academy
Castle Hill Academy
Prim. Sch.
GRAVEL HILL A212
Gravel Hill
Gilbert Scott Primary School & Red Gates School
CR2
John Ruskin College
KENT GATE WAY A2022
PARK A2022
Forestdale Prim. Sch.
NEWLANDS WOODS
Addington Well Pumping Sta.
Play. Fld.
FORESTDALE
ADDINGTON COURT GOLF COURSE
Fieldway
North Down
SELSDON
SPRING PARK
FOX HILL
CR0

171
159
172
HAYES
Hayes
HAYES COMMON
CONEY HALL
NASH
NEW ADDINGTON
BR2
BR4
A232
A2022
B251
B265
CROYDON ROAD
HAYES LANE
HAYES HILL
BASTON ROAD
PICKHURST LANE
WEST WICKHAM
Hayes Street Farm
Hayes Prim. Sch.
Playing Field
Bolds Wood
Brook Wood
Hawes Down Jun. & Inf. Schs.
Glebe Sch.
Youth Cen.
Sports Grounds
Sports Ground
Tennis Courts
Hayes Sch.
HAYES GROVE PRIORY HOSP.
Nash College
The Warren Bowl. Grn.
West Wickham Common
Sparrow's Den Playing Fields
Recreation Ground
Coney Hall Rec. Grd.
Court Sch.
The Emmaus Centre
Wickham Court Farm
The Cottages
The Bungalows
Hast Hill
Baston Manor
Keston Court Riding School
Miry Grove
Rouse Farm
Arlington Orchard
Well Wood
Elm Farm
Fox Hill Nursery
Cooper's Wood
Long Shaw
North Pole Farm
Nash Farm
Fuller's Wood
James's Wood
Waytes
Five Oaks
Baldwin Shaw
Bradmanshill Wood
Rushfield Shaw
Broomfieldbank Shaw
Metropolitan Police Dog Training Establishment
Electricity Sub Station
Castlehill Ruffs
Rowdown Wood
Milchden
Gorsewood
Play. Fld.
F
G
H
J
K
1
2
3
4
5
6
7

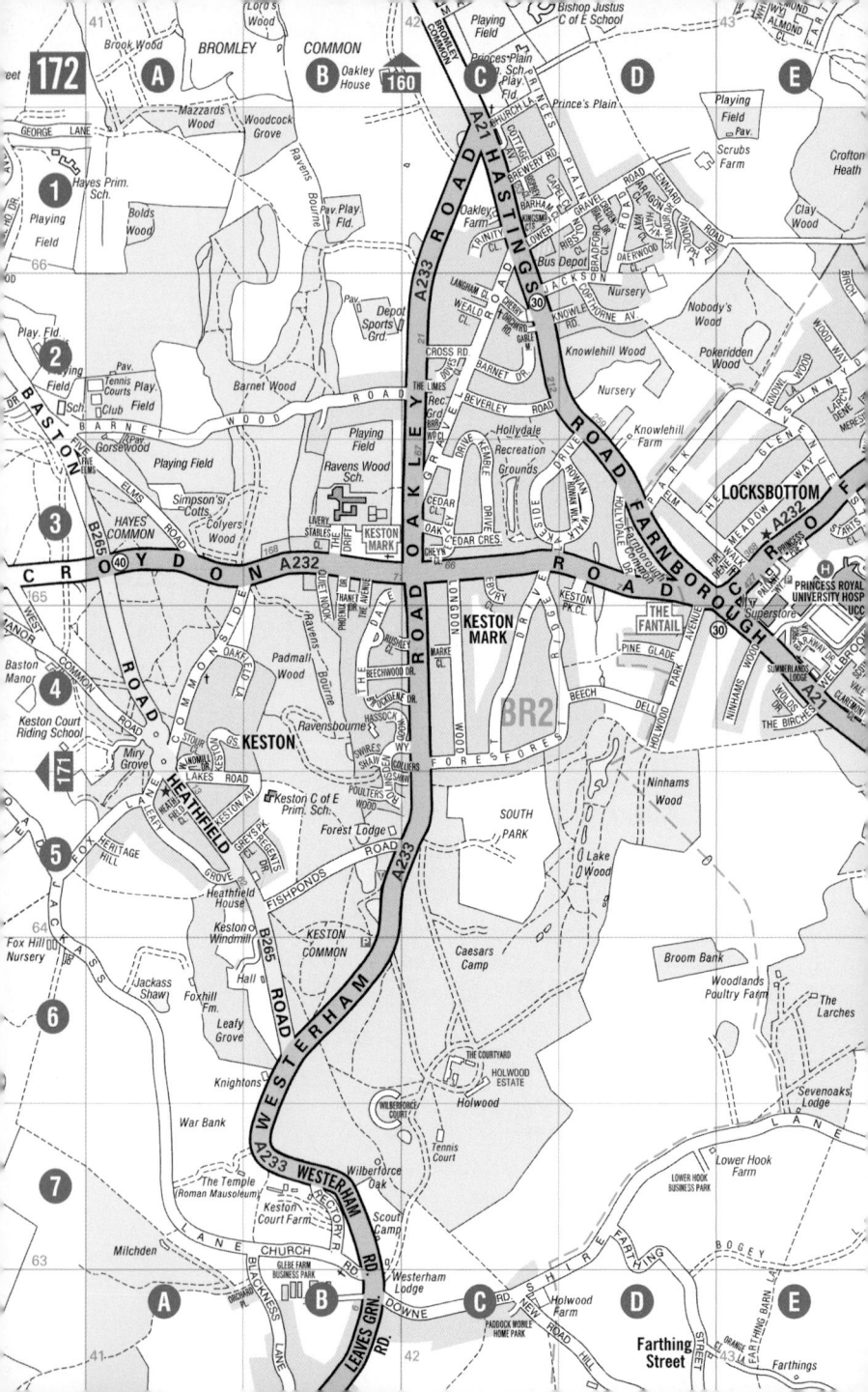
172
171
160
BROMLEY COMMON
Oakley House
Brook Wood
Mazzards Wood
Woodcock Grove
Hayes Prim. Sch.
Playing Field
Bolds Wood
Ravens Bourne
Barnet Wood
Gorsewood
Playing Field
Simpson's Cotts.
Colyers Wood
HAYES COMMON
CROYDON A232
CROYDON ROAD
BASTON
Baston Manor
Keston Court Riding School
Miry Grove
HEATHFIELD
KESTON
Keston C of E Prim. Sch.
Forest Lodge
Padmall Wood
Ravensbourne
Heathfield House
Keston Windmill
Fox Hill Nursery
Jackass Shaw
Foxhill Fm.
Leafy Grove
Knightons
War Bank
The Temple (Roman Mausoleum)
Keston Court Farm
Milchden
GLEBE FARM BUSINESS PARK
KESTON COMMON
Caesars Camp
SOUTH PARK
Lake Wood
Ninhams Wood
Broom Bank
Woodlands Poultry Farm
The Larches
Sevenoaks Lodge
Lower Hook Farm
LOWER HOOK BUSINESS PARK
Holwood Farm
PADDOCK MOBILE HOME PARK
Farthing Street
Farthings
Westerham Lodge
Scout Camp
Wilberforce Oak
WILBERFORCE COURT
Tennis Court
Holwood
HOLWOOD ESTATE
THE COURTYARD
WESTERHAM ROAD A233
OAKLEY ROAD A233
A21 HASTINGS ROAD
FARNBOROUGH ROAD
KESTON MARK
BR2
THE FANTAIL
Ravens Wood Sch.
Playing Field
Depot Sports Grd.
Oakley Farm
Bus Depot
Hollydale Recreation Grounds
Knowlehill Wood
Knowlehill Farm
Nursery
Nobody's Wood
Pokeridden Wood
LOCKSBOTTOM
PRINCESS ROYAL UNIVERSITY HOSP
Superstore
Crofton Heath
Clay Wood
Scrubs Farm
Prince's Plain
Bishop Justus C of E School
Playing Field
Lord's Wood
Farnborough Common

173
161
ORPINGTON
Orpington
CROFTON
FARNBOROUGH
GREEN STREET GREEN
Broom Hill
BR5
BR6
A232
STATION ROAD
A223
A21
B2158
FARNBOROUGH COMMON
HIGH STREET FARNBOROUGH
SEVENOAKS ROAD
SEVENOAKS WAY
HIGH ST.
Darrick Wood Swimming Pool
Darrick Wood School
Darrick Wood Sports Cen.
Darrick Wood Jun. & Inf. Schs.
Bromley Tennis Centre
Newstead Wood School
Tubbenden Prim. Sch.
Orpington Hospital
Hospice
Ontario Centre
Knoll Lawn Tennis Club
Crofton Halls
Crofton Inf. Sch.
Farnborough Prim. Sch.
Bromley Environmental Education Centre at High Elms (BEECHE)
HIGH ELMS COUNTRY PARK (Local Nature Reserve)
HIGH ELMS GOLF COURSE
High Elms Clockhouse
Chelsfield Hall
Glentrammon Rec. Grd.
Sparrow Wood
Recreation Ground
Roundabout Wood
Gumping Common
Newstead Wood
Darrick Wood
Ramus Wood
Cocksett Plantation
Whitelands Wood
Rounds Wood
Church Field Plantation
North End Farm
Blacklands
The Rookery
Club House
Scouts Hall
Club Sports Ground
The Manse
Mill Hill
Woodpiece
The Lodge
Cocksett Hill
Rec. Grd.
1
2
3
4
5
6
7
F
G
H
J
K
44
545
46
63
64
165
66

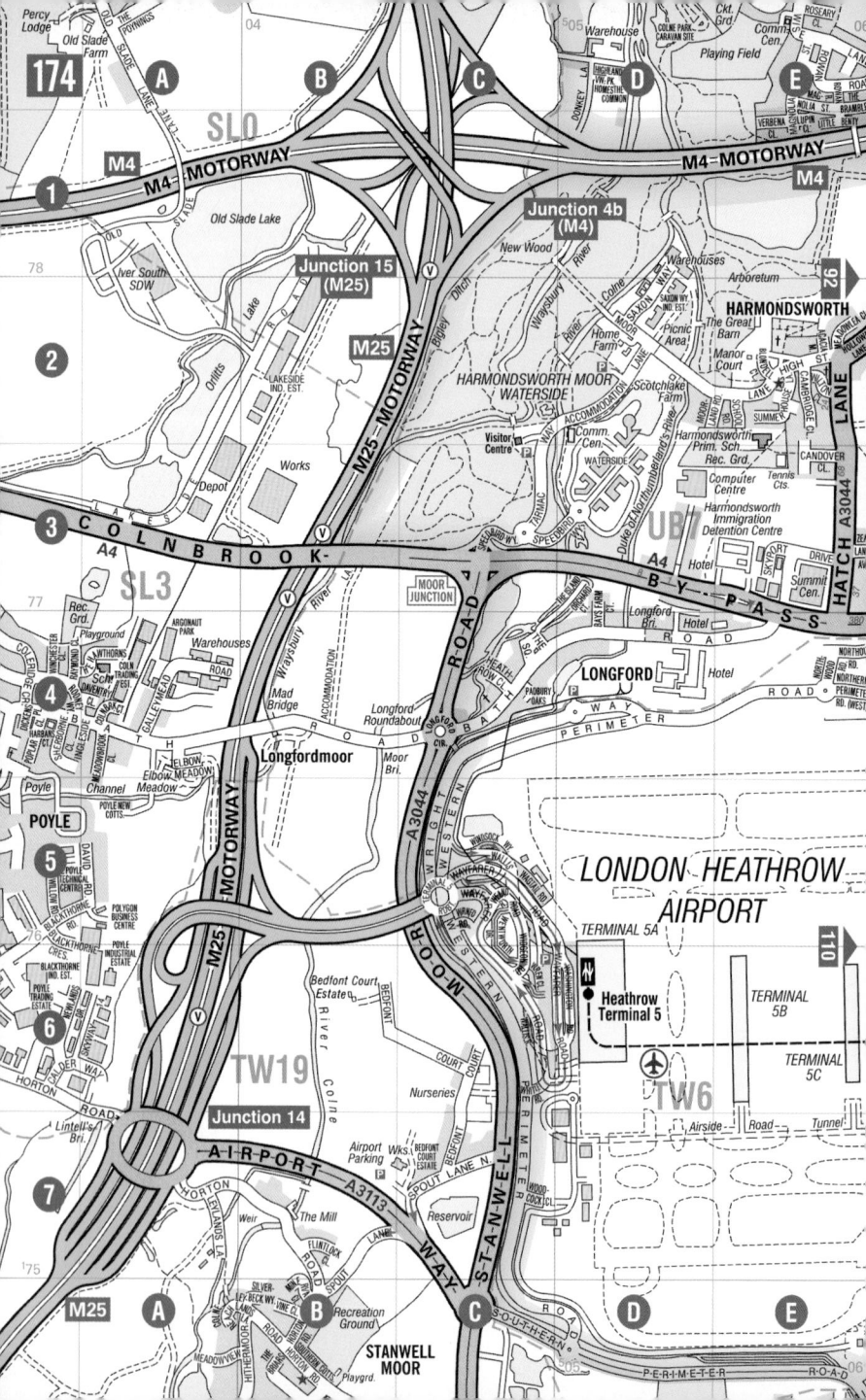

174
92
110
A
B
C
D
E
1
2
3
4
5
6
7
M4 MOTORWAY
M4
M25 MOTORWAY
M25
Junction 4b (M4)
Junction 15 (M25)
Junction 14
COLNBROOK BY-PASS
A4
A3044
A3113
SL0
SL3
UB7
TW19
TW6
Percy Lodge
Old Slade Farm
Old Slade Lake
Iver South SDW
Orlitts Lake
Lakeside Ind. Est.
Works
Depot
New Wood
Warehouses
Arboretum
HARMONDSWORTH
The Great Barn
Manor Court
HARMONDSWORTH MOOR WATERSIDE
Visitor Centre
Comm. Cen.
Harmondsworth Prim. Sch.
Rec. Grd.
Computer Centre
Harmondsworth Immigration Detention Centre
Hotel
Summit Cen.
MOOR JUNCTION
LONGFORD
Longford Roundabout
Longfordmoor
Moor Bri.
Mad Bridge
POYLE
Poyle Channel
Elbow Meadow
LONDON HEATHROW AIRPORT
TERMINAL 5A
TERMINAL 5B
TERMINAL 5C
Heathrow Terminal 5
Airside Road Tunnel
Bedfont Court Estate
Nurseries
Airport Parking
Reservoir
The Mill
Recreation Ground
STANWELL MOOR
AIRPORT WAY
STANWELL MOOR ROAD
PERIMETER ROAD
SOUTHERN PERIMETER ROAD
HATCH LANE

INDEX

Including Streets, Places & Areas, Industrial Estates, Selected Flats & Walkways,
Junction Names & Service Areas and Selected Places of Interest.

HOW TO USE THIS INDEX

1. Each street name is followed by its Postcode District (or, if outside the London Postcodes, by its Locality Abbreviation(s)) then by its map reference;
e.g. **Abbey Av.** HAO: Wemb . . . .2E **78** is in the HAO Postcode District and the Wembley Locality and is to be found in square 2E on page **78**. The page number being shown in bold type.

2. A strict alphabetical order is followed in which Av., Rd., St., etc. (though abbreviated) are read in full and as part of the street name;
e.g. **Alder M.** appears after **Aldermary Rd.** but before **Aldermoor Rd.**

3. Streets and a selection of flats and walkways that cannot be shown on the mapping, appear in the index with the thoroughfare to which they are connected shown in brackets;
e.g. **Abbey Ct.** NW8 . . . .2A **82** (off Abbey Rd.)

4. Addresses that are in more than one part are referred to as not continuous.

5. Places and areas are shown in the index in BLUE TYPE and the map reference is to the actual map square in which the town centre or area is located and not to the place name shown on the map;
e.g. ABBEY WOOD 4C **108**

6. An example of a selected place of interest is Barnet Mus. 4B **20**

7. Junction names and Service Areas are shown in the index in **BOLD CAPITAL TYPE**; e.g. **ANGEL** 2A **84**

8. Map references for entries that appear on large scale pages **4-19** are shown first, with small scale map references shown in brackets; e.g. **Abbey Orchard St.** SW1 . . . .1D **18** (3H **101**)

GENERAL ABBREVIATIONS

All. : Alley	**Cotts.** : Cottages	**Info.** : Information	**Quad.** : Quadrant
App. : Approach	**Ct.** : Court	**Intl.** : International	**Ri.** : Rise
Arc. : Arcade	**Cres.** : Crescent	**Junc.** : Junction	**Rd.** : Road
Ashford TW15	**Cft.** : Croft	**La.** : Lane	**Rdbt.** : Roundabout
Av. : Avenue	**Dpt.** : Depot	**Lit.** : Little	**Shop.** : Shopping
Bk. : Back	**Dr.** : Drive	**Lwr.** : Lower	**Sth.** : South
Blvd. : Boulevard	**E.** : East	**Mnr.** : Manor	**Sq.** : Square
Bri. : Bridge	**Emb.** : Embankment	**Mans.** : Mansions	**Sta.** : Station
B'way. : Broadway	**Ent.** : Enterprise	**Mkt.** : Market	**St.** : Street
Bldg. : Building	**Est.** : Estate	**Mdw.** : Meadow	**Ter.** : Terrace
Bldgs. : Buildings	**Fld.** : Field	**Mdws.** : Meadows	**Twr.** : Tower
Bus. : Business	**Flds.** : Fields	**M.** : Mews	**Trad.** : Trading
Cvn. : Caravan	**Gdn.** : Garden	**Mt.** : Mount	**Up.** : Upper
C'way. : Causeway	**Gdns.** : Gardens	**Mus.** : Museum	**Va.** : Vale
Cen. : Centre	**Gth.** : Garth	**Nth.** : North	**Vw.** : View
Chu. : Church	**Ga.** : Gate	**Pal.** : Palace	**Vs.** : Villas
Chyd. : Churchyard	**Gt.** : Great	**Pde.** : Parade	**Vis.** : Visitors
Circ. : Circle	**Grn.** : Green	**Pk.** : Park	**Wlk.** : Walk
Cir. : Circus	**Gro.** : Grove	**Pas.** : Passage	**W.** : West
Cl. : Close	**Hgts.** : Heights	**Pav.** : Pavilion	**Yd.** : Yard
Coll. : College	**Ho.** : House	**Pl.** : Place	
Comn. : Common	**Ho's.** : Houses	**Pct.** : Precinct	
Cnr. : Corner	**Ind.** : Industrial	**Prom.** : Promenade	
Cott. : Cottage			

LOCALITY ABBREVIATIONS

Addington: BR4,CR0 . . . . .Addtn	**Claygate**: KT10 . . . . .Clay	**Farnborough**: BR5,BR6 . . . . .Farnb	**Keston**: BR2 . . . . .Kes
Arkley: EN5 . . . . .Ark	**Cockfosters**: EN4,EN5 . . . . .Cockf	**Feltham**: TW13-14 . . . . .Felt	**Kew**: TW9 . . . . .Kew
Ashford: TW15 . . . . .Ashf	**Collier Row**: RM5,RM6,RM7 . . . . .Col R	**Greenford**: UB6 . . . . .G'frd	**Kingston upon Thames**: KT1,KT2 . . . . .King T
Barking: IG3,IG11,RM9 . . . . .Bark	**Colnbrook**: SL3 . . . . .Coln	**Hadley Wood**: EN4 . . . . .Had W	**Laleham**: TW18 . . . . .Lale
Barnet: EN4,EN5 . . . . .Barn	**Cowley**: UB8 . . . . .Cowl	**Ham**: TW10 . . . . .Ham	**London Heathrow Airport**: TW6 . . . . .H'row A
Beckenham: BR3 . . . . .Beck	**Cranford**: TW4,TW5,TW6,UB3 . . . . .Cran	**Hampton**: TW12 . . . . .Hamp	**Longford**: TW6,UB7 . . . . .Lford
Beddington: CR0,SM6 . . . . .Bedd	**Crayford**: DA1 . . . . .Cray	**Hampton Hill**: TW12 . . . . .Hamp H	**Loughton**: IG9,IG10 . . . . .Lough
Bedfont: TW14 . . . . .Bedf	**Croydon**: CR0 . . . . .C'don	**Hampton Wick**: KT1,TW11 . . . . .Hamp W	**Mawney**: RM7 . . . . .Mawney
Belvedere: DA7,DA17-18 . . . . .Belv	**Dagenham**: IG11,RM6,RM8,RM9,RM10 . . . . .Dag	**Hanworth**: TW13 . . . . .Hanw	**Mitcham**: CR0,CR4 . . . . .Mitc
Bexley: DA1,DA5,DA15 . . . . .Bexl	**Dartford**: DA1,DA5 . . . . .Dart	**Harefield**: UB9 . . . . .Hare	**Morden**: SM4 . . . . .Mord
Bexleyheath: DA5,DA6-7 . . . . .Bex	**Downe**: BR6 . . . . .Downe	**Harlington**: UB3,UB7 . . . . .Harl	**New Addington**: CR0 . . . . .New Ad
Brentford: TW7,TW8 . . . . .Bford	**East Barnet**: EN4 . . . . .E Barn	**Harmondsworth**: UB7 . . . . .Harm	**New Barnet**: EN5 . . . . .New Bar
Brimsdown: EN3 . . . . .Brim	**Eastcote**: HA4,HA5 . . . . .Eastc	**Harrow**: HA1-2,HA3 . . . . .Harr	**New Malden**: KT3 . . . . .N Mald
Bromley: BR1,BR2 . . . . .Brom	**East Molesey**: KT8,TW12 . . . . .E Mos	**Harrow Weald**: HA3 . . . . .Hrw W	**Northolt**: UB4,UB5 . . . . .N'olt
Buckhurst Hill: IG8,IG9 . . . . .Buck H	**Edgware**: HA8 . . . . .Edg	**Hatch End**: HA5 . . . . .Hat E	**Northwood**: HA6 . . . . .N'wood
Bushey: WD23 . . . . .Bush	**Elstree**: WD6 . . . . .E'tree	**Hayes**: BR2,BR4,UB3,UB4 . . . . .Hayes	**Orpington**: BR5,BR6 . . . . .Orp
Bushy Heath: WD23 . . . . .B Hea	**Enfield**: EN1-2 . . . . .Enf	**Heston**: TW5 . . . . .Hest	**Petts Wood**: BR5,BR6 . . . . .Pet W
Carshalton: CR4,SM5 . . . . .Cars	**Enfield Highway**: EN3 . . . . .Enf H	**Hextable**: BR8 . . . . .Hext	**Pinner**: HA5-6 . . . . .Pinn
Chadwell Heath: RM6,RM7 . . . . .Chad H	**Enfield Lock**: EN3 . . . . .Enf L	**Hillingdon**: UB8,UB8,UB10 . . . . .Hil	**Ponders End**: EN3 . . . . .Pond E
Cheam: SM2-3 . . . . .Cheam	**Enfield Wash**: EN3 . . . . .Enf W	**Hinchley Wood**: KT10 . . . . .Hin W	**Poyle**: SL3 . . . . .Poyle
Chelsfield: BR6 . . . . .Chels	**Epsom**: KT19 . . . . .Eps	**Hounslow**: TW3-4,TW7,TW14 . . . . .Houn	**Pratts Bottom**: BR6 . . . . .Prat B
Chertsey: KT16 . . . . .Chert	**Erith**: DA7-18,DA8,DA17 . . . . .Erith	**Ickenham**: UB10 . . . . .Ick	**Purley**: CR8 . . . . .Purl
Chessington: KT9 . . . . .Chess	**Esher**: KT10 . . . . .Esh	**Ilford**: IG1-2,IG3,IG4-6,IG8,RM6 . . . . .Ilf	**Rainham**: RM9,RM13 . . . . .Rain
Chigwell: IG6-7 . . . . .Chig	**Ewell**: KT17-19 . . . . .Ewe	**Isleworth**: TW1,TW3,TW5,TW7 . . . . .Isle	**Richings Park**: SL0,SL3 . . . . .Rich P
Chislehurst: BR7 . . . . .Chst		**Kenton**: HA3,HA7-9 . . . . .Kenton	**Richmond**: TW9,TW10 . . . . .Rich

Romford: RM1,RM5,RM7 ....Rom	South Croydon: CR2 ....S Croy	Thames Ditton: KT7,KT10 ....T Ditt	West Drayton: UB7 ....W Dray
Ruislip: HA4 ....Ruis	Staines: TW18,TW19 ....Staines	Thornton Heath: CR7 ....Thor H	West Molesey: KT8 ....W Mole
Rush Green: RM7,RM10 ....Rush G	Stanmore: HA3,HA7 ....Stan	Twickenham:	West Wickham: BR4 ....W W'ck
St Mary Cray: BR5,BR6 ....St M Cry	Stanwell: TW6,TW19 ....Stanw	TW1,TW2,TW7,TW13 ....Twick	Weybridge: KT13 ....Weyb
St Pauls Cray: BR5 ....St P	Stanwell Moor: TW19 ....Stanw M	Uxbridge: UB8,UB10 ....Uxb	Whitton: TW2 ....Whitt
Sanderstead: CR2 ....Sande	Stockley Park: UB11 ....Stock P	Waddon: CR0 ....Wadd	Wilmington: DA2 ....Wilm
Selsdon: CR0,CR2 ....Sels	Sunbury: TW16 ....Sun	Wallington: SM5,SM6 ....Wall	Woodford Green:
Shepperton: TW17,TW18 ....Shep	Surbiton: KT1-6,KT10 ....Surb	Walton-on-Thames: KT12 ....Walt T	IG4,IG8,IG9 ....Wfd G
Sidcup: BR5,BR7,DA14,DA15 .....Sidc	Sutton: SM1-2,SM3 ....Sutt	Wealdstone: HA3 ....W'stone	Worcester Park: KT4,SM3 .....Wor Pk
Sipson: UB7 ....Sip	Swanley: BR8,DA14 ....Swan	Welling: DA16 ....Well	Yeading: UB4 ....Yead
Southall: UB1-2 ....S'hall	Teddington: TW1,TW11 ....Tedd	Wembley: HA0,HA9 ....Wemb	Yiewsley: UB7 ....View

2 Temple Place 7A 84
  (off Temple Pl.)
2 Willow Road 3D 18
7/7 Memorial 5G 11 (1E 100)
10 Brock St. NW1 ....3A 6
18 Stafford Terrace
  The Sambourne Family Home
  ....3J 99
  (off Stafford Ter.)
60 St Martins La. WC2 ....2E 12
  (off St Martin's La.)
198 Contemporary Arts and Learning
  ....6B 120
  (off Railton Rd.)
201 Bishopsgate EC2 ....5H 9

A

Aaron Hill Rd. E6 ....5E 88
Abady Ho. SW1 ....3D 18
  (off Page St.)
Abberley M. SW4 ....3F 119
Abbess Cl. E6 ....5C 88
  SW2 ....1B 138
Abbeville M. SW4 ....4H 119
Abbeville Rd. N8 ....5H 47
  SW4 ....6G 119
Abbey Av. HA0: Wemb 2E 78
Abbey Cl. E5 ....4G 67
  HA5: Pinn 3K 39
  SW8 ....1H 119
  UB3: Hayes 1K 93
  UB5: N'olt 3D 76
Abbey Ct. NW8 ....2A 82
  (off Abbey Rd.)
  SE6 ....6C 122
  SE17 ....5C 102
  (off Macleod St.)
  TW12: Hamp 7E 130
Abbey Cres. DA17: Belv 4G 109
Abbeydale Rd. HA0: Wemb 1F 79
Abbey Dr. DA2: Wilm 2K 145
  SW17 ....5E 136
Abbey Est. NW8 ....1K 81
Abbeyfield Cl. CR4: Mitc 2C 154
Abbeyfield Est. SE16 ....4J 103
Abbeyfield Rd. SE16 ....4J 103
  (not continuous)
Abbeyfields Cl. NW10 ....3G 79
Abbey Gdns. BR7: Chst 1E 160
  NW8 ....2A 82
  SE16 ....4G 103
  SW1 ....1E 18
  (off Great College St.)
  TW15: Ashf 5D 128
  W6 ....6G 99
Abbey Gro. SE2 ....4B 108
Abbeyhill Rd. DA15: Sidc 2C 144
Abbey Ho. E15 ....2G 87
  (off Baker's Row)
  NW8 ....1A 4
Abbey Ind. Est. CR4: Mitc 5D 154
  HA0: Wemb 1F 79

Abbey La. BR3: Beck 7C 140
  E15 ....2E 86
  (not continuous)
Abbey La. Commercial Est. E15 ...2G 87
Abbey Leisure Cen. 1G 89
Abbey Life Ct. E16 ....5K 87
Abbey Lodge NW8 ....2D 4
Abbey Mansion M. SE24 ....5B 120
Abbey M. E17 ....5C 50
  TW7: Isle 1B 114
Abbey Mt. DA17: Belv 5F 109
Abbey Orchard St. SW1 ....1D 18 (3H 101)
Abbey Orchard St. Est.
  SW1 ....1D 18 (3H 101)
  (not continuous)
Abbey Pde. SW19 ....7A 136
  (off Merton High St.)
  W5 ....3F 79
Abbey Pk. BR3: Beck 7C 140
Abbey Pk. Ind. Est. IG11: Bark ..2G 89
Abbey Retail Pk. IG11: Bark ...7F 71
Abbey Rd. CR0: C'don 3B 168
  DA7: Bex 4E 126
  DA17: Belv 4D 108
  E15 ....2F 87
  EN1: Enf 5K 23
  IG2: Ilf 5H 53
  IG11: Bark 1F 89
  NW6 ....7K 63
  NW8 ....1A 4 (7K 63)
  NW10 ....1H 79
  SE2 ....4D 108
  SW19 ....7A 136
Abbey Rd. Apartments NW8 ......2A 82
  (off Abbey Rd.)
Abbey Sports Cen. 1G 89
Abbey St. E13 ....4J 87
  SE1 ....7H 15 (3E 102)
  SE16 ....7H 15 (3G 103)
Abbey Ter. SE2 ....4C 108
Abbey Trad. Est. SE26 ....5B 140
Abbey Vw. NW7 ....3G 29
Abbey Wlk. KT8: W Mole 3F 149
Abbey Wharf Ind. Est. IG11: Bark ..3H 89
ABBEY WOOD 4C 108
Abbey Wood Cvn. Club Site SE2 ...4C 108
Abbey Wood Rd. SE2 ....4B 108
Abbot Cl. HA4: Ruis 3B 58
Abbot Ct. SW8 ....7J 101
  (off Hartington Rd.)
Abbot Ho. E14 ....7H 86
  (off Smythe St.)
Abbotsbury NW1 ....7H 65
  (off Camley St.)
Abbotsbury Cl. E15 ....2E 86
  W14 ....2G 99
Abbotsbury Gdns. HA5: Eastc ...7A 40
Abbotsbury Ho. W14 ....2G 99
Abbotsbury M. SE15 ....3J 121
Abbotsbury Rd. BR2: Hayes 2H 171
  SM4: Mord 5K 153
  W14 ....2G 99
Abbots Cl. BR5: Farnb 1G 173
Abbots Ct. W8 ....2K 99
  (off Thackeray St.)
Abbots Dr. HA2: Harr 2E 58
Abbotsford Av. N15 ....4C 48
Abbotsford Gdns. IG8: Wfd G ...7D 36

Abbotsford Rd. IG3: Ilf 2A 72
Abbots Gdns. N2 ....4B 46
Abbots Grn. CR0: Addtn 6K 169
Abbotshade Rd. SE16 ....1K 103
Abbotshall Av. N14 ....3B 32
Abbotshall Rd. SE6 ....1F 141
Abbot's Ho. W14 ....3H 99
  (off St Mary Abbot's Ter.)
Abbotsleigh Cl. SM2: Sutt 7K 165
Abbotsleigh Rd. SW16 ....4G 137
Abbots Mnr. SW1 ....5J 17 (4F 101)
  (not continuous)
Abbots Pk. SW2 ....1A 138
Abbot's Pl. NW6 ....1K 81
Abbot's Rd. E6 ....1B 88
Abbots Rd. HA8: Edg 7D 28
Abbots Ter. N8 ....6J 47
Abbotstone Rd. SW15 ....3E 116
Abbot St. E8 ....6F 67
Abbots Wlk. W8 ....3K 99
Abbots Way BR3: Beck 5A 158
Abbotswell Rd. SE4 ....5B 122
Abbotswood Cl. DA17: Belv 3E 108
Abbotswood Gdns. IG5: Ilf 3D 52
Abbotswood Rd. SE22 ....4E 120
  SW16 ....3H 137
Abbotswood Way UB3: Hayes 1K 93
Abbott Av. SW20 ....1F 153
Abbott Cl. TW12: Hamp 6C 130
  UB5: N'olt 6D 58
Abbott Rd. E14 ....5E 86
  (not continuous)
Abbotts Cl. N1 ....6C 66
  RM7: Mawney 3H 55
  SE28 ....7C 90
Abbotts Cres. E4 ....4A 36
  EN2: Enf 2G 23
Abbotts Dr. HA0: Wemb 2B 60
Abbotts Ho. SW1 ....6C 18
  (off Aylesford St.)
Abbotts Mead TW10: Ham 4D 132
Abbotts Pk. Rd. E10 ....7E 50
Abbotts Rd. CR4: Mitc 4G 155
  EN5: New Bar 4E 20
  SM3: Cheam 4G 165
  UB1: S'hall 1C 94
Abbott's Wlk. DA7: Bex 7D 108
Abbott's Wharf E14 ....6C 86
  (off Stainsby Rd.)
Abbotts Wharf Moorings
  E14 ....6C 86
  (off Stainsby Rd.)
Abchurch La. EC4 ......2F 15 (7D 84)
  (not continuous)
Abchurch Yd. EC4 ......2E 14 (7D 84)
Abdale Rd. W12 ....1D 98
Abelard Pl. W5 ....3D 96
Abel Ho. SE11 ....7K 19
  (off Kennington Rd.)
Abenglen Ind. Est.
  UB3: Hayes 2F 93
Aberavon Rd. E3 ....3A 86
Abercairn Rd. SW16 ....7G 137
Aberconway Rd. SM4: Mord 4K 153
Abercorn Cl. NW7 ....7B 30
  NW8 ....3A 82

Abercorn Commercial Cen.
  HA0: Wemb 1D 78
Abercorn Cotts. NW8 ....3A 82
  (off Abercorn Pl.)
Abercorn Cres. HA2: Harr 1F 59
Abercorn Dell WD23: B Hea 2B 26
Abercorn Gdns. HA3: Kenton ...7D 42
  RM6: Chad H 6B 54
Abercorn Gro. HA4: Ruis 4F 39
Abercorn Mans. NW8 ....2A 82
  (off Abercorn Pl.)
Abercorn M. TW10: Rich 4F 115
Abercorn Pl. NW8 ....3A 82
Abercorn Rd. HA7: Stan 7H 27
  NW7 ....7B 30
Abercorn Wlk. NW8 ....3A 82
Abercorn Way SE1 ....5G 103
Abercrombie Dr. EN1: Enf 1B 24
Abercrombie Rd. E20 ....5D 68
Abercrombie St. SW11 ....2C 118
Aberdale Cl. SE16 ....2K 103
  (off Garter Way)
Aberdare Cl. BR4: W W'ck 2E 170
Aberdare Gdns. NW6 ....7K 63
  NW7 ....7A 30
Aberdare Rd. EN3: Pond E 4D 24
Aberdeen Cotts. HA7: Stan 7H 27
Aberdeen Ct. W9 ....4A 4
  (off Maida Vale)
Aberdeen La. N5 ....5C 66
Aberdeen Mans. WC1 ....3E 6
  (off Kenton St.)
Aberdeen Pde. N18 ....5C 34
  (off Aberdeen Rd.)
Aberdeen Pk. N5 ....5C 66
Aberdeen Pk. M. N5 ......4A 4 (4B 82)
Aberdeen Pl. NW8 ....4A 4 (4B 82)
Aberdeen Rd. CR0: C'don 4C 168
  HA3: W'stone 2K 41
  N5 ....4C 66
  N18 ....5B 34
  (not continuous)
  NW10 ....5B 62
Aberdeen Sq. E14 ....1B 104
Aberdeen Ter. SE3 ....2F 123
Aberdeen Wharf E1 ....1H 103
  (off Wapping High St.)
Aberdour Rd. IG3: Ilf 3B 72
Aberdour St. SE1 ....4E 102
Aberfeldy Ho. SE5 ....7B 102
  (not continuous)
Aberfeldy St. E14 ....5E 86
  (not continuous)
Aberford Gdns. SE18 ....1C 124
Aberfoyle Rd. SW16 ....6H 137
Abergeldie Rd. SE12 ....6K 123
Abernethy Ho. EC1 ....5C 84
  (off Bartholomew Cl.)
Abernethy Rd. SE13 ....4G 123
Abersham Rd. E8 ....5F 67
Abery St. SE18 ....4J 107
Ability Pl. E14 ....2D 104
Ability Plaza E8 ....7F 67
  (off Arbutus St.)
Ability Towers EC1 ....1C 8
  (off Macclesfield Rd.)
Abingdon W14 ....4H 99
  (off Kensington Village)

Abingdon Cl. KT4: Wor Pk 3D **164**	
NW1 ....6H **65**	
SE1 ....4F **103**	
(off Bushwood Dr.)	
SW19 ....6A **136**	
UB10: Hil 1B **74**	
Abingdon Ct. *W8* 3J **99**	
(off Abingdon Vs.)	
Abingdon Gdns. W8 ....3J **99**	
Abingdon Ho. BR1: Brom 7K **141**	
E2 ....3J **9**	
(off Boundary St.)	
Abingdon Lodge BR2: Brom 2H **159**	
(off Beckenham La.)	
W8 ....3J **99**	
Abingdon Mans. *W8* 3J **99**	
(off Pater St.)	
Abingdon Rd. N3 ....2A **46**	
SW16 ....2J **155**	
W8 ....3J **99**	
Abingdon St. SW1 ....1E **18** (3J **101**)	
Abingdon Vs. W8 ....3J **99**	
Abinger Cl. BR1: Brom 3C **160**	
CR0: New Ad 6E **170**	
IG11: Bark 4A **72**	
SM6: Wall 5J **167**	
Abinger Ct. *SM6: Wall* 5J **167**	
(off Abinger Cl.)	
W5 ....7C **78**	
Abinger Gdns. TW7: Isle 3J **113**	
Abinger Gro. SE8 ....6B **104**	
Abinger Ho. *SE1* 7E **14**	
(off Gt. Dover St.)	
Abinger M. W9 ....4J **81**	
Abinger Rd. W4 ....3A **98**	
Ablett St. SE16 ....5J **103**	
Abney Gdns. N16 ....2F **67**	
Abney Pk. Cemetery	
(Local Nature Reserve) 2E **66**	
Abney Pk. Ter. *N16* 2F **67**	
(off Cazenove St.)	
Aborfield NW5 ....5G **65**	
Aboyne Dr. SW20 ....2C **152**	
Aboyne Rd. NW10 ....3A **62**	
SW17 ....3B **136**	
Abraham Fisher Ho. E12 ....5E **70**	
Abyssinia Cl. SW11 ....4C **118**	
Abyssinia Ct. N8 ....5K **47**	
Abyssinia Rd. SW11 ....4C **118**	
Acacia Av. HA4: Ruis 1J **57**	
HA9: Wemb 5E **60**	
N17 ....7J **33**	
TW8: Bford 7B **96**	
TW17: Shep 5C **146**	
UB3: Hayes 6H **75**	
UB7: Yiew 7B **74**	
Acacia Bus. Cen. E11 ....3G **69**	
Acacia Cl. BR5: Pet W 5H **161**	
HA7: Stan 6D **26**	
SE8 ....4A **104**	
SE20 ....2G **157**	
Acacia Ct. HA1: Harr 5F **41**	
Acacia Dr. SM3: Sutt 1H **165**	
Acacia Gdns. BR4: W W'ck 2E **170**	
NW8 ....2B **82**	
Acacia Gro. KT3: N Mald 3K **151**	
SE21 ....2D **138**	
Acacia Ho. *N22* 1A **48**	
(off Douglas Rd.)	
Acacia M. UB7: Harm 2E **174**	
Acacia Pl. NW8 ....2B **82**	
Acacia Rd. BR3: Beck 3B **158**	
CR4: Mitc 3E **154**	
E11 ....2G **69**	
E17 ....6A **50**	
EN2: Enf 1J **23**	
N22 ....1A **48**	
NW8 ....2B **82**	
SW16 ....1J **155**	
TW12: Hamp 6E **130**	
W3 ....7J **79**	

Acacias, The EN4: E Barn 5G **21**	
Acacia Wlk. *SW10* 7A **100**	
(off Tadema Rd.)	
Acacia Way DA15: Sidc 1K **143**	
Academia Way N17 ....6K **33**	
Academy, The	
Middlesex County Cricket Club	
........2K **45**	
Academy, The SW8 ....7G **19** (6K **101**)	
Academy Apartments E8 ....5H **67**	
(off Dalston La.)	
Academy Bldgs. *N1* 1G **9**	
(off Fanshaw St.)	
Academy Ct. DA5: Bexl 2K **145**	
(off Beaconsfield Rd.)	
E2 ....3J **85**	
(off Kirkwall Pl.)	
NW6 ....1J **81**	
RM8: Dag 4A **72**	
Academy Gdns.	
CR0: C'don 1F **169**	
UB5: N'olt 2B **76**	
W8 ....2J **99**	
Academy Ho. *E3* 5D **86**	
(off Violet Rd.)	
Academy Pl. SE18 ....1D **124**	
TW7: Isle 1J **113**	
Academy Rd. SE18 ....1D **124**	
Academy Way E17 ....1C **50**	
RM8: Dag 4A **72**	
Acanthus Dr. SE1 ....5G **103**	
Acanthus Rd. SW11 ....3E **118**	
Accommodation La.	
UB7: Harm 2D **174**	
UB7: Lford 4B **174**	
Accommodation Rd.	
E4 ....3A **36**	
(off Ashwood Rd.)	
KT17: Ewe 5C **164**	
NW11 ....1H **63**	
AC Court KT7: T Ditt 6A **150**	
Ace Pde. KT9: Chess 3E **162**	
Acer Av. UB4: Yead 5C **76**	
Acer Ct. EN3: Enf H 3F **25**	
(off Enstone Rd.)	
Acer Rd. E8 ....7F **67**	
Acers BR7: Chst 7C **142**	
Aces Ct. TW3: Houn 2G **113**	
Acfold Rd. SW6 ....1K **117**	
Achilles Cl. SE1 ....5G **103**	
Achilles Ho. *E2* 2H **85**	
(off Old Bethnal Grn. Rd.)	
Achilles Rd. NW6 ....5J **63**	
Achilles Statue 5H **11** (1E **100**)	
Achilles St. SE14 ....7A **104**	
Achilles Way W1 ....5H **11** (1E **100**)	
Acklam Rd. W10 ....5G **81**	
(not continuous)	
Acklington Dr. NW9 ....1A **44**	
Ackmar Rd. SW6 ....1J **117**	
Ackroyd Dr. E3 ....5B **86**	
Ackroyd Rd. SE23 ....7K **121**	
Acland Cl. SE18 ....7H **107**	
Acland Cres. SE5 ....3D **120**	
Acland Ho. SW9 ....1K **119**	
Acland Rd. NW2 ....6D **62**	
Acle Cl. IG6: Ilf 1F **53**	
Acme Studios E14 ....5E **86**	
(Gillender St.)	
E14 ....5E **86**	
(off Leven Rd.)	
Acock Gro. UB5: N'olt 4F **59**	
Acol Cl. NW6 ....7J **63**	
Acol Cres. HA4: Ruis 5K **57**	
Acol Rd. NW6 ....7J **63**	
Aconbury Rd. RM9: Dag 1B **90**	
Acorn Cl. BR7: Chst 5G **143**	
E4 ....5J **35**	
EN2: Enf 1G **23**	
HA7: Stan 7G **27**	
TW12: Hamp 6F **131**	

Acorn Ct. E3 ....2C **86**	
(off Morville St.)	
E6 ....7C **70**	
IG2: Ilf 6J **53**	
Acorn Gdns. SE19 ....1F **157**	
W3 ....5K **79**	
Acorn Gro. HA4: Ruis 4H **57**	
UB3: Harl 7H **93**	
Acorn Pde. SE15 ....7H **103**	
Acorn Production Cen. N7 ....7J **65**	
Acorn Wlk. SE16 ....1A **104**	
Acorn Way BR3: Beck 5E **158**	
BR6: Farnb 4F **173**	
SE23 ....3K **139**	
Acqua Ho. TW9: Kew 7H **97**	
Acre Dr. SE22 ....4G **121**	
Acrefield Ho. *NW4* 4F **45**	
(off Belle Vue Est.)	
Acre La. SM5: Cars 4E **166**	
SM6: Wall 4E **166**	
SW2 ....4J **119**	
Acre Path *UB5: N'olt* 6C **58**	
(off Arnold Rd.)	
Acre Rd. KT2: King T 1E **150**	
RM10: Dag 7H **73**	
SW19 ....6B **136**	
Acre Way HA6: Nwood 1H **39**	
Acris St. SW18 ....5A **118**	
Acropolis Ho. *KT1: King T* 3F **151**	
(off Winery La.)	
ACTON 1J **97**	
Acton Apartments *N1* 1D **84**	
(off Branch Pl.)	
Acton Central Ind. Est. W3 ....1H **97**	
Acton Cl. N9 ....2B **34**	
ACTON GREEN 3J **97**	
Acton Hill M. W3 ....1H **97**	
Acton Ho. *E8* 1F **85**	
(off Lee St.)	
W3 ....6J **79**	
Acton La. NW10 ....3J **79**	
W3 ....2J **97**	
W4 ....4J **97**	
(not continuous)	
Acton M. E8 ....1F **85**	
Acton Pk. Est. W3 ....2K **97**	
Acton St. WC1 ....2G **7** (3K **83**)	
Acton Swimming Baths 1J **97**	
(off Salisbury St.)	
Acton Va. Ind. Pk. W3 ....2B **98**	
Acuba Rd. SW18 ....2K **135**	
Acworth Cl. N9 ....7D **24**	
Acworth Ho. *SE18* 6F **107**	
(off Barnfield Rd.)	
Ada Cl. N11 ....3J **31**	
Ada Ct. *N1* 1C **84**	
(off Packington St.)	
W9 ....2A **4** (3A **82**)	
Ada Gdns. E14 ....6F **87**	
E15 ....1H **87**	
Adagio Point *SE8* 6D **104**	
(off Copperas St.)	
Ada Ho. *E2* 1G **85**	
(off Ada Pl.)	
Adair Cl. SE25 ....3H **157**	
Adair Ho. SW3 ....7D **16**	
Adair Rd. W10 ....4G **81**	
Adair Twr. *W10* 4G **81**	
(off Appleford Rd.)	
Ada Kennedy Ct. SE10 ....7E **104**	
(off Greenwich Sth. St.)	
Ada Lewis Ho. HA9: Wemb 4F **61**	
Adam & Eve Ct. W1 ....7B **6**	
Adam & Eve M. W8 ....3J **99**	
Ada Maria Cl. *E1* 5A **86**	
(off James Voller Way)	
Adam Cl. NW7 ....6A **30**	
SE6 ....4B **140**	
Adam Ct. SE11 ....4K **19**	
SW7 ....4A **100**	
(off Gloucester Rd.)	

Adamfields NW3 ....7B **64**	
(off Adamson Rd.)	
Adam Rd. E4 ....6G **35**	
Adams Bri. Bus. Cen. HA9: Wemb 5H **61**	
Adams Cl. KT5: Surb 6F **151**	
N3 ....7D **30**	
NW9 ....2H **61**	
RM5: Col R 1J **55**	
Adams Ct. E17 ....6A **50**	
EC2 ....7F **9** (6E **84**)	
Adams Gdns. Est. SE16 ....2J **103**	
Adams Ho. *E14* 6F **87**	
(off Aberfeldy St.)	
Adams M. N22 ....7E **32**	
SW17 ....2D **136**	
Adamson Cl. N2 ....3C **46**	
Adamson Rd. E16 ....6J **87**	
NW3 ....7B **64**	
Adamson Way BR3: Beck 5E **158**	
Adams Pl. *E14* 1D **104**	
(off The Nth. Colonnade)	
N7 ....5K **65**	
Adams Quarter TW8: Bford 7C **96**	
Adamsrill Cl. EN1: Enf 6J **23**	
Adamsrill Rd. SE26 ....4K **139**	
Adams Rd. BR3: Beck 5A **158**	
N17 ....2D **48**	
Adam's Row W1 ....3H **11** (7E **82**)	
Adams Sq. DA6: Bex 3E **126**	
Adams Ter. *E3* 3C **86**	
(off Rainhill Way)	
Adams Wlk. KT1: King T 2E **150**	
Adams Way CR0: C'don 6F **157**	
SE25 ....5H **157**	
Adam Wlk. SW6 ....7E **98**	
Adana SE13 ....2E **122**	
Ada Pl. E2 ....1G **85**	
Adare Wlk. SW16 ....3K **137**	
Ada Rd. HA0: Wemb 3D **60**	
SE5 ....7E **102**	
Adastral Ho. *WC1* 5G **7**	
(off Harpur St.)	
Adastra Way SM6: Wall 6J **167**	
Ada St. E8 ....1H **85**	
Adcock Wlk. BR6: Orp 4K **173**	
Adderley Gdns. SE9 ....4E **142**	
Adderley Gro. SW11 ....5E **118**	
Adderley Rd. HA3: W'stone 1K **41**	
Adderley St. E14 ....6E **86**	
Addey Ho. SE8 ....7B **104**	
ADDINGTON 5C **170**	
Addington Ct. SW14 ....3K **115**	
Addington Court Golf Course 7C **170**	
Addington Dr. N12 ....6G **31**	
Addington Golf Course, The 4B **170**	
Addington Gro. SE26 ....4A **140**	
Addington Ho. *SW9* 2K **119**	
(off Stockwell Rd.)	
Addington Lofts SE5 ....7C **102**	
(off Bethwin Rd.)	
Addington Palace Golf Course 6A **170**	
Addington Rd. BR4: W W'ck 4E **170**	
CR0: C'don 1A **168**	
CR2: Sande, Sels 7K **169**	
E3 ....3C **86**	
E16 ....4G **87**	
N4 ....6A **48**	
Addington Sq. SE5 ....6D **102**	
(not continuous)	
Addington St. SE1 ....7H **13** (2K **101**)	
Addington Village Rd. CR0: Addtn 6B **170**	
(not continuous)	
Addis Cl. EN3: Enf H 1E **24**	
ADDISCOMBE 1G **169**	
Addiscombe Av. CR0: C'don 1G **169**	
Addiscombe Cl. HA3: Kenton 5C **42**	
Addiscombe Ct. Rd. CR0: C'don 1E **168**	
Addiscombe Gro. CR0: C'don 2E **168**	
Addiscombe Rd. CR0: C'don 2D **168**	
(not continuous)	

Addis Ho.—Aitman Dr.

Addis Ho. *E1* 5J **85**
(off Lindley St.)
Addisland Ct. *W14* 2G **99**
(off Holland Vs. Rd.)
Addison Av. N14 6A **22**
TW3: Houn 1G **113**
W11 1G **99**
Addison Bri. Pl. W14 4H **99**
Addison Cl. BR5: Pet W 6G **161**
HA6: Nwood 1J **39**
Addison Ct. *NW6* 1J **81**
(off Brondesbury Rd.)
Addison Cres. W14 3G **99**
(not continuous)
Addison Dr. SE12 5K **123**
Addison Gdns. KT5: Surb 4F **151**
W14 3F **99**
Addison Gro. W4 3A **98**
Addison Ho. NW8 1A **4**
Addison Pk. Mans. *W14* 3F **99**
(off Richmond Way)
Addison Pl. SE25 4G **157**
UB1: S'hall 7E **76**
W11 1G **99**
Addison Rd. BR2: Brom 5A **160**
E11 6J **51**
E17 5D **50**
EN3: Enf H 1D **24**
IG6: Ilf 1G **53**
SE25 4G **157**
TW11: Tedd 6B **132**
W14 2G **99**
Addisons Cl. CR0: C'don 2B **170**
Addison Ter. *W4* 4J **97**
(off Chiswick Rd.)
Addison Way HA6: Nwood 1H **39**
NW11 4H **45**
UB3: Hayes 6J **75**
Addle Hill EC4 1B **14** (6B **84**)
Addlestone Ho. *W10* 5E **80**
(off Sutton Way)
Addle St. EC2 7D **8** (6C **84**)
Addy Ho. SE16 4J **103**
Adecroft Way KT8: W Mole 3G **149**
Adela Av. KT3: N Mald 5D **152**
Adela Ho. *W6* 5E **98**
(off Queen Caroline St.)
Adelaide Av. SE4 4B **122**
Adelaide Cl. EN1: Enf 1K **23**
HA7: Stan 4F **27**
SW9 4A **120**
Adelaide Ct. BR3: Beck 7C **140**
E9 5A **68**
(off Kenworthy Rd.)
NW8 2A **82**
(off Abbey Rd.)
W7 2K **95**
Adelaide Gdns. RM6: Chad H 5E **54**
Adelaide Gro. W12 1C **98**
Adelaide Ho. E15 2H **87**
E17 2B **50**
SE5 2E **120**
W11 6H **81**
(off Portobello Rd.)
Adelaide Rd. BR7: Chst 5F **143**
E10 3D **68**
IG1: Ilf 2F **71**
KT6: Surb 5E **150**
NW3 7B **64**
SW18 5J **117**
TW5: Hest 1C **112**
TW9: Rich 4F **115**
TW11: Tedd 6K **131**
TW15: Ashf 5A **128**
UB2: S'hall 4C **94**
W13 1A **96**
Adelaide St. WC2 3E **12** (7J **83**)
(not continuous)
Adelaide Ter. TW8: Bford 5D **96**
Adela St. W10 4G **81**
Adelina Gro. E1 5J **85**
Adelina M. SW12 1H **137**
Adelina Yd. *E1* 5J **85**
(off Adelina Gro.)
Adeline Pl. WC1 6D **6** (5H **83**)
Adeliza Cl. IG11: Bark 7G **71**
Adelphi Ct. *E8* 7F **67**
(off Celandine Dr.)
SE16 2K **103**
(off Garter Way)
W4 6K **97**
Adelphi Cres.
UB4: Hayes 3G **75**
Adelphi Ter. WC2 3F **13** (7J **83**)
Adelphi Theatre 3F 13
(off Strand)
Adelphi Way UB4: Hayes 3H **75**
Adeney Cl. W6 6F **99**
Aden Gro. N16 4D **66**
Adenmore Rd. SE6 7C **122**
Aden Rd. EN3: Brim 4F **25**
IG1: Ilf 7G **53**
Aden Ter. N16 4D **66**
Adeyfield Ho. *EC1* 2F **9**
(off Cranwood St.)
Adie Rd. W6 3E **98**
Adine Rd. E13 4K **87**
Adler Ind. Est.
UB3: Hayes 2F **93**
Adler St. E1 6G **85**
Adley St. E5 5A **68**
Adlington Cl. N18 5J **33**
Admaston Rd. SE18 7G **107**
Admiral Ct. IG11: Bark 2B **90**
SE5 1E **120**
(off Havil St.)
SM5: Cars 1C **166**
SW10 1A **118**
(off Admiral Sq.)
W1 6G **5**
(off Blandford St.)
Admiral Ho. *SW1* 3B **18**
(off Willow Pl.)
TW11: Tedd 4A **132**
Admiral Hyson Ind. Est. SE16 5H **103**
Admiral M. SW19 7A **136**
W10 4F **81**
Admiral Pl. N8 4B **48**
SE16 1A **104**
Admirals Cl. E18 4K **51**
Admirals Ct. *E6* 6F **89**
(off Trader Rd.)
SE1 5J **15**
(off Horselydown La.)
Admiral Seymour Rd. SE9 4D **124**
Admiral's Ga. SE10 1D **122**
Admiral Sq. SW10 1A **118**
Admiral's Twr. *SE10* 6D **104**
(off Dowells St.)
Admiral St. SE8 2C **122**
Admirals Wlk. NW3 3A **64**
Admirals Way E14 2C **104**
Admiralty & Commercial Court
7J 7 (6A 84)
Admiralty Arch 4D 12 (1H 101)
Admiralty Bldg. *KT2: King T* 1D **150**
(off Down Hall Rd.)
Admiralty Cl. SE8 7C **104**
UB7: W Dray 2A **92**
Admiralty Rd. TW11: Tedd 6K **131**
Admiralty Way
TW11: Tedd 6K **131**
Admiral Wlk. W9 5J **81**
Adolf St. SE6 4D **140**
Adolphus Rd. N4 2B **66**
Adolphus St. SE8 7B **104**
Adomar Rd. RM8: Dag 3E **72**
Adpar St. W2 5A **4** (5B **82**)
Adrian Av. NW2 1D **62**
Adrian Boult Ho. *E2* 3H **85**
(off Mansford St.)
Adrian Cl. EN5: Barn 6A **20**
Adrian Ho. *E15* 7F **69**
(off Jupp Rd.)
N1 1K **83**
(off Barnsbury Est.)
SW8 7J **101**
(off Wyvil Rd.)
Adrian M. SW10 6K **99**
Adriatic Apartments *E16* 7J **87**
(off Western Gateway)
Adriatic Bldg. *E14* 7A **86**
(off Horseferry Rd.)
Adriatic Ho. *E1* 4K **85**
(off Ernest St.)
Adrienne Av. UB1: S'hall 4D **76**
Adrienne Bus. Cen. UB1: S'hall 3D **76**
Adron Ho. *SE16* 4J **103**
(off Millender Wlk.)
Adstock Ho. *N1* 7B **66**
(off The Sutton Est.)
Advance Rd. SE27 4C **138**
Adventure Kingdom 2K 159
(off Stockwell Cl.)
Adventurers Ct. *E14* 7F **87**
(off Newport Av.)
Advent Way N18 5D **34**
Adys Lawn NW2 6D **62**
Ady's Rd. SE15 3F **121**
Aegean Apartments *E16* 7J **87**
(off Western Gateway)
Aegon Ho. *E14* 3D **104**
(off Lanark Sq.)
Aerodrome Rd. NW4 2B **44**
NW9 2B **44**
Aerodrome Way TW5: Hest 6A **94**
Aeroville NW9 2A **44**
AFC Wimbledon 3G 151
Affleck St. N1 1G **7** (2K **83**)
Afghan Rd. SW11 2C **118**
Afsil Ho. *EC1* 6K **7**
(off Viaduct Bldgs.)
Aftab Ter. *E1* 4H **85**
(off Tent St.)
Agamemnon Rd. NW6 4H **63**
Agar Cl. KT6: Surb 2F **163**
Agar Gro. NW1 7G **65**
Agar Gro. Est. NW1 7H **65**
Agar Ho. *KT1: King T* 3E **150**
(off Denmark Rd.)
Agar Pl. NW1 7G **65**
Agar St. WC2 3E **12** (7J **83**)
Agate Cl. E16 6B **88**
NW10 3G **79**
Agate Rd. W6 3E **98**
Agatha Cl. E1 1H **103**
Agaton Path SE9 2G **143**
Agaton Rd. SE9 2G **143**
Agave Rd. NW2 4E **62**
Agdon St. EC1 3A **8** (4B **84**)
Ager Av. RM8: Dag 1D **72**
Agincourt Rd. NW3 4D **64**
Agnes Av. IG1: Ilf 4E **70**
Agnes Cl. E6 7E **88**
Agnesfield Cl. N12 6H **31**
Agnes Gdns. RM8: Dag 4D **72**
Agnes George Wlk. E16 1B **106**
Agnes Ho. *W11* 7F **81**
(off St Ann's Rd.)
Agnes Rd. W3 1B **98**
Agnes St. E14 6B **86**
Agnew Rd. SE23 7K **121**
Agricola Ct. *E3* 1B **86**
(off Parnell Rd.)
Agricola Pl. EN1: Enf 5A **24**
Ahoy Cen., The *SE8* 5C **104**
(off Stretton Mans.)
Aidan Cl. RM8: Dag 4E **72**
Aigburth Mans. *SW9* 7A **102**
(off Mowll St.)
Ailantus Ct. HA8: Edg 5A **28**
Aileen Wlk. E15 7H **69**
Ailsa Av. TW1: Twick 5A **114**
Ailsa Ho. *E16* 7E **88**
(off University Way)
Ailsa Rd. TW1: Twick 5B **114**
Ailsa St. E14 5E **86**
Ailsa Wlk. *E14* 2C **104**
(off Alpha Gro.)
Ainger M. *NW3* 7D **64**
(off Ainger Rd.)
Ainger Rd. NW3 7D **64**
Ainsdale *NW1* 1A **6**
(off Harrington St.)
Ainsdale Cl. BR6: Orp 1H **173**
Ainsdale Cres. HA5: Pinn 3E **40**
Ainsdale Dr. SE1 5G **103**
Ainsdale Rd. W5 4D **78**
Ainsley Av. RM7: Rom 6H **55**
Ainsley Cl. N9 1K **33**
Ainsley St. E2 3H **85**
Ainslie Ct. HA0: Wemb 2E **78**
Ainslie Wlk. SW12 7F **119**
Ainslie Wood Cres. E4 5J **35**
Ainslie Wood Gdns. E4 4J **35**
Ainslie Wood Nature Reserve 5J 35
Ainslie Wood Rd. E4 5H **35**
Ainsty Est. SE16 2K **103**
Ainsty St. SE16 2J **103**
Ainsworth Cl. NW2 3C **62**
SE15 2E **120**
Ainsworth Ct. *NW10* 3D **80**
(off Plough Cl.)
Ainsworth Ho. *NW8* 1K **81**
(off Ainsworth Way)
W10 3G **81**
(off Kilburn La.)
Ainsworth Rd. CR0: C'don 1B **168**
E9 7J **67**
Ainsworth Way NW8 1A **82**
Aintree Av. E6 1C **88**
Aintree Cl. UB8: Hil 6D **74**
Aintree Cres. IG6: Ilf 2G **53**
Aintree Est. SW6 7G **99**
Aintree Rd. UB6: G'frd 2B **78**
Aintree St. SW6 7G **99**
Airbourne Ho. *SM6: Wall* 4G **167**
(off Maldon Rd.)
Air Call Bus. Cen. NW9 3K **43**
Airco Cl. NW9 3K **43**
Aird Ho. *SE1* 3C **102**
(off Rockingham St.)
Airdrie Cl. N1 7K **65**
UB4: Yead 5C **76**
Airedale Av. W4 4B **98**
Airedale Av. Sth. W4 5B **98**
Airedale Rd. SW12 7D **118**
W5 3C **96**
Airedale Wlk. *E15* 7G **69**
(off Maiden Rd.)
Airlie Gdns. IG1: Ilf 1F **71**
W8 1J **99**
Airlinks Golf Course 5A 94
Air Links Ind. Est. TW13: Hanw 3C **130**
Airlinks Ind. Est. TW5: Cran 5A **94**
Air Pk. Way TW13: Felt 2K **129**
Airport Bowl 1G 111
Airport Ga. Bus. Cen. UB7: Sip 7B **92**
Airport Way TW19: Stanw M 7A **174**
Air Sea M. TW2: Twick 2H **131**
Air St. W1 3B **12** (7G **83**)
Airthrie Rd. IG3: Ilf 2B **72**
Aisgill Av. W14 5H **99**
(not continuous)
Aisher Rd. SE28 7C **90**
Aislibie Rd. SE12 4G **123**
Aiten Pl. W6 4C **98**
Aithan Ho. *E14* 6B **86**
(off Copenhagen Pl.)
Aitken Cl. CR4: Mitc 7D **154**
E8 1G **85**
HA4: Eastc 6J **39**
Aitken Rd. SE6 2D **140**
Aitman Dr. TW8: Bford 5G **97**

Aitons Ho.—Alcester Ct.

Aitons Ho. TW8: Bford .5E 96
Aits Vw. KT8: W Mole .3F 149
Ajax Av. NW9 .3A 44
Ajax Ho. E2 .2H 85
(off Old Bethnal Grn. Rd.)
Ajax Rd. NW6 .4H 63
Akabusi Cl. CR0: C'don .6G 157
Akbar Ho. E14 .4D 104
(off Cahir St.)
Akehurst St. SW15 .6C 116
Akenside Rd. NW3 .5B 64
Akerman Rd. KT6: Surb .6C 150
SW9 .2B 120
Akintaro Ho. SE8 .6B 104
(off Alverton St.)
Alabama St. SE18 .7H 107
Alacross Rd. W5 .2C 96
Alamaro Lodge SE10 .3H 105
(off Teal St.)
Alana Hgts. E4 .7J 25
Alan Coren Cl. NW2 .4E 62
Alandale Dr. HA5: Pinn .1K 39
Aland Ct. SE16 .3A 104
Alander M. E17 .4E 50
Alan Dr. EN5: Barn .6B 20
Alan Gdns. RM7: Rush G .7G 55
Alan Hocken Way E15 .2G 87
Alan Preece Ct. NW6 .7F 63
Alan Rd. SW19 .5G 135
Alanthus Cl. SE12 .6J 123
Alaska Apartments E16 .7J 87
(off Western Gateway)
Alaska Bldg. SE13 .1D 122
(off Deal's Gateway)
Alaska Bldgs. SE1 .3E 102
Alaska St. SE1 .5J 13 (1A 102)
Alastor Ho. E14 .3E 104
(off Strattondale Ho.)
Alba Cl. UB4: Yead .4B 76
Albacore Cres. SE13 .6D 122
Albacore Way UB3: Hayes .7H 75
Alba Gdns. NW11 .6G 45
Albain Cres. TW15: Ashf .2A 128
Alba M. SW18 .2J 135
Alban Highwalk EC2 .7D 8
(not continuous)
Albany, The .7C 104
Albany N12 .6E 30
W1 .3A 12 (7G 83)
Albany, The IG8: Wfd G .4C 36
Albany Cl. DA5: Bexl .7C 126
N15 .4B 48
SW14 .4H 115
UB10: Ick .5C 56
Albany Ct. E1 .6G 85
(off Plumber's Row)
E4 .6H 25
(Chelwood Cl.)
E4 .5G 35
(Westward Rd.)
E10 .7C 50
HA8: Edg .1K 43
NW8 .1A 4
(off Abbey Rd.)
NW10 .3D 80
(off Trenmar Gdns.)
TW15: Ashf .7E 128
Albany Courtyard W1 .3B 12 (7G 83)
Albany Cres. HA8: Edg .7B 28
Albany Mans. SW11 .7C 100
Albany M. BR1: Brom .6J 141
KT2: King T .6D 132
N1 .7A 66
SE5 .6C 102
SM1: Sutt .5K 165
Albany Pde. TW8: Bford .6E 96
Albany Pk. Av. EN3: Enf W .1D 24
Albany Pk. Rd. KT2: King T .6D 132
Albany Pas. TW10: Rich .5E 114
Albany Pl. TW8: Bford .6D 96
Albany Reach KT7: T Ditt .5K 149
Albany Rd. BR7: Chst .5F 143
DA5: Bexl .7C 126
DA17: Belv .6F 109
E10 .7C 50
E12 .4B 70
E17 .6A 50
KT3: N Mald .4K 151
N4 .6A 48
N18 .5D 34
RM6: Chad H .6F 55
SE5 .6D 102
SW19 .5K 135
TW8: Bford .6D 96
TW10: Rich .5F 115
W13 .7B 78
Albany St. NW1 .1K 5 (2F 83)
Albany Ter. NW1 .4K 5
TW10: Rich .5F 115
(off Albany Pas.)
Albany Vw. IG9: Buck H .1D 36
Albany Works E3 .1A 86
(off Gunmakers La.)
Alba Pl. W11 .6H 81
Albatross NW9 .2B 44
Albatross Cl. E6 .5D 88
Albatross St. SE18 .7J 107
Albatross Way SE16 .2K 103
Albemarle SW19 .2F 135
Albemarle App. IG2: Ilf .6F 53
Albemarle Av. TW2: Whitt .1D 130
Albemarle Ct. N17 .3H 49
(off Perkyn Sq.)
Albemarle Gdns. IG2: Ilf .6F 53
KT3: N Mald .4K 151
Albemarle Ho. SE8 .4B 104
(off Foreshore)
Albemarle Pk. BR3: Beck .1D 158
HA7: Stan .5H 27
Albemarle Rd. BR3: Beck .1D 158
EN4: E Barn .7H 21
Albemarle St. W1 .3K 11 (7F 83)
Albemarle Wlk. SW9 .3A 120
Albemarle Way EC1 .4A 8 (4B 84)
Alberon Gdns. NW11 .4H 45
Alberta Av. SM1: Sutt .4G 165
Alberta Est. SE17 .5B 102
(off Alberta St.)
Alberta Ho. UB4: Yead .3K 75
(off Ayles Rd.)
Alberta Rd. DA8: Erith .1J 127
EN1: Enf .6A 24
Alberta St. SE17 .5B 102
Albert Av. E4 .4H 35
SW8 .7K 101
Albert Barnes Ho. SE1 .3C 102
(off New Kent Rd.)
Albert Basin Way E16 .7G 89
Albert Bigg Point E15 .2E 86
(off Godfrey St.)
Albert Bri. SW3 .7D 16 (6C 100)
Albert Bri. Rd. SW11 .7C 100
Albert Carr Gdns. SW16 .5J 137
Albert Cl. E9 .1H 85
N22 .1H 47
Albert Cotts. E1 .5G 85
(off Deal St.)
Albert Ct. E7 .4J 69
SW7 .7A 10 (3B 100)
Albert Ct. Ga. SW1 .7E 10
(off Knightsbridge)
Albert Cres. E4 .4H 35
Albert Dane Cen. UB2: S'hall .3C 94
Albert Dr. SW19 .2G 135
Albert Emb. SE1 .1G 19 (3K 101)
(Lambeth Pal. Rd.)
SE1 .6F 19 (5J 101)
(Vauxhall Bri.)
Albert Gdns. E1 .6K 85
Albert Ga. SW1 .6F 11 (2D 100)
Albert Gray Ho. SW10 .7B 100
(off Worlds End Est.)
Albert Gro. SW20 .1F 153
Albert Hall Mans.
SW7 .7A 10 (2B 100)
Albert Ho. E18 .3K 51
(off Albert Rd.)
SE28 .3G 107
Albert Mans. CR0: C'don .1D 168
(off Lansdowne Rd.)
SW11 .1D 118
(off Albert Bri. Rd.)
Albert Memorial
Knightsbridge .7A 10 (2B 100)
Albert M. E14 .7A 86
(off Northey St.)
N4 .1K 65
SE4 .4A 122
W8 .3A 100
Albert Pal. Mans. SW11 .1F 119
(off Lurline Gdns.)
Albert Pl. N3 .1J 45
N17 .3F 49
W8 .3K 99
Albert Rd. BR2: Brom .5B 160
CR4: Mitc .3D 154
DA5: Bexl .6G 127
DA17: Belv .5F 109
E10 .2E 68
E16 .1C 106
E17 .5C 50
E18 .3K 51
EN4: E Barn .4F 21
HA2: Harr .3G 41
IG1: Ilf .3F 71
IG9: Buck H .2G 37
KT1: King T .2F 151
KT3: N Mald .4B 152
N4 .1K 65
N15 .6E 48
N22 .1G 47
NW4 .4F 45
NW6 .2H 81
NW7 .5G 29
RM8: Dag .1G 73
SE9 .3C 142
SE20 .6K 139
SE25 .4G 157
SM1: Sutt .5B 166
TW1: Twick .1K 131
TW3: Houn .4E 112
TW10: Rich .5E 114
TW11: Tedd .6K 131
TW12: Hamp H .5G 131
TW15: Ashf .5B 128
UB2: S'hall .3B 94
UB3: Hayes .3G 93
UB7: Yiew .1A 92
W5 .4B 78
Albert Rd. Est. DA17: Belv .5F 109
Alberts Ct. NW1 .3D 4
Albert Sleet Ct. N9 .3C 34
(off Colthurst Dr.)
Albert Sq. E15 .5G 69
SW8 .7K 101
Albert Starr Ho. SE8 .4K 103
(off Haddonfield)
Albert St. N12 .5F 31
NW1 .1F 83
Albert Studios SW11 .1D 118
Albert Ter. IG9: Buck H .2H 37
NW1 .1E 82
NW10 .1J 79
W5 .4B 78
W6 .5C 98
(off Beavor La.)
Albert Ter. M. NW1 .1E 82
Albert Victoria Ho. N22 .1A 48
Albert Wlk. E16 .2E 106
Albert Way SE15 .7H 103
Albert Westcott Ho. SE17 .5B 102
Albert Whicher Ho. E17 .4E 50
Albert Yd. SE19 .6F 139
Albery Ct. E8 .7F 67
(off Middleton Rd.)
Albion Av. N10 .1E 46
SW8 .2H 119
Albion Bldgs. N1 .2J 83
(off Albion Yd.)
Albion Cl. RM7: Rom .6K 55
W2 .2D 10 (7C 82)
Albion Ct. SE10 .4G 105
(off Azof St.)
SM2: Sutt .7B 166
W6 .4D 98
(off Albion Pl.)
Albion Dr. E8 .7F 67
Albion Est. SE16 .2K 103
Albion Gdns. W6 .4D 98
Albion Ga. W2 .2D 10
(not continuous)
Albion Gro. N16 .4E 66
Albion Ho. E16 .1F 107
(off Church St.)
SE8 .7C 104
(off Watsons St.)
Albion M. N1 .1A 84
NW6 .7H 63
W2 .2D 10 (7C 82)
W6 .4D 98
Albion Pde. N16 .4D 66
Albion Pl. EC1 .5A 8 (5B 84)
EC2 .6F 9 (5D 84)
W6 .4D 98
Albion Riverside Bldg. SW11 .7C 100
Albion Rd. DA6: Bex .4F 127
E17 .3E 50
KT2: King T .1J 151
N16 .4D 66
N17 .2G 49
SM2: Sutt .6B 166
TW2: Twick .1J 131
TW3: Houn .4E 112
UB3: Hayes .6G 75
Albion Sq. E8 .7F 67
(not continuous)
Albion St. CR0: C'don .1B 168
SE16 .2J 103
W2 .1D 10 (6C 82)
Albion Ter. E4 .4J 25
E8 .7F 67
Albion Vs. Rd. SE26 .3J 139
Albion Wlk. N1 .1F 7
(off York Way)
Albion Way EC1 .6C 8 (5C 84)
HA9: Wemb .3G 61
SE13 .4E 122
Albion Yd. E1 .5H 85
N1 .2J 83
Albon Ho. SW18 .6K 117
(off Neville Gill Cl.)
Albrighton Rd. SE22 .3E 120
Albuhera Cl. EN2: Enf .1F 23
Albuhera M. NW7 .5A 30
Albury Av. DA7: Bex .2E 126
TW7: Isle .7K 95
Albury Cl. TW12: Hamp .6F 131
Albury Ct. CR0: C'don .4C 168
(off Tanfield Rd.)
CR4: Mitc .2B 154
SE8 .6C 104
(off Albury St.)
SM1: Sutt .4A 166
UB5: N'olt .3A 76
(off Canberra Dr.)
Albury Dr. HA5: Pinn .1A 40, 1C 40
Albury Ho. SE1 .7B 14
(off Boyfield St.)
Albury M. E12 .2A 70
Albury Rd. KT9: Chess .5E 162
Albury St. SE8 .6C 104
Albyfield BR1: Brom .4D 160
Albyn Rd. SE8 .1C 122
Alcester Ct. SM6: Wall .4F 167

Alcester Cres.—Alfred Gdns.

Alcester Cres. E5 . . . . . 2H **67**
Alcester Rd. SM6: Wall 4F **167**
Alcock Cl. SM6: Wall 7H **167**
Alcock Rd. TW5: Hest 7B **94**
Alconbury DA6: Bex 5H **127**
Alconbury Rd. E5 . . . . . 2G **67**
Alcorn Cl. SM3: Sutt 2J **165**
Alcott Cl. TW14: Felt 1H **129**
W7 . . . . . 5K **77**
Alcuin Ct. HA7: Stan 7H **27**
Aldam Pl. N16 . . . . . 2F **67**
Aldborough Ct. *IG2: Ilf* *5K* ***53***
(off Aldborough Rd. Nth.)
ALDBOROUGH HATCH 4K 53
Aldborough Rd. RM10: Dag 6J **73**
Aldborough Rd. Nth. IG2: Ilf 5K **53**
Aldborough Rd. Sth. IG3: Ilf 1J **71**
Aldbourne Rd. W12 . . . . . 1B **98**
Aldbridge St. SE17 . . . . . 5E **102**
Aldburgh M. W1 . . . . . 7H **5** (6E **82**)
Aldbury Av. HA9: Wemb 7H **61**
Aldbury Ho. *SW3* *5C* ***16***
(off Cale St.)
Aldbury M. N9 . . . . . 7J **23**
Aldebert Ter. SW8 . . . . . 7J **101**
Aldeburgh Cl. E5 . . . . . 2H **67**
Aldeburgh Pl. IG8: Wfd G 4D **36**
SE10 . . . . . *4J* ***105***
(off Aldeburgh St.)
Aldeburgh St. SE10 . . . . . 5J **105**
Alden Av. E15 . . . . . 3H **87**
Alden Ct. CR0: C'don 3E **168**
Aldenham Dr. UB8: Hil 4D **74**
Aldenham Ho. *NW1* *1B* ***6***
(off Aldenham St.)
Aldenham St. NW1 . . . . . 1C **6** (2G **83**)
Alden Ho. *E8* *1H* ***85***
(off Duncan Rd.)
Aldensley Rd. W6 . . . . . 3D **98**
Alderbrook Rd. SW12 . . . . . 6F **119**
Alderbury Rd. SW13 . . . . . 6C **98**
Alder Cl. DA18: Erith 2F **109**
SE15 . . . . . 6F **103**
Alder Ct. E7 . . . . . 5J **69**
N11 . . . . . 6B **32**
Alder Gro. NW2 . . . . . 2C **62**
Aldergrove Gdns. TW3: Houn 2C **112**
Alder Ho. *E3* *1B* ***86***
(off Hornbeam Sq.)
NW3 . . . . . 6D **64**
SE4 . . . . . 3C **122**
SE15 . . . . . *6F* ***103***
(off Alder Cl.)
Alder Lodge SW6 . . . . . 1E **116**
Alderman Av. IG11: Bark 3A **90**
Aldermanbury EC2 . . . . . 7D **8** (6C **84**)
Aldermanbury Sq. EC2 . . . . . 6D **8** (5C **84**)
Alderman Judge Mall *KT1: King T* *2E* ***150***
(off Eden St.)
Aldermans Hill N13 . . . . . 4D **32**
Aldermans Ho. *E9* *5A* ***68***
(off Ward La.)
Aldermans Wlk. EC2 . . . . . 6G **9** (5E **84**)
Aldermary Rd. BR1: Brom 1J **159**
Alder M. N19 . . . . . 2G **65**
Aldermoor Rd. SE6 . . . . . 3B **140**
Alderney Av. TW5: Hest, Isle 7F **95**
Alderney Ct. *SE10* *6F* ***105***
(off Trafalgar Rd.)
Alderney Gdns. UB5: N'olt 7D **58**
Alderney Ho. EN3: Enf W 1E **24**
N1 . . . . . *6C* ***66***
(off Arran Wlk.)
Alderney M. SE1 . . . . . 3D **102**
Alderney Rd. E1 . . . . . 4K **85**
Alderney St. SW1 . . . . . 4K **17** (4F **101**)
Alder Rd. DA14: Sidc 3K **143**
SW14 . . . . . 3K **115**
Alders, The BR4: W W'ck 1D **170**
N21 . . . . . 6F **23**
SW16 . . . . . 4G **137**
Alders, The TW5: Hest 6D **94**
TW13: Hanw 4C **130**
Alders Av. IG8: Wfd G 6B **36**
ALDERSBROOK 2K 69
Aldersbrook Av. EN1: Enf 2K **23**
Aldersbrook Dr. KT2: King T 6F **133**
Aldersbrook La. E12 . . . . . 3D **70**
Aldersbrook Rd. E11 . . . . . 2K **69**
E12 . . . . . 2K **69**
Alders Cl. E11 . . . . . 2K **69**
HA8: Edg 5D **28**
W5 . . . . . 3D **96**
Aldersey Gdns. IG11: Bark 6H **71**
Aldersford Cl. SE4 . . . . . 5K **121**
Aldersgate Ct. *EC1* *6C* ***8***
(off Bartholomew Cl.)
Aldersgate St. EC1 . . . . . 5C **8** (5C **84**)
Alders Gro. KT8: E Mos 5H **149**
Aldersgrove Av. SE9 . . . . . 3B **142**
Aldershot Rd. NW6 . . . . . 1H **81**
Aldershot Ter. SE18 . . . . . 7E **106**
Aldersmead Av. CR0: C'don 6K **157**
Aldersmead Rd. BR3: Beck 7A **140**
Alderson Pl. UB2: S'hall 1G **95**
Alderson St. W10 . . . . . 4G **81**
Alders Rd. HA8: Edg 5D **28**
Alderton Cl. NW10 . . . . . 3K **61**
Alderton Ct. *KT8: W Mole* *4D* ***148***
(off Dunstable Rd.)
Alderton Cres. NW4 . . . . . 5D **44**
Alderton Rd. CR0: C'don 7F **157**
SE24 . . . . . 3C **120**
Alderton Way NW4 . . . . . 5D **44**
Alderville Rd. SW6 . . . . . 2H **117**
Alder Wlk. IG1: Ilf 5G **71**
Alderwick Ct. *N7* *6K* ***65***
(off Cornelia St.)
Alderwick Dr. TW3: Houn 3H **113**
Alderwood M. EN4: Had W 1F **21**
Alderwood Rd. SE9 . . . . . 6H **125**
Aldford Ho. *W1* *4G* ***11***
(off Park St.)
Aldford St. W1 . . . . . 4H **11** (1E **100**)
ALDGATE ***6F 85***
(off Aldgate High St.)
Aldgate *E1* *6F* ***85***
(off Whitechapel High St.)
EC3 . . . . . 1J **15** (6F **85**)
Aldgate Av. E1 . . . . . 7J **9** (6F **85**)
Aldgate Barrs E1 . . . . . 7K **9**
Aldgate High St. EC3 . . . . . 1J **15** (6F **85**)
Aldgate Pl. E1 . . . . . 7K **9** (6F **85**)
Aldgate Sq. EC3 . . . . . 1J **15** (6F **85**)
Aldgate Twr. E1 . . . . . 6F **85**
Aldham Ho. *SE4* *2B* ***122***
(off Malpas Rd.)
Aldine Ct. *W12* *2E* ***98***
(off Aldine St.)
Aldine Pl. W12 . . . . . 2E **98**
Aldine St. W12 . . . . . 2E **98**
Aldington Cl. RM8: Dag 1C **72**
Aldington Ct. *E8* *7G* ***67***
(off London Flds. W. Side)
Aldington Rd. SE18 . . . . . 3B **106**
Aldis M. SW17 . . . . . 5C **136**
Aldis St. SW17 . . . . . 5C **136**
Aldred Rd. NW6 . . . . . 5J **63**
Aldren Rd. SW17 . . . . . 3A **136**
Aldrich Cres. CR0: New Ad 7E **170**
Aldriche Way E4 . . . . . 6K **35**
Aldrich Gdns. SM3: Cheam 3H **165**
Aldrich Ter. SW18 . . . . . 2A **136**
Aldrick Ho. *N1* *1K* ***83***
(off Barnsbury Est.)
Aldridge Av. HA4: Ruis 2A **58**
HA7: Stan 1E **42**
HA8: Edg 3C **28**
Aldridge Ct. *W11* *5H* ***81***
(off Aldridge Rd. Vs.)
Aldridge Ri. KT3: N Mald 7A **152**
Aldridge Rd. Vs. W11 . . . . . 5H **81**
Aldridge Wlk. N14 . . . . . 7D **22**
Aldrington Rd. SW16 . . . . . 5G **137**
Aldsworth Cl. W9 . . . . . 4K **81**
Aldwick Cl. SE9 . . . . . 3H **143**
Aldwick Rd.
CR0: Bedd 3K **167**
Aldworth Gro. SE13 . . . . . 6E **122**
Aldworth Rd. E15 . . . . . 7G **69**
Aldwych WC2 . . . . . 2G **13** (6K **83**)
Aldwych Av. IG6: Ilf 4G **53**
Aldwych Bldgs. *WC2* *7F* ***7***
(off Parker M.)
Aldwych Ct. *E8* *7F* ***67***
(off Middleton Rd.)
Aldwych Theatre ***1G 13***
(off Aldwych)
Aldwyn Ho. *SW8* *7J* ***101***
(off Davidson Gdns.)
Alers Rd. DA6: Bex 5D **126**
Alesia Cl. N22 . . . . . 7D **32**
Alestan Beck Rd. E16 . . . . . 6B **88**
Alexa Ct. SM2: Sutt 6J **165**
W8 . . . . . 4J **99**
Alexander Av. NW10 . . . . . 7D **62**
Alexander Cl. BR2: Hayes 1J **171**
DA15: Sidc 6J **125**
EN4: E Barn 4G **21**
TW2: Twick 2J **131**
UB2: S'hall 1G **95**
Alexander Ct. BR3: Beck 1F **159**
HA7: Stan 3F **43**
TW16: Sun 6H **129**
Alexander Evans M. SE23 . . . . . 2K **139**
Alexander Fleming Laboratory Mus.
. . . . . **7B 4 (6B 82)**
Alexander Ho. *E14* *3C* ***104***
(off Tiller Rd.)
KT2: King T *1E* ***150***
(off Seven Kings Way)
SE15 . . . . . *2H* ***121***
(off Godman Rd.)
Alexander M. SW16 . . . . . 5G **137**
W2 . . . . . 6K **81**
Alexander Pl. SW7 . . . . . 3C **16** (4C **100**)
Alexander Rd. BR7: Chst 6F **143**
DA7: Bex 2D **126**
N19 . . . . . 3J **65**
Alexander Sq. SW3 . . . . . 3C **16** (4C **100**)
Alexander St. W2 . . . . . 6J **81**
Alexander Studios *SW11* *4B* ***118***
(off Haydon Way)
Alexander Ter. SE2 . . . . . 5B **108**
Alexandra Av. HA2: Harr 1D **58**
N22 . . . . . 1H **47**
SM1: Sutt 3J **165**
SW11 . . . . . 1E **118**
UB1: S'hall 7D **76**
W4 . . . . . 7K **97**
Alexandra Cl. HA2: Harr 3E **58**
SE8 . . . . . 6B **104**
TW15: Ashf 7F **129**
Alexandra Cotts. SE14 . . . . . 1B **122**
Alexandra Ct. HA9: Wemb 4F **61**
N14 . . . . . 5B **22**
SE5 . . . . . *6C* ***102***
(off Urlwin St.)
SW7 . . . . . 1A **16**
TW3: Houn 2F **113**
TW15: Ashf 6F **129**
UB6: G'frd 2F **77**
W2 . . . . . *7K* ***81***
(off Moscow Rd.)
W9 . . . . . *4A* ***82***
(off Maida Vale)
Alexandra Cres. BR1: Brom 6H **141**
Alexandra Dr. KT5: Surb 7G **151**
SE19 . . . . . 5E **138**
Alexandra Gdns. N10 . . . . . 4F **47**
SM5: Cars 7E **166**
TW3: Houn 2F **113**
W4 . . . . . 7A **98**
Alexandra Gro. N4 . . . . . 1B **66**
N12 . . . . . 5E **30**
Alexandra Ho. *E16* *1K* ***105***
(off Wesley Av.)
IG8: Wfd G 7K **37**
W6 . . . . . *5E* ***98***
(off Queen Caroline St.)
Alexandra Mans. *SW3* *7A* ***16***
(off King's Rd.)
W12 . . . . . *1E* ***98***
(off Stanlake Rd.)
Alexandra M. N2 . . . . . 3D **46**
N4 . . . . . 2B **66**
SW19 . . . . . 6H **135**
Alexandra Palace 2H **47**
Alexandra Pal. Way N8 . . . . . 4G **47**
N22 . . . . . 4G **47**
Alexandra Pde. HA2: Harr 4F **59**
Alexandra Pk. Rd. N10 . . . . . 2F **47**
N22 . . . . . 1G **47**
Alexandra Pl. CR0: C'don 1E **168**
NW8 . . . . . 1A **82**
SE25 . . . . . 5D **156**
Alexandra Rd. CR0: C'don 1E **168**
CR4: Mitc 7C **136**
E6 . . . . . 3E **88**
E10 . . . . . 3E **68**
E17 . . . . . 6B **50**
E18 . . . . . 3K **51**
EN3: Pond E 4E **24**
KT2: King T 7G **133**
KT7: T Ditt 5K **149**
N8 . . . . . 3A **48**
N9 . . . . . 7C **24**
N10 . . . . . 7A **32**
N15 . . . . . 5D **48**
NW4 . . . . . 4F **45**
NW8 . . . . . 1A **82**
RM6: Chad H 6E **54**
SE26 . . . . . 6K **139**
SW14 . . . . . 3K **115**
SW19 . . . . . 6H **135**
TW1: Twick 6C **114**
TW3: Houn 2F **113**
TW8: Bford 6D **96**
TW9: Kew 2F **115**
TW15: Ashf 7F **129**
W4 . . . . . 2K **97**
Alexandra Rd. Ind. Est. EN3: Pond E . . . 4E **24**
Alexandra Sq. SM4: Mord 5J **153**
Alexandra St. E16 . . . . . 5J **87**
SE14 . . . . . 7A **104**
Alexandra Ter. *E14* *5D* ***104***
(off Westferry Rd.)
Alexandra Wlk. SE19 . . . . . 5E **138**
Alexandra Wharf *E2* *1H* ***85***
(off Darwen Pl.)
Alexandra Yd. E9 . . . . . 1K **85**
Alexandria Apartments *SE17* *4E* ***102***
(off Townsend St.)
Alexandria Rd. W13 . . . . . 7A **78**
Alex Guy Gdns. RM8: Dag 1H **73**
Alexia Sq. E14 . . . . . 3D **104**
Alexis St. SE16 . . . . . 4G **103**
Alfan La. DA2: Wilm 5K **145**
Alfearn Rd. E5 . . . . . 4J **67**
Alford Ct. *N1* *1D* ***8***
(off Shepherdess Wlk.)
Alford Grn. CR0: New Ad 6F **171**
Alford Ho. N6 . . . . . 6G **47**
Alford Pl. N1 . . . . . 1D **8** (2C **84**)
Alford Rd. DA8: Erith 5J **109**
Alfoxton Av. N15 . . . . . 4B **48**
Alfreda St. SW11 . . . . . 1F **119**
Alfred Cl. W4 . . . . . 4K **97**
Alfred Ct. *SE16* *4H* ***103***
(off Bombay St.)
Alfred Dickens Ho. *E16* *6H* ***87***
(off Hallsville Rd.)
Alfred Finlay Ho. N22 . . . . . 2B **48**
Alfred Gdns. UB1: S'hall 7C **76**

180 A-Z London

Alfred Ho. *E9* .5A 68
(off Homerton Rd.)
E12 .7C 70
(off Tennyson Av.)
Alfred M. W1 .5C 6 (5H 83)
Alfred Nunn Ho. NW10 .1B 80
Alfred Pl. WC1 .5C 6 (5H 83)
Alfred Prior Ho. E12 .4E 70
Alfred Rd. DA17: Belv .5F 109
E15 .5H 69
IG9: Buck H .2G 37
KT1: King T .3E 150
SE25 .5G 157
SM1: Sutt .5A 166
TW13: Felt .2A 130
W2 .5J 81
W3 .1J 97
Alfred Salter Ho. *SE1* .4F 103
(off Fort Rd.)
Alfred's Gdns. IG11: Bark .2J 89
Alfred St. E3 .3B 86
Alfreds Way IG11: Bark .3F 89
Alfreds Way Ind. Est. IG11: Bark .2A 90
Alfred Vs. E17 .4E 50
Alfreton Cl. SW19 .3F 135
Alfriston KT5: Surb .6F 151
Alfriston Av. CR0: C'don .7J 155
HA2: Harr .6E 40
Alfriston Cl. KT5: Surb .5F 151
Alfriston Rd. SW11 .5D 118
Algar Cl. HA7: Stan .5E 26
TW7: Isle .3A 114
Algar Ho. SE1 .7A 14
Algar Rd. TW7: Isle .3A 114
Algarve Rd. SW18 .1K 135
Algernon Rd. NW4 .6C 44
NW6 .1J 81
SE13 .4D 122
Algiers Rd. SE13 .4C 122
Alibon Gdns. RM10: Dag .5G 73
Alibon Rd. RM9: Dag .5F 73
RM10: Dag .5F 73
Alice Cl. *EN5: New Bar* .4F 21
(off Station App.)
Alice Gilliatt Ct. *W14* .6H 99
(off Star Rd.)
Alice La. E3 .1B 86
Alice M. TW11: Tedd .5K 131
Alice Owen Technology Cen. *EC1* .1A 8
(off Goswell Rd.)
Alice Shepherd Ho. *E14* .2E 104
(off Manchester Rd.)
Alice St. SE1 .3E 102
(not continuous)
Alice Thompson Cl. SE12 .2A 142
Alice Walker Cl. SE24 .4B 120
Alice Way TW3: Houn .4F 113
Alicia Av. HA3: Kenton .4B 42
Alicia Cl. HA3: Kenton .4C 42
Alicia Gdns. HA3: Kenton .4B 42
Alicia Ho. DA16: Well .1B 126
Alie St. E1 .1K 15 (6F 85)
Alington Cres. NW9 .7J 43
Alington Gro. SM6: Wall .7G 167
Alison Cl. CR0: C'don .1K 169
E6 .6E 88
HA5: Eastc .6K 39
Aliwal M. SW11 .4C 118
Aliwal Rd. SW11 .4C 118
Alkerden Rd. W4 .5A 98
Alkham Rd. N16 .2F 67
Allan Barclay Cl. N15 .6F 49
Allan Cl. KT3: N Mald .5K 151
Allandale Av. N3 .3G 45
Allanson Ct. *E10* .2C 68
(off Leyton Grange Est.)
Allan Way W3 .5J 79
Allard Cres. WD23: B Hea .1B 26
Allard Gdns. SW4 .5H 119
Allard Ho. *NW9* .2B 44
(off Boulevard Dr.)
Allardyce St. SW4 .4K 119
Allbrook Cl.
TW11: Tedd .5J 131
Allcroft Rd. NW5 .5E 64
Allder Way CR2: S Croy .7B 168
Allenby Cl. UB6: G'frd .3E 76
Allenby Rd. SE23 .3A 140
SE28 .3G 107
UB1: S'hall .3E 76
Allen Cl. CR4: Mitc .1F 155
TW16: Sun .1K 147
Allen Ct. *E17* .6C 50
(off Yunus Khan Cl.)
UB6: G'frd .5K 59
Allendale Av. UB1: S'hall .6E 76
Allendale Cl. SE5 .2D 120
SE26 .5K 139
Allendale Rd.
HA0: Wemb .6B 60
UB6: G'frd .6B 60
Allen Edwards Dr. SW8 .1J 119
Allenford Ho. *SW15* .6B 116
(off Tunworth Cres.)
Allen Ho. *W8* .3J 99
(off Allen St.)
Allen Mans. *W8* .3J 99
(off Allen St.)
Allen Rd. BR3: Beck .2K 157
CR0: C'don .1A 168
E3 .2B 86
N16 .4E 66
TW16: Sun .1K 147
Allensbury Pl. NW1 .7H 65
Allens Rd. EN3: Pond E .5D 24
Allen St. W8 .3J 99
Allenswood SW19 .1G 135
Allenswood Rd. SE9 .3C 124
Allerford Ct.
HA2: Harr .5G 41
Allerford Rd. SE6 .3D 140
Allerton Ho. *N1* .1E 8
(off Provost St.)
Allerton Rd. N16 .2C 66
Allerton St. N1 .1E 8 (3D 84)
Allerton Wlk. N7 .2K 65
Allestree Rd. SW6 .7G 99
Alleyn Cres. SE21 .2D 138
Alleyndale Rd. RM8: Dag .2C 72
Alleyn Ho. *SE1* .3D 102
(off Burbage Cl.)
Alleyn Pk. SE21 .2D 138
UB2: S'hall .5E 94
Alleyn Rd. SE21 .3D 138
Alley Way UB8: Uxb .7A 56
Allfarthing La. SW18 .6K 117
Allgood Cl. SM4: Mord .6F 153
Allgood St. E2 .1K 9 (2F 85)
Allhallows La. EC4 .3E 14 (7D 84)
All Hallows Rd. N17 .1E 48
Allhallows Rd. E6 .5C 88
Alliance Cl. HA0: Wemb .4D 60
TW4: Houn .5D 112
Alliance Ct. TW15: Ashf .4E 128
W3 .5H 79
Alliance Rd. E13 .5A 88
SE18 .6A 108
W3 .4H 79
Allianz Pk. .7K 29
Allied Ct. *N1* .7E 66
(off Enfield Rd.)
Allied Ind. Est. W3 .2A 98
Allied Way W3 .2A 98
Allingham Cl. W7 .7K 77
Allingham Ct. BR2: Brom .4H 159
Allingham M. *N1* .2C 84
(off Allingham St.)
Allingham St. N1 .2C 84
Allington Av. N17 .6K 33
TW17: Shep .3G 147
Allington Cl. SW19 .5F 135
UB6: G'frd .7G 59
Allington Ct. *CR0: C'don* .6J 157
(off Chart Cl.)
EN3: Pond E .5E 24
SW8 .2G 119
Allington Rd. BR6: Orp .2H 173
HA2: Harr .5G 41
NW4 .5D 44
W10 .3G 81
Allington St. SW1 .2A 18 (3F 101)
Allison Cl. SE10 .1E 122
Allison Gro. SE21 .1E 138
Allison Rd. N8 .5A 48
W3 .6J 79
Alliston Ho. *E2* .2K 9
(off Gibraltar Wlk.)
Allitsen Rd. NW8 .2C 82
(not continuous)
All Nations Ho. *E8* .7H 67
(off Martello St.)
Allnutt Way SW4 .5H 119
Alloa Rd. IG3: Ilf .2A 72
SE8 .5K 103
Allom Ho. *W11* .7G 81
(off Clarendon Rd.)
Allonby Dr. HA4: Ruis .7D 38
Allonby Gdns. HA9: Wemb .1C 60
Allonby Ho. *E14* .5A 86
(off Aston St.)
Allotment Way NW2 .3F 63
Alloway Rd. E3 .3A 86
Allport Ho. *SE5* .3D 120
(off Champion Pk.)
Allport M. *E1* .4J 85
(off Hayfield Pas.)
All Saints Cl. N9 .2B 34
SW8 .1J 119
All Saint's Ct. *TW5: Hest* .1B 112
(off Springwell Rd.)
All Saints Ct. *E1* .7J 85
(off Johnson St.)
SW11 .7F 101
(off Prince of Wales Dr.)
All Saints Dr. SE3 .2G 123
(not continuous)
All Saints Ho. *W11* .5H 81
(off All Saints Rd.)
All Saints M. HA3: Hrw W .6D 26
All Saints Pas. SW18 .5J 117
All Saints Rd. SM1: Sutt .3K 165
SW19 .7A 136
(not continuous)
W3 .3J 97
W11 .5H 81
All Saints St. N1 .2K 83
Allsop Pl. NW1 .4F 5 (4D 82)
All Souls Av. NW10 .2D 80
All Souls' Pl. W1 .6K 5 (5F 83)
Allum Way N20 .1F 31
Alluvium Ct. *SE1* .7G 15
(off Long La.)
Allwood Cl. SE26 .4K 139
Alma Av. E4 .7K 35
Alma Birk Ho. NW6 .7G 63
Almack Rd. E5 .4J 67
Alma Cl. N10 .1F 47
Alma Ct. HA2: Harr .2H 59
Alma Cres. SM1: Sutt .5G 165
Alma Gro. SE1 .4F 103
Alma Ho. N9 .4B 34
TW8: Bford .6E 96
Almanza Pl. IG11: Bark .2B 90
Alma Pl. CR7: Thor H .5A 156
NW10 .3D 80
SE19 .7F 139
Alma Rd. DA14: Sidc .3A 144
EN3: Enf H, Pond E .5F 25
KT10: Esh .7J 149
N10 .7A 32
SM5: Cars .5C 166
SW18 .4A 118
UB1: S'hall .7C 76
Alma Rd. Ind. Est. EN3: Pond E .4E 24
Alma Row HA3: Hrw W .1H 41
Alma Sq. NW8 .2A 82
Alma St. E15 .6F 69
NW5 .6F 65
Alma Ter. *E3* .1B 86
(off Beale Rd.)
SW18 .7B 118
W8 .3J 99
Almeida St. N1 .1B 84
Almeida Theatre .1B 84
(off Almeida St.)
Almeric Rd. SW11 .4D 118
Almer Rd. SW20 .7C 134
Almington St. N4 .1K 65
Almond Av. SM5: Cars .2D 166
UB7: W Dray .3C 92
UB10: Ick .3D 56
W5 .3D 96
Almond Cl. BR2: Brom .7E 160
E17 .4A 50
HA4: Ruis .3H 57
SE15 .2G 121
TW13: Felt .1J 129
TW17: Shep .2E 146
UB3: Hayes .7G 75
Almond Gro. TW8: Bford .7B 96
Almond Ho. *E15* .3G 87
(off Teasel Way)
Almond Rd. N17 .7B 34
SE16 .4H 103
Almonds Av. IG9: Buck H .2D 36
Almond Way BR2: Brom .7E 160
CR4: Mitc .5H 155
HA2: Harr .2F 41
Almorah Rd. N1 .7D 66
TW5: Hest .1B 112
Almshouse La. KT9: Chess .7C 162
Alms Ho's., The IG11: Bark .6G 71
Alnmouth Ct. *UB1: S'hall* .6G 77
(off Fleming Rd.)
Alnwick N17 .7C 34
Alnwick Gro. SM4: Mord .4K 153
Alnwick Rd. E16 .6A 88
SE12 .6K 123
ALPERTON .2E 78
Alperton La. HA0: Wemb .3C 78
UB6: G'frd .3C 78
Alperton St. W10 .4H 81
Alphabet Gdns. SM5: Cars .6B 154
Alphabet Sq. E3 .5C 86
Alpha Bus. Cen. E17 .5B 50
Alpha Cl. NW1 .2D 4 (4C 82)
Alpha Est. UB3: Hayes .2G 93
Alpha Gro. E14 .2C 104
Alpha Ho. NW6 .2J 81
NW8 .4D 4
SW4 .4K 119
Alpha Pl. NW6 .2J 81
SM4: Mord .1F 165
SW3 .7D 16 (6C 100)
Alpha Rd. CR0: C'don .1E 168
E4 .3H 35
EN3: Pond E .4F 25
KT5: Surb .6F 151
N18 .6B 34
SE14 .1B 122
TW11: Tedd .5H 131
UB10: Hil .4D 74
Alpha St. SE15 .2G 121
Alphea Cl. SW19 .7C 136
Alpine Av. KT5: Surb .2J 163
Alpine Bus. Cen. E6 .5E 88
Alpine Cl. CR0: C'don .3E 168
KT19: Ewe .5J 163
Alpine Copse BR1: Brom .2E 160
Alpine Gro. E9 .7J 67
Alpine Rd. E10 .2D 68
KT12: Walt T .7J 147
NW9 .4G 43
SE16 .5K 103

Alpine Vw.—Ancaster Rd.

Alpine Vw. SM5: Cars 5C 166
Alpine Wlk. HA7: Stan 2D 26
Alpine Way E6 5E 88
Alric Av. KT3: N Mald 3A 152
NW10 7K 61
Alroy Rd. N4 7A 48
Alsace Rd. SE17 5E 102
Alscot Rd. SE1 4F 103
Alscot Way SE1 4F 103
Alsike Rd. DA18: Erith 3D 108
SE2 3D 108
Alsom Av. KT4: Wor Pk 4C 164
Alston Cl. KT6: Surb 7B 150
Alston Rd. EN5: Barn 3B 20
N18 5C 34
SW17 4B 136
Alston Works EN5: Barn 2B 20
Altair Cl. N17 6A 34
Altash Way SE9 2D 142
Altenburg Av. W13 3B 96
Altenburg Gdns. SW11 4D 118
Alt Gro. SW19 7H 135
Altham Ct. HA2: Harr 1F 41
Altham Rd. HA5: Pinn 1C 40
Althea St. SW6 2K 117
Althorne Gdns. E18 4H 51
Althorne Way RM10: Dag 2G 73
Althorp Cl. EN5: Ark 1H 29
Althorpe M. SW11 1B 118
Althorpe Rd. HA1: Harr 5G 41
Althorp Rd. SW17 1D 136
Altima Ct. *SE22 4G 121*
(off E. Dulwich Rd.)
Altior Ct. N6 6G 47
Altissima Ho. SW8 7F 101
Altitude Apartments *CR0: C'don 3D 168*
(off Altyre Rd.)
Altius Apartments *E3 2C 86*
(off Wick La.)
Altius Ct. E4 6K 35
Altius Wlk. E20 6E 68
Altmore Av. E6 7D 70
Alton Av. HA7: Stan 7E 26
Alton Cl. DA5: Bexl 1E 144
TW7: Isle 2K 113
Alton Gdns. BR3: Beck 7C 140
TW2: Whitt 7H 113
Alton Ho. *E3 3D 86*
(off Bromley High St.)
Alton Rd. CR0: Wadd 3A 168
N17 3D 48
SW15 1C 134
TW9: Rich 4E 114
Alton St. E14 5D 86
Altura Twr. SW11 2B 118
Altus Ho. SE6 4E 140
Altyre Cl. BR3: Beck 5B 158
Altyre Rd. CR0: C'don 2D 168
Altyre Way BR3: Beck 5B 158
Aluna Ct. SE15 3J 121
Alvanley Gdns. NW6 5K 63
Alverstone Av. EN4: E Barn 7H 21
SW19 2J 135
Alverstone Gdns. SE9 1G 143
Alverstone Ho. SE11 7J 19 (6A 102)
Alverstone Rd. E12 4E 70
HA9: Wemb 1F 61
KT3: N Mald 4B 152
NW2 7E 62
Alverston Gdns. SE25 5E 156
Alverton St. SE8 5B 104
(not continuous)
Alveston Av. HA3: Kenton 3B 42
Alveston Sq. E18 2J 51
Alvey St. SE17 5E 102
Alvia Gdns. SM1: Sutt 4A 166
Alvington Cres. E8 5F 67
Alway Av. KT19: Ewe 5K 163
Alwold Cres. SE12 6K 123
Alwyn Av. W4 5K 97
Alwyn Cl. CR0: New Ad 7D 170
Alwyne La. N1 7B 66
Alwyne Pl. N1 6C 66
Alwyne Rd. N1 7C 66
SW19 6H 135
W7 7J 77
Alwyne Sq. N1 6C 66
Alwyne Vs. N1 7B 66
Alwyn Gdns. NW4 4C 44
W3 6H 79
Alyth Gdns. NW11 6J 45
Alzette Ho. *E2 2K 85*
(off Mace St.)
Amalgamated Dr.
TW8: Bford 6B 96
Amanda Ct. *TW15: Ashf 2B 128*
(off Edward Way)
Amanda M. RM7: Rom 5J 55
Amar Ct. SE18 4K 107
Amar Deep Ct. SE18 5K 107
Amarelle Apartments
CR0: C'don 1D 168
(off Cherry Orchard Rd.)
Amazon Bldg. N8 4K 47
Amazon St. E1 6G 85
Ambassador Cl. TW3: Houn 2C 112
Ambassador Gdns. E6 5D 88
Ambassador Ho. NW8 1A 82
Ambassador's Ct. SW1 5B 12
Ambassadors Ct. *E8 7F 67*
(off Holly St.)
Ambassador Sq. E14 4D 104
Ambassadors Theatre 1D 12
(off West St.)
Amber Av. E17 1A 50
Amber Cl. EN5: New Bar 6E 20
Amber Ct. CR0: C'don 1E 168
E15 1E 86
(off Warton Rd.)
KT5: Surb 7F 151
N7 6A 66
(off Bride St.)
Amberden Av. N3 3J 45
Ambergate St. SE17 5B 102
Amber Gro. NW2 1F 63
Amber Ho. *E1 6K 85*
(off Aylward St.)
Amberley Cl. BR6: Chels 5K 173
HA5: Pinn 3D 40
Amberley Ct. BR3: Beck 7B 140
DA14: Sidc 5C 144
Amberley Gdns. EN1: Enf 7K 23
KT19: Ewe 4B 164
Amberley Gro. CR0: C'don 7F 157
SE26 5H 139
Amberley Rd. E10 7C 50
EN1: Enf 7A 24
IG9: Buck H 1F 37
N13 2E 32
SE2 6D 108
W9 5J 81
Amberley Way RM7: Mawney 4H 55
SM4: Mord 7H 153
TW4: Houn 5A 112
UB10: Uxb 2A 74
Amberlith Ho. *CR7: Thor H 5A 156*
(off Thornton Rd.)
Amber M. *N22 3A 48*
(off High Rd.)
Amberside Cl. TW7: Isle 6H 113
Amber Way W3 2A 98
Amber Wharf *E2 1F 85*
(off Nursery La.)
Amberwood Cl. SM6: Wall 5J 167
Amberwood Ri. KT3: N Mald 6A 152
Amblecote Cl. SE12 3K 141
Amblecote Mdws. SE12 3K 141
Amblecote Rd. SE12 3K 141
Ambler Rd. N4 3B 66
Ambleside BR1: Brom 6F 141
NW1 1K 5
SW19 1G 135
Ambleside Av. BR3: Beck 5A 158
KT12: Walt T 7A 148
SW16 4H 137
Ambleside Cl. E9 5J 67
E10 7D 50
N17 3F 49
Ambleside Cres. EN3: Enf H 3E 24
Ambleside Dr. TW14: Felt 1H 129
Ambleside Gdns.
HA9: Wemb 1D 60
IG4: Ilf 4C 52
SM2: Sutt 6A 166
SW16 5H 137
Ambleside Point *SE15 7J 103*
(off Tustin Est.)
Ambleside Rd. DA7: Bex 2G 127
NW10 7B 62
Ambleside Wlk. UB8: Uxb 1A 74
Ambrooke Rd. DA17: Belv 3G 109
Ambrosden Av.
SW1 2B 18 (3G 101)
Ambrose Av. NW11 7G 45
Ambrose Cl. BR6: Orp 3K 173
E6 5D 88
Ambrose Ct. *N18 6A 34*
(off Cannon Rd.)
Ambrose Ho. *E14 5C 86*
(off Selsey St.)
Ambrose M. SW11 2D 118
Ambrose St. SE16 4H 103
Ambrose Wlk. E3 2C 86
Ambulance Rd. E11 5F 51
AMC Bus. Cen. NW10 3H 79
Amelia Cl. W3 1H 97
Amelia Ho. *NW9 2B 44*
(off Boulevard Dr.)
TW9: Kew 7H 97
W6 5E 98
(off Queen Caroline St.)
Amelia Mans. *E20 6D 68*
(off Olympic Pk. Av.)
Amelia St. SE17 5C 102
Amen Corner EC4 1B 14 (6B 84)
SW17 6D 136
Amen Ct. EC4 1B 14 (6B 84)
Amenity Way SM4: Mord 7E 152
American International University
in London, The
Kensington Campus -
Ansdell Street 3K 99
(off Ansdell St.)
St Albans Grove 3K 99
Young Street 2K 99
Richmond Hill Campus 7E 114
American University of London, The
3K 65
America Sq. EC3 2J 15 (7F 85)
America St. SE1 5C 14 (1C 102)
Amerland Rd. SW18 5H 117
Amersham Av. N18 6J 33
Amersham Gro. SE14 7B 104
Amersham Rd. CR0: C'don 6C 156
SE14 1B 122
Amersham Va. SE14 7B 104
Amery Gdns. NW10 1E 80
Amery Ho. *SE17 5E 102*
(off Kinglake St.)
Amery Rd. HA1: Harr 2A 60
Amesbury Av. SW2 2J 137
Amesbury Cl. KT4: Wor Pk 1E 164
Amesbury Ct. EN2: Enf 2F 23
Amesbury Dr. E4 6J 25
Amesbury Rd. BR1: Brom 3B 160
RM9: Dag 7D 72
TW13: Felt 2B 130
Amesbury Twr. SW8 2G 119
Ames Cotts. *E14 5A 86*
(off Maroon St.)
Ames Ho. *E2 2K 85*
(off Mace St.)
Amethyst Cl. N11 7C 32
Amethyst Ct. *BR6: Chels 5J 173*
(off Farnborough Hill)
EN3: Enf H 3F 25
(off Enstone Rd.)
Amethyst Rd. E15 4F 69
Amherst Av. W13 6C 78
Amherst Dr. BR5: St M Cry 4K 161
Amherst Gdns. *W13 6C 78*
(off Amherst Rd.)
Amherst Ho. *SE16 2K 103*
(off Wolfe Cres.)
Amherst Rd. W13 6C 78
Amhurst Gdns. TW7: Isle 2A 114
Amhurst Pde. *N16 7F 49*
(off Amhurst Pk.)
Amhurst Pk. N16 7D 48
Amhurst Pas. E8 4G 67
Amhurst Rd. E8 5H 67
N16 4F 67
Amhurst Ter. E8 4G 67
Amhurst Wlk. SE28 1A 108
Amias Dr. HA8: Edg 4K 27
Amias Ho. *EC1 3C 8*
(off Central St.)
Amidas Gdns. RM8: Dag 4B 72
Amiel St. E1 4J 85
Amies St. SW11 3D 118
Amigo Ho. *SE1 1K 19*
(off Morley St.)
Amina Way SE16 3G 103
Amiot Ho. *NW9 2B 44*
(off Heritage Av.)
Amis Av. KT19: Ewe 6H 163
Amisha Ct. *SE1 3F 103*
(off Grange Rd.)
Amity Gro. SW20 1D 152
Amity Rd. E15 7H 69
Ammanford Grn. NW9 6A 44
Ammonite Ho. E15 7H 69
Amner Rd. SW11 6E 118
Amor Rd. W6 3E 98
Amory Ho. *N1 1K 83*
(off Barnsbury Est.)
Amott Rd. SE15 3G 121
Amoy Pl. E14 7C 86
(not continuous)
Ampere Way CR0: Wadd 7J 155
Ampleforth Rd. SE2 2B 108
Amport Pl. NW7 6B 30
Ampthill Est. NW1 1B 6 (2G 83)
Ampthill Sq. NW1 1B 6 (2G 83)
Ampton Pl. WC1 2G 7 (3K 83)
Ampton St. WC1 2G 7 (3K 83)
Amroth Cl. SE23 1H 139
Amroth Grn. NW9 6A 44
Amstel Ct. SE15 7F 103
Amsterdam Rd. E14 3E 104
Amundsen Ct. *E14 5C 104*
(off Napier Av.)
Amunsden Ho. *NW10 7K 61*
(off Stonebridge Pk.)
Amwell Cl. EN2: Enf 5J 23
Amwell Ct. Est. N4 2C 66
Amwell Ho. *WC1 1J 7*
(off Cruikshank St.)
Amwell St. EC1 1J 7 (3A 84)
Amyand Cotts. TW1: Twick 6B 114
Amyand La. TW1: Twick 7B 114
Amyand Pk. Gdns. TW1: Twick 7B 114
Amyand Pk. Rd. TW1: Twick 7A 114
Amy Cl. SM6: Wall 7J 167
Amy Johnson Ct. HA8: Edg 2H 43
Amyruth Rd. SE4 5C 122
Amy Warne Cl. E6 4C 88
Anastasia M. N12 5E 30
Anatola Rd. N19 2G 65
Anayah Apartments *SE8 5K 103*
(off Trundleys Rd.)
Ancaster Cres. KT3: N Mald 6C 152
Ancaster M. BR3: Beck 3K 157
Ancaster Rd. BR3: Beck 3K 157

182 A-Z London

Ancaster St. SE18 .7J **107**
Anchor SW18 .4K **117**
Anchorage Cl. SW19 .5J **135**
Anchorage Ho. *E14* .*7F* ***87***
(off Clove Cres.)
Anchorage Point *E14* .*2B* ***104***
(off Cuba St.)
Anchorage Point Ind. Est. SE7 .3A **106**
Anchor & Hope La. SE7 .3K **105**
Anchor Brewhouse SE1 .5J **15** (1F **103**)
Anchor Bus. Cen. CR0: Bedd .3J **167**
Anchor Cl. IG11: Bark .3B **90**
Anchor Ct. EN1: Enf .5K **23**
SW1 .*4C* ***18***
(off Vauxhall Bri. Rd.)
Anchor Dr. N15 .4E **48**
Anchor Ho. *E16* .*5H* ***87***
(off Barking Rd.)
E16 .*6A* ***88***
(off Prince Regent La.)
EC1 .*3C* ***8***
(off Old St.)
SW10 .*6B* ***100***
(off Cremorne Est.)
Anchor M. N1 .6E **66**
SW12 .6F **119**
Anchor Retail Pk. E1 .4J **85**
Anchor St. SE16 .4H **103**
Anchor Ter. E1 .4J **85**
SE1 .*4D* ***14***
(off Southwark Bri. Rd.)
Anchor Wharf *E3* .*5D* ***86***
(off Yeo St.)
Anchor Yd. EC1 .3D **8** (4C **84**)
Ancill Cl. W6 .6G **99**
Ancona Rd. NW10 .2C **80**
SE18 .5H **107**
Andace Pk. Gdns. BR1: Brom .1A **160**
Andalus Rd. SW9 .3J **119**
Ander Cl. HA0: Wemb .4D **60**
Anderson Cl. N21 .5E **22**
SM3: Sutt .1J **165**
W3 .6K **79**
Anderson Ct. NW2 .1E **62**
Anderson Dr. TW15: Ashf .4E **128**
Anderson Hgts. SW16 .2K **155**
Anderson Ho. *E14* .*7E* ***86***
(off Woolmore St.)
IG11: Bark .1H **89**
SW17 .5B **136**
Anderson Pl. TW3: Houn .4F **113**
Anderson Rd. E9 .6K **67**
IG8: Wfd G .3B **52**
Anderson Sq. *N1* .*1B* ***84***
(off Gaskin St.)
Anderson St. SW3 .5E **16** (5D **100**)
Anderson Way DA17: Belv .2H **109**
Anderton Cl. SE5 .3D **120**
Anderton Ct. N22 .2H **47**
Andora Ct. *NW6* .*7G* ***63***
(off Brondesbury Pk.)
Andora Ho. E10 .1A **68**
Andorra Ct. BR1: Brom .1A **160**
Andover Av. E16 .6B **88**
Andover Cl. TW14: Felt .1H **129**
UB6: G'frd .4F **77**
Andover Ct. *E2* .*4H* ***85***
(off Thee Colts La.)
TW19: Stanw .7A **110**
Andover Pl. NW6 .2K **81**
Andover Rd. BR6: Orp .1H **173**
N7 .2K **65**
TW2: Twick .1H **131**
Andoversford Ct. *SE15* .*6E* ***102***
(off Bibury Cl.)
Andover Ter. *W6* .*4D* ***98***
(off Raynham Rd.)
Andreck Ct. *BR3: Beck* .*2E* ***158***
(off Crescent Rd.)
Andre St. E8 .5G **67**
Andrew Cl. DA1: Cray .5K **127**
Andrew Ct. SE23 .2K **139**
Andrewes Gdns. E6 .6C **88**
Andrewes Highwalk EC2 .6D **8**
Andrewes Ho. EC2 .6D **8**
SM1: Sutt .4J **165**
Andrew Gibb Memorial, The .1H 123
Andrew Pl. SW8 .7H **101**
Andrew Reed Ho. *SW18* .*7G* ***117***
(off Linstead Way)
Andrews Cl. HA1: Harr .7H **41**
IG9: Buck H .2F **37**
KT4: Wor Pk .2E **164**
Andrews Crosse WC2 .1J **13**
Andrews Ga. TW17: Shep .2E **146**
Andrew's Ho. CR2: S Croy .6C **168**
Andrews Ho. *NW3* .*7D* ***64***
(off Fellows Rd.)
Andrews Pl. DA2: Wilm .2K **145**
SE9 .6F **125**
Andrew's Rd. E8 .1H **85**
Andrew St. E14 .6E **86**
Andrews Wlk. SE17 .6B **102**
Andringham Lodge *BR1: Brom* .*1K* ***159***
(off Palace Gro.)
Andrula Ct. N22 .1B **48**
Andwell Cl. SE2 .2B **108**
ANERLEY .1H 157
Anerley Gro. SE19 .7F **139**
Anerley Hill SE19 .6F **139**
Anerley Pk. SE20 .7G **139**
Anerley Pk. Rd. SE20 .7H **139**
Anerley Rd. SE19 .7G **139**
SE20 .7G **139**
Anerley Sta. Rd. SE20 .1H **157**
Anerley Va. SE19 .7F **139**
Aneurin Bevan Ct. NW2 .2D **62**
Aneurin Bevan Ho. N11 .7C **32**
Anfield Cl. SW12 .7G **119**
ANGEL .**2A 84**
Angela Carter Cl. SW9 .3A **120**
Angela Davies Ind. Est. SE24 .4B **120**
Angela Hooper Pl. *SW1* .*1B* ***18***
(off Victoria St.)
Angel All. E1 .7K **9**
Angel Bldg. N1 .1K **7** (2A **84**)
Angel Cl. N18 .5A **34**
TW12: Hamp H .5G **131**
Angel Cnr. Pde. N18 .4B **34**
Angel Ct. E15 .6F **69**
EC2 .7F **9** (6D **84**)
SW1 .5B **12** (1G **101**)
ANGEL EDMONTON .**5B 34**
Angelfield TW3: Houn .4F **113**
Angel Ga. EC1 .1B **8** (3B **84**)
(not continuous)
Angel Hill SM1: Sutt .3K **165**
Angel Hill Dr. SM1: Sutt .3K **165**
Angel Ho. *E3* .*3C* ***86***
(off Campbell Rd.)
Angelica Cl. UB7: Yiew .6A **74**
Angelica Dr. E6 .5E **88**
Angelica Gdns. CR0: C'don .1K **169**
Angelica Ho. *E3* .*1B* ***86***
(off Sycamore Av.)
Angelina Ho. *SE15* .*1G* ***121***
(off Goldsmith Rd.)
Angelis Apartments *N1* .*1B* ***8***
(off Graham St.)
Angel La. E15 .6F **69**
EC4 .3E **14** (7D **84**)
UB3: Hayes .5F **75**
Angell Pk. Gdns. SW9 .3A **120**
Angell Rd. SW9 .3A **120**
ANGELL TOWN .1A 120
Angell Town Est. SW9 .2A **120**
Angel M. E1 .7H **85**
N1 .2A **84**
SW15 .7C **116**
Angelo M. SW16 .3K **155**
Angel Pl. N18 .4B **34**
SE1 .6E **14** (2D **102**)
Angel Rd. HA1: Harr .6J **41**
KT7: T Ditt .7A **150**
N18 .5B **34**
Angel Rd. Works N18 .5D **34**
Angel Sq. EC1 .2B **84**
Angel St. EC1 .7C **8** (6C **84**)
Angel Wlk. W6 .4E **98**
Angel Way RM1: Rom .5K **55**
Angel Wharf N1 .2C **84**
Angel Yd. N6 .1E **64**
Angerstein Bus. Pk. SE10 .4J **105**
Angerstein La. SE3 .1H **123**
Anglais M. *NW9* .*4A* ***44***
(off Colin Cl.)
Anglebury *W2* .*6J* ***81***
(off Talbot Rd.)
Angle Cl. UB10: Hil .1C **74**
Angle Grn. RM8: Dag .1C **72**
Anglers, The *KT1: King T* .*3D* ***150***
(off High St.)
Anglers Cl. TW10: Ham .4C **132**
Angler's La. NW5 .6F **65**
Anglers Reach KT6: Surb .5D **150**
Anglesea Av. SE18 .4F **107**
Anglesea Ho. *KT1: King T* .*4D* ***150***
(off Anglesea Rd.)
Anglesea M. SE18 .4F **107**
Anglesea Rd. KT1: King T .4D **150**
SE18 .4F **107**
Anglesea Ter. *W6* .*3D* ***98***
(off Wellesley Av.)
Anglesey Cl. TW15: Ashf .3C **128**
Anglesey Ct. Rd. SM5: Cars .6E **166**
Anglesey Gdns. SM5: Cars .6E **166**
Anglesey Ho. *E14* .*6C* ***86***
(off Lindfield St.)
Anglesey Rd. EN3: Pond E .4C **24**
Anglesmede Cres. HA5: Pinn .3E **40**
Anglesmede Way HA5: Pinn .3E **40**
Angles Rd. SW16 .4J **137**
Anglia Cl. N17 .7C **34**
Anglia Ct. *RM8: Dag* .*1D* ***72***
(off Spring Cl.)
Anglia Ho. *E14* .*6A* ***86***
(off Salmon La.)
Anglian Ind. Est. IG11: Bark .4K **89**
Anglian Rd. E11 .3F **69**
Anglia Wlk. *E6* .*1E* ***88***
(off Napier Rd.)
Anglo Rd. E3 .2B **86**
Angrave Ct. *E8* .*1F* ***85***
(off Scriven St.)
Angrave Pas. E8 .1F **85**
Angus Cl. KT9: Chess .5G **163**
Angus Dr. HA4: Ruis .4A **58**
Angus Gdns. NW9 .1K **43**
Angus Ho. SW2 .7H **119**
Angus Rd. E13 .3A **88**
Angus St. SE14 .7A **104**
Anhalt Rd. SW11 .7C **100**
Ankerdine Cres. SE18 .7F **107**
Anlaby Rd. TW11: Tedd .5J **131**
Anley Rd. W14 .2F **99**
Anmersh Gro. HA7: Stan .1D **42**
Annabel Cl. E14 .6D **86**
Annabels M. W5 .4D **78**
Anna Cl. E8 .1F **85**
Annandale Gro. UB10: Ick .3E **56**
Annandale Rd. CR0: C'don .2G **169**
DA15: Sidc .7J **125**
SE10 .6H **105**
W4 .5A **98**
Anna Neagle Cl. E7 .4J **69**
Annan Way RM1: Rom .1K **55**
Anne Boleyn Ct. SE9 .6G **125**
Anne Boleyn's Wlk. KT2: King T .5E **132**
SM3: Cheam .7F **165**
Anne Case M. KT3: N Mald .3K **151**
Anne Compton M. SE12 .7H **123**
Anne Goodman Ho. *E1* .*6J* ***85***
(off Jubilee St.)
Anne Matthews Ct. *E14* .*5C* ***86***
(off Selsey St.)
Anne M. IG11: Bark .7G **71**
Anne of Cleeves Ct. SE9 .6H **125**
Annes Ct. NW1 .3D **4**
Annesley Av. NW9 .3K **43**
Annesley Cl. NW10 .3A **62**
Annesley Dr. CR0: C'don .3B **170**
Annesley Ho. SW9 .1A **120**
Annesley Pl. BR2: Brom .6C **160**
Annesley Rd. SE3 .1K **123**
Annesley Wlk. N19 .2G **65**
Annesmere Gdns. SE3 .3B **124**
Anne St. E13 .4J **87**
Anne Sutherland Ho. BR3: Beck .7K **139**
Annett Cl. TW17: Shep .4G **147**
Annette Cl. HA3: W'stone .2J **41**
Annette Cres. N1 .7C **66**
Annette Rd. N7 .3K **65**
(not continuous)
Annett Rd. KT12: Walt T .7J **147**
Anne Way KT8: W Mole .4F **149**
Annexe Mkt. *E1* .*5J* ***9***
(off Spital Sq.)
Annie Besant Cl. E3 .1B **86**
Annie Taylor Ho. *E12* .*4E* ***70***
(off Walton Rd.)
Anning St. EC2 .3H **9** (4E **84**)
Annington Rd. N2 .3D **46**
Annis Rd. E9 .6A **68**
Ann La. SW10 .6B **100**
Ann Moss Way SE16 .3J **103**
Ann's Cl. SW1 .7F **11**
Ann's Pl. E1 .6J **9**
Ann St. N1 .1C **84**
SE18 .5G **107**
(not continuous)
Ann Stroud Ct. SE12 .5J **123**
Annsworthy Av. CR7: Thor H .3D **156**
Annsworthy Cres. SE25 .2D **156**
Ansar Gdns. E17 .5B **50**
Ansdell Rd. SE15 .2J **121**
Ansdell St. W8 .3K **99**
Ansdell Ter. W8 .3K **99**
Ansell Gro. SM5: Cars .1E **166**
Ansell Ho. *E1* .*5J* ***85***
(off Mile End Rd.)
Ansell Rd. SW17 .3C **136**
Anselm Cl. CR0: C'don .3F **169**
Anselm Rd. HA5: Hat E .1D **40**
SW6 .6J **99**
Ansford Rd. BR1: Brom .5E **140**
Ansleigh Pl. W11 .7F **81**
Anson Cl. RM7: Mawney .2H **55**
Anson Ho. *E1* .*4A* ***86***
(off Shandy St.)
SW1 .*7A* ***18***
(off Churchill Gdns.)
Anson M. SW19 .7J **135**
Anson Pl. SE28 .2H **107**
Anson Rd. N7 .4G **65**
NW2 .4D **62**
Anson Ter. UB5: N'olt .6F **59**
Anstey Ct. W3 .2H **97**
Anstey Ho. *E9* .*1J* ***85***
(off Templecombe Rd.)
Anstey Rd. SE15 .3G **121**
Anstey Wlk. N15 .4B **48**
Anstice Cl. W4 .7A **98**
Anstridge Path SE9 .6H **125**
Anstridge Rd. SE9 .6H **125**
Antelope Rd. SE18 .3D **106**
Antelope Wlk.
KT6: Surb .5D **150**
Antenor Ho. *E2* .*2H* ***85***
(off Old Bethnal Grn. Rd.)
Anthems Way E20 .6D **68**
Anthony Cl. NW7 .4F **29**
Anthony Cope Ct. *N1* .*1F* ***9***
(off Chart St.)
Anthony Ct. W3 .2A **98**

Anthony Ho. *NW8* *4C 4*
(off Ashbridge St.)
Anthony Rd. DA16: Well 1A **126**
SE25 6G **157**
UB6: G'frd 3J **77**
Anthony St. E1 6H **85**
Anthony Way N18 6E **34**
Antigua M. E13 3K **87**
Antigua Wlk. SE19 5D **138**
Antila Ct. *E1* *3K 9*
(off Sclater St.)
Antilles Bay E14 2E **104**
Antill Rd. E3 3A **86**
N15 4G **49**
Antill Ter. E1 6K **85**
Antlers Hill E4 5J **25**
Antoinette M. NW2 6C **62**
Anton Cres. SM1: Sutt 3J **165**
Antoneys Cl. HA5: Pinn 2B **40**
Antonine Hgts. SE1 7G **15**
Anton Pl. HA9: Wemb 3H **61**
Anton St. E8 5G **67**
Antony Ho. *SE16* *4J 103*
(off Raymouth Rd.)
Antrim Gro. NW3 6D **64**
Antrim Rd. NW3 6D **64**
Antrobus Cl. SM1: Sutt 5H **165**
Antrobus Rd. W4 4J **97**
Antwerp Way E16 2E **106**
Anvil Cl. SW16 7G **137**
Anvil Rd. TW16: Sun 3J **147**
Anworth Cl. IG8: Wfd G 6E **36**
Apeldoorn Dr. SM6: Wall 7J **167**
Apex Cl. BR3: Beck 1D **158**
APEX CORNER
Feltham 3D 130
Mill Hill 4F 29
Apex Ct. W13 7A **78**
Apex Ho. *E1* *3K 9*
(off Bacon St.)
Apex Ind. Est. NW10 4B **80**
Apex Pde. *NW7* *4E 28*
(off Selvage La.)
Apex Retail Pk. TW13: Hanw 3D **130**
Aphrodite Ct. *E14* *4C 104*
(off Homer Dr.)
E15 *1E 86*
(off Warton Rd.)
Aplin Way TW7: Isle 1J **113**
Apollo Av. BR1: Brom 1K **159**
Apollo Bldg. E14 4C **104**
Apollo Bus. Cen. SE8 5K **103**
Apollo Ct. *E1* *7G 85*
(off Thomas More St.)
E15 *1E 86*
(off High St.)
SW9 *1A 120*
(off Southey Rd.)
Apollo Ho. *E2* *2H 85*
(off St Jude's Rd.)
E3 *2C 86*
(off Garrison Rd.)
N6 7D **46**
SW10 *7B 100*
(off Milman's St.)
Apollo Pl. E11 3G **69**
SW10 7B **100**
Apollo Theatre
Soho ***2C 12***
(off Shaftesbury Av.)
Apollo Victoria Theatre ***2A 18***
(off Wilton Rd.)
Apollo Way DA8: Erith 4K **109**
SE28 3H **107**
Apostle Ct. SE20 7K **139**
Apostles, The *SE23* *2K 139*
(off Church Ri.)
Apostle Way CR7: Thor H 2B **156**
Apothecary St.
EC4 1A **14** (6B **84**)
Appach Rd. SW2 5A **120**
Appian Ct. *E3* *2B 86*
(off Parnell Rd.)
Apple Blossom Ct. *SW8* *7H 101*
(off Pascal St.)
Appleby Cl. BR5: Pet W 7J **161**
E4 6K **35**
N15 5D **48**
TW2: Twick 2H **131**
UB8: Hil 6E **74**
Appleby Ct. *W3* *2J 97*
(off Newport Rd.)
Appleby Gdns. TW14: Felt 1H **129**
Appleby Rd. E8 7G **67**
E16 6H **87**
Appleby St. E2 2F **85**
Appledore Av. DA7: Bex 1J **127**
HA4: Ruis 3K **57**
Appledore Cl. BR2: Brom 5H **159**
HA8: Edg 1G **43**
SW17 2D **136**
Appledore Cres. DA14: Sidc 3J **143**
Appledore Way NW7 7A **30**
Appleford Ho. *W10* *4G 81*
(off Bosworth Rd.)
Appleford Rd. W10 4G **81**
Apple Gth. TW8: Bford 4D **96**
Applegarth CR0: New Ad 7D **170**
(not continuous)
KT10: Clay 5A **162**
Applegarth Dr. IG2: Ilf 4K **53**
Applegarth Ho. SE1 6B **14**
SE15 *7G 103*
(off Bird in Bush Rd.)
Applegarth Rd. SE28 1B **108**
W14 3F **99**
Applegate Ho. *E20* *5E 68*
(off Victory Pde.)
Apple Gro. EN1: Enf 3K **23**
HA2: Harr 1E **58**
KT9: Chess 4E **162**
TW1: Twick 6A **114**
Apple Mkt. *KT1: King T* *2D 150*
(off Market Pl.)
Apple Rd. E11 3G **69**
Appleshaw Ho. SE5 3E **120**
Appleton Cl. DA7: Bex 2J **127**
Appleton Gdns. KT3: N Mald 6C **152**
Appleton Rd. SE9 3C **124**
Appleton Sq. CR4: Mitc 1C **154**
Apple Tree Av. UB7: Yiew 5B **74**
UB8: Hil 5B **74**
Appletree Cl. SE20 1H **157**
Appletree Gdns. EN4: E Barn 4H **21**
Apple Tree La. RM13: Rain 2K **91**
APPLE TREE RDBT. **6B 74**
Apple Tree Yd. *E1* *3K 85*
(off Longnor Rd.)
SW1 4B **12** (1G **101**)
Applewood Cl. N20 1H **31**
NW2 3D **62**
UB10: Ick 4A **56**
Applewood Dr. E13 4K **87**
Appold St. EC2 5G **9** (5E **84**)
Apprentice Gdns. UB5: N'olt 3D **76**
Apprentice Way E5 4H **67**
Approach, The BR6: Orp 2K **173**
EN1: Enf 2C **24**
NW4 5F **45**
W3 6K **79**
Approach Cl. N16 4E **66**
Approach Rd. E2 2J **85**
EN4: E Barn 4G **21**
HA8: Edg 6B **28**
KT8: W Mole 5E **148**
SW20 2E **152**
TW15: Ashf 6E **128**
Apps Mdw. Cl. KT8: W Mole 4D **148**
Aprey Gdns. NW4 4E **44**
April Cl. BR6: Chels 5K **173**
TW13: Felt 3J **129**
W7 7J **77**
April Ct. *E2* *2G 85*
(off Teale St.)
April Glen SE23 3K **139**
April St. E8 4F **67**
Apsley Cen., The NW2 2C **62**
Apsley Cl. HA2: Harr 5G **41**
Apsley Ho. *E1* *5J 85*
(off Stepney Way)
NW8 *2B 82*
(off Finchley Rd.)
SW15 *6C 116*
(off Holford Way)
TW4: Houn 4D **112**
Apsley House (Wellington Mus.)
6H 11 (2E 100)
Apsley Rd. KT3: N Mald 3J **151**
SE25 4H **157**
Apsley Way NW2 2C **62**
W1 6H **11** (2E **100**)
(not continuous)
Aqua Ho. NW10 3G **79**
Aquarelle Ho. EC1 1C **8**
Aquarius TW1: Twick 1B **132**
Aquarius Bus. Pk. *NW2* *1C 62*
(off Priestley Way)
Aquarius Ct. HA8: Edg 7B **28**
Aquarius Golf Course **6J 121**
Aqua Vista Sq. *E3* *5C 86*
(off Bow Comn. La.)
Aquila St. NW8 2B **82**
Aquinas St. SE1 5K **13** (1A **102**)
Arabella Ct. *NW8* *2A 82*
(off Marlborough Pl.)
Arabella Dr. SW15 4A **116**
Arabella St. SE16 7K **15** (3G **103**)
Arabia Cl. E4 7K **25**, 1A **36**
Arabian Ho. *E1* *4A 86*
(off Ernest St.)
Arabin Rd. SE4 4A **122**
Arado Ho. *NW9* *2B 44*
(off Boulevard Dr.)
Aragon Av. KT7: T Ditt 5K **149**
Aragon Cl. BR2: Brom 1D **172**
EN2: Enf 1E **22**
TW16: Sun 6H **129**
Aragon Ct. KT8: E Mos 4G **149**
SE11 *5J 19*
(off Hotspur St.)
Aragon Dr. HA4: Ruis 1B **58**
Aragon Ho. *E16* *1J 105*
(off Capulet M.)
Aragon Pl. SM4: Mord 7G **153**
Aragon Rd. KT2: King T 5E **132**
SM4: Mord 6F **153**
Aragon Twr. SE8 4B **104**
Aral Ho. *E1* *4K 85*
(off Ernest St.)
Arandora Cres. RM6: Chad H 7B **54**
Aran Dr. HA7: Stan 4H **27**
Aran Lodge *NW6* *7J 63*
(off Woodchurch Rd.)
Aran M. *N7* *7A 66*
(off St Clements St.)
Arapiles Ho. *E14* *6F 87*
(off Blair St.)
Arbery Rd. E3 3A **86**
Arbon Ct. *N1* *1C 84*
(off Linton St.)
Arbor Cl. BR3: Beck 2D **158**
Arbor Ct. N16 2D **66**
Arboretum Ct. *N1* *6D 66*
(off Dove Rd.)
Arboretum Pl. *IG11: Bark* *7G 71*
(off Clockhouse Av.)
Arborfield Cl. SW2 1K **137**
Arborfield Ho. *E14* *7C 86*
(off E. India Dock Rd.)
Arbor Ho. *BR6: Orp* *2K 173*
(off Orchard Gro.)
TW8: Bford 7C **96**
Arbor Rd. E4 3A **36**
Arbour Ho. *E1* *6K 85*
(off Arbour Sq.)
Arbour Rd. EN3: Pond E 3E **24**
Arbour Sq. E1 6K **85**
Arbroath Rd. SE9 3C **124**
Arbury Ter. SE26 3G **139**
Arbuthnot La.
DA5: Bexl 6E **126**
Arbuthnot Rd. SE14 2K **121**
SM4: Mord 4A **154**
Arbutus St. E8 1F **85**
Arcade CR0: C'don 2C **168**
Arcade, The *CR0: C'don* *3C 168*
(off High St.)
E20 *6E 68*
(within Westfield Stratford City Shop. Cen.)
EC2 6G **9**
IG11: Bark 7G **71**
N7 *4J 65*
(off Macready Pl.)
SE9 *6E 124*
(off High St.)
Arcade Chambers SE9 6E **124**
Arcade Ct. N11 4A **32**
Arcade Pde. KT9: Chess 5D **162**
Arcadia Av. N3 2J **45**
Arcadia Cl. SM5: Cars 4E **166**
Arcadia Ct. E1 7J **9**
Arcadia M. KT3: N Mald 3A **152**
Arcadian Av. DA5: Bexl 6E **126**
Arcadian Cl. DA5: Bexl 6E **126**
Arcadian Gdns. N22 7E **32**
Arcadian Pl. SW18 7H **117**
Arcadian Rd. DA5: Bexl 6E **126**
Arcadia St. E14 6C **86**
Archangel St. SE16 2K **103**
Archbishop Lanfranc School Sports Cen.
6J 155
Archbishop's Pl. SW2 7K **119**
Archdale Ct. W12 1D **98**
Archdale Ho. *SE1* *7G 15*
(off Long La.)
Archdale Pl. KT3: N Mald 3H **151**
Archdale Rd. SE22 5F **121**
Archel Rd. W14 6H **99**
Archer Apartments *N1* *2E 84*
(off Fern Cl.)
Archer Cl. EN5: Barn 6C **20**
KT2: King T 7E **132**
Archer Ho. *N1* *1E 84*
(off Whitmore Est.)
SE14 1A **122**
SW11 1B **118**
W11 *7H 81*
(off Westbourne Gro.)
W13 *1B 96*
(off Sherwood Cl.)
Archer M. SW9 3J **119**
TW12: Hamp H 6G **131**
Archer Rd. BR5: St M Cry 5K **161**
SE25 4H **157**
Archers Ct. *CR2: S Croy* *5C 168*
(off Nottingham Rd.)
Archers Dr. EN3: Enf H 2D **24**
Archers Lodge *SE16* *5G 103*
(off Culloden Cl.)
Archer Sq. SE14 6A **104**
Archer St. W1 2C **12** (7H **83**)
Archer Ter. UB7: Yiew 7A **74**
Archery Cl. HA3: W'stone 3K **41**
W2 1D **10** (6C **82**)
Archery Flds. Ho. *WC1* *1H 7*
(off Wharton St.)
Archery La. BR2: Brom 6B **160**
Archery Rd. SE9 5D **124**
Archery Steps W2 2D **10**
Arches SW8 7F **19** (6J **101**)
Arches, The E16 4G **87**
HA2: Harr 2F **59**
NW1 7F **65**
SE8 6A **104**

Arches, The SW8 7H 101
WC2 4F 13
(off Villiers St.)
Arches Bus. Cen., The UB2: S'hall 2D 94
(off Merrick Rd.)
Archgate Bus. Cen. N12 5F 31
Archibald M. W1 3J 11 (7F 83)
Archibald Rd. N7 4H 65
Archibald St. E3 3C 86
Archie Cl. UB7: W Dray 2C 92
Archie St. SE1 7H 15 (2E 102)
Arc Ho. SE1 7J 15
Arch St. SE1 3C 102
ARCHWAY 2G 65
Archway Bus. Cen. N19 3H 65
Archway Cl. N19 2G 65
SM6: Bedd 3H 167
SW19 3K 135
W10 5F 81
Archway Leisure Cen. 2G 65
Archway Mall N19 2G 65
Archway M. SW15 4G 117
(off Putney Bri. Rd.)
Archway Rd. N6 6E 46
N19 6E 46
Archway St. SW13 3A 116
Arcola St. E8 5F 67
Arcola Theatre 5F 67
Arcon Dr. UB5: N'olt 4C 76
Arcon Ter. N9 7B 24
Arctic Ho. NW9 2B 44
(off Heritage Av.)
Arctic St. NW5 5F 65
Arcus Rd. BR1: Brom 6G 141
Ardbeg Rd. SE24 5D 120
Arden Cl. HA1: Harr 3H 59
SE28 6D 90
TW2: Whitt 7D 112
UB4: Yead 4K 75
Arden Ct. SE26 5J 139
Arden Ct. Gdns. N2 6B 46
Arden Cres. E14 4C 104
RM9: Dag 7C 72
Arden Est. N1 2E 84
Arden Grange N12 4F 31
Arden Gro. BR6: Farnb 4F 173
Arden Ho. N1 1G 9
SE11 4G 19
SE13 3D 122
(off Thurston Rd.)
SW9 2J 119
(off Grantham Rd.)
Arden M. E17 5D 50
Arden Mhor HA5: Eastc 4K 39
Arden Rd. N3 3H 45
W13 7C 78
Ardent Cl. SE25 3E 156
Ardent Ho. E3 2A 86
(off Roman Rd.)
Ardfern Av. SW16 3A 156
Ardfillan Rd. SE6 1F 141
Ardgowan Rd. SE6 7G 123
Ardilaun Rd. N5 4C 66
Ardingly Cl. CR0: C'don 3K 169
Ardleigh Ct. BR1: Brom 7H 141
(off London Rd.)
Ardleigh Gdns. SM3: Sutt 7J 153
Ardleigh Ho. IG11: Bark 1G 89
Ardleigh M. IG1: Ilf 3F 71
Ardleigh Rd. E17 1B 50
N1 6E 66
Ardleigh Ter. E17 1B 50
Ardley Cl. HA4: Ruis 7E 38
NW10 3A 62
SE6 3A 140
Ardlui Rd. SE27 2C 138
Ardmay Gdns. KT6: Surb 5E 150
Ardmere Rd. SE13 6F 123
Ardmore La. IG9: Buck H 1E 36
Ardmore Pl. IG9: Buck H 1E 36
Ardoch Rd. SE6 2F 141
Ardra Rd. N9 3E 34
Ardrossan Gdns. KT4: Wor Pk 3C 164
Ardshiel Cl. SW15 3F 117
Ardwell Av. IG6: Ilf 5G 53
Ardwell Rd. SW2 2J 137
Ardwick Rd. NW2 4J 63
Arena, The EN3: Enf L 1G 25
Arena Bus. Cen. N4 6C 48
Arena Ho. E3 2C 86
(off Lefevre Wlk.)
Arena Shop. Pk. N4 6B 48
Arena Sq. HA9: Wemb 4G 61
Ares Ct. E14 4C 104
(off Homer Dr.)
Arethusa Ho. E14 4C 104
(off Cahir St.)
Argali Ho. DA18: Erith 3E 108
(off Kale Rd.)
Argall Av. E10 7K 49
Argall Way E10 1K 67
Argan Cl. EN5: Barn 3C 20
Argenta Way HA9: Wemb 6G 61
NW10 7H 61
Argent Cen., The UB3: Hayes 2J 93
Argent Ct. E14 5C 86
(off Thomas Rd.)
EN5: New Bar 4F 21
(off Leicester Rd.)
KT6: Surb 3G 163
Argenton Twr. SW18 6K 117
(off Mapleton Cres.)
Argo Bus. Cen. NW6 3J 81
Argonaut Pk. SL3: Poyle 4A 174
Argon M. SW6 7J 99
Argon Rd. N18 5D 34
Argos Ct. SW9 1A 120
(off Caldwell St.)
Argos Ho. E2 2H 85
(off Old Bethnal Grn. Rd.)
Argosy Ho. SE8 4A 104
Argosy La. TW19: Stanw 7A 110
Argus Cl. RM7: Mawney 1H 55
Argus Way UB5: N'olt 3C 76
Argyle Av. TW3: Houn 6E 112
Argyle Cl. W13 4A 78
Argyle Ho. E14 3E 104
Argyle Pas. N17 1F 49
Argyle Pl. W6 4D 98
Argyle Rd. E1 4K 85
E15 4G 69
E16 6K 87
EN5: Barn 4A 20
HA2: Harr 6F 41
IG1: Ilf 2E 70
N12 5E 30
N17 1G 49
N18 4B 34
TW3: Houn 5F 113
UB6: G'frd 3K 77
W13 5A 78
Argyle Sq. WC1 1F 7 (3J 83)
(not continuous)
Argyle St. WC1 1E 6 (3J 83)
Argyle Wlk. WC1 2F 7 (3J 83)
Argyle Way SE16 5G 103
Argyll Av. UB1: S'hall 1F 95
Argyll Cl. SW9 3K 119
Argyll Ct. SW2 7J 119
(off New Pk. Rd.)
Argyll Gdns. HA8: Edg 2H 43
Argyll Mans. SW3 7B 16 (6B 100)
W14 4G 99
(off Hammersmith Rd.)
Argyll Rd. SE18 3G 107
W8 2J 99
Argyll St. W1 1A 12 (6G 83)
Aria Ct. IG2: Ilf 6G 53
Arica Ho. SE16 3H 103
(off Slippers Pl.)
Arica Rd. SE4 4A 122
Ariel Apartments E16 6J 87
Ariel Ct. SE11 4K 19 (4B 102)
Ariel Rd. NW6 6J 63
Ariel Way TW4: Houn 3K 111
W12 1E 98
Aristotle Rd. SW4 3H 119
Arizona Bldg. SE13 1D 122
(off Deal's Gateway)
Ark, The W6 5F 99
(off Talgarth Rd.)
Arkell Gro. SE19 7B 138
Arkindale Rd. SE6 3E 140
Arklay Cl. UB8: Hil 4B 74
Arkley Cres. E17 5B 50
Arkley Rd. E17 5B 50
Arklow Ho. SE17 6D 102
Arklow M. KT6: Surb 2E 162
Arklow Rd. SE14 6B 104
Arklow Rd. Trad. Est. SE14 6A 104
Arkwright Rd. CR2: Sande 7F 169
NW3 5A 64
Arlesey Cl. SW15 5G 117
Arlesford Rd. SW9 3J 119
Arlidge Ho. EC1 5K 7
(off Kirby St.)
Arlingford Rd. SW2 5A 120
Arlington N12 3D 30
Arlington Av. N1 2C 84
Arlington Bldg. E3 2C 86
Arlington Cl. DA15: Sidc 7J 125
SE13 5F 123
SM1: Sutt 2J 165
TW1: Twick 6C 114
Arlington Ct. W3 2H 97
(off Mill Hill Rd.)
Arlington Dr. HA4: Ruis 6F 39
SM5: Cars 2D 166
Arlington Gdns. IG1: Ilf 1E 70
W4 5J 97
Arlington Grn. NW7 7A 30
Arlington Ho. EC1 1K 7
(off Arlington Way)
SE8 6B 104
(off Evelyn St.)
SW1 4A 12 (1G 101)
TW9: Kew 7H 97
UB7: W Dray 2B 92
W12 1D 98
(off Tunis Rd.)
Arlington Lodge SW2 4K 119
Arlington M. SE13 5F 123
Arlington Pk. Mans. W4 5J 97
(off Sutton La. Nth.)
Arlington Pas. TW11: Tedd 4K 131
Arlington Pl. SE10 7E 104
Arlington Rd. IG8: Wfd G 1J 51
KT6: Surb 6D 150
N14 2A 32
NW1 1F 83
TW1: Twick 6C 114
TW10: Ham 2D 132
TW11: Tedd 4K 131
TW15: Ashf 5B 128
W13 6B 78
Arlington Sq. N1 1C 84
Arlington St. SW1 4A 12 (1G 101)
Arlington Way EC1 1K 7 (3A 84)
Arliss Ho. HA1: Harr 5K 41
Arliss Way UB5: N'olt 1A 76
Arlow Rd. N21 1F 33
Armada Ct. SE8 6C 104
Armadale Cl. N17 4H 49
Armadale Rd. SW6 7J 99
TW14: Felt 5J 111
Armada St. SE8 6C 104
Armada Way E6 5F 89
Armagh Rd. E3 1B 86
Arments Ct. SE5 6D 102
(off Albany Rd.)
Armfield Cl. KT8: W Mole 5D 148
Armfield Cres. CR4: Mitc 2D 154
Armfield Rd. EN2: Enf 1J 23
Arminger Rd. W12 1D 98
Armistice Gdns. SE25 3G 157
Armitage Ho. NW1 5D 4
(off Lisson Gro.)
Armitage Rd. NW11 1G 63
SE10 5H 105
Armour Cl. N7 6K 65
Armoury, The 4C 64
(off Pond St.)
Armoury Ho. E3 1A 86
(off Gunmakers La.)
Armoury Rd. SE8 2D 122
Armoury Way SW18 5J 117
Armsby Ho. E1 5J 85
(off Stepney Way)
Armstead Wlk. RM10: Dag 7G 73
Armstrong Av. IG8: Wfd G 6B 36
Armstrong Cl. BR1: Brom 3C 160
E6 6D 88
HA5: Eastc 6J 39
KT12: Walt T 6J 147
RM8: Dag 7D 54
SE3 4K 123
Armstrong Cres. EN4: Cockf 3G 21
Armstrong Ho. E14 6A 86
(off Commercial Rd.)
Armstrong Rd. NW10 7A 62
SE18 3G 107
SW7 2A 16 (3B 100)
TW13: Hanw 5C 130
W3 1B 98
Armstrong Way UB2: S'hall 2F 95
Armytage Rd. TW5: Hest 7B 94
Arnal Cres. SW18 7G 117
Arncliffe NW6 2K 81
Arncliffe Cl. N11 6K 31
Arncroft Ct. IG11: Bark 3B 90
Arndale Wlk. SW18 5K 117
Arne Gro. BR6: Orp 3K 173
Arne Ho. SE11 5G 19
Arne St. WC2 1F 13 (6J 83)
Arnett Sq. E4 6G 35
Arne Wlk. SE3 4H 123
Arneways Av. RM6: Chad H 3D 54
Arneway St. SW1 2D 18 (3H 101)
Arnewood Cl. SW15 1C 134
Arneys La. CR4: Mitc 6E 154
Arngask Rd. SE6 7F 123
Arnhem Pl. E14 3C 104
Arnhem Way SE22 5E 120
Arnhem Wharf E14 3B 104
Arnison Rd. KT8: E Mos 4H 149
Arnold Bennett Way N8 3A 48
Arnold Cir. E2 2J 9 (3F 85)
Arnold Cl. HA3: Kenton 7F 43
Arnold Ct. N22 7D 32
Arnold Cres. TW7: Isle 5H 113
Arnold Dr. KT9: Chess 6D 162
Arnold Est. SE1 7K 15 (2F 103)
(not continuous)
Arnold Gdns. N13 5G 33
Arnold Ho. SE3 7A 106
(off Shooters Hill Rd.)
SE17 5B 102
(off Doddington Gro.)
Arnold Mans. W14 6H 99
(off Queen's Club Gdns.)
Arnold Rd. E3 3C 86
N15 3F 49
RM9: Dag 7F 73
RM10: Dag 7F 73
SW17 7D 136
UB5: N'olt 6B 58
Arnold Ter. HA7: Stan 5E 26
Arnos Gro. N14 4C 32
Arnos Gro. Ct. N11 5B 32
(off Palmer's Rd.)
Arnos Rd. N11 5B 32
Arnos Swimming Pool 5C 32
Arnot Ho. SE5 7C 102
(off Comber Gro.)

Arnott Cl. SE28 1C 108
W4 4K 97
Arnould Av. SE5 4D 120
Arnsberg Way DA6: Bex 4G 127
DA7: Bex 4G 127
Arnside Gdns. HA9: Wemb 1D 60
Arnside Ho. *SE17* *6D 102*
(off Arnside St.)
Arnside Rd. DA7: Bex 1G 127
Arnside St. SE17 6D 102
Arnulf St. SE6 4D 140
Arnulls Rd. SW16 6B 138
Arodene Rd. SW2 6K 119
Arona Ho. BR3: Beck 2E 158
Arosa Rd. TW1: Twick 6D 114
Arpley Sq. *SE20* *7J 139*
(off High St.)
Arragon Gdns.
BR4: W W'ck 3D 170
SW16 7J 137
Arragon Rd. E6 1B 88
SW18 1J 135
TW1: Twick 7A 114
Arran Cl. DA8: Erith 6K 109
SM6: Wall 4F 167
Arran Ct. NW9 2B 44
NW10 3K 61
Arran Dr. E12 1B 70
Arran Ho. *E14* *1E 104*
(off Raleana Rd.)
Arran M. W5 1F 97
Arran Rd. SE6 2D 140
Arran Wlk. N1 7C 66
Arras Av. SM4: Mord 5A 154
Arrol Ho. SE1 3C 102
Arrol Rd. BR3: Beck 3J 157
Arrow Ct. *SW5* *4J 99*
(off W. Cromwell Rd.)
Arrowhead Quay E14 2C 104
Arrow Ho. *N1* *1E 84*
(off Wilmer Gdns.)
Arrow Rd. E3 3D 86
Arrowscout Wlk. *UB5: N'olt* *3C 76*
(off Argus Way)
Arrows Ho. *SE15* *7J 103*
(off Clifton Way)
Arrowsmith Ho. SE11 5G 19
Arsenal FC 4A 66
Arsenal Rd. SE9 2D 124
Arsenal Way SE18 3G 107
Arta Ho. *E1* *6J 85*
(off Devonport St.)
Artbrand Ho. *SE1* *7G 15*
(off Leathermarket St.)
Artemis SW11 2D 118
Artemis Ct. *E14* *4C 104*
(off Homer Dr.)
Artemis Pl. SW18 7H 117
Arterberry Rd. SW20 7E 134
Artesian Cl. NW10 7K 61
Artesian Gro. EN5: New Bar 4F 21
Artesian Ho. *SE1* *3F 103*
(off Grange Rd.)
Artesian Rd. W2 6J 81
Artesian Wlk. E11 3G 69
Arthaus Apartments *E8* *6H 67*
(off Richmond Rd.)
Arthingworth St. E15 1G 87
Arthouse
Crouch End 5J 47
Arthur Ct. *CR0: C'don* *3E 168*
(off Fairfield Path)
SW11 1E 118
W2 *6K 81*
(off Queensway)
W10 *6F 81*
(off Silchester Rd.)
Arthur Deakin Ho. *E1* *5K 9*
(off Hunton St.)
Arthurdon Rd. SE4 5C 122
Arthur Gro. SE18 4G 107
Arthur Henderson Ho. *SW6* *2H 117*
(off Fulham Rd.)
Arthur Horsley Wlk. *E7* *5H 69*
(off Tower Hamlets Rd.)
Arthur Ho. *N1* *1E 84*
(off Halcomb St.)
Arthur Lovell Ct. *E14* *6B 86*
(off Lovat Cl.)
Arthur Newton Ho.
SW11 *3B 118*
(off Winstanley Est.)
Arthur Rd. E6 2D 88
KT2: King T 7G 133
KT3: N Mald 5D 152
N7 4K 65
N9 2A 34
RM6: Chad H 6C 54
SW19 5H 135
Arthur St. EC4 2F 15 (7D 84)
Arthur Wade Ho. *E2* *1K 9*
(off Baroness Rd.)
Arthur Wallis Ho. *E12* *3E 70*
(off Grantham Rd.)
Artichoke Hill E1 7H 85
Artichoke M. *SE5* *1D 120*
(off Artichoke Pl.)
Artichoke Pl. SE5 1D 120
Artichoke Wlk.
TW9: Rich *5D 114*
(off Red Lion St.)
Artillery Bldg., The *E1* *6H 9*
(off Artillery La.)
Artillery Cl. IG2: Ilf 6G 53
Artillery Ho. *E3* *1A 86*
(off Barge La.)
E15 6G 69
SE18 *5E 106*
(off Connaught M.)
Artillery La. E1 6H 9 (5E 84)
W12 6C 80
Artillery Mans. SW1 1C 18
Artillery Pas. E1 6J 9
Artillery Pl.
HA3: Hrw W 7B 26
SE18 4D 106
SW1 2C 18 (3H 101)
Artillery Row SW1 2C 18 (3G 101)
Artillery Sq. *SE18* *3F 107*
(off No 1 St.)
Artington Cl. BR6: Farnb 4G 173
Artisan Cl. E6 6F 89
Artisan Ct. E8 6G 67
Artisan M. *NW10* *3F 81*
(off Warfield Rd.)
Artisan Pl. HA3: W'stone 2J 41
Artisan Quarter *NW10* *3F 81*
(off Wellington Rd.)
Artizan St. E1 7J 9
Arts Depot 5F 31
Arts La. SE16 3F 103
Arts Sq. E1 4A 86
Arts Theatre *2E 12*
(off Gt. Newport St.)
Arun Ct. SE25 5G 157
Arundale *KT1: King T* *4D 150*
(off Anglesea Rd.)
Arundel Av. SM4: Mord 4H 153
Arundel Bldgs. SE1 3E 102
Arundel Cl. CR0: Wadd 3B 168
DA5: Bexl 6F 127
E15 4G 69
SW11 5C 118
TW12: Hamp H 5F 131
Arundel Ct. BR2: Brom 2G 159
HA2: Harr 4E 58
N12 6H 31
N17 1G 49
SE16 *5H 103*
(off Verney Rd.)
SW3 *5D 16*
(off Jubilee Pl.)
Arundel Ct. *SW13* *6D 98*
(off Arundel Ter.)
W11 *7H 81*
(off Arundel Gdns.)
Arundel Dr. HA2: Harr 4D 58
IG8: Wfd G 7D 36
Arundel Gdns.
HA8: Edg 7E 28
IG3: Ilf 2A 72
N21 1F 33
W11 7H 81
Arundel Gt. Ct. WC2 2H 13 (7K 83)
Arundel Gro. N16 5E 66
Arundel Ho.
CR0: C'don *5D 168*
(off Heathfield Rd.)
E17 1B 50
W3 *2H 97*
(off Park Rd. Nth.)
Arundel Mans. *SW6* *1H 117*
(off Kelvedon Rd.)
Arundel Pl. N1 6A 66
Arundel Rd. CR0: C'don 6D 156
EN4: Cockf 3H 21
KT1: King T 2H 151
SM2: Cheam, Sutt 7H 165
(not continuous)
TW4: Houn 3A 112
Arundel Sq. N7 6A 66
Arundel St. WC2 2H 13 (7K 83)
Arundel Ter. SW13 6D 98
Arun Ho. KT2: King T 1D 150
Arvon Rd. N5 5A 66
(not continuous)
Asa Ct. UB3: Harl 3H 93
Asbaston Ter. IG1: Ilf 6G 71
Asbridge Ct. *W6* *3D 98*
(off Dalling Rd.)
Asbury Ct. *N21* *5D 22*
(off Pennington Dr.)
Ascalon Ho. *SW8* *7G 101*
(off Thessaly Rd.)
Ascalon St. SW8 7G 101
Ascensis Twr. SW18 4A 118
Ascent Ho. *NW9* *2B 44*
(off Boulevard Dr.)
Ascham Dr. E4 7J 35
Ascham End E17 1A 50
Ascham St. NW5 5G 65
Aschurch Rd. CR0: C'don 7F 157
Ascot Cl. UB5: N'olt 5E 58
Ascot Ct. DA5: Bexl 7F 127
NW8 2A 4
Ascot Gdns. UB1: S'hall 4D 76
Ascot Ho. *NW1* *1K 5*
(off Redhill St.)
W9 *4J 81*
(off Harrow Rd.)
Ascot Lodge NW6 1K 81
Ascot Pl. HA7: Stan 5H 27
Ascot Rd. BR5: St M Cry 4K 161
E6 3D 88
N15 5D 48
N18 4B 34
SW17 6E 136
TW14: Bedf 1C 128
Ascott Av. W5 2E 96
Ascott Cl. HA5: Eastc 4J 39
Ashanti M. E8 5J 67
Ashbee Ho. *E2* *3J 85*
(off Portman Pl.)
Ashbourne Av. DA7: Bex 7E 108
E18 4K 51
HA2: Harr 2H 59
N20 2J 31
NW11 5H 45
Ashbourne Cl. N12 4E 30
W5 5G 79
Ashbourne Ct. E5 4A 68
N12 *4E 30*
(off Ashbourne Cl.)
Ashbourne Gro. NW7 5E 28
SE22 4F 121
W4 5A 98
Ashbourne Pde. NW11 4H 45
W5 4F 79
Ashbourne Ri. BR6: Orp 4J 173
Ashbourne Rd. CR4: Mitc 7E 136
W5 4F 79
Ashbourne Ter. SW19 7H 135
Ashbourne Way NW11 4H 45
Ashbridge Rd. E11 7G 51
Ashbridge St. NW8 4C 4 (4C 82)
Ashbrook HA8: Edg 6A 28
Ashbrook Rd. N19 1H 65
RM10: Dag 3H 73
Ashburn Gdns. SW7 4A 100
Ashburnham Av. HA1: Harr 6K 41
Ashburnham Cl. N2 3B 46
Ashburnham Ct. BR3: Beck 2E 158
Ashburnham Gdns. HA1: Harr 6K 41
Ashburnham Gro. SE10 7D 104
Ashburnham Mans. *SW10* *7A 100*
(off Ashburnham Rd.)
Ashburnham Pl. SE10 7D 104
Ashburnham Retreat SE10 7D 104
Ashburnham Rd. DA17: Belv 4J 109
NW10 3E 80
SW10 7A 100
TW10: Ham 3B 132
Ashburnham Twr. *SW10* *7B 100*
(off Worlds End Est.)
Ashburn Pl. SW7 4A 100
Ashburton Av. CR0: C'don 1H 169
IG3: Ilf 5J 71
Ashburton Cl. CR0: C'don 1G 169
Ashburton Ent. Cen. SW15 6E 116
Ashburton Gdns. CR0: C'don 2G 169
ASHBURTON GROVE 4A 66
Ashburton Ho. *W9* *4H 81*
(off Fernhead Rd.)
Ashburton Memorial Homes
CR0: C'don 7H 157
Ashburton Rd. CR0: C'don 2G 169
E16 6J 87
HA4: Ruis 2J 57
Ashburton Ter. E13 2J 87
Ashburton Triangle N5 4A 66
Ashbury Dr. UB10: Ick 3D 56
Ashbury Gdns. RM6: Chad H 5D 54
Ashbury Pl. SW19 6A 136
Ashbury Rd. SW11 3D 118
Ashby Av. KT9: Chess 6G 163
Ashby Cl. BR4: W W'ck 3F 171
Ashby Ct. *NW8* *3B 4*
(off Pollitt Dr.)
Ashby Gro. N1 7C 66
(not continuous)
Ashby Ho. *N1* *7C 66*
(off Essex Rd.)
SW9 2B 120
UB5: N'olt *4D 76*
(off Waxlow Way)
Ashby M. SE4 2B 122
SW2 *5J 119*
(off Prague Pl.)
Ashby Rd. N15 5G 49
SE4 2B 122
Ashbys Ct. *E3* *2B 86*
(off Centurion La.)
Ashby St. EC1 2B 8 (3B 84)
Ashby Wlk. CR0: C'don 6C 156
Ashby Way UB7: Sip 7C 92
Ashchurch Gro. W12 3C 98
Ashchurch Pk. Vs. W12 3C 98
Ashchurch Ter. W12 3C 98
Ash Cl. BR5: Pet W 5H 161
DA14: Sidc 3B 144
HA7: Stan 6F 27
HA8: Edg 4D 28
KT3: N Mald 2K 151
RM5: Col R 1H 55

Ash Cl.—Askew Est.

Ash Cl. SE20 2J **157**
SM5: Cars 2D **166**
TW7: Isle 1K **113**
UB9: Hare 1A **38**
Ashcombe Av. KT6: Surb 7D **150**
Ashcombe Cl. TW15: Ashf 3A **128**
Ashcombe Ct. TW15: Ashf 2B **128**
Ashcombe Gdns.
HA8: Edg 4B **28**
Ashcombe Ho. *E3* *3D 86*
(off Bruce Rd.)
EN3: Pond E 3E **24**
Ashcombe Pk. NW2 3A **62**
Ashcombe Rd. SM5: Cars 6E **166**
SW19 5J **135**
Ashcombe Sq. KT3: N Mald 3J **151**
Ashcombe St. SW6 2K **117**
Ash Ct. KT19: Ewe 4J **163**
N11 6B **32**
SW19 7G **135**
Ashcroft HA5: Hat E 6A **26**
N14 2C **32**
Ashcroft Av. DA15: Sidc 6A **126**
Ashcroft Ct. N20 2G **31**
Ashcroft Cres. DA15: Sidc 6A **126**
Ashcroft Ho. *SW8* *1G 119*
(off Wadhurst Rd.)
Ashcroft Rd. KT9: Chess 3F **163**
Ashcroft Sq. W6 4E **98**
Ashcroft Theatre
Croydon *3D 168*
(within Fairfield Halls)
Ashdale Cl. TW2: Whitt 7G **113**
TW19: Stanw 2A **128**
Ashdale Gro. HA7: Stan 6E **26**
Ashdale Ho. N4 7D **48**
Ashdale Rd. SE12 1K **141**
Ashdale Way TW2: Whitt 7F **113**
Ashdene HA5: Pinn 3A **40**
SE15 7H **103**
Ashdene Cl. TW15: Ashf 7E **128**
Ashdon Cl. IG8: Wfd G 6E **36**
Ashdon Rd. NW10 1B **80**
Ashdown *W13* *5B 78*
(off Clivedon Ct.)
Ashdown Cl. BR3: Beck 2D **158**
DA5: Bexl 7J **127**
Ashdown Ct. E17 2E **50**
IG11: Bark 6F **71**
SM2: Sutt 6A **166**
Ashdown Cres. NW5 5E **64**
Ashdowne Ct. N17 1G **49**
Ashdown Pl. KT7: T Ditt 7A **150**
KT17: Ewe 7B **164**
Ashdown Rd. EN3: Enf H 2D **24**
KT1: King T 2E **150**
UB10: Hil 2C **74**
Ashdown Wlk. E14 4C **104**
RM7: Mawney 1H **55**
Ashdown Way SW17 2E **136**
Ashe Ho. TW1: Twick 6D **114**
Ashen E6 6E **88**
Ashenden Rd. E5 5A **68**
Ashen Gro. SW19 3J **135**
Ashentree Ct. EC4 1K **13**
Asher Loftus Way N11 6J **31**
Asher Way E1 7G **85**
Ashfield Av. TW13: Felt 1K **129**
WD23: Bush 1B **26**
Ashfield Cl. BR3: Beck 7C **140**
TW10: Ham 1E **132**
Ashfield Ct. *SW9* *2J 119*
(off Clapham Rd.)
Ashfield Ho. *W14* *5H 99*
(off W. Cromwell Rd.)
Ashfield La. BR7: Chst 6F **143**
(not continuous)
Ashfield Pde. N14 1C **32**
Ashfield Rd. N4 6C **48**
N14 3B **32**
W3 1B **98**
Ashfield St. E1 5H **85**
(not continuous)
Ashfield Yd. E1 5J **85**
ASHFORD 4B 128
Ashford Av. N8 4J **47**
TW15: Ashf 6D **128**
UB4: Yead 6B **76**
Ashford Bus. Complex TW15: Ashf 5E **128**
Ashford Cl. E17 6B **50**
TW15: Ashf 4A **128**
ASHFORD COMMON 7F 129
Ashford Ct. HA8: Edg 3C **28**
NW2 4F **63**
Ashford Cres. EN3: Enf H 2D **24**
TW15: Ashf 3A **128**
Ashford Ho. SE8 6B **104**
SW9 4B **120**
Ashford Ind. Est. TW15: Ashf 4E **128**
Ashford Manor Golf Course 6B 128
Ashford M. N17 1G **49**
Ashford Pas. NW2 4F **63**
Ashford Rd. E6 7E **70**
E18 2K **51**
NW2 4F **63**
TW13: Felt 4F **129**
TW15: Ashf 7E **128**
TW18: Lale, Staines 7A **128**
Ashford St. N1 1G **9** (3E **84**)
Ashford Tennis Club 4A 128
Ash Gro. BR4: W W'ck 2E **170**
E8 1H **85**
(not continuous)
EN1: Enf 7K **23**
HA0: Wemb 4A **60**
N10 4F **47**
N13 3H **33**
NW2 4F **63**
SE12 1J **141**
SE20 2J **157**
TW5: Hest 1B **112**
TW14: Felt 1G **129**
UB1: S'hall 5E **76**
UB3: Hayes 7F **75**
UB7: Yiew 7B **74**
UB9: Hare 1A **38**
W5 2E **96**
Ashgrove Ct. *W9* *5J 81*
(off Elmfield Way)
Ashgrove Ho. *SW1* *5D 18*
(off Lindsay Sq.)
Ashgrove Rd. BR1: Brom 6F **141**
IG3: Ilf 1K **71**
TW15: Ashf 5E **128**
Ash Hill Cl. WD23: Bush 1A **26**
Ash Hill Dr. HA5: Pinn 3A **40**
Ash Ho. *E14* *2E 104*
(off E. Ferry Rd.)
SE1 *4F 103*
(off Longfield Est.)
W10 *4G 81*
(off Heather Wlk.)
Ashingdon Cl. E4 3K **35**
Ashington Ho. *E1* *4H 85*
(off Barnsley St.)
Ashington Rd. SW6 2H **117**
Ash Island KT8: E Mos 3H **149**
Ashlake Rd. SW16 4J **137**
Ashland Pl. W1 5G **5** (5E **82**)
Ashlar Pl. SE18 4F **107**
Ashleigh Commercial Est. SE7 3A **106**
Ashleigh Ct. N14 7B **22**
W5 *4D 96*
(off Murray Rd.)
Ashleigh Gdns. SM1: Sutt 2K **165**
Ashleigh M. *SE15* *3F 121*
(off Oglander Rd.)
Ashleigh Point SE23 3K **139**
Ashleigh Rd. SE20 3H **157**
SW14 3A **116**
Ashley Av. IG6: Ilf 2F **53**
SM4: Mord 5J **153**
Ashley Cl. HA5: Pinn 2K **39**
NW4 2E **44**
Ashley Ct. EN5: New Bar 5F **21**
NW4 2E **44**
SW1 *2A 18*
(off Morpeth Ter.)
UB5: N'olt 1C **76**
Ashley Cres. N22 2A **48**
SW11 3E **118**
Ashley Dr. TW2: Whitt 7F **113**
TW7: Isle 6J **95**
Ashley Gdns.
BR6: Orp 5J **173**
HA9: Wemb 2E **60**
N13 4H **33**
SW1 2B **18** (3G **101**)
(not continuous)
TW10: Ham 2D **132**
Ashley La. CR0: Wadd 4B **168**
NW4 2E **44**
Ashley Pl. SW1 2A **18** (3G **101**)
(not continuous)
Ashley Rd. CR7: Thor H 4K **155**
E4 6H **35**
E7 7A **70**
EN3: Enf H 2D **24**
KT7: T Ditt 6K **149**
N17 3G **49**
N19 1J **65**
SW19 6K **135**
TW9: Rich 3E **114**
TW12: Hamp 1E **148**
Ashley Wlk. NW7 7K **29**
Ashling Rd. CR0: C'don 1G **169**
Ashlin Rd. E15 4F **69**
Ash Lodge KT12: Walt T 7J **147**
TW16: Sun *7H 129*
(off Forest Dr.)
Ashlone Rd. SW15 3E **116**
Ashlyns Way KT9: Chess 6D **162**
Ashmead N14 5B **22**
Ashmead Bus. Cen. E16 4F **87**
Ashmead Cl. TW15: Ashf 7E **128**
Ashmead Ga. BR1: Brom 1A **160**
Ashmead Ho. *E9* *5A 68*
(off Homerton Rd.)
W13 *1A 96*
(off Tewkesbury Rd.)
Ashmead M. SE8 2C **122**
Ashmead Rd. SE8 2C **122**
TW14: Felt 1J **129**
Ashmere Av. BR3: Beck 2F **159**
Ashmere Cl. SM3: Cheam 5F **165**
Ashmere Gro. SW2 4J **119**
Ash M. NW5 5G **65**
Ashmill St. NW1 5C **4** (5C **82**)
Ashmole Pl. SW8 6K **101**
Ashmole St. SW8 6K **101**
Ashmore *NW1* *7H 65*
(off Agar Gro.)
Ashmore Cl. SE15 7F **103**
Ashmore Ct. N11 6J **31**
TW5: Hest 6E **94**
Ashmore Gro. DA16: Well 3H **125**
Ashmore Ho. *W14* *3G 99*
(off Russell Rd.)
Ashmore Rd. SE18 7D **106**
W9 2H **81**
Ashmount Est. N19 7H **47**
Ashmount Rd. N15 5F **49**
N19 7G **47**
Ashmount Ter. W5 4D **96**
Ashmour Gdns.
RM1: Rom 2K **55**
Ashneal Gdns. HA1: Harr 3H **59**
Ashness Gdns.
UB6: G'frd 6B **60**
Ashness Rd. SW11 5D **118**
Ashpark Ho. *E14* *6B 86*
(off Norbiton Rd.)
Ashridge Cl. HA3: Kenton 6C **42**
Ashridge Ct. N3 3J **45**
N14 5B **22**
UB1: S'hall *6G 77*
(off Redcroft Rd.)
Ashridge Cres. SE18 7G **107**
Ashridge Gdns. HA5: Pinn 4C **40**
N13 5C **32**
Ashridge Way SM4: Mord 3H **153**
TW16: Sun 6J **129**
Ash Rd. BR6: Chels 7K **173**
CR0: C'don 2C **170**
E15 5G **69**
SM3: Sutt 7G **153**
TW17: Shep 4C **146**
Ash Row BR2: Brom 7E **160**
Ashtead Rd. E5 7G **49**
Ashton Cl. SM1: Sutt 4J **165**
Ashton Ct. E4 3B **36**
HA1: Harr 3K **59**
Ashton Gdns. RM6: Chad H 6E **54**
TW4: Houn 4D **112**
Ashton Hgts. SE23 1J **139**
Ashton Ho. SE11 5K **19**
SW9 7A **102**
Ashton Pl. KT10: Clay 7A **162**
Ashton Reach SE16 4A **104**
Ashton Rd. E15 5F **69**
Ashton St. E14 7E **86**
Ashtree Av. CR4: Mitc 2B **154**
Ash Tree Cl. CR0: C'don 6A **158**
KT6: Surb 2E **162**
Ashtree Cl. BR6: Farnb 4F **173**
Ash Tree Ct. *TW15: Ashf* *5D 128*
(off Feltham Hill Rd.)
Ash Tree Dell NW9 5J **43**
Ash Tree Ho. *SE5* *7C 102*
(off Pitman St.)
Ash Tree Way CR0: C'don 5K **157**
Ashurst Cl. SE20 1H **157**
Ashurst Dr. IG2: Ilf 6F **53**
IG6: Ilf 5G **53**
TW17: Shep 5A **146**
Ashurst Gdns. SW2 1A **138**
Ashurst Rd. EN4: Cockf 5J **21**
N12 5H **31**
Ashurst Wlk. CR0: C'don 2H **169**
Ashvale Ct. *E3* *2C 86*
(off Matilda Gdns.)
Ashvale Rd. SW17 5D **136**
Ashview Apartments *N4* *7C 48*
(off Katherine Cl.)
Ashview Cl. TW15: Ashf 5A **128**
Ashview Gdns. TW15: Ashf 5A **128**
Ashville Rd. E11 2F **69**
Ash Wlk. HA0: Wemb 4C **60**
Ashwater Rd. SE12 1J **141**
Ash Way IG8: Wfd G 2B **52**
Ashway Cen., The KT2: King T 1E **150**
Ashwell Cl. E6 6C **88**
Ashwell Ct. TW15: Ashf 2A **128**
Ashwin St. E8 6F **67**
Ashwood Av. UB8: Hil 6C **74**
Ashwood Gdns. CR0: New Ad 6E **170**
UB3: Harl 4H **93**
Ashwood Ho. *NW4* *4E 44*
(off Belle Vue Est.)
Ashwood Rd. E4 3A **36**
Ashworth Cl. SE5 2D **120**
Ashworth Est. CR0: Bedd 1J **167**
Ashworth Mans. *W9* *3K 81*
(off Elgin Av.)
Ashworth Rd. W9 3K **81**
Aske Ho. N1 1G **9**
Asker Ho. N7 4J **65**
Askern Cl. DA6: Bex 4D **126**
Aske St. N1 1G **9** (3E **84**)
Askew Bldg., The *EC1* *5C 84*
(off Bartholomew Cl.)
Askew Cres. W12 2B **98**
Askew Est. *W12* *1B 98*
(off Uxbridge Rd.)

Askew Rd.—Auckland Cl.

Askew Rd. W12 2B 98
Askham Ct. W12 1C 98
Askham Rd. W12 1C 98
Askill Dr. SW15 5G 117
Askwith Rd. RM13: Rain 3K 91
Asland Rd. E15 1G 87
Aslett St. SW18 7K 117
Asman Ho. N1 2B 84
(off Colebrooke Rd.)
Asmara Rd. NW2 5G 63
Asmuns Hill NW11 5J 45
Asmuns Pl. NW11 5H 45
Asolando Dr. SE17 4C 102
Aspect Ct. E14 2E 104
(off Manchester Rd.)
SW6 2A 118
Aspects SM1: Sutt 5K 165
Aspen Cl. KT1: Hamp W 1C 150
N19 2G 65
UB7: Yiew 1B 92
W5 2F 97
Aspen Copse BR1: Brom 2D 160
Aspen Ct. NW4 2G 45
Aspen Dr. HA0: Wemb 3A 60
Aspen Gdns. CR4: Mitc 5E 154
TW15: Ashf 5E 128
W6 5D 98
Aspen Grn. DA18: Erith 3F 109
Aspen Gro. HA5: Eastc 3H 39
Aspen Ho. DA15: Sidc 2A 144
E15 3G 87
(off Teasel Way)
SE15 6J 103
(off Sharratt St.)
Aspen La. UB5: N'olt 3C 76
Aspenlea Rd. W6 6F 99
Aspen Lodge W8 3K 99
(off Abbots Wlk.)
Aspen M. SE20 6J 139
Aspen Pl. WD23: B Hea 1D 26
Aspen Way E14 7D 86
TW13: Felt 3K 129
Aspern Gro. NW3 5C 64
Aspinall Rd. SE4 3K 121
(not continuous)
Aspinden Rd. SE16 4H 103
ASPIRE National Training Cen. 2G 27
Aspire Sport & Fitness Cen. 1K 33
Aspland Gro. E8 6H 67
Aspley Rd. SW18 5K 117
Asplins Rd. N17 1G 49
Asprey M. BR3: Beck 5B 158
Asprey Pl. BR1: Brom 2C 160
Asquith Cl. RM8: Dag 1C 72
Asquith Ho. SW1 2D 18
(off Monck St.)
Assam St. E1 6G 85
(off White Church La.)
Assata M. N1 6B 66
Assembly Apartments SE15 1J 121
(off York Gro.)
Assembly Pas. E1 5J 85
Assembly Wlk. SM5: Cars 7C 154
Ass Ho. La. HA3: Hrw W 4A 26
Astall Cl. HA3: Hrw W 1J 41
Astbury Bus. Pk. SE15 1J 121
Astbury Ho. SE11 2J 19
Astbury Rd. SE15 1J 121
Astell Ho. SW3 5D 16
(off Astell St.)
Astell Rd. SE3 4A 124
Astell St. SW3 5D 16 (5C 100)
Asten Way RM7: Mawney 2H 55
Aster Ct. E5 2J 67
(off Woodmill Rd.)
Asterid Hgts. E20 5E 68
(off Liberty Bri. Rd.)
Aster Pl. E9 7J 67
(off Frampton Pk. Rd.)
Aste St. E14 2E 104
Astey's Row N1 7C 66
Asthall Gdns. IG6: Ilf 4G 53
Astins Ho. E17 4D 50
Astleham Rd. TW17: Shep 3A 146
Astle St. SW11 2E 118
Astley Av. NW2 5E 62
Astley Ho. SE1 5F 103
(off Rowcross St.)
SW13 6D 98
(off Wyatt Dr.)
W2 5J 81
(off Alfred Rd.)
Aston Av. HA3: Kenton 7C 42
Aston Cl. DA14: Sidc 3A 144
Aston Ct. IG8: Wfd G 6D 36
Aston Grn. TW4: Cran 2A 112
Aston Ho. EC4 6J 7
(off Furnival St.)
RM8: Dag 4A 72
SW8 1H 119
W11 7H 81
(off Westbourne Gro.)
Aston M. RM6: Chad H 7C 54
W10 3F 81
Aston Pl. SW16 6B 138
Aston Rd. SW20 2E 152
W5 6D 78
Aston St. E14 5A 86
Aston Ter. SW12 6F 119
Astonville St. SW18 1J 135
Aston Webb Ho. SE1 5G 15
Astor Av. RM7: Rom 6J 55
Astor Cl. KT2: King T 6H 133
Astor Ct. E16 6A 88
(off Ripley Rd.)
SW6 7A 100
(off Maynard Cl.)
Astoria Ct. E8 7F 67
(off Queensbridge Rd.)
Astoria Ho. NW9 2B 44
(off Boulevard Dr.)
Astoria Mans. SW16 3J 137
Astoria Wlk. SW9 3A 120
Astra Ho. E3 3B 86
(off Alfred St.)
SE14 6B 104
(off Arklow Rd.)
Astral Ho. E1 6H 9
(off Middlesex Rd.)
SE6 4E 140
Astrid Ho. TW13: Felt 2A 130
Astrop M. W6 3E 98
Astrop Ter. W6 2E 98
Astwood M. SW7 4A 100
Asylum Rd. SE15 7H 103
Atalanta St. SW6 7F 99
Atbara Rd. TW11: Tedd 6B 132
Atcham Rd. TW3: Houn 4G 113
Atcost Rd. IG11: Bark 5A 90
Atcraft Cen. HA0: Wemb 1E 78
Atelier Ct. SE8 7C 104
(off Watson's St.)
Atelier Ct. Central E14 5E 86
(off Leven Rd.)
Atelier Ct. Nth. E14 5E 86
(off Leven Rd.)
Atelier Ct. Sth. E14 5E 86
(off Leven Rd.)
Atheldene Rd. SW18 1K 135
Athelney St. SE6 3C 140
Athelstane Gro. E3 2B 86
Athelstane M. N4 1A 66
Athelstan Gdns. NW6 7G 63
Athelstan Ho. E9 5B 68
(off Homerton Rd.)
KT1: King T 4F 151
(off Athelstan Rd.)
Athelstan Pl. TW2: Twick 1J 131
Athelstan Rd. KT1: King T 4F 151
Athelstone Rd. HA3: W'stone 2H 41
Athena Cl. HA2: Harr 2H 59
KT1: King T 3F 151
Athena Ct. SE1 7G 15
(off City Wlk.)
Athenaeum Ct. N5 4C 66
Athenaeum Pl. N10 3F 47
Athenaeum Rd. N20 1F 31
Athena Pl. HA6: Nwood 1H 39
Athene Pl. EC4 7K 7
(off Thavie's Inn)
Athenia Ho. E14 6F 87
(off Blair St.)
Athenlay Rd. SE15 5K 121
Athens Gdns. W9 4J 81
(off Harrow Rd.)
Atherden Rd. E5 4J 67
Atherfold Rd. SW9 3J 119
Atherley Way TW4: Houn 7D 112
Atherstone Ct. W2 5K 81
(off Delamere Ter.)
Atherstone M. SW7 4A 100
Atherton Dr. SW19 4F 135
Atherton Hgts.
HA0: Wemb 7C 60
Atherton Leisure Cen. 6H 69
Atherton M. E7 6H 69
Atherton Pl. HA2: Harr 3H 41
UB1: S'hall 7E 76
Atherton Rd. E7 6H 69
IG5: Ilf 2C 52
SW13 7C 98
Atherton St. SW11 2C 118
Athlone Cl. E5 5H 67
Athlone Ct. E17 3F 51
Athlone Ga. W10 5G 81
Athlone Ho. E1 6J 85
(off Sidney St.)
Athlone Pl. W10 5G 81
(off Athlone Ga.)
Athlone Rd. SW2 7K 119
Athlone St. NW5 6E 64
Athlon Ind. Est. HA0: Wemb 1D 78
Athlon Rd. HA0: Wemb 2D 78
Athol Cl. HA5: Pinn 1K 39
Athole Gdns. EN1: Enf 5K 23
Athol Gdns. HA5: Pinn 1K 39
Atholl Ho. W9 3A 82
(off Maida Vale)
Atholl Rd. IG3: Ilf 7A 54
Athol Rd. DA8: Erith 5J 109
Athol Sq. E14 6E 86
Athol Way UB10: Hil 3C 74
Atkin Bldg. WC1 5H 7
(off Raymond Bldgs.)
Atkins Ct. E3 1B 86
(off Willow Tree Cl.)
Atkins Dr. BR4: W W'ck 2F 171
Atkins Lodge W8 2J 99
(off Thornwood Gdns.)
Atkinson Cl. BR6: Chels 5K 173
SW20 7C 134
Atkinson Ct. E10 7D 50
(off Kings Cl.)
Atkinson Ho. E2 2G 85
(off Pritchards Rd.)
E13 4H 87
(off Sutton Rd.)
SE17 4D 102
(off Catesby St.)
SW11 1E 118
(off Austin Rd.)
Atkinson Morley Av. SW17 3B 136
Atkinson Rd. E16 5A 88
Atkins Rd. E10 6D 50
SW12 7G 119
Atkins Sq. E5 5H 67
Atlanta Bldg. SE13 1D 122
(off Deal's Gateway)
Atlanta Ct. CR7: Thor H 3C 156
Atlanta Ho. SE16 3A 104
(off Brunswick Quay)
Atlantic Apartments E16 7J 87
(off Seagull La.)
Atlantic Ct. E14 7F 87
(off Jamestown Way)
SW3 5E 16 (5D 100)
Atlantic Rd. SW9 4A 120
Atlantic Wharf E1 7K 85
Atlantis Av. E16 7F 89
Atlantis Cl. IG11: Bark 3B 90
Atlas Bus. Cen. NW2 1D 62
Atlas Cres. HA8: Edg 2C 28
Atlas Gdns. SE7 4A 106
Atlas M. E8 6F 67
N7 6K 65
SE13 4F 123
Atlas Rd. E13 2J 87
HA9: Wemb 4J 61
N11 7K 31
NW10 3A 80
Atlas Trade Pk. DA8: Erith 5K 109
Atlas Wharf E9 6C 68
Atlip Rd. HA0: Wemb 1E 78
Atlitude E1 6G 85
(off Alie St.)
Atney Rd. SW15 4G 117
Atrium, The IG9: Buck H 2G 37
W12 1F 99
Atrium Apartments N1 1D 84
(off Felton St.)
Atrium Hgts. SE8 6D 104
(off Creekside)
Atrium Ho. SE8 7B 104
Atterbury Rd. N4 6A 48
Atterbury St. SW1 4D 18 (4J 101)
Attewood Av. NW10 3A 62
Attewood Rd. UB5: N'olt 6C 58
Attfield Cl. N20 2G 31
Attfield Ct. KT1: King T 2F 151
(off Albert Rd.)
Attilburgh Ho. SE1 7J 15
(off St Saviour's Est.)
Attleborough Ct. SE23 2G 139
Attle Cl. UB10: Hil 2C 74
Attlee Cl. CR7: Thor H 5C 156
UB4: Yead 3K 75
UB5: N'olt 3K 75
Attlee Rd. SE28 7B 90
UB4: Yead 3J 75
Attlee Ter. E17 4D 50
Attneave St. WC1 2J 7 (3A 84)
Attock M. E17 5D 50
Atunbi Ct. NW1 7G 65
(off Farrier St.)
Atwater Cl. SW2 1A 138
Atwell Cl. E10 6D 50
Atwell Pl. KT7: T Ditt 7K 149
Atwell Rd. SE15 2G 121
Atwood Av. TW9: Kew 2G 115
Atwood Ho. W14 4H 99
(off Beckford Cl.)
Atwood Rd. W6 4D 98
Atwoods All. TW9: Kew 1G 115
Aube Ho. SE6 4E 140
Aubers Ridge Ct. E3 2B 86
(off Festubert Pl.)
Aubert Ct. N5 4B 66
Aubert Pk. N5 4B 66
Aubert Rd. N5 4B 66
Aubrey Beardsley Ho. SW1 4B 18
(off Vauxhall Bri. Rd.)
Aubrey Mans. NW1 5C 4
(off Lisson St.)
Aubrey Moore Point E15 2E 86
(off Abbey La.)
Aubrey Pl. NW8 2A 82
Aubrey Rd. E17 3C 50
N8 5J 47
W8 1H 99
Aubrey Wlk. W8 1H 99
Auburn Cl. SE14 7A 104
Aubyn Hill SE27 4C 138
Aubyn Sq. SW15 5C 116
Auckland Cl. SE19 1F 157

Auckland Ct.—Avondale Av.

Auckland Ct. UB4: Yead 4A **76**
Auckland Gdns. SE19 1E **156**
Auckland Hill SE27 4C **138**
Auckland Ho. *W12* *7D* ***80***
(off White City Est.)
Auckland Ri. SE19 1E **156**
Auckland Rd. E10 3D **68**
IG1: Ilf 1F **71**
KT1: King T 4F **151**
SE19 1F **157**
SW11 4C **118**
Auckland St. SE11 6G **19** (5K **101**)
Audax NW9 2B **44**
Auden Pl. NW1 1E **82**
SM3: Cheam 4E **164**
Audleigh Pl. IG7: Chig 6K **37**
Audley Cl. N10 7A **32**
SW11 3E **118**
Audley Ct. E18 4H **51**
HA5: Pinn 2A **40**
TW2: Twick 3H **131**
UB5: N'olt 3A **76**
Audley Dr. E16 1K **105**
Audley Gdns. IG3: Ilf 2K **71**
Audley Pl. SM2: Sutt 7K **165**
Audley Rd. EN2: Enf 2G **23**
NW4 5C **44**
TW10: Rich 5F **115**
W5 5F **79**
Audley Sq. W1 4H **11** (1E **100**)
Audrey Cl. BR3: Beck 6D **158**
Audrey Gdns. HA0: Wemb 2B **60**
Audrey Rd. IG1: Ilf 3F **71**
Audrey St. E2 2G **85**
Audric Cl. KT2: King T 1G **151**
Augurs La. E13 3K **87**
Augusta Cl. KT8: W Mole 3D **148**
Augusta Rd. TW2: Twick 2G **131**
Augustas La. N1 7A **66**
Augusta St. E14 6D **86**
Augusta Wlk. W5 5D **78**
Augustine Bell Twr. *E3* *2C* ***86***
(off Pancras Way)
Augustine Rd. HA3: Hrw W 1F **41**
W14 3F **99**
Augustus Bldg. *E1* *6H* ***85***
(off Tarling St.)
Augustus Cl. HA7: Stan 3J **27**
TW8: Bford 7C **96**
W12 2D **98**
Augustus Ct. *SE1* *4E* ***102***
(off Old Kent Rd.)
SW16 2H **137**
TW13: Hanw 4D **130**
Augustus Ho. *NW1* *1A* ***6***
(off Augustus St.)
Augustus La. BR6: Orp 2K **173**
Augustus Rd. SW19 1F **135**
Augustus St. NW1 1K **5** (2F **83**)
Aulay Ho. SE16 3F **103**
Aultone Way SM1: Sutt 2K **165**
SM5: Cars 3D **166**
Aultone Yd. Ind. Est. SM5: Cars 3D **166**
Aulton Pl. SE11 6K **19** (5A **102**)
Aura Ct. SE15 4H **121**
Aura Ho. TW9: Kew 1H **115**
Aurelia Gdns. CR0: C'don 5K **155**
Aurelia Ho. *E20* *5E* ***68***
(off Sunrise Cl.)
Aurelia Rd. CR0: C'don 6J **155**
Auriel Av. RM10: Dag 6K **73**
Auriga M. N1 5D **66**
Auriol Cl. KT4: Wor Pk 3A **164**
Auriol Dr. UB6: G'frd 7H **59**
UB10: Hil 6C **56**
Auriol Ho. *W12* *1D* ***98***
(off Ellerslie Rd.)
Auriol Mans. *W14* *4G* ***99***
(off Edith Rd.)
Auriol Pk. Rd. KT4: Wor Pk 3A **164**
Auriol Rd. W14 4G **99**
Aurora Apartments EC1 1C **8**
SW18 *5J* ***117***
(off Buckhold Rd.)
Aurora Bldg. *E14* *1E* ***104***
(off Blackwall Way)
Aurora Bldg., The *N1* *3D* ***84***
(off East Rd.)
Aurora Ho. *E14* *6D* ***86***
(off Kerbey St.)
SE6 4E **140**
Austell Gdns. NW7 3F **29**
Austell Hgts. *NW7* *3F* ***29***
(off Austell Gdns.)
Austen Apartments SE20 2H **157**
Austen Cl. SE28 1B **108**
Austen Ho. *NW6* *3J* ***81***
(off Cambridge Rd.)
SW17 *3B* ***136***
(off St George's Gro.)
Austen Rd. DA8: Erith 7H **109**
HA2: Harr 2F **59**
Austin Av. BR2: Brom 5C **160**
Austin Cl. SE23 7A **122**
TW1: Twick 5C **114**
Austin Ct. E6 1A **88**
EN1: Enf 5K **23**
SE15 *3G* ***121***
(off Peckham Rye)
Austin Friars EC2 7F **9** (6D **84**)
Austin Friars Pas. EC2 7F **9**
Austin Friars Sq. *EC2* *7F* ***9***
(off Austin Friars)
Austin Ho. *SE14* *7B* ***104***
(off Achilles St.)
Austin Rd. SW11 1E **118**
UB3: Hayes 2H **93**
Austin's La. HA4: Ruis 4F **57**
UB10: Ick 3E **56**
Austin St. E2 2J **9** (3F **85**)
Austin Ter. *SE1* *1K* ***19***
(off Morley St.)
Austral Cl. DA15: Sidc 3K **143**
Australian War Memorial ***6H 11***
(off Duke of Wellington Pl.)
Australia Rd. W12 7D **80**
Austral St. SE11 3K **19** (4B **102**)
Austyn Gdns. KT5: Surb 1H **163**
Autumn Cl. EN1: Enf 1B **24**
SW19 6A **136**
Autumn Gro. BR1: Brom 6K **141**
Autumn Lodge *CR2: S Croy* *4E* ***168***
(off South Pk. Hill Rd.)
Autumn St. E3 1C **86**
Autumn Way UB7: W Dray 2B **92**
Avalon Cl. EN2: Enf 2F **23**
SW20 2G **153**
W13 5A **78**
Avalon Ct. CR0: C'don 7F **157**
Avalon Rd. SW6 1K **117**
W13 4A **78**
Avante KT1: King T 3D **150**
Avantgarde Pl. *E1* *3K* ***9***
(off Sclater St.)
Avantgarde Twr. *E1* *3J* ***9***
(off Sclater St.)
Avard Gdns. BR6: Farnb 4G **173**
Avarn Rd. SW17 6D **136**
Avebury Ct. *N1* *1D* ***84***
(off Imber St.)
SE16 *4J* ***103***
(off Debnams Rd.)
Avebury Pk. KT6: Surb 7D **150**
Avebury Rd. BR6: Orp 3H **173**
E11 1F **69**
SW19 1H **153**
Avebury St. N1 1D **84**
Aveley Mans. *IG11: Bark* *7F* ***71***
(off Whiting Av.)
Aveley Rd. RM1: Rom 4K **55**
Aveline St. SE11 5H **19** (5A **102**)
Aveling Pk. Rd. E17 2C **50**
Ave Maria La. EC4 1B **14** (6B **84**)
Avenell Mans. N5 4B **66**
Avenell Rd. N5 3B **66**
Avenfield Ho. *W1* *2F* ***11***
(off Park La.)
Avening Rd. SW18 7J **117**
Avening Ter. SW18 7J **117**
Avenons Rd. E13 4J **87**
Aventine Av. CR4: Mitc 3F **155**
Avenue, The BR1: Brom 3B **160**
BR2: Kes 4B **172**
BR3: Beck 1D **158**
BR4: W W'ck 7E **158**
BR5: St P 7B **144**
BR6: Orp 2K **173**
CR0: C'don 3E **168**
DA5: Bexl 7D **126**
E3 *4D* ***86***
(off Devas St.)
E4 6A **36**
E11 6K **51**
EC2 7H **9** (6E **84**)
EN5: Barn 3B **20**
HA3: Hrw W 1K **41**
HA5: Pinn 6D **40**
HA9: Wemb 1E **60**
IG9: Buck H 2F **37**
KT4: Wor Pk 2B **164**
KT5: Surb 6F **151**
KT17: Ewe 7D **164**
N3 2J **45**
N8 3A **48**
N10 2G **47**
N11 5A **32**
N17 3D **48**
NW6 1F **81**
RM1: Rom 4K **55**
SE10 7F **105**
SM2: Cheam 7G **165**
SM3: Cheam 7E **164**
SM5: Cars 7E **166**
SW4 4E **118**
SW18 7C **118**
TW1: Twick 5B **114**
TW3: Houn 5F **113**
TW5: Cran 7J **93**
TW9: Kew 2F **115**
TW12: Hamp 6D **130**
TW16: Sun 1K **147**
UB10: Ick 4C **56**
W4 3A **98**
W13 6B **78**
Avenue Cl. N14 6B **22**
NW8 1C **82**
(not continuous)
TW5: Cran 1K **111**
UB7: W Dray 3A **92**
Avenue Ct. IG5: Ilf 3C **52**
N14 6B **22**
NW2 3H **63**
SW3 *4E* ***16***
(off Draycott Av.)
Avenue Cres. TW5: Cran 1K **111**
W3 2H **97**
Avenue Elmers KT6: Surb 5E **150**
Avenue Gdns. SE25 2G **157**
SW14 3A **116**
TW5: Cran 7K **93**
TW11: Tedd 7K **131**
W3 2H **97**
Avenue Ho. *NW6* *7G* ***63***
(off The Avenue)
NW8 *2C* ***82***
(off Allitsen Rd.)
NW10 *2D* ***80***
(off All Souls Av.)
Avenue Ind. Est. E4 6H **35**
Avenue Lodge *NW8* *7B* ***64***
(off Avenue Rd.)
Avenue Mans. *NW3* *5K* ***63***
(off Finchley Rd.)
Avenue M. N10 3F **47**
Avenue Pde. N21 7J **23**
TW16: Sun 3K **147**
Avenue Pk. Rd. SE27 2B **138**
Avenue Rd. BR3: Beck 2K **157**
DA7: Bex 3E **126**
DA8: Erith 7J **109**
DA17: Belv, Erith 4J **109**
E7 4K **69**
HA5: Pinn 3C **40**
IG8: Wfd G 6F **37**
KT1: King T 3E **150**
KT3: N Mald 4A **152**
N6 7G **47**
N12 4F **31**
N14 7B **22**
N15 5D **48**
NW3 7B **64**
NW8 7B **64**
NW10 2B **80**
RM6: Chad H 7B **54**
SE20 1J **157**
SE25 2F **157**
SM6: Wall 7G **167**
SW16 2H **155**
SW20 2D **152**
TW7: Isle 1K **113**
TW8: Bford 5C **96**
TW11: Tedd 7A **132**
TW12: Hamp 1F **149**
TW13: Felt 3H **129**
UB1: S'hall 1D **94**
W3 2H **97**
Avenue Sth. KT5: Surb 7G **151**
Avenue Studios *SW3* *4B* ***16***
(off Sydney Cl.)
Avenue Ter.
KT3: N Mald 3J **151**
Averil Gro. SW16 6B **138**
Averill St. W6 6F **99**
Avern Gdns. KT8: W Mole 4F **149**
Avern Rd. KT8: W Mole 4F **149**
Avershaw Ho. SW15 5F **117**
Avery Cl. BR3: Beck 6B **140**
Avery Farm Row SW1 4J **17** (4E **100**)
Avery Gdns. IG2: Ilf 5D **52**
AVERY HILL 6H 125
Avery Hill Rd. SE9 6H **125**
Avery Row W1 2J **11** (7F **83**)
Aviary Cl. E16 5H **87**
Aviation Dr. NW9 2C **44**
Aviemore Cl. BR3: Beck 5B **158**
Aviemore Way BR3: Beck 5A **158**
Avigdor M. N16 2D **66**
Avignon Rd. SE4 3K **121**
Avingdor Ct. *W3* *1J* ***97***
(off Horn La.)
Avington Ct. *SE1* *4E* ***102***
(off Old Kent Rd.)
Avington Gro. SE20 7J **139**
Avion Cres. NW9 1C **44**
Avis Sq. E1 6K **85**
Avoca Rd. SW17 4E **136**
Avocet Cl. SE1 5G **103**
Avocet M. SE28 3H **107**
Avon Cl. KT4: Wor Pk 2C **164**
SM1: Sutt 4A **166**
UB4: Yead 4A **76**
Avon Ct. E4 1K **35**
IG9: Buck H 1E **36**
N12 5E **30**
SW15 5G **117**
UB6: G'frd 4F **77**
W9 *5J* ***81***
(off Elmfield Way)
Avondale Av.
EN4: E Barn 1J **31**
KT4: Wor Pk 1B **164**
KT10: Hin W 3A **162**
N12 5E **30**
NW2 3A **62**

Avondale Ct.—Baines Cl.

Avondale Ct. E11 1G **69**
E16 5G **87**
E18 1K **51**
SM2: Sutt 7A ***166***
(off Brighton Rd.)
Avondale Cres.
EN3: Enf H 3F **25**
IG4: Ilf 5B **52**
Avondale Dr. UB3: Hayes 1J **93**
Avondale Gdns. TW4: Houn 5D **112**
Avondale Ho. *SE1 5G* ***103***
(off Avondale Sq.)
Avondale Mans. *SW6 1H* ***117***
(off Rostrevor Rd.)
Avondale Pk. Gdns. W11 7G **81**
Avondale Pk. Rd. W11 7G **81**
Avondale Pavement SE1 5G **103**
Avondale Ri. SE15 3F **121**
Avondale Rd. BR1: Brom 6G **141**
CR2: S Croy 6C **168**
DA16: Well 2C **126**
E16 5G **87**
E17 7C **50**
HA3: W'stone 3K **41**
N3 1A **46**
N13 2F **33**
N15 5B **48**
SE9 2C **142**
SW14 3A **116**
SW19 5K **135**
TW15: Ashf 3A **128**
Avondale Sq. SE1 5G **103**
Avonfield Ct. E17 3F **51**
Avongrove Ct. *EC1 1D* ***8***
(off Bollinder Pl.)
Avon Ho. KT2: King T 1D **150**
W8 3J ***99***
(off Allen St.)
W14 4H ***99***
(off Kensington Village)
Avonhurst Ho. NW2 7G **63**
Avonley Rd. SE14 7J **103**
Avon M. HA5: Hat E 1D **40**
Avonmore Gdns. W14 4H **99**
Avonmore Mans. *W14 4G* ***99***
(off Avonmore Rd.)
Avonmore Pl. W14 4G **99**
Avonmore Rd. W14 4G **99**
Avonmouth Apartments *SW11 4C* ***118***
(off Monarch Sq.)
Avonmouth St. SE1 7C **14** (3C **102**)
Avon Path CR2: S Croy 6C **168**
Avon Pl. SE1 7D **14** (2C **102**)
Avon Rd. E17 3F **51**
SE4 3C **122**
TW16: Sun 7H **129**
UB6: G'frd 4E **76**
Avonstowe Cl. BR6: Farnb 3G **173**
Avon Way E18 3J **51**
Avonwick Rd. TW3: Houn 2F **113**
Avril Way E4 5K **35**
Avro Ct. *E9 5A* ***68***
(off Mabley St.)
Avro Ho. *NW9 2B* ***44***
(off Boulevard Dr.)
SW8 7F ***101***
(off Havelock Ter.)
Avro Pl. TW5: Hest 7A **94**
Avro Way SM6: Wall 7J **167**
Awlfield Av. N17 1D **48**
Awliscombe Rd.
DA16: Well 2K **125**
Axe St. IG11: Bark 1G **89**
(not continuous)
Axholme Av. HA8: Edg 1G **43**
Axiom Apartments
BR2: Brom 4K ***159***
(off Masons Hill)
Axio Way E3 5C **86**
Axis Apartments *E1 3J* ***9***
(off Sclater St.)
Axis Ct. *SE10 6G* ***105***
(off Woodland Cres.)
SE16 2G ***103***
(off East La.)
Axis Ho. *SE13 4E* ***122***
(off Lewisham High St.)
Axminster Cres.
DA16: Well 1C **126**
Axminster Rd. N7 3J **65**
Axon Pl. IG1: Ilf 2G **71**
Aybrook St. W1 6G **5** (5E **82**)
Aycliffe Cl. BR1: Brom 4D **160**
Aycliffe Ho. *SE17 6D* ***102***
(off Portland St.)
Aycliffe Rd. W12 1C **98**
Ayerst Ct. E10 7E **50**
Aylands Cl. HA9: Wemb 2E **60**
Aylesbury Cl. E7 6H **69**
Aylesbury Ct. SM1: Sutt 3A **166**
Aylesbury Ho. *HA0: Wemb 1E* ***78***
(off Hatton Rd.)
SE15 6G ***103***
(off Friary Est.)
Aylesbury Rd. BR2: Brom 3J **159**
SE17 5D **102**
Aylesbury St. EC1 4A **8** (4B **84**)
NW10 3K **61**
Aylesford Av. BR3: Beck 5A **158**
Aylesford Ho. *SE1 7F* ***15***
(off Long La.)
Aylesford St. SW1 5C **18** (5H **101**)
Aylesham Cen. SE15 1G **121**
Aylesham Cl. NW7 7H **29**
Aylesham Rd. BR6: Orp 7K **161**
Ayles Rd. UB4: Yead 3K **75**
Aylestone Av. NW6 7F **63**
Aylett Rd. SE25 4H **157**
TW7: Isle 2J **113**
Ayley Cft. EN1: Enf 5B **24**
Ayliffe Cl. KT1: King T 2G **151**
Aylmer Cl. HA7: Stan 4F **27**
Aylmer Ct. N2 5D **46**
Aylmer Dr. HA7: Stan 4F **27**
Aylmer Ho. SE10 5F **105**
Aylmer Pde. N2 5D **46**
Aylmer Rd. E11 1H **69**
N2 5C **46**
RM8: Dag 3E **72**
W12 2B **98**
Ayloffe Rd. RM9: Dag 6F **73**
Aylsham Dr. UB10: Ick 2E **56**
Aylton Est. SE16 2J **103**
Aylward Rd. SE23 2K **139**
SW20 2H **153**
Aylwards Ri. HA7: Stan 4F **27**
Aylward St. E1 6J **85**
(Jamaica St.)
E1 6J **85**
(Jubilee St.)
Aylwin Est. SE1 3E **102**
Aynhoe Mans. *W14 4F* ***99***
(off Aynhoe Rd.)
Aynhoe Rd. W14 4F **99**
Aynscombe Path SW14 2J **115**
Ayr Ct. W3 5G **79**
Ayres Cl. E13 3J **87**
Ayres St. SE1 6D **14** (2C **102**)
Ayr Grn. RM1: Rom 1K **55**
Ayrsome Rd. N16 3E **66**
Ayrton Gould Ho. *E2 3K* ***85***
(off Roman Rd.)
Ayrton Rd. SW7 1A **16** (3B **100**)
Ayr Way RM1: Rom 1K **55**
Aysgarth Ct. SM1: Sutt 3K **165**
Aysgarth Rd. SE21 7E **120**
Ayston Ho. *SE16 4K* ***103***
(off Plough Way)
Aytoun Pl. SW9 2K **119**
Aytoun Rd. SW9 2K **119**
Azalea Cl. IG1: Ilf 5F **71**
W7 1K **95**
Azalea Ct. IG8: Wfd G 6B **36**
W7 1K **95**
Azalea Ho. *SE14 7B* ***104***
(off Achilles St.)
TW13: Felt 1K **129**
Azalea Wlk. HA5: Eastc 5K **39**
Azania M. NW5 6F **65**
Azenby Rd. SE15 2F **121**
Azof St. SE10 4G **105**
Azov Ho. *E1 4A* ***86***
(off Commodore St.)
Aztec Ho. IG1: Ilf 2H **71**
IG6: Ilf 1G **53**
Azura Ct. *E15 1E* ***86***
(off Warton Rd.)
Azure Bldg. *E15 7F* ***69***
(off Gt. Eastern Rd.)
Azure Ct. NW9 5G **43**
Azure Ho. *E2 3G* ***85***
(off Buckfast St.)
Azure Pl. TW3: Houn 4F **113**

B

Baalbec Rd. N5 5B **66**
Babbacombe Cl. KT9: Chess 5D **162**
Babbacombe Gdns. IG4: Ilf 4C **52**
Babbacombe Ho. *BR1: Brom 1J* ***159***
(off Babbacombe Rd.)
Babbacombe Rd. BR1: Brom 1J **159**
Babbage Ct. *SE17 6B* ***102***
(off Cook's Rd.)
Babell Ho. *N1 6B* ***66***
(off Canonbury Rd.)
Baber Bri. Cvn. Site TW14: Felt 5A **112**
Baber Bri. Pde. TW14: Felt 6A **112**
Baber Dr. TW14: Felt 6A **112**
Babington Ct. WC1 5G **7**
Babington Ho. *SE1 6D* ***14***
(off Disney St.)
Babington Ri. HA9: Wemb 6G **61**
Babington Rd. NW4 4D **44**
RM8: Dag 5C **72**
SW16 5H **137**
Babmaes St. SW1 3C **12** (7H **83**)
Bacchus Wlk. *N1 2E* ***84***
(off Regan Way)
Bache's St. N1 2F **9** (3D **84**)
Back All. EC3 1H **15**
Bk. Church La. E1 6G **85**
Back Hill EC1 4K **7** (4A **84**)
Backhouse Pl. SE17 4E **102**
Back La. DA5: Bexl 7G **127**
HA8: Edg 1J **43**
IG9: Buck H 2G **37**
N8 5J **47**
NW3 4A **64**
NW9 2K **43**
RM6: Chad H 7D **54**
TW8: Bford 6D **96**
TW10: Ham 3C **132**
Backley Gdns. SE25 6G **157**
Back Pas. *EC1 5B* ***8***
(off Long La.)
Back Rd. DA14: Sidc 4A **144**
E17 4E **50**
TW11: Tedd 7J **131**
Bacon Gro. SE1 3F **103**
Bacon La. HA8: Edg 1G **43**
NW9 4H **43**
(not continuous)
Bacon's College Sports Cen. 1A **104**
Bacons La. N6 1E **64**
Bacon St. E1 3K **9** (4F **85**)
E2 3K **9** (4F **85**)
Bacon Ter. RM8: Dag 5B **72**
Bacton NW5 5E **64**
Bacton St. E2 3J **85**
Baddeley Ho. *KT8: W Mole 5E* ***148***
(off Down St.)
Baddesley Ho. SE11 5H **19**
Baddow Cl. IG8: Wfd G 6F **37**
RM10: Dag 1G **91**
Baddow Wlk. *N1 1C* ***84***
(off New North Rd.)
Baden Dr. E4 4J **25**
Baden Pl. SE1 6E **14** (2D **102**)
Baden Powell Cl. KT6: Surb 2F **163**
RM9: Dag 1E **90**
Baden Powell Ho. *DA17: Belv 3G* ***109***
(off Ambrooke Rd.)
SW7 2A **16**
Baden Rd. IG1: Ilf 5F **71**
N8 4H **47**
Bader Ct. *NW9 2B* ***44***
(off Runway Cl.)
Bader Way SW15 6C **116**
UB10: Uxb 7A **56**
Badgemore Path *SE18 5H* ***107***
(off Tuscan Rd.)
Badger Cl. IG2: Ilf 6G **53**
TW4: Houn 3A **112**
TW13: Felt 3K **129**
Badger Ct. NW2 3E **62**
Badgers Cl. EN2: Enf 3G **23**
HA1: Harr 6H **41**
TW15: Ashf 5B **128**
UB3: Hayes 7G **75**
Badgers Copse BR6: Orp 2K **173**
KT4: Wor Pk 2B **164**
Badgers Cft. N20 7B **20**
SE9 3E **142**
Badgers Hole CR0: C'don 4K **169**
Badgers Wlk. KT3: N Mald 2A **152**
Badlis Rd. E17 3C **50**
Badma Cl. N9 3D **34**
Badminton Cl. HA1: Harr 4J **41**
UB5: N'olt 6E **58**
Badminton M. E16 1J **105**
Badminton Rd. SW12 6E **118**
Badric Ct. SW11 2B **118**
Badsworth Rd. SE5 1C **120**
Baffin Way E14 1E **104**
Bafton Ga. BR2: Hayes 1K **171**
Bagley Cl. UB7: W Dray 2A **92**
Bagley's La. SW6 1K **117**
Bagleys Spring RM6: Chad H 4E **54**
Bagnigge Ho. *WC1 2J* ***7***
(off Margery St.)
Bagshot Ct. SE18 1E **124**
Bagshot Ho. NW1 1K **5**
Bagshot Rd. EN1: Enf 7A **24**
Bagshot St. SE17 5E **102**
Bahram Ct. *E2 4H* ***85***
(off Three Colts La.)
Baildon *E2 2J* ***85***
(off Cyprus St.)
Baildon St. SE8 7B **104**
Bailes Pl. BR3: Beck 1A **158**
Bailey Cl. E4 4K **35**
N11 7C **32**
SE28 1J **107**
Bailey Cotts. *E14 5A* ***86***
(off Maroon St.)
Bailey Ct. *NW9 3A* ***44***
(off Lingard Av.)
Bailey Cres. KT9: Chess 7D **162**
Bailey Ho. *E3 3D* ***86***
(off Talwin St.)
SW10 7K ***99***
(off Coleridge Gdns.)
Bailey M. SW2 5A **120**
W4 6H **97**
Bailey Pl. N16 5E **66**
SE26 6K **139**
Bailey Twr. E1 7H **85**
Baillies Wlk. W5 2D **96**
Bainbridge Cl. TW10: Ham 5E **132**
Bainbridge Rd. RM9: Dag 4F **73**
Bainbridge St. WC1 7D **6** (6H **83**)
Baines Cl. CR2: S Croy 5D **168**

Baird Av. UB1: S'hall 7F 77
Baird Cl. E10 1C 68
NW9 6J 43
Baird Gdns. SE19 4E 138
Baird Ho. *W12* *7D 80*
(off White City Est.)
Baird Memorial Cotts. *N14* *2C 32*
(off Balaams La.)
Baird Rd. EN1: Enf 3C 24
Baird St. EC1 3D 8 (4C 84)
Bairny Wood App. IG8: Wfd G 6E 36
Baizdon Rd. SE3 2G 123
Bakehouse M. TW12: Hamp 7E 130
Baker Beal Ct. DA7: Bex 3H 127
Baker Ho. *E3* *3D 86*
(off Bromley High St.)
W7 1K 95
WC1 *4F 7*
(off Colonnade)
Baker La. CR4: Mitc 2E 154
Baker Pas. NW10 1A 80
Baker Pl. KT19: Ewe 6J 163
Baker Rd. NW10 1A 80
SE18 7C 106
Bakers Av. E17 6D 50
Bakers Ct. SE25 3E 156
Bakers End SW20 2G 153
Baker's Fld. N7 4H 65
Bakersfield Cl. KT19: Ewe 7K 163
Bakers Gdns. SM5: Cars 2C 166
Bakers Hall Ct. EC3 3G 15
Bakers Hill E5 1J 67
EN5: New Bar 2E 20
Bakers Ho. *W5* *1D 96*
(off The Grove)
Bakers La. N6 6D 46
Baker's M. W1 7G 5 (6E 82)
Bakers M. BR6: Chels 6K 173
Bakers Pas. *NW3* *4A 64*
(off Heath St.)
Baker's Rents E2 2J 9 (3F 85)
Baker's Row E15 2G 87
EC1 4J 7 (4A 84)
BAKER STREET 5D 82
Baker St. EN1: Enf 3J 23
NW1 4F 5 (4D 82)
W1 4F 5 (4D 82)
Baker's Yd. EC1 4J 7
Bakery Cl. SW9 7K 101
Bakery M. KT6: Surb 1G 163
Bakery Path *HA8: Edg* *5C 28*
(off St Margaret's Rd.)
Bakery Pl. SW11 4D 118
Bakewell Way KT3: N Mald 2A 152
Balaam Ho. SM1: Sutt 4J 165
Balaam Leisure Cen. 4J 87
Balaams La. N14 2C 32
Balaam St. E13 4J 87
Balaclava Rd. KT6: Surb 7C 150
SE1 4F 103
Bala Grn. *NW9* *6A 44*
(off Ruthin Cl.)
Balcaskie Rd. SE9 5D 124
Balchen Rd. SE3 2B 124
Balchier Rd. SE22 6H 121
Balcombe Cl. DA6: Bex 4D 126
Balcombe Ho. *NW1* *3E 4*
(off Taunton Pl.)
Balcombe St. NW1 3E 4 (4D 82)
Balcon Ct. W5 6F 79
Balcony, The W12 1F 99
Balcorne St. E9 7J 67
Balder Ri. SE12 2K 141
Balderton Flats *W1* *1H 11*
(off Balderton St.)
Balderton St. W1 1H 11 (6E 82)
Baldewyne Ct. N17 1G 49
Baldock St. E3 2D 86
Baldrey Ho. *SE10* *5H 105*
(off Blackwall La.)
Baldry Gdns. SW16 6J 137
Baldwin Cres. SE5 1C 120
Baldwin Gdns. TW3: Houn 1G 113
Baldwin Ho. SW2 1A 138
Baldwin Rd. SW11 6E 118
Baldwins Gdns. EC1 5J 7 (5A 84)
Baldwin St. EC1 2E 8 (3D 84)
Baldwin Ter. N1 2C 84
Baldwyn Gdns. W3 7K 79
Baldwyn's Pk. DA5: Bexl 2K 145
Baldwyn's Rd. DA5: Bexl 2K 145
Balearic Apartments *E16* *7J 87*
(off Western Gateway)
Bale Rd. E1 5A 86
Bales Ter. N9 3A 34
Balfern Gro. W4 5A 98
Balfern St. SW11 2C 118
Balfe St. N1 2J 83
Balfour Av. W7 1K 95
Balfour Bus. Cen. UB2: S'hall 3A 94
Balfour Gro. N20 3J 31
Balfour Ho. *SW11* *1E 118*
(off Forfar Rd.)
W10 *5F 81*
(off St Charles Sq.)
Balfour M. N9 3B 34
W1 4H 11 (1E 100)
Balfour Pl. SW15 4D 116
W1 3H 11 (7E 82)
Balfour Rd. BR2: Brom 5B 160
HA1: Harr 5H 41
IG1: Ilf 2F 71
N5 4C 66
SE25 5G 157
SM5: Cars 7D 166
SW19 7K 135
TW3: Houn 3F 113
UB2: S'hall 3B 94
W3 5J 79
W13 2A 96
Balfour St. SE17 4D 102
Balfour Ter. N3 2K 45
Balfron Twr. E14 6E 86
Balgonie Rd. E4 1A 36
Balgove Ct. *NW10* *6D 62*
(off Eden Gro.)
Balgowan Cl. KT3: N Mald 5A 152
Balgowan Rd. BR3: Beck 3A 158
Balgowan St. SE18 4K 107
BALHAM 1E 136
Balham Continental Mkt. *SW12* *1F 137*
(off Shipka Rd.)
Balham Gro. SW12 7E 118
Balham High Rd. SW12 3E 136
SW17 3E 136
Balham Hill SW12 7F 119
Balham Leisure Cen. 2F 137
Balham New Rd. SW12 7F 119
Balham Pk. Rd. SW12 1D 136
Balham Rd. N9 2B 34
Balham Sta. Rd. SW12 1F 137
Balin Ho. *SE1* *6E 14*
(off Long La.)
Balkan Wlk. E1 7H 85
Balladier Wlk. E14 5D 86
Ballamore Rd. BR1: Brom 3J 141
Ballance Rd. E9 6K 67
Ballantine St. SW18 4A 118
Ballantrae Ho. NW2 4H 63
Ballantyne Cl. SE9 4C 142
Ballard Cl. KT2: King T 7K 133
Ballard Ho. *SE10* *6D 104*
(off Thames St.)
Ballards Cl. RM10: Dag 1H 91
Ballards Farm Rd. CR0: C'don 6G 169
CR2: S Croy 6G 169
Ballards La. N3 1J 45
N12 1J 45
Ballards M. HA8: Edg 6B 28
Ballards Ri. CR2: Sels 6G 169
Ballards Rd. NW2 2C 62
RM10: Dag 2H 91
Ballards Way CR0: C'don 6G 169
CR2: Sels 6G 169
Ballast Quay SE10 5F 105
Ballater Rd. CR2: S Croy 5F 169
SW2 4J 119
Ball Ct. *EC3* *1F 15*
(off Birchin La.)
Balletica Apartments *WC2* *1F 13*
(off Long Acre)
Ball Ho. *NW9* *3B 44*
(off Aerodrome Rd.)
Ballina St. SE23 7K 121
Ballin Ct. *E14* *2E 104*
(off Stewart St.)
Ballingdon Rd. SW11 6E 118
Ballinger Point *E3* *3D 86*
(off Bromley High St.)
Ballinger Way UB5: N'olt 4C 76
Balliol Av. E4 4B 36
Balliol Rd. DA16: Well 2B 126
N17 1E 48
W10 6E 80
Balloch Rd. SE6 1F 141
Ballogie Av. NW10 4A 62
Ballow Cl. SE5 7E 102
Balls Pond Pl. N1 6D 66
Balls Pond Rd. N1 6D 66
Balmain Cl. W5 1D 96
Balmain Ct. TW3: Houn 1F 113
Balmain Lodge
KT5: Surb *4E 150*
(off Cranes Pk. Av.)
Balman Ho. *SE16* *4K 103*
(off Rotherhithe New Rd.)
Balmer Rd. E3 2B 86
Balmes Rd. N1 1D 84
Balmoral Apartments *W2* *6C 4*
(off Praed St.)
Balmoral Av. BR3: Beck 4A 158
N11 6K 31
Balmoral Cl. SW15 6F 117
Balmoral Ct. *BR3: Beck* *1E 158*
(off The Avenue)
HA9: Wemb 3F 61
KT4: Wor Pk 2D 164
NW8 *2B 82*
(off Queen's Ter.)
SE12 4K 141
SE16 *1K 103*
(off King & Queen Wharf)
SE17 *5D 102*
(off Merrow St.)
SE27 4C 138
SM2: Sutt 7J 165
Balmoral Cres. KT8: W Mole 3E 148
Balmoral Dr. UB1: S'hall 4D 76
UB4: Hayes 4G 75
Balmoral Gdns. DA5: Bexl 7F 127
IG3: Ilf 1K 71
W13 3A 96
Balmoral Gro. N7 6K 65
Balmoral Ho. *E14* *3D 104*
(off Lanark Sq.)
E16 *1K 105*
(off Keats Av.)
W14 *4G 99*
(off Windsor Way)
Balmoral M. W12 3B 98
Balmoral Rd. E7 4A 70
E10 2D 68
HA2: Harr 4E 58
KT1: King T 4F 151
KT4: Wor Pk 3D 164
NW2 6D 62
Balmoral Trad. Est. IG11: Bark 5K 89
Balmore Cl. E14 6E 86
Balmore Cres. EN4: Cockf 5K 21
Balmore St. N19 2F 65
Balmuir Gdns. SW15 4E 116
Balnacraig Av. NW10 4A 62
Balniel Ga. SW1 5D 18 (5H 101)
Balsam Ho. *E14* *7D 86*
(off E. India Dock Rd.)
Baltic Apartments *E16* *7J 87*
(off Western Gateway)
Baltic Av. TW8: Bford 5D 96
Baltic Cl. SW19 7B 136
Baltic Ct. *E1* *1J 103*
(off Clave St.)
SE16 2K 103
Baltic Ho. SE5 2C 120
Baltic Pl. N1 1E 84
Baltic St. E. EC1 4C 8 (4C 84)
Baltic St. W. EC1 4C 8 (4C 84)
Baltimore Cl. DA17: Belv 2H 109
Baltimore Ct. *SW1* *4C 18*
(off Vauxhall Bri. Rd.)
Baltimore Ho. SE11 5J 19
SW18 3A 118
Baltimore Pl. DA16: Well 2K 125
Baltimore Twr. E14 2D 104
Baltimore Wharf E14 3D 104
Balvaird Pl. SW1 6D 18 (5H 101)
Balvernie Gro. SW18 7H 117
Balvernie M. SW18 7J 117
Bamber Ho. IG11: Bark 1G 89
Bamber Rd. SE15 1F 121
Bamborough Gdns. W12 2E 98
Bamburgh N17 7C 34
Bamford Av. HA0: Wemb 1F 79
Bamford Rd. BR1: Brom 5E 140
IG11: Bark 6G 71
Bampfylde Cl. SM6: Wall 3G 167
Bampton Ct. W5 6D 78
Bampton Dr. NW7 7H 29
Bampton Rd. SE23 3K 139
Banavie Gdns. BR3: Beck 1E 158
Banbury Cl. EN2: Enf 1G 23
Banbury Ct. SM2: Sutt 7J 165
WC2 2E 12
Banbury Ho. E9 7K 67
Banbury Rd. E9 7K 67
E17 7E 34
Banbury St. SW11 2C 118
Banbury Wlk. *UB5: N'olt* *2E 76*
(off Brabazon Rd.)
Banchory Rd. SE3 7K 105
Bancroft Av. IG9: Buck H 2D 36
N2 5C 46
Bancroft Cl. TW15: Ashf 5C 128
Bancroft Ct. *SW8* *7J 101*
(off Allen Edwards Dr.)
UB5: N'olt 1A 76
Bancroft Gdns. BR6: Orp 1K 173
HA3: Hrw W 1G 41
Bancroft Ho. *E1* *4J 85*
(off Cephas St.)
Bancroft Rd. E1 3J 85
HA3: Hrw W 2G 41
Bandon Cl. UB10: Uxb 2B 74
BANDONHILL 5H 167
Bandon Ri. SM6: Wall 5H 167
Banfield Rd. SE15 3H 121
Banfor Ct. SM6: Wall 5G 167
Bangalore St. SW15 3E 116
Bangla Ho. *E8* *1F 85*
(off Clarissa St.)
Bangor Cl. UB5: N'olt 5F 59
Banim St. W6 4D 98
Banister Ho. E9 5K 67
SW8 *1G 119*
(off Wadhurst Rd.)
W10 *3G 81*
(off Bruckner St.)
Banister M. NW6 7K 63
Banister Rd. W10 3F 81
Bank, The N6 1F 65
Bank Av. CR4: Mitc 2B 154
Bank Bldgs. *E4* *6A 36*
(off The Avenue)
Bank Ct. E17 4E 50
Bank End SE1 4D 14 (1C 102)

Bankfoot Rd. BR1: Brom 4G **141**
Bankhurst Rd. SE6 7B **122**
Bank La. KT2: King T 7E **132**
SW15 5A **116**
Bank M. SM1: Sutt 6A **166**
Bank of England 1E **14** (6D **84**)
Bank of England Mus. 1F **15**
Bank of England Sports Cen. 5A **116**
Banks Ho. *SE1* *3C **102***
(off Rockingham St.)
Banksian Wlk. TW7: Isle 1J **113**
Banksia Rd. N18 5E **34**
Bankside CR2: S Croy 6F **169**
EN2: Enf 1G **23**
SE1 3C **14** (7C **84**)
(not continuous)
UB1: S'hall 1B **94**
Bankside Av. SE13 3E **122**
UB5: N'olt 2J **75**
Bankside Cl. DA5: Bexl 4K **145**
SM5: Cars 6C **166**
TW7: Isle 4K **113**
Bankside Dr. KT7: T Ditt 1B **162**
Bankside Gallery 3B **14** (7B **84**)
Bankside Lofts SE1 4B **14**
Bankside Mix SE1 4C **14** (1C **102**)
Bankside Pk. IG11: Bark 3A **90**
Bankside Pl. N4 6C **48**
Bankside Rd. IG1: Ilf 5G **71**
Bankside Way SE19 6E **138**
Banks La. DA6: Bex 4F **127**
Bank St. E14 1D **104**
Banks Way E12 4E **70**
Banks Yd. TW5: Hest 6D **94**
Bankton Rd. SW2 4A **120**
Bankwell Rd. SE13 4G **123**
Bannatyne Health Club
Chingford 6H **35**
Grove Park 2K **141**
Maida Vale ***2K 81***
(off Greville Rd.)
Orpington 7D **144**
Russell Square ***3D 6***
(off Woburn Pl.)
Banner Ct. *SE16* *4J **103***
(off Rotherhithe New Rd.)
Banner Ho. *EC1* *4D **8***
(off Roscoe St.)
Banner La. RM8: Dag 1E **72**
Bannerman Ho. SW8 7G **19** (6K **101**)
Banner St. EC1 4D **8** (4C **84**)
Banning St. SE10 5G **105**
Bannister Cl. SW2 1A **138**
UB6: G'frd 5H **59**
Bannister Ho. *HA3: W'stone* *3J **41***
(off Headstone Dr.)
SE14 *6K **103***
(off John Williams Cl.)
Bannister Sports Cen. 6B **26**
Bannockburn Rd. SE18 4J **107**
Bannon Ct. *SW6* *1K **117***
(off Michael Rd.)
Bannow Cl. KT19: Ewe 4A **164**
Banqueting House 5E **12** (1J **101**)
Banstead Ct. W12 7B **80**
Banstead Gdns. N9 3K **33**
Banstead Rd. SM5: Cars 7B **166**
Banstead Rd. Sth. SM2: Sutt 7B **166**
Banstead St. SE15 3J **121**
Banstead Way SM6: Wall 5J **167**
Banstock Rd. HA8: Edg 6C **28**
Bantam Ho. *NW9* *2B **44***
(off Heritage Av.)
Banting Dr. N21 5E **22**
Banting Ho. NW2 3C **62**
Bantock Ho. *W10* *3G **81***
(off Third Av.)
Banton Cl. EN1: Enf 2C **24**
Bantry Ho. *E1* *4K **85***
(off Ernest St.)
Bantry St. SE5 7D **102**
Banwell Rd. DA5: Bexl 6D **126**
Banyard Rd. SE16 3H **103**
Baptist Gdns. NW5 6E **64**
Baquba SE13 2D **122**
Barandon Rd. *W11* *7F **81***
(off Grenfell Rd.)
Barandon Wlk. W11 7F **81**
Barbanel Ho. *E1* *4J **85***
(off Cephas St.)
Barbara Brosnan Ct. NW8 1A **4** (2B **82**)
Barbara Castle Cl. SW6 6H **99**
Barbara Cl. TW17: Shep 5D **146**
Barbara Hucklesby Cl. N22 2B **48**
Barbauld Rd. N16 3E **66**
Barber Beaumont Ho. *E1* *3K **85***
(off Bancroft Rd.)
Barber Cl. N21 7F **23**
Barberry Ct. E15 6G **69**
Barbers All. E13 3K **87**
Barbers Rd. E15 2D **86**
Barbican EC2 5D **8**
Barbican Arts Cen. 5D **8** (5C **84**)
Barbican Cinema
Beech St. ***5D 8***
(within Arts Cen.)
Whitecross St. ***5C 84***
(off Whitecross St.)
Barbican Rd. UB6: G'frd 6F **77**
Barbican Theatre
Silk St. ***5D 8***
(within Arts Cen.)
Barb M. W6 3E **98**
Barbon All. *EC2* *7H **9***
(off Devonshire Sq.)
Barbon Cl. WC1 5F **7** (5K **83**)
Barbot Cl. N9 3B **34**
Barchard St. SW18 5K **117**
Barchester Cl. W7 1K **95**
Barchester Rd. HA3: Hrw W 2H **41**
Barchester St. E14 5D **86**
Barclay Cl. SW6 7J **99**
Barclay Ho. *E9* *7J **67***
(off Well St.)
Barclay Oval IG8: Wfd G 4D **36**
Barclay Path E17 5E **50**
Barclay Rd. CR0: C'don 3D **168**
E11 1H **69**
E13 4A **88**
E17 5E **50**
N18 6J **33**
SW6 7J **99**
Barcombe Av. SW2 2J **137**
Barcombe Cl. BR5: St P 3K **161**
Bardell Ho. *SE1* *7K **15***
(off Parkers Row)
Barden St. SE18 7J **107**
Bardfield Av. RM6: Chad H 3D **54**
Bardney Rd. SM4: Mord 4K **153**
Bardolph Rd. N7 4J **65**
TW9: Rich 3F **115**
Bard Rd. W10 7F **81**
Bardsey Pl. E1 4J **85**
Bardsey Wlk. *N1* *6C **66***
(off Douglas Rd. Nth.)
Bardsley Cl. CR0: C'don 3F **169**
Bardsley Ho. *SE10* *6E **104***
(off Bardsley La.)
Bardsley La. SE10 6E **104**
Barents Ho. *E1* *4K **85***
(off White Horse La.)
Barfett St. W10 4H **81**
Barfield Av. N20 2J **31**
Barfield Rd. BR1: Brom 3E **160**
E11 1H **69**
Barfleur La. SE8 4B **104**
Barford Cl. NW4 2C **44**
Barford Ho. *E3* *2B **86***
(off Tredegar Rd.)
Barford St. N1 1A **84**
Barforth Rd. SE15 3H **121**
Barfreston Way SE20 1H **157**
Bargate Cl. KT3: N Mald 7C **152**
SE18 5K **107**
Barge Dr. UB2: S'hall 3F **95**
Barge Ho. Rd. E16 2F **107**
Barge Ho. St. SE1 4K **13** (1A **102**)
Barge La. E3 1A **86**
Bargery Rd. SE6 1D **140**
Barge Wlk. KT1: Hamp W 3D **150**
KT1: King T 1D **150**
KT8: E Mos 6A **150**
(Boyle Farm Island)
KT8: E Mos 3H **149**
(Hampton Ct. Cres.)
SE10 3H **105**
Bargrove Cl. SE20 7G **139**
Bargrove Cres. SE6 2B **140**
Barham Cl. BR2: Brom 1C **172**
BR7: Chst 5F **143**
HA0: Wemb 6B **60**
RM7: Mawney 2H **55**
Barham Ct. *CR2: S Croy* *4C **168***
(off Barham Rd.)
Barham Ho. *SE17* *5E **102***
(off Kinglake Est.)
Barham Rd. BR7: Chst 5F **143**
CR2: S Croy 4C **168**
SW20 7C **134**
Baring Cl. SE12 2J **141**
Baring Ct. *N1* *1D **84***
(off Baring St.)
Baring Ho. *E14* *6C **86***
(off Canton St.)
Baring Rd. CR0: C'don 1G **169**
EN4: Cockf 4G **21**
SE12 7J **123**
Baring St. N1 1D **84**
Baritone Ct. *E15* *1H **87***
(off Church St.)
Barker Cl. HA6: Nwood 1H **39**
KT3: N Mald 4H **151**
TW9: Kew 2H **115**
Barker Dr. NW1 7G **65**
Barker Ho. *SE17* *4E **102***
(off Congreve St.)
Barker M. SW4 4F **119**
Barkers Arc. W8 2K **99**
Barker St. SW10 6A **100**
Barker Wlk. SW16 3H **137**
Barkham Rd. N17 7J **33**
Barkham Ter. SE1 1K **19**
BARKING 7G **71**
Barking Abbey 1G **89**
Barking Abbey School Leisure Cen. 6A **72**
Barking Bus. Cen. IG11: Bark 3A **90**
Barking Ind. Pk. IG11: Bark 1K **89**
Barking Northern Relief Rd.
IG11: Bark 7F **71**
BARKING RIVERSIDE 3B **90**
Barking Rd. E6 2A **88**
E13 2A **88**
E16 5G **87**
BARKINGSIDE 3G **53**
Barking Splash Pk. 5H **71**
Barkis Ho. W11 1F **99**
Bark Pl. W2 7K **81**
Barkston Gdns. SW5 4K **99**
Barkway Ct. N4 2C **66**
Barkway Dr. BR6: Farnb 4E **172**
Barkwith Ho. *SE14* *6K **103***
(off Cold Blow La.)
Barkwood Cl. RM7: Rom 5J **55**
Barkworth Rd. SE16 5H **103**
Barlborough St. SE14 7K **103**
Barlby Gdns. W10 4F **81**
Barlby Rd. W10 5E **80**
Barley Cl. HA0: Wemb 4D **60**
Barleycorn Way E14 7B **86**
(not continuous)
Barley Ct. E5 2J **67**
RM13: Rain *2K **91***
(off Lwr Mardyke Av.)
Barleyfields Cl. RM6: Chad H 6B **54**
Barley La. IG3: Ilf 7A **54**
RM6: Chad H 7A **54**
Barley Mow Pas. EC1 5B **8**
W4 5K **97**
Barley Mow Way TW17: Shep 4C **146**
Barley Shotts Bus. Pk. W10 5H **81**
Barling *NW1* *6F **65***
(off Castlehaven Rd.)
Barlow Cl. SM6: Wall 6J **167**
Barlow Dr. SE18 1C **124**
Barlow Ho. *N1* *1E **8***
(off Provost Est.)
SE16 *4H **103***
(off Rennie Est.)
W11 *7G **81***
(off Walmer Rd.)
Barlow Pl. W1 3K **11** (7F **83**)
Barlow Rd. NW6 6H **63**
TW12: Hamp 7E **130**
W3 1H **97**
Barlow St. SE17 4D **102**
Barlow Way RM13: Rain 5K **91**
Barmeston Rd. SE6 2D **140**
Barmor Cl. HA2: Harr 2F **41**
Barmouth Av. UB6: G'frd 2K **77**
Barmouth Rd. CR0: C'don 2K **169**
SW18 6A **118**
Barnabas Ct. EN2: Enf 4F **23**
Barnabas Ho. EC1 2C **8**
Barnabas Lodge *SW8* *1J **119***
(off Guildford Rd.)
Barnabas Rd. E9 5K **67**
Barnaby Cl. HA2: Harr 2G **59**
Barnaby Ct. NW9 3A **44**
SE16 *2G **103***
(off Scott Lidgett Cres.)
Barnaby Ho. SE15 6J **103**
Barnaby Pl. SW7 4A **16**
Barnaby Way IG7: Chig 3K **37**
Barnard Cl. BR7: Chst 1H **161**
SE18 3E **106**
SM6: Wall 7H **167**
TW16: Sun 7K **129**
Barnard Gdns. KT3: N Mald 4C **152**
UB4: Yead 4K **75**
Barnard Gro. E15 7H **69**
Barnard Hill N10 1F **47**
Barnard Ho. *E2* *3H **85***
(off Ellsworth St.)
Barnard Lodge EN5: New Bar 4F **21**
W9 *5J **81***
(off Admiral Wlk.)
Barnard M. SW11 4C **118**
Barnardo Dr. IG6: Ilf 4G **53**
Barnardo Gdns. E1 7K **85**
Barnardo St. E1 6K **85**
Barnardos Village IG6: Ilf 3G **53**
Barnardo Village Wlk. IG6: Ilf 3G **53**
Barnard Rd. CR4: Mitc 3E **154**
EN1: Enf 2C **24**
SW11 4C **118**
Barnards Ho. *SE16* *2B **104***
(off Wyatt Cl.)
Barnard's Inn EC1 6J **7**
Barnbrough *NW1* *1G **83***
(off Camden St.)
Barnby Sq. E15 1G **87**
Barnby St. E15 1G **87**
NW1 1B **6** (2G **83**)
Barn Cl. *NW5* *5H **65***
(off Torriano Av.)
TW15: Ashf 5D **128**
UB5: N'olt 2A **76**
Barn Cres. HA7: Stan 6H **27**
Barncroft Cl. UB8: Hil 5D **74**
Barneby Cl. TW2: Twick 1J **131**
BARNEHURST 3J **127**
Barnehurst Av. DA7: Bex 1J **127**
DA8: Erith 1J **127**
Barnehurst Cl. DA8: Erith 1J **127**

Barnehurst Golf Course . . . 3K **127**
Barnehurst Rd. DA7: Bex . . . 2J **127**
Barn Elms Athletics Track . . . 2D **116**
Barn Elms Cl. KT4: Wor Pk . . . 3B **164**
Barn Elms Pk. SW15 . . . 3E **116**
BARNES . . . 2B **116**
Barnes All. TW12: Hamp . . . 2G **149**
Barnes Av. SW13 . . . 7C **98**
UB2: S'hall . . . 4D **94**
Barnes Bri. W4 . . . 2A **116**
Barnes Cl. E12 . . . 4B **70**
HA8: Edg . . . 4A **28**
Barnes Common Nature Reserve . . . 3C **116**
Barnes Ct. CR7: Thor H . . . 3C **156**
E16 . . . 5A **88**
EN5: New Bar . . . 4E **20**
IG8: Buck H, Wfd G . . . 5G **37**
N1 . . . 7A **66**
Barnes End KT3: N Mald . . . 5C **152**
Barnes High St. SW13 . . . 2B **116**
Barnes Ho. *E2* . . . *2J* ***85***
(off Wadeson St.)
IG11: Bark . . . 1H **89**
SE14 . . . *6K* ***103***
(off John Williams Cl.)
Barnes Pikle W5 . . . 7D **78**
Barnes Rd. IG1: Ilf . . . 5G **71**
N18 . . . 4D **34**
Barnes St. E14 . . . 6A **86**
Barnes Ter. SE8 . . . 5B **104**
Barnes Wallis Ct. HA9: Wemb . . . 3J **61**
BARNET . . . 3B **20**
Barnet Burnt Oak Leisure Cen. . . . 1K **43**
Barnet Bus. Cen. EN5: Barn . . . 3B **20**
Barnet By-Pass NW4 . . . 2E **44**
NW7 . . . 6G **29**
Barnet Copthall Sports Cen. . . . 1D **44**
Barnet Dr. BR2: Brom . . . 2C **172**
Barnet FC . . . 1E **42**
Barnet Ga. La. EN5: Ark . . . 1H **29**
Barnet Gro. E2 . . . 1K **9** (3G **85**)
Barnet Hill EN5: Barn . . . 4C **20**
Barnet Ho. N20 . . . 2F **31**
Barnet La. EN5: Barn . . . 1C **30**
N20 . . . 1C **30**
Barnet Mus. . . . 4B **20**
Barnetts Ct. HA2: Harr . . . 3F **59**
Barnett St. E1 . . . 6H **85**
BARNET VALE . . . 5E **20**
Barnet Way NW7 . . . 3E **28**
Barnet Wood Rd. BR2: Brom . . . 2A **172**
Barney Cl. SE7 . . . 5A **106**
Barn Fld. NW3 . . . 5D **64**
Barnfield KT3: N Mald . . . 6A **152**
Barnfield Av. CR0: C'don . . . 2J **169**
CR4: Mitc . . . 4F **155**
KT2: King T . . . 4D **132**
Barnfield Cl. N4 . . . 7J **47**
SW17 . . . 3B **136**
Barnfield Gdns. KT2: King T . . . 4E **132**
SE18 . . . 6F **107**
Barnfield Pl. E14 . . . 4C **104**
Barnfield Rd. CR2: Sande . . . 7E **168**
DA17: Belv . . . 6F **109**
HA8: Edg . . . 1J **43**
SE18 . . . 6F **107**
(not continuous)
W5 . . . 4C **78**
Barnfield Wood Cl. BR3: Beck . . . 6F **159**
Barnfield Wood Rd. BR3: Beck . . . 6F **159**
Barnham Dr. SE28 . . . 1K **107**
(not continuous)
Barnham Rd. UB6: G'frd . . . 3G **77**
Barnham St. SE1 . . . 6H **15** (2E **102**)
Barn Hill HA9: Wemb . . . 1G **61**
Barnhill HA5: Eastc . . . 5A **40**
Barnhill Av. BR2: Brom . . . 5H **159**
Barnhill La. UB4: Yead . . . 3K **75**
Barnhill Rd. HA9: Wemb . . . 3J **61**
UB4: Yead . . . 3K **75**
Barningham Way NW9 . . . 6K **43**
Barnlea Cl. TW13: Hanw . . . 2C **130**
Barnmead Ct. RM9: Dag . . . 5F **73**
Barnmead Gdns. RM9: Dag . . . 5F **73**
Barnmead Rd. BR3: Beck . . . 1K **157**
RM9: Dag . . . 5F **73**
Barn M. HA2: Harr . . . 3E **58**
Barn Ri. HA9: Wemb . . . 1G **61**
BARNSBURY . . . 7K **65**
Barnsbury Cl. KT3: N Mald . . . 4J **151**
Barnsbury Cres. KT5: Surb . . . 1J **163**
Barnsbury Est. N1 . . . 1K **83**
(not continuous)
Barnsbury Gro. N7 . . . 7K **65**
Barnsbury Ho. SW4 . . . 6H **119**
Barnsbury La. KT5: Surb . . . 2H **163**
Barnsbury Pk. N1 . . . 7A **66**
Barnsbury Rd. N1 . . . 2A **84**
Barnsbury Sq. N1 . . . 7A **66**
Barnsbury St. N1 . . . 7A **66**
Barnsbury Ter. N1 . . . 7K **65**
Barnscroft SW20 . . . 3D **152**
Barnsdale Av. E14 . . . 4D **104**
Barnsdale Rd. W9 . . . 4H **81**
Barnsley St. E1 . . . 4H **85**
Barnstable La. SE13 . . . 4E **122**
Barnstaple Ho. *SE10* . . . *7D* ***104***
(off Devonshire Dr.)
SE12 . . . *5H* ***123***
(off Taunton Rd.)
Barnstaple Rd. HA4: Ruis . . . 3A **58**
Barnston Wlk. *N1* . . . *1C* ***84***
(off Popham St.)
Barn St. N16 . . . 2E **66**
Barn Theatre, The
Sidcup . . . 1A **144**
West Molesey . . . 4E **148**
Barn Way HA9: Wemb . . . 1G **61**
Barnwell Cl. HA8: Edg . . . 4A **28**
Barnwell Ho. *SE5* . . . *1E* ***120***
(off St Giles Rd.)
Barnwell Rd. SW2 . . . 5A **120**
Barnwood Cl. HA4: Ruis . . . 2F **57**
N20 . . . 1C **30**
W9 . . . 4K **81**
Baron Cl. N1 . . . 2A **84**
N11 . . . 5K **31**
Baroness Rd. E2 . . . 1K **9** (3F **85**)
Baronet Gro. N17 . . . 1G **49**
Baronet Rd. N17 . . . 1G **49**
Baron Gdns. IG6: Ilf . . . 3G **53**
Baron Gro. CR4: Mitc . . . 4C **154**
Baron Ho. SW19 . . . 1B **154**
Baron Rd. RM8: Dag . . . 1D **72**
Barons, The TW1: Twick . . . 6B **114**
Baronsclere Ct. N6 . . . 7G **47**
BARONS COURT . . . 5G **99**
Barons Ct. IG1: Ilf . . . 2H **71**
NW9 . . . 6K **43**
SM6: Bedd . . . 3H **167**
Baron's Ct. Rd. W14 . . . 5G **99**
Barons Court Theatre . . . *5G* ***99***
(off Comeragh Rd.)
Baronsfield Rd. TW1: Twick . . . 6B **114**
Barons Ga. EN4: E Barn . . . 6H **21**
W4 . . . 3J **97**
Barons Keep W14 . . . 5G **99**
Barons Lodge *E14* . . . *4F* ***105***
(off Manchester Rd.)
Barons Mead HA1: Harr . . . 4J **41**
Baronsmead Rd. SW13 . . . 1C **116**
Baronsmede W5 . . . 2F **97**
Baronsmere Ct. EN5: Barn . . . 4B **20**
Baronsmere Rd. N2 . . . 4C **46**
Baron's Pl. SE1 . . . 7K **13** (2A **102**)
Baron St. N1 . . . 2A **84**
Baron's Wlk. CR0: C'don . . . 6A **158**
Baron Wlk. CR4: Mitc . . . 4C **154**
E16 . . . 5H **87**
Baroque Ct. TW3: Houn . . . 3F **113**
Baroque Gdns. *SE8* . . . *4A* ***104***
(off Grand Canal Av.)
Barque M. SE8 . . . 6C **104**
Barquentine Hgts. SE10 . . . 3J **105**
Barrack Rd. TW4: Houn . . . 4B **112**
Barracks La. EN5: Barn . . . 3B **20**
Barracouta Ho. SE18 . . . 6K **107**
Barra Hall Cir. UB3: Hayes . . . 7G **75**
Barra Hall Rd. UB3: Hayes . . . 7G **75**
Barratt Av. N22 . . . 2K **47**
Barratt Ho. *N1* . . . *7B* ***66***
(off Sable St.)
Barratt Ind. Est. UB1: S'hall . . . 2E **94**
Barratt Ind. Pk. E3 . . . 4E **86**
Barratt Way HA3: W'stone . . . 2H **41**
Barra Wood Cl.
UB3: Hayes . . . 6G **75**
Barrenger Rd. N10 . . . 1D **46**
Barret Ho. NW6 . . . 1J **81**
SW9 . . . *3K* ***119***
(off Benedict Rd.)
Barrett Ct. *SE5* . . . *7D* ***102***
(off Dobson Wlk.)
Barrett Ho. *SE17* . . . *5C* ***102***
(off Browning St.)
Barrett Rd. E17 . . . 4E **50**
Barrett's Grn. Rd. NW10 . . . 3J **79**
Barrett's Gro. N16 . . . 5E **66**
Barrett St. W1 . . . 1H **11** (6E **82**)
Barrhill Rd. SW2 . . . 2J **137**
Barrie Ct. *EN5: New Bar* . . . *5F* ***21***
(off Lyonsdown Rd.)
Barriedale SE14 . . . 2A **122**
Barrie Est. W2 . . . 2A **10** (7B **82**)
Barrie Ho. *NW8* . . . *1C* ***82***
(off St Edmund's Ter.)
W2 . . . *7A* ***82***
(off Lancaster Ga.)
Barrier App. SE7 . . . 3B **106**
Barrier Point Rd. E16 . . . 1A **106**
Barringers Ct. HA4: Ruis . . . 7F **39**
Barringer Sq. SW17 . . . 4E **136**
Barrington Cl. IG5: Ilf . . . 1D **52**
NW5 . . . 5E **64**
Barrington Ct. N10 . . . 2E **46**
SW4 . . . 2J **119**
W3 . . . *2H* ***97***
(off Cheltenham Pl.)
Barrington Rd. DA7: Bex . . . 2D **126**
E12 . . . 6E **70**
N8 . . . 5H **47**
SM3: Sutt . . . 2J **165**
SW9 . . . 3B **120**
Barrington Vs. SE18 . . . 1E **124**
Barrington Wlk. SE19 . . . 6E **138**
Barrow Av. SM5: Cars . . . 7D **166**
Barrow Cl. N21 . . . 3G **33**
Barrow Ct. *SE6* . . . *1H* ***141***
(off Cumberland Pl.)
Barrowdene Cl. HA5: Pinn . . . 2C **40**
Barrowell Grn. N21 . . . 2G **33**
Barrowfield Cl. N9 . . . 3C **34**
Barrowgate Rd. W4 . . . 5J **97**
Barrow Hedges Cl. SM5: Cars . . . 7C **166**
Barrow Hedges Way SM5: Cars . . . 7C **166**
Barrow Hill KT4: Wor Pk . . . 2A **164**
Barrow Hill Cl. KT4: Wor Pk . . . 2A **164**
Barrow Hill Est. *NW8* . . . *2C* ***82***
(off Barrow Hill Rd.)
Barrow Hill Rd. NW8 . . . 1C **4** (2C **82**)
Barrow Point Av. HA5: Pinn . . . 2C **40**
Barrow Point La. HA5: Pinn . . . 2C **40**
Barrow Rd. CR0: Wadd . . . 5A **168**
SW16 . . . 6H **137**
Barrow Store Ct. *SE1* . . . *7G* ***15***
(off Decima St.)
Barrow Wlk. TW8: Bford . . . 6C **96**
Barrs Rd. NW10 . . . 7K **61**
Barry Av. DA7: Bex . . . 7E **108**
N15 . . . 6F **49**
Barry Blandford Way E3 . . . 4D **86**
Barry Cl. BR6: Orp . . . 3J **173**
Barrydene N20 . . . 1G **31**
Barry Ho. *SE16* . . . *4H* ***103***
(off Rennie Est.)
Barry Pde. SE22 . . . 5G **121**
Barry Rd. E6 . . . 6C **88**
NW10 . . . 7J **61**
SE22 . . . 6G **121**
Barry Ter. *TW15: Ashf* . . . *2B* ***128***
(off Orchard Way)
Barset Rd. SE15 . . . 3J **121**
(not continuous)
Barson Cl. SE20 . . . 7J **139**
Barston Rd. SE27 . . . 3C **138**
Barstow Cres. SW2 . . . 1K **137**
Barter St. WC1 . . . 6F **7** (5J **83**)
Barters Wlk. HA5: Pinn . . . 3C **40**
Barth M. SE18 . . . 4J **107**
Bartholomew Cl. EC1 . . . 6B **8** (5C **84**)
(not continuous)
SW18 . . . 4A **118**
Bartholomew Ct. *E14* . . . *7F* ***87***
(off Newport Av.)
EC1 . . . *3D* ***8***
(off Old St.)
HA8: Edg . . . 7J **27**
Bartholomew Ho. IG8: Wfd G . . . 1F **53**, 7K **37**
W10 . . . *4G* ***81***
(off Appleford Rd.)
Bartholomew La. EC2 . . . 1F **15** (6D **84**)
Bartholomew Pl. EC1 . . . 6C **8**
Bartholomew Rd. NW5 . . . 6G **65**
Bartholomew Sq. E1 . . . 4H **85**
EC1 . . . 3D **8** (3C **84**)
Bartholomew St. SE1 . . . 3D **102**
Bartholomew Vs. NW5 . . . 6G **65**
Barth Rd. SE18 . . . 4J **107**
Bartle Av. E6 . . . 2C **88**
Bartle Rd. W11 . . . 6G **81**
Bartlett Cl. E14 . . . 6C **86**
Bartlett Ct. EC4 . . . 7K **7** (6A **84**)
Bartlett Ho. *KT4: Wor Pk* . . . *2B* ***164***
(off The Avenue)
Bartlett Ho's. *RM10: Dag* . . . *7H* ***73***
(off Vicarage Rd.)
Bartlett M. E14 . . . 5D **104**
Bartletts Pas. *EC4* . . . *7K* ***7***
(off Fetter La.)
Bartlett St. CR2: S Croy . . . 5D **168**
Bartlow Gdns. RM5: Col R . . . 1K **55**
Bartok Ho. *W11* . . . *1H* ***99***
(off Lansdowne Wlk.)
Barton Av. RM7: Rush G . . . 1H **73**
Barton Cl. DA6: Bex . . . 5E **126**
E6 . . . 6D **88**
E9 . . . 5J **67**
NW4 . . . 5C **44**
SE15 . . . 3H **121**
TW17: Shep . . . 6D **146**
Barton Ct. *W14* . . . *5G* ***99***
(off Baron's Ct. Rd.)
Barton Grn. KT3: N Mald . . . 2K **151**
Barton Ho. *E3* . . . *3D* ***86***
(off Bow Rd.)
N1 . . . *7B* ***66***
(off Sable St.)
SW6 . . . *3K* ***117***
(off Wandsworth Bri. Rd.)
Barton Mdws. IG6: Ilf . . . 4F **53**
Barton M. E14 . . . 2D **104**
SW19 . . . 6A **136**
Barton Rd. DA14: Sidc . . . 6E **144**
W14 . . . 5G **99**
Barton St. SW1 . . . 1E **18** (3J **101**)
Bartonway *NW8* . . . *1B* ***82***
(off Queen's Ter.)
Bartram Cl. UB8: Hil . . . 4D **74**
Bartram Rd. SE4 . . . 5A **122**
Bartrams La. EN4: Had W . . . 1F **21**
Bartrip St. E9 . . . 6B **68**
Barts Cl. BR3: Beck . . . 5C **158**
Barville Cl. SE4 . . . 4A **122**
Barwell Bus. Pk. KT9: Chess . . . 7D **162**

Barwell Ct.—Bazalgette Gdns.

Barwell Ct. KT9: Chess 7B **162**
Barwell Ho. *E2* *4G **85***
(*off Menotti St.*)
Barwell La. KT9: Chess 7C **162**
Barwick Dr. UB8: Hil 5D **74**
Barwick Ho. *W3* *2J **97***
(*off Strafford Rd.*)
Barwick Rd. E7 . . . . . 4K **69**
Barwood Av. BR4: W W'ck 1D **170**
Bascombe Gro.
DA1: Bexl, Cray 7K **127**
Bascombe St. SW2 . . . . . 6A **120**
Basden Gro. TW13: Hanw 2E **130**
Basden Ho. TW13: Hanw 2E **130**
Basedale Rd. RM9: Dag 7B **72**
Baseing Cl. E6 . . . . . 7E **88**
Baseline Bus. Studios *W11* *7F **81***
(*off Barandon Wlk.*)
Basepoint Bus. Cen. RM13: Rain 4K **91**
Basevi Way SE8 . . . . . 6D **104**
Bashley Rd. NW10 . . . . . 4K **79**
Basil Av. E6 . . . . . 3C **88**
Basildene Rd. TW4: Houn 3B **112**
Basildon Av. IG5: Ilf 1E **52**
Basildon Cl. SM2: Sutt 7K **165**
Basildon Ct. *W1* *5H **5***
(*off Devonshire Rd.*)
Basildon Rd. SE2 . . . . . 5A **108**
Basil Gdns. CR0: C'don 1K **169**
SE27 . . . . . 5C **138**
Basil Ho. *E1* *6G **85***
(*off Henriques St.*)
SW8 . . . . . *7J **101***
(*off Wyvil Rd.*)
Basilica Pl. E3 . . . . . 2B **86**
Basil Mans. *SW3* *7E **10***
(*off Basil St.*)
Basilon Rd. DA7: Bex 2E **126**
Basil Spence Ho. N22 . . . . . 1K **47**
Basil St. SW3 . . . . . 1E **16** (3D **100**)
Basin App. E14 . . . . . 6A **86**
E16 . . . . . 7F **89**
Basing Cl. KT7: T Ditt 7K **149**
Basing Ct. SE15 . . . . . 1F **121**
Basingdon Way SE5 . . . . . 4D **120**
Basing Dr. DA5: Bexl 6F **127**
Basingfield Rd. KT7: T Ditt 7K **149**
Basinghall Av. EC2 . . . . . 7E **8** (6D **84**)
Basinghall Gdns. SM2: Sutt 7K **165**
Basinghall St. EC2 . . . . . 7E **8** (6D **84**)
Basing Hill HA9: Wemb 2F **61**
NW11 . . . . . 1H **63**
Basing Ho. Yd. E2 . . . . . 1H **9**
Basing Pl. E2 . . . . . 1H **9** (3E **84**)
Basing St. W11 . . . . . 6H **81**
Basing Way KT7: T Ditt 7K **149**
N3 . . . . . 3J **45**
Basin Mill Apartments *E2* *1F **85***
(*off Laburnum St.*)
Basin Sth. E16 . . . . . 1F **107**
Basire St. N1 . . . . . 1C **84**
Baskerville Gdns. NW10 . . . . . 4A **62**
Baskerville Rd. SW18 . . . . . 7C **118**
Basket Gdns. SE9 . . . . . 5C **124**
Baslow Cl. HA3: Hrw W 1H **41**
Baslow Wlk. E5 . . . . . 4K **67**
Basnett Rd. SW11 . . . . . 3E **118**
Basque Ct. *SE16* *2K **103***
(*off Garter Way*)
Bassano St. SE22 . . . . . 5F **121**
Bassant Rd. SE18 . . . . . 6K **107**
Bass Ct. *E15* *1H **87***
(*off Plaistow Rd.*)
Bassein Pk. Rd. W12 . . . . . 2B **98**
Bassett Gdns. TW7: Isle 7G **95**
Bassett Ho. SW19 . . . . . 5K **135**
Bassett Rd. W10 . . . . . 6F **81**
Bassett's Cl. BR6: Farnb 4F **173**
Bassett St. NW5 . . . . . 6E **64**
Bassett's Way BR6: Farnb 4F **173**
Bassett Way UB6: G'frd 6F **77**
Bassingbourn Ho. *N1* *7A **66***
(*off The Sutton Est.*)
Bassingham Rd. HA0: Wemb 6D **60**
SW18 . . . . . 7A **118**
Bassishaw Highwalk EC2 . . . . . 6E **8**
Bass M. SE22 . . . . . 4G **121**
Basswood Cl. SE15 . . . . . 3H **121**
Bastable Av. IG11: Bark 2J **89**
Basterfield Ho. *EC1* *4C **8***
(*off Golden La. Est.*)
Bastion Highwalk EC2 . . . . . 6C **8**
Bastion Ho. *EC2* *6D **8***
(*off London Wall*)
Bastion Rd. SE2 . . . . . 5A **108**
Baston Mnr. Rd. BR2: Hayes, Kes . . . 3K **171**
Baston Rd. BR2: Hayes 2K **171**
Bastwick St. EC1 . . . . . 3C **8** (4C **84**)
Basuto Rd. SW6 . . . . . 1J **117**
Batavia Cl. TW16: Sun 1K **147**
Batavia Ho. *SE14* *7A **104***
(*off Batavia Rd.*)
Batavia M. SE14 . . . . . 7A **104**
Batavia Rd. SE14 . . . . . 7A **104**
TW16: Sun 1K **147**
Batchelor St. N1 . . . . . 1A **84**
Bateman Cl. IG11: Bark 6G **71**
Bateman Ho. *SE17* *6B **102***
(*off Otto St.*)
Bateman M. SW4 . . . . . 6H **119**
Bateman Rd. E4 . . . . . 6H **35**
Bateman's Bldgs. W1 . . . . . 1C **12**
Bateman's Row EC2 . . . . . 3H **9** (4E **84**)
Bateman St. W1 . . . . . 1C **12** (6H **83**)
Bates Cres. CR0: Wadd 5A **168**
SW16 . . . . . 7G **137**
Bateson St. SE18 . . . . . 4J **107**
Bates Point *E13* *1J **87***
(*off Pelly Rd.*)
Bate St. E14 . . . . . 7B **86**
Bat Gdns. KT2: King T 6F **133**
Bath Cl. SE15 . . . . . 7H **103**
Bath Ct. EC1 . . . . . 2E **8**
(St Luke's Est.)
EC1 . . . . . 4J **7**
(Warner St.)
SE26 . . . . . *3G **139***
(*off Droitwich Cl.*)
Bathgate Ho. *SW9* *1B **120***
(*off Lothian Rd.*)
Bathgate Rd. SW19 . . . . . 3F **135**
Bath Gro. *E2* *2G **85***
(*off Horatio St.*)
Bath Ho. *E2* *4G **85***
(*off Ramsey St.*)
IG11: Bark 7G **71**
SE1 . . . . . *3C **102***
(*off Bath Ter.*)
Bath Ho. Rd. CR0: Bedd 1J **167**
Bath Pas. KT1: King T 2D **150**
Bath Pl. EC2 . . . . . 2G **9** (3E **84**)
EN5: Barn 3C **20**
W6 . . . . . *5E **98***
(*off Peabody Est.*)
Bath Rd. E7 . . . . . 6B **70**
N9 . . . . . 2C **34**
RM6: Chad H 6E **54**
SL3: Coln, Poyle 4A **174**
TW3: Houn 3F **113**
TW4: Houn 2B **112**
TW5: Cran 1G **111**
TW6: H'row A 1G **111**
UB3: Harl 1G **111**
UB7: Lford, Harm, Sip 4C **174**
W4 . . . . . 4A **98**
Baths Ct. W12 . . . . . 2D **98**
Baths Rd. BR2: Brom 4B **160**
Bath St. EC1 . . . . . 2D **8** (3C **84**)
Bath Ter. SE1 . . . . . 3C **102**
Bathurs Sq. N15 . . . . . 4E **48**
Bathurst Av. SW19 . . . . . 1K **153**
Bathurst Gdns. NW10 . . . . . 2D **80**
Bathurst Ho. *W12* *7D **80***
(*off White City Est.*)
Bathurst M. W2 . . . . . 2B **10** (6B **82**)
Bathurst Rd. IG1: Ilf 1F **71**
Bathurst St. W2 . . . . . 2B **10** (7B **82**)
Bathway SE18 . . . . . 4E **106**
Batley Cl. CR4: Mitc 7D **154**
Batley Pl. N16 . . . . . 3F **67**
Batley Rd. EN2: Enf 1H **23**
N16 . . . . . 3F **67**
Batman Cl. W12 . . . . . 1D **98**
Batoum Gdns. W6 . . . . . 3E **98**
Batsford Ho. *SW19* *4K **135***
(*off Durnsford Rd.*)
Batson Ho. *E1* *6G **85***
(*off Fairclough St.*)
Batson St. W12 . . . . . 2C **98**
Batsworth Rd. CR4: Mitc 3B **154**
Battenberg Wlk. SE19 . . . . . 6E **138**
Batten Cl. E6 . . . . . 6D **88**
Batten Cotts. *E14* *5A **86***
(*off Maroon St.*)
Batten Ho. SW4 . . . . . 5G **119**
W10 . . . . . *3G **81***
(*off Third Av.*)
Batten St. SW11 . . . . . 3C **118**
Battersby Rd. SE6 . . . . . 2F **141**
BATTERSEA 1E 118
Battersea Arts Cen. *3D 118*
(off Lavender Hill)
Battersea Bri. SW3 . . . . . 7B **100**
Battersea Bri. Rd. SW11 . . . . . 7C **100**
Battersea Bus. Cen. SW11 . . . . . 3E **118**
Battersea Bus. Pk. SW8 . . . . . 1G **119**
Battersea Church Rd. SW11 . . . . . 1B **118**
Battersea Dogs' Home 7F 101
Battersea High St. SW11 . . . . . 1B **118**
(not continuous)
BATTERSEA PARK 7F 101
Battersea Pk. 7D 100
Battersea Pk. Children's Zoo 7E 100
Battersea Pk. Rd. SW8 . . . . . 1E **118**
SW11 . . . . . 2C **118**
Battersea Power Station Development
SW8 . . . . . 6F **101**
Battersea Ri. SW11 . . . . . 5C **118**
Battersea Roof Gdns. SW8 . . . . . 7F **101**
Battersea Sports Cen. 3B 118
Battersea Sq. SW11 . . . . . 1B **118**
Battery Rd. SE28 . . . . . 2J **107**
Battilion Ho. *NW9* *2B **44***
(*off Heritage Av.*)
Battishill St. N1 . . . . . 7B **66**
Battlebridge Ct. *N1* *2J **83***
(*off Wharfdale Rd.*)
Battle Bri. La. SE1 . . . . . 5G **15** (1E **102**)
Battle Cl. SW19 . . . . . 6A **136**
Battledean Rd. N5 . . . . . 5B **66**
Battle Ho. *SE15* *6G **103***
(*off Haymerle Rd.*)
Battle Rd. DA8: Erith 4J **109**
DA17: Belv, Erith 4J **109**
Batty St. E1 . . . . . 6G **85**
Batwa Ho. SE16 . . . . . 5H **103**
Baudwin Rd. SE6 . . . . . 2G **141**
Baugh Rd. DA14: Sidc 5C **144**
Baulk, The SW18 . . . . . 7J **117**
Bavant Rd. SW16 . . . . . 2J **155**
Bavaria Rd. N19 . . . . . 2J **65**
Bavdene M. *NW4* *4D **44***
(*off The Burroughs*)
Bavent Rd. SE5 . . . . . 2C **120**
Bawdale Rd. SE22 . . . . . 5F **121**
Bawdsey Av. IG2: Ilf 4K **53**
Bawley Ct. E16 . . . . . 7G **89**
Bawley Ter. *E15* *1F **87***
(*off Rick Roberts Way*)
Bawtree Rd. SE14 . . . . . 7A **104**
Bawtry Rd. N20 . . . . . 3J **31**
Baxendale N20 . . . . . 2F **31**
Baxendale St. E2 . . . . . 3G **85**
Baxter Cl. BR1: Brom 3F **161**
UB2: S'hall 3F **95**
UB10: Hil 3D **74**
Baxter Ho. *E3* *3D **86***
(*off Bromley High St.*)
Baxter Rd. E16 . . . . . 6A **88**
IG1: Ilf 5F **71**
N1 . . . . . 6D **66**
N18 . . . . . 4C **34**
Baxter Wlk. SW16 . . . . . 2H **137**
Bayard Ct. DA6: Bex 4H **127**
Bay Ct. *E1* *4K **85***
(*off Frimley Way*)
W5 . . . . . 3E **96**
Baycroft Cl. HA5: Eastc 3A **40**
Baydon Ct. BR2: Brom 3H **159**
Bayer Ho. *EC1* *4C **8***
(*off Golden La. Est.*)
Bayes Cl. SE26 . . . . . 5J **139**
Bayes Ct. *NW3* *7D **64***
(*off Primrose Hill Rd.*)
Bayes Ho. *N1* *7A **66***
(*off Augustas La.*)
Bayfield Ho. *SE4* *4K **121***
(*off Coston Wlk.*)
Bayfield Rd. SE9 . . . . . 4B **124**
Bayford M. *E8* *7H **67***
(*off Bayford St.*)
Bayford Rd. NW10 . . . . . 3F **81**
Bayford St. E8 . . . . . 7H **67**
Bayford St. Bus. Cen. *E8* *7H **67***
(*off Sidworth St.*)
Baygrove M.
KT1: Hamp W 1C **150**
Bayham Pl. NW1 . . . . . 1G **83**
Bayham Rd. SM4: Mord 4K **153**
W4 . . . . . 3K **97**
W13 . . . . . 7B **78**
Bayham St. NW1 . . . . . 1G **83**
Bayhurst Wood Country Pk. 5B 38
Bayleaf Cl. TW12: Hamp H 5H **131**
Bayley St. WC1 . . . . . 6C **6** (5H **83**)
Bayley Wlk. SE2 . . . . . 6E **108**
Baylis M. TW1: Twick 7A **114**
Baylis Pl. BR1: Brom 3C **160**
Baylis Rd. SE1 . . . . . 7J **13** (2A **102**)
Bayliss Av. SE28 . . . . . 7D **90**
Bayliss Cl. N21 . . . . . 5D **22**
UB1: S'hall *6F **77***
(*off Whitecote Rd.*)
Bayne Cl. E6 . . . . . 6D **88**
Baynes Cl. EN1: Enf 1B **24**
Baynes M. NW3 . . . . . 6B **64**
Baynes St. NW1 . . . . . 7G **65**
Baynham Cl. DA5: Bexl 6F **127**
Bayonne Rd. W6 . . . . . 6G **99**
Bays Ct. HA8: Edg 5C **28**
Bays Farm Ct. UB7: Lford 4D **174**
Bayshill Ri. UB5: N'olt 6F **59**
Baysixty6 Skate Pk. *5H 81*
(off Acklam Rd.)
Bayston Rd. N16 . . . . . 3F **67**
BAYSWATER 7A 82
Bayswater Cl. N13 . . . . . 4G **33**
Bayswater Rd. W2 . . . . . 3A **10** (7K **81**)
Baythorne Ho. *E16* *6H **87***
(*off Turner St.*)
Baythorne St. E3 . . . . . 5B **86**
Bayton Ct. *E8* *7G **67***
(*off Lansdowne Dr.*)
Bay Tree Cl. BR1: Brom 1B **160**
Baytree Cl. DA15: Sidc 1K **143**
Baytree Ct. SW2 . . . . . 4K **119**
Bay Tree Ho. *EC1* *4J **7***
(*off Baker's Row*)
Baytree Ho. E4 . . . . . 7J **25**
Baytree M. SE17 . . . . . 4D **102**
Baytree Rd. SW2 . . . . . 4K **119**
Baywillow Av. SM5: Cars 1D **166**
Bazalgette Cl. KT3: N Mald 5K **151**
Bazalgette Gdns. KT3: N Mald 5K **151**

194 A-Z London

Bazalgette Ho. NW8 . . . 3B 4
(off Orchardson St.)
Bazalgette Way SE2 . . . 1C 108
Bazeley Ho. SE1 . . . 7A 14
(off Library St.)
Bazely St. E14 . . . 7E 86
Bazile Rd. N21 . . . 6E 23
BBC Broadcasting House . . . 6K 5 (5F 83)
BBC Maida Vale Studios . . . 4K 81
(off Delaware Rd.)
BBC Studios W12 . . . 1E 98
BBC Worldwide W12 . . . 1E 98
BDA Dental Mus. . . . 6J 5 (5F 83)
Beacham Cl. SE7 . . . 5B 106
Beachborough Rd. BR1: Brom . . . 4E 140
Beach Cl. SE9 . . . 6C 124
Beachcroft Av. UB1: S'hall . . . 1C 94
Beachcroft Rd. E11 . . . 3G 69
Beachcroft Way N19 . . . 1H 65
Beach Gro. TW13: Hanw . . . 2E 130
Beach Ho. SW5 . . . 5J 99
(off Philbeach Gdns.)
TW13: Hanw . . . 2E 130
Beachy Rd. E3 . . . 7C 68
Beacon Bingo
Cricklewood . . . 4F 63
Streatham . . . 2J 137
Beacon Cl. UB8: Uxb . . . 5A 56
Beacon Ga. SE14 . . . 3K 121
Beacon Gro. SM5: Cars . . . 4E 166
Beacon Hill N7 . . . 5J 65
Beacon Ho. E14 . . . 5D 104
(off Burrells Wharf Sq.)
SE5 . . . 7E 102
(off Southampton Way)
Beacon Pl. CR0: Bedd . . . 3J 167
Beacon Point SE10 . . . 6D 104
(off Dowells St.)
Beacon Rd. SE13 . . . 6F 123
TW6: H'row A . . . 6C 110
Beacons Cl. E6 . . . 5C 88
Beaconsfield WC1 . . . 2E 7
(off Red Lion St.)
Beaconsfield Cl. N11 . . . 5K 31
SE3 . . . 6J 105
W4 . . . 5J 97
Beaconsfield Pde. SE9 . . . 4C 142
Beaconsfield Rd. BR1: Brom . . . 3B 160
CR0: C'don . . . 6D 156
DA5: Bexl . . . 2K 145
E10 . . . 2E 68
E16 . . . 4H 87
E17 . . . 6B 50
KT3: N Mald . . . 2K 151
KT5: Surb . . . 7F 151
N9 . . . 3B 34
N11 . . . 3K 31
N15 . . . 4E 48
NW10 . . . 6B 62
SE3 . . . 7H 105
SE9 . . . 2C 142
SE17 . . . 5D 102
TW1: Twick . . . 6B 114
UB1: S'hall . . . 1B 94
UB4: Yead . . . 1A 94
W4 . . . 3K 97
W5 . . . 2C 96
Beaconsfield St. N1 . . . 1J 83
Beaconsfield Ter. RM6: Chad H . . . 6D 54
Beaconsfield Ter. Rd. W14 . . . 3G 99
Beaconsfield Wlk. E6 . . . 6E 88
SW6 . . . 1H 117
Beacontree Av. E17 . . . 1F 51
BEACONTREE HEATH . . . 1G 73
Beacontree Rd. E11 . . . 1H 69
Beadle's Pde. RM10: Dag . . . 6J 73
Beadlow Cl. SM5: Cars . . . 6B 154
Beadman Pl. SE27 . . . 4B 138
Beadman St. SE27 . . . 4B 138
Beadnell Ct. E1 . . . 7G 85
(off Cable St.)

Beadnell Rd. SE23 . . . 1K 139
Beadon Rd. BR2: Brom . . . 4J 159
W6 . . . 4E 98
Beaford Gro. SW20 . . . 3G 153
Beagle Cl. TW13: Felt . . . 4K 129
Beak St. W1 . . . 2B 12 (7G 83)
Beal Cl. DA16: Well . . . 1A 126
Beale Arboretum, The . . . 1J 21
Beale Cl. N13 . . . 5G 33
Beale Pl. E3 . . . 2B 86
Beale Rd. E3 . . . 1B 86
Beal Rd. IG1: Ilf . . . 2E 70
Beam Av. RM10: Dag . . . 1H 91
Beames Rd. NW10 . . . 1K 79
Beaminster Gdns. IG6: Ilf . . . 2F 53
Beaminster Ho. SW8 . . . 7K 101
(off Dorset Rd.)
Beamish Dr. WD23: B Hea . . . 1B 26
Beamish Ho. SE16 . . . 4H 103
(off Rennie Est.)
Beamish Rd. N9 . . . 1B 34
Beam Reach Bus. Pk. RM13: Rain . . . 3K 91
Beam Valley Country Pk. . . . 1J 91
Beamway RM10: Dag . . . 7K 73
Beanacre Cl. E9 . . . 6B 68
Bean Rd. DA6: Bex . . . 4D 126
Beanshaw SE9 . . . 4E 142
Beansland Gro. RM6: Chad H . . . 3E 54
Bear All. EC4 . . . 7A 8 (6B 84)
Bear Cl. RM7: Rom . . . 6H 55
Beardell St. SE19 . . . 6F 139
Beardow Gro. N14 . . . 6B 22
Beard Rd. KT2: King T . . . 5F 133
Beardsfield E13 . . . 2J 87
Beard's Hill TW12: Hamp . . . 1E 148
Beard's Hill Cl. TW12: Hamp . . . 1E 148
Beardsley Ter. RM8: Dag . . . 5B 72
(off Stonard Rd.)
Beardsley Way W3 . . . 2K 97
Beard's Rd. TW15: Ashf . . . 6G 129
Bearfield Rd. KT2: King T . . . 7E 132
Bear Gdns. SE1 . . . 4C 14 (1C 102)
Bear La. SE1 . . . 4B 14 (1B 102)
Bear Pit Apartments SE1 . . . 4C 14
(off New Globe Wlk.)
Bear Rd. TW13: Hanw . . . 4B 130
Bearstead Ri. SE4 . . . 5B 122
Bearsted Ter. BR3: Beck . . . 1C 158
Bear St. WC2 . . . 2D 12 (7H 83)
Beasley's Ait TW16: Sun . . . 6H 147
Beasley's Ait La. TW16: Sun . . . 6H 147
Beaton Cl. SE15 . . . 1F 121
Beatrice Av. HA9: Wemb . . . 5E 60
SW16 . . . 3K 155
Beatrice Cl. E13 . . . 4J 87
HA5: Eastc . . . 4J 39
Beatrice Ct. IG9: Buck H . . . 2G 37
Beatrice Ho. W6 . . . 5E 98
(off Queen Caroline St.)
Beatrice Pl. W8 . . . 3K 99
Beatrice Rd. E17 . . . 5C 50
N4 . . . 7A 48
N9 . . . 7D 24
SE1 . . . 4G 103
TW10: Rich . . . 5F 115
UB1: S'hall . . . 1D 94
Beatrice Webb Ho. E3 . . . 2A 86
(off Chisenhale Rd.)
Beatrix Apartments E3 . . . 4B 86
(off English St.)
Beatrix Ho. SW5 . . . 5K 99
(off Old Brompton Rd.)
Beatson Wlk. SE16 . . . 1A 104
(not continuous)
Beattie Cl. TW14: Felt . . . 7H 111
Beattie Ho. SW8 . . . 1G 119
Beattock Ri. N10 . . . 4F 47
Beatty Ho. E14 . . . 2C 104
(off Admirals Way)
SW1 . . . 6B 18
(off Dolphin Sq.)

Beatty Rd. HA7: Stan . . . 6H 27
N16 . . . 4E 66
Beatty St. NW1 . . . 2G 83
Beattyville Gdns. IG6: Ilf . . . 4E 52
Beauchamp Cl. W4 . . . 3J 97
Beauchamp Ct. EN5: Barn . . . 4C 20
(off Victors Way)
HA7: Stan . . . 5H 27
Beauchamp Pl. SW3 . . . 1D 16 (3C 100)
Beauchamp Rd. E7 . . . 7K 69
KT8: W Mole, E Mos . . . 5F 149
SE19 . . . 1D 156
SM1: Sutt . . . 4J 165
SW11 . . . 4C 118
TW1: Twick . . . 7A 114
Beauchamp St. EC1 . . . 6J 7 (5A 84)
Beauchamp Ter. SW15 . . . 3D 116
Beauclerc Ct. TW16: Sun . . . 2A 148
Beauclerc Rd. W6 . . . 3D 98
Beauclere Ho. SM2: Sutt . . . 6A 166
Beauclerk Cl. TW13: Felt . . . 1K 129
Beauclerk Ho. SW16 . . . 3J 137
Beau Ct. HA7: Stan . . . 7J 27
(off Hitchin La.)
Beaudesert M. UB7: W Dray . . . 2A 92
Beaufort E6 . . . 5E 88
Beaufort Av. HA3: Kenton . . . 4A 42
Beaufort Cl. E4 . . . 6J 35
RM7: Mawney . . . 4J 55
SW15 . . . 7D 116
W5 . . . 5F 79
Beaufort Ct. E14 . . . 2C 104
(off Admirals Way)
EN5: New Bar . . . 5F 21
N11 . . . 5A 32
(off The Limes Av.)
SW6 . . . 6J 99
TW10: Ham . . . 4C 132
Beaufort Dr. NW11 . . . 4J 45
Beaufort Gdns. E1 . . . 5K 85
IG1: Ilf . . . 1E 70
NW4 . . . 6E 44
SW3 . . . 1D 16 (3C 100)
SW16 . . . 7K 137
TW5: Hest . . . 1C 112
Beaufort Ho. E16 . . . 1K 105
(off Fairfax M.)
SW1 . . . 6C 18
(off Aylesford St.)
SW3 . . . 7B 16
(off Beaufort St.)
Beaufort Mans. SW3 . . . 7B 16 (6B 100)
Beaufort M. SW6 . . . 6H 99
Beaufort Pk. NW11 . . . 4J 45
Beaufort Rd. HA4: Ruis . . . 2F 57
KT1: King T . . . 4E 150
TW1: Twick . . . 7C 114
TW10: Ham . . . 4C 132
W5 . . . 5F 79
Beaufort Sq. NW9 . . . 2C 44
Beaufort St. SW3 . . . 7A 16 (6B 100)
Beaufort Ter. E14 . . . 5E 104
(off Ferry St.)
Beaufort Way KT17: Ewe . . . 7C 164
Beaufoy Ho. SE27 . . . 3B 138
SW8 . . . 7K 101
(off Rita Rd.)
Beaufoy Rd. N17 . . . 7K 33
(not continuous)
Beaufoy Wlk. SE11 . . . 4H 19 (4K 101)
SE26 . . . 4H 139
Beaulieu Av. E16 . . . 1K 105
Beaulieu Cl. CR4: Mitc . . . 1E 154
NW9 . . . 4A 44
SE5 . . . 3D 120
TW1: Twick . . . 6D 114
TW4: Houn . . . 5D 112
Beaulieu Dr. HA5: Pinn . . . 6B 40
Beaulieu Gdns. N21 . . . 7H 23
Beaulieu Hgts. SE25 . . . 1E 156

Beaulieu Lodge E14 . . . 3F 105
(off Schooner Cl.)
Beaulieu Pl. W4 . . . 3J 97
Beaumanor Gdns. SE9 . . . 4E 142
Beaumanor Mans. W2 . . . 7K 81
(off Queensway)
Beaumans Dr. E17 . . . 1B 50
Beaumaris Dr. IG8: Wfd G . . . 7G 37
Beaumaris Gdns. SE19 . . . 7C 138
Beaumaris Grn. NW9 . . . 6A 44
Beaumaris Twr. W3 . . . 2H 97
(off Park Rd. Nth.)
Beaumont W14 . . . 4H 99
(off Kensington Village)
Beaumont Av. HA0: Wemb . . . 5C 60
HA2: Harr . . . 6F 41
TW9: Rich . . . 3F 115
W14 . . . 5H 99
Beaumont Bldgs. WC2 . . . 1F 13
(off Martlett Ct.)
Beaumont Cl. KT2: King T . . . 7G 133
N2 . . . 4C 46
Beaumont Ct. E1 . . . 3K 85
E5 . . . 3H 67
HA0: Wemb . . . 5C 60
NW1 . . . 1H 83
NW9 . . . 2B 44
(off Cherry Cl.)
W1 . . . 5H 5
(off Beaumont St.)
W4 . . . 5J 97
Beaumont Cres. W14 . . . 5H 99
Beaumont Dr. KT4: Wor Pk . . . 7D 152
TW15: Ashf . . . 5F 129
Beaumont Gdns. NW3 . . . 3J 63
Beaumont Gro. E1 . . . 4K 85
Beaumont Ho. E10 . . . 7D 50
(off Skelton's La.)
W9 . . . 3H 81
(off Fernhead Rd.)
Beaumont Lodge E8 . . . 6G 67
(off Greenwood Rd.)
Beaumont M. HA5: Pinn . . . 3C 40
NW5 . . . 5H 65
(off Charlton King's Rd.)
W1 . . . 5H 5 (5E 82)
Beaumont Pl. EN5: Barn . . . 1C 20
TW7: Isle . . . 5K 113
UB10: Ick . . . 5C 56
N1 . . . 3B 6 (4G 83)
Beaumont Ri. N19 . . . 1H 65
Beaumont Rd. BR5: Pet W . . . 6H 161
E10 . . . 7D 50
(not continuous)
E13 . . . 3K 87
SE19 . . . 6C 138
SW19 . . . 7G 117
W4 . . . 3J 97
Beaumont Sq. E1 . . . 5K 85
Beaumont St. W1 . . . 5H 5 (5E 82)
Beaumont Ter. SE13 . . . 7G 123
(off Wellmeadow Rd.)
Beaumont Wlk. NW3 . . . 7D 64
Beauvais Ter. UB5: N'olt . . . 3B 76
Beauvale NW1 . . . 7E 64
(off Ferdinand St.)
Beauval Rd. SE22 . . . 6F 121
Beaux Arts Bldg., The N7 . . . 3J 65
Beaverbank Rd. SE9 . . . 1H 143
Beaver Cl. SE20 . . . 7G 139
SM4: Mord . . . 7E 152
TW12: Hamp . . . 1F 149
Beaver Gro. UB5: N'olt . . . 3C 76
Beaver Ind. Est. UB2: S'hall . . . 3A 94
Beavers Cres. TW4: Houn . . . 4A 112
Beavers La. Campsite
TW4: Houn . . . 4B 112
Beavers Lodge DA14: Sidc . . . 4K 143
Beaverwood Rd. BR7: Chst . . . 6J 143

Beavor Gro. W6 . . . . .5C 98
(off Beavor La.)
Beavor La. W6 . . . . .5C 98
Bebbington Rd. SE18 . . . . .4J 107
Beblets Cl. BR6: Chels 5K 173
Beccles Dr. IG11: Bark 6J 71
Beccles St. E14 . . . . .6B 86
Bec Cl. HA4: Ruis 3B 58
Bechervaise Ct. E10 . . . . .1D 68
(off Leyton Grange Est.)
Bechtel Ho. W6 . . . . .4F 99
(off Hammersmith Rd.)
Beck Cl. SE13 . . . . .1D 122
Beck Ct. BR3: Beck 3K 157
BECKENHAM 2C 158
Beckenham Bus. Cen. BR3: Beck . . .6A 140
Beckenham Crematorium
BR3: Beck 3J 157
Beckenham Gdns. N9 . . . . .3K 33
Beckenham Hill Est. BR3: Beck 5D 140
Beckenham Hill Rd. BR3: Beck 6D 140
SE6 . . . . .6D 140
Beckenham La. BR2: Brom 2G 159
Beckenham Pl. Pk. BR3: Beck 7D 140
Beckenham Place Pk. Golf Course . . .6D 140
Beckenham Place Pk. Local Nature Reserve
. . . . .6E 140
Beckenham Rd. BR3: Beck 1K 157
BR4: W W'ck 7D 158
Beckenham Theatre Cen., The 2D 158
Beckers, The N16 . . . . .4G 67
Becket Av. E6 . . . . .3E 88
Becket Cl. IG5: Ilf 1C 52
SE25 . . . . .6G 157
SW19 . . . . .1K 153
(off High Path)
Becket Fold HA1: Harr 5K 41
Becket Ho. E16 . . . . .1K 105
(off Constable Av.)
SE1 . . . . .7E 14
WC1 . . . . .3F 7
Becket Rd. N18 . . . . .4D 34
Becket St. SE1 . . . . .7E 14 (3D 102)
Beckett Cl. DA17: Belv 3F 109
NW10 . . . . .6A 62
SW16 . . . . .2H 137
Beckett Ho. E1 . . . . .5J 85
(off Jubilee St.)
SW9 . . . . .2J 119
Becketts Cl. BR6: Orp 3K 173
DA5: Bexl 1J 145
TW14: Felt 6K 111
Becketts Ho. IG1: Ilf 3E 70
Becketts Pl. KT1: Hamp W 1D 150
Becketts Wharf KT1: Hamp W 1D 150
(off Lwr. Teddington Rd.)
Beckett Wlk. BR3: Beck 6A 140
Beckfoot NW1 . . . . .1B 6
(off Ampthill Est.)
Beckford Cl. W14 . . . . .4H 99
Beckford Dr. BR5: Orp 7H 161
Beckford Ho. N16 . . . . .5E 66
Beckford Pl. SE17 . . . . .5C 102
Beckford Rd. CR0: C'don 6F 157
Beckham Ho. SE11 . . . .4H 19 (4K 101)
Beckhaven Ho. SE11 . . . . .4K 19
(off Gilbert Rd.)
Beck Ho. N18 . . . . .5C 34
(off Upton Rd.)
Beck La. BR3: Beck 3K 157
Beckley Ho. E3 . . . . .4B 86
(off Hamlets Way)
Becklow Gdns. W12 . . . . .2C 98
(off Becklow Rd.)
Becklow M. W12 . . . . .2C 98
(off Becklow Rd.)
Becklow Rd. W12 . . . . .2B 98
Beck River Pk. BR3: Beck 1B 158
Beck Rd. CR4: Mitc 6D 154
E8 . . . . .1H 85

Becks Rd. DA14: Sidc 3A 144
Beck Theatre, The 6H 75
BECKTON 5E 88
BECKTON ALPS 4D 88
BECKTON PARK 6D 88
Beckton Retail Pk. E6 . . . . .5E 88
Beckton Rd. E16 . . . . .5H 87
Beckton Triangle Retail Pk. E6 . . . . .4F 89
Beck Way BR3: Beck 3B 158
Beckway Rd. SW16 . . . . .2H 155
Beckway St. SE17 . . . . .4E 102
(not continuous)
Beckwith Cl. EN2: Enf 1G 23
Beckwith Ho. E2 . . . . .2H 85
(off Wadeson St.)
Beckwith Rd. SE24 . . . . .5D 120
Beclands Rd. SW17 . . . . .6E 136
Becmead Av. HA3: Kenton 5B 42
SW16 . . . . .4H 137
Becondale Rd. SE19 . . . . .5E 138
BECONTREE 4D 72
Becontree Av. RM8: Dag 4B 72
Becontree Heath Leisure Cen. 2G 73
Becontree Rd. E11 . . . . .1G 69
Becquerel Ct. SE10 . . . . .3H 105
(off West Parkside)
Bective Pl. SW15 . . . . .4H 117
Bective Rd. E7 . . . . .4J 69
SW15 . . . . .4H 117
Becton Pl. DA8: Erith 7H 109
Bedale Rd. EN2: Enf 1H 23
Bedale St. SE1 . . . . . .5E 14 (1D 102)
Beddalls Farm Ct. E6 . . . . .5B 88
BEDDINGTON 4J 167
BEDDINGTON CORNER 7E 154
Beddington Cross CR0: Bedd 7H 155
Beddington Farm Rd.
CR0: Bedd, Wadd 7J 155
Beddington Gdns. SM5: Cars 6E 166
SM6: Wall 6E 166
Beddington Grn. BR5: St P 1K 161
Beddington La. CR0: Bedd, C'don . .5G 155
Beddington Pk. 3F 167
Beddington Pk. Cotts. SM6: Bedd . .3H 167
Beddington Path BR5: St P 1K 161
Beddington Rd. BR5: St P 2J 161
IG3: Ilf 7K 53
Beddington Ter. CR0: C'don 7K 155
Beddington Trad. Est. CR0: Bedd . . .1J 167
Bede Cl. HA5: Pinn 1B 40
Bedefield WC1 . . . . .2F 7 (3J 83)
Bede Ho. SE14 . . . . .1B 122
(off Clare Rd.)
Bedens Rd. DA14: Sidc 6E 144
Bede Rd. RM6: Chad H 6C 54
Bede Sq. E3 . . . . .4B 86
(off Joseph St.)
Bedevere Rd. N9 . . . . .3B 34
Bedfont Cl. CR4: Mitc 2E 154
TW14: Bedf 6E 110
Bedfont Ct. TW19: Stanw M 6B 174
Bedfont Ct. Est. TW19: Stanw M . . .7C 174
Bedfont Grn. Cl. TW14: Bedf 1E 128
Bedfont Ind. Pk. TW15: Ashf 3E 128
Bedfont Ind. Pk. Nth. TW15: Ashf . .3E 128
Bedfont Lakes Country Pk. 2E 128
Bedfont Lakes Country Pk. Vis. Cen.
. . . . .3D 128
Bedfont La. TW13: Felt 7G 111
TW14: Felt 7G 111
Bedfont Rd. TW13: Felt 1E 128
TW14: Bedf 1E 128
TW19: Stanw 6A 110
Bedfont Trad. Est. TW14: Bedf 2F 129
Bedford Av. EN5: Barn 5C 20
UB4: Yead 6K 75
WC1 . . . . .6D 6 (5H 83)
Bedfordbury WC2 . . . . . .2E 12 (7J 83)
(not continuous)
Bedford Cl. N10 . . . . .7K 31
W4 . . . . .6A 98

Bedford Cnr. W4 . . . . .4A 98
(off South Pde.)
Bedford Ct. CR0: C'don 1D 168
(off Tavistock Rd.)
WC2 . . . . .3E 12 (7J 83)
Bedford Ct. Mans. WC1 . . . . .6D 6
Bedford Gdns. W8 . . . . .1J 99
Bedford Gdns. Ho. W8 . . . . .1J 99
(off Bedford Gdns.)
Bedford Ho. CR0: C'don 7B 156
SW4 . . . . .4J 119
(off Solon New Rd. Est.)
Bedford Hill SW12 . . . . .1F 137
SW16 . . . . .1F 137
Bedford Ho. CR0: C'don 7B 156
SW4 . . . . .4J 119
(off Solon New Rd. Est.)
Bedford M. N2 . . . . .3C 46
SE6 . . . . .2D 140
BEDFORD PARK 3K 97
Bedford Pk. CR0: C'don 1C 168
Bedford Pk. Cnr. W4 . . . . .4A 98
Bedford Pk. Mans. W4 . . . . .4K 97
Bedford Pas. SW6 . . . . .7G 99
(off Dawes Rd.)
W1 . . . . .5B 6 (5G 83)
Bedford Pl. CR0: C'don 1D 168
WC1 . . . . .5E 6 (5J 83)
Bedford Rd. DA15: Sidc 3J 143
E6 . . . . .1E 88
E17 . . . . .2C 50
E18 . . . . .2J 51
HA1: Harr 6G 41
HA4: Ruis 4H 57
IG1: Ilf 3F 71
KT4: Wor Pk 2E 164
N2 . . . . .3C 46
N8 . . . . .6H 47
N9 . . . . .7C 24
N15 . . . . .4E 48
N22 . . . . .2J 47
NW7 . . . . .2F 29
SW4 . . . . .4J 119
TW2: Twick 3H 131
W4 . . . . .3K 97
W13 . . . . .7B 78
Bedford Row SE1 . . . . . .7D 14 (3C 102)
WC1 . . . . .5H 7 (5K 83)
Bedford Sq. WC1 . . . . . .6C 6 (5H 83)
Bedford St. WC2 . . . . . .2E 12 (7J 83)
Bedford Ter. SM2: Sutt 6A 166
SW2 . . . . .5J 119
Bedford Way WC1 . . . . .4D 6 (4H 83)
Bedgebury Ct. E17 . . . . .2E 50
Bedgebury Gdns. SW19 . . . . .2G 135
Bedgebury Rd. SE9 . . . . .4B 124
Bedivere Rd. BR1: Brom 3J 141
Bedlam M. SE11 . . . . .3J 19
Bedlow Way CR0: Bedd 4K 167
Bedmond Ho. SW3 . . . . .5C 16
(off Cale St.)
Bedonwell Rd. DA7: Belv, Bex, Erith . .6F 109
DA17: Belv 6E 108
SE2 . . . . .6E 108
Bedser Cl. CR7: Thor H 3C 156
SE11 . . . . .7H 19 (6K 101)
Bedser Dr. UB6: G'frd 5H 59
Bedster Gdns. KT8: W Mole 2F 149
Bedwardine Rd. SE19 . . . . .7E 138
Bedwell Cl. CR0: C'don 5D 156
Bedwell Ct. RM6: Chad H 7D 54
(off Chapel La.)
Bedwell Gdns. UB3: Harl 5G 93
(not continuous)
Bedwell Ho. SW9 . . . . .2A 120
Bedwell Rd. DA17: Belv 5G 109
N17 . . . . .1E 48
Beeby Rd. E16 . . . . .5K 87
Beech Av. DA15: Sidc 7A 126
HA4: Ruis 1K 57
IG9: Buck H 2E 36
N20 . . . . .1H 31
TW8: Bford 7B 96
W3 . . . . .1A 98

Beech Cl. N9 . . . . .6B 24
SE8 . . . . .6C 104
SM5: Cars 2D 166
SW15 . . . . .7C 116
SW19 . . . . .6E 134
TW15: Ashf 5F 129
TW16: Sun 2B 148
UB7: W Dray 3C 92
Beech Copse BR1: Brom 1D 160
CR2: S Croy 5E 168
Beech Ct. BR1: Brom 1H 159
(off Blyth Rd.)
BR3: Beck 7B 140
E17 . . . . .3F 51
IG1: Ilf 3E 70
(off Riverdene Rd.)
KT6: Surb 7D 150
UB5: N'olt 1C 76
W9 . . . . .5J 81
(off Elmfield Way)
Beech Cres. Ct. N5 . . . . .4B 66
Beechcroft BR7: Chst 7E 142
Beechcroft Av. DA7: Bex 1K 127
HA2: Harr 7E 40
KT3: N Mald 1J 151
NW11 . . . . .7H 45
Beechcroft Cl. BR6: Orp 4H 173
SW16 . . . . .5K 137
TW5: Hest 7C 94
Beechcroft Ct. N12 . . . . .4E 30
NW11 . . . . .7H 45
(off Beechcroft Av.)
Beechcroft Gdns. HA9: Wemb 3F 61
Beechcroft Ho. W5 . . . . .5E 78
Beechcroft Lodge SM2: Sutt 7A 166
Beechcroft Rd. BR6: Orp 4H 173
E18 . . . . .2K 51
KT9: Chess 3F 163
SW14 . . . . .3J 115
SW17 . . . . .2C 136
Beechdale N21 . . . . .2E 32
Beechdale Rd. SW2 . . . . .6K 119
Beech Dell BR2: Kes 4D 172
Beechdene SE15 . . . . .1H 121
(off Carlton Gro.)
Beech Dr. N2 . . . . .2D 46
Beechen Cliff Way TW7: Isle 2K 113
Beechen Gro. HA5: Pinn 3D 40
Beechen Pl. SE23 . . . . .2K 139
Beeches, The CR2: S Croy 5D 168
(off Blunt Rd.)
E12 . . . . .7C 70
TW3: Houn 1F 113
Beeches Av. SM5: Cars 7C 166
Beeches Cl. SE20 . . . . .1J 157
Beeches Rd. SM3: Sutt 1G 165
SW17 . . . . .3C 136
Beeches Wlk. SM5: Cars 7B 166
Beechey Ho. E1 . . . . .1H 103
(off Watts St.)
Beechfield Cotts. BR1: Brom 1A 160
Beechfield Ct. CR2: S Croy 4C 168
(off Bramley Hill)
Beechfield Gdns. RM7: Rush G 7J 55
Beechfield Rd. BR1: Brom 2A 160
DA8: Erith 7K 109
N4 . . . . .6C 48
SE6 . . . . .1B 140
Beech Gdns. EC2 . . . . .5C 8
(off Beech St.)
RM10: Dag 7J 73
W5 . . . . .2E 96
Beech Gro. CR4: Mitc 5H 155
KT3: N Mald 3K 151
Beech Hall Cres. E4 . . . . .7A 36
Beech Hall Rd. E4 . . . . .7K 35
Beech Haven Ct. DA1: Cray 5K 127
(off London Rd.)
Beech Hill EN4: Had W 1G 21
Beech Hill Av. EN4: Had W 1F 21
Beechhill Rd. SE9 . . . . .5E 124

Beech Ho. CR0: New Ad 6D 170
   SE16 .2J 103
   (off Ainsty Est.)
Beech Ho. Rd. CR0: C'don 3D 168
Beech Hurst Cl. BR7: Chst 1G 161
Beeching Ct. W3 . . . . .3J 97
   (off Bollo Bri. Rd.)
Beech La. IG9: Buck H 2E 36
Beech Lawns N12 . . . . .5G 31
Beechmont Cl. BR1: Brom 5G 141
Beechmore Gdns. SM3: Cheam . . .2F 165
Beechmore Rd. SW11 . . . . .1D 118
Beechmount Av. W7 . . . . .5H 77
Beecholme N12 . . . . .5E 30
Beecholme Av. CR4: Mitc 1F 155
Beecholme Est. E5 . . . . .3H 67
Beecholme M. SW12 . . . . .6E 118
Beech Rd. N11 . . . . .6D 32
   SW16 . . . . .2J 155
   TW14: Bedf 7G 111
Beechrow TW10: Ham 4E 132
Beech St. EC2 . . . . .5C 8 (5C 84)
   RM7: Rom 4J 55
Beech Tree Cl. HA7: Stan 5H 27
   N1 . . . . .7A 66
Beech Tree Glade E4 . . . . .1C 36
Beech Tree Pl. SM1: Sutt 5K 165
Beechvale Cl. N12 . . . . .5H 31
Beech Wlk. N17 . . . . .3F 49
   NW7 .6F 29
Beech Way NW10 . . . . .7K 61
   TW2: Twick 3E 130
Beechway DA5: Bexl 6D 126
Beechwood Av. BR6: Chels 5J 173
   CR7: Thor H 4B 156
   HA2: Harr 3F 59
   HA4: Ruis 2H 57
   N3 . . . . .3H 45
   TW9: Kew 1G 115
   TW16: Sun 6J 129
   UB3: Hayes 7F 75
   UB6: G'frd 3F 77
   UB8: Hil 6C 74
Beechwood Cen., The BR2: Brom . . .1D 172
   (off Lwr. Gravel Rd.)
Beechwood Circ. HA2: Harr 3F 59
Beechwood Cl. KT6: Surb 7C 150
   N2 . . . . .3D 46
   NW7 .5F 29
Beechwood Cres. DA7: Bex 3D 126
Beechwood Dr. BR2: Kes 4B 172
   IG8: Wfd G 5C 36
Beechwood Gdns. HA2: Harr 3F 59
   IG5: Ilf 5D 52
   NW10 . . . . .3F 79
Beechwood Gro. KT6: Surb 7C 150
   W3 . . . . .7A 80
Beechwood Hall N3 . . . . .3H 45
Beechwood Ho. E2 . . . . .2G 85
   (off Teale St.)
Beechwood M. N9 . . . . .2B 34
Beechwood Pk. E18 . . . . .3J 51
Beechwood Ri. BR7: Chst 4F 143
Beechwood Rd. CR2: Sande 7E 168
   E8 . . . . .6F 67
   N8 . . . . .4H 47
Beechwoods Ct. SE19 . . . . .5F 139
Beechworth NW6 . . . . .7G 63
Beechworth Cl. NW3 . . . . .2J 63
Beecroft La. SE4 . . . . .5A 122
Beecroft M. SE4 . . . . .5A 122
Beecroft Rd. SE4 . . . . .5A 122
Beehive Cl. E8 . . . . .7F 67
   UB10: Uxb 7B 56
Beehive La. HA8: Edg 5C 28
   IG1: Ilf 6D 52
Beehive La. IG1: Ilf 5D 52
   IG4: Ilf 5D 52

Beehive Pas. EC3 . . . . .1G 15
   (off Lime St.)
Beehive Pl. SW9 . . . . .3A 120
Beeken Dene BR6: Farnb 4G 173
Beeleigh Rd. SM4: Mord 4K 153
Beemans Row SW18 . . . . .2A 136
Beeston Cl. E8 . . . . .5G 67
Beeston Ho. SE1 . . . . .3D 102
   (off Burbage Cl.)
Beeston Pl. SW1 . . . . .1K 17 (3F 101)
Beeston Rd. EN4: E Barn 6G 21
Beeston Way TW14: Felt 6A 112
Beethoven St. W10 . . . . .3G 81
Beeton Cl. HA5: Hat E 1E 40
Beeton Way SE27 . . . . .4D 138
Begbie Rd. SE3 . . . . .1A 124
BEGGAR'S HILL 6B 164
Beggar's Hill KT17: Ewe 7B 164
Beggars Roost La. SM1: Sutt 6J 165
Begonia Cl. E6 . . . . .5D 88
Begonia Pl. TW12: Hamp 6E 130
Begonia Wlk. W12 . . . . .6B 80
Beira St. SW12 . . . . .7F 119
Bejun Ct. EN5: New Bar 4F 21
Bekesbourne St. E14 . . . . .6A 86
Belcroft Cl. BR1: Brom 7H 141
Beldam Way TW3: Houn 3D 112
Beldanes Lodge NW10 . . . . .7C 62
Beldham Gdns. KT8: W Mole 2F 149
Belfairs Dr. RM6: Chad H 7C 54
Belfast Rd. N16 . . . . .2F 67
   SE25 . . . . .4H 157
Belfield Rd. KT19: Ewe 7K 163
Belfont Wlk. N7 . . . . .4J 65
   (not continuous)
Belford Gro. SE18 . . . . .4E 106
Belford Ho. E8 . . . . .1F 85
Belfort Rd. SE15 . . . . .2J 121
Belfry Cl. BR1: Brom 4F 161
   SE16 . . . . .5H 103
Belgrade Rd. N16 . . . . .4E 66
   TW12: Hamp 1F 149
Belgrave Ct. N14 . . . . .5B 22
   NW7 .5E 28
   W3 . . . . .2H 97
Belgrave Ct. E2 . . . . .2H 85
   (off Temple St.)
   E13 . . . . .4A 88
   E14 . . . . .7B 86
   (off Westferry Cir.)
   SW8 . . . . .7G 101
   (off Ascalon St.)
   W4 . . . . .5J 97
Belgrave Cres. TW16: Sun 1K 147
Belgrave Gdns. HA7: Stan 5H 27
   N14 . . . . .5C 22
   NW8 .1K 81
Belgrave Hgts. E11 . . . . .1J 69
Belgrave Ho. SW9 . . . . .7A 102
Belgrave Mans. NW8 . . . . .1K 81
   (off Belgrave Gdns.)
Belgrave M. Nth. SW1 . . . . .7G 11 (2E 100)
Belgrave M. Sth. SW1 . . . . .1H 17 (3E 100)
Belgrave M. W. SW1 . . . . . .1G 17 (3E 100)
Belgrave Pl. SW1 . . . . .1H 17 (3E 100)
Belgrave Rd. CR4: Mitc 3B 154
   E10 . . . . .1E 68
   E11 . . . . .2J 69
   E13 . . . . .4A 88
   E17 . . . . .5C 50
   IG1: Ilf 1D 70
   SE25 . . . . .4F 157
   SW1 . . . . .3K 17 (4F 101)
   SW13 . . . . .7B 98
   TW4: Houn 3D 112
   TW16: Sun 1K 147
Belgrave Sq. SW1 . . . . .1G 17 (3E 100)
Belgrave St. E1 . . . . .5K 85
Belgrave Ter. IG8: Wfd G 3D 36
Belgrave Wlk. CR4: Mitc 3B 154
Belgrave Yd. SW1 . . . . .2J 17

BELGRAVIA 2H 17 (3E 100)
Belgravia Cl. EN5: Barn 3C 20
Belgravia Ct. SW1 . . . . .2J 17
Belgravia Gdns. BR1: Brom 6G 141
Belgravia Ho. SW1 . . . . .1G 17
   (off Halkin Pl.)
   SW4 . . . . .6H 119
Belgravia M. KT1: King T 4D 150
Belgravia Workshops N19 . . . . .2J 65
   (off Marlborough Rd.)
Belgrove St. WC1 . . . . .1F 7 (3J 83)
Belham Wlk. SE5 . . . . .1D 120
Belinda Rd. SW9 . . . . .3B 120
Belitha Vs. N1 . . . . .7K 65
BELL, THE .3C 50
Bella Best Ho. SW1 . . . . .5K 17
   (off Westmoreland Ter.)
Bellamy Cl. E14 . . . . .2C 104
   HA8: Edg 2D 28
   UB10: Ick 3C 56
   W14 .5H 99
Bellamy Dr. HA7: Stan 1B 42
Bellamy Dr. HA7: Stan 1B 42
Bellamy Ho. SW17 . . . . .4B 136
   TW5: Hest 6E 94
Bellamy Rd. E4 . . . . .6J 35
   EN2: Enf 2J 23
Bellamy's Ct. SE16 . . . . .1K 103
   (off Abbotshade Rd.)
Bellasdy St. SW12 . . . . .7F 119
Bel La. TW13: Hanw 3C 130
Bellarmine Cl. SE28 . . . . .1K 107
Bellasis Av. SW2 . . . . .2J 137
Bell Av. UB7: W Dray 4B 92
Bell Brook Ri. N11 . . . . .4A 32
Bellclose Rd. UB7: W Dray 2A 92
Bell Cl. NW4 .4E 44
Bell Dr. SW18 . . . . .7G 117
Bellefields Rd. SW9 . . . . .3K 119
Bellegrove Cl. DA16: Well 2K 125
Bellegrove Pde. DA16: Well 3K 125
Bellegrove Rd. DA16: Well 2H 125
Bellenden Rd. SE15 . . . . .1F 121
Bellenden Rd. Retail Pk. SE15 . . . .1G 121
Bellestaines Pleasaunce E4 . . . . . . .2H 35
Belleville Ho. SE10 . . . . .7D 104
   (off Norman Rd.)
Belleville Rd. SW11 . . . . .5C 118
Belle Vue UB6: G'frd 1H 77
Belle Vue Est. NW4 . . . . .4F 45
Belle Vue La. WD23: B Hea 1C 26
Bellevue M. N11 . . . . .5K 31
Bellevue Pde. SW17 . . . . .1D 136
Belle Vue Pk. CR7: Thor H 3C 156
Bellevue Pl. E1 . . . . .4J 85
Belle Vue Rd. E17 . . . . .2F 51
   NW4 .4E 44
Bellevue Rd. DA6: Bex 5F 127
   KT1: King T 3E 150
   (not continuous)
   N11 . . . . .4K 31
   SW13 . . . . .2C 116
   SW17 . . . . .1C 136
   W13 .4B 78
Bellew St. SW17 . . . . .3A 136
Bellfield CR0: Sels 7A 170
Bellfield Av. HA3: Hrw W 6C 26
Bellfield Cl. SE3 . . . . .7K 105
Bellflower Cl. E6 . . . . .5C 88
Bell Gdns. E10 . . . . .1C 68
   (off Church Rd.)
Bellgate M. NW5 . . . . .4F 65
BELL GREEN 4B 140
Bell Grn. SE26 . . . . .4B 140
Bell Grn. La. SE26 . . . . .5B 140
Bell Grn. Retail Pk. SE6 . . . . .3B 140
Bell Grn. Trade City SE6 . . . . .3B 140

Bellhaven E15 . . . . .6F 69
Bell Hill CR0: C'don 2C 168
Bell Ho. HA9: Wemb 3E 60
   SE10 . . . . .6E 104
   (off Haddo St.)
Bellhouse Cotts. UB3: Hayes 7G 75
Bell Ho. Rd. RM7: Rush G 1J 73
Bellina M. NW5 . . . . .4F 65
Bell Ind. Est. W4 . . . . .4J 97
BELLINGHAM 3D 140
Bellingham N17 . . . . .7C 34
   (off Park La.)
Bellingham Ct. IG11: Bark 3B 90
Bellingham Grn. SE6 . . . . .3C 140
Bellingham Leisure & Lifestyle Cen.
    . . . . .3D 140
Bellingham Rd. SE6 . . . . .3D 140
Bellingham Trad. Est. SE6 . . . . .3D 140
Bell Inn Yd. EC3 . . . . .1F 15 (6D 84)
Bell La. E1 . . . . .6J 9 (5F 85)
   E16 . . . . .1H 105
   EN3: Enf H, Enf W 1E 24
   HA9: Wemb 2D 60
   NW4 .4F 45
   TW1: Twick 1A 132
   TW14: Bedf 7F 111
Bellmaker Ct. E3 . . . . .5C 86
Bell Moor NW3 . . . . .3A 64
Bello Cl. SE24 . . . . .7B 120
Bellot Gdns. SE10 . . . . .5G 105
   (off Bellot St.)
Bellot St. SE10 . . . . .5G 105
Bell Pde. BR4: W W'ck 2E 170
Bellring Cl. DA17: Belv 6G 109
Bell Rd. EN1: Enf 1J 23
   KT8: E Mos 5H 149
   TW3: Houn 3F 113
Bells All. SW6 . . . . .2J 117
Bells Hill EN5: Barn 5A 20
Bellsize Ct. NW3 . . . . .5B 64
Bell St. NW1 . . . . .5C 4 (5C 82)
   SE18 . . . . .1C 124
Belltrees Gro. SW16 . . . . .5K 137
Bell Vw. Mnr. HA4: Ruis 7F 39
Bell Water Ga. SE18 . . . . .3E 106
Bell Wharf La. EC4 . . . . .3D 14 (7D 84)
Bellwood Rd. SE15 . . . . .4K 121
Bell Yd. WC2 . . . . .1J 13 (6A 84)
Bell Yd. M. SE1 . . . . .7H 15
Belmarsh Rd. SE28 . . . . .2J 107
BELMONT
   HA3 .2A 42
   SM2 .7J 165
Belmont Av. DA16: Well 3J 125
   EN4: Cockf 5J 21
   HA0: Wemb 1F 79
   KT3: N Mald 5C 152
   N9 . . . . .1B 34
   N13 . . . . .5E 32
   N17 . . . . .3C 48
   UB2: S'hall 3D 94
Belmont Circ. HA3: Kenton 1B 42
Belmont Cl. E4 . . . . .5A 36
   EN4: Cockf 4J 21
   IG8: Wfd G 4E 36
   N20 . . . . .1E 30
   SW4 .3G 119
   UB8: Uxb 6A 56
Belmont Ct. N5 . . . . .4C 66
   NW11 . . . . .5H 45
Belmont Gro. SE13 . . . . .3F 123
   W4 . . . . .4K 97
Belmont Hall Ct. SE13 . . . . .3F 123
Belmont Hill SE13 . . . . .3E 123
Belmont La. BR7: Chst 5G 143
   HA7: Stan 1C 42
Belmont Lodge HA3: Hrw W 7C 26
Belmont M. SW19 . . . . .2F 135
Belmont Pde. BR7: Chst 5G 143
   NW11 . . . . .5H 45

Belmont Pk. SE13 4F 123
Belmont Pk. Cl. SE13 4G 123
Belmont Pk. Rd. E10 6D 50
Belmont Ri. SM2: Sutt 6H 165
Belmont Rd. BR3: Beck 2A 158
BR7: Chst 5F 143
DA8: Erith 7G 109
HA3: W'stone 3K 41
IG1: Ilf 3G 71
N15 4C 48
N17 4C 48
SE25 5H 157
SM6: Wall 5F 167
SW4 3G 119
TW2: Twick 2H 131
UB8: Uxb 7A 56
W4 4K 97
Belmont St. NW1 7E 64
Belmont Ter. W4 4K 97
Belmore Av. UB4: Hayes 6J 75
Belmore Ho. N7 5H 65
Belmore La. N7 5H 65
Belmore St. SW8 1H 119
Beloe Cl. SW15 4C 116
Belsham St. E9 6J 67
Belsize Av. N13 6E 32
NW3 6B 64
W13 3B 96
Belsize Ct. SM1: Sutt 4K 165
Belsize Ct. Garages NW3 5B 64
(off Belsize La.)
Belsize Cres. NW3 5B 64
Belsize Gdns. SM1: Sutt 4K 165
Belsize Gro. NW3 6C 64
Belsize La. NW3 6B 64
Belsize M. NW3 6B 64
Belsize Pk. NW3 6B 64
Belsize Pk. Gdns. NW3 6B 64
Belsize Pk. M. NW3 6B 64
Belsize Pl. NW3 5B 64
Belsize Rd. HA3: Hrw W 7C 26
NW6 1K 81
Belsize Sq. NW3 6B 64
Belsize Ter. NW3 6B 64
Belson Rd. SE18 4D 106
Beltane Dr. SW19 3F 135
Belthorn Cres. SW12 7G 119
Belton Rd. DA14: Sidc 4A 144
E7 7K 69
E11 4G 69
N17 3E 48
NW2 6C 62
Belton Way E3 5C 86
Beltran Rd. SW6 2K 117
Beltwood Rd. DA17: Belv 4J 109
BELVEDERE 4G 109
Belvedere, The SW10 1A 118
(off Chelsea Harbour)
Belvedere Av. IG5: Ilf 2F 53
SW19 5G 135
Belvedere Bldgs. SE1 7B 14 (2B 102)
Belvedere Bus. Pk. DA17: Belv 2H 109
Belvedere Cl. TW11: Tedd 5J 131
Belvedere Ct. DA17: Belv 3F 109
N1 1E 84
(off De Beauvoir Cres.)
N2 5B 46
NW2 6F 63
(off Willesden La.)
SW15 4E 116
Belvedere Dr. SW19 5G 135
Belvedere Gdns. KT8: W Mole 5D 148
Belvedere Gro. SW19 5G 135
Belvedere Ho. TW13: Felt 1J 129
(off Lemon Gro.)
Belvedere Ind. Est. DA17: Belv 1J 109
Belvedere Link Bus. Pk. DA8: Erith 3J 109
Belvedere M. SE3 7K 105
SE15 3J 121
Belvedere Pl. SE1 7B 14 (2B 102)
SW2 4K 119
Belvedere Rd. DA7: Bex 3F 127
E10 1A 68
SE1 7G 13 (2K 101)
SE19 7F 139
W7 3K 95
Belvedere Sq. SW19 5G 135
Belvedere Way HA3: Kenton 6E 42
Belvoir Cl. SE9 3C 142
Belvoir Ho. SW1 4G 101
Belvoir Rd. SE22 7G 121
Belvue Bus. Cen.
UB5: N'olt 7F 59
Belvue Cl. UB5: N'olt 7E 58
Belvue Rd. UB5: N'olt 7E 58
Belz Dr. N15 4E 48
Belz Ter. E5 7G 49
Bembridge Cl. NW6 7G 63
Bembridge Gdns. HA4: Ruis 2F 57
Bembridge Ho. KT2: King T 2G 151
(off Coombe Rd.)
SE8 4B 104
(off Longshore)
SW18 6K 117
(off Iron Mill Rd.)
Bemersyde Point E13 3K 87
(off Dongola Rd. W.)
Bemerton Est. N1 7J 65
Bemerton St. N1 1K 83
Bemish Rd. SW15 3F 117
Bempton Dr. HA4: Ruis 2K 57
Bemsted Rd. E17 3B 50
Benares Rd. SE18 4K 107
Benbow Ct. W6 3E 98
(off Benbow Rd.)
Benbow Ho. SE8 6C 104
(off Benbow St.)
Benbow M. E3 3B 86
(off Tredegar Sq.)
Benbow Rd. W6 3D 98
Benbow St. SE8 6C 104
Benbury Cl. BR1: Brom 5E 140
Bence Ho. SE8 4A 104
(off Rainsborough Av.)
Bench, The TW10: Ham 3C 132
Bench Fld. CR2: S Croy 6F 169
Bencroft Rd. SW16 7G 137
Bencurtis Pk. BR4: W W'ck 3F 171
Bendall Ho. NW1 5D 4
(off Penfold St.)
Bendall M. NW1 5D 4
Bendemeer Rd. SW15 3F 117
Benden Ho. SE13 5E 122
(off Monument Gdns.)
Bendish Point SE28 2G 107
Bendish Rd. E6 7C 70
Bendmore Av. SE2 5A 108
Bendon Valley SW18 7K 117
Benedict Cl. BR6: Orp 3J 173
DA17: Belv 3E 108
Benedict Ct. RM6: Chad H 6F 55
Benedict Dr. TW14: Bedf 7F 111
Benedict Rd. CR4: Mitc 3B 154
SW9 3K 119
Benedicts Wharf IG11: Bark 1F 89
Benedict Way N2 3A 46
Benedict Wharf CR4: Mitc 3C 154
Benenden Grn. BR2: Brom 5J 159
Benenden Ho. SE17 5E 102
(off Mina Rd.)
Benett Gdns. SW16 2J 155
Ben Ezra Ct. SE17 4C 102
(off Asolando Dr.)
Benfleet Cl. SM1: Sutt 3A 166
Benfleet Ct. E8 1F 85
Benfleet Way N11 2K 31
Bengal Ct. EC3 1F 15
(off Birchin La.)
Bengal Rd. IG1: Ilf 4F 71
Bengarth Dr. HA3: Hrw W 2H 41
Bengarth Rd. UB5: N'olt 1C 76
Bengeo Gdns. RM6: Chad H 6C 54
Bengeworth Rd. HA1: Harr 2A 60
SE5 3C 120
Ben Hale Cl. HA7: Stan 5G 27
Benham Cl. KT9: Chess 6C 162
SW11 3B 118
Benham Gdns. TW4: Houn 5D 112
Benham Ho. SW10 7K 99
(off Coleridge Gdns.)
Benham Rd. W7 5J 77
Benham's Pl. NW3 4A 64
Benhill Av. SM1: Sutt 4K 165
(not continuous)
Benhill Rd. SE5 7D 102
SM1: Sutt 3A 166
Benhill Wood Rd. SM1: Sutt 3A 166
BENHILTON 2K 165
Benhilton Gdns. SM1: Sutt 3K 165
Benhurst Ct. SW16 5A 138
Benhurst La. SW16 5A 138
Benina Cl. IG2: Ilf 5K 53
Benin Ho. WC1 6G 7
(off Procter St.)
Benin St. SE13 7F 123
Benjafield Cl. N18 4C 34
Benjamin Cl. E8 1G 85
Benjamin Ct. DA17: Belv 6F 109
TW15: Ashf 7E 128
Benjamin Franklin House 4E 12
(off Craven St.)
Benjamin M. SW12 7G 119
Benjamin St. EC1 5A 8 (5B 84)
Benjamin Truman Cl. E1 4G 85
Ben Jonson Ct. N1 2E 84
Ben Jonson Ho. EC2 5D 8
Ben Jonson Pl. EC2 5D 8
Ben Jonson Rd. E1 5K 85
Benkart M. SW15 6C 116
Benledi Rd. E14 6F 87
Benlow Works UB3: Hayes 2H 93
(off Silverdale Rd.)
Bennelong Cl. W12 7D 80
Bennerley Rd. SW11 5C 118
Bennet Cl. KT1: Hamp W 1C 150
Bennet M. N19 3H 65
(off Wedmore St.)
Bennets Courtyard SW19 1A 154
Bennets Fld. Rd. UB11: Stock P 1D 92
Bennet's Hill EC4 2B 14 (7C 84)
Bennets Lodge EN2: Enf 3G 23
Bennet St. SW1 4A 12 (1G 101)
Bennett Cl. DA16: Well 2A 126
HA6: Nwood 1H 39
TW4: Houn 5C 112
Bennett Ct. N7 3K 65
Bennett Gro. SE13 1D 122
Bennett Ho. SW1 3D 18
(off Page St.)
Bennett Pk. SE3 3H 123
Bennett Rd. E13 4A 88
N16 4E 66
RM6: Chad H 6E 54
SW9 2A 120
Bennetts Av. CR0: C'don 2A 170
UB6: G'frd 1J 77
Bennett's Castle La. RM8: Dag 2C 72
Bennetts Cl. CR4: Mitc 1F 155
N17 6A 34
Bennetts Copse BR7: Chst 6C 142
Bennett St. W4 6A 98
Bennetts Way CR0: C'don 2A 170
Bennett's Yd. SW1 2D 18 (3H 101)
Benning Dr. RM8: Dag 1E 72
Benningholme Rd. HA8: Edg 6F 29
Bennington Rd. IG8: Wfd G 7B 36
N17 1E 48
Benn's All. TW12: Hamp 2F 149
Benn St. E9 6A 68
Benns Wlk. TW9: Rich 4E 114
(off Michelsdale Dr.)
Benrek Cl. IG6: Ilf 1G 53
Bensbury Cl. SW15 7D 116
Bensham Cl. CR7: Thor H 4C 156
Bensham Gro. CR7: Thor H 2C 156
Bensham La. CR0: C'don 7B 156
CR7: Thor H 5B 156
Bensham Mnr. Rd. CR7: Thor H 4C 156
Bensham Mnr. Rd. Pas.
CR7: Thor H 4C 156
Bensley Cl. N11 5J 31
Ben Smith Way SE16 3G 103
Benson Av. E6 2A 88
Benson Cl. EN5: Barn 5C 20
TW3: Houn 4E 112
UB8: Hil 5A 74
Benson Ct. SW8 1J 119
(off Hartington Rd.)
Benson Ho. E2 3J 9
(off Ligonier St.)
SE1 5K 13
(off Hatfields)
W14 4H 99
(off Radnor Ter.)
Benson Quay E1 7J 85
Benson Rd. CR0: Wadd 3A 168
SE23 1J 139
Bentall Cen., The KT1: King T 2D 150
Bentfield Gdns. SE9 3B 142
Bentfield Ho. NW9 3B 44
(off Heritage Av.)
Benthal Rd. N16 2G 67
Bentham Ct. N1 7C 66
(off Ecclesbourne Rd.)
Bentham Ho. SE1 3D 102
(off Falmouth Rd.)
SE18 3F 107
Bentham Rd. E9 6K 67
SE28 7B 90
Bentham Wlk. NW10 5J 61
Ben Tillet Cl. E16 1D 106
IG11: Bark 7A 72
Ben Tillet Ho. N15 3B 48
Bentinck Cl. NW8 2C 82
Bentinck Ho. SW1 2D 18
(off Monck St.)
W12 7D 80
(off White City Est.)
Bentinck Mans. W1 7H 5
(off Bentinck St.)
Bentinck M. W1 7H 5 (6E 82)
Bentinck Rd. UB7: Yiew 1A 92
Bentinck St. W1 7H 5 (6E 82)
Bentley Cl. SW19 3J 135
W7 1K 95
Bentley Ct. SE13 4E 122
(off Whitburn Rd.)
Bentley Dr. IG2: Ilf 6G 53
NW2 3H 63
Bentley Ho. E3 4C 86
(off Wellington Way)
SE5 1E 120
(off Peckham Rd.)
Bentley Lodge WD23: B Hea 2D 26
Bentley M. EN1: Enf 6J 23
Bentley Priory Local Nature Reserve
4D 26
Bentley Priory Mus. 3D 26
Bentley Rd. N1 6E 66
Bentley Way EN5: New Bar 4F 21
HA7: Stan 5F 27
IG8: Buck H, Wfd G 2D 36
Benton Rd. IG1: Ilf 1H 71
Bentons La. SE27 4C 138
Benton's Ri. SE27 5D 138
Bentry Cl. RM8: Dag 2E 72
Bentry Rd. RM8: Dag 2E 72
Bentworth Ct. E2 3K 9
(off Granby St.)
Bentworth Rd. W12 6D 80
Ben Uri Gallery 1K 81
Benville Ho. SW8 7K 101
(off Dorset Rd.)
Benwell Cen. TW16: Sun 1J 147

Benwell Ct. TW16: Sun 1J 147
Benwell Rd. N7 4A 66
Benwick Cl. SE16 4H 103
Benwick M. SE20 1J 157
Benwood Ct. SM1: Sutt 3A 166
Benworth St. E3 3B 86
Benyon Ct. *N1* *1E 84*
(off De Beauvoir Est.)
Benyon Ho. *EC1* *1K 7*
(off Myddelton Pas.)
Benyon Rd. N1 1D 84
Benyon Wharf *E8* *1E 84*
(off Kingsland Rd.)
Berberis Ct. IG1: Ilf 6F 71
Berberis Ho. *E3* *5C 86*
(off Gale St.)
TW13: Felt 2J 129
Berberis Wlk.
UB7: W Dray 4A 92
Berber Pde. SE18 1C 124
Berber Pl. E14 7C 86
Berber Rd. SW11 5D 118
Berberry Cl. HA8: Edg 4D 28
Bercta Rd. SE9 2G 143
Berebinder Ho. *E3* *2B 86*
(off Tredegar Rd.)
Beregaria Ct. *SE11* *7K 19*
(off Kennington Pk. Rd.)
Berengers Ct. *RM6: Chad H* *7F 55*
(off Whalebone La. Sth.)
Berengers Pl. RM9: Dag 6B 72
Berenger Twr. *SW10* *7B 100*
(off Worlds End Est.)
Berenger Wlk. *SW10* *7B 100*
(off Worlds End Est.)
Berens Ct. DA14: Sidc 4K 143
Berens Rd. NW10 3F 81
Berens Way BR7: Chst 3K 161
Beresford Av. HA0: Wemb 1F 79
KT5: Surb 1H 163
N20 2J 31
TW1: Twick 6C 114
W7 5H 77
Beresford Ct. *E9* *5A 68*
(off Mabley St.)
Beresford Dr. BR1: Brom 3C 160
IG8: Wfd G 4F 37
Beresford Gdns. EN1: Enf 4K 23
RM6: Chad H 5E 54
TW4: Houn 5D 112
Beresford Rd. E4 1B 36
E17 1D 50
HA1: Harr 5H 41
KT2: King T 1F 151
KT3: N Mald 4J 151
N2 3C 46
N5 5D 66
N8 5A 48
SM2: Sutt 7H 165
UB1: S'hall 1B 94
Beresford Sq. SE18 4F 107
Beresford St. SE18 3F 107
Beresford Ter. N5 5C 66
Berestede Rd. W6 5B 98
Bere St. E1 7K 85
Bergen Ho. *SE5* *2C 120*
(off Carew St.)
Bergenia Ho. TW13: Felt 1J 129
Bergen Sq. SE16 3A 104
Berger Cl. BR5: Pet W 6H 161
Berger Rd. E9 6K 67
Berghem M. W14 3F 99
Bergholt Av. IG4: Ilf 5C 52
Bergholt Cres. N16 7E 48
Bergholt M. NW1 7H 65
Berglen Ct. E14 6A 86
Bergman Ho. *E17* *4C 50*
(off Hoe St.)
Bering Sq. E14 5C 104
Bering Wlk. E16 6B 88
Berisford M. SW18 6A 118
Berkeley Av. DA7: Bex 1D 126
IG5: Ilf 2E 52
RM5: Col R 1J 55
TW4: Cran 1J 111
UB6: G'frd 6H 59
(not continuous)
Berkeley Cl. BR5: Pet W 7J 161
HA4: Ruis 3J 57
KT2: King T 7E 132
Berkeley Ct. BR2: Brom 4K 159
CR0: C'don *4D 168*
(off Coombe Rd.)
KT6: Surb 7D 150
N3 1K 45
N14 6B 22
NW1 4F 5
NW10 4A 62
NW11 *7H 45*
(off Ravenscroft Av.)
SM6: Wall 3G 167
W5 7C 78
Berkeley Cres. EN4: E Barn 5G 21
Berkeley Dr. KT8: W Mole 3D 148
Berkeley Gdns. KT10: Clay 6A 162
KT12: Walt T 7H 147
N21 7J 23
W8 1J 99
Berkeley Ho. *E3* *3C 86*
(off Wellington Way)
SE8 *5B 104*
(off Grove St.)
TW8: Bford *6D 96*
(off Albany Rd.)
Berkeley M. TW16: Sun 3A 148
W1 1F 11 (6D 82)
Berkeley Pl. SW19 6F 135
Berkeley Rd. E12 5C 70
N8 5H 47
N15 6D 48
NW9 4G 43
SW13 1C 116
UB10: Hil 7E 56
Berkeleys, The SE25 4G 157
Berkeley Sq. W1 3K 11 (7F 83)
Berkeley St. W1 3K 11 (7F 83)
Berkeley Twr. *E14* *1B 104*
(off Westferry Cir.)
Berkeley Wlk. *N7* *2K 65*
(off Durham Rd.)
Berkeley Waye TW5: Hest 6B 94
Berkhampstead Rd. DA17: Belv 5G 109
Berkhamsted Av. HA9: Wemb 6F 61
Berkley Cl. *TW2: Twick* *3J 131*
(off Wellesley Rd.)
Berkley Gro. NW1 7E 64
Berkley Rd. NW1 7D 64
Berkshire Ct. *W7* *4K 77*
(off Copley Cl.)
Berkshire Gdns. N13 6F 33
N18 5C 34
Berkshire Ho. SE6 4C 140
Berkshire Rd. E9 6B 68
Berkshire Way CR4: Mitc 4J 155
Berley Rd. E17 1B 50
Berlin Ter. E15 5G 69
Bermans Way NW10 4A 62
BERMONDSEY 7K 15 (2G 103)
Bermondsey Exchange *SE1* *7H 15*
(off Bermondsey St.)
Bermondsey Sq. SE1 7H 15 (3E 102)
Bermondsey St. SE1 5G 15 (1E 102)
Bermondsey Trad. Est. SE16 5J 103
Bermondsey Wall E. SE16 2G 103
Bermondsey Wall W. SE16 2G 103
Bermuda Way *E1* *5A 86*
(off Dongola Rd.)
Bernal Cl. SE28 7D 90
Bernard Angell Ho. *SE10* *6F 105*
(off Trafalgar Rd.)
Bernard Ashley Dr. SE7 5K 105
Bernard Av. W13 3B 96
Bernard Cassidy St. E16 5H 87
Bernard Gdns. SW19 5H 135
Bernard Hegarty Lodge *E8* *7G 67*
(off Lansdowne Dr.)
Bernard Ho. E1 6J 9
Bernard Mans. *WC1* *4E 6*
(off Bernard St.)
Bernard Myers Ho. *SE5* *7E 102*
(off Havil St.)
Bernard Rd. N15 5F 49
RM7: Rush G 7J 55
SM6: Wall 4F 167
Bernard Shaw Ct. *NW1* *7G 65*
(off St Pancras Way)
Bernard Shaw Ho. *NW10* *1K 79*
(off Knatchbull Rd.)
Bernard St. WC1 4E 6 (4J 83)
Bernard Sunley Ho. *SW9* *7A 102*
(off Sth. Island Pl.)
Bernays Cl. HA7: Stan 6H 27
Bernays Gro. SW9 4K 119
Bernel Dr. CR0: C'don 3B 170
Berne Rd. CR7: Thor H 5C 156
Berners Dr. W13 7A 78
Berners Ho. *N1* *2A 84*
(off Barnsbury Est.)
Berners M. W1 6B 6 (5G 83)
Berners Pl. W1 7B 6 (6G 83)
Berners Rd. N1 1B 84
N22 1A 48
Berners St. W1 6B 6 (5G 83)
Berner Ter. *E1* *6G 85*
(off Fairclough St.)
Berney Ho. BR3: Beck 5A 158
Berney Rd. CR0: C'don 7D 156
Bernhard Baron Ho. *E1* *6G 85*
(off Henriques St.)
Bernhardt Cres. NW8 3C 4 (4C 82)
Bernhart Cl. HA8: Edg 7D 28
Bernie Grant Arts Cen. 4F 49
Bernville Way HA3: Kenton 5F 43
Bernwell Rd. E4 3B 36
Berridge Grn. HA8: Edg 7B 28
Berridge M. NW6 5J 63
Berridge Rd. SE19 5D 138
Berriman Rd. N7 3K 65
Berrington Ho. *W2* *7J 81*
(off Herrington Rd.)
Berriton Rd. HA2: Harr 1D 58
Berrybank Cl. E4 2K 35
Berry Cl. N21 1G 33
RM10: Dag 5G 73
Berry Cotts. *E14* *6A 86*
(off Maroon St.)
Berry Ct. TW4: Houn 5D 112
Berrydale Rd. UB4: Yead 4C 76
Berryfield Cl. BR1: Brom 1C 160
E17 4D 50
Berryfield Rd. SE17 5B 102
Berry Hill HA7: Stan 4J 27
Berryhill SE9 4F 125
Berryhill Gdns. SE9 4F 125
Berry Ho. *E1* *4H 85*
(off Headlam St.)
SW11 *2D 118*
(off Culvert Rd.)
BERRYLANDS 6G 151
Berrylands KT5: Surb 6F 151
SW20 3E 152
Berrylands Rd. KT5: Surb 6F 151
Berry La. SE21 4D 138
Berryman Cl. RM8: Dag 3C 72
Berryman's La. SE26 4K 139
Berrymead Gdns. W3 1J 97
Berrymede Rd. W4 3K 97
Berry Pl. EC1 2B 8 (3B 84)
Berryside Apartments *N4* *1C 66*
(off Swan La.)
Berry St. EC1 3B 8 (4B 84)
Berry Way W5 3E 96
Bertal Rd. SW17 4B 136
Bertelli Pl. TW13: Felt 1K 129
Bertha Hollamby Ct. *DA14: Sidc* *5C 144*
(off Sidcup Hill)
Bertha James Ct. BR2: Brom 4K 159
Berthons Gdns. *E17* *5F 51*
(off Wood St.)
Berthon St. SE8 7C 104
Bertie Rd. NW10 6C 62
SE26 6K 139
Bertram Cotts. SW19 7J 135
Bertram Rd. EN1: Enf 4B 24
KT2: King T 7G 133
NW4 6C 44
Bertram St. N19 2F 65
Bertrand Ho. *E16* *6K 87*
(off Russell Rd.)
SW16 *3J 137*
(off Leigham Av.)
Bertrand St. SE13 3D 122
Bertrand Way SE28 7B 90
Bert Rd. CR7: Thor H 5C 156
Bert Way EN1: Enf 4A 24
Berwick Av. UB4: Yead 6B 76
Berwick Cl. HA7: Stan 6E 26
TW2: Whitt 1E 130
Berwick Ct. SE1 7D 14
Berwick Cres. DA15: Sidc 7J 125
Berwick Gdns. SM1: Sutt 3A 166
Berwick Ho. BR6: Orp 1K 173
N2 2B 46
Berwick Rd. DA16: Well 1B 126
E16 6K 87
N22 1B 48
Berwick St. W1 7B 6 (6G 83)
Berwick Way BR6: Orp 1K 173
Berwyn Av. TW3: Houn 1F 113
Berwyn Rd. SE24 1B 138
TW10: Rich 4H 115
Beryl Av. E6 5C 88
Beryl Ho. *SE18* *5K 107*
(off Spinel Cl.)
Beryl Rd. W6 5F 99
Berystede KT2: King T 7H 133
Besant Cl. NW2 3G 63
Besant Ct. N1 5D 66
SE28 *1B 108*
(off Titmuss Av.)
Besant Ho. *NW8* *1A 82*
(off Boundary Rd.)
Besant Pl. SE22 4F 121
Besant Rd. NW2 4G 63
Besant Wlk. N7 2K 65
Besant Way NW10 5J 61
Besford Ho. *E2* *2G 85*
(off Pritchard's Rd.)
Besley St. SW16 6G 137
Bessant Dr. TW9: Kew 1H 115
Bessborough Gdns. SW1 5D 18 (5H 101)
Bessborough Pl. SW1 5D 18 (5H 101)
Bessborough Rd. HA1: Harr 1H 59
SW15 1C 134
Bessborough St. SW1 5C 18 (5H 101)
Bessemer Ct. *NW1* *7G 65*
(off Rochester Sq.)
Bessemer Pk. Ind. Est. SE24 4B 120
Bessemer Pl. SE10 3H 105
Bessemer Rd. SE5 2C 120
Bessie Lansbury Cl. E6 6E 88
Bessingby Rd. HA4: Ruis 2K 57
Bessingham Wlk. *SE4* *4K 121*
(off Aldersford Cl.)
Besson St. SE14 1J 121
Bessy St. E2 3J 85
Bestwood St. SE8 4K 103
Beswick M. NW6 6K 63
Beta Ct. *CR0: C'don* *1D 168*
(off Sydenham Rd.)
Betam Rd. UB3: Hayes 2F 93
Beta Pl. SW4 4K 119
Betchworth Cl. SM1: Sutt 5B 166
Betchworth Rd. IG3: Ilf 2J 71

Betchworth Way—Bingham Pl.

Betchworth Way CR0: New Ad 7E 170
Betham Rd. UB6: G'frd 3H 77
Bethany Waye TW14: Bedf 7G 111
Bethecar Rd. HA1: Harr 5J 41
Bethel Cl. NW4 5F 45
Bethell Av. E16 4H 87
IG1: Ilf 7E 52
Bethel Rd. DA16: Well 3C 126
Bethersden Cl. BR3: Beck 7B 140
Bethersden Ho. *SE17* *5E 102*
(off Kinglake Est.)
Bethlehem Cl. UB6: G'frd 2C 78
Bethlehem Ho. *E14* *7B 86*
(off Limehouse C'way.)
BETHNAL GREEN 3H 85
Bethnal Green Cen. For Sports & Performing Arts 2K 9 (3F 85)
Bethnal Grn. Rd. E1 3J 9 (4F 85)
E2 3J 9 (4F 85)
Bethune Av. N11 4J 31
Bethune Rd. N16 7D 48
NW10 4K 79
Bethwin Rd. SE5 7B 102
Betjeman Cl. HA5: Pinn 4E 40
Betjeman Ct. UB7: Yiew 1A 92
Betjeman M. N5 4C 66
Betony Cl. CR0: C'don 1K 169
Betoyne Av. E4 4B 36
Betsham Ho. *SE1* *6E 14*
(off Newcomen St.)
Betstyle Cir. N11 4A 32
Betstyle Ho. N10 7K 31
Betstyle Rd. N11 4A 32
Bettenson Cl. BR7: Chst 5D 142
Better Gym Greenwich 2G 105
Betterton Dr. DA14: Sidc 2E 144
Betterton Ho. *WC2* *1F 13*
(off Betterton St.)
Betterton Rd. RM13: Rain 3K 91
Betterton St. WC2 1E 12 (6J 83)
Bettons Pk. E15 1G 87
Bettridge Rd. SW6 2H 117
Betts Cl. BR3: Beck 2A 158
Betts Ho. *E1* *7H 85*
(off Betts St.)
Betts M. E17 6B 50
Betts Rd. E16 7K 87
Betts St. E1 7H 85
Betts Way KT6: Surb 1B 162
SE20 1H 157
Betty Brooks Ho. E11 3F 69
Betty May Gray Ho. *E14* *4E 104*
(off Pier St.)
Beulah Av. CR7: Thor H 2C 156
Beulah Cl. HA8: Edg 3C 28
Beulah Cres. CR7: Thor H 2C 156
Beulah Gro. CR0: C'don 6C 156
Beulah Hill SE19 6B 138
Beulah Path E17 5E 50
Beulah Rd. CR7: Thor H 3C 156
E17 5D 50
SM1: Sutt 4J 165
SW19 7H 135
Bevan Av. IG11: Bark 7A 72
Bevan Ct. CR0: Wadd 5A 168
E3 *2C 86*
(off Tredegar Rd.)
Bevan Ho. IG11: Bark 7B 72
N1 *1E 84*
(off Halcomb St.)
TW1: Twick 6D 114
WC1 *5F 7*
(off Boswell St.)
Bevan M. W12 2C 98
Bevan Rd. EN4: Cockf 4J 21
SE2 5B 108
Bevans Ho. *SW18* *4A 118*
(off Eltringham St.)
Bevan St. N1 1C 84
Bev Callender Cl. SW8 3F 119
Bevenden St. N1 1F 9 (3D 84)
Bevercote Wlk. *DA17: Belv* *6F 109*
(off Osborne Rd.)
Beveree Stadium 1F 149
Beveridge Ct. *N21* *5D 22*
(off Pennington Dr.)
SE28 *7B 90*
(off Saunders Way)
Beveridge M. E1 5J 85
Beveridge Rd. NW10 7A 62
Beverley Av. DA15: Sidc 7K 125
SW20 1B 152
TW4: Houn 4D 112
Beverley Cl. EN1: Enf 4K 23
KT9: Chess 4C 162
N21 1H 33
SW11 4B 118
SW13 2C 116
Beverley Cotts. SW15 3A 134
Beverley Ct. HA2: Harr 3H 41
HA3: Kenton 4C 42
N2 *4D 46*
(off Western Rd.)
N14 7B 22
NW6 *7A 64*
(off Fairfax Rd.)
SE4 3B 122
(not continuous)
TW4: Houn 4D 112
W4 5J 97
Beverley Cres. IG8: Wfd G 1K 51
Beverley Dr. HA8: Edg 3G 43
Beverley Gdns. HA7: Stan 1A 42
HA9: Wemb 1F 61
KT4: Wor Pk 1C 164
NW11 7G 45
SW13 3B 116
Beverley Ho. *BR1: Brom* *5F 141*
(off Brangbourne Rd.)
Beverley Hyrst CR0: C'don 2F 169
Beverley La. KT2: King T 7A 134
SW15 3B 134
Beverley Meads & Fishpond Woods Nature Reserve 6B 134
Beverley M. E4 6A 36
Beverley Path SW13 2B 116
Beverley Rd. BR2: Brom 2C 172
CR4: Mitc 4H 155
DA7: Bex 2J 127
E4 6A 36
E6 3B 88
HA4: Ruis 2J 57
KT1: Hamp W 1C 150
KT3: N Mald 4C 152
KT4: Wor Pk 2E 164
RM9: Dag 4E 72
SE20 2H 157
SW13 3B 116
TW16: Sun 1H 147
UB2: S'hall 4C 94
W4 5B 98
Beverley Trad. Est. SM4: Mord 7F 153
Beverley Way KT3: N Mald 1B 152
SW20 1B 152
Beversbrook Rd. N19 3H 65
Beverstone Rd. CR7: Thor H 4A 156
SW2 5K 119
Beverston M. W1 6E 4
Bevill Allen Cl. SW17 5D 136
Bevill Cl. SE25 3G 157
Bevin Cl. SE16 1A 104
Bevin Ct. WC1 1H 7 (3K 83)
Bevington Path SE1 7J 15
Bevington Rd. BR3: Beck 2D 158
W10 5G 81
Bevington St. SE16 2G 103
Bevin Ho. *E2* *3J 85*
(off Butler St.)
E3 *3C 86*
(off Alfred St.)
Bevin Rd. UB4: Yead 3J 75
Bevin Sq. SW17 3D 136
Bevin Way WC1 1J 7 (2A 84)
Bevis Marks EC3 7H 9 (6E 84)
Bewcastle Gdns. EN2: Enf 4D 22
Bew Ct. SE22 7G 121
Bewdley St. N1 7A 66
Bewick M. SE15 7H 103
Bewick St. SW8 2F 119
Bewley Ho. *E1* *7H 85*
(off Bewley St.)
Bewley St. E1 7J 85
SW19 6A 136
Bewlys Rd. SE27 5B 138
Bexhill Cl. TW13: Felt 2C 130
Bexhill Rd. N11 5C 32
SE4 6B 122
SW14 3J 115
Bexhill Wlk. E15 1G 87
BEXLEY 7G 127
Bexley Gdns. N9 3J 33
RM6: Chad H 5B 54
BEXLEYHEATH 4G 127
Bexleyheath Golf Course 5E 126
Bexleyheath Sports Club 4C 126
Bexley High St. DA5: Bexl 7G 127
Bexley Ho. SE4 4A 122
Bexley La. DA1: Cray 5K 127
DA14: Sidc 4C 144
Bexley Lawn Tennis, Squash & Racketball Club 7G 127
Bexley Mus. Collection, The 6J 127
Bexley Music & Dance Cen. *4A 144*
(off Station Rd.)
Bexley Rd. DA8: Erith 1J 127
SE9 5F 125
Beynon Rd. SM5: Cars 5D 166
Bezier Apartments EC2 3F 9 (4D 84)
BFI Southbank 4H 13
Bianca Ho. *N1* *1G 9*
(off Crondall St.)
Bianca Rd. SE15 6G 103
Bibsworth Rd. N3 2H 45
Bibury Cl. SE15 6E 102
(not continuous)
Bicester Rd. TW9: Rich 3G 115
Bickels Yd. *SE1* *7H 15*
(off Bermondsey St.)
Bickenhall Mans. W1 5F 5
(not continuous)
Bickenhall St. W1 5F 5 (5D 82)
Bickersteth Rd. SW17 6D 136
Bickerton Rd. N19 2G 65
BICKLEY 3C 160
Bickley Cres. BR1: Brom 4C 160
Bickley Pk. Rd. BR1: Brom 3C 160
Bickley Rd. BR1: Brom 2B 160
E10 7D 50
Bickley St. SW17 5C 136
Bicknell Ho. *E1* *6G 85*
(off Ellen St.)
Bicknell Rd. SE5 3C 120
Bicknoller Rd. EN1: Enf 1K 23
Bicknor Rd. BR6: Orp 7J 161
Bicycle M. SW4 3H 119
Bidborough Cl. BR2: Brom 5H 159
Bidborough St. WC1 2E 6 (3J 83)
Biddenden Way SE9 4E 142
Biddenham Ho. *SE16* *4K 103*
(off Plough Way)
Bidder St. E16 5G 87
(not continuous)
Biddesden Ho. *SW3* *4E 16*
(off Cadogan St.)
Biddestone Rd. N7 4K 65
Biddulph Ho. SE18 4D 106
Biddulph Mans. *W9* *3K 81*
(off Elgin Av.)
Biddulph Rd. W9 3K 81
Bideford Av. UB6: G'frd 2B 78
Bideford Cl. HA8: Edg 1G 43
TW13: Hanw 3D 130
Bideford Gdns. EN1: Enf 7K 23
Bideford Rd. BR1: Brom 3H 141
DA16: Well 7B 108
EN3: Enf L 1G 25
HA4: Ruis 3K 57
Bidwell Gdns. N11 7B 32
Bidwell St. SE15 1H 121
Big Ben 7F 13 (2J 101)
Bigbury Cl. N17 7J 33
Biggerstaff Rd. E15 1E 86
Biggerstaff St. N4 2A 66
Biggin Av. CR4: Mitc 1D 154
Biggin Hill SE19 7B 138
Biggin Hill Cl. KT2: King T 5C 132
Biggin Way SE19 7B 138
Bigginwood Rd. SW16 7B 138
Biggs Ct. *NW9* *2A 44*
(off Harvey Cl.)
Biggs Row SW15 3F 117
Biggs Sq. E9 6B 68
Big Hill E5 1H 67
Bigland St. E1 6H 85
Bignell Rd. SE18 5F 107
Bignold Rd. E7 4J 69
Bigsworth Ct. SE20 1H 157
Bigwood Ct. NW11 5K 45
Bigwood Rd. NW11 5K 45
Bike Shed, The *IG11: Bark* *7G 71*
(off Ripple Rd.)
Bilberry Ho. *E3* *5C 86*
(off Watts Gro.)
Billet Cl. RM6: Chad H 3D 54
Billet Rd. E17 1K 49
RM6: Chad H 3B 54
Billets Hart Cl. W7 2J 95
Bill Hamling Cl. SE9 2D 142
Billing Cl. RM9: Dag 7C 72
Billingford Cl. SE4 4K 121
Billing Ho. *E1* *6K 85*
(off Bower St.)
Billingley *NW1* *1G 83*
(off Pratt St.)
Billing Pl. SW10 7K 99
Billing Rd. SW10 7K 99
Billingsgate Market 1D 104
Billing St. SW10 7K 99
Billington M. *W3* *1H 97*
(off High St.)
Billington Rd. SE14 7K 103
Billinton Hill CR0: C'don 2D 168
Billiter Sq. EC3 1H 15
Billiter St. EC3 1H 15 (6E 84)
Bill Nicholson Way *N17* *7A 34*
(off High Rd.)
Billockby Cl. KT9: Chess 6F 163
Billson St. E14 4E 104
Bill Voisey Cl. *E14* *6A 86*
(off Repton St.)
Bilsby Gro. SE9 4B 142
Bilsby Lodge *HA9: Wemb* *3J 61*
(off Chalklands)
Bilton Cen., The UB6: G'frd 1B 78
Bilton Rd. UB6: G'frd 1A 78
Bilton Towers *W1* *1F 11*
(off Gt. Cumberland Pl.)
Bilton Way EN3: Enf L 1F 25
UB3: Hayes 2K 93
Bina Gdns. SW5 4A 100
Binbrook Ho. *W10* *5E 80*
(off Sutton Way)
Bincote Rd. EN2: Enf 3E 22
Binden Rd. W12 3B 98
Bindon Grn. SM4: Mord 4K 153
Binfield Rd. CR2: S Croy 5F 169
SW4 1J 119
Bingfield St. N1 1J 83
(not continuous)
Bingham Ct. *N1* *7B 66*
(off Halton Rd.)
Bingham Pl. W1 5G 5 (5E 82)

Bingham Point *SE18* 4F 107
(off Wilmount St.)
Bingham Rd. CR0: C'don 1G 169
Bingham St. N1 6D 66
Bingley Rd. E16 6A 88
TW16: Sun 7J 129
UB6: G'frd 4G 77
Binley Ho. SW15 6C 116
Binnacle Ho. *E1* 1H 103
(off Cobblestone Sq.)
Binney St. W1 1H 11 (6E 82)
Binnie Ho. *SE1* 3C 102
(off Bath Ter.)
Binnington Twr.
BR2: Brom 6C 160
Binns Rd. W4 5A 98
Binns Ter. W4 5A 98
Binsey Wlk. SE2 2C 108
(not continuous)
Binstead Cl. UB4: Yead 6C 76
Binyon Cres. HA7: Stan 5E 26
Bioko Ct. *E1* 5A 86
(off Ocean Est.)
Biraj Ho. E6 1D 88
Birbetts Rd. SE9 2D 142
Bircham Path *SE4* 4K 121
(off Aldersford Cl.)
Birchanger Rd. SE25 5G 157
Birch Av. N13 3H 33
UB7: Yiew 6B 74
Birch Cl. E16 5G 87
IG9: Buck H 3G 37
N19 2G 65
RM7: Mawney 3H 55
SE15 2G 121
TW3: Houn 2H 113
TW8: Bford 7B 96
TW11: Tedd 5A 132
TW17: Shep 2G 147
Birch Ct. N12 4E 30
RM6: Chad H 6C 54
SM1: Sutt 4A 166
SM6: Wall 4F 167
Birch Cres. UB10: Uxb 1B 74
Birchdale Gdns. RM6: Chad H 7D 54
Birchdale Rd. E7 5A 70
Birchdene Dr. SE28 1A 108
Birchdown Ho. *E3* 3D 86
(off Rainhill Way)
Birchen Cl. NW9 2K 61
Birchend Cl. CR2: S Croy 6D 168
Birchen Gro. NW9 2K 61
Birches, The *BR2: Brom* 4H 159
(off Durham Rd.)
BR6: Farnb 4E 172
E12 4C 70
N21 6E 22
SE5 2E 120
SE7 6K 105
TW4: Houn 7D 112
Birches Cl. CR4: Mitc 3D 154
HA5: Pinn 5C 40
Birchfield Ct.
KT12: Walt T 7K 147
(off Grove Cres.)
Birchfield Ho. *E14* 7C 86
(off Birchfield St.)
Birchfield St. E14 7C 86
Birch Gdns. RM10: Dag 3J 73
Birch Grn. NW9 7F 29
Birch Gro. DA16: Well 4A 126
E11 4G 69
SE12 7H 123
TW17: Shep 2G 147
W3 1G 97
Birchgrove Ho. TW9: Kew 7H 97
Birch Hill CR0: C'don 5K 169
Birch Ho. *N22* 1A 48
(off Acacia Rd.)
SE14 1B 122
SW2 6A 120
Birch Ho. *UB7: W Dray* 2B 92
(off Park Lodge Av.)
W10 4G 81
(off Droop St.)
Birchington Cl. DA7: Bex 1H 127
Birchington Ct. *NW6* 1K 81
(off West End La.)
Birchington Ho. E5 5H 67
Birchington Rd. KT5: Surb 7F 151
N8 6H 47
NW6 1J 81
Birchin La. EC3 1F 15 (6D 84)
Birchlands Av. SW12 7D 118
Birch Mead BR6: Farnb 2E 172
Birchmead Av. HA5: Pinn 4A 40
Birchmere Bus. Pk. SE28 2A 108
Birchmere Lodge *SE16* 5H 103
(off Sherwood Gdns.)
Birchmere Row SE3 2H 123
Birchmore Hall N5 3C 66
Birchmore Wlk. N5 3C 66
(not continuous)
Birch Pk. HA3: Hrw W 7B 26
Birch Rd. RM7: Mawney 3H 55
TW13: Hanw 5B 130
Birch Row BR2: Brom 7E 160
Birch Tree Av. BR4: W W'ck 5H 171
Birch Tree Way CR0: C'don 2H 169
Birch Va. Ct. *NW8* 3B 4
(off Pollitt Dr.)
Birch Vw. HA1: Harr 5H 41
Birchville Ct. WD23: B Hea 1D 26
Birch Wlk. CR4: Mitc 1F 155
DA8: Erith 6J 109
IG3: Ilf 4J 71
(off Loxford La.)
Birchway UB3: Hayes 1J 93
Birchwood Apartments *N4* 7C 48
(off Woodberry Gro.)
Birchwood Av. BR3: Beck 4B 158
DA14: Sidc 2B 144
N10 3E 46
SM6: Wall 3E 166
Birchwood Cl. SM4: Mord 4K 153
Birchwood Ct. HA8: Edg 2J 43
N13 5G 33
Birchwood Dr. DA2: Wilm 4K 145
NW3 3K 63
Birchwood Gro. TW12: Hamp 6E 130
Birchwood Pde. DA2: Wilm 4K 145
Birchwood Pk. Golf Course 7J 145
Birchwood Rd. BR5: Pet W 4H 161
BR8: Swan 7J 145
DA2: Wilm 7J 145
SW17 5F 137
Birdbrook Cl. RM10: Dag 7J 73
Birdbrook Ho. *N1* 7C 66
(off Popham Rd.)
Birdbrook Rd. SE3 4A 124
Birdcage Wlk. SW1 7A 12 (2G 101)
Birdham Cl. BR1: Brom 5C 160
Birdhurst Av. CR2: S Croy 4D 168
Birdhurst Ct. *SM6: Wall* 7G 167
(off Woodcote Av.)
Birdhurst Gdns. CR2: S Croy 4D 168
Birdhurst Ri. CR2: S Croy 5E 168
Birdhurst Rd. CR2: S Croy 5E 168
SW18 5A 118
SW19 6C 136
Bird in Bush BMX Track *7H 103*
(off Bird in Bush Rd.)
Bird in Bush Rd. SE15 7G 103
Bird in Hand La. BR1: Brom 2B 160
Bird-in-Hand M. *SE23* 2J 139
(off Bird-in-Hand Pas.)
Bird-in-Hand Pas. SE23 2J 139
Bird in Hand Path *CR0: C'don* 7D 156
(off Sydenham Rd.)
Bird in Hand Yd. NW3 4A 64
Birdsall Ho. SE5 3E 120
Birds Farm Av. RM5: Col R 1H 55
Birdsfield La. E3 1B 86
Birdsmouth Ct. *N15* 4E 48
(off Bathurst Sq.)
Bird St. W1 1H 11 (6E 82)
Bird Wlk. TW2: Whitt 1D 130
Birdwood Av. SE13 6F 123
Birdwood Cl. TW11: Tedd 4J 131
Birkbeck Av. UB6: G'frd 1G 77
W3 7J 79
Birkbeck Ct. W3 1K 97
Birkbeck Gdns. IG8: Wfd G 2D 36
Birkbeck Gro. W3 2K 97
Birkbeck Hill SE21 1B 138
Birkbeck M. E8 5F 67
W3 1K 97
Birkbeck Pl. SE21 2C 138
Birkbeck Rd. BR3: Beck 2J 157
DA14: Sidc 3A 144
E8 5F 67
EN2: Enf 1J 23
IG2: Ilf 5H 53
N8 4J 47
N12 5F 31
N17 1F 49
NW7 5G 29
RM7: Rush G 1K 73
SW19 5K 135
W3 1K 97
W5 4C 96
Birkbeck St. E2 3H 85
Birkbeck Way UB6: G'frd 1H 77
Birkdale Av. HA5: Pinn 3E 40
Birkdale Cl. BR6: Orp 7H 161
SE16 5H 103
SE28 6D 90
Birkdale Ct. *UB1: S'hall* 6G 77
(off Redcroft Rd.)
Birkdale Gdns. CR0: C'don 4K 169
Birkdale Rd. SE2 4A 108
W5 4E 78
Birkenhead Av. KT2: King T 2F 151
Birkenhead St. WC1 1F 7 (3J 83)
Birkhall Rd. SE6 1F 141
Birkwood Cl. SW12 7H 119
Birley Lodge *NW8* 2B 82
(off Acacia Rd.)
Birley Rd. N20 2F 31
Birley St. SW11 2E 118
Birling Rd. DA8: Erith 7K 109
Birnam Rd. N4 2K 65
Birnbeck Ct. EN5: Barn 4A 20
NW11 5H 45
Birrell Ho. *SW9* 2K 119
(off Stockwell Rd.)
Birse Cres. NW10 3A 62
Birstall Rd. N15 5E 48
Birtwhistle Ho. *E3* 1B 86
(off Parnell Rd.)
Biscay Ho. *E1* 4K 85
(off Mile End Rd.)
Biscayne Av. E14 1F 105
Biscay Rd. W6 5F 99
Biscoe Cl. TW5: Hest 6E 94
Biscoe Way SE13 3F 123
Biscott Ho. E3 4D 86
Bisenden Rd. CR0: C'don 2E 168
Bisham Cl. SM5: Cars 1D 166
Bisham Gdns. N6 1E 64
Bishop Butt Cl. BR6: Orp 3K 173
Bishop Ct. TW9: Rich 3E 114
Bishop Duppas Pk. TW17: Shep 7G 147
Bishop Fox Way KT8: W Mole 4D 148
Bishop Ken Rd. HA3: W'stone 2K 41
Bishop King's Rd. W14 4G 99
Bishop Ramsey Cl. HA4: Ruis 7H 39
Bishop Rd. N14 7A 22
Bishop's Av. E13 1K 87
SW6 2F 117
Bishops Av. BR1: Brom 2A 160
RM6: Chad H 6C 54
Bishops Av., The N2 7B 46
Bishop's Bri. Rd. W2 6A 4 (6K 81)
Bishop's Cl. N19 3G 65
SE9 2G 143
SM1: Sutt 3J 165
Bishops Cl. E17 4D 50
EN1: Enf 2C 24
EN5: Barn 6A 20
TW10: Ham 3D 132
UB10: Hil 2C 74
W4 5J 97
Bishop's Ct. EC4 7A 8
WC2 7J 7
Bishops Ct. CR0: C'don 2F 169
HA0: Wemb 4B 60
N2 5C 46
W2 6K 81
(off Bishop's Bri. Rd.)
Bishopsdale Ho. *NW6* 1J 81
(off Kilburn Vale)
Bishop's Dr. TW14: Bedf 6F 111
Bishops Dr. UB5: N'olt 1C 76
Bishopsford Ho. SM5: Cars 6C 154
Bishopsford Rd. SM4: Mord 7A 154
Bishopsgate EC2 1G 15 (6E 84)
Bishopsgate Arc. EC2 6H 9
Bishopsgate Chyd. EC2 7G 9 (5E 84)
Bishopsgate Institute & Libraries 6H 9
Bishopsgate Plaza *EC3* 6E 84
(off Bishopsgate)
Bishops Grn. BR1: Brom 1A 160
Bishop's Gro. TW12: Hamp 4D 130
Bishops Gro. N2 6C 46
Bishops Gro. Cvn. Site
TW12: Hamp, Hamp H 4E 130
Bishop's Hall KT1: King T 2D 150
Bishops Hill KT12: Walt T 7J 147
Bishops Ho. *SW8* 7J 101
(off Sth. Lambeth Rd.)
Bishop's Mans. SW6 2F 117
Bishops Mead *SE5* 7C 102
(off Camberwell Rd.)
Bishop's Pk. Rd. SW6 2F 117
Bishops Pk. Rd. SW16 1J 155
Bishops Pl. SM1: Sutt 5A 166
Bishop's Rd. CR0: C'don 7B 156
SW11 7C 100
UB3: Hayes 6E 74
Bishops Rd. N6 6E 46
SW6 1G 117
W7 2J 95
Bishops Sq. E1 5H 9 (5E 84)
Bishop's Ter. SE11 3K 19 (4A 102)
Bishopsthorpe Rd. SE26 4K 139
Bishop St. N1 1C 84
Bishops Vw. Ct. N10 4F 47
Bishops Wlk. BR7: Chst 1G 161
CR0: Addtn 5K 169
HA5: Pinn 3C 40
Bishop's Way E2 2H 85
Bishops Wharf Ho. *SW11* 7C 100
(off Parkgate Rd.)
Bishops Wood Almshouses *E5* 4H 67
(off Lwr. Clapton Rd.)
Bishopswood Rd. N6 7D 46
Bishop Wilfred Wood Cl. SE15 2G 121
Bishop Wilfred Wood Ct. *E13* 2A 88
(off Pragel St.)
Bisley Cl. KT4: Wor Pk 1E 164
Bison Ct. TW14: Felt 7K 111
Bispham Rd. NW10 3F 79
Bissagos Ct. *E1* 5A 86
(off Ocean Est.)
Bissextile Ho. SE13 2D 122
Bisson Rd. E15 2E 86
Bisterne Av. E17 3F 51
Bittacy Bus. Cen. NW7 7B 30
Bittacy Cl. NW7 6A 30
Bittacy Ct. NW7 7B 30
Bittacy Hill NW7 6A 30
Bittacy Pk. Av. NW7 5A 30
Bittacy Ri. NW7 6K 29

Bittacy Rd. NW7 . . . . 6A **30**
Bittern Cl. UB4: Yead 5B **76**
Bittern Ct. NW9 . . . . 2A **44**
SE8 . . . . 6C **104**
Bittern Ho. *SE1* *7C **14***
(off Gt. Suffolk St.)
Bittern Pl. N22 . . . . 2K **47**
Bittern St. SE1 . . . . 7C **14** (2C **102**)
Bittoms, The KT1: King T 3D **150**
Bittoms Ct. KT1: King T 3D **150**
Bixley Cl. UB2: S'hall 4D **94**
Blackall St. EC2 . . . . 3G **9** (4E **84**)
Blackberry Cl. E17 . . . . 3D **50**
TW17: Shep 4G **147**
Blackberry Ct. HA9: Wemb 7E **42**
Blackberry Farm Cl. TW5: Hest 7C **94**
Blackberry Fld. BR5: St P 7A **144**
Blackbird Ct. NW9 . . . . 3K **61**
Blackbird Hill NW9 . . . . 2J **61**
Blackbird Yd. E2 . . . . 1K **9** (3F **85**)
Blackborne Rd. RM10: Dag 6G **73**
Blackborough Ho. *IG9: Buck H* *2G **37***
(off Beatrice Ct.)
Black Boy La. N15 . . . . 5C **48**
Blackbrook La. BR1: Brom 5E **160**
BR2: Brom 5E **160**
Black Bull Yd. *EC1* *5K **7***
(off Hatton Wall)
Blackburn NW9 . . . . 2B **44**
Blackburne's M. W1 . . . . 2G **11** (7E **82**)
Blackburn Rd. NW6 . . . . 6K **63**
Blackburn Trad. Est. TW19: Stanw 6B **110**
Blackburn Way TW4: Houn 5C **112**
Blackbush Av. RM6: Chad H 5D **54**
Blackbush Cl. SM2: Sutt 7K **165**
Blackdown Cl. N2 . . . . 2A **46**
Blackdown Ter. SE18 . . . . 1D **124**
Blackett Apartments *E3* *4B **86***
(off Hamlets Way)
Blackett St. SW15 . . . . 3F **117**
Black Fan Cl. EN2: Enf 1H **23**
BLACKFEN 6A 126
Blackfen Pde. DA15: Sidc 6A **126**
Blackfen Rd. DA15: Sidc 5J **125**
Blackford Cl. CR2: S Croy 7B **168**
Blackford's Path SW15 . . . . 7C **116**
Blackfriars Bri. EC4 . . . . 2A **14** (7B **84**)
Blackfriars Ct. EC4 . . . . 2A **14**
Black Friars La. EC4 . . . . 2A **14** (6B **84**)
(not continuous)
Blackfriars Pas. EC4 . . . . 2A **14** (7B **84**)
Blackfriars Rd. SE1 . . . . 4A **14** (2B **102**)
Blackfriars Underpass
EC4 . . . . 2A **14** (7A **84**)
Black Gates HA5: Pinn 3D **40**
BLACKHEATH 2H 123
Blackheath Av. SE10 . . . . 7F **105**
Blackheath Bus. Cen. SE10 . . . . 1E **122**
Blackheath Bus. Est. *SE10* *1E **122***
(off Blackheath Hill)
Blackheath Concert Halls 3H **123**
Blackheath Gro. SE3 . . . . 2H **123**
Blackheath Hill SE10 . . . . 1E **122**
BLACKHEATH PARK 3J 123
Blackheath Pk. SE3 . . . . 3H **123**
Blackheath Ri. SE13 . . . . 2E **122**
(not continuous)
Blackheath Rd. SE10 . . . . 1D **122**
Blackheath RUFC 7K 105
BLACKHEATH VALE 2H 123
Blackheath Va. SE3 . . . . 2G **123**
Blackheath Village SE3 . . . . 2H **123**
Black Horse Ct. SE1 . . . . 3D **102**
Blackhorse La. CR0: C'don 7G **157**
E17 . . . . 2K **49**
Blackhorse M. E17 . . . . 3K **49**
Black Horse Pde. HA5: Eastc 5K **39**
BLACKHORSE ROAD **4K 49**
Blackhorse Rd. DA14: Sidc 4A **144**
E17 . . . . 4K **49**
SE8 . . . . 6A **104**
Blacklands Dr. UB4: Hayes 4E **74**
Blacklands Rd. SE6 . . . . 4E **140**
Blacklands Ter. SW3 . . . . 4E **16** (4D **100**)
Black Lion La. W6 . . . . 4C **98**
Black Lion M. W6 . . . . 4C **98**
Blackmans Yd. E2 . . . . 4G **85**
Blackmore Av. UB1: S'hall 1H **95**
Blackmore Dr. NW10 . . . . 7H **61**
Blackmore Ho. *N1* *1K **83***
(off Barnsbury Est.)
Blackmore Rd. IG9: Buck H 1H **37**
Blackmore's Gro. TW11: Tedd 6A **132**
Blackness La. BR2: Kes 7B **172**
Black Path E10 . . . . 7A **50**
Blackpool Gdns. UB4: Hayes 4G **75**
Blackpool Rd. SE15 . . . . 2H **121**
BLACK PRINCE INTERCHANGE **6H 127**
Black Prince Rd. SE1 . . . . 4G **19** (4K **101**)
SE11 . . . . 4G **19** (4K **101**)
Black Prince St. SE18 . . . . 6A **108**
Black Rd. E11 . . . . 6G **51**
Black Rod Cl. UB3: Hayes 3H **93**
Blackshaw Rd. SW17 . . . . 4A **136**
Blacksmiths Cl. RM6: Chad H 6C **54**
Blacksmiths Ho. *E17* *4C **50***
(off Gillards M.)
Blacks Rd. W6 . . . . 5E **98**
Blackstock M. N4 . . . . 2B **66**
Blackstock Rd. N4 . . . . 2B **66**
N5 . . . . 2B **66**
Blackstone Est. E8 . . . . 7G **67**
Blackstone Ho. *SW1* *6A **18***
(off Churchill Gdns.)
Blackstone Rd. NW2 . . . . 5E **62**
Black Swan Yd. SE1 . . . . 6H **15** (2E **102**)
Blackthorn Av. N7 . . . . 6A **66**
UB7: W Dray 4C **92**
Blackthorn Ct. *E15* *4F **69***
(off Hall Rd.)
TW5: Hest 7C **94**
Blackthorne Av. CR0: C'don 1J **169**
Blackthorne Ct. *SE15* *7F **103***
(off Cator St.)
TW15: Ashf 7E **128**
UB1: S'hall *1F **95***
(off Dormer's Wells La.)
Blackthorne Cres. SL3: Poyle 5A **174**
Blackthorne Dr. E4 . . . . 4A **36**
Blackthorne Ind. Est. SL3: Poyle 6A **174**
Blackthorne Rd. SL3: Poyle 5A **174**
Blackthorn Gro. DA7: Bex 3E **126**
Blackthorn Ho. *SE16* *2A **104***
(off Blondin Way)
Blackthorn Rd. IG1: Ilf 5H **71**
Blackthorn St. E3 . . . . 4C **86**
Blacktree M. SW9 . . . . 3A **120**
BLACKWALL 1E 104
Blackwall La. SE10 . . . . 5G **105**
Blackwall Trad. Est. E14 . . . . 5F **87**
Blackwall Tunnel E14 . . . . 1F **105**
(not continuous)
Blackwall Tunnel App. E14 . . . . 7E **86**
Blackwall Tunnel Northern App.
E3 . . . . 2C **86**
E14 . . . . 2C **86**
Blackwall Tunnel Southern App.
SE10 . . . . 3G **105**
Blackwall Way E14 . . . . 1E **104**
Blackwater Cl. E7 . . . . 4H **69**
RM13: Rain 5K **91**
Blackwater Ho. *NW8* *5B **4***
(off Church St.)
Blackwater St. SE22 . . . . 5F **121**
Blackwell Cl. E5 . . . . 4K **67**
HA3: Hrw W 7C **26**
N21 . . . . 5D **22**
Blackwell Gdns. HA8: Edg 4B **28**
Blackwell Ho. SW4 . . . . 6H **119**
Blackwood Av. N18 . . . . 5E **34**
Blackwood Ho. *E1* *4H **85***
(off Collingwood St.)
Blackwood St. SE17 . . . . 5D **102**
Blade M. SW15 . . . . 4H **117**
Bladen Ho. *E1* *6K **85***
(off Dunelm St.)
Blades Ct. SW15 . . . . 4H **117**
W6 . . . . *5D **98***
(off Lower Mall)
Blades Ho. *SE11* *7J **19***
(off Kennington Oval)
Bladindon Dr. DA5: Bexl 7C **126**
Bladon Ct. SW16 . . . . 6J **137**
Bladon Gdns. HA2: Harr 6F **41**
Blagdens Cl. N14 . . . . 2C **32**
Blagdens La. N14 . . . . 2B **32**
Blagdon Ct. W7 . . . . 7J **77**
Blagdon Rd. KT3: N Mald 4B **152**
SE13 . . . . 6D **122**
Blagdon Wlk. TW11: Tedd 6C **132**
Blagrove Cres. HA4: Eastc 6K **39**
Blagrove Rd. TW11: Hamp W 7B **132**
W10 . . . . 5G **81**
Blair Av. NW9 . . . . 7A **44**
Blair Cl. DA15: Sidc 5J **125**
N1 . . . . 6C **66**
UB3: Harl 4J **93**
Blair Ct. BR3: Beck 1D **158**
NW8 . . . . 1B **82**
SE6 . . . . 1H **141**
Blairderry Rd. SW2 . . . . 2J **137**
Blairgowrie Ct. *E14* *6F **87***
(off Blair St.)
Blair Ho. SW9 . . . . 2K **119**
Blair St. E14 . . . . 6E **86**
Blake Av. IG11: Bark 1J **89**
Blake Bldg. N8 . . . . 3K **47**
Blake Cl. DA16: Well 1J **125**
SM5: Cars 1C **166**
UB4: Hayes 2F **75**
W10 . . . . 5E **80**
Blake Ct. N21 . . . . 5E **22**
NW6 . . . . *3J **81***
(off Malvern Rd.)
SE16 . . . . *5H **103***
(off Stubbs Dr.)
Blakeden Dr. KT10: Clay 6A **162**
Blake Gdns. SW6 . . . . 1K **117**
Blake Hall Cres. E11 . . . . 1J **69**
Blake Hall Rd. E11 . . . . 7J **51**
Blakehall Rd. SM5: Cars 6D **166**
Blake Ho. *E14* *2C **104***
(off Admirals Way)
SE1 . . . . 1J **19** (3A **102**)
SE8 . . . . *6C **104***
(off New King St.)
Blake M. TW9: Kew 1G **115**
Blakemore Gdns. SW13 . . . . 6D **98**
Blakemore Rd. CR7: Thor H 5K **155**
SW16 . . . . 3J **137**
Blakemore Way DA17: Belv 3E **108**
Blakeney Av. BR3: Beck 1B **158**
Blakeney Cl. E8 . . . . 5G **67**
N20 . . . . 1F **31**
NW1 . . . . 7H **65**
Blakeney Rd. BR3: Beck 7B **140**
Blakenham Rd. SW17 . . . . 4D **136**
Blaker Ct. SE7 . . . . 7A **106**
(not continuous)
Blake Rd. CR0: C'don 2E **168**
CR4: Mitc 3C **154**
E16 . . . . 4H **87**
N11 . . . . 7B **32**
Blaker Rd. E15 . . . . 2E **86**
Blakes Av. KT3: N Mald 5B **152**
Blake's Grn. BR4: W W'ck 1E **170**
Blakes La. KT3: N Mald 5B **152**
Blakesley Av. W5 . . . . 6C **78**
Blakesley Ho. *E12* *3E **70***
(off Grantham Rd.)
Blakesley Wlk. SW20 . . . . 2H **153**
Blake's Rd. SE15 . . . . 7E **102**
Blakes Ter. KT3: N Mald 5C **152**
Blakesware Gdns. N9 . . . . 7J **23**
Blake Twr. *EC2* *5C **8***
(off Fann St.)
Blakewood Cl. TW13: Hanw 4A **130**
Blakewood Ct. *SE20* *7H **139***
(off Anerley Pk.)
Blanchard Cl. SE9 . . . . 3C **142**
Blanchard Ho. *TW1: Twick* *6D **114***
(off Clevedon Rd.)
Blanchard Way E8 . . . . 6G **67**
Blanch Cl. SE15 . . . . 7J **103**
Blanchedowne SE5 . . . . 4D **120**
Blanche St. E16 . . . . 4H **87**
Blanchland Rd. SM4: Mord 5K **153**
Blandfield Rd. SW12 . . . . 7E **118**
Blandford Av. BR3: Beck 2A **158**
TW2: Whitt 1F **131**
Blandford Cl. CR0: Bedd 3J **167**
N2 . . . . 4A **46**
RM7: Mawney 4H **55**
Blandford Ct. *N1* *7E **66***
(off St Peter's Way)
NW6 . . . . 7F **63**
Blandford Cres. E4 . . . . 7K **25**
Blandford Ho. *SW8* *7K **101***
(off Richborne Ter.)
Blandford Rd. BR3: Beck 2J **157**
TW11: Tedd 5H **131**
UB2: S'hall 4E **94**
W4 . . . . 3A **98**
W5 . . . . 2D **96**
Blandford Sq. NW1 . . . . 4D **4** (4C **82**)
Blandford St. W1 . . . . 7F **5** (6D **82**)
Blandford Waye UB4: Yead 6A **76**
Bland Ho. SE11 . . . . 5H **19**
Bland St. SE9 . . . . 4B **124**
Blaney Cres. E6 . . . . 3F **89**
Blanmerle Rd. SE9 . . . . 1F **143**
Blann Cl. SE9 . . . . 6B **124**
Blantyre St. SW10 . . . . 7B **100**
Blantyre Twr. *SW10* *7B **100***
(off Blantyre St.)
Blantyre Wlk. *SW10* *7B **100***
(off Worlds End Est.)
Blashford *NW3* *7D **64***
(off Adelaide Rd.)
Blashford St. SE13 . . . . 7F **123**
Blashill Ct. *E14* *7E **86***
(off Bullivant St.)
Blasker Wlk. E14 . . . . 5D **104**
Blaven Path E16 . . . . 4H **87**
Blawith Rd. HA1: Harr 4J **41**
Blaxland Ho. *W12* *7D **80***
(off White City Est.)
Blaydon Cl. HA4: Ruis 7G **39**
N17 . . . . 7C **34**
Blaydon Ct. UB5: N'olt 6E **58**
Blaydon Wlk. N17 . . . . 7C **34**
Blazer Ct. NW8 . . . . 2B **4**
Bleak Hill La. SE18 . . . . 6K **107**
Bleak Ho. La. *W4* *5K **97***
(off Chiswick High Rd.)
Blean Gro. SE20 . . . . 7J **139**
Bleasdale Av. UB6: G'frd 2A **78**
Blechynden Ho. *W10* *6F **81***
(off Kingsdown Cl.)
Blechynden St. W10 . . . . 7F **81**
Bledlow Cl. NW8 . . . . 4B **4** (4B **82**)
SE28 . . . . 7C **90**
Bledlow Ri. UB6: G'frd 2G **77**
Bleeding Heart Yd. EC1 . . . . 6K **7**
Blegborough Rd. SW16 . . . . 6G **137**
Blemundsbury *WC1* *5G **7***
(off Dombey St.)
BLENDON 6D 126
Blendon Dr. DA5: Bexl 6D **126**
Blendon Path BR1: Brom 7H **141**
Blendon Rd. DA5: Bexl 6D **126**
Blendon Row *SE17* *4D **102***
(off Orb St.)
Blendon Ter. SE18 . . . . 5G **107**

Blendworth Point SW15 1D **134**
Blenheim Av. IG2: Ilf 6E **52**
Blenheim Bus. Cen. *CR4: Mitc* *2D* ***154***
(off London Rd.)
Blenheim Cen., The TW3: Houn 3F **113**
Blenheim Cl. N21 1H **33**
RM7: Mawney 4J **55**
SE12 1K **141**
SM6: Wall 7G **167**
SW20 3E **152**
UB6: G'frd 2H **77**
Blenheim Ct. BR2: Brom 4H **159**
DA14: Sidc 3H **143**
HA3: Kenton 6A **42**
IG8: Wfd G 7E **36**
N7 6J **65**
N19 2J **65**
RM13: Rain *2K* ***91***
(off Lowen Rd.)
SE10 *5J* ***105***
(off Denham St.)
SE16 *1K* ***103***
(off King & Queen Wharf)
SM2: Sutt 6A **166**
Blenheim Cres. CR2: S Croy 7C **168**
HA4: Ruis 2F **57**
W11 7G **81**
Blenheim Dr. DA16: Well 1K **125**
Blenheim Gdns. HA9: Wemb 3E **60**
KT2: King T 7H **133**
NW2 6E **62**
SM6: Wall 6G **167**
SW2 6K **119**
Blenheim Gro. SE15 2G **121**
Blenheim Ho. *E16* *1K* ***105***
(off Constable Av.)
SE18 3G **107**
SW3 *6D* ***16***
(off Kings Rd.)
TW3: Houn 3E **112**
Blenheim Pde. UB10: Hil 4D **74**
Blenheim Pk. Rd. CR2: S Croy 7C **168**
Blenheim Pas. NW8 2A **82**
Blenheim Pl. TW11: Tedd 5K **131**
Blenheim Ri. N15 4F **49**
Blenheim Rd. BR1: Brom 4C **160**
DA15: Sidc 1C **144**
E6 3B **88**
E15 4G **69**
E17 3K **49**
EN5: Barn 3A **20**
HA2: Harr 6F **41**
NW8 2A **82**
SE20 7J **139**
SM1: Sutt 3J **165**
SW20 3E **152**
UB5: N'olt 6F **59**
W4 3A **98**
Blenheim Shop. Cen. SE20 7J **139**
Blenheim St. W1 1J **11** (6F **83**)
Blenheim Ter. NW8 2A **82**
Blenheim Twr. *SE14* *7A* ***104***
(off Batavia Rd.)
Blenheim Way TW7: Isle 1A **114**
Blenkarne Rd. SW11 6D **118**
Bleriot Rd. TW5: Hest 7A **94**
Blessbury Rd. HA8: Edg 1J **43**
Blessington Cl. SE13 3F **123**
Blessington Rd. SE13 3F **123**
Blessing Way IG11: Bark 3C **90**
Bletchingley Cl. CR7: Thor H 4B **156**
Bletchley Ct. *HA7: Stan* *7K* ***27***
(off Hitchin Way)
N1 1E **8**
Bletchley St. N1 1D **8** (2D **84**)
Bletchmore Cl. UB3: Harl 5F **93**
Bletsoe Wlk. N1 2C **84**
Blewbury Ho. SE2 2C **108**
(not continuous)
Blick Ho. *SE16* *3J* ***103***
(off Neptune St.)
Blincoe Cl. SW19 2F **135**
Bliss Cres. SE13 2D **122**
Blissett St. SE10 1E **122**
Bliss Ho. EN1: Enf 1B **24**
Bliss M. W10 3G **81**
Blisworth Cl. UB4: Yead 4C **76**
Blisworth Ho. *E2* *1G* ***85***
(off Whiston Rd.)
Blithbury Rd. RM9: Dag 6B **72**
Blithdale Rd. SE2 4A **108**
Blithehale Ct. *E2* *3H* ***85***
(off Withan St.)
Blithfield St. W8 3K **99**
Blockley Rd.
HA0: Wemb 2B **60**
Block Wharf *E14* *2C* ***104***
(off Cuba St.)
Bloemfontein Av. W12 1D **98**
Bloemfontein Rd. W12 7D **80**
Bloemfontein Way W12 1D **98**
Blomfield Ct. *W9* *3A* ***4***
(off Maida Vale)
Blomfield Mans. *W12* *1E* ***98***
(off Stanlake Rd.)
Blomfield Rd. W9 4A **4** (5K **81**)
Blomfield St. EC2 6F **9** (5D **84**)
Blomfield Vs. W2 5K **81**
Blomville Rd. RM8: Dag 3E **72**
Blondell Cl. UB7: Harm 2E **174**
Blondel St. SW11 2E **118**
Blondin Av. W5 4C **96**
Blondin Pk. & Nature Area 4B **96**
Blondin St. E3 2C **86**
Blondin Way SE16 2A **104**
Bloomberg Arc. EC4 6D **84**
Bloomberg Ct. *SW1* *4C* ***18***
(off Vauxhall Bri. Rd.)
Bloomburg St. SW1 4B **18** (4H **101**)
Bloomfield Ct. *E10* *3D* ***68***
(off Brisbane Rd.)
N6 6E **46**
Bloomfield Cres. IG2: Ilf 6F **53**
Bloomfield Ho. *E1* *5G* ***85***
(off Old Montague St.)
Bloomfield Pl. W1 2K **11**
Bloomfield Rd. BR2: Brom 5B **160**
KT1: King T 4E **150**
N6 6E **46**
SE18 6F **107**
Bloomfield Ter. SW1 5H **17** (5E **100**)
Bloom Gro. SE27 3B **138**
Bloomhall Rd. SE19 5D **138**
Bloom Pk. Rd. SW6 7H **99**
BLOOMSBURY 5E **6** (5J **83**)
Bloomsbury Cl. NW7 7H **29**
W5 7F **79**
Bloomsbury Ct. HA5: Pinn 3D **40**
TW5: Cran 1K **111**
WC1 6F **7**
Bloomsbury Ho. SW4 6H **119**
Bloomsbury Mans. *BR1: Brom* *1K* ***159***
(off Widmore Rd.)
Bloomsbury M. IG8: Wfd G 6H **37**
Bloomsbury Pl. SW18 5A **118**
WC1 5F **7** (5J **83**)
Bloomsbury Sq. WC1 6F **7** (5J **83**)
Bloomsbury St. WC1 6D **6** (5H **83**)
Bloomsbury Theatre 3C **6**
Bloomsbury Way WC1 6E **6** (5J **83**)
Blore Cl. SW8 1H **119**
Blore Ct. W1 1C **12**
Blore Ho. *SW10* *7K* ***99***
(off Coleridge Gdns.)
Blossom Av. HA2: Harr 2F **59**
Blossom Cl. CR2: S Croy 5F **169**
RM9: Dag 1F **91**
W5 2E **96**
Blossom Dr. BR6: Orp 2K **173**
Blossom La. EN2: Enf 1H **23**
Blossom Pl. SE28 3G **107**
Blossom St. E1 4H **9** (4E **84**)
Blossom Way UB7: W Dray 4C **92**
UB10: Hil 7B **56**
Blossom Waye TW5: Hest 6C **94**
Blount M. UB10: Uxb 2A **74**
Blount St. E14 6A **86**
Bloxam Gdns. SE9 5C **124**
Bloxhall Rd. E10 1B **68**
Bloxham Cres. TW12: Hamp 7D **130**
Bloxworth Cl. SM6: Wall 3G **167**
Blucher Rd. SE5 7C **102**
Blue Anchor All. TW9: Rich 4E **114**
Blue Anchor La. SE16 4G **103**
Blue Anchor Yd. E1 2K **15** (7G **85**)
Blue Ball Yd. SW1 5A **12** (1G **101**)
Bluebell Apartments *N4* *1C* ***66***
(off Swan La.)
Bluebell Av. E12 5B **70**
Bluebell Cl. BR6: Farnb 2G **173**
E9 1J **85**
RM7: Rush G 2K **73**
SE26 4F **139**
SM6: Wall 1F **167**
UB5: N'olt 6D **58**
Bluebell Ct. *NW9* *1A* ***44***
(off Heybourne Cres.)
Bluebell Ho. *SE16* *2A* ***104***
(off Bondin Way)
Bluebell Ter. UB7: W Dray 2B **92**
Bluebell Way IG1: Ilf 6F **71**
Blueberry Cl. IG8: Wfd G 6D **36**
Bluebird Cl. SW20 2E **152**
Bluebird Ho. IG11: Bark 3K **89**
Bluebird La. RM10: Dag 7G **73**
Bluebird Way SE28 2H **107**
Blue Bldg. *SE10* *5H* ***105***
(off Glenforth St.)
Blue Ct. *N1* *1D* ***84***
(off Sherborne St.)
Blue Elephant Theatre *7C* ***102***
(off Bethwin Rd.)
Bluefield Cl. TW12: Hamp 5E **130**
Blue Fin Bldg. SE1 4B **14**
Bluegate M. E1 7H **85**
Bluegates KT17: Ewe 7C **164**
Bluehouse Rd. E4 2B **36**
Blue Lion Pl. SE1 7G **15** (3E **102**)
Blueprint Apartments *SW12* *7F* ***119***
(off Balham Gro.)
Blue Riband Ind. Est. CR0: C'don 2B **168**
Blues St. E8 6F **67**
Blue Water SW18 4K **117**
Blumenthal Cl. TW7: Isle 7H **95**
Blundell Cl. E8 5G **67**
Blundell Rd. HA8: Edg 1K **43**
Blundell St. N7 7J **65**
Blunden Cl. RM8: Dag 1C **72**
Blunden Ct. *SW6* *7J* ***99***
(off Farm La.)
Blunt Rd. CR2: S Croy 5D **168**
Blunts Av. UB7: Sip 7C **92**
Blunts Rd. SE9 5E **124**
Blurton Rd. E5 4J **67**
Blydon Ct. *N21* *5E* ***22***
(off Chaseville Pk. Rd.)
Blyth Cl. E14 4F **105**
TW1: Twick 6K **113**
Blyth Ct. *BR1: Brom* *1H* ***159***
(off Blyth Rd.)
Blythe Cl. SE6 7B **122**
BLYTHE HILL 7B **122**
Blythe Hill BR5: St P 1K **161**
SE6 7B **122**
Blythe Hill La. SE6 7B **122**
Blythe Hill Pl. SE23 7A **122**
Blythe Ho. SE11 7J **19** (6A **102**)
Blythe M. W14 3F **99**
Blythendale Ho. *E2* *2G* ***85***
(off Mansford St.)
Blythe Rd. W14 3F **99**
Blythe St. E2 3H **85**
Blytheswood Pl. SW16 4K **137**
Blythe Va. SE6 1B **140**
Blyth Hill Pl. *SE23* *7A* ***122***
(off Brockley Pk.)
Blyth Ho. DA8: Erith 5K **109**
Blyth Rd. BR1: Brom 1H **159**
E17 7B **50**
SE28 7C **90**
UB3: Hayes 2G **93**
Blyth's Wharf E14 7A **86**
Blythswood Rd. IG3: Ilf 1A **72**
Blyth Wood Pk. BR1: Brom 1H **159**
Blythwood Rd. HA5: Pinn 1B **40**
N4 7J **47**
Boades M. NW3 4B **64**
Boadicea St. N1 1K **83**
Boakes Cl. NW9 4J **43**
Boardman Av. E4 5J **25**
Boardman Cl. EN5: Barn 5B **20**
Boardwalk Pl. E14 1E **104**
Boarley Ho. *SE17* *4E* ***102***
(off Massinger St.)
Boars Head Yd. TW8: Bford 7D **96**
Boatemah Wlk. *SW9* *2A* ***120***
(off Peckford Pl.)
Boathouse, The E14 6C **86**
Boathouse Cen., The *W10* *4F* ***81***
(off Canal Cl.)
Boathouse Wlk. SE15 7F **103**
(not continuous)
Boat La. E2 1F **85**
Boat Lifter Way SE16 4A **104**
Boat Quay E16 7A **88**
Boatyard Apartments E14 5D **104**
Bob Anker Cl. E13 3J **87**
Bobbin Cl. SW4 3G **119**
Bobby Moore Way IG11: Bark 1G **89**
N10 7J **31**
Bob Hope Theatre, The 6D **124**
Bob Marley Way SE24 4A **120**
Bockhampton Rd. KT2: King T 7F **133**
Bocking St. E8 1H **85**
Boddicott Cl. SW19 2G **135**
Boddington Gdns. W3 2G **97**
Boddington Ho. *SE14* *1J* ***121***
(off Pomeroy St.)
SW13 *6D* ***98***
(off Wyatt Dr.)
Bodeney Ho. *SE5* *1E* ***120***
(off Peckham Rd.)
Boden Ho. *E1* *5K* ***9***
(off Woodseer St.)
Bodiam Cl. EN1: Enf 2K **23**
Bodiam Rd. SW16 7H **137**
Bodiam Way NW10 3F **79**
Bodicea M. TW4: Houn 6D **112**
Bodington Ct. W12 2F **99**
Bodium Ct. *E17* *1B* ***50***
(off Thornbury Way)
Bodleian Ho. SE20 1G **157**
Bodley Cl. KT3: N Mald 5A **152**
Bodley Mnr. Way SW2 7A **120**
Bodley Rd. KT3: N Mald 6K **151**
Bodmin Cl. HA2: Harr 3D **58**
Bodmin Gro. SM4: Mord 5K **153**
Bodmin St. SW18 1J **135**
Bodnant Gdns. SW20 3C **152**
Bodney Rd. E8 5H **67**
Boeing Way UB2: S'hall 3K **93**
Boevey Path DA17: Belv 5F **109**
Bogart Ct. *E14* *7C* ***86***
(off Premiere Pl.)
Bogey La. BR6: Downe 7E **172**
Bognor Rd.
DA16: Well 1D **126**
Bohemia Pl. E8 6J **67**
Bohn Rd. E1 5A **86**
Bohun Gro. EN4: E Barn 6H **21**
Boileau Pde. *W5* *6F* ***79***
(off Boileau Rd.)
Boileau Rd. SW13 7C **98**
W5 6F **79**

Boisseau Ho. *E1* 5J 85
(off Stepney Way)
Bolanachi Bldg. SE16 . . . . 3F 103
Bolander Gro. Nth. *SW6* 6J 99
(off Seagrave Rd.)
Bolander Gro. Sth. *SW6* 6J 99
(off Seagrave Rd.)
Bolden St. SE8 . . . . 2D 122
Boldero Pl. NW8 . . . . 4C 4
Bolderwood Way
BR4: W W'ck 2D 170
Boldmere Rd. HA5: Eastc 7A 40
Boleyn Av. EN1: Enf 1C 24
Boleyn Cl. E17 . . . . 4C 50
Boleyn Ct. IG9: Buck H 1D 36
KT8: E Mos 4H 149
(off Bridge Rd.)
Boleyn Dr. HA4: Ruis 2B 58
KT8: W Mole 3D 148
Boleyn Gdns. BR4: W W'ck 2D 170
RM10: Dag 7J 73
Boleyn Gro. BR4: W W'ck 2E 170
Boleyn Ho. *E16* 1J 105
(off Southey M.)
Boleyn Rd. E6 . . . . 2B 88
E7 . . . . 7J 69
N16 . . . . 5E 66
Boleyn Way EN5: New Bar 3F 21
Bolina Rd. SE16 . . . . 5J 103
Bolingbroke Cl. EN4: Cockf 3J 21
Bolingbroke Gro. SW11 . . . . 4C 118
Bolingbroke Rd. W14 . . . . 3F 99
Bolingbroke Wlk. SW11 . . . . 1B 118
Bolingbroke Way UB3: Hayes 1F 93
Bolliger Ct. NW10 . . . . 4J 79
Bollinder Pl. EC1 . . . . 1C 8 (3C 84)
Bollo Bri. Rd. W3 . . . . 3H 97
Bollo La. W3 . . . . 2H 97
W4 . . . . 4J 97
Bolney Ga. SW7 . . . . 7C 10 (2C 100)
Bolney St. SW8 . . . . 7K 101
Bolney Way TW13: Hanw 3C 130
Bolsover St. W1 . . . . 4K 5 (4F 83)
Bolstead Rd. CR4: Mitc 1F 155
Bolster Gro. N22 . . . . 7C 32
Bolt Ct. EC4 . . . . 6A 84
Bolt Ho. *N1* 1E 84
(off Phillipp St.)
Boltmore Cl. NW4 . . . . 3F 45
Bolton Cl. KT9: Chess 6D 162
SE20 . . . . 2G 157
Bolton Cres. SE5 . . . . 7B 102
SE11 . . . . 7A 102
Bolton Dr. SM4: Mord 7A 154
Bolton Gdns. BR1: Brom 6H 141
NW10 . . . . 2F 81
SW5 . . . . 5K 99
TW11: Tedd 6A 132
Bolton Gdns. M. SW10 . . . . 5A 100
Bolton Ho. *SE10* 5G 105
(off Trafalgar Rd.)
SE11 . . . . 4B 102
(off George Mathers Rd.)
Bolton Pl. *NW8* 1K 81
(off Bolton Rd.)
Bolton Rd. E15 . . . . 6H 69
HA1: Harr 4G 41
KT9: Chess 6D 162
N18 . . . . 5A 34
NW8 . . . . 1K 81
NW10 . . . . 1A 80
W4 . . . . 7J 97
Boltons, The HA0: Wemb 4K 59
IG8: Wfd G 4D 36
SW10 . . . . 5A 100
Boltons Ct. *SW5* 5K 99
(off Old Brompton Rd.)
Bolton's La. UB3: Harl 1E 110
Boltons Pl. SW5 . . . . 5A 100
Bolton St. W1 . . . . 4K 11 (1F 101)
Bolton Studios SW10 . . . . 5A 100
Bolton Wlk. *N7* 2K 65
(off Durham Rd.)
Bombay Ct. *SE16* 2J 103
(off St Marychurch St.)
Bombay St. SE16 . . . . 4H 103
Bomer Cl. UB7: Sip 7C 92
Bomore Rd. W11 . . . . 7G 81
Bonar Pl. BR7: Chst 7C 142
Bonar Rd. SE15 . . . . 7G 103
Bonchester Cl. BR7: Chst 7E 142
Bonchurch Cl. SM2: Sutt 7K 165
Bonchurch Rd. W10 . . . . 5G 81
W13 . . . . 1B 96
Bond Cl. UB7: Yiew 6B 74
Bond Ct. EC4 . . . . 2E 14 (7D 84)
Bondfield Av. UB4: Yead 3J 75
Bondfield Rd. E6 . . . . 5D 88
Bond Gdns. SM6: Wall 4G 167
Bond Ho. *NW6* 2H 81
(off Rupert Rd.)
SE14 . . . . 7A 104
(off Goodwood Rd.)
TW8: Bford 5D 96
Bonding Yd. Wlk. SE16 . . . . 3A 104
Bond Rd. CR4: Mitc 2C 154
KT6: Surb 2F 163
Bond St. E15 . . . . 5G 69
W4 . . . . 4K 97
W5 . . . . 7D 78
Bondway SW8 . . . . 7F 19 (6J 101)
Bonesgate Open Space Local Nature Reserve
. . . . 6G 163
Boneta Rd. SE18 . . . . 3D 106
Bonfield Rd. SE13 . . . . 4E 122
Bonham Cl. DA17: Belv 5F 109
Bonham Gdns. RM8: Dag 2D 72
Bonham Ga. *KT12: Walt T* 7H 147
(off New Zealand Av.)
Bonham Ho. *W11* 1H 99
(off Boyne Ter. M.)
Bonham Rd. RM8: Dag 2D 72
SW2 . . . . 5K 119
Bonheur Rd. W4 . . . . 2K 97
Bonhill St. EC2 . . . . 4F 9 (4D 84)
Boniface Gdns. HA3: Hrw W 7A 26
Boniface Rd. UB10: Ick 3D 56
Boniface Wlk. HA3: Hrw W 7A 26
Bonington Ho. EN1: Enf 5B 24
Bonita M. SE4 . . . . 3K 121
Bon Marche Ter. M. *SE27* 4E 138
(off Gypsy Rd.)
Bonner Hill Rd. KT1: King T 2F 151
Bonner Rd. E2 . . . . 2J 85
Bonnersfield Cl. HA1: Harr 6K 41
Bonnersfield La. HA1: Harr 6K 41
(not continuous)
Bonner St. E2 . . . . 2J 85
Bonneville Gdns. SW4 . . . . 6G 119
Bonnington Ct. *UB5: N'olt* 2B 76
(off Gallery Gdns.)
Bonnington Ho. N1 . . . . 2K 83
Bonnington Sq. SW8 . . . . 7G 19 (6K 101)
Bonny St. NW1 . . . . 7G 65
Bonser Rd. TW1: Twick 2K 131
Bonsor Ho. SW8 . . . . 1G 119
Bonsor St. SE5 . . . . 7E 102
Bonville Gdns. NW4 . . . . 4D 44
Bonville Rd. BR1: Brom 5H 141
Bookbinders Cott. Homes N20 . . . . 3J 31
Bookbinders Ct. *E1* 4H 85
(off Cudworth St.)
Booker Cl. E14 . . . . 5B 86
Booker Rd. N18 . . . . 5B 34
Bookham Ct. CR4: Mitc 3B 154
Book Ho. N1 . . . . 1C 8 (2C 84)
Boone Ct. N9 . . . . 3D 34
Boones Rd. SE13 . . . . 4G 123
Boone St. SE13 . . . . 4G 123
Boord St. SE10 . . . . 3G 105
Boothby Ct. E4 . . . . 3K 35
Boothby Rd. N19 . . . . 2H 65
Booth Cl. E9 . . . . 1H 85
SE28 . . . . 1B 108
Booth Ct. SE13 . . . . 3D 122
Booth Dr. TW18: Staines 6A 128
Booth Ho. *TW8: Bford* 7C 96
(off High St.)
Booth La. EC4 . . . . 2C 14
Boothman Ho.
HA3: Kenton 3D 42
Booth Rd. CR0: C'don 2B 168
E16 . . . . 2A 106
NW9 . . . . 2K 43
Booth's Pl. W1 . . . . 6B 6 (5G 83)
Boot Pde. *HA8: Edg* 6B 28
(off High St.)
Boot St. N1 . . . . 2G 9 (3E 84)
Bordars Rd. W7 . . . . 5J 77
Bordars Wlk. W7 . . . . 5J 77
Bordeaux Ho. *E15* 5G 69
(off Luxembourg M.)
Borden Av. EN1: Enf 6J 23
Border Cres. SE26 . . . . 5H 139
Border Gdns. CR0: C'don 4D 170
Bordergate CR4: Mitc 1D 154
Border Rd. SE26 . . . . 5H 139
Bordesley Rd. SM4: Mord 5K 153
Bordeston Ct. *TW8: Bford* 7C 96
(off The Ham)
Bordon Wlk. SW15 . . . . 7C 116
Boreas Wlk. N1 . . . . 1B 8
Boreham Av. E16 . . . . 6J 87
Boreham Cl. E11 . . . . 1E 68
Boreham Rd. N22 . . . . 2C 48
Boreman Ho. *SE10* 6E 104
(off Thames St.)
Borgard Rd. SE18 . . . . 4D 106
Borkwood Pk. BR6: Orp 4K 173
Borkwood Way BR6: Orp 4J 173
Borland Rd. SE15 . . . . 4J 121
TW11: Tedd 7B 132
Borley Ct. TW19: Stanw 1A 128
Borneo St. SW15 . . . . 3E 116
BOROUGH, THE 7D 14 (2D 102)
Borough High St. SE1 . . . . 7D 14 (2C 102)
Borough Hill CR0: Wadd 3B 168
Borough Mkt. SE1 . . . . 5E 14
Borough Rd. CR4: Mitc 2C 154
KT2: King T 1G 151
SE1 . . . . 7B 14 (3B 102)
TW7: Isle 1J 113
Borough Sports Ground 4J 165
Borough Sq. SE1 . . . . 7C 14
Borrett Cl. SE17 . . . . 5C 102
Borrodaile Rd. SW18 . . . . 6K 117
Borrowdale *NW1* 2A 6
(off Robert St.)
Borrowdale Av. HA3: W'stone 2A 42
Borrowdale Cl. IG4: Ilf 4C 52
N2 . . . . 2A 46
Borrowdale Ct. EN2: Enf 1H 23
Borthwick M. E15 . . . . 4G 69
Borthwick Rd. E15 . . . . 4G 69
NW9 . . . . 6B 44
Borthwick St. SE8 . . . . 5C 104
Borwick Av. E17 . . . . 3B 50
Bosanquet Cl. UB8: Cowl 4A 74
Bosbury Rd. SE6 . . . . 3E 140
Boscastle Rd. NW5 . . . . 3F 65
Boscobel Cl.
BR1: Brom 2D 160
Boscobel Ho. E8 . . . . 6H 67
Boscobel Pl.
SW1 . . . . 3H 17 (4E 100)
Boscobel St. NW8 . . . . 4B 4 (4B 82)
Bosco Cl. BR6: Orp 4K 173
Boscombe Av. E10 . . . . 7F 51
Boscombe Cir. NW9 . . . . 1K 43
Boscombe Cl. E5 . . . . 5A 68
Boscombe Gdns. SW16 . . . . 6J 137
Boscombe Ho. *CR0: C'don* 1D 168
(off Sydenham Rd.)
Boscombe Rd. KT4: Wor Pk 1E 164
SW17 . . . . 6E 136
SW19 . . . . 1K 153
W12 . . . . 1C 98
Bose Cl. N3 . . . . 1G 45
Bosgrove E4 . . . . 2K 35
Boss Ho. *SE1* 6J 15
(off Boss St.)
Boss St. SE1 . . . . 6J 15 (2F 103)
Bostall Hill SE2 . . . . 5A 108
Bostall La. SE2 . . . . 4B 108
Bostall Mnr. Way SE2 . . . . 4B 108
Bostall Pk. Av. DA7: Bex 7E 108
Bostall Rd. BR5: St P 7B 144
Bostock Ho. TW5: Hest 6E 94
Boston Bus. Pk. W7 . . . . 3J 95
Boston Ct. SE25 . . . . 4F 157
SM2: Sutt 7A 166
Boston Gdns. TW8: Bford 4A 96
W4 . . . . 6A 98
W7 . . . . 4A 96
Boston Gro. HA4: Ruis 6E 38
Boston Ho. *SW5* 4K 99
(off Collingham Rd.)
BOSTON MANOR 4A 96
Boston Manor House 5B 96
Boston Mnr. Rd. TW8: Bford 4B 96
Boston Pde. W7 . . . . 3A 96
Boston Pk. Rd. TW8: Bford 5C 96
Boston Pl. NW1 . . . . 4E 4 (4D 82)
Boston Rd. CR0: C'don 6K 155
E6 . . . . 3C 88
E17 . . . . 6C 50
HA8: Edg 7D 28
W7 . . . . 1J 95
Bostonthorpe Rd. W7 . . . . 2J 95
Boston Va. W7 . . . . 4A 96
Bosun Cl. E14 . . . . 2C 104
Boswell Ct. *KT2: King T* 1F 151
(off Clifton Rd.)
NW9 . . . . 2A 44
(off Charcot Rd.)
W14 . . . . 3F 99
(off Blythe Rd.)
WC1 . . . . 5F 7 (5J 83)
Boswell Ho. *WC1* 5F 7
(off Boswell St.)
Boswell Path UB3: Harl 4H 93
Boswell Rd. CR7: Thor H 4C 156
Boswell St. WC1 . . . . 5F 7 (5J 83)
Boswood Ct. TW3: Houn 3D 112
Bosworth Cl. E17 . . . . 1B 50
Bosworth Ho. *W10* 4G 81
(off Bosworth Rd.)
Bosworth Rd. EN5: New Bar 3D 20
N11 . . . . 6C 32
RM10: Dag 3G 73
W10 . . . . 4G 81
Botany Bay La. BR7: Chst 3G 161
Botany Cl. EN4: E Barn 4H 21
Boteley Cl. E4 . . . . 2A 36
Botham Cl. HA8: Edg 7D 28
Botha Rd. E13 . . . . 5K 87
Bothwell Cl. E16 . . . . 5H 87
Bothwell St. W6 . . . . 6F 99
Botolph All. EC3 . . . . 2G 15
Botolph La. EC3 . . . . 3G 15 (7E 84)
Botsford Rd. SW20 . . . . 2G 153
Botts M. W2 . . . . 6J 81
Botwell Comn. Rd. UB3: Hayes 7F 75
Botwell Cres. UB3: Hayes 6G 75
Botwell Green Sports & Leisure Cen.
. . . . 1H 93
Botwell La. UB3: Hayes 7G 75
Boucher Cl. TW11: Tedd 5K 131
Bouchier Ho. *N2* 2B 46
(off The Grange)
Boughton Av. BR2: Hayes 7H 159
Boughton Ho. *SE1* 6E 14
(off Tennis St.)
Boughton Rd. SE28 . . . . 3J 107

Boulcott St.—Boyle St.

Boulcott St. E1 . . . . 6K **85**
Boulevard, The IG8: Wfd G 6K **37**
SW6 . . . . 1A **118**
SW17 . . . . 2E **136**
SW18 . . . . 4K **117**
Boulevard Dr. NW9 . . . . 2B **44**
Boulevard Walkway *E1* *1K 15*
(off Piazza Wlk.)
Boulogne Ho. *SE1* *7J 15*
(St Saviour's Est.)
Boulogne Rd. CR0: C'don 6C **156**
Boulter Cl. BR1: Brom 3E **160**
Boulter Ho. *SE14* *1J 121*
(off Kender St.)
Boulton Ho. TW8: Bford 5E **96**
Boulton Rd. RM8: Dag 2E **72**
Boultwood Rd. E6 . . . . 6D **88**
Bounces La. N9 . . . . 2C **34**
Bounces Rd. N9 . . . . 2C **34**
Boundaries Rd. SW12 . . . . 2D **136**
TW13: Felt 1A **130**
Boundary Av. E17 . . . . 7B **50**
Boundary Bus. Ct. CR4: Mitc 3B **154**
Boundary Cl. EN5: Barn 1C **20**
IG3: Ilf 4J **71**
KT1: King T 3H **151**
SE20 . . . . 2G **157**
UB2: S'hall 5E **94**
Boundary Ct. *N18* *6A 34*
(off Snells Pk.)
Boundary Ho. SE5 . . . . 7C **102**
W11 . . . . *1F 99*
(off Queensdale Cres.)
Boundary La. E13 . . . . 3B **88**
SE17 . . . . 6C **102**
Boundary Pas. E2 . . . . 3J **9** (4F **85**)
Boundary Rd. DA15: Sidc 5J **125**
E13 . . . . 2A **88**
E17 . . . . 7B **50**
HA5: Eastc 7B **40**
HA9: Wemb 3E **60**
IG11: Bark 2G **89**
(The Clarksons)
IG11: Bark 1H **89**
(King Edwards Rd.)
N2 . . . . 1B **46**
N9 . . . . 6D **24**
N22 . . . . 3B **48**
NW8 . . . . 1K **81**
SM5: Cars 6F **167**
SM6: Wall 6F **167**
SW19 . . . . 6B **136**
Boundary Row SE1 . . . . 6A **14** (2B **102**)
Boundary St. E2 . . . . 2J **9** (3F **85**)
Boundary Way CR0: Addtn 5C **170**
Boundfield Rd. SE6 . . . . 3G **141**
BOUNDS GREEN 6C 32
Bounds Grn. Ct. *N11* *6C 32*
(off Bounds Grn. Rd.)
Bounds Grn. Ind. Est. N11 . . . . 6B **32**
Bounds Grn. Rd. N11 . . . . 6B **32**
N22 . . . . 6B **32**
Bourbon Ho. SE6 . . . . 5E **140**
Bourbon La. W12 . . . . 1F **99**
Bourbon Rd. SW9 . . . . 1A **120**
Bourchier St. W1 . . . . 2C **12** (7H **83**)
Bourdon Pl. W1 . . . . 2K **11**
Bourdon Rd. SE20 . . . . 2J **157**
Bourdon St. W1 . . . . 3J **11** (7F **83**)
Bourke Cl. NW10 . . . . 6A **62**
SW4 . . . . 6J **119**
Bourlet Cl. W1 . . . . 6A **6** (5G **83**)
Bourn Av. EN4: E Barn 5G **21**
N15 . . . . 4D **48**
UB8: Hil 4C **74**
Bournbrook Rd. SE3 . . . . 3B **124**
Bourne, The N14 . . . . 1C **32**
Bourne Av. HA4: Ruis 5A **58**
N14 . . . . 2D **32**
UB3: Harl 3E **92**
Bournebrook Gro. RM7: Rush G 6K **55**
Bourne Cir. UB3: Harl 3E **92**
Bourne Cl. TW7: Isle 3J **113**
Bourne Ct. HA4: Ruis 5K **57**
IG8: Wfd G 3B **52**
W4 . . . . 6J **97**
Bourne Dr. CR4: Mitc 2B **154**
Bourne Est. EC1 . . . . 5J **7** (5A **84**)
Bourne Gdns. E4 . . . . 4J **35**
Bourne Hall Mus. 7B **164**
Bourne Hill N13 . . . . 2D **32**
Bourne Hill Cl. N13 . . . . 2E **32**
Bourne Ho. IG9: Buck H 3G **37**
TW15: Ashf 5C **128**
Bourne Ind. Pk. DA1: Cray 5K **127**
Bourne Mead DA5: Bexl 5K **127**
Bournemead Av. UB5: N'olt 2J **75**
Bournemead Cl. UB5: N'olt 3J **75**
Bournemead Way
UB5: N'olt 2K **75**
Bourne M. W1 . . . . 1H **11** (6E **82**)
Bournemouth Cl. SE15 . . . . 2G **121**
Bournemouth Rd. SE15 . . . . 2G **121**
SW19 . . . . 1J **153**
Bourne Pde. DA5: Bexl 7H **127**
Bourne Pl. W4 . . . . 5K **97**
Bourne Rd. BR2: Brom 4B **160**
DA1: Cray 6J **127**
DA5: Bexl, Dart 7H **127**
E7 . . . . 3H **69**
N8 . . . . 6J **47**
Bournes Ho. *N15* *6E 48*
(off Chisley Rd.)
Bourneside Cres. N14 . . . . 1C **32**
Bourneside Gdns. SE6 . . . . 5E **140**
Bourne St. CR0: C'don 2B **168**
SW1 . . . . 4G **17** (4E **100**)
Bourne Ter. W2 . . . . 5K **81**
Bourne Va. BR2: Hayes 1H **171**
Bournevale Rd. SW16 . . . . 4J **137**
Bourne Vw. UB6: G'frd 6K **59**
Bourneville Rd. SE6 . . . . 7C **122**
Bourne Way BR2: Hayes 2H **171**
KT19: Ewe 4J **163**
SM1: Sutt 5H **165**
Bournewood Rd. SE18 . . . . 7A **108**
Bournwell Cl. EN4: Cockf 3J **21**
Bourton Cl. UB3: Hayes 1J **93**
Bousfield Rd. SE14 . . . . 2K **121**
Boutflower Rd. SW11 . . . . 4C **118**
Boutique Hall SE13 . . . . 4E **122**
Bouton Pl. *N1* *7B 66*
(off Waterloo Ter.)
Bouverie Gdns. HA3: Kenton 6D **42**
Bouverie M. N16 . . . . 2E **66**
Bouverie Pl. W2 . . . . 7B **4** (6B **82**)
Bouverie Rd. HA1: Harr 6G **41**
N16 . . . . 2E **66**
Bouverie St. EC4 . . . . 1K **13** (6A **84**)
Bouvier Rd. EN3: Enf W 1D **24**
Boveney Rd. SE23 . . . . 7K **121**
Bovet Ct. *E1* *5A 86*
(off Ocean Est.)
Bovill Rd. SE23 . . . . 7K **121**
Bovingdon Av. HA9: Wemb 6G **61**
Bovingdon Cl. N19 . . . . 2G **65**
Bovingdon La. NW9 . . . . 1A **44**
Bovingdon Rd. SW6 . . . . 1K **117**
Bovril Ct. *SW6* *7K 99*
(off Fulham Rd.)
BOW 3B 86
Bowater Cl. NW9 . . . . 5K **43**
SW2 . . . . 6J **119**
Bowater Gdns. TW16: Sun 2A **148**
Bowater Ho. *EC1* *4C 8*
(off Golden La. Est.)
Bowater Pl. SE3 . . . . 7K **105**
Bowater Rd. HA9: Wemb 3H **61**
SE18 . . . . 3B **106**
Bow Bell Twr. *E3* *1C 86*
(off Pancras Way)
Bow Bri. Est. E3 . . . . 3D **86**
Bow Brook, The *E2* *2K 85*
(off Mace St.)
Bow Chyd. EC4 . . . . 1D **14**
BOW COMMON 5C 86
Bow Comn. La. E3 . . . . 4B **86**
Bow Creek Ecology Pk. 6G **87**
Bowden Cl.
TW14: Bedf 1G **129**
Bowden Ho. *E3* *3D 86*
(off Rainhill Way)
Bowden St. SE11 . . . . 6K **19** (5A **102**)
Bowditch SE8 . . . . 4B **104**
Bowdon Rd. E17 . . . . 7C **50**
Bowen Ct. *SE16* *4J 103*
(off Debnams Rd.)
Bowen Dr. SE21 . . . . 3E **138**
Bowen Rd. HA1: Harr 7G **41**
Bowen St. E14 . . . . 6D **86**
Bower Av. SE10 . . . . 1G **123**
Bower Cl. RM5: Col R 1K **55**
UB5: N'olt 2A **76**
Bower Ct. *E4* *1K 35*
(off The Ridgeway)
Bowerdean St. SW6 . . . . 1K **117**
Bowerden Ct. NW10 . . . . 2D **80**
Bowerman Av. SE14 . . . . 6A **104**
Bowerman Ct. *N19* *2H 65*
(off St John's Way)
Bower St. E1 . . . . 6K **85**
Bowers Wlk. E6 . . . . 6D **88**
Bowery Ct. RM10: Dag 6H **73**
Bowes Cl. DA15: Sidc 6B **126**
Bowe's Ho. IG11: Bark 7F **71**
Bowes-Lyon Hall *E16* *1J 105*
(off Wesley Av.)
BOWES PARK 6D 32
Bowes Rd. N11 . . . . 5B **32**
N13 . . . . 5B **32**
RM8: Dag 4C **72**
W3 . . . . 7A **80**
Bow Exchange *E3* *5D 86*
(off Yeo St.)
Bow Fair *E3* *2C 86*
(off Fairfield Rd.)
Bowfell Rd. W6 . . . . 6E **98**
Bowford Av. DA7: Bex 1E **126**
Bowhill Cl. SW9 . . . . 7A **102**
Bow Ho. *N1* *1E 84*
(off Wilmer Gdns.)
Bowie Cl. SW4 . . . . 7H **119**
BOW INTERCHANGE 2D **86**
Bowland Rd. IG8: Wfd G 6F **37**
SW4 . . . . 4H **119**
Bowland Yd. SW1 . . . . 7F **11**
Bow La. EC4 . . . . 1D **14** (6C **84**)
N12 . . . . 7F **31**
SM4: Mord 6G **153**
Bowlby Ho. *SE4* *4K 121*
(off Frendsbury Rd.)
Bowl Ct. EC2 . . . . 4H **9** (4E **84**)
Bowles Ct. N12 . . . . 7H **31**
Bowles Rd. SE1 . . . . 6G **103**
Bowley Cl. SE19 . . . . 6F **139**
Bowley Ho. SE16 . . . . 3G **103**
Bowley La. SE19 . . . . 5F **139**
Bowline Ct. SE10 . . . . 4G **105**
TW8: Bford 6C **96**
Bowling, The KT12: Walt T 7J **147**
Bowling Cl. UB10: Uxb 1B **74**
Bowling Grn. Cl. SW15 . . . . 7D **116**
Bowling Grn. Ct. HA9: Wemb 2F **61**
Bowling Grn. Ho. *SW10* *7B 100*
(off Riley St.)
Bowling Grn. La. EC1 . . . . 3K **7** (4A **84**)
Bowling Grn. Pl. SE1 . . . . 6E **14** (2D **102**)
Bowling Grn. Row SE18 . . . . 3D **106**
Bowling Grn. St. SE11 . . . . 7J **19** (6A **102**)
Bowling Grn. Wlk. N1 . . . . 1G **9** (3E **84**)
Bow Locks E3 . . . . 4E **86**
Bowls Cl. HA7: Stan 5G **27**
Bowman Av. E16 . . . . 7H **87**
Bowman Ho. *N1* *1E 84*
(off Nuttall St.)
Bowman M. SW18 . . . . 1H **135**
Bowman's Bldgs. *NW1* *5C 4*
(off Penfold Pl.)
Bowmans Cl. W13 . . . . 1B **96**
Bowmans Lea SE23 . . . . 7J **121**
Bowmans Mdw. SM6: Wall 3F **167**
Bowman's M. E1 . . . . 6G **85**
N7 . . . . 3J **65**
Bowman's Pl. N7 . . . . 3J **65**
Bowman Trad. Est. NW9 . . . . 3G **43**
Bowmead SE9 . . . . 2D **142**
Bowmore Wlk. NW1 . . . . 7H **65**
Bowness Cl. *E8* *6F 67*
(off Beechwood Rd.)
Bowness Cres. SW15 . . . . 5A **134**
Bowness Dr. TW4: Houn 4C **112**
Bowness Ho. *SE15* *7J 103*
(off Hillbeck Cl.)
Bowness Rd. DA7: Bex 2H **127**
SE6 . . . . 7D **122**
Bowood Rd. EN3: Enf H 2E **24**
SW11 . . . . 5E **118**
Bow Rd. E3 . . . . 3B **86**
Bowrons Av. HA0: Wemb 7D **60**
Bowry Ho. *E14* *5B 86*
(off Wallwood St.)
Bowsley Ct. TW13: Felt 2J **129**
Bowsprit Point *E14* *3C 104*
(off Westferry Rd.)
Bow St. E15 . . . . 5G **69**
WC2 . . . . 1F **13** (6J **83**)
Bow Triangle Bus. Cen. E3 . . . . 4C **86**
(not continuous)
Bowyer Cl. E6 . . . . 5D **88**
Bowyer Ho. *N1* *1E 84*
(off Whitmore Est.)
Bowyer Pl. SE5 . . . . 7C **102**
Bowyers Ct. TW1: Isle 4B **114**
Bowyer St. SE5 . . . . 7C **102**
Boxall Rd. SE21 . . . . 6E **120**
Boxelder Cl. HA8: Edg 5D **28**
Boxgrove Rd. SE2 . . . . 3C **108**
Box La. IG11: Bark 2B **90**
Boxley Rd. SM4: Mord 4A **154**
Boxley St. E16 . . . . 1K **105**
Boxmoor Ho. *E2* *1G 85*
(off Whiston Rd.)
W11 . . . . *1F 99*
(off Queensdale Cres.)
Boxmoor Rd. HA3: Kenton 4B **42**
Boxoll Rd. RM9: Dag 4F **73**
Boxted Cl. IG9: Buck H 1H **37**
Box Tree Ho. SE8 . . . . 6A **104**
Boxtree La. HA3: Hrw W 1G **41**
Boxtree Rd. HA3: Hrw W 7C **26**
Boxwood Cl. UB7: W Dray 2B **92**
Boxworth Cl. N12 . . . . 5G **31**
Boxworth Gro. N1 . . . . 1K **83**
Boyard Rd. SE18 . . . . 5F **107**
Boyce Ho. SW16 . . . . 5G **137**
W10 . . . . *3H 81*
(off Bruckner St.)
Boyce Way E13 . . . . 4J **87**
Boycroft Av. NW9 . . . . 6J **43**
Boyd Av. UB1: S'hall 1D **94**
Boyd Cl. KT2: King T 7G **133**
Boydell Ct. NW8 . . . . 7B **64**
(not continuous)
Boyden Ho. E17 . . . . 3E **50**
Boyd Rd. SW19 . . . . 6B **136**
Boyd St. E1 . . . . 6G **85**
Boyd Way SE3 . . . . 4A **124**
Boyfield St. SE1 . . . . 7B **14** (2B **102**)
Boyland Rd. BR1: Brom 5H **141**
Boyle Av. HA7: Stan 6F **27**
Boyle Cl. UB10: Uxb 2B **74**
Boyle Farm Island KT7: T Ditt 6A **150**
Boyle Farm Rd. KT7: T Ditt 6A **150**
Boyle St. W1 . . . . 2A **12** (7G **83**)

Boyne Av. NW4 4F **45**
Boyne Rd. RM10: Dag 3G **73**
SE13 3E **122**
Boyne Ter. M. W11 1H **99**
Boyseland Ct. HA8: Edg 2D **28**
Boyson Rd. SE17 6C **102**
(not continuous)
Boyson Wlk. SE17 6D **102**
Boyton Cl. E1 4J **85**
N8 3J **47**
Boyton Ho. *NW8* *2B* ***82***
(off Wellington Rd.)
Boyton Rd. N8 3J **47**
Brabant Ct. EC3 2G **15**
Brabant Rd. N22 2K **47**
Brabazon Av. SM6: Wall 7J **167**
Brabazon Ct. *SW1* *5C* ***18***
(off Moreton St.)
Brabazon Rd. TW5: Hest 7A **94**
UB5: N'olt 2E **76**
Brabazon St. E14 6D **86**
Brabner Ho. *E2* *1K* ***9***
(off Wellington Row)
Brabourne Cl. SE19 5E **138**
Brabourne Cres. DA7: Bex 6F **109**
Brabourne Hgts. NW7 3F **29**
Brabourne Ri. BR3: Beck 5E **158**
Brabourn Gro. SE15 2J **121**
Brabrook Ct. SM6: Wall 4F **167**
Brabstone Ho. UB6: G'frd 2K **77**
Bracer Ho. *N1* *2E* ***84***
(off Whitmore Est.)
Bracewell Av. UB6: G'frd 5K **59**
Bracewell Rd. W10 5E **80**
Bracewood Gdns. CR0: C'don 3F **169**
Bracey M. N4 2J **65**
Bracey St. N4 2J **65**
Bracken, The E4 2K **35**
Bracken Av. CR0: C'don 3D **170**
SW12 6E **118**
Brackenbridge Dr. HA4: Ruis 3B **58**
Brackenbury *N4* *1A* ***66***
(off Osborne Rd.)
Brackenbury Gdns. W6 3D **98**
Brackenbury Rd. N2 3A **46**
W6 3D **98**
Bracken Cl. E6 5D **88**
TW2: Whitt 7E **112**
TW16: Sun 6H **129**
Brackendale N21 2E **32**
Brackendale Cl. TW3: Houn 1F **113**
Brackendene DA2: Wilm 4K **145**
Bracken End TW7: Isle 5H **113**
Brackenfield Cl. E5 3H **67**
Bracken Gdns. SW13 2C **116**
Brackenhill HA4: Ruis 4C **58**
Bracken Hill Cl. BR1: Brom 1H **159**
Bracken Hill La. BR1: Brom 1H **159**
Bracken Ho. *E3* *5C* ***86***
(off Devons Rd.)
Bracken Ind. Est. IG6: Ilf 1J **53**
Bracken M. E4 1K **35**
RM7: Rom 6H **55**
Brackens BR3: Beck 7C **140**
Brackens, The EN1: Enf 7K **23**
Brackenwood TW16: Sun 1J **147**
Brackenwood Lodge *EN5: New Bar* *4D* ***20***
(off Prospect Rd.)
Brackley Av. SE15 3J **121**
Brackley Cl. SM6: Wall 7J **167**
Brackley Ct. *NW8* *3B* ***4***
(off Pollitt Dr.)
Brackley Rd. BR3: Beck 7B **140**
W4 5A **98**
Brackley Sq. IG8: Wfd G 7G **37**
Brackley St. EC1 5D **8** (4C **84**)
Brackley Ter. W4 5A **98**
Brackley Wlk. HA8: Edg 7C **28**
Bracklyn Ct. N1 2D **84**
(not continuous)
Bracklyn St. N1 2D **84**
Bracknell Cl. N22 1A **48**
Bracknell Gdns. NW3 4K **63**
Bracknell Ga. NW3 5K **63**
Bracknell Way NW3 4K **63**
Bracondale Rd. SE2 4A **108**
Bradbeer Ho. *E2* *3J* ***85***
(off Cornwall Av.)
Bradbourne Rd. DA5: Bexl 7G **127**
Bradbourne St. SW6 2J **117**
Bradbury Cl. UB2: S'hall 4D **94**
Bradbury M. N16 5E **66**
Bradbury St. N16 5E **66**
Bradby Ho. *NW8* *2K* ***81***
(off Hamilton Ter.)
Bradby's *HA1: Harr* *1J* ***59***
(off High St.)
Braddock Cl. TW7: Isle 2K **113**
Braddon Ct. EN5: Barn 3B **20**
Braddon Rd. TW9: Rich 3F **115**
Braddyll St. SE10 5G **105**
Bradenham Av. DA16: Well 4A **126**
Bradenham Cl. SE17 6D **102**
Bradenham Rd. HA3: Kenton 4B **42**
UB4: Hayes 3G **75**
Braden St. W9 4K **81**
Bradfield Ct. *NW1* *7F* ***65***
(off Hawley Rd.)
Bradfield Dr. IG11: Bark 5A **72**
Bradfield Ho. IG8: Wfd G 6K **37**
Bradfield Rd. E16 2J **105**
HA4: Ruis 5C **58**
Bradford Cl. BR2: Brom 1D **172**
N17 6A **34**
SE26 4H **139**
Bradford Dr. KT19: Ewe 6B **164**
Bradford Ho. *W14* *3F* ***99***
(off Spring Va. Ter.)
Bradford Rd. IG1: Ilf 1H **71**
W3 2A **98**
Bradfords Cl. IG9: Buck H 4G **37**
Bradgate Rd. SE6 6D **122**
Brading Cres. E11 2K **69**
Brading Rd. CR0: C'don 6K **155**
SW2 7K **119**
Brading Ter. W12 3C **98**
Bradiston Rd. W9 3H **81**
Bradley Cl. N7 6J **65**
Bradley Gdns. W13 6B **78**
Bradley Ho. *E3* *3D* ***86***
(off Bromley High St.)
IG8: Wfd G 7D **36**
SE16 *4J* ***103***
(off Raymouth Rd.)
Bradley M. SW17 1D **136**
Bradley Rd. N22 2K **47**
SE19 6C **138**
Bradley's Cl. N1 2A **84**
Bradley Stone Rd. E6 5D **88**
Bradman Ho. *NW8* *3A* ***82***
(off Abercorn Pl.)
Bradman Row HA8: Edg 7D **28**
Bradmead SW8 7F **101**
Bradmore Ct. *EN3: Enf H* *3F* ***25***
(off Enstone Rd.)
Bradmore Pk. Rd. W6 4D **98**
Bradshaw Cl. SW19 6J **135**
Bradshaw Cotts. *E14* *6A* ***86***
(off Repton St.)
Bradshaw Dr. NW7 7A **30**
Bradshawe Waye UB8: Hil 5B **74**
Bradshaws Cl. SE25 3G **157**
Bradstock Ho. E9 7K **67**
Bradstock Rd. E9 6K **67**
KT17: Ewe 5C **164**
Brad St. SE1 5K **13** (1A **102**)
Bradwell Av. RM10: Dag 2G **73**
Bradwell Cl. E18 4H **51**
Bradwell Ho. *NW6* *1K* ***81***
(off Mortimer Cres.)
Bradwell M. N18 4B **34**
Bradwell Rd. IG9: Buck H 1H **37**
Bradwell St. E1 3K **85**
Brady Ct. RM8: Dag 1D **72**
Brady Dr. BR1: Brom 3E **160**
Brady Ho. *SW8* *1G* ***119***
(off Corunna Rd.)
Bradymead E6 6E **88**
Brady St. E1 4H **85**
Braeburn Ct. *BR6: Orp* *2K* ***173***
(off Blossom Dr.)
EN4: E Barn 4G **21**
RM13: Rain *2K* ***91***
(off Broadis Way)
Brae Ct. KT2: King T 1G **151**
Braemar SW15 6F **117**
Braemar Av. CR2: S Croy 7C **168**
CR7: Thor H 3A **156**
DA7: Bex 4J **127**
HA0: Wemb 7D **60**
N22 1J **47**
NW10 3K **61**
SW19 2J **135**
Braemar Cl. *SE16* *5H* ***103***
(off Masters Dr.)
Braemar Ct. *SE6* *1H* ***141***
(off Cumberland Pl.)
Braemar Gdns.
BR4: W W'ck 1E **170**
DA15: Sidc 3H **143**
NW9 1K **43**
Braemar Ho. *W9* *3A* ***82***
(off Maida Vale)
Braemar Mans. *SW7* *3K* ***99***
(off Cornwall Gdns.)
Braemar Rd. E13 4H **87**
KT4: Wor Pk 3D **164**
N15 5E **48**
TW8: Bford 6D **96**
Braeside BR3: Beck 5C **140**
Braeside Av. SW19 1G **153**
Braeside Cres. DA7: Bex 4J **127**
Braeside Rd. SW16 7G **137**
Braes St. N1 7B **66**
Braesyde Cl. DA17: Belv 4F **109**
Brafferton Rd. CR0: C'don 4C **168**
Braganza St. SE17 5B **102**
Bragg Cl. RM8: Dag 6B **72**
Braham Ct. *E2* *4H* ***85***
(off Three Colts La.)
Braham Ho. SE11 6H **19** (5K **101**)
Braham St. E1 1K **15** (6F **85**)
Braid Av. W3 6A **80**
Braid Cl. TW13: Hanw 2D **130**
Braidwood Pas. *EC1* *5C* ***8***
(off Aldersgate St.)
Braidwood Rd. SE6 1F **141**
Braidwood St. SE1 5G **15** (1E **102**)
Brailsford Cl. CR4: Mitc 7C **136**
Brailsford Rd. SW2 5A **120**
Brainton Av. TW14: Felt 7K **111**
Braintree Av. IG4: Ilf 4C **52**
Braintree Ho. *E1* *4J* ***85***
(off Malcolm Rd.)
Braintree Rd. HA4: Ruis 4K **57**
RM10: Dag 3G **73**
Braintree St. E2 3J **85**
Braithwaite Av. RM7: Rush G 7G **55**
Braithwaite Gdns. HA7: Stan 1C **42**
Braithwaite Ho. *EC1* *3E* ***8***
(off Bunhill Row)
Braithwaite Rd. EN3: Brim 3G **25**
Braithwaite St. E1 4J **9** (4F **85**)
Braithwaite Twr. W2 5B **4**
Bramah Grn. *SW9* *1A* ***120***
(off Eythorne Rd.)
Bramah Ho. SW1 6J **17** (5F **101**)
Bramah Rd. SW9 1A **120**
Bramalea Cl. N6 6E **46**
Bramall Cl. E15 5H **69**
Bramall Ct. *N7* *6K* ***65***
(off Watkinson Rd.)
Bramber WC1 2E **6**
Bramber Ct. TW8: Bford 4E **96**
W14 *6H* ***99***
(off Bramber Rd.)
Bramber Ho. *KT2: King T* *1E* ***150***
(off Seven Kings Way)
Bramber Rd. N12 5H **31**
W14 6H **99**
Brambleacres Cl. SM2: Sutt 7J **165**
Bramblebury Rd. SE18 5G **107**
Bramble Cl. BR3: Beck 5E **158**
CR0: C'don 4C **170**
HA7: Stan 7J **27**
N15 4G **49**
SE19 1D **156**
TW17: Shep 3F **147**
UB8: Hil 6B **74**
Bramble Cft. DA8: Erith 4J **109**
Brambledown Cl. BR4: W W'ck 5G **159**
Brambledown Rd. CR2: Sande 7E **168**
SM5: Cars 7E **166**
SM6: Wall 7E **166**
Bramble Gdns. W12 7B **80**
Bramble Ho. *E3* *5C* ***86***
(off Devons Rd.)
Bramble La. TW12: Hamp 6D **130**
Brambles, The SM1: Sutt 2B **166**
SW19 *5H* ***135***
(off Woodside)
UB7: W Dray 4A **92**
Brambles Cl. TW7: Isle 7B **96**
Brambles Farm Dr. UB10: Hil 3C **74**
Bramblewood Cl. SM5: Cars 1C **166**
Brambling Ct. *SE8* *6B* ***104***
(off Abinger Gro.)
Bramblings, The E4 4A **36**
Bramcote Av. CR4: Mitc 4D **154**
Bramcote Ct. *CR4: Mitc* *4D* ***154***
(off Bramcote Av.)
Bramcote Gro. SE16 5J **103**
Bramcote Rd. SW15 4D **116**
Bramdean Cres. SE12 1J **141**
Bramdean Gdns. SE12 1J **141**
Bramerton *NW6* *7F* ***63***
(off Willesden La.)
Bramerton Rd. BR3: Beck 3B **158**
Bramerton St. SW3 7C **16** (6C **100**)
Bramfield Ct. *N4* *2C* ***66***
(off Queen's Dr.)
Bramfield Rd. SW11 6C **118**
Bramford Ct. N14 2C **32**
Bramford Rd. SW18 4A **118**
Bramham Gdns. KT9: Chess 4D **162**
SW5 5K **99**
Bramhope La. SE7 6K **105**
Bramlands Cl. SW11 3C **118**
Bramley Av. TW17: Shep 3G **147**
Bramley Bank Nature Reserve 6J **169**
Bramley Cl. BR6: Farnb 1F **173**
CR2: S Croy 5C **168**
E17 2A **50**
HA5: Eastc 3H **39**
IG8: Wfd G 7F **37**
N14 5A **22**
NW7 3F **29**
TW2: Whitt 6G **113**
UB3: Hayes 7J **75**
Bramley Ct. *BR6: Orp* *2K* ***173***
(off Blossom Dr.)
CR4: Mitc 2B **154**
DA16: Well 1B **126**
E4 *1K* ***35***
(off The Ridgeway)
EN4: E Barn 4H **21**
RM13: Rain *2K* ***91***
(off Broadis Way)
UB1: S'hall *7G* ***77***
(off Haldane Rd.)
Bramley Cres. IG2: Ilf 6E **52**
SW8 7H **101**
Bramley Hill
CR2: S Croy 5B **168**

Bramley Ho.—Brenton Ct.

Bramley Ho. *SW15* *6B* ***116***
(off Tunworth Cres.)
TW4: Houn 4D **112**
W10 . . . . 6F **81**
Bramley Hyrst CR2: S Croy 5C **168**
Bramley Lodge HA0: Wemb 4D **60**
Bramley Pde. N14 . . . . 4C **22**
Bramley Rd. N14 . . . . 5K **21**
SM1: Sutt 5B **166**
SM2: Cheam 7F **165**
W5 . . . . 3C **96**
W10 . . . . 6F **81**
Bramley Sports Ground 5K **21**
Bramley Way BR4: W W'ck 2D **170**
TW4: Houn 5D **112**
Brampton *WC1* *6G* ***7***
(off Red Lion Sq.)
Brampton Cl. E5 . . . . 2H **67**
Brampton Ct. NW4 . . . . 4D **44**
RM7: Rush G *6K* ***55***
(off Union Rd.)
Brampton Gro. HA3: Kenton 4A **42**
HA9: Wemb 1G **61**
NW4 . . . . 4D **44**
Brampton Ho. *SE16* *2J* ***103***
(off Albatross Way)
Brampton La. NW4 . . . . 4E **44**
Brampton Pk. Rd. N22 . . . . 3A **48**
Brampton Rd. CR0: C'don 7F **157**
DA7: Bex 3D **126**
E6 . . . . 3B **88**
N15 . . . . 5C **48**
NW9 . . . . 4G **43**
SE2 . . . . 6C **108**
UB10: Hil 2D **74**
Bramshaw Ri. KT3: N Mald 6A **152**
Bramshaw Rd. E9 . . . . 6K **67**
Bramshill Gdns. NW5 . . . . 3F **65**
Bramshill Rd. NW10 . . . . 2B **80**
Bramshot Av. SE7 . . . . 6J **105**
Bramshurst *NW8* *1K* ***81***
(off Abbey Rd.)
Bramston Rd. NW10 . . . . 2C **80**
SW17 . . . . 3A **136**
Bramwell Cl. TW16: Sun 2B **148**
Bramwell Ho. SE1 . . . . 3C **102**
SW1 . . . . *6A* ***18***
(off Churchill Gdns.)
Bramwell M. N1 . . . . 1K **83**
Bramwell Way E16 . . . . 1A **106**
Brancaster Dr. NW7 . . . . 7H **29**
Brancaster Ho. *E1* *3K* ***85***
(off Moody St.)
Brancaster Rd. E12 . . . . 4D **70**
IG2: Ilf 6J **53**
SW16 . . . . 3J **137**
Brancepeth Gdns. IG9: Buck H 2D **36**
Branch Hill NW3 . . . . 3A **64**
Branch Hill Ho. NW3 . . . . 3K **63**
Branch Pl. N1 . . . . 1D **84**
Branch Rd. E14 . . . . 7A **86**
Branch St. SE15 . . . . 7E **102**
Brancker Rd. HA3: Kenton 3D **42**
Brancroft Way EN3: Brim 1F **25**
Brand Av. UB10: Uxb 2A **74**
Brand Cl. N4 . . . . 1B **66**
Brandesbury Sq. IG8: Wfd G 7K **37**
Brandlehow Rd. SW15 . . . . 4H **117**
Brandon Ct. E16 . . . . 4H **87**
Brandon Est. SE17 . . . . 6B **102**
Brandon Ho. *BR3: Beck* *5D* ***140***
(off Beckenham Hill Rd.)
Brandon Mans. *W14* *6G* ***99***
(off Queen's Club Gdns.)
Brandon M. EC2 . . . . 6E **8**
SE17 . . . . *4C* ***102***
(off Brandon St.)
Brandon Rd. E17 . . . . 4E **50**
N7 . . . . 7J **65**
SM1: Sutt 4K **165**
UB2: S'hall 5D **94**
Brandon St. SE17 . . . . 4C **102**
(not continuous)
Brandram M. *SE13* *4G* ***123***
(off Brandram Rd.)
Brandram Rd. SE13 . . . . 3G **123**
Brandrams Wharf SE16 . . . . 2J **103**
Brandreth Ct. HA1: Harr 6K **41**
Brandreth Rd. E6 . . . . 6D **88**
SW17 . . . . 2F **137**
Brandries, The SM6: Bedd 3H **167**
Brands Ho. *NW6* *1H* ***81***
(off Lincoln M.)
Brand St. SE10 . . . . 7E **104**
Brandville Gdns. IG6: Ilf 4F **53**
Brandville Rd. UB7: W Dray 2A **92**
Brandy Way SM2: Sutt 7J **165**
Brangbourne Rd. BR1: Brom 5E **140**
Brangton Rd. SE11 . . . . 6H **19** (5K **101**)
Brangwyn Ct. *W14* *3G* ***99***
(off Blythe Rd.)
Brangwyn Cres. SW19 . . . . 1A **154**
Branham Ho. SE18 . . . . 5F **107**
Branksea St. SW6 . . . . 7G **99**
Branksome Av. N18 . . . . 6A **34**
Branksome Cl. TW11: Tedd 4H **131**
Branksome Ho. *SW8* *7K* ***101***
(off Meadow Rd.)
Branksome Rd. SW2 . . . . 5J **119**
SW19 . . . . 1J **153**
Branksome Way HA3: Kenton 6F **43**
KT3: N Mald 1J **151**
Branksone Ct. N2 . . . . 3A **46**
Brannigan Way HA8: Edg 4A **28**
Bransby Rd. KT9: Chess 6E **162**
Branscombe *NW1* *1G* ***83***
(off Plender St.)
Branscombe Ct. BR2: Brom 5H **159**
Branscombe Gdns. N21 . . . . 7F **23**
Branscombe St. SE13 . . . . 3D **122**
Bransdale Cl. NW6 . . . . 1J **81**
Bransgrove Rd. HA8: Edg 1F **43**
Branston Cres. BR5: Pet W 1H **173**
Branstone Rd. TW9: Kew 1F **115**
Brants Wlk. W7 . . . . 4J **77**
Brantwood Av. DA8: Erith 7J **109**
TW7: Isle 4A **114**
Brantwood Cl. E17 . . . . 3D **50**
Brantwood Gdns. EN2: Enf 4D **22**
IG4: Ilf 4C **52**
Brantwood Ho. *SE5* *7C* ***102***
(off Wyndam Est.)
Brantwood Rd. CR2: S Croy 7C **168**
DA7: Bex 2H **127**
N17 . . . . 6B **34**
SE24 . . . . 5C **120**
Branxholme Ct. *BR1: Brom* *1H* ***159***
(off Highland Rd.)
Braque Bldg. *SE1* *5C* ***14***
(off Union St.)
Brasenose Dr. SW13 . . . . 6E **98**
Brasher Cl. UB6: G'frd 5H **59**
Brassett Point *E15* *1G* ***87***
(off Abbey Rd.)
Brassey Cl. TW14: Felt 1J **129**
Brassey Ho. *E14* *4D* ***104***
(off Cahir St.)
Brassey Rd. NW6 . . . . 6H **63**
Brassey Sq. SW11 . . . . 3E **118**
Brassie Av. W3 . . . . 6A **80**
Brass Talley All. SE16 . . . . 2K **103**
Brasted Cl. BR6: Orp 2K **173**
DA6: Bex 5D **126**
SE26 . . . . 4J **139**
Brasted Lodge BR3: Beck 7C **140**
Brathay *NW1* *1B* ***6***
(off Ampthill Est.)
Brathway Rd. SW18 . . . . 7J **117**
Bratley St. E1 . . . . 4G **85**
Bratten Ct. CR0: C'don 6D **156**
Braund Av. UB6: G'frd 4F **77**
Braundton Av. DA15: Sidc 1K **143**
Braunston Dr. UB4: Yead 4C **76**
Braunston Ho. HA0: Wemb 1E **78**
Bravington Cl. TW17: Shep 5B **146**
Bravington Pl. W9 . . . . 4H **81**
Bravington Rd. W9 . . . . 2H **81**
Bravingtons Wlk. *N1* *1F* ***7***
(off York Way)
Brawne Ho. *SE17* *6B* ***102***
(off Brandon Est.)
Braxfield Rd. SE4 . . . . 4A **122**
Braxted Pk. SW16 . . . . 6K **137**
Bray NW3 . . . . 7C **64**
Brayards Rd. SE15 . . . . 2H **121**
Brayards Rd. Est. *SE15* *2H* ***121***
(off Caulfield Rd.)
Braybourne Dr. TW7: Isle 7K **95**
Braybrooke Gdns. SE19 . . . . 7E **138**
Braybrook St. W12 . . . . 5B **80**
Brayburne Av. SW4 . . . . 2G **119**
Bray Ct. *E2* *3K* ***85***
(off Meath Cres.)
SW16 . . . . 5J **137**
Braycourt Av. KT12: Walt T 7K **147**
Bray Cres. SE16 . . . . 2K **103**
Braydon Rd. N16 . . . . 1G **67**
Bray Dr. E16 . . . . 7H **87**
Brayfield Ter. N1 . . . . 7A **66**
Brayford Sq. E1 . . . . 6J **85**
Bray Pas. E16 . . . . 7J **87**
Bray Pl. SW3 . . . . 4E **16** (4D **100**)
Bray Rd. NW7 . . . . 6A **30**
Brayton Gdns. EN2: Enf 4C **22**
Braywood Rd. SE9 . . . . 4H **125**
Brazier Cres. UB5: N'olt 4D **76**
Brazil Cl. CR0: Bedd 7J **155**
Breach La. RM9: Dag 3G **91**
Bread St. EC4 . . . . 1D **14** (6C **84**)
(not continuous)
Breakspear Crematorium (Ruislip)
HA4: Ruis 5E **38**
Breakspear Ho. UB9: Hare 3A **38**
Breakspear M. UB9: Hare 3A **38**
Breakspear Rd. HA4: Ruis 7D **38**
Breakspear Rd. Nth. UB9: Hare 3A **38**
Breakspear Rd. Sth. UB9: Hare 3B **56**
UB10: Ick 3B **56**
Breakspears Dr. BR5: St P . . . 7A **144**, 1K **161**
Breakspears M. SE4 . . . . 2B **122**
Breakspears Rd. SE4 . . . . 4B **122**
(not continuous)
Breakwell Ct. *W10* *4G* ***81***
(off Wornington Rd.)
Bream Cl. N17 . . . . 4H **49**
Bream Gdns. E6 . . . . 3E **88**
Breamore Cl. SW15 . . . . 1C **134**
Breamore Ct. IG3: Ilf 2A **72**
Breamore Ho. *SE15* *7G* ***103***
(off Friary Est.)
Breamore Rd. IG3: Ilf 2K **71**
Bream's Bldgs. EC4 . . . . 7J **7** (6A **84**)
Bream St. E3 . . . . 7C **68**
Breamwater Gdns. TW10: Ham 3B **132**
Brearley Cl. HA8: Edg 7D **28**
UB8: Uxb 6A **56**
Breasley Cl. SW15 . . . . 4D **116**
Breasy Pl. *NW4* *4D* ***44***
(off Burroughs Gdns.)
Brechin Pl. SW7 . . . . 4A **100**
Brecknock Rd. N7 . . . . 5H **65**
N19 . . . . 4G **65**
Brecknock Rd. Est. N19 . . . . 4G **65**
Breckonmead BR1: Brom 2A **160**
Brecon Cl. CR4: Mitc 3J **155**
KT4: Wor Pk 2E **164**
Brecon Grn. NW9 . . . . 6A **44**
Brecon Ho. *E3* *2B* ***86***
(off Ordell Rd.)
UB5: N'olt *3D* ***76***
(off Taywood Rd.)
W2 . . . . *6A* ***82***
(off Hallfield Est.)
Brecon Lodge UB7: W Dray 2B **92**
Brecon M. N7 . . . . 5H **65**
Brecon Rd. EN3: Pond E 4D **24**
W6 . . . . 6G **99**
Brede Cl. E6 . . . . 3E **88**
Bredel Ho. *E14* *5C* ***86***
(off St Paul's Way)
Bredgar SE13 . . . . 5D **122**
Bredgar Rd. N19 . . . . 2G **65**
Bredhurst Cl. SE20 . . . . 6J **139**
Bredinghurst SE22 . . . . 7G **121**
Bredin Ho. *SW10* *7K* ***99***
(off Coleridge Gdns.)
Bredon Rd. CR0: C'don 7F **157**
Breer St. SW6 . . . . 3K **117**
Breezers Ct. *E1* *7G* ***85***
(off The Highway)
Breezer's Hill E1 . . . . 7G **85**
Bremans Rd. HA2: Harr 2G **59**
Bremer M. E17 . . . . 4D **50**
Bremner Rd. SW7 . . . . 1A **16** (3A **100**)
Brenchley Cl. BR2: Brom 6H **159**
BR7: Chst 1E **160**
Brenchley Gdns. SE23 . . . . 6J **121**
Brenchley Rd. BR5: St P 2K **161**
Brenda Rd. SW17 . . . . 2D **136**
Brende Gdns. KT8: W Mole 4F **149**
Brendon Av. NW10 . . . . 4A **62**
Brendon Cl. UB3: Harl 7E **92**
Brendon Ct. UB2: S'hall 4F **95**
Brendon Gdns. HA2: Harr 4F **59**
IG2: Ilf 5J **53**
Brendon Gro. N2 . . . . 2A **46**
Brendon Rd. RM8: Dag 1F **73**
SE9 . . . . 2H **143**
Brendon St. W1 . . . . 7D **4** (6C **82**)
Brendon Vs. N21 . . . . 1H **33**
Brendon Way EN1: Enf 7K **23**
Brenley Cl. CR4: Mitc 3E **154**
Brenley Gdns. SE9 . . . . 4B **124**
Brenley Ho. *SE1* *6E* ***14***
(off Tennis St.)
Brennand Ct. N19 . . . . 3G **65**
Brent Cl. DA5: Bexl 1E **144**
Brentcot Cl. W13 . . . . 4B **78**
Brent Ct. NW11 . . . . 7F **45**
W7 . . . . 7H **77**
Brent Cres. NW10 . . . . 2F **79**
BRENT CROSS 7E 44
Brent Cross Fly-Over NW2 . . . . 7F **45**
NW4 . . . . 7F **45**
Brent Cross Gdns. NW4 . . . . 6F **45**
BRENT CROSS INTERCHANGE **6E 44**
Brent Cross Shop. Cen. NW4 . . . . 7E **44**
Brentfield NW10 . . . . 7H **61**
Brentfield Cl. NW10 . . . . 6K **61**
Brentfield Gdns. NW2 . . . . 7F **45**
Brentfield Ho. NW10 . . . . 7K **61**
Brentfield Rd. NW10 . . . . 6K **61**
BRENTFORD 6D 96
Brentford Bus. Cen. TW8: Bford 7C **96**
Brentford Cl. UB4: Yead 4B **76**
BRENTFORD END 7B 96
Brentford FC 6D **96**
Brentford Fountain Leisure Cen. 5G **97**
Brentford Ho. TW1: Twick 7B **114**
Brent Grn. NW4 . . . . 5E **44**
Brent Grn. Wlk. HA9: Wemb 3J **61**
Brentham Club 3C **78**
Brentham Way W5 . . . . 4D **78**
Brent Ho. *E9* *6J* ***67***
(off Brenthouse Rd.)
Brenthouse Rd. E9 . . . . 7J **67**
Brenthurst Rd. NW10 . . . . 6B **62**
Brent Lea TW8: Bford 7C **96**
Brentmead Cl. W7 . . . . 7J **77**
Brentmead Gdns. NW10 . . . . 2F **79**
Brentmead Pl. NW11 . . . . 6F **45**
Brent New Ent. Cen. NW10 . . . . 6B **62**
Brenton Ct. *E9* *5A* ***68***
(off Mabley St.)

Brenton St. E14 . . . . .6A 86
Brent Pk. Ind. Est. UB2: S'hall 3K 93
Brent Pk. Rd. NW4 . . . . .7D 44
NW9 .7D 44
Brent Pl. EN5: Barn 5C 20
Brent Rd. CR2: Sels 7H 169
E16 . . . . .6J 87
SE18 .7F 107
TW8: Bford 6C 96
UB2: S'hall 3A 94
Brent Side TW8: Bford 6C 96
Brentside Cl. W13 . . . . .4A 78
Brentside Executive Cen.
TW8: Bford 6B 96
Brentside Ind. Pk. NW2 . . . . .1E 62
Brent St. NW4 . . . . .4E 44
Brent Ter. NW2 . . . . .2C 44
(not continuous)
Brent Trad. Cen. NW10 . . . . .5A 62
Brentvale Av. HA0: Wemb 1F 79
UB1: S'hall 1H 95
Brent Valley Golf Course 7J 77
Brent Vw. Rd. NW9 . . . . .6C 44
Brentwaters Bus. Pk. TW8: Bford . . .7C 96
Brent Way HA9: Wemb 6H 61
N3 . . . . .6D 30
TW8: Bford 7D 96
Brentwick Gdns. TW8: Bford 6C 96
Brentwood Cl. SE9 . . . . .1G 143
Brentwood Ho. SE18 . . . . .7B 106
(off Portway Gdns.)
Brentwood Lodge NW4 . . . . .5F 45
(off Holmdale Gdns.)
Brereton Rd. N17 . . . . .7A 34
Bressay Dr. NW7 . . . . .7H 29
Bressenden Pl. SW1 . . . .1K 17 (3F 101)
Bressey Av. EN1: Enf 1B 24
Bressey Gro. E18 . . . . .2H 51
Bresslaw Ct. E3 . . . . .5B 86
(off Wager St.)
Breton Highwalk EC2 . . . . .5D 8
(off Golden La.)
Breton Ho. EC2 . . . . .5D 8
SE1 .7J 15
(off St Saviour's Est.)
Brett Cl. N16 . . . . .2E 66
UB5: N'olt 3B 76
Brett Ct. N9 . . . . .2D 34
Brettell St. SE17 . . . . .5D 102
Brettenham Av. E17 . . . . .1C 50
Brettenham Rd. E17 . . . . .2C 50
N18 .4B 34
Brett Gdns. RM9: Dag 7E 72
Brett Ho. Cl. SW15 . . . . .7F 117
Brettinghurst SE1 . . . . .5G 103
(off Avondale Sq.)
Brett Pas. E8 . . . . .5H 67
Brett Rd. E8 . . . . .5H 67
Brewers Bldgs. EC1 . . . . .1A 8
(off Rawstorne St.)
Brewers Cl. W2 . . . . .5A 82
Brewer's Grn. SW1 . . . . .1C 18
Brewer's Hall Gdn. EC2 . . . . .6D 8
(off Aldermanbury Sq.)
Brewers La. TW9: Rich 5D 114
Brewer St. W1 . . . . .2B 12 (7G 83)
Brewery, The EC2 . . . . . .5E 8 (5C 84)
RM1: Rom 5K 55
Brewery Cl. HA0: Wemb 5A 60
Brewery Ind. Est., The N1 . . . . .1D 8
(off Wenlock Rd.)
Brewery La. TW1: Twick 7K 113
Brewery M. Cen. TW7: Isle 3A 114
Brewery Rd. BR2: Brom 1C 172
N7 . . . . .7J 65
SE18 .5H 107
Brewery Sq. EC1 . . . . . .3B 8 (4B 84)
SE1 .5J 15
Brewery Wlk. RM1: Rom 5K 55
Brewhouse La. E1 . . . . .1H 103
SW15 . . . . .3G 117

Brewhouse Rd. SE18 . . . . .4D 106
Brewhouse Wlk. SE16 . . . . .1A 104
Brewhouse Yd. EC1 . . . . . .3A 8 (4B 84)
Brewin Ter. UB4: Yead 5A 76
Brewood Rd. RM8: Dag 6B 72
Brewster Gdns. W10 . . . . .5E 80
Brewster Ho. E14 . . . . .7B 86
(off Three Colt St.)
SE1 .4F 103
(off Dunton Rd.)
Brewster Pl. KT1: King T 2J 151
Brewster Rd. E10 . . . . .1D 68
Brian Rd. RM6: Chad H 5C 54
Briant Ho. SE1 . . . . .2J 19
Briants Cl. HA5: Pinn 2D 40
Briant St. SE14 . . . . .1K 121
Briar Av. SW16 . . . . .7K 137
Briarbank Rd. W13 . . . . .6A 78
Briar Cl. IG9: Buck H 2G 37
N2 . . . . .3K 45
N13 .3F 33
TW7: Isle 5K 113
TW12: Hamp 5D 130
Briar Ct. E3 . . . . .2C 86
(off Morville St.)
SM3: Cheam 4E 164
SW15 . . . . .4D 116
Briar Cres. UB5: N'olt 6F 59
Briardale HA8: Edg 4E 28
Briardale Gdns. NW3 . . . . .3J 63
Briarfield Av. N3 . . . . .2K 45
(not continuous)
Briarfield Cl. DA7: Bex 2G 127
Briar Gdns. BR2: Hayes 1H 171
Briaris Cl. N17 . . . . .7C 34
Briar La. BR4: Addtn 4D 170
Briar Rd. DA5: Bexl 3K 145
HA3: Kenton 5C 42
NW2 .4E 62
SW16 . . . . .3J 155
TW2: Twick 1J 131
TW17: Shep 5B 146
Briars, The TW19: Stanw M 7B 174
WD23: B Hea 1D 26
Briarswood Way BR6: Chels 5K 173
Briar Wlk. HA8: Edg 7D 28
SW15 . . . . .4D 116
W10 .4G 81
Briar Way UB7: W Dray 2C 92
Briar Wood Cl. BR2: Brom 2C 172
Briarwood Cl. NW9 . . . . .6J 43
TW13: Felt 4G 129
Briarwood Ct. KT4: Wor Pk 1C 164
(off The Avenue)
Briarwood Dr. HA6: Nwood 2J 39
Briarwood Rd. KT17: Ewe 6C 164
SW4 .5H 119
Briary Cl. NW3 . . . . .7C 64
Briary Ct. DA14: Sidc 5B 144
E16 . . . . .6H 87
Briary Gdns. BR1: Brom 5K 141
Briary Gro. HA8: Edg 2H 43
Briary La. N9 . . . . .3A 34
Briary Lodge BR3: Beck 1E 158
Brickbarn Cl. SW10 . . . . .7A 100
(off King's Barn)
Brick Ct. EC4 . . . . .1J 13 (6A 84)
Brickett Cl. HA4: Ruis 5E 38
Brick Farm Cl. TW9: Kew 1H 115
Brickfield Cl. E9 . . . . .6J 67
TW8: Bford 7C 96
Brickfield Cotts. BR7: Chst 5E 142
SE18 .6K 107
Brickfield Farm Gdns.
BR6: Farnb 4G 173
Brickfield Ho. N1 . . . . .1E 84
(off Hertford Rd.)
Brickfield La. UB3: Harl 6F 93
Brickfield Rd. CR4: Mitc 3C 154
CR7: Thor H 1B 156
E3 . . . . .4D 86

Brickfield Rd. SW4 . . . . .6H 119
(off Parkfield Rd.)
SW19 . . . . .4K 135
Brickfields HA2: Harr 2H 59
(not continuous)
Brickfields Way UB7: W Dray 3B 92
Brick La. E1 . . . . .3K 9 (4F 85)
E2 . . . . .3F 85
EN1: Enf 2C 24
EN3: Enf H 2C 24
HA7: Stan 7J 27
UB5: N'olt 3D 76
Brick Lane Music Hall 1B 106
BRICKLAYER'S ARMS 4D 102
Bricklayers Arms Distribution Cen.
SE1 .4E 102
(not continuous)
Brick St. W1 . . . . .5J 11 (1F 101)
Brickwall La. HA4: Ruis 1G 57
Brickwood Cl. SE26 . . . . .3H 139
Brickwood Rd. CR0: C'don 2E 168
Brideale Cl. SE15 . . . . .6F 103
Bride La. EC4 . . . . .1A 14 (6B 84)
Bridel M. N1 . . . . .1B 84
(off Colebrook Row)
Brides M. N7 . . . . .6K 65
Brides Pl. N1 . . . . .7E 66
Bride St. N7 . . . . .6K 65
Bridewain St. SE1 . . . . . .7J 15 (3F 103)
Bridewell Pl. E1 . . . . .1H 103
EC4 . . . . .1A 14 (6B 84)
Bridford M. W1 . . . . .5K 5 (5F 83)
Bridge, The HA3: W'stone 4K 41
SW8 .7F 101
Bridge App. NW1 . . . . .7E 64
Bridge Av. W6 . . . . .4E 98
W7 . . . . .5H 77
Bridge Av. Mans. W6 . . . . .5E 98
(off Bridge Av.)
Bridge Bus. Cen., The UB2: S'hall . .2E 94
Bridge Cl. EN1: Enf 2C 24
KT12: Walt T 7H 147
TW11: Tedd 4K 131
W10 .6F 81
Bridge Ct. E10 . . . . .1B 68
E14 . . . . .7F 87
(off Newport Av.)
HA2: Harr 2G 59
KT12: Walt T 7H 147
(off Bridge St.)
Bridge Dr. N13 . . . . .4E 32
Bridge End E17 . . . . .1E 50
Bridge End Cl. KT2: King T 1G 151
Bridgefield Ho. W2 . . . . .6K 81
(off Queensway)
Bridgefield Rd. SM1: Sutt 6J 165
Bridgefoot SE1 . . . . .6F 19 (5J 101)
TW16: Sun 1H 147
Bridge Gdns. KT8: E Mos 4H 149
N16 .4D 66
TW15: Ashf 7E 128
Bridge Ga. N21 . . . . .7H 23
Bridgehill Cl. HA0: Wemb 1D 78
Bridge Ho. CR0: C'don 3C 168
(off Surrey St.)
E9 . . . . .6K 67
(off Shepherds La.)
NW3 .7E 64
(off Adelaide Rd.)
NW10 . . . . .2F 81
(off Chamberlayne Rd.)
SE4 . . . . .4B 122
SM2: Sutt 6K 165
(off Bridge Rd.)
SW1 .5J 17
(off Ebury Bri.)
UB7: W Dray 1A 92
W2 . . . . .6A 4
Bridgehouse Ct. SE1 . . . . .7A 14
(off Blackfriars Rd.)

Bridge Ho. Quay E14 . . . . .1E 104
Bridgeland Rd. E16 . . . . .7J 87
Bridgelands Cl. BR3: Beck 7B 140
Bridge La. NW11 . . . . .4G 45
SW11 . . . . .1C 118
Bridge Leisure Cen., The 4B 140
Bridgeman Ho. E9 . . . . .7J 67
(off Frampton Pk. Rd.)
W14 .4H 99
(off Radnor Ter.)
Bridgeman Rd. N1 . . . . .7K 65
TW11: Tedd 6A 132
Bridgeman St. NW8 . . . . .2C 82
Bridge Mdws. SE14 . . . . .6K 103
Bridge M. NW10 . . . . .6A 62
Bridgemount M. N4 . . . . .7K 47
BRIDGEN 7E 126
Bridgend Rd. SW18 . . . . .4A 118
Bridgenhall Rd. EN1: Enf 1A 24
Bridgen Ho. E1 . . . . .6H 85
(off Nelson St.)
Bridgen Rd. DA5: Bexl 7E 126
Bridge Pde. N21 . . . . .7H 23
(off Ridge Av.)
Bridgepark SW18 . . . . .5J 117
Bridge Pk. Community Leisure Cen.
. . . . .7H 61
Bridge Pl. CR0: C'don 1D 168
SW1 . . . . .3K 17 (4F 101)
Bridgepoint Lofts E7 . . . . .7A 70
Bridgepoint Pl. N6 . . . . .1G 65
(off Hornsey La.)
Bridgeport Pl. E1 . . . . .1G 103
Bridge Rd. BR3: Beck 7B 140
DA7: Bex 2E 126
E6 . . . . .7D 70
E11 . . . . .6F 51
E15 . . . . .7F 69
E17 . . . . .7B 50
HA9: Wemb 3G 61
KT8: E Mos 4H 149
KT9: Chess 5E 162
N9 . . . . .3B 34
N22 .1J 47
NW10 . . . . .6A 62
SM2: Sutt 6K 165
SM6: Wall 5F 167
TW1: Twick 6B 114
TW3: Houn, Isle 3H 113
TW7: Isle 3H 113
UB2: S'hall 2D 94
Bridge Rd. Depot E15 . . . . .1G 87
Bridge Row CR0: C'don 1D 168
Bridges Ct. Rd. SW11 . . . . .3B 118
Bridges Ho. SE5 . . . . .7D 102
(off Elmington Est.)
Bridgeside Lodge N1 . . . . .2C 84
(off Wharf Rd.)
Bridges La. CR0: Bedd 4J 167
Bridges Pl. SW6 . . . . .1H 117
Bridges Rd. HA7: Stan 5E 26
SW19 . . . . .6K 135
Bridges Rd. M. SW19 . . . . .6K 135
Bridge St. HA5: Pinn 3C 40
KT12: Walt T 7G 147
SW1 . . . . .7E 12 (2J 101)
TW9: Rich 5D 114
W4 . . . . .4K 97
Bridges Wharf SW11 . . . . .3B 118
Bridge Ter. E15 . . . . .7F 69
Bridgetown Cl. SE19 . . . . .5E 138
Bridge Vw. W6 . . . . .5E 98
Bridge Vw. Ct. SE1 . . . . .3E 102
(off Grange Rd.)
Bridge Wlk. IG1: Ilf 2F 71
(within The Exchange)
SE8 . . . . .6D 104
(off Copperas St.)
Bridgewalk Hgts. SE1 . . . . .6F 15
(off Weston St.)
Bridgewater Cl. BR7: Chst 3J 161

Bridgewater Gdns.
HA8: Edg .2F **43**
Bridgewater Highwalk EC2 . . . . .5C **8**
Bridgewater Rd. E15 . . . . .1E **86**
HA0: Wemb 6C **60**
Bridgewater Sq. EC2 . . . . . . .5C **8** (5C **84**)
Bridgewater St. EC2 . . . . . . .5C **8** (5C **84**)
Bridge Way N11 . . . . .3B **32**
NW11 .5H **45**
TW2: Whitt 7G **113**
UB10: Ick 5D **56**
Bridgeway HA0: Wemb 7E **60**
IG11: Bark 7K **71**
Bridgeway St. NW1 . . . . .2G **83**
Bridge Wharf E2 . . . . .2K **85**
N1 . . . . .2K **83**
(off Calshot St.)
Bridge Wharf Rd. TW7: Isle 3B **114**
Bridgewood Cl. SE20 . . . . .7H **139**
Bridgewood Rd. KT4: Wor Pk 4C **164**
SW16 .7H **137**
Bridge Yd. SE1 . . . . .4F **15** (1D **102**)
Bridgford St. SW18 . . . . .3A **136**
Bridgman Rd. W4 . . . . .3J **97**
Bridgnorth Ho. SE15 . . . . .6G **103**
(off Friary Est.)
Bridgwater Ho. W2 . . . . .6A **82**
(off Hallfield Est.)
Bridgwater Rd. HA4: Ruis 4J **57**
Bridle Cl. KT1: King T 4D **150**
KT19: Ewe 5K **163**
TW16: Sun 3J **147**
Bridle La. TW1: Twick 6B **114**
W1 . . . . .2B **12** (7G **83**)
Bridle M. EN5: Barn 4C **20**
Bridle Path CR0: Bedd 3J **167**
Bridle Path, The IG8: Wfd G 7B **36**
Bridlepath Way TW14: Bedf 7G **111**
Bridle Rd. CR0: C'don 3C **170**
CR2: Sande 7G **169**
HA5: Eastc 6X **39**
KT10: Clay 6B **162**
Bridle Way BR6: Farnb 4G **173**
CR0: C'don 5C **170**
Bridleway, The SM6: Wall 4G **167**
Bridlington Rd. N9 . . . . .7C **24**
Bridport SE17 . . . . .5D **102**
(off Cadiz St.)
Bridport Av. RM7: Rom 6H **55**
Bridport Ho. N1 . . . . .1D **84**
(off Bridport Pl.)
N18 . . . . .5B **34**
(off College Gdns.)
Bridport Pl. N1 . . . . .1D **84**
(not continuous)
Bridport Rd. CR7: Thor H 3A **156**
N18 . . . . .5K **33**
UB6: G'frd 1F **77**
Bridport Ter. SW8 . . . . .1H **119**
(off Deeley Rd.)
Bridstow Pl. W2 . . . . .6J **81**
Brief St. SE5 . . . . .1B **120**
Brierfield NW1 . . . . .1G **83**
(off Arlington Rd.)
Brierley CR0: New Ad 6D **170**
(not continuous)
Brierley Av. N9 . . . . .1D **34**
Brierley Cl. SE25 . . . . .4G **157**
Brierley Cl. W7 . . . . .7J **77**
Brierley Rd. E11 . . . . .4F **69**
SW12 . . . . .2G **137**
Brierly Gdns. E2 . . . . .2J **85**
Brigade Cl. HA2: Harr 2H **59**
Brigade St. SE3 . . . . .2H **123**
(off Tranquil Va.)
Brigadier Av. EN2: Enf 1H **23**
Brigadier Hill EN2: Enf 1H **23**
Brigadier Ho. NW9 . . . . .2B **44**
(off Heritage Av.)
Briggeford Cl. E5 . . . . .2G **67**
Briggs Cl. CR4: Mitc 1F **155**

Briggs Ho. E2 . . . . .1K **9**
(off Chambord St.)
Bright Cl. DA17: Belv 4D **108**
Brightfield Rd. SE12 . . . . .5G **123**
Brightling Rd. SE4 . . . . .6B **122**
Brightlingsea Pl. E14 . . . . .7B **86**
Brightman Rd. SW18 . . . . .1B **136**
Brighton Av. E17 . . . . .5B **50**
Brighton Bldgs. SE1 . . . . .3E **102**
(off Tower Bri. Rd.)
Brighton Cl. UB10: Hil 7D **56**
Brighton Dr. UB5: N'olt 6E **58**
Brighton Gro. SE14 . . . . .1A **122**
Brighton Ho. SE5 . . . . .1D **120**
(off Camberwell Grn.)
Brighton Rd. CR2: S Croy 5C **168**
E6 . . . . .3E **88**
(not continuous)
KT6: Surb 6C **150**
N2 . . . . .2A **46**
N16 . . . . .4E **66**
SM2: Sutt 7K **165**
Brighton Ter. SW9 . . . . .4K **119**
Brightside, The
EN3: Enf H 1E **24**
Brightside Rd. SE13 . . . . .6F **123**
Bright St. E14 . . . . .5D **86**
Brightwell Cl. CR0: C'don 1A **168**
Brightwell Ct. N7 . . . . .5K **65**
(off Mackenzie Rd.)
Brightwell Cres. SW17 . . . . .5D **136**
Brightwen Gro. HA7: Stan 2F **27**
Brig M. SE8 . . . . .6C **104**
Brigstock Ho. SE5 . . . . .2C **120**
Brigstock Rd. CR7: Thor H 5A **156**
DA17: Belv 4H **109**
Brill Pl. NW1 . . . . .1D **6** (2H **83**)
Brim Hill N2 . . . . .4A **46**
Brimpsfield Cl. SE2 . . . . .3B **108**
(not continuous)
BRIMSDOWN 2G **25**
Brimsdown Av. EN3: Enf H 2F **25**
Brimsdown Ho. E3 . . . . .4D **86**
Brimsdown Ind. Est. EN3: Brim 1G **25**
(Lockfield Av.)
EN3: Brim 2G **25**
(Stockingswater La.)
Brimstone Ho. E15 . . . . .7G **69**
(off Victoria St.)
Brindle Ga. DA15: Sidc 1J **143**
Brindlewick Gdns. BR3: Beck 6C **140**
Brindley Cl. DA7: Bex 3H **127**
HA0: Wemb 1D **78**
Brindley Ct. HA7: Stan 7J **27**
Brindley Ho. W2 . . . . .5J **81**
(off Alfred Rd.)
Brindley St. SE14 . . . . .1B **122**
Brindley Way BR1: Brom 5J **141**
UB1: S'hall 7F **77**
Brindwood Rd. E4 . . . . .3G **35**
Brine Ho. E3 . . . . .2A **86**
(off St Stephen's Rd.)
Brinkburn Cl. HA8: Edg 3H **43**
SE2 . . . . .4A **108**
Brinkburn Gdns. HA8: Edg 3G **43**
Brinkley KT1: King T 2G **151**
Brinkley Rd. KT4: Wor Pk 2D **164**
Brinklow Cres. SE18 . . . . .7F **107**
Brinklow Ho. W2 . . . . .5K **81**
(off Torquay St.)
Brinkworth Rd. IG5: Ilf 3C **52**
Brinkworth Way E9 . . . . .6B **68**
Brinsdale Rd. NW4 . . . . .3F **45**
Brinsley Ho. E1 . . . . .6J **85**
(off Tarling St.)
Brinsley Rd. HA3: Hrw W 2H **41**
Brinsworth Cl. TW2: Twick 1H **131**
Brinsworth Ho. TW2: Twick 2H **131**
Brinton Wlk. SE1 . . . . .5A **14**
Brion Pl. E14 . . . . .5E **86**
Brisbane Av. SW19 . . . . .1K **153**

Brisbane Ho. W12 . . . . .7D **80**
(off White City Est.)
Brisbane Rd. E10 . . . . .2D **68**
IG1: Ilf .7F **53**
W13 .2A **96**
Brisbane St. SE5 . . . . .7D **102**
Briscoe Cl. E11 . . . . .2H **69**
Briscoe M. TW2: Twick 2H **131**
Briscoe Rd. SW19 . . . . .6B **136**
Briset Rd. SE9 . . . . .3B **124**
Briset St. EC1 . . . . .5A **8** (4B **84**)
Briset Way N7 . . . . .2K **65**
Bristol Cl. SM6: Wall 7J **167**
TW4: Houn 7E **112**
TW19: Stanw 6A **110**
Bristol Ct. TW19: Stanw 6A **110**
Bristol Gdns. SW15 . . . . .7E **116**
W9 . . . . .4K **81**
Bristol Ho. IG11: Bark 7A **72**
(off Margaret Bondfield Av.)
SE11 .2J **19**
SW1 .5G **17**
(off Lwr. Sloane St.)
WC1 . . . . .5F **7**
(off Southampton Row)
Bristol M. W9 . . . . .4K **81**
Bristol Pk. Rd. E17 . . . . .4A **50**
Bristol Rd. E7 . . . . .6A **70**
SM4: Mord 5A **154**
UB6: G'frd 1F **77**
Bristol Wlk. NW6 . . . . .2J **81**
(off Alpha Pl.)
Briston Gro. N8 . . . . .6J **47**
Briston M. NW7 . . . . .7H **29**
Bristow Ct. E8 . . . . .1H **85**
(off Triangle Rd.)
Bristowe Cl. SW2 . . . . .6A **120**
Bristow Rd. CR0: Bedd 4J **167**
DA7: Bex 1E **126**
SE19 .5E **138**
TW3: Houn 3G **113**
Britannia Bldg. N1 . . . . .1E **8**
(off Ebenezer St.)
Britannia Bus. Cen. NW2 . . . . .4F **63**
Britannia Cl. SW4 . . . . .4H **119**
UB5: N'olt 3B **76**
Britannia Ct. KT2: King T 1D **150**
(off Skerne Wlk.)
W Dray 3A **92**
Britannia Ga. E16 . . . . .1J **105**
BRITANNIA JUNC. 1F **83**
Britannia La. TW2: Whitt 7G **113**
Britannia Leisure Cen. 1D **84**
Britannia Rd. E14 . . . . .4C **104**
IG1: Ilf .3F **71**
KT5: Surb 7F **151**
N12 . . . . .3F **31**
SW6 .7K **99**
Britannia Row N1 . . . . .1B **84**
Britannia St. WC1 . . . . .1G **7** (3K **83**)
Britannia Wlk. N1 . . . . . . .1E **8** (2D **84**)
(not continuous)
Britannia Way NW10 . . . . .4H **79**
SW6 .7K **99**
(off Britannia Rd.)
TW19: Stanw 7A **110**
Britannic Highwalk EC2 . . . . .6E **8**
(off Moor La.)
British Genius Site 7E **100**
British Gro. W4 . . . . .5B **98**
British Gro. Pas. W4 . . . . .5B **98**
British Gro. Sth. W4 . . . . .5B **98**
British Legion Rd. E4 . . . . .2C **36**
British Library 1D **6** (3H **83**)
British Mus. 6D **6** (5J **83**)
British St. E3 . . . . .3B **86**
British Telecom Cen. EC1 . . . . .7C **8**
British Wharf Ind. Est. SE14 . . . . . .5K **103**
Britley Ho. E14 . . . . .6B **86**
(off Copenhagen Pl.)
Brittain Ct. SE9 . . . . .1C **142**

Brittain Rd. RM8: Dag 3E **72**
Brittany Ho. EN2: Enf 1H **23**
Brittany Point SE11 . . . . . . .4J **19** (4A **102**)
Britten Cl. NW11 . . . . .1K **63**
Britten Ct. E15 . . . . .2F **87**
Brittenden Cl. BR6: Chels 6K **173**
Brittenden Pde. BR6: Chels 6K **173**
Britten Dr. UB1: S'hall 6E **76**
Britten Ho. SW3 . . . . .5D **16**
(off Britten St.)
Britten St. SW3 . . . . .6C **16** (5C **100**)
Britten Theatre 3B **100**
(off Prince Consort Rd.)
Brittidge Rd. NW10 . . . . .7A **62**
Britton St. EC1 . . . . .4A **8** (4B **84**)
Brixham Cres. HA4: Ruis 1J **57**
Brixham Gdns. IG3: Ilf 5J **71**
Brixham Rd. DA16: Well 1D **126**
Brixham St. E16 . . . . .1E **106**
BRIXTON .4K **119**
Brixton Hill SW2 . . . . .7J **119**
Brixton Hill Ct. SW2 . . . . .5K **119**
Brixton Hill Pl. SW2 . . . . .7J **119**
Brixton Oval SW2 . . . . .4A **120**
Brixton Recreation Cen. 3A **120**
(off Brixton Sta. Rd.)
Brixton Rd. SE11 . . . . .7J **19** (6A **102**)
SW9 .4A **120**
Brixton Sta. Rd. SW9 . . . . .3A **120**
Brixton Water La. SW2 . . . . .5K **119**
Broadacre Cl. UB10: Ick 3D **56**
Broadbent Cl. N6 . . . . .1F **65**
Broadbent St. W1 . . . . .2J **11** (7F **83**)
Broadberry Ct. N18 . . . . .6C **34**
Broadbridge Cl. SE3 . . . . .7J **105**
Broad Comn. Est. N16 . . . . .1G **67**
(off Osbaldeston Rd.)
Broadcoombe CR2: Sels 7J **169**
Broad Cl. WC2 . . . . .1F **13** (6J **83**)
Broadcroft Av. HA7: Stan 2D **42**
Broadcroft Rd. BR5: Pet W 7K **161**
Broadeaves Cl. CR2: S Croy 5E **168**
Broadfield NW6 . . . . .6K **63**
Broadfield Cl. CR0: Wadd 2K **167**
NW2 .3E **62**
Broadfield Ct. HA2: Harr 1F **41**
(off Broadfields)
WD23: B Hea 2D **26**
Broadfield La. NW1 . . . . .7J **65**
Broadfield Pde. HA8: Edg 3C **28**
(off Glengall Rd.)
Broadfield Rd. SE6 . . . . .7G **123**
Broadfields HA2: Harr 2F **41**
KT8: E Mos 6J **149**
Broadfields Av. HA8: Edg 4C **28**
N21 . . . . .6F **23**
Broadfields Hgts. HA8: Edg 4C **28**
Broadfield Sq. EN1: Enf 2C **24**
Broadfields Way NW10 . . . . .5B **62**
Broadfield Way IG9: Buck H 2E **37**
Broadford Ho. E1 . . . . .4A **86**
(off Commodore St.)
Broadgate EC2 . . . . .6F **9**
Broadgate Circle 6G **9** (5E **84**)
Broadgate Circ. EC2 . . . . . . .5G **9** (5E **84**)
Broadgate Ice Rink 5H **9** (5E **84**)
Broadgate Plaza EC2 . . . . .5E **84**
Broadgate Rd. E16 . . . . .6B **88**
Broadgates Av. EN4: Had W 1E **20**
Broadgates Ct. SE11 . . . . .6K **19**
(off Cleaver St.)
Broadgates Rd. SW18 . . . . .1B **136**
Broadgate Twr. EC2 . . . . . . .4H **9** (4E **84**)
BROAD GREEN 7B **156**
Broad Grn. Av. CR0: C'don 7B **156**
Broadhead Strand NW9 . . . . .1B **44**
Broadhinton Rd. SW4 . . . . .3G **119**
Broadhurst Av. HA8: Edg 4C **28**
IG3: Ilf .4K **71**

Broadhurst Cl. NW6 6A 64
TW10: Rich 5F 115
Broadhurst Gdns.
HA4: Ruis 2A 58
NW6 6K 63
Broadis Way RM13: Rain 2K 91
Broadlands E17 3A 50
TW13: Hanw 3E 130
Broadlands Av. EN3: Enf H 3C 24
SW16 2J 137
TW17: Shep 6E 146
Broadlands Cl. EN3: Enf H 3D 24
N6 7E 46
SW16 2J 137
Broadlands Ct. *TW9: Kew* *7G 97*
(*off Kew Gdns. Rd.*)
Broadlands Lodge N6 7D 46
Broadlands Rd. BR1: Brom 4K 141
N6 7D 46
Broadlands Way KT3: N Mald 6B 152
Broad La. EC2 5G 9 (5E 84)
N8 5K 47
N15 4F 49
N17 4G 49
TW12: Hamp 7D 130
Broad Lawn SE9 2E 142
Broadlawns Ct. HA3: Hrw W 1K 41
Broadley St. NW8 5B 4 (5B 82)
Broadley Ter. NW1 4D 4 (4C 82)
Broadmayne *SE17* *5D 102*
(*off Portland St.*)
Broadmead SE6 3C 140
W14 4G 99
Broadmead Av. KT4: Wor Pk 7C 152
Broadmead Cen. *IG8: Wfd G* *7F 37*
(*off Navestock Cres.*)
Broadmead Cl. HA5: Hat E 1C 40
TW12: Hamp 6E 130
Broadmead Ct. IG8: Wfd G 6D 36
Broadmead Rd. IG8: Wfd G 6D 36
(not continuous)
UB4: Yead 4C 76
UB5: N'olt 4C 76
Broad Oak IG8: Wfd G 5E 36
TW16: Sun 6H 129
Broad Oak Cl. E4 5H 35
Broadoak Ct. *SW9* *3A 120*
(*off Gresham Rd.*)
Broadoak Ho. *NW6* *1K 81*
(*off Mortimer Cres.*)
Broadoak Rd. DA8: Erith 7K 109
Broadoaks KT6: Surb 2H 163
Broadoaks Way BR2: Brom 5H 159
Broad Sanctuary SW1 7D 12 (2H 101)
Broadstone *NW1* *7H 65*
(*off Agar Gro.*)
Broadstone Ho. *SW8* *7K 101*
(*off Dorset Rd.*)
Broadstone Pl. W1 6G 5 (5E 82)
Broad St. RM10: Dag 7G 73
TW11: Tedd 6K 131
Broad St. Av. EC2 6G 9 (5E 84)
Broad St. Mkt. RM10: Dag 7G 73
Broad St. Pl. EC2 6F 9
Broadview NW9 6G 43
Broadview Pl. E5 1J 67
Broadview Rd. SW16 7H 137
Broad Wlk. N21 2E 32
NW1 1H 5 (1E 82)
SE3 2A 124
TW5: Hest 1B 112
TW9: Kew 7F 97
W1 3F 11 (7D 82)
Broad Wlk., The
KT8: E Mos 4K 149
W8 1K 99
Broadwalk E18 3H 51
HA2: Harr 5E 40
Broadwalk, The HA6: Nwood 2E 38
Broadwalk Ct. *W8* *1J 99*
(*off Palace Gdns. Ter.*)
Broadwalk Ho. EC2 5G 9
SW7 *2A 100*
(*off Hyde Pk. Ga.*)
Broad Wlk. La. NW11 7H 45
Broadwalk Shop. Cen. HA8: Edg 6C 28
Broadwall SE1 4K 13 (1A 102)
Broadwater Farm Est. N17 2D 48
Broadwater Gdns. BR6: Farnb 4F 173
Broadwater Rd. N17 1E 48
SE28 3H 107
SW17 4C 136
Broadway DA6: Bex 4E 126
(not continuous)
DA7: Bex 4H 127
E13 2K 87
E15 7F 69
IG11: Bark 1G 89
SW1 7C 12 (3H 101)
W7 1J 95
W13 1A 96
Broadway, The CR0: Bedd 4J 167
E4 6A 36
HA3: W'stone 2J 41
HA6: Nwood 2J 39
HA7: Stan 5H 27
HA9: Wemb 3E 60
IG8: Wfd G 6E 36
KT7: T Ditt 7J 149
N8 6J 47
N9 3B 34
N11 5J 31
N14 *1C 32*
(*off The Bourne*)
N22 2A 48
NW7 5F 29
RM8: Dag 1F 73
SM1: Sutt 5A 166
SM3: Cheam 6G 165
SW13 2A 116
SW19 6H 135
UB1: S'hall 7B 76
UB6: G'frd 4G 77
W3 *2G 97*
(*off Ridgeway Dr.*)
W5 7D 78
Broadway Arc. *W6* *4E 98*
(*off Hammersmith B'way.*)
Broadway Av. CR0: C'don 5D 156
TW1: Twick 6B 114
Broadway Cen., The W6 4E 98
Broadway Chambers *W6* *4E 98*
(*off Hammersmith B'way.*)
Broadway Cl. IG8: Wfd G 6E 36
Broadway Ct. BR3: Beck 3E 158
SW19 6J 135
Broadway Gdns. CR4: Mitc 4C 154
IG8: Wfd G 6E 36
Broadway Ho. *BR1: Brom* *5F 141*
(*off Bromley Rd.*)
BR1: Brom 3J 159
(High St.)
E8 *1H 85*
(*off Ada St.*)
Broadway Mans. *SW6* *7J 99*
(*off Fulham Rd.*)
Broadway Mkt. E8 1H 85
(not continuous)
IG6: Ilf 1H 53
(not continuous)
SW17 4D 136
Broadway Mkt. M. E8 1G 85
Broadway M. E5 7F 49
N13 5E 32
N21 1G 33
Broadway Pde. *E4* *6K 35*
(*off The Broadway*)
HA2: Harr 5F 41
N8 6J 47
UB3: Hayes 1J 93
Broadway Pl. SW19 6H 135
Broadway Retail Pk. NW2 4F 63
Broadway Shop. Cen. DA6: Bex 4G 127
Broadway Shop. Mall
SW1 1C 18 (3H 101)
Broadway Sq. DA6: Bex 4G 127
Broadway Theatre, The
Barking 1G 89
Catford 7D 122
Broadway W5, The W5 7D 78
Broadway Wlk. E14 2C 104
Broadwell Ct. *TW5: Hest* *1B 112*
(*off Springwell Rd.*)
Broadwell Pde. *NW6* *6K 63*
(*off Broadhurst Gdns.*)
Broadwick St. W1 2B 12 (7G 83)
Broadwood Av. HA4: Ruis 6F 39
Broadwood Ter. W8 4H 99
Broad Yd. EC1 4A 8 (4B 84)
Brocas Cl. NW3 7C 64
Brockbridge Ho. SW15 6B 116
Brockdene Dr. BR2: Kes 4B 172
Brockdish Av. IG11: Bark 5K 71
Brockenhurst KT8: W Mole 5D 148
Brockenhurst Av. KT4: Wor Pk 1A 164
Brockenhurst Gdns. IG1: Ilf 5G 71
NW7 5F 29
Brockenhurst M. N18 4B 34
Brockenhurst Rd. CR0: C'don 7H 157
Brockenhurst Way SW16 2H 155
Brocket Ho. SW8 2H 119
Brockham Cl. SW19 5H 135
Brockham Ct. CR2: S Croy 5C 168
Brockham Cres. CR0: New Ad 7F 171
Brockham Dr. IG2: Ilf 6F 53
SW2 7K 119
Brockham Ho. *NW1* *1G 83*
(*off Bayham Pl.*)
SW2 *7K 119*
(*off Brockham Dr.*)
Brockham St. SE1 7D 14 (3C 102)
Brockhurst Cl. HA7: Stan 6E 26
Brockill Cres. SE4 4A 122
Brocklebank Ho. *E16* *1E 106*
(*off Glenister St.*)
Brocklebank Rd. SE7 4K 105
SW18 7A 118
Brocklehurst St. SE14 7K 103
Brocklesby Rd. SE25 4H 157
BROCKLEY 4K 121
Brockley Av. HA7: Stan 3K 27
Brockley Cl. HA7: Stan 4K 27
Brockley Cres. RM5: Col R 1J 55
Brockley Cross SE4 3A 122
Brockley Cross Bus. Cen. SE4 3A 122
Brockley Footpath SE4 5A 122
(not continuous)
SE15 3J 121
Brockley Gdns. SE4 2B 122
Brockley Gro. SE4 5B 122
Brockley Hall Rd. SE4 5A 122
Brockley Hill HA7: Stan 1H 27
Brockley Jack Theatre 5A 122
Brockley M. SE4 5A 122
Brockley Pk. SE23 7A 122
Brockley Ri. SE23 1A 140
Brockley Rd. SE4 3B 122
Brockleyside HA7: Stan 4K 27
Brockley Vw. SE23 7A 122
Brockley Way SE4 5K 121
Brockman Ri. BR1: Brom 4F 141
Brockmer Ho. *E1* *7H 85*
(*off Crowder St.*)
Brock Pl. E3 4D 86
Brock Rd. E13 5K 87
Brocks Dr. SM3: Cheam 3G 165
Brockshot Cl. TW8: Bford 5D 96
Brock St. SE15 3J 121
Brockway Cl. E11 2G 69
Brockweir *E2* *2J 85*
(*off Cyprus St.*)
Brockwell Av. BR3: Beck 5D 158
Brockwell Cl. BR5: St M Cry 5K 161
Brockwell Ct. SW2 5A 120
Brockwell Ho. *SE11* *7H 19*
(*off Vauxhall St.*)
Brockwell Pk. 6B 120
Brockwell Pk. Gdns. SE24 7A 120
Brockwell Pk. Lido 6B 120
Brockwell Pk. Row SW2 7A 120
Brockwell Pas. SE24 6B 120
Brodia Rd. N16 3E 66
Brodick Ho. *E3* *2B 86*
(*off Saxon Rd.*)
Brodie Ho. *SE1* *5F 103*
(*off Cooper's Rd.*)
Brodie Rd. E4 1K 35
EN2: Enf 1H 23
Brodie St. SE1 5F 103
Brodlove La. E1 7K 85
Brodrick Gro. SE2 4B 108
Brodrick Rd. SW17 2C 136
Brody Ho. *E1* *6J 9*
(*off Strype St.*)
Brograve Gdns. BR3: Beck 2D 158
Broken Wharf EC4 2C 14 (7C 84)
Brokesley St. E3 3B 86
Broke Wlk. E8 1F 85
Bromar Rd. SE5 3E 120
Bromefield HA7: Stan 1C 42
Bromehead St. E1 6J 85
Bromell's Rd. SW4 4G 119
Brome Rd. SE9 3D 124
Bromfelde Rd. SW4 3H 119
Bromfelde Wlk. SW4 2H 119
Bromfield Ct. *SE16* *3G 103*
(*off Ben Smith Way*)
Bromfield St. N1 1A 84
Bromhall Rd. RM8: Dag 6B 72
RM9: Dag 6B 72
Bromhead Rd. *E1* *6J 85*
(*off Jubilee St.*)
Bromhedge SE9 3D 142
Bromholm Rd. SE2 3B 108
Bromleigh Ct. SE23 2G 139
Bromleigh Ho. *SE1* *7J 15*
(*off St Saviour's Est.*)
BROMLEY
BR1 2J 159
E3 3D 86
Bromley Av. BR1: Brom 7G 141
Bromley Coll. BR1: Brom 1J 159
BROMLEY COMMON 7C 160
Bromley Comn. BR2: Brom 4A 160
Bromley Cres. BR2: Brom 3H 159
HA4: Ruis 4H 57
Bromley Environmental Education Cen.
at High Elms (BEECHE) 6H 173
Bromley FC 5K 159
Bromley Gdns. BR2: Brom 3H 159
Bromley Golf Course 7C 160
Bromley Gro. BR2: Brom 2F 159
Bromley Hall Rd. E14 5E 86
Bromley High St. E3 3D 86
Bromley Hill BR1: Brom 6G 141
Bromley Ho. *BR1: Brom* *1J 159*
(*off North St.*)
Bromley Ind. Cen. BR1: Brom 3B 160
Bromley La. BR7: Chst 7G 143
Bromley Little Theatre 1J 159
BROMLEY PARK 1G 159
Bromley Pk. BR1: Brom 1H 159
Bromley Pl. W1 5A 6 (5G 83)
Bromley Rd. BR1: Brom 1D 140
BR2: Brom 2D 158
BR3: Beck 1D 158
BR7: Chst 1F 161
E10 6D 50
E17 3C 50
N17 1F 49
N18 3J 33
SE6 1D 140
Bromley Ski Cen. 7E 144
Bromley St. E1 5K 85

Bromley Tennis Cen. 3H 173
BROMPTON 2D 16 (3C 100)
Brompton Arc. SW3 7E 10
Brompton Cemetery 6K 99
Brompton Cl. SE20 2G 157
TW4: Houn 5D 112
Brompton Cotts. *SW10* 6A 100
(off Hollywood Rd.)
Brompton Ct. *BR1: Brom* 1J 159
(off Tweedy Rd.)
Brompton Gro. N2 4C 46
Brompton M. N12 6F 31
Brompton Oratory 2C 16 (3C 100)
Brompton Pk. Cres. SW6 6K 99
Brompton Pl. SW3 1D 16 (3C 100)
Brompton Rd. SW1 3C 16 (4C 100)
SW3 3C 16 (4C 100)
SW7 4C 100
Brompton Sq. SW3 1C 16 (3C 100)
Brompton Ter. SE18 1D 124
Brompton Vs. *SW6* 6J 99
(off Lillie Rd.)
Bromwich Av. N6 2E 64
Bromyard Av. W3 7A 80
Bromyard Ho. *SE15* 7H 103
(off Commercial Way)
Bromyward Ho. W3 1B 98
Bron Ct. NW6 1J 81
BRONDESBURY 7H 63
Brondesbury Ct. NW2 6F 63
Brondesbury M. NW6 7J 63
BRONDESBURY PARK 1E 80
Brondesbury Pk. NW2 6E 62
NW6 6E 62
Brondesbury Pk. Mans. *NW6* 1G 81
(off Salusbury Rd.)
Brondesbury Rd. NW6 2H 81
Brondesbury Vs. NW6 2H 81
Bronhill Ter. N17 1G 49
Bronsart Rd. SW6 7G 99
Bronson Rd. SW20 2F 153
Bronte Cl. DA8: Erith 7H 109
E7 4J 69
IG2: Ilf 4E 52
Bronte Ct. W3 2G 97
W14 3F 99
(off Girdler's Rd.)
Bronte Ho. N16 5E 66
SW4 7G 119
SW17 3B 136
(off Grosvenor Way)
Bronti Cl. SE17 5C 102
Bronwen Ct. *NW8* 2A 4
(off Grove End Rd.)
Bronze Age Way DA8: Erith 2H 109
DA17: Belv 2H 109
Bronze St. SE8 7C 104
Brook Av. HA8: Edg 6C 28
HA9: Wemb 2F 61
RM10: Dag 7H 73
Brookbank Av. W7 5H 77
Brookbank Rd. SE13 3C 122
Brook Cl. HA4: Ruis 7G 39
NW7 7B 30
SW17 2E 136
SW20 3D 152
TW19: Stanw 7B 110
W3 1G 97
Brook Ct. BR3: Beck 1B 158
E11 3G 69
E17 3A 50
EC4 2E 14
(off Laurence Pountney La.)
HA8: Edg 5C 28
IG11: Bark 1K 89
(Sebastian Ct.)
IG11: Bark 2G 89
(Spring Pl.)
SE12 3A 142
Brook Cres. E4 4H 35
N9 4C 34
Brookdale N11 4B 32
Brookdale Rd. DA5: Bexl 6E 126
E17 3C 50
SE6 7D 122
(Catford B'way.)
SE6 6D 122
(Medusa Rd.)
Brookdales NW11 4G 45
Brookdene Rd. SE18 4J 107
Brook Dr. HA1: Harr 4G 41
HA4: Ruis 7G 39
SE11 2K 19 (3A 102)
Brooke Av. HA2: Harr 3G 59
Brooke Cl. WD23: Bush 1B 26
Brooke Ct. *W10* 2G 81
(off Kilburn La.)
Brooke Ho. SE14 1A 122
WD23: Bush 1B 26
Brookehowse Rd. SE6 2C 140
Brookend Rd.
DA15: Sidc 1J 143
Brooke Rd. E5 3G 67
E17 4E 50
N16 3F 67
Brooke's Ct. EC1 6J 7 (5A 84)
Brooke's Mkt. EC1 5K 7
Brooke St. EC1 6J 7 (5A 84)
Brooke Way WD23: Bush 1B 26
Brookfield N6 3E 64
Brookfield Av. E17 4E 50
NW7 6J 29
SM1: Sutt 4B 166
W5 4D 78
Brookfield Cl. NW7 6J 29
Brookfield Ct. N12 4E 30
UB6: G'frd 3G 77
Brookfield Cres. HA3: Kenton 5E 42
NW7 6J 29
Brookfield Gdns. KT10: Clay 6A 162
Brookfield Pk. NW5 3F 65
Brookfield Path IG8: Wfd G 6B 36
Brookfield Rd. E9 6A 68
N9 3B 34
W4 2K 97
Brookfields EN3: Pond E 4E 24
Brookfields Av. CR4: Mitc 5C 154
Brook Gdns. E4 4J 35
KT2: King T 1J 151
SW13 3B 116
Brook Ga. W1 3F 11 (7D 82)
BROOK GREEN 4F 99
Brook Grn. W6 3F 99
Brook Grn. Flats *W14* 3F 99
(off Dunsany Rd.)
Brookhill Cl. EN4: E Barn 5H 21
SE18 5F 107
Brookhill Rd. EN4: E Barn 5H 21
SE18 6F 107
Brook Ho. *E1* 7G 85
(off Fletcher St.)
W6 4E 98
(off Shepherd's Bush Rd.)
Brookhouse Gdns. E4 4B 36
Brook Ho's. *NW1* 2G 83
(off Cranleigh St.)
Brook Ind. Est. UB4: Yead 1B 94
Brooking Cl. RM8: Dag 3C 72
Brooking Rd. E7 5J 69
Brookland Cl. NW11 4J 45
Brookland Gth. NW11 4J 45
Brookland Hill NW11 4K 45
Brookland Ri. NW11 4J 45
Brooklands, The TW7: Isle 1H 113
Brooklands App. RM1: Rom 4K 55
Brooklands Av. DA15: Sidc 2H 143
SW19 2K 135
Brooklands Cl. RM7: Rom 4K 55
TW16: Sun 1G 147
Brooklands Ct. CR4: Mitc 2B 154
KT1: King T 4D 150
(off Surbiton Rd.)
Brooklands Ct. N21 5J 23
NW6 7H 63
Brooklands Dr. UB6: G'frd 1C 78
Brooklands La. RM7: Rom 4K 55
(not continuous)
Brooklands Pk. SE3 3J 123
Brooklands Pas. SW8 1H 119
Brooklands Pl. TW12: Hamp H 5F 131
Brooklands Rd. KT7: T Ditt 1A 162
RM7: Rom 4K 55
Brooklands Ter. TW16: Sun 4J 147
Brook La. BR1: Brom 6J 141
DA5: Bexl, Bex 6D 126
SE3 2K 123
Brook La. Bus. Cen. TW8: Bford 5D 96
Brook La. Nth. TW8: Bford 5D 96
(not continuous)
Brooklea Cl. NW9 1A 44
Brook Lodge *NW11* 5F 45
(off Nth. Circular Rd.)
RM7: Rom 4K 55
(off Brooklands Rd.)
Brooklyn SE20 7G 139
Brooklyn Av. SE25 4H 157
Brooklyn Cl. SM5: Cars 2C 166
Brooklyn Ct. *W12* 1E 98
(off Frithville Gdns.)
Brooklyn Gro. SE25 4H 157
Brooklyn Pas. *W12* 2E 98
(off Lime Gro.)
Brooklyn Rd. BR2: Brom 5B 160
SE25 4H 157
Brookman Ho. *E3* 2B 86
(off Mostyn Gro.)
Brookmarsh Ind. Est. SE10 7D 104
Brook Mead KT19: Ewe 6A 164
Brookmead CR0: Bedd 6G 155
Brookmead Av. BR1: Brom 5D 160
Brookmead Ind. Est. CR0: Bedd 6G 155
Brook Mdw. N12 3E 30
Brook Mdw. Cl. IG8: Wfd G 6B 36
Brookmead Rd. CR0: C'don 6G 155
Brook M. IG7: Chig 3K 37
N13 5F 33
WC2 6H 83
Brook M. Nth. W2 2A 10 (7A 82)
Brookmill Rd. SE8 1C 122
Brook Pde. IG7: Chig 3K 37
Brook Pk. Cl. N21 5G 23
Brook Pl. EN5: Barn 5D 20
Brook Retail Pk. HA4: Ruis 5B 58
Brook Ri. IG7: Chig 3K 37
Brook Rd. CR7: Thor H 4C 156
IG2: Ilf 6J 53
IG9: Buck H, Wfd G 2D 36
KT6: Surb 2E 162
N8 4J 47
N22 3K 47
NW2 2B 62
TW1: Twick 6A 114
Brook Rd. Sth. TW8: Bford 6D 96
Brooks Apartments *E3* 5C 86
(off Geoff Cade Way)
Brooks Av. E6 4D 88
Brooksbank Ho. *E9* 6J 67
(off Retreat Pl.)
Brooksbank St. E9 6J 67
Brooksby Ho. *N1* 7A 66
(off Liverpool Rd.)
Brooksby M. N1 7A 66
Brooksby St. N1 7A 66
Brooksby's Wlk. E9 5K 67
Brooks Cl. SE9 2E 142
Brooks Ct. SW8 7G 101
Brookscroft E17 3D 50
Brookscroft Rd. E17 1D 50
(not continuous)
Brooks Farm 7D 50
Brookshill HA3: Hrw W 5C 26
Brookshill Av. HA3: Hrw W 5C 26
Brookshill Dr. HA3: Hrw W 5C 26
Brookshill Ga. HA3: Hrw W 5C 26
Brookside BR6: Orp 7K 161
EN4: E Barn 6H 21
N21 6E 22
SM5: Cars 5E 166
UB10: Uxb 7B 56
Brookside Cl. EN5: Barn 6B 20
HA2: Harr 4C 58
HA3: Kenton 5D 42
TW13: Felt 3J 129
Brookside Cres. KT4: Wor Pk 1C 164
Brookside Rd. N9 4C 34
(not continuous)
N19 2G 65
NW11 6G 45
UB4: Yead 7A 76
Brookside Sth. EN4: E Barn 7K 21
Brookside Wlk. N3 3G 45
N12 6D 30
NW11 4G 45
Brookside Way CR0: C'don 6K 157
Brooks La. W4 6G 97
Brooks Lodge N1 2E 84
Brook's M. W1 2J 11 (7F 83)
Brook Sq. SE18 1C 124
Brooks Rd. E13 1J 87
W4 5G 97
Brook St. DA8: Erith 5H 109
DA17: Belv, Erith 5H 109
KT1: King T 2E 150
N17 2F 49
W1 2H 11 (7F 83)
W2 2B 10 (7B 82)
Brooksville Av. NW6 1G 81
Brook Va. DA8: Erith 1H 127
Brookview Ct. EN1: Enf 5K 23
Brookview Rd. SW16 5G 137
Brookville Rd. SW6 7H 99
Brook Wlk. HA8: Edg 6E 28
N2 1B 46
Brook Way IG7: Chig 3K 37
Brookway SE3 3J 123
Brookwood Av. SW13 2B 116
Brookwood Cl. BR2: Brom 4H 159
Brookwood Ho. *SE1* 7B 14
(off Webber St.)
Brookwood Rd. SW18 1H 135
TW3: Houn 2F 113
Broom Cl. BR2: Brom 6C 160
TW11: Tedd 7D 132
Broomcroft Av. UB5: N'olt 3A 76
Broome Rd. TW12: Hamp 7D 130
Broome Way SE5 7D 102
Broomfield E17 7B 50
NW1 7E 64
(off Ferdinand St.)
TW16: Sun 1J 147
Broomfield Av. N13 5E 32
Broomfield Ct. N2 4C 46
Broomfield Ho. *HA7: Stan* 3F 27
(off Stanmore Hill)
SE17 4E 102
(off Massinger St.)
Broomfield La. N13 4D 32
Broomfield Pl. W13 1B 96
Broomfield Rd. BR3: Beck 3A 158
DA6: Bex 5G 127
KT5: Surb 1F 163
N13 5D 32
RM6: Chad H 7D 54
TW9: Kew 1F 115
TW11: Tedd 6C 132
W13 1B 96
Broomfield St. E14 5C 86
Broom Gdns. CR0: C'don 3C 170
Broomgrove Gdns. HA8: Edg 1G 43
Broomgrove Rd. SW9 2K 119
Broomhall Rd. CR2: Sande 7D 168
BROOM HILL 7K 161
Broomhill Ct. IG8: Wfd G 6D 36
Broomhill Ri. DA6: Bex 5G 127

Broomhill Rd. BR6: Orp 7K **161**
IG3: Ilf 2A **72**
IG8: Wfd G 6D **36**
(not continuous)
SW18 . . . . .5J **117**
Broomhill Wlk. IG8: Wfd G 6C **36**
Broomhouse La. SW6 . . . . .2J **117**
Broomhouse Rd. SW6 . . . . .2J **117**
Broomloan La. SM1: Sutt 2J **165**
Broom Lock TW11: Tedd 6C **132**
Broom Mead DA6: Bex 6G **127**
Broom Pk. TW11: Tedd 7D **132**
Broom Rd. CR0: C'don 3C **170**
TW11: Tedd 5B **132**
Broomsleigh Bus. Pk. SE26 . . . . .5B **140**
Broomsleigh St. NW6 . . . . .5H **63**
Broom Water TW11: Tedd 6C **132**
Broom Water W. TW11: Tedd 5C **132**
Broomwood Cl. CR0: C'don 5K **157**
DA5: Bexl 2K **145**
Broomwood Rd. SW4 . . . . .5E **118**
SW11 .6D **118**
Broseley Gro. SE26 . . . . .5A **140**
Brosse Way BR2: Brom 6C **160**
Broster Gdns. SE25 . . . . .3F **157**
Brotherstone Wlk. TW9: Kew 1H **115**
Brouard Ct. BR1: Brom 3J **159**
Brougham Rd. E8 . . . . .1G **85**
W3 . . . . .6J **79**
Brougham St. SW11 . . . . .2D **118**
Brough Cl. KT2: King T 5D **132**
SW8 . . . . .7J **101**
Broughton Av. N3 . . . . .3G **45**
TW10: Ham 3B **132**
Broughton Ct. W13 . . . . .7B **78**
Broughton Dr. SW9 . . . . .4A **120**
Broughton Gdns. N6 . . . . .6G **47**
Broughton Pl. E17 . . . . .1B **50**
Broughton Rd. BR6: Orp 2H **173**
CR7: Thor H 6A **156**
SW6 . . . . .2K **117**
W13 . . . . .7B **78**
Broughton Rd. App. SW6 . . . . .2K **117**
Broughton St. SW8 . . . . .2E **118**
Broughton St. Ind. Est. SW11 . . . . . . .2E **118**
Brouncker Rd. W3 . . . . .2J **97**
Browells La. TW13: Felt 2K **129**
(not continuous)
Brown Bear Ct. TW13: Hanw 4B **130**
Brown Cl. SM6: Wall 7J **167**
Browne Ho. *SE8* *7C* ***104***
(off Deptford Chu. St.)
Brownell Pl. W7 . . . . .2K **95**
Brownfield Area E14 . . . . .6D **86**
Brownfield St. E14 . . . . .6D **86**
Browngraves Rd. UB3: Harl 7E **92**
Brown Hart Gdns. W1 . . . . .2H **11** (7E **82**)
Brownhill Rd. SE6 . . . . .7D **122**
Browning Apartments *E3* *4B* ***86***
(off Hamlets Way)
Browning Av. KT4: Wor Pk 1D **164**
SM1: Sutt 4C **166**
W7 . . . . .6K **77**
Browning Cl. DA16: Well 1J **125**
E17 . . . . .4E **50**
RM5: Col R 1F **55**
TW12: Hamp 4D **130**
W9 . . . . .4A **4** (4A **82**)
Browning Ct. *W14* *6H* ***99***
(off Turneville Rd.)
Browning Ho. *N16* *4E* ***66***
(off Shakspeare Wlk.)
SE14 . . . .*1A* ***122***
(off Loring Rd.)
W12 . . . .*6E* ***80***
(off Wood La.)
Browning M. W1 . . . . .6H **5** (5F **83**)
Browning Rd. E11 . . . . .7H **51**
E12 . . . . .5D **70**
EN2: Enf 1J **23**
Browning St. SE17 . . . . .5C **102**
Browning Way TW5: Hest 1B **112**
Brownlea Gdns. IG3: Ilf 2A **72**
Brownlow Cl. EN4: E Barn 5G **21**
Brownlow Ct. N2 . . . . .5A **46**
N11 . . . .*6D* ***32***
(off Brownlow Rd.)
Brownlow Ho. *SE16* *2G* ***103***
(off George Row)
Brownlow M. WC1 . . . . .4H **7** (4K **83**)
Brownlow Rd. CR0: C'don 4E **168**
E7 . . . . .4J **69**
E8 . . . . .1F **85**
N3 . . . . .7E **30**
N11 . . . . .6D **32**
NW10 . . . . .7A **62**
W13 . . . . .1A **96**
Brownlow St. WC1 . . . . .6H **7** (5K **83**)
Brownrigg Rd. TW15: Ashf 4C **128**
Brown's Bldgs. EC3 . . . . .1H **15** (6E **84**)
Brownsea Wlk. NW7 . . . . .6A **30**
Browns La. NW5 . . . . .5F **65**
Brownspring Dr. SE9 . . . . .4F **143**
Brown's Rd. KT5: Surb 7F **151**
Browns Rd. E17 . . . . .3C **50**
Brown St. W1 . . . . .7E **4** (6D **82**)
Brownswell Rd. N2 . . . . .2B **46**
BROWNSWOOD PARK 2B 66
Brownswood Rd. N4 . . . . .3B **66**
Broxash Rd. SW11 . . . . .6E **118**
Broxbourne Av. E18 . . . . .4K **51**
Broxbourne Gdns. *BR6: Orp* *1K* ***173***
(off Broxbourne Rd.)
Broxbourne Ho. *E3* *4D* ***86***
(off Empson St.)
Broxbourne Rd. BR6: Orp 1K **173**
E7 . . . . .3J **69**
Broxholme Cl. SE25 . . . . .4D **156**
Broxholme Ho. *SW6* *1K* ***117***
(off Harwood Rd.)
Broxholm Rd. SE27 . . . . .3A **138**
Broxted Rd. SE6 . . . . .2B **140**
Broxwood Way NW8 . . . . .1C **82**
Bruce Av. TW17: Shep 6E **146**
Bruce Castle Ct. *N17* *1F* ***49***
(off Lordship La.)
Bruce Castle Mus. **1E 48**
Bruce Castle Rd. N17 . . . . .1F **49**
Bruce Cl.
DA16: Well 1B **126**
W10 . . . . .5F **81**
Bruce Ct. DA15: Sidc 4K **143**
Bruce Gdns. N20 . . . . .3J **31**
Bruce Gro. N17 . . . . .1E **48**
Bruce Hall M. SW17 . . . . .4E **136**
Bruce Ho. W10 . . . . .5F **81**
Bruce Rd. CR4: Mitc 7E **136**
E3 . . . . .3D **86**
EN5: Barn 3B **20**
HA3: W'stone 2J **41**
NW10 . . . . .7K **61**
SE25 . . . . .4D **156**
Bruckner St. W10 . . . . .3G **81**
Brudenell Rd. SW17 . . . . .3D **136**
Bruffs Mdw.
UB5: N'olt 6C **58**
Bruford Ct. SE8 . . . . .6C **104**
Bruges Pl. *NW1* *7G* ***65***
(off Randolph St.)
Brumfield Rd. KT19: Ewe 5J **163**
Brummel Cl. DA7: Bex 3J **127**
Brune Ho. E1 . . . . .6J **9**
Brunei Gallery **5D 6** (**5H 83**)
Brunel Cl. SE19 . . . . .6F **139**
TW5: Cran 7K **93**
UB5: N'olt 3D **76**
Brunel Ct. HA8: Edg 4A **28**
SE16 . . . .*2J* ***103***
(off Canon Beck Rd.)
SW13 . . . .*2B* ***116***
(off Westfields Av.)
Brunel Est. W2 . . . . .5J **81**
Brunel Ho. *BR2: Brom* *6C* ***160***
(off Wells Vw. Dr.)
E14 . . . .*5D* ***104***
(off Ship Yd.)
RM8: Dag 4A **72**
Brunel M. W10 . . . . .3F **81**
Brunel Mus. **2J 103**
Brunel Pl. UB1: S'hall 6F **77**
Brunel Rd. E17 . . . . .6A **50**
IG8: Wfd G 5J **37**
SE16 . . . . .2J **103**
W3 . . . . .5A **80**
Brunel Science Pk. UB8: Cowl 3A **74**
Brunel St. E16 . . . . .6H **87**
Brunel University
Indoor Athletics Cen. **3A 74**
Sports Pk. **4B 74**
Uxbridge Campus **3A 74**
Brunel Wlk. N15 . . . . .5E **48**
SW10 . . . .*7B* ***100***
(off Cheyne Rd.)
TW2: Whitt 7E **112**
Brune St. E1 . . . . .6J **9** (5F **85**)
Brunlees Ho. *SE1* *3C* ***102***
(off Bath Ter.)
Brunner Cl. NW11 . . . . .5K **45**
Brunner Ho. SE6 . . . . .4E **140**
Brunner Rd. E17 . . . . .5A **50**
W5 . . . . .4D **78**
Bruno Pl. NW9 . . . . .2J **61**
Brunswick Av. N11 . . . . .3K **31**
Brunswick Cen. WC1 . . . . .3E **6** (4J **83**)
Brunswick Cl. DA6: Bex 4D **126**
HA5: Pinn 6C **40**
KT7: T Ditt 1A **162**
TW2: Twick 3H **131**
Brunswick Cl. Est. EC1 . . . . . . .2A **8** (3B **84**)
Brunswick Ct. *EC1* *2A* ***8***
(off Tompion St.)
EN4: E Barn 5G **21**
SE1 . . . . .7H **15** (2E **102**)
SM1: Sutt 4K **165**
SW1 . . . .*4D* ***18***
(off Regency St.)
Brunswick Cres. N11 . . . . .3K **31**
Brunswick Flats *W11* *6J* ***81***
(off Westbourne Gro.)
Brunswick Gdns. IG6: Ilf 1G **53**
W5 . . . . .4E **78**
W8 . . . . .1J **99**
Brunswick Gro. N11 . . . . .3K **31**
Brunswick Ho. *E2* *2F* ***85***
(off Thurtle Rd.)
N3 . . . . .1H **45**
SE16 . . . .*3A* ***104***
(off Brunswick Quay)
W6 . . . .*5E* ***98***
(off Parrs Way)
Brunswick Ind. Pk. N11 . . . . .4A **32**
Brunswick Mans. *WC1* *3F* ***7***
(off Handel St.)
Brunswick M. SW16 . . . . .6H **137**
W1 . . . . .7F **5** (6D **82**)
BRUNSWICK PARK 3J 31
Brunswick Pk. SE5 . . . . .1E **120**
Brunswick Pk. Gdns.
N11 . . . . .2K **31**
Brunswick Pk. Rd. N11 . . . . .2K **31**
Brunswick Pl. N1 . . . . .2F **9** (3D **84**)
NW1 . . . . .4H **5** (4E **82**)
(not continuous)
SE19 . . . . .7G **139**
Brunswick Quay SE16 . . . . .3K **103**
Brunswick Rd. DA6: Bex 4D **126**
E10 . . . . .1E **68**
E14 . . . . .6E **86**
EN3: Enf L 1H **25**
KT2: King T 1G **151**
N15 . . . . .5E **48**
SM1: Sutt 4K **165**
W5 . . . . .4D **78**
Brunswick Sq. N17 . . . . .6A **34**
WC1 . . . . .3F **7** (4J **83**)
(not continuous)
Brunswick St. E17 . . . . .5E **50**
Brunswick Ter. BR3: Beck 1D **158**
Brunswick Vs. SE5 . . . . .1E **120**
Brunswick Way N11 . . . . .4A **32**
Brunton Pl. E14 . . . . .6A **86**
Brushfield St. E1 . . . . .5H **9** (5E **84**)
Brushwood Cl. E14 . . . . .5D **86**
Brussels Rd. SW11 . . . . .4B **118**
Bruton Cl. BR7: Chst 7D **142**
Bruton La. W1 . . . . .3K **11** (7F **83**)
Bruton Pl. W1 . . . . .3K **11** (7F **83**)
Bruton Rd.
SM4: Mord 4A **154**
Bruton St. W1 . . . . .3K **11** (7F **83**)
Bruton Way W13 . . . . .5A **78**
Brutus Ct. *SE11* *4B* ***102***
(off Kennington La.)
Bryan Av. NW10 . . . . .7D **62**
Bryan Cl. TW16: Sun 7J **129**
Bryan Ho. NW10 . . . . .7D **62**
SE16 . . . . .2B **104**
Bryan Rd. SE16 . . . . .2B **104**
Bryan's All. SW6 . . . . .2K **117**
Bryanston Av. TW2: Whitt 1F **131**
Bryanston Cl. UB2: S'hall 4D **94**
Bryanston Ct. W1 . . . . .7E **4**
(not continuous)
Bryanstone Ct. SM1: Sutt 3A **166**
Bryanstone Rd. N8 . . . . .5H **47**
Bryanston Mans. *W1* *5E* ***4***
(off York St.)
Bryanston M. E. W1 . . . . .6E **4** (5D **82**)
Bryanston M. W. W1 . . . . .6E **4** (5D **82**)
Bryanston Pl. W1 . . . . .6E **4** (5D **82**)
Bryanston Sq. W1 . . . . .6E **4** (6D **82**)
Bryanston St. W1 . . . . .1E **10** (6D **82**)
Bryan St. N1 .1K **83**
Bryant Cl. EN5: Barn 5C **20**
Bryant Ct. *E2* *1F* ***85***
(off Whiston Rd.)
W3 . . . . .1K **97**
Bryant Ho. *E3* *2C* ***86***
(off Thomas Fyre Dr.)
Bryant Rd. UB5: N'olt 3A **76**
Bryant St. E2 .1F **85**
E15 . . . . .7F **69**
Bryantwood Rd. N7 . . . . .5A **66**
Brycedale Cres. N14 . . . . .4C **32**
Bryce Ho. *SE14* *6K* ***103***
(off John Williams Cl.)
Bryce Rd. RM8: Dag 4C **72**
Brydale Ho. *SE16* *4K* ***103***
(off Rotherhithe New Rd.)
Bryden Cl. SE26 . . . . .5A **140**
Brydges Pl. WC2 . . . . .3E **12** (7J **83**)
Brydges Rd. E15 . . . . .5F **69**
Brydon Wlk. N1 . . . . .1J **83**
Bryer Ct. EC2 . . . . .5C **8**
Bryett Rd. N7 .3J **65**
Bryher Ct. SE11 . . . . .5J **19**
Brymay Cl. E3 .2C **86**
Brymcourt W9 .2K **81**
Brynmaer Rd. SW11 . . . . .1D **118**
Bryn-y-mawr Rd. EN1: Enf 4A **24**
Bryony Cl. UB8: Hil 5B **74**
Bryony Rd. W12 . . . . .7C **80**
Bryony Way TW16: Sun 6J **129**
Buccleugh Ho. E5 . . . . .7G **49**
Buchanan Cl. N21 . . . . .5E **22**
Buchanan Ct. *SE16* *4K* ***103***
(off Worgan St.)
Buchanan Gdns. NW10 . . . . .2D **80**
Buchan Ho. *W3* *2H* ***97***
(off Hanbury Rd.)
Buchan Rd. SE15 . . . . .3J **121**
Bucharest Rd. SW18 . . . . .7A **118**
Buckden Cl. N2 . . . . .4D **46**
SE12 . . . . .6J **123**

Buckfast Ct.—Burgess Pk.

Buckfast Ct. *W13* *7A 78*
(off Romsey Rd.)
Buckfast Ho. N14 .... 5B 22
Buckfast Rd. SM4: Mord 4K 153
Buckfast St. E2 .... 3G 85
Buck Hill Wlk. W2 .... 3B 10 (7B 82)
Buckhold Rd. SW18 .... 6J 117
Buckhurst Av. SM5: Cars 1C 166
Buckhurst Ct. IG9: Buck H 1G 37
BUCKHURST HILL 2G 37
Buckhurst Hill Ho.
IG9: Buck H 2E 36
Buckhurst Ho. N7 .... 5H 65
Buckhurst St. E1 .... 4H 85
Buckhurst Way IG9: Buck H 4G 37
Buckingham Arc. WC2 .... 3E 12
Buckingham Av. CR7: Thor H 1A 156
DA16: Well 4J 125
KT8: W Mole 2F 149
N20 .... 7F 21
TW14: Felt 6K 111
UB6: G'frd 1A 78
Buckingham Chambers *SW1* *3B 18*
(off Greencoat Pl.)
Buckingham Cl. BR5: Pet W 7J 161
EN1: Enf 2K 23
TW12: Hamp 5D 130
W5 .... 5C 78
Buckingham Ct. NW4 .... 3C 44
UB5: N'olt 2C 76
W7 .... *4K 77*
(off Copley Cl.)
W11 .... *7J 81*
(off Kensington Pk. Rd.)
Buckingham Dr. BR7: Chst 4G 143
Buckingham Gdns. CR7: Thor H 2A 156
HA8: Edg 7K 27
KT8: W Mole 2F 149
Buckingham Ga. SW1 .... 1A 18 (3G 101)
Buckingham Gro. UB10: Hil 2C 74
Buckingham La. SE23 .... 7A 122
Buckingham Mans. *NW6* *5K 63*
(off West End La.)
Buckingham M. N1 .... 6E 66
NW10 .... 2B 80
SW1 .... 1A 18
Buckingham Palace .... **7K 11 (2F 101)**
Buckingham Pal. Rd.
SW1 .... 4J 17 (4F 101)
Buckingham Pde. HA7: Stan 5H 27
Buckingham Pl. SW1 .... 1A 18 (3G 101)
Buckingham Rd. CR4: Mitc 4J 155
E10 .... 3D 68
E11 .... 5A 52
E15 .... 5H 69
E18 .... 1H 51
HA1: Harr 5H 41
HA8: Edg 7A 28
IG1: Ilf 2H 71
KT1: King T 4F 151
N1 .... 6E 66
N22 .... 1J 47
NW10 .... 2B 80
TW10: Ham 2D 132
TW12: Hamp 4D 130
Buckingham St. WC2 .... 4F 13 (7J 83)
Buckingham Way SM6: Wall 7G 167
Buckland Cl. NW7 .... 4H 29
Buckland Ct. *N1* *2E 84*
(off St John's Est.)
UB10: Ick 2E 56
Buckland Cres. NW3 .... 7B 64
Buckland Ho. *SW1* *5J 17*
(part of Abbots Mnr.)
Buckland Ri. HA5: Pinn 1A 40
Buckland Rd. BR6: Orp 4J 173
E10 .... 2E 68
KT9: Chess 5F 163
Bucklands Rd. TW11: Tedd 6C 132
Buckland St. N1 .... 2D 84
Buckland's Wharf KT1: King T 2D 150
Buckland Wlk. SM4: Mord 4A 154
W3 .... 2J 97
Buckland Way KT4: Wor Pk 1E 164
Buck La. NW9 .... 5K 43
Bucklebury *NW1* *3A 6*
(off Stanhope St.)
Buckleigh Av. SW20 .... 3G 153
Buckleigh Rd. SW16 .... 6H 137
Buckleigh Way SE19 .... 7F 139
Buckler Ct. N7 .... 5K 65
Buckler Gdns. SE9 .... 3D 142
Bucklers All. SW6 .... 6H 99
Bucklersbury EC4 .... 1E 14 (6D 84)
Bucklersbury Pas. EC4 .... 6D 84
Buckler's Way SM5: Cars 3D 166
Buckles Ct. DA17: Belv 4D 108
Buckle St. E1 .... 7K 9 (6F 85)
Buckley Cl. SE23 .... 7H 121
Buckley Ct. NW6 .... 7H 63
SE1 .... 3F 103
Buckley Ho. *W14* *2G 99*
(off Holland Pk. Av.)
Buckley Rd. NW6 .... 7H 63
Buckmaster Cl. *SW9* *3A 120*
(off Stockwell Pk. Rd.)
Buckmaster Ho. N7 .... 4K 65
Buckmaster Rd. SW11 .... 4C 118
Bucknall St. WC2 .... 7D 6 (6J 83)
Bucknall Way BR3: Beck 4D 158
Bucknell Cl. SW2 .... 4K 119
Buckner Rd. SW2 .... 4K 119
Bucknill Ho. *SW1* *5J 17*
(off Ebury Bri. Rd.)
Buckrell Rd. E4 .... 2A 36
Buckridge Ho. *EC1* *5J 7*
(off Portpool La.)
Buckshead Ho. *W2* *5J 81*
(off Gt. Western Rd.)
Buckstone Cl. SE23 .... 6J 121
Buckstone Rd. N18 .... 5B 34
Buck St. NW1 .... 7F 65
Buckters Rents SE16 .... 1A 104
Buckthorne Rd. SE4 .... 5A 122
Buckthorn Ho. *DA15: Sidc* *3K 143*
(off Longlands Rd.)
E15 .... *3G 87*
(off Manor Rd.)
Buck Wlk. E17 .... 4F 51
Buckwheat Ct. DA18: Erith 3D 108
Budd Cl. N12 .... 4E 30
Buddings Circ. HA9: Wemb 3J 61
Buddleia Ho. TW13: Felt 1J 129
Budd's All. TW1: Twick 5C 114
Bude Cl. E17 .... 5B 50
Budge La. CR4: Mitc 7D 154
Budge's Wlk. W2 .... 3A 10
Budleigh Cres. DA16: Well 1C 126
Budleigh Ho. *SE15* *7G 103*
(off Bird in Bush Rd.)
Budoch Ct. IG3: Ilf 2A 72
Budoch Dr. IG3: Ilf 2A 72
Buer Rd. SW6 .... 2G 117
Bugsby's Way SE7 .... 4H 105
SE10 .... 4H 105
Buick Ho. *E3* *4C 86*
(off Wellington Way)
KT2: King T 2F 151
Building 50 SE18 .... 3G 107
Bulbarrow *NW8* *1K 81*
(off Abbey Rd.)
Bulganak Rd. CR7: Thor H 4C 156
Bulinga St. SW1 .... 4E 18
Bullace Row SE5 .... 1D 120
Bull All. DA16: Well 3B 126
Bullard's Pl. E2 .... 3K 85
Bullbanks Rd. DA17: Belv 4J 109
Bulleid Way SW1 .... 4K 17 (4F 101)
Bullen Ho. *E1* *4H 85*
(off Collingwood St.)
Bullen St. SW11 .... 2C 118
Buller Cl. SE15 .... 7G 103
Buller Rd. CR7: Thor H 2D 156
IG11: Bark 7J 71
N17 .... 2G 49
N22 .... 2A 48
NW10 .... 3F 81
Bullers Cl. DA14: Sidc 5E 144
Bullers Wood Dr. BR7: Chst 7D 142
Bullescroft Rd. HA8: Edg 3B 28
Bullfinch Ho. *NW9* *6B 44*
(off Perryfield Way)
Bullingham Mans. *W8* *2J 99*
(off Pitt St.)
Bull Inn Ct. WC2 .... 3F 13
Bullivant St. E14 .... 7E 86
Bull La. BR7: Chst 7H 143
N18 .... 5K 33
RM10: Dag 3H 73
Bullman Cl. DA7: Bex 3H 127
Bull Rd. E15 .... 2H 87
Bullrush Cl. CR0: C'don 6E 156
SM5: Cars 2C 166
Bull's All. SW14 .... 2K 115
Bulls Bri. Cen. UB3: Hayes 3J 93
Bullsbridge Ind. Est. UB2: S'hall 4A 94
Bulls Bri. Rd. UB2: S'hall 4A 94
UB3: Hayes 3K 93
Bullsbrook Rd. UB4: Yead 1A 94
Bulls Gdns. SW3 .... 3D 16 (4C 100)
Bulls Head Pas. EC3 .... 1G 15
Bull Theatre, The **4C 20**
Bull Yd. SE15 .... 1G 121
Bulmer Gdns. HA3: Kenton 7D 42
Bulmer M. W11 .... 7J 81
Bulmer Pl. W11 .... 1J 99
Bulow Est. *SW6* *1K 117*
(off Pearscroft Rd.)
Bulstrode Av. TW3: Houn 2D 112
Bulstrode Gdns. TW3: Houn 3E 112
Bulstrode Pl. W1 .... 6H 5 (5E 82)
Bulstrode Rd. TW3: Houn 3E 112
Bulstrode St. W1 .... 7H 5 (6E 82)
Bulwark Ct. *E14* *4E 104*
(off Parkside Sq.)
Bulwer Ct. E11 .... 1F 69
Bulwer Ct. Rd. E11 .... 1F 69
Bulwer Gdns. EN5: New Bar 4F 21
Bulwer Rd. E11 .... 7F 51
EN5: New Bar 4E 20
N18 .... 4K 33
Bulwer St. W12 .... 1E 98
Bunbury Ho. *SE15* *7G 103*
(off Fenham Rd.)
Bunce's La. IG8: Wfd G 7C 36
Bungalow Rd. SE25 .... 4E 156
Bungalows, The E10 .... 6E 50
HA2: Harr 4D 58
IG6: Ilf 1J 53
SM6: Wall 5F 167
SW16 .... 7F 137
UB4: Yead 4B 76
Bunhill Row EC1 .... 3E 8 (4D 84)
Bunhouse Pl. SW1 .... 5H 17 (5E 100)
Bunkers Hill DA14: Sidc 3F 145
DA17: Belv 4G 109
NW11 .... 7A 46
Bunning Way N7 .... 7J 65
Bunns La. NW7 .... 6F 29
(not continuous)
Bunsen Ho. *E3* *2A 86*
(off Grove Rd.)
Bunsen St. E3 .... 2A 86
Buntingbridge Rd. IG2: Ilf 5H 53
Bunting Cl. CR4: Mitc 5D 154
N9 .... 1E 34
Bunting Ct. NW9 .... 2A 44
Bunting Ho. *UB10: Ick* *2E 56*
(off Coyle Dr.)
Bunton St. SE18 .... 3E 106
Bunwell Ho. *E3* *4B 86*
(off William Whiffin Sq.)
Bunyan Ct. EC2 .... 5C 8
Bunyan Rd. E17 .... 3A 50
Buonaparte M. SW1 .... 5C 18 (5H 101)
Burbage Cl. SE1 .... 3D 102
UB3: Hayes 6F 75
Burbage Ho. *N1* *1D 84*
(off Poole St.)
SE14 .... *6K 103*
(off Samuel Cl.)
Burbage Rd. SE21 .... 6C 120
SE24 .... 6C 120
Burberry Cl. KT3: N Mald 2A 152
Burbidge Rd. TW17: Shep 4C 146
Burbridge Way N17 .... 2G 49
Burcham Cl. TW12: Hamp 7E 130
Burcham St. E14 .... 6D 86
Burcharbro Rd. SE2 .... 6D 108
Burchell Ct. WD23: Bush 1B 26
Burchell Ho. *SE11* *5H 19*
(off Jonathan St.)
Burchell Rd. E10 .... 1D 68
SE15 .... 1H 121
Burcher Gale Gro. SE15 .... 7F 103
Burchetts Way TW17: Shep 6D 146
Burchett Way RM6: Chad H 6F 55
Burchwall Cl. RM5: Col R 1J 55
Burcote Rd. SW18 .... 7B 118
Burden Cl. TW8: Bford 5C 96
Burden Ho. *SW8* *7J 101*
(off Thorncroft St.)
Burdenshott Av. TW10: Rich 4H 115
Burden Way E11 .... 2K 69
Burder Cl. N1 .... 6E 66
Burder Rd. N1 .... 6E 66
Burdett Av. SW20 .... 1C 152
Burdett Cl. DA14: Sidc 5E 144
W7 .... 1K 95
Burdett M. NW3 .... 6B 64
W2 .... 6K 81
Burdett Rd. CR0: C'don 6D 156
E3 .... 4A 86
E14 .... 4A 86
TW9: Rich 2F 115
Burdetts Rd. RM9: Dag 1F 91
Burdock Cl. CR0: C'don 1K 169
Burdock Rd. N17 .... 3G 49
Burdon La. SM2: Cheam 7G 165
Burdon Pk. SM2: Cheam 7H 165
Bure Ct. EN5: New Bar 5E 20
Burfield Cl. SW17 .... 4B 136
Burford Cl. IG6: Ilf 4G 53
RM8: Dag 3C 72
UB10: Ick 4A 56
Burford Gdns. N13 .... 3E 32
Burford Ho. TW8: Bford 5D 96
Burford Rd. BR1: Brom 4C 160
E6 .... 3C 88
E15 .... 1F 87
KT4: Wor Pk 7B 152
SE6 .... 2B 140
SM1: Sutt 2J 165
TW8: Bford 5E 96
Burford Wlk. SW6 .... 7A 100
Burford Way CR0: New Ad 6E 170
Burford Wharf Apartments *E15* *1F 87*
(off Cam Rd.)
Burges Gro. SW13 .... 7D 98
Burges Rd. E6 .... 7C 70
Burgess Av. NW9 .... 6K 43
Burgess Bus. Pk. SE5 .... 7D 102
Burgess Cl. TW13: Hanw 4C 130
Burgess Ct. E6 .... 7E 70
SE6 .... 7C 122
UB1: S'hall *6F 77*
(off Fleming Rd.)
Burgess Hill NW2 .... 4J 63
Burgess Ho. *SE5* *7C 102*
(off Bethwin Rd.)
Burgess Lofts *SE5* *7C 102*
(off Bethwin Rd.)
Burgess M. SW19 .... 6K 135
Burgess Pk. **6D 102**

Burgess Pk. Kart Track 6D 102
Burgess Rd. E6 7E 70
E15 4G 69
SM1: Sutt 4K 165
Burgess St. E14 5C 86
Burge St. SE1 3D 102
Burgh House 4B 64
Burghill Rd. SE26 4A 140
Burghley Av. KT3: N Mald 1K 151
Burghley Hall Cl. SW19 1G 135
Burghley Ho. SW19 3G 135
Burghley Pas. *E11* *1G 69*
(off Burghley Rd.)
Burghley Pl. CR4: Mitc 5D 154
Burghley Rd. E11 1G 69
N8 3A 48
NW5 4F 65
SW19 4F 135
Burghley Twr. W3 7B 80
Burgh St. N1 2B 84
Burgoine Quay
KT1: Hamp W 1D 150
Burgon St. EC4 1B 14 (6B 84)
Burgos Cl. CR0: Wadd 6A 168
Burgos Gro. SE10 1D 122
Burgoyne Ho. *TW8: Bford* *5D 96*
(off Ealing Rd.)
Burgoyne Rd. N4 6B 48
SE25 4F 157
SW9 3K 119
TW16: Sun 6H 129
Burgundy Ho. *E20* *5E 68*
(off Liberty Bri. Rd.)
Burgundy Pl. W12 1F 99
Burham Cl. SE20 7J 139
Burhill Gro. HA5: Pinn 2C 40
Burke Cl. SW15 4A 116
Burke Lodge E13 3K 87
Burke St. E16 5H 87
(not continuous)
Burket Cl. UB2: S'hall 4C 94
Burland Rd. SW11 5D 118
Burleigh Av. DA15: Sidc 5K 125
SM6: Wall 3E 166
Burleigh Cl. RM7: Mawney 4H 55
Burleigh Gdns. N14 1B 32
TW15: Ashf 5E 128
Burleigh Ho. SW3 7B 16
W10 *5G 81*
(off St Charles Sq.)
WC1 2F 7
Burleigh Pde. N14 1C 32
Burleigh Pl. SW15 5F 117
Burleigh Rd. EN1: Enf 4K 23
SM3: Sutt 1G 165
UB10: Hil 1D 74
Burleigh St. WC2 2G 13 (7K 83)
Burleigh Wlk. SE6 1E 140
Burleigh Way EN2: Enf 3J 23
Burley Cl. E4 5H 35
SW16 2H 155
Burley Ho. *E1* *6K 85*
(off Chudleigh St.)
Burley Rd. E16 6A 88
Burlington Arc. W1 3A 12 (7G 83)
Burlington Av. RM7: Rom 6H 55
TW9: Kew 1G 115
Burlington Cl. BR6: Farnb 2F 173
E6 6C 88
HA5: Eastc 3K 39
TW14: Bedf 7F 111
W9 4J 81
Burlington Cnr. *NW1* *7G 65*
(off Camden Rd.)
Burlington Ct. *E1* *7G 85*
(off Cable St.)
Burlington Gdns. RM6: Chad H 7E 54
SW6 2G 117
W1 3A 12 (7G 83)
W3 1J 97
W4 5J 97
Burlington Ho. *N15* *6D 48*
(off Tewkesbury Rd.)
SE16 *2K 103*
(off Province Dr.)
UB7: W Dray *2B 92*
(off Park Lodge Av.)
Burlington La. W4 7J 97
Burlington M. SW15 5H 117
W3 1J 97
Burlington Pl. IG8: Wfd G 3E 36
SW6 2G 117
Burlington Ri. EN4: E Barn 1H 31
Burlington Rd.
CR7: Thor H 2C 156
EN2: Enf 1J 23
KT3: N Mald 4B 152
N10 3E 46
N17 1G 49
SW6 2G 117
TW7: Isle 1H 113
W4 5J 97
Burma M. N16 4D 66
Burma Rd. N16 4D 66
Burmarsh NW5 6E 64
Burmarsh Ct. SE20 1J 157
Burma Ter. SE19 5E 138
Burmester Rd. SW17 3A 136
Burnaby Cres. W4 6J 97
Burnaby Gdns. W4 6H 97
Burnaby St. SW10 7A 100
Burnand Ho. *W14* *3F 99*
(off Redan St.)
Burnbrae Cl. N12 6E 30
Burnbury Rd. SW12 1G 137
Burncroft Av. EN3: Enf H 2D 24
Burndell Way UB4: Yead 5B 76
Burne Jones Ho. W14 4G 99
Burnell Av. DA16: Well 2A 126
TW10: Ham 5C 132
Burnell Gdns. HA7: Stan 2D 42
Burnell Ho. *E20* *5D 68*
(off Peloton Av.)
Burnelli Bldg. *SW8* *7F 101*
(off Sopwith Way)
Burnell Rd. SM1: Sutt 4K 165
Burnell Wlk. *SE1* *5F 103*
(off Cadet Dr.)
Burnels Av. E6 3E 88
Burness Cl. N7 6K 65
Burne St. NW1 5C 4 (5C 82)
Burnett Cl. E9 5J 67
Burnett Ho. *SE13* *2E 122*
(off Lewisham Hill)
Burnett Rd. IG6: Ilf 7K 37
Burney Av. KT5: Surb 5F 151
Burney St. SE10 7E 104
Burnfoot Av. SW6 1G 117
Burnham NW3 7C 64
Burnham Av. UB10: Ick 4E 56
Burnham Cl. EN1: Enf 1K 23
HA3: W'stone 4A 42
NW7 7H 29
SE1 4F 103
Burnham Ct. *NW4* *4E 44*
(off Brent St.)
NW6 *7A 64*
(off Fairhazel Gdns.)
W2 *7K 81*
(off Moscow Rd.)
Burnham Cres. E11 4A 52
Burnham Dr. KT4: Wor Pk 2F 165
Burnham Est. *E2* *3J 85*
(off Burnham St.)
Burnham Gdns. CR0: C'don 7F 157
TW4: Cran 1K 111
UB3: Harl 3F 93
Burnham Rd. DA14: Sidc 2E 144
E4 5G 35
RM7: Rom 3K 55
RM9: Dag 7B 72
SM4: Mord 4K 153
Burnham St. E2 3J 85
KT2: King T 1G 151
Burnham Way SE26 5B 140
W13 4B 96
Burnhill Cl. SE15 7H 103
Burnhill Ho. *EC1* *2C 8*
(off Norman St.)
Burnhill Rd. BR3: Beck 2C 158
Burnley Rd. NW10 5B 62
SW9 2K 119
Burnsall St. SW3 6D 16 (5C 100)
Burns Av. DA15: Sidc 6B 126
RM6: Chad H 7C 54
TW14: Felt 6J 111
UB1: S'hall 7E 76
Burns Cl. DA16: Well 1K 125
E17 4E 50
SM5: Cars 7E 166
SW19 6B 136
UB4: Hayes 5H 75
Burns Ho. *E2* *3J 85*
(off Cornwall Av.)
SE17 *5B 102*
(off Doddington Gro.)
Burnside Av. E4 6G 35
Burnside Cl. EN5: New Bar 3D 20
SE16 1K 103
TW1: Twick 6A 114
Burnside Ct. SM5: Cars 3E 166
Burnside Cres. HA0: Wemb 1D 78
Burnside Rd. RM8: Dag 2C 72
Burns Rd. HA0: Wemb 2E 78
NW10 1B 80
SW11 2D 118
W13 2B 96
Burns Way TW5: Hest 2B 112
Burnt Ash Hgts. BR1: Brom 5K 141
Burnt Ash Hill SE12 6H 123
Burnt Ash La. BR1: Brom 7J 141
Burnt Ash Rd. SE12 5H 123
Burnthwaite Rd. SW6 7H 99
BURNT OAK 1H 43
Burnt Oak Apartments *E16* *6J 87*
(off Pacific Rd.)
Burnt Oak B'way. HA8: Edg 7B 28
Burnt Oak Flds. HA8: Edg 1J 43
Burnt Oak La. DA15: Sidc 6A 126
(not continuous)
Burntwood Cl. SW18 1C 136
Burntwood Grange Rd. SW18 1B 136
Burntwood La. SW17 3A 136
Burntwood Vw. SE19 5F 139
Buross St. E1 6H 85
Burpham Cl. UB4: Yead 5B 76
Burrage Ct. *SE16* *4K 103*
(off Worgan St.)
Burrage Gro. SE18 4G 107
Burrage Pl. SE18 5F 107
Burrage Rd. SE18 5G 107
Burrard Ho. *E2* *2J 85*
(off Bishop's Way)
Burrard Rd. E16 6K 87
NW6 5J 63
Burr Cl. DA7: Bex 3F 127
E1 4K 15 (1G 103)
Burreed M. RM13: Rain 2J 91
Burrell Cl. CR0: C'don 6A 158
HA8: Edg 2C 28
Burrell Row BR3: Beck 2C 158
Burrell St. SE1 4A 14 (1B 102)
Burrells Wharf Sq. E14 5D 104
Burrell Towers E10 7C 50
Burrhill Ct. *SE16* *3K 103*
(off Worgan St.)
Burritt Rd. KT1: King T 2G 151
Burroughs, The NW4 4D 44
Burroughs Club, The 4D 44
Burroughs Cotts. *E14* *5A 86*
(off Halley St.)
Burroughs Gdns. NW4 4D 44
Burroughs Pde. NW4 4D 44
Burrow Ho. *SW9* *2A 120*
(off Stockwell Pk. Rd.)
Burrow Rd. SE22 4E 120
Burrows M. SE1 6A 14 (2B 102)
Burrows Rd. NW10 3E 80
Burrow Wlk. SE21 7C 120
Burr Rd. SW18 1J 135
Bursar St. SE1 5G 15 (1E 102)
Bursdon Cl. DA15: Sidc 2K 143
Bursland Rd. EN3: Pond E 4E 24
Burslem St. E1 6G 85
Burstock Rd. SW15 4G 117
Burston Rd. SW15 5F 117
Burston Vs. *SW15* *5F 117*
(off St John's Av.)
Burstow Rd. SW20 1G 153
Burtenshaw Rd. KT7: T Ditt 7A 150
Burtley Cl. N4 1C 66
Burton Bank *N1* *7D 66*
(off Yeate St.)
Burton Cl. CR7: Thor H 3D 156
KT9: Chess 7D 162
Burton Ct. KT7: T Ditt 6A 150
SE20 2J 157
SW3 5F 17
(not continuous)
Burton Gdns. TW5: Hest 1D 112
Burton Gro. SE17 5D 102
Burtonhole Cl. NW7 4A 30
Burtonhole La. N12 4B 30
NW7 5K 29
Burton Ho. *SE16* *2H 103*
(off Cherry Gdn. St.)
Burton La. SW9 2A 120
(not continuous)
Burton M. SW1 4H 17 (4E 100)
Burton Pl. WC1 2D 6 (3H 83)
Burton Ridge Ct. *E3* *2B 86*
(off Festubert Pl.)
Burton Rd. E18 3K 51
KT2: King T 7E 132
NW6 7H 63
SW9 2B 120
(Akerman Rd.)
SW9 2A 120
(Evesham Wlk.)
Burtons Ct. E15 7F 69
Burton's Rd. TW12: Hamp H 4F 131
Burton St. WC1 2D 6 (3H 83)
Burtonwood Ho. N4 7D 48
Burtop Rd. Est. SW17 3A 136
Burt Rd. E16 1A 106
Burts Wharf DA17: Belv 7J 91
Burtt Ho. *N1* *1G 9*
(off Aske St.)
Burtwell La. SE27 4D 138
Burwash Ho. *SE1* *7F 15*
(off Kipling Est.)
Burwash Rd. SE18 5H 107
Burway Cl. CR2: S Croy 6E 168
Burwell *KT1: King T* *2G 151*
(off Excelsior Cl.)
Burwell Av. UB6: G'frd 6J 59
Burwell Cl. E1 6H 85
Burwell Rd. E10 1A 68
Burwell Rd. Ind. Est. E10 1A 68
Burwell Wlk. E3 4C 86
Burwood Av. BR2: Hayes 2K 171
HA5: Eastc 5K 39
Burwood Cl. KT6: Surb 1G 163
Burwood Ho. SW9 4B 120
Burwood Pl. EN4: Had W 1F 21
W2 7D 4 (6C 82)
Bury Av. HA4: Ruis 6E 38
UB4: Hayes 2G 75
Bury Cl. SE16 1K 103
Bury Ct. EC3 7H 9 (6E 84)
Buryfield Ct. *SE8* *4K 103*
(off Lower Rd.)
Bury Gro. SM4: Mord 5K 153
Bury Hall Vs. N9 7A 24

Bury Pl.—Bywell Pl.

Bury Pl. WC1 6E **6** (5J **83**)
Bury Rd. E4 1B **36**
N22 2A **48**
RM10: Dag 5H **73**
Buryside Cl. IG2: Ilf 4K **53**
Bury St. EC3 1H **15** (6E **84**)
HA4: Ruis 5E **38**
N9 7A **24**
SW1 4B **12** (1G **101**)
Bury St. W. N9 7J **23**
Bury Wlk. SW3 4C **16** (4C **100**)
Busbridge Ho. *E14* *5C **86***
(off Brabazon St.)
Busby Ho. SW16 4G **137**
Busby M. NW5 6H **65**
Busby Pl. NW5 6H **65**
Busch Cl. TW7: Isle 1B **114**
Bushbaby Cl. SE1 3E **102**
Bushberry Rd. E9 6A **68**
Bush Cl. IG2: Ilf 5H **53**
Bush Cotts. SW18 5J **117**
Bush Ct. N14 1B **32**
W12 2F **99**
Bushell Cl. SW2 2K **137**
Bushell Grn. WD23: B Hea 2C **26**
Bushell St. E1 1G **103**
Bushell Way BR7: Chst 5E **142**
BUSHEY 1C 26
Bushey Av. BR5: Pet W 7H **161**
E18 3H **51**
Bushey Cl. E4 3K **35**
UB10: Ick 2C **56**
Bushey Ct. SW20 3D **152**
Bushey Down SW12 2F **137**
Bushey Golf Course 1A **26**
BUSHEY HEATH 1C 26
Bushey Hill Rd. SE5 1E **120**
Bushey La. SM1: Sutt 4J **165**
Bushey Lees DA15: Sidc 6K **125**
BUSHEY MEAD 2F 153
Bushey Rd. CR0: C'don 2C **170**
E13 2A **88**
N15 6E **48**
SM1: Sutt 4J **165**
(not continuous)
SW20 3D **152**
UB3: Harl 4G **93**
UB10: Ick 2C **56**
Bushey Way BR3: Beck 6F **159**
Bush Fair Ct. N14 6A **22**
Bushfield Cl. HA8: Edg 2C **28**
Bushfield Cres. HA8: Edg 2C **28**
Bush Gro. HA7: Stan 1D **42**
NW9 7J **43**
Bushgrove Rd. RM8: Dag 4D **72**
Bush Hill N21 7H **23**
Bush Hill Pde. EN1: Enf 7J **23**
N9 7J **23**
BUSH HILL PARK 6A 24
Bush Hill Pk. Golf Course 5H **23**
Bush Hill Rd. HA3: Kenton 6F **43**
N21 6J **23**
Bush Ind. Est. N19 3G **65**
NW10 4K **79**
Bush La. EC4 2E **14** (7D **84**)
Bushmead Cl. N15 4F **49**
Bushmoor Cres. SE18 7F **107**
Bushnell Rd. SW17 2F **137**
Bush Rd. E8 1H **85**
E11 7H **51**
IG9: Buck H 4G **37**
SE8 4K **103**
TW9: Kew 6F **97**
TW17: Shep 5B **146**
Bush Theatre 2E **98**
Bushway RM8: Dag 4D **72**
Bushwood E11 7H **51**
Bushwood Dr. SE1 4F **103**
Bushwood Rd. TW9: Kew 6G **97**
Bushy Ct. *KT1: Hamp W* *1C **150***
(off Beverley Rd.)
Bushy Pk. 7H **131**
Bushy Pk. Gdns.
TW11: Tedd 5H **131**
Bushy Pk. Rd. TW11: Tedd 7B **132**
(not continuous)
Bushy Rd. TW11: Tedd 6K **131**
Bus. Design Cen. *N1* *1A **84***
(off Upper St.)
Buspace Studios *W10* *4G **81***
(off Conlan St.)
Butcher Row E14 7K **85**
Butchers M. *UB3: Hayes* *7H **75***
(off Hemmen La.)
Butchers Rd. E16 6J **87**
Bute Av. TW10: Ham 2E **132**
Bute Ct. SM6: Wall 5G **167**
Bute Gdns. SM6: Wall 5G **167**
TW10: Ham 1E **132**
W6 4F **99**
Bute Gdns. W. SM6: Wall 5G **167**
Bute M. NW11 5A **46**
Bute Rd. CR0: C'don 1A **168**
IG6: Ilf 5F **53**
SM6: Wall 4G **167**
Bute St. SW7 3A **16** (4B **100**)
Bute Wlk. N1 6D **66**
Butfield Ho. *E9* *6J **67***
(off Stevens Av.)
Butler Av. HA1: Harr 7H **41**
Butler Cl. HA8: Edg 2H **43**
Butler Ct. HA0: Wemb 4A **60**
RM8: Dag *2G **73***
(off Gosfield Rd.)
SW11 *1C **118***
(off Hyde La.)
Butler Farm Cl. TW10: Ham 4D **132**
Butler Ho. *E2* *3J **85***
(off Bacton St.)
E3 *5B **86***
(off Geoffrey Chaucer Way)
E14 *6B **86***
(off Burdett St.)
SW9 *1B **120***
(off Lothian Rd.)
Butler Pl. SW1 1C **18** (3H **101**)
Butler Rd. HA1: Harr 7G **41**
NW10 7B **62**
RM8: Dag 4B **72**
Butlers & Colonial Wharf *SE1* *6K **15***
(off Shad Thames)
Butlers Cl. TW4: Houn 3D **112**
Butlers Dr. E4 1K **25**
Butler St. E2 3J **85**
UB10: Hil 4D **74**
Butlers Wharf SE1 5K **15** (1F **103**)
Butlers Wharf W. *SE1* *5J **15***
(off Shad Thames)
Butley Ct. *E3* *2A **86***
(off Ford St.)
Buttercup Cl. UB5: N'olt 6D **58**
Butterfield Cl. N17 6H **33**
SE16 2H **103**
TW1: Twick 6K **113**
Butterfields E17 5E **50**
Butterfield Sq. E6 6D **88**
Butterfly Apartments *SW11* *4C **118***
(off Comyn Rd.)
Butterfly Ct. E6 3D **88**
N15 *4E **48***
(off Bathurst Sq.)
NW9 1A **44**
Butterfly La. SE9 6F **125**
Butterfly Wlk. *SE5* *1D **120***
(off Denmark Hill)
Butter Hill SM5: Cars 3E **166**
SM6: Wall 3E **166**
Butteridges Cl. RM9: Dag 1F **91**
Buttermere *NW1* *1K **5***
(off Augustus St.)
Buttermere Cl. E15 4F **69**
SE1 4F **103**
Buttermere Cl. SM4: Mord 6F **153**
TW14: Felt 1H **129**
Buttermere Ct. *NW8* *1B **82***
(off Boundary Rd.)
Buttermere Dr. SW15 5G **117**
Buttermere Ho. *E3* *3B **86***
(off Mile End Rd.)
Buttermere Wlk. E8 6F **67**
Butterwick W6 4F **99**
Butterworth Gdns. IG8: Wfd G 6D **36**
Butterworth Ter. *SE17* *5C **102***
(off Sutherland Wlk.)
Buttery M. N14 3D **32**
Buttesland St. N1 1F **9** (3D **84**)
Buttfield Cl. RM10: Dag 6H **73**
Buttmarsh Cl. SE18 5F **107**
Button Lodge E17 4C **50**
Buttonscroft Cl. CR7: Thor H 3C **156**
Butts, The TW8: Bford 6C **96**
TW16: Sun 3A **148**
Buttsbury Rd. IG1: Ilf 5G **71**
Butts Cotts TW13: Hanw 3C **130**
Butts Cres. TW13: Hanw 3E **130**
Buttsmead HA6: Nwood 1E **38**
Butts Piece UB5: N'olt 2K **75**
Butts Rd. BR1: Brom 5G **141**
Buxhall Cres. E9 6B **68**
Buxted Rd. E8 7F **67**
N12 5H **31**
SE22 4E **120**
Buxton Cl. IG8: Wfd G 6G **37**
N9 2D **34**
Buxton Ct. E11 7H **51**
N1 1D **8**
(not continuous)
Buxton Cres. SM3: Cheam 4G **165**
Buxton Dr. E11 4G **51**
KT3: N Mald 2K **151**
Buxton Gdns. W3 7H **79**
Buxton Ho. E11 4G **51**
Buxton M. SW4 2H **119**
Buxton Rd. CR7: Thor H 5B **156**
DA8: Erith 7K **109**
E4 1A **36**
E6 3C **88**
E15 5G **69**
E17 4A **50**
(not continuous)
IG2: Ilf 6J **53**
N19 1H **65**
NW2 6D **62**
SW14 3A **116**
TW15: Ashf 5A **128**
Buxton St. E1 4K **9** (4G **85**)
Buzzard Creek Ind. Est. IG11: Bark 5A **90**
Byam St. SW6 2A **118**
Byards Ct. *SE16* *4K **103***
(off Worgan St.)
Byards Cft. SW16 1H **155**
Byas Ho. *E3* *3B **86***
(off Benworth St.)
Byatt Wlk. TW12: Hamp 6C **130**
Bychurch End TW11: Tedd 5K **131**
Bycroft Rd. UB1: S'hall 4E **76**
Bycroft St. SE20 7K **139**
Bycullah Av. EN2: Enf 3G **23**
Bycullah Rd. EN2: Enf 2G **23**
Bye, The W3 6A **80**
Byegrove Rd. SW19 6B **136**
Byelands Cl. SE16 1K **103**
Bye Way, The HA3: W'stone 1J **41**
Byeway, The SW14 3J **115**
Byeways TW2: Twick 3F **131**
Byeways, The KT5: Surb 5G **151**
Byfeld Gdns. SW13 1C **116**
Byfield Cl. SE16 2B **104**
Byfield Rd. TW7: Isle 3A **114**
Byford Cl. E15 7G **69**
Byford Ho. EN5: Barn 4A **20**
HA2: Harr 1E **58**
Bygrove CR0: New Ad 6D **170**
Bygrove St. E14 6D **86**
(not continuous)
Byland Cl. N21 7E **22**
SM4: Mord 7A **154**
Bylands Cl. SE2 3B **108**
Byne Rd. SE26 6J **139**
SM5: Cars 2C **166**
Bynes Rd. CR2: S Croy 7D **168**
Byng Pl. WC1 4D **6** (4H **83**)
Byng Rd. EN5: Barn 2A **20**
Byng St. E14 2C **104**
Bynon Av. DA7: Bex 3F **127**
Byre Rd. N14 6A **22**
Byrne Cl. CR0: C'don 6C **156**
Byrne Rd. SW12 1F **137**
Byron Av. E12 6C **70**
E18 3H **51**
KT3: N Mald 5C **152**
NW9 4H **43**
SM1: Sutt 4B **166**
TW4: Cran 2J **111**
Byron Av. E. SM1: Sutt 4B **166**
Byron Cl. E8 1G **85**
KT12: Walt T 7C **148**
SE20 3H **157**
SE26 4A **140**
SE28 1C **108**
SW16 6J **137**
TW12: Hamp 4D **130**
Byron Ct. *E11* *4K **51***
(off Makepeace Rd.)
EN2: Enf 2G **23**
HA1: Harr 6J **41**
NW6 *7A **64***
(off Fairfax Rd.)
SE22 1G **139**
SW3 *4D **16***
(off Elystan St.)
W7 *4A **96***
(off Boston Rd.)
W9 *4J **81***
(off Lanhill Rd.)
WC1 *3G **7***
(off Mecklenburgh Sq.)
Byron Dr. DA8: Erith 7H **109**
N2 6B **46**
Byron Gdns. SM1: Sutt 4B **166**
Byron Hill Rd. HA2: Harr 1H **59**
Byron Ho. DA1: Cray 5K **127**
Byron M. NW3 4C **64**
W9 4J **81**
Byron Pde. UB10: Hil 4E **74**
Byron Rd. E10 1D **68**
E17 3C **50**
HA0: Wemb 2C **60**
HA1: Harr 6J **41**
HA3: W'stone 2K **41**
NW2 2D **62**
NW7 5H **29**
W5 1F **97**
Byron St. E14 6E **86**
Byron Ter. N9 6D **24**
SE7 7A **106**
Byron Way UB4: Hayes 4H **75**
UB5: N'olt 3C **76**
UB7: W Dray 4B **92**
Bysouth Cl. IG5: Ilf 1F **53**
N15 4D **48**
Bythorn St. SW9 3K **119**
Byton Rd. SW17 6D **136**
Byward Av. TW14: Felt 6A **112**
Byward St. EC3 3H **15** (7E **84**)
Bywater Ho. SE18 3C **106**
Bywater Pl. SE16 1A **104**
Bywater St.
SW3 5E **16** (5D **100**)
Byway E11 5A **52**
Byway, The KT19: Ewe 4B **164**
SM2: Sutt 7B **166**
Bywell Pl. E16 5H **87**
W1 6A **6**

Bywood Av. CR0: C'don 6J 157
Byworth Wlk. N19 . . . . .1J 65

C

Cabanel Pl. SE11 . . . . . . .4H 19 (4K 101)
Cabbell St. NW1 . . . . .6C 4 (5C 82)
Cabinet Ct. NW2 . . . . .3B 62
Cabinet Way E4 . . . . .6G 35
Cable Car .2H 105
Cable Ct. SE16 . . . . .4A 104
(off Rope St.)
Cable Ho. WC1 . . . . .1J 7
(off Gt. Percy St.)
Cable Pl. SE10 . . . . .1E 122
Cable St. E1 .7G 85
Cable Trade Pk. SE7 . . . . .4A 106
Cabot Cl. CR0: Wadd 3A 168
Cabot Ct. SE16 . . . . .4K 103
(off Worgan St.)
Cabot Sq. E14 . . . . .1C 104
Cabot Way E6 . . . . .1B 88
Cab Rd. SE1 .5H 13
Cabul Rd. SW11 . . . . .2C 118
Caci Ho. W14 . . . . .4H 99
(off Kensington Village)
Cactus Cl. SE15 . . . . .2E 120
Cactus Wlk. W12 . . . . .6B 80
Cadbury Cl. TW7: Isle 1A 114
TW16: Sun 7G 129
Cadbury Rd. TW16: Sun 7G 129
Cadbury Way SE16 . . . . .3F 103
Caddington Cl. EN4: E Barn 5H 21
Caddington Rd. NW2 . . . . .3G 63
Caddis Cl. HA7: Stan 7E 26
Cadell Cl. E2 . . . . .1K 9 (2F 85)
Cade Rd. SE10 . . . . .1F 123
Cader Rd. SW18 . . . . .6A 118
Cadet Dr. SE1 . . . . .4F 103
Cadet Ho. SE18 . . . . .3F 107
Cadiz Ct. RM10: Dag 7K 73
Cadiz Rd. RM10: Dag 7J 73
Cadiz St. SE17 . . . . .5C 102
Cadley Ter. SE23 . . . . .2J 139
Cadman Cl. SW9 . . . . .7B 102
Cadman Ct. W4 . . . . .5H 97
(off Chaseley Dr.)
Cadmer Cl. KT3: N Mald 4A 152
Cadmium Sq. E2 . . . . .3K 85
(off Palmer's Rd.)
Cadmore Ho. N1 . . . . .7B 66
(off The Sutton Est.)
Cadmus Cl. SW4 . . . . .3H 119
Cadmus Ct. SE16 . . . . .4A 104
(off Seafarer Way)
SW9 . . . . .1A 120
(off Southey Rd.)
Cadnam Lodge E14 . . . . .3E 104
(off Schooner Cl.)
Cadnam Point SW15 . . . . .1D 134
Cadogan Cl. BR3: Beck 1F 159
E9 . . . . .7B 68
HA2: Harr 4F 59
TW11: Tedd 5J 131
Cadogan Ct. E9 . . . . .7B 68
(off Cadogan Ter.)
SM2: Sutt 6K 165
SW3 . . . . .4E 16
(off Draycott Av.)
Cadogan Ct. Gdns. SW1 . . . . .3G 17
(off D'Oyley St.)
Cadogan Gdns. E18 . . . . .3K 51
N3 . . . . .1K 45
N21 . . . . .5F 23
SW3 . . . . .3F 17 (4D 100)
Cadogan Ga. SW1 . . . . .3F 17 (4D 100)
Cadogan Hall 3G 17
(off Sloane Ter.)
Cadogan Ho. IG8: Wfd G 7K 37
SW3 . . . . .7B 16

Cadogan La. SW1 . . . . .2G 17 (3E 100)
Cadogan Mans. SW3 . . . . .4F 17
(off Cadogan Gdns.)
Cadogan Pl. SW1 . . . . .1F 17 (3D 100)
Cadogan Rd. KT6: Surb 5D 150
SE18 . . . . .3G 107
Cadogan Sq. SW1 . . . . .2E 16 (3D 100)
Cadogan St. SW3 . . . . .4E 16 (4D 100)
Cadogan Ter. E9 . . . . .6B 68
Cadoxton Av. N15 . . . . .6F 49
Cadwal Apartments N1 . . . . .7J 65
(off Caledonian Rd.)
Cadwallon Rd. SE9 . . . . .2F 143
Caedmon Rd. N7 . . . . .4K 65
Caerleon Cl. DA14: Sidc 5C 144
KT10: Clay 7B 162
Caerleon Ter. SE2 . . . . .4B 108
Caernafon Ho. HA7: Stan 5F 27
Caernarvon Cl. CR4: Mitc 3J 155
Caernarvon Dr. IG5: Ilf 1E 52
Caernarvon Ho. E16 . . . . .1K 105
(off Audley Dr.)
W2 . . . . .6A 82
(off Hallfield Est.)
Caesar Ct. E2 . . . . .2K 85
(off Palmer's Rd.)
Caesars Wlk. CR4: Mitc 5D 154
Caesars Way TW17: Shep 6F 147
Café Gallery 3J 103
Cagney Ct. TW16: Sun 1J 147
Cahill St. EC1 . . . . .4D 8 (4C 84)
Cahir St. E14 . . . . .4D 104
Cain Ct. W5 .5C 78
(off Castlebar M.)
Caine Ho. W3 .2H 97
(off Hanbury Rd.)
Cain's La. TW14: Felt 5G 111
Caird St. W10 . . . . .3G 81
Cairn Av. W5 .1D 96
Cairncross M. N8 . . . . .6J 47
Cairndale Cl. BR1: Brom 7H 141
Cairnfield Av. NW2 . . . . .3A 62
Cairngorm Cl. TW11: Tedd 5A 132
Cairns Av. IG8: Wfd G 6H 37
SW16 . . . . .3G 155
Cairns M. SE18 . . . . .1C 124
Cairns Pl. SW16 . . . . .2C 155
Cairns Rd. SW11 . . . . .5C 118
Cairn Way HA7: Stan 6E 26
Cairo New Rd. CR0: C'don 2C 168
Cairo Rd. E17 . . . . .4C 50
Caisson Moor Ct. E3 . . . . .4E 86
(off Navigation Rd.)
Caister Ho. N7 . . . . .6K 65
Caistor Ho. E15 . . . . .1H 87
(off Caistor Pk. Rd.)
Caistor M. SW12 . . . . .7F 119
Caistor Pk. Rd. E15 . . . . .1H 87
Caistor Rd. SW12 . . . . .7F 119
Caithness Gdns. DA15: Sidc 6K 125
Caithness Ho. N1 . . . . .1K 83
(off Twyford St.)
Caithness Rd. CR4: Mitc 7F 137
W14 . . . . .3F 99
Calabria Rd. N5 . . . . .6B 66
Calais Ga. SE5 . . . . .1B 120
Calais St. SE5 . . . . .1B 120
Calbourne Rd. SW12 . . . . .7D 118
Calcott Ct. W14 . . . . .3G 99
(off Blythe Rd.)
Calcott Wlk. SE9 . . . . .4C 142
Calcraft Ho. E2 . . . . .2J 85
(off Bonner Rd.)
Caldbeck Av. KT4: Wor Pk 2C 164
Caldecote KT1: King T 2G 151
(off Excelsior Cl.)
Caldecote Gdns. WD23: Bush 1D 26
CALDECOTE HILL 1E 26
Caldecot Rd. SE5 . . . . .2C 120
Caldecott Way E5 . . . . .3K 67
Calder Av. UB6: G'frd 2K 77

Calder Cl. EN1: Enf 3K 23
Calder Ct. SE16 . . . . .1B 104
Calder Gdns. HA8: Edg 3G 43
Calderon Ho. NW8 . . . . .2C 82
(off Townshend Est.)
Calderon Pl. W10 . . . . .5E 80
Calderon Rd. E11 . . . . .4E 68
Caldervale Rd. SW4 . . . . .5H 119
Calder Way SL3: Poyle 6A 174
Calderwood Pl. EN4: Had W 1E 20
Calderwood St. SE18 . . . . .4E 106
Caldew St. SE5 . . . . .7D 102
Caldicot Grn. NW9 . . . . .6A 44
Caldon Ho. UB5: N'olt 4D 76
Caldwell Cl. SE18 . . . . .5E 106
Caldwell Ho. SW13 . . . . .7E 98
(off Trinity Chu. Rd.)
Caldwell St. SW9 . . . . .7K 101
Caldy Rd. DA17: Belv 3H 109
Caldy Wlk. N1 . . . . .7C 66
Caleb St. SE1 . . . . .6C 14 (2C 102)
Caledonia Ct. IG11: Bark 2C 90
(off Keel Cl.)
Caledonia Ho. E14 . . . . .6A 86
(off Salmon La.)
Caledonian Cl. IG3: Ilf 1B 72
Caledonian Ct. BR2: Brom 6D 160
(off Wells Vw. Dr.)
UB5: N'olt 4C 76
Caledonian Rd. N1 . . . . .1F 7 (2J 83)
N7 . . . . .4K 65
Caledonian Sq. NW1 . . . . .6H 65
Caledonian Wharf E14 . . . . .4F 105
Caledonia Rd. TW19: Stanw 1A 128
Caledonia St. N1 . . . . .1F 7 (2J 83)
Caledon Rd. E6 . . . . .1D 88
SM6: Wall 4E 166
Calendar M. KT6: Surb 6D 150
Cale St. SW3 . . . . .5C 16 (5C 100)
Caletock Way SE10 . . . . .5H 105
Calgarth NW1 .1G 83
(off Ampthill Est.)
Calgary Ct. RM7: Mawney 4H 55
SE16 . . . . .2J 103
(off Canada Est.)
Calia Ho. E20 . . . . .6E 68
(off Anthems Way)
Caliban Twr. N1 . . . . .2E 84
(off Arden Est.)
Calico Ct. SE16 . . . . .3G 103
(off Marine St.)
Calico Ho. E20 . . . . .6E 68
(off Mirabelle Gdns.)
EC4 . . . . .1D 14
(off Well Ct.)
SE1 . . . . .7G 15
(off Long La.)
Calico Row SW11 . . . . .3A 118
Calidore Cl. SW2 . . . . .6K 119
California Bldg. SE13 . . . . .1D 122
(off Deal's Gateway)
California La. WD23: B Hea 1C 26
California Pl. WD23: B Hea 1C 26
(off High Rd.)
California Rd. KT3: N Mald 4H 151
Callaby Ter. N1 . . . . .6D 66
Callaghan Cl. SE13 . . . . .4G 123
Callahan Cotts. E1 . . . . .5J 85
(off Lindley St.)
Callander Rd. SE6 . . . . .2D 140
Callanders, The WD23: B Hea 1D 26
Callard Av. N13 . . . . .4G 33
Callard Cl. W2 .4A 4
Callcott Ct. NW6 . . . . .7H 63
Callcott Rd. NW6 . . . . .7H 63
Callcott St. W8 . . . . .1J 99
Callendar Rd. SW7 . . . . .1A 16 (3B 100)
Callender Ct. CR0: C'don 6C 156
(off Harry Cl.)

Callingham Cl. E14 . . . . .5B 86
Callington M. TW2: Twick 2J 131
Callis Farm Cl. TW19: Stanw 6A 110
Callisons Pl. SE10 . . . . .5G 105
Callis Rd. E17 . . . . .6B 50
Calliston Ct. E16 . . . . .5J 87
(off Hammersley Rd.)
Callonfield E17 . . . . .4K 49
Callow St. SW3 . . . . .7A 16 (6B 100)
Cally Swimming Pool 1K 83
Calmont Rd. BR1: Brom 6F 141
Calne Av. IG5: Ilf 1F 53
Calonne Rd. SW19 . . . . .4F 135
Calshot Ho. N1 . . . . .2K 83
(off Calshot St.)
Calshot Rd. TW6: H'row A 2C 110
Calshot St. N1 . . . . .1G 7 (2K 83)
Calshot Way EN2: Enf 3G 23
TW6: H'row A 2C 110
Calstock NW1 .1G 83
(off Royal Coll. St.)
Calstock Ho. SE11 . . . . .5K 19
Calthorpe Gdns. HA8: Edg 5K 27
SM1: Sutt 3A 166
Calthorpe St. WC1 . . . . .3H 7 (4K 83)
Calton Av. SE21 . . . . .6E 120
Calton Rd. EN5: New Bar 6F 21
Calverley Cl. BR3: Beck 6D 140
Calverley Ct. KT19: Ewe 4K 163
Calverley Cres. RM10: Dag 2G 73
Calverley Gdns. HA3: Kenton 7D 42
Calverley Gro. N19 . . . . .1H 65
Calverley Rd. KT17: Ewe 6C 164
Calvert Av. E2 . . . . .2H 9 (3E 84)
Calvert Cl. DA14: Sidc 6E 144
DA17: Belv 4G 109
Calvert Ct. TW9: Rich 4F 115
Calvert Dr. DA2: Wilm 2K 145
Calvert Ho. W12 . . . . .7D 80
(off White City Est.)
Calverton SE5 . . . . .6E 102
(off Albany Rd.)
Calverton Pl. UB6: G'frd 6K 59
Calverton Rd. E6 . . . . .1E 88
Calvert Rd. EN5: Barn 2A 20
SE10 . . . . .5H 105
Calvert's Bldgs. SE1 . . . . . . .5E 14 (1D 102)
Calvert St. NW1 . . . . .1E 82
Calvin St. E1 . . . . .4J 9 (4F 85)
Calydon Rd. SE7 . . . . .5K 105
Calypso Cres. SE15 . . . . .7F 103
Calypso Way SE16 . . . . .3B 104
Camac Rd. TW2: Twick 1H 131
Camarthen Grn. NW9 . . . . .5A 44
Cambalt Rd. SW15 . . . . .5F 117
Cambay Ho. E1 . . . . .4A 86
(off Harford St.)
Camber Ho. SE15 . . . . .6J 103
Camberley Av. EN1: Enf 4K 23
SW20 . . . . .2D 152
Camberley Cl. SM3: Cheam 3F 165
Camberley Ho. NW1 . . . . .1K 5
Camberley Rd. TW6: H'row A 3C 110
Camberwell SE3 . . . . .4K 123
CAMBERWELL 1D 120
Camberwell Bus. Cen. SE5 . . . . .7D 102
Camberwell Chu. St. SE5 . . . . .1D 120
Camberwell Glebe SE5 . . . . .1E 120
CAMBERWELL GREEN 1C 120
Camberwell Grn. SE5 . . . . .1D 120
Camberwell Gro. SE5 . . . . .1D 120
Camberwell Leisure Cen. 1D 120
Camberwell New Rd. SE5 . . . . .6A 102
Camberwell Pl. SE5 . . . . .1C 120
Camberwell Rd. SE5 . . . . .6C 102
Camberwell Sta. Rd. SE5 . . . . .1C 120
Camberwell Trad. Est. SE5 . . . . .1B 120
Cambeys Rd. RM10: Dag 5H 73
Cambisgate SW19 . . . . .5G 135
Camborne Av. W13 . . . . .2B 96
Camborne Cl. TW6: H'row A 3C 110

Camborne Cres. TW6: H'row A ... 3C 110
(off Camborne Rd.)
Camborne M. SW18 ... 7J 117
W11 ... 6G 81
Camborne Rd. CR0: C'don ... 7G 157
DA14: Sidc ... 3C 144
DA16: Well ... 2K 125
SM2: Sutt ... 7J 165
SM4: Mord ... 5F 153
SW18 ... 7J 117
TW6: H'row A ... 3C 110
Camborne Way TW5: Hest ... 1E 112
TW6: H'row A ... 3C 110
Cambourne Av. N9 ... 7E 24
Cambourne Rd. HA8: Edg ... 4A 28
Cambourne Wlk. TW10: Rich ... 6D 114
Cambrai Ct. N13 ... 3D 32
Cambray Rd. BR6: Orp ... 7K 161
SW12 ... 1G 137
Cambria Cl. DA15: Sidc ... 1H 143
TW3: Houn ... 4E 112
Cambria Ct. E17 ... 3A 50
TW14: Felt ... 7K 111
Cambria Gdns. TW19: Stanw ... 7A 110
(not continuous)
Cambria Ho. E14 ... 6A 86
(off Salmon La.)
SE26 ... 4G 139
(off High Level Dr.)
Cambrian Av. IG2: Ilf ... 5J 53
Cambrian Cl. SE27 ... 3B 138
Cambrian Grn. NW9 ... 5A 44
(off Snowdon Dr.)
Cambrian Rd. E10 ... 7C 50
TW10: Rich ... 6F 115
Cambria Rd. SE5 ... 3C 120
Cambria St. SW6 ... 7K 99
Cambridge Arc. E9 ... 7J 67
Cambridge Av. DA16: Well ... 4K 125
KT3: N Mald ... 3A 152
(not continuous)
NW6 ... 2J 81
UB6: G'frd ... 5K 59
Cambridge Barracks Rd. SE18 ... 4D 106
Cambridge Cir. WC2 ... 1D 12 (6H 83)
Cambridge Cl. E17 ... 6B 50
EN4: E Barn ... 1K 31
N22 ... 1A 48
NW10 ... 3J 61
SW20 ... 1D 152
TW4: Houn ... 4C 112
UB7: Harm ... 2E 174
Cambridge Cotts. TW9: Kew ... 6G 97
Cambridge Ct. E2 ... 2H 85
(off Cambridge Heath Rd.)
N16 ... 7E 48
(off Amhurst Pk.)
NW6 ... 2J 81
(not continuous)
W2 ... 6C 4
(off Edgware Rd.)
W6 ... 4E 98
(off Shepherd's Bush Rd.)
Cambridge Cres. E2 ... 2H 85
TW11: Tedd ... 5A 132
Cambridge Dr. HA4: Ruis ... 2A 58
SE12 ... 5J 123
Cambridge Gdns. EN1: Enf ... 2B 24
KT1: King T ... 2G 151
N10 ... 1E 46
N17 ... 7J 33
N21 ... 7J 23
NW6 ... 2J 81
W10 ... 6F 81
Cambridge Ga. NW1 ... 3J 5 (4F 83)
Cambridge Ga. M. NW1 ... 3K 5 (4F 83)
Cambridge Grn. SE9 ... 1F 143
Cambridge Gro. SE20 ... 1H 157
W6 ... 4D 98
Cambridge Gro. Rd. KT1: King T ... 3G 151
(not continuous)
Cambridge Heath Rd. E1 ... 5H 85
E2 ... 5H 85
Cambridge Ho. W6 ... 4D 98
(off Cambridge Gro.)
W13 ... 6A 78
Cambridge Pde. EN1: Enf ... 1B 24
Cambridge Pk. E11 ... 7J 51
TW1: Twick ... 6C 114
Cambridge Pk. Ct. TW1: Twick ... 7D 114
Cambridge Pk. Rd. E11 ... 7J 51
(off Lonsdale Rd.)
Cambridge Pl. W8 ... 2K 99
Cambridge Rd. BR1: Brom ... 7J 141
CR4: Mitc ... 3G 155
DA14: Sidc ... 4J 143
E4 ... 1A 36
E11 ... 6H 51
HA2: Harr ... 5E 40
IG3: Ilf ... 1J 71
IG11: Bark ... 7G 71
KT1: King T ... 2F 151
KT2: King T ... 2F 151
KT3: N Mald ... 4K 151
KT8: W Mole ... 4D 148
KT12: Walt T ... 6K 147
NW6 ... 2J 81
(not continuous)
SE20 ... 3H 157
SM5: Cars ... 6C 166
SW11 ... 1D 118
SW13 ... 2B 116
SW20 ... 1C 152
TW1: Twick ... 6D 114
TW4: Houn ... 4C 112
TW9: Kew ... 7G 97
TW11: Tedd ... 4K 131
TW12: Hamp ... 7D 130
TW15: Ashf ... 7E 128
UB1: S'hall ... 1D 94
W7 ... 2K 95
Cambridge Rd. Nth. W4 ... 5H 97
Cambridge Rd. Sth. W4 ... 5H 97
Cambridge Row SE18 ... 5F 107
Cambridge Sq. W2 ... 7C 4 (6C 82)
Cambridge St. SW1 ... 4K 17 (4F 101)
Cambridge Ter. N9 ... 7K 23
NW1 ... 2J 5 (3F 83)
Cambridge Ter. M. NW1 ... 2K 5 (3F 83)
Cambridge Theatre ... 1E 12
(off Earlham St.)
Cambstone Cl. N11 ... 2K 31
Cambus Cl. UB4: Yead ... 5C 76
Cambus Rd. E16 ... 5J 87
Cam Ct. SE15 ... 6F 103
Camdale Rd. SE18 ... 7K 107
Camden Arts Cen. ... 5K 63
Camden Av. TW13: Felt ... 1A 130
UB4: Yead ... 7B 76
Camden Cl. BR7: Chst ... 1G 161
Camden Ct. DA17: Belv ... 5G 109
NW1 ... 7G 65
(off Rousden St.)
Camden Gdns. CR7: Thor H ... 3B 156
NW1 ... 7F 65
SM1: Sutt ... 5K 165
Camden Gro. BR7: Chst ... 6F 143
Camden High St. NW1 ... 7F 65
Camden Hill Rd. SE19 ... 6E 138
Camden Ho. SE8 ... 5B 104
Camdenhurst St. E14 ... 6A 86
Camden La. N7 ... 5H 65
Camden Lock Market ... 7F 65
Camden Lock Pl. NW1 ... 7F 65
Camden Markets ... 7F 65
Camden M. NW1 ... 7G 65
Camden Pk. Rd.
BR7: Chst ... 7D 142
NW1 ... 6H 65
Camden Pas. N1 ... 2B 84
Camden People's Theatre ... 3A 6
(off Hampstead Rd.)
Camden Rd. DA5: Bexl ... 1E 144
E11 ... 6K 51
E17 ... 6B 50
N7 ... 4J 65
NW1 ... 7G 65
SM1: Sutt ... 5K 165
SM5: Cars ... 4D 166
Camden Row HA5: Pinn ... 3A 40
SE3 ... 2G 123
Camden Sq. NW1 ... 7H 65
(not continuous)
SE15 ... 1F 121
Camden St. NW1 ... 7G 65
Camden Studios NW1 ... 1G 83
(off Camden St.)
Camden Ter. NW1 ... 6H 65
CAMDEN TOWN ... 1F 83
Camden Wlk. N1 ... 1B 84
Camden Way BR7: Chst ... 7D 142
CR7: Thor H ... 3B 156
Cameford Ct. SW2 ... 7J 119
Camelford NW1 ... 1G 83
(off Royal Coll. St.)
Camelford Ct. W11 ... 6G 81
Camelford Ho. SE1 ... 5F 19 (5J 101)
Camelford Wlk. W11 ... 6G 81
Camel Gro. KT2: King T ... 5D 132
Camellia Cl. E10 ... 2C 68
Camellia Ho. SE8 ... 7B 104
(off Idonia St.)
TW13: Felt ... 1J 129
(off Bedfont La.)
Camellia La. KT5: Surb ... 4H 151
Camellia Pl. TW2: Whitt ... 7F 113
Camellia St. SW8 ... 7J 101
(not continuous)
Camelot Cl. SE28 ... 2H 107
SW19 ... 4H 135
Camelot Ho. NW1 ... 6H 65
Camel Rd. E16 ... 1C 106
Camera Pl. SW10 ... 7A 16 (6B 100)
Camera Press Gallery, The ... 6J 15
(off Queen Elizabeth St.)
Cameret Ct. W11 ... 2F 99
(off Holland Rd.)
Cameron Cl. DA5: Bexl ... 3K 145
N18 ... 4C 34
N20 ... 2G 31
N22 ... 7E 32
Cameron Cres. HA8: Edg ... 1H 43
Cameron Ho. BR1: Brom ... 1H 159
NW8 ... 2C 82
(off St John's Wood Ter.)
SE5 ... 7C 102
Cameron Pl. E1 ... 6H 85
SW16 ... 2A 138
Cameron Rd. BR2: Brom ... 5J 159
CR0: C'don ... 6B 156
IG3: Ilf ... 1J 71
SE6 ... 2B 140
Cameron Sq. CR4: Mitc ... 1C 154
Cameron Ter. SE12 ... 3K 141
Camerton Cl. E8 ... 6F 67
Camgate Cen., The TW19: Stanw ... 6B 110
Camgate Mans. SE5 ... 6C 102
(off Camberwell Rd.)
Camilla Cl. TW16: Sun ... 6H 129
Camilla Rd. SE16 ... 4H 103
Camille Cl. SE25 ... 3G 157
Camlan Rd. BR1: Brom ... 4H 141
Camlet St. E2 ... 3J 9 (4F 85)
Camlet Way EN4: Barn, Had W ... 2D 20
Camley St. N1 ... 7H 65
Camley Street Natural Pk. ... 2J 83
Camley Street Natural Pk. Vis. Cen.
... 2H 83
Camm Gdns. KT1: King T ... 2F 151
KT7: T Ditt ... 7K 149
Camms Ter. RM10: Dag ... 5J 73
(off Cambeys Rd.)
Camomile Av. CR4: Mitc ... 1D 154
Camomile Rd. RM7: Rush G ... 2K 73
Camomile St. EC3 ... 7H 9 (6E 84)
Camomile Way UB7: Yiew ... 6A 74
Campaign Ct. W9 ... 4H 81
(off Chantry Cl.)
Campana Rd. SW6 ... 1J 117
Campania Bldg. E1 ... 7K 85
(off Jardine Rd.)
Campaspe Bus. Pk. TW16: Sun ... 5H 147
Campbell Av. IG6: Ilf ... 4F 53
Campbell Cl. HA4: Ruis ... 6J 39
SE18 ... 1E 124
SW16 ... 4H 137
TW2: Twick ... 1H 131
Campbell Ct. N17 ... 1F 49
NW9 ... 6J 43
SE22 ... 1G 139
SW7 ... 3A 100
(off Gloucester Rd.)
Campbell Cft. HA8: Edg ... 5B 28
Campbell Gordon Way NW2 ... 4D 62
Campbell Ho. SW1 ... 6A 18
(off Churchill Gdns.)
W2 ... 4A 4
(off Hall Pl.)
W12 ... 7D 80
(off White City Est.)
Campbell Rd. CR0: C'don ... 7B 156
E3 ... 3C 86
E6 ... 1C 88
E15 ... 4H 69
E17 ... 4B 50
KT8: E Mos ... 3J 149
N17 ... 1F 49
TW2: Twick ... 2H 131
W7 ... 7J 77
Campbell Wlk. N1 ... 1J 83
(off Outram Pl.)
Campdale Rd. N7 ... 3H 65
Campden Cres. HA0: Wemb ... 3B 60
RM8: Dag ... 4B 72
Campden Gro. W8 ... 2J 99
Campden Hill W8 ... 2J 99
Campden Hill Ct. W8 ... 2J 99
Campden Hill Gdns. W8 ... 1J 99
Campden Hill Ga. W8 ... 2J 99
Campden Hill Mans. W8 ... 1J 99
(off Edge St.)
Campden Hill Pl. W11 ... 1H 99
Campden Hill Rd. W8 ... 1J 99
Campden Hill Sq. W8 ... 1H 99
Campden Hill Towers W11 ... 1J 99
Campden Ho. NW6 ... 7B 64
(off Harben Rd.)
W8 ... 1J 99
(off Sheffield Ter.)
Campden Ho. Cl. W8 ... 2J 99
Campden Ho's. W8 ... 1J 99
Campden Ho. Ter. W8 ... 1J 99
(off Kensington Chu. St.)
Campden Mans. W8 ... 1J 99
(off Kensington Mall)
Campden Rd. CR2: S Croy ... 5E 168
UB10: Ick ... 3B 56
Campden St. W8 ... 1J 99
Campden Way RM8: Dag ... 4B 72
Campe Ho. N10 ... 7K 31
Campen Cl. SW19 ... 2G 135
Camperdown St. E1 ... 1K 15 (6F 85)
Campfield Rd. SE9 ... 7B 124
Campion Cl. CR0: C'don ... 4E 168
E6 ... 7D 88
HA3: Kenton ... 6F 43
RM7: Rush G ... 2K 73
UB8: Hil ... 5B 74
Campion Ct. HA0: Wemb ... 2E 78
Campion Gdns. IG8: Wfd G ... 5D 36
Campion Ho. E14 ... 6B 86
(off Frances Wharf)
SE16 ... 2A 104
(off Blondin Way)

Campion Pl. SE28 . . . . .1A **108**
Campion Rd. E10 . . . . .7D **50**
  SW15 . . . . .4E **116**
  TW7: Isle 1K **113**
Campion Ter. NW2 . . . . .3F **63**
Campion Way HA8: Edg 4D **28**
Camplin Rd. HA3: Kenton 5E **42**
Camplin St. SE14 . . . . .7K **103**
Camp Rd. SW19 . . . . .5D **134**
Campsbourne, The N8 . . . . .4J **47**
Campsbourne Ho. N8 . . . . .4J **47**
  (off Pembroke Rd.)
Campsbourne Pde. N8 . . . . .4J **47**
  (off High St.)
Campsbourne Rd. N8 . . . . .3J **47**
  (not continuous)
Campsey Gdns. RM9: Dag 7B **72**
Campsey Rd. RM9: Dag 7B **72**
Campsfield Rd. N8 . . . . .3J **47**
  (off Campsfield Rd.)
Campsfield Ho. N8 . . . . .3J **47**
  (off Campsfield Rd.)
Campshill Pl. SE13 . . . . .5E **122**
Campshill Rd. SE13 . . . . .5E **122**
Campus Av. RM8: Dag 4A **72**
Campus Ho. TW7: Isle 7J **95**
Campus Rd. E17 . . . . .6B **50**
Campus Way NW4 . . . . .3D **44**
Camp Vw. SW19 . . . . .5D **134**
Cam Rd. E15 . . . . .1F **87**
Camrose Av. Erith 6H **109**
  HA8: Edg 2E **42**
  TW13: Felt 4A **130**
Camrose Cl. CR0: C'don 7A **158**
  SM4: Mord 4J **153**
Camrose St. SE2 . . . . .5A **108**
Camwal Cl. CR4: Mitc 2C **154**
Canada Av. N18 . . . . .6H **33**
Canada Cres. W3 . . . . .5J **79**
Canada Est. SE16 . . . . .3J **103**
Canada Gdns. SE13 . . . . .5E **122**
Canada House 4D **12**
Canada Ho. SE16 . . . . .3J **103**
  (off Brunswick Quay)
  SW1 .1H **101**
  (off Trafalgar Sq.)
Canada Memorial 6A **12**
  (within Green Pk.)
Canada Pl. E14 . . . . .1D **104**
  (off Canada Sq.)
Canada Rd. W3 . . . . .5J **79**
Canada Sq. E14 . . . . .1D **104**
Canada St. SE16 . . . . .2K **103**
Canada Way W12 . . . . .7D **80**
Canada Wharf SE16 . . . . .1B **104**
Canadian Av. SE6 . . . . .1D **140**
Canal App. SE8 . . . . .5A **104**
Canal Blvd. NW1 . . . . .6H **65**
CANAL BRIDGE 6G **103**
Canal Bldg. N1 . . . . .2C **84**
Canal Cl. E1 . . . . .4A **86**
  W10 . . . . .4F **81**
Canal Cotts. E3 . . . . .1B **86**
  (off Parnell Rd.)
Canal Gro. SE15 . . . . .6H **103**
Canal Market 7F **65**
  (off Castlehaven Rd.)
Canal Path E2 . . . . .1F **85**
Canal Reach N1 . . . . .1H **83**
Canalside SE28 . . . . .7D **90**
Canalside Activity Cen. 4F **81**
Canalside Gdns. UB2: S'hall 4C **94**
Canalside Sq. N1 . . . . .2C **84**
  (off Arlington Av.)
Canal Side Studios NW1 . . . . .1H **83**
  (off St Pancras Way)
Canalside Studios N1 . . . . .1E **84**
  (off Orsman Rd.)
Canal St. SE5 . . . . .6D **102**
Canal Wlk. CR0: C'don 6E **156**
  E17 . . . . .3K **49**
  N1 . . . . .1D **84**

Canal Wlk. NW10 . . . . .7J **61**
  (off Westend Cl.)
  SE26 .5J **139**
Canal Way W10 . . . . .4F **81**
Canal Wharf E8 . . . . .1E **84**
  (off Kingsland Rd.)
  UB6: G'frd 1A **78**
Canary Vw. SE10 . . . . .6D **104**
  (off Dowells St.)
Canberra Cl. NW4 . . . . .3C **44**
  RM10: Dag 1K **91**
Canberra Cres. RM10: Dag 7K **73**
Canberra Dr. UB4: N'olt 3A **76**
  UB5: N'olt 3A **76**
Canberra Path E10 . . . . .7D **50**
  (off Whitney Rd.)
Canberra Pl. TW9: Rich 3G **115**
Canberra Rd. DA7: Bex 6D **108**
  E6 . . . . .1D **88**
  SE7 . . . . .6A **106**
  TW6: H'row A 3F **110**
  W13 . . . . .1A **96**
Canbury Av. KT2: King T 1F **151**
Canbury Bus. Cen. KT2: King T . . .1E **150**
Canbury Bus. Pk. KT2: King T 1E **150**
  (off Canbury Pk. Rd.)
Canbury Ct. KT2: King T 7D **132**
Canbury M. SE26 . . . . .3G **139**
Canbury Pk. Rd. KT2: King T 1E **150**
Canbury Pas. KT2: King T 1D **150**
Cancell Rd. SW9 . . . . .1A **120**
Candahar Rd. SW11 . . . . .2C **118**
Candida Cl. NW1 . . . . .7F **65**
  (off Trenmar Gdns.)
Candid Ho. NW10 . . . . .3D **80**
  (off Trenmar Gdns.)
Candle Gro. SE15 . . . . .3H **121**
Candlelight Ct. E15 . . . . .6H **69**
  (off Romford Rd.)
Candler M. TW1: Twick 7A **114**
Candler St. N15 . . . . .6D **48**
Candle St. E1 . . . . .5A **86**
C & L Golf Course 7K **57**
Candover St. W1 . . . . .6A **6** (5G **83**)
Candy St. E3 . . . . .1B **86**
Candy Wharf E3 . . . . .4A **86**
Caney M. NW2 . . . . .2F **63**
Canfield Dr. HA4: Ruis 5K **57**
Canfield Gdns. NW6 . . . . .7K **63**
Canfield Ho. N15 . . . . .6E **48**
  (off Albert Rd.)
Canfield Pl. NW6 . . . . .6A **64**
Canfield Rd. IG8: Wfd G 7H **37**
Canford Av. UB5: N'olt 1D **76**
Canford Cl. EN2: Enf 2F **23**
Canford Gdns. KT3: N Mald 6A **152**
Canford Pl. TW11: Tedd 6C **132**
Canford Rd. SW11 . . . . .5E **118**
Canham Gdns. TW4: Houn 7D **112**
Canham Rd. SE25 . . . . .3E **156**
  W3 . . . . .2A **98**
Canmore Gdns. SW16 . . . . .7G **137**
CANN HALL 4G **69**
Cann Hall Rd. E11 . . . . .4G **69**
Cann Ho. W14 . . . . .3G **99**
  (off Russell Rd.)
Canning Cres. N22 . . . . .1K **47**
Canning Cross SE5 . . . . .2E **120**
Canning Ho. W12 . . . . .7D **80**
  (off Australia Rd.)
Canning Pas. W8 . . . . .3A **100**
Canning Pl. W8 . . . . .3A **100**
Canning Pl. M. W8 . . . . .3A **100**
  (off Canning Pl.)
Canning Rd. CR0: C'don 2F **169**
  E15 . . . . .2G **87**
  E17 . . . . .4A **50**
  HA3: W'stone 3J **41**
  N5 . . . . .3B **66**
Canning Sq. EN1: Enf 1B **24**
Cannington Rd. RM9: Dag 6C **72**

CANNING TOWN 6H **87**
CANNING TOWN 5G **87**
Cannizaro Rd. SW19 . . . . .6E **134**
Cannock Ct. E17 . . . . .2E **50**
Cannock Ho. N4 . . . . .7C **48**
Cannonbury Av. HA5: Pinn 6B **40**
Cannon Cl. SW20 . . . . .3E **152**
  TW12: Hamp 6F **131**
Cannon Ct. EC1 . . . . .3B **8**
  (off Brewhouse Yd.)
Cannon Dr. E14 . . . . .7C **86**
Cannon Hill N14 . . . . .3D **32**
  NW6 . . . . .5J **63**
Cannon Hill La. SW20 . . . . .5F **153**
Cannon Hill M. N14 . . . . .3D **32**
Cannon Ho. SE11 . . . . .4H **19**
Cannon La. HA5: Pinn 5C **40**
  NW3 . . . . .3B **64**
Cannon Pl. NW3 . . . . .3B **64**
  SE7 . . . . .5C **106**
Cannon Retail Pk. SE28 . . . . .7A **90**
Cannon Rd. DA7: Bex 1E **126**
  N14 . . . . .3D **32**
  N18 . . . . .6A **34**
Cannons Health Club
  Richmond 4D **114**
Cannon St. EC4 . . . . .1C **14** (6C **84**)
Cannon St. Rd. E1 . . . . .6H **85**
Cannon Trad. Est. HA9: Wemb 4H **61**
Cannon Way KT8: W Mole 4E **148**
Cannon Wharf Bus. Cen. SE8 . . . .4A **104**
  (off Pell St.)
Cannon Wharf Development SE8 . . .4A **104**
  (off Yeoman St.)
Cannon Workshops E14 . . . . .7C **86**
  (off Cannon Dr.)
Canon All. EC4 . . . . .1C **14**
  (off Queen's Head Pas.)
Canon Av. RM6: Chad H 5C **54**
Canon Beck Rd. SE16 . . . . .2J **103**
Canonbie Rd. SE23 . . . . .7J **121**
CANONBURY 6C **66**
Canonbury Bus. Cen. N1 . . . . .1C **84**
Canonbury Cotts. EN1: Enf 1K **23**
Canonbury Ct. N1 . . . . .7B **66**
  (off Hawes St.)
Canonbury Cres. N1 . . . . .7C **66**
Canonbury Gro. N1 . . . . .7C **66**
Canonbury Hgts. N1 . . . . .6D **66**
  (off Dove Rd.)
Canonbury La. N1 . . . . .7B **66**
Canonbury Pk. Nth. N1 . . . . .6C **66**
Canonbury Pk. Sth. N1 . . . . .6C **66**
Canonbury Pl. N1 . . . . .6B **66**
  (not continuous)
Canonbury Rd. EN1: Enf 1K **23**
  N1 . . . . .6B **66**
Canonbury Sq. N1 . . . . .7B **66**
Canonbury St. N1 . . . . .7C **66**
Canonbury Vs. N1 . . . . .7B **66**
Canon Mohan Cl. N14 . . . . .6K **21**
Canon Rd. BR1: Brom 3A **160**
Canon Row SW1 . . . . .7E **12** (2J **101**)
  (not continuous)
Canon's Cl. N2 . . . . .7B **46**
Canons Cl. CR4: Mitc 4D **154**
  HA8: Edg 6A **28**
Canons Cnr. HA8: Edg 4K **27**
Canons Ct. E15 . . . . .4G **69**
  HA8: Edg 6A **28**
Canons Dr. HA8: Edg 6K **27**
Canonsleigh Rd. RM9: Dag 7B **72**
Canons Leisure Cen.
  Mitcham 4D **154**
CANONS PARK 7J **27**
Canons Pk. HA7: Stan 6J **27**
Canons Pk. Cl. HA8: Edg 7K **27**
Canon St. N1 . . . . .1C **84**
Canon's Wlk. CR0: C'don 3K **169**
Canopus Way TW19: Stanw 7A **110**
Canrobert St. E2 . . . . .2H **85**

Cantelowes Rd. NW1 . . . . .6H **65**
Canterbury Av. DA15: Sidc 2B **144**
  IG1: Ilf .7C **52**
Canterbury Cl.
  BR3: Beck 1D **158**
  E6 . . . . .6D **88**
  KT4: Wor Pk 2F **165**
  SE5 . . . . .2C **120**
  (off Lilford Rd.)
  UB6: G'frd 5F **77**
Canterbury Cr. CR2: S Croy 7C **168**
  (off St Augustine's Av.)
  NW6 . . . . .2J **81**
  (off Canterbury Rd.)
  NW9 . . . . .2A **44**
  SE5 . . . . .7A **102**
  SE12 .3K **141**
  TW15: Ashf 4B **128**
Canterbury Cres. SW9 . . . . .3A **120**
Canterbury Gro. SE27 . . . . .4A **138**
Canterbury Hall KT4: Wor Pk 7D **152**
Canterbury Ho. CR0: C'don 1D **168**
  (off Sydenham Rd.)
  E3 . . . . .3D **86**
  (off Bow Rd.)
  IG11: Bark 7A **72**
  (off Margaret Bondfield Av.)
  RM8: Dag 4A **72**
  (off Academy Way)
  SE1 . . . . .1H **19** (3K **101**)
  SE8 . . . . .5C **104**
  (off Wharf St.)
Canterbury Ind. Pk. SE15 . . . . .6J **103**
Canterbury Pl. SE17 . . . . .5B **102**
Canterbury Rd. CR0: C'don 7K **155**
  E10 . . . . .7E **50**
  HA1: Harr 5F **41**
  HA2: Harr 5F **41**
  NW6 . . . . .2H **81**
  (Carlton Va.)
  NW6 . . . . .2J **81**
  (Princess Rd.)
  SM4: Mord 7K **153**
  TW13: Hanw 2C **130**
Canterbury Ter. NW6 . . . . .2J **81**
Cantium Retail Pk. SE1 . . . . .6G **103**
Cantley Gdns. IG2: Ilf 6G **53**
  SE19 .1F **157**
Cantley Rd. W7 . . . . .3A **96**
Canto Ct. EC1 . . . . .3D **8**
  (off Old St.)
Canton St. E14 . . . . .6C **86**
Cantrell Rd. E3 . . . . .4B **86**
Cantwell Rd. SE18 . . . . .7F **107**
Canute Gdns. SE16 . . . . .4K **103**
Canvey St. SE1 . . . . .4C **14** (1C **102**)
Cape Cl. IG11: Bark 7F **71**
Cape Henry Ct. E14 . . . . .7F **87**
  (off Jamestown Way)
Cape Ho. E8 . . . . .6F **67**
  (off Dalston La.)
Capel Av. SM6: Wall 5K **167**
Capel Cl. BR2: Brom 1C **172**
  N20 . . . . .3F **31**
Capel Ct. EC2 . . . . .1F **15**
  (off Bartholomew La.)
  SE20 .1J **157**
Capel Cres. HA7: Stan 2F **27**
Capel Gdns. HA5: Pinn 4D **40**
  IG3: Bark, Ilf 4K **71**
Capel Ho. E9 . . . . .7J **67**
  (off Loddiges Rd.)
Capel Rd. E7 . . . . .4K **69**
  E12 . . . . .4K **69**
  EN4: E Barn 6H **21**
Capener's Cl. SW1 . . . . .7F **11**
Capern Rd. SW18 . . . . .1A **136**
Cape Rd. N17 . . . . .3G **49**
Cape Yd. E1 . . . . .1G **103**
Capital Bus. Cen. CR2: S Croy 7D **168**
  HA0: Wemb 2D **78**

Capital E. Apartments *E16* 7J **87**
(off Western Gateway)
Capital Ho. *SW15* 5G **117**
(off Plaza Gdns.)
Capital Ind. Est. CR4: Mitc 5D **154**
DA17: Belv 3H **109**
Capital Interchange Way
TW8: Bford 5G **97**
Capital Mill Apartments *E2* 1F **85**
(off Whiston Rd.)
Capital Trad. Est. IG11: Bark 2H **89**
Capital Wharf E1 1G **103**
Capitol Ind. Pk. NW9 3J **43**
Capitol Wlk. *SE23* 2J **139**
(off London Rd.)
Capitol Way NW9 3J **43**
Capland Ho. *NW8* 3B **4**
(off Capland St.)
Capland St. NW8 3B **4** (4B **82**)
Caple Ho. *SW10* 7A **100**
(off King's Rd.)
Caple Rd. NW10 2B **80**
Capper St. WC1 4B **6** (4G **83**)
Caprea Cl. UB4: Yead 5B **76**
Capricorn Cen. RM8: Dag 7F **55**
Capri Ho. E17 2B **50**
Capri Rd. CR0: C'don 1F **169**
Capstan Cl. RM6: Chad H 6B **54**
Capstan Ct. *E1* 7J **85**
(off Wapping Wall)
Capstan Ho. *E14* 7F **87**
(off Clove Cres.)
E14 4E **104**
(off Stebondale St.)
Capstan Ride EN2: Enf 2F **23**
Capstan Rd. SE8 4B **104**
Capstan Sq. E14 2E **104**
Capstan Way SE16 1A **104**
Capstone Rd. BR1: Brom 4H **141**
Captain Cook Statue 4D **12**
(on The Mall)
Capthorne Av. HA2: Harr 1C **58**
Capuchin Cl. HA7: Stan 6G **27**
Capulet M. E16 1J **105**
Capulet Sq. *E3* 3D **86**
(off Talwin St.)
Capworth St. E10 1C **68**
Caradoc Cl. W2 6J **81**
Caradoc Evans Cl. *N11* 5A **32**
(off Springfield Rd.)
Caradoc St. SE10 5G **105**
Caradon Cl. E11 1G **69**
Caradon Way N15 4D **48**
Cara Ho. *N1* 7A **66**
(off Liverpool Rd.)
Caramel Ct. *E3* 2D **86**
(off Taylor Pl.)
Caranday Vs. *W11* 1F **99**
(off Norland Rd.)
Carat Ho. *E14* 5C **86**
(off Ursula Gould Way)
Caravel Cl. E14 3C **104**
Caravelle Gdns. UB5: N'olt 3B **76**
Caravel M. SE8 6C **104**
Caraway Apartments *SE1* 6K **15**
(off Cayenne Ct.)
Caraway Cl. E13 5K **87**
Caraway Hgts. *E14* 7E **86**
(off Poplar High St.)
Caraway Pl. SM6: Wall 3F **167**
Carberry Rd. SE19 6E **138**
Carbery Av. W3 2F **97**
Carbis Cl. E4 1A **36**
Carbis Rd. E14 6B **86**
Carbrooke Ho. *E9* 1J **85**
(off Templecombe Rd.)
Carbuncle Pas. N17 2G **49**
Carburton St. W1 5K **5** (5F **83**)
Cardale St. E14 2E **104**
Cardamon Bldg. *SE1* 5K **15**
(off Shad Thames)
Carden Ct. KT8: W Mole 4F **149**
Carden Rd. SE15 3H **121**
Cardiff Ho. *SE15* 6G **103**
(off Friary Est.)
Cardiff Rd. EN3: Pond E 4C **24**
W7 3A **96**
Cardiff St. SE18 7J **107**
Cardigan Ct. *W7* 4K **77**
(off Copley Cl.)
Cardigan Gdns. IG3: Ilf 2A **72**
Cardigan Pl. SE3 2F **123**
Cardigan Rd. E3 2B **86**
SW13 2C **116**
SW19 6A **136**
TW10: Rich 6E **114**
Cardigan St. SE11 5J **19** (5A **102**)
Cardigan Wlk. *N1* 7C **66**
(off Ashby Gro.)
Cardinal Av. KT2: King T 5E **132**
SM4: Mord 6G **153**
Cardinal Bourne St. SE1 3D **102**
Cardinal Cap All. SE1 1C **102**
Cardinal Cl. BR7: Chst 1J **161**
HA8: Edg 7D **28**
KT4: Wor Pk 4C **164**
SM4: Mord 6G **153**
Cardinal Ct. *E1* 7G **85**
(off Thomas More St.)
Cardinal Cres. KT3: N Mald 2J **151**
Cardinal Hinsley Cl. NW10 2C **80**
Cardinal Mans. *SW1* 3A **18**
(off Carlisle Pl.)
Cardinal Pl. SW1 1A **18** (3G **101**)
(not continuous)
SW15 4F **117**
Cardinal Rd. HA4: Ruis 1B **58**
TW13: Felt 1K **129**
Cardinals Wlk. TW12: Hamp 7G **131**
TW16: Sun 6G **129**
Cardinals Way N19 1H **65**
Cardinal Wlk. SW1 2A **18**
Cardinal Way HA3: W'stone 3J **41**
Cardine M. SE15 7H **103**
Cardington Sq. TW4: Houn 4B **112**
Cardington St. NW1 1B **6** (3G **83**)
Cardinham Rd. BR6: Chels 4K **173**
Cardozo Rd. N7 5J **65**
Cardrew Av. N12 5G **31**
Cardrew Cl. N12 5H **31**
Cardrew Ct. N12 5G **31**
Cardross Ho. *W6* 3D **98**
(off Cardross St.)
Cardross St. W6 3D **98**
Cardwell Rd. N7 4J **65**
Cardwell Ter. *N7* 4J **65**
(off Cardwell Rd.)
Career Ct. *SE16* 2K **103**
(off Christopher Cl.)
Carew Cl. N7 2K **65**
Carew Ct. *RM6: Chad H* 6B **54**
(off Quarles Pk. Rd.)
SE14 6K **103**
(off Samuel Cl.)
SM2: Sutt 7K **165**
Carew Manor & Dovecote 3G **167**
Carew Mnr. Cotts. SM6: Bedd 3H **167**
Carew Rd. CR4: Mitc 2E **154**
CR7: Thor H 4B **156**
N17 2G **49**
SM6: Wall 6G **167**
TW15: Ashf 6E **128**
W13 2C **96**
Carew St. SE5 2C **120**
Carey Ct. DA6: Bex 5H **127**
SE5 7C **102**
Carey Gdns. SW8 1G **119**
Carey La. EC2 7C **8** (6C **84**)
Carey Mans. *SW1* 3C **18**
(off Rutherford St.)
Carey Pl. SW1 4C **18** (4H **101**)
Carey Rd. RM9: Dag 4E **72**
Carey St. WC2 1H **13** (6K **83**)
Carey Way HA9: Wemb 4H **61**
Carfax Ho. SE20 1G **157**
Carfax Pl. SW4 4H **119**
Carfax Rd. UB3: Harl 5H **93**
Carfree Cl. N1 7A **66**
Cargill Rd. SW18 1K **135**
Cargo Point TW19: Stanw 6B **110**
Cargreen Pl. *SE25* 4F **157**
(off Cargreen Rd.)
Cargreen Rd. SE25 4F **157**
Cargrey Ho. HA7: Stan 5H **27**
Carholme Rd. SE23 1B **140**
Carillon Ct. *E1* 5G **85**
(off Greatorex St.)
W5 7D **78**
Carina Ho. *E20* 5E **68**
(off Cheering La.)
Carinthia Ct. *SE16* 4A **104**
(off Plough Way)
Carisbrook N10 2F **47**
Carisbrook Cl. EN1: Enf 1A **24**
Carisbrooke Av. DA5: Bexl 1D **144**
Carisbrooke Cl. HA7: Stan 2D **42**
TW4: Houn 7C **112**
Carisbrooke Ct. SM2: Cheam 7H **165**
UB5: N'olt 1D **76**
(off Eskdale Av.)
W1 6H **5**
(off Weymouth St.)
W3 2J **97**
(off Brouncker Rd.)
Carisbrooke Gdns. SE15 7F **103**
Carisbrooke Ho. *KT2: King T* 1E **150**
(off Seven Kings Way)
TW10: Rich 5G **115**
UB7: W Dray 2B **92**
(off Park Lodge Av.)
Carisbrooke Rd. BR2: Brom 4A **160**
CR4: Mitc 4H **155**
E17 4A **50**
Carker's La. NW5 5F **65**
Carlcott Cl. KT12: Walt T 7K **147**
Carleton Av. SM6: Wall 7H **167**
Carleton Cl. KT10: Esh 7H **149**
Carleton Gdns. N19 5G **65**
Carleton Rd. N7 5H **65**
Carleton Vs. NW5 5G **65**
Carlile Cl. E3 2B **86**
Carlile Ho. *SE1* 3D **102**
(off Tabard St.)
Carlile Pl. TW10: Rich 6F **115**
Carlina Gdns. IG8: Wfd G 5E **36**
Carlingford Gdns. CR4: Mitc 7D **136**
Carlingford Rd. N15 3B **48**
NW3 4B **64**
SM4: Mord 6F **153**
Carlisle Av. EC3 1J **15** (6E **84**)
W3 6A **80**
Carlisle Cl. HA5: Pinn 7C **40**
KT2: King T 1G **151**
Carlisle Gdns. HA3: Kenton 7D **42**
IG1: Ilf 6C **52**
Carlisle Ho. IG1: Ilf 6C **52**
Carlisle La. SE1 2H **19** (3K **101**)
Carlisle Mans. *SW1* 3A **18**
(off Carlisle Pl.)
Carlisle M. KT2: King T 1G **151**
Carlisle Pl. N11 4A **32**
SW1 2A **18** (3G **101**)
Carlisle Rd. E10 1C **68**
N4 7A **48**
NW6 1G **81**
NW9 3J **43**
SM1: Sutt 6H **165**
TW12: Hamp 7F **131**
Carlisle St. W1 1C **12** (6H **83**)
Carlisle Wlk. E8 6F **67**
Carlisle Way SW17 5E **136**
Carlos Pl. W1 3H **11** (7E **82**)
Carlow St. NW1 2G **83**
Carlson Ct. SW15 4H **117**
Carlton Av. CR2: S Croy 7E **168**
HA3: Kenton 5B **42**
N14 5C **22**
TW14: Felt 6A **112**
UB3: Harl 4G **93**
Carlton Av. E. HA9: Wemb 2D **60**
Carlton Av. W. HA0: Wemb 2B **60**
Carlton Cl. HA8: Edg 5B **28**
KT9: Chess 6D **162**
NW3 2J **63**
UB5: N'olt 5G **59**
Carlton Ct. IG6: Ilf 3H **53**
N3 7D **30**
SE20 1H **157**
UB8: Cowl 5A **74**
W9 2K **81**
(off Maida Vale)
Carlton Cres. SM3: Cheam 4G **165**
Carlton Dr. IG6: Ilf 3H **53**
SW15 5F **117**
Carlton Gdns. SW1 5C **12** (1H **101**)
W5 6C **78**
Carlton Grn. DA14: Sidc 4K **143**
Carlton Gro. SE15 1H **121**
Carlton Hill NW8 2K **81**
Carlton Ho. *NW6* 2J **81**
(off Canterbury Ter.)
SE16 2K **103**
(off Wolfe Cres.)
TW3: Houn 6E **112**
TW14: Felt 6H **111**
Carlton Ho. Ter. SW1 5C **12** (1H **101**)
Carlton Lodge *N4* 7A **48**
(off Carlton Rd.)
Carlton Mans. N16 1F **67**
NW6 7J **63**
(off West End La.)
W9 3K **81**
W14 2G **99**
(off Holland Pk. Gdns.)
Carlton M. *NW6* 5J **63**
(off West Cotts.)
Carlton Pde. HA9: Wemb 2E **60**
Carlton Pk. Av. SW20 2F **153**
Carlton Rd. CR2: S Croy 6D **168**
DA8: Erith 6H **109**
DA14: Sidc 5K **143**
DA16: Well 3B **126**
E11 1H **69**
E12 4B **70**
E17 1A **50**
KT3: N Mald 2A **152**
KT12: Walt T 7K **147**
N4 7A **48**
N11 5K **31**
SW14 3J **115**
TW16: Sun 7H **129**
W4 2K **97**
W5 7C **78**
Carlton Sq. E1 4K **85**
(not continuous)
Carlton St. SW1 3C **12** (7H **83**)
Carlton Ter. E7 7A **70**
E11 5K **51**
(not continuous)
N18 3J **33**
SE26 3J **139**
Carlton Twr. Pl. SW1 1F **17** (3D **100**)
Carlton Towers
SM5: Cars 3D **166**
Carlton Va. NW6 2H **81**
Carlton Vs. SW15 5G **117**
Carlton Works, The
SE15 7H **103**
(off Asylum Rd.)
Carlwell St. SW17 5C **136**
Carlyle Av. BR1: Brom 3B **160**
UB1: S'hall 7D **76**
Carlyle Cl. KT8: W Mole 2F **149**
N2 6A **46**

Carlyle Ct. SW6 . . . . .1K 117
(off Imperial Rd.)
SW10 . . . . .1A 118
(off Chelsea Harbour Dr.)
Carlyle Gdns. UB1: S'hall 7D 76
Carlyle Ho. KT8: W Mole 5E 148
(off Down St.)
N16 . . . . .3E 66
SE5 . . . . .7C 102
(off Bethwin Rd.)
SW3 . . . . .7B 16
(off Old Church St.)
Carlyle Mans. SW3 . . . . .7C 16
(off Cheyne Wlk.)
W8 . . . . .1J 99
(off Kensington Mall)
Carlyle M. E1 . . . . .4K 85
Carlyle Pl. SW15 . . . . .4F 117
Carlyle Rd. CRO: C'don 2G 169
E12 . . . . .4C 70
NW10 .1K 79
SE28 . . . . .7B 90
W5 . . . . .4C 96
Carlyle's House 7C 16
Carlyle Sq. SW3 . . . . .6B 16 (5B 100)
Carly M. E2 . . . . .3G 85
(off Barnet Gro.)
Carlyon Av. HA2: Harr 4D 58
Carlyon Cl. HAO: Wemb 1E 78
Carlyon Rd. HAO: Wemb 2E 78
UB4: Yead 5A 76
(not continuous)
Carlys Cl. BR3: Beck 2K 157
Carmalt Gdns. SW15 . . . . .4E 116
Carmarthen Ct. W7 . . . . .4K 77
(off Copley Cl.)
Carmarthen Pl. SE1 . . . . .6G 15 (2E 102)
Carmel Ct. HA9: Wemb 2H 61
W8 . . . . .2K 99
(off Holland St.)
Carmelite Cl. HA3: Hrw W 1G 41
Carmelite Rd. HA3: Hrw W 1G 41
Carmelite St. EC4 . . . . . . .2K 13 (7A 84)
Carmelite Wlk. HA3: Hrw W 1G 41
Carmelite Way HA3: Hrw W 2G 41
Carmel Lodge SW6 . . . . .6J 99
(off Lillie Rd.)
Carmelo M. E1 . . . . .5K 85
(off Maria Ter.)
Carmel Way TW9: Rich 2H 115
Carmen St. E14 . . . . .6D 86
Carmichael Cl. HA4: Ruis 4J 57
SW11 . . . . .3B 118
Carmichael Ct. SW13 . . . . .2B 116
(off Grove Rd.)
Carmichael Ho. E14 . . . . .7E 86
(off Poplar High St.)
Carmichael M. SW18 . . . . .7B 118
Carmichael Rd. SE25 . . . . .5F 157
Carmine W2 . . . . .6B 4
Carmine Ct. BR1: Brom 7H 141
Carmine Wharf E14 . . . . .6B 86
Carminia Rd. SW17 . . . . .2F 137
Carnaby St. W1 . . . . . . .1A 12 (6G 83)
Carnac St. SE27 . . . . .4D 138
Carnanton Rd. E17 . . . . .1F 51
Carnarvon Av. EN1: Enf 3A 24
Carnarvon Dr. UB3: Harl 3E 92
Carnarvon Rd. E10 . . . . .5E 50
E15 . . . . .6H 69
E18 . . . . .1H 51
EN5: Barn 3B 20
Carnation Cl. RM7: Rush G 2K 73
Carnation St. SE2 . . . . .5B 108
Carnbrook M. SE3 . . . . .3B 124
Carnbrook Rd. SE3 . . . . .3B 124
Carnecke Gdns. SE9 . . . . .5C 124
Carnegie Cl. KT6: Surb 2F 163
Carnegie Pl. SW19 . . . . .3F 135
Carnegie Rd. HA1: Harr 7K 41
Carnegie St. N1 . . . . .1K 83

Carnell Apartments E14 . . . . .6B 86
(off St Anne's Row)
Carney Pl. SW9 . . . . .4A 120
Carnforth Cl. KT19: Ewe 6H 163
Carnforth Rd. SW16 . . . . .7H 137
(not continuous)
Carnie Lodge SW17 . . . . .3F 137
Carnival Ho. SE1 . . . . .6K 15
(off Gainsford St.)
Carnoustie Cl. SE28 . . . . .6D 90
Carnoustie Dr. N1 . . . . .7K 65
(not continuous)
Carnwath Rd. SW6 . . . . .3J 117
Caroe Ct. N9 . . . . .1C 34
Carol Cl. NW4 . . . . .4F 45
Carole Ho. NW1 . . . . .1D 82
(off Regent's Pk. Rd.)
Carolina Cl. E15 . . . . .5G 69
Carolina Rd. CR7: Thor H 2B 156
Caroline Cl. CR0: C'don 4E 168
N10 . . . . .2F 47
SW16 .3K 137
TW7: Isle 7H 95
UB7: W Dray 2A 92
W2 . . . . .7K 81
Caroline Cl. HA7: Stan 6F 27
SE6 . . . . .4F 141
TW15: Ashf 6D 128
Caroline Gdns. E2 . . . . . .1H 9 (3E 84)
SE15 .7H 103
(not continuous)
Caroline Ho. W2 . . . . .7K 81
(off Bayswater Rd.)
W6 . . . . .5E 98
(off Queen Caroline St.)
Caroline Pl. SW11 . . . . .2E 118
UB3: Harl 7G 93
W2 . . . . .7K 81
Caroline Pl. M. W2 . . . . .7K 81
Caroline Rd. SW19 . . . . .7H 135
Caroline St. E1 . . . . .6K 85
Caroline Ter. SW1 . . . . . .4G 17 (4E 100)
Caroline Wlk. W6 . . . . .6H 99
(off Lillie Rd.)
Carol St. NW1 . . . . .1G 83
Caronia Ct. SE16 . . . . .4A 104
(off Plough Way)
Caro Pl. KT3: N Mald 4B 152
Carpenter Gdns. N21 . . . . .2G 33
Carpenter Ho. E1 . . . . .5K 85
(off Trafalgar Gdns.)
E14 . . . . .5C 86
(off Burgess St.)
NW11 . . . . .6A 46
Carpenters Arms Apartments SE1 . . . .4G 103
(off Welsford St.)
Carpenters Arms Path SE9 . . . . .6D 124
(off Eltham High St.)
Carpenters Cl. EN5: New Bar 6E 20
Carpenters Ct. NW1 . . . . .1G 83
(off Pratt St.)
TW2: Twick 2J 131
Carpenters M. N7 . . . . .5J 65
Carpenters Pl. SW4 . . . . .4H 119
Carpenter's Rd. E15 . . . . .7E 68
E20 . . . . .6C 68
Carpenter St. W1 . . . . . . .3J 11 (7F 83)
Carp Ho. E3 . . . . .1B 86
(off Old Ford Rd.)
Carradale Ho. E14 . . . . .6E 86
(off St Leonard's Rd.)
Carrara Cl. SE24 . . . . .4A 120
SW9 . . . . .4B 120
Carrara M. E8 . . . . .6G 67
(off Dalston La.)
Carrara Wharf SW6 . . . . .3G 117
Carr Cl. HA7: Stan 6F 27
Carre M. SE5 . . . . .3B 120
(off Calais St.)
Carrera Twr. EC1 . . . . .1C 8
Carr Gro. SE18 . . . . .4C 106

Carr Ho. DA1: Cray 5K 127
Carriage Dr. E. SW11 . . . . .7E 100
Carriage Dr. Nth. SW11 . . . . .7H 17 (6E 100)
(Carriage Dr. E.)
SW11 .7D 100
(The Parade)
Carriage Dr. Sth. SW11 . . . . .1D 118
(not continuous)
Carriage Dr. W. SW11 . . . . .7D 100
Carriage M. IG1: Ilf 2G 71
Carriage Pl. N16 . . . . .3D 66
SW16 .5G 137
Carriage St. SE18 . . . . .3F 107
Carriage Way SE8 . . . . .7C 104
(off Deptford High St.)
Carrick Cl. TW7: Isle 3A 114
Carrick Dr. IG6: Ilf 1G 53
Carrick Gdns. N17 . . . . .7K 33
Carrick Ho. N7 . . . . .6K 65
(off Caledonian Rd.)
SE11 . . . . .5K 19 (5A 102)
Carrick M. SE8 . . . . .6C 104
Carrick Sq. TW8: Bford 7C 96
Carrill Way DA17: Belv 3D 108
Carrington Av. TW3: Houn 5F 113
Carrington Cl. CR0: C'don 7A 158
KT2: King T 5J 133
Carrington Ct. SW11 . . . . .4C 118
(off Barnard Rd.)
Carrington Gdns. E7 . . . . .4J 69
Carrington Ho. W1 . . . . .5J 11
(off Carrington St.)
Carrington Rd. TW10: Rich 4G 115
Carrington Sq. HA3: Hrw W 6B 26
Carrington St. W1 . . . . . . .5J 11 (1H 101)
Carrock Ct. RM7: Rush G 6K 55
(off Union Rd.)
Carrol Cl. NW5 . . . . .4F 65
Carroll Cl. E15 . . . . .5H 69
Carroll Ct. W3 . . . . .3H 97
(off Osborne Rd.)
Carroll Ho. W2 . . . . .2A 10
(off Craven Ter.)
Carronade Ct. N7 . . . . .5K 65
Carronade Pl. SE28 . . . . .3G 107
Carron Cl. E14 . . . . .6D 86
Carroun Rd. SW8 . . . . .7K 101
Carroway La. UB6: G'frd 3H 77
Carrow Rd. RM9: Dag 7B 72
Carr Rd. E17 . . . . .2B 50
UB5: N'olt 6E 58
Carrs La. N21 . . . . .5H 23
Carr St. E14 . . . . .5A 86
CARSHALTON 4E 166
Carshalton Athletic FC 4C 166
CARSHALTON BEECHES 7C 166
Carshalton Gro. SM1: Sutt 4B 166
CARSHALTON ON THE HILL 7E 166
Carshalton Pk. Rd. SM5: Cars 5D 166
Carshalton Pl. SM5: Cars 5E 166
Carshalton Rd. CR4: Mitc 4E 154
SM1: Sutt 5A 166
SM5: Cars 5A 166
Carslake Rd. SW15 . . . . .6E 116
Carson Rd. E16 . . . . .4J 87
EN4: Cockf 4J 21
SE21 . . . . .2D 138
Carson Ter. W11 . . . . .1G 99
(off Princes Pl.)
Carstairs M. SE6 . . . . .3E 140
Carston Cl. SE12 . . . . .5H 123
Carswell Cl. IG4: Ilf 4B 52
Carswell Rd. SE6 . . . . .7E 122
Carter Cl. EN5: Barn 5B 20
NW9 . . . . .6K 43
Carter Ct. EC4 . . . . .1A 14
Carter Dr. RM5: Col R 1H 55
Carteret Ho. W12 . . . . .7D 80
(off White City Est.)
Carteret St. SW1 . . . . . . .7C 12 (2H 101)
Carteret Way SE8 . . . . .4A 104

Carterhatch La. EN1: Enf 1A 24
Carterhatch Rd. EN3: Enf H 1D 24
Carter Ho. E1 . . . . .6J 9
Carter La. EC4 . . . . .1B 14 (6B 84)
Carter Pl. SE17 . . . . .5C 102
Carter Rd. E13 . . . . .1K 87
SW19 .6B 136
Carters Cl.
KT4: Wor Pk 2F 165
NW5 . . . . .5H 65
(off Torriano Av.)
Carters Hill Cl. SE9 . . . . .1A 142
Carters La. SE23 . . . . .2A 140
Carter Sq. E14 . . . . .6D 86
(off Bowen St.)
Carter St. SE17 . . . . .6C 102
Carter's Yd. SW18 . . . . .5J 117
Carthew Rd. W6 . . . . .3D 98
Carthew Vs. W6 . . . . .3D 98
Carthusian Ct EC1 . . . . .5C 8
(off Carthusian St.)
Carthusian St. EC1 . . . . . . .5C 8 (5C 84)
Cartier Circ. E14 . . . . .1D 104
Carting La. WC2 . . . . .3F 13 (7J 83)
Cart La. E4 .1B 36
Cart Lodge M. CR0: C'don 1E 168
Cartmel NW1 . . . . .1A 6
(off Harrington St.)
Cartmel Cl. N17 . . . . .7C 34
Cartmel Ct. UB5: N'olt 6C 58
Cartmel Gdns. SM4: Mord 5A 154
Cartmel Rd. DA7: Bex 1G 127
Carton Ho. W11 . . . . .7F 81
(off St Ann's Rd.)
Cartoon Mus. 6E 6
(off Lit. Russell St.)
Cartridge Pl. SE18 . . . . .3F 107
Cartwright Gdns. WC1 . . . . .2E 6 (3J 83)
Cartwright Ho. SE1 . . . . .3C 102
(off County St.)
Cartwright Rd. RM9: Dag 7F 73
Cartwright St. E1 . . . . .2K 15 (7F 85)
Cartwright Way SW13 . . . . .7D 98
Carvel Ho. E14 . . . . .5E 104
(off Manchester Rd.)
Carver Cl. W4 . . . . .3J 97
Carver Rd. SE24 . . . . .6C 120
Carville Cres. TW8: Bford 4E 96
Carville St. N4 . . . . .2A 66
Cary Av. SE16 . . . . .4A 104
Cary Rd. E11 . . . . .4G 69
Carysfort Rd. N8 . . . . .5H 47
N16 . . . . .3D 66
Casby Ho. SE16 . . . . .3G 103
(off Marine St.)
Cascade Av. N10 . . . . .4G 47
Cascade Cl. IG9: Buck H 2G 37
Cascade Ct. SW8 . . . . .7F 101
Cascade Rd. IG9: Buck H 2G 37
Cascades Ct. SW19 . . . . .7H 135
Cascades Twr. E14 . . . . .1B 104
Casel Ct. HA7: Stan 2F 27
(off Brightwen Gro.)
Casella Rd. SE14 . . . . .7K 103
Casewick Rd. SE27 . . . . .5A 138
Casey Av. UB5: N'olt 2D 76
Casey Cl. NW8 . . . . .2C 4 (3C 82)
Casey Ct. SE14 . . . . .1K 121
(off Besson St.)
Cashmere Ho. E8 . . . . .1F 85
(off Pamela St.)
Casimir Rd. E5 . . . . .2J 67
Casino Av. SE24 . . . . .5C 120
Caspian St. SE5 . . . . .7D 102
Caspian Wlk. E16 . . . . .6B 88
Caspian Wharf E3 . . . . .5D 86
(off Violet Rd.)
Cassander Pl. HA5: Pinn 1C 40
(off Holly Gro.)
Cassandra Cl. UB5: N'olt 4H 59
Casselden Rd. NW10 . . . . .7K 61

Cassell Ho. SW9 . . . 2K 119
(off Stockwell Gdns. Est.)
Cass Ho. E9 . . . 6K 67
(off Harrowgate Rd.)
Cassidy Rd. SW6 . . . 7J 99
(not continuous)
Cassilda Rd. SE2 . . . 4A 108
Cassilis Rd. E14 . . . 2C 104
TW1: Twick . . . 5B 114
Cassini Apartments E16 . . . 6J 87
Cassiobury Av. TW14: Felt . . . 7H 111
Cassiobury Rd. E17 . . . 5A 50
Cassland Rd. CR7: Thor H . . . 4D 156
E9 . . . 7K 67
Casslee Rd. SE6 . . . 7B 122
Cassocks Sq. TW17: Shep . . . 7F 147
Casson Apartments E14 . . . 6C 86
(off Upper Nth. St.)
Casson Ho. E1 . . . 5K 9
(off Hanbury St.)
Casson St. E1 . . . 5G 85
Castalia Sq. E14 . . . 2E 104
Castellain Mans. W9 . . . 4K 81
(off Castellain Rd.)
Castellain Rd. W9 . . . 4K 81
Castellane Cl. HA7: Stan . . . 7E 26
Castell Ho. SE8 . . . 7C 104
Castello Av. SW15 . . . 5E 116
CASTELNAU . . . 6D 98
Castelnau SW13 . . . 1C 116
Castelnau Gdns. SW13 . . . 6D 98
Castelnau Mans. SW13 . . . 6D 98
(off Castelnau)
Castelnau Row SW13 . . . 6D 98
Casterbridge NW6 . . . 1K 81
(off Abbey Rd.)
W11 . . . 6H 81
(off Dartmouth Cl.)
Casterbridge Rd. SE3 . . . 3J 123
Casterton St. E8 . . . 6H 67
Castile Rd. SE18 . . . 4E 106
Castillon Rd. SE6 . . . 2G 141
Castlands Rd. SE6 . . . 2B 140
Castleacre W2 . . . 1C 10
(off Hyde Pk. Cres.)
Castle Av. E4 . . . 5A 36
KT17: Ewe . . . 7D 164
UB7: Yiew . . . 7A 74
Castlebar Ct. W5 . . . 5C 78
Castlebar Hill W5 . . . 5C 78
Castlebar M. W5 . . . 5C 78
Castlebar Pk. W5 . . . 5B 78
Castlebar Rd. W5 . . . 5C 78
Castle Baynard St. EC4 . . . 2B 14 (7B 84)
Castlebrook Cl. SE11 . . . 4B 102
Castle Bus. Cen. TW12: Hamp . . . 1F 149
(off Castle M.)
Castle Climbing Cen., The . . . 2C 66
Castle Cl. BR2: Brom . . . 3G 159
E9 . . . 5A 68
SW19 . . . 3F 135
TW16: Sun . . . 7G 129
W3 . . . 2H 97
Castlecombe Dr. SW19 . . . 7F 117
Castlecombe Rd. SE9 . . . 4C 142
Castle Ct. EC3 . . . 1F 15
(off Birchin La.)
SE26 . . . 4A 140
SW15 . . . 3G 117
(off Brewhouse La.)
Castleden Ho. NW3 . . . 7B 64
(off Hilgrove Rd.)
Castledine Rd. SE20 . . . 7H 139
Castle Dr. IG4: Ilf . . . 6C 52
Castleford Av. SE9 . . . 1F 143
Castleford Cl. N17 . . . 6A 34
Castleford Ct. NW8 . . . 3B 4
(off Henderson Dr.)
Castlegate TW9: Rich . . . 3F 115
Castle Green Leisure Cen. . . . 1D 90
Castlehaven Rd. NW1 . . . 7F 65
Castle Hgts. RM9: Dag . . . 1B 90
Castle Hill Av. CR0: New Ad . . . 7D 170
Castle Hill Local Nature Reserve . . . 6G 163
Castle Hill Pde. W13 . . . 7B 78
(off The Avenue)
Castle Ho. SM2: Sutt . . . 6J 165
SW8 . . . 7J 101
(off Sth. Lambeth Rd.)
Castle Ind. Est. SE17 . . . 4C 102
Castle La. SW1 . . . 1B 18 (3G 101)
Castleleigh Ct. EN2: Enf . . . 5J 23
Castlemaine Av. CR2: S Croy . . . 5F 169
KT17: Ewe . . . 7D 164
Castlemain St. E1 . . . 5H 85
Castle Mead SE5 . . . 7C 102
Castle M. N12 . . . 5F 31
NW1 . . . 6F 65
SW17 . . . 4C 136
TW12: Hamp . . . 1F 149
(not continuous)
Castle Pde. KT17: Ewe . . . 7C 164
Castle Pl. NW1 . . . 6F 65
W4 . . . 4A 98
Castle Point E13 . . . 2A 88
(off Boundary Rd.)
Castlereagh Ho. HA7: Stan . . . 6G 27
Castlereagh St. W1 . . . 7E 4 (6D 82)
Castle Rd. EN3: Enf H . . . 1F 25
N12 . . . 5F 31
NW1 . . . 6F 65
RM9: Dag . . . 1B 90
TW7: Isle . . . 2K 113
UB2: S'hall . . . 3D 94
UB5: N'olt . . . 6F 59
Castle Row W4 . . . 5K 97
Castle St. E6 . . . 2A 88
KT1: King T . . . 2E 150
Castleton Av. DA7: Bex . . . 1K 127
HA9: Wemb . . . 4E 60
Castleton Cl. CR0: C'don . . . 6A 158
Castleton Gdns. HA9: Wemb . . . 3E 60
Castleton Ho. E14 . . . 4E 104
(off Pier St.)
Castleton Rd. CR4: Mitc . . . 4H 155
E17 . . . 2F 51
HA4: Ruis . . . 1B 58
IG3: Ilf . . . 1A 72
SE9 . . . 4B 142
Castletown Rd. W14 . . . 5G 99
Castleview Cl. N4 . . . 2C 66
Castleview Gdns. IG1: Ilf . . . 6C 52
Castle Wlk. TW16: Sun . . . 3A 148
Castle Way SW19 . . . 3F 135
TW13: Hanw . . . 4A 130
Castle Wharf E14 . . . 7G 87
(off Orchard Pl.)
Castlewood Dr. SE9 . . . 2D 124
Castlewood Rd. EN4: Cockf . . . 3G 21
N15 . . . 6G 49
N16 . . . 6G 49
Castle Yd. N6 . . . 7E 46
SE1 . . . 4B 14 (1B 102)
TW10: Rich . . . 5D 114
Castor La. E14 . . . 7D 86
Catalina Ho. E1 . . . 1K 15
Catalina Rd. TW6: H'row A . . . 2D 110
Catalpa Ct. SE13 . . . 6F 123
Caterham Av. IG5: Ilf . . . 2D 52
Caterham High School Fitness Cen. . . . 2D 52
Caterham Rd. SE13 . . . 3F 123
Catesby Ho. E9 . . . 7J 67
(off Frampton Pk. Rd.)
Catesby St. SE17 . . . 4D 102
CATFORD . . . 7D 122
Catford B'way. SE6 . . . 7D 122
CATFORD GYRATORY . . . 7D 122
Catford Hill SE6 . . . 1B 140
Catford Island SE6 . . . 7D 122
Catford M. SE6 . . . 7D 122
Catford Rd. SE6 . . . 7C 122
Catford Trad. Est. SE6 . . . 2D 140
Cathall Rd. E11 . . . 2F 69
Cathay Ho. SE16 . . . 2H 103
Cathay St. SE16 . . . 2H 103
Cathay Wlk. UB5: N'olt . . . 2E 76
(off Brabazon Rd.)
Cathcart Dr. BR6: Orp . . . 2J 173
Cathcart Hill N19 . . . 3G 65
Cathcart Ho. SW10 . . . 5A 100
(off Cathcart Rd.)
Cathcart Rd. SW10 . . . 6K 99
Cathcart St. NW5 . . . 6F 65
Cathedral Lodge EC1 . . . 5C 8
(off Aldersgate St.)
Cathedral Mans. SW1 . . . 3A 18
(off Vauxhall Bri. Rd.)
Cathedral Piazza SW1 . . . 2A 18 (3G 101)
Cathedral St. SE1 . . . 4E 14 (1D 102)
Cathedral Wlk. SW1 . . . 1A 18
Catherall Rd. N5 . . . 3C 66
Catherine Cl. NW4 . . . 4D 44
Catherine Ct. IG2: Ilf . . . 5G 53
N14 . . . 5B 22
SW3 . . . 7A 16
(off Callow St.)
SW19 . . . 5H 135
Catherine Dr. TW9: Rich . . . 4E 114
TW16: Sun . . . 6H 129
Catherine Gdns. TW3: Houn . . . 4H 113
Catherine Griffiths Ct. EC1 . . . 3K 7
(off Northampton Rd.)
Catherine Gro. SE10 . . . 1D 122
Catherine Ho. E3 . . . 2C 86
(off Thomas Fyre Dr.)
N1 . . . 1E 84
(off Whitmore Est.)
Catherine Howard Ct. SE9 . . . 6H 125
Catherine of Aragon Ct. SE9 . . . 6G 125
Catherine Parr Ct. SE9 . . . 6H 125
Catherine Pl. HA1: Harr . . . 5K 41
SW1 . . . 1A 18 (3G 101)
Catherine Rd. KT6: Surb . . . 5D 150
Catherine St. WC2 . . . 2G 13 (7K 83)
Catherine Wheel All. E1 . . . 6H 9 (5E 84)
Catherine Wheel Rd. TW8: Bford . . . 7D 96
Catherine Wheel Yd. SW1 . . . 5A 12
Catherwood Ct. N1 . . . 1E 8
Cat Hill EN4: E Barn . . . 6H 21
Cathles Rd. SW12 . . . 6F 119
Cathnor Rd. W12 . . . 2D 98
Catkin Cl. E14 . . . 6F 87
Catlin Cres. TW17: Shep . . . 5F 147
Catling Cl. SE23 . . . 3J 139
Catlin's La. HA5: Eastc . . . 3K 39
Catlin St. SE16 . . . 5G 103
Cator La. BR3: Beck . . . 1B 158
Cato Rd. SW4 . . . 3H 119
Cator Rd. SE26 . . . 6K 139
SM5: Cars . . . 5D 166
Cator St. SE15 . . . 7F 103
(Commercial Way)
SE15 . . . 6F 103
(Ebley Cl.)
Cato St. W1 . . . 6D 4 (5C 82)
Catsey La. WD23: Bush . . . 1B 26
Catsey Woods WD23: Bush . . . 1B 26
Catterick Cl. N11 . . . 6K 31
Cattistock Rd. SE9 . . . 5C 142
Cattley Cl. EN5: Barn . . . 4B 20
Catton St. WC1 . . . 6G 7 (5K 83)
Catwalk Pl. N15 . . . 6D 48
Caudwell Ter. SW18 . . . 6B 118
Caughley Ho. SE11 . . . 2J 19
Caulfield Ct. NW1 . . . 7G 65
(off Baynes St.)
Caulfield Gdns. HA5: Pinn . . . 2A 40
Caulfield Rd. E6 . . . 1C 88
SE15 . . . 2H 121
W3 . . . 3J 97
Causeway, The KT9: Chess . . . 4E 162
KT10: Clay . . . 7A 162
Causeway, The N2 . . . 4C 46
SM2: Sutt . . . 7A 166
SM5: Cars . . . 3E 166
SW18 . . . 5K 117
SW19 . . . 5E 134
TW4: Houn . . . 4J 111
TW11: Tedd . . . 6K 131
TW14: Felt, Houn . . . 4J 111
Causeyware Rd. N9 . . . 7D 24
Causton Cotts. E14 . . . 6A 86
(off Galsworthy Av.)
Causton Ho. SE5 . . . 6C 102
SW9 . . . 1K 119
Causton Rd. N6 . . . 7F 47
Causton Sq. RM10: Dag . . . 7G 73
Causton St. SW1 . . . 4D 18 (4H 101)
Cautley Av. SW4 . . . 5G 119
Cavalier Cl. RM6: Chad H . . . 4D 54
Cavalier Ct. KT5: Surb . . . 6F 151
Cavalier Gdns. UB3: Hayes . . . 6F 75
Cavalier Ter. SE7 . . . 6A 106
Cavalry Cres. TW4: Houn . . . 4B 112
Cavalry Gdns. SW15 . . . 5H 117
Cavalry Memorial . . . 1E 100
Cavalry Pl. E17 . . . 2K 49
Cavalry Sq. SW3 . . . 5F 17 (5D 100)
Cavan Pl. HA5: Hat E . . . 1D 40
Cavatina Point SE8 . . . 6D 104
(off Copperas St.)
Cavaye Ho. SW10 . . . 7A 16
(off Cavaye Pl.)
Cavaye Pl. SW10 . . . 6A 16 (5A 100)
Cavell Dr. EN2: Enf . . . 2F 23
Cavell Ho. N1 . . . 1E 84
(off Colville Est.)
Cavell Rd. N17 . . . 7J 33
Cavell St. E1 . . . 5H 85
Cavendish Av. DA8: Erith . . . 6J 109
DA15: Sidc . . . 7A 126
DA16: Well . . . 3K 125
HA1: Harr . . . 4H 59
HA4: Ruis . . . 5K 57
IG8: Wfd G . . . 1K 51
KT3: N Mald . . . 5C 152
N3 . . . 2J 45
NW8 . . . 1B 4 (2B 82)
W13 . . . 5A 78
Cavendish Cl. N18 . . . 5C 34
NW6 . . . 6H 63
NW8 . . . 1B 4 (3B 82)
TW16: Sun . . . 6H 129
UB4: Hayes . . . 5G 75
Cavendish Ct. EC3 . . . 7H 9
SE6 . . . 1D 140
(off Bromley Rd.)
SM6: Wall . . . 6F 167
TW16: Sun . . . 6H 129
Cavendish Dr. E11 . . . 1F 69
HA8: Edg . . . 6A 28
Cavendish Gdns.
IG1: Ilf . . . 1E 70
IG11: Bark . . . 5J 71
RM6: Chad H . . . 5E 54
SW4 . . . 6G 119
Cavendish Ho.
CR0: C'don . . . 1D 168
(off Tavistock Rd.)
NW8 . . . 1B 4
(off Wellington Rd.)
NW9 . . . 3B 44
SW1 . . . 2D 18
(off Monck St.)
UB7: W Dray . . . 2B 92
(off Park Lodge Av.)
W1 . . . 6A 6
(off Mortimer St.)
Cavendish Mans. EC1 . . . 4J 7
(off Rosebery Av.)
NW6 . . . 5J 63
Cavendish M. Nth. W1 . . . 5K 5 (5F 83)
Cavendish M. Sth. W1 . . . 6K 5 (5F 83)

Cavendish Pde. *SW4* *6F* ***119***
(off Clapham Comn. Sth. Side)
TW4: Houn 2C **112**
Cavendish Pl. BR1: Brom 4D **160**
NW2 6F **63**
SW4 5H **119**
W1 7K **5** (6F **83**)
Cavendish Rd. CR0: C'don 1B **168**
E4 6K **35**
EN5: Barn 3A **20**
KT3: N Mald 4B **152**
N4 6B **48**
N18 5C **34**
NW6 7G **63**
SM2: Sutt 7A **166**
SW12 6F **119**
SW19 7B **136**
TW16: Sun 6H **129**
W4 1J **115**
Cavendish Sq. W1 7K **5** (6F **83**)
Cavendish St. N1 2D **84**
Cavendish Ter. E3 3B **86**
TW13: Felt 2J **129**
Cavendish Way BR4: W W'ck 1D **170**
Cavenham Gdns. IG1: Ilf 3H **71**
Caverleigh Pl. BR1: Brom 2A **160**
Caverleigh Way KT4: Wor Pk 1C **164**
Cave Rd. E13 3K **87**
TW10: Ham 4C **132**
Caversham Av. N13 3F **33**
SM3: Cheam 2G **165**
Caversham Ct. *N11* *3K* ***31***
(off Brunswick Pk. Rd.)
Caversham Ho. *KT1: King T* *2E* ***150***
(off Lady Booth Rd.)
N15 *4C* ***48***
(off Caversham Rd.)
SE15 *6G* ***103***
(off Haymerle Rd.)
Caversham M. SW3 7E **16**
Caversham Rd. KT1: King T 2F **151**
N15 4C **48**
NW5 6G **65**
NW9 3C **44**
Caversham St. SW3 7E **16** (6D **100**)
Caverswall St. W12 6E **80**
Caveside Cl. BR7: Chst 1E **160**
Cavesson Ho. *E20* *5E* ***68***
(off Ribbons Wlk.)
Cavour Ho. *SE17* *5B* ***102***
(off Alberta Est.)
Cawdor Cres. W7 4A **96**
Cawdor Wlk. E14 6E **86**
Cawnpore St. SE19 5E **138**
Cawston Ct. BR1: Brom 7H **141**
Caxton Ct. SW11 2C **118**
Caxton Gro. E3 3C **86**
Caxton Hall *SW1* *3H* ***101***
(off Caxton St.)
Caxton M. TW8: Bford 6D **96**
Caxton Pl. IG1: Ilf 3E **70**
Caxton Rd. N22 2K **47**
SW19 5A **136**
UB2: S'hall 3B **94**
W12 2F **99**
Caxtons, The *SW9* *7B* ***102***
(off Langton Rd.)
Caxton St. SW1 1C **18** (3G **101**)
Caxton St. Nth. E16 6H **87**
Caxton Trad. Est.
UB3: Hayes 2G **93**
Caxton Wlk. WC2 1D **12** (6H **83**)
Cayenne Ct. SE1 5K **15** (2F **103**)
Caygill Cl. BR2: Brom 4H **159**
Cayley Rd. UB2: S'hall 3F **95**
Cayton Pl. EC1 2E **8**
Cayton Rd. UB6: G'frd 2J **77**
Cayton St. EC1 2E **8** (3D **84**)
Cazenove Rd. E17 1C **50**
N16 2F **67**
Cearns Ho. E6 1B **88**
Cecil Av. EN1: Enf 4A **24**
HA9: Wemb 5F **61**
IG11: Bark 7H **71**
Cecil Cl. KT9: Chess 4D **162**
TW15: Ashf 7E **128**
W5 5D **78**
Cecil Ct. CR0: C'don 2F **169**
EN2: Enf 4J **23**
EN5: Barn 3A **20**
NW6 7K **63**
SW10 *6A* ***100***
(off Fawcett St.)
WC2 3E **12** (7J **83**)
Cecile Pk. N8 6J **47**
Cecil Gro. NW8 1C **82**
Cecil Hepworth Playhouse, The *7H* ***147***
(off Hepworth Way)
Cecil Ho. E17 1C **50**
Cecilia Cl. N2 3A **46**
Cecilia Rd. E8 5F **67**
Cecil Manning Cl. UB6: G'frd 1A **78**
Cecil Mans. SW17 2E **136**
Cecil Pk. HA5: Pinn 4C **40**
Cecil Pl. CR4: Mitc 5D **154**
Cecil Rhodes Ho. *NW1* *2H* ***83***
(off Goldington St.)
Cecil Rd. CR0: C'don 6J **155**
E11 3H **69**
E13 1J **87**
E17 1C **50**
EN2: Enf 3H **23**
HA3: W'stone 3J **41**
IG1: Ilf 4F **71**
N10 2F **47**
N14 1B **32**
NW9 3A **44**
NW10 1A **80**
RM6: Chad H 7D **54**
SM1: Sutt 6H **165**
SW19 7K **135**
TW3: Houn 2G **113**
TW15: Ashf 7E **128**
W3 5J **79**
Cecil Rosen Ct. HA0: Wemb 3B **60**
WD23: B Hea 1D **26**
Cecil Sharp House *1E* ***82***
(off Gloucester Av.)
Cecil Way BR2: Hayes 1J **171**
Cedar Av. DA15: Sidc 7A **126**
EN3: Enf H 2D **24**
EN4: E Barn 7H **21**
HA4: Ruis 5A **58**
RM6: Chad H 5E **54**
TW2: Whitt 6F **113**
UB3: Hayes 6J **75**
UB7: Yiew 7B **74**
Cedar Cl. BR2: Brom 3C **172**
E3 1B **86**
IG1: Ilf 5H **71**
IG9: Buck H 2G **37**
KT8: E Mos 4J **149**
RM7: Rom 4J **55**
SE21 1C **138**
SM5: Cars 6D **166**
SW15 4K **133**
Cedar Copse BR1: Brom 2D **160**
Cedar Ct. E11 5K **51**
E18 1J **51**
N1 7C **66**
N10 2E **46**
N11 5B **32**
N20 1G **31**
SE1 *7G* ***15***
(off Royal Oak Yd.)
SE7 6A **106**
SE9 6C **124**
SE13 4F **123**
SM2: Sutt 6A **166**
SW19 3F **135**
TW8: Bford 6C **96**
Cedar Cres. BR2: Brom 3C **172**
Cedarcroft Rd. KT9: Chess 4F **163**
Cedar Dr. HA5: Hat E 6A **26**
N2 4C **46**
Cedar Gdns. SM2: Sutt 6A **166**
Cedar Grange EN1: Enf 5K **23**
Cedar Gro. DA5: Bexl 6D **126**
UB1: S'hall 5E **76**
W5 3E **96**
Cedar Hgts. NW2 6H **63**
TW10: Ham 1E **132**
Cedar Ho. *E2* *2H* ***85***
(off Mowlem St.)
E14 *2E* ***104***
(off Manchester Rd.)
N22 *1A* ***48***
(off Acacia Rd.)
SE14 1K **121**
SE16 *2K* ***103***
(off Woodland Cres.)
SW6 *2A* ***118***
(off Lensbury Av.)
TW9: Kew 1H **115**
TW16: Sun *7H* ***129***
(off Spelthorne Gro.)
UB4: Yead 4A **76**
W8 *3K* ***99***
(off Marloes Rd.)
Cedarhurst BR1: Brom 7G **141**
Cedarhurst Cotts. DA5: Bexl 7G **127**
Cedarhurst Dr. SE9 5A **124**
Cedarland Ter. SW20 7D **134**
Cedar Lawn Av. EN5: Barn 5B **20**
Cedar M. SE4 3B **122**
SW15 5F **117**
Cedar Mt. SE9 1B **142**
Cedarne Rd. SW6 7K **99**
Cedar Pk. IG7: Chig 4K **37**
Cedar Pk. Gdns. RM6: Chad H 7D **54**
SW19 5D **134**
Cedar Pk. Rd. EN2: Enf 1H **23**
Cedar Pl. SE7 5A **106**
Cedar Ri. N14 7K **21**
Cedar Rd. BR1: Brom 2A **160**
CR0: C'don 2D **168**
EN2: Enf 1G **23**
KT8: E Mos 4J **149**
N17 1F **49**
NW2 4E **62**
RM7: Rom 4J **55**
SM2: Sutt 6A **166**
TW4: Cran 2A **112**
TW11: Tedd 5A **132**
TW14: Bedf 1F **129**
Cedars, The *E9* *7K* ***67***
(off Banbury Rd.)
E15 7H **69**
IG9: Buck H 1D **36**
SM6: Wall 4G **167**
TW11: Tedd 6K **131**
W13 6C **78**
Cedars Av. CR4: Mitc 4E **154**
E17 5C **50**
Cedars Cl. NW4 3F **45**
SE13 3F **123**
Cedars Ct. N9 2K **33**
Cedars Dr. UB10: Hil 2B **74**
Cedars Ho. E17 3D **50**
Cedars M. SW4 4F **119**
(not continuous)
Cedars Rd. BR3: Beck 2A **158**
CR0: Bedd 3J **167**
E15 6G **69**
KT1: Hamp W 1C **150**
N9 2B **34**
N21 2G **33**
SM4: Mord 4J **153**
SW4 3F **119**
SW13 2C **116**
W4 5J **97**
Cedar Ter. TW9: Rich 4E **114**
Cedar Tree Gro. SE27 5B **138**
Cedar Vw. *KT1: King T* *3D* ***150***
(off Milner Rd.)
Cedarville Gdns. SW16 6K **137**
Cedar Way N1 7H **65**
TW16: Sun 7G **129**
Cedar Way Ind. Est. N1 7H **65**
Cedra Ct. N16 1G **67**
Cedric Chambers *NW8* *3A* ***4***
(off Northwick Cl.)
Cedric Rd. SE9 3G **143**
Celadon Cl. EN3: Enf H 3F **25**
Celandine Cl. E14 5C **86**
Celandine Ct. E4 3J **35**
Celandine Dr. E8 7F **67**
SE28 1B **108**
Celandine Gro. N14 5B **22**
Celandine Way E15 3G **87**
Celbridge M. W2 5K **81**
Celebration Av. E20 5E **68**
Celebration Way E4 6K **35**
Celestial Gdns. SE13 4F **123**
Celia Cres. TW15: Ashf 6A **128**
Celia Ho. *N1* *2E* ***84***
(off Arden Est.)
Celia Rd. N19 4G **65**
Celtic Av. BR2: Brom 3G **159**
Celtic St. E14 5D **86**
Cemetery La. SE7 6C **106**
TW17: Shep 7D **146**
Cemetery Rd. E7 5H **69**
N17 7K **33**
SE2 7B **108**
Cemetery Way E4 3H **35**
Cenacle Cl. NW3 3J **63**
Cenotaph 6E **12** (2J **101**)
Centaur Ct. TW8: Bford 5E **96**
Centaurs Bus. Pk. TW7: Isle 6A **96**
Centaur St. SE1 1H **19** (3K **101**)
Centenary Rd. EN3: Brim 4G **25**
Centenary Trad. Est. EN3: Brim 3G **25**
Centennial Av. WD6: E'tree 1H **27**
Centennial Ct. WD6: E'tree 1H **27**
Centennial Pk. WD6: E'tree 1H **27**
Central Apartments HA9: Wemb 5E **60**
Central Arc. *TW15: Ashf* *4B* ***128***
(off Woodthorpe Rd.)
Central Av. DA16: Well 2K **125**
E11 2F **69**
EN1: Enf 2C **24**
HA5: Pinn 6D **40**
KT8: W Mole 4D **148**
N2 2B **46**
N9 3K **33**
SM6: Wall 5J **167**
SW6 3A **118**
SW11 7D **100**
TW3: Houn 4G **113**
UB3: Hayes 1H **93**
Central Bus. Cen. NW10 5A **62**
Central Cir. NW4 5D **44**
Central Courtyard *EC2* *7H* ***9***
(off Cutlers Gdns.)
Central Criminal Court
Old Bailey 7B **8** (6B **84**)
Centrale Shop. Cen. CR0: C'don 2C **168**
Central Gallery *IG1: Ilf* *2F* ***71***
(within The Exchange)
Central Gdns. SM4: Mord 5K **153**
Central Hill SE19 5D **138**
Central Ho. E15 2D **86**
IG11: Bark 7G **71**
Central London Golf Course 2B **136**
Central Mall *SW18* *6K* ***117***
(within Southside Shop. Cen.)
Central Mans. *NW4* *5D* ***44***
(off Watford Way)
Central Markets (Smithfield) 6A **8**
Central Pde. DA15: Sidc 3A **144**
E17 4C **50**
EN3: Enf H 2D **24**
HA1: Harr 5K **41**

Central Pde. IG2: Ilf ... 6H **53**
KT6: Surb ... 6E **150**
KT8: W Mole ... 4D **148**
SE20 ... *7K* ***139***
(off High St.)
TW5: Hest ... 7D **94**
TW14: Felt ... 7A **112**
UB6: G'frd ... 3A **78**
W3 ... 2H **97**
Central Pk. NW10 ... 3J **79**
Central Pk. Av. RM10: Dag ... 3H **73**
Central Pk. Est. TW4: Houn ... 5B **112**
Central Pk. Rd. E6 ... 2B **88**
Central Pl. SE25 ... 5G **157**
Central Rd. HA0: Wemb ... 5B **60**
KT4: Wor Pk ... 1C **164**
SM4: Mord ... 6J **153**
Central St Giles Piazza WC2 ... 7E **6**
Central St Martins College of Art & Design
Byam Shaw Campus ... 2H **65**
Central School Path SW14 ... 3J **115**
Central Sq. *HA9: Wemb* ... *5E* ***60***
(off High Rd.)
KT8: W Mole ... 5D **148**
NW11 ... 6K **45**
Central St. EC1 ... 1C **8** (3C **84**)
Central Ter. BR3: Beck ... 3K **157**
Central Walkway *N19* ... *4H* ***65***
(off Pleshey Rd.)
Central Way NW10 ... 3J **79**
SE28 ... 1A **108**
SM5: Cars ... 7C **166**
TW14: Felt ... 5J **111**
Central W. UB6: G'frd ... 4G **77**
Central Wharf *E14* ... *6C* ***86***
(off Thomas Rd.)
Centre, The KT12: Walt T ... 7J **147**
TW3: Houn ... 3F **113**
TW13: Felt ... 1K **129**
Centre Av. W3 ... 1K **97**
Centre Comn. Rd. BR7: Chst ... 6G **143**
Centre Ct. Shop. Cen. SW19 ... 6H **135**
Cen. for the Magic Arts, The ... *3B* ***6***
(off Stephenson Way)
Cen. for Wildlife Gardening Vis. Cen.
... 3F **121**
Centre Hgts. *NW3* ... *7B* ***64***
(off Finchley Rd.)
Cen. of the Cell ... ***5H 85***
(off Newark St.)
Cen. Point SE1 ... 5G **103**
Centrepoint WC2 ... 7D **6**
Cen. Point Ho. *WC2* ... *7D* ***6***
(off St Giles High St.)
Centre Rd. E7 ... 2J **69**
E11 ... 2J **69**
RM10: Dag ... 2H **91**
Centre Sq. *SW18* ... *5J* ***117***
(off Buckhold Rd.)
Centre St. E2 ... 2H **85**
Centre Vw. Apartments *CR0: C'don* ... *3C* ***168***
(off Whitgift St.)
Centre Way E17 ... 7K **35**
N9 ... 2D **34**
Centreway *IG1: Ilf* ... *2G* ***71***
(off High Rd.)
Centreway Apartments *IG1: Ilf* ... *2G* ***71***
(off Axon Pl.)
Centric Cl. NW1 ... 1E **82**
Centrillion Point *CR0: C'don* ... *4C* ***168***
(off Mason's Av.)
Centro Ct. E6 ... 4D **88**
Centurion Bldg. SW8 ... 7J **17** (6F **101**)
Centurion Cl. N7 ... 7K **65**
Centurion Ct. SE18 ... 4E **106**
SM6: Wall ... 2F **167**
Centurion Ho. UB3: Hayes ... 6F **75**
Centurion La. E3 ... 1B **86**
Centurion Sq. SE18 ... 1C **124**
Centurion Way DA18: Erith ... 3F **109**
Century Cl. NW4 ... 5F **45**
Century Ct. NW8 ... 2B **4**
Century Ho. HA9: Wemb ... 2F **61**
SW15 ... 4F **117**
Century M. E5 ... 4J **67**
N5 ... *3B* ***66***
(off Conewood St.)
Century Plaza *HA8: Edg* ... *6B* ***28***
(off Station Rd.)
Century Rd. E17 ... 3A **50**
Century Way BR3: Beck ... 6B **140**
Century Yd. SE23 ... 2J **139**
(not continuous)
Cephas Av. E1 ... 4J **85**
Cephas Ho. *E1* ... *4J* ***85***
(off Doveton St.)
Cephas St. E1 ... 4J **85**
Ceres Rd. SE18 ... 4K **107**
Cerise Apartments *E3* ... *1A* ***86***
(off Gunmaker's La.)
Cerise Rd. SE15 ... 1G **121**
Cerne Cl. UB4: Yead ... 7A **76**
Cerne Rd. SM4: Mord ... 6A **154**
Cerney M. W2 ... 2A **10** (7B **82**)
Cervantes Ct. W2 ... 6K **81**
W11 ... *6G* ***81***
(off Rushton M.)
Cester St. E2 ... 1G **85**
Ceylon Rd. W14 ... 3F **99**
Ceylon Wharf Apartments *SE16* ... *2J* ***103***
(off St Marychurch St.)
CFGS Community Performing Arts &
Sports Cen. ... 3B **86**
Chabot Dr. SE15 ... 3H **121**
Chadacre Av. IG5: Ilf ... 3D **52**
Chadacre Ct. *E15* ... *1J* ***87***
(off Vicars Cl.)
Chadacre Ho. *SW9* ... *4B* ***120***
(off Loughborough Pk.)
Chadacre Rd. KT17: Ewe ... 6D **164**
Chadbourn St. E14 ... 5D **86**
Chadbury Ct. NW7 ... 1C **44**
Chad Cres. N9 ... 3D **34**
Chadd Dr. BR1: Brom ... 3C **160**
Chadd Grn. E13 ... 1J **87**
(not continuous)
Chadston Ho. *N1* ... *7B* ***66***
(off Halton Rd.)
Chadswell *WC1* ... *2F* ***7***
(off Cromer St.)
Chadview Ct. RM6: Chad H ... 7D **54**
Chadville Gdns. RM6: Chad H ... 5D **54**
Chadway RM8: Dag ... 1C **72**
Chadwell Av. RM6: Chad H ... 7B **54**
CHADWELL HEATH ... 7D **54**
Chadwell Heath Ind. Pk. RM8: Dag ... 1D **72**
Chadwell Heath La. RM6: Chad H ... 4B **54**
Chadwell Ho. *SE17* ... *5D* ***102***
(off Inville Rd.)
Chadwell La. N8 ... 3K **47**
Chadwell St. EC1 ... 1K **7** (3A **84**)
Chadwick Av. E4 ... 4A **36**
N21 ... 5E **22**
SW19 ... 6J **135**
Chadwick Cl. SW15 ... 7B **116**
TW11: Tedd ... 6A **132**
W7 ... 5K **77**
Chadwick Ct. *E14* ... *6C* ***86***
(off Jonzen Wlk.)
Chadwick Gdns. UB8: Uxb ... 7A **56**
Chadwick M. W4 ... 6H **97**
Chadwick Pl. KT6: Surb ... 7C **150**
Chadwick Rd. E11 ... 6G **51**
IG1: Ilf ... 3F **71**
NW10 ... 1B **80**
SE15 ... 2F **121**
Chadwick St. SW1 ... 2C **18** (3H **101**)
Chadwick Way SE28 ... 7D **90**
Chadwin Rd. E13 ... 5K **87**
Chadworth Ho. *EC1* ... *2C* ***8***
(off Lever St.)
N4 ... 1C **66**
Chaffinch Av. CR0: C'don ... 6K **157**
Chaffinch Bus. Pk. BR3: Beck ... 4K **157**
Chaffinch Cl. CR0: C'don ... 5K **157**
KT6: Surb ... 3G **163**
N9 ... 1E **34**
Chaffinch Rd. BR3: Beck ... 1A **158**
Chafford Way RM6: Chad H ... 4C **54**
Chagford Ho. *E3* ... *3D* ***86***
(off Talwin St.)
Chagford St. NW1 ... 4E **4** (4D **82**)
Chailey Av. EN1: Enf ... 2A **24**
Chailey Cl. TW5: Hest ... 1B **112**
Chailey Ind. Est. UB3: Hayes ... 2J **93**
Chailey St. E5 ... 3J **67**
Chalbury Wlk. N1 ... 2K **83**
Chalcombe Rd. SE2 ... 3B **108**
Chalcot Cl. SM2: Sutt ... 7J **165**
Chalcot Cres. NW1 ... 1D **82**
Chalcot Gdns. NW3 ... 6D **64**
Chalcot M. SW16 ... 3J **137**
Chalcot Rd. NW1 ... 7E **64**
Chalcot Sq. NW1 ... 7E **64**
(not continuous)
Chalcott Gdns. KT6: Surb ... 1C **162**
Chalcroft Rd. SE13 ... 5G **123**
Chaldon Ct. SE19 ... 2D **156**
Chaldon Path CR7: Thor H ... 4B **156**
Chaldon Rd. SW6 ... 7G **99**
Chale Rd. SW2 ... 6J **119**
Chalet Cl. DA5: Bexl ... 4K **145**
TW15: Ashf ... 6F **129**
Chalet Ct. CR7: Thor H ... 5C **156**
Chalet Est. NW7 ... 4H **29**
Chalfont Av. HA9: Wemb ... 6H **61**
Chalfont Ct. *HA1: Harr* ... *6K* ***41***
(off Northwick Pk. Rd.)
NW1 ... *4F* ***5***
(off Baker St.)
NW9 ... 3B **44**
Chalfont Grn. N9 ... 3K **33**
Chalfont Ho. *SE16* ... *3H* ***103***
(off Keetons Rd.)
Chalfont M. SW19 ... 1H **135**
UB10: Hil ... 7D **56**
Chalfont Rd. N9 ... 3K **33**
SE25 ... 3F **157**
UB3: Hayes ... 2J **93**
Chalfont Wlk. HA5: Pinn ... 2A **40**
Chalfont Way W13 ... 3B **96**
Chalford *NW6* ... *6A* ***64***
(off Finchley Rd.)
Chalford Cl. KT8: W Mole ... 4E **148**
Chalford Rd. SE21 ... 4D **138**
Chalford Wlk. IG8: Wfd G ... 1B **52**
Chalgrove Av. SM4: Mord ... 5J **153**
Chalgrove Cres. IG5: Ilf ... 2C **52**
Chalgrove Gdns. N3 ... 3G **45**
Chalgrove Rd. N17 ... 1H **49**
SM2: Sutt ... 7B **166**
Chalice Cl. SM6: Wall ... 6H **167**
Chalice Ct. N2 ... 4C **46**
SE19 ... 6D **138**
Chalkenden Cl. SE20 ... 7H **139**
CHALKER'S CORNER ... **3H 115**
CHALK FARM ... 7E **64**
Chalk Farm Pde. *NW3* ... *7E* ***64***
(off Adelaide Rd.)
Chalk Farm Rd. NW1 ... 7E **64**
Chalk Hill Rd. W6 ... 4F **99**
Chalkhill Rd. HA9: Wemb ... 3H **61**
Chalklands HA9: Wemb ... 3J **61**
Chalk La. EN4: Cockf ... 3J **21**
Chalkley Cl. CR4: Mitc ... 2D **154**
Chalkmill Dr. EN1: Enf ... 3C **24**
Chalk Pit Way SM1: Sutt ... 5A **166**
Chalk Rd. E13 ... 5K **87**
Chalkstone Cl. DA16: Well ... 1A **126**
Chalkwell Ho. *E1* ... *6K* ***85***
(off Pitsea St.)
Chalkwell Pk. Av. EN1: Enf ... 4K **23**
Challenge Cl. NW10 ... 1A **80**
Challenge Ct. TW2: Twick ... 7J **113**
Challenger Ho. *E14* ... *7A* ***86***
(off Victory Pl.)
Challenge Rd. TW15: Ashf ... 3F **129**
Challice Way SW2 ... 1K **137**
Challin St. SE20 ... 1J **157**
Challis Rd. TW8: Bford ... 5D **96**
Challoner Cl. N2 ... 2B **46**
Challoner Ct. BR2: Brom ... 2F **159**
W14 ... *5H* ***99***
(off Challoner St.)
Challoner Cres. W14 ... 5H **99**
Challoner Mans. *W14* ... *5H* ***99***
(off Challoner St.)
Challoners Cl. KT8: E Mos ... 4H **149**
Challoner St. W14 ... 5H **99**
Challoner Wlk. *E1* ... *6G* ***85***
(off Christian St.)
Chalmers Ho. E17 ... 5D **50**
Chalmers Rd. TW15: Ashf ... 5D **128**
Chalmers Rd. E. TW15: Ashf ... 4D **128**
Chalmers Wlk. *SE17* ... *6B* ***102***
(off Hillingdon St.)
Chalmers Way TW1: Isle ... 4B **114**
TW14: Felt ... 5K **111**
Chaloner Ct. SE1 ... 6E **14**
Chalsey Rd. SE4 ... 4B **122**
Chalton Dr. N2 ... 6B **46**
Chalton Ho. *NW1* ... *1C* ***6***
(off Chalton St.)
Chalton St. NW1 ... 1C **6** (2G **83**)
(not continuous)
Chamberlain Cl. IG1: Ilf ... 3G **71**
SE28 ... 3H **107**
UB3: Hayes ... 7H **75**
Chamberlain Cotts. SE5 ... 1D **120**
Chamberlain Ct. *SE16* ... *4J* ***103***
(off Silwood St.)
Chamberlain Cres. BR4: W W'ck ... 1D **170**
Chamberlain Gdns. TW3: Houn ... 1G **113**
Chamberlain Ho. *E1* ... *7J* ***85***
(off Cable St.)
EC2 ... *3G* ***9***
(off Blackall St.)
NW1 ... 1D **6**
SE1 ... *7J* ***13***
(off Westminster Bri. Rd.)
Chamberlain La. HA5: Eastc ... 3J **39**
Chamberlain Pl. E17 ... 3A **50**
Chamberlain Rd. N2 ... 2A **46**
W13 ... 2A **96**
Chamberlain St. NW1 ... 7D **64**
Chamberlain Wlk. TW13: Hanw ... 4C **130**
Chamberlain Way HA5: Eastc ... 3K **39**
KT6: Surb ... 7E **150**
Chamberlayne Av. HA9: Wemb ... 3E **60**
Chamberlayne Mans. *NW10* ... *3F* ***81***
(off Chamberlayne Rd.)
Chamberlayne Rd. NW10 ... 1E **80**
Chamberlens Garages *W6* ... *4D* ***98***
(off Dalling Rd.)
Chambers, The *SW10* ... *1A* ***118***
(off Chelsea Harbour Dr.)
Chambers Av. DA14: Sidc ... 6E **144**
Chambers Bus. Pk. UB7: Sip ... 6C **92**
Chambers Gdns. N2 ... 1B **46**
Chambers La. NW10 ... 7D **62**
Chambers Pl. CR2: S Croy ... 7D **168**
Chambers Rd. N7 ... 4J **65**
Chambers St. SE16 ... 2G **103**
Chamber St. E1 ... 2K **15** (7F **85**)
Chambers Wlk. HA7: Stan ... 5G **27**
Chambers Wharf SE16 ... 2G **103**
Chambon Pl. W6 ... 4C **98**
Chambord Ho. *E2* ... *2K* ***9***
(off Chambord St.)
Chambord St. E2 ... 2K **9** (3F **85**)
Chamomile Ct. *E17* ... *6C* ***50***
(off Yunus Khan Cl.)
Champa Cl. N17 ... 2F **49**
Champion Cres. SE26 ... 4A **140**

Champion Gro. SE5 3D 120
Champion Hill SE5 3D 120
Champion Hill Est. SE5 3E 120
Champion Hill Stadium 4E 120
Champion Ho. *SE7 6A 106*
(off Charlton Rd.)
Champion Pk. SE5 2D 120
Champion Rd. SE26 4A 140
Champions Wlk. E20 5E 68
Champions Way NW4 1D 44
NW7 1D 44
Champlain Ho. *W12 7D 80*
(off White City Est.)
Champness Cl. E17 3K 49
SE27 4D 138
Champness Rd. IG11: Bark 6K 71
Champneys Cl. SM2: Cheam 7H 165
Chancel Ct. *W1 7H 83*
(off Old Compton St.)
Chancel Ind. Est. NW10 5B 62
Chancellor Gdns. CR2: S Croy 7B 168
Chancellor Gro. SE21 2C 138
Chancellor Ho. *E1 1H 103*
(off Green Bank)
SW7 3A 100
(off Hyde Pk. Ga.)
Chancellor Pas. E14 1C 104
Chancellor Pl. NW9 2B 44
Chancellors Cl. BR3: Beck 7C 158
Chancellors Ct. WC1 5G 7
Chancellor's Rd. W6 5E 98
Chancellor's St. W6 5E 98
Chancellors Wharf W6 5E 98
Chancellor Way RM8: Dag 4A 72
Chancelot Rd. SE2 4B 108
Chancel St. SE1 5A 14 (1B 102)
Chancery Bldg. SW8 7D 18 (6H 101)
Chancery Bldgs. *E1 7H 85*
(off Lowood St.)
Chancerygate UB7: Yiew 1C 92
Chancerygate Bus. Cen. HA4: Ruis 4C 58
Chancery Ga. Bus. Pk. KT6: Surb 2F 163
Chancery La. BR3: Beck 2D 158
WC2 6H 7 (6A 84)
Chancery M. SW17 2C 136
Chance St. E1 3J 9 (4F 85)
E2 3J 9 (4F 85)
Chanctonbury Cl. SE9 3F 143
Chanctonbury Gdns. SM2: Sutt 7K 165
Chanctonbury Way N12 4C 30
Chandaria Ct. *CR0: C'don 3C 168*
(off Church Rd.)
Chandler Av. E16 5J 87
Chandler Cl. TW12: Hamp 1E 148
Chandler Ct. TW14: Felt 6J 111
Chandler Ho. *NW6 1H 81*
(off Willesden La.)
WC1 4F 7
(off Colonnade)
Chandlers Av. SE10 3H 105
Chandlers Cl. KT8: W Mole 5F 149
TW14: Felt 7H 111
Chandlers Ct. SE12 1K 141
Chandlers Dr. DA8: Erith 4K 109
Chandlers M. E14 2C 104
Chandler St. E1 1H 103
Chandlers Way SW2 7A 120
Chandler Way SE15 6E 102
Chandlery, The *SE1 1K 19*
(off Gerridge St.)
Chandlery Ho. *E1 6G 85*
(off Gower's Wlk.)
Chandon Lodge SM2: Sutt 7A 166
Chandos Av. E17 2C 50
N14 3B 32
N20 1F 31
W5 4C 96
Chandos Cl. IG9: Buck H 2E 36
Chandos Ct. HA7: Stan 6G 27
HA8: Edg 7A 28
N14 2C 32
Chandos Cres. HA8: Edg 7A 28
Chandos Pde. HA8: Edg 7A 28
Chandos Pl. WC2 3E 12 (7J 83)
Chandos Rd. E15 5F 69
HA1: Harr 5G 41
HA5: Eastc 7B 40
N2 2B 46
N17 2E 48
NW2 5E 62
NW10 4A 80
Chandos St. W1 6K 5 (5F 83)
Chandos Way NW11 1K 63
Change All. EC3 1F 15 (6D 84)
Chanin M. NW2 5E 62
Channel 4 TV 2C 18
Channel Cl. TW5: Hest 1E 112
Channel Ga. Rd. NW10 3A 80
Channel Ho. *E14 5A 86*
(off Aston St.)
SE16 2K 103
(off Water Gdns. Sq.)
Channel Islands Est. N1 6C 66
Channelsea Ho. E15 2F 87
Channelsea Path E15 1F 87
Channelsea Rd. E15 1F 87
Channon Ct. *KT6: Surb 5E 150*
(off Maple Rd)
Chantress Cl. RM10: Dag 1J 91
Chantrey Ho. SW1 3K 17
Chantrey Rd. SW9 3K 119
Chantry, The E4 1K 35
UB8: Hil 3B 74
Chantry Cl. DA14: Sidc 5E 144
EN2: Enf 1H 23
HA3: Kenton 5F 43
SE2 3C 108
TW16: Sun 7J 129
UB7: Yiew 7A 74
W9 4J 81
Chantry Ct. SM5: Cars 3C 166
Chantry Cres. NW10 6B 62
Chantry Ho. KT1: King T 4E 150
Chantry La. BR2: Brom 5B 160
Chantry Pl. HA3: Hrw W 1F 41
Chantry Rd. HA3: Hrw W 1F 41
KT9: Chess 5F 163
Chantry Sq. W8 3K 99
Chantry St. N1 1B 84
Chantry Way CR4: Mitc 3B 154
Chant Sq. E15 7F 69
Chant St. E15 7F 69
(not continuous)
Chapel, The SW15 6G 117
Chapel Cl. DA1: Cray 5K 127
NW10 5B 62
Chapel Ct. *E10 2D 68*
(off Rosedene Ter.)
N2 3C 46
RM7: Rush G 6K 55
SE1 6E 14 (2D 102)
SE18 6A 108
UB3: Hayes 7H 75
CHAPEL END 1D 50
Chapel Farm Rd. SE9 3D 142
Chapel Ga. M. *SW4 3J 119*
(off Bedford Rd.)
Chapel Ga. Pl. BR7: Chst 6F 143
Chapel Hill DA1: Cray 5K 127
Chapel Ho. St. E14 5D 104
Chapelier Ho. SW18 4J 117
Chapel La. HA5: Pinn 3B 40
RM6: Chad H 7D 54
UB8: Hil 6C 74
Chapel Mkt. N1 2A 84
Chapel M. IG8: Wfd G 6K 37
Chapel Mill Rd. KT1: King T 3F 151
Chapelmount Rd. IG8: Wfd G 6J 37
Chapel of St John the Evangelist *3J 15*
(within The Tower of London)
Chapel of St Peter & St Paul *6F 105*
(within University of Greenwich)
Chapel Path *E11 6K 51*
(off Woodbine Pl.)
Chapel Pl. EC2 2G 9 (3E 84)
N1 2A 84
N17 7A 34
W1 1J 11 (6F 83)
Chapel Rd. DA7: Bex 4G 127
IG1: Ilf 3E 70
SE27 4B 138
TW1: Twick 7B 114
TW3: Houn 3F 113
W13 1B 96
Chapel Side W2 7K 81
Chapel Stones N17 1F 49
Chapel St. EN2: Enf 3H 23
NW1 6C 4 (5C 82)
SW1 1H 17 (3E 100)
Chapel Vw. CR2: Sels 6J 169
Chapel Wlk. CR0: C'don 2C 168
NW4 4D 44
(not continuous)
Chapel Way N7 3K 65
Chapel Yd. *SW18 5K 117*
(off Wandsworth High St.)
Chaplin Cl. HA0: Wemb 6D 60
SE1 6K 13 (2A 102)
Chaplin Ct. *E3 4B 86*
(off Joseph St.)
SE14 1K 121
(off Besson St.)
SE17 6B 102
(off Royal Rd.)
Chaplin Cres. TW16: Sun 6G 129
Chaplin Ho. *DA14: Sidc 4A 144*
(off Sidcup High St.)
E17 4C 50
(off Hoe St.)
N1 1D 84
(off Shepperton Rd.)
W3 3J 97
(off All Saints Rd.)
Chaplin Rd. E15 2H 87
HA0: Wemb 6C 60
N17 3F 49
NW2 6C 62
RM9: Dag 7E 72
Chaplin Sq. N12 7G 31
Chapman Cl. UB7: W Dray 3B 92
Chapman Cres. HA3: Kenton 6E 42
Chapman Grn. N22 1A 48
Chapman Ho. *E1 6H 85*
(off Bigland St.)
Chapman Pl. N4 2B 66
Chapman Rd. CR0: C'don 1A 168
DA17: Belv 5G 109
E9 6B 68
Chapman's La. DA17: Belv 4D 108
SE2 4C 108
Chapmans Pk. Ind. Est. NW10 6B 62
Chapman Sq. SW19 2F 135
Chapman's Ter. N22 1B 48
Chapman St. E1 7H 85
Chapone Pl. W1 1C 12 (6H 83)
Chapter Chambers *SW1 4C 18*
(off Chapter St.)
Chapter Cl. UB10: Hil 7B 56
W4 3J 97
Chapter House 1C 14
Chapter Ho. *E2 4G 85*
(off Dunbridge St.)
Chapter Rd. NW2 5C 62
SE17 5B 102
Chapter St. SW1 4C 18 (4H 101)
Chapter Way SW19 1B 154
TW12: Hamp 4E 130
Chara Pl. W4 6K 97
Charcot Ho. SW15 6B 116
Charcot Rd. NW9 2A 44
Charcroft Ct. *W14 2F 99*
(off Minford Gdns.)
Charcroft Gdns. EN3: Pond E 4E 24
Chardin Ho. *SW9 1A 120*
(off Gosling Way)
Chardin Rd. W4 4A 98
Chardmore Rd. N16 1G 67
Chard Rd. TW6: H'row A 2D 110
Chardwell Cl. E6 6D 88
Charecroft Way W12 2F 99
W14 2F 99
Charfield Ct. *W9 4K 81*
(off Shirland Rd.)
Charford Rd. E16 5J 87
Chargeable La. E13 4H 87
Chargeable St. E16 4H 87
Chargrove Cl. SE16 2K 103
Charing Cl. BR6: Orp 4K 173
Charing Ct. BR2: Brom 2G 159
Charing Cross SW1 4E 12
Charing Cross Rd. WC2 7D 6 (6H 83)
Charing Cross Sports Club 6F 99
Charing Cross Theatre *4F 13*
(off Villiers St.)
Charing Cross Underground Shop. Cen.
WC2 3E 12
Charing Ho. *SE1 6K 13*
(off Windmill Wlk.)
Chariot Cl. E3 1C 86
Charis Ho. *E3 3D 86*
(off Grace St.)
Charlbert Ct. *NW8 2C 82*
(off Charlbert St.)
Charlbert St. NW8 2C 82
Charlbury Av. HA7: Stan 5J 27
Charlbury Gdns. IG3: Ilf 2K 71
Charlbury Gro. W5 6C 78
Charlbury Rd. UB10: Ick 3B 56
Charldane Rd. SE9 3F 143
Charlecote Gro. SE26 3H 139
Charlecote Rd. RM8: Dag 3E 72
Charlemont Rd. E6 4D 88
Charles II Pl. SW3 6E 16 (5D 100)
Charles II St. SW1 4C 12 (1H 101)
Charles Auffray Ho. *E1 5J 85*
(off Smithy St.)
Charles Babbage Cl. KT9: Chess 7C 162
Charles Baker Pl. SW17 1C 136
Charles Barry Cl. SW4 3G 119
Charles Bradlaugh Ho. *N17 7C 34*
(off Haynes Cl.)
Charles Burton Ct. *E5 5A 68*
(off Ashenden Rd.)
Charles Chu. Wlk. IG1: Ilf 6D 52
Charles Cl. DA14: Sidc 4B 144
Charles Cobb Gdns. CR0: Wadd 5A 168
Charles Coveney Rd. SE15 1F 121
Charles Cres. HA1: Harr 7H 41
(not continuous)
Charles Curran Ho. UB10: Ick 3D 56
Charles Darwin Ho. *E2 3H 85*
(off Canrobert St.)
Charles Dickens Ho. *E2 3G 85*
(off Mansford St.)
Charles Dickens Mus., The 4G 7
Charlesfield SE9 3A 142
Charles Flemwell M. E16 1J 105
Charles Gardner Ct. *N1 1F 9*
(off Haberdasher St.)
Charles Grinling Wlk. SE18 4E 106
Charles Gro. N14 1B 32
Charles Haller St. SW2 7A 120
Charles Harrod Ct. *SW13 6E 98*
(off Somerville Av.)
Charles Hocking Ho. *W3 2J 97*
(off Bollo Bri. Rd.)
Charles Ho. *N17 7A 34*
(off Love La.)
UB2: S'hall 2E 94
W14 4H 99
Charles Lamb Ct. *N1 2B 84*
(off Gerrard Rd.)
Charles La. NW8 2C 82
Charles Lesser Ho. KT9: Chess 5D 162

Charles Mackenzie Ho.—Chatsworth Ct.

Charles Mackenzie Ho. *SE16* ... 4G 103
(off Linsey St.)
Charlesmere Gdns. *SE28* ... 2J 107
(off Thames Reach)
Charles Nex M. SE21 ... 2C 138
Charles Pl. E4 ... 7K 25, 1A 36
NW1 ... 2B 6 (3G 83)
Charles Rd. E7 ... 7A 70
RM6: Chad H ... 6D 54
RM10: Dag ... 6K 73
SW19 ... 1J 153
TW18: Staines ... 6A 128
W13 ... 6A 78
Charles Rowan Ho. *WC1* ... 2J 7
(off Margery St.)
Charles Sevright Way NW7 ... 5A 30
Charles Simmons Ho. *WC1* ... 2J 7
(off Margery St.)
Charles Sq. N1 ... 2F 9 (3D 84)
Charles Sq. Est. N1 ... 2F 9
Charles St. CR0: C'don ... 3C 168
E16 ... 1A 106
EN1: Enf ... 5A 24
N19 ... 1J 65
SW13 ... 2A 116
TW3: Houn ... 2D 112
UB10: Hil ... 4D 74
W1 ... 4J 11 (1F 101)
Charles Talbot M. SE22 ... 1H 139
Charleston Cl. TW13: Felt ... 3J 129
Charleston St. SE17 ... 4C 102
Charles Townsend Ho. *EC1* ... 3A 8
(off Skinner St.)
Charles Uton Ct. E8 ... 4G 67
Charles Whincup Rd. E16 ... 1K 105
Charlesworth Ho. *E14* ... 6C 86
(off Dod St.)
Charlesworth Pl. SW13 ... 3A 116
Charleville Cir. SE26 ... 5G 139
Charleville Ct. *W14* ... 5H 99
(off Charleville Rd.)
Charleville Mans. *W14* ... 5G 99
(off Charleville Rd.)
Charleville M. TW7: Isle ... 4B 114
Charleville Rd. W14 ... 5G 99
CHARLIE BROWN'S RDBT. ... 2A 52
Charlie Chaplin Wlk.
SE1 ... 4H 13 (1K 101)
Charlieville Rd. DA8: Erith ... 7J 109
Charlmont Rd. SW17 ... 6C 136
Charlotte Cl. DA6: Bex ... 5E 126
IG6: Ilf ... 1G 53
Charlotte Ct. IG2: Ilf ... 6E 52
N8 ... 6H 47
SE1 ... 4E 102
(off Old Kent Rd.)
W6 ... 4C 98
Charlotte Despard Av. SW11 ... 1E 118
Charlotte Ho. *E16* ... 1K 105
(off Fairfax M.)
W6 ... 5E 98
(off Queen Caroline St.)
Charlotte M. W1 ... 5B 6 (5G 83)
W10 ... 6F 81
W14 ... 4G 99
Charlotte Pk. Av. BR1: Brom ... 3C 160
Charlotte Pl. NW9 ... 5J 43
SW1 ... 4A 18 (4G 101)
W1 ... 6B 6 (5G 83)
Charlotte Rd. EC2 ... 2G 9 (3E 84)
RM10: Dag ... 6H 73
SM6: Wall ... 6G 167
SW13 ... 1B 116
Charlotte Row SW4 ... 3G 119
Charlotte Sq. TW10: Rich ... 6F 115
Charlotte St. W1 ... 5B 6 (5G 83)
Charlotte Ter. N1 ... 1K 83
Charlow Cl. SW6 ... 2A 118
CHARLTON
SE7 ... 7B 106
TW17 ... 3E 146
Charlton Athletic FC ... 5A 106
Charlton Chu. La. SE7 ... 5A 106
Charlton Cl. UB10: Ick ... 2D 56
Charlton Ct. E2 ... 1F 85
NW5 ... 5H 65
Charlton Cres. IG11: Bark ... 2K 89
Charlton Dene SE7 ... 7A 106
Charlton Ga. Bus. Pk. SE7 ... 4A 106
Charlton Ho. TW8: Bford ... 6E 96
Charlton King's Rd. NW5 ... 5H 65
Charlton La. SE7 ... 4B 106
TW17: Shep ... 3E 146
(not continuous)
Charlton Lido ... 7B 106
Charlton Pk. La. SE7 ... 7B 106
Charlton Pk. Rd. SE7 ... 6B 106
Charlton Pl. N1 ... 2B 84
Charlton Riverside Pl. SE7 ... 4K 105
Charlton Rd. HA3: Kenton ... 4D 42
HA9: Wemb ... 1F 61
N9 ... 1E 34
NW10 ... 1A 80
SE3 ... 7J 105
SE7 ... 7J 105
TW17: Shep ... 3E 146
Charlton Ter. SE11 ... 6A 102
Charlton Way SE3 ... 1G 123
Charlwood CR0: Sels ... 7B 170
Charlwood Cl. HA3: Hrw W ... 6D 26
Charlwood Ho. *SW1* ... 4C 18
(off Vauxhall Bri. Rd.)
TW9: Kew ... 7H 97
Charlwood Ho's. *WC1* ... 2F 7
(off Midhope St.)
Charlwood Pl. SW1 ... 4B 18 (4G 101)
Charlwood Rd. SW15 ... 4F 117
Charlwood St. SW1 ... 6A 18 (5G 101)
(not continuous)
Charlwood Ter. SW15 ... 4F 117
Charmans Ho. *SW8* ... 7J 101
(off Wandsworth Rd.)
Charmeuse Ct. *E2* ... 2H 85
(off Silk Weaver Way)
Charmian Av. HA7: Stan ... 3D 42
Charmian Ho. *N1* ... 1G 9
(off Crondall St.)
Charminster Av. SW19 ... 2J 153
Charminster Ct. KT6: Surb ... 7D 150
Charminster Rd. KT4: Wor Pk ... 1F 165
SE9 ... 4B 142
Charmouth Ct. TW10: Rich ... 5F 115
Charmouth Ho. SW8 ... 7K 101
Charmouth Rd. DA16: Well ... 1C 126
Charnock Ho. *W12* ... 7D 80
(off White City Est.)
Charnock Rd. E5 ... 3H 67
Charnwood Av. SW19 ... 2J 153
Charnwood Cl. KT3: N Mald ... 4A 152
Charnwood Dr. E18 ... 3K 51
Charnwood Gdns. E14 ... 4C 104
Charnwood Pl. N20 ... 3F 31
Charnwood Rd. SE25 ... 5D 156
UB10: Hil ... 2C 74
Charnwood St. E5 ... 2H 67
Charrington Rd. CR0: C'don ... 2C 168
Charrington St. NW1 ... 2H 83
(not continuous)
Charsley Rd. SE6 ... 2D 140
Chart Cl. BR2: Brom ... 1G 159
CR0: C'don ... 6J 157
CR4: Mitc ... 4D 154
Charter Av. IG2: Ilf ... 1H 71
Charter Bldgs. *SE10* ... 1D 122
(off Catherine Gro.)
Charter Ct. KT3: N Mald ... 3A 152
N4 ... 1A 66
N22 ... 1H 47
UB1: S'hall ... 1E 94
Charter Cres. TW4: Houn ... 4C 112
Charter Dr. DA5: Bexl ... 7E 126
Charterhouse ... 4B 8
Charter Ho. *SM2: Sutt* ... 6K 165
(off Mulgrave Rd.)
WC2 ... 1F 13
(off Crown Ct.)
Charterhouse Apartments SW18 ... 4A 118
Charterhouse Av. HA0: Wemb ... 4C 60
Charterhouse Bldgs. EC1 ... 4B 8 (4C 84)
Charterhouse M. EC1 ... 5B 8 (5B 84)
Charterhouse Rd. BR6: Chels ... 3K 173
E8 ... 4G 67
Charterhouse Sq. EC1 ... 5B 8 (5B 84)
Charterhouse St. EC1 ... 6K 7 (5A 84)
Charteris Community Sports Cen. ... 1J 81
Charteris Rd. IG8: Wfd G ... 7E 36
N4 ... 1A 66
NW6 ... 1H 81
Charter Quay *KT1: King T* ... 2D 150
(off Wadbrook St.)
Charter Rd. KT1: King T ... 3H 151
Charter Rd., The IG8: Wfd G ... 6B 36
Charters Cl. SE19 ... 5E 138
Charter Sq. KT1: King T ... 2H 151
Charter Way N3 ... 4H 45
N14 ... 6B 22
Chartes Ho. *SE1* ... 7H 15
(off Stevens St.)
Chartfield Av. SW15 ... 5D 116
Chartfield Sq. SW15 ... 5F 117
Chartham Ct. *SW9* ... 3A 120
(off Canterbury Cres.)
Chartham Gro. SE27 ... 3B 138
Chartham Ho. *SE1* ... 7F 15
(off Weston St.)
Chartham Rd. SE25 ... 3H 157
Chart Hills Cl. SE28 ... 6E 90
Chart Ho. CR4: Mitc ... 2D 154
E14 ... 5D 104
(off Burrells Wharf Sq.)
Chartley Av. HA7: Stan ... 6E 26
NW2 ... 3A 62
Charton Cl. DA17: Belv ... 6F 109
Chartres Ct. UB6: G'frd ... 2H 77
Chartridge *SE17* ... 6D 102
(off Westmoreland Rd.)
Chart St. N1 ... 1F 9 (3D 84)
Chartwell Bus. Cen. BR1: Brom ... 3B 160
Chartwell Cl. CR0: C'don ... 1D 168
SE9 ... 2H 143
UB6: G'frd ... 1F 77
Chartwell Ct. EN5: Barn ... 4B 20
IG8: Wfd G ... 7C 36
NW2 ... 3C 62
UB3: Hayes ... 7H 75
Chartwell Dr. BR6: Farnb ... 5H 173
Chartwell Gdns. SM3: Cheam ... 4G 165
Chartwell Ho. *W11* ... 1H 99
(off Ladbroke Rd.)
Chartwell Lodge BR3: Beck ... 7C 140
Chartwell Pl. HA2: Harr ... 2H 59
SM3: Cheam ... 4G 165
Chartwell Way SE20 ... 1H 157
Charville Ct. *HA1: Harr* ... 6K 41
(off Gayton Rd.)
SE10 ... 6F 105
(off Trafalgar Gro.)
Charville La. UB4: Hayes ... 3E 74
Charville La. W. UB10: Hil ... 3D 74
(not continuous)
Charwood SW16 ... 4A 138
Chase, The BR1: Brom ... 3K 159
DA7: Bex ... 3H 127
E12 ... 4B 70
HA5: Eastc ... 6A 40
HA5: Pinn ... 4D 40
HA7: Stan ... 6F 27
HA8: Edg ... 1H 43
RM1: Rom ... 3K 55
RM6: Chad H ... 6E 54
RM7: Rush G ... 3K 73
SM6: Wall ... 5J 167
SW4 ... 3F 119
Chase, The SW16 ... 7K 137
SW20 ... 1G 153
TW16: Sun ... 1K 147
UB10: Ick ... 5C 56
Chase Bank Ct. *N14* ... 6B 22
(off Avenue Rd.)
Chase Cen., The NW10 ... 3K 79
Chase Ct. *SW3* ... 2E 16
(off Beaufort Gdns.)
SW20 ... 2G 153
TW7: Isle ... 2A 114
Chase Ct. Gdns. EN2: Enf ... 3H 23
Chase Cross Rd. RM5: Col R ... 1J 55
Chasefield Rd. SW17 ... 4D 136
Chase Gdns. E4 ... 4H 35
TW2: Whitt ... 7H 113
Chase Grn. EN2: Enf ... 3H 23
Chase Grn. Av. EN2: Enf ... 2G 23
Chase Hill EN2: Enf ... 3H 23
Chase Ho. *NW6* ... 3J 81
(off Hansel Rd.)
Chase La. IG2: Ilf ... 5H 53
IG6: Ilf ... 5H 53
Chaseley Dr. W4 ... 5H 97
Chaseley St. E14 ... 6A 86
Chasemore Cl. CR4: Mitc ... 7D 154
Chasemore Gdns. CR0: Wadd ... 5A 168
Chasemore Ho. *SW6* ... 7G 99
(off Williams Cl.)
Chase Ridings EN2: Enf ... 2F 23
Chase Rd. N14 ... 5B 22
NW10 ... 4K 79
Chase Rd. Trad. Est. NW10 ... 4K 79
CHASE SIDE ... 1J 23
Chase Side EN2: Enf ... 3H 23
N14 ... 5K 21
Chase Side Av. EN2: Enf ... 2H 23
SW20 ... 1G 153
Chase Side Cres. EN2: Enf ... 1H 23
Chase Side Pl. EN2: Enf ... 2H 23
Chaseville Pde. N21 ... 5E 22
Chaseville Pk. Rd. N21 ... 5D 22
Chase Way N14 ... 2A 32
Chaseway Lodge *E16* ... 6J 87
(off Butchers Rd.)
Chaseways Vs. RM5: Col R ... 1F 55
Chasewood Av. EN2: Enf ... 2G 23
Chasewood Ct. NW7 ... 5E 28
Chasewood Pk. HA1: Harr ... 3K 59
Chaston Pl. *NW5* ... 5E 64
(off Grafton Ter.)
Chater Ho. *E2* ... 3K 85
(off Roman Rd.)
Chatfield Rd. CR0: C'don ... 1B 168
SW11 ... 3A 118
Chatham Av. BR2: Hayes ... 7H 159
Chatham Cl. NW11 ... 5J 45
SE18 ... 3F 107
SM3: Sutt ... 7H 153
Chatham Ho. *SM6: Wall* ... 5F 167
(off Melbourne Rd.)
Chatham Pl. E9 ... 6J 67
Chatham Rd. E17 ... 3A 50
E18 ... 2H 51
KT1: King T ... 2G 151
SW11 ... 6D 118
Chatham St. SE17 ... 4D 102
Chatsfield Pl. W5 ... 6E 78
Chats Palace Arts Cen. ... 5K 67
Chatsworth Av. BR1: Brom ... 4K 141
DA15: Sidc ... 1A 144
HA9: Wemb ... 5F 61
NW4 ... 2E 44
SW20 ... 1G 153
Chatsworth Cl. BR4: W W'ck ... 2H 171
NW4 ... 2E 44
W4 ... 6J 97
Chatsworth Ct. HA7: Stan ... 5H 27
SW16 ... 3K 155
W8 ... 4J 99
(off Pembroke Rd.)

Chatsworth Cres.—Cherry Orchard Gdns.

Chatsworth Cres. TW3: Houn 4H 113
Chatsworth Dr. EN1: Enf 7B 24
Chatsworth Est. E5 . . . . 4K 67
Chatsworth Gdns. HA2: Harr 1F 59
KT3: N Mald 5B 152
W3 . . . . 1H 97
Chatsworth Ho. *BR2: Brom 4J 159*
(off Westmoreland Rd.)
E16 . . . . 1K 105
(off Wesley Av.)
SE1 . . . . 5J 15
(off Duchess Wlk.)
Chatsworth Lodge *W4 . . . . 5K 97*
(off Bourne Pl.)
Chatsworth M. DA14: Sidc 4K 143
Chatsworth Pde. BR5: Pet W 5G 161
Chatsworth Pl. CR4: Mitc 3D 154
TW11: Tedd 4A 132
Chatsworth Ri. W5 . . . . 4F 79
Chatsworth Rd. CR0: C'don 4D 168
E5 . . . . 3J 67
E15 . . . . 5H 69
NW2 . . . . 6E 62
SM3: Cheam 5F 165
UB4: Yead 4K 75
W4 . . . . 6J 97
W5 . . . . 4F 79
Chatsworth Way SE27 . . . . 3B 138
CHATTERN HILL 4D 128
Chattern Hill TW15: Ashf 4D 128
Chattern Rd. TW15: Ashf 4E 128
Chatterton Ct. TW9: Kew 2F 115
Chatterton M. *N4 . . . . 3B 66*
(off Chatterton Rd.)
Chatterton Rd. BR2: Brom 4B 160
N4 . . . . 3B 66
Chatto Rd. SW11 . . . . 5D 118
Chaucer Av. TW4: Cran 2K 111
TW9: Rich 3G 115
UB4: Hayes 5J 75
Chaucer Cl. N11 . . . . 5B 32
Chaucer Ct. EN5: New Bar 5E 20
N16 . . . . 4E 66
SW17 . . . . 3B 136
(off Lanesborough Way)
Chaucer Dr. SE1 . . . . 4F 103
Chaucer Gdns. SM1: Sutt 3J 165
Chaucer Grn. CR0: C'don 7H 157
Chaucer Ho. EN5: Barn 4A 20
SM1: Sutt 3J 165
(off Chaucer Gdns.)
SW1 . . . . 6A 18
(off Churchill Gdns.)
Chaucer Mans. *W14 . . . . 6G 99*
(off Queen's Club Gdns.)
Chaucer Rd. DA15: Sidc 1C 144
DA16: Well 1J 125
E7 . . . . 6J 69
E11 . . . . 6J 51
E17 . . . . 2E 50
SE24 . . . . 5A 120
SM1: Sutt 4J 165
TW15: Ashf 4A 128
W3 . . . . 1J 97
Chaucer Way SW19 . . . . 6B 136
Chaulden Ho. *EC1 . . . . 2F 9*
(off Cranwood St.)
Chauncey Cl. N9 . . . . 3B 34
Chaundrye Cl. SE9 . . . . 6D 124
Chauntler Cl. E16 . . . . 6K 87
Chaville Ct. N11 . . . . 4K 31
Chaville Way N3 . . . . 1J 45
Cheadle Ct. *NW8 . . . . 3B 4*
(off Henderson Dr.)
Cheadle Ho. *E14 . . . . 6B 86*
(off Copenhagen Pl.)
CHEAM 6G 165
Cheam Comn. Rd. KT4: Wor Pk 2D 164
Cheam Leisure Cen. 4F 165
Cheam Mans. SM3: Cheam 7G 165
Cheam Pk. Way SM3: Cheam 6G 165
Cheam Rd. SM1: Sutt 6H 165
SM2: Cheam 7F 165
Cheam St. SE15 . . . . 3J 121
CHEAM VILLAGE 6G 165
Cheapside EC2 . . . . 1D **14** (6C **84**)
N13 . . . . 4J 33
N22 . . . . 3A 48
Cheapside Pas. *EC2 . . . . 1C 14*
(off One New Change)
Cheddar Cl. N11 . . . . 6J 31
Cheddar Waye UB4: Yead 6K 75
Cheddington Ho. *E2 . . . . 1G 85*
(off Whiston Rd.)
Cheddington Rd. N18 . . . . 3K 33
Chedworth Cl. *E16 . . . . 6H 87*
(off Wouldham Rd.)
Chedworth Ho. *N15 . . . . 4D 48*
(off West Grn. Rd.)
Cheering La. E20 . . . . 5E 68
Cheesegrater, The 1G 15
Cheeseman Cl.
TW12: Hamp 6C 130
Cheesemans Ter. W14 . . . . 5H 99
(not continuous)
Cheffery Ct. TW15: Ashf 6D 128
Cheldon Av. NW7 . . . . 7A 30
Chelford Rd. BR1: Brom 5F 141
Chelmer Cres. IG11: Bark 2B 90
Chelmer Rd. E9 . . . . 5K 67
Chelmsford Cl. E6 . . . . 6D 88
W6 . . . . 6F 99
Chelmsford Ct. *N14 . . . . 7C 22*
(off Chelmsford Rd.)
Chelmsford Gdns. IG1: Ilf 7C 52
Chelmsford Ho. *N7 . . . . 4K 65*
(off Holloway Rd.)
Chelmsford Rd. E11 . . . . 1F 69
E17 . . . . 6C 50
E18 . . . . 1H 51
N14 . . . . 7B 22
Chelmsford Sq. NW10 . . . . 1E 80
Chelmsine Ct. HA4: Ruis 5E 38
CHELSEA 6D 16 (5C 100)
Chelsea Bri. SW1 . . . . 7J **17** (6F **101**)
Chelsea Bri. Rd. SW1 . . . . 5G **17** (5E **100**)
Chelsea Bri. Wharf SW8 . . . . 6F 101
Chelsea Cinema 6D **16** (5C **100**)
Chelsea Cloisters SW3 . . . . 4D **16** (4C **100**)
Chelsea Cl. HA8: Edg 2G 43
KT4: Wor Pk 7C 152
NW10 . . . . 1K 79
TW12: Hamp H 5G 131
Chelsea Ct. *BR1: Brom 3C 160*
(off Holmdene Ct.)
SW3 . . . . 7G 17
(off Embankment Gdns.)
Chelsea Cres. NW2 . . . . 6H 63
SW10 . . . . 1A 118
Chelsea Emb. SW3 . . . . 7D **16** (6C **100**)
Chelsea Farm Ho. Studios *SW10 . . . . 6B 100*
(off Cremorne Est.)
Chelsea FC 7K 99
Chelsea Flds. SW19 . . . . 1B 154
Chelsea Gdns. SM3: Cheam 4G 165
SW1 . . . . 6H **17** (5E **100**)
W13 . . . . 5K 77
Chelsea Ga. SW1 . . . . 6H 17
Chelsea Harbour SW10 . . . . 1A 118
Chelsea Harbour Design Cen.
SW10 . . . . 1A 118
(off Chelsea Harbour Dr.)
Chelsea Harbour Dr. SW10 . . . . 1A 118
Chelsea Lodge *SW3 . . . . 7F 17*
(off Tite St.)
Chelsea Mnr. Ct. SW3 . . . . 7D **16** (6C **100**)
Chelsea Mnr. Gdns. SW3 . . . . 6D **16** (5C **100**)
Chelsea Mnr. St. SW3 . . . . 6D **16** (5C **100**)
Chelsea Mnr. Studios *SW3 . . . . 6D 16*
(off Flood St.)
Chelsea Pk. Gdns. SW3 . . . . 7A **16** (6B **100**)
Chelsea Physic Garden 7E **16** (6D **100**)
Chelsea Reach Twr. *SW10 . . . . 7B 100*
(off Worlds End Est.)
Chelsea Sports Cen. 6D **16** (5C **100**)
Chelsea Sq. SW3 . . . . 5B **16** (5B **100**)
Chelsea Studios *SW6 . . . . 7K 99*
(off Fulham Rd.)
Chelsea Theatre, The 7A 100
Chelsea Towers SW3 . . . . 7D 16
Chelsea Village *SW6 . . . . 7K 99*
(off Fulham Rd.)
Chelsea Vista SW6 . . . . 1A 118
Chelsea Wharf *SW10 . . . . 7B 100*
(off Lots Rd.)
Chelsfield Av. N9 . . . . 7E 24
Chelsfield Gdns. SE26 . . . . 3J 139
Chelsfield Grn. N9 . . . . 7E 24
(not continuous)
Chelsfield Ho. *SE17 . . . . 4E 102*
(off Massinger St.)
Chelsfield Point *E9 . . . . 7K 67*
(off Penshurst Rd.)
Chelsham Rd. CR2: S Croy 7D 168
SW4 . . . . 3H 119
Chelsiter Ct. DA14: Sidc 4K 143
Chelston App. HA4: Ruis 2J 57
Chelston Ct. E11 . . . . 5K 51
Chelston Rd. HA4: Ruis 1J 57
Chelsworth Dr. SE18 . . . . 6H 107
Cheltenham Av. TW1: Twick 7A 114
Cheltenham Cl. KT3: N Mald 3J 151
UB5: N'olt 6F 59
Cheltenham Ct. *HA7: Stan 5H 27*
(off Marsh La.)
Cheltenham Gdns. E6 . . . . 2C 88
Cheltenham Ho. IG8: Wfd G 6K 37
UB3: Harl 3E 92
(off Skipton Dr.)
Cheltenham Pl. HA3: Kenton 4E 42
W3 . . . . 1H 97
Cheltenham Rd. BR6: Chels 3K 173
E10 . . . . 6E 50
SE15 . . . . 4J 121
Cheltenham Ter. SW3 . . . . 5F **17** (5D **100**)
Chelverton Rd. SW15 . . . . 4F 117
Chelwood N20 . . . . 2G 31
Chelwood Cl. E4 . . . . 6J 25
Chelwood Ct. CR2: S Croy 5C 168
SW11 . . . . 1B 118
(off Westbridge Rd.)
Chelwood Gdns. TW9: Kew 2G 115
Chelwood Gdns. Pas. TW9: Kew 2G 115
Chelwood Ho. *W2 . . . . 1B 10*
(off Gloucester Sq.)
Chelwood Wlk. SE4 . . . . 4A 122
Chenappa Cl. E13 . . . . 3J 87
Chenduit Way HA7: Stan 5E 26
Cheney Ct. SE23 . . . . 1K 139
Cheney Row E17 . . . . 1B 50
Cheneys Rd. E11 . . . . 3G 69
Cheney St. HA5: Eastc 4A 40
Chenies, The BR6: Pet W 6J 161
NW1 . . . . 2H 83
(off Pancras Rd.)
Chenies Ho. *W2 . . . . 7K 81*
(off Moscow Rd.)
W4 . . . . 7B 98
(off Corney Reach Way)
Chenies M. WC1 . . . . 4C **6** (4H **83**)
Chenies Pl. NW1 . . . . 2H 83
Chenies St. WC1 . . . . 5C **6** (5H **83**)
Cheniston Gdns. W8 . . . . 3K 99
Chenla SE13 . . . . 2D 122
Cheping Ho. *W10 . . . . 7F 81*
(off Shalfleet Dr.)
Chepstow Cl. SW15 . . . . 5G 117
Chepstow Cnr. *W2 . . . . 6J 81*
(off Chepstow Pl.)
Chepstow Ct. *W11 . . . . 7J 81*
(off Chepstow Vs.)
Chepstow Cres. IG3: Ilf 6J 53
W11 . . . . 7J 81
Chepstow Gdns. UB1: S'hall 6D 76
Chepstow Pl. W2 . . . . 6J 81
Chepstow Ri. CR0: C'don 3E 168
Chepstow Rd.
CR0: C'don 3E 168
W2 . . . . 6J 81
W7 . . . . 3A 96
Chepstow Vs. W11 . . . . 7H 81
Chequers IG9: Buck H 1E 36
Chequers, The HA5: Pinn 3B 40
Chequers Cl. BR5: St P 4K 161
NW9 . . . . 3A 44
Chequers Ct. DA17: Belv 4G 109
EC1 . . . . 4D 8
(off Chequer St.)
Chequers Ho. *NW8 . . . . 3C 4*
(off Jerome Cres.)
Chequers La. RM9: Dag 4F 91
(not continuous)
Chequers Pde. N13 . . . . 5H 33
RM9: Dag 1F 91
SE9 . . . . 6D 124
(off Eltham High St.)
Chequer St. EC1 . . . . 4D **8** (4C **84**)
(not continuous)
Chequers Way N13 . . . . 5G 33
Cherbury Cl. SE28 . . . . 6D 90
Cherbury Ct. *N1 . . . . 2D 84*
(off St John's Est.)
Cherbury St. N1 . . . . 2D 84
Cherchefelle M. HA7: Stan 5G 27
Cherimoya Gdns.
KT8: W Mole 3F 149
Cherington Rd. W7 . . . . 1J 95
Cheriton Av. BR2: Brom 5H 159
IG5: Ilf 2D 52
Cheriton Cl. EN4: Cockf 3J 21
W5 . . . . 5C 78
Cheriton Ct. SE12 . . . . 7J 123
SE25 . . . . 5E 156
Cheriton Dr. SE18 . . . . 7H 107
Cheriton Lodge HA4: Ruis 1H 57
Cheriton Sq. SW17 . . . . 2E 136
Cherry Av. UB1: S'hall 1B 94
Cherry Blossom Cl. N13 . . . . 5G 33
Cherry Cl. E17 . . . . 5D 50
HA0: Wemb 3D 60
HA4: Ruis 3H 57
NW9 . . . . 2A 44
SM4: Mord 4G 153
SM5: Cars 2D 166
SW2 . . . . 7A 120
W5 . . . . 3D 96
Cherrycot Hill BR6: Farnb 4G 173
Cherrycot Ri. BR6: Farnb 4G 173
Cherry Ct. HA5: Pinn 2B 40
IG6: Ilf 3F 53
W3 . . . . 1A 98
Cherry Cres. TW8: Bford 7B 96
Cherrydown Av. E4 . . . . 3G 35
Cherrydown Cl. E4 . . . . 3H 35
Cherrydown Rd. DA14: Sidc 2D 144
Cherrydown Wlk. RM7: Mawney 2H 55
Cherry Gdn. Ho. *SE16 . . . . 2H 103*
(off Cherry Gdn. St.)
Cherry Gdns. RM9: Dag 5F 73
UB5: N'olt 7F 59
Cherry Gdn. St. SE16 . . . . 2H 103
Cherry Gth. TW8: Bford 5D 96
Cherry Gro. UB3: Hayes 1K 93
UB8: Hil 5D 74
Cherry Hill EN5: New Bar 6E 20
HA3: Hrw W 6E 26
Cherry Hill Gdns. CR0: Wadd 4K 167
Cherrylands Cl. NW9 . . . . 2J 61
Cherry La. UB7: W Dray 4B 92
Cherry Laurel Wlk. SW2 . . . . 6K 119
Cherry Orchard SE7 . . . . 6A 106
UB7: W Dray 2A 92
Cherry Orchard Gdns. CR0: C'don 1D 168
KT8: W Mole 3D 148

Cherry Orchard Rd. BR2: Brom 2C **172**
CR0: C'don 2D **168**
KT8: W Mole 3E **148**
Cherry Pk. La. E20 7E **68**
Cherry Red Records Stadium (Kingsmeadow) 3H 151
Cherry Rd. EN3: Enf W 1D **24**
Cherry St. RM7: Rom 5K **55**
Cherry Tree Av. UB7: Yiew 6B **74**
Cherry Tree Cl. E9 1J **85**
HA0: Wemb 4A **60**
Cherry Tree Ct. *NW1 7G 65*
(off Camden Rd.)
NW9 4J **43**
SE7 6A **106**
Cherry Tree Dr. SW16 3J **137**
Cherry Tree Hill N2 5C **46**
Cherry Tree Ho. N22 7D **32**
Cherry Tree Ri. IG9: Buck H 4F **37**
Cherry Tree Rd. E15 5G **69**
N2 4D **46**
Cherry Tree Ter. *SE1 7H 15*
(off Whites Grounds)
Cherry Tree Wlk. BR3: Beck 4B **158**
BR4: W W'ck 4H **171**
EC1 4D **8** (4C **84**)
Cherry Tree Way E13 4B **88**
HA7: Stan 6G **27**
Cherry Wlk. BR2: Hayes 1J **171**
Cherry Way KT19: Ewe 6K **163**
TW17: Shep 4F **147**
Cherrywood Cl. E3 3A **86**
KT2: King T 7G **133**
Cherrywood Ct. TW11: Tedd 5A **132**
Cherrywood Dr. SW15 5F **117**
Cherrywood La. SM4: Mord 4G **153**
Cherrywood Lodge *SE13 6F 123*
(off Birdwood Av.)
Cherry Wood Way W5 5G **79**
Chertsey Bri. Rd. KT16: Chert 7A **146**
Chertsey Ct. SW14 3H **115**
Chertsey Dr. SM3: Cheam 2G **165**
Chertsey Ho. *E2 2J 9*
(off Arnold Cir.)
CHERTSEY MEADS 7A 146
Chertsey Meads Local Nature Reserve 7A 146
Chertsey Rd. E11 2F **69**
IG1: Ilf 4H **71**
TW1: Twick 6K **113**
TW2: Twick 2F **131**
TW13: Felt 3G **129**
TW15: Ashf 7F **129**
TW16: Sun 7F **129**
TW17: Shep 7A **146**
Chertsey St. SW17 5E **136**
Chervil Cl. TW13: Felt 3J **129**
Chervil M. SE28 1B **108**
Cherwell Ct. KT19: Ewe 4J **163**
Cherwell Ho. NW8 4B **4**
Cherwell M. SW11 4C **118**
Cherwell Way HA4: Ruis 6E **38**
Cheryls Cl. SW6 1K **117**
Cheseman St. SE26 3H **139**
Chesfield Rd. KT2: King T 7E **132**
Chesham Apartments E4 7J **35**
Chesham Av. BR5: Pet W 6F **161**
Chesham Cl. NW7 4F **29**
RM7: Rom 4K **55**
SW1 2G **17**
Chesham Cres. SE20 1J **157**
Chesham Flats *W1 2H 11*
(off Brown Hart Gdns.)
Chesham Ho. *SE8 1C 122*
(off Brookmill Rd.)
Chesham M. SW1 1G **17**
Chesham Pl. SW1 2G **17** (3E **100**)
(not continuous)
Chesham Rd. KT1: King T 2G **151**
SE20 2J **157**
SW19 5B **136**
Chesham St. NW10 3K **61**
SW1 2G **17** (3E **100**)
Chesham Ter. W13 2B **96**
Cheshire Cl. CR4: Mitc 3J **155**
E17 1D **50**
SE4 2B **122**
Cheshire Ct. *EC4 1K 13*
(off Fleet St.)
Cheshire Gdns. KT9: Chess 6D **162**
Cheshire Ho. N18 4C **34**
SM4: Mord 7K **153**
Cheshire Rd. N22 7E **32**
Cheshire St. E2 3K **9** (4F **85**)
Cheshir Ho. NW4 4E **44**
Chesholm Rd. N16 3E **66**
Cheshunt Ho. *NW6 1K 81*
(off Mortimer Cres.)
Cheshunt Rd. DA17: Belv 5G **109**
E7 6K **69**
Chesil Ct. E2 2J **85**
SW3 7D **16** (6C **100**)
Chesilton Rd. SW6 1H **117**
Chesil Way UB4: Hayes 3H **75**
Chesley Gdns. E6 2B **88**
Chesney Ct. *W9 4J 81*
(off Shirland Rd.)
Chesney Cres. CR0: New Ad 7E **170**
Chesney Ho. *SE13 4F 123*
(off Mercator Rd.)
Chesney St. SW11 1E **118**
Chesnut Gro. N17 3F **49**
Chesnut Rd. N17 3F **49**
Chesnut Row *N3 7D 30*
(off Nether St.)
Chessell Cl. CR7: Thor H 4B **156**
Chessholme Ct. *TW16: Sun 7G 129*
(off Scotts Av.)
Chessholme Rd. TW15: Ashf 6E **128**
Chessing Ct. *N2 3D 46*
(off Fortis Grn.)
CHESSINGTON 5E 162
Chessington Av. DA7: Bex 7E **108**
N3 3G **45**
Chessington Cl. KT19: Ewe 6J **163**
Chessington Ct. HA5: Pinn 4D **40**
N3 3H 45
(off Charter Way)
Chessington Hall Gdns.
KT9: Chess 7D **162**
Chessington Hill Pk. KT9: Chess 5G **163**
Chessington Ho. SW8 2H **119**
Chessington Lodge N3 3H **45**
Chessington Mans. E10 7C **50**
E11 7G **51**
Chessington Pde. KT9: Chess 6D **162**
Chessington Pk. KT9: Chess 4G **163**
Chessington Rd. KT17: Ewe 7B **164**
KT19: Ewe 6G **163**
Chessington Sports Cen. 7D 162
Chessington Trade Pk. KT9: Chess 4G **163**
Chessington Way BR4: W W'ck 2D **170**
Chesson Rd. W14 6H **99**
Chesswood Way HA5: Pinn 2B **40**
Chestbrook Ct. *EN1: Enf 5K 23*
(off Forsyth Pl.)
Chester Av. TW2: Whitt 1D **130**
TW10: Rich 6F **115**
Chester Cl. SM1: Sutt 2J **165**
SW1 7J **11** (2F **101**)
SW13 3D **116**
TW10: Rich 6F **115**
TW15: Ashf 5F **129**
UB8: Hil 6D **74**
Chester Cl. Nth.
NW1 1K **5** (3F **83**)
Chester Cl. Sth. NW1 2K **5** (3F **83**)
Chester Cotts. SW1 4G **17**
Chester Ct. *BR2: Brom 4H 159*
(off Durham Rd.)
NW1 1K **5** (3F **83**)
(not continuous)
Chester Ct. *SE5 7D 102*
(off Lomond Gro.)
SE8 5K **103**
W6 4F 99
(off Wolverton Gdns.)
Chester Cres. E8 5F **67**
Chester Dr. HA2: Harr 6D **40**
Chesterfield Cl. SE13 2F **123**
Chesterfield Ct. *KT5: Surb 5E 150*
(off Cranes Pk.)
Chesterfield Dr. KT10: Hin W 2A **162**
Chesterfield Flats *EN5: Barn 5A 20*
(off Bells Hill)
Chesterfield Gdns. N4 5B **48**
SE10 1F **123**
W1 4J **11** (1F **101**)
Chesterfield Gro. SE22 5F **121**
Chesterfield Hill W1 4J **11** (1F **101**)
Chesterfield Ho. *W1 4H 11*
(off Chesterfield Gdns.)
Chesterfield Lodge *N21 7E 22*
(off Church Hill)
Chesterfield M. N4 5B **48**
TW15: Ashf 4A **128**
Chesterfield Rd. E10 6E **50**
EN5: Barn 5A **20**
KT19: Ewe 7K **163**
N3 6D **30**
TW15: Ashf 4A **128**
W4 6J **97**
Chesterfield St. W1 4J **11** (1F **101**)
Chesterfield Wlk. SE10 1F **123**
Chesterfield Way SE15 7J **103**
UB3: Hayes 2J **93**
Chesterford Gdns. NW3 4K **63**
Chesterford Ho. *SE18 1B 124*
(off Tellson Av.)
Chesterford Rd. E12 5D **70**
Chester Gdns. EN3: Pond E 6C **24**
SM4: Mord 6A **154**
W13 6B **78**
Chester Ga. NW1 2J **5** (3F **83**)
Chester Ho. N10 2F **47**
SE8 6B **104**
SW1 3J 17
(off Eccleston Pl.)
SW9 7A 102
(off Cranmer Rd.)
Chesterman Ct. *W4 7A 98*
(off Corney Reach Way)
Chester M. E17 2C **50**
SW1 1J **17** (3F **101**)
Chester Pl. NW1 1J **5** (3F **83**)
Chester Rd. DA15: Sidc 5J **125**
E7 7B **70**
E11 6K **51**
E16 4G **87**
E17 5K **49**
HA6: Nwood 1H **39**
IG3: Ilf 1K **71**
IG7: Chig 3K **37**
N9 1C **34**
N17 3D **48**
N19 2F **65**
NW1 2H **5** (3E **82**)
SW19 6E **134**
TW4: Houn 3K **111**
TW6: H'row A 3C **110**
Chester Row SW1 4G **17** (4E **100**)
Chesters, The
KT3: N Mald 1A **152**
Chester Sq. SW1 3H **17** (4E **100**)
Chester Sq. M. SW1 2J **17**
Chester St. E2 4G **85**
SW1 1H **17** (3E **100**)
Chester Ter. IG11: Bark 6H **71**
NW1 1J **5** (3F **83**)
(not continuous)
Chesterton Cl.
SW18 5J **117**
UB6: G'frd 2F **77**
Chesterton Ct. *W3 3H 97*
(off Bollo Bri. Rd.)
W5 5D **78**
Chesterton Dr. TW19: Stanw 1B **128**
Chesterton Ho. *CR0: C'don 4D 168*
(off Heathfield Rd.)
SW11 3B 118
(off Ingrave St.)
W10 5G 81
(off Portobello Rd.)
Chesterton Rd. E13 3J **87**
W10 5F **81**
Chesterton Sq. W8 4J **99**
Chesterton Ter. E13 3J **87**
KT1: King T 2G **151**
Chester Way SE11 4K **19** (4A **102**)
Chesthunte Rd. N17 1C **48**
Chestlands Ct. UB10: Hil 6C **56**
Chestnut All. SW6 6H **99**
Chestnut Av. BR4: W W'ck 5G **171**
E7 4K **69**
HA0: Wemb 5B **60**
HA6: Nwood 2H **39**
HA8: Edg 6K **27**
IG9: Buck H 3G **37**
KT8: E Mos 3K **149**
KT10: Esh 7H **149**
KT19: Ewe 4A **164**
N8 5J **47**
SW14 3K **115**
TW8: Bford 4D **96**
TW11: Tedd 2K **149**
TW12: Hamp 7E **130**
UB7: Yiew 7B **74**
Chestnut Av. Nth. E17 4F **51**
Chestnut Av. Sth. E17 5E **50**
Chestnut Cl. BR6: Chels 5K **173**
DA15: Sidc 1A **144**
IG9: Buck H 3G **37**
N14 5B **22**
N16 2D **66**
SE6 5E **140**
SE14 1B **122**
SM5: Cars 1D **166**
SW16 4A **138**
TW15: Ashf 4D **128**
TW16: Sun 6H **129**
UB3: Hayes 7G **75**
UB7: Harl, Sip 7D **92**
Chestnut Ct. *CR2: S Croy 4C 168*
(off Bramley Hill)
N8 5J **47**
SW6 6H **99**
TW13: Hanw 5B **130**
TW19: Stanw 1A 128
(off Mulberry Av.)
W8 3K 99
(off Abbots Wlk.)
Chestnut Dr. DA7: Bex 3D **126**
E11 6J **51**
HA3: Hrw W 7E **26**
HA5: Pinn 6B **40**
Chestnut Gro.
CR2: Sels 7H **169**
CR4: Mitc 5H **155**
DA2: Wilm 4K **145**
EN4: E Barn 5J **21**
HA0: Wemb 5B **60**
KT3: N Mald 3K **151**
SE20 7H **139**
SW12 7E **118**
TW7: Isle 4A **114**
W5 3D **96**
Chestnut Ho. *E3 1B 86*
(off Sycamore Av.)
SW15 4B **116**
W4 4A 98
(off The Orchard)
Chestnut La. N20 1B **30**
Chestnut M. SW14 4J **115**
Chestnut Pl. SE26 4F **139**

Chestnut Plaza *E20* 6E *68*
(within Westfield Stratford City Shop. Cen.)
Chestnut Ri. SE18 . . . . .6H **107**
  WD23: Bush 1A **26**
Chestnut Rd. KT2: King T 7E **132**
  SE27 . . . . .3B **138**
  SW20 .2F **153**
  TW2: Twick 2J **131**
  TW15: Ashf 4D **128**
Chestnuts, The BR3: Beck 3K **157**
  HA5: Hat E 1D **40**
  N5 . . . . .4C *66*
    (off Highbury Grange)
  UB10: Uxb 7A **56**
Chestnut Ter. SM1: Sutt 4K **165**
Chestnut Wlk. IG8: Wfd G 5D **36**
  TW17: Shep 4G **147**
Chestnut Way TW13: Felt 3K **129**
Cheston Av. CR0: C'don 2A **170**
Chestwood Gro. UB10: Hil 7B **56**
Chesworth Ct. *E1* 5J *85*
    (off Fulneck Pl.)
Chettle Cl. *SE1* 3D **102**
    (off Spurgeon St.)
Chettle Ct. N8 . . . . .6A **48**
Chetwode Ho. NW6 . . . . .3C *4*
Chetwode Rd. SW17 . . . . .3D **136**
Chetwood Wlk. *E6* 5C *88*
    (off Greenwich Cres.)
Chetwynd Av. EN4: E Barn 1J **31**
Chetwynd Dr. UB10: Hil 2B **74**
Chetwynd Rd. NW5 . . . . .4F **65**
Chetwynd Vs. *NW5* 4F *65*
    (off Chetwynd Rd.)
Chevalier Cl. HA7: Stan 4K **27**
Cheval Pl. SW7 . . . . .1D **16** (3C **100**)
Cheval St. E14 . . . . .3C **104**
Cheveney Wlk. BR2: Brom 3J **159**
Chevening Rd. NW6 . . . . .2F **81**
  SE10 . . . . .5H **105**
  SE19 . . . . .6D **138**
Chevenings, The DA14: Sidc 3C **144**
Cheverell Ho. *E2* 2G *85*
    (off Pritchard's Rd.)
Cheverton Rd. N19 . . . . .1H **65**
Chevet St. E9 . . . . .5A **68**
Chevington NW2 . . . . .6H **63**
Cheviot *N17* 7C *34*
    (off Northumberland Gro.)
Cheviot Cl. DA7: Bex 2K **127**
  EN1: Enf .2J **23**
  UB3: Harl 7F **93**
Cheviot Ct. *SE14* 6J *103*
    (off Avonley Rd.)
  UB2: S'hall 4F **95**
Cheviot Gdns. NW2 . . . . .2F **63**
  SE27 . . . . .4B **138**
Cheviot Ga. NW2 . . . . .2G **63**
Cheviot Ho. *E1* 6H *85*
    (off Commercial Rd.)
Cheviot Rd. SE27 . . . . .5A **138**
Cheviot Way IG2: Ilf 4J **53**
Chevron Cl. E16 . . . . .6J **87**
Chevy Rd. UB2: S'hall 2G **95**
Chewton Rd. E17 . . . . .4A **50**
Cheylesmore Ho. *SW1* 5J *17*
    (off Ebury Bri. Rd.)
Cheyne Av. E18 . . . . .3H **51**
  TW2: Whitt 1D **130**
Cheyne Cl. BR2: Brom 3C **172**
  NW4 . . . . .5E *44*
Cheyne Ct. SW3 . . . . . . .7E **16** (6D **100**)
Cheyne Gdns. SW3 . . . . . .7D **16** (6C **100**)
Cheyne Hill KT5: Surb 4F **151**
Cheyne Ho. *SW3* 7E *16*
    (off Chelsea Emb.)
Cheyne M. SW3 . . . . .7D **16** (6C **100**)
Cheyne Pk. Dr. BR4: W W'ck 3E **170**
Cheyne Path W7 . . . . .5K **77**
Cheyne Pl. SW3 . . . . . . .7E **16** (6D **100**)
Cheyne Rd. TW15: Ashf 7F **129**

Cheyne Row SW3 . . . . .7C **16** (6C **100**)
Cheyne Wlk. CR0: C'don 2G **169**
  N21 . . . . .5G **23**
  NW4 . . . . .6E **44**
  SW3 . . . . .7C **16** (6B **100**)
  SW10 . . . . .7B **100**
Cheyneys Av. HA8: Edg 6J **27**
Chichele Gdns. CR0: C'don 4E **168**
Chichele Rd. NW2 . . . . .5F **63**
Chicheley Gdns. HA3: Hrw W 7B **26**
    (not continuous)
Chicheley Rd. HA3: Hrw W 7B **26**
Chicheley St. SE1 . . . . . . .6H **13** (2K **101**)
Chichester Av. HA4: Ruis 2F **57**
Chichester Cl. E6 . . . . .6C **88**
  SE3 . . . . .7A **106**
  TW12: Hamp 6D **130**
Chichester Ct. HA7: Stan 3E **42**
  HA8: Edg 6B *28*
    (off Whitchurch La.)
  KT17: Ewe 7B **164**
  NW1 . . . . .7G *65*
    (off Royal Coll. St.)
  TW19: Stanw 1A **128**
  UB5: N'olt 1D **76**
Chichester Gdns. IG1: Ilf 7C **52**
Chichester Ho. NW6 . . . . .2J **81**
  SW9 . . . . .7A *102*
    (off Cranmer Rd.)
Chichester M. SE27 . . . . .4A **138**
Chichester Rents WC2 . . . . .7J *7*
Chichester Rd. CR0: C'don 3E **168**
  E11 . . . . .3G **69**
  N9 . . . . .1B **34**
  NW6 . . . . .2J **81**
  W2 . . . . .5K **81**
Chichester St. SW1 . . . . . .6B **18** (5G **101**)
Chichester Way E14 . . . . .4F **105**
  TW14: Felt 7A **112**
Chickenshed Theatre 5K **21**
Chicksand Ho. *E1* 5K *9*
    (off Chicksand St.)
Chicksand St. E1 . . . . .6K **9** (5F **85**)
    (not continuous)
Chiddingfold N12 . . . . .3D **30**
Chiddingstone SE13 . . . . .5E **122**
Chiddingstone Av. DA7: Bex 7F **109**
Chiddingstone St. SW6 . . . . .2J **117**
Chieveley Pde. DA7: Bex 3H **127**
Chieveley Rd. DA7: Bex 4H **127**
Chignell Pl. W13 . . . . .1A **96**
CHIGWELL 3K **37**
Chigwell Ct. *E9* 6A *68*
    (off Ballance Rd.)
Chigwell Golf Course 4K **37**
Chigwell Hill E1 . . . . .7H **85**
Chigwell Hurst Ct. HA5: Pinn 3B **40**
Chigwell Pk. IG7: Chig 4K **37**
Chigwell Pk. Dr. IG7: Chig 4K **37**
Chigwell Ri. IG7: Chig 2K **37**
Chigwell Rd. E18 . . . . .3K **51**
  IG8: Wfd G 2A **52**
Chilcombe Ho. *SW15* 7C *116*
    (off Fontley Way)
Chilcot Cl. E14 . . . . .6D **86**
Chilcott Cl. HA0: Wemb 4C **60**
Childebert Rd. SW17 . . . . .2F **137**
Childeric Rd. SE14 . . . . .7A **104**
Childerley *KT1: King T* 3G *151*
    (off Burritt Rd.)
Childerley St. SW6 . . . . .1G **117**
Childers, The IG8: Wfd G 5J **37**
Childers St. SE8 . . . . .6A **104**
Child La. SE10 . . . . .3H **105**
Childs Cl. UB3: Hayes 7J **75**
CHILD'S HILL 3H **63**
Childs Hill Wlk. *NW2* 3H *63*
    (off Cricklewood La.)
Child's La. SE19 . . . . .6E **138**
Child's M. *SW5* 4J *99*
    (off Child's Pl.)

Child's Pl. SW5 . . . . .4J **99**
Child's St. SW5 . . . . .4J **99**
Child's Wlk. *SW5* 4J *99*
    (off Child's St.)
Childs Way NW11 . . . . .5H **45**
Chilham Cl. DA5: Bexl 7F **127**
  UB6: G'frd 2A **78**
Chilham Ho. SE1 . . . . .3D **102**
  SE15 . . . . .6J **103**
Chilham Rd. SE9 . . . . .4C **142**
Chilham Way BR2: Hayes 7J **159**
Chilianwallah Memorial 7G **17** (6E **100**)
Chillerton Rd. SW17 . . . . .5E **136**
Chillingford Ho. SW17 . . . . .4A **136**
Chillington Dr. SW11 . . . . .4B **118**
Chillingworth Gdns. TW1: Twick . . .3K **131**
Chillingworth Rd. N7 . . . . .5A **66**
Chilmark Gdns. KT3: N Mald 6C **152**
  SE15 . . . . .2H **155**
Chiltern Av. TW2: Whitt 1E **130**
Chiltern Cl. CR0: C'don 3E **168**
  DA7: Bex 1K **127**
  KT4: Wor Pk 1E **164**
  UB10: Ick 2C **56**
Chiltern Ct. BR2: Brom 2C *172*
    (off Gravel Rd.)
  EN5: New Bar 5F **21**
  HA1: Harr 5H **41**
  N10 . . . . .2E **46**
  NW1 . . . . .4F *5*
    (off Baker St.)
  SE14 . . . . .7J *103*
    (off Avonley Rd.)
  UB8: Hil 4D **74**
Chiltern Dene EN2: Enf 4E **22**
Chiltern Dr. KT5: Surb 6G **151**
Chiltern Gdns. BR2: Brom 4H **159**
  NW2 . . . . .3F **63**
Chiltern Hgts. *N1* 7K *65*
    (off Caledonian Rd.)
Chiltern Ho. N9 . . . . .3B **34**
  SE17 . . . . .6D *102*
    (off Portland St.)
  W5 . . . . .5E **78**
  W10 . . . . .5G *81*
    (off Telford Rd.)
Chiltern Rd. E3 . . . . .4C **86**
  HA5: Eastc 5A **40**
  IG2: Ilf 5J **53**
Chilterns, The *BR1: Brom* 2K *159*
    (off Murray Av.)
Chiltern St. W1 . . . . .5G **5** (5E **82**)
Chiltern Way IG8: Wfd G 3D **36**
Chilthorne Cl. SE6 . . . . .7B **122**
Chilton Av. W5 . . . . .4D **96**
Chilton Ct. *N22* 7D *32*
    (off Truro Rd.)
Chilton Gro. SE8 . . . . .4K **103**
Chiltonian Ind. Est. SE12 . . . . .6H **123**
Chiltonian M. SE13 . . . . .5F **123**
Chilton Rd. HA8: Edg 6B **28**
  TW9: Rich 3G **115**
Chiltons, The E18 . . . . .2J **51**
Chilton St. E2 . . . . .3K **9** (4F **85**)
Chilvers Cl. TW2: Twick 2J **131**
Chilver St. SE10 . . . . .5H **105**
Chilworth Ct. SW19 . . . . .1F **135**
Chilworth Gdns. SM1: Sutt 3A **166**
Chilworth M. W2 . . . . .1A **10** (6B **82**)
Chilworth Pl. IG11: Bark 4A **90**
Chilworth St. W2 . . . . .1A **10** (6A **82**)
Chimes Av. N13 . . . . .5F **33**
Chimes Ho. BR3: Beck 1A **158**
Chimes Ter. N8 . . . . .5J **47**
Chimney Ct. *E1* 1H *103*
    (off Brewhouse La.)
China Ct. *E1* 1H *103*
    (off Asher Way)
China Hall M. SE16 . . . . .3J **103**
China M. SW2 . . . . .7K **119**
China Town .2D **12**

China Wharf SE1 . . . . .6K **15** (2G **103**)
Chinbrook Cres. SE12 . . . . .3K **141**
Chinbrook Rd. SE12 . . . . .3K **141**
Chinchilla Dr. TW4: Houn 2A **112**
Chine, The HA0: Wemb 5B **60**
  N10 . . . . .4G **47**
  N21 . . . . .6G **23**
Ching Ct. *WC2* 1E *12*
    (off Monmouth St.)
Chingdale Rd. E4 . . . . .3B **36**
CHINGFORD .1K **35**
Chingford Av. E4 . . . . .3H **35**
Chingford Fitness & Wellbeing Cen.
  . . . . .4K **35**
Chingford Golf Range 1H **35**
CHINGFORD GREEN 1A **36**
CHINGFORD HATCH 4A **36**
Chingford Ind. Cen. E4 . . . . .5F **35**
Chingford La. IG8: Wfd G 4B **36**
Chingford Leisure Cen. 4K **35**
CHINGFORD MOUNT 4H **35**
Chingford Mt. Rd. E4 . . . . .4H **35**
Chingford Rd. E4 . . . . .6H **35**
  E17 . . . . .1D **50**
Chingley Cl. BR1: Brom 6G **141**
Chingstone Ter. E4 . . . . .1K **35**
Ching Way E4 . . . . .6G **35**
    (not continuous)
Chinnery Cl. EN1: Enf 1A **24**
Chinnock's Wharf *E14* 7A *86*
    (off Narrow St.)
Chinnor Cres. UB6: G'frd 2F **77**
Chipka St. E14 . . . . .2E **104**
    (not continuous)
Chipley St. SE14 . . . . .6A **104**
Chipmunk Gro. UB5: N'olt 3C **76**
Chippendale All. UB8: Uxb 7A **56**
Chippendale Ho. *SW1* 6K *17*
    (off Churchill Gdns.)
Chippendale St. E5 . . . . .3K **67**
Chippendale Waye UB8: Uxb 7A **56**
Chippenham *KT1: King T* 2F *151*
    (off Excelsior Cl.)
Chippenham Av. HA9: Wemb 5H **61**
Chippenham Cl. HA5: Eastc 4H **39**
Chippenham Gdns. NW6 . . . . .3J **81**
Chippenham M. W9 . . . . .4J **81**
Chippenham Rd. W9 . . . . .4J **81**
Chipperfield Ho. *SW3* 5C *16*
    (off Cale St.)
Chipperfield Rd. BR5: St P 7A **144**
    (not continuous)
CHIPPING BARNET 4B **20**
Chipping Cl. EN5: Barn 3B **20**
Chipstead Av. CR7: Thor H 4B **156**
Chipstead Cl. SE19 . . . . .7F **139**
  SM2: Sutt 7K **165**
Chipstead Gdns. NW2 . . . . .2D **62**
Chipstead St. SW6 . . . . .1J **117**
Chip St. SW4 . . . . .3H **119**
Chirk Cl. UB4: Yead 4C **76**
Chisenhale Rd. E3 . . . . .2A **86**
Chisholm Ct. W6 . . . . .5C **98**
Chisholm Rd. CR0: C'don 2E **168**
  TW10: Rich 6F **115**
Chisledon Wlk. *E9* 6B *68*
    (off Osborne Rd.)
CHISLEHURST 6F **143**
Chislehurst Av. N12 . . . . .7F **31**
Chislehurst Caves 1E **160**
Chislehurst Golf Course 7F **143**
Chislehurst Rd. BR1: Brom 2B **160**
  BR5: Pet W 4J **161**
  BR6: Orp, Pet W, St M Cry 4J **161**
  BR7: Chst 2B **160**
  DA14: Sidc 5A **144**
  TW10: Rich 5E **114**
CHISLEHURST WEST 6E **142**
Chislet Cl. BR3: Beck 7C **140**
Chisley Rd. N15 . . . . .6E **48**
Chiswell Sq. SE3 . . . . .2K **123**

Chiswell St. EC1 . . . . .5E **8** (5C **84**)
   SE5 . . . . .7D **102**
    (off Edmund St.)
CHISWICK 5K **97**
Chiswick Bri. SW14 . . . . .2J **115**
Chiswick Cl. CRO: Bedd 3K **167**
Chiswick Comn. Rd. W4 . . . . .4K **97**
Chiswick Community Sports Hall . . .7K **97**
Chiswick Ct. HA5: Pinn 3D **40**
   W4 . . . . .4H **97**
Chiswick High Rd. TW8: Bford 5G **97**
   W4 . . . . .5G **97**
Chiswick House & Gdns. 6K **97**
Chiswick Ho. Grounds W4 . . . . . . .6A **98**
Chiswick La. W4 . . . . .5A **98**
Chiswick La. Sth. W4 . . . . .6B **98**
Chiswick Lifeboat Station 7B **98**
Chiswick Mall W4 . . . . .6B **98**
   W6 . . . . .6B **98**
Chiswick Pk. W4 . . . . .4H **97**
Chiswick Plaza W4 . . . . .6J **97**
Chiswick Quay W4 . . . . .1J **115**
Chiswick Rd. N9 . . . . .2B **34**
   W4 . . . . .4J **97**
CHISWICK RDBT. 5G **97**
Chiswick Sq. W4 . . . . .6A **98**
Chiswick Staithe W4 . . . . .1J **115**
Chiswick Ter. W4 . . . . .4J **97**
    (off Chiswick High Rd.)
Chiswick Village W4 . . . . .6G **97**
Chiswick Wharf W4 . . . . .6B **98**
Chitterfield Ga. UB7: Sip 7C **92**
Chitty's La. RM8: Dag 2D **72**
Chitty St. W1 . . . . .5B **6** (5G **83**)
Chivalry Rd. SW11 . . . . .5C **118**
Chivelston SW19 . . . . .1F **135**
Chivenor Gro. KT2: King T 5D **132**
Chivers Rd. E4 . . . . .3J **35**
Choats Mnr. Way RM9: Dag 2E **90**
Choats Rd. IG11: Bark 2C **90**
   RM9: Dag 2C **90**
Chobham Academy Sports Cen. . . .5E **68**
Chobham Gdns. SW19 . . . . .2F **135**
CHOBHAM MANOR 5D **68**
Chobham Rd. E15 . . . . .5F **69**
Chocolate Factory 1, The 2K **47**
    (off Clarendon Rd.)
Chocolate Factory 2, The 2K **47**
    (off Coburg Rd.)
Chocolate Studios N1 . . . . .1E **8**
    (off Shepherdess Pl.)
Choice Vw. IG1: Ilf 2G **71**
    (off Axon Pl.)
Cholmeley Cl. N6 . . . . .7F **47**
Cholmeley Cres. N6 . . . . .7F **47**
Cholmeley Lodge N6 . . . . .1F **65**
Cholmeley Pk. N6 . . . . .1F **65**
Cholmley Gdns. NW6 . . . . .5J **63**
Cholmley Rd. KT7: T Ditt 6B **150**
Cholmley Ter. KT7: T Ditt 7B **150**
    (off Portsmouth Rd.)
Cholmley Vs. KT7: T Ditt 6B **150**
    (off Portsmouth Rd.)
Cholmondeley Av. NW10 . . . . .2C **80**
Cholmondeley Wlk. TW9: Rich 5C **114**
Choppin's Ct. E1 . . . . .1H **103**
Chopwell Cl. E15 . . . . .7F **69**
Chorleywood Cres. BR5: St P 2K **161**
Choudhury Mans. N1 . . . . .7J **65**
    (off Pembroke St.)
Choumert Gro. SE15 . . . . .2G **121**
Choumert M. SE15 . . . . .2G **121**
Choumert Rd. SE15 . . . . .3F **121**
Choumert Sq. SE15 . . . . .2G **121**
Chow Sq. E8 . . . . .5F **67**
Chrisp Ho. SE10 . . . . .6G **105**
    (off Maze Hill)
Chrisp St. E14 . . . . .5D **86**
    (not continuous)
Chris Pullen Way N7 . . . . .6J **65**
Christabel Cl. TW7: Isle 3J **113**

Christabel Pankhurst Cl. SE5 . . . . .7D **102**
    (off Brisbane St.)
Christchurch Av. DA8: Erith 6K **109**
   HA0: Wemb 6E **60**
   HA3: Kenton, W'stone 4K **41**
   N12 . . . . .6F **31**
   NW6 . . . . .1F **81**
   TW11: Tedd 5A **132**
Christchurch Cl. EN2: Enf 2H **23**
   N12 . . . . .7G **31**
   SW19 . . . . .7B **136**
Christ Church Ct. NW10 . . . . .1A **80**
Christchurch Ct. EC4 . . . . .7B **8**
    (off Warwick La.)
   NW6 . . . . .7G **63**
    (off Willesden La.)
   UB4: Yead 4A **76**
    (off Dunedin Way)
Christchurch Flats TW9: Rich 3E **114**
Christchurch Gdns. HA3: W'stone . . .4A **42**
Christchurch Grn. HA0: Wemb 6E **60**
Christchurch Hill NW3 . . . . .3B **64**
Christchurch Ho. RM8: Dag 5B **72**
   SW2 . . . . .1K **137**
    (off Christchurch Rd.)
Christchurch La. EN5: Barn 2B **20**
Christchurch Lodge EN4: Cockf 4J **21**
Christchurch Pk. SM2: Sutt 7A **166**
Christchurch Pas. EN5: Barn 2B **20**
   NW3 . . . . .3A **64**
Christchurch Path UB3: Harl 3E **92**
Christchurch Pl. SW8 . . . . .2H **119**
Christ Chu. Rd. BR3: Beck 2C **158**
   KT5: Surb 6F **151**
Christchurch Rd. DA15: Sidc 4K **143**
   IG1: Ilf .1F **71**
   N8 . . . . .6J **47**
   SW2 . . . . .1K **137**
   SW14 . . . . .5H **115**
   SW19 . . . . .7B **136**
   TW6: H'row A 3C **110**
Christchurch Sq. E9 . . . . .1J **85**
Christchurch St. SW3 . . . . .7E **16** (6D **100**)
Christchurch Ter. SW3 . . . . .7E **16**
Christchurch Way SE10 . . . . .5G **105**
Christian Cl. SE16 . . . . .1B **104**
Christian Flds. SW16 . . . . .7A **138**
Christian Pl. E1 . . . . .6G **85**
    (off Burslem St.)
Christian St. E1 . . . . .6G **85**
Christie Ct. N19 . . . . .2J **65**
Christie Dr. CRO: C'don 5G **157**
Christie Gdns. RM6: Chad H 6B **54**
Christie Ho. E16 . . . . .5J **87**
    (off Hammersley Rd.)
   SE10 . . . . .5H **105**
    (off Blackwall La.)
   W12 . . . . .6D **80**
    (off Du Cane Rd.)
Christie Rd. E9 . . . . .6A **68**
Christina Sq. N1 . . . . .1B **66**
Christina St. EC2 . . . . .3G **9** (4E **84**)
Christine Worsley Cl. N21 . . . . .1G **33**
Christopher Av. W7 . . . . .3A **96**
Christopher Bell Twr. E3 . . . . .2C **86**
    (off Pancras Way)
Christopher Cl. DA15: Sidc 5K **125**
   SE16 . . . . .2K **103**
Christopher Ct. DA15: Sidc 2A **144**
    (off Station Rd.)
   E1 . . . . .1K **15**
   TW15: Ashf 5A **128**
Christopher Gdns. RM9: Dag 5D **72**
Christopher Pl. N22 . . . . .7D **32**
    (off Myddleton Rd.)
   NW1 . . . . .1D **6** (3H **83**)
Christopher Rd. UB2: S'hall 4K **93**
Christophers M. W11 . . . . .1G **99**
Christopher St. EC2 . . . . . .4F **9** (4D **84**)
Chroma Mans. E20 . . . . .6E **68**
    (off Penny Brookes St.)

Chronicle Twr. N1 . . . . .1C **8**
Chryssell Rd. SW9 . . . . .7A **102**
Chubworthy St. SE14 . . . . .6A **104**
Chudleigh DA14: Sidc 4B **144**
Chudleigh Cres. IG3: Ilf 4J **71**
Chudleigh Gdns.
   SM1: Sutt 3A **166**
Chudleigh Rd. NW6 . . . . .7F **63**
   SE4 . . . . .5B **122**
   TW2: Twick 6J **113**
Chudleigh St. E1 . . . . .6K **85**
Chudleigh Way HA4: Ruis 1J **57**
Chulsa Rd. SE26 . . . . .5H **139**
Chumleigh Gdns. SE5 . . . . .5E **102**
    (off Chumleigh St.)
Chumleigh St. SE5 . . . . .5E **102**
Chumleigh Wlk. KT5: Surb 4F **151**
Church All. CRO: C'don 1A **168**
Church App. SE21 . . . . .3D **138**
Church Av. BR3: Beck 1C **158**
   DA14: Sidc 5A **144**
   E4 . . . . .6A **36**
    (not continuous)
   HA4: Ruis 1F **57**
   HA5: Pinn 6C **40**
   N14 . . . . .6F **65**
   NW1 . . . . .6F **65**
   SW14 . . . . .3K **115**
   UB3: S'hall 3C **94**
   UB5: N'olt 7D **58**
Churchbank E17 . . . . .4C **50**
    (off Eastfield Rd.)
Churchbury Cl. EN1: Enf 2K **23**
Churchbury La. EN1: Enf 3J **23**
Churchbury Rd. EN1: Enf 2K **23**
   SE9 . . . . .7B **124**
Church Cloisters EC3 . . . . .3G **15**
Church Cl. HA6: Nwood 1H **39**
   HA8: Edg 5D **28**
   N20 . . . . .3H **31**
   TW3: Houn 2C **112**
   UB4: Hayes 5F **75**
   UB7: W Dray 3A **92**
   W8 . . . . .2K **99**
Church Ct. EC4 . . . . .6A **84**
   SE16 . . . . .2B **104**
    (off Rotherhithe St.)
   TW9: Rich 5D **114**
Church Cres. E9 . . . . .7K **67**
   N3 . . . . .1H **45**
   N10 . . . . .4F **47**
   N20 . . . . .3H **31**
Churchcroft Cl. SW12 . . . . .7E **118**
Churchdown BR1: Brom 4G **141**
Church Dr. BR4: W W'ck 3G **171**
   HA2: Harr 6E **40**
   NW9 . . . . .1K **61**
Church Elm La. RM10: Dag 6G **73**
CHURCH END
   N3 . . . . .1H **45**
   NW10 . . . . .7A **62**
   NW4 . . . . .3D **44**
Church Entry EC4 . . . . .1B **14**
Church Est. Almshouses TW9: Rich . . .4F **115**
    (off Sheen Rd.)
Church Farm La. SM3: Cheam 6G **165**
Church Farm Pool 7J **21**
Church Farm Way N12 . . . . .6G **31**
Churchfield Cl. HA2: Harr 4G **41**
   UB3: Hayes 7H **75**
Churchfield Ho. W2 . . . . .4A **4**
    (off Hall Pl.)
Churchfield Mans. SW6 . . . . .2H **117**
    (off New Kings Rd.)
Churchfield Pl.
   TW17: Shep 7D **146**
Churchfield Rd. DA16: Well 3A **126**
   KT12: Walt T 7J **147**
   W3 . . . . .1J **97**
   W7 . . . . .2J **95**
   W13 . . . . .1B **96**

Churchfields E18 . . . . .1J **51**
   KT8: W Mole 3E **148**
   SE10 . . . . .6E **104**
Churchfields Av. TW13: Hanw 3D **130**
Churchfields Rd. BR3: Beck 2K **157**
Churchfield Way N12 . . . . .6F **31**
Church Gdns. HA0: Wemb 4A **60**
   W5 . . . . .2D **96**
Church Gth. N19 . . . . .2H **65**
    (off St John's Gro.)
Church Ga. SW6 . . . . .3G **117**
Church Grn. SW9 . . . . .1A **120**
   UB3: Hayes 6H **75**
Church Gro. KT1: Hamp W 1C **150**
   SE13 . . . . .5D **122**
Church Hill DA1: Cray 4K **127**
   E17 . . . . .4C **50**
   HA1: Harr 1J **59**
   N21 . . . . .7E **22**
   SE18 . . . . .3D **106**
   SM5: Cars 5D **166**
   SW19 . . . . .5H **135**
Church Hill Rd. E17 . . . . .4D **50**
   EN4: E Barn 6H **21**
   KT6: Surb 5E **150**
   SM3: Cheam 3F **165**
Church Hill Wood BR5: St M Cry . . .5K **161**
Church Ho. EC1 . . . . .3B **8**
    (off Compton St.)
   SW1 . . . . .1D **18**
    (off Gt. Smith St.)
Church Hyde SE18 . . . . .6J **107**
Churchill Av. HA3: Kenton 6C **42**
   UB10: Hill 3D **74**
Churchill Cl. TW14: Felt 1H **129**
   UB10: Hill 3D **74**
Churchill Ct. BR6: Farnb 5G **173**
   HA2: Harr 2F **59**
    (Eastcote Av.)
   HA2: Harr 5F **41**
    (Montrose Ct.)
   HA5: Hat E 1C **40**
   N4 . . . . .7A **48**
   N9 . . . . .1K **33**
   SE18 . . . . .4D **106**
   UB5: N'olt 5E **58**
    (off Newmarket Av.)
   W5 . . . . .4F **79**
Churchill Gdns. SW1 . . . . .6A **18**
    (not continuous)
   W3 . . . . .6G **79**
Churchill Gdns. Rd. SW1 . . . .6K **17** (5F **101**)
Churchill Lodge IG6: Ilf 4G **53**
Churchill Pl. E14 . . . . .1D **104**
   HA1: Harr 4J **41**
Churchill Rd. CR2: S Croy 7C **168**
   E16 . . . . .6A **88**
   HA8: Edg 6A **28**
   NW2 . . . . .6D **62**
   NW5 . . . . .4F **65**
   UB10: Uxb 2A **74**
Churchills M. IG8: Wfd G 6C **36**
Churchill Ter. E4 . . . . .4H **35**
Churchill Theatre 2J **159**
Churchill War Rooms 6D **12** (2H **101**)
Churchill Way BR1: Brom 2J **159**
   TW16: Sun 5J **129**
Churchlands Way KT4: Wor Pk 2F **165**
Church La. BR2: Brom 1C **172**
   BR7: Chst 1G **161**
   E11 . . . . .1G **69**
   E17 . . . . .4D **50**
   EN1: Enf 3J **23**
   HA3: W'stone 1K **41**
   HA5: Pinn 3C **40**
   KT7: T Ditt 6K **149**
   KT9: Chess 6F **163**
   N2 . . . . .3B **46**
   N8 . . . . .4K **47**
   N9 . . . . .2B **34**

Church La. N17 ....1E **48**
  NW9 ....6J **43**
  RM10: Dag 7J **73**
  SM6: Bedd 3H **167**
    (not continuous)
  SW17 ....5D **136**
  SW19 ....1H **153**
  TW1: Twick 1A **132**
  TW10: Ham 1E **132**
  TW11: Tedd 5K **131**
  W5 ....2C **96**
Churchley Rd. SE26 ....4H **139**
Church Manorway DA8: Erith 4K **109**
  DA17: Belv 2J **109**
  SE2 ....5A **108**
Church Mead SE5 ....7C **102**
    (off Camberwell Rd.)
Churchmead Cl. EN4: E Barn 6H **21**
Church Mdw. KT6: Surb 2C **162**
Churchmead Rd. NW10 ....6C **62**
Churchmore Rd. SW16 ....1G **155**
Church Mt. N2 ....5B **46**
Church Paddock Cl. SM6: Bedd 3H **167**
Church Pde. TW15: Ashf 4B **128**
Church Pas. EC2 ....7D **8**
    (off Gresham St.)
  EN5: Barn 3B **20**
  KT6: Surb 5E **150**
  TW1: Twick 1B **132**
Church Path CRO: C'don 2C **168**
  CR4: Mitc 3C **154**
    (not continuous)
  E11 ....5J **51**
  E17 ....4D **50**
  N5 ....5B **66**
  N8 ....5K **47**
    (off Tottenham La.)
  N12 ....3F **31**
    (Woodside La.)
  N12 ....4F **31**
    (Woodside Pk. Rd.)
  N17 ....7K **33**
  NW10 ....7A **62**
  SW14 ....3K **115**
    (not continuous)
  SW19 ....2H **153**
  UB1: S'hall 1E **94**
  UB2: S'hall 3D **94**
    (not continuous)
  W3 ....2J **97**
    (not continuous)
  W4 ....3J **97**
Church Pl. CR4: Mitc 3C **154**
  SW1 ....3B **12** (7G **83**)
  UB10: Ick 3E **56**
  W5 ....2D **96**
Church Ri. KT9: Chess 6F **163**
  SE23 ....2K **139**
Church Rd. BR2: Brom 2J **159**
    (Edison Rd.)
  BR2: Brom 3G **159**
    (Hazelwood Ho's.)
  BR2: Kes 7B **172**
  BR6: Farnb 5G **173**
  CRO: C'don 3C **168**
    (not continuous)
  CR4: Mitc 1B **154**
  DA7: Bex 2F **127**
  DA8: Erith 5K **109**
  DA14: Sidc 4A **144**
  DA16: Well 2B **126**
  E10 ....1C **68**
  E12 ....5C **70**
  E17 ....2A **50**
  EN3: Pond E 6D **24**
  HA6: Nwood 1H **39**
  HA7: Stan 5G **27**
  IG2: Ilf 6J **53**
  IG9: Buck H 1E **36**
  IG11: Bark 6G **71**
  KT1: King T 2F **151**

Church Rd. KT4: Wor Pk 1A **164**
  KT6: Surb 1C **162**
  KT8: E Mos 4H **149**
  KT10: Clay 7A **162**
  KT19: Ewe 7K **163**
  N1 ....6C **66**
  N6 ....6E **46**
  N17 ....1E **48**
    (not continuous)
  NW4 ....4D **44**
  NW10 ....7A **62**
  SE19 ....1E **156**
  SM3: Cheam 6G **165**
  SM6: Bedd 3H **167**
  SW13 ....2B **116**
  SW19 ....5G **135**
    (Courthorpe Rd.)
  SW19 ....1B **154**
    (Reynolds Cl.)
  TW5: Cran 5K **93**
  TW5: Hest 7E **94**
  TW7: Isle 1H **113**
  TW9: Rich 4E **114**
  TW10: Ham 4D **132**
  TW10: Rich 5E **114**
  TW11: Tedd 4J **131**
  TW13: Hanw 5B **130**
  TW15: Ashf 3B **128**
  TW17: Shep 7D **146**
  UB2: S'hall 3D **94**
  UB3: Hayes 1H **93**
  UB5: N'olt 2B **76**
  UB7: W Dray 3A **92**
  UB8: Cowl 4A **74**
  W3 ....1J **97**
  W7 ....7H **77**
Church Rd. Almshouses E10 ......2D **68**
    (off Church Rd.)
Church Rd. Ind. Est. E10 ....1C **68**
Church Row BR7: Chst 1G **161**
  NW3 ....4A **64**
  SW6 ....6H **99**
    (off Moore Pk. Rd.)
Church Row M. BR7: Chst 7G **143**
Church Sq. TW17: Shep 7D **146**
Church St. CRO: C'don 3B **168**
  E15 ....1G **87**
  E16 ....1F **107**
  EN2: Enf 3H **23**
  KT1: King T 2D **150**
  KT12: Walt T 7J **147**
  KT17: Ewe 7C **164**
  N9 ....7J **23**
  NW8 ....5B **4** (5B **82**)
  RM10: Dag 6H **73**
  SM1: Sutt 5K **165**
  TW1: Twick 1A **132**
  TW7: Isle 3B **114**
  TW12: Hamp 1G **149**
  TW16: Sun 3K **147**
  W2 ....5B **4** (5B **82**)
    (not continuous)
  W4 ....6B **98**
Church St. Est. NW8 ....4A **4** (4B **82**)
Church St. Nth. E15 ....1G **87**
Church St. Pas. E15 ....1G **87**
    (off Church St.)
Church Stretton Rd. TW3: Houn ...5G **113**
Church Ter. NW4 ....3D **44**
  SE13 ....3G **123**
  TW10: Rich 5D **114**
Church Va. N2 ....3D **46**
  SE23 ....2K **139**
Church Vw. TW10: Rich 5E **114**
Church Vw. Gro. SE26 ....6K **139**
Churchview Rd. TW2: Twick 1H **131**
Church Wlk. EN2: Enf 3J **23**
  KT7: T Ditt 6K **149**
  KT12: Walt T 7J **147**
    (not continuous)
  N6 ....3E **64**

Church Wlk. N16 ....3D **66**
    (not continuous)
  NW2 ....3H **63**
  NW4 ....3E **44**
  NW9 ....1K **61**
  SW13 ....1C **116**
  SW15 ....5D **116**
  SW16 ....2G **155**
  SW20 ....3E **152**
  TW8: Bford 6C **96**
    (not continuous)
  TW9: Rich 5D **114**
  UB3: Hayes 6G **75**
Churchward Ho. SE17 ....6B **102**
    (off Lorrimore Sq.)
  W14 ....5H **99**
    (off Ivatt Pl.)
Church Way EN4: Cockf 4J **21**
  HA8: Edg 6B **28**
  N20 ....3H **31**
Churchway NW1 ....1D **6** (3H **83**)
Churchwell Path E9 ....5J **67**
Churchwood Gdns. IG8: Wfd G 4D **36**
  SE23 ....7J **121**
Churchyard Pas. SE5 ....2D **120**
Churchyard Row SE11 ....4B **102**
Church Yd. Wlk. W2 ....5A **4**
    (off St Mary's Sq.)
Churston Av. E13 ....1K **87**
Churston Cl. SW2 ....1A **138**
Churston Dr. SM4: Mord 5F **153**
Churston Gdns. N11 ....6B **32**
Churston Mans. WC1 ....4H **7**
    (off Gray's Inn Rd.)
Churton Pl. SW1 ....4B **18** (4G **101**)
Churton St. SW1 ....4B **18** (4G **101**)
Chusan Pl. E14 ....6B **86**
Chute Ho. SW9 ....2A **120**
    (off Stockwell Pk. Rd.)
Chuter Ede Ho. SW6 ....6H **99**
    (off Clem Attlee Ct.)
Chyngton Cl. DA15: Sidc 3K **143**
Cibber Rd. SE23 ....2K **139**
Cicada Rd. SW18 ....6A **118**
Cicely Ct. CRO: Wadd 5A **168**
Cicely Ho. NW8 ....2B **82**
    (off Cochrane St.)
Cicely Rd. SE15 ....1G **121**
Cinderella Path NW11 ....1K **63**
Cinderford Way BR1: Brom 4G **141**
Cine Lumiere 3A **16**
    (off Queensberry Pl.)
Cineworld Cinema
  Bexleyheath 4H **127**
  Chelsea -
    Fulham Rd. 5A **100**
    King's Rd. 6B **100**
  Enfield 4B **24**
  Feltham 2K **129**
  Haymarket 3C **12**
    (off Haymarket)
  Ilford 3F **71**
    (off Clements Rd.)
  The O2 ....1G **105**
    (within The O2)
  Shaftesbury Av. 3C **12**
    (off Shaftesbury Av.)
  Staples Corner 1D **62**
  Wandsworth 5K **117**
  Wembley 4G **61**
  West India Quay 7C **86**
  Wood Green 2A **48**
    (within Wood Green Shop. City)
Cinnabar Wharf Central
  E1 ....1G **103**
    (off Wapping High St.)
Cinnabar Wharf E. E1 ....1G **103**
    (off Wapping High St.)
Cinnabar Wharf W. E1 ....1G **103**
    (off Wapping High St.)

Cinnamon Cl. CRO: C'don 7J **155**
  SE15 ....7F **103**
Cinnamon M. N13 ....2F **33**
Cinnamon Row SW11 ....3A **118**
Cinnamon St. E1 ....1H **103**
Cinnamon Wharf SE1 ....6K **15**
    (off Shad Thames)
Cintra Pk. SE19 ....7F **139**
Cipher Ct. NW2 ....3C **62**
Circa Apartments NW1 ....7E **64**
Circle, The NW2 ....3A **62**
  NW7 ....6E **28**
  SE1 ....6J **15**
    (off Queen Elizabeth St.)
Circle Gdns. SW19 ....2J **153**
Circuits, The HA5: Pinn 4A **40**
Circular Rd. N17 ....3F **49**
Circular Way SE18 ....6D **106**
Circus Lodge NW8 ....1A **4**
Circus M. W1 ....5E **4**
Circus Pl. EC2 ....6F **9** (5D **84**)
Circus Rd. NW8 ....1A **4** (3B **82**)
Circus Rd. E. SW8 ....7K **17** (7F **101**)
Circus Rd. W. SW8 ....7F **101**
Circus St. SE10 ....7E **104**
Circus W. SW8 ....7K **17** (6F **101**)
Cirencester St. W2 ....5K **81**
Cirrus Apartments E1 ....3K **9**
    (off Bacon St.)
Cirrus Cl. SM6: Wall 7J **167**
Cissbury Ho. SE26 ....3G **139**
Cissbury Ring Nth. N12 ....5C **30**
Cissbury Ring Sth.
  N12 ....5C **30**
Cissbury Rd. N15 ....5D **48**
Citadel Pl. SE11 ....5G **19** (5K **101**)
Citius Apartments E3 ....2C **86**
    (off Tredegar La.)
Citius Ct. E4 ....6K **35**
Citius Wlk. E20 ....6E **68**
Citizen Ho. N7 ....4A **66**
Citizen Rd. N7 ....4A **66**
Citrine Apartments E3 ....1A **86**
    (off Gunmaker's La.)
Citrus Ho. SE8 ....5B **104**
    (off Alverton St.)
CITY AIRPORT 1C **106**
City Apartments E1 ....7K **9**
    (off White Church La.)
City Bus. Cen. SE16 ....3J **103**
City Ct. CRO: C'don 7B **156**
City Cross Bus. Pk. SE10 ....4G **105**
City E. Bldg. E1 ....7H **85**
    (off Cable St.)
City Forum EC1 ....1C **8** (3C **84**)
City Gdn. Row N1 ....1C **8** (2B **84**)
City Ga. Ho. IG2: Ilf 6E **52**
    (off Eastern Av.)
City Gateway E1 ....7G **85**
    (off Ensign St.)
City Hall 5H **15** (1E **102**)
City Harbour E14 ....3D **104**
    (off Selsdon Way)
City Hgts. E8 ....1F **85**
    (off Kingsland Rd.)
City Ho. BR2: Brom 6C **160**
City Island E14 ....6G **87**
City Lights Ct. SE11 ....5K **19**
    (off Bowden St.)
City Mill Apartments E8 ....1F **85**
    (off Lovelace St.)
City Mill River Path E15 ....1E **86**
CITY OF LONDON 1E **14** (6D **84**)
City of London Almshouses SW9 ...4K **119**
City of London Crematorium E12 ...3C **70**
City of London Distillery 6B **84**
City of London Point N7 ....6H **65**
    (off York Way)
City of London Police Mus. 6C **84**
City of Westminster College
  Paddington Green Campus 5A **4**

City Pavilion, The
   Marks Gate 2F 69
City Pav. EC1 .5A 8
   (off Britton St.)
City Pl. Ho. EC2 . . . . .6D 8
   (off Basinghall St.)
Citypoint EC2 .5E 8
City Pride Development E14 . . . . . .1C 104
City Rd. EC1 . . . . .1A 8 (2B 84)
City Twr. EC2 .6E 8
   (off Basinghall St.)
   SW8 . . . . .7E 18 (6J 101)
City University London
   Goswell Pl. 3B 84
   Northampton Square Campus
   . . . . .2A 8 (3B 84)
   Saddlers Sports Cen., The
   . . . . .3B 8 (4B 84)
City Vw. IG1: Ilf 2G 71
   (off Axon Pl.)
Cityview SE7 . . . . .6A 106
City Vw. Apartments N1 . . . . .7C 66
   (off Essex Rd.)
   N4 . . . . .7D 48
   (off Devan Gro.)
City Vw. Ct. SE22 . . . . .7G 121
City Wlk. SE1 . . . . .7G 15 (2E 102)
City Wlk. Apartments EC1 . . . . .2C 8
   (off Seward St.)
City Wharf Ho. KT7: T Ditt 6B 150
Civic Way HA4: Ruis 5B 58
   IG6: Ilf 4G 53
Civil and Family Courts
   Barnet 1J 45
Civil Justice Cen.
   Central London 4J 5
Clabon M. SW1 . . . . .2E 16 (3D 100)
Clack La. HA4: Ruis 1E 56
Clack St. SE16 . . . . .2J 103
Clacton Rd. E6 . . . . .3B 88
   E17 .6A 50
   N17 .2F 49
Claigmar Gdns. N3 . . . . .1K 45
Claire Ct. HA5: Hat E 1D 40
   N12 .3F 31
   NW2 .6G 63
   WD23: B Hea 1C 26
Claire Gdns. HA7: Stan 5H 27
Claire Ho. IG1: Ilf 4F 71
Claire Pl. E14 . . . . .3C 104
Clairvale Rd. TW5: Hest 1B 112
Clairview Rd. SW16 . . . . .5F 137
Clairville Gdns. W7 . . . . .1J 95
Clairville Point SE23 . . . . .3K 139
   (off Dacres Rd.)
Clamp Hill HA7: Stan 4C 26
Clancarty Rd. SW6 . . . . .2J 117
Clandon Cl. KT17: Ewe 6B 164
   W3 .2H 97
Clandon Gdns. N3 . . . . .3J 45
Clandon Ho. SE1 . . . . .7B 14
   (off Webber St.)
Clandon Rd. IG3: Ilf 2J 71
Clandon St. SE8 . . . . .2C 122
Clandon Ter. SW20 . . . . .2F 153
Clanricarde Gdns. W2 . . . . .7J 81
CLAPHAM .4G 119
CLAPHAM COMMON 4H 119
Clapham Comn. Nth. Side SW4 . . . . .4D 118
Clapham Comn. Sth. Side SW4 . . . . .6F 119
Clapham Comn. W. Side SW4 . . . . . .4D 118
   (not continuous)
Clapham Cres. SW4 . . . . .4H 119
Clapham High St. SW4 . . . . .4H 119
CLAPHAM JUNCTION 3C 118
Clapham Leisure Cen. 3H 119
Clapham Mnr. Ct. SW4 . . . . .3G 119
Clapham Mnr. St. SW4 . . . . .3G 119
CLAPHAM PARK 7H 119
Clapham Pk. Est. SW4 . . . . .6H 119
Clapham Pk. Rd. SW4 . . . . .4G 119

Clapham Pk. Ter. SW2 . . . . .5J 119
   (off Lyham Rd.)
Clapham Picturehouse 4G 119
Clapham Rd. SW9 . . . . .3J 119
Clapham Rd. Est. SW4 . . . . .3J 119
Clap La. RM10: Dag, Rush G 2H 73
Claps Ga. La. E6 . . . . .4E 88
Clapton Comn. E5 . . . . .7F 49
   (not continuous)
CLAPTON PARK 4K 67
Clapton Pk. Est. E5 . . . . .4K 67
Clapton Pas. E5 . . . . .5J 67
Clapton Sq. E5 . . . . .5J 67
Clapton Ter. E5 . . . . .1G 67
Clapton Way E5 . . . . .4G 67
Clara Grant Ho. E14 . . . . .3C 104
   (off Mellish St.)
Clara Nehab Ho. NW11 . . . . .5H 45
   (off Leeside Cres.)
Clara Pl. SE18 . . . . .4E 106
Clare Cl. N2 . . . . .3A 46
Clare Cnr. SE9 . . . . .7F 125
Clare Ct. W11 . . . . .7G 81
   (off Clarendon Rd.)
   WC1 . . . . .2F 7
   (off Judd St.)
Claredale Ho. E2 . . . . .2H 85
   (off Claredale St.)
Claredale St. E2 . . . . .2G 85
Clare Gdns. E7 . . . . .4J 69
   IG11: Bark 6K 71
   W11 .6G 81
Clare Ho. E3 . . . . .1B 86
   E16 . . . . .7E 88
   (off University Way)
   HA8: Edg 2J 43
   (off Burnt Oak B'way.)
   SE1 . . . . .5F 103
   (off Cooper's Rd.)
Clare La. N1 . . . . .7C 66
Clare Lawn Av. SW14 . . . . .5K 115
Clare Mkt. WC2 . . . . .1H 13 (6K 83)
Clare M. SW6 . . . . .7K 99
Claremont TW17: Shep 6D 146
   (off Laleham Rd.)
Claremont Av. HA3: Kenton 5E 42
   KT3: N Mald 5C 152
   TW16: Sun 1K 147
Claremont Cl. BR6: Farnb 4E 172
   E16 . . . . .1E 106
   N1 . . . . .1K 7 (2A 84)
   SW2 .1J 137
Claremont Ct. E2 . . . . .2H 85
   (off Cambridge Heath Rd.)
   E2 . . . . .2G 85
   (off Claredale St.)
   W2 . . . . .6K 81
   (off Queensway)
   W9 . . . . .2H 81
   (off Claremont Rd.)
Claremont Dr. TW17: Shep 6D 146
Claremont Gdns. IG3: Ilf 2J 71
   KT6: Surb 5E 150
Claremont Gro. IG8: Wfd G 6F 37
   W4 . . . . .7A 98
Claremont Ho. SM2: Sutt 7K 165
Claremont Pk. N3 . . . . .1G 45
Claremont Pl. KT10: Clay 6A 162
Claremont Rd. BR1: Brom 4C 160
   CR0: C'don 1G 169
   E7 . . . . .5K 69
   E11 . . . . .3F 69
   E17 . . . . .2A 50
   HA3: W'stone 2J 41
   KT6: Surb 5E 150
   N6 . . . . .7G 47
   NW2 .7F 45
   TW1: Twick 6B 114
   TW11: Tedd 5K 131
   W9 . . . . .2G 81
   W13 .5A 78

Claremont Sq. N1 . . . . .1J 7 (2A 84)
Claremont St. E16 . . . . .2E 106
   N18 .6B 34
   SE10 . . . . .6D 104
Claremont Ter. KT7: T Ditt 7B 150
Claremont Vs. SE5 . . . . .7D 102
   (off Southampton Way)
Claremont Way NW2 . . . . .1E 62
   (not continuous)
Claremont Way Ind. Est.
   NW2 .1E 62
Clarence Av. BR1: Brom 4C 160
   IG2: Ilf 6E 52
   KT3: N Mald 2J 151
   SW4 .7H 119
Clarence Cl. EN4: E Barn 5G 21
   WD23: B Hea 1E 26
Clarence Ct. NW7 . . . . .5F 29
   W6 . . . . .4D 98
   (off Cambridge Gro.)
Clarence Cres. DA14: Sidc 3B 144
   SW4 .6H 119
Clarence Gdns. NW1 . . . . . .2K 5 (3F 83)
Clarence Ga. IG8: Ilf, Wfd G 6K 37
Clarence Ga. Gdns. NW1 . . . . .4F 5
   (off Glentworth St.)
Clarence House 6B 12
Clarence Ho. SE17 . . . . .6D 102
   (off Merrow St.)
Clarence La. SW15 . . . . .6A 116
Clarence M. E5 . . . . .5H 67
   SE16 . . . . .1K 103
   SW12 . . . . .7F 119
Clarence Pk. Cres. HA7: Stan 3D 26
Clarence Pl. E5 . . . . .5H 67
   CR0: C'don 7D 156
Clarence Rd. BR1: Brom 3B 160
   DA6: Bex 4E 126
   DA14: Sidc 3B 144
   E5 . . . . .4H 67
   E12 . . . . .4A 70
   E16 . . . . .4G 87
   E17 . . . . .2K 49
   EN3: Pond E 5C 24
   N15 .5C 48
   N22 .7D 32
   NW6 .7H 63
   SE8 .6D 104
   SE9 .2C 142
   SM1: Sutt 5K 165
   SM6: Wall 5F 167
   SW19 . . . . .6K 135
   TW9: Kew 1F 115
   TW11: Tedd 6K 131
   W4 . . . . .5G 97
Clarence St. KT1: King T 2D 150
   TW9: Rich 4E 114
   UB2: S'hall 3B 94
Clarence Ter. NW1 . . . . . .3F 5 (4D 82)
   TW3: Houn 4F 113
Clarence Wlk. SW4 . . . . .2J 119
Clarence Way NW1 . . . . .7F 65
Clarendon Cl. BR5: St P 3K 161
   E9 . . . . .7J 67
   W2 . . . . .2C 10 (7C 82)
Clarendon Ct. BR3: Beck 1D 158
   (off Albemarle Rd.)
   NW2 .7E 62
   NW11 . . . . .4H 45
   TW5: Cran 1J 111
   TW9: Kew 1F 115
   W9 . . . . .3A 4
   (off Maida Vale)
Clarendon Cres. TW2: Twick 3H 131
Clarendon Cross W11 . . . . .7G 81
Clarendon Dr. SW15 . . . . .4E 116
Clarendon Flats W1 . . . . .1H 11
   (off Balderton St.)
Clarendon Gdns. HA9: Wemb 3D 60
   IG1: Ilf 7D 52

Clarendon Gdns. NW4 . . . . .3C 44
   W9 . . . . .4A 82
Clarendon Grn. BR5: St P 4K 161
Clarendon Gro. CR4: Mitc 3D 154
   NW1 . . . . .1C 6 (3H 83)
Clarendon Ho. KT2: King T 1E 150
   (off Cowleaze Rd.)
   NW1 . . . . .1B 6
   (off Werrington St.)
   W2 . . . . .2C 10
   (off Strathearn Pl.)
Clarendon Lodge W11 . . . . .7G 81
   (off Clarendon Rd.)
Clarendon M. DA5: Bexl 1H 145
   W2 . . . . .2C 10 (7C 82)
Clarendon Path BR5: St P 4K 161
   (not continuous)
Clarendon Pl. W2 . . . . . . .2C 10 (7C 82)
Clarendon Ri. SE13 . . . . .4E 122
Clarendon Rd. CR0: C'don 2B 168
   E11 . . . . .1F 69
   E17 . . . . .6D 50
   E18 . . . . .3J 51
   HA1: Harr 6J 41
   N8 . . . . .3K 47
   N15 .4C 48
   N18 .6B 34
   N22 .2K 47
   SM6: Wall 6G 167
   SW19 . . . . .7C 136
   TW15: Ashf 4B 128
   UB3: Hayes 2H 93
   W5 . . . . .3E 78
   W11 .7G 81
Clarendon St. SW1 . . . . . .5K 17 (5F 101)
Clarendon Ter. W9 . . . . . .3A 4 (4A 82)
Clarendon Wlk. W11 . . . . .6G 81
Clarendon Way BR5: St P 3K 161
   BR7: Chst 3K 161
   N21 .6H 23
Clarens St. SE6 . . . . .2B 140
Clare Pl. SW15 . . . . .7B 116
Clare Point NW2 . . . . .1F 63
   (off Whitefield Av.)
Clare Rd. E11 . . . . .6F 51
   NW10 . . . . .7C 62
   SE14 . . . . .1B 122
   TW4: Houn 3D 112
   TW19: Stanw 1A 128
   UB6: G'frd 6H 59
Clare St. E2 .2H 85
Clare Ter. SW25 . . . . .3E 156
Clareville Ct. SW7 . . . . .4A 16
   (off Clareville St.)
Clareville Gro. SW7 . . . . . . .4A 16 (4A 100)
Clareville Gro. M. SW7 . . . . .4A 16 (4A 100)
Clareville Rd. BR5: Farnb 2G 173
Clareville St. SW7 . . . . .4A 16 (4A 100)
Clare Way DA7: Bex 1E 126
Clearwood Ct. W1 . . . . .6E 4
   (off Seymour Pl.)
Clearwood Wlk. SW9 . . . . .4A 120
Clarges M. W1 . . . . .4J 11 (1F 101)
Clarges St. W1 . . . . .4K 11 (1F 101)
Claribel Rd. SW9 . . . . .2B 120
Clarice Way SM6: Wall 7J 167
Claridge Ct. SW6 . . . . .2H 117
Claridge Rd. RM8: Dag 1D 72
Clarinet Cl. HA8: Edg 7C 28
Clarion Ho. E3 . . . . .2A 86
   (off Roman Rd.)
   SW1 . . . . .5B 18
   (off Moreton Pl.)
   W1 . . . . .1C 12
   (off St Anne's Ct.)
Clarissa Ho. E14 . . . . .6D 86
   (off Cordela St.)
Clarissa Rd. RM6: Chad H 7D 54
Clarissa St. E8 . . . . .1F 85
Clarke Apartments E3 . . . . .4B 86
   (off Heath Pl.)

Clarke Cl. CR0: C'don 6C 156
Clarke Mans. *IG11: Bark* *7K 71*
(off Upney La.)
Clarke M. N9 3C 34
Clarke Path N16 1G 67
Clarkes Av. KT4: Wor Pk 1F 165
Clarkes Dr. UB8: Hil 5A 74
Clarke's M. W1 5H 5 (5E 82)
Clark Gro. IG3: Ilf 4J 71
Clark Ho. *SW10* *7A 100*
(off Coleridge Gdns.)
Clarks Mead WD23: Bush 1B 26
Clarkson Rd. E16 6H 87
Clarkson Row *NW1* *2G 83*
(off Mornington Ter.)
Clarksons, The IG11: Bark 2G 89
Clarkson St. E2 3H 85
Clarks Rd. IG1: Ilf 2H 71
Clark St. E1 5H 85
(not continuous)
Clark Way TW5: Hest 7B 94
Clarnico Rd. E20 6C 68
Clarson Ho. *SE5* *7B 102*
(off Midnight Av.)
SE8 6A 104
Classic Mans. *E9* *7H 67*
(off Wells St.)
Classon Cl. UB7: W Dray 2A 92
Claude Rd. E10 2E 68
E13 1K 87
SE15 2H 121
Claude St. E14 4C 104
Claudia Jones Ho. N17 1C 48
Claudia Jones Way SW2 6J 119
Claudia Pl. SW19 1G 135
Claudius Cl. HA7: Stan 3J 27
Claughton Rd. E13 2A 88
Clauson Av. UB5: N'olt 5F 59
Clavell St. SE10 6E 104
Claverdale Rd. SW2 7K 119
Clavering Av. SW13 6D 98
Clavering Cl. TW1: Twick 4A 132
Clavering Ho. *SE13* *4F 123*
(off Blessington Rd.)
Clavering Pl. SW12 6E 118
Clavering Rd. E12 1B 70
Claverings Ind. Est. *N9* *2D 34*
(off Centre Way)
Claverley Gro. N3 1K 45
Claverley Vs. N3 7E 30
Claverton St. SW1 6B 18 (5G 101)
Clave St. E1 1J 103
Claxton Gro. W6 5F 99
Claxton Path *SE4* *4K 121*
(off Coston Wlk.)
Clay Av. CR4: Mitc 2F 155
Claybank Gro. SE13 3D 122
Claybourne M. SE19 7E 138
Claybridge Rd. SE12 4A 142
Claybrook Cl. N2 3B 46
Claybrook Rd. W6 6F 99
Claybury WD23: Bush 1A 26
Claybury B'way. IG5: Ilf 3C 52
Claybury Hall IG8: Wfd G 7J 37
Claybury Rd. IG8: Wfd G 7H 37
Clay Ct. E17 3F 51
SE1 *7G 15*
(off Long La.)
Claydon Dr. CR0: Bedd 4J 167
Claydon Ho. *NW4* *2F 45*
(off Holders Hill Rd.)
Claydown M. SE18 5E 106
Clayfarm Rd. SE9 2G 143
CLAYGATE 7A 162
Claygate Common (Local Nature Reserve)
7A 162
Claygate Cres. CR0: New Ad 6E 170
Claygate La. KT7: T Ditt 1A 162
KT10: Clay, Hin W 2A 162
Claygate Rd. W13 3B 96
CLAYHALL 3C 52
Clayhall Av. IG5: Ilf 3C 52
Clayhall Ct. *E3* *2B 86*
(off St Stephen's Rd.)
Clay Hill EN2: Enf 1K 23
Clayhill KT5: Surb 5G 151
Clayhill Cres. SE9 4B 142
Claylands Pl. SW8 7A 102
Claylands Rd. SW8 7H 19 (6K 101)
Clay La. HA3: Kenton 4D 42
HA8: Edg 2B 28
TW19: Stanw 7B 110
WD23: B Hea 1D 26
Claymill Ho. SE18 5G 107
Claymore Cl. SM4: Mord 7J 153
Clay Path E17 2C 50
Claypole Ct. *E17* *5C 50*
(off Yunus Khan Cl.)
Claypole Dr. TW5: Hest 1C 112
Claypole Rd. E15 2E 86
Clayponds Av. TW8: Bford 4D 96
Clayponds Gdns. W5 4D 96
(not continuous)
Clayponds La.
TW8: Bford 5E 96
(not continuous)
Clay St. W1 6F 5 (5D 82)
Clayton Av. HA0: Wemb 7E 60
Clayton Bus. Cen. UB3: Hayes 2G 93
Clayton Cl. E6 6D 88
Clayton Cres. N1 1J 83
TW8: Bford 5D 96
Clayton Dr. SE8 5A 104
Clayton Fld. NW9 7F 29
Clayton Ho. *E9* *7J 67*
(off Frampton Pk. Rd.)
KT7: T Ditt 1B 162
SW13 *7E 98*
(off Trinity Chu. Rd.)
Clayton M. SE10 1F 123
Clayton Rd. KT9: Chess 4C 162
RM7: Rush G 1J 73
SE15 1G 121
TW7: Isle 3J 113
UB3: Hayes 2G 93
Clayton St. SE11 7J 19 (6A 102)
Clayton Ter. UB4: Yead 5C 76
Claytonville Ter. DA17: Belv 2J 109
Clay Wood Cl. BR6: Orp 7J 161
Clayworth Cl. DA15: Sidc 6B 126
Cleanthus Cl. SE18 1F 125
Cleanthus Rd. SE18 2F 125
(not continuous)
Clearbrook Way E1 6J 85
Clearwater Pl. KT6: Surb 6C 150
Clearwater Ter. W11 2F 99
Clearwater Yd. *NW1* *1F 83*
(off Inverness St.)
Clearwell Dr. W9 4K 81
Cleave Av. BR6: Chels 6J 173
UB3: Harl 4G 93
Cleaveland Rd. KT6: Surb 5D 150
Cleaverholme Cl. SE25 6H 157
Cleaver Ho. *NW3* *7D 64*
(off Adelaide Rd.)
Cleaver Sq. SE11 6K 19 (5A 102)
Cleaver St. SE11 5K 19 (5A 102)
Cleaves Almshouses *KT2: King T* *2E 150*
(off London Rd.)
Cleeve Ct. TW14: Bedf 1G 129
Cleeve Hill SE23 1H 139
Cleeve Ho. *E2* *2H 9*
(off Calvert Av.)
Cleeve Pk. Gdns. DA14: Sidc 2B 144
Cleeve Way SM1: Sutt 1K 165
SW15 7B 116
Cleeve Workshops *E2* *2H 9*
(off Boundary Rd.)
Clegg Ho. *SE16* *3J 103*
(off Moodkee St.)
Clegg St. E1 1H 103
E13 2J 87
Cleland Ho. *E2* *2J 85*
(off Sewardstone Rd.)
Clematis Apartments *E3* *3B 86*
(off Merchant St.)
Clematis Gdns. IG8: Wfd G 5D 36
Clematis St. W12 7C 80
Clem Attlee Ct. SW6 6H 99
Clem Attlee Pde. *SW6* *6H 99*
(off North End Rd.)
Clemence Rd. RM10: Dag 1J 91
Clemence St. E14 5B 86
Clement Av. SW4 4H 119
Clement Cl. NW6 7E 62
W4 4K 97
Clement Danes Ho. W12 6D 80
Clement Gdns. UB3: Harl 4G 93
Clementhorpe Rd. RM9: Dag 6C 72
Clement Ho. SE8 4A 104
W10 *5E 80*
(off Dalgarno Gdns.)
Clementina Ct. *E3* *4A 86*
(off Copperfield Rd.)
Clementina Rd. E10 1B 68
Clementine Cl. W13 2B 96
Clementine Wlk. IG8: Wfd G 7D 36
Clement Rd. BR3: Beck 2K 157
SW19 5G 135
Clement's Av. E16 7J 87
Clements Cl. N12 4E 30
Clements Ct. IG1: Ilf 3F 71
TW4: Houn 4B 112
Clement's Inn WC2 1H 13 (6K 83)
Clement's Inn Pas. WC2 1H 13
Clements La. EC4 2F 15 (7D 84)
IG1: Ilf 3F 71
Clements Pl. TW8: Bford 5D 96
Clements Rd. E6 7C 70
IG1: Ilf 3F 71
SE16 3G 103
Clemson Ho. E8 1F 85
Clendon Way SE18 4H 107
Clennam St. SE1 6D 14 (2C 102)
Clensham Ct. SM1: Sutt 2J 165
Clensham La. SM1: Sutt 2J 165
Clenston M. W1 7E 4 (6D 82)
Cleopatra Cl. HA7: Stan 3J 27
Cleopatra's Needle 4G 13 (1J 101)
Clephane Rd. N1 6C 66
Clephane Rd. Nth. N1 6C 66
Clere Pl. EC2 3F 9 (4D 84)
Clere St. EC2 3F 9 (4D 84)
Clerics Wlk. TW17: Shep 7F 147
CLERKENWELL 4K 7 (4A 84)
Clerkenwell Cl. EC1 3K 7 (4A 84)
(not continuous)
Clerkenwell Ct. *N1* *2B 84*
(off Duncan St.)
Clerkenwell Grn. EC1 4K 7 (4A 84)
Clerkenwell Rd. EC1 4J 7 (4A 84)
Clerk's Pl. EC2 7G 9 (6E 84)
Clermont Rd. E9 1J 85
Clevedon Cl. N16 3F 67
Clevedon Ct. CR2: S Croy 5E 168
SW11 *1C 118*
(off Bolingbroke Wlk.)
Clevedon Gdns. TW5: Cran 1K 111
UB3: Harl 3F 93
Clevedon Ho. SM1: Sutt 4A 166
Clevedon Mans. NW5 4E 64
Clevedon Pas. N16 2F 67
Clevedon Rd. KT1: King T 2G 151
SE20 1K 157
TW1: Twick 6D 114
Cleve Ho. NW6 7K 63
Cleveland Av. SW20 2H 153
TW12: Hamp 7D 130
W4 4B 98
Cleveland Ct. W13 5B 78
Cleveland Gdns. KT4: Wor Pk 2A 164
N4 5C 48
NW2 2F 63
Cleveland Gdns. SW13 2B 116
W2 6A 82
Cleveland Gro. E1 4J 85
Cleveland Ho. *N2* *2B 46*
(off The Grange)
Cleveland Mans. *NW6* *7H 63*
(off Willesden La.)
SW9 *7A 102*
(off Mowll St.)
W9 4J 81
Cleveland M. W1 5A 6 (5G 83)
Cleveland Pk. TW19: Stanw 6A 110
Cleveland Pk. Av. E17 4C 50
Cleveland Pk. Cres. E17 4C 50
Cleveland Pl. SW1 4B 12 (1G 101)
Cleveland Ri. SM4: Mord 7F 153
Cleveland Rd. DA16: Well 2K 125
E18 3J 51
IG1: Ilf 3F 71
KT3: N Mald 4A 152
KT4: Wor Pk 2A 164
N1 7D 66
N9 7C 24
SW13 2B 116
TW7: Isle 4A 114
W4 3J 97
W13 5A 78
Cleveland Row SW1 5A 12 (1G 101)
Cleveland Sq. W2 6A 82
Cleveland St. W1 4K 5 (4F 83)
Cleveland Ter. W2 6A 82
Cleveland Way E1 4J 85
Cleveley Cl. SE7 4B 106
Cleveley Ct. *SE16* *4A 104*
(off Ashton Reach)
Cleveley Cres. W5 2E 78
Cleveleys Rd. E5 3H 67
Cleverly Est. W12 1C 98
Cleve Rd. DA14: Sidc 3D 144
NW6 7J 63
Cleves Av. KT17: Ewe 7D 164
Cleves Ho. *E16* *1J 105*
(off Southey M.)
Cleves Rd. E6 1B 88
TW10: Ham 3C 132
Cleves Wlk. IG6: Ilf 1G 53
Cleves Way HA4: Ruis 1B 58
TW12: Hamp 7D 130
TW16: Sun 6H 129
Clewer Ct. *E10* *1C 68*
(off Leyton Grange Est.)
Clewer Cres. HA3: Hrw W 1H 41
Clewer Ho. *SE2* *2D 108*
(off Wolvercote Rd.)
Cley Ho. SE4 4K 121
Clichy Est. E1 5J 85
Clichy Ho. *E1* *5J 85*
(off Stepney Way)
Clifden M. E5 4K 67
Clifden Rd. E5 5J 67
TW1: Twick 1K 131
TW8: Bford 6D 96
Cliffe Ho. *SE10* *5H 105*
(off Blackwall La.)
Cliffe Rd. CR2: S Croy 5D 168
Cliffe Wlk. *SM1: Sutt* *5A 166*
(off Greyhound Rd.)
Clifford Av.
BR7: Chst 6D 142
IG5: Ilf 1F 53
SM6: Wall 4G 167
SW14 3H 115
Clifford Cl. UB5: N'olt 1C 76
Clifford Ct. *W2* *5K 81*
(off Westbourne Pk. Vs.)
Clifford Dr. SW9 4B 120
Clifford Gdns. NW10 2E 80
UB3: Harl 4G 93
Clifford Gro.
TW15: Ashf 4C 128
Clifford Haigh Ho. SW6 7F 99

Clifford Ho. *BR3: Beck* *6D* ***140***
(off Calverley Cl.)
W14 . . . . *4H* ***99***
(off Edith Vs.)
Clifford Rd. E16 . . . . 4H **87**
E17 . . . . 2E **50**
EN5: New Bar 3E **20**
HA0: Wemb 7D **60**
N1 . . . . 1E **84**
N9 . . . . 6D **24**
SE25 . . . . 4G **157**
TW4: Houn 3B **112**
TW10: Ham 2D **132**
Clifford's Inn EC4 . . . . 1J **13**
Clifford's Inn Pas. EC4 . . . . . . 1J **13** (6A **84**)
Clifford St. W1 . . . . 3A **12** (7G **83**)
Clifford Way NW10 . . . . 4B **62**
Cliff Rd. NW1 . . . . 6H **65**
Cliffsend Ho. *SW9* *1A* ***120***
(off Cowley Rd.)
Cliff Ter. SE8 . . . . 2C **122**
Cliffview Rd. SE13 . . . . 3C **122**
Cliff Vs. NW1 . . . . 6H **65**
Cliff Wlk. E16 . . . . 5H **87**
Clifton Av. E17 . . . . 3K **49**
HA7: Stan 2B **42**
HA9: Wemb 6F **61**
N3 . . . . 1H **45**
TW13: Felt 3A **130**
W12 . . . . 1B **98**
Clifton Cl. BR6: Farnb 5G **173**
Clifton Ct. BR3: Beck 1D **158**
IG8: Wfd G 6D **36**
KT5: Surb 7F **151**
N4 . . . . 2A **66**
NW8 . . . . 3A **4**
SE15 . . . . 7H **103**
TW19: Stanw 6A **110**
Clifton Cres. SE15 . . . . 7H **103**
Clifton Est. SE15 . . . . 1H **121**
Clifton Gdns. EN2: Enf 4D **22**
N15 . . . . 6F **49**
NW11 . . . . 6H **45**
UB10: Hil 2D **74**
W4 . . . . 4K **97**
(not continuous)
W9 . . . . 4A **82**
Clifton Ga. SW10 . . . . 6A **100**
Clifton Gro. E8 . . . . 6G **67**
Clifton Hill NW8 . . . . 2K **81**
Clifton Hill Studios NW8 . . . . 2A **82**
Clifton Ho. *E2* *3J* ***9***
(off Club Row)
E11 . . . . 2G **69**
Clifton M. SE25 . . . . 4E **156**
Clifton Pde. TW13: Felt 3A **130**
Clifton Pk. Av. SW20 . . . . 2E **152**
Clifton Pl. SE16 . . . . 2J **103**
SW10 . . . . *6A* ***100***
(off Hollywood Rd.)
W2 . . . . 1B **10** (6B **82**)
Clifton Ri. SE14 . . . . 7A **104**
(not continuous)
Clifton Rd. DA14: Sidc 4J **143**
DA16: Well 3C **126**
E7 . . . . 6B **70**
E16 . . . . 5G **87**
HA3: Kenton 4F **43**
IG2: Ilf 6H **53**
KT2: King T 7F **133**
N1 . . . . 6C **66**
N3 . . . . 1A **46**
N8 . . . . 6H **47**
N22 . . . . 1G **47**
NW10 . . . . 2C **80**
SE25 . . . . 4E **156**
SM6: Wall 5F **167**
SW19 . . . . 6F **135**
TW7: Isle 2J **113**
TW11: Tedd 4J **131**
UB2: S'hall 4C **94**
Clifton Rd. UB6: G'frd 4G **77**
W9 . . . . 3A **4** (4A **82**)
Clifton St. EC2 . . . . 4G **9** (4E **84**)
Clifton Ter. N4 . . . . 2A **66**
Clifton Vs. W9 . . . . 5A **82**
Cliftonville Ct. SE12 . . . . 1J **141**
Clifton Wlk. *W6* *4D* ***98***
(off King St.)
Clifton Way HA0: Wemb 1E **78**
SE15 . . . . 7H **103**
TW6: H'row A 3C **110**
Climsland Ho. SE1 . . . . 4K **13** (1A **102**)
Cline Rd. N11 . . . . 6B **32**
Clinger Ct. *N1* *1E* ***84***
(off Hobbs Pl. Est.)
Clink Prison Mus. **4E 14**
Clink St. SE1 . . . . 4D **14** (1D **102**)
Clink Wharf *SE1* *4E* ***14***
(off Clink St.)
Clinton Av. DA16: Well 4A **126**
KT8: E Mos 4G **149**
Clinton Ho. *KT6: Surb* *7D* ***150***
(off Lovelace Gdns)
Clinton Rd. E3 . . . . 3A **86**
E7 . . . . 4J **69**
N15 . . . . 4D **48**
Clinton Ter. *SE8* *6C* ***104***
(off Watergate St.)
SM1: Sutt 4A **166**
Clipper Apartments *SE10* *6E* ***104***
(off Welland St.)
Clipper Cl. SE16 . . . . 2K **103**
Clipper Ho. *E14* *5E* ***104***
(off Manchester Rd.)
Clipper Way SE13 . . . . 4E **122**
Clippesby Cl. KT9: Chess 6F **163**
Clipstone M. W1 . . . . 5A **6** (5G **83**)
Clipstone Rd. TW3: Houn 3E **112**
Clipstone St. W1 . . . . 5K **5** (5F **83**)
Clissold Cl. N2 . . . . 3D **46**
Clissold Ct. N4 . . . . 2C **66**
Clissold Cres. N16 . . . . 3D **66**
Clissold Leisure Cen. **3D 66**
Clissold Rd. N16 . . . . 3D **66**
Clitheroe Av. HA2: Harr 1E **58**
Clitheroe Rd. SW9 . . . . 2J **119**
Clitherow Av. W7 . . . . 3A **96**
Clitherow Ct. TW8: Bford 5C **96**
Clitherow Pas. TW8: Bford 5C **96**
Clitherow Rd. TW8: Bford 5B **96**
Clitterhouse Cres. NW2 . . . . 1E **62**
Clitterhouse Rd. NW2 . . . . 1E **62**
Clive Av. N18 . . . . 6B **34**
Clive Ct. W9 . . . . 4A **82**
Cliveden Cl. N12 . . . . 4F **31**
Cliveden Ho. *E16* *1J* ***105***
(off Fitzwilliam M.)
SW1 . . . . *3G* ***17***
(off Cliveden Pl.)
Cliveden Pl. SW1 . . . . 3G **17** (4E **100**)
TW17: Shep 6E **146**
Cliveden Rd. SW19 . . . . 1H **153**
Clivedon Ct. W13 . . . . 5B **78**
Clivedon Rd. E4 . . . . 5B **36**
Clive Ho. *SE10* *6E* ***104***
(off Haddo St.)
Clive Lloyd Ho. *N15* *5C* ***48***
(off Woodlands Pk. Rd.)
Clive Lodge NW4 . . . . 6F **45**
Clive Pas. SE21 . . . . 3D **138**
Clive Rd. DA17: Belv 4G **109**
EN1: Enf 4B **24**
SE21 . . . . 3D **138**
SW19 . . . . 6C **136**
TW1: Twick 4K **131**
TW14: Felt 6J **111**
Clivesdale Dr. UB3: Hayes 1K **93**
Clive Way EN1: Enf 4B **24**
Cloak La. EC4 . . . . 2D **14** (7C **84**)
Clochar Ct. NW10 . . . . 1B **80**
Clock Ct. E11 . . . . 4K **51**
Clock Ho. E3 . . . . 3E **86**
E17 . . . . *4F* ***51***
(off Wood St.)
Clockhouse, The SW19 . . . . 3E **134**
Clockhouse Av. IG11: Bark 1G **89**
Clockhouse Cl. SW19 . . . . 2E **134**
Clockhouse Ct. BR3: Beck 2A **158**
CLOCKHOUSE JUNC. **5E 32**
Clockhouse La. RM5: Col R 1H **55**
TW14: Bedf 4C **128**
TW15: Ashf 4C **128**
Clock Ho. Pde. E11 . . . . 6K **51**
Clockhouse Pde. N13 . . . . 5F **33**
Clockhouse Pl. SW15 . . . . 6G **117**
Clock Ho. Rd. BR3: Beck 3A **158**
CLOCKHOUSE RDBT. **1D 128**
Clock Pde. EN2: Enf 5J **23**
Clock Pl. *SE1* *4B* ***102***
(off Newington Butts)
Clock Twr. Ind. Est. TW7: Isle 3K **113**
Clock Twr. M. N1 . . . . 1C **84**
SE28 . . . . 7B **90**
W7 . . . . 1J **95**
Clock Twr. Rd. TW7: Isle 3K **113**
Clock Vw. Cres. N7 . . . . 6J **65**
(not continuous)
Clockwork Apartments *EC4* *1B* ***14***
(off Ludgate Sq.)
Clockwork M. E9 . . . . 5K **67**
Cloister Cl. TW11: Tedd 5B **132**
Cloister Gdns. HA8: Edg 5D **28**
SE25 . . . . 6H **157**
Cloister Rd. NW2 . . . . 3H **63**
W3 . . . . 5J **79**
Cloisters, The **1E 18**
Cloisters, The E1 . . . . 4J **9**
SW9 . . . . 1A **120**
TW7: Isle *3A* ***114***
(off Pulteney Cl.)
Cloisters Av. BR2: Brom 5D **160**
Cloisters Bus. Cen. *SW8* *7F* ***101***
(off Battersea Pk. Rd.)
Cloisters Ct. DA7: Bex 3H **127**
Cloisters Mall KT1: King T 2E **150**
Clonard Way HA5: Hat E 6A **26**
Clonbrock Rd. N16 . . . . 4E **66**
Cloncurry St. SW6 . . . . 2F **117**
Clonmel Cl. HA2: Harr 2H **59**
Clonmell Rd. N17 . . . . 3D **48**
Clonmel Rd. SW6 . . . . 7H **99**
TW11: Tedd 4H **131**
Clonmore St. SW18 . . . . 1H **135**
Cloonmore Av. BR6: Chels 4K **173**
Clorane Gdns. NW3 . . . . 3J **63**
Close, The BR3: Beck 4A **158**
BR5: Pet W 6J **161**
CR4: Mitc 4D **154**
DA5: Bexl 6G **127**
DA14: Sidc 4B **144**
E4 . . . . 7K **35**
EN4: E Barn 6J **21**
HA0: Wemb 6E **60**
HA2: Harr 2G **41**
HA5: Eastc 7A **40**
HA5: Pinn 7D **40**
HA9: Wemb 3J **61**
IG2: Ilf 6J **53**
KT3: N Mald 2J **151**
KT6: Surb 6E **150**
N10 . . . . 2F **47**
N14 . . . . 2C **32**
N20 . . . . 2C **30**
RM6: Chad H 6E **54**
SE3 . . . . 2F **123**
SE25 . . . . 6G **157**
SM3: Sutt 7H **153**
SM5: Cars 7C **166**
TW7: Isle 2H **113**
TW9: Rich 3H **115**
UB10: Hil 1C **74**
Cloth Ct. EC1 . . . . 6B **8**
Cloth Fair EC1 . . . . 6B **8** (5B **84**)
Cloth Ho. *EC1* *5C* ***8***
(off Cloth St.)
Clothier St. E1 . . . . 7H **9** (6E **84**)
Cloth St. EC1 . . . . 5C **8** (5C **84**)
Clothworkers Rd. SE18 . . . . 7H **107**
Cloudesdale Rd. SW17 . . . . 2F **137**
Cloudeseley Cl. DA14: Sidc 4K **143**
Cloudesley Ho. *N1* *1A* ***84***
(off Cloudesley St.)
Cloudesley Mans. *N1* *1A* ***84***
(off Cloudesley Pl.)
Cloudesley Pl. N1 . . . . 1A **84**
Cloudesley Rd. DA7: Bex 1F **127**
N1 . . . . 1A **84**
(not continuous)
Cloudesley Sq. N1 . . . . 1A **84**
Cloudesley St. N1 . . . . 1A **84**
Clouston Cl. SM6: Wall 5J **167**
Clova Rd. E7 . . . . 6H **69**
Clove Cres. E14 . . . . 7E **86**
Clove Hitch Quay SW11 . . . . 3A **118**
Clovelly Av. NW9 . . . . 4B **44**
UB10: Ick 4E **56**
Clovelly Cl. HA5: Eastc 3K **39**
UB10: Ick 4E **56**
Clovelly Ct. NW2 . . . . 5E **62**
Clovelly Gdns. EN1: Enf 7K **23**
RM7: Mawney 1H **55**
SE19 . . . . 1F **157**
Clovelly Ho. *W2* *6A* ***82***
(off Hallfield Est.)
Clovelly Rd. DA7: Bex 6E **108**
N8 . . . . 4H **47**
TW3: Houn 2E **112**
W4 . . . . 2K **97**
W5 . . . . 2C **96**
Clovelly Way BR6: St M Cry 6K **161**
E1 . . . . 6J **85**
HA2: Harr 2D **58**
Clover Cl. E11 . . . . 2F **69**
Cloverdale Ct. SM6: Wall 6F **167**
Cloverdale Gdns. DA15: Sidc 6K **125**
Clover M. SW3 . . . . 7F **17** (6D **100**)
Clover Way SM6: Wall 1E **166**
Clove St. E13 . . . . 4J **87**
Clowders Rd. SE6 . . . . 3B **140**
Clowser Cl. SM1: Sutt 5A **166**
Cloysters Grn. E1 . . . . 1G **103**
Cloyster Wood HA8: Edg 7J **27**
Club Gdns. Rd. BR2: Hayes 7J **159**
Clubhouse, The E14 . . . . 6C **86**
Clubhouse La. UB10: Ick 4C **56**
Club Row E1 . . . . 3J **9** (4F **85**)
E2 . . . . 3J **9** (4F **85**)
Clumps, The TW15: Ashf 4F **129**
Clunbury Av. UB2: S'hall 5D **94**
Clunbury St. N1 . . . . 2D **84**
Clunie Ho. *SW1* *1F* ***17***
(off Hans Pl.)
Cluny Est. SE1 . . . . 7G **15** (3E **102**)
Cluny M. SW5 . . . . 4J **99**
Cluny Pl. SE1 . . . . 7G **15** (3E **102**)
Cluse Ct. *N1* *2C* ***84***
(off St Peters St.)
Cluster Ho. W3 . . . . 1B **98**
Clutton St. E14 . . . . 5D **86**
Clydach Rd. EN1: Enf 4A **24**
Clyde Cir. N15 . . . . 4E **48**
Clyde Ct. *NW1* *2H* ***83***
(off Hampden Cl.)
Clyde Flats *SW6* *7H* ***99***
(off Rylston Rd.)
Clyde Ho. KT2: King T 1D **150**
SW18 . . . . *4J* ***117***
(off Enterprise Way)
Clyde Pl. E10 . . . . 7D **50**
Clyde Rd. CR0: C'don 2F **169**
N15 . . . . 4E **48**
(not continuous)
N22 . . . . 1H **47**

Clyde Rd. SM1: Sutt .5J 165
SM6: Wall .6G 167
TW19: Stanw .1A 128
Clydesdale EN3: Pond E .4E 24
Clydesdale Av. HA7: Stan .3D 42
Clydesdale Cl. TW7: Isle .3K 113
Clydesdale Ct. N20 .1G 31
Clydesdale Gdns.
TW10: Rich .4H 115
Clydesdale Ho. *DA18: Erith .2E 108*
(off Kale Rd.)
W11 .6H 81
(off Clydesdale Rd.)
Clydesdale Rd. W11 .6H 81
Clydesdale Way DA17: Belv .2H 109
Clyde St. SE8 .6B 104
Clyde Ter. SE23 .2J 139
Clyde Va. SE23 .2J 139
Clyde Way RM1: Rom .1K 55
Clyde Wharf E16 .1J 105
Clydon Cl. DA8: Erith .6K 109
Clyfford Rd. HA4: Ruis .4H 57
Clymping Dene TW14: Felt .7K 111
Clynes Ho. *E2 .3K 85*
(off Knottisford St.)
RM10: Dag .3G 73
(off Uvedale Rd.)
Clyston St. SW8 .2G 119
Coach & Horses Yd. W1 .2K 11 (7G 83)
Coach Ho. La. N5 .4B 66
SW19 .4F 135
Coach Ho. M. *SE1 .7G 15*
(off Long La.)
SE23 .6K 121
SM2: Sutt .6K 165
Coachhouse M. SE20 .7H 139
Coach Ho. Yd. *NW3 .4A 64*
(off Heath St.)
SW18 .4K 117
Coachmaker M. *SW4 .3J 119*
(off Bedford Rd.)
W4 .3K 97
(off Berrymede Rd.)
Coach Yd. M. N19 .1J 65
Coalbrookdale Gates .6A 10 (2B 100)
Coaldale Wlk. SE21 .7C 120
Coal Drops N1 .1J 83
Coalecroft Rd. SW15 .4E 116
Coalport Ho. SE11 .2J 19
Coal Post Cl. BR6: Chels .6K 173
Coalstore Ct. E1 .5A 86
Coatbridge Ho. *N1 .7K 65*
(off Carnoustie Dr.)
Coates Av. SW18 .6C 118
Coates Cl. CR7: Thor H .3C 156
Coates Hill Rd. BR1: Brom .2E 160
Coate St. E2 .2G 85
Coates Wlk. TW8: Bford .6E 96
Cobalt SE28 .2A 108
Cobalt Bldg., The *EC2 .5C 8*
(off Bridgewater Sq.)
Cobalt Cl. BR3: Beck .4K 157
NW9 .1B 44
Cobalt Pl. SW11 .1B 118
Cobalt Sq. SW8 .7G 19
Cobbett Rd. SE9 .3C 124
TW2: Whitt .1E 130
Cobbetts Av. IG4: Ilf .5B 52
Cobbett St. SW8 .7K 101
Cobble La. N1 .7B 66
Cobble M. N5 .3C 66
N6 .1E 64
(off Highgate West Hill)
Cobble Path *E17 .5C 50*
(off Cedars Av.)
Cobblers Wlk. KT1: Hamp W .1A 150
KT8: E Mos .1A 150
TW11: Tedd .1A 150
TW12: Hamp .1G 149
Cobblestone Pl. CR0: C'don .1C 168
Cobblestone Sq. E1 .1H 103
Cobbold Ct. *SW1 .3C 18*
(off Elverton St.)
Cobbold Ind. Est. NW10 .6B 62
Cobbold M. W12 .2B 98
Cobbold Rd. E11 .3H 69
NW10 .6B 62
W12 .2A 98
Cobb's Ct. EC4 .1B 14
Cobb's Hall *SW6 .6F 99*
(off Fulham Pal. Rd.)
Cobb's Rd. TW4: Houn .4D 112
Cobbsthorpe Vs. SE26 .4K 139
Cobb St. E1 .6J 9 (5F 85)
Cobden Bldgs. *WC1 .1G 7*
(off King's Cross Rd.)
Cobden Ct. BR2: Brom .4A 160
Cobden Ho. *E2 .3G 85*
(off Nelson Gdns.)
NW1 .2G 83
(off Arlington Rd.)
Cobden M. SE26 .5H 139
Cobden Rd. BR6: Farnb .4H 173
E11 .3G 69
SE25 .5G 157
Cobham Av. KT3: N Mald .5C 152
Cobham Cl. BR2: Brom .7C 160
DA15: Sidc .6B 126
EN1: Enf .3B 24
HA8: Edg .2H 43
SM6: Wall .6J 167
SW11 .6C 118
Cobham Ct. CR4: Mitc .2B 154
Cobham M. NW1 .7H 65
Cobham Pl. DA6: Bex .5E 126
Cobham Rd. E17 .1E 50
IG3: Ilf .2J 71
KT1: King T .2G 151
N22 .3B 48
TW5: Hest .7A 94
Cobland Rd. SE12 .4A 142
Coborn M. *E3 .3B 86*
(off Coborn St.)
Coborn Rd. E3 .2B 86
Coborn St. E3 .3B 86
Cobourg Rd. SE5 .6F 103
Cobourg St. NW1 .2B 6 (3G 83)
Coburg Cl. SW1 .3B 18 (4G 101)
Coburg Cres. SW2 .1K 137
Coburg Dwellings *E1 .6J 85*
(off Hardinge St.)
Coburg Gdns. IG5: Ilf .2B 52
Coburg Rd. N22 .3K 47
Cochrane Cl. NW8 .1B 4
Cochrane Ct. *E10 .1C 68*
(off Leyton Grange Est.)
Cochrane Ho. *E14 .2C 104*
(off Admirals Way)
Cochrane M. NW8 .2B 82
Cochrane Rd. SW19 .7G 135
Cochrane St. NW8 .1B 4 (2B 82)
Cockburn Ho. *SW1 .6D 18*
(off Aylesford St.)
COCKCROW HILL .1D 162
Cockerell Rd. E17 .7A 50
COCKFOSTERS .4J 21
Cockfosters Pde. EN4: Cockf .4K 21
Cockfosters Rd. EN4: Cockf, Had W .1H 21
Cock Hill E1 .6H 9 (5E 84)
Cock La. EC1 .6A 8 (5B 84)
Cockpit Steps SW1 .7C 12
Cockpit Theatre .4C 4
(off Gateforth St.)
Cockpit Yd. WC1 .5H 7 (5K 83)
Cocks Cres. KT3: N Mald .4B 152
Cocksett Av. BR6: Chels .6J 173
Cockspur Ct. SW1 .4D 12 (1H 101)
Cockspur St. SW1 .4D 12 (1H 101)
Cocksure La. DA14: Sidc .3G 145
Coda Cen., The SW6 .7G 99
Code Ct. NW2 .3C 62
Code St. E1 .4K 9
Codicote Ho. *SE8 .4K 103*
(off Chilton Gro.)
Codicote Ter. N4 .2C 66
Codling Cl. E1 .1G 103
Codling Way HA0: Wemb .4D 60
Codrington Ct. E1 .4H 85
SE16 .7A 86
Codrington Hill SE23 .7A 122
Codrington M. W11 .6G 81
Cody Cl. HA3: Kenton .3D 42
SM6: Wall .7H 167
Cody Rd. E16 .4F 87
Coe Av. SE25 .6G 157
Coe's All. EN5: Barn .4B 20
Coffey St. SE8 .7C 104
Cogan Av. E17 .1A 50
Coin St. SE1 .4J 13 (1A 102)
(not continuous)
Coity Rd. NW5 .6E 64
Cokers La. SE21 .1D 138
Coke St. E1 .6G 85
Colas M. NW6 .1J 81
Colbeck M. SW7 .4K 99
Colbeck Rd. HA1: Harr .7G 41
Colberg Pl. N16 .7F 49
Colbert *SE5 .1E 120*
(off Sceaux Gdns.)
Colborne Ho. *E14 .7C 86*
(off E. India Dock Rd.)
Colborne Way KT4: Wor Pk .3E 164
Colbrook Av. UB3: Harl .3F 93
Colbrook Cl. UB3: Harl .3F 93
Colburn Way SM1: Sutt .3B 166
Colby M. SE19 .5E 138
Colby Rd. KT12: Walt T .7J 147
SE19 .5E 138
Colchester Av. E12 .4D 70
Colchester Dr. HA5: Pinn .5B 40
Colchester Ho. *E3 .1B 86*
(off Parnell Rd.)
Colchester Rd. E10 .7E 50
E17 .6C 50
HA6: Nwood .2J 39
HA8: Edg .7D 28
Colclough Ct. *CR0: C'don .6C 156*
(off Simpson Cl.)
Coldbath Sq. EC1 .3J 7 (4A 84)
Coldbath St. SE13 .1D 122
COLDBLOW .1J 145
Cold Blow Cres. DA5: Bexl .1K 145
Cold Blow La. SE14 .7K 103
(not continuous)
Cold Blows CR4: Mitc .3D 154
Coldershaw Rd. W7 .1A 96
W13 .1A 96
Coldfall Av. N10 .2E 46
Coldham Ct. N22 .1B 48
Coldharbour E14 .2E 104
Coldharbour Crest SE9 .3E 142
Coldharbour Ind. Est. SE5 .2C 120
Coldharbour La. SE5 .3C 120
SW9 .4A 120
UB3: Hayes .1J 93
Coldharbour Leisure Cen. .2D 142
Coldharbour Pl. SE5 .2C 120
Coldharbour Rd. CR0: Wadd .5A 168
Coldharbour Way CR0: Wadd .5A 168
Coldstream Gdns. SW18 .6H 117
Colebeck M. N1 .6B 66
Colebert Av. E1 .4J 85
Colebert Ho. *E1 .4J 85*
(off Colebert Av.)
Colebrook Cl. NW7 .6A 30
SW15 .7F 117
Colebrook Ct. *SW3 .4D 16*
(off Makins St.)
Colebrooke Av. W13 .6B 78
Colebrooke Ct. DA14: Sidc .3B 144
Colebrooke Dr. E11 .7A 52
Colebrooke Pl. N1 .1B 84
Colebrooke Ri. BR2: Brom .2G 159
Colebrooke Row N1 .2B 84
Colebrook Ho. *E14 .6D 86*
(off Ellesmere St.)
SE18 .7E 106
Colebrook Rd. SW16 .1J 155
Colebrook Way N11 .5A 32
Coleby Path SE5 .7D 102
Colechurch Ho. *SE1 .5G 103*
(off Avondale Sq.)
Cole Cl. SE28 .1B 108
Cole Ct. TW1: Twick .7A 114
Coledale Dr. HA7: Stan .1C 42
Colefax Bldgs. *E1 .6G 85*
(off Plumber's Row)
Coleford Rd. SW18 .5A 118
Cole Gdns. TW5: Cran .7J 93
Colegrave Rd. E15 .5F 69
Colegrove Rd. SE15 .6F 103
Coleherne Ct. SW5 .5K 99
Coleherne Mans. *SW5 .5K 99*
(off Old Brompton Rd.)
Coleherne M. SW10 .5K 99
Coleherne Rd. SW10 .5K 99
Colehill Gdns. SW6 .2G 117
Colehill La. SW6 .1G 117
Cole Ho. *SE1 .7K 13*
(off Baylis Rd.)
Coleman Cl. SE25 .2G 157
Coleman Ct. SW18 .7J 117
Coleman Flds. N1 .1C 84
Coleman Mans. N8 .7J 47
Coleman Rd. DA17: Belv .4G 109
RM9: Dag .6E 72
SE5 .7E 102
Colemans Heath SE9 .3E 142
Coleman St. EC2 .7E 8 (6D 84)
Coleman St. Bldgs. EC2 .7E 8
Colenso Dr. NW7 .7H 29
Colenso Rd. E5 .4J 67
IG2: Ilf .1J 71
COLE PARK .6A 114
Cole Pk. Gdns. TW1: Twick .5A 114
Cole Pk. Rd. TW1: Twick .6A 114
Cole Pk. Vw. TW1: Twick .6A 114
Colepits Wood Rd. SE9 .5H 125
Coleraine Rd. N8 .3A 48
SE3 .6H 105
Coleridge Av. E12 .6C 70
SM1: Sutt .4C 166
Coleridge Cl. SW8 .2F 119
Coleridge Ct. *EN5: New Bar .5E 20*
(off Station Rd.)
N1 .1C 84
(off Dibden St.)
SW1 .3C 18
(off Regency St.)
W14 .3F 99
(off Blythe Rd.)
Coleridge Cres. SL3: Poyle .4A 174
Coleridge Dr. HA4: Ruis .6K 39
Coleridge Gdns. NW6 .7A 64
SW10 .7K 99
Coleridge Ho. *SE17 .5C 102*
(off Browning St.)
SW1 .6B 18
(off Churchill Gdns.)
Coleridge La. N8 .6J 47
Coleridge Rd. CR0: C'don .7J 157
E17 .4B 50
N4 .2A 66
N8 .6H 47
N12 .5F 31
TW15: Ashf .4A 128
Coleridge Sq. *SW10 .7A 100*
(off Coleridge Gdns.)
W13 .6A 78
Coleridge Wlk. NW11 .4J 45
Coleridge Way UB4: Hayes .6J 75
UB7: W Dray .4A 92
Cole Rd. TW1: Twick .6A 114
Colesburg Rd. BR3: Beck .3B 158

Coles Cres. HA2: Harr . . . 2F **59**
Coles Grn. WD23: B Hea . . . 1B **26**
Coles Grn. Ct. NW2 . . . 2C **62**
Coles Grn. Rd. NW2 . . . 1C **62**
Coleshill Flats SW1 . . . 4H **17**
Coleshill Rd.
TW11: Tedd . . . 6J **131**
Colestown St. SW11 . . . 2C **118**
Cole St. SE1 . . . 7D **14** (2C **102**)
Colesworth Ho. *HA8: Edg . . . 2J 43*
(off Burnt Oak B'way.)
Colet Cl. N13 . . . 6G **33**
Colet Ct. *W6 . . . 4F 99*
(off Hammersmith Rd.)
Colet Flats *E1 . . . 6A 86*
(off Troon St.)
Colet Gdns. W14 . . . 4F **99**
Colet Ho. *SE17 . . . 5B 102*
(off Doddington Gro.)
Colette Ct. *SE16 . . . 2K 103*
(off Eleanor Cl.)
Coley St. WC1 . . . 4H **7** (4K **83**)
Colfe & Hatcliffe Glebe *SE13 . . . 5D 122*
(off Lewisham High St.)
Colfe Rd. SE23 . . . 1A **140**
Colfes Leisure Cen. . . . 6J 123
Colham Av. UB7: Yiew . . . 1A **92**
COLHAM GREEN . . . 5C 74
Colham Grn. Rd. UB8: Hil . . . 5C **74**
Colham Mill Rd. UB7: W Dray . . . 2A **92**
Colham Rd. UB8: Hil . . . 4B **74**
COLHAM RDBT. . . . **6C 74**
Colina M. N15 . . . 4B **48**
Colina Rd. N15 . . . 5B **48**
Colin Cl. BR4: W W'ck . . . 3H **171**
CR0: C'don . . . 3B **170**
NW9 . . . 4A **44**
Colin Ct. SE6 . . . 7B **122**
Colin Cres. NW9 . . . 4B **44**
COLINDALE . . . 3K 43
Colindale Av. NW9 . . . 3K **43**
Colindale Bus. Pk. NW9 . . . 3J **43**
Colindale Retail Pk. NW9 . . . 4K **43**
Colindeep Gdns. NW4 . . . 4C **44**
Colindeep La. NW4 . . . 3A **44**
NW9 . . . 3A **44**
Colin Dr. NW9 . . . 5B **44**
Colinette Rd. SW15 . . . 4E **116**
Colin Gdns. NW9 . . . 4B **44**
Colin Pde. NW9 . . . 4A **44**
Colin Pk. Rd. NW9 . . . 4A **44**
Colin Pond Ct. RM6: Chad H . . . 4D **54**
Colin Rd. NW10 . . . 6C **62**
Colinsdale *N1 . . . 1B 84*
(off Camden Wlk.)
Colinton Rd. IG3: Ilf . . . 2B **72**
Colin Winter Ho. *E1 . . . 4J 85*
(off Nicholas Rd.)
Coliseum Theatre . . . *3E 12*
(off St Martin's La.)
Coliston Pas. *SW18 . . . 7J 117*
(off Coliston Rd.)
Coliston Rd. SW18 . . . 7J **117**
Collamore Av. SW18 . . . 1C **136**
Collapit Cl. HA1: Harr . . . 6F **41**
Collard Pl. NW1 . . . 7F **65**
Collards Almshouses *E17 . . . 5E 50*
(off Maynard Rd.)
Collection Pl. *NW8 . . . 1K 81*
(off Bolton Pl.)
College App. SE10 . . . 6E **104**
College Av.
HA3: Hrw W . . . 1J **41**
College Cl. E9 . . . 5J **67**
HA3: Hrw W . . . 7D **26**
N18 . . . 5A **34**
TW2: Twick . . . 1H **131**
College Ct. EN3: Pond E . . . 5D **24**
NW3 . . . 6B 64
(off College Cres.)
SW3 . . . 6F **17**
College Ct. W5 . . . 7E **78**
W6 . . . 5E 98
(off Queen Caroline St.)
College Cres. NW3 . . . 6A **64**
College Cross N1 . . . 7A **66**
College Dr. HA4: Ruis . . . 7J **39**
KT7: T Ditt . . . 7J **149**
College E. E1 . . . 6K **9** (5F **85**)
College Flds. Bus. Cen. SW19 . . . 1C **154**
College Gdns. E4 . . . 7J **25**
EN2: Enf . . . 1J **23**
IG4: Ilf . . . 5C **52**
KT3: N Mald . . . 5B **152**
N18 . . . 5B **34**
SE21 . . . 1E **138**
SW17 . . . 2C **136**
College Grn. SE19 . . . 7E **138**
College Gro. NW1 . . . 1G **83**
College Hill EC4 . . . 2D **14** (7C **84**)
College Hill Rd. HA3: Hrw W . . . 7D **26**
College Ho. SW15 . . . 5F **117**
TW7: Isle . . . 7J **95**
College La. NW5 . . . 4F **65**
College Mans. *NW6 . . . 1G 81*
(off Salusbury Rd.)
College M. *N1 . . . 7A 66*
(off College Cross)
SW1 . . . 1E **18**
SW18 . . . 5K **117**
College of Arms . . . 2C 14
College Pde. *NW6 . . . 1G 81*
(off Salusbury Rd.)
COLLEGE PARK . . . 3D 80
College Pk. Cl. SE13 . . . 4F **123**
College Pk. Rd. N17 . . . 6A **34**
College Pl. E17 . . . 4G **51**
NW1 . . . 1G **83**
SW10 . . . 7A **100**
College Point E15 . . . 6H **69**
College Rd. BR1: Brom . . . 1J **159**
BR8: Hext . . . 7K **145**
CR0: C'don . . . 2D **168**
E17 . . . 5E **50**
EN2: Enf . . . 2J **23**
HA1: Harr . . . 6J **41**
HA3: Hrw W . . . 1J **41**
HA9: Wemb . . . 1D **60**
N17 . . . 6A **34**
N21 . . . 2F **33**
NW10 . . . 2E **80**
SE19 . . . 5F **139**
SE21 . . . 7E **120**
SW19 . . . 6B **136**
TW7: Isle . . . 1K **113**
W13 . . . 6B **78**
COLLEGE RDBT. . . . **3E 150**
College Row E9 . . . 5K **67**
College Slip BR1: Brom . . . 1J **159**
College St. EC4 . . . 2D **14** (7C **84**)
College Ter. E3 . . . 3B **86**
N3 . . . 2H **45**
College Vw. SE9 . . . 1B **142**
College Wlk. KT1: King T . . . 3E **150**
College Way RM8: Dag . . . 4A **72**
TW15: Ashf . . . 4B **128**
UB3: Hayes . . . 7J **75**
College Yd. NW5 . . . 4F **65**
NW6 . . . 1G **81**
Collendale Rd. E17 . . . 3K **49**
Collent St. E9 . . . 6J **67**
Collerston Ho. *SE10 . . . 5H 105*
(off Armitage Rd.)
Colless Rd. N15 . . . 5F **49**
Collett Rd. SE16 . . . 3G **103**
Collett Way UB2: S'hall . . . 2F **95**
Collier Cl. E6 . . . 7F **89**
KT19: Ewe . . . 6G **163**
Collier Dr. HA8: Edg . . . 2G **43**
COLLIER ROW . . . 1H 55
Collier Row La. RM5: Col R . . . 1H **55**
Collier Row Rd. RM5: Col R . . . 1F **55**
Colliers Ct. *CR0: C'don . . . 4D 168*
(off St Peter's Rd.)
Colliers Shaw BR2: Kes . . . 4B **172**
Collier St. N1 . . . 2K **83**
Colliers Water La. CR7: Thor H . . . 5A **156**
COLLIERS WOOD . . . 7B 136
COLLIERS WOOD . . . **7B 136**
Collindale Av. DA8: Erith . . . 7H **109**
DA15: Sidc . . . 1A **144**
Collingbourne Rd. W12 . . . 1D **98**
Collingham Gdns. SW5 . . . 4K **99**
Collingham Pl. SW5 . . . 4K **99**
Collingham Rd. SW5 . . . 4K **99**
Collings Cl. N22 . . . 6E **32**
Collington St. SE10 . . . 5F **105**
Collingtree Rd. SE26 . . . 4J **139**
Collingwood Av. KT5: Surb . . . 1J **163**
N10 . . . 3E **46**
Collingwood Cl. SE20 . . . 1H **157**
TW2: Whitt . . . 7E **112**
Collingwood Ct. EN5: New Bar . . . 5E **20**
W5 . . . 5F **79**
Collingwood Ho. *E1 . . . 4H 85*
(off Darling Row)
SE16 . . . 2H 103
(off Cherry Gdn. St.)
SW1 . . . 6C 18
(off Dolphin Sq.)
W1 . . . 5A 6
(off Clipstone St.)
Collingwood Rd. CR4: Mitc . . . 3C **154**
E17 . . . 6C **50**
N15 . . . 4E **48**
SM1: Sutt . . . 3J **165**
UB8: Hil . . . 4D **74**
Collingwood St. E1 . . . 4H **85**
Collins Av. HA7: Stan . . . 2E **42**
Collins Ct. E8 . . . 6G **67**
Collins Dr. HA4: Ruis . . . 2A **58**
Collins Ho. *E14 . . . 7E 86*
(off Newby Pl.)
SE10 . . . 5H 105
(off Armitage Rd.)
Collinson Ct. *SE1 . . . 7C 14*
(off Gt. Suffolk St.)
Collinson Ho. *SE3 . . . 4K 123*
(off Wallace Ct.)
SE15 . . . 7G 103
(off Peckham Pk. Rd.)
Collinson St. SE1 . . . 7C **14** (2C **102**)
Collinson Wlk. SE1 . . . 7C **14** (2C **102**)
Collins Path TW12: Hamp . . . 6D **130**
Collins Rd. N5 . . . 4C **66**
Collins Sq. SE3 . . . 2H **123**
Collins St. SE3 . . . 2G **123**
(not continuous)
Collin's Yd. N1 . . . 1B **84**
Collinwood Av. EN3: Enf H . . . 3D **24**
Collinwood Gdns. IG5: Ilf . . . 5D **52**
Collis All. TW2: Twick . . . 1J **131**
Collison Pl. N16 . . . 1E **66**
Coll's Rd. SE15 . . . 1J **121**
Collyer Av. CR0: Bedd . . . 4J **167**
Collyer Pl. SE15 . . . 1G **121**
Collyer Rd. CR0: Bedd . . . 4J **167**
Colman Ct. HA7: Stan . . . 6G **27**
N12 . . . 6F **31**
Colman Pde. EN1: Enf . . . 3K **23**
Colman Rd. E16 . . . 5A **88**
Colmans Wharf *E14 . . . 5D 86*
(off Morris Rd.)
Colmar Cl. E1 . . . 4K **85**
Colmer Pl. HA3: Hrw W . . . 7C **26**
Colmer Rd. SW16 . . . 1J **155**
Colmore M. SE15 . . . 1H **121**
Colmore Rd. EN3: Pond E . . . 4D **24**
Colnbrook By-Pass
SL3: Coln . . . 3A **174**
UB7: Harm . . . 3A **174**
Colnbrook Ct. SL3: Poyle . . . 4A **174**
Colnbrook St. SE1 . . . 3B **102**
Colne Ct. KT19: Ewe . . . 4J **163**
W7 . . . 6H 77
(off High La.)
Colnedale Rd. UB8: Uxb . . . 5A **56**
Colne Ho. IG11: Bark . . . 7F **71**
NW8 . . . 4B 4
(off Penfold St.)
Colne Pk. Cvn. Site UB7: W Dray . . . 1D **174**
Colne Reach TW19: Stanw M . . . 7A **174**
Colne Rd. E5 . . . 4A **68**
N21 . . . 7J **23**
TW1: Twick . . . 1J **131**
TW2: Twick . . . 1J **131**
Colne St. E13 . . . 3J **87**
COLNEY HATCH . . . 6J 31
Colney Hatch La. N10 . . . 6J **31**
N11 . . . 6J **31**
Colnmore Ct. *E2 . . . 3K 85*
(off Meath Cres.)
Coln Trad. Est. SL3: Poyle . . . 4A **174**
Cologne Rd. SW11 . . . 4B **118**
Coloma Ct. BR4: W W'ck . . . 4G **171**
Colombo Rd. IG1: Ilf . . . 1G **71**
Colombo St. SE1 . . . 5A **14** (1B **102**)
Colombo Street Sports & Community Cen.
. . . **5A 14**
Colomb St. SE10 . . . 5G **105**
Colonel's Wlk. EN2: Enf . . . 3G **23**
Colonial Av. TW2: Whitt . . . 6G **113**
Colonial Ct. N7 . . . 3K **65**
Colonial Dr. W4 . . . 4J **97**
Colonial Rd. TW14: Felt . . . 7G **111**
Colonnade WC1 . . . 4F **7** (4J **83**)
Colonnade, The *SE1 . . . 6J 13*
(off Waterloo Rd.)
SE8 . . . 4B **104**
Colonnades, The W2 . . . 6K **81**
Colonnades Leisure Pk., The . . . **6A** 168
Colonnade Wlk. SW1 . . . 4J **17** (4F **101**)
Colony Mans. *SW5 . . . 5K 99*
(off Earl's Ct. Rd.)
Colony M. *N1 . . . 5D 66*
(off Mildmay Gro. Nth.)
Colorado Apartments *N8 . . . 3K 47*
(off Gt. Amwell La.)
Colorado Bldg. *SE13 . . . 1D 122*
(off Deal's Gateway)
Colosseum Apartments *E2 . . . 2K 85*
(off Palmers Rd.)
Colosseum Ter. NW1 . . . 2K **5**
Colour Ct. SW1 . . . 5B **12**
Colour Ho. *SE1 . . . 7H 15*
(off Bell Yd M.)
Colour House Theatre
Merton . . . 1A 154
Colroy Ct. NW11 . . . 5G **45**
Colson Rd. CR0: C'don . . . 2E **168**
Colson Way SW16 . . . 4G **137**
Colstead Ho. *E1 . . . 6H 85*
(off Watney Mkt.)
Colsterworth Rd. N15 . . . 4F **49**
(not continuous)
Colston Av. SM5: Cars . . . 4C **166**
Colston Ct. SM5: Cars . . . 4D **166**
Colston Rd. E7 . . . 6B **70**
SW14 . . . 4J **115**
Coltash Ct. *EC1 . . . 3D 8*
(off Whitecross St.)
Colthurst Cres. N4 . . . 2B **66**
Colthurst Dr. N9 . . . 3C **34**
Coltman Ho. *SE10 . . . 6E 104*
(off Welland St.)
Coltman St. E14 . . . 5A **86**
Coltness Cres. SE2 . . . 5B **108**
Colton Gdns. N17 . . . 3C **48**
Colton Rd. HA1: Harr . . . 5J **41**
Coltsfoot Dr. UB7: Yiew . . . 6A **74**
Columbas Dr. NW3 . . . 1B **64**
Columbia Av. HA4: Ruis . . . 1K **57**
HA8: Edg . . . 1H **43**
KT4: Wor Pk . . . 7B **152**

Columbia Gdns. Nth. SW6 . . . . 6J 99
(off Rickett St.)
Columbia Gdns. Sth. SW6 . . . . 6J 99
(off Rickett St.)
Columbia Ho. E3 . . . . 4H 87
(off Hamlets Way)
Columbia Point SE16 . . . . 3J 103
(off Canada Est.)
Columbia Rd. E2 . . . . 1J 9 (3F 85)
E13 . . . . 4H 87
Columbia Road Flower Market 1K 9
(off Columbia Rd.)
Columbia Sq. SW14 . . . . 4J 115
Columbia Wharf
EN3: Pond E 6F 25
Columbine Av. CR2: S Croy 7B 168
E6 . . . . 5C 88
Columbine Way SE13 . . . . 2E 122
Columbus Ct. SE16 . . . . 1J 103
(off Rotherhithe St.)
Columbus Courtyard E14 . . . . 1C 104
Columbus Gdns. HA6: Nwood 1J 39
Colva Wlk. N19 . . . . 2F 65
Colvern Ho. RM7: Rom 5J 55
Colverson Ho. E1 . . . . 5J 85
(off Lindley St.)
Colvestone Cres. E8 . . . . 5F 67
Colview Ct. SE9 . . . . 1B 142
Colville Est. N1 . . . . 1E 84
Colville Est. W. E2 . . . . 2K 9
Colville Gdns. W11 . . . . 6H 81
(not continuous)
Colville Ho. E2 . . . . 2J 85
(off Waterloo Gdns.)
Colville Ho's. W11 . . . . 6H 81
Colville Mans. E20 . . . . 5D 68
(off Victory Pde.)
Colville M. W11 . . . . 6H 81
Colville Pl. W1 . . . . 6B 6 (5H 83)
Colville Rd. E11 . . . . 3E 68
E17 . . . . 2A 50
N9 . . . . 1C 34
W3 . . . . 3H 97
W11 . . . . 6H 81
Colville Sq. W11 . . . . 6H 81
Colville Ter. W11 . . . . 6H 81
Colvin Cl. SE26 . . . . 5J 139
Colvin Gdns. E4 . . . . 3K 35
E11 . . . . 4K 51
IG6: Ilf 1G 53
Colvin Ho. W10 . . . . 6F 81
(off Kingsdown Cl.)
Colvin Rd. CR7: Thor H 5A 156
E6 . . . . 7C 70
Colwall Gdns. IG8: Wfd G 5D 36
Colwell Rd. SE22 . . . . 5F 121
Colwick Cl. N6 . . . . 7H 47
Colwith Rd. W6 . . . . 6E 98
Colwood Gdns. SW19 . . . . 7B 136
Colworth Gro. SE17 . . . . 4C 102
Colworth Rd. CR0: C'don 1G 169
E11 . . . . 6G 51
Colwyn Av. UB6: G'frd 2K 77
Colwyn Cl. SW16 . . . . 5G 137
Colwyn Cres. TW3: Houn 1G 113
Colwyn Grn. NW9 . . . . 6A 44
(off Snowdon Dr.)
Colwyn Ho. SE1 . . . . 2J 19 (3A 102)
Colwyn Rd. NW2 . . . . 3D 62
Colyer Cl. SE9 . . . . 2F 143
Colyers Cl. DA8: Erith 1K 127
Colyers La. DA8: Erith 1J 127
Colyers Wlk. DA8: Erith 1K 127
Colyton Cl. DA16: Well 1D 126
HA0: Wemb 6C 60
Colyton La. SW16 . . . . 5A 138
Colyton Rd. SE22 . . . . 5H 121
Colyton Way N18 . . . . 5B 34
Combe, The NW1 . . . . 2K 5 (3F 83)
Combe Av. SE3 . . . . 7H 105
Combedale Rd. SE10 . . . . 5J 105

Combe Ho. W2 . . . . 5J 81
(off Gt. Western Rd.)
Combemartin Rd. SW18 . . . . 7G 117
Combe M. SE3 . . . . 7H 105
Comber Cl. NW2 . . . . 3D 62
Comber Gro. SE5 . . . . 7C 102
Comber Ho. SE5 . . . . 7C 102
Combermere Rd. SM4: Mord 6K 153
SW9 . . . . 3K 119
Comberton KT1: King T 2G 151
(off Eureka Rd.)
Comberton Rd. E5 . . . . 2H 67
Combeside SE18 . . . . 7K 107
Combwell Cres. SE2 . . . . 3A 108
Comedy Store 3C 12
(off Oxendon St.)
Comely Bank Rd. E17 . . . . 5E 50
Comeragh M. W14 . . . . 5G 99
Comeragh Rd. W14 . . . . 5G 99
Comer Cres. UB2: S'hall 2G 95
(off Windmill Av.)
Comerell Pl. SE10 . . . . 5H 105
Comerford Rd. SE4 . . . . 4A 122
Comet Cl. E12 . . . . 4B 70
Comet Ho. UB3: Harl 7E 92
Comet Pl. SE8 . . . . 7C 104
(not continuous)
Comet Rd. TW19: Stanw 7A 110
Comet St. SE8 . . . . 7C 104
Comfort St. SE15 . . . . 6E 102
Commander Av. NW9 . . . . 3C 44
Commerce Pk. CR0: Wadd 2K 167
Commerce Rd. N22 . . . . 1K 47
TW8: Bford 6C 96
Commerce Way CR0: Wadd 2K 167
Commercial Dock Path SE16 . . . . 3B 104
(off Gulliver St.)
Commercial Rd. E1 . . . . 7K 9 (6G 85)
E14 . . . . 6G 85
N18 . . . . 5K 33
Commercial Rd. Ind. Est. N18 . . . . . . 6A 34
Commercial St. E1 . . . . 4J 9 (4F 85)
Commercial Way NW10 . . . . 2H 79
SE10 . . . . 4H 105
SE15 . . . . 7F 103
Commercial Wharf E8 . . . . 1E 84
(off Kingsland Rd.)
Commerell St. SE10 . . . . 5G 105
Commodity Quay E1 . . . . . 3K 15 (7F 85)
Commodore Ct. SE8 . . . . 1C 122
(off Albyn Rd.)
Commodore Ho. E14 . . . . 7E 86
(off Poplar High St.)
SW18 . . . . 3A 118
Commodore Sq. SW10 . . . . 1A 118
Commodore St. E1 . . . . 4A 86
Common, The E15 . . . . 6G 69
HA7: Stan 2D 26
UB2: S'hall 4A 94
UB7: W Dray 1D 174
W5 . . . . 7E 78
(not continuous)
Commondale SW15 . . . . 2E 116
Commonfield La. SW17 . . . . 5C 136
Common La. KT10: Clay 7A 162
Common Mile Cl. SW4 . . . . 5H 119
Common Rd. HA7: Stan 4C 26
KT10: Clay 6A 162
SW13 . . . . 3D 116
Commonside BR2: Kes 4A 172
Commonside E. CR4: Mitc 3E 154
Commonside W. CR4: Mitc 3D 154
Commonwealth Av. UB3: Hayes 6F 75
W12 . . . . 7D 80
(not continuous)
Commonwealth Rd. N17 . . . . 7B 34
Commonwealth Secretariat 5B 12
Commonwealth Way SE2 . . . . 5B 108
Community Cl. TW5: Cran 1K 111
UB10: Ick 3D 56

Community La. N7 . . . . 5H 65
Community Rd. E15 . . . . 5F 69
UB6: G'frd 1G 77
Como Rd. SE23 . . . . 2A 140
Como St. RM7: Rom 5K 55
Compass Bus. Pk. 4G 163
Compass Cl. HA8: Edg 4A 28
TW15: Ashf 7E 128
Compass Ct. SE1 . . . . 5J 15
(off Shad Thames)
Compass Hill TW10: Rich 6D 114
Compass Ho. E1 . . . . 1H 103
(off Raine St.)
SW18 . . . . 4K 117
Compass La. BR1: Brom 1J 159
(off North St.)
Compass Point E14 . . . . 7B 86
(off Grenade St.)
Compass Theatre 3E 56
Compayne Gdns. NW6 . . . . 7K 63
Compayne Mans. NW6 . . . . 6K 63
(off Fairhazel Gdns.)
Compter Pas. EC2 . . . . 1D 14
Compton Av. E6 . . . . 2B 88
HA0: Wemb 4C 60
N1 . . . . 6B 66
N6 . . . . 7C 46
Compton Cl. E3 . . . . 5C 86
HA8: Edg 7D 28
NW1 . . . . 2K 5
NW11 . . . . 3F 63
SE15 . . . . 7G 103
W13 . . . . 6A 78
Compton Ct. SE19 . . . . 6E 138
SM1: Sutt 4A 166
Compton Cres. KT9: Chess 5E 162
N17 . . . . 7H 33
UB5: N'olt 1B 76
W4 . . . . 6J 97
Compton Ho. E20 . . . . 5D 68
(off Peloton Av.)
SW11 . . . . 1C 118
Compton Leisure Cen. 6H 31
Compton Pas. EC1 . . . . 3B 8 (4B 84)
Compton Pl. WC1 . . . . 3E 6 (4J 83)
Compton Ri. HA5: Pinn 5C 40
Compton Rd. CR0: C'don 1H 169
N1 . . . . 6B 66
N21 . . . . 1G 33
NW10 . . . . 3F 81
SW19 . . . . 6H 135
UB3: Hayes 7G 75
Compton St. EC1 . . . . 3A 8 (4B 84)
Compton Ter. N1 . . . . 6B 66
N21 . . . . 1F 33
Comreddy Cl. EN2: Enf 1G 23
Comus Ho. SE17 . . . . 4E 102
(off Comus Pl.)
Comus Pl. SE17 . . . . 4E 102
Comyn Rd. SW11 . . . . 4C 118
Comyns, The WD23: B Hea 1B 26
Comyns Cl. E16 . . . . 5H 87
Comyns Rd. RM9: Dag 7G 73
Conant Ho. SE11 . . . . 7K 19
(off St Agnes Pl.)
Conant M. E1 . . . . 7G 85
Concanon Rd. SW2 . . . . 4K 119
Concert Hall App. SE1 . . . . . 5H 13 (1K 101)
Concord Bus. Cen. W3 . . . . 4H 79
Concord Cl. UB5: N'olt 3B 76
Concord Ct. KT1: King T 3F 151
(off Winery La.)
Concorde Cl. TW3: Houn 2F 113
Concorde Dr. E6 . . . . 5D 88
Concord Ho. CR0: C'don 1H 169
KT3: N Mald 3A 152
N17 . . . . 7A 34
(off Park La.)

Concordia Wharf E14 . . . . 1E 104
(off Coldharbour)
Concord Rd. EN3: Pond E 5C 24
W3 . . . . 4H 79
Concord Ter. HA2: Harr 2F 59
(off Coles Cres.)
Concourse, The N9 . . . . 2B 34
(within Edmonton Grn. Shop. Cen.)
NW9 . . . . 1B 44
(off Quakers Course)
Condell Rd. SW8 . . . . 1G 119
Conder St. E14 . . . . 6A 86
Condor Path UB5: N'olt 2E 76
(off Union Rd.)
Condover Cres. SE18 . . . . 7F 107
Condray Pl. SW11 . . . . 7C 100
Conduit Av. SE10 . . . . 1F 123
Conduit Ct. WC2 . . . . 2E 12
Conduit La.
CR0: C'don 5G 169
CR2: S Croy 5G 169
EN3: Pond E 6F 25
N18 . . . . 5D 34
Conduit M. SE18 . . . . 5F 107
W2 . . . . 1A 10 (6B 82)
Conduit Pas. W2 . . . . 1A 10
Conduit Pl. W2 . . . . 1A 10 (6B 82)
Conduit Rd. SE18 . . . . 5F 107
Conduit St. W1 . . . . 2K 11 (7F 83)
Conduit Way NW10 . . . . 7J 61
Conewood St. N5 . . . . 3B 66
Coney Acre SE21 . . . . 1C 138
Coney Burrows E4 . . . . 2B 36
Coney Gro. UB8: Hil 3C 74
Coneygrove Path UB5: N'olt 6C 58
(off Arnold Rd.)
CONEY HALL 3G 171
Coney Hall Pde. BR4: W W'ck 3G 171
Coney Hill Rd. BR4: W W'ck 2G 171
Coney Way SW8 . . . . 6K 101
Conference Cl. E4 . . . . 2K 35
Conference Rd. SE2 . . . . 4C 108
Confluence Plaza SE13 . . . . 3E 122
(off Station Rd.)
Congers Ho. SE8 . . . . 7C 104
Congleton Gro. SE18 . . . . 5G 107
Congo Dr. N9 . . . . 3D 34
Congo Rd. SE18 . . . . 5H 107
Congress Rd. SE2 . . . . 4C 108
Congreve Ho. N16 . . . . 5E 66
Congreve Rd. SE9 . . . . 3D 124
Congreve St. SE17 . . . . 4E 102
Congreve Wlk. E16 . . . . 5B 88
(off Fulmer Rd.)
Conical Cnr. EN2: Enf 2H 23
Conifer Cl. BR6: Orp 4H 173
Conifer Ct. TW15: Ashf 5B 128
(off The Crescent)
Conifer Gdns. EN1: Enf 6K 23
SM1: Sutt 2K 165
SW16 . . . . 3K 137
Conifer Ho. SE4 . . . . 4B 122
(off Brockley Rd.)
Conifers Cl. TW11: Tedd 7B 132
Conifer Way HA0: Wemb 3C 60
UB3: Hayes 7J 75
Coniger Rd. SW6 . . . . 2J 117
Coningham Ct. SW10 . . . . 7A 100
(off King's Rd.)
Coningham M. W12 . . . . 1C 98
Coningham Rd. W12 . . . . 2D 98
Coningsby Av. NW9 . . . . 2A 44
Coningsby Cotts. W5 . . . . 2D 96
Coningsby Ct. CR4: Mitc 2E 154
Coningsby Gdns. E4 . . . . 6J 35
Coningsby Rd. CR2: S Croy 7C 168
N4 . . . . 7B 48
W5 . . . . 2D 96
Conington Rd. SE13 . . . . 2D 122
Conisbee Ct. N14 . . . . 5B 22
Conisborough Cres. SE6 . . . . 3E 140

Conisbrough *NW1* 1G **83**
(off Bayham St.)
Conisclife Cl. BR7: Chst 1E **160**
Conisclife Rd. N13 3H **33**
Coniston *NW1* 1A **6**
(off Harrington St.)
Coniston Av. DA16: Well 3J **125**
IG11: Bark 7J **71**
UB6: G'frd 3B **78**
Coniston Cl. DA7: Bex 1J **127**
DA8: Erith 7K **109**
IG11: Bark 7J **71**
N20 3F **31**
SW13 7B **98**
SW20 6F **153**
W4 7J **97**
Coniston Ct. *NW7* 7B **30**
(off Langstone Way)
SE16 2K **103**
(off Eleanor Cl.)
SM6: Wall 4F **167**
TW15: Ashf 3A **128**
W2 1D **10**
(off Kendal St.)
Conistone Way N7 7J **65**
Coniston Gdns. HA5: Eastc 4J **39**
HA9: Wemb 1C **60**
IG4: Ilf 4C **52**
N9 1D **34**
NW9 5K **43**
SM2: Sutt 6B **166**
Coniston Ho. *E3* 4B **86**
(off Southern Gro.)
SE5 7C **102**
(off Wyndham Rd.)
Coniston Rd. BR1: Brom 6G **141**
CR0: C'don 7G **157**
DA7: Bex 1J **127**
N10 2F **47**
N17 6B **34**
TW2: Whitt 6F **113**
Coniston Wlk. E9 5J **67**
Coniston Way KT9: Chess 3E **162**
Conlan St. W10 4G **81**
Conley Rd. NW10 6A **62**
Conley St. SE10 5G **105**
Connaught Av. E4 7K **25**, 1A **36**
EN1: Enf 2K **23**
EN4: E Barn 1J **31**
SW14 3J **115**
TW4: Houn 4C **112**
TW15: Ashf 4A **128**
Connaught Bri. E16 1B **106**
Connaught Bus. Cen. CR0: Wadd 6K **167**
CR4: Mitc 5D **154**
NW9 5B **44**
Connaught Cl. E10 2A **68**
EN1: Enf 2K **23**
SM1: Sutt 2B **166**
UB8: Hil 4E **74**
W2 1D **10** (6C **82**)
Connaught Club, The 1C **36**
Connaught Ct. *E17* 4D **50**
(off Orford Rd.)
W2 1E **10**
(off Connaught St.)
Connaught Dr. NW11 4J **45**
Connaught Gdns. N10 5F **47**
N13 4G **33**
SM4: Mord 4A **154**
Connaught Hgts. *E16* 1B **106**
(off Agnes George Wlk.)
UB10: Hil 4E **74**
(off Uxbridge Rd.)
Connaught Ho. *NW10* 3D **80**
(off Trenmar Gdns.)
W1 3J **11**
(off Davies St.)
Connaught La. IG1: Ilf 2G **71**
Connaught Lodge *N4* 7A **48**
(off Connaught Rd.)
Connaught M. NW3 4C **64**
SE18 5E **106**
SW6 1G **117**
Connaught Pl. W2 2E **10** (7D **82**)
Connaught Rd. E4 1B **36**
E11 1F **69**
E16 1B **106**
E17 5C **50**
EN5: Barn 6A **20**
HA3: W'stone 1K **41**
IG1: Ilf 2H **71**
KT3: N Mald 4A **152**
N4 7A **48**
NW10 1A **80**
SE18 5E **106**
SM1: Sutt 2B **166**
TW10: Rich 5F **115**
TW11: Tedd 5H **131**
W13 7B **78**
CONNAUGHT RDBT. 7B **88**
(off Victoria Dock Rd.)
Connaught Sq. W2 1D **10** (6D **82**)
Connaught St. W2 1D **10** (6C **82**)
Connaught Way N13 4G **33**
Connaught Works *E3* 1A **86**
(off Old Ford Rd.)
Connect La. IG6: Ilf 2G **53**
Connell Ct. *SE14* 6K **103**
(off Myers La.)
Connell Cres. W5 4F **79**
Connersville Way CR0: Wadd 3A **168**
Conniffe Ct. SE9 5F **125**
Conningham Ct. SE9 5A **124**
Connington Cres. E4 3A **36**
Connolly Ct. *RM7: Rush G* 6K **55**
(off Union Rd.)
Connor Cl. E11 7G **51**
IG6: Ilf 1G **53**
Connor Ct. SW11 1F **119**
Connor Rd. RM9: Dag 4F **73**
Connor St. E9 1K **85**
Conolly Dell *W7* 1J **95**
(off Conolly Rd.)
Conolly Rd. W7 1J **95**
Conrad Ct. *NW9* 2A **44**
(off Needleman Cl.)
SE16 4A **104**
(off Cary Av.)
Conrad Dr. KT4: Wor Pk 1E **164**
Conrad Ho. E8 6G **67**
E14 7A **86**
(off Victory Pl.)
E16 1K **105**
(off Wesley Av.)
N16 5E **66**
(off Matthias Rd.)
SW8 7J **101**
(off Wyvil Rd.)
Conrad Twr. W3 3H **97**
Consfield Av. KT3: N Mald 4C **152**
Consort Ct. *W8* 3K **99**
(off Wright's La.)
Consort Ho. *E14* 5D **104**
(off St Davids Sq.)
SW6 2A **118**
(off Lensbury Av.)
W2 7K **81**
(off Queensway)
Consort Lodge *NW8* 1D **82**
(off Prince Albert Rd.)
Consort M. TW7: Isle 5H **113**
Consort Rd. SE15 1H **121**
Cons St. SE1 6K **13** (2A **102**)
Constable Av. E16 1K **105**
Constable Cl. N11 5J **31**
NW11 6K **45**
UB4: Hayes 2E **74**
Constable Ct. *SE16* 5H **103**
(off Stubbs Dr.)
W4 5H **97**
(off Chaseley Dr.)
Constable Cres. N15 5G **49**
Constable Gdns. HA8: Edg 1G **43**
TW7: Isle 5H **113**
Constable Ho. NW3 7D **64**
UB5: N'olt 2B **76**
(off Gallery Gdns.)
Constable Ho's. *E14* 2C **104**
(off Cassilis Rd.)
Constable M. BR1: Brom 2K **159**
RM8: Dag 4B **72**
Constable Wlk. SE21 3E **138**
Constance Allen Ho. *W10* 6F **81**
(off Bridge Cl.)
Constance Cl. SW15 4K **133**
Constance Cres. BR2: Hayes 7H **159**
Constance Rd. CR0: C'don 7B **156**
EN1: Enf 6K **23**
SM1: Sutt 4A **166**
TW2: Whitt 7F **113**
Constance St. E16 1C **106**
Constant Ho. *E14* 7D **86**
(off Harrow La.)
Constantine Ct. *E1* 6G **85**
(off Fairclough St.)
Constantine Ho. UB3: Hayes 6F **75**
Constantine Pl. UB10: Hil 1B **74**
Constantine Rd. NW3 4C **64**
Constitution Hill SW1 6J **11** (2F **101**)
Constitution Ri. SE18 1E **124**
Consul Av. RM9: Dag, Rain 3J **91**
RM13: Rain 3J **91**
Consul Ho. *E3* 4C **86**
(off Wellington Way)
Content St. SE17 4D **102**
Contessa Cl. BR6: Farnb 5J **173**
Control Twr. Rd. TW6: H'row A 3C **110**
Convair Wlk. UB5: N'olt 3B **76**
Convent Cl. BR3: Beck 7E **140**
EN5: Barn 2C **20**
Convent Gdns. W5 4C **96**
W11 6G **81**
Convent Hill SE19 6C **138**
Convent Rd. TW15: Ashf 5D **128**
Convent Way UB2: S'hall 4A **94**
Conway Cl. BR3: Beck 1A **158**
HA7: Stan 6F **27**
Conway Cres. RM6: Chad H 6C **54**
UB6: G'frd 2J **77**
Conway Dr. SM2: Sutt 6K **165**
TW15: Ashf 6E **128**
UB3: Harl 3E **92**
Conway Gdns. CR4: Mitc 4J **155**
EN2: Enf 1K **23**
HA9: Wemb 7C **42**
Conway Gro. W3 5K **79**
Conway Ho. *E14* 4C **104**
(off Cahir St.)
SW3 6F **17**
(off Ormonde Ga.)
Conway M. W1 4A **6**
Conway Rd. N14 3D **32**
N15 5B **48**
NW2 2E **62**
SE18 4H **107**
SW20 1E **152**
TW4: Houn 7D **112**
TW6: H'row A 3D **110**
TW13: Hanw 5B **130**
Conway St. W1 4A **6** (4G **83**)
(not continuous)
Conway Wlk. TW12: Hamp 6D **130**
Conybeare NW3 7C **64**
Conyers Cl. IG8: Wfd G 6B **36**
Conyer's Rd. SW16 5H **137**
Conyer St. E3 2A **86**
Cooden Cl. BR1: Brom 7K **141**
Cook Ct. *SE8* 5A **104**
(off Evelyn St.)
SE16 1J **103**
(off Rotherhithe St.)
Cooke Cl. SE2 3C **108**
Cookes Cl. E11 2H **69**
Cookes La. SM3: Cheam 6G **165**
Cooke St. IG11: Bark 1G **89**
(not continuous)
Cookham Cl. UB2: S'hall 3F **95**
Cookham Cres. SE16 2K **103**
Cookham Dene Cl. BR7: Chst 1H **161**
Cookham Ho. *E2* 3J **9**
(off Montclare St.)
Cookham Rd. BR8: Swan 7G **145**
Cookhill Rd. SE2 2B **108**
Cook Rd. RM9: Dag 1E **90**
Cook's Cl. RM5: Col R 1J **55**
Cooks Cl. *E14* 1C **104**
(off Cabot Sq.)
Cooks Hole Rd. EN2: Enf 1H **23**
Cookson Gro. DA8: Erith 7H **109**
Cook's Rd. E15 2D **86**
Cooks Rd. SE17 6B **102**
Coolfin Rd. E16 6J **87**
Coolgardie Av. E4 5A **36**
IG7: Chig 3K **37**
Coolgardie Rd. TW15: Ashf 5E **128**
Coolhurst Rd. N8 6H **47**
Coolhurst Tennis & Squash Club 6H **47**
Cool Oak La. NW9 7A **44**
Coomassie Rd. W9 4H **81**
COOMBE 7J 133
Coombe Av. CR0: C'don 4E **168**
Coombe Bank KT2: King T 1A **152**
Coombe Cl. HA8: Edg 2F **43**
TW3: Houn 4E **112**
Coombe Cnr. N21 1G **33**
Coombe Ct. *CR0: C'don* 4D **168**
(off Coombe Rd.)
Coombe Cres. TW12: Hamp 7D **130**
Coombe Dene *BR2: Brom* 4H **159**
(off Cumberland Rd.)
Coombe Dr. HA4: Ruis 1K **57**
Coombe End KT2: King T 7K **133**
Coombefield Cl. KT3: N Mald 5A **152**
Coombe Gdns. KT3: N Mald 4B **152**
SW20 2C **152**
Coombe Hill Glade KT2: King T 7A **134**
Coombe Hill Golf Course 7K **133**
Coombe Hill Rd. KT2: King T 7A **134**
Coombe Ho. N7 5H **65**
Coombe Ho. Chase KT3: N Mald 1K **151**
Coombehurst Cl. EN4: Cockf 2J **21**
COOMBE LANE 1B **152**
Coombe La. CR0: C'don 5H **169**
SW20 1B **152**
Coombe La. Flyover SW20 1B **152**
Coombe La. W. KT2: King T 1H **151**
Coombe Lea BR1: Brom 3C **160**
Coombe Lodge SE7 6A **106**
Coombe Neville KT2: King T 7K **133**
Coombe Pk. KT2: King T 5J **133**
Coombe Pl. KT2: King T 5J **133**
Coomber Ho. *SW6* 3K **117**
(off Wandsworth Bri. Rd.)
Coombe Ridings KT2: King T 5J **133**
Coombe Ri. KT2: King T 1J **151**
Coombe Rd. CR0: C'don 4D **168**
KT2: King T 1G **151**
KT3: N Mald 2A **152**
N22 2A **48**
NW10 3K **61**
SE26 4H **139**
TW12: Hamp 6D **130**
W4 5A **98**
W13 3B **96**
Coomber Way CR0: Bedd 7H **155**
Coombes Rd. RM9: Dag 1F **91**
Coombe Wlk. SM1: Sutt 3K **165**
Coombewood Dr.
RM6: Chad H 6F **55**
Coombe Wood Golf Course 7H **133**
Coombe Wood Local Nature Reserve
7B **134**
Coombe Wood Rd. KT2: King T 5J **133**

Coombrook Ct.—Cornelia St.

Coombrook Ct. *SE16* ... *2A* **104**
(off Elgar St.)
Coombs St. N1 ... 1B **8** (2B **84**)
Coomer M. SW6 ... 6H **99**
Coomer Pl. SW6 ... 6H **99**
Coomer Rd. SW6 ... 6H **99**
Cooms Wlk. HA8: Edg ... 1J **43**
Coope Ct. *RM7: Rush G* ... *6K* **55**
(off Union Rd.)
Cooperage, The *SE1* ... *6J* **15**
(off Gainsford St.)
SW8 ... *7K* **101**
(off Regent's Bri. Gdns.)
Cooperage Cl. N17 ... 6A **34**
Co-operative Ho. SE15 ... 3G **121**
Cooper Av. E17 ... 1A **50**
Cooper Cl. SE1 ... 7K **13** (2A **102**)
Cooper Ct. SE18 ... 6F **107**
Cooper Cres. SM5: Cars ... 3D **166**
Cooper Ho. *NW8* ... *4A* **4**
(off Lyons Pl.)
SE4 ... *5K* **121**
(off St Norbert Rd.)
TW4: Houn ... 3D **112**
Cooper La. N16 ... 4D **66**
Cooper Rd. CR0: Wadd ... 4B **168**
NW4 ... 6F **45**
NW10 ... 5C **62**
Coopersale Cl. IG8: Wfd G ... 7F **37**
Coopersale Rd. E9 ... 5K **67**
Coopers Cl. E1 ... 4J **85**
RM10: Dag ... 6H **73**
Coopers Ct. *E3* ... *4B* **86**
(off Eric St.)
TW7: Isle ... *2K* **113**
(off Woodlands Rd.)
W3 ... *1J* **97**
(off Church Rd.)
Cooper's La. SE12 ... 2K **141**
Coopers La. E10 ... 1D **68**
NW1 ... 2H **83**
Coopers Lodge *SE1* ... *6J* **15**
(off Tooley St.)
Coopers M. BR3: Beck ... 2C **158**
Cooper's Rd. SE1 ... 5F **103**
Coopers Row EC3 ... 2J **15** (7F **85**)
Cooper St. E16 ... 5H **87**
Coopers Wlk. E15 ... 5G **69**
Cooper's Yd. SE19 ... 6E **138**
Coopers Yd. *N1* ... *7B* **66**
(off Upper St.)
Coote Gdns. RM8: Dag ... 3F **73**
Coote Rd. DA7: Bex ... 1F **127**
RM8: Dag ... 3F **73**
Cope Ho. EC1 ... 2D **8**
Copeland Dr. E14 ... 4C **104**
Copeland Ho. SE11 ... 2H **19**
SW17 ... 4B **136**
Copeland Rd. E17 ... 6D **50**
SE15 ... 2G **121**
Copeman Cl. SE26 ... 5J **139**
Copenhagen Ct. *SE8* ... *4A* **104**
(off Pell St.)
Copenhagen Gdns. W4 ... 2K **97**
Copenhagen Ho. *N1* ... *1K* **83**
(off Barnsbury Est.)
Copenhagen Pl. E14 ... 6B **86**
(not continuous)
Copenhagen St. N1 ... 1J **83**
Cope Pl. W8 ... 3J **99**
Copers Cope Rd. BR3: Beck ... 7B **140**
Cope St. SE16 ... 4K **103**
Copford Cl. IG8: Wfd G ... 6H **37**
Copford Wlk. *N1* ... *1C* **84**
(off Popham St.)
Copgate Path SW16 ... 6K **137**
Copinger Wlk. HA8: Edg ... 1H **43**
Copland Av. HA0: Wemb ... 5D **60**
Copland Cl. HA0: Wemb ... 5C **60**
Copland M. HA0: Wemb ... 6E **60**
Copland Rd. HA0: Wemb ... 6E **60**
Copleston M. SE15 ... 2F **121**
Copleston Pas. SE5 ... 2F **121**
Copleston Rd. SE15 ... 3F **121**
Copley Cl. SE17 ... 6C **102**
W7 ... 4K **77**
Copley Dene BR1: Brom ... 1B **160**
Copley Pk. SW16 ... 6K **137**
Copley Rd. HA7: Stan ... 5H **27**
Copley St. E1 ... 5K **85**
Coppard Gdns. KT9: Chess ... 6C **162**
Coppelia Rd. SE3 ... 4H **123**
Coppen Rd. RM8: Dag ... 7F **55**
Copperas St. SE8 ... 6D **104**
Copper Beech Cl. IG5: Ilf ... 1E **52**
Copperbeech Cl. NW3 ... 5B **64**
Copper Beeches Ct. TW7: Isle ... 1H **113**
Copper Box Arena ... 6C **68**
Copper Cl. N17 ... 7C **34**
SE19 ... 7F **139**
Copper Ct. E5 ... 2J **67**
Copperdale Rd. UB3: Hayes ... 2J **93**
Copperfield Av. UB8: Hil ... 5C **74**
Copperfield Dr. N15 ... 4F **49**
Copperfield Ho. *SE1* ... *7K* **15**
(off Wolseley St.)
W1 ... *5H* **5**
(off Marylebone High St.)
W11 ... *1F* **99**
(off St Ann's Rd.)
Copperfield M. *E2* ... *2G* **85**
(off Claredale St.)
N18 ... 4K **33**
Copperfield Rd. E3 ... 4A **86**
SE28 ... 6C **90**
Copperfields BR3: Beck ... 1E **158**
HA1: Harr ... 7J **41**
TW16: Sun ... 6H **129**
Copperfields Ct. W3 ... 2G **97**
Copperfield St. SE1 ... 6B **14** (2B **102**)
Copperfield Way BR7: Chst ... 6G **143**
HA5: Pinn ... 4D **40**
Coppergate Cl. BR1: Brom ... 1K **159**
Copperlight Apartments *SW18* ... *5J* **117**
(off Buckhold Rd.)
Coppermead Cl. NW2 ... 3E **62**
Copper M. W4 ... 3J **97**
Copper Mill Dr. TW7: Isle ... 2K **113**
Coppermill Hgts. *N17* ... *3H* **49**
(off Daneland Wlk.)
Copper Mill La. SW17 ... 4A **136**
Coppermill La. E17 ... 6J **49**
Copper Row SE1 ... 5J **15**
Copperwood Pl. SE10 ... 1E **122**
Copperworks, The *N1* ... *2J* **83**
(off Railway St.)
Coppetts Cen. N12 ... 7J **31**
Coppetts Cl. N12 ... 7H **31**
Coppetts Rd. N10 ... 7J **31**
Coppetts Wood & Glebelands
Local Nature Reserve ... 6J **31**
Coppice, The DA5: Bexl ... 3K **145**
EN2: Enf ... 4G **23**
EN5: New Bar ... *6E* **20**
(off Great Nth. Rd.)
TW15: Ashf ... 6D **128**
UB7: Yiew ... 6A **74**
Coppice Cl. BR3: Beck ... 4D **158**
HA4: Ruis ... 6F **39**
HA7: Stan ... 6E **26**
SW20 ... 3E **152**
Coppice Dr. SW15 ... 6D **116**
Coppice Wlk. N20 ... 3D **30**
Coppice Way E18 ... 4H **51**
Coppies Gro. N11 ... 4A **32**
Copping Cl. CR0: C'don ... 4E **168**
Coppins, The CR0: New Ad ... 6D **170**
HA3: Hrw W ... 6D **26**
Coppock Cl. SW11 ... 2C **118**
Coppsfield KT8: W Mole ... 3E **148**
Copse, The E4 ... 1C **36**
N2 ... 3D **46**
Copse Av. BR4: W W'ck ... 2D **170**
Copse Cl. HA6: Nwood ... 2E **38**
SE7 ... 6K **105**
Copse Glade KT6: Surb ... 7D **150**
COPSE HILL ... 7C 134
Copse Hill SM2: Sutt ... 7K **165**
SW20 ... 1C **152**
Copse Vw. CR2: Sels ... 7K **169**
Copsewood Cl. DA15: Sidc ... 6J **125**
Copse Wood Way HA6: Nwood ... 1D **38**
Coptain Ho. SW18 ... 4J **117**
Coptefield Dr. DA17: Belv ... 3D **108**
Copthall Av. EC2 ... 7F **9** (6D **84**)
(not continuous)
Copthall Bldgs. EC2 ... 7F **9**
Copthall Cl. EC2 ... 7E **8** (6D **84**)
Copthall Dr. NW7 ... 7H **29**
Copthall Gdns. NW7 ... 7H **29**
TW1: Twick ... 1K **131**
Copthall Leisure Cen. ... 7J **29**
Copthall Rd. E. UB10: Ick ... 2C **56**
Copthall Rd. W. UB10: Ick ... 2C **56**
Copthorne Av. BR2: Brom ... 2D **172**
SW12 ... 7H **119**
Copthorne Chase TW15: Ashf ... 4B **128**
Copthorne Cl. TW17: Shep ... 6E **146**
Copthorne M. UB3: Harl ... 4G **93**
Coptic St. WC1 ... 6E **6** (5J **83**)
Copt Pl. NW7 ... 6B **30**
Copwood Cl. N12 ... 4G **31**
Coral Apartments *E16* ... *7J* **87**
(off Western Gateway)
Coral Cl. RM6: Chad H ... 3D **54**
Coral Ho. *E1* ... *4A* **86**
(off Harford St.)
NW10 ... 3G **79**
Coraline Cl. UB1: S'hall ... 3D **76**
Coralline Wlk. SE2 ... 3C **108**
Coral Mans. *NW6* ... *1J* **81**
(off Kilburn High Rd.)
Coral Row SW11 ... 3A **118**
Coral St. SE1 ... 7K **13** (2A **102**)
Coram Ho. *W4* ... *5A* **98**
(off Wood St.)
WC1 ... 3E **6**
Coram Mans. *WC1* ... *4G* **7**
(off Millman St.)
Coram St. WC1 ... 4E **6** (4J **83**)
Coran Cl. N9 ... 7E **24**
Corban Rd. TW3: Houn ... 3E **112**
Corbar Cl. EN4: Had W ... 1G **21**
Corbden Cl. SE15 ... 1F **121**
Corben M. SW8 ... 2G **119**
Corbet Cl. SM6: Wall ... 1E **166**
Corbet Ct. EC3 ... 1F **15** (6D **84**)
Corbet Ho. *N1* ... *2A* **84**
(off Barnsbury Est.)
SE5 ... *7C* **102**
(off Wyndham Rd.)
Corbet Pl. E1 ... 5J **9** (5F **85**)
Corbett Ct. SE26 ... 4B **140**
Corbett Gro. N22 ... 7D **32**
Corbett Ho. *SW10* ... *6A* **100**
(off Cathcart Rd.)
Corbett Rd. E11 ... 6A **52**
E17 ... 3E **50**
Corbetts La. SE16 ... 4J **103**
(not continuous)
Corbetts Pas. *SE16* ... *4J* **103**
(off Corbetts La.)
Corbetts Wharf *SE16* ... *2H* **103**
(off Bermondsey Wall E.)
Corbicum E11 ... 7G **51**
Corbidge Ct. SE8 ... 6D **104**
Corbiere Ct. SW19 ... 6F **135**
Corbiere Ho. *N1* ... *1D* **84**
(off De Beauvoir Est.)
Corbin Ho. *E3* ... *3D* **86**
(off Bromley High St.)
Corbins La. HA2: Harr ... 3F **59**
Corbould Cl. SM5: Cars ... 6D **166**
Corbridge N17 ... 7C **34**
Corbridge Cres. E2 ... 2H **85**
Corby Cres. EN2: Enf ... 4D **22**
Corbylands Rd. DA15: Sidc ... 7J **125**
Corbyn St. N4 ... 1J **65**
Corby Rd. NW10 ... 2K **79**
Corby Way E3 ... 4C **86**
Cordage Ho. *E1* ... *1H* **103**
(off Cobblestone Sq.)
Cordelia Cl. SE24 ... 4B **120**
Cordelia Gdns. TW19: Stanw ... 7A **110**
Cordelia Ho. *N1* ... *2E* **84**
(off Arden Est.)
Cordelia Rd. TW19: Stanw ... 7A **110**
Cordelia St. E14 ... 6D **86**
Cordell Ho. *N15* ... *5F* **49**
(off Newton Rd.)
Cordingley Rd. HA4: Ruis ... 2F **57**
Cording St. E14 ... 5D **86**
Cordwainer Ho. E8 ... 1H **85**
Cordwainers Ct. *E9* ... *7J* **67**
(off St Thomas's Sq.)
Cordwainers Wlk. E13 ... 2J **87**
Cord Way E14 ... 3C **104**
Cordwell Rd. SE13 ... 5G **123**
Corefield Cl. N11 ... 2K **31**
Corelli Ct. SE1 ... 4H **103**
SW5 ... *4J* **99**
(off W. Cromwell Rd.)
Corelli Rd. SE3 ... 2C **124**
Corfe Av. HA2: Harr ... 4E **58**
Corfe Cl. TW4: Houn ... 1C **130**
UB4: Yead ... 6A **76**
Corfe Ho. *SW8* ... *7K* **101**
(off Dorset Rd.)
Corfe Twr. W3 ... 2H **97**
Corfield Rd. N21 ... 5E **22**
Corfield St. E2 ... 3H **85**
Corfton Lodge W5 ... 5E **78**
Corfton Rd. W5 ... 6E **78**
Coriander Av. E14 ... 6F **87**
Coriander Ct. *SE1* ... *6K* **15**
(off Gainsford St.)
Cories Cl. RM8: Dag ... 2D **72**
Corinium Cl. HA9: Wemb ... 4F **61**
Corinne Rd. N19 ... 4G **65**
Corinthian Manorway DA8: Erith ... 4K **109**
Corinthian Rd. DA8: Erith ... 4K **109**
Corinthian Way TW19: Stanw ... 7A **110**
Corkers Path IG1: Ilf ... 2G **71**
Corker Wlk. N7 ... 2K **65**
Cork Ho. SW19 ... 4K **135**
Corkran Rd. KT6: Surb ... 7D **150**
Corkscrew Hill BR4: W W'ck ... 2E **170**
Cork Sq. E1 ... 1H **103**
Cork St. W1 ... 3A **12** (7G **83**)
Cork St. M. W1 ... 3A **12**
Cork Tree Ho. *SE27* ... *5B* **138**
(off Lakeview Rd.)
Cork Tree Retail Pk. E4 ... 5F **35**
Cork Tree Way E4 ... 5F **35**
Corlett St. NW1 ... 5C **4** (5C **82**)
Cormont Rd. SE5 ... 1B **120**
Cormorant Cl. E17 ... 7F **35**
Cormorant Ct. *SE8* ... *6B* **104**
(off Pilot Cl.)
Cormorant Ho.
EN3: Pond E ... 5E **24**
Cormorant Lodge *E1* ... *1G* **103**
(off Thomas More St.)
Cormorant Pl.
SM1: Sutt ... 5H **165**
Cormorant Rd. E7 ... 5H **69**
Cornbury Ho. *SE8* ... *6B* **104**
(off Evelyn St.)
Cornbury Rd. HA8: Edg ... 7J **27**
Cornel Ho. DA15: Sidc ... 3A **144**
Cornelia Dr. UB4: Yead ... 4A **76**
Cornelia Ho. *TW1: Twick* ... *6D* **114**
(off Denton Rd.)
Cornelia St. N7 ... 6K **65**

Cornell Bldg.—Cottrill Gdns.

Cornell Bldg. *E1* 6G 85
(off Coke St.)
Cornell Cl. DA14: Sidc 6E 144
Cornell Ct. EN3: Enf H 3F 25
Cornell Gdns.
EN4: E Barn 5K 21
Cornell Ho. HA2: Harr 3D 58
Cornell Sq. SW8 1H 119
Corner, The W5 1E 96
Corner Ct. *E2* 4H 85
(off Three Colts La.)
Cornercroft *SM3: Cheam* 5F 165
(off Wickham Av.)
Corner Fielde SW2 1K 137
Corner Grn. SE3 2J 123
Corner Ho. *NW6* 2K 81
(off Oxford Rd.)
Corner House Arts Cen., The 1F 163
Corner Ho. St. WC2 4E 12
Corner Mead NW9 7G 29
Cornerside TW15: Ashf 7E 128
Cornerstone Ho.
CR0: C'don 7C 156
Corney Reach Way W4 7A 98
Corney Rd. W4 6A 98
Cornfield Cl. UB8: Uxb 2A 74
Cornflower La. CR0: C'don 1K 169
Cornflower Ter. SE22 6H 121
Cornford Cl.
BR2: Brom 5J 159
Cornford Gro. SW12 2F 137
Cornhill EC3 1F 15 (6D 84)
Cornick Ho. *SE16* 3H 103
(off Slippers Pl.)
Cornish Ct. N9 7C 24
Cornish Gro. SE20 1H 157
Cornish Ho. *SE17* 6B 102
(off Brandon Est.)
TW8: Bford 5F 97
Corn Mill Dr. BR6: Orp 7K 161
Cornmill Ho. *SE8* 5C 104
(off Wharf St.)
Cornmill La. SE13 3E 122
Cornmow Dr. NW10 5B 62
Cornshaw Rd. RM8: Dag 1D 72
Cornthwaite Rd. E5 3J 67
Cornwall Av. DA16: Well 3J 125
E2 3J 85
KT10: Clay 7A 162
N3 7D 30
N22 1J 47
UB1: S'hall 5D 76
Cornwall Cl. IG11: Bark 6K 71
Cornwall Ct. HA5: Hat E 1D 40
W7 4K 77
(off Copley Cl.)
Cornwall Cres. W11 6G 81
Cornwall Dr. BR5: St P 7C 144
Cornwall Gdns. NW10 6D 62
SE25 4F 157
SW7 3K 99
Cornwall Gdns. Wlk. SW7 3K 99
Cornwall Gro. W4 5A 98
Cornwall Ho. *SW7* 3K 99
(off Cornwall Gdns.)
Cornwallis Av. N9 2C 34
SE9 2H 143
Cornwallis Ct. *SW8* 1J 119
(off Lansdowne Grn.)
Cornwallis Gro. N9 2C 34
Cornwallis Ho. *SE16* 2H 103
(off Cherry Gdn. St.)
W12 7D 80
(off India Way)
Cornwallis Rd. E17 4K 49
N9 2C 34
N19 2J 65
RM9: Dag 4D 72
SE18 3G 107
Cornwallis Sq. N19 2J 65
Cornwallis Wlk. SE9 3D 124
Cornwall Mans. *SW10* 7A 100
(off Cremorne Rd.)
W8 2K 99
(off Kensington Ct.)
W14 3F 99
(off Blythe Rd.)
Cornwall M. Sth. SW7 3A 100
Cornwall M. W. SW7 3K 99
Cornwall Pl. E4 4J 25
Cornwall Rd. CR0: C'don 2B 168
HA1: Harr 6G 41
HA4: Ruis 3H 57
HA5: Hat E 1D 40
N4 7A 48
N15 5D 48
N18 5B 34
SE1 4J 13 (1A 102)
SM2: Sutt 7H 165
TW1: Twick 7A 114
UB8: Uxb 6A 56
Cornwall Sq. SE11 5K 19
Cornwall St. E1 7H 85
Cornwall Ter. NW1 4F 5 (4D 82)
Cornwall Ter. M. NW1 4F 5
Corn Way E11 3F 69
Cornwells Gdns. E10 7C 50
Cornwood Cl. N2 5B 46
Cornwood Dr. E1 6J 85
Cornworthy Rd. RM8: Dag 5C 72
Corona Bldg. *E14* 1E 104
(off Blackwall Way)
Corona Rd. SE12 7J 123
Coronation Av. N16 4F 67
Coronation Cl. DA5: Bexl 6D 126
IG6: Ilf 4G 53
Coronation Ct. DA8: Erith 7K 109
E15 6H 69
KT1: King T 4E 150
(off Surbiton Rd.)
W10 5E 80
(off Brewster Gdns.)
Coronation Rd. E13 3A 88
NW10 3G 79
UB3: Harl 4H 93
Coronation Vs. NW10 4H 79
Coronation Wlk. TW2: Whitt 1E 130
Coroner's Court
City of London 2E 14 (7D 84)
North London 4C 20
Poplar 7D 86
(off Poplar High St.)
St Pancras 1H 83
South London 3D 168
(off Barclay Rd.)
Southwark 2D 102
West London 1A 118
Westminster 3D 18 (4H 101)
Coronet Pde. HA0: Wemb 6E 60
Coronet St. N1 2G 9 (3E 84)
Coronet Theatre 3C 102
(off New Kent Rd.)
Corporate Dr. TW13: Felt 3K 129
Corporate Ho. HA3: Hrw W 1H 41
Corporation Av. TW4: Houn 4C 112
Corporation Row EC1 3K 7 (4A 84)
Corporation St. E15 2G 87
N7 5J 65
Corrance Rd. SW2 4J 119
Corri Av. N14 4C 32
Corrib Ct. N13 3E 32
Corrib Dr. SM1: Sutt 5C 166
Corrigan Cl. NW4 3E 44
Corringham Ct. NW11 7J 45
Corringham Ho. *E1* 6K 85
(off Pitsea St.)
Corringham Rd. HA9: Wemb 2G 61
NW11 7J 45
Corringway NW11 7K 45
W5 4G 79
Corris Grn. NW9 5A 44
Corry Dr. SW9 4B 120
Corry Ho. *E14* 7D 86
(off Wade's Pl.)
Corsair Cl. TW19: Stanw 7A 110
Corsair Rd. TW19: Stanw 7A 110
Corscombe Cl. KT2: King T 5J 133
Corsehill St. SW16 6G 137
Corsellis Sq. *TW1: Isle* 4B 114
(off Varley Dr.)
Corsham St. N1 2F 9 (3D 84)
Corsica St. N5 6B 66
Corsley Way E9 6B 68
Cortayne Ct.
TW2: Twick 2J 131
Cortayne Rd. SW6 2H 117
Cortina Dr. RM13: Rain 2J 91
Cortis Rd. SW15 6D 116
Cortis Ter. SW15 6D 116
Cortland Cl. IG8: Wfd G 1A 52
Corunna Rd. SW8 1G 119
Corunna Ter. SW8 1G 119
Corvette Sq. SE10 6F 105
Corwell Gdns. UB8: Hil 6E 74
Corwell La. UB8: Hil 6E 74
Coryton Path *W9* 4H 81
(off Ashmore Rd.)
Cosbycote Av. SE24 5C 120
Cosdach Av. SM6: Wall 7H 167
Cosedge Cres. CR0: Wadd 5A 168
Cosgrove Cl. N21 2H 33
UB4: Yead 4B 76
Cosgrove Ho. *E2* 1G 85
(off Whiston Rd.)
HA0: Wemb 1E 78
(off Hatton Rd.)
Cosmo Pl. WC1 5F 7 (5J 83)
Cosmopolitan Ct. EN1: Enf 5B 24
Cosmur Cl. W12 3B 98
Cossall Wlk. SE15 2H 121
Cossar M. SW2 5A 120
Cosser St. SE1 1J 19 (3A 102)
Costa St. SE15 2G 121
Costemonger Bldg. *SE16* 3F 103
(off Arts La.)
Costons Av. UB6: G'frd 3H 77
Costons La. UB6: G'frd 3H 77
(not continuous)
Coston Wlk. SE4 4K 121
Cosway Mans. *NW1* 5D 4
(off Shroton St.)
Cosway St. NW1 5D 4 (5C 82)
Cotall St. E14 5C 86
Coteford Cl. HA5: Eastc 5J 39
Coteford St. SW17 4D 136
Cotelands CR0: C'don 3E 168
Cotesbach Rd. E5 3J 67
Cotes Ho. *NW8* 4C 4
(off Broadley St.)
Cotesmore Gdns. RM8: Dag 4C 72
Cotford Rd. CR7: Thor H 4C 156
Cotham St. SE17 4C 102
Cotherstone Ct. *E2* 4H 85
(off Three Colts La.)
Cotherstone Rd. SW2 1K 137
Cotleigh Av. DA5: Bexl 2D 144
Cotleigh Rd. NW6 7J 63
RM7: Rom 6K 55
Cotman Cl. NW11 6A 46
SW15 6F 117
Cotman Gdns. HA8: Edg 2G 43
Cotman Ho. *NW8* 2C 82
(off Townshend Est.)
UB5: N'olt 2B 76
(off Academy Gdns.)
Cotman M. *RM8: Dag* 5C 72
(off Highgrove Rd.)
Cotmans Cl. UB3: Hayes 1J 93
Coton Dr. UB10: Ick 3E 56
Coton Rd. DA16: Well 3A 126
Cotsford Av. KT3: N Mald 5J 151
Cotswold Cl. DA7: Bex 2K 127
KT2: King T 6J 133
Cotswold Cl. KT10: Hin W 2A 162
N11 4K 31
Cotswold Ct. EC1 3C 8
UB6: G'frd 2K 77
(off Hodder Dr.)
Cotswold Gdns. E6 3B 88
IG2: Ilf 7H 53
NW2 2F 63
Cotswold Ga. NW2 1G 63
Cotswold Grn. EN2: Enf 4E 22
Cotswold M. SW11 1B 118
Cotswold Ri. BR6: St M Cry 6K 161
Cotswold Rd. TW12: Hamp 5E 130
Cotswold St. SE27 4B 138
Cotswold Way EN2: Enf 3E 22
KT4: Wor Pk 2E 164
Cottage Av. BR2: Brom 1C 172
Cottage Cl. *E1* 4J 85
(off Mile End Rd.)
HA2: Harr 2H 59
HA4: Ruis 1F 57
Cottage Fld. Cl. DA14: Sidc 1C 144
Cottage Grn. SE5 7D 102
Cottage Gro. KT6: Surb 6D 150
SW9 3J 119
Cottage Pl. SW3 1C 16 (3C 100)
Cottage Rd. KT19: Ewe 7K 163
N7 5K 65
(not continuous)
Cottages, The UB10: Ick 2A 56
Cottage St. E14 7D 86
Cottage Wlk. N16 3F 67
Cottenham Dr. NW9 3B 44
SW20 7D 134
Cottenham Pde. SW20 2D 152
COTTENHAM PARK 1D 152
Cottenham Pk. Rd. SW20 1C 152
(not continuous)
Cottenham Pl. SW20 7D 134
Cottenham Rd. E17 4B 50
Cotterill Rd. KT6: Surb 2E 162
Cottesbrook St. SE14 7A 104
Cottesloe Ho. NW8 3C 4
Cottesloe M. *SE1* 1K 19
(off Emery St.)
Cottesmore Av. IG5: Ilf 2E 52
Cottesmore Ct. *W8* 3K 99
(off Stanford Rd.)
Cottesmore Gdns. W8 3K 99
Cottesmore Ho. UB10: Ick 2E 56
Cottimore Av. KT12: Walt T 7K 147
Cottimore Cres. KT12: Walt T 7K 147
Cottimore La. KT12: Walt T 7K 147
Cottimore Ter. KT12: Walt T 7K 147
Cottingham Chase HA4: Ruis 3J 57
Cottingham Rd. SE20 7K 139
SW8 7K 101
Cottington Rd. TW13: Hanw 4B 130
Cottington St. SE11 5K 19 (5A 102)
Cottle Way *SE16* 2H 103
(off Paradise St.)
Cotton Apartments *E1* 5K 85
(off Killick Way)
Cotton Av. W3 6K 79
Cotton Cl. CR4: Mitc 3C 154
E11 2G 69
RM9: Dag 7C 72
Cottongrass Cl. CR0: C'don 1K 169
Cottonham Cl. N12 5G 31
Cotton Hill BR1: Brom 4E 140
Cotton Ho. SW2 7J 119
Cotton Row SW11 3A 118
Cottons App. RM7: Rom 5K 55
Cottons Cen. SE1 4G 15 (1E 102)
Cottons Ct. RM7: Rom 5K 55
Cotton's Gdns. E2 1H 9 (3E 84)
Cottons La. SE1 4F 15 (1D 102)
Cotton St. E14 7E 86
Cottrell Ct. *SE10* 4H 105
(off Hop St.)
Cottrill Gdns. E8 6H 67

A-Z London 239

Cotts Cl. W7 5K **77**
Couchmore Av. IG5: Ilf 2D **52**
Coulgate St. SE4 3A **122**
Coulson Cl. RM8: Dag 1C **72**
Coulson St. SW3 5E **16** (5D **100**)
Coulter Cl. UB4: Yead 4C **76**
Coulter Rd. W6 3D **98**
Coulthurst Ct. *SW16* *7J* ***137***
(off Heybridge Av.)
Councillor St. SE5 7C **102**
Counter Ct. *SE1* *5E* ***14***
(off Borough High St.)
Counters Ct. *W14* *3G* ***99***
(off Holland Rd.)
Counter St. SE1 5G **15** (1E **102**)
Countess Rd. NW5 5G **65**
Countisbury Av. EN1: Enf 7A **24**
Country Way TW13: Hanw 6K **129**
County Court
Brentford 6D **96**
Bromley 1J **159**
Central London 4J **5**
Clerkenwell and Shoreditch
3C **8** (4C **84**)
Croydon 2D **168**
Edmonton 6B **34**
Kingston upon Thames 2D **150**
Uxbridge 5H **75**
Wandsworth 5G **117**
West London *5F* ***99***
(off Talgarth Rd.)
Willesden 2B **80**
Woolwich 3E **106**
County Gdns. TW7: Isle 4H **113**
County Ga. EN5: New Bar 6E **20**
SE9 3G **143**
County Ground, The
Beckenham 6C **140**
County Gro. SE5 1C **120**
County Hall Apartments SE1 6G **13**
County Hall (Former) *6G* ***13***
(off Westminster Bri. Rd.)
County Ho. BR3: Beck 1A **158**
SW9 *1A* ***120***
(off Brixton Rd.)
County Pde. TW8: Bford 7D **96**
County Rd. CR7: Thor H 2B **156**
E6 5F **89**
County St. SE1 3C **102**
Coupland Pl. SE18 5G **107**
Courage Stadium 5K **159**
Courcy Rd. N8 3A **48**
Courier Rd. RM9: Dag 4J **91**
Courland Gro. SW8 1H **119**
Courland St. SW8 1H **119**
Course, The SE9 3E **142**
Court, The HA4: Ruis 4C **58**
Court Annexe 7D **14** (2C **102**)
Courtauld Cl. SE28 1A **108**
Courtauld Gallery 2G **13**
Courtauld Ho. *E2* *1G* ***85***
(off Goldsmiths Row)
Courtauld Rd. N19 1J **65**
Court Av. DA17: Belv 5F **109**
Court Cl. HA3: Kenton 3E **42**
NW8 *7B* ***64***
(off Boydell Ct.)
SM6: Wall 7H **167**
TW2: Twick 3F **131**
Court Cl. Av. TW2: Twick 3F **131**
Court Cres. KT9: Chess 5D **162**
Court Downs Rd. BR3: Beck 2D **158**
Court Dr. CR0: Wadd 4K **167**
HA7: Stan 4K **27**
SM1: Sutt 4C **166**
UB10: Hil 1B **74**
Courtenay Av. HA3: Hrw W 7B **26**
N6 7C **46**
SM2: Sutt 7J **165**
Courtenay Dr. BR3: Beck 2F **159**
Courtenay Gdns. HA3: Hrw W 2G **41**
Courtenay Ho. *CR0: C'don* *7C* ***156***
(off Oakfield Rd.)
Courtenay M. E17 5A **50**
Courtenay Pl. E17 5A **50**
Courtenay Rd. E11 3H **69**
E17 4K **49**
HA9: Wemb 3D **60**
KT4: Wor Pk 3E **164**
SE20 6K **139**
Courtenay Sq. SE11 6J **19** (5A **102**)
Courtenay St. SE11 5J **19** (5A **102**)
Courtens M. HA7: Stan 7H **27**
Court Farm Av. KT19: Ewe 5K **163**
Court Farm La. UB5: N'olt 7E **58**
Court Farm Rd. SE9 2B **142**
UB5: N'olt 7E **58**
Courtfield W5 5C **78**
Courtfield Av. HA1: Harr 5K **41**
Courtfield Cres. HA1: Harr 5K **41**
Courtfield Gdns. HA4: Ruis 2H **57**
SW5 4K **99**
W13 6A **78**
Courtfield Ho. *EC1* *5J* ***7***
(off Baldwins Gdns.)
Courtfield M. SW5 4A **100**
Courtfield Ri. BR4: W W'ck 3F **171**
Courtfield Rd. SW7 4A **100**
TW15: Ashf 6D **128**
Court Gdns. N1 6A **66**
N7 6A **66**
Courtgate Cl. NW7 6G **29**
Courthill Rd. SE13 4E **122**
Courthope Ho. *SE16* *3J* ***103***
(off Lower Rd.)
SW8 *7J* ***101***
(off Hartington Rd.)
Courthope Rd. NW3 4D **64**
SW19 5G **135**
UB6: G'frd 2H **77**
Courthope Vs. SW19 7G **135**
Courthouse, The *SW1* *2D* ***18***
(off Horseferry Rd.)
Courthouse Gdns. N3 6D **30**
Courthouse La. N16 4F **67**
Courthouse Rd. N12 6E **30**
Courtland Av. E4 2C **36**
IG1: Ilf 2D **70**
NW7 3E **28**
SW16 7K **137**
Courtland Gro. SE28 6D **90**
Courtland Rd. E6 1C **88**
Courtlands KT12: Walt T 7J **147**
TW10: Rich 5G **115**
Courtlands Av. BR2: Hayes 1G **171**
SE12 5K **123**
TW9: Kew 2H **115**
TW12: Hamp 6D **130**
Courtlands Cl. HA4: Ruis 7H **39**
Courtlands Dr. KT19: Ewe 6A **164**
Courtlands Rd. KT5: Surb 7G **151**
Court La. SE21 6E **120**
Court La. Gdns. SE21 7E **120**
Courtleet Dr. DA8: Erith 1H **127**
Courtleigh NW11 5H **45**
Courtleigh Gdns. NW11 4G **45**
Court Lodge DA17: Belv 5G **109**
SW1 *4G* ***17***
(off Sloane Sq.)
Courtman Rd. N17 7H **33**
Court Mead UB5: N'olt 3D **76**
Courtmead Cl. SE24 6C **120**
Courtnell St. W2 6J **81**
Courtney Cl. SE19 6E **138**
Courtney Ct. N7 5A **66**
Courtney Cres.
SM5: Cars 7D **166**
Courtney Ho. *NW4* *3E* ***44***
(off Mulberry Cl.)
W14 *3G* ***99***
(off Russell Rd.)
Courtney Pl. CR0: Wadd 3A **168**
Courtney Rd. CR0: Wadd 3A **168**
N7 5A **66**
SW19 7C **136**
TW6: H'row A 3C **110**
Courtney Way TW6: H'row A 2C **110**
Court Pde. HA0: Wemb 3B **60**
Courtrai Rd. SE23 6A **122**
Court Rd. SE9 6D **124**
SE25 2F **157**
UB2: S'hall 4D **94**
UB10: Ick 5D **56**
Court Royal SW15 5G **117**
Courtside N8 6H **47**
SE26 3H **139**
Court St. BR1: Brom 2J **159**
E1 5H **85**
Courtville Ho. *W10* *3G* ***81***
(off Third Av.)
Court Way NW9 4A **44**
TW2: Twick 7K **113**
W3 5J **79**
Courtway IG6: Ilf 3G **53**
IG8: Wfd G 5F **37**
Courtwood La. CR0: Sels 7B **170**
Court Yd. SE9 6D **124**
Courtyard *SW3* *5E* ***16***
(off Smith St.)
Courtyard, The BR2: Kes 6C **172**
E2 *1K* ***9***
(off Ezra St.)
EC3 *1F* ***15***
(within Royal Exchange)
N1 7K **65**
NW1 7E **64**
SE14 *1K* ***121***
(off Besson St.)
SW3 *7B* ***16***
(off Trident Pl.)
Courtyard Apartments *E1* *3K* ***9***
(off Sclater St.)
Courtyard Ho. *SW6* *2A* ***118***
(off Lensbury Av.)
Courtyard M. BR5: St P 7A **144**
Courtyard Theatre
Shoreditch 2G **9** (3E **84**)
Cousin La. EC4 3E **14** (7D **84**)
Cousins Cl. UB7: Yiew 7A **74**
Couthurst Rd. SE3 6K **105**
Coutts Av. KT9: Chess 5E **162**
Coutt's Cres. NW5 3E **64**
Couzens Ho. *E3* *5B* ***86***
(off Weatherley Cl.)
Coval Gdns. SW14 4H **115**
Coval La. SW14 4H **115**
Coval Pas. SW14 4J **115**
Coval Rd. SW14 4H **115**
Covelees Wall E6 6E **88**
Covell Ct. *EN2: Enf* *1E* ***22***
(off The Ridgeway)
SE8 7C **104**
COVENT GARDEN 2F **13** (7J **83**)
Covent Garden 2F **13** (7J **83**)
Covent Gdn. WC2 2F **13** (7J **83**)
Coventry Cl. E6 6D **88**
NW6 2J **81**
Coventry Hall SW16 5J **137**
Coventry Rd. E1 4H **85**
E2 4H **85**
IG1: Ilf 2F **71**
SE25 4G **157**
Coventry St. W1 3C **12** (7H **83**)
Coverack Cl. CR0: C'don 7A **158**
N14 6B **22**
Coverdale Cl. HA7: Stan 5G **27**
Coverdale Gdns. CR0: C'don 3F **169**
Coverdale Rd. N11 6K **31**
NW2 7F **63**
W12 2D **98**
Coverdales, The IG11: Bark 2H **89**
Coverham Ho. *SE4* *4K* ***121***
(off Billingford Cl.)
Coverley Cl. E1 5G **85**
Coverley Point SE11 4G **19**
Covert, The BR6: Pet W 6J **161**
HA6: Nwood 1E **38**
SE19 *7F* ***139***
(off Fox Hill)
Coverton Rd. SW17 5C **136**
Covert Way EN4: Had W 2F **21**
Covet Wood Cl. BR5: St M Cry 6K **161**
Covey Cl. SW19 2K **153**
Covey Rd. KT4: Wor Pk 2F **165**
Covington Gdns. SW16 7B **138**
Covington Way SW16 6K **137**
(not continuous)
Cowan Cl. E6 5C **88**
Cowbridge La. IG11: Bark 7F **71**
Cowbridge Rd. HA3: Kenton 4F **43**
Cowcross St. EC1 5A **8** (5B **84**)
Cowdenbeath Path N1 1K **83**
Cowden Rd. BR6: Orp 7K **161**
Cowden St. SE6 4C **140**
Cowdray Rd. UB10: Hil 1E **74**
Cowdrey Cl. EN1: Enf 2K **23**
Cowdrey M. SE6 4C **140**
Cowdrey Rd. SW19 5K **135**
Cowen Av. HA2: Harr 2H **59**
Cowgate Rd. UB6: G'frd 3H **77**
Cowick Rd. SW17 4D **136**
Cowings Mead UB5: N'olt 6C **58**
Cowland Av. EN3: Pond E 4D **24**
Cow La. UB6: G'frd 2H **77**
Cow Leaze E6 6E **88**
Cowleaze Rd. KT2: King T 1E **150**
COWLEY 4A **74**
Cowley La. E11 3G **69**
COWLEY PEACHEY 6A **74**
Cowley Pl. NW4 5E **44**
Cowley Rd. E11 5K **51**
IG1: Ilf 7D **52**
SW9 1A **120**
(not continuous)
SW14 3A **116**
W3 1B **98**
Cowley St. SW1 1E **18** (3J **101**)
Cowling Cl. W11 1G **99**
Cowper Av. E6 7C **70**
SM1: Sutt 4B **166**
Cowper Cl. BR2: Brom 4B **160**
DA16: Well 5A **126**
Cowper Gdns. N14 6A **22**
SM6: Wall 6G **167**
Cowper Ho. *SE17* *5C* ***102***
(off Browning St.)
SW1 *6C* ***18***
(off Aylesford St.)
Cowper Rd. BR2: Brom 4B **160**
DA17: Belv 4G **109**
KT2: King T 5F **133**
N14 1A **32**
N16 5E **66**
N18 5B **34**
SW19 6A **136**
W3 1K **97**
W7 7K **77**
Cowper's Ct. *EC3* *1F* ***15***
(off Birchin La.)
Cowper St. EC2 3F **9** (4D **84**)
Cowper Ter. W10 5F **81**
Cowslip Cl. UB10: Uxb 7A **56**
Cowslip Rd. E18 2K **51**
Cowthorpe Rd. SW8 1H **119**
Cox Ct. EN4: E Barn 4H **21**
Coxe Pl. HA3: W'stone 4A **42**
Cox Ho. *W6* *6G* ***99***
(off Field Rd.)
Cox La. KT9: Chess 4F **163**
KT19: Ewe 5H **163**
(not continuous)
Coxmount Rd. SE7 5B **106**
Coxs Av. TW17: Shep 3G **147**
Coxson Way SE1 7J **15** (2F **103**)

Cox's Wlk.—Crawshay Rd.

Cox's Wlk. SE21 1G 139
Coxwell Rd. SE18 5H 107
SE19 7E 138
Coxwold Path KT9: Chess 7E 162
Coyle Dr. UB10: Ick 2E 56
Crabbs Cft. Cl. BR6: Farnb 5G 173
Crab Hill BR3: Beck 7F 141
Crabtree Av. HA0: Wemb 2E 78
RM6: Chad H 4D 54
Crabtree Cl. E2 2F 85
Crabtree Ct. EN5: New Bar 4E 20
Crabtree Hall SW6 7E 98
(off Crabtree La.)
Crabtree La. SW6 7E 98
(not continuous)
Crabtree Manorway Nth.
DA17: Belv, Erith 2J 109
Crabtree Manorway Sth.
DA17: Belv 3J 109
Crabtree Pl. W1 6C 6 (5G 83)
Crabtree Wlk. CR0: C'don 1G 169
Crace St. NW1 1C 6 (3H 83)
Craddock Rd. EN1: Enf 3A 24
Craddock St. NW5 6E 64
Cradford Ho. Nth. E2 3K 85
Cradford Ho. Sth. E2 3K 85
Cradley Rd. SE9 1H 143
Crafts Council & Gallery 2A 84
Cragie Ho. SE1 4F 103
(off Balaclava Rd.)
Craig Dr. UB8: Hil 6D 74
Craigen Av. CR0: C'don 1H 169
Craigen Gdns. IG3: Ilf 4J 71
Craigerne Rd. SE3 7K 105
Craig Gdns. E18 2H 51
Craigholm SE18 2E 124
Craig Ho. E17 4C 50
(off High St.)
Craigmore Ct. HA6: Nwood 1G 39
Craigmuir Pk. HA0: Wemb 1F 79
Craignair Rd. SW2 7A 120
Craignish Av. SW16 2K 155
Craig Pk. Rd. N18 4C 34
Craig Rd. TW10: Ham 4C 132
Craig's Ct. SW1 4E 12 (1J 101)
Craigton Rd. SE9 4D 124
Craigweil Cl. HA7: Stan 5J 27
Craigweil Dr. HA7: Stan 5J 27
Craigwell Av. TW13: Felt 3J 129
Craik Ct. NW6 2H 81
(off Carlton Vale)
Crail Row SE17 4D 102
Crales Ho. SE18 3C 106
Cramer St. W1 6H 5 (5E 82)
Crammond Cl. W6 6G 99
Cramond Ct. TW14: Bedf 1G 129
Cramonde Ct. DA16: Well 2A 126
Crampton Ho. SW8 1G 119
Crampton Rd. SE20 6J 139
Crampton St. SE17 4C 102
Cranberry Cl. UB5: N'olt 2B 76
Cranberry Ent. Pk. N17 7A 34
(off White Hart La.)
Cranberry La. E16 4G 87
Cranborne Av. KT6: Surb 3G 163
UB2: S'hall 4E 94
Cranborne Rd. IG11: Bark 1H 89
Cranborne Waye UB4: Yead 6K 75
(not continuous)
Cranbourn All. WC2 2D 12
(off Cranbourn St.)
Cranbourne NW1 7H 65
(off Agar Gro.)
Cranbourne Av. E11 4K 51
Cranbourne Cl. SW16 3J 155
Cranbourne Ct. SW11 7C 100
(off Albert Bri. Rd.)
Cranbourne Dr. HA5: Pinn 5B 40
Cranbourne Gdns. IG6: Ilf 3G 53
NW11 5G 45
Cranbourne Pas. SE16 2H 103
Cranbourne Rd. E12 5C 70
E15 4E 68
HA6: Nwood 3H 39
N10 2F 47
Cranbourn Ho. SE16 2H 103
(off Marigold St.)
Cranbourn St. WC2 2D 12 (7H 83)
CRANBROOK 1D 70
Cranbrook NW1 1G 83
(off Camden St.)
Cranbrook Castle Tennis Club 7D 52
Cranbrook Cl. BR2: Hayes 6J 159
Cranbrook Ct. CR2: S Croy 5E 168
TW8: Bford 6C 96
Cranbrook Dr. KT10: Esh 7G 149
TW2: Whitt 1F 131
Cranbrook Est. E2 2K 85
Cranbrook La. N11 4A 32
Cranbrook M. E17 5B 50
Cranbrook Pk. N22 1A 48
Cranbrook Ri. IG1: Ilf 6D 52
Cranbrook Rd. CR7: Thor H 2C 156
DA7: Bex 1F 127
EN4: E Barn 6G 21
IG1: Ilf 7E 52
IG2: Ilf 5E 52
IG6: Ilf 5E 52
SE8 1C 122
SW19 7G 135
TW4: Houn 4D 112
W4 5A 98
Cranbrook St. E2 2K 85
Cranbury Rd. SW6 2K 117
Crandley Ct. SE8 4A 104
(not continuous)
Crane Av. TW7: Isle 5A 114
W3 7J 79
Cranebank M. TW1: Twick 4A 114
Cranebank (Nature Reserve) 2J 111
Cranebrook TW2: Twick 2G 131
Crane Cl. HA2: Harr 3G 59
RM10: Dag 6G 73
Crane Ct. EC4 6A 84
KT19: Ewe 4J 163
SW14 4J 115
Craneford Cl. TW2: Twick 7K 113
Craneford Way TW2: Twick 7J 113
Crane Gdns. UB3: Harl 4H 93
Crane Gro. N7 6A 66
Crane Hgts. N17 3H 49
(off Waterside Way)
Crane Ho. E3 2A 86
(off Roman Rd.)
SE15 1F 121
TW13: Hanw 3E 130
Crane Lodge Rd. TW5: Cran 6K 93
Crane Mead SE16 5J 103
Crane Mead Ct. TW1: Twick 7K 113
Crane Pk. Island Nature Reserve 2D 130
Crane Pk. Rd. TW2: Whitt 2F 131
Crane Rd. TW2: Twick 1J 131
TW19: Stanw 6C 110
Cranesbill Cl. NW9 3K 43
SW16 2H 155
Cranes Dr. KT5: Surb 4E 150
Cranes Pk. KT5: Surb 4E 150
Cranes Pk. Av. KT5: Surb 4E 150
Cranes Pk. Cres. KT5: Surb 4F 151
Crane St. SE10 5F 105
SE15 1F 121
Craneswater UB3: Harl 7H 93
Craneswater Pk. UB2: S'hall 5D 94
Crane Way TW2: Whitt 7G 113
Cranfield Cl. SE27 3C 138
Cranfield Ct. W1 6D 4
Cranfield Dr. NW9 7F 29
Cranfield Ho. WC1 5E 6
Cranfield Rd. SE4 3B 122
Cranfield Rd. E. SM5: Cars 7E 166
Cranfield Rd. W. SM5: Cars 7E 166
Cranfield Row SE1 1K 19
Cranfield Wlk. SE3 3K 123
CRANFORD 7J 93
Cranford Av. N13 5D 32
TW19: Stanw 7A 110
Cranford Cl. SW20 7D 134
TW19: Stanw 7A 110
Cranford Community College Sports Cen.
6K 93
Cranford Cotts. E1 7K 85
(off Cranford St.)
Cranford Dr. UB3: Harl 4H 93
Cranford La. TW5: Cran, Hest 7K 93
TW6: H'row A 1H 111
(Bath Rd.)
TW6: H'row A 3H 111
(Elmdon Rd.)
UB3: Cran, Harl 6F 93
Cranford M. BR2: Brom 5C 160
Cranford Pk. Rd. UB3: Harl 4H 93
Cranford St. E1 7K 85
Cranford Way N8 4K 47
Cranhurst Rd. NW2 5E 62
Cranleigh W11 1H 99
(off Ladbroke Rd.)
Cranleigh Cl. BR6: Chels 3K 173
DA5: Bexl 6H 127
SE20 2H 157
Cranleigh Ct. CR4: Mitc 3B 154
TW9: Rich 3G 115
UB1: S'hall 6D 76
Cranleigh Gdns. HA3: Kenton 5E 42
IG11: Bark 7H 71
KT2: King T 6F 133
N21 5F 23
SE25 3E 156
SM1: Sutt 2K 165
UB1: S'hall 6D 76
Cranleigh Gdns. Ind. Est.
UB1: S'hall 6D 76
Cranleigh Ho's. NW1 2G 83
(off Cranleigh St.)
Cranleigh M. SW11 2C 118
Cranleigh Rd. N15 5C 48
SW19 3J 153
TW13: Felt 4H 129
Cranleigh St. NW1 2G 83
Cranley Dene Ct. N10 4F 47
Cranley Dr. HA4: Ruis 2H 57
IG2: Ilf 7G 53
CRANLEY GARDENS 4F 47
Cranley Gdns. N10 4F 47
N13 3E 32
SM6: Wall 7G 167
SW7 5A 16 (5A 100)
Cranley M. SW7 5A 16 (5A 100)
Cranley Pde. SE9 4C 142
(off Beaconsfield Rd.)
Cranley Pl. SW7 4A 16 (4B 100)
Cranley Rd. E13 5K 87
IG2: Ilf 6G 53
Cranmer Av. W13 3B 96
Cranmer Cl. HA4: Ruis 1B 58
HA7: Stan 7H 27
SM4: Mord 6F 153
Cranmer Ct. N3 2G 45
SW3 4D 16 (4C 100)
SW4 3H 119
TW12: Hamp H 5F 131
Cranmere Ct. EN2: Enf 2F 23
Cranmer Farm Cl. CR4: Mitc 4D 154
Cranmer Gdns. RM10: Dag 4J 73
Cranmer Ho. SW9 7A 102
(off Cranmer Rd.)
SW11 1C 118
(off Surrey La. Est.)
Cranmer Rd. CR0: C'don 3B 168
CR4: Mitc 4D 154
E7 4K 69
HA8: Edg 3C 28
KT2: King T 5E 132
SW9 7A 102
Cranmer Rd. TW12: Hamp H 5F 131
UB3: Hayes 6F 75
Cranmer Ter. SW17 5B 136
Cranmore Av. TW7: Isle 7G 95
Cranmore Rd. BR1: Brom 3H 141
BR7: Chst 5D 142
Cranmore Way N10 4G 47
Cranston Cl. TW3: Houn 2C 112
UB10: Ick 2F 57
Cranston Est. N1 2D 84
Cranston Gdns. E4 6J 35
Cranston Rd. SE23 1A 140
Cranswick Rd. SE16 5H 103
Crantock Rd. SE6 2D 140
Cranwell Gro. TW17: Shep 4B 146
Cranwell Rd. TW6: H'row A 2D 110
Cranwich Av. N21 7J 23
Cranwich Rd. N16 7D 48
Cranwood Ct. EC1 2F 9
Cranwood St. EC1 2E 8 (3D 84)
Cranworth Cres. E4 1A 36
Cranworth Gdns. SW9 1A 120
Craster Rd. SW2 7K 119
Crathie Rd. SE12 6K 123
Cravan Av. TW13: Felt 2J 129
Craven Av. UB1: S'hall 5D 76
W5 7C 78
Craven Cl. N16 7G 49
UB4: Hayes 6J 75
Craven Cottage 2F 117
Craven Ct. NW10 1A 80
RM6: Chad H 6E 54
Craven Gdns. IG6: Ilf 2H 53
IG11: Bark 2J 89
SW19 5J 135
Craven Hill W2 7A 82
Craven Hill Gdns. W2 7A 82
(not continuous)
Craven Hill M. W2 7A 82
Craven Ho. N2 2B 46
(off High Rd. E. Finchley)
Craven Lodge SW6 1F 117
(off Harbord St.)
W2 7A 82
(off Craven Hill)
Craven M. SW11 3E 118
Craven Pk. NW10 1K 79
Craven Pk. M. NW10 7A 62
Craven Pk. Rd. N15 6F 49
NW10 1A 80
Craven Pas. WC2 4E 12
(off Craven St.)
Craven Rd. CR0: C'don 1H 169
KT2: King T 1F 151
NW10 1K 79
W2 1A 10 (7A 82)
W5 7C 78
Craven St. WC2 4E 12 (1J 101)
Craven Ter. W2 2A 10 (7A 82)
Craven Wlk. N16 7G 49
Crawford Av. HA0: Wemb 5D 60
Crawford Bldgs. W1 6D 4
(off Homer St.)
Crawford Cl. TW7: Isle 2J 113
Crawford Ct. NW9 3A 44
(off Charcot Rd.)
Crawford Est. SE5 2C 120
Crawford Gdns. N13 3G 33
UB5: N'olt 3D 76
Crawford Mans. W1 6D 4
(off Crawford St.)
Crawford M. W1 6E 4 (5D 82)
Crawford Pas. EC1 4K 7 (4A 84)
Crawford Pl. W1 7D 4 (6C 82)
Crawford Rd. SE5 1C 120
Crawford St. NW10 7K 61
W1 6E 4 (5C 82)
Crawley Rd. E10 1D 68
EN1: Enf 7K 23
N22 2C 48
Crawshay Rd. SW9 1A 120

Crawthew Gro. SE22 4F 121
Craybrooke Rd. DA14: Sidc 4B 144
Craybury End SE9 2G 143
Crayfields Bus. Pk. BR5: St P 7C 144
CRAYFORD 5K 127
Crayford Cl. E6 6C 88
Crayford Ho. *SE1* *7F 15*
(off Long La.)
Crayford M. N7 4J 65
Crayford Rd. N7 4H 65
Cray Ho. *NW8* *5B 4*
(off Penfold St.)
Crayke Hill KT9: Chess 7E 162
Crayle Ho. *EC1* *3B 8*
(off Malta St.)
Crayleigh Ter. DA14: Sidc 6C 144
Crayonne Cl. TW16: Sun 1G 147
Cray Rd. DA14: Sidc 6C 144
DA17: Belv 6G 109
Cray Valley Golf Course 7E 144
Cray Valley Rd. BR5: St M Cry 5K 161
Cray Wanderers FC 5K 159
Crayzee Barn 2F 145
Crealock Gro. IG8: Wfd G 5C 36
Crealock St. SW18 6K 117
Creasy Est. SE1 3E 102
Creative Ho. *SW8* *7F 101*
(off Prince of Wales Dr.)
Creative Rd. SE8 7D 104
Crebor St. SE22 6G 121
Crecy Ct. *SE11* *5J 19*
(off Hotspur St.)
Credenhall Dr. BR2: Brom 1D 172
Credenhill Ho. SE15 7H 103
Credenhill St. SW16 6G 137
Crediton Hgts. *NW10* *1F 81*
(off Okehampton Rd.)
Crediton Hill NW6 5K 63
Crediton Rd. E16 6J 87
NW10 1F 81
Crediton Way KT10: Clay 5A 162
Credon Rd. E13 2A 88
SE16 5H 103
Creechurch La. EC3 1H 15 (6E 84)
(not continuous)
Creechurch Pl. EC3 1H 15
Creed Ct. E1 3A 86
EC4 1B 14
Creed La. EC4 1B 14 (6B 84)
Creek, The TW16: Sun 5J 147
Creek Cotts. *KT8: E Mos* *4J 149*
(off Creek Rd.)
Creek Ho. *W14* *3G 99*
(off Russell Rd.)
CREEKMOUTH 4K 89
Creekmouth Ind. Pk. IG11: Bark 4K 89
Creek Rd. IG11: Bark 3K 89
KT8: E Mos 4J 149
SE8 6C 104
SE10 6C 104
Creekside SE8 7D 104
Creekside Discovery Cen. 7D 104
Creekside Foyer *SE8* *6D 104*
(off Stowage)
Creek Way RM13: Rain 5K 91
Creeland Gro. SE6 1B 140
Crefeld Cl. W6 6G 99
Creffield Rd. W3 7F 79
W5 7F 79
Creighton Av. E6 2B 88
N2 3C 46
N10 3C 46
Creighton Cl. W12 7C 80
Creighton Rd. N17 7K 33
NW6 2F 81
W5 3D 96
Cremer Bus. Cen. *E2* *1J 9*
(off Cremer St.)
Cremer Ho. *SE8* *7C 104*
(off Deptford Chu. St.)
Cremer St. E2 1J 9 (2F 85)
Cremorne Est. SW10 6B 100
(not continuous)
Cremorne Riverside Cen. 7B 100
Cremorne Rd. SW10 7A 100
Creon Ct. *SW9* *7A 102*
(off Caldwell St.)
Crescent EC3 2J 15 (7F 85)
Crescent, The BR3: Beck 1C 158
BR4: W W'ck 6G 159
CR0: C'don 5D 156
DA5: Bexl 7C 126
DA14: Sidc 4K 143
E17 6A 50
EN5: New Bar 2E 20
HA0: Wemb 2B 60
HA2: Harr 1G 59
IG2: Ilf 6E 52
KT3: N Mald 3J 151
KT6: Surb 5E 150
KT8: W Mole 4E 148
N9 2C 34
N11 4J 31
NW2 3D 62
SE8 *1C 122*
(off Seager Pl.)
SM1: Sutt 5B 166
SW13 2B 116
SW19 3J 135
TW15: Ashf 5B 128
TW17: Shep 7H 147
UB1: S'hall 2D 94
UB3: Harl 7E 92
W3 6A 80
W12 1E 98
Crescent Arc. *SE10* *6E 104*
(off Creek Rd.)
Crescent Ct. KT6: Surb 5D 150
SW4 *5H 119*
(off Park Hill)
Crescent Ct. Bus. Cen. E16 4F 87
Crescent Dr. BR5: Pet W 5F 161
Crescent E. EN4: Had W 1F 21
Crescent Gdns. HA4: Ruis 7K 39
SW19 3J 135
Crescent Gro. CR4: Mitc 4C 154
SW4 4G 119
Crescent Ho. *EC1* *4C 8*
(off Golden La. Est.)
SE13 2D 122
Crescent La. SW4 4G 119
Crescent Mans. *SW3* *4C 16*
(off Fulham Rd.)
W11 *7G 81*
(off Elgin Cres.)
Crescent M. N22 1J 47
Crescent Pde. UB10: Hil 3C 74
Crescent Pl. SW3 3D 16 (4C 100)
Crescent Ri. EN4: E Barn 5H 21
N3 1H 45
N22 1H 47
Crescent Rd. BR1: Brom 7J 141
BR3: Beck 2D 158
DA15: Sidc 3K 143
E4 1B 36
E6 1A 88
E10 2D 68
E13 1J 87
E18 1A 52
EN2: Enf 4G 23
EN4: E Barn 4G 21
KT2: King T 7G 133
N3 1H 45
N8 6H 47
N9 1B 34
N11 4J 31
N15 3B 48
N22 1H 47
RM10: Dag 3H 73
SE18 5F 107
SW20 1F 153
TW17: Shep 5E 146
Crescent Row EC1 4C 8 (4C 84)
Crescent Stables SW15 5G 117
Crescent St. N1 7K 65
Crescent Way BR6: Orp 5J 173
N12 6H 31
SE4 3C 122
SW16 6K 137
Crescent W. EN4: Had W 1F 21
Crescent Wharf E16 2K 105
(not continuous)
Crescent Wood Rd. SE26 3G 139
Cresford Rd. SW6 1K 117
Crespigny Rd. NW4 6D 44
Cressage Cl. UB1: S'hall 4E 76
Cressage Ho. *TW8: Bford* *6E 96*
(off Ealing Rd.)
Cressal Ho. *E14* *3C 104*
(off Tiller Rd.)
Cresset Ho. E9 6J 67
Cresset Rd. E9 6J 67
Cresset St. SW4 3H 119
Cressfield Cl. NW5 5E 64
Cressida Rd. N19 1G 65
Cressingham Gro. SM1: Sutt 4A 166
Cressingham Rd. HA8: Edg 6E 28
SE13 3E 122
Cressington Cl. N16 5E 66
Cress M. BR1: Brom 5F 141
Cresswell Gdns. SW5 5A 100
Cresswell Ho. HA9: Wemb 3E 60
TW19: Stanw *6A 110*
(off Douglas Rd.)
Cresswell Pk. SE3 3H 123
Cresswell Pl. SW10 5A 100
Cresswell Rd. SE25 4G 157
TW1: Twick 6D 114
TW13: Hanw 3C 130
Cresswell Way N21 7F 23
Cressy Ct. E1 5J 85
W6 3D 98
Cressy Ho. SW15 3D 116
Cressy Ho's. *E1* *5J 85*
(off Hannibal Rd.)
Cressy Pl. E1 5J 85
Cressy Rd. NW3 5D 64
Crest, The KT5: Surb 5G 151
N13 4F 33
NW4 5E 44
Cresta Ct. W5 4F 79
Cresta Ho. *E3* *4C 86*
(off Dimson Cres.)
NW3 *7B 64*
(off Finchley Rd.)
Crestbrook Av. N13 3G 33
Crestbrook Pl. *N13* *3G 33*
(off Green Lanes)
Crest Ct. NW4 5E 44
Crest Dr. EN3: Enf W 1D 24
Crested Ct. NW9 7B 44
Crestfield St. WC1 1F 7 (3J 83)
Crest Gdns. HA4: Ruis 3A 58
Creston Way KT4: Wor Pk 1F 165
Crest Rd. BR2: Hayes 7H 159
CR2: Sels 7H 169
NW2 2B 62
Crest Vw. HA5: Pinn 4B 40
Crest Vw. Dr. BR5: Pet W 5F 161
Crest Way E18 2A 52
Crestway SW15 6C 116
Crestwood Way TW4: Houn 5C 112
Creswell Dr. BR3: Beck 5D 158
Creswick Ct. W3 7H 79
Creswick Rd. W3 7H 79
Creswick Wlk. E3 3C 86
NW11 4H 45
Creton St. SE18 3E 106
Creukhorne Rd. NW10 7A 62
Crewdson Rd. SW9 7A 102
Crewe Pl. NW10 3B 80
Crewkerne Ct. *SW11* *1B 118*
(off Bolingbroke Wlk.)
Crews St. E14 4C 104
Crewys Rd. NW2 2H 63
SE15 2H 121
Crichton Av. SM6: Bedd 5H 167
Crichton Ho. DA14: Sidc 6D 144
Crichton Rd. SM5: Cars 6D 166
Crichton St. SW8 2G 119
Crick Ct. *IG11: Bark* *2G 89*
(off Spring Pl.)
Cricketers Arms Rd. EN2: Enf 2H 23
Cricketers Cl. DA8: Erith 5K 109
KT9: Chess 4D 162
N14 7B 22
Cricketers Ct. *SE11* *4B 102*
(off Kennington La.)
Cricketers M. SW18 5K 117
Cricketers Ter. SM5: Cars 3C 166
Cricketers Wlk. SE26 5J 139
Cricketfield Rd. E5 4H 67
Cricket Grn. CR4: Mitc 3D 154
Cricket Ground Rd. BR7: Chst 1F 161
Cricket La. BR3: Beck 6A 140
TW12: Hamp H 6G 131
Cricklade Av. SW2 2J 137
Cricklefield Pl. IG1: Ilf 2J 71
CRICKLEWOOD 4F 63
Cricklewood B'way. NW2 3E 62
Cricklewood La. NW2 4F 63
Cridland St. E15 1H 87
Crieff Ct. TW11: Tedd 7C 132
Crieff Rd. SW18 6A 118
Criffel Av. SW2 2H 137
Crimscott St. SE1 3E 102
Crimsworth Rd. SW8 1H 119
Crinan St. N1 2J 83
Cringle St. SW8 7G 101
Crinoline M. E1 5F 85
Cripplegate St. EC2 5D 8 (5C 84)
Cripps Grn. UB4: Yead 4K 75
Crispe Ho. IG11: Bark 2H 89
N1 *1K 83*
(off Barnsbury Est.)
Crispen Rd. TW13: Hanw 4C 130
Crispian Cl. NW10 4A 62
Crispin Cl. CR0: Bedd 2J 167
Crispin Ct. SE17 4E 102
Crispin Cres. CR0: Bedd 3H 167
Crispin Ind. Cen. N18 5D 34
Crispin Lodge N11 5J 31
Crispin M. NW11 5H 45
Crispin Pl. E1 5J 9 (5F 85)
Crispin Rd. HA8: Edg 6D 28
Crispin St. E1 6J 9 (5F 85)
Crispin Way UB8: Hil 4B 74
Crisp Rd. W6 5E 98
Cristie Ct. E16 4H 87
Cristowe Rd. SW6 2H 117
Criterion Bldgs. *KT7: T Ditt* *7B 150*
(off Portsmouth Rd.)
Criterion Ct. *E8* *7F 67*
(off Middleton Rd.)
Criterion M. N19 2H 65
SE24 *5B 120*
(off Shakespeare Rd.)
Criterion Theatre *3C 12*
(off Piccadilly Cir.)
CRITTALLS CORNER 7C 144
Crockerton Rd. SW17 2D 136
Crockham Way SE9 4E 142
Crocus Cl. CR0: C'don 1K 169
Crocus Fld. EN5: Barn 6C 20
Croft, The CR0: C'don 3F 169
E4 2B 36
EN5: Barn 4B 20
HA0: Wemb 5C 60
HA4: Ruis 4A 58
HA5: Pinn 7D 40
HA8: Edg 7C 28
NW10 2B 80
TW5: Hest 6C 94
W5 5E 78

Croft Av. BR4: W W'ck 1E **170**
Croft Cl. BR7: Chst 5D **142**
  DA17: Belv 5F **109**
  NW7 ....3F **29**
  UB3: Harl 7E **92**
  UB10: Hil 7C **56**
Croft Ct. HA4: Ruis 1H **57**
  SE13 ....6E **122**
  SM1: Sutt 2B **166**
Croftdown Rd. NW5 ....3E **64**
Croft End Cl. KT9: Chess 3F **163**
Crofters Cl. TW7: Isle 5H **113**
Crofters Ct. SE8 ....4A **104**
      (off Croft St.)
Crofters Mead CR0: Sels 7B **170**
Crofters Way NW1 ....1H **83**
Croft Gdns. HA4: Ruis 1H **57**
  W7 ....2A **96**
Croft Ho. E17 ....4D **50**
  NW9 ....3B **44**
  W10 ....3G **81**
      (off Third Av.)
Croft Lodge Cl. IG8: Wfd G 6E **36**
Croft M. N12 ....3F **31**
CROFTON 2G **173**
Crofton Av. BR6: Farnb 2G **173**
  DA5: Bexl 7D **126**
  W4 ....7J **97**
Croftongate Way SE4 ....5A **122**
Crofton Gro. E4 ....4A **36**
Crofton Ho. SW3 ....7C **16**
      (off Old Church St.)
Crofton La. BR5: Farnb, Orp, Pet W ...2H **173**
  BR6: Pet W 7H **161**
CROFTON PARK 5B **122**
Crofton Pk. Rd. SE4 ....6B **122**
Crofton Rd. BR6: Farnb, Orp 3E **172**
  E13 ....4K **87**
  SE5 ....1E **120**
Crofton Roman Villa 2J **173**
Crofton Ter. 5A **68**
  TW9: Rich 4F **115**
Crofton Way EN2: Enf 2F **23**
  EN5: New Bar 6E **20**
Croft Rd. BR1: Brom 6J **141**
  EN3: Enf H 1F **25**
  SM1: Sutt 5C **166**
  SW16 ....1A **156**
  SW19 ....7A **136**
Crofts, The TW17: Shep 4G **147**
Crofts Ho. E2 ....2G **85**
      (off Teale St.)
Croftside, The SE25 ....3G **157**
Crofts La. N22 ....7F **33**
Crofts Rd. HA1: Harr 6A **42**
Croft St. E1 ....3K **15** (7G **85**)
Croft St. SE8 ....4A **104**
Crofts Vs. HA1: Harr 6A **42**
Croft Way BR5: Sidc 3J **143**
Croftway NW3 ....4J **63**
  TW10: Ham 3B **132**
Crogsland Rd. NW1 ....7E **64**
Croham Cl. CR2: S Croy 7E **168**
Croham Hurst Golf Course 6F **169**
Croham Mnr. Rd. CR2: S Croy 7E **168**
Croham Mt. CR2: S Croy 7E **168**
Croham Pk. Av. CR2: S Croy 5E **168**
Croham Rd. CR2: S Croy 5D **168**
Croham Valley Rd. CR2: Sels 6G **169**
Croindene Rd. SW16 ....1J **155**
Crokesley Ho. HA8: Edg 2J **43**
      (off Burnt Oak B'way.)
Cromartie Rd. N19 ....7H **47**
Cromarty Ct. SW2 ....5K **119**
Cromarty Ho. E1 ....5A **86**
      (off Ben Jonson Rd.)
Cromarty Rd. HA8: Edg 2C **28**
Cromberdale Ct. N17 ....1G **49**
      (off Spencer Rd.)
Crombie Cl. IG4: Ilf 5D **52**
Crombie M. SW11 ....2C **118**

Crombie Rd. DA15: Sidc 1H **143**
Crome Ho. UB5: N'olt 2C **76**
      (off Parkfield Dr.)
Cromer Cl. UB8: Hil 6E **74**
Cromer Hyde
  SM4: Mord 5K **153**
Crome Rd. NW10 ....6A **62**
Cromer Pl. BR6: Orp 1J **173**
Cromer Rd. E10 ....7F **51**
  EN5: New Bar 4F **21**
  IG8: Wfd G 4D **36**
  N17 ....2G **49**
  RM6: Chad H 6E **54**
  RM7: Rom 6K **55**
  SE25 ....3H **157**
  SW17 ....6E **136**
  TW6: H'row A 2C **110**
Cromer St. WC1 ....2E **6** (3J **83**)
Cromer Ter. E8 ....5G **67**
  RM6: Chad H 5B **54**
Cromer Vs. Rd. SW18 ....6H **117**
Cromford Cl. BR6: Orp 3J **173**
Cromford Path E5 ....4K **67**
Cromford Rd. SW18 ....5J **117**
Cromford Way KT3: N Mald 1K **151**
Cromie Cl. N13 ....3F **33**
Cromlix Cl. BR7: Chst 2F **161**
Crompton Ct. BR2: Brom 3J **159**
      (off St Mark's Sq.)
  SW3 ....3C **16** (4C **100**)
Crompton Ho. SE1 ....3C **102**
      (off County St.)
  W2 ....4A **4**
      (off Hall Pl.)
Crompton Pl. EN3: Enf L 1H **25**
Crompton St. W2 ....4A **4** (4B **82**)
Cromwell Av. BR2: Brom 4K **159**
  KT3: N Mald 5B **152**
  N6 ....1F **65**
  W6 ....5D **98**
Cromwell Cen. IG11: Bark 3A **90**
  NW10 ....3K **79**
Cromwell Cen., The RM8: Dag 7F **55**
      (off Coppen Rd.)
Cromwell Cl. BR2: Brom 4K **159**
  E1 ....1G **103**
  KT12: Walt T 7K **147**
  N2 ....4B **46**
  W3 ....1J **97**
      (not continuous)
  W4 ....5H **97**
      (off Harvard Rd.)
Cromwell Ind. Est. E10 ....1A **68**
Cromwell Cres. SW5 ....4J **99**
Cromwell Gdns. SW7 ....2B **16** (3B **100**)
Cromwell Gro. W6 ....3E **98**
Cromwell Highwalk EC2 ....5D **8**
Cromwell Ho. CR0: C'don 3B **168**
  SW11 ....1E **118**
      (off Charlotte Despard Av.)
Cromwell Lodge DA6: Bex 5E **126**
  E1 ....4J **85**
      (off Cleveland Gro.)
  IG11: Bark 5J **71**
Cromwell Mans. SW5 ....4J **99**
      (off Cromwell Rd.)
Cromwell M. SW7 ....3B **16** (4B **100**)
Cromwell Pl. EC2 ....5D **8**
      (off Silk St.)
  N6 ....1F **65**
  SW7 ....3B **16** (4B **100**)
  SW14 ....3J **115**
Cromwell Rd. BR3: Beck 2A **158**
  CR0: C'don 7D **156**
  E7 ....7A **70**
  E17 ....5E **50**
  HA0: Wemb 2E **78**
  KT2: King T 1E **150**
  KT4: Wor Pk 3K **163**
  N3 ....1A **46**

Cromwell Rd. N10 ....7K **31**
      (not continuous)
  SW5 ....4J **99**
  SW7 ....3A **16** (4J **99**)
  SW9 ....1A **120**
  SW19 ....5J **135**
  TW3: Houn 4E **112**
  TW11: Tedd 6A **132**
  TW13: Felt 1K **129**
  UB3: Hayes 6F **75**
Cromwell St. TW3: Houn 4E **112**
Cromwell Twr. EC2 ....5D **8**
Cromwell Trad. Cen. IG11: Bark ...3J **89**
Crondace Rd. SW6 ....1J **117**
Crondall Ct. N1 ....1F **9**
Crondall Ho. SW15 ....7C **116**
Crondall St. N1 ....1F **9** (2D **84**)
Crone Ct. NW6 ....2H **81**
      (off Denmark Rd.)
Cronin St. SE15 ....7F **103**
CROOKED BILLET 7H **35**
Crooked Billet SW19 ....6E **134**
Crooked Billet Yd. E2 ....1H **9**
Crooked Usage N3 ....3G **45**
Crooke Rd. SE8 ....5A **104**
Crookham Rd. SW6 ....1H **117**
Crook Log DA6: Bex 3D **126**
Crook Log Leisure Cen. 3D **126**
Crookston Rd. SE9 ....3E **124**
Croombs Rd. E16 ....5A **88**
Croom's Hill SE10 ....7E **104**
Croom's Hill Gro. SE10 ....7E **104**
Cropley Ct. N1 ....2D **84**
      (off Cropley St.)
Cropley St. N1 ....1E **8** (2D **84**)
Croppath Rd. RM10: Dag 4G **73**
Cropthorne Ct. W9 ....3A **82**
Crosbie Ho. E17 ....3E **50**
      (off Prospect Hill)
Crosby Cl. TW13: Hanw 4C **130**
Crosby Ct. SE1 ....6E **14** (2D **102**)
Crosby Gdns. UB8: Uxb 7A **56**
Crosby Ho. BR1: Brom 2J **159**
      (off Elmfield Rd.)
  E7 ....6J **69**
  E14 ....3E **104**
      (off Manchester Rd.)
Crosby Rd. E7 ....6J **69**
  RM10: Dag 2H **91**
Crosby Row SE1 ....7E **14** (2D **102**)
Crosby Sq. EC3 ....1G **15** (6E **84**)
Crosby Wlk. E8 ....6F **67**
  SW2 ....7A **120**
Crosby Way SW2 ....7A **120**
Crosier Cl. SE3 ....1C **124**
Crosier Rd. UB10: Ick 4E **56**
Crosier Way HA4: Ruis 3G **57**
Crosland Pl. SW11 ....3E **118**
Cross Av. SE10 ....6F **105**
Crossbones Graveyard 5D **14**
      (off Redcross Way)
Crossbow Ho. N1 ....1E **84**
      (off Whitmore Est.)
  W13 ....1B **96**
      (off Sherwood Cl.)
Crossbrook Rd. SE3 ....2C **124**
Cross Cl. SE15 ....2H **121**
Cross Ct. SE28 ....7B **90**
      (off Titmuss Av.)
Cross Deep TW1: Twick 2K **131**
Cross Deep Gdns. TW1: Twick ...2K **131**
Crossfield Cl. W10 ....6F **81**
      (off Cambridge Gdns.)
Crossfield Ho. W11 ....7G **81**
      (off Mary Pl.)
Crossfield Rd. N17 ....3C **48**
  NW3 ....6B **64**
Crossfield St. SE8 ....7C **104**
      (not continuous)
Crossford St. SW9 ....2K **119**
Cross Ga. HA8: Edg 3B **28**

Crossgate UB6: G'frd 6B **60**
Cross Keys Cl. N9 ....2B **34**
  W1 ....6H **5** (5E **82**)
Cross Keys Sq. EC1 ....6C **8**
      (off Little Britain)
Cross Lances Rd. TW3: Houn 4F **113**
Crossland Rd. CR7: Thor H 6B **156**
Crosslands Av. UB2: S'hall 5D **94**
  W5 ....1F **97**
Crosslands Rd. KT19: Ewe 6K **163**
Cross La. DA5: Bexl 7F **127**
  EC3 ....3G **15** (7E **84**)
      (not continuous)
  N8 ....3K **47**
Crossleigh Ct. SE14 ....7B **104**
      (off New Cross Rd.)
Crosslet St. SE17 ....4D **102**
Crosslet Va. SE10 ....1D **122**
Crossley St. N7 ....6A **66**
Crossmead SE9 ....1D **142**
Crossmead Av. UB6: G'frd 3E **76**
Crossmount Ho. SE5 ....7C **102**
      (off Bowyer St.)
Crossness Footpath DA18: Erith ...1F **109**
Crossness La. SE2 ....7E **90**
Crossness Nature Reserve 1G **109**
Crossness Pumping Station, The ...6F **91**
Crossness Rd. IG11: Bark 3K **89**
Crosspoint Ho. SE8 ....7C **104**
      (off Watson's St.)
Crossrail Pl. E14 ....1D **104**
Crossrail Wlk. E14 ....1D **104**
Cross Rd. BR2: Brom 2C **172**
  CR0: C'don 1D **168**
  DA14: Sidc 4B **144**
  E4 ....1A **36**
  EN1: Enf 4K **23**
  HA1: Harr 4H **41**
  HA2: Harr 3F **59**
  HA3: W'stone 2A **42**
  IG8: Wfd G 6J **37**
  KT2: King T 7F **133**
  N11 ....5A **32**
  N22 ....7F **33**
  RM6: Chad H 7C **54**
  RM7: Mawney 4G **55**
  SE5 ....2E **120**
  SM1: Sutt 5B **166**
  SW19 ....7J **135**
  TW13: Hanw 4C **130**
Cross St. N1 ....1B **84**
  N18 ....5B **34**
  SE5 ....3D **120**
  SW13 ....2A **116**
  TW12: Hamp H 5G **131**
Crossthwaite Av. SE5 ....4D **120**
Crosstrees Ho. E14 ....3C **104**
      (off Cassilis Rd.)
Crosswall EC3 ....2J **15** (7F **85**)
Cross Way NW10 ....7C **62**
Cross Way, The HA3: W'stone ...2J **41**
Crossway BR5: Pet W 4H **161**
  EN1: Enf 7K **23**
  HA4: Ruis 4A **58**
  HA5: Pinn 2C **40**
  IG8: Wfd G 4F **37**
  N12 ....6G **31**
  N16 ....5E **66**
  NW9 ....4B **44**
  RM8: Dag 3C **72**
  SE28 ....6B **90**
  SW20 ....4E **152**
  UB3: Hayes 1J **93**
  W13 ....4A **78**
Crossway, The N22 ....7G **33**
Crossway, The 2B **142**
  UB10: Hil 2B **74**
Crossway Ct. SE4 ....2A **122**
Crossway Pde. N22 ....7G **33**
      (off The Crossway)

Crossways CR2: Sels 7A **170**
  N21 . . . . .6H **23**
  SM2: Sutt 7B **166**
  TW16: Sun 7H **129**
Crossways, The HA9: Wemb 2G **61**
  KT5: Surb 1H **163**
  TW5: Hest 7D **94**
Crossways Rd. BR3: Beck 4C **158**
  CR4: Mitc 3F **155**
Crossways Ter. E5 . . . . .4J **67**
Cresswell Cl.
  TW17: Shep 2E **146**
Croston St. E8 . . . . .1G **85**
Crothall Cl. N13 . . . . .3E **32**
Crouch Av. IG11: Bark 2B **90**
Crouch Cl. BR3: Beck 6C **140**
Crouch Cft. SE9 . . . . .3E **142**
CROUCH END 7H **47**
Crouch End Hill N8 . . . . .7H **47**
Crouch Hall Cl. N19 . . . . .1J **65**
Crouch Hall Rd. N8 . . . . .6H **47**
Crouch Hill N4 . . . . .6J **47**
  N8 . . . . .6J **47**
Crouchman's Cl. SE26 . . . . .3F **139**
Crouch Rd. NW10 . . . . .7K **61**
Crowborough Rd. SW17 . . . . .6E **136**
Crowden Way SE28 . . . . .7C **90**
Crowder Cl. N12 . . . . .1A **46**
Crowder St. E1 . . . . .7H **85**
Crowfield Ho. N5 . . . . .4C **66**
Crowfoot Cl. E9 . . . . .5B **68**
  SE28 . . . . .1J **107**
Crowhurst Cl. SW9 . . . . .2A **120**
Crowhurst Ho. SW9 . . . . .2K **119**
                     (off Aytoun Rd.)
Crowland Av. UB3: Harl 4G **93**
Crowland Gdns. N14 . . . . .7D **22**
Crowland Ho. NW8 . . . . .1A **82**
             (off Springfield Rd.)
Crowland Rd. CR7: Thor H 4D **156**
  N15 . . . . .5F **49**
CROWLANDS 7H **55**
Crowlands Av. RM7: Rom 6H **55**
Crowlands Heath Golf Course 1H **73**
Crowland Ter. N1 . . . . .7D **66**
Crowland Wlk. SM4: Mord 6K **153**
Crow La. RM7: Rush G 7F **55**
Crowley Cres. CR0: Wadd 5A **168**
Crowline Wlk. N1 . . . . .6C **66**
Crowmarsh Gdns. SE23 . . . . .7J **121**
Crown All. SE9 . . . . .6D **124**
                 (off Court Yd.)
Crown Apartments HA4: Ruis 1J **57**
Crown Arc. KT1: King T 2D **150**
Crownbourne Ct. SM1: Sutt 4K **165**
            (off St Nicholas Way)
Crown Bldgs. E4 . . . . .1K **35**
Crown Cl. E3 . . . . .1C **86**
  IG9: Buck H 1E **36**
  KT12: Walt T 7A **148**
  N22 . . . . .1A **48**
  NW6 . . . . .6K **63**
  NW7 . . . . .2G **29**
  UB3: Hayes 2H **93**
Crown Cl. Bus. Cen. E3 . . . . .1C **86**
               (off Crown Cl.)
Crown Cotts. RM5: Col R 1G **55**
Crown Court
  Blackfriars 6B **14** (2B **102**)
  Croydon 2D **168**
  Harrow .3H **41**
  Inner London 7C **14** (3C **102**)
  Isleworth 1J **113**
  Kingston upon Thames . . .3D **150**
  Snaresbrook 5H **51**
  Southwark 4G **15** (1E **102**)
  Wood Green 1A **48**
  Woolwich 2J **107**
Crown Cl. EC2 . . . . .1D **14**
  N10 . . . . .7K **31**

Crown Ct. NW8 . . . . .2D **4**
                (off Park Rd.)
  SE12 . . . . .6K **123**
  WC2 . . . . .1F **13** (6J **83**)
Crown Dale SE19 . . . . .6B **138**
            (not continuous)
Crowndale Ct. NW1 . . . . .2H **83**
          (off Crowndale Rd.)
Crowndale Pl. E17 . . . . .2E **50**
Crowndale Rd. NW1 . . . . .2G **83**
Crown Dr. RM7: Rush G 6K **55**
Crownfield Av. IG2: Ilf 6J **53**
Crownfield Rd. E15 . . . . .4F **69**
Crowngate Ho. E3 . . . . .2B **86**
            (off Hereford Rd.)
Crown Grn. M. HA9: Wemb 2E **60**
Crown Hill CR0: C'don 2C **168**
Crownhill Rd. IG8: Wfd G 7H **37**
  NW10 .1B **80**
Crown Ho. KT3: N Mald 3J **151**
  NW10 .2G **79**
Crown La. BR2: Brom 5B **160**
  BR7: Chst 1G **161**
  N14 . . . . .1B **32**
  SM4: Mord 4J **153**
  SW16 .5A **138**
Crown La. Gdns. SW16 . . . . .5A **138**
Crown La. Spur BR2: Brom 6B **160**
Crown Lodge SW3 . . . . .4D **16**
Crown Mdw. Cl. BR2: Brom 6C **160**
Crownmead Way RM7: Mawney . . .4H **55**
Crown M. E1 . . . . .5K **85**
          (off White Horse La.)
  E13 . . . . .1A **88**
  TW13: Felt 1K **129**
  W6 . . . . .4C **98**
Crown Mill CR4: Mitc 5C **154**
Crown Office Row EC4 . . . . .2J **13** (7A **84**)
Crown Pde. N14 . . . . .1B **32**
  SM4: Mord 3J **153**
Crown Pas. KT1: King T 2D **150**
            (off Church St.)
  SW1 . . . . .5B **12** (1G **101**)
Crown Pl. EC2 . . . . .5G **9** (5E **84**)
  NW5 . . . . .6F **65**
  SE16 . . . . .5H **103**
Crown Point SE19 . . . . .6B **138**
Crown Point Pde. SE19 . . . . .6B **138**
             (off Crown Dale)
Crown Reach SW1 . . . . . . .6D **18** (5H **101**)
Crown Rd. EN1: Enf 3B **24**
  HA4: Ruis 5B **58**
            (not continuous)
  IG6: Ilf .4H **53**
  KT3: N Mald 1J **151**
  N10 . . . . .7K **31**
  SM1: Sutt 4K **165**
  SM4: Mord 4K **153**
  TW1: Twick 6B **114**
Crownstone Cl. SW2 . . . . .5A **120**
Crownstone Rd. SW2 . . . . .5A **120**
Crown St. HA2: Harr 1H **59**
  RM10: Dag 6J **73**
            (not continuous)
  SE5 . . . . .7C **102**
  W3 . . . . .1H **97**
Crown Ter. N14 . . . . .1C **32**
            (off Crown La.)
  TW9: Rich 4F **115**
Crown Trad. Cen.
  UB3: Hayes 2C **92**
Crowntree Cl. TW7: Isle 6K **95**
Crown Wlk. HA9: Wemb 3F **61**
Crown Way UB7: Yiew 1B **92**
Crown Wharf E14 . . . . .1E **104**
            (off Coldharbour)
  SE8 . . . . .5B **104**
             (off Grove St.)
Crown Woods SE18 . . . . .2F **125**
Crown Woods Sports Cen. 5G **125**
Crown Woods Way SE9 . . . . .5H **125**

Crown Yd. E2 . . . . .2H **85**
  SW6 . . . . .2J **117**
  TW3: Houn 3G **113**
Crowshott Av. HA7: Stan 2C **42**
Crows Rd. E3 . . . . .3F **87**
  E15 . . . . .3F **87**
  IG11: Bark 6F **71**
Crowther Av. TW8: Bford 4E **96**
Crowther Cl. SW6 . . . . .6H **99**
          (off Bucklers All.)
Crowther Rd. SE25 . . . . .5G **157**
Crowthorne Cl. SW18 . . . . .7H **117**
Crowthorne Rd. W10 . . . . .6F **81**
Croxall Ho. KT12: Walt T 6A **148**
Croxden Cl. HA8: Edg 3G **43**
Croxden Wlk. SM4: Mord 6A **154**
Croxford Gdns. N22 . . . . .7G **33**
Croxford Way RM7: Rush G 1K **73**
Croxley Grn. BR5: St P 7B **144**
Croxley Rd. W9 . . . . .3H **81**
Croxted Cl. SE21 . . . . .7C **120**
Croxted M. SE24 . . . . .6C **120**
Croxted Rd. SE21 . . . . .7C **120**
  SE24 . . . . .7C **120**
Croxteth Ho. SW8 . . . . .2H **119**
Croyde Av. UB3: Harl 4G **93**
  UB6: G'frd 3G **77**
Croyde Cl. DA15: Sidc 7H **125**
CROYDON .2C **168**
Croydon N17 . . . . .2D **48**
          (off Gloucester Rd.)
Croydon Airport Ind. Est.
  CR0: Wadd 6K **167**
Croydon Airport Vis. Cen. 6A **168**
Croydon Clocktower 3C **168**
          (off Katharine St.)
Croydon Crematorium CR0: C'don . .5K **155**
Croydon Flyover, The CR0: C'don . .4B **168**
Croydon Gro. CR0: C'don 1B **168**
Croydon Ho. SE1 . . . . .6K **13**
           (off Wootton St.)
Croydon Rd. BR2: Hayes, Kes 3G **171**
  BR3: Beck 4K **157**
  BR4: Hayes, W W'ck 3G **171**
  CR0: Bedd, Wadd 4F **167**
  CR0: C'don 4E **154**
  CR4: Mitc 4E **154**
  E13 . . . . .4H **87**
  SE20 . . . . .2H **157**
  SM6: Bedd, Wall 4F **167**
  TW6: H'row A 2D **110**
Croydon Rd. Ind. Est. BR3: Beck . . .4K **157**
Croydon Sailing Club 2F **157**
Croydon Sports Arena 5J **157**
Croydon Valley Trade Pk.
  CR0: Bedd 7J **155**
          (off Therapia La.)
Croyland Rd. N9 . . . . .1B **34**
Croylands Dr. KT6: Surb 7E **150**
Crozier Ho. SW8 . . . . .7K **101**
          (off Wilkinson St.)
Crozier Ter. E9 . . . . .5K **67**
           (not continuous)
Crucible Cl. RM6: Chad H 6B **54**
Crucifix La. SE1 . . . . .6H **15** (2E **102**)
Cruden Ho. E3 . . . . .2B **86**
            (off Vernon Rd.)
  SE17 . . . . .6B **102**
          (off Brandon Est.)
Cruden St. N1 . . . . .1B **84**
Cruikshank Ho. NW8 . . . . .2C **82**
          (off Townshend Rd.)
Cruikshank Rd. E15 . . . . .4G **69**
Cruikshank St. WC1 . . . . . . .1J **7** (3A **84**)
Crummock Gdns. NW9 . . . . .5A **44**
Crumpsall St. SE2 . . . . .4C **108**
Crundale Av. NW9 . . . . .5G **43**
Crunden Rd. CR2: S Croy 7D **168**
Crusader Gdns. CR0: C'don 3E **168**
Crusader Ind. Est. N4 . . . . .6C **48**
Crusoe M. N16 . . . . .2D **66**

Crusoe Rd. CR4: Mitc 7D **136**
  DA8: Erith 5K **109**
Crutched Friars EC3 . . . . . . .2H **15** (7E **84**)
Crutchley Rd. SE6 . . . . .2G **141**
Crypt, The .1D **120**
Crystal, The 7J **87**
Crystal Ct. E8 . . . . .1H **85**
  SE19 . . . . .5F **139**
          (off College Rd.)
Crystal Ho. SE18 . . . . .5K **107**
CRYSTAL PALACE 6F **139**
Crystal Palace Athletics Stadium . . .6G **139**
Crystal Palace Dinosaurs 6G **139**
Crystal Palace FC 4E **156**
Crystal Palace Indoor Bowling Club
  . . . . .1H **157**
Crystal Palace Mus. 6F **139**
Crystal Palace National Sports Cen.
  . . . . .5G **139**
Crystal Palace Pde. SE19 . . . . .6F **139**
Crystal Palace Pk. 5G **139**
Crystal Palace Pk. Farm 6G **139**
Crystal Palace Pk. Rd. SE26 . . . . .5G **139**
Crystal Palace Rd. SE22 . . . . .6F **121**
Crystal Palace Sta. Rd.
  SE19 . . . . .6G **139**
Crystal Pl. KT4: Wor Pk 2D **164**
Crystal Ter. SE19 . . . . .6D **138**
Crystal Vw. Ct. BR1: Brom 4F **141**
Crystal Way HA1: Harr 5K **41**
  RM8: Dag 1C **72**
Crystal Wharf N1 . . . . .2B **84**
Cuba Dr. EN3: Enf H 2D **24**
Cuba St. E14 . . . . .2C **104**
Cube, The
  North East London Gymnastic Club
  . . . . .4D **66**
Cube Ho. SE16 . . . . .3F **103**
Cubitt Apartments SW11 . . . . .3A **118**
          (off Chatfield Rd.)
Cubitt Bldg. SW1 . . . . .7J **17** (5F **101**)
Cubitt Ct. NW1 . . . . .1A **6**
          (off Park Village E.)
Cubitt Ho. SW4 . . . . .6G **119**
Cubitt Sq. UB2: S'hall 1G **95**
Cubitt Steps E14 . . . . .1C **104**
Cubitt St. WC1 . . . . .2H **7** (3K **83**)
Cubitt's Yd. WC2 . . . . .2F **13**
Cubitt Ter. SW4 . . . . .3G **119**
CUBITT TOWN 4E **104**
Cuckoo Av. W7 . . . . .4J **77**
Cuckoo Dene W7 . . . . .5H **77**
Cuckoo Hall La. N9 . . . . .7D **24**
Cuckoo Hall Rd. N9 . . . . .7D **24**
Cuckoo Hill HA5: Eastc, Pinn 3A **40**
Cuckoo Hill Dr. HA5: Pinn 3A **40**
Cuckoo Hill Rd. HA5: Pinn 4A **40**
Cuckoo La. W7 . . . . .7J **77**
Cuckoo Pound TW17: Shep 5G **147**
Cudas Cl. KT19: Ewe 4B **164**
Cuddington Av. KT4: Wor Pk 3B **164**
Cudham La. Nth. BR6: Downe 7J **173**
Cudham St. SE6 . . . . .7E **122**
Cudworth Ho. SW8 . . . . .1G **119**
Cudworth St. E1 . . . . .4H **85**
Cuff Cres. SE9 . . . . .6B **124**
Cuffley Ho. W10 . . . . .5E **80**
          (off Sutton Way)
Cuff Point E2 . . . . .1J **9**
          (off Columbia Rd.)
Culand Ho. SE17 . . . . .4E **102**
          (off Congreve St.)
Culford Gdns. SW3 . . . . .4F **17** (4D **100**)
Culford Gro. N1 . . . . .6E **66**
Culford Mans. SW3 . . . . .4F **17**
          (off Culford Gdns.)
Culford M. N1 . . . . .6E **66**
Culford Rd. N1 . . . . .7E **66**
Culford Ter. N1 . . . . .6E **66**
          (off Balls Pond Rd.)
Culgaith Gdns. EN2: Enf 4D **22**

Culham Ho. E2 2J 9
(off Palissy St.)
W2 5J 81
(off Gt. Western Rd.)
Cullen Way NW10 4J 79
Culling Rd. DA17: Belv 3J 109
SE16 3J 103
Cullington Cl.
HA3: W'stone 4A 42
Cullingworth Rd. NW10 5C 62
Culloden Cl. SE7 6K 105
SE16 5G 103
Culloden Ho. SE14 7A 104
(off Batavia Rd.)
Culloden Rd. EN2: Enf 2G 23
Cullum St. EC3 2G 15 (7E 84)
Cullum Welch Ct. N1 1F 9
(off Haberdasher St.)
Cullum Welch Ho. EC1 4C 8
(off Golden La. Est.)
Culmington Pde. W13 1C 96
(off Uxbridge Rd.)
Culmington Rd. CR2: S Croy 7C 168
W13 1C 96
Culmore Rd. SE15 7H 103
Culmstock Rd. SW11 5E 118
Culpepper Cl. N18 5C 34
Culpepper Ct. SE11 3J 19
Culross Cl. N15 4C 48
Culross Ho. W10 6F 81
(off Bridge Cl.)
Culross St. W1 3G 11 (7E 82)
Culsac Rd. KT6: Surb 2E 162
Culverden Rd. SW12 2G 137
Culver Gro. HA7: Stan 2C 42
Culverhouse WC1 6G 7
(off Red Lion Sq.)
Culverhouse Gdns. SW16 3K 137
Culverlands Cl. HA7: Stan 4G 27
Culverley Rd. SE6 1D 140
Culvers Av. SM5: Cars 2D 166
Culvers Retreat SM5: Cars 1D 166
Culverstone Cl. BR2: Brom 6H 159
Culvers Way SM5: Cars 2D 166
Culvert Dr. E3 3E 86
Culvert Pl. SW11 2E 118
Culvert Rd. N15 5E 48
(not continuous)
SW11 2D 118
Culworth Ho. NW8 2C 82
(off Allitsen Rd.)
Culworth St. NW8 2C 82
Culzean Cl. SE27 3B 138
Cumberland Av. DA16: Well 3J 125
NW10 3H 79
Cumberland Bus. Pk. NW10 3H 79
Cumberland Cl. E8 6F 67
IG6: Ilf 1G 53
SW20 7F 135
TW1: Twick 6B 114
Cumberland Ct. CR0: C'don 1D 168
DA16: Well 2J 125
HA1: Harr 3J 41
(off Princes Dr.)
SW1 5K 17
(off Cumberland St.)
W1 1F 11
(off Gt. Cumberland Pl.)
Cumberland Cres. W14 4G 99
(not continuous)
Cumberland Dr. DA7: Bex 7E 108
KT9: Chess 3E 162
KT10: Hin W 2A 162
Cumberland Gdns. NW4 2G 45
WC1 1J 7 (3A 84)
Cumberland Ga. W1 2E 10 (7D 82)
Cumberland Ho. E16 1J 105
(off Wesley Av.)
KT2: King T 7H 133
N9 1D 34
(off Cumberland Rd.)
Cumberland Ho. SE28 2G 107
W8 2K 99
(off Kensington Ct.)
Cumberland Mans. W1 7E 4
Cumberland Mkt. NW1 1K 5 (3F 83)
Cumberland M. SE11 6K 19 (5A 102)
Cumberland Mills Sq. E14 5F 105
Cumberland Pk. W3 7J 79
Cumberland Pk. Ind. Est.
NW10 3C 80
Cumberland Pl. NW1 1J 5 (3F 83)
SE6 1H 141
TW16: Sun 4J 147
Cumberland Rd. BR2: Brom 4G 159
E12 4B 70
E13 5K 87
E17 2A 50
HA1: Harr 5F 41
HA7: Stan 3F 43
N9 1D 34
N22 2K 47
SE25 6H 157
SW13 1B 116
TW9: Kew 7G 97
TW15: Ashf 3A 128
W3 7J 79
W7 2K 95
Cumberland St. SW1 5K 17 (5F 101)
Cumberland Ter. NW1 1J 5 (2F 83)
Cumberland Ter. M. NW1 1J 5
(not continuous)
Cumberland Vs. W3 7J 79
(off Cumberland Rd.)
Cumberland Wharf SE16 2J 103
(off Rotherhithe St.)
Cumberlow Av. SE25 3F 157
Cumbernauld Gdns. TW16: Sun 5H 129
Cumberton Rd. N17 1D 48
Cumbrae Gdns. KT6: Surb 2D 162
Cumbrian Gdns. NW2 2F 63
Cumbrian Way UB8: Uxb 7A 56
Cumming St. N1 1H 7 (2K 83)
Cumnor Cl. SW9 2K 119
(off Robsart St.)
Cumnor Gdns. KT17: Ewe 6C 164
Cumnor Rd. SM2: Sutt 6A 166
Cunard Ct. HA7: Stan 2F 27
(off Brightwen Gro.)
Cunard Cres. N21 6J 23
Cunard Pl. EC3 1H 15 (6E 84)
Cunard Rd. NW10 3K 79
Cunard Wlk. SE16 4K 103
Cundy Rd. E16 6A 88
Cundy St. SW1 4H 17 (4E 100)
Cunio M. NW7 5B 30
Cunliffe Pde. KT19: Ewe 4B 164
Cunliffe Rd. KT19: Ewe 4B 164
Cunliffe St. SW16 6G 137
Cunningham Cl. BR4: W W'ck 2D 170
RM6: Chad H 5C 54
Cunningham Ct. E10 3D 68
(off Oliver Rd.)
W9 4A 4
(off Maida Vale)
Cunningham Ho. SE5 7D 102
(off Elmington Est.)
Cunningham Pk. HA1: Harr 5G 41
Cunningham Pl. NW8 3A 4 (4B 82)
Cunningham Rd. N15 4G 49
Cunnington St. W4 3J 97
Cupar Rd. SW11 1E 118
Cupola Cl. BR1: Brom 5K 141
Cureton St.
SW1 4D 18 (4H 101)
Curfew Ho. IG11: Bark 1G 89
Curfew Tower, The 1G 89
Curie Ct. HA1: Harr 7B 42
Curie Gdns. NW9 2A 44
Curlew Cl. SE28 7D 90
Curlew Ct. KT6: Surb 3G 163
W13 4K 77
Curlew Ho. EN3: Pond E 5E 24
SE4 4A 122
(off St Norbert Rd.)
SE15 1F 121
Curlew St. SE1 6K 15 (2F 103)
Curlew Way UB4: Yead 5B 76
Curness St. SE13 4E 122
Curnick's La. SE27 4C 138
Curran Av. DA15: Sidc 5K 125
SM6: Wall 3E 166
Curran Ho. SW3 4C 16
(off Lucan Pl.)
Currey Rd. UB6: G'frd 6H 59
Curricle St. W3 1A 98
Currie Hill Cl. SW19 4H 135
Curry Ri. NW7 6A 30
Cursitor St. EC4 7J 7 (6A 84)
Curtain Pl. EC2 3H 9 (3E 84)
Curtain Rd. EC2 2H 9 (4E 84)
Curthwaite Gdns. EN2: Enf 4C 22
Curtis & Staub Health Club
Golders Green 7H 45
Curtis Dr. W3 6K 79
Curtis Fld. Rd. SW16 4K 137
Curtis Ho. SE17 5D 102
(off Morecambe St.)
Curtis La. HA0: Wemb 6E 60
Curtis Rd. KT19: Ewe 4J 163
TW4: Houn 7D 112
Curtiss Ho. NW9 3B 44
Curtis St. SE1 4F 103
Curtis Way SE1 4F 103
SE28 7B 90
Curtlington Ho. HA8: Edg 2J 43
(off Burnt Oak B'way.)
Curve, The W12 7C 80
Curwen Av. E7 4K 69
Curwen Rd. W12 2C 98
Curzon Av. EN3: Pond E 5E 24
HA7: Stan 1A 42
Curzon Cinema
Bloomsbury 4J 83
Mayfair 5J 11
(off Curzon St.)
Richmond 5D 114
Soho 2D 12
(off Shaftesbury Av.)
Curzon Cl. BR6: Orp 4H 173
Curzon Ct. SW6 1A 118
(off Imperial Rd.)
Curzon Cres. IG11: Bark 2K 89
NW10 7A 62
Curzon Ga. W1 5H 11 (1E 100)
Curzon Pl. HA5: Eastc 5A 40
Curzon Rd. CR7: Thor H 6A 156
N10 2F 47
W5 4B 78
Curzon Sq. W1 5H 11 (1E 100)
Curzon St. W1 5H 11 (1E 100)
Cusack Cl. TW1: Tedd 4K 131
Custance Ho. N1 1E 8
(off Provost St.)
Custance St. N1 1E 8 (3D 84)
CUSTOM HOUSE 6A 88
Custom Ho. EC3 3G 15 (7E 84)
Custom Ho. Reach SE16 2B 104
Custom Ho. Wlk. EC3 3G 15 (7E 84)
Cut, The SE1 6K 13 (2A 102)
Cutbush Ho. N7 5H 65
Cutcombe Rd. SE5 2C 120
Cuthberga Cl. IG11: Bark 7G 71
Cuthbert Bell Twr. E3 2C 86
(off Pancras Way)
Cuthbert Gdns. SE25 3E 156
Cuthbert Harrowing Ho. EC1 4C 8
(off Golden La. Est.)
Cuthbert Ho. W2 5A 4
(off Hall Pl.)
Cuthbert Rd. CR0: C'don 2B 168
E17 3E 50
N18 5B 34
Cuthbert St. W2 5A 4 (5B 82)
Cuthill Wlk. SE5 1D 120
Cutlers Gdns. EC2 6H 9 (5E 84)
Cutlers Gdns. Arc. EC2 7H 9
(off Devonshire Sq.)
Cutlers Sq. E14 4C 104
Cutlers Ter. N1 6E 66
(off Balls Pond Rd.)
Cutler St. E1 7H 9 (6E 84)
Cutter Ho. DA8: Erith 4K 109
Cutter La. SE10 2G 105
Cutthroat All.
TW10: Ham 2C 132
Cutty Sark 6E 104
Cutty Sark Gdns. SE10 6E 104
(off King William Wlk.)
Cutty Sark Hall SE10 6E 104
(off Welland St.)
Cuxton BR5: Pet W 5G 161
Cuxton Cl. DA6: Bex 5E 126
Cuxton Ho. SE17 5E 102
(off Mina Rd.)
Cyan Apartments E3 1A 86
(off Gunmaker's La.)
Cyclamen Cl. TW12: Hamp 6E 130
Cyclamen Way
KT19: Ewe 5J 163
Cyclops M. E14 4C 104
Cygnet Av. TW14: Felt 7A 112
Cygnet Cl. NW10 5K 61
Cygnet Ho. SE15 6G 103
SW3 6D 16
(off King's Rd.)
Cygnet Ho. Nth. E14 6D 86
(off Chrisp St.)
Cygnet Ho. Sth. E14 6D 86
(off Chrisp St.)
Cygnets, The
TW13: Hanw 4C 130
Cygnet St. E1 3K 9 (4F 85)
Cygnet Way UB4: Yead 5B 76
Cygnus Bus. Cen. NW10 5B 62
Cymbeline Ct.
HA1: Harr 6K 41
Cynthia St. N1 1H 7 (2K 83)
Cyntra Pl. E8 7H 67
Cypress Av. TW2: Whitt 7G 113
Cypress Cl. E5 2G 67
KT19: Eps 7K 163
Cypress Ct. E15 4F 69
(off Langthorne Rd.)
NW9 4G 43
(off Alpine Rd.)
SM1: Sutt 5J 165
Cypress Gdns. SE4 5A 122
Cypress Ho. SE14 1K 121
SE16 2K 103
(off Woodland Cres.)
Cypress Pl. W1 4B 6 (4G 83)
Cypress Rd.
HA3: Hrw W 2H 41
SE25 2E 156
Cypress Tree Cl.
DA15: Sidc 1K 143
CYPRUS 7E 88
Cyprus Av. N3 2G 45
Cyprus Cl. N4 6B 48
Cyprus Gdns. N3 2G 45
Cyprus Pl. E2 2J 85
E6 7E 88
Cyprus Rd. N3 2H 45
N9 2A 34
Cyprus St. E2 2J 85
(not continuous)
Cyrena Rd. SE22 6F 121
Cyril Lodge DA14: Sidc 4A 144
Cyril Mans. SW11 1D 118
Cyril Rd. BR6: Orp 7K 161
DA7: Bex 2E 126
Cyrus Ho. EC1 3B 8
Cyrus St. EC1 3B 8

Cyrus Ter. *UB10: Ick* 3E 56
(off Pentland Way)
Czar St. SE8 6C 104

D

Dabbs Hill La. UB5: N'olt 6D 58
(not continuous)
Dabbs La. *EC1* 4K 7
(off Farringdon Rd.)
Dabin Cres. SE10 1E 122
Dacca St. SE8 6B 104
Dace Rd. E3 1C 86
Dacre Av. IG5: Ilf 2E 52
Dacre Cl. UB6: G'frd 2F 77
Dacre Gdns. SE13 4G 123
Dacre Ho. SW3 7B 16
Dacre Pk. SE13 3G 123
Dacre Pl. SE13 3G 123
Dacre Rd. CR0: C'don 7J 155
E11 1H 69
E13 1K 87
Dacres Est. SE23 3K 139
Dacres Ho. SW4 3F 119
Dacres Rd. SE23 2K 139
Dacre St. SW1 1C 18 (3H 101)
Dade Way UB2: S'hall 5D 94
Daerwood Cl. BR2: Brom 1D 172
Daffodil Cl. CR0: C'don 1K 169
Daffodil Gdns. IG1: Ilf 5F 71
Daffodil Pl. TW12: Hamp 6E 130
Daffodil St. W12 7B 80
Dafforne Rd. SW17 3E 136
Da Gama Pl. E14 5C 104
DAGENHAM 6G 73
Dagenham & Redbridge FC 5H 73
Dagenham Av. RM9: Dag 1E 90
(not continuous)
Dagenham Bowl 1E 90
Dagenham Leisure Pk. 1D 90
Dagenham Pk. Leisure Cen. 7G 73
Dagenham Rd. E10 1B 68
RM7: Rush G 7K 55
RM10: Dag 4J 73
RM13: Rain 7K 73
Dagmar Av. HA9: Wemb 4F 61
Dagmar Ct. E14 3E 104
Dagmar Gdns. NW10 2F 81
Dagmar M. *UB2: S'hall* 3C 94
(off Dagmar Rd.)
Dagmar Pas. *N1* 1B 84
(off Cross St.)
Dagmar Rd. KT2: King T 1F 151
N4 7A 48
N15 4D 48
N22 1H 47
RM10: Dag 7J 73
SE5 1E 120
SE25 5E 156
UB2: S'hall 3C 94
Dagmar Ter. N1 1B 84
Dagnall Pk. SE25 6E 156
Dagnall Rd. SE25 5E 156
Dagnall St. SW11 2D 118
Dagnan Rd. SW12 7F 119
Dagobert Ho. *E1* 5J 85
(off Smithy St.)
Dagonet Gdns. BR1: Brom 3J 141
Dagonet Rd. BR1: Brom 3J 141
Dahlia Gdns. CR4: Mitc 4H 155
IG1: Ilf 6F 71
Dahlia Rd. SE2 4B 108
Dahomey Rd. SW16 6G 137
Daimler Ho. *E3* 4C 86
(off Wellington Way)
Daimler Way SM6: Wall 7J 167
Dain Ct. *W8* 4J 99
(off Lexham Gdns.)
Daines Cl. E12 3D 70
Dainford Cl. BR1: Brom 5F 141
Dainton Cl. BR1: Brom 1K 159
Dainton Ho. *W2* 5J 81
(off Gt. Western Rd.)
Daintry Cl. HA3: W'stone 4A 42
Daintry Way E9 6B 68
Dairsie Ct. BR1: Brom 1A 160
Dairsie Rd. SE9 3E 124
Dairy Cl. BR1: Brom 7K 141
CR7: Thor H 2C 156
NW10 1C 80
SW6 1J 117
UB6: G'frd 2H 77
Dairy La. SE18 4D 106
Dairyman Cl. NW2 3F 63
Dairy M. N2 4C 46
RM6: Chad H 7D 54
SW9 3J 119
Dairy Wlk. SW19 4G 135
Daisy Cl. CR0: C'don 1K 169
NW9 2J 61
Daisy Dobbings Wlk. *N19* 7J 47
(off Jessie Blythe La.)
Daisy La. SW6 3J 117
Daisy Rd. E16 4G 87
E18 2K 51
Dakin Pl. E1 5A 86
Dakota Bldg. *SE13* 1D 122
(off Deal's Gateway)
Dakota Cl. SM6: Wall 7K 167
Dakota Gdns. E6 4C 88
UB5: N'olt 3C 76
Dakota Ho. CR7: Thor H 6B 156
Dalberg Rd. SW2 4A 120
(not continuous)
Dalberg Way SE2 3D 108
Dalby Rd. SW18 4A 118
Dalbys Cres. N17 6K 33
Dalby St. NW5 6F 65
Dalcross Rd. TW4: Houn 2C 112
Dale, The BR2: Kes 4B 172
Dale Av. HA8: Edg 1F 43
TW4: Houn 3C 112
Dalebury Pl. TW5: Hest 5E 94
Dalebury Rd. SW17 2D 136
Dale Cl. E4 3K 35
EN5: New Bar 6E 20
HA5: Pinn 1K 39
SE3 3J 123
Dale Ct. EN2: Enf 1H 23
KT2: King T 7F 133
(off York Rd.)
Dale Dr. UB4: Hayes 4H 75
Dalefield *IG9: Buck H* 1F 37
(off Roebuck La.)
Dale Gdns. IG8: Wfd G 4E 36
Dale Grn. Rd. N11 3A 32
Dale Gro. N12 5F 31
Daleham Dr. UB8: Hil 6D 74
Daleham Gdns. NW3 5B 64
Daleham M. NW3 6B 64
Dalehead *NW1* 1A 6
(off Hampstead Rd.)
Dale Ho. *N1* 1E 84
(off Halcomb St.)
NW8 1A 82
(off Boundary Rd.)
SE4 4A 122
Dale Lodge N6 6G 47
Dalemain M. E16 1J 105
Dale Pk. Av. SM5: Cars 2D 166
Dale Pk. Rd. SE19 1C 156
Dale Rd. KT12: Walt T 7H 147
NW5 5E 64
SE17 6B 102
SM1: Sutt 4H 165
TW16: Sun 7H 129
UB6: G'frd 5F 77
Dale Row W11 6G 81
Daleside Rd. KT19: Ewe 6K 163
SW16 5F 137
Dale St. W4 5A 98
Dale Vw. Av. E4 2K 35
Dale Vw. Cres. E4 2K 35
Dale Vw. Gdns. E4 3A 36
Daleview Rd. N15 6E 48
Dalewood Gdns. KT4: Wor Pk 2D 164
Dale Wood Rd. BR6: Orp 7J 161
Daleworth Cl. BR3: Beck 6C 140
Daley Ho. W12 6D 80
Daley St. E9 6K 67
Daley Thompson Way SW8 2F 119
Dalgarno Gdns. W10 5E 80
Dalgarno Way W10 4E 80
Dalgleish St. E14 6A 86
Daling Way E3 1A 86
Dalkeith Ct. *SW1* 3D 18
(off Vincent St.)
Dalkeith Gro. HA7: Stan 5J 27
Dalkeith Ho. *SW9* 1B 120
(off Lothian Rd.)
Dalkeith Rd. IG1: Ilf 3G 71
SE21 1C 138
Dallas Rd. NW4 7C 44
SE26 3H 139
SM3: Cheam 6G 165
W5 5F 79
Dallas Ter. UB3: Harl 3H 93
Dallega Cl. UB3: Hayes 7F 75
Dallinger Rd. SE12 6H 123
Dalling Rd. W6 4D 98
Dallington Sq. *EC1* 3B 8
(off Dallington St.)
Dallington St. EC1 3B 8 (4B 84)
Dallin Rd. DA6: Bex 4D 126
SE18 7F 107
Dalmain Rd. SE23 1K 139
Dalmally Rd. CR0: C'don 7F 157
Dalmany Pas. CR0: C'don 7F 157
Dalmeny Av. N7 4H 65
SW16 2A 156
Dalmeny Cl. HA0: Wemb 6C 60
Dalmeny Cres. TW3: Houn 4H 113
Dalmeny Rd. DA8: Erith 1H 127
EN5: New Bar 6F 21
KT4: Wor Pk 3D 164
N7 3H 65
(not continuous)
SM5: Cars 7E 166
Dalmeyer Rd. NW10 6B 62
Dalmore Rd. SE21 2C 138
Dalo Lodge *E3* 5C 86
(off Gale St.)
Dalrymple Cl. N14 7C 22
Dalrymple Rd. SE4 4A 122
DALSTON 6F 67
Dalston Gdns. HA7: Stan 1E 42
Dalston La. E8 6F 67
Dalston Sq. E8 6F 67
(not continuous)
Dalton Av. CR4: Mitc 2C 154
Dalton Cl. BR6: Orp 3J 173
UB4: Hayes 4F 75
Dalton Ho. *E3* 2A 86
(off Ford St.)
HA7: Stan 5F 27
SE14 6K 103
(off John Williams Cl.)
SW1 5J 17
(off Ebury Bri. Rd.)
Dalton Rd. HA3: W'stone 2H 41
Dalton St. SE27 3B 138
Dalwood St. SE5 1E 120
Daly Dr. BR1: Brom 3E 160
Dalyell Rd. SW9 3K 119
Damascene Wlk. SE21 1C 138
Damask Ct. SM1: Sutt 1K 165
Damask Cres. E16 4G 87
Damer Ter. SW10 7A 100
Dames Rd. E7 3J 69
Dame St. N1 2C 84
Damien Ct. *E1* 6H 85
(off Damien St.)
Damien St. E1 6H 85
Damon Cl. DA14: Sidc 3B 144
Damory Ho. *SE16* 4H 103
(off Abbeyfield Est.)
Damsel Ho. *SE4* 3A 122
(off Dragonfly Pl.)
Damson Dr. UB3: Hayes 7J 75
Damson Way SM5: Cars 7D 166
Damsonwood Rd. UB2: S'hall 3E 94
Danbrook Rd. SW16 1J 155
Danbury Cl. RM6: Chad H 3D 54
Danbury Mans. *IG11: Bark* 7F 71
(off Whiting Av.)
Danbury M. SM6: Wall 4F 167
Danbury St. N1 2B 84
Danbury Way IG8: Wfd G 6F 37
Danby Ct. EN2: Enf 3H 23
Danby Ho. *E9* 7J 67
(off Frampton Pk. Rd.)
W10 3G 81
(off Bruckner St.)
Danby St. SE15 3F 121
Dance Ho. *SE4* 5K 121
(off St Norbert Rd.)
Dancer Rd. SW6 1H 117
TW9: Rich 3G 115
Dancers Way SE8 6D 104
Dance Sq. EC1 2C 8 (3C 84)
Dan Ct. NW10 3G 79
Dandridge Cl. SE10 5H 105
Dandridge Ho. *E1* 5J 9
(off Lamb St.)
Danebury CR0: New Ad 6E 170
Danebury Av. SW15 6A 116
Daneby Rd. SE6 3D 140
Dane Cl. BR6: Farnb 5H 173
DA5: Bexl 7G 127
Danecourt Gdns. CR0: C'don 3F 169
Danecroft Rd. SE24 5C 120
Danehill Wlk. DA14: Sidc 3A 144
Danehurst TW8: Bford 7C 96
Danehurst Gdns. IG4: Ilf 5C 52
Danehurst St. SW6 1G 117
Daneland EN4: E Barn 6J 21
Daneland Wlk. N17 3H 49
Danemead Gro. UB5: N'olt 5F 59
Danemere St. SW15 3E 116
Dane Pl. E3 2A 86
Dane Rd. IG1: Ilf 5G 71
N18 3D 34
SW19 1A 154
TW15: Ashf 6E 128
UB1: S'hall 7C 76
W13 1C 96
Danesbury Rd. TW13: Felt 1K 129
Danescombe SE12 1J 141
Danes Ct. HA9: Wemb 3H 61
NW8 1D 82
(off St Edmund's Ter.)
Danescourt Cres. SM1: Sutt 2A 166
Danescroft NW4 5F 45
Danescroft Av. NW4 5F 45
Danescroft Gdns. NW4 5F 45
Danesdale Rd. E9 6A 68
Danesfield *SE5* 6E 102
(off Albany Rd.)
Danes Ga. HA1: Harr 3J 41
Danes Ho. *W10* 5E 80
(off Sutton Way)
Danes Rd. RM7: Rush G 7J 55
Dane St. WC1 6G 7 (5K 83)
Daneswood Av. SE6 3E 140
Danethorpe Rd. HA0: Wemb 6D 60
Danetree Cl. KT19: Ewe 7J 163
Danetree Rd. KT19: Ewe 7J 163
Danette Gdns.
RM10: Dag 2G 73
Daneville Rd. SE5 1D 120
Danewood Dr. N2 7B 46
Dangan Rd. E11 6J 51
Daniel Bolt Cl. E14 5D 86

Daniel Cl. N18 . . . . .4D 34
  SW17 .6C 136
  TW4: Houn 7D 112
Daniel Ct. NW9 . . . . .1A 44
Daniel Gdns. SE15 . . . . .7F 103
Daniell Ho. N1 . . . . .2D 84
  (off Cranston Est.)
Daniell Way CRO: Wadd 1J 167
Daniel Pl. NW4 . . . . .7D 44
Daniel Rd. W5 . . . . .7F 79
Daniels Rd. SE15 . . . . .3J 121
Danleigh Ct. N14 . . . . .7C 22
Dan Leno Wlk. SW6 . . . . .7K 99
Dan Mason Dr. W4 . . . . .2J 115
Danny Fiszman Bri. N5 . . . . .4A 66
  N7 . . . . .4A 66
Dansey Pl. W1 . . . . .2C 12
Dansington Rd. DA16: Well 4A 126
Danson Cres. DA16: Well 3B 126
Danson House 4C 126
DANSON INTERCHANGE 5D 126
Danson La. DA16: Well 4B 126
Danson Mead DA16: Well 3C 126
Danson Pk. 5C 126
Danson Pk. Watersports Cen. 4C 126
Danson Rd. DA5: Bexl, Bex 6C 126
  DA6: Bex 5D 126
  SE17 .5B 102
Danson Underpass DA15: Sidc 6C 126
Dante Pl. SE11 . . . . .4B 102
Dante Rd. SE11 . . . . .4B 102
Danube Apartments N8 . . . . .3K 47
  (off Gt. Amwell La.)
Danube Cl. N9 . . . . .3D 34
Danube Ct. SE15 . . . . .7F 103
  (off Daniel Gdns.)
Danube St. SW3 . . . . .5D 16 (5C 100)
Danvers Av. SW11 . . . . .4C 118
Danvers Ho. E1 . . . . .6G 85
  (off Christian St.)
Danvers Rd. N8 . . . . .4H 47
Danvers St. SW3 . . . . .7B 16 (6B 100)
Dao Ct. E13 . . . . .1K 87
Da Palma Ct. SW6 . . . . .6J 99
  (off Anselm Rd.)
Daphne Ct. KT4: Wor Pk 2A 164
Daphne Gdns. E4 . . . . .3K 35
Daphne Ho. N22 . . . . .1A 48
  (off Acacia Rd.)
Daphne St. SW18 . . . . .6A 118
Daplyn St. E1 . . . . .5K 9 (5G 85)
Darbishire Pl. E1 . . . . .2K 15
D'Arblay St. W1 . . . . .1B 12 (6G 83)
Darby Cres. TW16: Sun 2A 148
Darby Gdns. TW16: Sun 2A 148
Darcy Av. SM6: Wall 4G 167
Darcy Cl. N20 . . . . .2G 31
D'Arcy Dr. HA3: Kenton 4D 42
D'Arcy Gdns. HA3: Kenton 4D 42
Darcy Gdns. RM9: Dag 1F 91
Darcy Ho. E8 . . . . .1H 85
  (off London Flds. E. Side)
  RM9: Dag 1G 91
D'Arcy Pl. BR2: Brom 4J 159
D'Arcy Rd. SM3: Cheam 4F 165
Darcy Rd. SW16 . . . . .2J 155
  TW7: Isle 1A 114
Dare Gdns. RM8: Dag 3E 72
Darell Rd. TW9: Rich 3G 115
Darent Ho. BR1: Brom 5F 141
  NW8 . . . . .5B 4
  (off Church St. Est.)
Darenth Rd. DA16: Well 1A 126
  N16 . . . . .7F 49
Darfield NW1 . . . . .1G 83
  (off Bayham St.)
Darfield Rd. SE4 . . . . .5B 122
Darfield Way W10 . . . . .6F 81
Darfur St. SW15 . . . . .3F 117
Dargate Cl. SE19 . . . . .7F 139
Darien Rd. SW11 . . . . .3B 118

Daring Ho. E3 . . . . .2A 86
  (off Roman Rd.)
Dark Ho. Wlk. EC3 . . . . .3F 15 (7D 84)
Darlands Dr. EN5: Barn 5A 20
Darlan Rd. SW6 . . . . .7H 99
Darlaston Rd. SW19 . . . . .7F 135
Darley Cl. CRO: C'don 6A 158
Darley Dr. KT3: N Mald 2K 151
Darley Gdns. SM4: Mord 6A 154
Darley Ho. SE11 . . . . .6G 19
Darley Rd. N9 . . . . .1A 34
  SW11 .6D 118
Darling Ho. TW1: Twick 6D 114
Darling Rd. SE4 . . . . .3C 122
Darling Row E1 . . . . .4H 85
Darlington Ct. SE6 . . . . .1H 141
Darlington Ho. SW8 . . . . .7H 101
  (off Hemans St.)
Darlington Rd. SE27 . . . . .5B 138
Darmaine Cl. CR2: S Croy 7C 168
Darnall Ho. SE10 . . . . .1E 122
  (off Royal Hill)
Darnaway Pl. E14 . . . . .5E 86
  (off Aberfeldy St.)
Darnay Apartments E15 . . . . .6F 69
Darndale Cl. E17 . . . . .2B 50
Darnley Cl. DA15: Sidc 5K 125
Darnley Ho. E14 . . . . .6A 86
  (off Camdenhurst St.)
Darnley Rd. E9 . . . . .6J 67
  IG8: Wfd G 1J 51
Darnley Ter. W11 . . . . .1F 99
Darrell Charles Ct. UB8: Uxb 7A 56
Darrell Rd. SE22 . . . . .5G 121
Darren Cl. N4 . . . . .7K 47
Darren Ct. N7 . . . . .4J 65
Darrick Wood Rd. BR6: Orp 2H 173
Darrick Wood Sports Cen. 3G 173
Darrick Wood Swimming Pool 3G 173
Darris Cl. UB4: Yead 4C 76
Darsley Dr. SW8 . . . . .1H 119
Dartford Av. N9 . . . . .6D 24
Dartford By-Pass DA5: Bexl, Dart . . .7K 127
Dartford Gdns. RM6: Chad H 5B 54
Dartford Ho. SE1 . . . . .4F 103
  (off Longfield Est.)
Dartford Rd. DA5: Bexl 1J 145
Dartford St. SE17 . . . . .6C 102
Dartington NW1 . . . . .1G 83
  (off Plender St.)
Dartington Ho. SW8 . . . . .2H 119
  (off Union Gro.)
  W2 . . . . .5K 81
  (off Senior St.)
Dartle Ct. SE16 . . . . .2G 103
  (off Scott Lidgett Cres.)
Dartmoor Wlk. E14 . . . . .4C 104
  (off Severnake Cl.)
Dartmouth Cl. W11 . . . . .6H 81
Dartmouth Ct. SE10 . . . . .1E 122
Dartmouth Gro. SE10 . . . . .1E 122
Dartmouth Hill SE10 . . . . .1E 122
Dartmouth Ho. KT2: King T 1E 150
  (off Seven Kings Way)
  SE10 .1D 122
  (off Catherine Gro.)
DARTMOUTH PARK 3F 65
Dartmouth Pk. Av. NW5 . . . . .3F 65
Dartmouth Pk. Hill N19 . . . . .1F 65
  NW5 . . . . .1F 65
Dartmouth Pk. Rd. NW5 . . . . .4F 65
Dartmouth Pl. SE23 . . . . .2J 139
  W4 . . . . .6A 98
Dartmouth Rd. BR2: Hayes 7J 159
  HA4: Ruis 3J 57
  NW2 . . . . .6F 63
  NW4 . . . . .6C 44
  SE23 . . . . .3H 139
  SE26 . . . . .3H 139
Dartmouth Row SE10 . . . . .1E 122
Dartmouth St. SW1 . . . . . .7D 12 (2H 101)

Dartmouth Ter. SE10 . . . . .1F 123
Dartnell Rd. CRO: C'don 7F 157
Darton Ct. W3 . . . . .1J 97
Dartrey Twr. SW10 . . . . .7A 100
  (off Worlds End Est.)
Dartrey Wlk. SW10 . . . . .7A 100
Dart St. W10 . . . . .3G 81
Darvell Ho. SE17 . . . . .5D 102
  (off Inville Rd.)
Darville Rd. N16 . . . . .3F 67
Darwell Cl. E6 . . . . .2E 88
Darwen Pl. E2 . . . . .2H 85
Darwin Cl. BR6: Farnb 5H 173
  N11 . . . . .3A 32
Darwin Ct. CR2: S Croy 5B 168
  (off Warham Rd.)
  E13 . . . . .3K 87
  NW1 . . . . .1F 83
  (not continuous)
  SE17 . . . . .4D 102
  (off Barlow St.)
Darwin Dr. UB1: S'hall 6F 77
Darwin Ho. SE20 . . . . .1G 157
  SW1 . . . . .7A 18
Darwin Rd. DA16: Well 3K 125
  N22 . . . . .1B 48
  W5 . . . . .5C 96
Darwin St. SE17 . . . . .4D 102
  (not continuous)
Darwood Ct. NW6 . . . . .7A 64
  (off Belsize Rd.)
Daryngton Dr. UB6: G'frd 2H 77
Daryngton Ho. SW8 . . . . .7J 101
  (off Hankey Pl.)
  SW8 . . . . .7J 101
  (off Hartington Rd.)
Dashwood Cl. DA6: Bex 5G 127
Dashwood Rd. N8 . . . . .6K 47
Dashwood Studios SE17 . . . . .4C 102
  (off Walworth Rd.)
Dassett Rd. SE27 . . . . .5B 138
Data Point Bus. Cen. E16 . . . . .4F 87
Datchelor Pl. SE5 . . . . .1D 120
Datchet Ho. E2 . . . . .3F 85
  (off Virginia Rd.)
  NW1 . . . . .1K 5
  (off Augustus St.)
Datchet Rd. SE6 . . . . .2B 140
Datchworth Ct. EN1: Enf 5K 23
Datchworth Ho. N1 . . . . .7B 66
  (off The Sutton Est.)
Date St. SE17 . . . . .5D 102
Daubeney Gdns. N17 . . . . .7H 33
Daubeney Pl. TW12: Hamp 1G 149
  (off High St.)
Daubeney Rd. E5 . . . . .4A 68
  N17 . . . . .7H 33
Daubeney Twr. SE8 . . . . .5B 104
  (off Bowditch)
Dault Rd. SW18 . . . . .6A 118
Dauncey Ho. SE1 . . . . .7A 14
Dave Adams Ho. E3 . . . . .2B 86
  (off Norman Gro.)
Davema Cl. BR7: Chst 1E 160
Davenant Ho. E1 . . . . .5G 85
  (off Old Montague St.)
Davenant Rd. CRO: C'don 4B 168
  N19 . . . . .2H 65
Davenant St. E1 . . . . .5G 85
Davenport Cen. IG11: Bark 1B 90
Davenport Ct. TW11: Tedd 6A 132
Davenport Cl. CRO: C'don 7B 156
Davenport Ho. SE11 . . . . .3J 19
  (off Walnut Tree Wlk.)
Davenport Lodge TW5: Hest 7C 94
Davenport Rd. DA14: Sidc 2E 144
  SE6 . . . . .6D 122
Daventer Dr. HA7: Stan 7E 26
Daventry Av. E17 . . . . .6C 50
Daventry Cl. SL3: Poyle 4A 174

Daventry St. NW1 . . . . .5C 4 (5C 82)
Daver Cl. SW3 . . . . .5D 16 (5C 100)
  W5 . . . . .4D 78
Davern Cl. SE10 . . . . .4H 105
Davey Cl. N7 . . . . .6K 65
  N13 . . . . .5E 32
Davey Gdns. IG11: Bark 4A 90
Davey Rd. E9 . . . . .7C 68
Davey's Cl. WC2 . . . . .2E 12
Davey St. SE15 . . . . .6F 103
David Av. UB6: G'frd 3J 77
David Cl. UB3: Harl 7G 93
David Coffer Ct. DA17: Belv 4H 109
David Ct. E14 . . . . .5D 86
  (off Hillary M.)
  N20 . . . . .3F 31
Davidge Ho. SE1 . . . . .7K 13
  (off Coral St.)
Davidge St. SE1 . . . . .7A 14 (2B 102)
David Hewitt Ho. E3 . . . . .5D 86
  (off Watts Gro.)
David Ho. DA15: Sidc 3A 144
  SW8 . . . . .7J 101
  (off Wyvil Rd.)
David Lean Cinema
  Croydon 3D 168
  (within Fairfield Halls)
David Lee Point E15 . . . . .1G 87
  (off Leather Gdns.)
David Lloyd Leisure
  Barnet .7G 31
  Beckenham 4B 158
  Cheam 7F 165
  Chigwell 1J 37
  Enfield .2B 24
  Fulham .7J 99
  (within Fulham Broadway Shop.)
  Hampton 3E 130
  Hounslow 5A 94
  Kidbrooke 4K 123
  Kingston upon Thames 2E 150
  (within The Rotunda Cen.)
  Raynes Park 3F 153
  Sidcup .5C 144
  South Kensington 4K 99
  (off Point West)
  Sudbury Hill 5H 59
David M. SE10 . . . . .7E 104
  W1 . . . . .5F 5 (5D 82)
David Rd. RM8: Dag 2E 72
  SL3: Poyle 5A 174
Davidson Gdns. SW8 . . . . .7J 101
Davidson La. HA1: Harr 7K 41
Davidson Rd. CRO: C'don 7E 157
Davidson Terraces E7 . . . . .5K 69
  (off Claremont Rd.)
David's Rd. SE23 . . . . .1J 139
David St. E15 . . . . .6F 69
David Twigg Cl. KT2: King T 1E 150
David Wildman La. NW7 . . . . .6B 30
Davies Cl. CRO: C'don 6G 157
Davies La. E11 . . . . .2G 69
Davies M. W1 . . . . .2J 11 (7F 83)
Davies St. W1 . . . . .1J 11 (6F 83)
Davies Wlk. TW7: Isle 1H 113
Da Vinci Cl. SE16 . . . . .3H 103
  (off Rossetti Rd.)
Da Vinci Lodge SE10 . . . . .3H 105
  (off West Parkside)
Da Vinci Torre SE13 . . . . .3D 122
  (off Loampit Va.)
Davington Gdns. RM8: Dag 5B 72
Davington Rd. RM8: Dag 6B 72
Davinia Cl. IG8: Wfd G 6J 37
Davis Ho. W12 . . . . .7D 80
  (off White City Est.)
Davis Rd. KT9: Chess 4G 163
  W3 . . . . .1B 98
Davis Rd. Ind. Pk. KT9: Chess 4G 163
Davis St. E13 . . . . .2A 88
Davisville Rd. W12 . . . . .2C 98

Davis Way DA14: Sidc 6E 144
Davmor Cl. TW8: Bford 5C 96
Dawburn Pl. TW5: Hest 7B 94
Dawes Av. TW7: Isle 5A 114
Dawes Cl. UB10: Uxb 2A 74
Dawes Ho. SE17 ....4D 102
　　　　　　　　　(off Orb St.)
Dawe's Rd. UB10: Uxb 2A 74
Dawes Rd. SW6 ....7G 99
Dawes St. SE17 ....5D 102
Dawkins Ct. SE1 ....3D 102
Dawley Av. UB8: Hil 5E 74
Dawley Pde. UB3: Hayes 7E 74
Dawley Pk. UB3: Hayes 2F 93
Dawley Rd. UB3: Harl, Hayes 7E 74
Dawlish Av. N13 ....4D 32
　SW18 ....2K 135
　UB6: G'frd 2A 78
Dawlish Dr. HA4: Ruis 2J 57
　HA5: Pinn 5C 40
　IG3: Ilf 4J 71
Dawlish Rd. E10 ....1E 68
　N17 ....3G 49
　NW2 ....6F 63
Dawnay Gdns. SW18 ....2B 136
Dawnay Rd. SW18 ....2A 136
Dawn Cl. TW4: Houn 3C 112
Dawn Cres. E15 ....1F 87
Dawpool Rd. NW2 ....2B 62
Daws Hill E4 ....2K 25
Daws La. NW7 ....5G 29
Dawson Av. IG11: Bark 7K 71
Dawson Cl. SE18 ....4G 107
　UB3: Hayes 5F 75
Dawson Ct. W3 ....3J 97
　　　　　　　(off Palmerston Rd.)
Dawson Gdns. IG11: Bark 7K 71
Dawson Ho. E2 ....3J 85
　　　　　　　　(off Sceptre Rd.)
Dawson Pl. W2 ....7J 81
Dawson Rd. KT1: King T 3F 151
　NW2 ....5E 62
Dawson St. E2 ....1K 9 (2F 85)
Dawson Ter. N9 ....7D 24
Dax Ct. TW16: Sun 3A 148
Daybrook Rd. SW19 ....2K 153
Day Dr. RM8: Dag 1D 72
Day Ho. SE5 ....7C 102
　　　　　　　　(off Bethwin Rd.)
Daylesford Av. SW15 ....4C 116
Daymer Gdns. HA5: Eastc 4K 39
Daynor Ho. NW6 ....1J 81
　　　　　　　　(off Quex Ho.)
Daysbrook Rd. SW2 ....1K 137
Days La. DA15: Sidc 7J 125
Dayton Gro. SE15 ....1J 121
Deaconess Ct. N15 ....4F 49
　　　　　　　(off Tottenham Grn. E.)
Deacon Estate, The E4 ....6G 35
Deacon Ho. SE11 ....4H 19
　　　　　　　　(off Black Prince Rd.)
Deacon M. N1 ....7D 66
Deacon Rd. KT2: King T 1F 151
　NW2 ....5C 62
Deacons Cl. HA5: Pinn 2K 39
Deacons Ct. TW1: Twick 2K 131
Deacons Leas BR6: Orp 4H 173
Deacon's Ri. N2 ....5B 46
Deacons Ter. N1 ....6C 66
　　　　　　　　(off Harecourt Rd.)
Deacons Wlk. TW12: Hamp 4E 130
Deacon Way IG8: Wfd G 7J 37
Deal Ct. NW9 ....1A 44
　　　　　　　　(off Hazel Cl.)
　UB1: S'hall 6B 77
　　　　　　　　(off Haldane Rd.)
Deal Ho. SE15 ....6K 103
　　　　　　　　(off Lovelinch La.)
　SE17 ....5E 102
　　　　　　　　(off Mina Rd.)
Deal M. W5 ....4D 96

Deal Porters Wlk. SE16 ....2K 103
Deal Porters Way SE16 ....3J 103
Deal Rd. SW17 ....6E 136
Deal's Gateway SE13 ....1C 122
Dealtry Rd. SW15 ....4E 116
Deal Wlk. SW9 ....7A 102
Dean Abbott Ho. SW1 ....3C 18
　　　　　　　　(off Vincent St.)
Dean Bradley St. SW1 .....2E 18 (3J 101)
Dean Cl. E9 ....5J 67
　SE16 ....1K 103
　UB10: Hil 7B 56
Dean Ct. HA0: Wemb 3B 60
　HA8: Edg 6C 28
　RM7: Rom 5K 55
　SW8 ....7J 101
　　　　　　　　(off Thorncroft St.)
　W3 ....6K 79
Dean Dr. HA7: Stan 2E 42
Deancross St. E1 ....6J 85
Deane Av. HA4: Ruis 5A 58
Deane Ct. HA6: Nwood 1G 39
Deane Cft. Rd. HA5: Eastc 6A 40
Deanery Cl. N2 ....4C 46
Deanery M. W1 ....4H 11
Deanery Rd. E15 ....6G 69
Deanery St. W1 ....4H 11 (1E 100)
Deane Way HA4: Ruis 6K 39
Dean Farrar St. SW1 ......1D 18 (3H 101)
Deanfield Gdns. CR0: C'don 4D 168
Dean Gdns. E17 ....4F 51
Deanhill Ct. SW14 ....4H 115
Deanhill Rd. SW14 ....4H 115
Dean Ho. E1 ....6J 85
　　　　　　　　(off Tarling St.)
　SE14 ....7A 104
　　　　　　　　(off New Cross Rd.)
Dean Path IG11: Bark 4A 72
Deal Rd. CR0: C'don 4D 168
　NW2 ....6E 62
　SE28 ....1A 108
　TW3: Houn 5F 113
　TW12: Hamp 5E 130
Dean Ryle St. SW1 ....3E 18 (4J 101)
Deansbrook Cl. HA8: Edg 7D 28
Deansbrook Rd. HA8: Edg 7C 28
Dean's Bldgs. SE17 ....4D 102
Deans Cl. CR0: C'don 3F 169
　HA8: Edg 6D 28
　W4 ....6H 97
　　　　　　　　(off Deans Cl.)
Dean's Ct. EC4 ....1B 14 (6B 84)
Deanscroft Av. NW9 ....1J 61
Deans Dr. HA8: Edg 5E 28
　N13 ....6G 33
Deans Ga. Cl. SE23 ....3K 139
Deanshanger Ho. SE8 ....4K 103
　　　　　　　　(off Chilton Gro.)
Deans La. HA8: Edg 6D 28
　W4 ....6H 97
　　　　　　　　(off Deans Cl.)
Dean's M. W1 ....7K 5 (6F 83)
Deans Rd. SM1: Sutt 3K 165
　W7 ....1K 95
Dean Stanley St. SW1 .....2E 18 (3J 101)
Deanston Wharf E16 ....2K 105
　　　　　　　　(not continuous)
Dean St. E7 ....5J 69
　W1 ....7C 6 (6H 83)
Deans Way HA8: Edg 5D 28
Deansway N2 ....4B 46
　N9 ....3K 33
Deanswood N11 ....6C 32
Dean's Yd. SW1 ....1D 18 (3H 101)
Dean Trench St. SW1 ......2E 18 (3J 101)
Dean Wlk. HA8: Edg 6D 28
Dean Way UB2: S'hall 2F 95
Dearne Cl. HA7: Stan 5G 27
De'Arn Gdns. CR4: Mitc 3C 154
Dearsley Ho. RM13: Rain 2K 91
Dearsley Rd. EN1: Enf 3B 24

Death Trap, London's 7G 13
Deauville Ct. SE16 ....2K 103
　　　　　　　　(off Eleanor Cl.)
　SW4 ....6G 119
De Barowe M. N5 ....4B 66
Debdale Ho. E2 ....1G 85
　　　　　　　　(off Whiston Rd.)
Debden N17 ....2D 48
　　　　　　　　(off Gloucester Rd.)
Debden Cl. IG8: Wfd G 7G 37
　KT2: King T 5D 132
　NW9 ....1A 44
De Beauvoir Ct. N1 ....7D 66
　　　　　　　(off Northchurch Rd.)
De Beauvoir Cres. N1 ....1E 84
De Beauvoir Est. N1 ....1E 84
De Beauvoir Pl. N1 ....6E 66
De Beauvoir Rd. N1 ....1E 84
De Beauvoir Sq. N1 ....7E 66
DE BEAUVOIR TOWN 1E 84
De Beauvoir Wharf N1 ....1E 84
　　　　　　　　(off Hertford Rd.)
Debenham Ct. E8 ....1G 85
　　　　　　　　(off Pownall Rd.)
Debham Ct. NW2 ....3E 62
Deblin Dr. UB10: Uxb 2A 74
Debnams Rd. SE16 ....4J 103
De Bohun Av. N14 ....6A 22
Deborah Cl. TW7: Isle 1J 113
Deborah Ct. E18 ....3K 51
　　　　　　　　(off Victoria Rd.)
Deborah Cres. HA4: Ruis 7F 39
Deborah Lodge HA8: Edg 1H 43
Debrabant Cl. DA8: Erith 6K 109
De Brome Rd. TW13: Felt 1A 130
De Bruin Ct. E14 ....5E 104
　　　　　　　　(off Ferry St.)
Deburgh Rd. SW19 ....7A 136
Debussy NW9 ....2B 44
Decima St. SE1 ....7G 15 (3E 102)
Decima Studios SE1 ....7G 15
　　　　　　　　(off Decima St.)
Decimus Cl. CR7: Thor H 4D 156
Deck Cl. SE16 ....1K 103
De Coubertin St. E20 ....6E 68
Decoy Av. NW11 ....5G 45
De Crespigny Pk. SE5 ....2D 120
Dee Ho. E14 ....6H 77
　　　　　　　　(off Hobbayne Rd.)
Dee Ho. KT2: King T 1D 150
　　　　　　　　(off May Bate Av.)
Deeley Rd. SW8 ....1H 119
Deena Cl. W3 ....6F 79
Deen City Farm 2A 154
Deepak Ho. SW17 ....4C 136
Deepdale SW19 ....4F 135
Deepdale Av. BR2: Brom 4H 159
Deepdale Cl. N11 ....6K 31
Deepdale Ct. CR2: S Croy 4D 168
　　　　　　　　(off Birdhurst Av.)
Deep Dene W5 ....4F 79
Deepdene Av. CR0: C'don 3F 169
Deepdene Cl. E11 ....4J 51
Deepdene Ct. BR2: Brom 3G 159
　N21 ....6G 23
Deepdene Gdns. SW2 ....7K 119
Deepdene Mans. SW6 ....1H 117
　　　　　　　(off Rostrevor Rd.)
Deepdene Point SE23 ....3K 139
Deepdene Rd. DA16: Well 3A 126
　SE5 ....4D 120
Deepwell Cl. TW7: Isle 1A 114
Deepwood La. UB6: G'frd 3H 77
Deerbrook Rd. SE24 ....2B 138
Deerdale Rd. SE24 ....4C 120
Deerfield Cl. NW9 ....5B 44
Deerfield Cotts. NW9 ....5B 44
Deerhurst Cl. TW13: Felt 4K 129
Deerhurst Ct. CR0: C'don 1B 168
　　　　　　　　(off Parson's Mead)
Deerhurst Cres. TW12: Hamp H 5G 131

Deerhurst Ho. SE15 ....6G 103
　　　　　　　　(off Haymerle Rd.)
Deerhurst Rd. NW2 ....6F 63
　SW16 ....5K 137
Deering Ho. SE3 ....4A 124
Deerings Dr. HA5: Eastc 5J 39
Deerleap Gro. E4 ....5J 25
Dee Rd. TW9: Rich 4F 115
Deer Pk. Cl. KT2: King T 7H 133
Deer Pk. Gdns. CR4: Mitc 4B 154
Deer Pk. Rd. SW19 ....2K 153
Deer Pk. Way BR4: W W'ck 2H 171
Deeside Rd. SW17 ....3B 136
Dee St. E14 ....6E 86
Defence Cl. SE28 ....1J 107
Defiance Wlk. SE18 ....3D 106
Defiant Way SM6: Wall 7J 167
Defoe Av. TW9: Kew 7G 97
Defoe Cl. SE16 ....2B 104
　SW17 ....6C 136
Defoe Ho. EC2 ....5D 8
　　　　　　　　(off Beech St.)
　SW17 ....4D 136
Defoe Rd. N16 ....3E 66
De Frene Rd. SE26 ....4K 139
Degema Rd. BR7: Chst 5F 143
Dehar Cres. NW9 ....7B 44
Dehavilland Cl. UB5: N'olt 3B 76
De Havilland Ct. N17 ....3H 49
De Havilland Dr. SE18 ....6F 107
De Havilland Rd. HA8: Edg 2G 43
　TW5: Hest 7A 94
Dehavilland Studios E5 ....2J 67
　　　　　　　　(off Theydon Rd.)
De Havilland Way TW19: Stanw 6A 110
Dekker Ho. SE5 ....7D 102
　　　　　　　(off Elmington St.)
Dekker Rd. SE21 ....6E 120
Delacourt Rd. SE3 ....7K 105
Delafield Ho. E1 ....6G 85
　　　　　　　　(off Christian St.)
Delafield Rd. SE7 ....5K 105
Delaford Rd. SE16 ....5H 103
Delaford St. SW6 ....7G 99
Delahay Ho. SW3 ....7E 16
　　　　　　　　(off Chelsea Emb.)
Delamare Cres. CR0: C'don 6J 157
Delamere Ct. E17 ....2E 50
Delamere Gdns. NW7 ....6E 28
Delamere Rd. SW20 ....1F 153
　UB4: Yead 7B 76
　W5 ....2C 96
Delamere St. W2 ....5K 81
Delamere Ter. W2 ....5K 81
Delancey Pas. NW1 ....1F 83
　　　　　　　　(off Delancey St.)
Delancey St. NW1 ....1F 83
Delancey Studios NW1 ....1F 83
Delany Ho. SE10 ....6E 104
　　　　　　　　(off Thames St.)
Delarch Ho. SE1 ....7A 14
De Laune St. SE17 ......6K 19 (5B 102)
Delaware Mans. W9 ....4K 81
　　　　　　　　(off Delaware Rd.)
Delaware Rd. W9 ....4K 81
Delawyk Cres. SE24 ....6C 120
Delcombe Av. KT4: Wor Pk 1E 164
Delderfield Ho. RM1: Rom 2K 55
　　　　　　　　(off Portnoi Cl.)
Delft Ho. KT2: King T 7F 133
　　　　　　　　(off Acre Rd.)
Delft Way SE22 ....5E 120
Delhi Rd. EN1: Enf 7A 24
Delhi St. N1 ....1J 83
Delia St. SW18 ....7K 117
Delisle Rd. SE28 ....1J 107
Delius Gro. E15 ....2F 87
Dell, The DA5: Bexl 1K 145
　HA0: Wemb 5B 60

Dell, The HA5: Pinn 2B **40**
IG8: Wfd G 3E **36**
SE2 5A **108**
SE19 1F **157**
TW8: Bford 6C **96**
TW14: Felt 7K **111**
Della Path E5 3G **67**
Dellbow Rd. TW14: Felt 5K **111**
Dell Cl. E15 1F **87**
IG8: Wfd G 3E **36**
SM6: Wall 4G **167**
Dell Farm Rd. HA4: Ruis 5F **39**
Dellfield Cl. BR3: Beck 1E **158**
Dell La. KT17: Ewe 5C **164**
Dellors Cl. EN5: Barn 5A **20**
Dellow Cl. IG2: Ilf 7H **53**
Dellow Ho. *E1 7H* ***85***
(off Dellow St.)
Dellow St. E1 7H **85**
Dell Rd. KT17: Ewe 6C **164**
UB7: W Dray 4B **92**
Dells Cl. E4 7J **25**
TW11: Tedd 6K **131**
Dell's M. SW1 4B **18**
Dell Wlk. KT3: N Mald 2A **152**
Dell Way W13 6C **78**
Dellwood Gdns. IG5: Ilf 3E **52**
Delmare Cl. SW9 4K **119**
Delme Cres. SE3 2K **123**
Delmerend Ho. *SW3 5C* ***16***
(off Cale St.)
Delmey Cl. CR0: C'don 3F **169**
Deloraine Ho. SE8 1C **122**
Delorme St. W6 6F **99**
Delroy Ct. N20 7F **21**
Delta Bldg. *E14 6E* ***86***
(off Ashton St.)
Delta Bldg., The RM7: Rush G 6K **55**
Delta Cen. HA0: Wemb 1F **79**
Delta Cl. KT4: Wor Pk 3B **164**
Delta Ct. NW2 2C **62**
SE8 6A ***104***
(off Trundleys Rd.)
Delta Gro. UB5: N'olt 3B **76**
Delta Ho. *N1 1E* ***8***
(off Nile St.)
Delta Pk. SW18 4K **117**
Delta Pk. Ind. Est. EN3: Brim 3G **25**
Delta Point *CR0: C'don 1C* ***168***
(off Wellesley Rd.)
E2 3G ***85***
(off Delta St.)
Delta Rd. KT4: Wor Pk 3A **164**
Delta St. E2 3G **85**
De Luci Rd. DA8: Erith 5J **109**
De Lucy St. SE2 4B **108**
Delvan Cl. SE18 7E **106**
Delvers Mead RM10: Dag 4J **73**
Delverton Ho. *SE17 5B* ***102***
(off Delverton Rd.)
Delverton Rd. SE17 5B **102**
Delvino Rd. SW6 1J **117**
Demesne Rd. SM6: Wall 4H **167**
Demeta Cl. HA9: Wemb 3J **61**
De Montfort Pde. SW16 3J **137**
De Montfort Rd. SW16 3J **137**
De Morgan Rd. SW6 3K **117**
Dempsey Ct. SE6 7C **122**
Dempster Cl. KT6: Surb 1C **162**
Dempster Rd. SW18 5A **118**
Den, The **5J 103**
Denbar Pde. RM7: Rom 4J **55**
Denberry Dr. DA14: Sidc 3B **144**
Denbigh Cl. BR7: Chst 6D **142**
HA4: Ruis 2H **57**
SM1: Sutt 5H **165**
UB1: S'hall 6D **76**
W11 7H **81**
Denbigh Ct. E6 3B **88**
W7 5K ***77***
(off Copley Cl.)
Denbigh Dr. UB3: Harl 2E **92**
Denbigh Gdns. TW10: Rich 5F **115**
Denbigh Ho. *SW1 1F* ***17***
(off Hans Pl.)
W11 7H ***81***
(off Westbourne Gro.)
Denbigh M. SW1 4A **18**
Denbigh Pl. SW1 5A **18** (5G **101**)
Denbigh Rd. E6 3B **88**
TW3: Houn 2F **113**
UB1: S'hall 6D **76**
W11 7H **81**
W13 7B **78**
Denbigh St. SW1 4A **18** (4G **101**)
(not continuous)
Denbigh Ter. W11 7H **81**
Denbridge Rd. BR1: Brom 2D **160**
Denbury Ho. *E3 3D* ***86***
(off Talwin St.)
Denby Ct. SE11 3H **19**
Dence Ho. *E2 2K* ***9***
(off Turin St.)
Denchworth Ho. SW9 2A **120**
Dencliffe TW15: Ashf 5C **128**
Den Cl. BR3: Beck 3F **159**
Dencora Cen., The EN3: Brim 3F **25**
Dene, The CR0: C'don 4K **169**
HA9: Wemb 4E **60**
KT8: W Mole 5D **148**
W13 5B **78**
Dene Av. DA15: Sidc 7B **126**
TW3: Houn 3D **112**
Dene Cl. BR2: Hayes 1H **171**
DA2: Wilm 4K **145**
E10 2D **68**
KT4: Wor Pk 2B **164**
SE4 3A **122**
Dene Ct. *CR2: S Croy 5C* ***168***
(off Warham Rd.)
W5 5C **78**
Denecroft Cres. UB10: Hil 1D **74**
Dene Gdns. HA7: Stan 5H **27**
KT7: T Ditt 2A **162**
Dene Ho. N14 7C **22**
Denehurst Gdns. IG8: Wfd G 4E **36**
NW4 6E **44**
TW2: Twick 7H **113**
TW10: Rich 4G **115**
W3 1H **97**
Dene Rd. IG9: Buck H 1G **37**
N11 1J **31**
Denesmead SE24 5C **120**
Denewood EN5: New Bar 5F **21**
Denewood Rd. N6 6D **46**
Denford St. *SE10 5H* ***105***
(off Glenforth St.)
Dengie Wlk. *N1 1C* ***84***
(off Basire St.)
Denham Cl. DA16: Well 3C **126**
Denham Ct. *NW6 7A* ***64***
(off Fairfax Rd.)
SE26 3H ***139***
(off Kirkdale)
UB1: S'hall 7G ***77***
(off Baird Av.)
Denham Cres. CR4: Mitc 4D **154**
Denham Dr. IG2: Ilf 6G **53**
Denham Ho. *UB7: W Dray 2B* ***92***
(off Park Lodge Av.)
W12 7D ***80***
(off White City Est.)
Denham Rd. N20 3J **31**
TW14: Felt 7A **112**
Denham St. SE10 5J **105**
Denham Way IG11: Bark 1J **89**
Denholme Rd. W9 3H **81**
Denison Cl. N2 3A **46**
Denison Ho. E14 3D **104**
Denison Rd. SW19 6B **136**
TW13: Felt 4H **129**
W5 4C **78**
Deniston Av. DA5: Bexl 1E **144**
Denis Way SW4 3H **119**
Denland Ho. *SW8 7K* ***101***
(off Dorset Rd.)
Denleigh Gdns. KT7: T Ditt 6J **149**
N21 1F **33**
Denman Dr. KT10: Clay 5A **162**
NW11 5J **45**
TW15: Ashf 6D **128**
Denman Dr. Nth. NW11 5J **45**
Denman Dr. Sth. NW11 5J **45**
Denman Ho. N16 2E **66**
Denman Pl. W1 2C **12**
Denman Rd. SE15 1F **121**
Denman St. W1 3C **12** (7H **83**)
Denmark Av. SW19 7G **135**
Denmark Ct. SM4: Mord 6J **153**
Denmark Gdns. SM5: Cars 3D **166**
Denmark Gro. N1 2A **84**
DENMARK HILL 3C **120**
Denmark Hill SE5 1D **120**
Denmark Hill Dr. NW9 3C **44**
Denmark Hill Est. SE5 4D **120**
Denmark Ho. SE7 4C **106**
Denmark Mans. *SE5 2C* ***120***
(off Coldharbour La.)
Denmark Path SE25 5H **157**
Denmark Pl. E3 3C **86**
WC2 7D **6** (6H **83**)
Denmark Rd. BR1: Brom 1K **159**
KT1: King T 3E **150**
N8 4A **48**
NW6 2H **81**
SE5 1C **120**
SE25 5G **157**
SM5: Cars 3D **166**
SW19 6F **135**
TW2: Twick 3H **131**
W13 7B **78**
Denmark St. E11 3G **69**
E13 5K **87**
N17 1H **49**
WC2 7D **6** (6H **83**)
Denmark Ter. N2 3D **46**
Denmark Wlk. SE27 4C **138**
Denmead Ho. SW15 6B **116**
Denmead Rd. CR0: C'don 1B **168**
Denmore Ct. SM6: Wall 5F **167**
Dennan Rd. KT6: Surb 1F **163**
Dennard Way BR6: Farnb 4F **173**
Denner Rd. E4 2H **35**
Denne Ter. E8 1F **85**
Dennett Rd. CR0: C'don 1A **168**
Dennett's Gro. SE14 2K **121**
Dennett's Rd. SE14 1J **121**
Denning Av. CR0: Wadd 4A **168**
Denning Cl. NW8 1A **4** (3A **82**)
TW12: Hamp 5D **130**
Denning M. SW12 6E **118**
Denning Point *E1 7K* ***9***
(off Commercial St.)
Denning Rd. NW3 4B **64**
Dennington Cl. E5 2J **67**
Dennington Pk. Rd. NW6 6J **63**
Denningtons, The KT4: Wor Pk 2A **164**
Dennis Av. HA9: Wemb 5F **61**
Dennis Cl. TW15: Ashf 7F **129**
Dennis Gdns. HA7: Stan 5H **27**
Dennis Ho. *E3 2B* ***86***
(off Roman Rd.)
SM1: Sutt 4K **165**
Dennis La. HA7: Stan 3G **27**
Dennison Point E15 7E **68**
Dennis Pde. N14 1C **32**
Dennis Pk. Cres. SW20 1G **153**
Dennis Reeve Cl. CR4: Mitc 1D **154**
Dennis Rd. KT8: E Mos 4G **149**
Dennis Severs' House **5H 9 (5E 84)**
Dennis Way SW4 3H **119**
Denny Cl. E6 5C **88**
Denny Cres. SE11 5K **19** (5A **102**)
Denny Gdns. RM9: Dag 7B **72**
Denny Rd. N9 1C **34**
Denny St. SE11 5K **19** (5A **102**)
Den Rd. BR2: Brom 3F **159**
Densham Ho. *NW8 1B* ***4***
(off Cochrane St.)
Densham Rd. E15 1G **87**
Densole Cl. BR3: Beck 1A **158**
Denstone Ho. *SE15 6G* ***103***
(off Haymerle Rd.)
Densworth Gro. N9 2D **34**
Dent Ho. *SE17 4E* ***102***
(off Peacock St.)
Denton NW1 6E **64**
Denton Ho. *N1 7B* ***66***
(off Halton Rd.)
Denton Rd. DA5: Bexl 2K **145**
DA16: Well 7C **108**
N8 5K **47**
N18 4K **33**
TW1: Twick 6D **114**
Denton St. SW18 6K **117**
Denton Ter. DA5: Bexl 2K **145**
Denton Way E5 3K **67**
Dents Rd. SW11 6D **118**
Denver Cl. BR6: Pet W 6J **161**
Denver Rd. N16 7E **48**
Denwood SE23 3K **139**
Denyer St. SW3 4D **16** (4C **100**)
Denys Ho. *EC1 5J* ***7***
(off Bourne Est.)
Denziloe Av. UB10: Hil 3D **74**
Denzil Rd. NW10 5B **62**
Deodar Rd. SW15 4G **117**
Deodora Cl. N20 3H **31**
Department for Communities **1A 18**
De Pass Gdns. IG11: Bark 4A **90**
Depot App. NW2 4F **63**
Depot Rd. TW3: Houn 3H **113**
W12 7E **80**
Depot St. SE5 6D **102**
DEPTFORD 7C **104**
Deptford Bri. SE8 1C **122**
Deptford B'way. SE8 1C **122**
Deptford Bus. Pk. SE15 6J **103**
Deptford Chu. St. SE8 6C **104**
Deptford Creek Bri. *SE8 6D* ***104***
(off Creek Rd.)
Deptford Ferry Rd. E14 4C **104**
Deptford Grn. SE8 6C **104**
Deptford High St. SE8 6C **104**
Deptford Pk. Bus. Cen. SE8 5A **104**
Deptford Strand SE8 4B **104**
Deptford Trad. Est. SE8 5A **104**
Deptford Wharf SE8 4B **104**
De Quincey Ho. *SW1 6A* ***18***
(off Lupus St.)
De Quincey M. E16 1J **105**
De Quincey Rd. N17 1D **48**
Derby Av. HA3: Hrw W 1H **41**
N12 5F **31**
RM7: Rom 6J **55**
Derby Ga. SW1 6E **12** (2J **101**)
(not continuous)
Derby Hill SE23 2J **139**
Derby Hill Cres. SE23 2J **139**
Derby Ho. HA5: Pinn 2B **40**
SE11 3J **19**
Derby Lodge N3 2H **45**
WC1 1G ***7***
(off Britannia St.)
Derby Rd. CR0: C'don 1B **168**
E7 7B **70**
E9 1K **85**
E18 1H **51**
EN3: Pond E 5C **24**
KT5: Surb 1G **163**
N18 5D **34**
SM1: Sutt 6H **165**
SW14 4H **115**
SW19 7J **135**

Derby Rd. TW3: Houn 4F 113
UB6: G'frd 1F 77
Derby Rd. Ind. Est. TW3: Houn 4F 113
Derbyshire St. E2 3G 85
(not continuous)
Derby St. W1 5H 11 (1E 100)
Dere Cl. SW6 1G 117
Dereham Ho. SE4 4K 121
(off Frendsbury Rd.)
Dereham Pl. EC2 2H 9 (3E 84)
Dereham Rd. IG11: Bark 5K 71
Derek Av. HA9: Wemb 7H 61
KT19: Ewe 6G 163
SM6: Wall 4F 167
Derek Cl. KT19: Ewe 5H 163
Derek Walcott Cl. SE24 5B 120
Dericote St. E8 1H 85
Deri Dene Cl. TW19: Stanw 6A 110
Derifall Cl. E6 5D 88
Dering Pl. CR0: C'don 4C 168
Dering Rd. CR0: C'don 4C 168
Dering St. W1 1K 11 (6F 83)
Dering Yd. W1 1K 11 (6F 83)
Derinton Rd. SW17 4D 136
Derley Rd. UB2: S'hall 3A 94
Dermody Gdns. SE13 5F 123
Dermody Rd. SE13 5F 123
Deronda Rd. SE24 1B 138
Deroy Cl. SM5: Cars 6D 166
Derrick Gdns. SE7 3A 106
Derrick Rd. BR3: Beck 3B 158
Derrycombe Ho. W2 5J 81
(off Gt. Western Rd.)
Derry Ho. NW8 4B 4
(off Church St. Est.)
Derry M. N19 2J 65
Derry Rd. CR0: Bedd 3J 167
Derry St. W8 2K 99
Dersingham Av. E12 4D 70
Dersingham Rd. NW2 3G 63
Derwent NW1 2A 6
(off Robert St.)
Derwent Av. EN4: E Barn 1J 31
N18 5J 33
NW7 6E 28
NW9 5A 44
SW15 4A 134
UB10: Ick 2C 56
Derwent Cl. TW14: Felt 1H 129
Derwent Ct. SE16 2K 103
(off Eleanor Cl.)
Derwent Cres. DA7: Bex 2G 127
HA7: Stan 2C 42
N20 3F 31
Derwent Dr. BR5: Pet W 7H 161
UB4: Hayes 5G 75
Derwent Gdns. HA9: Wemb 7C 42
IG4: Ilf 4C 52
Derwent Gro. SE22 4F 121
Derwent Ho. E3 4B 86
(off Southern Gro.)
KT2: King T 1D 150
(off May Bate Av.)
SW7 3A 16
(off Cromwell Rd.)
Derwent Lodge KT4: Wor Pk 2D 164
TW7: Isle 2H 113
Derwent Point EC1 1A 8
(off Goswell Rd.)
Derwent Ri. NW9 6A 44
Derwent Rd. N13 4E 32
SE20 2G 157
SW20 6F 153
TW2: Whitt 6F 113
UB1: S'hall 6D 76
W5 3C 96
Derwent St. SE10 5G 105
Derwent Wlk. SM6: Wall 7F 167
Derwentwater Rd. W3 1J 97
Derwent Yd. W5 3C 96
(off Derwent Rd.)
De Salis Rd. UB10: Hil 4E 74
Des Barres Ct. SE10 3J 105
Desborough Cl. TW17: Shep 7C 146
W2 5K 81
Desborough Ho. W14 6H 99
(off North End Rd.)
Desborough Sailing Club 7D 146
Desborough St. W2 5K 81
(off Cirencester St.)
Desenfans Rd. SE21 6E 120
Desford Rd. E16 4G 87
Desford Way TW15: Ashf 2B 128
Design Mus.
Kensington 3H 99
Desmond Ho. EN4: E Barn 6H 21
Desmond St. SE14 6A 104
Desmond Tutu Dr. SE23 1B 140
Despard Rd. N19 1G 65
Desvignes Dr. SE13 6F 123
Dethick Ct. E3 1A 86
Detling Ho. SE17 4E 102
(off Congreve St.)
Detling Rd. BR1: Brom 5J 141
DA8: Erith 7K 109
Detmold Rd. E5 2J 67
Dettingen Pl. IG11: Bark 2B 90
Devalls Cl. E6 7F 89
Devana End SM5: Cars 3D 166
Devane Way SE27 3B 138
Devan Gro. N4 7D 48
Devas Rd. SW20 1E 152
Devas St. E3 4D 86
Devenay Rd. E15 7H 69
Devenish Rd. SE2 2A 108
Deventer Cres. SE22 5E 120
Deveraux Cl. BR3: Beck 5E 158
De Vere Cl. SM6: Wall 7J 167
De Vere Cotts. W8 3A 100
(off Canning Pl.)
De Vere Gdns. IG1: Ilf 2D 70
W8 2A 100
Deverell St. SE1 3D 102
De Vere M. W8 3A 100
(off Canning Pl.)
Devereux Ct. WC2 1J 13
Devereux La. SW13 7D 98
Devereux Rd. SW11 6D 118
Deveron Way RM1: Rom 1K 55
Devey Cl. KT2: King T 7B 134
Devitt Ho. E14 7D 86
(off Wade's Pl.)
Devizes St. N1 1D 84
Devon Av. TW2: Twick 1G 131
Devon Cl. IG9: Buck H 2E 36
N17 3F 49
UB6: G'frd 1C 78
Devon Ct. TW12: Hamp 7E 130
W7 5K 77
(off Copley Cl.)
Devoncroft Gdns. TW1: Twick 7A 114
Devon Gdns. N4 6B 48
Devon Ho. E17 2B 50
N1 2B 84
(off Upper St.)
Devonhurst Pl. W4 5K 97
Devonia Gdns. N18 6H 33
Devonia Rd. N1 2B 84
Devon Mans. HA3: Kenton 5C 42
(off Woodcock Hill)
SE1 6J 15
(off Tooley St.)
Devon Pde. HA3: Kenton 5C 42
Devonport W2 1C 10 (6C 82)
Devonport Gdns. IG1: Ilf 6D 52
Devonport Ho. W2 5J 81
(off Gt. Western Rd.)
Devonport M. W12 2D 98
Devonport Rd. W12 1D 98
(not continuous)
Devonport St. E1 6J 85
Devon Ri. N2 4B 46
Devon Rd. IG11: Bark 1J 89
SM2: Cheam 7G 165
Devons Est. E3 3D 86
Devonshire Av. SM2: Sutt 7A 166
Devonshire Cl. E15 4G 69
N13 3F 33
W1 5J 5 (5F 83)
Devonshire Ct. E1 3J 85
(off Bancroft Rd.)
HA5: Hat E 1D 40
(off Devonshire Rd.)
N17 6H 33
TW13: Felt 2K 129
WC1 5F 7
(off Boswell St.)
Devonshire Cres. NW7 7A 30
Devonshire Dr. KT6: Surb 1D 162
SE10 7D 104
Devonshire Gdns. N17 6H 33
N21 7H 23
W4 7J 97
Devonshire Gro. SE15 6H 103
Devonshire Hall E9 6J 67
(off Frampton Pk. Rd.)
Devonshire Hill La. N17 6G 33
Devonshire Ho. E14 4C 104
(off Westferry Rd.)
IG8: Wfd G 7K 37
NW6 6H 63
(off Kilburn High Rd.)
SE1 3C 102
(off Bath Ter.)
SM2: Sutt 7A 166
SW1 5D 18
(off Lindsay Sq.)
SW15 5F 117
W2 5B 4
(off Adpar St.)
Devonshire Ho. Bus. Cen.
BR2: Brom 4K 159
(off Devonshire Sq.)
Devonshire M. N13 4F 33
SW10 7A 16
(off Park Wlk.)
W4 5A 98
Devonshire M. Nth. W1 5J 5 (5F 83)
Devonshire M. Sth. W1 5J 5 (5F 83)
Devonshire M. W. W1 4H 5 (4E 82)
Devonshire Pas. W4 5A 98
Devonshire Pl. NW2 3J 63
W1 4H 5 (4E 82)
W8 3K 99
Devonshire Pl. M. W1 4H 5 (5E 82)
Devonshire Point TW15: Ashf 3E 128
Devonshire Rd. BR6: Orp 7K 161
CR0: C'don 7D 156
DA6: Bex 4E 126
E16 6K 87
E17 6C 50
HA1: Harr 6H 41
HA5: Eastc 6A 40
HA5: Hat E 1D 40
IG2: Ilf 7J 53
N9 1D 34
N13 4E 32
N17 6H 33
NW7 7A 30
SE9 2C 142
SE23 1J 139
SM2: Sutt 7A 166
SM5: Cars 4E 166
SW19 7C 136
TW13: Hanw 3C 130
UB1: S'hall 5E 76
W4 5A 98
W5 3C 96
Devonshire Road Nature Reserve 7K 121
Devonshire Road Nature Reserve Vis. Cen.
7K 121
Devonshire Row EC2 6H 9 (5E 84)
Devonshire Row M. W1 4K 5
Devonshire Sq. BR2: Brom 4K 159
EC2 6H 9 (6E 84)
Devonshire St. W1 5H 5 (5E 82)
W4 5A 98
Devonshire Ter. W2 6A 82
Devonshire Way CR0: C'don 2A 170
UB4: Yead 6K 75
Devons Rd. E3 3D 86
Devon St. SE15 6H 103
Devon Way KT9: Chess 5C 162
KT19: Ewe 5H 163
UB10: Hil 2B 74
Devon Waye TW5: Hest 7D 94
De Walden Ho. NW8 2C 82
(off Allitsen Rd.)
De Walden St. W1 6H 5 (5E 82)
Dewar St. SE15 3G 121
Dewberry Gdns. E6 5C 88
Dewberry St. E14 5E 86
Dewey Ct. BR1: Brom 3J 159
Dewey La. SW2 6A 120
(off Tulse Hill)
Dewey Rd. N1 2A 84
RM10: Dag 6H 73
Dewey St. SW17 5D 136
Dewhurst Ct. TW3: Houn 4E 112
Dewhurst Rd. W14 3F 99
Dewsbury Cl. HA5: Pinn 6C 40
Dewsbury Ct. W4 4J 97
Dewsbury Gdns. KT4: Wor Pk 3C 164
Dewsbury Rd. NW10 5C 62
Dewsbury Ter. NW1 1F 83
Dews Farm Sand Pits Nature Reserve
6A 38
De Wyndsor Ct. SE16 3G 103
(off Jamaica Rd.)
Dexter Apartments SE15 1H 121
(off Queen's Rd.)
Dexter Ho. DA18: Erith 3E 108
(off Kale Rd.)
Dexter Rd. EN5: Barn 6A 20
Deyncourt Rd. N17 1C 48
Deynecourt Gdns. E11 4A 52
D'Eynsford Rd. SE5 1D 120
Dhonau Ho. SE1 4F 103
(off Longfield Est.)
Diadem Ct. W1 7C 6
Dial Wlk., The W8 2K 99
Diameter Rd. BR5: Pet W 7F 161
Diamond Cl. RM8: Dag 1C 72
Diamond Est. SW17 3C 136
Diamond Gdns. E3 5B 86
Diamond Ho. E3 2A 86
(off Roman Rd.)
Diamond Jubilee Way SM5: Cars 7D 166
Diamond Rd. HA4: Ruis 4B 58
Diamond St. NW10 7K 61
SE15 7E 102
Diamond Ter. SE10 1E 122
Diamond Way SE8 6C 104
Diana Cl. DA14: Sidc 2E 144
E18 1K 51
SE8 6B 104
Diana Gdns. KT6: Surb 2F 163
Diana Ho. SW13 1B 116
Diana, Princess of Wales
Memorial Playground 1K 99
Diana, Princess of Wales Memorial Walk
1A 100
(within Kensington Gdns.)
Diana Rd. E17 3B 50
Dianne Ct. SE12 1J 141
Dianne Way EN4: E Barn 4H 21
Dianthus Cl. SE2 5B 108
Dibden Ho. SE5 7E 102
Dibden St. N1 1C 84
Dibdin Cl. SM1: Sutt 3J 165
Dibdin Ho. W9 2K 81
Dibdin Rd. SM1: Sutt 3J 165
Dibdin Row SE1 1K 19 (3A 102)
Dicey Av. NW2 4E 62

Dickens Av. N3 1A 46
UB8: Hil 6D 74
Dickens Cl. DA8: Erith 7H 109
TW10: Ham 2E 132
UB3: Harl 4G 93
Dickens Ct. *E11 4J 51*
(off Makepeace Rd.)
SW17 3B 136
(off Grosvenor Way)
Dickens Dr. BR7: Chst 6G 143
Dickens Est. SE1 2G 103
SE16 3G 103
Dickens Ho. *NW6 3J 81*
(off Malvern Rd.)
NW8 3B 4
SE17 5B 102
(off Doddington Gro.)
SE19 7E 138
WC1 3E 6
Dickens La. N18 5K 33
Dickens M. *EC1 5A 8*
(off Turnmill St.)
Dickenson Cl. N9 1B 34
Dickenson Rd. N8 7J 47
TW13: Hanw 5A 130
Dickensons La. SE25 5G 157
(not continuous)
Dickensons Pl. SE25 6G 157
Dickens Pl. SL3: Poyle 4A 174
Dickens Ri. IG7: Chig 3K 37
Dickens Rd. E6 2B 88
Dickens Sq. SE1 7D 14 (3C 102)
Dickens St. SW8 2F 119
Dickenswood Cl. SE19 7B 138
Dickerage La. KT3: N Mald 3J 151
Dickerage Rd. KT1: King T 1J 151
KT3: N Mald 1J 151
Dickinson Ct. *EC1 3B 8*
(off Brewhouse Yd.)
Dicksee Ho. *NW8 4A 4*
(off Lyons Pl.)
Dickson Fold HA5: Pinn 4B 40
Dickson Ho. *E1 6H 85*
(off Philpot St.)
N1 7A 66
(off Drummond Way)
Dickson Rd. SE9 3C 124
Dick Turpin Way TW14: Felt 4H 111
Didsbury Cl. E6 1D 88
Dieppe Cl. W14 5H 99
Digby Bus. Cen. *E9 6K 67*
(off Digby Rd.)
Digby Cres. N4 2C 66
Digby Gdns. RM10: Dag 1G 91
Digby Mans. *W6 5D 98*
(off Hammersmith Bri. Rd.)
Digby Pl. CR0: C'don 3F 169
Digby Rd. E9 6K 67
IG11: Bark 7K 71
Digby St. E2 3J 85
Diggon St. E1 5K 85
Dighton Ct. SE5 6C 102
Dighton Rd. SW18 5A 118
Dignum St. N1 2A 84
Digswell St. N7 6A 66
Dilhorne Cl. SE12 3K 141
Dilke St. SW3 7F 17 (6D 100)
Dilloway La. UB2: S'hall 2C 94
Dillwyn Cl. SE26 4A 140
Dilston Cl. UB5: N'olt 3A 76
Dilston Gro. SE16 4J 103
Dilton Gdns. SW15 1C 134
Dilwyn Ct. E17 2A 50
Dimes Pl. W6 4D 98
Dimmock Dr. UB6: G'frd 5H 59
Dimond Cl. E7 4J 69
Dimsdale Dr. EN1: Enf 7B 24
NW9 1J 61
Dimsdale Hgts. *E1 6H 85*
(off Spencer Way)
Dimsdale Wlk. E13 2J 87
Dimson Cres. E3 3C 86
Dinerman Ct. NW8 1A 82
Dingle, The UB10: Hil 3D 74
Dingle Gdns. E14 7C 86
Dingle Rd. TW15: Ashf 5D 128
Dingles Ct. HA5: Pinn 1B 40
Dingley La. SW16 2H 137
Dingley Pl. EC1 1D 8 (3C 84)
Dingley Rd. EC1 2C 8 (3C 84)
Dingwall Av. CR0: C'don 2C 168
Dingwall Gdns. NW11 6J 45
Dingwall Rd. CR0: C'don 1D 168
SM5: Cars 7D 166
SW18 7A 118
Dinmont Est. E2 2G 85
Dinmont Ho. *E2 2G 85*
(off Pritchard's Rd.)
Dinmont St. E2 2H 85
Dinmore Ho. *E9 1J 85*
(off Templecombe Rd.)
Dinnington Ho. *E1 4H 85*
(off Coventry Rd.)
Dinsdale Gdns. EN5: New Bar 5E 20
SE25 5E 156
Dinsdale Rd. SE3 6H 105
Dinsmore Rd. SW12 7F 119
Dinton Ho. *NW8 3D 4*
(off Lilestone St.)
Dinton Rd. KT2: King T 7F 133
SW19 6B 136
Diploma Av. N2 4C 46
Diploma Ct. N2 4C 46
Diprose Lodge SW17 4B 136
Dirleton Rd. E15 1H 87
Dirty La. SE1 1C 102
Disbrowe Rd. W6 6G 99
Discover
Stratford 7F 69
Discover Greenwich Vis. Cen. 6E 104
Discovery Bus. Pk. *SE16 3G 103*
(off St James's Rd.)
Discovery Cen. (Beckton), The 3G 89
Discovery Dock Apartments E. *E14 2D 104*
(off Sth. Quay Sq.)
Discovery Dock Apartments W.
E14 2D 104
(off Sth. Quay Sq.)
Discovery Ho. *E14 7E 86*
(off Newby Pl.)
Discovery Wlk. E1 1H 103
Dishforth La. NW9 7F 29
Disley Ct. *UB1: S'hall 6F 77*
(off Howard Rd.)
Disney Pl. SE1 6D 14 (2C 102)
Disney St. SE1 6D 14 (2C 102)
Dison Cl. EN3: Enf H 1E 24
Disraeli Cl. SE28 1C 108
W4 3K 97
Disraeli Gdns. SW15 4H 117
Disraeli Rd. E7 6J 69
NW10 2K 79
SW15 4G 117
W5 1D 96
Diss St. E2 1J 9 (3F 85)
Distaff La. EC4 2C 14 (7C 84)
Distillery La. W6 5E 98
Distillery Rd. W6 5E 98
Distillery Twr. SE8 1C 122
Distillery Wlk. TW8: Bford 6E 96
Distillery Wharf W6 6E 98
Distin St. SE11 4J 19 (4A 102)
District Rd. HA0: Wemb 5B 60
Ditch All. SE13 1D 122
Ditchburn St. E14 7E 86
Ditchfield Rd. UB4: Yead 4C 76
Ditchley Ct. *W7 5K 77*
(off Templeman Rd.)
Dittisham Rd. SE9 4C 142
Ditton Cl. KT7: T Ditt 7A 150
Dittoncroft Cl. CR0: C'don 4E 168
Ditton Grange Cl. KT6: Surb 1D 162
Ditton Grange Dr. KT6: Surb 1D 162
Ditton Hill KT6: Surb 1C 162
Ditton Hill Rd. KT6: Surb 1C 162
Ditton Lawn KT7: T Ditt 1A 162
Ditton Pl. SE20 1H 157
Ditton Reach KT7: T Ditt 6B 150
Ditton Rd. DA6: Bex 5D 126
KT6: Surb 2D 162
UB2: S'hall 5D 94
Diversity Av. RM13: Rain 2K 91
Divine Way UB3: Hayes 6F 75
Divis Way *SW15 6D 116*
(off Dover Pk. Dr.)
Dixon Clark Ct. N1 6B 66
Dixon Cl. E6 6D 88
Dixon Ho. *W10 6F 81*
(off Darfield Way)
Dixon Pl. BR4: W W'ck 1D 170
Dixon Rd. SE14 1A 122
SE25 3E 156
Dixon's All. SE16 2H 103
Dixon Way NW10 7A 62
Dobbin Cl. HA3: Kenton 2A 42
Dobell Rd. SE9 5D 124
Dobree Av. NW10 7D 62
Dobson Cl. NW6 7B 64
Dobson Ho. *SE14 6K 103*
(off John Williams Cl.)
Dobson Wlk. SE5 7D 102
Doby Ct. EC4 2D 14
Dock Cotts. *E1 7J 85*
(off The Highway)
Dockers Tanner Rd. E14 3C 104
Dockett Eddy KT16: Chert 7A 146
Dockett Eddy La. TW17: Shep 7B 146
Dockett Moorings KT16: Chert 7A 146
Dockhead SE1 7K 15 (2F 103)
Dockhead Wharf *SE1 7K 15*
(off Shad Thames)
Dock Hill Av. SE16 1K 103
Docklands Ct. *E14 6B 86*
(off Wharf La.)
Docklands Equestrian Cen., The 4E 88
Docklands Sailing & Watersports Cen.
3C 104
Dockland St. E16 1E 106
(not continuous)
Dockley Rd. SE16 3G 103
Dockley Rd. Ind. Est. *SE16 3G 103*
(off Dockley Rd.)
Dock Mdw. Reach W7 3J 95
Dock Offices *SE16 3J 103*
(off Surrey Quays Rd.)
Dock Rd. E16 7H 87
IG11: Bark 2G 89
TW8: Bford 7D 96
Dockside Ct. E5 2J 67
Dockside Rd. E16 7B 88
Dock St. E1 7G 85
Dockwell Cl. TW14: Felt 4J 111
Dockwell's Ind. Est. TW14: Felt 5K 111
Doctor Johnson Av. SW17 3F 137
Dr Johnson's House *1K 13*
(off Pemberton Row)
Doctors Cl. SE26 5J 139
Docura Ho. N7 2K 65
Docwra's Bldgs. N1 6E 66
Dodbrooke Rd. SE27 3A 138
Dodd Ho. *SE16 4H 103*
(off Rennie Est.)
Doddington Gro. SE17 6B 102
Doddington Pl. SE17 6B 102
Dodsley Pl. N9 3D 34
Dodson St. SE1 7K 13 (2A 102)
Dod St. E14 6B 86
Doebury Wlk. *SE18 7A 108*
(off Prestwood Cl.)
Doel Cl. SW19 7A 136
Dog & Duck Yd. WC1 5H 7
Doggett Rd. SE6 7C 122
Doggetts Cl. EN4: E Barn 5H 21
Doghurst Av. UB3: Harl 7D 92
Doghurst Dr. UB7: Sip 7D 92
Dog Kennel Hill SE22 3E 120
Dog Kennel Hill Est. *SE22 3E 120*
(off Albrighton Rd.)
Dog La. NW10 4A 62
Doherty Rd. E13 4J 87
Dokal Ind. Est. UB2: S'hall 2C 94
Dolben Ct. *SW1 4D 18*
(off Montaigne Cl.)
Dolben St. SE1 5A 14 (1B 102)
(not continuous)
Dolby Rd. SW6 2H 117
Dolland Ho. SE11 6H 19
Dolland St. SE11 6H 19 (5K 101)
Dollar Bay E14 2E 104
Dollary Pde. *KT1: King T 3H 151*
(off Kingston Rd.)
Dolliffe Cl. CR4: Mitc 2C 154
Dollis Av. N3 1H 45
Dollis Brook Wlk. EN5: Barn 6B 20
Dollis Cres. HA4: Ruis 1A 58
Dolliscroft NW7 7B 30
DOLLIS HILL 2D 62
Dollis Hill Av. NW2 3D 62
Dollis Hill La. NW2 4B 62
Dollis M. N3 1J 45
Dollis Pk. N3 1H 45
Dollis Rd. N3 7B 30
NW7 7B 30
Dollis Valley Dr. EN5: Barn 6C 20
Dollis Valley Way EN5: Barn 6C 20
Dolman Cl. N3 2A 46
Dolman Rd. W4 4K 97
Dolman St. SW4 4K 119
Dolphin Cl. KT6: Surb 5D 150
SE16 2K 103
SE28 6D 90
Dolphin Ct. NW11 6G 45
Dolphin Est. TW16: Sun 1G 147
Dolphin Ho. *SW6 2A 118*
(off Lensbury Av.)
SW18 4K 117
Dolphin La. E14 7D 86
Dolphin Rd. TW16: Sun 1G 147
UB5: N'olt 2D 76
Dolphin Rd. Nth. TW16: Sun 1G 147
Dolphin Rd. Sth. TW16: Sun 1G 147
Dolphin Rd. W. TW16: Sun 1G 147
Dolphin Sq. SW1 6B 18 (5G 101)
W4 7A 98
Dolphin St. KT1: King T 2E 150
Dolphin Twr. *SE8 6B 104*
(off Abinger Gro.)
Dombey Ho. *SE1 7K 15*
(off Wolseley St.)
W11 1F 99
(off St Ann's Rd.)
Dombey St. WC1 5G 7 (5K 83)
(not continuous)
Domecq Ho. *EC1 3B 8*
(off Dallington St.)
Dome Hill Pk. SE26 4F 139
Domelton Ho. *SW18 6K 117*
(off Iron Mill Rd.)
Domett Cl. SE5 4D 120
Domfe Pl. E5 4J 67
Domingo St. EC1 3C 8 (4C 84)
Dominica Cl. E13 2B 88
Dominion Bus. Pk. N9 2E 34
Dominion Cen., The UB2: S'hall 2C 94
Dominion Cl. TW3: Houn 2H 113
Dominion Ct. *E8 7F 67*
(off Middleton Rd.)
Dominion Dr. SE16 2K 103
Dominion Ho. *E14 5D 104*
(off St Davids Sq.)
EC1 5C 84
(off Bartholomew Cl.)
Dominion Ind. Est. *UB2: S'hall 2C 94*
(off Feather Rd.)

Dominion Pde. HA1: Harr 5K **41**
Dominion Rd. CR0: C'don 7F **157**
UB2: S'hall 2C **94**
Dominion St. EC2 5F **9** (5D **84**)
Dominion Theatre *7D 6*
(off Tottenham Ct. Rd.)
Dominion Wlk. *E14* *7F 87*
(off Fairmont Av.)
Domonic Dr. SE9 4F **143**
Domville Cl. N20 2G **31**
Domville Ct. *SE17* *5E 102*
(off Bagshott St.)
Donald Dr. RM6: Chad H 5C **54**
Donald Hunter Ho. *E7* *5K 69*
(off Woodgrange Rd.)
Donald Rd. CR0: C'don 7A **156**
E13 1K **87**
Donaldson Rd. NW6 1H **81**
SE18 1E **124**
Donald Woods Gdns.
KT5: Surb 2H **163**
Donato Dr. SE15 6E **102**
Doncaster Dr. UB5: N'olt 5D **58**
Doncaster Gdns. N4 6C **48**
UB5: N'olt 5D **58**
Doncaster Rd. N9 7C **24**
Donegal Ho. *E1* *4H 85*
(off Cambridge Heath Rd.)
Donegal St. N1 2K **83**
Doneraile Ho. *SW1* *5J 17*
(off Ebury Bri. Rd.)
Doneraile St. SW6 2F **117**
Dongola Rd. E1 5A **86**
E13 3K **87**
N17 3E **48**
Dongola Rd. W. E13 3K **87**
Don Gratton Ho. *E1* *5G 85*
(off Old Montague St.)
Donington Av. IG2: Ilf 5G **53**
IG6: Ilf 5G **53**
Donkey All. SE22 7G **121**
Donkey La. EN1: Enf 2B **24**
UB7: W Dray 1D **174**
Donkin Ho. *SE16* *4H 103*
(off Rennie Est.)
Donmar Warehouse Theatre *1E 12*
(off Earlham St.)
Donnatt's Rd. SE14 1B **122**
Donne Ct. SE24 6C **120**
Donnefield Av. HA8: Edg 7K **27**
Donne Ho. *E14* *6C 86*
(off Dod St.)
SE14 *6K 103*
(off Samuel Cl.)
Donnelly Ct. *SW6* *7G 99*
(off Dawes Rd.)
Donnelly Ho. *SE1* *3A 102*
(off McAuley Cl.)
Donne Pl. CR4: Mitc 4F **155**
SW3 3D **16** (4C **100**)
Donne Rd. RM8: Dag 2C **72**
Donnington Ct. *NW1* *7F 65*
(off Castlehaven Rd.)
NW10 *7D 62*
(off Donnington Rd.)
Donnington Mans. *NW10* *1E 80*
(off Donnington Rd.)
Donnington Rd. HA3: Kenton 5D **42**
KT4: Wor Pk 2C **164**
NW10 7D **62**
Donnybrook Ct. *E3* *1B 86*
(off Old Ford Rd.)
Donnybrook Rd. SW16 7G **137**
Donoghue Bus. Pk. NW2 3F **63**
Donoghue Cotts. *E14* *5A 86*
(off Galsworthy Av.)
Donoghue Ct. *E3* *4D 86*
(off Barry Blandford Way)
Donovan Av. N10 2F **47**
Donovan Ct. *SW10* *6A 16*
(off Drayton Gdns.)
Donovan Ho. *E1* *7J 85*
(off Cable St.)
Donovan Pl. N21 5E **22**
Don Phelan Cl. SE5 1D **120**
Dons Ct. *BR1: Brom* *1H 159*
(off London Rd.)
Doone Cl. TW11: Tedd 6A **132**
Doon St. SE1 5J **13** (1A **102**)
Dora Ho. *E14* *6B 86*
(off Rhodeswell Rd.)
W11 *7F 81*
(off St Ann's Rd.)
Doral Way SM5: Cars 5D **166**
Doran Ct. E6 2D **88**
Dorando Cl. W12 7D **80**
Doran Gro. SE18 7J **107**
Doran Mnr. *N2* *5D 46*
(off Great Nth. Rd.)
Doran Wlk. E15 7E **68**
Dora Rd. SW19 5J **135**
Dora St. E14 6B **86**
Dora Way SW9 2A **120**
Dorchester Av. DA5: Bexl 1D **144**
HA2: Harr 6G **41**
N13 4H **33**
Dorchester Cl. BR5: St P 7B **144**
KT10: Hin W 2A **162**
UB5: N'olt 5F **59**
Dorchester Ct. *E18* *1H 51*
(off Buckingham Rd.)
N1 *7E 66*
(off Englefield Rd.)
N10 3F **47**
N14 7A **22**
NW2 3F **63**
SE24 5C **120**
SW1 *2F 17*
(off Sloane St.)
Dorchester Dr. SE24 5C **120**
TW14: Bedf 6G **111**
Dorchester Gdns. E4 4H **35**
NW11 4J **45**
Dorchester Gro. W4 5A **98**
Dorchester Ho. TW9: Kew 7H **97**
Dorchester M. KT3: N Mald 4K **151**
TW1: Twick 6C **114**
Dorchester Rd. KT4: Wor Pk 1E **164**
SM4: Mord 7K **153**
UB5: N'olt 5F **59**
Dorchester Ter. *NW2* *3F 63*
(off Needham Ter.)
Dorchester Way HA3: Kenton 6F **43**
Dorchester Waye UB4: Yead 6K **75**
(not continuous)
Dorcis Av. DA7: Bex 2E **126**
Dordrecht Rd. W3 1A **98**
Dore Av. E12 5E **70**
Doreen Av. NW9 1K **61**
Doreen Capstan Ho. *E11* *3G 69*
(off Apollo Pl.)
Dore Gdns. SM4: Mord 7K **153**
Dorell Cl. UB1: S'hall 5D **76**
Dorey Ho. *TW8: Bford* *7C 96*
(off High St.)
Dorfman Theatre *4H 13*
(within National Theatre)
Doria Rd. SW6 2H **117**
Doric Ho. *E2* *2K 85*
(off Mace St.)
Doric Way NW1 1C **6** (3H **83**)
Dorie M. *N12* *4E 30*
(off Ashbourne Cl.)
Dorien Rd. SW20 2F **153**
Doris Ashby Cl. UB6: G'frd 1A **78**
Doris Av. DA8: Erith 1J **127**
Doris Emmerton Ct. SW11 4A **118**
Doris Rd. E7 7J **69**
TW15: Ashf 6F **129**
Dorking Cl.
KT4: Wor Pk 2F **165**
SE8 6B **104**
Dorking Ct. *N17* *1G 49*
(off Hampden La.)
Dorking Ho. SE1 3D **102**
Dorlcote Rd. SW18 7C **118**
Dorly Cl. TW17: Shep 5G **147**
Dorman Pl. N9 2B **34**
Dormans Cl. HA6: Nwood 1F **39**
Dorman Wlk. NW10 5K **61**
Dorman Way NW8 1B **82**
Dorma Trad. Pk. E10 1K **67**
Dormay St. SW18 5K **117**
Dormer Cl. E15 6H **69**
EN5: Barn 5A **20**
Dormer's Av. UB1: S'hall 6E **76**
Dormers Ri. UB1: S'hall 7F **77**
DORMER'S WELLS 6E **76**
Dormer's Wells La. UB1: S'hall 6E **76**
Dormers Wells Leisure Cen. 6F **77**
Dormstone Ho. *SE17* *4E 102*
(off Congreve St.)
Dormywood HA4: Ruis 5H **39**
Dornberg Cl. SE3 7J **105**
Dornberg Rd. SE3 7K **105**
Dorncliffe Rd. SW6 2G **117**
Dorney NW3 7C **64**
Dorney Ri. BR5: St M Cry 4K **161**
Dorney Way TW4: Houn 5C **112**
Dornfell St. NW6 5H **63**
Dornoch Ho. *E3* *2B 86*
(off Anglo Rd.)
Dornton Rd. CR2: S Croy 5D **168**
SW12 2F **137**
Dorothy Av. HA0: Wemb 7E **60**
Dorothy Evans Cl. DA7: Bex 4H **127**
Dorothy Gdns. RM8: Dag 4B **72**
Dorothy Pettingell Ho. *SM1: Sutt* *3K 165*
(off Vermont Rd.)
Dorothy Rd. SW11 3D **118**
Dorothy Smith La. N17 7J **33**
Dorrell Pl. SW9 3A **120**
Dorrien Wlk. SW16 2H **137**
Dorrington Ct. SE25 2E **156**
Dorrington Point *E3* *3D 86*
(off Bromley High St.)
Dorrington St. EC1 5J **7** (5A **84**)
Dorrington Way BR3: Beck 5E **158**
Dorrit Ho. *W11* *1F 99*
(off St Ann's Rd.)
Dorrit M. N18 5K **33**
Dorrit St. SE1 6D **14** (2C **102**)
Dorrit Way BR7: Chst 6G **143**
Dorryn Ct. SE26 5K **139**
Dors Cl. NW9 1K **61**
Dorset Av. DA16: Well 4K **125**
RM1: Rom 4K **55**
UB2: S'hall 4E **94**
UB4: Hayes 3G **75**
Dorset Bldgs. EC4 1A **14** (6B **84**)
Dorset Cl. KT9: Chess 4D **162**
NW1 5E **4** (5D **82**)
UB4: Hayes 3G **75**
Dorset Ct. HA6: Nwood 1H **39**
N1 *7E 66*
(off Hertford Rd.)
UB5: N'olt 3C **76**
W7 *5K 77*
(off Copley Cl.)
Dorset Dr. HA8: Edg 6A **28**
Dorset Gdns. CR4: Mitc 4K **155**
HA0: Wemb 5C **60**
Dorset Ho. *NW1* *5F 5*
(off Gloucester Pl.)
Dorset Mans. *SW6* *6F 99*
(off Lillie Rd.)
Dorset M. N3 1J **45**
SW1 1J **17** (3F **101**)
Dorset Pl. E15 6F **69**
Dorset Ri. EC4 1A **14** (6B **84**)
Dorset Rd. BR3: Beck 3K **157**
CR4: Mitc 2C **154**
E7 7A **70**
Dorset Rd. HA1: Harr 6G **41**
N15 4D **48**
N22 1J **47**
SE9 2C **142**
SW8 7J **101**
SW19 1J **153**
TW15: Ashf 3A **128**
W5 3C **96**
Dorset Sq. NW1 4E **4** (4D **82**)
Dorset St. W1 6F **5** (5D **82**)
Dorset Way TW2: Twick 1H **131**
UB10: Hil 2B **74**
Dorset Waye TW5: Hest 7D **94**
Dorset Wharf *W6* *7E 98*
(off Rainville Rd.)
Dorsey Ho. *N1* *6B 66*
(off Canonbury Rd.)
Dorton Cl. SE15 7E **102**
Dorton Vs. UB7: Sip 7C **92**
Dorville Cres. W6 3D **98**
Dorville Rd. SE12 5H **123**
Dothill Rd. SE18 7G **107**
Douai Gro. TW12: Hamp 1G **149**
Doughty Ct. *E1* *1H 103*
(off Prusom St.)
Doughty Ho. *SW10* *6A 100*
(off Netherton Gro.)
Doughty M. WC1 4G **7** (4K **83**)
Doughty St. WC1 3G **7** (4K **83**)
Douglas Av. E17 1B **50**
HA0: Wemb 7E **60**
KT3: N Mald 4D **152**
Douglas Bader Ho. TW7: Isle 3H **113**
Douglas Cl. HA7: Stan 5F **27**
IG6: Ilf 7K **37**
SM6: Wall 6J **167**
Douglas Ct. *KT1: King T* *4E 150*
(off Geneva Rd.)
N3 2K **45**
NW6 *7J 63*
(off Quex Rd.)
Douglas Cres. UB4: Yead 4A **76**
Douglas Dr. CR0: C'don 3C **170**
Douglas Est. *N1* *6C 66*
(off Oransay Rd.)
Douglas Eyre Sports Cen. 5K **49**
Douglas Ho. KT6: Surb 1F **163**
Douglas Johnstone Ho. *SW6* *6H 99*
(off Clem Attlee Ct.)
Douglas Mans. TW3: Houn 3F **113**
Douglas M. NW2 3G **63**
Douglas Path *E14* *5E 104*
(off Manchester Rd.)
Douglas Rd. DA16: Well 1B **126**
E4 1B **36**
E16 5J **87**
IG3: Ilf 7A **54**
KT1: King T 2H **151**
KT6: Surb 2F **163**
N1 7C **66**
N22 1A **48**
NW6 1H **81**
TW3: Houn 3F **113**
TW19: Stanw 6A **110**
Douglas Rd. Nth. N1 6C **66**
Douglas Rd. Sth. N1 6C **66**
Douglas Robinson Ct. *SW16* *7J 137*
(off Streatham High Rd.)
Douglas Sq. SM4: Mord 6J **153**
Douglas St. SW1 4C **18** (4H **101**)
Douglas Ter. E17 1B **50**
Douglas Waite Ho. NW6 7J **63**
Douglas Way SE8 7B **104**
(Stanley St.)
SE8 7C **104**
(Watsons St.)
Doulton Ho. SE11 2H **19**
Doulton M. NW6 6K **63**
Dounesforth Gdns. SW18 1K **135**
Douro Pl. W8 3K **99**
Douro St. E3 2C **86**

Douthwaite Sq. E1 .... 1G **103**
Dove App. E6 .... 5C **88**
Dove Cl. SM6: Wall 7K **167**
UB5: N'olt 4B **76**
Dove Commercial Cen. NW5 .... 5G **65**
Dovecot Cl. HA5: Eastc 5A **40**
Dovecote Av. N22 .... 3A **48**
Dovecote Gdns. SW14 .... 3K **115**
Dovecote Ho. *SE16* *2K* ***103***
(off Water Gdns. Sq.)
Dovecote M. UB9: Hare 3A **38**
Dove Ct. TW19: Stanw 7A **110**
Dovedale Av. HA3: Kenton 6C **42**
IG5: Ilf 2E **52**
Dovedale Bus. Est. *SE15* *2G* ***121***
(off Blenheim Gro.)
Dovedale Cl. DA16: Well 2A **126**
Dovedale Ri. CR4: Mitc 7D **136**
Dovedale Rd. SE22 .... 5H **121**
Dovedon Cl. N14 .... 2D **32**
Dovehouse Ct. *UB5: N'olt* *3B* ***76***
(off Delta Gro.)
Dove Ho. Gdns. E4 .... 2H **35**
Dovehouse Mead IG11: Bark 2H **89**
Dovehouse St. SW3 .... 5B **16** (5B **100**)
Dove M. SW5 .... 4A **100**
Dove Pk. HA5: Hat E 1E **40**
Dover Cl. NW2 .... 2F **63**
RM5: Col R 2J **55**
Dover Ct. *EC1* *3A* ***8***
(off St John St.)
N1 .... *7D* ***66***
(off Southgate Rd.)
Dovercourt Av. CR7: Thor H 5A **156**
Dovercourt Est. N1 .... 6D **66**
Dovercourt Gdns. HA7: Stan 5K **27**
Dovercourt La. SM1: Sutt 3A **166**
Dovercourt Rd. SE22 .... 6E **120**
Doverfield Rd. SW2 .... 7J **119**
Dover Flats SE1 .... 4E **102**
Dover Gdns. SM5: Cars 3D **166**
Dover Ho. N18 .... 5A **34**
SE15 .... 6J **103**
Dover Ho. Rd. SW15 .... 4C **116**
Doveridge Gdns. N13 .... 4G **33**
Dove Rd. N1 .... 6D **66**
Dove Row E2 .... 1G **85**
Dover Pk. Dr. SW15 .... 6D **116**
Dover Patrol SE3 .... 2K **123**
Dover Rd. E12 .... 2A **70**
N9 .... 2D **34**
RM6: Chad H 6E **54**
SE19 .... 6D **138**
Dover St. W1 .... 3K **11** (7F **83**)
Dover Ter. *TW9: Rich* *2F* ***115***
(off Sandycombe Rd.)
Dover Yd. W1 .... 4A **12**
Doves Cl. BR2: Brom 2C **172**
Doves Yd. N1 .... 1A **84**
Dovet Ct. SW9 .... 1K **119**
Doveton Ho. *E1* *4J* ***85***
(off Doveton St.)
Doveton Rd. CR2: S Croy 5D **168**
Doveton St. E1 .... 4J **85**
Dove Wlk. SW1 .... 5G **17** (5E **100**)
Dovey Lodge *N1* *7A* ***66***
(off Bewdley St.)
Dovoll Ct. *SE16* *3G* ***103***
(off Old Jamaica Rd.)
Dowanhill Rd. SE6 .... 1F **141**
Dowd Cl. N11 .... 2K **31**
Dowdeswell Cl. SW15 .... 4A **116**
Dowding Dr. SE9 .... 5A **124**
Dowding Ho. *N6* *7E* ***46***
(off Hillcrest)
Dowding Pl. HA7: Stan 6F **27**
Dowding Rd. UB10: Uxb 7B **56**
Dowdney Cl. NW5 .... 5G **65**
Dowe Ho. SE3 .... 3G **123**
Dowells St. SE10 .... 6D **104**
Dower Av. SM6: Wall 7F **167**
Dower Ct. *SE16* *4J* ***103***
(off Silwood Rd.)
Dowes Ho. SW16 .... 3J **137**
Dowgate Hill EC4 .... 2E **14** (7D **84**)
Dowland St. W10 .... 3G **81**
Dowlas St. SE5 .... 7E **102**
Dowler Ct. KT2: King T 1E **150**
Dowler Ho. *E1* *6G* ***85***
(off Burslem St.)
Dowlerville Rd. BR6: Chels 6K **173**
Dowling Ho. DA17: Belv 3F **109**
Dowman Cl. SW19 .... 7K **135**
Downage NW4 .... 3E **44**
(not continuous)
Downalong WD23: B Hea 1C **26**
Downbank Av. DA7: Bex 1K **127**
Down Barns Rd. HA4: Ruis 3B **58**
Downbarton Ho. *SW9* *1A* ***120***
(off Gosling Way)
Downbury M. SW18 .... 5J **117**
Down Cl. UB5: N'olt 2K **75**
Downderry Rd. BR1: Brom 3F **141**
Downe Cl. DA16: Well 7C **108**
Downend SE18 .... 7F **107**
Downend Ct. *SE15* *6E* ***102***
(off Bibury Cl.)
Downe Rd. BR2: Kes 7C **172**
CR4: Mitc 2D **154**
Downer's Cott. SW4 .... 4G **119**
Downesbury *NW3* *6D* ***64***
(off Steele's Rd.)
Downes Cl. TW1: Twick 6B **114**
Downes Ct. N21 .... 1F **33**
Downes Ho. *CR0: Wadd* *4B* ***168***
(off Violet La.)
Downe Ter. TW10: Rich 6E **114**
Downey Ho. *E1* *4K* ***85***
(off Globe Rd.)
Downfield KT4: Wor Pk 1B **164**
Downfield Cl. W9 .... 4K **81**
Down Hall Rd. KT2: King T 1D **150**
DOWNHAM 5F **141**
Downham Cl. RM5: Col R 1G **55**
Downham Ct. *N1* *7D* ***66***
(off Downham Rd.)
Downham Ent. Cen. SE6 .... 2H **141**
Downham Health & Leisure Cen. 4H **141**
Downham La. BR1: Brom 5F **141**
Downham Rd. N1 .... 7D **66**
Downham Way BR1: Brom 5F **141**
Downham Wharf *N1* *1E* ***84***
(off Downham Rd.)
Downhills Av. N17 .... 3D **48**
Downhills Pk. Rd. N17 .... 3C **48**
Downhills Way N17 .... 3C **48**
Downhurst Av. NW7 .... 5E **28**
Downhurst Ct. NW4 .... 3E **44**
Downing Cl. HA2: Harr 3G **41**
Downing Ct. *WC1* *4F* ***7***
(off Grenville St.)
Downing Dr. UB6: G'frd 1H **77**
Downing Ho. *W10* *6F* ***81***
(off Cambridge Gdns.)
Downing Rd. RM9: Dag 7F **73**
Downings E6 .... 6E **88**
Downing St. SW1 .... 6E **12** (2J **101**)
Downland Cl. N20 .... 1F **31**
Downland Ct. E11 .... 2G **69**
Downleys Cl. SE9 .... 2C **142**
Downman Rd. SE9 .... 3C **124**
Down Pl. W6 .... 4D **98**
Down Rd. TW11: Tedd 6B **132**
Downs, The SW20 .... 7F **135**
Downs Av. BR7: Chst 5D **142**
HA5: Pinn 6C **40**
Downs Bri. Rd. BR3: Beck 1F **159**
Downs Ct. UB6: G'frd 3A **78**
Downs Ct. Pde. *E8* *5H* ***67***
(off Amhurst Rd.)
Downsell Rd. E15 .... 4E **68**
Downsfield Rd. E17 .... 6A **50**
Downshall Av. IG3: Ilf 6J **53**
Downs Hill BR3: Beck 7F **141**
Downshire Hill NW3 .... 4B **64**
Downside TW1: Twick 3K **131**
TW16: Sun 1J **147**
Downside Cl. SW19 .... 6A **136**
Downside Cres. NW3 .... 5C **64**
W13 .... 4A **78**
Downside Rd. SM2: Sutt 6B **166**
Downside Wlk. *TW8: Bford* *6D* ***96***
(off Windmill Rd.)
UB5: N'olt 3D **76**
Downs La. E5 .... 4H **67**
Downs Pk. Rd. E5 .... 5F **67**
E8 .... 5F **67**
Downs Rd. BR3: Beck 2D **158**
CR7: Thor H 1C **156**
E5 .... 4G **67**
EN1: Enf 4K **23**
Down St. KT8: W Mole 5E **148**
W1 .... 5J **11** (1F **101**)
Down St. M. W1 .... 5J **11** (1F **101**)
Downs Vw. TW7: Isle 1K **113**
Downsview Gdns. SE19 .... 7B **138**
Downsview Rd. SE19 .... 7C **138**
Downsway BR6: Orp 5J **173**
Downsway, The SM2: Sutt 7A **166**
Downton Av. SW2 .... 2J **137**
Downtown Rd. SE16 .... 2A **104**
Down Way UB5: N'olt 3K **75**
Downy Ho. W3 .... 1A **98**
Dowrey St. N1 .... 1A **84**
Dowsett Rd. N17 .... 2F **49**
Dowson Cl. SE5 .... 4D **120**
Dowson Ho. *E1* *6K* ***85***
(off Bower St.)
Doyce St. SE1 .... 6C **14** (2C **102**)
Doyle Gdns. NW10 .... 1C **80**
Doyle Ho. *SW13* *7E* ***98***
(off Trinity Chu. Rd.)
Doyle Rd. SE25 .... 4G **157**
D'Oyley St. SW1 .... 3G **17** (4E **100**)
Doynton St. N19 .... 2F **65**
Draco Ga. SW15 .... 3E **116**
Draco St. SE17 .... 6C **102**
Dragmore St. SW4 .... 6H **119**
Dragonfly Cl. E13 .... 3K **87**
KT5: Surb 1J **163**
Dragonfly Ct. *NW9* *1A* ***44***
(off Heybourne Cres.)
Dragonfly Pl. SE4 .... 3A **122**
Dragon Rd. SE15 .... 6E **102**
Dragons Way EN5: Barn 5C **20**
Dragon Yd. WC1 .... 7F **7** (6J **83**)
Dragoon Rd. SE8 .... 5B **104**
Dragor Rd. NW10 .... 4J **79**
Drake Cl. IG11: Bark 4A **90**
SE16 .... 2K **103**
Drake Ct. *KT5: Surb* *4E* ***150***
(off Cranes Pk. Av.)
SE1 .... *7D* ***14***
(off Swan St.)
SE19 .... 5F **139**
W12 .... *2E* ***98***
(off Scott's Rd.)
Drake Cres. SE28 .... 6C **90**
Drakefell Rd. SE4 .... 2K **121**
SE14 .... 2K **121**
Drakefield Rd. SW17 .... 3E **136**
Drake Hall *E16* *1K* ***105***
(off Wesley Av.)
Drake Ho. *E1* *5J* ***85***
(off Stepney Way)
E14 .... *7A* ***86***
(off Victory Pl.)
SW1 .... *7C* ***18***
(off Dolphin Sq.)
Drakeland Ho. *W9* *4H* ***81***
(off Fernhead Rd.)
Drakeley Ct. N5 .... 4B **66**
Drake M. BR2: Brom 4A **160**
Drake Rd. CR0: C'don 7K **155**
CR4: Mitc 6E **154**
HA2: Harr 2D **58**
KT9: Chess 5G **163**
SE4 .... 3C **122**
Drakes, The SE8 .... 6C **104**
Drakes Ct. SE23 .... 1J **139**
Drakes Courtyard NW6 .... 7H **63**
Drakes Dr. HA6: Nwood 1D **38**
Drake St. EN2: Enf 1J **23**
WC1 .... 6G **7** (5K **83**)
Drakes Wlk. E6 .... 1D **88**
Drakewood Rd. SW16 .... 7H **137**
Draper Cl. DA17: Belv 4F **109**
TW7: Isle 2H **113**
Draper Ct. BR1: Brom 4C **160**
Draper Ho. *SE1* *4B* ***102***
(off Newington Butts)
Draper Pl. *N1* *1B* ***84***
(off Dagmar Ter.)
Drapers Almshouses *E3* *3D* ***86***
(off Rainhill Way)
Drapers Cott. Homes NW7 .... 4G **29**
(not continuous)
Draper's Ct. *SW11* *1E* ***118***
(off Battersea Pk. Rd.)
Drapers Gdns. EC2 .... 7F **9** (6D **84**)
Drapers Rd. E15 .... 4F **69**
EN2: Enf 2G **23**
N17 .... 3F **49**
Drappers Way SE16 .... 4G **103**
Draven Cl. BR2: Hayes 7H **159**
Drawell Cl. SE18 .... 5J **107**
Drax Av. SW20 .... 7C **134**
Draxmont SW19 .... 6G **135**
Draycot Rd. E11 .... 6K **51**
KT6: Surb 1G **163**
Draycott Av. HA3: Kenton 6B **42**
SW3 .... 3D **16** (4C **100**)
Draycott Cl. HA3: Kenton 6B **42**
NW2 .... 3F **63**
SE5 .... 7D **102**
(not continuous)
Draycott Ct. *SW11* *1C* ***118***
(off Westbridge Rd.)
Draycott M. *SW6* *2H* ***117***
(off Laurel Bank Gdns.)
Draycott Pl. SW3 .... 4E **16** (4D **100**)
Draycott Ter. SW3 .... 4F **17** (4D **100**)
Dray Ct. *HA0: Wemb* *5A* ***60***
(off Brewery Cl.)
Drayford Cl. W9 .... 4H **81**
Dray Gdns. SW2 .... 5K **119**
Draymans M. SE15 .... 2F **121**
Draymans Way TW7: Isle 3K **113**
Drayside M. UB2: S'hall 2D **94**
Drayson M. W8 .... 2J **99**
Drayton Av. BR6: Farnb 1F **173**
W13 .... 7A **78**
Drayton Bri. Rd. W7 .... 7K **77**
W13 .... 7K **77**
Drayton Cl. IG1: Ilf 1H **71**
TW4: Houn 5D **112**
Drayton Ct. UB7: W Dray 4B **92**
Drayton Gdns. N21 .... 7G **23**
SW10 .... 6A **16** (5A **100**)
UB7: W Dray 2A **92**
W13 .... 7A **78**
Drayton Grn. W13 .... 7A **78**
Drayton Grn. Rd. W13 .... 7B **78**
Drayton Gro. W13 .... 7A **78**
Drayton Ho. E11 .... 1F **69**
SE5 .... *7D* ***102***
(off Elmington Rd.)
Drayton Pk. N5 .... 4A **66**
Drayton Pk. M. N5 .... 5A **66**
Drayton Rd. CR0: C'don 2B **168**
E11 .... 1F **69**
N17 .... 2E **48**
NW10 .... 1B **80**
W13 .... 7A **78**

Drayton Waye HA3: Kenton 6B **42**
Dray Wlk. E1 . . . . .4K **9** (4F **85**)
Dreadnought Cl. SW19 . . . . .2B **154**
Dreadnought St. SE10 . . . . .3G **105**
Dreadnought Wlk. SE10 . . . . .6D **104**
Drenon Sq. UB3: Hayes 7H **75**
Dresden Cl. NW6 . . . . .6K **63**
Dresden Ho. SE11 . . . . .3H **19**
SW11 . . . .*2E **118***
(off Dagnall St.)
Dresden Rd. N19 . . . . .1G **65**
Dressington Av. SE4 . . . . .6C **122**
Drewery Ct. SE3 . . . . .3G **123**
Drewett Ho. *E1* *6G **85***
(off Christian St.)
Drew Gdns. UB6: G'frd 6K **59**
Drew Ho. SE8 . . . . .5C **104**
SW16 .3J **137**
Drew Rd. E16 . . . . .1B **106**
(not continuous)
Drewstead La. SW16 . . . . .2H **137**
Drewstead Rd. SW16 . . . . .2H **137**
Drey Ct. *KT4: Wor Pk* *2C **164***
(off The Avenue)
Driffield Ct. *NW9* *1A **44***
(off Pageant Av.)
Driffield Rd. E3 . . . . .2A **86**
Drift, The BR2: Brom 3B **172**
Drift Ct. E16 . . . . .7F **89**
Driftway, The
CR4: Mitc 1E **154**
Driftway Ho. *E3* *2B **86***
(off Stafford Rd.)
Drinkwater Ho. *SE5* *7D **102***
(off Picton St.)
Drinkwater Rd. HA2: Harr 2F **59**
Drive, The BR3: Beck 2C **158**
BR4: W W'ck 7F **159**
BR6: Orp 2K **173**
BR7: Chst 3K **161**
CR7: Thor H 4D **156**
DA5: Bexl 6C **126**
DA8: Erith 7H **109**
DA14: Sidc 3B **144**
E4 . . . . .1A **36**
E17 . . . . .3D **50**
E18 . . . . .4J **51**
EN2: Enf 1J **23**
EN5: Barn 3B **20**
EN5: New Bar 6F **21**
HA2: Harr 7E **40**
HA6: Nwood 2G **39**
HA8: Edg 5B **28**
HA9: Wemb 2J **61**
IG1: Ilf .6C **52**
IG9: Buck H 1F **37**
IG11: Bark 7K **71**
KT2: King T 7J **133**
KT6: Surb 7E **150**
KT10: Esh 7G **149**
KT19: Ewe 6B **164**
N3 . . . . .7D **30**
N6 . . . . .5D **46**
N7 . . . . .6K **65**
(not continuous)
N11 . . . . .6B **32**
NW10 . . . . .1B **80**
NW11 . . . . .7G **45**
RM5: Col R 1J **55**
SM4: Mord 5A **154**
SW6 . . . . .2G **117**
SW20 . . . . .7E **134**
TW3: Houn 2H **113**
TW7: Isle 2H **113**
TW14: Felt 7A **112**
TW15: Ashf 7F **129**
UB10: Ick 4A **56**
W3 . . . . .6J **79**
Drive Ct. HA8: Edg 5B **28**
Drive Mans. *SW6* *2G **117***
(off Fulham Rd.)
Driveway, The *E17* *6D **50***
(off Hoe St.)
Droitwich Cl. SE26 . . . . .3G **139**
Dromey Gdns. HA3: Hrw W 7E **26**
Dromore Rd. SW15 . . . . .6G **117**
Dronfield Gdns. RM8: Dag 5C **72**
Dron Ho. *E1* *5J **85***
(off Adelina Gro.)
Droop St. W10 . . . . .3F **81**
Drovers Ct. *KT1: King T* *2E **150***
(off Fairfield E.)
Drovers Pl. SE15 . . . . .7J **103**
Drovers Rd. CR2: S Croy 5D **168**
Drovers Way N7 . . . . .6J **65**
Druce Rd. SE21 . . . . .6E **120**
Druid St. SE1 . . . . .6H **15** (2E **102**)
(not continuous)
Druids Way BR2: Brom 4F **159**
Drumaline Ridge KT4: Wor Pk 2A **164**
Drum Ct. *N1* *7J **65***
(off Gifford St.)
Drummer Stagpole M. NW7 . . . . .5B **30**
Drummond Av. RM7: Rom 4K **55**
Drummond Ct. N12 . . . . .7H **31**
W3 . . . .*3J **97***
(off Palmerston Rd.)
Drummond Cres. NW1 . . . . .1C **6** (3H **83**)
Drummond Dr. HA7: Stan 7E **26**
Drummond Ga. SW1 . . . . .5D **18** (5H **101**)
Drummond Ho. *E2* *2G **85***
(off Goldsmiths Row)
N2 . . . .*2A **46***
(off Font Hills)
Drummond Pl. TW1: Twick 7B **114**
Drummond Rd. CR0: C'don 2C **168**
E11 . . . . .6A **52**
RM7: Rom 4K **55**
SE16 . . . . .3H **103**
Drummonds, The IG9: Buck H 2E **36**
Drummonds Pl. TW9: Rich 4E **114**
Drummond St. NW1 . . . . .3A **6** (4G **83**)
Drummond Way N1 . . . . .7A **66**
Druries *HA1: Harr* *1J **59***
(off High St.)
Drury Cl. SW15 . . . . .6C **116**
Drury Cres. CR0: Wadd 2A **168**
Drury Ho. SW8 . . . . .1G **119**
Drury La. WC2 . . . . .7F **7** (6J **83**)
Drury Lane Theatre Royal **2G 13**
(off Catherine St.)
Drury Rd. HA1: Harr 7G **41**
Drury Way NW10 . . . . .5K **61**
Drury Way Ind. Est. NW10 . . . . .5J **61**
Dryad St. SW15 . . . . .3F **117**
Dryburgh Gdns. NW9 . . . . .3G **43**
Dryburgh Ho. *SW1* *5K **17***
(part of Abbots Mnr.)
Dryburgh Rd. SW15 . . . . .3D **116**
Dryden Av. W7 .6K **77**
Dryden Bldg. *E1* *6G **85***
(off Commercial Rd.)
Dryden Cl. SW4 . . . . .5H **119**
Dryden Ct. SE11 . . . . .4K **19** (4A **102**)
Dryden Mans. *W14* *6G **99***
(off Queen's Club Gdns.)
Dryden Rd. DA16: Well 1K **125**
EN1: Enf 6K **23**
HA3: W'stone 1K **41**
SW19 . . . . .6A **136**
Dryden St. WC2 . . . . .1F **13** (6J **83**)
Dryfield Cl. NW10 . . . . .6J **61**
Dryfield Rd. HA8: Edg 6D **28**
Dryfield Wlk. SE8 . . . . .6C **104**
Dryhill Rd. DA17: Belv 6F **109**
Dryland Av. BR6: Orp 4K **173**
Drylands Rd. N8 . . . . .6J **47**
Drysdale Av. E4 . . . . .7J **25**
Drysdale Dwellings *E8* *5F **67***
(off Dunn St.)
Drysdale Pl. N1 . . . . .1H **9** (3E **84**)
Drysdale St. N1 . . . . .1H **9** (3E **84**)
Dublin Av. E8 . . . . .1G **85**
Dublin Ct. *HA2: Harr* *2H **59***
(off Northolt Rd.)
Du Burstow Ter. W7 . . . . .2J **95**
Ducaine Apartments *E3* *3B **86***
(off Merchant St.)
Ducal St. E2 . . . . .2K **9** (3F **85**)
Du Cane Cl. W12 . . . . .6E **80**
Du Cane Ct. SW17 . . . . .1E **136**
Du Cane Rd. W12 . . . . .6B **80**
Ducavel Ho. SW2 . . . . .1K **137**
Duchess Cl. N11 . . . . .5A **32**
SM1: Sutt 4A **166**
Duchess Cres. HA7: Stan 3E **26**
Duchess Gro. IG9: Buck H 2E **36**
Duchess M. W1 . . . . .6K **5** (5F **83**)
Duchess of Bedford Ho. *W8* *2J **99***
(off Duchess of Bedford's Wlk.)
Duchess of Bedford's Wlk. W8 . . . . . . .2J **99**
Duchess St. W1 . . . . .6K **5** (5F **83**)
Duchess Theatre **2G 13**
(off Catherine St.)
Duchess Wlk. SE1 . . . . .1F **103**
Duchy Rd. EN4: Had W 1G **21**
Duchy St. SE1 . . . . .4K **13** (1A **102**)
(not continuous)
Ducie St. SW4 .4K **119**
Duckett M. N4 . . . . .6B **48**
Duckett Rd. N4 .6B **48**
Duckett's Apartments *E3* *7B **68***
(off Wick La.)
Duckett St. E1 .4K **85**
Duck La. W1 . . . . .1C **12**
Duck Lees La. EN3: Pond E 4F **25**
Duck's Hill Rd. HA4: Ruis 2D **38**
HA6: Nwood 1D **38**
DUCKS ISLAND **6A 20**
Ducks Wlk. TW1: Twick 5C **114**
Du Cros Dr. HA7: Stan 6J **27**
Du Cros Rd. W3 . . . . .1A **98**
DUDDEN HILL **5D 62**
Dudden Hill La. NW10 . . . . .4B **62**
Dudden Hill Pde. NW10 . . . . .4B **62**
Duddington Cl. SE9 . . . . .4B **142**
Dudley Av. HA3: Kenton 3C **42**
Dudley Ct. NW11 . . . . .4H **45**
W1 . . . .*1E **10***
(off Up. Berkeley St.)
WC2 . . . . .7E **6** (6J **83**)
Dudley Dr. HA4: Ruis 5K **57**
SM4: Mord 1G **165**
Dudley Gdns. HA2: Harr 1H **59**
W13 . . . . .2B **96**
Dudley Ho. *W2* *6A **4***
(off Nth. Wharf Rd.)
Dudley M. SW2 . . . . .6A **120**
Dudley Pl. TW19: Stanw 6B **110**
UB3: Harl 4F **93**
Dudley Rd. E17 .2C **50**
HA2: Harr 2G **59**
IG1: Ilf 4F **71**
KT1: King T 3F **151**
KT12: Walt T 6J **147**
N3 . . . . .2K **45**
NW6 . . . . .2G **81**
SW19 . . . . .6J **135**
TW9: Rich 2F **115**
TW14: Bedf 1E **128**
TW15: Ashf 5B **128**
UB2: S'hall 2B **94**
Dudley St. W2 . . . . .6A **4** (5B **82**)
Dudlington Rd. E5 . . . . .2J **67**
Dudmaston M. SW3 . . . . .5B **16**
Dudrich Cl. N11 .6J **31**
Dudrich M. EN2: Enf 1F **23**
SE22 . . . . .5F **121**
Dudsbury Rd. DA14: Sidc 6B **144**
Dudset La. TW5: Cran 1J **111**
Duett Ct. TW5: Hest 7C **94**
Duffell Ho. SE11 . . . . .6H **19**
Dufferin Av. EC1 . . . . .4E **8**
Dufferin Ct. *EC1* *4E **8***
(off Dufferin St.)
Dufferin St. EC1 . . . . .4D **8** (4C **84**)
Duffield Cl. HA1: Harr 5K **41**
Duffield Dr. N15 . . . . .4F **49**
Duff St. E14 . . . . .6D **86**
Dufour's Pl. W1 . . . . .1B **12** (6G **83**)
Dufton Dwellings *E15* *4G **69***
(off High Rd. Leyton)
Dugard Way SE11 . . . . .4B **102**
Dugdale Cen.
Enfield .4J **23**
Dugdale Ct. *NW10* *3D **80***
(off Harrow Rd.)
Duggan Dr. BR7: Chst 6C **142**
Dugolly Av. HA9: Wemb 3H **61**
Duke Ct. TW3: Houn 4D **112**
Duke Gdns. IG6: Ilf 4H **53**
Duke Humphrey Rd. SE3 . . . . .1G **123**
Duke of Cambridge Cl. TW2: Whitt . . .6H **113**
Duke of Clarence Ct. *SE17* *5C **102***
(off Manor Pl.)
Duke of Edinburgh Rd. SM1: Sutt 2B **166**
Duke of Wellington Av. SE18 . . . . .3F **107**
Duke of Wellington Pl.
SW1 . . . . .6H **11** (2E **100**)
Duke of York Column (Memorial) **5C 12**
Duke of York Sq. SW3 . . . . . . .4F **17** (5D **100**)
Duke of York's Theatre **3E 12**
(off St Martin's La.)
Duke of York St. SW1 . . . . . . .4B **12** (1G **101**)
Duke Rd. IG6: Ilf 4H **53**
W4 . . . . .5K **97**
Duke's Av. HA8: Edg 6A **28**
N10 . . . . .3F **47**
W4 . . . . .5K **97**
Dukes Av. HA1: Harr 4J **41**
HA2: Harr 6D **40**
KT2: King T 4C **132**
KT3: N Mald 3A **152**
N3 . . . . .1K **45**
TW4: Houn 4C **112**
TW10: Ham 4C **132**
UB5: N'olt 7C **58**
Dukes Cl. TW12: Hamp 5D **130**
TW15: Ashf 4E **128**
Dukes Ct. E6 . . . . .1E **88**
(not continuous)
SE13 . . . . .2E **122**
SW14 . . . . .2K **115**
W2 . . . .*7K **81***
(off Moscow Rd.)
Dukes Ga. W4 . . . . .4J **97**
Dukes Grn. Av. TW14: Felt 5J **111**
Dukes Head Pas. TW12: Hamp 7G **131**
Duke's Head Yd. N6 . . . . .1F **65**
Duke Shore Wharf E14 . . . . .7B **86**
Duke's Ho. *SW1* *3D **18***
(off Vincent St.)
Dukes La. W8 . . . . .2K **99**
Duke's La. Chambers *W8* *2K **99***
(off Dukes La.)
Duke's La. Mans. *W8* *2K **99***
(off Dukes La.)
Dukes Lodge *W8* *1H **99***
(off Holland Wlk.)
Dukes Meadow Golf & Tennis **2K 115**
Duke's Meadow Golf Course **2K 115**
Duke's Meadows **2K 115**
Duke's M. W1 . . . . .7H **5**
Dukes M. N10 . . . . .3F **47**
Dukes Orchard DA5: Bexl 1J **145**
Duke's Pas. E17 . . . . .4E **50**
Duke's Pl. EC3 . . . . .1H **15** (6E **84**)
Dukes Point *N6* *1F **65***
(off Dukes Head Yd.)
Dukes Ride UB10: Ick 4A **56**
Duke's Rd. WC1 . . . . .2D **6** (3H **83**)
Dukes Rd. E6 . . . . .1E **88**
W3 . . . . .4G **79**
Dukesthorpe Rd. SE26 . . . . .4K **139**

Duke St. SM1: Sutt 4B **166**
TW9: Rich 4D **114**
W1 7H **5** (6E **82**)
Duke St. Hill SE1 4F **15** (1D **102**)
Duke St. Mans. *W1* *1H* ***11***
(off Duke St.)
Duke St. St James's
SW1 4B **12** (1G **101**)
Dukes Way BR4: W W'ck 3G **171**
HA9: Wemb 5E **60**
Duke's Yd. W1 2H **11** (7E **82**)
Dulas St. N4 1K **65**
Dulford St. W11 7G **81**
Dulka Rd. SW11 5D **118**
Dulverton *NW1* *1G* ***83***
(off Royal College St.)
Dulverton Mans. WC1 4H **7**
Dulverton Rd. HA4: Ruis 1J **57**
SE9 2G **143**
DULWICH 2E 138
Dulwich & Sydenham Hill Golf Course
2F 139
Dulwich Bus. Cen. SE23 1K **139**
Dulwich Comn. SE21 1E **138**
SE22 1E **138**
Dulwich Hamlet FC 4E 120
Dulwich Lawn Cl. SE22 5F **121**
Dulwich Leisure Cen. 4G 121
Dulwich Oaks, The SE21 3F **139**
Dulwich Picture Gallery 7D 120
Dulwich Ri. Gdns. SE22 5F **121**
Dulwich Rd. SE24 5A **120**
Dulwich Upper Wood Nature Pk. 5F 139
DULWICH VILLAGE 7E 120
Dulwich Village SE21 6D **120**
Dulwich Wood Av. SE19 4E **138**
Dulwich Wood Pk. SE19 4E **138**
Dumain Ct. *SE11* *4B* ***102***
(off Opal St.)
Dumbarton Ct. SW2 6J **119**
Dumbarton Rd. SW2 6J **119**
Dumbleton Cl. KT1: King T 1H **151**
Dumbreck Rd. SE9 4D **124**
Dumont Rd. N16 3E **66**
Dumpton Pl. NW1 7E **64**
Dumsey Eyot KT16: Chert 7A **146**
Dunally Pk. TW17: Shep 7F **147**
Dunbar Av. BR3: Beck 4A **158**
RM10: Dag 3G **73**
SW16 2A **156**
Dunbar Cl. UB4: Hayes 5K **75**
Dunbar Ct. *BR2: Brom* *3H* ***159***
(off Durham Rd.)
SM1: Sutt 5B **166**
Dunbar Gdns. RM10: Dag 5G **73**
Dunbar Rd. E7 6J **69**
KT3: N Mald 4J **151**
N22 1A **48**
Dunbar St. SE27 3C **138**
Dunbar Twr. *E8* *6F* ***67***
(off Dalston Sq.)
Dunbar Wharf *E14* *7B* ***86***
(off Narrow St.)
Dunblane Cl. HA8: Edg 2C **28**
Dunblane Rd. SE9 3C **124**
Dunboe Pl. TW17: Shep 7E **146**
Dunboyne Rd. NW3 5D **64**
Dunbridge Ho. SW15 6B **116**
Dunbridge St. E2 4G **85**
Duncan Cl. EN5: New Bar 4F **21**
Duncan Ct. *E14* *5E* ***86***
(off Teviot St.)
N21 1G **33**
Duncan Gro. W3 6A **80**
Duncan Ho. *NW3* *7D* ***64***
(off Fellows Rd.)
SW1 *6B* ***18***
(off Dolphin Sq.)
Duncannon Ho. *SW1* *6D* ***18***
(off Lindsay Sq.)
Duncannon St. WC2 3E **12** (7J **83**)
Duncan Rd. E8 1H **85**
TW9: Rich 4E **114**
Duncan St. N1 2B **84**
Duncan Ter. N1 2B **84**
(not continuous)
Dunch St. E1 6H **85**
Dunchurch Ho. RM10: Dag 7G **73**
Duncombe Hill SE23 7A **122**
Duncombe Rd. N19 1H **65**
Duncrievie Rd. SE13 6F **123**
Duncroft SE18 7J **107**
Dundalk Ho. *E1* *6J* ***85***
(off Clark St.)
Dundalk Rd. SE4 3A **122**
Dundas Ct. *SE10* *6D* ***104***
(off Dowells St.)
Dundas Gdns. KT8: W Mole 3F **149**
Dundas Ho. *E2* *2J* ***85***
(off Bishop's Way)
Dundas Rd. SE15 2J **121**
SW9 1A **120**
Dundee Ct. *E1* *1H* ***103***
(off Wapping High St.)
SE1 *7G* ***15***
(off Long La.)
Dundee Ho. *W9* *3A* ***82***
(off Maida Vale)
Dundee Rd. E13 2K **87**
SE25 5H **157**
Dundee St. E1 1H **103**
Dundee Way EN3: Brim 3F **25**
Dundee Wharf E14 7B **86**
Dundela Gdns. KT4: Wor Pk 4D **164**
Dundonald Cl. E6 6C **88**
Dundonald Rd. NW10 1F **81**
SW19 7G **135**
Dundry Ho. SE26 3G **139**
Dunedin Ho. *E16* *1D* ***106***
(off Manwood St.)
Dunedin M. SW2 1J **137**
Dunedin Rd. E10 4E **68**
IG1: Ilf 1G **71**
Dunedin Way UB4: Yead 4A **76**
Dunelm Gro. SE27 3C **138**
Dunelm St. E1 6K **85**
Dunfield Gdns. SE6 5D **140**
Dunfield Rd. SE6 5D **140**
(not continuous)
Dunford Ct. HA5: Hat E 1D **40**
Dunford Rd. N7 4K **65**
Dungannon Ho. *SW6* *7J* ***99***
(off Vanston Pl.)
Dungarvan Av. SW15 4C **116**
Dunheved Cl. CR7: Thor H 6A **156**
Dunheved Rd. Nth. CR7: Thor H 6A **156**
Dunheved Rd. Sth. CR7: Thor H 6A **156**
Dunheved Rd. W. CR7: Thor H 6A **156**
Dunhill Point SW15 1C **134**
Dunholme Grn. N9 3A **34**
Dunholme La. N9 3A **34**
Dunholme Rd. N9 3A **34**
Dunkeld Rd. RM8: Dag 2B **72**
SE25 4D **156**
Dunkery Rd. SE9 4B **142**
Dunkirk Ho. SE1 2D **102**
Dunkirk St. SE27 4C **138**
Dunlace Rd. E5 4J **67**
Dunleary Cl. TW4: Houn 7D **112**
Dunley Dr. CR0: New Ad 7D **170**
Dunlin Ho. *SE16* *4K* ***103***
(off Tawny Way)
Dunloe Av. N17 3D **48**
Dunloe Ct. E2 2F **85**
Dunloe Pas. *E2* *2F* ***85***
(off Dunloe St.)
Dunloe St. E2 2F **85**
Dunlop Pl. SE16 3F **103**
Dunmore Point *E2* *2J* ***9***
(off Gascoigne Pl.)
Dunmore Rd. NW6 1G **81**
SW20 1E **152**
Dunmow Cl. RM6: Chad H 5C **54**
TW13: Hanw 3C **130**
Dunmow Ho. *SE11* *5H* ***19***
(off Newburn St.)
Dunmow Rd. E15 4F **69**
Dunmow Wlk. *N1* *1C* ***84***
(off Popham St.)
Dunnage Cres. SE16 4A **104**
(not continuous)
Dunnell Cl. TW16: Sun 1J **147**
Dunnett Ho. *E3* *2B* ***86***
(off Vernon Rd.)
Dunnico Ho. *SE17* *5E* ***102***
(off East St.)
Dunn Mead NW9 7G **29**
Dunnock Cl. N9 1E **34**
Dunnock Ho. NW9 6B **44**
Dunnock M. E5 3G **67**
Dunnock Rd. E6 6C **88**
Dunn's Pas. WC1 7F **7**
Dunn St. E8 5F **67**
Dunollie Pl. NW5 5G **65**
Dunollie Rd. NW5 5G **65**
Dunoon Gdns. SE23 7K **121**
Dunoon Ho. *N1* *1K* ***83***
(off Bemerton Est.)
Dunoon Rd. SE23 7J **121**
Dunoran Home BR1: Brom 1C **160**
Dunraven Dr. EN2: Enf 2F **23**
Dunraven Rd. W12 1C **98**
Dunraven St. W1 2F **11** (7D **82**)
Dunsany Rd. W14 3F **99**
Dunsfold Cl. *SM2: Sutt* *7K* ***165***
(off Blackbush Cl.)
Dunsfold Way CR0: New Ad 7D **170**
Dunsford Way SW15 6D **116**
Dunsmore Cl. UB4: Yead 4B **76**
Dunsmore Rd. KT12: Walt T 6K **147**
Dunsmure Rd. N16 1E **66**
Dunspring La. IG5: Ilf 2F **53**
Dunstable M. W1 5H **5** (5E **82**)
Dunstable Rd. KT8: W Mole 4D **148**
TW9: Rich 4E **114**
Dunstall Rd. SW20 6D **134**
Dunstall Way KT8: W Mole 3F **149**
Dunstall Welling Est. DA16: Well 2B **126**
Dunstan Cl. N2 3A **46**
Dunstan Glade BR5: Pet W 6H **161**
Dunstan Gro. SE20 7H **139**
Dunstan Ho's. *E1* *5J* ***85***
(off Stepney Grn.)
Dunstan M. EN1: Enf 3K **23**
Dunstan Rd. NW11 1H **63**
Dunstan's Gro. SE22 6H **121**
Dunstan's Rd. SE22 7G **121**
Dunster Av. SM4: Mord 1F **165**
Dunster Cl. EN5: Barn 4A **20**
RM5: Col R 2J **55**
Dunster Ct. EC3 2H **15** (7E **84**)
Dunster Dr. NW9 1J **61**
Dunster Gdns. NW6 7H **63**
Dunster Ho. SE6 3E **140**
Dunsterville Way SE1 7F **15** (2D **102**)
Dunster Way HA2: Harr 3C **58**
SM6: Wall 1E **166**
Dunstone Ct. SE6 7C **122**
Dunston Rd. E8 1F **85**
SW11 2E **118**
Dunston St. E8 1E **84**
Dunton Cl. KT6: Surb 1E **162**
Dunton Ct. SE23 2H **139**
Dunton Rd. E10 7D **50**
RM1: Rom 4K **55**
SE1 5F **103**
Duntshill Rd. SW18 1K **135**
Dunvegan Cl. KT8: W Mole 4E **148**
Dunvegan Rd. SE9 4D **124**
Dunwich Ct. *RM6: Chad H* *5B* ***54***
(off Glandford Way)
Dunwich Rd. DA7: Bex 1F **127**
Dunworth M. W11 6H **81**
Duplex Ride SW1 7F **11** (2D **100**)
Dupont Rd. SW20 2F **153**
Duppas Av. CR0: Wadd 4B **168**
Duppas Cl. TW17: Shep 5F **147**
Duppas Ct. *CR0: C'don* *3B* ***168***
(off Duppas Hill Ter.)
Duppas Hill La. CR0: C'don 4B **168**
Duppas Hill Rd. CR0: Wadd 4A **168**
Duppas Hill Ter. CR0: C'don 3B **168**
Duppas Rd. CR0: Wadd 3A **168**
Dupree Rd. SE7 5K **105**
Dura Den Cl. BR3: Beck 7D **140**
Durand Gdns. SW9 1K **119**
Durands Wlk. SE16 2B **104**
Durand Way NW10 7J **61**
Durants Pk. 3D 24
Durants Pk. Av. EN3: Pond E 4E **24**
Durants Rd. EN3: Pond E 4D **24**
Durant St. E2 2G **85**
Durban Ct. E7 7B **70**
Durban Gdns. RM10: Dag 7J **73**
Durban Ho. *W12* *7D* ***80***
(off White City Est.)
Durban Rd. BR3: Beck 2B **158**
E15 3G **87**
E17 1B **50**
IG2: Ilf 1J **71**
N17 6K **33**
SE27 4C **138**
Durbin Rd. KT9: Chess 4E **162**
Durdan Cotts. *UB1: S'hall* *6D* ***76***
(off Denbigh Rd.)
Durdans Ho. *NW1* *7F* ***65***
(off Farrier St.)
Durdans Rd. UB1: S'hall 6D **76**
Durell Gdns. RM9: Dag 5D **72**
Durell Ho. *SE16* *2K* ***103***
(off Wolfe Cres.)
Durell Rd. RM9: Dag 5D **72**
Durfey Pl. SE5 7D **102**
Durford Cres. SW15 1D **134**
Durham Av. BR2: Brom 4H **159**
IG8: Buck H, Wfd G 5G **37**
TW5: Hest 5D **94**
Durham Cl. SW20 2D **152**
Durham Ct. *NW6* *2J* ***81***
(off Kilburn Pk. Rd.)
TW11: Tedd 4J **131**
Durham Hill BR1: Brom 4H **141**
Durham Ho. BR2: Brom 4G **159**
IG11: Bark *7A* ***72***
(off Margaret Bondfield Av.)
NW8 *2D* ***4***
(off Lorne Cl.)
RM10: Dag 5J **73**
Durham Ho. St. WC2 3F **13**
Durham Pl. IG1: Ilf 4G **71**
SW3 6E **16** (5D **100**)
Durham Ri. SE18 5G **107**
Durham Rd. BR2: Brom 3H **159**
DA14: Sidc 5B **144**
E12 4B **70**
E16 4G **87**
HA1: Harr 5F **41**
N2 3C **46**
N7 2K **65**
N9 2B **34**
RM10: Dag 5J **73**
SW20 1D **152**
TW14: Felt 7A **112**
W5 3D **96**
Durham Row E1 5A **86**
Durham St. SE11 6G **19** (5K **101**)
Durham Ter. W2 6K **81**
Durham Wharf Dr. TW8: Bford 7C **96**
Durham Yd. E2 3H **85**
Durley Av. HA5: Pinn 7C **40**
Durley Rd. N16 7E **48**
Durlston Rd. E5 2G **67**
KT2: King T 6E **132**
Durnford Ho. SE6 3E **140**

Durnford St. N15 . . . . .5E 48
  SE10 . . . . .6E 104
Durning Rd. SE19 . . . . .5D 138
Durnsford Av. SW19 . . . . .2J 135
Durnsford Ct. EN3: Enf H 3F 25
       (off Enstone Rd.)
Durnsford Rd. N11 . . . . .1H 47
  SW19 . . . . .2J 135
Durrant Ct. HA3: Hrw W 2J 41
Durrant Ho. EC1 . . . . .5E 8
      (off Chiswell St.)
Durrant Way BR6: Farnb 5H 173
Durrell Rd. SW6 . . . . .1H 117
Durrell Way TW17: Shep 6F 147
Durrels Ho. W14 . . . . .4H 99
      (off Warwick Gdns.)
Durrington Av. SW20 . . . . .7E 134
Durrington Pk. Rd. SW20 . . . . .1E 152
Durrington Rd. E5 . . . . .4A 68
Durrington Twr. SW8 . . . . .2G 119
Durrisdeer Ho. NW2 . . . . .4H 63
      (off Lyndale)
Dursley Cl. SE3 . . . . .2A 124
Dursley Gdns. SE3 . . . . .1B 124
Dursley Rd. SE3 . . . . .2A 124
Durward Ho. W8 . . . . .2K 99
      (off Kensington Ct.)
Durward St. E1 . . . . .5H 85
Durweston M. W1 . . . . .5F 5
Durweston St. W1 . . . . .6F 5 (5D 82)
Dury Falls Cl. RM11: Col R 2J 55
Dury Rd. EN5: Barn 1C 20
Dutch Barn Cl. TW19: Stanw 6A 110
Dutch Gdns. KT2: King T 6H 133
Dutch Yd. SW18 . . . . .5J 117
Dutton St. SE10 . . . . .1E 122
Duval Ho. N19 . . . . .2H 65
      (off Ashbrook Rd.)
Duxberry Av. TW13: Felt 3A 130
Duxberry Cl. BR2: Brom 5C 160
Duxford Ho. SE2 . . . . .2D 108
      (off Wolvercote Rd.)

DW Fitness
  Waldorf Hotel 2G 13
Dyas Rd. TW16: Sun 1J 147
Dye Ho. La. E3 . . . . .1C 86
Dyer Ho. TW12: Hamp 1F 149
Dyer's Bldgs. EC1 . . . . .6J 7 (5A 84)
Dyers Hall Rd. E11 . . . . .1G 69
Dyers Hill Rd. E11 . . . . .2F 69
Dyers La. SW15 . . . . .4D 116
Dykes Way BR2: Brom 3H 159
Dykewood Cl. DA5: Bexl 3K 145
Dylan Rd. DA17: Belv 3G 109
  SE24 . . . . .4B 120
Dylways SE5 . . . . .4D 120
Dymchurch Cl. BR6: Orp 4J 173
  IG5: Ilf 2E 52
Dymes Path SW19 . . . . .2F 135
Dymock St. SW6 . . . . .3K 117
Dyneley Rd. SE12 . . . . .3A 142
Dyne Rd. NW6 . . . . .7G 63
Dynevor Rd. N16 . . . . .3E 66
  TW10: Rich 5E 114
Dynham Rd. NW6 . . . . .7J 63
Dyott St. WC1 . . . . .7D 6 (6H 83)
Dysart Av. KT2: King T 5C 132
Dysart St. EC2 . . . . .4G 9 (4D 84)
Dyson Ct. HA0: Wemb 4A 60
  NW2 . . . . .1E 62
Dyson Ho. SE10 . . . . .5H 105
      (off Blackwall La.)
Dyson Rd. E11 . . . . .6G 51
  E15 .6H 69
Dysons Rd. N18 . . . . .5C 34

E

Eade Rd. N4 . . . . .7C 48
Eagans Cl. N2 . . . . .3B 46

Eagle Av. RM6: Chad H 6E 54
Eagle Cl. EN3: Pond E 4D 24
  SE16 . . . . .5J 103
  SM6: Wall 6J 167
Eagle Ct. E11 . . . . .4J 51
  EC1 . . . . .5A 8 (5B 84)
Eagle Dr. NW9 . . . . .2A 44
Eagle Dwellings EC1 . . . . .1D 8
      (off City Rd.)
Eagle Hgts. SW11 . . . . .3C 118
Eagle Hill SE19 . . . . .6D 138
Eagle Ho. E1 . . . . .4H 85
      (off Headlam St.)
  EC1 . . . . .2E 8
      (off City Rd.)
  N1 . . . . .2D 84
      (off Eagle Wharf Rd.)
Eagle Ho. M. SW4 . . . . .5G 119
Eagle La. E11 . . . . .4J 51
Eagle Lodge NW11 . . . . .7H 45
Eagle Mans. N16 . . . . .5F 67
      (off Salcombe Rd.)
Eagle M. N1 . . . . .6E 66
Eagle Pl. SW1 . . . . .3B 12
  SW7 . . . . .5A 100
Eagle Point EC1 . . . . .2E 8
      (off City Rd.)
Eagle Rd. HA0: Wemb 7D 60
  TW6: H'row A 3H 111
Eaglesfield Rd. SE18 . . . . .1F 125
Eagle St. WC1 . . . . .6G 7 (5K 83)
Eagle Ter. IG8: Wfd G 7F 36
Eagle Trad. Est. CR4: Mitc 6D 154
Eagle Wharf Ct. SE1 . . . . .5J 15
      (off Lafone St.)
Eagle Wharf E. E14 . . . . .7A 86
      (off Narrow St.)
Eagle Wharf Rd. N1 . . . . .2C 84
Eagle Wharf W. E14 . . . . .7A 86
      (off Narrow St.)
Eagle Works E. E1 . . . . .4K 9
Eagle Works W. E1 . . . . .4J 9
Eagling Cl. E3 . . . . .3C 86
Ealdham Sq. SE9 . . . . .4A 124
EALING 7D 78
Ealing B'way. Cen. W5 . . . . .7D 78
EALING COMMON 7F 79
Ealing Golf Course 3B 78
Ealing Grn. W5 . . . . .1D 96
Ealing Pk. Gdns. W5 . . . . .4C 96
Ealing Pk. Mans. W5 . . . . .3D 96
      (off Sth. Ealing Rd.)
Ealing Rd. HA0: Wemb 6E 60
  TW8: Bford 5D 96
  UB5: N'olt 1E 76
Ealing Squash & Fitness Club 6E 78
Ealing Studios 1D 96
Ealing Village W5 . . . . .6E 78
Eamont Cl. HA4: Ruis 7D 38
Eamont Ct. NW8 . . . . .2C 82
      (off Eamont St.)
Eamont St. NW8 . . . . .2C 82
Eardley Cres. SW5 . . . . .5J 99
Eardley Point SE18 . . . . .4F 107
      (off Wilmount St.)
Eardley Rd. DA17: Belv 5G 109
  SW16 . . . . .5G 137
Earhart Ho. NW9 . . . . .3C 44
      (off East Dr.)
Earhart Way TW6: Cran, H'row A 3J 111
Earldom Rd. SW15 . . . . .4E 116
Earle Gdns. KT2: King T 7E 132
Earle Ho. SW1 . . . . .4D 18
      (off Montaigne Cl.)
Earlham Ct. E11 . . . . .7H 51
Earlham Gro. E7 . . . . .5H 69
  N22 .7E 32
Earlham St. WC2 . . . . .1D 12 (6J 83)
Earl Ho. NW1 . . . . .4D 4
      (off Lisson Gro.)

Earlom Ho. WC1 . . . . .2J 7
      (off Margery St.)
Earl Ri. SE18 . . . . .5H 107
Earl Rd. SW14 . . . . .4J 115
Earlsbury Gdns. HA8: Edg 4B 28
EARL'S COURT 4K 99
Earl's Ct. Gdns. SW5 . . . . .4K 99
Earl's Ct. Rd. SW5 . . . . .3J 99
  W8 .3J 99
Earl's Ct. Sq. SW5 . . . . .5K 99
Earls Cres. HA1: Harr 4J 41
Earlsdown Ho. IG11: Bark 2H 89
Earlsferry Way N1 . . . . .7J 65
      (not continuous)
EARLSFIELD 1A 136
Earlsfield Ho. KT2: King T 1D 150
      (off Seven Kings Way)
Earlsfield Rd. SW18 . . . . .1A 136
Earlshall Rd. SE9 . . . . .4D 124
Earls Ho. TW9: Kew 7H 97
Earlsmead HA2: Harr 4D 58
Earlsmead Rd. N15 . . . . .5F 49
  NW10 . . . . .3E 80
Earlsmead Stadium 4D 58
Earlsthorpe M. SW12 . . . . .6E 118
Earlsthorpe Rd. SE26 . . . . .4K 139
Earlstoke St. EC1 . . . . .1A 8 (3B 84)
Earlston Gro. E9 . . . . .1H 85
Earl St. EC2 . . . . .5G 9 (5D 84)
Earl's Wlk. RM8: Dag 4B 72
Earls Wlk. W8 . . . . .3J 99
Earls Way SE1 . . . . .5E 14
      (off Queen Elizabeth St.)
Earlswood Av. CR7: Thor H 5A 156
Earlswood Cl. SE10 . . . . .6G 105
Earlswood Gdns. IG5: Ilf 3E 52
Earlswood St. SE10 . . . . .5G 105
Early M. NW1 . . . . .1F 83
Early Rivers Ho. E20 . . . . .5E 68
      (off Ellis Way)
Earnshaw Ho. EC1 . . . . .2B 8
      (off Percival St.)
Earnshaw St. WC2 . . . . . . .7D 6 (6H 83)
Earsby St. W14 . . . . .4G 99
      (not continuous)
Easby Cres. SM4: Mord 6K 153
Easebourne Rd. RM8: Dag 5C 72
Easedale Ho. TW7: Isle 5K 113
Eashing Point SW15 . . . . .1D 134
      (off Wanborough Dr.)
Easleys M. W1 . . . . .7H 5 (6E 82)
East 10 Ent. Pk. E10 . . . . .1A 68
East Acton .7B 80
E. Acton Arc. W3 . . . . .6A 80
E. Acton Ct. W3 . . . . .7A 80
E. Acton La. W3 . . . . .1A 98
E. Arbour St. E1 . . . . .6K 85
East Av. E12 . . . . .7C 70
  E17 .4D 50
  SM6: Wall 5K 167
  UB1: S'hall 7D 76
  UB3: Hayes 1H 93
East Bank N16 . . . . .7E 48
Eastbank Cl. E17 . . . . .5D 50
Eastbank Rd. TW12: Hamp H 5G 131
EAST BARNET 6H 21
East Barnet Golf Course 3F 21
E. Barnet Rd. EN4: E Barn 4G 21
E. Bay La. E20 . . . . .5C 68
E. Beckton District Cen. E6 . . . . .5D 88
EAST BEDFONT 7G 111
E. Block SE1 . . . . .6K 13
      (off York Rd.)
Eastbourne Av. W3 . . . . .6K 79
Eastbourne Gdns. SW14 . . . . .3J 115
Eastbourne M. W2 . . . . .7A 4 (6A 82)
Eastbourne Rd. E6 . . . . .3E 88
      (not continuous)
  E15 .1G 87
  N15 .6E 48

Eastbourne Rd. SW17 . . . . .6E 136
  TW8: Bford 5C 96
  TW13: Felt 2B 130
  W4 .6J 97
Eastbourne Ter. W2 . . . . . . .7A 4 (6A 82)
Eastbournia Av. N9 . . . . .3C 34
Eastbrook Av. N9 . . . . .7D 24
  RM10: Dag 4J 73
Eastbrook Cl. RM10: Dag 4J 73
Eastbrook Dr. RM7: Rush G 3K 73
Eastbrookend Country Pk. 3K 73
Eastbrook Rd. SE3 . . . . .1K 123
Eastbury Av. EN1: Enf 1A 24
  IG11: Bark 1J 89
Eastbury Ct. EN5: New Bar 5F 21
      (off Lyonsdown Rd.)
  IG11: Bark 1J 89
Eastbury Gro. W4 . . . . .5A 98
Eastbury Manor House 1K 89
Eastbury Rd. BR5: Pet W 6H 161
  E6 . . . . .4E 88
  KT2: King T 7E 132
  RM7: Rom 6K 55
Eastbury Sq. IG11: Bark 1K 89
Eastbury Ter. E1 . . . . .4K 85
E. Carriage Ho. SE18 . . . . .3F 107
      (off Royal Carriage M.)
Eastcastle St. W1 . . . . .7A 6 (6G 83)
Eastcheap EC3 . . . . .2G 15 (7E 84)
E. Churchfield Rd. W3 . . . . .1K 97
Eastchurch Rd. TW6: H'row A 2G 111
East Cl. EN4: Cockf 4K 21
  UB6: G'frd 2G 77
  W5 .4G 79
Eastcombe Av. SE7 . . . . .6K 105
EASTCOTE .7K 39
Eastcote BR6: Orp 1K 173
Eastcote Av. HA2: Harr 2F 59
  KT8: W Mole 5D 148
  UB6: G'frd 6K 59
Eastcote Hockey & Badminton Club . . .6H 39
Eastcote Ind. Est. HA4: Ruis 7A 40
Eastcote La. HA2: Harr 4C 58
  UB5: N'olt 5D 58
      (not continuous)
Eastcote La. Nth. UB5: N'olt 6D 58
Eastcote Pl. HA5: Eastc 6K 39
Eastcote Rd. DA16: Well 2H 125
  HA2: Harr 3G 59
  HA4: Ruis 7G 39
  HA5: Pinn 5B 40
Eastcote St. SW9 . . . . .2K 119
Eastcote Vw. HA5: Pinn 4A 40
EASTCOTE VILLAGE 5K 39
Eastcott Cl. KT2: King T 5J 133
East Ct. HA0: Wemb 2C 60
East Cres. EN1: Enf 5A 24
  N11 .4J 31
Eastcft Ho. HA2: Harr 2G 59
Eastcroft Rd. KT19: Ewe 7A 164
E. Cross Route E3 . . . . .7B 68
  E9 . . . . .5B 68
      (Crowfoot Cl.)
  E9 . . . . .5B 68
      (Wansbeck Rd.)
  E10 .5B 68
Eastdown Cl. SE13 . . . . .4F 123
Eastdown Ho. E8 . . . . .4G 67
Eastdown Pk. SE13 . . . . .4F 123
East Dr. NW9 . . . . .3C 44
  SM5: Cars 7C 166
E. Duck Lees La.
  EN3: Pond E 4F 25
EAST DULWICH 4F 121
      (off Albrighton Rd.)
E. Dulwich Gro. SE22 . . . . .5E 120
E. Dulwich Rd. SE15 . . . . .4F 121
  SE22 . . . . .4F 121
      (not continuous)
E. End Farm HA5: Pinn 3D 40

E. End Rd. N2 ....3K 45
N3 ....2J 45
E. End Way HA5: Pinn 3C 40
East Entrance RM10: Dag 2H 91
Eastern App. IG11: Bark 1A 90
Eastern Av. E11 ....6K 51
HA5: Pinn 7B 40
IG2: Ilf 6F 53
IG4: Ilf 6C 52
RM6: Chad H 4A 54
Eastern Av. E. RM1: Rom 3K 55
Eastern Av. Retail Pk. RM7: Rom ..4J 55
Eastern Av. W. RM1: Rom 4E 54
RM5: Rom 4E 54
RM6: Chad H 4E 54
RM7: Chad H, Mawney, Rom 4E 54
Eastern Bus. Pk. TW6: H'row A 2G 111
Eastern Ct. E15 ....6G 69
(off Gt. Eastern Rd.)
Eastern Gateway E16 ....7A 88
Eastern Ho. E2 ....3H 85
(off Bethnal Grn. Rd.)
Eastern Ind. Est. DA18: Erith 2G 109
Eastern Perimeter Rd.
TW6: H'row A 2H 111
Eastern Quay Apartments E16 .....1K 105
(off Portsmouth M.)
Eastern Rd. E13 ....2K 87
E17 ....5E 50
N2 ....3D 46
N22 ....1J 47
SE4 ....4C 122
EASTERN RDBT. 2G 71
Easternville Gdns. IG2: Ilf 6G 53
Eastern Way DA17: Belv 2A 108
DA18: Erith 2A 108
SE2 ....2A 108
SE28 ....2A 108
E. Ferry Rd. E14 ....4D 104
Eastfield Gdns. RM10: Dag 4G 73
Eastfield Rd. E17 ....4C 50
EN3: Enf W 1E 24
N8 ....3J 47
RM9: Dag 4F 73
RM10: Dag 4F 73
Eastfields HA5: Eastc 5A 40
Eastfields Av. SW18 ....4J 117
Eastfields Rd. CR4: Mitc 2E 154
W3 ....5J 79
Eastfield St. E14 ....5A 86
EAST FINCHLEY 4C 46
East Gdns. SW17 ....6C 136
Eastgate Bus. Pk. E10 ....1A 68
Eastgate Cl. SE28 ....6D 90
Eastglade HA5: Pinn 3D 40
EAST HAM 2D 88
East Ham & Barking By-Pass
IG11: Bark 2H 89
Eastham Cl. BR1: Brom 5B 20
East Ham Ind. Est. E6 ....4C 88
East Ham Leisure Cen. 1D 88
East Ham Mnr. Way E6 ....6E 88
East Ham Nature Reserve 4D 88
East Ham Nature Reserve Vis. Cen.
...............................4D 88
E. Handyside Canopy N1 ....1J 83
E. Harding St. EC4 ....7K 7 (6A 84)
E. Heath Rd. NW3 ....3A 64
East Hill HA9: Wemb 2G 61
SW18 ....5K 117
Eastholm NW11 ....4K 45
East Holme DA8: Erith 1K 127
Eastholme UB3: Hayes 1J 93
E. India Bldgs. E14 ....7C 86
(off Saltwell St.)
E. India Ct. SE16 ....2J 103
(off St Marychurch St.)
East India Dock Basin Nature Reserve
...............................7G 87
E. India Dock Ho. E14 ....6E 86
E. India Dock Rd. E14 ....6C 86

E. India Way CRO: C'don 1F 169
Eastlake Ho. NW8 ....4B 4
Eastlake Rd. SE5 ....2C 120
Eastlands Cres. SE21 ....6F 121
East La. HA0: Wemb 3B 60
HA9: Wemb 3B 60
KT1: King T 3D 150
SE16 ....2G 103
(Chambers St.)
SE16 ....2C 103
(Scott Lidgett Cres.)
East La. Bus. Pk.
HA9: Wemb 2D 60
Eastlea M. E16 ....4G 87
Eastleigh Av. HA2: Harr 2F 59
Eastleigh Cl. NW2 ....3A 62
SM2: Sutt 7K 165
Eastleigh Rd. DA7: Bex 3J 127
E17 ....2B 50
Eastleigh Wlk. SW15 ....7C 116
Eastleigh Way TW14: Felt 1J 129
East Lodge E16 ....1J 105
(off Wesley Av.)
E. London Crematorium E13 .....3H 87
East London Gymnastic Cen. 6D 88
Eastman Ho. SW4 ....6G 119
Eastman Rd. W3 ....2K 97
East Mead HA4: Ruis 3B 58
Eastmead Av. UB6: G'frd 3F 77
Eastmead Cl. BR1: Brom 2C 160
Eastmearn Rd. SE21 ....2C 138
EAST MOLESEY 4H 149
Eastmoor Pl. SE7 ....3B 106
Eastmoor St. SE7 ....3B 106
East Mt. St. E1 ....5H 85
(not continuous)
Eastney Rd. CRO: C'don 1B 168
Eastney St. SE10 ....5F 105
Eastnor Rd. SE9 ....1G 143
Eastone Apartments E1 ....6K 9
(off Lolesworth Cl.)
Easton St. WC1 ....3J 7 (4A 84)
East Pk. Cl. RM6: Chad H 5E 54
East Parkside SE10 ....2G 105
East Pas. EC1 ....5C 8
East Pl. SE27 ....4C 138
East Point SE1 ....5G 103
E. Pole Cotts. N14 ....4C 22
E. Poultry Av. EC1 ....6A 8 (5B 84)
East Ramp TW6: H'row A 1D 110
East Rd. DA16: Well 2B 126
E15 ....1J 87
EN3: Enf W 1D 24
EN4: E Barn 1K 31
HA1: Harr 7B 42
HA8: Edg 1H 43
KT2: King T 1E 150
N1 ....2E 8 (3D 84)
RM6: Chad H 5E 54
RM7: Rush G 7K 55
SW3 ....6G 16 (5E 100)
SW19 ....6A 136
TW14: Bedf 7F 111
UB7: W Dray 4B 92
E. Rochester Way DA5: Bexl 6F 127
DA15: Sidc 5J 125
East Row E11 ....6J 51
W10 ....4G 81
Eastry Av. BR2: Hayes 6H 159
Eastry Ho. SW8 ....7J 101
(off Hartington Rd.)
W11 ....7G 81
(off Walmer Rd.)
Eastry Rd. DA8: Erith 7G 109
EAST SHEEN 4J 115
E. Sheen Av. SW14 ....5K 115
East Shop. Cen. E7 ....7K 69
East Side W12 ....2E 98
(off Shepherd's Bush Mkt.)
Eastside Halls SW7 ....1B 16
(off Prince's Gdns.)

Eastside M. E3 ....2C 86
(off Morville St.)
Eastside Rd. NW11 ....4H 45
East Smithfield E1 ....3K 15 (7F 85)
East Sq. E10 ....7D 50
East Stand N5 ....3B 66
East St. BR1: Brom 2J 159
DA7: Bex 4G 127
IG11: Bark 1G 89
SE17 ....5C 102
(not continuous)
E. Surrey Gro. SE15 ....7F 103
E. Tenter St. E1 ....1K 15 (6F 85)
East Ter. DA15: Sidc 1J 143
E. Thamesmead Bus. Pk.
DA18: Erith 2F 109
East Twr. E14 ....2D 104
(off Pan Peninsula Sq.)
East Towers HA5: Pinn 5B 40
East Va. W3 ....1B 98
East Vw. E4 ....5K 35
EN5: Barn 2C 20
Eastview Av. SE18 ....7J 107
EAST VILLAGE 5E 68
Eastville Av. NW11 ....6H 45
East Wlk.
EN4: E Barn 7K 21
UB3: Hayes 1J 93
East Way BR2: Hayes 7J 159
CRO: C'don 2A 170
E11 ....5K 51
HA4: Ruis 1J 57
UB3: Hayes 1J 93
Eastway E9 ....6B 68
(not continuous)
SM4: Mord 5F 153
SM6: Wall 4G 167
Eastway Cres. HA2: Harr 2F 59
Eastwell Cl. BR3: Beck 7A 140
Eastwood Ho. SE1 ....7F 15
EAST WICKHAM 1C 126
East Wintergarden 1D 104
(off Bank St.)
Eastwood Cl. E18 ....2J 51
N7 ....5A 66
N17 ....7C 34
Eastwood Ho. E3 ....5C 86
(off Bow Comn. La.)
Eastwood Rd. E18 ....2J 51
IG3: Ilf 1A 72
N10 ....2E 46
UB7: W Dray 2C 92
East Woodside DA5: Bexl 7E 126
Eastwood St. SW16 ....6G 137
easyGym
Fulham 6H 99
Eatington Rd. E10 ....5F 51
Eaton Cl. HA7: Stan 4G 27
SW1 ....4G 17 (4E 100)
Eaton Ct. E18 ....2J 51
HA8: Edg 4B 28
Eaton Dr. KT2: King T 7G 133
RM5: Col R 1H 55
SW9 ....4B 120
Eaton Gdns. RM9: Dag 7E 72
Eaton Ga. SW1 ....3G 17 (4E 100)
Eaton Ho. E14 ....7B 86
(off Westferry Cir.)
SW11 ....1B 118
Eaton La. SW1 ....2K 17 (3E 100)
Eaton Mans. SW1 ....4G 17
(off Bourne St.)
Eaton M. Nth. SW1 ....3G 17 (4E 100)
Eaton M. Sth. SW1 ....3H 17 (4E 100)
Eaton M. W. SW1 ....3H 17 (4E 100)
Eaton Pk. Rd. N13 ....2F 33
Eaton Pl. SW1 ....2G 17 (4E 100)
Eaton Ri. E11 ....5A 52
W5 ....5D 78
Eaton Rd. DA14: Sidc 2D 144
EN1: Enf 4K 23

Eaton Rd. NW4 ....5E 44
SM2: Sutt 6B 166
TW3: Houn 4H 113
Eaton Row SW1 ....2J 17 (3F 101)
Eatons Mead E4 ....2H 35
Eaton Sq. SW1 ....3G 17 (4E 100)
Eaton Ter. E3 ....3A 86
SW1 ....3G 17 (4E 100)
Eaton Ter. M. SW1 ....3G 17
Eatonville Rd. SW17 ....2D 136
Eatonville Vs. SW17 ....2D 136
Ebb Ct. E16 ....7G 89
Ebbett Ct. W3 ....5K 79
Ebbisham Dr. SW8 ....7G 19 (6K 101)
Ebbisham Rd. KT4: Wor Pk 2E 164
Ebbsfleet Rd. NW2 ....5G 63
Ebdon Way SE3 ....3K 123
Ebenezer Ho. SE11 ....4K 19 (4B 102)
Ebenezer Mussel Ho. E2 ....2J 85
(off Patriot Sq.)
Ebenezer St. N1 ....1E 8 (3D 84)
Ebenezer Wlk. SW16 ....1G 155
Ebley Cl. SE15 ....6F 103
Ebner St. SW18 ....5K 117
Ebony Cres. EN4: E Barn 5K 21
Ebony Ho. E2 ....3G 85
(off Buckfast St.)
Ebor Cotts. SW15 ....3A 134
Ebor St. E1 ....3J 9 (4F 85)
Ebrington Rd. HA3: Kenton 6D 42
Ebsworth St. SE23 ....7K 121
Eburne Rd. N7 ....3J 65
Ebury Bri. SW1 ....5J 17 (5F 101)
Ebury Bri. Est. SW1 .....5J 17 (5F 101)
Ebury Bri. Rd. SW1 ......6H 17 (5E 100)
Ebury Cl. BR2: Kes 3C 172
Ebury M. N5 ....3C 66
SE27 ....3B 138
SW1 ....3J 17 (4F 101)
Ebury M. E. SW1 ....2J 17 (3F 101)
Ebury Sq. SW1 ....4H 17 (4E 100)
Ebury St. SW1 ....4H 17 (4E 100)
Ecclesbourne Apartments N1 .....7D 66
(off Ecclesbourne Rd.)
Ecclesbourne Cl. N13 ....5F 33
Ecclesbourne Gdns. N13 ....5F 33
Ecclesbourne Rd. CR7: Thor H ..5C 156
N1 ....7C 66
Eccleshill BR2: Brom 4H 159
(off Durham Rd.)
Eccles Rd. SW11 ....4D 118
Eccleston Bri. SW1 ......3K 17 (4F 101)
Eccleston Cl. BR6: Orp 1H 173
EN4: Cockf 4J 21
Eccleston Cres. RM6: Chad H 7B 54
Ecclestone Ct. HA9: Wemb 5E 60
Ecclestone M. HA9: Wemb 5E 60
Ecclestone Pl. HA9: Wemb 5F 61
Eccleston Ho. SW2 ....6A 120
Eccleston M. SW1 ....2H 17 (3E 100)
Eccleston Pl. SW1 ....3J 17 (4F 101)
Eccleston Rd. W13 ....7A 78
Eccleston Sq. SW1 ....4K 17 (4F 101)
(not continuous)
Eccleston Sq. M. SW1 ....4A 18 (4F 101)
Eccleston St. SW1 ....2J 17 (3F 101)
Echelforde Dr. TW15: Ashf 4C 128
Echo Hgts. E4 ....1J 35
Eckford St. N1 ....2A 84
Eckington Cl. SE14 ....7K 103
Eckington Ho. N15 ....6D 48
(off Fladbury Rd.)
Eckington La. SE14 ....7K 103
Eckstein Rd. SW11 ....4C 118
Eclipse Bldg. N1 ....6A 66
(off Laycock St.)
Eclipse Ho. N22 ....2K 47
(off Station Rd.)
Eclipse Rd. E13 ....5K 87
Ecology Cen. & Arts Pavilion 3A 86
Eco Va. SE23 ....6H 121

Ector Rd. SE6 . . . . 2G **141**
Edam Ct. DA15: Sidc 3A **144**
Edans Ct. W12 . . . . 2B **98**
Edar Ho. CR0: New Ad 6D **170**
Edbrooke Rd. W9 . . . . 4J **81**
Eddington Ct. *E16* *5H* ***87***
(off Silvertown Sq.)
Eddinton Cl. CR0: New Ad 6E **170**
Eddisbury Ho. SE26 . . . . 3G **139**
Eddiscombe Rd. SW6 . . . . 2H **117**
Eddy Cl. RM7: Rom 6H **55**
Eddystone Rd. SE4 . . . . 5A **122**
Eddystone Twr. SE8 . . . . 5A **104**
Eddystone Wlk. TW19: Stanw 7A **110**
Ede Cl. TW3: Houn 3D **112**
Eden Apartments *E14* *4E* ***104***
(off Glengarnock Av.)
Edenbridge Cl. *SE16* *5H* ***103***
(off Masters Dr.)
Edenbridge Rd. E9 . . . . 7K **67**
EN1: Enf 6K **23**
Eden Cl. DA5: Bexl 4K **145**
HA0: Wemb 1D **78**
NW3 . . . . 2J **63**
W8 . . . . 3J **99**
Eden Ct. IG6: Ilf 1H **53**
Edencourt Rd. SW16 . . . . 6F **137**
Edendale W3 . . . . 7H **79**
Edendale Rd. DA7: Bex 1K **127**
Edenfield Gdns. KT4: Wor Pk 3B **164**
Eden Gro. E17 . . . . 5D **50**
N7 . . . . 5K **65**
NW10 . . . . 6D **62**
Edenham Way W10 . . . . 4H **81**
Eden Ho. *NW8* *4C* ***4***
(off Church St.)
SE8 . . . . *7C* ***104***
(off Deptford High St.)
SE16 . . . . *2K* ***103***
(off Water Gdns. Sq.)
Edenhurst Av. SW6 . . . . 3H **117**
Eden Lodge NW6 . . . . 7F **63**
Eden M. SW17 . . . . 3A **136**
EDEN PARK 5C 158
Eden Pk. Av. BR3: Beck 4A **158**
Eden Rd. BR3: Beck 4A **158**
CR0: C'don 4D **168**
DA5: Bexl 4J **145**
E17 . . . . 5D **50**
SE27 . . . . 4B **138**
Edensor Gdns. W4 . . . . 7A **98**
Edensor Rd. W4 . . . . 7A **98**
Eden St. KT1: King T 2D **150**
Edenvale Cl. CR4: Mitc 7E **136**
Edenvale Rd. CR4: Mitc 7E **136**
Edenvale St. SW6 . . . . 2A **118**
Eden Wlk. KT1: King T 2E **150**
Eden Way BR3: Beck 5B **158**
E3 . . . . 1B **86**
Ederline Av. SW16 . . . . 3K **155**
Edgar Ct. KT3: N Mald 2A **152**
Edgar Ho. *E9* *5A* ***68***
(off Homerton Rd.)
E11 . . . . 7J **51**
SW8 . . . . *7J* ***101***
(off Wyvil Rd.)
Edgar Kail Way SE22 . . . . 4E **120**
Edgarley Ter. SW6 . . . . 1G **117**
Edgar Myles Ho. *E16* *5H* ***87***
(off Ordnance Rd.)
Edgar Rd. E3 . . . . 3D **86**
RM6: Chad H 7D **54**
TW4: Houn 7D **112**
UB7: Yiew 7A **74**
Edgar Wallace Cl. SE15 . . . . 7E **102**
Edgar Wright Ct. *SW6* *7H* ***99***
(off Dawes Rd.)
Edgcott Ho. *W10* *5E* ***80***
(off Sutton Way)
Edge, The *SE8* *7B* ***104***
(off Glenville Gro.)
Edge Apartments E15 . . . . 7F **69**
Edgeborough Way BR1: Brom 7B **142**
Edgebury BR7: Chst 4F **143**
Edgebury Wlk. BR7: Chst 4G **143**
Edge Bus. Cen., The NW2 . . . . 2D **62**
Edgecombe Ho. SE5 . . . . 2E **120**
SW19 . . . . 1G **135**
Edgecoombe CR2: Sels 7J **169**
Edgecoombe Cl. KT2: King T 7K **133**
Edgecote Cl. W3 . . . . 1J **97**
Edgecot Gro. N15 . . . . 5E **48**
Edgefield Av. IG11: Bark 7K **71**
Edgefield Cl. BR3: Beck 6C **140**
Edgefield Ct. *IG11: Bark* *7K* ***71***
(off Edgefield Av.)
Edge Hill SE18 . . . . 6F **107**
SW19 . . . . 7F **135**
Edge Hill Av. N3 . . . . 4J **45**
Edge Hill Ct. DA14: Sidc 4K **143**
SW19 . . . . 7F **135**
Edgehill Gdns. RM10: Dag 4G **73**
Edgehill Ho. SW9 . . . . 2B **120**
Edgehill Rd. BR7: Chst 3G **143**
CR4: Mitc 1F **155**
W13 . . . . 5C **78**
Edgeley La. SW4 . . . . 3H **119**
Edgeley Rd. SW4 . . . . 3H **119**
Edgel St. SW18 . . . . 4K **117**
Edge Point Cl. SE27 . . . . 5B **138**
Edge St. W8 . . . . 1J **99**
Edgewood Dr. BR6: Chels 5K **173**
Edgewood Grn. CR0: C'don 1K **169**
Edgeworth Av. NW4 . . . . 5C **44**
Edgeworth Cl. NW4 . . . . 5C **44**
Edgeworth Ct. *EN4: Cockf* *4H* ***21***
(off Fordham Rd.)
Edgeworth Cres. NW4 . . . . 5C **44**
Edgeworth Ho. *NW8* *1A* ***82***
(off Boundary Rd.)
Edgeworth Rd. EN4: Cockf 4H **21**
SE9 . . . . 4A **124**
Edgington Rd. SW16 . . . . 6H **137**
Edgington Way DA14: Sidc 7C **144**
Edgson Ho. *SW1* *5J* ***17***
(off Ebury Bri. Rd.)
EDGWARE 6B 28
EDGWARE BURY 1A 28
Edgwarebury Gdns. HA8: Edg 5B **28**
Edgwarebury La. HA8: Edg 1A **28**
(not continuous)
WD6: E'tree 1A **28**
Edgware Ct. HA8: Edg 6B **28**
Edgware Rd. NW2 . . . . 1D **62**
NW9 . . . . 2J **43**
W2 . . . . 4A **4** (4B **82**)
Edgware Way HA8: Edg 4A **28**
NW7 . . . . 4A **28**
WD6: E'tree 1J **27**
Edicule Sq. E3 . . . . 3A **86**
Edinburgh Cl. E2 . . . . 2J **85**
HA5: Pinn 7B **40**
UB10: Ick 4D **56**
Edinburgh Ct. DA8: Erith 7K **109**
KT1: King T *3E* ***150***
(off Watersplash Cl.)
SE16 . . . . *1K* ***103***
(off Rotherhithe St.)
SW20 . . . . 5F **153**
Edinburgh Dr. UB10: Ick 4D **56**
Edinburgh Ga. SW1 . . . . 7E **10** (2D **100**)
Edinburgh Ho. NW4 . . . . 3E **44**
W9 . . . . *3K* ***81***
(off Maida Vale)
Edinburgh Rd. E13 . . . . 2K **87**
E17 . . . . 5C **50**
N18 . . . . 5B **34**
SM1: Sutt 2A **166**
W7 . . . . 2K **95**
Edington NW5 . . . . 6E **64**
Edington Rd. EN3: Enf H 2D **24**
SE2 . . . . 3B **108**
Edison Bldg. E14 . . . . 2C **104**
Edison Cl. E17 . . . . 5C **50**
UB7: W Dray 2B **92**
Edison Ct. *CR0: C'don* *7B* ***156***
(off Campbell Rd.)
SE10 . . . . *3H* ***105***
(off Schoolbank Rd.)
W3 . . . . 2A **98**
Edison Dr. HA9: Wemb 3E **60**
UB1: S'hall 6F **77**
Edison Gro. SE18 . . . . 7K **107**
Edison Hgts. *E1* *3K* ***9***
(off Cygnet St.)
Edison Ho. *HA9: Wemb* *3J* ***61***
(off Barnhill Rd.)
SE1 . . . . *4D* ***102***
(off New Kent Rd.)
Edison M. SW18 . . . . 6K **117**
Edison Rd. BR2: Brom 2J **159**
DA16: Well 1K **125**
EN3: Brim 2G **25**
N8 . . . . 6H **47**
Edis St. NW1 . . . . 1E **82**
Editha Mans. *SW10* *6A* ***100***
(off Edith Gro.)
Edith Brinson Ho. *E14* *6F* ***87***
(off Oban St.)
Edith Cavell Cl. N19 . . . . 7J **47**
Edith Cavell Ho. *E14* *6D* ***86***
(off Sturry St.)
Edith Cavell Way SE18 . . . . 1C **124**
Edith Gdns. KT5: Surb 7H **151**
Edith Gro. SW10 . . . . 6A **100**
Edith Ho. *W6* *5E* ***98***
(off Queen Caroline St.)
Edithna St. SW9 . . . . 3J **119**
Edith Nesbit Wlk. SE9 . . . . 5D **124**
Edith Neville Cotts. *NW1* *1C* ***6***
(off Drummond Cres.)
Edith Ramsay Ho. *E1* *5A* ***86***
(off Duckett St.)
Edith Rd. E6 . . . . 7B **70**
E15 . . . . 5F **69**
N11 . . . . 7C **32**
RM6: Chad H 7D **54**
SE25 . . . . 5D **156**
SW19 . . . . 6K **135**
W14 . . . . 4G **99**
Edith Row SW6 . . . . 1K **117**
Edith St. E2 . . . . 2G **85**
Edith Summerskill Ho. *SW6* *7H* ***99***
(off Clem Attlee Ct.)
Edith Ter. SW10 . . . . 7A **100**
Edith Vs. W14 . . . . 4H **99**
Edith Yd. SW10 . . . . 7A **100**
Edmansons Cl. N17 . . . . 1F **49**
Edmeston Cl. E9 . . . . 6A **68**
Edmond Ct. SE14 . . . . 1J **121**
Edmonds Ct. KT8: W Mole 5F **149**
Edmonscote W13 . . . . 5A **78**
EDMONTON 3B 34
Edmonton Ct. *SE16* *3J* ***103***
(off Canada Est.)
Edmonton Grn. Shop. Cen. N9 . . . . 2B **34**
Edmonton Leisure Cen. 3B 34
Edmund Gro. TW13: Hanw 2D **130**
Edmund Halley Way SE10 . . . . 2G **105**
Edmund Ho. SE17 . . . . 6B **102**
Edmund Hurst Dr. E6 . . . . 5F **89**
Edmund Rd. CR4: Mitc 3C **154**
DA16: Well 3A **126**
Edmundsbury Ct. Est. SW9 . . . . 4K **119**
Edmunds Cl. UB4: Yead 5A **76**
Edmund St. SE5 . . . . 7D **102**
Edmunds Wlk. N2 . . . . 4C **46**
Ednam Ho. *SE15* *6G* ***103***
(off Haymerle Rd.)
Edna Rd. SW20 . . . . 2F **153**
Edna St. SW11 . . . . 1C **118**
Edred Ho. *E9* *4A* ***68***
(off Lindisfarne Way)
Edrich Ho. SW4 . . . . 1J **119**
Edric Ho. *SW1* *3D* ***18***
(off Page St.)
Edrick Rd. HA8: Edg 6D **28**
Edrick Wlk. HA8: Edg 6D **28**
Edric Rd. SE14 . . . . 7K **103**
Edridge Rd. CR0: C'don 3C **168**
Education Sq. *E1* *6G* ***85***
(off Alder St.)
Edward VII Mans. *NW10* *3F* ***81***
(off Chamberlayne Rd.)
Edward Alderton Theatre 3D 126
Edward Av. E4 . . . . 6J **35**
SM4: Mord 5B **154**
Edward Bond Ho. *WC1* *2F* ***7***
(off Cromer St.)
Edward Clifford Ho. *SE17* *4D* ***102***
(off Elsted St.)
Edward Cl. N9 . . . . 7A **24**
NW2 . . . . 4F **63**
TW12: Hamp H 5G **131**
Edward Ct. E16 . . . . 5J **87**
Edward Dodd Ct. *N1* *1F* ***9***
(off Chart St.)
Edward Edward's Ho. SE1 . . . . 5A **14**
Edwardes Pl. W8 . . . . 3H **99**
Edwardes Sq. W8 . . . . 3H **99**
Edward Gro. EN4: E Barn 5G **21**
Edward Heylin Ct. *E15* *2D* ***86***
(off High St.)
Edward Heylyn Ho. *E3* *2C* ***86***
(off Thomas Fyre Dr.)
Edward Ho. SE11 . . . . 5H **19**
W2 . . . . *4A* ***4***
(off Hall Pl.)
Edward Kennedy Ho. *W10* *4G* ***81***
(off Wornington Rd.)
Edward Mann Cl. *E1* *6K* ***85***
(off Pitsea St.)
Edward M. NW1 . . . . 1K **5** (3F **83**)
Edward Mills Way E14 . . . . 6C **86**
Edward Pl. SE8 . . . . 6B **104**
Edward Rd. BR1: Brom 7K **141**
BR7: Chst 5F **143**
CR0: C'don 7E **156**
E17 . . . . 4K **49**
EN4: E Barn 5G **21**
HA2: Harr 3G **41**
RM6: Chad H 6E **54**
SE20 . . . . 7K **139**
TW12: Hamp H 5G **131**
TW14: Felt 5F **111**
UB5: N'olt 2A **76**
Edward's Av. HA4: Ruis 6K **57**
Edwards Cl. KT4: Wor Pk 2F **165**
Edward's Cotts. N1 . . . . 6B **66**
Edwards Ct. *CR0: C'don* *4E* ***168***
(off South Pk. Hill Rd.)
Edwards Dr. N11 . . . . 7C **32**
Edward's La. N16 . . . . 2E **66**
Edwards Mans. *IG11: Bark* *7K* ***71***
(off Upney La.)
Edwards M. N1 . . . . 7B **66**
W1 . . . . 1G **11** (6E **82**)
Edwards Pas. *E1* *5J* ***85***
(off Trinity Grn.)
Edward Sq. N1 . . . . 1K **83**
SE16 . . . . 1A **104**
Edwards Rd. DA17: Belv 4G **109**
Edward St. E16 . . . . 4J **87**
(not continuous)
SE8 . . . . 6B **104**
SE14 . . . . 7A **104**
Edwards Yd. HA0: Wemb 1E **78**
Edward Temme Av. E15 . . . . 7H **69**
Edward Tyler Rd. SE12 . . . . 2A **142**
Edward Way TW15: Ashf 2B **128**
Edwina Gdns. IG4: Ilf 5C **52**
Edwin Arnold Ct. DA14: Sidc 4K **143**
Edwin Av. E6 . . . . 2E **88**
(not continuous)

Edwin Cl. DA7: Bex 6F 109
Edwin Hall Pl. SE13 6F 123
Edwin Ho. SE15 7G 103
Edwin Pl. *CR0: C'don* *1E 168*
(off Leslie Gro.)
Edwin Rd. HA8: Edg 6E 28
TW1: Twick 1K 131
TW2: Twick 1J 131
Edwin's Mead E9 4A 68
Edwin Stray Ho. TW13: Hanw 2E 130
Edwin St. E1 4J 85
E16 5J 87
Edwin Ware Ct. HA5: Pinn 2A 40
Edwy Ho. *E9* *4B 68*
(off Homerton Rd.)
Edwyn Cl. EN5: Barn 6A 20
Edwyn Ho. *SW18* *6K 117*
(off Neville Gill Cl.)
Eel Brook Cl. SW6 1K 117
Eel Pie Island TW1: Twick 1A 132
Effie Pl. SW6 7J 99
Effie Rd. SW6 7J 99
Effingham Cl. SM2: Sutt 7K 165
Effingham Lodge KT1: King T 4D 150
Effingham Rd. CR0: C'don 7K 155
KT6: Surb 7B 150
N8 5A 48
SE12 5G 123
Effort St. SW17 5C 136
Effra Cl. SW19 6K 135
Effra Ct. *SW2* *5K 119*
(off Brixton Hill)
Effra Pde. SW2 5A 120
Effra Rd. SW2 4A 120
SW19 6K 135
Effra Rd. Retail Pk. SW2 5A 120
Egan Way UB3: Hayes 7G 75
Egbert Ho. *E9* *5A 68*
(off Homerton Rd.)
Egbert St. NW1 1E 82
Egbury Ho. *SW15* *6B 116*
(off Tangley Gro.)
Egeremont Rd. SE13 2D 122
Egerton Cl. DA17: Belv 5J 109
HA5: Eastc 4J 39
Egerton Ct. E11 7F 51
Egerton Cres. SW3 3D 16 (4C 100)
Egerton Dr. SE10 1D 122
Egerton Gdns. IG3: Ilf 3K 71
NW4 4D 44
NW10 1E 80
SW3 2C 16 (4C 100)
W13 6B 78
Egerton Gdns. M. SW3 2D 16 (3C 100)
Egerton Pl. SW3 2D 16 (3C 100)
Egerton Rd. HA0: Wemb 7F 61
KT3: N Mald 4B 152
N16 7F 49
SE25 3E 156
TW2: Twick 7J 113
Egerton Ter. SW3 2D 16 (3C 100)
Egerton Way UB3: Harl 7D 92
Eggardon Ct. UB5: N'olt 6F 59
Egham Cl. SM3: Cheam 2G 165
SW19 2G 135
Egham Cres. SM3: Cheam 3G 165
Egham Rd. E13 5K 87
Eglantine Rd. SW18 5A 118
Egleston Rd. SM4: Mord 6K 153
Egleton Ho. SW15 7C 116
Eglington Ct. SE17 6C 102
Eglington Rd. E4 7K 25
Eglinton Hill SE18 6F 107
Eglinton Rd. SE18 6E 106
Egliston M. SW15 3E 116
Egliston Rd. SW15 3E 116
Eglon M. NW1 7D 64
Egmont Av. KT6: Surb 1F 163
Egmont Ct. *KT12: Walt T* *7K 147*
(off Egmont Rd.)
Egmont M. KT19: Ewe 4K 163
Egmont Rd. KT3: N Mald 4B 152
KT6: Surb 1F 163
KT12: Walt T 7K 147
SM2: Sutt 7A 166
Egmont St. SE14 7K 103
Egremont Ho. *E20* *5E 68*
(off Medals Way)
SE13 *2D 122*
(off Russett Way)
Egremont Rd. SE27 3A 138
Egret Hgts. *N17* *3H 49*
(off Waterside Way)
Egret Ho. *SE16* *4K 103*
(off Tawny Way)
Egret Way UB4: Yead 5B 76
Eider Cl. E7 5H 69
UB4: Yead 5B 76
Eider Ct. *SE8* *6B 104*
(off Pilot Cl.)
Eighteenth Rd. CR4: Mitc 4J 155
Eighth Av. E12 4D 70
UB3: Hayes 1J 93
Eileen Rd. SE25 5D 156
Eindhoven Cl. SM5: Cars 1E 166
Einstein Ho. HA9: Wemb 3J 61
Eisenhower Dr. E6 5C 88
Ekarro Ho. *SW8* *1J 119*
(off Guildford Rd.)
Elaine Gro. NW5 5E 64
Elam Cl. SE5 2B 120
Elam St. SE5 2B 120
Elan Ct. E1 5H 85
Eland Pl. CR0: Wadd 3B 168
Eland Rd. CR0: Wadd 3B 168
SW11 3D 118
Elba Pl. SE17 4C 102
Elberon Av. CR0: Bedd 6G 155
Elbe St. SW6 2A 118
Elborough Rd. SE25 5G 157
Elborough St. SW18 1J 135
Elbourne Ct. *SE16* *3K 103*
(off Worgan St.)
Elbourne Trad. Est. DA17: Belv 3H 109
Elbourn Ho. *SW3* *5C 16*
(off Cale St.)
Elbow Mdw. SL3: Poyle 4A 174
Elbury Dr. E16 6J 87
Elcho St. SW11 7C 100
Elcot Av. SE15 7H 103
Elden Ho. *SW3* *3C 16*
(off Sloane Av.)
Eldenwall Ind. Est. RM8: Dag 1E 72
Elder Av. N8 5J 47
Elderberry Gro. SE27 4C 138
Elderberry Rd. W5 2E 96
Elderberry Way E6 3D 88
Elder Cl. DA15: Sidc 1K 143
N20 2E 30
UB7: Yiew 7A 74
Elder Ct. WD23: B Hea 2D 26
Elderfield Ho. *E14* *7C 86*
(off Pennyfields)
Elderfield Pl. SW17 4F 137
Elderfield Rd. E5 4K 67
Elderfield Wlk. E11 5K 51
Elderflower Way E15 7G 69
Elder Gdns. SE27 5C 138
Elder Ho. *E15* *3G 87*
(off Manor Rd.)
KT1: King T *1D 150*
(off Water La.)
Elder Oak Cl. SE20 1H 157
Elder Oak Ct. *SE20* *1H 157*
(off Anerley Rd.)
Elder Pl. CR2: S Croy 6B 168
Elder Rd. SE27 5C 138
Elderslie Cl. BR3: Beck 5C 158
Elderslie Rd. SE9 5E 124
Elder St. E1 5J 9 (4F 85)
(not continuous)
Elderton Rd. SE26 4A 140
Eldertree Pl. CR4: Mitc 1G 155
Eldertree Way CR4: Mitc 1G 155
Elder Wlk. *N1* *1B 84*
(off Popham St.)
SE13 3E 122
Elderwood Pl. SE27 5C 138
Eldon Av. CR0: C'don 2J 169
TW5: Hest 7E 94
Eldon Ct. NW6 1J 81
Eldon Gro. NW3 5B 64
Eldon Ho. *NW9* *3C 44*
(off East Dr.)
Eldon Pk. SE25 4H 157
Eldon Rd. E17 4B 50
N9 1D 34
N22 1B 48
W8 3K 99
Eldons Pas. *E1* *7G 85*
(off Cable St.)
Eldon St. EC2 6F 9 (5D 84)
Eldon Way NW10 3H 79
Eldred Rd. IG11: Bark 1J 89
Eldrick Ct. TW14: Bedf 1F 129
Eldridge Cl. TW14: Felt 1J 129
Eldridge Ct. RM10: Dag 6H 73
SE16 3G 103
Eleanor Cl. N15 3F 49
SE16 2K 103
Eleanor Ct. *E2* *1G 85*
(off Whiston Rd.)
Eleanor Cres. NW7 5A 30
Eleanor Gdns. EN5: Barn 5A 20
RM8: Dag 2F 73
Eleanor Gro. SW13 3A 116
UB10: Ick 3D 56
Eleanor Ho. *W6* *5E 98*
(off Queen Caroline St.)
Eleanor Rathbone Ho. *N6* *7H 47*
(off Avenue Rd.)
Eleanor Rd. E8 6H 67
E15 6H 69
N11 6D 32
SW9 1A 120
Eleanor St. E3 3C 86
Eleanor Wlk. SE18 4C 106
Electra Av. TW6: H'row A 3H 111
Electra Bus. Pk. E16 5F 87
Electric Av. SW9 4A 120
Electric Cinema 6H 81
Electric Empire, The *SE14* *1K 121*
(off New Cross Rd.)
Electric Ho. *E3* *3C 86*
(off Bow Rd.)
Electric La. SW9 4A 120
(not continuous)
Electric Pde. *E18* *2J 51*
(off George La.)
IG3: Ilf 2J 71
KT6: Surb 6D 150
Elektron Twr. E14 7F 87
Eleonora Ter. *SM1: Sutt* *5A 166*
(off Lind Rd.)
ELEPHANT & CASTLE 3B 102
Elephant & Castle SE1 4B 102
Elephant & Castle Leisure Cen. 4B 102
Elephant & Castle Shop. Cen. SE1 4C 102
Elephant La. SE16 2J 103
Elephant Rd. SE17 4C 102
Elers Rd. UB3: Harl 4F 93
W13 2C 96
Eley Rd. N18 4E 34
Eley Rd. Retail Pk. N18 5D 34
Eleys Est. N18 4E 34
(not continuous)
Elfindale Rd. SE24 5C 120
Elfin Gro. TW11: Tedd 5K 131
Elfin Oak 1K 99
Elford Cl. SE3 4A 124
Elford M. SW4 5G 119
Elfort Rd. N5 4A 66
Elfrida Cl. IG8: Wfd G 7D 36
Elfrida Cres. SE6 4C 140
Elf Row E1 7J 85
Elfwine Rd. W7 5J 77
Elgal Cl. BR6: Farnb 5F 173
Elgar *N8* *3J 47*
(off Boyton Cl.)
Elgar Av. KT5: Surb 1G 163
NW10 6K 61
(not continuous)
SW16 3J 155
W5 2E 96
Elgar Cl. E13 2A 88
IG9: Buck H 2G 37
SE8 7C 104
UB10: Ick 2C 56
Elgar Ct. NW6 3J 81
W14 *3G 99*
(off Blythe Rd.)
Elgar Ho. *NW6* *7A 64*
(off Fairfax Rd.)
SW1 *6K 17*
(off Churchill Gdns.)
Elgar St. SE16 3A 104
Elgin Av. HA3: Kenton 2B 42
TW15: Ashf 6E 128
W9 4H 81
W12 2C 98
Elgin Cl. W12 2D 98
Elgin Ct. *CR2: S Croy* *4C 168*
(off Bramley Hill)
W9 4K 81
Elgin Cres. TW6: H'row A 2G 111
W11 7G 81
Elgin Dr. HA6: Nwood 1G 39
Elgin Est. *W9* *4J 81*
(off Elgin Av.)
Elgin Ho. *E14* *6D 86*
(off Ricardo St.)
RM6: Chad H *6F 55*
(off High Rd.)
Elgin Mans. W9 3K 81
Elgin M. W11 6G 81
Elgin M. Nth. W9 3K 81
Elgin M. Sth. W9 3K 81
Elgin Rd. CR0: C'don 2F 169
IG3: Ilf 1J 71
N22 2G 47
SM1: Sutt 3A 166
SM6: Wall 6G 167
Elgood Cl. W11 7G 81
Elgood Ho. *NW8* *2B 82*
(off Wellington Rd.)
SE1 *7E 14*
(off Tabard St.)
Elham Cl. BR1: Brom 7B 142
Elham Ho. E5 5H 67
Elia M. N1 1A 8 (2B 84)
Elias Pl. SW8 6A 102
Elia St. N1 1B 8 (2B 84)
Elibank Rd. SE9 4D 124
Elim Est. SE1 7G 15 (3E 102)
Elim St. SE1 7G 15 (3D 102)
(not continuous)
Elim Way E13 3H 87
Eliot Bank SE23 2H 139
Eliot Cotts. SE3 2G 123
Eliot Ct. SW18 6K 117
Eliot Dr. HA2: Harr 2F 59
Eliot Gdns. SW15 4C 116
Eliot Hill SE13 2E 122
Eliot M. NW8 2A 82
Eliot Pk. SE13 2E 122
Eliot Pl. SE3 2G 123
Eliot Rd. RM9: Dag 4D 72
Eliot Va. SE3 2F 123
Elis David Almshouses CR0: C'don 3B 168
Elis Way E20 5E 68
Elizabethan Cl. TW19: Stanw 7A 110
Elizabethan Way TW19: Stanw 7A 110
Elizabeth Av. EN2: Enf 3G 23
IG1: Ilf 2H 71

Elizabeth Av. N1 ... 1C **84**
TW18: Staines ... 7A **128**
Elizabeth Barnes Ct. *SW6 ... 2K 117*
(off Marinefield Rd.)
Elizabeth Bates Ct. *E1 ... 5J 85*
(off Fulneck Pl.)
Elizabeth Blackwell Ho. *N22 ... 1A 48*
(off Progress Way)
Elizabeth Blount Ct. *E14 ... 6A 86*
(off Carr St.)
Elizabeth Bri. SW1 ... 4J **17** (4F **101**)
Elizabeth Cl. E14 ... 6D **86**
EN5: Barn ... 3A **20**
RM7: Mawney ... 1H **55**
SM1: Sutt ... 4H **165**
W9 ... 4A **82**
Elizabeth Clyde Cl. N15 ... 4E **48**
Elizabeth Cotts. TW9: Kew ... 1F **115**
Elizabeth Ct. *BR1: Brom ... 1H 159*
(off Highland Rd.)
CR0: C'don ... 3E 168
(off The Avenue)
E4 ... 5G **35**
E10 ... 7D **50**
IG8: Wfd G ... 7F **37**
KT2: King T ... 1E **150**
NW1 ... 3D **4**
SW1 ... 2D **18**
SW10 ... 6B 100
(off Milman's St.)
TW11: Tedd ... 5J **131**
TW16: Sun ... 3A 148
(off Elizabeth Gdns.)
Elizabeth Croll Ho. *WC1 ... 1H 7*
(off Penton Ri.)
Elizabeth Fry Apartments *IG11: Bark ... 7G 71*
(off Kings Rd.)
Elizabeth Fry Ho. UB3: Harl ... 4H **93**
Elizabeth Fry M. E8 ... 7H **67**
Elizabeth Fry Pl. SE18 ... 1C **124**
Elizabeth Gdns. HA7: Stan ... 6H **27**
TW7: Isle ... 4A **114**
TW16: Sun ... 3A **148**
W3 ... 1B **98**
Elizabeth Garrett Anderson Ho.
DA17: Belv ... 3G 109
(off Ambrooke Rd.)
Elizabeth Ho. *E3 ... 3D 86*
(off St Leonard's St.)
SE11 ... 4K 19
(off Reedworth St.)
SM3: Cheam ... 6G 165
(off Park La.)
W6 ... 5E 98
(off Queen Caroline St.)
Elizabeth Ind. Est. SE14 ... 6K **103**
Elizabeth M. *E2 ... 2G 85*
(off Kay St.)
HA1: Harr ... 6J **41**
NW3 ... 6C **64**
Elizabeth Newcomen Ho. *SE1 ... 6E 14*
(off Newcomen St.)
Elizabeth Pl. N15 ... 4D **48**
Elizabeth Ride N9 ... 7C **24**
Elizabeth Rd. E6 ... 1B **88**
N15 ... 5E **48**
Elizabeth Sq. *SE16 ... 7A 86*
(off Sovereign Cres.)
Elizabeth St. SW1 ... 3H **17** (4E **100**)
Elizabeth Ter. SE9 ... 6D **124**
Elizabeth Way SE19 ... 7D **138**
TW13: Hanw ... 4A **130**
Elkanette M. N20 ... 2F **31**
Elkington Point SE11 ... 4J **19**
Elkington Rd. E13 ... 4K **87**
Elkstone Rd. W10 ... 5H **81**
Ella Cl. BR3: Beck ... 2C **158**
Ellacott M. SW16 ... 2H **137**
Ellaline Rd. W6 ... 6F **99**
Ella M. NW3 ... 4D **64**
Ellanby Cres. N18 ... 4C **34**
Elland Cl. EN5: New Bar ... 5G **21**
Elland Ho. *E14 ... 6B 86*
(off Copenhagen Pl.)
Elland Rd. SE15 ... 4J **121**
Ella Rd. N8 ... 7J **47**
Ellement Cl. HA5: Pinn ... 5B **40**
Ellena Ct. *N14 ... 3D 32*
(off Conway Rd.)
Ellenborough Ho. *W12 ... 7D 80*
(off White City Est.)
Ellenborough Pl. SW15 ... 4C **116**
Ellenborough Rd. DA14: Sidc ... 5D **144**
N22 ... 1C **48**
Ellenbridge Way CR2: Sande ... 7E **168**
Ellen Cl. BR1: Brom ... 3B **160**
Ellen Ct. *E4 ... 1K 35*
(off The Ridgeway)
N9 ... 2D **34**
Ellen Julia Ct. *E1 ... 6J 85*
(off James Voller Way)
Ellen St. E1 ... 6G **85**
Ellen Terry Ct. *NW1 ... 7F 65*
(off Farrier St.)
Ellen Webb Dr. HA3: W'stone ... 3J **41**
Ellen Wilkinson Ho. *E2 ... 3K 85*
(off Usk St.)
RM10: Dag ... 3G **73**
SW6 ... 6H 99
(off Clem Attlee Ct.)
Elleray Rd. TW11: Tedd ... 6K **131**
Ellerby St. SW6 ... 1F **117**
Ellerdale Cl. NW3 ... 4A **64**
Ellerdale Rd. NW3 ... 5A **64**
Ellerdale St. SE13 ... 4D **122**
Ellerdine Rd. TW3: Houn ... 4G **113**
Ellerker Gdns. TW10: Rich ... 6E **114**
Ellerman Av. TW2: Whitt ... 1D **130**
Ellerslie Gdns. NW10 ... 1C **80**
Ellerslie Rd. W12 ... 1D **98**
Ellerslie Sq. Ind. Est. SW2 ... 5J **119**
Ellerton Gdns. RM9: Dag ... 7C **72**
Ellerton Lodge N3 ... 2J **45**
Ellerton Rd. KT6: Surb ... 2F **163**
RM9: Dag ... 7C **72**
SW13 ... 1C **116**
SW18 ... 1B **136**
SW20 ... 7C **134**
Ellery Ho. SE17 ... 4D **102**
Ellery Rd. SE19 ... 7D **138**
Ellery St. SE15 ... 2H **121**
Ellesmere Av. BR3: Beck ... 2E **158**
NW7 ... 3E **28**
Ellesmere Cl. E11 ... 5H **51**
HA4: Ruis ... 7E **38**
Ellesmere Ct. SE12 ... 1J **141**
W4 ... 5K **97**
Ellesmere Gdns. IG4: Ilf ... 5C **52**
Ellesmere Gro. EN5: Barn ... 5C **20**
Ellesmere Ho. *SW10 ... 6A 100*
(off Fulham Rd.)
Ellesmere Mans. *NW6 ... 6A 64*
(off Canfield Gdns.)
Ellesmere Rd. E3 ... 2A **86**
NW10 ... 5C **62**
TW1: Twick ... 6C **114**
UB6: G'frd ... 4G **77**
W4 ... 6K **97**
Ellesmere St. E14 ... 6D **86**
Ellie M. E13 ... 2A **88**
Ellies M. TW15: Ashf ... 2A **128**
Ellingfort Rd. E8 ... 7H **67**
Ellingham Rd. E15 ... 4F **69**
KT9: Chess ... 6D **162**
W12 ... 2C **98**
Ellington Ct. N14 ... 2C **32**
Ellington Ho. SE1 ... 3C **102**
SE18 ... 7E **106**
Ellington Rd. N10 ... 4F **47**
TW3: Houn ... 2F **113**
TW13: Felt ... 4H **129**
Ellington St. N7 ... 6A **66**
Elliot Cl. E15 ... 7G **69**
IG8: Wfd G ... 6G **37**
Elliot Ho. *SW17 ... 3B 136*
(off Grosvenor Way)
W1 ... 6D 4
(off Cato St.)
Elliot Rd. NW4 ... 6D **44**
Elliott Av. HA4: Ruis ... 2K **57**
Elliott Cl. HA9: Wemb ... 3F **61**
Elliott Gdns. TW17: Shep ... 4C **146**
Elliott Rd. BR2: Brom ... 4B **160**
CR7: Thor H ... 4B **156**
HA7: Stan ... 6F **27**
SW9 ... 1B **120**
W4 ... 4A **98**
Elliott's Pl. N1 ... 1B **84**
Elliott Sq. NW3 ... 7C **64**
Elliotts Row SE11 ... 4B **102**
Ellis Av. RM8: Dag ... 1E **72**
Ellis Cl. HA4: Eastc ... 6J **39**
HA8: Edg ... 6F **29**
NW10 ... 6D **62**
SE9 ... 2G **143**
Elliscombe Mt. SE7 ... 6A **106**
Elliscombe Rd. SE7 ... 6A **106**
Ellis Ct. *E1 ... 6J 85*
(off James Voller Way)
W7 ... 5K **77**
Ellisfield Dr. SW15 ... 7C **116**
Ellis Franklin Ct. *NW8 ... 2A 82*
(off Abbey Rd.)
Ellis Ho. *SE17 ... 5D 102*
(off Brandon St.)
Ellison Apartments *E3 ... 3C 86*
(off Merchant St.)
Ellison Gdns. UB2: S'hall ... 4D **94**
Ellison Ho. *SE13 ... 2D 122*
(off Lewisham Rd.)
Ellison Rd. DA15: Sidc ... 1H **143**
SW13 ... 2B **116**
SW16 ... 7H **137**
Ellis Rd. CR4: Mitc ... 6D **154**
UB2: S'hall ... 1G **95**
Ellis St. SW1 ... 3F **17** (4E **100**)
Ellis Ter. SE11 ... 7A **102**
Elliston Ho. *SE18 ... 4E 106*
(off Wellington St.)
Ellora Rd. SW16 ... 5H **137**
Ellswood Ct. KT6: Surb ... 7D **150**
Ellsworth St. E2 ... 3H **85**
Ellwood Ct. *W9 ... 4K 81*
(off Clearwell Dr.)
Elmar Rd. N15 ... 4D **48**
Elm Av. HA4: Ruis ... 1J **57**
TW19: Stanw ... 2A **128**
W5 ... 1E **96**
Elmbank N14 ... 7D **22**
Elmbank Av. EN5: Barn ... 4A **20**
Elm Bank Dr. BR1: Brom ... 2B **160**
Elm Bank Gdns. SW13 ... 2A **116**
Elmbank Way W7 ... 5H **77**
Elmbourne Dr. DA17: Belv ... 4H **109**
Elmbourne Rd. SW17 ... 3F **137**
Elmbridge Av. KT5: Surb ... 5H **151**
Elmbridge Cl. HA4: Ruis ... 6J **39**
Elmbridge Dr. HA4: Ruis ... 5H **39**
Elmbridge Sports Hub ... 5K **147**
Elmbridge Wlk. E8 ... 7G **67**
Elmbridge Xcel Leisure Complex ... 5K **147**
Elmbrook Cl. TW16: Sun ... 1K **147**
Elmbrook Gdns. SE9 ... 4C **124**
Elmbrook Rd. SM1: Sutt ... 4H **165**
Elm Cl. CR2: S Croy ... 6E **168**
E11 ... 6K **51**
HA2: Harr ... 6F **41**
IG9: Buck H ... 2G **37**
KT5: Surb ... 7J **151**
N19 ... 2G **65**
NW4 ... 5F **45**
RM7: Mawney ... 1H **55**
SM5: Cars ... 1D **166**
Elm Cl. SW20 ... 4E **152**
TW2: Twick ... 2F **131**
UB3: Hayes ... 6J **75**
Elmcote HA5: Pinn ... 2B **40**
Elm Cotts. CR4: Mitc ... 2D **154**
Elm Ct. CR4: Mitc ... 2D **154**
EC4 ... 1J **13**
EN4: E Barn ... 7H **21**
KT8: W Mole ... 4F **149**
SE1 ... 7G 15
(off Royal Oak Yd.)
SE13 ... 3F **123**
SW9 ... 1A 120
(off Cranworth Gdns.)
TW16: Sun ... 7H 129
(off Grangewood Dr.)
W9 ... 5J 81
(off Admiral Wlk.)
Elmcourt Rd. SE27 ... 2B **138**
Elm Cres. KT2: King T ... 1E **150**
W5 ... 1E **96**
Elmcroft N6 ... 7G **47**
N8 ... 5K **47**
Elmcroft Av. DA15: Sidc ... 7K **125**
E11 ... 5K **51**
N9 ... 6C **24**
NW11 ... 7H **45**
Elmcroft Cl. E11 ... 4K **51**
KT9: Chess ... 3E **162**
TW14: Felt ... 6H **111**
W5 ... 6D **78**
Elmcroft Cres. HA2: Harr ... 3E **40**
NW11 ... 7G **45**
Elmcroft Dr. KT9: Chess ... 3E **162**
TW15: Ashf ... 5C **128**
Elmcroft Gdns. NW9 ... 4G **43**
Elmcroft St. E5 ... 4J **67**
Elmcroft Ter. UB8: Hil ... 6C **74**
Elmdale Rd. N13 ... 5E **32**
Elmdene KT5: Surb ... 1J **163**
Elmdene Cl. BR3: Beck ... 6B **158**
Elmdene Rd. SE18 ... 5F **107**
Elmdon Rd. TW4: Houn ... 2B **112**
TW6: H'row A ... 3H **111**
Elm Dr. HA2: Harr ... 6F **41**
TW16: Sun ... 2A **148**
Elmer Cl. EN2: Enf ... 3E **22**
Elmer Gdns. HA8: Edg ... 7C **28**
TW7: Isle ... 3H **113**
Elmer Ho. *NW8 ... 5C 4*
(off Penfold St.)
Elmer Rd. SE6 ... 7E **122**
Elmers Dr. TW11: Tedd ... 6B **132**
ELMERS END ... 4A **158**
Elmers End Rd. BR3: Beck ... 2J **157**
SE20 ... 2J **157**
Elmerside Rd. BR3: Beck ... 4A **158**
Elmers Lodge BR3: Beck ... 4K **157**
Elmers Rd. SE25 ... 7G **157**
Elmfield HA1: Harr ... 7K **41**
Elmfield Av. CR4: Mitc ... 1E **154**
N8 ... 5J **47**
TW11: Tedd ... 5K **131**
Elmfield Cl. HA1: Harr ... 2J **59**
Elmfield Ct. DA16: Well ... 1B **126**
Elmfield Ho. *N2 ... 2B 46*
(off The Grange)
NW8 ... 2K 81
(off Carlton Hill)
W9 ... 4J 81
(off Goldney Rd.)
Elmfield Pk. BR1: Brom ... 3J **159**
Elmfield Rd. BR1: Brom ... 2J **159**
E4 ... 2K **35**
E17 ... 6K **49**
N2 ... 3B **46**
SW17 ... 2E **136**
UB2: S'hall ... 3C **94**
Elmfield Way CR2: Sande ... 7F **169**
W9 ... 5J **81**
Elm Friars Wlk. NW1 ... 7H **65**

Elm Gdns. CR4: Mitc 4H 155
KT10: Clay 6A 162
N2 3A 46
Elmgate Av. TW13: Felt 3K 129
Elmgate Gdns. HA8: Edg 5D 28
Elm Grn. W3 6A 80
Elmgreen Cl. E15 1G 87
Elm Gro. BR6: Orp 1K 173
DA8: Erith 7K 109
HA2: Harr 7E 40
IG8: Wfd G 5C 36
KT2: King T 1E 150
N8 6J 47
NW2 4F 63
SE15 2F 121
SM1: Sutt 4K 165
SW19 7G 135
UB7: Yiew 7B 74
Elmgrove Cres. HA1: Harr 5K 41
Elmgrove Gdns. HA1: Harr 5A 42
Elm Gro. Pde. SM6: Wall 3E 166
Elmgrove Point SE18 4H 107
Elm Gro. Rd. SW13 1C 116
W5 2E 96
Elmgrove Rd. CR0: C'don 7H 157
HA1: Harr 5K 41
HA3: W'stone 5A 42
Elm Hall Gdns. E11 5K 51
(not continuous)
Elm Ho. *E3* *1B 86*
(off Sycamore Av.)
E14 *2E 104*
(off E. Ferry Rd.)
KT2: King T *7F 133*
(off Elm Rd.)
W10 *4G 81*
(off Briar Wlk.)
Elmhurst DA17: Belv 6E 108
Elmhurst Av. CR4: Mitc 7F 137
N2 3B 46
Elmhurst Ct. CR0: C'don 4D 168
Elmhurst Dr. E18 2J 51
Elmhurst Lodge SM2: Sutt 7A 166
Elmhurst Mans. SW4 3H 119
Elmhurst Rd. E7 7K 69
N17 2F 49
SE9 2C 142
Elmhurst St. SW4 3H 119
Elmington Cl. DA5: Bexl 6H 127
Elmington Est. SE5 7D 102
Elmington Rd. SE5 7D 102
Elmira St. SE13 3D 122
Elm La. SE6 2B 140
Elm Lawn Cl. UB8: Uxb 7A 56
Elmlea Dr. UB3: Hayes 5G 75
Elm Lea Trad. Est. N17 6C 34
Elmlee Cl. BR7: Chst 6D 142
Elmley Cl. E6 5C 88
Elmley St. SE18 5H 107
(not continuous)
Elm Lodge SW6 1E 116
Elmore Cl. HA0: Wemb 2E 78
Elmore Ho. *N1* *7D 66*
(off Elmore St.)
SW9 2B 120
Elmore Rd. E11 3E 68
EN3: Enf W 1E 24
Elmore St. N1 7C 66
Elm Pde. DA14: Sidc 4A 144
Elm Pk. HA7: Stan 5G 27
SW2 6K 119
Elm Pk. Av. N15 5F 49
Elm Pk. Chambers *SW10* *6A 16*
(off Fulham Rd.)
Elm Pk. Ct. HA5: Pinn 3A 40
Elm Pk. Gdns. NW4 5F 45
SW10 6A 16 (5B 100)
Elm Pk. Ho. SW10 6A 16 (5B 100)
Elm Pk. La. SW3 6A 16 (5B 100)
Elm Pk. Mans.
SW10 7A 16 (6A 100)
Elm Pk. Rd. E10 1A 68
HA5: Pinn 2A 40
N3 7C 30
N21 7H 23
SE25 3F 157
SW3 7A 16 (6B 100)
Elm Pas. EN5: Barn 4C 20
Elm Pl. SW7 5A 16 (5B 100)
TW15: Ashf 5C 128
Elm Quay Ct. SW8 7C 18 (6H 101)
Elm Rd. BR3: Beck 2B 158
BR6: Chels 7K 173
CR7: Thor H 4D 156
DA14: Sidc 4A 144
E7 6H 69
E11 2F 69
E17 5E 50
EN5: Barn 4C 20
HA9: Wemb 5E 60
KT2: King T 1F 151
KT3: N Mald 2K 151
KT9: Chess 4E 162
KT17: Ewe 6B 164
N22 1B 48
RM7: Mawney 2H 55
SM6: Wall 1E 166
SW14 3J 115
TW14: Bedf 1F 129
Elm Rd. W. SM3: Sutt 7H 153
Elm Row NW3 3A 64
Elms, The *CR0: C'don* *1C 168*
(off Tavistock Rd.)
E12 6B 70
KT10: Clay 7A 162
SW13 3B 116
TW15: Ashf 5C 128
Elms Av. N10 3F 47
NW4 5F 45
Elmscott Gdns. N21 6H 23
Elmscott Rd. BR1: Brom 5G 141
Elms Ct. HA0: Wemb 4A 60
Elms Cres. SW4 6G 119
Elmsdale Rd. E17 4B 50
Elms Gdns. HA0: Wemb 4A 60
RM9: Dag 4F 73
Elmshaw Rd. SW15 5C 116
Elmshurst Cres. N2 4B 46
Elmside CR0: New Ad 6D 170
Elmside Rd. HA9: Wemb 3G 61
Elms La. HA0: Wemb 3A 60
Elmsleigh Av. HA3: Kenton 4B 42
Elmsleigh Ct. SM1: Sutt 3K 165
Elmsleigh Ho. *TW2: Twick* *2H 131*
(off Staines Rd.)
Elmsleigh Rd. TW2: Twick 2H 131
Elmslie Cl. IG8: Wfd G 6J 37
Elmslie Point *E3* *5B 86*
(off Leopold St.)
Elms M. W2 2A 10 (7B 82)
Elms Pk. Av. HA0: Wemb 4A 60
Elms Rd. HA3: Hrw W 7D 26
SW4 5G 119
ELMSTEAD 6D 142
Elmstead Av. BR7: Chst 5D 142
HA9: Wemb 1E 60
Elmstead Cl. KT19: Ewe 5A 164
N20 2D 30
Elmstead Gdns. KT4: Wor Pk 3C 164
Elmstead Glade BR7: Chst 6D 142
Elmstead La. BR7: Chst 7C 142
Elmstead Rd. DA8: Erith 1K 127
IG3: Ilf 2J 71
Elmsted Cres. DA16: Well 6C 108
Elmstone Rd. SW6 1J 117
Elm St. WC1 4H 7 (4K 83)
Elmsway TW15: Ashf 5C 128
Elmsworth Av. TW3: Houn 2F 113
Elm Ter. HA3: Hrw W 1H 41
NW2 3J 63
NW3 4C 64
SE9 6E 124
Elmton Ct. *NW8* *3A 4*
(off Cunningham Pl.)
Elm Tree Av. KT10: Esh 7H 149
Elm Tree Cl. NW8 1A 4 (3B 82)
TW15: Ashf 5D 128
UB5: N'olt 2D 76
Elm Tree Ct. NW8 1A 4
SE7 6A 106
Elm Tree Rd. NW8 1A 4 (3B 82)
Elmtree Rd. TW11: Tedd 4J 131
Elm Vw. Ct. UB2: S'hall 4E 94
Elm Vw. Ho. UB3: Harl 4F 93
Elm Wlk. BR6: Farnb 3D 172
NW3 2J 63
SW20 4E 152
Elm Way KT4: Wor Pk 3E 164
KT19: Ewe 5K 163
N11 6K 31
NW10 4A 62
Elmwood Av. HA3: Kenton 5A 42
N13 5D 32
TW13: Felt, Hanw 2J 129
Elmwood Cl. KT17: Ewe 7C 164
SM6: Wall 2F 167
Elmwood Ct. *E10* *1C 68*
(off Goldsmith Rd.)
HA0: Wemb 3A 60
SW11 1F 119
Elmwood Cres. NW9 4J 43
Elmwood Dr. DA5: Bexl 7E 126
KT17: Ewe 6C 164
Elmwood Gdns. W7 6J 77
Elmwood Ho. *NW10* *2D 80*
(off All Souls Av.)
Elmwood Rd. CR0: C'don 7B 156
CR4: Mitc 3D 154
SE24 5D 120
W4 6J 97
Elmworth Gro. SE21 2D 138
Elnathan M. W9 4K 81
Elphinstone Ct. SW16 6J 137
Elphinstone Rd. E17 2B 50
Elphinstone St. N5 4B 66
Elrington Rd. E8 6G 67
IG8: Wfd G 5D 36
Elsa Cotts. *E14* *5A 86*
(off Halley St.)
Elsa Ct. BR3: Beck 1B 158
Elsa Rd. DA16: Well 2B 126
Elsa St. E1 5A 86
Elsdale St. E9 6J 67
Elsden M. E2 2J 85
Elsden Rd. N17 1F 49
Elsenham Rd. E12 5E 70
Elsenham St. SW18 1H 135
Elsham Rd. E11 3G 69
W14 2G 99
Elsham Ter. *W14* *3G 99*
(off Elsham Rd.)
Elsiedene Rd. N21 7H 23
Elsie La. Ct. *W2* *5J 81*
(off Westbourne Pk. Vs.)
Elsiemaud Rd. SE4 5B 122
Elsie Rd. SE22 4F 121
Elsinore Av. TW19: Stanw 7A 110
Elsinore Gdns. NW2 3G 63
Elsinore Ho. *N1* *1A 84*
(off Denmark Gro.)
SE5 *2C 120*
(off Denmark Rd.)
SE7 4C 106
W6 *5F 99*
(off Fulham Pal. Rd.)
Elsinore Rd. SE23 1A 140
Elsinore Way TW9: Rich 3H 115
Elsley Ct. HA9: Wemb 6H 61
Elsley Rd. SW11 3D 118
Elspeth Rd. HA0: Wemb 5E 60
SW11 4D 118
Elsrick Av. SM4: Mord 5J 153
Elstan Way CR0: C'don 7A 158
Elstar Ct. *RM13: Rain* *2K 91*
(off Lowen Rd.)
Elstead Ct. SM3: Sutt 1G 165
Elstead Ho. *SW2* *7K 119*
(off Redlands Way)
Elsted St. SE17 4D 102
Elstow Cl. HA4: Ruis 7B 40
SE9 5D 124
(not continuous)
Elstow Gdns. RM9: Dag 1E 90
Elstow Grange NW6 7F 63
Elstow Rd. RM9: Dag 1E 90
Elstree Gdns. DA17: Belv 4E 108
IG1: Ilf 5G 71
N9 1C 34
Elstree Hill BR1: Brom 7G 141
Elstree Hill Sth. WD6: E'tree 1H 27
Elstree Rd. WD23: B Hea 1C 26
Elswick Rd. SE13 2D 122
Elswick St. SW6 2A 118
Elsworth Cl. TW14: Bedf 1G 129
Elsworthy KT7: T Ditt 6J 149
Elsworthy Ct. *NW3* *7D 64*
(off Primrose Hill Rd.)
Elsworthy Ri. NW3 7C 64
Elsworthy Rd. NW3 1C 82
Elsworthy Ter. NW3 7C 64
Elsynge Rd. SW18 5B 118
ELTHAM 6D 124
Eltham Cen. 5E 124
Eltham Crematorium SE9 4H 125
Eltham Grn. SE9 5B 124
Eltham Grn. Rd. SE9 4A 124
Eltham High St. SE9 6D 124
Eltham Hill SE9 5B 124
Eltham Palace & Gdns. 7C 124
Eltham Pal. Rd. SE9 6A 124
ELTHAM PARK 4E 124
Eltham Pk. Gdns. SE9 4E 124
Eltham Rd. SE9 5H 123
SE12 5H 123
Eltham Warren Golf Course 5F 125
Elthiron Rd. SW6 1J 117
Elthorne Av. W7 2K 95
Elthorne Ct. TW13: Felt 1A 130
ELTHORNE HEIGHTS 5J 77
Elthorne Pk. Rd. W7 2K 95
Elthorne Rd. N19 2H 65
NW9 7K 43
Elthorne Sports Cen. 3K 95
Elthorne Way NW9 6K 43
Elthruda Rd. SE13 6F 123
Eltisley Rd. IG1: Ilf 4F 71
Elton Av. EN5: Barn 5C 20
HA0: Wemb 5B 60
UB6: G'frd 6J 59
Elton Cl. KT1: Hamp W 7C 132
Elton Ho. *E3* *1B 86*
(off Candy St.)
Elton Pl. N16 5E 66
Elton Rd. KT2: King T 1F 151
Eltringham St. SW18 4A 118
Eluna Apartments *E1* *7H 85*
(off Wapping La.)
Elvaston M. SW7 2A 16 (3A 100)
Elvaston Pl. SW7 2A 16 (3A 100)
Elveden Ho. SE24 5B 120
Elveden Pl. NW10 2G 79
Elveden Rd. NW10 2G 79
Elvedon Rd. TW13: Felt 3H 129
Elvendon Rd. N13 6D 32
Elven M. SE15 1J 121
Elver Gdns. E2 3G 85
Elverson Rd. SE8 2D 122
Elverton St. SW1 3C 18 (4H 101)
Elvin Ct. NW9 7J 43
Elvington Grn. BR2: Brom 5H 159
Elvington La. NW9 1A 44
Elvino Rd. SE26 5A 140
Elvis Rd. NW2 6E 62
Elwill Way BR3: Beck 4E 158

Elwin St. E2 . . . . .1K 9 (3G 85)
Elwood Cl. EN5: New Bar 4F 21
Elwood St. N5 . . . . .3B 66
Elworth Ho. SW8 . . . . .7K 101
. . . .(off Oval Pl.)
Elwyn Gdns. SE12 . . . . .7J 123
Ely Cl. KT3: N Mald 2B 152
Ely Ct. EC1 .6K 7
. . . KT1: King T 2G 151
Ely Gdns. IG1: Ilf 7C 52
. . . RM10: Dag 3J 73
Ely Ho. SE15 . . . . .7C 103
. . . .(off Friary Est.)
Elyne Rd. N4 . . . . .6A 48
Ely Pl. EC1 . . . . .6K 7 (5A 84)
. . . IG8: Wfd G 6K 37
. . . SW8 . . . . .7K 101
Ely Rd. CR0: C'don 5D 156
. . . E10 . . . . .6E 50
. . . TW4: Houn 3A 112
. . . TW6: H'row A 2H 111
. . . .(off Esher Cres.)
Elysian Av. BR5: St M Cry 6K 161
Elysian M. N7 . . . . .6K 65
Elysian Pl. CR2: S Croy 7C 168
Elysium Apartments E1 . . . . .4J 85
. . . .(off Theven St.)
Elysium Pl. SW6 . . . . .2H 117
. . . .(off Elysium St.)
Elysium St. SW6 . . . . .2H 117
Elystan Bus. Cen. UB4: Yead 7A 76
Elystan Cl. SM6: Wall 7G 167
Elystan Ho. SW3 . . . . .4C 16
. . . .(off Elystan St.)
Elystan Pl. SW3 . . . . .5D 16 (5C 100)
Elystan St. SW3 . . . . .4C 16 (4C 100)
Elystan Wlk. N1 . . . . .1A 84
Ely's Yd. E1 . . . . .5K 9 (5F 85)
Emanuel Av. W3 . . . . .6J 79
Emanuel Dr. TW12: Hamp 5D 130
Emanuel Ho. SW1 . . . . .3H 101
. . . . .2F 117
Embankment SW15 . . . . .2F 117
Embankment, The TW1: Twick 1A 132
Embankment Galleries 2H 13
. . . .(within Somerset House)
Embankment Gdns. SW3 . . . .7F 17 (6D 100)
Embankment Pl. WC2 . . . . . . .4F 13 (1J 101)
Embassy Apartments SE5 . . . . .2C 120
. . . .(off Coldharbour La.)
Embassy Ct. DA14: Sidc 3B 144
. . . DA16: Well 3B 126
. . . E2 . . . . .4H 85
. . . .(off Brady St.)
. . . N11 . . . . .6C 32
. . . .(off Bounds Grn. Rd.)
. . . NW8 . . . . .1B 4
. . . SM6: Wall 6F 167
. . . W5 . . . . .7F 79
Embassy Gdns. BR3: Beck 1B 158
Embassy Ho. NW6 . . . . .7K 63
Embassy Lodge N3 . . . . .2H 45
. . . .(off Cyprus Rd.)
Embassy Theatre
. . . Central School of Speech & Drama
. . . . .7B 64
Embassy Way SW8 . . . . .6H 101
Emba St. SE16 . . . . .2G 103
Ember Cl. BR5: Pet W 7G 161
Ember Ct. NW9 . . . . .2B 44
Embercourt Rd. KT7: T Ditt 6J 149
Ember Farm Av. KT8: E Mos 6H 149
Ember Farm Way KT8: E Mos 6H 149
Ember Gdns. KT7: T Ditt 7J 149
Ember La. KT8: E Mos 7H 149
. . . KT10: Esh 7H 149
Emberton SE5 . . . . .6E 102
. . . .(off Albany Rd.)
Emberton Ct. EC1 . . . . .2A 8
. . . .(off Tompion St.)
Embleton Rd. SE13 . . . . .4D 122
Embleton Wlk. TW12: Hamp 5D 130

Embroidery World Bus. Cen.
. . . IG8: Wfd G 2B 52
Embry Cl. HA7: Stan 4F 27
Embry Dr. HA7: Stan 6F 27
Embry Rd. SE9 . . . . .4A 124
Emden Cl. UB7: W Dray 2B 92
Emden St. SW6 . . . . .1K 117
Emerald Cl. E16 . . . . .6B 88
Emerald Gdns. RM8: Dag 1G 73
Emerald Rd. NW10 . . . . .1K 79
Emerald Sq. SW15 . . . . .5C 116
. . . UB2: S'hall 3B 94
Emerald St. WC1 . . . . .5G 7 (5K 83)
Emerson Apartments N8 . . . . .3K 47
Emerson Gdns. HA3: Kenton 6F 43
Emerson M. KT3: N Mald 4A 152
Emerson Rd. IG1: Ilf 7F 52
Emerson St. SE1 . . . . .4C 14 (1C 102)
Emerton Cl. DA6: Bex 4E 126
Emery Hill St. SW1 . . . . .2B 18 (3G 101)
Emery St. SE1 . . . . .1K 19 (3A 102)
Emery Theatre 6D 86
. . . .(off Annabel Cl.)
Emery Walker Trust 5C 98
. . . .(off Hammersmith Ter.)
Emes Rd. DA8: Erith 7J 109
Emilia Cl. EN3: Pond E 5C 24
Emily Bowes Ct. N17 . . . . .3H 49
Emily Ct. SE1 . . . . .7C 14
. . . .(off Sudrey St.)
Emily Duncan Pl. E7 . . . . .4K 69
Emily Ho. W10 . . . . .6H 81
. . . .(off Kensal Rd.)
Emily St. E16 . . . . .6H 87
. . . .(off Jude St.)
Emirates Air Line 2H 105
Emirates Stadium 4A 66
Emlyn Gdns. W12 . . . . .2A 98
Emlyn Rd. W12 . . . . .2A 98
Emma Ho. RM1: Rom 4K 55
Emma St. E2 . . . . .2H 85
Emmanuel Ho. SE11 . . . . . . .4J 19 (4A 102)
Emmanuel Rd. HA6: Nwood 1H 39
. . . SW12 . . . . .1G 137
Emma Rd. E13 . . . . .2H 87
Emmanuel Pl. SE2 . . . . .2H 85
Emmaus Way IG7: Chig 5K 37
Emmeline Cl. KT12: Walt T 7A 148
Emminster NW6 . . . . .1K 81
. . . .(off Abbey Rd.)
Emmott Av. IG6: Ilf 5G 53
Emmott Cl. E1 . . . . .4A 86
. . . NW11 .6A 46
Emms Pas. KT1: King T 2D 150
Emperor Ho. E20 . . . . .5E 68
. . . .(off Napa Cl.)
. . . SE4 .3A 122
. . . .(off Dragonfly Pl.)
Emperor's Ga. SW7 . . . . .3A 100
Empingham Ho. SE8 . . . . .4K 103
. . . .(off Chilton Gro.)
Empire Av. N18 . . . . .5H 33
Empire Cinema
. . . Bromley 2J 159
. . . .(off High St.)
. . . Leicester Square 2D 12
. . . .(off Leicester Sq.)
. . . Sutton 5K 165
. . . Walthamstow 4C 50
Empire Cl. SE7 . . . . .6K 105
Empire Ct. HA9: Wemb 3H 61
Empire Ho. N18 . . . . .6J 33
. . . SW7 .2C 16
. . . SW16 . . . . .5J 137
Empire Pde.
. . . HA9: Wemb 3G 61
. . . N18 . . . . .6J 33
Empire Reach SE10 . . . . .6D 104
. . . .(off Dowells St.)
Empire Rd. UB6: G'frd 1B 78

Empire Sq. N7 . . . . .3J 65
. . . SE1 . . . . .7E 14
. . . .(off Tabard St.)
. . . SE20 .7K 139
. . . .(off High St.)
Empire Sq. E. SE1 . . . . .7E 14
Empire Sq. Sth. SE1 . . . . .7E 14
Empire Sq. W. SE1 . . . . .7E 14
Empire Way HA9: Wemb 4F 61
Empire Wharf E3 . . . . .1A 86
. . . .(off Old Ford Rd.)
Empire Wharf Rd. E14 . . . . .4F 105
Empress App. SW6 . . . . .5J 99
Empress Av. E4 . . . . .7J 35
. . . E12 . . . . .2A 70
. . . IG1: Ilf 2D 70
. . . IG8: Wfd G 7C 36
Empress Dr. BR7: Chst 6F 143
Empress M. SE5 . . . . .2C 120
Empress Pde. E4 . . . . .7H 35
Empress Pl. SW6 . . . . .5J 99
Empress State Bldg. SW6 . . . . .5J 99
Empress St. SE17 . . . . .6C 102
Empson St. E3 . . . . .4D 86
Emsworth Cl. N9 . . . . .1D 34
Emsworth Ct. SW16 . . . . .3J 137
Emsworth Rd. IG6: Ilf 2F 53
Emsworth St. SW2 . . . . .2K 137
EMT House E6 . . . . .5E 88
Emu Rd. SW8 . . . . .2F 119
Enard Ho. E3 . . . . .2B 86
. . . .(off Cardigan Rd.)
Ena Rd. SW16 . . . . .3J 155
Enbrook St. W10 . . . . .3G 81
Enclave, The SW13 . . . . .2B 116
Enclave Ct. EC1 . . . . .3B 8
. . . .(off Dallington St.)
Endale Cl. SM5: Cars 2C 166
Endeavour Ho. E14 . . . . .2C 104
. . . .(off Cuba St.)
. . . SE16 . . . . .4A 104
. . . .(off Ashton Reach)
Endeavour Way CR0: Bedd 7J 155
. . . IG11: Bark 2A 90
. . . SW19 . . . . .4K 135
Endell St. WC2 . . . . .7E 6 (6J 83)
Enderby St. SE10 . . . . .5F 105
Enderley Cl. HA3: Hrw W 2J 41
Enderley Rd. HA3: Hrw W 1J 41
Enders Cl. EN2: Enf 1F 23
Endersleigh Gdns. NW4 . . . . .4C 44
Endlebury Rd. E4 . . . . .2K 35
Endlesham Rd. SW12 . . . . .7E 118
Endsleigh Cl. WC1 . . . . .3D 6
Endsleigh Gdns. IG1: Ilf 2D 70
. . . KT6: Surb 6C 150
. . . WC1 . . . . .3C 6 (4H 83)
Endsleigh Ind. Est. UB2: S'hall 4C 94
Endsleigh Pl. WC1 . . . . .3D 6 (4H 83)
Endsleigh Rd. UB2: S'hall 4C 94
. . . W13 . . . . .7A 78
Endsleigh St. WC1 . . . . .3D 6 (4H 83)
Endway KT5: Surb 7H 151
Endwell Rd. SE4 . . . . .2A 122
Endymion Rd. N4 . . . . .7A 48
. . . SW2 .6K 119
Energen Cl. NW10 . . . . .6A 62
Energize Fitness Club
. . . Hammersmith 5G 99
. . . .(off Gliddon Rd.)
Energy Cen., The N1 . . . . .1G 9
. . . .(off Bowling Grn. Wlk.)
ENFIELD 3J 23
Enfield Bus. Cen. EN3: Enf H 2D 24
Enfield Cloisters N1 . . . . .1G 9
. . . .(off Fanshaw St.)
Enfield Golf Course 4G 23
ENFIELD HIGHWAY 3D 24
Enfield Ho. SW9 . . . . .2J 119
. . . .(off Stockwell Rd.)
ENFIELD ISLAND VILLAGE 1H 25

ENFIELD LOCK 1G 25
Enfield Lock EN3: Enf L 1H 25
Enfield Mus. .4J 23
. . . .(off London Rd.)
Enfield Retail Pk. EN1: Enf 3B 24
Enfield Rd. EN2: Enf 4C 22
. . . N1 . . . . .7E 66
. . . TW6: H'row A 2G 111
. . . TW8: Bford 5D 96
. . . W3 . . . . .2H 97
ENFIELD ROAD RDBT. 2G 111
ENFIELD TOWN 4J 23
Enfield Town FC 2A 24
Enfield Wlk.
. . . TW8: Bford 5D 96
ENFIELD WASH 1F 25
Enford St. W1 . . . . .5E 4 (5D 82)
Engadine Cl.
. . . CR0: C'don 3F 169
Engadine St. SW18 . . . . .1H 135
Engate St. SE13 . . . . .4E 122
Engel Pk. NW7 . . . . .6K 29
Engine Ct. SW1 . . . . .5B 12
. . . .(off Ambassador's Ct.)
Engineer Cl. SE18 . . . . .6E 106
Engineers Row SE18 . . . . .4E 106
. . . .(off Woolwich New Rd.)
Engineers Way HA9: Wemb 4G 61
Engineers Wharf UB5: N'olt 4D 76
England's La. NW3 . . . . .6D 64
England Way KT3: N Mald 4H 151
Englefield NW1 . . . . .2A 6
. . . .(off Clarence Gdns.)
Englefield Cl. BR5: St M Cry 5K 161
. . . CR0: C'don 6C 156
. . . EN2: Enf 2F 23
Englefield Cres. BR5: St M Cry 4K 161
Englefield Path BR5: St M Cry 4K 161
Englefield Rd. N1 . . . . .7D 66
Engleheart Dr. TW14: Felt 6H 111
Engleheart Rd. SE6 . . . . .7D 122
Englewood Rd. SW12 . . . . .6F 119
English Grounds SE1 . . . . .5G 15 (1E 102)
English St. E3 . . . . .4B 86
Enid St. SE16 . . . . .7K 15 (3F 103)
Enmore Av. SE25 . . . . .5G 157
Enmore Gdns. SW14 . . . . .5K 115
Enmore Rd. SE25 . . . . .5G 157
. . . SW15 .4E 116
. . . UB1: S'hall 4E 76
Ennerdale NW1 . . . . .1A 6
. . . .(off Varndell St.)
Ennerdale Av. HA7: Stan 3C 42
Ennerdale Cl. SM1: Sutt 4H 165
. . . TW14: Felt 1H 129
Ennerdale Ct. E11 . . . . .7J 51
. . . .(off Cambridge Rd.)
Ennerdale Dr. NW9 . . . . .5A 44
Ennerdale Gdns. HA9: Wemb 1C 60
Ennerdale Ho. E3 . . . . .4B 86
Ennerdale Rd. DA7: Bex 1G 127
. . . TW9: Kew, Rich 2F 115
Ennersdale Rd. SE13 . . . . .5F 123
Ennis Ho. E14 . . . . .6D 86
. . . .(off Vesey Path)
Ennismore Av. UB6: G'frd 6J 59
. . . W4 . . . . .4B 98
Ennismore Gdns. KT7: T Ditt 6C 150
. . . SW7 . . . . .7C 10 (2C 100)
Ennismore Gdns. M. SW7 . .1C 16 (3C 100)
Ennismore M. SW7 . . . . .7C 10 (3C 100)
Ennismore St. SW7 . . . . .1C 16 (3C 100)
Ennis Rd. N4 . . . . .1A 66
. . . SE18 . . . . .6G 107
Ennor Cl. SM3: Cheam 4E 164
Ensbury Ho. SW8 . . . . .7K 101
. . . .(off Carroun Rd.)
Ensham Ho. SW17 . . . . .5D 136
Ensign Cl. TW6: H'row A 3G 111
. . . TW19: Stanw 1A 128
Ensign Dr. N13 . . . . .3H 33

Ensign Ho. *E14* 2C **104**
(off Admirals Way)
NW9 3C **44**
(off East Dr.)
SW18 3A **118**
Ensign St. E1 7G **85**
SE3 4K **123**
Ensign Way SM6: Wall 7J **167**
TW19: Stanw 1A **128**
Enslin Rd. SE9 6E **124**
Ensor M. SW7 5A **16** (5B **100**)
Enstone Rd. EN3: Enf H 3F **25**
UB10: Ick 3B **56**
Enterprise Bus. Pk. E14 2D **104**
Enterprise Cen., The
BR3: Beck 5A **140**
(off Cricket La.)
Enterprise Cl. CR0: C'don 1A **168**
Enterprise Ho. E4 7K **25**
E9 7J **67**
(off Tudor Gro.)
E14 5D **104**
(off St Davids Sq.)
IG11: Bark 3K **89**
KT12: Walt T 7K **147**
Enterprise Ind. Est. SE16 5J **103**
Enterprise Row N15 5F **49**
Enterprise Trad. Est. UB2: S'hall 2F **95**
Enterprise Way NW10 3B **80**
SW18 4J **117**
TW11: Tedd 6K **131**
Enterprize Way SE8 4B **104**
Entertainment Av. SE10 1G **105**
Envoy Av. TW6: H'row A 3H **111**
Envoy Ho. *NW9* 3C **44**
(off East Dr.)
ENVOY RDBT. **3H 111**
Epcot M. NW10 3F **81**
Epirus M. SW6 7J **99**
Epirus Rd. SW6 7H **99**
Epping Cl. E14 4C **104**
RM7: Mawney 3H **55**
Epping Glade E4 6K **25**
Epping New Rd. IG9: Buck H 3D **36**
Epping Pl. N1 6A **66**
Epping Way E4 6J **25**
Epple Rd. SW6 1H **117**
Epsom Cl. DA7: Bex 3H **127**
UB5: N'olt 5D **58**
Epsom Rd. CR0: Wadd 4A **168**
E10 6E **50**
IG3: Ilf 6K **53**
SM3: Sutt 7H **153**
SM4: Mord 7H **153**
Epsom Sq. TW6: H'row A 2H **111**
Epstein Ct. *N1* 1B **84**
(off Gaskin St.)
Epstein Rd. SE28 1A **108**
Epstein Sq. *E14* 6C **86**
(off Upper Nth. St.)
Epworth Rd. TW7: Isle 7B **96**
Epworth St. EC2 4F **9** (4D **84**)
Equana Apartments *SE8* 5A **104**
(off Evelyn St.)
Equiano Ho. *SW9* 1K **119**
(off Lett Rd.)
Equinox Ct. IG2: Ilf 5F **53**
Equinox Ho. *IG11: Bark* 6G **71**
(off Wakering Rd.)
Equinox Sq. E14 6D **86**
Equity M. W5 1D **96**
Equity Sq. *E2* 2K **9**
(off Shacklewell St.)
Erasmus St. SW1 4D **18** (4H **101**)
Erconwald St. W12 6B **80**
Erebus Dr. SE28 3G **107**
Eresby Dr. BR3: Beck 1C **170**
Eresby Ho. *SW7* 7D **10**
(off Rutland Ga.)
Eresby Pl. NW6 7J **63**
Erica Gdns. CR0: C'don 3D **170**
Erica Ho. *N22* 1A **48**
(off Acacia Rd.)
SE4 3B **122**
Erica St. W12 7C **80**
Eric Clarke La.
IG11: Bark 4F **89**
Eric Cl. E7 4J **69**
Ericcson Cl. SW18 5J **117**
Eric Fletcher Ct. *N1* 7C **66**
(off Essex Rd.)
Erickson Gdns. BR2: Brom 6C **160**
Eric Liddell Sports Cen. 2B **142**
Eric Rd. E7 4J **69**
NW10 6B **62**
RM6: Chad H 7D **54**
Eric Shipman Ter. *E13* 4J **87**
(off Balaam St.)
Ericson Ho. *SE13* 4F **123**
(off Blessington Rd.)
Eric St. E3 4B **86**
(not continuous)
Eric Wilkins Ho. *SE1* 5G **103**
(off Old Kent Rd.)
Eridge Rd. W4 3K **97**
Erin Cl. BR1: Brom 7G **141**
IG3: Ilf 6A **54**
SW6 7J **99**
Erindale SE18 6H **107**
Erindale Ter. SE18 6H **107**
Erin M. N22 1B **48**
Erin's Vs. *SE14* 1K **121**
(off New Cross Rd.)
ERITH 5K **109**
Erith Cres. RM5: Col R 1J **55**
Erith Quarry DA8: Erith 6J **109**
Erith Rd. DA7: Bex 4H **127**
DA8: Erith 5G **109**
(Picardy Rd.)
DA8: Erith 4H **127**
(Watling St.)
DA17: Belv, Erith 5G **109**
Erith School Community Sports Cen.
7J **109**
Erlanger Rd. SE14 1K **121**
Erlesmere Gdns. W13 3A **96**
Erlich Cotts. *E1* 5J **85**
(off Sidney St.)
Ermine Cl. TW4: Houn 2A **112**
Ermine Ho. *E3* 1B **86**
(off Parnell Rd.)
N17 7A **34**
(off Moselle St.)
Ermine M. E2 1F **85**
Ermine Rd. N15 6F **49**
SE13 4D **122**
Ermine Side EN1: Enf 5B **24**
Ermington Rd. SE9 2G **143**
Ernald Av. E6 2C **88**
Erncroft Way TW1: Twick 6K **113**
Ernest Av. SE27 4B **138**
Ernest Cl. BR3: Beck 5C **158**
Ernest Cotts. KT17: Ewe 7B **164**
Ernest Gdns. W4 6H **97**
Ernest Gro. BR3: Beck 5B **158**
Ernest Harriss Ho. *W9* 4J **81**
(off Elgin Av.)
Ernest Rd. KT1: King T 2H **151**
Ernest Shackleton Lodge *SE10* 4G **105**
(off Christchurch Way)
Ernest Sq. KT1: King T 2H **151**
Ernest St. E1 4K **85**
Ernle Rd. SW20 7D **134**
Ernshaw Pl. SW15 5G **117**
Ernst Bldg. *SE1* 5C **14**
(off Union St.)
Eros **3C 12 (7H 83)**
Eros Ho. Shops *SE6* 7D **122**
(off Brownhill Rd.)
Erpingham Rd. SW15 3E **116**
Erridge Rd. SW19 2J **153**
Errington Rd. W9 4H **81**
Errol Gdns. KT3: N Mald 4C **152**
UB4: Yead 4K **75**
Errol St. EC1 4D **8** (4C **84**)
Erskine Cl. SM1: Sutt 3C **166**
Erskine Cres. N17 4H **49**
Erskine Hill NW11 4J **45**
Erskine Ho. *SW1* 6A **18**
(off Churchill Gdns.)
Erskine M. *NW3* 7D **64**
(off Erskine Rd.)
Erskine Rd. E17 4B **50**
NW3 7D **64**
SM1: Sutt 4B **166**
Erwin Ho. *NW9* 3C **44**
(off Commander Av.)
Erwood Rd. SE7 5C **106**
Esam Way SW16 5A **138**
Escot Rd. TW16: Sun 7G **129**
Escott Gdns. SE9 4C **142**
Escreet Gro. SE18 4E **106**
Esher Av. KT12: Walt T 7J **147**
RM7: Rom 6J **55**
SM3: Cheam 3F **165**
Esher By-Pass KT9: Chess 7B **162**
KT10: Clay 7B **162**
Esher Cl. DA5: Bexl 1E **144**
Esher Cres.
TW6: H'row A 2H **111**
Esher Gdns. SW19 2F **135**
Esher M. CR4: Mitc 3E **154**
Esher Rd. IG3: Ilf 3J **71**
KT8: E Mos 6H **149**
Eskdale *NW1* 1A **6**
(off Stanhope St.)
Eskdale Av. UB5: N'olt 1D **76**
Eskdale Cl. HA9: Wemb 2D **60**
Eskdale Rd. DA7: Bex 2G **127**
Esk Ho. *E3* 4B **86**
(off British St.)
Eskmont Ridge SE19 7D **138**
Esk Rd. E13 4J **87**
Esk Way RM1: Rom 1K **55**
Esmar Cres. NW9 7C **44**
Esmat Cl. E11 5K **51**
Esmeralda Rd. SE1 4G **103**
Esmond Ct. *W8* 3K **99**
(off Thackeray St.)
Esmond Gdns. W4 4K **97**
Esmond Rd. NW6 1H **81**
W4 4K **97**
Esmond St. SW15 4G **117**
Esparto St. SW18 7K **117**
Esprit Ct. *E1* 6J **9**
(off Brune St.)
Esquiline La. CR4: Mitc 3F **155**
Essan Ho. W5 5B **78**
Essence *E3* 2B **86**
(off Cardigan Rd.)
Essence Ct. HA9: Wemb 2F **61**
Essenden Rd. CR2: S Croy 7E **168**
DA17: Belv 5G **109**
Essendine Mans. W9 3J **81**
Essendine Rd. W9 3J **81**
Essex Av. TW7: Isle 3J **113**
Essex Cl. E17 4A **50**
HA4: Ruis 1B **58**
RM7: Mawney 4H **55**
SM4: Mord 7F **153**
Essex Ct. EC4 1J **13**
SW13 2B **116**
W6 3E **98**
(off Hammersmith Gro.)
Essex Gdns. N4 6B **48**
Essex Gro. SE19 6D **138**
Essex Hall E17 1K **49**
Essex Ho. *E14* 6D **86**
(off Girauld St.)
Essex Mans. E11 7F **51**
Essex M. SE19 6E **138**
Essex Pk. N3 6E **30**
Essex Pk. M. W3 1A **98**
Essex Pl. W4 4J **97**
(not continuous)
Essex Pl. Sq. W4 4K **97**
Essex Rd. E4 1B **36**
E10 6E **50**
E12 5C **70**
E17 6A **50**
E18 2K **51**
EN2: Enf 4J **23**
IG11: Bark 7H **71**
N1 1B **84**
NW10 7A **62**
RM6: Chad H 7C **54**
RM7: Mawney 4H **55**
RM10: Dag 5J **73**
W3 7J **79**
W4 4K **97**
Essex Rd. Sth. E11 7F **51**
Essex St. E7 5J **69**
WC2 1J **13** (6A **84**)
Essex Twr. *SE20* 1H **157**
(off Jasmine Gro.)
Essex Vs. W8 2J **99**
Essex Wharf E5 2K **67**
Essian St. E1 5A **86**
Essoldo Way HA8: Edg 3F **43**
Estate Way E10 1B **68**
Estcourt Rd. SE25 6H **157**
SW6 7H **99**
Estella Apartments *E15* 6F **69**
(off Grove Cres. Rd.)
Estella Av. KT3: N Mald 4D **152**
Estella Ho. *W11* 7F **81**
(off St Ann's Rd.)
Estelle Rd. NW3 4D **64**
Esterbrooke St. SW1 4C **18** (4H **101**)
Este Rd. SW11 3C **118**
Esther Anne Pl. N1 1B **84**
Esther Cl. N21 7F **23**
Esther M. *BR1: Brom* 1K **159**
(off Freelands Rd.)
Esther Randall Ct. *NW1* 3K **5**
(off Lit. Albany St.)
Esther Rd. E11 7G **51**
Estoria Cl. SW2 7A **120**
Estorick Collection of Modern Italian Art
6B **66**
Estreham Rd. SW16 6H **137**
Estridge Cl. TW3: Houn 4E **112**
Estuary Cl. IG11: Bark 3B **90**
Estuary Ho. *E16* 1B **106**
(off Agnes George Wlk.)
Eswyn Rd. SW17 4D **136**
Etal Ho. *N1* 7B **66**
(off The Sutton Est.)
Etcetera Theatre *7F 65*
(off Camden High St.)
Etchingham Ct. N3 7E **30**
Etchingham Pk. Rd. N3 7E **30**
Etchingham Rd. E15 4E **68**
Eternit Wlk. SW6 1E **116**
Etfield Gro. DA14: Sidc 5B **144**
Ethelbert Cl. BR1: Brom 2J **159**
Ethelbert Ct. *BR1: Brom* 3J **159**
(off Ethelbert Rd.)
Ethelbert Gdns. IG2: Ilf 5D **52**
Ethelbert Ho. *E9* 4A **68**
(off Homerton Rd.)
Ethelbert Rd. BR1: Brom 3J **159**
DA8: Erith 7J **109**
SW20 1F **153**
Ethelbert St. SW12 1F **137**
Ethel Brooks Ho. SE18 6F **107**
Ethelburga St. SW11 1C **118**
Ethelburga Twr. *SW11* 1C **118**
(off Rosenau Rd.)
Etheldene Av. N10 4G **47**
Ethelden Rd. W12 1D **98**
Ethelred Ct. HA3: Kenton 5G **43**
Ethel Rd. E16 6K **87**
TW15: Ashf 5A **128**

Ethel St. SE17 . . . . .4C **102**
Etheridge Rd. NW4 . . . . .7E **44**
  (not continuous)
Etherley Rd. N15 . . . . .5C **48**
Etherow St. SE22 . . . . .7G **121**
Etherstone Grn.
  SW16 . . . . .4A **138**
Etherstone Rd. SW16 . . . . .4A **138**
Ethnard Rd. SE15 . . . . .6H **103**
Ethos Sport Imperial . . .7B **10** (2B **100**)
Ethronvi Rd. DA7: Bex 3E **126**
Etloe Ho. E10 . . . . .1C **68**
Etloe Rd. E10 . . . . .2C **68**
Eton Av. EN4: E Barn 6H **21**
  HA0: Wemb 4B **60**
  KT3: N Mald 5K **151**
  N12 . . . . .7F **31**
  NW3 .7B **64**
  TW5: Hest 6D **94**
Eton Cl. SW18 . . . . .7K **117**
Eton Coll. Rd. NW3 . . . . .6D **64**
Eton Ct. HA0: Wemb 4C **60**
  NW3 .7B **64**
Eton Garages NW3 . . . . .6C **64**
Eton Gro. NW9 . . . . .3G **43**
  SE13 . . . . .3G **123**
Eton Hall NW3 . . . . .6D **64**
Eton Ho. N5 . . . . .4B **66**
  (off Leigh Rd.)
  UB7: W Dray 2B **92**
ETON MANOR 4D **68**
Eton Mnr. Cl. E10 . . . . .2C **68**
  (off Leyton Grange Est.)
Eton Pl. NW3 . . . . .7E **64**
Eton Ri. NW3 . . . . .6D **64**
Eton Rd. IG1: Ilf 4G **71**
  NW3 .7D **64**
  UB3: Harl 7H **93**
Eton St. TW9: Rich 5E **114**
Eton Vs. NW3 . . . . .6D **64**
Etta St. SE8 . . . . .6A **104**
Ettrick St. E14 . . . . .6E **86**
  (not continuous)
Etwell Pl. KT5: Surb 6F **151**
Eucalyptus M. SW16 . . . . .6H **137**
Euesden Cl. N9 . . . . .3C **34**
Eugene Cotter Ho. SE17 . . . . .4D **102**
  (off Tatum St.)
Eugenia Rd. SE16 . . . . .4J **103**
Eugenie M. BR7: Chst 1F **161**
Eureka Rd. KT1: King T 2G **151**
Euro Cl. NW10 . . . . .6C **62**
Eurolink Bus. Cen. SW2 . . . . .4A **120**
Europa Pl. EC1 . . . . .2C **8** (3C **84**)
Europa Trade Pk. E16 . . . . .4G **87**
Europa Trad. Est. DA8: Erith 5K **109**
European Bus. Cen. NW9 . . . . .3J **43**
  (not continuous)
European Design Cen. NW9 . . . . . . .3K **43**
Europe Rd. SE18 . . . . .3D **106**
Euro Trade Cen. DA17: Belv 2J **109**
Eustace Bldg. SW8 . . . . .6F **101**
Eustace Ho. SE11 . . . . .3G **19**
Eustace Pl. SE18 . . . . .4D **106**
Eustace Rd. E6 . . . . .3C **88**
  RM6: Chad H 7D **54**
  SW6 .7J **99**
Euston Cir. NW1 . . . . .3B **6** (4G **83**)
Euston Gro. NW1 . . . . .2C **6**
Euston Rd. CR0: C'don 1A **168**
  N1 . . . . .4A **6** (3H **83**)
  NW1 . . . . .4A **6** (4F **83**)
Euston Sq. NW1 . . . . .2C **6** (3H **83**)
  (not continuous)
Euston Sta. Colonnade NW1 . . .2C **6** (3H **83**)
Euston St. NW1 . . . . .2B **6** (3G **83**)
Euston Twr. NW1 . . . . .3A **6** (4G **83**)
EUSTON UNDERPASS 4G **83**
Eva Ct. CR2: S Croy 6E **168**
Evan Cook Cl. SE15 . . . . .1J **121**
Evandale Rd. SW9 . . . . .2A **120**

Evangelist Ho. EC4 . . . . .1A **14**
  (off Black Friars La.)
Evangelist Rd. NW5 . . . . .4F **65**
Evan Ho. E16 . . . . .5J **87**
  (off Exeter Rd.)
Evans Apartments E2 . . . . .3K **85**
Evans Cl. E8 . . . . .6F **67**
Evans Gro.
  TW13: Hanw 2E **130**
Evans Ho. SW8 . . . . .7H **101**
  (off Wandsworth Rd.)
  TW13: Hanw 2E **130**
  W12 .7D **80**
  (off White City Est.)
Evans Rd. SE6 . . . . .2G **141**
Evanston Av. E4 . . . . .7K **35**
Evanston Gdns. IG4: Ilf 6C **52**
Eva Rd. RM6: Chad H 7C **54**
Evedon Ho. N1 . . . . .1E **84**
  (off Halcomb St.)
Evelina Mans. SE5 . . . . .7D **102**
Evelina Rd. SE15 . . . . .3J **121**
  SE20 . . . . .7J **139**
Eveline Lowe Est. SE16 . . . . .3G **103**
Eveline Rd. CR4: Mitc 1D **154**
Evelyn Av. HA4: Ruis 7G **39**
  NW9 .4K **43**
Evelyn Cl. E3 . . . . .5B **86**
  (off Burdett Rd.)
  E8 . . . . .4G **67**
  N1 . . . . .1E **8**
  (off Evelyn Wlk.)
Evelyn Cres. TW16: Sun 1H **147**
Evelyn Denington Ct. N1 . . . . .7B **66**
  (off The Sutton Est.)
Evelyn Denington Rd. E6 . . . . .4C **88**
Evelyn Dr. HA5: Pinn 1B **40**
Evelyn Fox Ct. W10 . . . . .5E **80**
Evelyn Gdns. SW7 . . . . . .6A **16** (5A **100**)
  TW9: Rich 4E **114**
Evelyn Gro. UB1: S'hall 6D **76**
  W5 . . . . .1F **97**
Evelyn Ho. SE14 . . . . .1A **122**
  (off Loring Rd.)
  W8 . . . . .2K **99**
  (off Hornton Pl.)
  W12 .2B **98**
  (off Cobbold Rd.)
Evelyn Mans. SW1 . . . . .2A **18**
  (off Carlisle Pl.)
  W14 .5G **99**
  (off Queen's Club Gdns.)
Evelyn Rd. E16 . . . . .1J **105**
  E17 . . . . .4E **50**
  EN4: Cockf 4J **21**
  SW19 . . . . .5K **135**
  TW9: Rich 3E **114**
  TW10: Ham 3C **132**
  W4 . . . . .3K **97**
Evelyns Cl. UB8: Hil 6C **74**
Evelyn St. SE8 . . . . .4A **104**
Evelyn Ter. TW9: Rich 3E **114**
Evelyn Wlk. N1 . . . . .1E **8** (2D **84**)
Evelyn Way SM6: Bedd 4H **167**
  TW16: Sun 1H **147**
Evelyn Yd. W1 . . . . .7C **6** (6H **83**)
Evening Hill BR3: Beck 7E **140**
Evenlode Ho. SE2 . . . . .2C **108**
Evenwood Cl. SW15 . . . . .5G **117**
Everall Ct. E4 . . . . .6G **35**
Everard Av. BR2: Hayes 1J **171**
Everard Cl. N13 . . . . .3E **32**
Everard Ho. E1 . . . . .6G **85**
  (off Boyd St.)
Everard Way HA9: Wemb 3E **60**
Everatt Cl. SW18 . . . . .6H **117**
Everdon Rd. SW13 . . . . .6C **98**
Everest Pl. E14 . . . . .5E **86**
Everest Rd. SE9 . . . . .5D **124**
  TW19: Stanw 7A **110**

Everett Cl. HA5: Eastc 3H **39**
  WD23: B Hea 1D **26**
Everett Ho. SE17 . . . . .5D **102**
  (off East St.)
Everett Wlk. DA17: Belv 5F **109**
  (off Osborne Rd.)
Everglade Ho. E17 . . . . .2B **50**
Everglades, The TW3: Houn 3G **113**
Everglade Strand NW9 . . . . .1B **44**
Evergreen Apartments
  IG8: Wfd G 1H **51**
  (off High Rd. Woodford Grn.)
Evergreen Cl. SE20 . . . . .7J **139**
Evergreen Dr. UB7: W Dray 2B **92**
  UB10: Hil 2D **74**
Evergreen Sq. E8 . . . . .7F **67**
Evergreen Way UB3: Hayes 7H **75**
Everilda St. N1 . . . . .1K **83**
Evering Rd. E5 . . . . .3F **67**
  N16 . . . . .3F **67**
Everington Rd. N10 . . . . .2D **46**
Everington St. W6 . . . . .6F **99**
Everitt Rd. NW10 . . . . .3K **79**
Everleigh St. N4 . . . . .1K **65**
Eve Rd. E11 . . . . .4G **69**
  E15 . . . . .2G **87**
  N17 . . . . .3E **48**
  TW7: Isle 4A **114**
Eversfield Gdns. NW7 . . . . .6F **29**
Eversfield Rd. TW9: Kew 2F **115**
Evershed Ho. E1 . . . . .7K **9**
  (off Old Castle St.)
Evershed Wlk. W4 . . . . .3J **97**
Eversholt Ct. EN5: New Bar 5F **21**
Eversholt St. NW1 . . . . . .1B **6** (2G **83**)
Evershot Rd. N4 . . . . .1K **65**
Eversleigh Ct. N3 . . . . .7C **30**
Eversleigh Pl. BR3: Beck 6C **140**
Eversleigh Rd. E6 . . . . .1B **88**
  EN5: New Bar 5F **21**
  N3 . . . . .7C **30**
  SW11 . . . . .3D **118**
Eversley Av. DA7: Bex 2K **127**
  HA9: Wemb 2G **61**
Eversley Cl. N21 . . . . .6E **22**
Eversley Cres. HA4: Ruis 2G **57**
  N21 . . . . .6E **22**
  TW7: Isle 1H **113**
Eversley Ho. E2 . . . . .2K **9**
  (off Gosset St.)
Eversley Mt. N21 . . . . .6E **22**
Eversley Pk. SW19 . . . . .6D **134**
Eversley Pk. Rd. N21 . . . . .6E **22**
Eversley Rd. KT5: Surb 4F **151**
  SE7 . . . . .6K **105**
  SE19 . . . . .7D **138**
Eversley Way CR0: C'don 3C **170**
Everthorpe Rd. SE15 . . . . .3F **121**
Everton Ct. HA7: Stan 3E **42**
  (off Honeypot La.)
Everton Dr. HA7: Stan 3E **42**
Everton M. NW1 . . . . .2A **6** (3G **83**)
Everton Rd. CR0: C'don 1G **169**
Everyman Cinema
  Baker Street 5F **5**
  (off Baker St.)
  Belsize Pk. 5C **64**
Evesham Av. E17 . . . . .2B **50**
Evesham Cl. SM2: Sutt 7J **165**
  UB6: G'frd 2F **77**
Evesham Ct. TW10: Rich 6F **115**
  W13 .1A **96**
  (off Tewkesbury Rd.)
Evesham Grn.
  SM4: Mord 6K **153**
Evesham Ho. E2 . . . . .2J **85**
  (off Old Ford Rd.)
  NW8 .1A **82**
  (off Abbey Rd.)
  SW1 .6K **17**
  (part of Abbots Mnr.)

Evesham Rd. E15 . . . . .7H **69**
  N11 . . . . .5B **32**
  SM4: Mord 6K **153**
Evesham St. W11 . . . . .7F **81**
Evesham Ter. KT6: Surb 6D **150**
Evesham Wlk. SE5 . . . . .2D **120**
  SW9 .2A **120**
Evesham Way IG5: Ilf 3E **52**
  SW11 . . . . .3E **118**
Evette M. IG5: Ilf 1E **52**
Evry Rd. DA14: Sidc 6C **144**
Ewald Rd. SW6 . . . . .2H **117**
Ewanrigg Ter. IG8: Wfd G 5F **37**
Ewart Gro. N22 . . . . .1K **47**
Ewart Ho. HA1: Harr 5A **42**
Ewart Pl. E3 . . . . .2B **86**
Ewart Rd. SE23 . . . . .7K **121**
Ewe Cl. N7 .6J **65**
EWELL 7C **164**
Ewell By-Pass KT17: Ewe 7C **164**
Ewell Ct. Av. KT19: Ewe 5A **164**
Ewellhurst Rd. IG5: Ilf 2C **52**
Ewell Pk. Gdns. KT17: Ewe 7C **164**
Ewell Pk. Way KT17: Ewe 6C **164**
Ewell Rd. KT6: Surb 7B **150**
  (Mount Holme)
  KT6: Surb 6E **150**
  (South Ter.)
  SM3: Cheam 6F **165**
Ewelme Rd. SE23 . . . . .1J **139**
Ewen Cres. SW2 . . . . .7A **120**
Ewen Henderson Ct. SE14 . . . . .7A **104**
  (off Goodwood Rd.)
Ewen Ho. N1 . . . . .1K **83**
  (off Barnsbury Est.)
Ewer St. SE1 . . . . .5C **14** (1C **102**)
Ewhurst Av. CR2: Sande 7F **169**
Ewhurst Cl. E1 . . . . .5J **85**
  CR4: Mitc 3B **154**
Ewhurst Ho. SE4 . . . . .6B **122**
Exbury Ho. E9 . . . . .7J **67**
  SW1 .5C **18**
  (off Rampayne St.)
Exbury Rd. SE6 . . . . .2C **140**
ExCeL 7K **87**
Excel Ct. WC2 . . . . .3D **12**
Excel Marina E16 . . . . .7J **87**
Excelsior Cl. KT1: King T 2G **151**
Excelsior Gdns. SE13 . . . . .2E **122**
Excelsior Ind. Est. SE15 . . . . .6J **103**
Excel Waterfront E16 . . . . .7K **87**
Exchange, The CR0: C'don 3C **168**
  (off Surrey St.)
  IG1: Ilf .2F **71**
Exchange Apartments BR2: Brom . . .4K **159**
  (off Sparkes Cl.)
Exchange Arc. EC2 . . . . .5H **9** (5E **84**)
Exchange Bldg. E1 . . . . .4J **9**
  (off Commercial St.)
Exchange Cl. N11 . . . . .2K **31**
Exchange Ct. WC2 . . . . . . .3F **13** (7J **83**)
Exchange Garages N13 . . . . .4F **33**
Exchange Ho. EC2 . . . . .5H **9**
  NW10 . . . . .7D **62**
  SW1 .4C **18**
  (off Vauxhall Bri. Rd.)
Exchange Mans. NW11 . . . . .7H **45**
Exchange Pl. EC2 . . . . .5G **9** (5E **84**)
Exchange Sq. EC2 . . . . .5G **9** (5E **84**)
Exchange St. EC1 . . . . .2C **8** (3C **84**)
  RM1: Rom 5K **55**, 6K **55**
Exchange Wlk.
  HA5: Pinn 1A **40**
Exeforde Av. TW15: Ashf 4C **128**
Exeter Cl. E6 . . . . .6D **88**
Exeter Ct.
  KT6: Surb 5E **150**
  (off Maple Rd.)
  NW6 .2J **81**
  (off Cambridge Rd.)
Exeter Gdns. IG1: Ilf 1C **70**

Exeter Ho.—Fairmark Dr.

Exeter Ho. *E14* *5E* ***86***
(off St Ives Pl.)
IG11: Bark *7A* ***72***
(off Margaret Bondfield Av.)
N1 *1E* ***84***
(off New Era Est.)
RM8: Dag 4A **72**
SE15 *6G* ***103***
(off Friary Est.)
SW15 6E **116**
TW13: Hanw *2D* ***130***
(off Watermill Way)
W2 *6A* ***82***
(off Hallfield Est.)
Exeter Mans. NW2 6G **63**
Exeter M. NW6 6K **63**
SW6 7J **99**
Exeter Rd. CR0: C'don 7E **156**
DA16: Well 2K **125**
E16 5J **87**
E17 5C **50**
EN3: Pond E 3E **24**
HA2: Harr 2C **58**
N9 2D **34**
N14 1A **32**
NW2 5G **63**
RM10: Dag 6H **73**
TW6: H'row A 3F **111**
TW13: Hanw 3D **130**
Exeter St. WC2 2F **13** (7J **83**)
Exeter Way SE14 7B **104**
TW6: H'row A 2G **111**
Exford Ct. *SW11* *1B* ***118***
(off Bolingbroke Wlk.)
Exford Gdns. SE12 1K **141**
Exford Rd. SE12 2K **141**
Exhibition Cl. W12 7E **80**
Exhibition Grounds HA9: Wemb 4H **61**
Exhibition Rd. SW7 7B **10** (2B **100**)
Exhibition Way HA9: Wemb 4G **61**
Exit Rd. N2 2B **46**
Exmoor Cl. IG6: Ilf 1G **53**
Exmoor Ho. DA17: Belv 2H **109**
E3 *2A* ***86***
(off Gernon Rd.)
Exmoor St. W10 4F **81**
Exmouth Ho. *E14* *4D* ***104***
(off Cahir St.)
EC1 *3J* ***7***
(off Pine St.)
Exmouth Mkt. EC1 3J **7** (4A **84**)
Exmouth M. NW1 2B **6** (3G **83**)
Exmouth Pl. E8 7H **67**
Exmouth Rd. DA16: Well 1C **126**
E17 5B **50**
HA4: Ruis 3A **58**
UB4: Hayes 3G **75**
Exmouth St. E1 6J **85**
Exning Rd. E16 4G **87**
Exonbury *NW8* *1K* ***81***
(off Abbey Rd.)
Exon St. SE17 5E **102**
Explorer Av. TW19: Stanw 1A **128**
Explorers Ct. *E14* *7F* ***87***
(off Newport Av.)
Export Ho. *SE1* *7H* ***15***
(off Tower Bri. Rd.)
Express Dr. IG3: Ilf 1B **72**
Express Ho. *SE8* *6A* ***104***
(off Rolt St.)
Express Newspapers *SE1* *4A* ***14***
(off Blackfriars Rd.)
Express Wharf *E14* *2C* ***104***
(off Hutchings St.)
Exton Gdns. RM8: Dag 5C **72**
Exton Rd. NW10 7J **61**
Exton St. SE1 5J **13** (1A **102**)
Eyebright Cl. CR0: C'don 1K **169**
Eyhurst Cl. NW2 2C **62**
Eylewood Rd. SE27 5C **138**
Eynella Rd. SE22 7F **121**
Eynham Rd. W12 6E **80**
Eynsford Cl. BR5: Pet W 7G **161**
Eynsford Cres. DA5: Bexl 1C **144**
Eynsford Ho. *SE1* *7E* ***14***
(off Crosby Row)
SE15 6J **103**
SE17 *4E* ***102***
(off East St.)
Eynsford Rd. IG3: Ilf 2J **71**
Eynsford Ter. UB7: Yiew 6B **74**
Eynsham Dr. SE2 4A **108**
Eynswood Dr. DA14: Sidc 5B **144**
Eyot Gdns. W6 5B **98**
Eyot Grn. W4 5B **98**
Eyot Ho. *SE16* *3G* ***103***
(off Frean St.)
Eyre Ct. NW8 2B **82**
Eyre St. Hill EC1 4J **7** (4A **84**)
Eysham Ct. EN5: New Bar 5E **20**
Eythorne Rd. SW9 1A **120**
Ezra St. E2 1K **9** (3F **85**)

F

Faber Gdns. NW4 5C **44**
Fabian Bell Twr. *E3* *2C* ***86***
(off Pancras Way)
Fabian Rd. SW6 7H **99**
Fabian St. E6 4D **88**
Fable Apartments N1 1C **8**
Facade, The SE23 2J **139**
Factory La. CR0: C'don 1A **168**
N17 2F **49**
Factory Rd. E16 1B **106**
Factory Yd. W7 1J **95**
Faggs Rd. TW14: Felt 4H **111**
Fairacre HA5: Eastc 4J **39**
KT3: N Mald 3A **152**
Fairacre Ct. HA6: Nwood 1G **39**
Fair Acres BR2: Brom 5J **159**
CR0: Sels 7B **170**
Fairacres HA4: Ruis 7H **39**
SW15 4B **116**
Fairbain Grn. SW9 1B **120**
Fairbank Av. BR6: Farnb 2F **173**
Fairbank Est. N1 1F **9** (2D **84**)
Fairbanks Ct. HA0: Wemb 1E **78**
Fairbanks Rd. N17 3F **49**
Fairbourne Ho. UB3: Harl 3E **92**
Fairbourne Rd. N17 3E **48**
SW4 6H **119**
Fairbriar Residence *SW7* *4A* ***100***
(off Stanhope Gdns.)
Fairbridge Rd. N19 2H **65**
Fairbrook Cl. N13 5F **33**
Fairbrook Rd. N13 6F **33**
Fairburn Ct. SW15 5G **117**
Fairburn Ho. *W14* *5H* ***99***
(off Ivatt Pl.)
Fairby Ho. *SE1* *4F* ***103***
(off Longfield Est.)
Fairby Rd. SE12 5K **123**
Fairchild Cl. SW11 2B **118**
Fairchild Ho. *E2* *2H* ***85***
(off Cambridge Cres.)
E9 *7J* ***67***
(off Frampton Pk. Rd.)
N1 *1G* ***9***
(off Fanshaw St.)
N3 1J **45**
Fairchild Pl. EC2 4H **9**
Fairchild St. EC2 3H **9** (4E **84**)
Fair Cl. WD23: Bush 1A **26**
Fairclough Cl. UB5: N'olt 4D **76**
Fairclough St. E1 6G **85**
Faircroft Ct. TW11: Tedd 6A **132**
FAIR CROSS 5J **71**
Faircross Av. IG11: Bark 6G **71**
RM5: Col R 1K **55**
Faircross Pde. IG11: Bark 5J **71**
Fairdale Gdns. SW15 4D **116**
UB3: Hayes 2J **93**
Fairey Av. UB3: Harl 4H **93**
Fairfax Av. KT17: Ewe 7D **164**
Fairfax Cl. KT12: Walt T 7K **147**
Fairfax Ct. *NW6* *7A* ***64***
(off Fairfax Rd.)
Fairfax Gdns. SE3 1A **124**
Fairfax Ho. *KT1: King T* *3F* ***151***
(off Livesey Cl.)
Fairfax Mans. *NW6* *7A* ***64***
(off Finchley Rd.)
Fairfax M. E16 1K **105**
N8 4B **48**
SW15 4E **116**
Fairfax Pl. NW6 7A **64**
W14 3G **99**
Fairfax Rd. N8 4A **48**
NW6 7A **64**
TW11: Tedd 6A **132**
W4 3A **98**
Fairfax Way N10 7K **31**
Fairfield *E1* *5J* ***85***
(off Redman's Rd.)
KT1: King T 2F **151**
N20 7G **21**
NW1 *1G* ***83***
(off Arlington Rd.)
Fairfield Av. HA4: Ruis 7E **38**
HA8: Edg 6C **28**
NW4 6D **44**
TW2: Whitt 1F **131**
Fairfield Cl. CR4: Mitc 7C **136**
DA15: Sidc 6K **125**
EN3: Pond E 4E **24**
KT19: Ewe 5A **164**
N12 4F **31**
Fairfield Ct. HA4: Ruis 1F **57**
HA6: Nwood 2J **39**
NW10 1C **80**
Fairfield Cres. HA8: Edg 6C **28**
Fairfield Dr. HA2: Harr 3G **41**
SW18 5K **117**
UB6: G'frd 1C **78**
Fairfield E. KT1: King T 2E **150**
Fairfield Gdns. N8 5J **47**
Fairfield Gro. SE7 6B **106**
Fairfield Halls
Croydon 3D **168**
Fairfield Nth. KT1: King T 2E **150**
Fairfield Path CR0: C'don 3D **168**
Fairfield Pl. KT1: King T 3E **150**
Fairfield Rd. BR1: Brom 7J **141**
BR3: Beck 2C **158**
BR5: Pet W 6H **161**
CR0: C'don 3D **168**
DA7: Bex 2F **127**
E3 2C **86**
E17 2A **50**
IG1: Ilf 6F **71**
IG8: Wfd G 6D **36**
KT1: King T 2E **150**
N8 5J **47**
N18 4B **34**
UB1: S'hall 6D **76**
UB7: Yiew 7A **74**
UB8: Uxb 6A **56**
Fairfields Cl. NW9 5J **43**
Fairfields Cres. NW9 4J **43**
Fairfield Sth. KT1: King T 2E **150**
Fairfields Rd. TW3: Houn 3G **113**
Fairfield St. SW18 5K **117**
Fairfield Trade Pk. KT1: King T 3F **151**
Fairfield Way EN5: Barn 5D **20**
KT19: Ewe 5A **164**
Fairfield W. KT1: King T 2E **150**
Fairfoot Rd. E3 4C **86**
Fairford SE6 1C **140**
Fairford Av. CR0: C'don 5K **157**
DA7: Bex 1K **127**
Fairford Cl. CR0: C'don 5A **158**
Fairford Ct. SM2: Sutt 7K **165**
Fairford Gdns. KT4: Wor Pk 2B **164**
Fairford Ho. SE11 4K **19** (4A **102**)
Fairgreen EN4: Cockf 3J **21**
Fairgreen Ct. EN4: Cockf 3J **21**
Fairgreen E. EN4: Cockf 3J **21**
Fairgreen Rd. CR7: Thor H 5B **156**
Fairhall Ct. KT5: Surb 7F **151**
Fairhaven Av. CR0: C'don 6K **157**
Fairhaven Ct. *CR2: S Croy* *5C* ***168***
(off Warham Rd.)
Fairhazel Gdns. NW6 6K **63**
Fairhazel Mans. *NW6* *7A* ***64***
(off Fairhazel Gdns.)
Fairholme TW14: Bedf 7F **111**
Fairholme Cl. N3 4G **45**
Fairholme Cres. UB4: Hayes 4H **75**
Fairholme Gdns. N3 3G **45**
Fairholme Rd. CR0: C'don 7A **156**
HA1: Harr 5K **41**
IG1: Ilf 7D **52**
SM1: Sutt 6H **165**
TW15: Ashf 5A **128**
W14 5G **99**
Fairholt Cl. N16 1E **66**
Fairholt Rd. N16 1D **66**
Fairholt St. SW7 1D **16** (3C **100**)
Fairland Ho. BR2: Brom 4K **159**
Fairland Rd. E15 6H **69**
Fairlands Av. CR7: Thor H 4K **155**
IG9: Buck H 2D **36**
SM1: Sutt 2J **165**
Fairlands Ct. SE9 6E **124**
Fairlawn KT2: King T 6J **133**
SE7 7A **106**
Fairlawn Av. DA7: Bex 2D **126**
N2 4C **46**
W4 4J **97**
Fairlawn Cl. KT2: King T 6J **133**
KT10: Clay 6A **162**
N14 6B **22**
TW13: Hanw 4D **130**
Fairlawn Ct. SE7 7A **106**
(not continuous)
W4 4J **97**
Fairlawn Dr. IG8: Wfd G 7D **36**
Fairlawnes SM6: Wall 5F **167**
Fairlawn Gdns. UB1: S'hall 7D **76**
Fairlawn Gro. W4 4J **97**
Fairlawn Mans. SE14 1K **121**
Fairlawn Pk. SE26 5A **140**
Fairlawn Rd. SW19 7H **135**
Fairlawns HA5: Pinn 2B **40**
TW1: Twick 6C **114**
TW16: Sun 3J **147**
Fairlead Ho. *E14* *3C* ***104***
(off Alpha Gro.)
Fairlea Pl. W5 4C **78**
Fairlie Ct. *E3* *3D* ***86***
(off Stroudley Wlk.)
Fairlie Gdns. SE23 7J **121**
Fairlight TW12: Hamp H 5F **131**
Fairlight Av. E4 2A **36**
IG8: Wfd G 6D **36**
NW10 2A **80**
Fairlight Cl. E4 2A **36**
KT4: Wor Pk 4E **164**
Fairlight Ct. NW10 2A **80**
UB6: G'frd 2G **77**
Fairlight Rd. SW17 4B **136**
Fairline Ct.
BR3: Beck 2E **158**
FAIRLOP 1J **53**
Fairlop Ct. E11 1F **69**
Fairlop Gdns. IG6: Ilf 1G **53**
Fairlop Rd. E11 7F **51**
IG6: Ilf 2G **53**
Fairlop Sailing Cen. 1K **53**
Fairlop Waters Country Pk. 2K **53**
Fairlop Waters Golf Course 1J **53**
Fairmark Dr. UB10: Hil 6C **56**

Fairmead BR1: Brom 4D **160**
KT5: Surb 1H **163**
Fairmead Cl. BR1: Brom 4D **160**
KT3: N Mald 3K **151**
TW5: Hest 7B **94**
Fairmead Ct. TW9: Rich 2H **115**
Fairmead Cres. HA8: Edg 3D **28**
Fairmead Gdns. IG4: Ilf 5C **52**
Fairmead Ho. E9 4A **68**
Fairmead Rd. CR0: C'don 7K **155**
N19 3H **65**
Fairmile Av. SW16 5H **137**
Fairmile Ho. TW11: Tedd 4A **132**
Fairmont Av. E14 1F **105**
Fairmont Cl. DA17: Belv 5F **109**
Fairmont Ho. *E3* *4C* ***86***
(off Wellington Way)
SE16 *2K* ***103***
(off Needleman St.)
Fairmont M. NW2 2J **63**
Fairmount Rd. SW2 6K **119**
Fairoak Cl. BR5: Pet W 7F **161**
Fairoak Dr. SE9 5H **125**
Fairoak Gdns. RM1: Rom 2K **55**
Fair Oak Pl. IG6: Ilf 2G **53**
Fairseat Cl. WD23: B Hea 2D **26**
Fairstead Lodge *IG8: Wfd G* *6D* ***36***
(off Snakes La. W.)
Fairstead Wlk. *N1* *1C* ***84***
(off Popham St.)
Fair St. SE1 6H **15** (2E **102**)
TW3: Houn 3G **113**
Fairthorne Vs. *SE7* *5J* ***105***
(off Felltram Way)
Fairthorn Rd. SE7 5J **105**
Fairview HA4: Ruis 4A **58**
Fairview Av. HA0: Wemb 6D **60**
Fairview Cl. E17 1A **50**
SE26 5A **140**
Fairview Ct. NW4 2F **45**
TW15: Ashf 5C **128**
Fairview Cres. HA2: Harr 1E **58**
Fairview Dr. BR6: Orp 4H **173**
TW17: Shep 5B **146**
Fairview Est. NW10 3J **79**
Fairview Gdns. IG8: Wfd G 1K **51**
Fairview Ho. SW2 7K **119**
Fairview Ind. Pk. RM13: Rain 5K **91**
Fairview Pl. SW2 7K **119**
Fairview Rd. EN2: Enf 1F **23**
N15 5F **49**
SM1: Sutt 5B **166**
SW16 1K **155**
Fairview Vs. E4 7H **35**
Fairview Way HA8: Edg 4B **28**
Fairwall Ho. SE5 1E **120**
Fairwater Av. DA16: Well 4A **126**
Fairwater Dr. TW17: Shep 5E **146**
Fairwater Ho. TW11: Tedd 4A **132**
Fairway BR5: Pet W 5H **161**
DA6: Bex 5E **126**
IG8: Wfd G 5F **37**
SW20 3E **152**
Fairway, The
BR1: Brom 5D **160**
EN5: New Bar 6E **20**
HA0: Wemb 3B **60**
HA4: Ruis 4A **58**
KT3: N Mald 1K **151**
KT8: W Mole 3F **149**
N13 3H **33**
N14 6A **22**
NW7 3E **28**
UB5: N'olt 6G **59**
UB10: Hil 3B **74**
W3 6A **80**
Fairway Av. NW9 3H **43**
Fairway Cl. CR0: C'don 5A **158**
KT10: Surb 3B **162**
KT19: Ewe 4J **163**
NW11 7A **46**
Fairway Cl. TW4: Houn 5A **112**
(Amberley Way)
TW4: Houn 5B **112**
(Islay Gdns.)
Fairway Ct. *E3* *3E* ***86***
(off Culvert Dr.)
EN5: New Bar 6E **20**
NW7 3E **28**
SE16 *2K* ***103***
(off Christopher Cl.)
Fairway Dr. SE28 6D **90**
UB6: G'frd 7F **59**
Fairway Gdns. BR3: Beck 6F **159**
IG1: Ilf 5G **71**
Fairways E17 4E **50**
HA7: Stan 2E **42**
TW7: Isle 1H **113**
TW11: Tedd 7D **132**
TW15: Ashf 6D **128**
Fairways Bus. Pk. E10 2A **68**
Fairway Trad. Est. TW4: Houn 5A **112**
Fairweather Cl. DA16: Well 5A **126**
N15 4E **48**
Fairweather Ct. N13 3E **32**
Fairweather Ho. N7 4J **65**
Fairweather Rd. N16 6G **49**
Fairwyn Rd. SE26 4A **140**
Faith Ct. *E3* *2C* ***86***
(off Lefevre Wlk.)
SE1 *5F* ***103***
(off Cooper's Rd.)
Faith M. E12 4B **70**
Fakenham Cl. NW7 7H **29**
UB5: N'olt 6D **58**
Fakruddin St. E1 4G **85**
Falcon *WC1* *5F* ***7***
(off Old Gloucester St.)
Falcon Av. BR1: Brom 4C **160**
Falconberg M. W1 7D **6** (6H **83**)
Falcon Cl. HA6: Nwood 1G **39**
W4 6J **97**
Falcon Ct. *E18* *3K* ***51***
(off Albert Rd.)
EC4 1K **13** (6A **84**)
EN5: New Bar 4F **21**
HA4: Ruis 2G **57**
N1 *1B* ***8***
(off City Gdn. Row)
Falcon Cres. EN3: Pond E 5E **24**
Falcondal Ct. NW10 3G **79**
Falcon Dr. TW19: Stanw 6A **110**
Falconer Ct. *N17* *7H* ***33***
(off Compton Cres.)
Falconer Wlk. N7 2K **65**
Falconet Ct. *E1* *1H* ***103***
(off Wapping High St.)
Falcon Gro. SW11 3C **118**
Falcon Highwalk EC2 6C **8**
Falcon Ho. BR1: Brom 1H **159**
E14 *5D* ***104***
(off St Davids Sq.)
NW6 *1K* ***81***
(off Springfield Wlk.)
SW5 *5K* ***99***
(off Old Brompton Rd.)
Falcon La. SW11 3C **118**
Falcon Lodge *W9* *5J* ***81***
(off Admiral Wlk.)
Falcon Pk. Ind. Est. NW10 4A **62**
Falcon Point SE1 3B **14** (7B **84**)
Falcon Rd. EN3: Pond E 5E **24**
SW11 2C **118**
TW12: Hamp 7D **130**
Falconry Ct. *KT1: King T* *3E* ***150***
(off Fairfield Sth.)
Falcon St. E13 4J **87**
Falcon Ter. SW11 3C **118**
Falcon Way E11 4J **51**
E14 4D **104**
HA3: Kenton 5E **42**
NW9 2A **44**
Falcon Way TW14: Felt 5K **111**
TW16: Sun 2G **147**
Falcon Wharf SW11 2B **118**
FALCONWOOD 4K 125
FALCONWOOD 4H 125
Falconwood Av. DA16: Well 2H **125**
Falconwood Ct. *SE3* *2H* ***123***
(off Montpelier Row)
Falconwood Pde. DA16: Well 4J **125**
Falconwood Rd. CR0: Sels 7B **170**
Falcourt Cl. SM1: Sutt 5K **165**
Falkirk Ct. *SE16* *1K* ***103***
(off Rotherhithe St.)
Falkirk Ho. *W9* *2K* ***81***
(off Maida Vale)
Falkirk St. N1 1H **9** (2E **84**)
Falkland Av. N3 7D **30**
N11 4A **32**
Falkland Ho. SE6 4E **140**
W8 3K **99**
W14 *5H* ***99***
(off Edith Vs.)
Falkland Pk. Av. SE25 3E **156**
Falkland Pl. NW5 5G **65**
Falkland Rd. EN5: Barn 2B **20**
N8 4A **48**
NW5 5G **65**
Fallaize Av. IG1: Ilf 4F **71**
Falling La. UB7: Yiew 7A **74**
Falloden Way NW11 4J **45**
Fallodon Ho. *W11* *5H* ***81***
(off Tavistock Cres.)
FALLOW CORNER 7F 31
Fallow Ct. *SE16* *5G* ***103***
(off Argyle Way)
Fallow Ct. Av. N12 7F **31**
Fallowfield HA7: Stan 4F **27**
Fallowfield Ct. HA7: Stan 3F **27**
Fallowfields Dr. N12 6H **31**
Fallowhurst Path N3 7F **31**
Fallow Pl. TW11: Tedd 5J **131**
Fallows Cl. N2 2B **46**
Fallsbrook Rd. SW16 6F **137**
Falman Cl. N9 1B **34**
Falmer Rd. E17 3D **50**
EN1: Enf 4K **23**
N15 5C **48**
Falmouth Av. E4 5A **36**
Falmouth Cl. N22 7E **32**
SE12 5H **123**
Falmouth Gdns. IG4: Ilf 4B **52**
Falmouth Ho. HA5: Hat E 1D **40**
KT2: King T *1D* ***150***
(off Skerne Rd.)
SE11 *5K* ***19***
(off Seaton Cl.)
W2 *2C* ***10***
(off Clarendon Pl.)
Falmouth Rd. SE1 7E **14** (3C **102**)
Falmouth St. E15 5F **69**
Falmouth Wlk. SW15 6C **116**
Falmouth Way E17 5B **50**
Falstaff Bldg. *E1* *7H* ***85***
(off Cannon St. Rd.)
Falstaff Cl. DA1: Cray 7K **127**
Falstaff Ct. *SE11* *4B* ***102***
(off Opal St.)
Falstaff Ho. *N1* *1G* ***9***
(off Regan Way)
Falstaff M. *TW12: Hamp H* *5H* ***131***
(off High St.)
Fambridge Cl. SE26 4B **140**
Fambridge Ct. *RM7: Rom* *5K* ***55***
(off Marks Rd.)
Fambridge Rd. RM8: Dag 1G **73**
Family Court
East London 1C **104**
West London 6J **111**
Fancourt M. BR1: Brom 3E **160**
Fane St. W14 6H **99**
Fan Mus., The 7E **104**
Fann St. EC1 4C **8** (4C **84**)
EC2 4C **8** (4C **84**)
(not continuous)
Fanshawe Av. IG11: Bark 6G **71**
Fanshawe Cres. RM9: Dag 5E **72**
Fanshawe Rd. TW10: Ham 4C **132**
Fanshaw St. N1 1G **9** (3E **84**)
FANTAIL, THE 3D 172
Fantail Cl. SE28 6C **90**
Fanthorpe St. SW15 3E **116**
Faraday Av. DA14: Sidc 2A **144**
Faraday Bldg. E14 6G **87**
Faraday Cl. N7 6K **65**
Faraday Ho. *E14* *7B* ***86***
(off Brightlingsea Pl.)
HA9: Wemb 3J **61**
SE1 *7E* ***14***
(off Cole St.)
W10 *5G* ***81***
(off Wornington Rd.)
Faraday Lodge SE10 3H **105**
Faraday Mans. *W14* *6G* ***99***
(off Queen's Club Gdns.)
Faraday Mus., The 3A 12 (7G 83)
Faraday Pl. KT8: W Mole 4E **148**
Faraday Rd. DA16: Well 3A **126**
E15 6H **69**
KT8: W Mole 4E **148**
SW19 6J **135**
UB1: S'hall 7F **77**
W3 7J **79**
W10 5G **81**
Faraday Way CR0: Wadd 1K **167**
SE18 3B **106**
Fareham Rd. TW14: Felt 7A **112**
Farewell Pl. CR4: Mitc 1C **154**
Fari Ct. *E17* *4C* ***50***
(off Tower M.)
Faringdon Av. BR2: Brom 7E **160**
Faringford Rd. E15 7G **69**
Farjeon Ho. *NW6* *7B* ***64***
(off Hilgrove Rd.)
Farjeon Rd. SE3 1B **124**
Farleigh Av. BR2: Hayes 7H **159**
Farleigh Ct. CR2: S Croy 5C **168**
Farleigh Ho. *N1* *7B* ***66***
(off Halton Rd.)
Farleigh Pl. N16 4F **67**
Farleigh Rd. N16 4F **67**
Farley Ct. *NW1* *4G* ***5***
(off Allsop Pl.)
W14 3H **99**
Farley Dr. IG3: Ilf 1J **71**
Farley Ho. SE26 3H **139**
Farley M. SE6 7E **122**
Farley Pl. SE25 4G **157**
Farley Rd. CR2: Sels 7H **169**
SE6 7D **122**
Farlington Pl. SW15 7D **116**
Farlow Rd. SW15 3F **117**
Farlton Rd. SW18 1K **135**
Farman Gro. UB5: N'olt 3B **76**
Farman Ter. HA3: Kenton 4D **42**
Farm Av. HA0: Wemb 6C **60**
HA2: Harr 7D **40**
NW2 3G **63**
SW16 4J **137**
Farmborough Cl. HA1: Harr 7H **41**
Farm Cl. BR4: W W'ck 3H **171**
IG9: Buck H 3F **37**
RM10: Dag 7J **73**
SM2: Sutt 7B **166**
SW6 7J **99**
TW17: Shep 7C **146**
UB1: S'hall 7F **77**
UB10: Ick 2D **56**
Farmcote Rd. SE12 1J **141**
Farm Ct. NW4 3C **44**
Farmdale Rd. SE10 5J **105**
SM5: Cars 7C **166**
Farm Dr. CR0: C'don 2B **170**

Farm End HA6: Nwood 1D **38**
Farmer Rd. E10 1D **68**
Farmer's Rd. SE5 7B **102**
Farmer St. W8 1J **99**
Farmfield Rd. BR1: Brom 5G **141**
Farm Ho. Ct. NW7 7H **29**
Farmhouse Rd. SW16 7G **137**
Farmilo Rd. E17 7B **50**
Farmington Av. SM1: Sutt 3B **166**
Farmlands EN2: Enf 1F **23**
HA5: Eastc 4J **39**
Farmlands, The UB5: N'olt 6D **58**
Farmland Wlk. BR7: Chst 5F **143**
Farm La. CR0: C'don 2B **170**
N14 7A **22**
SW6 6J **99**
Farmleigh N14 7B **22**
Farmleigh Ho. SW9 5B **120**
Farm M. CR4: Mitc 2F **155**
Farm Pl. W8 1J **99**
Farm Rd. HA8: Edg 6C **28**
N21 1H **33**
NW10 1K **79**
SM2: Sutt 7B **166**
SM4: Mord 5K **153**
TW4: Houn 1C **130**
Farmstead Ct. *SM6: Wall* *5F* ***167***
(off Melbourne Rd.)
Farmstead Rd. HA3: Hrw W 1H **41**
SE6 4D **140**
Farm St. W1 3J **11** (7F **83**)
Farm Va. DA5: Bexl 6H **127**
Farm Wlk. NW11 5H **45**
Farm Way IG9: Buck H 4F **37**
KT4: Wor Pk 3E **164**
Farmway RM8: Dag 3C **72**
Farnaby Ho. *W10* *3H* ***81***
(off Bruckner St.)
Farnaby Rd. BR1: Brom 7F **141**
BR2: Brom 7F **141**
SE9 4A **124**
Farnan Av. E17 2C **50**
Farnan Lodge SW16 5J **137**
Farnan Rd. SW16 5J **137**
FARNBOROUGH 5G 173
Farnborough Av. CR2: Sels 7K **169**
E17 3A **50**
Farnborough Cl. HA9: Wemb 2H **61**
Farnborough Comn. BR6: Farnb 3D **172**
Farnborough Cres. BR2: Hayes 1H **171**
CR2: Sels 7A **170**
Farnborough Hill
BR6: Chels, Farnb 5H **173**
Farnborough Ho. SW15 1C **134**
Farnborough Way
BR6: Chels, Farnb 5G **173**
Farncombe St. SE16 2G **103**
Farndale Av. N13 2G **33**
Farndale Ct. SE18 7C **106**
Farndale Cres. UB6: G'frd 3G **77**
Farndale Ho. *NW6* *1K* ***81***
(off Kilburn Vale)
Farnell M. SW5 5K **99**
Farnell Pl. W3 7H **79**
Farnell Rd. TW7: Isle 3H **113**
Farnfield Ct. CR2: S Croy 5B **168**
Farnham Cl. N20 7F **21**
Farnham Ct. SM3: Cheam 6G **165**
UB1: S'hall *7G* ***77***
(off Redcroft Rd.)
Farnham Gdns. SW20 2D **152**
Farnham Ho. NW1 4D **4**
SE1 *5C* ***14***
(off Union St.)
Farnham Pl. SE1 5B **14** (1B **102**)
Farnham Rd. DA16: Well 2C **126**
IG3: Ilf 7K **53**
Farnham Royal SE11 6H **19** (5K **101**)
Farningham Ct. SW16 7H **137**
Farningham Ho. N4 7D **48**
Farningham Rd. N17 7B **34**
Farnley Ho. SW8 2H **119**
Farnley Rd. E4 1B **36**
SE25 4D **156**
Farnsworth Ct. *SE10* *3H* ***105***
(off West Parkside)
Farnworth Ho. *E14* *4F* ***105***
(off Manchester Rd.)
Faro Cl. BR1: Brom 2E **160**
Faroe Rd. W14 3F **99**
Farorna Wlk. EN2: Enf 1F **23**
Farquhar Rd. SE19 5F **139**
SW19 3J **135**
Farquharson Rd. CR0: C'don 1C **168**
Farrance Rd. RM6: Chad H 7E **54**
Farrance St. E14 6C **86**
Farrans Ct. HA3: Kenton 7B **42**
Farrant Av. N22 2A **48**
Farrant Cl. BR6: Chels 7K **173**
Farr Av. IG11: Bark 2A **90**
Farrell Ho. *E1* *6J* ***85***
(off Ronald St.)
Farren Rd. SE23 2A **140**
Farrer Ct. TW1: Twick 7D **114**
Farrer Ho. SE8 7C **104**
Farrer M. N8 4G **47**
Farrer Rd. HA3: Kenton 5E **42**
N8 4G **47**
Farrer's Pl. CR0: C'don 4K **169**
Farrier Cl. BR1: Brom 3B **160**
TW16: Sun 4J **147**
UB8: Hil 6C **74**
Farrier Ct. *E1* *5K* ***85***
(off White Horse La.)
RM13: Rain *2K* ***91***
(off Lowen Rd.)
Farrier Pl. SM1: Sutt 3K **165**
Farrier Rd. UB5: N'olt 2E **76**
Farriers Ho. *EC1* *4D* ***8***
(off Errol St.)
Farriers M. SE15 3J **121**
Farrier St. NW1 7F **65**
Farrier Wlk. SW10 6A **100**
Farringdon Ho. TW9: Kew 7H **97**
UB7: W Dray 2B **92**
Farringdon La. EC1 4K **7** (4A **84**)
Farringdon Rd. EC1 3J **7** (4A **84**)
Farringdon St. EC4 6A **8** (5B **84**)
Farrington Ct. *BR1: Brom* *2K* ***159***
(off Widmore Rd.)
Farrington Pl. BR7: Chst 7H **143**
Farrins Rents SE16 1A **104**
Farrow La. SE14 7J **103**
Farrow Pl. SE16 3A **104**
Farr Rd. EN2: Enf 1J **23**
Farthingale Wlk. E15 7F **69**
Farthing All. SE1 7K **15** (2G **103**)
Farthing Barn La. BR6: Downe 7E **172**
Farthing Ct. NW7 7B **30**
Farthing Flds. E1 1H **103**
Farthings, The KT2: King T 1G **151**
Farthings Cl. E4 3B **36**
HA5: Eastc 6K **39**
FARTHING STREET 7D 172
Farthing St. BR6: Downe 7D **172**
Farwell Rd. DA14: Sidc 4B **144**
Farwig La. BR1: Brom 1H **159**
Fashion & Textile Mus. 6H **15** (2E **102**)
Fashion St. E1 6K **9** (5F **85**)
Fashoda Rd. BR2: Brom 4B **160**
Fassett Rd. E8 6G **67**
KT1: King T 4E **150**
Fassett Sq. E8 6G **67**
Fathom Ct. *E16* *7F* ***89***
(off Basin App.)
Fauconberg Ct. *W4* *6J* ***97***
(off Fauconberg Rd.)
Fauconberg Rd. W4 6J **97**
Faulkner Cl. RM8: Dag 7D **54**
Faulkner Ho. BR7: Chst 1H **161**
W6 6E **98**
Faulkner M. E17 1A **50**
Faulkners All. EC1 5A **8** (5B **84**)
Faulkner St. SE14 1J **121**
Fauna Cl. HA7: Stan 4J **27**
RM6: Chad H 6C **54**
Faunce Ho. *SE17* *6B* ***102***
(off Doddington Gro.)
Faunce St. SE17 5B **102**
Favart Rd. SW6 1J **117**
Faversham Av. E4 1B **36**
EN1: Enf 6J **23**
Faversham Ho. *NW1* *1G* ***83***
(off Bayham Pl.)
SE17 *5E* ***102***
(off Kinglake St.)
Faversham Rd. BR3: Beck 2B **158**
SE6 7B **122**
SM4: Mord 6K **153**
Fawcett Cl. SW11 2B **118**
SW16 5A **138**
Fawcett Ct. *SW10* *6A* ***100***
(off Fawcett St.)
Fawcett Est. E5 1G **67**
Fawcett Rd. CR0: C'don 3C **168**
NW10 7B **62**
Fawcett St. SW10 6A **100**
Fawe Pk. M. SW15 4H **117**
Fawe Pk. Rd. SW15 4H **117**
Fawe St. E14 5D **86**
Fawkham Ho. *SE1* *4F* ***103***
(off Longfield Est.)
Fawley Lodge *E14* *4F* ***105***
(off Millennium Dr.)
Fawley Rd. NW6 5K **63**
Fawnbrake Av. SE24 5B **120**
Fawn Hgts. *IG9: Buck H* *2E* ***36***
(off Stag La.)
Fawn Rd. E13 2A **88**
Fawns Mnr. Cl. TW14: Bedf 1E **128**
Fawns Mnr. Rd. TW14: Bedf 1F **129**
Fawood Av. NW10 7J **61**
Faygate Cres. DA6: Bex 5G **127**
Faygate Rd. SW2 2K **137**
Fayland Av. SW16 5G **137**
Fazeley Ct. *W9* *5J* ***81***
(off Elmfield Way)
Fazeley Ho. *UB5: N'olt* *3D* ***76***
(off Taywood Rd.)
Fearnley Cres. TW12: Hamp 5C **130**
Fearnley Ho. SE5 2E **120**
Fearns Ho. W13 1A **96**
Fearon St. SE10 5J **105**
Featherbed La. CR0: Sels 7B **170**
Feather M. E1 5G **85**
Feathers Pl. SE10 6F **105**
Featherstone Av. SE23 2H **139**
Featherstone Ct. UB2: S'hall 3B **94**
Featherstone Ho. UB4: Yead 5A **76**
Featherstone Ind. Est. *UB2: S'hall* *3C* ***94***
(off Feather Rd.)
Featherstone Rd. NW7 6J **29**
UB2: S'hall 3C **94**
Featherstone Sports Cen. 4B **94**
Featherstone St. EC1 3E **8** (4D **84**)
Featherstone Ter. UB2: S'hall 3C **94**
Featley Rd. SW9 3B **120**
Federal Rd. UB6: G'frd 1C **78**
Federation Rd. SE2 4B **108**
Fee Farm Rd. KT10: Clay 7A **162**
Feeny Cl. NW10 4B **62**
Felbridge Av. HA7: Stan 1A **42**
Felbridge Cl. SM2: Sutt 7K **165**
SW16 4A **138**
Felbridge Ct. *TW13: Felt* *1K* ***129***
(off High St.)
UB3: Harl 6F **93**
Felbridge Ho. SE22 3E **120**
Felbrigge Rd. IG3: Ilf 2K **71**
Felday Rd. SE13 6D **122**
Felden Cl. HA5: Hat E 1C **40**
Felden St. SW6 1H **117**
Feldman Cl. N16 1G **67**
Feldspar Ct. *EN3: Enf H* *3F* ***25***
(off Enstone Rd.)
Feldspar M. N13 5G **33**
Felgate M. W6 4D **98**
Felhampton Rd. SE9 2F **143**
Felhurst Cres. RM10: Dag 4H **73**
Feline Ct. EN4: E Barn 6H **21**
Felix Av. N8 6J **47**
Felix Ct. E17 5D **50**
NW9 2A **44**
Felix Ho. *E16* *7E* ***88***
(off University Way)
Felix La. TW17: Shep 6G **147**
Felix Mnr. BR7: Chst 6J **143**
Felix Neubergh Ho. EN1: Enf 4K **23**
Felix Pl. *SW2* *5A* ***120***
(off Talma Rd.)
Felix Point *E14* *6C* ***86***
(off Upper Nth. St.)
Felix Rd. KT12: Walt T 6J **147**
W13 7A **78**
Felixstowe Ct. E16 1F **107**
Felixstowe Rd. N9 3B **34**
N17 3F **49**
NW10 3D **80**
SE2 3B **108**
Felix St. E2 2H **85**
Fellbrigg Rd. SE22 5F **121**
Fellbrigg St. E1 4H **85**
Fellbrook TW10: Ham 3B **132**
Fellmongers Path SE1 7J **15**
Fellmongers Yd. CR0: C'don 3C **168**
Fellowes Cl. UB4: Yead 4B **76**
Fellowes Rd. SM5: Cars 3C **166**
Fellows Ct. E2 1J **9** (2F **85**)
(not continuous)
Fellowship Cl. RM8: Dag 4A **72**
Fellows Rd. NW3 7B **64**
Fell Rd. CR0: C'don 3C **168**
Felltram M. SE7 5J **105**
Felltram Way SE7 5J **105**
Fell Wlk. HA8: Edg 1J **43**
Felmersham Cl. SW4 4J **119**
Felmingham Rd. SE20 2J **157**
Felnex Trad. Est. NW10 2K **79**
SM6: Wall 2E **166**
Felsberg Rd. SW2 6J **119**
Fels Cl. RM10: Dag 3H **73**
Fels Farm Av. RM10: Dag 3J **73**
Felsham M. *SW15* *3F* ***117***
(off Felsham Rd.)
Felsham Rd. SW15 3E **116**
Felspar Cl. SE18 5K **107**
Felstead Av. IG5: Ilf 1E **52**
Felstead Cl. N13 5F **33**
Felstead Gdns. E14 5E **104**
Felstead Rd. E9 6B **68**
E11 7J **51**
Felstead St. E9 6B **68**
Felstead Wharf E14 5E **104**
Felsted Rd. E16 6B **88**
FELTHAM 1K 129
Feltham Av. KT8: E Mos 4J **149**
Felthambrook Ind. Est. TW13: Felt 3K **129**
Felthambrook Way TW13: Felt 3K **129**
Feltham Bus. Complex TW13: Felt 2K **129**
Feltham Corporate Cen.
TW13: Felt 3K **129**
FELTHAMHILL 5H 129
Feltham Hill Rd. TW15: Ashf 5C **128**
Feltham Rd. CR4: Mitc 2D **154**
TW15: Ashf 4C **128**
Felton Cl. BR5: Pet W 6F **161**
Felton Gdns. IG11: Bark 1J **89**
Felton Hall Ho. SE16 7K **15**
Felton Ho. *N1* *1D* ***84***
(off Colville Est.)
Felton Lea DA14: Sidc 5K **143**
Felton Rd. IG11: Bark 2J **89**
W13 2C **96**
Felton St. N1 1D **84**

Fencepiece Rd. IG6: Chig, Ilf 1G **53**
Fenchurch Av. EC3 . . . . 1G **15** (6E **84**)
Fenchurch Bldgs. EC3 . . . . 1H **15** (6E **84**)
Fenchurch Ho. *EC3* *1J 15*
(off Minories)
Fenchurch M. *E3* *5B 86*
(off St Paul's Way)
Fenchurch Pl. EC3 . . . . 2H **15** (6E **84**)
Fenchurch St. EC3 . . . . 2G **15** (7E **84**)
Fen Ct. EC3 . . . . 2G **15** (6E **84**)
Fendall Rd. KT19: Ewe 5J **163**
Fendall St. SE1 . . . . 3E **102**
(not continuous)
Fendt Cl. E16 . . . . 6H **87**
Fendyke Rd. DA17: Belv 4D **108**
Fenelon Pl. W14 . . . . 4H **99**
Fengate Cl. KT9: Chess 6D **162**
Fen Gro. DA15: Sidc 5K **125**
Fenham Rd. SE15 . . . . 7G **103**
Fenland Ho. E5 . . . . 2J **67**
Fen La. SW13 . . . . 1D **116**
Fenman Ct. N17 . . . . 1H **49**
Fenman Gdns. IG3: Ilf 1B **72**
Fenn Cl. BR1: Brom 6J **141**
Fennel Apartments *SE1* *5J 15*
(off Cayenne Ct.)
Fennel Cl. CR0: C'don 1K **169**
E16 . . . . 4G **87**
Fennells Mead KT17: Ewe 7B **164**
Fennell St. SE18 . . . . 6E **106**
Fenner Cl. SE16 . . . . 4H **103**
Fenner Ho. *E1* *1H 103*
(off Watts St.)
Fenner Sq. SW11 . . . . 3B **118**
Fenn Ho. TW7: Isle 1B **114**
Fennings Rd. SW4 . . . . 6H **119**
Fenning St. SE1 . . . . 6G **15** (2E **102**)
Fenn St. E9 . . . . 5K **67**
Fenstanton *N4* *1K 65*
(off Marquis Rd.)
Fenstanton Av. N12 . . . . 6G **31**
Fen St. E16 . . . . 7H **87**
Fenswood Cl. DA5: Bexl 6G **127**
Fentiman Rd. SW8 . . . . 7F **19** (6J **101**)
Fentiman Way HA2: Harr 2F **59**
Fenton Cl. BR7: Chst 5D **142**
E8 . . . . 6F **67**
SW9 . . . . 2K **119**
Fenton House *3A 64*
(off Hampstead Gro.)
Fenton Ho. SE14 . . . . 7A **104**
TW5: Hest 6E **94**
Fenton Pde. *SE10* *5H 105*
(off Woolwich Rd.)
Fenton Rd. N17 . . . . 7H **33**
Fentons Av. E13 . . . . 3K **87**
Fenton St. E1 . . . . 6H **85**
Fenwick Cl. SE18 . . . . 6E **106**
Fenwick Gro. SE15 . . . . 3G **121**
Fenwick Pl. CR2: S Croy 7B **168**
SW9 . . . . 3J **119**
Fenwick Rd. SE15 . . . . 3G **121**
Ferby Ct. *DA14: Sidc* *4K 143*
(off Main Rd.)
Ferdinand Ct. *SE6* *7C 122*
(off Adenmore Rd.)
Ferdinand Dr. SE15 . . . . 7E **102**
Ferdinand Ho. *NW1* *7E 64*
(off Ferdinand Pl.)
Ferdinand Pl. NW1 . . . . 7E **64**
Ferdinand St. NW1 . . . . 7E **64**
Ferguson Av. KT5: Surb 5F **151**
Ferguson Cen., The E17 . . . . 6A **50**
Ferguson Cl. BR2: Brom 3F **159**
E14 . . . . 4C **104**
Ferguson Dr. W3 . . . . 6K **79**
Fergus Rd. N5 . . . . 5B **66**
Ferial Ct. *SE15* *7G 103*
(off Fenham Rd.)
Fermain Ct. E. *N1* *1E 84*
(off Hertford Rd.)
Fermain Ct. Nth. *N1* *1E 84*
(off De Beauvoir Est.)
Fermain Ct. W. *N1* *1E 84*
(off De Beauvoir Est.)
Ferme Pk. Rd. N4 . . . . 5J **47**
N8 . . . . 5J **47**
Fermor Rd. SE23 . . . . 1A **140**
Fermoy Ho. *W9* *4H 81*
(off Fermoy Rd.)
Fermoy Rd. UB6: G'frd 4F **77**
W9 . . . . 4H **81**
(not continuous)
Fern Av. CR4: Mitc 4H **155**
Fernbank IG9: Buck H 1E **36**
Fernbank Av. HA0: Wemb 4K **59**
KT12: Walt T 7C **148**
Fernbank M. SW12 . . . . 6G **119**
Fernbrook Av. DA15: Sidc 5J **125**
Fernbrook Cres. *SE13* *6G 123*
(off Leahurst Rd.)
Fernbrook Dr. HA2: Harr 7F **41**
Fernbrook Rd. SE13 . . . . 5G **123**
Ferncliff Rd. E8 . . . . 5G **67**
Fern Cl. N1 . . . . 2E **84**
Fern Ct. DA7: Bex 4G **127**
RM7: Rom 5K **55**
SE14 . . . . 2K **121**
Ferncroft Av. HA4: Ruis 2A **58**
N12 . . . . 6J **31**
NW3 . . . . 3J **63**
Ferndale BR1: Brom 2A **160**
Ferndale Av. E17 . . . . 5F **51**
TW4: Houn 3C **112**
Ferndale Cl. DA7: Bex 1E **126**
Ferndale Community Sports Cen. . . . 3K **119**
Ferndale Cres. SM5: Cars 1D **166**
Ferndale Rd. E7 . . . . 7K **69**
E11 . . . . 2G **69**
N15 . . . . 6F **49**
RM5: Col R 2J **55**
SE25 . . . . 5H **157**
SW4 . . . . 4J **119**
SW9 . . . . 4J **119**
TW15: Ashf 5A **128**
Ferndale St. E6 . . . . 7F **89**
Ferndale Ter. HA1: Harr 4K **41**
Ferndale Way BR6: Farnb 5H **173**
Ferndell Av. DA5: Bexl 3K **145**
Fern Dene W13 . . . . 5B **78**
Ferndene Rd. SE24 . . . . 4C **120**
Fernden Way RM7: Rom 6H **55**
Ferndown HA6: Nwood 2J **39**
NW1 . . . . *7H 65*
(off Camley St.)
Ferndown Av. BR6: Orp 1H **173**
Ferndown Cl. HA5: Pinn 1C **40**
SM2: Sutt 6B **166**
Ferndown Ct. *UB1: S'hall* *6G 77*
(off Haldane Rd.)
Ferndown Lodge *E14* *3E 104*
(off Manchester Rd.)
Ferndown Rd. SE9 . . . . 7B **124**
Ferney Meade Way TW7: Isle 2A **114**
Ferney Rd. EN4: E Barn 7K **21**
Fern Gro. TW14: Felt 7K **111**
Fernhall Dr. IG4: Ilf 5B **52**
Fernham Rd. CR7: Thor H 3C **156**
Fernhead Rd. W9 . . . . 3H **81**
Fernheath Way DA2: Wilm 5K **145**
Fernhill Ct. E17 . . . . 2F **51**
Fernhill Gdns. KT2: King T 5D **132**
Fern Hill Pl. BR6: Farnb 5G **173**
Fernhill St. E16 . . . . 1D **106**
Fernholme Rd. SE15 . . . . 5K **121**
Fernhurst Gdns. HA8: Edg 6B **28**
Fernhurst Rd. CR0: C'don 7H **157**
SW6 . . . . 1G **117**
TW15: Ashf 4E **128**
Fern La. TW5: Hest 5D **94**
Fernlea Rd. CR4: Mitc 2E **154**
SW12 . . . . 1F **137**
Fernleigh Cl. CR0: Wadd 4A **168**
W9 . . . . 3H **81**
Fernleigh Ct. HA2: Harr 2F **41**
HA9: Wemb 2E **60**
RM7: Rom 5J **55**
Fernleigh Rd. N21 . . . . 2F **33**
Fernly Cl. HA5: Eastc 4J **39**
Fernsbury St. WC1 . . . . 2J **7** (3A **84**)
Fernshaw Cl. SW10 . . . . 6A **100**
Fernshaw Mans. *SW10* *6A 100*
(off Fernshaw Rd.)
Fernshaw Rd. SW10 . . . . 6A **100**
Fernside IG9: Buck H 1E **36**
KT7: T Ditt 1B **162**
NW11 . . . . 2J **63**
Fernside Av. NW7 . . . . 3E **28**
TW13: Felt 4K **129**
Fernside Ct. NW4 . . . . 2F **45**
Fernside Rd. SW12 . . . . 1D **136**
Ferns Rd. E15 . . . . 6H **69**
Fern St. E3 . . . . 4C **86**
Fernthorpe Rd. SW16 . . . . 6G **137**
Ferntower Rd. N5 . . . . 5D **66**
Fern Wlk. SE16 . . . . 5G **103**
TW15: Ashf 5A **128**
Fernways IG1: Ilf 4F **71**
Fernwood SW19 . . . . 1H **135**
Fernwood Av. HA0: Wemb 6C **60**
SW16 . . . . 4H **137**
Fernwood Cl. BR1: Brom 2A **160**
Fernwood Ct. N14 . . . . 7B **22**
Fernwood Cres. N20 . . . . 3J **31**
Fernwood Pl. KT10: Hin W 2A **162**
Ferny Hill EN4: Had W 1J **21**
Ferranti Cl. SE18 . . . . 3B **106**
Ferraro Cl. TW5: Hest 6E **94**
Ferrers Av. SM6: Bedd 4H **167**
UB7: W Dray 2A **92**
Ferrers Rd. SW16 . . . . 5H **137**
Ferrestone Rd. N8 . . . . 4K **47**
Ferrey M. SW9 . . . . 2A **120**
Ferriby Cl. N1 . . . . 7A **66**
Ferrier Ind. Est. *SW18* *4K 117*
(off Ferrier St.)
Ferrier Point *E16* *5J 87*
(off Forty Acre La.)
Ferrier St. SW18 . . . . 4K **117**
Ferring Cl. HA2: Harr 1G **59**
Ferrings SE21 . . . . 3E **138**
Ferris Av. CR0: C'don 3B **170**
Ferris Rd. SE22 . . . . 4G **121**
Ferron Rd. E5 . . . . 3H **67**
Ferry App. SE18 . . . . 3E **106**
Ferrybridge Ho. SE11 . . . . 2H **19**
Ferrydale Lodge *NW4* *4E 44*
(off Parson St.)
Ferry Ho. *E5* *1H 67*
(off Harrington Hill)
Ferry Island Retail Pk. N17 . . . . 3G **49**
Ferry La. N17 . . . . 4G **49**
SW13 . . . . 6B **98**
TW8: Bford 6E **96**
TW9: Kew 6F **97**
TW17: Shep 7C **146**
Ferry La. Ind. Est. E17 . . . . 4K **49**
Ferryman's Quay SW6 . . . . 2A **118**
Ferrymead Av. UB6: G'frd 3E **76**
Ferrymead Dr. UB6: G'frd 2E **76**
Ferrymead Gdns. UB6: G'frd 2G **77**
Ferrymoor TW10: Ham 3B **132**
Ferry Pl. SE18 . . . . 3E **106**
Ferry Quays TW8: Bford 6E **96**
(Ferry La.)
TW8: Bford *7D 96*
(off Point Wharf La.)
Ferry Rd. KT7: T Ditt 6B **150**
KT8: W Mole 3E **148**
SW13 . . . . 7C **98**
TW1: Twick 1B **132**
TW11: Tedd 5B **132**
Ferry Sq. TW8: Bford 7E **96**
Ferry St. E14 . . . . 5E **104**
Ferry Wharf TW8: Bford 7E **96**
Festing Rd. SW15 . . . . 3F **117**
Festival Cl. DA5: Bexl 1D **144**
UB10: Hil 1D **74**
Festival Ct. *E8* *7F 67*
(off Holly St.)
SM1: Sutt 7K **153**
Festival Wlk.
SM5: Cars 4D **166**
Festival Way E4 . . . . 6K **35**
Festive Mans. *E20* *5E 68*
(off Napa Cl.)
Festoon Way E16 . . . . 7B **88**
Festubert St. E3 . . . . 2B **86**
Festuca Ho. *E20* *5E 68*
(off Mirabelle Gdns.)
Fetherstone Ct. *RM6: Chad H* *6F 55*
(off High Rd.)
Fetherton Ct. *IG11: Bark* *2G 89*
(off Spring Pl.)
Fetter La. EC4 . . . . 1K **13** (6A **84**)
Fetter La. Apartments *EC4* *1J 13*
(off Fetter La.)
Fettes Ho. *NW8* *2B 82*
(off Wellington Rd.)
Fews Lodge RM6: Chad H 4D **54**
Ffinch St. SE8 . . . . 7C **104**
Fidelis Ho. *E1* *6J 9*
(off Gun St.)
Fidgeon Cl. BR1: Brom 3E **160**
Field Cl. BR1: Brom 2A **160**
E4 . . . . 6J **35**
HA4: Ruis 1E **56**
IG9: Buck H 3F **37**
KT8: W Mole 5F **149**
KT9: Chess 5C **162**
NW2 . . . . 2C **62**
TW4: Cran 1K **111**
UB3: Harl 7E **92**
UB10: Ick 2D **56**
FIELDCOMMON 7D 148
Fieldcommon La. KT12: Walt T 7C **148**
Field Ct. SW19 . . . . 3J **135**
WC1 . . . . 6H **7** (5K **83**)
Field End HA4: Ruis 6A **58**
UB5: N'olt 6B **58**
Fieldend TW1: Twick 4K **131**
Fld. End Rd. HA4: Ruis 5K **39**
HA5: Eastc 5K **39**
Fieldend Rd. SW16 . . . . 1G **155**
Fielder Apartments *E3* *4B 86*
(off Heath Pl.)
Fielders Cl. EN1: Enf 4K **23**
HA2: Harr 1G **59**
Fieldfare Rd. SE28 . . . . 7C **90**
Fieldgate La. CR4: Mitc 2C **154**
Fieldgate Mans. *E1* *5G 85*
(off Fieldgate St.)
Fieldgate St. E1 . . . . 5G **85**
Field Ho. *NW6* *3F 81*
(off Harvist Rd.)
SM4: Mord *5K 153*
(off School Ga. Dr.)
Fieldhouse Cl. E18 . . . . 1J **51**
Fieldhouse Rd. SW12 . . . . 1G **137**
Fielding Av. TW2: Twick 3G **131**
Fielding Ct. *WC2* *1E 12*
(off Earlham St.)
Fielding Ho. *NW8* *1A 82*
(off Ainsworth Way)
W4 . . . . *6A 98*
(off Devonshire Rd.)
Fielding La. BR2: Brom 4A **160**
Fielding M. SW13 . . . . 6D **98**
Fielding Rd. W4 . . . . 3K **97**
W14 . . . . 3F **99**
Fieldings, The SE23 . . . . 1J **139**
Fielding St. SE17 . . . . 6C **102**
Fielding Ter. W5 . . . . 7F **79**
Fielding Wlk. W13 . . . . 3B **96**

Field La. TW8: Bford 7C 96
TW11: Tedd 5A 132
Fld. Maple M. RM5: Col R 1G 55
Field Mead NW7 7F 29
NW9 7F 29
Fieldpark Gdns. CR0: C'don 1A 170
Field Pl. KT3: N Mald 6B 152
Field Point E7 4J 69
Field Rd. E7 4H 69
N17 3D 48
TW14: Felt 6K 111
W6 5G 99
Fieldsend Rd. SM3: Cheam 5G 165
Fields Est. E8 7G 67
Fieldside Cl. BR6: Farnb 4G 173
Fieldside Rd. BR1: Brom 5F 141
Fields Pk. Cres. RM6: Chad H 5D 54
Field St. WC1 1G 7 (3K 83)
Fieldsway Ho. N5 5A 66
Field Vw. TW13: Felt 4F 129
Fieldview SW18 1B 136
Field Vw. Cl. RM7: Mawney 3G 55
Fieldview Cotts. *N14* *2C 32*
(off Balaams La.)
Field Way HA4: Ruis 1E 56
NW10 7J 61
UB6: G'frd 1F 77
Fieldway BR5: Pet W 6H 161
CR0: New Ad 7D 170
RM8: Dag 3C 72
Fieldway Cres. N5 5A 66
Fiennes Cl. RM8: Dag 1C 72
Fifehead Cl. TW15: Ashf 6A 128
Fife Rd. E16 5J 87
KT1: King T 2E 150
N22 7G 33
SW14 5J 115
Fife Ter. N1 2K 83
Fifield Path SE23 3K 139
Fifth Av. E12 4D 70
UB3: Hayes 1H 93
W10 3G 81
Fifth Cross Rd. TW2: Twick 2H 131
Fifth Way HA9: Wemb 4H 61
Figges Rd. CR4: Mitc 7E 136
Fight for Peace Academy 1E 106
Fig Tree Cl. NW10 1A 80
Figure Ct. SW3 6F 17
Filament Wlk. *SW18* *5J 117*
(off Spectrum Way)
Filanco Ct. W7 1K 95
Filby Rd. KT9: Chess 6F 163
Filey Av. N16 1G 67
Filey Cl. SM2: Sutt 7A 166
Filey Waye HA4: Ruis 2J 57
Filigree Ct. SE16 1B 104
Fillebrook Av. EN1: Enf 2K 23
Fillebrook Rd. E11 1F 69
Filmer Chambers *SW6* *1G 117*
(off Filmer Rd.)
Filmer Ho. *SW6* *1H 117*
(off Filmer Rd.)
Filmer M. SW6 1H 117
Filmer Rd. SW6 1G 117
Filston Rd. DA8: Erith 5J 109
Filton Cl. NW9 1A 44
Filton Ct. *SE14* *7J 103*
(off Farrow La.)
Finborough Ho. *SW10* *6A 100*
(off Finborough Rd.)
Finborough Rd. SW10 5K 99
SW17 6D 136
Finborough Theatre, The *6K 99*
(off Finborough Rd.)
Finchale Rd. SE2 3A 108
Fincham Cl. UB10: Ick 3E 56
Finch Av. SE27 4D 138
Finch Cl. EN5: Barn 5D 20
NW10 6K 61
Finch Ct. DA14: Sidc 3B 144
Finchdean Ho. SW15 7B 116
Finch Dr. TW14: Felt 7B 112
Finch Gdns. E4 5H 35
Finch Ho. *E3* *1B 86*
(off Jasmine Sq.)
SE8 *7D 104*
(off Bronze St.)
Finchingfield Av.
IG8: Wfd G 7F 37
Finch La. EC3 1F 15 (6D 84)
FINCHLEY 1J 45
Finchley Ct. N3 6E 30
Finchley Golf Course 6C 30
Finchley Ind. Est. N12 4F 31
Finchley La. NW4 4E 44
Finchley Lido 7G 31
Finchley Manor Club 1H 45
Finchley Pk. N12 4F 31
Finchley Pl. NW8 2B 82
Finchley Rd. NW2 4H 45
NW3 4H 45
NW8 1B 82
NW11 4H 45
Finchley Way N3 7D 30
Finch Lodge *W9* *5J 81*
(off Admiral Wlk.)
Finch M. SE15 1F 121
Finch's Ct. E14 7D 86
Finch's Ct. M. *E14* *7D 86*
(off Finch's Ct.)
Finden Rd. E7 5A 70
Findhorn Av. UB4: Yead 5K 75
Findhorn St. E14 6E 86
Findlay Ho. *E3* *3C 86*
(off Trevithick Way)
Findon Cl. HA2: Harr 3F 59
SW18 6J 117
Findon Rd. N9 1C 34
W12 2C 98
Fine Bush La. UB9: Hare 6D 38
Fingal St. SE10 5H 105
Fingest Ho. *NW8* *3C 4*
(off Lilestone St.)
Finians Cl. UB10: Uxb 7B 56
Finland Rd. SE4 3A 122
Finland St. SE16 3A 104
Finlays Cl. KT9: Chess 5G 163
Finlay St. SW6 1F 117
Finley Ct. *SE5* *7C 102*
(off Redcar St.)
Finmere Ho. N4 7C 48
Finnemore Ho. *N1* *1C 84*
(off Britannia Row)
Finney La. TW7: Isle 1A 114
Finn Ho. *N1* *1F 9*
(off Bevenden St.)
Finnis St. E2 3H 85
Finnymore Rd. RM9: Dag 7E 72
FINSBURY 3C 8 (3A 84)
Finsbury Av. EC2 6F 9 (5D 84)
Finsbury Av. Sq. EC2 5G 9 (5E 84)
Finsbury Cir. EC2 6F 9 (5D 84)
Finsbury Cotts. N22 7D 32
Finsbury Est. EC1 2K 7 (3A 84)
Finsbury Ho. N22 1J 47
Finsbury Leisure Cen. 3C 8 (3C 84)
Finsbury Mkt. EC2 4G 9 (4E 84)
(not continuous)
FINSBURY PARK 1A 66
Finsbury Pk. Av. N4 6C 48
Finsbury Pk. Rd. N4 2B 66
Finsbury Pavement EC2 5F 9 (5D 84)
Finsbury Rd. N22 7E 32
(not continuous)
Finsbury Sq. EC2 4F 9 (4D 84)
Finsbury St. EC2 5E 8 (5D 84)
Finsbury Way DA5: Bexl 6F 127
Finsen Rd. SE5 4C 120
Finstock Rd. W10 6F 81
Finucane Ct. *TW9: Rich* *3F 115*
(off Lwr. Mortlake Rd.)
Finucane Ri. WD23: B Hea 2B 26
Finwhale Ho. *E14* *3D 104*
(off Glengall Gro.)
Fiona Ct. EN2: Enf 3G 23
NW6 2J 81
Firbank Cl. E16 5B 88
EN2: Enf 4H 23
Firbank Rd. SE15 2H 121
Fir Cl. KT12: Walt T 7J 147
Fircroft Gdns. HA1: Harr 3J 59
Fircroft Rd. KT9: Chess 4F 163
SW17 2D 136
Fir Dene BR6: Farnb 3D 172
Firdene KT5: Surb 1J 163
Fire Bell All. KT6: Surb 6E 150
Firecrest Dr. NW3 3K 63
Firefly Cl. UB3: Hayes 7H 75
UB5: N'olt 3B 76
Firefly Gdns. E6 4C 88
Firehorn Ho. *E15* *3G 87*
(off Teasel Way)
Firemans Flats N22 7D 32
Firepower (The Royal Artillery Mus.)
3F 107
Fire Station All. EN5: Barn 3B 20
Fire Station M. BR3: Beck 1C 158
Firestone Ho. TW8: Bford 5E 96
Firethorn Cl. HA8: Edg 4D 28
Firewatch Ct. *E1* *5A 86*
(off Candle St.)
Fir Gro. KT3: N Mald 6B 152
Firgrove Ct. SE6 7C 122
Fir Gro. Rd. SW9 2A 120
Firhill Rd. SE6 4C 140
Fir Ho. *W10* *4G 81*
(off Droop St.)
Firle Ho. *W10* *5E 80*
(off Sutton Way)
Firman Cl. KT3: N Mald 4A 152
Firmans Ct. E17 4F 51
Fir Rd. SM3: Sutt 1H 165
TW13: Hanw 5B 130
Firs, The DA5: Bexl 1K 145
DA15: Sidc 2K 143
E6 7C 70
HA8: Edg *4E 28*
(off Stoneyfields La.)
IG8: Wfd G 7F 37
N20 1G 31
SE26 5H 139
(Border Rd.)
SE26 5J 139
(Waverley Ct.)
W5 5D 78
Firs Av. N10 3E 46
N11 6J 31
SW14 4J 115
Firsby Av. CR0: C'don 1K 169
Firsby Rd. N16 1G 67
Firs Cl. CR4: Mitc 2F 155
N10 4E 46
SE23 7A 122
Firscroft N13 3H 33
Firs Dr. TW5: Cran 7K 93
Firs Ho. *N22* *1A 48*
(off Acacia Rd.)
Firside Gro. DA15: Sidc 1K 143
Firs La. N13 3H 33
N21 7H 23
Firs Pk. Av. N21 1J 33
Firs Pk. Gdns. N21 1H 33
First Av. DA7: Bex 7C 108
E12 4C 70
E13 3J 87
E17 5C 50
EN1: Enf 5A 24
HA9: Wemb 2D 60
KT8: W Mole 4D 148
KT12: Walt T 6K 147
KT19: Ewe 7A 164
N18 4D 34
NW4 4E 44
First Av. RM6: Chad H 5C 54
RM10: Dag 2H 91
SW14 3A 116
UB3: Hayes 1H 93
W3 1B 98
W10 4H 81
First Central Bus. Pk. NW10 3F 79
First Cl. KT8: W Mole 3G 149
First Cross Rd. TW2: Twick 2J 131
First Dr. NW10 7J 61
First St. SW3 3D 16 (4C 100)
First Way HA9: Wemb 4H 61
Firstway SW20 2E 152
Firs Wlk. IG8: Wfd G 5D 36
Firswood Av. KT19: Ewe 5A 164
Firth Gdns. SW6 1G 117
Firth Ho. *E2* *3G 85*
(off Turin St.)
Fir Tree Av. UB7: W Dray 3C 92
Firtree Av. CR4: Mitc 2E 154
Fir Tree Cl. BR6: Chels 5K 173
KT19: Ewe 4B 164
RM1: Rom 3K 55
SW16 5G 137
W5 6E 78
Fir Tree Gdns. CR0: C'don 4C 170
Fir Tree Gro. SM5: Cars 7D 166
Firtree Ho. *SE13* *7F 123*
(off Birdwood Av.)
Fir Tree Pl. TW15: Ashf 5C 128
Fir Tree Rd. TW4: Houn 4C 112
Fir Trees Cl. SE16 1A 104
Fir Tree Wlk. EN1: Enf 3J 23
RM10: Dag 3J 73
Fir Wlk. SM3: Cheam 6F 165
Fisher Cl. CR0: C'don 1F 169
E9 5K 67
SE16 1K 103
UB6: G'frd 3E 76
Fisher Ho. *E1* *7J 85*
(off Cable St.)
N1 *1A 84*
(off Barnsbury Est.)
Fisherman Cl. TW10: Ham 4B 132
Fishermans Dr. SE16 2K 103
Fisherman's Pl. W4 6B 98
Fisherman's Wlk. E14 1C 104
Fishermans Wlk. SE28 2J 107
Fisher Rd. HA3: W'stone 2K 41
Fisher's Cl. SW16 3H 137
Fishers Ct. SE14 1K 121
Fishersdene KT10: Clay 7A 162
Fisher's La. W4 4K 97
Fisher St. E16 5J 87
WC1 6G 7 (5K 83)
Fishers Way DA17: Belv 1J 109
HA0: Wemb 5B 60
Fisherton St. NW8 4A 4 (4B 82)
Fishguard Way E16 1F 107
Fishmongers Hall Wharf EC4 3E 14
Fishponds Rd. BR2: Kes 5B 172
SW17 4C 136
Fish St. Hill EC3 3F 15 (7D 84)
Fish Wharf EC3 3F 15 (7D 84)
Fisk Cl. TW16: Sun 6H 129
Fiske Ct. IG11: Bark 2H 89
N17 1G 49
SM2: Sutt 7A 166
Fit4less
Tower Hill *2K 15*
(off Mansell St.)
Fitch Ct. SW2 5A 120
Fitness4Less
Canning Town 5G 87
Sutton 6J 165
Fitness First
America Square 2J 15
Angel 1A 8 (2B 84)
Baker Street 6F 5 (5D 82)
Beckenham 5B 140
Berkeley Square 3K 11 (7F 83)

Fitness First
Bloomsbury 4E 6
Brixton 3A 120
Camden 1F 83
Chancery Lane 6K 7
Clapham Junction 4C 118
Covent Garden 3F 13
(off Bedford St.)
Fetter Lane 1K 13
(off Fetter La.)
Gracechurch Street 2F 15
(off Gracechurch St.)
Great Marlborough Street 1A 12
Hammersmith 4E 98
Harrow 6J 41
(within St George's Shop. & Leisure Cen.)
Highbury 3B 66
High Holborn 6G 7
(off High Holborn)
Ilford 2G 71
Kilburn 1H 81
Kingly Street 2A 12
Kingsbury 5G 43
Leyton Mills 3E 68
London Bridge 5F 15
(off London Bri. St.)
North Finchley 5F 31
Paternoster Square 7B 8
Pinner 3B 40
Queen Victoria Street 2C 14
(off Queen Victoria St.)
South Kensington 3A 16
(off Harrington Rd.)
Streatham 2J 137
Thomas More Square 7G 85
(off Thomas More Sq.)
Tooting Bec 3E 136
Victoria 1A 18 (3G 101)
Walworth Road 5C 102
Wembley 5E 60
FitSpace Gym 3F 107
Fittleton Gdns. E3 4D 86
Fitzalan Rd. N3 3G 45
Fitzalan St. SE11 3H 19 (4A 102)
Fitzclarence Ho. W11 2G 99
(off Holland Park Av.)
Fitzgeorge Av. KT3: N Mald 1K 151
W14 4G 99
Fitzgerald Av. SW14 3A 116
Fitzgerald Ct. E10 1D 68
(off Leyton Grange Est.)
Fitzgerald Ho. E14 6D 86
(off E. India Dock Rd.)
SW9 2A 120
SW17 3B 136
UB3: Hayes 1K 93
Fitzgerald Rd. E11 5J 51
KT7: T Ditt 6A 150
SW14 3K 115
Fitzhardinge Ho. W1 7G 5
(off Portman Sq.)
Fitzhardinge St. W1 7G 5 (6E 82)
Fitzherbert Cl. IG5: Ilf 1C 52
Fitzherbert Wlk. UB1: S'hall 2H 95
Fitzhugh Gro. SW18 6B 118
Fitzjames Av. CR0: C'don 2G 169
W14 4G 99
Fitzjohn Av. EN5: Barn 5B 20
Fitzjohn's Av. NW3 4A 64
Fitzmaurice Ho. SE16 4H 103
(off Rennie Est.)
Fitzmaurice Pl. W1 4K 11 (1F 101)
Fitzneal St. W12 6B 80
Fitzpatrick Rd. SW9 1B 120
FITZROVIA 5K 5
Fitzrovia Apartments W1 4K 5
(off Bolsover St.)
Fitzroy Bri. NW1 1E 82
Fitzroy Bus. Pk.
BR5: St P 7D 144
Fitzroy Cl. N6 1D 64
Fitzroy Ct. CR0: C'don 7D 156
N6 6G 47
W1 4B 6
Fitzroy Cres. W4 7K 97
Fitzroy Gdns. SE19 7E 138
Fitzroy Ho. E14 5B 86
(off Wallwood St.)
SE1 5F 103
(off Cooper's Rd.)
Fitzroy House Mus. 4A 6 (4G 83)
Fitzroy M. W1 4A 6
Fitzroy Pk. N6 1D 64
Fitzroy Rd. NW1 1E 82
Fitzroy Sq. W1 4A 6 (4G 83)
Fitzroy St. W1 4A 6 (4G 83)
(not continuous)
Fitzroy Yd. NW1 1E 82
Fitzstephen Rd. RM8: Dag 5B 72
Fitzwarren Gdns. N19 1G 65
Fitzwilliam Av. TW9: Rich 2F 115
Fitzwilliam Cl. N20 1K 31
Fitzwilliam Hgts. SE23 2J 139
Fitzwilliam Ho. TW9: Rich 4D 114
Fitzwilliam M. E16 1J 105
Fitzwilliam Rd. SW4 3G 119
Fitz Wygram Cl. TW12: Hamp H 5G 131
Five Acre NW9 2B 44
Fiveacre Cl. CR7: Thor H 6A 156
Five Arches Bus. Pk. DA14: Sidc 5D 144
Five Bell All. E14 6B 86
(off Three Colt St.)
Five Elms BR2: Hayes 3K 171
Five Elms Rd. BR2: Hayes 3K 171
RM9: Dag 3F 73
Five Oaks M. BR1: Brom 3J 141
Fives Ct. SE11 3B 102
FIVEWAYS 2F 143
Five Ways Bus. Cen. TW13: Felt 3K 129
FIVEWAYS CORNER
Croydon 4A 168
Hendon 1C 44
Fiveways Rd. SW9 2A 120
Flack Ct. E10 7D 50
Fladbury Rd. N15 6D 48
Fladgate Rd. E11 6G 51
Flag Cl. CR0: C'don 1K 169
Flagon Ct. CR0: C'don 4C 168
(off St Andrew's Rd.)
Flag Wlk. HA5: Eastc 6J 39
Flambard Rd. HA1: Harr 6A 42
Flamborough Ho. SE15 1G 121
(off Clayton Rd.)
Flamborough Rd. HA4: Ruis 3J 57
Flamborough St. E14 6A 86
Flamborough Wlk. E14 6A 86
(off Flamborough St.)
Flamingo Ct. SE8 7C 104
(off Hamilton St.)
SE17 5C 102
(off Crampton St.)
Flamingo Gdns. UB5: N'olt 3C 76
Flamstead Gdns. RM9: Dag 7C 72
Flamstead Ho. SW3 5C 16
(off Cale St.)
Flamstead Rd. RM9: Dag 7C 72
Flamsted Av. HA9: Wemb 6G 61
Flamsteed Rd. SE7 5C 106
Flanaghan Apartments E3 4B 86
(off Portia Way)
Flanchford Rd. W12 3B 98
Flanders Ct. E17 7A 50
Flanders Cres. SW17 7D 136
Flanders Mans. W4 4B 98
Flanders Rd. E6 2D 88
W4 4A 98
Flanders Way E9 6K 67
Flandrian Cl. EN3: Enf L 1J 25
Flank St. E1 7G 85
Flannery Ct. SE16 3H 103
Flansham Ho. E14 6B 86
(off Clemence St.)
Flask Wlk. NW3 4A 64
Flatford Ho. SE6 4E 140
Flather Cl. SW16 5G 137
Flat Iron Sq. SE1 5D 14
(off Southwark Bri. Rd.)
Flatiron Yd. SE1 5D 14
(off Ayres St.)
Flavell M. SE10 5G 105
Flaxen Cl. E4 3J 35
Flaxen Rd. E4 3J 35
Flaxley Ho. SW1 5J 17
(part of Abbots Mnr.)
Flaxley Rd. SM4: Mord 7K 153
Flaxman Ct. DA17: Belv 5G 109
(off Hoddesdon Rd.)
W1 1C 12 (6H 83)
WC1 2D 6
(off Flaxman Ter.)
Flaxman Ho. SE1 3B 102
(off London Rd.)
W4 5A 98
(off Devonshire St.)
Flaxman Rd. SE5 3B 120
Flaxman Sports Cen. 2C 120
Flaxman Ter. WC1 2D 6 (3H 83)
Flaxton Rd. SE18 7H 107
Flecker Cl. HA7: Stan 5E 26
Flecker Ho. SE5 7D 102
(off Lomond Gro.)
Fleece Dr. N9 4B 34
Fleece Rd. KT6: Surb 1C 162
Fleece Wlk. N7 6J 65
Fleeming Cl. E17 2B 50
Fleeming Rd. E17 2B 50
Fleetbank Ho. EC4 1K 13
(off Salisbury Sq.)
Fleet Cl. HA4: Ruis 6E 38
KT8: W Mole 5D 148
Fleetfield WC1 1F 7
(off Birkenhead St.)
Fleet Ho. E14 7A 86
(off Victory Pl.)
Fleet La. KT8: W Mole 6D 148
Fleet Pl. EC4 7A 8 (6B 84)
Fleet Rd. IG11: Bark 1F 89
NW3 5C 64
Fleetside KT8: W Mole 5D 148
Fleet Sq. WC1 2H 7 (3K 83)
Fleet St. EC4 1J 13 (6A 84)
Fleetway WC1 1F 7
(off Birkenhead St.)
Fleetway W. UB6: G'frd 2B 78
Fleetwood Cl. CR0: C'don 3F 169
E16 5B 88
KT9: Chess 7D 162
Fleetwood Ct. E6 5D 88
(off Evelyn Dennington Rd.)
TW19: Stanw 6A 110
(off Douglas Rd.)
Fleetwood Rd. KT1: King T 3H 151
NW10 5C 62
Fleetwood Sq. KT1: King T 3H 151
Fleetwood St. N16 2E 66
Fleming N8 3J 47
(off Boyton Cl.)
Fleming Cl. SW10 7A 16
(off Winterton Pl.)
W9 4J 81
Fleming Collection, The 7F 83
(off Berkeley St.)
Fleming Ct. CR0: Wadd 5A 168
W2 5A 4
Fleming Dr. N21 5E 22
Fleming Ho. HA9: Wemb 3J 61
(off Barnhill Rd.)
N4 1C 66
SE16 2G 103
(off George Row)
SW17 3B 136
Fleming Lodge W9 5J 81
(off Admiral Wlk.)
Fleming Mead CR4: Mitc 7C 136
Fleming Rd. SE17 6B 102
UB1: S'hall 6F 77
Fleming Wlk. NW9 3A 44
Fleming Way SE28 7D 90
TW7: Isle 4K 113
Flemming Av.
HA4: Ruis 1K 57
Flempton Rd. E10 1A 68
Fletcher Bldgs. WC2 1F 13
(off Martlett Ct.)
Fletcher Cl. E6 6F 89
Fletcher Ct. NW9 3A 44
Fletcher Ho. N1 1E 84
(off Nuttall St.)
SE15 7J 103
(off Clifton Way)
Fletcher La. E10 7E 50
Fletcher Path SE8 7C 104
Fletcher Rd. W4 3J 97
Fletchers Cl. BR2: Brom 4K 159
Fletcher St. E1 7G 85
Fletching Rd. E5 3J 67
SE7 6A 106
Fletton Rd. N11 7D 32
Fleur de Lis St. E1 4H 9 (4F 85)
Fleur Gates SW19 7F 117
Flexmere Gdns. N17 1D 48
Flexmere Rd. N17 1D 48
Flight App. NW9 2B 44
Flight Ho. N1 1E 84
(off Phillipp St.)
Flimwell Cl. BR1: Brom 5G 141
Flinders Ho. E1 1H 103
(off Green Bank)
Flint Cl. BR6: Chels 6K 173
CR0: C'don 6K 155
E15 7H 69
Flintlock Cl. TW19: Stanw M 7B 174
Flintlock St. E1 6H 85
Flintmill Cres. SE3 2C 124
Flinton St. SE17 5E 102
Flint St. SE17 4D 102
Flitcroft St. WC2 1D 12 (6H 83)
Flitton Ho. N1 7B 66
(off The Sutton Est.)
Floathaven Cl. SE28 1A 108
Flock Mill Pl. SW18 1K 135
Flockton St. SE16 2G 103
Flodden Rd. SE5 1C 120
Flood La. TW1: Twick 1A 132
Flood Pas. SE18 3C 106
Flood St. SW3 6D 16 (5C 100)
Flood Wlk. SW3 7D 16 (6C 100)
Flora Cl. E14 6D 86
HA7: Stan 3K 27
Flora Gdns. RM6: Chad H 6C 54
W6 4D 98
(off Albion Gdns.)
Flora Ho. E3 1C 86
(off Garrison Rd.)
Floral Pl. N1 5D 66
Floral St. WC2 2E 12 (7J 83)
Flora St. DA17: Belv 5F 109
Florence Av. EN2: Enf 3H 23
SM4: Mord 5A 154
Florence Cantwell Wlk. N19 7J 47
(off Jessie Blythe La.)
Florence Cl. KT2: King T 5F 133
KT12: Walt T 7K 147
Florence Ct. E11 4K 51
N1 7B 66
(off Florence St.)
SW19 6G 135
W9 3A 82
(off Maida Vale)
Florence Dr. EN2: Enf 3H 23
Florence Elson Cl. E12 4E 70
Florence Gdns.
RM6: Chad H 7C 54
W4 6J 97

Florence Ho.—Forge Dr.

Florence Ho. *KT2: King T* 7F **133**
(off Florence Rd)
SE16 .5H **103**
(off Rotherhithe New Rd.)
W11 . . . . .7F **81**
(off St Ann's Rd.)
Florence Mans. *NW4* 5D **44**
(off Vivian Av.)
SW6 .1H **117**
(off Rostrevor Rd.)
Florence Nightingale Mus.
. . . . .7G 13 (2K 101)
Florence Rd. BR1: Brom 1J **159**
BR3: Beck 2A **158**
CR2: Sande 7D **168**
E6 . . . . .1A **88**
E13 . . . . .2J **87**
KT2: King T 7F **133**
KT12: Walt T 7K **147**
N4 . . . . .7K **47**
(not continuous)
SE2 . . . . .4C **108**
SE14 .1B **122**
SW19 .6K **135**
TW13: Felt 1K **129**
UB2: S'hall 4B **94**
W4 . . . . .3K **97**
W5 . . . . .7E **78**
Florence Root Ho. IG4: Ilf 5C **52**
Florence Sq. E3 . . . . .4D **86**
Florence St. E16 . . . . .4H **87**
N1 . . . . .7B **66**
NW4 . . . . .4E **44**
Florence Ter. SE14 . . . . .1B **122**
SW15 .3A **134**
Florence Way SW12 . . . . .1D **136**
Florey Lodge *W9* 5J **81**
(off Admiral Wlk.)
Florey Sq. N21 . . . . .5E **22**
Florfield Pas. *E8* 6H **67**
(off Reading La.)
Florfield Rd. E8 . . . . .6H **67**
Florian SE5 . . . . .1E **120**
Florian Av. SM1: Sutt 4B **166**
Florian Ct. *E16* 5J **87**
(off Hastings Rd.)
Florian Rd. SW15 . . . . .4G **117**
Florida Cl. WD23: B Hea 2C **26**
Florida Ct. *BR2: Brom* 4H **159**
(off Westmoreland Rd.)
Florida Rd. CR7: Thor H 1B **156**
Florida St. E2 .3G **85**
Florin Ct. EC1 .5C **8**
N18 . . . . .4K **33**
SE1 . . . . .7J **15**
(off Tanner St.)
Floris Pl. SW4 . . . . .3G **119**
Floriston Av. UB10: Hil 7E **56**
Floriston Cl. HA7: Stan 1B **42**
Floriston Ct. UB5: N'olt 5F **59**
Floriston Gdns. HA7: Stan 1B **42**
Florys Ct. SW19 . . . . .1G **135**
Floss St. SW15 . . . . .2E **116**
Flotilla Ho. SW18 . . . . .3A **118**
Flounder Ho. *SE8* 7D **104**
(off Creative Rd.)
Flower & Dean Wlk. E1 . . . . .6K **9** (5F **85**)
Flowerdown Ct. *HA4: Eastc* 6J **39**
(off Lidgould Gro.)
Flower La. NW7 . . . . .5G **29**
Flower M. NW11 . . . . .6G **45**
Flower Pot Cl. N15 . . . . .6F **49**
Flowers Av. HA4: Eastc, Ruis 6J **39**
Flowers Cl. NW2 . . . . .3C **62**
Flowersmead SW17 . . . . .2E **136**
Flowers M. N19 . . . . .2G **65**
Flower Wlk., The SW7 . . . . .6A **10** (2A **100**)
Floyd Rd. SE7 . . . . .5A **106**
Floyer Cl. TW10: Rich 5F **115**
Fludyer St. SE13 . . . . .4G **123**
Flutemakers M. SW4 . . . . .5H **119**
Flying Angel Ho. *E16* 7K **87**
(off Victoria Dock Rd.)
Flynn Ct. *E14* .7C **86**
(off Garford St.)
Foley Ho. *E1* 6J **85**
(off Tarling St.)
Foley St. W1 . . . . .6A **6** (5G **83**)
Folgate St. E1 . . . . .5H **9** (5E **84**)
(not continuous)
Foliot Ho. *N1* .2K **83**
(off Priory Grn. Est.)
Foliot St. W12 . . . . .6B **80**
Folkestone Ct. *UB5: N'olt* 5F **59**
(off Newmarket Av.)
Folkestone Ho. *SE17* 5E **102**
(off Upnor Way)
Folkestone Rd. E6 . . . . .2E **88**
E17 . . . . .4D **50**
N18 . . . . .4B **34**
Folkingham La. NW9 . . . . .1K **43**
Folkington Cnr. N12 . . . . .5C **30**
Folland *NW9* 2B **44**
(off Hundred Acre)
Follett Ho. *SW10* 7B **100**
(off Worlds End Est.)
Follett St. E14 .6E **86**
Follingham Ct. *N1* 1H **9**
(off Drysdale Pl.)
Folly Brook & Darland's Lake Nature Reserve
. . . . .3B 30
Folly La. E4 . . . . .6G **35**
E17 . . . . .1A **50**
Folly M. W11 . . . . .6H **81**
Folly Wall E14 . . . . .2E **104**
Fonda Ct. *E14* .7C **86**
(off Premiere Pl.)
Fondant Ct. *E3* 2D **86**
(off Taylor Pl.)
Fontaine Ho. *E17* 4C **50**
(off Hoe St.)
Fontaine Rd. SW16 . . . . .7K **137**
Fontarabia Rd. SW11 . . . . .4E **118**
Fontayne Av. RM1: Rom 2K **55**
Fontenelle SE5 . . . . .1E **120**
Fontenoy Ho. *SE11* 4B **102**
(off Kennington La.)
Fontenoy Rd. SW12 . . . . .2F **137**
Fonteyne Gdns. IG8: Wfd G 2B **52**
Fonthill Cl. SE20 . . . . .2G **157**
Fonthill Ho. *SW1* 5K **17**
(part of Abbots Mnr.)
W14 . . . . .3G **99**
(off Russell Rd.)
Fonthill M. N4 .2K **65**
Fonthill Rd. N4 . . . . .1K **65**
Font Hills N2 . . . . .2A **46**
Fontley Way SW15 . . . . .7C **116**
Fontmell Cl. TW15: Ashf 5C **128**
Fontmell Pk. TW15: Ashf 5B **128**
Fontwell Cl. HA3: Hrw W 7D **26**
UB5: N'olt 6E **58**
Fontwell Dr. BR2: Brom 5E **160**
Football La. HA1: Harr 1K **59**
Footpath, The SW15 . . . . .6C **116**
FOOTS CRAY .6C 144
Foots Cray High St. DA14: Sidc 6C **144**
Foots Cray La. DA14: Sidc 1C **144**
Foots Cray Meadows (Nature Reserve)
. . . . .4D 144
Footscray Rd. SE9 . . . . .6E **124**
Forber Ho. *E2* 3J **85**
(off Cornwall Av.)
Forbes Cl. NW2 .3C **62**
Forbes Ho. *E7* 5A **70**
(off Romford Rd.)
W4 . . . . .5G **97**
(off Stonehill Rd.)
Forbes St. E1 . . . . .6G **85**
Forbes Way HA4: Ruis 2K **57**
Forburg Rd. N16 . . . . .1G **67**
Fordbridge Ct. TW15: Ashf 6A **128**
Fordbridge Pk. TW16: Sun 6H **147**
Fordbridge Rd. TW15: Ashf 6A **128**
TW16: Sun 6G **147**
TW17: Shep 6G **147**
FORDBRIDGE RDBT. **6A 128**
Ford Cl. CR7: Thor H 5B **156**
E3 . . . . .2A **86**
HA1: Harr 7H **41**
TW15: Ashf 6A **128**
TW17: Shep 4C **146**
Forde Av. BR1: Brom 3A **160**
Fordel Rd. SE6 . . . . .1E **140**
Ford End IG8: Wfd G 6E **36**
Fordgate Bus. Pk. DA17: Belv 2J **109**
Fordham *KT1: King T* 2G **151**
(off Excelsior Cl.)
Fordham Cl. EN4: Cockf 3H **21**
KT4: Wor Pk 1D **164**
Fordham Ho. *SE14* 7A **104**
(off Angus St.)
Fordham Rd. EN4: Cockf 3G **21**
Fordham St. E1 . . . . .6G **85**
Fordhook Av. W5 . . . . .1F **97**
Ford Ho. EN5: New Bar 5E **20**
Fordie Ho. *SW1* 2F **17**
(off Sloane St.)
Ford Ind. Pk. RM9: Dag 4H **91**
Fordingley Rd. W9 . . . . .3H **81**
Fordington Ho. SE26 . . . . .3G **139**
Fordington Rd. N6 . . . . .5D **46**
Ford Lodge RM7: Rom 4K **55**
Fordmill Rd. SE6 . . . . .2C **140**
Ford Rd. E3 . . . . .2B **86**
RM9: Dag 7F **73**
RM10: Dag 7F **73**
TW15: Ashf 4B **128**
Fords Gro. N21 . . . . .1H **33**
Fords Pk. Rd. E16 . . . . .5J **87**
Fords Pl. HA6: Nwood 2J **39**
Ford Sq. E1 . . . . .5H **85**
Ford St. E3 . . . . .1A **86**
E16 . . . . .6H **87**
Fordview Ind. Est. RM13: Rain 3K **91**
Fordwich Cl. BR6: Orp 7K **161**
Fordwych Rd. NW2 . . . . .4G **63**
Fordyce Rd. SE13 . . . . .6E **122**
Fordyke Rd. RM8: Dag 2F **73**
Foreign St. SE5 . . . . .2B **120**
Foreland Ct. NW4 . . . . .1F **45**
Foreland Ho. *W11* 7G **81**
(off Walmer Rd.)
Foreland St. SE18 . . . . .4H **107**
Forelle Way SM5: Cars 7D **166**
Foreman Ct. TW1: Twick 1K **131**
Foreman Ho. *SE4* 4K **121**
(off Billingford Cl.)
Foreshore SE8 . . . . .4B **104**
Forest, The E11 . . . . .4G **51**
Forest App. E4 . . . . .1B **36**
IG8: Wfd G 7D **36**
Forest Av. E4 .1B **36**
IG7: Chig 5K **37**
Forest Bus. Pk. E10 . . . . .7K **49**
Forest Cl. BR7: Chst 1E **160**
E11 . . . . .5J **51**
IG8: Wfd G 3E **36**
N10 . . . . .1F **47**
NW6 . . . . .7G **63**
Forest Ct. E4 .1C **36**
E11 . . . . .4G **51**
N12 . . . . .5E **30**
Forest Cft. SE23 . . . . .2H **139**
FORESTDALE 7B 170
Forestdale N14 . . . . .4C **32**
Forestdale Cen., The CR0: Sels 7B **170**
Forest Dene Ct. SM2: Sutt 6A **166**
Forest Dr. BR2: Kes 4C **172**
BR3: Beck 7B **158**
E12 . . . . .3B **70**
IG8: Wfd G 7A **36**
TW16: Sun 7H **129**
Forest Dr. E. E11 . . . . .7F **51**
Forest Dr. W. E11 . . . . .7E **50**
Forest Edge IG9: Buck H 4F **37**
Forester Ho. *E14* 7A **86**
(off Victory Pl.)
Forester Rd. SE15 . . . . .3H **121**
Foresters Cl. SM6: Wall 7H **167**
Foresters Cres. DA7: Bex 4H **127**
Foresters Dr. E17 . . . . .4F **51**
SM6: Wall 7H **167**
Forest Gdns. N17 . . . . .2F **49**
FOREST GATE 5J 69
Forest Ga. NW9 . . . . .4A **44**
Forest Ga. Retreat *E7* 5J **69**
(off Odessa Rd.)
Forest Glade E4 . . . . .4B **36**
E11 . . . . .6G **51**
Forest Gro. E8 .6F **67**
Forest Hgts. IG9: Buck H 2D **36**
FOREST HILL .2J 139
Forest Hill Bus. Cen. *SE23* 2J **139**
(off Clyde Va.)
Forest Hill Ind. Est. SE23 . . . . .2J **139**
Forest Hill Pool 2J 139
Forest Hill Rd. SE22 . . . . .5H **121**
SE23 .5H **121**
Forest Hill School Sports Cen. 3K 139
Forestholme Cl. SE23 . . . . .2J **139**
Forest Ind. Pk. IG6: Ilf 1J **53**
Forest La. E7 . . . . .5G **69**
E15 . . . . .5G **69**
IG7: Chig 5K **37**
Forest Lodge *SE23* 3J **139**
(off Dartmouth Rd.)
Forest Mt. Rd. IG8: Wfd G 7A **36**
Forest Point *E7* 5K **69**
(off Windsor Rd.)
Fore St. EC2 . . . . .6D **8** (5C **84**)
HA5: Eastc 4H **39**
N9 . . . . .4B **34**
N18 . . . . .6A **34**
Fore St. Av. EC2 . . . . .6E **8** (5D **84**)
Forest Ridge BR2: Kes 4C **172**
BR3: Beck 3C **158**
Forest Ri. E17 .3F **51**
Forest Rd. E7 . . . . .4J **69**
E8 . . . . .6F **67**
E11 . . . . .7F **51**
E17 . . . . .4A **50**
IG6: Chig, Ilf 2H **53**
IG8: Wfd G 3D **36**
N9 . . . . .1C **34**
N17 . . . . .4J **49**
RM7: Mawney 3H **55**
SM3: Sutt 1J **165**
TW9: Kew 7G **97**
TW13: Felt 2A **130**
Forest Side E4 .1C **36**
E7 . . . . .4K **69**
IG9: Buck H 1F **37**
KT4: Wor Pk 1B **164**
Forest St. E7 . . . . .5J **69**
Forest Ter. IG7: Chig 5K **37**
Forest Trad. Est. E17 . . . . .3K **49**
Forest Vw. E4 . . . . .7K **25**, 1B **36**
E11 . . . . .7H **51**
Forest Vw. Av. E10 . . . . .5F **51**
Forest Vw. Rd. E12 . . . . .4C **70**
E17 . . . . .1E **50**
Forest Wlk. N10 . . . . .1F **47**
Forest Way
BR5: St M Cry 5K **161**
DA15: Sidc 7H **125**
IG8: Wfd G 4E **36**
N19 . . . . .2G **65**
Forfar Rd. N22 .1B **48**
SW11 .1E **118**
Forge Cl. BR2: Hayes 1J **171**
UB3: Harl 6F **93**
Forge Cotts. W5 . . . . .1D **96**
Forge Dr. KT10: Clay 7A **162**

Forge La. HA6: Nwood 1G 39
  SM3: Cheam 7G 165
  TW10: Ham 1E 132
  TW13: Hanw 5C 130
  TW16: Sun 3J 147
Forge M. CRO: Addtn 5C 170
  TW16: Sun 5D 68
    (off Forge La.)
Forge Pl. NW1 . . . . .6E 64
Forge Sq. E14 . . . . .4D 104
Forlong Path UB5: N'olt 6C 58
    (off Cowings Mead)
Forman Pl. N16 . . . . .4F 67
Formation, The E16 . . . . .2F 107
    (off Woolwich Mnr. Way)
Formby Av. HA7: Stan 3C 42
Formby Cl. N7 . . . . .5A 66
    (off Morgan Rd.)
Formosa Ho. E1 . . . . .4A 86
    (off Ernest St.)
Formosa St. W9 . . . . .4K 81
Formunt Cl. E16 . . . . .5H 87
Forres Gdns. NW11 . . . . .6J 45
Forrester Path SE26 . . . . . . .4J 139
Forresters Apartments IG11: Bark . .7G 71
    (off Linton Rd.)
Forrest Gdns. SW16 . . . . . . .3K 155
Forris Av. UB3: Hayes 1H 93
Forset Ct. W2 . . . . .7D 4
    (off Edgware Rd.)
Forset St. W1 . . . . .7D 4 (6C 82)
    (not continuous)
Forstal Cl. BR2: Brom 3J 159
Forster Cl. IG8: Wfd G 7A 36
Forster Ho. BR1: Brom 4F 141
  SW17 . . . . .3B 136
    (off Grosvenor Way)
Forster Rd. BR3: Beck 3A 158
  E17 . . . . .6A 50
  N17 . . . . .3F 49
  SW2 . . . . .7J 119
Forsters Cl. RM6: Chad H 6F 55
Forsters Way UB4: Yead 6K 75
Forston St. N1 . . . . .2C 84
Forsyte Cres. SE19 . . . . .1E 156
Forsyte Ho. SW3 . . . . .6D 16
Forsythe Shades Cl. BR3: Beck . . .1E 158
Forsyth Gdns. SE17 . . . . .6B 102
Forsyth Ho. E9 . . . . .7J 67
    (off Frampton Pk. Rd.)
  SW1 . . . . .5B 18
    (off Tachbrook St.)
Forsythia Cl. IG1: Ilf 5F 71
Forsyth Pl. EN1: Enf 5K 23
Forterie Gdns. IG3: Bark, Ilf 3A 72
Fortescue Av. E8 . . . . .7H 67
  TW2: Twick 3G 131
Fortescue Ho. HA8: Edg 1K 43
  SW19 . . . . .7B 136
Fortess Gro. NW5 . . . . .5G 65
Fortess Rd. NW5 . . . . .5F 65
Fortess Wlk. NW5 . . . . .5F 65
Fortess Yd. NW5 . . . . .4F 65
Forthbridge Rd. SW11 . . . . . . .4E 118
Forth Ho. E3 . . . . .2B 86
    (off Tredegar Rd.)
Fortis Cl. E16 . . . . .6A 88
Fortis Ct. N10 . . . . .3E 46
FORTIS GREEN 4D 46
Fortis Grn. N2 . . . . .4C 46
  N10 . . . . .4C 46
Fortis Grn. Av. N2 . . . . .3D 46
Fortis Grn. Rd. N10 . . . . .3E 46
Fortismere Av. N10 . . . . .3E 46
Fortius Apartments E3 . . . . . . .2C 86
    (off Tredegar La.)
Fortius Wlk. E20 . . . . .6E 68
Fortnam Rd. N19 . . . . .2H 65
Fortnum's Acre HA7: Stan 6E 26
Fort Rd. SE1 . . . . .4F 103
  UB5: N'olt 7E 58

Fortrose Cl. E14 . . . . .6F 87
Fortrose Gdns. SW2 . . . . . . .1J 137
    (not continuous)
Fort St. E1 . . . . .6H 9 (5E 84)
  E16 . . . . .1K 105
Fortuna Cl. N7 . . . . .6K 65
Fortuna Ho. E20 . . . . .5D 68
    (off Scarlet Cl.)
Fortune Av. HA8: Edg 1H 43
Fortune Cl. E18 . . . . .7F 67
    (off Queensbridge Rd.)
  IG11: Bark 2C 90
Fortunegate Rd. NW10 . . . . . .1A 80
FORTUNE GREEN 5J 63
Fortune Grn. Rd. NW6 . . . . . . .4J 63
Fortune Ho. EC1 . . . . .4D 8
    (off Fortune St.)
  SE11 . . . . .4J 19
Fortune Pl. SE1 . . . . .5F 103
Fortunes Mead UB5: N'olt 6C 58
Fortune St. EC1 . . . . . .4D 8 (4C 84)
Fortunes Wlk. E20 . . . . .5E 68
Fortune Theatre 1F 13
    (off Russell St.)
Fortune Wlk. SE28 . . . . .3H 107
    (off Broadwater Rd.)
Fortune Way NW10 . . . . .3C 80
Forty Acre La. E16 . . . . .5J 87
Forty Av. HA9: Wemb 3F 61
Forty Cl. HA9: Wemb 3F 61
Forty Footpath SW14 . . . . . . .3J 115
Forty Foot Way SE9 . . . . .7G 125
FORTY HILL 1K 23
Forty Hill EN2: Enf 1K 23
Forty La. HA9: Wemb 2H 61
Forum, The KT8: W Mole 4F 149
Forum Cl. E3 . . . . .1C 86
Forum Ho. HA9: Wemb 4G 61
Forum Magnum Sq. SE1 . . . . . .6H 13
    (off York Rd.)
Forumside HA8: Edg 6B 28
Forum Way HA8: Edg 6B 28
Forval Cl. CR4: Mitc 5D 154
Forward Bus. Cen., The E16 . . . .4F 87
Forward Dr. HA3: W'stone 4K 41
Fosbrooke Ho. SW8 . . . . .7J 101
    (off Davidson Gdns.)
Fosbury M. W2 . . . . .7K 81
Foscote Ct. W9 . . . . .4J 81
    (off Amberley Rd.)
Foscote M. W9 . . . . .4J 81
Foscote Rd. NW4 . . . . .6D 44
Foskett Ho. N2 . . . . .2B 46
    (off The Grange)
Foskett M. E8 . . . . .5F 67
Foskett Rd. SW6 . . . . .2H 117
Foss Av. CRO: Wadd 5A 168
Fossdene Rd. SE7 . . . . .5K 105
Fossdyke Cl. UB4: Yead 5C 76
Fosset Lodge DA7: Bex 1J 127
Fosse Way W13 . . . . .5A 78
Foss Ho. NW8 . . . . .2K 81
    (off Carlton Hill)
Fossil Ct. SE1 . . . . .7G 15
    (off Long La.)
Fossil Rd. SE13 . . . . .3C 122
Fossington Rd. DA17: Belv 4D 108
Foss Rd. SW17 . . . . .4B 136
Fossway RM8: Dag 2C 72
Foster Cl. E16 . . . . .7H 87
    (off Tarling Rd.)
  NW1 . . . . .7G 65
    (off Royal College St.)
  NW4 . . . . .4E 44
Foster Ho. SE14 . . . . .1B 122
Foster La. EC2 . . . . . .7C 8 (6C 84)
Foster Rd. E13 . . . . .4J 87
  W3 . . . . .7A 80
  W4 . . . . .5K 97
Fosters Cl. BR7: Chst 5D 142
  E18 . . . . .1K 51

Foster St. NW4 . . . . .4E 44
Foster's Way SW18 . . . . .1K 135
Foster Wlk. NW4 . . . . .4E 44
Fothergill Cl. E13 . . . . .2J 87
Fothergill Dr. N21 . . . . .5D 22
Fotheringham Rd.
  EN1: Enf 4A 24
    (not continuous)
Foubert's Pl. W1 . . . . . .1A 12 (6G 83)
Foulden Rd. N16 . . . . .4F 67
Foulden Ter. N16 . . . . .4F 67
Foulis Ter. SW7 . . . . .5B 16 (5B 100)
Foulser Rd. SW17 . . . . .3D 136
Foulsham Rd. CR7: Thor H 3C 156
Foundary Bldg. E14 . . . . .6G 87
Foundation Pl. SE9 . . . . .5E 124
    (off Archery Rd.)
Founder Cl. E6 . . . . .6F 89
Founders Cl. UB5: N'olt 3D 76
Founders Ct. EC2 . . . . .7E 8
Founders Gdns. SE19 . . . . .7C 138
Founders Ho. SW1 . . . . .6C 18
    (off Aylesford St.)
Foundling Ct. WC1 . . . . .3E 6
    (off Brunswick Cen.)
Foundling Mus., The 3F 7
Foundry, The EC2 . . . . .2H 9
    (off Dereham Pl.)
Foundry Cl. SE16 . . . . .1A 104
Foundry Ho. E14 . . . . .5D 86
    (off Morris Rd.)
  SW8 . . . . .1F 119
    (off Lockington Rd.)
Foundry M. E17 . . . . .3E 50
  NW1 . . . . .3B 6 (4G 83)
  TW3: Houn 4F 113
Foundry Pl. E1 . . . . .5J 85
    (off Jubilee St.)
  SW18 . . . . .7K 117
Fountain Cl. SE18 . . . . .5F 107
  UB8: Hil 5E 74
Fountain Ct. DA15: Sidc 6B 126
  EC4 . . . . .2J 13 (7A 84)
  SE23 . . . . .2K 139
  SW1 . . . . .2F 99
    (off Buckingham Pal. Rd.)
  W11 . . . . .2F 99
    (off Clearwater Ter.)
Fountain Dr. SE19 . . . . .4F 139
  SM5: Cars 7D 166
Fountain Grn. Sq. SE16 . . . . . . .2G 103
Fountain Ho. CR4: Mitc 2D 154
  E2 . . . . .3J 9
    (off Redchurch St.)
  NW6 . . . . .7G 63
  SE16 . . . . .2G 103
    (off Bermondsey Wall E.)
  SW6 . . . . .2A 118
  W1 . . . . .4G 11
    (off Park St.)
Fountain M. N5 . . . . .4C 66
    (off Highbury Grange)
  NW3 . . . . .6D 64
Fountain Pl. SW9 . . . . .1A 120
Fountain Rd. CR7: Thor H 3C 156
  SW17 . . . . .5B 136
FOUNTAIN RDBT. 4A 152
Fountains, The N3 . . . . .3J 7
    (off Ballards La.)
Fountains Av. TW13: Hanw 3D 130
Fountains Cl. TW13: Hanw 2D 130
    (not continuous)
Fountains Cres. N14 . . . . .7D 22
Fountain Sq. SW1 . . .3K 17 (4F 101)
Fountayne Bus. Cen. N15 . . . . . .4G 49
Fountayne Rd. N15 . . . . .4G 49
  N16 . . . . .2G 67
Fount St. SW8 . . . . .7H 101
Fouracre Path SE25 . . . . .6E 156
Four Acres N12 . . . . .3E 30
Fouracres EN3: Enf H 1F 25

Four Dials E20 . . . . .6E 68
  (within Westfield Stratford City Shop. Cen.)
Fourland Wlk. HA8: Edg 6D 28
Fournier St. E1 . . . . .5J 9 (5F 85)
Fourscore Mans. E8 . . . . .7G 67
    (off Shrubland Rd.)
Four Seasons Cl. E3 . . . . .2C 86
Four Seasons Cres. SM3: Sutt . . .2H 165
Four Sq. Ct. TW3: Houn 6E 112
Fourth Av. E12 . . . . .4D 70
  RM7: Rush G 1K 73
  UB3: Hayes 1H 93
  W10 . . . . .4G 81
Fourth Cross Rd. TW2: Twick 2H 131
Four Wents, The E4 . . . . .1A 36
Fovant Ct. SW8 . . . . .2G 119
Fowey Av. IG4: Ilf 5B 52
Fowey Cl. E1 . . . . .1H 103
Fowey Ho. SE11 . . . . .5K 19
Fowler Cl. SW11 . . . . .3B 118
Fowler Ho. N15 . . . . .5D 48
    (off South Gro.)
Fowler Rd. CR4: Mitc 2E 154
  E7 . . . . .4J 69
  N1 . . . . .1B 84
Fowlers Cl. DA14: Sidc 5E 144
Fowlers M. N19 . . . . .2G 65
    (off Holloway Rd.)
Fowler's Wlk. W5 . . . . .4D 78
Fownes St. SW11 . . . . .3C 118
Fox & Knot St. EC1 . . . . .5B 8
Foxberry Rd. SE4 . . . . .3A 122
Foxborough Gdns. SE4 . . . . . . .5C 122
Foxbourne Rd. SW17 . . . . .2E 136
Foxbury Av. BR7: Chst 6H 143
Foxbury Cl. BR1: Brom 6K 141
Foxbury Ho. BR1: Brom 6J 141
Fox Cl. BR6: Chels 5K 173
  E1 . . . . .4J 85
  E16 . . . . .5J 87
Foxcombe CRO: New Ad 6D 170
    (not continuous)
Foxcombe Cl. E6 . . . . .2B 88
Foxcombe Rd. SW15 . . . . .1C 134
Foxcote SE5 . . . . .5E 102
Foxcroft WC1 . . . . .1H 7
    (off Penton Ri.)
Foxcroft Rd. SE18 . . . . .1F 125
Foxdene Cl. E18 . . . . .3K 51
Foxearth Spur CR2: Sels 7J 169
Foxes Dale BR2: Brom 3F 159
  SE3 . . . . .3J 123
Foxfield NW1 . . . . .1F 83
    (off Arlington Rd.)
Foxfield Rd. BR6: Orp 2H 173
Foxglove Cl. DA15: Sidc 6A 126
  N9 . . . . .1D 34
  UB1: S'hall 7C 76
Foxglove Ct. E3 . . . . .2C 86
    (off Four Seasons Cl.)
  HA0: Wemb 2E 78
Foxglove Gdns. E11 . . . . .4A 52
Foxglove La. KT9: Chess 4G 163
Foxglove Path SE28 . . . . .1J 107
    (off Martins Pl.)
Foxglove Rd. RM7: Rush G 2K 73
Foxglove St. W12 . . . . .7B 80
Foxglove Way SM6: Wall 1F 167
Fox Gro. KT12: Walt T 7K 147
Foxgrove N14 . . . . .3D 32
Foxgrove Av. BR3: Beck 7D 140
Foxgrove Rd. BR3: Beck 7D 140
Foxham Rd. N19 . . . . .3H 65
Fox Hill SE19 . . . . .7F 139
Fox Hill Gdns. SE19 . . . . .7F 139
Foxhole Rd. SE9 . . . . .5C 124
Fox Hollow Cl. SE18 . . . . .5J 107
Fox Hollow Dr. DA7: Bex 3D 126

Foxholt Gdns. NW10 7J **61**
Foxhome Cl. BR7: Chst 6E **142**
Fox Ho. Rd. DA17: Belv 5H **109**
(not continuous)
Foxlands Cres. RM10: Dag 5J **73**
Foxlands La. RM10: Dag 5K **73**
Foxlands Rd. RM10: Dag 5J **73**
Fox La. BR2: Kes 5K **171**
N13 2E **32**
W5 4E **78**
Foxleas Ct. BR1: Brom 7G **141**
Foxlees HA0: Wemb 4A **60**
Foxley Cl. E8 5G **67**
Foxley Ct. SM2: Sutt 7A **166**
Foxley Ho. *E3 3D **86***
(off Bow Rd.)
Foxley Rd. CR7: Thor H 4B **156**
SW9 7A **102**
Foxley Sq. SW9 7B **102**
Foxmead Cl. EN2: Enf 3E **22**
Foxmore St. SW11 1D **118**
Fox Rd. E16 5H **87**
Fox's Path CR4: Mitc 2C **154**
Fox's Yd. E2 3K **9**
Foxton Gro. CR4: Mitc 2B **154**
Foxton Ho. *E16 2E **106***
(off Albert Rd.)
Foxton M. TW10: Rich 6E **114**
Foxwarren KT10: Clay 7A **162**
Foxwell M. SE4 3A **122**
Foxwell St. SE4 3A **122**
Foxwood Cl. NW7 4F **29**
TW13: Felt 3K **129**
Foxwood Grn. Cl. EN1: Enf 6K **23**
Fox Wood Nature Reserve 4E **78**
Foxwood Rd. SE3 4H **123**
Foyle Rd. N17 1G **49**
SE3 6H **105**
Framfield Cl. N12 3D **30**
Framfield Ct. *EN1: Enf 6K **23***
(off Queen Anne's Gdns.)
Framfield Rd. CR4: Mitc 7E **136**
N5 5B **66**
W7 6J **77**
Framlingham Cl. E5 2J **67**
Framlingham Ct. *RM6: Chad H 5B **54***
(off Norwich Cres.)
Framlingham Cres. SE9 4C **142**
Frampton *NW1 7H **65***
(off Wrotham Rd.)
Frampton Cl. IG6: Ilf 4H **53**
SM2: Sutt 7J **165**
Frampton Ct. *W3 2J **97***
(off Avenue Rd.)
Frampton Ho. *NW8 4B **4***
(off Frampton St.)
Frampton Pk. Est. E9 7J **67**
Frampton Pk. Rd. E9 6J **67**
Frampton Rd. TW4: Houn 5C **112**
Frampton St. NW8 4B **4** (4B **82**)
Frampton Ter. SE9 3F **143**
Francemary Rd. SE4 5C **122**
Frances Ct. E17 6C **50**
SE25 3F **157**
Frances Rd. E4 6H **35**
Frances St. SE18 3D **106**
Frances Wharf E14 6B **86**
Franche Ct. Rd. SW17 3A **136**
Francis & Dick James Ct. NW7 7B **30**
Francis Av. DA7: Bex 2G **127**
IG1: Ilf 2H **71**
TW13: Felt 3J **129**
Francis Bacon Ct. *SE16 4H **103***
(off Galleywall Rd.)
Francis Barber Cl. SW16 5K **137**
Francis Bentley M. SW4 3G **119**
Franciscan Rd. SW17 5D **136**
Francis Chichester Way SW11 1E **118**
Francis Cl. E14 4F **105**
KT19: Ewe 4K **163**
TW17: Shep 4C **146**
Francis Ct. EC1 5A **8**
*KT5: Surb 4E **150***
(off Cranes Pk. Av.)
*NW7 5G **29***
(off Watford Way)
*SE14 6K **103***
(off Myers La.)
Francis Crick Institute 2H **83**
Francis Gro. SW19 6H **135**
Francis Harvey Way SE8 1B **122**
Francis Ho. *N1 1E **84***
(off Colville Est.)
*SW10 7K **99***
(off Coleridge Gdns.)
*SW18 4A **118***
(off Eltringham St.)
Francis M. SE12 7J **123**
Francis Pl. *N6 7F **47***
(off Shepherd's Cl.)
Francis Rd. CR0: C'don 7B **156**
E10 1E **68**
HA1: Harr 5A **42**
HA5: Eastc 5A **40**
IG1: Ilf 2H **71**
N2 4D **46**
SM6: Wall 6G **167**
TW4: Houn 2B **112**
UB6: G'frd 2B **78**
Francis St. E15 5G **69**
IG1: Ilf 2H **71**
SW1 3A **18** (4G **101**)
Francis Ter. N19 3G **65**
Francis Ter. M. N19 3G **65**
Francis Wlk. N1 1K **83**
Francklyn Gdns. HA8: Edg 3B **28**
Franconia Rd. SW4 5H **119**
Frank Bailey Wlk. E12 6E **70**
Frank Beswick Ho. *SW6 6H **99***
(off Clem Attlee Ct.)
Frank Burton Cl. SE7 5K **105**
Frank Dixon Cl. SE21 7E **120**
Frank Dixon Way SE21 1E **138**
Frankfurt Rd. SE24 5C **120**
Frank Godley Ct. DA14: Sidc 5B **144**
Frankham Ho. *SE8 7C **104***
(off Frankham St.)
Frankham St. SE8 7C **104**
Frank Ho. *SW8 7J **101***
(off Wyvil Rd.)
Frankland Cl. IG8: Wfd G 5F **37**
SE16 3H **103**
Frankland Rd. E4 5H **35**
SW7 2A **16** (3B **100**)
Franklin Bldg. E14 2C **104**
Franklin Cl. KT1: King T 3G **151**
N20 7F **21**
SE13 1D **122**
SE27 3B **138**
Franklin Cotts. HA7: Stan 4G **27**
Franklin Cres. CR4: Mitc 4G **155**
Franklin Ho. BR2: Brom 3G **159**
*E1 1H **103***
(off Watts St.)
*E14 6F **87***
(off E. India Dock Rd.)
*NW6 3J **81***
(off Carlton Va.)
Franklin Ind. Est. *SE20 1J **157***
(off Franklin Rd.)
Franklin Pas. SE9 3C **124**
Franklin Pl. SE13 1D **122**
Franklin Rd. DA7: Bex 1E **126**
SE20 7J **139**
Franklins M. HA2: Harr 2G **59**
Franklin Sq. W14 5H **99**
Franklin's Row SW3 5F **17** (5D **100**)
Franklin St. E3 3D **86**
N15 6E **48**
Franklin Way CR0: Wadd 7J **155**
Franklyn Rd. KT12: Walt T 6J **147**
NW10 6B **62**
Frank M. SE1 4H **103**
Franks Av. KT3: N Mald 4J **151**
Frank Soskice Ho. *SW6 6H **99***
(off Clem Attlee Ct.)
Frank St. E13 4J **87**
Franks Wood Av. BR5: Pet W 5F **161**
Frankswood Av. UB7: Yiew 6B **74**
Frank Towell Ct. TW14: Felt 7J **111**
Frank Whipple Pl. *E14 6A **86***
(off Repton St.)
Frank Whymark Ho. *SE16 2J **103***
(off Rupack St.)
Franlaw Cres. N13 4H **33**
Fransfield Gro. SE26 3H **139**
Frans Hals Ct. E14 3F **105**
Franshams *WD23: B Hea 2D **26***
(off Hartsbourne Rd.)
Frant Cl. SE20 7J **139**
Franthorne Way SE6 2D **140**
Frant Rd. CR7: Thor H 5B **156**
Fraserburgh Ho. *E3 2B **86***
(off Vernon Rd.)
Fraser Cl. DA5: Bexl 1J **145**
E6 6C **88**
Fraser Ct. *E14 5E **104***
(off Ferry St.)
SE1 7D **14**
*SW11 1C **118***
(off Surrey La. Est.)
Fraser Ho. TW8: Bford 5F **97**
Fraser Rd. DA8: Erith 5K **109**
E17 5D **50**
N9 3C **34**
UB6: G'frd 1B **78**
Fraser St. W4 5A **98**
Frating Cres. IG8: Wfd G 6E **36**
Frazer Av. HA4: Ruis 5A **58**
Frazier St. SE1 7J **13** (2A **102**)
Frean St. SE16 3G **103**
Frearson Ho. *WC1 1H **7***
(off Penton Ri.)
Freda Corbett Cl. SE15 7G **103**
Freda St. SE16 7K **15** (3G **103**)
Frederica Ct. SW2 1B **138**
Frederica Rd. E4 1A **36**
Frederica St. N7 7K **65**
Frederick Charrington Ho. *E1 4J **85***
(off Wickford St.)
Frederick Cl. SM1: Sutt 4H **165**
W2 2D **10** (7D **82**)
Frederick Ct. *SW3 4F **17***
(off Duke of York Sq.)
Frederick Cres. EN3: Enf H 2D **24**
SW9 7B **102**
Frederick Dobson Ho. *W11 7G **81***
(off Cowling Cl.)
Frederick Gdns. CR0: C'don 6B **156**
SM1: Sutt 5H **165**
Frederick Ho. *SE18 4C **106***
(off Pett St.)
Frederick Pl. *N8 6H **47***
(off Crouch Hall Rd.)
SE18 5F **107**
Frederick Rd. RM13: Rain 2K **91**
SE17 6B **102**
SM1: Sutt 5H **165**
Frederick's Pl. EC2 1E **14** (6D **84**)
Fredericks Pl. N12 4F **31**
Frederick Sq. *SE16 7A **86***
(off Sovereign Cres.)
Frederick's Row EC1 1A **8** (3B **84**)
Frederick St. WC1 2G **7** (3K **83**)
Frederick Ter. E8 7F **67**
Frederick Vs. *W7 1J **95***
(off Lwr. Boston Rd.)
Frederic M. SW1 7F **11**
Frederic St. E17 5A **50**
Fredora Av. UB4: Hayes 4H **75**
Fred Styles Ho. SE7 6A **106**
Fred Tibble Ct. RM9: Dag 4E **72**
Fred White Wlk. N7 6J **65**
Freedom Cl. E17 4A **50**
Freedom Rd. N17 2D **48**
Freedom St. SW11 2D **118**
Freegrove Rd. N7 5J **65**
(not continuous)
Freehold Ind. Est. TW4: Houn 5A **112**
Freeland Ct. DA15: Sidc 3A **144**
Freeland Pk. NW4 2G **45**
Freeland Rd. W5 7F **79**
Freelands Av. CR2: Sels 7K **169**
Freelands Gro. BR1: Brom 1K **159**
Freelands Rd. BR1: Brom 1K **159**
Freeling Ho. *NW8 1B **82***
(off Dorman Way)
Freeling St. N1 7K **65**
(Carnoustie Dr.)
N1 7J **65**
(Pembroke St.)
Freeman Cl. TW17: Shep 4G **147**
UB5: N'olt 7C **58**
Freeman Ct. N7 3J **65**
SW16 2J **155**
Freeman Dr. KT8: W Mole 3D **148**
Freeman Ho. *SE11 4B **102***
(off George Mathers Rd.)
Freeman Rd. SM4: Mord 5B **154**
Freemans La. UB3: Hayes 7G **75**
Freemantle Av. EN3: Pond E 5E **24**
Freemantle St. SE17 5E **102**
Freeman Wlk. SE9 5A **124**
Freemasons' Hall 7F **7**
Freemasons Pl. *CR0: C'don 1E **168***
(off Freemasons Rd.)
Freemasons Rd. CR0: C'don 1E **168**
E16 5K **87**
Freesia Cl. BR6: Chels 5K **173**
Freethorpe Cl. SE19 7D **138**
Free Trade Wharf E1 7K **85**
Freezeland Way UB10: Hil 6D **56**
Freight La. N1 7H **65**
Freightliners City Farm 6A **66**
Freke Rd. SW11 3E **118**
Fremantle Ho. *E1 4H **85***
(off Somerford St.)
Fremantle Rd. DA17: Belv 4G **109**
IG6: Ilf 2F **53**
Fremantle Way UB3: Hayes 7H **75**
Fremont St. E9 1H **85**
(not continuous)
French Horn Yd. WC1 6G **7**
French Ordinary Ct. EC3 2H **15**
French Pl. E1 2H **9** (3E **84**)
French St. TW16: Sun 2A **148**
Frendsbury Rd. SE4 4A **122**
Frensham Cl. UB1: S'hall 4D **76**
Frensham Ct. SW19 3A **154**
Frensham Dr. CR0: New Ad 7E **170**
SW15 3B **134**
Frensham Rd. SE9 2H **143**
Frensham St. SE15 6G **103**
Frere St. SW11 2C **118**
Fresham Ho. *BR2: Brom 3H **159***
(off Durham Rd.)
Freshfield Av. E8 7F **67**
Freshfield Cl. SE13 4F **123**
Freshfield Dr. N14 7A **22**
Freshfields CR0: C'don 1B **170**
Freshford St. SW18 3A **136**
Freshill La. UB1: S'hall 4E **76**
Freshwater Cl. SW17 6E **136**
Freshwater Ct. UB1: S'hall 3E **76**
*W1 6D **4***
(off Crawford St.)
Freshwater Rd. RM8: Dag 1D **72**
SW17 6E **136**
Freshwell Av. RM6: Chad H 4C **54**
Fresh Wharf Est. IG11: Bark 2F **89**
Fresh Wharf Rd. IG11: Bark 1F **89**
Freshwood Cl. BR3: Beck 1D **158**
Freshwood Way SM6: Wall 7F **167**
Freston Gdns. EN4: Cockf 5K **21**

Freston Pk. N3 . . . . .2H 45
Freston Rd. W10 . . . . .7F 81
W11 . . . . .7F 81
Freswick Ho. SE8 . . . . .4A 104
(off Chilton Gro.)
Freta Rd. DA6: Bex 5F 127
Freud Mus. 6A 64
Frewell Ho. EC1 . . . . .5J 7
(off Bourne Est.)
Frewin Rd. SW18 . . . . .1B 136
Friar M. SE27 . . . . .3B 138
Friar Rd. BR5: St M Cry 5K 161
UB4: Yead .4B 76
Friars Av. N20 . . . . .3H 31
SW15 . . . . .3B 134
Friars Cl. E4 .3K 35
IG1: Ilf 1H 71
SE1 . . . . .5B 14
UB5: N'olt .3B 76
Friars Ct. E17 . . . . .1B 50
RM7: Rush G 6K 55
SM6: Wall .4F 167
Friars Gdns. W3 . . . . .6K 79
Friarsgate NW10 . . . . .2H 79
Friars Ga. Cl. IG8: Wfd G 4D 36
Friars La. TW9: Rich 5D 114
Friars Mead E14 . . . . .3E 104
Friars M. SE9 . . . . .5E 124
Friars Pl. La. W3 . . . . .7K 79
Friars Rd. E6 .1B 88
Friars Stile Pl. TW10: Rich 6E 114
Friars Stile Rd. TW10: Rich 6E 114
Friar St. EC4 . . . . .1B 14 (6B 84)
Friars Wlk. N14 . . . . .7A 22
SE2 . . . . .5D 108
Friars Way W3 . . . . .6K 79
Friars Wood CRO: Sels 7A 170
Friary Cl. N12 . . . . .5H 31
Friary Ct. SW1 . . . . .5B 12
Friary Est. SE15 . . . . .6G 103
(not continuous)
Friary La. IG8: Wfd G 4D 36
Friary Pk. W3 .6K 79
Friary Pk. Ct. W3 . . . . .6J 79
Friary Rd. N12 . . . . .4G 31
N20 . . . . .4G 31
SE15 . . . . .7G 103
W3 . . . . .6J 79
Friary Way N12 . . . . .4H 31
FRIDAY HILL .2B 36
Friday Hill E4 .2B 36
Friday Hill E. E4 . . . . .3B 36
Friday Hill W. E4 . . . . .2B 36
Friday Rd. CR4: Mitc 7D 136
DA8: Erith .5K 109
Friday St. EC4 . . . . .2C 14 (7C 84)
Frideswide Pl. NW5 . . . . .5G 65
Friendly Pl. SE13 . . . . .1D 122
Friendly St. SE8 . . . . .2C 122
Friendly St. M. SE8 . . . . .2C 122
Friendship Ho. SE1 . . . . .7B 14
(off Belvedere Pl.)
Friendship Wlk. UB5: N'olt 3B 76
Friendship Way E15 . . . . .1E 86
Friends Rd. CRO: C'don 3D 168
Friend St. EC1 . . . . .1A 8 (3B 84)
FRIERN BARNET 5J 31
Friern Barnet La. N11 . . . . .2G 31
N20 . . . . .2G 31
Friern Barnet Rd. N11 . . . . .5J 31
Friern Bri. Retail Pk. N11 . . . . .6A 32
Friern Ct. N20 . . . . .3G 31
Friern Mt. Dr. N20 . . . . .7F 21
Friern Pk. N12 . . . . .5F 31
Friern Rd. SE22 . . . . .7G 121
(not continuous)
Friern Watch Av. N12 . . . . .4F 31
Frigate Ho. E14 . . . . .4E 104
(off Stebondale St.)
Frigate M. SE8 . . . . .6C 104
Frimley Av. SM6: Wall 5J 167

Frimley Cl. CRO: New Ad 7E 170
SW19 . . . . .2G 135
Frimley Ct. DA14: Sidc 5C 144
Frimley Cres. CRO: New Ad 7E 170
Frimley Gdns. CR4: Mitc 3C 154
Frimley Rd. IG3: Ilf 3J 71
KT9: Chess .5D 162
Frimley St. E1 .4K 85
(off Frimley Way)
Frimley Way E1 . . . . .4K 85
Fringewood Cl. HA6: Nwood 1D 38
Frinstead Ho. W10 . . . . .7F 81
(off Freston Rd.)
Frinsted Rd. DA8: Erith 7K 109
Frinton Ct. W13 . . . . .5B 78
(off Hardwick Grn.)
Frinton Dr. IG8: Wfd G 7A 36
Frinton M. IG2: Ilf 6E 52
Frinton Rd. DA14: Sidc 2E 144
E6 . . . . .3B 88
N15 . . . . .6E 48
SW17 . . . . .6E 136
Friston St. SW6 . . . . .2K 117
Friswell Pl. DA6: Bex 4G 127
Fritham Cl. KT3: N Mald 6A 152
Frith Ct. NW7 .7B 30
Frith Ho. NW8 .4B 4
(off Frampton St.)
Fryent Cl. NW9 . . . . .6G 43
Frith La. NW7 .7B 30
Frith Rd. CRO: C'don 2C 168
E11 . . . . .4E 68
Frith St. W1 . . . . .1C 12 (6H 83)
Frithville Ct. W12 . . . . .1E 98
(off Frithville Gdns.)
Frithville Gdns. W12 . . . . .1E 98
Frizlands La. RM10: Dag 2H 73
Frobisher Cl. HA5: Pinn 7B 40
Frobisher Ct. NW9 . . . . .2A 44
SE8 . . . . .5A 104
(off Evelyn St.)
SE10 . . . . .6F 105
(off Old Woolwich Rd.)
SE23 . . . . .2H 139
SM3: Cheam 7G 165
W12 . . . . .2E 98
(off Lime Gro.)
Frobisher Cres. EC2 . . . . .5D 8
(off Silk St.)
TW19: Stanw 7A 110
Frobisher Gdns. E10 . . . . .7D 50
TW19: Stanw 7A 110
Frobisher Ho. E1 . . . . .1H 103
(off Watts St.)
SW1 . . . . .7C 18
(off Dolphin Sq.)
Frobisher M. EN2: Enf 4J 23
Frobisher Pas. E14 . . . . .1C 104
Frobisher Pl. SE15 . . . . .1J 121
Frobisher Rd. E6 . . . . .6D 88
N8 . . . . .4A 48
Frobisher St. SE10 . . . . .6G 105
Frog La. RM13: Rain 6K 91
Frogley Rd. SE22 . . . . .4F 121
Frogmore SW18 . . . . .5J 117
Frogmore Av. UB4: Hayes 4G 75
Frogmore Cl. SM3: Cheam 3F 165
Frogmore Ct. UB2: S'hall 4D 94
Frogmore Gdns. SM3: Cheam 4G 75
UB4: Hayes .4G 75
Frogmore Ind. Est. N5 . . . . .5C 66
NW10 . . . . .3J 79
UB3: Hayes .2G 93
Frognal NW3 .4A 64
Frognal Av. DA14: Sidc 6A 144
HA1: Harr 4K 41
Frognal Cl. NW3 . . . . .5A 64
FROGNAL CORNER 6K 143
Frognal Ct. NW3 . . . . .6A 64
Frognal Gdns. NW3 . . . . .4A 64
Frognal La. NW3 . . . . .5K 63
Frognal Pde. NW3 . . . . .6A 64

Frognal Pl. DA14: Sidc 6A 144
Frognal Ri. NW3 . . . . .3A 64
Frognal Way NW3 . . . . .4A 64
Frogwell Cl. N15 . . . . .6D 48
Froissart Rd. SE9 . . . . .5B 124
Frome Ho. SE15 . . . . .4H 121
Frome Rd. N22 . . . . .3B 48
Frome St. N1 .2C 84
Fromondes Rd.
SM3: Cheam 5G 165
Frontenac NW10 . . . . .7D 62
Frontier Works N17 . . . . .6K 33
Frost Ct. NW9 .2A 44
(off Salk Cl.)
Frostic Wlk. E1 . . . . .6K 9 (5G 85)
Froude St. SW8 . . . . .2F 119
Fruen Rd. TW14: Felt 7H 111
Fruiterers Pas. EC4 . . . . .3D 14
(off Queen St. Pl.)
Fryatt Rd. N17 .7J 33
(not continuous)
Fryday Gro. M. SW12 . . . . .7G 119
(off Weir Rd.)
Frye Ct. E3 . . . . .3B 86
(off Benworth St.)
Frye Ho. E20 . . . . .6E 68
(off Penny Brookes St.)
Fryent Cl. NW9 . . . . .6G 43
Fryent Country Pk. (Local Nature Reserve)
. . . . .7G 43
Fryent Cres. NW9 . . . . .6A 44
Fryent Flds. NW9 . . . . .6A 44
Fryent Gro. NW9 . . . . .6A 44
Fryent Way NW9 . . . . .5G 43
Fryers Vw. SE4 . . . . .4K 121
(off Frendsbury Rd.)
Fry Ho. E6 . . . . .7A 70
Frying Pan Alley E1 . . . . .6J 9
Frying Pan Rd. E1 . . . . .7B 70
NW10 . . . . .1B 80
Frys Ct. SE10 .6E 104
(off Durnford St.)
Fryston Av. CRO: C'don 2G 169
Fuchsia Cl. RM7: Rush G 2K 73
Fuchsia St. SE2 . . . . .5B 108
Fulbeck Dr. NW9 . . . . .1A 44
Fulbeck Ho. N7 . . . . .6K 65
(off Sutterton St.)
Fulbeck Rd. N19 . . . . .4G 65
Fulbeck Wlk. HA8: Edg 2C 28
Fulbeck Way HA2: Harr 2G 41
Fulbourn KT1: King T 2G 151
(off Eureka Rd.)
Fulbourne Rd. E17 . . . . .1E 50
Fulbourne St. E1 . . . . .5H 85
Fulbrook M. N19 . . . . .4G 65
Fulcher Ho. N1 . . . . .1E 84
(off Colville Est.)
SE8 . . . . .5B 104
Fulford Rd. KT19: Ewe 7K 163
Fulford Rd. KT19: Ewe 7K 163
Fulford St. SE16 . . . . .2H 103
FULHAM 2G 117
FULHAM BROADWAY 7J 99
Fulham B'way. SW6 . . . . .7J 99
Fulham Bus. Exchange SW6 . . . . . .1A 118
(off The Boulevard)
Fulham B'way Shop. Cen. SW6 . . . . . . .7J 99
Fulham Cl. UB10: Hil 4E 74
Fulham Ct. SW6 . . . . .1J 117
Fulham FC 1F 117
Fulham High St. SW6 . . . . .2G 117
Fulham Island SW6 . . . . .7J 99
(off Fulham Rd.)
Fulham Palace 2G 117
Fulham Pal. Rd. SW6 . . . . .5E 98
W6 . . . . .5E 98
Fulham Pk. Gdns. SW6 . . . . .2H 117
Fulham Pk. Rd. SW6 . . . . .2H 117
Fulham Pools
Virgin Active 6G 99

Fulham Rd. SW3 . . . . .7A 16 (7K 99)
SW6 . . . . .2G 117
(not continuous)
SW10 . . . . .7A 16 (7K 99)
Fullbrooks Av. KT4: Wor Pk 1B 164
Fuller Cl. BR6: Chels 5K 173
E2 . . . . .4G 85
(off Cheshire St.)
WD23: Bush .1C 26
Fuller Ct. N8 . . . . .5H 47
Fuller Rd. RM8: Dag 3B 72
Fullers Av. IG8: Wfd G 7C 36
KT6: Surb 2F 163
Fullers Griffin Brewery & Vis. Cen. 6B 98
Fullers La. RM5: Col R 1J 55
Fullers Rd. E18 . . . . .7C 36
Fuller St. NW4 .4E 44
Fullers Way Nth. KT6: Surb 3F 163
Fullers Way Sth. KT9: Chess 4E 162
Fuller's Wood CRO: C'don 5C 170
Fullerton Cl. TW11: Tedd 6A 132
Fullerton Rd. CRO: C'don 7F 157
SM5: Cars .7C 166
SW18 . . . . .5K 117
Fuller Way UB3: Harl 5H 93
Fullwell Av. IG5: Ilf 1D 52
IG6: Ilf 1F 53
FULLWELL CROSS 2G 53
Fullwell Cross IG6: Ilf 2H 53
Fullwell Cross Leisure Cen. 2G 53
Fullwell Pde. IG5: Ilf 1E 52
Fullwood's M. N1 . . . . .1F 9 (3D 84)
Fulmar Cl. KT5: Surb 6F 151
Fulmar Ho. SE16 . . . . .4K 103
(off Tawny Way)
Fulmead St. SW6 . . . . .1K 117
Fulmer Cl. TW12: Hamp 5C 130
Fulmer Ho. NW8 . . . . .4D 4
(off Mallory St.)
UB8: Uxb 6A 56
Fulmer Rd. E16 . . . . .5B 88
Fulmer Way W13 . . . . .3B 96
Fulneck Pl. E1 .4J 85
Fulready Rd. E10 . . . . .5K 51
Fulstone Cl. TW4: Houn 4D 112
Fulthorp Rd. SE3 . . . . .2H 123
Fulton M. W2 .7A 82
Fulton Rd. HA9: Wemb 3G 61
FULWELL 4H 131
Fulwell Cl. IG5: Ilf 1E 52
UB1: S'hall 7G 77
(off Baird Av.)
Fulwell Golf Course 4H 131
Fulwell Pk. Av. TW2: Twick 2F 131
Fulwell Rd. TW11: Tedd 4H 131
Fulwood Av. HA0: Wemb 2F 79
Fulwood Cl. UB3: Hayes 6H 75
Fulwood Ct. HA3: Kenton 6A 42
Fulwood Gdns. TW1: Twick 6K 113
Fulwood Pl. WC1 . . . . .6H 7 (5K 83)
Fulwood Wlk. SW19 . . . . .1G 135
Funky Footprints Nature Reserve 6C 146
Furber St. W6 .3D 98
Furham Fld. HA5: Hat E 7A 26
Furley Ho. SE15 . . . . .7G 103
(off Peckham Pk. Rd.)
Furley Rd. SE15 . . . . .7G 103
Furlong Av. CR4: Mitc 3C 154
Furlong Cl. SM6: Wall 1F 167
Furlong Rd. N7 . . . . .6A 66
Furmage St. SW18 . . . . .7K 117
Furneaux Av. SE27 . . . . .5B 138
Furness Ho. SW1 . . . . .5J 17
(part of Abbots Mnr.)
Furness Rd. HA2: Harr 7F 41
NW10 . . . . .2C 80
SM4: Mord .6K 153
SW6 . . . . .2K 117
Furnival Ct. E3 .2C 86
(off Four Seasons Cl.)

Furnival Mans.—Garbutt Pl.

Furnival Mans. W1 . . . 6A 6 (off Wells St.)
Furnival St. EC4 . . . 7J 7 (6A 84)
Furrow La. E9 . . . 5J 67
Fursby Av. N3 . . . 6D 30
Fursecroft W1 . . . 7E 4
Furtherfield Cl. CR0: C'don . . . 6A 156
Further Grn. Rd. SE6 . . . 7G 123
FURZEDOWN . . . 5F 137
Furzedown Dr. SW17 . . . 5F 137
Furzedown Recreation Cen. . . . 5F 137
Furzedown Rd. SW17 . . . 5F 137
Furze Farm Cl. RM6: Chad H . . . 2E 54
Furzefield Cl. BR7: Chst . . . 6F 143
Furzefield Rd. SE3 . . . 6K 105
Furzeground Way
UB11: Stock P . . . 1E 92
Furzeham Rd. UB7: W Dray . . . 2A 92
Furze Rd. CR7: Thor H . . . 3C 156
Furze St. E3 . . . 5C 86
Furzewood TW16: Sun . . . 1J 147
Fusiliers Way TW4: Houn . . . 3A 112 (not continuous)
Fye Foot La. EC4 . . . 2C 14 (off Queen Victoria St.)
Fyfe Apartments N8 . . . 3K 47
Fyfe Way BR1: Brom . . . 2J 159
Fyfield N4 . . . 2A 66 (off Six Acres Est.)
Fyfield Cl. BR2: Brom . . . 4F 159
Fyfield Ct. E7 . . . 6J 69
Fyfield Ho. E6 . . . 1C 88 (off Ron Leighton Way)
Fyfield Rd. E17 . . . 3F 51
EN1: Enf . . . 3K 23
IG8: Wfd G . . . 7F 37
SW9 . . . 3A 120
Fynes St. SW1 . . . 3C 18 (4H 101)

G

Gable Cl. HA5: Hat E . . . 1E 40
Gable Ct. SE26 . . . 4H 139
Gable M. BR2: Brom . . . 2C 172
Gables, The BR1: Brom . . . 7K 141
HA9: Wemb . . . 3G 61
IG11: Bark . . . 6G 71
N10 . . . 3E 46 (off Fortis Grn.)
Gables Av. TW15: Ashf . . . 5B 128
Gables Cl. SE5 . . . 1E 120
SE12 . . . 1J 141
Gables Lodge EN4: Had W . . . 1F 21
Gabriel Cl. TW13: Hanw . . . 4C 130
Gabriel Ho. N1 . . . 1B 84 (off Islington Grn.)
SE11 . . . 3G 19 (4K 101)
SE16 . . . 3B 104 (off Odessa St.)
Gabrielle Cl. HA9: Wemb . . . 3F 61
Gabrielle Ct. NW3 . . . 6B 64
Gabriel M. NW2 . . . 2H 63
Gabriel's M. BR3: Beck . . . 1K 157
Gabriel St. SE23 . . . 7K 121
Gabriels Wharf SE1 . . . 4J 13 (1A 102)
Gad Cl. E13 . . . 3K 87
Gaddesden Av. HA9: Wemb . . . 6F 61
Gaddesden Ho. EC1 . . . 2F 9 (off Cranwood St.)
Gadebridge Ho. SW3 . . . 5C 16 (off Cale St.)
Gade Cl. UB3: Hayes . . . 1K 93
Gadesden Rd. KT19: Ewe . . . 6J 163
Gadsbury Cl. NW9 . . . 6B 44
Gadsden Ho. W10 . . . 4G 81 (off Hazlewood Cres.)
Gadwall Cl. E16 . . . 6K 87
Gadwall Ho. NW9 . . . 6C 44 (off Perryfield Way)
Gadwall Way SE28 . . . 2H 107
Gage Brown Ho. W10 . . . 6F 81 (off Bridge Cl.)
Gage M. CR2: S Croy . . . 5B 168
Gage Rd. E16 . . . 5G 87
Gage St. WC1 . . . 5F 7 (5J 83)
Gainford Ho. E2 . . . 3H 85 (off Ellsworth St.)
Gainford St. N1 . . . 1A 84
Gainsboro Gdns. UB6: G'frd . . . 5J 59
Gainsborough Av. E12 . . . 5E 70
Gainsborough Cl. BR3: Beck . . . 7C 140
KT10: Esh . . . 7J 149
Gainsborough Ct. BR2: Brom . . . 4A 160
KT19: Ewe . . . 6B 164
N12 . . . 5E 30
SE16 . . . 5H 103 (off Stubbs Dr.)
SE21 . . . 2E 138
W4 . . . 5H 97 (off Chaseley Dr.)
W12 . . . 2E 98
Gainsborough Gdns. HA8: Edg . . . 2F 43
NW3 . . . 3B 64
NW11 . . . 7H 45
TW7: Isle . . . 5H 113
Gainsborough Ho. E14 . . . 2C 104 (off Cassilis Rd.)
E14 . . . 7A 86 (off Victory Pl.)
EN1: Enf . . . 5B 24
RM8: Dag . . . 4B 72 (off Longbridge Rd.)
SW1 . . . 4D 18 (off Erasmus St.)
Gainsborough Lodge HA1: Harr . . . 5K 41 (off Hindes Rd.)
Gainsborough Mans. W14 . . . 6G 99 (off Queen's Club Gdns.)
Gainsborough M. SE26 . . . 3H 139
Gainsborough Rd. E11 . . . 7G 51
E15 . . . 3G 87
IG8: Wfd G . . . 6H 37
KT3: N Mald . . . 6K 151
N12 . . . 5E 30
RM8: Dag . . . 4B 72
TW9: Rich . . . 2F 115
UB4: Hayes . . . 2E 74
W4 . . . 4B 98
Gainsborough Sq. DA6: Bex . . . 3D 126
Gainsborough St. E9 . . . 6B 68
Gainsborough Studios E. N1 . . . 1D 84 (off Poole St.)
Gainsborough Studios Nth. N1 . . . 1D 84 (off Poole St.)
Gainsborough Studios Sth. N1 . . . 1D 84 (off Poole St.)
Gainsborough Studios W. N1 . . . 1D 84 (off Poole St.)
Gainsborough Ter. SM2: Sutt . . . 7H 165 (off Belmont Ri.)
Gainsborough Twr. UB5: N'olt . . . 2B 76 (off Academy Gdns.)
Gainsfield Ct. E11 . . . 3G 69
Gainsford Rd. E17 . . . 4B 50
Gainsford St. SE1 . . . 6J 15 (2F 103)
Gairloch Ho. NW1 . . . 7H 65 (off Stratford Vs.)
Gairloch Rd. SE5 . . . 2E 120
Gaisford St. NW5 . . . 6G 65
Gaitskell Ct. SW11 . . . 2C 118
Gaitskell Ho. E6 . . . 1B 88
E17 . . . 3D 50
SE17 . . . 6E 102 (off Villa St.)
Gaitskell Rd. SE9 . . . 1G 143
Gaitskell Way SE1 . . . 6C 14 (off Weller St.)
Gala Bingo
Acton . . . 1K 97 (off High St.)
Bexleyheath . . . 4H 127
Gala Bingo
Camberwell . . . 7C 102
East Ham . . . 1C 88
Enfield . . . 4B 24
Feltham . . . 2K 129
Harrow . . . 5K 41
Hounslow . . . 4E 112
Leyton . . . 1B 68
Stratford . . . 1F 87
Surrey Quays . . . 3K 103
Tooting . . . 5C 136
Gala Ct. CR7: Thor H . . . 5A 156
Galahad M. E3 . . . 2B 86
Galahad Rd. BR1: Brom . . . 4J 141
N9 . . . 3B 34
Galata Rd. SW13 . . . 7C 98
Galatea Sq. SE15 . . . 3H 121
Galaxy Bldg. E14 . . . 4C 104 (off Crews St.)
Galaxy Ho. EC2 . . . 3F 9 (off Leonard St.)
Galba Ct. TW8: Bford . . . 7D 96
Galbraith St. E14 . . . 3E 104
Galdana Av. EN5: New Bar . . . 3F 21
Galeborough Av. IG8: Wfd G . . . 7A 36
Gale Cl. CR4: Mitc . . . 3B 154
TW12: Hamp . . . 6C 130
Galena Arches W6 . . . 4D 98 (off Galena Rd.)
Galena Hgts. E20 . . . 6E 68 (off Mirabelle Gdns.)
Galena Ho. SE18 . . . 5K 107 (off Grosmont Rd.)
Galena Rd. W6 . . . 4D 98
Galen Pl. WC1 . . . 6F 7 (5J 83)
Galesbury Rd. SW18 . . . 6A 118
Gales Gdns. E2 . . . 3H 85
Gale St. E3 . . . 5C 86
RM9: Dag . . . 5C 72
Gales Way IG8: Wfd G . . . 7H 37
Galgate Cl. SW19 . . . 1F 135
Gallants Farm Rd. EN4: E Barn . . . 7H 21
Galleon Cl. DA8: Erith . . . 4K 109
SE16 . . . 2K 103
Galleon Ho. E14 . . . 4E 104 (off Glengarnock Av.)
Galleons Dr. IG11: Bark . . . 3A 90
Galleons Vw. E14 . . . 2E 104
Galleria Ct. SE15 . . . 6F 103
Galleria Shop. Mall, The E18 . . . 2J 51
Galleries, The NW8 . . . 1A 4 (off Abbey Rd.)
Gallery, The . . . 1G 89 (off Clockhouse Av.)
Gallery, The E20 . . . 6E 68 (within Westfield Stratford City Shop. Cen.)
SE14 . . . 7B 104 (off New Cross Rd.)
Gallery Apartments E1 . . . 6J 85 (off Commercial Rd.)
SE1 . . . 7G 15 (off Lamb Wlk.)
Gallery at London Glassblowing, The . . . 6G 15
Gallery Ct. E17 . . . 2E 50 (off Fulbourne Rd.)
SE1 . . . 7E 14 (off Pilgrimage St.)
SW10 . . . 6A 100 (off Gunter Gro.)
Gallery Gdns. UB5: N'olt . . . 2B 76
Gallery Ho. E8 . . . 6H 67 (off Hackney Gro.)
Gallery Rd. SE21 . . . 1D 138
Galley, The E16 . . . 7F 89
Galleymead Rd. SL3: Poyle . . . 4A 174
Galleywall Rd. SE16 . . . 4H 103
Galleywall Rd. Trad. Est. SE16 . . . 4H 103
Galleywood Ho. W10 . . . 5E 80 (off Sutton Way)
Galliard Cl. N9 . . . 6D 24
Galliard Ct. N9 . . . 6B 24
Galliard Rd. N9 . . . 1B 34
Gallia Rd. N5 . . . 5B 66
Gallica Ct. SM1: Sutt . . . 1K 165
Gallions Cl. IG11: Bark . . . 3A 90
Gallions Entrance E16 . . . 1G 107
Gallions Reach Shop. Pk. E6 . . . 5G 89
Gallions Rd. E16 . . . 7F 89
SE7 . . . 4K 105 (not continuous)
GALLIONS RDBT. . . . 7F 89
Gallions Vw. Rd. SE28 . . . 2J 107
Gallipoli Pl. RM9: Dag . . . 1B 90
Gallon Cl. SE7 . . . 4A 106
Gallop, The CR2: Sels . . . 7H 169
SM2: Sutt . . . 7B 166
Gallosson Rd. SE18 . . . 4J 107
Galloway Path CR0: C'don . . . 4D 168
Galloway Rd. W12 . . . 1C 98
Gallus Cl. N21 . . . 6E 22
Gallus Sq. SE3 . . . 3K 123
Galpins Rd. CR7: Thor H . . . 5J 155
Galsworthy Av. E14 . . . 6A 86
RM6: Chad H . . . 7B 54
Galsworthy Cl. NW2 . . . 4G 63
SE28 . . . 1B 108
Galsworthy Ct. W3 . . . 3H 97 (off Bollo Bri. Rd.)
Galsworthy Cres. SE3 . . . 7A 106
Galsworthy Ho. W11 . . . 6G 81 (off Elgin Cres.)
Galsworthy Rd. KT2: King T . . . 7H 133
NW2 . . . 4G 63
Galsworthy Ter. N16 . . . 3D 66
Galton Ct. NW9 . . . 3A 44 (off Joslin Av.)
Galton St. W10 . . . 3G 81
Galva Cl. EN4: Cockf . . . 4K 21
Galvani Way CR0: Wadd . . . 1K 167
Galveston Ho. E1 . . . 4A 86 (off Harford St.)
Galveston Rd. SW15 . . . 5H 117
Galway Cl. SE16 . . . 5H 103 (off Masters Dr.)
Galway Ho. E1 . . . 5K 85 (off White Horse La.)
EC1 . . . 2D 8
Galway St. EC1 . . . 2D 8 (3C 84)
Gambado
Beckenham . . . 6C 140
Chelsea . . . 1A 118 (off Station Ct.)
Gambetta St. SW8 . . . 2F 119
Gambia St. SE1 . . . 5B 14 (1B 102)
Gambier Ho. EC1 . . . 2D 8 (off Mora St.)
Gambole Rd. SW17 . . . 4C 136
Games Rd. EN4: Cockf . . . 3H 21
Gamlen Rd. SW15 . . . 4F 117
Gamma Ct. CR0: C'don . . . 1D 168 (off Sydenham Rd.)
Gamuel Cl. E17 . . . 6C 50
Gander Grn. Cres. TW12: Hamp . . . 1E 148
Gander Grn. La. SM1: Sutt . . . 3H 165
SM3: Cheam . . . 2G 165
Gandhi Cl. E17 . . . 6C 50
Gandolfi St. SE15 . . . 6E 102
Ganley Ct. SW11 . . . 3B 118 (off Winstanley Est.)
Ganton St. W1 . . . 2A 12 (7G 83)
GANTS HILL . . . 6E 52
GANTS HILL . . . 6E 52
Gants Hill IG2: Ilf . . . 6E 52
Gantshill Cres.
IG2: Ilf . . . 5E 52
Gap Rd. SW19 . . . 5J 135
Garage Rd. W3 . . . 6G 79
Garand Ct. N7 . . . 5K 65
Garbett Ho. SE17 . . . 6B 102 (off Doddington Gro.)
Garbutt Pl. W1 . . . 5H 5 (5E 82)

A-Z London 275

Garda Ho.—Gateway Arc.

Garda Ho. *SE10* *4G 105*
(off Cable Wlk.)
Garden Av. CR4: Mitc 7F **137**
DA7: Bex 3F **127**
Garden City HA8: Edg 6B **28**
Garden Cl. E4 5H **35**
HA4: Ruis 2G **57**
KT3: N Mald 4A **152**
SE12 3K **141**
SM6: Wall 5J **167**
SW15 7E **116**
TW12: Hamp 5D **130**
TW15: Ashf 6E **128**
UB5: N'olt 1C **76**
Garden Ct. CR0: C'don 2F **169**
EC4 2J **13**
HA7: Stan 5H **27**
N12 5E **30**
NW8 *1A 4*
(off Garden Rd.)
TW9: Kew 1F **115**
TW12: Hamp 5D **130**
W4 3J **97**
W11 *7G 81*
(off Clarendon Rd.)
Gardener Gro. TW13: Hanw 2D **130**
Gardeners Cl. N11 2K **31**
SE9 3C **142**
Gardeners Rd. CR0: C'don 1B **168**
Garden Ho. *N2* *2B 46*
(off The Grange)
NW6 *2K 81*
(off Oxford Rd.)
SW7 *3K 99*
(off Cornwall Gdns.)
Garden Ho's., The *W6* *6F 99*
(off Bothwell St.)
Gardenia Rd. BR1: Brom 3E **160**
EN1: Enf 6K **23**
Gardenia Way IG8: Wfd G 6D **36**
Garden La. BR1: Brom 6K **141**
SW2 1K **137**
Garden M. W2 7J **81**
Garden Mus., The 2G **19** (3K **101**)
Garden Pl. E8 1F **85**
Garden Rd. BR1: Brom 7K **141**
KT12: Walt T 6K **147**
NW8 1A **4** (3A **82**)
SE20 1J **157**
TW9: Rich 3G **115**
Garden Row SE1 3B **102**
Garden Royal SW15 6F **117**
Gardens, The BR3: Beck 1E **158**
E5 7F **49**
HA1: Harr 6G **41**
HA5: Pinn 6D **40**
N8 4J **47**
(not continuous)
SE22 4G **121**
TW14: Felt 5F **111**
Garden Sq. SW1 6H **17** (5E **100**)
Garden St. E1 5K **85**
Garden Ter. SW1 5C **18** (5H **101**)
SW7 7D **10**
Garden Wlk. BR3: Beck 1B **158**
EC2 2G **9** (3E **84**)
Garden Way NW10 6J **61**
Gardiner Av. NW2 5E **62**
Gardiner Cl. EN3: Pond E 6E **24**
RM8: Dag 4D **72**
Gardiner Ct. CR2: S Croy 6D **168**
Gardiner Ho. SW11 1C **118**
Gardner Cl. E11 6K **51**
Gardner Ct. *EC1* *3A 8*
(off Brewery Sq.)
N5 4C **66**
Gardner Ho. TW13: Hanw 2D **130**
UB1: S'hall *7B 76*
(off The Broadway)
Gardner Ind. Est. BR3: Beck 5B **140**
Gardner Pl. TW14: Felt 6K **111**
Gardner Rd. E13 4K **87**
Gardners La. EC4 2C **14** (7C **84**)
Gardnor Rd. NW3 4B **64**
Gard St. EC1 1B **8** (3B **84**)
Garendon Gdns. SM4: Mord 7K **153**
Garendon Rd. SM4: Mord 7K **153**
Garenne Ct. E4 1K **35**
Gareth Cl. KT4: Wor Pk 2F **165**
Gareth Ct. SW16 3H **137**
Gareth Dr. N9 2B **34**
Gareth Gro. BR1: Brom 4J **141**
Garfield *EN2: Enf* *5J 23*
(off London Rd.)
Garfield Ct. *NW6* *7G 63*
(off Willesden La.)
Garfield M. SW11 3E **118**
Garfield Rd. E4 1A **36**
E13 4H **87**
EN3: Pond E 4D **24**
SW11 3E **118**
SW19 5A **136**
TW1: Twick 1A **132**
Garford St. E14 7C **86**
Garganey Ct. *NW10* *6K 61*
(off Elgar Av.)
Garganey Wlk. SE28 7C **90**
Garibaldi St. SE18 4J **107**
Garland Cl. SE1 3C **102**
Garland Ct. *E14* *7C 86*
(off Premiere Pl.)
SE17 *4C 102*
(off Wansey St.)
Garland Dr. TW3: Houn 2G **113**
Garland Ho. *KT2: King T* *1E 150*
(off Skerne Rd.)
UB7: W Dray 2B **92**
Garland Rd. HA7: Stan 1E **42**
SE18 7H **107**
Garlands Ct. *CR0: C'don* *4D 168*
(off Chatsworth Rd.)
Garlands Ho. *NW8* *2A 82*
(off Carlton Hill)
Garlands La. HA1: Harr 1K **59**
Garlick Hill EC4 2D **14** (7C **84**)
Garlies Rd. SE23 3A **140**
Garlinge Ho. *SW9* *1A 120*
(off Gosling Way)
Garlinge Rd. NW2 6H **63**
Garman Cl. N18 5J **33**
Garman Rd. N17 7C **34**
(not continuous)
Garnault M. EC1 2K **7**
Garnault Pl. EC1 2K **7** (3A **84**)
Garnault Rd. EN1: Enf 1A **24**
Garner Cl. RM8: Dag 1D **72**
Garner Ct. *TW19: Stanw* *6A 110*
(off Douglas Rd.)
Garner Rd. E17 1E **50**
Garner St. E2 2G **85**
Garnet Ho. *E1* *1J 103*
(off Garnet St.)
Garnet Rd. CR7: Thor H 4C **156**
NW10 6A **62**
Garnet St. E1 7J **85**
Garnett Cl. SE9 3D **124**
Garnett Rd. NW3 5D **64**
Garnett Way *E17* *1A 50*
(off McEntee Av.)
Garnet Wlk. E6 5C **88**
Garnham Cl. N16 2F **67**
Garnham St. N16 2F **67**
Garnies Cl. SE15 7F **103**
Garrad's Rd. SW16 3H **137**
Garrard Cl. BR7: Chst 5F **143**
DA7: Bex 3G **127**
Garrard Wlk. NW10 6A **62**
Garratt Cl. CR0: Bedd 4J **167**
Garratt Ct. SW18 7K **117**
Garratt La. SW17 6K **117**
SW18 6K **117**
Garratt Rd. HA8: Edg 7B **28**
Garratts Rd. WD23: Bush 1B **26**
Garratt Ter. SW17 4C **136**
Garraway Ct. *SW13* *7E 98*
(off Wyatt Dr.)
Garrett Cl. W3 5K **79**
Garrett Ho. *SE1* *6A 14*
(off Burrows M.)
Garrett St. EC1 3D **8** (4C **84**)
Garrick Av. NW11 6G **45**
Garrick Cl. SW18 4A **118**
TW9: Rich 5D **114**
W5 4E **78**
Garrick Ct. *E8* *7F 67*
(off Jacaranda Gro.)
Garrick Cres. CR0: C'don 2E **168**
Garrick Dr. NW4 2E **44**
SE28 3H **107**
Garrick Gdns. KT8: W Mole 3E **148**
Garrick Ho. *KT1: King T* *4E 150*
(off Surbiton Rd.)
W1 5J **11**
W4 6A **98**
Garrick Ind. Cen. NW9 5B **44**
Garrick Pk. NW4 2F **45**
Garrick Rd. NW9 6B **44**
TW9: Rich 2G **115**
UB6: G'frd 4F **77**
Garricks Ho. *KT1: King T* *2D 150*
(off Wadbrook St.)
Garrick St. WC2 2E **12** (7J **83**)
Garrick Theatre *3E 12*
(off Charing Cross Rd.)
Garrick Way NW4 4F **45**
Garrick Yd. WC2 2E **12**
Garrison Cl. SE18 7E **106**
TW4: Houn 5D **112**
Garrison La. KT9: Chess 7D **162**
Garrison Rd. E3 1C **86**
Garrison Sq. SW1 5H **17** (5E **100**)
Garrowsfield EN5: Barn 6C **20**
Garry Way RM1: Rom 1K **55**
Garsdale Cl. N11 6K **31**
Garsdale Ter. *W14* *5H 99*
(off Aisgill Av.)
Garside Cl. SE28 3H **107**
TW12: Hamp 6F **131**
Garside Ct. TW11: Hamp W 1C **150**
Garsington M. SE4 3B **122**
Garson Ho. *W2* *2A 10*
(off Gloucester Ter.)
Garston Ho. *N1* *7B 66*
(off The Sutton Est.)
Garter Way SE16 2K **103**
Garth, The HA3: Kenton 6F **43**
TW12: Hamp H 6F **131**
Garth Cl. HA4: Ruis 1B **58**
KT2: King T 5F **133**
SM4: Mord 7F **153**
Garth Ct. *HA1: Harr* *6K 41*
(off Northwick Pk. Rd.)
W4 5K **97**
Garth Ho. NW2 2H **63**
Garth M. W5 4E **78**
Garthorne Rd. SE23 7K **121**
Garthorne Road Nature Reserve 7K **121**
Garth Rd. KT2: King T 5F **133**
NW2 2H **63**
SM4: Mord 6E **152**
W4 5K **97**
Garth Rd. Ind. Cen., The
SM4: Mord 1F **165**
Garthside TW10: Ham 5E **132**
Garthway N12 6H **31**
Gartmoor Gdns. SW19 1H **135**
Gartmore Rd. IG3: Ilf 2K **71**
Garton Pl. SW18 6A **118**
Gartons Cl. EN3: Pond E 4D **24**
Gartons Way SW11 3A **118**
Garvary Rd. E16 6K **87**
Garway Ct. *E3* *2C 86*
(off Matilda Gdns.)
Garway Rd. W2 6K **81**
Garwood Cl. N17 1H **49**
Gascoigne Cl. N17 1F **49**
Gascoigne Gdns. IG8: Wfd G 7B **36**
Gascoigne Pl. E2 1J **9** (3F **85**)
(not continuous)
Gascoigne Rd. CR0: New Ad 7F **171**
IG11: Bark 1G **89**
Gascony Av. NW6 7J **63**
Gascony Pl. W12 1F **99**
Gascoyne Ho. E9 7A **68**
Gascoyne Rd. E9 7K **67**
Gaselee St. *E14* *1E 104*
(off Baffin Way)
Gasholder Pk. 1H **83**
Gaskarth Rd. HA8: Edg 1J **43**
SW12 6F **119**
Gaskell Ct. SE20 7K **139**
Gaskell Rd. N6 6D **46**
Gaskell St. SW4 2J **119**
Gaskin St. N1 1B **84**
Gaspar Cl. SW5 4K **99**
Gaspar M. SW5 4K **99**
Gassiot Rd. SW17 4D **136**
Gassiot Way SM1: Sutt 3B **166**
Gasson Ho. *SE14* *6K 103*
(off John Williams Cl.)
Gastein Rd. W6 6F **99**
Gastigny Ho. EC1 2D **8**
Gaston Bell Cl. TW9: Rich 3F **115**
Gaston Bri. Rd. TW17: Shep 6F **147**
Gaston Rd. CR4: Mitc 3E **154**
Gaston Way TW17: Shep 5F **147**
Gataker Ho. *SE16* *3H 103*
(off Slippers Pl.)
Gataker St. SE16 3H **103**
Gatcombe Ct. BR3: Beck 7C **140**
Gatcombe Ho. SE22 3E **120**
Gatcombe M. W5 7F **79**
Gatcombe Rd. E16 1J **105**
N19 3H **65**
Gatcombe Way EN4: Cockf 3J **21**
Gateacre Ct. DA14: Sidc 4B **144**
Gate Cen., The TW8: Bford 7A **96**
Gate Cinema *1J 99*
(off Notting Hill Ga.)
Gateforth St. NW8 4C **4** (4C **82**)
Gate Hill Ct. *W11* *1H 99*
(off Ladbroke Ter.)
Gate Ho. *E3* *1A 86*
(off Gunmakers La.)
N1 *7D 66*
(off Ufton Rd.)
NW6 *2K 81*
(off Oxford Rd.)
Gatehouse Cl. KT2: King T 7J **133**
Gatehouse Sq. SE1 4D **14**
Gateley Ho. *SE4* *4K 121*
(off Coston Wlk.)
Gateley Rd. SW9 3K **119**
Gate Lodge *W9* *5J 81*
(off Admiral Wlk.)
Gately Ct. SE15 7F **103**
Gate M. SW7 7D **10**
Gater Dr. EN2: Enf 1J **23**
Gatesborough St. EC2 3G **9** (4E **84**)
Gates Ct. SE17 5C **102**
Gatesden WC1 2G **7** (3J **83**)
Gates Grn. Rd. BR2: Kes 3H **171**
BR4: W W'ck 3H **171**
Gateside Rd. SW17 3D **136**
Gatestone Ct. *SE19* *6E 138*
(off Central Hill)
Gatestone Rd. SE19 6E **138**
Gate St. WC2 7G **7** (6K **83**)
Gate Theatre, The
London *1J 99*
(off Pembridge Rd.)
Gateway SE17 6C **102**
Gateway Arc. *N1* *2B 84*
(off Upper St.)

276 A-Z London

Gateway Bus. Cen. SE26 . . . . .6A 140
SE28 . . . . .3H 107
Gateway Ct. IG2: Ilf 6E 52
(off Parham Dr.)
Gateway Ind. Est. NW10 . . . . .3B 80
Gateway M. E8 . . . . .5F 67
N11 . . . . .6B 32
Gateway Retail Pk. E6 . . . . .4F 89
Gateway Rd. E10 . . . . .3D 68
Gateways KT6: Surb 5E 150
(off Surbiton Hill Rd.)
Gateways, The SW3 . . . . .4D 16 (4C 100)
TW9: Rich 4D 114
(off Park La.)
Gateways Ct. SM6: Wall 5F 167
Gatfield Gro. TW13: Hanw 2E 130
Gatfield Ho. TW13: Hanw 2D 130
Gathorne Rd. N22 . . . . .2A 48
Gathorne St. E2 . . . . .2K 85
Gatley Av. KT19: Ewe 5H 163
Gatliff Cl. SW1 . . . . .6H 17
Gatliff Rd. SW1 . . . . . .6J 17 (5F 101)
Gatling Rd. SE2 . . . . .5A 108
Gatonby St. SE15 . . . . .1F 121
Gatting Cl. HA8: Edg 7D 28
Gatting Way UB8: Uxb 6A 56
Gattis Wharf N1 . . . . .2J 83
(off New Wharf Rd.)
Gatton Cl. SM2: Sutt 7K 165
Gatton Rd. SW17 . . . . .4C 136
Gattons Way DA14: Sidc 4F 145
Gatward Cl. N21 . . . . .6G 23
Gatward Grn. N9 . . . . .2A 34
Gatward Pl. IG11: Bark 3K 89
Gatwick Ho. E14 . . . . .6B 86
(off Clemence St.)
Gatwick Rd. SW18 . . . . .7H 117
Gauden Cl. SW4 . . . . .3H 119
Gauden Rd. SW4 . . . . .2H 119
Gaudi Apartments N8 . . . . .3K 47
(off Gt. Amwell La.)
Gaugin Ct. SE16 . . . . .5H 103
(off Stubbs Dr.)
Gaumont Ter. W12 . . . . .2E 98
(off Lime Gro.)
Gaumont Twr. E8 . . . . .6F 67
(off Dalston Sq.)
Gauntlet NW9 . . . . .2B 44
(off Five Acre)
Gauntlet Cl. UB5: N'olt 7C 58
Gauntlett Cl. HA0: Wemb 5B 60
Gauntlett Rd. SM1: Sutt 5B 166
Gaunt St. SE1 . . . . .3C 102
Gautrey Rd. SE15 . . . . .2J 121
Gautrey Sq. E6 . . . . .6D 88
Gavel St. SE17 . . . . .4D 102
Gaverick M. E14 . . . . .4C 104
Gavestone Cres. SE12 . . . . .7A 124
Gavestone Rd. SE12 . . . . .7K 123
Gaviller Pl. E5 . . . . .4H 67
Gavina Cl. SM4: Mord 5C 154
Gavin Ho. SE18 . . . . .4J 107
Gawain Wlk. N9 . . . . .3B 34
Gawber St. E2 . . . . .3J 85
Gawsworth Cl. E15 . . . . .5H 69
Gawthorne Cl. E3 . . . . .2C 86
Gay Cl. NW2 . . . . .5D 62
Gaydon Ho. W2 . . . . .5K 81
(off Bourne St.)
Gaydon La. NW9 . . . . .1A 44
Gayfere Pl. SE25 . . . . .2E 156
(off Grange Hill)
Gayfere Rd. IG5: Ilf 3D 52
KT17: Ewe 5C 164
Gayfere St. SW1 . . . . . .2E 18 (3J 101)
Gayford Rd. W12 . . . . .2B 98
Gay Gdns. RM10: Dag 4J 73
Gay Ho. N16 . . . . .5E 66
Gayhurst SE17 . . . . .6D 102
(off Hopwood Rd.)

Gayhurst Ct. UB5: N'olt 3A 76
Gayhurst Ho. NW8 . . . . .3C 4
(off Mallory Cl.)
Gayhurst Rd. E8 . . . . .7G 67
Gaylor Rd. UB5: N'olt 5D 58
Gaymead NW8 . . . . .1K 81
(off Abbey Rd.)
Gaynesford Rd. SE23 . . . . .2K 139
SM5: Cars 7D 166
Gaynes Hill Rd. IG8: Wfd G 6H 37
Gay Rd. E15 . . . . .2F 87
Gaysham Av. IG2: Ilf 5E 52
Gaysham Hall IG5: Ilf 3F 53
Gaysley Ho. SE11 . . . . .4J 19
Gay St. SW15 . . . . .3F 117
Gayton HA1: Harr 7J 41
(off Grove Hill)
Gayton Ct. HA1: Harr 6K 41
Gayton Cres. NW3 . . . . .4B 64
Gayton Ho. E3 . . . . .4C 86
(off Chiltern Rd.)
Gayton Rd. HA1: Harr 6K 41
NW3 . . . . .4B 64
SE2 . . . . .3C 108
Gayville Rd. SW11 . . . . .6D 118
Gaywood Cl. SW2 . . . . .1K 137
Gaywood Rd. E17 . . . . .3C 50
Gaywood St. SE1 . . . . .3B 102
Gaza St. SE17 . . . . .5B 102
Gaze Ho. E14 . . . . .6F 87
(off Blair St.)
Gazelle Ho. E15 . . . . .6G 69
Gean Ct. E11 . . . . .4F 69
N11 . . . . .6B 32
(off Cline Rd.)
Geariesville Gdns. IG6: Ilf 4F 53
Gearing Cl. SW17 . . . . .4E 136
Geary Rd. NW10 . . . . .5C 62
Geary St. N7 . . . . .5K 65
Geddes Pl. DA6: Bex 4G 127
(off Arnsberg Way)
Gedeney Rd. N17 . . . . .1C 48
Gedling Ct. SE1 . . . . .7K 15
(off Sweeney Cres.)
Gedling Pl. SE1 . . . . .7K 15 (3F 103)
Geere Rd. E15 . . . . .1H 87
Gees Ct. W1 . . . . .1H 11 (6E 82)
Gee St. EC1 . . . . .3C 8 (4C 84)
Geffery's Ct. SE9 . . . . .3C 142
Geffrye Ct. N1 . . . . .2E 84
Geffrye Est. N1 . . . . .2E 84
Geffrye Mus. 1J 9 (2F 85)
Geffrye St. E2 . . . . .1J 9 (2F 85)
Geldart Rd. SE15 . . . . .7H 103
Geldeston Rd. E5 . . . . .2G 67
Gellatly Rd. SE14 . . . . .2J 121
Gell Cl. UB10: Ick 3B 56
Gelsthorpe Rd. RM5: Col R 1H 55
Gem Ct. SE10 . . . . .7D 104
(off Merryweather Pl.)
Gemini Apartments E1 . . . . .3K 9
(off Sclater St.)
Gemini Bus. Cen. E16 . . . . .4F 87
Gemini Bus. Est. SE14 . . . . .5K 103
Gemini Bus. Pk. E6 . . . . .5H 89
Gemini Ct. E1 . . . . .7G 85
(off Vaughan Way)
Gemini Gro. UB5: N'olt 3C 76
Gemini Ho. E3 . . . . .1C 86
(off Garrison Rd.)
Gemini Pl. TW15: Ashf 6G 129
Genas Cl. IG6: Ilf 1F 53
General Gordon Pl. SE18 . . . . .4F 107
General Gordon Sq. SE18 . . . . .4F 107
(off Woolwich New Rd.)
General Wolfe Rd. SE10 . . . . .1F 123
Genesis Bus. Pk. NW10 . . . . .2H 79
Genesis Ct. TW19: Stanw 1B 128
Genesta Rd. SE18 . . . . .6F 107
Geneva Cl. TW17: Shep 2G 147
Geneva Ct. NW9 . . . . .5B 44

Geneva Dr. SW9 . . . . .4A 120
Geneva Gdns. RM6: Chad H 5E 54
Geneva Rd. CR7: Thor H 5C 156
KT1: King T 4E 150
Genever Cl. E4 . . . . .5H 35
Genista Rd. N18 . . . . .5C 34
Genoa Av. SW15 . . . . .5E 116
Genoa Ho. E1 . . . . .4K 85
(off Ernest St.)
SW18 . . . . .3A 118
Genoa Rd. SE20 . . . . .1J 157
Genotin Rd. EN1: Enf 3J 23
Genotin Ter. EN1: Enf 3J 23
Gentian Row SE10 . . . . .1E 122
Gentlemans Row EN2: Enf 3H 23
Gentry Gdns. E13 . . . . .4J 87
Geoff Cade Way E3 . . . . .5B 86
Geoffrey Chaucer Way E3 . . . . .5B 86
Geoffrey Cl. SE5 . . . . .2C 120
Geoffrey Ct. SE4 . . . . .2B 122
Geoffrey Gdns. E6 . . . . .2C 88
Geoffrey Ho. SE1 . . . . .7F 15
(off Pardoner St.)
Geoffrey Jones Ct. NW10 . . . . .1C 80
Geoffrey Rd. SE4 . . . . .3B 122
George V Av. HA5: Pinn 2D 40
George V Cl. HA5: Pinn 3E 40
George V Way UB6: G'frd 1B 78
George Beard Rd. SE8 . . . . .4B 104
George Belt Ho. E2 . . . . .3K 85
(off Smart St.)
George Comberton Wlk. E12 . . . . . . .5E 70
George Ct. TW15: Ashf 4B 128
(off Church Rd.)
UB3: Hayes 5H 75
WC2 . . . . .3F 13
George Cres. N10 . . . . .7K 31
George Davies Lodge IG6: Ilf 5G 53
(off Veronique Gdns.)
George Downing Est. N16 . . . . .2F 67
George Eliot Ho. SE17 . . . . .5C 102
(off Thrush St.)
SW1 . . . . .4B 18
(off Vauxhall Bri. Rd.)
George Elliston Ho. SE1 . . . . .5G 103
(off Old Kent Rd.)
George Eyre Ho. NW8 . . . . .2B 82
(off Cochrane St.)
George Furness Ho. NW10 . . . . .6D 62
(off Grange Rd.)
George Gange Way HA3: W'stone 3J 41
George Gillett Ct. EC1 . . . . .3D 8
George Groves Rd. SE20 . . . . .1G 157
George Hilsdon Ct. E14 . . . . .6A 86
(off Repton St.)
George Ho. NW6 . . . . .2H 81
(off Albert Rd.)
George Hudson Twr. E15 . . . . .2D 86
(off High St.)
George Inn Yd. SE1 . . . . .5E 14 (1D 102)
George La. BR2: Hayes 1K 171
E18 . . . . .2J 51
SE6 . . . . .6D 122
SE13 . . . . .6D 122
George Lansbury Ho. E3 . . . . .3B 86
(off Bow Rd.)
N22 . . . . .1A 48
(off Progress Way)
NW10 . . . . .7A 62
George Leybourne Ho. E1 . . . . .7G 85
(off Fletcher St.)
George Lindgren Ho. SW6 . . . . .7H 99
(off Clem Attlee Ct.)
George Loveless Ho. E2 . . . . .1K 9
(off Diss St.)
George Lowe Ct. W2 . . . . .5K 81
(off Bourne Ter.)
George Mathers Rd. SE11 . . . . .4B 102
George M. EN2: Enf 3J 23
NW1 . . . . .2B 6
SW9 . . . . .2A 120

George Padmore Ho. E8 . . . . .1G 85
(off Brougham Rd.)
George Peabody Ct. NW1 . . . . .5C 4
(off Burne St.)
George Peabody St. E13 . . . . .2A 88
George Pl. N17 . . . . .3E 48
George Potter Ho. SW11 . . . . .2B 118
(off George Potter Way)
George Potter Way SW11 . . . . .2B 118
George Rd. E4 . . . . .6H 35
KT2: King T 7H 133
KT3: N Mald 4B 152
George Row SE16 . . . . .2G 103
George Scott Ho. E1 . . . . .6K 85
(off W. Arbour St.)
George Sq. SW19 . . . . .3J 153
George's Rd. N7 . . . . .5K 65
George's Sq. SW6 . . . . .6H 99
(off North End Rd.)
George St. CR0: C'don 2C 168
E16 . . . . .6H 87
IG11: Bark 7G 71
TW3: Houn 2D 112
TW9: Rich 5D 114
UB2: S'hall 4C 94
W1 . . . . .7E 4 (6D 82)
W7 . . . . .1J 95
Georgetown Cl. SE19 . . . . .5E 138
Georgette Pl. SE10 . . . . .7E 104
George Vale Ho. E2 . . . . .2G 85
(off Mansford St.)
George Vw. Ho. SW18 . . . . .1K 135
(off Knaresborough Dr.)
Georgeville Gdns. IG6: Ilf 4F 53
George Walter Ct. SE16 . . . . .4J 103
(off Millender Wlk.)
George Wyver Cl. SW19 . . . . .7G 117
George Yd. EC3 . . . . .1F 15 (6D 84)
W1 . . . . .2H 11 (7E 82)
Georgia Cl. SE16 . . . . .3G 103
(off Priter Rd.)
Georgiana St. NW1 . . . . .1G 83
Georgian Cl. BR2: Hayes 1K 171
HA7: Stan 7F 27
UB10: Ick 4A 56
Georgian Ct. CR0: C'don 1D 168
(off Cross Rd.)
E9 . . . . .1J 85
EN5: New Bar 4F 21
HA9: Wemb 6G 61
N3 . . . . .1H 45
NW4 . . . . .5D 44
SW16 . . . . .4J 137
Georgian Ho. E16 . . . . .1J 105
(off Capulet M.)
N1 . . . . .1E 84
(off Hertford Rd.)
Georgian Way HA1: Harr 2H 59
Georgia Rd. CR7: Thor H 1B 156
KT3: N Mald 4J 151
Georgina Gdns. E2 . . . . . .1K 9 (3F 85)
Geraint Rd. BR1: Brom 4J 141
Geraldine Rd. SW18 . . . . .5A 118
W4 . . . . .6G 97
Geraldine St. SE11 . . . . .2K 19 (3B 102)
Gerald M. SW1 . . . . .3H 17
Gerald Pl. E8 . . . . .6F 67
(off Dalston Sq.)
Gerald Rd. E16 . . . . .4H 87
RM8: Dag 1F 73
SW1 . . . . .3H 17 (4E 100)
Gerard Av. TW4: Houn 7E 112
Gerard Gdns. RM13: Rain 2K 91
Gerard Pl. E9 . . . . .7K 67
Gerard Rd. HA1: Harr 6A 42
SW13 . . . . .1B 116
Gerards Cl. SE16 . . . . .5J 103
Gerards Pl. SW4 . . . . .4H 119
Gerda Rd. SE9 . . . . .2G 143
Germander Way E15 . . . . .3G 87
Gernigan Ho. SW18 . . . . .6B 118

Gernon Rd. E3 2A 86
Geron Way NW2 1D 62
Gerrard Gdns. HA5: Eastc 5J 39
Gerrard Ho. *SE14* *7J 103*
(off Briant St.)
Gerrard Pl. W1 2D 12 (7H 83)
Gerrard Rd. N1 2B 84
Gerrards Cl. N14 5B 22
Gerrards Ct. W5 3D 96
Gerrard St. W1 2D 12 (7H 83)
Gerrard Way SE3 4A 124
Gerridge Ct. *SE1* *1K 19*
(off Gerridge St.)
Gerridge St. SE1 1K 19 (3A 102)
Gerry Raffles Sq. E15 6F 69
Gertrude Rd.
DA17: Belv 4G 109
Gertrude St. SW10 7A 16 (6A 100)
Gervase Cl. HA9: Wemb 3J 61
Gervase Rd. HA8: Edg 1J 43
Gervase St. SE15 7H 103
Gervis Ct. TW7: Isle 7G 95
Ghent St. SE6 2C 140
Ghent Way E8 6F 67
Gherkin, The 1H 15
Giant Arches Rd. SE24 7C 120
Giant Tree Hill WD23: B Hea 1C 26
Gibbfield Cl. RM6: Chad H 3E 54
Gibbings Ho. *SE1* *7B 14*
(off King James St.)
Gibbins Rd. E15 7E 68
Gibbon Ho. *NW8* *4B 4*
(off Fisherton St.)
Gibbon Rd. KT2: King T 1E 150
SE15 2J 121
W3 7A 80
Gibbons M. NW11 5H 45
Gibbon's Rents SE1 5G 15
Gibbons Rd. NW10 6A 62
Gibbon Wlk. SW15 4C 116
Gibbs Av. SE19 5D 138
Gibbs Cl. SE19 6D 138
Gibbs Grn. HA8: Edg 4D 28
W14 5H 99
(not continuous)
Gibbs Ho. *BR1: Brom* *1H 159*
(off Longfield)
Gibb's Rd. N18 4D 34
Gibbs Sq. SE19 5D 138
Gibney Ter. BR1: Brom 4H 141
Gibraltar Wlk. E2 2K 9
Gibson Cl. E1 4J 85
KT9: Chess 5C 162
N21 6F 23
TW7: Isle 3J 113
Gibson Ct. SE9 5A 124
Gibson Gdns. N16 2F 67
Gibson Ho. SM1: Sutt 4J 165
Gibson M. TW1: Twick 6C 114
Gibson Rd. RM8: Dag 1C 72
SE11 4H 19 (4K 101)
SM1: Sutt 5K 165
UB10: Ick 4B 56
Gibsons Hill SW16 7A 138
(not continuous)
Gibson Sq. N1 1A 84
Gibson Sq. Gdns. *N1* *1A 84*
(off Gibson Sq.)
Gibson St. SE10 5G 105
Gideon Cl. DA17: Belv 4H 109
HA8: Edg 6B 28
Gideon M. W5 2D 96
Gideon Rd. SW11 3E 118
Gielgud Theatre *2C 12*
(off Shaftesbury Av.)
Giesbach Rd. N19 2H 65
Giffard Rd. N18 6K 33
Giffin Sq. Mkt. *SE8* *7C 104*
(off Giffin St.)
Giffin St. SE8 7C 104
Gifford Gdns. W7 5H 77
Gifford Ho. *SE10* *5F 105*
(off Eastney St.)
SW1 *6A 18*
(off Churchill Gdns.)
Gifford Rd. NW10 7A 62
Gifford St. N1 7J 65
Gift La. E15 1G 87
GIGGSHILL 7A 150
Giggs Hill BR5: St P 2K 161
Giggs Hill Gdns. KT7: T Ditt 1A 162
Giggs Hill Rd. KT7: T Ditt 7A 150
Gilbert Bri. *EC2* *5D 8*
(off Wood St.)
Gilbert Cl. SE18 1D 124
SW19 *1K 153*
(off Morden Rd.)
Gilbert Ct. *W5* *6F 79*
(off Green Va.)
Gilbert Gro. HA8: Edg 1K 43
Gilbert Ho. *E2* *3K 85*
(off Usk St.)
E17 3E 50
EC2 5D 8
SE8 6C 104
SW1 *6K 17*
(off Churchill Gdns.)
SW8 *7J 101*
(off Wyvil Rd.)
SW13 *7D 98*
(off Trinity Chu. Rd.)
Gilbert Pl. WC1 6E 6 (5J 83)
Gilbert Rd. BR1: Brom 7J 141
DA17: Belv 3G 109
HA5: Pinn 4B 40
SE11 4K 19 (4A 102)
SW19 7A 136
UB9: Hare 2A 38
Gilbert Scott Bldg. SW15 6G 117
Gilbert Scott Cl. HA0: Wemb 5D 60
Gilbert Sheldon Ho. *W2* *5B 4*
(off Edgware Rd.)
Gilbertson Ho. *E14* *3C 104*
(off Mellish St.)
Gilbert St. E15 4G 69
TW3: Houn 3G 113
W1 1H 11 (6E 82)
Gilbert Way CR0: Wadd 2K 167
Gilbert White Cl. UB6: G'frd 1A 78
Gilbey Cl. UB10: Ick 4D 56
Gilbey Ho. NW1 7F 65
Gilbey Rd. SW17 4C 136
Gilbeys Yd. NW1 7E 64
Gilbourne Rd. SE18 6K 107
Gilby Ho. E9 6K 67
Gilda Av. EN3: Pond E 5F 25
Gilda Ct. NW7 1C 44
Gilda Cres. N16 1G 67
Gildea Cl. HA5: Hat E 1E 40
Gildea St. W1 6K 5 (5F 83)
Gilden Cres. NW5 5E 64
Gildersome St. SE18 6E 106
Gilders Rd. KT9: Chess 7F 163
Giles Coppice SE19 4F 139
Giles Cres. *UB10: Uxb* *1B 74*
(off St Andrews Rd.)
Giles Ho. *W11* *6J 81*
(off Westbourne Gro.)
Gilesmead SE5 1D 120
Gilford Ho. *IG1: Ilf* *2F 71*
(off Clements Rd.)
Gilfrid Cl. UB8: Hil 6D 74
Gilkes Cres. SE21 6E 120
Gilkes Pl. SE21 6E 120
Gillan Ct. SE12 3K 141
Gillan Grn. WD23: B Hea 2B 26
Gillards M. E17 4C 50
Gillards Way E17 4C 50
Gill Av. E16 6J 87
Gillender St. E3 4E 86
E14 4E 86
Gillespie Pk. Local Nature Reserve 3A 66
Gillespie Rd. N5 3A 66
Gillett Av. E6 2C 88
GILLETTE CORNER 7A 96
Gillett Ho. *N8* *3J 47*
(off Campsfield Rd.)
Gillett Pl. N16 5E 66
Gillett Rd. CR7: Thor H 4D 156
Gillett Sq. *N16* *5E 66*
(off Gillett St.)
Gillett St. N16 5E 66
Gillfoot *NW1* *1A 6*
(off Hampstead Rd.)
Gillham Ter. N17 6B 34
Gillian Ho. HA3: Hrw W 6D 26
Gillian Pk. Rd. SM3: Sutt 1H 165
Gillian St. SE13 5D 122
Gillies Ho. *NW6* *7B 64*
(off Hilgrove Rd.)
Gillies St. NW5 5E 64
Gilling Ct. NW3 6C 64
Gillingham M. SW1 3A 18 (4G 101)
Gillingham Rd. NW2 3G 63
Gillingham Row SW1 3A 18 (4G 101)
Gillingham St. SW1 3A 18 (4G 101)
Gillings Ct. *EN5: Barn* *4B 20*
(off Wood St.)
Gillison Wlk. SE16 3H 103
Gillis Sq. SW15 6C 116
Gillman Dr. E15 1H 87
Gillman Ho. *E2* *2G 85*
(off Pritchard's Rd.)
Gillray Ho. *SW10* *6B 100*
(off Ann La.)
Gill St. E14 6B 86
Gillum Cl. EN4: E Barn 1J 31
Gilman Ho. *N1* *7A 66*
(off Drummond Way)
Gilmore Cl. UB10: Ick 3C 56
Gilmore Ct. N11 5J 31
Gilmore Cres. TW15: Ashf 5C 128
Gilmore Rd. SE13 4F 123
Gilmour Ho. NW9 2C 44
Gilpin Av. SW14 4K 115
Gilpin Cl. CR4: Mitc 2C 154
W2 *5A 4*
(off Porteus Rd.)
Gilpin Cres. N18 5A 34
TW2: Whitt 7F 113
Gilpin Rd. E5 4A 68
Gilpin Way UB3: Harl 7F 93
Gilray Ho. *W2* *2A 10*
(off Gloucester Ter.)
Gilsland Pl. CR7: Thor H 4D 156
Gilsland Rd. CR7: Thor H 4D 156
Gilson Pl. N10 7J 31
Gilstead Rd. SW6 2K 117
Gilston Rd. SW10 7A 16 (5A 100)
Gilton Rd. SE6 3G 141
Giltspur St. EC1 7B 8 (6B 84)
Gilwell Cl. E4 4J 25
Gilwell La. E4 4K 25
(not continuous)
GILWELL PARK 4K 25
Gilwell Pk. E4 3K 25
Ginger Apartments *SE1* *6K 15*
(off Cayenne Ct.)
Ginsburg Yd. NW3 4A 64
Gippeswyck Cl. HA5: Pinn 1B 40
Gipsy Hill SE19 4E 138
Gipsy La. SW15 3D 116
Gipsy Rd. DA16: Well 7D 108
SE27 4C 138
Gipsy Rd. Gdns. SE27 4C 138
Giralda Cl. E16 5B 88
Giraud St. E14 6D 86
Girdler's Rd. W14 4F 99
Girdlestone Wlk. N19 2G 65
Girdwood Rd. SW18 7G 117
Girling Ho. *N1* *1E 84*
(off Colville Est.)
Girling Way TW14: Felt 3J 111
Gironde Rd. SW6 7H 99
Girtin Ho. *UB5: N'olt* *2B 76*
(off Academy Gdns.)
Girton Av. NW9 3G 43
Girton Cl. UB5: N'olt 6G 59
Girton Gdns. CR0: C'don 3C 170
Girton Rd. SE26 5K 139
UB5: N'olt 6G 59
Girton Vs. W10 6F 81
Gisbourne Cl. SM6: Bedd 3H 167
Gisburn Ho. *SE15* *6G 103*
(off Friary Est.)
Gisburn Rd. N8 4K 47
Gissing Wlk. N1 7A 66
Gittens Cl. BR1: Brom 4H 141
Given Wilson Wlk. E13 2H 87
Giverny Ho. *SE16* *2K 103*
(off Water Gdns. Sq.)
Glacier Way HA0: Wemb 2D 78
Gladbeck Way EN2: Enf 4G 23
Gladding Rd. E12 4B 70
Glade, The BR1: Brom 2B 160
BR4: W W'ck 3D 170
CR0: C'don 5K 157
E8 6G 67
EN2: Enf 3F 23
IG5: Ilf 1D 52
IG8: Wfd G 3E 36
KT17: Ewe 6C 164
N12 3G 31
N21 6E 22
SE7 7A 106
SM2: Cheam 7G 165
W12 *2D 98*
(off Coningham Rd.)
Glade Apartments *E14* *4E 104*
(off Stebondale St.)
Glade Cl. KT6: Surb 2D 162
Glade Ct. IG5: Ilf 1D 52
Glade Gdns. CR0: C'don 7A 158
Glade La. UB2: S'hall 2F 95
Glades, The BR1: Brom 2J 159
KT6: Surb 7E 150
Gladeside CR0: C'don 6K 157
N21 6E 22
Gladeside Cl. KT9: Chess 7D 162
Gladesmore Community School & Sports Cen. 5G 49
Gladesmore Rd. N15 6F 49
Glades Pl. BR1: Brom 2J 159
Gladeswood Rd. DA17: Belv 4H 109
Glade Wlk. E20 6D 68
Gladiator St. SE23 7A 122
Glading Ter. N16 3F 67
Gladioli Cl. TW12: Hamp 6E 130
Gladsdale Dr. HA5: Eastc 4J 39
Gladsmuir Rd. EN5: Barn 2B 20
N19 1G 65
Gladstone Av. E12 7C 70
N22 2A 48
TW2: Twick 1H 131
TW14: Felt 6J 111
Gladstone Ct. *NW6* *7A 64*
(off Fairfax Rd.)
SW1 *4D 18*
(off Regency St.)
Gladstone Ct. Bus. Cen. *SW8* *1F 119*
(off Pagden St.)
Gladstone Gdns. TW3: Houn 1G 113
Gladstone Ho. CR4: Mitc 2D 154
E14 *6C 86*
(off E. India Dock Rd.)
Gladstone M. N22 2A 48
NW6 *7H 63*
(off Cavendish Rd.)
SE20 7J 139
Gladstone Pde. NW2 2E 62
Gladstone Pk. Gdns. NW2 4D 62
Gladstone Pl. E3 2B 86
EN5: Barn 4A 20
KT8: E Mos 5J 149

Gladstone Rd.—Glen Rd.

Gladstone Rd. BR6: Farnb 5G 173
CR0: C'don 7D 156
IG9: Buck H 1F 37
KT1: King T 3G 151
KT6: Surb 2D 162
SW19 7J 135
UB2: S'hall 2C 94
W4 3K 97
Gladstone St. SE1 3B 102
Gladstone Ter. *SE27 5C 138*
(off Bentons La.)
SW8 1F 119
Gladstone Way
HA3: W'stone 3J 41
Gladwell Rd. BR1: Brom 6J 141
N8 6K 47
Gladwin Ho. *NW1 1B 6*
(off Werrington St.)
Gladwyn Rd. SW15 3F 117
Gladys Dimson Ho. E7 5H 69
Gladys Rd. NW6 7J 63
Glaisher St. SE8 6C 104
Glamis Ct. W3 2H 97
Glamis Cres. UB3: Harl 3E 92
Glamis Pl. E1 7J 85
Glamis Rd. E1 7J 85
Glamis Way UB5: N'olt 6G 59
Glamorgan Cl. CR4: Mitc 3J 155
Glamorgan Ct. *W7 5K 77*
(off Copley Cl.)
Glamorgan Rd. KT1: Hamp W 7C 132
Glandford Way RM6: Chad H 5B 54
Glanfield Rd. BR3: Beck 4B 158
Glanleam Rd. HA7: Stan 4J 27
Glanville M. HA7: Stan 5F 27
Glanville Rd. BR2: Brom 3K 159
SW2 5J 119
Glasbrook Av. TW2: Whitt 1D 130
Glasbrook Rd. SE9 7B 124
Glaserton Rd. N16 7E 48
Glasford St. SW17 6D 136
Glasfryn Ct. *HA2: Harr 2H 59*
(off Roxeth Hill)
Glasfryn Ho. *HA2: Harr 2H 59*
(off Roxeth Hill)
Glasgow Ho. *W9 2K 81*
(off Maida Vale)
Glasgow Rd. E13 2K 87
N18 5C 34
Glasgow Ter. SW1 6A 18 (5G 101)
Glasier Ct. E15 7G 69
Glaskin M. E9 6A 68
Glass Bldg., The *NW1 1F 83*
(off Jamestown Rd.)
Glasse Cl. W13 7A 78
Glass Foundry Yd. *E13 5K 87*
(off Denmark St.)
Glasshill St. SE1 6B 14 (2B 102)
Glass Ho. *WC2 1E 12*
(off Shaftesbury Av.)
Glass Ho., The *SE1 7G 15*
(off Royal Oak Yd.)
Glasshouse Cl. UB8: Hil 5D 74
Glasshouse Flds. E1 7K 85
(not continuous)
Glasshouse St. W1 3B 12 (7G 83)
Glasshouse Wlk. SE11 5F 19 (5J 101)
Glasshouse Yd. EC1 4C 8 (4C 84)
Glasslyn Rd. N8 5H 47
Glassmill La. BR2: Brom 2H 159
Glass Mill Leisure Cen. 3E 122
Glass St. E2 4H 85
Glassworks Studios *E2 1H 9*
(off Basing Pl.)
Glass Yd. SE18 3E 106
Glastonbury Av.
IG8: Wfd G 7G 37
Glastonbury Ct. *SE14 7J 103*
(off Farrow La.)
W13 1A 96
(off Talbot Rd.)
Glastonbury Ho. *SE12 5H 123*
(off Wantage Rd.)
SW1 5J 17
(part of Abbots Mnr.)
Glastonbury Pl. E1 6J 85
Glastonbury Rd. N9 1B 34
SM4: Mord 7J 153
Glastonbury St. NW6 5H 63
Glaston Ct. *W5 1D 96*
(off Grange Rd.)
Glaucus St. E3 5D 86
Glazbury Rd. W14 4G 99
Glazebrook Cl. SE21 2D 138
Glazebrook Rd. TW11: Tedd 7K 131
Glebe, The BR7: Chst 1G 161
KT4: Wor Pk 1B 164
SE3 3G 123
SW16 4H 137
UB7: W Dray 4B 92
Glebe Av. CR4: Mitc 2C 154
EN2: Enf 3G 23
HA3: Kenton 4E 42
HA4: Ruis 6K 57
IG8: Wfd G 6D 36
UB10: Ick 3E 56
Glebe Cl. UB10: Ick 4E 56
W4 5A 98
Glebe Cotts. *TW13: Hanw 3E 130*
(off Twickenham Rd.)
Glebe Ct. CR4: Mitc 3D 154
E3 3D 86
(off Rainhill Way)
HA7: Stan 5H 27
N13 3F 33
SE3 3G 123
W5 1D 96
W7 7H 77
Glebe Cres. HA3: Kenton 3E 42
NW4 4E 44
Glebe Farm Bus. Pk. BR2: Kes 7B 172
Glebe Gdns. KT3: N Mald 7A 152
Glebe Ho. *SE16 3H 103*
(off Slippers Pl.)
Glebe Ho. Dr. BR2: Hayes 1K 171
Glebe Hyrst SE19 4E 138
Glebe Knoll BR2: Brom 2H 159
Glebeland Gdns. TW17: Shep 6E 146
Glebelands E10 2D 68
KT8: W Mole 5F 149
Glebelands Av. E18 2J 51
IG2: Ilf 7H 53
Glebelands Cl. N12 1B 46
SE5 3E 120
Glebelands Rd. TW14: Felt 1J 129
Glebe La. HA3: Kenton 4E 42
Glebe M. DA15: Sidc 6K 125
Glebe Path CR4: Mitc 3D 154
Glebe Pl. SW3 7C 16 (6C 100)
Glebe Rd. BR1: Brom 1J 159
E8 7F 67
HA7: Stan 5H 27
N3 1A 46
N8 4K 47
NW10 6C 62
RM10: Dag 6H 73
SM2: Cheam 7G 165
SM5: Cars 6D 166
SW13 2C 116
UB3: Hayes 1H 93
Glebe Side TW1: Twick 6K 113
Glebe Sq. CR4: Mitc 3D 154
Glebe St. W4 5A 98
Glebe Ter. W4 5A 98
Glebe Way BR4: W W'ck 2E 170
IG8: Wfd G 5F 37
TW13: Hanw 3E 130
Gledhow Gdns. SW5 4A 100
Gledstanes Rd. W14 5G 99
Gledwood Av. UB4: Hayes 5H 75
Gledwood Ct. UB4: Hayes 5H 75
Gledwood Cres. UB4: Hayes 5H 75
Gledwood Dr. UB4: Hayes 5H 75
Gledwood Gdns.
UB4: Hayes 5H 75
Gleed Av. WD23: B Hea 2C 26
Gleeson Dr. BR6: Chels 5K 173
Glegg Pl. SW15 4F 117
Glen, The BR2: Brom 2G 159
BR6: Farnb 3D 172
CR0: C'don 3K 169
EN2: Enf 4G 23
HA5: Eastc 5K 39
HA5: Pinn 7C 40
HA9: Wemb 4E 60
UB2: S'hall 5D 94
Glenaffric Av. E14 4E 104
Glen Albyn Rd. SW19 2F 135
Glenallan Ho. *W14 4H 99*
(off North End Cres.)
Glenalla Rd. HA4: Ruis 7H 39
Glenalmond Ho. TW15: Ashf 3A 128
Glenalmond Rd. HA3: Kenton 4E 42
Glenalvon Way SE18 4C 106
Glena Mt. SM1: Sutt 4A 166
Glenarm Rd. E5 4J 67
Glen Av. TW15: Ashf 4C 128
Glenavon Cl. KT10: Clay 6A 162
Glenavon Ct. KT4: Wor Pk 2D 164
Glenavon Lodge BR3: Beck 7C 140
Glenavon Rd. E15 7G 69
Glenbarr Cl. SE9 3F 125
Glenbow Rd. BR1: Brom 6G 141
Glenbrook Nth. EN2: Enf 4E 22
Glenbrook Rd. NW6 5J 63
Glenbrook Sth. EN2: Enf 4E 22
Glenbuck Ct. KT6: Surb 6E 150
Glenbuck Rd. KT6: Surb 6D 150
Glenburnie Rd. SW17 3D 136
Glencairn Dr. W5 4C 78
Glencairne Cl. E16 5B 88
Glencairn Rd. SW16 1J 155
Glencar Ct. SE19 6B 138
Glen Cl. TW17: Shep 4C 146
Glencoe Av. IG2: Ilf 7H 53
Glencoe Dr. RM10: Dag 4G 73
Glencoe Mans. *SW9 7A 102*
(off Mowll St.)
Glencoe Rd. UB4: Yead 5B 76
Glen Ct. *BR1: Brom 7H 141*
(off Bromley Av.)
DA15: Sidc 4A 144
Glen Cres. IG8: Wfd G 6E 36
Glendale Av. HA8: Edg 4A 28
N22 7F 33
RM6: Chad H 7C 54
Glendale Cl. SE9 3E 124
Glendale Dr. SW19 5H 135
Glendale Gdns. HA9: Wemb 1D 60
Glendale M. BR3: Beck 1D 158
Glendale Rd. DA8: Erith 4J 109
Glendale Way SE28 7C 90
Glendall St. SW9 4K 119
Glendarvon St. SW15 3F 117
Glendevon Cl. HA8: Edg 3C 28
Glendish Rd. N17 1H 49
Glendor Gdns. NW7 4E 28
Glendower Gdns. SW14 3K 115
Glendower Pl. SW7 3A 16 (4B 100)
Glendower Rd. E4 1A 36
SW14 3K 115
Glendown Ho. E8 5G 67
Glendown Rd. SE2 5A 108
Glendun Ct. W3 7A 80
Glendun Rd. W3 7A 80
Gleneagle M. SW16 5H 137
Gleneagle Rd. SW16 5H 137
Gleneagles HA7: Stan 7G 27
W13 5B 78
(off Malvern Way)
Gleneagles Cl. BR6: Orp 1H 173
SE16 5H 103
Gleneagles Grn. BR6: Orp 1H 173
Gleneagles Twr. *UB1: S'hall 6G 77*
(off Fleming Rd.)
Gleneldon M. SW16 4J 137
Gleneldon Rd. SW16 4J 137
Glenelg Rd. SW2 5J 119
Glenesk Rd. SE9 3E 124
Glenfarg Rd. SE6 1E 140
Glenfield Cres. HA4: Ruis 7F 39
Glenfield Rd. SW12 1G 137
TW15: Ashf 6D 128
W13 2B 96
Glenfield Ter. W13 2B 96
Glenfinlas Way SE5 7B 102
Glenforth St. SE10 5H 105
Glengall Bus. Cen. SE15 6F 103
Glengall Gro. E14 3D 104
Glengall Pas. *NW6 1J 81*
(off Priory Pk. Rd.)
Glengall Rd. DA7: Bex 3E 126
HA8: Edg 3C 28
IG8: Wfd G 6D 36
NW6 1H 81
SE15 5F 103
Glengall Ter. SE15 6F 103
Glen Gdns. CR0: Wadd 3A 168
Glengariff Mans. *SW9 7A 102*
(off Sth. Island Pl.)
Glengarnock Av. E14 4E 104
Glengarry Rd. SE22 5E 120
Glenham Dr. IG2: Ilf 5F 53
Glenhead Cl. SE9 3F 125
Glenhill Cl. N3 2J 45
Glen Ho. *E16 1E 106*
(off Storey St.)
Glenhouse Rd. SE9 5E 124
Glenhurst BR3: Beck 1E 158
Glenhurst Av. DA5: Bexl 1F 145
HA4: Ruis 7E 38
NW5 4E 64
Glenhurst Ct. SE19 5F 139
Glenhurst Ri. SE19 7C 138
Glenhurst Rd. N12 5G 31
TW8: Bford 6C 96
Glenilla Rd. NW3 6C 64
Glenister Gdns. UB3: Hayes 2K 93
Glenister Ho. *UB3: Hayes 1K 93*
(off Avondale Dr.)
Glenister Pk. Rd. SW16 7H 137
Glenister Rd. SE10 5H 105
Glenister St. E16 1E 106
Glenkerry Ho. *E14 6E 86*
(off Burcham St.)
Glenlea Rd. SE9 5D 124
Glenloch Rd. EN3: Enf H 2D 24
NW3 6C 64
Glenluce Rd. SE3 6J 105
Glenlyon Rd. SE9 5E 124
Glenmead IG9: Buck H 1F 37
Glenmere Av. NW7 7H 29
Glenmere Row SE12 6J 123
Glen M. E17 5B 50
Glenmill TW12: Hamp 5D 130
Glenmore Lawns W13 6A 78
Glenmore Lodge BR3: Beck 1D 158
Glenmore Pde. HA0: Wemb 1E 78
Glenmore Rd. DA16: Well 7K 107
NW3 6C 64
Glenmore Way IG11: Bark 2A 90
Glenmount Path SE18 5G 107
Glennie Ct. SE22 1G 139
Glennie Rd. SE27 3A 138
Glenny Rd. IG11: Bark 6G 71
Glenorchy Cl. UB4: Yead 5C 76
Glenpark Ct. W13 7A 78
Glenparke Rd. E7 6K 69
Glenridding *NW1 1B 6*
(off Ampthill Est.)
Glen Ri. IG8: Wfd G 6E 36
Glen Rd. E13 4A 88
E17 5B 50
KT9: Chess 4F 163

Glen Rd. End SM6: Wall 7F 167
Glenrosa St. SW6 2A 118
Glenrose Ct. DA14: Sidc 5B 144
SE1 *7G 15*
(off Long La.)
Glenroy St. W12 6E 80
Glensdale Rd. SE4 3B 122
Glenshaw Mans. *SW9* *7A 102*
(off Brixton Rd.)
Glenshiel Rd. SE9 5E 124
Glentanner Way SW17 3B 136
Glen Ter. *E14* *2E 104*
(off Manchester Rd.)
Glentham Gdns. SW13 6D 98
Glentham Rd. SW13 6C 98
Glenthorne Av. CR0: C'don 1H 169
Glenthorne Cl. SM3: Sutt 1J 165
UB10: Hil 3C 74
Glenthorne Gdns. IG6: Ilf 3E 52
SM3: Sutt 1J 165
Glenthorne M. W6 4D 98
Glenthorne Rd. E17 5A 50
KT1: King T 4F 151
N11 5J 31
W6 4D 98
Glenthorpe Av. SW15 4C 116
Glenthorpe Gdns. HA7: Stan 3E 26
Glenthorpe Rd. SM4: Mord 5F 153
Glenton M. SE15 2J 121
Glenton Rd. SE13 4G 123
Glentrammon Av. BR6: Chels 6K 173
Glentrammon Cl. BR6: Chels 5K 173
Glentrammon Gdns. BR6: Chels 6K 173
Glentrammon Rd. BR6: Chels 6K 173
Glentworth St. NW1 4F 5 (4D 82)
Glenure Rd. SE9 5E 124
Glenvern Ct. *TW7: Isle* *2A 114*
(off White Lodge Cl.)
Glenview SE2 6D 108
Glenview Rd. BR1: Brom 2B 160
Glenville Av. EN2: Enf 1H 23
Glenville Gro. SE8 7B 104
Glenville M. SW18 7K 117
Glenville M. Ind. Est. SW18 7J 117
Glenville Rd. KT2: King T 1G 151
Glen Wlk. TW7: Isle 5H 113
(not continuous)
Glenwood Av. NW9 1A 62
Glenwood Cl. HA1: Harr 5K 41
Glenwood Ct. DA14: Sidc 4A 144
E18 3J 51
Glenwood Gdns. IG2: Ilf 5E 52
Glenwood Gro. NW9 1J 61
Glenwood Rd. KT17: Ewe 6C 164
N15 5B 48
NW7 3F 29
SE6 1B 140
TW3: Houn 3H 113
Glenwood Way CR0: C'don 6K 157
Glenworth Av. E14 4F 105
Gliddon Dr. E5 4H 67
Gliddon Rd. W14 4G 99
Glimpsing Grn. DA18: Erith 3E 108
Glisson Rd. UB10: Hil 2C 74
Global App. E3 2E 86
Globe Apartments *SE8* *6B 104*
(off Evelyn St.)
Globe Pond Rd. SE16 1A 104
Globe Rd. E1 3J 85
E2 3J 85
E15 5H 69
IG8: Wfd G 6F 37
Globe Rope Wlk. *E14* *4D 104*
(off E. Ferry Rd.)
Globe St. SE1 7E 14 (3D 102)
Globe Ter. E2 3J 85
GLOBE TOWN 3K 85
Globe Town Mkt. E2 3K 85
Globe Vw. *EC4* *2C 14*
(off High Timber St.)
Globe Wharf SE16 7K 85
Globe Yd. W1 1J 11
Glossop Rd. CR2: Sande 7D 168
Gloster Ridley Ct. *E14* *6B 86*
(off St Anne's Row)
Gloster Rd. KT3: N Mald 4A 152
Gloucester *W14* *4H 99*
(off Kensington Village)
Gloucester Arc. SW7 4A 100
Gloucester Av. DA15: Sidc 2J 143
DA16: Well 4K 125
NW1 7E 64
Gloucester Cir. SE10 7E 104
Gloucester Cl. KT7: T Ditt 1A 162
NW10 7K 61
Gloucester Ct. CR4: Mitc 5J 155
EC3 3H 15 (7E 84)
HA1: Harr 3J 41
NW11 *7H 45*
(off Golders Grn. Rd.)
SE1 *5F 103*
(off Rolls Rd.)
SE1 *7D 14*
(off Swan St.)
SE22 1G 139
TW9: Kew 7G 97
W7 *5K 77*
(off Copley Cl.)
Gloucester Cres. NW1 1F 83
TW18: Staines 6A 128
Gloucester Dr. N4 2B 66
NW11 4J 45
Gloucester Gdns.
EN4: Cockf 4K 21
IG1: Ilf 7C 52
NW11 7H 45
SM1: Sutt 2K 165
W2 6A 82
Gloucester Ga. NW1 2F 83
(not continuous)
Gloucester Ga. Bri. *NW1* *1F 83*
(off Gloucester Gate)
Gloucester Ga. M. NW1 2F 83
Gloucester Gro. HA8: Edg 1K 43
Gloucester Ho. *E16* *1J 105*
(off Gatcombe Rd.)
NW6 *2J 81*
(off Cambridge Rd.)
SW9 7A 102
TW10: Rich 5G 115
Gloucester M. E10 7C 50
W2 1A 10 (6A 82)
Gloucester M. W. W2 6A 82
Gloucester Pde. DA15: Sidc 5A 126
UB3: Harl 3E 92
Gloucester Pk. Apartments *SW7* *4A 100*
(off Ashburn Pl.)
Gloucester Pl. NW1 4E 4 (4D 82)
W1 4E 4 (4D 82)
Gloucester Pl. M. W1 6F 5 (5D 82)
Gloucester Rd.
CR0: C'don 1D 168
DA17: Belv 5F 109
E10 7C 50
E11 5K 51
E12 3D 70
E17 2K 49
EN2: Enf 1H 23
EN5: New Bar 5E 20
HA1: Harr 5F 41
KT1: King T 2G 151
N17 2D 48
N18 5A 34
SW7 4A 16 (3A 100)
TW2: Twick 1G 131
TW4: Houn 4C 112
TW9: Kew 7G 97
TW11: Tedd 5J 131
TW12: Hamp 7F 131
TW13: Felt 1A 130
W3 2J 97
W5 2C 96
Gloucester Sq. E2 1G 85
W2 1B 10 (6B 82)
(not continuous)
Gloucester St. SW1 6A 18 (5G 101)
Gloucester Ter. *N14* *1C 32*
(off Crown La.)
W2 1A 10 (6K 81)
Gloucester Wlk. W8 2J 99
Gloucester Way EC1 2K 7 (3A 84)
Glover Cl. SE2 4C 108
Glover Dr. N18 6D 34
Glover Ho. *NW6* *7A 64*
(off Harben Rd.)
SE15 4H 121
Glover Rd. HA5: Pinn 6B 40
Glovers Gro. HA4: Ruis 7D 38
Gloxinia Wlk. TW12: Hamp 6E 130
Glycena Rd. SW11 3D 118
Glyn Av. EN4: E Barn 4G 21
Glyn Cl. SE25 2E 156
Glyn Ct. HA7: Stan 6G 27
SW16 3A 138
Glyndale Grange SM2: Sutt 6K 165
Glyndebourne Ct. *UB5: N'olt* *3A 76*
(off Canberra Dr.)
Glyndebourne Pk. BR6: Farnb 2F 173
Glynde M. SW3 2D 16
Glynde Reach WC1 2F 7
Glynde Rd. DA7: Bex 3D 126
Glynde St. SE4 6B 122
Glyndon Rd. SE18 4G 107
(not continuous)
Glyn Dr. DA14: Sidc 4B 144
Glynfield Rd. NW10 7A 62
Glyn Mans. *W14* *4G 99*
(off Hammersmith Rd.)
Glynne Rd. N22 2A 48
Glyn Rd. E5 3K 67
EN3: Pond E 4D 24
KT4: Wor Pk 2F 165
Glyn St. SE11 6G 19 (5K 101)
Glynswood Pl. HA6: Nwood 1D 38
Glynwood Ct. SE23 2J 139
Goals Soccer Cen.
Bexleyheath 3F 127
Chingford 6H 35
Dagenham 1D 90
Eltham 6A 124
Gillette Corner 6K 95
Hayes 1A 94
Heathrow 4E 92
Ruislip 5B 58
Sutton 3F 165
Tolworth 2J 163
Wimbledon 3C 152
Go Ape
Trent Park 3K 21
Goater's All. *SW6* *7H 99*
(off Dawes Rd.)
Goat Ho. Bri. SE25 3G 157
Goat La. EN1: Enf 1A 24
Goat Rd. CR4: Cars, Mitc 7D 154
Goat Wharf TW8: Bford 6E 96
Gobions Av. RM5: Col R 1K 55
Goby Ho. *SE8* *7D 104*
(off Creative Rd.)
Godalming Av. SM6: Wall 5J 167
Godalming Rd. E14 5D 86
Godbold Rd. E15 4G 87
Goddard Cl. TW17: Shep 3B 146
Goddard Ct. HA3: Kenton 2A 42
Goddard Ho. *SE11* *4B 102*
(off George Mathers Rd.)
Goddard Pl. N19 3G 65
Goddard Rd. BR3: Beck 4K 157
Goddards Way IG1: Ilf 1H 71
Goddarts Ho. E17 3C 50
Goddington La.
BR6: Chels 3K 173
Godfree Ct. *SE1* *6E 14*
(off Long La.)
Godfrey Av. TW2: Whitt 7H 113
UB5: N'olt 1C 76
Godfrey Hill SE18 4C 106
Godfrey Ho. EC1 2E 8
Godfrey Pl. *E2* *2J 9*
(off Austin St.)
Godfrey Rd. SE18 4D 106
Godfrey St. E15 2E 86
SW3 5D 16 (5C 100)
Godfrey Way TW4: Houn 7C 112
Goding St. SE11 5F 19 (5J 101)
Godley Cl. SE14 1J 121
Godley Rd. SW18 1B 136
Godliman St. EC4 1B 14 (6B 84)
Godman Rd. SE15 2H 121
Godolphin Cl. N13 6G 33
Godolphin Ho. *NW3* *7C 64*
(off Fellows Rd.)
Godolphin Pl. W3 7K 79
Godolphin Rd. W12 1D 98
(not continuous)
Godric Cres. CR0: New Ad 7F 171
Godson Rd. CR0: Wadd 3A 168
Godson St. N1 2A 84
Godson Yd. *NW6* *3J 81*
(off Kilburn Pk. Rd.)
Godstone Ho. *SE1* *7F 15*
(off Pardoner St.)
Godstone Rd. SM1: Sutt 4A 166
TW1: Twick 6B 114
Godstow Rd. SE2 2B 108
Godward Sq. E1 4K 85
Godwin Cl. E4 1K 25
KT19: Ewe 6J 163
N1 2C 84
Godwin Ct. *NW1* *2G 83*
(off Chalton St.)
Godwin Ho. *E2* *2F 85*
(off Thurtle Rd.)
NW6 *2K 81*
(off Tollgate Gdns.)
SE1 *5J 15*
(off Still Wlk.)
Godwin Rd. BR2: Brom 3A 160
E7 4K 69
Goffers Rd. SE3 1G 123
Goffs Rd. TW15: Ashf 6F 129
Goidel Cl. SM6: Bedd 4H 167
Golborne Gdns. W10 4G 81
(not continuous)
Golborne M. W10 5G 81
Golborne Rd. W10 5G 81
Golda Cl. EN5: Barn 6A 20
Golda Ct. N3 2H 45
Goldbeaters Gro. HA8: Edg 6F 29
Goldbeaters Ho. *W1* *1D 12*
(off Manette St.)
Goldcliff Cl. SM4: Mord 7J 153
Goldcrest Cl. E16 5B 88
SE28 7C 90
Goldcrest M. N16 3G 67
W5 5D 78
Goldcrest Way CR0: New Ad 7F 171
WD23: Bush 1B 26
Golden Bus. Pk. E10 1A 68
Golden Ct. EN4: E Barn 4H 21
TW7: Isle 2H 113
TW9: Rich 5D 114
Golden Cres. UB3: Hayes 1H 93
Golden Cross M. *W11* *6H 81*
(off Portobello Rd.)
Golden Hinde 4E 14 (1D 102)
Golden Hind Pl. *SE8* *4B 104*
(off Grove St.)
Golden Jubilee Bridges 5G 13
Golden La. BR4: W W'ck 3E 170
EC1 3C 8 (4C 84)
Golden La. Campus EC1 4D 8
Golden La. Est. EC1 4C 8 (4C 84)
Golden Lane Leisure Cen. 4C 8
Golden Mnr. W7 7J 77

Golden M. SE20 1J 157
Golden Mile Ho. TW8: Bford 5E 96
(off Clayponds La.)
Golden Pde. E17 3E 50
(off Wood St.)
Golden Plover Cl. E16 6J 87
Golden Sq. W1 2B 12 (7G 83)
Golden Yd. NW3 4A 64
(off Holly Mt.)
Golders Cl. HA8: Edg 5C 28
Golders Ct. NW11 7H 45
Golders Gdns. NW11 7G 45
GOLDERS GREEN 6G 45
Golders Grn. Crematorium
NW11 7J 45
Golders Grn. Cres. NW11 7H 45
Golders Grn. Rd. NW11 6G 45
Goldersleа NW11 1J 63
Golders Mnr. Dr. NW11 6F 45
Golders Pk. Cl. NW11 1J 63
Golders Ri. NW4 5F 45
Golders Way NW11 7H 45
Golderton NW4 4D 44
(off Prince of Wales Cl.)
Goldfinch Ct. E3 2C 86
(off Four Seasons Cl.)
Goldfinch Rd. SE28 3H 107
Goldhawk Ho. NW9 3B 44
(off Caversham Rd.)
Goldhawk Ind. Est. W6 3D 98
Goldhawk M. W12 2D 98
Goldhawk Rd. W6 4B 98
W12 4B 98
Goldhaze Cl. IG8: Wfd G 7F 37
Gold Hill HA8: Edg 6E 28
Goldhurst Ho. W6 6E 98
Goldhurst Mans. NW6 6A 64
(off Goldhurst Ter.)
Goldhurst Ter. NW6 7K 63
Goldie Ho. N19 7H 47
Goldie Leigh Hospital SE2 7B 108
Golding Cl. KT9: Chess 6C 162
N18 6J 33
Golding Ct. IG1: Ilf 3E 70
Golding St. E1 6G 85
(not continuous)
Golding Ter. E1 6G 85
(off Rope Wlk. Gdns.)
SW11 2E 118
Goldington Bldgs. NW1 1H 83
(off Royal College St.)
Goldington Cres. NW1 2H 83
Goldington St. NW1 2H 83
Gold La. HA8: Edg 6E 28
Goldman Cl. E2 3K 9 (4G 85)
Goldney Rd. W9 4J 81
Goldrill Dr. N11 2K 31
Goldsboro' Rd. SW8 1H 119
Goldsborough Cres. E4 2J 35
Goldsborough Ho. E14 5D 104
(off St Davids Sq.)
Goldsdown Cl. EN3: Enf H 2F 25
Goldsdown Rd. EN3: Enf H 2E 24
Goldsmid St. SE18 5J 107
Goldsmith Av. E12 6C 70
NW9 5A 44
RM7: Rush G 7G 55
W3 7K 79
Goldsmith Cl. HA2: Harr 1E 58
Goldsmith Ct. WC2 7F 7
(off Stukeley St.)
Goldsmith Est. SE15 1G 121
Goldsmith La. NW9 4H 43
Goldsmith Rd. E10 1C 68
E17 2K 49
N11 5J 31
SE15 1G 121
W3 1K 97
Goldsmith's Bldgs. W3 1K 97
Goldsmiths Cl. W3 1K 97
Goldsmiths College 1A 122
Goldsmith's Pl. NW6 1K 81
(off Springfield La.)
Goldsmith's Row E2 2G 85
Goldsmith's Sq. E2 2G 85
Goldsmith St. EC2 7D 8 (6C 84)
Goldsworthy Gdns.
SE16 5J 103
Goldthorpe NW1 1G 83
(off Camden St.)
Goldwell Ho. SE22 3E 120
(off Quorn Rd.)
Goldwell Rd. CR7: Thor H 4K 155
Goldwin Cl. SE14 1J 121
Goldwing Cl. E16 6J 87
Golf Cl. CR7: Thor H 1A 156
HA7: Stan 7H 27
Golf Club Dr. KT2: King T 7K 133
Golfe Rd. IG1: Ilf 3H 71
Golf Kingdom
Barking 5F 55
Golf Rd. BR1: Brom 3E 160
W5 6F 79
Golf Side TW2: Twick 3H 131
Golfside Cl. KT3: N Mald 2A 152
N20 3H 31
Gollogly Ter. SE7 5A 106
Gomer Gdns. TW11: Tedd 6A 132
Gomer Pl. TW11: Tedd 6A 132
Gomm Rd. SE16 3J 103
Gomshall Av. SM6: Wall 5J 167
Gondar Gdns. NW6 5H 63
Gonson St. SE8 6D 104
Gonston Cl. SW19 2G 135
Gonville Cres. UB5: N'olt 6F 59
Gonville Rd. CR7: Thor H 5K 155
Gonville St. SW6 3G 117
Gooch Ho. E5 3H 67
EC1 5J 7
(off Portpool La.)
Goodall Ho. SE4 4K 121
Goodall Rd. E11 3E 68
Goodchild Rd. N4 1C 66
Gooden Ct. HA1: Harr 3J 59
Goodenough Rd. SW19 7H 135
Goodey Rd. IG11: Bark 7K 71
Goodfaith Ho. E14 7D 86
(off Simpson's Rd.)
Goodge Pl. W1 6B 6 (5G 83)
Goodge St. W1 6B 6 (5G 83)
Goodhall Cl. HA7: Stan 6F 27
Goodhall St. NW10 3B 80
(not continuous)
Goodhart Pl. E14 7A 86
Goodhart Way BR4: W W'ck 7G 159
Goodhew Rd. CR0: C'don 6G 157
Goodhope Ho. E14 7D 86
(off Poplar High St.)
Gooding Cl. KT3: N Mald 4J 151
Goodinge Cl. N7 6J 65
Gooding Ho. SE7 5A 106
Goodman Cres. CR0: C'don 6B 156
SW2 2J 137
Goodman Rd. E10 7E 50
Goodman's Ct. E1 2J 15 (7F 85)
Goodmans Ct. HA0: Wemb 4D 60
Goodman's Stile E1 6G 85
Goodmans Yd. E1 2J 15 (7F 85)
GOODMAYES 2A 72
Goodmayes Av. IG3: Ilf 1A 72
Goodmayes La. IG3: Ilf 4A 72
Goodmayes Lodge RM8: Dag 4A 72
Goodmayes Retail Pk. RM6: Chad H 1B 72
Goodmayes Rd. IG3: Ilf 1A 72
Goodrich Ct. W10 6F 81
Goodrich Ho. E2 2J 85
(off Sewardstone Rd.)
Goodrich Rd. SE22 6F 121
Goodridge Ho. E4 7K 35
Goodson Ho. SM4: Mord 7A 154
(off Green La.)
Goodson Rd. NW10 7A 62
Goodspeed Ho. E14 7D 86
(off Simpson's Rd.)
Goods Way N1 2J 83
Goodway Gdns. E14 6F 87
Goodwill Dr. HA2: Harr 1E 58
Goodwill Ho. E14 7D 86
(off Simpson's Rd.)
Goodwin Cl. CR4: Mitc 3B 154
SE16 3F 103
Goodwin Ct. EN4: E Barn 6H 21
N8 3J 47
(off Campsbourne Rd.)
SW19 7C 136
Goodwin Dr. DA14: Sidc 3D 144
Goodwin Gdns. CR0: Wadd 6B 168
Goodwin Ho. N9 1D 34
Goodwin Rd. CR0: Wadd 5B 168
N9 1E 34
W12 2C 98
Goodwins Ct. WC2 2E 12 (7J 83)
Goodwin St. N4 2A 66
Goodwood Apartments E4 7J 35
Goodwood Cl. HA7: Stan 5H 27
SM4: Mord 4J 153
Goodwood Ct. W1 5K 5
(off Devonshire St.)
Goodwood Dr. UB5: N'olt 6E 58
Goodwood Ho. SE14 7A 104
(off Goodwood Rd.)
Goodwood Pde. BR3: Beck 4A 158
Goodwood Rd. SE14 7A 104
Goodwyn Av. NW7 5F 29
Goodwyns Va. N10 1E 46
Goodyear Ho. N2 2B 46
(off The Grange)
Goodyear Pl. SE5 6C 102
Goodyer Ho. SW1 5C 18
(off Tachbrook St.)
Goodyers Gdns. NW4 5F 45
Goosander Way SE28 3H 107
Gooseacre La. HA3: Kenton 5D 42
Goose Grn. Trad. Est. SE22 4F 121
Gooseley La. E6 4F 89
(Claps Ga. La.)
E6 3E 88
(Folkestone Rd.)
Goosens Cl. SM1: Sutt 5A 166
Goose Sq. E6 6D 88
Gophir La. EC4 2E 14 (7D 84)
Gopsall St. N1 1D 84
Gordon Av. E4 6B 36
HA7: Stan 7E 26
SW14 4A 116
TW1: Twick 5A 114
Gordonbrock Rd. SE4 5C 122
Gordon Cl. E17 6C 50
N19 1G 65
Gordon Cotts. W8 2K 99
(off Dukes La.)
Gordon Ct. HA8: Edg 5A 28
Gordon Cres. CR0: C'don 1E 168
UB3: Hayes 4J 93
Gordondale Rd. SW19 2J 135
Gordon Dr. TW17: Shep 7F 147
Gordon Gdns. HA8: Edg 2H 43
Gordon Gro. SE5 2B 120
Gordon Hill EN2: Enf 1H 23
Gordon Ho. E1 7J 85
(off Glamis Rd.)
SW1 2B 18
(off Greencoat Pl.)
W5 3E 78
Gordon Ho. Rd. NW5 4E 64
Gordon Mans. W14 3F 99
(off Addison Gdns.)
WC1 4C 6
(off Torrington Pl.)
Gordon Pl. W8 2J 99
Gordon Rd. BR3: Beck 3B 158
DA15: Sidc 5J 125
DA17: Belv 4J 109
Gordon Rd. E4 1B 36
E11 6J 51
E15 4E 68
E18 1K 51
EN2: Enf 1H 23
HA3: W'stone 3J 41
IG1: Ilf 3H 71
IG11: Bark 1J 89
KT2: King T 1F 151
KT5: Surb 7F 151
N3 7C 30
N9 2C 34
N11 7C 32
RM6: Chad H 6F 55
SE15 2H 121
SM5: Cars 6D 166
TW3: Houn 4G 113
TW9: Rich 2F 115
TW15: Ashf 3A 128
TW17: Shep 6F 147
UB2: S'hall 4C 94
UB7: Yiew 7A 74
W4 6H 97
W5 7B 78
W13 7B 78
Gordon Sq. WC1 3C 6 (4H 83)
Gordon St. E13 3J 87
WC1 3C 6 (4H 83)
Gordon Way BR1: Brom 1J 159
EN5: Barn 4C 20
Gore Ct. NW9 5G 43
Gorefield Ho. NW6 2J 81
(off Gorefield Pl.)
Gorefield Pl. NW6 2J 81
Gore Ho. N1 7A 66
(off Drummond Way)
Gore Rd. E9 1J 85
SW20 2E 152
GORESBROOK INTERCHANGE 2F 91
Goresbrook Rd. RM9: Dag 1B 90
Gore St. SW7 3A 100
Gorham Ho. SE16 2K 103
(off Wolfe Cres.)
Gorham Pl. W11 7G 81
Goring Cl. RM5: Col R 1J 55
Goring Gdns. RM8: Dag 4C 72
Goring Rd. N11 6D 32
RM10: Dag 6K 73
Goring St. EC3 7H 9
Goring Way UB6: G'frd 2G 77
Gorleston Rd. N15 5D 48
Gorleston St. W14 4G 99
(not continuous)
Gorman Rd. SE18 4D 106
Gorringe Pk. Av. CR4: Mitc 7D 136
Gorse Cl. E16 6J 87
Gorsefield Ho. E14 7C 86
(off E. India Dock Rd.)
Gorse Ri. SW17 5E 136
Gorse Rd. CR0: C'don 4C 170
Gorse Wlk. UB7: Yiew 6A 74
Gorseway RM7: Rush G 1K 73, 2K 73
Gorst Rd. NW10 4J 79
SW11 6D 118
Gorsuch Pl. E2 1J 9 (3F 85)
Gorsuch St. E2 1J 9 (2F 85)
Gosberton Rd. SW12 1D 136
Gosbury Hill KT9: Chess 4E 162
Gosfield Rd. RM8: Dag 2G 73
Gosfield St. W1 6A 6 (5G 83)
Gosford Gdns. IG4: Ilf 5D 52
Gosford Ho. E3 2B 86
(off Tredegar Rd.)
Goshawk Ct. NW9 7B 44
Goshawk Gdns. UB4: Hayes 3G 75
Goslett Yd. WC2 1D 12 (6H 83)
Gosling Cl. UB6: G'frd 3E 76
Gosling Ho. E1 7J 85
(off Sutton St.)
Gosling Way SW9 1A 120
Gospatrick Rd. N17 7H 33

GOSPEL OAK 4E 64
Gosport Rd. E17 5B 50
Gosport Wlk. N17 4H 49
Gossage Rd. SE18 5H 107
UB10: Uxb 7B 56
Gosse Ct. N1 1E 84
(off Downham Rd.)
Gosset St. E2 1K 9 (3F 85)
Gosshill Rd. BR7: Chst 2E 160
Gossington Cl. BR7: Chst 4F 143
Gosterwood St. SE8 6A 104
Gostling Rd. TW2: Whitt 1E 130
Goston Gdns. CR7: Thor H 3A 156
Goston Ga. SW8 1K 119
(off Hampson Way)
Goswell Pl. EC1 2B 8
Goswell Rd. EC1 1A 8 (2B 84)
Gothic Cotts. EN2: Enf 2H 23
(off Chase Grn. Av.)
Gothic Ct. SE5 7C 102
(off Wyndham Rd.)
UB3: Harl 6F 93
Gothic Rd. TW2: Twick 2H 131
Gottfried M. NW5 4G 65
Goudhurst Rd. BR1: Brom 5G 141
Gough Ho. KT1: King T 2E 150
(off Eden St.)
N1 1B 84
(off Windsor St.)
Gough Rd. E15 4H 69
EN1: Enf 2C 24
Gough Sq. EC4 1K 13 (6A 84)
Gough St. WC1 3H 7 (4K 83)
Gough Wlk. E14 6C 86
Goulden Ho. SW11 2C 118
Goulden Ho. App. SW11 2C 118
Goulding Gdns. CR7: Thor H 2C 156
Gouldman Ho. E1 4J 85
(off Wyllen Cl.)
Gould Rd. TW2: Twick 1J 131
TW14: Felt 7G 111
GOULDS GREEN 5D 74
Gould's Grn. UB8: Hil 7D 74
Gould Ter. E8 5H 67
Gould Way HA8: Edg 7C 28
Goulston St. E1 7J 9 (6F 85)
Goulton Rd. E5 4H 67
Gourley Pl. N15 5E 48
Gourley St. N15 5E 48
Gourock Rd. SE9 5E 124
Govan St. E2 1G 85
Gover Ct. SW4 2J 119
Govett Av. TW17: Shep 5E 146
Govier Cl. E15 7G 69
Gowan Av. SW6 1G 117
Gowan Ho. E2 2K 9
(off Chambord St.)
Gowan Rd. NW10 6D 62
Gower Cl. SW4 6G 119
Gower Ct. WC1 3C 6 (4H 83)
Gower Ho. E17 3D 50
SE17 5C 102
(off Morecambe St.)
Gower M. WC1 6D 6 (5H 83)
Gower M. Mans. WC1 5D 6
(off Gower M.)
Gower Pl. WC1 3B 6 (4H 83)
Gower Rd. E7 6J 69
TW7: Isle 6K 95
Gower St. WC1 3B 6 (4G 83)
Gower's Wlk. E1 6G 85
Gowland Pl. BR3: Beck 2B 158
Gowlett Rd. SE15 3G 121
Gowlland Cl. CR0: C'don 7G 157
Gowrie Rd. SW11 3E 118
Graburn Way KT8: E Mos 3H 149
Grace Av. DA7: Bex 2F 127
Grace Bus. Cen. CR4: Mitc 6D 154
Gracechurch St. EC3 2F 15 (7D 84)
Grace Cl. HA8: Edg 7D 28
SE9 3B 142
Grace Ct. CR0: C'don 3B 168
(off Waddon Rd.)
SM2: Sutt 7K 165
Gracedale Rd. SW16 5F 137
Gracefield Gdns. SW16 3J 137
Gracehill E1 5J 85
(off Hannibal Rd.)
Grace Ho. SE11 7H 19
Grace Jones Cl. E8 6G 67
Grace M. BR3: Beck 6C 140
SE20 2J 157
(off Marlow Rd.)
Grace Path SE26 4J 139
Grace Pl. E3 3D 86
Grace Rd. CR0: C'don 6C 156
Graces All. E1 7G 85
Grace's M. SE5 2D 120
Graces M. NW8 2A 82
Grace's Rd. SE5 2E 120
Grace St. E3 3D 86
Gradient, The SE26 4G 139
Graduate Pl. SE1 7F 15
Graeme Rd. EN1: Enf 2J 23
Graemesdyke Av. SW14 3H 115
Grafton Chambers NW1 2D 6
(off Grafton Pl.)
Grafton Cl. KT4: Wor Pk 3A 164
TW4: Houn 1C 130
W13 6A 78
Grafton Ct. TW14: Bedf 1F 129
Grafton Cres. NW1 6F 65
Grafton Gdns. N4 6C 48
RM8: Dag 2E 72
Grafton Ho. E3 3C 86
(off Wellington Way)
SE8 5B 104
Grafton M. W1 4A 6 (4G 83)
Grafton Pk. Rd. KT4: Wor Pk 2A 164
Grafton Pl. NW1 2D 6 (3H 83)
Grafton Rd. CR0: C'don 1A 168
EN2: Enf 3E 22
HA1: Harr 5G 41
KT3: N Mald 3A 152
KT4: Wor Pk 3K 163
NW5 5E 64
RM8: Dag 2E 72
W3 7J 79
Graftons, The NW2 3J 63
Grafton Sq. SW4 3G 119
Grafton St. W1 3K 11 (7F 83)
Grafton Ter. NW5 5D 64
Grafton Way KT8: W Mole 4D 148
W1 4A 6 (4G 83)
(not continuous)
WC1 4A 6 (4G 83)
Grafton Yd. NW5 6F 65
Graham Av. CR4: Mitc 1E 154
W13 2B 96
Graham Cl. CR0: C'don 2C 170
Graham Ct. SE14 6K 103
(off Myers La.)
UB5: N'olt 5C 58
GRAHAME PARK 1A 44
Grahame Pk. Way NW7 7G 29
NW9 2B 44
Grahame Twr. W3 3H 97
(off Hanbury Rd.)
Grahame White Ho. HA3: Kenton 3D 42
Graham Gdns. KT6: Surb 1E 162
Graham Ho. N9 1D 34
(off Cumberland Rd.)
Graham Lodge NW4 6D 44
Graham Mans. IG11: Bark 7A 72
(off Lansbury Av.)
Graham Rd. CR4: Mitc 1E 154
DA6: Bex 4F 127
E8 6G 67
E13 4J 87
HA3: W'stone 3J 41
N15 3B 48
NW4 6D 44
Graham Rd. SW19 7H 135
TW12: Hamp H 4E 130
W4 3K 97
Graham St. N1 1B 8 (2B 84)
Graham Ter. DA15: Sidc 6B 126
(off Westerham Dr.)
SW1 4G 17 (4E 100)
Grainger Cl. UB5: N'olt 5F 59
Grainger Ct. SE5 7C 102
Grainger Rd. N22 1C 48
TW7: Isle 2K 113
Grainstore, The E16 7J 87
Gramer Cl. E11 2F 69
Grampian Cl. BR6: St M Cry 6K 161
SM2: Sutt 7A 166
UB3: Harl 7F 93
Grampian Gdns. NW2 1G 63
Grampians, The W6 2F 99
(off Shepherd's Bush Rd.)
Gramsci Way SE6 3D 140
Granada St. SW17 5D 136
Granard Av. SW15 5D 116
Granard Bus. Cen. NW7 6F 29
Granard Ho. E9 6K 67
Granard Rd. SW12 7D 118
Granary Cl. N9 7D 24
Granary Ct. E15 6F 69
(off Millstone Cl.)
Granary Mans. SE28 2G 107
Granary Rd. E1 4H 85
Granary Sq. N1 1J 83
Granary St. NW1 1H 83
Granby Pl. SE1 7J 13
(off Lower Marsh)
Granby Rd. SE9 2D 124
Granby St. E2 3K 9 (4G 85)
(not continuous)
Granby Ter. NW1 1A 6 (2G 83)
Grand Arc. N12 5F 31
Grand Av. EC1 5B 8 (5B 84)
(not continuous)
HA9: Wemb 5G 61
KT5: Surb 5H 151
N10 4E 46
Grand Av. E. HA9: Wemb 5H 61
Grand Canal Apartments N1 1E 84
(off De Beauvoir Cres.)
Grand Canal Av. SE16 4A 104
Grand Connaught Rooms 7G 7
Grand Courts RM8: Dag 3E 72
Grand Depot Rd. SE18 5E 106
Grand Dr. SW20 2E 152
UB2: S'hall 2G 95
Granden Rd. SW16 2J 155
Grandfield Ct. W4 6K 97
Grandison Rd. KT4: Wor Pk 2E 164
SW11 5D 118
Grand Junc. Wharf E2 3K 85
N1 2C 84
Grand Pde. HA9: Wemb 2G 61
KT6: Surb 1G 163
N4 5B 48
SW14 4J 115
(off Up. Richmond Rd. W.)
Grand Pde. M. SW15 5G 117
Grand Regent Twr. E2 3K 85
(off Palmer's Rd.)
Grandstand Way UB5: N'olt 5D 58
Grand Twr. SW15 5G 117
(off Plaza Gdns.)
Grand Union Canal Wlk. W10 4E 80
(off Canal Way)
Grand Union Cen. W10 4F 81
(off West Row)
Grand Union Cl. W9 5H 81
Grand Union Cres. E8 1G 85
Grand Union Ent. Pk. UB2: S'hall 3E 94
Grand Union Hgts. HA0: Wemb 1D 78
Grand Union Ho. N1 1E 84
(off Hertford Rd.)
Grand Union Ind. Est. NW10 2H 79
Grand Union Village UB5: N'olt 3D 76
Grand Union Wlk. NW1 7F 65
(off Kentish Town Rd.)
Grand Union Way UB2: S'hall 2E 94
Grand Vitesse Ind. Cen. SE1 5B 14
(off Gt. Suffolk St.)
Grand Wlk. E1 4A 86
Granfield St. SW11 1B 118
Grange, The CR0: C'don 2B 170
E17 5A 50
(off Lynmouth Rd.)
HA0: Wemb 7G 61
KT3: N Mald 5B 152
KT4: Wor Pk 4K 163
N2 2B 46
N20 1F 31
(Grangeview Rd.)
N20 1G 31
(Oxford Gdns.)
SE1 3F 103
SW19 6F 135
W3 2H 97
W4 5H 97
W13 5C 78
W14 4H 99
Grange Av. EN4: E Barn 1H 31
HA7: Stan 2B 42
IG8: Wfd G 6D 36
N12 5F 31
N20 7B 20
SE25 2E 156
TW2: Twick 2J 131
Grangecliffe Gdns. SE25 2E 156
Grange Cl. DA15: Sidc 3A 144
HA8: Edg 5D 28
IG8: Wfd G 7D 36
KT8: W Mole 4F 149
TW5: Hest 6D 94
UB3: Hayes 5G 75
Grange Ct. HA1: Harr 4K 59
HA5: Pinn 3C 40
NW10 3A 62
(off Neasden La.)
SM2: Sutt 7K 165
SM6: Wall 3F 167
TW17: Shep 4C 146
UB5: N'olt 2A 76
WC2 1H 13 (6K 83)
Grangecourt Rd. N16 1E 66
Grange Cres. SE28 6C 90
Grangedale Cl. HA6: Nwood 1G 39
Grange Dr. BR7: Chst 6C 142
Grange Farm Cl. HA2: Harr 2G 59
Grangefield NW1 7H 65
(off Marquis Rd.)
Grange Gdns. HA5: Pinn 3C 40
N14 1C 32
NW3 3K 63
SE25 2E 156
Grange Gro. N1 6C 66
Grange Hill HA8: Edg 5D 28
SE25 2E 156
Grangehill Pl. SE9 3D 124
Grangehill Rd. SE9 4D 124
Grange Ho. NW10 7D 62
SE1 3F 103
Grange La. SE21 2F 139
Grange Lodge SW19 6F 135
Grange Mans. KT17: Ewe 7B 164
Grange M. N21 6G 23
TW13: Felt 4J 129
Grangemill Rd. SE6 3C 140
Grangemill Way SE6 2C 140
GRANGE PARK 6G 23
Grange Pk. W5 1E 96
Grange Pk. Av. N21 6H 23
Grange Pk. Pl. SW20 7D 134
Grange Pk. Rd.
CR7: Thor H 4D 156
E10 1D 68
Grange Pl. NW6 7J 63

Grange Rd.—Gt. Newport St.

Grange Rd. BR6: Orp . . . 2H **173**
CR2: S Croy . . . 7C **168**
CR7: Thor H . . . 4D **156**
E10 . . . 1C **68**
E13 . . . 3H **87**
E17 . . . 5A **50**
(not continuous)
HA1: Harr . . . 5A **42**
HA2: Harr . . . 2H **59**
HA8: Edg . . . 6E **28**
IG1: Ilf . . . 4F **71**
KT1: King T . . . 3E **150**
KT8: W Mole . . . 4F **149**
KT9: Chess . . . 4E **162**
N6 . . . 6E **46**
N17 . . . 6B **34**
N18 . . . 6B **34**
NW10 . . . 6D **62**
SE1 . . . 3E **102**
SE19 . . . 4D **156**
SE25 . . . 4D **156**
SM2: Sutt . . . 7J **165**
SW13 . . . 1C **116**
UB1: S'hall . . . 2C **94**
UB3: Hayes . . . 6G **75**
W4 . . . 5H **97**
W5 . . . 1D **96**
Grange St. N1 . . . 1D **84**
Grange Va. SM2: Sutt . . . 7K **165**
Grange Vw. Rd. N20 . . . 1F **31**
Grange Wlk. SE1 . . . 3E **102**
Grange Wlk. M. *SE1* . . . *3E* ***102***
(off Grange Wlk.)
Grange Way NW6 . . . 7J **63**
Grangeway IG8: Wfd G . . . 4F **37**
N12 . . . 4E **30**
Grangeway, The N21 . . . 6G **23**
Grangeway Gdns. IG4: Ilf . . . 5C **52**
Grangewood DA5: Bexl . . . 1F **145**
Grangewood Cl. HA5: Eastc . . . 5J **39**
Grangewood Dr. TW16: Sun . . . 7H **129**
Grangewood La. BR3: Beck . . . 6B **140**
Grangewood St. E6 . . . 1B **88**
Grangewood Ter. SE25 . . . 2D **156**
Grange Yd. SE1 . . . 3F **103**
Granham Gdns. N9 . . . 2A **34**
Granite Apartments E15 . . . 6G **69**
SE10 . . . 5G **105**
Granite St. SE18 . . . 5K **107**
Granleigh Rd. E11 . . . 2G **69**
Gransden Av. E8 . . . 7H **67**
Gransden Ho. SE8 . . . 5B **104**
Gransden Rd. W12 . . . 2B **98**
Grantbridge St. N1 . . . 2B **84**
Grantchester *KT1: King T* . . . *2G* ***151***
(off St Peters Rd.)
Grantchester Cl. HA1: Harr . . . 3K **59**
Grant Cl. DA17: Belv . . . 5F **109**
N14 . . . 7B **22**
N17 . . . 2E **48**
TW17: Shep . . . 6D **146**
Grant Ct. *E4* . . . *1K* ***35***
(off The Ridgeway)
NW9 . . . *2B* ***44***
(off Hazel Cl.)
Grantham Cl. HA8: Edg . . . 3K **27**
Grantham Ct. KT2: King T . . . 5D **132**
RM6: Chad H . . . 7F **55**
SE16 . . . *2K* ***103***
(off Eleanor Cl.)
Grantham Gdns.
RM6: Chad H . . . 6F **55**
Grantham Ho. *SE15* . . . *6G* ***103***
(off Friary Est.)
TW16: Sun . . . 7G **129**
UB5: N'olt . . . *3D* ***76***
(off Taywood Rd.)
Grantham Pl. W1 . . . 5J **11** (1F **101**)
Grantham Rd. E12 . . . 4E **70**
SW9 . . . 2J **119**
W4 . . . 7A **98**
Grant Ho. *E17* . . . *4C* ***50***
(off High St.)
SW9 . . . *1K* ***119***
(off Liberty St.)
Grantley Ho. *SE14* . . . *6K* ***103***
(off Myers La.)
Grantley Rd. TW4: Cran . . . 2A **112**
Grantley St. E1 . . . 3K **85**
Grant Mus. of Zoology . . . 4C **6**
Grantock Rd. E17 . . . 1F **51**
Granton Rd. DA14: Sidc . . . 6C **144**
IG3: Ilf . . . 1A **72**
SW16 . . . 1G **155**
Grant Pl. CR0: C'don . . . 1F **169**
Grant Rd. CR0: C'don . . . 1F **169**
HA3: W'stone . . . 3K **41**
SW11 . . . 4B **118**
Grants Cl. NW7 . . . 7K **29**
Grants Quay Wharf EC3 . . . 3F **15** (7D **84**)
Grant St. E13 . . . 3J **87**
N1 . . . 2A **84**
Grant Ter. *N16* . . . *7G* ***49***
(off Castlewood Rd.)
Grantully Rd. W9 . . . 3K **81**
Grant Way TW7: Isle . . . 6A **96**
Granville Arc. SW9 . . . 4A **120**
Granville Av. N9 . . . 3D **34**
TW3: Houn . . . 5E **112**
TW13: Felt . . . 2J **129**
Granville Cl. CR0: C'don . . . 2E **168**
Granville Ct. N1 . . . 1E **84**
N4 . . . 6K **47**
SE14 . . . *7A* ***104***
(off Nynehead St.)
Granville Gdns. SW16 . . . 1K **155**
W5 . . . 1F **97**
Granville Gro. SE13 . . . 3E **122**
Granville Ho. *E14* . . . *6C* ***86***
(off E. India Dock Rd.)
Granville Mans. *W12* . . . *2E* ***98***
(off Shepherd's Bush Grn.)
Granville M. DA14: Sidc . . . 4A **144**
Granville Pk. SE13 . . . 3E **122**
Granville Pl. HA5: Pinn . . . 3B **40**
N12 . . . 7F **31**
SW6 . . . 7K **99**
W1 . . . 1G **11** (6E **82**)
Granville Point NW2 . . . 2H **63**
Granville Rd. DA14: Sidc . . . 4A **144**
DA16: Well . . . 3C **126**
E17 . . . 6D **50**
E18 . . . 2K **51**
EN5: Barn . . . 4A **20**
IG1: Ilf . . . 1F **71**
N4 . . . 6K **47**
N12 . . . 7F **31**
N13 . . . 6E **32**
N22 . . . 1B **48**
NW2 . . . 2H **63**
NW6 . . . 2J **81**
(not continuous)
SW18 . . . 7H **117**
SW19 . . . 7J **135**
UB3: Harl . . . 4H **93**
UB10: Hil . . . 6D **56**
Granville Sq. SE15 . . . 7E **102**
WC1 . . . 2H **7** (3K **83**)
Granville St. WC1 . . . 2H **7** (3K **83**)
Granwood Ct. TW7: Isle . . . 1J **113**
Grape St. WC2 . . . 7E **6** (6J **83**)
Graphite Apartments, The *N1* . . . *1E* ***8***
(off Provost St.)
Graphite Point *E2* . . . *3K* ***85***
(off Palmer's Rd.)
Graphite Sq. SE11 . . . 5G **19** (5K **101**)
Grapsome Cl.
KT9: Chess . . . 7C **162**
Grasdene Rd. SE18 . . . 7A **108**
Grasgarth Cl. W3 . . . 7J **79**
Grasmere *NW1* . . . *2K* ***5***
(off Osnaburgh St.)
Grasmere Av. BR6: Farnb . . . 3F **173**
HA4: Ruis . . . 7E **38**
HA9: Wemb . . . 7C **42**
SW15 . . . 4K **133**
SW19 . . . 3J **153**
TW3: Houn . . . 6F **113**
W3 . . . 7K **79**
Grasmere Cl. TW14: Felt . . . 1H **129**
Grasmere Ct. N22 . . . 6E **32**
SE26 . . . 5G **139**
SM2: Sutt . . . 6A **166**
SW13 . . . *6C* ***98***
(off Verdun Rd.)
Grasmere Gdns. BR6: Farnb . . . 3F **173**
HA3: W'stone . . . 2A **42**
IG4: Ilf . . . 5D **52**
Grasmere Point *SE15* . . . *7J* ***103***
(off Old Kent Rd.)
Grasmere Rd. BR1: Brom . . . 1H **159**
BR6: Farnb . . . 3F **173**
DA7: Bex . . . 2J **127**
E13 . . . 2J **87**
N10 . . . 1F **47**
N17 . . . 6B **34**
SE25 . . . 6H **157**
SW16 . . . 5J **137**
Graspan Royal Marines Memorial . . . *4D* ***12***
(on The Mall)
Grasshaven Way SE28 . . . 1K **107**
(not continuous)
Grassington Cl. N11 . . . 6K **31**
Grassington Rd. DA14: Sidc . . . 4A **144**
Grassmount SE23 . . . 2H **139**
Grass Pk. N3 . . . 1H **45**
Grassway SM6: Wall . . . 4G **167**
Grasvenor Av. EN5: Barn . . . 5D **20**
Gratton Rd. W14 . . . 3G **99**
Gratton Ter. NW2 . . . 3F **63**
Gravel Hill CR0: Addtn . . . 6K **169**
DA6: Bex . . . 4H **127**
N3 . . . 2H **45**
UB8: Uxb . . . 5A **56**
Gravel Hill Cl. DA6: Bex . . . 5H **127**
Gravel La. E1 . . . 7J **9** (6F **85**)
Gravel Pit La. SE9 . . . 5F **125**
Gravel Pit Way BR6: Orp . . . 2K **173**
Gravel Rd. BR2: Brom . . . 3C **172**
TW2: Twick . . . 1J **131**
Gravelwood Cl. BR7: Chst . . . 3G **143**
Gravely Ho. *SE8* . . . *4A* ***104***
(off Chilton Gro.)
Gravenel Gdns. *SW17* . . . *5C* ***136***
(off Nutwell St.)
Graveney Gro. SE20 . . . 7J **139**
Graveney Rd. SW17 . . . 4C **136**
Gravesend Rd. W12 . . . 7C **80**
Gravesham Way BR3: Beck . . . 7B **158**
Gray Av. RM8: Dag . . . 1F **73**
Gray Ct. E1 . . . 5A **86**
HA5: Pinn . . . 4C **40**
Grayham Cres. KT3: N Mald . . . 4K **151**
Grayham Rd. KT3: N Mald . . . 4K **151**
Gray Ho. *SE17* . . . *5C* ***102***
(off King & Queen St.)
Grayland Cl. BR1: Brom . . . 1B **160**
Grayling Cl. E16 . . . 4G **87**
Grayling Ct. *W5* . . . *1D* ***96***
(off Grange Rd.)
Grayling Rd. N16 . . . 2D **66**
Grayling Sq. *E2* . . . *3G* ***85***
(off Nelson Gdns.)
Grayscroft Rd. SW16 . . . 7H **137**
Grays Farm Rd. BR5: St P . . . 7B **144**
Grayshott Rd. SW11 . . . 2E **118**
Gray's Inn . . . 5H **7** (5K **83**)
Gray's Inn Bldgs. *EC1* . . . *4J* ***7***
(off Rosebery Av.)
Gray's Inn Pl. WC1 . . . 6H **7** (5K **83**)
Gray's Inn Rd. WC1 . . . 1F **7** (3J **83**)
Gray's Inn Sq. WC1 . . . 5J **7** (5K **83**)
Grays La. TW15: Ashf . . . 4D **128**
Grayson Ho. EC1 . . . 2D **8**
Grays Rd. UB10: Uxb . . . 7A **56**
Grays Ter. E7 . . . 6A **70**
Grayston Ho. SE3 . . . 4A **124**
Gray St. SE1 . . . 7K **13** (2A **102**)
Grayswood Gdns. SW20 . . . 2D **152**
Grayswood Point SW15 . . . 1C **134**
Gray's Yd. W1 . . . 1H **11**
Graywood Ct. N12 . . . 7F **31**
Grazebrook Rd. N16 . . . 2D **66**
Grazeley Cl. DA6: Bex . . . 5J **127**
Grazeley Ct. SE19 . . . 5E **138**
Gt. Acre Ct. SW4 . . . 4H **119**
Gt. Amwell La. N8 . . . 3K **47**
Gt. Arthur Ho. *EC1* . . . *4C* ***8***
(off Golden La. Est.)
Gt. Bell All. EC2 . . . 7E **8** (6D **84**)
Great Benty UB7: W Dray . . . 4A **92**
Great Brownings SE21 . . . 4F **139**
Gt. Bushey Dr. N20 . . . 1E **30**
Gt. Cambridge Ind. Est. EN1: Enf . . . 5C **24**
GREAT CAMBRIDGE JUNC. . . . **4J 33**
Gt. Cambridge Rd. EN1: Enf . . . 4J **33**
N9 . . . 4J **33**
N17 . . . 5J **33**
N18 . . . 4J **33**
Gt. Castle St. W1 . . . 7K **5** (6F **83**)
Gt. Central Av. HA4: Ruis . . . 5A **58**
Gt. Central St. NW1 . . . 5E **4** (5D **82**)
Gt. Central Way HA9: Wemb . . . 4J **61**
NW10 . . . 5A **62**
Gt. Chapel St. W1 . . . 7C **6** (6H **83**)
Gt. Chart St. SW11 . . . 4B **118**
Gt. Chertsey Rd. TW2: Twick . . . 3D **130**
TW13: Hanw, Twick . . . 3D **130**
W4 . . . 1J **115**
(not continuous)
Gt. Church La. W6 . . . 4F **99**
Gt. College St. SW1 . . . 1E **18** (3J **101**)
Great Cft. *WC1* . . . *2F* ***7***
(off Cromer St.)
Gt. Cross Av. SE10 . . . 7F **105**
Gt. Cumberland M. W1 . . . 1E **10** (6D **82**)
Gt. Cumberland Pl. W1 . . . 7E **4** (6D **82**)
Gt. Dover St. SE1 . . . 7D **14** (2C **102**)
Greatdown Rd. W7 . . . 4K **77**
Gt. Eastern Ent. Cen. E14 . . . 2D **104**
Gt. Eastern Market *E20* . . . *6E* ***68***
(within Westfield Stratford City Shop. Cen.)
Gt. Eastern Rd. E15 . . . 7F **69**
Gt. Eastern St. EC2 . . . 2G **9** (3E **84**)
Gt. Eastern Wlk. EC2 . . . 6H **9**
Gt. Eastern Wharf SW11 . . . 7C **100**
Gt. Elms Rd. BR2: Brom . . . 4A **160**
Greater London Ho. *NW1* . . . *2G* ***83***
(off Hampstead Rd.)
Great Fld. NW9 . . . 1A **44**
Greatfield NW5 . . . 5G **65**
Greatfield Av. E6 . . . 4D **88**
Greatfield Cl. N19 . . . 4G **65**
SE4 . . . 4C **122**
Greatfields Dr. UB8: Hil . . . 5C **74**
Greatfields Rd. IG11: Bark . . . 1H **89**
Gt. Fleete Way IG11: Bark . . . 2C **90**
Gt. Galley Cl. IG11: Bark . . . 3B **90**
Gt. Gatton Cl. CR0: C'don . . . 7A **158**
Gt. George St. SW1 . . . 7D **12** (2H **101**)
Gt. Guildford Bus. Sq.
SE1 . . . 5C **14** (1C **102**)
Gt. Guildford St. SE1 . . . 4C **14** (1C **102**)
Great Hall . . . 6F **17** (5D **100**)
Great Hall *SW11* . . . *1E* ***118***
(off Battersea Pk. Rd.)
Greatham Wlk. SW15 . . . 1C **134**
Gt. Harry Dr. SE9 . . . 3E **142**
Gt. James St. WC1 . . . 5G **7** (5K **83**)
Gt. Marlborough St. W1 . . . 1A **12** (6G **83**)
Gt. Maze Pond SE1 . . . 6F **15** (2D **102**)
Gt. Minster Ho. *SW1* . . . *3D* ***18***
(off Marsham St.)
Gt. Newport St. WC2 . . . 2E **12** (7J **83**)

A-Z London 283

Gt. New St. *EC4* *7K 7*
(off New Fetter La.)
Great Nth. Leisure Pk. N12 7G 31
Great Nth. Rd. EN5: Barn 1C 20, 2C 20
EN5: New Bar 5D 20
N2 5C 46
N6 5C 46
Great Nth. Way NW4 2D 44
Greatorex Ho. *E1* *5G 85*
(off Greatorex St.)
Greatorex St. E1 5G 85
Gt. Ormond St. WC1 5F 7 (5J 83)
Gt. Owl Rd. IG7: Chig 3K 37
Great Pk. Cl. UB10: Hil 7C 56
Gt. Percy St. WC1 1H 7 (3K 83)
Gt. Peter St. SW1 2C 18 (3H 101)
Gt. Portland St. W1 4K 5 (4F 83)
Gt. Pulteney St. W1 2B 12 (7G 83)
Gt. Queen St. WC2 1F 13 (6J 83)
Gt. Russell Mans. *WC1* *6E 6*
(off Gt. Russell St.)
Gt. Russell St. WC1 7D 6 (6H 83)
Gt. St Helen's EC3 7G 9 (6E 84)
Gt. St Thomas Apostle EC4 2D 14 (7C 84)
Gt. Scotland Yd. SW1 5E 12 (1J 101)
Gt. Smith St. SW1 1D 18 (3H 101)
Great Sth. W. Rd. TW4: Houn 4H 111
TW14: Bedf, Felt 7E 110
Great Spilmans SE22 5E 120
Great Strand NW9 1B 44
Gt. Suffolk St. SE1 5B 14 (1B 102)
Gt. Sutton St. EC1 4B 8 (4B 84)
Gt. Swan All. EC2 7E 8 (6D 84)
Great Thrift BR5: Pet W 4G 161
Gt. Titchfield St. W1 4K 5 (4F 83)
Gt. Tower St. EC3 2G 15 (7E 84)
Gt. Trinity La. EC4 2D 14 (7C 84)
Gt. Turnstile WC1 6H 7 (5K 83)
Gt. Turnstile Ho. *WC1* *6H 7*
(off Great Turnstile)
Gt. Western Ind. Pk. UB2: S'hall 2F 95
Gt. Western Rd. W9 5H 81
W11 5H 81
Gt. West Rd. TW5: Hest 2B 112
TW7: Bford, Isle 2B 112
TW8: Bford 2B 112
W4 5H 97
(Cedars Rd.)
W4 6B 98
(Dorchester Gro.)
W6 6B 98
Great W. Trad. Est. TW8: Bford 6B 96
Gt. Winchester St. EC2 7F 9 (6D 84)
Gt. Windmill St. W1 2C 12 (7H 83)
Greatwood BR7: Chst 7E 142
Great Yd. SE1 6H 15
Greaves Cl. IG11: Bark 7H 71
Greaves Cotts. *E14* *5A 86*
(off Maroon St.)
Greaves Pl. SW17 4C 136
Greaves Twr. *SW10* *7A 100*
(off Worlds End Est.)
Grebe Av. UB4: Yead 6B 76
Grebe Cl. E7 5H 69
E17 7F 35
IG11: Bark 4A 90
Grebe Ct. *E14* *2E 104*
(off River Barge Cl.)
SE8 *6B 104*
(off Dorking Cl.)
SM1: Sutt 5H 165
Grebe Ter. KT1: King T 3E 150
Grecian Cres. SE19 6B 138
Greek Ct. W1 1D 12 (6H 83)
Greek St. W1 1D 12 (6H 83)
Green, The BR1: Brom 3J 141
(not continuous)
BR2: Hayes 7J 159
BR5: St P 7B 144
CR0: Sels 7B 170
DA7: Bex 1G 127
Green, The DA14: Sidc 4A 144
DA16: Well 4J 125
E4 1K 35
E11 6K 51
E15 6G 69
HA0: Wemb 2A 60
IG8: Wfd G 5D 36
IG9: Buck H 1E 36
KT3: N Mald 3K 151
N9 2B 34
N14 2C 32
N17 6H 33
N21 7F 23
SM1: Sutt 3K 165
SM4: Mord 4G 153
SM5: Cars 4E 166
SM6: Wall 2E 166
SW14 3J 115
SW19 5F 135
TW2: Twick 1J 131
TW5: Hest 6E 94
TW9: Rich 5D 114
TW13: Felt 2K 129
TW17: Shep 4G 147
UB2: S'hall 3C 94
UB7: W Dray 3A 92
UB10: Ick 2E 56
W3 6A 80
W5 1D 96
Greenacre Cl. EN5: Barn 1C 20
UB5: N'olt 5D 58
Greenacre Gdns. E17 4E 50
Greenacre Pl. SM6: Wall 2F 167
Green Acres CR0: C'don 3F 169
DA14: Sidc 4A 144
Greenacres N3 2H 45
SE9 6E 124
WD23: B Hea 2C 26
Greenacres Av. UB10: Ick 3B 56
Greenacres Cl. BR6: Farnb 4G 173
Greenacres Dr. HA7: Stan 6G 27
Greenacres Ho. *SW18* *1K 135*
(off Knaresborough Dr.)
Greenacre Sq. SE16 2K 103
Greenacre Wlk. N14 3C 32
Greenan Ct. *E2* *3K 85*
(off Meath Cres.)
Grn. Arbour Ct. EC1 7A 8
Green Av. NW7 4E 28
W13 3B 96
Greenaway Av. N18 6E 34
Greenaway Gdns. NW3 4K 63
Greenaway Ho. *NW8* *1A 82*
(off Boundary Rd.)
WC1 *2J 7*
(off Fernsbury St.)
Greenaway Ter. *TW19: Stanw* *1A 128*
(off Victory Cl.)
Green Bank E1 1H 103
N12 4E 30
Greenbank Av. HA0: Wemb 5A 60
Greenbank Cl. E4 2K 35
Greenbank Ct. *TW7: Isle* *2K 113*
(off Lanadron Cl.)
Greenbank Cres. NW4 4G 45
Greenbank Lodge *BR7: Chst* *2E 160*
(off Forest Cl.)
Greenbanks HA1: Harr 4J 59
Greenbanks Cl. SE13 3D 122
Greenbay Rd. SE7 7B 106
Greenberry St. NW8 1C 4 (2C 82)
Greenbrook Av. EN4: Had W 1F 21
Green Cl. BR2: Brom 3G 159
NW9 6J 43
NW11 7A 46
SM5: Cars 2D 166
TW13: Hanw 5C 130
Greencoat Mans. *SW1* *2B 18*
(off Greencoat Row)
Greencoat Pl. SW1 3B 18 (4G 101)
Greencoat Row SW1 2B 18 (3G 101)
Green Ct. TW16: Sun 6H 129
Greencourt Av. CR0: C'don 2H 169
HA8: Edg 1H 43
Greencourt Gdns. CR0: C'don 1H 169
Greencourt Ho. *E1* *4K 85*
(off Mile End Rd.)
Greencourt Rd. BR5: Pet W 5H 161
Greencrest Pl. NW2 3C 62
Greencroft HA8: Edg 5D 28
Greencroft Av. HA4: Ruis 2A 58
Greencroft Cl. E6 5B 88
Greencroft Gdns. EN1: Enf 3K 23
NW6 7K 63
Greencroft Rd. TW5: Hest 1D 112
Green Dale SE5 4D 120
SE22 5E 120
Greendale NW7 4F 29
Grn. Dale Cl. SE22 5E 120
Grn. Dragon Ct. SE1 4E 14
Grn. Dragon Ho. *WC2* *7F 7*
(off Stukeley St.)
Grn. Dragon La. N21 6F 23
TW8: Bford 5E 96
Grn. Dragon Yd. E1 6K 9 (5G 85)
Green Dr. UB1: S'hall 1E 94
Greene Ct. *SE14* *6K 103*
(off Samuel Cl.)
Greene Ho. *SE1* *3D 102*
(off Burbage Cl.)
Green End KT9: Chess 4E 162
N21 2G 33
Greenend Rd. W4 2A 98
Greener Ct. *CR0: C'don* *6C 156*
(off Goodman Cres.)
Greener Ho. SW4 3H 119
Grn. Farm Cl. BR6: Chels 5K 173
Greenfell Mans. SE8 6D 104
Grn. Ferry Way *E17* *4K 49*
(off Forest Rd.)
Greenfield Av. KT5: Surb 7H 151
Greenfield Dr. BR1: Brom 2A 160
N2 4D 46
Greenfield Gdns. BR5: Pet W 7H 161
NW2 2G 63
RM9: Dag 1D 90
Greenfield Ho. SW19 1F 135
Greenfield Pl. UB3: Hayes 7H 75
Greenfield Rd. DA2: Wilm 5K 145
E1 5G 85
N15 5E 48
RM9: Dag 1C 90
Greenfields UB1: S'hall 6E 76
Greenfield Way HA2: Harr 3F 41
GREENFORD 3E 76
Greenford Av. UB1: S'hall 7D 76
W7 4J 77
Greenford Bus. Cen. UB6: G'frd 7H 59
Greenford Gdns. UB6: G'frd 3F 77
GREENFORD GREEN 6J 59
Greenford Ind. Est. UB6: G'frd 7F 59
Greenford Pk. UB6: G'frd 7H 59
Greenford Rd. HA1: Harr 2H 77
SM1: Sutt 4K 165
(not continuous)
UB1: S'hall 7G 77
UB6: G'frd 2H 77
GREENFORD RDBT. 2H 77
Greenford Sports Cen. 3E 76
Green Gdns. BR6: Farnb 5G 173
Greengate UB6: G'frd 6B 60
Greengate Lodge *E13* *2K 87*
(off Hollybush St.)
Greengate Pde. IG2: Ilf 6H 53
Greengate St. E13 2K 87
Greenhalgh Wlk. N2 4A 46
Greenham Cl. SE1 7J 13 (2A 102)
Greenham Cres. E4 6G 35
Greenham Ho. *E9* *1J 85*
(off Templecombe Rd.)
TW7: Isle 3H 113
Greenham Rd. N10 2E 46
Greenhaven Dr. SE28 6B 90
Green Hedges TW1: Twick 5C 114
Greenheys Cl. HA6: Nwood 1G 39
Greenheys Dr. E18 3H 51
GREENHILL 5J 41
Green Hill SE18 5D 106
Greenhill HA9: Wemb 2H 61
IG9: Buck H 1F 37
NW3 4B 64
SM1: Sutt 2A 166
Greenhill Ct.
EN5: New Bar 5E 20
SE18 5D 106
Greenhill Gdns. UB5: N'olt 2D 76
Greenhill Gro. E12 4C 70
Greenhill Pde. EN5: New Bar 5E 20
Greenhill Pk. EN5: New Bar 5E 20
NW10 1A 80
Greenhill Rd. HA1: Harr 6J 41
NW10 1A 80
Greenhill's Rents EC1 5A 8 (5B 84)
Greenhills Ter. N1 6D 66
Greenhill Ter. SE18 5D 106
UB5: N'olt 2D 76
Greenhill Way HA1: Harr 6J 41
HA9: Wemb 2H 61
Greenhithe Cl. DA15: Sidc 7J 125
Greenholm Rd. SE9 5F 125
Green Hundred Rd. SE15 6G 103
Greenhurst Rd. SE27 5A 138
Greening St. SE2 4C 108
Greenland Cres. UB2: S'hall 3A 94
Greenland Ho. *E1* *4A 86*
(off Ernest St.)
Greenland M. SE8 5K 103
Greenland Pl. NW1 1F 83
Greenland Quay SE16 4K 103
Greenland Rd. EN5: Barn 6A 20
NW1 1G 83
Greenlands KT19: Ewe 5H 163
Greenlands La. NW4 1D 44
Greenland St. NW1 1F 83
Greenland Way CR0: Bedd 7H 155
Green La. BR7: Chst 1F 143
CR7: Thor H 7K 137
HA1: Harr 3J 59
HA7: Stan 4G 27
HA8: Edg 4A 28
(not continuous)
IG1: Ilf 2H 71
IG3: Ilf 2H 71
KT3: N Mald 5J 151
KT4: Wor Pk 1C 164
KT8: W Mole 5F 149
KT9: Chess 7D 162
NW4 4F 45
RM8: Dag 2H 71
SE9 1F 143
SE20 7K 139
SM4: Mord 6J 153
(Central Rd.)
SM4: Mord 7E 152
(Lwr. Morden La.)
SW16 7K 137
TW4: Houn 3K 111
TW13: Hanw 5C 130
TW16: Sun 7H 129
TW17: Shep 6E 146
UB8: Hil 5E 74
W7 2J 95
Green La. Bus. Pk. SE9 2E 142
Green La. Cotts. HA7: Stan 4G 27
Green La. Gdns. CR7: Thor H 2C 156
Green Lanes KT19: Ewe 7A 164
N4 1C 66
N8 3B 48
N13 6E 32
N15 3B 48
N16 1C 66
N21 3F 33
Grn. Lanes Wlk. N4 1C 66

Greenlaw Ct. W5 6D 78
(off Mount Pk. Rd.)
Greenlaw Gdns. KT3: N Mald 7B 152
Greenlawn La. TW8: Bford 4D 96
Green Lawns HA4: Ruis 1A 58
Greenlawns N12 6E 30
Greenlawns, The SE18 4F 107
(off Vincent Rd.)
Greenlaw St. SE18 3E 106
Green Leaf Av. SM6: Bedd 4H 167
Greenleaf Cl. SW2 7A 120
Greenleafe Dr. IG6: Ilf 3F 53
Greenleaf Rd. E6 1A 88
E17 3B 50
Greenleaf Way HA3: W'stone 3K 41
Greenlea Pk. SW19 7B 136
Green Leas KT1: King T 3E 150
(off Mill St.)
TW16: Sun 6H 129
Green Leas Cl. TW16: Sun 6H 129
Greenleaves Ct. TW15: Ashf 6D 128
Greenlink Wlk. TW9: Kew 1H 115
Green Man Gdns. W13 7A 78
Green Man La. TW14: Felt 4J 111
(not continuous)
W13 7A 78
Green Man Pas. W13 7B 78
(not continuous)
GREEN MAN RDBT. 7H 51
Greenman St. N1 7C 66
Greenmead DA18: Erith 3E 108
Greenmead Cl. SE25 5G 157
Green M. N1 3D 84
Green Moor Link N21 7G 23
Greenmoor Rd. EN3: Enf H 2D 24
Greenoak Pl. EN4: Cockf 2J 21
Green Oaks UB2: S'hall 4B 94
Greenoak Way SW19 4F 135
Greenock Rd. SW16 1H 155
W3 3H 97
Greeno Cres. TW17: Shep 5C 146
Green Pde. TW3: Houn 5F 113
Green Pk.
London 6K 11 (2F 101)
Greenpark Ct. HA0: Wemb 7C 60
Green Pk. Way UB6: G'frd 7J 59
Green Pl. SE10 2G 105
Green Point E15 6G 69
Grn. Pond Cl. E17 3B 50
Grn. Pond Rd. E17 3A 50
Green Rd. N14 6A 22
N20 3F 31
Green Rd. Nth. EN3: Pond E 4F 25
Greenrod Pl. TW8: Bford 5E 96
(off Clayponds La.)
Greenroof Way SE10 3H 105
Green's Ct. W1 2C 12
W11 1H 99
(off Lansdowne M.)
Green's End SE18 4F 107
Greenshank Cl. E17 7F 35
Greenshank Ho. NW9 6B 44
Greenshields Ind. Est. E16 2J 105
Greenside DA5: Bexl 1E 144
RM8: Dag 1C 72
Greenside Cl. N20 2G 31
SE6 2F 141
Greenside Rd. CR0: C'don 7A 156
W12 3C 98
Greenslade Rd. IG11: Bark 7H 71
Greenstead Av. IG8: Wfd G 7F 37
Greenstead Cl. IG8: Wfd G 6F 37
Greenstead Gdns. IG8: Wfd G 6F 37
SW15 5D 116
Greensted Rd. IG10: Lough 1H 37
Greenstone M. E11 6J 51
Green St. E7 6K 69
E13 6K 69
EN3: Brim, Enf H 2D 24
TW16: Sun 1J 147
W1 2G 11 (7E 82)
GREEN STREET GREEN 6K 173
Greenstreet Hill SE14 2K 121
Green Ter. EC1 2K 7 (3A 84)
Green Va. DA6: Bex 5D 126
W5 6F 79
Greenvale Rd. SE9 4D 124
Green Verges HA7: Stan 7J 27
Green Vw. KT9: Chess 7F 163
Greenview Av. BR3: Beck 6A 158
CR0: C'don 6A 158
Greenview Cl. W3 1A 98
Greenview Ct. TW15: Ashf 4B 128
Greenview Dr. SW20 3E 152
Green Wlk. HA4: Ruis 1H 57
IG8: Wfd G 6H 37
IG10: Lough 1H 37
NW4 5F 45
SE1 3E 102
TW12: Hamp 6D 130
UB2: S'hall 5E 94
Green Wlk., The E4 1A 36
Green Way BR2: Brom 6C 160
SE9 5B 124
TW16: Sun 4J 147
Greenway BR7: Chst 5E 142
E6 4E 88
E15 2F 87
E20 1D 86
HA3: Kenton 5E 42
HA5: Pinn 2K 39
IG8: Wfd G 5F 37
N14 2D 32
N20 2D 30
RM8: Dag 2C 72
SM6: Wall 4G 167
SW20 4E 152
UB4: Yead 3J 75
Greenway, The HA3: W'stone 1J 41
HA5: Pinn 6D 40
NW9 2K 43
TW4: Houn 4D 112
UB8: Uxb 2A 74
UB10: Ick 2D 56
Greenway Av. E17 4F 51
Greenway Cl. N4 2C 66
N11 6K 31
N15 4F 49
N20 2D 30
NW9 2K 43
Greenway Ct. IG1: Ilf 1E 70
Greenway Gdns. CR0: C'don 3B 170
HA3: W'stone 2J 41
NW9 2K 43
UB6: G'frd 3E 76
Greenways BR3: Beck 3C 158
Greenways, The TW1: Twick 6A 114
Greenways Dr. TW4: Houn 4C 112
Greenwell St. W1 4K 5 (4F 83)
GREENWICH 7E 104
Greenwich Bus. Pk. SE10 7D 104
Greenwich Cen., The SE10 5H 105
(off Lambarde Sq.)
Greenwich Chu. St. SE10 6E 104
Greenwich Ct. E1 6H 85
(off Cavell St.)
Greenwich Cres. E6 5C 88
Greenwich Foot Tunnel SE10 5E 104
Greenwich Hgts. SE18 7C 106
Greenwich Heritage Cen. 3F 107
Greenwich High Rd. SE10 1D 122
Greenwich Ho. SE13 6F 123
Greenwich Mkt. SE10 6E 104
GREENWICH MILLENNIUM VILLAGE
3H 105
Greenwich Pk. 7F 105
Greenwich Pk. St. SE10 6F 105
Greenwich Peninsula Ecology Pk. 3J 105
Greenwich Peninsula Golf Driving Range
2F 105
Greenwich Picturehouse 7E 104
Greenwich Quay SE8 6D 104
Greenwich Shop. Pk. SE7 4K 105
Greenwich Sth. St. SE10 1D 122
Greenwich Theatre 7E 104
Greenwich Vw. Pl. E14 3D 104
Greenwich Yacht Club 3J 105
Greenwood NW5 5G 65
(off Osney Cres.)
Greenwood Av. EN3: Enf H 2F 25
RM10: Dag 4H 73
Greenwood Bus. Cen. CR0: C'don 7F 157
Greenwood Cl. BR5: Pet W 6J 161
DA15: Sidc 2A 144
KT7: T Ditt 1A 162
SM4: Mord 4G 153
UB3: Hayes 1J 93
WD23: B Hea 1D 26
Greenwood Dr. E4 5A 36
Greenwood Gdns. IG6: Ilf 1G 53
N13 3G 33
Greenwood Ho. EC1 2J 7
(off Rosebery Av.)
N22 1K 47
SE4 4K 121
Greenwood La. TW12: Hamp H 5F 131
Greenwood Mans. IG11: Bark 7A 72
(off Lansbury Av.)
Greenwood Pk. KT2: King T 7A 134
Greenwood Pl. NW5 5F 65
Greenwood Rd. CR0: C'don 7B 156
CR4: Mitc 3H 155
DA5: Bexl 4K 145
E8 6G 67
E13 2H 87
KT7: T Ditt 1A 162
TW7: Isle 3K 113
Greenwoods, The HA2: Harr 3G 59
Greenwood Ter. NW10 1K 79
Greenwood Theatre 2D 102
Grn. Wrythe Cres. SM5: Cars 1C 166
Grn. Wrythe La. SM5: Cars 6B 154
Green Yd. WC1 3H 7 (4K 83)
Green Yd., The EC3 1G 15
Greer Rd. HA3: Hrw W 1G 41
Greet Ho. SE1 7K 13
Greet St. SE1 5K 13 (1A 102)
Greg Cl. E10 6E 50
Gregor M. SE3 7J 105
Gregory Cl. BR2: Brom 4G 159
Gregory Cres. SE9 7B 124
Gregory Pl. W8 2K 99
Gregory Rd. RM6: Chad H 4D 54
UB2: S'hall 3E 94
Greig Cl. N8 5J 47
Greig Ter. SE17 6B 102
Grenaby Av. CR0: C'don 7D 156
Grenaby Rd. CR0: C'don 7D 156
Grenada Ho. E14 7B 86
(off Limehouse C'way.)
Grenada Rd. SE7 7A 106
Grenade St. E14 7B 86
Grenadier St. E16 1E 106
Grena Gdns. TW9: Rich 4F 115
Grenard Cl. SE15 7G 103
Grena Rd. TW9: Rich 4F 115
Grendon Gdns. HA9: Wemb 2G 61
Grendon Ho. E9 7J 67
(off Shore Pl.)
N1 2K 83
(off Calshot St.)
Grendon Lodge HA8: Edg 2D 28
Grendon St. NW8 3C 4 (4C 82)
Grenfell Ct. E3 4D 86
(off Barry Blandford Way)
NW7 6J 29
Grenfell Gdns. HA3: Kenton 7E 42
IG3: Ilf 5K 53
Grenfell Ho. SE5 7C 102
Grenfell Rd. CR4: Mitc 6D 136
W11 7F 81
Grenfell Twr. W11 7F 81
Grenfell Wlk. W11 7F 81
Grenier Apartments SE15 7H 103
Grennell Cl. SM1: Sutt 2B 166
Grennell Rd. SM1: Sutt 2A 166
Grenoble Gdns. N13 6F 33
Grenville Cl. KT5: Surb 1J 163
N3 1G 45
Grenville Ct. W13 5B 78
Grenville Gdns. IG8: Wfd G 1A 52
Grenville Ho. E3 2A 86
(off Arbery Rd.)
SE8 6C 104
(off New King St.)
SW1 7C 18
(off Dolphin Sq.)
Grenville M. N19 1J 65
SW7 4A 100
TW12: Hamp H 5F 131
Grenville Pl. NW7 5E 28
SW7 3A 100
Grenville Rd. N19 1J 65
Grenville St. WC1 4F 7 (4J 83)
Gresham Av. N20 4J 31
Gresham Cl. DA5: Bexl 6E 126
EN2: Enf 3H 23
Gresham Dr. RM6: Chad H 5B 54
Gresham Gdns. NW11 1G 63
Gresham Lodge E17 5D 50
Gresham Pl. N19 2H 65
Gresham Rd. BR3: Beck 2A 158
E6 2D 88
E16 6K 87
HA8: Edg 6A 28
NW10 5K 61
SE25 4G 157
SW9 3A 120
TW3: Houn 1G 113
TW12: Hamp 6E 130
UB10: Hil 2C 74
Gresham St. EC2 7C 8 (6C 84)
Gresham Way SW19 3K 135
Gresham Way Ind. Est. SW19 3K 135
(off Gresham Way)
Gresley Cl. E17 6A 50
N15 4D 48
Gresley Rd. N19 1G 65
Gressenhall Rd. SW18 6H 117
Gresse St. W1 6C 6 (6H 83)
Gresswell Cl. DA14: Sidc 3A 144
Greswell St. SW6 1F 117
Gretton Ho. E2 3J 85
(off Globe Rd.)
Gretton Rd. N17 7A 34
Greville Cl. TW1: Twick 7B 114
Greville Ct. E5 3H 67
(off Napoleon Rd.)
HA1: Harr 4J 59
Greville Hall NW6 2K 81
Greville Ho. SW1 1G 17
(off Kinnerton St.)
Greville Lodge E13 1K 87
HA8: Edg 4C 28
(off Broadhurst Av.)
N12 5E 30
Greville M. NW6 1K 81
(off Greville Rd.)
Greville Pl. NW6 2K 81
Greville Rd. E17 4E 50
NW6 2K 81
TW10: Rich 6F 115
Greville St. EC1 6J 7 (5A 84)
(not continuous)
Grey Cl. NW11 6A 46
Greycoat Gdns. SW1 2C 18
(off Greycoat St.)
Greycoat Pl. SW1 2C 18 (3H 101)
Greycoat St. SW1 2C 18 (3H 101)
Greycot Rd. BR3: Beck 5C 140
Grey Eagle St. E1 4K 9 (4F 85)
Greyfell Cl. HA7: Stan 5G 27
Greyfriars SE26 3G 139
(off Wells Pk. Rd.)

Greyfriars Pas.—Grove Mill Pl.

Greyfriars Pas. EC1 7B **8** (6B **84**)
Greyhound Ct. WC2 2H **13** (7K **83**)
Greyhound Hill NW4 3C **44**
Greyhound La. SW16 6H **137**
Greyhound Mans. *W6* *6G* ***99***
(off Greyhound Rd.)
Greyhound Rd. N17 3E **48**
NW10 3D **80**
SM1: Sutt 5A **166**
W6 6F **99**
W14 6F **99**
Greyhound Ter. SW16 1G **155**
Grey Ho. *W12* *7D* ***80***
(off White City Est.)
Greyladies Gdns. SE10 2E **122**
Greys Pk. Cl. BR2: Kes 5B **172**
Greystead Rd. SE23 7J **121**
Greystoke Av. HA5: Pinn 3E **40**
Greystoke Ct. W5 4E **78**
Greystoke Dr. HA4: Ruis 6D **38**
Greystoke Gdns. EN2: Enf 4C **22**
W5 4E **78**
Greystoke Ho. *SE15* *6G* ***103***
(off Peckham Pk. Rd.)
W5 4E **78**
Greystoke Lodge *W5* *4F* ***79***
(off Hanger La.)
Greystoke Pk. Ter. W5 3D **78**
Greystoke Pl. EC4 7J **7** (6A **84**)
Greystone Gdns. HA3: Kenton 6C **42**
IG6: Ilf 2G **53**
Greyswood Av. N18 6E **34**
Greyswood St. SW16 6F **137**
Grey Turner Ho. W12 6C **80**
Grierson Ho. SW16 4G **137**
Grierson Rd. SE23 7K **121**
Griffen Ct. BR3: Beck 1D **158**
Griffin Cen. TW14: Felt 5K **111**
Griffin Cen., The *KT1: King T* *2D* ***150***
(off Market Pl.)
Griffin Cl. NW10 5D **62**
Griffin Ct. TW8: Bford 6E **96**
W4 5B **98**
Griffin Ho. CR0: C'don 7B **156**
E14 *6D* ***86***
(off Ricardo St.)
N1 *1E* ***84***
(off Halcomb St.)
W6 *4F* ***99***
(off Hammersmith Rd.)
Griffin Mnr. Way SE28 3H **107**
Griffin M. SW12 1G **137**
Griffin Pk. 6D **96**
Griffin Rd. N17 2E **48**
SE18 5H **107**
Griffins Cl. N21 7J **23**
Griffin Way TW16: Sun 2J **147**
Griffith Cl. E17 1F **51**
RM8: Dag 7C **54**
Griffiths Cl. KT4: Wor Pk 2D **164**
Griffiths Rd. SW19 7J **135**
Griggs App. IG1: Ilf 2G **71**
Griggs Cl. IG3: Ilf 4J **71**
Griggs Ct. *SE1* *3E* ***102***
(off Grigg's Pl.)
Grigg's Pl. SE1 3E **102**
Griggs Rd. E10 6E **50**
Grilse Cl. N9 4C **34**
Grimaldi Ho. *N1* *2K* ***83***
(off Calshot St.)
Grimsby Gro. E16 2F **107**
Grimsby St. E2 4K **9** (4F **85**)
Grim's Dyke Golf Course 5A **26**
Grimsdyke Rd. HA5: Hat E 1D **40**
Grimsel Path SE5 7B **102**
Grimshaw Cl. N6 7E **46**
Grimston Rd. SW6 2H **117**
Grimthorpe Ho. EC1 3A **8**
Grimwade Av. CR0: C'don 3G **169**
Grimwade Cl. SE15 3J **121**
Grimwood Rd. TW1: Twick 7K **113**
Grindall Cl. CR0: Wadd 4B **168**
Grindall Ho. *E1* *4H* ***85***
(off Darling Row)
Grindal St. SE1 7J **13** (2A **102**)
Grindleford Av. N11 2K **31**
Grindley Gdns. CR0: C'don 6F **157**
Grindley Ho. *E3* *5B* ***86***
(off Leopold St.)
Grinling Pl. SE8 6C **104**
Grinstead Rd. SE8 5A **104**
Grisedale *NW1* *1A* ***6***
(off Cumberland Mkt.)
Grittleton Av. HA9: Wemb 6H **61**
Grittleton Rd. W9 4J **81**
Grizedale Ter. SE23 2H **139**
Grocer's Hall Ct. EC2 1E **14** (6D **84**)
Grocer's Hall Gdns. EC2 1E **14**
Grogan Cl. TW12: Hamp 6D **130**
Groombridge Cl.
DA16: Well 5A **126**
Groombridge Ho. *SE17* *5E* ***102***
(off Upnor Way)
Groombridge Rd. E9 7K **67**
Groom Cl. BR2: Brom 4K **159**
Groom Cres. SW18 7B **118**
Groome Ho. SE11 4H **19** (4K **101**)
Groomfield Cl. SW17 4E **136**
Groom Pl. SW1 1H **17** (3E **100**)
Grooms Dr. HA5: Eastc 5J **39**
Grosmont Rd. SE18 5K **107**
Grosse Way SW15 6D **116**
Grosvenor Av. HA2: Harr 6F **41**
N5 5C **66**
SM5: Cars 6D **166**
SW14 3A **116**
TW10: Rich 5E **114**
UB4: Hayes 2H **75**
Grosvenor Cotts. SW1 3G **17** (4E **100**)
Grosvenor Ct. E10 1D **68**
E14 *6B* ***86***
(off Wharf La.)
N14 7B **22**
NW6 1F **81**
NW7 *5E* ***28***
(off Hale La.)
SE5 6C **102**
SM2: Sutt 6K **165**
SM4: Mord 4J **153**
TW11: Tedd 6A **132**
W3 1G **97**
W5 *7E* ***78***
(off The Grove)
W14 *3F* ***99***
(off Irving Rd.)
Grosvenor Ct. Mans. *W2* *1E* ***10***
(off Edgware Rd.)
Grosvenor Cres. NW9 4G **43**
SW1 7H **11** (2E **100**)
UB10: Hil 7D **56**
Grosvenor Cres. M. SW1 7G **11** (2E **100**)
Grosvenor Est. SW1 3D **18** (4H **101**)
Grosvenor Gdns. E6 3B **88**
IG8: Wfd G 6D **36**
KT2: King T 6D **132**
N10 3G **47**
N14 4C **22**
NW2 6E **62**
NW11 6H **45**
SM6: Wall 7G **167**
SW1 1J **17** (3F **101**)
SW14 3A **116**
Grosvenor Gdns. M. E. SW1 1K **17**
Grosvenor Gdns. M. Nth. SW1 2J **17**
Grosvenor Gdns. M. Sth. SW1 2K **17**
Grosvenor Ga. W1 3G **11** (7E **82**)
Grosvenor Hill SW19 6G **135**
W1 2J **11** (7F **83**)
Grosvenor Hill Ct. *W1* *2J* ***11***
(off Bourdon St.)
Grosvenor Ho. *SM1: Sutt* *5K* ***165***
(off West St.)
Grosvenor Pde. *W5* *1G* ***97***
(off Uxbridge Rd.)
Grosvenor Pk. SE5 7C **102**
Grosvenor Pk. Rd. E17 5C **50**
Grosvenor Pl. SW1 7H **11** (2E **100**)
Grosvenor Ri. E. E17 5D **50**
Grosvenor Rd. BR4: W W'ck 1D **170**
BR5: St M Cry 6J **161**
DA6: Bex 5D **126**
DA17: Belv 6G **109**
E6 1B **88**
E7 6K **69**
E10 1E **68**
E11 5K **51**
IG1: Ilf 3G **71**
N3 7C **30**
N9 1C **34**
N10 1F **47**
RM7: Rush G 7K **55**
RM8: Dag 1F **73**
SE25 4F **157**
SM6: Wall 6F **167**
SW1 7J **17** (6F **101**)
TW1: Twick 1A **132**
TW3: Houn 3D **112**
TW8: Bford 6D **96**
TW10: Rich 5E **114**
UB2: S'hall 3D **94**
W4 5H **97**
W7 1A **96**
Grosvenor Sq. W1 2H **11** (7E **82**)
Grosvenor St. W1 2J **11** (7F **83**)
Grosvenor Studios *SW1* *3G* ***17***
(off Eaton Ter.)
Grosvenor Ter. SE5 7C **102**
Grosvenor Va. HA4: Ruis 2H **57**
Grosvenor Way E5 2J **67**
SW17 3B **136**
Grosvenor Wharf Rd. E14 4F **105**
Grotes Bldgs. SE3 2G **123**
Grote's Pl. SE3 2G **123**
Groton Rd. SW18 2K **135**
Grotto Ct. SE1 6B **14** (2B **102**)
Grotto Pas. W1 5H **5** (5E **82**)
Grotto Rd. TW1: Twick 2K **131**
GROVE, THE 1G **139**
Grove, The BR4: W W'ck 3D **170**
DA6: Bex 4D **126**
DA14: Sidc 5E **144**
E15 6G **69**
EN2: Enf 2F **23**
HA1: Harr 7J **41**
HA7: Stan 2F **27**
HA8: Edg 4C **28**
KT12: Walt T 7K **147**
N3 1J **45**
N4 7K **47**
N6 1E **64**
N8 5H **47**
N13 4F **33**
(not continuous)
N14 5B **22**
NW9 5K **43**
NW11 7G **45**
TW1: Twick 6B **114**
TW7: Isle 1J **113**
TW11: Tedd 4A **132**
UB6: G'frd 6G **77**
UB10: Ick 5C **56**
W5 1D **96**
Grove Av. HA5: Pinn 4C **40**
N3 7D **30**
N10 2G **47**
SM1: Sutt 6J **165**
TW1: Twick 1K **131**
W7 7J **77**
Grovebury Cl. DA8: Erith 6K **109**
Grovebury Ct.
DA6: Bex 5H **127**
N14 7C **22**
Grovebury Rd. SE2 2B **108**
Grove Cl. BR2: Hayes 2J **171**
KT1: King T 4F **151**
N14 7B **22**
SE23 1A **140**
TW13: Hanw 4C **130**
UB10: Ick 5C **56**
Grove Cotts. SW3 7D **16**
W4 6A **98**
Grove Ct. *EN5: Barn* *3C* ***20***
(off Hadley Ridge)
KT1: King T *3E* ***150***
(off Grove Cres.)
KT8: E Mos 5H **149**
NW8 1A **4**
SE15 *7E* ***102***
(off Peckham Rd.)
SW10 *6A* ***16***
(off Drayton Gdns.)
TW3: Houn 4E **112**
W5 1E **96**
Grove Cres. E18 2H **51**
KT1: King T 3E **150**
KT12: Walt T 7K **147**
NW9 4J **43**
TW13: Hanw 4C **130**
Grove Cres. Rd. E15 6F **69**
Grovedale Rd. N19 2H **65**
Grove Dwellings E1 5J **85**
Grove End E18 2H **51**
NW5 4F **65**
Grove End Gdns. NW8 2B **82**
Grove End Ho. NW8 2A **4**
Grove End La. KT10: Esh 7H **149**
Grove End Rd. NW8 1A **4** (2B **82**)
Grove Farm Retail Pk. RM6: Chad H 7C **54**
Grovefield *N11* *4A* ***32***
(off Coppies Gro.)
Grove Footpath KT5: Surb 4E **150**
Grove Gdns. EN3: Enf W 1E **24**
NW4 5C **44**
NW8 2D **4** (3C **82**)
RM10: Dag 3J **73**
TW10: Rich 6F **115**
TW11: Tedd 4A **132**
Grove Grn. Rd. E11 3E **68**
Grove Hall Ct. *E3* *2C* ***86***
(off Jebb St.)
NW8 1A **4** (3A **82**)
Grove Hill E18 2H **51**
HA1: Harr 7J **41**
Grovehill Ct. BR1: Brom 6H **141**
Grove Hill Rd. HA1: Harr 7K **41**
SE5 3E **120**
Grove Ho. N3 3F **45**
SW3 *7D* ***16***
(off Chelsea Mnr. St.)
Grove Ho. Rd. N8 4J **47**
Groveland Av. SW16 7K **137**
Groveland Ct. EC4 1D **14**
Groveland Rd. BR3: Beck 3B **158**
Grovelands *KT1: King T* *4D* ***150***
(off Palace Rd.)
KT8: W Mole 4E **148**
Grovelands Cl. HA2: Harr 3F **59**
SE5 2E **120**
Grovelands Ct. N14 7C **22**
Grovelands Rd. BR5: St P 7A **144**
N13 4E **32**
N15 6G **49**
Groveland Way KT3: N Mald 5J **151**
Grove La. KT1: King T 4E **150**
SE5 1D **120**
UB8: Hil 4B **74**
Grove La. Ter. SE5 2D **120**
Groveley Rd. TW13: Felt 5H **129**
TW16: Sun 5G **129**
Grove Mans. *W6* *2E* ***98***
(off Hammersmith Gro.)
Grove Mkt. Pl. SE9 6D **124**
Grove M. W6 3E **98**
Grove Mill Pl. SM5: Cars 3E **166**

Grove Nature Reserve, The 4B 74
GROVE PARK
  SE12 .3K 141
  W4 . . . . .1J 115
Grove Pk. E11 . . . . .6K 51
  NW9 .4J 43
  SE5 .2E 120
Grove Pk. Av. E4 . . . . .7J 35
Grove Pk. Bri. W4 . . . . .7J 97
Grove Pk. Gdns. W4 . . . . .7J 97
Grove Pk. Ind. Est. NW9 . . . . .3K 43
Grove Pk. M. W4 . . . . .7J 97
Grove Pk. Nature Reserve 1H 141
Grove Pk. Rd. N15 . . . . .4E 48
  SE9 . . . . .3A 142
  W4 . . . . .7H 97
Grove Pk. Ter. W4 . . . . .7H 97
Grove Pas. E2 . . . . .2H 85
Grove Pl. IG11: Bark 7G 71
  NW3 . . . . .3B 64
  SW12 . . . . .7F 119
  W3 . . . . .1J 97
Grover Ct. SE13 . . . . .2D 122
Grover Ho. SE11 . . . . . . .6H 19 (5K 101)
Grove Rd. CR4: Mitc 3E 154
  (not continuous)
  CR7: Thor H 4A 156
  DA7: Bex 4J 127
  DA17: Belv 6F 109
  E3 . . . . .1K 85
  E4 . . . . .4K 35
  E11 . . . . .7H 51
  E17 . . . . .6D 50
  E18 . . . . .2H 51
  EN4: Cockf 3H 21
  HA5: Pinn 5D 40
  HA8: Edg 6B 28
  KT6: Surb 5D 150
  KT8: E Mos 4H 149
  N11 . . . . .5A 32
  N12 . . . . .5G 31
  N15 . . . . .5E 48
  NW2 . . . . .6E 62
  RM6: Chad H 7B 54
  SM1: Sutt 6J 165
  SW13 . . . . .2B 116
  SW19 . . . . .7A 136
  TW2: Twick 3H 131
  TW3: Houn 4E 112
  TW7: Isle 1J 113
  TW8: Bford 5C 96
  TW10: Rich 6F 115
  TW17: Shep 6E 146
  UB8: Uxb 7A 56
  W3 . . . . .1J 97
  W5 . . . . .7D 78
Groveside Cl. SM5: Cars 2C 166
  W3 . . . . .5G 79
Groveside Ct. SW11 . . . . .2B 118
Groveside Rd. E4 . . . . .2B 36
Grovestile Waye TW14: Bedf 7F 111
Grove St. N18 . . . . .5A 34
  SE8 . . . . .4B 104
Grove Ter. NW5 . . . . .3F 65
  TW11: Tedd 4A 132
  UB1: S'hall 7E 76
Grove Ter. M. NW5 . . . . .3F 65
Grove Va. BR7: Chst 6E 142
  SE22 .4F 121
Grove Vs. E14 . . . . .7D 86
Grove Way HA9: Wemb 5H 61
  KT10: Esh 7G 149
  UB8: Uxb 7A 56
Groveway RM8: Dag 3D 72
  SW9 .1K 119
Grovewood TW9: Kew 1G 115
Grove Wood Cl. BR1: Brom 3E 160
Grovewood Pl. IG8: Wfd G 6J 37
Grummant Rd. SE15 . . . . .1F 121
Grundy St. E14 . . . . .6D 86
Gruneisen Rd. N3 . . . . .7E 30

Grunwick Cl. NW2 . . . . .5C 62
Gtec Ho. E15 . . . . .2F 87
  (off Canning Rd.)
Guardhouse Way NW7 . . . . .5A 30
Guardian Ct. SE12 . . . . .5G 123
Guards Memorial 5D 12 (1H 101)
Guards' Mus., The 7B 12 (2G 101)
Gubyon Av. SE24 . . . . .5B 120
Guerin Sq. E3 . . . . .3B 86
Guernsey Cl. TW5: Hest 7E 94
Guernsey Gro. SE24 . . . . .7C 120
Guernsey Ho. EN3: Enf W 1E 24
  (off Eastfield Rd.)
  N1 . . . . .6C 66
  (off Channel Island Est.)
Guernsey Rd. E11 . . . . .1F 69
Guglielmo Marconi M. E3 . . . . .2B 86
Guibal Rd. SE12 . . . . .7K 123
Guildable Mnr. Wlk. SE1 . . . . .4F 15
  (off London Bri. St.)
Guildersfield Rd. SW16 . . . . .7J 137
Guildford Av. TW13: Felt 2H 129
Guildford Ct. SW8 . . . . .7J 101
  (off Guildford Rd.)
Guildford Gro. SE10 . . . . .1D 122
Guildford Rd. CR0: C'don 6D 156
  E6 . . . . .6D 88
  E17 . . . . .1E 50
  IG3: Ilf .2J 71
  SW8 .1J 119
Guildford Way SM6: Wall 5J 167
Guildhall
  City 7E 8
Guildhall Art Gallery 7E 8
  (off Aldermanbury)
Guildhall Bldgs. EC2 . . . . .7E 8
Guildhall Library 7D 8
Guildhall Offices EC2 . . . . .7D 8
Guildhouse St. SW1 . . . . .3A 18 (4G 101)
Guildown Av. N12 . . . . .4E 30
Guild Rd. SE7 . . . . .6B 106
Guildsway E17 . . . . .1B 50
Guilford Av. KT5: Surb 5F 151
Guilford Pl. WC1 . . . . .4G 7 (4K 83)
Guilford St. WC1 . . . . .4E 6 (4J 83)
Guilfoyle NW9 . . . . .2B 44
Guillemot Ct. SE8 . . . . .6B 104
  (off Alexandra Cl.)
Guillemot Pl. N22 . . . . .2K 47
Guinea Ct. E1 . . . . .7G 85
  (off Royal Mint St.)
Guinea Point E14 . . . . .6A 86
  (off Repton St.)
Guinness Cl. E9 . . . . .7A 68
  UB3: Harl 3F 93
Guinness Ct. CR0: C'don 2F 169
  E1 . . . . .1J 15
  EC1 . . . . .2D 8
  SE1 . . . . .6G 15
  SW3 . . . . .4E 16 (4D 100)
Guinness Sq. SE1 . . . . .4E 102
Guinness Trust SW3 . . . . .4E 16
  (off Cadogan St.)
Guinness Trust Bldgs. SE11 . . . . . .5B 102
  W6 . . . . .5F 99
  (off Fulham Pal. Rd.)
Guinness Trust Est., The N16 . . . . . .1E 66
Guion Rd. SW6 . . . . .2H 117
Gulland Wlk. N1 . . . . .6C 66
  (off Church Rd.)
Gullane Ho. E3 . . . . .2B 86
  (off Shetland Rd.)
Gulliver Cl. UB5: N'olt 1D 76
Gulliver Rd. DA15: Sidc 2H 143
Gulliver's Ho. EC1 . . . . .4C 8
Gulliver St. SE16 . . . . .3A 104
Gulston Wlk. SW3 . . . . .4F 17
Gumleigh Rd. W5 . . . . .4C 96
Gumley Gdns. TW7: Isle 3A 114
Gumping Rd. BR5: Farnb 2G 173

Gundulph Rd. BR2: Brom 3A 160
Gun Ho. E1 . . . . .7H 85
  (off Wapping High St.)
Gunmakers La. E3 . . . . .1A 86
Gun M. IG9: Buck H 4G 37
Gunnell Cl. CR0: C'don 6G 157
  SE25 .6G 157
  (off Backley Gdns.)
Gunner La. SE18 . . . . .5E 106
GUNNERSBURY 5H 97
Gunnersbury Av. W3 . . . . .1F 97
  W4 . . . . .1F 97
  W5 . . . . .1F 97
Gunnersbury Cl. W4 . . . . .5H 97
Gunnersbury Ct. W3 . . . . .2H 97
Gunnersbury Cres. W3 . . . . .2G 97
Gunnersbury Dr. W5 . . . . .2F 97
Gunnersbury Gdns. W3 . . . . .2G 97
Gunnersbury La. W3 . . . . .3G 97
Gunnersbury Mnr. W5 . . . . .1F 97
Gunnersbury M. W4 . . . . .5H 97
GUNNERSBURY PARK 3G 97
Gunnersbury Pk. Mus. 3G 97
Gunnersbury Triangle Nature Reserve
  . . . . .4J 97
Gunners Gro. E4 . . . . .3K 35
Gunners Rd. SW18 . . . . .2B 136
Gunnery Ter. SE18 . . . . .3G 107
Gunning St. SE18 . . . . .4J 107
Gunpowder Sq. EC4 . . . . .7K 7
  (off E. Harding St.)
Gunstor Rd. N16 . . . . .4E 66
Gun St. E1 . . . . .6J 9 (5F 85)
Gunter Gro. HA8: Edg 1K 43
  SW10 . . . . .6A 100
Gunter Hall Studios SW10 . . . . . . .6A 100
  (off Gunter Gro.)
Gunterstone Rd. W14 . . . . .4G 99
Gunthorpe St. E1 . . . . .6K 9 (5F 85)
Gunton M. SE13 . . . . .5F 123
Gunton Rd. E5 . . . . .3H 67
  SW17 . . . . .6E 136
Gunwhale Cl. SE16 . . . . .1K 103
Gun Wharf E1 . . . . .1J 103
  (off Wapping High St.)
Gunyard M. SE18 . . . . .7C 106
Gurdon Ho. E14 . . . . .6C 86
  (off Dod St.)
Gurdon Rd. SE7 . . . . .5J 105
Gurnard Cl. UB7: Yiew 7A 74
Gurnell Gro. W13 . . . . .4K 77
Gurnell Leisure Cen. 3K 77
Gurney Cl. E15 . . . . .5G 69
  E17 . . . . .1K 49
  IG11: Bark 6F 71
Gurney Cres. CR0: C'don 1K 167
Gurney Dr. N2 . . . . .4A 46
Gurney Ho. E2 . . . . .2G 85
  (off Goldsmiths Row)
  UB3: Harl 5G 93
Gurney Rd. E15 . . . . .5G 69
  SM5: Cars 4E 166
  SW6 .3A 118
  UB5: N'olt 3K 75
Gutenberg Ct. SE1 . . . . .3F 103
  (off Grange Rd.)
Guthrie Ct. SE1 . . . . .7K 13
Guthrie St. SW3 . . . . .5C 16 (5B 100)
Gutter La. EC2 . . . . .7C 8 (6C 84)
Guyatt Gdns. CR4: Mitc 2E 154
Guy Barnett Gro. SE3 . . . . .3J 123
Guy Rd. SM6: Bedd 3H 167
Guyscliff Rd. SE13 . . . . .5E 122
Guys Retreat IG9: Buck H 1F 37
Guy St. SE1 . . . . .6F 15 (2D 102)
Guy Townsley Sq. E3 . . . . .5D 86
Gwalior Ho. N14 . . . . .6B 22
Gwalior Rd. SW15 . . . . .4F 117
Gwendolen Av. SW15 . . . . .4F 117
Gwendolen Cl. SW15 . . . . .5F 117

Gwendolen Ho. TW19: Stanw 1A 128
  (off Yeoman Dr.)
Gwendoline Av. E13 . . . . .1K 87
Gwendwr Rd. W14 . . . . .5G 99
Gweneth Cotts. HA8: Edg 6B 28
Gwen Morris Ho. SE5 . . . . .7C 102
Gwent Ct. SE16 . . . . .1K 103
  (off Rotherhithe St.)
Gwillim Cl. DA15: Sidc 5A 126
Gwilym Maries Ho. E2 . . . . .3H 85
  (off Blythe St.)
Gwydor Rd. BR3: Beck 3K 157
Gwydyr Rd. BR2: Brom 3H 159
Gwyn Cl. SW6 . . . . .7A 100
Gwynne Av. CR0: C'don 7K 157
Gwynne Cl. W4 . . . . .6B 98
Gwynne Ho. E1 . . . . .5H 85
  (off Turner St.)
  SW1 . . . . .5G 17
  (off Lwr. Sloane St.)
  WC1 . . . . .2J 7
  (off Lloyd Baker St.)
Gwynne Pk. Av. IG8: Wfd G 6J 37
Gwynne Pl. WC1 . . . . .2H 7 (3K 83)
Gwynne Rd. SW11 . . . . .2B 118
Gylcote Cl. SE5 . . . . .4D 120
Gyles Pk. HA7: Stan 1C 42
Gyllyngdune Gdns. IG3: Ilf 2K 71
Gym, The
  Hounslow 3F 113
Gymnasium, The N1 . . . . .2J 83
GYPSY CORNER 5K 79

H

Haarlem Rd. W14 . . . . .3F 99
Haberdasher Est. N1 . . . . . .1F 9 (3D 84)
Haberdasher Pl. N1 . . . . . . .1F 9 (3D 84)
Haberdashers Ct. SE14 . . . . .3K 121
Haberdasher St. N1 . . . . . . .1F 9 (3D 84)
Habitat Cl. SE15 . . . . .2H 121
Habitat Sq. SE10 . . . . .3H 105
  (off Teal St.)
Haccombe Rd. SW19 . . . . .6A 136
HACKBRIDGE 1E 166
Hackbridge Pk. Gdns. SM5: Cars . . .2D 166
Hackbridge Rd. SM6: Wall 2E 166
Hackford Rd. SW9 . . . . .1K 119
Hackford Wlk. SW9 . . . . .1K 119
Hackington Cres. BR3: Beck 6C 140
HACKNEY .6H 67
Hackney City Farm 2G 85
Hackney Empire Theatre 6H 67
Hackney Fashion Hub E9 . . . . .6J 67
Hackney Gro. E8 . . . . .6H 67
Hackney Mus. 6H 67
Hackney Picturehouse 6H 67
  (off Mare St.)
Hackney Rd. E2 . . . . .2J 9 (3F 85)
HACKNEY WICK 6B 68
HACKNEY WICK 6A 68
Hackworth Point E3 . . . . .3D 86
  (off Rainhill Way)
Hacon Sq. E8 . . . . .7H 67
  (off Mare St.)
Hadar Cl. N20 . . . . .1D 30
Hadden Rd. SE28 . . . . .3J 107
Hadden Way UB6: G'frd 6H 59
Haddington Rd. BR1: Brom 3F 141
Haddo Ho. SE10 . . . . .6D 104
  (off Haddo St.)
Haddon Cl. EN1: Enf 6B 24
  KT3: N Mald 5B 152
Haddon Ct. NW4 . . . . .3E 44
  W3 . . . . .7B 80
Haddonfield SE8 . . . . .4K 103
Haddon Gro.
  DA15: Sidc 7K 125
Haddon Hall St. SE1 . . . . .3D 102
  (off Rephidim St.)

Haddon Rd. SM1: Sutt 4K 165
(not continuous)
Haddo St. SE10 6D 104
Haden Ct. N4 2A 66
Haden La. N11 4B 32
Hadfield Cl. UB1: S'hall 3D 76
Hadfield Ho. *E1 6G 85*
(off Ellen St.)
Hadleigh Cl. E1 4J 85
HA2: Harr 4E 58
SW20 2H 153
Hadleigh Ct. E4 1B 36
NW2 6E 62
Hadleigh Ho. *E1 4J 85*
(off Hadleigh Cl.)
Hadleigh Lodge *IG8: Wfd G 6D 36*
(off Snakes La. W.)
Hadleigh Rd. N9 7C 24
Hadleigh St. E2 3J 85
Hadleigh Wlk. E6 6C 88
HADLEY 3C 20
Hadley Cl. N21 6F 23
Hadley Comn. EN5: Barn, New Bar 2D 20
Hadley Ct. EN5: New Bar 3E 20
N16 1G 67
SL3: Poyle 4A 174
(off Coleridge Cres.)
Hadley Gdns. UB2: S'hall 5D 94
W4 5K 97
Hadley Grn. EN5: Barn 2C 20
Hadley Grn. Rd. EN5: Barn 2C 20
Hadley Grn. W. EN5: Barn 2C 20
Hadley Gro. EN5: Barn 2B 20
Hadley Highstone EN5: Barn 1C 20
Hadley M. EN5: Barn 3C 20
Hadley Pde. *EN5: Barn 3B 20*
(off High St.)
Hadley Ridge EN5: Barn 3C 20
Hadley Rd. CR4: Mitc 4H 155
DA17: Belv 4F 109
EN2: Enf 1A 22
EN4: Had W 1K 21
EN5: New Bar 2E 20
Hadley St. NW1 6F 65
(not continuous)
Hadley Way N21 6F 23
HADLEY WOOD 1F 21
Hadley Wood Golf Course 1H 21
Hadley Wood Lawn Tennis Club 1F 21
Hadley Wood Nature Reserve 2F 21
Hadley Wood Rd. EN4: Cockf 2F 21
EN5: Cockf, New Bar 2F 21
Hadlow Ho. *SE17 5E 102*
(off Kinglake Est.)
Hadlow Pl. SE19 7G 139
Hadlow Rd. DA14: Sidc 4A 144
DA16: Well 7C 108
Hadrian Cl. *E3 1C 86*
(off Garrison Rd.)
TW19: Stanw 7A 110
Hadrian Ct. SM2: Sutt 7K 165
Hadrian Est. E2 2G 85
Hadrian M. CR4: Mitc 3F 155
N7 7K 65
Hadrians Ride EN1: Enf 5A 24
Hadrian St. SE10 5G 105
Hadrian Way TW19: Stanw 7A 110
(not continuous)
Hadstock Ho. *NW1 1D 6*
(off Ossulston St.)
Hadyn Pk. Ct. *W12 2C 98*
(off Curwen Rd.)
Hadyn Pk. Rd. W12 2C 98
Hafer Rd. SW11 4D 118
Hafton Rd. SE6 1G 141
Haggard Rd. TW1: Twick 7B 114
Hagger Ct. E17 3F 51
HAGGERSTON 7F 67
Haggerston Rd. E8 7F 67
Haggerston Studios *E8 1F 85*
(off Kingsland Rd.)
Hague St. E2 3G 85
Ha Ha Rd. SE18 6D 106
Haig Ho. *E2 1K 9*
(off Shipton St.)
Haig Pl. SM4: Mord 6J 153
Haig Rd. HA7: Stan 5H 27
UB8: Hil 5D 74
Haig Rd. E. E13 3A 88
Haig Rd. W. E13 3A 88
Haigville Gdns. IG6: Ilf 4F 53
Hailes Cl. CR0: Bedd 2H 167
SW19 6A 136
Haileybury Av. EN1: Enf 6A 24
Hailey Rd. DA18: Erith 2G 109
Hailey Rd. Bus. Pk. DA18: Erith 2G 109
Hailing M. *BR2: Brom 3K 159*
(off Wendover Rd.)
Hailsham Av. SW2 2K 137
Hailsham Cl. KT6: Surb 7D 150
Hailsham Dr. HA1: Harr 3H 41
Hailsham Ho. *NW8 4C 4*
(off Salisbury St.)
Hailsham Rd. SW17 6E 136
Hailsham Ter. N18 5J 33
Haimo Rd. SE9 5B 124
Hainault Bri. Pde. *IG1: Ilf 2F 71*
(off Hainault St.)
Hainault Ct. *E17 4F 51*
(off Forest Ri.)
Hainault Gore RM6: Chad H 5E 54
Hainault Rd. E11 1E 68
RM5: Col R, Rom 2J 55
RM6: Chad H 1B 54
(Forest Rd.)
RM6: Chad H 6F 55
(Sylvan Av.)
Hainault St. IG1: Ilf 2G 71
SE9 1F 143
Haines Cl. N1 7E 66
Haines St. SW8 7G 101
Haines Wlk. SM4: Mord 7K 153
Hainford Cl. SE4 4K 121
Haining Cl. W4 5G 97
Hainthorpe Rd. SE27 3B 138
Hainton Cl. E1 6H 85
Halberd M. E5 2H 67
Halbutt Gdns. RM9: Dag 3F 73
Halbutt St. RM9: Dag 4F 73
Halcomb St. N1 1E 84
Halcot Av. DA6: Bex 5H 127
Halcrow St. E1 5H 85
Halcyon *EN1: Enf 5K 23*
(off Private Rd.)
Halcyon Cl. SW13 3C 116
Halcyon Wharf *E1 1G 103*
(off Hermitage Wall)
Haldane Cl. N10 7A 32
Haldane Pl. SW18 1K 135
Haldane Rd. E6 3B 88
SE28 7D 90
SW6 7H 99
UB1: S'hall 7G 77
Haldan Rd. E4 6K 35
Haldon Rd. SW18 6H 117
HALE, THE 5E 28
Hale, The E4 7A 36
N17 3G 49
Hale Cl. BR6: Farnb 4G 173
E4 3K 35
HA8: Edg 5D 28
Hale Ct. HA8: Edg 5D 28
Hale Dr. NW7 6D 28
HALE END 6B 36
Hale End Cl. HA4: Ruis 6J 39
Hale End Rd. E4 6A 36
E17 1E 50
IG8: Wfd G 7A 36
Halefield Rd. N17 1H 49
Hale Gdns. N17 4G 49
W3 1G 97
Hale Gro. Gdns. NW7 5F 29
Hale Ho. *SW1 5D 18*
(off Lindsay Sq.)
Hale La. HA8: Edg 5C 28
NW7 5E 28
Hale Path SE27 4B 138
Hale Rd. E6 4C 88
N17 3G 49
Halesowen Rd. SM4: Mord 7K 153
Hales Prior *N1 1G 7*
(off Calshot St.)
Hales St. SE8 7C 104
Hale St. E14 7D 86
Halesworth Cl. E5 2J 67
Halesworth Rd. SE13 3D 122
Hale Wlk. W7 5J 77
Haley Rd. NW4 6E 44
Half Acre HA7: Stan 5H 27
TW8: Bford 6D 96
Half Acre Rd. W7 1J 95
Half Moon Ct. CR0: C'don 7B 156
EC1 6C 8
Half Moon Cres. N1 2K 83
(not continuous)
Half Moon La. SE24 6C 120
Half Moon Pas. E1 1K 15 (6F 85)
(not continuous)
Half Moon St. W1 4K 11 (1F 101)
Halford Cl. HA8: Edg 2H 43
Halford Pl. W7 1K 95
Halford Rd. E10 5F 51
SW6 6J 99
TW10: Rich 5E 114
UB10: Ick 4C 56
Halfway St. DA15: Sidc 7H 125
Haliburton Rd. TW1: Twick 5A 114
Haliday Ho. *N1 6D 66*
(off Mildmay St.)
Haliday Wlk. N1 6D 66
Halidon Cl. E9 5J 67
Halifax NW9 2B 44
Halifax Cl. TW11: Tedd 6J 131
Halifax Rd. EN2: Enf 2H 23
UB6: G'frd 1F 77
Halifax St. SE26 3H 139
Halifield Dr. DA17: Belv 3E 108
Haling Down Pas. CR8: Purl 7C 168
Haling Gro. CR2: S Croy 7C 168
Haling Pk. Gdns. CR2: S Croy 6B 168
Haling Pk. Rd. CR2: S Croy 5B 168
Haling Rd. CR2: S Croy 6D 168
Haliwell Ho. *NW6 1K 81*
(off Mortimer Cres.)
Halkett Ho. *E2 1J 85*
(off Waterloo Gdns.)
Halkin Arc. SW1 1F 17 (3D 100)
Halkin M. SW1 1G 17 (3E 100)
Halkin Pl. SW1 1G 17 (3E 100)
Halkin St. SW1 7H 11 (2E 100)
Hall, The SE3 3J 123
Hallam Cl. BR7: Chst 5D 142
Hallam Ct. *W1 5K 5*
(off Hallam St.)
Hallam Gdns. HA5: Hat E 1C 40
Hallam Ho. *SW1 6B 18*
(off Churchill Gdns.)
Hallam M. W1 5K 5 (5F 83)
Hallam Rd. N15 4B 48
SW13 3D 116
Hallam St. W1 4K 5 (5F 83)
Hallane Ho. SE27 5C 138
Hall Apartments *E3 5B 86*
(off Geoff Cade Way)
Hall Cl. W5 5E 78
Hall Ct. TW11: Tedd 5K 131
Hall Dr. SE26 5J 139
W7 6J 77
Halley Gdns. SE13 4F 123
Halley Ho. *E2 2G 85*
(off Pritchards Rd.)
SE10 5H 105
(off Armitage Rd.)
Halley Rd. E7 6A 70
E12 6A 70
Halley St. E14 5A 86
Hall Farm Cl. HA7: Stan 4G 27
Hall Farm Dr. TW2: Whitt 7H 113
Hallfield Est. W2 6A 82
(not continuous)
Hall Gdns. E4 4G 35
Hall Ga. NW8 1A 4 (3B 82)
Halliards, The KT12: Walt T 6J 147
Halliday Ho. *E1 6G 85*
(off Christian St.)
Halliday Sq. UB2: S'hall 1H 95
Halliford Cl. TW17: Shep 4F 147
Halliford Rd. TW16: Sun 5G 147
TW17: Shep 5G 147
Halliford St. N1 7C 66
Hallingbury Ct. E17 3D 50
Halling Ho. *SE1 7F 15*
(off Long La.)
Hallings Wharf Studios E15 1F 87
Halliwell Ct. SE22 5G 121
Halliwell Rd. SW2 6K 119
Halliwick Ct. Pde. *N12 6J 31*
(off Woodhouse Rd.)
Halliwick Rd. N10 1E 46
HALL LANE 5E 34
Hall La. E4 5F 35
NW4 1C 44
UB3: Harl 7F 93
Hallmark Ho. *E14 5C 86*
(off Ursula Gould Way)
Hallmark Trad. Est. HA9: Wemb 4J 61
Hallmead Rd. SM1: Sutt 3K 165
Hall Oak Wlk. NW6 6H 63
Hallowell Av. CR0: Bedd 4J 167
Hallowell Cl. CR4: Mitc 3E 154
Hallowell Gdns. CR7: Thor H 2C 156
Hallowell Rd. HA6: Nwood 1G 39
Hallowfield Way CR4: Mitc 3B 154
Hallows Gro. TW16: Sun 5H 129
Hall Pl. W2 4A 4 (4B 82)
(not continuous)
Hall Place & Gdns. 6J 127
Hall Pl. Cres. DA5: Bexl 5J 127
Hall Place Sports Pavilion 6J 127
Hall Rd. E6 1D 88
E15 4F 69
NW8 1A 4 (3A 82)
RM6: Chad H 6C 54
SM6: Wall 7F 167
TW7: Isle 5H 113
Hallside Rd. EN1: Enf 1A 24
Halls Ter. UB10: Hil 4D 74
Hall St. EC1 1B 8 (3B 84)
N12 5F 31
Hallsville Rd. E16 6H 87
Hallswelle Pde. NW11 5H 45
Hallswelle Rd. NW11 5H 45
Hall Twr. W2 5B 4
Hall Vw. SE9 2B 142
Hallywell Cres. E6 5D 88
Halo E15 1E 86
Halons Rd. SE9 7E 124
Halpin Pl. SE17 4D 102
Halsbrook Rd. SE3 3A 124
Halsbury Cl. HA7: Stan 4G 27
Halsbury Ct. HA7: Stan 5G 27
Halsbury Ho. *N7 4K 65*
(off Biddestone Rd.)
Halsbury Rd. W12 1D 98
Halsbury Rd. E. UB5: N'olt 4G 59
Halsbury Rd. W. UB5: N'olt 5F 59
Halsend UB3: Hayes 1K 93
Halsey Ho. *WC1 6G 7*
(off Red Lion Sq.)
Halsey M. SW3 3E 16 (4D 100)
Halsey St. SW3 3E 16 (4D 100)
Halsham Cres. IG11: Bark 5K 71
Halsmere Rd. SE5 1B 120
Halstead Cl. CR0: C'don 3C 168

Halstead Ct. E17 7B 50
N1 1F 9
(off Murray Gro.)
Halstead Gdns. N21 1J 33
Halstead Rd. E11 5J 51
EN1: Enf 4K 23
N21 1H 33
Halston Cl. SW11 6D 118
Halstow Rd. NW10 3F 81
SE10 5J 105
Halsway UB3: Hayes 1J 93
Halton Cl. N11 6J 31
Halton Ct. SE3 3K 123
Halton Cross St. N1 1B 84
Halton Ho. N1 7B 66
(off Halton Rd.)
Halton Mans. N1 7B 66
Halton Pl. N1 1C 84
Halton Rd. N1 7B 66
Halt Robin La. DA17: Belv 4H 109
Halt Robin Rd. DA17: Belv 4G 109
(not continuous)
Halyard Ho. E14 3E 104
(off Manchester Rd.)
Halyard St. RM9: Dag 4E 90
HAM 3C 132
Ham, The TW8: Bford 7C 96
Hamara Ghar E13 1A 88
Hambalt Rd. SW4 5G 119
Hamble Cl. HA4: Ruis 2G 57
Hambledon SE17 6D 102
(off Villa St.)
Hambledon Cl. UB8: Hil 4D 74
Hambledon Ct. SE22 4E 120
W5 7E 78
Hambledon Gdns. SE25 3F 157
Hambledon Pl. SE21 1E 138
Hambledon Rd. SW18 7H 117
Hambledown Rd. DA15: Sidc 7H 125
Hamble Dr. UB3: Hayes 7H 75
Hamblehyrst BR3: Beck 2D 158
Hamble St. SW6 3K 117
Hambleton Cl. KT4: Wor Pk 2E 164
Hamble Wlk. UB5: N'olt 2E 76
(off Brabazon Rd.)
Hambley Ho. SE16 4H 103
(off Camilla Rd.)
Hamblin Ho. UB1: S'hall 7C 76
(off The Broadway)
Hambridge Way SW2 7A 120
Hambro Av. BR2: Hayes 1J 171
Hambrook Rd. SE25 3H 157
Hambro Rd. SW16 6H 137
Hambrough Ho. UB4: Yead 5A 76
Hambrough Rd. UB1: S'hall 1C 94
Ham Cl. TW10: Ham 3C 132
(not continuous)
Ham Comn. TW10: Ham 3D 132
Ham Common (Nature Reserve) 4E 132
Ham Ct. NW9 2A 44
Ham Cft. Cl. TW13: Felt 3J 129
Hamden Cres. RM10: Dag 3H 73
Hamel Cl. HA3: Kenton 4D 42
Hamella Ho. E9 5A 68
(off Sadler Pl.)
Hameway E6 3E 88
Ham Farm Rd. TW10: Ham 4D 132
Ham Flds. TW10: Ham 3B 132
Hamfrith Rd. E15 6H 69
Ham Ga. Av. TW10: Ham 3D 132
Ham House & Garden 1C 132
Hamilton Av. IG6: Ilf 4F 53
KT6: Surb 2G 163
N9 7B 24
RM1: Rom 2K 55
SM3: Cheam 2G 165
Hamilton Cl. EN4: Cockf 4H 21
HA7: Stan 2D 26
N17 3F 49
NW8 2A 4 (3B 82)
SE16 2A 104
Hamilton Cl. TW11: Tedd 6B 132
TW13: Felt 5H 129
Hamilton Ct. CR0: C'don 1G 169
SE6 1H 141
SW15 3G 117
TW3: Houn 4F 113
(off Hanworth Rd.)
W5 7E 78
W9 3A 82
(off Maida Vale)
Hamilton Cres. HA2: Harr 3D 58
N13 4F 33
TW3: Houn 5F 113
Hamilton Gdns. NW8 1A 4 (3A 82)
Hamilton Hall NW8 2A 82
(off Hamilton Ter.)
Hamilton Ho. E3 3B 86
(off British St.)
E14 5D 104
(off St Davids Sq.)
E14 7B 86
(off Victory Pl.)
NW8 1A 4
W4 6A 98
W8 2K 99
(off Vicarage Ga.)
Hamilton La. N5 4B 66
Hamilton Lodge E1 4J 85
(off Cleveland Gro.)
Hamilton M. SW18 1J 135
SW19 7J 135
W1 6J 11 (2F 101)
Hamilton Pde. TW13: Felt 4H 129
Hamilton Pk. N5 4B 66
Hamilton Pk. W. N5 4B 66
Hamilton Pl. N19 3H 65
TW16: Sun 7K 129
W1 5H 11 (1E 100)
Hamilton Rd. CR7: Thor H 3D 156
DA7: Bex 2E 126
DA15: Sidc 4A 144
E15 3G 87
E17 2A 50
EN4: Cockf 4H 21
HA1: Harr 5J 41
IG1: Ilf 4F 71
N2 3A 46
N9 7B 24
NW10 5C 62
NW11 7F 45
SE27 4D 138
SW19 7K 135
TW2: Twick 1J 131
TW8: Bford 6D 96
TW13: Felt 4H 129
UB1: S'hall 1D 94
UB3: Hayes 7K 75
W4 2A 98
W5 7E 78
Hamilton Rd. Ind. Est. SE27 4D 138
Hamilton Rd. M. SW19 7K 135
Hamilton Sq. N12 6G 31
SE1 6F 15 (2D 102)
Hamilton St. SE8 6C 104
Hamilton Ter. NW8 2A 4 (2K 81)
Hamilton Way N3 6D 30
N13 4G 33
SM6: Wall 7H 167
Ham Lands Nature Reserve 2A 132
Hamlea Cl. SE12 5J 123
Hamlet, The SE5 3D 120
Hamlet Cl. RM5: Col R 1G 55
SE6 7D 122
SE13 4G 123
Hamlet Ct. E3 3C 86
(off Tomlin's Gro.)
EN1: Enf 5K 23
SE11 5B 102
(off Opal St.)
W6 4C 98
Hamlet Gdns. W6 4C 98
Hamlet Ind. Est. E9 7C 68
Hamlet Intl. Ind. Est. DA8: Erith 5K 109
Hamlet Lodge UB10: Hil 6D 56
Hamlet M. SE21 1D 138
Hamleton Ter. RM9: Dag 7C 72
(off Flamstead Rd.)
Hamlet Rd. RM5: Col R 1G 55
SE19 7F 139
Hamlet Sq. NW2 3G 63
Hamlets Way E3 4B 86
Hamlet Way SE1 6F 15 (2D 102)
Hamlin Cres. HA5: Eastc 5A 40
Hamlyn Cl. HA8: Edg 3K 27
Hamlyn Gdns. SE19 7E 138
Hamlyn Ho. TW13: Felt 1K 129
Hammelton Ct. BR1: Brom 1H 159
(off London Rd.)
Hammelton Rd. BR1: Brom 1H 159
Hammerfield Ho. SW3 5D 16
(off Cale St.)
Hammers La. NW7 5H 29
Hammersley Ho. SE14 7J 103
(off Pomeroy St.)
Hammersley Rd. E16 5J 87
HAMMERSMITH 4E 98
Hammersmith Apollo
The Eventim Apollo 5E 98
Hammersmith Bri. SW13 6D 98
Hammersmith Bri. Rd. W6 5E 98
HAMMERSMITH BROADWAY 4E 98
Hammersmith B'way. W6 4E 98
Hammersmith Emb. W6 6E 98
Hammersmith Fitness & Squash Cen. 4F 99
(off Chalk Hill Rd.)
HAMMERSMITH FLYOVER 5E 98
Hammersmith Flyover W6 5E 98
Hammersmith Gro. W6 2E 98
Hammersmith Rd. W6 4F 99
W14 4F 99
Hammersmith Ter. W6 5C 98
Hammet Cl. UB4: Yead 5B 76
Hammett St. EC3 2J 15 (7F 85)
Hammond Av. CR4: Mitc 2F 155
Hammond Cl. EN5: Barn 5B 20
TW12: Hamp 1E 148
UB6: G'frd 5H 59
Hammond Ct. E10 2D 68
(off Leyton Grange Est.)
E17 5A 50
(off Maude Rd.)
SE11 5J 19
(off Hotspur St.)
Hammond Ho. E14 3C 104
(off Tiller Rd.)
SE14 7J 103
(off Lubbock St.)
Hammond Lodge W9 5J 81
(off Admiral Wlk.)
Hammond Rd. EN1: Enf 2C 24
UB2: S'hall 3C 94
Hammonds Cl. RM8: Dag 3C 72
Hammond St. NW5 6G 65
Hammond Way SE28 7B 90
Hamond Cl. CR2: S Croy 7B 168
Hamonde Cl. HA8: Edg 2C 28
Hamond Sq. N1 2E 84
Ham Pk. Rd. E7 7H 69
E15 7H 69
Hampden Av. BR3: Beck 2A 158
Hampden Cl. NW1 2H 83
Hampden Ct. N10 7K 31
Hampden Gurney St. W1 1E 10 (6D 82)
Hampden Ho. SW9 2A 120
(off Overton Rd.)
Hampden La. N17 1F 49
Hampden Rd. BR3: Beck 2A 158
HA3: Hrw W 1G 41
KT1: King T 3G 151
N8 4A 48
N10 7K 31
Hampden Rd. N17 1G 49
N19 2H 65
RM5: Col R 1H 55
Hampden Sq. N14 1A 32
Hampden Way N14 1A 32
Hampshire Cl. N18 5C 34
Hampshire Hog La. W6 5D 98
Hampshire Rd. N22 7E 32
Hampshire St. NW5 6H 65
Hampson Way SW8 1K 119
HAMPSTEAD 4B 64
Hampstead Av. IG8: Wfd G 7K 37
Hampstead Cl. SE28 1B 108
Hampstead Gdns. NW11 6J 45
RM6: Chad H 5B 54
HAMPSTEAD GARDEN SUBURB 5A 46
Hampstead Ga. NW3 5A 64
Hampstead Golf Course 7B 46
Hampstead Grn. NW3 5C 64
Hampstead Gro. NW3 3A 64
Hampstead Heath 2B 64
Hampstead Hgts. N2 3A 46
Hampstead High St. NW3 4B 64
Hampstead Hill Gdns. NW3 4B 64
Hampstead Ho. NW1 2A 6
(off William Rd.)
Hampstead La. N6 1B 64
NW3 1B 64
Hampstead Lodge NW1 5C 4
(off Bell St.)
Hampstead M. BR3: Beck 4D 158
Hampstead Mus. 4B 64
(off New End Sq.)
Hampstead Rd. NW1 1A 6 (2G 83)
Hampstead Sq. NW3 3A 64
Hampstead Theatre 7B 64
Hampstead Wlk. E3 1B 86
Hampstead Way NW11 5H 45
Hampstead W. NW6 6J 63
HAMPTON 1F 149
Hampton & Richmond Borough FC 1F 149
Hampton Bus. Pk. TW13: Hanw 3C 130
Hampton Cl. N11 5A 32
NW6 3J 81
SW20 7E 134
HAMPTON COURT 4J 149
HAMPTON COURT 3J 149
Hampton Ct. N1 6B 66
N22 1G 47
SE14 7A 104
(off Batavia Rd.)
SE16 7K 85
(off King & Queen Wharf)
Hampton Ct. Av. KT8: E Mos 6H 149
Hampton Ct. Bri. KT8: E Mos 4J 149
Hampton Ct. Cres. KT8: E Mos 3H 149
Hampton Ct. Est. KT7: T Ditt 4J 149
Hampton Ct. M. KT8: E Mos 4J 149
(off Feltham Av.)
Hampton Court Palace 4K 149
Hampton Court Palace Golf Course 5C 150
Hampton Ct. Pde. KT8: E Mos 4J 149
Hampton Ct. Rd. KT1: Hamp W 3K 149
KT8: E Mos 3K 149
TW12: E Mos, Hamp 2G 149
Hampton Ct. Way KT7: T Ditt 7J 149
KT8: E Mos 7J 149
Hampton Golf Course 3E 130
Hampton Grange
BR1: Brom 7A 142
HAMPTON HILL 5G 131
Hampton Hill Bus. Pk.
TW12: Hamp H 5G 131
(off High St.)
Hampton Hill Playhouse Theatre 5G 131
Hampton Ho. DA7: Bex 2H 127
(off Erith Rd.)
SW8 7G 101
(off Ascalon St.)
Hampton La. TW13: Hanw 4C 130

Hampton M. EN3: Enf H 3D **24**
NW10 . . . . . 3K **79**
WD23: B Hea 1B **26**
Hampton Open Air Pool 7G 131
Hampton Ri. HA3: Kenton 6E **42**
Hampton Rd. CR0: C'don 6C **156**
E4 . . . . . 5G **35**
E7 . . . . . 5K **69**
E11 . . . . . 1F **69**
HA7: Stan 3D **26**
IG1: Ilf 4G **71**
KT4: Wor Pk 2C **164**
TW2: Twick 3H **131**
TW11: Tedd 5H **131**
TW12: Hamp H 5H **131**
Hampton Rd. E. TW13: Hanw 4D **130**
Hampton Rd. Ind. Pk. CR0: C'don 6C **156**
Hampton Rd. W. TW13: Hanw 3C **130**
Hampton Sports & Fitness Cen. 5E 130
Hampton St. SE1 . . . . . 4C **102**
SE17 . . . . . 4B **102**
HAMPTON WICK 1C 150
Hampton Youth Project (Sports Hall)
. . . . . 6D 130
Ham Ridings TW10: Ham 5F **133**
Hamshades Cl. DA15: Sidc 3K **143**
Hamston Ho. *W8* *3K 99*
(off Kensington Ct. Pl.)
Ham St. TW10: Ham 1B **132**
Ham Vw. CR0: C'don 6A **158**
Ham Yd. W1 . . . . . 2C **12** (7H **83**)
Hanah Ct. SW19 . . . . . 7F **135**
Hanameel St. E16 . . . . . 1K **105**
Hana M. E5 . . . . . 4H **67**
Hanbury Cl. NW4 . . . . . 3E **44**
Hanbury Ct. HA1: Harr 6K **41**
Hanbury Dr. E11 . . . . . 7H **51**
N21 . . . . . 5E **22**
Hanbury Ho. *E1* *5G 85*
(off Hanbury St.)
SW8 . . . . . *7J 101*
(off Regent's Bri. Gdns.)
Hanbury M. N1 . . . . . 1C **84**
Hanbury Rd. N17 . . . . . 2H **49**
W3 . . . . . 2H **97**
Hanbury St. E1 . . . . . 5K **9** (5F **85**)
Hanbury Wlk. DA5: Bexl 3K **145**
Hancock Nunn Ho. *NW3* *6D 64*
(off Fellows Rd.)
Hancock Rd. E3 . . . . . 3E **86**
SE19 . . . . . 6D **138**
Handa Wlk. N1 . . . . . 6D **66**
Hand Ct. WC1 . . . . . 6H **7** (5K **83**)
Handcroft Rd. CR0: C'don 7B **156**
Handel Bus. Cen. SW8 . . . . . 7E **18** (6J **101**)
Handel Cl. HA8: Edg 6A **28**
Handel House Mus. *2J 11*
(off Brook St.)
Handel Mans. SW13 . . . . . 7E **98**
WC1 . . . . . *3F 7*
(off Handel St.)
Handel Pde. *HA8: Edg* *7B 28*
(off Whitchurch La.)
Handel Pl. NW10 . . . . . 6K **61**
Handel St. WC1 . . . . . 3E **6** (4J **83**)
Handel Way HA8: Edg 7B **28**
Handen Rd. SE12 . . . . . 5G **123**
Handforth Rd. IG1: Ilf 3F **71**
SW9 . . . . . 7A **102**
Handley Dr. SE3 . . . . . 3K **123**
Handley Gro. NW2 . . . . . 3F **63**
Handley Page Rd. SM6: Wall 7K **167**
Handley Rd. E9 . . . . . 7J **67**
Handowe Cl. NW4 . . . . . 4C **44**
Handside Cl. KT4: Wor Pk 1F **165**
Hands Wlk. E16 . . . . . 6J **87**
Handsworth Av. E4 . . . . . 6A **36**
Handsworth Rd. N17 . . . . . 3D **48**
Handtrough Way IG11: Bark 2F **89**
Handyside St. N1 . . . . . 1H **83**
Hanford Cl. SW18 . . . . . 1J **135**
Hanford Row SW19 . . . . . 6E **134**
Hanger Ct. W5 . . . . . 4F **79**
Hanger Grn. W5 . . . . . 4G **79**
HANGER HILL 4F 79
HANGER LANE **3E 78**
Hanger La. W5 . . . . . 2E **78**
Hanger Va. La. W5 . . . . . 6F **79**
(not continuous)
Hanger Vw. Way W3 . . . . . 6G **79**
Hanging Sword All.
EC4 . . . . . 1K **13**
Hankey Ho. *SE1* *7F 15*
(off Hankey Pl.)
Hankey Pl. SE1 . . . . . 7F **15** (2D **102**)
Hankins Ho. SE10 . . . . . 3J **105**
Hankins La. NW7 . . . . . 2F **29**
Hanley Gdns. N4 . . . . . 1K **65**
Hanley Pl. BR3: Beck 7C **140**
Hanley Rd. N4 . . . . . 1J **65**
Hanmer Wlk. N7 . . . . . 2K **65**
Hannaford Wlk. E3 . . . . . 4D **86**
Hannah Barlow Ho. SW8 . . . . . 1K **119**
Hannah Bldg. *E1* *6H 85*
(off Watney St.)
Hannah Cl. BR3: Beck 3E **158**
NW10 . . . . . 4J **61**
Hannah Ct. E15 . . . . . 2H **87**
Hannah Mary Way SE1 . . . . . 4G **103**
Hannah M. SM6: Wall 7G **167**
Hannay Ho. SW15 . . . . . 6G **117**
Hannay La. N8 . . . . . 7H **47**
Hannay Wlk. SW16 . . . . . 2H **137**
Hannell Rd. SW6 . . . . . 7G **99**
Hannen Rd. SE27 . . . . . 3B **138**
Hannibal Rd. E1 . . . . . 5J **85**
TW19: Stanw 7A **110**
Hannibal Way CR0: Wadd 5K **167**
Hannington Rd. SW4 . . . . . 3F **119**
Hanno Cl. SM6: Wall 7H **167**
Hanover Av. E16 . . . . . 1J **105**
TW13: Felt 1J **129**
Hanover Circ. UB3: Hayes 6E **74**
Hanover Cl. SM3: Cheam 4G **165**
TW9: Kew 7G **97**
TW15: Ashf 4A **128**
Hanover Ct. *E8* *1F 85*
(off Stean St.)
HA4: Ruis 3J **57**
NW9 . . . . . 3A **44**
SE19 . . . . . *7G 139*
(off Anerley Rd.)
SW15 . . . . . 4B **116**
W12 . . . . . *1C 98*
(off Uxbridge Rd.)
Hanover Dr. BR7: Chst 4G **143**
Hanover Flats *W1* *2H 11*
(off Binney St.)
Hanover Gdns. IG6: Ilf 1G **53**
SE11 . . . . . 6A **102**
Hanover Ga. NW1 . . . . . 2D **4** (3C **82**)
Hanover Ga. Mans. NW1 . . . . . 3D **4** (4C **82**)
Hanover Ho. *E14* *1B 104*
(off Westferry Cir.)
NW8 . . . . . *2C 82*
(off St John's Wood High St.)
SE16 . . . . . *2K 103*
(off Dominion Dr.)
SW9 . . . . . 3A **120**
Hanover Mans. *SW2* *5A 120*
(off Barnwell Rd.)
Hanover Mead NW11 . . . . . 5G **45**
Hanover Pk. SE15 . . . . . 1G **121**
Hanover Pl. E3 . . . . . 3B **86**
WC2 . . . . . 1F **13** (6J **83**)
Hanover Rd. N15 . . . . . 4F **49**
NW10 . . . . . 7E **62**
SW19 . . . . . 7A **136**
Hanover Sq. W1 . . . . . 1K **11** (6F **83**)
Hanover Steps W2 . . . . . 1D **10**
Hanover St. CR0: C'don 3B **168**
W1 . . . . . 1K **11** (6F **83**)
Hanover Ter. NW1 . . . . . 2E **4** (3D **82**)
TW7: Isle 1A **114**
Hanover Ter. M. NW1 . . . . . 2D **4** (3C **82**)
Hanover Trad. Est. N7 . . . . . 5J **65**
Hanover Way DA6: Bex 3D **126**
Hanover W. Ind. Est. NW10 . . . . . 3K **79**
Hanover Yd. *N1* *2C 84*
(off Noel Rd.)
Hansa Cl. UB2: S'hall 3A **94**
Hansard M. W14 . . . . . 2F **99**
Hansart Way EN2: Enf 1F **23**
Hanscomb M. SW4 . . . . . 4G **119**
Hans Ct. SW3 . . . . . 1E **16**
Hans Cres. SW1 . . . . . 1E **16** (3D **100**)
Hanseatic Wlk. EC4 . . . . . 3E **14**
Hanselin Cl. HA7: Stan 5E **26**
Hansel Rd. NW6 . . . . . 3J **81**
Hansen Dr. N21 . . . . . 5E **22**
Hanshaw Dr. HA8: Edg 1K **43**
Hansler Ct. *SW19* *1G 135*
(off Princes Way)
Hansler Gro. KT8: E Mos 4H **149**
Hansler Rd. SE22 . . . . . 5F **121**
Hansol Rd. DA6: Bex 5E **126**
Hansom M. SE11 . . . . . 5H **19** (5K **101**)
Hansom Ter. *BR1: Brom* *1K 159*
(off Freelands Gro.)
Hanson Cl. BR3: Beck 6D **140**
SW12 . . . . . 7F **119**
SW14 . . . . . 3J **115**
UB7: W Dray 3B **92**
Hanson Ct. E17 . . . . . 6D **50**
Hanson Gdns. UB1: S'hall 2C **94**
Hanson Ho. *E1* *7G 85*
(off Pinchin St.)
Hanson St. W1 . . . . . 5A **6** (5G **83**)
Hans Pl. SW1 . . . . . 1F **17** (3D **100**)
Hans Rd. SW3 . . . . . 1E **16** (3D **100**)
Hans St. SW1 . . . . . 2F **17** (3D **100**)
Hanway Pl. W1 . . . . . 7C **6** (6H **83**)
Hanway Rd. W7 . . . . . 6H **77**
Hanway St. W1 . . . . . 7C **6** (6H **83**)
HANWELL 1K 95
Hanwell Ho. *W2* *5J 81*
(off Gt. Western Rd.)
HANWORTH 4B 130
Hanworth Air Pk. Leisure Cen. 2B 130
Hanworth Ho. SE5 . . . . . 7B **102**
Hanworth Rd. TW3: Houn 1C **130**
TW4: Houn 1C **130**
TW12: Hamp 4D **130**
TW13: Felt 1K **129**
TW16: Sun 7J **129**
(not continuous)
Hanworth Ter. TW3: Houn 4F **113**
Hanworth Trad. Est. TW13: Hanw 3C **130**
Hapgood Cl. UB6: G'frd 5H **59**
Harad's Pl. E1 . . . . . 7G **85**
Harbans Ct. SL3: Poyle 4A **174**
Harben Pde. *NW3* *7A 64*
(off Finchley Rd.)
Harben Rd. NW6 . . . . . 7A **64**
Harberson Rd. E15 . . . . . 1H **87**
SW12 . . . . . 1F **137**
Harberton Rd. N19 . . . . . 1G **65**
Harbet Rd. E4 . . . . . 5F **35**
N18 . . . . . 5F **35**
W2 . . . . . 6B **4** (5B **82**)
Harbex Cl. DA5: Bexl 7H **127**
Harbinger Rd. E14 . . . . . 4D **104**
Harbledown Ho. *SE1* *7E 14*
(off Manciple St.)
Harbledown Rd. SW6 . . . . . 1J **117**
Harbord Cl. SE5 . . . . . 2D **120**
Harbord Ho. *SE16* *4K 103*
(off Cope St.)
Harbord St. SW6 . . . . . 1F **117**
Harborough Av. DA15: Sidc 7J **125**
Harborough Ho. *UB5: N'olt* *3D 76*
(off Taywood Rd.)
Harborough Rd. SW16 . . . . . 4K **137**
Harbour Av. SW10 . . . . . 1A **118**
Harbour Cl. CR4: Mitc 1E **154**
Harbour Club, The
Chelsea 2A 118
Harbour Club Notting Hill 5J 81
Harbour Exchange Sq. E14 . . . . . 2D **104**
Harbour Quay E14 . . . . . 1E **104**
Harbour Reach SW6 . . . . . 1A **118**
Harbour Rd. SE5 . . . . . 3C **120**
Harbour Yd. SW10 . . . . . 1A **118**
Harbridge Av. SW15 . . . . . 7B **116**
Harbury Rd. SM5: Cars 7C **166**
Harbut Rd. SW11 . . . . . 4B **118**
Harcombe Rd. N16 . . . . . 3E **66**
Harcourt Av. DA15: Sidc 6C **126**
E12 . . . . . 4D **70**
HA8: Edg 3D **28**
SM6: Wall 4F **167**
Harcourt Bldgs. EC4 . . . . . 2J **13**
Harcourt Cl. TW7: Isle 3A **114**
Harcourt Fld. SM6: Wall 4F **167**
Harcourt Ho. W1 . . . . . 7J **5**
Harcourt Lodge SM6: Wall 4F **167**
Harcourt Rd. CR7: Thor H 6K **155**
DA6: Bex 4E **126**
E15 . . . . . 2H **87**
N22 . . . . . 1H **47**
SE4 . . . . . 3B **122**
SM6: Wall 4F **167**
SW19 . . . . . 7J **135**
Harcourt St. W1 . . . . . 6D **4** (5C **82**)
Harcourt Ter. SW10 . . . . . 5K **99**
Hardcastle Cl. CR0: C'don 6G **157**
Hardcastle Ho. *SE14* *1A 122*
(off Loring Rd.)
Hardcourts Cl. BR4: W W'ck 3D **170**
Hardegray Cl. SM2: Sutt 7J **165**
Hardel Ri. SW2 . . . . . 1B **138**
Hardel Wlk. SW2 . . . . . 7A **120**
Harden Ct. SE7 . . . . . 4C **106**
Harden Ho. SE5 . . . . . 2E **120**
Harden's Manorway SE7 . . . . . 3B **106**
(not continuous)
Harders Rd. SE15 . . . . . 2H **121**
Hardess St. SE24 . . . . . 3C **120**
Hardie Cl. NW10 . . . . . 5K **61**
Hardie Rd. RM10: Dag 3J **73**
Harding Cl. CR0: C'don 3F **169**
SE17 . . . . . 6C **102**
Harding Dr. RM8: Dag 1E **72**
Hardinge Cl. UB8: Hil 5D **74**
Hardinge Cres. SE18 . . . . . 3G **107**
Hardinge La. E1 . . . . . 6J **85**
(not continuous)
Hardinge Rd. N18 . . . . . 6K **33**
NW10 . . . . . 1D **80**
Hardinge St. E1 . . . . . 7J **85**
(Johnson St.)
E1 . . . . . 6J **85**
(Steel's La.)
Harding Ho. *SW13* *6D 98*
(off Wyatt Dr.)
UB3: Hayes 6K **75**
Harding Rd. DA7: Bex 2F **127**
Harding's Cl. KT2: King T 1F **151**
Hardings La. SE20 . . . . . 6K **139**
Hardington *NW1* *7E 64*
(off Belmont St.)
Hardman Rd. KT2: King T 2E **150**
SE7 . . . . . 5K **105**
Hardwick Cl. HA7: Stan 5H **27**
Hardwick Ct. DA8: Erith 6K **109**
Hardwicke Av. TW5: Hest 1E **112**
Hardwicke M. WC1 . . . . . 2H **7**
Hardwicke Rd. N13 . . . . . 6D **32**
TW10: Ham 4C **132**
W4 . . . . . 4K **97**
Hardwicke St. IG11: Bark 1G **89**
Hardwick Grn. W13 . . . . . 5B **78**
Hardwick Ho. *NW8* *3D 4*
(off Lilestone St.)

Hardwick Pl. SW16 7G 137
Hardwicks Sq. SW18 5J 117
Hardwick St. EC1 2K 7 (3A 84)
Hardwidge St.
SE1 6G 15 (2E 102)
Hardy Av. E16 1J 105
HA4: Ruis 5K 57
Hardy Cl. EN5: Barn 6B 20
HA5: Pinn 7B 40
SE16 2K 103
Hardy Cotts. SE10 6F 105
Hardy Ct. SW17 3B 136
(off Grosvenor Way)
W3 3J 97
(off Bollo Bri. Rd.)
Hardy Ho. SW4 7G 119
SW18 7K 117
Hardying Ho. E17 4A 50
Hardy Pas. N22 1K 47
Hardy Rd. E4 6G 35
SE3 7H 105
SW19 7K 135
Hardy's M. KT8: E Mos 4J 149
Hardy Way EN2: Enf 1F 23
Hare & Billet Rd. SE3 1F 123
Harebell Dr. E6 5E 88
Harecastle Cl. UB4: Yead 4C 76
Hare Ct. EC4 1J 13
Harecourt Rd. N1 6C 66
Harecroft La. UB10: Ick 3E 56
Haredale Ho. SE16 2G 103
(off East La.)
Haredale Rd. SE24 4C 120
Haredon Cl. SE23 7K 121
HAREFIELD 1A 38
Harefield Cl. EN2: Enf 1F 23
Harefield Grn. NW7 6K 29
Harefield M. SE4 3B 122
Harefield Rd. DA14: Sidc 3D 144
N8 5H 47
SE4 3B 122
SW16 7K 137
UB8: Uxb 5A 56
Hare Marsh E2 4G 85
Harepit Cl. CR2: S Croy 7B 168
Hare Pl. EC4 1K 13
(off Fleet St.)
Hare Row E2 2H 85
Haresfield Rd. RM10: Dag 6G 73
Hare St. SE18 3E 106
Hare Wlk. N1 2E 84
(not continuous)
Harewood Av. NW1 4D 4 (4C 82)
UB5: N'olt 7D 58
Harewood Cl. UB5: N'olt 7D 58
Harewood Dr. IG5: Ilf 2D 52
Harewood Pl. W1 1K 11 (6F 83)
Harewood Rd. CR2: S Croy 6E 168
SW19 6C 136
TW7: Isle 7K 95
Harewood Row NW1 5D 4 (5C 82)
Harewood Ter. UB2: S'hall 4D 94
Harfield Gdns. SE5 3E 120
Harfield Rd. TW16: Sun 2B 148
Harfleur Ct. SE11 4B 102
(off Opal St.)
Harford Cl. E4 7J 25
Harford Ho. SE5 6C 102
(off Bethwin Rd.)
W11 5H 81
Harford M. N19 3H 65
Harford Rd. E4 7J 25
Harford St. E1 4A 86
Harford Wlk. N2 4B 46
Harfst Way BR8: Swan 7J 145
Hargood Cl. HA3: Kenton 6E 42
Hargood Rd. SE3 1A 124
Hargrave Mans. N19 2H 65
Hargrave Pk. N19 2G 65
Hargrave Pl. N7 5H 65
Hargrave Rd. N19 2G 65
Hargraves Ho. W12 7D 80
(off White City Est.)
Hargwyne St. SW9 3K 119
Hari Cl. UB5: N'olt 5F 59
Haringey Independent Cinema 4C 48
Haringey Pk. N8 6J 47
Haringey Pas. N8 4A 48
Haringey Rd. N8 4J 47
Harington Ter. N9 3J 33
N18 3J 33
Harkett Cl. HA3: W'stone 2K 41
Harkett Ct. HA3: W'stone 2K 41
Harkness Ct.
SM1: Sutt 1K 165
(off Cleeve Way)
Harkness Ho. E1 6G 85
(off Christian St.)
Harland Av. CR0: C'don 3F 169
DA15: Sidc 3H 143
Harland Cl. SW19 3K 153
Harland Rd. SE12 7J 123
Harlands Gro. BR6: Farnb 4F 173
Harlech Gdns. HA5: Pinn 7B 40
TW5: Hest 6A 94
Harlech Rd. N14 3D 32
Harlech Twr. W3 2J 97
Harlequin Av. TW8: Bford 6A 96
Harlequin Cl. IG11: Bark 4A 90
TW7: Isle 5J 113
UB4: Yead 5B 76
Harlequin Ct. E1 7G 85
(off Thomas More St.)
NW10 6K 61
(off Mitchellbrook Way)
W5 7C 78
Harlequin Ho. DA18: Erith 3E 108
(off Kale Rd.)
Harlequin Rd. TW11: Tedd 7B 132
Harlequins RUFC 7J 113
Harlescott Rd. SE15 4K 121
HARLESDEN 2B 80
Harlesden Gdns. NW10 1B 80
Harlesden La. NW10 1C 80
Harlesden Plaza NW10 2B 80
Harlesden Rd. NW10 1C 80
Harleston Cl. E5 2J 67
Harley Cl. HA0: Wemb 6D 60
Harley Ct. E11 7J 51
HA1: Harr 4H 41
N20 3F 31
Harley Cres. HA1: Harr 4H 41
Harleyford BR1: Brom 1K 159
Harleyford Ct. SE11 7G 19
Harleyford Mnr. W3 1J 97
(off Edgecote Cl.)
Harleyford Rd. SE11 7G 19 (6K 101)
Harleyford St. SE11 7J 19 (6A 102)
Harley Gdns. BR6: Orp 4J 173
SW10 5A 100
Harley Gro. E3 3B 86
Harley Ho. E11 7F 51
E14 6B 86
(off Frances Wharf)
NW1 4H 5
Harley Pl. W1 6J 5 (5F 83)
Harley Rd. HA1: Harr 4H 41
NW3 7B 64
NW10 2A 80
Harley St. W1 4J 5 (4F 83)
Harley Vs. NW10 2A 80
Harlie Ct. SE6 6C 122
Harling Ct. SW11 2D 118
Harlinger St. SE18 3C 106
HARLINGTON 6F 93
Harlington Cl. UB3: Harl 7E 92
HARLINGTON CORNER 1F 111
Harlington Rd. DA7: Bex 3E 126
UB8: Hil 3C 74
Harlington Rd. E. TW13: Felt 7K 111
TW14: Felt 7K 111
Harlington Rd. W. TW14: Felt 6K 111
Harlington Sports Cen., The 4F 93
(off Pinkwell La.)
Harlow Mans. IG11: Bark 7F 71
(off Whiting Av.)
Harlow Rd. N13 3J 33
Harlyn Dr. HA5: Eastc 3K 39
Harlynwood SE5 7C 102
(off Wyndham Rd.)
Harman Av. IG8: Wfd G 6C 36
Harman Cl. E4 4A 36
NW2 3G 63
SE1 5G 103
Harman Dr. DA15: Sidc 6K 125
NW2 3G 63
Harman Ri. IG3: Ilf 4J 71
Harman Rd. EN1: Enf 5A 24
HARMONDSWORTH 2E 174
Harmondsworth La. UB7: Harm, Sip 6A 92
Harmondsworth Moor Waterside 2C 174
Harmondsworth Moor Waterside Vis. Cen. 2C 174
Harmondsworth Rd. UB7: W Dray 5A 92
Harmon Ho. SE8 4B 104
Harmont Ho. W1 6J 5
(off Harley St.)
Harmony Apartments BR1: Brom 2J 159
(off High St.)
Harmony Cl. NW11 5G 45
(not continuous)
SM6: Wall 7J 167
Harmony Pl. SE1 5F 103
SE8 6D 104
(off Dancers Way)
Harmony Ter. HA2: Harr 1F 59
Harmony Way BR1: Brom 2J 159
NW4 4E 44
Harmood Gro. NW1 7F 65
Harmood Ho. NW1 7F 65
(off Harmood St.)
Harmood Pl. NW1 7F 65
Harmood St. NW1 6F 65
Harmsworth M. SE11 2K 19 (3A 102)
Harmsworth St. SE17 6K 19 (5B 102)
Harmsworth Way N20 1C 30
Harold Av. DA17: Belv 5F 109
UB3: Hayes 3H 93
Harold Ct. SE16 2K 103
(off Christopher Cl.)
Harold Est. SE1 3E 102
Harold Gibbons Ct. SE7 6A 106
Harold Ho. E2 2K 85
(off Mace St.)
Harold Laski Ho. EC1 2B 8
(off Percival St.)
Harold Maddison Ho. SE17 5B 102
(off Penton Pl.)
Harold Mugford Ter. E6 6E 88
(off Pearl Cl.)
Harold Pinter Theatre 3C 12
(off Panton St.)
Harold Pl. SE11 6J 19 (5A 102)
Harold Rd. E4 4K 35
E11 1G 69
E13 1K 87
IG8: Wfd G 1J 51
N8 5K 47
N15 5F 49
NW10 3K 79
SE19 7D 138
SM1: Sutt 4B 166
Haroldstone Rd. E17 5K 49
Harold Wilson Ho. SE28 1B 108
SW6 6H 99
(off Clem Attlee Ct.)
Harp All. EC4 7A 8 (6B 84)
Harp Bus. Cen., The NW2 2C 62
Harpenden Rd. E12 2A 70
SE27 3B 138
Harpenmead Point NW2 2H 63
Harper Cl. N14 5B 22
Harper Ho. SW9 3B 120
Harper M. SW17 3A 136
Harper Rd. E6 6D 88
SE1 7C 14 (3C 102)
Harper's Yd. N17 1F 49
Harpers Yd. TW7: Isle 2J 113
(off Rennels Way)
Harp Island Cl. NW10 2K 61
Harp La. EC3 3G 15 (7E 84)
Harpley Sq. E1 4K 85
Harpour Rd. IG11: Bark 6G 71
Harp Rd. W7 4K 77
Harpsden St. SW11 1E 118
Harpur M. WC1 5G 7 (5K 83)
Harpur St. WC1 5G 7 (5K 83)
Harraden Rd. SE3 1A 124
Harrier Av. E11 6K 51
Harrier Cen., The 6K 163
Harrier Ct. TW4: Houn 3C 112
Harrier M. SE28 2H 107
Harrier Rd. NW9 2A 44
Harriers Cl. W5 7E 78
Harrier Way E6 5D 88
Harries Rd. UB4: Yead 4A 76
Harriet Cl. E8 1G 85
Harriet Gdns. CR0: C'don 2G 169
Harriet Ho. SW6 7K 99
(off Wandon Rd.)
Harriet M. DA16: Well 2B 126
Harriet St. SW1 7F 11 (2D 100)
Harriet Tubman Cl. SW2 7K 119
Harriet Wlk. SW1 7F 11 (2D 100)
Harriet Way WD23: Bush 1C 26
HARRINGAY 5B 48
Harringay Gdns. N8 4B 48
Harringay Rd. N15 5B 48
(not continuous)
Harrington Cl. CR0: Bedd 2J 167
NW10 3K 61
Harrington Ct. CR0: C'don 2D 168
SW7 3B 16
(off Harrington Rd.)
W10 3H 81
Harrington Gdns. SW7 4K 99
Harrington Hill E5 1H 67
Harrington Ho. NW1 1A 6
(off Harrington St.)
UB10: Ick 4D 56
Harrington Rd. E11 1G 69
SE25 4G 157
SW7 3A 16 (4B 100)
Harrington Sq. NW1 2G 83
Harrington St. NW1 1A 6 (2G 83)
(not continuous)
Harrington Way SE18 3B 106
Harriott Cl. SE10 4H 105
Harriott Ho. E1 5J 85
(off Jamaica St.)
Harris Bldgs. E1 6G 85
(off Burslem St.)
Harris Cl. EN2: Enf 1G 23
N11 5J 31
TW3: Houn 1E 112
Harris Ct. HA9: Wemb 3F 61
Harris Ho. E3 3C 86
(off Alfred St.)
E11 1G 69
SW9 3A 120
(off St James's Cres.)
Harris Lodge SE6 1E 140
Harrison Cl. N20 1H 31
RM7: Mawney 3G 55
Harrison Ct. E18 1J 51
(off Queen Mary Av.)
Harrison Dr. BR1: Brom 4E 160
Harrison Ho. E1 6H 85
SE17 5D 102
(off Brandon St.)
Harrison Rd. NW10 1K 79
RM10: Dag 6H 73
Harrisons Ct. SE14 6K 103
(off Myers La.)

Harrison's Ri.—Hastings Ct.

Harrison's Ri. CR0: Wadd 3B 168
Harrison St. WC1 2F 7 (3J 83)
Harrison Way TW17: Shep 5D 146
Harris Rd. DA7: Bex 1E 126
RM9: Dag 5F 73
Harris Sports Cen. 5J 121
Harris St. E17 7B 50
SE5 7D 102
Harris Way TW16: Sun 1G 147
Harrod Ct. NW9 4J 43
Harrods 1E 16 (3D 100)
Harrogate Ct. N11 6K 31
SE12 7J 123
SE26 *3G 139*
(off Droitwich Cl.)
Harrold Ho. NW3 7B 64
Harrold Rd. RM8: Dag 5B 72
Harrovian Bus. Village HA1: Harr 7J 41
HARROW 6J 41
Harrow Arts Cen. 7A 26
Harrow Av. EN1: Enf 6A 24
Harroway Rd. SW11 2B 118
Harrow Borough FC 4D 58
Harrowby Ho. *W1* *7E 4*
(off Harrowby St.)
Harrowby St. W1 7D 4 (6C 82)
Harrow Cl. KT9: Chess 7D 162
Harrow Club W10 7F 81
Harrowdene Cl. HA0: Wemb 4D 60
Harrowdene Gdns. TW11: Tedd 6A 132
Harrowdene Rd. HA0: Wemb 3D 60
Harrow Dr. N9 1A 34
Harrowes Meade HA8: Edg 3B 28
Harrow Flds. Gdns. HA1: Harr 3J 59
Harrow Gdns. KT8: E Mos 3H 149
Harrowgate Ho. E9 6K 67
Harrowgate Rd. E9 6A 68
Harrow Grn. E11 3G 69
Harrow Hill Golf Course 7K 41
Harrow La. E14 7D 86
Harrow Leisure Cen. 3K 41
Harrow Lodge *NW8* *3A 4*
(off Northwick Ter.)
Harrow Mnr. Way SE2 1C 108
SE28 7C 90
Harrow Mus. 3G 41
HARROW ON THE HILL 1J 59
Harrow Pk. HA1: Harr 2J 59
Harrow Pl. E1 7H 9 (6E 84)
HARROW ROAD 7H 61
Harrow Rd. E6 1C 88
E11 3G 69
HA0: Wemb 4K 59
HA9: Wemb 5G 61
IG1: Ilf 4G 71
IG11: Bark 1J 89
NW10 3D 80
SM5: Cars 6C 166
TW14: Bedf 2C 128
W2 6A 4 (5A 82)
(not continuous)
W9 4F 81
W10 4G 81
Harrow Rd. Bri. W2 5A 82
Harrow Safari Cinema 5K 41
Harrow School Golf Course 2K 59
Harrow Sports Hall 7A 42
Harrow St. NW1 5D 4
Harrow Vw. HA1: Harr 2G 41
HA2: Harr 2G 41
UB3: Hayes 6J 75
UB10: Hil 3E 74
Harrow Vw. Rd. W5 4B 78
Harrow Way TW17: Shep 2E 146
HARROW WEALD 1J 41
Harrow Weald Lawn Tennis Club 1J 41
Harrow Weald Pk. HA3: Hrw W 6C 26
Harry Cl. CR0: C'don 6C 156
Harry Day M. SE27 3C 138
Harry Hinkins Ho. *SE17* *5C 102*
(off Bronti Cl.)
Harry Lambourn Ho. *SE15* *7H 103*
(off Gervase St.)
Harry Zeital Way E5 2J 67
Harston Wlk. E3 4D 86
Hartcliff Ct. W7 2K 95
Hart Cl. CR0: C'don 3B 168
Hart Ct. E6 7E 70
Harte Rd. TW3: Houn 2D 112
Hartfield Av. UB5: N'olt 2K 75
Hartfield Cres.
BR4: W W'ck 3J 171
SW19 7H 135
Hartfield Gro. SE20 1J 157
Hartfield Ho. *UB5: N'olt* *2K 75*
(off Hartfield Av.)
Hartfield Rd. BR4: W W'ck 4J 171
KT9: Chess 5D 162
SW19 7H 135
Hartfield Ter. E3 2C 86
Hartford Av. HA3: Kenton 3A 42
Hartford Rd. DA5: Bexl 6G 127
KT19: Ewe 6H 163
Hart Gro. UB1: S'hall 5E 76
W5 1G 97
Hart Gro. Ct. W5 1G 97
Hartham Cl. N7 5J 65
TW7: Isle 1A 114
Hartham Rd. N7 5J 65
N17 2F 49
TW7: Isle 1K 113
Harting Rd. SE9 3C 142
Hartington Cl. BR6: Farnb 5G 173
HA1: Harr 4J 59
Hartington Ct. SW8 1J 119
W4 7H 97
Hartington Ho. *SW1* *5D 18*
(off Drummond Ga.)
Hartington Rd. E16 6K 87
E17 6A 50
SW8 1J 119
TW1: Twick 7B 114
UB2: S'hall 3C 94
W4 7H 97
W13 7B 78
Hartismere Rd. SW6 7H 99
Hartlake Rd. E9 6K 67
Hartland *NW1* *1G 83*
(off Royal College St.)
Hartland Cl. HA8: Edg 2B 28
N21 6H 23
Hartland Ct. *N11* *5J 31*
(off Hartland Rd.)
Hartland Dr. HA4: Ruis 3K 57
HA8: Edg 2B 28
Hartland Rd. E15 7H 69
N11 5J 31
NW1 7F 65
NW6 2H 81
SM4: Mord 7J 153
TW7: Isle 3A 114
TW12: Hamp H 4F 131
Hartlands, The TW5: Cran 6K 93
Hartlands Cl. DA5: Bexl 6F 127
Hartland Way CR0: C'don 3A 170
SM4: Mord 7H 153
Hartlepool Ct. E16 1F 107
Hartley Av. E6 1C 88
NW7 5G 29
Hartley Cl. BR1: Brom 2D 160
NW7 5G 29
Hartley Ho. *SE1* *4F 103*
(off Longfield Est.)
Hartley Rd. CR0: C'don 7C 156
DA16: Well 7C 108
E11 1H 69
Hartley St. E2 3J 85
(not continuous)
Hart Lodge EN5: Barn 3B 20
Hartmann Rd. E16 1B 106
Hartnoll St. N7 5K 65
Harton Cl. BR1: Brom 1B 160
Harton Lodge *SE8* *1C 122*
(off Harton St.)
Harton Rd. N9 2C 34
Harton St. SE8 1C 122
Hartop Point *SW6* *7G 99*
(off Pellant Rd.)
Hartsbourne Av. WD23: B Hea 2B 26
Hartsbourne Cl. WD23: B Hea 2C 26
Hartsbourne Country Club & Golf Course 2B 26
Hartsbourne Ct. *UB1: S'hall* *6G 77*
(off Fleming Rd.)
Hartsbourne Pk. WD23: B Hea 2D 26
Hartsbourne Rd. WD23: B Hea 2C 26
Harts Gro. IG8: Wfd G 5D 36
Hartshill Cl. UB10: Hil 7D 56
Hartshorn All. EC3 1H 15
Hartshorn Gdns. E6 4E 88
Hart's La. SE14 1A 122
Harts La. IG11: Bark 6F 71
Hartslock Dr. SE2 2D 108
Hartsmead Rd. SE9 2D 142
Hart Sq. SM4: Mord 6J 153
Hart St. EC3 2H 15 (7E 84)
Hartsway EN3: Pond E 4D 24
Hartswood Gdns. W12 3B 98
Hartswood Grn. WD23: B Hea 2C 26
Hartswood Rd. W12 2B 98
Hartsworth Cl. E13 2H 87
Hartville Rd. SE18 4J 107
Hartwell Cl. SW2 1K 137
Hartwell Dr. E4 6K 35
Hartwell Ho. *SE7* *5K 105*
(off Troughton Rd.)
Hartwell St. E8 6F 67
Harvard Ct. NW6 5K 63
Harvard Hill W4 6H 97
Harvard Ho. *SE17* *6B 102*
(off Doddington Gro.)
Harvard La. W4 5J 97
Harvard Rd. SE13 5E 122
TW7: Isle 1J 113
W4 5H 97
Harvel Cl. BR5: St P 3K 161
Harvel Cres. SE2 5D 108
Harvest Bank Rd. BR4: W W'ck 3H 171
Harvest Ct. *RM13: Rain* *2K 91*
(off Broadis Way)
TW17: Shep 4C 146
Harvesters Cl. TW7: Isle 5H 113
Harvest La. KT7: T Ditt 6A 150
Harvest Rd. TW13: Felt 4J 129
Harvey Cl. NW9 2A 44
Harvey Ct. E17 5C 50
Harvey Dr. TW12: Hamp 1F 149
Harvey Gdns. E11 1H 69
SE7 5A 106
Harvey Ho. *E1* *4H 85*
(off Brady St.)
N1 *1D 84*
(off Colville Est.)
RM6: Chad H 4D 54
SW1 *6D 18*
(off Aylesford St.)
TW8: Bford 5E 96
Harvey Lodge *W9* *5J 81*
(off Admiral Wlk.)
Harvey M. *N8* *5K 47*
(off Harvey Rd.)
Harvey Rd. E11 1G 69
IG1: Ilf 5F 71
KT12: Walt T 7H 147
N8 5K 47
SE5 1D 120
(not continuous)
TW4: Houn 7D 112
UB5: N'olt 7A 58
UB10: Hil 2C 74
Harvey's Bldgs. WC2 3F 13 (7J 83)
Harveys La. RM7: Rush G 2K 73
Harvey St. N1 1D 84
Harvil Ct. *NW9* *3A 44*
(off Mornington Cl.)
Harvill Rd. DA14: Sidc 5E 144
Harvil Rd. UB9: Hare 6A 38
UB10: Ick 6A 38
Harvington Wlk. E8 7G 67
Harvist Est. N7 4A 66
Harvist Rd. NW6 2F 81
Harwell Cl. HA4: Ruis 1F 57
Harwell Pas. N2 4D 46
Harwicke Ho. *E3* *3D 86*
(off Bow Rd.)
Harwood Av. BR1: Brom 2K 159
CR4: Mitc 3C 154
Harwood Cl. HA0: Wemb 4D 60
N12 6H 31
Harwood Ct. *N1* *1D 84*
(off Colville Est.)
SW15 4E 116
Harwood Dr. UB10: Hil 1B 74
Harwood M. SW6 7J 99
Harwood Point SE16 2B 104
Harwood Rd. SW6 7J 99
Harwoods Yd. N21 7F 23
Harwood Ter. SW6 1K 117
Hascombe Ter. *SE5* *2D 120*
(off Love Wlk.)
Haselbury Rd. N9 4K 33
N18 4K 33
Haseley End SE23 7J 121
Haselrigge Rd. SW4 4H 119
Haseltine Rd. SE26 4B 140
Haselwood Dr. EN2: Enf 4G 23
Haskard Rd. RM9: Dag 4D 72
Hasker St. SW3 3D 16 (4C 100)
Haslam Av. SM3: Sutt 1G 165
Haslam Cl. N1 7A 66
UB10: Ick 2E 56
Haslam Ct. N11 4A 32
Haslam Ho. *N1* *7C 66*
(off Canonbury Rd.)
Haslam St. SE15 7F 103
Haslemere Av. CR4: Mitc 2B 154
EN4: E Barn 1J 31
NW4 6F 45
SW18 2K 135
TW5: Cran 2A 112
W7 3A 96
W13 3A 96
Haslemere Bus. Cen. EN1: Enf 4C 24
Haslemere Cl. SM6: Wall 5J 167
TW12: Hamp 5D 130
Haslemere Gdns. N3 3H 45
Haslemere Heathrow Est., The
TW4: Cran 2K 111
Haslemere Ind. Est. SW18 2K 135
Haslemere Rd. CR7: Thor H 5B 156
DA7: Bex 2F 127
IG3: Ilf 2K 71
N8 7H 47
N21 2G 33
Hasler Cl. SE28 7B 90
Haslers Wharf *E3* *1A 86*
(off Old Ford Rd.)
Haslett Rd. TW17: Shep 2G 147
Hasluck Gdns. EN5: New Bar 6E 20
Hassard St. E2 1K 9 (2F 85)
Hassendean Rd. SE3 7K 105
Hassett Rd. E9 6K 67
Hassocks Cl. SE26 3H 139
Hassocks Rd. SW16 1H 155
Hassock Wood BR2: Kes 4B 172
Hassop Rd. NW2 4F 63
Hassop Wlk. SE9 4C 142
Hasted Rd. SE7 5B 106
Haste Hill Golf Course 2G 39
Hastings Av. IG6: Ilf 4G 53
Hastings Cl. EN5: New Bar 4F 21
HA0: Wemb 4C 60
SE15 7G 103
Hastings Ct. TW11: Tedd 5H 131

Hastings Dr. KT6: Surb 6C **150**
Hastings Ho. EN3: Enf H 2D **24**
*SE18 . . . . .4D **106***
(off Mulgrave Rd.)
*W12 . . . . .7D **80***
(off White City Est.)
W13 . . . . .7B **78**
*WC1 . . . . .2E **6***
(off Hastings St.)
Hastings Pl. *CR0: C'don 1F **169***
(off Hastings Rd.)
Hastings Rd. BR2: Brom 1C **172**
CR0: C'don 1F **169**
E16 . . . . .5J **87**
N11 . . . . .5B **32**
N17 . . . . .3D **48**
W13 . . . . .7B **78**
Hastings St. SE18 . . . . .3G **107**
WC1 . . . . .2E **6** (3J **83**)
Hastingwood Ct. E17 . . . . .5D **50**
Hastingwood Trad. Est. N18 . . . . .6E **34**
Hastoe Cl. UB4: Yead 4C **76**
Hasty Cl. CR4: Mitc 1F **155**
Hat & Mitre Ct. EC1 . . . . .4B **8**
Hatch, The EN3: Enf H 1E **24**
Hatcham Mews Bus. Cen.
*SE14 . . . . .1K **121***
(off Hatcham Pk. Rd.)
Hatcham Pk. M. SE14 . . . . .1K **121**
Hatcham Pk. Rd. SE14 . . . . .1K **121**
Hatcham Rd. SE15 . . . . .6J **103**
Hatchard Rd. N19 . . . . .2H **65**
Hatchcroft NW4 . . . . .3D **44**
HATCH END .7A **26**
Hatch End Lawn Tennis Club 6A **26**
Hatch End Swimming Pool 7A **26**
Hatchers M. SE1 . . . . .7H **15**
Hatchett Rd. TW14: Bedf 1E **128**
Hatchfield Ho. *N15 . . . . .6E **48***
(off Albert Rd.)
Hatch Gro. RM6: Chad H 4E **54**
Hatch La. E4 . . . . .4A **36**
UB7: Harm 3E **174**
Hatch Pl. KT2: King T 5F **133**
Hatch Rd. SW16 . . . . .2J **155**
Hatch Side IG7: Chig 5K **37**
Hatchwood Cl. IG8: Wfd G 4C **36**
Hatcliffe Almshouses *SE10 . . . . .5G **105***
(off Tuskar St.)
Hatcliffe Cl. SE3 . . . . .3H **123**
Hatcliffe St. SE10 . . . . .5H **105**
Hatfeild Cl. CR4: Mitc 4B **154**
Hatfeild Mead SM4: Mord 5J **153**
Hatfield Cl. IG6: Ilf 3F **53**
SE14 . . . . .7K **103**
Hatfield Ct. SE3 . . . . .7J **105**
*UB5: N'olt 3A **76***
(off Canberra Dr.)
Hatfield Ho. EC1 . . . . .4C **8**
SE10 . . . . .7D **104**
Hatfield M. RM9: Dag 7E **72**
Hatfield Rd. E15 . . . . .5G **69**
RM9: Dag 6E **72**
W4 . . . . .2K **97**
W13 . . . . .1A **96**
Hatfields SE1 . . . . .4K **13** (1A **102**)
Hathaway Cl. BR2: Brom 1D **172**
HA4: Ruis .4H **57**
HA7: Stan .5F **27**
Hathaway Cres. E12 . . . . .6D **70**
Hathaway Gdns. RM6: Chad H 5D **54**
W13 . . . . .5K **77**
Hathaway Ho. N1 . . . . .1G **9** (2E **84**)
Hathaway Rd. CR0: C'don 7B **156**
Hatherleigh Cl. KT9: Chess 5D **162**
NW7 . . . . .6A **30**
SM4: Mord 4J **153**
Hatherleigh Rd. HA4: Ruis 2J **57**
Hatherley Ct. *W2 . . . . .6K **81***
(off Hatherley Gro.)
Hatherley Cres. DA14: Sidc 2A **144**
Hatherley Gdns. E6 . . . . .3B **88**
N8 . . . . .6J **47**
Hatherley Gro. W2 . . . . .6K **81**
Hatherley Ho. E17 . . . . .4C **50**
Hatherley M. E17 . . . . .4C **50**
Hatherley Rd. DA14: Sidc 4A **144**
E17 . . . . .4B **50**
TW9: Kew .1F **115**
Hatherley St. SW1 . . . . .4B **18** (4G **101**)
Hathern Gdns. SE9 . . . . .4E **142**
Hatherop Rd. TW12: Hamp 7D **130**
Hathersage Ct. N1 . . . . .5D **66**
Hathorne Cl. SE15 . . . . .2H **121**
Hathway St. SE14 . . . . .2K **121**
Hathway Ter. *SE14 . . . . .2K **121***
(off Hathway St.)
Hatley Av. IG6: Ilf 4G **53**
Hatley Cl. N11 .5J **31**
Hatley Rd. N4 .2K **65**
Hatteraick St. SE16 . . . . .2J **103**
Hattersfield Cl. DA17: Belv 4F **109**
HATTON 4H **111**
Hatton Cl. SE18 . . . . .7H **107**
HATTON CROSS 4H **111**
Hatton Cross Cen. TW6: H'row A 3H **111**
Hatton Gdn. EC1 . . . . .5K **7** (5A **84**)
Hatton Gdns. CR4: Mitc 5D **154**
Hatton Grn. TW14: Felt 4J **111**
Hatton Gro. UB7: W Dray 2A **92**
Hatton Ho. *E1 .7G **85***
(off Hindmarsh Cl.)
*KT1: King T 2F **151***
(off Victoria Rd.)
Hatton Pl. EC1 . . . . .5K **7** (5A **84**)
Hatton Rd. CR0: C'don 1A **168**
HA0: Wemb 1E **78**
TW14: Bedf, Felt 7E **110**
Hatton Rd. Sth. TW14: Felt 4H **111**
Hatton Row NW8 . . . . .4B **4**
Hatton St. NW8 . . . . .4B **4** (4B **82**)
Hatton Wlk. *EN2: Enf 4J **23***
(off London Rd.)
Hatton Wall EC1 . . . . .5K **7** (5A **84**)
Haughmond N12 . . . . .4E **30**
Haunch of Venison Yd. W1 . . . .1J **11** (6F **83**)
Hauteville Ct. Gdns. *W6 . . . . .3B **98***
(off South Side)
Havana Rd. SW19 . . . . .2J **135**
Havanna Dr. NW11 . . . . .5G **45**
Havannah St. E14 . . . . .2C **104**
Havant Rd. E17 . . . . .3E **50**
Havelock Cl. W12 . . . . .7D **80**
Havelock Ct. *UB2: S'hall 3D **94***
(off Havelock Rd.)
Havelock Ho. *SE1 . . . . .4F **103***
(off Fort Rd.)
SE23 . . . . .1J **139**
Havelock Pl. HA1: Harr 6J **41**
Havelock Rd. BR2: Brom 4A **160**
CR0: C'don 2F **169**
DA17: Belv 4F **109**
HA3: W'stone 3J **41**
N17 . . . . .2G **49**
SW19 . . . . .5A **136**
UB2: S'hall 3C **94**
Havelock St. IG1: Ilf 2F **71**
N1 . . . . .1J **83**
Havelock Ter. SW8 . . . . .1F **119**
Havelock Ter. Arches *SW8 . . . . .1F **119***
(off Havelock Ter.)
Havelock Wlk. SE23 . . . . .1J **139**
Haven, The TW9: Rich 3G **115**
TW16: Sun 7J **129**
Haven Cl. DA14: Sidc 6C **144**
SE9 . . . . .3D **142**
SW19 . . . . .3F **135**
UB4: Hayes 4G **75**
Haven Ct. BR3: Beck 2E **158**
KT5: Surb .6F **151**
Haven Grn. W5 .6D **78**
Haven Grn. Ct. W5 . . . . .6D **78**
Havenhurst Ri. EN2: Enf 2F **23**
Haven La. W5 . . . . .6E **78**
Haven Lodge *EN1: Enf 6K **23***
(off Village Rd.)
*SE18 . . . . .4F **107***
(off Vincent Rd.)
Haven M. E3 . . . . .5B **86**
N1 . . . . .7A **66**
Haven Pl. W5 . . . . .7D **78**
Havenpool *NW8 . . . . .1K **81***
(off Abbey Rd.)
Haven Rd. TW15: Ashf 4D **128**
Haven St. NW1 .7F **65**
Haven Way SE1 . . . . .3F **103**
Havenwood HA9: Wemb 3H **61**
Haverfield Gdns. TW9: Kew 7G **97**
Haverfield Rd. E3 . . . . .3A **86**
Haverford Way HA8: Edg 1F **43**
Haverhill Rd. E4 . . . . .1K **35**
SW12 . . . . .1G **137**
Havering *NW1 .7F **65***
(off Castlehaven Rd.)
Havering Dr. RM1: Rom 4K **55**
Havering Gdns. RM6: Chad H 5C **54**
Havering Mus. .5K **55**
Havering Rd. RM1: Rom 3K **55**
Havering St. E1 .6K **85**
Havering Way IG11: Bark 3B **90**
Haversham Cl. TW1: Twick 6D **114**
Haversham Ct. UB6: G'frd 6K **59**
Haversham Pl. N6 . . . . .2D **64**
Haverstock Cl. HA1: Harr 7G **41**
Haverstock Hill NW3 . . . . .5C **64**
Haverstock Pl. *N1 . . . . .1B **8***
(off Haverstock St.)
Haverstock Rd. NW5 . . . . .5E **64**
Haverstock St. N1 . . . . .1B **8** (2B **84**)
Haverthwaite Rd. BR6: Orp 2H **173**
Havilland Ct. HA8: Edg 4A **28**
Havilland M. W12 . . . . .2D **98**
Havil St. SE5 . . . . .7E **102**
Havisham Apartments *E15 . . . . .6F **69***
(off Grove Cres. Rd.)
Havisham Ho. SE16 . . . . .2G **103**
Havisham Pl. SE19 . . . . .7B **138**
Hawarden Gro. SE24 . . . . .7C **120**
Hawarden Hill NW2 . . . . .3C **62**
Hawarden Rd. E17 . . . . .4K **49**
Hawbridge Rd. E11 . . . . .1F **69**
Hawbush Ct. RM6: Ilf 4B **54**
Hawes Ho. E17 .4K **49**
Hawes La. BR4: W W'ck 1E **170**
Hawes Rd. BR1: Brom 1K **159**
(not continuous)
N18 . . . . .6C **34**
Hawes St. N1 . . . . .7B **66**
Haweswater Ho. TW7: Isle 5K **113**
Hawfinch Ho. NW9 . . . . .7B **44**
Hawgood St. E3 . . . . .5C **86**
Hawkdene E4 . . . . .6J **25**
Hawke Ct. *UB4: Yead 4A **76***
(off Perth Av.)
Hawke Ho. *E1 .4K **85***
(off Ernest St.)
Hawke Pk. Rd. N22 . . . . .3B **48**
Hawke Pl. SE16 . . . . .2K **103**
Hawker *NW9 . . . . .1B **44***
(off Everglade Strand)
Hawker Ct. *KT1: King T 2F **151***
(off Church Rd.)
Hawke Rd. SE19 . . . . .6D **138**
Hawker Pl. E17 .2E **50**
Hawker Rd. CR0: Wadd 6A **168**
Hawkesbury Rd. SW15 . . . . .5D **116**
Hawkesfield Rd. SE23 . . . . .2A **140**
Hawkesley Cl. TW1: Twick 4A **132**
Hawkes Rd. CR4: Mitc 1D **154**
TW14: Felt 7J **111**
Hawkesworth Cl. HA6: Nwood 1G **39**
Hawkes Yd. KT7: T Ditt 6K **149**
Hawke Twr. SE14 . . . . .6A **104**
Hawkewood Rd. TW16: Sun 3J **147**
Hawkfield Ct. TW7: Isle 2J **113**
Hawkhurst Gdns. KT9: Chess 4E **162**
Hawkhurst Rd. SW16 . . . . .1H **155**
Hawkhurst Way BR4: W W'ck 2D **170**
KT3: N Mald 5K **151**
Hawkinge *N17 .2D **48***
(off Gloucester Rd.)
Hawkins Cl. HA1: Harr 7H **41**
NW7 . . . . .5E **28**
Hawkins Ct. SE18 . . . . .4C **106**
Hawkins Ho. *SE8 . . . . .6C **104***
(off New King St.)
*SW1 . . . . .7B **18***
(off Dolphin Sq.)
Hawkins Rd. NW10 . . . . .7A **62**
TW11: Tedd 6B **132**
Hawkins Ter. SE7 . . . . .5C **106**
Hawkins Way SE6 . . . . .5C **140**
Hawkley Gdns. SE27 . . . . .2B **138**
Hawkridge Cl. RM6: Chad H 6C **54**
Hawksbrook La. BR3: Beck 6D **158**
Hawkshaw Cl. SW2 . . . . .7J **119**
Hawkshead NW1 . . . . .1A **6**
Hawkshead Cl. BR1: Brom 7G **141**
Hawkshead Rd. NW10 . . . . .7B **62**
W4 . . . . .2A **98**
Hawkslade Rd. SE15 . . . . .5K **121**
Hawksley Rd. N16 . . . . .3E **66**
Hawks M. SE10 . . . . .7E **104**
Hawksmoor Cl. E6 . . . . .6C **88**
SE18 . . . . .5J **107**
Hawksmoor Gro. BR2: Brom 6B **160**
Hawksmoor M. E1 . . . . .7H **85**
Hawksmoor Pl. *E2 . . . . .3K **9***
(off Cheshire St.)
Hawksmoor St. W6 . . . . .6F **99**
Hawksmouth E4 . . . . .7K **25**
Hawks Pas. *KT1: King T 2F **151***
(off Minerva Rd.)
Hawks Rd. KT1: King T 2F **151**
Hawkstone Rd. SE16 . . . . .4J **103**
Hawksworth Ho. BR1: Brom 2J **159**
Hawkwell Ct. E4 . . . . .3K **35**
Hawkwell Ho. RM8: Dag 1G **73**
Hawkwell Wlk. *N1 . . . . .1C **84***
(off Maldon Cl.)
Hawkwood Cres. E4 . . . . .6J **25**
Hawkwood La. BR7: Chst 1G **161**
Hawkwood Mt. E5 . . . . .1H **67**
Hawlands Dr. HA5: Pinn 7C **40**
Hawley Cl. TW12: Hamp 6D **130**
Hawley Cres. NW1 . . . . .7F **65**
Hawley M. NW1 . . . . .7F **65**
Hawley Rd. N18 . . . . .5E **34**
NW1 . . . . .7F **65**
(not continuous)
Hawley St. NW1 . . . . .7F **65**
Hawley Way TW15: Ashf 5C **128**
Hawstead Rd. SE6 . . . . .6D **122**
Hawsted IG9: Buck H 1E **36**
Hawthorn Av. CR7: Thor H 1B **156**
E3 . . . . .1B **86**
N13 . . . . .5D **32**
Hawthorn Cen., The HA1: Harr 5K **41**
Hawthorn Cl. BR5: Pet W 6H **161**
TW5: Cran 7K **93**
TW12: Hamp 5E **130**
Hawthorn Cotts. *DA16: Well 3A **126***
(off Hook La.)
Hawthorn Ct. *HA5: Pinn 2A **40***
(off Rickmansworth Rd.)
TW9: Kew 1H **115**
TW15: Ashf 7E **128**
Hawthorn Cres. SW17 . . . . .5E **136**
Hawthornden Cl. N12 . . . . .6H **31**
Hawthorndene Cl. BR2: Hayes 2H **171**
Hawthorndene Rd.
BR2: Hayes 2H **171**
Hawthorn Dr. BR4: W W'ck 4G **171**
HA2: Harr .6E **40**

Hawthorne Av. CR4: Mitc 2B **154**
HA3: Kenton 6A **42**
HA4: Ruis 6K **39**
SM5: Cars 7E **166**
Hawthorne Cl. BR1: Brom 3D **160**
N1 .... 6E **66**
SM1: Sutt 2A **166**
Hawthorne Ct.
HA6: Nwood 2J **39**
W5 .... 1E **96**
Hawthorne Cres. SE10 .... 5H **105**
UB7: W Dray 2B **92**
Hawthorne Gro. NW9 .... 7J **43**
Hawthorne Ho. N15 .... 5G **49**
SW1 .... *6B* ***18***
(off Churchill Gdns.)
Hawthorne M. UB6: G'frd 6G **77**
Hawthorne Pl. UB3: Hayes 7H **75**
Hawthorne Rd. BR1: Brom 3C **160**
E17 .... 3C **50**
Hawthorne Way N9 .... 2A **34**
Hawthorn Farm Av. UB5: N'olt 1C **76**
Hawthorn Gdns. W5 .... 3D **96**
Hawthorn Gro. EN2: Enf 1J **23**
SE20 .... 7H **139**
Hawthorn Hatch TW8: Bford 7B **96**
Hawthorn Ho. *SE16* *2A* ***104***
(off Blondin Way)
Hawthorn M. NW7 .... 1G **45**
Hawthorn Rd. DA6: Bex 4F **127**
IG9: Buck H 4G **37**
N8 .... 3H **47**
N18 .... 6A **34**
NW10 .... 7C **62**
SM1: Sutt 6C **166**
SM6: Wall 7F **167**
TW8: Bford 7B **96**
TW13: Felt 1J **129**
Hawthorns *CR2: S Croy* *4C* ***168***
(off Bramley Hill)
IG8: Wfd G 3D **36**
Hawthorns, The KT17: Ewe 7B **164**
SL3: Poyle 4A **174**
Hawthorn Ter. DA15: Sidc 5K **125**
N19 .... *1H* ***65***
(off Calverley Gro.)
Hawthorn Wlk. W10 .... 4G **81**
Hawthorn Way TW17: Shep 4F **147**
Hawtrey Av. UB5: N'olt 2B **76**
Hawtrey Dr. HA4: Ruis 7J **39**
Hawtrey Rd. NW3 .... 7C **64**
Haxted Rd. BR1: Brom 1K **159**
Hay Cl. E15 .... 7G **69**
Haycroft Gdns. NW10 .... 1C **80**
Haycroft Rd. KT6: Surb 2D **162**
SW2 .... 5J **119**
Hay Currie St. E14 .... 6D **86**
Hayday Rd. E16 .... 5J **87**
(not continuous)
Hayden Ct. TW13: Felt 4G **129**
Hayden Piper Ho. *SW3* *7E* ***16***
(off Caversham St.)
Haydens M. W3 .... 6J **79**
Hayden's Pl. W11 .... 6H **81**
Hayden Way RM5: Col R 2J **55**
Haydock Av. UB5: N'olt 6E **58**
Haydock Grn. UB5: N'olt 6E **58**
Haydock Grn. Flats *UB5: N'olt* *6E* ***58***
(off Haydock Grn.)
Haydon Cl. EN1: Enf 6K **23**
NW9 .... 4J **43**
Haydon Ct. NW9 .... 4J **43**
Haydon Dr. HA5: Eastc 4J **39**
Haydon Pk. Rd. SW19 .... 5J **135**
Haydon Rd. RM8: Dag 2C **72**
Haydons Rd. SW19 .... 5K **135**
Haydon St. E1 .... 6F **85**
EC3 .... 2J **15** (7F **85**)
Haydon Wlk. E1 .... 1K **15** (6F **85**)
Haydon Way SW11 .... 4B **118**
Hay Dr. CR4: Mitc 2C **154**

HAYES
BR2 .... 1J 171
UB3 .... 6G 75
Hayes & Yeading United FC 1A 94
Hayes Bri. Retail Pk. UB4: Yead 7A **76**
Hayes Chase BR4: W W'ck 6F **159**
Hayes Cl. BR2: Hayes 2J **171**
Hayes Ct. BR2: Hayes 3J **171**
HA0: Wemb 1E **78**
SE5 .... *7C* ***102***
(off Camberwell New Rd.)
SW2 .... 1J **137**
Hayes Cres. NW11 .... 5H **45**
SM3: Cheam 4F **165**
HAYES END 4F 75
Hayes End Cl. UB4: Hayes 4F **75**
Hayes End Dr. UB4: Hayes 4F **75**
Hayes End Rd. UB4: Hayes 4F **75**
Hayesens Ho. SW17 .... 4A **136**
Hayesford Pk. Dr. BR2: Brom 5H **159**
Hayes Gdn. BR2: Hayes 1J **171**
Hayes Gro. SE22 .... 3F **121**
Hayes Hill BR2: Hayes 1G **171**
Hayes Hill Rd. BR2: Hayes 1H **171**
Hayes La. BR2: Brom, Hayes 5K **159**
BR3: Beck 3E **158**
Hayes Mead Rd. BR2: Hayes 1G **171**
Hayes Metro Cen. UB4: Yead 7A **76**
Hayes Pk. Lodge UB4: Hayes 4F **75**
Hayes Pl. NW1 .... 4D **4** (4C **82**)
Hayes Rd. BR2: Brom 4J **159**
UB2: S'hall 4K **93**
Hayes St. BR2: Hayes 1K **171**
Hayes Swimming Pool 1H 93
HAYES TOWN 2H 93
Hayes Way BR3: Beck 4E **158**
Hayes Wood Av. BR2: Hayes 1K **171**
Hayfield Pas. E1 .... 4J **85**
Hayfield Yd. E1 .... 4J **85**
Haygarth Pl. SW19 .... 5F **135**
Haygreen Cl. KT2: King T 6H **133**
Hay Hill W1 .... 3K **11** (7F **83**)
Hayhurst Ct. *N1* *1B* ***84***
(off Dibden St.)
Hayland Cl. NW9 .... 4K **43**
Haylands Ct. TW8: Bford 6C **96**
Hay La. NW9 .... 4J **43**
Hayles Bldgs. *SE11* *4B* ***102***
(off Elliotts Row)
Hayles St. SE11 .... 4B **102**
Haylett Gdns. KT1: King T 4D **150**
Hayling Av. TW13: Felt 3J **129**
Hayling Cl. N16 .... 5E **66**
Hayling Ct. SM3: Cheam 4E **164**
Hayling Way HA8: Edg 4A **28**
Haymaker Cl. UB10: Uxb 7B **56**
Hayman Cres. UB4: Hayes 2F **75**
Haymans Point SE11 .... 5G **19** (4K **101**)
Hayman St. N1 .... 7B **66**
Haymarket SW1 .... 3C **12** (7H **83**)
Haymarket Arc. SW1 .... 3C **12**
Haymarket Ct. *E8* *7F* ***67***
(off Jacaranda Gro.)
Haymarket Theatre Royal *3D 12*
(off Haymarket)
Haymer Gdns. KT4: Wor Pk 3C **164**
Haymerle Ho. *SE15* *6G* ***103***
(off Haymerle Rd.)
Haymerle Rd. SE15 .... 6G **103**
Hay M. NW3 .... 6D **64**
Haymill Cl. UB6: G'frd 3K **77**
Hayne Ho. *W11* *1G* ***99***
(off Penzance Pl.)
Hayne Rd. BR3: Beck 2B **158**
Haynes Cl. N11 .... 3K **31**
N17 .... 7C **34**
SE3 .... 3G **123**
Haynes Dr. N9 .... 3C **34**
Haynes La. SE19 .... 6E **138**
Haynes Rd. HA0: Wemb 7E **60**
Hayne St. EC1 .... 5B **8** (5B **84**)

Haynt Wlk. SW20 .... 3G **153**
Hayre Dr. UB2: S'hall 5C **94**
Hay's Ct. *SE16* *2J* ***103***
(off Rotherhithe St.)
Hay's Galleria SE1 .... 4G **15** (1E **102**)
Hays La. SE1 .... 4G **15** (1E **102**)
Haysleigh Gdns. SE20 .... 2G **157**
Hay's M. W1 .... 4J **11** (1F **101**)
Haysoms Cl. RM1: Rom 4K **55**
Haystall Cl. UB4: Hayes 2G **75**
Hay St. E2 .... 1G **85**
Hayter Ct. E11 .... 2K **69**
Hayter Rd. SW2 .... 5J **119**
Hayton Cl. E8 .... 6F **67**
Hayward Cl. DA1: Cray 5K **127**
SW19 .... 7K **135**
Hayward Ct. *SW9* *2J* ***119***
(off Studley Rd.)
Hayward Gallery 5H 13 (1K 101)
Hayward Gdns. SW15 .... 6E **116**
Hayward Ho. *N1* *2A* ***84***
(off Penton St.)
Hayward M. SE4 .... 5B **122**
Hayward Rd. KT7: T Ditt 7K **149**
N20 .... 2F **31**
Haywards Cl. RM6: Chad H 5B **54**
Hayward's Pl. EC1 .... 3A **8** (4B **84**)
Haywood Cl. HA5: Pinn 2B **40**
Haywood Lodge *N11* *6D* ***32***
(off York Rd.)
Haywood Ri. BR6: Orp 5J **173**
Haywood Rd. BR2: Brom 4B **160**
Hazel Av. UB7: W Dray 3C **92**
Hazel Bank SE25 .... 2E **156**
Hazelbank KT5: Surb 1J **163**
Hazelbank Rd. SE6 .... 2F **141**
Hazelbourne Rd. SW12 .... 6F **119**
Hazelbury Cl. SW19 .... 2J **153**
Hazelbury Grn. N9 .... 3K **33**
Hazelbury La. N9 .... 3K **33**
Hazel Cl. CR0: C'don 7K **157**
CR4: Mitc 4H **155**
N13 .... 3J **33**
N19 .... 2G **65**
NW9 .... 2A **44**
SE15 .... *2G* ***121***
(off Bournemouth Cl.)
TW2: Whitt 7G **113**
TW8: Bford 7B **96**
Hazel Ct. W5 .... 7E **78**
Hazelcroft HA5: Hat E 6A **26**
Hazelcroft Cl. UB10: Hil 7B **56**
Hazeldean Rd. NW10 .... 7K **61**
Hazeldene Dr. HA5: Pinn 3A **40**
Hazeldene Gdns. UB10: Hil 1E **74**
Hazeldene Rd. DA16: Well 2C **126**
IG3: Ilf 2B **72**
Hazeldon Rd. SE4 .... 5A **122**
Hazeleigh Gdns. IG8: Wfd G 5H **37**
Hazel Gdns. HA8: Edg 4C **28**
Hazelgreen Cl. N21 .... 1G **33**
Hazel Gro. BR6: Farnb 2F **173**
EN1: Enf 6B **24**
HA0: Wemb 1E **78**
RM6: Chad H 3E **54**
SE26 .... 4K **139**
TW13: Felt 1J **129**
Hazel Ho. *E3* *1B* ***86***
(off Barge La.)
Hazelhurst BR3: Beck 1F **159**
Hazelhurst Ct. *SE6* *5E* ***140***
(off Beckenham Hill Rd.)
Hazelhurst Rd. SW17 .... 4A **136**
Hazel La. IG6: Ilf 6K **37**
SE10 .... 5H **105**
TW10: Ham 2E **132**
Hazell Cres. RM5: Col R 1H **55**
Hazellville Rd. N19 .... 7H **47**
Hazelmere Cl. TW14: Felt 6G **111**
UB5: N'olt 2D **76**
Hazelmere Ct. SW2 .... 1K **137**

Hazelmere Dr. UB5: N'olt 2D **76**
Hazelmere Rd. BR5: Pet W 4G **161**
NW6 .... 1H **81**
UB5: N'olt 2D **76**
Hazelmere Wlk. UB5: N'olt 2D **76**
(not continuous)
Hazelmere Way BR2: Hayes 6J **159**
Hazel M. *N22* *3A* ***48***
(off High Rd.)
Hazel Rd. E15 .... 5G **69**
NW10 .... 3D **80**
(not continuous)
Hazeltree La. UB5: N'olt 3C **76**
Hazel Wlk. BR2: Brom 6E **160**
Hazel Way E4 .... 6G **35**
SE1 .... 4F **103**
Hazelwood Av. SM4: Mord 4K **153**
Hazelwood Cl. HA2: Harr 4F **41**
W5 .... 2E **96**
Hazelwood Ct. KT6: Surb 6E **150**
N13 .... *4F* ***33***
(off Hazelwood La.)
NW10 .... 3A **62**
Hazelwood Cres. N13 .... 4F **33**
Hazelwood Dr. HA5: Pinn 2K **39**
TW16: Sun 3J **147**
Hazelwood Ho. SE8 .... 4A **104**
TW16: Sun 1J **147**
Hazelwood Ho's. BR2: Brom 3G **159**
Hazelwood La. N13 .... 4F **33**
Hazelwood Rd. E17 .... 5A **50**
EN1: Enf 6A **24**
Hazelwood Sports Club 7H 23
Hazlebury Rd. SW6 .... 2K **117**
Hazledean Rd. CR0: C'don 2D **168**
Hazledene Rd. W4 .... 6J **97**
Hazlemere Gdns. KT4: Wor Pk 1C **164**
Hazlewell Rd. SW15 .... 5E **116**
Hazlewood Cl. E5 .... 3A **68**
Hazlewood Cres. W10 .... 4G **81**
Hazlewood M. SW9 .... 3J **119**
Hazlewood Twr. *W10* *4G* ***81***
(off Golborne Gdns.)
Hazlitt Cl. TW13: Hanw 4C **130**
Hazlitt M. W14 .... 3G **99**
Hazlitt Rd. W14 .... 3G **99**
Heacham Av. UB10: Ick 3E **56**
Headbourne Ho. *E17* *3A* ***50***
(off Sutherland Rd.)
SE1 .... 7F **15** (3D **102**)
Headcorn Pl. CR7: Thor H 4K **155**
Headcorn Rd. BR1: Brom 5H **141**
CR7: Thor H 4K **155**
N17 .... 7A **34**
Headfort Pl. SW1 .... 7H **11** (2E **100**)
Headingley Dr. BR3: Beck 6C **140**
Headington Ct. *CR0: C'don* *4C* ***168***
(off Tanfield Rd.)
Headington Rd. SW18 .... 2A **136**
Headlam Rd. SW4 .... 6H **119**
(not continuous)
Headlam St. E1 .... 4H **85**
Headley App. IG2: Ilf 5F **53**
Headley Av. SM6: Wall 5K **167**
Headley Cl. KT19: Ewe 6G **163**
Headley Ct. SE26 .... 5J **139**
Headley Dr. CR0: New Ad 7D **170**
IG2: Ilf 6F **53**
Head's M. W11 .... 6J **81**
HEADSTONE 4G 41
Headstone Dr. HA1: Harr 3H **41**
HA3: W'stone 3J **41**
Headstone Gdns. HA2: Harr 4G **41**
Headstone La. HA2: Harr 4E **40**
HA3: Hrw W 7A **26**
Headstone Manor 3G 41
Headstone Pde. HA1: Harr 4H **41**
Headstone Rd. HA1: Harr 5J **41**
Head St. E1 .... 6K **85**
(not continuous)
Headway Cl. TW10: Ham 4C **132**

Headway Gdns. E17 . . . . . 1C **50**
Heald St. SE14 . . . . . 1C **122**
Healey Ho. *E3* *4C 86*
(off Wellington Way)
SW9 . . . . . 7A **102**
Healey St. NW1 . . . . . 6F **65**
Healy Ct. EN5: Barn 6A **20**
Healy Dr. BR6: Orp 4K **173**
Hearne Rd. W4 . . . . . 6G **97**
Hearn Ri. UB5: N'olt 1B **76**
Hearn's Bldgs. SE17 . . . . . 4D **102**
Hearnshaw St. E14 . . . . . 6A **86**
Hearn St. EC2 . . . . . 4H **9** (4E **84**)
Hearnville Rd. SW12 . . . . . 1E **136**
Heart, The KT12: Walt T 7J **147**
Heath, The W7 . . . . . 1J **95**
Heatham Pk. TW2: Twick 7K **113**
Heath Av. DA7: Bex 6D **108**
Heathbourne Rd. HA7: Stan 2D **26**
WD23: B Hea 1D **26**
Heath Brow NW3 . . . . . 3A **64**
Heath Bus. Cen. TW3: Houn 4G **113**
Heath Cl. CR2: S Croy 6B **168**
NW11 . . . . . 7K **45**
UB3: Harl 7F **93**
W5 . . . . . 4F **79**
Heathcock Ct. *WC2* *3F 13*
(off Exchange Ct.)
Heathcote Av. IG5: Ilf 2D **52**
Heathcote Ct. IG5: Ilf 1D **52**
(not continuous)
Heathcote Ga. SW6 . . . . . 3J **117**
Heathcote Gro. E4 . . . . . 3K **35**
Heathcote Rd. TW1: Twick 6B **114**
Heathcote St. WC1 . . . . . 3G **7** (4K **83**)
Heath Ct. *CR0: C'don* *4D 168*
(off Heathfield Rd.)
SE9 . . . . . 1G **143**
TW4: Houn 4D **112**
UB8: Uxb 7A **56**
Heath Cft. NW11 . . . . . 1K **63**
Heathcroft W5 . . . . . 4F **79**
Heathcroft Av. TW16: Sun 7H **129**
Heathcroft Gdns. E17 . . . . . 1F **51**
Heathdale Av. TW4: Houn 3C **112**
Heathdene Dr. DA17: Belv 4H **109**
Heathdene Rd. SM6: Wall 7F **167**
SW16 . . . . . 7K **137**
Heath Dr. NW3 . . . . . 4K **63**
SM2: Sutt 7A **166**
SW20 . . . . . 4E **152**
Heathedge SE26 . . . . . 2H **139**
Heath End Rd. DA5: Bexl 1K **145**
Heather Av. RM1: Rom 2K **55**
Heatherbank BR7: Chst 2E **160**
SE9 . . . . . 2D **124**
Heather Cl. E6 . . . . . 6E **88**
N7 . . . . . 3K **65**
RM1: Rom 1K **55**
SE13 . . . . . 7F **123**
SW8 . . . . . 3F **119**
TW7: Isle 5H **113**
TW12: Hamp 1D **148**
UB8: Hil 5B **74**
Heather Ct. DA14: Sidc 6D **144**
Heatherdale Cl. KT2: King T 6G **133**
Heatherdene Cl. CR4: Mitc 4B **154**
N12 . . . . . 7F **31**
Heather Dr. EN2: Enf 2G **23**
RM1: Rom 2K **55**
Heatherfold Way HA5: Eastc 3H **39**
Heather Gdns. NW11 . . . . . 6G **45**
RM1: Rom 2K **55**
SM2: Sutt 6J **165**
Heather Glen RM1: Rom 2K **55**
Heather Ho. *E14* *6E 86*
(off Dee St.)
Heatherlands TW16: Sun 6J **129**
Heather La. UB7: Yiew 6A **74**
Heatherlea Gro. KT4: Wor Pk 1D **164**
Heatherley Ct. E5 . . . . . 3G **67**
Heatherley Dr. IG5: Ilf 3C **52**
Heather Pk. Dr. HA0: Wemb 7G **61**
Heather Pk. Pde. *HA0: Wemb* *7F 61*
(off Heather Pk. Dr.)
Heather Rd. E4 . . . . . 6G **35**
NW2 . . . . . 2B **62**
SE12 . . . . . 2J **141**
Heathers, The TW19: Stanw 7B **110**
Heatherset Gdns. SW16 . . . . . 7K **137**
Heatherside Rd. DA14: Sidc 3C **144**
KT19: Ewe 7K **163**
Heatherton Ter. N3 . . . . . 2K **45**
Heather Wlk. HA8: Edg 5C **28**
TW2: Whitt *7E 112*
(off Stephenson Rd.)
W10 . . . . . 4G **81**
Heather Way CR2: Sels 7K **169**
HA7: Stan 6E **26**
RM1: Rom 2K **55**
Heatherwood Cl. E12 . . . . . 2A **70**
Heatherwood Dr. UB4: Hayes 2F **75**
Heathfield BR7: Chst 6G **143**
E4 . . . . . 3K **35**
HA1: Harr 7K **41**
Heathfield Av. SW18 . . . . . 7B **118**
Heathfield Cl. BR2: Kes 5A **172**
E16 . . . . . 5B **88**
Heathfield Ct. *E3* *2C 86*
(off Tredegar Rd.)
SE14 . . . . . 7J **103**
SE20 . . . . . 7J **139**
TW15: Ashf 3A **128**
W4 . . . . . 5K **97**
Heathfield Dr. CR4: Mitc 1C **154**
Heathfield Gdns. CR0: C'don 4D **168**
NW11 . . . . . 6F **45**
SE3 . . . . . *2G 123*
(off Baizdon Rd.)
SW18 . . . . . 6B **118**
W4 . . . . . 5J **97**
Heathfield Ho. SE3 . . . . . 2G **123**
Heathfield La. BR7: Chst 6G **143**
Heathfield Nth. TW2: Twick 7J **113**
Heathfield Pk. NW2 . . . . . 6E **62**
Heathfield Pk. Dr. RM6: Chad H 5B **54**
Heathfield Ri. HA4: Ruis 7E **38**
Heathfield Rd. BR1: Brom 7H **141**
BR2: Kes 5A **172**
CR0: C'don 4D **168**
DA6: Bex 4F **127**
SW18 . . . . . 6A **118**
W3 . . . . . 2H **97**
Heathfields Ct. TW4: Houn 5C **112**
Heathfield Sth. TW2: Twick 7K **113**
Heathfield Sq. SW18 . . . . . 7B **118**
Heathfield Ter. SE18 . . . . . 6J **107**
W4 . . . . . 5J **97**
Heathfield Va. CR2: Sels 7K **169**
Heath Gdns. TW1: Twick 1K **131**
Heathgate NW11 . . . . . 6K **45**
Heathgate Pl. NW3 . . . . . 5D **64**
Heath Gro. SE20 . . . . . 7J **139**
TW16: Sun 7H **129**
Heath Ho. DA15: Sidc 4K **143**
Heath Hurst Rd. NW3 . . . . . 4C **64**
Heathhurst Rd. CR2: Sande 7E **168**
Heathland Rd. N16 . . . . . 1E **66**
Heathlands Cl. TW1: Twick 2K **131**
TW16: Sun 2J **147**
Heathlands Way TW4: Houn 5C **112**
Heath La. SE3 . . . . . 2F **123**
(not continuous)
Heathlee Rd. SE3 . . . . . 4H **123**
Heathley End BR7: Chst 6G **143**
Heath Lodge WD23: B Hea 1D **26**
Heathmans Rd. SW6 . . . . . 1H **117**
Heath Mead SW19 . . . . . 3F **135**
Heath Pk. Dr. BR1: Brom 3C **160**
Heathpark Golf Course 3C **92**
Heath Pas. NW3 . . . . . 2K **63**
Heath Pl. E3 . . . . . 4B **86**
Heathpool Ct. E1 . . . . . 4H **85**
Heath Ri. BR2: Hayes 6H **159**
SW15 . . . . . 6F **117**
Heath Rd. CR7: Thor H 3C **156**
DA5: Bexl 1J **145**
HA1: Harr 7G **41**
RM6: Chad H 7D **54**
SW8 . . . . . 2F **119**
TW1: Twick 1K **131**
TW2: Twick 1K **131**
TW3: Houn, Isle 4F **113**
TW7: Isle 4F **113**
UB10: Hil 4E **74**
Heathrow Academy 1E **110**
HEATHROW AIRPORT
Terminals 1, 2, 3 . . . . . 3C **110**
Terminal 4 . . . . . 5D **110**
Terminal 5 . . . . . 6D **174**
Heathrow Blvd. UB7: Sip 7B **92**
(not continuous)
Heathrow Causeway Cen.
TW4: Houn 3K **111**
Heathrow Cl. UB7: Lford 4C **174**
Heathrow Gateway TW4: Houn 7C **112**
Heathrow Interchange UB4: Yead 1A **94**
Heathrow Intl. Trad. Est.
TW4: Houn 3K **111**
Heathrow Prologis Pk. UB3: Harl 3D **92**
Heath Royal SW15 . . . . . 6F **117**
Heaths Cl. EN1: Enf 2K **23**
Heath Side BR5: Pet W 1G **173**
NW3 . . . . . 4B **64**
Heathside NW11 . . . . . 1J **63**
SE13 . . . . . 2E **122**
TW4: Houn 7D **112**
Heathside Av. DA7: Bex 1E **126**
Heathside Cl. IG2: Ilf 5H **53**
Heathstan Rd. W12 . . . . . 6C **80**
Heath St. NW3 . . . . . 3A **64**
Heath Ter. RM6: Chad H 7D **54**
Heath Vw. N2 . . . . . 4A **46**
Heathview NW5 . . . . . 4E **64**
Heath Vw. Cl. N2 . . . . . 4A **46**
Heathview Dr. SE2 . . . . . 6D **108**
Heathview Gdns. SW15 . . . . . 7E **116**
Heathview Rd. CR7: Thor H 4A **156**
Heath Vs. NW3 . . . . . 3B **64**
SE18 . . . . . 5K **107**
Heathville Rd. N19 . . . . . 7J **47**
Heathwall St. SW11 . . . . . 3D **118**
HEATHWAY 1G **91**
Heath Way DA8: Erith 1J **127**
Heathway CR0: C'don 3B **170**
IG8: Wfd G 5F **37**
RM9: Dag 3F **73**
RM10: Dag 3F **73**
SE3 . . . . . 7J **105**
UB2: S'hall 4B **94**
Heathway Ct. NW3 . . . . . 2J **63**
Heathway Ind. Est. RM10: Dag 4H **73**
Heathwood Gdns. SE7 . . . . . 4C **106**
Heathwood Point SE23 . . . . . 3K **139**
Heathwood Wlk. DA5: Bexl 1K **145**
Heaton Cl. E4 . . . . . 3K **35**
Heaton Ho. *SW10* *6A 100*
(off Fulham Rd.)
Heaton Rd. CR4: Mitc 7E **136**
SE15 . . . . . 2H **121**
Heaven Tree Cl. N1 . . . . . 6C **66**
Heaver Rd. SW11 . . . . . 3B **118**
Heavitree Cl. SE18 . . . . . 5H **107**
Heavitree Rd. SE18 . . . . . 5H **107**
(not continuous)
Hebden Ter. N17 . . . . . 6K **33**
Hebdon Rd. SW17 . . . . . 3C **136**
Heber Mans. *W14* *6G 99*
(off Queen's Club Gdns.)
Heber Rd. NW2 . . . . . 5F **63**
SE22 . . . . . 6F **121**
Hebrides Ct. *E1* *5A 86*
(off Ocean Est.)
Hebron Rd. W6 . . . . . 3E **98**
Hecham Cl. E17 . . . . . 2A **50**
Heckfield Pl. SW6 . . . . . 7J **99**
Heckford Ho. *E14* *6D 86*
(off Grundy St.)
Heckford St. E1 . . . . . 7K **85**
Heckford St. Bus. Cen. *E1* *7K 85*
(off Heckford St.)
Hector *NW9* *1B 44*
(off Five Acre)
Hector Cl. N9 . . . . . 2B **34**
Hector Ct. *SW9* *7A 102*
(off Caldwell St.)
Hector Ho. *E2* *2H 85*
(off Old Bethnal Grn. Rd.)
Hector St. SE18 . . . . . 4J **107**
Heddington Gro. N7 . . . . . 5K **65**
Heddon Cl. TW7: Isle 4A **114**
Heddon Ct. Av. EN4: Cockf 5J **21**
Heddon Ct. Pde. EN4: Cockf 5K **21**
Heddon Rd. EN4: Cockf 5J **21**
Heddon St. W1 . . . . . 2A **12** (7G **83**)
Hedera Pl. TW4: Houn 4D **112**
Hedgegate Ct. *W11* *6H 81*
(off Powis Ter.)
Hedge Hill EN2: Enf 1G **23**
Hedge La. N13 . . . . . 3G **33**
Hedgeley IG4: Ilf 4D **52**
Hedgemans Rd. RM9: Dag 7D **72**
Hedgemans Way RM9: Dag 6E **72**
Hedgerley Gdns. UB6: G'frd 2G **77**
Hedgerow Ct. *E6* *1D 88*
(off Nelson St.)
Hedgers Gro. E9 . . . . . 6A **68**
Hedger St. SE11 . . . . . 4B **102**
Hedges Cl. TW14: Felt 6K **111**
Hedge Wlk. SE6 . . . . . 5D **140**
Hedgewood Gdns. IG5: Ilf 5E **52**
Hedgley M. SE12 . . . . . 5H **123**
Hedgley St. SE12 . . . . . 5H **123**
Hedingham Cl. N1 . . . . . 7C **66**
Hedingham Ho. *KT2: King T* *1E 150*
(off Royal Quarter)
Hedingham Rd. RM8: Dag 5B **72**
Hedley Cl. RM1: Rom 5K **55**
Hedley Ho. *E14* *3E 104*
(off Stewart St.)
Hedley Rd. TW2: Whitt 7E **112**
Hedley Row N5 . . . . . 5D **66**
Hedsor Ho. *E2* *3J 9*
(off Ligonier St.)
Heenan Cl. IG11: Bark 6G **71**
Heene Rd. EN2: Enf 1J **23**
Heer M. *E2* *2G 85*
(off Hackney Rd.)
Hega Ho. *E14* *5E 86*
(off Ullin St.)
Heidegger Cres. SW13 . . . . . 7D **98**
Heigham Rd. E6 . . . . . 7C **70**
Heighton Gdns. CR0: Wadd 5B **168**
Heights, The BR3: Beck 7E **140**
(not continuous)
SE7 . . . . . 5A **106**
UB5: N'olt 5D **58**
Heights Cl. SW20 . . . . . 7D **134**
Heiron St. SE17 . . . . . 6B **102**
Helby Rd. SW4 . . . . . 6H **119**
Heldar Ct. SE1 . . . . . 7F **15** (2D **102**)
Helder Gro. SE12 . . . . . 7H **123**
Helder St. CR2: S Croy 6D **168**
Heldmann Cl.
TW3: Houn 4H **113**
Helegan Cl. BR6: Chels 4K **173**
Helena Ct. *NW6* *7K 63*
(off Compayne Gdns.)
W5 . . . . . 5D **78**
Helena Pl. E9 . . . . . 1H **85**
Helena Rd. E13 . . . . . 2H **87**
E17 . . . . . 5C **50**
NW10 . . . . . 5D **62**
W5 . . . . . 5D **78**

Helena Sq. *SE16* 7A 86
(off Sovereign Cres.)
Helen Av. TW14: Felt 7K 111
Helen Cl. KT8: W Mole 4F 149
N2 3A 46
Helen Gladstone Ho. *SE1* 6A 14
(off Surrey Row)
Helen Ho. *E2* 2H 85
(off Old Bethnal Grn. Rd.)
Helen Mackay Ho. *E14* 6F 87
(off Blair St.)
Helen Peele Cotts. *SE16* 3J 103
(off Lower Rd.)
Helenslea Av. NW11 1J 63
Helen's Pl. E2 3J 85
Helen St. SE18 4F 107
Helen Taylor Ho. *SE16* 3G 103
(off Evelyn Lowe Est.)
Helford Cl. HA4: Ruis 2G 57
Helgiford Gdns. TW16: Sun 7G 129
Heligan Ho. *SE16* 2K 103
(off Water Gdns. Sq.)
Helios, The W12 7E 80
Helios Rd. SM6: Wall 1E 166
Heliport Ind. Est. SW11 2B 118
Helix Ct. *W11* 1F 99
(off Swanscombe Rd.)
Helix Gdns. SW2 6K 119
Helix Rd. SW2 6K 119
Helix Ter. SW19 2F 135
Hellings St. E1 1G 103
Helm, The E16 7F 89
Helme Cl. SW19 5H 135
Helmet Row EC1 2D 8 (4C 84)
Helmore Rd. IG11: Bark 7K 71
Helmsdale Cl. UB4: Yead 4C 76
Helmsdale Ho. *NW6* 2K 81
(off Carlton Vale)
Helmsdale Rd. SW16 1H 155
Helmsley Pl. E8 7H 67
Helmsley St. E8 7H 67
Helperby Rd. NW10 7A 62
Helsby Ct. *NW8* 3A 4
(off Pollitt Dr.)
Helsinki Sq. SE16 3A 104
Helston *NW1* 1G 83
(off Camden St.)
Helston Cl. HA5: Hat E 1D 40
Helston Ct. *N15* 5E 48
(off Culvert Rd.)
Helston Ho. *SE11* 5K 19
(off Kennings Way)
Helvetia St. SE6 2B 140
Helwys Ct. E4 6J 35
Hemans St. SW8 7H 101
Hemans St. Est. SW8 7J 101
Hemberton Rd. SW9 3J 119
Hemery Rd. UB6: G'frd 5H 59
Hemingford Cl. N12 5G 31
Hemingford Rd. N1 1K 83
SM3: Cheam 4E 164
Heming Rd. HA8: Edg 7C 28
Hemington Av. N11 5J 31
Hemingway Cl. NW5 4E 64
Hemlock Cl. SW16 2G 155
Hemlock Rd. W12 7B 80
(not continuous)
Hemmen La. UB3: Hayes 6H 75
Hemming Cl. TW12: Hamp 1E 148
Hemmings Cl. DA14: Sidc 2B 144
Hemmings Mead KT19: Ewe 6J 163
Hemming St. E1 4G 85
Hempstead Cl. IG9: Buck H 2D 36
Hempstead Rd. E17 3F 51
Hemp Wlk. SE17 4D 102
Hemsby Rd. KT9: Chess 6F 163
Hemstal Rd. NW6 7J 63
Hemsted Rd. DA8: Erith 7K 109
Hemswell Dr. NW9 1A 44
Hemsworth Ct. N1 2E 84
Hemsworth St. N1 2E 84
Hemus Pl. SW3 6D 16 (5C 100)
Hen & Chicken Ct. *EC4* 1J 13
(off Fleet St.)
Hen & Chickens Theatre 6B 66
(off St Paul's Rd.)
Henchman St. W12 6B 80
Hendale Av. NW4 3D 44
Henderson Cl. NW10 6J 61
Henderson Ct. N12 4E 30
NW3 5B 64
(off Fitzjohn's Av.)
SE14 6K 103
(off Myers La.)
Henderson Dr. NW8 3A 4 (4B 82)
Henderson Ho. *RM10: Dag* 3G 73
(off Kershaw Rd.)
Henderson Rd. CR0: C'don 6D 156
E7 6A 70
N9 1C 34
SW18 7C 118
UB4: Yead 3J 75
Hendfield Ct. SM6: Wall 6F 167
Hendham Rd. SW17 2C 136
HENDON 4E 44
Hendon Av. N3 1G 45
Hendon Crematorium NW7 1F 45
Hendon FC 4D 58
Hendon Golf Course 7K 29
Hendon Hall Ct. NW4 3F 45
Hendon Ho. NW4 5F 45
Hendon La. N3 3G 45
Hendon Leisure Cen. 7F 45
Hendon Lodge NW4 3D 44
Hendon Pk. Mans. NW4 5E 44
Hendon Pk. Row NW11 6H 45
Hendon Rd. N9 2B 34
Hendon Ter. TW15: Ashf 6F 129
Hendon Way NW2 7F 45
NW4 6D 44
Hendon Wood La. NW7 1G 29
Hendre Ho. *SE1* 4E 102
(off Hendre Rd.)
Hendren Cl. UB6: G'frd 5H 59
Hendre Rd. SE1 4E 102
Hendrick Av. SW12 7D 118
Heneage La. EC3 1H 15 (6E 84)
Heneage Pl. EC3 1H 15 (6E 84)
Heneage St. E1 5K 9 (5F 85)
Henera's Ct. *BR1: Brom* 3E 160
(off Brady Dr.)
Henfield Cl. DA5: Bexl 6G 127
N19 1G 65
Henfield Rd. SW19 1H 153
Hengelo Gdns. CR4: Mitc 4B 154
Hengest Av. KT10: Surb 3A 162
Hengist Rd. DA8: Erith 7H 109
SE12 7K 123
Hengist Way BR2: Brom 4G 159
SM6: Wall 7H 167
Hengrave Rd. SE23 6J 121
Hengrove Ct. DA5: Bexl 1E 144
Hengrove Cres. TW15: Ashf 3A 128
Henham Ct. RM5: Col R 1J 55
Henley Av. SM3: Cheam 3G 165
Henley Cl. *SE16* 2J 103
(off St Marychurch St.)
TW7: Isle 1K 113
UB6: G'frd 2G 77
Henley Ct. N14 7B 22
NW2 6F 63
Henley Dr. KT2: King T 7B 134
SE1 4F 103
Henley Gdns.
HA5: Eastc 3K 39
RM6: Chad H 5E 54
Henley Hgts. *N1* 7K 65
(off Caledonian Rd.)
Henley Ho. *E2* 3K 9
(off Swanfield St.)
Henley Prior *N1* 1G 7
(off Affleck St.)
Henley Rd. E16 2D 106
IG1: Ilf 4G 71
N18 4K 33
NW10 1E 80
Henley St. SW11 2E 118
Henley Way TW13: Hanw 5B 130
Henlow Pl. TW10: Ham 2D 132
HENLYS CORNER 4H 45
HENLYS RDBT. 2A 112
Hennel Cl. SE23 3J 139
Hennesse M. RM8: Dag 1E 72
Hennessy Ct. E10 6E 50
Hennessy Rd. N9 2D 34
Henniker Gdns. E6 3B 88
Henniker M. SW3 7A 16 (6B 100)
Henniker Point *E15* 5G 69
(off Leytonstone Rd.)
Henniker Rd. E15 5F 69
Henningham Rd. N17 1D 48
Henning St. SW11 1C 118
Henrietta Barnet Wlk. NW11 6J 45
Henrietta Cl. SE8 6C 104
Henrietta Ct. *TW1: Twick* 7C 114
(off Richmond Rd.)
Henrietta Gdns. N21 1F 33
Henrietta Ho. *N15* 6E 48
(off St Ann's Rd.)
W6 5E 98
(off Queen Caroline St.)
Henrietta M. WC1 3F 7 (4J 83)
Henrietta Pl. W1 1J 11 (6F 83)
Henrietta St. WC2 2F 13 (7J 83)
Henriques St. E1 6G 85
Henry Addlington Cl. E6 5F 89
Henry Chester Bldg. SW15 2E 116
Henry Cl. EN2: Enf 1K 23
Henry Cooper Way SE9 3B 142
Henry Ct. HA7: Stan 7J 27
Henry Darlot Dr. NW7 6A 30
Henry Dent Cl. SE5 3D 120
Henry Dickens Ct. W11 7F 81
Henry Doulton Dr. SW17 4E 136
Henry Hatch Ct. SM2: Sutt 7A 166
Henry Ho. SE1 5J 13 (1A 102)
SW8 7J 101
(off Wyvil Rd.)
Henry Hudson Apartments *SE10* 5G 105
(off Banning St.)
Henry Jackson Rd. SW15 3F 117
Henry Macaulay Av. KT2: King T 1D 150
Henry Moore Ct. SW3 6C 16 (5C 100)
Henry Peters Dr. *TW11: Tedd* 5J 131
(off Somerset Gdns.)
Henry Purcell Ho. *E16* 1K 105
(off Evelyn Rd.)
Henry Rd. E6 2C 88
EN4: E Barn 5G 21
N4 1C 66
SW9 1A 120
Henrys Av. IG8: Wfd G 5C 36
Henryson Rd. SE4 5C 122
Henry St. BR1: Brom 1K 159
Henry's Wlk. IG6: Ilf 1H 53
Henry Tate M. SW16 5K 137
Henry Tudor Ct. SE9 7G 125
Henry Wise Ho. *SW1* 4B 18
(off Vauxhall Bri. Rd.)
Hensford Gdns. SE26 4H 139
Henshall Point *E3* 3D 86
(off Bromley High St.)
Henshall St. N1 6D 66
Henshawe Rd. RM8: Dag 3D 72
Henshaw St. SE17 4D 102
Henslowe Rd. SE22 5G 121
Henslow Ho. *SE15* 7G 103
(off Peckham Pk. Rd.)
Henson Av. NW2 5E 62
Henson Cl. BR6: Farnb 2F 173
Henson Path HA3: Kenton 3D 42
Henson Pl. UB5: N'olt 1A 76
Henstridge Pl. NW8 1C 82
Henty Cl. SW11 7C 100
Henty Wlk. SW15 5D 116
Henville Rd. BR1: Brom 1K 159
Henwick Rd. SE9 3B 124
Henwood Side IG8: Wfd G 6J 37
Hepburn Gdns.
BR2: Hayes 1G 171
Hepburn M. SW11 5D 118
Hepburn Pl. W3 7H 79
Hepdon M. SW17 5B 136
Hepple Cl. TW7: Isle 2B 114
Hepplestone Cl. SW15 6D 116
Hepscott Rd. E9 6C 68
Hepworth Ct. *N1* 1B 84
(off Gaskin St.)
NW3 5C 64
SM3: Sutt 1J 165
SW1 6J 17 (5F 101)
Hepworth Gdns. IG11: Bark 5A 72
Hepworth Rd. SW16 7J 137
Hepworth Way KT12: Walt T 7H 147
Hera Av. EN5: Barn 5C 20
Heracles *NW9* 1B 44
(off Five Acre)
Hera Ct. *E14* 4C 104
(off Homer Dr.)
Herald Gdns. SM6: Wall 2F 167
Herald's Pl. SE11 3K 19 (4B 102)
Herald St. E2 4H 85
Herbal Hill EC1 4K 7 (4A 84)
Herbal Hill Gdns. *EC1* 4K 7
(off Herbal Hill)
Herbal Pl. EC1 4K 7
Herbert Cres. SW1 1F 17 (3D 100)
Herbert Gdns. NW10 2D 80
RM6: Chad H 7D 54
W4 6H 97
Herbert Ho. *E1* 7J 9
(off Old Castle St.)
Herbert M. SW2 6A 120
Herbert Morrison Ho. *SW6* 6H 99
(off Clem Attlee Ct.)
Herbert Pl. SE18 6F 107
TW7: Isle 2H 113
Herbert Rd. BR2: Brom 5B 160
DA7: Bex 2E 126
E12 4C 70
E17 7B 50
IG3: Ilf 2J 71
KT1: King T 3F 151
N11 7D 32
N15 5F 49
NW9 6C 44
SE18 7E 106
(not continuous)
SW19 7H 135
(not continuous)
UB1: S'hall 1D 94
Herbert St. E13 2J 87
NW5 6E 64
Herbrand Est. WC1 3E 6 (4J 83)
Herbrand St. WC1 3E 6 (4J 83)
Hercies Rd. UB10: Hil 7B 56
Hercules Ct. SE14 6A 104
Hercules Pl. N7 3J 65
(not continuous)
Hercules Rd. SE1 2H 19 (3K 101)
Hercules St. N7 3J 65
Hercules Wharf *E14* 7G 87
(off Orchard Pl.)
Hercules Yd. N7 3J 65
Here East E20 5C 68
Hereford Av. EN4: E Barn 1J 31
Hereford Bldgs. *SW3* 7B 16
(off Old Church St.)
Hereford Ct. HA1: Harr 4J 41
SM2: Sutt 7J 165
W7 5K 77
(off Copley Cl.)
Hereford Gdns. HA5: Pinn 5C 40
IG1: Ilf 7C 52

Hereford Gdns. SE13 . . . . . 5G **123**
TW2: Twick 1G **131**
Hereford Ho. *N18* *5C 34*
(off Cameron Cl.)
NW6 . . . . . *2J 81*
(off Carlton Vale)
SW3 . . . . . *1D 16*
(off Ovington Gdns.)
SW10 . . . . . *7K 99*
(off Fulham Rd.)
Hereford Mans. *W2* *6J 81*
(off Hereford Rd.)
Hereford M. W2 . . . . . 6J **81**
Hereford Pl. SE14 . . . . . 7B **104**
Hereford Retreat SE15 . . . . . 7G **103**
Hereford Rd. E3 . . . . . 2B **86**
E11 . . . . . 5K **51**
TW13: Felt 1A **130**
W2 . . . . . 6J **81**
W3 . . . . . 7H **79**
W5 . . . . . 3C **96**
Hereford Sq. SW7 . . . . . 4A **100**
Hereford St. E2 . . . . . 4G **85**
Hereford Way
KT9: Chess 5C **162**
Herent Dr. IG5: Ilf 4C **52**
Herent Gdns. IG5: Ilf 4D **52**
Hereward Gdns. N13 . . . . . 5F **33**
Hereward Rd. SW17 . . . . . 4D **136**
Herga Ct. HA1: Harr 3J **59**
Herga Rd. HA3: W'stone 4K **41**
Heriot Av. E4 . . . . . 2H **35**
Heriot Rd. NW4 . . . . . 5E **44**
Heriots Cl. HA7: Stan 4F **27**
Heritage Av. NW9 . . . . . 3B **44**
Heritage Cl. SW9 . . . . . 3B **120**
TW16: Sun 1J **147**
Heritage Ct. SE8 . . . . . 5K **103**
Heritage Hill BR2: Kes 5A **172**
Heritage La. NW6 . . . . . 6J **63**
Heritage Pl. SW18 . . . . . 1A **136**
Heritage Vw. HA1: Harr 3K **59**
Herlwyn Av. HA4: Ruis 2G **57**
Herlwyn Gdns. SW17 . . . . . 4D **136**
Her Majesty's Theatre ***4C 12***
(off Haymarket)
Herm Cl. TW7: Isle 7G **95**
Hermes Cl. W9 . . . . . 4J **81**
Hermes Ct. SW2 . . . . . 6K **119**
SW9 . . . . . *1A 120*
(off Southey Rd.)
Hermes St. N1 . . . . . 1J **7** (2A **84**)
Hermes Wlk. UB5: N'olt 2E **76**
Herm Ho. EN3: Enf W 1E **24**
N1 . . . . . *6C 66*
(off Clifton Rd.)
Hermiston Av. N8 . . . . . 5J **47**
Hermitage, The KT1: King T 4D **150**
SE13 . . . . . 2E **122**
SE23 . . . . . 1J **139**
SW13 . . . . . 1B **116**
TW10: Rich 5E **114**
TW13: Felt 3H **129**
UB8: Uxb 6A **56**
Hermitage Cl. E18 . . . . . 4H **51**
EN2: Enf 2G **23**
KT10: Clay 6A **162**
SE2 . . . . . 3C **108**
TW17: Shep 4C **146**
Hermitage Ct. *E1* *1G 103*
(off Knighten St.)
E18 . . . . . 4J **51**
NW2 . . . . . 3J **63**
Hermitage Gdns. NW2 . . . . . 3J **63**
SE19 . . . . . 7C **138**
Hermitage Grn. SW16 . . . . . 1J **155**
Hermitage Ho. *N1* *2B 84*
(off Gerrard Rd.)
Hermitage La. CR0: C'don 7G **157**
N18 . . . . . 5J **33**
NW2 . . . . . 3J **63**
Hermitage La. SE25 . . . . . 6G **157**
SW16 . . . . . 7K **137**
Hermitage Moorings E1 . . . . . 1G **103**
Hermitage Path SW16 . . . . . 1J **155**
Hermitage Rd. N4 . . . . . 7B **48**
N15 . . . . . 7B **48**
SE19 . . . . . 7C **138**
Hermitage Row E8 . . . . . 5G **67**
Hermitage St. W2 . . . . . 6A **4** (5B **82**)
Hermitage Vs. *SW6* *6J 99*
(off Lillie Rd.)
Hermitage Wlk. E18 . . . . . 4H **51**
Hermitage Wall E1 . . . . . 1G **103**
Hermitage Waterside *E1* *1G 103*
(off Thomas More St.)
Hermitage Way HA7: Stan 1A **42**
Hermit Pl. NW6 . . . . . 1K **81**
Hermit Rd. E16 . . . . . 5H **87**
Hermit St. EC1 . . . . . 1A **8** (3B **84**)
Hermon Gro. UB3: Hayes 1J **93**
Hermon Hill E11 . . . . . 5J **51**
E18 . . . . . 5J **51**
Herndon Rd. SW18 . . . . . 5A **118**
Herne Cl. NW10 . . . . . 5K **61**
UB3: Hayes 6H **75**
Herne Ct. WD23: Bush 1B **26**
HERNE HILL 5C **120**
Herne Hill SE24 . . . . . 6C **120**
Herne Hill Ho. *SE24* *6B 120*
(off Railton Rd.)
Herne Hill Rd. SE24 . . . . . 3C **120**
Herne Hill Stadium 6D **120**
Herne M. N18 . . . . . 4B **34**
Herne Pl. SE24 . . . . . 5B **120**
Herne Rd. KT6: Surb 2D **162**
Heron Cl. E17 . . . . . 2B **50**
IG9: Buck H 1D **36**
NW10 . . . . . 6A **62**
SM1: Sutt 5H **165**
Heron Ct. BR2: Brom 4A **160**
E14 . . . . . *3E 104*
(off New Union Cl.)
HA4: Ruis 2F **57**
KT1: King T 3E **150**
NW9 . . . . . 2A **44**
TW19: Stanw 1A **128**
Heron Cres. DA14: Sidc 3J **143**
Herondale Av. SW18 . . . . . 1B **136**
Heron Dr. N4 . . . . . 2C **66**
Herongate *N1* *1C 84*
(off Ridgewell Cl.)
Herongate Rd. E12 . . . . . 2A **70**
Heron Hill DA17: Belv 5F **109**
Heron Ho. DA14: Sidc 3B **144**
E3 . . . . . *1B 86*
(off Sycamore Av.)
E6 . . . . . 7C **70**
NW8 . . . . . *1C 4*
(off Newcourt St.)
SW11 . . . . . *7C 100*
(off Searles Cl.)
W13 . . . . . 4A **78**
Heron Mead EN3: Enf L 1H **25**
Heron M. IG1: Ilf 2F **71**
Heron Pl. *E16* *1A 106*
(off Bramwell Way)
SE16 . . . . . 1A **104**
W1 . . . . . *7H 5*
(off Thayer St.)
Heron Quay E14 . . . . . 1C **104**
Heron Rd. CR0: C'don 2E **168**
SE24 . . . . . 4C **120**
TW1: Twick 4A **114**
Herons, The E11 . . . . . 6H **51**
Heronsforde W13 . . . . . 6C **78**
Heronsgate HA8: Edg 5B **28**
Heron's Lea N6 . . . . . 6D **46**
Heronslea Dr. HA7: Stan 5K **27**
Heron's Pl. TW7: Isle 3B **114**
Heron Sq. TW9: Rich 5D **114**
Herons Ri. EN4: E Barn 4H **21**
Heron Tower 7H **9**
Heron Trad. Est. W3 . . . . . 5H **79**
Heron Vw. *TW8: Bford* *7C 96*
(off Commerce Rd.)
Heron Way SM6: Wall 7H **167**
TW14: Felt 4J **111**
Heronway IG8: Wfd G 4F **37**
Herrick Ct. *W3* *3J 97*
(off Bollo Bri. Rd.)
Herrick Ho. *N16* *4D 66*
(off Howard Rd.)
SE5 . . . . . *7D 102*
(off Elmington Est.)
Herrick Rd. N5 . . . . . 3C **66**
Herrick St. SW1 . . . . . 4D **18** (4H **101**)
Herries St. W10 . . . . . 2G **81**
Herringham Rd. SE7 . . . . . 3A **106**
Herron Ct. BR2: Brom 4H **159**
Herrongate Cl. EN1: Enf 2A **24**
Hersant Cl. NW10 . . . . . 1C **80**
Herschell M. SE5 . . . . . 3C **120**
Herschell Rd. SE23 . . . . . 7A **122**
Hersham Cl. SW15 . . . . . 7C **116**
Hershell Ct. SW14 . . . . . 4H **115**
Hertford Av. SW14 . . . . . 5K **115**
Hertford Cl. EN4: Cockf 3G **21**
Hertford Ct. E6 . . . . . 3D **88**
N13 . . . . . 3F **33**
Hertford Ho. UB5: N'olt 4D **76**
Hertford Lock Ho. *E3* *1B 86*
(off Parnell Rd.)
Hertford Pl. W1 . . . . . 4B **6** (4G **83**)
Hertford Rd. EN3: Enf H, Enf W 3D **24**
EN4: Cockf 3F **21**
IG2: Ilf 6J **53**
IG11: Bark 7E **70**
N1 . . . . . 1E **84**
(not continuous)
N2 . . . . . 3C **46**
N9 . . . . . 2C **34**
Hertford St. W1 . . . . . 5J **11** (1F **101**)
Hertford Wlk. DA17: Belv 5G **109**
Hertford Way CR4: Mitc 4J **155**
Hertford Wharf *N1* *1E 84*
(off Hertford Rd.)
Hertslet Rd. N7 . . . . . 3K **65**
Hertsmere Ho. *E14* *7C 86*
(off Hertsmere Rd.)
Hertsmere Rd. E14 . . . . . 1C **104**
Hertswood Ct. EN5: Barn 4B **20**
Hervey Cl. N3 . . . . . 1J **45**
Hervey Pk. Rd. E17 . . . . . 4A **50**
Hervey Rd. SE3 . . . . . 1K **123**
Hervey Way N3 . . . . . 1J **45**
Hesa Rd. UB3: Hayes 6J **75**
Hesewall Cl. SW4 . . . . . 2G **119**
Hesketh Pl. W11 . . . . . 7G **81**
Hesketh Rd. E7 . . . . . 3J **69**
Heslop Rd. SW12 . . . . . 1D **136**
Hesper M. SW5 . . . . . 4K **99**
Hesperus Cres. E14 . . . . . 4D **104**
Hessel Rd. W13 . . . . . 2A **96**
Hessel St. E1 . . . . . 6H **85**
Hestercombe Av. SW6 . . . . . 2G **117**
Hesterman Way CR0: Wadd 1K **167**
Hester Rd. N18 . . . . . 5B **34**
SW11 . . . . . 7C **100**
Hester Ter. TW9: Rich 3G **115**
Hestia Ho. SE1 . . . . . 7G **15**
HESTON 7E **94**
Heston Av. TW5: Hest 6C **94**
Heston Cen., The TW5: Cran 5A **94**
Heston Community Sports Hall 7E **94**
Heston Grange TW5: Hest 6D **94**
Heston Grange La. TW5: Hest 6D **94**
Heston Ho. SE8 . . . . . 1C **122**
Heston Ind. Mall TW5: Hest 7D **94**
Heston Phoenix Distribution Pk.
TW5: Hest 6A **94**
Heston Pool 6D **94**
Heston Rd. TW5: Hest 6E **94**
HESTON SERVICE AREA 6B **94**
Heston St. SE14 . . . . . 1C **122**
Hetherington Rd. SW4 . . . . . 4J **119**
TW17: Shep 2E **146**
Hetherington Way UB10: Ick 4A **56**
Hethpool Ho. W2 . . . . . 4A **4**
Hetley Gdns. SE19 . . . . . 7F **139**
Hetley Rd. W12 . . . . . 1D **98**
Heton Gdns. NW4 . . . . . 4D **44**
Hevelius Cl. SE10 . . . . . 5H **105**
Hever Cft. SE9 . . . . . 4E **142**
Hever Gdns. BR1: Brom 2E **160**
Heverham Rd. SE18 . . . . . 4J **107**
Hever Ho. *SE15* *6K 103*
(off Lovelinch Cl.)
Hever Pl. KT8: E Mos 3G **149**
Heversham Ho. SE15 . . . . . 6J **103**
Heversham Rd. DA7: Bex 2G **127**
Hevingham Dr. RM6: Chad H 5C **54**
Hewens Rd. UB4: Hil 4E **74**
UB10: Hil 4E **74**
Hewer St. W10 . . . . . 5F **81**
Hewett Cl. HA7: Stan 4G **27**
Hewett Rd. RM8: Dag 5D **72**
Hewetts Quay IG11: Bark 1F **89**
Hewett St. EC2 . . . . . 4H **9** (4E **84**)
Hewish Rd. N18 . . . . . 4K **33**
Hewison St. E3 . . . . . 2B **86**
Hewitt Av. N22 . . . . . 2B **48**
Hewitt Cl. CR0: C'don 3C **170**
Hewitt Rd. N8 . . . . . 5A **48**
Hewlett Ho. *SW8* *7F 101*
(off Havelock Ter.)
Hewlett Rd. E3 . . . . . 2A **86**
Hexagon, The N6 . . . . . 1D **64**
Hexagon Bus. Cen. UB4: Yead 7A **76**
Hexal Rd. SE6 . . . . . 3G **141**
Hexham Gdns. TW7: Isle 7A **96**
UB5: N'olt 5D **58**
Hexham Rd. EN5: New Bar 4E **20**
SE27 . . . . . 2C **138**
SM4: Mord 1K **165**
Heybourne Cres. NW9 . . . . . 1A **44**
Heybourne Rd. N17 . . . . . 7C **34**
Heybridge *NW1* *6F 65*
(off Lewis St.)
Heybridge Av. SW16 . . . . . 7J **137**
Heybridge Dr. IG6: Ilf 2H **53**
Heybridge Way E10 . . . . . 7A **50**
Heydon Ct. *BR4: W W'ck* *2G 171*
(off Deer Pk. Way)
Heydon Ho. *SE14* *1J 121*
(off Kender St.)
Heyford Av. SW8 . . . . . 7J **101**
SW20 . . . . . 3H **153**
Heyford Rd. CR4: Mitc 2C **154**
Heyford Ter. SW8 . . . . . 7J **101**
Heygate St. SE17 . . . . . 4C **102**
Heylyn Sq. E3 . . . . . 3B **86**
Heynes Rd. RM8: Dag 4C **72**
Heysham La. NW3 . . . . . 3K **63**
Heysham Rd. N15 . . . . . 6D **48**
Heythorp St. SW18 . . . . . 1H **135**
Heythrop Dr. UB10: Ick 4B **56**
Heywood Av. NW9 . . . . . 1A **44**
Heywood Ct. HA7: Stan 5H **27**
Heywood Ho. *SE14* *6K 103*
(off Myers La.)
Heyworth Rd. E5 . . . . . 4H **67**
E15 . . . . . 5H **69**
Hibbert Ho. *E14* *3C 104*
(off Tiller Rd.)
Hibbert Rd. E17 . . . . . 7B **50**
HA3: W'stone 2K **41**
Hibbert St. SW11 . . . . . 3B **118**
Hibernia Gdns.
TW3: Houn 4E **112**
Hibernia Point *SE2* *2D 108*
(off Wolvercote Rd.)
Hibernia Rd. TW3: Houn 4E **112**
Hibiscus Cl. HA8: Edg 4D **28**

Hibiscus Ho. E17 . . . 3D **50**
TW13: Felt . . . 1J **129**
Hibiscus Lodge *E15* . . . *7G 69*
(off Glenavon Rd.)
Hichisson Rd. SE15 . . . 5J **121**
Hicken Rd. SW2 . . . 5K **119**
Hickes Ho. NW6 . . . 7B **64**
Hickey's Almshouses TW9: Rich . . . 4F **115**
Hickin Cl. SE7 . . . 4B **106**
Hickin St. E14 . . . 3E **104**
Hickleton *NW1* . . . *1G 83*
(off Camden St.)
Hickling Ho. *SE16* . . . *3H 103*
(off Slippers Pl.)
Hickling Rd. IG1: Ilf . . . 5F **71**
Hickman Av. E4 . . . 6K **35**
Hickman Cl. E16 . . . 5B **88**
Hickman Rd. RM6: Chad H . . . 7C **54**
Hickmore Wlk. SW4 . . . 3H **119**
Hickory Cl. N9 . . . 7B **24**
Hicks Av. UB6: G'frd . . . 3H **77**
Hicks Bolton Ho. *NW6* . . . *2H 81*
(off Denmark Ho.)
Hicks Cl. SW11 . . . 3C **118**
Hicks Ct. RM10: Dag . . . 3H **73**
Hicks Gallery . . . 5J 135
Hicks Ho. *SE16* . . . *3G 103*
(off Spa Rd.)
Hicks St. SE8 . . . 5A **104**
Hidcote Apartments *SW11* . . . *4C 118*
(off Danvers Av.)
Hidcote Gdns. SW20 . . . 3D **152**
Hidden Cl. KT8: W Mole . . . 4G **149**
Hide E6 . . . 6E **88**
Hide Pl. SW1 . . . 4C **18** (4H **101**)
Hider Ct. SE3 . . . 7A **106**
Hide Rd. HA1: Harr . . . 4G **41**
Hides St. N7 . . . 6K **65**
Hide Twr. *SW1* . . . *4C 18*
(off Regency St.)
Hierro Ct. *E1* . . . *5A 86*
(off Ocean Est.)
Higgins Ho. *N1* . . . *1E 84*
(off Colville Est.)
Higginson Ho. *NW3* . . . *7D 64*
(off Fellows Rd.)
Higgins Wlk. *TW12: Hamp* . . . *6C 130*
(off Abbott Cl.)
Higgs Ind. Est. SE24 . . . 3B **120**
High Acres EN2: Enf . . . 3G **23**
HIGHAM HILL . . . 2A 50
Higham Hill Rd. E17 . . . 1A **50**
Higham M. UB5: N'olt . . . 4D **76**
Higham Path E17 . . . 3A **50**
Higham Pl. E17 . . . 3A **50**
Higham Rd. IG8: Wfd G . . . 6D **36**
N17 . . . 3D **48**
Highams, The E17 . . . 1E **50**
Highams Ct. E4 . . . 3K **35**
Highams Lodge Bus. Cen. E17 . . . 3K **49**
HIGHAMS PARK . . . 6A 36
Higham Sta. Av. E4 . . . 6H **35**
Higham St. E17 . . . 3A **50**
High Ashton KT2: King T . . . 7H **133**
Highbanks Cl. DA16: Well . . . 7B **108**
Highbanks Rd. HA5: Hat E . . . 6A **26**
Highbank Way N8 . . . 6A **48**
HIGH BARNET . . . 2A 20
Highbarrow Rd. CR0: C'don . . . 1G **169**
High Beech CR2: S Croy . . . 7E **168**
N21 . . . 6E **22**
High Beeches DA14: Sidc . . . 5E **144**
High Birch Ct. *EN4: E Barn* . . . *4H 21*
(off Park Rd.)
High Bri. SE10 . . . 5F **105**
Highbridge Ct. *SE14* . . . *7J 103*
(off Farrow La.)
Highbridge Rd. IG11: Bark . . . 1F **89**
High Bri. Wharf *SE10* . . . *5F 105*
(off High Bri.)
Highbrook Rd. SE3 . . . 3B **124**
High Broom Cres. BR4: W W'ck . . . 7D **158**
HIGHBURY . . . 4B 66
Highbury Av. CR7: Thor H . . . 2A **156**
Highbury Cl. BR4: W W'ck . . . 2D **170**
KT3: N Mald . . . 4J **151**
HIGHBURY CORNER . . . **6B 66**
Highbury Cres. N5 . . . 5B **66**
Highbury Est. N5 . . . 5C **66**
Highbury Gdns. IG3: Ilf . . . 2J **71**
N7 . . . 5A **66**
Highbury Grange N5 . . . 4C **66**
Highbury Gro. N5 . . . 5B **66**
Highbury Gro. Ct. N5 . . . 6C **66**
Highbury Hill N5 . . . 3A **66**
Highbury Mans. *N1* . . . *7B 66*
(off Upper St.)
Highbury New Pk. N5 . . . 5C **66**
Highbury Pk. N5 . . . 3B **66**
Highbury Pl. N5 . . . 6B **66**
Highbury Pool . . . 6B 66
Highbury Quad. N5 . . . 3C **66**
Highbury Rd. SW19 . . . 5G **135**
Highbury Sq. N14 . . . 1B **32**
Highbury Stadium Sq. N5 . . . 3B **66**
Highbury Sta. Rd. N1 . . . 6A **66**
Highbury Ter. N5 . . . 5B **66**
Highbury Ter. M. N5 . . . 5B **66**
High Cedar Dr. SW20 . . . 7E **134**
Highclere Rd. KT3: N Mald . . . 3K **151**
Highclere St. SE26 . . . 4A **140**
Highcliffe *W13* . . . *5B 78*
(off Clivedon Ct.)
Highcliffe Dr. SW15 . . . 6B **116**
Highcliffe Gdns. IG4: Ilf . . . 5C **52**
Highcombe SE7 . . . 6K **105**
Highcombe Cl. SE9 . . . 1B **142**
High Coombe Pl. KT2: King T . . . 6K **133**
Highcroft NW9 . . . 5A **44**
Highcroft Av. HA0: Wemb . . . 7G **61**
Highcroft Est. N19 . . . 7J **47**
Highcroft Gdns. NW11 . . . 6H **45**
Highcroft Rd. N19 . . . 7J **47**
High Cross Cen., The N15 . . . 4G **49**
High Cross Rd. N17 . . . 3G **49**
Highcross Way SW15 . . . 1C **134**
Highdaun Dr. SW16 . . . 4K **155**
Highdown KT4: Wor Pk . . . 2A **164**
Highdown Rd. SW15 . . . 6D **116**
High Dr. KT3: N Mald . . . 1J **151**
High Elms IG8: Wfd G . . . 5D **36**
High Elms Country Pk.
(Local Nature Reserve) . . . 7H 173
High Elms Golf Course . . . 7G 173
High Elms Rd. BR6: Downe . . . 7G **173**
Highfield WD23: B Hea . . . 2D **26**
Highfield Av. BR6: Chels . . . 5K **173**
DA8: Erith . . . 6H **109**
HA5: Pinn . . . 5D **40**
HA9: Wemb . . . 3F **61**
NW9 . . . 5J **43**
NW11 . . . 7F **45**
UB6: G'frd . . . 5J **59**
Highfield Cl. HA6: Nwood . . . 1G **39**
KT6: Surb . . . 1C **162**
N22 . . . 1A **48**
NW9 . . . 5J **43**
SE13 . . . 6F **123**
Highfield Ct. N14 . . . 6B **22**
NW11 . . . 6G **45**
Highfield Cres. HA6: Nwood . . . 1G **39**
Highfield Dr. BR2: Brom . . . 4G **159**
BR4: W W'ck . . . 2D **170**
KT19: Ewe . . . 6B **164**
UB10: Ick . . . 4A **56**
Highfield Gdns. NW11 . . . 6G **45**
Highfield Hill SE19 . . . 7D **138**
Highfield M. *NW6* . . . *7K 63*
(off Compayne Gdns.)
Highfield Rd. BR1: Brom . . . 4D **160**
BR7: Chst . . . 3K **161**
DA6: Bex . . . 5F **127**
Highfield Rd. HA6: Nwood . . . 1G **39**
IG8: Wfd G . . . 7H **37**
KT5: Surb . . . 7J **151**
KT12: Walt T . . . 7J **147**
N21 . . . 2G **33**
NW11 . . . 6G **45**
SM1: Sutt . . . 5C **166**
TW7: Isle . . . 1K **113**
TW13: Felt . . . 2J **129**
TW16: Sun . . . 5H **147**
W3 . . . 5H **79**
Highfields SM1: Sutt . . . 2J **165**
Highfields Gro. N6 . . . 1D **64**
High Foleys KT10: Clay . . . 7B **162**
High Gables BR2: Brom . . . 2G **159**
HIGHGATE . . . 6E 46
Highgate Av. N6 . . . 7F **47**
Highgate Cemetery N6 . . . 1E **64**
Highgate Cl. N6 . . . 7E **46**
Highgate Edge N2 . . . 5C **46**
Highgate Golf Course . . . 6C 46
Highgate Hgts. N6 . . . 6G **47**
Highgate High St. N6 . . . 1E **64**
Highgate Hill N6 . . . 1F **65**
N19 . . . 1F **65**
Highgate Ho. SE26 . . . 3G **139**
Highgate Rd. NW5 . . . 3E **64**
Highgate Spinney N8 . . . 6H **47**
Highgate Wlk. SE23 . . . 2J **139**
Highgate West Hill N6 . . . 1E **64**
High Gro. BR1: Brom . . . 1B **160**
SE18 . . . 7H **107**
Highgrove Cl. BR7: Chst . . . 1C **160**
N11 . . . 5K **31**
Highgrove Ct. BR3: Beck . . . 7C **140**
SM1: Sutt . . . 6J **165**
Highgrove Ho. HA4: Ruis . . . 6J **39**
Highgrove M. SM5: Cars . . . 3D **166**
Highgrove Rd. RM8: Dag . . . 5C **72**
Highgrove Swimming Pool . . . 6J 39
Highgrove Ter. E4 . . . 2A **36**
Highgrove Way HA4: Ruis . . . 6J **39**
High Hill Est. E5 . . . 1H **67**
High Hill Ferry E5 . . . 1H **67**
High Holborn WC1 . . . 7E **6** (6J **83**)
Highland Av. RM10: Dag . . . 3J **73**
W7 . . . 6J **77**
Highland Cotts. SM6: Wall . . . 4G **167**
Highland Ct. BR1: Brom . . . 1H **159**
E18 . . . 1K **51**
Highland Cft. BR3: Beck . . . 5D **140**
Highland Dr. WD23: Bush . . . 1A **26**
Highland Pk. TW13: Felt . . . 4H **129**
Highland Rd. BR1: Brom . . . 1H **159**
BR2: Brom . . . 1H **159**
DA6: Bex . . . 5G **127**
HA6: Nwood . . . 2H **39**
SE19 . . . 6E **138**
Highlands N20 . . . 2G **31**
Highlands, The EN5: New Bar . . . 4D **20**
HA8: Edg . . . 2H **43**
Highlands Av. N21 . . . 5E **22**
W3 . . . 7J **79**
Highlands Cl. N4 . . . 7J **47**
TW3: Houn . . . 1F **113**
Highlands Ct. SE19 . . . 6E **138**
Highlands Gdns. IG1: Ilf . . . 1D **70**
Highlands Heath SW15 . . . 7E **116**
Highlands Rd. EN5: New Bar . . . 5D **20**
HIGHLANDS VILLAGE . . . 5E 22
Highland Ter. *SE13* . . . *3D 122*
(off Algernon Rd.)
Highland Vw. Pk. Homes
UB7: W Dray . . . 1D **174**
High La. W7 . . . 5H **77**
Highlawn Hall HA1: Harr . . . 3J **59**
Highlea Cl. NW9 . . . 7F **29**
High Level Dr. SE26 . . . 4G **139**
Highlever Rd. W10 . . . 5E **80**
High Mead BR4: W W'ck . . . 2F **171**
HA1: Harr . . . 5J **41**
Highmead SE18 . . . 7K **107**
Highmead Cres. HA0: Wemb . . . 7F **61**
High Mdw. Cl. HA5: Eastc . . . 4A **40**
Highmeadow Cres. NW9 . . . 5K **43**
High Meads Rd. E16 . . . 6B **88**
Highmore Rd. SE3 . . . 7G **105**
High Mt. NW4 . . . 6C **44**
High Oaks EN2: Enf . . . 1E **22**
High Pde., The SW16 . . . 3J **137**
High Pk. Av. TW9: Kew . . . 1G **115**
High Pk. Rd. TW9: Kew . . . 1G **115**
High Path SW19 . . . 1K **153**
High Point N6 . . . 7E **46**
SE9 . . . 3F **143**
High Ridge N10 . . . 1F **47**
High Rd. E18 . . . 1J **51**
HA0: Wemb . . . 5D **60**
HA3: Hrw W . . . 7D **26**
HA5: Eastc . . . 6J **39**
HA9: Wemb . . . 5D **60**
IG1: Ilf . . . 3F **71**
(not continuous)
IG3: Ilf . . . 1K **71**
IG7: Chig . . . 5K **37**
IG9: Buck H . . . 2E **36**
N11 . . . 5A **32**
N15 . . . 4F **49**
N17 . . . 2F **49**
N22 . . . 7E **32**
NW10 . . . 6A **62**
RM6: Chad H . . . 7D **54**
UB4: Hayes . . . 5G **75**
UB10: Ick . . . 3D **56**
WD23: B Hea . . . 1C **26**
High Rd. E. Finchley N2 . . . 1B **46**
High Rd. Leyton E10 . . . 6D **50**
E15 . . . 2D **68**
High Rd. Leytonstone E11 . . . 3G **69**
E15 . . . 4G **69**
High Rd. Nth. Finchley N12 . . . 3F **31**
(not continuous)
High Rd. Whetstone N20 . . . 7F **21**
High Rd. Woodford Grn. E18 . . . 1J **51**
IG8: Wfd G . . . 6C **36**
High Sheldon N6 . . . 6D **46**
Highshore Rd. SE15 . . . 2F **121**
(not continuous)
Highstead Cres. DA8: Erith . . . 1K **127**
Highstone Av. E11 . . . 6J **51**
Highstone Ct. *E11* . . . *6H 51*
(off New Wanstead)
Highstone Mans. *NW1* . . . *7G 65*
(off Camden Rd.)
High St. BR1: Brom . . . 2J **159**
(not continuous)
BR3: Beck . . . 2C **158**
BR4: W W'ck . . . 1D **170**
BR6: Chels . . . 7K **173**
BR6: Farnb . . . 5F **173**
BR6: Orp . . . 2K **173**
BR7: Chst . . . 6F **143**
CR0: C'don . . . 3C **168**
CR7: Thor H . . . 4C **156**
E11 . . . 5J **51**
E13 . . . 2J **87**
E15 . . . 2E **86**
E17 . . . 5A **50**
EN3: Pond E . . . 6D **24**
EN5: Barn . . . 3B **20**
HA1: Harr . . . 1J **59**
HA3: Hrw W, W'stone . . . 2J **41**
HA4: Ruis . . . 7G **39**
HA5: Pinn . . . 3C **40**
HA6: Nwood . . . 1H **39**
HA8: Edg . . . 6B **28**
HA9: Wemb . . . 4F **61**
IG6: Ilf . . . 3G **53**
KT1: Hamp W . . . 1C **150**
KT1: King T . . . 3D **150**
KT3: N Mald . . . 4A **152**
KT7: T Ditt . . . 6A **150**

High St. KT8: W Mole 4E 148
  KT12: Walt T 7J 147
  KT17: Ewe 7B 164
  N8 . . . .4J 47
  N14 . . . .1C 32
  NW7 . . . .5J 29
  RM1: Rom 5K 55
  SE20 . . . .6J 139
  SE25 . . . .4F 157
  SM1: Sutt 4K 165
  SM3: Cheam 6G 165
  SM5: Cars 5E 166
  SW19 . . . .5F 135
  TW2: Whitt 7G 113
  TW3: Houn 3F 113
  TW5: Cran 1J 111
  TW8: Bford 7C 96
  TW11: Tedd 5K 131
  TW12: Hamp, Hamp H 1G 149
  TW13: Felt 3H 129
  TW17: Shep 6D 146
  TW19: Stanw 3A 110
  UB1: S'hall 1D 94
  UB3: Harl 6F 93
  UB7: Harm 2E 174
  UB7: Yiew 7A 74
  UB8: Uxb 1A 74
  W3 . . . .1H 97
  W5 . . . .1D 96
High St. Colliers Wood SW19 . . . .7B 136
High St. Harlesden NW10 . . . .2B 80
High St. M. SW19 . . . .5G 135
High St. Nth. E6 . . . .1C 88
  E12 . . . .5C 70
High St. Sth. E6 . . . .2D 88
High Timber St. EC4 . . . .2C 14 (7C 84)
High Tor Cl. BR1: Brom 7K 141
High Tor Vw. SE28 . . . .1J 107
High Trees CRO: C'don 1A 170
  EN4: E Barn 5H 21
  N20 . . . .3F 31
  SW2 . . . .1A 138
Hightrees Cl. W7 . . . .7J 77
Hightrees Ho. SW12 . . . .6E 118
High Vw. HA5: Pinn 4A 40
Highview N6 . . . .6G 47
  NW7 . . . .3E 28
  UB5: N'olt 3C 76
Highview Av. HA8: Edg 4D 28
  SM6: Wall 5K 167
High Vw. Cl. SE19 . . . .2F 157
High Vw. Ct. HA3: Hrw W 7D 26
Highview Gdns. HA8: Edg 4D 28
  N3 . . . .3G 45
  N11 . . . .5B 32
Highview Ho. RM6: Chad H 4E 54
Highview Lodge EN2: Enf 3G 23
  (off The Ridgeway)
High Vw. Pde. IG4: Ilf 5D 52
High Vw. Rd. E18 . . . .2H 51
  SE19 . . . .6D 138
Highview Rd. DA14: Sidc 4B 144
  W13 . . . .5A 78
Highway, The E1 . . . .7G 85
  HA7: Stan 1K 41
  SM2: Sutt 7A 166
Highway Trad. Cen., The E1 . . . .7K 85
  (off Heckford St.)
Highwood BR2: Brom 3F 159
Highwood Av. N12 . . . .4F 31
Highwood Cl. BR6: Farnb 2G 173
  SE22 . . . .1G 139
Highwood Ct. EN5: New Bar 5D 20
  N12 . . . .3F 31
Highwood Dr. BR6: Farnb 2G 173
Highwood Gdns. IG5: Ilf 5D 52
Highwood Gro. NW7 . . . .5E 28
HIGHWOOD HILL 3G 29
Highwood Hill NW7 . . . .2G 29
Highwood Rd. N19 . . . .3J 65
High Worple HA2: Harr 7D 40

Highworth Rd. N11 . . . .6C 32
Highworth St. NW1 . . . .5D 4
Hi-Gloss Cen. SE8 . . . .5A 104
Hilary Av. CR4: Mitc 3E 154
Hilary Cl. DA8: Erith 1H 127
  SW6 . . . .7K 99
Hilary Dennis Ct. E11 . . . .4J 51
Hilary Rd. W12 . . . .6B 80
  (not continuous)
Hilberry Ct. WD23: Bush 1A 26
Hilbert Rd. SM3: Cheam 3F 165
Hilborough Ct. SW19 . . . .7A 136
Hilborough Ct. E8 . . . .7F 67
Hilborough Way BR6: Farnb 5H 173
Hilda Ct. KT6: Surb 7D 150
Hilda Lockert Wlk. SW9 . . . .2B 120
  (off Loughborough Rd.)
Hilda Rd. E6 . . . .7B 70
  E16 . . . .4G 87
Hilda Ter. SW9 . . . .2A 120
Hilda Va. Cl. BR6: Farnb 4F 173
Hilda Va. Rd. BR6: Farnb 4E 172
Hildenborough Gdns. BR1: Brom 6G 141
Hildenborough Ho. BR3: Beck 7B 140
  (off Bethersden Cl.)
Hildenlea Pl. BR2: Brom 2F 159
Hilderley Ho. KT1: King T 3F 151
  (off Winery La.)
Hildreth St. SW12 . . . .1F 137
Hildreth St. M. SW12 . . . .1F 137
Hildyard Rd. SW6 . . . .6J 99
Hiley Rd. NW10 . . . .3E 80
Hilgrove Rd. NW6 . . . .7A 64
Hiliary Gdns. HA7: Stan 2C 42
Hillary N8 . . . .3J 47
  (off Boyton Cl.)
Hillary Ct. TW19: Stanw 1A 128
  (off Explorer Av.)
  W12 . . . .2E 98
  (off Titmuss St.)
Hillary Cres. KT12: Walt T 7A 148
Hillary Dr. TW7: Isle 5K 113
Hillary M. E14 . . . .5D 86
Hillary Ri. EN5: New Bar 4D 20
Hillary Rd. UB2: S'hall 3E 94
Hillbeck Cl. SE15 . . . .7J 103
  (not continuous)
Hillbeck Way UB6: G'frd 1H 77
Hillborne Cl. UB3: Harl 5J 93
Hillboro Ct. E11 . . . .7F 51
Hillbrook Rd. SW17 . . . .3D 136
Hill Brow BR1: Brom 1B 160
Hillbrow KT3: N Mald 3B 152
Hillbrow Cl. DA5: Bexl 4K 145
Hillbrow Rd. BR1: Brom 7G 141
Hillbury Av. HA3: Kenton 5B 42
Hillbury Rd. SW17 . . . .3F 137
Hill Cl. BR7: Chst 5F 143
  HA1: Harr 3J 59
  HA7: Stan 4G 27
  NW2 . . . .3D 62
  NW11 . . . .6J 45
Hillcote Av. SW16 . . . .7A 138
Hill Ct. EN4: E Barn 4H 21
  UB5: N'olt 5E 58
  W5 . . . .4F 79
Hillcourt Av. N12 . . . .6E 30
Hillcourt Est. N16 . . . .1D 66
Hillcourt Rd. SE22 . . . .6H 121
Hill Cres. DA5: Bexl 1J 145
  HA1: Harr 5A 42
  KT4: Wor Pk 2E 164
  KT5: Surb 5F 151
  N20 . . . .2E 30
Hill Crest DA15: Sidc 7A 126
  KT6: Surb 7E 150
Hillcrest N6 . . . .7E 46
  N21 . . . .7F 23
  SE24 . . . .4D 120
  W11 . . . .7H 81
  (off St John's Gdns.)

Hillcrest Av. HA5: Pinn 4B 40
  HA8: Edg 4B 28
  NW11 . . . .5H 45
Hillcrest Cl. BR3: Beck 6B 158
  SE26 . . . .4G 139
Hillcrest Ct. RM5: Col R 1K 55
  SM2: Sutt 6B 166
  (off Eaton Rd.)
Hillcrest Gdns. KT10: Hin W 3A 162
  N3 . . . .4G 45
  NW2 . . . .3C 62
Hillcrest Rd. BR1: Brom 5J 141
  BR6: Chels 2K 173
  E17 . . . .2F 51
  E18 . . . .2H 51
  W3 . . . .1H 97
  W5 . . . .5E 78
Hillcrest Vw. BR3: Beck 6B 158
Hillcroft Av. HA5: Pinn 6D 40
Hillcroft Cres. HA4: Ruis 3B 58
  HA9: Wemb 4G 61
  W5 . . . .6D 78
Hillcroft Rd. E6 . . . .5F 89
Hillcroome Rd. SM2: Sutt 6B 166
Hillcross Av. SM4: Mord 6F 153
Hilldale Rd. SM1: Sutt 4H 165
Hilldown Ct. SW16 . . . .7J 137
Hilldown Rd. BR2: Hayes 1G 171
  SW16 . . . .7J 137
Hill Dr. NW9 . . . .1J 61
  SW16 . . . .3K 155
Hilldrop Cres. N7 . . . .5H 65
Hilldrop Est. N7 . . . .5H 65
  (not continuous)
Hilldrop La. N7 . . . .5H 65
Hilldrop Rd. BR1: Brom 6K 141
  N7 . . . .5H 65
Hill End BR6: Orp 2K 173
Hillend SE18 . . . .1E 124
Hillersdon Ho. SW1 . . . .5J 17
  (off Ebury Bri. Rd.)
Hillersdon Av. HA8: Edg 5A 28
  SW13 . . . .2C 116
Hillery Cl. SE17 . . . .4D 102
Hill Farm Cotts. HA4: Ruis 7E 38
Hill Farm Rd. UB10: Ick 4F 57
  W10 . . . .5E 80
Hillfield Av. HA0: Wemb 7E 60
  N8 . . . .5J 47
  NW9 . . . .5A 44
  SM4: Mord 6C 154
Hillfield Cl. HA2: Harr 4G 41
Hillfield Ct. NW3 . . . .5C 64
Hillfield Ho. N5 . . . .5C 66
Hillfield M. N8 . . . .4K 47
Hillfield Pde. SM4: Mord 6B 154
Hillfield Pk. N10 . . . .4F 47
  N21 . . . .2F 33
Hillfield Pk. M. N10 . . . .4F 47
Hill Fld. Rd. TW12: Hamp 7D 130
Hillfield Rd. NW6 . . . .5H 63
Hillfoot Av. RM5: Col R 1J 55
Hillfoot Rd. RM5: Col R 1J 55
Hillgate Pl. SW12 . . . .7F 119
  W8 . . . .1J 99
Hillgate St. W8 . . . .1J 99
Hill Ga. Wlk. N6 . . . .6G 47
Hill Gro. RM1: Rom 3K 55
  TW13: Hanw 2D 130
Hill Ho. BR2: Brom 2H 159
  E5 . . . .1H 67
  (off Harrington Hill)
  N19 . . . .2G 65
  (off Highgate Hill)
  SE28 . . . .1H 107
Hill Ho. Apartments N1 . . . .1H 7
  (off Pentonville Rd.)
Hill Ho. Av. HA7: Stan 7E 26
Hill Ho. Cl. N21 . . . .7F 23
Hill Ho. Dr. TW12: Hamp 1E 148
Hill Ho. M. BR2: Brom 2H 159

Hill Ho. Rd. SW16 . . . .5K 137
Hilliard Ho. E1 . . . .1H 103
  (off Prusom St.)
Hilliard Rd. HA6: Nwood 1H 39
Hilliards Ct. E1 . . . .1J 103
Hillier Cl. EN5: New Bar 6E 20
Hillier Gdns. CRO: Wadd 5A 168
Hillier Ho. NW1 . . . .7H 65
  (off Camden Sq.)
Hillier Lodge TW11: Tedd 5H 131
Hillier Pl. KT9: Chess 6D 162
Hillier Rd. SW11 . . . .6D 118
Hilliers Av. UB8: Hil 3C 74
Hilliers La. CRO: Bedd 3J 167
HILLINGDON 3C 74
Hillingdon Athletic Club 5F 39
Hillingdon Athletics Stadium 6A 56
Hillingdon Av. TW19: Stanw 1A 128
HILLINGDON CIRCUS 6D 56
Hillingdon Ct. HA3: Kenton 4D 42
Hillingdon Cycling Circuit 1A 94
Hillingdon Golf Course 2B 74
HILLINGDON HEATH 4D 74
Hillingdon Hill UB10: Hil 2A 74
Hillingdon Pde. UB10: Hil 4D 74
  (off Uxbridge Rd.)
  UB8: Uxb 1A 74
  UB10: Uxb 1A 74
Hillingdon Sports & Leisure Complex 6A 56
Hillingdon St. SE17 . . . .6B 102
Hillington Gdns. IG8: Wfd G 2B 52
Hill La. HA4: Ruis 1E 56
Hillman Cl.
  UB8: Uxb 5A 56
Hillman Dr. W10 . . . .4E 80
Hillman St. E8 . . . .6H 67
Hillmarton Rd. N7 . . . .5J 65
Hillmarton Ter. N7 . . . .5J 65
  (off Hillmarton Rd.)
Hillmead Dr. SW9 . . . .4B 120
Hillmore Ct. SE13 . . . .3F 123
  (off Belmont Hill)
Hillmore Gro. SE26 . . . .5A 140
Hill Path SW16 . . . .5K 137
Hillreach SE18 . . . .5D 106
Hill Ri. HA4: Ruis 1E 56
  KT10: Hin W 2B 162
  N9 . . . .6C 24
  NW11 . . . .4K 45
  SE23 . . . .1H 139
  TW10: Rich 5D 114
  UB6: G'frd 7G 59
Hillrise KT12: Walt T 7H 147
Hillrise Mans. N19 . . . .7J 47
  (off Warltersville Rd.)
Hillrise Rd. N19 . . . .7J 47
Hill Rd. CR4: Mitc 1F 155
  HA0: Wemb 3B 60
  HA1: Harr 5K 41
  HA5: Pinn 5C 40
  N10 . . . .1D 46
  NW8 . . . .2A 82
  SM1: Sutt 5K 165
  SM5: Cars 6C 166
Hillsboro' Rd. SE22 . . . .5E 120
Hillsborough Ct. NW6 . . . .1K 81
  (off Mortimer Cres.)
Hillsgrove Cl.
  DA16: Well 7C 108
HILLSIDE 4J 109
Hillside DA8: Erith 4J 109
  EN5: New Bar 5F 21
  N8 . . . .6H 47
  NW5 . . . .3E 64
  NW9 . . . .4K 43
  NW10 . . . .7J 61
  SE10 . . . .7F 105
  (off Croom's Hill)
  SW19 . . . .6F 135

Hillside Av. HA9: Wemb 4F 61
IG8: Wfd G 6F 37
N11 6J 31
Hillside Cl. IG8: Wfd G 5F 37
NW8 2K 81
SM4: Mord 4G 153
Hillside Cres. HA2: Harr 1G 59
HA6: Nwood 1J 39
Hillside Dr. HA8: Edg 6B 28
Hillside Gdns. E17 3F 51
EN5: Barn 4B 20
HA3: Kenton 7E 42
HA6: Nwood 1J 39
HA8: Edg 4A 28
N6 6F 47
N11 6B 32
SM6: Wall 7G 167
SW2 2A 138
Hillside Gro. N14 7C 22
NW7 7H 29
Hillside Ho. *CR0: Wadd* 4B 168
(off Duppas Av.)
Hillside La. BR2: Hayes 2H 171
(not continuous)
Hillside Mans. EN5: Barn 4C 20
Hillside Pas. SW2 2K 137
Hillside Ri. HA6: Nwood 1J 39
Hillside Rd. BR2: Brom 3H 159
CR0: Wadd 5B 168
HA5: Pinn 1K 39
HA6: Nwood 1J 39
KT5: Surb 4F 151
N15 7E 48
SM2: Sutt 7H 165
SW2 2K 137
UB1: S'hall 4E 76
W5 5E 78
Hills La. HA6: Nwood 1G 39
Hillsleigh Rd. W8 1H 99
Hills M. W5 7E 78
Hills Pl. W1 1A 12 (6G 83)
Hills Rd. IG9: Buck H 1E 36
Hillstone Ct. *E3* 4D 86
(off Empson St.)
Hillstowe St. E5 3J 67
Hill St. TW9: Rich 5D 114
W1 4H 11 (1E 100)
Hill Top NW11 4K 45
SM3: Sutt 7H 153
SM4: Mord 6J 153
Hilltop E17 3D 50
Hilltop Av. NW10 7J 61
(not continuous)
Hill Top Ct. IG8: Wfd G 6J 37
Hilltop Ct. *NW8* 7A 64
(off Alexandra Rd.)
Hilltop Gdns. BR6: Orp 2J 173
NW4 2D 44
Hilltop Ho. N6 7H 47
Hilltop Rd. NW6 7J 63
Hill Top Vw. IG8: Wfd G 6J 37
Hilltop Way HA7: Stan 3F 27
Hill Vw. *NW3* 1D 82
(off Ainger Rd.)
Hillview SW20 7D 134
Hillview Av. HA3: Kenton 5E 42
Hillview Cl. HA9: Wemb 2F 61
Hill Vw. Cres. IG1: Ilf 6D 52
Hillview Cres. BR6: Orp 1J 173
Hill Vw. Dr. DA16: Well 2J 125
SE28 1J 107
Hill Vw. Gdns. NW9 5K 43
Hillview Gdns. HA2: Harr 3E 40
NW4 4F 45
Hill Vw. Rd. KT10: Clay 7A 162
TW1: Twick 6A 114
Hillview Rd. BR6: Orp 1K 173
BR7: Chst 5E 142
HA5: Hat E 1D 40
NW7 4A 30
SM1: Sutt 3A 166
Hillway N6 2E 64
NW9 1A 62
Hill-Wood Ho. *NW1* 1B 6
(off Polygon Rd.)
Hillworth BR3: Beck 2D 158
Hillworth Rd. SW2 7A 120
Hillyard Ho. SW9 1A 120
Hillyard Rd. W7 5J 77
Hillyard St. SW9 1A 120
Hillyfield E17 2A 50
Hillyfield Cl. E9 5A 68
Hilly Flds. Cres. SE4 3C 122
SE13 3C 122
Hilsea Point SW15 1D 134
Hilsea St. E5 4J 67
Hilton W13 6C 78
Hilton Av. N12 5G 31
Hilton Ho. SE4 4K 121
Hilton's Wharf *SE10* 6D 104
(off Norman Rd.)
Hilversum Cres. SE22 5E 120
Himalaya Palace Cinema 1D 94
Himley Rd. SW17 5C 136
Hinchinbrook Ho. *NW6* 1K 81
(off Mortimer Cres.)
Hinchley Cl. KT10: Hin W 4A 162
Hinchley Dr. KT10: Hin W 3A 162
Hinchley Mnr. KT10: Hin W 3A 162
Hinchley Way KT10: Hin W 3A 162
HINCHLEY WOOD 3A 162
Hinckley Rd. SE15 4G 121
Hind Ct. EC4 1K 13 (6A 84)
Hind Cres. DA8: Erith 6K 109
Hinde Ho. *W1* 7H 5
(off Hinde St.)
Hinde M. W1 7H 5
Hindes Rd. HA1: Harr 5H 41
Hinde St. W1 7H 5 (6E 82)
Hind Gro. E14 6C 86
Hindhead Cl. N16 1E 66
UB8: Hil 5D 74
Hindhead Gdns. UB5: N'olt 1C 76
Hindhead Point SW15 1D 134
Hindhead Way SM6: Wall 5J 167
Hind Ho. N7 4A 66
SE14 6K 103
(off Myers La.)
Hindle Ho. E8 5F 67
Hindlip Ho. SW8 1H 119
Hindmans Rd. SE22 5G 121
Hindmans Way RM9: Dag 4F 91
Hindmarsh Cl. E1 7G 85
Hindon Ct. SW1 3A 18
Hindrey Rd. E5 5H 67
Hindsley's Pl. SE23 2J 139
Hinkler Rd. HA3: Kenton 3D 42
Hinksey Path SE2 2D 108
Hinstock *NW6* 1K 81
(off Belsize Rd.)
Hinstock Rd. SE18 6G 107
Hinton Av. TW4: Houn 4B 112
Hinton Cl. SE9 1C 142
Hinton Ct. *E10* 2D 68
(off Leyton Grange Est.)
Hinton Rd. N18 4K 33
SE24 3C 120
SM6: Wall 6G 167
SW9 3B 120
Hippisley Ct. TW7: Isle 3K 113
Hippodrome M. W11 7G 81
Hippodrome Pl. W11 7G 81
Hiroshima Prom. SE7 3A 106
Hirst Ct. SW1 7J 17 (6F 101)
Hirst Cres. HA9: Wemb 3E 60
Hitcham Rd. E17 7B 50
Hitchcock Cl. TW17: Shep 3B 146
Hitchcock La. E20 6E 68
Hitchin La. HA7: Stan 7J 27
Hitchin Rd. HA7: Stan 7K 27
Hitchin Sq. E3 2A 86
Hitch St. RM9: Dag 3E 90
Hithe Gro. SE16 3J 103
Hitherbroom Rd. UB3: Hayes 1J 93
Hither Farm Rd. SE3 3A 124
Hitherfield Rd. RM8: Dag 2E 72
SW16 2K 137
HITHER GREEN 6F 123
Hither Green Crematorium SE6 2H 141
Hither Grn. La. SE13 5E 122
Hithermoor Rd. TW19: Stanw M 7B 174
Hitherwell Dr. HA3: Hrw W 1H 41
Hitherwood Ct. *NW9* 2A 44
(off Charcot Rd.)
Hitherwood Dr. SE19 4F 139
Hittard Ct. *SE17* 6D 102
(off Red Lion Row)
Hive, The 1E 42
Hive Cl. WD23: B Hea 2C 26
Hive Football & Fitness Cen., The 1E 42
Hive Rd. WD23: B Hea 2C 26
HMP Belmarsh SE28 2J 107
HMP Brixton SW2 6J 119
HMP Isis SE28 2K 107
HMP Pentonville N7 6K 65
HMP Thameside SE28 3J 107
HMP Wandsworth SW18 7B 118
HMP Wormwood Scrubs W12 6C 80
HMS Belfast 4H 15 (1E 102)
HMYOI Feltham TW13: Felt 3F 129
Hoadly Ho. *SE1* 5C 14
(off Union St.)
Hoadly Rd. SW16 3H 137
Hobart Cl. N20 2H 31
UB4: Yead 4B 76
Hobart Ct. *CR2: S Croy* 5D 168
(off South Pk. Hill Rd.)
IG8: Wfd G 4C 36
Hobart Dr. UB4: Yead 4B 76
Hobart Gdns. CR7: Thor H 3D 156
Hobart La. UB4: Yead 4B 76
Hobart Pl. SW1 1J 17 (3F 101)
TW10: Rich 7F 115
Hobart Rd. IG6: Ilf 2G 53
KT4: Wor Pk 3D 164
RM9: Dag 4D 72
UB4: Yead 4B 76
Hobbayne Rd. W7 6H 77
Hobbes Wlk. SW15 5D 116
Hobbs Ct. *SE1* 6K 15
(off Mill St.)
Hobbs Grn. N2 3A 46
Hobbs M. IG3: Ilf 2K 71
Hobbs Pl. N1 1E 84
Hobbs Pl. Est. *N1* 2E 84
(off Hobbs Pl.)
Hobbs Rd. SE27 4C 138
Hobby Ho. SE1 4H 103
Hobby St. EN3: Pond E 5E 24
Hobday St. E14 6D 86
Hobhouse Ct. *SW1* 3D 12
(off Suffolk St.)
Hobill Wlk. KT5: Surb 6F 151
Hoblands End BR7: Chst 6J 143
Hobson's Pl. E1 5G 85
Hobury St. SW10 7A 16 (6A 100)
Hocker St. E2 2J 9 (3F 85)
Hockett Cl. SE8 4A 104
Hockington Ct. EN5: New Bar 4E 20
Hockley Av. E6 2C 88
Hockley Ct. E18 1J 51
Hockley M. IG11: Bark 3J 89
Hockliffe Ho. *W10* 5E 80
(off Sutton Way)
Hockney Ct. *SE16* 5H 103
(off Rossetti Rd.)
Hocroft Av. NW2 3H 63
Hocroft Ct. NW2 3H 63
Hocroft Rd. NW2 4H 63
Hocroft Wlk. NW2 3H 63
Hodder Dr. UB6: G'frd 2K 77
Hoddesdon Rd. DA17: Belv 5G 109
Hodes Row NW3 4E 64
Hodford Rd. NW11 1H 63
Hodgkin Cl. SE28 7D 90
Hodgkin Ct. *SE5* 7D 102
(off Dobson Wlk.)
Hodgkins M. HA7: Stan 5G 27
Hodister Cl. SE5 7C 102
Hodnet Gro. SE16 4K 103
Hodson Cl. HA2: Harr 3D 58
Hoecroft Ct. *EN3: Enf W* 1D 24
(off Hoe La.)
Hoe La. EN1: Enf 1B 24
EN3: Enf W 1C 24
Hoe St. E17 4C 50
Hoever Ho. SE6 4E 140
Hoey Ct. *E3* 4D 86
(off Barry Blandford Way)
Hoffmann Gdns.
CR2: Sels 7H 169
Hoffman Sq. N1 1F 9
Hoffmans Rd. E17 3K 49
Hofland Rd. W14 3G 99
Hogan M. W2 5A 4 (5A 82)
Hogan Way E5 2G 67
Hogarth Av. TW15: Ashf 6E 128
Hogarth Bus. Pk. W4 6A 98
Hogarth Cl. E16 5B 88
W5 5E 78
Hogarth Ct. *E1* 6G 85
(off Batty St.)
EC3 2H 15 (6E 84)
NW1 7G 65
(off St Pancras Way)
SE19 4F 139
TW5: Hest 7C 94
Hogarth Cres. CR0: C'don 7C 156
SW19 1B 154
Hogarth Gdns. TW5: Hest 7E 94
Hogarth Health Club, The 4B 98
Hogarth Hill NW11 4H 45
Hogarth Ho. *EC1* 5B 84
(off Bartholomew Cl.)
SW1 4D 18
(off Erasmus St.)
UB5: N'olt 2B 76
(off Gallery Gdns.)
Hogarth Ind. Est. NW10 4C 80
Hogarth La. W4 6A 98
Hogarth Pl. *SW5* 4K 99
(off Hogarth Rd.)
Hogarth Rd. HA8: Edg 2G 43
RM8: Dag 5B 72
SW5 4K 99
HOGARTH RDBT. 6A 98
Hogarth's House 6A 98
(off Hogarth La.)
Hogarth Ter. W4 6A 98
Hogarth Way TW12: Hamp 1G 149
Hog Hill Rd. RM5: Col R 1F 55
Hogshead Pas. *E1* 7H 85
(off Tobacco Dock)
Hogsmill Ho. *KT1: King T* 3F 151
(off Vineyard Cl.)
Hogsmill La. KT1: King T 3F 151
Hogsmill Local Nature Reserve 5H 163
Hogsmill Wlk. *KT1: King T* 3E 150
(off Penrhyn Rd.)
Hogsmill Way KT19: Ewe 5J 163
Holbeach Cl. NW9 1A 44
Holbeach Gdns. DA15: Sidc 6J 125
Holbeach M. SW12 1F 137
Holbeach Rd. SE6 7C 122
Holbeck Row SE15 7G 103
Holbein Ho. *SW1* 5G 17
(off Holbein M.)
Holbein M. SW1 5G 17 (5E 100)
Holbein Pl. SW1 4G 17 (4E 100)
Holbein Ter. *RM8: Dag* 4C 72
(off Marlborough Rd.)
Holberton Gdns. NW10 3D 80
HOLBORN 7F 7 (6J 83)
Holborn EC1 6J 7 (5A 84)

Holborn Bars *EC1* 6J 7
(off Holborn)
Holborn Cir. EC1 6K 7 (5A 84)
Holborn Cl. NW7 4G 29
Holborn Ho. W12 6D 80
Holborn Pl. WC1 6G 7 (5K 83)
Holborn Rd. E13 4K 87
Holborn Viaduct EC1 6K 7 (5B 84)
Holborn Way CR4: Mitc 2D 154
Holbrook Cl. EN1: Enf 1A 24
N19 1F 65
Holbrooke Ct. N7 4J 65
Holbrooke Pl. TW10: Rich 5D 114
Holbrook Ho. BR7: Chst 1H 161
Holbrook La. BR7: Chst 7H 143
Holbrook Rd. E15 2H 87
Holbrook Way BR2: Brom 6D 160
Holburne Cl. SE3 1A 124
Holburne Gdns. SE3 1B 124
Holburne Rd. SE3 1A 124
Holcombe Hill NW7 3H 29
Holcombe Ho. *SW9* 3J 119
(off Landor Rd.)
Holcombe Pl. *SE4* 3A 122
(off St Asaph Rd.)
Holcombe Rd. IG1: Ilf 7E 52
N17 3F 49
Holcombe St. W6 4D 98
Holcote Cl. DA17: Belv 3E 108
Holcroft Ct. W1 5A 6
Holcroft Ho. SW11 3B 118
Holcroft Rd. E9 7J 67
Holden Av. N12 5E 30
NW9 1J 61
Holdenby Rd. SE4 5A 122
Holden Cl. RM8: Dag 3B 72
Holden Ho. *N1* 1C 84
(off Prebend St.)
SE8 7C 104
Holdenhurst Av. N12 7F 31
Holden Point *E15* 6F 69
(off Waddington St.)
Holden Rd. N12 5E 30
Holden St. SW11 2E 118
Holder Cl. N3 7E 30
Holdernesse Cl. TW7: Isle 1A 114
Holdernesse Rd. SW17 3D 136
Holderness Ho. SE5 3E 120
Holderness Way SE27 5B 138
HOLDERS HILL 2F 45
Holder's Hill Av. NW4 2F 45
Holders Hill Cir. NW7 7B 30
Holders Hill Cres. NW4 2F 45
Holders Hill Dr. NW4 3F 45
Holder's Hill Gdns. NW4 2G 45
Holders Hill Pde. NW7 1G 45
Holders Hill Rd. NW4 2F 45
NW7 2F 45
Holford Ho. *SE16* 4H 103
(off Camilla Rd.)
WC1 1H 7
(off Gt. Percy St.)
Holford M. WC1 1J 7
Holford Pl. WC1 1H 7 (3K 83)
Holford Rd. NW3 3A 64
Holford St. WC1 1J 7 (3K 83)
Holford Way SW15 6C 116
Holford Yd. *WC1* 1J 7
(off Cruikshank St.)
Holgate Av. SW11 3B 118
Holgate Gdns. RM10: Dag 6G 73
Holgate Rd. RM10: Dag 5G 73
Holgate St. SE7 3B 106
Holinser Ter. W5 1D 96
Hollam Ho. N8 4K 47
Holland Av. SM2: Sutt 7J 165
SW20 1B 152
Holland Cl. BR2: Hayes 2H 171
EN5: New Bar 7G 21
HA7: Stan 5G 27
RM7: Rom 5J 55
Holland Ct. *E17* 4E 50
(off Evelyn Rd.)
KT6: Surb 7D 150
NW7 6H 29
Holland Dr. SE23 3A 140
Holland Dwellings *WC2* 7F 7
(off Newton St.)
Holland Gdns. TW8: Bford 6E 96
W14 3G 99
Holland Grn. Pl. W8 3J 99
Holland Gro. SW9 7A 102
Holland Ho. E4 4K 35
NW10 2D 80
(off Holland Rd.)
HOLLAND PARK 1H 99
Holland Pk. 2H 99
Holland Pk. W11 1G 99
Holland Pk. Av. IG3: Ilf 6J 53
W11 2G 99
Holland Pk. Ct. *W14* 2G 99
(off Holland Pk. Gdns.)
Holland Pk. Gdns. W14 2G 99
Holland Pk. Mans. *W14* 1G 99
(off Holland Pk. Gdns.)
Holland Pk. M. W11 1G 99
Holland Pk. Rd. W14 3H 99
HOLLAND PARK RDBT. 2F 99
Holland Pk. Ter. *W11* 1G 99
(off Portland Rd.)
Holland Pk. Theatre (Open Air) 2H 99
Holland Pas. *N1* 1C 84
(off Basire St.)
Holland Pl. *W8* 2K 99
(off Kensington Chu. St.)
Holland Pl. Chambers *W8* 2K 99
(off Holland Pl.)
Holland Ri. Ho. *SW9* 7K 101
(off Clapham Rd.)
Holland Rd. E6 1D 88
E15 3G 87
HA0: Wemb 6D 60
NW10 1C 80
SE25 5G 157
W14 2F 99
Hollands, The KT4: Wor Pk 1B 164
TW13: Hanw 4B 130
Holland St. SE1 4B 14 (1B 102)
W8 2J 99
Holland Vs. Rd. W14 2G 99
Holland Wlk. HA7: Stan 5F 27
N19 1H 65
W8 1H 99
Holland Way BR2: Hayes 2H 171
Hollar Rd. N16 3F 67
Hollen St. W1 7C 6 (6H 83)
Holles Cl. TW12: Hamp 6E 130
Holles Ho. SW9 2A 120
Holles St. W1 7K 5 (6F 83)
Holley Rd. W3 2A 98
Hollickwood Av. N12 6J 31
Holliday Sq. *SW11* 3B 118
(off Fowler Cl.)
Hollidge Way RM10: Dag 7H 73
Hollies, The *E11* 5J 51
(off New Wanstead)
HA3: W'stone 4A 42
N20 1G 31
Hollies Av. DA15: Sidc 2K 143
Hollies Cl. SW16 6A 138
TW1: Twick 2K 131
Hollies End NW7 5J 29
Hollies Rd. W5 4C 96
Hollies Way SW12 7E 118
Holligrave Rd. BR1: Brom 1J 159
Hollingbourne Av. DA7: Bex 1F 127
Hollingbourne Gdns. W13 5B 78
Hollingbourne Rd. SE24 5C 120
Hollingsworth Ct. KT6: Surb 7D 150
Hollingsworth Rd. CR0: C'don 6H 169
Hollington Ct. BR7: Chst 6F 143
Hollington Cres. KT3: N Mald 6B 152
Hollington Rd. E6 3D 88
N17 2G 49
Hollingworth Cl. KT8: W Mole 4D 148
Hollingworth Rd. BR5: Pet W 6F 161
Hollins Ho. N7 4J 65
Hollisfield *WC1* 2F 7
(off Cromer St.)
Hollister Ho. *NW6* 3J 81
(off Kilburn Pk. Rd.)
Hollman Gdns. SW16 6B 138
Hollow, The IG8: Wfd G 4C 36
HOLLOWAY 3J 65
Holloway Cl. UB7: Harm 5A 92
Holloway Ho. *NW2* 3E 62
(off Stoll Cl.)
Holloway La. UB7: Harm, W Dray 2E 174
Holloway Rd. E6 3D 88
E11 3F 69
N7 4K 65
N19 2H 65
Holloway St. TW3: Houn 3F 113
Hollowfield Wlk. UB5: N'olt 6C 58
Hollows, The TW8: Bford 6F 97
Holly Av. HA7: Stan 2E 42
KT12: Walt T 7B 148
Hollybank Cl. TW12: Hamp 5E 130
Hollyberry La. NW3 4A 64
Hollybrake Cl. BR7: Chst 7H 143
Hollybush Cl. E11 5J 51
HA3: Hrw W 1J 41
Hollybush Gdns. E2 3H 85
Holly Bush Hill NW3 4A 64
Hollybush Hill E11 6H 51
Hollybush Ho. E2 3H 85
Holly Bush La. TW12: Hamp 7D 130
Hollybush Pl. E2 3H 85
Hollybush Rd. KT2: King T 5E 132
Holly Bush Steps *NW3* 4A 64
(off Holly Mt.)
Hollybush St. E13 3K 87
Holly Bush Va. NW3 4A 64
Hollybush Wlk. SW9 4B 120
Holly Cl. BR3: Beck 4E 158
IG9: Buck H 3G 37
KT19: Eps 7K 163
SM6: Wall 7F 167
TW13: Hanw 5C 130
TW16: Sun 3K 147
Holly Cott. M. UB8: Hil 5C 74
Holly Ct. *DA14: Sidc* 4B 144
(off Sidcup Hill)
N15 4E 48
SE10 3H 105
SM2: Sutt 7J 165
Holly Cres. BR3: Beck 5B 158
IG8: Wfd G 7A 36
Hollycroft Av. HA9: Wemb 2F 61
NW3 3J 63
Hollycroft Cl. CR2: S Croy 5E 168
UB7: Sip 6C 92
Hollycroft Gdns. UB7: Sip 6C 92
Hollydale Cl. UB5: N'olt 4F 59
Hollydale Dr. BR2: Brom 3D 172
Hollydale Rd. SE15 1J 121
Hollydene *BR2: Brom* 1H 159
(off Beckenham La.)
SE13 6F 123
SE15 1H 121
Hollydown Way E11 3F 69
Holly Dr. E4 7J 25
Holly Farm Rd. UB2: S'hall 5C 94
Hollyfield Av. N11 5J 31
Hollyfield Rd. KT5: Surb 7F 151
Holly Gdns. DA7: Bex 4J 127
UB7: W Dray 2B 92
Holly Gro. HA5: Pinn 1C 40
NW9 7J 43
SE15 2F 121
Hollygrove WD23: Bush 1C 26
Hollygrove Cl. TW3: Houn 4D 112
Holly Hedge Ter. SE13 5F 123
Holly Hill N21 6E 22
NW3 4A 64
Holly Hill Rd. DA8: Erith 5H 109
DA17: Belv, Erith 5H 109
Holly Ho. TW8: Bford 6C 96
W10 4G 81
(off Hawthorn Wlk.)
Holly La. IG3: Ilf 2A 72
Holly Lodge HA1: Harr 5H 41
W8 2J 99
(off Thornwood Gdns.)
Holly Lodge Gdns. N6 2E 64
Holly Lodge Mans. N6 2E 64
Hollymead SM5: Cars 3D 166
Holly M. SW10 6A 16 (5A 100)
Holly Mt. NW3 4A 64
Hollymount Cl. SE10 1E 122
Holly Pde. *TW13: Felt* 3H 129
(off High St.)
Holly Pk. N3 3H 45
N4 7J 47
(not continuous)
Holly Pk. Est. N4 7K 47
Holly Pk. Gdns. N3 3J 45
Holly Pk. Rd. N11 5K 31
W7 1K 95
Holly Pl. *NW3* 4A 64
(off Holly Berry La.)
Holly Rd. E11 7H 51
TW1: Twick 1K 131
TW3: Houn 4F 113
TW12: Hamp H 6G 131
W4 4K 97
Holly St. E8 7F 67
Holly Ter. N6 1E 64
N20 2F 31
Holly Tree Cl. SW19 1F 135
Holly Tree Ho. *SE4* 3B 122
(off Brockley Rd.)
Hollytree Pde. *DA14: Sidc* 6C 144
(off Sidcup Hill)
Hollyview Cl. NW4 6C 44
Holly Village N6 2F 65
Holly Vs. *W6* 3D 98
(off Wellesley Av.)
Holly Wlk. EN2: Enf 3H 23
NW3 4A 64
Holly Way CR4: Mitc 4H 155
Hollywood Bowl
Finchley 7G 31
Surrey Quays 3K 103
Tolworth 2H 163
Hollywood Ct. *SW10* 6A 100
(off Hollywood Rd.)
W5 7F 79
Hollywood Gdns. UB4: Yead 6K 75
Hollywood M. SW10 6A 100
Hollywood Rd. E4 5F 35
SW10 6A 100
Hollywood Way IG8: Wfd G 7A 36
Holman Ct. KT17: Ewe 7C 164
Holman Ho. *E2* 3K 85
(off Roman Rd.)
Holman Hunt Ho. *W6* 5G 99
(off Field Rd.)
Holman Rd. KT19: Ewe 5J 163
SW11 2B 118
Holmbank Dr. TW17: Shep 4G 147
Holmbridge Gdns. EN3: Pond E 4E 24
Holmbrook *NW1* 2G 83
(off Eversholt St.)
Holmbrook Dr. NW4 5F 45
Holmbury Ct. CR2: S Croy 5E 168
SW17 3D 136
SW19 7C 136
Holmbury Gdns. UB3: Hayes 1H 93
Holmbury Gro. CR0: Sels 7B 170
Holmbury Ho. SE24 5B 120
Holmbury Mnr. DA14: Sidc 4A 144
Holmbury Pk. BR1: Brom 7C 142
Holmbury Vw. E5 1H 67

Holmbush Rd. SW15 .6G **117**
Holmcote Gdns. N5 .5C **66**
Holm Ct. SE12 .3K **141**
Holmcroft Ho. E17 .4D **50**
Holmcroft Way BR2: Brom .5D **160**
Holmdale Gdns. NW4 .5F **45**
Holmdale Rd. BR7: Chst .5G **143**
NW6 .5J **63**
Holmdale Ter. N15 .6E **48**
Holmdene N12 .5E **30**
Holmdene Av. HA2: Harr .3F **41**
NW7 .6H **29**
SE24 .5C **120**
Holmdene Cl. BR3: Beck .2E **158**
Holmdene Ct. BR1: Brom .3C **160**
Holmead Rd. SW6 .7K **99**
Holmebury Cl. WD23: B Hea .2D **26**
Holme Ct. TW7: Isle .3A **114**
Holmefield Ho. *W10* .*4G* ***81***
(off Hazlewood Cres.)
Holme Ho. *SE15* .*7H* ***103***
(off Studholme St.)
Holme Lacey Rd. SE12 .6H **123**
Holmeoak Av. RM13: Rain .2K **91**
Holme Rd. E6 .1C **88**
Holmes Av. E17 .3B **50**
Holmes Cl. SE22 .4G **121**
Holmesdale Av. SW14 .3H **115**
Holmesdale Cl. SE25 .3F **157**
Holmesdale Ho. *NW6* .*1J* ***81***
(off Kilburn Vale)
Holmesdale Rd. CR0: C'don .5D **156**
DA7: Bex .2D **126**
N6 .7F **47**
SE25 .5D **156**
TW9: Kew .1F **115**
TW11: Tedd .7C **132**
Holmesley Rd. SE23 .6A **122**
Holmes Pl. SW10 .6A **100**
Holmes Rd. NW5 .5F **65**
SW19 .7A **136**
TW1: Twick .2K **131**
Holmes Ter. SE1 .6J **13**
Holmeswood SM2: Sutt .6K **165**
Holmeswood Ct. N22 .2A **48**
Holme Way HA7: Stan .6E **26**
Holmewood Gdns. SW2 .7K **119**
Holmewood Rd. SE25 .3E **156**
SW2 .7K **119**
Holmfield Av. NW4 .5F **45**
Holmfield Ct. NW3 .5C **64**
Holm Gro. UB10: Hil .7C **56**
Holmhurst SE13 .6F **123**
Holmhurst Rd. DA17: Belv .5H **109**
Holmlea Ct. *CR0: C'don* .*4D* ***168***
(off Chatsworth Rd.)
Holmleigh Ct. EN3: Pond E .4D **24**
Holmleigh Rd. N16 .1E **66**
Holmleigh Rd. Est. N16 .1E **66**
Holm Oak Cl. SW15 .6H **117**
Holm Oak M. SW4 .5J **119**
Holmoaks Ho. BR3: Beck .2E **158**
Holmsdale Ho. *E14* .*7D* ***86***
(off Poplar High St.)
N11 .*4A* ***32***
(off Coppies Gro.)
Holmshaw Cl. SE26 .4A **140**
Holmside Rd. SW12 .6E **118**
Holmsley Cl. KT3: N Mald .6B **152**
Holmsley Ho. *SW15* .*7B* ***116***
(off Tangley Gro.)
Holmstall Av. HA8: Edg .3J **43**
Holmstall Pde. HA8: Edg .2J **43**
Holmstead Ct. CR2: S Croy .5D **168**
Holm Wlk. SE3 .2J **123**
Holmwood Cl. HA2: Harr .3G **41**
SM2: Cheam .7F **165**
UB5: N'olt .6F **59**
Holmwood Gdns. N3 .2J **45**
SM6: Wall .6F **167**
Holmwood Gro. NW7 .5E **28**
Holmwood Rd. IG3: Ilf .2J **71**
KT9: Chess .5D **162**
SM2: Cheam .7E **164**
Holmwood Vs. SE7 .5J **105**
Holne Chase N2 .6A **46**
SM4: Mord .6H **153**
Holness Rd. E15 .6H **69**
Holocaust Memorial .2D **100**
Holocaust Memorial Garden, The .6F **11**
Holroyd Rd. KT10: Clay .7A **162**
SW15 .4E **116**
Holsgrove Ho. W3 .1A **98**
Holst Ct. *SE1* .*1J* ***19***
(off Kennington Rd.)
Holstein Way DA18: Erith .3D **108**
Holst Ho. *W12* .*6D* ***80***
(off Du Cane Rd.)
Holst Mans. SW13 .6E **98**
Holstock Rd. IG1: Ilf .2G **71**
Holsworth Cl. HA2: Harr .5G **41**
Holsworthy Ho. *E3* .*3D* ***86***
(off Talwin St.)
Holsworthy Sq. WC1 .4H **7**
Holsworthy Way KT9: Chess .5C **162**
Holt, The SM4: Mord .4J **153**
SM6: Wall .4G **167**
Holt Cl. BR7: Chst .5D **142**
DA14: Sidc .4E **144**
N10 .4E **46**
SE28 .7B **90**
Holt Ct. *SE10* .*6E* ***104***
(off Horseferry Pl.)
Holt Ho. SW2 .6A **120**
Holton St. E1 .4K **85**
Holt Rd. E16 .1C **106**
HA0: Wemb .3B **60**
Holtwhite Av. EN2: Enf .2H **23**
Holtwhite's Hill EN2: Enf .1G **23**
Holwell Pl. HA5: Pinn .4C **40**
Holwood Est. BR2: Kes .6C **172**
Holwood Pk. Av. BR6: Farnb .4D **172**
Holwood Pl. SW4 .4H **119**
Holybourne Av. SW15 .7C **116**
Holycross Cl. SM4: Mord .7J **153**
Holyhead Cl. E6 .5D **88**
Holyhead Ct. *KT1: King T* .*4D* ***150***
(off Anglesea Rd.)
Holyoake Ct. SE16 .2B **104**
Holyoake Ho. W5 .4C **78**
Holyoake Wlk. N2 .3A **46**
W5 .4C **78**
Holyoak Rd. SE11 .4B **102**
Holyport Rd. SW6 .7F **99**
Holyrood Av. HA2: Harr .4C **58**
Holyrood Ct. *NW1* .*1F* ***83***
(off Gloucester Av.)
Holyrood Gdns. HA8: Edg .3H **43**
Holyrood M. E16 .1J **105**
Holyrood Rd. EN5: New Bar .6F **21**
Holyrood St. SE1 .5G **15** (1E **102**)
Holywell Cl. BR6: Chels .4K **173**
SE3 .6J **105**
SE16 .5H **103**
TW19: Stanw .1A **128**
Holywell La. EC2 .3H **9** (4E **84**)
Holywell Row EC2 .4G **9** (4E **84**)
Holywell Way TW19: Stanw .1A **128**
Homan Ct. N12 .4G **31**
Homebush Ho. E4 .7J **25**
Homecedars Ho. WD23: B Hea .1C **26**
Home Cl. SM5: Cars .2D **166**
UB5: N'olt .3D **76**
Home Ct. KT6: Surb .5D **150**
Homecroft Rd. N22 .1C **48**
SE26 .5J **139**
Home Farm Cl. KT7: T Ditt .7K **149**
TW17: Shep .4G **147**
Homefarm Rd. W7 .6J **77**
Home Fld. EN5: Barn .5C **20**
Homefield SM4: Mord .4J **153**
Homefield Av. IG2: Ilf .5J **53**
Homefield Cl. NW10 .6J **61**
UB4: Yead .4B **76**
Homefield Gdns. CR4: Mitc .2A **154**
N2 .3B **46**
Homefield Ho. SE23 .3J **139**
Homefield M. BR3: Beck .1C **158**
Homefield Pk. SM1: Sutt .6K **165**
Homefield Pl. CR0: C'don .2F **169**
Homefield Rd. BR1: Brom .1A **160**
HA0: Wemb .4A **60**
HA8: Edg .6E **28**
KT12: Walt T .7C **148**
SW19 .6F **135**
W4 .5B **98**
Homefield St. N1 .1G **9** (2E **84**)
Homefirs Ho. HA9: Wemb .3F **61**
Home Gdns. RM10: Dag .3J **73**
Homeheather Ho. IG4: Ilf .5D **52**
Homeland Dr. SM2: Sutt .7K **165**
Homelands Dr. SE19 .7E **138**
Home Lea BR6: Chels .5K **173**
Homeleigh Ct. SW16 .3J **137**
Homeleigh Rd. SE15 .5K **121**
Home Mead HA7: Stan .1C **42**
Home Mdw. M. SE22 .5G **121**
Homemead Rd. BR2: Brom .5D **160**
CR0: C'don .6G **155**
Home Pk. Ct. *KT1: King T* .*4D* ***150***
(off Palace Rd.)
Home Pk. Pde.
KT1: Hamp W .*2D* ***150***
(off High St.)
Home Pk. Rd. SW19 .4H **135**
Home Pk. Ter. *KT1: Hamp W* .*2D* ***150***
(off Hampton Ct. Rd.)
Home Pk. Wlk. KT1: King T .4D **150**
Homer Cl. DA7: Bex .1J **127**
Homer Dr. E14 .4C **104**
Home Rd. SW11 .2C **118**
Homer Rd. CR0: C'don .6K **157**
E9 .6A **68**
Homer Row W1 .6D **4** (5C **82**)
Homersham Rd. KT1: King T .2G **151**
Homer St. W1 .6D **4** (5C **82**)
HOMERTON .5K 67
Homerton Gro. E9 .5K **67**
Homerton High St. E9 .5K **67**
Homerton Rd. E9 .5A **68**
Homerton Row E9 .5J **67**
Homerton Ter. E9 .6J **67**
(not continuous)
Homesdale Cl. E11 .5J **51**
Homesdale Rd. BR1: Brom .4A **160**
BR2: Brom .4A **160**
BR5: Pet W .7J **161**
Homesfield NW11 .5J **45**
Homestall Rd. SE22 .5J **121**
Homestead Ct. EN5: New Bar .5D **20**
Homestead Paddock N14 .5A **22**
Homestead Pk. NW2 .3B **62**
Homestead Rd. RM8: Dag .2F **73**
SW6 .7H **99**
Homesteads, The N11 .4A **32**
Homevale Cl. BR2: Hayes .7H **159**
Homewalk Ho. SE26 .4H **139**
Homewaters Av. TW16: Sun .1H **147**
Homewillow Cl. N21 .6G **23**
Homewood Cl. TW12: Hamp .6D **130**
Homewood Cres. BR7: Chst .6J **143**
Homewoods SW12 .7G **119**
Homildon Ho. SE26 .3G **139**
Honduras St. EC1 .3C **8** (4C **84**)
Honeybourne Rd. NW6 .5K **63**
Honeybourne Way BR5: Pet W .1H **173**
Honeybrook Rd. SW12 .7G **119**
Honey Cl. RM10: Dag .6H **73**
Honeycroft Hill UB10: Uxb .7A **56**
Honeyden Rd. DA14: Sidc .6E **144**
Honeyfield M. SE23 .3K **139**
Honey Hill UB10: Uxb .7B **56**
Honey La. EC2 .1D **14**
Honey La. Ho. *SW10* .*6K* ***99***
(off Finborough Rd.)
Honeyman Cl. NW6 .7F **63**
Honeymead *N8* .*3J* ***47***
(off Campsfield Rd.)
Honey M. RM7: Rom .5J **55**
SE27 .*4C* ***138***
(off Norwood High St.)
Honeypot Bus. Cen. HA7: Stan .1E **42**
Honeypot Cl. NW9 .4F **43**
Honeypot La. HA7: Stan .7J **27**
NW9 .1D **42**
Honeysett Rd. N17 .2F **49**
Honeysuckle Cl. UB1: S'hall .7C **76**
Honeysuckle Ct. IG1: Ilf .6F **71**
IG9: Buck H .3G **37**
Honeysuckle Gdns. CR0: C'don .7K **157**
E17 .3C **50**
Honeysuckle La. N22 .2C **48**
Honeywell Rd. SW11 .6D **118**
Honeywood Ho. *SE15* .*1G* ***121***
(off Goldsmith Rd.)
Honeywood Mus. .5D **166**
Honeywood Rd. NW10 .2B **80**
TW7: Isle .4A **114**
Honeywood Wlk. SM5: Cars .4D **166**
Honister Cl. HA7: Stan .1B **42**
Honister Gdns. HA7: Stan .7G **27**
Honister Pl. HA7: Stan .1B **42**
Honiton Gdns. NW7 .7A **30**
SE15 .*2J* ***121***
(off Gibbon Rd.)
Honiton Ho. EN3: Pond E .3E **24**
Honiton Rd. DA16: Well .2K **125**
NW6 .2H **81**
RM7: Rom .6K **55**
Honley Rd. SE6 .7D **122**
Honnor Gdns. TW7: Isle .2H **113**
HONOR OAK .6J 121
Honor Oak Crematorium SE23 .5K **121**
HONOR OAK PARK .7A 122
Honor Oak Pk. SE23 .6J **121**
Honor Oak Ri. SE23 .6J **121**
Honor Oak Rd. SE23 .1J **139**
Honour Gdns. RM8: Dag .4A **72**
Honour Lea Av. E20 .5D **68**
Hood Av. N14 .6A **22**
SW14 .5J **115**
Hood Cl. CR0: C'don .1B **168**
Hoodcote Gdns. N21 .7G **23**
Hood Ct. EC4 .1K **13**
Hood Ho. *SE5* .*7D* ***102***
(off Elmington Est.)
SW1 .*6C* ***18***
(off Dolphin Sq.)
Hood Point *SE16* .*2B* ***104***
(off Rotherhithe St.)
Hood Rd. SW20 .7B **134**
Hood Wlk. RM7: Mawney .1H **55**
HOOK .4D 162
Hook, The EN5: New Bar .6G **21**
Hooke Ct. *SE10* .*1E* ***122***
(off Winforton St.)
Hooke Ho. *E3* .*2A* ***86***
(off Gernon Rd.)
Hookers Rd. E17 .3K **49**
Hook Farm Rd. BR2: Brom .5B **160**
Hookham Ct. SW8 .1H **119**
Hooking Grn. HA2: Harr .5F **41**
HOOK JUNC. .**3E 162**
Hook La. DA16: Well .4K **125**
Hook Ri. Nth. KT6: Surb .3E **162**
Hook Ri. Sth. KT6: Surb .3E **162**
Hook Ri. Sth. Ind. Pk. KT6: Surb .3F **163**
Hook Rd. KT6: Surb .2E **162**
KT9: Chess .5D **162**
KT19: Eps, Ewe .7J **163**
Hooks Cl. SE15 .1H **121**
Hooks Hall Dr. RM10: Dag .3J **73**
Hookstone Way IG8: Wfd G .7G **37**
Hook Wlk. HA8: Edg .6D **28**

Hool Cl. NW9 . . . .5J 43
Hooper Dr. UB8: Hil 5D 74
Hooper Ho.
  TW15: Ashf 3A 128
Hooper Rd. E16 . . . .6H 69
Hooper's Ct. SW3 . . . .7E 10 (2D 100)
Hooper's M. W3 . . . .1J 97
Hoopers M.
  WD23: Bush 1A 26
Hooper Sq. E1 . . . .6G 85
  (off Hooper St.)
Hooper St. E1 . . . .6G 85
Hoopers Yd. E1 . . . .6G 85
  (off Hooper St.)
  NW6 . . . .1H 81
  (off Kimberley Rd.)
Hoop La. NW11 . . . .7H 45
Hop Ct. HA0: Wemb 5A 60
  (off Brewery Cl.)
Hope Cl. IG8: Wfd G 6F 37
  N1 . . . .6C 66
  RM6: Chad H 4D 54
  SE12 . . . .3K 141
  SM1: Sutt 5A 166
  TW8: Bford 5E 96
Hope Ct. NW10 . . . .3F 81
  (off Chamberlayne Rd.)
  SE1 . . . .5G 103
  (off Avocet Cl.)
Hopedale Rd. SE7 . . . .6K 105
Hopefield Av. NW6 . . . .2G 81
Hope Gdns. W3 . . . .2H 97
Hope Ho. CR0: C'don 4E 168
  (off Steep Hill)
Hope La. SE9 . . . .2F 143
Hope Pk. BR1: Brom 7H 141
Hopes Cl. TW5: Hest 6E 94
Hope Sq. EC2 . . . .6G 9
Hope St. SW11 . . . .3B 118
Hopetown St. E1 . . . .6K 9 (5F 85)
Hopewell St. SE5 . . . .7D 102
Hopewell Yd. SE5 . . . .7D 102
  (off Hopewell St.)
Hope Wharf SE16 . . . .2J 103
Hop Gdns. WC2 . . . .3E 12 (7J 83)
Hopgood St. W12 . . . .1E 98
Hopground Ho. E20 . . . .6E 68
  (off De Coubertin St.)
Hopkins Cl. N10 . . . .7K 31
Hopkins Ho. E14 . . . .6C 86
  (off Canton St.)
Hopkins M. E15 . . . .1H 87
Hopkinsons Pl. NW1 . . . .1E 82
Hopkins Rd. E10 . . . .7D 50
Hopkins St. W1 . . . .1B 12 (6G 83)
Hoppers Rd. N13 . . . .2F 33
  N21 . . . .2F 33
Hoppett Rd. E4 . . . .2B 36
Hopping La. N1 . . . .6B 66
Hoppingwood Av. KT3: N Mald 3A 152
Hoppner Rd. UB4: Hayes 2F 75
Hop St. SE10 . . . .4H 105
Hopton Ct. BR2: Hayes 1K 171
Hopton Gdns. KT3: N Mald 6C 152
Hopton Rd. SE18 . . . .3F 107
  SW16 . . . .5J 137
Hopton's Gdns. SE1 . . . .4B 14
Hopton St. SE1 . . . .3A 14 (7B 84)
Hoptree Cl. N12 . . . .5E 30
Hopwood Cl. SW17 . . . .3A 136
Hopwood Rd. SE17 . . . .6D 102
Hopwood Wlk. E8 . . . .7G 67
Horace Av. RM7: Rush G 1J 73
Horace Bldg. SW8 . . . .7F 101
Horace Jones Ho. SE1 . . . .1H 15
  (off Duchess Wlk.)
Horace Rd. E7 . . . .4K 69
  IG6: Ilf 3G 53
  KT1: King T 3F 151
Horatio Ct. SE16 . . . .1J 103
  (off Rotherhithe St.)

Horatio Ho. E2 . . . .2F 85
  (off Horatio St.)
  W6 . . . .5F 99
  (off Fulham Pal. Rd.)
Horatio Pl. E14 . . . .1E 104
  (off Managers St.)
  SW19 . . . .1J 153
Horatio St. E2 . . . .2F 85
Horatius Way CR0: Wadd 5K 167
Horbury Cres. W11 . . . .7J 81
Horbury M. W11 . . . .7H 81
Horder Rd. SW6 . . . .1G 117
Hordle Prom. E. SE15 . . . .7F 103
Hordle Prom. Sth. SE15 . . . .7F 103
  (off Quarley Way)
Horizon Bldg. E14 . . . .7C 86
  (off Hertsmere Rd.)
Horizon Bus. Cen. N9 . . . .2E 34
  (off Goodwin Rd.)
Horizon Cl. SM2: Cheam 7G 165
  (off Up. Mulgrave Rd.)
Horizon Ho. SW18 . . . .3A 118
  (off Juniper Dr.)
Horizon Ind. Est. SE15 . . . .6G 103
Horle Wlk. SE5 . . . .2B 120
Horley Cl. DA6: Bex 5G 127
Horley Rd. SE9 . . . .4C 142
Hormead Rd. W9 . . . .4H 81
Hornbeam Cl. IG1: Ilf 5H 71
  IG9: Buck H 3G 37
  IG11: Bark 3A 90
  NW7 . . . .3G 29
  SE11 . . . .3J 19 (4A 102)
  UB5: N'olt 5D 58
Hornbeam Cres. TW8: Bford 7B 96
Hornbeam Gdns. KT3: N Mald 6C 152
Hornbeam Gro. E4 . . . .3B 36
Hornbeam Ho. IG9: Buck H 3H 37
  SE14 . . . .7B 104
  (off Manor Rd.)
Hornbeam La. DA7: Bex 2J 127
  E4 . . . .6K 19
Hornbeam Rd. IG9: Buck H 3G 37
  UB4: Yead 5A 76
Hornbeam Sq. E3 . . . .1B 86
Hornbeams Ri. N11 . . . .6K 31
Hornbeam Ter. SM5: Cars 1C 166
Hornbeam Wlk. TW10: Rich 2F 133
Hornbeam Way BR2: Brom 6E 160
Hornbean Ho. E15 . . . .3G 87
  (off Manor Rd.)
Hornblower Cl. SE16 . . . .3A 104
Hornbuckle Cl. HA2: Harr 2H 59
Hornby Cl. NW3 . . . .7B 64
Hornby Cl. NW10 . . . .6B 62
Hornby Ho. SE11 . . . .7J 19
Horncastle Cl. SE12 . . . .7J 123
Horncastle Rd. SE12 . . . .7J 123
Hornchurch N17 . . . .2D 48
  (off Gloucester Rd.)
Hornchurch Cl. KT2: King T 4D 132
Horndean Cl. SW15 . . . .1C 134
Horndon Cl. RM5: Col R 1J 55
Horndon Grn. RM5: Col R 1J 55
Horndon Rd. RM5: Col R 1J 55
Horner Ho. N1 . . . .1E 84
  (off Nuttall St.)
Horner La. CR4: Mitc 2B 154
Horne Rd. TW17: Shep 4C 146
Horner Sq. E1 . . . .5J 9
  (within Old Spitalfields Market)
Hornet Way E6 . . . .5H 89
Horne Way SW15 . . . .2E 116
Hornfair Rd. SE7 . . . .6A 106
Horniman Dr. SE23 . . . .1H 139
Horniman Gdns. 1H 139
Horniman Mus. 1H 139
Horning Cl. SE9 . . . .4C 142
Horn La. IG8: Wfd G 6D 36
  SE10 . . . .5J 105
  (not continuous)
  W3 . . . .7J 79
  (not continuous)
Horn Link Way SE10 . . . .4J 105

HORN PARK 5K 123
Horn Pk. Cl. SE12 . . . .5K 123
Horn Pk. La. SE12 . . . .5K 123
Hornscroft Cl. IG11: Bark 7J 71
Horns End Pl. HA5: Eastc 4A 40
HORNSEY 4J 47
Hornsey N8 . . . .4J 47
Hornsey Cricket Club 5H 47
Hornsey La. N6 . . . .1F 65
Hornsey La. Est. N19 . . . .7H 47
Hornsey La. Gdns. N6 . . . .7G 47
Hornsey Pk. Rd. N8 . . . .3K 47
Hornsey Ri. N19 . . . .7H 47
Hornsey Ri. Gdns. N19 . . . .7H 47
Hornsey Rd. N7 . . . .1J 65
  N19 . . . .1J 65
Hornsey St. N7 . . . .5K 65
HORNSEY VALE 5K 47
Hornshay St. SE15 . . . .6J 103
Horns Rd. IG2: Ilf 5G 53
  IG6: Ilf 4H 53
Hornton Cl. W8 . . . .2J 99
  (off Kensington High St.)
Hornton Pl. W8 . . . .2K 99
Hornton St. W8 . . . .2J 99
Horsa Rd. DA8: Erith 7H 109
  SE12 . . . .7A 124
Horse & Dolphin Yd. W1 . . . .2D 12
Horsebridges Cl. RM9: Dag 1E 90
Horsecroft Rd. HA8: Edg 7E 28
Horse Fair KT1: King T 2D 150
Horseferry Pl. SE10 . . . .6E 104
Horseferry Rd. E14 . . . .7A 86
  SW1 . . . .2C 18 (3H 101)
Horse Guards Av. SW1 . . . .5E 12 (1J 101)
Horse Guards Parade 5E 12 (1H 101)
Horse Guards Rd. SW1 . . . .5D 12 (1H 101)
Horse Leaze E6 . . . .6E 88
Horseley Ct. E1 . . . .5A 86
Horsell Rd. BR5: St P 7B 144
  N5 . . . .5A 66
  (not continuous)
Horselydown La. SE1 . . . .6J 15 (2F 103)
Horselydown Mans. SE1 . . . .6J 15
  (off Lafone St.)
Horsemongers M. SE1 . . . .7D 14
Horsenden Av. UB6: G'frd 5K 59
Horsenden Cres. UB6: G'frd 5K 59
Horsenden Hill Golf Course 7A 60
Horsenden La. Nth. UB6: G'frd 6J 59
Horsenden La. Sth. UB6: G'frd 1A 78
Horse Ride SW1 . . . .5C 12 (1G 101)
Horseshoe Cl. E14 . . . .5E 104
  NW2 . . . .2D 62
Horseshoe Ct. EC1 . . . .3B 8
  (off Brewhouse Yd.)
Horse Shoe Cres. UB5: N'olt 2E 76
Horseshoe Dr. UB8: Hil 6C 74
Horse Shoe Grn. SM1: Sutt 2K 165
Horseshoe La. EN2: Enf 3H 23
  N20 . . . .1A 30
Horseshoe M. SW2 . . . .4J 119
Horseshoe Wharf SE1 . . . .4E 14
  (off Clink St.)
Horse Yd. N1 . . . .1B 84
  (off Essex Rd.)
Horsfeld Gdns. SE9 . . . .5C 124
Horsfeld Rd. SE9 . . . .5B 124
Horsfield Ho. N1 . . . .7C 66
  (off Northampton St.)
Horsford Rd. SW2 . . . .5K 119
Horsham Av. N12 . . . .5H 31
Horsham Ct. N17 . . . .1G 49
  (off Lansdowne Rd.)
Horsham Rd. DA6: Bex 5G 127
  TW14: Bedf 6E 110
Horsley Ct. SW1 . . . .4D 18
  (off Vincent St.)
Horsley Dr. CR0: New Ad 7E 170
  KT2: King T 5D 132

Horsley Rd. BR1: Brom 1K 159
  E4 . . . .2K 35
Horsley St. SE17 . . . .6D 102
Horsman Ho. SE5 . . . .6C 102
  (off Bethwin Rd.)
Horsman St. SE5 . . . .6C 102
Horsmonden Cl. BR6: Orp 7K 161
Horsmonden Rd. SE4 . . . .5B 122
Hortensia Ho. SW10 . . . .7A 100
  (off Gunter Gro.)
Hortensia Rd. SW10 . . . .7A 100
Horticultural Pl. W4 . . . .5K 97
Horton Av. NW2 . . . .4G 63
Horton Bri. Rd. UB7: Yiew 1B 92
Horton Cl. UB7: Yiew 1C 92
Horton Country Pk. Local Nature Reserve
  . . . .7G 163
Horton Halls SW17 . . . .3B 136
Horton Ho. SE15 . . . .6J 103
  SW8 . . . .7K 101
  W6 . . . .5G 99
  (off Field Rd.)
Horton Ind. Pk. UB7: Yiew 1B 92
Horton La. KT19: Eps 7H 163
Horton Pde. UB7: Yiew 1A 92
Horton Pk. Golf Course 7J 163
Horton Rd. E8 . . . .6H 67
  SL3: Poyle 6A 174
  TW19: Stanw M 6A 174
  UB7: Yiew 1A 92
  UB11: Stock P 1A 92
Horton Rd. Ind. Est. UB7: Yiew 1B 92
Horton Way CR0: C'don 5K 157
Hortus Rd. E4 . . . .2K 35
  UB2: S'hall 2D 94
Horwood Ho. E2 . . . .3H 85
  (off Pott St.)
  NW8 . . . .3D 4
  (off Paveley St.)
Hosack Rd. SW17 . . . .2E 136
Hoser Av. SE12 . . . .2J 141
Hosier La. EC1 . . . .6A 8 (5B 84)
Hoskins Cl. E16 . . . .6A 88
  UB3: Harl 5H 93
Hoskins St. SE10 . . . .5F 105
Hospital Bri. Rd.
  TW2: Twick, Whitt 7F 113
HOSPITAL BRIDGE RDBT. 2F 131
Hospital Rd. E9 . . . .5K 67
  E11 . . . .5F 51
  TW3: Houn 3E 112
Hospital Way SE13 . . . .7F 123
Hotham Cl. KT8: W Mole 3E 148
Hotham Rd. SW15 . . . .3E 116
  SW19 . . . .7A 136
Hotham Rd. M. SW19 . . . .7A 136
Hotham St. E15 . . . .1G 87
Hothfield Pl. SE16 . . . .3J 103
Hotspur Ind. Est. N17 . . . .6C 34
Hotspur Rd. UB5: N'olt 2E 76
Hotspur St. SE11 . . . .5J 19 (4A 102)
Houblon Rd.
  TW10: Rich 5E 114
Houghton Cl. E8 . . . .6F 67
  TW12: Hamp 6C 130
Houghton Ct. EC1 . . . .4B 8
  (off Glasshouse Yd.)
Houghton Rd. N15 . . . .4F 49
Houghton Sq. SW9 . . . .2J 119
  (off Clapham Rd.)
Houghton St. WC2 . . . .1H 13 (6K 83)
  (not continuous)
Houlder Cres. CR0: Wadd 6B 168
Houlton Ho. SW3 . . . .5E 16
  (off Walpole St.)
Houlton Pl. E3 . . . .4B 86
  (off Hamlets Way)
Houndsden Rd. N21 . . . .6E 22
Houndsditch EC3 . . . .7H 9 (6E 84)
Houndsfield Rd. N9 . . . .7C 24
HOUNSLOW 3F 113

Hounslow and District Indoor Bowls Club
...............................2D 112
Hounslow Av. TW3: Houn 5F 113
Hounslow Bus. Pk. TW3: Houn ...4E 112
Hounslow Cen. TW3: Houn 3F 113
Hounslow Gdns. TW3: Houn 5F 113
Hounslow Heath Golf Course 5A 112
Hounslow Heath Nature Reserve ...6C 112
Hounslow Rd. TW2: Whitt 6F 113
  TW13: Hanw 4B 130
  TW14: Felt 1K 129
Hounslow Urban Farm 5J 111
HOUNSLOW WEST 3C 112
Household Cavalry Mus., The
  Whitehall 5D 12 (1H 101)
Houseman Way SE5 ....7D 102
House Mill, The 3E 86
Houses of Parliament 1F 19 (3J 101)
Houston Bus. Pk.
  UB4: Yead 1A 94
Houston Pl. KT10: Esh 7J 149
Houston Rd. KT6: Surb 6B 150
  SE23 ....2A 140
Houstoun Ct. TW5: Hest 7D 94
Hove Av. E17 ....5B 50
Hoveden Rd. NW2 ....5G 63
Hove Gdns. SM1: Sutt 1K 165
Hove St. SE15 ....7J 103
  (off Culmore Rd.)
Hoveton Rd. SE28 ....6C 90
Hoveton Way IG6: Ilf 1F 53
Howard Av. DA5: Bexl 1C 144
Howard Bldg. SW8 ....7J 17 (6F 101)
Howard Cl. N11 ....2K 31
  NW2 ....4G 63
  TW12: Hamp 7G 131
  TW16: Sun 6H 129
  W3 ....6H 79
  WD23: B Hea 1D 26
Howard Ct. IG11: Bark 1H 89
Howard Ho. E16 ....1K 105
  (off Wesley Av.)
  SE8 ....6B 104
  (off Evelyn St.)
  SW1 ....6B 18
  (off Dolphin Sq.)
  SW9 ....3B 120
  (off Barrington Rd.)
  W1 ....4K 5
  (off Cleveland St.)
Howard M. N5 ....4B 66
Howard Rd. BR1: Brom 7J 141
  E6 ....2D 88
  E11 ....3G 69
  E17 ....3C 50
  HA7: Stan 1D 42
  IG1: Ilf 4F 71
  IG11: Bark 1H 89
  KT3: N Mald 3A 152
  KT5: Surb 6F 151
  N15 ....6E 48
  N16 ....4D 66
  NW2 ....4F 63
  SE20 ....1J 157
  SE25 ....5G 157
  TW7: Isle 3K 113
  UB1: S'hall 6F 77
Howards Cl. HA5: Pinn 2K 39
Howards Crest Cl. BR3: Beck ...2E 158
Howard's La. SW15 ....4D 116
Howards Rd. E13 ....3J 87
Howard St. KT7: T Ditt 7B 150
Howard Wlk. N2 ....4A 46
Howard Way EN5: Barn 5A 20
Howarth Rd. SE2 ....5A 108
Howberry Cl. HA8: Edg 6J 27
Howberry Rd. CR7: Thor H ...1D 156
  HA7: Stan 6J 27
  HA8: Edg 6J 27
Howbury Rd. SE15 ....3J 121
Howcroft Cres. N3 ....7D 85

Howcroft Ho. E3 ....3B 86
  (off Benworth St.)
Howcroft La. UB6: G'frd 3H 77
Howden Cl. SE28 ....7D 90
Howden Rd. SE25 ....2F 157
Howden St. SE15 ....3G 121
Howe Cl. RM7: Mawney 1G 55
Howell Cl. RM6: Chad H 5D 54
Howell Ct. E10 ....7D 50
Howell Wlk. SE1 ....4B 102
Howerd Way SE18 ....1C 124
  (not continuous)
Howes Cl. N3 ....3J 45
Howeth Ct. N11 ....6J 31
  (off Ribblesdale Av.)
Howfield Pl. N17 ....3F 49
Howgate Rd. SW14 ....3K 115
Howick Pl. SW1 ......2B 18 (3G 101)
Howie St. SW11 ....7C 100
Howitt Cl. N16 ....4E 66
  NW3 ....6C 64
Howitt Rd. NW3 ....6C 64
Howland Est. SE16 ....3J 103
Howland Ho. SW16 ....3J 137
Howland M. E. W1 ....5B 6 (5G 83)
Howland St. W1 ......5A 6 (5G 83)
Howland Way SE16 ....2A 104
Howlett Apartments N1 ......7J 65
  (off Caledonian Rd.)
Howletts La. HA4: Ruis 5E 38
Howlett's Rd. SE24 ....6C 120
Howley Pl. W2 ....5A 4 (5A 82)
Howley Rd. CR0: C'don 3B 168
Howsman Rd. SW13 ....6C 98
Howson Rd. SE4 ....4A 122
Howson Ter. TW10: Rich 6E 114
How's St. E2 ....2F 85
Howton Pl. WD23: B Hea 1C 26
HOXTON 2E 84
Hoxton Hall Theatre 2E 84
  (off Hoxton St.)
Hoxton Mkt. N1 ....2G 9
Hoxton Sq. N1 ....2G 9 (3E 84)
Hoxton St. N1 ....2H 9 (1E 84)
Hoylake Cres. UB10: Ick 2C 56
Hoylake Gdns. CR4: Mitc 3G 155
  HA4: Ruis 1K 57
Hoylake Rd. W3 ....6A 80
Hoyland Cl. SE15 ....7H 103
Hoyle Rd. SW17 ....5C 136
Hoy St. E16 ....6H 87
HQS Wellington 3J 13
Hub, The
  Westminster 1F 5 (2D 82)
Hubbard Ct. IG10: Lough 1H 37
Hubbard Dr. KT9: Chess 6D 162
Hubbard Ho. SW10 ....7B 100
  (off World's End Pas.)
Hubbard Rd. SE27 ....4C 138
Hubbards Cl. UB8: Hil 6D 74
Hubbard St. E15 ....1G 87
Hubbinet Ind. Est. RM7: Mawney ...3J 55
Huberd Ho. SE1 ....7F 15
  (off Manciple St.)
Hubert Gro. SW9 ....3J 119
Hubert Ho. NW8 ....4C 4
  (off Ashbridge St.)
Hubert Rd. E6 ....3B 88
Hucknall Ct. NW8 ....3A 4
  (off Cunningham Pl.)
Huddart St. E3 ....5B 86
  (not continuous)
Huddleston Cl. E2 ....2J 85
Huddlestone Rd. E7 ....4H 69
  NW2 ....6D 62
Huddleston Rd. N7 ....3G 65
Hudson NW9 ....4C 44
  (off Five Acre)
Hudson Apartments N8 ......3K 47
Hudson Bldg. E1 ....6K 9
  (off Chicksand St.)

Hudson Cl. E15 ....1J 87
  W12 ....7D 80
Hudson Ct. E14 ....5C 104
  (off Maritime Quay)
Hudson Gdns. BR6: Chels ...6K 173
Hudson Ho. SW10 ....7A 100
  (off Hortensia Rd.)
  W11 ....6G 81
  (off Ladbroke Gro.)
Hudson Pl. SE18 ....5G 107
Hudson Rd. DA7: Bex 2F 127
  UB3: Harl 6F 93
Hudson's Pl. SW1 ...3A 18 (4F 101)
Hudson Way N9 ....3D 34
  NW2 ....3F 63
Huggin Cl. EC4 ....2D 14
Huggin Hill EC4 ......2C 14 (7C 84)
Huggins Ho. E3 ....3C 86
  (off Alfred St.)
Huggins Pl. SW2 ....1K 137
Hughan Rd. E15 ....5F 69
Hugh Astor Ct. SE1 ....7B 14
  (off Keyworth St.)
Hugh Clark Ho. W13 ....1A 96
  (off Singapore Rd.)
Hugh Cubitt Ho. N1 ....2K 83
  (off Collier St.)
Hugh Dalton Av. SW6 ......6H 99
Hughenden Av. HA3: Kenton ...5B 42
Hughenden Gdns. UB5: N'olt ...3A 76
  (not continuous)
Hughenden Ho. NW8 ....3C 4
Hughenden Rd. KT4: Wor Pk ...7C 152
Hughendon EN5: New Bar 4E 20
Hughendon Ct. UB3: Hayes ...7H 75
  (off Chamberlain Cl.)
Hughenden Ter. E15 ....4E 68
Hughes Cl. N12 ....5F 31
Hughes Cl. N7 ....5H 65
Hughes Ho. E2 ....3K 85
  (off Sceptre Ho.)
  E3 ....3C 86
  (off Trevithick Way)
  SE5 ....1C 120
  (off Flodden Rd.)
  SE8 ....6C 104
  (off Benbow St.)
  SE17 ....4B 102
  (off Peacock St.)
Hughes Mans. E1 ....4G 85
Hughes Rd. TW15: Ashf 7E 128
  UB3: Hayes 7K 75
Hughes Ter. SW9 ....3B 120
  (off Styles Gdns.)
Hughes Wlk. CR0: C'don 7C 156
Hugh Gaitskell Cl. SW6 ......6H 99
Hugh Gaitskell Ho. N16 ......2F 67
Hugh Herland Ho. KT1: King T ...3E 150
Hugh M. SW1 ....4K 17 (4F 101)
Hugh Platt Ho. E2 ....2H 85
  (off Patriot Sq.)
Hugh St. SW1 ....4K 17 (4F 101)
Hugo Ho. SW1 ....1F 17
  (off Sloane St.)
Hugon Rd. SW6 ....3K 117
Hugo Rd. N19 ....5A 65
Huguenot Pl. E1 .....5K 9 (5F 85)
  SW18 ....5A 118
Huguenot Sq. SE15 ....3H 121
Hullbridge M. N1 ....1D 84
Hull Cl. SE16 ....2K 103
Hull Pl. E16 ....1G 107
Hull St. EC1 ....2C 8 (3C 84)
Hulme Pl. SE1 ....7D 14 (2C 102)
Hulse Av. IG11: Bark 6H 71
  RM7: Mawney 1H 55
Hult International Studios ...6G 85
  (off Alder St.)
Hult Twr. E1 ....6G 85
  (off Alder St.)
Hulverston Cl. SM2: Sutt ...7K 165

Humber Cl. UB7: W Dray 1A 92
Humber Ct. W7 ....6H 77
  (off Hobbayne Rd.)
Humber Dr. W10 ....4F 81
Humber Rd. NW2 ....2D 62
  SE3 ....6H 105
Humberstone Rd. E13 ......3A 88
Humberton Cl. E9 ....5A 68
Humber Trad. Est. NW2 ......2D 62
Humbolt Rd. W6 ....6G 99
Hume Ct. N1 ....7B 66
  (off Hawes St.)
Hume Ho. W11 ....1F 99
  (off Queensdale Cres.)
Humes Av. W7 ....3J 95
Hume Ter. E16 ....5K 87
Hume Way HA4: Ruis 6J 39
Humphrey Cl. IG5: Ilf 1D 52
Humphrey St. SE1 ....5F 103
Humphries Cl.
  RM9: Dag 4F 73
Hundred Acre NW9 ....2B 44
Hungerdown E4 ....1K 35
Hungerford Ho. SW1 ......7B 18
  (off Churchill Gdns.)
Hungerford La. WC2 ....4F 13
  (not continuous)
Hungerford Rd. N7 ....6H 65
Hungerford St. E1 ....6H 85
Hunsdon Cl. RM9: Dag 6E 72
Hunsdon Rd. SE14 ....7K 103
Hunslett St. E2 ....3J 85
Hunstanton Ho. NW1 ......5D 4
  (off Cosway St.)
Hunston Rd. SM4: Mord 1K 165
Hunt Cl. W11 ....1F 99
Hunt Ct. N14 ....7A 22
  RM7: Rush G 6K 55
  (off Union Rd.)
  UB5: N'olt 2B 76
  (off Gallery Gdns.)
Hunter Cl. SE1 ....3D 102
  SM6: Wall 7J 167
  SW12 ....1E 136
Hunter Ho. SE1 ....7B 14
  (off King James St.)
  SW5 ....5J 99
  (off Old Brompton Rd.)
  SW8 ....7H 101
  (off Fount St.)
  TW13: Felt 1J 129
  (off Hazel Gro.)
  WC1 ....3F 7
  (off Hunter St.)
Hunterian Mus., The 7H 7
  (off Portugal St.)
Hunter Lodge W9 ....5J 81
  (off Admiral Wlk.)
Hunter Rd. CR7: Thor H 3D 156
  IG1: Ilf 5F 71
  SW20 ....1E 152
Hunters Cl. DA5: Bexl 3K 145
Hunter's Way CR0: C'don 4E 168
Hunters Ct. TW9: Rich 5D 114
Hunters Gro. BR6: Farnb 4G 173
  HA3: Kenton 4C 42
  UB3: Hayes 1J 93
Hunters Hall Rd. RM10: Dag ...4G 73
Hunters Hill HA4: Ruis 3A 58
Hunters Mdw. SE19 ....4E 138
Hunters Rd. KT9: Chess 3E 162
Hunters Sq. RM10: Dag 4G 73
Hunter St. WC1 ....3F 7 (4J 83)
Hunters Way CR0: C'don 4E 168
Hunters Way EN2: Enf 1F 23
Hunter Wlk. E13 ....2J 87
Huntingdon Cl. CR4: Mitc ...3J 155
  UB5: N'olt 6E 58
Huntingdon Gdns. KT4: Wor Pk ...3E 164
  W4 ....7J 97
Huntingdon Rd. N2 ....3C 46
  N9 ....2D 34

Huntingdon St. E16 . . . . .6H 87
  N1 . . . . .7K 65
Huntingfield CR0: Sels 7B 170
Huntingfield Rd. SW15 . . . . . . .4C 116
Hunting Ga. Cl. EN2: Enf 3F 23
Hunting Ga. Dr. KT9: Chess 7E 162
Hunting Ga. M. SM1: Sutt 3K 165
  TW2: Twick 1J 131
Hunting Pl. TW5: Hest 6D 94
Huntings Farm IG1: Ilf 2J 71
Huntings Rd. RM10: Dag 6G 73
Huntington Cl. DA5: Bexl 1H 145
Huntley Cl. TW19: Stanw 7A 110
Huntley St. WC1 . . . . . 4B 6 (4G 83)
Huntley Way SW20 . . . . .2C 152
Huntloe Ho. SE14 . . . . .1J 121
  (off Kender St.)
Huntly Dr. N3 . . . . .6D 30
Huntly Rd. SE25 . . . . .4E 156
Hunton St. E1 . . . . .4K 9 (5G 85)
Hunt Rd. UB2: S'hall 3E 94
Hunt's Cl. SE3 . . . . .2J 123
Hunt's Ct. WC2 . . . . . .3D 12 (7H 83)
Huntshaw Ho. E3 . . . . .3D 86
  (off Devons Rd.)
Hunts La. E15 . . . . .2E 86
Huntsmans Cl. TW13: Felt 4K 129
Huntsman St. SE17 . . . . .4E 102
Hunts Mead EN3: Enf H 3E 24
Hunts Mead Cl. BR7: Chst 7D 142
Huntsmoor Rd. KT19: Ewe 5K 163
Huntspill St. SW17 . . . . .3A 136
Hunts Slip Rd. SE21 . . . . .3E 138
Huntsworth M. NW1 . . . . 3E 4 (4D 82)
Hurdwick Ho. NW1 . . . . .2G 83
  (off Harrington Sq.)
Hurdwick Pl. NW1 . . . . .2G 83
  (off Hampstead Rd.)
Hurleston Ho. SE8 . . . . .5B 104
Hurley Ct. SW17 . . . . .6E 136
  (off Mitcham Rd.)
  W5 . . . . .6C 78
Hurley Cres. SE16 . . . . .2K 103
Hurley Ho. SE11 . . . . .4K 19 (4B 102)
  UB7: W Dray 2B 92
  (off Park Lodge Av.)
Hurley Rd. UB6: G'frd 6F 77
HURLINGHAM 3K 117
Hurlingham Bus. Pk. SW6 . . . . .3J 117
Hurlingham Club, The 3J 117
Hurlingham Ct. SW6 . . . . .3H 117
Hurlingham Gdns. SW6 . . . . . . .3H 117
Hurlingham Pk. 2H 117
Hurlingham Retail Pk. SW6 . . . . .3K 117
Hurlingham Rd. DA7: Bex 7F 109
  SW6 . . . . .2H 117
Hurlingham Sq. SW6 . . . . .3J 117
Hurlingham Yacht Club 3G 117
Hurlock St. N5 . . . . .3B 66
Hurlstone Rd. SE25 . . . . .5E 156
Hurn Cl. TW4: Houn 2B 112
Hurn Cl. Rd. TW4: Houn 2B 112
Huron Cl. BR6: Chels 6J 173
Huron Rd. SW17 . . . . .2E 136
Hurren Cl. SE3 . . . . .3G 123
Hurricane Rd. SM6: Wall 7J 167
Hurricane Trad. Cen. NW9 . . . . . .1C 44
Hurry Cl. E15 . . . . .7G 69
Hurst Av. E4 . . . . .4H 35
  N6 . . . . .6G 47
Hurstbourne KT10: Clay 6A 162
Hurstbourne Gdns. IG11: Bark . . .6J 71
Hurstbourne Ho. SW15 . . . . . . .6B 116
  (off Tangley Gro.)
Hurstbourne Rd. SE23 . . . . .1A 140
Hurst Cl. BR2: Hayes 1H 171
  E4 . . . . .3H 35
  KT9: Chess 5G 163
  NW11 . . . . .6K 45
  UB5: N'olt 6D 58
Hurstcombe IG9: Buck H 2D 36

Hurst Ct. DA15: Sidc 2A 144
  E6 . . . . .5B 88
  (off Tollgate Rd.)
  IG8: Wfd G 6E 36
  (off Snakes La. W.)
Hurstcourt Rd. SM1: Sutt 2K 165
Hurstdene Av. BR2: Hayes 1H 171
Hurstdene Gdns. N15 . . . . .7E 48
Hurstfield BR2: Brom 5J 159
Hurstfield Cres. UB4: Hayes 4G 75
Hurstfield Rd. KT8: W Mole 3E 148
Hurst Gro. KT12: Walt T 7H 147
Hurst Ho. WC1 . . . . .1H 7
  (off Penton Ri.)
Hurst La. KT8: E Mos 4G 149
  SE2 . . . . .5D 108
Hurst La. Est. SE2 . . . . .5D 108
Hurstleigh Gdns. IG5: Ilf 1D 52
Hurstmead Ct. HA8: Edg 4C 28
HURST PARK 2G 149
Hurst Pl. HA6: Nwood 1D 38
Hurst Pool 3F 149
Hurst Ri. EN5: New Bar 3D 20
Hurst Rd. CR0: C'don 5D 168
  DA5: Bexl 1D 144
  DA8: Erith 1J 127
  DA15: Bexl, Sidc 2A 144
  E17 . . . . .3D 50
  IG9: Buck H 1G 37
  KT8: W Mole, E Mos 3F 149
  KT12: Walt T 5A 148
  N21 . . . . .1F 33
Hurst Springs DA5: Bexl 1E 144
Hurst St. SE24 . . . . .6B 120
Hurstview Grange CR2: S Croy . . .7B 168
Hurst Vw. Rd. CR2: S Croy 7E 168
Hurst Way CR2: S Croy 6E 168
Hurstway Rd. W11 . . . . .7F 81
  (off Hurstway Wlk.)
Hurstway Wlk. W11 . . . . .7F 81
Hurstwood Av. DA5: Bexl 1E 144
  E18 . . . . .4K 51
Hurstwood Ct. N12 . . . . .6H 31
  NW11 . . . . .4H 45
  (off Finchley Rd.)
Hurstwood Dr. BR1: Brom 3D 160
Hurstwood Rd. NW11 . . . . .4G 45
Hurtwood Rd. KT12: Walt T 7D 148
Husborne Ho. SE8 . . . . .4A 104
  (off Chilton Gro.)
Huson Cl. NW3 . . . . .7C 64
Hussain Cl. HA1: Harr 4K 59
Hussars Cl. TW4: Houn 3C 112
Husseywell Cres. BR2: Hayes 1J 171
Hutchings St. E14 . . . . .2C 104
Hutchings Wlk. NW11 . . . . .4K 45
Hutchings Wharf E14 . . . . .2C 104
  (off Hutchings St.)
Hutchins Cl. E15 . . . . .7E 68
Hutchinson Ct. RM6: Chad H 4D 54
Hutchinson Ho. NW3 . . . . .7D 64
  SE14 . . . . .7J 103
Hutchinson Ter. HA9: Wemb 3D 60
Hutchins Rd. SE28 . . . . .7A 90
Hutton Cl. IG8: Wfd G 6E 36
  UB6: G'frd 5H 59
Hutton Ct. N4 . . . . .1K 65
  (off Victoria Rd.)
  N9 . . . . .7D 24
  (off Tramway Av.)
  W5 . . . . .5B 78
Hutton Gdns. HA3: Hrw W 7B 26
Hutton Gro. N12 . . . . .5E 30
Hutton La. HA3: Hrw W 7B 26
Hutton M. SW15 . . . . .5D 116
Hutton Row HA8: Edg 7D 28
Hutton St. EC4 . . . . . .2K 13 (6B 84)
Hutton Wlk. HA3: Hrw W 7B 26
Huxbear St. SE4 . . . . .5B 122
Huxley Cl. UB5: N'olt 2C 76
  UB8: Cowl 4A 74

Huxley Dr. RM6: Chad H 7B 54
Huxley Gdns. NW10 . . . . .3F 79
Huxley Ho. NW8 . . . . .4B 4
  (off Fisherton St.)
Huxley Pde. N18 . . . . .5J 33
Huxley Pl. N13 . . . . .3G 33
Huxley Rd. DA16: Well 3K 125
  E10 . . . . .2E 68
  N18 . . . . .4J 33
Huxley Sayze N18 . . . . .5J 33
Huxley Sth. N18 . . . . .5J 33
Huxley St. W10 . . . . .3G 81
Hyacinth Cl. IG1: Ilf 6F 71
  TW12: Hamp 6E 130
Hyacinth Dr. UB10: Uxb 7A 56
Hyacinth Ho. E17 . . . . .3D 50
  (off Vine St.)
Hyacinth Rd. SW15 . . . . .1C 134
Hybrid Ho. W3 . . . . .1A 98
HYDE, THE 5B 44
Hyde, The NW9 . . . . .4A 44
  (not continuous)
Hyde Cl. E13 . . . . .2J 87
  EN5: Barn 3C 20
  TW15: Ashf 6G 129
Hyde Cl. N20 . . . . .3G 31
Hyde Cres. NW9 . . . . .5A 44
Hyde Est. Rd. NW9 . . . . .5B 44
Hyde Farm M. SW12 . . . . .1H 137
Hydefield Cl. N21 . . . . .1J 33
Hydefield Ct. N9 . . . . .2K 33
Hyde Ho. E3 . . . . .5C 86
  (off Furze St.)
  TW3: Houn 3G 113
  UB8: Uxb 6A 56
  W13 . . . . .1A 96
  (off Singapore Rd.)
Hyde Ind. Est., The NW9 . . . . . . .5B 44
Hyde La. SW11 . . . . .1C 118
Hyde Pk. 4D 10 (1D 100)
Hyde Pk. Av. N21 . . . . .2H 33
HYDE PARK CORNER 2F 101
Hyde Pk. Cnr. W1 . . . . .6H 11 (2E 100)
Hyde Pk. Cres. W2 . . . . .1C 10 (6C 82)
Hyde Pk. Gdns. N21 . . . . .1H 33
  W2 . . . . .2B 10 (7B 82)
  (not continuous)
Hyde Pk. Gdns. M. W2 . . .2B 10 (7B 82)
Hyde Pk. Ga. SW7 . . . . .2A 100
  (not continuous)
Hyde Pk. Ga. M. SW7 . . . . .2A 100
Hyde Pk. Mans. NW1 . . . . .6C 4
  (off Cabbell St.)
Hyde Pk. Pl. W2 . . . . . .2D 10 (7C 82)
Hyde Pk. Sq. W2 . . . . . .1C 10 (6C 82)
Hyde Pk. Sq. M. W2 . . . . .1C 10
Hyde Pk. St. W2 . . . . . .1C 10 (6C 82)
Hyde Pk. Towers W2 . . . . .7A 82
Hyderabad Way E15 . . . . .7G 69
Hyde Rd. DA7: Bex 2F 127
  N1 . . . . .1E 84
  TW10: Rich 5F 115
Hydeside Gdns. N9 . . . . .2A 34
Hyde's Pl. N1 . . . . .7B 66
Hyde St. SE8 . . . . .6C 104
Hyde Ter. TW15: Ashf 6G 129
Hydethorpe Av. N9 . . . . .2A 34
Hydethorpe Rd. SW12 . . . . .1G 137
Hyde Va. SE10 . . . . .7E 104
Hyde Wlk. SM4: Mord 7J 153
Hyde Way N9 . . . . .2A 34
  UB3: Harl 4H 93
Hydon Ct. N11 . . . . .5J 31
Hydra Bldg., The EC1 . . . . .2K 7
Hylands Rd. E17 . . . . .2F 51
Hylton St. SE18 . . . . .4K 107
Hyndewood SE23 . . . . .3K 139
Hyndman Ho. RM10: Dag 3G 73
  (off Kershaw Rd.)
Hyndman St. SE15 . . . . .6H 103
Hynton Rd. RM8: Dag 2C 72

Hyperion Cl. E16 . . . . .5J 87
  (off Robertson Rd.)
Hyperion Ho. E3 . . . . .2A 86
  (off Arbery Rd.)
  SW2 . . . . .6K 119
Hyrstdene CR2: S Croy 4B 168
Hyson Rd. SE16 . . . . .5H 103
Hythe Av. DA7: Bex 7E 108
Hythe Cl. N18 . . . . .4B 34
Hythe Ho. SE16 . . . . .2J 103
  (off Swan Rd.)
  W6 . . . . .4E 98
  (off Shepherd's Bush Rd.)
Hythe Rd. CR7: Thor H 2D 156
  KT8: Surb 6E 150
  NW10 . . . . .3B 80
Hythe Rd. Ind. Est. NW10 . . . . . .3C 80

I

Ian Bowater Ct. N1 . . . . .1F 9
  (off East Rd.)
Ian Ct. SE23 . . . . .2J 139
Ian Sq. EN3: Enf H 1E 24
Ibberton Ho. SW8 . . . . .7K 101
  (off Meadow Rd.)
  W14 . . . . .3G 99
  (off Russell Rd.)
Ibbotson Av. E16 . . . . .6H 87
Ibbott St. E1 . . . . .4J 85
Iberia Ho. N19 . . . . .7H 47
Iberian Av. SM6: Bedd 4H 167
Ibex Ho. E15 . . . . .5G 69
  (off Forest La.)
Ibis Ct. BR3: Beck 1F 159
  (off Albemarle Rd.)
  SE8 . . . . .6B 104
  (off Edward Pl.)
Ibis La. W4 . . . . .1J 115
Ibis Way UB4: Yead 6B 76
Ibrox Ct. IG9: Buck H 2F 37
Ibscott Cl. RM10: Dag 6J 73
Ibsley Gdns. SW15 . . . . .1C 134
Ibsley Way EN4: Cockf 5H 21
ICA Cinema 4D 12
  (within ICA)
Icarus Ho. E3 . . . . .3B 86
  (off British St.)
ICA Theatre 4D 12
  (within ICA)
Iceland Rd. E3 . . . . .1C 86
Iceland Wharf SE16 . . . . .4A 104
Iceni Ct. E3 . . . . .1B 86
  (off Parnell Rd.)
  IG9: Buck H 1E 36
Ice Wharf N1 . . . . .2J 83
Ice Wharf Marina N1 . . . . .2J 83
  (off New Wharf Rd.)
Ice Works, The NW1 . . . . .7F 65
  (off Jamestown Rd.)
Ickburgh Est. E5 . . . . .2H 67
Ickburgh Rd. E5 . . . . .3H 67
ICKENHAM 3D 56
Ickenham Cl. HA4: Ruis 2F 57
Ickenham Grn. UB10: Ick 1D 56
Ickenham Rd. HA4: Ruis 2E 56
Ickleton Rd. SE9 . . . . .4C 142
Icknield Dr. IG2: Ilf 5F 53
Icknield Ho. SW3 . . . . .5D 16
  (off Cale St.)
Ickworth Pk. Rd. E17 . . . . .4A 50
Icon Apartments SE1 . . . . .7G 15
  (off Cluny Pl.)
Icona Point E15 . . . . .1E 86
  (off Warton Rd.)
Iconia Ho.
  BR2: Brom 4A 160
Idaho Bldg. SE13 . . . . .1D 122
  (off Deal's Gateway)
Ida Rd. N15 . . . . .4D 48

Ida St. E14 6E 86
(not continuous)
Ide Mans. *E1* *7K 85*
(off Cable St.)
Iden Cl. BR2: Brom 3G 159
Idlecombe Rd. SW17 6E 136
Idmiston Rd. E15 4H 69
KT4: Wor Pk 7B 152
SE27 3C 138
Idmiston Sq. KT4: Wor Pk 7B 152
Idol La. EC3 3G 15 (7E 84)
Idonia St. SE8 7C 104
Iffley Cl. UB8: Uxb 7A 56
Iffley Rd. W6 3D 98
Ifield Ho. *SE17* *5E 102*
(off Madron St.)
Ifield Rd. SW10 6K 99
Ifor Evans Pl. E1 4K 85
Ightham Ho. *BR3: Beck* *7B 140*
(off Bethersden Cl.)
SE17 *4E 102*
(off Beckway St.)
Ightham Rd. DA8: Erith 7G 109
Ikon Ho. *E1* *7J 85*
(off Devonport St.)
Ilbert St. W10 3F 81
Ilchester Gdns. W2 7K 81
Ilchester Mans. *W8* *3J 99*
(off Abingdon Rd.)
Ilchester Pl. W14 3H 99
Ilchester Rd. RM8: Dag 5B 72
Ildersly Gro. SE21 2D 138
Ilderton Rd. SE15 5J 103
SE16 5J 103
Ilderton Wharf *SE15* *6J 103*
(off Rollins St.)
Ilex Cl. TW16: Sun 2A 148
Ilex Rd. NW10 6B 62
Ilex Way SW16 5A 138
ILFORD 3F 71
Ilford Bldg. IG1: Ilf 3E 70
Ilford Golf Course 1D 70
Ilford Hill IG1: Ilf 3E 70
Ilford Ho. *N1* *6D 66*
(off Dove Rd.)
Ilford La. IG1: Ilf 3F 71
Ilford Sports Club 2J 71
Ilfracombe Flats *SE1* *6D 14*
(off Marshalsea Rd.)
Ilfracombe Gdns. RM6: Chad H 7B 54
Ilfracombe Rd. BR1: Brom 3H 141
Iliffe St. SE17 5B 102
Iliffe Yd. *SE17* *5B 102*
(off Crampton St.)
Ilkeston Ct. *E5* *4K 67*
(off Overbury St.)
Ilkley Cl. SE19 6D 138
Ilkley Rd. E16 5A 88
Illingworth Cl. CR4: Mitc 3B 154
Illingworth Way EN1: Enf 5K 23
Illumina Ho. *SW18* *5J 117*
(off Broomhill Rd.)
Ilmington Rd. HA3: Kenton 6D 42
Ilminster Gdns. SW11 4C 118
Ilsley Ct. SW8 2G 119
Images IG2: Ilf 6E 52
Imani Mans. SW11 2B 118
IMAX (BFI) 5J 13 (1A 102)
Imber Cl. N14 7B 22
Imber Court 7H 149
Imber Ct. Trad. Est. KT8: E Mos 6H 149
Imber Cross KT7: T Ditt 6K 149
Imber Gro. KT10: Esh 7H 149
Imber Pk. Rd. KT10: Esh 7H 149
Imber St. N1 1D 84
Impact Bus. Pk.
UB6: G'frd 2B 78
Impact Ct. SE20 2H 157
Imperial Av. N16 4E 66
Imperial Cl. HA2: Harr 6E 40
NW2 5D 62
Imperial College London
Chelsea & Westminster Campus
6A 100
(within Chelsea & Westminster Hospital)
Royal Brompton Campus 6C 16
St Mary's *6B 82*
(off Norfolk Pl.)
Sth. Kensington Campus
1A 16 (3B 100)
Imperial Coll. Rd. SW7 2A 16 (3B 100)
Imperial Ct. HA2: Harr 7E 40
N6 6G 47
N20 3F 31
NW8 *2C 82*
(off Prince Albert Rd.)
SE11 6J 19 (5A 102)
Imperial Cres. SW6 2A 118
Imperial Dr. HA2: Harr 7E 40
Imperial Gdns. CR4: Mitc 3F 155
Imperial Gro. EN4: Had W 1E 20
Imperial Hgts. *E18* *1J 51*
(off Queen Mary Av.)
Imperial Ho. *E3* *3A 86*
(off Grove Rd.)
E14 *7B 86*
(off Victory Pl.)
Imperial M. E6 2B 88
SW9 *4K 119*
(off Brighton Ter.)
Imperial Pl. BR7: Chst 1E 160
Imperial Rd. N22 7D 32
SW6 1K 117
TW14: Felt 7G 111
Imperial Sq. SW6 1K 117
Imperial St. E3 3E 86
Imperial War Mus.
All Saints Annexe *3K 19*
(off Austral St.)
Lambeth Rd. 2K 19 (3A 102)
Imperial Way BR7: Chst 3G 143
CR0: Wadd 6K 167
HA3: Kenton 6E 42
Imperial Wharf *E2* *2H 85*
(off Darwen Pl.)
SW6 2A 118
Imperium Ho. *E1* *6H 85*
(off Cannon St. Rd.)
Imre Cl. W12 1D 98
Inca Dr. SE9 7F 125
Inca Ter. N15 3B 48
Inchmery Rd. SE6 2D 140
Inchwood BR4: Addtn 4D 170
Independence Ho. *SW19* *1B 154*
(off Chapter Way)
Independent Ind. Est. UB7: Yiew 1A 92
Independent Pl. E8 5F 67
Independents Rd. SE3 3H 123
Inderwick Rd. N8 5K 47
Indescon Ct. E14 2D 104
Indescon Sq. E14 2C 104
India Gdns.
UB5: N'olt 7A 58
India Ho. *WC2* *7K 83*
(off Aldwych)
Indiana Bldg. *SE13* *1C 122*
(off Deal's Gateway)
India Pl. WC2 2G 13
India St. EC3 1J 15 (6F 85)
India Way SW15 6C 116
W12 7D 80
IndigO2 1G 105
Indigo M. E14 7E 86
N16 3D 66
Indigo Wlk. N6 4D 46
Indus Ct. *SE15* *7F 103*
(off Amstel Ct.)
Indus Rd. SE7 7A 106
Infirmary Ct. SW3 7F 17
Inforum M. SE15 7G 103
Ingal Rd. E13 4J 87
Ingate Pl. SW8 1F 119
Ingatestone Rd. E12 1A 70
IG8: Wfd G 7E 36
SE25 4H 157
Ingelow Ho. *W8* *2K 99*
(off Holland St.)
Ingelow Rd. SW8 2F 119
Ingersoll Rd. EN3: Enf W 1D 24
W12 1D 98
Ingestre Pl. W1 1B 12 (6G 83)
Ingestre Rd. E7 4J 69
NW5 4F 65
Ingham Cl. CR2: Sels 7K 169
Ingham Rd. CR2: Sels 7J 169
NW6 4J 63
Inglebert St. EC1 1J 7 (3A 84)
Ingleborough St. SW9 2A 120
Ingleby Dr. HA1: Harr 3H 59
Ingleby Rd. IG1: Ilf 1F 71
N7 3J 65
RM10: Dag 6H 73
Ingleby Way BR7: Chst 5E 142
SM6: Wall 7H 167
Ingle Cl. HA5: Pinn 3C 40
Ingledew Rd. SE18 5H 107
Inglefield Sq. *E1* *1H 103*
(off Prusom St.)
Inglehurst Gdns. IG4: Ilf 5D 52
Inglemere Rd. CR4: Mitc 7D 136
SE23 3K 139
Ingle M. EC1 1J 7 (3A 84)
Inglesham Wlk. E9 6B 68
Ingleside SL3: Poyle 4A 174
Ingleside Cl. BR3: Beck 7C 140
Ingleside Gro. SE3 6H 105
Inglethorpe St. SW6 1F 117
Ingleton Av. DA16: Well 5A 126
Ingleton Rd. N18 6B 34
SM5: Cars 7C 166
Ingleton St. SW9 2A 120
Ingleway N12 6G 31
Inglewood BR7: Chst 6H 143
CR0: Sels 7A 170
Inglewood Cl. E14 4C 104
Inglewood Copse BR1: Brom 2C 160
Inglewood Ct. BR1: Brom 7G 141
Inglewood M. KT6: Surb 1G 163
SE27 *5C 138*
(off Elder Rd.)
Inglewood Rd. DA7: Bex 4K 127
NW6 5J 63
Inglis Barracks NW7 6A 30
Inglis Rd. CR0: C'don 1F 169
W5 7F 79
Inglis St. SE5 1B 120
Inglis Way NW7 6A 30
Ingoldisthorpe Gro. SE15 6F 103
Ingot Twr. *E14* *5C 86*
(off Ursula Gould Way)
Ingram Av. NW11 7A 46
Ingram Cl. HA7: Stan 5H 27
SE11 3H 19 (4K 101)
Ingram Ct. CR0: C'don 1B 168
Ingram Ho. E3 1A 86
Ingram Rd. CR7: Thor H 1C 156
N2 4C 46
Ingram Way UB6: G'frd 1H 77
Ingrave Rd. RM1: Rom 4K 55
Ingrave St. SW11 3B 118
Ingrebourne Apartments SW6 3K 117
Ingrebourne Ct. E4 3J 35
Ingrebourne Ho. *BR1: Brom* *5F 141*
(off Brangbourne Rd.)
NW8 *5B 4*
(off Broadley St.)
Ingress St. W4 5A 98
Inigo Jones Rd. SE7 7C 106
Inigo Pl. WC2 2E 12
Ink Bldg. W10 5F 81
Inkerman Rd. NW5 6F 65
Inkerman Ter. *W8* *3J 99*
(off Allen St.)
Inks Grn. E4 5K 35
Inkster Ho. SW11 3C 118
Inkwell Cl. N12 3F 31
Ink Works Ct. *SE1* *2E 102*
(off Bell Yd. M.)
Inman Rd. NW10 1A 80
SW18 7A 118
Inmans Row IG8: Wfd G 4D 36
Inner Circ. NW1 2G 5 (3E 82)
Inner Ct. SW3 7C 16 (6C 100)
Innerd Ct. *CR0: C'don* *6C 156*
(off Harry Cl.)
Inner Pk. Rd. SW19 1F 135
Inner Ring E. TW6: H'row A 3D 110
Inner Ring W. TW6: H'row A 3C 110
Inner Temple La. EC4 1J 13
Innes Cl. SW20 2G 153
Innes Gdns. SW15 6D 116
Innes St. SE15 7E 102
Innes Yd. CR0: C'don 3C 168
Innis Ho. *SE17* *5E 102*
(off East St.)
Inniskilling Rd. E13 2A 88
Innova Ct. CR0: C'don 1E 168
Innova Pas. *E1* *3J 9*
(off Sclater St.)
Innovation Cen., The *E14* *2E 104*
(off Marsh Wall)
Innovation Cl. HA0: Wemb 1E 78
Inns of Court & City Yeomanry Mus.
6H 7 (5K 83)
Inskip Cl. E10 2D 68
Inskip Rd. RM8: Dag 1D 72
Insley Ho. *E3* *3D 86*
(off Bow Rd.)
Institute of Archaeology Collections
4H 83
Institute of Contemporary Arts 5D 12
Institute Pl. E8 5H 67
Integer Gdns. E11 7F 51
Interchange, The *NW1* *7F 65*
(off Camden Lock Pl.)
Interface Ho. *TW3: Houn* *3E 112*
(off Staines Rd.)
International Av. TW5: Cran 5A 94
International Bus. Pk. E15 1F 87
International Ho. *E1* *3K 15*
(off St Katharine's Way)
TW8: Bford *5E 96*
(off Gt. West Rd.)
INTERNATIONAL QUARTER, THE 6E 68
International Sq. *E20* *6E 68*
(within Westfield Stratford City Shop. Cen.)
International Trad. Est. UB2: S'hall 3K 93
International Way E20 6E 68
TW16: Sun 1G 147
INTU Bromley BR1: Brom 2J 159
Inverary Pl. SE18 6H 107
Inver Cl. E5 2J 67
Inverclyde Gdns. RM6: Chad H 4C 54
(not continuous)
Inver Ct. W2 6K 81
W6 3C 98
Inveresk Gdns. KT4: Wor Pk 3C 164
Inverforth Cl. NW3 2A 64
Inverforth Rd. N11 5A 32
Invergarry Ho. *NW6* *2K 81*
(off Carlton Vale)
Inverine Rd. SE7 5K 105
Invermead Cl. W6 3C 98
Invermore Pl. SE18 4G 107
Inverness Av. EN1: Enf 1K 23
Inverness Ct. SE6 1H 141
Inverness Gdns. W8 1K 99
Inverness M. E16 1G 107
W2 7K 81
Inverness Pl. W2 7K 81
Inverness Rd. KT4: Wor Pk 1F 165
N18 5C 34
TW3: Houn 4D 112
UB2: S'hall 4C 94

Inverness St.—Jacklin Grn.

Inverness St. NW1 . . . 1F **83**
Inverness Ter. W2 . . . 6K **81**
Inverton Rd. SE15 . . . 4K **121**
Invicta Cen., The IG11: Bark . . . 1A **90**
Invicta Cl. BR7: Chst . . . 5E **142**
E3 . . . 5C **86**
TW14: Felt . . . 1H **129**
Invicta Gro. UB5: N'olt . . . 3D **76**
Invicta Pde. DA14: Sidc . . . 4B **144**
Invicta Plaza SE1 . . . 4A **14** (1B **102**)
Invicta Rd. SE3 . . . 7J **105**
Inville Rd. SE17 . . . 5D **102**
(not continuous)
Inville Wlk. SE17 . . . 5D **102**
Invito IG2: Ilf . . . 6E **52**
Inwen Ct. SE8 . . . 5A **104**
(not continuous)
Inwood Av. TW3: Houn . . . 3G **113**
Inwood Bus. Pk. TW3: Houn . . . 4F **113**
Inwood Cl. CR0: C'don . . . 2A **170**
Inwood Ct. *NW1* . . . *7G* ***65***
(off Rochester Sq.)
Inwood Ho. *N1* . . . *1B* ***84***
(off Elliott's Pl.)
Inwood Rd. TW3: Houn . . . 4F **113**
Inworth St. SW11 . . . 2C **118**
Inworth Wlk. *N1* . . . *1C* ***84***
(off Popham St.)
IO Centre SE18 . . . 3G **107**
(not continuous)
Iona Cl. SE6 . . . 7C **122**
SM4: Mord . . . 7K **153**
Ion Ct. E2 . . . 2G **85**
Ionian Bldg. *E14* . . . *7A* ***86***
(off Narrow St.)
Ionian Ho. *E1* . . . *4K* ***85***
(off Duckett St.)
Ion Sq. E2 . . . 2G **85**
IO Trade Cen. CR0: Bedd . . . 4K **167**
Ipsden Bldgs. SE1 . . . 5K **13**
Ipswich Rd. SW17 . . . 6E **136**
Ira Ct. SE27 . . . 2B **138**
Ireland Cl. E6 . . . 5D **88**
Ireland Pl. N22 . . . 7D **32**
Ireland Yd. EC4 . . . 1B **14** (6B **84**)
Irene M. *W7* . . . *1K* ***95***
(off Uxbridge Rd.)
Irene Rd. BR6: Orp . . . 7K **161**
SW6 . . . 1J **117**
Ireton Cl. N10 . . . 7K **31**
Ireton Ho. *SW15* . . . *5G* ***117***
(off Stamford Sq.)
Ireton St. E3 . . . 4C **86**
Iris Av. DA5: Bexl . . . 5E **126**
Iris Cl. CR0: C'don . . . 1K **169**
E6 . . . 5C **88**
KT6: Surb . . . 7F **151**
N14 . . . 7C **22**
Iris Ct. *SE14* . . . *1J* ***121***
(off Briant St.)
Iris Cres. DA7: Bex . . . 6F **109**
Iris Gdns. KT7: T Ditt . . . 7J **149**
Iris M. TW4: Houn . . . 6E **112**
Iris Rd. KT19: Ewe . . . 5H **163**
Iris Wlk. HA8: Edg . . . 4D **28**
Iris Way E4 . . . 6G **35**
Irkdale Av. EN1: Enf . . . 1A **24**
Iron Bri. Cl. NW10 . . . 5A **62**
Ironbridge Cl. UB2: S'hall . . . 1G **95**
Iron Bri. Ho. NW1 . . . 7D **64**
Iron Bri. Rd. Nth. UB11: Stock P . . . 2C **92**
Iron Bri. Rd. Sth. UB7: W Dray . . . 2C **92**
Iron Mill Pl. SW18 . . . 6K **117**
Iron Mill Rd. SW18 . . . 6K **117**
Ironmonger La. EC2 . . . 1D **14** (6C **84**)
Ironmonger Pas. *EC1* . . . *2D* ***8***
(off Ironmonger Row)
Ironmonger Row EC1 . . . 2D **8** (3C **84**)
Ironmonger Row Baths . . . 2C 8
Ironmongers Pl. E14 . . . 4C **104**
Ironside Cl. SE16 . . . 2K **103**
Ironside Ct. CR2: S Croy . . . 6D **168**
TW11: Hamp W . . . 1C **150**
Ironside Ho. E9 . . . 4A **68**
Irons Way RM5: Col R . . . 1J **55**
Iron Works E3 . . . 1C **86**
Ironworks, The *N1* . . . *2J* ***83***
(off Albion Wlk.)
Irvine Av. HA3: Kenton . . . 3A **42**
Irvine Cl. E14 . . . 5D **86**
N20 . . . 2H **31**
Irvine Ct. *W1* . . . *4B* ***6***
(off Whitfield St.)
Irvine Ho. *N7* . . . *6K* ***65***
(off Caledonian Rd.)
Irvine Way BR6: Orp . . . 7K **161**
Irving Av. UB5: N'olt . . . 1B **76**
Irving Gro. SW9 . . . 2K **119**
Irving Ho. *SE17* . . . *5B* ***102***
(off Doddington Gro.)
Irving Mans. *W14* . . . *6G* ***99***
(off Queen's Club Gdns.)
Irving M. N1 . . . 6C **66**
Irving Rd. W14 . . . 3F **99**
Irving St. WC2 . . . 3D **12** (7H **83**)
Irving Way NW9 . . . 5C **44**
Irwell Ct. *W7* . . . *6H* ***77***
(off Hobbayne Rd.)
Irwell Est. SE16 . . . 3J **103**
Irwin Av. SE18 . . . 7J **107**
Irwin Cl. UB10: Ick . . . 3C **56**
Irwin Gdns. NW10 . . . 1D **80**
Isaac Way *SE1* . . . *6D* ***14***
(off Sanctuary St.)
Isabel Hill Cl. TW12: Hamp . . . 1F **149**
Isabella Cl. N14 . . . 7B **22**
Isabella Ct. *TW10: Rich* . . . *6F* ***115***
(off Kingsmead)
Isabella Dr. BR6: Farnb . . . 4G **173**
Isabella Ho. SE11 . . . 5K **19**
W6 . . . *5E* ***98***
(off Queen Caroline St.)
Isabella Pl. KT2: King T . . . 5F **133**
Isabella Plantation Garden . . . 3H 133
Isabella Rd. E9 . . . 5J **67**
Isabella St. SE1 . . . 5A **14** (1B **102**)
Isabel St. SW9 . . . 1K **119**
Isambard M. E14 . . . 3E **104**
Isambard Pl. SE16 . . . 1J **103**
Isel Way SE22 . . . 5E **120**
Isham Rd. SW16 . . . 2J **155**
Isis Cl. HA4: Ruis . . . 6E **38**
SW15 . . . 4E **116**
Isis Ct. W4 . . . 7H **97**
Isis Ho. N18 . . . 6A **34**
NW8 . . . *4B* ***4***
(off Church St. Est.)
SE20 . . . 7G **139**
Isis St. SW18 . . . 2A **136**
Island, The KT7: T Ditt . . . 6A **150**
UB7: Lford . . . 3D **174**
Island Apartments N1 . . . 1C **84**
Island Barn Reservoir Sailing Club
. . . 6F 149
Island Farm Av. KT8: W Mole . . . 5D **148**
Island Farm Rd. KT8: W Mole . . . 5D **148**
Island Ho. E3 . . . 3E **86**
Island Rd. CR4: Mitc . . . 7D **136**
SE16 . . . 4K **103**
Island Row E14 . . . 6B **86**
Isla Rd. SE18 . . . 6G **107**
Islay Gdns. TW4: Houn . . . 5B **112**
Islay Wlk. *N1* . . . *6C* ***66***
(off Douglas Rd. Sth.)
Isleden Ho. *N1* . . . *1C* ***84***
(off Prebend St.)
Isledon Rd. N7 . . . 3A **66**
ISLEDON VILLAGE . . . 3A 66
Islehurst Cl. BR7: Chst . . . 1E **160**
ISLE OF DOGS . . . 2D 104
ISLEWORTH . . . 3A 114
Isleworth Ait Nature Reserve . . . 3B 114
Isleworth Bus. Complex
TW7: Isle . . . 2K **113**
Isleworth Prom. TW1: Twick . . . 4B **114**
Isleworth Recreation Cen. . . . 4K 113
Isley Ct. SW8 . . . 2G **119**
ISLINGTON . . . 7B 66
Islington Bus. Cen. *N1* . . . *1C* ***84***
(off Coleman Flds.)
Islington Crematorium N2 . . . 1D **46**
Islington Ecology Cen., The . . . 3A 66
Islington Grn. N1 . . . 1B **84**
(not continuous)
Islington High St. N1 . . . 2A **84**
(not continuous)
Islington Mus. . . . 2A 8 (3B 84)
Islington Pk. M. N1 . . . 7B **66**
Islington Pk. St. N1 . . . 7A **66**
Islington Pl. N1 . . . 1A **84**
Islington Sq. N1 . . . 1B **84**
Islington Tennis Cen. . . . 6J 65
Islip Gdns. HA8: Edg . . . 7E **28**
UB5: N'olt . . . 7C **58**
Islip Mnr. Rd. UB5: N'olt . . . 7C **58**
Islip St. NW5 . . . 5G **65**
Ismailia Rd. E7 . . . 7K **69**
Isobel Ho. HA1: Harr . . . 5K **41**
Isobel Pl. N15 . . . 4F **49**
Isola Ct. *N1* . . . *1C* ***84***
(off Popham Rd.)
Isom Cl. E13 . . . 3K **87**
Issa Rd. TW3: Houn . . . 4D **112**
Issigonis Ho. *W3* . . . *1B* ***98***
(off Cowley Rd.)
Istra Ho. *E20* . . . *5E* ***68***
(off Logan Cl.)
Italia Conti Academy of Theatre Arts
Avondale . . . *3J 119*
(off Landor Rd.)
Itaska Cotts. WD23: B Hea . . . 1D **26**
Ithell Ct. HA0: Wemb . . . 5D **60**
Ivanhoe Cl. UB8: Cowl . . . 5A **74**
Ivanhoe Dr. HA3: Kenton . . . 3A **42**
Ivanhoe Ho. *E3* . . . *2A* ***86***
(off Grove Rd.)
Ivanhoe Rd. SE5 . . . 3F **121**
TW4: Houn . . . 3B **112**
Ivaro Cl. RM5: Col R . . . 1J **55**
Ivatt Pl. W14 . . . 5H **99**
Ivatt Way N17 . . . 3B **48**
Iveagh Av. NW10 . . . 2G **79**
Iveagh Cl. E9 . . . 1K **85**
HA6: Nwood . . . 1D **38**
NW10 . . . 2G **79**
Iveagh Ct. BR3: Beck . . . 3E **158**
E1 . . . 1J **15**
Iveagh Ho. SW9 . . . 2B **120**
SW10 . . . *7A* ***100***
(off King's Rd.)
Iveagh Ter. *NW10* . . . *2G* ***79***
(off Iveagh Av.)
Ivedon Rd. DA16: Well . . . 2C **126**
Ive Farm Cl. E10 . . . 2C **68**
Ive Farm La. E10 . . . 2C **68**
Iveley Rd. SW4 . . . 2G **119**
Ivere Dr. EN5: New Bar . . . 6E **20**
Iver Ho. *N1* . . . *1E* ***84***
(off Halcomb St.)
Iverhurst Cl. DA6: Bex . . . 5D **126**
Iverna Ct. W8 . . . 3J **99**
Iverna Gdns. TW14: Felt . . . 5F **111**
W8 . . . 3J **99**
Iverson Rd. NW6 . . . 6H **63**
Ivers Way CR0: New Ad . . . 7D **170**
Ives Rd. E16 . . . 5G **87**
Ives St. SW3 . . . 3D **16** (4C **100**)
Ivestor Ter. SE23 . . . 7J **121**
Ivimey St. E2 . . . 3G **85**
Ivinghoe Cl. EN1: Enf . . . 1K **23**
Ivinghoe Ho. N7 . . . 5H **65**
Ivinghoe Rd. RM8: Dag . . . 5B **72**
Ivo Pl. N19 . . . 3H **65**
Ivor Ct. N8 . . . 6J **47**
NW1 . . . *3E* ***4***
(off Gloucester Pl.)
Ivor Gro. SE9 . . . 1F **143**
Ivories, The *N1* . . . *7C* ***66***
(off Northampton St.)
Ivor Pl. NW1 . . . 4E **4** (4D **82**)
Ivor St. NW1 . . . 7G **65**
Ivory Ct. E18 . . . 1J **51**
TW13: Felt . . . 1J **129**
Ivorydown BR1: Brom . . . 4J **141**
Ivory Ho. E1 . . . 3K **15** (1F **103**)
Ivory Pl. *W11* . . . *7G* ***81***
(off Treadgold St.)
Ivory Sq. SW11 . . . 3A **118**
Ivybridge Cl. TW1: Twick . . . 7A **114**
UB8: Uxb . . . 3A **74**
Ivybridge Ct. *BR7: Chst* . . . *1E* ***160***
(off Old Hill)
NW1 . . . *7F* ***65***
(off Lewis St.)
Ivybridge La. WC2 . . . 3F **13** (7J **83**)
Ivy Bri. Retail Pk. TW7: Isle . . . 5K **113**
Ivychurch Cl. SE20 . . . 7J **139**
Ivychurch La. SE17 . . . 5F **103**
Ivy Cl. HA2: Harr . . . 4D **58**
HA5: Eastc . . . 7A **40**
TW16: Sun . . . 2A **148**
Ivy Cotts. E14 . . . 7E **86**
UB10: Hil . . . 3C **74**
Ivy Ct. *SE16* . . . *5G* ***103***
(off Argyle Way)
Ivy Cres. W4 . . . 4J **97**
Ivydale Rd. SE15 . . . 3K **121**
SM5: Cars . . . 2D **166**
Ivyday Gro. SW16 . . . 3K **137**
Ivydene KT8: W Mole . . . 5D **148**
Ivydene Cl. SM1: Sutt . . . 4A **166**
Ivydene Ct. *IG9: Buck H* . . . *2F* ***37***
(off Queen's Rd.)
Ivy Gdns. CR4: Mitc . . . 3H **155**
N8 . . . 6J **47**
Ivy Ho. Rd. UB10: Ick . . . 3D **56**
Ivyhouse Rd. RM9: Dag . . . 6D **72**
Ivy La. TW4: Houn . . . 4D **112**
Ivy Lodge *W11* . . . *1J* ***99***
(off Notting Hill Ga.)
Ivymount Rd. SE27 . . . 3A **138**
Ivy Rd. E16 . . . 6J **87**
E17 . . . 6C **50**
KT6: Surb . . . 1G **163**
N14 . . . 7B **22**
NW2 . . . 4E **62**
SE4 . . . 4B **122**
SW17 . . . 5C **136**
TW3: Houn . . . 4F **113**
Ivy St. N1 . . . 2E **84**
Ivy Wlk. HA6: Nwood . . . 1G **39**
RM9: Dag . . . 6E **72**
Ixworth Pl. SW3 . . . 5C **16** (5C **100**)
Izane Rd. DA6: Bex . . . 4F **127**

J

Jacana Ct. *E1* . . . *3K* ***15***
(off Star Pl.)
Jacaranda Cl. KT3: N Mald . . . 3A **152**
Jacaranda Gro. E8 . . . 7F **67**
Jackass La. BR2: Kes . . . 5K **171**
Jack Barnett Way N22 . . . 2K **47**
Jack Clow Rd. E15 . . . 2G **87**
Jack Cook Ho. IG11: Bark . . . 7F **71**
Jack Cornwell St. E12 . . . 4E **70**
Jack Dash Way E6 . . . 4C **88**
Jack Dimmer Cl. SW16 . . . 2G **155**
Jackets La. HA6: Nwood . . . 1D **38**
Jack Goodchild Way
KT1: King T . . . 3H **151**
Jack Jones Way RM9: Dag . . . 1F **91**
Jacklin Grn. IG8: Wfd G . . . 4D **36**

Jackman Ho. E1 . . . .1H 103
(off Watts St.)
Jackman M. NW2 . . . .3A 62
Jackman St. E8 . . . .1H 85
Jacks Farm Way E4 . . . .6K 35
Jackson & Joseph Bldg. E1 . . . .5K 9
(off Princelet St.)
Jackson Cl. E9 . . . .7J 67
UB10: Uxb 7A 56
Jackson Ct. E7 . . . .6K 69
Jackson Ho. N11 . . . .5B 32
Jackson Rd. BR2: Brom 2D 172
EN4: E Barn 6H 21
IG11: Bark 1H 89
N7 . . . .4K 65
UB10: Uxb 7A 56
Jacksons La. N6 . . . .7E 46
Jacksons Lane Theatre 6F 47
(off Archway Rd.)
Jackson St. SE18 . . . .6E 106
Jackson's Way CRO: C'don . . .3C 170
Jackson Way UB2: S'hall 2F 95
Jacks Pl. E1 . . . .5J 9
(off Corbet Pl.)
Jack the Ripper Mus. 7G 85
Jack Walker Ct. N5 . . . .4B 66
Jacob Ho. DA18: Erith 2D 108
(off Kale Rd.)
Jacobin Lodge N7 . . . .5J 65
Jacob Mans. E1 . . . .6H 85
(off Commercial Rd.)
Jacob M. HA7: Stan 2F 27
Jacobs Cl. RM10: Dag 4H 73
Jacobs Ct. E1 . . . .6G 85
(off Plumber's Row)
Jacobs Ho. E13 . . . .3A 88
(off New City Rd.)
Jacobs Island Ho. SE16 . . . .3F 103
(off Spa Rd.)
Jacobs Island Pier SE16 . . . .2G 103
(off Bermondsey Wall W.)
Jacobs M. SW15 . . . .4G 117
Jacob St. SE1 . . . .6K 15 (2G 103)
Jacob's Well M. W1 . . .6H 5 (5E 82)
Jacotts Ho. W10 . . . .4E 80
(off Sutton Way)
Jacqueline Cl. UB5: N'olt 1C 76
Jacqueline Creft Ter. N6 . . . .6E 46
(off Grange Rd.)
Jacqueline Ho. NW1 . . . .1D 82
(off Regent's Pk. Rd.)
Jacqueline Vs. E17 . . . .5E 50
(off Shernhall St.)
Jade Cl. E16 . . . .6B 88
NW2 . . . .7F 45
RM8: Dag 1C 72
Jade Ter. NW6 . . . .7A 64
Jaffe Rd. IG1: Ilf 1H 71
Jaffray Pl. SE27 . . . .4B 138
Jaffray Rd. BR2: Brom 4B 160
Jaggard Way SW12 . . . .7D 118
Jagger Ho. SW11 . . . .1D 118
(off Rosenau Rd.)
Jago Cl. SE18 . . . .6G 107
Jago Wlk. SE5 . . . .7D 102
Jake Russell Wlk. E16 . . . .7A 88
Jamaica Rd. CR7: Thor H 6B 156
SE1 . . . .7K 15 (2F 103)
SE16 . . . .7K 15 (2F 103)
Jamaica St. E1 . . . .5J 85
James Allens School Swimming Pool
. . . .5E 120
James Anderson Ct. E2 . . . .2E 84
(off Kingsland Rd.)
James Av. NW2 . . . .5E 62
RM8: Dag 1F 73
James Bedford Cl. HA5: Pinn 2A 40
James Boswell Cl. SW16 . . . .4K 137
James Brine Ho. E2 . . . .1K 9
(off Ravenscroft St.)

James Campbell Ho. E2 . . . .2J 85
(off Old Ford Rd.)
James Clavell Sq. SE18 . . . .3F 107
(off No 1 St.)
James Cl. E13 . . . .2J 87
NW11 . . . .6G 45
James Collins Cl. W9 . . . .4H 81
James Ct. HA6: N'wood 1H 39
N1 . . . .1C 84
(off Raynor Pl.)
NW9 . . . .2A 44
UB5: N'olt 2C 76
(off Church Rd.)
James Docherty Ho. E2 . . . .2H 85
(off Patriot Sq.)
James Dudson Ct. NW10 . . . .7J 61
James Est. CR4: Mitc 2D 154
James Gdns. N22 . . . .7G 33
James Hammett Ho. E2 . . . .1K 9
(off Ravenscroft St.)
James Hill Ho. W10 . . . .4G 81
(off Kensal Rd.)
James Ho. E1 . . . .4A 86
(off Solebay St.)
SE16 . . . .2K 103
(off Wolfe Cres.)
SW8 . . . .7J 101
(off Wyvil Rd.)
W10 . . . .4G 81
James Joyce Wlk. SE24 . . . .4B 120
James La. E10 . . . .7E 50
E11 . . . .7F 51
James Leal Cen.
Woodford 5G 37
James Lighthill Ho. WC1 . . . .1H 7
(off Penton Ri.)
James Lind Ho. SE8 . . . .4B 104
(off Grove St.)
James Middleton Ho. E2 . . . .3H 85
(off Middleton St.)
James Morgan M. N1 . . . .1C 84
James Newman Ct. SE9 . . . .3E 142
Jameson Cl. W3 . . . .2J 97
Jameson Ct. E2 . . . .2J 85
(off Russia La.)
Jameson Ho. SE11 . . . .5G 19
(off Glasshouse Wlk.)
Jameson Lodge N6 . . . .6G 47
Jameson St. W8 . . . .1J 99
James Pl. N17 . . . .1F 49
James Riley Point E15 . . . .1E 86
(off Carpenters Rd.)
James's Cotts. TW9: Kew 7G 97
James Stewart Ho. NW6 . . . .7H 63
James St. EN1: Enf 5A 24
IG11: Bark 7G 71
TW3: Houn 3H 113
W1 . . . .1H 11 (6E 82)
WC2 . . . .1F 13 (7J 83)
James Stroud Ho. SE17 . . . .5C 102
(off Walworth Pl.)
James Ter. SW14 . . . .3K 115
(off Church Path)
Jameston Lodge HA4: Ruis . . .1H 57
Jamestown Rd. NW1 . . . .1F 83
Jamestown Way E14 . . . .7F 87
James Voller Way E1 . . . .6J 85
James Yd. E4 . . . .6A 36
Jam Factory, The SE1 . . . .3E 102
(off Green Wlk.)
Jamieson Ho. TW4: Houn . . .6D 112
Jamilah Ho. E16 . . . .7E 88
(off University Way)
Jamuna Cl. E14 . . . .5A 86
Jane Austen Hall E16 . . . .1K 105
(off Wesley Av.)
Jane Austen Ho. SW1 . . . .6A 18
(off Churchill Gdns.)
Jane Seymour Ct. SE9 . . . .7H 125
Jane St. E1 . . . .6H 85
Janet Adegoke Swimming Pool 7C 80

Janet St. E14 . . . .3C 104
Janeway Pl. SE16 . . . .2H 103
Janeway St. SE16 . . . .2G 103
Janice M. IG1: Ilf 2F 71
Jansen Wlk. SW11 . . . .3B 118
Janson Cl. E15 . . . .5G 69
NW10 . . . .3A 62
Janson Rd. E15 . . . .5G 69
Jansons Rd. N15 . . . .3E 48
Japan Cres. N4 . . . .7K 47
Japan Rd. RM6: Chad H 6D 54
Jaquard Ct. E2 . . . .2J 85
(off Bishop's Way)
Jardine Rd. E1 . . . .7K 85
Jarman Ho. E1 . . . .5J 85
(off Jubilee St.)
SE16 . . . .4K 103
(off Hawkstone Rd.)
Jarret Ho. E3 . . . .3C 86
(off Bow Rd.)
Jarrett Cl. SW2 . . . .1B 138
Jarrow Cl. SM4: Mord 5K 153
Jarrow Rd. N17 . . . .4H 49
RM6: Chad H 6C 54
SE16 . . . .4J 103
Jarrow Way E9 . . . .4B 68
Jarvis Cl. EN5: Barn 5A 20
IG11: Bark 1H 89
Jarvis Ho. SE15 . . . .1G 121
(off Goldsmith Rd.)
Jarvis Rd. CR2: S Croy 6D 168
SE22 . . . .4E 120
Jashoda Ho. SE18 . . . .5E 106
(off Connaught M.)
Jasmin Cl. HA6: N'wood 1H 39
Jasmin Ct. SE12 . . . .6J 123
Jasmine Cl. BR6: Farnb 2F 173
IG1: Ilf 5F 71
UB1: S'hall 7C 76
Jasmine Gdns. CRO: C'don . . .3D 170
HA2: Harr 2E 58
Jasmine Gro. SE20 . . . .1H 157
Jasmine Ho. SW18 . . . .3A 118
Jasmine Rd. RM7: Rush G . . .2K 73
Jasmine Sq. E3 . . . .1B 86
(off Hawthorn Av.)
Jasmine Ter. UB7: W Dray 2C 92
Jasmine Way KT8: E Mos 4J 149
Jasmine Lodge SE16 . . . .5H 103
(off Sherwood Gdns.)
Jason Ct. SW9 . . . .1A 120
(off Southey Rd.)
W1 . . . .7H 5
Jason Wlk. SE9 . . . .4E 142
Jasper Av. W7 . . . .2K 95
Jasper Cl. EN3: Enf W 1D 24
Jasper Pas. SE19 . . . .6F 139
Jasper Rd. E16 . . . .6B 88
SE19 . . . .5F 139
Jasper Wlk. N1 . . . .3D 84
Java Wharf SE1 . . . .6K 15
(off Shad Thames)
Javelin Ct. HA7: Stan 5G 27
(off William Dr.)
Javelin Way UB5: N'olt 3B 76
Jaycroft EN2: Enf 1F 23
Jay Gdns. BR7: Chst 4D 142
Jay Ho. E3 . . . .1B 86
(off Hawthorn Av.)
Jay M. SW7 . . . .7A 10 (2A 100)
Jays St. N1 . . . .1K 83
Jazzfern Ter. HA0: Wemb 5A 60
Jean Batten Cl. SM6: Wall 7K 167
Jean Brown Indoor Arena, The 1H 53
Jean Darling Ho. SW10 . . . .6B 100
(off Milman's St.)
Jean Ho. SW17 . . . .5C 136
Jean Pardies Ho. E1 . . . .5J 85
(off Jubilee St.)

Jebb Av. SW2 . . . .6J 119
(not continuous)
Jebb St. E3 . . . .2C 86
Jedburgh Rd. E13 . . . .3A 88
Jedburgh St. SW11 . . . .4E 118
Jeddo M. W12 . . . .2B 98
Jeddo Rd. W12 . . . .2B 98
Jeeyas Apartments E16 . . . .5H 87
Jefferson Bldg. E14 . . . .2C 104
Jefferson Cl. IG2: Ilf 5F 53
W13 . . . .3B 96
Jefferson Ho. TW8: B'ford 6E 96
UB7: W Dray 2B 92
(off Park Lodge Av.)
Jefferson Pl. BR2: Brom . . .6B 160
Jefferson Plaza E3 . . . .4E 86
(off Hannaford Wlk.)
Jefferson Wlk. SE18 . . . .6E 106
Jeffrey Row SE12 . . . .5K 123
Jeffrey's Pl. NW1 . . . .7G 65
Jeffreys Rd. EN3: Brim 4F 25
SW4 . . . .2J 119
Jeffrey's St. NW1 . . . .7G 65
Jeffreys Wlk. SW4 . . . .2J 119
Jeffs Cl. TW12: Hamp 6F 131
Jeffs Rd. SM1: Sutt 4H 165
Jeger Av. E2 . . . .1F 85
Jeken Rd. SE9 . . . .4A 124
Jelf Rd. SW2 . . . .5A 120
Jelico Point SE16 . . . .2B 104
(off Rotherhithe St.)
Jellicoe Gdns. HA7: Stan 6E 26
Jellicoe Ho. E2 . . . .2G 85
(off Ropley St.)
Jellicoe Rd. E13 . . . .4J 87
N17 . . . .7J 33
Jemma Knowles Cl. SW2 . . .1A 138
(off Tulse Hill)
Jemmett Cl. KT2: King T 1H 151
Jemotts Ct. SE14 . . . .6K 103
(off Myers La.)
Jenkins Rd. E13 . . . .4K 87
Jenner Av. W3 . . . .5K 79
Jenner Cl. DA14: Sidc 4A 144
Jenner Ct. N21 . . . .5D 22
(off Pennington Dr.)
Jenner Ho. WC1 . . . .3F 7
(off Hunter St.)
Jenner Pl. SW13 . . . .6D 98
Jenner Rd. N16 . . . .3F 67
Jennett Rd. CRO: Wadd 3A 168
Jennifer Ho. E14 . . . .6K 86
SE11 . . . .4K 19
(off Reedworth St.)
Jennifer Rd. BR1: Brom 3H 141
Jenningsbury Ho. SW3 . . . .5D 16
(off Cale St.)
Jennings Cl. KT6: Surb 7C 150
RM8: Dag 1E 72
Jennings Ho. SE10 . . . .5F 105
(off Old Woolwich Rd.)
Jennings Rd. SE22 . . . .6F 121
Jennings Way EN5: Barn 3A 20
Jenningtree Way DA17: Belv . . .2J 109
Jenny Hammond Cl. E11 . . . .3H 69
Jensen Ho. E3 . . . .4C 86
(off Wellington Way)
Jenson Hgts. N1 . . . .7K 65
(off Caledonian Rd.)
Jenson Way SE19 . . . .7F 139
Jenton Av. DA7: Bex 1E 126
Jephson Ct. SW4 . . . .2J 119
Jephson Ho. SE17 . . . .6B 102
(off Doddington Gro.)
Jephson Rd. E7 . . . .7A 70
Jephson St. SE5 . . . .1D 120

Jephtha Rd. SW18 . . . . .6J 117
Jeppos La. CR4: Mitc 4D 154
Jepson Ho. SW6 . . . . .1K 117
(off Pearscroft Rd.)
Jerdan Ho. SW6 . . . . .7J 99
(off North End Rd.)
Jerdan Pl. SW6 . . . . .7J 99
Jeremiah St. E14 . . . . .6D 86
Jeremy Bentham Ho. E2 . . . . .3G 85
(off Mansford St.)
Jeremy's Grn. N18 . . . . .4C 34
Jermyn St. SW1 . . . . . . .4A 12 (1G 101)
Jermyn Street Theatre 3C 12
(off Jermyn St.)
Jerningham Av. IG5: Ilf 2F 53
Jerningham Ct. SE14 . . . . .1A 122
Jerningham Rd. SE14 . . . . .2A 122
Jerome Cres. NW8 . . . . .3C 4 (4C 82)
Jerome Ho. KT1: Hamp W 2D 150
(off Old Bridge St.)
NW1 . . . . .5D 4
(off Lisson Gro.)
SW7 . . . . .3A 16
(off Glendower Pl.)
Jerome Pl. KT1: King T 2D 150
(off Wadbrook St.)
Jerome St. E1 . . . . .5J 9 (4F 85)
Jerome Twr. W3 . . . . .2H 97
Jerrard St. SE13 . . . . .3D 122
Jerrold St. N1 . . . . .1H 9 (2E 84)
Jersey Av. HA7: Stan 2B 42
Jersey Dr. BR5: Pet W 6H 161
Jersey Ho. EN3: Enf W 1E 24
(off Eastfield Rd.)
N1 . . . . .6C 66
(off Jersey Rd.)
Jersey Rd. E11 . . . . .1F 69
E16 . . . . .6A 88
IG1: Ilf 4F 71
N1 . . . . .6C 66
SW17 . . . . .6F 137
TW3: Houn 1F 113
TW5: Hest 1F 113
TW7: Isle 7H 95
W7 . . . . .2A 96
Jersey St. E2 .3H 85
Jerusalem Pas. EC1 . . . . . . .4A 8 (4B 84)
Jervis Bay Ho. E14 . . . . .6F 87
(off Blair St.)
Jervis Ct. RM10: Dag 6H 73
SE10 . . . . .1E 122
(off Blissett St.)
W1 . . . . .1K 11
Jervis Rd. SW6 . . . . .6H 99
Jerviston Gdns. SW16 . . . . .6A 138
Jerwood Space Art Gallery 6C 14
Jesmond Av. HA9: Wemb 6F 61
Jesmond Cl. CR4: Mitc 3F 155
Jesmond Dene NW3 . . . . .6A 64
Jesmond Rd. CR0: C'don 7F 157
Jesmond Way HA7: Stan 5K 27
Jessam Av. E5 . . . . .1H 67
Jessamine Rd. W7 . . . . .1K 95
Jessel Ho. SW1 . . . . .3D 18
(off Page St.)
WC1 . . . . .2E 6
(off Judd St.)
Jessel Mans. W14 . . . . .6G 99
(off Queen's Club Gdns.)
Jesse Rd. E10 . . . . .1E 68
Jessett Cl. DA8: Erith 4K 109
Jessica Rd. SW18 . . . . .6A 118
Jessie Blythe La. N19 . . . . .7J 47
Jessie Duffett Ho. SE5 . . . . .7C 102
(off Pitman St.)
Jessie Wood Ct. SW9 . . . . .7A 102
(off Caldwell St.)
Jessiman Ter. TW17: Shep 5C 146
Jesson Ho. SE17 . . . . .4D 102
(off Orb St.)
Jessop Av. UB2: S'hall 4D 94

Jessop Ct. N1 .2B 84
Jessop Ho. W4 . . . . .4K 97
(off Kirton Cl.)
Jessop Pl. W7 .3J 95
Jessop Rd. SE24 . . . . .4B 120
Jessop Sq. E14 . . . . .1C 104
Jessops Way CR0: Bedd, Mitc 6G 155
Jessup Cl. SE18 . . . . .4G 107
Jetstar Way UB5: N'olt 3C 76
Jevington Way SE12 . . . . .1K 141
Jevons Ho. NW8 . . . . .7B 64
(off Hilgrove Rd.)
Jewel Rd. E17 . . . . .3C 50
Jewel Tower 1E 18
(off College M.)
Jewish Military Mus. 4E 44
(off Harmony Way)
Jewish Mus.
Camden Town 1F 83
Jewry St. EC3 . . . . .1J 15 (6F 85)
Jew's Row SW18 . . . . .4K 117
Jews' Wlk. SE26 . . . . .4H 139
Jeymer Av. NW2 . . . . .5D 62
Jeymer Dr. UB6: G'frd 1F 77
(not continuous)
Jeypore Rd. SW18 . . . . .7A 118
Jeypore Rd. Pas. SW18 . . . . .6A 118
Jhumat Pl. IG1: Ilf 3E 70
(off Roden St.)
Jigger Mast Ho. SE18 . . . . .3E 106
Jillian Cl. TW12: Hamp 7E 130
Jim Bradley Cl. SE18 . . . . .4E 106
Jim Griffiths Ho. SW6 . . . . .6H 99
(off Clem Attlee Ct.)
Jim Veal Dr. N7 . . . . .6J 65
Joan Cres. SE9 . . . . .7B 124
Joan Gdns. RM8: Dag 2E 72
Joanna Ho. W6 . . . . .5E 98
(off Queen Caroline St.)
Joan Rd. RM8: Dag 2E 72
Joan St. SE1 . . . . .5A 14 (1B 102)
Job Drain Pl. IG11: Bark 2A 90
Jocelin Ho. N1 . . . . .1K 83
(off Barnsbury Est.)
Jocelyn Rd. TW9: Rich 3E 114
Jocelyn St. SE15 . . . . .1G 121
Jockey's Flds. WC1 . . . . .5H 7 (5K 83)
Jodane St. SE8 . . . . .4B 104
Jodrell Cl. TW7: Isle 1A 114
Jodrell Rd. E3 .1B 86
Joe Hunte Ct. SE27 . . . . .5B 138
Joel St. HA5: Eastc 3J 39
HA6: Nwood 2J 39
Johanna St. SE1 . . . . . . .7J 13 (2A 102)
John Adams Ct. N9 . . . . .2A 34
John Adam St. WC2 . . . . .3F 13 (7J 83)
John Aird Ct. W2 . . . . .5A 4
(not continuous)
John Archer Way SW18 . . . . .6B 118
John Ashby Cl. SW2 . . . . .6J 119
John Austin Cl. KT2: King T 1F 151
John Baird Ct. SE26 . . . . .4J 139
John Barker Cl. NW6 . . . . .7G 63
John Barnes Wlk. E15 . . . . .6H 69
John Bell Twr. E. E3 . . . . .2C 86
(off Pancras Way)
John Bell Twr. W. E3 . . . . .2C 86
(off Pancras Way)
John Betts' Ho. W12 . . . . .3B 98
John Bond Ho. E3 . . . . .2B 86
(off Wright's Rd.)
John Bowles Ct. E1 . . . . .7K 85
(off Schoolhouse La.)
John Bradshaw Rd. N14 . . . . .1C 32
John Brent Ho. SE8 . . . . .4K 103
(off Haddonfield)
John Buck Ho. NW10 . . . . .1B 80
John Bull Pl. W4 . . . . .4H 97
John Burns Dr. IG11: Bark 7J 71
John Campbell Rd. N16 . . . . .5E 66
John Carpenter St. EC4 . . . .2A 14 (7B 84)

John Cartwright Ho. E2 . . . . .3H 85
(off Old Bethnal Grn. Rd.)
John Crane St. SE17 . . . . .6D 102
John Donne Way SE10 . . . . .7D 104
(off Norman Rd.)
John Drinkwater Cl. E11 . . . . .7H 51
John Fearon Wlk. W10 . . . . .3G 81
(off Dart St.)
John Felton Rd. SE16 . . . . .2G 103
John Fielden Ho. E2 . . . . .3H 85
(off Canrobert St.)
John Fisher St. E1 . . . . . . .2K 15 (7G 85)
John Goddard Way TW13: Felt 2K 129
John Gooch Dr. EN2: Enf 1G 23
John Harrison Way SE10 . . . . .3H 105
John Horner M. N1 . . . . .2C 84
John Islip St. SW1 . . . . . . .5D 18 (4H 101)
John Kaye Ct. TW17: Shep 5C 146
John Keats Ho. N22 . . . . .7E 32
John Keats Lodge EN2: Enf 1J 23
John Kennedy Cl. N1 . . . . .6D 66
(off Newington Grn. Rd.)
John Kennedy Ho. SE16 . . . . .4K 103
(off Rotherhithe Old Rd.)
John Knight Lodge SW6 . . . . .7J 99
John Lamb Ct. HA3: W'stone 1J 41
John McDonald Ho. E14 . . . . .3E 104
(off Glengall Gro.)
John McKenna Wlk. SE16 . . . . .3G 103
John Masefield Ho. N15 . . . . .6D 48
(off Fladbury Rd.)
John Maurice Cl. SE17 . . . . .4D 102
John Milton Pas. EC4 . . . . .1D 14
(off Bow La.)
John Nash M. E14 . . . . .6A 86
(off Commercial Rd.)
John Newton Cl. DA16: Well 3B 126
Johnny Andrews Ho. E1 . . . . .6K 85
(off Boulcott St.)
John Orwell Sports Cen. 1H 103
John Parker Cl. RM10: Dag 7H 73
John Parker Sq. SW11 . . . . .3B 118
John Parry Ct. N1 . . . . .2E 84
(off Hare Wlk.)
John Penn Ho. SE14 . . . . .7B 104
(off Amersham Va.)
John Penn St. SE13 . . . . .1D 122
John Penry Ho. SE1 . . . . .5G 103
(off Marlborough Gro.)
John Perrin Pl. HA3: Kenton 7E 42
John Prince's St. W1 . . . . . . .7K 5 (6F 83)
John Pritchard Ho. E1 . . . . .4G 85
(off Buxton St.)
John Ratcliffe Ho. NW6 . . . . .3J 81
(off Chippenham Gdns.)
John Rennie Wlk. E1 . . . . .7H 85
John Riley Ho. E3 . . . . .5B 86
(off Geoffrey Chaucer Way)
John Roll Way SE16 . . . . .3G 103
John Ruskin St. SE5 . . . . .7B 102
John's Av. NW4 . . . . .4E 44
John Sayer Ct.
IG11: Bark 3K 89
John's Cl. TW15: Ashf 4E 128
John Scurr Ho. E14 . . . . .6A 86
(off Ratcliffe La.)
John Silkin La. SE8 . . . . .5K 103
John's La. SM4: Mord 5A 154
John's M. WC1 . . . . .4H 7 (4K 83)
John Smith Av. SW6 . . . . .7H 99
John Smith M. E14 . . . . .7F 87
Johnson Cl. E8 . . . . .1G 85
Johnson Ct. SE9 . . . . .4A 124
Johnson Ho. E2 . . . . .2G 85
(off Roberta St.)
NW1 . . . . .2G 83
(off Cranleigh St.)
NW3 . . . . .7D 64
(off Adelaide Rd.)
SW1 . . . . .4H 17
(off Cundy St.)

Johnson Ho. SW8 . . . . .7H 101
(off Wandsworth Rd.)
W8 . . . . .2J 99
(off Campden Hill)
Johnson Lock Ct. E1 . . . . .5A 86
Johnson Lodge W9 . . . . .5J 81
(off Admiral Wlk.)
Johnson Mans. W14 . . . . .6G 99
(off Queen's Club Gdns.)
Johnson Rd. BR2: Brom 5B 160
CR0: C'don 7D 156
NW10 .1K 79
TW5: Hest 7A 94
Johnsons Cl. SM5: Cars 2D 166
Johnson's Ct. EC4 . . . . .6A 84
Johnsons Dr. TW12: Hamp 1G 149
Johnsons Ind. Est. UB3: Hayes 2H 93
Johnson's Pl. SW1 . . . . . . .6A 18 (5G 101)
Johnson St. E1 . . . . .7J 85
UB2: S'hall 3A 94
Johnsons Way NW10 . . . . .4H 79
John Spencer Sq. N1 . . . . .6B 66
John's Pl. E1 . . . . .6H 85
John's Ter. CR0: C'don 1E 168
Johnston Cl. SW9 . . . . .1K 119
Johnston Ct. E10 . . . . .3D 68
Johnstone Ho. SE13 . . . . .3F 123
(off Belmont Hill)
Johnston Dr. 3D 88
Johnston Rd. IG8: Wfd G 6D 36
Johnston Ter. NW2 . . . . .3F 63
John Strachey Ho. SW6 . . . . .6H 99
(off Clem Attlee Ct.)
John St. E15 . . . . .1H 87
EN1: Enf 5A 24
SE25 . . . . .4G 157
TW3: Houn 2C 112
WC1 . . . . .4H 7 (4K 83)
John Strype Ct. E10 . . . . .1D 68
John Trundle Ct. EC2 . . . . .5C 8
John Trundle Highwalk EC2 . . . . .5C 8
(off Aldersgate St.)
John Tucker Ho. E14 . . . . .3C 104
(off Mellish St.)
John Watkin Cl. KT19: Eps 7A 163
John Wesley Cl. E6 . . . . .3D 88
John Wesley St. TW1: Twick 1A 132
John Wesley Highwalk EC2 . . . . .6C 8
(off Aldersgate St.)
John Wetherby Ct. E15 . . . . .2D 86
(off High St.)
John Wetherby Ct. E. E15 . . . . .2D 86
(off High St.)
John Wetherby Ct. W. E15 . . . . .2D 86
(off High St.)
John Wheatley Ho. SW6 . . . . .6H 99
(off Clem Attlee Ct.)
John Williams Cl. KT2: King T 1D 150
SE14 . . . . .6K 103
John Wilson St. SE18 . . . . .3E 106
John Woolley Cl. SE13 . . . . .4G 123
Joiners Arms Yd. SE5 . . . . .1D 120
Joiners Pl. N5 .4D 66
Joiner St. SE1 . . . . .5F 15 (1D 102)
Joiners Yd. N1 .1F 7
(off Caledonia St.)
Jolles Ho. E3 . . . . .3D 86
(off Bromley High St.)
Jolly M. SW16 .2G 155
Jollys La. HA2: Harr 1H 59
UB4: Yead 5B 76
Jonathan St. SE11 . . . . .5G 19 (5K 101)
Jones Ho. E14 .6F 87
(off Blair St.)
Jones M. SW15 . . . . .4G 117
Jones Rd. E13 .4K 87
Jones St. W1 . . . . .3J 11 (7F 83)
Jones Wlk. TW10: Rich 6F 115
Jonquil Gdns. TW12: Hamp 6E 130
Jonson Cl. CR4: Mitc 4F 155
UB4: Hayes 5J 75

Jonson Ho. SE1 . . . . .3D 102
   (off Burbage Cl.)
Jonzen Wlk. E14 . . . . .6C 86
Jordan Cl. HA2: Harr 3D 58
Jordan Cl. SW15 . . . . .4F 117
Jordan Ho. N1 . . . . .1D 84
   (off Colville Est.)
SE4 . . . . .4K 121
   (off St Norbert Rd.)
Jordan Rd. UB6: G'frd 1B 78
TW7: Isle 1J 113
Jordans Cl. RM10: Dag 4H 73
Jordans Ho. NW8 . . . . .3C 4
   (off Capland St.)
Jordans M. TW2: Twick 2J 131
Joscoyne Ho. E1 . . . . .6H 85
   (off Philpot St.)
Joseph Av. W3 . . . . .6K 79
Joseph Cl. N4 . . . . .2B 66
Joseph Conrad Ho. SW1 . . . . . . .4B 18
   (off Tachbrook St.)
Joseph Ct. N16 . . . . .6E 48
   (off Amhurst Pk.)
Josephine Av. SW2 . . . . .5K 119
Joseph Irwin Ho. E14 . . . . .7B 86
   (off Gill St.)
Joseph Lister Ct. E7 . . . . .7J 69
Joseph M. N7 . . . . .6A 66
   (off Westbourne Rd.)
SE15 . . . . .5K 121
Joseph Powell Cl. SW12 . . . . . . .6G 119
Joseph Priestley Ho. E2 . . . . .3H 85
   (off Canrobert St.)
Joseph Ray Rd. E11 . . . . .2G 69
Joseph St. E3 . . . . .4B 86
Joseph Trotter Cl. EC1 . . . . .2K 7
Joshua Cl. CR2: S Croy 7B 168
N10 . . . . .7A 32
Joshua Pedley M. E3 . . . . .2C 86
   (off Douro St.)
Joshua St. E14 . . . . .6E 86
Josiah Dr. UB10: Ick 2E 56
Joslin Av. NW9 . . . . .3A 44
Joslings Cl. W12 . . . . .7C 80
Joslyn Cl. EN3: Enf L 1H 25
Jossiline Ct. E3 . . . . .2A 86
   (off Ford St.)
Joubert Mans. SW3 . . . . .5D 16
   (off Jubilee Pl.)
Joubert St. SW11 . . . . .2D 118
Jowett St. SE15 . . . . .7F 103
Jowitt Ho. E2 . . . . .3K 85
   (off Morpeth St.)
Joyce Av. N18 . . . . .5A 34
Joyce Butler Ho. N22 . . . . .1K 47
Joyce Dawson Way SE28 . . . . . . .7A 90
Joyce Latimore Ct. N9 . . . . .3C 34
   (off Colthurst Dr.)
Joyce Page Cl. SE7 . . . . .6B 106
Joyce Wlk. SW2 . . . . .6A 120
JOYDENS WOOD 4K 145
Joydens Wood 4H 145
Joydens Wood Rd. BA5: Bexl 4K 145
Joydon Dr. RM6: Chad H 6B 54
Joyners Cl. RM9: Dag 4F 73
Joy of Life Fountain 1D 100
Joystone Ct. EN4: E Barn 4H 21
   (off Park Rd.)
Jubb Powell Ho. N15 . . . . .6E 48
Jubilee, The SE10 . . . . .7D 104
Jubilee Av. E4 . . . . .6K 35
RM7: Rom 5H 55
TW2: Whitt 1G 131
Jubilee Bldgs. NW8 . . . . .1B 82
Jubilee Cl. HA5: Pinn 2A 40
KT1: Hamp W 1C 150
NW9 . . . . .6K 43
NW10 . . . . .2A 80
RM7: Rom 5H 55
Jubilee Country Pk. 4F 161

Jubilee Country Pk. Local Nature Reserve
. . . . .5F 161
Jubilee Ct. BR4: W W'ck 1E 170
E16 . . . . .5H 87
   (off Rathbone St.)
E18 . . . . .1J 51
HA3: Kenton 7E 42
N10 . . . . .3E 46
SE10 . . . . .6D 104
   (off Dowells St.)
TW3: Houn 3F 113
   (off Bristow Rd.)
Jubilee Cres. E14 . . . . .3E 104
N9 . . . . .1B 34
Jubilee Dr. HA4: Ruis 4B 58
Jubilee Gdns. UB1: S'hall 5E 76
Jubilee Hall Gym 2F 13
   (within Jubilee Hall)
Jubilee Hgts. SE10 . . . . .1E 122
   (off Parkside Av.)
Jubilee Ho. HA7: Stan 5J 27
SE11 . . . . .4K 19
   (off Reedworth St.)
WC1 . . . . .3G 7
   (off Jubilee St.)
Jubilee Mans. E1 . . . . .6J 85
   (off Jubilee St.)
Jubilee Mkt. IG8: Wfd G 6F 37
WC2 . . . . .2F 13
   (off Covent Gdn.)
Jubilee Pde. IG8: Wfd G 6F 37
Jubilee Pl. SW3 . . . . . .5D 16 (5C 100)
Jubilee Pl. Shop. Mall E14 . . . . . .1D 104
   (off Bank St.)
Jubilee Rd. SM3: Cheam 7F 165
UB6: G'frd 1B 78
Jubilee Sports Cen.
London 3H 81
Jubilee St. E1 . . . . .6J 85
Jubilee Vs. KT10: Esh 7H 149
Jubilee Walkway SE1 . . .3B 14 (7B 84)
Jubilee Way DA14: Sidc 2A 144
KT9: Chess 4G 163
SW19 .1K 153
TW14: Felt 1J 129
Jubilee Way Training Track 3H 163
Jubilee Yd. SE1 . . . . .6J 15
Judd Apartments N8 . . . . .3K 47
   (off Gt. Amwell La.)
Judd St. WC1 . . . . .2E 6 (3J 83)
Jude St. E16 . . . . .6H 87
Judge Heath La. UB3: Hayes 6E 74
UB8: Hill 6E 74
Judges Wlk. NW3 . . . . .3A 64
Juer St. SW11 . . . . .7C 100
Jules Thorn Av. EN1: Enf 4B 24
Julia Cl. E17 . . . . .5D 50
Julia Gdns. IG11: Bark 2D 90
Julia Garfield M. E16 . . . . .1K 105
   (not continuous)
Juliana Cl. N2 . . . . .2A 46
Julian Av. W3 . . . . .7H 79
Julian Cl. EN5: New Bar 3E 20
Julian Ct. NW1 . . . . .7G 65
   (off Rochester Sq.)
Julian Hill HA1: Harr 2J 59
Julian Ho. SE21 . . . . .4E 138
Julian Pl. E14 . . . . .5D 104
Julian Taylor Path SE23 . . . . .2H 139
St. Ju St. NW5 . . . . .4F 65
Julien Rd. W5 . . . . .3C 96
Juliet Ho. N1 . . . . .2E 84
   (off Arden Est.)
Juliette Rd. E13 . . . . .2J 87
Julius Caesar Way HA7: Stan 3J 27
Julius Ho. E14 . . . . .6F 87
   (off E. India Dock Rd.)
Julius Nyerere Cl. N1 . . . . .1K 83
   (off Copenhagen St.)
Junction App. SE13 . . . . .3E 122
SW11 .3C 118

Junction M. W2 . . . . .7C 4 (6C 82)
Junction Pl. W2 . . . . .7B 4
Junction Rd. CR2: S Croy 5D 168
E13 . . . . .2K 87
HA1: Harr 6H 41
   (not continuous)
N9 . . . . .1B 34
N17 . . . . .3G 49
N19 . . . . .4G 65
TW8: Bford 4C 96
TW15: Ashf 5E 128
W5 . . . . .4C 96
Junction Rd. E. RM6: Chad H 7E 54
Junction Rd. W. RM6: Chad H 7E 54
Junction Shop. Cen., The SW11 . . .4C 118
Juniper Cl. EN5: Barn 5A 20
HA2: Harr 2F 59
HA8: Wemb 5G 61
KT9: Chess 5F 163
TW13: Felt 3K 129
Juniper Cl. HA3: Hrw W 1K 41
HA6: Nwood 1J 39
KT8: W Mole 4F 149
RM6: Chad H 6B 54
TW3: Houn 4F 113
   (off Grove Rd.)
W8 . . . . .3K 99
   (off St Mary's Pl.)
Juniper Cres. NW1 . . . . .7E 64
Juniper Dr. SW18 . . . . .4A 118
Juniper Gdns. SW16 . . . . .1G 155
TW16: Sun 6H 129
Juniper Ho. SE14 . . . . .7J 103
TW9: Kew 1H 115
W10 . . . . .4G 81
   (off Fourth Av.)
Juniper La. E6 . . . . .5C 88
Juniper Rd. IG1: Ilf 3E 70
Juniper St. E1 . . . . .7J 85
Juniper Way UB3: Hayes 7F 75
Juno Ct. SW9 . . . . .7A 102
   (off Caldwell St.)
Juno Ent. Cen. SE14 . . . . .6K 103
Juno Ho. E3 . . . . .1C 86
   (off Garrison Rd.)
Juno Way SE14 . . . . .6K 103
Juno Way Ind. Est. SE14 . . . . .6K 103
Jupiter Ct. E3 . . . . .2C 86
   (off Four Seasons Cl.)
SW9 . . . . .7A 102
   (off Caldwell St.)
UB5: N'olt 3B 76
   (off Seasprite Cl.)
Jupiter Hgts. UB10: Uxb 1B 74
Jupiter Ho. E14 . . . . .5D 104
   (off St Davids Sq.)
E16 . . . . .6H 87
   (off Turner St.)
HA2: Harr 1E 58
Jupiter Way N7 . . . . .6K 65
Jupp Rd. E15 . . . . .7F 69
Jupp Rd. W. E15 . . . . .1F 87
Jura Ho. SE16 . . . . .4K 103
   (off Plough Way)
Jurassic Encounter 3C 152
Jurston Ct. SE1 . . . . .7K 13
Justice Apartments E1 . . . . .6K 85
   (off Aylward St.)
Justice Wlk. SW3 . . . . .7C 16 (6C 100)
Justin Cl. TW8: Bford 7D 96
Justines Pl. E2 . . . . .3K 85
Justin Pl. N22 . . . . .7E 32
Justin Plaza CR4: Mitc 4C 154
Justin Rd. E4 . . . . .6G 35
Jute La. EN3: Brim 2F 25
Jutland Cl. N19 . . . . .1J 65
Jutland Ho. SE5 . . . . .2C 120
SE18 . . . . .4C 106
   (off Prospect Va.)
Jutland Rd. E13 . . . . .4J 87
SE6 . . . . .7E 122

Jutsums Av. RM7: Rom 6H 55
Jutsums Cl. RM7: Rom 6H 55
Jutsums La.
RM7: Rom, Rush G 6H 55
Juxon Cl. HA3: Hrw W 1F 41
Juxon Ho. EC4 . . . . .1B 14
   (off St Paul's Chyd.)
Juxon St. SE11 . . . . .3H 19 (4K 101)
JVC Bus. Pk. NW2 . . . . .1C 62

K

Kaduna Cl. HA5: Eastc 5J 39
Kaine Pl. CR0: C'don 7A 158
Kaleidoscope Ho. E20 . . . . .5E 68
   (off Mirabelle Gdns.)
Kale Rd. DA18: Erith 2D 108
Kambala Rd. SW11 . . . . .3B 118
Kamen Ho. SE1 . . . . .5G 15
   (off Magdalen St.)
Kamrans Pl. HA8: Edg 2F 43
Kangley Bri. Rd. SE26 . . . . .6B 140
Kangley Bus. Cen. SE26 . . . . .5B 140
Kaplan Dr. N21 . . . . .5E 22
Kapuvar Cl. SE15 . . . . .2G 121
Karachi Ho. E15 . . . . .6G 69
   (off Well St.)
Karanjia Cl. NW2 . . . . .6E 62
Kara Way NW2 . . . . .4F 63
Karen Cl. BR1: Brom 1H 159
Karen Ter. E11 . . . . .2H 69
Karenza Ct. HA9: Wemb 7C 42
Kariba Cl. N9 . . . . .3D 34
Karim M. E17 . . . . .4A 50
Karma Way HA2: Harr 1E 58
Karner Ho. E20 . . . . .5D 68
   (off Logan Cl.)
Karoline Gdns. UB6: G'frd 2H 77
Kashgar Rd. SE18 . . . . .4K 107
Kashmir Rd. SE7 . . . . .7B 106
Kassala Rd. SW11 . . . . .1D 118
Katella Trad. Est. IG11: Bark 3J 89
Katharine Ho. CR0: C'don 3C 168
   (off Katharine St.)
Katharine St. CR0: C'don 3C 168
Katherine Bell Twr. E3 . . . . .2C 86
   (off Pancras Way)
Katherine Cl. N4 . . . . .7C 48
NW7 . . . . .7K 29
SE16 . . . . .1K 103
Katherine Ct. SE23 . . . . .1H 139
Katherine Gdns. SE9 . . . . .4B 124
Katherine Ho. W10 . . . . .4G 81
   (off Portobello Rd.)
Katherine Rd. E6 . . . . .5A 70
E7 . . . . .5A 70
TW1: Twick 1A 132
Katherine Sq. W11 . . . . .1G 99
Kathleen Av. HA0: Wemb 7E 60
W3 . . . . .5J 79
Kathleen Godfree Ct. SW19 . . . . . .6J 135
Kathleen Rd. SW11 . . . . .3D 118
Kavan Gdns. TW5: Cran 7J 93
Kavsan Pl. TW5: Cran 7J 93
Kayani Av. N4 . . . . .1C 66
Kayani Ho. E16 . . . . .6K 87
   (off Burrard Rd.)
Kayemoor Rd. SM2: Sutt 6B 166
Kay Rd. SW9 . . . . .2J 119
Kays Ter. E18 . . . . .1H 51
Kay St. DA16: Well 1B 126
E2 . . . . .2G 85
E15 . . . . .7F 69
   (off New Mount St.)
Kean Cres. RM8: Dag 1E 72
Kean Ho. SE17 . . . . .6B 102
TW1: Twick 6D 114
   (off Arosa Rd.)
Kean St. WC2 . . . . .1G 13 (6K 83)
Keatley Grn. E4 . . . . .6G 35

Keats—Kenilworth Cres.

Keats *CR0: C'don 1C 168*
(off Saffron Central Sq.)
Keats Apartments *E3 4B 86*
(off Wraxall Rd.)
Keats Av. E16 1K **105**
Keats Cl. E11 5K **51**
EN3: Pond E 5E **24**
NW3 4C **64**
SE1 4F **103**
SE7 7A **106**
SW19 6B **136**
UB4: Hayes 5J **75**
Keats Est. *N16 2F 67*
(off Kyverdale Rd.)
Keats Gro. NW3 4C **64**
Keats House 4C 64
Keats Ho. *E2 3J 85*
(off Roman Rd.)
HA2: Harr 2J **59**
SE5 7C 102
(off Elmington Est.)
SW1 7K 17
(off Churchill Gdns.)
Keats Pde. *N9 2B 34*
(off Church St.)
Keats Pl. *EC2 6E 8*
(off Moorfields)
Keats Rd. DA16: Well 1J **125**
DA17: Belv 3J **109**
E10 7D **50**
Keats Way CR0: C'don 6J **157**
UB6: G'frd 5F **77**
UB7: W Dray 4B **92**
Kebbell Ter. *E7 5K 69*
(off Claremont Rd.)
Keble Cl. KT4: Wor Pk 1B **164**
UB5: N'olt 5G **59**
Keble Pl. SW13 6D **98**
Keble St. SW17 4A **136**
Kebony Cl. UB7: W Dray 2C **92**
Kechill Gdns. BR2: Hayes 7J **159**
Kedeston Ct. SM1: Sutt 1K **165**
Kedge Ho. *E14 3C 104*
(off Tiller Rd.)
Kedleston Dr. BR5: St M Cry 5K **161**
Kedleston Wlk. E2 3H **85**
Kedyngton Ho. *HA8: Edg 2J 43*
(off Burnt Oak B'way.)
Keeble Cl. SE18 6F **107**
Keedonwood Rd. BR1: Brom 5G **141**
Keel Cl. IG11: Bark 2C **90**
N18 6K **33**
SE16 1K **103**
Keel Ct. *E14 7F 87*
(off Newport Av.)
Keele Ho. RM8: Dag 4A **72**
Keeley Rd. CR0: C'don 2C **168**
Keeley St. WC2 1G **13** (6K **83**)
Keeling Ho. *E2 2H 85*
(off Claredale St.)
Keeling Rd. SE9 5B **124**
Keelson Ho. *E14 3C 104*
(off Mellish St.)
Keely Cl. EN4: E Barn 5H **21**
Keemor Cl. SE18 7E **106**
Keens Cl. SW16 5H **137**
Keens Rd. CR0: C'don 4C **168**
Keen's Yd. N1 6B **66**
Keep, The KT2: King T 6F **133**
SE3 2J **123**
Keepers Ct. *CR2: S Croy 5C 168*
(off Warham Rd.)
Keepers M. TW11: Tedd 6C **132**
Keepier Wharf *E14 7K 85*
(off Narrow St.)
Keeping Ct. *BR2: Brom 3J 159*
(off St Mark's Sq.)
Keeton's Rd. SE16 3H **103**
(not continuous)
Keevil Dr. SW19 7F **117**
Keighley Cl. N7 5J **65**
Keightley Dr. SE9 1G **143**
Keilder Cl. UB10: Hil 2C **74**
Keildon Rd. SW11 4D **118**
Keiller Ho. *E16 1D 106*
(off Kennard St.)
Keir, The SW19 5E **134**
Keir Hardie Est. E5 1H **67**
Keir Hardie Ho. N19 7H **47**
NW10 7B **62**
W6 6F 99
(off Fulham Pal. Rd.)
Keir Hardie Way IG11: Bark 7A **72**
UB4: Yead 3J **75**
Keirin Rd. E20 5D **68**
Keith Connor Cl. SW8 3F **119**
Keith Gro. W12 2C **98**
Keith Ho. *NW6 2K 81*
(off Carlton Vale)
SW8 7J 101
(off Wheatsheaf La.)
Keith Pk. Rd. UB10: Uxb 7B **56**
Keith Rd. E17 1B **50**
IG11: Bark 2H **89**
UB3: Hayes 3G **93**
Kelbrook Rd. SE3 2C **124**
Kelby Ho. *N7 6K 65*
(off Sutterton St.)
Kelby Path SE9 3F **143**
Kelceda Cl. NW2 2C **62**
Kelday Hgts. *E1 6H 85*
(off Spencer Way)
Kelf Gro. UB3: Hayes 6H **75**
Kelfield Ct. W10 6F **81**
Kelfield Gdns. W10 6E **80**
Kelfield M. W10 6F **81**
Kelland Cl. N8 5H **47**
Kelland Rd. E13 4J **87**
Kellaway Rd. SE3 2B **124**
Keller Cres. E12 4B **70**
Kellerton Rd. SE13 5G **123**
Kellet Ho's. *WC1 2F 7*
(off Tankerton St.)
Kellett Ho. *N1 1E 84*
(off Colville Est.)
Kellett Rd. SW2 4A **120**
Kelling Gdns. CR0: C'don 7B **156**
Kellino St. SW17 4D **136**
Kellner Rd. SE28 3K **107**
Kellogg Twr. UB6: G'frd 5J **59**
Kellow Ho. *SE1 6E 14*
(off Tennis St.)
Kell St. SE1 7B **14** (3B **102**)
Kelly Av. SE15 7F **103**
Kelly Cl. NW10 3K **61**
TW17: Shep 2G **147**
Kelly Ct. *E14 7C 86*
(off Garford St.)
Kelly M. W9 4H **81**
Kelly St. NW1 6F **65**
Kelly Ter. E17 4C **50**
Kelly Way RM6: Chad H 5E **54**
Kelman Cl. SW4 2H **119**
Kelmore Gro. SE22 4G **121**
Kelmscott Cl. E17 1B **50**
Kelmscott Gdns. W12 3C **98**
Kelmscott House 5D 98
Kelmscott Rd. SW11 5C **118**
Kelross Pas. N5 4C **66**
Kelross Rd. N5 4C **66**
Kelsall Cl. SE3 2K **123**
Kelsall M. TW9: Kew 1H **115**
Kelsey Cl. KT9: Chess 7D **162**
Kelsey Ga. BR3: Beck 2D **158**
Kelsey La. BR3: Beck 2C **158**
Kelsey Pk. Av. BR3: Beck 2D **158**
Kelsey Pk. Rd. BR3: Beck 2C **158**
Kelsey Sq. BR3: Beck 2C **158**
Kelsey St. E2 4G **85**
Kelsey Way BR3: Beck 3C **158**
Kelson Ho. E14 3E **104**
Kelso Pl. W8 3K **99**
Kelso Rd. SM5: Cars 7A **154**
Kelston Rd. IG6: Ilf 2F **53**
Kelvedon Cl. KT2: King T 6G **133**
Kelvedon Ho. SW8 1J **119**
Kelvedon Rd. SW6 7H **99**
Kelvedon Way IG8: Wfd G 6J **37**
Kelvin Av. N13 6E **32**
TW11: Tedd 6J **131**
Kelvinbrook KT8: W Mole 3F **149**
Kelvin Cl. KT19: Ewe 6G **163**
Kelvin Ct. SE20 1H **157**
TW7: Isle 2J **113**
W11 7J 81
(off Kensington Pk. Rd.)
Kelvin Cres. HA3: Hrw W 7D **26**
Kelvin Dr. TW1: Twick 6B **114**
Kelvin Gdns. CR0: Wadd 7J **155**
UB1: S'hall 6E **76**
Kelvin Gro. KT9: Chess 3D **162**
SE26 3H **139**
Kelvington Cl. CR0: C'don 7A **158**
Kelvington Rd. SE15 5K **121**
Kelvin Ho. *SE26 4B 140*
(off Worsley Bri. Rd.)
Kelvin Ind. Est. UB6: G'frd 7F **59**
Kelvin Pde. BR6: Orp 1J **173**
Kelvin Rd. DA16: Well 3A **126**
N5 4C **66**
Kelway Ho. W14 5H **99**
Kember St. N1 7K **65**
Kemble Dr. BR2: Brom 3C **172**
Kemble Ho. *SW9 3B 120*
(off Barrington Rd.)
Kemble Rd. CR0: Wadd 3B **168**
N17 1G **49**
SE23 1K **139**
Kemble St. WC2 1G **13** (6K **83**)
Kemerton Rd. BR3: Beck 2D **158**
CR0: C'don 7F **157**
SE5 3C **120**
Kemey's St. E9 5A **68**
Kemmel Rd. RM9: Dag 1B **90**
Kemnal Rd. BR7: Chst 4H **143**
Kemp *NW9 1B 44*
(off Quakers Course)
Kemp Ct. *SW8 7J 101*
(off Hartington Rd.)
Kempe Ho. *SE1 3D 102*
(off Burbage Cl.)
Kempe Rd. NW6 2F **81**
Kemp Gdns. CR0: C'don 6C **156**
Kemp Ho. *E2 2K 85*
(off Sewardstone Rd.)
E6 6E **70**
W1 2C 12
(off Berwick St.)
Kempis Way SE22 5E **120**
Kemplay Rd. NW3 4B **64**
Kemp Rd. RM8: Dag 1D **72**
Kemps Ct. *W1 1B 12*
(off Hopkins St.)
Kemps Dr. E14 7C **86**
HA6: Nwood 1H **39**
Kempsford Gdns. SW5 5J **99**
Kempsford Rd. SE11 4K **19** (4B **102**)
(not continuous)
Kemps Gdns. SE13 5E **122**
Kempshott Rd. SW16 7H **137**
Kempson Rd. SW6 1J **117**
Kempthorne Rd. SE8 4B **104**
Kempton Av. TW16: Sun 1K **147**
UB5: N'olt 6E **58**
Kempton Cl. DA8: Erith 6J **109**
UB10: Ick 4E **56**
Kempton Ct. E1 5H **85**
TW16: Sun 1K **147**
Kempton Ga. TW12: Hamp 1D **148**
Kempton Ho. *N1 1E 84*
(off Hoxton St.)
Kempton Nature Reserve 6B 130
Kempton Pk. Racecourse 7K 129
Kempton Rd. E6 1D **88**
Kemptons, The TW15: Ashf 2C **128**
Kempton Wlk. CR0: C'don 6A **158**
Kempt St. SE18 6E **106**
Kemsing Cl. BR2: Hayes 2H **171**
CR7: Thor H 4C **156**
DA5: Bexl 7E **126**
Kemsing Ho. *SE1 7F 15*
(off Long La.)
Kemsing Rd. SE10 5J **105**
Kemsley SE13 5D **122**
Kemsley Ct. W13 1C **96**
Kenbrook Ho. NW5 5G **65**
W14 3H **99**
Kenbury Cl. UB10: Ick 3C **56**
Kenbury Gdns. SE5 2C **120**
Kenbury Mans. *SE5 2C 120*
(off Kenbury St.)
Kenbury St. SE5 2C **120**
Kenchester Cl. SW8 7J **101**
Kencot Way DA18: Erith 2F **109**
Kendal *NW1 1K 5*
(off Augustus St.)
Kendal Av. IG11: Bark 1J **89**
N18 4J **33**
W3 4G **79**
Kendal Cl. IG8: Wfd G 2C **36**
N20 2H **31**
SW9 7B **102**
TW14: Felt 1H **129**
UB4: Hayes 2G **75**
Kendal Ct. W3 5G **79**
Kendale Rd. BR1: Brom 5G **141**
Kendal Gdns. N18 4J **33**
SM1: Sutt 2A **166**
Kendal Ho. E9 1J **85**
N1 2K 83
(off Priory Grn. Est.)
SE20 2G 157
(off Derwent Rd.)
Kendall Av. BR3: Beck 2A **158**
CR2: Sande 7D **168**
Kendall Ct. DA15: Sidc 3A **144**
SW19 6B **136**
Kendall Lodge *BR1: Brom 1K 159*
(off Willow Tree Wlk.)
Kendall Mnr. HA6: Nwood 1D **38**
Kendall Pl. W1 6G **5** (5E **82**)
Kendall Rd. BR3: Beck 2A **158**
SE18 1C **124**
TW7: Isle 2A **114**
Kendalmere Cl. N10 1F **47**
Kendal Pde. N18 4J **33**
Kendal Pl. SW15 5H **117**
Kendal Rd. NW10 4C **62**
Kendal Steps W2 1D **10**
Kendal St. W2 1D **10** (6C **82**)
Kender Est. *SE14 1J 121*
(off Queen's Rd.)
Kender St. SE14 7J **103**
Kendoa Rd. SW4 4H **119**
Kendon Cl. E11 5K **51**
Kendon Ho. *E15 7F 69*
(off Bryant St.)
Kendra Hall Rd.
CR2: S Croy 7B **168**
Kendrey Gdns. TW2: Whitt 7J **113**
Kendrick Ct. *SE15 1H 121*
(off Colmore M.)
Kendrick M. SW7 3A **16** (4B **100**)
Kendrick Pl. SW7 4A **16** (4B **100**)
Kenelm Cl. HA1: Harr 3A **60**
Kenerne Dr. EN5: Barn 5B **20**
Ken Friar Bri. N7 4A **66**
Kenilford Rd. SW12 7F **119**
Kenilworth Av. E17 2C **50**
HA2: Harr 4D **58**
SW19 5J **135**
Kenilworth Ct. *SW15 3G 117*
(off Lwr. Richmond Rd.)
Kenilworth Cres. EN1: Enf 1K **23**

Kenilworth Gdns. IG3: Ilf 2K 71
SE18 2F 125
UB1: S'hall 3D 76
UB4: Hayes 5H 75
Kenilworth Rd. BR5: Pet W 6G 161
E3 2A 86
HA8: Edg 3D 28
KT17: Ewe 5C 164
NW6 1H 81
SE20 1K 157
TW15: Ashf 3A 128
W5 1E 96
Kenley *N17* *2D 48*
(off Gloucester Rd.)
Kenley Av. NW9 1A 44
Kenley Cl. BR7: Chst 3J 161
DA5: Bexl 7G 127
EN4: E Barn 4H 21
Kenley Gdns. CR7: Thor H 4B 156
Kenley Rd. KT1: King T 2H 151
SW19 2J 153
TW1: Twick 6B 114
Kenley Wlk. SM3: Cheam 4F 165
W11 7G 81
Kenlor Rd. SW17 5B 136
Kenmare Cl. UB10: Ick 2F 57
Kenmare Dr. CR4: Mitc 7D 136
N17 2F 49
Kenmare Gdns. N13 4H 33
Kenmare Rd. CR7: Thor H 6A 156
Kenmere Gdns. HA0: Wemb 1G 79
Kenmere Rd. DA16: Well 2C 126
Kenmont Gdns. NW10 3D 80
(not continuous)
Kenmore Av. HA3: Kenton, W'stone 4A 42
Kenmore Cl. TW9: Kew 7G 97
Kenmore Ct. *NW6* *7K 63*
(off Acol Rd.)
Kenmore Cres. UB4: Hayes 3H 75
Kenmore Gdns. HA8: Edg 2H 43
Kenmore Rd. HA3: Kenton 3D 42
Kenmure Rd. E8 5H 67
Kenmure Yd. E8 5H 67
Kennacraig Cl. E16 1J 105
Kennard Ho. SW11 2E 118
Kennard Rd. E15 7F 69
N11 5J 31
Kennard St. E16 1D 106
SW11 1E 118
Kennedy Av. EN3: Pond E 6D 24
Kennedy Cl. BR5: Pet W 1H 173
CR4: Mitc 1E 154
E13 2J 87
Kennedy Ct. TW15: Ashf 5E 128
WD23: B Hea 2C 26
Kennedy Cox Ho. *E16* *5H 87*
(off Burke St.)
Kennedy Ho. *SE11* *5G 19*
(off Vauxhall Wlk.)
Kennedy Path W7 4K 77
Kennedy Rd. IG11: Bark 1J 89
W7 5J 77
Kennedy Wlk. *SE17* *4D 102*
(off Elsted St.)
Kennet Cl. SW11 4B 118
Kennet Ct. *W9* *5J 81*
(off Elmfield Way)
Kenneth Av. IG1: Ilf 4F 71
Kenneth Campbell Ho. *NW8* *3B 4*
(off Orchardson St.)
Kenneth Chambers Ct. IG8: Wfd G 6H 37
Kenneth Ct. SE11 3K 19 (4A 102)
Kenneth Cres. NW2 5D 62
Kenneth Gdns. HA7: Stan 6F 27
Kenneth Moore Rd. IG1: Ilf 3F 71
Kenneth More Theatre 3F 71
Kennet Ho. *NW8* *4B 4*
(off Church St. Est.)
SW18 *4J 117*
(off Enterprise Way)
Kenneth Rd. RM6: Chad H 7D 54
Kenneth Robbins Ho. N17 7C 34
Kenneth Younger Ho. *SW6* *6H 99*
(off Clem Attlee Ct.)
Kennet Rd. TW7: Isle 3K 113
W9 4H 81
Kennet Sq. CR4: Mitc 1C 154
Kennet St. E1 1G 103
Kennett Ct. W4 7H 97
Kennett Dr. UB4: Yead 5C 76
Kennett Wharf La.
EC4 3D 14 (7C 84)
KENNINGHALL 5D 34
Kenninghall Rd. E5 3G 67
N18 5D 34
Kenning Ho. *N1* *1E 84*
(off Colville Est.)
Kenning St. SE16 2J 103
Kennings Way SE11 5K 19 (5A 102)
KENNINGTON 7K 19 (6A 102)
Kennington Grn. SE11 6J 19 (5A 102)
Kennington La. SE11 6G 19 (5K 101)
KENNINGTON OVAL 6A 102
Kennington Oval SE11 7H 19 (6K 101)
Kennington Pal. Ct. SE11 5J 19
Kennington Pk. Gdns.
SE11 7K 19 (6B 102)
Kennington Pk. Ho. SE11 6K 19
Kennington Pk. Pl. SE11 7K 19 (6A 102)
Kennington Pk. Rd. SE11 7K 19 (6A 102)
Kennington Rd. SE1 1J 19 (3A 102)
SE11 1J 19 (3A 102)
Kennistoun Ho. NW5 5G 65
Kennoldes *SE21* *2D 138*
(off Croxted Rd.)
Kenny Dr. SM5: Cars 7E 166
Kennyland Ct. *NW4* *6D 44*
(off Hendon Way)
Kenrick Pl. W1 6G 5 (5E 82)
KENSAL GREEN 3E 80
Kensal Ho. *W10* *4F 81*
(off Ladbroke Gro.)
KENSAL RISE 2F 81
Kensal Rd. W10 4G 81
KENSAL TOWN 4G 81
Kensal Wharf W10 4F 81
KENSINGTON 3J 99
Kensington Arc. *W8* *2K 99*
(off Kensington High St.)
Kensington Av. CR7: Thor H 1A 156
E12 6C 70
Kensington Cen. W14 4G 99
(not continuous)
Kensington Chu. Ct. W8 2K 99
Kensington Chu. St. W8 1J 99
Kensington Chu. Wlk. W8 2K 99
(not continuous)
Kensington Cl. N11 6K 31
Kensington Ct. *SE16* *1K 103*
(off King & Queen Wharf)
W8 2K 99
Kensington Ct. Gdns. *W8* *3K 99*
(off Kensington Ct. Pl.)
Kensington Ct. Mans. *W8* *2K 99*
(off Kensington Ct.)
Kensington Ct. M. *W8* *3K 99*
(off Kensington Ct. Pl.)
Kensington Ct. Pl. W8 3K 99
Kensington Dr. IG8: Wfd G 2B 52
Kensington Gdns. 4A 10 (1A 100)
Kensington Gdns.
IG1: Ilf 1D 70
KT1: King T 3D 150
Kensington Gdns. Sq. W2 6K 81
Kensington Ga. W8 3A 100
Kensington Gore SW7 7A 10 (2A 100)
Kensington Hall Gdns. W14 5H 99
Kensington Hgts. *HA1: Harr* *6K 41*
(off Sheepcote Rd.)
W8 1J 99
Kensington High St. W8 3H 99
W14 3H 99
Kensington Ho. IG8: Wfd G 7K 37
UB7: W Dray *2B 92*
(off Park Lodge Av.)
W8 *2K 99*
(off Kensington Ct.)
W14 2F 99
Kensington Leisure Cen. 7G 81
Kensington Mall W8 1J 99
Kensington Mans. *SW5* *5J 99*
(off Trebovir Rd.)
Kensington Palace 1K 99
Kensington Pal. Gdns. W8 1K 99
Kensington Pk. Gdns. W11 7H 81
Kensington Pk. M. W11 6H 81
Kensington Pk. Rd. W11 6H 81
Kensington Path *E10* *2D 68*
(off Osborne Rd.)
Kensington Pl. W8 1J 99
Kensington Rd. RM7: Rom 6J 55
SW7 2B 100
UB5: N'olt 3E 76
W8 2K 99
Kensington Sq. W8 3K 99
Kensington Ter. CR2: S Croy 7D 168
Kensington Village W14 4H 99
Kensington W. W14 4G 99
Kensworth Ho. *EC1* *2F 9*
(off Cranwood St.)
Kent Av. DA16: Well 5K 125
RM9: Dag 4G 91
W13 5B 78
Kent Cl. BR6: Chels 6J 173
CR4: Mitc 4J 155
Kent Ct. E2 2F 85
NW9 2A 44
Kent Dr. EN4: Cockf 4K 21
TW11: Tedd 5J 131
Kentford Way UB5: N'olt 1C 76
Kent Gdns. HA4: Ruis 6J 39
W13 5B 78
Kent Ga. Way CR0: Addtn 6B 170
Kent Ho. SE1 5F 103
SW1 *5C 18*
(off Aylesford St.)
W4 *5A 98*
(off Devonshire St.)
W8 *2K 99*
(off Kensington Ct.)
W11 *1H 99*
(off Boyne Ter. M.)
Kent Ho. App. Rd. BR3: Beck 1A 158
Kent Ho. La. BR3: Beck 6A 140
Kent Ho. Rd. BR3: Beck 1K 157
SE26 5A 140
Kentish Bldgs. SE1 5E 14 (2D 102)
Kentish Pl. SE2 3A 108
Kentish Rd. DA17: Belv 4G 109
KENTISH TOWN 5F 65
Kentish Town Ind. Est. NW5 5F 65
Kentish Town Rd. NW1 7F 65
NW5 7F 65
Kentish Town Sports Cen. 6F 65
Kentish Way BR1: Brom 2K 159
BR2: Brom 2K 159
Kentlea Rd. SE28 2J 107
Kentmere Ho. SE15 6J 103
Kentmere Mans. W5 4B 78
Kentmere Rd. SE18 4J 107
KENTON 5C 42
Kenton Av. HA1: Harr 7K 41
TW16: Sun 2B 148
UB1: S'hall 7E 76
Kenton Ct. HA3: Kenton 6B 42
SE26 *4A 140*
(off Adamsrill Rd.)
TW1: Twick 6D 114
W14 3H 99
Kentone Ct. SE25 4H 157
Kenton Gdns. HA3: Kenton 5C 42
Kenton Ho. *E1* *4J 85*
(off Mantus Cl.)
Kentonian Cl. HA3: Kenton 5B 42
Kenton La.
HA3: Hrw W, Kenton, W'stone 6E 26
Kenton Pk. Av. HA3: Kenton 5D 42
Kenton Pk. Cl. HA3: Kenton 4C 42
Kenton Pk. Cres. HA3: Kenton 4D 42
Kenton Pk. Mans. *HA3: Kenton* *5C 42*
(off Kenton Rd.)
Kenton Pk. Pde. HA3: Kenton 5C 42
Kenton Pk. Rd. HA3: Kenton 4C 42
Kenton Rd. E9 6K 67
HA1: Harr 7K 41
HA3: Kenton 6A 42
Kenton St. WC1 3E 6 (4J 83)
Kenton Way UB4: Hayes 3G 75
Kent Pk. Ind. Est. SE15 6H 103
Kent Pas. NW1 3E 4 (4D 82)
Kent Rd. BR4: W W'ck 1D 170
KT1: King T 3D 150
KT8: E Mos 4G 149
N21 1J 33
RM10: Dag 5H 73
TW9: Kew 7G 97
W4 3J 97
Kent's Pas. TW12: Hamp 1D 148
Kent St. E2 2F 85
E13 3A 88
Kent Ter. NW1 2D 4 (3C 82)
Kent Vw. Gdns. IG3: Ilf 2J 71
Kent Wlk. SW9 4B 120
Kent Way KT6: Surb 3E 162
Kentwell Cl. SE4 4A 122
Kent Wharf *SE8* *7D 104*
(off Creekside)
Kentwode Grn. SW13 7C 98
Kent Yd. SW7 7D 10 (2C 100)
Kenver Av. N12 6G 31
Kenward Rd. SE9 5A 124
Kenward Way SW11 2E 118
Ken Way HA9: Wemb 3J 61
Kenway RM5: Col R 2J 55
Kenway Rd. SW5 4K 99
Ken Wilson Ho. *E2* *2G 85*
(off Pritchards Rd.)
Kenwood Av. N14 5C 22
Kenwood Cl. NW3 1B 64
UB7: Sip 6C 92
Kenwood Ct. *NW9* *4J 43*
(off Elmwood Cres.)
Kenwood Dr. BR3: Beck 3E 158
Kenwood Gdns. E18 3K 51
IG2: Ilf 5E 52
IG5: Ilf 4E 52
Kenwood House 1C 64
Kenwood Ho. SW9 4B 120
Kenwood Pl. N6 1D 64
Kenwood Rd. N6 6D 46
N9 1B 34
Kenworthy Rd. E9 5A 68
Kenwrick Ho. *N1* *1K 83*
(off Barnsbury Est.)
Kenwyn Dr. NW2 2A 62
Kenwyn Lodge N2 4D 46
Kenwyn Rd. SW4 4H 119
SW20 1E 152
Kenya Rd. SE7 7B 106
Kenyngton Ct. TW16: Sun 5J 129
Kenyngton Dr. TW16: Sun 5J 129
Kenyngton Pl. HA3: Kenton 5C 42
Kenyon Ho. *SE5* *7C 102*
(off Camberwell Rd.)
Kenyon Mans. *W14* *6G 99*
(off Queen's Club Gdns.)
Kenyon St. SW6 1F 117
Keogh Rd. E15 6G 69
Kepler Ho. *SE10* *5H 105*
(off Armitage Rd.)
Kepler Rd. SW4 4J 119
Keppel Ho. SE8 5B 104
SW3 *4C 16*
(off Elystan St.)

Keppel Rd. E6 . . . . .7D **70**
   RM9: Dag 4E **72**
Keppel Row SE1 . . . . .5C **14** (1C **102**)
Keppel St. WC1 . . . . .5D **6** (5H **83**)
Kepplestone M. BR3: Beck 2E **158**
Kerbela St. E2 . . . . .3K **9** (4G **85**)
Kerbey St. E14 . . . . .6D **86**
Kerfield Cres. SE5 . . . . .1D **120**
Kerfield Pl. SE5 . . . . .1D **120**
Kerlin Vw. SW16 . . . . .2G **155**
Kerr Cl. CR2: Sels 7A **170**
Kerridge Ct. N1 . . . . .6E **66**
   (off Balls Pond Rd.)
Kerrier Ho. SW10 . . . . .7A **100**
   (off Stadium St.)
Kerrington Ct. W10 . . . . .4G **81**
   (off Wornington Rd.)
   W12 . . . . .2E **98**
   (off Uxbridge Rd.)
Kerris Ho. SE11 . . . . .5K **19**
   (off Tavy Cl.)
Kerrison Pl. W5 . . . . .1D **96**
Kerrison Rd. E15 . . . . .1F **87**
   SW11 . . . . .3C **118**
   W5 . . . . .1D **96**
Kerrison Vs. W5 . . . . .1D **96**
Kerry Av. HA7: Stan 4H **27**
Kerry Cl. E16 . . . . .6K **87**
   N13 . . . . .2E **32**
Kerry Ct. HA7: Stan 4J **27**
Kerry Ho. E1 . . . . .6J **85**
   (off Sidney St.)
Kerry Path SE14 . . . . .6B **104**
Kerry Rd. SE14 . . . . .6B **104**
Kerscott Ho. E3 . . . . .2C **86**
   (off Rainhill Way)
Kersey Gdns. SE9 . . . . .4C **142**
Kersfield Ho. SW15 . . . . .6F **117**
Kersfield Rd. SW15 . . . . .6F **117**
Kershaw Cl. SW18 . . . . .6B **118**
Kershaw Rd. RM10: Dag 3G **73**
Kersley M. SW11 . . . . .1D **118**
Kersley Rd. N16 . . . . .2E **66**
Kersley St. SW11 . . . . .2D **118**
Kerstin Cl. UB3: Hayes 7H **75**
Kerswell Cl. N15 . . . . .5E **48**
Kerwick Cl. N7 . . . . .7J **65**
Keslake Mans. NW10 . . . . .2F **81**
   (off Station Ter.)
Keslake Rd. NW6 . . . . .2F **81**
Kessock Cl. N17 . . . . .5H **49**
Kestlake Rd. DA5: Bexl 6C **126**
KESTON 5A **172**
Keston Av. BR2: Kes 5A **172**
Keston Cl. DA16: Well 7C **108**
   N18 . . . . .3J **33**
Keston Ct. DA5: Bexl 7F **127**
   KT5: Surb 5F **151**
   (off Cranes Pk.)
Keston Gdns.
   BR2: Kes 4A **172**
Keston Ho. SE17 . . . . .5E **102**
   (off Kinglake Est.)
KESTON MARK 4C **172**
KESTON MARK **3C 172**
Keston Pk. Cl. BR2: Kes 3D **172**
Keston Rd.
   CR7: Thor H 6A **156**
   N17 . . . . .3D **48**
   SE15 . . . . .3G **121**
Kestrel Av. E6 . . . . .5C **88**
   SE24 . . . . .5B **120**
Kestrel Cl. KT2: King T 4D **132**
   NW9 . . . . .2A **44**
   NW10 . . . . .5K **61**
Kestrel Ct. CR2: S Croy 6C **168**
   E3 . . . . .2C **86**
   (off Four Seasons Cl.)
   E17 . . . . .2K **49**
   HA4: Ruis 2G **57**
   SM6: Wall 5G **167**

Kestrel Ho. EC1 . . . . .1C **8**
   (off Pickard Cl.)
   EN3: Pond E 5F **25**
   SE10 . . . . .1E **122**
   (off Parkside Av.)
Kestrel Pl. SE14 . . . . .6A **104**
Kestrel Way CRO: New Ad 7F **171**
   UB3: Hayes 2F **93**
Keswick Av. SW15 . . . . .5A **134**
   SW19 . . . . .2J **153**
   TW17: Shep 3G **147**
Keswick B'way. SW15 . . . . .5H **117**
   (off Up. Richmond Rd.)
Keswick Cl. SM1: Sutt 4A **166**
   Keswick Cl. BR2: Brom 4H **159**
   SE6 . . . . .1H **141**
   SE13 . . . . .5D **122**
Keswick Gdns. HA4: Ruis 6F **39**
   HA9: Wemb 4E **60**
   IG4: Ilf 4C **52**
Keswick Ho. SE5 . . . . .2C **120**
Keswick M. W5 . . . . .1E **96**
Keswick Rd. BR4: W W'ck 2G **171**
   BR6: Orp 1K **173**
   DA7: Bex 1G **127**
   SW15 . . . . .5G **117**
   TW2: Whitt 6G **113**
Kettering Ct. CR7: Thor H 4C **156**
Kettering St. SW16 . . . . .6G **137**
Kett Gdns. SW2 . . . . .5K **119**
Kettlebaston Rd. E10 . . . . .1B **68**
Kettleby Ho. SW9 . . . . .3B **120**
   (off Barrington Rd.)
Kettlewell Cl. N11 . . . . .6K **31**
Ketton Ho. W10 . . . . .4E **80**
   (off Sutton Way)
Kevan Ct. E17 . . . . .4C **50**
Kevan Ho. SE5 . . . . .7C **102**
Kevelioc Rd. N17 . . . . .1C **48**
Kevin Cl. TW4: Houn 2B **112**
Kevington Cl. BR5: St P 4K **161**
Kevington Dr. BR5: St P 4K **161**
   BR7: Chst 4K **161**
KEW 1G **115**
KEW BRIDGE 5F **97**
Kew Bri. TW8: Bford 6G **97**
Kew Bri. Arches TW8: Kew 6G **97**
Kew Bri. Ct. W4 . . . . .5G **97**
Kew Bri. Distribution Cen.
   TW8: Bford 6G **97**
Kew Bri. Rd. TW8: Bford 6F **97**
Kew Cl. KT2: King T 1E **150**
Kew Cres. SM3: Cheam 3G **165**
Kew Foot Rd. TW9: Rich 4E **114**
Kew Gdns. 7E **96**
Kew Gdns. Rd. TW9: Kew 7F **97**
KEW GREEN 7G **97**
Kew Grn. TW9: Kew 6F **97**
Kew Mdw. Path TW9: Kew 2J **115**
   (Clifford Av.)
   TW9: Kew 1H **115**
   (Magnolia Ct.)
Kew Retail Pk. TW9: Kew 1H **115**
Kew Riverside Pk. TW9: Kew 7H **97**
Kew Rd. TW9: Kew, Rich 6G **97**
Keybridge Ho. SW8 . . . . .7F **19**
   (off Miles St.)
Key Cl. E1 . . . . .4J **85**
Keyes Ho. SW1 . . . . .6C **18**
   (off Dolphin Sq.)
Keyes Rd. NW2 . . . . .5F **63**
Keyham Ho. W2 . . . . .5J **81**
   (off Westbourne Pk. Rd.)
Key Ho. SE11 . . . . .7K **19** (6A **102**)
Keymer Rd. SW2 . . . . .2K **137**
Keynes Cl. N2 . . . . .4D **46**
Keynes Ct. SE28 . . . . .7B **90**
   (off Attlee Rd.)
Keynsham Av.
   IG8: Wfd G 4B **36**
Keynsham Gdns. SE9 . . . . .5C **124**

Keynsham Rd. SE9 . . . . .5B **124**
   SM4: Mord 1K **165**
Keynsham Wlk. SM4: Mord 1K **165**
Keys Cl. CRO: C'don 3D **168**
   (off Beech Ho. Rd.)
Keyse Rd. SE1 . . . . .3F **103**
Keysham Av. TW5: Cran 1J **111**
Keystone Cres. N1 . . . . . . .1F **7** (2J **83**)
Key W. Ct. IG7: Chig 4K **37**
Keywood Dr. TW16: Sun 6J **129**
Keyworth Cl. E5 . . . . .4A **68**
Keyworth Pl. SE1 . . . . .7B **14**
Keyworth St. SE1 . . . . . .7B **14** (3B **102**)
Kezia M. SE8 . . . . .5A **104**
Kezia St. SE8 . . . . .5A **104**
Khalsa Ct. N22 . . . . .1B **48**
Khama Rd. SW17 . . . . .4C **136**
Khartoum Rd. E13 . . . . .3K **87**
   IG1: Ilf 5F **71**
   SW17 . . . . .4B **136**
Khyber Rd. SW11 . . . . .2C **118**
Kia Oval 7H **19** (6K **101**)
Kibble Cl. RM6: Chad H 7C **54**
Kibworth St. SW8 . . . . .7K **101**
KIDBROOKE 2K **123**
Kidbrooke Est. SE3 . . . . .3A **124**
Kidbrooke Gdns. SE3 . . . . .2J **123**
Kidbrooke Green Nature Reserve . . .3A **124**
Kidbrooke Gro. SE3 . . . . .1J **123**
Kidbrooke La. SE9 . . . . .4C **124**
Kidbrooke Pk. Cl. SE3 . . . . .1K **123**
Kidbrooke Pk. Rd. SE3 . . . . .1K **123**
Kidbrooke Way SE3 . . . . .2K **123**
Kidderminster Pl. CRO: C'don 1B **168**
Kidderminster Rd. CRO: C'don 1B **168**
Kidderpore Av. NW3 . . . . .4J **63**
Kidderpore Gdns. NW3 . . . . .4J **63**
Kidd Pl. SE7 . . . . .5C **106**
Kidspace
   Croydon 6A **168**
Kierbeck Bus. Complex E16 . . . . . .2K **105**
   (not continuous)
Kiffen St. EC2 . . . . .3F **9** (4D **84**)
Kilberry Cl. TW7: Isle 1H **113**
Kilbrennan Ho. E14 . . . . .6E **86**
   (off Findhorn St.)
KILBURN 2H **81**
Kilburn Bri. NW6 . . . . .1J **81**
Kilburn Ga. NW6 . . . . .2K **81**
Kilburn High Rd. NW6 . . . . .7H **63**
Kilburn Ho. W9 . . . . .2H **81**
   (off Malvern Rd.)
Kilburn La. W9 . . . . .3F **81**
   W10 . . . . .3F **81**
Kilburn Pk. Rd. NW6 . . . . .3J **81**
Kilburn Pl. NW6 . . . . .1J **81**
Kilburn Priory NW6 . . . . .1K **81**
Kilburn Sq. NW6 . . . . .1J **81**
Kilburn Va. NW6 . . . . .1K **81**
Kilburn Va. Est. NW6 . . . . .1K **81**
   (off Kilburn Vale)
Kilby Ct. SE10 . . . . .3H **105**
   (off Greenroof Way)
Kildare Cl. HA4: Ruis 1A **58**
Kildare Ct. W2 . . . . .6J **81**
   (off Kildare Ter.)
Kildare Gdns. W2 . . . . .6J **81**
Kildare Rd. E16 . . . . .5J **87**
Kildare Ter. W2 . . . . .6J **81**
Kildare Wlk. E14 . . . . .6C **86**
Kildoran Rd. SW2 . . . . .5J **119**
Kildowan Rd. IG3: Ilf 1A **72**
Kilgour Rd. SE23 . . . . .6A **122**
Kilkie St. SW6 . . . . .2A **118**
Killarney Rd. SW18 . . . . .6A **118**
Killburns Mill Cl. SM6: Wall 2F **167**
Killearn Rd. SE6 . . . . .1F **141**
Killester Gdns. KT4: Wor Pk 4D **164**
Killick Ho. SM1: Sutt 4K **165**
Killick M. SM3: Cheam 6G **165**
Killick St. N1 . . . . .1G **7** (2K **83**)

Killick Way E1 . . . . .5K **85**
Killieser Av. SW2 . . . . .2J **137**
Killigarth Ct. DA14: Sidc 4A **144**
Killigrew Ho. TW16: Sun 7G **129**
Killip Cl. E16 . . . . .6H **87**
Killoran Ho. E14 . . . . .3E **104**
   (off Galbraith St.)
Killowen Av. UB5: N'olt 5G **59**
Killowen Rd. E9 . . . . .6K **67**
Killyon Rd. SW8 . . . . .2G **119**
Killyon Ter. SW8 . . . . .2G **119**
Kilmaine Rd. SW6 . . . . .7G **99**
Kilmarnock Gdns. RM8: Dag 3C **72**
Kilmarsh Rd. W6 . . . . .4E **98**
Kilmartin Av. SW16 . . . . .3A **156**
Kilmartin Rd. IG3: Ilf 2A **72**
Kilmington Rd. SW13 . . . . .6C **98**
Kilmiston Av. TW17: Shep 6E **146**
Kilmiston Ho. TW17: Shep 6E **146**
Kilmore Ho. E14 . . . . .6D **86**
   (off Vesey Path)
Kilmorey Gdns. TW1: Twick 5B **114**
Kilmorey Rd. TW1: Twick 4B **114**
Kilmorie Rd. SE23 . . . . .1A **140**
Kilmuir Ho. SW1 . . . . .4H **17**
   (off Bury St.)
Kiln Cl. UB3: Harl 6F **93**
Kiln Ct. E14 . . . . .7B **86**
   (off Newell St.)
Kilner Ho. E16 . . . . .5K **87**
   (off Freemasons Rd.)
   SE11 . . . . .7J **19**
Kilner St. E14 . . . . .5C **86**
Kiln Ho. E1 . . . . .5K **85**
   (off Duckett St.)
Kiln M. SW17 . . . . .5B **136**
Kiln Pl. NW5 . . . . .5E **64**
Kilnside KT10: Clay 7A **162**
Kilpatrick Way UB4: Yead 5C **76**
Kilravock St. W10 . . . . .3G **81**
Kilronan W3 . . . . .6K **79**
Kilross Rd. TW14: Bedf 1F **129**
Kilsby Wlk. RM9: Dag 6B **72**
Kilsha Rd. KT12: Walt T 6A **148**
Kimbell Gdns. SW6 . . . . .1G **117**
Kimbell Pl. SE3 . . . . .4A **124**
Kimber Ct. SE1 . . . . .7G **15**
   (off Long La.)
Kimberley Av. E6 . . . . .2C **88**
   IG2: Ilf 7H **53**
   RM7: Rom 6J **55**
   SE15 . . . . .2H **121**
Kimberley Ct. NW6 . . . . .1G **81**
   (off Kimberley Rd.)
Kimberley Dr. DA14: Sidc 2D **144**
Kimberley Gdns. EN1: Enf 3A **24**
   N4 . . . . .5B **48**
Kimberley Ga. BR1: Brom 7G **141**
Kimberley Ho. E14 . . . . .3E **104**
   (off Galbraith St.)
Kimberley Rd. BR3: Beck 2K **157**
   CRO: C'don 6B **156**
   E4 . . . . .1B **36**
   E11 . . . . .2F **69**
   E16 . . . . .4H **87**
   E17 . . . . .1A **50**
   N17 . . . . .2G **49**
   N18 . . . . .5C **34**
   NW6 . . . . .1G **81**
   SW9 . . . . .2J **119**
Kimberley Wlk. KT12: Walt T 7K **147**
Kimberley Way E4 . . . . .1B **36**
Kimber Pl. TW4: Houn 7D **112**
   (Conway Rd.)
   TW4: Houn 4D **112**
   (Marryat Cl.)
Kimber Rd. SW18 . . . . .7J **117**
Kimble Cres. WD23: Bush 1B **26**
Kimble Ho. NW8 . . . . .3D **4**
Kimble Rd. SW19 . . . . .6B **136**
Kimbolton Cl. SE12 . . . . .6H **123**

Kimbolton Ct. SW3 . . . . .4C 16
    (off Fulham Rd.)
Kimbolton Row SW3 . . . . .4C 16
    (off Fulham Rd.)
Kimmeridge Gdns. SE9 . . . . .4C 142
Kimmeridge Rd. SE9 . . . . .4C 142
Kimmins Ct. SE16 . . . . .7K 15
    (off Old Jamaica Rd.)
Kimpton Ho. SW15 . . . . .7C 116
Kimpton Ind. Est. SM3: Sutt 2H 165
Kimpton Link Bus. Cen. SM3: Sutt . .2H 165
Kimpton Pk. Way SM1: Sutt 2G 165
    SM3: Sutt 2G 165
Kimpton Rd. SE5 . . . . .1D 120
    SM3: Sutt 2H 165
Kimpton Trade & Bus. Cen.
    SM3: Sutt 2H 165
Kinburn St. SE16 . . . . .2K 103
Kincaid Rd. SE15 . . . . .7H 103
Kincardine Gdns. W9 . . . . .4J 81
    (off Harrow Rd.)
Kincha Lodge KT2: King T 1F 151
    (off Elm Rd.)
Kinch Gro. HA9: Wemb 7F 43
Kinder Cl. SE28 . . . . .7D 90
Kinder Ho. N1 . . . . .2D 84
    (off Cranston Est.)
Kindersley Ho. E1 . . . . .6G 85
    (off Pinchin St.)
Kinder St. E1 . . . . .6H 85
Kinderton Cl. N14 . . . . .1B 32
Kinefold Ho. N7 . . . . .6J 65
    (off York Way Est.)
Kinesis Gym & Fitness Cen 4C 124
    (off Well Hall Rd.)
Kinfauns Rd. IG3: Ilf 1A 72
    SW2 . . . . .2A 138
King Alfred Av. SE6 . . . . .4C 140
    (not continuous)
King & Queen Cl. SE9 . . . . .4C 142
King & Queen St. SE17 . . . . .5C 102
King & Queen Wharf SE16 . . . . .7K 85
King Arthur Cl. SE15 . . . . .7J 103
KING CHARLES I ISLAND 4E 12
King Charles Ct. SE17 . . . . .6B 102
    (off Royal Rd.)
King Charles Cres. KT5: Surb 7F 151
King Charles Ho. SW6 . . . . .7K 99
    (off Wandon Rd.)
King Charles Rd. KT5: Surb 5F 151
    (Park Row)
King Charles St. SW1 . . . . . . .6D 12 (2H 101)
King Charles Ter. E1 . . . . .7H 85
    (off Sovereign Cl.)
King Charles Wlk. SW19 . . . . .1G 135
King Ct. E10 . . . . .7D 50
Kingcup Cl. CR0: C'don 7K 157
King David La. E1 . . . . .7J 85
Kingdom St. W2 . . . . .5A 82
Kingdon Ho. E14 . . . . .3E 104
    (off Galbraith St.)
Kingdon Rd. NW6 . . . . .6J 63
King Edward III M. SE16 . . . . .2H 103
King Edward Bldg. EC1 . . . . .7B 8
    (off King Edward St.)
King Edward Ct. HA9: Wemb 5E 60
    (off Elm Rd.)
King Edward Dr. KT9: Chess 3E 162
King Edward Mans. E8 . . . . .1H 85
    (off Mare St.)
King Edward M. SW13 . . . . .1C 116
King Edward Rd. E10 . . . . .1E 68
    E17 . . . . .3A 50
    EN5: New Bar 4D 20
King Edward's Gdns. W3 . . . . .1G 97
King Edwards Gro.
    TW11: Tedd 6B 132
King Edwards Mans. SW6 . . . . .7J 99
    (off Fulham Rd.)
King Edward's Pl. W3 . . . . .1G 97

King Edward's Rd. E9 . . . . .1H 85
    EN3: Pond E 4E 24
    HA4: Ruis 1F 57
    N9 . . . . .7C 24
King Edwards Rd.
    IG11: Bark 1H 89
King Edward St. EC1 . . . . .7C 8 (6C 84)
King Edward Wlk. SE1 . . . . . .1K 19 (3A 102)
Kingfield Rd. W5 . . . . .4D 78
Kingfield St. E14 . . . . .4E 104
Kingfisher Av. E11 . . . . .6K 51
Kingfisher Cl. HA3: Hrw W 7E 26
    HA6: Nwood 1D 38
    SE28 . . . . .7C 90
Kingfisher Ct. CR0: C'don 3C 168
    (off Wandle Rd.)
    E14 . . . . .2E 104
    (off River Barge Cl.)
    EN2: Enf 1E 22
    KT8: E Mos 4J 149
    SE1 . . . . .7D 14
    (off Swan St.)
    SM1: Sutt 5H 165
    SW19 . . . . .2F 135
    TW3: Houn 5F 113
    TW7: Isle 2H 113
Kingfisher Dr. TW10: Ham 4B 132
Kingfisher Hgts. E16 . . . . .1A 106
    (off Bramwell Way)
    N17 . . . . .3H 49
    (off Waterside Way)
Kingfisher Ho. SW18 . . . . .3A 118
    W14 . . . . .3H 99
    (off Melbury Rd.)
Kingfisher Leisure Cen.
    Kingston upon Thames 2E 150
Kingfisher M. SE13 . . . . .4C 122
Kingfisher Pl. N22 . . . . .2K 47
Kingfisher Sq. SE8 . . . . .6B 104
    (off Clyde St.)
Kingfisher St. E6 . . . . .5C 88
Kingfisher Wlk. NW9 . . . . .2A 44
Kingfisher Way BR3: Beck 5K 157
    NW10 . . . . .6K 61
King Frederick IX Twr. SE16 . . . . . . .3B 104
King Gdns. CR0: Wadd 5B 168
King George IV Ct. SE17 . . . . .5D 102
    (off Dawes St.)
King George VI Av. CR4: Mitc 4D 154
King George VI Memorial 5C 12
King George Av. E16 . . . . .6A 88
    IG2: Ilf 5H 53
    TW16: Sun 5G 129
King George Cres. HA0: Wemb 5D 60
King George M. SW17 . . . . .5D 136
King George's Dr. UB1: S'hall 5D 76
King George Sq. TW10: Rich 6F 115
King George's Sailing Club 6H 25
King George's Trad. Est.
    KT9: Chess 4G 163
King George St. SE10 . . . . .7E 104
King George Way E4 . . . . .4J 25
Kingham Cl. SW18 . . . . .7A 118
    W11 . . . . .2G 99
King Harolds Way DA7: Belv, Bex 7D 108
    DA17: Belv 7D 108
King Henry Lodge E4 . . . . .4H 35
King Henry M. BR6: Chels 5K 173
    HA2: Harr 1J 59
King Henry's Dr. CR0: New Ad 7D 170
King Henry's Reach W6 . . . . .6E 98
King Henry's Rd. KT1: King T 3H 151
    NW3 . . . . .7C 64
King Henry's Stairs E1 . . . . .1H 103
King Henry St. N16 . . . . .5E 66
King Henry's Wlk. N1 . . . . .6E 66
King Henry Ter. E1 . . . . .7H 85
    (off Sovereign Cl.)
Kinghorn St. EC1 . . . . .6C 8 (5C 84)
King Ho. W12 . . . . .6D 80

Kingisholt Ct. NW10 . . . . .3F 81
    (off Wellington Rd.)
King James Ct. SE1 . . . . .7B 14
King James St. SE1 . . . . . . .7B 14 (2B 102)
King John Ct. EC2 . . . . .3H 9 (4E 84)
King John St. E1 . . . . .5K 85
King John's Wlk. SE9 . . . . .7C 124
Kinglake Est. SE17 . . . . .5E 102
Kinglake St. SE17 . . . . .5E 102
    (not continuous)
Kinglet Cl. E7 . . . . .6J 69
Kingly Ct. W1 . . . . .2B 12
Kingly St. W1 . . . . .1A 12 (6G 83)
Kingsand Rd. SE12 . . . . .2J 141
Kings Arbour UB2: S'hall 5C 94
King's Arms All.
    TW8: Bford 6D 96
Kings Arms Ct. E1 . . . . .5G 85
King's Arms Yd. SW18 . . . . .5K 117
Kings Arms Yd. EC2 . . . . .7E 8 (6D 84)
Kingsash Dr. UB4: Yead 4C 76
King's Av. IG8: Wfd G 6E 36
    IG9: Buck H 6E 36
    (The Broadway)
    IG9: Buck H 2G 37
    (Langfords)
    N10 . . . . .3E 46
    SM5: Cars 7C 166
    TW16: Sun 5H 129
    UB6: G'frd 5F 77
Kings Av. BR1: Brom 6H 141
    KT3: N Mald 4A 152
    N21 . . . . .1G 33
    RM6: Chad H 6F 55
    SW4 . . . . .1H 137
    SW12 . . . . .1H 137
    TW3: Houn 1F 113
King's Bench St. SE1 . . . . . . .6B 14 (2B 102)
King's Bench Wlk.
    EC4 . . . . .1K 13 (6A 84)
King's Blvd. N1 . . . . .2J 83
Kingsbridge Av. W3 . . . . .2F 97
Kingsbridge Ct. E14 . . . . .3C 104
    (off Dockers Tanner Rd.)
    NW1 . . . . .7F 65
    (off Castlehaven Rd.)
Kingsbridge Cres. UB1: S'hall 5D 76
Kingsbridge Dr. NW7 . . . . .7A 30
Kingsbridge Rd. IG11: Bark 2H 89
    KT12: Walt T 7K 147
    SM4: Mord 6F 153
    UB2: S'hall 4D 94
    W10 . . . . .6E 80
Kingsbridge Way UB4: Hayes 3G 75
Kingsbridge Wharf IG11: Bark 3J 89
KINGSBURY .5H 43
Kingsbury Circ. NW9 . . . . .5G 43
KINGSBURY GREEN 6K 43
Kingsbury Rd. N1 . . . . .6E 66
    NW9 . . . . .5G 43
Kingsbury Ter. N1 . . . . .6E 66
Kingsbury Trad. Est. NW9 . . . . .6K 43
Kings Chase KT8: E Mos 3G 149
Kings Chase Vw. EN2: Enf 2F 23
Kingsclere Cl. SW15 . . . . .7C 116
Kingsclere Ct. N12 . . . . .5H 31
Kingsclere Pl. EN2: Enf 2H 23
Kingscliffe Gdns. SW19 . . . . .1H 135
King's Cl. DA1: Cray 4K 127
    NW4 . . . . .4F 45
Kings Cl. E10 . . . . .7D 50
    KT7: T Ditt 6A 150
    KT12: Walt T 7K 147
    TW18: Staines 7A 128
Kings Club, The 6E 134
Kings Coll. Ct. NW3 . . . . .7C 64
King's College London
    Denmark Hill Campus 2D 120
    Guy's Campus 1D 102
    Maughan Library 7J 7 (6A 84)

King's College London
    St Thomas' Campus -
      Lambeth Pal. Rd. 2F 19
      St Thomas' House 1G 19
    Strand Campus 2H 13 (7K 83)
    Waterloo Campus 5J 13 (1A 102)
King's Coll. Rd. NW3 . . . . .7C 64
Kings Coll. Rd. HA4: Ruis 6H 39
King's College School of
    Medicine & Dentistry 2C 120
Kingscote Rd. CR0: C'don 7H 157
    KT3: N Mald 3K 151
    W4 . . . . .3K 97
Kingscote St. EC4 . . . . .2A 14 (7B 84)
King's Ct. E13 . . . . .1K 87
    SE1 . . . . .6B 14 (2B 102)
Kings Ct. HA9: Wemb 2H 61
    IG9: Buck H 2G 37
    N7 . . . . .7K 65
    (off Caledonian Rd.)
    NW8 . . . . .1D 82
    (off Prince Albert Rd.)
    W6 . . . . .4C 98
Kings Ct. Mans. SW6 . . . . .1H 117
    (off Fulham Rd.)
Kings Ct. M. KT8: E Mos 5H 149
Kings Ct. Nth. SW3 . . . . . . .6C 16 (5C 100)
Kingscourt Rd. SW16 . . . . .3H 137
King's Ct. Sth. SW3 . . . . .6C 16
King's Cres. N4 . . . . .3C 66
Kings Cres. Est. N4 . . . . .2C 66
Kingscroft SW4 . . . . .6J 119
Kingscroft Rd. NW2 . . . . .6H 63
KING'S CROSS 2J 83
King's Cross Bri. N1 . . . . .1F 7
King's Cross Rd. WC1 . . . . . . .1G 7 (3K 83)
King's Cross Sq. N1 . . . . .3J 83
    (off Euston Rd.)
Kingsdale Gdns. W11 . . . . .1F 99
Kingsdale Rd. SE18 . . . . .7K 107
    SE20 . . . . .7K 139
Kingsdown Av.
    CR2: S Croy 7C 168
    W3 . . . . .7A 80
    W13 . . . . .2B 96
Kingsdown Cl. SE16 . . . . .5H 103
    (off Masters Dr.)
    W10 . . . . .6F 81
Kingsdowne Rd. KT6: Surb 7E 150
Kingsdown Ho. E8 . . . . .5G 67
Kingsdown Point SW2 . . . . .2A 138
Kingsdown Rd. E11 . . . . .3G 69
    N19 . . . . .2J 65
    SM3: Cheam 5G 165
Kingsdown Way BR2: Hayes 7J 159
King's Dr. HA8: Edg 4A 28
Kings Dr. HA9: Wemb 2H 61
    KT5: Surb 7G 151
    KT7: T Ditt 7B 150
    TW11: Tedd 5H 131
Kingsend HA4: Ruis 1F 57
Kingsend Ct. HA4: Ruis 1G 57
Kings Farm E17 . . . . .1D 50
Kings Farm Av. TW10: Rich 4G 115
Kingsfield Av. HA2: Harr 4F 41
Kingsfield Ho. SE9 . . . . .3B 142
Kingsfield Rd. HA1: Harr 7H 41
Kingsfield Ter. HA1: Harr 1H 59
Kingsford St. NW5 . . . . .5D 64
King's Gdns. NW6 . . . . .7J 63
Kings Gdns. IG1: Ilf 1H 71
    KT12: Walt T 7K 147
Kings Gth. M. SE23 . . . . .2J 139
Kingsgate HA9: Wemb 3J 61
Kingsgate Av. N3 . . . . .3J 45
Kingsgate Bus. Cen. KT2: King T 1E 150
    (off Kingsgate Rd.)
Kingsgate Cl. DA7: Bex 1E 126
Kingsgate Est. N1 . . . . .6E 66
Kingsgate Ho. SW9 . . . . .1A 120

Kingsgate Mans. WC1 . . . . .6G 7
(off Red Lion Sq.)
Kings Ga. M. N8 . . . . .5K 47
(off Spencer Rd.)
Kingsgate Pde. SW1 . . . . .2B 18
Kingsgate Pl. NW6 . . . . .7J 63
Kingsgate Rd. KT1: King T 1E 150
KT2: King T 1E 150
NW6 . . . . .7J 63
Kings Ga. Wlk. SW1 . . . . .1B 18
(off Victoria St.)
Kings Grange HA4: Ruis 1H 57
Kingsground SE9 . . . . .7B 124
King's Gro. SE15 . . . . .7H 103
(not continuous)
Kingsgrove Cl. DA14: Sidc 4K 143
Kings Hall Leisure Cen. 5J 67
Kings Hall M. SE13 . . . . .3E 122
Kings Hall Rd. BR3: Beck 7A 140
Kings Head Hill E4 . . . . .7J 25
Kingshead Ho. NW7 . . . . .4J 29
Kings Head Pas. SW4 . . . . .4H 119
(off Clapham Pk. Rd.)
Kings Head Theatre 1B 84
(off Upper St.)
King's Head Yd. SE1 . . . .5E 14 (1D 102)
King's Highway SE18 . . . . .6J 107
Kingshill Av. HA3: Kenton 4B 42
KT4: Wor Pk 7C 152
UB4: Hayes, Yead 3G 75
UB5: N'olt 3G 75
Kingshill Cl. UB4: Hayes 3U 75
Kingshill Cl. EN5: Barn 4B 20
Kingshill Dr. HA3: Kenton 2B 42
Kingshold Rd. E9 . . . . .7J 67
Kingsholm Gdns. SE9 . . . . .4B 124
King's Ho. SW10 . . . . .7A 16
(off King's Rd.)
Kings Ho. SW8 . . . . .7J 101
(off Sth. Lambeth Rd.)
King's Ho. Studios SW10 . . . . .7A 16
(off Lamont Rd. Pas.)
Kingshurst Rd. SE12 . . . . .7J 123
Kingside SE18 . . . . .3C 106
Kings Keep BR2: Brom 2G 159
KT1: King T 4E 150
SW15 . . . . .5F 117
KINGSLAND 6E 66
Kingsland NW8 . . . . .1C 82
Kingsland Grn. E8 . . . . .6E 66
Kingsland High St. E8 . . . . .6F 67
Kingsland Pas. E8 . . . . .6E 66
Kingsland Rd. E2 . . . . . . .2H 9 (3E 84)
E8 . . . . .3E 84
E13 . . . . .3A 88
Kingsland Shop. Cen. E8 . . . . .6F 67
Kings La. SM1: Sutt 6B 166
Kingslawn Cl. SW15 . . . . .5D 116
Kingslee Cl. SM2: Sutt 7K 165
Kingsleigh Cl. TW8: Bford 6D 96
Kingsleigh Pl. CR4: Mitc 3D 154
Kingsleigh Wlk. BR2: Brom 4H 159
Kingsley Av. SM1: Sutt 4B 166
TW3: Houn 2G 113
UB1: S'hall 7E 76
W13 . . . . .5A 78
Kingsley Cl. N2 . . . . .5A 46
RM10: Dag 4H 73
Kingsley Ct. DA6: Bex 4G 127
HA8: Edg 3C 28
KT4: Wor Pk 2B 164
(off The Avenue)
NW2 . . . . .6D 62
Kingsley Dr. KT4: Wor Pk 2B 164
Kingsley Flats SE1 . . . . .4E 102
(off Old Kent Rd.)
Kingsley Gdns. E4 . . . . .5H 35
Kingsley Ho. SW3 . . . . .6B 100
(off Beaufort St.)
W14 . . . . .4G 99
(off Avonmore Pl.)

Kingsley Mans. W14 . . . . .6G 99
(off Greyhound Rd.)
Kingsley M. BR7: Chst 6F 143
E1 . . . . .7H 85
W8 . . . . .3K 99
Kingsley Pl. N6 . . . . .7E 46
Kingsley Rd. BR6: Chels 7K 173
CR0: C'don 1A 168
E7 . . . . .7J 69
E17 . . . . .2E 50
HA2: Harr 4G 59
HA5: Pinn 4D 40
IG6: Ilf 1G 53
N13 . . . . .4F 33
NW6 . . . . .1H 81
SW19 . . . . .5K 135
TW3: Houn 1F 113
Kingsley St. SW11 . . . . .3D 118
Kingsley Way N2 . . . . .5A 46
Kingsley Wood Dr. SE9 . . . . .3D 142
Kings Lodge HA4: Ruis 1G 57
(off Pembroke Rd.)
N12 . . . . .6F 31
Kingslyn Cres. SE19 . . . . .1E 156
Kings Mall W6 . . . . .4E 98
Kingsman Pde. SE18 . . . . .3D 106
Kings Mans. SW3 . . . . .7C 16
(off Lawrence St.)
Kingsman St. SE18 . . . . .3D 106
Kingsmead EN5: New Bar 4D 20
TW10: Rich 6F 115
Kingsmead Av. CR4: Mitc 3G 155
KT4: Wor Pk 2D 164
KT6: Surb 2G 163
N9 . . . . .1C 34
NW9 . . . . .7K 43
TW16: Sun 2A 148
Kingsmead Cl. DA15: Sidc 2A 144
KT19: Ewe 7K 163
TW11: Tedd 6B 132
Kingsmead Cotts. BR2: Brom 1C 172
Kingsmead Ct. N6 . . . . .7H 47
Kingsmead Dr. UB5: N'olt 7D 58
Kingsmead Ho. E9 . . . . .4A 68
Kingsmead Lodge SM2: Sutt 6B 166
Kingsmeadow 3G 151
Kingsmeadow Athletics Cen. 3G 151
Kingsmead Rd. SW2 . . . . .2A 138
Kingsmead Way E9 . . . . .4A 68
Kingsmere Cl. SW15 . . . . .3F 117
Kingsmere Pk. NW9 . . . . .1H 61
Kingsmere Pl. N16 . . . . .1D 66
Kingsmere Rd. SW19 . . . . .2F 135
King's M. SW4 . . . . .5J 119
WC1 . . . . .4H 7 (4K 83)
Kingsmill NW8 . . . . .2B 82
(off Kingsmill Ter.)
Kingsmill Bus. Cen. KT1: King T 3F 151
Kingsmill Gdns. RM9: Dag 5F 73
Kingsmill Ho. SW3 . . . . .5D 16
(off Cale St.)
Kingsmill Rd. RM9: Dag 5F 73
Kingsmill Ter. NW8 . . . . .2B 82
Kingsnorth Ho. W10 . . . . .6F 81
Kingsnympton Pk. KT2: King T 7H 133
Kings Oak RM7: Mawney 3G 55
King's Orchard SE9 . . . . .6C 124
King's Paddock TW12: Hamp 1G 149
King's Pde. HA8: Edg 5B 28
(off Edgwarebury La.)
SM5: Cars 3D 166
(off Wrythe La.)
Kings Pde. N17 . . . . .3F 49
NW10 . . . . .1E 80
W12 . . . . .3C 98
Kingspark Bus. Cen. KT3: N Mald . . .4J 151
Kingspark Ct. E18 . . . . .3J 51
King's Pas. KT2: King T 1D 150
King's Pas. E11 . . . . .7G 51
KT1: King T 2D 150
Kings Place 2J 83

King's Pl. SE1 . . . . .7C 14
W4 . . . . .5J 97
Kings Pl. IG9: Buck H 2F 37
King Sq. EC1 . . . . .2C 8 (3C 84)
Kings Quarter Apartments N1 . . . . . .1K 83
(off Copenhagen St.)
King's Quay SW10 . . . . .1A 118
(off Chelsea Harbour Dr.)
Kings Reach Twr. SE1 . . . . .4A 14
Kings Ride Ga. TW10: Rich 4G 115
Kingsridge SW19 . . . . .2G 135
King's Rd. BR6: Orp 4K 173
E6 . . . . .1A 88
KT2: King T 7E 132
KT6: Surb 1C 162
N17 . . . . .1F 49
SW3 . . . . .6D 16 (7K 99)
SW6 . . . . .7K 99
SW10 . . . . .7A 16 (7K 99)
SW19 . . . . .6J 135
TW11: Tedd 5H 131
UB7: W Dray 2B 92
Kings Rd. CR4: Mitc 3E 154
E11 . . . . .1A 36
E14 . . . . .7G 51
EN5: Barn 3A 20
HA2: Harr 2D 58
IG11: Bark 7G 71
KT12: Walt T 7K 147
N18 . . . . .5B 34
N22 . . . . .1K 47
NW10 . . . . .7D 62
SE25 . . . . .3G 157
SW14 . . . . .3K 115
TW1: Twick 6B 114
TW10: Rich 6F 115
TW13: Felt 1A 130
W5 . . . . .5D 78
King's Scholars' Pas. SW1 . . . . .2A 18
King Stairs Cl. SE16 . . . . .2H 103
King's Ter. NW1 . . . . .1G 83
TW7: Isle 4A 114
Kingsthorpe Rd. SE26 . . . . .4K 139
Kingston Av. SM3: Cheam 3G 165
TW14: Felt 6G 111
UB7: Yiew 7B 74
(Ash Gro.)
UB7: Yiew 1B 92
(Whitethorn Av.)
Kingston Bri. KT1: King T 2D 150
Kingston Bus. Cen. KT9: Chess 3E 162
Kingston By-Pass KT3: N Mald 5A 152
KT6: Surb 3D 162
SW15 . . . . .4A 134
SW20 . . . . .2C 152
Kingston By-Pass Rd. KT6: Surb 3B 162
KT10: Hin W, Surb 3A 162
Kingston Cl. RM6: Chad H 3E 54
(not continuous)
TW11: Tedd 6B 132
UB5: N'olt 1D 76
Kingston Crematorium KT1: King T . . .3G 151
Kingston Cres. BR3: Beck 1B 158
Kingston Gdns. CR0: Bedd 3J 167
Kingston Hall Rd. KT1: King T 3D 150
Kingston Hill KT2: King T 1G 151
Kingston Hill Av. RM6: Chad H 3E 54
Kingston Hill Pl. KT2: King T 4J 133
Kingston Ho. KT1: King T 4D 150
(off Surbiton Rd.)
NW1 . . . . .1G 83
(off Camden St.)
NW6 . . . . .7G 63
Kingston Ho. E. SW7 . . . . .7C 10
(off Prince's Ga.)
Kingston Ho. Est. KT6: Surb 6B 150
Kingston Ho. Nth. SW7 . . . . .7C 10
(off Prince's Ga.)
Kingston Ho. Sth. SW7 . . . . .7C 10
(off Ennismore Gdns.)
Kingstonian FC 3G 151

Kingston La. TW11: Tedd 5A 132
UB7: W Dray 2B 92
UB8: Hil 3A 74
Kingston Lodge KT3: N Mald 4A 152
Kingston Mans. SW9 . . . . .1K 119
(off Clapham Rd.)
Kingston Pl. HA3: Hrw W 7E 26
Kingston Rd. EN4: E Barn 5G 21
IG1: Ilf 4F 71
KT1: King T 3H 151
KT3: N Mald 3H 151
KT4: Wor Pk 2H 163
KT5: Surb 2H 163
KT17: Ewe 7B 164
KT19: Ewe 2H 163
N9 . . . . .2B 34
SW15 . . . . .2C 134
SW19 . . . . .2C 134
(Norstead Pl.)
SW19 . . . . .2H 153
(Rothesay Av.)
SW20 . . . . .2F 153
TW11: Tedd 5B 132
TW15: Ashf 6A 128
UB2: S'hall 2D 94
Kingston University
Kingston Hill Campus 5K 133
Knights Pk. Campus 3E 150
Penrhyn Road Campus 4E 150
Roehampton Vale Cen. 3B 134
KINGSTON UPON THAMES 2D 150
Kingston upon Thames Art Gallery & Mus.
. . . . .2E 150
KINGSTON VALE 4A 134
Kingston Va. SW15 . . . . .4K 133
Kingstown St. NW1 . . . . .1E 82
(not continuous)
King St. E13 . . . . .4J 87
EC2 . . . . .1D 14 (6C 84)
N2 . . . . .3B 46
N17 . . . . .2F 49
SW1 . . . . .5B 12 (1G 101)
TW1: Twick 1A 132
TW9: Rich 5D 114
UB2: S'hall 3C 94
W3 . . . . .1J 97
W6 . . . . .4C 98
WC2 . . . . .2E 12 (7J 83)
King St. Cloisters W6 . . . . .4D 98
(off King St.)
King St. M. N2 . . . . .3B 46
King St. Pde. TW1: Twick 1A 132
(off King St.)
Kings Wlk. Shop. Cen.
SW3 . . . . .5E 16 (5D 100)
Kingswater Pl. SW11 . . . . .7C 100
King's Way CR0: Wadd 5K 167
Kings Way HA1: Harr 4J 41
Kingsway BR4: W W'ck 3G 171
BR5: Pet W 5H 161
EN3: Pond E 5C 24
HA9: Wemb 4E 60
IG8: Wfd G 5F 37
KT3: N Mald 4E 152
N12 . . . . .6F 31
SW14 . . . . .3H 115
TW19: Stanw 1A 128
UB3: Hayes 5E 74
WC2 . . . . .7G 7 (6K 83)
Kingsway Bus. Pk.
TW12: Hamp 1D 148
Kingsway Cres. HA2: Harr 4G 41
Kingsway Est. N18 . . . . .6E 34
Kingsway Mans. WC1 . . . . .5G 7
(off Red Lion Sq.)
Kingsway Pde. N16 . . . . .3D 66
(off Albion Rd.)
Kingsway Pl. EC1 . . . . .3K 7
(off Sans Wlk.)
Kingsway Rd. SM3: Cheam 7G 165

Kingswear Rd.—Knole, The

Kingswear Rd. HA4: Ruis . . . 2J 57
NW5 . . . 3F 65
King's Wharf *SE10* . . . *6D 104*
(off Wood Wharf)
Kings Wharf *E8* . . . *1E 84*
(off Kingsland Rd.)
Kingswood *E2* . . . *2J 85*
(off Cyprus St.)
Kingswood Av. BR2: Brom . . . 3G 159
CR7: Thor H . . . 5A 156
DA17: Belv . . . 4F 109
NW6 . . . 1G 81
TW3: Houn . . . 1D 112
TW12: Hamp . . . 6F 131
Kingswood Cl. BR6: Orp . . . 7J 161
EN1: Enf . . . 5K 23
KT3: N Mald . . . 6B 152
KT6: Surb . . . 7E 150
N20 . . . 7F 21
SW8 . . . 7J 101
TW15: Ashf . . . 5F 129
Kings Wood Ct. TW10: Rich . . . 5F 115
Kingswood Ct. E4 . . . 5H 35
NW6 . . . *7J 63*
(off West End La.)
SE13 . . . 6F 123
Kingswood Dr. SE19 . . . 4E 138
SM2: Sutt . . . 7K 165
SM5: Cars . . . 1D 166
Kingswood Est. SE21 . . . 4E 138
Kingswood Hgts. *E18* . . . *1J 51*
(off Queen Mary Av.)
Kingswood M. N15 . . . 4B 48
Kingswood Pk. N3 . . . 2H 45
Kingswood Pl. SE13 . . . 4G 123
UB3: Hayes . . . 5G 75
Kingswood Rd. BR2: Brom . . . 4F 159
E11 . . . 7G 51
HA9: Wemb . . . 3G 61
IG3: Ilf . . . 1A 72
SE20 . . . 6J 139
SW2 . . . 6J 119
SW19 . . . 7H 135
W4 . . . 3J 97
Kingswood Ter. W4 . . . 3J 97
Kingswood Way SM6: Wall . . . 5J 167
Kingsworth Cl. BR3: Beck . . . 5A 158
Kingsworthy Cl. KT1: King T . . . 3F 151
Kings Yd. *SW15* . . . *3E 116*
(off Lwr. Richmond Rd.)
Kingthorpe Rd. NW10 . . . 7K 61
Kingthorpe Ter. NW10 . . . 6K 61
Kington Ho. *NW6* . . . *1K 81*
(off Mortimer Cres.)
Kingward Ho. *E1* . . . *5G 85*
(off Hanbury St.)
King Wardrobe Apartments *EC4* . . . *1B 14*
(off Carter La.)
Kingweston Cl. NW2 . . . 3G 63
King William IV Gdns. SE20 . . . 6J 139
King William La. SE10 . . . 5G 105
King William's Ct. *SE10* . . . *6F 105*
(off Park Row)
King William St. EC4 . . . 1F 15 (6D 84)
King William Wlk. SE10 . . . 6E 104
(not continuous)
Kingwood Gdns. *E1* . . . *1K 15*
(off Piazza Wlk.)
Kingwood Rd. SW6 . . . 1G 117
Kinlet Rd. SE18 . . . 1G 125
Kinloch Dr. NW9 . . . 7K 43
Kinloch St. N7 . . . 3K 65
Kinloss Ct. N3 . . . 4H 45
Kinloss Gdns. N3 . . . 3H 45
Kinloss Rd. SM5: Cars . . . 7A 154
Kinnaird Av. BR1: Brom . . . 6H 141
W4 . . . 7J 97
Kinnaird Cl. BR1: Brom . . . 6H 141
Kinnaird Ho. SE17 . . . 4D 102
Kinnaird Way IG8: Wfd G . . . 6J 37
Kinnear Apartments N8 . . . 3K 47
Kinnear Rd. W12 . . . 2B 98
Kinnerton Pl. Nth. SW1 . . . 7F 11
Kinnerton Pl. Sth. SW1 . . . 7F 11
Kinnerton St. SW1 . . . 7G 11 (2E 100)
Kinnerton Yd. SW1 . . . 7G 11
Kinnoul Rd. W6 . . . 6G 99
Kinross Av. KT4: Wor Pk . . . 2C 164
Kinross Cl. HA3: Kenton . . . 5F 43
HA8: Edg . . . 2C 28
TW16: Sun . . . 5H 129
Kinross Ct. *BR1: Brom* . . . *1H 159*
(off Highland Rd.)
SE6 . . . 1H 141
Kinross Dr. TW16: Sun . . . 5H 129
Kinross Ho. *N1* . . . *1K 83*
(off Bemerton Est.)
Kinross Ter. E17 . . . 2B 50
Kinsale Cl. NW7 . . . 6A 30
Kinsale Rd. SE15 . . . 3G 121
Kinsella Gdns. SW19 . . . 5D 134
Kinsham Ho. *E2* . . . *4G 85*
(off Ramsey St.)
Kinsheron Pl. KT8: E Mos . . . 4G 149
Kintore Way SE1 . . . 4F 103
Kintyre Cl. SW16 . . . 2K 155
Kintyre Ct. SW2 . . . 7J 119
Kintyre Ho. *E14* . . . *1E 104*
(off Coldharbour)
Kinveachy Gdns. SE7 . . . 5C 106
Kinver Ho. N19 . . . 2H 65
Kinver Rd. SE26 . . . 4J 139
Kipling Ct. W7 . . . 7K 77
Kipling Dr. SW19 . . . 6B 136
Kipling Est. SE1 . . . 7F 15 (2D 102)
Kipling Ho. *N19* . . . *1J 65*
(off Charles St.)
SE5 . . . *7D 102*
(off Elmington Est.)
Kipling Pl. HA7: Stan . . . 6E 26
Kipling Rd. DA7: Bex . . . 1E 126
Kipling St. SE1 . . . 7F 15 (2D 102)
Kipling Ter. N9 . . . 3J 33
Kipling Twr. *W3* . . . *3J 97*
(off Palmerston Rd.)
Kippington Dr. SE9 . . . 1B 142
Kira Bldg. E3 . . . 3B 86
Kiran Apartments *E1* . . . *6K 9*
(off Chicksand St.)
Kirby Cl. KT19: Ewe . . . 5B 164
Kirby Est. SE16 . . . 3H 103
UB7: Yiew . . . 7A 74
Kirby Gro. SE1 . . . 6G 15 (2E 102)
Kirby St. EC1 . . . 5K 7 (5A 84)
Kirby Way KT12: Walt T . . . 6A 148
UB8: Hil . . . 4B 74
Kirchen Rd. W13 . . . 7B 78
Kirkby Apartments *E3* . . . *5B 86*
(off St Paul's Way)
Kirkby Cl. N11 . . . 6K 31
Kirkdale SE26 . . . 2H 139
Kirkdale Cnr. SE26 . . . 4J 139
Kirkdale Rd. E11 . . . 1G 69
Kirkeby Ho. *EC1* . . . *5J 7*
(off Leather La.)
Kirkfield Cl. W13 . . . 1B 96
Kirkham Apartments *IG11: Bark* . . . *7G 71*
(off Linton Rd.)
Kirkham Rd. E6 . . . 6C 88
Kirkham St. SE18 . . . 6J 107
Kirk Ho. HA9: Wemb . . . 3E 60
Kirkland Av. IG5: Ilf . . . 2E 52
Kirkland Cl. DA15: Sidc . . . 6J 125
Kirkland Dr. EN2: Enf . . . 1H 23
Kirkland Ho. *E14* . . . *5D 104*
(off St Davids Sq.)
E14 . . . *5D 104*
(off Westferry Rd.)
Kirkland Ter. BR3: Beck . . . 6C 140
Kirkland Wlk. E8 . . . 6F 67
Kirk La. SE18 . . . 6G 107
Kirkleas Rd. KT6: Surb . . . 1E 162
Kirklees Rd. CR7: Thor H . . . 5A 156
RM8: Dag . . . 5C 72
Kirkley Rd. SW19 . . . 1J 153
Kirkman Pl. W1 . . . 6C 6
Kirkmichael Rd. E14 . . . 6E 86
Kirk Ri. SM1: Sutt . . . 3K 165
Kirk Rd. E17 . . . 6B 50
Kirkside Rd. SE3 . . . 6J 105
Kirk's Place . . . 5B 86
Kirkstall Av. N17 . . . 4D 48
Kirkstall Gdns. SW2 . . . 1J 137
Kirkstall Ho. *SW1* . . . *5J 17*
(part of Abbots Mnr.)
Kirkstall Rd. SW2 . . . 1H 137
Kirkstead Ct. E5 . . . 4K 67
Kirksted Rd. SM4: Mord . . . 1K 165
Kirkstone *NW1* . . . *1A 6*
(off Harrington St.)
Kirkstone Way BR1: Brom . . . 7G 141
Kirk St. WC1 . . . 4G 7
Kirkton Rd. N15 . . . 4E 48
Kirkwall Pl. E2 . . . 3J 85
Kirkwood Pl. NW1 . . . 7E 64
Kirkwood Rd. SE15 . . . 2H 121
Kirn Rd. W13 . . . 7B 78
Kirrane Cl. KT3: N Mald . . . 5B 152
Kirtley Ho. SW8 . . . 1G 119
Kirtley Rd. SE26 . . . 4A 140
Kirtling St. SW8 . . . 7G 101
Kirton Cl. W4 . . . 4K 97
Kirton Gdns. E2 . . . 2K 9 (3F 85)
(not continuous)
Kirton Lodge SW18 . . . 6K 117
Kirton Rd. E13 . . . 2A 88
Kirton Wlk. HA8: Edg . . . 7D 28
Kirwyn Way SE5 . . . 7B 102
Kitcat Ter. E3 . . . 3C 86
Kitchen Ct. E10 . . . 2D 68
Kitchener Ho. SE18 . . . 7E 106
Kitchener Rd. CR7: Thor H . . . 3D 156
E7 . . . 6K 69
E17 . . . 1D 50
N2 . . . 3C 46
N17 . . . 3E 48
RM10: Dag . . . 6H 73
Kite Ho. SE1 . . . 4H 103
SE3 . . . 4K 123
Kite Pl. *E2* . . . *3G 85*
(off Warner Pl.)
Kite Yd. *SW11* . . . *1D 118*
(off Cambridge Rd.)
Kitley Gdns. SE19 . . . 1F 157
Kitson Rd. SE5 . . . 7D 102
SW13 . . . 1C 116
Kittiwake Ct. *SE1* . . . *7D 14*
(off Gt. Dover St.)
SE8 . . . *6B 104*
(off Abinger Gro.)
Kittiwake Pl. SM1: Sutt . . . 5H 165
Kittiwake Rd. UB5: N'olt . . . 3B 76
Kittiwake Way UB4: Yead . . . 5B 76
Kitto Rd. SE14 . . . 2K 121
Kitts End Rd. EN5: Barn . . . 1C 20
Kiver Rd. N19 . . . 2H 65
Klea Av. SW4 . . . 6G 119
Kleine Wharf N1 . . . 1E 84
Klein's Wharf *E14* . . . *3C 104*
(off Westferry Rd.)
Knapdale Cl. SE23 . . . 2H 139
Knapmill Rd. SE6 . . . 2C 140
Knapmill Way SE6 . . . 2D 140
Knapp Cl. NW10 . . . 6A 62
Knapp Rd. E3 . . . 4C 86
TW15: Ashf . . . 4B 128
Knapton M. SW17 . . . 6E 136
Knaresborough Dr. SW18 . . . 1K 135
Knaresborough Pl. SW5 . . . 4K 99
Knatchbull Rd. NW10 . . . 1K 79
SE5 . . . 2B 120
Knebworth Av. E17 . . . 1C 50
Knebworth Cl. EN5: New Bar . . . 4E 20
Knebworth Ho. SW8 . . . 2H 119
Knebworth Rd. N16 . . . 4E 66
Knee Hill SE2 . . . 4C 108
Knee Hill Cres. SE2 . . . 4C 108
Kneller Gdns. TW7: Isle . . . 6H 113
Kneller Ho. *UB5: N'olt* . . . *2B 76*
(off Academy Gdns.)
Kneller Rd. KT3: N Mald . . . 7A 152
SE4 . . . 4A 122
TW2: Whitt . . . 6G 113
Knevett Ter. TW3: Houn . . . 4E 112
Knight Cl. RM8: Dag . . . 2C 72
Knight Ct. *E4* . . . *1K 35*
(off The Ridgeway)
N15 . . . 5E 48
Knighten St. E1 . . . 1H 103
Knighthead Point E14 . . . 2C 104
Knight Ho. *SE17* . . . *4E 102*
(off Tatum St.)
Knightland Rd. E5 . . . 2H 67
Knightleas Ct. NW2 . . . 6E 62
Knightleys Ct. *E10* . . . *1A 68*
(off Wellington Rd.)
Knightley Wlk. SW18 . . . 4J 117
Knighton Cl. CR2: S Croy . . . 7B 168
IG8: Wfd G . . . 4E 36
RM7: Rom . . . 6K 55
Knighton Dr. IG8: Wfd G . . . 4E 36
Knighton Grn. IG9: Buck H . . . 2E 36
Knighton La. IG9: Buck H . . . 2E 36
Knighton Pk. Rd. SE26 . . . 5K 139
Knighton Pl. *IG9: Buck H* . . . *2E 36*
(off Knighton La.)
Knighton Rd. E7 . . . 3J 69
RM7: Rom . . . 6J 55
Knightrider Ct. EC4 . . . 2B 14
Knightrider St. EC4 . . . 2B 14 (6B 84)
Knights Arc. SW1 . . . 7E 10
Knights Av. W5 . . . 2E 96
KNIGHTSBRIDGE . . . 7D 10 (2C 100)
Knightsbridge SW1 . . . 7D 10 (2D 100)
SW7 . . . 7D 10 (2D 100)
Knightsbridge Apartments, The
SW7 . . . *7E 10*
(off Knightsbridge)
Knightsbridge Ct. *BR2: Brom* . . . *6C 160*
(off Wells Vw. Dr.)
SW1 . . . 7F 11
Knightsbridge Gdns. RM7: Rom . . . 5K 55
Knightsbridge Grn. SW1 . . . 7E 10 (2D 100)
(not continuous)
Knights Cl. E9 . . . 5J 67
KT8: W Mole . . . 5D 148
Knightscote Cl. UB9: Hare . . . 2A 38
Knights Ct. BR1: Brom . . . 3H 141
KT1: King T . . . 3E 150
RM6: Chad H . . . *6E 54*
(off High Rd.)
WD23: B Hea . . . 1C 26
Knights Hill SE27 . . . 5B 138
Knight's Hill Sq. SE27 . . . 4B 138
Knight's Ho. *SW10* . . . *7A 100*
(off Hortensia Rd.)
W14 . . . *5H 99*
(off Baron's Ct. Rd.)
Knights Ho. *SW8* . . . *7J 101*
(off Sth. Lambeth Rd.)
Knight's Pk. KT1: King T . . . 3E 150
Knight's Pl. TW2: Twick . . . 1J 131
Knight's Rd. E16 . . . 2J 105
Knights Rd. HA7: Stan . . . 4H 27
Knights Twr. SE8 . . . 5C 104
Knight's Wlk. SE11 . . . 4K 19 (4B 102)
(not continuous)
Knightswood Cl. HA8: Edg . . . 2D 28
Knightswood Ct. N6 . . . 7H 47
Knightswood Ho. N12 . . . 6F 31
Knightwood Cres. KT3: N Mald . . . 6A 152
Knivet Rd. SW6 . . . 6J 99
Knockholt Rd. SE9 . . . 5B 124
Knole, The SE9 . . . 4E 142

Knole Cl. CR0: C'don 6J 157
Knole Ct. *UB5: N'olt* *3A 76*
(off Broomcroft Av.)
Knole Ga. DA15: Sidc 3J 143
Knoll, The BR2: Hayes 2J 171
BR3: Beck 1D 158
HA1: Harr 1K 59
W13 5C 78
Knoll Ct. *SE19* *5F 139*
(off Farquhar Rd.)
Knoll Cres. HA6: Nwood 2G 39
(not continuous)
Knoll Dr. N14 7K 21
Knoll Ho. *NW8* *2A 82*
(off Carlton Hill)
Knollmead KT5: Surb 1J 163
Knoll Ri. BR6: Orp 1K 173
Knoll Rd. DA5: Bexl 7G 127
DA14: Sidc 5B 144
SW18 5A 118
Knolls Cl.
KT4: Wor Pk 3D 164
Knollys Cl. SW16 3A 138
Knolly's Ho. *WC1* *3E 6*
(off Tavistock Pl.)
Knollys Rd. SW16 3K 137
Knot Ho. *SE1* *5J 15*
(off Brewery Sq.)
Knotley Way BR4: W W'ck 2D 170
Knottisford St. E2 3J 85
Knotts Grn. M. E10 6D 50
Knotts Grn. Rd. E10 6D 50
Knowlden Ho. *E1* *7J 85*
(off Cable St.)
Knowle Av. DA7: Bex 7E 108
Knowle Cl. SW9 3A 120
Knowledge Ct. SW16 3K 155
Knowle Rd. BR2: Brom 2D 172
TW2: Twick 1J 131
Knowles Cl. UB7: Yiew 1A 92
Knowles Ct. HA1: Harr 6K 41
Knowles Hill Cres. SE13 5F 123
Knowles Ho. *SW18* *6K 117*
(off Neville Gill Cl.)
Knowles Wlk. SW4 3G 119
Knowles Wharf *NW1* *1G 83*
(off St Pancras Way)
Knowlton Grn. BR2: Brom 5H 159
Knowlton Ho. *SW9* *1A 120*
(off Cowley Rd.)
Knowl Wood La. BR6: Farnb 2E 172
Knowsley Av. UB1: S'hall 1F 95
Knowsley Rd. SW11 2D 118
Knox Ct. SW4 2J 119
Knox Rd. E7 6H 69
Knox St. W1 5E 4 (5D 82)
Knoyle Ho. *W14* *3G 99*
(off Russell Rd.)
Knoyle St. SE14 6A 104
Koblenz Ho. *N8* *3J 47*
(off Newland Rd.)
Kohat Rd. SW19 5K 135
Koops Mill M. SE1 7K 15 (3F 103)
Korda Cl. TW17: Shep 3B 146
Kossuth St. SE10 5G 105
Kotata Ho. *E20* *6E 68*
(off Ravens Wlk.)
Kotree Way SE1 4G 103
Kramer M. SW5 5J 99
Kreedman Wlk. E8 5G 67
Kreisel Wlk. TW9: Kew 6F 97
Kristina Ct. *SM2: Sutt* *6J 165*
(off Overton Rd.)
Krithia Rd. RM9: Dag 1B 90
Krupnik Pl. *EC2* *3H 9*
(shown as Curtain Pl.)
Kuala Gdns. SW16 1K 155
Kubrick Bus. Est. *E7* *4K 69*
(off Station App.)
Kuhn Way E7 5J 69
Kurdish Mus. 4C 98
Kwame Ho. *E16* *7F 89*
(off University Way)
Kwesi M. SE27 5A 138
Kydbrook Cl.
BR5: Pet W 7G 161
Kyle Ho. NW6 1J 81
Kylemore Cl. E6 2B 88
Kylemore Rd. NW6 7J 63
Kylestrome Ho. *SW1* *4H 17*
(off Cundy St.)
Kymberley Rd. HA1: Harr 6J 41
Kymes Ct. HA2: Harr 2H 59
Kynance Gdns. HA7: Stan 1C 42
Kynance M. SW7 3K 99
Kynance Pl. SW7 3A 100
Kynaston Av. CR7: Thor H 5C 156
N16 3F 67
Kynaston Cl. HA3: Hrw W 7C 26
Kynaston Cres. CR7: Thor H 5C 156
Kynaston Rd. BR1: Brom 5J 141
CR7: Thor H 5C 156
EN2: Enf 1J 23
N16 3E 66
Kynaston Wood HA3: Hrw W 7C 26
Kynersley Cl. SM5: Cars 3D 166
Kynoch Rd. N18 4D 34
Kyrle Rd. SW11 6E 118
Kyverdale Rd. N16 7F 49

L

Laban Cen. 6D 104
Laban Wlk. *SE8* *6D 104*
(off Copperas St.)
Laboratory Spa and Health Club, The
3G 47
Labrun Sq. SE3 3K 123
Laburnham Cl. EN5: Barn 3C 20
Laburnham La. E2 2F 85
Laburnum Av. N9 2A 34
N17 7J 33
SM1: Sutt 3C 166
UB7: Yiew 7B 74
Laburnum Cl. E4 6G 35
HA0: Wemb 1G 79
N11 6K 31
SE15 7J 103
Laburnum Ct. E2 1F 85
HA1: Harr 5F 41
HA7: Stan 4H 27
SE16 *2J 103*
(off Albion St.)
Laburnum Cres. TW16: Sun 1K 147
Laburnum Gdns. CR0: C'don 7K 157
N21 2H 33
Laburnum Gro. HA4: Ruis 6F 39
KT3: N Mald 2K 151
N21 2H 33
NW9 7J 43
TW3: Houn 4D 112
UB1: S'hall 4D 76
Laburnum Ho. BR2: Brom 1F 159
RM10: Dag 2G 73
Laburnum Lodge N3 2H 45
Laburnum Pl. SE9 5E 124
Laburnum Rd. CR4: Mitc 2E 154
SW19 7A 136
UB3: Harl 4H 93
Laburnums, The E6 4C 88
Laburnum St. E2 1F 85
Laburnum Way BR2: Brom 7E 160
TW19: Stanw 1B 128
Labyrinth Twr. *E8* *6F 67*
(off Dalston Sq.)
Lacebark Cl.
DA15: Sidc 7K 125
Lace Ct. *E1* *5K 85*
(off Master's St.)
Lacewing Cl. E13 3J 87
Lacey Cl. N9 2B 34
Lacey Dr. HA8: Edg 4K 27
RM8: Dag 3C 72
TW12: Hamp 1D 148
Lacey Gro. UB10: Uxb 2A 74
Lacey M. E3 2C 86
Lacine Ct. *SE16* *2K 103*
(off Christopher Cl.)
Lackington St. EC2 5F 9 (5D 84)
Lackland Ho. *SE1* *5F 103*
(off Rowcross St.)
Lacland Ho. *SW10* *7B 100*
(off Worlds End Est.)
Lacock Cl. SW19 6A 136
Lacock Ct. W13 1A 96
Lacon Ho. *WC1* *5G 7*
(off Theobald's Rd.)
Lacon Rd. SE22 4G 121
Lacrosse Way SW16 1H 155
Lacy Rd. SW15 4F 117
Ladas Rd. SE27 4C 138
Ladbroke Ct. E1 6F 85
Ladbroke Cres. W11 6G 81
Ladbroke Gdns. W11 7H 81
Ladbroke Gro. W10 4F 81
W11 4F 81
Ladbroke Gro. Ho. *W11* *7H 81*
(off Ladbroke Gro.)
Ladbroke Grove Memorial 4F 81
(off Canal Way)
Ladbroke M. W11 1G 99
Ladbroke Rd. EN1: Enf 6A 24
W11 1H 99
Ladbroke Sq. W11 7H 81
Ladbroke Ter. W11 7H 81
Ladbroke Wlk. W11 1H 99
Ladbrook Cl. BR1: Brom 6G 141
HA5: Pinn 5D 40
Ladbrooke Cres. DA14: Sidc 3D 144
Ladbrook Rd. SE25 4D 156
Ladderstile Ride
KT2: King T 5H 133
Ladderswood Way N11 5B 32
Ladlands SE22 7G 121
Lady Anne Ct. *E18* *1J 51*
(off Queen Mary Av.)
Lady Aylesford Av. HA7: Stan 5F 27
Lady Booth Rd. KT1: King T 2E 150
Lady Craig Ct. UB8: Hil 5D 74
Ladycroft Gdns. BR6: Farnb 5G 173
Ladycroft Rd. SE13 3D 122
Ladycroft Wlk. HA7: Stan 1D 42
Ladycroft Way BR6: Farnb 5G 173
Lady Dock Path SE16 2A 104
Lady Elizabeth Ho. SW14 3J 115
Ladyfern Ho. *E3* *5C 86*
(off Gail St.)
Lady Florence Courtyard *SE8* *7C 104*
(off Reginald Sq.)
Lady Forsdyke Way KT19: Eps 7G 163
Ladygate La. HA4: Ruis 6D 38
Lady Harewood Way KT19: Eps 7G 163
Lady Hay KT4: Wor Pk 2B 164
Lady Jane Ct. *KT2: King T* *2F 151*
(off Cambridge Rd.)
Lady Margaret Ho. *SE17* *6D 102*
(off Queen's Row)
Lady Margaret Rd. N19 5G 65
NW5 5G 65
UB1: S'hall 7D 76
Lady May Ho. *SE5* *7C 102*
(off Pitman St.)
Lady Micos Almshouses *E1* *6J 85*
(off Aylward St.)
Lady Sarah Cohen Ho.
N11 *6J 31*
(off Asher Loftus Way)
Lady Shaw Ct. N13 2E 32
Ladyship Ter. SE22 7G 121
Ladysmith Av. E6 2C 88
IG2: Ilf 7J 53
Ladysmith Cl. NW7 7H 29
Ladysmith Rd. E16 3H 87
EN1: Enf 3K 23
(not continuous)
HA3: W'stone 2J 41
N17 2G 49
N18 5C 34
SE9 6E 124
Lady Somerset Rd. NW5 4F 65
LADYWELL 5D 122
Ladywell Arena (Running Track) 6C 122
Ladywell Cl. SE4 5C 122
Ladywell Hgts. SE4 6B 122
Ladywell Rd. SE13 5C 122
Ladywell St. E15 1H 87
Ladywood Av. BR5: Pet W 5J 161
Ladywood Rd. KT6: Surb 2G 163
Lafone Av. TW13: Felt 2A 130
Lafone St. SE1 6J 15 (2F 103)
Lagado M. SE16 1K 103
Lagare Apartments *SE1* *6B 14*
(off Surrey Row)
Lagonda Ho. *E3* *4C 86*
(off Tidworth Rd.)
Lagonier Ho. *EC1* *2D 8*
(off Ironmonger Row)
Laidlaw Dr. N21 5E 22
Laing Dean UB5: N'olt 1A 76
Laing Ho. SE5 7C 102
Laings Av. CR4: Mitc 2D 154
Lainlock Pl. TW3: Houn 1F 113
Lainson St. SW18 7J 117
Lairdale Cl. SE21 1C 138
Laird Ho. *SE5* *7C 102*
(off Redcar St.)
Lairs Cl. N7 5J 65
Lait Ho. BR3: Beck 1D 158
Laitwood Rd. SW12 1F 137
Lakanal *SE5* *1E 120*
(off Sceaux Gdns.)
Lake, The WD23: B Hea 1C 26
Lake Av. BR1: Brom 6J 141
Lake Bus. Cen. N17 7B 34
Lake Cl. RM8: Dag 3D 72
SW19 5H 135
Lakedale Ct. IG11: Bark 4B 90
Lakedale Rd. SE18 6J 107
Lake Dr. WD23: B Hea 2C 26
Lake Farm Country Pk. 1G 93
Lakefield Cl. SE20 7H 139
Lakefield Rd. N22 2B 48
Lake Gdns. RM10: Dag 5G 73
SM6: Wall 3F 167
TW10: Ham 2B 132
Lakehall Gdns.
CR7: Thor H 5B 156
Lakehall Rd. CR7: Thor H 5B 156
Lake Ho. *SE1* *7C 14*
(off Southwark Bri. Rd.)
Lake Ho. Rd. E11 3J 69
Lakehurst Rd. KT19: Ewe 5A 164
Lakeland Cl. HA3: Hrw W 6C 26
Lakenham Pl. E3 4B 86
Lakenheath N14 5B 22
Laker Ct. SW4 1J 119
Laker Ind. Est.
BR3: Beck 5A 140
Lake Rd. CR0: C'don 2B 170
E10 7D 50
RM6: Chad H 4D 54
RM9: Dag 3H 91
SW19 5H 135
Laker Pl. SW15 6G 117
Lakeside BR3: Beck 3D 158
EN2: Enf 4C 22
KT2: King T 7H 133
KT19: Ewe 6A 164
N3 2K 45
SM6: Wall 4F 167
W13 6C 78
Lakeside Av. IG4: Ilf 4B 52
SE28 1A 108

Lakeside Cl.—Landscape Rd.

Lakeside Cl. DA15: Sidc . . . 5C 126
HA4: Ruis . . . 4F 39
SE25 . . . 2G 157
Lakeside Ct. N4 . . . 2C 66
Lakeside Cres. EN4: E Barn . . . 5J 21
Lakeside Dr. BR2: Brom . . . 3C 172
NW10 . . . 3F 79
Lakeside Ind. Est. SL3: Coln . . . 2B 174
Lakeside Rd. N13 . . . 4E 32
SL0: Rich P . . . 3A 174
SL3: Coln, Rich P . . . 3A 174
W14 . . . 3F 99
Lakeside Ter. EC2 . . . 5D 8
Lakeside Way HA9: Wemb . . . 4G 61
Lakes Rd. BR2: Kes . . . 5A 172
Lakeswood Rd. BR5: Pet W . . . 6F 161
Lake Vw. HA8: Edg . . . 5A 28
Lakeview Ct. SE28 . . . 7B 90
Lake Vw. Est. E3 . . . 2A 86
Lakeview Rd. DA16: Well . . . 4B 126
SE27 . . . 5A 138
Lake Vw. Ter. *N18* . . . *4A 34*
(off Sweet Briar Wlk.)
Lakin Cl. SM5: Cars . . . 4E 166
Lakis Cl. NW3 . . . 4A 64
Laleham Av. NW7 . . . 3E 28
Laleham Ct. SM1: Sutt . . . 5A 166
Laleham Ho. *E2* . . . *3J 9*
(off Camlet St.)
Laleham Rd. SE6 . . . 7E 122
TW17: Shep . . . 4B 146
Lalor St. SW6 . . . 2G 117
Lambarde Av. SE9 . . . 4E 142
Lambarde Sq. SE10 . . . 5H 105
Lambard Ho. *SE10* . . . *7E 104*
(off Langdale Rd.)
Lamb Cl. UB5: N'olt . . . 3C 76
Lamb Ct. *E14* . . . *7A 86*
(off Narrow St.)
Lamberhurst Ho. SE15 . . . 6J 103
Lamberhurst Rd. RM8: Dag . . . 1F 73
SE27 . . . 4A 138
Lambert Av. TW9: Rich . . . 3G 115
Lambert Ct. *DA8: Erith* . . . *6J 109*
(off Park Cres.)
Lambert Jones M. EC2 . . . 5C 8
Lambert Lodge *TW8: Bford* . . . *5D 96*
(off Layton Rd.)
Lambert Rd. E16 . . . 6K 87
N12 . . . 5G 31
SW2 . . . 5J 119
Lambert's Pl. CR0: C'don . . . 1D 168
Lamberts Rd. KT5: Surb . . . 5E 150
Lambert St. N1 . . . 7A 66
Lambert Wlk. HA9: Wemb . . . 3E 60
Lambert Way N12 . . . 5F 31
LAMBETH . . . 3G 19 (3K 101)
Lambeth Bri. SW1 . . . 3F 19 (4J 101)
Lambeth Crematorium SW17 . . . 4A 136
Lambeth High St. SE1 . . . 4G 19 (4K 101)
Lambeth Hill EC4 . . . 2C 14 (7C 84)
Lambeth Palace . . . 2G 19 (3K 101)
Lambeth Pal. Rd. SE1 . . . 2G 19 (3K 101)
Lambeth Rd. CR0: C'don . . . 7A 156
SE1 . . . 3G 19 (4K 101)
SE11 . . . 3G 19 (4K 101)
Lambeth Towers SE11 . . . 2J 19
Lambeth Wlk. SE11 . . . 4H 19 (4K 101)
(not continuous)
Lambfold Ho. *N7* . . . *6J 65*
(off North Rd.)
Lamb Ho. *SE5* . . . *7C 102*
(off Elmington Est.)
SE10 . . . *6E 104*
(off Haddo St.)
Lambkins M. E17 . . . 4E 50
Lamb La. E8 . . . 7H 67
Lamble St. NW5 . . . 5E 64
Lambley Rd. RM9: Dag . . . 6B 72
Lambolle Pl. NW3 . . . 6C 64
Lambolle Rd. NW3 . . . 6C 64
Lambourn Cl. CR2: S Croy . . . 7B 168
NW5 . . . 4G 65
W7 . . . 2K 95
Lambourne Av. SW19 . . . 4H 135
Lambourne Ct. IG8: Wfd G . . . 7F 37
Lambourne Gdns. E4 . . . 2H 35
EN1: Enf . . . 2A 24
IG11: Bark . . . 7K 71
Lambourne Gro. SE16 . . . 5K 103
Lambourne Ho. *NW8* . . . *5B 4*
(off Broadley St.)
Lambourne Pl. SE3 . . . 1K 123
Lambourne Rd. E11 . . . 7E 50
IG3: Ilf . . . 2J 71
IG11: Bark . . . 7J 71
Lambourn Gro. KT1: King T . . . 2H 151
Lambourn Rd. SW4 . . . 3F 119
Lambrook Ho. SE15 . . . 1G 121
Lambrook Ter. SW6 . . . 1G 117
Lamb's Bldgs. EC1 . . . 4E 8 (4D 84)
Lamb's Cl. N9 . . . 2B 34
Lamb's Conduit Pas. WC1 . . . 5G 7 (5K 83)
Lamb's Conduit St. WC1 . . . 4G 7 (4K 83)
(not continuous)
Lambscroft Av. SE9 . . . 3A 142
Lambs Mdw. IG8: Wfd G . . . 2B 52
Lamb's M. N1 . . . 1B 84
Lambs Pas. EC1 . . . 5E 8 (4D 84)
Lambs Ter. N9 . . . 2J 33
Lamb St. E1 . . . 5J 9 (5F 85)
Lamb's Wlk. EN2: Enf . . . 2H 23
Lambton M. *N19* . . . *1J 65*
(off Lambton Rd.)
Lambton Pl. W11 . . . 7H 81
Lambton Rd. N19 . . . 1J 65
SW20 . . . 1E 152
Lamb Wlk. SE1 . . . 7G 15 (2E 102)
LAMDA . . . 5F 99
Lamerock Rd. BR1: Brom . . . 4H 141
Lamerton Rd. IG6: Ilf . . . 2F 53
Lamerton St. SE8 . . . 6C 104
Lamford Cl. N17 . . . 7J 33
Lamington St. W6 . . . 4D 98
Lamlash St. SE11 . . . 4B 102
Lamley Ho. *SE10* . . . *7D 104*
(off Ashburnham Pl.)
Lammas Av. CR4: Mitc . . . 2E 154
Lammas Grn. SE26 . . . 3H 139
Lammas Pk. Gdns. W5 . . . 1C 96
Lammas Pk. Rd. W5 . . . 2D 96
Lammas Rd. E9 . . . 7K 67
E10 . . . 2A 68
TW10: Ham . . . 4C 132
Lammermoor Rd. SW12 . . . 7F 119
Lamont Rd. SW10 . . . 7A 16 (6B 100)
Lamont Rd. Pas. SW10 . . . 7A 16
LAMORBEY . . . 1K 143
Lamorbey Cl. DA15: Sidc . . . 1K 143
Lamorbey Pk. . . . 1B 144
Lamorna Cl. BR6: Orp . . . 7K 161
E17 . . . 2E 50
Lamorna Gro. HA7: Stan . . . 1D 42
Lampard Gro. N16 . . . 1F 67
Lampern Sq. E2 . . . 3G 85
Lampeter Cl. NW9 . . . 6A 44
Lampeter Sq. W6 . . . 6G 99
Lamplighter Cl. E1 . . . 4J 85
Lampmead Rd. SE12 . . . 5H 123
Lamp Office Ct. WC1 . . . 4G 7
Lamport Cl. SE18 . . . 4D 106
LAMPTON . . . 1F 113
Lampton Av. TW3: Houn . . . 1F 113
Lampton Ct. TW3: Houn . . . 1F 113
Lampton Ho. Cl. SW19 . . . 4F 135
Lampton Pk. Rd. TW3: Houn . . . 2F 113
Lampton Rd. TW3: Houn . . . 2F 113
Lampton Sports Cen. . . . 2E 112
Lanacre Av. NW9 . . . 1K 43
Lanadron Cl. TW7: Isle . . . 2K 113
Lanain Ct. SE12 . . . 7H 123
Lanark Cl. W5 . . . 5C 78
Lanark Ct. *UB5: N'olt* . . . *5E 58*
(off Newmarket Av.)
Lanark Ho. *SE1* . . . *5G 103*
(off Old Kent Rd.)
Lanark Mans. *W9* . . . *4A 82*
(off Lanark Rd.)
W12 . . . *2E 98*
(off Pennard Rd.)
Lanark M. W9 . . . 3A 82
Lanark Pl. W9 . . . 3A 4 (4A 82)
Lanark Rd. W9 . . . 2K 81
Lanark Sq. E14 . . . 3D 104
Lanata Wlk. *UB4: Yead* . . . *4B 76*
(off Alba Cl.)
Lanbury Rd. SE15 . . . 4K 121
Lancashire Ct. W1 . . . 2K 11 (7F 83)
Lancaster Av. CR4: Mitc . . . 5J 155
E18 . . . 4K 51
EN4: Had W . . . 1F 21
IG11: Bark . . . 7J 71
SE27 . . . 2B 138
SW19 . . . 5F 135
Lancaster Cl. BR2: Brom . . . 4H 159
KT2: King T . . . 5D 132
N1 . . . 7E 66
N17 . . . 7B 34
NW9 . . . 7G 29
TW15: Ashf . . . 4A 128
TW19: Stanw . . . 6A 110
W2 . . . *7K 81*
(off St Petersburgh Pl.)
Lancaster Cotts. TW10: Rich . . . 6E 114
Lancaster Ct. KT12: Walt T . . . 7J 147
SE27 . . . 2B 138
SM2: Sutt . . . *7J 165*
(off Mulgrave Rd.)
SW6 . . . 7H 99
TW19: Stanw . . . 1A 128
W2 . . . *2A 10*
(off Lancaster Ga.)
Lancaster Dr. E14 . . . 1E 104
NW3 . . . 6C 64
Lancaster Gdns. BR1: Brom . . . 5C 160
KT2: King T . . . 5D 132
SW19 . . . 5G 135
W13 . . . 2B 96
Lancaster Ga. W2 . . . 2A 10 (7A 82)
Lancaster Gro. NW3 . . . 6B 64
Lancaster Hall *E16* . . . *1J 105*
(off Wesley Av.)
Lancaster House . . . 6A 12
Lancaster Ho. E11 . . . 2H 69
EN2: Enf . . . 1J 23
RM8: Dag . . . 4B 72
TW7: Isle . . . 7K 95
Lancaster Lodge *W11* . . . *6G 81*
(off Lancaster Rd.)
Lancaster M. SW18 . . . 5K 117
TW10: Rich . . . 6E 114
W2 . . . 2A 10 (7A 82)
Lancaster Pk. TW10: Rich . . . 5E 114
Lancaster Pl. IG1: Ilf . . . 5G 71
SW19 . . . 5F 135
TW1: Twick . . . 6A 114
TW4: Houn . . . 2A 112
WC2 . . . 2G 13 (7K 83)
Lancaster Rd. E7 . . . 7J 69
E11 . . . 2G 69
E17 . . . 2K 49
EN2: Enf . . . 1J 23
EN4: E Barn . . . 5G 21
HA2: Harr . . . 5E 40
N4 . . . 7K 47
N11 . . . 6C 32
N18 . . . 5A 34
NW10 . . . 5C 62
SE25 . . . 2F 157
SW19 . . . 5F 135
UB1: S'hall . . . 7C 76
UB5: N'olt . . . 6G 59
W11 . . . 6G 81
Lancaster Rd. Ind. Est. EN4: E Barn . . . 5G 21
Lancaster Stables NW3 . . . 6C 64
Lancaster St. SE1 . . . 7A 14 (2B 102)
Lancaster Ter. W2 . . . 2A 10 (7B 82)
Lancaster Wlk. UB3: Hayes . . . 6E 74
W2 . . . 3A 10 (1A 100)
Lancaster Way KT4: Wor Pk . . . 7D 152
Lancastrian Rd. SM6: Wall . . . 7J 167
Lancefield Ho. SE15 . . . 4H 121
Lancefield St. W10 . . . 3H 81
Lancell St. N16 . . . 2F 67
Lancelot Av. HA0: Wemb . . . 4D 60
Lancelot Cres. HA0: Wemb . . . 4D 60
Lancelot Gdns. EN4: E Barn . . . 7K 21
Lancelot Pl. SW7 . . . 7E 10 (2D 100)
Lancelot Rd. DA16: Well . . . 4A 126
HA0: Wemb . . . 4D 60
Lance Rd. HA1: Harr . . . 7G 41
Lancer Sq. *W8* . . . *2K 99*
(off Kensington Chu. St.)
Lancey Cl. SE7 . . . 4C 106
Lanchester Ct. *W2* . . . *1E 10*
(off Seymour St.)
Lanchester Rd. N6 . . . 5D 46
Lanchester Way SE14 . . . 1J 121
Lancing Gdns. N9 . . . 1A 34
Lancing Ho. *CR0: C'don* . . . *4D 168*
(off Coombe Rd.)
Lancing Rd. CR0: C'don . . . 7K 155
IG2: Ilf . . . 6H 53
TW13: Felt . . . 2H 129
W13 . . . 7B 78
Lancing St. NW1 . . . 2C 6 (3H 83)
Lancresse Ct. *N1* . . . *1E 84*
(off De Beauvoir Est.)
Landale Ho. *SE16* . . . *3J 103*
(off Lower Rd.)
Landau Apartments SW6 . . . 6J 99
Landau Ct. *CR2: S Croy* . . . *5C 168*
(off Warham Rd.)
Landcroft Rd. SE22 . . . 5F 121
Landells Rd. SE22 . . . 6F 121
Landford Rd. SW15 . . . 3E 116
Landgrove Rd. SW19 . . . 5J 135
Landin Ho. *E14* . . . *6C 86*
(off Thomas Rd.)
Landleys Fld. *N7* . . . *5H 65*
(off Long Mdw.)
Landmann Ho. *SE16* . . . *4H 103*
(off Rennie Est.)
Landmann Point SE10 . . . 3J 105
Landmann Way SE14 . . . 5K 103
Landmark Arts Cen. . . . 5B 132
Landmark Commercial Cen. N18 . . . 6K 33
Landmark East Twr. *E14* . . . *2C 104*
(off Marsh Wall)
Landmark Hgts. E5 . . . 4A 68
Landmark Ho. *W6* . . . *5E 98*
(off Hammersmith Bri. Rd.)
Landmark Pl. UB10: Hil . . . 2D 74
Landmark Sq. E14 . . . 2C 104
Landmark West Twr. *E14* . . . *2C 104*
(off Marsh Wall)
Landon Pl. SW1 . . . 1E 16 (3D 100)
Landon's Cl. E14 . . . 1E 104
Landon Wlk. E14 . . . 7D 86
Landon Way TW15: Ashf . . . 6D 128
Landor Ho. *SE5* . . . *7D 102*
(off Elmington Est.)
W2 . . . *5J 81*
(off Westbourne Pk. Rd.)
Landor Rd. SW9 . . . 3J 119
Landor Theatre . . . 3J 119
Landor Wlk. W12 . . . 2C 98
Landra Gdns. N21 . . . 6G 23
Landrake *NW1* . . . *1G 83*
(off Plender St.)
Landridge Dr. EN1: Enf . . . 1C 24
Landridge Rd. SW6 . . . 2H 117
Landrock Rd. N8 . . . 6J 47
Landscape Rd. IG8: Wfd G . . . 7E 36

Landsdown Cl.
EN5: New Bar 4F 21
Landsdowne Ct. *N19* 1J 65
(off Fairbridge Rd.)
Landseer Av. E12 5E 70
Landseer Cl. HA8: Edg 2G 43
SW19 1A 154
Landseer Ct. UB4: Hayes 2F 75
Landseer Ho. *NW8* 3B 4
(off Frampton St.)
SW1 4D 18
(off Herrick St.)
SW11 1E 118
UB5: N'olt 2B 76
(off Parkfield Dr.)
Landseer Rd. EN1: Enf 5B 24
KT3: N Mald 7K 151
N19 3J 65
(not continuous)
SM1: Sutt 6J 165
Landstead Rd. SE18 7H 107
Landulph Ho. *SE11* 5K 19
(off Kennings Way)
Landward Ct. *W1* 7D 4
(off Harrowby St.)
Lane, The NW8 2A 82
SE3 3J 123
Lane Cl. NW2 3D 62
Lane End DA7: Bex 3H 127
SW15 6F 117
Lane Gdns. WD23: B Hea 1D 26
Lane M. E12 3D 70
Lanercost Cl. SW2 2A 138
Lanercost Gdns. N14 7D 22
Lanercost Rd. SW2 2A 138
Lanesborough Ct. *N1* 1G 9
(off Fanshaw St.)
Lanesborough Pl. SW1 6H 11
Lanesborough Way SW17 3B 136
Laneside BR7: Chst 5F 143
HA8: Edg 5D 28
Laneside Av. RM8: Dag 7F 55
Laneway SW15 5D 116
Laney Ho. *EC1* 5J 7
(off Leather La.)
Lanfranc Ct. HA1: Harr 3K 59
Lanfranc Rd. E3 2A 86
Lanfrey Pl. W14 5H 99
Langbourne Av. N6 2E 64
Langbourne Ct. E17 6A 50
Langbourne Mans. N6 2E 64
Langbourne Pl. E14 5D 104
Langbourne Way KT10: Clay 6A 162
Langbrook Rd. SE3 3B 124
Langcroft Cl. SM5: Cars 3D 166
Langdale *NW1* 1A 6
(off Stanhope St.)
Langdale Av. CR4: Mitc 3D 154
Langdale Cl. BR6: Farnb 3F 173
RM8: Dag 1C 72
SE17 6C 102
SW14 4H 115
Langdale Cres. DA7: Bex 7G 109
Langdale Dr. UB4: Hayes 2G 75
Langdale Gdns. UB6: G'frd 3B 78
Langdale Ho. *SW1* 6A 18
(off Churchill Gdns.)
Langdale Pde. CR4: Mitc 3D 154
Langdale Rd. CR7: Thor H 4A 156
SE10 7E 104
Langdale St. E1 6H 85
Langdon Ct. *EC1* 1B 8
(off City Rd.)
NW10 1A 80
Langdon Cres. E6 2E 88
Langdon Dr. NW9 1J 61
Langdon Ho. *E14* 6E 86
(off Ida St.)
Langdon Pk. TW11: Tedd 7C 132
Langdon Pk. Rd. N6 7G 47
Langdon Pl. SW14 3J 115
Langdon Rd. BR2: Brom 3K 159
E6 1E 88
SM4: Mord 5A 154
Langdons Ct. UB2: S'hall 3E 94
Langdon Shaw DA14: Sidc 5K 143
Langdon Wlk. SM4: Mord 5A 154
Langdon Way SE1 4G 103
Langford Cl. E8 5G 67
NW8 2A 82
W3 2H 97
Langford Ct. *NW8* 2A 82
(off Abbey Rd.)
Langford Cres. EN4: Cockf 4J 21
Langford Grn. SE5 3E 120
Langford Ho. SE8 6C 104
Langford M. N1 7A 66
SW11 4B 118
(off St John's Hill)
Langford Pl. DA14: Sidc 3A 144
NW8 2A 82
Langford Rd. EN4: Cockf 4J 21
IG8: Wfd G 6F 37
SW6 2K 117
Langfords IG9: Buck H 2G 37
Langham Cl. BR2: Brom 2C 172
N15 3B 48
(off Langham Rd.)
Langham Ct. HA4: Ruis 5K 57
NW4 5F 45
SW20 2E 152
Langham Dr. RM6: Chad H 6B 54
Langham Gdns. HA0: Wemb 2C 60
HA8: Edg 7D 28
N21 5F 23
TW10: Ham 4C 132
W13 7B 78
Langham Ho. Cl. TW10: Ham 4D 132
Langham Mans. *SW5* 5K 99
(off Earl's Ct. Sq.)
Langham Pk. Pl. BR2: Brom 4H 159
Langham Pl. N15 3B 48
W1 6K 5 (5F 83)
W4 6A 98
Langham Rd. HA8: Edg 6D 28
N15 3B 48
SW20 1E 152
TW11: Tedd 5B 132
Langham St. W1 6K 5 (5F 83)
Langhedge Cl. N18 6A 34
Langhedge La. N18 6A 34
Langhedge La. Ind. Est. N18 6A 34
Langholm Cl. SW12 7H 119
Langholme WD23: Bush 1B 26
Langhorn Dr. TW2: Twick 7J 113
Langhorne Ct. *NW8* 7B 64
(off Dorman Way)
Langhorne Rd. RM10: Dag 7G 73
Langhorne St. SE18 7D 106
Lang Ho. *SW8* 7J 101
(off Hartington Rd.)
TW19: Stanw 1A 128
Langland Cres. HA7: Stan 2D 42
Langland Dr. HA5: Pinn 1C 40
Langland Gdns. CR0: C'don 2B 170
NW3 5K 63
Langland Ho. *SE5* 7D 102
(off Edmund St.)
Langler Rd. NW10 2E 80
Langley Av. HA4: Ruis 2K 57
KT4: Wor Pk 1F 165
KT6: Surb 1D 162
Langley Ct. WC2 2E 12 (7J 83)
Langley Cres. E11 7A 52
HA8: Edg 3D 28
RM9: Dag 7C 72
UB3: Harl 7H 93
Langley Dr. E11 7K 51
W3 2H 97
Langley Gdns. BR2: Brom 4A 160
BR5: Pet W 6F 161
RM9: Dag 7D 72
Langley Gro. KT3: N Mald 2A 152
Langley Ho. *W2* 5J 81
(off Alfred Rd.)
Langley La. SW8 7F 19 (6K 101)
Langley Mans. SW8 7F 19
Langley M. RM9: Dag 7D 72
Langley Pk. NW7 6F 29
Langley Pk. Golf Course 6F 159
Langley Pk. Rd. SM1: Sutt 5A 166
SM2: Sutt 5A 166
Langley Pk. Sports Cen. 6E 158
Langley Rd. BR3: Beck 4A 158
DA16: Well 6C 108
KT6: Surb 7E 150
SW19 1H 153
TW7: Isle 2K 113
Langley Row EN5: Barn 1C 20
Langley St. WC2 1E 12 (6J 83)
Langley Way BR4: W W'ck 1F 171
Langmead Dr. WD23: B Hea 1D 26
Langmead Ho. *E3* 3D 86
(off Bruce Rd.)
Langmead St. SE27 4B 138
Langmore Ct. DA6: Bex 3D 126
Langmore Ho. *E1* 6G 85
(off Stutfield St.)
Langport Ct. KT12: Walt T 7A 148
Langport Ho. SW9 2B 120
Langridge M. TW12: Hamp 6D 130
Langroyd Rd. SW17 2D 136
Langside Av. SW15 4C 116
Langside Cres. N14 3C 32
Langstone Way NW7 7A 30
Langston Hughes Cl. SE24 4B 120
Lang St. E1 4J 85
Langthorn Ct. EC2 7E 8 (6D 84)
Langthorne Ct. BR1: Brom 4E 140
Langthorne Ho. *E3* 3B 86
(off Merchant St.)
UB3: Harl 4G 93
Langthorne Rd. E11 3E 68
(not continuous)
Langthorne St. SW6 7F 99
Langton Av. E6 3E 88
N20 7F 21
Langton Cl. WC1 3H 7 (4K 83)
Langton Ho. SE11 3H 19
Langton Pl. SW18 1J 135
Langton Ri. SE23 7H 121
Langton Rd. HA3: Hrw W 7B 26
KT8: W Mole 4G 149
NW2 3E 62
SW9 7B 102
Langton St. SW10 6A 100
Langton Way CR0: C'don 3E 168
SE3 1H 123
Langtry Ct. TW7: Isle 2K 113
Langtry Ho. *KT2: King T* 1G 151
(off London Rd.)
Langtry Pl. SW6 6J 99
Langtry Rd. NW8 1K 81
UB5: N'olt 2B 76
Langtry Wlk. NW8 1K 81
Langwood Chase TW11: Tedd 6C 132
Langworth Dr. UB4: Yead 6K 75
Lanhill Rd. W9 4J 81
Lanier Rd. SE13 6F 123
Lanigan Dr. TW3: Houn 5F 113
Lankaster Gdns. N2 1B 46
Lankers Dr. HA2: Harr 6D 40
Lankton Cl. BR3: Beck 1E 158
Lannock Rd. UB3: Hayes 1H 93
Lannoy Point *SW6* 7G 99
(off Pellant Rd.)
Lannoy Rd. SE9 1G 143
Lanrick Rd. E14 6F 87
Lanridge Rd. SE2 3D 108
Lansbury Av. IG11: Bark 7A 72
N18 5J 33
RM6: Chad H 5E 54
TW14: Felt 6K 111
Lansbury Cl. NW10 5J 61
Lansbury Ct. *SE28* 7B 90
(off Saunders Way)
Lansbury Dr. UB4: Hayes 2G 75
Lansbury Est. E14 6D 86
Lansbury Gdns. E14 6F 87
Lansbury Rd. EN3: Enf H 1E 24
Lansbury Way N18 5K 33
Lanscombe Wlk. SW8 1J 119
Lansdell Ho. SW2 6A 120
Lansdell Rd. CR4: Mitc 2E 154
Lansdowne Av. BR6: Farnb 1F 173
DA7: Bex 7D 108
Lansdowne Cl. KT6: Surb 2H 163
SW20 7F 135
TW1: Twick 1K 131
Lansdowne Ct. IG5: Ilf 3C 52
KT4: Wor Pk 2C 164
W11 7G 81
(off Lansdowne Ri.)
Lansdowne Cres. W11 7G 81
Lansdowne Dr. E8 6G 67
Lansdowne Gdns. SW8 1J 119
Lansdowne Grn. SW8 1J 119
Lansdowne Gro. NW10 4A 62
Lansdowne Hill SE27 3B 138
Lansdowne Ho. *W11* 1H 99
(off Ladbroke Rd.)
Lansdowne La. SE7 6B 106
Lansdowne M. SE7 5B 106
W11 1H 99
Lansdowne Pl. SE1 3D 102
SE19 7F 139
Lansdowne Ri. W11 7G 81
Lansdowne Rd. BR1: Brom 7J 141
CR0: C'don 2D 168
E4 2H 35
E11 2H 69
E17 6C 50
E18 3J 51
HA1: Harr 7J 41
HA7: Stan 6H 27
IG3: Ilf 1K 71
KT19: Ewe 7J 163
N3 7D 30
N10 2G 47
N17 1F 49
SW20 7E 134
TW3: Houn 3F 113
UB8: Hil 6E 74
W11 7G 81
Lansdowne Row W1 4K 11 (1F 101)
Lansdowne Ter. WC1 4F 7 (4J 83)
Lansdowne Wlk. W11 1H 99
Lansdowne Way SW8 1H 119
Lansdowne Wood Cl. SE27 3B 138
Lansdowne Workshops
SE7 5A 106
Lansdown Rd. DA14: Sidc 3B 144
E7 7A 70
Lansfield Av. N18 4B 34
Lanson Apartments SW8 7F 101
Lantern *SE1* 6C 14
(off Lant St.)
Lantern Cl. BR6: Farnb 4F 173
HA0: Wemb 5D 60
SW15 4C 116
Lantern Ho. *UB3: Harl* 3E 92
(off Nine Acres Cl.)
Lanterns Way E14 2C 104
Lantern Way UB7: W Dray 2A 92
Lant Ho. *SE1* 7C 14
(off Toulmin St.)
Lantry Ct. W3 1H 97
Lant St. SE1 6C 14 (2C 102)
Lanvanor Rd. SE15 2J 121
Lanward Apartments *N1* 7K 65
(off Caledonian Rd.)
Lanyard Ho. SE8 4B 104
Lapford Cl. W9 4H 81
Lapis Cl. NW10 3G 79

Lapis M. E15 1E **86**
Lapponum Wlk. UB4: Yead 4B **76**
Lapse Wood Wlk. SE23 1H **139**
Lapstone Gdns.
HA3: Kenton 6C **42**
Lapwing Ct. KT6: Surb 3G **163**
*SE1 7D **14***
(off Swan St.)
Lapwing Ter. E7 5B **70**
Lapwing Twr. *SE8 6B **104***
(off Taylor Cl.)
Lapwing Way UB4: Yead 6B **76**
Lapworth *N11 4A **32***
(off Coppies Gro.)
Lapworth Ct. *W2 5K **81***
(off Delamere Ter.)
Lara Cl. KT9: Chess 7E **162**
SE13 6E **122**
Larbert Rd. SW16 7G **137**
Larch Av. W3 1A **98**
Larch Cl. E13 4K **87**
N11 7K **31**
N19 2G **65**
SE8 6B **104**
SW12 2F **137**
Larch Ct. *SE1 7G **15***
(off Royal Oak Yd.)
*W9 5J **81***
(off Admiral Wlk.)
Larch Cres. KT19: Ewe 6H **163**
UB4: Yead 4A **76**
Larch Dene BR6: Farnb 2E **172**
Larch Dr. W4 5G **97**
Larches, The N13 3H **33**
UB10: Hil 3D **74**
Larches Av. SW14 4K **115**
Larch Grn. NW9 1A **44**
Larch Gro. DA15: Sidc 1K **143**
Larch Ho. BR2: Brom 1G **159**
*SE16 2J **103***
(off Ainsty Est.)
UB4: Yead 5A **76**
*W10 4G **81***
(off Rowan Wlk.)
Larch Rd. E10 2C **68**
NW2 4E **62**
Larch Tree Way CR0: C'don 3C **170**
Larchvale Ct. SM2: Sutt 7K **165**
Larch Way BR2: Brom 7E **160**
Larchwood Ho. *UB7: W Dray 2B **92***
(off Park Lodge Av.)
Larchwood Rd. SE9 2F **143**
Larcombe Cl. CR0: C'don 4F **169**
Larcombe Ct. *SM2: Sutt 7K **165***
(off Worcester Rd.)
Larcom St. SE17 4C **102**
Larden Rd. W3 1A **98**
Largewood Av. KT6: Surb 2G **163**
Larissa St. SE17 5D **102**
Larkbere Rd. SE26 4A **140**
Lark Ct. *NW9 1A **44***
(off Lanacre Av.)
Larken Cl. WD23: Bush 1B **26**
Larken Dr. WD23: Bush 1B **26**
Larkfield Av. HA3: Kenton 3B **42**
Larkfield Cl. BR2: Hayes 2H **171**
Larkfield Rd. DA14: Sidc 3K **143**
TW9: Rich 4E **114**
Larkhall La. SW4 2H **119**
Larkhall Ri. SW4 3G **119**
(not continuous)
Larkham Cl. TW13: Felt 3G **129**
Lark Hill Ter. *SE18 7E **106***
(off Prince Imperial Rd.)
Lark Row E2 1J **85**
Larksfield Gro. EN1: Enf 1C **24**
Larks Gro. IG11: Bark 7J **71**
Larkshall Ct.
RM7: Mawney 2J **55**
Larkshall Cres. E4 4K **35**
Larkshall Rd. E4 5K **35**
Larkspur Cl. E6 5C **88**
HA4: Ruis 7E **38**
N17 7J **33**
NW9 5H **43**
Larkspur Gro. HA8: Edg 4D **28**
Larkspur Lodge DA14: Sidc 3B **144**
Larkspur Way KT19: Ewe 5J **163**
Larkswood Ct. E4 5A **36**
Larkswood Ri. HA5: Eastc 4A **40**
Larkswood Rd. E4 4H **35**
Lark Way SM5: Cars 7C **154**
Larkway Cl. NW9 4K **43**
Larnach Rd. W6 6F **99**
Larne Rd. HA4: Ruis 7H **39**
Larpent Av. SW15 5E **116**
Larson Wlk. E14 3C **104**
Larwood Cl. UB6: G'frd 5H **59**
Lascar Cl. TW3: Houn 3D **112**
Lascar Wharf Bldg. *E14 6A **86***
(off Parnham St.)
Lascelles Av. HA1: Harr 7H **41**
Lascelles Cl. E11 2F **69**
Lascelles Ho. NW1 4D **4**
Lascotts Rd. N22 6E **32**
Laseron Ho. *N15 4F **49***
(off Tottenham Grn. E.)
Las Palmas Est. TW17: Shep 7E **146**
Lassa Rd. SE9 5C **124**
Lassell St. SE10 5F **105**
Lasseter Pl. SE3 6H **105**
Latchett Rd. E18 1K **51**
Latchingdon Ct. E17 4K **49**
Latchingdon Gdns. IG8: Wfd G 6H **37**
Latchmere Cl. TW10: Ham 5E **132**
Latchmere La. KT2: King T 6F **133**
TW10: Ham 6F **133**
Latchmere Leisure Cen. 2D **118**
Latchmere Pas. SW11 2C **118**
Latchmere Pl. TW15: Ashf 2A **128**
Latchmere Rd. KT2: King T 7E **132**
SW11 2D **118**
Latchmere St. SW11 2D **118**
Lateward Rd. TW8: Bford 6D **96**
Latham Cl. E6 5C **88**
TW1: Twick 7A **114**
Latham Ct. *N11 6D **32***
(off Brownlow Rd.)
*SW5 4J **99***
(off W. Cromwell Rd.)
*UB5: N'olt 3B **76***
(off Delta Gro.)
Latham Ho. *E1 6K **85***
(off Chudleigh St.)
Latham Rd. DA6: Bex 5G **127**
TW1: Twick 7K **113**
Latham's Way CR0: Wadd 1K **167**
Lathkill Cl. EN1: Enf 7B **24**
Lathkill Ct. BR3: Beck 1B **158**
Lathom Rd. E6 7C **70**
Latimer Av. E6 1D **88**
Latimer Cl. HA5: Pinn 1A **40**
KT4: Wor Pk 4D **164**
Latimer Ct. *BR2: Brom 4H **159***
(off Durham Rd.)
Latimer Gdns. HA5: Pinn 1A **40**
Latimer Ho. E9 6K **67**
*W11 7H **81***
(off Kensington Pk. Rd.)
Latimer Ind. Est. W10 6E **80**
Latimer Pl. W10 6E **80**
Latimer Rd. CR0: C'don 3B **168**
E7 4K **69**
EN5: New Bar 3E **20**
N15 6E **48**
SW19 6K **135**
TW11: Tedd 5K **131**
W10 5E **80**
(not continuous)
Latitude Apartments
*CR0: C'don 3D **168***
(off Fairfield Rd.)
Latitude Ct. E16 7G **89**
Latitude Ho. *NW1 1F **83***
(off Oval Rd.)
Latona Ct. *SW9 7A **102***
(off Caldwell St.)
Latona Rd. SE15 6G **103**
La Tourne Gdns. BR6: Farnb 3G **173**
Lattimer Pl. W4 7A **98**
Latton Cl. KT12: Walt T 7C **148**
Latvia Ct. *SE17 5C **102***
(off Macleod St.)
Latymer Ct. W6 4F **99**
Latymer Gdns. N3 2G **45**
Latymer Rd. N9 1A **34**
Latymer Way N9 2K **33**
Laubin Cl. TW1: Twick 4B **114**
Lauder Cl. UB5: N'olt 2B **76**
Lauder Ct. N14 7D **22**
Lauderdale Dr. TW10: Ham 3D **132**
Lauderdale House 1F **65**
Lauderdale Ho. *SW9 1A **120***
(off Gosling Way)
Lauderdale House Community Arts Cen.
1F **65**
Lauderdale Mans. *W9 3K **81***
(off Lauderdale Rd.)
Lauderdale Pde. W9 4K **81**
Lauderdale Pl. *EC2 5C **8***
(off Beech St.)
Lauderdale Rd. W9 3K **81**
Lauderdale Twr. EC2 5C **8**
Laud St. CR0: C'don 3C **168**
SE11 5G **19** (5K **101**)
Laugan Wlk. SE17 5C **102**
Laughton Rd. UB5: N'olt 1B **76**
Launcelot Rd. BR1: Brom 4J **141**
Launcelot St. SE1 7J **13** (2A **102**)
Launceston Gdns. UB6: G'frd 1C **78**
Launceston Pl. W8 3A **100**
Launceston Rd. UB6: G'frd 1C **78**
Launch St. E14 3E **104**
Launders Ga. W3 2H **97**
Laundress La. N16 3G **67**
Laundry La. N1 1C **84**
Laundry M. SE23 7A **122**
Laundry Rd. W6 6G **99**
Launton Dr. DA6: Bex 4D **126**
Laura Cl. E11 5A **52**
EN1: Enf 5K **23**
Lauradale Rd. N2 4D **46**
Laura Pl. E5 4J **67**
Laura Ter. N4 2B **66**
Laurel Apartments
*SE17 4E **102***
(off Townsend St.)
Laurel Av. TW1: Twick 1K **131**
Laurel Bank N12 4F **31**
Laurel Bank Gdns. SW6 2H **117**
Laurel Bank Rd.
EN2: Enf 1H **23**
Laurel Bank Vs. *W7 2J **95***
(off Lwr. Boston Rd.)
Laurel Cl. DA14: Sidc 3A **144**
N19 2G **65**
SW17 5C **136**
Laurel Ct. *CR2: S Croy 4E **168***
(off South Pk. Hill Rd.)
HA0: Wemb 2E **78**
*SE1 3D **102***
(off Garland Cl.)
Laurel Cres. CR0: C'don 3C **170**
RM7: Rush G 1K **73**
Laurel Dr. N21 7F **23**
Laurel Gdns. BR1: Brom 4C **160**
E4 7J **25**
NW7 3E **28**
TW4: Houn 4C **112**
TW15: Ashf 5E **128**
W7 1J **95**
Laurel Gro. SE20 7J **139**
SE26 4K **139**
Laurel Ho. BR2: Brom 1G **159**
*E3 1B **86***
(off Hornbeam Sq.)
SE8 6B **104**
Laurel La. UB7: W Dray 4A **92**
Laurel Mnr. SM2: Sutt 7A **166**
Laurel M. *SE5 3C **120***
(off Harbour Rd.)
Laurel Pk. HA3: Hrw W 7E **26**
Laurel Rd. SW13 2C **116**
SW20 1D **152**
TW12: Hamp H 5H **131**
Laurels, The BR1: Brom 1K **159**
BR2: Brom 4J **159**
IG9: Buck H 1F **37**
NW10 1D **80**
*SW9 7B **102***
(off Langton Rd.)
WD23: B Hea 2D **26**
Laurel St. E8 6F **67**
Laurel Vw. N12 3E **30**
Laurel Way E18 4H **51**
N20 3D **30**
Laurence Calvert Cl. IG11: Bark 2J **89**
Laurence Ct. E10 7D **50**
*W11 7G **81***
(off Lansdowne Rd.)
Laurence M. W12 2C **98**
Laurence Pountney Hill EC4 2E **14** (7D **84**)
Laurence Pountney La. EC4 2E **14** (7D **84**)
Laurence Rd. TW3: Houn 3G **113**
Laurie Gro. SE14 1A **122**
Laurie Ho. *SE1 3B **102***
(off St George's Rd.)
*W8 1J **99***
(off Airlie Gdns.)
Laurie Rd. W7 5J **77**
Laurier Rd. CR0: C'don 7F **157**
NW5 3F **65**
Laurimel Cl. HA7: Stan 6G **27**
Laurino Pl. WD23: B Hea 2B **26**
Lauriston Ho. *E9 7J **67***
(off Lauriston Rd.)
Lauriston Rd. E9 7J **67**
SW19 6F **135**
Lausanne Rd. N8 4A **48**
SE15 1J **121**
Laval Ho. *TW8: Bford 5E **96***
(off Ealing Rd.)
Lavell St. N16 4D **66**
Lavender Av. CR4: Mitc 1C **154**
KT4: Wor Pk 3E **164**
NW9 1J **61**
Lavender Cl. BR2: Brom 6C **160**
E4 4H **35**
SM5: Cars 4F **167**
SW3 7B **16** (6B **100**)
Lavender Ct. KT8: W Mole 3F **149**
SM2: Sutt 7A **166**
TW14: Felt 6K **111**
Lavender Gdns. EN2: Enf 1G **23**
HA3: Hrw W 6D **26**
SW11 4D **118**
Lavender Gro. CR4: Mitc 1C **154**
E8 7G **67**
Lavender Hill EN2: Enf 1F **23**
SW11 4C **118**
Lavender Ho. *SE16 1K **103***
(off Rotherhithe St.)
TW9: Kew 1H **115**
Lavender Pl. IG1: Ilf 5F **71**
Lavender Pond Nature Pk. 1A **104**
Lavender Ri. UB7: W Dray 2C **92**
Lavender Rd. CR0: C'don 6K **155**
EN2: Enf 1J **23**
KT19: Ewe 5H **163**
SE16 1A **104**
SM1: Sutt 4B **166**
SM5: Cars 4E **166**
SW11 3B **118**
UB8: Hil 5B **74**

Lavender Sq. *SW9* 1K **119**
(*off Printers Rd.*)
Lavender St. E15 6G **69**
Lavender Sweep SW11 4D **118**
Lavender Ter. SW11 3C **118**
Lavender Va. SM6: Wall 6H **167**
Lavender Wlk. CR4: Mitc 3E **154**
SW11 4D **118**
Lavender Way CR0: C'don 6K **157**
Lavendon Ho. *NW8* *3D* ***4***
(*off Paveley St.*)
Lavengro Rd. SE27 2C **138**
Lavenham Rd. SW18 2H **135**
Lavernock Rd. DA7: Bex 2G **127**
Lavers Rd. N16 3E **66**
Laverstoke Gdns. SW15 7B **116**
Laverton M. SW5 4K **99**
Laverton Pl. SW5 4K **99**
Lavette Ho. *E3* *3C* ***86***
(*off Rainhill Way*)
Lavidge Rd. SE9 2C **142**
Lavina Gro. N1 2K **83**
Lavington Cl. E9 6B **68**
Lavington Rd. CR0: Bedd 3K **167**
W13 1B **96**
Lavington St. SE1 5B **14** (1B **102**)
Lavisham Ho. BR1: Brom 5K **141**
Lawdons Gdns.
CR0: Wadd 4B **168**
Lawes Ho. *W10* *3H* ***81***
(*off Lancefield St.*)
Lawes Way IG11: Bark 3K **89**
Lawford Rd. N1 7E **66**
NW5 6G **65**
W4 7J **97**
Lawfords Wharf *NW1* *7G* ***65***
(*off Lyme St.*)
Law Ho. IG11: Bark 2A **90**
Lawless Ho. *E14* *7E* ***86***
(*off Bazely St.*)
Lawless St. E14 7D **86**
Lawley Ho. TW1: Twick 6D **114**
Lawley Rd. N14 7A **22**
Lawley St. E5 4J **67**
Lawlor Cl. TW16: Sun 1K **147**
Lawn, The UB2: S'hall 5E **94**
Lawn Cl. BR1: Brom 6K **141**
HA4: Ruis 3H **57**
KT3: N Mald 2A **152**
N9 7A **24**
Lawn Cres. TW9: Kew 2G **115**
Lawn Farm Gro. RM6: Chad H 4E **54**
Lawnfield Ct. *NW6* *7F* ***63***
(*off Coverdale Rd.*)
Lawn Gdns. W7 1J **95**
Lawn Ho. Cl. E14 2E **104**
Lawn La. SW8 7F **19** (6K **101**)
Lawn Rd. BR3: Beck 7B **140**
NW3 5D **64**
Lawns, The DA14: Sidc 4B **144**
E4 5H **35**
HA5: Hat E 7A **26**
SE3 3H **123**
SE19 1D **156**
SM2: Cheam 7G **165**
SW19 5H **135**
Lawns Ct. HA9: Wemb 2F **61**
Lawnside SE3 4H **123**
Lawns Way RM5: Col R 1J **55**
Lawnswood EN5: Barn 5B **20**
Lawn Ter. SE3 3G **123**
Lawn Va. HA5: Pinn 2C **40**
Lawrence Av. E12 4E **70**
E17 1K **49**
KT3: N Mald 6K **151**
N13 4G **33**
NW7 4F **29**
NW10 1K **79**
Lawrence Bldgs. N16 3F **67**
Lawrence Campe Cl.
N20 3G **31**
Lawrence Cl. E3 3C **86**
N15 4E **48**
W12 7D **80**
Lawrence Ct. N10 3G **47**
N16 *3F* ***67***
(*off Smalley Rd. Est.*)
NW7 5F **29**
SE6 6C **122**
W3 *3J* ***97***
(*off Stanley Rd.*)
Lawrence Cres. HA8: Edg 2G **43**
RM10: Dag 3H **73**
Lawrence Dr. UB10: Ick 4E **56**
Lawrence Est. TW4: Houn 4A **112**
Lawrence Gdns. NW7 3G **29**
Lawrence Gro. UB10: Uxb 2A **74**
Lawrence Hill E4 2H **35**
Lawrence Ho. *NW1* *7F* ***65***
(*off Hawley Cres.*)
SW1 *4D* ***18***
(*off Cureton St.*)
Lawrence La. EC2 7D **8** (6C **84**)
Lawrence Mans. *SW3* *7C* ***16***
(*off Lordship Pl.*)
Lawrence M. SW15 4E **116**
Lawrence Pde. *TW7: Isle* *3B* ***114***
(*off Lower Sq.*)
Lawrence Pl. *N1* *1J* ***83***
(*off Brydon Wlk.*)
Lawrence Rd. BR4: W W'ck 4J **171**
DA8: Erith 7H **109**
E6 1C **88**
E13 1K **87**
HA5: Pinn 6B **40**
N15 4E **48**
N18 4C **34**
(not continuous)
SE25 4F **157**
TW4: Houn 4A **112**
TW10: Ham 4C **132**
TW12: Hamp 7D **130**
UB4: Hayes 2E **74**
W5 4D **96**
Lawrence St. E16 5H **87**
NW7 5G **29**
SW3 7C **16** (6C **100**)
Lawrence Trad. Est. SE10 4G **105**
Lawrence Way NW10 3J **61**
Lawrence Weaver Cl. SM4: Mord 6J **153**
Lawrence Yd. N15 4E **48**
Lawrie Ho. *SW19* *5K* ***135***
(*off Durnsford Rd.*)
Lawrie Pk. Av. SE26 5H **139**
Lawrie Pk. Cres. SE26 5H **139**
Lawrie Pk. Gdns. SE26 4H **139**
Lawrie Pk. Rd. SE26 6H **139**
Laws Cl. SE25 4D **156**
Lawson Cl. E16 5A **88**
IG1: Ilf 5H **71**
SW19 3F **135**
Lawson Ct. KT6: Surb 7D **150**
N4 *1K* ***65***
(*off Lorne Rd.*)
N11 *6B* ***32***
(*off Ring Way*)
Lawson Gdns. HA5: Eastc 3K **39**
Lawson Ho. *SE18* *6E* ***106***
(*off Nightingale Pl.*)
W12 *7D* ***80***
(*off White City Est.*)
Lawson Rd. EN3: Enf H 1D **24**
UB1: S'hall 4E **76**
Lawson Ter. SE15 4J **121**
Law St. SE1 3D **102**
Lawton Rd. E3 3A **86**
(not continuous)
E10 1E **68**
EN4: Cockf 3G **21**
LAX by PureGym
London Wall 6E **8**
South Kensington 3C **16** (4C **100**)
Laxcon Cl. NW10 5K **61**
Laxey Rd. BR6: Chels 6K **173**
Laxfield Ct. *E8* *1G* ***85***
(*off Pownall Rd.*)
Laxford Ho. *SW1* *4H* ***17***
(*off Cundy St.*)
Laxley Cl. SE5 7B **102**
Laxton Ct. CR7: Thor H 4C **156**
Laxton Pl. NW1 3K **5** (4F **83**)
Layard Rd. CR7: Thor H 2D **156**
EN1: Enf 1A **24**
SE16 4H **103**
Layard Sq. SE16 4H **103**
Laybourne Ho. *E14* *2C* ***104***
(*off Admirals Way*)
Laybrook Lodge E18 4H **51**
Laycock St. N1 6A **66**
Layer Gdns. W3 7G **79**
Layfield Cl. NW4 7D **44**
Layfield Cres. NW4 7D **44**
Layfield Ho. *SE10* *5J* ***105***
(*off Kemsing Rd.*)
Layfield Rd. NW4 7D **44**
Layhams Rd. BR2: Kes 4G **171**
BR4: W W'ck 4G **171**
Laymarsh Cl. DA17: Belv 3F **109**
Laymead Cl. UB5: N'olt 6C **58**
Laystall Ct. *WC1* *4J* ***7***
(*off Mt. Pleasant*)
Laystall St. EC1 4J **7** (4A **84**)
Layton Ct. TW8: Bford 5D **96**
Layton Cres. CR0: Wadd 5A **168**
Layton Pl. TW9: Kew 1G **115**
Layton Rd. TW3: Houn 4F **113**
TW8: Bford 5D **96**
Layton's La. TW16: Sun 2H **147**
Layzell Wlk. SE9 1B **142**
Lazar Wlk. N7 2K **65**
Lazenby Ct. WC2 2E **12**
Leabank Cl. HA1: Harr 3J **59**
Leabank Sq. E9 6C **68**
Leabank Vw. N15 6G **49**
Lea Bon Ct. *E15* *1H* ***87***
(*off Plaistow Gro.*)
Leabourne Rd. N16 7G **49**
LEA BRIDGE 3K **67**
Lea Bri. Ind. Cen. E10 1A **68**
Lea Bri. Rd. E5 3J **67**
E10 7C **50**
E17 5F **51**
Lea Cl. TW2: Whitt 7D **112**
Lea Ct. E4 2K **35**
E13 3J **87**
N15 4G **49**
Lea Cres. HA4: Ruis 4H **57**
Leacroft Av. SW12 7D **118**
Leacroft Cl. N21 2G **33**
UB7: Yiew 6A **74**
Leadale Av. E4 2H **35**
Leadale Rd. N15 6G **49**
N16 6G **49**
Leadbeaters Cl. N11 5J **31**
Leadbetter Ct. *NW10* *7K* ***61***
(*off Melville Rd.*)
Leadenhall Mkt. EC3 1G **15** (6E **84**)
Leadenhall Pl. EC3 1G **15** (6E **84**)
Leadenhall St. EC3 1G **15** (6E **84**)
Leadenham Ct. E3 4C **86**
Leader Av. E12 5E **70**
Leadings, The HA9: Wemb 3J **61**
Leadmill La. E20 4D **68**
Leaf Cl. HA6: Nwood 1F **39**
KT7: T Ditt 5J **149**
Leaf Gro. SE27 5A **138**
Leaf Ho. *HA1: Harr* *5K* ***41***
(*off Catherine Pl.*)
Leafield Cl. SW16 6B **138**
Leafield La. DA14: Sidc 3F **145**
Leafield Rd. SM1: Sutt 2J **165**
SW20 3H **153**
Leaf Wlk. N7 4H **65**
Leafy Gro. BR2: Kes 5A **172**
Leafy Oak Rd. SE12 4A **142**
Leafy Way CR0: C'don 2F **169**
Lea Gdns. HA9: Wemb 4F **61**
Leagrave St. E5 3J **67**
Lea Hall Gdns. E10 1C **68**
Lea Hall Rd. E10 1C **68**
Leaholme Way HA4: Ruis 6E **38**
Lea Ho. *NW8* *4C* ***4***
(*off Salisbury St.*)
Leahurst Rd. SE13 5F **123**
LEA INTERCHANGE **5C 68**
Leake Ct. SE1 7H **13** (2K **101**)
Leake St. SE1 6H **13** (2K **101**)
(not continuous)
Lealand Rd. N15 6F **49**
Leamington Av. BR1: Brom 5A **142**
BR6: Orp 4J **173**
E17 5C **50**
SM4: Mord 4G **153**
Leamington Cl. BR1: Brom 4A **142**
E12 5C **70**
TW3: Houn 5G **113**
Leamington Ct. SE3 6G **105**
Leamington Cres. HA2: Harr 3C **58**
Leamington Gdns. IG3: Ilf 2K **71**
Leamington Ho. HA8: Edg 5A **28**
W11 *5H* ***81***
(*off Tavistock Rd.*)
Leamington Pk. W3 5K **79**
Leamington Pl. UB4: Hayes 4H **75**
Leamington Rd. UB2: S'hall 4B **94**
Leamington Rd. Vs. W11 5H **81**
Leamore Ct. E2 3K **85**
Leamore St. W6 4E **98**
LEAMOUTH 7G **87**
Leamouth Rd. E6 5C **88**
E14 6F **87**
Leander Ct. *E9* *7K* ***67***
(*off Lauriston Rd.*)
KT6: Surb 7D **150**
NW9 1A **44**
SE8 1C **122**
Leander Rd. CR7: Thor H 4K **155**
SW2 6K **119**
UB5: N'olt 2E **76**
Lea Pk. Trad. Est. E10 7B **50**
Learner Dr. HA2: Harr 2E **58**
Lea Rd. BR3: Beck 2C **158**
EN2: Enf 1J **23**
UB2: S'hall 4C **94**
Learoyd Gdns. E6 7E **88**
Leary Ho. SE11 5K **101**
Leas Cl. KT9: Chess 7F **163**
Leas Dale SE9 3E **142**
Leas Grn. BR7: Chst 6K **143**
Leaside Av. N10 3E **46**
Leaside Bus. Cen. EN3: Brim 2G **25**
Leaside Ct. UB10: Hil 3D **74**
Leaside Mans. *N10* *3E* ***46***
(*off Fortis Grn.*)
Leaside Rd. E5 1J **67**
Leasowes Rd. E10 1C **68**
Lea Sq. E3 1B **86**
Leatherbottle Grn. DA18: Erith 3F **109**
Leather Bottle La. DA17: Belv 4E **108**
Leather Cl. CR4: Mitc 2E **154**
Leatherdale St. E1 3K **85**
Leather Gdns. E15 1G **87**
Leatherhead Cl. N16 1F **67**
Leatherhead Rd. KT9: Chess 7D **162**
Leather La. EC1 5J **7** (5A **84**)
(not continuous)
Leathermarket, The SE1 7G **15**
Leathermarket Ct. SE1 7G **15** (2E **102**)
Leathermarket St. SE1 7G **15** (2E **102**)
Leather Rd. SE16 4K **103**
Leathersellers Cl. *EN5: Barn* *3B* ***20***
(*off The Avenue*)
Leather St. E1 7K **85**
Leathsail Rd. HA2: Harr 3F **59**

Leathwaite Rd. SW11 . . . . .4D 118
Leathwell Rd. SE8 . . . . .2D 122
Lea Va. DA1: Cray 4K 127
Lea Valley Bus. Pk. E10 . . . . .2A 68
Lea Valley Rd. E4 . . . . .5F 25
EN3: Pond E 5F 25
Lea Valley Trad. Est. N18 . . . . .6E 34
Lea Valley Viaduct E4 . . . . .5E 34
N18 . . . . .5E 34
Leaveland Cl. BR3: Beck 4C 158
Leaver Gdns. UB6: G'frd 2H 77
Leavesden Rd. HA7: Stan 6F 27
Leaves Grn. Rd. BR2: Kes 7B 172
Lea Vw. Ho. E5 . . . . .1H 67
Leaway E10 . . . . .1K 67
Lebanon Av. TW13: Hanw 5B 130
Lebanon Ct. TW1: Twick 7B 114
Lebanon Gdns. SW18 . . . . .6J 117
Lebanon Pk. TW1: Twick 7B 114
Lebanon Rd. CR0: C'don 1E 168
SW18 .5J 117
Lebus Ho. *NW8* *1C 4*
(off Cochrane St.)
Lebus St. N17 . . . . .3H 49
Le Chateau *CR0: C'don* *3D 168*
(off Chatsworth Rd.)
Lechmere App. IG8: Wfd G 2A 52
Lechmere Av. IG8: Wfd G 2B 52
Lechmere Rd. NW2 . . . . .6D 62
Leckford Rd. SW18 . . . . .2A 136
Leckhampton Pl. SW2 . . . . .7A 120
Leckwith Av. DA7: Bex 6E 108
Lecky St. SW7 . . . . .5A 16 (5B 100)
Leconfield Av. SW13 . . . . .3B 116
Leconfield Ho. SE5 . . . . .4E 120
Leconfield Rd. N5 . . . . .4D 66
Le Cordon Bleu
London *5J 83*
(off Bloomsbury Sq.)
London Culinary Arts Institute
. . . .*6H 5*
(off Marylebone La.)
Leda Av. EN3: Enf W 1E 24
Leda Ct. *SW9* *7A 102*
(off Caldwell St.)
Ledam Ho. *EC1* *5J 7*
(off Bourne Est.)
Leda Rd. SE18 . . . . .3D 106
Ledbury Ho. SE22 . . . . .3E 120
W11 . . . .*6H 81*
(off Colville Rd.)
Ledbury M. Nth. W11 . . . . .7J 81
Ledbury M. W. W11 . . . . .7J 81
Ledbury Pl. CR0: C'don 4C 168
Ledbury Rd. CR0: C'don 4D 168
W11 . . . . .6H 81
Ledbury St. SE15 . . . . .7G 103
Ledger M. E17 . . . . .6C 50
Ledrington Rd. SE19 . . . . .6G 139
Ledway Dr. HA9: Wemb 7F 43
LEE 6J 123
Lee Av. RM6: Chad H 6E 54
Lee Bri. SE13 . . . . .3E 122
Leechcroft Av. DA15: Sidc 5K 125
Leechcroft Rd. SM6: Wall 3E 166
Lee Chu. St. SE13 . . . . .4G 123
Lee Cl. E17 . . . . .1K 49
EN5: New Bar 4F 21
Lee Conservancy Rd. E9 . . . . .5B 68
Lee Ct. *E3* *4E 86*
(off Navigation Rd.)
SE13 . . . .*4F 123*
(off Lee High Rd.)
Leecroft Rd. EN5: Barn 5B 20
Leeds Ct. *EC1* *3A 8*
(off St John St.)
Leeds Pl. N4 . . . . .1K 65
Leeds Rd. IG1: Ilf 1H 71
Leeds St. N18 .5B 34
Leefern Rd. W12 . . . . .2C 98
Leegate SE12 . . . . .5H 123
LEE GREEN **5H 123**
Lee Gro. IG7: Chig 2K 37
Lee High Rd. SE12 . . . . .3E 122
SE13 . . . . .3E 122
Leeke St. WC1 . . . . .1G 7 (3K 83)
Leeland Rd. W13 . . . . .1A 96
Leeland Ter. W13 . . . . .1A 96
Leeland Way NW10 . . . . .4B 62
Lee M. BR3: Beck 3A 158
Leemount Ho. NW4 . . . . .4F 45
Lee Pk. SE3 . . . . .4H 123
Lee Pk. Way N9 . . . . .4E 34
N18 . . . . .4E 34
Leerdam Dr. E14 . . . . .3E 104
Lee Rd. EN1: Enf 6B 24
NW7 . . . . .7A 30
SE3 . . . . .3H 123
SW19 . . . . .1K 153
UB6: G'frd 1C 78
Lees, The CR0: C'don 2B 170
Lees Av. HA6: Nwood 1H 39
Lees Ct. *W1* *2G 11*
(off Lees Pl.)
Lees Ho. *SE17* *5D 102*
(off Inville Rd.)
Leeside EN5: Barn 5B 20
Leeside Ct. *SE16* *1K 103*
(off Rotherhithe St.)
Leeside Cres. NW11 . . . . .6G 45
Leeside Ind. Est. N17 . . . . .7D 34
Leeside Rd. N17 . . . . .6C 34
Leeside Works N17 . . . . .7D 34
Leeson Ho. TW1: Twick 7B 114
Leeson Rd. SE24 . . . . .4A 120
Leesons Hill BR5: St P 3J 161
BR7: Chst 3J 161
Leeson's Way BR5: St P 2K 161
Lees Pde. UB10: Hil 4D 74
Lees Pl. W1 . . . . .2G 11 (7E 82)
Lees Rd. UB8: Hil 4D 74
Lee St. E8 . . . . .1F 85
Lee Ter. SE3 . . . . .3G 123
SE13 . . . . .3G 123
Lee Valley Athletics Cen. 1E 34
Lee Valley Golf Course 7F 25
Lee Valley Hockey & Tennis Cen. 4D 68
Lee Valley Ice Cen. 2K 67
Lee Valley Pk. 7E 34
Lee Valley Technopark N17 . . . . .3G 49
Lee Valley VeloPark 5D 68
Leeve Ho. *W10* *3H 81*
(off Lancefield St.)
Lee Vw. EN2: Enf 1G 23
Leeward Ct. E1 . . . . .7G 85
SE8 . . . .*4A 104*
(off Yeoman St.)
Leeward Gdns. SW19 . . . . .5G 135
Leeward Ho. *N1* *1E 84*
(off Halcomb St.)
Leeway SE8 . . . . .5B 104
Leeway Cl. HA5: Hat E 1D 40
Leeways, The SM3: Cheam 6G 165
Leewood Cl. SE12 . . . . .6J 123
Lefa Bus. & Ind. Pk. DA14: Sidc 6D 144
Lefevre Wlk. E3 . . . . .2C 86
Leff Ho. NW6 . . . . .1G 81
Lefroy Ho. *SE1* *7C 14*
(off Southwark Bri. Rd.)
Lefroy Rd. W12 . . . . .2B 98
Left Side *N14* *1C 32*
(off Stationе Pde.)
Legard Rd. N5 .3B 66
Legatt Rd. SE9 . . . . .5B 124
Leggatt Rd. E15 . . . . .2E 86
Legge St. SE13 . . . . .5E 122
Leghorn Rd. NW10 . . . . .2B 80
SE18 . . . . .5H 107
Legion Cl. N1 . . . . .7A 66
Legion Ct. SM4: Mord 6J 153
Legion Rd. UB6: G'frd 1G 77
Legion Ter. E3 .1B 86
Legion Way N12 . . . . .7H 31
Leg O'Mutton Local Nature Reserve
. . . . .7B 98
Legon Av. RM7: Rush G 1J 73
Legrace Av. TW4: Houn 2B 112
Leicester Av. CR4: Mitc 4J 155
Leicester Cl. KT4: Wor Pk 4E 164
Leicester Ct. *TW1: Twick* *6D 114*
(off Clevedon Rd.)
W9 . . . .*5J 81*
(off Elmfield Way)
WC2 . . . . .2D 12
Leicester Flds. WC2 . . . . .3D 12
Leicester Gdns. IG3: Ilf 7J 53
Leicester Ho. *N18* *5C 34*
(off Cavendish Cl.)
SW9 . . . .*3B 120*
(off Loughborough Rd.)
Leicester M. N2 . . . . .3C 46
Leicester Pl. WC2 . . . . .2D 12 (7H 83)
Leicester Rd. CR0: C'don 7E 156
E11 . . . . .5K 51
EN5: New Bar 5E 20
N2 . . . . .3C 46
NW10 . . . . .7K 61
Leicester Sq. WC2 . . . . .3D 12 (7H 83)
Leicester Square Theatre *7H 83*
(off Leicester Pl.)
Leicester St. WC2 . . . . .2D 12 (7H 83)
Leigh, The KT2: King T 7A 134
Leigham Av. SW16 . . . . .3J 137
Leigham Cl. SW16 . . . . .3K 137
Leigham Ct. SM6: Wall 6G 167
Leigham Ct. Rd. SW16 . . . . .2J 137
Leigham Dr. TW7: Isle 7J 95
Leigham Hall Pde. *SW16* *3J 137*
(off Streatham High Rd.)
Leigham Va. SW2 . . . . .3K 137
SW16 . . . . .3K 137
Leigh Av. IG4: Ilf 4B 52
Leigh Cl. KT3: N Mald 4J 151
Leigh Cl. Ind. Est. KT3: N Mald 4K 151
Leigh Ct. HA2: Harr 1J 59
W14 . . . .*4H 99*
(off Avonmore Pl.)
Leigh Cres. CR0: New Ad 7D 170
Leigh Gdns. NW10 . . . . .2E 80
Leigh Hunt Dr. N14 . . . . .1C 32
Leigh Orchard Cl. SW16 . . . . .3K 137
Leigh Pl. DA16: Well 2A 126
EC1 . . . . .5J 7 (5A 84)
TW13: Felt 1A 130
Leigh Rd. E6 . . . . .6E 70
E10 . . . . .7E 50
N5 . . . . .4B 66
TW3: Houn 4H 113
Leigh St. WC1 . . . . .2E 6 (3J 83)
Leighton Av. E12 . . . . .5E 70
HA5: Pinn 3C 40
Leighton Cl. HA8: Edg 2G 43
Leighton Cres. NW5 . . . . .5G 65
Leighton Gdns. CR0: C'don 1B 168
NW10 . . . . .2D 80
Leighton Gro. NW5 . . . . .5G 65
Leighton Ho. *SW1* *4D 18*
(off Herrick St.)
Leighton House Mus. 3H 99
Leighton Mans. *W14* *6G 99*
(off Greyhound Rd.)
Leighton Pl. NW5 . . . . .5G 65
Leighton Rd. EN1: Enf 5A 24
HA3: Hrw W 2H 41
NW5 . . . . .5G 65
W13 . . . . .2A 96
Leighton St. CR0: C'don 1B 168
Leila Parnell Pl. SE7 . . . . .6A 106
Leinster Av. SW14 . . . . .3J 115
Leinster Gdns. W2 . . . . .6A 82
Leinster M. EN5: Barn 3B 20
W2 . . . . .7A 82
Leinster Pl. W2 . . . . .6A 82
Leinster Rd. N10 . . . . .4F 47
Leinster Sq. W2 . . . . .6J 81
(not continuous)
Leinster Ter. W2 . . . . .7A 82
Leirum St. N1 .1K 83
Leisure Way N12 . . . . .7G 31
Leisure W. TW13: Felt 2K 129
Leitch Ho. *NW8* *7B 64*
(off Hilgrove Rd.)
Leith Cl. NW9 . . . . .1K 61
Leithcote Gdns. SW16 . . . . .4K 137
Leithcote Path SW16 . . . . .3K 137
Leith Hill BR5: St P 1K 161
Leith Hill Grn. BR5: St P 1K 161
Leith Mans. *W9* *3K 81*
(off Grantully Rd.)
Leith Rd. N22 . . . . .1B 48
Leith Towers SM2: Sutt 7K 165
Leith Yd. *NW6* *1J 81*
(off Quex Rd.)
Lela Av. TW4: Houn 2A 112
Lelitia Cl. E8 .1G 85
Lely Ho. *UB5: N'olt* *2B 76*
(off Academy Gdns.)
Leman Pas. *E1* *6G 85*
(off Leman St.)
Leman St. E1 . . . . .7K 9 (6F 85)
Lemark Cl. HA7: Stan 6H 27
Le May Av. SE12 . . . . .3K 141
Lemmon Rd. SE10 . . . . .6G 105
Lemna Rd. E11 .7H 51
Le Moal Ho. *E1* *5J 85*
(off Stepney Way)
Lemonade Bldg.
IG11: Bark *7G 71*
(off Ripple Rd.)
Lemon Gro. TW13: Felt 1J 129
Lemon Tree Ho. *E3* *3B 86*
(off Bow Rd.)
Lemonwell Dr. SE9 . . . . .5G 125
Lemsford Cl. N15 . . . . .6G 49
Lemsford Ct. N4 . . . . .2C 66
Lemuel St. SW18 . . . . .6A 118
Lena Cres. N9 .2D 34
Lena Gdns. W6 .3E 98
Lena Kennedy Cl. E4 . . . . .6K 35
Lenanton Steps *E14* *2C 104*
(off Manilla St.)
Len Bishop Ct. *E1* *7K 85*
(off Schoolhouse La.)
Len Clifton Ho. *SE18* *4D 106*
(off Cambridge Barracks Rd.)
Lendal Ter. SW4 . . . . .3H 119
Lendy Pl. TW16: Sun 4J 147
Lenelby Rd. KT6: Surb 1G 163
Len Freeman Pl. SW6 . . . . .6H 99
W6 . . . .*4B 98*
(off Goldhawk Rd.)
Lenham Ho. *SE1* *7F 15*
(off Staple St.)
Lenham Rd. CR7: Thor H 2D 156
DA7: Bex 6F 109
SE12 . . . . .4H 123
SM1: Sutt 4K 165
Lennard Av.
BR4: W W'ck 2G 171
Lennard Cl. BR4: W W'ck 2G 171
Lennard Rd. BR2: Brom 1D 172
BR3: Beck 6K 139
CR0: C'don 1C 168
SE20 . . . . .6K 139
Lennon Rd. NW2 . . . . .5E 62
Lennox Gdns. CR0: Wadd 4B 168
IG1: Ilf .1D 70
NW10 . . . . .4B 62
SW1 . . . . .2E 16 (3D 100)
Lennox Gdns. M. SW1 . . . . . .2E 16 (3D 100)
Lennox Ho. *DA17: Belv* *3G 109*
(off Ambrooke Rd.)
TW1: Twick *6D 114*
(off Clevedon Rd.)

Lennox Rd. E17 . . . . . . 6B **50**
N4 . . . . . . 2K **65**
SW9 . . . . . . 1B **120**
Lenor Cl. DA6: Bex 4E **126**
Lensbury Av. SW6 . . . . . . 2A **118**
Lensbury Way SE2 . . . . . . 3C **108**
Lens Rd. E7 . . . . . . 7A **70**
Len Taylor Cl. UB4: Hayes 4G **75**
Lenthall Ho. *SW1* *6B* ***18***
(off Churchill Gdns.)
Lenthall Rd. E8 . . . . . . 7G **67**
Lenthorp Rd. SE10 . . . . . . 4H **105**
Lentmead Rd. BR1: Brom 3H **141**
Lenton Path SE18 . . . . . . 6H **107**
Lenton Ri. TW9: Rich 3E **114**
Lenton St. SE18 . . . . . . 4H **107**
Lenton Ter. N4 . . . . . . 2A **66**
Len Williams Ct. NW6 . . . . . . 2J **81**
Leo Ct. TW8: Bford 7D **96**
Leof Cres. SE6 . . . . . . 5D **140**
Leominster Rd. SM4: Mord 6A **154**
Leominster Wlk. SM4: Mord 6A **154**
Leonard Av. RM7: Rush G 1K **73**
SM4: Mord 5A **154**
Leonard Ct. HA3: Hrw W 1J **41**
W8 . . . . . . 3J **99**
WC1 . . . . . . 3D **6** (4H **83**)
Leonard Pl. N16 . . . . . . 4E **66**
Leonard Rd. E4 . . . . . . 6H **35**
E7 . . . . . . 4J **69**
N9 . . . . . . 3A **34**
SW16 . . . . . . 1G **155**
UB2: S'hall 3B **94**
Leonard Robbins Path *SE28* *7B* ***90***
(off Tawney Rd.)
Leonard St. E16 . . . . . . 1C **106**
EC2 . . . . . . 3F **9** (4D **84**)
Leonora Ho. *W9* *4A* ***82***
(off Lanark Rd.)
Leonora Tyson M. SE21 . . . . . . 2D **138**
Leontine Cl. SE15 . . . . . . 7G **103**
Leopards Ct. EC1 . . . . . . 5J **7**
Leopold Av. SW19 . . . . . . 5H **135**
Leopold Bldgs. *E2* *1J* ***9***
(off Columbia Rd.)
Leopold M. E9 . . . . . . 1J **85**
Leopold Rd. E17 . . . . . . 5C **50**
N2 . . . . . . 3B **46**
N18 . . . . . . 5C **34**
NW10 . . . . . . 7A **62**
SW19 . . . . . . 4H **135**
W5 . . . . . . 1F **97**
Leopold St. E3 . . . . . . 5B **86**
Leopold Ter. SW19 . . . . . . 5H **135**
Leopold Wlk. *SE11* *6G* ***19***
(off Tyers St.)
Leo St. SE15 . . . . . . 7H **103**
Leo Yd. EC1 . . . . . . 4B **8**
Leppoc Rd. SW4 . . . . . . 5H **119**
Leroy St. SE1 . . . . . . 4E **102**
Lerry Cl. W14 . . . . . . 6H **99**
Lerwick Ct. EN1: Enf 5K **23**
Lescombe Cl. SE23 . . . . . . 3A **140**
Lescombe Rd. SE23 . . . . . . 3A **140**
Lescot Pl. BR2: Brom 6C **160**
Lesley Cl. DA5: Bexl 7H **127**
Lesley Ct. *SW1* *2C* ***18***
(off Strutton Ground)
Leslie Foster Cl. IG11: Bark 2K **89**
Leslie Gdns. SM2: Sutt 6J **165**
Leslie Gro. CR0: C'don 1E **168**
Leslie Gro. Pl. CR0: C'don 1E **168**
Leslie Ho. *SW8* *7J* ***101***
(off Wheatsheaf La.)
Leslie Pk. Rd. CR0: C'don 1E **168**
Leslie Prince Ct. SE5 . . . . . . 7D **102**
Leslie Rd. E11 . . . . . . 4E **68**
E16 . . . . . . 6K **87**
N2 . . . . . . 3B **46**
Leslie Smith Sq. SE18 . . . . . . 6E **106**
Lesnes Abbey 4D **108**
Lesnes Abbey Woods (Nature Reserve) 4D **108**
Lesney Av. E20 . . . . . . 5C **68**
Lesney Farm Est. DA8: Erith 7K **109**
Lesney Pk. DA8: Erith 6K **109**
Lesney Pk. Rd. DA8: Erith 6K **109**
Lessar Av. SW4 . . . . . . 6G **119**
Lessingham Av. IG5: Ilf 3E **52**
SW17 . . . . . . 4D **136**
Lessing St. SE23 . . . . . . 7A **122**
Lessington Av. RM7: Rom 6J **55**
Lessness Av. DA7: Bex 7D **108**
LESSNESS HEATH 5G 109
Lessness Pk. DA17: Belv 5F **109**
Lessness Rd. DA17: Belv 6G **109**
SM4: Mord 6A **154**
Lester Av. E15 . . . . . . 4G **87**
Lester Ct. *E3* *3D* ***86***
(off Bruce Rd.)
Lestock Cl. *SE25* *3G* ***157***
(off Manor Rd.)
Leswin Pl. N16 . . . . . . 3F **67**
Leswin Rd. N16 . . . . . . 3F **67**
Letchford Gdns. NW10 . . . . . . 3C **80**
Letchford Ho. *E3* *2C* ***86***
(off Thomas Fyre Dr.)
Letchford M. NW10 . . . . . . 3C **80**
Letchford Ter. HA3: Hrw W 1F **41**
Letchmore Ho. *W10* *4E* ***80***
(off Sutton Way)
Letchworth Av. TW14: Felt 7H **111**
Letchworth Cl. BR2: Brom 5J **159**
Letchworth Dr. BR2: Brom 5J **159**
Letchworth Rd. HA7: Stan 7K **27**
Letchworth St. SW17 . . . . . . 4D **136**
Lethbridge Cl. SE10 . . . . . . 1E **122**
Letterstone Rd. SW6 . . . . . . 7H **99**
Lettice St. SW6 . . . . . . 1H **117**
Lett Rd. E15 . . . . . . 7F **69**
SW9 . . . . . . 1K **119**
Lettsom St. SE5 . . . . . . 2E **120**
Lettsom Wlk. E13 . . . . . . 2J **87**
Leucha Rd. E17 . . . . . . 5A **50**
Levana Cl. SW19 . . . . . . 1G **135**
Levant Ho. *E1* *4K* ***85***
(off Ernest St.)
Levehurst Ho. SE27 . . . . . . 5C **138**
Levendale Rd. SE23 . . . . . . 2A **140**
Levenhurst Way SW4 . . . . . . 2J **119**
Leven Rd. E14 . . . . . . 5E **86**
Leven Way UB3: Hayes 6G **75**
Leverett St. SW3 . . . . . . 3D **16** (4C **100**)
Leverholme Gdns. SE9 . . . . . . 4E **142**
Leverington Pl. N1 . . . . . . 2F **9** (3D **84**)
Leverson St. SW16 . . . . . . 6G **137**
Leverstock Ho. *SW3* *5D* ***16***
(off Cale St.)
Lever St. EC1 . . . . . . 2B **8** (3B **84**)
Leverton Cl. N22 . . . . . . 1K **47**
Leverton Pl. NW5 . . . . . . 5G **65**
Leverton St. NW5 . . . . . . 5G **65**
Levett Gdns. IG3: Ilf 4K **71**
Levett Rd. IG11: Bark 6J **71**
Levine Gdns. IG11: Bark 2D **90**
Levison Way N19 . . . . . . 1H **65**
Levita Ho. NW1 . . . . . . 1D **6**
(not continuous)
Levyne Ct. *EC1* *3J* ***7***
(off Pine St.)
Lewen Cl. CR0: C'don 1D **168**
Lewes Cl. UB5: N'olt 6E **58**
Lewes Ct. *CR4: Mitc* *3D* ***154***
(off Chatsworth Pl.)
Lewesdon Cl. SW19 . . . . . . 1F **135**
Lewes Ho. *SE1* *6H* ***15***
(off Druid St.)
SE15 . . . . . . *6G* ***103***
(off Friary Est.)
Lewes Rd. BR1: Brom 2B **160**
N12 . . . . . . 5H **31**
Leweston Pl. N16 . . . . . . 7F **49**
Lew Evans Ho. SE22 . . . . . . 5G **121**
Lewey Ho. *E3* *4B* ***86***
(off Joseph St.)
Lewgars Av. NW9 . . . . . . 6J **43**
Lewing Cl. BR6: Orp 1J **173**
Lewington Apartments *SE16* *4J* ***103***
(off Alpine Rd.)
Lewington Cen. *SE16* *4J* ***103***
(off Alpine Rd.)
Lewin Rd. DA6: Bex 4E **126**
SW14 . . . . . . 3K **115**
SW16 . . . . . . 6H **137**
Lewin Ter. TW14: Bedf 7F **111**
Lewis Av. E17 . . . . . . 1C **50**
Lewis Cl. N14 . . . . . . 7B **22**
Lewis Ct. *SE16* *5H* ***103***
(off Stubbs Dr.)
Lewis Cres. NW10 . . . . . . 5K **61**
Lewis Cubitt Pk. 1J **83**
Lewis Cubitt Sq. N1 . . . . . . 1J **83**
Lewis Gdns. N2 . . . . . . 2B **46**
N16 . . . . . . 6F **49**
Lewis Gro. SE13 . . . . . . 3E **122**
LEWISHAM 3E 122
Lewisham Cen. SE13 . . . . . . 4E **122**
Lewisham Hgts. SE23 . . . . . . 1J **139**
Lewisham High St. SE13 . . . . . . 3E **122**
(not continuous)
Lewisham Hill SE13 . . . . . . 2E **122**
Lewisham Indoor Bowls Cen. 5B 140
Lewisham Lions Cen. 5J 103
Lewisham Model Mkt. *SE13* *4E* ***122***
(off Lewisham High St.)
Lewisham Pk. SE13 . . . . . . 5E **122**
Lewisham Rd. SE13 . . . . . . 1D **122**
Lewisham St. SW1 . . . . . . 7D **12** (2H **101**)
Lewisham Way SE4 . . . . . . 1B **122**
SE14 . . . . . . 1B **122**
Lewis Ho. *E14* *1E* ***104***
(off Coldharbour)
N1 . . . . . . *6B* ***66***
(off Canonbury Rd.)
Lewis M. BR7: Chst 5D **142**
Lewis Pl. E8 . . . . . . 5G **67**
Lewis Rd. CR4: Mitc 2B **154**
DA14: Sidc 3C **144**
DA16: Well 3C **126**
SM1: Sutt 4K **165**
TW10: Rich 5D **114**
UB1: S'hall 2C **94**
Lewis Silkin Ho. *SE15* *6J* ***103***
(off Lovelinch Cl.)
Lewis Sports and Leisure Cen. 1F 157
Lewis St. NW1 . . . . . . 6F **65**
(not continuous)
Lewiston Cl. KT4: Wor Pk 7D **152**
Lewis Way RM10: Dag 6H **73**
Lexden Dr. RM6: Chad H 6B **54**
Lexden Rd. CR4: Mitc 4H **155**
W3 . . . . . . 7H **79**
Lexham Gdns. W8 . . . . . . 4J **99**
Lexham Gdns. M. W8 . . . . . . 3K **99**
Lexham Ho. *W8* *4K* ***99***
(off Lexham Gdns.)
Lexham M. W8 . . . . . . 4J **99**
Lexham Wlk. W8 . . . . . . 3K **99**
Lexington Apartments EC1 . . . . . . 3F **9** (4D **84**)
Lexington Bldg. E3 . . . . . . 2C **86**
Lexington Ho. *UB7: W Dray* *2B* ***92***
(off Park Lodge Av.)
Lexington Pl.
KT1: Hamp W 7D **132**
Lexington St. W1 . . . . . . 2B **12** (7G **83**)
Lexington Way EN5: Barn 4A **20**
Lexton Gdns. SW12 . . . . . . 1H **137**
Leyborne Av. W13 . . . . . . 2B **96**
Leyborne Pk. TW9: Kew 1G **115**
Leybourne Cl. BR2: Brom 6J **159**
Leybourne Ho. *E14* *6B* ***86***
(off Dod St.)
SE15 . . . . . . 6J **103**
Leybourne Rd. E11 . . . . . . 1H **69**
NW1 . . . . . . 7F **65**
NW9 . . . . . . 5G **43**
UB10: Hil 1E **74**
Leybourne St. NW1 . . . . . . 7F **65**
Leybridge Ct. SE12 . . . . . . 5J **123**
Leyburn Cl. E17 . . . . . . 4D **50**
Leyburn Gdns. CR0: C'don 2E **168**
Leyburn Gro. N18 . . . . . . 6B **34**
Leyburn Rd. N18 . . . . . . 6B **34**
Leydenhatch La. BR8: Swan 7J **145**
Leyden Mans. N19 . . . . . . 7J **47**
Leyden St. E1 . . . . . . 6J **9** (5F **85**)
Leydon Cl. SE16 . . . . . . 1K **103**
Leyes Rd. E16 . . . . . . 6B **88**
Leyfield KT4: Wor Pk 1A **164**
Ley Ho. *SE1* *7C* ***14***
(off Scovell Rd.)
Leyland Av. EN3: Enf H 2F **25**
Leyland Gdns. IG8: Wfd G 5F **37**
Leyland Ho. *E14* *7D* ***86***
(off Hale St.)
Leyland Rd. SE12 . . . . . . 5J **123**
Leylands SW18 . . . . . . 6H **117**
Leylands La. TW19: Stanw M 7A **174**
(not continuous)
Leylang Rd. SE14 . . . . . . 7K **103**
Leys, The HA3: Kenton 6F **43**
N2 . . . . . . 4A **46**
Leys Av. RM10: Dag 1J **91**
Leys Cl. HA1: Harr 5H **41**
RM10: Dag 7J **73**
Leys Ct. SW9 . . . . . . 2A **120**
Leysdown Av. DA7: Bex 4J **127**
Leysdown Ho. *SE17* *5E* ***102***
(off Madron St.)
Leysdown Rd. SE9 . . . . . . 2C **142**
Leysfield Rd. W12 . . . . . . 3C **98**
Leys Gdns. EN4: Cockf 5K **21**
Leyspring Rd. E11 . . . . . . 1H **69**
Leys Rd. E. EN3: Enf H 1F **25**
Leys Rd. W. EN3: Enf H 1F **25**
Leys Sq. N3 . . . . . . 1K **45**
Ley St. IG1: Ilf 2F **71**
IG2: Ilf 2G **71**
Leyswood Dr. IG2: Ilf 5J **53**
Leythe Rd. W3 . . . . . . 2J **97**
LEYTON 2E 68
Leyton Bus. Cen. E10 . . . . . . 2C **68**
Leyton Ct. SE23 . . . . . . 1J **139**
Leyton Grange E10 . . . . . . 1C **68**
Leyton Grn. Rd. E10 . . . . . . 6E **50**
Leyton Grn. Twr. *E10* *6E* ***50***
(off Leyton Grn. Rd.)
Leyton Ho. *E2* *2J* ***9***
(off Calvert Av.)
Leyton Ind. Village E10 . . . . . . 7K **49**
Leyton Leisure Cen. 7E 50
Leyton Link Est. E10 . . . . . . 7A **50**
Leyton Mills E10 . . . . . . 3E **68**
Leyton Orient FC
Brisbane Road Stadium 3D 68
Leyton Pk. Rd. E10 . . . . . . 3E **68**
Leyton Rd. E15 . . . . . . 5E **68**
SW19 . . . . . . 7A **136**
LEYTONSTONE 1G 69
Leytonstone Ho. *E11* *7H* ***51***
(off Hanbury Dr.)
Leytonstone Leisure Cen. 2G 69
Leytonstone Rd. E15 . . . . . . 6G **69**
Leyton Way E11 . . . . . . 7G **51**
Leywick St. E15 . . . . . . 2G **87**
Lezayre Rd. BR6: Chels 6K **173**
Lianne Gro. SE9 . . . . . . 3A **142**
Liardet St. SE14 . . . . . . 6A **104**
Libari Mans. *E20* *5E* ***68***
(off Victory Pde.)
Liberia Rd. N5 . . . . . . 6B **66**
Liberty Av. SW19 . . . . . . 1B **154**
Liberty Bri. Rd. E15 . . . . . . 5E **68**
E20 . . . . . . 5E **68**

Liberty Cen. HA0: Wemb 1F **79**
Liberty Cl. KT4: Wor Pk 1E **164**
N18 4A **34**
Liberty Ct. BR1: Brom 3B **160**
IG11: Bark 2B **90**
Liberty Ho. *CR7: Thor H 5A **156***
(off Thornton Rd.)
*E1 7G **85***
(off Ensign St.)
E13 2J **87**
Liberty M. N22 1B **48**
SW12 6F **119**
Liberty Point *CR0: C'don 7G **157***
(off Blackhorse La.)
Liberty St. SW9 1K **119**
Libra Mans. *E3 2B **86***
(off Libra Rd.)
Libra Rd. E3 1B **86**
E13 2J **87**
Library Ct. N17 3F **49**
Library Mans. *W12 2E **98***
(off Pennard Rd.)
Library M. TW12: Hamp H 6G **131**
Library Pde. *NW10 1A **80***
(off Craven Pk. Rd.)
Library Pl. E1 7H **85**
Library Sq. E1 4A **86**
Library St. SE1 7A **14** (2B **102**)
Library Way TW2: Whitt 7G **113**
Libro Ct. E4 4H **35**
Lichfield Cl. EN4: Cockf 3J **21**
Lichfield Ct. *KT6: Surb 5E **150***
(off Claremont Rd.)
TW9: Rich 5E **114**
Lichfield Gdns. TW9: Rich 4E **114**
Lichfield Gro. N3 1J **45**
Lichfield La. TW2: Whitt 1G **131**
Lichfield Rd. E3 3A **86**
E6 3B **88**
HA6: Nwood 3J **39**
IG8: Wfd G 4B **36**
N9 2B **34**
NW2 4G **63**
RM8: Dag 4B **72**
TW4: Houn 3A **112**
TW9: Kew 1F **115**
Lichfield Ter. *TW9: Rich 5E **114***
(off Sheen Rd.)
Lichlade Cl. BR6: Orp 4K **173**
Lickey Ho. *W14 6H **99***
(off North End Rd.)
Lidcote Gdns. SW9 2K **119**
Liddall Way UB7: Yiew 1B **92**
Liddell Cl. HA3: Kenton 3D **42**
Liddell Gdns. NW10 2E **80**
Liddell Rd. NW6 6J **63**
Liddiard Ho. *W11 7G **81***
(off Lansdowne Rd.)
Lidding Rd. HA3: Kenton 5D **42**
Liddington Rd. E15 1H **87**
Liddon Rd. BR1: Brom 3A **160**
E13 3K **87**
Liden Cl. E17 7B **50**
Lidfield Rd. N16 4D **66**
Lidgate Rd. SE15 7F **103**
Lidgould Gro. HA4: Ruis 6J **39**
Lidiard Rd. SW18 2A **136**
Lidlington Pl. NW1 2G **83**
Lido Sq. N17 2D **48**
Lidyard Rd. N19 1G **65**
Lifestyle Club @ Charlton, The 7B **106**
Liffler Rd. SE18 5J **107**
Liffords Pl. SW13 2B **116**
Lifford St. SW15 4F **117**
Lightcliffe Rd. N13 4F **33**
Lighterage Ct. TW8: Bford 6E **96**
Lighter Cl. SE16 4A **104**
Lighterman Ho. E14 7E **86**
Lighterman M. E1 6K **85**
Lighterman Point *E14 6F **87***
(off New Village Av.)
Lightermans Rd. E14 2C **104**
Lightermans Wlk. SW18 4J **117**
Lightfoot Rd. N8 5J **47**
Lightfoot Vs. *N1 7A **66***
(off Augustas La.)
Light Horse Ct. SW3 6G **17**
Lighthouse Apartments *E1 6J **85***
(off Commercial Rd.)
Lighthouse Bldg. E14 6G **87**
Lightley Cl. HA0: Wemb 1E **78**
Ligonier St. E2 3J **9** (4F **85**)
Lilac Cl. E4 6G **35**
Lilac Ct. E13 1A **88**
TW11: Tedd 4K **131**
Lilac Gdns.
CR0: C'don 3C **170**
RM7: Rush G 1K **73**
UB3: Hayes 6G **75**
W5 3D **96**
Lilac Ho. SE4 3C **122**
Lilac M. *N22 3A **48***
(off High Rd.)
Lilac Pl. SE11 4G **19** (4K **101**)
UB7: Yiew 7B **74**
Lilac St. W12 7C **80**
Lilah M. BR2: Brom 2G **159**
Lilburne Gdns. SE9 5C **124**
Lilburne Rd. SE9 5C **124**
Lilburne Wlk. NW10 6J **61**
Lile Cres. W7 5J **77**
Lilestone Ho. *NW8 3B **4***
(off Frampton St.)
Lilestone St. NW8 3C **4** (4C **82**)
Lilford Ho. SE5 2C **120**
Lilford Rd. SE5 2B **120**
Lilian Barker Cl. SE12 5J **123**
Lilian Board Way
UB6: G'frd 5H **59**
Lilian Cl. N16 3E **66**
Lilian Gdns. IG8: Wfd G 1K **51**
Lilian Knowles Ho. *E1 6J **9***
(off Crispin St.)
Lilian Rd. SW16 1G **155**
Lilium M. E10 7C **50**
Lillechurch Rd. RM8: Dag 6B **72**
Lilleshall Rd. SM4: Mord 6B **154**
Lilley Cl. E1 1G **103**
Lilley La. NW7 5E **28**
Lillian Av. W3 2G **97**
Lillian Rd. SW13 6C **98**
Lillie Bri. Dpt. *W14 5H **99***
(off Aisgill Av.)
Lillie Mans. *SW6 6G **99***
(off Lillie Rd.)
Lillie Rd. SW6 6G **99**
Lillie Road Fitness Cen. 7F 99
Lillieshall Rd. SW4 3F **119**
Lillie Sq. SW6 6J **99**
Lillie Yd. SW6 6J **99**
Lillingston Ho. N7 4A **66**
Lillington Gdns. Est. SW1 4B **18**
Lilliput Av. UB5: N'olt 1C **76**
Lilliput Ct. SE12 5K **123**
Lilliput Rd. E15 1G **87**
RM7: Rush G 7K **55**
Lily Cl. HA5: Pinn 2A **40**
W14 4F **99**
Lily Gdns. HA0: Wemb 2C **78**
Lily M. SE11 4B **102**
Lily Nichols Ho. *E16 1B **106***
(off Connaught Rd.)
Lily Pl. EC1 5K **7** (5A **84**)
Lily Rd. E17 6C **50**
Lilyville Rd. SW6 1H **117**
Limasol St. SE16 3F **103**
Limborough Ho. *E14 5C **86***
(off Thomas Rd.)
Limbourne Av. RM8: Dag 7F **55**
Limburg Rd. SW11 4C **118**
Lime Av. UB7: Yiew 7B **74**
Limeburner La. EC4 1A **14** (6B **84**)
Lime Cl. BR1: Brom 4C **160**
E1 1G **103**
HA3: W'stone 2A **42**
HA5: Eastc 3H **39**
IG9: Buck H 2G **37**
RM7: Rom 4J **55**
SM5: Cars 2D **166**
Lime Ct. CR4: Mitc 2B **154**
*E11 2G **69***
(off Trinity Cl.)
E17 5E **50**
*HA1: Harr 6K **41***
(off Gayton Rd.)
HA4: Ruis 7K **39**
SE9 2F **143**
Lime Cres. TW16: Sun 2A **148**
Limecroft Cl. KT19: Ewe 7K **163**
Limedene Cl. HA5: Pinn 1B **40**
Lime Gro. BR6: Farnb 2F **173**
DA15: Sidc 6K **125**
E4 6G **35**
HA4: Ruis 6K **39**
KT3: N Mald 3K **151**
N20 1C **30**
TW1: Twick 6K **113**
UB3: Hayes 7F **75**
W12 2E **98**
Limeharbour E14 3D **104**
LIMEHOUSE 6B 86
Lime Ho. TW9: Kew 1H **115**
Limehouse C'way. E14 7B **86**
Lime Ho. Ct. *E14 6B **86***
(off Wharf La.)
Limehouse Ct. E14 6C **86**
Limehouse Cut *E14 5D **86***
(off Morris Rd.)
Limehouse Flds. Est. E14 5A **86**
Limehouse Link E14 6A **86**
Limehouse Lodge *E5 2J **67***
(off Harry Zeital Way)
Lime Kiln Dr. SE7 6K **105**
Limekiln Pl. SE19 7F **139**
Limekiln Wharf E14 7B **86**
Limelight Ho. *SE11 4B **102***
(off Dugard Way)
Lime Lodge *TW16: Sun 7H **129***
(off Forest Dr.)
Lime Quay E14 4E **86**
Limerick Cl. SW12 7G **119**
Limerick M. N2 3C **46**
Lime Rd. TW9: Rich 4F **115**
Lime Row DA18: Erith 3F **109**
Limerston St. SW10 7A **16** (6A **100**)
Limes, The BR2: Brom 2C **172**
KT8: W Mole 4F **149**
SW18 6J **117**
W2 7J **81**
Limes Av. CR0: Wadd 3A **168**
E11 4K **51**
N12 4F **31**
NW7 6F **29**
NW11 7G **45**
SE20 7H **139**
SM5: Cars 1D **166**
SW13 2B **116**
Limes Av., The N11 5A **32**
Limes Cl. N11 5B **32**
TW15: Ashf 5C **128**
Limes Ct. BR3: Beck 2D **158**
*NW6 7G **63***
(off Brondesbury Pk.)
Limesdale Gdns. HA8: Edg 2J **43**
Limes Fld. Rd. SW13 3A **116**
Limesford Rd. SE15 4K **121**
Limes Gdns. SW18 6J **117**
Limes Gro. SE13 4E **122**
Limes Pl. CR0: C'don 7D **156**
Limes Rd. BR3: Beck 2D **158**
CR0: C'don 7D **156**
Limes Row BR6: Farnb 5F **173**
Limestone Wlk. DA18: Erith 2D **108**
Lime St. E17 4A **50**
EC3 2G **15** (7E **84**)
Lime St. Pas. EC3 1G **15** (6E **84**)
Limes Wlk. SE15 4J **121**
W5 2D **96**
Lime Ter. W7 7J **77**
Lime Tree Av. KT7: T Ditt 7H **149**
KT10: Esh 7H **149**
Lime Tree Cl. E18 4A **52**
Limetree Cl. SW2 1K **137**
Lime Tree Ct. CR2: S Croy 6C **168**
*E3 5C **86***
(off Whitehorn St.)
*SE17 5C **102***
(off Walworth Rd.)
Lime Tree Gro. CR0: C'don 3B **170**
Lime Tree Pl. CR4: Mitc 1F **155**
Lime Tree Rd. TW5: Hest 1F **113**
Lime Trees Pk. Golf Course 1A **76**
Limetree Ter. DA16: Well 3A **126**
SE6 1B **140**
Lime Tree Wlk. BR4: W W'ck 4H **171**
EN2: Enf 1H **23**
WD23: B Hea 1D **26**
Limetree Wlk. SW17 5E **136**
Lime View Apartments *E14 6A **86***
(off Commerical Rd.)
Lime Wlk. E15 1G **87**
KT8: E Mos 4K **149**
Limewood Cl. BR3: Beck 5E **158**
E17 4B **50**
W13 6B **78**
Limewood Ct. IG4: Ilf 5D **52**
Limewood M. *SE20 7G **139***
(off Lullington Rd.)
Limewood Rd. DA8: Erith 7J **109**
Limpsfield Av. CR7: Thor H 5K **155**
SW19 2F **135**
Limscott Ho. *E3 3D **86***
(off Bruce Rd.)
Linacre Cl. SE15 3H **121**
Linacre Ct. W6 5F **99**
Linacre Rd. NW2 6D **62**
Linale Ho. N1 1E **8**
Linberry Wlk. SE8 4B **104**
Linchmere Rd. SE12 7H **123**
Lincoln Av. N14 3B **32**
RM7: Rush G 2K **73**
SW19 3F **135**
TW2: Twick 2G **131**
Lincoln Cl. HA2: Harr 5D **40**
SE25 6G **157**
UB6: G'frd 1G **77**
Lincoln Ct. *CR2: S Croy 5C **168***
(off Warham Rd.)
IG2: Ilf 6G **53**
N16 7D **48**
SE12 3K **141**
Lincoln Cres. EN1: Enf 5K **23**
Lincoln Gdns. IG1: Ilf 7C **52**
Lincoln Grn. Rd.
BR5: St M Cry 5K **161**
Lincoln Ho. SE5 7A **102**
SW3 2D **100**
*TW8: Bford 5D **96***
(off Ealing Rd.)
Lincoln M. N15 4C **48**
NW6 1H **81**
SE21 2D **138**
Lincoln Pde. HA9: Wemb 1E **60**
*N2 3C **46***
(off Lincoln Rd.)
Lincoln Plaza *E14 2D **104***
(off Lightermans Rd.)
Lincoln Rd. CR4: Mitc 5J **155**
DA14: Sidc 5B **144**
E7 6B **70**
E13 4K **87**
E18 1J **51**
EN1: Enf 4K **23**
EN3: Pond E 5B **24**

Lincoln Rd. HA0: Wemb 6D 60
HA2: Harr 5D 40
HA6: Nwood 3H 39
KT3: N Mald 3J 151
KT4: Wor Pk 1D 164
N2 3C 46
SE25 3H 157
TW13: Hanw 3D 130
Lincolns, The NW7 3G 29
Lincoln's Inn Flds.
WC2 7G 7 (6K 83)
Lincoln's Inn Hall 7H 7 (6K 83)
Lincoln St. E11 2G 69
SW3 4E 16 (4D 100)
Lincoln Ter. SM2: Sutt 7J 165
Lincoln Way EN1: Enf 5C 24
TW16: Sun 1G 147
Lincombe Rd. BR1: Brom 3H 141
Lindal Ct. E18 1H 51
Lindal Cres. EN2: Enf 4D 22
Lindale Cl. IG4: Ilf 5D 52
Lindales, The N17 6B 34
(off Grasmere Rd.)
Lindal Rd. SE4 5B 122
Lindbergh Rd. SM6: Wall 7J 167
Linden Av. CR7: Thor H 4B 156
EN1: Enf 1B 24
HA4: Ruis 1J 57
HA9: Wemb 5F 61
NW10 2F 81
TW3: Houn 5F 113
Linden Cl. HA4: Ruis 1J 57
HA7: Stan 5G 27
KT7: T Ditt 7K 149
N14 6B 22
Linden Ct. DA14: Sidc 4J 143
SE20 7H 139
(off Anerley Pk.)
W12 1E 98
Linden Cres. IG8: Wfd G 6E 36
KT1: King T 2F 151
UB6: G'frd 6K 59
Lindenfield BR7: Chst 2F 161
Linden Gdns. EN1: Enf 1B 24
W2 7J 81
W4 5A 98
Linden Gro. KT3: N Mald 3A 152
SE15 3H 121
SE26 6J 139
TW11: Tedd 5K 131
Linden Ho. SE8 6B 104
(off Abinger Gro.)
TW12: Hamp 6E 130
Linden Lawns HA9: Wemb 4F 61
Linden Lea N2 5A 46
Linden Leas BR4: W W'ck 2F 171
Linden Mans. N6 1F 65
(off Hornsey La.)
Linden M. N1 5D 66
W2 7J 81
Linden Pl. CR4: Mitc 4C 154
Linden Rd. N10 4F 47
N11 2J 31
N15 4C 48
TW12: Hamp 7E 130
Lindens, The CR0: New Ad 6E 170
E17 4D 50
(off Prospect Hill)
N12 5G 31
W4 1J 115
Linden St. RM7: Rom 4K 55
Linden Wlk. N19 2G 65
Linden Way N14 6B 22
TW17: Shep 5E 146
Linder's Field Local Nature Reserve
1G 37
Lindeth Cl. HA7: Stan 6G 27
Lindfield Gdns. NW3 5K 63
Lindfield Rd. CR0: C'don 6F 157
W5 4C 78
Lindfield St. E14 6C 86
Lindhill Cl. EN3: Enf H 2E 24
Lindholme Ct. NW9 1A 44
(off Pageant Av.)
Lindie Gdns. UB8: Uxb 7A 56
Lindisfarne Ct. HA8: Edg 4A 28
Lindisfarne Rd. RM8: Dag 3C 72
SW20 7C 134
Lindisfarne Way E9 4A 68
Lindley Ct. KT1: Hamp W 1C 150
Lindley Est. SE15 7G 103
Lindley Ho. E1 5J 85
(off Lindley St.)
SE15 7G 103
(off Peckham Pk. Rd.)
Lindley Pl. TW9: Kew 1G 115
Lindley Rd. E10 2E 68
Lindley St. E1 5J 85
Lindop Ho. E1 4A 86
(off Mile End Rd.)
Lindore Rd. SW11 4D 118
Lindores Rd. SM5: Cars 7A 154
Lindo St. SE15 2J 121
Lind Rd. SM1: Sutt 5A 166
Lindrop St. SW6 2A 118
Lindsay Cl. KT9: Chess 7E 162
TW19: Stanw 5A 110
Lindsay Ct. CR0: C'don 4D 168
(off Eden Rd.)
SE13 3D 122
(off Loampit Va.)
SW11 1B 118
(off Battersea High St.)
Lindsay Dr. HA3: Kenton 6E 42
TW17: Shep 6F 147
Lindsay Ho. SW7 3A 100
(off Gloucester Rd.)
Lindsay Rd. KT4: Wor Pk 2D 164
TW12: Hamp H 4F 131
Lindsay Sq. SW1 5D 18 (5H 101)
Lindsell St. SE10 1E 122
Lindsey Cl. BR1: Brom 3B 160
CR4: Mitc 4J 155
Lindsey Ct. N13 3F 33
(off Green Lanes)
Lindsey Gdns. TW14: Bedf 7F 111
Lindsey Ho. W5 4D 96
Lindsey M. N1 7C 66
Lindsey Rd. RM8: Dag 4C 72
Lindsey St. EC1 5B 8 (5B 84)
Lind St. SE8 2C 122
Lindum Rd. TW11: Tedd 7C 132
Lindway SE27 5B 138
Lindwood Cl. E6 6D 88
Linen Ho., The W10 2G 81
Linfield WC1 2G 7
(off Sidmouth St.)
Linfield Cl. NW4 3E 44
Linford Christie Stadium 5C 80
Linford Ho. E2 1G 85
(off Whiston Rd.)
E16 5J 87
(off Hammersley Rd.)
Linford Rd. E17 3E 50
Linford St. SW8 1G 119
Linford St. Bus. Est. SW8 1G 119
(off Linford St.)
Lingard Av. NW9 2A 44
Lingard Ho. E14 3E 104
(off Marshfield St.)
Lingards Rd. SE13 4E 122
Lingey Cl. DA15: Sidc 2K 143
Lingfield Apartments E4 7J 35
Lingfield Av. KT1: King T 4E 150
Lingfield Cl. EN1: Enf 6K 23
HA6: Nwood 1G 39
Lingfield Ct. UB5: N'olt 2E 76
Lingfield Cres. SE9 4H 125
Lingfield Gdns. N9 7C 24
Lingfield Ho. SE1 7B 14
Lingfield Rd. KT4: Wor Pk 3E 164
SW19 5F 135
Lingham Ct. SW9 2J 119
Lingham St. SW9 2J 119
Lingholm Way EN5: Barn 5A 20
Ling Rd. DA8: Erith 6J 109
E16 5J 87
Lingrove Gdns.
IG9: Buck H 2E 36
Lings Coppice SE21 2D 138
Lingwell Rd. SW17 3C 136
Lingwood DA7: Bex 2H 127
Lingwood Ct. N2 3C 46
(off Norfolk Cl.)
Lingwood Gdns. TW7: Isle 7J 95
Lingwood Rd. E5 7G 49
Linhope St. NW1 3E 4 (4D 82)
Link, The EN3: Enf H 1F 25
HA0: Wemb 1C 60
HA5: Eastc 7A 40
NW2 1C 62
SE9 3E 142
(off William Barefoot Dr.)
UB5: N'olt 5D 58
W3 6H 79
Linkenholt Mans. W6 4B 98
(off Stamford Brook Av.)
Linkfield BR2: Hayes 6J 159
KT8: W Mole 3F 149
Linkfield Rd. TW7: Isle 2K 113
Link Ho. E3 2D 86
W10 6F 81
(off Kingsdown Cl.)
Link La. SM6: Wall 6H 167
Linklea Cl. NW9 7F 29
Link Rd. E1 2K 15 (7G 85)
N11 4K 31
RM9: Dag 2H 91
SM6: Wall 1E 166
TW14: Felt 7H 111
Links, The E17 4A 50
Links Av. SM4: Mord 4J 153
Linkscroft Av. TW15: Ashf 6D 128
Links Dr. N20 1D 30
Links Gdns. SW16 7A 138
Linkside KT3: N Mald 2A 152
N12 6D 30
Linkside Cl. EN2: Enf 3E 22
Linkside Gdns. EN2: Enf 3E 22
Links Rd. BR4: W W'ck 1E 170
IG8: Wfd G 5D 36
NW2 2B 62
SW17 6E 136
TW15: Ashf 5A 128
W3 6G 79
Links Side EN2: Enf 3E 22
Link St. E9 6J 67
Links Vw. N3 7C 30
Linksview N2 5D 46
(off Great Nth. Rd.)
Links Vw. Cl. HA7: Stan 7F 27
Linksview Ct.
TW12: Hamp H 4H 131
Links Vw. Rd. CR0: C'don 3C 170
TW12: Hamp H 5G 131
Links Way BR3: Beck 6C 158
Linksway HA6: Nwood 1E 38
NW4 2F 45
Links Yd. E1 5K 9
Link Way BR2: Brom 7C 160
HA5: Pinn 1B 40
Linkway N4 7C 48
RM8: Dag 4C 72
SW20 3D 152
TW10: Ham 2B 132
Linkway, The EN5: Barn 6E 20
Linkwood Wlk. NW1 7H 65
Linley Ct. SM1: Sutt 4A 166
Linley Cres.
RM7: Mawney 3H 55
Linley Rd. N17 2E 48
Linnell Cl. NW11 6K 45
Linnell Dr. NW11 6K 45
Linnell Ho. E1 5J 9
(off Folgate St.)
NW8 1A 82
(off Ainsworth Way)
Linnell Rd. N18 5B 34
SE5 2E 120
Linnet Cl. N9 1E 34
SE28 7C 90
WD23: Bush 1B 26
Linnet Ct. SW15 6E 116
Linnet M. SW12 7E 118
Linnett Cl. E4 4K 35
Linom Rd. SW4 4J 119
Linscott Rd. E5 4J 67
Linsdell Rd. IG11: Bark 1G 89
Linsey Ct. E10 1C 68
(off Grange Rd.)
Linsey St. SE16 4G 103
(not continuous)
Linslade Cl. HA5: Eastc 4K 39
TW4: Houn 5C 112
Linslade Ho. E2 1G 85
NW8 3D 4
(off Paveley St.)
Linslade Rd. BR6: Chels 6K 173
Linstead St. NW6 7J 63
Linstead Way SW18 7G 117
Linsted Ct. SE9 6J 125
Lintaine Cl. W6 6G 99
Linthorpe Av. HA0: Wemb 6C 60
Linthorpe Rd. EN4: Cockf 3H 21
N16 7E 48
Linton Cl. CR4: Mitc 7D 154
DA16: Well 1B 126
SE7 5A 106
Linton Ct. NW1 7G 65
(off Agar Gro.)
RM1: Rom 2K 55
Linton Gdns. E6 6C 88
Linton Gro. SE27 5B 138
Linton Ho. E3 5C 86
(off St Paul's Way)
Linton Rd. IG11: Bark 7G 71
Linton St. N1 1C 84
(not continuous)
Lintott Ct. TW19: Stanw 6A 110
Linver Rd. SW6 2J 117
Linwood Cl. SE5 2F 121
Linwood Cres. EN1: Enf 1B 24
Linzee Rd. N8 4J 47
Lion Apartments SE16 5H 103
(off Rotherhithe New Rd.)
Lion Av. TW1: Twick 1K 131
Lion Cl. SE4 6C 122
TW17: Shep 3A 146
Lion Ct. E1 7K 85
(off The Highway)
N1 1K 83
(off Copenhagen St.)
SE1 5G 15
(off Magdalen St.)
Lionel Gdns. SE9 5B 124
Lionel Ho. W10 5G 81
(off Portobello Rd.)
Lionel Mans. W14 3F 99
(off Haarlem Rd.)
Lionel M. W10 5G 81
Lionel Rd. SE9 5B 124
Lionel Rd. Nth. TW8: Bford 3E 96
Lionel Rd. Sth. TW8: Bford 5F 97
Liongate Ent. Pk. CR4: Mitc 4B 154
Lion Ga. Gdns. TW9: Rich 3F 115
Lion Ga. M. SW18 7J 117
Liongate M. KT8: E Mos 3K 149
Lion Head Ct. CR0: C'don 4C 168
(off St Andrew's Rd.)
Lion Mills E2 2G 85
Lion Pk. Av. KT9: Chess 4G 163
Lion Rd. CR0: C'don 5C 156
DA6: Bex 4E 126
E6 5D 88

Lion Rd. N9 .2B 34
TW1: Twick .1K 131
Lions Cl. SE9 .3A 142
Lion Way TW8: Bford .7D 96
Lion Wharf Rd. TW7: Isle .3B 114
Lion Yd. SW4 .4H 119
Liphook Cres. SE23 .7J 121
Lipton Cl. SE28 .7C 90
Lipton Rd. E1 .6K 85
Lisbon Av. TW2: Twick .2G 131
Lisbon Cl. E17 .2B 50
Lisburne Rd. NW3 .4D 64
Lisford St. SE15 .1F 121
Lisgar Ter. W14 .4H 99
Liskeard Cl. BR7: Chst .6G 143
Liskeard Gdns. SE3 .1J 123
Liskeard Ho. *SE11* .*5K 19*
(off Kennings Way)
Lisle Cl. SW17 .4F 137
Lisle Ct. NW2 .3G 63
Lisle St. WC2 .2D 12 (7H 83)
Lismore *SW19* .*5H 135*
(off Woodside)
Lismore Cir. NW5 .5E 64
Lismore Cl. TW7: Isle .2A 114
Lismore Rd. CR2: S Croy .6E 168
N17 .3D 48
Lismore Wlk. *N1* .*6C 66*
(off Clephane Rd. Nth.)
Lissant Cl. KT6: Surb .7D 150
Lisselton Ho. *NW4* .*4F 45*
(off Belle Vue Est.)
Lissenden Gdns. NW5 .4E 64
(not continuous)
Lissenden Mans. NW5 .4E 64
Lisson Grn. Est. *NW8* .*3C 4*
(off Tresham Cres.)
LISSON GROVE .5B 4 (5C 82)
Lisson Gro. NW1 .3B 4 (4B 82)
NW8 .3B 4 (4B 82)
Lisson Ho. *NW1* .*5C 4*
(off Lisson St.)
Lisson St. NW1 .5C 4 (5C 82)
Lister Cl. CR4: Mitc .1C 154
W3 .5K 79
Lister Ct. HA1: Harr .7B 42
N16 .2E 66
NW9 .2A 44
Lister Gdns. N18 .5H 33
Listergate Ct. SW15 .4E 116
Lister Ho. *E1* .*5G 85*
(off Lomas St.)
HA9: Wemb .*3J 61*
(off Barnhill Rd.)
UB3: Harl .4G 93
Lister Lodge *W9* .*5J 81*
(off Admiral Wlk.)
Lister Rd. E11 .1G 69
Lister Wlk. SE28 .7D 90
Liston Rd. N17 .1G 49
SW4 .3G 119
Liston Way IG8: Wfd G .7F 37
Listowel Cl. SW9 .7A 102
Listowel Rd. RM10: Dag .3G 73
Listria Pk. N16 .2E 66
Litcham Ho. *E1* .*3K 85*
(off Longnor Rd.)
Litchfield Av. E15 .6G 69
SM4: Mord .7H 153
Litchfield Ct. E17 .6C 50
Litchfield Gdns. NW10 .6C 62
Litchfield Rd. SM1: Sutt .4A 166
Litchfield St. WC2 .2D 12 (7H 83)
Litchfield Way NW11 .5K 45
Lithgow's Rd. TW6: H'row A .4G 111
Lithos Rd. NW3 .6K 63
Litten Nature Reserve .3G 77
Little Acre BR3: Beck .3C 158
Lit. Albany St. NW1 .3K 5
Little Angel Theatre .*1B 84*
(off Dagmar Ter.)
Lit. Argyll St. W1 .1A 12 (6G 83)
Little Benty UB7: W Dray .1E 174
Little Birches DA15: Sidc .2J 143
Lit. Boltons, The SW5 .5K 99
SW10 .5K 99
Little Bornes SE21 .4E 138
Littlebourne SE13 .7G 123
Littlebourne Ho. *SE17* .*5E 102*
(off Upnor Way)
Lit. Brights Rd. DA17: Belv .2H 109
Little Britain EC1 .6B 8 (5B 84)
Littlebrook Cl. CR0: C'don .6K 157
Little Brownings SE23 .2H 139
Littlebury Rd. SW4 .3H 119
Lit. Bury St. N9 .1J 33
Lit. Bushey La. WD23: Bush .1C 26
Little Cedars N12 .4F 31
Lit. Chelsea Ho. *SW10* .*6A 100*
(off Edith Gro.)
Lit. Chester St. SW1 .1J 17 (3F 101)
Little Cloisters SW1 .1E 18 (3J 101)
Lit. College La. *EC4* .*2E 14*
(off College St.)
Lit. College St. SW1 .1E 18 (3J 101)
Littlecombe SE7 .6K 105
Littlecombe Cl. SW15 .6F 117
Little Comn. HA7: Stan .3F 27
Littlecote Cl. SW19 .7G 117
Littlecote Pl. HA5: Hat E .1C 40
Lit. Cottage Pl. SE10 .7D 104
Little Ct. BR4: W W'ck .2G 171
Littlecroft SE9 .3E 124
Littledale SE2 .6A 108
Lit. Dean's Yd. SW1 .1E 18
Little Dimocks SW12 .2F 137
Lit. Dorrit Ct. SE1 .6D 14 (2C 102)
LITTLE EALING .3D 96
Lit. Ealing La. W5 .4C 96
Lit. Edward St. NW1 .1K 5 (3F 83)
Little Elms UB3: Harl .7F 93
Lit. Essex St. WC2 .2J 13
Lit. Ferry Rd. TW1: Twick .1B 132
Littlefield Cl. KT1: King T .2E 150
N19 .4G 65
Littlefield Ho. *KT1: King T* .*2E 150*
(off Littlefield Cl.)
Littlefield Rd. HA8: Edg .7D 28
Lit. Friday Rd. E4 .2B 36
Little Gearies IG6: Ilf .4F 53
Lit. George St. SW1 .7E 12 (2J 101)
Little Gn. St. NW5 .4F 65
Little Grange UB6: G'frd .3A 78
Little Green TW9: Rich .4D 114
Littlegrove EN4: E Barn .6H 21
Little Halliards KT12: Walt T .6J 147
LITTLE HEATH .5B 54
Little Heath RM6: Chad H .4B 54
SE7 .6C 106
Lit. Heath Rd. DA7: Bex .1F 127
Littleheath Rd. CR2: Sels .7H 169
Little Holland House .7D 166
Little Holt E11 .5J 51
LITTLE ILFORD .5D 70
Lit. Ilford La. E12 .4D 70
Littlejohn Rd. W7 .6K 77
Little Larkins EN5: Barn .6B 20
Lit. London Cl. UB8: Hil .5D 74
Lit. London Ct. *SE1* .*7K 15*
(off Wolseley St.)
Lit. Marlborough St. W1 .1A 12
Littlemede SE9 .3D 142
Littlemoor Rd. IG1: Ilf .3H 71
Littlemore Rd. SE2 .2A 108
Lit. Moss La. HA5: Pinn .2C 40
Lit. Newport St. WC2 .2D 12 (7H 83)
Lit. New St. EC4 .7K 7 (6A 84)
Lit. Oaks Cl. TW17: Shep .4B 146
Lit. Orchard Cl. HA5: Pinn .2C 40
Little Pk. Dr. TW13: Felt .2C 130
Little Pk. Gdns. EN2: Enf .3H 23
Lit. Pluckett's Way IG9: Buck H .1G 37
Lit. Portland St. W1 .7K 5 (6G 83)
Little Potters WD23: Bush .1C 26
Lit. Queen's Rd. TW11: Tedd .6K 131
Little Redlands BR1: Brom .2C 160
Little Rd. UB3: Hayes .2H 93
Littlers Cl. SW19 .1B 154
Lit. Russell St. WC1 .6E 6 (5J 83)
Lit. St James's St. SW1 .5A 12 (1G 101)
Lit. St Leonard's SW14 .3J 115
Lit. Sanctuary SW1 .7D 12 (2H 101)
Lit. Smith St. SW1 .1D 18 (3H 101)
Lit. Somerset St. E1 .1J 15 (6F 85)
Little Sth. St. SE5 .1E 120
LITTLE STANMORE .7A 28
Littlestone Cl. BR3: Beck .6C 140
Little Strand NW9 .2B 44
Lit. Thames Wlk. *SE8* .*6D 104*
(off Dancers Way)
Little Thrift BR5: Pet W .4G 161
Lit. Titchfield St. W1 .6A 6 (5G 83)
LITTLETON .3C 146
Littleton Av. E4 .1C 36
LITTLETON COMMON .7E 128
Littleton Cres. HA1: Harr .2K 59
Littleton Ho. *SW1* .*6A 18*
(off Lupus St.)
Littleton La. TW17: Shep .7A 146
Littleton Rd. HA1: Harr .2K 59
TW15: Ashf .7E 128
Littleton St. SW18 .2A 136
Lit. Trinity La. EC4 .2D 14 (7C 84)
Little Turnstile WC1 .6G 7 (5K 83)
Little Venice .5A 82
Little Venice Sports Cen. .5A 4 (5B 82)
Littlewood SE13 .6E 122
Littlewood Cl. W13 .3B 96
Lit. Wood St. KT1: King T .2D 150
Livermere Ct. *E8* .*1F 85*
(off Queensbridge Rd.)
Livermere Rd. E8 .1F 85
Liverpool Gro. SE17 .5C 102
Liverpool Rd. CR7: Thor H .3C 156
E10 .6E 50
E16 .5G 87
KT2: King T .7G 133
N1 .5A 66
N7 .5A 66
W5 .2D 96
Liverpool St. EC2 .6G 9 (5E 84)
Livery Stables Cl. BR2: Brom .3B 172
Livesey Cl. KT1: King T .3F 151
SE28 .3G 107
Livesey Pl. SE15 .6G 103
Livingstone Ct. E10 .6E 50
EN5: Barn .*2B 20*
(off Church La.)
HA3: W'stone .3K 41
TW19: Stanw .*1A 128*
(off Explorer Av.)
Livingstone Ho. NW10 .7K 61
SE5 .*7C 102*
(off Wyndham Rd.)
Livingstone Lodge *W9* .*5J 81*
(off Admiral Wlk.)
Livingstone Mans. *W14* .*6G 99*
(off Queen's Club Gdns.)
Livingstone Pl. E14 .5E 104
Livingstone Rd. CR7: Thor H .2C 156
E17 .6D 50
N13 .6D 32
SW11 .3B 118
TW3: Houn .4G 113
UB1: S'hall .7B 76
LivingWell Health Club
London Heathrow Hilton .6E 110
Wembley .4G 61
Livonia St. W1 .1B 12 (6G 83)
Lizard St. EC1 .2D 8 (3C 84)
Lizban St. SE3 .7K 105
Lizmans Ter. *W8* .*3J 99*
(off Earl's Ct. Rd.)
Llandovery Ho. *E14* .*2E 104*
(off Chipka St.)
Llanelly Rd. NW2 .2H 63
Llanover Rd. HA9: Wemb .3D 60
SE18 .6E 106
Llanthony Rd. SM4: Mord .5B 154
Llanvanor Rd. NW2 .2H 63
Llewellyn Ct. SE20 .1J 157
Llewellyn Mans. *W14* .*4G 99*
(off Hammersmith Rd.)
Llewellyn St. SE16 .2G 103
Lloyd Av. SW16 .1J 155
Lloyd Baker St. WC1 .2H 7 (3K 83)
(not continuous)
Lloyd Ct. HA5: Pinn .5B 40
Lloyd Ho. BR3: Beck .6D 140
CR0: C'don .*1D 168*
(off Tavistock Rd.)
Lloyd M. EN3: Enf L .1H 25
Lloyd Pk. Av.
CR0: C'don .4F 169
Lloyd Pk. Ho. E17 .3C 50
Lloyd Rd. E6 .1D 88
E17 .4K 49
KT4: Wor Pk .3E 164
RM9: Dag .7F 73
Lloyd's Av. EC3 .1H 15 (6E 84)
Lloyd's Building .1G 15 (6E 84)
Lloyds Lanes Raynes Pk. .3F 153
Lloyd's Pl. SE3 .2G 123
Lloyd Sq. WC1 .1J 7 (3A 84)
Lloyd's Row EC1 .2K 7 (3A 84)
Lloyd St. WC1 .1J 7 (3A 84)
Lloyds Way BR3: Beck .5A 158
Lloyds Wharf SE1 .6K 15
Lloyd Thomas Ct. N22 .7E 32
Lloyd Vs. E6 .4C 88
SE4 .2C 122
Loampit Hill SE13 .2C 122
LOAMPIT VALE .3E 122
Loampit Va. SE13 .3D 122
Loanda Cl. E8 .1F 85
Loats Rd. SW2 .6J 119
Lobelia Cl. E6 .5C 88
Locarno Ct. SW16 .5G 137
Locarno Rd. UB6: G'frd .4H 77
W3 .1J 97
Lochaber Rd. SE13 .4G 123
Lochaline St. W6 .6E 98
Lochan Cl. UB4: Yead .4C 76
Loch Cres. HA8: Edg .4A 28
Lochinvar St. SW12 .7F 119
Lochleven Ho. *N2* .*2B 46*
(off The Grange)
Lochmere Cl. DA8: Erith .6H 109
Lochmore Ho. *SW1* .*4H 17*
(off Cundy St.)
Lochnagar St. E14 .5E 86
Lockbridge Ct. *W9* .*5J 81*
(off Woodfield Rd.)
Lock Bldg., The E15 .2E 86
Lock Chase SE3 .3G 123
Lock Cl. UB2: S'hall .2G 95
Lock Cotts. UB1: S'hall .2H 95
Lock Ct. E5 .2K 67
Locke Hgts. *N1* .*7K 65*
(off Caledonian Rd.)
Locke Ho. *SW8* .*1G 119*
(off Wadhurst Rd.)
Lockesfield Pl. E14 .5D 104
Lockesley Dr. BR5: St M Cry .6K 161
Lockesley Sq. KT6: Surb .6D 150
Locket Rd. HA3: W'stone .3J 41
Locket Rd. M. HA3: W'stone .2J 41
Lockfield Av. EN3: Brim .2F 25
Lockgate Cl. E9 .5B 68
Lockhart Cl. EN3: Pond E .5C 24
N7 .6K 65
Lockhart St. E3 .4B 86
Lockhouse, The NW1 .1E 82
Lockhurst St. E5 .4K 67

Lockie Pl. SE25 . . . . 3G 157
Lockier Wlk. HA9: Wemb 3D 60
Lockington Rd. SW8 . . . . 1F 119
Lock Keepers Hgts. SE16 . . . . . . 3K 103
(off Brunswick Quay)
Lockmead Rd. N15 . . . . 6G 49
SE13 . . . . 3E 122
Lock M. NW1 . . . . 6H 65
(off Northpoint Sq.)
Lock Rd. TW10: Ham 4C 132
LOCKSBOTTOM 3E 172
Locksfields SE17 . . . . 4D 102
(off Catesby St.)
Lockside E14 . . . . 1E 154
(off Narrow St.)
Locks La. CR4: Mitc 1E 154
Locksley Est. E14 . . . . 6B 86
Locksley St. E14 . . . . 5B 86
Locksmeade Rd. TW10: Ham 4C 132
Locksons Cl. E14 . . . . 5D 86
Lockswood Cl. EN4: Cockf 4J 21
Lockton St. W10 . . . . 7F 81
(off Bramley Rd.)
Lock Vw. Ct. E14 . . . . 7A 86
(off Narrow St.)
Lockwell Rd. RM10: Dag 3G 73
Lockwood Cl. SE26 . . . . 4K 139
Lockwood Ho. E5 . . . . 2J 67
SE11 . . . . 7J 19 (6A 102)
Lockwood Ind. Pk. N17 . . . . 3H 49
Lockwood Pl. E4 . . . . 6H 35
Lockwood Sq. SE16 . . . . 3H 103
Lockwood Way E17 . . . . 2K 49
KT9: Chess 5G 163
Lockyer Est. SE1 . . . . 7F 15
(not continuous)
Lockyer Ho. SE10 . . . . 5H 105
(off Armitage Rd.)
SW8 . . . . 7H 101
(off Wandsworth Rd.)
SW15 . . . . 3F 117
Lockyer M. EN3: Enf L 1J 25
Lockyer St. SE1 . . . . 7F 15 (2D 102)
Locomotive Dr. TW14: Felt 1J 129
Locton Grn. E3 . . . . 1B 86
Loddiges Ho. E9 . . . . 7J 67
Loddiges Rd. E9 . . . . 7J 67
Loddon Ho. NW8 . . . . 4B 4
(off Church St. Est.)
Loder St. SE15 . . . . 7J 103
Lodge, The W12 . . . . 2F 99
(off Richmond Way)
Lodge Av. CR0: Wadd 3A 168
HA3: Kenton 4E 42
RM8: Dag 6B 72
RM9: Dag 1A 90
SW14 . . . . 3A 116
LODGE AVENUE FLYOVER JUNC. 1A 90
Lodge Cl. HA8: Edg 6A 28
N18 . . . . 5H 33
SM6: Wall 1E 166
TW7: Isle 1B 114
Lodge Ct. HA0: Wemb 5E 60
(off Station Gro.)
Lodge Dr. N13 . . . . 4F 33
Lodge Gdns. BR3: Beck 5B 158
Lodge Hill DA16: Well 7B 108
IG4: Ilf 4C 52
SE2 . . . . 7B 108
Lodgehill Pk. Cl.
HA2: Harr 2F 59
Lodge La. CR0: New Ad 6C 170
DA5: Bexl 6D 126
N12 . . . . 5F 31
RM5: Col R 1G 55
Lodge Pl. SM1: Sutt 5K 165
Lodge Rd. BR1: Brom 7A 142
CR0: C'don 6B 156
NW4 . . . . 4E 44
NW8 . . . . 2B 4 (3B 82)
SM6: Wall 5F 167

Lodge Vs. IG8: Wfd G 6C 36
Lodge Way TW15: Ashf 2A 128
TW17: Shep 2E 146
Lodore Gdns. NW9 . . . . 5A 44
Lodore Grn. UB10: Ick 3A 56
Lodore St. E14 . . . . 6E 86
Loft, The W12 . . . . 1F 99
Loft Ho. E1 . . . . 7J 9
(off Middlesex St.)
Lofthouse Pl. KT9: Chess 6C 162
Loftie St. SE16 . . . . 2G 103
Lofting Ho. N1 . . . . 7A 66
(off Liverpool Rd.)
Lofting Rd. N1 . . . . 7K 65
Lofts on the Park E9 . . . . 6K 67
(off Cassland Rd.)
Loftus Road 1D 98
Loftus Rd. IG11: Bark 6G 71
W12 . . . . 1D 98
Loftus Vs. W12 . . . . 1D 98
(off Loftus Rd.)
Logan Cl. E20 . . . . 5E 68
EN3: Enf H 1E 24
TW4: Houn 3D 112
Logan M. RM1: Rom 5K 55
W8 . . . . 4J 99
Logan Pl. W8 . . . . 4J 99
Loggetts SE21 . . . . 2E 138
Logs Hill BR1: Brom 7C 142
BR7: Chst 7C 142
Logs Hill Cl.
BR7: Chst 1C 160
Lohmann Ho. SE11 . . . . 7J 19
Lois Dr. TW17: Shep 5D 146
Lolesworth Cl. E1 . . . . . . 6J 9 (5F 85)
Lolland Ho. SE7 . . . . 4C 106
Lollard St. SE11 . . . . . . 3H 19 (4K 101)
(not continuous)
Loman St. SE1 . . . . 6B 14 (2B 102)
Lomas Cl. CR0: New Ad 7E 170
Lomas Dr. E8 . . . . 7F 67
Lomas St. E1 . . . . 5G 85
Lombard Av. EN3: Enf H 1D 24
IG3: Ilf 1J 71
Lombard Bus. Pk. CR0: C'don 7K 155
SW19 . . . . 2K 153
Lombard Ct. EC3 . . . . . . 2F 15 (7D 84)
RM7: Rom 4J 55
W3 . . . . 1H 97
Lombard La. EC4 . . . . . . 1K 13 (6A 84)
Lombard Pl. E3 . . . . 2A 86
Lombard Rd. N11 . . . . 5A 32
SW11 . . . . 2B 118
SW19 . . . . 2K 153
LOMBARD RDBT. 7K 155
Lombard St. EC3 . . . . . . 1F 15 (6D 84)
Lombard Trad. Est. SE7 . . . . 4K 105
Lombard Wall SE7 . . . . 3K 105
Lombard Wharf SW11 . . . . 2B 118
Lombardy Cl. IG6: Ilf 7K 37
Lombardy Pl. W2 . . . . 7K 81
Lombardy Retail Pk. UB3: Hayes . . 7K 75
Lomond Cl. HA0: Wemb 7F 61
N15 . . . . 5E 48
Lomond Gdns. CR2: Sels 7A 170
Lomond Gro. SE5 . . . . 7D 102
Lomond Ho. SE5 . . . . 7D 102
Loncroft Rd. SE5 . . . . 6F 103
Londesborough Rd. N16 . . . . 4E 66
Londinium Twr. E1 . . . . 2K 15
(off W. Tenter St.)
LONDON 4E 12 (1J 101)
London Ambulance Service Mus. . . 5K 53
London Aquatics Cen.
Queen Elizabeth Olympic Pk.
. . . . 7E 68
London Bri. SE1 . . . . . . 4F 15 (1D 102)
London Bridge Experience 4F 15
(off Tooley St.)

London Bri. St. SE1 . . . . . . 5F 15 (1D 102)
London Bri. Wlk. SE1 . . . . 4F 15
(off Duke St. Hill)
London Broncos RLFC 1E 42
London Business School 3E 4 (4D 82)
London Canal Mus. 2J 83
LONDON CITY AIRPORT 1C 106
London City College 5J 13
(off Waterloo Rd.)
London Coliseum 3E 12
(off St Martin's La.)
London College of Fashion, The
Hackney 7J 67
Londonderry Pde. DA8: Erith 7K 109
London Designer Outlet
HA9: Wemb 4G 61
London Dungeon 6G 13 (2K 101)
London Eye 6G 13 (2K 101)
London Flds. East Side E8 . . . . . . 7H 67
London Fields Lido 7H 67
London Flds. West Side E8 . . . . . . 7G 67
London Film Mus. 2F 13
London Fire Brigade Mus. . . 6C 14 (2C 102)
London Fruit Exchange E1 . . . . . . 6J 9
(off Brushfield St.)
LONDON GATEWAY SERVICE AREA . . . 1D 28
London Group Bus. Pk. NW2 . . . . 1B 62
LONDON HEATHROW AIRPORT
Terminals 1, 2, 3 . . . . 3C 110
Terminal 4 . . . . 5D 110
Terminal 5 . . . . 6D 174
London Heliport, The 2A 118
London Ho. EC1 . . . . 6C 8
(off Aldersgate St.)
NW8 . . . . 2C 82
(off Avenue Rd.)
WC1 . . . . 3G 7 (4K 83)
London Ind. Pk., The E6 . . . . 5F 89
(not continuous)
London Irish RFC (Hazelwood) 3H 147
London La. BR1: Brom 7H 141
E8 . . . . 7H 67
London Master Bakers Almshouses
E10 . . . . 6D 50
London Mercantile Court 7J 7 (6A 84)
London Metropolitan Archives 3K 7
London Metropolitan University
Calcutta House & Goulston St.
. . . . 7K 9 (6F 85)
Central House 7K 9
Commercial Rd. 6G 85
Jewry St. 1J 15
(off Jewry St.)
Moorgate 6E 8
Tower Hill 2J 15
North London Campus -
Eden Grove 5K 65
Stapleton House 5K 65
Tower Bldg. & Graduate Cen.
. . . . 5A 66
London M. W2 . . . . 7B 4 (6B 82)
London Mill Apartments
. . . . 2F 85
(off Whiston Rd.)
London Motorcycle Mus.
(Ravenor Farm) 3G 77
London Motor Mus. 3H 93
London Palladium 1A 12
(off Argyll St.)
London Pavilion 3C 12
(off Shaftesbury Av.)
London Plane Ho. E15 . . . . 4B 88
(off Teasel Way)
London Regatta Cen. 7B 88
London Rd. BR1: Brom 7H 141
CR0: C'don 7B 156
CR4: Mitc 5C 154
(Brookfields Av.)
CR4: Mitc 7E 154
(Mill Grn. Rd.)

London Rd. CR7: Thor H 1K 155
DA1: Bexl, Cray 5K 127
E13 . . . . 2J 87
EN2: Enf 3J 23
HA1: Harr 2J 59
HA7: Stan 5H 27
HA9: Wemb 5E 60
IG11: Bark 7F 71
KT2: King T 2F 151
KT17: Ewe 7B 164
RM6: Chad H 6G 55
RM7: Chad H, Rom 6G 55
SE1 . . . . 7A 14 (3B 102)
SE23 . . . . 1H 139
SM3: Cheam 3F 165
SM4: Mord 5J 153
SM6: Wall 4F 167
SW16 . . . . 1K 155
SW17 . . . . 7D 136
TW1: Twick 7A 114
TW3: Houn 3G 113
TW7: Bford, Isle 5A 114
TW7: Isle, Twick 5A 114
TW8: Bford 6G 113
TW14: Bedf 2A 128
TW15: Ashf 2A 128
LONDON ROAD RDBT. 6A 114
London School of Economics &
Political Science, The
. . . . 1G 13 (6K 83)
London Scottish & Richmond
Rugby Football Ground 3D 114
London Scottish Golf Course 3D 134
London's Death Trap 7G 13
London Shootfighters Gym 4G 79
London South Bank University
Keyworth St. 7B 14 (3B 102)
London Rd. 7A 14
Southwark Campus . . . 7B 14 (3B 102)
London South Bank University Sports Cen.
. . . . 7B 14
(off London Rd.)
London South Bank University Technopark
. . . . 3B 102
(off London Rd.)
London's Roman Amphitheatre 7E 8
(off Aldermanbury)
London Stadium
Queen Elizabeth Olympic Pk.
. . . . 7D 68
London Stile W4 . . . . 5G 97
London Stock Exchange 7C 8
London St. EC3 . . . . 2H 15 (7E 84)
W2 . . . . 7A 4 (6B 82)
London Telecom Tower, The . . . 5A 6 (5G 83)
London Television Cen., The
. . . . 4J 13 (7A 84)
London Ter. E2 . . . . 2G 85
London Transport Mus. 2F 13 (7J 83)
London Transport Mus. Depot 2G 97
London Trocadero 2C 12 (7H 83)
London Underwriting Cen. 2H 15
London Wall EC2 . . . . . . 6D 8 (5C 84)
London Wall Bldgs. EC2 . . . . 6F 9
London Wall Pl. EC2 . . . . 6D 8
(off Fore St.)
London Wetland Cen. 1D 116
London Wetland Cen. Vis. Cen. . . . 1D 116
London Wharf E2 . . . . 1H 85
(off Wharf Pl.)
London Zoo 2E 82
LONESOME 1G 155
Lonesome Cvn. Site SW16 . . . . . . 1F 155
Lonesome Way SW16 . . . . 1F 155
Long Acre WC2 . . . . 2E 12 (7J 83)
Long Acre Ct. W13 . . . . 5A 78
Longacre Pl. SM5: Cars 6E 166
Longacre Rd. E17 . . . . 1F 51
Longbeach Rd. SW11 . . . . 3D 118
Longberrys NW2 . . . . 3H 63
Longboat Row UB1: S'hall 6D 76

Longbow Ho. EC1 . . . . .5E **8**
    (off Chiswell St.)
Longbridge Ho. E16 . . . . .7F **89**
    (off University Way)
  RM8: Dag 4B **72**
    (off Longbridge Rd.)
Longbridge Rd.
  IG11: Bark 6H **71**
  RM8: Dag 6H **71**
Longbridge Way SE13 . . . . . . .5E **122**
Longcourt M. E11 . . . . .4A **52**
Longcroft SE9 . . . . .3D **142**
Longcrofte Rd. HA8: Edg 7J **27**
Long Deacon Rd. E4 . . . . .1B **36**
LONG DITTON 1C **162**
Longdon Wood BR2: Kes 3C **172**
Longdown Rd. SE6 . . . . .4C **140**
Long Dr. HA4: Ruis 5A **58**
  UB6: G'frd 1F **77**
  UB7: W Dray 2A **92**
  W3 .6A **80**
Long Elmes HA3: Hrw W 1F **41**
Longfellow Rd. E17 . . . . .6B **50**
  KT4: Wor Pk 2C **164**
Longfellow Way SE1 . . . . .4F **103**
Long Fld. NW9 . . . . .7F **29**
Longfield BR1: Brom 1H **159**
Longfield Av. E17 . . . . .4A **50**
  HA9: Wemb 1E **60**
  NW7 . . . . .7H **29**
  SM6: Wall 1E **166**
  W5 .7C **78**
Longfield Cres. SE26 . . . . .3J **139**
Longfield Dr. CR4: Mitc 1C **154**
  SW14 . . . . .5H **115**
Longfield Est. SE1 . . . . .4F **103**
Longfield Ho. E17 . . . . .5B **50**
  W5 .7C **78**
Longfield Rd. W5 . . . . .6C **78**
Longfield St. SW18 . . . . .7J **117**
Longfield Wlk. W5 . . . . .6C **78**
LONGFORD 4C **174**
Longford Av. TW14: Felt 6G **111**
  TW19: Stanw 1A **128**
  UB1: S'hall 7F **77**
Longford Cir. UB7: Lford 4C **174**
Longford Cl. TW12: Hamp H . . .4E **130**
  TW13: Hanw 3C **130**
  UB4: Yead 7B **76**
Longford Ct. E5 . . . . .4K **67**
    (off Pedro St.)
  KT19: Ewe 4J **163**
  NW4 . . . . .4F **45**
  TW12: Hamp H 6F **131**
  UB1: S'hall 1E **94**
    (off Uxbridge Rd.)
Longford Gdns. SM1: Sutt 3A **166**
  UB4: Yead 7B **76**
Longford Ho. BR1: Brom 5F **141**
    (off Brangbourne Rd.)
  E1 . . . . .6J **85**
    (off Jubilee St.)
  TW12: Hamp H 4E **130**
Longford Ind. Est. TW12: Hamp . . .6F **131**
LONGFORDMOOR 4B **174**
Longford Rd. TW2: Whitt 1E **130**
Longford St. NW1 . . . . .3K **5** (4F **83**)
Longford Wlk. SW2 . . . . .7A **120**
Longford Way TW19: Stanw . . .1A **128**
Longhayes Av. RM6: Chad H . . .4D **54**
Longhayes Ct. RM6: Chad H . . .4D **54**
Longheath Gdns. CR0: C'don . . .5J **157**
Longhedge Ho. SE26 . . . . .4G **139**
    (off High Level Dr.)
Long Hedges TW3: Houn 2E **112**
Longhedge St. SW11 . . . . .2E **118**
Longhill Rd. SE6 . . . . .2F **141**
Longhook Gdns. UB5: N'olt 2J **75**
Longhope Cl. SE15 . . . . .6E **102**
Longhurst Ho. W10 . . . . .3H **81**
    (off Lancefield St.)

Longhurst Rd. CR0: C'don 6H **157**
  SE13 . . . . .5F **123**
Longitude Apartments CR0: C'don . .2D **168**
    (off Addiscombe Gro.)
Longland Ct. E9 . . . . .5A **68**
    (off Mabley St.)
  SE1 . . . . .5G **103**
Longland Dr. N20 . . . . .3E **30**
LONGLANDS 3G **143**
Longlands Cl. CR4: Mitc 1E **154**
  DA15: Sidc 2K **143**
  W11 .1H **81**
Longlands Pk. Cres.
  DA15: Sidc 3J **143**
Longlands Rd. DA15: Sidc 3J **143**
Long La. CR0: C'don 6J **157**
  DA7: Bex 7D **108**
  EC1 . . . . .6B **8** (5B **84**)
  N2 . . . . .7E **30**
  N3 . . . . .7E **30**
  SE1 . . . . .7E **14** (2D **102**)
  TW19: Stanw 2B **128**
  UB10: Hil, Ick 3C **74**
Longleat Ho. SW1 . . . . .5C **18**
    (off Rampayne St.)
Longleat Rd. EN1: Enf 5K **23**
Longleat Way TW14: Bedf 7F **111**
Longleigh Ho. SE5 . . . . .1E **120**
    (off Peckham Rd.)
Longleigh La. DA7: Bex 6C **108**
  SE2 . . . . .6C **108**
Long Lents Ho. NW10 . . . . .1K **79**
    (off Shrewsbury Rd.)
Longley Av. HA0: Wemb 1F **79**
Longley Ct. SW8 . . . . .1J **119**
Longley Rd. CR0: C'don 7B **156**
  HA1: Harr 5G **41**
  SW17 . . . . .6C **136**
Long Leys E4 . . . . .6J **35**
Longley St. SE1 . . . . .4G **103**
Longley Way NW2 . . . . .3E **62**
Longman Ho. E2 . . . . .2K **85**
    (off Mace St.)
  E8 . . . . .1F **85**
    (off Haggerston Rd.)
Long Mark Rd. E16 . . . . .5B **88**
Longmarsh La. SE28 . . . . .1J **107**
Long Mead NW9 . . . . .1B **44**
Longmead BR7: Chst 2E **160**
Longmead Dr. DA14: Sidc 2D **144**
Longmead Ho. SE27 . . . . .5C **138**
Long Mdw. NW5 . . . . .5H **65**
Long Mdw. Cl. BR4: W W'ck . . .7E **158**
Longmeadow Rd. DA15: Sidc . . .1J **143**
Longmead Rd. KT7: T Ditt 7J **149**
  SW17 . . . . .5D **136**
  UB3: Hayes 7H **75**
Long Mill SE10 . . . . .1D **122**
    (off Greenwich High Rd.)
Longmoore St. SW1 . . . .4A **18** (4G **101**)
Longmoor Point SW15 . . . . . . .1D **134**
    (off Norley Va.)
Longmore Av. EN4: E Barn 6F **21**
  EN5: New Bar 6F **21**
Longmore Gdns. Est. SW1 . . . .4B **18**
Longmore St. SW1 . . . . .4B **18**
Longnor Est. E1 . . . . .3K **85**
Longnor Rd. E1 . . . . .3K **85**
Long Pond Rd. SE3 . . . . .1G **123**
Longreach Ct. IG11: Bark 2H **89**
Long Reach Rd. IG11: Bark 4K **89**
Lorac Ct. SM2: Sutt 7J **165**
Longridge Ho. SE1 . . . . .3C **102**
Longridge La. UB1: S'hall 6F **77**
Longridge Rd. IG11: Bark 7G **71**
  SW5 . . . . .4J **99**
Long Ridges N2 . . . . .5A **46**
    (off Fortis Grn.)
Long Rd. SW4 . . . . .4F **119**
Long's Ct. WC2 . . . . .3D **12**
Longs Ct. TW9: Rich 4F **115**
Longshaw Rd. E4 . . . . .3A **36**
Longshore SE8 . . . . .4B **104**

Longshott Cl. SW5 . . . . .4J **99**
    (off W. Cromwell Rd.)
Longstaff Cres. SW18 . . . . . . .6J **117**
Longstaff Rd. SW18 . . . . .6J **117**
Longstone Av. NW10 . . . . .7B **62**
Longstone Ct. SE1 . . . . .7E **14**
    (off Gt. Dover St.)
Longstone Rd. SW17 . . . . .5F **137**
Long St. E2 . . . . .1J **9** (3F **85**)
Longthornton Rd. SW16 . . . . .2G **155**
Longthorpe Ct. W6 . . . . .4C **98**
Longton Av. SE26 . . . . .4G **139**
Longton Gro. SE26 . . . . .4H **139**
Longview Vs. RM5: Col R 1F **55**
Longview Way RM5: Col R 1K **55**
Longville Rd. SE11 . . . . .4B **102**
Long Wlk. KT3: N Mald 3J **151**
  SE1 . . . . .3E **102**
  SE18 . . . . .5F **107**
  SW13 . . . . .2A **116**
Longwalk Rd. UB11: Stock P . . .1D **92**
Long Wall E15 . . . . .3F **87**
Longwater Ho. KT1: King T 3D **150**
    (off Portsmouth Rd.)
Longwood Bus. Pk.
  TW16: Sun 5H **147**
Longwood Dr. SW15 . . . . .6C **116**
Longwood Gdns. IG5: Ilf 4D **52**
  IG6: Ilf 4D **52**
Longworth Cl. SE28 . . . . .6D **90**
Long Yd. WC1 . . . . .4G **7** (4K **83**)
Loning, The NW9 . . . . .4A **44**
Lonsdale Av. E6 . . . . .4B **88**
  HA9: Wemb 5E **60**
  RM7: Rom 6J **55**
Lonsdale Cl. E6 . . . . .4C **88**
  HA5: Hat E 1C **40**
  HA8: Edg 5A **28**
  SE9 .3B **142**
  UB8: Hil 5E **74**
Lonsdale Ct. KT6: Surb 7D **150**
Lonsdale Cres. IG2: Ilf 6F **53**
Lonsdale Dr. EN2: Enf 4C **22**
Lonsdale Dr. Nth. EN2: Enf 5D **22**
Lonsdale Gdns. CR7: Thor H . . .4K **155**
Lonsdale Ho. W11 . . . . .6H **81**
    (off Lonsdale Rd.)
Lonsdale M. TW9: Kew 1G **115**
  W11 .6H **81**
    (off Colville M.)
Lonsdale Pl. N1 . . . . .7A **66**
Lonsdale Rd. DA7: Bex 2F **127**
  E11 . . . . .6H **51**
  NW6 . . . . .2J **81**
  SE25 . . . . .4H **157**
  SW13 . . . . .1B **116**
  UB2: S'hall 3B **94**
  W4 .4B **98**
  W11 .6H **81**
Lonsdale Sq. N1 . . . . .7A **66**
Lonsdale Yd. W11 . . . . .7J **81**
Loobert Rd. N15 . . . . .3E **48**
Looe Gdns. IG6: Ilf 3F **53**
Lookout Education Cen., The
    . . . . .4E **10** (1D **100**)
Loop Ct. SE10 . . . . .4G **105**
    (off Telegraph Av.)
Loop Rd. BR7: Chst 6C **143**
Lopen Rd. N18 . . . . .4K **33**
Lopez Ho. SW9 . . . . .3J **119**
Loraine Cl. EN3: Pond E 5D **24**
Loraine Cotts. N7 . . . . .4K **65**
Loraine Ct. BR7: Chst 5F **143**
Loraine Ho. SM6: Wall 4F **167**
Loraine Rd. N7 . . . . .4K **65**
  W4 .6H **97**
Lord Admiral's Vw. SE18 . . . . . .4D **106**
    (off Frances St.)
Lord Amory Way E14 . . . . .2E **104**
Lord Av. IG5: Ilf 4D **52**

Lord Chancellor Wlk. KT2: King T . . .1J **151**
Lord Cl. IG5: Ilf 4D **52**
Lordell Pl. SW19 . . . . .6E **134**
Lorden Wlk. E2 . . . . .2K **9** (3G **85**)
Lord Gdns. IG5: Ilf 4D **52**
Lord Graham M. N18 . . . . .5B **34**
Lord Hills Bri. W2 . . . . .5K **81**
Lord Hills Rd. W2 . . . . .5K **81**
Lord Holland La. SW9 . . . . . . .2A **120**
Lord Kensington Ho. W14 . . . . . .4H **99**
    (off Radnor St.)
Lord Knyvetts Ct. TW19: Stanw . .6A **110**
Lord Napier Pl. W6 . . . . .5C **98**
Lord Nth. St. SW1 . . . . . .2E **18** (3J **101**)
Lord Roberts M. SW6 . . . . .7K **99**
Lord Robert's Ter. SE18 . . . . . .5E **106**
Lord's 2B **4** (3B **82**)
Lords Cl. SE21 . . . . .2C **138**
  TW13: Hanw 2C **130**
Lordship Gro. N16 . . . . .2D **66**
Lordship La. N17 . . . . .1D **48**
  N22 .2A **48**
  SE22 . . . . .4F **121**
Lordship La. Est. SE21 . . . . . . .7G **121**
Lordship Pk. N16 . . . . .2C **66**
Lordship Pk. M. N16 . . . . .2C **66**
Lordship Pl. SW3 . . . . . . .7C **16** (6C **100**)
Lordship Rd. N16 . . . . .1D **66**
  UB5: N'olt 7C **58**
Lordship Ter. N16 . . . . .2D **66**
Lordsmead Rd. N17 . . . . .1E **48**
Lord St. E16 . . . . .1C **106**
Lords Vw. NW8 . . . . .2C **4** (3B **82**)
    (not continuous)
Lordswood Cl. DA6: Bex 5E **126**
Lord Warwick St. SE18 . . . . . . .3D **106**
Loreburn Ho. N7 . . . . .4K **65**
Lorenzo Ho. IG3: Ilf 6A **54**
Lorenzo St. WC1 . . . . .1G **7** (3K **83**)
Loretto Gdns. HA3: Kenton 4E **42**
Lorian Cl. N12 . . . . .4E **30**
Lorimer Row BR2: Brom 6B **160**
Loring Rd. N20 . . . . .2H **31**
  SE14 . . . . .1A **122**
  TW7: Isle 2K **113**
Loris Rd. W6 . . . . .3E **98**
Lorn Ct. SW9 . . . . .2A **120**
Lorne Av. CR0: C'don 7K **157**
Lorne Cl. NW8 . . . . .2D **4** (3C **82**)
Lorne Gdns. CR0: C'don 7K **157**
  E11 . . . . .4A **52**
  W11 .2F **99**
Lorne Ho. E1 . . . . .5A **86**
    (off Ben Jonson Rd.)
Lorne Rd. E7 . . . . .4K **69**
  E17 . . . . .5C **50**
  HA3: W'stone 2K **41**
  N4 . . . . .1K **65**
  TW10: Rich 5F **115**
Lorne Ter. N3 . . . . .2H **45**
Lorn Rd. SW9 . . . . .2K **119**
Lorraine Ct. NW1 . . . . .7F **65**
Lorraine Pk. HA3: Hrw W 7D **26**
Lorrimore Rd. SE17 . . . . .6B **102**
Lorrimore Sq. SE17 . . . . .6B **102**
Lorton Ho. NW6 . . . . .1J **81**
    (off Kilburn Vale)
Lost Theatre 1H **119**
Lothair Rd. W5 . . . . .2D **96**
Lothair Rd. Nth. N4 . . . . .6B **48**
Lothair Rd. Sth. N4 . . . . .7A **48**
Lothair St. SW11 . . . . .3C **118**
Lothbury EC2 . . . . .7E **8** (6D **84**)
Lothian Av. UB4: Yead 5K **75**
Lothian Cl. HA0: Wemb 3A **60**
Lothian Rd. SW9 . . . . .1B **120**
Lothrop St. W10 . . . . .3G **81**
Lots Rd. SW10 . . . . .7A **100**
Lotus Cl. SE21 . . . . .3D **138**
Lotus M. N19 . . . . .2J **65**
Loubet St. SW17 . . . . .6D **136**

Loudoun Av. IG6: Ilf 5F **53**
Loudoun Rd. NW8 . . . . 1A **82**
Loudwater Cl. TW16: Sun 4J **147**
Loudwater Rd. TW16: Sun 4J **147**
Loughborough Est. SW9 . . . . 3B **120**
Loughborough Ho. *RM8: Dag* *4A* ***72***
(off Academy Way)
Loughborough Pk. SW9 . . . . 4B **120**
Loughborough Rd. SW9 . . . . 2A **120**
Loughborough St. SE11 . . . . 5H **19** (5K **101**)
Lough Rd. N7 . . . . 5K **65**
Loughton Way IG9: Buck H 1G **37**
Louisa Cl. E9 . . . . 1K **85**
Louisa Ct. TW2: Twick 2J **131**
Louisa Gdns. E1 . . . . 4K **85**
Louisa Ho. IG3: Ilf 6A **54**
Louisa Oakes Cl. E4 . . . . 4G **35**
Louisa St. E1 . . . . 4K **85**
Louise Aumonier Wlk. *N19* *7J* ***47***
(off Jessie Blythe La.)
Louise Bennett Cl. SE24 . . . . 4B **120**
Louise Ct. E11 . . . . 5K **51**
N22 . . . . 1A **48**
Louise De Marillac Ho. *E1* *5J* ***85***
(off Smithy St.)
Louise Rd. E15 . . . . 6G **69**
Louise White Ho. N19 . . . . 1H **65**
Louis Gdns. BR7: Chst 4D **142**
Louis M. N10 . . . . 1F **47**
Louisville Rd. SW17 . . . . 3E **136**
Lousada Lodge *N14* *6B* ***22***
(off Avenue Rd.)
Louvaine Rd. SW11 . . . . 4B **118**
Lovage App. E6 . . . . 5C **88**
Lovat Cl. E14 . . . . 6B **86**
NW2 . . . . 3B **62**
Lovat La. EC3 . . . . 2G **15** (7E **84**)
Lovatt Cl. HA8: Edg 6C **28**
Lovatt Ct. SW12 . . . . 1F **137**
Lovatt Dr. HA4: Ruis 5J **39**
Lovat Wlk. TW5: Hest 7C **94**
Loveday Rd. W13 . . . . 2B **96**
Lovegrove St. SE1 . . . . 5G **103**
Lovegrove Wlk. E14 . . . . 1E **104**
Lovekyn Cl. KT2: King T 2E **150**
Lovelace Av. BR2: Brom 6E **160**
Lovelace Gdns. IG11: Bark 4A **72**
KT6: Surb 7D **150**
Lovelace Grn. SE9 . . . . 3D **124**
Lovelace Ho. W13 . . . . 7B **78**
Lovelace Rd. EN4: E Barn 7H **21**
KT6: Surb 7C **150**
SE21 . . . . 2C **138**
Lovelace St. E8 . . . . 1F **85**
Lovelace Vs. *KT7: T Ditt* *7B* ***150***
(off Portsmouth Rd.)
Loveland Ct. *SE1* *7K* ***15***
(off Jamaica Rd.)
Loveland Mans. *IG11: Bark* *7K* ***71***
(off Upney La.)
Love La. BR1: Brom 3K **159**
CR4: Mitc 3C **154**
(not continuous)
DA5: Bexl 6F **127**
EC2 . . . . 7D **8** (6C **84**)
HA5: Pinn 2B **40**
IG8: Wfd G 6J **37**
KT6: Surb 2C **162**
N17 . . . . 7A **34**
SE18 . . . . 4F **107**
SE25 . . . . 3H **157**
SM1: Sutt 6H **165**
SM3: Cheam, Sutt 6G **165**
SM4: Mord 7J **153**
Lovel Av. DA16: Well 2A **126**
Lovelinch Cl. SE15 . . . . 6J **103**
Lovell Ho. *E8* *1G* ***85***
(off Shrubland Rd.)
Lovell Pl. SE16 . . . . 3A **104**
Lovell Rd. TW10: Ham 3C **132**
UB1: S'hall 6F **77**
Loveridge M. NW6 . . . . 6H **63**
Loveridge Rd. NW6 . . . . 6H **63**
Lovers Wlk. N3 . . . . 7D **30**
(not continuous)
NW7 . . . . 6C **30**
SE10 . . . . 6F **105**
Lovers' Wlk. W1 . . . . 4G **11** (1E **100**)
Lovett Dr. SM5: Cars 7A **154**
Lovett's Pl. SW18 . . . . 4K **117**
Lovett Way NW10 . . . . 5J **61**
Love Wlk. SE5 . . . . 2D **120**
Lovibond La. *SE10* *7D* ***104***
(off Norman Rd.)
Lovibonds Av. BR6: Farnb 4F **173**
UB7: Yiew 6B **74**
Lowbrook Rd. IG1: Ilf 4F **71**
Low Cross Wood La. SE21 . . . . 3F **139**
Lowdell Cl. UB7: Yiew 6A **74**
Lowden Rd. N9 . . . . 1C **34**
SE24 . . . . 4B **120**
UB1: S'hall 7C **76**
Lowder Ho. *E1* *1H* ***103***
(off Wapping La.)
Lowe Av. E16 . . . . 5J **87**
Lowell Ho. *SE5* *7C* ***102***
(off Wyndham Est.)
Lowell St. E14 . . . . 6A **86**
Lowen Rd. RM13: Rain 2K **91**
Lwr. Addiscombe Rd. CR0: C'don 1E **168**
Lwr. Addison Gdns. W14 . . . . 2G **99**
Lwr. Ash Est. TW17: Shep 6H **147**
Lwr. Belgrave St. SW1 . . . . 2J **17** (3F **101**)
Lwr. Boston Rd. W7 . . . . 1J **95**
Lwr. Broad St. RM10: Dag 1G **91**
Lower Camden BR7: Chst 7D **142**
Lwr. Church St. CR0: C'don 2B **168**
LOWER CLAPTON 4H 67
Lwr. Clapton Rd. E5 . . . . 3H **67**
Lwr. Clarendon Wlk. *W11* *6G* ***81***
(off Clarendon Rd.)
Lwr. Common Sth. SW15 . . . . 3D **116**
Lwr. Coombe St. CR0: C'don 4C **168**
Lwr. Downs Rd. SW20 . . . . 1F **153**
Lwr. Drayton Pl. CR0: C'don 2B **168**
LOWER EDMONTON 2B 34
LOWER FELTHAM 3J 129
Lower Fosters *NW4* *5E* ***44***
(off New Brent St.)
Lwr. George St. TW9: Rich 5D **114**
Lwr. Gravel Rd. BR2: Brom 1C **172**
Lower Grn. Gdns. KT4: Wor Pk 1C **164**
Lower Grn. W. CR4: Mitc 3C **154**
Lwr. Grosvenor Pl. SW1 . . . . 1K **17** (3F **101**)
Lower Gro. Rd. TW10: Rich 6F **115**
LOWER HALLIFORD 7F 147
Lwr. Hall La. E4 . . . . 5F **35**
(not continuous)
Lwr. Hampton Rd. TW16: Sun 3A **148**
Lwr. Ham Rd. KT2: King T 5D **132**
LOWER HOLLOWAY 5K 65
Lwr. Hook Bus. Pk. BR6: Downe 7D **172**
Lwr. James St. W1 . . . . 2B **12** (7G **83**)
Lwr. John St. W1 . . . . 2B **12** (7G **83**)
Lwr. Kenwood Av. EN2: Enf 5D **22**
Lwr. King's Rd. KT2: King T 1E **150**
Lwr. Lea Crossing E14 . . . . 7G **87**
E16 . . . . 7G **87**
Lwr. Maidstone Rd. N11 . . . . 6B **32**
Lower Mall W6 . . . . 5D **98**
Lwr. Mardyke Av. RM13: Rain 2J **91**
Lower Marsh SE1 . . . . 7J **13** (2A **102**)
Lwr. Marsh La. KT1: King T 4F **151**
Lwr. Merton Ri. NW3 . . . . 7C **64**
Lower Mill KT17: Ewe 7B **164**
Lwr. Morden La. SM4: Mord 6E **152**
Lwr. Mortlake Rd. TW9: Rich 4E **114**
Lwr. New Change Pas. *EC4* *1D* ***14***
(off One New Change)
Lower Pk. Rd. DA17: Belv 4G **109**
N11 . . . . 5B **32**
Lwr. Park Trad. Est. NW10 . . . . 4J **79**
LOWER PLACE 2J 79
Lower Pl. Bus. Cen. *NW10* *2K* ***79***
(off Steele Rd.)
Lwr. Queen's Rd. IG9: Buck H 2G **37**
Lwr. Richmond Rd. SW14 . . . . 3G **115**
SW15 . . . . 3D **116**
TW9: Rich 3G **115**
Lower Rd. DA8: Erith 3H **109**
DA17: Belv 3H **109**
HA2: Harr 1H **59**
SE1 . . . . 6J **13** (2A **102**)
SE8 . . . . 4K **103**
SE16 . . . . 2J **103**
(not continuous)
SM1: Sutt 4A **166**
Lwr. Robert St. *WC2* *3F* ***13***
(off Robert St.)
Lwr. Sand Hills KT6: Surb 7C **150**
Lwr. Sloane St. SW1 . . . . 4G **17** (4E **100**)
Lower Sq. TW7: Isle 3B **114**
Lower Sq., The *SM1: Sutt* *5K* ***165***
(off St Nicholas Way)
Lower Strand NW9 . . . . 2B **44**
Lwr. Sunbury Rd. TW12: Hamp 2D **148**
LOWER SYDENHAM 4K 139
Lwr. Sydenham Ind. Est. SE26 . . . . 5B **140**
Lwr. Teddington Rd. KT1: Hamp W 1D **150**
Lower Ter. NW3 . . . . 3A **64**
SE27 . . . . *5B* ***138***
(off Woodcote Pl.)
Lwr. Thames St. EC3 . . . . 3F **15** (7D **84**)
Lowerwood Ct. *W11* *6G* ***81***
(off Westbourne Pk. Rd.)
Lwr. Wood Rd. KT10: Clay 6B **162**
Lowestoft Cl. *E5* *2J* ***67***
(off Theydon Rd.)
Lowestoft M. E16 . . . . 2F **107**
Loweswater Cl. HA9: Wemb 2D **60**
Loweswater Ho. E3 . . . . 4B **86**
Lowfield Rd. NW6 . . . . 7J **63**
W3 . . . . 6H **79**
Low Hall Cl. E4 . . . . 7J **25**
Low Hall La. E17 . . . . 6A **50**
Low Hall Mnr. Bus. Cen. E17 . . . . 6A **50**
Lowick Rd. HA1: Harr 4J **41**
Lowlands Gdns. RM7: Rom 6H **55**
Lowlands Rd. HA1: Harr 6J **41**
HA5: Eastc 7A **40**
Lowman Rd. N7 . . . . 4K **65**
Lownde M. SW16 . . . . 2J **137**
Lowndes Cl. SW1 . . . . 2H **17** (3E **100**)
Lowndes Ct. SW1 . . . . 1F **17** (3D **100**)
W1 . . . . *1A* ***12***
(off Carnaby St.)
Lowndes Lodge *SW1* *1F* ***17***
(off Cadogan Pl.)
Lowndes M. SW16 . . . . 2J **137**
Lowndes Pl. SW1 . . . . 2G **17** (3E **100**)
Lowndes Sq. SW1 . . . . 7F **11** (2D **100**)
Lowndes St. SW1 . . . . 1F **17** (3E **100**)
Lownds Ct. BR1: Brom 2J **159**
Lowood Ct. *SE19* *5F* ***139***
(off Farquhar Rd.)
Lowood Ho. *E1* *7J* ***85***
(off Bewley St.)
Lowood St. E1 . . . . 7H **85**
Lowry Cl. DA8: Erith 4K **109**
Lowry Ct. *SE16* *5H* ***103***
(off Stubbs Dr.)
Lowry Cres. CR4: Mitc 2C **154**
Lowry Ho. *E14* *2C* ***104***
(off Cassilis Rd.)
N17 . . . . *1F* ***49***
(off Pembury Rd.)
W3 . . . . *3J* ***97***
(off Palmerston Rd.)
Lowry Rd. RM8: Dag 5B **72**
Lowshoe La. RM5: Col R 1G **55**
Lowswood Cl. HA6: Nwood 1E **38**
Lowther Dr. EN2: Enf 4D **22**
Lowther Hill SE23 . . . . 7A **122**
Lowther Ho. *SW1* *6B* ***18***
(off Churchill Gdns.)
Lowther Rd. E17 . . . . 2A **50**
HA7: Stan 3F **43**
KT2: King T 1F **151**
N7 . . . . 5A **66**
SW13 . . . . 1B **116**
Lowth Rd. SE5 . . . . 1C **120**
LOXFORD 5G 71
Loxford Av. E6 . . . . 2B **88**
Loxford Gdns. N5 . . . . 4B **66**
Loxford La. IG1: Ilf 5G **71**
IG3: Ilf 5G **71**
Loxford Rd. IG11: Bark 6F **71**
Loxford Ter. IG11: Bark 6G **71**
Loxham Rd. E4 . . . . 7J **35**
Loxham St. WC1 . . . . 2F **7** (3J **83**)
Loxley Cl. SE26 . . . . 5K **139**
Loxley Ho. HA9: Wemb 3E **60**
Loxley Rd. SW18 . . . . 1B **136**
TW12: Hamp 4D **130**
Loxton Rd. SE23 . . . . 1K **139**
Loxwood Cl. TW14: Bedf 1F **129**
Loxwood Rd. N17 . . . . 3E **48**
LSO St Lukes ***3D 8***
(off Old St.)
Lubbock Ho. *E14* *7D* ***86***
(off Poplar High St.)
Lubbock Rd. BR7: Chst 7D **142**
Lubbock St. SE14 . . . . 7J **103**
Lucan Ho. *N1* *1D* ***84***
(off Colville Est.)
Lucan Pl. SW3 . . . . 4C **16** (4C **100**)
Lucan Rd. EN5: Barn 3B **20**
Lucas Av. E13 . . . . 1K **87**
HA2: Harr 2E **58**
Lucas Cl. NW10 . . . . 7C **62**
Lucas Ct. SE26 . . . . 5A **140**
SW11 . . . . 1E **118**
Lucas Gdns. N2 . . . . 2A **46**
Lucas Ho. *SW10* *7K* ***99***
(off Coleridge Gdns.)
WC1 . . . . *3J* ***83***
(off Argyle Wlk.)
Lucas Rd. SE20 . . . . 6J **139**
Lucas Sq. NW11 . . . . 6J **45**
Lucas St. SE8 . . . . 1C **122**
Lucent Ho. *SW18* *5J* ***117***
(off Hardwicks Sq.)
Lucerne Cl. N13 . . . . 3D **32**
Lucerne Ct. DA18: Erith 3E **108**
Lucerne Gro. E17 . . . . 4F **51**
Lucerne M. W8 . . . . 1J **99**
Lucerne Rd. BR6: Orp 1K **173**
CR7: Thor H 5B **156**
N5 . . . . 4B **66**
Lucey Rd. SE16 . . . . 3G **103**
Lucey Way SE16 . . . . 3G **103**
Lucia Hgts. *E20* *5E* ***68***
(off Logan Cl.)
Lucie Av. TW15: Ashf 6D **128**
Lucien Rd. SW17 . . . . 4E **136**
SW19 . . . . 2K **135**
Lucinda Ct. E17 . . . . 2K **49**
EN1: Enf 4K **23**
Lucknow St. SE18 . . . . 7J **107**
Lucorn Cl. SE12 . . . . 6H **123**
Luctons Av. IG9: Buck H 1F **37**
Lucy Brown Ho. SE1 . . . . 5D **14**
Lucy Cres. W3 . . . . 5J **79**
Lucy Gdns. RM8: Dag 3F **73**
Luddesdon Rd.
DA8: Erith 7G **109**
Ludford Cl. CR0: Wadd 3B **168**
Ludgate B'way. EC4 . . . . 1A **14** (6B **84**)
Ludgate Cir. EC4 . . . . 1A **14** (6B **84**)
Ludgate Hill EC4 . . . . 1A **14** (6B **84**)
Ludgate Sq. EC4 . . . . 1B **14** (6B **84**)
Ludham NW5 . . . . 5D **64**
Ludham Cl. IG6: Ilf 1G **53**
SE28 . . . . 6C **90**

Ludlow Cl. BR2: Brom 3J **159**
HA2: Harr 4D **58**
Ludlow Ct. W3 2J **97**
Ludlow Rd. TW13: Felt 4J **129**
W5 4C **78**
Ludlow St. EC1 3C **8** (4C **84**)
Ludlow Way N2 4A **46**
Ludovick Wlk. SW15 4A **116**
Ludwell Ho. *W14* *3G* ***99***
(off Russell Rd.)
Ludwick M. SE14 7A **104**
Luffield Rd. SE2 3B **108**
Luffman Rd. SE12 3K **141**
Lugard Ho. *W12* *1D* ***98***
(off Bloemfontein Rd.)
Lugard Rd. SE15 2H **121**
Lugg App. E12 3E **70**
Luke Allsopp Sq. RM10: Dag 3H **73**
Luke Ho. *E1* *6H* ***85***
(off Tillman St.)
Lukes Cl. NW2 2C **62**
Luke St. EC2 3G **9** (4E **84**)
Lukin Cres. E4 3A **36**
Lukin St. E1 6J **85**
Luli Ct. SE14 6B **104**
Lullingstone Cl. BR5: St P 7B **144**
Lullingstone Cres. BR5: St P 7A **144**
Lullingstone Ho. *SE15* *6J* ***103***
(off Lovelinch Cl.)
Lullingstone La. SE13 6F **123**
Lullingstone Rd. DA17: Belv 6F **109**
Lullington Gth. BR1: Brom 7G **141**
N12 5C **30**
Lullington Rd. RM9: Dag 7E **72**
SE20 7G **139**
Lulot Gdns. N19 2F **65**
Lulsgate M. E3 4B **86**
Lulworth *NW1* *7H* ***65***
(off Wrotham Rd.)
SE17 *5D* ***102***
(off Portland St.)
Lulworth Av. HA9: Wemb 7C **42**
TW5: Hest 1F **113**
Lulworth Cl. HA2: Harr 3D **58**
Lulworth Ct. *N1* *7E* ***66***
(off St Peter's Way)
Lulworth Cres. CR4: Mitc 2C **154**
Lulworth Dr. HA5: Pinn 6B **40**
Lulworth Gdns. HA2: Harr 2C **58**
Lulworth Ho. SW8 7K **101**
Lulworth Rd. DA16: Well 2K **125**
SE9 2C **142**
SE15 2H **121**
Lulworth Waye UB4: Yead 6K **75**
Lumen Rd. HA9: Wemb 2D **60**
Lumiere Apartments SW11 4B **118**
Lumiere Bldg., The *E7* *5B* ***70***
(off Romford Rd.)
Lumiere Ct. SW17 2E **136**
Lumina Bldgs. *E14* *1E* ***104***
(off Prestons Rd.)
Lumina Bus. Pk. EN1: Enf 5B **24**
Lumina Loft Apartments *SE1* *7H* ***15***
(off Tower Bri. Rd.)
Lumina Way EN1: Enf 5B **24**
Luminosity Ct. W13 7B **78**
Lumley Cl. DA17: Belv 5G **109**
Lumley Ct. WC2 3F **13** (7J **83**)
Lumley Flats *SW1* *5G* ***17***
(off Holbein Pl.)
Lumley Gdns. SM3: Cheam 5G **165**
Lumley Rd. SM3: Cheam 5G **165**
Lumley St. W1 1H **11** (6E **82**)
Lumsdon *NW8* *1K* ***81***
(off Abbey Rd.)
Luna Ho. SE16 2G **103**
Lunan Ho. *E3* *2B* ***86***
(off Shetland Rd.)
Lunaria Ho. *E20* *5E* ***68***
(off Elis Way)
Luna Rd. CR7: Thor H 3C **156**
Lund Point E15 1E **86**
Lundy Dr. UB3: Harl 4G **93**
Lundy Wlk. N1 6C **66**
Lunham Rd. SE19 6E **138**
Luntley Pl. *E1* *6K* ***9***
(off Chicksand St.)
Lupin Cl. CR0: C'don 1K **169**
RM7: Rush G 2K **73**
SW2 2B **138**
UB7: W Dray 1E **174**
Lupin Cres. IG1: Ilf 6F **71**
Lupin M. E17 3E **50**
Lupino Ct. SE11 3H **19** (4K **101**)
Lupin Point SE1 7K **15**
Lupton Cl. SE12 3K **141**
Lupton St. NW5 4G **65**
(not continuous)
Lupus St. SW1 6K **17** (5F **101**)
Luralda Wharf E14 5F **105**
Lurgan Av. W6 6F **99**
Lurline Gdns. SW11 1E **118**
Luscombe Ct. BR2: Brom 2G **159**
Luscombe Way SW8 7J **101**
Lushington Ho.
KT12: Walt T 6A **148**
Lushington Rd. NW10 2D **80**
SE6 4D **140**
Lushington Ter. E8 5G **67**
Lutea Ho. *SM2: Sutt* *7A* ***166***
(off Walnut M.)
Luther Cl. HA8: Edg 2D **28**
Luther King Cl. E17 6B **50**
Luther M. TW11: Tedd 5K **131**
Luther Rd. TW11: Tedd 5K **131**
Luton Ho. *E13* *4J* ***87***
(off Luton Rd.)
Luton Pl. SE10 7E **104**
Luton Rd. DA14: Sidc 3C **144**
E13 4J **87**
E17 3B **50**
Luton St. NW8 4B **4** (4B **82**)
Lutton Ter. *NW3* *4A* ***64***
(off Lakis Cl.)
Luttrell Av. SW15 5D **116**
Lutwyche M. SE6 2B **140**
Lutwyche Rd. SE6 2B **140**
Lutyens Ho. *SW1* *6A* ***18***
(off Churchill Gdns.)
Lux Apartments *SW18* *5J* ***117***
(off Broomhill Rd.)
Luxborough Ho. *W1* *5G* ***5***
(off Luxborough St.)
Luxborough La. IG7: Chig 3H **37**
Luxborough St. W1 5G **5** (5E **82**)
Luxborough Twr. W1 5G **5**
Luxembourg M. E15 5G **69**
Luxemburg Gdns. W6 4F **99**
Luxfield Rd. SE9 1C **142**
Luxford St. SE16 4K **103**
Luxmore St. SE4 1B **122**
Luxor St. SE5 3C **120**
Lyall Av. SE21 4E **138**
Lyall M. SW1 2G **17** (3E **100**)
Lyall M. W. SW1 2G **17** (3E **100**)
Lyall St. SW1 2G **17** (3E **100**)
Lyal Rd. E3 2A **86**
Lycett Pl. W12 2C **98**
Lyceum Theatre
Covent Garden 2G **13**
Lychgate Mnr. HA1: Harr 7J **41**
Lych Ga. Wlk. UB3: Hayes 7H **75**
(not continuous)
Lyconby Gdns. CR0: C'don 7A **158**
Lydd Cl. DA14: Sidc 3J **143**
Lydden Ct. SE9 6J **125**
Lydden Gro. SW18 7K **117**
Lydden Rd. SW18 7K **117**
Lydd Rd. DA7: Bex 7F **109**
Lydeard Rd. E6 7D **70**
Lydford *NW1* *1G* ***83***
(off Royal College St.)
Lydford Cl. *N16* *5E* ***66***
(off Pellerin Rd.)
Lydford Rd. N15 5D **48**
NW2 6E **62**
W9 4H **81**
Lydhurst Av. SW2 2K **137**
Lydia Ct. *KT1: King T* *3E* ***150***
(off Grove Cres.)
N12 6F **31**
Lydney Cl. SW19 2G **135**
Lydon Rd. SW4 3G **119**
Lydstep Rd.
BR7: Chst 4E **142**
Lyford Rd. SW18 7B **118**
Lyford St. SE7 4C **106**
Lygon Ho. *E2* *1K* ***9***
(off Gosset St.)
SW6 *1G* ***117***
(off Fulham Pal. Rd.)
Lygon Pl. SW1 2J **17** (3F **101**)
Lyham Cl. SW2 6J **119**
Lyham Rd. SW2 5J **119**
Lyle Cl. CR4: Mitc 7E **154**
Lyle Ct. SM4: Mord 6B **154**
Lyly Ho. *SE1* *3D* ***102***
(off Burbage Cl.)
Lyme Farm Rd. SE12 4J **123**
Lyme Gro. E9 7J **67**
Lyme Gro. Ho. *E9* *7J* ***67***
(off Lyme Gro.)
Lymer Av. SE19 5F **139**
Lyme Rd. DA16: Well 1B **126**
Lymescote Gdns. SM1: Sutt 2J **165**
Lyme St. NW1 7G **65**
Lyme Ter. NW1 7G **65**
Lyminge Cl. DA14: Sidc 4K **143**
Lyminge Gdns. SW18 1C **136**
Lymington Av. N22 2A **48**
Lymington Cl. E6 5D **88**
SW16 2H **155**
Lymington Ct. SM1: Sutt 3K **165**
Lymington Dr. HA4: Ruis 2F **57**
Lymington Gdns. KT19: Ewe 5B **164**
Lymington Lodge *E14* *3F* ***105***
(off Schooner Cl.)
Lymington Rd. NW6 6K **63**
RM8: Dag 1D **72**
Lyminster Cl. UB4: Yead 5C **76**
Lympne *N17* *2D* ***48***
(off Gloucester Rd.)
Lympstone Gdns. SE15 7G **103**
Lynbridge Gdns. N13 4G **33**
Lynbrook Cl. RM13: Rain 2K **91**
Lynbrook Gro. SE15 7E **102**
Lynch Cl. SE3 2H **123**
Lynchen Cl. TW5: Cran 1K **111**
Lynch Wlk. *SE8* *6B* ***104***
(off Prince St.)
Lyncott Cres. SW4 4F **119**
Lyncourt SE3 2F **123**
Lyncroft Av. HA5: Pinn 5C **40**
Lyncroft Gdns. NW6 5J **63**
TW3: Houn 5G **113**
W13 2C **96**
Lyncroft Mans. NW6 5J **63**
Lyndale KT7: T Ditt 7J **149**
NW2 4H **63**
Lyndale Av. NW2 3H **63**
Lyndale Cl. SE3 6H **105**
Lyndean Ind. Est. SE2 3C **108**
Lynde Ho. KT12: Walt T 6A **148**
SW4 3H **119**
Lynden Ho. *E1* *3K* ***85***
(off Westfield Way)
Lynden Hyrst CR0: C'don 2F **169**
Lyndhurst Av. HA5: Pinn 1K **39**
KT5: Surb 1H **163**
N12 6J **31**
NW7 6F **29**
SW16 2H **155**
TW2: Whitt 1D **130**
Lyndhurst Av. TW16: Sun 3J **147**
UB1: S'hall 1F **95**
Lyndhurst Cl. BR6: Farnb 4F **173**
CR0: C'don 3F **169**
DA7: Bex 3H **127**
NW10 3K **61**
Lyndhurst Ct. E18 1J **51**
NW8 *1B* ***82***
(off Finchley Rd.)
SM2: Sutt *7J* ***165***
(off Grange Rd.)
Lyndhurst Dr. E10 7E **50**
KT3: N Mald 7A **152**
Lyndhurst Gdns. EN1: Enf 4K **23**
HA5: Pinn 1K **39**
IG2: Ilf 6H **53**
IG11: Bark 6J **71**
N3 1G **45**
NW3 5B **64**
Lyndhurst Gro. SE15 2E **120**
Lyndhurst Lodge *E14* *4F* ***105***
(off Millennium Dr.)
Lyndhurst Ri. IG7: Chig 4K **37**
Lyndhurst Rd.
CR7: Thor H 4A **156**
DA7: Bex 3H **127**
E4 7K **35**
N18 4B **34**
N22 6F **33**
NW3 5B **64**
UB6: G'frd 4F **77**
Lyndhurst Sq. SE15 1F **121**
Lyndhurst Ter. NW3 5B **64**
Lyndhurst Way SE15 1F **121**
SM2: Sutt 7J **165**
Lyndon Av. DA15: Sidc 5K **125**
SM6: Wall 3E **166**
Lyndon Ho. *E18* *1J* ***51***
(off Queen Mary Av.)
Lyndon Rd. DA17: Belv 4G **109**
Lyndon Yd. SW17 4A **136**
Lyne Cres. E17 1B **50**
Lynegrove Av. TW15: Ashf 5E **128**
Lyneham Dr. NW9 1A **44**
Lyneham Wlk. E5 5A **68**
HA5: Eastc 3H **39**
Lynette Av. SW4 6F **119**
Lynford Cl. HA8: Edg 1J **43**
Lynford Ct. *CR2: S Croy* *4E* ***168***
(off Coombe Rd.)
Lynford French Ho. *SE17* *5C* ***102***
(off Thrush St.)
Lynford Gdns. HA8: Edg 3C **28**
IG3: Ilf 2K **71**
Lynford Ter. N9 1A **34**
Lynhurst Cres. UB10: Hil 7E **56**
Lynhurst Rd. UB10: Hil 7E **56**
Lynmere Rd. DA16: Well 2B **126**
Lyn M. E3 3B **86**
N16 4E **66**
Lynmouth Av. EN1: Enf 6A **24**
SM4: Mord 6F **153**
Lynmouth Dr. HA4: Ruis 2K **57**
Lynmouth Gdns. TW5: Hest 7B **94**
UB6: G'frd 1B **78**
Lynmouth Rd. E17 6A **50**
N2 3D **46**
N16 1F **67**
UB6: G'frd 1B **78**
Lynn Cl. HA3: Hrw W 2H **41**
TW15: Ashf 5F **129**
Lynne Cl. BR6: Chels 6K **173**
SE23 7B **122**
Lynne Ct. *CR2: S Croy* *4E* ***168***
(off Birdhurst Rd.)
NW6 *7K* ***63***
(off Priory Rd.)
Lynnett Ct. *E9* *6A* ***68***
(off Annis Rd.)
Lynnett Rd. RM8: Dag 2D **72**
Lynne Way UB5: N'olt 2B **76**

Lynn Ho. *SE15* *6H* ***103***
(off Friary Est.)
Lynn M. E11 2G **69**
Lynn Rd. E11 2G **69**
IG2: Ilf 7H **53**
SW12 7F **119**
Lynn St. EN2: Enf 1J **23**
Lynscott Way CR2: S Croy 7B **168**
Lynstead Ct. BR3: Beck 2A **158**
Lynsted Cl. BR1: Brom 2A **160**
DA6: Bex 5H **127**
Lynsted Gdns. SE9 4B **124**
Lynton Av. N12 4G **31**
NW9 4B **44**
RM7: Mawney 1G **55**
W13 6A **78**
Lynton Cl. KT9: Chess 4E **162**
NW10 5A **62**
TW7: Isle 4K **113**
Lynton Cres. IG2: Ilf 6F **53**
Lynton Est. SE1 4G **103**
Lynton Gdns. EN1: Enf 7K **23**
N11 6C **32**
Lynton Grange N2 3D **46**
Lynton Ho. *IG1: Ilf* *2G* ***71***
(off High Rd.)
W2 *6A* ***82***
(off Hallfield Est.)
Lynton Mans. *SE1* *1J* ***19***
(off Westminster Bri. Rd.)
Lynton Mead N20 3D **30**
Lynton Rd. CR0: C'don 6A **156**
E4 5J **35**
HA2: Harr 2C **58**
KT3: N Mald 5K **151**
N8 5H **47**
(not continuous)
NW6 2H **81**
SE1 4F **103**
W3 7G **79**
Lynton Ter. W3 6J **79**
Lynton Wlk. UB4: Hayes 3G **75**
Lynwood Cl. E18 1A **52**
HA2: Harr 3C **58**
Lynwood Ct. KT1: King T 2H **151**
Lynwood Dr. HA6: Nwood 1H **39**
KT4: Wor Pk 2C **164**
Lynwood Gdns. CR0: Wadd 4K **167**
UB1: S'hall 6D **76**
Lynwood Gro. BR6: Orp 7J **161**
N21 1F **33**
Lynwood Rd. KT7: T Ditt 2A **162**
SW17 3D **136**
W5 3D **78**
Lynx Way E16 7B **88**
Lyon Bus. Pk. IG11: Bark 2J **89**
Lyon Ct. HA4: Ruis 1H **57**
Lyon Ho. *NW8* *4C* ***4***
(off Broadley St.)
Lyon Ind. Est. NW2 2D **62**
Lyon Meade HA7: Stan 1C **42**
Lyon Pk. Av. HA0: Wemb 6E **60**
(not continuous)
Lyon Rd. HA1: Harr 6K **41**
SW19 1A **154**
LYONSDOWN 5F **21**
Lyonsdown Av. EN5: New Bar 6F **21**
Lyonsdown Rd. EN5: New Bar 6F **21**
Lyons Pl. HA7: Stan 3D **26**
NW8 4A **4** (4B **82**)
Lyon St. N1 7K **65**
Lyons Wlk. W14 4G **99**
Lyon Way UB6: G'frd 1J **77**
Lyoth Rd. BR5: Farnb 2G **173**
Lyric Ct. *E8* *7F* ***67***
(off Holly St.)
Lyric Dr. UB6: G'frd 4F **77**
Lyric M. SE26 4J **139**
Lyric Rd. SW13 1B **116**
Lyric Sq. *W6* *4E* ***98***
(off King St.)
Lyric Theatre
Hammersmith 4E 98
Westminster *2C 12*
(off Shaftesbury Av.)
Lysander NW9 1B **44**
Lysander Gdns. KT6: Surb 6F **151**
Lysander Gro. N19 1H **65**
Lysander Ho. *E2* *2H* ***85***
(off Temple St.)
Lysander M. N19 1G **65**
Lysander Rd. CR0: Wadd 6K **167**
HA4: Ruis 2F **57**
Lysander Way BR6: Farnb 3G **173**
Lysia Ct. *SW6* *7F* ***99***
(off Lysia St.)
Lysias Rd. SW12 6F **119**
Lysia St. SW6 7F **99**
Lysons Wlk. SW15 4C **116**
Lytchet Rd. BR1: Brom 7J **141**
Lytchet Way EN3: Enf H 1D **24**
Lytchgate Cl. CR2: S Croy 7E **168**
Lytcott Dr. KT8: W Mole 3D **148**
Lytcott Gro. SE22 5E **120**
Lytham Cl. SE28 6E **90**
Lytham Gro. W5 3F **79**
Lytham St. SE17 5D **102**
Lyttelton Cl. NW3 7C **64**
Lyttelton Ct. N2 5A **46**
Lyttelton Ho. *E9* *7J* ***67***
(off Well St.)
Lyttelton Rd. E10 3D **68**
N2 5A **46**
Lyttelton Theatre *4H 13*
(within National Theatre)
Lyttleton Ct. *UB4: Yead* *4A* ***76***
(off Dunedin Way)
Lyttleton Rd. N8 3A **48**
Lytton Av. EN3: Enf L 1F **25**
N13 2F **33**
Lytton Cl. N2 6B **46**
UB5: N'olt 7D **58**
Lytton Ct. *WC1* *6F* ***7***
(off Barter St.)
Lytton Gdns. SM6: Bedd 4H **167**
Lytton Gro. SW15 5F **117**
Lytton Rd. E11 7G **51**
EN5: New Bar 4F **21**
HA5: Pinn 1C **40**
Lytton Strachey Path SE28 7B **90**
Lytton Ter. E12 6D **70**
Lyveden Rd. SE3 7K **105**
SW17 6D **136**

M

Mabbett Ho. *SE18* *6E* ***106***
(off Nightingale Pl.)
Mabel Evetts Ct. UB3: Hayes 7K **75**
Maberley Cres. SE19 7G **139**
Maberley Rd. BR3: Beck 3K **157**
SE19 1F **157**
Mabledon Pl. WC1 2D **6** (3H **83**)
Mablethorpe Rd. SW6 7G **99**
Mabley St. E9 5A **68**
Mablin Lodge IG9: Buck H 1F **37**
McAdam Dr. EN2: Enf 2G **23**
McAllister Gro. IG11: Bark 3A **90**
Macaret Cl. N20 7E **20**
Macarthur Cl. DA8: Erith 5K **109**
E7 6J **69**
HA9: Wemb 6H **61**
Macarthur Ter. SE7 6B **106**
Macartney Ho. *SE10* *7F* ***105***
(off Chesterfield Wlk.)
SW9 *1A* ***120***
(off Gosling Way)
Macaulay Ct. SW4 3F **119**
Macaulay Rd. E6 2B **88**
SW4 3F **119**
Macaulay Sq. SW4 4F **119**
Macaulay Wlk. *SW9* *1K* ***119***
(off Lett Rd.)
Macaulay Way SE28 1B **108**
McAuley Cl. SE1 1J **19** (3A **102**)
SE9 5F **125**
Macauley Ho. *W10* *5G* ***81***
(off Portobello Rd.)
Macauley M. SE13 2E **122**
McAusland Ho. *E3* *2B* ***86***
(off Wright's Rd.)
Macbean St. SE18 3F **107**
Macbeth Ho. N1 2E **84**
Macbeth St. W6 5D **98**
McBride Ho. *E3* *2B* ***86***
(off Libra Rd.)
McCabe Ct. *E16* *5H* ***87***
(off Barking Rd.)
McCall Cl. SW4 2J **119**
McCall Cres. SE7 5C **106**
McCall Ho. N7 4J **65**
McCarthy Rd. TW13: Hanw 5B **130**
Macclesfield Apartments *N1* *1D* ***84***
(off Branch Pl.)
Macclesfield Ho. *EC1* *2C* ***8***
(off Central St.)
Macclesfield Rd. EC1 1C **8** (3C **84**)
SE25 5J **157**
Macclesfield St. W1 2D **12** (7H **83**)
McCoid Way SE1 7C **14** (2C **102**)
McCrone M. NW3 6B **64**
McCullum Rd. E3 1B **86**
McDermott Cl. SW11 3C **118**
McDermott Rd. SE15 3G **121**
Macdonald Av.
RM10: Dag 3H **73**
Macdonald Ho. *SW11* *2E* ***118***
(off Dagnall St.)
McDonald Ho. *NW6* *3J* ***81***
(off Malvern Rd.)
Macdonald Rd. E7 4J **69**
E17 2E **50**
(not continuous)
N11 5J **31**
N19 2G **65**
McDonough Cl. KT9: Chess 4E **162**
McDougall Ct. TW9: Rich 2G **115**
McDowall Cl. E16 5H **87**
McDowall Rd. SE5 1C **120**
Macduff Rd. SW11 1E **118**
Mace Cl. E1 1H **103**
Mace Ho. TW7: Isle 1B **114**
McEntee Av. E17 1A **50**
Mace St. E2 2K **85**
McEwan Ho. *E3* *2B* ***86***
(off Roman Rd.)
McEwen Way *E15* *1F* ***87***
(off Rokeby St.)
Macey Ho. SW11 1C **118**
Macey St. *SE10* *6E* ***104***
(off Thames St.)
McFadden Ct. *E10* *3D* ***68***
(off Buckingham Rd.)
Macfarland Gro. SE15 7E **102**
Macfarlane La. TW7: Isle 6K **95**
Macfarlane Rd. W12 1E **98**
Macfarren Pl. NW1 4H **5** (4E **82**)
Macfarron Ho. *W10* *3G* ***81***
(off Parry Rd.)
McGlashon Ho. *E1* *4K* ***9***
(off Hunton St.)
McGrath Rd. E15 5H **69**
McGregor Ct. N1 1H **9**
Macgregor Rd. E16 5A **88**
McGregor Rd. W11 6H **81**
Machell Rd. SE15 3J **121**
McIndoe Ct. *N1* *1D* ***84***
(off Sherborne St.)
McIntosh Cl. RM1: Rom 3K **55**
SM6: Wall 7J **167**
Macintosh Ho. *W1* *5H* ***5***
(off Beaumont St.)
McIntosh Ho. *SE16* *4J* ***103***
(off Millender Wlk.)
McIntosh Rd. RM1: Rom 3K **55**
McIntyre Ct. *SE18* *4C* ***106***
(off Prospect Va.)
Mackay Ho. *W12* *7D* ***80***
(off White City Est.)
Mackay Rd. SW4 3F **119**
McKay Rd. SW20 7D **134**
McKeever Ho. *E16* *5J* ***87***
(off Hammersley Rd.)
McKellar Cl. WD23: B Hea 2B **26**
McKenna Ho. *E3* *2B* ***86***
(off Wright's Rd.)
Mackennal St. NW8 2C **82**
Mackenzie Cl. W12 7D **80**
Mackenzie Ho. *N8* *4J* ***47***
(off Pembroke Rd.)
NW2 3C **62**
Mackenzie Rd. BR3: Beck 2J **157**
N7 6K **65**
Mackenzie Wlk. E14 1C **104**
McKerrell Rd. SE15 1G **121**
Mackeson Rd. NW3 4D **64**
Mackie Rd. SW2 7A **120**
McKillop Way DA14: Sidc 7C **144**
Mackintosh La. E9 5K **67**
Mackintosh St. BR2: Brom 6B **160**
Macklin St. WC2 7F **7** (6J **83**)
Mackonochie Ho. *EC1* *5J* ***7***
(off Baldwins Gdns.)
Mackrow Wlk. E14 7E **86**
Mack's Rd. SE16 4G **103**
Mackworth Ho. *NW1* *1A* ***6***
(off Augustus St.)
Mackworth St. NW1 1A **6** (3G **83**)
McLaren Ho. *SE1* *7A* ***14***
(off St Georges Cir.)
Maclaren M. SW15 4E **116**
Maclean Rd. SE23 6A **122**
McLeod Ct. SE22 1G **139**
Macleod Rd. N21 5D **22**
McLeod Rd. SE2 4B **108**
McLeod's M. SW7 4K **99**
Macleod St. SE17 5C **102**
Maclise Ho. *SW1* *4E* ***18***
(off Marsham St.)
Maclise Rd. W14 3G **99**
Macmillan Ct. HA2: Harr 1E **58**
UB6: G'frd 4H **77**
Macmillan Ho. *NW8* *2D* ***4***
(off Lorne Cl.)
McMillan Ho. *SE4* *3A* ***122***
(off Arica Rd.)
SE14 1A **122**
McMillan St. SE8 6C **104**
McMillan Student Village SE8 6C **104**
Macmillan Way SW17 4F **137**
McNair Rd. UB2: S'hall 3F **95**
Macnamara Ho. *SW10* *7B* ***100***
(off Worlds End Est.)
McNeil Rd. SE5 2E **120**
McNicol Dr. NW10 2J **79**
Macoma Rd. SE18 6H **107**
Macoma Ter. SE18 6H **107**
Maconochies Rd. E14 5D **104**
MacOwan Theatre 4J **99**
Macquarie Way E14 4D **104**
McRae La. CR4: Mitc 7D **154**
Macready Ho. *W1* *6E* ***4***
(off Crawford St.)
Macready Pl. N7 4J **65**
(not continuous)
Macrea Ho. *E3* *3B* ***86***
(off Bow Rd.)
Macroom Ho. *W9* *3H* ***81***
(off Macroom Rd.)
Macroom Rd. W9 3H **81**
Macs Ho. E17 3D **50**
Mac's Pl. EC4 7J **7**
Madame Tussaud's 4G **5** (4E **82**)

Mada Rd. BR6: Farnb 3F **173**
Maddams St. E3 ....4D **86**
Madderfields Ct. N11 ....1H **47**
Maddison Cl. N2 ....2A **46**
  TW11: Tedd 6K **131**
Maddison Ct. E16 ....5J **87**
  (off Hastings Rd.)
Maddocks Cl. DA14: Sidc 5E **144**
Maddocks Ho. E1 ....7H **85**
  (off Cornwall St.)
Maddock Way SE17 ....6B **102**
Maddox St. W1 ....2K **11** (7F **83**)
Madeira Av. BR1: Brom 7G **141**
Madeira Gro. IG8: Wfd G 6F **37**
Madeira Rd. CR4: Mitc 4D **154**
  E11 ....1F **69**
  N13 ....4G **33**
  SW16 ....5J **137**
Madeleine Cl.
  RM6: Chad H 6C **54**
Madeleine Ct. HA7: Stan 7K **27**
  (off Letchworth Rd.)
Madeley Ho. W5 ....6D **78**
Madeline Gro. IG1: Ilf 5H **71**
Madeline Rd. SE20 ....7G **139**
Madge Gill Way E6 ....1C **88**
  (off High St. Nth.)
Madge Hill W7 ....7J **77**
Madinah Rd. E8 ....6G **67**
Madison, The SE1 ....6E **14**
  (off Long La.)
Madison Bldg. SE10 ....1D **122**
  (off Blackheath Rd.)
Madison Cl. SM2: Sutt 7B **166**
Madison Ct. RM10: Dag 6H **73**
Madison Cres. DA7: Bex 7C **108**
Madison Gdns. BR2: Brom 3H **159**
  DA7: Bex 7C **108**
Madison Ho. E14 ....7B **86**
  (off Victory Pl.)
Madison Way E20 ....5D **68**
Madoc Cl. NW2 ....2J **63**
Madras Pl. N7 ....6A **66**
Madras Rd. IG1: Ilf 4F **71**
Madrid Rd. SW13 ....1C **116**
Madrigal La. SE5 ....7B **102**
Madron St. SE17 ....5E **102**
Mafeking Av. E6 ....2C **88**
  IG2: Ilf 7H **53**
  TW8: Bford 6E **96**
Mafeking Rd. E16 ....4H **87**
  EN1: Enf 3A **24**
  N17 ....2G **49**
Magazine Ga. W2 ....4D **10** (1C **100**)
Magdala Av. N19 ....2G **65**
Magdala Rd. CR2: S Croy 7D **168**
  TW7: Isle 3A **114**
Magdalene Cl. SE15 ....2H **121**
Magdalene Gdns. E6 ....4E **88**
  N20 ....1J **31**
Magdalene Ho. TW17: Shep 4B **146**
Magdalen Ho. E16 ....1K **105**
  (off Keats Av.)
Magdalen M. NW3 ....6A **64**
  (off Frognal)
Magdalen Pas. E1 ......2K **15** (7F **85**)
Magdalen Rd. SW18 ....1A **136**
Magdalen St. SE1 ......5G **15** (1E **102**)
Magee St. SE11 ......7J **19** (6A **102**)
Magellan Blvd. E16 ....7G **89**
Magellan Ct. NW10 ....7K **61**
  (off Brentfield Rd.)
Magellan Ho. E1 ....4K **85**
  (off Ernest St.)
Magellan Pl. E14 ....4C **104**
Magistrates' Court
  Barkingside 3G **53**
  Belmarsh 2J **107**
  Bexley 4G **127**
  Bromley 1H **159**
  Camberwell Green 1D **120**

Magistrates' Court
  City of London 1E **14**
  Croydon 3D **168**
  Ealing 1A **96**
    (off Green Man La.)
  Hammersmith 5F **99**
  Hendon 6B **44**
  Highbury Corner 6A **66**
  Lavender Hill 3D **118**
  Richmond-upon-Thames 4D **114**
  Stratford 7F **69**
  Thames 3C **86**
  Westminster 5D **4** (5C **82**)
  Willesden 6B **62**
  Wimbledon 6J **135**
Magna Sq. SW14 ....3J **115**
  (off Moore Cl.)
Magnaville Rd. WD23: B Hea ...1D **26**
Magnet Rd. HA9: Wemb 2D **60**
Magnin Cl. E8 ....1G **85**
Magnolia Cl. E10 ....2C **68**
  KT2: King T 6H **133**
Magnolia Ct. HA3: Kenton 7F **43**
  SM2: Sutt 7J **165**
    (off Grange Rd.)
  SM6: Wall 5F **167**
  TW9: Kew 1H **115**
  TW13: Felt 1J **129**
    (off Plum Cl.)
  UB5: N'olt 4C **76**
  UB10: Hil 6D **56**
Magnolia Gdns. E10 ....2C **68**
  HA8: Edg 4D **28**
Magnolia Ho. SE8 ....6B **104**
    (off Evelyn St.)
  TW16: Sun 7H **129**
Magnolia Lodge E4 ....3J **35**
  W8 ....3K **99**
    (off St Mary's Ga.)
Magnolia Pl. HA2: Harr 2H **41**
  SW4 ....5J **119**
  W5 ....5D **78**
Magnolia Rd. W4 ....6H **97**
Magnolia St. UB7: W Dray 4A **92**
Magnolia Way KT19: Ewe 5J **163**
Magnolia Wharf W4 ....6G **97**
Magpie All. EC4 ......1K **13** (6A **84**)
Magpie Cl. E7 ....5H **69**
  EN1: Enf 1B **24**
  NW9 ....2A **44**
Magpie Hall Cl. BR2: Brom 6C **160**
Magpie Hall La. BR2: Brom 5D **160**
Magpie Hall Rd. WD23: B Hea ...2D **26**
Magpie Ho. E3 ....1B **86**
    (off Sycamore Av.)
Magpie Pl. SE14 ....5H **103**
Magri Wlk. E1 ....5J **85**
Maguire Apartments E3 ....5B **86**
    (off Geoff Cade Way)
Maguire Dr.
  TW10: Ham 4C **132**
Maguire St. SE1 ......6K **15** (2F **103**)
Maha Bldg. E3 ....3C **86**
    (off Merchant St.)
Mahatma Gandhi Ind. Est.
  SE24 ....4B **120**
Mahlon Av. HA4: Ruis 5K **57**
    (not continuous)
Mahogany Cl. SE16 ....1A **104**
Mahon Cl. EN1: Enf 1A **24**
Mahoney Ho. SE14 ....1B **122**
    (off Heald St.)
Maibeth Gdns. BR3: Beck 4A **158**
Maida Av. E4 ....7J **25**
  W2 ....4A **4** (5A **82**)
MAIDA HILL 4H **81**
Maida Rd. DA17: Belv 3G **109**
MAIDA VALE 4K **81**
Maida Va. W9 ....3A **4** (2K **81**)
Maida Way E4 ....7J **25**
Maiden Erlegh Av. DA5: Bexl ...1E **144**

Maiden La. NW1 ....7H **65**
  SE1 ....5D **14** (1C **102**)
  WC2 ....3F **13** (7J **83**)
Maiden Pl. NW5 ....3G **65**
Maiden Rd. E15 ....7G **69**
Maidenstone Hill SE10 ....1E **122**
Maids of Honour Row TW9: Rich ...5D **114**
Maidstone Av. RM5: Col R 2J **55**
Maidstone Bldgs. M. SE1 ...5D **14** (1C **102**)
Maidstone Ho. E14 ....6D **86**
    (off Carmen St.)
Maidstone Rd. DA14: Sidc, Swan ...6D **144**
  N11 ....6B **32**
Main Av. EN1: Enf 5A **24**
Main Dr. HA9: Wemb 3D **60**
Main Mill SE10 ....7D **104**
    (off Greenwich High St.)
Mainridge Rd. BR7: Chst 4E **142**
Main Rd. DA14: Sidc 3H **143**
  TW13: Hanw 5B **130**
Mainwaring Cl. CR4: Mitc 2E **154**
Mais Ho. SE26 ....2H **139**
Maismore St. SE15 ....6G **103**
Maisonettes, The SM1: Sutt ...5H **165**
Maitland Cl. SE10 ....7D **104**
  TW4: Houn 3D **112**
Maitland Ct. W2 ....2A **10**
    (off Lancaster Ter.)
Maitland Ho. E2 ....2J **85**
    (off Waterloo Gdns.)
  SW1 ....7A **18**
    (off Churchill Gdns.)
Maitland Pk. Est. NW3 ....6D **64**
Maitland Pk. Rd. NW3 ....6D **64**
Maitland Pk. Vs. NW3 ....6D **64**
Maitland Pl. E5 ....4H **67**
Maitland Rd. E15 ....6H **69**
  SE26 ....6K **139**
Maitland Yd. W13 ....1A **96**
Maize Row E14 ....7B **86**
Majendie Rd. SE18 ....5H **107**
Majestic Way CR4: Mitc 2D **154**
Major Cl. SW9 ....3B **120**
Major Draper St. SE18 ....3F **107**
Major Rd. E15 ....5F **69**
  SE16 ....3G **103**
Makepeace Av. N6 ....2E **64**
Makepeace Mans. N6 ....2E **64**
Makepeace Rd. E11 ....4J **51**
  UB5: N'olt 2C **76**
Makers' Yd. E20 ....5C **68**
Makinen Ho. IG9: Buck H 1F **37**
Makins St. SW3 ......4D **16** (4C **100**)
Malabar Ct. W12 ....7D **80**
    (off India Way)
Malabar St. E14 ....2C **104**
Malam Ct. SE11 ......4J **19** (4A **102**)
Malam Gdns. E14 ....7D **86**
Malbrook Rd. SW15 ....4D **116**
Malcolm Cl. SE20 ....7J **139**
Malcolm Ct. E7 ....6H **69**
  HA7: Stan 5H **27**
  NW4 ....6C **44**
Malcolm Cres. NW4 ....6C **44**
Malcolm Dr.
  KT6: Surb 1E **162**
Malcolm Ho. N1 ....2E **84**
    (off Arden Est.)
Malcolm Pl. E2 ....4J **85**
Malcolm Rd. E1 ....4J **85**
  SE20 ....7J **139**
  SE25 ....6G **157**
  SW19 ....6G **135**
  UB10: Ick 4B **56**
Malcolm Sargent Ho. E16 .....1K **105**
    (off Evelyn Rd.)
Malcolmson Ho. SW1 ....6C **18**
    (off Aylesford St.)
Malcolms Way N14 ....5B **22**
Malcolm Way E11 ....5J **51**

Malden Av. SE25 ....4H **157**
  UB6: G'frd 5J **59**
Malden Ct. KT3: N Mald 3D **152**
  N4 ....6C **48**
Malden Cres. NW1 ....6E **64**
Malden Golf Course 2A **152**
MALDEN GREEN 1C **164**
Malden Grn. Av. KT4: Wor Pk ...1B **164**
Malden Grn. M. KT4: Wor Pk ...1C **164**
Malden Hill KT3: N Mald 3B **152**
Malden Hill Gdns. KT3: N Mald ...3B **152**
MALDEN JUNC. 5B **152**
Malden Pk. KT3: N Mald 6B **152**
Malden Pl. NW5 ....5E **64**
Malden Rd. KT3: N Mald 5A **152**
  KT4: Wor Pk 6B **152**
  NW5 ....5D **64**
  SM3: Cheam 4F **165**
Malden Way KT3: N Mald 6K **151**
Maldon Cl. E15 ....5G **69**
  N1 ....1C **84**
  SE5 ....3E **120**
Maldon Cl. E6 ....1E **88**
  SM6: Wall 5G **167**
Maldon District Society
  of Model Engineers, The ...1A **162**
Maldon Rd. N9 ....3A **34**
  RM7: Rush G 7J **55**
  SM6: Wall 5F **167**
  W3 ....7J **79**
Maldon Wlk. IG8: Wfd G 6F **37**
Malet Pl. WC1 ....4C **6** (4H **83**)
Malet St. WC1 ....4C **6** (4H **83**)
Maley Av. SE27 ....2B **138**
Malford Ct. E18 ....2J **51**
Malford Gro. E18 ....4H **51**
Malfort Rd. SE5 ....3E **120**
Malham Cl. N11 ....6K **31**
Malham Rd. SE23 ....1K **139**
Malham Rd. Ind. Est. SE23 ...1K **139**
Malham Ter. N18 ....5C **34**
Malibu Ct. SE26 ....3H **139**
Mall, The BR1: Brom 3J **159**
  CR0: C'don 2C **168**
  DA6: Bex 4G **127**
  E15 ....7F **69**
  HA3: Kenton 6F **43**
  KT6: Surb 5D **150**
  N14 ....3D **32**
  RM10: Dag 6G **73**
  SW1 ....6B **12** (2G **101**)
  SW14 ....5J **115**
  TW8: Bford 6D **96**
  W5 ....7E **78**
Mallams M. SW9 ....3B **120**
Mallard Cl. E9 ....6B **68**
  EN5: New Bar 6G **21**
  NW6 ....2J **81**
  TW2: Whitt 7E **112**
  W7 ....2J **95**
Mallard Ct. E17 ....3F **51**
Mallard Ho. NW8 ....2C **82**
    (off Bridgeman St.)
  SW6 ....1A **118**
    (off Station Ct.)
Mallard Path SE28 ....3H **107**
Mallard Pl. N22 ....2K **47**
  TW1: Twick 2A **132**
Mallard Point E3 ....3D **86**
    (off Rainhill Way)
Mallards E11 ....7J **51**
    (off Blake Hall Rd.)
Mallards Rd. IG8: Wfd G 7E **36**
  IG11: Bark 4A **90**
Mallard Wlk. BR3: Beck 5K **157**
  DA14: Sidc 6C **144**
Mallard Way NW9 ....7J **43**
  SM6: Wall 1G **167**
Mall Chambers W8 ....1J **99**
    (off Kensington Mall)
Mallet Dr. UB5: N'olt 5D **58**

Mallet Rd. SE13 . . . 6F 123
Mall Galleries . . . 4D 12
Malling SE13 . . . 5D 122
Malling Cl. CR0: C'don . . . 6J 157
Malling Gdns. SM4: Mord . . . 6A 154
Malling Way BR2: Hayes . . . 7H 159
Mallinson Rd. CR0: Bedd . . . 3H 167
SW11 . . . 5C 118
Mallinson Sports Cen. . . . 7D 46
Mallon Gdns. *E1* . . . *7K 9*
(off Commercial St.)
Mallord St. SW3 . . . 7B 16 (6B 100)
Mallory Bldgs. *EC1* . . . *4A 8*
(off St John St.)
Mallory Cl. E14 . . . 5D 86
SE4 . . . 4A 122
Mallory Ct. *N17* . . . *6A 34*
(off Cannon Rd.)
SE12 . . . 7K 123
Mallory Gdns. EN4: E Barn . . . 7K 21
Mallory St. NW8 . . . 3D 4 (4C 82)
Mallory Way SE3 . . . 4K 123
Mallow Cl. CR0: C'don . . . 1K 169
Mallow Mead NW7 . . . 7B 30
Mallows, The UB10: Ick . . . 3D 56
Mallow St. EC1 . . . 3E 8 (4D 84)
Mall Rd. W6 . . . 5D 98
Mall Vs. *W6* . . . *5D 98*
(off Mall Rd.)
Malmains Cl. BR3: Beck . . . 4F 159
Malmains Way BR3: Beck . . . 4E 158
Malmesbury *E2* . . . *2J 85*
(off Cyprus St.)
Malmesbury Cl. HA5: Eastc . . . 4H 39
Malmesbury Rd. E3 . . . 3B 86
E16 . . . 5G 87
E18 . . . 1H 51
SM4: Mord . . . 7A 154
Malmesbury Ter. E16 . . . 5H 87
Malmsey Ho. SE11 . . . 5H 19 (5K 101)
Malmsmead Ho. *E9* . . . *5B 68*
(off Homerton Rd.)
Malory Cl. BR3: Beck . . . 2A 158
Malpas Dr. HA5: Pinn . . . 5B 40
Malpas Rd. E8 . . . 5H 67
RM9: Dag . . . 6D 72
SE4 . . . 2B 122
Malswick Ct. *SE15* . . . *7E 102*
(off Tower Mill Rd.)
Malta Rd. E10 . . . 1C 68
Malta St. EC1 . . . 3A 8 (4B 84)
Maltby Cl. BR6: Orp . . . 1K 173
Maltby Dr. EN1: Enf . . . 1C 24
Maltby Ho. *SE1* . . . *7J 15*
(off Maltby St.)
SE3 . . . 4A 124
Maltby Rd. KT9: Chess . . . 6G 163
Maltby St. SE1 . . . 7J 15 (2F 103)
Malthouse Ct. *TW8: Bford* . . . *6E 96*
(off High St.)
Malthouse Dr. TW13: Hanw . . . 5B 130
W4 . . . 6B 98
Malthouse Pas. *SW13* . . . *2B 116*
(off Clevelands Gdns.)
Malthus Path SE28 . . . 1C 108
Malting Ho. *E14* . . . *7B 86*
(off Oak La.)
Maltings, The BR6: Orp . . . 1K 173
W4 . . . *5G 97*
(off Spring Gro.)
Maltings Cl. E3 . . . 3E 86
SW13 . . . 2B 116
Maltings Lodge *W4* . . . *6A 98*
(off Corney Reach Way)
Maltings M. DA15: Sidc . . . 3A 144
Maltings Pl. SE1 . . . 7H 15
SW6 . . . 1K 117
Malting Way TW7: Isle . . . 3K 113
Malton M. SE18 . . . 6J 107
W10 . . . 6G 81
Malton Rd. W10 . . . 6G 81
Malton St. SE18 . . . 6J 107
Maltravers St. WC2 . . . 2H 13 (7K 83)
Malt St. SE1 . . . 6G 103
Malva Cl. SW18 . . . 5K 117
Malvern Av. DA7: Bex . . . 7E 108
E4 . . . 7A 36
HA2: Harr . . . 3C 58
Malvern Cl. CR4: Mitc . . . 3G 155
KT6: Surb . . . 1E 162
SE20 . . . 2G 157
UB10: Ick . . . 2C 56
W10 . . . 5H 81
Malvern Ct. SM2: Sutt . . . 7J 165
SW7 . . . 3B 16
W12 . . . *2C 98*
(off Hadyn Pk. Rd.)
Malvern Dr. IG3: Bark, Ilf . . . 4K 71
IG8: Wfd G . . . 5F 37
TW13: Hanw . . . 5B 130
Malvern Gdns. HA3: Kenton . . . 4E 42
NW2 . . . 2G 63
Malvern Ho. N16 . . . 1F 67
SE17 . . . *5C 102*
(off Liverpool Gro.)
Malvern M. NW6 . . . 3J 81
Malvern Pl. NW6 . . . 3H 81
Malvern Rd. CR7: Thor H . . . 4A 156
E6 . . . 1C 88
E8 . . . 7G 67
E11 . . . 2G 69
KT6: Surb . . . 2E 162
N8 . . . 3K 47
N17 . . . 3G 49
NW6 . . . 2H 81
(not continuous)
TW12: Hamp . . . 7E 130
UB3: Harl . . . 7G 93
Malvern Ter. N1 . . . 1A 84
N9 . . . 1A 34
Malvern Way W13 . . . 5B 78
Malwood Rd. SW12 . . . 6F 119
Malyons, The TW17: Shep . . . 6F 147
Malyons Rd. SE13 . . . 6D 122
Malyons Ter. SE13 . . . 5D 122
Managers St. E14 . . . 1E 104
Manatee Pl. SM6: Bedd . . . 3H 167
Manaton Cl. SE15 . . . 3H 121
Manaton Cres. UB1: S'hall . . . 6E 76
Manbey Gro. E15 . . . 6G 69
Manbey M. E15 . . . 6G 69
Manbey Pk. Rd. E15 . . . 6G 69
Manbey Rd. E15 . . . 6G 69
Manbey St. E15 . . . 6G 69
Manbre Rd. W6 . . . 6E 98
Manbrough Av. E6 . . . 3D 88
Manchester Ct. *E16* . . . *6K 87*
(off Garvary Rd.)
Manchester Dr. W10 . . . 4G 81
Manchester Gro. E14 . . . 5E 104
Manchester Ho. *SE17* . . . *5C 102*
(off East St.)
Manchester M. W1 . . . 6G 5
Manchester Rd. CR7: Thor H . . . 3C 156
E14 . . . 5E 104
N15 . . . 6D 48
Manchester Sq. W1 . . . 7G 5 (6E 82)
Manchester St. W1 . . . 6G 5 (5E 82)
Manchester Way
RM10: Dag . . . 4H 73
Manchuria Rd. SW11 . . . 6E 118
Manciple St. SE1 . . . 7E 14 (2D 102)
Mancroft Ct. *NW8* . . . *1B 82*
(off St John's Wood Pk.)
Mandalay Rd. SW4 . . . 5G 119
Mandara Pl. *SE8* . . . *4A 104*
(off Yeoman St.)
Mandarin Ct. *NW10* . . . *6K 61*
(off Mitchellbrook Way)
SE8 . . . 6B 104
Mandarin St. E14 . . . 7C 86
Mandarin Way UB4: Yead . . . 6B 76
Mandarin Wharf *N1* . . . *1E 84*
(off De Beauvoir Cres.)
Mandela Cl. NW10 . . . 7J 61
W12 . . . 7D 80
Mandela Ho. *E2* . . . *2J 9*
(off Virginia Rd.)
SE5 . . . 2B 120
Mandela Rd. E16 . . . 6J 87
Mandela St. NW1 . . . 1G 83
SW9 . . . 7A 102
(not continuous)
Mandela Way SE1 . . . 4E 102
Mandel Ho. SW18 . . . 4J 117
Manderley *W14* . . . *3H 99*
(off Oakwood La.)
Mandeville Cl. SE3 . . . 7H 105
SW20 . . . 7G 135
Mandeville Ct. E4 . . . 5F 35
Mandeville Dr. KT6: Surb . . . 1D 162
Mandeville Ho. *SE1* . . . *5F 103*
(off Rolls Rd.)
SW4 . . . 5G 119
Mandeville M. SW4 . . . 4J 119
Mandeville Pl. W1 . . . 7H 5 (6E 82)
Mandeville Rd. N14 . . . 2A 32
TW7: Isle . . . 2A 114
TW17: Shep . . . 5C 146
UB5: N'olt . . . 7E 58
Mandeville St. E5 . . . 3A 68
Mandrake Rd. SW17 . . . 3D 136
Mandrake Way E15 . . . 7G 69
Mandrell Rd. SW2 . . . 5J 119
Manesty Ct. *N14* . . . *7C 22*
(off Ivy Rd.)
Manette St. W1 . . . 1D 12 (6H 83)
Manfred Rd. SW15 . . . 5H 117
Manger Rd. N7 . . . 6J 65
Mangold Way DA18: Erith . . . 3D 108
Manhattan Bldg. E3 . . . 2C 86
Manhattan Bus. Pk. W5 . . . 3E 78
Manhattan Loft Gdns. E20 . . . 6E 68
Manilla Ct. *RM6: Chad H* . . . *6B 54*
(off Quarles Pk. Rd.)
Manilla St. E14 . . . 2C 104
Manilla Wlk. SE10 . . . 4G 105
Manister Rd. SE2 . . . 3A 108
Manitoba Ct. *SE16* . . . *2J 103*
(off Canada Est.)
Manitoba Gdns. BR6: Chels . . . 6K 173
Manley Ct. N16 . . . 3F 67
Manley Ho. SE11 . . . 5J 19 (4A 102)
Manley St. NW1 . . . 1E 82
Manna Ho. *E20* . . . *6E 68*
(off Glade Wlk.)
Mannan Ho. *E3* . . . *2B 86*
(off Roman Rd.)
Mann Cl. CR0: C'don . . . 3C 168
Manneby Prior *N1* . . . *1H 7*
(off Cumming St.)
Mannequin Ho. E17 . . . 3K 49
Manning Ct. *SE28* . . . *1B 108*
(off Titmuss Av.)
Manningford Cl. EC1 . . . 1A 8 (3B 84)
Manning Gdns. CR0: C'don . . . 7H 157
HA3: Kenton . . . 7D 42
Manning Ho. *W11* . . . *6G 81*
(off Westbourne Pk. Rd.)
Manning Pl. TW10: Rich . . . 6F 115
Manning Rd. E17 . . . 5A 50
RM10: Dag . . . 6G 73
Manningtree Cl. SW19 . . . 1G 135
Manningtree Rd.
HA4: Ruis . . . 4K 57
Manningtree St. E1 . . . 6G 85
Mannin Rd. RM6: Chad H . . . 7B 54
Mannock Cl. NW9 . . . 3K 43
Mannock M. E18 . . . 1A 52
Mannock Rd. N22 . . . 3B 48
Mann's Cl. TW7: Isle . . . 5K 113
Manns Rd. HA8: Edg . . . 6B 28
Manns Ter. SE27 . . . 3C 138
Manny Shinwell Ho. *SW6* . . . *6H 99*
(off Clem Attlee Ct.)
Manoel Rd. TW2: Twick . . . 2G 131
Manor, The IG8: Wfd G . . . 7K 37
Manor Av. SE4 . . . 2B 122
TW4: Houn . . . 3B 112
UB5: N'olt . . . 7D 58
Manorbrook SE3 . . . 4J 123
MANOR CIRCUS . . . 3G 115
Manor Cl. DA1: Cray . . . 4K 127
E17 . . . 1A 50
EN5: Barn . . . 4B 20
HA4: Ruis . . . 1H 57
KT4: Wor Pk . . . 1A 164
NW7 . . . 5E 28
NW9 . . . 5H 43
RM10: Dag . . . 6K 73
SE28 . . . 7C 90
Manor Cotts. HA6: Nwood . . . 1H 39
N2 . . . *2A 46*
(off Manor Cotts. App.)
Manor Cotts. App. N2 . . . 2A 46
Manor Ct. BR4: W W'ck . . . 1D 170
DA7: Bex . . . 4H 127
E4 . . . 1B 36
E10 . . . 1D 68
HA1: Harr . . . 6K 41
HA9: Wemb . . . 5E 60
IG11: Bark . . . 7K 71
KT2: King T . . . 1G 151
KT8: W Mole . . . 4E 148
N2 . . . 5D 46
N14 . . . 2C 32
N20 . . . *3J 31*
(off York Way)
SM5: Cars . . . 3E 166
SW2 . . . 5K 119
SW3 . . . *6D 16*
(off Hemus Pl.)
SW6 . . . 1K 117
SW16 . . . 3J 137
TW2: Twick . . . 2G 131
W3 . . . 4G 97
Manor Ct. Rd. W7 . . . 7J 77
Manor Cres. KT5: Surb . . . 6G 151
Manor Dene SE28 . . . 6C 90
Manordene Cl. KT7: T Ditt . . . 1A 162
Manordene Rd. SE28 . . . 6C 90
Manor Dr. HA9: Wemb . . . 4F 61
KT5: Surb . . . 6F 151
KT10: Hin W . . . 2A 162
KT19: Ewe . . . 6A 164
N14 . . . 1A 32
N20 . . . 4J 31
NW7 . . . 5E 28
TW13: Hanw . . . 5B 130
TW16: Sun . . . 2J 147
Manor Dr., The KT4: Wor Pk . . . 1A 164
Manor Dr. Nth. KT3: N Mald . . . 7K 151
KT4: Wor Pk . . . 1A 164
Manor Est. SE16 . . . 4H 103
Manor Farm
Ruislip . . . 7G 39
Mnr. Farm Av. TW17: Shep . . . 6D 146
Mnr. Farm Cl. KT4: Wor Pk . . . 1A 164
Mnr. Farm Ct. E6 . . . 3D 88
Mnr. Farm Dr. E4 . . . 3B 36
Mnr. Farm Rd. HA0: Wemb . . . 2D 78
SW16 . . . 2A 156
Manorfield Cl. *N19* . . . *4G 65*
(off Fulbrook M.)
Manor Flds. SW15 . . . 6F 117
Manorfields Cl. BR7: Chst . . . 3K 161
Manor Gdns. CR2: S Croy . . . 6F 169
HA4: Ruis . . . 5A 58
N7 . . . 3J 65
SW4 . . . *2G 119*
(off Larkhall Ri.)
SW20 . . . 2H 153
TW9: Rich . . . 4F 115
TW12: Hamp . . . 7F 131

Manor Gdns. TW16: Sun 1J 147
W3 4G 97
W4 5A 98
Manor Ga. UB5: N'olt 7C 58
Manorgate Rd. KT2: King T 1G 151
Manor Gro. BR3: Beck 2D 158
SE15 6J 103
TW9: Rich 4G 115
Mnr. Hall Av. NW4 2F 45
Mnr. Hall Dr. NW4 2F 45
Manorhall Gdns. E10 1C 68
MANOR HOUSE 7D 48
MANOR HOUSE 7C 48
Manor Ho. *NW1 5D 4*
(off Lisson Gro.)
UB2: S'hall 3C 94
Manor Ho. Ct. TW17: Shep 7D 146
W9 4A 82
(off Warrington Gdns.)
Manor Ho. Dr. HA6: Nwood 1D 38
NW6 7F 63
Manor Ho. Est. HA7: Stan 6G 27
Manor Ho. Gdn. E11 6K 51
Manor Ho. Way TW7: Isle 3B 114
Manor La. SE12 5G 123
SE13 5G 123
SM1: Sutt 5A 166
TW13: Felt 2J 129
TW16: Sun 2J 147
UB3: Harl 6F 93
Manor La. Ter. SE13 4G 123
Manor Lodge *NW6 7F 63*
(off Willesden La.)
Manor M. *NW6 2J 81*
(off Cambridge Av.)
SE4 2B 122
Manor Mt. SE23 1J 139
Manor Pde. HA1: Harr 6K 41
N16 2F 67
NW10 2B 80
(off High St. Harlesden)
MANOR PARK 4B 70
Manor Pk. BR7: Chst 2H 161
SE13 4F 123
TW9: Rich 4F 115
TW13: Felt 2J 129
Manor Pk. Cl. BR4: W W'ck 1D 170
Manor Pk. Crematorium E7 4A 70
Manor Pk. Cres. HA8: Edg 6B 28
Manor Pk. Dr. HA2: Harr 3F 41
Manor Pk. Gdns. HA8: Edg 5B 28
Manor Pk. Pde. *SE13 4F 123*
(off Lee High Rd.)
Manor Pk. Rd. BR4: W W'ck 1D 170
BR7: Chst 1G 161
E12 4B 70
(not continuous)
N2 3A 46
NW10 1B 80
SM1: Sutt 5A 166
Manor Pl. BR1: Brom 1C 160
BR7: Chst 2H 161
CR4: Mitc 3G 155
KT12: Walt T 7H 147
(not continuous)
SE17 5B 102
SM1: Sutt 4K 165
TW14: Felt 1J 129
Manor Rd. BR3: Beck 2D 158
BR4: W W'ck 2D 170
CR4: Mitc 4G 155
DA1: Cray 4K 127
DA5: Bexl 1H 145
DA15: Sidc 3K 143
E10 7C 50
E15 2G 87
E16 2G 87
E17 2A 50
EN2: Enf 2H 23
EN5: Barn 4B 20
HA1: Harr 6A 42
Manor Rd. HA4: Ruis 1F 57
IG7: Chig 6J 37
IG8: Wfd G 6J 37
IG11: Bark 6K 71
KT8: E Mos 4H 149
KT12: Walt T 7H 147
N16 2D 66
N17 1G 49
N22 6D 32
RM6: Chad H 6D 54
RM10: Dag 6J 73
SE25 4G 157
SM2: Cheam 7H 165
SM6: Wall 4F 167
SW20 2H 153
TW2: Twick 2G 131
TW9: Rich 4G 115
TW11: Tedd 5A 132
(not continuous)
TW15: Ashf 5B 128
UB3: Hayes 6J 75
W13 7A 78
Manor Rd. Ho. HA1: Harr 6A 42
Manor Rd. Nth. KT7: T Ditt 3A 162
KT10: Hin W, T Ditt 3A 162, 3A 162
SM6: Wall 4F 167
Manorside EN5: Barn 4B 20
Manorside Cl. SE2 4C 108
Manor Sq. RM8: Dag 2C 72
Manor Va. TW8: Bford 5C 96
Manor Vw. N3 2K 45
Manor Way BR2: Brom 6C 160
BR3: Beck 2C 158
BR5: Pet W 4G 161
CR2: S Croy 6E 168
CR4: Mitc 3G 155
DA5: Bexl 1G 145
DA7: Bex 3K 127
E4 4A 36
HA2: Harr 4F 41
HA4: Ruis 7G 39
KT4: Wor Pk 1A 164
NW9 4A 44
RM13: Rain 4K 91
SE3 4H 123
SE23 7J 121
UB2: S'hall 4B 94
Manor Way, The SM6: Wall 4F 167
Manorway EN1: Enf 7K 23
IG8: Wfd G 5F 37
Manor Way Bus. Cen. RM13: Rain 5K 91
Manor Waye UB8: Uxb 1A 74
Manpreet Ct. E12 5D 70
Manresa Rd. SW3 6C 16 (5C 100)
Mansard Beeches SW17 5E 136
Mansard Cl. HA5: Pinn 3B 40
Manse Cl. UB3: Harl 6F 93
Mansel Gro. E17 1C 50
Mansell Rd. UB6: G'frd 5F 77
W3 2K 97
Mansell St. E1 1K 15 (6F 85)
EC3 7F 85
Mansel Rd. SW19 6G 135
Manser Ct. RM13: Rain 3K 91
Mansergh Cl. SE18 7C 106
Manse Rd. N16 3F 67
Manser Rd. RM13: Rain 3K 91
Mansfield Av. EN4: E Barn 6J 21
HA4: Ruis 1K 57
N15 4D 48
Mansfield Cl. N9 6B 24
Mansfield Ct. *E2 1F 85*
(off Whiston Rd.)
SE15 7F 103
(off Sumner Rd.)
Mansfield Dr. UB4: Hayes 4G 75
Mansfield Hgts. N2 5C 46
Mansfield Hill E4 7J 25
Mansfield Ho. *N1 1E 84*
(off Halcomb St.)
Mansfield M. W1 6J 5 (5F 83)
Mansfield Pl. CR2: S Croy 6D 168
NW3 4A 64
Mansfield Rd. CR2: S Croy 6D 168
E11 6K 51
E17 4B 50
IG1: Ilf 2E 70
KT9: Chess 5C 162
NW3 5D 64
W3 4H 79
Mansfield St. W1 6J 5 (5F 83)
Mansford St. E2 2G 85
Manship Rd. CR4: Mitc 7E 136
Mansion Cl. SW9 1A 120
(not continuous)
Mansion Gdns. NW3 3K 63
Mansion House 1E 14 (6D 84)
Mansion Ho. Dr. HA7: Stan 2D 26
Mansion Ho. Pl. EC4 1E 14 (6D 84)
Mansion Ho. St. EC4 1E 14
Mansion Lock Ho. *NW1 7F 65*
(off Hawley Cres.)
Mansions, The SW5 5K 99
(Earl's Ct. Rd.)
SW5 5K 99
(off Old Brompton Rd.)
Mansion Vw. *E15 1F 87*
(off High St.)
Manson Ho. *N1 7A 66*
(off Drummond Way)
Manson M. SW7 4A 16 (4B 100)
Manson Pl. SW7 4A 16 (4B 100)
Mansted Gdns. RM6: Chad H 7C 54
Manston *N17 2D 48*
(off Adams Rd.)
NW1 7G 65
(off Agar Gro.)
Manston Av. UB2: S'hall 4E 94
Manston Cl. SE20 1J 157
Manston Ct. E17 1B 50
Manstone Rd. NW2 5G 63
Manston Gro. KT2: King T 5D 132
Manston Ho. *W14 3G 99*
(off Russell Rd.)
Manthorp Rd. SE18 5G 107
Mantilla Rd. SW17 4E 136
Mantle Ct. *SW18 6K 117*
(off Mapleton Rd.)
Mantle Rd. SE4 3A 122
Mantlet Cl. SW16 7G 137
Mantle Way E15 7G 69
Manton Av. W7 2K 95
Manton Cl. UB3: Hayes 7G 75
Manton Rd. EN3: Enf L 1H 25
SE2 4A 108
Manton Way EN3: Enf L 1J 25
Mantua St. SW11 3B 118
Mantus Cl. E1 4J 85
Mantus Rd. E1 4J 85
Manuka Cl. W7 1A 96
Manuka Hgts. *E20 5E 68*
(off Napa Cl.)
Manus Way N20 2F 31
Manville Gdns. SW17 3F 137
Manville Rd. SW17 2E 136
Manwood Rd. SE4 5B 122
Manwood St. E16 1D 106
Manygate La. TW17: Shep 7E 146
Manygate Pk. *TW17: Shep 6F 147*
(off Mitre Cl.)
Manygates SW12 2F 137
Mapesbury Ct. NW2 5G 63
Mapesbury M. NW4 6C 44
Mapesbury Rd. NW2 7G 63
Mapeshill Pl. NW2 6E 62
Mapes Ho. NW6 7G 63
Mape St. E2 4H 85
(not continuous)
Maple Av. E4 5G 35
HA2: Harr 2F 59
UB7: Yiew 7A 74
W3 1A 98
Maple Cl. BR5: Pet W 5H 161
CR4: Mitc 1F 155
HA4: Ruis 6K 39
IG9: Buck H 3G 37
N3 6D 30
N16 6G 49
SW4 6H 119
TW12: Hamp 6D 130
UB4: Yead 3B 76
Maple Ct. *CR0: C'don 4C 168*
(off Lwr. Coombe St.)
CR0: C'don 4C 168
(off The Waldrons)
E3 2C 86
(off Four Seasons Cl.)
E6 5E 88
KT3: N Mald 3K 151
SE6 1D 140
TW15: Ashf 7F 129
Maple Cres. DA15: Sidc 6A 126
Maplecroft Cl. E6 6B 88
Mapledale Av. CR0: C'don 2G 169
Mapledene BR7: Chst 6G 143
Mapledene Est. E8 7G 67
Mapledene Rd. E8 7F 67
Maple Gdns. HA8: Edg 7F 29
TW19: Stanw 2A 128
Maple Gro. NW9 7J 43
TW8: Bford 7B 96
UB1: S'hall 5D 76
W5 3D 96
Maple Gro. Bus. Cen.
TW4: Houn 4A 112
Maple Ho. E17 3D 50
KT1: King T 5E 150
(off Maple Rd.)
N19 3G 65
SE8 7B 104
(off Idonia St.)
TW9: Kew 1H 115
Maplehurst BR2: Brom 2G 159
Maplehurst Cl. KT1: King T 4E 150
Maple Ind. Est. TW13: Felt 3J 129
Maple Leaf Dr. DA15: Sidc 1K 143
Mapleleafe Gdns. IG6: Ilf 3F 53
Maple Leaf Sq. SE16 2K 103
Maple Lodge *W8 3K 99*
(off Abbots Wlk.)
Maple M. NW6 2K 81
SE16 2K 103
SW16 5K 137
Maple Pl. N17 7B 34
UB7: Yiew 1A 92
W1 5B 6 (4G 83)
Maple Rd. E11 6G 51
KT6: Surb 6D 150
SE20 1H 157
UB4: Yead 3A 76
Maples, The KT1: Hamp W 7C 132
KT10: Clay 7A 162
Maples Pl. E1 5H 85
Maplestead Rd. RM9: Dag 1B 90
SW2 7K 119
Maple St. E2 2H 85
RM7: Rom 4J 55
W1 5A 6 (5G 83)
Maplethorpe Rd. CR7: Thor H 4A 156
Mapleton Cl. BR2: Brom 6J 159
Mapleton Cres. EN3: Enf W 1D 24
SW18 6K 117
Mapleton Rd. E4 3K 35
EN1: Enf 2C 24
SW18 6J 117
(not continuous)
Maple Tree Pl. SE3 1C 124
Maple Wlk. W10 3F 81
Maple Way TW13: Felt 3J 129
Maplewood Apartments *N4 7C 48*
(off Katherine Cl.)
Maplewood Ct. TW15: Ashf 4A 128
Maplin Cl. N21 6E 22

Maplin Ho.—Marlborough Cl.

Maplin Ho. *SE2* *2D 108*
(off Wolvercote Rd.)
Maplin Rd. E16 .... 6J 87
Maplin St. E3 .... 3B 86
Mapperley Cl. E11 .... 6H 51
Mapperley Dr. IG8: Wfd G 7B 36
Marabou Cl. E12 .... 5C 70
Mara Ho. *E20* *5D 68*
(off Victory Pde.)
Maran Way DA18: Erith 2D 108
Maraschino Apartment *CR0: C'don* *1D 168*
(off Cherry Orchard Rd.)
Marathon Ho. *NW1* *5E 4*
(off Marylebone Rd.)
Marathon Way SE28 .... 2K 107
Marbaix Gdns. TW7: Isle 1H 113
Marban Rd. W9 .... 3H 81
Marble Arch 2F 11
MARBLE ARCH 7D 82
Marble Arch W1 .... 2E 10 (7D 82)
Marble Arch Apartments *W1* *7E 4*
(off Harrowby St.)
Marble Cl. W3 .... 1H 97
Marble Dr. NW2 .... 1F 63
Marble Hill Cl. TW1: Twick 7B 114
Marble Hill Gdns. TW1: Twick 7B 114
Marble Hill House 7C 114
Marble Ho. SE18 .... 5K 107
W9 .... 4H 81
Marble Quay E1 .... 4K 15 (1G 103)
Marbles Ho. *SE5* *6C 102*
(off Grosvenor Ter.)
Marbrook Ct. SE12 .... 3A 142
Marcella Rd. SW9 .... 2A 120
Marcellina Way BR6: Orp 3J 173
March *NW9* *1B 44*
(off Long Mead)
Marchant Cl. NW7 .... 6F 29
Marchant Ho. *N1* *1E 84*
(off Halcomb St.)
Marchant Rd. E11 .... 2F 69
Marchant St. SE14 .... 6A 104
Marchbank Rd. W14 .... 6H 99
March Ct. SW15 .... 4D 116
Marchmont Gdns. TW10: Rich 5F 115
Marchmont Rd. SM6: Wall 7G 167
TW10: Rich 5F 115
Marchmont St. WC1 .... 3E 6 (4J 83)
March Rd. TW1: Twick 7A 114
Marchside Cl. TW5: Hest 1B 112
Marchwood Cl. SE5 .... 7E 102
Marchwood Cres. W5 .... 6C 78
Marcia Ct. *SE1* *4E 102*
(off Marcia Rd.)
Marcia Rd. SE1 .... 4E 102
Marcilly Rd. SW18 .... 5B 118
Marco Dr. HA5: Hat E 1D 40
Marcon Ct. *E8* *5H 67*
(off Amhurst Rd.)
Marconi Pl. N11 .... 4A 32
Marconi Rd. E10 .... 1C 68
Marconi Way UB1: S'hall 6F 77
Marcon Pl. E8 .... 6H 67
Marco Rd. W6 .... 3E 98
Marcourt Lawns W5 .... 4E 78
Marcus Ct. E15 .... 1G 87
Marcus Garvey M. SE22 .... 6H 121
Marcus Garvey Way SE24 .... 4A 120
Marcus St. E15 .... 1H 87
SW18 .... 6K 117
Marcus Ter. SW18 .... 6K 117
Mardale Ct. NW7 .... 7H 29
Mardale Dr. NW9 .... 5K 43
Mardell Rd. CR0: C'don 5K 157
Marden Av. BR2: Hayes 6J 159
Marden Cres. CR0: C'don 6K 155
DA5: Bexl 5J 127
Marden Ho. E8 .... 5H 67
Marden Rd. CR0: C'don 6K 155
N17 .... 2E 48
Marden Sq. SE16 .... 3H 103
Marder Rd. W13 .... 2A 96
Mardyke Cl. RM13: Rain 2J 91
Mardyke Ho. *SE17* *4D 102*
(off Mason St.)
Marechal Niel Av. DA15: Sidc 3H 143
Marechal Niel Pde. *DA14: Sidc* *3H 143*
(off Main Rd.)
Maresby Ho. E4 .... 2J 35
Maresfield CR0: C'don 3E 168
Maresfield Gdns. NW3 .... 5A 64
Mare St. E8 .... 5H 67
Marfleet Cl. SM5: Cars 2C 166
Margaret Av. E4 .... 6J 25
Margaret Bondfield Av. IG11: Bark 7A 72
Margaret Bondfield Ho. *E3* *2A 86*
(off Driffield Rd.)
Margaret Cl. E11 .... 6G 51
Margaret Ct. EN4: E Barn 4G 21
W1 .... 7A 6
Margaret Gardner Dr. SE9 .... 2D 142
Margaret Herbison Ho. *SW6* *6H 99*
(off Clem Attlee Ct.)
Margaret Ho. *W6* *5E 98*
(off Queen Caroline St.)
Margaret Ingram Cl. SW6 .... 6H 99
Margaret Lockwood Cl. KT1: King T 4F 151
Margaret McMillan Ho. E16 .... 6A 88
Margaret Rd. DA5: Bexl 6D 126
EN4: E Barn 4G 21
N16 .... 1F 67
Margaret Rutherford Pl. SW12 .... 1G 137
Margaret St. W1 .... 7K 5 (6F 83)
Margaretta Ter. SW3 .... 7C 16 (6C 100)
Margaretting Rd. E12 .... 1A 70
Margaret Way IG4: Ilf 6C 52
Margaret White Ho. *NW1* *1D 6*
(off Chalton St.)
Margate Rd. SW2 .... 5J 119
Margery Fry Ct. N7 .... 3J 65
Margery Pk. Rd. E7 .... 6J 69
Margery Rd. RM8: Dag 3D 72
Margery St. WC1 .... 2J 7 (3A 84)
Margery Ter. *E7* *6J 69*
(off Margery Pk. Rd.)
Margin Dr. SW19 .... 5F 135
Margravine Gdns. W6 .... 5F 99
Margravine Rd. W6 .... 5F 99
Marham Dr. NW9 .... 1A 44
Marham Gdns. SM4: Mord 6A 154
SW18 .... 1C 136
Mar Ho. NW9 .... 3K 43
Maria Cl. SE1 .... 4H 103
Maria Ct. SE25 .... 2E 156
Marian Cl. UB4: Yead 4B 76
Marian Ct. E9 .... 5J 67
SM1: Sutt 5K 165
Marian Gdns. BR1: Brom 7A 142
Marianne Cl. SE5 .... 1E 120
Marian Pl. E2 .... 2H 85
Marian Rd. SW16 .... 1G 155
Marian St. E2 .... 2H 85
Marian Way NW10 .... 7B 62
Maria Ter. E1 .... 5K 85
Maria Theresa Cl. KT3: N Mald 5K 151
Maribor *SE10* *7E 104*
(off Burney St.)
Maricas Av. HA3: Hrw W 1H 41
Marie Curie SE5 .... 1F 121
Marie Lloyd Gdns. N19 .... 7J 47
Marie Lloyd Ho. *N1* *1E 8*
(off Murray Gro.)
Marie Lloyd Wlk. E8 .... 6F 67
Marien Ct. E4 .... 5A 36
Mariette Way SM6: Wall 7J 167
Marigold All. SE1 .... 3A 14 (7B 84)
Marigold Cl. UB1: S'hall 7C 76
Marigold Rd. N17 .... 7D 34
Marigold St. SE16 .... 2H 103
Marigold Way CR0: C'don 1K 169
Marina App. UB4: Yead 5C 76
Marina Av. KT3: N Mald 5D 152
Marina Cl. BR2: Brom 3J 159
Marina Ct. *E3* *3B 86*
(off Alfred St.)
SW6 .... 2A 118
Marina Dr. DA16: Well 2J 125
Marina Gdns. RM7: Rom 5J 55
Marina One *N1* *2J 83*
(off New Wharf Rd.)
Marina Pl. KT1: Hamp W 1D 150
Marina Point *E14* *3D 104*
(off Lanark Sq.)
Marina Way TW11: Tedd 7D 132
Marine Ct. E11 .... 2G 69
Marine Dr. IG11: Bark 4A 90
SE18 .... 4D 106
Marinefield Rd. SW6 .... 2K 117
Marinel Ho. SE5 .... 7C 102
Mariner Bus. Cen.
CR0: Wadd 5A 168
Mariner Gdns. TW10: Ham 3C 132
Marine Rd. RM9: Dag 1B 90
Mariner Rd. E12 .... 4E 70
Mariners Cl. EN4: E Barn 5G 21
Mariners M. E14 .... 4F 105
Mariners Pl. *SE16* *4A 104*
(off Plough Way)
Marine St. SE16 .... 3G 103
Marine Twr. *SE8* *6B 104*
(off Abinger Gro.)
Marion Av. TW17: Shep 5D 146
Marion Gro. IG8: Wfd G 5B 36
Marion Ho. *NW1* *1D 82*
(off Regent's Pk. Rd.)
Marion M. SE21 .... 3D 138
Marion Rd. CR7: Thor H 5C 156
NW7 .... 5H 29
Marischal Rd. SE13 .... 3F 123
Maritime Ho. SE18 .... 4F 107
Maritime Quay E14 .... 5C 104
Maritime St. E3 .... 4B 86
Marius Mans. SW17 .... 2E 136
Marius Rd. SW17 .... 2E 136
Marjorie Gro. SW11 .... 4D 118
Marjorie M. E1 .... 6K 85
Mark Av. E4 .... 6J 25
Mark Cl. DA7: Bex 1E 126
UB1: S'hall 7F 77
Marke Cl. BR2: Kes 4C 172
Market, The SM1: Sutt 1A 166
SM5: Cars 1A 166
Market App. W12 .... 2E 98
Market Chambers *EN2: Enf* *3J 23*
(off Church St.)
Market Ct. W1 .... 7A 6
Market Dr. W4 .... 7A 98
Market Entrance SW8 .... 7G 101
Market Est. N7 .... 6J 65
Market Hall N22 .... 2A 48
Market Hill SE18 .... 3E 106
Market La. HA8: Edg 1J 43
W12 .... 2E 98
Market Link RM1: Rom 4K 55
Market M. W1 .... 5J 11 (1F 101)
Market Pde. *BR1: Brom* *1J 159*
(off East St.)
DA14: Sidc 4B 144
E10 .... *6E 50*
(off High Rd. Leyton)
E17 .... *3B 50*
(off Higham Hill Rd.)
N9 .... *2B 34*
(off Winchester Rd.)
N16 .... *1G 67*
(off Oldhill St.)
SE25 .... 4G 157
TW13: Hanw 3C 130
Market Pav. E10 .... 3C 68
Market Pl. DA6: Bex 4G 127
EN2: Enf 3J 23
KT1: King T 2D 150
N2 .... 3B 46
Market Pl. SE16 .... 4G 103
(not continuous)
TW8: Bford 7C 96
UB1: S'hall 1D 94
W1 .... 7A 6 (6G 83)
W3 .... 1J 97
Market Pl., The NW11 .... 4A 46
Market Rd. N7 .... 6J 65
TW9: Rich 3G 115
Market Row SW9 .... 4A 120
Market Sq. BR1: Brom 2J 159
(not continuous)
E14 .... 6D 86
KT1: King T *2D 150*
(off Market Pl.)
Market Square, The *N9* *2C 34*
(within Edmonton Grn. Shop. Cen.)
Market St. E1 .... 5J 9 (5F 85)
E6 .... 2D 88
SE18 .... 4E 106
Market Ter. *TW8: Bford* *6E 96*
(off Albany Rd.)
Market Trad. Est. UB2: S'hall 4K 93
Market Way E14 .... 6D 86
HA0: Wemb 5E 60
Market Yd. SE8 .... 7C 104
Market Yd. M. SE1 .... 7G 15 (2E 102)
Markfield Beam Engine & Mus. 5G 49
Markfield Gdns. E4 .... 7J 25
Markfield Rd. N15 .... 4G 49
Markham Ho. *RM10: Dag* *3G 73*
(off Uvedale Rd.)
Markham Pl. SW3 .... 5E 16 (5D 100)
Markham Sq. SW3 .... 5E 16 (5D 100)
Markham St. SW3 .... 5D 16 (5C 100)
Markhole Cl. TW12: Hamp 7D 130
Mark Ho. *E2* *2K 85*
(off Sewardstone Rd.)
Markhouse Av. E17 .... 6A 50
Markhouse Pas. *E17* *6B 50*
(off Downsfield Rd.)
Markhouse Rd. E17 .... 6B 50
Markland Ho. *W10* *7F 81*
(off Darfield Way)
Mark La. EC3 .... 2H 15 (7E 84)
Mark Lodge *EN4: Cockf* *4H 21*
(off Edgeworth Rd.)
Markmanor Av. E17 .... 7A 50
Mark Rd. N22 .... 2B 48
Marksbury Av. TW9: Rich 3G 115
MARKS GATE 1E 54
Mark Sq. EC2 .... 3G 9 (4E 84)
Marks Rd. RM7: Rom 5J 55
(not continuous)
Markstone Ho. *SE1* *7A 14*
(off Lancaster St.)
Mark St. E15 .... 7G 69
EC2 .... 3G 9 (4E 84)
Mark Wade Cl. E12 .... 1B 70
Markway TW16: Sun 2A 148
Markwell Cl. SE26 .... 4H 139
Markyate Ho. *W10* *4E 80*
(off Sutton Way)
Markyate Rd.
RM8: Dag 5B 72
Marland Ho. *SW1* *1F 17*
(off Sloane St.)
Marlands Rd. IG5: Ilf 3C 52
Marlborough *SW19* *1F 135*
(off Inner Pk. Rd.)
W9 .... *3A 82*
(off Maida Vale)
Marlborough Av. E8 .... 1G 85
(not continuous)
HA4: Ruis 6E 38
HA8: Edg 3C 28
N14 .... 3B 32
Marlborough Cl. BR6: Orp 6K 161
N20 .... 3J 31
SE17 .... 4C 102
SW19 .... 6C 136

Marlborough Ct.—Martineau Est.

Marlborough Ct. *CR2: S Croy* 4E **168**
(off Birdhurst Rd.)
EN1: Enf 5K **23**
HA1: Harr 4H **41**
HA6: Nwood 1H **39**
IG9: Buck H 2F **37**
N17 1G **49**
(off Kemble Rd.)
SM6: Wall 7G **167**
W1 1B **12**
(off Carnaby St.)
W8 4J **99**
(off Pembroke Rd.)
Marlborough Cres. UB3: Harl 7F **93**
W4 3K **97**
Marlborough Dr. IG5: Ilf 3C **52**
Marlborough Flats SW3 3D **16**
Marlborough Gdns. KT6: Surb 7D **150**
N20 3J **31**
Marlborough Ga. Ho. *W2* 2A **10**
(off Elms M.)
Marlborough Gro. SE1 5G **103**
Marlborough Hill HA1: Harr 4H **41**
NW8 2A **82**
MARLBOROUGH HOUSE 5B **12** (1G **101**)
Marlborough Ho. *E16* 1J **105**
(off Hardy Av.)
UB7: W Dray 2B **92**
(off Park Lodge Av.)
Marlborough La. SE7 6A **106**
Marlborough Lodge *NW8* 2A **82**
(off Hamilton Ter.)
Marlborough Mans. *NW6* 5K **63**
(off Canon Hill)
Marlborough M. SW2 4K **119**
Marlborough Pde. *HA8: Edg* 3C **28**
(off Marlborough Av.)
UB10: Hil 4D **74**
Marlborough Pk. Av. DA15: Sidc 7A **126**
Marlborough Pl. NW8 2A **82**
Marlborough Rd. BR2: Brom 4A **160**
CR2: S Croy 7C **168**
DA7: Bex 3D **126**
E4 6J **35**
E7 7A **70**
E15 4G **69**
E18 2J **51**
N9 1B **34**
N19 2H **65**
N22 7D **32**
RM7: Mawney 4G **55**
RM8: Dag 4B **72**
SE18 3F **107**
SE28 3G **107**
SM1: Sutt 3J **165**
SW1 5B **12** (1G **101**)
SW19 6C **136**
TW7: Isle 1B **114**
TW10: Rich 6F **115**
TW12: Hamp 6E **130**
TW13: Felt 2B **130**
TW15: Ashf 5A **128**
UB2: S'hall 3A **94**
UB10: Hil 4D **74**
W4 5J **97**
W5 2D **96**
Marlborough St. SW3 4C **16** (4C **100**)
Marlborough Yd. N19 2H **65**
Marlbury *NW8* 1K **81**
(off Abbey Rd.)
Marler Rd. SE23 1A **140**
Marley Av. DA7: Bex 6D **108**
Marley Cl. N15 4B **48**
UB6: G'frd 3E **76**
Marley Ho. *E16* 7F **89**
(off University Way)
W11 7F **81**
(off St Ann's Rd.)
Marley St. SE16 4K **103**
Marley Wlk. NW2 5E **62**
Marl Fld. Cl. KT4: Wor Pk 1C **164**
Marlin Cl. TW16: Sun 6G **129**
Marling Ct. TW12: Hamp 6D **130**
Marlingdene Cl. TW12: Hamp 6E **130**
MARLING PARK 7D **130**
Marlings Cl. BR7: Chst 4J **161**
Marlings Pk. Av. BR7: Chst 4J **161**
Marlin Pk. TW14: Felt 5K **111**
Marlins Cl. SM1: Sutt 5A **166**
Marloes Cl. HA0: Wemb 4D **60**
Marloes Rd. W8 3K **99**
Marlow Cl. SE20 3H **157**
Marlow Ct. N14 7B **22**
NW6 7F **63**
NW9 3B **44**
Marlow Cres. TW1: Twick 6K **113**
Marlow Dr. SM3: Cheam 2F **165**
Marlowe Cl. BR7: Chst 6H **143**
IG6: Ilf 1G **53**
Marlowe Ct. SE19 5F **139**
SW3 4D **16**
(off Petyward)
Marlowe Gdns. SE9 6E **124**
Marlowe Ho. IG8: Wfd G 7K **37**
KT1: King T 4D **150**
(off Portsmouth Rd.)
Marlowe Path SE8 6C **104**
Marlowe Rd. E17 4E **50**
Marlowes, The DA1: Cray 4K **127**
NW8 1B **82**
Marlowe Sq. CR4: Mitc 4G **155**
Marlowe Way CR0: Bedd 2J **167**
Marlow Gdns. UB3: Harl 3F **93**
Marlow Ho. *E2* 2J **9**
(off Calvert Av.)
KT5: Surb 5E **150**
(off Cranes Pk.)
SE1 7J **15**
(off Abbey St.)
TW11: Tedd 4A **132**
W2 6K **81**
(off Hallfield Est.)
Marlow Rd. E6 3D **88**
SE20 3H **157**
UB2: S'hall 3D **94**
Marlow Way SE16 2K **103**
Marlow Workshops *E2* 2J **9**
(off Virginia Rd.)
Marl Rd. SW18 4A **118**
Marlston NW1 2K **5**
Marlton St. SE10 5H **105**
Marlu Ct. *SE14* 1K **121**
(off Hatcham Pk. M.)
Marlu Ho. *SE14* 1K **121**
(off Hatcham Pk. M.)
Marlwood Cl. DA15: Sidc 2J **143**
Marmadon Rd. SE18 4K **107**
Marmara Apartments *E16* 7J **87**
(off Western Gateway)
Marmion App. E4 4H **35**
Marmion Av. E4 4G **35**
Marmion Cl. E4 4G **35**
Marmion M. SW11 3E **118**
Marmion Rd. SW11 4E **118**
Marmont Rd. SE15 1G **121**
Marmora Rd. SE22 6J **121**
Marmot Rd. TW4: Houn 3B **112**
Marne Av. DA16: Well 3A **126**
N11 4A **32**
Marnell Way TW4: Houn 3B **112**
Marner Point E3 4E **86**
Marne St. W10 3G **81**
Marney Rd. SW11 4E **118**
Marnfield Cres. SW2 1A **138**
Marnham Av. NW2 4G **63**
Marnham Ct. HA0: Wemb 5C **60**
Marnham Cres. UB6: G'frd 3F **77**
Marnock Ho. *SE17* 5D **102**
(off Brandon St.)
Marnock Rd. SE4 5B **122**
Maroon St. E14 5A **86**
Maroons Way SE6 5C **140**
Marqueen Ct. *W8* 2K **99**
(off Kensington Chu. St.)
Marqueen Towers SW16 7K **137**
Marquess Hgts. E18 1K **51**
Marquess Rd. N1 6D **66**
Marquis Cl. HA0: Wemb 7F **61**
Marquis Ct. IG11: Bark 5J **71**
KT1: King T 4D **150**
(off Anglesea Rd.)
N4 1K **65**
(off Marquis Rd.)
TW19: Stanw 1A **128**
Marquis Rd. N4 1K **65**
N22 6E **32**
NW1 6H **65**
Marrabon Cl. DA15: Sidc 1A **144**
Marrick Cl. SW15 4C **116**
Marrick Ho. *NW6* 1K **81**
(off Mortimer Cres.)
Marriett Ho. SE6 4E **140**
Marrilyne Av. EN3: Enf L 1G **25**
Marriner Ct. *UB3: Hayes* 7G **75**
(off Barra Hall Rd.)
Marriott Cl. TW14: Felt 6F **111**
Marriott Rd. E15 1G **87**
EN5: Barn 3A **20**
N4 1K **65**
N10 1D **46**
Marriotts Cl. NW9 6B **44**
Marryat Cl. TW4: Houn 4D **112**
Marryat Ho. *SW1* 6A **18**
(off Churchill Gdns.)
Marryat Pl. SW19 4G **135**
Marryat Rd. SW19 5F **135**
Marryat Sq. SW6 1G **117**
Marsala Rd. SE13 4D **122**
Marsalis Ho. *E3* 3C **86**
(off Rainhill Way)
Marsden Rd. N9 2C **34**
SE15 3F **121**
Marsden St. NW5 6E **64**
Marsden Way BR6: Orp 4K **173**
Marshall Bldg. *W2* 6A **4**
(off Hermitage St.)
Marshall Cl. HA1: Harr 7H **41**
SW18 6A **118**
TW4: Houn 5D **112**
Marshall Ct. *NW6* 7F **63**
(off Coverdale Rd.)
SE20 7H **139**
(off Anerley Pk.)
Marshall Dr. UB4: Hayes 5H **75**
Marshall Est. NW7 4H **29**
Marshall Ho. *N1* 2D **84**
(off Cranston Est.)
SE1 3E **102**
(off Page's Wlk.)
SE17 5D **102**
(off East St.)
Marshall Path SE28 7B **90**
Marshall Rd. E10 3D **68**
N17 1D **48**
Marshalls Cl. N11 4A **32**
Marshalls Dr. RM1: Rom 3K **55**
Marshalls Gro. SE18 4C **106**
Marshall's Pl. SE16 3F **103**
Marshall's Rd. SM1: Sutt 4K **165**
Marshalls Rd. RM7: Rom 4K **55**
Marshall St. NW10 7K **61**
W1 1B **12** (6G **83**)
Marshall Street Leisure Cen. 1B **12** (6G **83**)
Marshalsea Rd. SE1 6D **14** (2C **102**)
Marsham Cl. BR7: Chst 5F **143**
Marsham Ct. SW1 3D **18** (4H **101**)
Marsham St. SW1 2D **18** (3H **101**)
Marsh Av. CR4: Mitc 2D **154**
Marshbrook Cl. SE3 3B **124**
Marsh Cen., The *E1* 7K **9**
(off Whitechapel High St.)
Marsh Cl. NW7 3G **29**
Marsh Ct. E8 6G **67**
SW19 1A **154**
Marsh Dr. NW9 6B **44**
Marsh Farm Rd. TW2: Twick 1K **131**
Marshfield St. E14 3E **104**
Marshgate Bus. Cen. E15 1E **86**
Marshgate La. E15 2E **86**
E20 7C **68**
Marshgate Path SE28 3G **107**
Marsh Grn. Rd. RM10: Dag 1G **91**
Marsh Hall HA9: Wemb 3F **61**
Marsh Hill E9 5A **68**
Marsh Ho. *SW1* 6D **18**
(off Aylesford St.)
SW8 1G **119**
Marsh La. E10 2B **68**
HA7: Stan 5H **27**
N17 7C **34**
NW7 3F **29**
Marsh Rd. HA0: Wemb 3D **78**
HA5: Pinn 4C **40**
Marshside Cl. N9 1D **34**
Marsh St. E14 4D **104**
Marsh Wall E14 1C **104**
Marsh Way RM13: Rain 3K **91**
Marshwood Ho. *NW6* 1J **81**
(off Kilburn Vale)
Marsland Cl. SE17 5B **102**
Marsom Ho. *N1* 1E **8**
(off Provost St.)
Marston Av. KT9: Chess 6E **162**
RM10: Dag 2G **73**
Marston Cl. NW6 7A **64**
RM10: Dag 3G **73**
Marston Ho. SW9 2A **120**
Marston Rd. IG5: Ilf 1C **52**
TW11: Tedd 5B **132**
Marston Way SE19 7B **138**
Marsworth Av. HA5: Pinn 1B **40**
Marsworth Cl. UB4: Yead 5C **76**
Marsworth Ho. *E2* 1G **85**
(off Whiston Rd.)
HA0: Wemb 1E **78**
Martaban Rd. N16 2F **67**
Martara M. SE17 5C **102**
Marta Rose Ct. *SE20* 2H **157**
(off Wadhurst Cl.)
Martello St. E8 7H **67**
Martello Ter. E8 7H **67**
Martell Rd. SE21 3D **138**
Martel Pl. E8 6F **67**
Marten Rd. E17 2C **50**
Martens Av. DA7: Bex 4H **127**
Martens Cl. DA7: Bex 4J **127**
Martham Cl. IG6: Ilf 1F **53**
SE28 7D **90**
Martha Rd. E15 6G **69**
Martha's Bldgs. EC1 3E **8** (4D **84**)
Martha St. E1 6J **85**
Marthorne Cres. HA3: Hrw W 2H **41**
Martin Bowes Rd. SE9 3D **124**
Martinbridge Trad. Est. EN1: Enf 5B **24**
Martin Cl. N9 1E **34**
UB10: Uxb 2A **74**
Martin Ct. *CR2: S Croy* 5E **168**
(off Birdhurst Rd.)
E14 2E **104**
(off River Barge Cl.)
Martin Cres. CR0: C'don 1A **168**
Martindale SW14 5J **115**
Martindale Av. BR6: Chels 5K **173**
E16 7J **87**
Martindale Ho. *E14* 7D **86**
(off Poplar High St.)
Martin Dale Ind. Est. EN1: Enf 3C **24**
Martindale Rd. SW12 7F **119**
TW4: Houn 3C **112**
Martin Dene DA6: Bex 5F **127**
Martin Dr. UB5: N'olt 5D **58**
Martineau Dr. TW1: Twick 4B **114**
Martineau Est. E1 7J **85**

Martineau Ho. SW1 . . . 6A 18
(off Churchill Gdns.)
Martineau M. N5 . . . 4B 66
Martineau Rd. N5 . . . 4B 66
Martineau Sq. E1 . . . 7G 85
Martingale Cl. TW16: Sun . . . 4J 147
Martingale Ho. E1 . . . 1H 103
(off Raine St.)
Martingales Cl. TW10: Ham . . . 3D 132
Martin Gdns. RM8: Dag . . . 4C 72
Martin Gro. SM4: Mord . . . 3J 153
Martin Ho. E3 . . . 1B 86
(off Old Ford Rd.)
SE1 . . . 3C 102
SW8 . . . 7J 101
(off Wyvil Rd.)
Martin Kinggett Gdns.
RM9: Dag . . . 1E 90
Martin La. EC4 . . . 2F 15 (7D 84)
(not continuous)
Martin Ri. DA6: Bex . . . 5F 127
Martin Rd. RM8: Dag . . . 4C 72
Martins, The HA9: Wemb . . . 3F 61
SE26 . . . 5H 139
Martins Cl. BR4: W W'ck . . . 1F 171
Martin's Mt. EN5: New Bar . . . 4D 20
Martins Pl. SE28 . . . 1J 107
Martin's Rd. BR2: Brom . . . 2G 159
Martin St. SE28 . . . 1J 107
Martins Wlk. N10 . . . 1E 46
N22 . . . 3A 48
SE28 . . . 1J 107
Martin Way SM4: Mord . . . 2F 153
SW20 . . . 2F 153
Martlesham N17 . . . 2E 48
(off Adams Rd.)
Martlesham Wlk. NW9 . . . 2A 44
Martlet Gro. UB5: N'olt . . . 3B 76
Martlett Ct. WC2 . . . 1F 13 (6J 83)
Martley Dr. IG2: Ilf . . . 5F 53
Martock Cl. HA3: W'stone . . . 4A 42
Martock Gdns. N11 . . . 5J 31
Marton Cl. SE6 . . . 3C 140
Marton Rd. N16 . . . 2E 66
Martynside NW9 . . . 1B 44
Martys Yd. NW3 . . . 4B 64
Marvell Av. UB4: Hayes . . . 5J 75
Marvell Ct. RM6: Chad H . . . 6B 54
(off Quarles Pk. Rd.)
Marvell Ho. SE5 . . . 7D 102
(off Camberwell Rd.)
Marvels Cl. SE12 . . . 2K 141
Marvels La. SE12 . . . 2K 141
Marville Rd. SW6 . . . 7H 99
Marvin St. E8 . . . 6H 67
Marwell Cl. BR4: W W'ck . . . 2H 171
Marwood Cl. DA16: Well . . . 3B 126
Marwood Dr. NW7 . . . 7A 30
Mary Adelaide Cl. SW15 . . . 4A 134
Mary Ann Gdns. SE8 . . . 6C 104
Maryatt Av. HA2: Harr . . . 2F 59
Marybank SE18 . . . 4D 106
Mary Bayly Ho. W11 . . . 1G 99
(off Wilsham St.)
Mary Boast Wlk. SE5 . . . 2D 120
Mary Cl. HA7: Stan . . . 4F 43
Mary Datchelor Cl. SE5 . . . 1D 120
Mary Datchelor Ho. SE5 . . . 1D 120
(off Grove La.)
Maryfield Cl. DA5: Bexl . . . 3K 145
Mary Flux Ct. SW5 . . . 5K 99
(off Bramham Gdns.)
Mary Grn. NW8 . . . 1K 81
Mary Holben Ho. SW16 . . . 5G 137
Mary Ho. W6 . . . 5E 98
(off Queen Caroline St.)
Mary Jones Ct. E14 . . . 7C 86
(off Garford St.)
Maryland Ind. Est. E15 . . . 5G 69
Maryland Pk. E15 . . . 5G 69
(not continuous)
Maryland Point E15 . . . 6G 69
(off The Grove)
Maryland Rd. CR7: Thor H . . . 1B 156
E15 . . . 5F 69
N22 . . . 6E 32
Maryland Sq. E15 . . . 5G 69
Marylands Rd. W9 . . . 4J 81
(not continuous)
Maryland St. E15 . . . 5F 69
Maryland Wlk. N1 . . . 1C 84
(off Popham St.)
Maryland Way TW16: Sun . . . 2J 147
Mary Lawrenson Pl. SE3 . . . 7J 105
MARYLEBONE . . . 5H 5 (5E 82)
Marylebone Cricket Club . . . 2B 4
MARYLEBONE FLYOVER . . . 5C 82
Marylebone Fly-Over NW1 . . . 5B 82
W2 . . . 6B 4 (5B 82)
Marylebone Gdns. TW9: Rich . . . 4G 115
Marylebone High St. W1 . . . 5H 5 (5E 82)
Marylebone La. W1 . . . 6H 5 (5E 82)
Marylebone M. W1 . . . 6J 5 (5F 83)
Marylebone Pas. W1 . . . 7B 6 (6G 83)
Marylebone Rd. NW1 . . . 5D 4 (5C 82)
Marylebone St. W1 . . . 6H 5 (5E 82)
Marylee Way SE11 . . . 4H 19 (4K 101)
Mary Macarthur Ho. E2 . . . 3K 85
(off Warley St.)
RM10: Dag . . . 3G 73
(off Wythenshawe Rd.)
W6 . . . 6G 99
Mary Neuner Rd. N8 . . . 3K 47
N22 . . . 3K 47
Maryon Gro. SE7 . . . 4C 106
Maryon Ho. NW6 . . . 7A 64
(off Goldhurst Ter.)
Maryon M. NW3 . . . 4C 64
Maryon Rd. SE7 . . . 4C 106
SE18 . . . 4C 106
Mary Peters Dr. UB6: G'frd . . . 5H 59
Mary Pl. W11 . . . 7G 81
Mary Rose Cl. TW12: Hamp . . . 1E 148
Mary Rose Mall E6 . . . 5D 88
Mary Rose Sq. SE16 . . . 4A 104
(off Cary Av.)
Maryrose Way N20 . . . 1G 31
Marys Ct. NW1 . . . 3D 4
Mary Seacole Cl. E8 . . . 1F 85
Mary Seacole Ho. W6 . . . 3C 98
(off Invermead Cl.)
Mary Smith Ct. SW5 . . . 4J 99
(off Trebovir Rd.)
Marysmith Ho. SW1 . . . 5D 18
(off Cureton St.)
Mary's Ter. TW1: Twick . . . 7A 114
Mary St. E16 . . . 5H 87
N1 . . . 1C 84
Mary Ter. NW1 . . . 1F 83
Maryville DA16: Well . . . 2K 125
Mary Wallace Theatre
Twickenham . . . 1A 132
Mary Wharrie Ho. NW3 . . . 7D 64
(off Fellows Rd.)
Marzell Ho. W14 . . . 5H 99
(off North End Rd.)
Marzena Ct. TW3: Houn . . . 6G 113
Masault Ct. TW9: Rich . . . 4E 114
(off Kew Foot Rd.)
Masbro' Rd. W14 . . . 3F 99
Mascalls Ct. SE7 . . . 6A 106
Mascalls Rd. SE7 . . . 6A 106
Mascotte Rd. SW15 . . . 4F 117
Mascotts Cl. NW2 . . . 3D 62
Masefield Av. HA7: Stan . . . 5E 26
UB1: S'hall . . . 7E 76
Masefield Ct. EN5: New Bar . . . 4F 21
KT6: Surb . . . 7D 150
Masefield Cres. N14 . . . 5B 22
Masefield Gdns. E6 . . . 4E 88
Masefield Ho. NW6 . . . 3J 81
(off Stafford Rd.)
Masefield La. UB4: Yead . . . 4K 75
Masefield Rd. TW12: Hamp . . . 4D 130
Masefield Vw. BR6: Farnb . . . 3G 173
Masefield Way TW19: Stanw . . . 1B 128
Masey M. SW2 . . . 5A 120
Masham Ho. DA18: Erith . . . 2D 108
(off Kale Rd.)
Mashie Rd. W3 . . . 6A 80
Mashiters Hill RM1: Rom . . . 1K 55
Maskall Cl. SW2 . . . 1A 138
Maskani Wlk. SW16 . . . 7G 137
Maskell Rd. SW17 . . . 3A 136
Maskelyne Cl. SW11 . . . 1C 118
Mason Cl. DA7: Bex . . . 3H 127
E16 . . . 7J 87
SE16 . . . 5G 103
SW20 . . . 1F 153
TW12: Hamp . . . 1D 148
Mason Ho. E9 . . . 7J 67
(off Frampton Pk. Rd.)
SE1 . . . 4G 103
(off Simms Rd.)
Mason Rd. IG8: Wfd G . . . 4B 36
SM1: Sutt . . . 5K 165
Masonry Ho. SE14 . . . 1K 121
(off Fishers Ct.)
Mason's Arms M. W1 . . . 1K 11 (6F 83)
Mason's Av. CR0: C'don . . . 3C 168
EC2 . . . 7E 8 (6D 84)
Masons Av. HA3: W'stone . . . 4K 41
Masons Grn. La. W3 . . . 4G 79
W5 . . . 4G 79
Masons Hill BR1: Brom . . . 3J 159
BR2: Brom . . . 3K 159
SE18 . . . 4F 107
Masons Pl. CR4: Mitc . . . 1D 154
EC1 . . . 1B 8 (3C 84)
Mason St. SE17 . . . 4D 102
Mason's Yd. SW1 . . . 4B 12 (1G 101)
SW19 . . . 5F 135
Masons Yd. EC1 . . . 1B 8 (3B 84)
Massey Cl. N11 . . . 5A 32
Massey Ct. E6 . . . 1A 88
(off Florence Rd.)
Massie Rd. E8 . . . 6G 67
Massingberd Way SW17 . . . 4F 137
Massinger St. SE17 . . . 4E 102
Massingham St. E1 . . . 4K 85
Masson Av. HA4: Ruis . . . 6A 58
Masson Ho. TW8: Bford . . . 6F 97
Mast, The E16 . . . 7G 89
Mast Ct. SE16 . . . 4A 104
(off Boat Lifter Way)
Master Gunner Pl. SE18 . . . 7C 106
Masterman Ho. SE5 . . . 7D 102
(off Elmington Est.)
Masterman Rd. E6 . . . 3C 88
Masters Cl. SW16 . . . 6G 137
Masters Dr. SE16 . . . 5H 103
Masters Lodge E1 . . . 6J 85
(off Johnson St.)
Masters St. E1 . . . 5K 85
Mast Ho. Ter. E14 . . . 4C 104
(not continuous)
Mastmaker Ct. E14 . . . 2C 104
Mastmaker Rd. E14 . . . 2C 104
Mast Quay SE18 . . . 3D 106
MASWELL PARK . . . 5G 113
Maswell Pk. Cres. TW3: Houn . . . 5G 113
Maswell Pk. Rd. TW3: Houn . . . 5F 113
Matcham Ct. TW1: Twick . . . 6D 114
(off Clevedon Rd.)
Matcham Rd. E11 . . . 3G 69
Match Ct. E3 . . . 2C 86
(off Blondin St.)
Matching Ct. E3 . . . 3B 86
(off Merchant St.)
Matchless Dr. SE18 . . . 7E 106
Matfield Cl. BR2: Brom . . . 5J 159
Matfield Rd. DA17: Belv . . . 6G 109
Matha Ct. BR1: Brom . . . 1A 160
Matham Gro. SE22 . . . 4F 121
Matham Rd. KT8: E Mos . . . 5H 149
Matheson Lang Ho. SE1 . . . 7J 13
Matheson Rd. W14 . . . 4H 99
Mathews Av. E6 . . . 2E 88
Mathews Pk. Av. E15 . . . 6H 69
Mathews Yd. WC2 . . . 1E 12 (6J 83)
Mathieson Ct. SE1 . . . 7B 14
(off King James St.)
Mathison Ho. SW10 . . . 7A 100
(off Coleridge Gdns.)
Matilda Cl. SE19 . . . 7D 138
Matilda Gdns. E3 . . . 2C 86
Matilda Ho. E1 . . . 1G 103
(off St Katherine's Way)
Matilda St. N1 . . . 1K 83
Matisse Ct. EC1 . . . 3E 8
Matisse Rd. TW3: Houn . . . 3F 113
Matlock Cl. EN5: Barn . . . 5A 20
SE24 . . . 4C 120
Matlock Ct. NW8 . . . 2A 82
(off Abbey Rd.)
SE5 . . . 4D 120
W11 . . . 7J 81
(off Kensington Pk. Rd.)
Matlock Cres. SM3: Cheam . . . 4G 165
Matlock Gdns. SM3: Cheam . . . 4G 165
Matlock Pl. SM3: Cheam . . . 4G 165
Matlock Rd. E10 . . . 6E 50
Matlock St. E14 . . . 6A 86
Matlock Way KT3: N Mald . . . 1K 151
Maton Ho. SW6 . . . 7H 99
(off Estcourt Rd.)
Matrimony Pl. SW8 . . . 2G 119
Matson Ct. IG8: Wfd G . . . 7B 36
Matson Ho. SE16 . . . 3H 103
Matthew Cl. W10 . . . 4F 81
Matthew Ct. CR4: Mitc . . . 5H 155
E17 . . . 3E 50
Matthew Parker St. SW1 . . . 7D 12 (2H 101)
Matthews Cl. HA9: Wemb . . . 3G 61
Matthews Ct. E17 . . . 1C 50
(off Chingford Rd.)
Matthews Ho. E14 . . . 5C 86
(off Burgess St.)
Matthews Rd. UB6: G'frd . . . 5H 59
Matthews St. SW11 . . . 2D 118
Matthews Yd. CR0: C'don . . . 3C 168
(off Surrey St.)
Matthias Apartments N1 . . . 7D 66
(off Northchurch Rd.)
Matthias Ct. TW10: Rich . . . 5E 114
Matthias Rd. N16 . . . 5E 66
Mattison Rd. N4 . . . 6A 48
Mattock La. W5 . . . 1B 96
W13 . . . 1B 96
Maud Cashmore Way SE18 . . . 3D 106
Maud Chadburn Pl. SW4 . . . 6F 119
Maude Ho. E2 . . . 2G 85
(off Ropley St.)
Maude Rd. E17 . . . 5A 50
SE5 . . . 1E 120
Maude Ter. E17 . . . 5A 50
Maud Gdns. E13 . . . 1H 87
IG11: Bark . . . 2K 89
Maudlins Grn. E1 . . . 4K 15 (1G 103)
Maud Rd. E10 . . . 3E 68
E13 . . . 2H 87
Maudslay Rd. SE9 . . . 3D 124
Maudsley Ho. TW8: Bford . . . 5E 96
Maud St. E16 . . . 5H 87
Maudsville Cotts. W7 . . . 1J 95
Maud Wilkes Cl. NW5 . . . 5G 65
Maugham Way W3 . . . 3J 97
Mauleverer Rd. SW2 . . . 5J 119
Maundeby Wlk. NW10 . . . 6A 62
Maunder Rd. W7 . . . 1K 95
Maunsel St. SW1 . . . 3C 18 (4H 101)
Maureen Campbell Ct.
TW17: Shep . . . 5D 146
(off Harrison Way)

Maureen Ct. BR3: Beck 2J 157
Maurer Ct. SE10 . . . . .3H 105
Mauretania Bldg. E1 . . . . .7K 85
(off Jardine Rd.)
Maurice Av. N22 . . . . .2B 48
Maurice Browne Av. NW7 . . . . .6A 30
Maurice Ct. E1 . . . . .3K 85
N22 . . . . .1K 47
TW8: Bford 7D 96
Maurice Drummond Ho. SE10 . . . . . .1D 122
(off Catherine Gro.)
Maurice St. W12 . . . . .6D 80
Maurice Wlk. NW11 . . . . .4A 46
Maurier Cl. UB5: N'olt 1A 76
Mauritius Rd. SE10 . . . . .4G 105
Maury Rd. N16 . . . . .2G 67
Mauveine Gdns. TW3: Houn 4E 112
Mavelstone Cl. BR1: Brom 1C 160
Mavelstone Rd. BR1: Brom 1B 160
Maverton Rd. E3 . . . . .1C 86
Mavery Ct. BR1: Brom 7H 141
(off Bromley Av.)
Mavis Av. KT19: Ewe 5A 164
Mavis Cl. KT19: Ewe 5A 164
Mavis Wlk. E6 . . . . .5C 88
(off Greenwich Cres.)
Mavor Ho. N1 . . . . .1K 83
(off Barnsbury Est.)
Mawbey Ho. SE1 . . . . .5G 103
Mawbey Pl. SE1 . . . . .5F 103
Mawbey Rd. SE1 . . . . .5F 103
Mawbey St. SW8 . . . . .7J 101
Mawdley Ho. SE1 . . . . .7A 14
MAWNEY 3H 55
Mawney Cl. RM7: Mawney 2H 55
Mawney Rd. RM7: Mawney, Rom 2H 55
Mawson Cl. SW20 . . . . .2G 153
Mawson Ct. N1 . . . . .1D 84
(off Gopsall St.)
Mawson Ho. EC1 . . . . .5J 7
(off Baldwins Gdns.)
Mawson La. W4 . . . . .6B 98
Maxden Ct. SE15 . . . . .3F 121
Maxey Gdns. RM9: Dag 4E 72
Maxey Rd. RM9: Dag 4E 72
SE18 . . . . .4G 107
Maxfield Cl. N20 . . . . .7F 21
Maxilla Wlk. W10 . . . . .6F 81
Maxim Apartments BR2: Brom 4K 159
(off Tiger La.)
Maximfeldt Rd. DA8: Erith 5K 109
Maxim Rd. DA8: Erith 4K 109
N21 . . . . .6F 23
Maxted Pk. HA1: Harr 7J 41
Maxted Rd. SE15 . . . . .3F 121
Maxwell Cl. CR0: Wadd 1J 167
UB3: Hayes 7J 75
Maxwell Ct. SE22 . . . . .1G 139
SW4 . . . . .5H 119
Maxwell Gdns. BR6: Orp 3K 173
Maxwell Rd. DA16: Well 3K 125
HA6: Nwood 1F 39
RM7: Rush G 6K 55
SW6 . . . . .7K 99
TW15: Ashf 6E 128
UB7: W Dray 4B 92
Maxwelton Av. NW7 . . . . .5E 28
Maxwelton Cl. NW7 . . . . .5E 28
Maya Angelou Cl. E4 . . . . .4K 35
Maya Apartments E20 . . . . .5E 68
(off Victory Pde.)
Maya Cl. SE15 . . . . .2H 121
Mayall Cl. EN3: Enf L 1H 25
Mayall Rd. SE24 . . . . .5B 120
Maya Pl. N11 . . . . .7C 32
Maya Rd. N2 . . . . .4A 46
Maybank Av. E18 . . . . .2K 51
HA0: Wemb 5K 59
Maybank Gdns. HA5: Eastc 5J 39
Maybank Rd. E18 . . . . .1K 51
May Bate Av. KT2: King T 1D 150

Maybells Commercial Est.
IG11: Bark 2D 90
Mayberry Cl. BR3: Beck 7B 140
(off Copers Cope Rd.)
Mayberry Pl. KT5: Surb 7F 151
Maybourne Cl. SE26 . . . . .6H 139
Maybourne Rd. BR5: Pet W 5F 161
EN1: Enf .1C 24
Maybury Cl. CR2: S Croy 5B 168
(off Haling Pk. Rd.)
HA1: Harr 6H 41
W1 . . . . .1F 5
(off Marylebone St.)
Maybury Gdns. NW10 . . . . .6D 62
Maybury M. N6 . . . . .7G 47
Maybury Rd. E13 . . . . .4A 88
IG11: Bark 2K 89
Maybury St. SW17 . . . . .5C 136
Maychurch Cl. HA7: Stan 7J 27
May Cl. KT9: Chess 6F 163
May Ct. SW19 . . . . .1A 154
(off Pincott Rd.)
Maycroft HA5: Pinn 2K 39
Maycross Av. SM4: Mord 4H 153
Mayday Gdns. SE3 . . . . .2C 124
Mayday Rd. CR7: Thor H 6B 156
Maydeb Ct. RM6: Chad H 6F 55
Maydew Ho. SE16 . . . . .4J 103
(off Abbeyfield Est.)
Maydwell Ho. E14 . . . . .5C 86
(off Thomas Rd.)
Mayerne Rd. SE9 . . . . .5B 124
Mayesbrook Pk. Arena 5A 72
Mayesbrook Rd. IG3: Ilf 3A 72
IG11: Bark 1K 89
RM8: Dag 3A 72
Mayes Cl. CR0: New Ad 7F 171
Mayesford Rd. RM6: Chad H 7C 54
Mayes Rd. N22 . . . . .2K 47
Mayeswood Rd. SE12 . . . . .4A 142
MAYFAIR 3J 11 (7F 83)
Mayfair Av. DA7: Bex 1D 126
IG1: Ilf 2D 70
KT4: Wor Pk 1C 164
RM6: Chad H 6D 54
TW2: Whitt 7G 113
Mayfair Cl. BR3: Beck 1D 158
KT6: Surb 1E 162
Mayfair Ct. HA8: Edg 5A 28
Mayfair Gdns. IG8: Wfd G 7D 36
N17 . . . . .6H 33
Mayfair M. NW1 . . . . .7D 64
(off Regents Pk. Rd.)
SW12 . . . . .1H 137
Mayfair Pl. W1 . . . . .4K 11 (1F 101)
Mayfair Ter. N14 . . . . .7C 22
Mayfield DA7: Bex 3F 127
HA3: Kenton 5B 42
IG8: Wfd G 6D 36
N12 . . . . .4F 31
N14 . . . . .2C 32
W4 . . . . .4A 98
W13 . . . . .3B 96
Mayfield Cl. E8 . . . . .6F 67
KT7: T Ditt 1B 162
SE20 . . . . .1H 157
SW4 . . . . .5H 119
TW15: Ashf 6D 128
UB10: Hil 3D 74
Mayfield Cres. CR7: Thor H 4K 155
N9 . . . . .6C 24
Mayfield Dr. HA5: Pinn 4D 40
Mayfield Gdns. NW4 . . . . .6F 45
W7 . . . . .6H 77
Mayfield Ho. E2 . . . . .2H 85
(off Cambridge Heath Rd.)
Mayfield Mans. SW15 . . . . .5H 117
Mayfield Rd. BR1: Brom 5C 160
CR2: Sande 7D 168
CR7: Thor H 4K 155

Mayfield Rd. DA17: Belv 4J 109
E4 . . . . .2K 35
E8 . . . . .7F 67
E13 . . . . .4H 87
E17 . . . . .2B 50
EN3: Enf H 2E 24
N8 . . . . .5K 47
RM8: Dag 1C 72
SM2: Sutt 6B 166
SW19 . . . . .1H 153
W3 . . . . .7H 79
W12 . . . . .2A 98
Mayfield Rd. Flats N8 . . . . .6K 47
Mayfields HA9: Wemb 2G 61
Mayfields Cl. HA9: Wemb 2G 61
Mayfield Vs. DA14: Sidc 6C 144
Mayflower Cl. HA4: Ruis 6E 38
SE16 . . . . .4K 103
Mayflower Ho. E14 . . . . .2C 104
(off Westferry Rd.)
IG11: Bark 2A 90
(off Westbury Rd.)
Mayflower Rd. SW9 . . . . .3J 119
Mayflower St. SE16 . . . . .2J 103
Mayfly Cl. HA5: Eastc 7A 40
Mayfly Gdns.
UB5: N'olt 3B 76
Mayford NW1 . . . . .2G 83
(not continuous)
Mayford Cl. BR3: Beck 3K 157
SW12 . . . . .7D 118
Mayford Rd. SW12 . . . . .7D 118
May Gdns. HA0: Wemb 3C 78
Maygood Ho. N1 . . . . .2K 83
(off Maygood St.)
Maygood St. N1 . . . . .2A 84
Maygrove Rd. NW6 . . . . .6H 63
Mayhew Cl. E4 . . . . .3H 35
Mayhew Ct. SE5 . . . . .4D 120
Mayhill Ct. SE15 . . . . .7E 102
(off Tower Mill Rd.)
Mayhill Rd. EN5: Barn 6B 20
SE7 . . . . .6K 105
May Ho. E3 . . . . .2C 86
(off Thomas Fyre Dr.)
Mayland Mans. IG11: Bark 7F 71
(off Whiting Av.)
Maylands Dr. DA14: Sidc 3D 144
UB8: Uxb 6A 56
Maylands Ho. SW3 . . . . .4D 16
(off Cale St.)
May La. HA3: Kenton 7F 43
Maylie Ho. SE16 . . . . .2H 103
(off Marigold St.)
Maynard Cl. N15 . . . . .5E 48
SW6 . . . . .7K 99
Maynard Path E17 . . . . .5E 50
Maynard Rd. E17 . . . . .5E 50
Maynards Quay E1 . . . . .7J 85
Mayne Ct. SE26 . . . . .5H 139
Maynooth Gdns. SM5: Cars 7D 154
Mayo Cl. W13 . . . . .3B 96
Mayo Ho. E1 .5J 85
(off Lindley St.)
Mayola Rd. E5 . . . . .4J 67
Mayo Rd. CR0: C'don 5D 156
KT12: Walt T 7J 147
NW10 . . . . .6A 62
Mayor's & City of London Court, The . . .7E 8
Mayow Rd. SE23 . . . . .4K 139
SE26 . . . . .4K 139
Mayplace Cl. DA7: Bex 3H 127
Mayplace La. SE18 . . . . .6E 107
(not continuous)
Mayplace Rd. E. DA1: Cray 3J 127
DA7: Bex 3H 127
Mayplace Rd. W. DA7: Bex 4G 127
MAYPOLE 1K 145
Maypole Ct.
UB2: S'hall 2D 94
(off Merrick Rd.)

May Rd. E4 . . . . .6H 35
E13 . . . . .2J 87
TW2: Twick 1J 131
Mayroyd Av. KT6: Surb 2G 163
May's Bldgs. M. SE10 . . . . .7E 104
May's Ct. SE10 . . . . .7F 105
Mays Ct. WC2 . . . . .3E 12 (7J 83)
Mays Hill Rd. BR2: Brom 2G 159
Mays La. EN5: Ark, Barn 6A 20, 1H 29
Maysoule Rd. SW11 . . . . .4B 118
Mays Rd. TW11: Tedd 5H 131
Mayston M. SE10 . . . . .5J 105
(off Ormiston Rd.)
May St. W14 .5H 99
(Kelway Ho.)
W14 . . . . .5H 99
(Orchard Sq.)
Mayswood Gdns. RM10: Dag 6J 73
Maythorne Cotts. SE13 . . . . .5F 123
Mayton St. N7 . . . . .3K 65
Maytree Cl. HA8: Edg 3D 28
Maytree Ct. CR4: Mitc 3E 154
UB5: N'olt 3C 76
Maytree Gdns. W5 . . . . .2D 96
May Tree Ho. SE4 . . . . .3B 122
(off Wickham Rd.)
Maytree La. HA7: Stan 7F 27
Maytree Wlk. SW2 . . . . .2A 138
Mayville Est. N16 . . . . .5E 66
Mayville Rd. E11 . . . . .2G 69
(not continuous)
IG1: Ilf 5F 71
May Wlk. E13 .3K 87
Mayward Ho. SE5 . . . . .1E 120
(off Peckham Rd.)
Maywood Cl. BR3: Beck 7D 140
May Wynne Ho. E16 . . . . .7K 87
(off Murray Sq.)
Maze Hill SE3 . . . . .7H 105
SE10 . . . . .6G 105
Maze Hill Lodge SE10 . . . . .6F 105
(off Park Vista)
Mazenod Av. NW6 . . . . .7J 63
Maze Rd. TW9: Kew 7G 97
MCC Cricket Mus. & Tours . . .2A 4 (3B 82)
Mead, The BR3: Beck 1E 158
BR4: W W'ck 1F 171
N2 . . . . .2A 46
SM6: Wall 6H 167
UB10: Ick 2C 56
W13 . . . . .5B 78
Meadbank Studios SW11 . . . . .7C 100
(off Parkgate Rd.)
Mead Cl. HA3: Hrw W 1H 41
NW1 . . . . .6E 64
Mead Cl. NW9 . . . . .5J 43
Mead Cres. E4 . . . . .4K 35
SM1: Sutt 3C 166
Meadcroft Rd. SE11 . . . . .7K 19 (6B 102)
(not continuous)
SE17 . . . . .6B 102
Meade Cl. W4 . . . . .6G 97
Meade M. SW1 . . . . .5D 18
(off Causton St.)
Meader Ct. SE14 . . . . .7K 103
Mead Fld. HA2: Harr 3D 58
Meadfield HA8: Edg 2C 28
(not continuous)
Meadfoot Rd. SW16 . . . . .7G 137
Meadgate Av. IG8: Wfd G 5H 37
Mead Gro. RM6: Chad H 3D 54
Mead Ho. W11 . . . . .1H 99
(off Ladbroke Rd.)
Mead Ho. La. UB4: Hayes 4F 75
Meadhurst Club 5H 129
Meadhurst Pk. TW16: Sun 6G 129
Meadlands Dr. TW10: Ham 2D 132
Mead Lodge W4 . . . . .2A 97
Meadow, The BR7: Chst 6G 143
N10 . . . . .3E 46

Meadow Av. CR0: C'don 6K 157
Meadow Bank N21 6E 22
Meadowbank KT5: Surb 6F 151
NW3 7D 64
SE3 3H 123
Meadowbank Cl. SW6 7E 98
TW7: Isle 1J 113
Meadowbank Gdns. TW5: Cran 1J 111
Meadowbank Rd. NW9 7K 43
Meadowbridge Ct. CR0: C'don 5D 156
(off Princess Rd.)
Meadowbrook Cl. SL3: Poyle 4A 174
Meadowbrook Ct. TW7: Isle 3J 113
Meadow Cl. BR7: Chst 5F 143
DA6: Bex 5F 127
E4 1J 35
E9 6B 68
EN3: Enf W 1F 25
EN5: Barn 6C 20
HA4: Ruis 6H 39
IG11: Bark 7A 72
KT10: Hin W 3A 162
SE6 5C 140
SM1: Sutt 2A 166
SW20 4E 152
TW4: Houn 6E 112
TW10: Ham 1E 132
UB5: N'olt 2E 76
Meadow Ct. E16 1A 106
(off Booth Rd.)
N1 2E 84
TW3: Houn 6F 113
Meadowcourt Rd. SE3 4H 123
Meadowcroft BR1: Brom 3D 160
W4 5G 97
(off Brooks Rd.)
Meadowcroft Cl. E10 7D 50
N13 2F 33
Meadowcroft M. E1 7G 85
(off Cable St.)
SE6 6D 122
Meadowcroft Rd. N13 2F 33
Meadow Dr. N10 3F 47
NW4 2E 44
Meadowford Cl. SE28 7A 90
Meadow Gdns. HA8: Edg 6C 28
Meadow Gth. NW10 6J 61
Meadow Ga. HA2: Harr 3F 59
Meadowgate Cl. NW7 5G 29
Meadow Hill KT3: N Mald 6A 152
Meadow La. SE12 3K 141
Meadowlark Ho. NW9 7B 44
Meadowlea Cl. UB7: Harm 2E 174
Meadow M. SW8 6K 101
Meadow Pl. SW8 7J 101
W4 7A 98
Meadow Rd. BR2: Brom 2G 159
HA5: Pinn 4B 40
IG11: Bark 7K 71
RM7: Rush G 1J 73
RM9: Dag 6F 73
SM1: Sutt 4C 166
SW8 7H 19 (7K 101)
SW19 7A 136
TW13: Felt 2C 130
TW15: Ashf 5F 129
UB1: S'hall 7D 76
Meadow Row SE1 3C 102
Meadows, The E4 4A 36
Meadows Cl. E10 2C 68
Meadows Ct. DA14: Sidc 6B 144
Meadows End TW16: Sun 1J 147
Meadowside SE3 4A 124
SE9 4A 124
TW1: Twick 7D 114
Meadow Stile CR0: C'don 3C 168
Meadows Way SE4 3A 122
Meadowsweet Cl. E16 5B 88
SW20 4E 152
Meadow Vw. DA15: Sidc 7B 126
HA1: Harr 1J 59
Meadowview TW19: Stanw M 7A 174
Meadow Vw. Rd. CR7: Thor H 5B 156
SW20 4E 152
UB4: Hayes 4F 75
Meadowview Rd. DA5: Bexl 6E 126
KT19: Ewe 7A 164
SE6 5B 140
Meadow Wlk. E18 4J 51
KT17: Ewe 7B 164
KT19: Ewe 6A 164
RM9: Dag 6F 73
SM6: Wall 3F 167
Meadow Walks
EN5: New Bar 6E 20
Meadow Way BR6: Farnb 3E 172
HA4: Ruis 6K 39
HA9: Wemb 4D 60
KT9: Chess 5E 162
NW9 5K 43
Meadow Way, The HA3: Hrw W 1J 41
Meadow Waye TW5: Hest 6C 94
Mead Path SW17 4A 136
Mead Pl. CR0: C'don 1C 168
E9 6J 67
Mead Plat NW10 6J 61
Mead Rd. BR7: Chst 6G 143
HA8: Edg 6B 28
TW10: Ham 3C 132
Mead Row SE1 1J 19 (3A 102)
Meads, The HA8: Edg 6E 28
SM3: Cheam 3G 165
SM4: Mord 5C 154
UB8: Cowl 4A 74
Meads Ct. E15 6H 69
Meadside Cl. BR3: Beck 1A 158
Meads La. IG3: Ilf 7J 53
Meads Rd. EN3: Enf H 1F 25
N22 2B 48
Mead Ter. HA9: Wemb 4D 60
Meadvale Rd. CR0: C'don 7F 157
W5 4B 78
Mead Way BR2: Hayes 6H 159
CR0: C'don 2A 170
HA4: Ruis 6F 39
Meadway BR3: Beck 1E 158
EN5: Barn, New Bar 4D 20
IG3: Bark, Ilf 4J 71
IG8: Wfd G 5F 37
KT5: Surb 1J 163
N14 2C 32
NW11 6J 45
SW20 4E 152
TW2: Twick 1H 131
TW15: Ashf 4C 128
Meadway, The
IG9: Buck H 1G 37
SE3 2F 123
Meadway Cl. EN5: Barn 4D 20
HA5: Hat E 6A 26
NW11 6K 45
Meadway Ct. RM8: Dag 2F 73
TW11: Tedd 5C 132
W5 4F 79
Meadway Gdns.
HA4: Ruis 6F 39
Meadway Ga. NW11 6J 45
Meaford Way SE20 7H 139
Meakin Est. SE1 3E 102
Meander Ho. E20 5D 68
(off Logan Cl.)
Meanley Rd. E12 4C 70
Meard St. W1 1C 12 (6H 83)
(not continuous)
Mears Cl. E1 5G 85
(off Settles St.)
Meath Cres. E2 3K 85
Meath Ho. SE24 6B 120
(off Dulwich Rd.)
Meath Rd. E15 2H 87
IG1: Ilf 3G 71
Meath St. SW11 1F 119
Mecca Bingo
Burnt Oak 2J 43
Camden 1F 83
(off Arlington Rd.)
Catford 7D 122
Chadwell Heath 7D 54
Croydon 2C 168
Dagenham 1E 90
Hayes 6K 75
Morden 7A 154
Wandsworth 1K 135
Wood Green 2A 48
(off Lordship La.)
Mecklenburgh Pl. WC1 3G 7 (4K 83)
Mecklenburgh Sq. WC1 3G 7 (4K 83)
Mecklenburgh St.
WC1 3G 7 (4K 83)
Medals Way E20 5E 68
Medburn St. NW1 2H 83
Medcroft Gdns. SW14 4J 115
Medebourne Cl. SE3 3J 123
Mede Ho. BR1: Brom 5K 141
(off Pike Cl.)
Medesenge Way N13 6G 33
Medfield St. SW15 7C 116
Medhurst Cl. E3 2A 86
(not continuous)
Medhurst Dr.
BR1: Brom 5G 141
Median Rd. E5 5J 67
Medici Cl. IG3: Ilf 6A 54
(not continuous)
Medina Gro. N7 3A 66
Medina Rd. N7 3A 66
Medland Cl.
SM6: Wall 1E 166
Medland Ho. E14 7A 86
Medlar Cl. UB5: N'olt 2B 76
Medlar Ho. DA15: Sidc 3A 144
Medlar St. SE5 1C 120
Medley Rd. NW6 6J 63
Medora Rd. RM7: Rom 4K 55
SW2 7K 119
Medusa Rd. SE6 6D 122
Medway Bldgs. E3 2A 86
(off Medway Rd.)
Medway Cl. CR0: C'don 6J 157
IG1: Ilf 5G 71
RM7: Mawney 1H 55
Medway Ct. NW11 6K 45
WC1 2E 6
(off Judd St.)
Medway Dr. UB6: G'frd 2K 77
Medway Gdns. HA0: Wemb 4A 60
Medway Ho. KT2: King T 1D 150
NW8 4C 4
(off Penfold St.)
SE1 7F 15
(off Hankey Pl.)
Medway M. E3 2A 86
Medway Pde. UB6: G'frd 2K 77
Medway Rd. E3 2A 86
Medway St. SW1 2D 18 (3H 101)
Medwin St. SW4 4K 119
Meerbrook Rd. SE3 3A 124
Meeson Rd. E15 7H 69
Meeson St. E5 4A 68
Meeson's Wharf E15 2E 86
Meeting Fld. Path E9 6J 67
Meeting Ho. All. E1 1H 103
Meeting Ho. La. SE15 1H 121
Megelish M. UB1: S'hall 3E 76
Mehetabel Rd. E9 5J 67
Meister Cl. IG1: Ilf 1H 71
Melancholy Wlk. TW10: Ham 2C 132
Melanda Cl. BR7: Chst 5D 142
Melanie Cl. DA7: Bex 1E 126
Melba Way SE13 1D 122
Melbourne Av. HA5: Pinn 3F 41
N13 6E 32
W13 1A 96
Melbourne Cl. BR6: Orp 7J 161
SE20 7G 139
SM6: Wall 5G 167
UB10: Ick 4C 56
Melbourne Ct. E5 4A 68
(off Daubeney Rd.)
N10 7A 32
W9 4A 82
(off Randolph Av.)
Melbourne Gdns. RM6: Chad H 5E 54
Melbourne Gro. SE22 4E 120
Melbourne Ho. UB4: Yead 4A 76
W8 1J 99
(off Kensington Pl.)
Melbourne Mans. W14 6G 99
(off Musard Rd.)
Melbourne M. SE6 7E 122
SW9 1A 120
Melbourne Pl. WC2 1H 13 (6K 83)
Melbourne Rd. E6 2D 88
E10 7D 50
E17 4A 50
IG1: Ilf 1F 71
SM6: Wall 5F 167
SW19 1J 153
TW11: Tedd 6C 132
Melbourne Sq. SW9 1A 120
Melbourne Ter. SW6 7K 99
(off Moore Pk. Rd.)
Melbourne Way EN1: Enf 6A 24
Melbourne Yd. SE19 6E 138
Melbray M. SW6 2H 117
Melbreak Ho. SE22 3E 120
Melbury Av. UB2: S'hall 3F 95
Melbury Cl. BR7: Chst 6C 142
KT10: Clay 6B 162
Melbury Ct. W8 3H 99
Melbury Dr. SE5 7E 102
Melbury Gdns. SW20 1D 152
Melbury Ho. SW8 7K 101
(off Richborne Ter.)
Melbury Rd. HA3: Kenton 5F 43
W14 3H 99
Melchester W11 6H 81
(off Ledbury Rd.)
Melchester Ho. N19 3H 65
(off Wedmore St.)
Melcombe Ct. NW1 5E 4
(off Melcombe Pl.)
Melcombe Gdns. HA3: Kenton 6F 43
Melcombe Ho. SW8 7K 101
(off Dorset Rd.)
Melcombe Pl. NW1 5E 4 (5D 82)
Melcombe Regis Ct. W1 6H 5
(off Weymouth St.)
Melcombe St. NW1 4F 5 (4D 82)
Meldex Cl. NW7 6K 29
Meldon Cl. SW6 1K 117
Meldone Cl. KT5: Surb 7H 151
Meldrum Rd. IG3: Ilf 2A 72
Melfield Gdns. SE6 4E 140
Melford Av. IG11: Bark 6J 71
Melford Cl. KT9: Chess 5F 163
Melford Ct. SE1 3E 102
(off Fendall St.)
SE22 1G 139
(not continuous)
Melford Pas. SE22 7G 121
Melford Rd. E6 4D 88
E11 2G 69
E17 4A 50
IG1: Ilf 2H 71
SE22 7G 121
Melfort Av. CR7: Thor H 3B 156
Melfort Rd. CR7: Thor H 3B 156
Melgund Rd. N5 5A 66
Melina Cl. UB3: Hayes 5F 75
Melina Ct. NW8 2A 4
SW15 3C 116
Melina Pl. NW8 2A 4 (3B 82)
Melina Rd. W12 2D 98

Melior Ct. N6 ....6G 47
Melior Pl. SE1 ....6G 15 (2E 102)
Melior St. SE1 ....6G 15 (2E 102)
Meliot Rd. SE6 ....2F 141
Meller Cl. CR0: Bedd 3J 167
Meller Ho. E20 ....6E 68
(off Champions Wlk.)
Mellifont Cl. SM5: Cars 7B 154
Melling Dr. EN1: Enf 1B 24
Melling St. SE18 ....6J 107
Mellish Cl. IG11: Bark 1K 89
Mellish Flats E10 ....7C 50
Mellish Gdns. IG8: Wfd G 5D 36
Mellish Ho. E1 ....6H 85
(off Varden St.)
Mellish Ind. Est. SE18 ....3B 106
Mellish St. E14 ....3C 104
Mellison Rd. SW17 ....5C 136
Melliss Av. TW9: Kew 1H 115
Mellitus St. W12 ....5B 80
Mellor Cl. KT12: Walt T 7D 148
Mellow La. E. UB4: Hayes 3E 74
Mellow La. W. UB10: Hil 3E 74
Mellows Rd. IG5: Ilf 3D 52
SM6: Wall 5H 167
Mells Cres. SE9 ....4D 142
Mell St. SE10 ....5G 105
Melody La. N5 ....5C 66
Melody Rd. SW18 ....5A 118
Melon Pl. W8 ....2J 99
Melon Rd. E11 ....3G 69
SE15 ....1G 121
Melrose Av. CR4: Mitc 7F 137
DA1: Cray 7K 127
N22 ....1B 48
NW2 ....5D 62
SW16 ....3K 155
SW19 ....2H 135
TW2: Whitt 7F 113
UB6: G'frd 2F 77
Melrose Cl. SE12 ....1J 141
UB4: Hayes 5J 75
UB6: G'frd 2F 77
Melrose Ct. W13 ....1A 96
(off Williams Rd.)
Melrose Cres. BR6: Orp 4H 173
Melrose Dr. UB1: S'hall 1E 94
Melrose Gdns. HA8: Edg 3H 43
KT3: N Mald 3K 151
W6 ....3E 98
Melrose Ho. NW6 ....3J 81
(off Carlton Vale)
SW1 ....5J 17
(part of Abbots Mnr.)
Melrose Rd. HA5: Pinn 4D 40
SW13 ....2B 116
SW18 ....6H 117
SW19 ....2J 153
W3 ....3J 97
Melrose Ter. W6 ....3E 98
Melrose Tudor SM6: Wall 5J 167
(off Plough La.)
Melsa Rd. SM4: Mord 6A 154
Melthorne Dr. HA4: Ruis 3A 58
Melthorpe Gdns. SE3 ....1C 124
Melton Cl. HA4: Ruis 1A 58
Melton Ct. SM2: Sutt 7A 166
SW7 ....4B 16 (4B 100)
Melton St. NW1 ....2B 6 (3G 83)
Melville Av. CR2: S Croy 5F 169
SW20 ....7C 134
UB6: G'frd 5K 59
Melville Cl. UB10: Ick 2F 57
Melville Ct. SE8 ....4A 104
W4 ....5G 97
(off Haining Cl.)
W12 ....2G 98
(off Goldhawk Rd.)
Melville Gdns. N13 ....5G 33
Melville Ho. EN5: New Bar 5G 21
Melville Pl. N1 ....7C 66

Melville Rd. DA14: Sidc 2C 144
E17 ....3B 50
NW10 ....7K 61
RM5: Col R 1H 55
SW13 ....1C 116
Melville Vs. Rd. W3 ....1J 97
Melvin Rd. SE20 ....1J 157
Melwood Ho. E1 ....6H 85
(off Watney Mkt.)
Melyn Cl. N7 ....4G 65
Memel Ct. EC1 ....4C 8
Memel St. EC1 ....4C 8 (4C 84)
Memess Path SE18 ....6E 106
Memorial Av. E15 ....3G 87
Memorial Cl. TW5: Hest 6D 94
Memorial Hgts. IG2: Ilf 6F 53
Menai Pl. E3 ....2C 86
(off Blondin St.)
Menard Ct. EC1 ....2D 8
(off Galway St.)
Mendez Way SW15 ....6C 116
Mendham Ho. SE1 ....7G 15
(off Cluny Pl.)
Mendip Cl. KT4: Wor Pk 1E 164
SE26 ....4J 139
UB3: Harl 7F 93
Mendip Ct. SE14 ....6J 103
(off Avonley Rd.)
Mendip Dr. NW2 ....2G 63
SW11 ....3A 118
Mendip Ho. N9 ....2B 34
(within Edmonton Grn. Shop. Cen.)
Mendip Ho's. E2 ....3J 85
(off Welwyn St.)
Mendip Rd. DA7: Bex 1K 127
IG2: Ilf 5J 53
SW11 ....3A 118
Mendora Rd. SW6 ....7G 99
Menelik Rd. NW2 ....4G 63
Menier Chocolate Factory 5D 14
(off Southwark St.)
Menlo Gdns. SE19 ....7D 138
Menlo Lodge N13 ....3E 32
(off Crothall Cl.)
Menon Dr. N9 ....3C 34
Menotti St. E2 ....4G 85
Menteath Ho. E14 ....6C 86
(off Dod St.)
Mentmore Cl. HA3: Kenton 6C 42
Mentmore Ter. E8 ....7H 67
Mentone Mans. SW10 ....7K 99
(off Fulham Rd.)
Meon Ct. TW7: Isle 2J 113
Meon Rd. W3 ....2J 97
Meopham Rd. CR4: Mitc 1G 155
Mepham Cres. HA3: Hrw W 7B 26
Mepham Gdns. HA3: Hrw W 7B 26
Mepham St. SE1 ....5H 13 (1A 102)
Mera Dr. DA7: Bex 4G 127
Meranti Ho. E1 ....6G 85
(off Goodman's Stile)
Merantun Way SW19 ....1K 153
Merbury Cl. SE13 ....5E 122
SE28 ....1H 107
Merbury Rd. SE28 ....1H 107
Mercator Pl. E14 ....5C 104
Mercator Rd. SE13 ....4F 123
Mercer Bldg. EC2 ....3H 9
(off New Inn Yd.)
Mercer Cl. KT7: T Ditt 7K 149
Mercer Ct. E1 ....5A 86
Mercer Ho. SW1 ....5J 17
(off Ebury Bri. Rd.)
Merceron Ho's. E2 ....3J 85
(off Globe Rd.)
Merceron St. E1 ....4H 85
Mercer Pl. HA5: Pinn 2A 40
Mercers Cl. SE10 ....4H 105
Mercer's Cotts. E1 ....6A 86
(off White Horse Rd.)
Mercers M. N19 ....3H 65

Mercers Pl. W6 ....4F 99
Mercers Rd. N19 ....3H 65
(not continuous)
Mercer St. WC2 ....1E 12 (6J 83)
Merchant Cl. KT19: Ewe 5K 163
Merchant Ct. E1 ....1J 103
(off Wapping Wall)
Merchant Ho. E14 ....3D 104
(off Selsdon Way)
Merchant Ind. Ter. NW10 ....4J 79
Merchant Navy (Tower Hill) Memorial
..........................3H 15 (7F 85)
Merchants Cl. SE25 ....4G 157
Merchants Ho. E14 ....4H 87
(off New Village Av.)
SE10 ....5F 105
(off Collington St.)
Merchants Lodge E17 ....4C 50
(off Westbury Rd.)
Merchant Sq. W2 ....6B 4
Merchants Row SE10 ....5F 105
(off Hoskins St.)
Merchant St. E3 ....3B 86
Merchiston Rd. SE6 ....2F 141
Mercia Gro. SE13 ....4E 122
Mercia Ho. SE5 ....2C 120
(off Denmark Rd.)
TW15: Ashf 1E 146
Mercier Rd. SW15 ....5G 117
Mercury NW9 ....1B 44
(off Quakers Course)
Mercury Cen.
TW14: Felt 5J 111
Mercury Ct. E14 ....4C 104
(off Homer Dr.)
SW9 ....1A 120
(off Southey Rd.)
Mercury Ho. E3 ....1C 86
(off Garrison Rd.)
E16 ....6H 87
(off Jude St.)
TW8: Bford 6C 96
(off Glenhurst Rd.)
W5 ....4F 79
Mercury Rd. TW8: Bford 6C 96
Mercury Way SE14 ....6K 103
Mercy Ter. SE13 ....5D 122
Merebank La. CR0: Wadd 5K 167
Mere Cl. BR6: Farnb 2E 172
SW15 ....7F 117
Meredith Av. NW2 ....5E 62
Meredith Cl. HA5: Pinn 1B 40
Meredith Ho. N16 ....5E 66
Meredith M. SE4 ....4B 122
Meredith St. E13 ....3J 87
EC1 ....2A 8 (3B 84)
Meredith Twr. W3 ....3H 97
(off Hanbury Rd.)
Meredyth Rd. SW13 ....2C 116
Mere End CR0: C'don 7K 157
Mere Rd. SE2 ....2D 108
TW17: Shep 6D 146
Mereside BR6: Farnb 2E 172
Mereside Pk. TW15: Ashf 4E 128
Meretone Cl. SE4 ....4A 122
Mereton Mans. SE8 ....1C 122
(off Brookmill Rd.)
Merevale Cres. SM4: Mord 6A 154
Mereway Rd. TW2: Twick 1H 131
Merewood Cl. BR1: Brom 2E 160
Merewood Gdns. CR0: C'don ...7K 157
Merewood Rd. DA7: Bex 2J 127
Mereworth Cl. BR2: Brom 5H 159
Mereworth Dr. SE18 ....7F 107
Mereworth Ho. SE15 ....6J 103
Merganser Ct. E1 ....3K 15
(off Star Pl.)
SE8 ....6B 104
(off Edward St.)
Merganser Gdns. SE28 ....3H 107

Meriden Cl. BR1: Brom 7B 142
IG6: Ilf 1G 53
Meriden Ct. SW3 ....6C 16
Meriden Ho. N1 ....1E 84
(off Wilmer Gdns.)
Merideth Ct. KT1: King T 2F 151
Meridia Ct. E15 ....1E 86
(off Biggerstaff Rd.)
Meridian Bus. Pk. EN3: Pond E ..6F 25
Meridian Cl. NW7 ....4E 28
Meridian Ct. SE15 ....7H 103
(off Gervase St.)
SE16 ....2G 103
(off East La.)
UB4: Yead 4A 76
Meridian Ga. E14 ....2D 104
Meridian Ho. NW1 ....7H 65
(off Baynes St.)
SE10 ....4G 105
(off Azof St.)
SE10 ....7E 104
(off Royal Hill)
SW18 ....4A 118
(off Juniper Dr.)
Meridian Pl. E14 ....2D 104
Meridian Point SE8 ....6D 104
Meridian Rd. SE7 ....7B 106
Meridian Sq. E15 ....7F 69
Meridian Trad. Est. SE7 ......4K 105
Meridian Wlk. N17 ....6K 33
N9 ....4D 34
N18 ....5D 34
Merifield Rd. SE9 ....4A 124
Merino Cl. E11 ....4A 52
Merino Ct. EC1 ....2D 8
(off Lever St.)
Merino Pl. DA15: Sidc 6A 126
Merioneth Ct. W7 ....5K 77
(off Copley Cl.)
Merita Ho. E1 ....1G 103
(off Nesham St.)
Merivale Rd. HA1: Harr 7G 41
SW15 ....4G 117
Merle Mans. E20 ....6E 68
(off Glade Wlk.)
Merlewood Dr. BR7: Chst 1D 160
Merley Cl. NW9 ....1J 61
Merlin NW9 ....1B 44
(off Near Acre)
Merlin Cl. CR0: C'don 4E 168
CR4: Mitc 3C 154
SM6: Wall 6K 167
UB5: N'olt 3A 76
UB5: BR2: Brom 3H 159
HA4: Ruis 2F 57
HA7: Stan 5G 27
(off William Dr.)
SE3 ....4K 123
Merlin Cres. HA8: Edg 1F 43
Merlin Gdns. BR1: Brom 3H 143
Merling Cl. KT9: Chess 5C 162
Merlin Gro. BR3: Beck 4B 158
Merlin Hgts. N17 ....3H 49
(off Daneland Wlk.)
Merlin Ho. EN3: Pond E 5E 24
Merlin Rd. DA16: Well 4A 126
E12 ....2A 70
Merlin Rd. Nth. DA16: Well 4A 126
Merlins Av. HA2: Harr 3D 58
Merlins Ct. WC1 ....2J 7
(off Margery St.)
Merlin St. WC1 ....2J 7 (3A 84)
Mermaid Ct. E8 ....7F 67
(off Celandine Dr.)
SE1 ....6E 14 (2D 102)
SE16 ....1B 104
Mermaid Ho. E14 ....7E 86
(off Bazely St.)
Mermaid Twr. SE8 ....6B 104
(off Abinger Gro.)

Meroe Ct.—Midhurst Hill

Meroe Ct. N16 2E **66**
Merredene St. SW2 6K **119**
Merriam Av. E9 6B **68**
Merriam Cl. E4 5K **35**
Merrick Rd. UB2: S'hall 2D **94**
Merrick Sq. SE1 7E **14** (3D **102**)
Merridene N21 6G **23**
Merrielands Cres. RM9: Dag 2F **91**
Merrielands Retail Pk. RM9: Dag 1F **91**
Merrilands Rd. KT4: Wor Pk 1E **164**
Merrilees Rd. DA15: Sidc 7J **125**
Merrilyn Cl. KT10: Clay 6A **162**
Merriman Rd. SE3 1A **124**
Merrington Rd. SW6 6J **99**
Merrion Av. HA7: Stan 5J **27**
Merrion Ct. *HA4: Ruis* *1H **57***
(off Pembroke Rd.)
Merritt Gdns. KT9: Chess 6C **162**
Merritt Rd. SE4 5B **122**
Merrivale N14 6C **22**
NW1 *1G **83***
(off Camden St.)
Merrivale Av. IG4: Ilf 4B **52**
Merrivale M. HA8: Edg 1J **43**
Merrow Bldgs. *SE1* *6B **14***
(off Rushworth St.)
Merrow Ct. CR4: Mitc 2B **154**
Merrow Rd. SM2: Cheam 7F **165**
Merrow St. SE17 5D **102**
Merrow Wlk. SE17 5D **102**
Merrow Way CR0: New Ad 6E **170**
Merrydown Way BR7: Chst 1C **160**
Merryfield SE3 2H **123**
Merryfield Gdns. HA7: Stan 5H **27**
Merryfield Ho. *SE9* *3A **142***
(off Grove Pk. Rd.)
Merryfields UB8: Uxb 2A **74**
Merryfields Way SE6 7D **122**
MERRY HILL 1A **26**
Merryhill Cl. E4 7J **25**
Merry Hill Mt. WD23: Bush 1A **26**
Merry Hill Rd. WD23: Bush 1A **26**
Merryhills Ct. N14 5B **22**
Merryhills Dr. EN2: Enf 4C **22**
Merryweather Ct. KT3: N Mald 5A **152**
N19 3G **65**
Merryweather Pl. SE10 7D **104**
Mersea Ho. IG11: Bark 6F **71**
Mersey Ct. *KT2: King T* *1D **150***
(off Samuel Gray Gdns.)
Mersey Rd. E17 3B **50**
Mersey Wlk. UB5: N'olt 2E **76**
Mersham Dr. NW9 5G **43**
Mersham Pl. *CR7: Thor H* *2D **156***
(off Livingstone Rd.)
SE20 1H **157**
Mersham Rd. CR7: Thor H 3D **156**
Merten Rd. RM6: Chad H 7E **54**
Merthyr Ter. SW13 6D **98**
MERTON 7A **136**
Merton Abbey Mills SW19 1A **154**
Merton Av. UB5: N'olt 5G **59**
UB10: Hil 7D **56**
W4 4B **98**
Merton Ct. DA16: Well 2B **126**
IG1: Ilf 6C **52**
Merton Gdns.
BR5: Pet W 5F **161**
Merton Hall Gdns. SW20 1G **153**
Merton Hall Rd. SW19 7G **135**
Merton High St. SW19 7K **135**
Merton Ind. Pk. SW19 1K **153**
Merton La. N6 2D **64**
Merton Lodge
EN5: New Bar 5F **21**
Merton Mans. SW20 2F **153**
MERTON PARK 2J **153**
Merton Pk. Pde. SW19 1H **153**
Merton Pl. *SW19* *1A **154***
(off Nelson Gro. Rd.)
Merton Ri. NW3 7C **64**
Merton Rd. E17 5E **50**
EN2: Enf 1J **23**
HA2: Harr 1G **59**
IG3: Ilf 7K **53**
IG11: Bark 7K **71**
SE25 5F **157**
SW18 6J **117**
SW19 7K **135**
Merton's Intergenerational Cen. 2F **155**
Merton Way KT8: W Mole 4F **149**
UB10: Hil 7D **56**
Mertoun Ter. *W1* *7E **4***
(off Seymour Pl.)
Merttins Rd. SE15 5K **121**
Meru Cl. NW5 4E **64**
Mervan Rd. SW2 4A **120**
Mervyn Av. SE9 3G **143**
Mervyn Rd. TW17: Shep 7E **146**
W13 3A **96**
Messaline Av. W3 6J **79**
Messenger Ct. *SE16* *3G **103***
(off Spa Rd.)
Messent Rd. SE9 5A **124**
Messeter Pl. SE9 6E **124**
Messina Av. NW6 7J **63**
Messina Way RM9: Dag 2F **91**
Messiter Ho. *N1* *1K **83***
(off Barnsbury Est.)
Metcalfe Ct. SE10 3H **105**
Metcalf Rd. TW15: Ashf 5D **128**
Metcalf Wlk. TW13: Hanw 4C **130**
Meteor St. SW11 4E **118**
Meteor Way SM6: Wall 7J **167**
Methley St. SE11 6K **19** (5A **102**)
Methuen Cl. HA8: Edg 7B **28**
Methuen Pk. N10 3F **47**
Methuen Rd. DA6: Bex 4F **127**
DA17: Belv 4H **109**
HA8: Edg 7B **28**
Methven Ct. *N9* *3B **34***
(off The Broadway)
Methwold Rd. W10 5F **81**
Metro Bus. Cen. SE26 6B **140**
Metro Central Hgts. *SE1* *3C **102***
(off Newington C'way.)
Metro Golf Cen. 7K **29**
Metro Ind. Cen. TW7: Isle 2J **113**
Metropolis *SE11* *3B **102***
(off Oswin St.)
Metropolitan Bus. Cen. *N1* *7E **66***
(off Enfield Rd.)
Metropolitan Cen., The UB6: G'frd 1F **77**
Metropolitan Cl. E14 5C **86**
Metropolitan Ho. TW8: Bford 6F **97**
Metropolitan Police FC 6H **149**
Metropolitan Sta. Bldgs. *W6* *4E **98***
(off Beadon Rd.)
Metropolitan Wharf E1 1J **103**
Metro Trad. Est. HA9: Wemb 4H **61**
Mews, The DA14: Sidc 4A **144**
IG4: Ilf 5B **52**
N1 1C **84**
N8 3A **48**
RM1: Rom 4K **55**
TW1: Twick 6B **114**
TW12: Hamp H 6G **131**
Mews Pl. IG8: Wfd G 4D **36**
Mews St. E1 4K **15** (1G **103**)
Mexborough NW1 1G **83**
Mexfield Rd. SW15 5H **117**
Meyer Grn. EN1: Enf 1B **24**
Meyer Rd. DA8: Erith 6K **109**
Meymott St. SE1 5A **14** (1B **102**)
Meynell Cres. E9 7K **67**
Meynell Gdns. E9 7K **67**
Meynell Rd. E9 7K **67**
Meyrick Ho. *E14* *5C **86***
(off Burgess St.)
Meyrick Rd. NW10 6C **62**
SW11 3B **118**
MFA Bowl
Lewisham 3E **122**
Miah Ter. E1 1G **103**
Miall Wlk. SE26 4A **140**
Mia M. N13 5F **33**
Mica Ho. N1 7A **66**
Micawber Av. UB8: Hil 4C **74**
Micawber Ct. *N1* *1D **8***
(off Windsor Ter.)
Micawber Ho. *SE16* *2G **103***
(off Llewellyn St.)
Micawber St. N1 1D **8** (3C **84**)
Michael Cliffe Ho. EC1 2A **8**
Michael Cl. E3 4B **86**
Michael Edwards Studio Theatre, The 6E **104**
(within Cutty Sark)
Michael Faraday Ho. *SE17* *5E **102***
(off Beaconsfield Rd.)
Michael Gaynor Cl. W7 1K **95**
Michael Haines Ho. *SW9* *7A **102***
(off Sth. Island Pl.)
Michael Manley Ind. Est. SW8 1G **119**
Michaelmas Cl. SW20 3E **152**
Michael Rd. E11 1G **69**
SE25 3E **156**
SW6 1K **117**
Michaels Cl. SE13 4G **123**
Michael Stewart Ho. *SW6* *6H **99***
(off Clem Attlee Ct.)
Michelangelo Ct. *SE16* *5H **103***
(off Stubbs Dr.)
Micheldever Rd. SE12 6G **123**
Michelham Gdns. TW1: Twick 3K **131**
Michelle Ct. *BR1: Brom* *1H **159***
(off Blyth Rd.)
N12 5F **31**
W3 7K **79**
Michelsdale Dr. TW9: Rich 4E **114**
Michelson Ho. SE11 4H **19**
Michel's Row *TW9: Rich* *4E **114***
(off Michelsdale Dr.)
Michel Wlk. SE18 5F **107**
Michigan Av. E12 4D **70**
Michigan Bldg. *E14* *1F **105***
(off Biscayne Av.)
Michigan Ho. E14 3C **104**
Michleham Down N12 4C **30**
Mickledore *NW1* *1B **6***
(off Ampthill Est.)
Mickleham Cl. BR5: St P 2K **161**
Mickleham Gdns. SM3: Cheam 6G **165**
Mickleham Rd. BR5: St P 1K **161**
Mickleham Way CR0: New Ad 7F **171**
Micklethwaite Rd. SW6 6J **99**
Mickleton Ho. *W2* *5J **81***
(off Westbourne Pk. Rd.)
Midas Bus. Cen. RM10: Dag 4H **73**
Midas Metropolitan Ind. Est.
SM4: Mord 7E **152**
MID BECKTON 5D **88**
Midcroft HA4: Ruis 1G **57**
Middle Dartrey Wlk. *SW10* *7A **100***
(off Dartrey Wlk.)
Middle Dene NW7 3E **28**
Middlefield NW8 1B **82**
Middlefielde W13 5B **78**
Middlefield Gdns. IG2: Ilf 6F **53**
Middle Grn. Cl.
KT5: Surb 6F **151**
Middleham Gdns. N18 6B **34**
Middleham Rd. N18 6B **34**
Middle La. N8 5J **47**
TW11: Tedd 6K **131**
Middle La. M. N8 5J **47**
Middle Mill Halls of Residence
KT1: King T 3F **151**
Middle New St. *EC4* *7K **7***
(off Pemberton Row)
Middle Pk. Av. SE9 6B **124**
Middle Path HA2: Harr 1H **59**
Middle Rd. E13 2J **87**
EN4: E Barn 6H **21**
HA2: Harr 2H **59**
SW16 2H **155**
Middle Row W10 4G **81**
Middlesborough Rd. N18 6B **34**
Middlesex Bldg., The *E1* *6H **9***
(off Artillery La.)
Middlesex Bus. Cen. UB2: S'hall 2E **94**
Middlesex CCC 1B **4** (3B **82**)
Middlesex Cl. UB1: S'hall 4F **77**
Middlesex Ct. HA1: Harr 5K **41**
TW8: Bford *5C **96***
(off Glenhurst Rd.)
W4 4B **98**
Middlesex Filter Beds Nature Reserve 3K **67**
Middlesex Guildhall *7E **12***
(off Lit. George St.)
Middlesex Ho. HA0: Wemb 1D **78**
Middlesex Pas. EC1 6B **8**
Middlesex Pl. *E9* *6J **67***
(off Elsdale St.)
Middlesex Rd. CR4: Mitc 5J **155**
Middlesex St. E1 6H **9** (5E **84**)
Middlesex University
Archway Campus 1G **65**
Hendon Campus 4D **44**
Middlesex Wharf E5 2J **67**
Middle St. CR0: C'don 2C **168**
(not continuous)
EC1 5C **8** (5C **84**)
Middle Temple La. EC4 1J **13** (6A **84**)
Middleton Av. DA14: Sidc 6B **144**
E4 4G **35**
UB6: G'frd 2H **77**
Middleton Cl. E4 3G **35**
Middleton Dr. HA5: Eastc 3J **39**
SE16 2K **103**
Middleton Gdns. IG2: Ilf 6F **53**
Middleton Gro. IG11: Bark 3A **90**
N7 5J **65**
Middleton Ho. E8 7G **67**
SE1 *3D **102***
(off Burbage Cl.)
SW1 *4D **18***
(off Causton St.)
Middleton M. N7 5J **65**
Middleton Pl. W1 6A **6**
Middleton Rd. E8 7F **67**
NW11 7J **45**
SM4: Mord 6K **153**
SM5: Cars 6A **154**
UB3: Hayes 5F **75**
Middleton St. E2 3H **85**
Middleton Way SE13 4F **123**
Middle Way DA18: Erith 3E **108**
SW16 2H **155**
UB4: Yead 4A **76**
Middle Way, The HA3: W'stone 2K **41**
Middleway NW11 5K **45**
Middle Yd. SE1 4G **15** (1E **102**)
Midfield Av. DA7: Bex 3J **127**
Midfield Pde. DA7: Bex 3J **127**
Midfield Way BR5: St P 7A **144**
Midford Ho. *NW4* *4E **44***
(off Belle Vue Est.)
Midford Pl. W1 4B **6** (4G **83**)
Midholm HA9: Wemb 1G **61**
NW11 4K **45**
Midholm Cl. NW11 4K **45**
Midholm Rd.
CR0: C'don 2A **170**
Midhope Ho. *WC1* *2F **7***
(off Midhope St.)
Midhope St. WC1 2F **7** (3J **83**)
Midhurst SE26 6J **139**
Midhurst Av. CR0: C'don 7A **156**
N10 3E **46**
Midhurst Gdns. UB10: Hil 1E **74**
Midhurst Hill DA6: Bex 6G **127**

Midhurst Ho. *E14* *6B 86*
(off Salmon La.)
Midhurst Pde. *N10* *3E 46*
(off Fortis Grn.)
Midhurst Rd. W13 . . . . 2A **96**
Midhurst Way E5 . . . . 4G **67**
Midland Goods Shed *N1* *1J 83*
(off Handyside St.)
Midland Pde. NW6 . . . . 6K **63**
Midland Pl. E14 . . . . 5E **104**
Midland Rd. E10 . . . . 7E **50**
NW1 . . . . 1D **6** (2H **83**)
Midland Ter. NW2 . . . . 3F **63**
NW10 . . . . 4A **80**
Midleton Rd. KT3: N Mald 3J **151**
Midlothian Rd. *E3* *4B 86*
(off Burdett Rd.)
Midmoor Rd. SW12 . . . . 1G **137**
SW19 . . . . 1F **153**
Midnight Av. SE5 . . . . 7B **102**
Midship Cl. SE16 . . . . 1K **103**
Midship Point *E14* *2C 104*
(off The Quarterdeck)
Midstrath Rd. NW10 . . . . 4A **62**
Midsummer Av. TW4: Houn 4D **112**
Midway SM3: Sutt 7H **153**
Midway Ho. EC1 . . . . 1A **8**
Midwinter Cl. DA16: Well 3A **126**
Midwood Cl. NW2 . . . . 3D **62**
Miers Cl. E6 . . . . 1E **88**
Mighell Av. IG4: Ilf 5B **52**
Mikardo Ct. *E14* *7E 86*
(off Poplar High St.)
Milan Ct. N11 . . . . 1H **47**
Milan Rd. UB1: S'hall 2D **94**
Milborne Gro. SW10 . . . . 6A **16** (5A **100**)
Milborne St. E9 . . . . 6J **67**
Milborough Cres. SE12 . . . . 6G **123**
Milbourne Ho. *KT1: King T* *1G 151*
(off Coombe Rd.)
Milbourne Pl. KT19: Ewe 4K **163**
Milburn Dr. UB7: Yiew 7A **74**
Milcote St. SE1 . . . . 7A **14** (2B **102**)
Mildenhall Rd. E5 . . . . 4J **67**
Mildmay Av. N1 . . . . 6D **66**
Mildmay Gro. Nth. N1 . . . . 5D **66**
Mildmay Gro. Sth. N1 . . . . 5D **66**
Mildmay Pk. N1 . . . . 5D **66**
Mildmay Pl. N16 . . . . 5E **66**
Mildmay Rd. IG1: Ilf 3F **71**
N1 . . . . 5D **66**
RM7: Rom 5J **55**
Mildmay St. N1 . . . . 6D **66**
Mildred Av. UB3: Harl 4F **93**
UB5: N'olt 5F **59**
Mildred Ct. CR0: C'don 1G **169**
Mildred Rd. DA8: Erith 5K **109**
Mildrose Ct. *NW6* *3J 81*
(off Malvern M.)
Mildura Ct. N8 . . . . 4K **47**
MILE END 4B 86
Mile End, The E17 . . . . 1K **49**
Mile End Climbing Wall 3A 86
Mile End Pk. 2A 86
Mile End Pk. Leisure Cen. 5A 86
Mile End Pl. E1 . . . . 4K **85**
Mile End Rd. E1 . . . . 5J **85**
E3 . . . . 5J **85**
Mile End Stadium 5B 86
Mile Rd. SM6: Bedd, Wall 1F **167**
(not continuous)
Miles Bldgs. *NW1* *5C 4*
(off Penfold Pl.)
Miles Cl. SE28 . . . . 1H **107**
Miles Ct. *CR0: C'don* *2B 168*
(off Cuthbert Rd.)
E1 . . . . *6H 85*
(off Tillman St.)
Miles Dr. SE28 . . . . 1J **107**
Miles Ho. *SE10* *5G 105*
(off Tuskar St.)
Miles Lodge *E15* *5F 69*
(off Colegrave Rd.)
HA1: Harr 5H **41**
Milespit Hill NW7 . . . . 5J **29**
Miles Pl. KT5: Surb 4F **151**
NW8 . . . . 5B **4**
Miles Rd. CR4: Mitc 3C **154**
N8 . . . . 3J **47**
Miles St. SW8 . . . . 7E **18** (6J **101**)
(not continuous)
Milestone Cl. N9 . . . . 2B **34**
SM2: Sutt 6B **166**
Milestone Ct. E10 . . . . 7D **50**
MILESTONE GREEN **4J 115**
Milestone Ho. *KT1: King T* *3D 150*
(off Surbiton Rd.)
Milestone Rd. SE19 . . . . 6F **139**
Miles Way N20 . . . . 2H **31**
Milfoil St. W12 . . . . 7C **80**
Milford Cl. SE2 . . . . 6E **108**
Milford Ct. UB1: S'hall 1E **94**
Milford Gdns. CR0: C'don 5J **157**
HA0: Wemb 4D **60**
HA8: Edg 7B **28**
Milford Gro. SM1: Sutt 4A **166**
Milford La. WC2 . . . . 2H **13** (7A **84**)
Milford M. SW16 . . . . 3K **137**
Milford Rd. UB1: S'hall 7E **76**
W13 . . . . 1B **96**
Milford Towers SE6 . . . . 7D **122**
Milk St. BR1: Brom 6K **141**
E16 . . . . 1F **107**
EC2 . . . . 7D **8** (6C **84**)
Milkwell Gdns.
IG8: Wfd G 7E **36**
Milkwell Yd. SE5 . . . . 1C **120**
Milkwood Rd. SE24 . . . . 5B **120**
Milk Yd. E1 . . . . 7J **85**
Millais Av. E12 . . . . 5E **70**
Millais Ct. *UB5: N'olt* *2B 76*
(off Academy Gdns.)
Millais Cres. KT19: Ewe 5A **164**
Millais Gdns. HA8: Edg 2G **43**
Millais Ho. *SW1* *4E 18*
(off Marsham St.)
Millais Rd. E11 . . . . 4E **68**
EN1: Enf 5A **24**
KT3: N Mald 7A **152**
Millais Way KT19: Ewe 4J **163**
Millard Cl. N16 . . . . 5E **66**
Millard Rd. SE8 . . . . 5B **104**
Millard Ter. RM10: Dag 6G **73**
Millbank SM6: Wall 5H **167**
SW1 . . . . 2E **18** (3J **101**)
Millbank Ct. SW1 . . . . 3E **18**
Millbank Twr. SW1 . . . . 4E **18** (4J **101**)
Millbank Way SE12 . . . . 5J **123**
Millbourne Rd. TW13: Hanw 4C **130**
Mill Bri. EN5: Barn 6C **20**
Millbroke M. IG8: Wfd G 6B **36**
Millbrook Av. DA16: Well 4H **125**
Millbrooke Ct. *SW15* *5G 117*
(off Keswick Rd.)
Millbrook Gdns. RM6: Chad H 6F **55**
Millbrook Ho. *SE15* *6G 103*
(off Peckham Pk. Rd.)
Millbrook Pas. SW9 . . . . 3B **120**
Millbrook Pl. *NW1* *2G 83*
(off Hampstead Rd.)
Millbrook Rd. N9 . . . . 1C **34**
SW9 . . . . 3B **120**
Mill Cl. NW7 . . . . 1G **45**
SM5: Cars 2E **166**
Mill Cnr. EN5: Barn 1C **20**
Mill Ct. E5 . . . . 2J **67**
E10 . . . . 3E **68**
SE28 . . . . *7B 90*
(off Titmuss Av.)
Millcroft Ho. *SE6* *4E 140*
(off Melfield Gdns.)
Mill Dr. HA4: Ruis 7F **39**
Millender Wlk. *SE16* *4J 103*
(off New Rotherhithe Rd.)
Millennium Arena 7E 100
Millennium Bridge 3C 14 (7C 84)
Millennium Bri. Ho. *EC4* *2C 14*
(off Up. Thames St.)
Millennium Bus. Cen. NW2 . . . . 2D **62**
Millennium Cen., The 4K 73
Millennium Cl. E16 . . . . 6K **87**
Millennium Dr. E14 . . . . 4F **105**
Millennium Ho. E17 . . . . 5K **49**
SW15 . . . . *5G 117*
(off Plaza Gdns.)
Millennium Pl. E2 . . . . 2H **85**
Millennium Sq. SE1 . . . . 6K **15** (2F **103**)
Millennium Way SE10 . . . . 2G **105**
Miller Av. EN3: Enf L 1H **25**
Miller Cl. BR1: Brom 5K **141**
CR4: Mitc 7D **154**
HA5: Pinn 2A **40**
RM5: Col R 1G **55**
Miller Ct. DA7: Bex 3J **127**
Miller Ho. *E1* *5K 85*
(off Shandy St.)
W10 . . . . *4H 81*
(off Harrow Rd.)
Miller Rd. CR0: C'don 1K **167**
SW19 . . . . 6B **136**
Miller's Av. E8 . . . . 5F **67**
Millers Cl. NW7 . . . . 4H **29**
Millers Ct. *HA0: Wemb* *2E 78*
(off Vicars Bri. Cl.)
Millers Grn. Cl. EN2: Enf 3G **23**
Millers Mdw. Cl. SE3 . . . . 4H **123**
Miller's Ter. E8 . . . . 5F **67**
Miller St. NW1 . . . . 2G **83**
(not continuous)
Millers Way W6 . . . . 2E **98**
Millers Wharf Ho. *E1* *5K 15*
(off St Katherine's Way)
Millers Yd. N3 . . . . 1K **45**
Miller Wlk. SE1 . . . . 5K **13** (1A **102**)
Milles Sq. SW9 . . . . 4A **120**
Millet Rd. UB6: G'frd 2F **77**
Mill Farm Av. TW16: Sun 7G **129**
Mill Farm Bus. Pk. TW4: Houn 7C **112**
Mill Farm Cl. HA5: Pinn 2A **40**
Mill Farm Cres. TW4: Houn 1C **130**
Millfield KT1: King T 3F **151**
N4 . . . . 2A **66**
TW16: Sun 1F **147**
Millfield Av. E17 . . . . 1A **50**
Millfield La. N6 . . . . 1C **64**
Millfield Pl. N6 . . . . 2E **64**
Millfield Rd. HA8: Edg 2J **43**
TW4: Houn 1C **130**
Millfields Rd. E5 . . . . 4J **67**
Millfield Theatre 4J 33
Mill Gdns. SE26 . . . . 3H **139**
Mill Grn. CR4: Mitc 7E **154**
Mill Grn. Bus. Pk. CR4: Mitc 7E **154**
Mill Grn. Rd. CR4: Mitc 7D **154**
Millgrove St. SW11 . . . . 1E **118**
Millharbour E14 . . . . 2D **104**
Millhaven Cl. RM6: Chad H 6B **54**
MILL HILL 5F 29
Mill Hill SW13 . . . . 2C **116**
MILL HILL CIRCUS **5G 29**
Mill Hill Cir. NW7 . . . . 5G **29**
Mill Hill Golf Course 2F 29
Mill Hill Gro. W3 . . . . 1J **97**
Mill Hill Ind. Est. NW7 . . . . 6G **29**
Mill Hill Old Railway Nature Reserve
. . . . 6D 28
Mill Hill Rd. SW13 . . . . 2C **116**
W3 . . . . 2H **97**
Mill Hill School Sports Cen. 4H 29
Mill Hill Ter. W3 . . . . 1H **97**
Mill Ho. IG8: Wfd G 5C **36**
Millhouse Pl. SE27 . . . . 4B **138**
Millicent Fawcett Ct. N17 . . . . 1F **49**
Millicent Gro. N13 . . . . 5G **33**
Millicent Preston Ho. *IG11: Bark* *1H 89*
(off Ripple Rd.)
Millicent Rd. E10 . . . . 1B **68**
Milligan St. E14 . . . . 7B **86**
Milliner Ho. *SW10* *7A 100*
(off Hortensia Rd.)
Milliners Ho. *SE1* *7H 15*
(off Bermondsey St.)
SW18 . . . . 4J **117**
Milling Rd. HA8: Edg 7E **28**
Millington Ho. N16 . . . . 3D **66**
Millington Rd. UB3: Harl 3G **93**
Mill La. CR0: Wadd 3K **167**
E4 . . . . 3J **25**
IG8: Wfd G 5C **36**
KT17: Ewe 7B **164**
NW6 . . . . 5H **63**
RM6: Chad H 6E **54**
SE8 . . . . *1C 122*
(off Deptford Bri.)
SE18 . . . . 5E **106**
SM5: Cars 4D **166**
Mill La. Trad. Est. CR0: Wadd 3K **167**
Millman Ct. *WC1* *4G 7*
(off Millman St.)
Millman M. WC1 . . . . 4G **7** (4K **83**)
Millman Pl. *WC1* *4G 7*
(off Millman St.)
Millman Rd. E16 . . . . 7D **88**
Millman St. WC1 . . . . 4G **7** (4K **83**)
Millmark Gro. SE14 . . . . 2A **122**
Millmarsh La. EN3: Brim 2F **25**
Millmead Ind. Cen. N17 . . . . 2H **49**
Mill Mead Rd. N17 . . . . 3H **49**
MILL MEADS 2F 87
Mill Pl. BR7: Chst 1E **160**
E14 . . . . 6A **86**
KT1: King T 3F **151**
Mill Plat TW7: Isle 2A **114**
(not continuous)
Mill Plat Av. TW7: Isle 2A **114**
Mill Pond Cl. SW8 . . . . 7H **101**
Millpond Est. SE16 . . . . 2H **103**
Millpond Pl. SM5: Cars 3E **166**
Mill Ridge HA8: Edg 5A **28**
Mill River Trad. Est. EN3: Pond E 3F **25**
Mill Rd. DA8: Erith 7J **109**
E16 . . . . 1K **105**
IG1: Ilf 3E **70**
SW19 . . . . 7A **136**
TW2: Twick 2G **131**
Mill Row DA5: Bexl 1H **145**
N1 . . . . 1E **84**
Mills Cl. UB10: Hil 2C **74**
Mills Ct. EC2 . . . . 3G **9**
Mills Gro. E14 . . . . 6E **86**
NW4 . . . . 3F **45**
Millshott Cl. SW6 . . . . 1E **116**
Mills Ho. *SW8* *1G 119*
(off Thessaly Rd.)
Millside SM5: Cars 2D **166**
Millside Pl. TW7: Isle 2B **114**
Millson Cl. N20 . . . . 2G **31**
Mills Row W4 . . . . 4K **97**
Millstone Cl. E15 . . . . 6F **69**
Millstream Cl. N13 . . . . 5F **33**
Millstream Ho. *SE16* *2H 103*
(off Jamaica Rd.)
Millstream Rd. SE1 . . . . 7J **15** (2F **103**)
Mill St. KT1: King T 3E **150**
SE1 . . . . 7K **15** (2F **103**)
W1 . . . . 2A **12** (7F **83**)
Mills Yd. SW6 . . . . 3K **117**
Mill Trad. Est., The NW10 . . . . 3J **79**
Mill Va. BR2: Brom 2H **159**
Mill Vw. Cl. KT17: Ewe 7B **164**
Mill Vw. Gdns. CR0: C'don 3K **169**
MILLWALL 4D 104
Millwall Dock Rd. E14 . . . . 3C **104**
Millwall FC 5J 103

Millwall Pk.—MODA

Millwall Pk. 4E 104
Mill Way TW14: Felt 5K 111
Millway NW7 4F 29
Millway Gdns. UB5: N'olt 6D 58
Millwood Rd. TW3: Houn 5G 113
Millwood St. W10 5G 81
Mill Yd. E1 7G 85
Mill Yd. Ind. Est. HA8: Edg 1H 43
Milman Cl. HA5: Pinn 3B 40
Milman Rd. NW6 2F 81
Milman's Ho. *SW10* *6B 100*
(off Milman's St.)
Milman's St. SW10 6B 100
Milne Ct. E18 1J 51
Milne Gdns. SE9 5C 124
Milne Ho. *SE18* *4D 106*
(off Ogilby St.)
Milner Ct. *SE15* *7F 103*
(off Colegrove Rd.)
Milner Dr. TW2: Whitt 7H 113
Milner Pl. N1 1A 84
SM5: Cars 4E 166
Milner Rd. CR7: Thor H 3D 156
E15 3G 87
KT1: King T 3D 150
RM8: Dag 2C 72
SM4: Mord 5B 154
SW19 1K 153
Milner Sq. N1 7B 66
Milner St. SW3 3E 16 (4D 100)
Milner Wlk. SE9 2H 143
Milnthorpe Rd. W4 6K 97
Milo Gdns. SE22 6F 121
Milo Rd. SE22 6F 121
Milrood Ho. *E1* *5K 85*
(off Stepney Grn.)
Milroy Wlk. SE1 4A 14 (1B 102)
Milson Rd. W14 3F 99
Milstead Ho. E5 5H 67
Milton Av. CR0: C'don 7D 156
E6 7B 70
EN5: Barn 5C 20
N6 7G 47
NW9 3J 43
NW10 1J 79
SM1: Sutt 3B 166
Milton Cl. N2 5A 46
SE1 4F 103
SM1: Sutt 3B 166
UB4: Hayes 6J 75
Milton Ct. E17 4C 50
EC2 5E 8 (5D 84)
RM6: Chad H 7C 54
SE14 6B 104
(not continuous)
SW18 5J 117
TW2: Twick 3J 131
UB10: Ick 3D 56
Milton Court Concert Hall *5D 84*
(off Milton Ct.)
Milton Ct. Rd. SE14 6A 104
Milton Cres. IG2: Ilf 7F 53
Milton Dr. TW17: Shep 4A 146
Milton Gdn. Est. N16 4D 66
Milton Gdns. TW19: Stanw 1B 128
Milton Gro. N11 5B 32
N16 4D 66
Milton Ho. *E2* *3J 85*
(off Roman Rd.)
E17 4C 50
SE5 *7D 102*
(off Elmington Est.)
SM1: Sutt 3J 165
Milton Lodge
DA14: Sidc 4A 144
TW1: Twick 7K 113
Milton Mans. *W14* *6G 99*
(off Queen's Club Gdns.)
Milton Pk. N6 7G 47
Milton Pl. *N7* *5A 66*
(off Eastwood Cl.)
Milton Rd. CR0: C'don 7D 156
CR4: Mitc 7E 136
DA16: Well 1K 125
DA17: Belv 4G 109
E17 4C 50
HA1: Harr 4J 41
N6 7G 47
N15 4B 48
NW7 5H 29
NW9 7C 44
SE24 5B 120
SM1: Sutt 3J 165
SM6: Wall 6G 167
SW14 3K 115
SW19 6A 136
TW12: Hamp 7E 130
UB10: Ick 4D 56
W3 1K 97
W7 7K 77
Milton St. EC2 5E 8 (5D 84)
Milton Way UB7: W Dray 4B 92
Milverton Dr. UB10: Ick 4E 56
Milverton Gdns. IG3: Ilf 2K 71
Milverton Ho. SE6 3A 140
Milverton Pl. BR1: Brom 5A 142
Milverton Rd. NW6 7E 62
Milverton St. SE11 6K 19 (5A 102)
Milverton Way SE9 4E 142
Milward St. E1 5H 85
Milward Wlk. SE18 6E 106
Mimosa Ho. *E20* *5E 68*
(off Liberty Bri. Rd.)
UB4: Yead 5A 76
Mimosa Lodge NW10 5B 62
Mimosa Rd. UB4: Yead 5A 76
Mimosa St. SW6 1H 117
Minard Rd. SE6 7G 123
Mina Rd. SE17 5E 102
SW19 1J 153
Minchenden Ct. N14 2C 32
Minchenden Cres. N14 3B 32
Minchin Ho. *E14* *6C 86*
(off Dod St.)
Mincing La. EC3 2G 15 (7E 84)
Minden Gdns. IG11: Bark 3B 90
Minden Rd. SE20 1H 157
SM3: Sutt 2G 165
Minehead Rd. HA2: Harr 3E 58
SW16 5K 137
Mineral Cl. EN5: Barn 6A 20
Mineral St. SE18 4J 107
Minera M. SW1 3G 17 (4E 100)
Minerva Cl. DA14: Sidc 3J 143
SW9 7A 102
TW19: Stanw M 7B 174
Minerva Ct. *EC1* *4K 7*
(off Bowling Grn. La.)
Minerva Lodge N7 6K 65
Minerva Rd. E4 7J 35
KT1: King T 2F 151
NW10 4J 79
Minerva St. E2 2H 85
Minerva Wlk. EC1 7B 8 (6B 84)
Minerva Way EN5: Barn 5C 20
Minet Av. NW10 2A 80
Minet Country Pk. 2A 94
Minet Dr. UB3: Hayes 1J 93
Minet Gdns. NW10 2A 80
UB3: Hayes 1K 93
Minet Rd. SW9 2B 120
Minford Gdns. W14 2F 99
Minford Ho. *W14* *2F 99*
(off Minford Gdns.)
Mingard Wlk. N7 2K 65
Ming St. E14 7C 86
Minimax Cl. TW14: Felt 6J 111
Minima Yacht Club *3D 150*
(off High St.)
Ministry Way SE9 2D 142
Miniver Pl. EC4 2D 14
Mink Ct. TW4: Houn 2A 112
Minniedale KT5: Surb 5F 151
Minnow St. SE17 4E 102
Minnow Wlk. SE17 4E 102
Minories EC3 1J 15 (6F 85)
Minshaw Ct. DA14: Sidc 4K 143
Minshill St. SW8 1H 119
Minshull Pl. BR3: Beck 7C 140
Minson Rd. E9 1K 85
Minstead Gdns. SW15 7B 116
Minstead Way KT3: N Mald 6A 152
Minster Av. SM1: Sutt 2J 165
Minster Ct. EC3 2H 15
W5 4E 78
Minster Dr. CR0: C'don 4E 168
Minster Gdns. KT8: W Mole 4D 148
Minsterley Av. TW17: Shep 4G 147
Minster Pavement *EC3* *2H 15*
(off Mincing La.)
Minster Rd. BR1: Brom 7K 141
NW2 5G 63
Minster Wlk. N8 4J 47
Minstrel Gdns. KT5: Surb 4F 151
Mint Bus. Pk. E16 5K 87
Mint Cl. UB10: Hil 3D 74
Mintern Cl. N13 3G 33
Minterne Av. UB2: S'hall 4E 94
Minterne Rd. HA3: Kenton 5F 43
Minterne Waye UB4: Yead 6A 76
Mintern St. N1 2D 84
Minter Rd. IG11: Bark 4A 90
Minton Ho. SE11 3J 19
Minton M. NW6 6K 63
Mint Rd. SM6: Wall 4F 167
Mint St. *E2* *4H 85*
(off Three Colts La.)
SE1 6C 14 (2C 102)
Mint Wlk. CR0: C'don 3C 168
Mirabelle Gdns. E20 5E 68
Mirabel Rd. SW6 7H 99
Mira Ho. *E20* *5E 68*
(off Prize Wlk.)
Miranda Cl. E1 5J 85
Miranda Ct. W3 6F 79
Miranda Ho. *N1* *1G 9*
(off Crondall St.)
Miranda Rd. N19 1G 65
Mirfield St. SE7 4B 106
Miriam Rd. SE18 5J 107
Mirravale Trad. Est. RM8: Dag 7E 54
Mirren Cl. HA2: Harr 4D 58
Mirror Path SE9 3A 142
Misbourne Rd. UB10: Hil 1C 74
Missenden *SE17* *5D 102*
(off Roland Way)
Missenden Cl. TW14: Felt 1H 129
Missenden Gdns. SM4: Mord 6A 154
Missenden Ho. NW8 3C 4
Mission, The *E14* *6B 86*
(off Commercial Rd.)
Mission Gro. E17 5A 50
Mission Pl. SE15 1G 121
Mission Sq. TW8: Bford 6E 96
Missouri Ct. HA5: Eastc 6A 40
Mistletoe Cl. CR0: C'don 1K 169
Mistral SE5 1E 120
Misty's Fld. KT12: Walt T 7A 148
Mitali Pas. E1 6G 85
MITCHAM 3D 154
Mitcham Gdn. Village CR4: Mitc 5E 154
Mitcham Golf Course 5E 154
Mitcham Ho. SE5 1C 120
Mitcham Ind. Est. CR4: Mitc 1E 154
Mitcham La. SW16 6G 137
Mitcham Pk. CR4: Mitc 4C 154
Mitcham Rd. CR0: C'don 6J 155
E6 3C 88
IG3: Ilf 7K 53
SW17 5D 136
Mitchell *NW9* *1B 44*
(off Quakers Course)
Mitchellbrook Way NW10 6K 61
Mitchell Cl. DA17: Belv 3J 109
SE2 4C 108
Mitchell Ho. *N1* *7B 66*
(off College Cross)
W12 *7D 80*
(off White City Est.)
Mitchell Rd. BR6: Orp 4K 173
N13 5H 33
Mitchell's Pl. *SE21* *6E 120*
(off Aysgarth Rd.)
Mitchell St. EC1 3C 8 (4C 84)
(not continuous)
Mitchell Wlk. *E6* *5C 88*
(off Allhallows Rd.)
E6 5D 88
(Elmley Cl.)
Mitchell Way BR1: Brom 1J 159
NW10 6J 61
Mitchison Ct. *TW16: Sun* *1J 147*
(off Downside)
Mitchison Rd. N1 6D 66
Mitchley Rd. N17 3G 49
Mitford Bldgs. *SW6* *7J 99*
(off Dawes Rd.)
Mitford Cl. KT9: Chess 6C 162
Mitford Rd. N19 2J 65
Mitre, The E14 7B 86
Mitre Av. E17 3C 50
Mitre Bri. Ind. Pk. W10 4D 80
(not continuous)
Mitre Cl. BR2: Brom 2H 159
SM2: Sutt 7A 166
TW17: Shep 6F 147
Mitre Ho. *SW3* *5E 16*
(off King's Rd.)
Mitre Pas. *EC3* *1H 15*
(off Mitre Sq.)
SE10 2G 105
Mitre Rd. E15 2G 87
SE1 6K 13 (2A 102)
Mitre Sq. EC3 1H 15 (6E 84)
Mitre St. EC3 1H 15 (6E 84)
Mitre Way W10 4D 80
Mitre Yd. SW3 3D 16 (4C 100)
Mitten Ho. *SE8* *7D 104*
(off Creative Rd.)
Mizen Ct. *E14* *2C 104*
(off Alpha Gro.)
Mizzen Mast Ho. SE18 3D 106
Moat, The KT3: N Mald 1A 152
Moat Cl. BR6: Chels 6K 173
Moat Ct. DA15: Sidc 3K 143
SE9 6D 124
Moat Cres. N3 3K 45
Moat Cft. DA16: Well 3C 126
Moat Dr. E13 2A 88
HA1: Harr 4G 41
HA4: Ruis 7G 39
Moat Farm Rd. UB5: N'olt 6D 58
Moatfield NW6 7G 63
Moatlands Ho. *WC1* *2F 7*
(off Cromer St.)
Moat La. KT8: E Mos 3K 149
Moat Lodge, The HA2: Harr 2J 59
Moat Pl. SW9 3K 119
W3 6H 79
Moat Side EN3: Pond E 4E 24
TW13: Hanw 4A 130
Moberly Rd. SW4 7H 119
Moberly Sports & Education Cen. *3F 81*
(off Chamberlayne Rd.)
Mobil Ct. *WC2* *1H 13*
(off Clement's Inn)
MOBY DICK 4E 54
Mocatta Ho. *E1* *4H 85*
(off Brady St.)
Mocha Ct. *E3* *2D 86*
(off Taylor Pl.)
MODA
Mus. of Domestic Design & Architecture 2B 44

Modbury Gdns. NW5 . . . . .6E **64**
Modder Pl. SW15 . . . . .4F **117**
Model Cotts. SW14 . . . . .4J **115**
   W13 . . . . .2B **96**
Model Farm Cl. SE9 . . . . .3C **142**
Modern Ct. EC4 . . . . .7A **8**
Modling Ho. E2 . . . . .2K **85**
   (off Mace St.)
Moelwyn N7 . . . . .5H **65**
Moelyn M. HA1: Harr 5A **42**
Moffat Cl. SW19 . . . . .5J **135**
Moffat Ho. SE5 . . . . .7C **102**
Moffat Rd. CR7: Thor H 2C **156**
   N13 . . . . .6D **32**
   SW17 .4D **136**
Mogden La. TW7: Isle 5K **113**
Mohammedi Pk. UB5: N'olt 1E **76**
Mohawk Ho. E3 . . . . .2A **86**
   (off Gernon Rd.)
Mohmmad Khan Rd. E11 . . . . .1H **69**
Moineau NW9 . . . . .1B **44**
   (off Long Mead)
Moira Cl. N17 . . . . .2E **48**
Moira Ho. SW9 . . . . .1A **120**
   (off Gosling Way)
Moira Rd. SE9 . . . . .4D **124**
Mokswell Ct. N10 . . . . .1E **46**
Molasses Ho. SW11 . . . . .3A **118**
   (off Clove Hitch Quay)
Molasses Row SW11 . . . . .3A **118**
Mole Abbey Gdns. KT8: W Mole . . .3F **149**
Mole Cl. KT19: Ewe 4J **163**
Mole Ho. NW8 . . . . .4B **4**
   (off Church St. Est.)
Molember Ct. KT8: E Mos 4J **149**
Molember Rd. KT8: E Mos 5J **149**
Mole Pl. KT8: W Mole 4F **149**
Molescroft SE9 . . . . .3G **143**
Molesey Av. KT8: W Mole 5D **148**
Molesey Dr. SM3: Cheam 2G **165**
Molesey Heath Local Nature Reserve
   . . . . .6E **148**
Molesey Pk. Av. KT8: W Mole 5F **149**
Molesey Pk. Cl. KT8: E Mos 5G **149**
Molesey Pk. Rd.
   KT8: W Mole, E Mos 5F **149**
Molesey Rd. KT8: W Mole 5C **148**
   KT12: Walt T 7C **148**
Molesford Rd. SW6 . . . . .1J **117**
Molesham Cl. KT8: W Mole 3F **149**
Molesham Way KT8: W Mole 3F **149**
Molesworth Ho. SE17 . . . . .6B **102**
   (off Brandon St.)
Molesworth St. SE13 . . . . .4E **122**
Moliner Ct. BR3: Beck 7C **140**
Mollis Ho. E3 . . . . .5C **86**
   (off Gale St.)
Mollison Av.
   EN3: Brim, Enf L, Enf W, Pond E
   . . . . .4F **25**
Mollison Dr. SM6: Wall 7H **167**
Mollison Sq. SM6: Wall 7H **167**
   (off Mollison Dr.)
Mollison Way HA8: Edg 2F **43**
Molly Huggins Cl. SW12 . . . . .7G **119**
Molton Ho. N1 . . . . .1K **83**
   (off Barnsbury Est.)
Molyneux Dr. SW17 . . . . .4F **137**
Molyneux St. W1 . . . . .6D **4** (5C **82**)
Monarch Cl. BR4: W W'ck 4H **171**
   TW14: Felt 7G **111**
Monarch Ct. HA7: Stan 7J **27**
   (off Howard Rd.)
   N2 . . . . .5B **46**
Monarch Dr. E16 . . . . .5B **88**
   UB3: Hayes 7H **75**
Monarch Ho. W8 . . . . .3J **99**
   (off Kensington High St.)
Monarch M. E17 . . . . .6D **50**
   SW16 .5A **138**
Monarch Pde. CR4: Mitc 2D **154**

Monarch Pl. IG9: Buck H 2F **37**
Monarch Point SW6 . . . . .2A **118**
Monarch Rd. DA17: Belv 3G **109**
Monarch Sq. SW11 . . . . .4C **118**
Monarchs Way HA4: Ruis 1F **57**
Monarch Way IG2: Ilf 6H **53**
Mona Rd. SE15 . . . . .2J **121**
Mona St. E16 . . . . .5H **87**
Monastery Gdns. EN2: Enf 2J **23**
Mona St. E16 . . . . .5H **87**
Monaveen Gdns. KT8: W Mole 3F **149**
Monck Ho. SE1 . . . . .7D **14**
   (off Cole St.)
Moncks Row SW18 . . . . .6H **117**
Monck St. SW1 . . . . .2D **18** (3H **101**)
Monckton Ct. W14 . . . . .3H **99**
   (off Strangways Ter.)
Monclar Rd. SE5 . . . . .4D **120**
Moncorvo Cl. SW7 . . . . . .7C **10** (2C **100**)
Moncrieff Cl. E6 . . . . .6C **88**
Moncrieff Pl. SE15 . . . . .2G **121**
Moncrieff St. SE15 . . . . .2G **121**
Monday All. N16 . . . . .2F **67**
   (off High St.)
Mondial Way UB3: Harl 7E **92**
Mondragon Ho. SW8 . . . . .1J **119**
   (off Guildford Rd.)
Monega Rd. E7 . . . . .6A **70**
   E12 . . . . .6A **70**
Monet Ct. SE16 . . . . .5H **103**
   (off Stubbs Dr.)
Moneyer Ho. N1 . . . . .1E **8**
   (off Provost St.)
Money La. UB7: W Dray 3A **92**
Mongers Almshouses E9 . . . . .7K **67**
   (off Church Cres.)
Monica Cl. EN1: Enf 5K **23**
Monica James Ho. DA14: Sidc 3A **144**
Monica Shaw Ct. NW1 . . . . .1D **6**
   (off Purchese St.)
Monier Rd. E3 . . . . .7C **68**
Monivea Rd. BR3: Beck 7B **140**
Monk Ct. W12 . . . . .1C **98**
Monk Dr. E16 . . . . .7J **87**
MONKEN HADLEY 2C **20**
Monkfrith Av. N14 . . . . .6A **22**
Monkfrith Cl. N14 . . . . .7A **22**
Monkfrith Way N14 . . . . .7K **21**
Monkham's Av. IG8: Wfd G 5E **36**
Monkham's Dr. IG8: Wfd G 5E **36**
Monkham's La. IG8: Wfd G 5D **36**
   IG9: Buck H 3E **36**
Monkleigh Rd. SM4: Mord 3G **153**
Monk Pas. E16 . . . . .7J **87**
   (off Monk Dr.)
Monks Av. EN5: New Bar 6F **21**
   KT8: W Mole 5D **148**
Monks Cl. EN2: Enf 2H **23**
   HA2: Harr 2F **59**
   HA4: Ruis 4B **58**
   SE2 . . . . .4D **108**
Monks Cres. KT12: Walt T 7K **147**
Monksdene Gdns. SM1: Sutt 3K **165**
Monks Dr. W3 . . . . .5G **79**
Monks Orchard Rd. BR3: Beck 1C **170**
Monks Pk. HA9: Wemb 6H **61**
Monks Pk. Gdns. HA9: Wemb 7H **61**
Monks Rd. EN2: Enf 2G **23**
Monk St. SE18 . . . . .4E **106**
Monks Way BR3: Beck 6C **158**
   BR5: Farnb 1G **173**
   NW11 .4H **45**
   UB7: Harm 6A **92**
Monkswood Gdns. IG5: Ilf 3E **52**
Monkton Ho. E5 . . . . .5H **67**
   SE16 . . . . .2K **103**
   (off Wolfe Cres.)
Monkton Rd. DA16: Well 2K **125**
Monkton St. SE11 . . . . . . .3K **19** (4A **102**)
Monkville Av. NW11 . . . . .4H **45**
Monkville Pde. NW11 . . . . .4H **45**

Monkwell Sq. EC2 . . . . . . .6D **8** (5C **84**)
Monmouth Av. E18 . . . . .3K **51**
   KT1: Hamp W 7C **132**
Monmouth Cl. CR4: Mitc 4J **155**
   DA16: Well 4A **126**
   W4 . . . . .3J **97**
Monmouth Ct. W7 . . . . .5K **77**
   (off Copley Cl.)
Monmouth Gro. TW8: Bford 4E **96**
Monmouth Pl. W2 . . . . .6K **81**
   (off Monmouth Rd.)
Monmouth Rd. E6 . . . . .3D **88**
   N9 . . . . .2C **34**
   RM9: Dag 5F **73**
   UB3: Harl 4G **93**
   W2 . . . . .6J **81**
Monmouth St. WC2 . . . . . .1E **12** (6J **83**)
Monnery Rd. N19 . . . . .3G **65**
Monnow Rd. SE1 . . . . .5G **103**
Mono La. TW13: Felt 2K **129**
Monoux Almshouses E17 . . . . .4D **50**
Monoux Gro. E17 . . . . .1C **50**
Monro Ct. E16 . . . . .4H **87**
Monroe Cres. EN1: Enf 1C **24**
Monroe Dr. SW14 . . . . .5H **115**
Monroe Ho. NW8 . . . . .2D **4**
   (off Lorne Cl.)
Monro Gdns. HA3: Hrw W 7D **26**
Monro Way E5 . . . . .4G **67**
Monsell Ct. N4 . . . . .3B **66**
Monsell Rd. N4 . . . . .3A **66**
Monsey Pl. E1 . . . . .4A **86**
Monson Rd. NW10 . . . . .2C **80**
   SE14 .7K **103**
Mons Way BR2: Brom 6C **160**
Montacute Rd. CR0: New Ad 7E **170**
   SE6 . . . . .7B **122**
   SM4: Mord 6B **154**
   WD23: B Hea 1E **26**
Montagu Cl. W1 . . . . .6F **5**
   (off Montagu Pl.)
Montagu Cres. N18 . . . . .4C **34**
Montague Av. SE4 . . . . .4B **122**
   W7 . . . . .1K **95**
Montague Cl. EN5: Barn 4C **20**
   KT12: Walt T 7K **147**
   SE1 . . . . .4E **14** (1D **102**)
Montague Ct. DA15: Sidc 3A **144**
   N7 . . . . .7A **66**
   (off St Clements St.)
Montague Gdns. W3 . . . . .7G **79**
Montague Ho. E16 . . . . .1K **105**
   (off Wesley Av.)
   IG3: Ilf .1A **72**
   N1 . . . . .1E **84**
   (off Halcomb St.)
Montague M. E3 . . . . .3B **86**
   (off Tredegar Ter.)
   SE20 . . . . .6J **139**
Montague Pas. UB8: Uxb 7A **56**
Montague Pl. WC1 . . . . . . .5D **6** (5H **83**)
Montague Rd. CR0: C'don 1B **168**
   E8 . . . . .5G **67**
   E11 . . . . .2H **69**
   N8 . . . . .5K **47**
   N15 . . . . .4G **49**
   SW19 .7K **135**
   TW3: Houn 3F **113**
   TW10: Rich 6E **114**
   UB2: S'hall 4C **94**
   UB8: Uxb 7A **56**
   W7 . . . . .1K **95**
   W13 . . . . .6B **78**
Montague Sq. SE15 . . . . .7J **103**
Montague St. EC1 . . . . . . .6C **8** (5C **84**)
   WC1 . . . . .5E **6** (5J **83**)
Montague Ter. BR2: Brom 4H **159**
Montague Walks HA0: Wemb 1F **79**
Montague Waye UB2: S'hall 3C **94**
Montagu Gdns. N18 . . . . .4C **34**
   SM6: Wall 4G **167**

Montagu Ind. Est. N18 . . . . .4D **34**
Montagu Mans. W1 . . . . . .5F **5** (5D **82**)
Montagu M. Nth. W1 . . . . .6F **5** (5D **82**)
Montagu M. Sth. W1 . . . . .7F **5** (6D **82**)
Montagu M. W. W1 . . . . . .7F **5** (6D **82**)
Montagu Pl. W1 . . . . .6E **4** (5D **82**)
Montagu Rd. N9 . . . . .4C **34**
   N18 . . . . .5C **34**
   NW4 . . . . .6C **44**
Montagu Row W1 . . . . . . .6F **5** (5D **82**)
Montagu Sq. W1 . . . . .6F **5** (5D **82**)
Montagu St. W1 . . . . .7F **5** (6D **82**)
Montaigne Cl. SW1 . . . . . .4D **18** (4H **101**)
Montalt Rd.
   IG8: Wfd G 4C **36**
Montana Bldg. SE13 . . . . .1D **122**
   (off Deal's Gateway)
Montana Gdns. SE26 . . . . .5B **140**
   SM1: Sutt 5A **166**
Montana Rd. SW17 . . . . .3E **136**
   SW20 .1E **152**
Montanaro Ct. N1 . . . . .1C **84**
   (off Coleman Flds.)
Montbelle Rd. SE9 . . . . .3F **143**
Montcalm Cl.
   BR2: Hayes 6J **159**
   UB4: Yead 3K **75**
Montcalm Ho. E14 . . . . .4B **104**
Montcalm Rd. SE7 . . . . .7B **106**
Montclare St. E2 . . . . .3J **9** (4F **85**)
Monteagle Av. IG11: Bark 6G **71**
Monteagle Ho. N1 . . . . .2E **84**
Monteagle Way E5 . . . . .3G **67**
   SE15 . . . . .3H **121**
Montefiore Ct. N16 . . . . .1F **67**
Montefiore St. SW8 . . . . .2F **119**
Montego Cl. SE24 . . . . .4A **120**
Montem Rd. KT3: N Mald 4A **152**
   SE23 . . . . .7B **122**
Montem St. N4 . . . . .1K **65**
Montenotte Rd. N8 . . . . .5G **47**
Monterey Apartments N15 . . . . .5D **48**
Monterey Cl. DA5: Bexl 2J **145**
   NW7 . . . . .5F **29**
   (off The Broadway)
   UB10: Hil 7C **56**
Monterey Studios W10 . . . . .2G **81**
Montesole Ct. HA5: Pinn 2A **40**
Montevetro SW11 . . . . .1B **118**
Montfichet Rd. E20 . . . . .7E **68**
Montford Pl. SE11 . . . . . . .6J **19** (5A **102**)
Montford Rd. TW16: Sun 4J **147**
Montfort Ho. E2 . . . . .2J **85**
   (off Victoria Pk. Sq.)
   E14 . . . . .3E **104**
   (off Galbraith St.)
Montfort Pl. SW19 . . . . .1F **135**
Montgolfier Wlk. UB5: N'olt 3C **76**
Montgomerie M. SE23 . . . . .7J **121**
Montgomery Cl. CR4: Mitc 4J **155**
   DA15: Sidc 6K **125**
Montgomery Ct. CR2: S Croy 5E **168**
   (off Birdhurst Rd.)
   W4 . . . . .7J **97**
Montgomery Gdns. SM2: Sutt 7B **166**
Montgomery Ho. UB5: N'olt 3D **76**
   (off Taywood Rd.)
   W2 . . . . .6A **4**
   (off Harrow Rd.)
Montgomery Lodge E1 . . . . .4J **85**
   (off Cleveland Gro.)
Montgomery Rd. HA8: Edg 6A **28**
   W4 . . . . .4J **97**
Montgomery Sq. E14 . . . . .1D **104**
Montgomery St. E14 . . . . .1D **104**
Montholme Rd. SW11 . . . . .6D **118**
Monthope Rd. E1 . . . . .6K **9** (5G **85**)
Montieu Gdns. SW15 . . . . .5D **116**
Montolieu Gdns. SW15 . . . . .5D **116**
Montpelier Av. DA5: Bexl 7D **126**
   W5 . . . . .5C **78**
Montpelier Cl. UB10: Hil 1C **74**

Montpelier Ct. *BR2: Brom* *4H 159*
(off Westmoreland Rd.)
W5 . . . . 5D 78
Montpelier Gdns. E6 . . . . 3B 88
RM6: Chad H 7C 54
Montpelier Gro. NW5 . . . . 5G 65
Montpelier M. SW7 . . . . 1D 16 (3C 100)
Montpelier Pl. E1 . . . . 6J 85
SW7 . . . . 1D 16 (3C 100)
Montpelier Ri. HA9: Wemb 1D 60
NW11 . . . . 7G 45
(not continuous)
Montpelier Rd. N3 . . . . 1A 46
SE15 . . . . 1H 121
SM1: Sutt 4A 166
W5 . . . . 5D 78
Montpelier Row SE3 . . . . 2H 123
TW1: Twick 7C 114
Montpelier Sq. SW7 . . . . 7D 10 (2C 100)
Montpelier St. SW7 . . . . 1D 16 (3C 100)
Montpelier Ter. SW7 . . . . 7D 10 (2C 100)
Montpelier Va. SE3 . . . . 2H 123
Montpelier Wlk. SW7 . . . . . . 1D 16 (3C 100)
Montpelier Way NW11 . . . . 7G 45
Montpellier Ct. KT12: Walt T 6J 147
Montrave Rd. SE20 . . . . 6J 139
Montreal Ho. *SE16* *2K 103*
(off Maple M.)
UB4: Yead *3K 75*
(off Ayles Rd.)
Montreal Pl. WC2 . . . . 2G 13 (7K 83)
Montreal Rd. IG1: Ilf 7G 53
Montrell Rd. SW2 . . . . 1J 137
Montrose Av. DA15: Sidc 7A 126
DA16: Well 3H 125
HA8: Edg 2J 43
NW6 . . . . 2G 81
TW2: Whitt 7F 113
Montrose Cl. DA16: Well 3K 125
IG8: Wfd G 4D 36
TW15: Ashf 6E 128
Montrose Ct. HA1: Harr 5F 41
NW9 . . . . 2J 43
NW11 . . . . 4H 45
SE6 . . . . 2H 141
SW7 . . . . 7B 10 (2B 100)
Montrose Cres. HA0: Wemb 6E 60
N12 . . . . 6F 31
Montrose Gdns. CR4: Mitc 2D 154
SM1: Sutt 2K 165
Montrose Ho. E14 . . . . 3C 104
SW1 . . . . *7H 11*
(off Montrose Pl.)
Montrose Pl. SW1 . . . . 7H 11 (2E 100)
Montrose Rd. HA3: W'stone 2J 41
TW14: Bedf 6F 111
Montrose Wlk. HA7: Stan 6G 27
Montrose Way SE23 . . . . 1K 139
Montserrat Av. IG8: Wfd G 7A 36
Montserrat Cl. SE19 . . . . 5D 138
Montserrat Rd. SW15 . . . . 4G 117
Monument, The 3F 15
Monument Gdns. SE13 . . . . 5E 122
Monument St. EC3 . . . . 2F 15 (7D 84)
Monument Way N17 . . . . 3F 49
Monza St. E1 . . . . 7J 85
Moodkee St. SE16 . . . . 3J 103
Moody Rd. SE15 . . . . 1F 121
Moody St. E1 . . . . 3K 85
Moon Ct. SE12 . . . . 4J 123
Moon Ho. HA1: Harr 4J 41
Moon La. EN5: Barn 3C 20
Moonlight Dr. SE23 . . . . 7H 121
Moonraker Point *SE1* *6B 14*
(off Pocock St.)
Moon St. N1 . . . . 1B 84
Moorcroft HA8: Edg 1H 43
Moorcroft Gdns. BR2: Brom 5C 160
Moorcroft La. UB8: Hil 5C 74
Moorcroft Rd. SW16 . . . . 3J 137
Moorcroft Way HA5: Pinn 5C 40
Moordown SE18 . . . . 7F 107
Moore Cl. CR4: Mitc 2F 155
SW14 . . . . 3J 115
Moore Ct. HA0: Wemb 6E 60
HA7: Stan 1D 42
N1 . . . . *1B 84*
(off Gaskin St.)
Moore Cres. RM9: Dag 1B 90
Moorefield Rd. N17 . . . . 2F 49
Moore Ho. *E1* *7J 85*
(off Cable St.)
E2 . . . . *3J 85*
(off Roman Rd.)
E14 . . . . 2C 104
N8 . . . . *4J 47*
(off Pembroke Rd.)
SE10 . . . . *5H 105*
(off Armitage Rd.)
SW1 . . . . 6J 17
Mooreland Rd. BR1: Brom 7H 141
Moore Pk. Rd. SW6 . . . . 7J 99
Moore Rd. SE19 . . . . 6C 138
Moore St. SW3 . . . . 3E 16 (4D 100)
Moore Wlk. E7 . . . . 4J 69
Moore Way SM2: Sutt 7J 165
Moorey Cl. E15 . . . . 1H 87
Moorfield Av. W5 . . . . 4D 78
Moorfield Rd. EN3: Enf H 1D 24
KT9: Chess 5E 162
UB8: Cowl 6A 74
Moorfields EC2 . . . . 6E 8 (5D 84)
Moorfields Highwalk *EC2* *6E 8*
(off New Union St.)
Moorgate EC2 . . . . 7E 8 (6D 84)
Moorgate Pl. EC2 . . . . 7E 8
Moorgreen Ho. EC1 . . . . 1A 8
Moorhead Way SE3 . . . . 3J 123
Moorhen Dr. NW9 . . . . 6B 44
Moorhen Ho. *E3* *1B 86*
(off Old Ford Rd.)
Moorhouse NW9 . . . . 1B 44
Moorhouse Rd. HA3: Kenton 3D 42
W2 . . . . 6J 81
Moorings, The *E16* *5A 88*
(off Prince Regent La.)
Moorings Ho. TW8: Bford 7C 96
MOOR JUNC. **3C 174**
Moorland Cl. RM5: Col R 1H 55
TW2: Whitt 7E 112
Moorland Rd. SW9 . . . . 4B 120
UB7: Harm 2D 174
Moorlands UB5: N'olt 1C 76
Moorlands Av. NW7 . . . . 6J 29
Moor La. EC2 . . . . 6E 8 (5D 84)
(not continuous)
KT9: Chess 4E 162
UB7: Harm 2D 174
Moormead Dr. KT19: Ewe 5A 164
Moor Mead Rd. TW1: Twick 6A 114
Moor Pk. Gdns. KT2: King T 7A 134
Moor Pl. EC2 . . . . 6E 8 (5D 84)
Moorside Rd. BR1: Brom 3G 141
Moor St. W1 . . . . 1D 12 (6H 83)
Moot Ct. NW9 . . . . 5G 43
Moran Ho. *E1* *1H 103*
(off Wapping La.)
Morant Pl. N22 . . . . 1K 47
Morant St. E14 . . . . 7C 86
Mora Rd. NW2 . . . . 4E 62
Mora St. EC1 . . . . 2D 8 (3C 84)
Morat St. SW9 . . . . 1K 119
Moravian Cl. SW10 . . . . 7A 16 (6B 100)
Moravian Pl. SW10 . . . . 6B 100
Moravian St. E2 . . . . 2J 85
Moray Av. UB3: Hayes 1H 93
Moray Cl. HA8: Edg 2C 28
RM1: Rom 1K 55
Moray Ct. *CR2: S Croy* *5C 168*
(off Warham Rd.)
Moray Ho. *E1* *4A 86*
(off Harford St.)
Moray M. N7 . . . . 2K 65
Moray Rd. N4 . . . . 2K 65
Moray Way RM1: Rom 1K 55
Mordaunt Gdns. RM9: Dag 7E 72
Mordaunt Ho. *NW10* *1K 79*
(off Stracey Rd.)
Mordaunt Rd. NW10 . . . . 1K 79
Mordaunt St. SW9 . . . . 3K 119
MORDEN 3K 153
Morden Ct. SM4: Mord 4K 153
Morden Ct. Pde. SM4: Mord 4K 153
Morden Gdns. CR4: Mitc 4B 154
UB6: G'frd 5K 59
Morden Hall Pk. 3A 154
Morden Hall Rd. SM4: Mord 3K 153
Morden Hill SE13 . . . . 2E 122
Morden Ho. SM4: Mord 4J 153
Morden La. SE13 . . . . 2E 122
MORDEN PARK 6G 153
Morden Pk. Pools 6H 153
Morden Rd. CR4: Mitc 4A 154
RM6: Chad H 7E 54
SE3 . . . . 2J 123
SM4: Mord 4A 154
SW19 . . . . 1K 153
Morden Rd. M. SE3 . . . . 2J 123
Morden St. SE13 . . . . 1D 122
Morden Way SM3: Sutt 7J 153
Morden Wharf *SE10* *3G 105*
(off Morden Wharf Rd.)
Morden Wharf Rd. SE10 . . . . 3G 105
Mordern Ho. NW1 . . . . 3D 4
Mordon Rd. IG3: Ilf 7K 53
Mordred Rd. SE6 . . . . 2G 141
Morea M. N5 . . . . 5C 66
Morecambe Cl. E1 . . . . 5K 85
Morecambe Gdns. HA7: Stan 4J 27
Morecambe St. SE17 . . . . 4C 102
More Cl. E16 . . . . 6H 87
W14 . . . . 4F 99
Morecoombe Cl. KT2: King T 7H 133
More Copper Ho. *SE1* *5G 15*
(off Magdalen St.)
Moree Way N18 . . . . 4B 34
Moreland Cotts. *E3* *2C 86*
(off Fairfield Rd.)
Moreland Ct. NW2 . . . . 3J 63
Moreland St. EC1 . . . . 1B 8 (3B 84)
Moreland Way E4 . . . . 3J 35
Morella Rd. SW12 . . . . 7D 118
Morell Cl. EN5: New Bar 3F 21
Morello Av. UB8: Hil 5D 74
Morel M. RM8: Dag 1D 72
More London Pl. SE1 . . . . . . 5G 15 (1E 102)
(not continuous)
More London Riverside
SE1 . . . . 5H 15 (1E 102)
(not continuous)
Moremead Rd. SE6 . . . . 4B 140
Morena St. SE6 . . . . 7D 122
Moresby Av. KT5: Surb 7H 151
Moresby Rd. E5 . . . . 1H 67
Moresby Wlk. SW8 . . . . 2G 119
More's Gdn. *SW3* *6B 100*
(off Cheyne Wlk.)
Moreton Av. TW7: Isle 1J 113
Moreton Cl. E5 . . . . 2H 67
N15 . . . . 6D 48
NW7 . . . . 6K 29
SW1 . . . . 5B 18
Moreton Gdns. IG8: Wfd G 5H 37
Moreton Ho. SE16 . . . . 3H 103
Moreton Pl. SW1 . . . . 5B 18 (5G 101)
Moreton Rd. CR2: S Croy 5D 168
KT4: Wor Pk 2C 164
N15 . . . . 6D 48
Moretons HA1: Harr 1J 59
Moreton St. SW1 . . . . 5B 18 (5G 101)
Moreton Ter. SW1 . . . . 5B 18 (5G 101)
Moreton Ter. M. Nth. SW1 . . 5B 18 (5G 101)
Moreton Ter. M. Sth. SW1 . . 5B 18 (5G 101)
Moreton Twr. W3 . . . . 1H 97
Morford Cl. HA4: Ruis 7K 39
Morford Way HA4: Ruis 7K 39
Morgan Av. E17 . . . . 4F 51
Morgan Cl. RM10: Dag 7G 73
Morgan Ct. SM5: Cars 4D 166
TW15: Ashf 5D 128
Morgan Cres. RM8: Dag 1E 72
Morgan Ho. *SW1* *4B 18*
(off Vauxhall Bri. Rd.)
SW8 . . . . *1G 119*
(off Wadhurst Rd.)
Morgan Mans. *N7* *5A 66*
(off Morgan Rd.)
Morgan Rd. BR1: Brom 7J 141
N7 . . . . 5A 66
W10 . . . . 5H 81
Morgan's La. UB3: Hayes 5F 75
Morgans La. *SE1* *5G 15*
(off Tooley St.)
Morgan St. E3 . . . . 3A 86
(not continuous)
E16 . . . . 5H 87
Morgan Wlk. BR3: Beck 4D 158
Morgan Way IG8: Wfd G 6H 37
Moriarty Cl. BR1: Brom 4E 160
Moriatry Cl. N7 . . . . 4J 65
Morie St. SW18 . . . . 5K 117
Morieux Rd. E10 . . . . 1B 68
Moring Rd. SW17 . . . . 4E 136
Morkyns Wlk. SE21 . . . . 3E 138
Morland Av. CR0: C'don 1E 168
Morland Cl. CR4: Mitc 3C 154
NW11 . . . . 1K 63
TW12: Hamp 5D 130
Morland Ct. *W12* *2D 98*
(off Coningham Rd.)
Morland Est. E8 . . . . 7G 67
Morland Gdns. NW10 . . . . 7K 61
UB1: S'hall 1F 95
Morland Ho. *NW1* *1B 6*
(off Werrington St.)
NW6 . . . . 1J 81
SW1 . . . . *3E 18*
(off Marsham St.)
W11 . . . . *6G 81*
(off Lancaster Rd.)
Morland M. N1 . . . . 7A 66
Morland Pl. N15 . . . . 4E 48
Morland Rd. CR0: C'don 1E 168
E17 . . . . 5K 49
HA3: Kenton 5E 42
IG1: Ilf 2F 71
RM10: Dag 7G 73
SE20 . . . . 6K 139
SM1: Sutt 5A 166
Morley Av. E4 . . . . 7A 36
N18 . . . . 4B 34
N22 . . . . 2A 48
Morley Cl. BR6: Farnb 2F 173
Morley Ct. BR2: Brom 4H 159
E4 . . . . 5G 35
Morley Cres. HA4: Ruis 2A 58
HA8: Edg 2D 28
Morley Cres. E. HA7: Stan 2C 42
Morley Cres. W. HA7: Stan 3C 42
Morley Hill EN2: Enf 1J 23
Morley Ho. *SE15* *7F 103*
(off Commercial Way)
Morley Rd. BR7: Chst 1G 161
E10 . . . . 1E 68
E15 . . . . 2H 87
IG11: Bark 1H 89
RM6: Chad H 5E 54
SE13 . . . . 4E 122
SM3: Sutt 1H 165
TW1: Twick 6D 114
Morley St. SE1 . . . . 1K 19 (3A 102)
Morna Rd. SE5 . . . . 2C 120
Morning La. E9 . . . . 6J 67
Morningside Rd. KT4: Wor Pk 2E 164

Mornington Av. BR1: Brom 3A 160
IG1: Ilf 7E 52
W14 4H 99
Mornington Av. Mans. *W14* *4H 99*
(off Mornington Av.)
Mornington Cl. IG8: Wfd G 4D 36
NW9 3A 44
Mornington Ct. DA5: Bexl 1K 145
NW1 *2G 83*
(off Mornington Cres.)
Mornington Cres. NW1 2G 83
TW5: Cran 1K 111
Mornington Gro. E3 3C 86
Mornington M. SE5 1C 120
Mornington Pl. NW1 2G 83
SE8 *7B 104*
(off Mornington Rd.)
Mornington Rd. E4 7K 25, 1A 36
E11 7H 51
IG8: Wfd G 4C 36
SE8 7B 104
TW15: Ashf 5E 128
UB6: G'frd 5F 77
Mornington St. NW1 2F 83
Mornington Ter. NW1 1F 83
Mornington Wlk.
TW10: Ham 4C 132
Moro Apartments *E14* *6C 86*
(off New Festival Av.)
Morocco St. SE1 7G 15 (2E 102)
Morocco Wharf *E1* *1H 103*
(off Wapping High St.)
Morpeth Gro. E9 1K 85
Morpeth Mans. *SW1* *2A 18*
(off Morpeth Ter.)
Morpeth Rd. E9 1K 85
Morpeth St. E2 3J 85
Morpeth Ter. SW1 2A 18 (3G 101)
Morpeth Wlk. N17 7C 34
Morphou Rd. NW7 6B 30
Morrab Gdns. IG3: Ilf 3K 71
Morrel Ct. *E2* *2G 85*
(off Goldsmiths Row)
Morrells Yd. *SE11* *5K 19*
(off Cleaver St.)
Morris Av. E12 5D 70
UB8: Uxb 6A 56
Morris Blitz Ct. N16 4F 67
Morris Cl. BR6: Orp 3J 173
CR0: C'don 5A 158
Morris Ct. E4 3J 35
Morris Dr. DA17: Belv 4J 109
Morris Gdns. SW18 7J 117
Morris Ho. *E2* *3J 85*
(off Roman Rd.)
NW8 *4C 4*
(off Salisbury St.)
W3 2B 98
Morrish Rd. SW2 7J 119
Morris M. SW19 5A 136
Morrison Av. E4 6H 35
N17 3E 48
Morrison Bldgs. Nth. *E1* *6G 85*
(off Commercial Rd.)
Morrison Ct. *EN5: Barn* *4B 20*
(off Manor Way)
N12 7H 31
SW1 *3H 101*
(off Gt. Smith St.)
Morrison Ho. *SW2* *1A 138*
(off Tulse Hill)
Morrison Rd. IG11: Bark 2E 90
RM9: Bark, Dag 2E 90
SW9 2A 120
UB4: Yead 3K 75
Morrison St. SW11 3E 118
Morris Pl. N4 2A 66
Morris Rd. E14 5D 86
E15 4G 69
RM8: Dag 2F 73
TW7: Isle 3K 113
Morriss Ho. *SE16* *2H 103*
(off Cherry Gdn. St.)
Morris St. E1 6H 85
Morritt Ho. *HA0: Wemb* *5D 60*
(off Talbot Rd.)
Morse Cl. E13 3J 87
Morshead Mans. *W9* *3J 81*
(off Morshead Rd.)
Morshead Rd. W9 3J 81
Morson Rd. EN3: Pond E 6F 25
Morston Gdns. SE9 4D 142
Mortain Ho. *SE16* *4H 103*
(off Roseberry St.)
Morten Cl. SW4 6H 119
Morteyne Rd. N17 1D 48
Mortgramit Sq. SE18 3E 106
Mortham St. E15 1G 87
Mortimer Cl. NW2 2H 63
SW16 2H 137
Mortimer Ct. *NW8* *1A 4*
(off Abbey Rd.)
Mortimer Cres. KT4: Wor Pk 3K 163
NW6 1K 81
Mortimer Dr. EN1: Enf 5K 23
Mortimer Est. *NW6* *1K 81*
(off Mortimer Pl.)
Mortimer Ho. W11 1F 99
W14 *4G 99*
(off North End Rd.)
Mortimer Mkt. WC1 4B 6 (4G 83)
Mortimer Pl. NW6 1K 81
Mortimer Rd. CR4: Mitc 1D 154
DA8: Erith 6K 109
E6 3D 88
N1 7E 66
(not continuous)
NW10 3E 80
W13 6C 78
Mortimer Sq. W11 7F 81
Mortimer St. W1 7K 5 (6G 83)
Mortimer Ter. NW5 4F 65
MORTLAKE 3K 115
Mortlake Cl. CR0: Bedd 3J 167
Mortlake Crematorium TW9: Kew 2H 115
Mortlake Dr. CR4: Mitc 1C 154
Mortlake High St. SW14 3K 115
Mortlake Rd. E16 6K 87
IG1: Ilf 4G 71
TW9: Kew, Rich 7G 97
Mortlake Ter. *TW9: Kew* *7G 97*
(off Mortlake Rd.)
Mortlock Cl. SE15 1H 121
Mortlock Ct. E7 4B 70
Morton Cl. E1 6J 85
SM6: Wall 7K 167
UB8: Hil 4B 74
Morton Ct. UB5: N'olt 5G 59
Morton Cres. N14 4C 32
Morton Gdns. SM6: Wall 5G 167
Morton Ho. SE17 6B 102
Morton M. SW5 4K 99
Morton Pl. SE1 2J 19 (3A 102)
Morton Rd. E15 7H 69
N1 7C 66
SM4: Mord 5B 154
Morton Way N14 3B 32
Morvale Cl. DA17: Belv 4F 109
Morval Rd. SW2 5A 120
Morven Rd. SW17 3D 136
Morville Ho. *SW18* *6B 118*
(off Fitzhugh Gro.)
Morville St. E3 2C 86
Morwell St. WC1 6C 6 (5H 83)
Moscow Mans. *SW5* *4J 99*
(off Cromwell Rd.)
Moscow Pl. W2 7K 81
Moscow Rd. W2 7J 81
Mosedale *NW1* *2K 5*
(off Cumberland Mkt.)
Moseley Row SE10 4H 105
Moselle Av. N22 2A 48
Moselle Cl. N8 3K 47
Moselle Ho. *N17* *7A 34*
(off William St.)
Moselle Pl. N17 7A 34
Moselle St. N17 7A 34
Mosque Ter. *E1* *5G 85*
(off Whitechapel Rd.)
Mosque Twr. *E1* *5G 85*
(off Fieldgate St.)
E3 *2A 86*
(off Ford St.)
Mosquito Cl. SM6: Wall 7J 167
Mossborough Cl. N12 6E 30
Mossbury Rd. SW11 3C 118
Moss Cl. E1 5G 85
HA5: Pinn 2D 40
N9 1B 34
Mossdown Cl. DA17: Belv 4G 109
Mossford Ct. IG6: Ilf 3F 53
Mossford Grn. IG6: Ilf 3F 53
Mossford La. IG6: Ilf 2F 53
Mossford St. E3 4B 86
Moss Gdns. CR2: Sels 7K 169
TW13: Felt 2J 129
Moss Hall Ct. N12 6E 30
Moss Hall Cres. N12 6E 30
Moss Hall Gro. N12 6E 30
Mossington Gdns. SE16 4J 103
Moss La. HA5: Pinn 1C 40
Mosslea Rd. BR2: Brom 5B 160
BR6: Farnb 3G 173
SE20 6J 139
(not continuous)
Mossop St. SW3 3D 16 (4C 100)
Moss Rd. RM10: Dag 7G 73
Mossville Gdns. SM4: Mord 3H 153
Mosswell Ho. N10 1E 46
Moston Cl. UB3: Harl 5H 93
Mostyn Av. HA9: Wemb 5F 61
Mostyn Gdns. NW10 3F 81
Mostyn Gro. E3 2C 86
Mostyn Rd. HA8: Edg 7F 29
SW9 1A 120
SW19 1H 153
Mosul Way BR2: Brom 6C 160
Motcomb St. SW1 1G 17 (3E 100)
Moth Cl. SM6: Wall 7J 167
Mothers Sq. E5 4H 67
Motley Av. EC2 4G 9
MOTSPUR PARK 6C 152
Motspur Pk. KT3: N Mald 6B 152
MOTTINGHAM 2C 142
Mottingham Gdns. SE9 1B 142
Mottingham La. SE9 1A 142
SE12 1A 142
Mottingham Rd. N9 6E 24
SE9 2C 142
Mottisfont Rd. SE2 3A 108
Mottistone Gro. SM2: Sutt 7K 165
Motts La. RM8: Dag 2F 73
Mott St. E4 1K 25
Moules Ct. SE5 7C 102
Moulins Rd. E9 7J 67
Moulsford Ho. N7 5H 65
W2 *5J 81*
(off Westbourne Pk. Rd.)
Moulton Av. TW3: Houn 2C 112
Mound, The SE9 3E 142
Moundfield Rd. N16 6G 49
Mounsey Ho. *W10* *3G 81*
(off Third Av.)
Mount, The BR1: Brom 1C 160
CR2: S Croy *5C 168*
(off Warham Rd.)
DA6: Bex 5H 127
E5 2H 67
(not continuous)
HA9: Wemb 2H 61
KT3: N Mald 3B 152
KT4: Wor Pk 4D 164
N20 2F 31
Mount, The NW3 3A 64
UB5: N'olt 5F 59
W3 1J 97
W8 *1J 99*
(off Bedford Gdns.)
Mountacre Cl. SE26 4F 139
Mt. Adon Pk. SE22 7G 121
Mountague Pl. E14 7E 86
Mountain Ho. SE11 4H 19 (4K 101)
Mt. Angelus Rd. SW15 7B 116
Mt. Ararat Rd. TW10: Rich 5E 114
Mt. Arlington
BR2: Brom *2G 159*
(off Park Hill Rd.)
Mt. Ash Rd. SE26 3H 139
Mount Av. E4 3H 35
UB1: S'hall 6E 76
W5 5C 78
Mountbatten Cl. SE18 6J 107
SE19 5E 138
Mountbatten Ct. IG9: Buck H 2G 37
SE16 *1J 103*
(off Rotherhithe St.)
Mountbatten Gdns. BR3: Beck 4A 158
Mountbatten Ho. *N6* *7E 46*
(off Hillcrest)
Mountbatten M. SW18 7A 118
Mountbel Rd. HA7: Stan 1A 42
Mt. Carmel Chambers *W8* *2J 99*
(off Dukes La.)
Mount Cl. BR1: Brom 1C 160
EN4: Cockf 4K 21
SM5: Cars 7E 166
W5 5C 78
Mountcombe Cl. KT6: Surb 7E 150
Mount Ct. BR4: W W'ck 2G 171
SW15 3G 117
Mt. Culver Av. DA14: Sidc 6D 144
Mount Dr. DA6: Bex 5E 126
HA2: Harr 5D 40
HA9: Wemb 2J 61
Mountearl Gdns. SW16 3K 137
Mt. Eaton Ct. *W5* *5C 78*
(off Mount Av.)
Mt. Echo Av. E4 2J 35
Mt. Echo Dr. E4 1J 35
Mt. Ephraim La. SW16 3H 137
Mt. Ephraim Rd. SW16 3H 137
Mount Felix KT12: Walt T 7H 147
Mountfield Cl. SE6 7F 123
Mountfield Rd. E6 2E 88
N3 3H 45
W5 6D 78
Mountfield Ter. SE6 7F 123
Mountford Mans. *SW11* *1E 118*
(off Battersea Pk. Rd.)
Mountfort Cres. N1 7A 66
Mountfort Ho. *N1* *7A 66*
(off Barnsbury Sq.)
Mountfort Ter. N1 7A 66
Mount Gdns. SE26 3H 139
Mount Gro. HA8: Edg 3D 28
Mountgrove Rd. N5 3B 66
Mount Holme KT7: T Ditt 7B 150
Mounthurst Rd. BR2: Hayes 7H 159
Mountington Pk. Cl. HA3: Kenton 6D 42
Mountjoy Cl. *EC2* *6D 8*
(off Monkwell Sq.)
SE2 2B 108
Mountjoy Ho. EC2 6C 8
Mount Lodge N6 6G 47
Mount M. TW12: Hamp 1F 149
Mount Mills EC1 2B 8 (3B 84)
Mt. Nod Rd. SW16 3K 137
Mt. Olive Ct. W7 2J 95
Mount Pde. EN4: Cockf 4H 21
Mount Pk. SM5: Cars 7E 166
Mount Pk. Av.
CR2: S Croy 7B 168
HA1: Harr 2H 59
Mount Pk. Cres. W5 6D 78

Mount Pk. Rd. HA1: Harr 3H 59
  HA5: Eastc 5J 39
  W5 . . . . .5D 78
Mount Pl. W3 . . . . .1H 97
Mt. Pleasant EN4: Cockf 4H 21
  HA0: Wemb 1E 78
  HA4: Ruis 2A 58
  IG1: Ilf 5G 71
  SE27 . . . . .4C 138
  WC1 . . . . .4J 7 (4A 84)
Mt. Pleasant Cotts. N14 . . . . .7C 22
              (off The Wells)
Mt. Pleasant Cres. N4 . . . . .1K 65
Mt. Pleasant Hill E5 . . . . .2H 67
Mt. Pleasant La. E5 . . . . .1H 67
Mt. Pleasant M. N4 . . . . .1K 65
       (off Mt. Pleasant Cres.)
Mt. Pleasant Rd. E17 . . . . .3A 50
  KT3: N Mald 3J 151
  N17 .2E 48
  NW10 . . . . .7E 62
  SE13 . . . . .6D 122
  W5 . . . . .4C 78
Mt. Pleasant Vs. N4 . . . . .7K 47
Mt. Pleasant Wlk. DA5: Bexl 5J 127
Mount Rd. CR4: Mitc 2B 154
  DA6: Bex 5D 126
  EN4: E Barn 5H 21
  KT3: N Mald 3K 151
  KT9: Chess 5F 163
  NW2 .3D 62
  NW4 .6C 44
  RM8: Dag 1F 73
  SE19 . . . . .6D 138
  SW19 . . . . .2J 135
  TW13: Hanw 3C 130
  UB3: Hayes 2J 93
Mount Row W1 . . . . . .3J 11 (7F 83)
Mountsfield Ct. SE13 . . . . .6F 123
Mountsfield Ho. SE10 . . . . .1E 122
          (off Primrose Way)
Mountside HA7: Stan 1A 42
Mounts Pond Rd. SE3 . . . . .2F 123
        (not continuous)
Mount Sq., The NW3 . . . . .3A 64
Mt. Stewart Av. HA3: Kenton 7D 42
Mount St. W1 . . . . . .3G 11 (7E 82)
Mount St. M. W1 . . . . .3J 11 (7F 83)
Mountstuart Ct. TW11: Hamp W . . .1B 150
Mount Ter. E1 . . . . .5H 85
Mount Vernon NW3 . . . . .4A 64
Mount Vw. EN2: Enf 1E 22
  NW7 .3E 28
  UB2: S'hall 4B 94
  W5 . . . . .4D 78
Mountview Academy of Theatre Arts
  . . . . .2K 47
         (off Clarendon Rd.)
Mountview Cl. NW11 . . . . .1K 63
Mountview Ct. N8 . . . . .4B 48
Mount Vw. Rd. E4 . . . . . . .7K 25, 1A 36
  KT10: Clay 7B 162
  N4 . . . . .7J 47
  NW9 .5K 43
Mountview Rd. BR6: Orp, St M Cry . . .7K 161
        (not continuous)
Mount Vs. SE27 . . . . .3B 138
Mount Way SM5: Cars 7E 166
Mountwood KT8: W Mole 3F 149
MOVERS LANE 2J 89
Movers La. IG11: Bark 1H 89
Mowat Ct. KT4: Wor Pk 2B 164
          (off The Avenue)
Mowatt Cl. N19 . . . . .1H 65
Mowbray Ct. N22 . . . . .1A 48
  SE19 . . . . .7F 139
Mowbray Gdns. UB5: N'olt 1E 76
Mowbray Ho. N2 . . . . .2B 46
          (off The Grange)
Mowbray Pde. HA8: Edg 4B 28

Mowbray Rd. EN5: New Bar 5F 21
  HA8: Edg 4B 28
  NW6 .7G 63
  SE19 . . . . .1F 157
  TW10: Ham 3C 132
Mowbrays Cl. RM5: Col R 1J 55
Mowbrays Rd.
  RM5: Col R 2J 55
Mowlem St. E2 . . . . .2H 85
Mowlem Trad. Est. N17 . . . . .7D 34
Mowll St. SW9 . . . . .7A 102
Moxon Cl. E13 . . . . .2H 87
Moxon Pl. UB10: Uxb 1B 74
Moxon St.
  EN5: Barn 3C 20
  W1 . . . . .6G 5 (5E 82)
Moye Cl. E2 . . . . .2G 85
Moyers Rd. E10 . . . . .7E 50
Moylan Rd. W6 . . . . .6G 99
Moyle Ho. DA17: Belv 2H 109
  SW1 .6B 18
        (off Churchill Gdns.)
Moyne Ho. SW9 . . . . .5B 120
Moyne Pl. NW10 . . . . .2G 79
Moynihan Dr. N21 . . . . .5D 22
Moys Cl. CR0: C'don 6J 155
Moyser Rd. SW16 . . . . .5F 137
Mozart St. W10 . . . . .3H 81
Mozart Ter. SW1 . . . . . .4H 17 (4E 100)
MTV Europe 7F 65
Muchelney Rd. SM4: Mord 6A 154
Mudchute Farm 4E 104
Mudlarks Blvd. SE10 . . . . .3H 105
Mudlarks Way SE10 . . . . .3J 105
Muffin La. E2 . . . . .2G 85
Muggeridge Cl. CR2: S Croy 5D 168
Muggeridge Rd. RM10: Dag 4H 73
Muirdown Av. SW14 . . . . .4K 115
Muir Dr. SW18 . . . . .6C 118
Muirfield W3 . . . . .6A 80
Muirfield Cl. SE16 . . . . .5H 103
Muirfield Cres. E14 . . . . .3D 104
Muirhead Quay IG11: Bark 2G 89
Muirkirk Rd. SE6 . . . . .1E 140
Muir Rd. E5 . . . . .3G 67
Muir St. E16 . . . . .1C 106
        (not continuous)
Mulberry Apartments N4 . . . . .1C 66
          (off Coster Av.)
Mulberry Av. TW19: Stanw 1A 128
Mulberry Cl. E4 . . . . .2H 35
  EN4: E Barn 4G 21
  N8 . . . . .5J 47
  NW3 .4B 64
  NW4 .3E 44
  SE7 .6B 106
  SE22 . . . . .5G 121
  SW3 .6B 100
         (off Beaufort St.)
  SW16 . . . . .4G 137
  TW13: Felt 3K 129
  UB5: N'olt 2C 76
Mulberry Ct. DA1: Cray 5K 127
  E11 . . . . .4F 69
      (off Langthorne Rd.)
  EC1 . . . . .2B 8
        (off Tompion St.)
  IG11: Bark 6K 71
  KT6: Surb 7D 150
  N2 . . . . .3C 46
       (off Bedford Rd.)
  SW3 . . . . .7B 16 (6B 100)
        (not continuous)
  TW1: Twick 3K 131
  W9 . . . . .3H 81
        (off Ashmore Rd.)
Mulberry Cres. TW8: Bford 7B 96
  UB7: W Dray 2C 92
Mulberry Ho. BR2: Brom 1G 159
  E2 . . . . .3J 85
      (off Victoria Pk. Sq.)

Mulberry Ho. SE8 . . . . .6B 104
  SE10 . . . . .1E 122
         (off Parkside Av.)
Mulberry Housing Co-operative
  SE1 . . . . .4K 13
Mulberry La. CR0: C'don 1F 169
Mulberry M. SE14 . . . . .1B 122
  SM6: Wall 6G 167
Mulberry Pde. UB7: W Dray 3C 92
Mulberry Pl. E14 . . . . .7E 86
         (off Clove Cres.)
  HA2: Harr 2H 41
  SE9 .4B 124
  W6 . . . . .5C 98
Mulberry Rd. E8 . . . . .7F 67
Mulberry St. E1 . . . . .6G 85
Mulberry Tree M. W4 . . . . .2J 97
Mulberry Trees TW17: Shep 7F 147
Mulberry Wlk. SW3 . . . . . .7B 16 (6B 100)
Mulberry Way DA17: Belv 2J 109
  E18 . . . . .2K 51
  IG6: Ilf 4G 53
Mulgrave Ct. SM2: Sutt 6K 165
         (off Mulgrave Rd.)
Mulgrave Rd. CR0: C'don 3D 168
  HA1: Harr 2A 60
  NW10 . . . . .4B 62
  SE18 . . . . .4D 106
  SM2: Sutt 7H 165
  SW6 .6H 99
  W5 . . . . .5D 78
Mulholland Cl. CR4: Mitc 2F 155
Mulkern Rd. N19 . . . . .1H 65
        (not continuous)
Mullards Cl. CR4: Mitc 1D 166
Mullen Twr. WC1 . . . . .4J 7
       (off Mt. Pleasant)
Muller Ho. SE18 . . . . .5E 106
Muller Rd. SW4 . . . . .6H 119
Mullet Gdns. E2 . . . . .2G 85
Mulletsfield WC1 . . . . .2F 7
        (off Cromer St.)
Mull Ho. E3 . . . . .2B 86
       (off Stafford Rd.)
Mulligans Apartments NW6 . . . . . . .7J 63
      (off Kilburn High Rd.)
Mullins Path SW14 . . . . .3K 115
Mullins Pl. SW4 . . . . .7J 119
Mullion Cl. HA3: Hrw W 1F 41
Mull Wlk. N1 . . . . .6C 66
        (off Clephane Rd.)
Mulready Ho. SW1 . . . . .4E 18
        (off Marsham St.)
Mulready St. NW8 . . . . . .4C 4 (4C 82)
Multi Way W3 . . . . .2A 98
Multon Ho. E9 . . . . .7J 67
Multon Rd. SW18 . . . . .7B 118
        (not continuous)
Mulvaney Way SE1 . . . . . .7F 15 (2D 102)
        (not continuous)
Mumford Mills SE10 . . . . .1D 122
      (off Greenwich High Rd.)
Mumford Rd. SE24 . . . . .5B 120
Muncaster Cl. TW15: Ashf 4C 128
Muncaster Rd. SW11 . . . . .5D 118
  TW15: Ashf 5D 128
Muncies M. SE6 . . . . .2E 140
Mundania Ct. SE22 . . . . .6H 121
Mundania Rd. SE22 . . . . .6H 121
Munday Ho. SE1 . . . . .3D 102
        (off Burbage Cl.)
Munday Rd. E16 . . . . .7J 87
Munden Ho. E3 . . . . .3D 86
      (off Bromley High St.)
Munden St. W14 . . . . .4G 99
Mundford Rd. E5 . . . . .2J 67
Mundon Gdns. IG1: Ilf 1H 71
Mund St. W14 . . . . .5H 99
Mundy Ho. W10 . . . . .3G 81
        (off Dart St.)
Mundy St. N1 . . . . .1G 9 (3E 84)
Mungo Pk. Cl. WD23: B Hea 2B 26

Munkenbeck Bldg. W2 . . . . .6A 4
        (off Hermitage St.)
Munnery Way BR6: Farnb 3E 172
Munnings Gdns. TW7: Isle 5H 113
Munnings Ho. E16 . . . . .1K 105
      (off Portsmouth M.)
Munro Dr. N11 . . . . .6B 32
Munro Ho. SE1 . . . . .7J 13 (2A 102)
Munro M. W10 . . . . .5G 81
        (not continuous)
Munro Ter. SW10 . . . . .7B 100
Munslow Gdns. SM1: Sutt 4B 166
Munster Av. TW4: Houn 5C 112
Munster Ct. SW6 . . . . .2H 117
  TW11: Tedd 6C 132
Munster Gdns. N13 . . . . .4G 33
Munster M. SW6 . . . . .7G 99
Munster Rd. SW6 . . . . .7G 99
  TW11: Tedd 6B 132
Munster Sq. NW1 . . . . . . .2K 5 (3F 83)
Munster Ter. E13 . . . . .3A 88
Munton Rd. SE17 . . . . .4C 102
Muratori Ho. WC1 . . . . .2J 7
        (off Margery St.)
Murchison Av. DA5: Bexl 1D 144
Murchison Ho. W10 . . . . .5G 81
        (off Ladbroke Gro.)
Murchison Rd. E10 . . . . .2E 68
Murdoch Ho. SE16 . . . . .3J 103
       (off Moodkee St.)
Murdock Cl. E16 . . . . .6H 87
Murdock St. SE15 . . . . .6H 103
Murfett Cl. SW19 . . . . .2G 135
Muriel St. N1 . . . . .2K 83
        (not continuous)
Murillo Rd. SE13 . . . . .4F 123
Muro Ct. SE1 . . . . .7B 14
       (off Milcote St.)
Murphy Ho. SE1 . . . . .7B 14
       (off Borough Rd.)
Murphy St. SE1 . . . . .7J 13 (2A 102)
Murray Av. BR1: Brom 3K 159
  TW3: Houn 5F 113
Murray Cl. SE28 . . . . .1J 107
Murray Ct. E3 . . . . .5B 86
       (off Geoff Cade Way)
  HA1: Harr 6K 41
  TW2: Twick 2H 131
  W7 . . . . .2J 95
Murray Cres. HA5: Pinn 1B 40
Murray Gro. N1 . . . . .1D 8 (2C 84)
Murray Ho. SE18 . . . . .4D 106
        (off Rideout St.)
Murray M. NW1 . . . . .7H 65
Murray Rd. HA6: Nwood 1G 39
  SW19 . . . . .6F 135
  TW10: Ham 2B 132
  W5 . . . . .4C 96
Murray Sq. E16 . . . . .6J 87
Murray St. NW1 . . . . .7G 65
Murrays Yd. SE18 . . . . .4F 107
Murray Ter. NW3 . . . . .4A 64
  W5 . . . . .4D 96
Mursell Est. SW8 . . . . .1K 119
Musard Rd. W6 . . . . .6G 99
  W14 .6G 99
Musbury St. E1 . . . . .6J 85
Muscal W6 . . . . .6G 99
        (off Field Rd.)
Muscatel Pl. SE5 . . . . .1E 120
Muschamp Rd. SE15 . . . . .3F 121
  SM5: Cars 2C 166
Muscott Ho. E2 . . . . .1G 85
       (off Whiston Rd.)
Muscovy Ho. DA18: Erith 2E 108
         (off Kale Rd.)
Muscovy St. EC3 . . . . .2H 15 (7E 84)
Mus. Chambers WC1 . . . . .6E 6
        (off Bury Pl.)
Museum Ho. E2 . . . . .3J 85
       (off Burnham St.)

Museum La. SW7 . . . . .2B 16 (3B 100)
Museum Mans. WC1 . . . . .6E 6
(off Gt. Russell St.)
Mus. of Brands, Packaging & Advertising
. . . . .6G 81
(off Lancaster Rd.)
Mus. of Childhood
Bethnal Green 3J 85
Mus. of Croydon 3C 168
(off High St.)
Mus. of Domestic Design & Architecture
MODA 2B 44
Mus. of Freemasonry 7F 7
(within Freemasons' Hall)
Mus. of London 6C 8 (5C 84)
Mus. of London Docklands 7C 86
Mus. of Richmond 5D 114
Mus. of the Order of St John 4A 8
(off St John's La.)
Mus. of Water & Steam 5F 97
Mus. of Wimbledon 6G 135
Museum Pas. E2 . . . . .3J 85
Museum St. WC1 . . . . . . .6E 6 (5J 83)
Museum Way W3 . . . . .2G 97
Musgrave Cl. EN4: Had W 1F 21
Musgrave Ct. SW11 . . . . .1C 118
Musgrave Cres. SW6 . . . . .7J 99
Musgrave Rd. TW7: Isle 1K 113
Musgrove Rd. SE14 . . . . .1K 121
Musical Mus., The 6E 96
Musjid Rd. SW11 . . . . .2B 118
Musket Cl. E4: E Barn 6G 21
Musquash Way TW4: Houn 2A 112
Mustang Ho. N1 . . . . .6B 66
(off Canonbury Rd.)
Muston Rd. E5 . . . . .2H 67
Mustow Pl. SW6 . . . . .2H 117
Muswell Av. N10 . . . . .1F 47
MUSWELL HILL 3F 47
Muswell Hill N10 . . . . .3F 47
Muswell Hill B'way. N10 . . . . .3F 47
Muswell Hill Golf Course 1G 47
Muswell Hill Pl. N10 . . . . .4F 47
Muswell Hill Rd. N6 . . . . .6E 46
N10 . . . . .6E 46
Muswell M. N10 . . . . .3F 47
Muswell Rd. N10 . . . . .3F 47
Mutrix Rd. NW6 . . . . .1J 81
Mutton Pl. NW1 . . . . .6E 64
Muybridge Rd. KT3: N Mald 2J 151
Muybridge Yd. KT5: Surb 7F 151
Myatt Rd. SW9 . . . . .1B 120
Myatts Fld. Sth. SW9 . . . . .2A 120
Mycenae Rd. SE3 . . . . .7J 105
Myddelton Av. EN1: Enf 1K 23
Myddelton Cl. EN1: Enf 1A 24
Myddelton Gdns. N21 . . . . .7H 23
Myddelton Pk. N20 . . . . .3G 31
Myddelton Pas. EC1 . . . . . .1K 7 (3A 84)
Myddelton Rd. N8 . . . . .4J 47
(not continuous)
Myddelton Sq. EC1 . . . . . . .1K 7 (3A 84)
Myddelton St. EC1 . . . . . . .2K 7 (3A 84)
Myddleton Av. N4 . . . . .2C 66
Myddleton Cl. HA7: Stan 2F 27
Myddleton Ho. N1 . . . . .1J 7
Myddleton M. N22 . . . . .7D 32
Myddleton Rd. N22 . . . . .7D 32
Myers Ho. SE5 . . . . .7C 102
(off Bethwin Rd.)
Myers La. SE14 . . . . .6K 103
Myles Ct. SE16 . . . . .3J 103
(off Neptune St.)
Mylis Cl. SE26 . . . . .4H 139
Mylius Cl. SE14 . . . . .7J 103
Mylne Cl. W6 . . . . .5C 98
Mylne St. EC1 . . . . .1J 7 (2A 84)
Myra St. SE2 . . . . .4A 108
Myrdle Ct. E1 . . . . .6G 85
(off Myrdle St.)
Myrdle St. E1 . . . . .5G 85

Myrna Cl. SW19 . . . . .7C 136
Myron Pl. SE13 . . . . .3E 122
Myrtle Av. HA4: Ruis 7J 39
TW14: Felt 5G 111
Myrtleberry Cl. E8 . . . . .6F 67
(off Beechwood Rd.)
Myrtle Cl. EN4: E Barn 1J 31
UB7: W Dray 3B 92
UB8: Hil 5B 74
Myrtledene Rd. SE2 . . . . .5A 108
Myrtle Gdns. W7 . . . . .1J 95
Myrtle Gro. EN2: Enf 1J 23
KT3: N Mald 2J 151
Myrtle Rd. CR0: C'don 3C 170
E6 .1D 88
E17 . . . . .6A 50
IG1: Ilf 2F 71
N13 . . . . .3H 33
SM1: Sutt 5A 166
TW3: Houn 2G 113
TW12: Hamp H 6G 131
W3 . . . . .1J 97
Myrtle Wlk. N1 . . . . .1G 9 (2E 84)
Mysore Rd. SW11 . . . . .3D 118
Myton Rd. SE21 . . . . .3D 138
Mytton Ho. SW8 . . . . .7K 101
(off St Stephens Ter.)

N

N1 Shop. Cen. N1 . . . . .2A 84
Nacton Ct. RM6: Chad H 5C 54
(off Hevingham Dr.)
Nadine Ct. SM6: Wall 7G 167
Nadine St. SE7 . . . . .5A 106
Nagasaki Wlk. SE7 . . . . .3K 105
Nagle Cl. E17 . . . . .2F 51
NAG'S HEAD 3J 65
Nags Head Cl. EC1 . . . . .4D 8
Nags Head La. DA16: Well 3B 126
Nags Head Rd. EN3: Pond E 4D 24
Nags Head Shop. Cen. N7 . . . . .4K 65
Nainby Ho. SE11 . . . . .4J 19
Nairne Gro. SE24 . . . . .5D 120
Nairn Rd. HA4: Ruis 6A 58
Nairn St. E14 . . . . .5E 86
Naldera Gdns. SE3 . . . . .6J 105
Nallhead Rd. TW13: Hanw 5A 130
Nalton Ho. NW6 . . . . .7A 64
(off Belsize Rd.)
Namba Roy Cl. SW16 . . . . .4K 137
Namco Funscape
Romford 6K 55
Namton Dr.
CR7: Thor H 4K 155
Nan Clark's La. NW7 . . . . .2F 29
Nankin St. E14 . . . . .6C 86
Nansen Ho. NW10 . . . . .7K 61
(off Stonebridge Pk.)
Nansen Rd. SW11 . . . . .3E 118
Nansen Village N12 . . . . .4E 30
Nant Cl. NW2 . . . . .2H 63
Nantes Cl. SW18 . . . . .4A 118
Nantes Pas. E1 . . . . .5J 9 (5F 85)
Nant Rd. NW2 . . . . .2C 64
Nant St. E2 . . . . .3H 85
Naomi St. SE8 . . . . .4A 104
Naoroji St. WC1 . . . . .2J 7 (3A 84)
Napa Cl. E20 . . . . .5E 68
Napier Av. E14 . . . . .5C 104
SW6 . . . . .3H 117
Napier Cl. SE8 . . . . .7B 104
UB7: W Dray 3B 92
W14 . . . . .3G 99
Napier Ct. BR2: Brom 4K 159
(off Napier Rd.)
N1 . . . . .2D 84
(off Cropley St.)
SE12 . . . . .3K 141

Napier Ct. SW6 . . . . .3H 117
(off Ranelagh Gdns.)
UB4: Yead 4A 76
(off Dunedin Way)
Napier Gro. N1 . . . . .2C 84
Napier Ho. E3 . . . . .3C 86
(off Campbell Rd.)
SE17 . . . . .6B 102
(off Cooks Rd.)
W3 . . . . .2A 98
Napier Lodge TW15: Ashf 6F 129
Napier PI. W14 . . . . .3H 99
Napier Rd. BR2: Brom 4K 159
CR2: S Croy 7D 168
DA17: Belv 4F 109
E6 .1E 88
E11 . . . . .4G 69
E15 . . . . .2G 87
(not continuous)
EN3: Pond E 5E 24
HA0: Wemb 6D 60
N17 . . . . .3E 48
NW10 . . . . .3D 80
SE25 . . . . .4H 157
TW7: Isle 4A 114
TW15: Ashf 7F 129
W14 . . . . .3H 99
Napier St. SE8 . . . . .7B 104
(off Napier Cl.)
Napier Ter. N1 . . . . .7B 66
Napier Wlk. TW15: Ashf 7F 129
Napoleon La. SE18 . . . . .7D 106
Napoleon Rd. E5 . . . . .3H 67
TW1: Twick 7B 114
Napton Cl. UB4: Yead 4C 76
Nara SE13 . . . . .2D 122
Narbonne Av. SW4 . . . . .5G 119
Narborough Cl. UB10: Ick 2E 56
Narborough St. SW6 . . . . .2K 117
Narcissus Rd. NW6 . . . . .5J 63
Nardini NW9 . . . . .1B 44
(off Long Mead)
Naresby Fold HA7: Stan 6H 27
Nares Cl. TW19: Stanw 1A 128
Narford Rd. E5 . . . . .3G 67
Narrowboat Av. TW8: Bford 7C 96
Narrow Boat Cl. SE28 . . . . .2H 107
Narrow St. E14 . . . . .7A 86
W3 . . . . .1H 97
Narrow Way BR2: Brom 6C 160
Narvic Ho. SE5 . . . . .2C 120
Narwhal Inuit Art Gallery 4K 97
Nascot St. W12 . . . . .6E 80
Naseby Cl. NW6 . . . . .7A 64
TW7: Isle 1J 113
Naseby Ct. DA14: Sidc 4K 143
Naseby Rd. IG5: Ilf 1D 52
RM10: Dag 3G 73
SE19 . . . . .6D 138
NASH 6J 171
Nash Cl. SM1: Sutt 3B 166
Nash Ct. HA3: Kenton 6B 42
Nashe Ho. SE1 . . . . .3D 102
(off Burbage Cl.)
Nash Grn. BR1: Brom 6J 141
Nash Ho. E14 . . . . .2C 104
(off Alpha Gro.)
E17 . . . . .3D 50
NW1 . . . . .2F 83
(off Park Village E.)
SW1 . . . . .6K 17
(off Lupus St.)
Nash La. BR2: Kes 7J 171
Nash Pl. E14 . . . . .1D 104
Nash Rd. N9 . . . . .2D 34
RM6: Chad H 4D 54
SE4 . . . . .4A 122
Nash St. NW1 . . . . .1K 5 (3F 83)
Nash Way HA3: Kenton 6B 42
Nasmyth St. W6 . . . . .3D 98
Nassau Path SE28 . . . . .1C 108

Nassau Rd. SW13 . . . . .1B 116
Nassau St. W1 . . . . .6A 6 (5G 83)
Nassington Rd. NW3 . . . . .4D 64
Natalie Cl. TW14: Bedf 7F 111
Natalie M. N22 . . . . .6D 32
TW2: Twick 3H 131
Natal Rd. CR7: Thor H 3D 156
IG1: Ilf 4F 71
N11 . . . . .6D 32
SW16 . . . . .6H 137
Natasha M. SE15 . . . . .4J 121
Nathan Ct. N9 . . . . .7D 24
(off Causeyware Rd.)
Nathan Ho. SE11 . . . . .4K 19
(off Reedworth St.)
Nathaniel Cl. E1 . . . . .6K 9 (5F 85)
Nathaniel Ct. E17 . . . . .7A 50
Nathans Rd. HA0: Wemb 1C 60
Nathan Way SE28 . . . . .4J 107
National Archives, The 7H 97
National Army Mus. 7F 17 (6D 100)
National Gallery 3D 12 (7H 83)
National Maritime Mus. 6F 105
National Portrait Gallery 3D 12
National Tennis Cen. 5A 116
National Ter. SE16 . . . . .2H 103
(off Bermondsey Wall E.)
National Theatre 4H 13 (1A 102)
National Works TW4: Houn 3D 112
Nation Way E4 . . . . .1K 35
Natural History Mus.
Knightsbridge 2A 16 (3B 100)
Nautical Ho. SW18 . . . . .4A 118
(off Juniper St.)
Nautilus Building, The EC1 . . . . .1K 7
(off Myddelton Pas.)
Naval Ho. E14 . . . . .7F 87
(off Quixley St.)
SE18 . . . . .3F 107
Naval Row E14 . . . . .7E 86
Naval Wlk. BR1: Brom 2J 159
(off Mitre Cl.)
Navarino Gro. E8 . . . . .6G 67
Navarino Mans. E8 . . . . .6G 67
Navarino Rd. E8 . . . . .6G 67
Navarre Rd. E6 . . . . .2C 88
SW9 . . . . .3B 120
Navarre St. E2 . . . . .3J 9 (4F 85)
Navenby Wlk. E3 . . . . .4C 86
Navestock Cl. E4 . . . . .3K 35
Navestock Cres. IG8: Wfd G 7F 37
Navigation Cl. E16 . . . . .7G 89
Navigation Dr. EN3: Enf L 1H 25
Navigation Ho. SE16 . . . . .4A 104
(off Grand Canal Av.)
Navigation Rd. E3 . . . . .4E 86
Navigator Dr. UB2: S'hall 2G 95
Navigator Pk. UB2: S'hall 4A 94
Navy St. SW4 . . . . .3H 119
Naxos Bldg. E14 . . . . .2B 104
Nayim Pl. E8 . . . . .5H 67
Nayland Ho. SE6 . . . . .4E 140
Naylor Bldg. E. E1 . . . . .6G 85
(off Assam St.)
Naylor Bldg. W. E1 . . . . .6G 85
(off Adler St.)
Naylor Gro. EN3: Pond E 5E 24
Naylor Ho. SE17 . . . . .4D 102
(off Flint St.)
W10 . . . . .3G 81
(off Dart St.)
Naylor Rd. N20 . . . . .2F 31
SE15 . . . . .7H 103
Nazareth Gdns. SE15 . . . . .2H 121
Nazrul St. E2 . . . . .1J 9 (3F 85)
NCR Bus. Cen. NW10 . . . . .5A 62
Neagle Ho. NW2 . . . . .3E 62
(off Stoll Cl.)
Neal Av. UB1: S'hall 4D 76
Neal Cl. HA6: Nwood 1J 39
Nealden St. SW9 . . . . .3K 119

Neale Cl. N2 3A **46**
Neale Ct. RM9: Dag 6B **72**
Neal St. WC2 1E **12** (6J **83**)
Neal's Yd. WC2 1E **12** (6J **83**)
Neap Ct. *E3 4E **86***
(off Navigation Rd.)
Near Acre NW9 1B **44**
NEASDEN 3A **62**
Neasden Cl. NW10 5A **62**
NEASDEN JUNC. **4A 62**
Neasden La. NW10 3A **62**
Neasden La. Nth. NW10 3K **61**
Neasham Rd. RM8: Dag 5B **72**
Neate Ho. *SW1 6B **18***
(off Lupus St.)
Neate St. SE5 6E **102**
Neath Gdns. SM4: Mord 6A **154**
Neathouse Pl. SW1 3A **18** (4G **101**)
Neats Acre HA4: Ruis 7F **39**
Neatscourt Rd. E6 5B **88**
Nebraska Bldg. *SE13 1D **122***
(off Deal's Gateway)
Nebraska St. SE1 7E **14** (2D **102**)
Nebula SW11 2D **118**
Nebula Ct. *E13 2J **87***
(off Umbriel Pl.)
Neckinger SE16 7K **15** (3F **103**)
Neckinger Est. SE16 3F **103**
Neckinger St. SE1 7K **15** (2F **103**)
Nectarine Way SE13 2D **122**
Needham Ho. SE11 4J **19**
Needham Rd. W11 6J **81**
Needham Ter. NW2 3F **63**
Needleman Cl. NW9 2A **44**
Needleman St. SE16 2K **103**
Needwood Ho. N4 1C **66**
Neela Cl. UB10: Ick 4D **56**
Neeld Cres. HA9: Wemb 5G **61**
NW4 5D **44**
Neeld Pde. HA9: Wemb 5F **61**
Neeld Pl. W9 5H **81**
Neil Cl. TW15: Ashf 5E **128**
Neil Wates Cres. SW2 1A **138**
Nelgarde Rd. SE6 7C **122**
Nella Rd. W6 6F **99**
Nelldale Rd. SE16 4J **103**
Nellgrove Rd. UB10: Hil 4D **74**
Nell Gwynn Av. TW17: Shep 6F **147**
Nell Gwynn Ho. SW3 4D **16** (4C **100**)
Nello James Gdns. SE27 4D **138**
Nelson Arc. *SE10 6E **104***
(off Nelson Rd.)
Nelson Cl. CR0: C'don 1B **168**
KT12: Walt T 7K **147**
NW6 3J **81**
RM7: Mawney 1H **55**
TW14: Felt 1H **129**
UB10: Hil 3D **74**
Nelson Ct. *SE16 1J **103***
(off Brunel Rd.)
Nelson Gdns. E2 3G **85**
TW3: Houn 6E **112**
Nelson Gro. Rd. SW19 1K **153**
Nelson Ho. *SW1 7B **18***
(off Dolphin Sq.)
Nelson La. UB10: Hil 3D **74**
Nelson Mandela Cl. N10 2E **46**
Nelson Mandela Ho. N16 2G **67**
Nelson Mandela Rd. SE3 3A **124**
Nelson Pas. EC1 1D **8** (3C **84**)
Nelson Pl. DA14: Sidc 4A **144**
N1 1B **8** (2B **84**)
Nelson Rd. BR2: Brom 4A **160**
DA14: Sidc 4A **144**
DA17: Belv 5F **109**
E4 6J **35**
E11 4J **51**
EN3: Pond E 6E **24**
HA1: Harr 1H **59**
HA7: Stan 6H **27**
KT3: N Mald 5K **151**
Nelson Rd. N8 5K **47**
N9 2C **34**
N15 4E **48**
SE10 6E **104**
SW19 7K **135**
TW2: Whitt 7F **113**
TW3: Houn 6E **112**
TW6: H'row A 1B **110**
TW15: Ashf 5A **128**
UB10: Hil 3D **74**
Nelson Rd. M. *SW19 7K **135***
(off Nelson Rd.)
Nelson's Column 4E **12** (1H **101**)
Nelson Sq. SE1 6A **14** (2B **102**)
Nelson's Row SW4 4H **119**
Nelson St. E1 6H **85**
E6 2D **88**
(not continuous)
E16 6H **87**
Nelsons Yd. *NW1 2G **83***
(off Mornington Cres.)
Nelson Ter. N1 1B **8** (2B **84**)
Nelson Trad. Est. SW19 1K **153**
Nelson Wlk. E3 4D **86**
KT19: Eps 7G **163**
SE16 1A **104**
Nemoure Rd. W3 7J **79**
Nemus Apartments SE8 4K **103**
Nene Gdns. TW13: Hanw 3D **130**
Nene Rd. TW6: H'row A 1D **110**
NENE ROAD RDBT. **1D 110**
Nepaul Rd. SW11 2C **118**
Nepean St. SW15 6C **116**
Neptune Ct. *E14 4C **104***
(off Homer Dr.)
*E16 5J **87***
(off Hammersley Rd.)
Neptune Ho. *E3 1C **86***
(off Garrison Rd.)
*SE16 3J **103***
(off Moodkee St.)
Neptune Rd. HA1: Harr 6H **41**
TW6: H'row A 1F **111**
Neptune St. SE16 3J **103**
Neptune Wlk. DA8: Erith 4K **109**
Nero Ct. TW8: Bford 7D **96**
Nero Ho. *E20 6E **68***
(off Anthems Way)
Nesbit Ct. *SE17 6B **102***
(off Cook's Rd.)
Nesbit Rd. SE9 4B **124**
Nesbitt Cl. SE3 3G **123**
Nesbitts All. EN5: Barn 3C **20**
Nesbitt Sq. SE19 7E **138**
Nesham Ho. *N1 1E **84***
(off Hoxton St.)
Nesham St. E1 7G **85**
Ness St. SE16 3G **103**
Nesta Rd. IG8: Wfd G 6B **36**
Nestles Av. UB3: Hayes 3H **93**
Nestor Av. N21 6G **23**
Nestor Ho. *E2 2H **85***
(off Old Bethnal Grn. Rd.)
Netheravon Rd. W4 4B **98**
W7 1K **95**
Netheravon Rd. Sth. W4 5B **98**
Netherbury Rd. W5 3D **96**
Netherby Gdns. EN2: Enf 4D **22**
Netherby Rd. SE23 7J **121**
Nether Cl. N3 7D **30**
Nethercott Ho. *E3 3D **86***
(off Bruce Rd.)
Nethercourt Av. N3 6D **30**
Netherfield Gdns. IG11: Bark 6H **71**
Netherfield Rd. N12 5E **30**
SW17 3E **136**
Netherford Rd. SW4 2G **119**
Netherhall Gdns. NW3 6A **64**
Netherhall Way NW3 5A **64**
Netherheys Dr. CR2: S Croy 7B **168**
Netherlands Rd. EN5: New Bar 6G **21**
Netherleigh Cl. N6 1F **65**
Nether St. N3 7D **30**
N12 5F **31**
(not continuous)
Netherton Gro. SW10 6A **100**
Netherton Rd. N15 6D **48**
TW1: Twick 5A **114**
Netherwood N2 2B **46**
Netherwood Pl. *W14 3F **99***
(off Netherwood Rd.)
Netherwood Rd. W14 3F **99**
Netherwood St. NW6 7H **63**
Nethewode Ct. *DA17: Belv 3H **109***
(off Lower Pk. Rd.)
Netley *SE5 1E **120***
(off Redbridge Gdns.)
Netley Cl. CR0: New Ad 7E **170**
SM3: Cheam 5F **165**
Netley Dr. KT12: Walt T 7D **148**
Netley Gdns.
SM4: Mord 7A **154**
Netley Rd. E17 5B **50**
IG2: Ilf 5H **53**
SM4: Mord 7A **154**
TW8: Bford 6E **96**
Netley St. NW1 2A **6** (3G **83**)
Nettlecombe *NW1 7H **65***
(off Agar Gro.)
Nettleden Av. HA9: Wemb 6G **61**
Nettleden Ho. *SW3 4D **16***
(off Cale St.)
Nettlefold Pl. SE27 3B **138**
TW16: Sun 5J **147**
Nettlefold Wlk.
KT12: Walt T 7H **147**
Nettlestead Cl. BR3: Beck 7B **140**
Nettleton Ct. *EC2 6C **8***
(off London Wall)
Nettleton Rd. SE14 1K **121**
TW6: H'row A 1D **110**
UB10: Ick 4B **56**
Nettlewood Rd. SW16 7H **137**
Neuchatel Rd. SE6 2B **140**
Neutron Twr. E14 7F **87**
Nevada Bldg. *SE10 1D **122***
(off Blackheath Rd.)
Nevada Cl. KT3: N Mald 4J **151**
Nevada St. SE10 6E **104**
Nevern Mans. *SW5 5J **99***
(off Warwick Rd.)
Nevern Pl. SW5 4J **99**
Nevern Rd. SW5 4J **99**
Nevern Sq. SW5 4J **99**
Nevil Ho. *SW9 2B **120***
(off Loughborough Est.)
Nevill Ct. *SW10 7A **100***
(off Edith Ter.)
Neville Av. KT3: N Mald 1K **151**
Neville Cl. DA15: Sidc 4K **143**
E11 3H **69**
NW1 2H **83**
NW6 2H **81**
SE15 1G **121**
TW3: Houn 2F **113**
W3 2J **97**
Neville Ct. NW8 1A **4**
Neville Dr. N2 6A **46**
Neville Gdns. RM8: Dag 3D **72**
Neville Gill Cl. SW18 6J **117**
Neville Ho. N11 4K **31**
*N22 1K **47***
(off Neville Pl.)
*NW6 2H **81***
(off Denmark Rd.)
Neville Ho. Yd. KT1: King T 2E **150**
Neville Pl. N22 1K **47**
Neville Rd. CR0: C'don 7D **156**
E7 7J **69**
IG6: Ilf 1G **53**
KT1: King T 2G **151**
NW6 2H **81**
Neville Rd. RM8: Dag 3D **72**
TW10: Ham 3C **132**
W5 4D **78**
Nevilles Ct. NW2 3C **62**
Neville St. SW7 5A **16** (5B **100**)
Neville Ter. SW7 5A **16** (5B **100**)
Neville Wlk.
SM5: Cars 7C **154**
Nevill La. EC4 7K **7**
Nevill Rd. N16 4E **66**
Nevin Dr. E4 1J **35**
Nevin Ho. UB3: Harl 3E **92**
Nevinson Cl. SW18 6B **118**
Nevis Cl. E13 2K **87**
Nevis Rd. SW17 2E **136**
Nevitt Ho. *N1 2D **84***
(off Cranston Est.)
New Acres Rd. SE28 2J **107**
NEW ADDINGTON 7F **171**
Newall Cl. UB10: Uxb 1B **74**
Newall Ho. *SE1 3C **102***
(off Bath Ter.)
Newall Rd. TW6: H'row A 1E **110**
Newark Cres. NW10 3K **79**
Newark Ho. SW9 2B **120**
Newark Knok E6 6E **88**
Newark Rd.
CR2: S Croy 6D **168**
Newark St. E1 5H **85**
(not continuous)
Newark Way NW4 4C **44**
New Ash Cl. N2 3B **46**
New Atlas Wharf *E14 3C **104***
(off Arnhem Pl.)
New Baltic Wharf *SE8 5A **104***
(off Evelyn St.)
New Barn Cl. SM6: Wall 6K **167**
NEW BARNET 4G **21**
New Barn Rd. BR8: Swan 7K **145**
New Barns Av. CR4: Mitc 4H **155**
New Barn St. E13 4J **87**
New Barns Way
IG7: Chig 3K **37**
Newbeck Ct. BR3: Beck 7B **140**
NEW BECKENHAM 6B **140**
New Bell Yd. *EC4 1B **14***
(off Knightrider St.)
New Bentham Ct. *N1 7C **66***
(off Ecclesbourne Rd.)
Newbery Ho. *N1 7C **66***
(off Northampton St.)
Newbold Cotts. E1 6J **85**
Newbolt Av. SM3: Cheam 5E **164**
Newbolt Ho. *SE17 5D **102***
(off Brandon St.)
Newbolt Rd. HA7: Stan 5E **26**
New Bond St. W1 1J **11** (6F **83**)
Newborough Grn. KT3: N Mald 4K **151**
New Brent St. NW4 5E **44**
Newbridge Point *SE23 3K **139***
(off Windrush La.)
New Bri. St. EC4 1A **14** (6B **84**)
New Broad St. EC2 6G **9** (5E **84**)
New Broadway TW12: Hamp H 5H **131**
UB10: Hil 3D **74**
W5 7D **78**
New Broadway Bldgs. W5 7D **78**
Newburgh Rd. W3 1J **97**
Newburgh St. W1 1B **12** (6G **83**)
New Burlington M. W1 2A **12** (7G **83**)
New Burlington Pl. W1 2A **12** (7G **83**)
New Burlington St. W1 2A **12** (7G **83**)
Newburn Ho. *SE11 5H **19***
(off Newburn St.)
Newburn St. SE11 5H **19** (5K **101**)
Newbury Cl. RM10: Dag 2G **73**
UB5: N'olt 6D **58**
Newbury Ct. DA14: Sidc 4K **143**
*E5 5A **68***
(off Daubeney Rd.)
Newbury Gdns. KT19: Ewe 4B **164**

Newbury Ho.—New Rd.

Newbury Ho. N22 1J 47
SW9 2B 120
W2 6K 81
(off Hallfield Est.)
Newbury M. NW5 6E 64
NEWBURY PARK 5H 53
Newbury Rd. BR2: Brom 3J 159
E4 6K 35
IG2: Ilf 6J 53
TW6: H'row A 1B 110
Newbury St. EC1 6C 8 (5C 84)
Newbury Way UB5: N'olt 6C 58
New Bus. Cen., The NW10 3B 80
New Butt La. SE8 7C 104
New Butt La. Nth. SE8 7C 104
(off Hales St.)
Newby NW1 2A 6
(off Robert St.)
Newby Cl. EN1: Enf 2K 23
Newby Ho. E14 7E 86
(off Newby Pl.)
Newby Pl. E14 7E 86
Newby St. SW8 3F 119
New Caledonian Mkt. SE1 7H 15
(off Bermondsey Sq.)
New Caledonian Wharf SE16 3B 104
Newcastle Cl. EC4 7A 8 (6B 84)
Newcastle Ct. EC4 2D 14
(off College Hill)
Newcastle Ho. W1 5G 5
(off Luxborough St.)
Newcastle Pl. W2 5B 4 (5B 82)
Newcastle Row EC1 4K 7 (4A 84)
New Cavendish St. W1 6H 5 (5E 82)
New Century Ho. E16 6H 87
(off Jude St.)
New Change EC4 1C 14 (6C 84)
New Change Pas. EC4 1C 14
(off New Change)
New Chapel Sq. TW13: Felt 1K 129
New Charles St. EC1 1B 8 (3B 84)
NEW CHARLTON 4A 106
New Chiswick Pool 7A 98
New Church Rd. SE5 7C 102
(not continuous)
New City Rd. E13 3A 88
New Claremont Apartments SE1 4F 103
(off Setchell Rd.)
New Clock Twr. Pl. N7 6J 65
New Cl. SW19 3A 154
TW13: Hanw 5C 130
New Colebrooke Ct. SM5: Cars 7D 166
New College Ct. NW3 6A 64
(off College Cres.)
New College M. N1 7A 66
New College Pde. NW3 6B 64
(off Finchley Rd.)
Newcombe Gdns. SW16 4J 137
TW4: Houn 4D 112
Newcombe Ho. E5 3H 67
Newcombe Pk. HA0: Wemb 1F 79
NW7 5F 29
Newcombe Ri. UB7: Yiew 6A 74
Newcombe St. W8 1J 99
Newcomen Rd. E11 3H 69
SW11 3B 118
Newcomen St. SE1 6E 14 (2D 102)
New Compton St. WC2 1D 12 (6H 83)
New Concordia Wharf SE1 6K 15 (2G 103)
New Ct. EC4 2J 13
UB5: N'olt 5F 59
Newcourt Ho. E2 3H 85
(off Pott St.)
Newcourt St. NW8 1C 4 (2C 82)
New Covent Garden Market 7D 18 (7H 101)
New Crane Pl. E1 1J 103
New Crane Wharf E1 1J 103
(off New Crane Pl.)
New Cres. Yd. NW10 2B 80
Newcroft Cl. UB8: Hil 5B 74
Newcroft Ho. CR0: C'don 2F 169
(off Homefield Pl.)
NEW CROSS 7B 104
NEW CROSS 1B 122
NEW CROSS GATE 1K 121
NEW CROSS GATE 1K 121
New Cross Rd. SE14 7J 103
Newdales Cl. N9 2B 34
Newdene Av. UB5: N'olt 2B 76
Newdigate Ho. E14 6B 86
(off Norbiton Rd.)
New Diorama Theatre 4F 83
Newell St. E14 6B 86
NEW ELTHAM 2G 143
New End NW3 3A 64
New End Sq. NW3 4B 64
New England Ind. Est. IG11: Bark 2G 89
Newent Cl. SE15 7E 102
SM5: Cars 1D 166
New Era Est. N1 1E 84
(off Halcomb St.)
New Era Ho. N1 1E 84
(off Halcomb St.)
New Farm Av. BR2: Brom 4J 159
New Farm La. HA6: Nwood 1G 39
New Festival Av. E14 6C 86
New Fetter La. EC4 7K 7 (6A 84)
Newfield Cl. TW12: Hamp 1E 148
Newfield Ri. NW2 3C 62
New Forest La. IG7: Chig 6K 37
Newgale Gdns. HA8: Edg 1F 43
New Gdn. Dr. UB7: W Dray 2A 92
New Gdn. Quarter E15 6F 69
Newgate CR0: C'don 1C 168
Newgate Cl. TW13: Hanw 2C 130
Newgate St. E4 3B 36
(not continuous)
EC1 7B 8 (6B 84)
New Globe Wlk. SE1 4C 14 (1C 102)
New Goulston St. E1 7J 9 (6F 85)
New Grn. Pl. SE19 6E 138
New Gun Wharf E3 1A 86
(off Gunmaker's La.)
Newhall Ct. N1 1C 84
(off Popham Rd.)
Newham City Farm 6B 88
Newham Dockside E16 7C 88
Newham Leisure Cen. 4A 88
Newham's Row SE1 7H 15 (3E 102)
Newham Way E6 5A 88
E16 5H 87
Newhaven Cl. UB3: Harl 4H 93
Newhaven Cres. TW15: Ashf 5F 129
Newhaven Gdns. SE9 4B 124
Newhaven La. E16 4H 87
Newhaven Rd. SE25 5D 156
New Heston Rd. TW5: Hest 7D 94
New Hope Ct. NW10 3D 80
New Horizons Ct. TW8: Bford 6A 96
Newhouse Av. RM6: Chad H 3D 54
Newhouse Cl. KT3: N Mald 7A 152
Newhouse Wlk. SM4: Mord 7A 154
Newick Cl. DA5: Bexl 6H 127
Newick Rd. E5 4H 67
Newing Grn. BR1: Brom 7B 142
NEWINGTON 3C 102
Newington Barrow Way N7 3K 65
Newington Butts SE1 4B 102
SE11 4B 102
Newington C'way. SE1 7C 14 (3B 102)
Newington Ct. N16 4C 66
(off Green Lanes)
Newington Ct. Bus. Cen. SE1 7C 14
Newington Grn. N1 5D 66
N16 5D 66
Newington Grn. Community Gdns.
N16 5D 66
(off Newington Grn.)
Newington Grn. Mans. N16 5D 66
Newington Grn. Rd. N1 6D 66
Newington Ind. Est. SE17 4B 102
New Inn B'way. EC2 3H 9 (4E 84)
New Inn Pas. WC2 1H 13
New Inn Sq. EC2 3H 9
New Inn St. EC2 3H 9 (4E 84)
New Inn Yd. EC2 3H 9 (4E 84)
New Jubilee Ct. IG8: Wfd G 7D 36
New Jubilee Wharf E1 1J 103
(off Wapping Wall)
New Kelvin Av. TW11: Tedd 6J 131
New Kent Rd. SE1 3C 102
New Kings Rd. SW6 2H 117
New King St. SE8 6C 104
Newland Ct. EC1 2E 8
HA9: Wemb 2G 61
Newland Dr. EN1: Enf 1C 24
Newland Gdns. W13 2A 96
Newland Ho. N8 3J 47
(off Newland Rd.)
SE14 6K 103
(off John Williams Cl.)
Newland Rd. N8 3J 47
NEWLANDS
HA8 3K 27
SE23 5K 121
Newlands HA1: Harr 1J 59
NW1 1A 6
(off Harrington St.)
Newlands, The KT7: T Ditt 7J 149
SM6: Wall 7G 167
Newlands Av. KT7: T Ditt 7J 149
Newlands Cl. HA0: Wemb 6C 60
HA8: Edg 3K 27
UB2: S'hall 5C 94
Newlands Ct. SE9 6E 124
Newlands Dr. SL3: Poyle 6A 174
Newlands Pk. SE26 6J 139
Newlands Pl. EN5: Barn 5A 20
Newlands Quay E1 7J 85
Newlands Rd. IG8: Wfd G 2C 36
SW16 2J 155
Newland St. E16 1C 106
Newlands Way KT9: Chess 5C 162
Newlands Woods CR0: Sels 7B 170
Newling Cl. E6 6D 88
New London Performing Arts Cen. 4F 47
New London St. EC3 2H 15
New London Theatre 7F 7
(off Parker St.)
New Lydenburg Commercial Est.
SE7 3A 106
New Lydenburg St. SE7 3A 106
Newlyn NW1 1G 83
(off Plender St.)
Newlyn Cl. BR6: Chels 4K 173
UB8: Hil 5C 74
Newlyn Gdns. HA2: Harr 7D 40
Newlyn Ho. HA5: Hat E 1D 40
Newlyn Rd. DA16: Well 2K 125
EN5: Barn 4C 20
N17 1F 49
NEW MALDEN 4A 152
Newman Cl. NW10 6D 62
SE26 4J 139
Newman Ct. BR1: Brom 1J 159
(off North St.)
TW15: Ashf 6D 128
Newman Ho. SE1 3B 102
Newman Pas. W1 6B 6 (5G 83)
Newman Rd. BR1: Brom 1J 159
CR0: C'don 1K 167
E13 3K 87
E17 5K 49
UB3: Hayes 7K 75
Newman Rd. Ind. Est. CR0: C'don 7K 155
Newman's Ct. EC3 1F 15
Newmans La. KT6: Surb 6D 150
Newman's Row WC2 6H 7 (5K 83)
Newman St. W1 6B 6 (5G 83)
Newman's Way EN4: Had W 1F 21
Newman Yd. W1 7C 6 (6G 83)
Newmarket Av. UB5: N'olt 5E 58
Newmarket Grn. SE9 7B 124
Newmarsh Rd. SE28 1K 107
Newmill Ho. E3 4E 86
New Mill Rd. SW8 6H 101
Newminster Rd. SM4: Mord 6A 154
New Mossford Way IG6: Ilf 4G 53
New Mt. St. E15 7F 69
Newnes Path SW15 4D 116
Newnham Av. HA4: Ruis 1A 58
Newnham Cl. CR7: Thor H 2C 156
UB5: N'olt 6G 59
Newnham Gdns. UB5: N'olt 6G 59
Newnham Grn. N22 1A 48
(off Highfield Cl.)
Newnham Lodge DA17: Belv 5G 109
(off Erith Rd.)
Newnham M. N22 7F 33
Newnham Rd. N22 1K 47
Newnhams Cl. BR1: Brom 3D 160
Newnham Ter. SE1 1J 19 (3A 102)
Newnham Way HA3: Kenton 5E 42
New Nth. Pl. EC2 3G 9 (4E 84)
New Nth. Rd. IG6: Ilf 1G 53
N1 1F 9 (7C 66)
New Nth. St. WC1 5G 7 (5K 83)
Newnton Cl. N4 7D 48
New Oak Rd. N2 2A 46
New Orleans Wlk. N19 7H 47
New Oxford St. WC1 7D 6 (6H 83)
New Pde. TW15: Ashf 4B 128
UB7: Yiew 1A 92
New Paragon Wlk. SE17 4D 102
New Pk. Av. N13 3H 33
New Pk. Cl. UB5: N'olt 6C 58
New Pk. Est. N18 5D 34
New Pk. Ho. N13 4E 32
New Pk. Pde. SW2 7J 119
(off New Pk. Rd.)
New Pk. Rd. SW2 1H 137
TW15: Ashf 5E 128
New Pl. CR0: Addtn 6C 170
New Pl. Sq. SE16 3H 103
New Plaistow Rd. E15 1G 87
New Pond Pde. HA4: Ruis 3J 57
Newport Av. E13 4K 87
E14 7F 87
Newport Ct. WC2 2D 12 (7H 83)
Newport Ho. E3 3A 86
(off Strahan Rd.)
Newport Lodge EN1: Enf 5K 23
(off Village Rd.)
Newport Pl. WC2 2D 12 (7H 83)
Newport Rd. E10 2E 68
E17 4A 50
SW13 1C 116
TW6: H'row A 1C 110
UB4: Hayes 5F 75
W3 2J 97
Newport St. SE11 4G 19 (4K 101)
Newport Street Gallery 3H 19 (4K 101)
New Priory Ct. NW6 7J 63
(off Mazenod Av.)
New Providence Wharf E14 1F 105
Newquay Cres. HA2: Harr 2C 58
Newquay Ho. SE11 5J 19 (5A 102)
Newquay Rd. SE6 2D 140
New Quebec St. W1 1F 11 (6D 82)
New Ride SW1 2C 100
SW7 6C 10 (2C 100)
New River Av. N8 3K 47
New River Ct. N5 4C 66
New River Cres. N13 4G 33
New River Head EC1 1K 7 (3A 84)
New River Wlk. N1 6C 66
(not continuous)
New River Way N4 7D 48
New Rd. CR4: Mitc 1D 166
DA16: Well 2B 126
E1 5H 85
E4 4J 35
HA1: Harr 4K 59

350 A-Z London

New Rd. IG3: Ilf 2J 71
KT2: King T 7G 133
KT8: W Mole 4E 148
N8 5J 47
N9 2C 34
N17 1F 49
N22 1C 48
NW7 7B 30
RM9: Dag 2G 91
RM10: Dag 2G 91
RM13: Rain 2G 91
SE2 4D 108
TW3: Houn 4F 113
TW8: Bford 6D 96
TW10: Ham 4C 132
TW13: Hanw 5C 130
TW14: Bedf 6F 111
TW14: Felt 1K 129
TW17: Shep 3C 146
UB3: Harl 7E 92
UB8: Hil 4E 74
New Rd. Hill BR2: Kes 7C 172
BR6: Downe 7C 172
New Rochford St. NW5 5D 64
New Row NW2 3E 62
WC2 2E 12 (7J 83)
Newry Rd. TW1: Twick 5A 114
Newsam Av. N15 5D 48
Newsholme Dr. N21 5E 22
NEW SOUTHGATE 5A 32
New Southgate Crematorium N11 3A 32
New Southgate Ind. Est. N11 5B 32
New Spitalfields Mkt. E10 3C 68
New Spring Gdns. Wlk.
SE11 6F 19 (5J 101)
New Sq. TW14: Bedf 1E 128
WC2 7J 7 (6A 84)
New Sq. Pk. TW14: Bedf 1E 128
New Sq. Pas. WC2 7J 7
Newstead Av. BR6: Orp 3H 173
Newstead Cl. N12 6H 31
Newstead Ct. UB5: N'olt 3C 76
Newstead Ho. *N1* 2A 84
(off Tolpuddle St.)
Newstead Rd. SE12 7H 123
Newstead Wlk. SM5: Cars 7A 154
Newstead Way SW19 4F 135
New St. EC2 6H 9 (5E 84)
New St. Hill BR1: Brom 5K 141
New St. Sq. EC4 7K 7 (6A 84)
(not continuous)
Newton Av. N10 1E 46
W3 2J 97
Newton Cl. E17 6A 50
HA2: Harr 2E 58
Newton Ct. E3 5C 86
NW6 7A 64
(off Fairfax Rd.)
SW17 3B 136
(off Grosvenor Way)
W8 2J 99
(off Kensington Chu. St.)
Newton Gro. W4 4A 98
Newton Ho. *E1* 7H 85
(off Cornwall St.)
E17 3D 50
(off Prospect Hill)
EN3: Enf H 3E 24
NW8 1K 81
(off Abbey Rd.)
SE20 7K 139
Newton Ind. Est. RM6: Chad H 4D 54
Newton Lodge *SE10* 3H 105
(off Teal St.)
Newton Mans. *W14* 6G 99
(off Queen's Club Gdns.)
Newton Pk. Pl. BR7: Chst 7D 142
Newton Pl. E14 4C 104
Newton Rd. DA16: Well 3A 126
E15 5F 69
HA0: Wemb 7F 61
Newton Rd. HA3: Hrw W 2J 41
N15 5G 49
NW2 4E 62
SW19 7G 135
TW7: Isle 2K 113
W2 6K 81
Newton St. WC2 7F 7 (6J 83)
Newton's Yd. SW18 5J 117
Newton Ter. BR2: Brom 6B 160
Newton Wlk. HA8: Edg 1H 43
Newton Way N18 5H 33
New Tower Bldgs. E1 1H 103
Newtown St. SW11 1F 119
New Trinity Rd. N2 3B 46
New Turnstile WC1 6G 7
New Union Cl. E14 3E 104
New Union Sq. SW8 6H 101
New Union St. EC2 6E 8 (5D 84)
New Village Av. E14 6F 87
New Wanstead E11 6H 51
New Way Rd. NW9 4A 44
New Wharf Rd. N1 2J 83
New Willow Ho. *E13* 2J 87
(off Plaistow Rd.)
NEWYEARS GREEN 7B 38
New Years Grn. La. UB9: Hare 6A 38
New Zealand Av. KT12: Walt T 7H 147
New Zealand War Memorial 2E 100
(off Hyde Pk. Cnr.)
New Zealand Way W12 7D 80
Nexus Apartments *BR1: Brom* 3K 159
(off Elmfield Rd.)
Nexus Cl. TW14: Felt 5J 111
Nexus Ct. E11 1G 69
NW6 3J 81
Niagara Av. W5 4C 96
Niagara Cl. N1 2C 84
Niagra Ct. *SE16* 3J 103
(off Canada Est.)
Nibthwaite Rd. HA1: Harr 5J 41
Nice Bus. Pk. SE15 6H 103
Nicholas Cl. UB6: G'frd 2F 77
Nicholas Ct. E13 3K 87
N7 5K 65
SE12 1J 141
W4 6A 98
(off Corney Reach Way)
Nicholas Gdns. W5 2D 96
Nicholas La. EC4 2F 15 (7D 84)
(not continuous)
Nicholas M. W4 6A 98
Nicholas Pas. EC4 2F 15
Nicholas Rd. CR0: Bedd 4J 167
E1 4J 85
RM8: Dag 2F 73
W11 7F 81
Nicholas Stacey Ho. *SE7* 5K 105
(off Frank Burton Cl.)
Nicholas Way HA6: Nwood 1E 38
Nicholay Rd. N19 1H 65
(not continuous)
Nichol Cl. N14 1C 32
Nicholes Rd. TW3: Houn 4E 112
Nichol La. BR1: Brom 7J 141
Nicholl Ho. N4 1C 66
Nicholls Av. UB8: Hil 4C 74
Nichollsfield Wlk. N7 5K 65
Nicholls M. SW16 4J 137
Nicholls Point *E15* 1J 87
(off Park Gro.)
Nicholl St. E2 1G 85
Nichols Cl. KT9: Chess 6C 162
N4 1A 66
(off Osborne Rd.)
Nichols Ct. E2 2F 85
Nichols Grn. W5 5E 78
Nicholson Ct. E17 4K 49
N17 3F 49
Nicholson Ho. SE17 5D 102
Nicholson M. KT1: King T 4E 150
Nicholson Rd. CR0: C'don 1F 169
Nicholson St. SE1 5A 14 (1B 102)
Nickelby Apartments *E15* 6F 69
(off Grove Cres. Rd.)
Nickelby Cl. SE28 6C 90
Nickleby Cl. UB8: Hil 6D 74
Nickleby Ho. *SE16* 7K 15
(off Parkers Row)
W11 1F 99
(off St Ann's Rd.)
Nickols Wlk. SW18 4K 117
Nicola Cl. CR2: S Croy 6C 168
HA3: Hrw W 2H 41
Nicola Ter. DA7: Bex 1E 126
Nicol Cl. TW1: Twick 6B 114
Nicoll Cir. NW7 6B 30
Nicoll Ct. N10 7A 32
NW10 1A 80
Nicoll Pl. NW4 6D 44
Nicoll Rd. NW10 1A 80
Nicolson NW9 1A 44
Nicolson Dr. WD23: B Hea 1B 26
Nicosia Rd. SW18 7C 118
Niederwald Rd. SE26 4A 140
Nield Rd. UB3: Hayes 2H 93
Nigel Cl. UB5: N'olt 1C 76
Nigel Ct. N3 7E 30
Nigel Fisher Way KT9: Chess 7C 162
Nigel Ho. *EC1* 5J 7
(off Portpool La.)
Nigel M. IG1: Ilf 4F 71
Nigel Playfair Av. W6 4D 98
Nigel Rd. E7 5A 70
SE15 3G 121
Nigeria Rd. SE7 7A 106
Nighthawk NW9 1B 44
Nightingale Av. E4 5B 36
HA1: Harr 7B 42
Nightingale Cl. E4 4A 36
HA5: Eastc 5A 40
SM5: Cars 2E 166
W4 6J 97
Nightingale Ct. BR2: Brom 2G 159
E14 2E 104
(off Ovex Cl.)
HA1: Harr 6K 41
N4 2K 65
(off Tollington Pk.)
SM1: Sutt 5A 166
SW6 1K 117
(off Maltings Pl.)
Nightingale Dr. KT19: Ewe 6H 163
Nightingale Gro. SE13 5F 123
Nightingale Hgts. SE18 6F 107
Nightingale Ho. *E1* 1G 103
(off Thomas More St.)
E2 1E 84
(off Kingsland Rd.)
NW8 4C 4
(off Samford St.)
SE18 5E 106
(off Connaught M.)
UB7: W Dray 2B 92
W12 6E 80
(off Du Cane Rd.)
Nightingale La. BR1: Brom 2A 160
E11 4K 51
N8 4J 47
SW4 7D 118
SW12 7D 118
TW10: Rich 7E 114
Nightingale Lodge *W9* 5J 81
(off Admiral Wlk.)
Nightingale M. E3 2K 85
E11 5J 51
KT1: King T 3D 150
(off South La.)
SE11 3K 19 (4B 102)
Nightingale Pl. SE18 6E 106
SW10 7A 16 (6A 100)
Nightingale Rd. BR5: Pet W 6G 161
E5 3H 67
Nightingale Rd. KT8: W Mole 5F 149
KT12: Walt T 7A 148
N1 6C 66
N9 6D 24
N22 1J 47
NW10 2B 80
SM5: Cars 3D 166
TW12: Hamp 5E 130
W7 1K 95
Nightingales, The TW19: Stanw 1B 128
Nightingale Sq. SW12 7E 118
Nightingale Va. SE18 6E 106
Nightingale Wlk. N1 6C 66
SW4 6F 119
Nightingale Way E6 5C 88
Nile Cl. N16 3F 67
Nile Dr. N9 2D 34
Nile Ho. *N1* 1E 8
(off Nile St.)
Nile Path SE18 6E 106
Nile Rd. E13 2A 88
Nile St. N1 1D 8 (3C 84)
Nile Ter. SE15 5F 103
Nimegen Way SE22 5E 120
Nimmo Dr. WD23: B Hea 1C 26
Nimrod NW9 1A 44
Nimrod Cl. UB5: N'olt 3B 76
Nimrod Ho. *E16* 5K 87
(off Vanguard Cl.)
Nimrod Pas. N1 6E 66
Nimrod Rd. SW16 6F 137
Nina Mackay Cl. E15 1G 87
Nine Acres Cl. E12 5C 70
UB3: Harl 3E 92
NINE ELMS 7G 101
Nine Elms Cl. TW14: Felt 1H 129
Nine Elms La. SW8 7C 18 (7G 101)
Nineteenth Rd. CR4: Mitc 4J 155
Ninhams Wood BR6: Farnb 4E 172
Ninth Av. UB3: Hayes 7J 75
Nipper All. *KT1: King T* 2E 150
(off Clarence St.)
Nipponzan Myohoji Peace Pagoda 6D 100
Nisbet Ho. E9 5K 67
Nisbett Wlk. *DA14: Sidc* 4A 144
(off Sidcup High St.)
Nita Ct. SE12 1J 141
Nithdale Rd. SE18 7F 107
Nithsdale Gro. UB10: Ick 3E 56
Niton Cl. EN5: Barn 6A 20
Niton Rd. TW9: Rich 3G 115
Niton St. SW6 7F 99
Niveda Cl. W12 2C 98
No 1 St. SE18 3F 107
Noah Cl. EN3: Enf W 1D 24
Noah's Yd. N1 2J 83
Nobel Cl. NW9 2K 43
Nobel Dr. UB3: Harl 1F 111
Nobel Ho. SE5 2C 120
Nobel Rd. N18 4D 34
Noble Cnr. TW5: Hest 1E 112
Noble Ct. CR4: Mitc 2B 154
E1 7H 85
Noblefield Hgts. N2 5C 46
Noble M. *N16* 3D 66
(off Albion Rd.)
Noble St. EC2 7C 8 (6C 84)
Noble Yd. *N1* 1B 84
(off Camden Pas.)
Nocavia Ho. *SW6* 2A 118
(off Townmead Rd.)
Noel NW9 1A 44
Noel Ct. CR0: C'don 7D 156
TW4: Houn 3D 112
Noel Coward Ho. *SW1* 4B 18
(off Vauxhall Bri. Rd.)
Noel Coward Theatre 2E 12
(off St Martin's La.)
Noel Ho. *NW6* 7B 64
(off Harben Rd.)
NOEL PARK 2B 48

Noel Pk. Rd. N22 2A **48**
Noel Rd. E6 4C **88**
N1 2B **84**
W3 7G **79**
Noel Sq. RM8: Dag 4C **72**
TW11: Tedd 5K **131**
Noel St. W1 1B **12** (6G **83**)
Noel Ter. DA14: Sidc 4B **144**
SE23 2J **139**
Noko W10 3F **81**
Nolands Cl. RM5: Col R 2J **55**
Nolan Mans. *E20* *5D **68***
(off Honour Lea Av.)
Nolan Way E5 4G **67**
Noll Ho. *N7* *2K **65***
(off Tomlins Wlk.)
Nolton Pl. HA8: Edg 1F **43**
Nonsuch Ho. *SW19* *1B **154***
(off Chapter Way)
Nonsuch Pl. *SM3: Cheam* *7F **165***
(off Ewell Rd.)
Nonsuch Wlk. SM2: Cheam 7F **165**
Nook Apartments *E1* *1K **15***
(off Scarborough St.)
Nora Gdns. NW4 4F **45**
Nora Leverton Ct. *NW1* *7G **65***
(off Randolph St.)
NORBITON 2G **151**
Norbiton Av. KT1: King T 1G **151**
Norbiton Comn. Rd. KT1: King T 3H **151**
Norbiton Hall KT2: King T 2F **151**
Norbiton Ho. *NW1* *1G **83***
(off Camden St.)
Norbiton Rd. E14 6B **86**
Norbreck Gdns. NW10 3F **79**
Norbreck Pde. NW10 3E **78**
Norbroke St. W12 7B **80**
Norburn St. W10 5G **81**
NORBURY 1K **155**
Norbury Av. CR7: Thor H 1K **155**
SW16 1K **155**
TW3: Houn 4H **113**
Norbury Cl. SW16 1A **156**
Norbury Ct. Rd. SW16 3J **155**
Norbury Cres. SW16 1K **155**
Norbury Cross SW16 3J **155**
Norbury Gdns. RM6: Chad H 5D **54**
Norbury Gro. NW7 3F **29**
Norbury Hill SW16 7A **138**
Norbury Ri. SW16 3J **155**
Norbury Rd. CR7: Thor H 2C **156**
E4 5H **35**
TW13: Felt 3H **129**
Norbury Trad. Est. SW16 2K **155**
Norcombe Gdns. HA3: Kenton 6C **42**
Norcombe Ho. *N19* *3H **65***
(off Wedmore St.)
Norcott Cl. UB4: Yead 4A **76**
Norcott Rd. N16 2G **67**
Norcroft Gdns. SE22 7G **121**
Norcutt Rd. TW2: Twick 1J **131**
Nordenfeldt Rd. DA8: Erith 5K **109**
Norden Ho. *E2* *3H **85***
(off Pott St.)
Norfield Rd. DA2: Wilm 4J **145**
Norfolk Apartments E4 7J **35**
Norfolk Av. N13 6G **33**
N15 6F **49**
Norfolk Cl. EN4: Cockf 4K **21**
N2 3C **46**
N13 6G **33**
TW1: Twick 6B **114**
Norfolk Ct. EN5: Barn 4B **20**
RM6: Chad H *5B **54***
(off Norwich Cres.)
Norfolk Cres. DA15: Sidc 7J **125**
W2 7C **4** (6C **82**)
Norfolk Gdns. DA7: Bex 1F **127**
Norfolk Ho. *BR2: Brom* *4H **159***
(off Westmoreland Rd.)
EC4 2C **14**
Norfolk Ho. *SE8* *1C **122***
(off Brookmill Rd.)
SE20 1J **157**
SW1 *3D **18***
(off Page St.)
Norfolk Ho. Rd. SW16 3H **137**
Norfolk Mans. *SW11* *1D **118***
(off Prince of Wales Dr.)
Norfolk M. *W10* *5G **81***
(off Blagrove Rd.)
Norfolk Pl. DA16: Well 2A **126**
W2 7B **4** (6B **82**)
(not continuous)
Norfolk Rd. CR7: Thor H 3C **156**
E6 1D **88**
E17 2K **49**
EN3: Pond E 6C **24**
EN5: New Bar 3D **20**
HA1: Harr 5F **41**
IG3: Ilf 1J **71**
IG11: Bark 7J **71**
NW8 1B **82**
NW10 7A **62**
RM7: Rom 6J **55**
RM10: Dag 5H **73**
SW19 7C **136**
TW13: Felt 1A **130**
UB8: Uxb 6A **56**
Norfolk Row SE1 3G **19** (4K **101**)
Norfolk Sq. W2 1B **10** (6B **82**)
Norfolk Sq. M. W2 1B **10**
Norfolk St. E7 5J **69**
Norfolk Ter. W6 5G **99**
Norgrove St. SW12 7E **118**
Norhyrst Av. SE25 3F **157**
Norland Ho. *W11* *1F **99***
(off Queensdale Cres.)
Norland Pl. W11 1G **99**
Norland Rd. W11 1F **99**
Norlands Cres. BR7: Chst 1F **161**
Norlands Ga. BR7: Chst 1F **161**
Norland Sq. W11 1G **99**
Norland Sq. Mans. *W11* *1G **99***
(off Norland Sq.)
Norlem Ct. *SE8* *4A **104***
(off Seafarer Way)
Norley Va. SW15 1C **134**
Norlington Rd. E10 1E **68**
E11 1E **68**
Norman Av. N22 1B **48**
TW1: Twick 7C **114**
TW13: Hanw 2C **130**
UB1: S'hall 7C **76**
Norman Butler Ho. *W10* *4G **81***
(off Ladbroke Gro.)
Normanby Cl. SW15 5H **117**
Normanby Rd. NW10 4B **62**
Norman Cl. BR6: Farnb 3G **173**
N22 1C **48**
RM5: Col R 1H **55**
Norman Ct. IG2: Ilf 7H **53**
N3 *1J **45***
(off Nether St.)
N4 7A **48**
NW10 7C **62**
W13 *1B **96***
(off Kirkfield Cl.)
Norman Cres. HA5: Pinn 1A **40**
TW5: Hest 7B **94**
Normand Gdns. *W14* *6G **99***
(off Greyhound Rd.)
Normand Mans. *W14* *6G **99***
(off Normand M.)
Normand M. W14 6G **99**
Normand Rd. W14 6H **99**
Normandy Av. EN5: Barn 5C **20**
Normandy Cl. SE26 3A **140**
Normandy Dr. UB3: Hayes 6E **74**
Normandy Ho. *E14* *2E **104***
(off Plevna St.)
EN2: Enf 1H **23**
Normandy Pl. W12 1F **99**
Normandy Rd. SW9 1A **120**
Normandy Ter. E16 6K **87**
Normandy Way DA8: Erith 1K **127**
Norman Gro. E3 2A **86**
Norman Hay Trad. Est., The
UB7: Sip 7B **92**
Norman Ho. *SE1* *7H **15***
(off Riley Rd.)
SW8 *7J **101***
(off Wyvil Rd.)
TW13: Hanw *2D **130***
(off Watermill Way)
Normanhurst TW15: Ashf 5C **128**
Normanhurst Av. DA7: Bex 1D **126**
Normanhurst Dr. TW1: Twick 5A **114**
Normanhurst Rd. SW2 2K **137**
Norman Leddy Memorial Gdns. 6H **75**
Norman Pde. DA14: Sidc 2D **144**
Norman Pk. Athletics Track 6K **159**
Norman Rd. CR7: Thor H 5B **156**
DA17: Belv 3H **109**
(not continuous)
E6 4D **88**
E11 2F **69**
IG1: Ilf 5F **71**
N15 5F **49**
SE10 7D **104**
SM1: Sutt 5J **165**
SW19 7A **136**
TW15: Ashf 6F **129**
Norman's Cl. NW10 6K **61**
Normans Cl. UB8: Hil 5B **74**
Normansfield Av. TW11: Tedd 7C **132**
Normanshire Dr. E4 4H **35**
Norman's Mead NW10 6K **61**
Norman St. EC1 2D **8** (3C **84**)
Norman Ter. NW6 5H **63**
Normanton Av. SW19 2J **135**
Normanton Ct. *CR2: S Croy* *5E **168***
(off Croham Rd.)
Normanton Pk. E4 2B **36**
Normanton Rd. CR2: S Croy 5E **168**
Normanton St. SE23 2K **139**
Norman Way N14 2D **32**
W3 5H **79**
Normington Cl. SW16 5A **138**
Norrice Lea N2 5B **46**
Norris *NW9* *1B **44***
(off Withers Mead)
Norris Ho. *E9* *1J **85***
(off Handley Rd.)
N1 *1E **84***
(off Colville Est.)
SE8 *5B **104***
(off Grove St.)
TW7: Isle 2A **114**
Norris St. SW1 3C **12** (7H **83**)
Norroy Rd. SW15 4F **117**
Norry's Cl. EN4: Cockf 4J **21**
Norry's Rd. EN4: Cockf 4J **21**
Norseman Cl. IG3: Ilf 1B **72**
Norseman Way UB6: G'frd 1F **77**
Norstead Pl. SW15 2C **134**
Nth. Access Rd. E17 6K **49**
North Acre NW9 1A **44**
NORTH ACTON 4K **79**
Nth. Acton Bus. Pk. W3 5K **79**
Nth. Acton Rd. NW10 2K **79**
Northall Rd. DA7: Bex 2J **127**
Northampton Gro. N1 5D **66**
Northampton Pk. N1 6C **66**
Northampton Rd.
CR0: C'don 2G **169**
EC1 3K **7** (4A **84**)
EN3: Pond E 4F **25**
Northampton Row EC1 3K **7**
Northampton Sq. EC1 2A **8** (3B **84**)
Northampton St. N1 7C **66**
Northanger Rd. SW16 6J **137**
Nth. Audley St. W1 1G **11** (7E **82**)
North Av. HA2: Harr 6F **41**
N18 4B **34**
SM5: Cars 7E **166**
TW9: Kew 1G **115**
UB1: S'hall 7D **76**
UB3: Hayes 7J **75**
W13 5B **78**
Northaw Ho. *W10* *4E **80***
(off Sutton Way)
North Bank NW8 2C **4** (3C **82**)
Northbank Rd. E17 2E **50**
NORTH BECKTON 5D **88**
Nth. Birkbeck Rd. E11 3F **69**
North Block *SE1* *6H **13***
(off Chicheley St.)
Northborough Rd. SW16 3H **155**
Northbourne BR2: Hayes 7J **159**
Northbourne Rd. SW4 5H **119**
Northbrook Dr. HA6: Nwood 1G **39**
Northbrook Rd. CR0: C'don 5D **156**
EN5: Barn 6B **20**
IG1: Ilf 2E **70**
N22 7D **32**
SE13 5G **123**
Northburgh St. EC1 4B **8** (4B **84**)
Northbury Cl. IG11: Bark 7G **71**
Nth. Carriage Dr. W2 2C **10**
NORTH CHEAM 3E **164**
Northchurch SE17 5D **102**
(not continuous)
Northchurch Ho. *E2* *1G **85***
(off Whiston Rd.)
Northchurch Rd. HA9: Wemb 6G **61**
N1 7D **66**
(not continuous)
Northchurch Ter. N1 7E **66**
Nth. Circular Rd. E4 6G **35**
E12 3E **70**
E18 2H **51**
IG1: Ilf 4E **70**
IG11: Bark 4E **70**
N3 4H **45**
N12 4H **45**
N13 5F **33**
NW2 3A **62**
NW4 7E **44**
NW10 2F **79**
NW11 7E **44**
Northcliffe Cl. KT4: Wor Pk 3A **164**
Northcliffe Dr. N20 1C **30**
North Cl. DA6: Bex 4D **126**
RM10: Dag 1G **91**
SM4: Mord 4G **153**
TW14: Bedf 6F **111**
Nth. Colonnade, The E14 1C **104**
(not continuous)
North Comn. Rd. UB8: Uxb 5A **56**
W5 7E **78**
Northcote HA5: Pinn 2A **40**
Northcote Av. KT5: Surb 7H **151**
TW7: Isle 5A **114**
UB1: S'hall 7C **76**
W5 7E **78**
Northcote Rd. CR0: C'don 6D **156**
DA14: Sidc 4J **143**
E17 4A **50**
KT3: N Mald 3J **151**
NW10 7A **62**
SW11 5C **118**
TW1: Twick 5A **114**
Northcott Av. N22 1J **47**
Nth. Countess Rd. E17 2B **50**
North Ct. *BR1: Brom* *1K **159***
(off Palace Gro.)
SE24 3B **120**
SW1 *2E **18***
(off Gt. Peter St.)
W1 5B **6** (5G **83**)
NORTH CRAY 5E **144**
Nth. Cray Rd. DA5: Bexl 1H **145**
DA14: Sidc 6E **144**

North Cray Woods 4D 144
North Cres. E16 4F 87
N3 2H 45
WC1 5C 6 (5H 83)
Northcroft Ct. W12 2C 98
Northcroft Rd.
KT19: Ewe 7A 164
W13 2B 96
North Crofts SE23 1H 139
Northcroft Ter. W13 2B 96
Nth. Cross Rd. IG6: Ilf 4G 53
SE22 5F 121
Northdale Ct. SE25 3F 157
North Dene NW7 3E 28
TW3: Houn 1F 113
Northdene Gdns. N15 6F 49
Northdown Cl. HA4: Ruis 3H 57
Northdown Gdns. IG2: Ilf 5J 53
Northdown Rd. DA16: Well 2B 126
Northdown St. N1 1G 7 (2J 83)
North Dr. BR3: Beck 4D 158
BR6: Orp 4J 173
HA4: Ruis 7G 39
SW16 4G 137
TW3: Houn 2G 113
Nth. E. Surrey Crematorium
SM4: Mord 6E 152
NORTH END 2A 64
North End CR0: C'don 2C 168
IG9: Buck H 1F 37
NW3 2A 64
Nth. End Av. NW3 2A 64
Nth. End Cres. W14 4H 99
Nth. End Ho. W14 4G 99
Nth. End La. BR6: Downe 7F 173
Nth. End Pde. *W14* *4G 99*
(off North End Rd.)
Nth. End Rd. HA9: Wemb 3G 61
NW11 1J 63
SW6 4G 99
W14 4G 99
Nth. End Way NW3 2A 64
Northern Av. N9 2K 33
Northernhay Wlk. SM4: Mord 4G 153
Northern Hgts. *N8* *7H 47*
(off Crescent Rd.)
Northern La. *E2* *2G 85*
(off Kay St.)
Northern Perimeter Rd.
TW6: H'row A 1D 110
Northern Perimeter Rd. (W.)
TW6: H'row A 4E 174
Northern Rd. E13 2K 87
Northesk Ho. *E1* *4H 85*
(off Tent St.)
Nth. Eyot Gdns. W6 5B 98
Northey St. E14 7A 86
NORTH FELTHAM 6K 111
Nth. Feltham Trad. Est. TW14: Felt 5K 111
Northfield Av. HA5: Pinn 4B 40
W5 1B 96
W13 1B 96
Northfield Cl. BR1: Brom 1C 160
UB3: Harl 3H 93
Northfield Cres. SM3: Cheam 4G 165
Northfield Gdns. RM9: Dag 4F 73
Northfield Ho. SE15 6G 103
Northfield Pde. UB3: Harl 3G 93
Northfield Pk. UB3: Harl 3H 93
Northfield Path RM9: Dag 4F 73
Northfield Recreation Grd. W5 4B 96
Northfield Rd. E6 7D 70
EN3: Pond E 5C 24
EN4: Cockf 3H 21
N16 7E 48
RM9: Dag 4F 73
TW5: Hest 6B 94
W13 2B 96
NORTHFIELDS 3B 96
Northfields SW18 4J 117
Northfields Ind. Est. HA0: Wemb 1G 79
Northfields Prospect Bus. Cen.
SW18 4J 117
Northfields Rd. W3 5H 79
NORTH FINCHLEY 5F 31
Northfleet Ho. *SE1* *6E 14*
(off Tennis St.)
Northflock St. SE16 2G 103
Nth. Flower Wlk. W2 3A 10
North Gdn. E14 1B 104
North Gdns. SW19 7B 136
North Ga. NW8 1C 4
Northgate HA6: Nwood 1E 38
Northgate Bus. Cen. EN1: Enf 3C 24
Northgate Ct. SW9 3A 120
Northgate Dr. NW9 6A 44
Northgate Ho. *E14* *7C 86*
(off E. India Dock Rd.)
Northgate Ind. Pk.
RM5: Col R 1F 55
North Gates *N12* *1A 46*
(off Bow La.)
Nth. Glade, The DA5: Bexl 7F 127
Nth. Gower St. NW1 2B 6 (3G 83)
North Grn. NW9 7F 29
North Gro. N6 7E 46
N15 5D 48
NORTH HARROW 5F 41
Nth. Hatton Rd. TW6: H'row A 1F 111
North Hill N6 6D 46
North Hill Av. N6 6E 46
NORTH HILLINGDON 7E 56
North Ho. SE8 5B 104
Nth. Hyde Gdns. UB3: Harl, Hayes 4J 93
Nth. Hyde La. TW5: Hest 5C 94
UB2: S'hall 5B 94
Nth. Hyde Rd. UB3: Harl, Hayes 3G 93
Northiam N12 4D 30
(not continuous)
WC1 *2F 7*
(off Cromer St.)
Northiam St. E9 1H 85
Northington St. WC1 4H 7 (4K 83)
NORTH KENSINGTON 5E 80
North Kent Indoor Bowls Club 3H 109
Northlands Av. BR6: Orp 4J 173
Northlands St. SE5 2C 120
North La. TW11: Tedd 6K 131
Northleigh Ho. *E3* *3D 86*
(off Powis Rd.)
North Lodge *E16* *1K 105*
(off Wesley Av.)
EN5: New Bar 5F 21
Nth. Lodge Cl. SW15 5F 117
Nth. London Bus. Pk. N11 2K 31
North Mall *N9* *2C 34*
(within Edmonton Grn. Shop. Cen.)
SW18 *5K 117*
(off Southside Shop. Cen.)
North M. WC1 4H 7 (4K 83)
North Middlesex Golf Course 3G 31
North Mill Apartments *E8* *1F 85*
(off Lovelace St.)
North Mt. *N20* *2F 31*
(off High Rd.)
Northolm HA8: Edg 4E 28
Northolme Gdns. HA8: Edg 1G 43
Northolme Ri. BR6: Orp 2J 173
Northolme Rd. N5 4C 66
NORTHOLT 7E 58
Northolt *N17* *2E 48*
(off Griffin Rd.)
Northolt Av. HA4: Ruis 5K 57
Northolt Gdns. UB6: G'frd 5K 59
Northolt Golf Course 2C 76
Northolt Leisure Cen. 6E 58
Northolt Rd. HA2: Harr 4F 59
TW6: H'row A 1A 110
(not continuous)
Northolt Trad. Est.
UB5: N'olt 7F 59
Northover BR1: Brom 3H 141
North Pde. HA8: Edg 2G 43
KT9: Chess 5F 163
UB1: S'hall *6E 76*
(off North Rd.)
North Pk. SE9 6D 124
North Pas. SW18 5J 117
North Pl. CR4: Mitc 7D 136
TW11: Tedd 6K 131
North Point N8 5K 47
Northpoint Cl. SM1: Sutt 3A 166
Northpoint Ho. *N1* *6D 66*
(off Essex Rd.)
Northpoint Sq. NW1 6H 65
Nth. Pole La. BR2: Kes 6H 171
Nth. Pole Rd. W10 5E 80
Northport St. N1 1D 84
North Quay Pl. E14 7D 86
North Ride W2 3C 10 (7C 82)
North Ri. W2 1D 10 (6C 82)
North Rd. BR1: Brom 1K 159
BR4: W W'ck 1D 170
DA17: Belv 3H 109
HA1: Harr 7A 42
HA8: Edg 1H 43
IG3: Ilf 2J 71
KT6: Surb 6D 150
N6 7E 46
N7 6J 65
N9 1C 34
RM6: Chad H 5E 54
SE18 4J 107
SW19 6A 136
TW5: Hest 6A 94
TW8: Bford 6E 96
TW9: Kew, Rich 3G 115
TW14: Bedf 6F 111
UB1: S'hall 6E 76
UB3: Hayes 5F 75
UB7: W Dray 3B 92
W5 3D 96
Northrop Rd. TW6: H'row A 1G 111
North Row W1 2F 11 (7D 82)
Nth. Row Bldgs. *W1* *2G 11*
(off North Row)
North Several SE3 2F 123
NORTH SHEEN 3G 115
Northside Rd. BR1: Brom 1J 159
Northside Studios *E8* *1H 85*
(off Andrew's Rd.)
Nth. Side Wandsworth Comn.
SW18 5B 118
Northspur Rd. SM1: Sutt 3J 165
North Sq. *N9* *2C 34*
(off New Rd.)
NW11 5J 45
North Stand N5 3B 66
Northstead Rd. SW2 2A 138
North St. BR1: Brom 1J 159
DA7: Bex 4G 127
E13 2K 87
IG11: Bark 6F 71
NW4 5E 44
RM1: Rom 3K 55
RM5: Rom 3K 55
SM5: Cars 3D 166
SW4 3G 119
TW7: Isle 3A 114
North St. Pas. E13 2K 87
Nth. Tenter St. E1 1K 15 (6F 85)
North Ter. SW3 2C 16 (3C 100)
WC2 4E 12
Northumberland All. EC3 1H 15 (6E 84)
(not continuous)
Northumberland Av. DA16: Well 4H 125
E12 1A 70
EN1: Enf 1C 24
TW7: Isle 1K 113
WC2 4E 12 (1J 101)
Northumberland Cl. DA8: Erith 7J 109
TW19: Stanw 6A 110
Northumberland Cres. TW14: Felt 6G 111
Northumberland Gdns. BR1: Brom 4E 160
CR4: Mitc 5H 155
N9 3A 34
TW7: Isle 7A 96
Northumberland Gro. N17 7C 34
NORTHUMBERLAND HEATH 7J 109
Northumberland Ho. IG8: Wfd G 7K 37
SW1 *4E 12*
(off Northumberland Av.)
Northumberland Pk. DA8: Erith 7J 109
N17 7A 34
Northumberland Pk. Ind. Est. N17 7C 34
Northumberland Pk. School Sports Cen.
7B 34
Northumberland Pl. TW10: Rich 5D 114
W2 6J 81
Northumberland Rd. E6 6C 88
E17 7C 50
EN5: New Bar 6F 21
HA2: Harr 5D 40
Northumberland St. WC2 4E 12 (1J 101)
Northumberland Way DA8: Erith 1J 127
Northumbria St. E14 6C 86
Nth. Verbena Gdns. W6 5C 98
North Vw. HA5: Eastc 7A 40
SW19 5E 134
W5 4C 78
North Vw. Cvn. Site IG6: Ilf 1A 54
Northview Cres. NW10 4B 62
North Vw. Dr. IG8: Wfd G 2B 52
Northview Pde. N7 3J 65
North Vw. Rd. N8 4H 47
North Vs. NW1 6H 65
North Wlk. CR0: New Ad 6D 170
(not continuous)
W2 3A 10 (7K 81)
W8 *7K 81*
(off The Broad Wlk.)
Northwall Rd. E20 5C 68
North Way HA5: Pinn 4B 40
N9 2E 34
N11 6B 32
NW9 3H 43
UB10: Uxb 7A 56
Northway NW11 5K 45
SM4: Mord 3G 153
SM6: Wall 4G 167
Northway Cir. NW7 4E 28
Northway Ct. NW7 4F 29
Northway Cres. NW7 4E 28
Northway Gdns. NW11 5K 45
Northway Rd. CR0: C'don 6F 157
SE5 3C 120
Northways *NW3* *7B 64*
(off College Cres.)
Northways Pde. *NW3* *7B 64*
(off College Cres.)
Northweald La. KT2: King T 5D 132
NORTH WEMBLEY 3D 60
Northwest Pl. N1 2A 84
North Wharf *E14* *1E 104*
(off Coldharbour)
Nth. Wharf Rd. W2 6A 4 (5B 82)
Northwick Av. HA3: Kenton 6A 42
Northwick Circ. HA3: Kenton 6C 42
Northwick Cl. HA1: Harr 1B 60
NW8 3A 4 (4B 82)
Northwick Ho. NW8 3A 4
Northwick Pk. Playgolf 1A 60
Northwick Pk. Rd. HA1: Harr 6K 41
NORTHWICK PARK RDBT. 7A 42
Northwick Rd. HA0: Wemb 1D 78
Northwick Ter. NW8 3A 4 (4B 82)
Northwick Wlk. HA1: Harr 7K 41
Northwold Dr. HA5: Pinn 2A 40
Northwold Rd. E5 2F 67
N16 2F 67
NORTHWOOD 1H 39
Northwood Club, The 2H 39
Nth. Wood Ct. SE25 3G 157
Northwood Est. E5 2G 67

Northwood Gdns. IG5: Ilf 4E **52**
N12 . . . . 5G **31**
UB6: G'frd 5K **59**
Northwood Golf Course 1F 39
Northwood Hall N6 . . . . 7G **47**
NORTHWOOD HILLS 2J 39
Northwood Hills Cir. HA6: Nwood 1J **39**
Northwood Ho. *KT2: King T* *2G* ***151***
(off Coombe Rd.)
SE27 . . . . 4D **138**
Northwood Pl. DA18: Erith 3F **109**
Northwood Rd. CR7: Thor H 2B **156**
N6 . . . . 7F **47**
SE23 . . . . 1B **140**
SM5: Cars 6E **166**
TW6: H'row A 4E **174**
UB9: Hare 1A **38**
Northwood Way HA6: Nwood 1J **39**
SE19 . . . . 6D **138**
UB9: Hare 1A **38**
NORTH WOOLWICH 2E 106
Nth. Woolwich Rd. E16 . . . . 1H **105**
Nth. Worple Way SW14 . . . . 3K **115**
Norton Av. KT5: Surb 7H **151**
Norton Cl. E4 . . . . 5H **35**
EN1: Enf 2C **24**
Norton Ct. BR3: Beck 1B **158**
Norton Folgate E1 . . . . 5H **9** (5E **84**)
Norton Folgate Ho. *E1* *5J* ***9***
(off Puma Ct.)
Norton Gdns. SW16 . . . . 2J **155**
Norton Ho. *E1* *6H* ***85***
(off Bigland St.)
E2 . . . . *2K* ***85***
(off Mace St.)
SW1 . . . . *2D* ***18***
(off Arneway St.)
SW9 . . . . *2K* ***119***
(off Aytoun Rd.)
Norton Rd. E10 . . . . 1B **68**
HA0: Wemb 6D **60**
RM10: Dag 6K **73**
Norval Rd. HA0: Wemb 2B **60**
Norway Ga. SE16 . . . . 3A **104**
Norway Ho. *N1* *1E* ***84***
(off Hertford Rd.)
Norway Pl. E14 . . . . 6B **86**
Norway St. SE10 . . . . 6D **104**
Norway Wharf E14 . . . . 6B **86**
Norwegian War Memorial . . . 5D 10 (1C 100)
Norwich Cres. RM6: Chad H 5B **54**
Norwich Ho. *E14* *6D* ***86***
(off Cordelia St.)
Norwich M. IG3: Ilf 1A **72**
Norwich Pl. DA6: Bex 4G **127**
Norwich Rd. CR7: Thor H 3C **156**
E7 . . . . 5J **69**
HA6: Nwood 3H **39**
RM9: Dag 2G **91**
UB6: G'frd 1F **77**
Norwich St. EC4 . . . . 7J **7** (6A **84**)
Norwich Wlk. HA8: Edg 7D **28**
NORWOOD 6E 138
Norwood Av. HA0: Wemb 1F **79**
RM7: Rush G 7K **55**
Norwood Cl. NW2 . . . . 3G **63**
TW2: Twick 2H **131**
UB2: S'hall 4E **94**
Norwood Dr. HA2: Harr 6D **40**
Norwood Gdns. UB2: S'hall 4D **94**
UB4: Yead 4A **76**
NORWOOD GREEN 4D 94
Norwood Grn. Rd. UB2: S'hall 4E **94**
Norwood High St. SE27 . . . . 3B **138**
Norwood Ho. *E14* *7D* ***86***
(off Poplar High St.)
NORWOOD NEW TOWN 6C 138
Norwood Pk. Rd. SE27 . . . . 5C **138**
Norwood Rd. SE24 . . . . 1B **138**
SE27 . . . . 2B **138**
UB2: S'hall 3C **94**
Norwood Ter. UB2: S'hall 4F **95**
Nota M. N3 . . . . 1J **45**
Notley Pl. SW4 . . . . 7J **119**
Notley St. SE5 . . . . 7D **102**
Notson Rd. SE25 . . . . 4H **157**
Notting Barn Rd. W10 . . . . 4F **81**
Nottingdale Sq. W11 . . . . 1G **99**
Nottingham Av. E16 . . . . 5A **88**
Nottingham Ct. WC2 . . . . 1E **12** (6J **83**)
Nottingham Ho. *WC2* *1E* ***12***
(off Shorts Gdns.)
Nottingham Pl. W1 . . . . 4G **5** (5E **82**)
Nottingham Rd. CR2: S Croy 4C **168**
E10 . . . . 6E **50**
SW17 . . . . 1D **136**
TW7: Isle 2K **113**
Nottingham St. W1 . . . . 5G **5** (5E **82**)
Nottingham Ter. NW1 . . . . 4G **5**
NOTTING HILL 7H 81
Notting Hill Ga. W11 . . . . 1J **99**
Nottingwood Ho. *W11* *7G* ***81***
(off Clarendon Rd.)
Nova Bldg. E14 . . . . 4C **104**
Nova Ct. E. *E14* *1E* ***104***
(off Yabsley St.)
Nova Ct. W. *E14* *1E* ***104***
(off Yabsley St.)
Nova M. SM3: Sutt 1G **165**
Novar Cl. BR6: Orp 7K **161**
Nova Rd. CR0: C'don 1B **168**
Novar Rd. SE9 . . . . 1G **143**
Novello Ct. *N1* *1C* ***84***
(off Dibden St.)
Novello St. SW6 . . . . 1J **117**
Novello Theatre
Covent Garden ***7K 83***
(off Aldwych)
Novem Ho. *E1* *6K* ***9***
(off Chicksand St.)
Nowell Rd. SW13 . . . . 6C **98**
Nower Ct. HA5: Pinn 4D **40**
Nower Hill HA5: Pinn 4D **40**
Noyna Rd. SW17 . . . . 3D **136**
Nubia Way BR1: Brom 3G **141**
Nuding Cl. SE13 . . . . 3C **122**
Nuffield Ct. TW5: Hest 7D **94**
Nuffield Health
Battersea ***2D 118***
(within Latchmere Leisure Cen.)
Bloomsbury ***3G 7***
(off Mecklenburgh Pl.)
Bromley 5K 159
Cannon Street 3E 14
Cheam 7G 165
Covent Garden ***1F 13***
(off Endell St.)
Croydon 6A 168
Fulham 1F 117
Norbury 2K 155
Paddington 5A 82
Surbiton 6C 150
Twickenham 7J 113
Wandsworth 7K 117
Willesden Green 7E 62
Wimbledon 6H 135
Nuffield Lodge N6 . . . . 6G **47**
W9 . . . . *5J* ***81***
(off Admiral Wlk.)
Nugent Rd. N19 . . . . 1J **65**
SE25 . . . . 3F **157**
Nugents Ct. HA5: Pinn 1C **40**
Nugent's Pk. HA5: Hat E 1C **40**
Nugent Ter. NW8 . . . . 2A **82**
Numa Ct. TW8: Bford 7D **96**
Number One EC1 . . . . 4D **8** (4C **84**)
Nun Ct. EC2 . . . . 7E **8**
Nuneaton Rd. RM9: Dag 7E **72**
NUNHEAD 3H 121
Nunhead Cemetery Nature Reserve
. . . . 4J 121
Nunhead Cres. SE15 . . . . 3H **121**
Nunhead Est. SE15 . . . . 4H **121**
Nunhead Grn. SE15 . . . . 3H **121**
Nunhead Gro. SE15 . . . . 3H **121**
Nunhead La. SE15 . . . . 3H **121**
Nunhead Pas. SE15 . . . . 3G **121**
Nunnington Cl. SE9 . . . . 3C **142**
Nunns Rd. EN2: Enf 2H **23**
Nupton Dr. EN5: Barn 6A **20**
Nurse Cl. HA8: Edg 1J **43**
Nursery App. N12 . . . . 6H **31**
Nursery Av. CR0: C'don 2K **169**
DA7: Bex 3F **127**
N3 . . . . 2A **46**
Nursery Cl. BR6: Orp 7K **161**
CR0: C'don 2K **169**
EN3: Enf H 1E **24**
IG8: Wfd G 5E **36**
RM6: Chad H 6D **54**
SE4 . . . . 2B **122**
SW15 . . . . 4F **117**
TW14: Felt 7K **111**
(not continuous)
Nursery Ct. N17 . . . . 7A **34**
W13 . . . . 5A **78**
Nursery Gdns. BR7: Chst 6F **143**
EN3: Enf H 1E **24**
TW4: Houn 5D **112**
TW12: Hamp 4D **130**
TW16: Sun 2H **147**
Nursery La. E2 . . . . 1F **85**
E7 . . . . 6J **69**
UB8: Cowl 4A **74**
W10 . . . . 5E **80**
Nurserymans Rd. N11 . . . . 2K **31**
Nursery Rd. CR4: Mitc 3C **154**
CR7: Thor H 4D **156**
E9 . . . . 6J **67**
HA5: Pinn 3A **40**
N2 . . . . 1B **46**
N14 . . . . 7B **22**
SM1: Sutt 4A **166**
SW9 . . . . 4K **119**
SW19 . . . . 7G **135**
(Elm Gro.)
SW19 . . . . 2K **153**
(Parkleigh Rd.)
TW16: Sun 2G **147**
Nursery Row EN5: Barn 3B **20**
SE17 . . . . 4D **102**
Nursery St. N17 . . . . 7A **34**
Nursery Wlk. NW4 . . . . 3E **44**
RM7: Rush G 7K **55**
Nursery Waye UB8: Uxb 1A **74**
Nurstead Rd. DA8: Erith 7G **109**
Nutbourne St. W10 . . . . 3G **81**
Nutbrook St. SE15 . . . . 3G **121**
Nutbrowne Rd. RM9: Dag 1F **91**
Nutcroft Rd. SE15 . . . . 7H **103**
Nutfield Cl. N18 . . . . 6B **34**
SM5: Cars 3C **166**
Nutfield Ct. BR1: Brom 3J **159**
Nutfield Gdns. IG3: Ilf 2K **71**
UB5: N'olt 2A **76**
Nutfield Pas. *CR7: Thor H* *4B* ***156***
(off Nutfield Rd.)
Nutfield Rd. CR7: Thor H 4B **156**
E15 . . . . 4E **68**
NW2 . . . . 3C **62**
SE22 . . . . 4F **121**
Nutfield Way BR6: Farnb 2F **173**
Nutford Pl. W1 . . . . 7D **4** (6D **82**)
Nuthatch Cl. TW19: Stanw 1B **128**
Nuthatch Gdns. SE28 . . . . 2H **107**
(not continuous)
Nuthatch Row KT10: Clay 6A **162**
Nuthurst Av. SW2 . . . . 2K **137**
Nutkin Wlk. UB8: Uxb 7A **56**
Nutley Ter. NW3 . . . . 6A **64**
Nutmead Cl. DA5: Bexl 1J **145**
Nutmeg Cl. E16 . . . . 4G **87**
Nutmeg La. E14 . . . . 6F **87**
Nuttall St. N1 . . . . 2E **84**
Nutter La. E11 . . . . 6A **52**
Nutt Gro. HA8: Edg 2J **27**
Nutt St. SE15 . . . . 7F **103**
Nutty La. TW17: Shep 3E **146**
Nutwell St. SW17 . . . . 5C **136**
Nuxley Rd. DA17: Belv 6F **109**
Nyanza St. SE18 . . . . 6H **107**
Nye Bevan Est. E5 . . . . 3K **67**
Nye Bevan Ho. *SW6* *7H* ***99***
(off St Thomas's Way)
Nyland Ct. *SE8* *4A* ***104***
(off Naomi St.)
Nylands Av. TW9: Kew 1G **115**
Nymans Gdns. SW20 . . . . 3D **152**
Nynehead St. SE14 . . . . 7A **104**
Nyon Gro. SE6 . . . . 2B **140**
Nyssa Cl. IG8: Wfd G 6J **37**
Nyton Cl. N19 . . . . 1J **65**

O

O2, The 1G 105
O2 Brixton Academy 3A 120
O2 Cen. NW3 . . . . 6A **64**
O2 Forum Kentish Town 5F 65
O2 Shepherd's Bush Empire Theatre
. . . . 2E 98
Oak Apple Ct. SE12 . . . . 1J **141**
Oak Av. CR0: C'don 1C **170**
EN2: Enf 1E **22**
N8 . . . . 4J **47**
N10 . . . . 7A **32**
N17 . . . . 7J **33**
TW5: Hest 7B **94**
TW12: Hamp 5C **130**
UB7: W Dray 3C **92**
UB10: Ick 2D **56**
Oak Avenue Local Nature Reserve . . . 5C 130
Oak Bank CR0: New Ad 6E **170**
Oakbank Av. KT12: Walt T 7D **148**
Oakbank Gro. SE24 . . . . 4C **120**
Oakbark Ho. *TW8: Bford* *7C* ***96***
(off High St.)
Oakbrook Cl. BR1: Brom 4K **141**
Oakbury Rd. SW6 . . . . 2K **117**
Oak Cl. N14 . . . . 7A **22**
SM1: Sutt 2A **166**
Oakcombe Cl. KT3: N Mald 1A **152**
Oak Cott. Cl. SE6 . . . . 1H **141**
Oak Cotts. W7 . . . . 2J **95**
Oak Ct. *SE15* *7F* ***103***
(off Sumner Rd.)
Oak Cres. E16 . . . . 5G **87**
Oakcroft Bus. Cen. KT9: Chess 4F **163**
Oakcroft Cl. HA5: Pinn 2K **39**
Oakcroft Rd. KT9: Chess 4F **163**
SE13 . . . . 2F **123**
Oakcroft Vs. KT9: Chess 4F **163**
Oakdale N14 . . . . 1A **32**
Oakdale Av. HA3: Kenton 5E **42**
HA6: Nwood 2J **39**
Oakdale Ct. E4 . . . . 5K **35**
Oakdale Gdns. E4 . . . . 5K **35**
Oakdale Rd. E7 . . . . 7K **69**
E11 . . . . 2F **69**
E18 . . . . 2K **51**
KT19: Ewe 7K **163**
N4 . . . . 6C **48**
SE15 . . . . 3J **121**
SW16 . . . . 5J **137**
Oakdale Way CR4: Mitc 7E **154**
Oak Dene W13 . . . . 5B **78**
Oakdene SE15 . . . . 1H **121**
Oakdene Av. BR7: Chst 5E **142**
DA8: Erith 6J **109**
KT7: T Ditt 1A **162**
Oakdene Cl. HA5: Hat E 1D **40**
Oakdene Dr. KT5: Surb 7J **151**
Oakdene M. SM3: Sutt 1H **165**

Oakdene Pk. N3 7C **30**
Oakdene Rd. BR5: St M Cry 5K **161**
UB10: Hil 2D **74**
Oakden St. SE11 3K **19** (4A **102**)
Oake Ct. SW15 5G **117**
Oakeford Ho. *W14 3G 99*
(off Russell Rd.)
Oakenholt Ho. SE2 1D **108**
Oakenshaw Cl. KT6: Surb 7E **150**
Oakes Cl. E6 6D **88**
Oakeshott Av. N6 2E **64**
Oakes M. *E14 5E 86*
(off Nairn St.)
Oakey La. SE1 1J **19** (3A **102**)
Oakfield E4 5J **35**
Oakfield Av. HA3: Kenton 3B **42**
Oakfield Cl. HA4: Ruis 6H **39**
KT3: N Mald 5B **152**
Oakfield Ct. N8 7J **47**
NW2 7F **45**
Oakfield Gdns. BR3: Beck 5D **158**
N18 4K **33**
SE19 5E **138**
(not continuous)
SM5: Cars 1C **166**
UB6: G'frd 4H **77**
Oakfield Ho. *E3 5C 86*
(off Gale St.)
Oakfield La. BR2: Kes 4A **172**
Oakfield Lodge *IG1: Ilf 3F 71*
(off Albert Rd.)
Oakfield Rd. CR0: C'don 1C **168**
E6 1C **88**
E17 2A **50**
IG1: Ilf 3F **71**
N3 1K **45**
N4 6A **48**
N14 2D **32**
SE20 7H **139**
SW19 3F **135**
TW15: Ashf 5D **128**
Oakfield Rd. Ind. Est. SE20 7H **139**
Oakfields Rd. NW11 6G **45**
Oakfield St. SW10 6A **100**
Oakford Rd. NW5 4G **65**
Oak Gdns. CR0: C'don 2C **170**
HA8: Edg 2J **43**
Oak Glade HA6: Nwood 1D **38**
Oak Gro. BR4: W W'ck 1E **170**
HA4: Ruis 7K **39**
NW2 4G **63**
TW16: Sun 7K **129**
Oak Gro. Rd. SE20 1J **157**
Oakhall Ct. E11 6K **51**
TW16: Sun 5H **129**
Oakhall Dr. TW16: Sun 5H **129**
Oak Hall Rd. E11 6K **51**
Oakham Cl. EN4: Cockf 3J **21**
SE6 2B **140**
Oakham Dr. BR2: Brom 4H **159**
Oakham Ho. *W10 4E 80*
(off Sutton Way)
Oakhampton Rd. NW7 7A **30**
Oak Hill IG8: Wfd G 7A **36**
KT6: Surb 7E **150**
Oakhill KT10: Clay 6A **162**
Oakhill Av. HA5: Pinn 2C **40**
NW3 4K **63**
Oak Hill Cl. IG8: Wfd G 7A **36**
Oak Hill Ct. IG8: Wfd G 7A **36**
Oakhill Ct. SE23 6J **121**
SW19 7F **135**
Oak Hill Cres. IG8: Wfd G 7A **36**
KT6: Surb 7E **150**
Oakhill Dr. KT6: Surb 7E **150**
Oak Hill Gdns. IG8: Wfd G 1G **51**
Oak Hill Gro. KT6: Surb 6E **150**
Oak Hill Pk. NW3 4K **63**
Oak Hill Pk. M. NW3 4A **64**
Oak Hill Path KT6: Surb 6E **150**
Oakhill Pl. SW15 5J **117**
Oak Hill Rd. KT6: Surb 6E **150**
Oakhill Rd. BR3: Beck 2E **158**
BR6: Orp 1K **173**
SM1: Sutt 3K **165**
SW15 5H **117**
SW16 1K **155**
Oak Hill Way NW3 4K **63**
(not continuous)
Oak Hill Woods Nature Reserve 6J **21**
Oak Ho. *E14 2E 104*
(off Stewart St.)
N2 2B **46**
RM7: Rom 5K **55**
TW9: Kew 1H **115**
W10 4G 81
(off Sycamore Wlk.)
Oakhouse Rd. DA6: Bex 5G **127**
Oakhurst Av. DA7: Bex 7E **108**
EN4: E Barn 7H **21**
Oakhurst Cl. BR7: Chst 1D **160**
E17 4G **51**
IG6: Ilf 1G **53**
KT2: King T 6F **133**
TW11: Tedd 5J **131**
Oakhurst Ct. *E17 4G 51*
(off Woodford New Rd.)
Oakhurst Gdns. DA7: Bex 7E **108**
E4 1C **36**
E17 4G **51**
Oakhurst Gro. SE22 4G **121**
Oakhurst Rd. KT19: Ewe 6J **163**
Oakington Av. HA2: Harr 7E **40**
HA9: Wemb 3F **61**
UB3: Harl 4F **93**
Oakington Cl. TW16: Sun 2A **148**
Oakington Ct. EN2: Enf 2G **23**
Oakington Dr. TW16: Sun 2A **148**
Oakington Mnr. Dr. HA9: Wemb 5G **61**
Oakington Rd. W9 4J **81**
Oakington Way N8 7J **47**
Oakland Pl. IG9: Buck H 2D **36**
Oakland Quay E14 3D **104**
Oakland Rd. E15 4F **69**
Oaklands BR3: Beck 1D **158**
N21 2E **32**
W13 5A **78**
Oaklands Av. BR4: W W'ck 3D **170**
CR7: Thor H 4A **156**
DA15: Sidc 7K **125**
KT10: Esh 7H **149**
N9 6C **24**
TW7: Isle 6K **95**
Oaklands Cl. BR5: Pet W 6J **161**
DA6: Bex 5F **127**
HA0: Wemb 5D **60**
KT9: Chess 4C **162**
Oaklands Ct. HA0: Wemb 5D **60**
NW10 1A 80
(off Nicoll Rd.)
SE20 7J 139
(off Chestnut Gro.)
Oaklands Dr. TW2: Whitt 7G **113**
Oaklands Est. SW4 6G **119**
Oaklands Gro. W12 1C **98**
Oaklands M. *NW2 4F 63*
(off Oaklands Rd.)
Oaklands Pk. Av. IG1: Ilf 2G **71**
Oaklands Pas. *NW2 4F 63*
(off Oaklands Rd.)
Oaklands Pl. SW4 4G **119**
Oaklands Rd. BR1: Brom 7G **141**
DA6: Bex 4F **127**
N20 7C **20**
NW2 4F **63**
SW14 3K **115**
W7 2K **95**
(not continuous)
W13 2K **95**
Oaklands Way
SM6: Wall 7H **167**
Oakland Way KT19: Ewe 6A **164**
Oak La. E14 7B **86**
IG8: Wfd G 4C **36**
N2 2B **46**
N11 6C **32**
TW1: Twick 7A **114**
TW7: Isle 4J **113**
Oakleafe Gdns. IG6: Ilf 3F **53**
Oaklea Lodge IG3: Ilf 3A **72**
Oaklea Pas. KT1: King T 3D **150**
Oakleigh Av. HA8: Edg 2H **43**
KT6: Surb 1G **163**
N20 2G **31**
Oakleigh Cl. N20 3J **31**
Oakleigh Ct. EN4: E Barn 6H **21**
HA8: Edg 2J **43**
N1 1E **8**
UB1: S'hall 1D **94**
Oakleigh Cres. N20 2H **31**
Oakleigh Gdns. BR6: Orp 4J **173**
HA8: Edg 5A **28**
N20 1F **31**
Oakleigh M. N20 1F **31**
OAKLEIGH PARK 1F 31
Oakleigh Pk. Av. BR7: Chst 1E **160**
Oakleigh Pk. Nth. N20 1G **31**
Oakleigh Pk. Sth. N20 7H **21**
Oakleigh Rd. UB10: Hil 7E **56**
Oakleigh Rd. Nth. N20 2G **31**
Oakleigh Rd. Sth. N11 3K **31**
Oakleigh Way CR4: Mitc 1F **155**
KT6: Surb 1G **163**
Oakley Av. CR0: Bedd 4K **167**
IG11: Bark 7K **71**
W5 7G **79**
Oakley Cl. E4 3K **35**
E6 6C **88**
TW7: Isle 1H **113**
W7 7J **77**
Oakley Ct. CR4: Mitc 7E **154**
Oakley Cres. EC1 2B **84**
Oakley Dr. BR2: Brom 3C **172**
SE9 1H **143**
SE13 6F **123**
Oakley Gdns. N8 5K **47**
SW3 7D **16** (6C **100**)
Oakley Grange HA1: Harr 2H **59**
Oakley Ho. *SE11 4J 19*
(off Hotspur St.)
SW1 2F **17** (4D **100**)
W5 7G **79**
Oakley Pk. DA5: Bexl 7C **126**
Oakley Pl. SE1 5F **103**
Oakley Rd. BR2: Brom 3C **172**
HA1: Harr 6J **41**
N1 7D **66**
SE25 5H **157**
Oakley Sq. NW1 2G **83**
Oakley St. SW3 7C **16** (6C **100**)
Oakley Studios *SW3 7C 16*
(off Up. Cheyne Row)
Oakley Wlk. W6 6F **99**
Oakley Yd. E2 3K **9** (4F **85**)
Oak Lock M. W4 5A **98**
Oak Lodge E11 6J **51**
SM1: Sutt 4A **166**
TW16: Sun 7H 129
(off Forest Dr.)
W8 3K 99
(off Chantry Sq.)
Oak Lodge Cl. HA7: Stan 5H **27**
Oak Lodge Dr. BR4: W W'ck 7D **158**
Oaklodge Way NW7 5G **29**
Oakman Ho. SW19 1F **135**
Oakmead Av. BR2: Hayes 6J **159**
Oakmead Ct. HA7: Stan 4H **27**
Oakmeade HA5: Hat E 6A **26**
Oakmead Gdns. HA8: Edg 4E **28**
Oakmead Pl. CR4: Mitc 1C **154**
Oakmead Rd. CR0: C'don 6H **155**
SW12 1E **136**
Oakmede EN5: Barn 4A **20**
Oakmere Rd. SE2 6A **108**
Oakmont Pl. BR6: Orp 1H **173**
Oak Pk. Gdns. SW19 1F **135**
Oak Pk. M. N16 3F **67**
Oak Pl. SW18 5K **117**
Oakridge Dr. N2 3B **46**
Oakridge La. BR1: Brom 5F **141**
Oakridge Rd.
BR1: Brom 4F **141**
Oak Ri. IG9: Buck H 3G **37**
Oak Rd. BR6: Chels 7K **173**
DA8: Erith 7J **109**
KT3: N Mald 2K **151**
W5 7D **78**
Oak Row SW16 2G **155**
Oaks, The BR2: Brom 6E **160**
EN2: Enf 3G **23**
HA4: Ruis 7F **39**
IG8: Wfd G 6B **36**
N12 4E **30**
NW6 7F 63
(off Brondesbury Pk.)
NW10 7D **62**
SE18 5G **107**
SM4: Mord 4G **153**
TW13: Felt 2B **130**
UB4: Hayes 2E **74**
Oaks Av. KT4: Wor Pk 3D **164**
RM5: Col R 2J **55**
SE19 5E **138**
TW13: Felt 2C **130**
Oaks Cvn. Pk., The KT9: Chess 3C **162**
Oaksford Av. SE26 3H **139**
Oaks Gro. E4 2B **36**
Oakshade Rd. BR1: Brom 4F **141**
Oakshaw Rd. SW18 7K **117**
Oakshott Ct. NW1 1C **6** (2H **83**)
(not continuous)
Oakside Ct. IG6: Ilf 2H **53**
Oakside Ter. NW10 3K **61**
Oaks La. CR0: C'don 3H **169**
IG2: Ilf 5J **53**
Oaks Pavilion M. SE19 5E **138**
Oak Sq. SW9 2K **119**
Oaks Rd. CR0: C'don 5H **169**
TW19: Stanw 5A **110**
Oaks Shop. Cen., The W3 1J **97**
Oak St. RM7: Rom 5J **55**
Oaks Way KT6: Surb 1D **162**
SM5: Cars 7D **166**
Oakthorpe Ct. N13 5H **33**
Oakthorpe Est. N13 5H **33**
Oakthorpe Rd. N13 5F **33**
Oaktree Av. N13 3G **33**
Oak Tree Cl. HA7: Stan 7H **27**
KT19: Ewe 6H **163**
W5 6C **78**
Oak Tree Ct. UB5: N'olt 2A **76**
W3 7H **79**
Oak Tree Dell NW9 5J **43**
Oak Tree Dr. N20 1E **30**
Oak Tree Gdns. BR1: Brom 5K **141**
Oaktree Gdns. SE9 3F **143**
Oaktree Gro. IG1: Ilf 5H **71**
Oak Tree Ho. *W9 4J 81*
(off Shirland Rd.)
Oak Tree M. NW2 6C **62**
Oak Tree Rd. NW8 2B **4** (3C **82**)
Oakview Apartments SM1: Sutt 4B **166**
Oakview Gdns. N2 4B **46**
Oakview Gro. CR0: C'don 1A **170**
Oakview Lodge *NW11 7H 45*
(off Beechcroft Av.)
Oakview Rd. SE6 5D **140**
Oak Village NW5 4E **64**
Oak Vs. *NW11 6H 45*
(off Hendon Pk. Row)
Oakville Ho. *SE16 2K 103*
(off Dominion Dr.)
Oak Wlk. *SM6: Wall 1E 166*
(off Helios Rd.)

Oak Way CR0: C'don 6K 157
N14 . . . . .7A 22
TW14: Felt 1G 129
W3 . . . . .1A 98
Oakway BR2: Brom 2F 159
SW20 . . . . .4E 152
Oakway Cl. DA5: Bexl 6E 126
Oakways SE9 . . . . .6F 125
OAKWOOD 4C 22
Oakwood SM6: Wall 7F 167
Oakwood Av. BR2: Brom 3K 159
BR3: Beck 2E 158
CR4: Mitc 2B 154
N14 .7C 22
UB1: S'hall 7E 76
Oakwood Bus. Pk. NW10 . . . . . .4K 79
Oakwood Cl. BR7: Chst 6D 142
IG8: Wfd G 6H 37
N14 .6B 22
SE13 . . . . .6F 123
Oakwood Ct. E6 . . . . .1C 88
HA1: Harr 6H 41
W14 .3H 99
Oakwood Cres. N21 . . . . .6D 22
UB6: G'frd 6A 60
Oakwood Dr. DA7: Bex 4J 127
HA8: Edg 6D 28
SE19 . . . . .6D 138
Oakwood Gdns. BR6: Farnb 2G 173
IG3: Ilf 2K 71
SM1: Sutt 2J 165
Oakwood Ho. E9 . . . . .6J 67
(off Frampton Pk. Rd.)
Oakwood La. W14 . . . . .3H 99
Oakwood Lodge N14 . . . . .6B 22
(off Avenue Rd.)
Oakwood Mans. W14 . . . . .3H 99
(off Oakwood Ct.)
Oakwood Pde. N14 . . . . .5B 22
Oakwood Pk. Rd. N14 . . . . .7C 22
Oakwood Pl. CR0: C'don 6A 156
Oakwood Rd. BR6: Farnb 2G 173
CR0: C'don 6A 156
HA5: Pinn 2K 39
NW11 . . . . .4J 45
SW20 . . . . .1C 152
Oakwood Vw. N14 . . . . .6C 22
Oakworth Rd. W10 . . . . .5E 80
Oarsman Pl. KT8: E Mos 4J 149
Oasis, The BR1: Brom 2A 160
Oasis Academy Sports Hall 1E 24
Oasis Sports Cen. 7E 6 (6J 83)
Oast Ct. E14 . . . . .7B 86
(off Newell St.)
Oast Lodge W4 . . . . .7A 98
(off Corney Reach Way)
Oates Cl. BR2: Brom 3F 159
Oatfield Ho. N15 . . . . .6E 48
(off Perry Ct.)
Oatfield Rd. BR6: Orp 1K 173
Oatland Ri. E17 . . . . .2A 50
Oatlands Dr. KT13: Weyb 7G 147
Oatlands Rd. EN3: Enf H 1D 24
Oat La. EC2 . . . . .7C 8 (6C 84)
Oatwell Ho. SW3 . . . . .4D 16
(off Cale St.)
Oban Cl. E13 . . . . .4A 88
Oban Ho. E14 . . . . .6F 87
(off Oban St.)
IG11: Bark 2H 89
Oban Rd. E13 . . . . .3A 88
SE25 . . . . .4D 156
Oban St. E14 . . . . .6F 87
Oberon Ct. E6 . . . . .7B 70
Oberon Ho. N1 . . . . .2E 9
(off Arden Est.)
Oberon Way TW17: Shep 3A 146
Oberstein Rd. SW11 . . . . .4B 118
Oborne Cl. SE24 . . . . .5B 120
O'Brien Ho. E2 . . . . .3K 85
(off Roman Rd.)

Observatory Gdns. W8 . . . . .2J 99
Observatory M. E14 . . . . .4F 105
Observatory Rd. SW7 . . .2A 16 (3B 100)
SW14 . . . . .4J 115
Occupation La. SE18 . . . . .1F 125
W5 . . . . .4D 96
Occupation Rd. KT19: Ewe 7K 163
SE17 . . . . .5C 102
W13 .2B 96
Ocean Est. E1 . . . . .5A 86
(Ben Jonson Rd.)
E1 . . . . .4K 85
(Ernest St.)
Oceanis Apartments E16 . . . . . . .7J 87
(off Seagull La.)
Ocean St. E1 . . . . .5K 85
Ocean Wharf E14 . . . . .2B 104
Ockbrook E1 . . . . .5J 85
(off Hannibal Rd.)
Ockendon M. N1 . . . . .6D 66
Ockendon Rd. N1 . . . . .6D 66
Ockham Bldg. SE16 . . . . .3F 103
(off Arts La.)
Ockham Dr. BR5: St P 7A 144
UB6: G'frd 7G 59
Ockley Ct. DA14: Sidc 3J 143
SM1: Sutt 4A 166
Ockley Rd. CR0: C'don 7K 155
SW16 . . . . .4J 137
Octagon, The SW10 . . . . .7K 99
(off Coleridge Gdns.)
Octagon Arc. EC2 . . . . . . .6G 9 (5E 84)
Octagon Ct. SE16 . . . . .1K 103
(off Rotherhithe St.)
Octavia Cl. CR4: Mitc 5C 154
Octavia Ho. SW1 . . . . .2C 18
(off Medway St.)
W10 .4G 81
Octavia M. W9 . . . . .4H 81
Octavia Rd. TW7: Isle 3J 113
Octavia St. SW11 . . . . .1C 118
Octavia Way SE28 . . . . .7B 90
Octavius St. SE8 . . . . .7C 104
October Pl. NW4 . . . . .3F 45
Odard Rd. KT8: W Mole 4E 148
Oddmark Ho. IG11: Bark 2H 89
Odelia Ct. E15 . . . . .7F 69
(off Biggerstaff Rd.)
Odell Cl. IG11: Bark 7K 71
Odell Ho. E14 . . . . .6C 86
(off New Festival Av.)
Odell Wlk. SE13 . . . . .3E 122
Odeon, The IG11: Bark 7H 71
Odeon Cinema
Barnet 5D 20
Beckenham 2C 158
Camden Town 1F 83
(off Parkway)
Covent Garden 6H 83
(off Shaftesbury Av.)
Edmonton 7E 24
Greenwich 4H 105
Holloway 3J 65
IMAX (BFI) 5J 13 (1A 102)
Kingston upon Thames 2E 150
(within The Rotunda Cen.)
Leicester Square 3D 12
(off Leicester Sq.)
Marble Arch 6D 82
(off Marble Arch)
Muswell Hill 4F 47
Panton Street 3D 12
(off Panton St.)
Richmond upon Thames -
Hill Street 5D 114
Red Lion Street 5D 114
South Woodford 2J 51
Streatham 3J 137
Surrey Quays 3K 103
Swiss Cottage 7B 64

Odeon Cinema
Tottenham Court Road 5H 83
(off Tottenham Ct. Rd.)
Uxbridge 7A 56
West End 3D 12
(off Leicester Sq.)
Whiteleys 6K 81
Wimbledon 6H 135
Odeon Ct. E16 . . . . .5J 87
NW10 . . . . .1A 80
(off St Albans Rd.)
Odeon Pde. SE9 . . . . .4C 124
(off Well Hall Rd.)
UB6: G'frd 6B 60
(off Allendale Rd.)
W3 . . . . .2G 97
(off Allendale Rd.)
Odessa Rd. E7 . . . . .3H 69
NW10 . . . . .2C 80
Odessa St. SE16 . . . . .2B 104
Odessa Wharf SE16 . . . . .3B 104
(off Odessa St.)
Odette Duval Ho. E1 . . . . .5J 85
(off Stepney Way)
Odger St. SW11 . . . . .2D 118
Odhams Wlk. WC2 . . . . . . .1F 13 (6J 83)
Odin Ho. SE5 . . . . .2C 120
O'Donnell Ct. WC1 . . . . . .3F 7 (4J 83)
O'Driscoll Ho. W12 . . . . .6D 80
Odyssey Bus. Pk. HA4: Ruis 5K 57
Offa's Mead E9 . . . . .4B 68
Offenbach Ho. E2 . . . . .2K 85
(off Mace St.)
Offenham Rd. SE9 . . . . .4D 142
SW9 . . . . .1A 120
Offers Ct. KT1: King T 3F 151
Offerton Rd. SW4 . . . . .3G 119
Offham Ho. SE17 . . . . .4E 102
(off Beckway St.)
Offham Slope N12 . . . . .5C 30
Offley Pl. TW7: Isle 2H 113
Offley Rd. SW9 . . . . .7A 102
Offord Cl. N17 . . . . .6B 34
Offord Rd. N1 . . . . .7K 65
Offord St. N1 . . . . .7K 65
Ogden Ho. TW13: Hanw 3C 130
Ogilby St. SE18 . . . . .4D 106
Ogilvie Ho. E1 . . . . .6K 85
(off Stepney C'way.)
Oglander Rd. SE15 . . . . .4F 121
Ogle St. W1 . . . . .5A 6 (5G 83)
Oglethorpe Rd. RM10: Dag 3F 73
O'Gorman Ho. SW10 . . . . .7A 100
(off King's Rd.)
O'Grady Ho. E17 . . . . .3D 50
Ohio Bldg. SE13 . . . . .1D 122
(off Deal's Gateway)
Ohio Rd. E13 . . . . .4H 87
Oil Mill La. W6 . . . . .5C 98
Okeburn Rd. SW17 . . . . .5E 136
Okehampton Cl. N12 . . . . .5G 31
Okehampton Cres. DA16: Well 1B 126
Okehampton Rd. NW10 . . . . .1E 80
Olaf Ct. W8 . . . . .2J 99
(off Kensington Chu. St.)
Olaf St. W11 . . . . .7F 81
Oldacre M. SW12 . . . . .7E 118
Old Aeroworks, The NW8 . . . . .4B 4
(off Hatton St.)
Old Bailey
Central Criminal Court
. . . . .7B 8 (6B 84)
Old Bailey EC4 . . . . . . .1B 14 (6B 84)
Old Barge Ho. All. SE1 . . . . .3K 13
Old Barn Cl. SM2: Cheam 7G 165
Old Barn Way DA7: Bex 3K 127
Old Barracks W8 . . . . .2K 99
Old Barrack Yd. SW1 . . . .7G 11 (2E 100)
(not continuous)
Old Barrowfield E15 . . . . .1G 87
Old Bellgate Pl. E14 . . . . .3C 104

Oldberry Rd. HA8: Edg 6E 28
Old Bethnal Grn. Rd. E2 . . . . .3G 85
OLD BEXLEY 7H 127
Old Bexley Bus. Pk. DA5: Bexl 7H 127
Old Bexley La. DA5: Bexl, Dart 2K 145
Old Billingsgate Mkt. EC3 . . . . . . .3F 15
Old Billingsgate Wlk. EC3 . .3G 15 (7E 84)
Old Bond St. W1 . . . . .3A 12 (7G 83)
Oldborough Rd. HA0: Wemb 3C 60
OLD BRENTFORD 7D 96
Old Brewer's Yd. WC2 . . . . .1E 12 (6J 83)
Old Brewery M. NW3 . . . . .4B 64
Old Bri. Cl. UB5: N'olt 2E 76
Old Bridge St. KT1: Hamp W 2D 150
Old Broad St. EC2 . . . . . . .7F 9 (6D 84)
Old Bromley Rd. BR1: Brom 5F 141
Old Brompton Rd. SW5 . . . . .5J 99
SW7 . . . . .4A 16 (5J 99)
Old Buildings WC2 . . . . .7J 7
Old Burlington St. W1 . . . . .2A 12 (7G 83)
Oldbury Ct. E9 . . . . .5A 68
(off Mabley St.)
Oldbury Ho. W2 . . . . .5K 81
(off Harrow Rd.)
Oldbury Pl. W1 . . . . .5H 5 (5E 82)
Oldbury Rd. EN1: Enf 2B 24
Old Canal M. SE15 . . . . .5F 103
(off Trafalgar Av.)
Old Castle St. E1 . . . . .7J 9 (6F 85)
Old Cavendish St. W1 . . . . .7J 5 (6F 83)
Old Change Ct. EC4 . . . . .1C 14
Old Chapel Pl. SW9 . . . . .2A 120
Old Charlton Rd. TW17: Shep 5E 146
Old Chelsea M. SW3 . . . . . .7C 16 (6C 100)
Old Chiswick Yd. W4 . . . . .6A 98
(off Pumping Sta. Rd.)
Old Church Ct. N11 . . . . .5A 32
Oldchurch Gdns. RM7: Rush G 7K 55
Old Church La. HA7: Stan 5G 27
NW9 .2K 61
UB6: G'frd 3A 78
Oldchurch Ri. RM7: Rush G 7K 55
Old Church Rd. E1 . . . . .6K 85
E4 . . . . .4H 35
Oldchurch Rd. RM7: Rush G 7K 55
Old Church St. SW3 . . . . . .6B 16 (5B 100)
Old Claygate La. KT10: Clay 6A 162
Old Clem Sq. SE18 . . . . .6E 106
(off Woolwich Comn.)
Old Coal Yd. SE28 . . . . .4H 107
Old College Ct. DA17: Belv 5H 109
Old Compton St. W1 . . . . . .2C 12 (7H 83)
Old Cople La. SE19 . . . . .5F 139
Old Cote Dr. TW5: Hest 6E 94
Old Ct. Ho. W8 . . . . .2K 99
(off Old Court Pl.)
Old Ct. Pl. W8 . . . . .2K 99
Old Courtyard, The BR1: Brom 1K 159
Old Curiosity Shop 7G 7
(off Portsmouth St.)
Old Dairy N15 . . . . .6E 48
Old Dairy Gro. UB2: S'hall 5E 94
Old Dairy M. NW5 . . . . .6F 65
SW4 .4J 119
(off Tintern St.)
SW12 . . . . .1E 136
Old Dairy Sq. N21 . . . . .7F 23
(off Wade Hill)
Old Deer Pk. 2C 114
Old Deer Pk. Gdns. TW9: Rich 3E 114
Old Devonshire Rd. SW12 . . . . . . .7F 119
Old Dock Cl. TW9: Kew 6G 97
Old Dover Rd. SE3 . . . . .7J 105
Oldegate Ho. E6 . . . . .7B 70
Old Farm Av. DA15: Sidc 1H 143
N14 . . . . .7B 22
Old Farm Cl. SW17 . . . . .2C 136
TW4: Houn 4D 112
Old Farm La. SW19 . . . . .5K 135
Old Farm Pas.
TW12: Hamp 1G 149

Old Farm Rd. N2 . . . . .1B **46**
TW12: Hamp 6D **130**
UB7: W Dray 2A **92**
Old Farm Rd. E. DA15: Sidc 2A **144**
Old Farm Rd. W. DA15: Sidc 2K **143**
Oldfield Cl. BR1: Brom 4D **160**
HA7: Stan 5F **27**
UB6: G'frd 5J **59**
Oldfield Ct. *KT5: Surb 4F* ***151***
(off Cranes Pk. Cres.)
Oldfield Farm Gdns. UB6: G'frd 1H **77**
Oldfield Gro. SE16 . . . . .4K **103**
Oldfield Ho. *W4 . . . . .5A* ***98***
(off Devonshire Rd.)
Oldfield La. Nth. UB6: G'frd 2H **77**
Oldfield La. Sth. UB6: G'frd 4G **77**
Oldfield M. N6 . . . . .7G **47**
Oldfield Rd. BR1: Brom 4D **160**
DA7: Bex 2E **126**
N16 . . . . .3E **66**
NW10 .7B **62**
SW19 . . . . .6G **135**
TW12: Hamp 1D **148**
W3 . . . . .2B **98**
Oldfields Cir. UB5: N'olt 6G **59**
Oldfields Rd. SM1: Sutt 3H **165**
Old Fire Station, The SE18 . . . . .7F **107**
Old Fish St. Hill *EC4 . . . . .2C* ***14***
(off Queen Victoria St.)
Old Fleet La. EC4 . . . . .7A **8** (6B **84**)
Old Fold Cl. EN5: Barn 1C **20**
Old Fold La. EN5: Barn 1C **20**
Old Fold Manor Golf Course 1B **20**
Old Fold Vw. EN5: Barn 3A **20**
OLD FORD .1B **86**
OLD FORD .1C **86**
Old Ford Rd. E2 . . . . .3J **85**
E3 . . . . .2A **86**
Old Ford Trading Cen. *E3 . . . . .1C* ***86***
(off Maverton Rd.)
Old Forge Cl. HA7: Stan 4F **27**
Old Forge Cres. TW17: Shep 6D **146**
Old Forge M. W12 . . . . .2D **98**
Old Forge Rd. EN1: Enf 1A **24**
N19 . . . . .2H **65**
Old Forge Way DA14: Sidc 4B **144**
Old Gloucester St. WC1 . . . . .5F **7** (5J **83**)
Old Goods Yd., The W2 . . . . .5A **82**
Old Hall Cl. HA5: Pinn 1C **40**
Old Hall Dr. HA5: Pinn 1C **40**
Oldham Ter. W3 . . . . .1J **97**
(not continuous)
Old Hatch Mnr. HA4: Ruis 7H **39**
Old Highwayman Pl. SW15 . . . . .1D **134**
Old Hill BR6: Downe 6H **173**
BR7: Chst 1E **160**
Oldhill St. N16 . . . . .1G **67**
Old Homesdale Rd. BR2: Brom 4A **160**
Old Hospital Cl. SW12 . . . . .1D **136**
Old Ho. Cl. SW19 . . . . .5G **135**
Old Ho. Gdns. TW1: Twick 6C **114**
Old Howlett's La. HA4: Ruis 6F **39**
OLD ISLEWORTH 3B **114**
Old Jamaica Bus. Est.
SE16 . . . . .7K **15** (3F **103**)
Old Jamaica Rd. SE16 . . . . . .7K **15** (3G **103**)
Old James St. SE15 . . . . .3H **121**
Old Jewry EC2 . . . . .1E **14** (6D **84**)
Old Kenton La. NW9 . . . . .5H **43**
Old Kent Rd. SE1 . . . . .4E **102**
SE15 . . . . .4E **102**
Old Kingston Rd. KT4: Wor Pk 2J **163**
Old Laundry, The BR7: Chst 1G **161**
Old Library Ct. HA4: Ruis 2J **57**
Old Library Ho. *E3 . . . . .2A* ***86***
(off Roman Rd.)
Old Lodge Pl. TW1: Twick 6B **114**
Old Lodge Way HA7: Stan 5F **27**
Old London Rd. DA14: Sidc, Swan . . .7G **145**
KT2: King T 2E **150**
Old Lyonian Sports Club 5G **41**
Old Maidstone Rd. DA14: Sidc 7F **145**
OLD MALDEN 1A **164**
Old Malden La. KT4: Wor Pk 2K **163**
Old Mnr. Ct. NW8 . . . . .2A **82**
Old Mnr. Dr. TW7: Isle 6G **113**
Old Mnr. Ho. M. TW17: Shep 3C **146**
Old Mnr. Rd. UB2: S'hall 4B **94**
Old Mnr. Way BR7: Chst 5D **142**
DA7: Bex 2K **127**
Old Manor Yd. SW5 . . . . .4K **99**
Old Mkt. Ct. SM1: Sutt 4K **165**
Old Mkt. Sq. E2 . . . . .1J **9** (3F **85**)
Old Marylebone Rd. NW1 . . . . . .6D **4** (5C **82**)
Oldmead Ho. RM10: Dag 6H **73**
Old M. HA1: Harr 5J **41**
Old Mill Ct. E18 . . . . .3A **52**
Old Mill Pl. RM7: Rom 6K **55**
Old Mill Rd. SE18 . . . . .6H **107**
Old Mitre Ct. EC4 . . . . .1K **13** (6A **84**)
Old Montague St. E1 . . . . .6K **9** (5G **85**)
Old Nichol St. E2 . . . . .3J **9** (4F **85**)
Old North St. WC1 . . . . .5G **7**
Old Nursery Ct. *E2 . . . . .2F* ***85***
(off Dawson St.)
Old Nursery Pl. TW15: Ashf 5D **128**
Old Oak Cl. KT9: Chess 4F **163**
OLD OAK COMMON 5A **80**
Old Oak Comn. La. NW10 . . . . .5A **80**
W3 . . . . .5A **80**
Old Oak La. NW10 . . . . .3A **80**
Old Oak Rd. W3 . . . . .7B **80**
Old Operating Theatre Mus. & Herb Garret
. . . . .5F **15**
Old Orchard TW16: Sun 2A **148**
Old Orchard, The NW3 . . . . .4D **64**
Old Orchard Cl. EN4: Had W 1G **21**
UB8: Hil 6C **74**
Old Palace La. TW9: Rich 5C **114**
Old Palace Rd. CR0: C'don 3B **168**
Old Palace Ter. TW9: Rich 5D **114**
Old Palace Yd. SW1 . . . . .1E **18** (3J **101**)
TW9: Rich 5C **114**
Old Paradise St. SE11 . . . . . .3G **19** (4K **101**)
Old Pk. Av. EN2: Enf 4H **23**
SW12 .6E **118**
Old Pk. Gro. EN2: Enf 4H **23**
Old Pk. La. W1 . . . . .5J **11** (1F **101**)
Old Pk. M. TW5: Hest 7D **94**
Old Pk. Ridings N21 . . . . .6G **23**
Old Pk. Rd. EN2: Enf 3G **23**
N13 . . . . .4E **32**
SE2 . . . . .5A **108**
Old Pk. Rd. Sth. EN2: Enf 4G **23**
Old Pk. Vw. EN2: Enf 3F **23**
Old Pearson St. SE10 . . . . .7D **104**
Old Perry St. BR7: Chst 6J **143**
Old Police Station, The SW17 . . . . . . .2D **136**
Old Police Station M. SE20 . . . . .7K **139**
Old Post Office La. SE3 . . . . .3K **123**
Old Post Office Wlk. *KT6: Surb 6D* ***150***
(off Victoria Rd.)
Old Pound Cl. TW7: Isle 1A **114**
Old Priory UB9: Hare 7D **38**
Old Pye St. SW1 . . . . .1C **18** (3H **101**)
Old Pye St. Est. *SW1 . . . . .2C* ***18***
(off Old Pye St.)
Old Quebec St. W1 . . . . .1F **11** (6D **82**)
(not continuous)
Old Queen St. SW1 . . . . .7D **12** (2H **101**)
Old Railway Wlk. *SE16 . . . . .2J* ***103***
(off Brunel Rd.)
Old Rectory Gdns. HA8: Edg 6B **28**
Old Redding HA3: Hrw W 5A **26**
Old Red Lion Theatre *1K* ***7***
(off St John St.)
Oldridge Rd. SW12 . . . . .7E **118**
Old Rd. DA1: Cray 5K **127**
EN3: Enf H 1D **24**
SE13 . . . . .4G **123**
Old Rope Wlk. TW16: Sun 3K **147**
Old Royal Free Pl. N1 . . . . .1A **84**
Old Royal Free Sq. N1 . . . . .1A **84**
Old Royal Naval College 5F **105**
Old Ruislip Rd. UB5: N'olt 2A **76**
Old School, The *WC1 . . . . .5H* ***7***
(off Princeton St.)
Old School Cl. BR3: Beck 2K **157**
SE10 .3G **105**
SW19 .2J **153**
Old School Ct. N17 . . . . .3F **49**
Old School Cres. E7 . . . . .6J **69**
Old School Pl. CR0: Wadd 4A **168**
Old School Rd. UB8: Hil 4B **74**
Old Schools La. KT17: Ewe 7B **164**
Old School Sq. *E14 . . . . .6C* ***86***
(off Pelling St.)
KT7: T Ditt 6K **149**
Old School Ter. SM3: Cheam 7F **165**
Old Seacoal La. EC4 . . . . .7A **8** (6B **84**)
Old Slade La. SL0: Rich P 1A **174**
SL3: Coln 1A **174**
Old Sth. Cl. HA5: Pinn 1B **40**
Old Sth. Lambeth Rd. SW8 . . . . .7J **101**
Old Speech Room Gallery 1J **59**
Old Spitalfields Market 5J **9** (5F **85**)
Old Sq. WC2 . . . . .7J **7** (6K **83**)
Old Stable M. N5 . . . . .3C **66**
Old Stable Row *SE18 . . . . .4E* ***106***
(off Woolwich New Rd.)
Old Stables Ct. *SE5 . . . . .1C* ***120***
(off Camberwell New Rd.)
Old Station Gdns. *TW11: Tedd 6A* ***132***
(off Victoria Rd.)
Old Station Ho. SE17 . . . . .5C **102**
Old Station Pas. *TW9: Rich 4D* ***114***
(off Little Green)
Old Station Rd. UB3: Harl 3H **93**
Old Station Way *SW4 . . . . .3H* ***119***
(off Voltaire Rd.)
Old Station Yd., The E17 . . . . .4E **50**
Oldstead Rd. BR1: Brom 4E **140**
Old Stockley Rd. UB7: W Dray 2D **92**
OLD STREET 4D **84**
Old St. E13 . . . . .2K **87**
EC1 . . . . .3C **8** (4C **84**)
Old Studio Cl. CR0: C'don 7D **156**
Old Sungate Cotts. RM5: Col R 1F **55**
Old Sun Wharf *E14 . . . . .7A* ***86***
(off Narrow St.)
Old Swan Wharf SW11 . . . . .1B **118**
Old Swan Yd. SM5: Cars 4D **166**
Old Theatre Ct. SE1 . . . . .4D **14**
Old Town CR0: C'don 3B **168**
SW4 . . . . .3G **119**
Old Town Hall Apartments SE16 . . . . .3F **103**
Old Tramyard SE18 . . . . .4J **107**
Old Twelve Cl. W7 . . . . .4J **77**
Old Vic Theatre, The 6K **13**
Old Watermen's Walk *EC3 . . . . .3F* ***15***
(off Lower Thames St.)
Old Willow Cl. E3 . . . . .3C **86**
Old Woolwich Rd. SE10 . . . . .6F **105**
Old York Rd. SW18 . . . . .5K **117**
Oleander Cl. BR6: Farnb 5H **173**
Oleander Ho. SE15 . . . . .5F **103**
O'Leary Sq. E1 . . . . .5J **85**
Olga St. E3 . . . . .2A **86**
Olinda Rd. N16 . . . . .6F **49**
Oliphant St. *E14 . . . . .7E* ***86***
(off Bullivant St.)
W10 . . . . .3F **81**
Olive Blythe Ho. *W10 . . . . .4G* ***81***
(off Ladbroke Gro.)
Olive Ct. *E5 . . . . .2J* ***67***
(off Woodmill Rd.)
N1 . . . . .1A ***84***
(off Liverpool Rd.)
Olive Gro. N15 . . . . .4C **48**
Olive Haines Lodge SW15 . . . . .5H **117**
Olive Ho. *EC1 .3K* ***7***
(off Bowling Grn. La.)
Oliver Av. SE25 . . . . .3F **157**
Oliver Bus. Pk. NW10 . . . . .2J **79**
Oliver Cl. W4 .6H **97**
Oliver Ct. SE18 . . . . .4G **107**
Oliver Gdns. E6 . . . . .5C **88**
Oliver Goldsmith Est. SE15 . . . . .1G **121**
Oliver Gro. SE25 . . . . .4F **157**
Oliver Ho. *SE14 . . . . .7B* ***104***
(off New Cross Rd.)
SE16 .2G ***103***
(off George Row)
SW8 . . . . .7J ***101***
(off Wyvil Rd.)
Oliver M. SE15 . . . . .2G **121**
Olive Rd. E13 .3A **88**
NW2 . . . . .4D **62**
SW19 .7A **136**
W5 . . . . .3D **96**
Oliver Rd. E10 . . . . .2D **68**
E17 . . . . .5E **50**
KT3: N Mald 2J **151**
NW10 . . . . .2J **79**
SM1: Sutt 4B **166**
Olivers Wharf *E1 . . . . .1H* ***103***
(off Wapping High St.)
Olivers Yd. EC1 . . . . .3F **9** (4D **84**)
Olive St. RM7: Rom 5K **55**
Olive Tree Ho. *SE15 . . . . .6J* ***103***
(off Sharratt St.)
Olivette St. SW15 . . . . .3F **117**
Olive Waite Ho. NW6 . . . . .7J **63**
Olivia Ct. *CR0: C'don 7C* ***156***
(off Whitehorse Rd.)
EN2: Enf 1H ***23***
(off Chase Side)
Olivia M. HA3: Hrw W 7D **26**
Olivier Theatre *4H* ***13***
(within National Theatre)
Ollerton Grn. E3 . . . . .1B **86**
Ollerton Rd. N11 . . . . .5C **32**
Olley Cl. SM6: Wall 7J **167**
Ollgar Cl. W12 . . . . .1B **98**
Olliffe St. E14 . . . . .3E **104**
Olmar St. SE1 . . . . .6G **103**
Olney Ho. *NW8 . . . . .3D* ***4***
(off Tresham Cres.)
Olney Rd. SE17 . . . . .6B **102**
(not continuous)
Olron Cres. DA6: Bex 5D **126**
Olven Rd. SE18 . . . . .6G **107**
Olveston Wlk. SM5: Cars 6B **154**
Olwen M. HA5: Pinn 2B **40**
Olyffe Av. DA16: Well 1A **126**
Olyffe Dr. BR3: Beck 1E **158**
Olympia 3G **99**
Olympia Ind. Est. N22 . . . . .3K **47**
Olympia M. W2 . . . . .7K **81**
Olympian Ct. *E3 . . . . .2C* ***86***
(off Wick La.)
E14 . . . . .4C ***104***
(off Homer Dr.)
Olympian Way SE10 . . . . .1G **105**
(not continuous)
Olympia Way W14 . . . . .3G **99**
Olympic Ho. N16 . . . . .4F **67**
Olympic M. SW18 . . . . .5A **118**
Olympic Pk. Av. E20 . . . . .5D **68**
Olympic Sq. HA9: Wemb 3G **61**
Olympic Way HA9: Wemb 3G **61**
UB6: G'frd 1G **77**
Olympus Gro. N22 . . . . .1A **48**
Olympus Sq. E5 . . . . .3G **67**
O'Mahoney Ct. SW17 . . . . .3A **136**
Oman Av. NW2 . . . . .4E **62**
O'Meara St. SE1 . . . . .5D **14** (1C **102**)
Omega Cl. E14 . . . . .3D **104**
Omega Ct. RM7: Rom 5K **55**
Omega Ho. *SW10 . . . . .7A* ***100***
(off King's Rd.)
Omega Pl. N1 .1F **7**
Omega St. SE14 . . . . .1C **122**
Omega Works E3 . . . . .7C **68**

Ommaney Rd. SE14 . . . .1K 121
Omnibus Ho. N22 . . . .2A 48
(off Lordship La.)
Omnibus Way E17 . . . .2C 50
Omnium Ct. WC1 . . . .5G 7
(off Princeton St.)
Ondine Rd. SE15 . . . .4F 121
Onedin Ct. E1 . . . .7G 85
(off Ensign St.)
Onega Ga. SE16 . . . .3A 104
One Hyde Pk. SW1 . . . .7E 10 (2D 100)
O'Neill Ho. NW8 . . . .1D 82
(off Cochrane St.)
O'Neill Path SE18 . . . .4E 106
One New Change EC4 . . . .1C 14 (6C 84)
One Owen St. EC1 . . . .1A 8
(off Goswell St.)
One The Elephant SE1 . . . .4B 102
(off Brook Dr.)
One Tree Cl. SE23 . . . .5J 121
One Tree Hill Local Nature Reserve
. . . .6J 121
Ongar Cl. RM6: Chad H 5C 54
Ongar Rd. SW6 . . . .6J 99
Onra Rd. E17 . . . .7C 50
Onslow Av. TW10: Rich 5E 114
Onslow Cl. E4 . . . .2K 35
　KT7: T Ditt 7J 149
　W10 . . . .3H 81
Onslow Ct. SW10 . . . .6A 16
(off Montpelier Rd.)
Onslow Cres. BR7: Chst 1F 161
　SW7 . . . .4B 16 (4B 100)
Onslow Dr. DA14: Sidc 2D 144
Onslow Gdns. E18 . . . .3K 51
　KT7: T Ditt 7J 149
　N10 . . . .5F 47
　N21 . . . .5F 23
　SM6: Wall 6G 167
　SW7 . . . .4A 16 (4B 100)
Onslow Ho. KT2: King T 1F 151
(off Acre Rd.)
Onslow M. E. SW7 . . . .4A 16 (4B 100)
Onslow M. W. SW7 . . . .4A 16 (4B 100)
Onslow Pde. N14 . . . .1A 32
Onslow Rd. CR0: C'don 7K 155
　KT3: N Mald 4C 152
　TW10: Rich 5E 114
Onslow Sq. SW7 . . . .3B 16 (4B 100)
Onslow St. EC1 . . . .4K 7 (4A 84)
Onslow Way KT7: T Ditt 7J 149
Ontario Point SE16 . . . .2J 103
(off Surrey Quays Rd.)
Ontario St. SE1 . . . .3B 102
Ontario Twr. E14 . . . .7F 87
Ontario Way E14 . . . .7C 86
(not continuous)
Onyx M. E15 . . . .6H 69
Opal Apartments W2 . . . .6J 81
(off Hereford Rd.)
Opal Cl. E16 . . . .6B 88
Opal Ct. E15 . . . .1E 86
Opal M. IG1: Ilf 2F 71
　NW6 . . . .1H 81
Opal St. SE11 . . . .5K 19 (5B 102)
Open Air Stage 1C 64
Openshaw Rd. SE2 . . . .4B 108
Openview SW18 . . . .1A 136
Opera Ct. N19 . . . .3H 65
(off Wedmore St.)
Ophelia Gdns. NW2 . . . .3G 63
Ophelia Ho. W6 . . . .5F 99
(off Fulham Pal. Rd.)
Ophir Ter. SE15 . . . .1G 121
Opie Ho. NW8 . . . .2C 82
(off Townshend Est.)
Opossum Way TW4: Houn 3A 112
Oppenheim Rd. SE13 . . . .2E 122
Oppidan Apartments NW6 . . . .7J 63
(off Netherwood St.)
Oppidans Rd. NW3 . . . .7D 64
Opulens Pl. HA6: Nwood 1E 38

Orange Ct. La. BR6: Downe 7E 172
Orange Gro. E11 . . . .3G 69
Orange Hill Rd. HA8: Edg 7D 28
Orange Pl. SE16 . . . .3J 103
Orangery, The TW10: Ham 2C 132
Orangery Gallery, The 2H 99
Orangery La. SE9 . . . .5D 124
Orange St. WC2 . . . .3D 12 (7H 83)
Orange Tree Ct. SE5 . . . .7E 102
(off Havil St.)
Orange Tree Theatre 4E 114
Orange Yd. W1 . . . .1D 12
Oransay Rd. N1 . . . .6C 66
Oratory La. SW3 . . . .5B 16 (5B 100)
Orbain Rd. SW6 . . . .7G 99
Orbel St. SW11 . . . .1C 118
Orbis Wharf SW11 . . . .3B 118
Orbit, The 7D 68
Orbital Cen. IG8: Wfd G 2B 52
Orb St. SE17 . . . .4D 102
Orchard, The KT17: Ewe 7B 164
　N14 . . . .5A 22
　N20 . . . .1E 30
　N21 . . . .6J 23
　NW11 . . . .5J 45
　SE3 . . . .2F 123
　TW3: Houn 2G 113
　W4 . . . .4K 97
　W5 . . . .5D 78
Orchard Av. CR0: C'don 2A 170
　CR4: Mitc 1E 166
　DA17: Belv 6E 108
　KT3: N Mald 2A 152
　KT7: T Ditt 1A 162
　N3 . . . .3J 45
　N14 . . . .6B 22
　N20 . . . .2G 31
　TW5: Hest 7C 94
　TW14: Felt 5F 111
　TW15: Ashf 6E 128
　UB1: S'hall 1D 94
Orchard Bldg. E14 . . . .6G 87
Orchard Bus. Cen. SE26 . . . .5B 140
Orchard Cl. DA7: Bex 1E 126
　E4 . . . .4H 35
　E11 . . . .4K 51
　HA0: Wemb 1E 78
　HA4: Ruis 7E 38
　HA8: Edg 6K 27
　KT6: Surb 1B 162
　KT12: Walt T 7K 147
　KT19: Ewe 6H 163
　N1 . . . .7C 66
　NW2 . . . .3C 62
　SE23 . . . .6J 121
　SW20 . . . .4E 152
　TW15: Ashf 6E 128
　UB5: N'olt 6G 59
　W10 . . . .5H 81
　WD23: B Hea 1C 26
Orchard Cotts. KT2: King T 1F 151
　UB3: Hayes 2G 93
Orchard Ct. E10 . . . .1D 68
　EN5: New Bar 3E 20
　HA8: Edg 5A 28
　KT4: Wor Pk 1C 164
　KT12: Walt T 7H 147
(off Bridge St.)
　N14 . . . .1A 22
　SE26 . . . .4B 140
　SM6: Wall 5F 167
　TW2: Twick 2H 131
　TW7: Isle 1H 113
　UB7: Lford 3D 174
　UB8: Uxb 2A 74
(off The Greenway)
　W1 . . . .7G 5
(off Fitzhardinge St.)
Orchard Cres. EN1: Enf 1A 24
　HA8: Edg 5D 28

Orchard Dr. HA8: Edg 5A 28
　SE3 . . . .2F 123
　TW17: Shep 3G 147
Orchard Gdns. KT9: Chess 4E 162
　SM1: Sutt 5J 165
Orchard Ga. KT10: Esh 7H 149
　NW9 . . . .4A 44
　UB6: G'frd 6B 60
Orchard Grn. BR6: Orp 2J 173
Orchard Gro. BR6: Orp 2K 173
　CR0: C'don 7A 158
　HA3: Kenton 5F 43
　HA8: Edg 1G 43
　SE20 . . . .7G 139
Orchard Hill DA1: Cray 5K 127
　SE13 . . . .2D 122
　SM5: Cars 5D 166
Orchard Ho. SE5 . . . .1C 120
(off County Gro.)
　SE16 . . . .3J 103
　SW6 . . . .7H 99
(off Varna Rd.)
　W12 . . . .1C 98
Orchard La. IG8: Wfd G 4F 37
　KT8: E Mos 6H 149
　SW20 . . . .1D 152
Orchardleigh Av. EN3: Enf H 2D 24
Orchard Mead Ho. NW2 . . . .2J 63
Orchardmede N21 . . . .6J 23
Orchard M. N1 . . . .7D 66
　N6 . . . .7F 47
　SW17 . . . .3A 136
Orchard Pl. BR2: Kes 7A 172
　E5 . . . .5H 67
　E14 . . . .7G 87
(not continuous)
　N17 . . . .7A 34
　W4 . . . .4A 98
Orchard Ri. CR0: C'don 1A 170
　HA5: Eastc 3H 39
　KT2: King T 1J 151
　TW10: Rich 4G 115
Orchard Ri. E. DA15: Sidc 5K 125
Orchard Ri. W. DA15: Sidc 5J 125
Orchard Rd. BR1: Brom 1A 160
　BR6: Farnb 5F 173
　CR4: Mitc 1E 166
　DA14: Sidc 4J 143
　DA16: Well 3B 126
　DA17: Belv 4G 109
　EN3: Pond E 5D 24
　EN5: Barn 4C 20
　KT1: King T 2E 150
　KT9: Chess 4E 162
　N6 . . . .7F 47
　RM7: Mawney 1H 55
　RM10: Dag 1G 91
　SE3 . . . .2G 123
　SE18 . . . .4H 107
　SM1: Sutt 5J 165
　TW1: Twick 5D 114
　TW4: Houn 5D 112
　TW8: Bford 6C 96
　TW9: Rich 3G 115
　TW12: Hamp 7D 130
　TW13: Felt 1J 129
　TW16: Sun 7K 129
　UB3: Hayes 7J 75
Orchardson Ho. NW8 . . . .4A 4
Orchardson St. NW8 . . . .4A 4 (4B 82)
Orchard Sq. SW1 . . . .5H 17 (5E 100)
　W14 . . . .5H 99
Orchard St. E17 . . . .4A 50
　W1 . . . .1G 11 (6E 82)
Orchard Studios W6 . . . .4F 99
(off Brook Grn.)
Orchard Ter. EN1: Enf 6B 24
　NW10 . . . .4B 62
Orchard Vs. DA14: Sidc 6C 144
Orchard Wlk. KT2: King T 1G 151
(off Gordon Rd.)

Orchard Way BR3: Beck 7C 158
(Monks Orchard Rd.)
　BR3: Beck 1A 170
(Orchard Av.)
　CR0: C'don 1A 170
　EN1: Enf 3K 23
　SM1: Sutt 4B 166
　TW15: Ashf 2B 128
Orchard Waye UB8: Uxb 2A 74
Orchard Wharf E14 . . . .7G 87
(off Orchard Pl.)
Orchestra Ct. HA8: Edg 7C 28
Orchid Cl. E6 . . . .5C 88
　KT9: Chess 7C 162
　SE13 . . . .5F 123
　UB1: S'hall 7C 76
Orchid Ct. HA9: Wemb 2E 60
Orchid Gdns. TW3: Houn 4D 112
Orchid Grange N14 . . . .7B 22
Orchid Rd. N14 . . . .7B 22
Orchid St. W12 . . . .7C 80
Orde NW9 . . . .1B 44
Orde Hall St. WC1 . . . .4G 7 (4K 83)
Ordell Ct. E3 . . . .2B 86
(off Ordell Rd.)
Ordell Rd. E3 . . . .2B 86
Ordnance Cl. TW13: Felt 2J 129
Ordnance Cres. SE10 . . . .2G 105
Ordnance Dock Pl. UB2: S'hall 4B 94
Ordnance Hill NW8 . . . .1B 82
Ordnance M. NW8 . . . .2B 82
Ordnance Rd. E16 . . . .5H 87
　SE18 . . . .6E 106
Oregano Cl. UB7: View 6A 74
Oregano Dr. E14 . . . .6F 87
Oregon Av. E12 . . . .4D 70
Oregon Bldg. SE13 . . . .1D 122
(off Deal's Gateway)
Oregon Cl. KT3: N Mald 4J 151
Oregon M. W5 . . . .5C 78
Oregon Sq. BR6: Orp 1H 173
Oreily St. SE1 . . . .4F 103
(off Willow Wlk.)
Orestes M. NW6 . . . .5J 63
Orford Ct. HA7: Stan 6H 27
　SE27 . . . .2B 138
Orford Gdns. TW1: Twick 2K 131
Orford Rd. E17 . . . .5C 50
　E18 . . . .3K 51
　SE6 . . . .3D 140
ORGAN CROSSROADS 7C 164
Organ La. E4 . . . .2K 35
Oriana Ho. E10 . . . .2D 68
(off Grange Pk. Rd.)
　E14 . . . .7B 86
(off Victory Pl.)
Oriel Cl. CR4: Mitc 4H 155
Oriel Ct. CR0: C'don 1D 168
　NW3 . . . .4A 64
Oriel Dr. SW13 . . . .6E 98
Oriel Gdns. IG5: Ilf 3D 52
Oriel Ho. NW6 . . . .1J 81
(off Priory Rd.)
　RM7: Rom 6K 55
Oriel M. E18 . . . .2J 51
Oriel Pl. NW3 . . . .4A 64
(off Heath St.)
Oriel Rd. E9 . . . .6K 67
Oriel Way UB5: N'olt 7F 59
Oriens M. E20 . . . .5E 68
Oriental Rd. E16 . . . .1B 106
Oriental St. E14 . . . .7C 86
(off Pennyfields)
Orient Ho. SW6 . . . .1A 118
(off Station Ct.)
Orient Ind. Pk. E10 . . . .2C 68
Orient St. SE11 . . . .4B 102
Orient Way E5 . . . .3K 67
　E10 . . . .1A 68
Orient Wharf E1 . . . .1H 103
(off Wapping High St.)

Origin Bus. Pk. NW10 . . . . .3G 79
Oriole Way SE28 . . . . .7B 90
Orion E14 . . . . .4C 104
　　　　　　　　　　　　　(off Crews St.)
Orion Bus. Cen. SE14 . . . . .5K 103
Orion Cen., The CR0: Bedd 2J 167
Orion Ho. E1 .4H 85
　　　　　　　　　　　　　(off Coventry St.)
Orion M. SM4: Mord 4J 153
Orion Pk. RM9: Dag 2F 91
Orion Rd. N11 . . . . .7K 31
Orissa Rd SE18 . . . . .5J 107
Orkney Ct. E1 .5A 86
　　　　　　　　　　　　　(off Ocean Est.)
Orkney Ho. N1 . . . . .1K 83
　　　　　　　　　　　　(off Bemerton Est.)
Orkney St. SW11 . . . . .2C 118
Orlando Rd. SW4 . . . . .3G 119
Orleans Ct. TW1: Twick 7B 114
Orleans Pk. School Sports Cen. 7B 114
Orleans Rd. SE19 . . . . .6D 138
　　TW1: Twick 7B 114
Orleston M. N7 . . . . .6A 66
Orleston Rd. N7 . . . . .6A 66
Orley Ct. HA1: Harr 4K 59
Orley Farm Rd. HA1: Harr 3J 59
Orlop St. SE10 . . . . .5G 105
Ormanton Rd. SE26 . . . . .4G 139
Orme Ct. W2 .7K 81
Orme Ct. M. W2 . . . . .7K 81
　　　　　　　　　　　　　(off Orme La.)
Orme Ho. E8 .1F 85
Orme La. W2 .7K 81
Ormeley Rd. SW12 . . . . .1F 137
Orme Rd. KT1: King T 2H 151
　　SM1: Sutt 6K 165
Ormerod Gdns. CR4: Mitc 2E 154
Ormesby Cl. SE28 . . . . .7D 90
Ormesby Way HA3: Kenton 6F 43
Orme Sq. W2 .7K 81
Ormiston Gro. W12 . . . . .1D 98
Ormiston Rd. SE10 . . . . .5J 105
Ormond Av. TW10: Rich 5D 114
　　TW12: Hamp 1F 149
Ormond Cl. WC1 . . . . .5F 7 (5J 83)
Ormond Cres. TW12: Hamp 1F 149
Ormond Dr. TW12: Hamp 7F 131
Ormonde Av. BR6: Farnb 2G 173
Ormonde Ct. NW8 . . . . .1D 82
　　　　　　　　　　　(off St Edmund's Cl.)
　　SW15 . . . . .4E 116
Ormonde Ga. SW3 . . . . .6F 17 (5D 100)
　　　　　　　　　　　　　(not continuous)
Ormonde Mans. WC1 . . . . .5F 7
　　　　　　　　　　　　(off Southampton Row)
Ormonde Pl. SW1 . . . . .4G 17 (4E 100)
Ormonde Ri. IG9: Buck H 1F 37
Ormonde Rd. SW14 . . . . .3J 115
Ormonde Ter. NW8 . . . . .1D 82
Ormond Ho. N16 . . . . .2D 66
Ormond M. WC1 . . . . .4F 7 (4J 83)
Ormond Rd. N19 . . . . .1J 65
　　TW10: Rich 5D 114
Ormond Yd. SW1 . . . . .4B 12 (1G 101)
Ormrod Ct. W11 . . . . .6G 81
　　　　　　　　　　　(off Westbourne Pk. Rd.)
Ormsby SM2: Sutt 7K 165
Ormsby Gdns. UB6: G'frd 2G 77
Ormsby Lodge W4 . . . . .3A 98
Ormsby Pl. N16 . . . . .3F 67
Ormsby Point SE18 . . . . .4F 107
　　　　　　　　　　　　　(off Vincent Rd.)
Ormsby St. E2 . . . . .2F 85
Ormside St. SE15 . . . . .6J 103
Ornan Rd. NW3 . . . . .5C 64
Orpen Ho. SW5 . . . . .4J 99
　　　　　　　　　　　　　(off Trebovir Rd.)
Orpen Wlk. N16 . . . . .3E 66
Orpheus Ho. W10 . . . . .4H 81
　　　　　　　　　　　　　(off Harrow Rd.)

Orpheus St. SE5 . . . . .1D 120
ORPINGTON .1K 173
Orpington Gdns. N18 . . . . .3K 33
Orpington Mans. N21 . . . . .1G 33
Orpington Rd. BR7: Chst 3J 161
　　N21 . . . . .1G 33
Orpwood Cl.
　　TW12: Hamp 6D 130
Orsett M. W2 .6K 81
　　　　　　　　　　　　　(not continuous)
Orsett St. SE11 . . . . .5H 19 (5K 101)
Orsett Ter. IG8: Wfd G 7F 37
　　W2 . . . . .6K 81
Orsman Rd. N1 . . . . .1E 84
Orton Gro. EN1: Enf 1B 24
Orton Pl. SW19 . . . . .7K 135
Orton St. E1 .1G 103
Orville Rd. SW11 . . . . .2B 118
Orwell Cl. RM13: Rain 5K 91
　　UB3: Hayes 7G 75
Orwell Ct. E8 .1G 85
　　　　　　　　　　　　　(off Pownall Rd.)
　　N5 . . . . .4C 66
　　SE13 . . . . .3D 122
　　SW17 . . . . .3B 136
　　　　　　　　　　　　(off Grosvenor Way)
Orwell Rd. E13 . . . . .2A 88
Osbaldeston Rd. N16 . . . . .2G 67
Osberton Rd. SE12 . . . . .5J 123
Osbert St. SW1 . . . . .4C 18 (4H 101)
Osborn Cl. E8 .1G 85
Osborne Av. TW19: Stanw 1A 128
Osborne Cl. BR3: Beck 4A 158
　　EN4: Cockf 3J 21
　　TW13: Hanw 5B 130
Osborne Ct. E10 . . . . .7D 50
　　HA2: Harr 4F 41
　　W5 . . . . .5E 78
Osborne Gdns. CR7: Thor H 2C 156
Osborne Gro. E17 . . . . .4B 50
Osborne Ho. E16 . . . . .1J 105
　　　　　　　　　　　　　(off Wesley Av.)
Osborne M. E17 . . . . .4B 50
Osborne Pl. SM1: Sutt 5B 166
Osborne Rd. CR7: Thor H 2C 156
　　DA17: Belv 5F 109
　　E7 . . . . .5K 69
　　E9 . . . . .6B 68
　　E10 . . . . .2D 68
　　EN3: Enf H 2F 25
　　IG9: Buck H 1E 36
　　KT2: King T 7E 132
　　KT12: Walt T 7J 147
　　N4 . . . . .1A 66
　　N13 . . . . .3F 33
　　NW2 . . . . .6D 62
　　RM9: Dag 5F 73
　　TW3: Houn 3D 112
　　UB1: S'hall 6G 77
　　W3 . . . . .3H 97
Osborne Sq. RM9: Dag 4F 73
Osborne Ter. SW17 . . . . .5D 136
　　　　　　　　　　　　　(off Church La.)
Osborne Way KT9: Chess 5F 163
Osborn Gdns. NW7 . . . . .7A 30
Osborn La. SE23 . . . . .7A 122
Osborn St. E1 . . . . .6K 9 (5F 85)
Osborn Ter. SE3 . . . . .4H 123
Osbourne Ho.
　　IG8: Wfd G 7K 37
　　TW2: Twick 2G 131
Oscar Ct. SE16 . . . . .2A 104
Oscar Faber Pl. N1 . . . . .7E 66
Oscar St. SE8 . . . . .2C 122
　　　　　　　　　　　　　(not continuous)
Oseney Cres. NW5 . . . . .5G 65
Osgood Av. BR6: Chels 5K 173
Osgood Gdns.
　　BR6: Chels 5K 173
OSIDGE 1A 32
Osidge La. N14 . . . . .1K 31

Osier Ct. E1 . . . . .4K 85
　　　　　　　　　　　　　(off Osier St.)
　　RM7: Rom 6K 55
　　TW8: Bford 6E 96
　　　　　　　　　　　　　(off Ealing Rd.)
Osier Cres. N10 . . . . .1D 46
Osier La. SE10 . . . . .3H 105
Osier M. W4 .6A 98
Osiers Ct. KT1: King T 1D 150
　　　　　　　　　　　　　(off Steadfast Rd.)
Osiers Rd. SW18 . . . . .4J 117
Osiers Twr. SW18 . . . . .4J 117
　　　　　　　　　　　　(off Enterprise Way)
Osier St. E1 . . . . .4J 85
Osier Way CR4: Mitc 5D 154
　　E10 . . . . .3D 68
Oslac Rd. SE6 . . . . .5D 140
Oslo Ct. NW8 . . . . .2C 82
　　　　　　　　　　　　(off Prince Albert Rd.)
Oslo Ho. E9 . . . . .6B 68
　　　　　　　　　　　　　(off Felstead St.)
　　SE5 . . . . .2C 120
　　　　　　　　　　　　　(off Carew St.)
Oslo Sq. SE16 . . . . .3A 104
Oslo Twr. SE8 . . . . .4A 104
　　　　　　　　　　　　　(off Naomi St.)
Osman Cl. N15 . . . . .6D 48
Osmani Youth Cen. 5G 85
Osman Rd. N9 . . . . .3B 34
　　W6 . . . . .3E 98
Osmington Ho. SW8 . . . . .7K 101
　　　　　　　　　　　　　(off Dorset Rd.)
Osmond Cl. HA2: Harr 2G 59
Osmond Gdns. SM6: Wall 5G 167
Osmunda Ct. E1 . . . . .6G 85
　　　　　　　　　　　　　(off Myrdle St.)
Osmund St. W12 . . . . .5B 80
Osnaburgh St. NW1 . . . . .4K 5 (4F 83)
　　　　　　　　　　　　　(Euston Rd.)
　　NW1 . . . . .2K 5
　　　　　　　　　　　　　(Robert St.)
Osnaburgh Ter. NW1 . . . . . . .3K 5 (4F 83)
Osney Ho. SE2 . . . . .2D 108
Osney Wlk. SM5: Cars 6B 154
Osprey NW9 .1B 44
Osprey Cl. BR2: Brom 1C 172
　　E6 . . . . .5C 88
　　E11 . . . . .4J 51
　　E17 . . . . .7F 35
　　SM1: Sutt 5H 165
　　UB7: W Dray 2A 92
Osprey Ct. BR3: Beck 7C 140
　　CR0: C'don 3C 168
　　　　　　　　　　　　　(off Innes Yd.)
　　E1 . . . . .3K 15
　　　　　　　　　　　　　(off Star Pl.)
Osprey Est. SE16 . . . . .4K 103
Osprey Ho. E14 . . . . .7A 86
　　　　　　　　　　　　　(off Victory Pl.)
　　SE1 . . . . .5H 103
　　　　　　　　　　　　　(off Lynton Rd.)
Osprey La. HA2: Harr 2F 59
Osprey M. EN3: Pond E 5D 24
Ospringe Cl. SE20 . . . . .7J 139
Ospringe Ct. SE9 . . . . .6H 125
Ospringe Ho. SE1 . . . . .6K 13
　　　　　　　　　　　　　(off Wootton St.)
Ospringe Rd. NW5 . . . . .4G 65
Osram Ct. W6 . . . . .3E 98
Osram Rd. HA9: Wemb 3D 60
Osric Path N1 . . . . .2E 84
Ossel Ct. SE10 . . . . .4G 105
Ossian M. N4 . . . . .7K 47
Ossian Rd. N4 . . . . .7K 47
OSSIE GARVIN RDBT. 7K 75
Ossington Bldgs. W1 . . . . . . .5G 5 (5E 82)
Ossington Cl. W2 . . . . .7J 81
Ossington St. W2 . . . . .7J 81
Ossory Rd. SE1 . . . . .6G 103
Ossulston St. NW1 . . . . .1D 6 (2H 83)
Ossulton Pl. N2 . . . . .3A 46

Ossulton Way N2 . . . . .4A 46
Ostade Rd. SW2 . . . . .7K 119
Ostell Cres. EN3: Enf L 1H 25
Ostend Pl. SE1 . . . . .4C 102
Osten M. SW7 . . . . .3K 99
OSTERLEY 7H 95
Osterley Av. TW7: Isle 7H 95
Osterley Cl. BR5: St P 1K 161
Osterley Ct. TW7: Isle 7H 95
　　UB5: N'olt 3A 76
　　　　　　　　　　　　　(off Canberra Dr.)
Osterley Cres. TW7: Isle 1J 113
Osterley Gdns. CR7: Thor H 2C 156
　　TW7: Isle 2G 95
Osterley Ho. E14 . . . . .6D 86
　　　　　　　　　　　　　(off Giraud St.)
Osterley La. TW7: Isle 4G 95
　　UB2: S'hall 5E 94
Osterley Lodge TW7: Isle 7J 95
　　　　　　　　　　　　　(off Church Rd.)
Osterley Pk. .6G 95
Osterley Pk. House 6G 95
Osterley Pk. Rd. UB2: S'hall 3D 94
Osterley Pk. Vw. Rd. W7 . . . . .2J 95
Osterley Rd. N16 . . . . .4E 66
　　TW7: Isle 7J 95
Osterley Sports & Athletics Cen. . . .7J 95
Osterley Sports Club 3G 95
Osterley Views UB2: S'hall 2H 95
Oster Ter. E17 . . . . .5K 49
Ostlers Dr. TW15: Ashf 5E 128
Ostliffe Rd. N13 . . . . .5H 33
Oswald Bldg. SW8 . . . . .6F 101
Oswald Rd. UB1: S'hall 1C 94
Oswald's Mead E9 . . . . .4E 68
Oswald St. E5 . . . . .3K 67
Oswald Ter. NW2 . . . . .3E 62
Oswald CR0: Sels 7B 170
　　　　　　　　　　　　　(not continuous)
Oswald Pl. N9 . . . . .2C 34
Osward SW17 . . . . .2D 136
Oswell Ho. E1 . . . . .1H 103
　　　　　　　　　　　　(off Farthing Flds.)
Oswin St. SE11 . . . . .4B 102
Oswyth Rd. SE5 . . . . .2E 120
Otford Cl. BR1: Brom 3E 160
　　DA5: Bexl 6H 127
　　SE20 . . . . .1J 157
Otford Cres. SE4 . . . . .6B 122
Otford Ho. SE1 . . . . .7F 15
　　　　　　　　　　　　　(off Staple St.)
　　SE15 . . . . .6J 103
　　　　　　　　　　　　　(off Lovelinch Cl.)
Othello Cl. SE11 . . . . .5K 19 (5B 102)
Otho Ct. TW8: Bford 7D 96
Otis St. E3 . . . . .3E 86
Otley App. IG2: Ilf 6F 53
Otley Dr. IG2: Ilf 5F 53
Otley Ho. N5 .3A 66
Otley Rd. E16 . . . . .6A 88
Otley Ter. E5 .3K 67
Ottawa Gdns. RM10: Dag 7K 73
Ottawa Ho. SE16 . . . . .3J 103
　　　　　　　　　　　　　(off Province Dr.)
　　UB4: Yead 3K 75
　　　　　　　　　　　　　(off Ayles Rd.)
Ottaway St. E5 . . . . .3G 67
Otterbourne Rd. CR0: C'don 2C 168
　　E4 . . . . .3A 36
Otterburn Gdns. TW7: Isle 7H 95
Otterburn Ho. SE5 . . . . .7C 102
　　　　　　　　　　　　　(off Sultan St.)
Otterburn St. SW17 . . . . .6D 136
Otter Cl. E15 .1E 86
Otterden Cl. BR6: Orp 3J 173
Otterden St. SE6 . . . . .4C 140
Otterden Ter. SE1 . . . . .4F 103
　　　　　　　　　　　　　(off Lynton Rd.)
Otter Dr. SM5: Cars 1D 166
Otterfield Rd. UB7: Yiew 7A 74
Otter Rd. UB6: G'frd 4G 77

Otter Way UB7: Yiew 1A 92
Ottley Dr. SE3 4A 124
Otto Cl. SE26 3H 139
Otto St. SE17 6B 102
Ott's Yard *N19* *4G 65*
(off Southcote Rd.)
Otway Gdns. WD23: Bush 1D 26
Oulton Cl. E5 2J 67
SE28 6C 90
Oulton Cres. IG11: Bark 5K 71
Oulton Rd. N15 5D 48
Ouseley Rd. SW12 1D 136
Outer Circ. NW1 1D 4, 1J 5 (2C 82)
Outgate Rd. NW10 7B 62
Outram Pl. N1 1J 83
Outram Rd. CR0: C'don 2F 169
E6 1C 88
N22 1H 47
Outwich St. EC3 7H 9
Outwood Ho. *SW2* *7K 119*
(off Deepdene Gdns.)
Oval, The 7H 19 (6K 101)
Oval, The DA15: Sidc 7A 126
E2 2H 85
Oval Ct. HA8: Edg 7D 28
Oval Ho. *CR0: C'don* *1E 168*
(off Oval Rd.)
Ovalhouse Theatre 6A 102
Oval Mans. SE11 7H 19 (6K 101)
Oval Pl. SW8 7K 101
Oval Rd. CR0: C'don 2D 168
NW1 1F 83
Oval Rd. Nth. RM10: Dag 1H 91
Oval Rd. Sth. RM10: Dag 2H 91
Oval Way SE11 6H 19 (5K 101)
Ovanna M. N1 6E 66
Overbrae BR3: Beck 6C 140
Overbrook Wlk. HA8: Edg 7B 28
(not continuous)
Overbury Av. BR3: Beck 3D 158
Overbury Rd. N15 6D 48
Overbury St. E5 4K 67
Overcliff Rd. SE13 3C 122
Overcourt Cl. DA15: Sidc 6B 126
Overdale Av. KT3: N Mald 2J 151
Overdale Rd. W5 3C 96
Overdown Rd. SE6 4C 140
Overhill Rd. SE22 7G 121
Overhill Way BR3: Beck 5F 159
Overlea Rd. E5 7G 49
Overmead DA15: Sidc 7H 125
Oversley Ho. *W2* *5J 81*
(off Alfred Rd.)
Overstand Cl. BR3: Beck 5C 158
Overstone Gdns. CR0: C'don 7B 158
Overstone Ho. *E14* *6C 86*
(off E. India Dock Rd.)
Overstone Rd. W6 3E 98
Overstrand Mans. SW11 1D 118
Overton Cl. NW10 6J 61
TW7: Isle 1K 113
Overton Ct. E11 7J 51
SM2: Sutt 7J 165
Overton Dr. E11 7J 51
RM6: Chad H 7C 54
Overton Ho. *SW15* *7B 116*
(off Tangley Gro.)
Overton Rd. E10 1A 68
N14 5D 22
SE2 3C 108
SM2: Sutt 6J 165
SW9 2A 120
Overton Rd. E. SE2 3D 108
Overton's Yd. CR0: C'don 3C 168
Overy Ho. SE1 7A 14 (2B 102)
Ovesdon Av. HA2: Harr 1D 58
Ovett Cl. SE19 6E 138
Ovex Cl. E14 2E 104
Ovington Ct. *SW3* *2D 16*
(off Brompton Rd.)
Ovington Gdns. SW3 2D 16 (3C 100)
Ovington M. SW3 2D 16
Ovington Sq. SW3 2D 16 (3C 100)
Ovington St. SW3 3D 16 (4C 100)
Owen Cl. CR0: C'don 6D 156
SE28 1C 108
TW16: Sun 1G 147
UB5: N'olt 6C 58
(Arnold Rd.)
UB5: N'olt 3K 75
(Attlee Rd.)
Owen Gdns. IG8: Wfd G 6H 37
Owen Ho. TW1: Twick 7B 114
TW14: Felt 7J 111
Owenite St. SE2 4B 108
Owen Mans. *W14* *6G 99*
(off Queen's Club Gdns.)
Owen Rd. N13 5H 33
UB4: Yead 3K 75
Owens M. E11 2G 69
Owen's Row EC1 1A 8 (3B 84)
Owen St. EC1 1A 8 (2B 84)
Owens Way SE23 7A 122
Owen Wlk. SE20 1G 157
Owen Way NW10 6J 61
Owgan Cl. SE5 7D 102
Oxberry Av. SW6 2G 117
Oxborough Ho. *SW18* *4A 118*
(off Eltringham St.)
Oxendon St. SW1 3C 12 (7H 83)
Oxenford St. SE15 3F 121
Oxenham Ho. *SE8* *6C 104*
(off Benbow St.)
Oxenholme *NW1* *1A 6*
(off Hampstead Rd.)
Oxenpark Av. HA9: Wemb 7E 42
Oxestall's Rd. SE8 5A 104
Oxford & Cambridge Mans. *NW1* *6D 4*
(off Old Marylebone Rd.)
Oxford Av. N14 1B 32
SW20 2G 153
TW5: Hest 5E 94
UB3: Harl 7H 93
Oxford Cir. W1 1A 12
Oxford Cir. Av. W1 1A 12 (6G 83)
Oxford Cl. CR4: Mitc 3G 155
N9 2C 34
TW15: Ashf 7E 128
Oxford Ct. EC4 2E 14
KT6: Surb *5E 150*
(off Avenue Elmers)
TW13: Hanw 4B 130
W3 6G 79
W4 5H 97
W7 *5K 77*
(off Copley Cl.)
W9 *5J 81*
(off Elmfield Way)
Oxford Cres. KT3: N Mald 6K 151
Oxford Dr. HA4: Ruis 2A 58
SE1 5G 15 (1E 102)
Oxford Gdns. N20 1G 31
N21 7H 23
W4 5G 97
W10 6E 80
Oxford Ga. W6 4F 99
Oxford Ho. *BR2: Brom* *6B 160*
(off Wells Vw. Dr.)
E3 *5B 86*
(off William Whiffin Sq.)
NW6 *2J 81*
(off Oxford Rd.)
RM8: Dag 4A 72
Oxford M. DA5: Bexl 7G 127
Oxford Pl. *NW10* *3K 61*
(off Press Rd.)
Oxford Rd. DA14: Sidc 5B 144
E15 6F 69
(not continuous)
EN3: Pond E 5C 24
HA1: Harr 6G 41
HA3: W'stone 3K 41
Oxford Rd. IG1: Ilf 5G 71
IG8: Wfd G 5G 37
N4 1A 66
N9 2C 34
NW6 2J 81
SE19 6D 138
SM5: Cars 6C 166
SM6: Wall 5G 167
SW15 4G 117
TW11: Tedd 5H 131
W5 7D 78
Oxford Rd. Nth. W4 5H 97
Oxford Rd. Sth. W4 5G 97
Oxford Row TW16: Sun 3A 148
Oxford Sq. W2 1D 10 (6C 82)
Oxford St. W1 1G 11 (6E 82)
Oxford Ter. *NW6* *2K 81*
(off Oxford Rd.)
Oxford Wlk. UB1: S'hall 1D 94
Oxford Way TW13: Hanw 4B 130
Oxgate Cen. NW2 2D 62
Oxgate Ct. NW2 2C 62
Oxgate Ct. Pde. NW2 2C 62
Oxgate Gdns. NW2 3D 62
Oxgate La. NW2 2D 62
Oxgate Pde. NW2 2C 62
Oxhawth Cres.
BR2: Brom 5E 160
Oxhey La. HA3: Hrw W 5A 26
HA5: Hat E 5A 26
Oxleas E6 6F 89
Oxleas Cl. DA16: Well 2H 125
Oxleay Rd. HA2: Harr 1E 58
Oxleigh Cl. KT3: N Mald 5A 152
Oxley Cl. SE1 5F 103
Oxley Sq. *E3* *4D 86*
(off Truman Wlk.)
Oxleys Rd. NW2 3D 62
Oxlip Cl. CR0: C'don 1K 169
Oxlow La. RM9: Dag 4F 73
RM10: Dag 4F 73
Oxonian St. SE22 4F 121
Oxo Tower Wharf SE1 3K 13 (7A 84)
Oxted Cl. CR4: Mitc 3B 154
Oxtoby Way SW16 1H 155
Oxygen, The E16 7J 87
OYO Bus. Units DA17: Belv 2J 109
RM9: Dag 4F 91
Oystercatcher Cl. E16 6K 87
Oyster Cl. EN5: Barn 6B 20
Oyster Ct. *SE17* *4C 102*
(off Crampton St.)
Oystergate Wlk. EC4 3E 14
Oyster M. E7 6B 70
Oyster Row E1 6J 85
Oyster Wharf SW11 2B 118
Ozolins Way E16 6J 87

P

Pablo Neruda Cl. SE24 4B 120
Pace Pl. E1 6H 85
Pacific Cl. TW14: Felt 1H 129
Pacific Ct. E1 5J 85
Pacific Ho. *E1* *4K 85*
(off Ernest St.)
Pacific M. SW9 4A 120
Pacific Rd. E16 6J 87
Pacific Wharf SE16 1K 103
Packenham Ho. *E2* *1K 9*
(off Wellington Row)
W10 *7F 81*
(off Shalfleet Dr.)
Packham Ct. KT4: Wor Pk 3E 164
Packington Rd. W3 3J 97
Packington Sq. N1 1C 84
(not continuous)
Packington St. N1 1B 84
Packmores Rd. SE9 5H 125
Packwell Pl. TW5: Hest 6A 94
Padbury *SE17* *5E 102*
(off Bagshot St.)
Padbury Cl. TW14: Bedf 1F 129
Padbury Ct. E2 2K 9 (3F 85)
Padbury Ho. *NW8* *3D 4*
(off Tresham Cres.)
Padbury Oaks UB7: Lford 4C 174
Padcroft Rd. UB7: Yiew 1A 92
Paddenswick Rd. W6 3C 98
PADDINGTON 7A 4 (6B 82)
Paddington Cl. UB4: Yead 4B 76
Paddington Ct. *W7* *5K 77*
(off Copley Cl.)
Paddington Grn. W2 5A 4 (5B 82)
Paddington Sports Club 4K 81
Paddington St. W1 5G 5 (5E 82)
Paddock, The N10 3E 46
NW9 5G 43
UB10: Ick 4D 56
Paddock Cl. BR6: Farnb 4F 173
KT4: Wor Pk 1A 164
SE3 2J 123
SE26 4K 139
UB5: N'olt 2E 76
Paddock Gdns. SE19 6E 138
Paddock Lodge *EN1: Enf* *5K 23*
(off Village Rd.)
Paddock Mobile Home Pk.
BR2: Kes 7C 172
Paddock Pas. *SE19* *6E 138*
(off Paddock Gdns.)
Paddock Rd. DA6: Bex 4E 126
HA4: Ruis 3B 58
NW2 3C 62
Paddocks, The CR0: Addtn 6C 170
EN4: Cockf 3J 21
HA9: Wemb 2H 61
W5 *3D 96*
(off Popes La.)
Paddocks Cl. HA2: Harr 4F 59
Paddocks Grn. NW9 1H 61
Paddock Way BR7: Chst 7H 143
SW15 7E 116
Padelford La. HA7: Stan 2F 27
Padfield Ct. HA9: Wemb 3F 61
Padfield Rd. SE5 3C 120
Padley Cl. KT9: Chess 5F 163
Padnall Ct. RM6: Chad H 3D 54
Padnall Rd. RM6: Chad H 3D 54
Padstone Ho. *E3* *3D 86*
(off Talwin St.)
Padstow Cl. BR6: Chels 4K 173
Padstow Ho. *E14* *7B 86*
(off Three Colt St.)
Padstow Rd. EN2: Enf 1G 23
Padstow Wlk. TW14: Felt 1H 129
Padua Rd. SE20 1J 157
Pagden St. SW8 1F 119
Pageant Av. NW9 1K 43
Pageant Cres. SE16 1A 104
Pageantmaster Ct. EC4 1A 14
Pageant Wlk. CR0: C'don 3E 168
Page Av. HA9: Wemb 3J 61
Page Cl. HA3: Kenton 6F 43
RM9: Dag 5E 72
TW12: Hamp 6C 130
Page Ct. NW7 7J 29
Page Cres. CR0: Wadd 5B 168
Page Grn. Rd. N15 5G 49
Page Grn. Ter. N15 5F 49
Page Heath La. BR1: Brom 3B 160
Page Heath Vs. BR1: Brom 3B 160
Page High *N22* *2A 48*
(off Lymington Av.)
Page Ho. *SE10* *6E 104*
(off Welland St.)
Pagehurst Rd. CR0: C'don 7H 157
Page Mdw. NW7 7J 29
Page M. SW11 2E 118
Page Rd. TW14: Bedf 6F 111
Pages Hill N10 2E 46

Pages La. N10 . . . . .2E 46
Page St. NW7 . . . . .1C 44
    SW1 . . . . .3D 18 (4H 101)
Page's Wlk. SE1 . . . . .4E 102
Pages Yd. W4 . . . . .6B 98
Paget Av. SM1: Sutt 3B 166
Paget Cl.
    TW12: Hamp H 4H 131
Paget Gdns. BR7: Chst 1F 161
Paget Ho. E2 . . . . .2J 85
                        (off Bishop's Way)
Paget La. TW7: Isle 3H 113
Paget Pl. KT2: King T 6J 133
    KT7: T Ditt 1A 162
Paget Ri. SE18 . . . . .6E 106
Paget Rd. IG1: Ilf 4F 71
    N16 . . . . .1D 66
    UB10: Hil 4E 74
Paget St. EC1 . . . . .1A 8 (3B 84)
Paget Ter. SE18 . . . . .6F 107
Pagham Ho. W10 . . . . .4E 80
                        (off Sutton Way)
Pagin Ho. N15 . . . . .5E 48
                        (off Braemar Rd.)
Pagitts Gro. EN4: Had W 1E 20
Pagnell St. SE14 . . . . .7B 104
Pagoda Av. TW9: Rich 3F 115
Pagoda Gdns. SE3 . . . . .2F 123
Pagoda Gro. SE27 . . . . .2C 138
Paignton Rd.
    HA4: Ruis 3J 57
    N15 . . . . .6E 48
Paines Cl. HA5: Pinn 3C 40
Paines La. HA5: Pinn 1C 40
Pain's Cl. CR4: Mitc 2F 155
Painsthorpe Rd. N16 . . . . .3E 66
Painted Hall
    Greenwich 6F 105
Painters M. SE16 . . . . .4G 103
Painters Rd. IG2: Ilf 3K 53
Paisley Rd. N22 . . . . .1B 48
    SM5: Cars 1B 166
Paisley Ter. SM5: Cars 7B 154
Pakefield M. SW2 . . . . .1K 137
Pakeman Ho. SE1 . . . . .6B 14
                        (off Surrey Row)
Pakeman St. N7 . . . . .3K 65
Pakenham Cl. SW12 . . . . .1E 136
Pakenham St. WC1 . . . . .2H 7 (3K 83)
Pakington Ho. SW9 . . . . .2J 119
                        (off Stockwell Gdns. Est.)
Palace Av. W8 . . . . .2K 99
Palace Bingo Club 4C 102
                        (within Elephant & Castle Shop. Cen.)
Palace Cl. E9 .6B 68
Palace Ct. BR1: Brom 1K 159
                        (off Palace Gro.)
    HA3: Kenton 6E 42
    NW3 . . . . .5K 63
    W2 . . . . .7K 81
                        (not continuous)
Palace Ct. Gdns. N10 . . . . .3G 47
Palace Exchange EN2: Enf 4J 23
Palace Gdns. IG9: Buck H 1G 37
Palace Gdns. M. W8 . . . . .1K 99
Palace Gdns. Shop. Cen. EN2: Enf 4J 23
Palace Gdns. Ter. W8 . . . . .1J 99
Palace Ga. W8 . . . . .2A 100
Palace Gates M. N8 . . . . .4J 47
                        (off The Campsbourne)
Palace Gates Rd. N22 . . . . .1H 47
Palace Grn. CR0: Sels 7B 170
    W8 . . . . .1K 99
Palace Gro. BR1: Brom 1K 159
    SE19 . . . . .7F 139
Palace Ice Rink, The 2H 47
Palace Mans.
    KT1: King T 4D 150
                        (off Palace Rd.)
    W14 . . . . .4G 99
                        (off Hammersmith Rd.)

Palace M. E17 . . . . .4B 50
    EN2: Enf 3J 23
    SW1 . . . . .4H 17
    SW6 . . . . .7H 99
Palace Pde. E17 . . . . .4B 50
Palace Pl. SW1 . . . . .1A 18 (3G 101)
Palace Pl. Mans. W8 . . . . .2K 99
                        (off Kensington Ct.)
Palace Rd. BR1: Brom 1K 159
    HA4: Ruis 4C 58
    KT1: King T 4D 150
    KT8: E Mos 3G 149
    N8 . . . . .5H 47
                        (not continuous)
    N11 . . . . .7D 32
    SE19 . . . . .7F 139
    SW2 . . . . .1K 137
Palace Sq. SE19 . . . . .7F 139
Palace St. SW1 . . . . .1A 18 (3G 101)
Palace Superbowl 4C 102
                        (off Elephant & Castle Shop. Cen.)
Palace Theatre
    Soho 1D 12
                        (off Shaftesbury Av.)
Palace Vw. BR1: Brom 3K 159
                        (not continuous)
    CR0: C'don 4B 170
    SE12 . . . . .2J 141
Palace Vw. Rd. E4 . . . . .5J 35
Palace Wharf W6 . . . . .7E 98
                        (off Rainville Rd.)
Palamos Rd. E10 . . . . .1C 68
Palatine Av. N16 . . . . .4E 66
Palatine Rd. N16 . . . . .4E 66
Palazzo Apartments N1 . . . . .7E 66
                        (off Ardleigh Rd.)
Palemead Cl. SW6 . . . . .1F 117
Palermo Rd. NW10 . . . . .2C 80
Palestine Gro. SW19 . . . . .1B 154
Palestra Ho. SE1 . . . . .5A 14
                        (off Blackfriars Rd.)
Palewell Comn. Dr. SW14 . . . . .5K 115
Palewell Pk. SW14 . . . . .5K 115
Palfrey Pl. SW8 . . . . .7K 101
Palgrave Av. UB1: S'hall 7E 76
Palgrave Ct. TW11: Hamp W 7C 132
Palgrave Gdns. NW1 . . . . . .3D 4 (4C 82)
Palgrave Ho. SE5 . . . . .7C 102
                        (off Wyndham Est.)
    TW2: Whitt 7G 113
Palgrave Rd. W12 . . . . .3B 98
Palissy St. E2 . . . . .2J 9 (3F 85)
                        (not continuous)
Palladino Ho. SW17 . . . . .5C 136
                        (off Laurel Cl.)
Palladio Cl. SW18 . . . . .6K 117
                        (off Mapleton Cres.)
Palladium Cl. E8 . . . . .7F 67
                        (off Queensbridge Rd.)
Pallant Ho. SE1 . . . . .3D 102
                        (off Tabard St.)
Pallant Way BR6: Farnb 3E 172
Pallet Way SE18 . . . . .1C 124
Palliser Ct. W14 . . . . .5G 99
                        (off Palliser Rd.)
Palliser Ho. E1 . . . . .4K 85
                        (off Ernest St.)
    SE10 . . . . .6F 105
                        (off Trafalgar Rd.)
Palliser Rd. W14 . . . . .5G 99
Pallister Ter. SW15 . . . . .3B 134
Pall Mall SW1 . . . . .5B 12 (1G 101)
Pall Mall E. SW1 . . . . .4D 12 (1H 101)
Pall Mall Pl. SW1 . . . . .5B 12
Palmadium Cl. N13 . . . . .3F 33
Palmar Cres. DA7: Bex 3G 127
Palmar Rd. DA7: Bex 2G 127
Palm Av. DA14: Sidc 6D 144
Palm Cl. E10 .3D 68
Palm Ct. SE15 . . . . .7F 103
                        (off Garnies Cl.)

Palmeira Rd. DA7: Bex 3D 126
Palmer Av. SM3: Cheam 4E 164
Palmer Cl. BR4: W W'ck 3F 171
    TW5: Hest 1E 112
    UB5: N'olt 6C 58
Palmer Cres. KT1: King T 3E 150
Palmer Dr. BR1: Brom 4F 161
Palmer Gdns. EN5: Barn 5A 20
Palmer Ho. SE14 . . . . .7K 103
                        (off Lubbock St.)
Palmer Pl. N7 . . . . .5A 66
Palmer Rd. E13 . . . . .4K 87
    RM8: Dag 1D 72
Palmer's Cl. N11 . . . . .5B 32
                        (off Palmer's Rd.)
PALMERS GREEN 3F 33
Palmers Gro. KT8: W Mole 4E 148
Palmers La. EN1: Enf 1C 24
    EN3: Enf H 1C 24
Palmers Pas. SW14 . . . . .3J 115
                        (off Little St Leonard's)
Palmer's Rd. E2 . . . . .2K 85
    N11 . . . . .5B 32
Palmers Rd. SW14 . . . . .3J 115
    SW16 . . . . .2K 155
Palmerston Cen. HA3: W'stone 3K 41
Palmerston Cl. E3 . . . . .2K 85
                        (off Old Ford Rd.)
    IG9: Buck H 1F 37
    KT6: Surb 7D 150
Palmerston Cres. N13 . . . . .5E 32
    SE18 . . . . .6G 107
Palmerston Gro. SW19 . . . . .7J 135
Palmerston Ho. SE1 . . . . .7J 13
                        (off Westminster Bri. Rd.)
    W8 . . . . .1J 99
                        (off Kensington Pl.)
Palmerston Mans. W14 . . . . .6G 99
                        (off Queen's Club Gdns.)
Palmerston Rd. BR6: Farnb 4G 173
    CR0: C'don 5D 156
    E7 . . . . .6K 69
    E17 . . . . .3B 50
    HA3: W'stone 3J 41
    IG9: Buck H 2E 36
    N22 . . . . .7E 32
    NW6 . . . . .7H 63
                        (not continuous)
    SM1: Sutt 5A 166
    SM5: Cars 4D 166
    SW14 . . . . .4J 115
    SW19 . . . . .7J 135
    TW2: Twick 6J 113
    TW3: Houn 1G 113
    W3 . . . . .3J 97
Palmerston Way SW8 . . . . .7F 101
Palmer St. SW1 . . . . .1C 18 (3H 101)
                        (not continuous)
Palmers Wharf KT1: King T 2D 150
                        (off Emms Pas.)
Palm Gro. W5 . . . . .3E 96
Palm Rd. RM7: Rom 5J 55
Palyn Ho. EC1 .2D 8
                        (off Radnor St.)
Pamela Ct. N12 . . . . .6E 30
Pamela Gdns. HA5: Eastc 5K 39
Pamela St. E8 .1F 85
Pamela Wlk. E8 . . . . .1G 85
                        (off Marlborough Av.)
Pampisford Rd. CR2: S Croy 7B 168
Pams Way KT19: Ewe 5K 163
Panama Ho. E1 . . . . .5K 85
                        (off Beaumont Sq.)
Pancras La. EC4 . . . . .1E 14 (6C 84)
Pancras Rd. N1 . . . . .1E 6 (2J 83)
    NW1 . . . . .2H 83
Pancras Sq. N1 . . . . .2J 83
Pancras Square Leisure Cen. 2J 83
Pancras Way E3 . . . . .2C 86
Pandangle Ho. E8 . . . . .1F 85
                        (off Kingsland Rd.)

Pandian Way NW1 . . . . .6H 65
Pandora Ct. E16 . . . . .5J 87
                        (off Robertson Rd.)
Pandora Rd. NW6 . . . . .6J 63
'Pan' (Epstein) 2D 100
                        (within Hyde Pk.)
Panfield M. IG2: Ilf 6E 52
Panfield Rd. SE2 . . . . .3A 108
Pangbourne NW1 . . . . .2A 6
                        (off Stanhope St.)
Pangbourne Av. W10 . . . . .5E 80
Pangbourne Dr. HA7: Stan 5J 27
Panhard Pl. UB1: S'hall 7F 77
Pank Av. EN5: New Bar 5F 21
Pankhurst Av. E16 . . . . .1K 105
Pankhurst Cl. SE14 . . . . .7K 103
    TW7: Isle 3K 113
Pankhurst Ho. W12 . . . . .6D 80
Pankhurst Rd. KT12: Walt T 7A 148
Panmuir Rd. SW20 . . . . .1D 152
Panmure Cl. N5 . . . . .4B 66
Panmure Ct. SE26 . . . . .3H 139
                        (off Osborne Rd.)
    UB1: S'hall 6G 77
Panmure Rd. SE26 . . . . .3H 139
Pannells Ct. TW5: Hest 6E 94
Panorama Ct. N6 . . . . .6G 47
Panoramic Twr. E14 . . . . .6D 86
                        (off Burcham St.)
Pan Peninsula Sq. E14 . . . . .2D 104
Pansy Gdns. W12 . . . . .7C 80
Panther Dr. NW10 . . . . .5K 61
Pantiles, The BR1: Brom 3C 160
    DA7: Bex 7F 109
    NW11 . . . . .4H 45
    WD23: B Hea 1C 26
Pantiles Cl. N13 . . . . .5G 33
Panton Cl. CR0: C'don 1B 168
Panton St. SW1 . . . . .3C 12 (7H 83)
Panyer All. EC1 . . . . .7C 8
                        (off Newgate St.)
Panyers Gdns. RM10: Dag 3H 73
Paper Bldgs. EC4 . . . . .2K 13
Papermill Cl. SM5: Cars 4E 166
Papermill Pl. E17 . . . . .2A 50
Paper Mill Wharf E14 . . . . .7A 86
Papillons Wlk. SE3 . . . . .2J 123
Papworth Gdns. N7 . . . . .5K 65
Papworth Way SW2 . . . . .7A 120
Papyrus Ho. N1 . . . . .1C 8
Parabola Cl. KT8: E Mos 4G 149
Parade, The CR0: C'don 6J 155
    KT2: King T 2E 150
                        (off London Rd.)
    KT4: Wor Pk 4B 164
    N4 . . . . .1A 66
    SE4 . . . . .2B 122
                        (off Up. Brockley Rd.)
    SE26 . . . . .3H 139
                        (off Wells Pk. Rd.)
    SM1: Sutt 3H 165
    SM5: Cars 5D 166
                        (off Beynon Rd.)
    SW11 . . . . .7D 100
    TW12: Hamp H 5H 131
    TW16: Sun 7H 129
    UB6: G'frd 5B 60
Parade Gdns. E4 . . . . .7J 35
Parade Ground Path SE18 . . . . .7D 106
Parade Mans. NW4 . . . . .5D 44
    SE4 . . . . .2B 138
Paradise Pas. N7 . . . . .5A 66
Paradise Path SE28 . . . . .1A 108
Paradise Pl. SE18 . . . . .4C 106
Paradise Rd. SW4 . . . . .2J 119
    TW9: Rich 5D 114
Paradise Row E2 . . . . .3H 85
Paradise St. SE16 . . . . .2H 103
Paradise Wlk. SW3 . . . . .7F 17 (6D 100)
Paragon TW8: Bford 5C 96
                        (off Boston Pk. Rd.)

Paragon, The SE3 2H **123**
Paragon Cl. E16 6J **87**
Paragon Gro. KT5: Surb 6F **151**
Paragon M. SE1 4D **102**
Paragon Pl. KT5: Surb 6F **151**
SE3 2H **123**
Paragon Rd. E9 6J **67**
Paramount Bldg. *EC1* *3A* ***8***
(off St John St.)
Paramount Ct. WC1 4B **6**
Parbury Ri. KT9: Chess 6E **162**
Parbury Rd. SE23 6A **122**
Parchmore Rd. CR7: Thor H 2B **156**
Parchmore Way CR7: Thor H 2B **156**
Pardoe Rd. E10 7D **50**
Pardoner Ho. *SE1* *3D* ***102***
(off Pardoner St.)
Pardoner St. SE1 7F **15** (3D **102**)
(not continuous)
Pardon St. EC1 3B **8** (4B **84**)
Parent Shop. Mall *E18* *2J* ***51***
(off Marlborough Rd.)
Parfett St. E1 5G **85**
(not continuous)
Parfitt Cl. NW3 1A **64**
Parfrey St. W6 6E **98**
Pargraves Ct. HA9: Wemb 2G **61**
Parham Dr. IG2: Ilf 6F **53**
Parham Way N10 2G **47**
Paris Corte *SE13* *3D* ***122***
(off Loampit Va.)
Paris Gdn. SE1 4A **14** (1B **102**)
Parish Ct. KT6: Surb 5E **150**
Parish Ga. Dr. DA15: Sidc 6J **125**
Parish La. SE20 6K **139**
Parish M. SE20 7K **139**
Paris Ho. *E2* *2H* ***85***
(off Old Bethnal Grn. Rd.)
Parish Wharf Pl. SE18 4C **106**
Parison Cl. TW9: Rich 3G **115**
Park, The DA14: Sidc 5A **144**
HA1: Harr 1J **59**
N6 6E **46**
NW11 1K **63**
SE23 1J **139**
SM5: Cars 5D **166**
W5 1D **96**
Park App. DA16: Well 4B **126**
SE16 3H **103**
Park Av. BR1: Brom 6H **141**
BR4: W W'ck 2E **170**
BR6: Chels 2K **173**
BR6: Farnb 3D **172**
CR4: Mitc 7F **137**
E6 1E **88**
E15 6G **69**
EN1: Enf 5J **23**
HA4: Ruis 6F **39**
IG1: Ilf 1E **70**
IG8: Wfd G 5E **36**
IG11: Bark 6G **71**
N3 1K **45**
N13 3F **33**
N18 4B **34**
N22 2J **47**
NW2 5D **62**
NW10 2F **79**
(Brent Cres., not continuous)
NW10 5D **62**
(Park Av. Nth.)
NW11 1K **63**
SM5: Cars 6E **166**
SW14 4K **115**
TW3: Houn 6F **113**
TW17: Shep 3G **147**
UB1: S'hall 2D **94**
Park Av. E. KT17: Ewe 6C **164**
Park Av. M. CR4: Mitc 7F **137**
Park Av. Nth. N8 3H **47**
NW10 5D **62**
Park Av. Rd. N17 7C **34**
Park Av. Sth. N8 4H **47**
Park Av. W. KT17: Ewe 6C **164**
Park Central Bldg. E3 2C **86**
Park Chase HA9: Wemb 4F **61**
Park Cl. E9 1J **85**
HA3: Hrw W 1J **41**
KT2: King T 1G **151**
N12 3G **31**
NW2 3D **62**
NW10 3F **79**
SM5: Cars 6D **166**
SW1 7E **10** (2D **100**)
TW3: Houn 5G **113**
TW12: Hamp 1G **149**
W4 6K **97**
W14 3H **99**
Park Club, The
Acton 1A 98
Park Ct. *CR2: S Croy* *5C* ***168***
(off Warham Rd.)
E4 2K **35**
E17 5D **50**
HA3: Kenton 7E **42**
HA9: Wemb 5E **60**
KT1: Hamp W 1C **150**
KT3: N Mald 4K **151**
N11 7C **32**
N17 7B **34**
SE21 3C **138**
SE26 6H **139**
SM6: Wall 5J **167**
SW11 1F **119**
UB8: Uxb 1A **74**
W6 4C **98**
Park Cres. DA8: Erith 6J **109**
EN2: Enf 4J **23**
HA3: Hrw W 1J **41**
N3 7F **31**
TW2: Twick 1H **131**
W1 4J **5** (4F **83**)
Park Cres. M. E. W1 4K **5** (4F **83**)
Park Cres. M. W. W1 4J **5** (4F **83**)
Park Cres. Rd. DA8: Erith 6K **109**
Park Cft. HA8: Edg 1J **43**
Parkcroft Rd. SE12 7H **123**
Parkdale N11 6C **32**
Parkdale Cres. KT4: Wor Pk 3K **163**
Parkdale Rd. SE18 5J **107**
Park Dr. HA2: Harr 7E **40**
HA3: Hrw W 6C **26**
N21 6H **23**
NW11 1K **63**
RM1: Rom 4K **55**
RM10: Dag 3J **73**
SE7 6C **106**
SW14 5K **115**
W3 3G **97**
Park Dwellings NW3 5D **64**
Park E. Bldg. *E3* *2C* ***86***
(off Fairfield Rd.)
Park End BR1: Brom 1H **159**
NW3 4C **64**
Parker Bldg. *SE16* *7K* ***15***
(off Old Jamaica Rd.)
Parker Cl. E16 1C **106**
SM5: Cars 6D **166**
Parker Ct. *N1* *1C* ***84***
(off Basire St.)
Parker Ho. *E14* *2C* ***104***
(off Admirals Way)
Parker M. WC2 7F **7** (6J **83**)
Parke Rd. SW13 1C **116**
TW16: Sun 4J **147**
Parker Rd. CR0: C'don 4C **168**
Parkers Row SE1 7K **15** (2G **103**)
Parker St. E16 1C **106**
WC2 7F **7** (6J **83**)
Parkes St. E20 6C **68**
Park Farm Cl. HA5: Eastc 5K **39**
N2 3A **46**
Park Farm Ct. UB3: Hayes 7G **75**
Park Farm Rd. BR1: Brom 1B **160**
KT2: King T 7E **132**
Parkfield TW7: Isle 1J **113**
Parkfield Av. HA2: Harr 2G **41**
SW14 4A **116**
TW13: Felt 3J **129**
UB5: N'olt 2B **76**
UB10: Hil 3D **74**
Parkfield Cl. HA8: Edg 6C **28**
UB5: N'olt 2C **76**
Parkfield Ct. *SE14* *1B* ***122***
(off Parkfield Rd.)
Parkfield Cres. HA2: Harr 2G **41**
HA4: Ruis 2C **58**
TW13: Felt 3J **129**
Parkfield Dr. UB5: N'olt 2B **76**
Parkfield Gdns. HA2: Harr 3F **41**
Parkfield Ho. HA2: Harr 1F **41**
Parkfield Ind. Est. SW11 2E **118**
Parkfield Pde. TW13: Felt 3J **129**
Parkfield Rd. HA2: Harr 3G **59**
NW10 7D **62**
SE14 1B **122**
SW4 6H **119**
(not continuous)
TW13: Felt 3J **129**
UB5: N'olt 2C **76**
UB10: Ick 2D **56**
Parkfields CR0: C'don 1B **170**
SW15 4E **116**
Parkfields Av. NW9 1K **61**
SW20 1D **152**
Parkfields Cl. SM5: Cars 4E **166**
Parkfields Rd. KT2: King T 5F **133**
Parkfield St. N1 2A **84**
Parkfield Way BR2: Brom 6D **160**
Park Gdns. DA8: Erith 4K **109**
E10 1C **68**
KT2: King T 5F **133**
NW9 3H **43**
Park Ga. N2 3B **46**
N21 7E **22**
W5 5D **78**
Parkgate *N1* *1D* ***84***
(off Southgate Rd.)
SE3 3H **123**
Parkgate Av. EN4: Had W 1F **21**
Parkgate Cl. KT2: King T 6H **133**
Park Ga. Ct. TW12: Hamp H 6G **131**
Parkgate Cres. EN4: Had W 1F **21**
Parkgate Gdns. SW14 5K **115**
Parkgate M. N6 7G **47**
Parkgate Rd. SM6: Wall 5E **166**
SW11 7C **100**
Park Gates HA2: Harr 4E **58**
Park Gro. BR1: Brom 1K **159**
DA7: Bex 4J **127**
E15 1J **87**
HA8: Edg 5A **28**
N11 7C **32**
Park Gro. Rd. E11 2G **69**
Park Hall *SE10* *7F* ***105***
(off Croom's Hill)
Park Hall Rd. N2 4C **46**
SE21 3C **138**
Park Hall Trad. Est. SE21 3C **138**
Parkham Ct. BR2: Brom 2G **159**
Parkham St. SW11 1C **118**
Park Hgts. Ct. *E14* *6B* ***86***
(off Wharf La.)
Park Hill BR1: Brom 4C **160**
SE23 2H **139**
SM5: Cars 6C **166**
SW4 5H **119**
TW10: Rich 6F **115**
W5 5D **78**
Park Hill Cl.
SM5: Cars 5C **166**
Park Hill Ct. SW17 3D **136**
Park Hill M. CR2: S Croy 5D **168**
Park Hill Ri. CR0: C'don 2E **168**
Park Hill Rd. BR2: Brom 2G **159**
CR0: C'don 2E **168**
SM6: Wall 7F **167**
Parkhill Rd. DA5: Bexl 7F **127**
DA14: Sidc 3H **143**
DA15: Sidc 3H **143**
E4 1K **35**
NW3 5D **64**
Parkhill Wlk. NW3 5D **64**
Parkholme Rd. E8 6G **67**
Park Ho. *E9* *7J* ***67***
(off Shore Rd.)
N21 7E **22**
SE5 *1D* ***120***
(off Camberwell Grn.)
W1 1G **11**
Park Ho. Gdns.
TW1: Twick 5C **114**
Park Ho. Pas. N6 7E **46**
Parkhouse St. SE5 7D **102**
Parkhurst Ct. N7 4J **65**
Parkhurst Gdns. DA5: Bexl 7G **127**
Parkhurst Rd. DA5: Bexl 7G **127**
E12 4E **70**
E17 4A **50**
N7 4J **65**
N11 5K **31**
N17 2G **49**
N22 6E **32**
SM1: Sutt 4B **166**
Parkinson Ct. *N1* *2F* ***9***
(off Charles Sq. Est.)
Parkinson Ho. *E9* *7J* ***67***
(off Frampton Pk. Rd.)
SW1 *5C* ***18***
(off Tachbrook St.)
Parkland Ct. *E15* *5G* ***69***
(off Maryland Pk.)
W14 *2G* ***99***
(off Holland Pk. Av.)
Parkland Gdns. SW19 1F **135**
Parkland Gro. TW15: Ashf 3C **128**
Parkland Mead BR1: Brom 3F **161**
(not continuous)
Parkland M. BR7: Chst 7H **143**
Parkland Rd. IG8: Wfd G 7E **36**
N22 2K **47**
TW15: Ashf 4C **128**
Parklands KT5: Surb 5F **151**
N6 7F **47**
Parklands Cl. EN4: Had W 1G **21**
IG2: Ilf 7G **53**
SW14 5J **115**
Parklands Ct. TW5: Hest 2B **112**
Parklands Dr. N3 3G **45**
Parklands Gro. TW7: Isle 1K **113**
Parklands Pde. *TW5: Hest* *2B* ***112***
(off Parklands Ct.)
Parklands Rd. SW16 5F **137**
Parklands Way KT4: Wor Pk 2A **164**
Parkland Walk Local Nature Reserve
7J 47
Park La. CR0: C'don 3D **168**
E15 1F **87**
HA2: Harr 3F **59**
HA7: Stan 3F **27**
HA9: Wemb 5E **60**
N9 3K **33**
(not continuous)
N17 7A **34**
(not continuous)
RM6: Chad H 6D **54**
SM3: Cheam 6G **165**
SM5: Cars 4E **166**
SM6: Wall 5E **166**
TW5: Cran 7J **93**
TW9: Rich 4D **114**
TW11: Tedd 6K **131**
UB4: Hayes 5G **75**
W1 2F **11** (7D **82**)
Park La. Cl. N17 7B **34**

Park La. Mans. *CR0: C'don* *3D 168*
(off Park La.)
PARK LANGLEY 4E 158
Parklangley Club, The 4E 158
Parklea Cl. NW9 . . . . 1A **44**
Park Lee Ct. N16 . . . . 7E **48**
Parkleigh Rd. SW19 . . . . 2K **153**
Parkleys TW10: Ham 4D **132**
Parkleys Pde. TW10: Ham 4D **132**
Park Lodge NW8 . . . . 7B **64**
W14 . . . . *3H 99*
(off Melbury Rd.)
Park Lodge Av. UB7: W Dray 2B **92**
Park Lofts *SW2* *5J 119*
(off Lyham Rd.)
Park Lorne *NW8* *2D 4*
(off Park Rd.)
Park Mnr. *SM2: Sutt* *7A 166*
(off Christchurch Pk.)
Park Mans. NW4 . . . . 5D **44**
NW8 . . . . *2C 82*
(off Allitsen Rd.)
SW1 . . . . *7E 10*
(off Knightsbridge)
SW8 . . . . 7F **19** (6J **101**)
SW11 . . . . *1D 118*
(off Prince of Wales Dr.)
Park Mead DA15: Sidc 5B **126**
HA2: Harr 3F **59**
Parkmead SW15 . . . . 6D **116**
Parkmead Cl. CR0: C'don 6K **157**
Parkmead Gdns. NW7 . . . . 6G **29**
Park M. BR7: Chst 6F **143**
N8 . . . . 6J **47**
SE10 . . . . 5H **105**
SE24 . . . . 7C **120**
TW19: Stanw 7B **110**
W10 . . . . 2G **81**
Parkmore Cl. IG8: Wfd G 4D **36**
Park Pde. NW10 . . . . 2B **80**
UB3: Hayes 6G **75**
W3 . . . . 3G **97**
Park Piazza SE13 . . . . 6F **123**
Park Pl. *BR1: Brom* *1K 159*
(off Park Rd.)
E14 . . . . 1C **104**
HA9: Wemb 4F **61**
N1 . . . . *7D 66*
(off Downham Rd.)
SW1 . . . . 5A **12** (1G **101**)
TW12: Hamp H 6G **131**
W3 . . . . 4G **97**
W5 . . . . 1D **96**
Park Pl. Dr. W3 . . . . 3G **97**
Park Pl. Vs. W2 . . . . 5A **4** (5A **82**)
Park Ridings N8 . . . . 3A **48**
Park Ri. HA3: Hrw W 1J **41**
SE23 . . . . 1A **140**
Park Ri. Rd. SE23 . . . . 1A **140**
Park Rd. BR1: Brom 1K **159**
BR3: Beck 7B **140**
BR7: Chst 6F **143**
E6 . . . . 1A **88**
E10 . . . . 1C **68**
E12 . . . . 1K **69**
E15 . . . . 1J **87**
E17 . . . . 5B **50**
EN4: E Barn 4G **21**
EN5: Barn 4C **20**
HA0: Wemb 6E **60**
IG1: Ilf 3H **71**
KT1: Hamp W 1C **150**
KT2: King T 5F **133**
KT3: N Mald 4K **151**
KT5: Surb 6F **151**
KT8: E Mos 4G **149**
N2 . . . . 3B **46**
N8 . . . . 4G **47**
N11 . . . . 7C **32**
N14 . . . . 1C **32**
N15 . . . . 4B **48**
Park Rd. N18 . . . . 4B **34**
NW1 . . . . 2D **4** (4D **82**)
NW4 . . . . 7C **44**
NW8 . . . . 2D **4** (3C **82**)
NW9 . . . . 7K **43**
NW10 . . . . 1A **80**
SE25 . . . . 4E **156**
SM3: Cheam 6G **165**
SM6: Wall 5F **167**
(Clifton Rd.)
SM6: Wall 2F **167**
(Elmwood Cl.)
SW19 . . . . 6B **136**
TW1: Twick 6C **114**
TW3: Houn 5F **113**
TW7: Isle 1B **114**
TW10: Rich 6F **115**
TW11: Tedd 6K **131**
TW12: Hamp H 4F **131**
TW13: Hanw 4B **130**
TW15: Ashf 5D **128**
TW16: Sun 7K **129**
UB4: Hayes 5G **75**
UB8: Uxb 1A **74**
W4 . . . . 7J **97**
W7 . . . . 7K **77**
Park Rd. E. UB10: Uxb 2A **74**
W3 . . . . 2H **97**
Park Rd. Ho. KT2: King T 7G **133**
Pk. Road Leisure Cen. 5H 47
Park Rd. Nth. W3 . . . . 2H **97**
W4 . . . . 5K **97**
Park Row SE10 . . . . 6F **105**
SW2 . . . . 6A **120**
PARK ROYAL 3H 79
Park Royal NW10 . . . . 3G **79**
PARK ROYAL JUNC. **1G 79**
Park Royal Metro Cen. NW10 . . . . . . 4H **79**
Pk. Royal Rd. NW10 . . . . 3J **79**
W3 . . . . 3J **79**
Pk. St James *NW8* *1D 82*
(off St James's Ter. M.)
Parkshot TW9: Rich 4D **114**
Park Side NW2 . . . . 3C **62**
Parkside DA14: Sidc 2B **144**
IG9: Buck H 2E **36**
N3 . . . . 1K **45**
NW7 . . . . 6H **29**
SE3 . . . . 7H **105**
SM3: Cheam 6G **165**
SW1 . . . . 6F **11**
SW19 . . . . 3F **135**
TW12: Hamp H 5H **131**
UB3: Hayes 7G **75**
W3 . . . . 1A **98**
W5 . . . . 7E **78**
Parkside Av. BR1: Brom 4C **160**
DA7: Bex 2K **127**
RM1: Rom 3K **55**
SE10 . . . . 1E **122**
SW19 . . . . 5F **135**
Parkside Bus. Est. SE8 . . . . 6A **104**
Parkside Cl. SE20 . . . . 7J **139**
Parkside Ct. *E11* *6J 51*
(off Wanstead Pl.)
E16 . . . . *2A 106*
(off Booth Rd.)
N22 . . . . 6E **32**
Parkside Cres. KT5: Surb 6J **151**
N7 . . . . 3A **66**
Parkside Cross DA7: Bex 2K **127**
Parkside Dr. HA8: Edg 3B **28**
Parkside Est. E9 . . . . 1J **85**
(not continuous)
Parkside Gdns. EN4: E Barn 1J **31**
SW19 . . . . 4F **135**
Parkside Ho. RM10: Dag 3J **73**
Parkside Lodge DA17: Belv 5J **109**
Parkside Rd. DA17: Belv 4H **109**
SW11 . . . . 1E **118**
TW3: Houn 5F **113**
Parkside Sq. E14 . . . . 4E **104**
SE10 . . . . 1E **122**
Parkside Ter. *BR6: Farnb* *3F 173*
(off Willow Wlk.)
N18 . . . . 4J **33**
Parkside Way HA2: Harr 4F **41**
Parks Info. Cen. 4D **10** (1C **100**)
Park Sth. *SW11* *1E 118*
(off Austin Rd.)
Park Sq. E. NW1 . . . . 3J **5** (4F **83**)
Park Sq. M. NW1 . . . . 4J **5** (4F **83**)
Park Sq. W. NW1 . . . . 3J **5** (4F **83**)
Parkstead Rd. SW15 . . . . 5C **116**
Park Steps W2 . . . . 2D **10**
Parkstone Av. N18 . . . . 6A **34**
Parkstone Rd. E17 . . . . 3E **50**
SE15 . . . . 2G **121**
Park St. CR0: C'don 2C **168**
SE1 . . . . 4C **14** (1C **102**)
SW6 . . . . 1A **118**
TW11: Tedd 6J **131**
W1 . . . . 2G **11** (7E **82**)
Park Ter. EN3: Enf H 1F **25**
KT4: Wor Pk 1C **164**
SM5: Cars 3C **166**
Park Theatre 2A 66
Parkthorne Cl. HA2: Harr 6F **41**
Parkthorne Dr. HA2: Harr 6E **40**
Parkthorne Rd. SW12 . . . . 7H **119**
Park Towers *W1* *5J 11*
(off Brick St.)
Park Vw. HA5: Hat E 1D **40**
HA9: Wemb 5H **61**
KT3: N Mald 3B **152**
N5 . . . . 4C **66**
N21 . . . . 7E **22**
RM6: Chad H 6D **54**
SE8 . . . . *5K 103*
(off Trundleys Rd.)
UB7: Yiew 7A **74**
W3 . . . . 5J **79**
Parkview DA18: Erith 3D **108**
UB6: G'frd *3A 78*
(off Perivale La.)
Pk. View Academy Sports Cen. 4C 48
Park Vw. Apartments *SE16* *3H 103*
(off Banyard Rd.)
Parkview Apartments *E14* *6D 86*
(off Chrisp St.)
Parkview Cl. SM5: Cars 7D **166**
Park Vw. Ct. E3 . . . . 5C **86**
N12 . . . . 4H **31**
SE12 . . . . 3A **142**
SE20 . . . . 1H **157**
Parkview Ct. HA3: Hrw W 7D **26**
IG2: Ilf 6J **53**
SW6 . . . . 2G **117**
SW18 . . . . 6J **117**
Park Vw. Cres. N11 . . . . 4A **32**
Parkview Cres. KT4: Wor Pk 7E **152**
Park Vw. Dr. CR4: Mitc 2B **154**
Park Vw. Est. E2 . . . . 2K **85**
Park Vw. Gdns. IG4: Ilf 4D **52**
N22 . . . . 1A **48**
NW4 . . . . 5E **44**
Park Vw. Ho. E4 . . . . 5H **35**
SE24 . . . . *6B 120*
(off Hurst St.)
Parkview Ho. N9 . . . . 7C **24**
Park Vw. Mans. *E20* *5D 68*
(off Olympic Pk. Av.)
N4 . . . . 6B **48**
Park Vw. M. SW9 . . . . 2K **119**
Park View Road 3C 126
Park Vw. Rd. DA16: Well 3C **126**
N3 . . . . 1K **45**
N17 . . . . 3G **49**
NW10 . . . . 4B **62**
UB1: S'hall 1E **94**
UB8: Hil 6B **74**
W5 . . . . 5E **78**
Parkview Rd. CR0: C'don 1G **169**
SE9 . . . . 1F **143**
Pk. Village E. NW1 . . . . 1K **5** (2F **83**)
Pk. Village W. NW1 . . . . 2F **83**
Park Vs. RM6: Chad H 6D **54**
Parkville Rd. SW6 . . . . 7H **99**
Park Vista SE10 . . . . 6F **105**
Park Wlk. EN4: Cockf 3G **21**
IG1: Ilf *2F 71*
(within The Exchange)
N6 . . . . 7E **46**
SE10 . . . . 7F **105**
SW10 . . . . 7A **16** (6A **100**)
Park Way EN2: Enf 2F **23**
HA4: Ruis 1J **57**
HA8: Edg 1H **43**
KT8: W Mole 3F **149**
N20 . . . . 4J **31**
NW11 . . . . 5G **45**
TW14: Felt 7K **111**
W3 . . . . 3G **97**
Parkway DA18: Erith 3E **108**
IG3: Ilf 3K **71**
IG8: Wfd G 5F **37**
N14 . . . . 2D **32**
NW1 . . . . 1F **83**
SW20 . . . . 4F **153**
UB10: Hil 7C **56**
Parkway, The TW4: Cran 2K **111**
TW5: Cran 5J **93**
UB2: S'hall 5J **93**
UB3: Hayes 3K **93**
UB4: Yead 3K **93**
UB5: N'olt 3K **93**
Pk. Way Ct. HA4: Ruis 1H **57**
Parkway Cres. E15 . . . . 5E **68**
Parkway Trad. Est. TW5: Hest 6A **94**
Park W. W2 . . . . 7D **4**
Park W. Bldg. E3 . . . . 2C **86**
Park W. Pl. W2 . . . . 7D **4** (6C **82**)
Park Wharf *SE8* *5A 104*
(off Evelyn St.)
Parkwood BR3: Beck 7C **140**
N20 . . . . 3K **31**
NW8 . . . . *1D 82*
(off St Edmund's Ter.)
Parkwood Av. KT10: Esh 7G **149**
Park Wood Ct. HA4: Ruis 4E **38**
Parkwood Flats N20 . . . . 3J **31**
Parkwood Gro. TW16: Sun 3J **147**
Parkwood M. N6 . . . . 6F **47**
Parkwood Rd. DA5: Bexl 7F **127**
SW19 . . . . 5H **135**
TW7: Isle 1K **113**
Parliament Ct. E1 . . . . 6H **9**
Parliament Hill 3D 64
Parliament Hill NW3 . . . . 4C **64**
Parliament Hill Fields 3E 64
Parliament Hill Lido 4E 64
Parliament Hill Mans. NW5 . . . . 4E **64**
Parliament M. SW14 . . . . 2J **115**
Parliament Sq. SW1 . . . . 7E **12** (2J **101**)
Parliament St. SW1 . . . . 6E **12** (2J **101**)
Parliament Vw. SE1 . . . . 3G **19** (4K **101**)
Parma Cres. SW11 . . . . 4D **118**
Parmiter St. E2 . . . . 2H **85**
Parmoor Ct. EC1 . . . . 3C **8**
Parndon Ho.
IG10: Lough 1H **37**
Parnell Cl. HA8: Edg 4C **28**
W12 . . . . 3D **98**
Parnell Ho. WC1 . . . . 6D **6** (5H **83**)
Parnelli Ho. *N1* *6B 66*
(off Canonbury Rd.)
Parnell Rd. E3 . . . . 1B **86**
Parnell Way HA3: Stan 1B **42**
Parnham Cl. BR1: Brom 3F **161**
Parnham St. E14 . . . . 6A **86**
(not continuous)
Parolles Rd. N19 . . . . 1G **65**
Paroma Rd. DA17: Belv 4G **109**

Parr Cl. N9 .4C 34
　　N18 . . . . .4C 34
Parr Ct. N1 .2D 84
　　　　　　　　　(off New North Rd.)
　　TW13: Hanw 4A 130
Parr Ho. E16 . . . . .1K 105
　　　　　　　　　　(off Beaulieu Av.)
Parrington Ho. SW4 . . . . .6H 119
Parr Rd. E6 .1B 88
　　HA7: Stan 1D 42
Parrs Cl. CR2: Sande 7D 168
Parrs Pl.
　　TW12: Hamp 7E 130
Parr St. N1 .2D 84
Parrs Way W6 . . . . .6E 98
Parry Av. E6 . . . . .6D 88
Parry Cl. KT17: Ewe 7D 164
Parry Ho. E1 . . . . .1H 103
　　　　　　　　　　(off Green Bank)
Parry Pl. SE18 . . . . .4F 107
Parry Rd. SE25 . . . . .3E 156
　　W10 . . . . .3G 81
Parry St. SW8 . . . . .7F 19 (6J 101)
Parsifal Rd. NW6 . . . . .5J 63
Parsley Gdns. CR0: C'don 1K 169
Parsloes Av. RM9: Dag 4D 72
Parsonage Cl. UB3: Hayes 6H 75
Parsonage Gdns. EN2: Enf 2H 23
Parsonage La. DA14: Sidc 4F 145
　　EN1: Enf 2H 23
　　EN2: Enf 2H 23
Parsonage Manorway DA17: Belv . .6G 109
Parsonage St. E14 . . . . .4E 104
Parsons Cl. SM1: Sutt 3K 165
Parson's Cres. HA8: Edg 3B 28
Parsons Ga. M. SW6 . . . . .2J 117
PARSONS GREEN 2H 117
Parson's Grn. SW6 . . . . .1J 117
Parson's Grn. La. SW6 . . . . .1J 117
Parson's Grn. Rd. HA8: Edg 3B 28
Parsons Hill SE18 . . . . .3E 106
　　　　　　　　　　　(off Powis St.)
Parsons Ho. W2 . . . . .4A 4
Parsons Lodge NW6 . . . . .7K 63
　　　　　　　　　　(off Priory Rd.)
Parson's Mead CR0: C'don 1B 168
Parsons Mead KT8: E Mos 3G 149
Parsons M. SW18 . . . . .5A 118
Parson's Rd. E13 . . . . .2A 88
Parson St. NW4 . . . . .4E 44
Parthenia Dr. TW7: Isle 3A 114
Parthenia Rd. SW6 . . . . .1J 117
Partingdale La. NW7 . . . . .5A 30
Partington Cl. N19 . . . . .1H 65
Partridge Cl. E16 . . . . .5B 88
　　EN5: Barn 6A 20
　　HA7: Stan 4K 27
　　UB10: Uxb 1B 74
　　WD23: Bush 1B 26
Partridge Ct. EC1 . . . . .3A 8
Partridge Dr. BR6: Farnb 3G 173
Partridge Grn. SE9 . . . . .3E 142
Partridge Ho. E3 . . . . .2B 86
　　　　　　　　　　(off Stafford Rd.)
Partridge Rd. DA14: Sidc 3J 143
　　TW12: Hamp 6D 130
Partridge Sq. E6 . . . . .5C 88
Partridge Way N22 . . . . .1J 47
Pasadena Cl. UB3: Hayes 2J 93
Pasadena Cl. Trad. Est. UB3: Hayes . .2K 93
Pascall Ho. SE17 . . . . .6C 102
　　　　　　　　　　(off Draco St.)
Pascal M. SE19 . . . . .7G 139
Pascal Rd. UB1: S'hall 6F 77
Pascal St. SW8 . . . . .7H 101
Pascoe Rd. SE13 . . . . .5F 123
Pasley Cl. SE17 . . . . .5B 102
Pasquier Rd. E17 . . . . .3A 50
Passage, The TW9: Rich 5E 114
Passey Pl. SE9 . . . . .6D 124
Passfield Dr. E14 . . . . .5D 86

Passfield Hall WC1 . . . . .3D 6
　　　　　　　　　　(off Endsleigh Pl.)
Passfield Path SE28 . . . . .7B 90
Passfields SE6 . . . . .3D 140
　　W14 . . . . .5H 99
　　　　　　　　　　　(off Star Rd.)
Passing All. EC1 . . . . .4B 8
Passingham Ho. TW5: Hest 6E 94
Passmore Ct. E14 . . . . .6C 86
　　　　　　　　　(off New Festival Av.)
Passmore Edwards Ho. N11 . . . . . . .6C 32
Passmore Gdns. N11 . . . . .6C 32
Passmore Ho. E2 . . . . .1F 85
　　　　　　　　　　(off Kingsland Rd.)
Passmore St. SW1 . . . . . .5G 17 (5E 100)
Pastel Ct. E1 . . . . .5K 85
　　　　　　　　　　(off Shandy St.)
Pasteur Cl. NW9 . . . . .2A 44
Pasteur Ct. HA1: Harr 1B 60
Pasteur Gdns. N18 . . . . .5G 33
Paston Cl. E5 . . . . .3K 67
　　SM6: Wall 3G 167
Paston Cres. SE12 . . . . .7K 123
Pastor Ct. N6 . . . . .6G 47
Pastor St. SE11 . . . . .4B 102
Pasture Cl. HA0: Wemb 3B 60
Pasture Rd. HA0: Wemb 2B 60
　　RM9: Dag 5F 73
　　SE6 . . . . .1H 141
Pastures, The N20 . . . . .1C 30
Pastures Mead UB10: Hil 6C 56
Pastures Path E11 . . . . .1H 69
Patcham Ter. SW8 . . . . .1F 119
Patch Cl. UB10: Uxb 1B 74
Patching Way UB4: Yead 5C 76
Patent Ho. E14 . . . . .5D 86
　　　　　　　　　　(off Morris Rd.)
Paternoster La. EC4 . . . . . .1B 14 (6B 84)
Paternoster Row EC4 . . . .1C 14 (6C 84)
Paternoster Sq. EC4 . . . . . .1B 14 (6B 84)
Paterson Ct. EC1 . . . . .2E 8
Pater St. W8 . . . . .3J 99
Pates Mnr. Dr. TW14: Bedf 7F 111
Path, The SW19 . . . . .1K 153
Pathfield Rd. SW16 . . . . .6H 137
Patience Rd. SW11 . . . . .2C 118
Patina Mans. E20 . . . . .5E 68
　　　　　　　　　(off Mirabelle Gdns.)
Patio Cl. SW4 . . . . .6H 119
Patmore Est. SW8 . . . . .1G 119
Patmore Ho. N16 . . . . .5E 66
Patmore St. SW8 . . . . .1G 119
Patmos Lodge SW9 . . . . .1B 120
　　　　　　　　　　(off Elliott Rd.)
Patmos Rd. SW9 . . . . .7B 102
Paton Cl. E3 . . . . .3C 86
Paton Ho. SW9 . . . . .2K 119
　　　　　　　　　　(off Stockwell Rd.)
Paton St. EC1 . . . . .2C 8 (3C 84)
Patricia Ct. BR7: Chst 1H 161
　　DA16: Well 7B 108
Patrick Coman Ho. EC1 . . . . .2A 8
　　　　　　　　　　(off St John St.)
Patrick Connolly Gdns. E3 . . . . .3D 86
Patrick Ct. SE1 . . . . .7B 14
　　　　　　　　　　(off Webber St.)
Patrick Cres. RM8: Dag 1E 72
Patrick Pas. SW11 . . . . .2C 118
Patrick Rd. E13 . . . . .3A 88
Patriot Sq. E2 . . . . .2H 85
Patrol Pl. SE6 . . . . .6D 122
Patroni Ct. E15 . . . . .3G 87
　　　　　　　　　　(off Durban Rd.)
Pat Shaw Ho. E1 . . . . .4K 85
　　　　　　　　　　(off Globe Rd.)
Patshull Pl. NW5 . . . . .6G 65
Patshull Rd. NW5 . . . . .6G 65
Patten All. TW10: Rich 5D 114
Pattenden Rd. SE6 . . . . .1B 140
Patten Ho. N4 . . . . .1C 66
Patten Rd. SW18 . . . . .7C 118

Patterdale NW1 . . . . .2K 5
　　　　　　　　　　(off Osnaburgh St.)
Patterdale Cl. BR1: Brom 6H 141
Patterdale Rd. SE15 . . . . .7J 103
Pattern Ho. EC1 . . . . .3A 8 (4B 84)
Patterson Ct. SE19 . . . . .7F 139
Patterson Rd. SE19 . . . . .6F 139
Pattina Wlk. SE16 . . . . .1A 104
　　　　　　　　　　(off Silver Wlk.)
Pattison Ho. E1 . . . . .6K 85
　　　　　　　　　　(off Wellesley St.)
　　SE1 . . . . .6D 14
　　　　　　　　　　(off Redcross Way)
Pattison Rd. NW2 . . . . .3J 63
Pattison Wlk. SE18 . . . . .5G 107
Paul Byrne Ho. N2 . . . . .3A 46
Paul Cl. E15 . . . . .1G 87
Paul Ct. N18 . . . . .4B 34
　　　　　　　　　　(off Fairfield Rd.)
　　RM7: Rom 5J 55
Paul Daisley Cl. NW6 . . . . .7G 63
　　　　　　　　　(off Christchurch Av.)
Paulet Rd. SE5 . . . . .2B 120
Paulet Way HA0: Wemb 7A 62
Paul Gdns. CR0: C'don 2F 169
Paulhan Rd. HA3: Kenton 4D 42
Paul Ho. W10 . . . . .4G 81
　　　　　　　　　　(off Ladbroke Gro.)
Paulin Dr. N21 . . . . .7F 23
Pauline Cres. TW2: Whitt 1G 131
Pauline Ho. E1 . . . . .5G 85
　　　　　　　　　(off Old Montague St.)
Paul Julius Cl. E14 . . . . .7F 87
Paul Robeson Cl. E6 . . . . .3E 88
Paul Robeson Ho. WC1 . . . . .1H 7
　　　　　　　　　　(off Penton Ri.)
Paul Robeson Theatre, The 3F 113
Paul St. E15 . . . . .1G 87
　　EC2 . . . . .4F 9 (4D 84)
Paul's Wlk. EC4 . . . . .2B 14 (7C 84)
Paultons Ho. SW3 . . . . .7B 16
　　　　　　　　　　(off Paultons Sq.)
Paultons Sq. SW3 . . . . . . .7B 16 (6B 100)
Paultons St. SW3 . . . . .6B 100
Paulton St. N19 . . . . .1G 65
Pavan Ct. E2 . . . . .3J 85
　　　　　　　　　　(off Sceptre Rd.)
Paved Ct. TW9: Rich 5D 114
Paveley Ct. NW7 . . . . .7B 30
　　　　　　　　　(off Langstone Way)
Paveley Dr. SW11 . . . . .7C 100
Paveley Ho. N1 . . . . .2K 83
　　　　　　　　　(off Priory Grn. Est.)
Paveley St. NW8 . . . . .2C 4 (3C 82)
Pavement, The E11 . . . . .1E 68
　　　　　　　　　　(off Hainault Rd.)
　　SW4 . . . . .4G 119
　　SW19 .6H 135
　　　　　　　　　　(off Worple Rd.)
　　TW7: Isle 3A 114
　　　　　　　　　　(off South St.)
　　TW11: Tedd 7B 132
　　W5 . . . . .3E 96
Pavement M. RM6: Chad H 7D 54
Pavement Sq. CR0: C'don 1G 169
Pavert Ho. RM10: Dag 6H 73
Pavilion, The SW8 . . . . .7H 101
Pavilion Apartments NW8 . . . .2B 4 (3B 82)
Pavilion Cl. NW6 . . . . .3J 81
　　　　　　　　　　(off Stafford Rd.)
Pavilion La. BR3: Beck 6B 140
Pavilion Leisure Cen. 2J 159
Pavilion Lodge HA2: Harr 1H 59
Pavilion M. N3 . . . . .3J 45
Pavilion Pde. W12 . . . . .6E 80
　　　　　　　　　　(off Wood La.)
Pavilion Rd. IG1: Ilf 7D 52
　　SW1 . . . . .7F 11 (3D 100)
　　SW3 . . . . .1F 17 (4D 100)
Pavilion Sports & Fitness Club, The
　　. . . . . .3G 149

Pavilion Sq. SW17 . . . . .3D 136
Pavilion St. E13 . . . . .2A 88
　　SW1 . . . . .2F 17 (3D 100)
Pavilion Ter. IG2: Ilf 5J 53
　　W12 . . . . .6E 80
　　　　　　　　　　(off Wood La.)
Pavilion Way HA4: Ruis 2A 58
　　HA8: Edg 7C 28
　　SE10 . . . . .2G 105
Pavillion Ho. SE16 . . . . .2K 103
　　　　　　　　　(off Water Gdns. Sq.)
Pavillion M. N4 . . . . .2K 65
　　　　　　　　　　(off Tollington Pl.)
Pawleyne Cl. SE20 . . . . .7J 139
Pawsey Cl. E13 . . . . .1K 87
Pawsons Rd. CR0: C'don 6C 156
Paxfold HA7: Stan 5J 27
Paxford Rd.
　　HA0: Wemb 2B 60
Paxton Cl. KT12: Walt T 7A 148
　　TW9: Kew 2F 115
Paxton Ct. CR4: Mitc 2D 154
　　　　　　　　　　(off Armfield Cres.)
　　N7 . . . . .6A 66
　　　　　　　　　(off Westbourne St.)
　　SE12 . . . . .3A 142
　　SE26 . . . . .4A 140
　　　　　　　　　　(off Adamsrill Rd.)
Paxton Ho. SE17 . . . . .5D 102
　　　　　　　　　　(off Morecambe St.)
Paxton M. SE19 . . . . .7E 138
　　　　　　　　　　(off Westow St.)
Paxton Pl. SE27 . . . . .4E 138
Paxton Point SE10 . . . . .7D 104
Paxton Rd. BR1: Brom 7J 141
　　N17 . . . . .7A 34
　　SE23 . . . . .3A 140
　　W4 . . . . .6A 98
Paxton Ter. SW1 . . . . .7K 17 (6F 101)
Paymal Ho. E1 . . . . .5J 85
　　　　　　　　　　(off Stepney Way)
Payne Cl. IG11: Bark 7J 71
Payne Ho. N1 . . . . .1K 83
　　　　　　　　　　(off Barnsbury Est.)
Paynell Ct. SE3 . . . . .3G 123
Payne Rd. E3 . . . . .2D 86
Paynesfield Av. SW14 . . . . .3K 115
Paynesfield Rd. WD23: B Hea 1E 26
Payne St. SE8 . . . . .7B 104
Paynes Wlk. W6 . . . . .6G 99
Payzes Gdns. IG8: Wfd G 6C 36
　　　　　　　　　　(off Ashingdon Cl.)
Peabody Av. SW1 . . . . .5J 17 (5F 101)
Peabody Bldgs. E1 . . . . .7G 85
　　　　　　　　　　(off John Fisher St.)
　　EC1 . . . . .4D 8
　　　　　　　　　　(off Banner St.)
　　SW3 . . . . .7C 16
Peabody Cl. CR0: C'don 1J 169
　　SE10 . . . . .1D 122
　　SW1 . . . . .7K 17 (5F 101)
Peabody Cotts. N17 . . . . .1E 48
Peabody Ct. EC1 . . . . .4D 8
　　　　　　　　　　(off Roscoe St.)
　　SE5 . . . . .1D 120
　　　　　　　　　　(off Kimpton Rd.)
Peabody Est. E1 . . . . .7K 85
　　　　　　　　　　(off Brodlove La.)
　　E2 . . . . .2H 85
　　　　　　　　　　(off Minerva St.)
　　EC1 . . . . .4D 8
　　　　　　　　　　(off Dufferin St.)
　　EC1 . . . . .4K 7
　　　　　　　　　(off Farringdon La.)
　　N1 . . . . .1E 84
　　SE1 . . . . .5K 13 (1A 102)
　　　　　　　　　　　(Duchy St.)
　　SE1 . . . . .6D 14
　　　　　　　　　(Marshalsea Rd.)
　　SE1 . . . . .5C 14 (1C 102)
　　　　　　　　　　(Southwark St.)

Peabody Est. *SE5* 1D 120
(off Camberwell Grn.)
SE24 . . . . . 7B 120
SW1 . . . . . 3B 18
SW3 . . . . . 7D 16 (6C 100)
SW6 . . . . . *6J 99*
(off Lillie Rd.)
SW11 . . . . . 4C 118
W6 . . . . . 5E 98
W10 . . . . . 5E 80
Peabody Hill SE21 . . . . . 1B 138
Peabody Ho. *N1* *1C 84*
(off Greenman St.)
Peabody Sq. SE1 . . . . . 7A 14 (2B 102)
(not continuous)
Peabody Ter. *EC1* *4K 7*
(off Farringdon La.)
Peabody Twr. *EC1* *4D 8*
(off Golden La.)
Peabody Trust SE17 . . . . . 4D 102
Peabody Yd. N1 . . . . . 1C 84
Peace Cl. N14 . . . . . 5A 22
SE25 . . . . . 4E 156
UB6: G'frd 1H 77
Peace Ct. *SE1* *5G 103*
(off Harmony Pl.)
Peace Gro. HA9: Wemb 3H 61
Peace St. SE18 . . . . . 6E 106
Peaches Cl. SM2: Cheam 7G 165
Peachey Ho. *SW18* *4A 118*
(off Eltringham St.)
Peachey La. UB8: Cowl 5A 74
Peach Gro. E11 . . . . . 3F 69
Peach Rd. TW13: Felt 1J 129
W10 . . . . . 3F 81
Peach Tree Av. UB7: Yiew 6B 74
Peachum Rd. SE3 . . . . . 6H 105
Peachwalk M. E3 . . . . . 2K 85
Peachy Cl. HA8: Edg 6B 28
Peacock Av. TW14: Bedf 1F 129
Peacock Cl. E4 . . . . . 7G 35
NW7 . . . . . 5B 30
RM8: Dag 1C 72
Peacock Ho. *SE5* *1E 120*
(off St Giles Rd.)
Peacock Ind. Est. N17 . . . . . 7A 34
Peacock Pl. N1 . . . . . 6A 66
Peacock St. SE17 . . . . . 4B 102
Peacock Theatre **1G 13**
(off Portugal St.)
Peacock Wlk. *E16* *6K 87*
(off Mortlake Rd.)
N6 . . . . . 7F 47
Peacock Yd. *SE17* *5B 102*
(off Iliffe St.)
Peak, The SE26 . . . . . 3J 139
Peaketon Av. IG4: Ilf 4B 52
Peak Hill SE26 . . . . . 4J 139
Peak Hill Av. SE26 . . . . . 4J 139
Peak Hill Gdns. SE26 . . . . . 4J 139
Peal Gdns. W13 . . . . . 4A 78
Peall Rd. CR0: C'don 6K 155
Peall Rd. Ind. Est. CR0: C'don 6K 155
Pearce Cl. CR4: Mitc 2E 154
Pearcefield Av. SE23 . . . . . 1J 139
Pearce Ho. *SW1* *4D 18*
(off Causton St.)
Pear Cl. NW9 . . . . . 4K 43
SE14 . . . . . 7A 104
Pear Ct. *SE15* *7F 103*
(off Thruxton Way)
Pearcroft Rd. E11 . . . . . 2F 69
Peardon St. SW8 . . . . . 2F 119
Peareswood Gdns. HA7: Stan 1D 42
Pearfield Rd. SE23 . . . . . 3A 140
Pearing Cl. KT4: Wor Pk 2F 165
Pearl Cl. E6 . . . . . 6E 88
NW2 . . . . . 7F 45
Pearl Rd. E17 . . . . . 3C 50
Pearl St. E1 . . . . . 1H 103
Pearmain Cl. TW17: Shep 5D 146
Pearman St. SE1 . . . . . 1K 19 (3A 102)
Pear Pl. SE1 . . . . . 6J 13 (2A 102)
Pear Rd. E11 . . . . . 3F 69
Pears Av. TW17: Shep 3G 147
Pearscroft Ct. SW6 . . . . . 1K 117
Pearscroft Rd. SW6 . . . . . 1K 117
Pearse St. SE15 . . . . . 6E 102
Pearson Cl. EN5: New Bar 3E 20
SE5 . . . . . *1C 120*
(off Camberwell New Rd.)
Pearson M. *SW4* *3H 119*
(off Edgeley Rd.)
Pearson's Av. SE14 . . . . . 1C 122
Pearson Sq. W1 . . . . . 6B 6 (5G 83)
Pearson St. E2 . . . . . 2F 85
Pearson Way CR4: Mitc 1E 154
Pears Rd. TW3: Houn 3G 113
Peartree SE26 . . . . . 5A 140
Pear Tree Av. UB7: Yiew 6B 74
Peartree Av. SW17 . . . . . 3A 136
Pear Tree Cl. BR2: Brom 5B 160
CR4: Mitc 2C 154
E2 . . . . . 1F 85
KT9: Chess 5G 163
KT19: Eps 7K 163
Peartree Cl. DA8: Erith 1K 127
Pear Tree Ct. E18 . . . . . 1K 51
EC1 . . . . . 4K 7 (4A 84)
SE26 . . . . . 3B 140
Peartree Gdns. RM7: Mawney 2H 55
RM8: Dag 4B 72
Pear Tree Ho. SE4 . . . . . 3B 122
Pear Tree La. RM13: Rain 2K 91
Peartree La. E1 . . . . . 7J 85
Pear Tree Rd. TW15: Ashf 5E 128
Peartree Rd. EN1: Enf 3K 23
Peartrees UB7: Yiew 7A 74
Pear Tree St. EC1 . . . . . 3B 8 (4C 84)
Peartree Way SE10 . . . . . 4J 105
Peary Ho. NW10 . . . . . 7K 61
Peary Pl. E2 . . . . . 3J 85
Peasmead Ter. E4 . . . . . 4K 35
Peatfield Cl. DA15: Sidc 3J 143
Pebble Way *W3* *1H 97*
(off Steyne Rd.)
Pebworth Rd. HA1: Harr 2A 60
Peckarmans Wood SE26 . . . . . 3G 139
Peckett Sq. N5 . . . . . 4C 66
Peckford Pl. SW9 . . . . . 2A 120
PECKHAM 1G 121
Peckham Gro. SE15 . . . . . 7E 102
Peckham High St. SE15 . . . . . 1G 121
Peckham Hill St. SE15 . . . . . 7G 103
Peckham Pk. Rd. SE15 . . . . . 7G 103
Peckham Pulse Health & Leisure Cen. 1G 121
Peckham Rd. SE5 . . . . . 1E 120
SE15 . . . . . 1E 120
Peckham Rye SE15 . . . . . 3G 121
SE22 . . . . . 4G 121
Peckham Sq. SE15 . . . . . 1G 121
Pecks Yd. *E1* *5J 9*
(off Hanbury St.)
Peckwater St. NW5 . . . . . 5G 65
Pedlar's Wlk. N7 . . . . . 5K 65
Pedley Rd. RM8: Dag 1C 72
Pedley St. E1 . . . . . 4G 85
Pedro St. E5 . . . . . 3K 67
Pedworth Gdns. SE16 . . . . . 4J 103
Peebles Ct.
UB1: S'hall *6G 77*
(off Haldane Rd.)
Peebles Ho. *NW6* *2K 81*
(off Carlton Vale)
Peek Cres. SW19 . . . . . 5F 135
Peel Cl. E4 . . . . . 2J 35
N9 . . . . . 3B 34
Peel Dr. IG5: Ilf 3C 52
NW9 . . . . . 3B 44
Peel Gro. E2 . . . . . 2J 85
Peel Pas. W8 . . . . . 1J 99
Peel Pl. IG5: Ilf 2C 52
SE18 . . . . . 1D 124
SW6 . . . . . 6J 99
Peel Pct. NW6 . . . . . 2J 81
Peel Rd. BR6: Farnb 5G 173
E18 . . . . . 1H 51
HA3: W'stone 3K 41
HA9: Wemb 3D 60
Peel St. W8 . . . . . 1J 99
Peel Way UB8: Hil 5A 74
Peerglow Est.
EN3: Pond E 5D 24
Peerless St. EC1 . . . . . 2E 8 (3D 84)
Pegamoid Rd. N18 . . . . . 3D 34
Pegasus Cl. N16 . . . . . 4D 66
Pegasus Ct. KT1: King T 3D 150
N21 . . . . . 7H 23
NW10 . . . . . *3D 80*
(off Trenmar Gdns.)
TW8: Bford 5F 97
W3 . . . . . *6J 79*
(off Horn La.)
Pegasus Ho. *E1* *4K 85*
(off Beaumont Sq.)
E13 . . . . . 3K 87
Pegasus Pl. SE11 . . . . . 7J 19 (6A 102)
SW6 . . . . . 1J 117
Pegasus Rd. CR0: Wadd 6A 168
Pegasus Way N11 . . . . . 6A 32
Peggotty Way UB8: Hil 6D 74
Pegg Rd. TW5: Hest 7B 94
Pegley Gdns. SE12 . . . . . 2J 141
Pegswood Ct. *E1* *7G 85*
(off Cable St.)
Pegwell St. SE18 . . . . . 7J 107
Pekin Cl. *E14* *6C 86*
(off Pekin St.)
Pekin St. E14 . . . . . 6C 86
Pelabon Ho. *TW1: Twick* *6D 114*
(off Clevedon Rd.)
Peldon Ct. TW9: Rich 4F 115
Peldon Pas. TW10: Rich 4F 115
Peldon Wlk. *N1* *1B 84*
(off Popham St.)
Pelham Av. IG11: Bark 1K 89
Pelham Cl. SE5 . . . . . 3E 120
Pelham Cotts. DA5: Bexl 1H 145
Pelham Ct. DA14: Sidc 3A 144
SW3 . . . . . *4C 16*
(off Fulham Rd.)
Pelham Cres. SW7 . . . . . 4C 16 (4C 100)
Pelham Ho. *SW1* *2D 18*
(off Gt. Peter St.)
W14 . . . . . *4H 99*
(off Mornington Av.)
Pelham Pl. SW7 . . . . . 4C 16 (4C 100)
W13 . . . . . 4K 77
Pelham Rd. BR3: Beck 2J 157
DA7: Bex 3G 127
E18 . . . . . 3K 51
IG1: Ilf 2H 71
N15 . . . . . 4F 49
N22 . . . . . 2A 48
SW19 . . . . . 7J 135
Pelham St. SW7 . . . . . 3B 16 (4B 100)
Pelican Dr. HA2: Harr 2F 59
Pelican Est. SE15 . . . . . 1F 121
Pelican Ho. SE5 . . . . . 1F 121
SE8 . . . . . 4B 104
Pelican Pas. E1 . . . . . 4J 85
Pelican Wlk. SW9 . . . . . 4B 120
Pelican Wharf *E1* *1J 103*
(off Wapping Wall)
Pelier St. SE17 . . . . . 6C 102
Pelinore Rd. SE6 . . . . . 2G 141
Pella Ho. SE11 . . . . . 5H 19 (5K 101)
Pellant Rd. SW6 . . . . . 7G 99
Pellatt Gro. N22 . . . . . 1A 48
Pellatt Rd. HA9: Wemb 2D 60
SE22 . . . . . 5F 121
Pellerin Rd. N16 . . . . . 5E 66
Pellew Ho. *E1* *4H 85*
(off Somerford St.)
Pellings Cl. BR2: Brom 3G 159
Pelling St. E14 . . . . . 6C 86
Pellipar Cl. N13 . . . . . 3F 33
Pellipar Gdns. SE18 . . . . . 5D 106
Pellipar Rd. SE18 . . . . . 5D 106
Pellow Cl. EN5: Barn 6C 20
Pell St. SE8 . . . . . 4A 104
Pelly Rd. E13 . . . . . 1J 87
(not continuous)
Peloton Av. E20 . . . . . 5D 68
Pelter St. E2 . . . . . 1J 9 (3F 85)
Pelton Rd. SE10 . . . . . 5G 105
Pembar Av. E17 . . . . . 3A 50
Pemberley Chase
KT19: Ewe 5H 163
Pemberley Cl. KT19: Ewe 5H 163
Pemberley Ho. *KT19: Ewe* *5H 163*
(off Pemberley Chase)
Pember Rd. NW10 . . . . . 3F 81
Pemberton Cl.
TW19: Stanw 1A 128
Pemberton Ct. *E1* *3K 85*
(off Portelet Rd.)
EN1: Enf 3K 23
Pemberton Gdns. N19 . . . . . 3G 65
RM6: Chad H 5E 54
Pemberton Ho. *SE26* *4G 139*
(off High Level Dr.)
Pemberton Pl. E8 . . . . . 7H 67
Pemberton Rd. KT8: E Mos 4G 149
N4 . . . . . 5A 48
Pemberton Row EC4 . . . . . 7K 7 (6A 84)
Pemberton Ter. N19 . . . . . 3G 65
Pembridge Av. TW2: Whitt 1D 130
Pembridge Cres. W11 . . . . . 7J 81
Pembridge Gdns. W2 . . . . . 7J 81
Pembridge M. W11 . . . . . 7J 81
Pembridge Pl. SW15 . . . . . 5J 117
W2 . . . . . 7J 81
Pembridge Rd. W11 . . . . . 7J 81
Pembridge Sq. W2 . . . . . 7J 81
Pembridge Studios *W11* *7J 81*
(off Pembridge Vs.)
Pembridge Vs. W2 . . . . . 7J 81
W11 . . . . . 7J 81
Pembroke *W14* *4H 99*
(off Kensington Village)
Pembroke Av. EN1: Enf 1C 24
HA3: Kenton 3A 42
HA5: Pinn 1B 58
KT5: Surb 5H 151
N1 . . . . . 1J 83
Pembroke Bldgs. NW10 . . . . . 3C 80
Pembroke Bus. Cen. BR8: Swan 7K 145
Pembroke Cen., The HA4: Ruis 1H 57
Pembroke Cl. SW1 . . . . . 7H 11 (2E 100)
Pembroke Cotts. *W8* *3J 99*
(off Pembroke Sq.)
Pembroke Ct. *W7* *6K 77*
(off Copley Cl.)
W8 . . . . . *3J 99*
(off Sth. Edwardes Sq.)
Pembroke Gdns. HA4: Ruis 1H 57
RM10: Dag 3H 73
SW14 . . . . . 4H 115
W8 . . . . . 4H 99
Pembroke Gdns. Cl. W8 . . . . . 3J 99
Pembroke Hall *NW4* *3E 44*
(off Mulberry Cl.)
Pembroke Ho. RM8: Dag 5A 72
SW1 . . . . . *2G 17*
(off Chesham St.)
W2 . . . . . *6K 81*
(off Hallfield Est.)
W3 . . . . . *2J 97*
(off Park Rd. E.)
Pembroke Lodge HA7: Stan 6J 27
Pembroke Mans. *NW6* *6A 64*
(off Canfield Gdns.)

Pembroke M. E3 3A 86
N10 1E 46
W8 3J 99
Pembroke Pde. DA8: Erith 5J 109
Pembroke Pl. HA8: Edg 7B 28
TW7: Isle 2J 113
W8 3J 99
Pembroke Rd.
BR1: Brom 2A 160
CR4: Mitc 2E 154
DA8: Erith 5J 109
E6 5D 88
E17 5D 50
HA4: Ruis 1G 57
HA9: Wemb 3D 60
IG3: Ilf 1K 71
N8 4J 47
N10 1E 46
N13 3H 33
N15 5F 49
SE25 4E 156
UB6: G'frd 4F 77
W8 4H 99
Pembroke Sq. W8 3J 99
Pembroke St. N1 7J 65
(not continuous)
Pembroke Studios W8 3H 99
Pembroke Ter. *NW8* *1B 82*
(off Queen's Ter.)
Pembroke Vs. TW9: Rich 4D 114
W8 4J 99
Pembroke Wlk. W8 4J 99
Pembroke Way UB3: Harl 3E 92
Pembrook M. SW11 4B 118
Pembry Cl. SW9 1A 120
Pembury Av. KT4: Wor Pk 1C 164
Pembury Cl. BR2: Hayes 7H 159
E5 5H 67
Pembury Ct. UB3: Harl 6F 93
Pembury Cres. DA14: Sidc 2E 144
Pembury Pl. E5 5H 67
Pembury Rd. DA7: Bex 7E 108
E5 5H 67
N17 1F 49
SE25 4G 157
Pemdevon Rd. CR0: C'don 7A 156
Pemell Cl. E1 4J 85
Pemell Ho. *E1* *4J 85*
(off Pemell Cl.)
Pemerich Cl. UB3: Harl 5H 93
Pempath Pl. HA9: Wemb 2D 60
Penally Pl. N1 1D 84
Penang Ho. *E1* *1H 103*
(off Prusom St.)
Penang St. E1 1H 103
Penard Rd. UB2: S'hall 3F 95
Penart Ct. SM2: Sutt 7A 166
Penarth Cen. SE15 6J 103
Penarth St. SE15 6J 103
Penberth Rd. SE6 2E 140
Penbury Rd. UB2: S'hall 4D 94
Pencombe M. W11 7H 81
Pencraig Way SE15 6H 103
Pendall Cl. EN4: E Barn 4H 21
Penda Rd. DA8: Erith 7H 109
Pendarves Rd. SW20 1E 152
Penda's Mead E9 4A 68
Pendell Av. UB3: Harl 7H 93
Pendennis Ho. SE8 4A 104
Pendennis Rd. N17 3D 48
SW16 4J 137
Penderel Rd. TW3: Houn 5E 112
Penderry Ri. SE6 2F 141
Penderyn Way N7 4H 65
Pendlebury Ct. *KT5: Surb* *4E 150*
(off Cranes Pk.)
Pendle Ct. UB10: Hil 1D 74
Pendle Ho. SE26 3G 139
Pendle Rd. SW16 6F 137
Pendlestone Rd. E17 5D 50
Pendlewood Cl. W5 5C 78
Pendley Ho. *E2* *1G 85*
(off Whiston Rd.)
Pendolino Way NW10 7G 61
Pendragon Rd. BR1: Brom 3H 141
Pendragon Wlk. NW9 6A 44
Pendrell Ho. *WC2* *1D 12*
(off New Compton St.)
Pendrell Rd. SE4 2A 122
Pendrell St. SE18 6H 107
Pendula Dr. UB4: Yead 4B 76
Pendulum M. E8 5F 67
Penerley Rd. SE6 1D 140
Penfield Lodge *W9* *5J 81*
(off Admiral Wlk.)
Penfields Ho. *N7* *6J 65*
(off York Way Est.)
Penfold Cl. CR0: Wadd 3A 168
Penfold La. DA5: Bexl 2D 144
(not continuous)
Penfold Pl. NW1 5C 4 (5C 82)
Penfold Rd. N9 1E 34
Penfold St. NW1 4B 4 (4B 82)
NW8 4B 4 (4B 82)
Penford Gdns. SE9 3B 124
Penford St. SE5 2B 120
Pengarth Rd. DA5: Bexl 5D 126
PENGE 7J 139
Penge Ho. SW11 3B 118
Penge La. SE20 7J 139
Pengelly Apartments *E14* *5D 104*
(off Bartlett M.)
Penge Rd. E13 1A 88
SE20 3G 157
SE25 3G 157
Penhale Cl. BR6: Chels 4K 173
Penhall Rd. SE7 4B 106
Penhill Rd. DA5: Bexl 6C 126
Penhurst Mans. *SW6* *1H 117*
(off Rostrevor Rd.)
Penhurst Pl. SE1 1H 19
Penhurst Rd. IG6: Ilf 1F 53
Penifather La. UB6: G'frd 3H 77
Peninsula Apartments *N1* *1C 84*
(off Basire St.)
W2 *6C 4*
(off Praed St.)
Peninsula Ct. *E14* *3D 104*
(off E. Ferry Rd.)
N1 *1C 84*
(off Basire St.)
Peninsula Hgts. SE1 5F 19 (5J 101)
Peninsular Cl. NW7 5B 30
TW14: Felt 6F 111
Peninsular Pk. SE7 4J 105
Peninsular Pk. Rd. SE7 4J 105
Peninsula Sq. SE10 2G 105
Penistone Rd. SW16 7J 137
Penketh Dr. HA1: Harr 3H 59
Penley Ct. WC2 2H 13 (7K 83)
Penmayne Ho. *SE11* *5K 19*
(off Kennings Way)
Penmon Rd. SE2 3A 108
Pennack Rd. SE15 6F 103
Penn Almshouses *SE10* *1E 122*
(off Greenwich Sth. St.)
Pennant M. W8 4K 99
Pennant Ter. E17 2B 50
Pennard Mans. *W12* *2E 98*
(off Goldhawk Rd.)
Pennard Rd. W12 2E 98
Pennards, The TW16: Sun 3A 148
Penn Cl. HA3: Kenton 4C 42
UB6: G'frd 2F 77
Penn Ct. NW9 3K 43
Penner Cl. SW19 2G 135
Penners Gdns. KT6: Surb 7E 150
Pennethorne Cl. E9 1J 85
Pennethorne Ho. SW11 3B 118
Pennethorne Rd. SE15 7H 103
Penn Gdns. BR7: Chst 2F 161
RM5: Col R 1G 55
Penn Ho. *NW8* *4C 4*
(off Mallory St.)
Pennine Dr. NW2 2F 63
Pennine Ho. *N9* *3B 34*
(off Plevna Rd.)
Pennine La. NW2 2G 63
Pennine Pde. NW2 2G 63
Pennine Way DA7: Bex 1K 127
UB3: Harl 7F 93
Pennington Cl. SE27 4D 138
Pennington Ct. SE16 1A 104
Pennington Dr. N21 5D 22
Pennington Lodge *KT5: Surb* *5E 150*
(off Cranes Dr.)
Pennington St. E1 7H 85
Pennington Way SE12 2K 141
Penniston Cl. N17 2C 48
Penniwell Cl. HA8: Edg 4A 28
Penn La. DA5: Bexl 5D 126
Penn Rd. N7 5J 65
Penn St. N1 1D 84
Penny Brookes St. E15 6F 69
E20 6E 68
Penny Cl. E4 3B 36
Pennycroft CR0: Sels 7A 170
Pennyfather La. EN2: Enf 3H 23
Pennyfields E14 7C 86
(not continuous)
Penny Flds. Ho. *SE8* *1B 122*
(off Francis Harvey Way)
Pennyford Ct. *NW8* *3A 4*
(off St John's Wood Rd.)
Penny La. TW17: Shep 7G 147
Penny M. SW12 7F 119
Pennymoor Wlk. *W9* *4H 81*
(off Fernhead Rd.)
Penny Rd. NW10 3H 79
Penny Royal SM6: Wall 6H 167
Pennyroyal Av. E6 6E 88
Pennyroyal Dr. UB7: W Dray 2B 92
Penpoll Rd. E8 6H 67
Penpool La. DA16: Well 3B 126
Penrhyn Av. E17 1B 50
Penrhyn Cres. E17 1C 50
SW14 4J 115
Penrhyn Gdns. KT1: King T 4D 150
Penrhyn Gro. E17 1C 50
Penrhyn Rd. KT1: King T 4E 150
Penrith Cl. BR3: Beck 1D 158
SW15 5G 117
UB8: Uxb 7A 56
Penrith Pl. SE27 2B 138
Penrith Rd. CR7: Thor H 2C 156
KT3: N Mald 4K 151
N15 5D 48
Penrith St. SW16 6G 137
Penrose Ct. SW12 1E 136
Penrose Gro. SE17 5C 102
Penrose Ho. N21 5E 22
SE17 5C 102
Penrose St. SE17 5C 102
Penrose Way SE10 1G 105
Penryn Ho. *SE11* *5B 102*
(off Seaton Cl.)
Penryn St. NW1 2H 83
Penry St. SE1 4E 102
Pensbury Pl. SW8 2G 119
Pensbury St. SW8 2G 119
Pensford Av. TW9: Kew 2G 115
Penshurst NW5 6E 64
Penshurst Av. DA15: Sidc 6A 126
Penshurst Gdns. HA8: Edg 5C 28
Penshurst Grn. BR2: Brom 5H 159
Penshurst Ho. *SE15* *6J 103*
(off Lovelinch Cl.)
Penshurst Rd. CR7: Thor H 5B 156
DA7: Bex 1F 127
E9 7K 67
N17 7A 34
Penshurst Wlk. BR2: Brom 5H 159
Penshurst Way SM2: Sutt 7J 165
Pensilver Cl. EN4: E Barn 4H 21
Penstemon Cl. N3 6D 30
Penstock Footpath N8 3K 47
N22 3K 47
Pentagram Yd. *W11* *6J 81*
(off Needham Rd.)
Pentavia Retail Pk. NW7 7G 29
Pentelow Gdns. TW14: Felt 6J 111
Pentire Rd. E17 1F 51
Pentland Av. HA8: Edg 2C 28
TW17: Shep 5C 146
Pentland Cl. N9 2D 34
NW11 2G 63
Pentland Gdns. SW18 6A 118
Pentland Pl. UB5: N'olt 1C 76
Pentland Rd. NW6 3J 81
Pentlands Cl. CR4: Mitc 3F 155
Pentland St. SW18 6A 118
Pentland Way UB10: Ick 3E 56
Pentlow St. SW15 3E 116
Pentlow Way IG9: Buck H 1H 37
Pentney Rd. E4 1A 36
SW12 1G 137
SW19 1G 153
Penton Gro. N1 2A 84
Penton Ho. *N1* *1J 7*
(off Pentonville Rd.)
SE2 1D 108
Penton Pl. SE17 5B 102
Penton Ri. WC1 1H 7 (3K 83)
Penton St. N1 2A 84
PENTONVILLE 2K 83
Pentonville Rd. N1 1F 7 (2J 83)
Pentrich Av. EN1: Enf 1B 24
Pentridge St. SE15 7F 103
Pentyre Av. N18 5J 33
Penwerris Av. TW7: Isle 7G 95
Penwerris Ct. TW5: Hest 7G 95
Penwith Rd. SW18 2J 135
Penwood Ct. HA5: Pinn 4D 40
Penwood Ho. SW15 6B 116
Penwortham Ct. *N22* *2A 48*
(off Mayes Rd.)
Penwortham Rd. SW16 6F 137
Penylan Pl. HA8: Edg 7B 28
Penywern Rd. SW5 5J 99
Penzance Pl. W11 1G 99
Penzance St. W11 1G 99
Peony Ct. IG8: Wfd G 7B 36
SW10 7A 16 (6A 100)
Peony Gdns. W12 7C 80
Peperfield *WC1* *2G 7*
(off Cromer St.)
Pepler Ho. *W10* *4G 81*
(off Wornington Rd.)
Pepler M. SE5 5F 103
Peploe Rd. NW6 2F 81
Peplow Cl. UB7: Yiew 1A 92
Pepper Cl. E6 5D 88
Peppercorn Cl. CR7: Thor H 2D 156
Peppermead Sq. SE13 5C 122
Peppermint Cl. CR0: C'don 7J 155
Peppermint Pl. E11 3G 69
Pepper St. E14 3D 104
SE1 6C 14 (2C 102)
Peppie Cl. N16 2E 66
Pepys Cl. UB10: Ick 4D 56
Pepys Cres. E16 1J 105
EN5: Barn 5A 20
Pepys Ho. *E2* *3J 85*
(off Kirkwall Pl.)
Pepys Ri. BR6: Orp 1K 173
Pepys Rd. SE14 1K 121
SW20 1E 152
Pepys St. EC3 2H 15 (7E 84)
Perceval Av. NW3 5C 64
Perceval Ct. UB5: N'olt 5E 58
Perceval Ho. W5 7C 78
Percheron Cl. TW7: Isle 3K 113
Perch St. E8 4F 67
Percival Av. NW9 2B 44

Percival Ct. N17 ... 7A 34
Percival Gdns. RM6: Chad H ... 6C 54
Percival M. SE11 ... 7G 19 (6K 101)
Percival Rd. BR6: Farnb ... 2F 173
EN1: Enf ... 4A 24
SW14 ... 4J 115
TW13: Felt ... 2H 129
Percival St. EC1 ... 3A 8 (4B 84)
Percival Way KT19: Ewe ... 4K 163
Percy Av. TW15: Ashf ... 5C 128
Percy Bilton Ct. TW5: Hest ... 1F 113
(off Skinners La.)
Percy Bryant Rd. TW16: Sun ... 7G 129
Percy Bush Rd. UB7: W Dray ... 3B 92
Percy Cir. WC1 ... 1H 7 (3K 83)
Percy Gdns. EN3: Pond E ... 5E 24
KT4: Wor Pk ... 1K 163
TW7: Isle ... 3B 114
UB4: Hayes ... 3G 75
Percy Laurie Ho. SW15 ... 4F 117
(off Nursery Cl.)
Percy M. W1 ... 6C 6
Percy Pas. W1 ... 6C 6
Percy Rd. CR4: Mitc ... 7E 154
DA7: Bex ... 2E 126
E11 ... 7G 51
E16 ... 5G 87
IG3: Ilf ... 7A 54
N12 ... 5F 31
N21 ... 7H 23
RM7: Mawney ... 3H 55
SE20 ... 1K 157
SE25 ... 5G 157
TW2: Whitt ... 1F 131
TW7: Isle ... 4A 114
TW12: Hamp ... 7E 130
W12 ... 2C 98
Percy St. W1 ... 6C 6 (5H 83)
Percy Ter. BR1: Brom ... 3F 161
Percy Way TW2: Whitt ... 1G 131
Percy Yd. WC1 ... 1H 7 (3K 83)
Peregrine Cl. NW10 ... 5K 61
Peregrine Ct. DA16: Well ... 1K 125
SE8 ... 6C 104
(off Edward St.)
SW16 ... 4K 137
Peregrine Gdns. CR0: C'don ... 2A 170
Peregrine Ho. EC1 ... 1B 8
Peregrine Rd. N17 ... 7H 33
TW16: Sun ... 2H 147
Peregrine Way SW19 ... 7E 134
Perendale Dr. TW17: Shep ... 1E 146
Perham Rd. W14 ... 5G 99
Peridot Ct. E2 ... 2J 9
(off Virginia Rd.)
Peridot St. E6 ... 5C 88
Perifield SE21 ... 1C 138
Perilla Ho. E1 ... 6G 85
(off Boulevard Walkway)
Perimeade Rd. UB6: G'frd ... 2C 78
Periton Rd. SE9 ... 4B 124
PERIVALE ... 1C 78
Perivale Gdns. W13 ... 4B 78
Perivale Grange UB6: G'frd ... 3A 78
Perivale La. UB6: G'frd ... 3A 78
Perivale Lodge UB6: G'frd ... 3A 78
(off Perivale La.)
Perivale New Bus. Cen. UB6: G'frd ... 2C 78
Perivale Pk. UB6: G'frd ... 2B 78
Perivale Pk. Athletics Track ... 3J 77
Perivale Pk. Golf Course ... 3J 77
Perivale Wood Local Nature Reserve
... 1K 77
Periwood Cres. UB6: G'frd ... 1A 78
Perkin Cl. HA0: Wemb ... 5B 60
TW3: Houn ... 4E 112
Perkins Ct. TW15: Ashf ... 5B 128
Perkins Gdns. UB10: Ick ... 2E 56
Perkins Ho. E14 ... 5B 86
(off Wallwood St.)
Perkin's Rents SW1 ... 2C 18 (3H 101)
Perkins Rd. IG2: Ilf ... 5H 53
Perkins Sq. SE1 ... 4D 14 (1C 102)
Perks Cl. SE3 ... 3G 123
Perkyn Sq. N17 ... 3H 49
Perley Ho. E3 ... 5B 86
(off Weatherley Cl.)
Perpins Rd. SE9 ... 6J 125
Perran Rd. SW2 ... 1B 138
Perran Wlk.
TW8: Bford ... 5E 96
Perren St. NW5 ... 6F 65
Perrers Rd. W6 ... 4D 98
Perrin Apartments N1 ... 7J 65
(off Caledonian Rd.)
Perrin Cl. TW15: Ashf ... 5B 128
WD23: B Hea ... 1D 26
Perrin Ct. TW15: Ashf ... 4C 128
Perring Est. E3 ... 5C 86
(off Gale St.)
Perrin Ho. NW6 ... 3J 81
Perrin Rd. HA0: Wemb ... 4B 60
Perrin's Ct. NW3 ... 4A 64
Perrin's La. NW3 ... 4A 64
Perrin's Wlk. NW3 ... 4A 64
Perronet Ho. SE1 ... 3B 102
(off Princess St.)
Perrott St. SE18 ... 4G 107
Perry Av. W3 ... 6K 79
Perry Cl. IG2: Ilf ... 6H 53
UB8: Hil ... 6D 74
Perry Ct. E14 ... 5C 104
(off Maritime Quay)
KT1: King T ... 2E 150
(off Old London Rd.)
N15 ... 6E 48
Perryfield Way NW9 ... 6B 44
TW10: Ham ... 3B 132
Perry Gdns. N9 ... 3J 33
Perry Gth. UB5: N'olt ... 1A 76
Perry Hall Rd. BR6: St M Cry ... 6K 161
Perry Hill SE6 ... 3B 140
Perry How KT4: Wor Pk ... 1B 164
Perry Lodge E12 ... 1B 70
Perryman Ho. IG11: Bark ... 1G 89
(off The Shaftesburys)
Perrymans Farm Rd. IG2: Ilf ... 6H 53
Perry Mead EN2: Enf ... 2G 23
Perrymead St. SW6 ... 1J 117
Perryn Ct. TW1: Twick ... 6A 114
Perryn Ho. W3 ... 7A 80
Perryn Rd. SE16 ... 3H 103
W3 ... 1K 97
Perry Ri. SE23 ... 3A 140
Perry Rd. RM9: Dag ... 5F 91
Perry's Pl. W1 ... 7C 6 (6H 83)
Perry St. BR7: Chst ... 6H 143
DA1: Cray ... 4K 127
Perry St. Gdns. BR7: Chst ... 6J 143
Perry St. Shaw BR7: Chst ... 7J 143
Perry Va. SE23 ... 2J 139
Persant Rd. SE6 ... 2G 141
Perseverance Pl. SW9 ... 7A 102
TW9: Rich ... 4E 114
Perseverance Works E2 ... 1H 9
(off Kingsland Rd.)
Pershore Cl. IG2: Ilf ... 5F 53
Pershore Gro. SM5: Cars ... 6B 154
Pershore Ho. W13 ... 1A 96
(off Singapore Rd.)
Pert Cl. N10 ... 7A 32
Perth Av. NW9 ... 7K 43
UB4: Yead ... 4A 76
Perth Cl. SE5 ... 4D 120
SW20 ... 2B 152
UB5: N'olt ... 5E 58
Perth Ho. N1 ... 7K 65
(off Bemerton Est.)
Perth Rd. BR3: Beck ... 2E 158
E10 ... 1A 68
E13 ... 2K 87
IG2: Ilf ... 6E 52
Perth Rd. IG11: Bark ... 2H 89
N4 ... 1A 66
N22 ... 1B 48
Perth Ter. IG2: Ilf ... 7G 53
Perwell Av. HA2: Harr ... 1D 58
Perystreete SE23 ... 2J 139
Petavel Rd. TW11: Tedd ... 6J 131
Peter Av. NW10 ... 7D 62
Peter Best Ho. E1 ... 6H 85
(off Nelson St.)
Peterboat Cl. SE10 ... 4G 105
Peterborough Ct. EC4 ... 1K 13 (6A 84)
Peterborough Gdns. IG1: Ilf ... 7C 52
Peterborough M. SW6 ... 2J 117
Peterborough Rd. E10 ... 5E 50
HA1: Harr ... 1J 59
SM5: Cars ... 6C 154
SW6 ... 2J 117
Peterborough Vs. SW6 ... 1K 117
Peter Butler Ho. SE1 ... 7K 15
(off Wolseley St.)
Peterchurch Ho. SE15 ... 6H 103
(off Commercial Way)
Petergate SW11 ... 4A 118
Peter Harrison Planetarium ... 7F 105
Peterhead Ct. UB1: S'hall ... 6G 77
(off Osborne Rd.)
Peter Heathfield Ho. E15 ... 1F 87
(off Wise Rd.)
Peter Hills Ho. SE16 ... 4G 103
(off Alexis St.)
Peter Ho. SW8 ... 7J 101
(off Luscombe Way)
Peter James Bus. Cen. UB3: Hayes ... 2J 93
Peter James Ent. Cen. NW10 ... 3J 79
Peter Kennedy Ct. CR0: C'don ... 6B 158
Peterley Bus. Cen. E2 ... 2H 85
Peter Lyell Ct. HA4: Ruis ... 2K 57
Peter May Sports Cen. ... 7K 35
Peter Pan Statue ... 4A 10 (1B 100)
Peters Cl. DA16: Well ... 2J 125
HA7: Stan ... 6J 27
RM8: Dag ... 1D 72
Peters Ct. W2 ... 6K 81
(off Porchester Rd.)
Petersfield Cl. N18 ... 5H 33
Petersfield Ri. SW15 ... 1D 134
Petersfield Rd. W3 ... 2J 97
Petersgate KT2: King T ... 6J 133
(off Warren Rd.)
PETERSHAM ... 1E 132
Petersham Cl. SM1: Sutt ... 5J 165
TW10: Ham ... 2D 132
Petersham Dr. BR5: St P ... 2K 161
Petersham Gdns. BR5: St P ... 2K 161
Petersham Ho. SW7 ... 3A 16
(off Kendrick M.)
Petersham La. SW7 ... 3A 100
Petersham M. SW7 ... 3A 100
Petersham Pl. SW7 ... 3A 100
Petersham Rd. TW10: Rich, Ham ... 6D 114
Petersham Ter. CR0: Bedd ... 3J 167
(off Richmond Grn.)
Peter's Hill EC4 ... 2C 14 (7C 84)
Peter Shore Ct. E1 ... 5K 85
(off Beaumont Sq.)
Peter's La. EC1 ... 5B 8 (5B 84)
(not continuous)
Peter's Path SE26 ... 4H 139
Peterstone Rd. SE2 ... 2B 108
Peterstow Cl. SW19 ... 2G 135
Peter St. W1 ... 2C 12 (7H 83)
Peterwood Pk. CR0: Wadd ... 2K 167
Peterwood Way CR0: Wadd ... 2K 167
Petherton Ct. HA1: Harr ... 6K 41
(off Gayton Rd.)
NW10 ... 1F 81
(off Tiverton Rd.)
Petherton Rd. N5 ... 5C 66
Petiver Cl. E9 ... 7J 67
Petley Rd. W6 ... 6F 99
Peto Pl. NW1 ... 3K 5 (4F 83)
Peto St. Nth. E16 ... 6H 87
Petrie Cl. NW2 ... 6G 63
Petrie Ho. SE18 ... 6E 106
(off Woolwich Comn.)
Petrie Mus. of Egyptian Archaeology
... 4C 6 (4H 83)
Petros Gdns. NW3 ... 6K 63
Pettacre Cl. SE28 ... 3G 107
Petticoat La. E1 ... 6J 9 (5E 84)
Petticoat Lane Market ... 7J 9
(in Wentworth St.)
Petticoat Sq. E1 ... 7J 9 (6F 85)
Petticoat Twr. E1 ... 7J 9
Pettits Cl. RM1: Rom ... 2K 55
Pettits La. Nth. RM1: Rom ... 1K 55
Pettits Pl. RM10: Dag ... 5G 73
Pettits Rd. RM10: Dag ... 5G 73
Pettiward Cl. SW15 ... 4E 116
Pettley Gdns. RM7: Rom ... 5K 55
Pettman Cres. SE28 ... 3H 107
Pettsgrove Av. HA0: Wemb ... 5C 60
Pett's Hill UB5: N'olt ... 5F 59
Petts La. TW17: Shep ... 4C 146
Pett St. SE18 ... 4C 106
PETTS WOOD ... 5H 161
Petts Wood Rd. BR5: Pet W ... 5G 161
Petty France SW1 ... 1B 18 (3G 101)
Petty Wales EC3 ... 3H 15 (7E 84)
Petworth Cl. UB5: N'olt ... 7D 58
Petworth Gdns. SW20 ... 3D 152
UB10: Hil ... 1E 74
Petworth Rd. DA6: Bex ... 5G 127
N12 ... 5H 31
Petworth St. SW11 ... 1C 118
Petyt Pl. SW3 ... 6C 100
Petyward SW3 ... 4D 16 (4C 100)
Pevensey Av. EN1: Enf ... 2K 23
N11 ... 5C 32
Pevensey Cl. TW7: Isle ... 7G 95
Pevensey Ct. SW16 ... 3A 138
W3 ... 2H 97
Pevensey Ho. E1 ... 5K 85
(off Ben Jonson Rd.)
Pevensey Rd. E7 ... 4H 69
SW17 ... 4B 136
TW13: Felt ... 1C 130
Peverel E6 ... 6E 88
Peverel Ho. RM10: Dag ... 2G 73
Peveret Cl. N11 ... 5A 32
Peveril Dr. TW11: Tedd ... 5H 131
Peveril Ho. SE1 ... 3D 102
(off Rephidim St.)
Pewsey Cl. E4 ... 5H 35
Peyton Pl. SE10 ... 7E 104
Pharamond NW2 ... 6F 63
Pharaoh Cl. CR4: Mitc ... 7D 154
Pheasant Cl. E16 ... 6K 87
Pheasantry Ho. SW3 ... 5D 16
(off Jubilee Pl.)
Pheasantry Welcome Cen., The ... 1K 149
Phelps La. NW7 ... 5B 30
Phelps Lodge N1 ... 1K 83
Phelp St. SE17 ... 6D 102
Phelps Way UB3: Harl ... 4H 93
Phene St. SW3 ... 7D 16 (6C 100)
Philadelphia Ct. SW10 ... 7A 100
(off Uverdale Rd.)
Philbeach Gdns. SW5 ... 5J 99
Phil Brown Pl.
SW8 ... 3F 119
(off Daley Thompson Way)
Philchurch Pl. E1 ... 6G 85
Philia Ho. NW1 ... 7G 65
(off Farrier St.)
Philimore Cl. SE18 ... 5J 107
Philip Av. RM7: Rush G ... 1K 73
Philip Cl. RM7: Rush G ... 1K 73
Philip Ct. W2 ... 5A 4
(off Hall Pl.)
Philip Gdns. CR0: C'don ... 2B 170

Philip Ho. NW6 . . . . . 1K 81
(off Mortimer Pl.)
Philip Jones Ct. N4 . . . . . 1K 65
Philip La. N15 . . . . . 4D 48
Philip Mole Ho. W9 . . . . . 4J 81
(off Chippenham Rd.)
Philipot Path SE9 . . . . . 6D 124
Philippa Gdns. SE9 . . . . . 5B 124
Philip Rd. N15 . . . . . 4D 48
TW18: Staines 6A 128
Philips Cl. SM5: Cars 1E 166
Philip Sq. SW8 . . . . . 2F 119
Philip St. E13 . . . . . 4J 87
Philip Wlk. SE15 . . . . . 3G 121
(not continuous)
Phillimore Ct. W8 . . . . . 2J 99
(off Kensington High St.)
Phillimore Gdns. NW10 . . . . . 1E 80
W3 . . . . . 1G 97
W8 . . . . . 2J 99
Phillimore Gdns. Cl. W8 . . . . . 3J 99
Phillimore Pl. W8 . . . . . 2J 99
Phillimore Ter. W8 . . . . . 3J 99
(off Allen St.)
Phillimore Wlk. W8 . . . . . 3J 99
Phillip Ho. E1 . . . . . 6K 9
(off Heneage St.)
Phillipp St. N1 . . . . . 1E 84
Phillips Ct. HA8: Edg 6B 28
Philpot La. EC3 . . . . . 2G 15 (7E 84)
Philpot Path IG1: Ilf 3G 71
Philpots Cl. UB7: Yiew 7A 74
Philpot Sq. SW6 . . . . . 3K 117
Philpot St. E1 . . . . . 6H 85
Phineas Pett Rd. SE9 . . . . . 3C 124
Phipps Bri. Rd. CR4: Mitc 3B 154
SW19 . . . . . 2A 154
Phipps Hatch La. EN2: Enf 1H 23
Phipps Ho. SE7 . . . . . 5K 105
(off Woolwich Rd.)
W12 . . . . . 7D 80
(off White City Est.)
Phipp's M. SW1 . . . . . 3F 101
(off Buckingham Palace Rd.)
Phipp St. EC2 . . . . . 3G 9 (4E 84)
Phoebeth Rd. SE4 . . . . . 5C 122
Phoebe Wlk. E16 . . . . . 6K 87
Phoenix Av. SE10 . . . . . 2G 105
Phoenix Cen. 7J 167
Phoenix Cinema
East Finchley 4C 46
Phoenix Cl. BR4: W W'ck 2F 171
CR4: Mitc 3B 154
E8 . . . . . 1F 85
E17 . . . . . 2B 50
W12 . . . . . 7D 80
Phoenix Ct. CR2: S Croy 5F 169
E1 . . . . . 4H 85
(off Buckhurst St.)
E4 . . . . . 3J 35
E14 . . . . . 4C 104
KT3: N Mald 3B 152
NW1 . . . . . 1D 6
(off Purchese St.)
SE14 . . . . . 6A 104
(off Chipley St.)
TW3: Houn 3E 112
TW4: Houn 5B 112
TW8: Bford 5E 96
TW13: Felt 4G 129
Phoenix Dr. BR2: Kes 4B 172
Phoenix Hgts. E. E14 . . . . . 2C 104
(off Byng St.)
Phoenix Hgts. W. E14 . . . . . 2C 104
(off Mastmaker Ct.)
Phoenix Ho. SM1: Sutt 4K 165
Phoenix Ind. Est. HA1: Harr 4K 41
Phoenix Lodge Mans. W6 . . . . . 4F 99
(off Brook Grn.)
Phoenix Pk. NW2 . . . . . 2C 62
Phoenix Pl. WC1 . . . . . 3H 7 (4K 83)

Phoenix Point SE28 . . . . . 1C 108
Phoenix Rd. NW1 . . . . . 1C 6 (2H 83)
SE20 . . . . . 6J 139
Phoenix Sports Cen.
Hammersmith 7C 80
Phoenix St. WC2 . . . . . 1D 12 (6H 83)
Phoenix Theatre 1D 12
(off Charing Cross Rd.)
Phoenix Trad. Est. UB6: G'frd 1C 78
Phoenix Trad. Pk. TW8: Bford 5D 96
Phoenix Way E16 . . . . . 5H 87
(off Barking Rd.)
SW18 . . . . . 5A 118
TW5: Hest 6B 94
Phoenix Wharf E1 . . . . . 1H 103
(off Wapping High St.)
Phoenix Wharf Rd. SE1 . . . . . 7K 15
Phoenix Yd. WC1 . . . . . 2H 7
Photographers Gallery 1A 12
(off Ramillies St.)
Phyllis Av. KT3: N Mald 5D 152
Phyllis Hodges Ho. NW1 . . . . . 1C 6
(off Aldenham St.)
Phyllis Ho. CR0: Wadd 4B 168
(off Ashley La.)
Physical Energy Statue 5A 10 (1A 100)
Physic Pl. SW3 . . . . . 7E 16 (6D 100)
Piano La. N16 . . . . . 3D 66
Piano Works IG11: Bark 7G 71
(off Ripple Rd.)
Piano Yd. NW5 . . . . . 5F 65
Piazza, The UB8: Uxb 7A 56
WC2 . . . . . 2F 13
(not continuous)
Piazza Wlk. E1 . . . . . 1K 15 (6G 85)
Picardy Ho. EN2: Enf 1H 23
Picardy Manorway DA17: Belv 3H 109
Picardy Rd. DA17: Belv 5G 109
Picardy St. DA17: Belv 3G 109
Piccadilly W1 . . . . . 5K 11 (1F 101)
Piccadilly Arc. SW1 . . . . . 4A 12
Piccadilly Circus 3C 12 (7H 83)
Piccadilly Cir. W1 . . . . . 3C 12 (7H 83)
Piccadilly Ct. N7 . . . . . 6K 65
(off Caledonian Rd.)
Piccadilly Pl. W1 . . . . . 3B 12
Piccadilly Theatre 2B 12
(off Denman St.)
Pickard Cl. N14 . . . . . 1C 32
Pickard Gdns. E3 . . . . . 5B 86
Pickard St. EC1 . . . . . 1B 8 (3B 84)
Pickering Av. E6 . . . . . 2E 88
Pickering Cl. E9 . . . . . 7K 67
Pickering Gdns. CR0: C'don 6F 157
N11 . . . . . 6K 31
Pickering Ho. W2 . . . . . 6A 82
(off Hallfield Est.)
W5 . . . . . 4C 96
(off Windmill Rd.)
Pickering La. BR5: Farnb 1H 173
Pickering M. W2 . . . . . 6K 81
Pickering Pl. SW1 . . . . . 5B 12
Pickering Rd. IG11: Bark 6G 71
Pickering St. N1 . . . . . 1B 84
Pickets Cl. WD23: B Hea 1C 26
Pickets St. SW12 . . . . . 7F 119
Pickett Cft. HA7: Stan 1D 42
Picketts Lock La. N9 . . . . . 2D 34
Picketts Lock La. Ind. Est. N9 . . . . . 2F 35
Picketts Ter. SE22 . . . . . 5G 121
Pickford Cl. DA7: Bex 2E 126
Pickford La. DA7: Bex 2E 126
Pickford Rd. DA7: Bex 3E 126
Pickfords Wharf N1 . . . . . 2C 84
SE1 . . . . . 4E 14 (1D 102)
Pickhurst Grn. BR2: Hayes 7H 159
Pickhurst La. BR2: Hayes 5G 159
BR4: W W'ck 5G 159
Pickhurst Mead BR2: Hayes 7H 159
Pickhurst Pk. BR2: Brom 5G 159
Pickhurst Ri. BR4: W W'ck 7E 158

Pickle M. SW9 . . . . . 7A 102
Pickwick Cl. TW4: Houn 5C 112
Pickwick Ct. SE9 . . . . . 1C 142
Pickwick Ho. SE16 . . . . . 2G 103
(off George Row)
W11 . . . . . 1F 99
(off St Ann's Rd.)
Pickwick M. N18 . . . . . 4K 33
Pickwick Pl. HA1: Harr 7J 41
Pickwick Rd. SE21 . . . . . 7D 120
Pickwick St. SE1 . . . . . 7C 14 (2C 102)
Pickwick Way
BR7: Chst 6G 143
Pickworth Cl. SW8 . . . . . 7J 101
Picton Pl. KT6: Surb 1G 163
W1 . . . . . 1H 11 (6E 82)
Picton St. SE5 . . . . . 7D 102
Picture Ho. SW16 . . . . . 2J 137
Picturehouse Central 7H 83
(of Shaftesbury Av.)
Pied Bull Ct. WC1 . . . . . 6E 6
(off Bury Pl.)
Pied Bull Yd. N1 . . . . . 1B 84
(off Theberton St.)
WC1 . . . . . 6E 6
Piedmont Rd. SE18 . . . . . 5H 107
(not continuous)
PIELD HEATH 4B 74
Pield Heath Av. UB8: Hil 4C 74
Pield Heath Rd. UB8: Cowl, Hil 4A 74
Pierce Campion Ct. E17 . . . . . 3B 50
Pier Head E1 . . . . . 1H 103
(not continuous)
Pierhead Wharf E1 . . . . . 1H 103
(off Wapping High St.)
Pier Ho. SW3 . . . . . 7D 16 (6C 100)
Pieris Ho. TW13: Felt 2J 129
(off High St.)
Piermont Grn. SE22 . . . . . 5H 121
Piermont Pl. BR1: Brom 2C 160
Piermont Rd. SE22 . . . . . 5H 121
Pier Pde. E16 . . . . . 1E 106
(off Pier Rd.)
Pierpoint Bldg. E14 . . . . . 2B 104
Pierrepoint Rd. W3 . . . . . 7H 79
Pierrepont Arc. N1 . . . . . 2B 84
(off Islington High St.)
Pierrepont Row N1 . . . . . 2B 84
(off Camden Pas.)
Pier Rd. E16 . . . . . 1E 106
TW14: Felt 5K 111
Pier St. E14 . . . . . 4E 104
(not continuous)
Pier Ter. SW18 . . . . . 4K 117
Pier Wlk. SE10 . . . . . 2G 105
Pier Way SE28 . . . . . 2G 107
Pietra Lara Bldg. EC1 . . . . . 3C 8
(off Pear Tree St.)
Pigeon La. TW12: Hamp 4E 130
Piggott Ho. E2 . . . . . 2K 85
(off Sewardstone Rd.)
Piggott St. E14 . . . . . 6C 86
Pike Cl. BR1: Brom 5K 141
UB10: Uxb 1B 74
Pikemans Ct. SW5 . . . . . 4J 99
(off W. Cromwell Rd.)
Pike Rd. NW7 . . . . . 4E 28
Pike's End HA5: Eastc 4K 39
Pikestone Cl. UB4: Yead 4C 76
Pikethorne SE23 . . . . . 2K 139
Pilgrimage St. SE1 . . . . . 7E 14 (2D 102)
Pilgrim Cl. SM4: Mord 7K 153
Pilgrim Hill SE27 . . . . . 4C 138
Pilgrim Ho. SE1 . . . . . 3D 102
(off Tabard St.)
SE16 . . . . . 2J 103
(off Brunel Rd.)
Pilgrims Cloisters SE5 . . . . . 7E 102
(off Sedgmoor Pl.)
Pilgrims Cl. N13 . . . . . 4E 32
UB5: N'olt 5G 59

Pilgrims Cnr. NW6 . . . . . 2J 81
(off Chichester Rd.)
Pilgrims Ct. EN1: Enf 2J 23
Pilgrim's La. NW3 . . . . . 4B 64
Pilgrims M. E14 . . . . . 7G 87
Pilgrims Ri. EN4: E Barn 5H 21
Pilgrim's Pl. NW3 . . . . . 4B 64
Pilgrim St. EC4 . . . . . 1A 14 (6B 84)
Pilgrim's Way HA9: Wemb 1H 61
Pilgrims Way CR2: S Croy 6F 169
E6 . . . . . 1C 88
N19 . . . . . 1H 65
Pilkington Rd. BR6: Farnb 3G 173
SE15 . . . . . 2H 121
Pill Box Studios E2 . . . . . 4H 85
(off Coventry Rd.)
Pillfold Ho. SE11 . . . . . 3G 19
(off Old Paradise St.)
Pillions La. UB4: Hayes 4F 75
Pilot Cl. SE8 . . . . . 6B 104
Pilot Ind. Cen. NW10 . . . . . 4K 79
Pilot Wlk. SE10 . . . . . 3H 105
Pilsdon Cl. SW19 . . . . . 1F 135
Pilton Est., The CR0: C'don 2B 168
Pilton Pl. SE17 . . . . . 5C 102
Pimento Ct. W5 . . . . . 3D 96
PIMLICO 6B 18 (5G 101)
Pimlico Ho. SW1 . . . . . 5J 17
(off Ebury Bri. Rd.)
Pimlico Rd. SW1 . . . . . 5G 17 (5E 100)
Pimlico Sq. SW1 . . . . . 5G 17 (5E 100)
Pimlico Wlk. N1 . . . . . 1G 9
Pimp Hall Nature Reserve 2A 36
Pinchbeck Rd. BR6: Chels 6K 173
Pinchin & Johnsons Yd. E1 . . . . . 7G 85
(off Pinchin St.)
Pinchin St. E1 . . . . . 7G 85
Pincombe Ho. SE17 . . . . . 5D 102
(off Orb St.)
Pincott Pl. SE4 . . . . . 3K 121
Pincott Rd. DA6: Bex 5G 127
SW19 . . . . . 7A 136
Pindar St. EC2 . . . . . 5G 9 (5E 84)
Pindock M. W9 . . . . . 4K 81
Pindoria M. E1 . . . . . 4J 9
Pineapple Ct. SW1 . . . . . 1B 18
Pine Av. BR4: W W'ck 1D 170
E15 . . . . . 5F 69
Pine Cl. E10 . . . . . 2D 68
HA7: Stan 4G 27
N14 . . . . . 7B 22
N19 . . . . . 2G 65
SE20 . . . . . 1J 157
Pine Coombe CR0: C'don 4K 169
Pine Ct. N21 . . . . . 5E 22
UB5: N'olt 4C 76
Pinecrest Gdns. BR6: Farnb 4F 173
Pinecroft DA16: Well 7A 108
Pinecroft Cres. EN5: Barn 4B 20
Pinedene SE15 . . . . . 1H 121
Pinefield Cl. E14 . . . . . 7C 86
Pine Gdns. HA4: Ruis 1K 57
KT5: Surb 6G 151
Pine Glade BR6: Farnb 4D 172
Pine Gro. N4 . . . . . 2J 65
N20 . . . . . 1C 30
SW19 . . . . . 5H 135
Pine Ho. E3 . . . . . 1A 86
(off Barge La.)
SE16 . . . . . 2J 103
(off Ainsty Est.)
W10 . . . . . 4G 81
(off Droop St.)
Pinehurst Ct. W11 . . . . . 6H 81
(off Colville Gdns.)
Pinehurst Wlk. BR6: Orp 1H 173
Pinelands Cl. SE3 . . . . . 7H 105
Pinemartin Cl. NW2 . . . . . 3E 62
Pine M. NW10 . . . . . 2F 81
(off Clifford Gdns.)
Pine Pl. UB4: Hayes 4H 75

Pine Ridge SM5: Cars 7E **166**
Pineridge Ct. EN5: Barn 4A **20**
Pine Rd. N11 .2K **31**
NW2 . . . . .4E **62**
Pines, The IG8: Wfd G 3C **36**
KT9: Chess 3E **162**
N14 . . . . .5B **22**
SE19 .6B **138**
TW16: Sun 3J **147**
Pines Rd. BR1: Brom 2C **160**
Pine St. EC1 . . . . .3K **7** (4A **84**)
Pine Tree Cl. TW5: Cran 1K **111**
Pine Tree Lodge BR2: Brom 4H **159**
Pine Trees Dr. UB10: Ick 4A **56**
Pine Tree Way SE13 . . . . .3D **122**
Pineview Ct. E4 . . . . .1K **35**
Pine Wlk. KT5: Surb 6G **151**
Pine Wood TW16: Sun 1J **147**
Pinewood Av. DA15: Sidc 1J **143**
HA5: Hat E 6A **26**
UB8: Hil .6B **74**
Pinewood Cl. BR6: Orp 1H **173**
CR0: C'don 3A **170**
HA5: Hat E 6A **26**
Pinewood Ct. EN2: Enf 3G **23**
SW4 . . . . .6H **119**
Pinewood Dr. BR6: Orp 5J **173**
Pinewood Gro. W5 . . . . .6C **78**
Pinewood Lodge WD23: B Hea 1C **26**
Pinewood Pl. DA2: Wilm 2K **145**
KT19: Ewe 4K **163**
Pinewood Rd. BR2: Brom 4J **159**
SE2 . . . . .6D **108**
TW13: Felt 3K **129**
Pinfold Rd. SW16 . . . . .4J **137**
Pinglestone Cl. UB7: Harm 7A **92**
Pinkcoat Cl. TW13: Felt 3K **129**
Pinkerton Pl. SW16 . . . . .4H **137**
Pinkham Mans. W4 . . . . .5G **97**
Pinkham Way N11 . . . . .7K **31**
Pinkwell Av. UB3: Harl 4F **93**
Pinkwell La. UB3: Harl 4E **92**
Pinley Gdns. RM9: Dag 1B **90**
Pinnace Ho. *E14* *3E* ***104***
(off Manchester Rd.)
Pinnacle, The EC2 . . . . .1G **15**
Pinnacle Apartments *CR0: C'don* *1C* ***168***
(off Saffron Central Sq.)
Pinnacle Hill DA7: Bex 4H **127**
Pinnacle Hill Nth. DA7: Bex 4H **127**
Pinnacle Ho. *EN1: Enf* *3K* ***23***
(off Colman Pde.)
NW9 . . . .*2B* ***44***
(off Heritage Av.)
SW18 .4A **118**
Pinnacle Pl. HA7: Stan 4G **27**
Pinnacle Way *E14* *6A* ***86***
(off Commercial Rd.)
Pinnata Cl. EN2: Enf 1H **23**
Pinnell Rd. SE9 . . . . .4B **124**
PINNER 4C 40
Pinner Ct. HA5: Pinn 4E **40**
NW8 . . . . .3A **4**
PINNER GREEN 2A 40
Pinner Grn. HA5: Pinn 2A **40**
Pinner Gro. HA5: Pinn 4C **40**
Pinner Hill Farm HA5: Pinn 1K **39**
Pinner Hill Golf Course 1A **40**
Pinner Hill Rd. HA5: Pinn 1K **39**
Pinner Pk. 1E **40**
Pinner Pk. HA5: Pinn 2E **40**
Pinner Pk. Av. HA2: Harr 3F **41**
Pinner Pk. Gdns. HA2: Harr 2G **41**
Pinner Rd. HA1: Harr 4E **40**
HA2: Harr 4E **40**
HA5: Pinn 4D **40**
HA6: Nwood, Pinn 1H **39**
HA6: Pinn 1H **39**
Pinners Cl. SM5: Cars 2C **166**
Pinners Pas. *EC2* *7F* ***9***
(off Old Broad St.)
Pinner Vw. HA1: Harr 4G **41**
HA2: Harr 3G **41**
PINNERWOOD PARK 1A 40
Pinn Way HA4: Ruis 7F **39**
Pintail Cl. E6 .5C **88**
Pintail Ct. *SE8* *6B* ***104***
(off Pilot Cl.)
Pintail Rd. IG8: Wfd G 7E **36**
Pintail Way UB4: Yead 5B **76**
Pinter Ho. *SW9* *2J* ***119***
(off Grantham Rd.)
Pinto Way SE3 . . . . .4K **123**
Pioneer Cen., The SE15 . . . . .1J **121**
Pioneer Cl. E14 . . . . .5D **86**
Pioneer Ct. *E16* *5J* ***87***
(off Hammersley Rd.)
Pioneer Ho. *WC1* *1G* ***7***
(off Britannia St.)
Pioneer Pl. CR0: Sels 7C **170**
Pioneer Point IG1: Ilf 3F **71**
Pioneers Ind. Pk. CR0: Bedd 1J **167**
Pioneer St. SE15 . . . . .1G **121**
Pioneer Way W12 . . . . .6D **80**
Piper Bldg., The SW6 . . . . .3K **117**
Piper Cl. N7 . . . . .6K **65**
Piper Rd. KT1: King T 3G **151**
Piper's Gdns. CR0: C'don 7A **158**
Pipers Grn. NW9 . . . . .5J **43**
Pipers Grn. La. HA8: Edg 3K **27**
(not continuous)
Pipers Ho. *SE10* *5F* ***105***
(off Collington St.)
Piper Way IG1: Ilf 1H **71**
Pipewell Rd. SM5: Cars 6C **154**
Pipit Dr. SW15 . . . . .6E **116**
Pippenhall SE9 . . . . .6F **125**
Pippin Cl. CR0: C'don 1B **170**
NW2 . . . . .3C **62**
TW13: Hanw 3D **130**
Pippin Ct. *SW8* *7G* ***19***
(off Vauxhall Gro.)
Pippin Ho. *W10* *7F* ***81***
(off Freston Rd.)
Pippin Mans. *E20* *5E* ***68***
(off Mirabelle Gdns.)
Pippins Cl. UB7: W Dray 3A **92**
Pippins Ct. TW15: Ashf 6D **128**
Pique M. *E1* *7K* ***85***
(off Glasshouse Flds.)
Piquet Rd. SE20 . . . . .2J **157**
Pirbright Cres. CR0: New Ad 6E **170**
Pirbright Rd. SW18 . . . . .1H **135**
Pirie Cl. SE5 .3D **120**
Pirie St. E16 . . . . .1K **105**
Pirin Ct. E4 . . . . .4H **35**
Pisces Ct. HA8: Edg 7B **28**
Pissaro Ho. *N1* *7A* ***66***
(off Augustas La.)
Pitcairn Cl. RM7: Mawney 4G **55**
Pitcairn Ho. E9 . . . . .7J **67**
Pitcairn Rd. CR4: Mitc 7D **136**
Pitcairn's Path HA2: Harr 3G **59**
Pitchford St. E15 . . . . .7F **69**
Pitfield Cres. SE28 . . . . .1A **108**
Pitfield Est. N1 . . . . .1G **9** (3E **84**)
Pitfield St. N1 . . . . .1G **9** (3E **84**)
Pitfield Way EN3: Enf H 1D **24**
NW10 . . . . .6J **61**
Pitfold Cl. SE12 . . . . .6K **123**
Pitfold Rd. SE12 . . . . .6J **123**
Pitlake CR0: C'don 2B **168**
Pitlochry Ho. *SE27* *2B* ***138***
(off Elmcourt Rd.)
Pitman Bldg. *SE16* *7K* ***15***
(off Old Jamaica Rd.)
Pitman Ho. SE8 . . . . .1C **122**
Pitman St. SE5 . . . . .7C **102**
Pitmaston Ho. *SE13* *2E* ***122***
(off Lewisham Rd.)
Pitmaston Rd. SE13 . . . . .2E **122**
Pitsea Pl. E1 . . . . .6K **85**
Pitsea St. E1 . . . . .6K **85**
Pitshanger La. W5 . . . . .4B **78**
Pitt Cres. SW19 . . . . .4K **135**
Pittman Gdns. IG1: Ilf 5G **71**
Pitt Rd. BR6: Farnb 4G **173**
CR0: C'don 5C **156**
CR7: Thor H 5C **156**
HA2: Harr 2G **59**
Pitt's Head M. W1 . . . . .5H **11** (1E **100**)
Pittsmead Av. BR2: Hayes 7J **159**
Pitt St. W8 . . . . .2J **99**
Pittville Gdns. SE25 . . . . .3G **157**
Pitwell M. E8 . . . . .6G **67**
Pixfield Ct. *BR2: Brom* *2H* ***159***
(off Beckenham La.)
Pixley St. E14 .6B **86**
Pixton Way CR0: Sels 7A **170**
Place, The 3H **83**
Place, The SE1 . . . . .5F **15** (1D **102**)
Place Farm Av. BR6: Orp 1H **173**
Plaisterers Highwalk *EC2* *6C* ***8***
(off London Wall)
PLAISTOW
BR1 . . . . .7J 141
E13 . . . . .2J 87
Plaistow Gro. BR1: Brom 7K **141**
E15 . . . . .1H **87**
Plaistow La. BR1: Brom 7J **141**
Plaistow Pk. Rd. E13 . . . . .2K **87**
(not continuous)
Plaistow Rd. E13 . . . . .1H **87**
E15 . . . . .1H **87**
Plaistow Wharf E16 . . . . .2J **105**
Plane Ho. BR2: Brom 2G **159**
Plane St. SE26 . . . . .3H **139**
Planetree Ct. *W6* *4F* ***99***
(off Brook Grn.)
Plane Tree Cres. TW13: Felt 3K **129**
Plane Tree Ho. *SE8* *6A* ***104***
(off Etta St.)
W8 . . . .*2H* ***99***
(off Duchess of Bedford's Wlk.)
Plane Tree Wlk. N2 . . . . .3C **46**
SE19 . . . . .6E **138**
Plantagenet Cl. KT4: Wor Pk 4K **163**
Plantagenet Gdns. RM6: Chad H 7D **54**
Plantagenet Ho. *SE18* *3D* ***106***
(off Leda Rd.)
Plantagenet Pl. RM6: Chad H 7D **54**
Plantagenet Rd. EN5: New Bar 4F **21**
Plantain Gdns. *E11* *3F* ***69***
(off Hollydown Way)
Plantain Pl. SE1 . . . . .6E **14** (2D **102**)
Plantation, The SE3 . . . . .2J **123**
Plantation Cl. SW4 . . . . .5J **119**
Plantation La. EC3 . . . . .2G **15**
Plantation Pl. EC3 . . . . .2G **15**
Plantation Wharf SW11 . . . . .3A **118**
Plantree Path *E17* *4C* ***50***
(off Selborne Rd.)
Plasel Ct. *E13* *1K* ***87***
(off Pawsey Cl.)
PLASHET 6C 70
Plashet Gro. E6 . . . . .1A **88**
Plashet Rd. E13 . . . . .1J **87**
Plassy Rd. SE6 . . . . .7D **122**
Plate Ho. *E14* *5D* ***104***
(off Burrells Wharf Sq.)
Platform Theatre 1J **83**
Platina St. EC2 . . . . .3F **9**
Platinum Ct. *E1* *4J* ***85***
(off Cephas Av.)
RM7: Mawney 3H **55**
Platinum M. N15 . . . . .5F **49**
Plato Rd. SW2 .4J **119**
Platt, The SW15 . . . . .3F **117**
Platt Halls NW9 . . . . .2B **44**
Platt's Eyot TW12: Hamp 2E **148**
Platt's La. NW3 . . . . .4J **63**
Platts Rd. EN3: Enf H 1D **24**
Platt St. NW1 . . . . .2H **83**
Plawsfield Rd. BR3: Beck 1K **157**
Plaxdale Ho. *SE17* *4E* ***102***
(off Congreve St.)
Plaxtol Cl. BR1: Brom 1A **160**
Plaxtol Rd. DA8: Erith 7G **109**
Plaxton Ct. E11 . . . . .3H **69**
Playfair Ho. *E14* *6C* ***86***
(off Saracen St.)
Playfair Mans. *W14* *6G* ***99***
(off Queen's Club Gdns.)
Playfair St. W6 . . . . .5E **98**
Playfield Av. RM5: Col R 1J **55**
Playfield Cres. SE22 . . . . .5F **121**
Playfield Rd. HA8: Edg 2J **43**
Playford Rd. N4 . . . . .2K **65**
(not continuous)
Playgreen Way SE6 . . . . .3C **140**
Playground Cl. BR3: Beck 2K **157**
Playhouse Ct. *SE1* *6C* ***14***
(off Southwark Bri. Rd.)
Playhouse Theatre ***4F 13***
(off Northumberland Av.)
Playhouse Yd. EC4 . . . . .1A **14** (6B **84**)
Plaza Bus. Cen. EN3: Brim 2G **25**
Plaza Gdns. SW15 . . . . .5G **117**
Plaza Hgts. E10 . . . . .3E **68**
Plaza Pde. *HA0: Wemb* *6E* ***60***
(off Ealing Rd.)
NW6 . . . . .2K **81**
Plaza Shop. Cen., The W1 . . . . .7B **6** (6G **83**)
Plaza Wlk. NW9 . . . . .3J **43**
Pleasance, The SW15 . . . . .4D **116**
Pleasance Rd. SW15 . . . . .5D **116**
Pleasance Theatre
London ***6J 65***
(off Carpenters M.)
Pleasant Gro. CR0: C'don 3B **170**
Pleasant Pl. N1 . . . . .7B **66**
Pleasant Row NW1 . . . . .1F **83**
Pleasant Vw. Pl. BR6: Farnb 5F **173**
Pleasant Way HA0: Wemb 2C **78**
Pleasaunce Mans. *SE10* *5J* ***105***
(off Halstow Rd.)
Plender Ct. *NW1* *1G* ***83***
(off College Pl.)
Plender St. NW1 . . . . .1G **83**
Pleshey Rd. N7 . . . . .4H **65**
Plesman Way SM6: Wall 7J **167**
Plessey Bldg. *E14* *6C* ***86***
(off Dod St.)
Plevna Cres. N15 . . . . .6E **48**
Plevna Rd. N9 .3B **34**
TW12: Hamp 1F **149**
Plevna St. E14 .3E **104**
Pleydell Av. SE19 . . . . .7F **139**
W6 . . . . .4B **98**
Pleydell Ct. *EC4* *1K* ***13***
(off Pleydell St.)
Pleydell Est. EC1 . . . . .2D **8**
Pleydell Gdns. *SE19* *6F* ***139***
(off Anerley Hill)
Pleydell Ho. *EC4* *6A* ***84***
(off Pleydell St.)
Pleydell St. EC4 . . . . .1K **13**
Plimley Pl. *W12* *2F* ***99***
(off Shepherd's Bush Pl.)
Plimsoll Cl. E14 . . . . .6D **86**
Plimsoll Rd. N4 . . . . .3A **66**
Plough Cl. NW10 . . . . .3D **80**
Plough Ct. EC3 . . . . .2F **15** (7D **84**)
RM13: Rain *2K* ***91***
(off Broadis Way)
Plough Farm Cl. HA4: Ruis 6F **39**
Plough La. CR8: Purl 7J **167**
SE22 . . . . .6F **121**
SM6: Bedd, Wall 4J **167**
SW17 .5K **135**
SW19 .5K **135**
TW11: Tedd 5A **132**
Plough La. Cl. SM6: Bedd 5J **167**
Ploughmans Cl. NW1 . . . . .1H **83**

Ploughmans End TW7: Isle 5H **113**
Ploughmans Wlk. *N2* *2A* ***46***
(off Long La.)
Plough M. SW11 . . . . 4B **118**
Plough Pl. EC4 . . . . 7K **7** (6A **84**)
Plough Rd. KT19: Ewe 7K **163**
SW11 . . . . 3B **118**
Plough St. E1 . . . . 7K **9**
Plough Ter. SW11 . . . . 4B **118**
Plough Way SE16 . . . . 4K **103**
Plough Yd. EC2 . . . . 4H **9** (4E **84**)
Plover Ho. *SW9* *7A* ***102***
(off Brixton Rd.)
Plover Way SE16 . . . . 3A **104**
UB4: Yead 6B **76**
Plowden Bldgs. EC4 . . . . 2J **13**
Plowman Cl. N18 . . . . 5J **33**
Plowman Way RM8: Dag 1C **72**
Plumber's Row E1 . . . . 5G **85**
Plumbridge St. SE10 . . . . 1E **122**
Plum Cl. TW13: Felt 1J **129**
Plume Ho. *SE10* *6D* ***104***
(off Creek Rd.)
Plum Gth. TW8: Bford 4D **96**
Plum La. RM13: Rain 2K **91**
SE18 . . . . 7F **107**
Plummer La. CR4: Mitc 2D **154**
Plummer Rd. SW4 . . . . 7H **119**
Plumpton Cl. UB5: N'olt 6E **58**
Plumpton Way SM5: Cars 3C **166**
PLUMSTEAD 4J 107
PLUMSTEAD COMMON 6F 107
Plumstead Comn. Rd. SE18 . . . . 6F **107**
Plumstead High St. SE18 . . . . 4H **107**
Plumstead Rd. SE18 . . . . 4F **107**
(not continuous)
Plumtree Cl. RM10: Dag 6H **73**
SM6: Wall 7H **167**
Plumtree Ct. EC4 . . . . 7A **8** (6B **84**)
Plymen Ho. KT8: W Mole 5E **148**
Plymouth Ct. *KT5: Surb* *4E* ***150***
(off Cranes Pk. Av.)
Plymouth Ho. *IG11: Bark* *7A* ***72***
(off Margaret Bondfield Av.)
SE10 . . . . *1D* ***122***
(off Devonshire Dr.)
Plymouth Rd. BR1: Brom 1K **159**
E16 . . . . 5J **87**
Plymouth Ter. *NW2* *6E* ***62***
(off Sidmouth Rd.)
Plymouth Wharf E14 . . . . 4F **105**
Plympton Av. NW6 . . . . 7H **63**
Plympton Cl. DA17: Belv 3E **108**
Plympton Pl. NW8 . . . . 4C **4** (4C **82**)
Plympton Rd. NW6 . . . . 7H **63**
Plympton St. NW8 . . . . 4C **4** (4C **82**)
Plymstock Rd. DA16: Well 7C **108**
PM Gallery & House 1D 96
Pocklington Cl. NW9 . . . . 2A **44**
W12 . . . . *3C* ***98***
(off Ashchurch Pk. Vs.)
Pocklington Ct. SW15 . . . . 1C **134**
Pocklington Lodge W12 . . . . 3C **98**
Pocock Av. UB7: W Dray 3B **92**
Pocock St. SE1 . . . . 6A **14** (2B **102**)
Podmore Rd. SW18 . . . . 4A **118**
Poet Ct. *E1* *5K* ***85***
(off Shandy St.)
Poets Ct. SE25 . . . . 4G **157**
W3 . . . . 1J **97**
Poet's Rd. N5 . . . . 5D **66**
Poets Way HA1: Harr 4J **41**
Point, The *E17* *4C* ***50***
(off Tower M.)
HA4: Ruis 4J **57**
W2 . . . . 6A **4**
Pointalls Cl. N3 . . . . 2A **46**
Point Cl. SE10 . . . . 1E **122**
Pointer Cl. SE28 . . . . 6D **90**
Pointers Cl. E14 . . . . 5D **104**
Pointers Cotts. TW10: Ham 2C **132**
Point Hill SE10 . . . . 7E **104**
Point Pl. HA9: Wemb 7H **61**
Point Pleasant SW18 . . . . 4J **117**
Point Ter. *E7* *5K* ***69***
(off Claremont Rd.)
Point W. SW7 . . . . 4K **99**
Point Wharf TW8: Bford 7E **96**
Point Wharf La. TW8: Bford 7D **96**
Poland St. W1 . . . . 1B **12** (6G **83**)
Polar Pk. UB7: Harm 7B **92**
Poldo Ho. *SE10* *4G* ***105***
(off Cable Wlk.)
Polebrook Rd. SE3 . . . . 3A **124**
Pole Cat All. BR2: Hayes 2H **171**
Polecroft La. SE6 . . . . 2B **140**
Polehamptons, The
TW12: Hamp 7G **131**
Pole Hill Rd. E4 . . . . 7K **25**
UB4: Hayes 4D **74**
UB10: Hil 4D **74**
Polesden Gdns. SW20 . . . . 2D **152**
Polesworth Ho. *W2* *5J* ***81***
(off Alfred Rd.)
Polesworth Rd. RM9: Dag 7D **72**
Police Sta. La. WD23: Bush 1A **26**
POLISH WAR MEMORIAL **7A 58**
Polka Theatre for Children 6K 135
Pollard Cl. E16 . . . . 7J **87**
N7 . . . . 4K **65**
Pollard Ho. KT4: Wor Pk 4E **164**
N1 . . . . *1G* ***7***
(off Northdown St.)
SE16 . . . . *3F* ***103***
(off Spa Rd.)
Pollard Rd. N20 . . . . 2H **31**
SM4: Mord 5B **154**
Pollard Row E2 . . . . 3G **85**
Pollards Cres. SW16 . . . . 3J **155**
Pollards Hill E. SW16 . . . . 3K **155**
Pollards Hill Nth. SW16 . . . . 3J **155**
Pollards Hill Sth. SW16 . . . . 3J **155**
Pollards Hill W. SW16 . . . . 3K **155**
Pollard St. E2 . . . . 3G **85**
Pollards Wood Rd. SW16 . . . . 3J **155**
Pollard Wlk. DA14: Sidc 6C **144**
Pollen St. W1 . . . . 1A **12** (6G **83**)
Pollitt Dr. NW8 . . . . 3B **4** (4B **82**)
Pollock Ho. *W10* *4G* ***81***
(off Kensal Rd.)
Pollock's Toy Mus. 5B 6 (5G 83)
Polo M. BR7: Chst 5H **143**
Polperro Cl. BR6: St M Cry 6K **161**
Polperro Ho. *W2* *5J* ***81***
(off Westbourne Pk. Rd.)
Polperro M. SE11 . . . . 3K **19** (4B **102**)
Polsted Rd. SE6 . . . . 7B **122**
Polthorne Est. *SE18* *4H* ***107***
(off Polthorne Gro.)
Polthorne Gro. SE18 . . . . 4G **107**
Polworth Rd. SW16 . . . . 5J **137**
Polychrome Ct. *SE1* *7A* ***14***
(off Waterloo Rd.)
Polydamas Cl. E3 . . . . 2C **86**
Polygon, The *NW8* *1B* ***82***
(off Avenue Rd.)
SW4 . . . . 4G **119**
Polygon Bus. Cen. SL3: Poyle 5A **174**
Polygon Rd. NW1 . . . . 1C **6** (2H **83**)
(not continuous)
Polytechnic St. SE18 . . . . 4E **106**
Pomell Way E1 . . . . 7K **9** (6F **85**)
Pomeroy Cl. TW1: Twick 4B **114**
Pomeroy Ho. *E2* *2K* ***85***
(off St James's Av.)
W11 . . . . *6G* ***81***
(off Lancaster Rd.)
Pomeroy St. SE14 . . . . 7J **103**
Pomfret Pl. *E14* *7E* ***86***
(off Bullivant St.)
Pomfret Rd. SE5 . . . . 3B **120**
Pomoja La. N19 . . . . 2J **65**
Pomona Ho. *SE8* *4A* ***104***
(off Evelyn St.)
Pompadour Way IG11: Bark 2B **90**
Pond Cl. N12 . . . . 6H **31**
SE3 . . . . 2J **123**
Pond Cott. La. BR4: W W'ck 1C **170**
Pond Cotts. SE21 . . . . 1E **138**
PONDERS END 5D 24
Ponders End Ind. Est.
EN3: Pond E 5F **25**
Ponder St. N7 . . . . 7K **65**
Pond Farm Est. E5 . . . . 3J **67**
Pondfield Ho. SE27 . . . . 5C **138**
Pondfield Rd. BR2: Hayes 1G **171**
BR6: Farnb 3F **173**
RM10: Dag 5H **73**
Pond Grn. HA4: Ruis 2G **57**
Pond Hill Gdns. SM3: Cheam 6G **165**
Pond Ho. HA7: Stan 6G **27**
SW3 . . . . 4C **16** (4C **100**)
Pond Lees Cl. RM10: Dag 7K **73**
Pond Mead SE21 . . . . 6D **120**
Pond Path BR7: Chst 6F **143**
Pond Pl. SW3 . . . . 4C **16** (4C **100**)
Pond Rd. E15 . . . . 2G **87**
SE3 . . . . 2H **123**
Pondside Av. KT4: Wor Pk 1E **164**
Pondside Cl. UB3: Harl 6F **93**
Pond Sq. N6 . . . . 1E **64**
Pond St. NW3 . . . . 5C **64**
Pond Way TW11: Tedd 6C **132**
Pondwood Ri. BR6: Orp 7J **161**
Ponler St. E1 . . . . 6H **85**
Ponsard Rd. NW10 . . . . 3D **80**
Ponsford St. E9 . . . . 6J **67**
Ponsonby Ho. *E2* *2J* ***85***
(off Bishop's Way)
Ponsonby Pl. SW1 . . . . 5D **18** (5H **101**)
Ponsonby Rd. SW15 . . . . 7D **116**
Ponsonby Ter. SW1 . . . . 5D **18** (5H **101**)
Ponsonby Vs. *E2* *2J* ***85***
(off Lark Row)
Pontefract Ct. *UB5: N'olt* *5F* ***59***
(off Newmarket Av.)
Pontefract Rd. BR1: Brom 5H **141**
Pontes Av. TW3: Houn 4D **112**
Pontifex Apartments *SE1* *4E* ***14***
(off Stoney St.)
Ponton Rd. SW8 . . . . 7C **18** (6H **101**)
Pontoon Rd. E16 . . . . 1K **105**
Pont St. SW1 . . . . 2E **16** (3D **100**)
Pont St. M. SW1 . . . . 2E **16** (3D **100**)
Pontypool Pl. SE1 . . . . 6A **14** (2B **102**)
Pooja Ct. *NW1* *7G* ***65***
(off Agar Gro.)
Pool Cl. BR3: Beck 5C **140**
KT8: W Mole 5D **148**
Pool Ct. SE6 . . . . 2C **140**
Poole Cl. HA4: Ruis 2G **57**
Poole Ct. *N1* *7E* ***66***
(off St Peter's Way)
TW4: Houn 2C **112**
Poole Ct. Rd. TW4: Houn 2C **112**
Poole Ho. SE11 . . . . 2H **19**
POOL END 5C 146
Pool End Cl. TW17: Shep 5C **146**
Poole Rd. E9 . . . . 6K **67**
KT19: Ewe 6K **163**
Pooles Bldgs. WC1 . . . . 4J **7**
Pooles Cotts. TW10: Ham 2D **132**
Pooles La. RM9: Dag 2E **90**
SW10 . . . . 7A **100**
Pooles Pk. N4 . . . . 2A **66**
Poole St. N1 . . . . 1D **84**
Poole Way UB4: Hayes 3G **75**
Pooley Dr. SW14 . . . . 3J **115**
Pooley Ho. E1 . . . . 3K **85**
E18 . . . . 1J **51**
Pool Ho. *NW8* *5C* ***4***
(off Penfold St.)
Poolmans St. SE16 . . . . 2K **103**
Pool Rd. HA1: Harr 7H **41**
KT8: W Mole 5D **148**
Poolsford Rd. NW9 . . . . 4A **44**
Poolside Manor 1H 45
Pools on the Pk. 4D 114
Pool St. E20 . . . . 7E **68**
Poonah St. E1 . . . . 6J **85**
Pope Cl. SW19 . . . . 6B **136**
TW14: Felt 1H **129**
Pope Ho. *SE5* *7D* ***102***
(off Elmington Est.)
SE16 . . . . *4H* ***103***
(off Manor Est.)
Pope Rd. BR2: Brom 5B **160**
Popes Av. TW2: Twick 2J **131**
Popes Ct. TW2: Twick 2J **131**
Popes Dr. N3 . . . . 1J **45**
Popes Gro. CR0: C'don 3B **170**
TW1: Twick 2K **131**
TW2: Twick 2K **131**
Pope's Head All. EC3 . . . . 1F **15** (6D **84**)
Popes La. W5 . . . . 3D **96**
Pope's Rd. SW9 . . . . 3A **120**
Pope St. SE1 . . . . 7H **15** (2E **102**)
Popham Cl. TW13: Hanw 3D **130**
Popham Gdns.
TW9: Rich 3G **115**
Popham Rd. N1 . . . . 1C **84**
Popham St. N1 . . . . 1B **84**
(not continuous)
Pop in Commercial Cen.
HA9: Wemb 5H **61**
Popinjays Row *SM3: Cheam* *5F* ***165***
(off Netley Cl.)
POPLAR 7D 86
Poplar Av. BR6: Farnb 2F **173**
CR4: Mitc 1D **154**
UB2: S'hall 3F **95**
UB7: Yiew 7B **74**
Poplar Bath St. E14 . . . . 6D **86**
Poplar Bus. Pk. E14 . . . . 7E **86**
Poplar Cl. E9 . . . . 5B **68**
HA5: Pinn 1B **40**
SL3: Poyle 4A **174**
Poplar Ct. SW19 . . . . 5J **135**
TW1: Twick 6C **114**
UB5: N'olt 2A **76**
Poplar Cres. KT19: Ewe 6J **163**
Poplar Farm Cl. KT19: Ewe 6J **163**
Poplar Gdns. KT3: N Mald 2K **151**
SE28 . . . . 7C **90**
Poplar Gro. HA9: Wemb 3J **61**
KT3: N Mald 2K **151**
N11 . . . . 6K **31**
W6 . . . . 2E **98**
Poplar High St. E14 . . . . 7D **86**
Poplar Ho. *SE4* *4B* ***122***
(off Wickham Rd.)
SE16 . . . . *2K* ***103***
(off Woodland Cres.)
Poplar Leisure Cen. 7D 86
Poplar M. W12 . . . . 1E **98**
Poplar Mt. DA17: Belv 4H **109**
Poplar Pl. SE28 . . . . 7C **90**
UB3: Hayes 7J **75**
W2 . . . . 7K **81**
Poplar Rd. KT10: Surb 3B **162**
SE24 . . . . 4C **120**
SM3: Sutt 1H **165**
SW19 . . . . 2J **153**
TW15: Ashf 5E **128**
Poplar Rd. Sth. SW19 . . . . 3J **153**
Poplars, The N14 . . . . 5A **22**
Poplars Av. NW2 . . . . 6E **62**
Poplars Cl. HA4: Ruis 1G **57**
Poplars Rd. E17 . . . . 6D **50**
Poplar St. RM7: Rom 4J **55**
Poplar Vw. HA9: Wemb 2D **60**
Poplar Wlk. CR0: C'don 2C **168**
SE24 . . . . 3C **120**
(not continuous)

Poplar Way IG6: Ilf 4G 53
TW13: Felt 3J 129
Poppins Ct. EC4 . . . . 1A 14 (6B 84)
Poppleton Rd. E11 . . . . 6G 51
Poppy Cl. DA17: Belv 3H 109
EN5: New Bar 6F 21
SM6: Wall 1E 166
UB5: N'olt 6D 58
Poppy Dr. EN3: Pond E 4C 24
Poppy La. CR0: C'don 7J 157
Poppy M. SE22 . . . . 5G 121
Porchester Cl. SE5 . . . . 4C 120
Porchester Ct. *W2* 7K 81
(off Porchester Gdns.)
Porchester Gdns. W2 . . . . 7K 81
Porchester Gdns. M. W2 . . . . 6K 81
Porchester Ga. *W2* 7K 81
(off Bayswater Rd.)
Porchester Ho. *E1* 6H 85
(off Philpot St.)
Porchester Leisure Cen. 6K 81
Porchester Mead BR3: Beck 6D 140
Porchester Pl. W2 . . . . 1D 10 (6C 82)
Porchester Rd. KT1: King T 2H 151
W2 . . . . 6K 81
Porchester Sq. W2 . . . . 6K 81
Porchester Sq. M. W2 . . . . 6K 81
Porchester Ter. W2 . . . . 7A 82
Porchester Ter. Nth. W2 . . . . 6K 81
Porchester Wlk. *W2* 6K 81
(off Porchester Ter. Nth.)
Porch Way N20 . . . . 3J 31
Porcupine Cl. SE9 . . . . 2C 142
Porden Rd. SW2 . . . . 4K 119
Porlock Av. HA2: Harr 1G 59
Porlock Ho. SE26 . . . . 3G 139
Porlock Rd. EN1: Enf 7A 24
Porlock St. SE1 . . . . 6F 15 (2D 102)
Porrington Cl. BR7: Chst 1D 160
Portal Cl. HA4: Ruis 4J 57
SE27 . . . . 3A 138
UB10: Uxb 7A 56
Portal Way W3 . . . . 5K 79
Portbury Cl. SE15 . . . . 1G 121
Port Cres. E13 . . . . 4K 87
Portcullis Ho. SW1 . . . . 7E 12
Portcullis Lodge Rd. EN1: Enf 3J 23
Port East Apartments *E14* 7C 86
(off Hertsmere Rd.)
Portelet Ct. *N1* 1E 84
(off De Beauvoir Est.)
Portelet Rd. E1 . . . . 3K 85
Porten Ho's. *W14* 3G 99
(off Porten Rd.)
Porten Rd. W14 . . . . 3G 99
Porter Rd. E6 . . . . 6D 88
Porters & Walters Almshouses *N22* . . . 7E 32
(off Nightingale Rd.)
Porters Av. RM8: Dag 6B 72
RM9: Dag 6B 72
Porters Lodge, The *SW10* 7A 100
(off Coleridge Gdns.)
Porters M. RM9: Dag 6B 72
Porter Sq. N19 . . . . 1J 65
Porter St. SE1 . . . . 4D 14 (1C 102)
W1 . . . . 5F 5 (5D 82)
Porters Wlk. *E1* 7H 85
(off Tobacco Dock)
Porters Way N12 . . . . 6H 31
UB7: W Dray 3B 92
Porteus Pl. SW4 . . . . 3G 119
Porteus Rd. W2 . . . . 5A 4 (5A 82)
Portfleet Pl. *N1* 1E 84
(off De Beauvoir Rd.)
Portgate Cl. W9 . . . . 4H 81
Porthallow Cl. BR6: Chels 4K 173
Porthcawe Rd. SE26 . . . . 4A 140
Porthkerry Av.
DA16: Well 4A 126
Port Ho. *E14* 5D 104
(off Burrells Wharf Sq.)
Portia Ct. IG11: Bark 7A 72
SE11 . . . . 5B 102
(off Opal St.)
Portia Way E3 . . . . 4B 86
Porticos, The SW3 . . . . 7A 16
Portinscale Rd. SW15 . . . . 5G 117
Portishead Ho. *W2* 5J 81
(off Westbourne Pk. Rd.)
Portland Av. DA15: Sidc 6A 126
KT3: N Mald 7B 152
N16 . . . . 7F 49
Portland Cl. KT4: Wor Pk 7D 152
RM6: Chad H 5E 54
Portland Commercial Est.
IG11: Bark 2C 90
Portland Cotts. CR0: Bedd 7H 155
Portland Ct. *N1* 7E 66
(off St Peter's Way)
SE1 . . . . 7E 14
(off Gt. Dover St.)
SE14 . . . . 6A 104
(off Whitcher Cl.)
Portland Cres. HA7: Stan 2D 42
SE9 . . . . 2C 142
TW13: Felt 4F 129
UB6: G'frd 4F 77
Portland Dr. EN2: Enf 1K 23
Portland Gdns. N4 . . . . 6B 48
RM6: Chad H 5D 54
Portland Gro. SW8 . . . . 1K 119
Portland Ho. SW1 . . . . 1A 18
SW15 . . . . 5F 117
Portland Mans. *W14* 4H 99
(off Addison Bri. Pl.)
Portland M. W1 . . . . 1B 12 (6G 83)
Portland Pl. *SE25* 4G 157
(off Sth. Norwood Hill)
W1 . . . . 4J 5 (5F 83)
Portland Ri. N4 . . . . 1B 66
(not continuous)
Portland Rd. BR1: Brom 4A 142
CR4: Mitc 2C 154
KT1: King T 3E 150
N15 . . . . 4F 49
SE9 . . . . 2C 142
SE25 . . . . 4G 157
TW15: Ashf 3A 128
UB2: S'hall 3D 94
UB4: Hayes 3G 75
W11 . . . . 7G 81
Portland Sq. E1 . . . . 1H 103
Portland St. SE17 . . . . 5D 102
Portland Ter. HA8: Edg 7B 28
TW9: Rich 4D 114
Portland Wlk. SE17 . . . . 6D 102
Portman Av. SW14 . . . . 3K 115
Portman Cl. DA5: Bexl 1K 145
DA7: Bex 3E 126
W1 . . . . 7F 5 (6D 82)
Portman Dr. IG8: Wfd G 2B 52
Portman Gdns. NW9 . . . . 2K 43
UB10: Hil 7C 56
Portman Ga. NW1 . . . . 4D 4 (4C 82)
Portman Mans. *W1* 5F 5
(off Chiltern St.)
Portman M. Sth. W1 . . . . 1G 11 (6E 82)
Portman Pl. E2 . . . . 3J 85
Portman Rd. KT1: King T 2F 151
Portman Sq. W1 . . . . 7G 5 (6E 82)
Portman St. W1 . . . . 1G 11 (6E 82)
Portman Towers W1 . . . . 7F 5 (6D 82)
Portmeadow Wlk. SE2 . . . . 2D 108
Portmeers Cl. E17 . . . . 6B 50
Portnall Ho. *W9* 3H 81
(off Portnall Rd.)
Portnall Rd. W9 . . . . 2H 81
Portnoi Cl. RM1: Rom 2K 55
Portobello Ct. W11 . . . . 6H 81
Portobello Grn. *W10* 5G 81
(off Portobello Rd.)
Portobello Ho. BR2: Brom 6B 160
Portobello Lofts *W10* 4G 81
(off Kensal Rd.)
Portobello M. W11 . . . . 7J 81
Portobello Rd. W10 . . . . 5G 81
W11 . . . . 6H 81
Portobello Road Market 7H 81
(off Portobello Rd.)
Porton Ct. KT6: Surb 6C 150
Portpool La. EC1 . . . . 5J 7 (5A 84)
Portree Cl. N22 . . . . 7E 32
Portree St. E14 . . . . 6F 87
Portrush Ct. *UB1: S'hall* 6G 77
(off Whitecote Rd.)
Portsdown HA8: Edg 5B 28
Portsdown Av. NW11 . . . . 6H 45
Portsdown M. NW11 . . . . 6H 45
Portsea Hall *W2* 1D 10
(off Portsea Pl.)
Portsea M. W2 . . . . 1D 10
Portsea Pl. W2 . . . . 1D 10 (6C 82)
Portslade Rd. SW8 . . . . 2G 119
Portsmouth Av. KT7: T Ditt 7A 150
Portsmouth M. E16 . . . . 1K 105
Portsmouth Rd. KT1: King T 7A 150
KT6: Surb 7A 150
KT7: T Ditt 1A 162
SW15 . . . . 7D 116
Portsmouth St. WC2 . . . . 1G 13 (6K 83)
Portsoken St. E1 . . . . 2J 15 (7F 85)
Portswood Pl. SW15 . . . . 6B 116
Portugal Gdns. TW2: Twick 2G 131
Portugal St. WC2 . . . . 1G 13 (6K 83)
Portway E15 . . . . 1H 87
Portway Gdns. SE18 . . . . 7B 106
Pory Ho. SE11 . . . . 4H 19 (4K 101)
Poseidon Ct. *E14* 4C 104
(off Homer Dr.)
POSK 4C 98
(off King St.)
Postal Mus., The 3H 7 (4K 83)
Postern, The EC2 . . . . 6D 8
Postern Grn. EN2: Enf 2F 23
Post La. TW2: Twick 1H 131
Postmasters Lodge HA5: Pinn 7C 40
Postmill Cl. CR0: C'don 3J 169
Post Office All. *W4* 6H 97
(off Thames Rd.)
Post Office App. E7 . . . . 5K 69
Post Office Ct. *EC3* 1F 15
(off King William St.)
Post Office Way SW8 . . . . 7H 101
Post Rd. UB2: S'hall 3F 95
Postway M. IG1: Ilf 3F 71
(not continuous)
Potier St. SE1 . . . . 3D 102
Potter Cl. CR4: Mitc 2F 155
SE15 . . . . 7E 102
Potter Ho. *E1* 5K 85
(off Beaufort Gdns.)
Potteries, The EN5: Barn 5D 20
Potterne Cl. SW19 . . . . 7F 117
Potters Cl. CR0: C'don 1A 170
Potters Ct. *SM1: Sutt* 6H 165
(off Rosebery Rd.)
Potters Fld. *EN1: Enf* 4K 23
(off Lincoln Rd.)
Potters Flds. SE1 . . . . 5H 15 (1E 102)
Potters Gro. KT3: N Mald 4J 151
Potters Hgts. Cl. HA5: Pinn 1K 39
Potter's La. SW16 . . . . 6H 137
Potters La. EN5: New Bar 4D 20
Potters Lodge *E14* 5E 104
(off Ferry St.)
Potter's Rd. EN5: New Bar 4E 20
Potters Rd. SW6 . . . . 2A 118
Potters Row *E20* 5D 68
(off Keirin Rd.)
Potter St. HA5: Pinn 1K 39
HA6: Nwood 1J 39
Potter St. Hill HA5: Pinn 1K 39
Pottery Cl. SE25 . . . . 3G 157
Pottery Ga. N11 . . . . 6C 32
Pottery La. W11 . . . . 1G 99
Pottery Rd. DA5: Bexl 2J 145
TW8: Bford 6E 96
Pottery St. SE16 . . . . 2H 103
Pott St. E2 . . . . 3H 85
Poulett Gdns. TW1: Twick 1A 132
Poulett Rd. E6 . . . . 2D 88
Poulter Pk. 6C 154
Poulters Wood BR2: Kes 5B 172
Poulton Av. SM1: Sutt 3B 166
Poulton Cl. E8 . . . . 6H 67
Poulton Ho. *W3* 5K 79
(off Victoria Rd.)
Poultry EC2 . . . . 1E 14 (6D 84)
Pound Cl. BR6: Orp 2H 173
KT6: Surb 1C 162
Pound Ct. Dr. BR6: Orp 2H 173
Pound Farm Cl. KT10: Esh 7G 149
Pound Grn. DA5: Bexl 7G 127
Pound La. NW10 . . . . 6C 62
Pound Pk. Rd. SE7 . . . . 4B 106
Pound Pl. SE9 . . . . 6E 124
Pound St. SM5: Cars 5D 166
Pound Way BR7: Chst 7G 143
Pountney Rd. SW11 . . . . 3E 118
POVEREST 4K 161
Poverest Rd. BR5: St M Cry 5K 161
Povey Ho. *SE17* 4E 102
(off Beckway St.)
Powder Mill La. TW2: Whitt 7D 112
Powell Cl. HA8: Edg 6A 28
KT9: Chess 5D 162
Powell Ct. *CR2: S Croy* 4B 168
(off Bramley Hill)
E17 . . . . 3D 50
Powell Dr. E4 . . . . 4J 25
Powell Gdns. RM10: Dag 4G 73
Powell Ho. *EN1: Enf* 4K 23
(off Dunstan M.)
W2 . . . . 2A 10
(off Gloucester Ter.)
Powell Rd. E5 . . . . 3H 67
IG9: Buck H 1F 37
Powell's Wlk. W4 . . . . 6A 98
Powergate Bus. Pk. NW10 . . . . 3K 79
Powerhouse, The 2G 93
Powerleague
Barking 3G 89
Colney Hatch 7K 31
Croydon 6K 167
Ilford 1K 53
Mill Hill 7J 29
Tottenham 6C 34
Power Rd. W4 . . . . 4G 97
Powers Ct. TW1: Twick 7D 114
Powerscroft Rd.
DA14: Sidc 6C 144
(not continuous)
E5 . . . . 4J 67
Powis Ct. *W11* 6H 81
(off Powis Gdns.)
WD23: B Hea 1C 26
(off Rutherford Way)
Powis Gdns. NW11 . . . . 7H 45
W11 . . . . 6H 81
Powis Ho. *WC2* 7F 7
(off Macklin St.)
Powis M. W11 . . . . 6H 81
Powis Pl. WC1 . . . . 4F 7 (4J 83)
Powis Rd. E3 . . . . 3D 86
Powis Sq. W11 . . . . 6H 81
(not continuous)
Powis St. SE18 . . . . 3E 106
Powis Ter. W11 . . . . 6H 81
Powlesland Ct. *E1* 6A 86
(off White Horse Rd.)
Powlett Ho. *NW1* 6F 65
(off Powlett Pl.)
Powlett Pl. NW1 . . . . 7E 64
Pownall Gdns. TW3: Houn 4F 113

Pownall Rd. E8 1F **85**
TW3: Houn 4F **113**
Pownsett Ter. IG1: Ilf 5G **71**
Powster Rd. BR1: Brom 5J **141**
Powys Cl. DA7: Bex 6D **108**
Powys Ct. N11 5D **32**
Powys La. N13 4D **32**
N14 4D **32**
POYLE 4A 174
Poyle Ind. Est. SL3: Poyle 6A **174**
Poyle New Cotts. SL3: Poyle 5A **174**
Poyle Technical Cen. SL3: Poyle 5A **174**
Poyle Trad. Est. SL3: Poyle 6A **174**
Poynders Ct. SW4 6G **119**
Poynders Gdns. SW4 7G **119**
Poynders Pde. SW4 6H **119**
Poynders Rd. SW4 6G **119**
Poynings, The SL0: Rich P 1A **174**
Poynings Rd. N19 3G **65**
Poynings Way N12 5D **30**
Poyntell Cres. BR7: Chst 1H **161**
Poynter Ct. *UB5: N'olt 2B **76***
(off Gallery Gdns.)
Poynter Ho. *NW8 3A **4***
(off Fisherton St.)
*W11 1F **99***
(off Queensdale Cres.)
Poynter Rd. EN1: Enf 5B **24**
Poynton Rd. N17 2G **49**
Poyntz Rd. SW11 2D **118**
Poyser St. E2 2H **85**
Prado Path *TW1: Twick 1K **131***
(off Laurel Av.)
Praed M. W2 7B **4** (6B **82**)
Praed St. W2 1A **10** (6B **82**)
Pragel St. E13 2A **88**
Pragnell Rd. SE12 2K **141**
Prague Pl. SW2 5J **119**
Prah Rd. N4 2A **66**
Prairie St. SW8 2E **118**
Praline Ct. *E3 2D **86***
(off Taylor Pl.)
Pratt M. NW1 1G **83**
Pratts Pas. KT1: King T 2E **150**
Pratt St. NW1 1G **83**
Pratt Wlk. SE11 3H **19** (4K **101**)
Prayle Gro. NW2 1F **63**
Preachers Ct. *EC1 5B **8***
(off Charterhouse Sq.)
Prebend Gdns. W4 4B **98**
W6 4B **98**
(not continuous)
Prebend Mans. *W4 4B **98***
(off Chiswick High Rd.)
Prebend St. N1 1C **84**
Precinct Rd. UB3: Hayes 7J **75**
Precincts, The SM4: Mord 6J **153**
Premier Cinema
Peckham 2G 121
Premier Cnr. W9 2H **81**
Premier Ct. EN3: Enf W 1D **24**
Premiere Pl. E14 7C **86**
Premier Ho. *N1 7B **66***
(off Waterloo Ter.)
Premier Pk. NW10 1H **79**
(not continuous)
Premier Pk. Rd. NW10 2H **79**
Premier Pl. SW15 4G **117**
Prendergast Rd. SE3 3G **123**
Prentice Ct. SW19 5H **135**
Prentis Rd. SW16 4H **137**
Prentiss Ct. SE7 4B **106**
Presburg Rd. KT3: N Mald 5A **152**
Presburg St. E5 3K **67**
Prescelly Pl. HA8: Edg 1F **43**
Prescot St. E1 2K **15** (7F **85**)
Prescott Av. BR5: Pet W 6F **161**
Prescott Cl. SW16 7J **137**
Prescott Ho. *SE17 6B **102***
(off Hillingdon St.)
Prescott Pl. SW4 3H **119**
Presentation M. SW2 2K **137**
Preshaw Cres. CR4: Mitc 3C **154**
President Dr. E1 1H **103**
President Ho. EC1 2B **8** (3B **84**)
President Quay E1 4K **15**
President St. EC1 1C **8**
Prespa Cl. N9 2D **34**
Press Ct. SE1 5G **103**
Press Ho. BR5: Pet W 5G **161**
*E1 5K **85***
(off Trafalgar Gdns.)
NW10 3K **61**
Press Rd. NW10 3K **61**
Prestage Way E14 7E **86**
Prestbury Rd. E7 7A **70**
Prestbury Sq. SE9 4D **142**
Prested Rd. SW11 4C **118**
Prestige Way NW4 5E **44**
PRESTON 1E 60
Preston Av. E4 6A **36**
Preston Cl. SE1 4E **102**
TW2: Twick 3J **131**
Preston Ct. *DA14: Sidc 4K **143***
(off The Crescent)
EN5: New Bar 4F **21**
Preston Dr. DA7: Bex 1D **126**
E11 5A **52**
KT19: Ewe 6A **164**
Preston Gdns. IG1: Ilf 6C **52**
NW10 6B **62**
Preston Hill HA3: Kenton 7E **42**
Preston Ho. *RM10: Dag 3G **73***
(off Uvedale Rd.)
*SE1 4E **102***
(off Preston Cl.)
*SE1 7J **15***
(off St Saviour's Est.)
Preston Pl. NW2 6C **62**
TW10: Rich 5E **114**
Preston Rd. E11 6G **51**
HA3: Kenton 1E **60**
HA9: Wemb 1E **60**
SE19 6B **138**
SW20 7B **134**
TW17: Shep 5C **146**
Preston's Rd. E14 7E **86**
Prestons Rd. BR2: Hayes 3J **171**
Preston St. E2 2K **85**
Preston Waye HA3: Kenton 1E **60**
Prestwich Ter. SW4 5G **119**
Prestwick Cl. UB2: S'hall 5C **94**
Prestwick Ct. *UB1: S'hall 7G **77***
(off Baird Av.)
Prestwood Av. HA3: Kenton 4B **42**
Prestwood Cl. HA3: Kenton 4B **42**
SE18 6A **108**
Prestwood Gdns. CR0: C'don 7C **156**
Prestwood Ho. *SE16 3H **103***
(off Drummond Rd.)
Prestwood St. N1 1D **8** (2C **84**)
Pretoria Av. E17 4A **50**
Pretoria Cres. E4 1K **35**
Pretoria Rd. E4 1K **35**
E11 1F **69**
E16 4H **87**
IG1: Ilf 5F **71**
N17 7A **34**
RM7: Rom 4J **55**
SW16 6F **137**
Pretoria Rd. Nth. N18 6A **34**
Prevost Rd. N11 2K **31**
Priam Ho. *E2 2H **85***
(off Old Bethnal Grn. Rd.)
Price Cl. SW17 3D **136**
Price Ho. *N1 1C **84***
(off Britannia Row)
Price Rd. CR0: Wadd 5B **168**
Price's Ct. SW11 3B **118**
Price's M. N1 1K **83**
Price's St. SE1 5B **14** (1B **102**)
Price Way TW12: Hamp 6C **130**
Prichard Ct. N7 5K **65**
Prichard Ho. *SE11 4J **19***
(off Kennington Rd.)
Pricklers Hill EN5: New Bar 6E **20**
Prickley Wood BR2: Hayes 1H **171**
Priddy's Yd. CR0: C'don 2C **168**
Prideaux Ho. *WC1 1H **7***
(off Prideaux Pl.)
Prideaux Pl. W3 7K **79**
WC1 1H **7** (3K **83**)
Prideaux Rd. SW9 3J **119**
Pridham Rd. CR7: Thor H 4D **156**
Priest Cl. TW12: Hamp 4E **130**
Priestfield Rd. SE23 3A **140**
Priestlands Pk. Rd.
DA15: Sidc 3K **143**
Priestley Cl. N16 7F **49**
Priestley Gdns. RM6: Chad H 6B **54**
Priestley Ho. *EC1 3D **8***
(off Old St.)
*HA9: Wemb 3J **61***
(off Barnhill Rd.)
Priestley Rd. CR4: Mitc 2E **154**
Priestley Way E17 3K **49**
NW2 1C **62**
Priestman Point *E3 3D **86***
(off Rainhill Way)
Priest Pk. Av. HA2: Harr 2E **58**
Priests Av. RM1: Rom 2K **55**
Priests Bri. SW14 3A **116**
SW15 3A **116**
Priest's Ct. EC2 7C **8**
Prima Rd. SW9 7A **102**
Prime Meridian Line 7F **105**
Prime Meridian Wlk. E14 7F **87**
Primeplace M. CR7: Thor H 2C **156**
Primezone M. N8 6J **47**
Primrose Av. EN2: Enf 1J **23**
RM6: Chad H 7B **54**
Primrose Cl. E3 2C **86**
HA2: Harr 3D **58**
N3 2K **45**
SE6 5E **140**
SM6: Wall 7F **155**
Primrose Ct. *NW8 2D **82***
(off Prince Albert Rd.)
SW12 7H **119**
Primrose Gdns. HA4: Ruis 5A **58**
NW3 6C **64**
WD23: Bush 1A **26**
PRIMROSE HILL 1E 82
Primrose Hill EC4 1K **13** (6A **84**)
Primrose Hill Ct. NW3 7D **64**
Primrose Hill Rd. NW3 7D **64**
Primrose Hill Studios NW1 1E **82**
Primrose Ho. *SE15 1G **121***
(off Peckham Hill St.)
*SE16 2A **104***
(off Blondin Way)
Primrose La. CR0: C'don 1J **169**
Primrose Mans. SW11 1E **118**
Primrose M. *NW1 7D **64***
(off Sharpleshall St.)
SE3 7J **105**
Primrose Pl. TW7: Isle 2K **113**
Primrose Rd. E10 1D **68**
E18 2K **51**
Primrose Sq. E9 7J **67**
Primrose St. EC2 5G **9** (5E **84**)
Primrose Wlk. KT17: Ewe 7B **164**
SE14 7A **104**
Primrose Way HA0: Wemb 2D **78**
SE10 2E **122**
Primula St. W12 6C **80**
Prince Albert Ct. *NW8 1D **82***
(off Prince Albert Rd.)
TW16: Sun 7H **129**
Prince Albert Rd. NW1 1C **4** (3C **82**)
NW8 1C **4** (3C **82**)
Prince Arthur M. NW3 4A **64**
Prince Arthur Rd. NW3 5A **64**
Prince Charles Cinema ***2D 12***
(off Leicester Pl.)
Prince Charles Dr. NW4 7E **44**
Prince Charles Rd. SE3 2H **123**
Prince Charles Way SM6: Wall 3F **167**
Prince Consort Dr. BR7: Chst 1H **161**
Prince Consort Rd. SW7 1A **16** (3A **100**)
Princedale Rd. W11 1G **99**
Prince Edward Mans. *W2 7J **81***
(off Moscow Rd.)
Prince Edward Rd. E9 6B **68**
Prince Edward Theatre ***1D 12***
(off Old Compton St.)
Prince George Av. N14 5C **22**
Prince George Rd. N16 4E **66**
Prince George's Av. SW20 2E **152**
Prince George's Rd. SW19 1B **154**
Prince Henry Rd. SE7 7B **106**
Prince Imperial Rd. BR7: Chst 1F **161**
SE18 1D **124**
Prince John Rd. SE9 5C **124**
Princelet St. E1 5K **9** (5F **85**)
Prince of Orange Ct. *SE16 3J **103***
(off Lower Rd.)
Prince of Orange La. SE10 7E **104**
Prince of Wales Cl. NW4 4D **44**
Prince of Wales Dr. SW8 7F **101**
SW11 1C **118**
Prince of Wales Mans. SW11 1E **118**
Prince of Wales Pas. NW1 2A **6**
Prince of Wales Rd. E16 6A **88**
NW5 6E **64**
SE3 2H **123**
SM1: Sutt 2B **166**
Prince of Wales Ter. W4 5A **98**
W8 2K **99**
Prince of Wales Theatre ***3C 12***
(off Coventry St.)
Prince Regent Ct. *NW8 2C **82***
(off Avenue Rd.)
*SE16 7A **86***
(off Edward Sq.)
Prince Regent La. E13 3K **87**
E16 3K **87**
Prince Regent M. NW1 2A **6**
Prince Regent Rd. TW3: Houn 3F **113**
Prince Rd. SE25 5E **156**
Prince Rupert Rd. SE9 4D **124**
Princes Arc. SW1 4B **12**
Prince's Av. UB6: G'frd 6F **77**
Princes Av. BR5: Pet W 5J **161**
IG8: Wfd G 4E **36**
KT6: Surb 1G **163**
N3 1J **45**
N10 3F **47**
N13 5F **33**
N22 1H **47**
NW9 4G **43**
SM5: Cars 7D **166**
W3 3G **97**
Princes Cir. WC2 7E **6** (6J **83**)
Prince's Cl. TW11: Tedd 4H **131**
Princes Cl. DA14: Sidc 3D **144**
HA8: Edg 5B **28**
N4 1B **66**
NW9 4G **43**
SW4 3G **119**
Prince's Ct. SE16 3B **104**
*SW3 1E **16***
(off Brompton Rd.)
Princes Ct. HA9: Wemb 5E **60**
Princes Ct. Bus. Cen. E1 7H **85**
Princes Dr. HA1: Harr 3J **41**
Prince's Gdns. SW7 1B **16** (3B **100**)
Princes Gdns. W3 5G **79**
W5 4C **78**
Prince's Ga. SW7 7B **10** (2B **100**)
(not continuous)
Prince's Ga. Ct. SW7 7B **10** (2B **100**)
Prince's Ga. M. SW7 1B **16** (3B **100**)
Princes Ho. W11 7H **81**

Princes La. N10 . . . . .3F **47**
Prince's M. W2 . . . . .7K **81**
Princes M. TW3: Houn 4E **112**
   W6 . . . . .5D **98**
               (off Down Pl.)
Princes Pde. NW11 . . . . .6G **45**
       (off Golders Grn. Rd.)
Princes Pk. Av. NW11 . . . . .6G **45**
   UB3: Hayes 7F **75**
Princes Pk. Circ. UB3: Hayes 7F **75**
Princes Pk. Cl. UB3: Hayes 7F **75**
Princes Pk. La. UB3: Hayes 7F **75**
Princes Pk. Pde. UB3: Hayes 7F **75**
Princes Pl. SW1 . . . . .4B **12**
   W11 . . . . .1G **99**
Prince's Plain BR2: Brom 7C **160**
Prince's Ri. SE13 . . . . .2E **122**
Princes Riverside Rd. SE16 . . . . . .1K **103**
Prince's Rd. SW19 . . . . .6J **135**
   TW11: Tedd 4H **131**
Princes Rd. IG6: Ilf 4H **53**
   IG9: Buck H 2F **37**
   KT2: King T 7G **133**
   N18 . . . . .4D **34**
   SE20 . . . . .6K **139**
   SW14 .3K **115**
   TW9: Kew 1F **115**
   TW10: Rich 5F **115**
   TW13: Felt 2H **129**
   TW15: Ashf 5B **128**
   W13 . . . . .1B **96**
Princessa Ct. EN2: Enf 5J **23**
Princess Alice Ho. W10 . . . . .4E **80**
Princess Alice Way SE28 . . . . .2H **107**
Princess Av. HA9: Wemb 2E **60**
Princess Av. E. HA9: Wemb 2E **60**
Princess Cl. SE28 . . . . .6D **90**
Princess Ct. KT1: King T 3F **151**
          (off Horace Rd.)
   N6 . . . . .7G **47**
   NW6 . . . . .6K **63**
       (off Compayne Gdns.)
   W1 . . . . .6E **4**
         (off Bryanston Pl.)
   W2 . . . . .7K **81**
           (off Queensway)
Princess Cres. N4 . . . . .2B **66**
Princess La. HA4: Ruis 1G **57**
Princess Louise Bldg. SE8 . . . . . . .7C **104**
            (off Hales St.)
Princess Louise Cl. W2 . . . .5B **4** (5B **82**)
Princess Louise Wlk. W10 . . . . . . .5F **81**
         (off Vincent St.)
Princess Mary Ho. SW1 . . . . .3D **18**
Princess May Rd. N16 . . . . .4E **66**
Princess M. KT1: King T 3F **151**
   NW3 . . . . .5B **64**
Princess of Wales Memorial Fountain
   . . . . .6B **10** (2B **100**)
Princess Pde. BR6: Farnb 3E **172**
   RM10: Dag 2G **91**
Princess Pk. Mnr. N11 . . . . .5K **31**
Princes Sq. W2 . . . . .7K **81**
        (not continuous)
Princess Rd. CR0: C'don 6C **156**
   NW1 . . . . .1E **82**
   NW6 . . . . .2J **81**
Princess St. SE1 . . . . .3B **102**
Prince's St. EC2 . . . . .1E **14** (6D **84**)
Princes St. DA7: Bex 3F **127**
   N17 . . . . .6K **33**
   SM1: Sutt 4B **166**
   TW9: Rich 4E **114**
   W1 . . . . .1K **11** (6F **83**)
Princes Ter. E13 . . . . .1K **87**
Prince's Twr. SE16 . . . . .2J **103**
       (off Elephant La.)
Prince St. SE8 . . . . .6B **104**
Princes Way BR4: W W'ck 4H **171**
   CR0: Wadd 5K **167**
   HA4: Ruis 4C **58**

Princes Way IG9: Buck H 2F **37**
   SW19 .7F **117**
   W3 . . . . .3G **97**
Prince's Yd. W11 . . . . .1G **99**
Princethorpe Ho. W2 . . . . .5K **81**
       (off Woodchester Sq.)
Princethorpe Rd. SE26 . . . . .4K **139**
Princeton Ct. SW15 . . . . .3F **117**
Princeton M. KT2: King T 1G **151**
Princeton St. WC1 . . . . .6G **7** (5K **83**)
Prince William Ct. TW15: Ashf 5B **128**
       (off Clarendon Rd.)
Principal Cl. N14 . . . . .1B **32**
Principal Pl. EC2 . . . . .4H **9**
Principal Sq. E9 . . . . .5K **67**
Pringle Gdns. SW16 . . . . .4G **137**
        (not continuous)
Printers Inn Ct. EC4 . . . . .6A **84**
Printers M. E3 . . . . .1A **86**
Printers Rd. SW9 . . . . .1K **119**
Printer St. EC4 . . . . .7K **7** (6A **84**)
Printing Ho. La. UB3: Hayes 2G **93**
Printing Ho. Yd. E2 . . . . . . .1H **9** (3E **84**)
Printon Ho. E14 . . . . .5B **86**
        (off Wallwood St.)
Print Room, The 6J **81**
        (off Hereford Rd.)
Print Room Cinema, The 1J **99**
       (off Notting Hill Ga.)
Print Village SE15 . . . . .2F **121**
Printwork Apartments SE1 . . . . . . .7G **15**
        (off Long La.)
   SE5 . . . . .2C **120**
       (off Coldharbour La.)
Priolo Rd. SE7 . . . . .5A **106**
Prior Av. SM2: Sutt 7C **166**
Prior Bolton St. N1 . . . . .6B **66**
Prior Ct. KT8: W Mole 5D **148**
Prioress Ho. E3 . . . . .3D **86**
       (off Bromley High St.)
Prioress Rd. SE27 . . . . .3B **138**
Prioress St. SE1 . . . . .3E **102**
Prior Rd. IG1: Ilf 3E **70**
Priors, The NW3 . . . . .3B **64**
Priors Cft. E17 . . . . .3A **50**
Priors Farm La. UB5: N'olt 6C **58**
Priors Fld. UB5: N'olt 6C **58**
Priors Gdns. HA4: Ruis 5A **58**
Priors Mead EN1: Enf 1K **23**
Prior St. SE10 . . . . .7E **104**
Priors Wood KT10: Hin W 2A **162**
Priory, The CR0: Wadd 4A **168**
   N8 . . . . .4H **47**
   SE3 . . . . .4H **123**
Priory Apartments, The SE6 . . . . .1D **140**
Priory Av. BR5: Pet W 6H **161**
   E4 . . . . .3G **35**
   E17 . . . . .5C **50**
   HA0: Wemb 4K **59**
   N8 . . . . .4H **47**
   SM3: Cheam 4F **165**
   W4 . . . . .4A **98**
Priory Cl. BR3: Beck 3A **158**
   BR7: Chst 1D **160**
   E4 . . . . .3G **35**
   E18 . . . . .1J **51**
   HA0: Wemb 4K **59**
   HA4: Ruis 1H **57**
   HA7: Stan 3E **26**
   N3 . . . . .1H **45**
   N14 . . . . .5A **22**
   N20 . . . . .1C **30**
   SW19 .1K **153**
   TW12: Hamp 1D **148**
   TW16: Sun 7J **129**
   UB3: Hayes 7K **75**
Priory Ct. E6 . . . . .1A **88**
   E9 . . . . .5K **67**
   E17 . . . . .2B **50**
   EC4 . . . . .1B **14**
        (off Pilgrim St.)

Priory Ct. HA0: Wemb 2E **78**
   KT1: King T 3F **150**
       (off Denmark Rd.)
   KT17: Ewe 7B **164**
   SM3: Cheam 4G **165**
   SW8 . . . . .1H **119**
   TW3: Houn 3F **113**
   WD23: Bush 1B **26**
       (off Sparrows Herne)
Priory Ct. Est. E17 . . . . .2B **50**
Priory Cres. HA0: Wemb 3A **60**
   SE19 .7C **138**
   SM3: Cheam 4F **165**
Priory Dr. HA7: Stan 3E **26**
   SE2 . . . . .5D **108**
Priory Fld. Dr. HA8: Edg 4C **28**
Priory Gdns.
   HA0: Wemb 4A **60**
   N6 . . . . .2K **63**
   NW10 . . . . .3E **78**
   SE25 . . . . .4F **157**
   SW13 .3B **116**
   TW12: Hamp 7D **130**
   TW15: Ashf 5F **129**
   W4 . . . . .4A **98**
   W5 . . . . .3E **78**
Priory Grange N2 . . . . .3D **46**
        (off Fortis Grn.)
Priory Grn. N1 . . . . .2K **83**
Priory Grn. Est. N1 . . . . .2K **83**
Priory Gro. EN5: Barn 5D **20**
   SW8 . . . . .1J **119**
Priory Hgts. N1 . . . . .2K **83**
        (off Wynford Rd.)
Priory Hill HA0: Wemb 4A **60**
Priory Ho. E1 . . . . .5J **9**
        (off Folgate St.)
   EC1 . . . . .3A **8**
        (off Sans Wlk.)
   SW1 . . . . .5C **18**
        (off Rampayne St.)
Priory La. KT8: W Mole 4F **149**
   SW15 .6A **116**
Priory Leas SE9 . . . . .1C **142**
Priory Lodge W4 . . . . .5G **97**
        (off Kew Bri. Ct.)
Priory Mans. SW10 . . . . .5A **100**
        (off Drayton Gdns.)
Priory M. SW8 . . . . .1J **119**
Priory Pk. SE3 . . . . .3H **123**
Priory Pk. Rd. HA0: Wemb 4A **60**
   NW6 . . . . .1H **81**
Priory Retail Pk. SW19 . . . . .7B **136**
Priory Rd. CR0: C'don 7A **156**
   E6 . . . . .1B **88**
   IG11: Bark 7H **71**
   KT9: Chess 3E **162**
   N8 . . . . .4G **47**
   NW6 . . . . .1K **81**
   SM3: Cheam 4F **165**
   SW19 .7B **136**
   TW3: Houn 5G **113**
   TW9: Kew 6G **97**
   TW12: Hamp 7D **130**
   W4 . . . . .3K **97**
Priory St. E3 . . . . .3D **86**
Priory Ter. NW6 . . . . .1K **81**
   TW16: Sun 7J **129**
Priory Vw. WD23: B Hea 1D **26**
Priory Vs. N11 . . . . .6J **31**
       (off Colney Hatch La.)
Priory Wlk. SW10 . . . . .5A **100**
   TW16: Sun 7J **129**
Priory Way HA2: Harr 4F **41**
   UB2: S'hall 3B **94**
   UB7: Harm 6A **92**
Priscilla Cl. N15 . . . . .5C **48**
Pritchard Ho. E2 . . . . .2H **85**
        (off Ada Pl.)
Pritchard's Rd. E2 . . . . .1G **85**
Priter Rd. SE16 . . . . .3G **103**

Priter Rd. Hostel SE16 . . . . .3G **103**
        (off Dockley Rd.)
Priter Way SE16 . . . . .3G **103**
Private Rd. EN1: Enf 5J **23**
Prize Wlk. E20 . . . . .5E **68**
Probert Rd. SW2 . . . . .5A **120**
Probyn Ho. SW1 . . . . .3D **18**
        (off Page St.)
Probyn Rd. SW2 . . . . .2B **138**
Procter Ho. SE1 . . . . .5G **103**
        (off Avondale Sq.)
   SE5 . . . . .7D **102**
        (off Picton St.)
Procter St. WC1 . . . . .6G **7** (5K **83**)
Proctor Cl. CR4: Mitc 1E **154**
Proctors Ct. TW14: Felt 1J **129**
Progress Bus. Pk. CR0: Wadd 2K **167**
Progress Cen., The EN3: Pond E . . .3E **24**
Progress Way CR0: Wadd 2K **167**
   EN1: Enf 5B **24**
   N22 . . . . .1A **48**
Project Ho. E16 . . . . .4F **87**
Prologis Pk. CR0: Bedd 7H **155**
   E3 . . . . .4E **86**
   TW4: Houn 4A **112**
Promenade, The HA8: Edg 5B **28**
   W4 . . . . .2A **116**
Promenade App. Rd. W4 . . . . .7A **98**
Propeller Cres. CR0: Wadd 5A **168**
Propeller Way NW9 . . . . .3C **44**
Prospect Cl. DA17: Belv 4G **109**
   HA4: Ruis 7B **40**
   SE26 . . . . .4H **139**
   TW3: Houn 1D **112**
Prospect Cotts. SW18 . . . . .4J **117**
Prospect Cres. TW2: Whitt 6G **113**
Prospect E. E15 . . . . .1F **69**
Prospect Hill E17 . . . . .4D **50**
Prospect Ho. E3 . . . . .3C **86**
       (off Campbell Rd.)
   E17 . . . . .3E **50**
       (off Prospect Hill)
   N1 . . . . .2A **84**
        (off Donegal St.)
   SE1 . . . . .3B **102**
        (off Gaywood St.)
   SE16 . . . . .3G **103**
        (off Frean St.)
   SW19 .1B **154**
       (off Chapter Way)
   W10 . . . . .6F **81**
        (off Bridge Cl.)
Prospect Pl. BR2: Brom 3K **159**
   CR2: S Croy 6C **168**
   E1 . . . . .1J **103**
        (not continuous)
   N2 . . . . .4B **46**
   N7 . . . . .4J **65**
   N17 . . . . .7K **33**
   NW2 . . . . .3H **63**
   NW3 . . . . .4A **64**
   RM5: Col R 2J **55**
   SE8 . . . . .6B **104**
        (off Evelyn St.)
   SW8 . . . . .7F **101**
   SW20 .7D **134**
   W4 . . . . .5K **97**
Prospect Quay SW18 . . . . .4J **117**
       (off Lightermans Wlk.)
Prospect Ring N2 . . . . .3B **46**
Prospect Rd. EN5: New Bar 4D **20**
   IG8: Wfd G 6F **37**
   KT6: Surb 6C **150**
   NW2 . . . . .3H **63**
Prospect St. SE16 . . . . .3H **103**
Prospect Va. SE18 . . . . .4C **106**
Prospect Wharf E1 . . . . .7J **85**
Prospero Ho. E1 . . . . .2J **15**
       (off Portsoken St.)
Prospero Rd. N19 . . . . .1H **65**
Protea Cl. E16 . . . . .4H **87**

Protea Pl. *E9* 7J **67**
      (off Lyme Gro.)
Protheroe Ho. *N17* 3F **49**
Prothero Gdns. *NW4* 5D **44**
Prothero Ho. *NW10* 7K **61**
      (off Fawood Av.)
Prothero Rd. *SW6* 7G **99**
Proton Twr. *E14* 7F **87**
Proud Ho. *E1* 6H **85**
      (off Amazon St.)
Prout Gro. NW10 . . . . .4A **62**
Prout Rd. E5 . . . . .3H **67**
Provence St. N1 . . . . .2C **84**
Providence Av. HA1: Harr 1E **58**
Providence Cl. E9 . . . . .1K **85**
Providence Ct. W1 . . . .2H **11** (7E **82**)
Providence Ho. *E14* 6B **86**
      (off Three Colt St.)
Providence La. UB3: Harl 7F **93**
Providence Pl. N1 . . . . .1B **84**
    RM5: Col R 1F **55**
    SE10 . . . . .5G **105**
Providence Rd. UB7: Yiew 1A **92**
Providence Row *N1* 2K **83**
      (off Pentonville Rd.)
Providence Row Cl. E2 . . . . .3H **85**
Providence Sq. SE1 . . . .6K **15** (2G **103**)
Providence Twr. *E14* 7F **87**
      (off Fairmont Av.)
    SE16 . . . . .2G **103**
      (off Bermondsey Wall W.)
Providence Yd. *E2* 1K **9**
      (off Ezra St.)
Provident Ind. Est. UB3: Hayes 2J **93**
Province Dr. SE16 . . . . .2J **103**
Province Sq. *E14* 1E **104**
      (off Blackwall Way)
Provincial Ter. SE20 . . . . .7K **139**
Provost Cl. *NW3* 6D **64**
      (off Eton Rd.)
Provost Est. N1 . . . . .1E **8**
Provost Rd. NW3 . . . . .7D **64**
Provost St. N1 . . . . .1E **8** (2D **84**)
Provost Way RM8: Dag 4A **72**
Prowse Av. WD23: B Hea 1B **26**
Prowse Cl. *N18* 5B **34**
      (off Lord Graham M.)
Prowse Pl. NW1 . . . . .7G **65**
Proyers Path HA1: Harr 7B **42**
Prudence La. BR6: Farnb 4E **172**
Pruden Cl. N14 . . . . .2B **32**
Prudent Pas. EC2 . . . . .7D **8**
Prusom's Island *E1* 1J **103**
      (off Wapping High St.)
Prusom St. E1 . . . . .1H **103**
Pryce Ho. *E3* 3C **86**
      (off Campbell Rd.)
Puccinia Ct. *TW19: Stanw* 1A **128**
      (off Yeoman Dr.)
Pucknells Cl. BR8: Swan 7J **145**
Pudding La. EC3 . . . . .3F **15** (7D **84**)
Pudding Mill La. E15 . . . . .1D **86**
Puddle Dock EC4 . . . . .2A **14** (7B **84**)
      (not continuous)
Puffin Cl. BR3: Beck 5K **157**
    IG11: Bark 3B **90**
Pugin Cl. SW19 . . . . .4K **135**
Pugin Ct. *N1* 7A **66**
      (off Liverpool Rd.)
Pulborough Rd. SW18 . . . . .7H **117**
Pulborough Way TW4: Houn 4A **112**
Pulford Rd. N15 . . . . .6D **48**
Pulham Av. N2 . . . . .4A **46**
Pulham Ho. *SW8* 7K **101**
      (off Dorset Rd.)
Pullen's Bldgs. *SE17* 5B **102**
      (off Iliffe St.)
Puller Rd. EN5: Barn 2B **20**
Pulleyns Av. E6 . . . . .3C **88**
Pullman Cl. SW2 . . . . .1J **137**
Pullman Gdns. SW15 . . . . .6E **116**

Pullman M. SE12 . . . . .3K **141**
Pullman Pl. SE9 . . . . .5C **124**
Pulross Rd. SW9 . . . . .3K **119**
Pulse Apartments *NW6* 5K **63**
      (off Lymington Rd.)
Pulse Ct. RM7: Rush G 6K **55**
Pulteney Cl. E3 . . . . .1B **86**
    TW7: Isle 3A **114**
Pulteney Gdns. E18 . . . . .3J **51**
Pulteney Rd. E18 . . . . .3K **51**
Pulteney Ter. N1 . . . . .1K **83**
      (not continuous)
Pultney St. N1 . . . . .1K **83**
Pulton Ho. *SE4* 4A **122**
      (off Turnham Rd.)
Pulton Pl. SW6 . . . . .7J **99**
Puma Ct. E1 . . . . .5J **9** (5F **85**)
Pump All. TW8: Bford 7D **96**
Pump Cl. UB5: N'olt 2E **76**
Pump Ct. EC4 . . . . .1J **13** (6A **84**)
Pumphandle Path *N2* 2B **46**
      (off Oak La.)
Pumphouse, The N8 . . . . .4K **47**
Pump Ho. Cl. BR2: Brom 2G **159**
    SE16 .2J **103**
Pump Ho. Cres. TW8: Bford 5E **96**
Pumphouse Educational Mus., The
    . . . . .1A **104**
Pump House Gallery 7E **100**
Pump Ho. La. SW8 . . . . .7G **101**
Pump Ho. M. *E1* 7G **85**
      (off Hooper St.)
Pump House Steam & Transport Mus.
    . . . . .6A **50**
Pumping Ho. *E14* 7F **87**
      (off Naval Row)
Pumping Station Rd. W4 . . . . .7A **98**
Pump La. SE14 . . . . .7J **103**
    UB3: Hayes 2J **93**
Pump Pail Nth. CR0: C'don 3C **168**
Pump Pail Sth. CR0: C'don 3C **168**
Punchard Cres. EN3: Enf L 1J **25**
Punderson's Gdns. E2 . . . . .3H **85**
Purbeck Av. KT3: N Mald 6B **152**
Purbeck Dr. NW2 . . . . .2F **63**
Purbeck Ho. *SW8* 7K **101**
      (off Bolney St.)
Purbrook Est. SE1 . . . . .7H **15** (2E **102**)
Purbrook St. SE1 . . . . . .7H **15** (3E **102**)
Purcell Cres. SW6 . . . . .7F **99**
Purcell Ho. EN1: Enf 1B **24**
    SW10 . . . . .6B **100**
      (off Milman's St.)
Purcell Mans. *W14* 6G **99**
      (off Queen's Club Gdns.)
Purcell M. NW10 . . . . .7A **62**
Purcell Rd. UB6: G'frd 5F **77**
Purcell Room 4H **13**
      (within Southbank Cen.)
Purcells Av. HA8: Edg 5B **28**
Purcell St. N1 . . . . .2E **84**
Purchese St. NW1 . . . . . .1D **6** (2H **83**)
Purday Ho. *W10* 3G **81**
      (off Bruckner St.)
Purdon Ho. *SE15* 1G **121**
      (off Oliver Goldsmith Est.)
Purdy Ct. KT4: Wor Pk 2C **164**
Purdy St. E3 . . . . .4D **86**
PureGym
    Bayswater 7K **81**
      (off Moscow Pl.)
    Canary Wharf 7C **86**
    Edgeware 6B **28**
    Finchley 3K **45**
    Hallam St. 5K **5**
      (off Hallam St.)
    Holborn 5G **7**
      (off Theobald's Rd.)
    Marylebone, Balcombe St.
    . . . . .5E **4** (5D **82**)

PureGym
    Muswell Hill 4F **47**
    New Barnet 4G **21**
    Northolt 1E **76**
    Piccadilly 3C **12**
      (off Regent St.)
    St Paul's 6C **8**
      (off Little Britain)
    Southgate 1C **32**
    Sydenham 4J **139**
Purelake M. *SE13* 3F **123**
      (off Marischal Rd.)
Purkis Cl. UB8: Hil 7E **74**
Purland Cl. RM8: Dag 1F **73**
Purland Rd. SE28 . . . . .2K **107**
      (not continuous)
Purleigh Av. IG8: Wfd G 6H **37**
Purley Av. NW2 . . . . .2G **63**
Purley Cl. IG5: Ilf 3E **52**
Purley Pl. N1 . . . . .7B **66**
Purley Rd. CR2: S Croy 7D **168**
    N9 . . . . .3K **33**
Purley Vw. Ter. *CR2: S Croy* 7D **168**
Purley Way Cen., The CR0: Wadd . . .2A **168**
Purley Way CR0: C'don, Wadd 7K **155**
Purley Way Cres. CR0: C'don 7K **155**
Purneys Rd. SE9 . . . . .4B **124**
Purrett Rd. SE18 . . . . .5K **107**
Purser Ho. SW2 . . . . .6A **120**
Pursers Cross Rd. SW6 . . . . .1H **117**
Pursewardens Cl. W13 . . . . .1C **96**
Pursley Rd. NW7 . . . . .7J **29**
Purves Rd. NW10 . . . . .3D **80**
Purvis Ho. CR0: C'don 7D **168**
Pusey Ho. *E14* 6C **86**
      (off Saracen St.)
Puteaux Ho. *E2* 2K **85**
      (off Mace St.)
PUTNEY 4F **117**
Putney Arts Theatre 4F **117**
Putney Bri. SW15 . . . . .3G **117**
Putney Bri. App. SW6 . . . . .3G **117**
Putney Bri. Rd. SW15 . . . . .4G **117**
    SW18 . . . . .4G **117**
Putney Comn. SW15 . . . . .3E **116**
Putney Exchange (Shop. Cen.)
    SW15 . . . . .4F **117**
Putney Gdns. RM6: Chad H 5B **54**
PUTNEY HEATH 6E **116**
Putney Heath SW15 . . . . .7D **116**
Putney Heath La. SW15 . . . . .6F **117**
Putney High St. SW15 . . . . .4F **117**
Putney Hill SW15 . . . . .7F **117**
      (not continuous)
Putney Leisure Cen. 4E **116**
Putney Pk. Av. SW15 . . . . .4C **116**
Putney Pk. La. SW15 . . . . .4D **116**
      (not continuous)
PUTNEY VALE 3C **134**
Putney Va. Crematorium SW19 . . . .2D **134**
Putney Wharf SW15 . . . . .3G **117**
Putt in the Pk. 4H **117**
Pycroft Way N9 . . . . .4A **34**
Pyecombe Cnr. N12 . . . . .4C **30**
Pylbrook Rd. SM1: Sutt 3J **165**
Pylon Way CR0: Bedd 1J **167**
Pym Cl. EN4: E Barn 5G **21**
Pymers Mead SE21 . . . . .1C **138**
Pymmes Brook Dr. EN4: E Barn 4H **21**
Pymmes Brook Ho. N10 . . . . .7K **31**
Pymmes Cl. N13 . . . . .5E **32**
    N17 . . . . .1H **49**
Pymmes Gdns. Nth. N9 . . . . .3A **34**
Pymmes Gdns. Sth. N9 . . . . .3A **34**
Pymmes Grn. Rd. N11 . . . . .4A **32**
Pymmes Rd. N13 . . . . .6D **32**
Pynchester Cl. UB10: Ick 2C **56**
Pyne Rd. KT6: Surb 1G **163**
Pynfolds SE16 . . . . .2H **103**
Pynham Cl. SE2 . . . . .3B **108**

Pynnacles Cl. HA7: Stan 5G **27**
Pynnersmead SE24 . . . . .5C **120**
Pyramid Ct. *KT1: King T* 2F **151**
      (off Cambridge Rd.)
Pyramid Ho. TW4: Houn 2C **112**
Pyrford Ho. SW9 . . . . .4B **120**
Pyrland Rd. N5 . . . . .5D **66**
    TW10: Rich 6F **115**
Pyrmont Gro. SE27 . . . . .3B **138**
Pyrmont Rd. W4 . . . . .6G **97**
Pytchley Cres. SE19 . . . . .6C **138**
Pytchley Rd. SE22 . . . . .3E **120**

Q

Q Bldg., The *E15* 6G **69**
      (off The Grove)
Quad Cl. *SE1* 3E **102**
      (off Grigg's Pl.)
Quadrangle, The E15 . . . . .6G **69**
    SE24 . . . . .5C **120**
    SW6 .7G **99**
    SW10 . . . . .1A **118**
    W2 . . . . .7C **4** (6C **82**)
Quadrangle Cl. SE1 . . . . .4E **102**
Quadrangle M. HA7: Stan 7H **27**
Quadrant, The DA7: Bex 7D **108**
    HA2: Harr 3H **41**
    HA8: Edg 6B **28**
      (off Manor Pk. Cres.)
    NW4 .4E **44**
    SM2: Sutt 6A **166**
    SW20 . . . . .1G **153**
    TW9: Rich 4D **114**
    W10 .3F **81**
Quadrant Arc. W1 . . . . .3B **12**
Quadrant Bus. Cen. NW6 . . . . .1G **81**
Quadrant Cl. NW4 . . . . .5D **44**
Quadrant Ct. HA9: Wemb 4G **61**
Quadrant Gro. NW5 . . . . .5D **64**
Quadrant Ho. *E1* 7G **85**
      (off Nesham St.)
    E15 . . . . .3G **87**
      (off Durban Rd.)
    SE1 . . . . .4A **14**
Quadrant Rd. CR7: Thor H 4B **156**
    TW9: Rich 4D **114**
Quadrant Wlk. *E14* 3D **104**
      (off Lanterns Way)
Quad Rd. HA9: Wemb 3D **60**
Quaggy Wlk. SE3 . . . . .4J **123**
Quain Mans. *W14* 6G **99**
      (off Queen's Club Gdns.)
Quainton St. NW10 . . . . .3K **61**
Quaker Cl. *E1* 4J **9**
      (off Quaker St.)
    EC1 . . . . .3E **8**
Quaker La. UB2: S'hall 3E **94**
Quakers Course NW9 . . . . .1B **44**
Quakers La. TW7: Isle 7A **96**
Quakers Pl. E7 . . . . .5B **70**
Quaker St. E1 . . . . .4J **9** (4F **85**)
Quakers Wlk. N21 . . . . .5J **23**
Quality Ct. WC2 . . . . .7J **7**
Quant Bldg. E17 . . . . .4C **50**
Quantock Cl. UB3: Harl 7F **93**
Quantock Dr. KT4: Wor Pk 2E **164**
Quantock Gdns. NW2 . . . . .2F **63**
Quantock Ho. N16 . . . . .1F **67**
Quantock M. SE15 . . . . .2G **121**
Quantum Ct. *E1* 7J **85**
      (off King David La.)
Quarles Pk. Rd. RM6: Chad H 6B **54**
Quarrendon St. SW6 . . . . .2J **117**
Quarr Rd. SM5: Cars 6B **154**
Quarry Pk. Rd. SM1: Sutt 6H **165**
Quarry Ri. SM1: Sutt 6H **165**
Quarry Rd. SW18 . . . . .6A **118**
Quarterdeck, The E14 . . . . .2C **104**
Quarter Ho. SW18 . . . . .4A **118**

Quartermaster La.—Queens St.

Quartermaster La. NW7 5B **30**
Quarters Apartments *CR0: C'don* *2D 168*
(off Wellesley Rd.)
Quartz Ho. HA2: Harr 1E **58**
Quastel Ho. *SE1* *7E 14*
(off Long La.)
Quatre Ports E4 5A **36**
Quay Ho. *E14* *2C 104*
(off Admirals Way)
Quayside Cotts. *E1* *4K 15*
(off Mews St.)
Quayside Ct. *SE16* *1K 103*
(off Abbotshade Rd.)
Quayside Ho. E14 1B **104**
E16 *6H 87*
(off Tarling Rd.)
W10 4G **81**
Quayside Wlk. *KT1: King T* *2D 150*
(off Wadbrook St.)
Quay Vw. Apartments *E14* *3C 104*
(off Arden Cres.)
Quebec M. W1 1F **11** (6D **82**)
Quebec Rd. IG1: Ilf 7F **53**
IG2: Ilf 7F **53**
UB4: Yead 6A **76**
Quebec Way SE16 2K **103**
Quebec Way Ind. Est. SE16 2A **104**
(not continuous)
Quebec Wharf *E8* *1E 84*
(off Kingsland Rd.)
E14 6C **86**
Quedgeley Ct. *SE15* *6F 103*
(off Ebley Cl.)
Queen Adelaide Ct. SE20 6J **139**
Queen Adelaide Rd. SE20 6J **139**
Queen Alexandra Mans. *WC1* *2E 6*
(off Bidborough St.)
Queen Alexandra's Ct. SW19 5H **135**
Queen Anne Alcove 3A **10**
Queen Anne Av. BR2: Brom 3H **159**
Queen Anne Ho. *E16* *1J 105*
(off Hardy Av.)
Queen Anne M. W1 6K **5** (5F **83**)
Queen Anne Rd. E9 6K **67**
Queen Anne's Cl. TW2: Twick 3H **131**
Queen Anne's Ct. *SE10* *5F 105*
(off Park Row)
Queen Anne's Gdns. CR4: Mitc 3D **154**
EN1: Enf 6K **23**
W4 3A **98**
W5 2E **96**
Queen Anne's Ga. DA7: Bex 3D **126**
SW1 7C **12** (2H **101**)
Queen Anne's Gro. EN1: Enf 7J **23**
W4 3A **98**
W5 2E **96**
Queen Anne's Pl. EN1: Enf 6K **23**
Queen Annes Sq. *SE1* *4G 103*
(off Monnow Rd.)
Queen Anne St. W1 7J **5** (6F **83**)
Queen Anne's Wlk. WC1 4F **7**
Queen Anne Ter. *E1* *7H 85*
(off Sovereign Cl.)
Queenborough Gdns. BR7: Chst 6H **143**
IG2: Ilf 4E **52**
Queen Caroline St. W6 5E **98**
Queen Catherine Ho. *SW6* *7K 99*
(off Wandon Rd.)
Queen Ct. *WC1* *4F 7*
(off Queen Sq.)
Queen Elizabeth II Stadium 2A **24**
Queen Elizabeth Bldgs. EC4 2J **13**
Queen Elizabeth Ct. EN5: Barn 3D **20**
Queen Elizabeth Gdns. SM4: Mord 4J **153**
Queen Elizabeth Hall 4H **13** (1K **101**)
Queen Elizabeth Ho. SW12 7E **118**
Queen Elizabeth II Conference Cen. 7D **12** (2H **101**)
Queen Elizabeth Olympic Pk. 7D **68**
Queen Elizabeth Rd. E17 3A **50**
KT2: King T 2F **151**
Queen Elizabeth's Cl. N16 2D **66**
Queen Elizabeth's Coll. SE10 7E **104**
Queen Elizabeth's Dr.
CR0: New Ad 7F **171**
N14 1D **32**
Queen Elizabeth's Hunting Lodge 1C **36**
Queen Elizabeth Sports Cen. 4C **20**
Queen Elizabeth St. SE1 6J **15** (2E **102**)
Queen Elizabeth's Wlk. N16 1D **66**
SM6: Bedd 4H **167**
Queen Elizabeth Wlk. SW13 1C **116**
Queenhithe EC4 2D **14** (7C **84**)
Queen Isabella Way EC1 7B **8**
Queen Margaret Flats *E2* *3H 85*
(off St Jude's Rd.)
Queen Margaret's Gro. N1 5E **66**
Queen Mary Av. E18 1J **51**
SM4: Mord 5F **153**
Queen Mary Cl. KT6: Surb 3G **163**
Queen Mary Ct. TW19: Stanw 1A **128**
Queen Mary Ho. *E16* *1K 105*
(off Wesley Av.)
E18 1K **51**
Queen Mary Rd. SE19 6B **138**
TW17: Shep 2E **146**
Queen Mary's Av. SM5: Cars 7D **166**
Queen Marys Bldgs. *SW1* *3B 18*
(off Stillington St.)
Queen Mary's Ct. *SE10* *6F 105*
(off Park Row)
Queen Mary's Ho. SW15 6C **116**
Queen Mary University of London
Charterhouse Square 4B **8** (4B **84**)
Lincoln's Inn Fields Campus *7G 7*
(off Remnant St.)
Mile End Campus 4A **86**
West Smithfield Campus 6B **8**
Queen Mother Memorial 5C **12**
Queen Mother Sports Cen., The 3A **18**
Queen of Denmark Ct. SE16 3B **104**
Queens Acre SM3: Cheam 7F **165**
Queen's Av. UB6: G'frd 6F **77**
Queens Av. HA7: Stan 3C **42**
IG8: Wfd G 5E **36**
N3 7F **31**
N10 3E **46**
N20 2G **31**
N21 1G **33**
TW13: Hanw 4A **130**
Queensberry Ho. TW9: Rich 5C **114**
Queensberry M. W. SW7 3A **16** (4B **100**)
Queensberry Pl. E12 5B **70**
SW7 3A **16** (4B **100**)
TW9: Rich *5D 114*
(off Friars La.)
Queensberry Way SW7 3A **16** (4B **100**)
Queensborough Ct. *N3* *4H 45*
(off Tillingbourne Gdns.)
Queensborough M. W2 7A **82**
Queensborough Pas. *W2* *7A 82*
(off Queensborough M.)
Queensborough Studios *W2* *7A 82*
(off Queensborough M.)
Queensborough Ter. W2 7K **81**
Queensbridge Ct. *E2* *1F 85*
(off Queensbridge Rd.)
Queensbridge Pk. TW7: Isle 5J **113**
Queensbridge Rd. E2 6F **67**
E8 6F **67**
Queensbridge Sports & Community Cen. 7F **67**
QUEENSBURY 3E **42**
Queensbury Circ. Pde. HA3: Kenton 3E **42**
HA7: Kenton 3E **42**
Queensbury Rd. HA0: Wemb 2F **79**
NW9 7K **43**
Queensbury Sta. Pde. HA8: Edg 3F **43**
Queensbury St. N1 7C **66**
Queen's Cir. SW8 7F **101**
Queens Cl. HA8: Edg 5B **28**
SM6: Wall 5F **167**
Queen's Club Gdns. W14 6G **99**
Queen's Club, The (Tennis Courts) 5G **99**
Queens Club Ter. *W14* *6H 99*
(off Normand Rd.)
Queen's Ct. *NW8* *2B 82*
(off Queen's Ter.)
Queens Ct. *CR2: S Croy* *5C 168*
(off Warham Rd.)
CR7: Thor H 5A **156**
E11 7G **51**
HA3: Kenton 2B **42**
IG9: Buck H 2G **37**
NW6 5K **63**
NW11 5H **45**
SE16 7K **15**
SE23 2J **139**
TW10: Rich 6F **115**
W2 *7K 81*
(off Queensway)
Queenscourt HA9: Wemb 4E **60**
Queen's Cres. NW5 6E **64**
TW10: Rich 5F **115**
Queenscroft Rd. SE9 5B **124**
Queensdale Cres. W11 1F **99**
(not continuous)
Queensdale Pl. W11 1G **99**
Queensdale Rd. W11 1F **99**
Queensdale Wlk. W11 1G **99**
Queensdown Rd. E5 4H **67**
Queen's Dr. KT5: Surb 7G **151**
KT7: T Ditt 6A **150**
N4 2B **66**
Queens Dr. E10 7C **50**
W3 6F **79**
W5 6F **79**
Queen's Elm Pde. *SW3* *5B 16*
(off Old Church St.)
Queen's Elm Sq. SW3 6B **16** (5B **100**)
Queensferry Wlk. N17 4H **49**
Queensfield Ct. SM3: Cheam 4E **164**
Queen's Gallery 7K **11** (2F **101**)
Queen's Gdns. NW4 5E **44**
RM13: Rain 2K **91**
TW5: Hest 1C **112**
W2 7A **82**
W5 4C **78**
Queen's Ga. SW7 7A **10** (2A **100**)
Queensgate Ct. N12 5E **30**
Queen's Ga. Gdns. SW7 3A **100**
Queens Ga. Gdns. BR7: Chst 1H **161**
SW15 4D **116**
Queensgate Ho. *E3* *2B 86*
(off Hereford Rd.)
Queen's Ga. M. SW7 3A **100**
Queensgate M. BR3: Beck 1A **158**
Queen's Ga. Pl. SW7 3A **100**
Queensgate Pl. NW6 7J **63**
Queen's Ga. Pl. M. SW7 2A **16** (3A **100**)
Queen's Ga. Ter. SW7 1A **16** (3A **100**)
Queens Ga. Vs. E9 7A **68**
Queen's Gro. NW8 1B **82**
Queens Gro. Rd. E4 1A **36**
Queen's Gro. Studios NW8 1B **82**
Queen's Head Pas. EC4 7C **8** (6C **84**)
Queen's Head St. N1 1B **84**
Queen's Head Yd. SE1 5E **14**
Queen's House, The ***6F 105***
(within National Maritime Mus.)
Queens Ho. *SE17* *6D 102*
(off Merrow St.)
SW8 *7J 101*
(off Sth. Lambeth Rd.)
TW11: Tedd 6K **131**
W2 *7K 81*
(off Queensway)
Queenshurst Sq. KT2: King T 1E **150**
Queen's Ice & Bowl 7K **81**
Queen's Keep TW1: Twick 6C **114**
Queensland Av. N18 6H **33**
SW19 1K **153**
Queensland Cl. E17 2B **50**
Queensland Ho. *E16* *1E 106*
(off Rymill St.)
Queensland Rd. N7 4A **66**
Queens La. N10 3F **47**
Queen's Mans. *W6* *4F 99*
(off Brook Grn.)
Queen's Mkt. E13 1A **88**
Queens Mead HA8: Edg 6A **28**
Queensmead NW8 1B **82**
Queens Mead Rd. BR2: Brom 2H **159**
Queensmead Sports Cen. 4B **58**
Queensmere Cl. SW19 2F **135**
Queensmere Ct. SW13 7B **98**
Queensmere Rd. SW19 2F **135**
Queen's M. W2 7K **81**
Queensmill Rd. SW6 7F **99**
Queen's Pde. *N11* *5J 31*
(off Friern Barnet Rd.)
NW2 *6E 62*
(off Willesden La.)
Queens Pde. N8 4B **48**
NW4 *5E 44*
(off Queens Rd.)
W5 6F **79**
Queen's Pde. Cl. N11 5J **31**
QUEENS PARK 2G **81**
Queens Pk. Ct. W10 3F **81**
Queen's Pk. Gdns. TW13: Felt 3H **129**
Queen's Pk. Rangers FC 1D **98**
Queens Pas. BR7: Chst 6F **143**
Queens Pl. SM4: Mord 4J **153**
Queen's Prom. KT1: King T, Surb 4D **150**
Queen Sq. WC1 4F **7** (4J **83**)
Queen Sq. Pl. WC1 4F **7**
Queen's Quay *EC4* *2C 14*
(off Up. Thames St.)
Queens Reach KT1: King T 2D **150**
KT8: E Mos 4J **149**
Queens Ride SW13 3C **116**
SW15 3C **116**
Queens Ri. TW10: Rich 6F **115**
Queen's Rd. CR4: Mitc 3B **154**
DA16: Well 2B **126**
E17 6B **50**
EN1: Enf 4K **23**
IG9: Buck H 2E **36**
KT7: T Ditt 5K **149**
SE14 1H **121**
SE15 1H **121**
SW14 3K **115**
TW3: Houn 3F **113**
TW10: Rich 7F **115**
TW11: Tedd 6K **131**
TW12: Hamp H 4F **131**
TW13: Felt 1K **129**
W5 6E **78**
Queens Rd. BR1: Brom 2J **159**
BR3: Beck 2A **158**
BR7: Chst 6F **143**
CR0: C'don 6B **156**
E11 7F **51**
E13 1K **87**
EN5: Barn 3A **20**
IG11: Bark 6G **71**
KT2: King T 7G **133**
KT3: N Mald 4B **152**
N3 1A **46**
N9 3C **34**
N11 7D **32**
NW4 5E **44**
SM4: Mord 4J **153**
SM6: Wall 5F **167**
SW19 6H **135**
TW1: Twick 1A **132**
UB2: S'hall 2B **94**
UB3: Hayes 6G **75**
UB7: W Dray 2B **92**
Queens Rd. Est. EN5: Barn 3A **20**
Queens Rd. W. E13 2J **87**
Queen's Row SE17 6D **102**
Queens St. TW15: Ashf 4B **128**

A-Z London 375

Queen's Ter.—Railway Arches

Queen's Ter. E13 ... 1K **87**
NW8 ... 1B **82**
Queens Ter. *E1* ... *4J **85***
(off Cephas St.)
KT7: T Ditt ... *6A **150***
(off Queens Dr.)
TW7: Isle ... 4A **114**
Queen's Ter. Cotts. W7 ... 2J **95**
Queen's Theatre
Westminster ... *2C **12***
(off Shaftesbury Av.)
Queensthorpe M. SE26 ... 4K **139**
Queensthorpe Rd. SE26 ... 4K **139**
Queens Tower ... *3B **100***
(within Imperial College London)
Queenstown M. SW8 ... 2F **119**
Queenstown Rd. SW8 ... 7J **17** (6F **101**)
Queen St. CR0: C'don ... 4C **168**
DA7: Bex ... 3F **127**
EC4 ... 2D **14** (7C **84**)
(not continuous)
N17 ... 6K **33**
RM7: Rom ... 6K **55**
W1 ... 4J **11** (1F **101**)
Queen St. Pl. EC4 ... 2D **14** (7C **84**)
Queensville Rd. SW12 ... 7H **119**
Queen's Wlk. N5 ... 5B **66**
SW1 ... 5A **12** (1G **101**)
TW15: Ashf ... 4A **128**
W5 ... 4C **78**
Queen's Wlk., The
SE1 ... 3K **13** (7A **84**)
(Oxo Tower Wharf)
SE1 ... 4F **15** (1E **102**)
(Tooley St.)
SE1 ... 4H **13** (1K **101**)
(Waterloo Rd.)
Queens Wlk. E4 ... 1A **36**
HA1: Harr ... 4J **41**
HA4: Ruis ... 2A **58**
NW9 ... 2J **61**
Queens Wlk. Ter. HA4: Ruis ... 3A **58**
Queen's Way NW4 ... 5E **44**
Queens Way TW13: Hanw ... 4A **130**
Queensway BR4: W W'ck ... 3G **171**
BR5: Pet W ... 5G **161**
CR0: Wadd ... 6K **167**
EN3: Pond E ... 4C **24**
TW16: Sun ... 2K **147**
W2 ... 6K **81**
Queensway Bus. Cen. EN3: Pond E ... 4C **24**
Queensway Ind. Est. EN3: Pond E ... 4D **24**
Queensway M. *BR1: Brom* ... *4E **140***
(off Whitefoot La.)
Queenswell Av. N20 ... 3H **31**
Queenswood Av. CR7: Thor H ... 5A **156**
E17 ... 1E **50**
SM6: Bedd ... 4H **167**
TW3: Houn ... 2D **112**
TW12: Hamp ... 6F **131**
Queenswood Ct. KT2: King T ... 1G **151**
SE27 ... 4D **138**
SW4 ... 5J **119**
Queenswood Gdns. E11 ... 1K **69**
Queenswood Pk. N3 ... 2G **45**
Queens Wood Rd. N10 ... 6F **47**
Queenswood Rd. DA15: Sidc ... 5K **125**
SE23 ... 3K **139**
Queen's Yd. WC1 ... 4B **6** (5G **83**)
Queens Yd. E9 ... 6C **68**
QUEEN VICTORIA ... **4F 165**
Queen Victoria Av. HA0: Wemb ... 7D **60**
Queen Victoria Memorial ... 7A **12** (2G **101**)
Queen Victoria Seaman's Rest
E14 ... *6D **86***
(off E. India Dock Rd.)
Queen Victoria Statue ... 1K **99**
Queen Victoria St. EC4 ... 2A **14** (7B **84**)
Queen Victoria Ter. *E1* ... *7H **85***
(off Sovereign Cl.)
Quemerford Rd. N7 ... 5K **65**
Quendon Ho. *W10* ... *4E **80***
(off Sutton Way)
Quenington Ct. SE15 ... 6F **103**
Quentin Ho. *SE1* ... *6A **14***
(off Chaplin Cl.)
Quentin Pl. SE13 ... 3G **123**
Quentin Rd. SE13 ... 3G **123**
Quernmore Cl. BR1: Brom ... 6J **141**
Quernmore Rd.
BR1: Brom ... 6J **141**
N4 ... 6A **48**
Querrin St. SW6 ... 2A **118**
Quest, The *W11* ... *7G **81***
(off Clarendon Rd.)
Quested Ct. *E8* ... *5H **67***
(off Brett Rd.)
Questors Theatre, The ... 7C **78**
Quex Ct. *NW6* ... *1K **81***
(off West End La.)
Quex M. NW6 ... 1J **81**
Quex Rd. NW6 ... 1J **81**
Quiberon Ct.
TW16: Sun ... 3J **147**
Quick Rd. W4 ... 5A **98**
Quicks Rd. SW19 ... 7K **135**
Quick St. N1 ... 2B **84**
Quick St. M. N1 ... 2B **84**
Quickswood NW3 ... 7C **64**
Quiet Nook
BR2: Hayes ... 3B **172**
Quill Ho. *E2* ... *3K **9***
(off Cheshire St.)
Quill La. SW15 ... 4F **117**
Quill St. N4 ... 3A **66**
W5 ... 3E **78**
Quilp St. SE1 ... 6C **14** (2C **102**)
(not continuous)
Quilters Pl. SE9 ... 1G **143**
Quilter St. E2 ... 1K **9** (3G **85**)
SE18 ... 5K **107**
Quilting Ct. *SE16* ... *2K **103***
(off Garter Way)
Quince Ho. *SE13* ... *2D **122***
(off Quince Rd.)
Quince Rd. SE13 ... 2D **122**
Quinn Cl. E2 ... 2J **85**
Quinnell Cl. SE18 ... 5K **107**
Quinta Dr. EN5: Barn ... 5A **20**
Quintain Ho. *KT1: King T* ... *2D **150***
(off Wood St.)
Quintet, The KT12: Walt T ... 7J **147**
Quintin Av. SW20 ... 1H **153**
Quintin Cl. HA5: Eastc ... 4K **39**
Quinton Cl. BR3: Beck ... 3E **158**
SM6: Wall ... 4F **167**
TW5: Cran ... 7K **93**
Quinton Ct. *SE16* ... *4A **104***
(off Plough Way)
Quinton Ho. *SW8* ... *7J **101***
(off Wyvil Rd.)
Quinton Rd. KT7: T Ditt ... 1A **162**
Quinton St. SW18 ... 2A **136**
Quixley St. E14 ... 7F **87**
Quorn Rd. SE22 ... 4E **120**

R

Rabbit Row W8 ... 1J **99**
Rabbits Rd. E12 ... 4C **70**
Rabournmead Dr. UB5: N'olt ... 5C **58**
Raby Rd. KT3: N Mald ... 4K **151**
Raby St. E14 ... 6A **86**
Raccoon Way TW4: Houn ... 2A **112**
Rachel Cl. IG6: Ilf ... 3H **53**
Racine *SE5* ... *1E **120***
(off Sceaux Gdns.)
Rackham Cl. DA16: Well ... 2B **126**
Rackham M. SW16 ... 6G **137**
Rackstraw Ho. NW3 ... 7D **64**
Racton Rd. SW6 ... 6J **99**
RADA
Chenies St. ... ***5C 6***
(off Chenies St.)
Gower St. ... 5C **6**
RADA Studios ... ***5C 6***
(off Chenies St.)
Radbourne Av. W5 ... 4C **96**
Radbourne Cl. E5 ... 4K **67**
Radbourne Ct. HA3: Kenton ... 6B **42**
Radbourne Cres. E17 ... 2F **51**
Radbourne Rd. SW12 ... 7G **119**
Radcliff Ct. *E3* ... *4B **86***
(off Jospeh St.)
Radcliffe Av. EN2: Enf ... 1H **23**
NW10 ... 2C **80**
Radcliffe Gdns. SM5: Cars ... 7C **166**
Radcliffe Ho. *SE16* ... *4H **103***
(off Anchor St.)
SE20 ... 1G **157**
Radcliffe M.
TW12: Hamp H ... 5G **131**
Radcliffe Path SW8 ... 2F **119**
Radcliffe Rd. CR0: C'don ... 2F **169**
HA3: W'stone ... 2A **42**
N21 ... 1G **33**
SE1 ... 3E **102**
Radcliffe Sq. SW15 ... 6F **117**
Radcliffe Way UB5: N'olt ... 3B **76**
Radcot Point SE23 ... 3K **139**
Radcot St. SE11 ... 6K **19** (5A **102**)
Raddington Rd. W10 ... 5G **81**
Raddon Twr. *E8* ... *6F **67***
(off Dalston Sq.)
Radfield Way DA15: Sidc ... 7H **125**
Radford Ct. *SE15* ... *7H **103***
(off Old Kent Rd.)
Radford Est. NW10 ... 3A **80**
Radford Ho. *E14* ... *5D **86***
(off St Leonard's Rd.)
N7 ... 5K **65**
Radford Rd. SE13 ... 6E **122**
Radford Way IG11: Bark ... 3K **89**
Radipole Rd. SW6 ... 1H **117**
Radisson Ct. *SE1* ... *7G **15***
(off Long La.)
Radius Apartments *N1* ... *1G **7***
(off Omega Pl.)
Radius Pk. TW14: Felt ... 4H **111**
Radland Rd. E16 ... 6H **87**
Radleigh Pl. BR3: Beck ... 6C **140**
Radlet Av. SE26 ... 3H **139**
Radlett Cl. E7 ... 6H **69**
Radlett Pl. NW8 ... 1C **82**
Radley Av. IG3: Bark, Ilf ... 4A **72**
Radley Cl. TW14: Felt ... 1H **129**
Radley Ct. SE16 ... 2K **103**
Radley Gdns. HA3: Kenton ... 4E **42**
Radley Ho. *NW1* ... *3E **4***
(off Gloucester Pl.)
SE2 ... *2D **108***
(off Wolvercote Rd.)
Radley M. W8 ... 3J **99**
Radley Rd. N17 ... 2E **48**
Radley's La. E18 ... 2J **51**
Radleys Mead RM10: Dag ... 6H **73**
Radley Sq. E5 ... 2J **67**
Radley Ter. *E16* ... *5H **87***
(off Hermit Rd.)
Radlix Rd. E10 ... 1C **68**
Radnor Av. DA16: Well ... 5B **126**
HA1: Harr ... 5J **41**
Radnor Cl. BR7: Chst ... 6J **143**
CR4: Mitc ... 4J **155**
Radnor Ct. HA3: Hrw W ... 1K **41**
W7 ... *6K **77***
(off Copley Cl.)
Radnor Cres. IG4: Ilf ... 5D **52**
SE18 ... 7A **108**
Radnor Gdns. EN1: Enf ... 1K **23**
TW1: Twick ... 2K **131**
Radnor Gro. UB10: Hil ... 2C **74**
Radnor Ho. *EC1* ... *2D **8***
(off Radnor St.)
SW16 ... 2K **155**
Radnor Lodge *W2* ... *1B **10***
(off Sussex Pl.)
Radnor M. W2 ... 1B **10** (6B **82**)
Radnor Pl. W2 ... 1C **10** (6C **82**)
Radnor Rd. HA1: Harr ... 5H **41**
NW6 ... 1G **81**
SE15 ... 7G **103**
TW1: Twick ... 1K **131**
Radnor St. EC1 ... 2D **8** (3C **84**)
Radnor Ter. SM2: Sutt ... 7J **165**
W14 ... 4H **99**
Radnor Wlk. CR0: C'don ... 6A **158**
E14 ... *4C **104***
(off Barnsdale Av.)
SW3 ... 6D **16** (5C **100**)
Radnor Way NW10 ... 4H **79**
Radstock Av. HA3: Kenton ... 3A **42**
Radstock Cl. N11 ... 6K **31**
Radstock St. SW11 ... 7C **100**
(not continuous)
Radway Ho. *W2* ... *5J **81***
(off Alfred Rd.)
Raeburn Av. KT5: Surb ... 1H **163**
Raeburn Cl. KT1: Hamp W ... 7D **132**
NW11 ... 6A **46**
Raeburn Ho. *UB5: N'olt* ... *2B **76***
(off Academy Gdns.)
Raeburn Rd. DA15: Sidc ... 6J **125**
HA8: Edg ... 1G **43**
UB4: Hayes ... 2F **75**
Raeburn St. SW2 ... 4J **119**
RAF Bomber Command Memorial
... **6J 11 (2F 101)**
Raffles Ho. NW4 ... 4D **44**
Rafford Way BR1: Brom ... 2K **159**
RAF Mus. London ... 2C **44**
RAF Northolt Aerodrome ... 6H **57**
RAF Uxbridge, Battle of Britain Bunker
... 1B **74**
Ragged School Mus. ... 5A **86**
Raggleswood BR7: Chst ... 1E **160**
Raglan Cl. TW4: Houn ... 5D **112**
Raglan Ct. CR2: S Croy ... 5B **168**
E17 ... 5E **50**
HA9: Wemb ... 4F **61**
SE12 ... 5J **123**
Raglan Rd. BR2: Brom ... 4A **160**
DA17: Belv ... 4F **109**
E17 ... 5E **50**
EN1: Enf ... 7A **24**
SE18 ... 5G **107**
Raglan St. NW5 ... 6F **65**
Raglan Ter. HA2: Harr ... 4F **59**
Raglan Way UB5: N'olt ... 6G **59**
Ragley Cl. W3 ... 2J **97**
Ragwort Ct. SE26 ... 5H **139**
Rahere Ct. *E1* ... *4A **86***
(off Toby La.)
Raider Cl. RM7: Mawney ... 1G **55**
Railey M. NW5 ... 5G **65**
Railshead Rd. TW1: Isle ... 4B **114**
TW7: Isle ... 4B **114**
Railton Rd. SE24 ... 4A **120**
Railway App. HA1: Harr ... 4K **41**
HA3: Harr ... 4K **41**
N4 ... 6A **48**
RM7: Rush G ... 6K **55**
SE1 ... 5F **15** (1D **102**)
SM6: Wall ... 5F **167**
TW1: Twick ... 7A **114**
Railway Arches *E1* ... *6K **85***
(off Barnardo St.)
E1 ... *7H **85***
(off Chapman St.)
E2 ... *1J **9***
(off Cremer St.)
E2 ... *2F **85***
(off Geffrye St.)

376 A-Z London

Railway Arches E2 1F 85
(off Laburnum St.)
E3 4B 86
(off Cantrell Rd.)
E7 4J 69
(off Winchelsea Rd.)
E8 7H 67
(off Mentmore Ter.)
E10 1E 68
E11 1F 69
(off Grove Grn. Rd.)
E16 1J 105
W6 3E 98
W12 2E 98
(off Shepherd's Bush Mkt.)
Railway Av. SE16 2J 103
(not continuous)
Railway Children Wlk.
BR1: Brom 2J 141
SE12 2J 141
Railway Cotts. E15 2G 87
(off Baker's Row)
SW19 4K 135
W6 2E 98
(off Sulgrave Rd.)
Railway Fields Local Nature Reserve 6B 48
Railway Gro. SE14 7B 104
Railway M. W10 6G 81
Railway Pas. TW11: Tedd 6A 132
Railway Pl. DA17: Belv 3G 109
Railway Ri. SE22 4E 120
Railway Rd. TW11: Tedd 4J 131
Railway Side SW13 3A 116
Railway Sidings Rd. SE16 3G 103
Railway St. N1 2J 83
RM6: Chad H 7C 54
Railway Ter. E17 1E 50
SE13 5D 122
TW13: Felt 1J 129
Railway Wharf KT1: King T 1D 150
(off Thames Side)
Rainborough Cl. NW10 6J 61
Rainbow Av. E14 5D 104
Rainbow Ct. SE14 6A 104
(off Chipley St.)
Rainbow Ind. Est. SW20 2D 152
UB7: Yiew 7A 74
Rainbow Quay SE16 3A 104
(not continuous)
Rainbow St. SE5 7E 102
Raine Gdns. IG8: Wfd G 4D 36
Rainer Apartment CR0: C'don 1D 168
(off Cherry Orchard Rd.)
Raines Est. Ct. N16 2F 67
Raine St. E1 1H 103
Rainham Cl. SE9 6J 125
SW11 6C 118
Rainham Ho. NW1 1G 83
(off Bayham Pl.)
Rainham Rd. NW10 3E 80
Rainham Rd. Nth. RM10: Dag 2G 73
Rainham Rd. Sth. RM10: Dag 4H 73
Rainhill Way E3 3C 86
(not continuous)
Rainsborough Av. SE8 4A 104
Rainsborough Ho. SW15 5G 117
(off Stamford Sq.)
Rainsborough Sq. SW6 6J 99
Rainsford Cl. HA7: Stan 5H 27
Rainsford Rd. NW10 3G 79
Rainsford St. W2 7C 4 (6C 82)
Rainton Rd. SE7 5J 105
Rainville Rd. W6 6E 98
Raisins Hill HA5: Eastc 3A 40
Raith Av. N14 3C 32
Rajsee Apartments E2 3G 85
(off Bethnal Grn. Rd.)
Raleana Rd. E14 1E 104
Raleigh Av. SM6: Bedd 4H 167
UB4: Yead 5K 75
Raleigh Cl. HA4: Ruis 2H 57
HA5: Pinn 7B 40
NW4 5E 44
Raleigh Ct. BR3: Beck 1D 158
SE8 5A 104
(off Evelyn St.)
SE16 1K 103
(off Clarence M.)
SM6: Wall 6F 167
W12 2E 98
(off Scott's Rd.)
W13 5B 78
Raleigh Dr. KT5: Surb 1J 163
N20 3H 31
Raleigh Gdns. CR4: Mitc 3D 154
(not continuous)
SW2 6K 119
Raleigh Ho.
BR1: Brom 1J 159
(off Hammelton Rd.)
CR0: C'don 7K 155
(off Mitcham Rd.)
E14 2D 104
(off Admirals Way)
SW1 7C 18
(off Dolphin Sq.)
Raleigh M. BR6: Chels 5K 173
N1 1B 84
(off Packington St.)
Raleigh Rd. EN2: Enf 4J 23
N8 4A 48
SE20 7K 139
TW9: Rich 3F 115
TW13: Felt 3H 129
UB2: S'hall 5C 94
Raleigh St. N1 1B 84
Raleigh Way N14 1C 32
TW13: Hanw 5A 130
Rale La. E4 1A 36
Ralph Bayer Ct. E3 5C 86
(off Geoff Cade Way)
Ralph Brook Ct. N1 1F 9
(off Chart St.)
Ralph Ct. W2 6K 81
(off Queensway)
Ralph Perring Ct. BR3: Beck 4C 158
Ralston St. SW3 6E 16 (5D 100)
Ramac Ind. Est. SE7 4K 105
Rama Cl. SW16 7J 137
Rama Ct. HA1: Harr 2J 59
Ramac Way SE7 4K 105
Rama La. SE19 7F 139
Ramar Ho. E1 5G 85
(off Hanbury St.)
Rambert 4J 13
(off Upper Ground)
Rambler Cl. SW16 4G 137
Rame Cl. SW17 5E 136
Ramilles Cl. SW2 6J 119
Ramillies Pl. W1 1A 12 (6G 83)
Ramillies Rd. DA15: Sidc 6B 126
NW7 2F 29
W4 4K 97
Ramillies St. W1 1A 12 (6G 83)
Ramones Ter. CR4: Mitc 4J 155
(off Yorkshire Rd.)
Rampart St. E1 6H 85
Ram Pas. KT1: King T 2D 150
Rampayne St. SW1 5C 18 (5H 101)
Ram Pl. E9 6J 67
Rampton Cl. E4 3H 35
Ram Quarter SW18 5K 117
Ramsay Ho. NW8 2C 82
(off Townshend Est.)
Ramsay M. SW3 7C 16 (6C 100)
Ramsay Rd. E7 4G 69
W3 3J 97
Ramscroft Cl. N9 7K 23
Ramsdale Rd. SW17 5E 136
Ramsden Dr.
RM5: Col R 1G 55
Ramsden Rd. DA8: Erith 7K 109
N11 5J 31
SW12 6E 118
Ramsey Cl. NW9 6B 44
UB6: G'frd 5H 59
Ramsey Ct. CR0: C'don 2B 168
(off Church St.)
Ramsey Ho. SW9 7A 102
Ramsey Rd. CR7: Thor H 6K 155
Ramsey St. E2 4G 85
Ramsey Wlk. N1 6D 66
Ramsey Way N14 7B 22
Ramsfort Ho. SE16 4H 103
(off Camilla Rd.)
Ramsgate Cl. E16 1K 105
Ramsgate St. E8 6F 67
Ramsgill App. IG2: Ilf 4K 53
Ramsgill Dr. IG2: Ilf 5K 53
Rams Gro. RM6: Chad H 4E 54
Ram St. SW18 5K 117
Ram Twr. SW18 5K 117
Ramulis Dr. UB4: Yead 4B 76
Ramuswood Av. BR6: Chels 5J 173
Rancliffe Gdns. SE9 4C 124
Rancliffe Rd. E6 2C 88
Randall Av. NW2 2A 62
Randall Cl. DA8: Erith 6J 109
SW11 1C 118
Randall Ct. NW7 7H 29
Randall Pl. SE10 7E 104
Randall Rd. SE11 4G 19 (5K 101)
Randall Row SE11 4G 19 (4K 101)
Randalls Rents SE16 3B 104
(off Gulliver St.)
Randell's Rd. N1 1J 83
Randisbourne Gdns. SE6 3D 140
Randle Rd. TW10: Ham 4C 132
Randlesdown Rd. SE6 4C 140
(not continuous)
Randolph App. E16 6A 88
Randolph Av. W9 4A 4 (2K 81)
Randolph Cl. DA7: Bex 3J 127
KT2: King T 5J 133
Randolph Ct. NW8 1A 82
Randolph Cres. W9 4A 82
Randolph Gdns. NW6 2K 81
Randolph Gro. RM6: Chad H 5C 54
Randolph M. W9 4A 82
Randolph Rd. BR2: Brom 1D 172
E17 5D 50
UB1: S'hall 2D 94
W9 4A 82
Randolph St. NW1 7G 65
Randon Cl. HA2: Harr 2F 41
Ranelagh Av. SW6 3H 117
SW13 2C 116
Ranelagh Bri. W2 5K 81
Ranelagh Cl. HA8: Edg 4B 28
Ranelagh Cotts. SW1 5J 17
(off Ebury Bri. Rd.)
Ranelagh Dr. HA8: Edg 4B 28
TW1: Twick 4B 114
Ranelagh Gdns. E11 5A 52
IG1: Ilf 1D 70
SW6 3G 117
(not continuous)
W4 7J 97
W6 4B 98
Ranelagh Gdns. Mans. SW6 3G 117
(off Ranelagh Gdns.)
Ranelagh Gro. SW1 5H 17 (5E 100)
Ranelagh Ho. SW3 5E 16
(off Elystan Pl.)
Ranelagh M. W5 2D 96
Ranelagh Pl. KT3: N Mald 5A 152
Ranelagh Rd. E6 1E 88
E11 4G 69
E15 2G 87
HA0: Wemb 6D 60
N17 3E 48
N22 1K 47
Ranelagh Rd. NW10 2B 80
SW1 6B 18 (5G 101)
UB1: S'hall 1B 94
W5 2D 96
Ranfurly Rd. SM1: Sutt 2J 165
Rangbourne Ho. N7 5J 65
Rangefield Rd. BR1: Brom 5G 141
Rangemoor Rd. N15 5F 49
Ranger's House 1F 123
Ranger's Rd. E4 1B 36
Rangers Sq. SE10 1F 123
Range Way TW17: Shep 7C 146
Rangeworth Pl. DA15: Sidc 3K 143
Rangoon St. EC3 1J 15
Rankin Cl. NW9 3A 44
Rankine Ho. SE1 3C 102
(off Bath Ter.)
Ranleigh Gdns. DA7: Bex 7F 109
Ranmere St. SW12 1F 137
Ranmoor Cl. HA1: Harr 4H 41
Ranmoor Gdns. HA1: Harr 4H 41
Ranmore Av. CR0: C'don 3F 169
Ranmore Ct. KT6: Surb 5D 150
Ranmore Path BR5: St M Cry 4K 161
Ranmore Rd. SM2: Cheam 7F 165
Rannoch Cl. HA8: Edg 2C 28
Rannoch Rd. W6 6E 98
Rannock Av. NW9 7K 43
Ransome's Dock Bus. Cen. SW11 7C 100
Ransom Rd. SE7 4A 106
Ranston St. NW1 5C 4 (5C 82)
Ranulf Rd. NW2 4H 63
Ranwell Cl. E3 1B 86
Ranwell Ho. E3 1B 86
(off Ranwell Cl.)
Ranworth Rd. N9 2D 34
Ranyard Cl. KT9: Chess 3F 163
Raphael Cl. KT1: King T 4D 150
Raphael Ct. SE16 5H 103
(off Stubbs Dr.)
Raphael Dr. KT7: T Ditt 7K 149
Raphael St. SW7 7E 10 (2D 100)
Raphen Apartments E3 2A 86
(off Medway Rd.)
Rapley Ho. E2 2K 9
(off Turin St.)
Raquel Ct. SE1 6G 15
(off Snowfields)
Rashleigh Ct. SW8 2F 119
Rashleigh Ho. WC1 2E 6
(off Thanet St.)
Rashleigh St. SW8 2F 119
(off Peardon St.)
Rasper Rd. N20 2F 31
Rastell Av. SW2 2H 137
RATCLIFF 5A 86
Ratcliffe Cl. SE12 7J 123
Ratcliffe Ct. SE1 7D 14
(off Gt. Dover St.)
Ratcliffe Cross St. E1 6K 85
Ratcliffe Ho. E14 6A 86
(off Barnes St.)
Ratcliffe La. E14 6A 86
Ratcliffe Orchard E1 7K 85
Ratcliff Rd. E7 5A 70
Rathbone Ho. E16 6H 87
(off Rathbone St.)
NW6 1J 81
Rathbone Mkt. E16 5H 87
Rathbone Pl. W1 6C 6 (5H 83)
Rathbone Sq. CR0: C'don 4C 168
Rathbone St. E16 6H 87
W1 6B 6 (5G 83)
Rathcoole Av. N8 5K 47
Rathcoole Gdns. N8 5K 47
Rathfern Rd. SE6 1B 140
Rathgar Av. W13 1B 96
Rathgar Cl. N3 2H 45
Rathgar Rd. SW9 3B 120
Rathmell Dr. SW4 6H 119
Rathmore Rd. SE7 5K 105

Rathnew Ct. E2 . . . . .3K **85**
(off Meath Cres.)
Rathore Cl. RM6: Chad H 5D **54**
Rattray Cl. SE6 . . . . .2H **141**
Rattray Rd. SW2 . . . . .4A **120**
Raul Rd. SE15 . . . . .2G **121**
Raveley St. NW5 . . . . .4G **65**
(not continuous)
Raven Cl. NW9 . . . . .2A **44**
RM7: Rush G 7G **55**
Ravendale Rd. TW16: Sun 2H **147**
Ravenet St. SW8 . . . . .1F **119**
SW11 . . . . .1F **119**
(not continuous)
Ravenfield Rd. SW17 . . . . .3D **136**
Ravenhill Rd. E13 . . . . .2A **88**
Raven Ho. SE16 . . . . .4K **103**
(off Tawny Way)
Ravenings Pde. IG3: Ilf 1A **72**
Ravenna Rd. SW15 . . . . .5F **117**
Ravenor Cl. UB6: G'frd 4F **77**
Ravenor Pk. Rd. UB6: G'frd 3F **77**
Raven Rd. E18 . . . . .2A **52**
Raven Row E1 . . . . .5H **85**
Raven Row Contemporary Art Cen. . . .5F **85**
Raven's Ait 5D **150**
Ravensbourne Apartments SW6 . . .3A **118**
(off Central Av.)
Ravensbourne Av. BR2: Brom 7F **141**
BR3: Beck 7F **141**
TW19: Stanw 1A **128**
Ravensbourne Ct. SE6 . . . . .7C **122**
Ravensbourne Gdns. IG5: Ilf 1E **52**
W13 . . . . .5B **78**
Ravensbourne Ho. BR1: Brom 5F **141**
NW8 . . . . .5C **4**
(off Broadley St.)
Ravensbourne Mans. SE8 . . . . .6C **104**
(off Berthon St.)
Ravensbourne Pk. SE6 . . . . .7C **122**
Ravensbourne Pk. Cres. SE6 . . . . .7B **122**
Ravensbourne Pl. SE8 . . . . .1C **122**
SE13 . . . . .2D **122**
Ravensbourne Rd. BR1: Brom 3J **159**
SE6 .7B **122**
TW1: Twick 6C **114**
Ravensbourne Ter. TW19: Stanw . . .1A **128**
Ravensbury Av. SM4: Mord 5A **154**
Ravensbury Ct. CR4: Mitc 4B **154**
(off Ravensbury Gro.)
Ravensbury Gro. CR4: Mitc 4B **154**
Ravensbury La. CR4: Mitc 4B **154**
Ravensbury Path CR4: Mitc 4B **154**
Ravensbury Rd. BR5: St P 3K **161**
SW18 . . . . .2K **135**
Ravensbury Ter. SW18 . . . . .2K **135**
Ravenscar NW1 . . . . .1G **83**
(off Bayham St.)
Ravenscar Rd. BR1: Brom 4G **141**
KT6: Surb 2F **163**
Ravens Cl. BR2: Brom 2H **159**
EN1: Enf 2K **23**
KT6: Surb 6D **150**
Ravens Ct. KT1: King T 5D **150**
(off Uxbridge Rd.)
Ravenscourt TW16: Sun 1H **147**
Ravenscourt Av. W6 . . . . .4C **98**
Ravenscourt Cl. HA4: Ruis 7E **38**
Ravenscourt Gdns. W6 . . . . .4C **98**
Ravenscourt Pk. EN5: Barn 4A **20**
W6 .3C **98**
Ravenscourt Pk. Mans. W6 . . . . . . .3D **98**
(off Paddenswick Rd.)
Ravenscourt Pl. W6 . . . . .4D **98**
Ravenscourt Rd. W6 . . . . .4D **98**
Ravenscourt Sq. W6 . . . . .3C **98**
Ravenscraig Rd. N11 . . . . .4B **32**
Ravenscroft Av. HA9: Wemb 1E **60**
NW11 . . . . .7H **45**
(not continuous)
Ravenscroft Cl. E16 . . . . .5J **87**

Ravenscroft Cotts.
EN5: New Bar 4D **20**
Ravenscroft Cres. SE9 . . . . .3D **142**
Ravenscroft Pk. E2 . . . . .3F **85**
(off Baroness Rd.)
EN5: Barn 3A **20**
Ravenscroft Rd. BR3: Beck 2J **157**
E16 .5J **87**
W4 .4J **97**
Ravenscroft St. E2 . . . . .1K **9** (2F **85**)
Ravensdale Av. N12 . . . . .4F **31**
Ravensdale Gdns. SE19 . . . . .7D **138**
TW4: Houn 3C **112**
Ravensdale Ind. Est. N16 . . . . .6G **49**
Ravensdale Mans. N8 . . . . .6J **47**
(off Haringey Pk.)
Ravensdale Rd. N16 . . . . .7F **49**
TW4: Houn 3C **112**
Ravens Dene BR7: Chst 5D **142**
Ravensdon St. SE11 . . . . . .6K **19** (5A **102**)
Ravensfield Cl. RM9: Dag 4D **72**
Ravensfield Gdns. KT19: Ewe 5A **164**
Ravens Ga. M. BR2: Brom 2G **159**
Ravenshaw St. NW6 . . . . .5H **63**
Ravenshill BR7: Chst 1F **161**
Ravenshurst Av. NW4 . . . . .4E **44**
Ravenside KT1: King T 5D **150**
(off Portsmouth Rd.)
Ravenside Cl. N18 . . . . .5E **34**
Ravenside Retail Pk. N18 . . . . .5E **34**
Ravenslea Rd. SW12 . . . . .7D **118**
Ravensleigh Gdns. BR1: Brom 5K **141**
Ravensmead Rd. BR2: Brom 7F **141**
Ravensmede Way W4 . . . . .4B **98**
Ravens M. SE12 . . . . .5J **123**
Ravenstone SE17 . . . . .5E **102**
Ravenstone Rd. N8 . . . . .3A **48**
NW9 . . . . .6B **44**
Ravenstone St. SW12 . . . . .1E **136**
Ravens Wlk. E20 . . . . .6D **68**
Ravens Way SE12 . . . . .5J **123**
Ravenswood DA5: Bexl 1E **144**
Ravenswood Av. BR4: W W'ck 1E **170**
KT6: Surb 2F **163**
Ravenswood Cl. KT2: King T 6H **133**
Ravenswood Cres. BR4: W W'ck 1E **170**
HA2: Harr 2D **58**
Ravenswood Gdns. TW7: Isle 1J **113**
Ravenswood Ind. Est. E17 . . . . .4E **50**
Ravenswood Rd. CR0: Wadd 3B **168**
E17 .4E **50**
SW12 . . . . .7F **119**
Ravensworth Cl. SW6 . . . . .7J **99**
(off Fulham Rd.)
Ravensworth Rd. NW10 . . . . .3D **80**
SE9 .3D **142**
Raven Wharf SE1 . . . . .6J **15**
(off Lafone St.)
Ravey St. EC2 . . . . .3G **9** (4E **84**)
Ravine Gro. SE18 . . . . .6J **107**
Rav Pinter Cl. N16 . . . . .7E **48**
Rawchester Cl. SW18 . . . . .1H **135**
Rawlings Cl. BR3: Beck 5E **158**
BR6: Chels 5K **173**
Rawlings Cres. HA9: Wemb 3H **61**
Rawlings St. SW3 . . . . .3E **16** (4D **100**)
Rawlins Cl. CR2: Sels 7B **170**
N3 . . . . .3G **45**
Rawlinson Cl. NW2 . . . . .7E **44**
Rawlinson Ho. SE13 . . . . .4F **123**
(off Mercator Rd.)
Rawlinson Ter. N17 . . . . .3F **49**
Rawnsley Av. CR4: Mitc 5B **154**
Rawreth Wlk. N1 . . . . .1C **84**
(off Basire St.)
Rawson St. SW11 . . . . .1E **118**
(not continuous)
Rawsthorne Cl. E16 . . . . .1D **106**
Rawsthorne Cl. TW4: Houn 4D **112**
Rawstone Wlk. E13 . . . . .2J **87**
Rawstorne Pl. EC1 . . . . .1A **8** (3B **84**)

Rawstorne St. EC1 . . . . .1A **8** (3B **84**)
(not continuous)
Raybell Ct. TW7: Isle 2K **113**
Rayburne Cl. IG9: Buck H 1F **37**
W14 .3G **99**
Ray Cl. KT9: Chess 6C **162**
Raydean Rd. EN5: New Bar 5E **20**
Raydons Gdns. RM9: Dag 5E **72**
Raydons Rd. RM9: Dag 5E **72**
Raydon St. N19 . . . . .2F **65**
Rayfield Cl. BR2: Brom 6C **160**
Rayford Av. SE12 . . . . .7H **123**
Ray Gdns. HA7: Stan 5G **27**
IG11: Bark 2A **90**
Ray Gunter Ho. SE17 . . . . .5B **102**
(off Marsland Cl.)
Ray Ho. N1 . . . . .1E **84**
(off Colville Est.)
W10 .6F **81**
(off Cambridge Gdns.)
Rayleas Cl. SE18 . . . . .1F **125**
Rayleigh Av. TW11: Tedd 6J **131**
Rayleigh Cl. N13 . . . . .3J **33**
Rayleigh Ct. KT1: King T 2G **151**
N22 . . . . .1C **48**
Rayleigh Ri. CR2: S Croy 6E **168**
Rayleigh Rd. E16 . . . . .1K **105**
IG8: Wfd G 6F **37**
N13 . . . . .3H **33**
SW19 . . . . .1H **153**
Ray Lodge Rd. IG8: Wfd G 6F **37**
Ray Massey Way E6 . . . . .1C **88**
(off High St. Nth.)
Raymead Av. CR7: Thor H 5A **156**
Raymead Pas. CR7: Thor H 5A **156**
(off Raymead Av.)
Raymede Towers W10 . . . . .5F **81**
(off Treverton St.)
Raymere Gdns. SE18 . . . . .7H **107**
Raymond Av. E18 . . . . .3H **51**
W13 . . . . .3A **96**
Raymond Bldgs. WC1 . . . . . . .5H **7** (5K **83**)
Raymond Chadburn Ho. E7 . . . . . . .4K **69**
Raymond Cl. SE26 . . . . .5J **139**
SL3: Poyle 4A **174**
Raymond Ct. N10 . . . . .7A **32**
Raymond Postgate Ct. SE28 . . . . . .7B **90**
Raymond Rd. BR3: Beck 4A **158**
E13 .1A **88**
IG2: Ilf 7H **53**
SW19 . . . . .6G **135**
Raymond Way KT10: Clay 6A **162**
Raymouth Rd. SE16 . . . . .4H **103**
Raynald Ho. SW16 . . . . .3J **137**
Rayne Cl. E18 . . . . .4H **51**
Rayne Ho. SW12 . . . . .6E **118**
W9 . . . . .4K **81**
(off Delaware Rd.)
Rayner Cl. SM5: Cars 5D **166**
Rayner Ct. W12 . . . . .2E **98**
(off Bamborough Gdns.)
Rayners Cl. HA0: Wemb 5D **60**
Rayners Cres. UB5: N'olt 3K **75**
Rayners Gdns. UB5: N'olt 2K **75**
RAYNERS LANE 1D **58**
Rayners La. HA2: Harr 1E **58**
HA5: Pinn 5D **40**
Rayners Rd. SW15 . . . . .5G **117**
Rayners Ter. E14 . . . . .6A **86**
(off Carr St.)
Rayner Towers E10 . . . . .7C **50**
(off Albany Rd.)
Raynes Av. E11 . . . . .7A **52**
RAYNES PARK 4E **152**
Raynes Pk. Bri. SW20 . . . . .2E **152**
Raynes Pk. School Sports Cen. 3D **152**
Raynham W2 . . . . .7D **4**
(off Norfolk Cres.)
Raynham Av. N18 . . . . .6B **34**
Raynham Ho. E1 . . . . .4K **85**
(off Harpley Sq.)

Raynham Rd. N18 . . . . .5B **34**
W6 . . . . .4D **98**
Raynham Ter. N18 . . . . .5B **34**
Raynor Cl. UB1: S'hall 1D **94**
Raynor Pl. N1 . . . . .7C **66**
Raynton Cl. HA2: Harr 1C **58**
UB4: Hayes 4H **75**
Raynton Dr. UB4: Hayes 4H **75**
Ray Rd. KT8: W Mole 5F **149**
Rays Av. N18 . . . . .4D **34**
Rays Rd. BR4: W W'ck 7E **158**
N18 .4D **34**
Ray St. EC1 . . . . .4K **7** (4A **84**)
Ray St. Bri. EC1 . . . . .4K **7**
Ray Wlk. N7 . . . . .2K **65**
Raywood Cl. UB3: Harl 7E **92**
Raywood Mans. E20 . . . . .6E **68**
(off West Pk. Wlk.)
Razia M. E12 . . . . .5D **70**
Reachview Cl. NW1 . . . . .7G **65**
Read Cl. KT7: T Ditt 7A **150**
Read Ct. E17 . . . . .6C **50**
Reade Ct. W3 . . . . .3J **97**
(off Stanley Rd.)
Reader Ho. SE5 . . . . .1C **120**
(off Badsworth Rd.)
Read Ho. SE11 . . . . .7J **19**
Reading Cl. SE22 . . . . .6G **121**
Reading Ho. SE15 . . . . .6G **103**
(off Friary Est.)
W2 . . . . .6A **82**
(off Hallfield Est.)
Reading La. E8 . . . . .6H **67**
Reading Rd. SM1: Sutt 5A **166**
UB5: N'olt 5F **59**
Readman Ct. SE20 . . . . .1H **157**
Reads Cl. IG1: Ilf 3F **71**
Ream Apartments SE23 . . . . .2J **139**
(off Clyde Ter.)
Reapers Cl. NW1 . . . . .1H **83**
Reapers Way TW7: Isle 5H **113**
Reardon Ct. N21 . . . . .2G **33**
Reardon Ho. E1 . . . . .1H **103**
(off Reardon St.)
Reardon Path E1 . . . . .1H **103**
(not continuous)
Reardon St. E1 . . . . .1H **103**
Reaston St. SE14 . . . . .7K **103**
Rebecca Ct. DA14: Sidc 4B **144**
Rebecca Ho. E3 . . . . .4B **86**
(off Brokesley St.)
N12 .4E **30**
(off Woodside Pk. Rd.)
Reckitt Rd. W4 . . . . .5A **98**
Record St. SE15 . . . . .6J **103**
Recovery St. SW17 . . . . .5C **136**
Recreation Av. RM7: Rom 5J **55**
Recreation Rd. BR2: Brom 2H **159**
DA15: Sidc 3J **143**
SE26 . . . . .4K **139**
UB2: S'hall 4C **94**
Recreation Way CR4: Mitc 3H **155**
Rector St. N1 . . . . .1C **84**
Rectory Bus. Cen. DA14: Sidc 4B **144**
Rectory Chambers SW3 . . . . .7C **16**
(off Old Church St.)
Rectory Cl. DA14: Sidc 4B **144**
E4 . . . . .3H **35**
HA7: Stan 5G **27**
KT6: Surb 1C **162**
N3 . . . . .1H **45**
SW20 . . . . .3E **152**
TW17: Shep 3C **146**
Rectory Cl. E18 . . . . .1H **51**
SM6: Wall 4G **167**
TW13: Felt 4A **130**
Rectory Cres. E11 . . . . .6A **52**
(not continuous)
Rectory Farm Rd. EN2: Enf 1E **22**
(not continuous)
Rectory Field 7K **105**

Rectory Fld. Cres.—Regatta La.

Rectory Fld. Cres. SE7 7A 106
Rectory Gdns. *BR3: Beck* *1C 158*
(off Rectory Rd.)
N8 4J 47
SW4 3G 119
UB5: N'olt 1D 76
Rectory Grn. BR3: Beck 1B 158
Rectory Gro. CR0: C'don 2B 168
SW4 3G 119
TW12: Hamp 4D 130
Rectory La. DA14: Sidc 4B 144
HA7: Stan 5G 27
HA8: Edg 6B 28
KT6: Surb 1B 162
SM6: Wall 4G 167
SW17 6E 136
Rectory Orchard SW19 4G 135
Rectory Pk. Av. UB5: N'olt 3D 76
Rectory Pl. SE18 4E 106
Rectory Rd. BR2: Kes 7B 172
BR3: Beck 1C 158
E12 5D 70
E17 4D 50
N16 2F 67
RM10: Dag 6H 73
SM1: Sutt 3J 165
SW13 2C 116
TW4: Cran 2A 112
UB2: S'hall 3D 94
UB3: Hayes 6J 75
W3 1H 97
Rectory Sq. E1 5K 85
Rectory Way UB10: Ick 2D 56
Reculver Ho. *SE15* *6J 103*
(off Lovelinch Cl.)
Reculver M. N18 4B 34
Reculver Rd. SE16 5K 103
Red Anchor Cl. SW3 6B 100
Redan Pl. W2 6K 81
Redan St. W14 3F 99
Redan Ter. SE5 2B 120
Red Barracks Rd. SE18 4D 106
Redberry Gro. SE26 3J 139
Redbourne Av. N3 1J 45
Redbourne Dr. SE28 6D 90
(not continuous)
Redbourne Ho. *E14* *6B 86*
(off Norbiton Rd.)
Redbourn Ho. *W10* *4E 80*
(off Sutton Way)
REDBRIDGE 6C 52
Redbridge Ent. Cen. IG1: Ilf 2G 71
Redbridge Foyer *IG1: Ilf* *2G 71*
(off Sylvan Rd.)
Redbridge Gdns. SE5 7E 102
Redbridge Ho. *E16* *7F 89*
(off University Way)
Redbridge La. E. IG4: Ilf 6B 52
Redbridge La. W. E11 6K 51
REDBRIDGE RDBT. 6B 52
Redbridge Sports & Leisure Cen. 1H 53
Redburn Ind. Est. EN3: Pond E 6E 24
Redburn St. SW3 7E 16 (6D 100)
Redcar Cl. UB5: N'olt 5F 59
Redcar St. SE5 7C 102
Redcastle Cl. E1 7J 85
Red Cedars Rd. BR6: Orp 7J 161
Redchurch St. E2 3J 9 (4F 85)
Redcliffe Cl. *SW5* *5K 99*
(off Old Brompton Rd.)
Redcliffe Ct. *E5* *3H 67*
(off Napoleon Rd.)
Redcliffe Gdns. IG1: Ilf 1E 70
SW10 5K 99
W4 7H 97
Redcliffe M. SW10 5K 99
Redcliffe Pl. SW10 6A 100
Redcliffe Rd. SW10 5A 100
Redcliffe Sq. SW10 5K 99
Redcliffe St. SW10 6K 99
Redclose Av. SM4: Mord 5J 153
Redclyffe Rd. E6 1A 88
Redclyf Ho. *E1* *4J 85*
(off Cephas St.)
Redcourt CR0: C'don 3E 168
Red Cow La. EC1 3C 8 (4C 84)
Redcroft Rd. UB1: S'hall 7G 77
Red Cross Cotts. *SE1* *6D 14*
(off Ayres St.)
Redcross Way SE1 6D 14 (2C 102)
Redding Ho. SE18 3C 106
Reddings, The NW7 3G 29
Reddings Cl. NW7 4G 29
Reddins Rd. SE15 6G 103
Reddons Rd. BR3: Beck 7A 140
Redenham Ho. *SW15* *7C 116*
(off Ellisfield Dr.)
Rede Pl. W2 6J 81
Redesdale Gdns. TW7: Isle 7A 96
Redesdale St. SW3 7D 16 (6C 100)
Redfern Av. TW4: Houn 7E 112
Redfern Ho. *E13* *1H 87*
(off Redriffe Rd.)
NW8 *1B 82*
(off Dorman Way)
Redfern Rd. NW10 7A 62
SE6 7E 122
Redfield La. SW5 4J 99
Redfield M. SW5 4K 99
Redford Av. CR7: Thor H 4K 155
SM6: Wall 6J 167
Redford Cl. TW13: Felt 2H 129
Redford Wlk. *N1* *1C 84*
(off Popham St.)
Redgate Dr. BR2: Hayes 2K 171
Redgate Ter. SW15 6F 117
Redgrave Cl. CR0: C'don 6F 157
Redgrave Rd. SW15 3F 117
Redgrave Ter. *E2* *3G 85*
(off Derbyshire St.)
Red Hill BR7: Chst 5F 143
Redhill Ct. SW2 2A 138
Redhill Dr. HA8: Edg 2H 43
Redhill St. NW1 1K 5 (2F 83)
Red House 4E 126
Red Ho. *SE20* *7H 139*
(off Anerley Pk.)
Red Ho. La. DA6: Bex 4D 126
Redhouse Rd. CR0: C'don 6H 155
Red Ho. Sq. N1 7C 66
Redif Ho. RM10: Dag 4H 73
Redington Gdns. NW3 4K 63
Redington Ho. *N1* *2K 83*
(off Priory Grn. Est.)
Redington Rd. NW3 3K 63
Redknap Ho. TW10: Ham 3C 132
Redland Gdns. KT8: W Mole 4D 148
Redlands N15 4D 48
TW11: Tedd 6A 132
Redlands, The BR3: Beck 2D 158
Redlands Ct. BR1: Brom 7H 141
Redlands Rd. EN3: Enf H 1F 25
Redlands Way SW2 7K 119
Red La. KT10: Clay 6A 162
Redleaf Cl. DA17: Belv 6G 109
Redleaves Av. TW15: Ashf 6D 128
Redlees Cl. TW7: Isle 4A 114
Red Leys UB8: Uxb 7A 56
Red Lion Bus. Pk. KT6: Surb 3F 163
Red Lion Cl. *SE17* *6D 102*
(off Red Lion Row)
Red Lion Ct. EC4 1K 13 (6A 84)
SE1 4D 14 (1C 102)
TW3: Houn *3F 113*
(off Alexandra Rd.)
Red Lion Hill N2 2B 46
(not continuous)
Red Lion La. SE18 7E 106
Red Lion Pde. HA5: Pinn 3C 40
Red Lion Pl. SE18 1E 124
Red Lion Rd. KT6: Surb 2F 163
Red Lion Row SE17 6C 102
Red Lion Sq. SW18 5J 117
WC1 6G 7 (5K 83)
Red Lion St. TW9: Rich 5D 114
WC1 5G 7 (5K 83)
Red Lion Wlk. *TW3: Houn* *3F 113*
(off High St.)
Red Lion Yd. W1 4H 11
Red Lodge BR4: W W'ck 1E 170
Red Lodge Cres. DA5: Bexl 3K 145
Red Lodge Rd. BR4: W W'ck 1E 170
DA5: Bexl 3K 145
Redlynch Ct. *W14* *2G 99*
(off Addison Cres.)
Redlynch Ho. *SW9* *1A 120*
(off Gosling Way)
Redman Cl. UB5: N'olt 2A 76
Redman Ho. *EC1* *5J 7*
(off Bourne Est.)
SE1 *7D 14*
(off Borough High St.)
Redman's Rd. E1 5J 85
Redmead La. E1 1G 103
Redmead Rd. UB3: Harl 4G 93
Redmill Ho. *E1* *4H 85*
(off Headlam St.)
Redmond Ho. *N1* *1K 83*
(off Barnsbury Est.)
Redmore Rd. W6 4D 98
Red Oak Cl. BR6: Farnb 3F 173
CR0: C'don 2C 170
Redo Ho. *E12* *5E 70*
(off Dore Av.)
Red Path E9 6A 68
Redpath Way SE10 2G 105
Red Pl. W1 2G 11 (7E 82)
Redpoll Way DA18: Erith 3D 108
Red Post Hill SE21 4D 120
SE24 4D 120
Red Post Ho. E6 7B 70
Redriffe Rd. E13 1H 87
Redriff Est. SE16 3B 104
Redriff Rd. RM7: Mawney 2H 55
SE16 4K 103
Redroofs Cl. BR3: Beck 1D 158
Redrose Trad. Cen. EN4: E Barn 5G 21
RED ROVER 4C 116
Redrup Ho. *SE14* *6K 103*
(off John Williams Cl.)
Redruth Cl. N22 7E 32
Redruth Gdns. KT10: Clay 7A 162
Redruth Ho. SM2: Sutt 7K 165
Redruth Rd. E9 1J 85
Redsan Cl. CR2: S Croy 7D 168
Redshank Ho. *SE1* *5F 103*
(off Avocet Cl.)
Red Sq. N16 3D 66
Redstart Cl. E6 5C 88
SE14 7A 104
Redstart Mans. *IG1: Ilf* *3E 70*
(off Mill Rd.)
Redston Rd. N8 4H 47
Redvers Rd. N22 2A 48
Redvers St. N1 1H 9 (3E 84)
Redwald Rd. E5 4K 67
Redway Dr. TW2: Whitt 7G 113
Redwing Ct. *SE1* *7D 14*
(off Swan St.)
Redwing M. SE5 2C 120
Redwing Path SE28 2H 107
Redwing Rd. SM6: Wall 7J 167
Redwood Cl. DA15: Sidc 1A 144
E3 2C 86
N14 7C 22
SE16 1A 104
UB10: Hil 2D 74
Redwood Ct. KT6: Surb 7D 150
N19 7H 47
NW6 7G 63
UB5: N'olt 3C 76
Redwood Est. TW5: Cran 6K 93
Redwood Gdns. E4 6J 25
Redwood Gro. W5 3B 96
Redwood Ho. *EC1* *2C 8*
(off Bollinder Pl.)
Redwood Mans. *W8* *3K 99*
(off Chantry Sq.)
Redwood M. SW4 3F 119
TW15: Ashf *7F 129*
(off Staines Rd. W.)
Redwoods SW15 1C 134
Redwoods Cl.
IG9: Buck H 2E 36
Redwood Wlk. KT6: Surb 1D 162
Redwood Way EN5: Barn 5A 20
Reece M. SW7 3A 16 (4B 100)
Reed Av. BR6: Orp 3J 173
Reed Cl. E16 5J 87
SE12 5J 123
Reede Gdns. RM10: Dag 5H 73
Reede Rd. RM10: Dag 6G 73
Reede Way RM10: Dag 6H 73
Reedham Cl. N17 4H 49
Reedham St. SE15 2G 121
Reedholm Vs. N16 4D 66
Reed Ho. SW19 4K 135
Reed Pl. SW4 4H 119
Reed Rd. N17 2F 49
Reedsfield Cl. TW15: Ashf 3D 128
Reedsfield Rd.
TW15: Ashf 4D 128
Reed's Pl. NW1 7G 65
Reedworth St. SE11 4K 19 (4A 102)
Reef Ho. *E14* *3E 104*
(off Manchester St.)
Reef St. RM9: Dag 3E 90
Reenglass Rd. HA7: Stan 4J 27
Rees Dr. HA7: Stan 4K 27
Rees Gdns. CR0: C'don 6F 157
Reesland Cl. E12 6E 70
Rees St. N1 1C 84
Reets Farm Cl. NW9 6A 44
Reeves Av. NW9 7K 43
Reeves Cnr. CR0: C'don 2B 168
Reeves Ho. *SE1* *7J 13*
(off Baylis Rd.)
Reeves M. W1 3G 11 (7E 82)
Reeves Rd. E3 4D 86
SE18 6F 107
Reflection, The *E16* *2F 107*
(off Woolwich Mnr. Way)
Reflection Ho. *E2* *4G 85*
(off Cheshire St.)
Reflex Apartments *BR2: Brom* *4K 159*
(off Wheeler Pl.)
Reform Row N17 2F 49
Reform St. SW11 2D 118
Regal Bldg. W10 3F 81
Regal Cl. E1 5G 85
W5 5D 78
Regal Ct. CR4: Mitc 3D 154
N18 5A 34
NW6 *2H 81*
(off Malvern Rd.)
SW6 *7J 99*
(off Dawes Rd.)
Regal Cres. SM6: Wall 3F 167
Regal Dr. N11 5A 32
Regal Ho. IG2: Ilf 6H 53
Regal Ho., The SW6 2A 118
Regalia Point *E2* *3K 85*
(off Palmer's Rd.)
Regal La. NW1 1E 82
Regal Pl. E3 3B 86
SW6 7K 99
Regal Row SE15 1J 121
Regal Way HA3: Kenton 6E 42
Regal Wharf Apartments *N1* *1E 84*
(off De Beauvoir Cres.)
Regan Ho. N18 6A 34
Regan Way N1 1G 9 (2E 84)
Regatta Ho. TW11: Tedd 4A 132
Regatta La. W6 6E 98

Regatta Point *E14* 2C 104
(off Westferry Rd.)
TW8: Bford 6F 97
Regenct Ct. *HA7: Stan* 7J 27
(off Unwin Way)
Regency Cl. TW12: Hamp 5D 130
W5 6E 78
Regency Ct. BR2: Brom 6B 160
E3 2B 86
(off Norman Gro.)
E9 1J 85
(off Park Cl.)
E18 2J 51
EN1: Enf 5J 23
SE8 7B 104
(off Glenville Gro.)
SM1: Sutt 4A 166
TW11: Tedd 6B 132
Regency Cres. NW4 2F 45
Regency Dr. HA4: Ruis 1G 57
Regency Gdns. KT12: Walt T 7A 148
Regency Ho. *E16* 1J 105
(off Pepys Cres.)
N3 2H 45
SW1 3D 18
(off Regency St.)
SW6 1A 118
(off The Boulevard)
Regency Lawn NW5 3F 65
Regency Lodge IG9: Buck H 2G 37
NW3 7B 64
(off Adelaide Rd.)
Regency M. BR3: Beck 1E 158
NW10 6C 62
SW9 7B 102
TW7: Isle 5J 113
Regency Pde. *NW3* 7B 64
(off Finchley Rd.)
Regency Pl. SW1 3D 18 (4H 101)
Regency St. NW10 4A 80
SW1 3D 18 (4H 101)
Regency Ter. SW7 5A 16
Regency Wlk. CR0: C'don 6B 158
TW10: Rich 5E 114
(off The Vineyard)
Regency Way DA6: Bex 3D 126
Regeneration House 1J 83
Regeneration Rd. SE16 4K 103
Regent Av. UB10: Hil 7D 56
Regent Bus. Cen. UB3: Hayes 2K 93
Regent Cl. HA3: Kenton 6E 42
N12 5F 31
TW4: Cran 1K 111
Regent Ct. N3 7E 30
N20 2G 31
NW6 7H 63
(off Cavendish Rd.)
NW8 2C 4
W8 3K 99
(off Wright's La.)
Regent Gdns. IG3: Ilf 7A 54
Regent Ho. *W14* 4G 99
(off Windsor Way)
Regent Pde. SM2: Sutt 6A 166
Regent Pl. CR0: C'don 1F 169
SW19 5A 136
W1 2B 12 (7G 83)
Regent Rd. KT5: Surb 5F 151
SE24 6B 120
Regents Av. N13 5F 33
Regent's Bri. Gdns. SW8 7J 101
Regents Canal Ho. *E14* 6A 86
(off Commercial Rd.)
Regents Cl. CR2: S Croy 6E 168
HA8: Edg 4K 27
UB4: Hayes 5H 75
Regents Ct. BR1: Brom 7H 141
E8 1G 85
HA5: Pinn 2B 40
KT2: King T 1E 150
(off Sopwith Way)
Regents Dr. BR2: Kes 5B 172
IG8: Wfd G 6K 37
Regents Ga. Ho. *E14* 7A 86
(off Horseferry Rd.)
Regents Ho. *E3* 5C 86
(off Bow Common La.)
Regents M. NW8 2A 82
REGENT'S PARK 2K 5 (3F 83)
Regent's Pk. 1F 5 (2D 82)
Regent's Pk. Barracks 1K 5
Regents Pk. Est. NW1 1A 6
Regent's Pk. Gdns. M. NW1 1D 82
Regent's Pk. Ho. *NW8* 2D 4
(off Park Rd.)
Regent's Pk. Open Air Theatre
2G 5 (3E 82)
Regent's Pk. Rd. NW1 7D 64
(not continuous)
Regents Pk. Rd. N3 3H 45
Regent's Pk. Ter. NW1 1F 83
Regent's Pl. SE3 2J 123
Regents Pl. NW1 3A 6 (4G 83)
Regent's Pl. Plaza NW1 4G 83
Regents Plaza *NW6* 2K 81
(off Kilburn High Rd.)
Regent Sq. DA17: Belv 4H 109
E3 3D 86
WC1 2F 7 (3J 83)
Regent's Row E8 1G 85
Regents Studios E8 1H 85
Regent St. NW10 3F 81
SW1 3C 12 (7H 83)
W1 7K 5 (6F 83)
W4 5G 97
Regent's University London 3F 5 (4D 82)
Regents Wharf *E2* 1H 85
(off Wharf Pl.)
N1 2K 83
Regent Ter. SW8 6J 101
Regiment Hill NW7 6B 30
Regina Cl. EN5: Barn 3A 20
Regina Ho. SE20 1K 157
Reginald Ellingworth St. RM9: Dag 1B 90
Reginald Pl. *SE8* 7C 104
(off Deptford High St.)
Reginald Rd. E7 7J 69
HA6: Nwood 1H 39
SE8 7C 104
Reginald Sorenson Ho. E11 7F 51
Reginald Sq. SE8 7C 104
Regina Point *SE16* 3J 103
(off Canada Est.)
Regina Rd. N4 1K 65
SE25 3G 157
UB2: S'hall 4C 94
W13 1A 96
Regina Ter. W13 1B 96
Regis Ct. CR4: Mitc 1C 154
N8 4K 47
NW1 5E 4
(off Melcombe Pl.)
Regis Ho. *W1* 5H 5
(off Beaumont St.)
Regis Pl. SW2 4K 119
Regis Rd. NW5 5F 65
Regnart Bldgs. NW1 3B 6
Regnas Ho. *E15* 6H 69
(off Carnarvon Rd.)
Regnolruf Ct. KT12: Walt T 7J 147
Regnum Apartments *E1* 4J 9
(off Wheler St.)
Reid Bldg. *E3* 4B 86
(off Eric St.)
Reid Cl. HA5: Eastc 4J 39
UB3: Hayes 6G 75
Reidhaven Rd. SE18 4J 107
Reigate Av. SM1: Sutt 1J 165
Reigate Rd. BR1: Brom 3H 141
IG3: Ilf 2K 71
Reigate Way SM6: Wall 5J 167
Reighton Rd. E5 3G 67
Reindeer Cl. E13 1J 87
Reinickendorf Av. SE9 6G 125
Reis Pl. *N15* 4F 49
(off Blenheim Ri.)
Reizel Cl. N16 1F 67
Relf Rd. SE15 3G 121
Reliance Arc. SW9 4A 120
Reliance Wharf N1 1E 84
Relko Gdns. SM1: Sutt 5B 166
Relton M. SW7 1D 16 (3C 100)
Rembrandt Cl. E14 3F 105
SW1 4G 17
Rembrandt Ct. KT19: Ewe 6B 164
SE16 5H 103
(off Stubbs Dr.)
Rembrandt Rd. HA8: Edg 2G 43
SE13 4G 123
Reminder La. SE10 3H 105
Remington Rd. E6 6C 88
N15 6D 48
Remington St. N1 1B 8 (2B 84)
Remnant St. WC2 7G 7 (6K 83)
Remsted Ho. *NW6* 1K 81
(off Mortimer Cres.)
Remus Bldg., The *EC1* 2K 7
(off Hardwick St.)
Remus Rd. E3 7C 68
Renaissance Ct. SM1: Sutt 1A 166
TW3: Houn 3G 113
(off Prince Regent Rd.)
Renaissance Wlk. *SE10* 3H 105
(off Teal St.)
Renbold Ho. *SE10* 1E 122
(off Blissett St.)
Rendalls *HA1: Harr* 1J 59
(off Grove Hill)
Rendle Cl. CR0: C'don 5F 157
Rendle Ho. *W10* 4G 81
(off Wornington Rd.)
Rendlesham Rd. E5 4G 67
EN2: Enf 1G 23
Renforth St. SE16 3J 103
Renfree Way TW17: Shep 7C 146
Renfrew Cl. E6 7E 88
Renfrew Ct. TW4: Houn 2C 112
Renfrew Ho. E17 2B 50
NW6 2K 81
(off Carlton Vale)
Renfrew Rd. KT2: King T 7H 133
SE11 3K 19 (4B 102)
TW4: Houn 2B 112
Renmuir St. SW17 6D 136
Rennell St. SE13 3E 122
Rennels Way TW7: Isle 2J 113
Renness Rd. E17 3A 50
Rennets Cl. SE9 5J 125
Rennets Wood Rd. SE9 5H 125
Rennie Cotts. *E1* 4J 85
(off Pemell Cl.)
Rennie Ct. EN3: Enf L 1H 25
SE1 4A 14
Rennie Est. SE16 4H 103
Rennie Ho. *SE1* 3C 102
(off Bath Ter.)
Rennie St. SE1 4A 14 (1B 102)
(not continuous)
Renoir Ct. *SE16* 5H 103
(off Stubbs Dr.)
Renovation, The *E16* 2F 107
(off Woolwich Mnr. Way)
Renown Cl. CR0: C'don 1B 168
RM7: Mawney 1G 55
Rensburg Rd. E17 5K 49
Renshaw Cl. DA17: Belv 6F 109
SE6 7C 122
Renters Av. NW4 6E 44
Renton Cl. SW2 6K 119
Renwick Dr. BR2: Brom 6B 160
Renwick Ind. Est. IG11: Bark 2B 90
Renwick Rd. IG11: Bark 4B 90
Repens Way UB4: Yead 4B 76
Rephidim St. SE1 3E 102
Replingham Rd. SW18 1H 135
Reporton Rd. SW6 7G 99
Repository Rd. SE18 6D 106
Repton Av. HA0: Wemb 4C 60
UB3: Harl 4F 93
Repton Cl. SM5: Cars 5C 166
Repton Ct. BR1: Brom 6B 142
BR3: Beck 1D 158
IG5: Ilf 1D 52
Repton Gro. IG5: Ilf 1D 52
Repton Ho. E4 6K 35
SW1 4B 18
(off Charlwood St.)
REPTON PARK 7K 37
Repton Rd. BR6: Chels 3K 173
HA3: Kenton 4F 43
Repton St. E14 6A 86
Repulse Cl. RM5: Col R 1G 55
Reservoir Cl.
CR7: Thor H 3D 156
Reservoir Rd. HA4: Ruis 4E 38
N14 5B 22
SE4 2A 122
Reservoir Studios *E1* 6K 85
(off Cable St.)
Resham Cl. UB2: S'hall 3A 94
Residence Twr. *N4* 7C 48
(off Goodchild Rd.)
Resolution Plaza E1 7K 9
Resolution Wlk. SE18 3D 106
Resolution Way *SE8* 7C 104
(off Deptford High St.)
Restell Cl. SE3 6G 105
Restmor Way SM6: Wall 2E 166
Reston Pl. SW7 2A 100
Restons Cres. SE9 6H 125
Restoration Sq. SW11 1B 118
Restormel Cl. TW3: Houn 5E 112
Restormel Ho. SE11 4J 19
Retcar Pl. N19 2F 65
Retford St. N1 1H 9 (2E 84)
Retingham Way E4 2J 35
Retles Ct. HA1: Harr 7J 41
Retreat, The CR7: Thor H 4D 156
HA2: Harr 7E 40
KT4: Wor Pk 2D 164
KT5: Surb 6F 151
NW9 5K 43
SW14 3A 116
Retreat Cl. HA3: Kenton 5C 42
Retreat Ho. E9 6J 67
Retreat Mobile Home Pk., The
IG9: Buck H 2D 36
Retreat Pl. E9 6J 67
Retreat Rd. TW9: Rich 5D 114
Reubens Ct. *W4* 5H 97
(off Chaseley Dr.)
Reunion Row E1 7H 85
Reuters Plaza *E14* 1D 104
(off The South Colonnade)
Reveley Sq. SE16 2A 104
Revell Ri. SE18 6K 107
Revell Rd. KT1: King T 2H 151
SM1: Sutt 6H 165
Revelon Rd. SE4 4A 122
Revelstoke Rd. SW18 2H 135
Reventlow Rd. SE9 1G 143
Reverdy Rd. SE1 4G 103
Reverend Cl. HA2: Harr 3F 59
Revesby Rd. SM5: Cars 6B 154
Review Lodge RM10: Dag 1H 91
Review Rd. NW2 2B 62
RM10: Dag 1H 91
Rewell St. SW6 7A 100
Rewley Rd. SM5: Cars 6B 154
Rex Av. TW15: Ashf 6C 128
Rex Cl. RM5: Col R 1H 55
Rex Pl. W1 3H 11 (7E 82)
Reydon Av. E11 5A 52
Reynard Bus. Pk. TW8: Bford 5C 96

Reynard Cl.—Ridgway Pl.

Reynard Cl. BR1: Brom 3E **160**
SE4 3A **122**
Reynard Dr. SE19 7F **139**
Reynard Pl. SE14 6A **104**
Reynardson Rd. N17 7H **33**
Reynolah Gdns. SE7 5K **105**
Reynolds Av. E12 5E **70**
KT9: Chess 7E **162**
RM6: Chad H 7C **54**
Reynolds Cl. NW11 7K **45**
SM5: Cars 1D **166**
SW19 1B **154**
Reynolds Ct. RM6: Chad H 3D **54**
Reynolds Dr. HA8: Edg 3F **43**
Reynolds Ho. *E2* *2J* ***85***
(off Approach Rd.)
NW8 *2B* ***82***
(off Wellington Rd.)
SW1 *4D* ***18***
(off Erasmus St.)
Reynolds Pl. SE3 7K **105**
TW10: Rich 6F **115**
Reynolds Rd. KT3: N Mald 7K **151**
SE15 4J **121**
UB4: Yead 4A **76**
W4 3J **97**
Reynolds Sports Cen. 1G **97**
Reynolds Way CR0: C'don 4E **168**
Rheidol M. N1 2C **84**
Rheidol Ter. N1 1C **84**
Rheingold Way SM6: Wall 7J **167**
Rhein Ho. *N8* *3J* ***47***
(off Campsfield Rd.)
Rheola Cl. N17 1F **49**
Rhoda St. E2 3K **9** (4F **85**)
Rhodes Av. N22 1G **47**
Rhodes Ho. *N1* *1E* ***8***
(off Provost St.)
Rhodesia Rd. E11 2F **69**
SW9 2J **119**
Rhodes Moorhouse Ct. SM4: Mord 6J **153**
Rhodes St. N7 5K **65**
Rhodeswell Rd. E14 5A **86**
(not continuous)
Rhodium Ct. *E14* *5C* ***86***
(off Thomas Rd.)
Rhodrons Av. KT9: Chess 5E **162**
Rhondda Gro. E3 3A **86**
Rhyl Rd. UB6: G'frd 2K **77**
Rhyl St. NW5 6E **64**
Rhys Av. N11 7C **32**
Rialto Rd. CR4: Mitc 2E **154**
Ribble Cl. IG8: Wfd G 6F **37**
Ribblesdale Av. N11 6K **31**
UB5: N'olt 6F **59**
Ribblesdale Ho. *NW6* *1J* ***81***
(off Kilburn Vale)
Ribblesdale Rd. N8 4K **47**
SW16 6F **137**
Ribbon Dance M. SE5 1D **120**
Ribbons Wlk. E20 5E **68**
Ribchester Av. UB6: G'frd 3K **77**
Ribston Cl. BR2: Brom 1D **172**
Ricardo Path SE28 1C **108**
Ricardo St. E14 6D **86**
Ricards Rd. SW19 5H **135**
Riccall Ct. *NW9* *1A* ***44***
(off Pageant Av.)
Rice Pde. BR5: Pet W 5H **161**
Riceyman Ho. *WC1* *2J* ***7***
(off Lloyd Baker St.)
Richard Anderson Ct. *SE14* *7K* ***103***
(off Monson Rd.)
Richard Burbidge Mans. *SW13* *6E* ***98***
(off Brasenose Dr.)
Richard Burton Ct. *IG9: Buck H* *2F* ***37***
(off Palmerston Rd.)
Richard Challoner Sports Cen. 7K **151**
Richard Cl. SE18 4C **106**
Richard Fell Ho. *E12* *4E* ***70***
(off Walton Rd.)
Richard Fielden Ho. E1 3A **86**
Richard Ho. *SE16* *4J* ***103***
(off Silwood St.)
Richard Ho. Dr. E16 6B **88**
Richard Neale Ho. *E1* *7H* ***85***
(off Cornwall St.)
Richard Neve Ho. *SE18* *4J* ***107***
(off Plumstead High St.)
Richard Robert Residence, The *E15* *6F* ***69***
(off Salway Rd.)
Richard Ryan Pl. RM9: Dag 1E **90**
Richards Av. RM7: Rom 6J **55**
Richards Cl. HA1: Harr 5A **42**
UB3: Harl 6F **93**
UB10: Hil 1C **74**
WD23: Bush 1C **26**
Richards Fld. KT19: Ewe 7K **163**
Richard Sharples Ct. SM2: Sutt 7A **166**
Richardson Cl. E8 1F **85**
Richardson Ct. *SW4* *2J* ***119***
(off Studley Rd.)
Richardson Gdns. RM10: Dag 6H **73**
Richardson Rd. E15 2G **87**
Richardson's M. W1 4A **6**
Richard's Pl. SW3 3D **16** (4C **100**)
Richards Pl. E17 3C **50**
Richard St. E1 6H **85**
Richbell *WC1* *5F* ***7***
(off Boswell St.)
Richbell Pl. WC1 5G **7** (5K **83**)
Richborne Ter. SW8 7K **101**
Richborough Ho. *SE15* *6J* ***103***
(off Sharratt St.)
Richborough Rd. NW2 4G **63**
Richbourne Ct. *W1* *7D* ***4***
(off Harrowby St.)
Richens Cl. TW3: Houn 2H **113**
Riches Rd. IG1: Ilf 2G **71**
Richfield Rd. WD23: Bush 1B **26**
Richford Ga. W6 3E **98**
Richford Rd. E15 1H **87**
Richford St. W6 2E **98**
Rich Ind. Est. SE1 3E **102**
SE15 6H **103**
Richland Ho. *SE15* *1G* ***121***
(off Goldsmith Rd.)
Richlands Av. KT17: Ewe 4C **164**
Rich La. SW5 5K **99**
Richman Ho. *SE8* *5B* ***104***
(off Grove St.)
Richmix Sq. *E1* *3K* ***9***
(off Bethnal Grn. Rd.)
RICHMOND 5D 114
Richmond,
The American International
University in London
Kensington Campus -
Ansdell Street ***3K 99***
(off Ansdell St.)
St Albans Grove **3K 99**
Young Street **2K 99**
Richmond Hill Campus **7E 114**
Richmond & London Scottish RUFC
3D 114
Richmond Athletic Ground **3D 114**
Richmond Av. E4 5A **36**
N1 1K **83**
NW10 6E **62**
SW20 1G **153**
TW14: Felt 6G **111**
UB10: Hil 6D **56**
Richmond Bri. TW1: Twick 6D **114**
Richmond Bldgs. W1 1C **12** (6H **83**)
RICHMOND CIRCUS **4E 114**
Richmond Cl. E17 6B **50**
Richmond Cotts. *W14* *4G* ***99***
(off Hammersmith Rd.)
Richmond Ct. CR4: Mitc 3B **154**
E8 *7H* ***67***
(off Mare St.)
HA9: Wemb 3F **61**
Richmond Ct. *N11* *6K* ***31***
(off Pickering Gdns.)
NW6 *7F* ***63***
(off Willesden La.)
SW1 *7F* ***11***
(off Sloane St.)
W14 *4G* ***99***
(off Hammersmith Rd.)
Richmond Cres. E4 5A **36**
N1 1K **83**
N9 1B **34**
Richmond Cricket Ground **3E 114**
Richmond Dr. IG8: Wfd G 7K **37**
TW17: Shep 6F **147**
Richmond Gdns. HA3: Hrw W 7E **26**
NW4 5C **44**
Richmond Golf Course **2E** 132
Richmond Grn. CR0: Bedd 3J **167**
Richmond Gro. KT5: Surb 6F **151**
N1 7B **66**
(not continuous)
Richmond Hill TW10: Rich 6E **114**
Richmond Hill Ct. TW10: Rich 6E **114**
Richmond Ho. *E3* *5C* ***86***
(off Bow Common La.)
NW1 *1K* ***5***
(off Park Village E.)
SE17 *5D* ***102***
(off Portland St.)
Richmond Mans. *SW5* *5K* ***99***
(off Old Brompton Rd.)
TW1: Twick 6D **114**
Richmond M. SE6 1D **140**
TW11: Tedd 5K **131**
W1 1C **12** (6H **83**)
Richmond Pde. *TW1: Twick* *6C* ***114***
(off Richmond Rd.)
Richmond Pk. Golf Course **7A** 116
Richmond Pk. (National Nature Reserve)
1G 133
Richmond Pk. Rd. KT2: King T 1E **150**
SW14 5J **115**
Richmond Pl. SE18 4G **107**
Richmond Rd. CR0: Bedd 3J **167**
CR7: Thor H 3B **156**
E4 1A **36**
E7 5K **69**
E8 7F **67**
E11 2F **69**
EN5: New Bar 5E **20**
IG1: Ilf 3G **71**
KT2: King T 5D **132**
N2 2A **46**
N11 6D **32**
N15 6E **48**
SW20 1D **152**
TW1: Twick 7B **114**
TW7: Isle 3A **114**
W5 2E **96**
Richmond St. E13 2J **87**
Richmond Ter. SW1 6E **12** (2J **101**)
Richmond Theatre **4D 114**
Richmond Way E11 2J **69**
W12 2F **99**
W14 3F **99**
Richmount Gdns. SE3 3J **123**
Rich St. E14 7B **86**
Rickard Cl. NW4 4D **44**
SW2 1A **138**
Rickards Cl. KT6: Surb 2E **162**
Rickett St. SW6 6J **99**
Rickman Ho. *E1* *3J* ***85***
(off Rickman St.)
Rickman St. E1 4J **85**
Rickmansworth Rd. HA5: Pinn 2K **39**
HA6: Nwood 1F **39**
Rick Roberts Way E15 1E **86**
Rickthorne Rd. N19 2J **65**
Rickyard Path SE9 4C **124**
Riddell Ct. *SE5* *5F* ***103***
(off Albany Rd.)
Ridding La. UB6: G'frd 5K **59**
Riddons Rd. SE12 3A **142**
Ride, The EN3: Pond E 3D **24**
TW8: Bford 5B **96**
Rideout St. SE18 4D **106**
Rider Cl. DA15: Sidc 6J **125**
Rideway Dr. W3 3G **97**
Ridgdale St. E3 2D **86**
Ridge, The BR6: Orp 2H **173**
DA5: Bexl 7F **127**
EN5: Barn 5C **20**
KT5: Surb 5G **151**
TW2: Whitt 7H **113**
Ridge Av. N21 7H **23**
Ridgebrook Rd. SE3 3B **124**
Ridge Cl. NW4 2F **45**
NW9 4K **43**
SE28 2H **107**
Ridge Ct. SE22 7G **121**
Ridge Crest EN2: Enf 1E **22**
Ridgecroft Cl. DA5: Bexl 1J **145**
Ridge Hill NW11 1G **63**
Ridgemead Cl. N14 2D **32**
Ridgemont Gdns. HA8: Edg 4D **28**
Ridgemount Av. CR0: C'don 1K **169**
Ridgemount Cl. SE20 7H **139**
Ridgemount Gdns. EN2: Enf 3G **23**
Ridge Rd. CR4: Mitc 7F **137**
N8 6K **47**
N21 1H **33**
NW2 3H **63**
SM3: Sutt 1G **165**
(not continuous)
Ridges Yd. CR0: C'don 3B **168**
Ridgeview Cl. EN5: Barn 6A **20**
Ridgeview Rd. N20 3E **30**
Ridge Way SE19 6E **138**
TW13: Hanw 3C **130**
Ridgeway BR2: Hayes 2J **171**
IG8: Wfd G 4F **37**
Ridgeway, The CR0: Wadd 3K **167**
E4 2J **35**
EN2: Enf 1E **22**
HA2: Harr 5D **40**
(not continuous)
HA3: Kenton 6C **42**
HA4: Ruis 7J **39**
HA7: Stan 6H **27**
KT12: Walt T 7H **147**
N3 7E **30**
N11 4J **31**
N14 2D **32**
NW7 3H **29**
NW9 4K **43**
NW11 7G **45**
W3 3G **97**
Ridgeway Av. EN4: E Barn 6J **21**
Ridgeway Cres. BR6: Orp 3J **173**
Ridgeway Cres. Gdns. BR6: Orp 2J **173**
Ridgeway Dr. BR1: Brom 4K **141**
Ridgeway E. DA15: Sidc 5K **125**
Ridgeway Gdns. IG4: Ilf 5C **52**
N6 7G **47**
Ridgeway Rd. TW7: Isle 7J **95**
Ridgeway Rd. Nth. TW7: Isle 6J **95**
Ridgeway Wlk. *UB5: N'olt* *6C* ***58***
(off Cowings Mead)
Ridgeway W. DA15: Sidc 5J **125**
Ridgewell Cl. N1 1C **84**
RM10: Dag 1H **91**
SE26 4B **140**
Ridgmount Gdns. WC1 5C **6** (5H **83**)
Ridgmount Pl. WC1 5C **6** (5H **83**)
Ridgmount Rd. SW18 5K **117**
Ridgmount St. WC1 5C **6** (5H **83**)
Ridgway SW19 7E **134**
TW10: Rich 6E **114**
Ridgway, The SM2: Sutt 7B **166**
Ridgway Ct. SW19 6F **135**
Ridgway Gdns. SW19 7F **135**
Ridgway Pl. SW19 6G **135**

A-Z London 381

Ridgway Rd. SW9 . . . 3B 120
Ridgwell Rd. E16 . . . 5A 88
Riding, The NW11 . . . 7H 45
Riding Ho. St. W1 . . . 6K 5 (5F 83)
Ridings, The E11 . . . 5J 51
EN4: E Barn . . . 7G 21
KT5: Surb . . . 5G 151
KT17: Ewe . . . 7B 164
TW16: Sun . . . 1J 147
W5 . . . 4F 79
Ridings Av. N21 . . . 4G 23
Ridings Cl. N6 . . . 7G 47
Ridler Rd. EN1: Enf . . . 1K 23
Ridley Av. W13 . . . 3B 96
Ridley Cl. IG11: Bark . . . 7K 71
Ridley Ct. SW16 . . . 6J 137
Ridley Ho. SW1 . . . 2D 18
(off Monck St.)
Ridley Rd. BR2: Brom . . . 3H 159
DA16: Well . . . 1B 126
E7 . . . 4A 70
E8 . . . 5F 67
NW10 . . . 2C 80
SW19 . . . 7K 135
Ridsdale Rd. SE20 . . . 7H 139
Riefield Rd. SE9 . . . 4G 125
Riesco Dr. CR0: C'don . . . 6J 169
Riffel Rd. NW2 . . . 5E 62
Rifle Ct. SE11 . . . 7K 19 (6A 102)
Rifle St. E14 . . . 5D 86
Riga M. E1 . . . 7K 9
Rigault Rd. SW6 . . . 2G 117
Rigby Cl. CR0: Wadd . . . 3A 168
Rigby La. UB3: Hayes . . . 2E 92
Rigby M. IG1: Ilf . . . 2E 70
Rigden St. E14 . . . 6D 86
Rigeley Rd. NW10 . . . 3C 80
Rigg App. E10 . . . 1K 67
Rigge Pl. SW4 . . . 4H 119
Riggindale Rd. SW16 . . . 5H 137
Riley Ho. E3 . . . 4C 86
(off Ireton St.)
SW10 . . . 7B 100
(off Riley St.)
Riley Rd. EN3: Enf W . . . 1D 24
SE1 . . . 7H 15 (3F 103)
Riley St. SW10 . . . 6B 100
Rill Ct. IG11: Bark . . . 2G 89
(off Spring Pl.)
Rill Ho. SE5 . . . 7D 102
(off Harris St.)
Rill La. HA8: Edg . . . 6E 28
Rima Ho. SW3 . . . 7A 16
(off Callow St.)
Rinaldo Rd. SW12 . . . 7F 119
Ring, The SW7 . . . 7B 10 (2B 100)
W2 . . . 2C 10 (7B 82)
Ring Cl. BR1: Brom . . . 7K 141
Ring Ct. SE1 . . . 2B 102
(off The Cut)
Ringcroft St. N7 . . . 5A 66
Ringers Ct. BR1: Brom . . . 3J 159
(off Ringers Rd.)
Ringers Rd. BR1: Brom . . . 3J 159
Ringford Rd. SW18 . . . 5H 117
Ring Ho. E1 . . . 7J 85
(off Sage St.)
Ringles Ct. E6 . . . 1D 88
Ringlet Cl. E16 . . . 5K 87
Ringlewell Cl. EN1: Enf . . . 2C 24
Ringmer Av. SW6 . . . 1G 117
Ringmer Gdns. N19 . . . 2J 65
Ringmer Pl. N21 . . . 5J 23
Ringmer Way BR1: Brom . . . 5C 160
Ringmore Ri. SE23 . . . 7H 121
Ringmore Vw. SE23 . . . 7H 121
Ring Rd. W12 . . . 1E 98
(not continuous)
Ringsfield Ho. SE17 . . . 5C 102
(off Bronti Cl.)
Ringside Ct. SE28 . . . 1C 108
Ringslade Rd. N22 . . . 2K 47
Ringstead Rd. SE6 . . . 7D 122
SM1: Sutt . . . 4B 166
Ring Way N11 . . . 6B 32
Ringway UB2: S'hall . . . 5B 94
Ringwold Cl. BR3: Beck . . . 7A 140
Ringwood Av. CR0: C'don . . . 7J 155
N2 . . . 2D 46
Ringwood Cl. HA5: Pinn . . . 3A 40
Ringwood Gdns. E14 . . . 4C 104
SW15 . . . 1C 134
Ringwood Rd. E17 . . . 6B 50
Ringwood Way N21 . . . 1G 33
TW12: Hamp H . . . 4E 130
Rio Cinema
Dalston . . . 5E 66
(off Kingsland High St.)
Ripley Bldgs. SE1 . . . 6B 14
(off Rushworth St.)
Ripley Cl. BR1: Brom . . . 5D 160
CR0: New Ad . . . 6E 170
Ripley Ct. CR4: Mitc . . . 2B 154
Ripley Gdns. SM1: Sutt . . . 4A 166
(not continuous)
SW14 . . . 3K 115
Ripley Ho. SW1 . . . 7A 18
(off Churchill Gdns.)
Ripley M. E11 . . . 6G 51
Ripley Rd. DA17: Belv . . . 4G 109
E16 . . . 6A 88
EN2: Enf . . . 1H 23
IG3: Ilf . . . 2K 71
TW12: Hamp . . . 7E 130
Ripley's Believe It or Not . . . 3C 12
(off Shaftesbury Av.)
Ripley Vs. W5 . . . 6C 78
Ripon Cl. UB5: N'olt . . . 5E 58
Ripon Ct. N11 . . . 6K 31
(off Ribblesdale Av.)
Ripon Gdns. IG1: Ilf . . . 6C 52
KT9: Chess . . . 5D 162
Ripon Rd. N9 . . . 7C 24
N17 . . . 3D 48
SE18 . . . 6F 107
Rippersley Rd. DA16: Well . . . 1A 126
Ripple Nature Reserve, The . . . 3B 90
Ripple Rd. IG11: Bark, Dag . . . 7G 71
RM9: Dag . . . 1B 90
RIPPLESIDE . . . 1B 90
Rippleside Commercial Est.
IG11: Bark . . . 2C 90
Ripplevale Gro. N1 . . . 7K 65
Rippolson Rd. SE18 . . . 5K 107
Ripston Rd. TW15: Ashf . . . 5F 129
Risborough Cl. N10 . . . 3F 47
Risborough Dr. KT4: Wor Pk . . . 7C 152
Risborough Ho. NW8 . . . 3D 4
(off Mallory St.)
Risborough St. SE1 . . . 6B 14 (2B 102)
Risdon Ho. SE16 . . . 2J 103
(off Risdon St.)
Risdon St. SE16 . . . 3J 103
Rise, The DA5: Bexl . . . 7C 126
E11 . . . 5J 51
HA0: Wemb . . . 5A 60
HA8: Edg . . . 5C 28
IG9: Buck H . . . 1G 37
N13 . . . 4F 33
NW7 . . . 6G 29
NW10 . . . 4K 61
UB6: G'frd . . . 5A 60
UB10: Hil . . . 2B 74
Risedale Rd. DA7: Bex . . . 3J 127
Riseholme Ct. E9 . . . 6B 68
Riseldine Rd. SE23 . . . 6A 122
RISE PARK . . . 2K 55
Rise Pk. Pde. RM1: Rom . . . 2K 55
Risinghill St. N1 . . . 2K 83
Risingholme Cl. HA3: Hrw W . . . 1J 41
WD23: Bush . . . 1A 26
Risingholme Rd. HA3: Hrw W . . . 2J 41
Risings, The E17 . . . 4F 51
Rising Sun Ct. EC1 . . . 5B 8
Risley Av. N17 . . . 1C 48
Risley Cl. SM4: Mord . . . 5K 153
Rita Rd. SW8 . . . 6J 101
Ritches Rd. N15 . . . 5C 48
Ritchie Ho. E14 . . . 6F 87
(off Blair St.)
N19 . . . 1H 65
SE16 . . . 3J 103
(off Howland Est.)
Ritchie Rd. CR0: C'don . . . 6H 157
Ritchie St. N1 . . . 2A 84
Ritchings Av. E17 . . . 4A 50
Ritherdon Rd. SW17 . . . 2E 136
Ritson Ho. N1 . . . 1K 83
(off Barnsbury Est.)
Ritson Rd. E8 . . . 6G 67
Ritter St. SE18 . . . 6E 106
Ritz Pde. W5 . . . 4F 79
Ritzy Picturehouse . . . 4A 120
(off Coldharbour La.)
Riva Bldg., The SE13 . . . 4F 123
Rivaz Pl. E9 . . . 6J 67
Riven Ct. W2 . . . 6K 81
(off Inverness Ter.)
Rivenhall Gdns. E18 . . . 4H 51
River App. HA8: Edg . . . 1J 43
RIVER ASH ESTATE . . . 7H 147
River Av. KT7: T Ditt . . . 7A 150
N13 . . . 3G 33
River Av. Ind. Est. N13 . . . 5F 33
River Bank KT7: T Ditt . . . 5K 149
KT8: E Mos . . . 3J 149
N21 . . . 7H 23
TW12: Hamp . . . 3E 148
Riverbank Rd. BR1: Brom . . . 3J 141
Riverbank Way TW8: Bford . . . 6C 96
River Barge Cl. E14 . . . 2E 104
River Brent Bus. Pk. W7 . . . 3J 95
River Cl. E11 . . . 6A 52
HA4: Ruis . . . 6H 39
UB2: S'hall . . . 2G 95
River Ct. KT6: Surb . . . 5D 150
(off Portsmouth Rd.)
SE1 . . . 3A 14 (7B 84)
TW17: Shep . . . 7E 146
Rivercourt Rd. W6 . . . 4D 98
River Crane Way TW13: Hanw . . . 2D 130
(off Watermill Way)
Riverdale SE13 . . . 4E 122
Riverdale Cl. IG11: Bark . . . 4B 90
Riverdale Ct. N21 . . . 5J 23
Riverdale Dr. SW18 . . . 1K 135
Riverdale Gdns. TW1: Twick . . . 6C 114
Riverdale Ho. SE13 . . . 4E 122
Riverdale Rd. DA5: Bexl . . . 7F 127
DA8: Erith . . . 5H 109
SE18 . . . 5K 107
TW1: Twick . . . 6C 114
TW13: Hanw . . . 4C 130
Riverdale Shop. Cen. SE13 . . . 3E 122
Riverdene HA8: Edg . . . 3D 28
Riverdene Rd. IG1: Ilf . . . 3E 70
Riverfleet WC1 . . . 1F 7
(off Birkenhead St.)
Riverford Ho. W2 . . . 5J 81
(off Westbourne Pk. Rd.)
River Front EN1: Enf . . . 3K 23
River Gdns. SM5: Cars . . . 2E 166
TW14: Felt . . . 5K 111
River Gdns. Bus. Cen. TW14: Felt . . . 5K 111
River Gdns. Wlk. SE10 . . . 5G 105
River Gro. Pk. BR3: Beck . . . 1B 158
Riverhead Cl. E17 . . . 2K 49
River Hgts. E15 . . . 1E 86
N17 . . . 1F 49
Riverhill KT4: Wor Pk . . . 2K 163
Riverhill M. KT4: Wor Pk . . . 3K 163
Riverhill Mobile Home Pk.
KT4: Wor Pk . . . 2K 163
Riverholme Dr. KT19: Ewe . . . 7K 163
Riverhope Mans. SE18 . . . 3C 106
River Ho. SE26 . . . 3H 139
Riverhouse Barn . . . 7H 147
River La. TW10: Ham . . . 7D 114
Riverleigh Ct. E4 . . . 5G 35
Riverlight Quay SW8 . . . 6G 101
River Lodge SW1 . . . 7B 18
(off Grosvenor Rd.)
Rivermead KT1: King T . . . 5D 150
KT8: E Mos . . . 3G 149
Rivermead Cl. TW11: Tedd . . . 5B 132
Rivermead Ct. SW6 . . . 3H 117
Rivermead Ho. E9 . . . 5A 68
TW16: Sun . . . 3A 148
(off Thames St.)
Rivermead Rd. N18 . . . 6E 34
River Meads Av. TW2: Twick . . . 3E 130
River Mt. KT12: Walt T . . . 7H 147
Rivernook Cl. KT12: Walt T . . . 5A 148
River Pk. Gdns. BR2: Brom . . . 7F 141
River Pk. Rd. N22 . . . 2K 47
River Pl. N1 . . . 7C 66
River Reach TW11: Tedd . . . 5C 132
River Rd. IG9: Buck H . . . 1H 37
IG11: Bark . . . 2J 89
River Rd. Bus. Pk.
IG11: Bark . . . 3K 89
Rivers Apartments N17 . . . 6A 34
(off Cannon Rd.)
Riversdale Gdns. N22 . . . 1A 48
Riversdale Rd. KT7: T Ditt . . . 5A 150
N5 . . . 3B 66
RM5: Col R . . . 1H 55
Riversfield Rd. EN1: Enf . . . 3K 23
Rivers Ho. TW7: Isle . . . 4B 114
(off Richmond Rd.)
TW8: Bford . . . 5G 97
(off Aitman Dr.)
Riverside E3 . . . 1C 86
NW4 . . . 7D 44
SE7 . . . 3K 105
SW11 . . . 7C 100
TW1: Twick . . . 1B 132
TW9: Rich . . . 5D 114
TW10: Rich . . . 5D 114
TW16: Sun . . . 2B 148
TW17: Shep . . . 7G 147
W6 . . . 6E 98
WC1 . . . 1F 7
(off Birkenhead St.)
Riverside, The KT8: E Mos . . . 3H 149
Riverside Apartments N4 . . . 7D 48
(off Goodchild Rd.)
N13 . . . 5E 32
Riverside Arts Cen. . . . 3A 148
Riverside Av. KT8: E Mos . . . 5H 149
Riverside Bus. Cen. SW18 . . . 1K 135
Riverside Bus. Pk. SW19 . . . 1A 154
Riverside Cl. E5 . . . 1J 67
KT1: King T . . . 4D 150
RM1: Rom . . . 4K 55
SM6: Wall . . . 3F 167
W7 . . . 4J 77
Riverside Cotts. IG11: Bark . . . 2H 89
Riverside Ct. E4 . . . 6H 25
SE3 . . . 4H 123
SW8 . . . 7D 18 (6H 101)
TW7: Isle . . . 2K 113
(off Woodlands Rd.)
TW14: Felt . . . 7G 111
Riverside Dr. CR4: Mitc . . . 5C 154
NW11 . . . 6G 45
TW10: Ham . . . 3B 132
W4 . . . 7K 97
Riverside Gdns. EN2: Enf . . . 2H 23
HA0: Wemb . . . 2E 78
N3 . . . 3G 45
W6 . . . 5D 98
Riverside Ho. N1 . . . 7C 66
(off Canonbury St.)

Riverside Ind. Est. EN3: Pond E 6F 25
IG11: Bark 3A 90
Riverside Mans. E1 1J 103
(off Milk Yd.)
Riverside M. CR0: Bedd 3J 167
Riverside Pl. N11 3B 32
TW19: Stanw 6A 110
Riverside Rd. DA14: Sidc 3E 144
E15 2E 86
N15 6G 49
SW17 4K 135
TW19: Stanw 5A 110
Riverside Studios 5E 98
Riverside Twr. SW6 2A 118
(off The Boulevard)
Riverside Vs. KT6: Surb 6C 150
Riverside Wlk. BR4: W W'ck 1D 170
EN5: Barn 6A 20
(not continuous)
KT1: King T 3D 150
N12 6D 30
(not continuous)
N20 3E 30
SW6 3G 117
TW7: Isle 3J 113
W4 6B 98
(off Chiswick Wharf)
Riverside Wharf E3 1C 86
Riverside Works IG11: Bark 7F 71
Riverside Yd. SW17 4A 136
Riverstone Cl. HA2: Harr 1H 59
Riverstone Ct. KT2: King T 1F 151
River St. EC1 1J 7 (3A 84)
River St. M. EC1 1J 7
River Ter. WC2 3G 13
River Thames Vis. Cen. 6D 114
Riverton Cl. W9 3H 81
River Twr. SW8 7E 18 (6J 101)
River Vw. EN2: Enf 3H 23
Riverview Ct. E14 3B 104
River Vw. Gdns. TW1: Twick 2K 131
Riverview Gdns. SW13 6D 98
Riverview Gro. W4 6H 97
River Vw. Hgts. SE16 2G 103
(off Bermondsey Wall W.)
Riverview Pk. SE6 2C 140
Riverview Rd. KT19: Ewe 4J 163
W4 7H 97
Riverview Wlk. SE6 3B 140
River Wlk. E4 7K 35
KT12: Walt T 6J 147
SW6 2A 118
W6 7E 98
Riverwalk SW1 5J 101
Riverwalk Apartments SW6 3A 118
(off Central Av.)
Riverwalk Bus. Pk. EN3: Brim 4G 25
River Wlk. Rd. EN3: Brim 4G 25
River Way BR3: Beck 1C 170
KT19: Ewe 5K 163
SE10 3H 105
TW2: Twick 2F 131
Riverway N13 5F 33
River Wharf Bus. Pk. DA17: Belv 1K 109
Riverwood La. BR7: Chst 1H 161
Rivet Ho. SE1 5F 103
(off Cooper's Rd.)
Riviera Ct. E1 1G 103
(off St Katharine's Way)
Rivington Av. IG8: Wfd G 2B 52
Rivington Ct. NW10 1C 80
RM10: Dag 6H 73
Rivington Cres. NW7 7G 29
Rivington Pl. EC2 2H 9 (3E 84)
Rivington St. EC2 2G 9 (3E 84)
Rivington Wlk. E8 1G 85
Rivulet Apartments N4 7D 48
Rivulet Rd. N17 7H 33
Rixon Ho. SE18 6F 107
Rixon St. N7 3A 66
Rixsen Rd. E12 5C 70
Roach Rd. E3 7C 68
Roads Pl. N19 2J 65
Roan Gdns. CR4: Mitc 1D 154
Roan St. SE10 6E 104
Robarts Cl. HA5: Eastc 5K 39
Robbins Hall EN3: Pond E 6E 24
Robb Rd. HA7: Stan 6F 27
Robert Adam St. W1 7G 5 (6E 82)
Roberta St. E2 3G 85
Robert Bell Ho. SE16 4G 103
(off Rouel Rd.)
Robert Burns Ho. N17 7C 34
(off Northumberland Pk.)
Robert Burns M. SE24 5B 120
Robert Clack Leisure Cen. 1G 73
Robert Cl. W9 4A 4 (4A 82)
Robert Ct. SE15 2G 121
Robert Dashwood Way SE17 4C 102
Robert Gentry Ho. W14 5G 99
(off Gledstanes Rd.)
Robert Jones Ho. SE16 4G 103
(off Rouel Rd.)
Robert Keen Cl. SE15 1G 121
Robert Lowe Cl. SE14 7K 103
Robert Morton Ho. NW8 7A 64
Roberton Dr. BR1: Brom 1A 160
Robert Owen Ho. E2 1K 9
(off Baroness Rd.)
N22 1A 48
(off Progress Way)
SW6 1F 117
Robert Runcie Ct. SW2 4K 119
Roberts All. W5 2D 96
Robertsbridge Rd. SM5: Cars 1A 166
Roberts Cl. CR7: Thor H 3D 156
IG11: Bark 6G 71
(off Tanner St.)
SE9 1H 143
SE16 2K 103
SM3: Cheam 7F 165
UB7: Yiew 1A 92
Roberts Ct. KT9: Chess 5D 162
N1 1B 84
(off Essex Rd.)
NW10 6A 62
SE20 1J 157
(off Maple Rd.)
Roberts M. SW1 1G 17 (3E 100)
Robertson Gro. SW17 5C 136
Robertson Rd. E16 5J 87
Robertson St. SW8 3F 119
Roberts Pl. EC1 3K 7 (4A 84)
RM10: Dag 6G 73
Roberts Rd. DA17: Belv 5G 109
E17 1D 50
Robert St. CR0: C'don 3C 168
E16 1F 107
NW1 2K 5 (3F 83)
SE18 5H 107
(not continuous)
WC2 3F 13 (7J 83)
Robert Sutton Ho. E1 6J 85
(off Tarling St.)
Robeson St. E3 5B 86
Robina Cl. DA6: Bex 4D 126
HA6: Nwood 1H 39
Robin Cl. NW7 3F 29
RM5: Col R 1K 55
TW12: Hamp 5C 130
Robin Ct. E14 2E 104
SE16 4G 103
SM6: Wall 5G 167
Robin Cres. E6 5B 88
Robin Gro. HA3: Kenton 6F 43
N6 2E 64
TW8: Bford 6C 96
Robin Hill Dr. BR7: Chst 6C 142
ROBIN HOOD 3A 134
Robinhood Cl. CR4: Mitc 3G 155
Robin Hood Ct. EC4 7K 7
(off Shoe La.)
Robin Hood Dr.
HA3: Hrw W 7E 26
Robin Hood Gdns. E14 7E 86
(off Woolmore St.)
Robin Hood Grn.
BR5: St M Cry 5K 161
Robin Hood La. DA6: Bex 5E 126
E14 7E 86
SM1: Sutt 5J 165
SW15 3A 134
Robinhood La. CR4: Mitc 3G 155
Robin Hood Rd. SW19 5C 134
Robin Hood Way SW15 3A 134
SW20 3A 134
UB6: G'frd 6K 59
Robin Ho. NW8 2C 82
(off Newcourt St.)
Robin Howard Dance Theatre 2D 6
(off Duke's Rd.)
Robinia Cl. SE20 1G 157
(off Sycamore Gro.)
Robinia Cres. E10 2D 68
Robinia Ho. SE16 2A 104
(off Blondin Way)
Robin La. NW4 3F 45
Robin's Ct. BR3: Beck 2F 159
Robins Ct. CR2: S Croy 4E 168
(off Birdhurst Rd.)
SE12 3A 142
Robinscroft M. SE10 1E 122
Robins Gro. BR4: W W'ck 3J 171
Robinson Cl. E11 3G 69
EN2: Enf 3H 23
Robinson Ct.
CR7: Thor H 6B 156
N1 1B 84
(off St Mary's Path)
TW9: Rich 4F 115
Robinson Cres. WD23: B Hea 1B 26
Robinson Ho. E14 5C 86
(off Selsey St.)
W10 6F 81
(off Bramley Rd.)
Robinson Rd. E2 2J 85
RM10: Dag 4G 73
SW17 6C 136
Robinson's Cl. W13 5A 78
Robinson St. SW3 7E 16 (6D 100)
Robinson Way SE14 7K 103
Robinswood Gdns. E17 1B 50
Robinswood M. N5 5B 66
Robinwood Gro. UB8: Hil 4B 74
Robinwood Pl. SW15 4K 133
Robsart St. SW9 2K 119
Robson Av. NW10 7C 62
Robson Cl. E6 6C 88
EN2: Enf 2G 23
Robson Rd. SE27 3C 138
Roby Ho. EC1 3C 8
(off Mitchell St.)
Roca Ct. E11 5J 51
Rocastle Rd. SE4 5A 122
Roch Av. HA8: Edg 2F 43
Rochdale Rd. E17 7C 50
SE2 5B 108
Rochdale Way SE8 7C 104
(not continuous)
Roche Ho. E14 7B 86
(off Beccles St.)
Rochelle Cl. SW11 4B 118
Rochelle St. E2 2J 9 (3F 85)
(not continuous)
Rochemont Wlk. E8 1G 85
(off Pownell Rd.)
Roche Rd. SW16 1K 155
Rochester Av. BR1: Brom 2K 159
E13 1A 88
TW13: Felt 2H 129
Rochester Cl. DA15: Sidc 6B 126
EN1: Enf 1K 23
SW16 7J 137
Rochester Ct. E2 4H 85
(off Wilmot St.)
NW1 7G 65
(off Rochester Sq.)
Rochester Dr. DA5: Bexl 6F 127
HA5: Pinn 5B 40
Rochester Gdns. CR0: C'don 3E 168
IG1: Ilf 7D 52
Rochester Ho. SE1 7F 15
(off Manciple St.)
SE15 6J 103
(off Sharratt St.)
Rochester M. NW1 7G 65
W5 4C 96
Rochester Pde. TW13: Felt 2J 129
Rochester Pl. NW1 6G 65
Rochester Rd. HA6: Nwood 3H 39
NW1 6G 65
SM5: Cars 4D 166
Rochester Row SW1 3B 18 (4G 101)
Rochester Sq. NW1 7G 65
Rochester St. SW1 2C 18 (3H 101)
Rochester Ter. NW1 6G 65
Rochester Wlk. SE1 4E 14 (1D 102)
Rochester Way DA1: Dart 7K 127
SE3 1K 123
SE9 3D 124
Rochester Way Relief Rd. SE3 1K 123
SE9 4A 124
Roche Wlk. SM5: Cars 6B 154
Rochford N17 2E 48
(off Griffin Rd.)
Rochford Av. RM6: Chad H 5C 54
Rochford Cl. E6 2B 88
Rochford Wlk. E8 7G 67
Rochford Way CR0: C'don 6J 155
Rochfort Ho. SE8 5B 104
Rock Av. SW14 3K 115
Rockbourne M. SE23 1K 139
Rockbourne Rd. SE23 1K 139
Rock Cl. CR4: Mitc 2B 154
Rockell's Pl. SE22 6H 121
Rockfield Ho. NW4 4F 45
(off Belle Vue Est.)
SE10 6E 104
(off Welland St.)
Rockford Av. UB6: G'frd 2A 78
Rock Gdns. RM10: Dag 5H 73
Rock Gro. Way SE16 4G 103
(not continuous)
Rockhall Rd. NW2 4F 63
Rockhall Way NW2 3F 63
Rockhampton Cl. SE27 4A 138
Rockhampton Rd. CR2: S Croy 6E 168
SE27 4A 138
Rock Hill SE26 4F 139
(not continuous)
Rockingham Cl. SW15 4B 116
Rockingham St. SE1 3C 102
Rockland Rd. SW15 4G 117
Rocklands Dr. CR2: S Croy 6D 168
HA7: Stan 2B 42
Rockley Ct. W14 2F 99
(off Rockley Rd.)
Rockley Rd. W14 2F 99
Rockmount Rd. SE18 5K 107
SE19 6D 138
Rocks La. SW13 1C 116
Rock St. N4 2A 66
Rockware Av. UB6: G'frd 1H 77
Rockware Av. Bus. Cen.
UB6: G'frd 1H 77
Rockwell Gdns. SE19 5E 138
Rockwell Rd. RM10: Dag 5H 73
Rockwood Pl. W12 2E 98
Rocliffe St. N1 2B 84
Rocombe Cres. SE23 7J 121
Rocque Ho. SW6 7H 99
(off Estcourt Rd.)
Rocque La. SE3 3H 123
Rodale Mans. SW18 6K 117

Rodborough Ct. W9 . . . . .4J 81
    (off Hermes Cl.)
Rodborough Rd. NW11 . . . . .1J 63
Rodd Est. TW17: Shep 5E 146
Roden Ct. N6 . . . . .7H 47
Roden Gdns. CRO: C'don 6E 156
Rodenhurst Rd. SW4 . . . . .6G 119
Roden St. IG1: Ilf 3E 70
   N7 . . . . .3K 65
Roden Way IG1: Ilf 3E 70
    (off Roden St.)
Roderick Ho. SE16 . . . . .4J 103
    (off Raymouth Rd.)
Roderick Rd. NW3 . . . . .4D 64
Rodgers Ho. SW4 . . . . .7H 119
    (off Clapham Pk. Est.)
Rodin Ct. N1 . . . . .1B 84
    (off Essex Rd.)
Roding Av. IG8: Wfd G 6H 37
Roding Ho. N1 . . . . .1A 84
    (off Barnsbury Est.)
Roding La. IG7: Chig 2K 37
   IG9: Buck H 2K 37
Roding La. Nth. IG8: Wfd G 6H 37
Roding La. Sth.
   IG8: Ilf, Wfd G 4B 52
    (not continuous)
   IG8: Wfd G 4B 52
Roding M. E1 . . . . .1G 103
Roding Rd. E5 . . . . .4K 67
   E6 . . . . .5F 89
Rodings, The IG8: Wfd G 6F 37
Rodings Row EN5: Barn 4B 20
    (off Leecroft Rd.)
Roding Trad. Est. IG11: Bark 7F 71
Roding Valley Meadows Nature Reserve
   . . . . .1K 37
Roding Vw. IG9: Buck H 1G 37
Rodmarton St. W1 . . . . . . .6F 5 (5D 82)
Rodmell WC1 . . . . .2F 7
    (off Regent Sq.)
Rodmell Cl. UB4: Yead 4C 76
Rodmell Slope N12 . . . . .5C 30
Rodmere St. SE10 . . . . .5G 105
Rodmill La. SW2 . . . . .7J 119
Rodney Cl. CRO: C'don 1B 168
   HA5: Pinn 7C 40
   KT3: N Mald 5A 152
Rodney Ct. EN5: Barn 3C 20
   W9 . . . . .3A 4 (4A 82)
Rodney Gdns. BR4: W W'ck 4J 171
   HA5: Eastc 5K 39
Rodney Ho. E14 . . . . .4D 104
    (off Cahir St.)
   N1 . . . . .2K 83
    (off Donegal St.)
   SW1 . . . . .6B 18
    (off Dolphin Sq.)
   W11 .7J 81
    (off Pembridge Cres.)
Rodney Pl. E17 . . . . .2A 50
   SE17 . . . . .4C 102
   SW19 . . . . .1A 154
Rodney Point SE16 . . . . .2B 104
    (off Rotherhithe St.)
Rodney Rd. CR4: Mitc 3C 154
   E11 . . . . .4K 51
   KT3: N Mald 5A 152
   SE17 . . . . .4C 102
    (not continuous)
   TW2: Whitt 6E 112
Rodney St. N1 . . . . .1H 7 (2K 83)
Rodney Way RM7: Mawney 1H 55
   SL3: Poyle 4A 174
Rodway Rd. BR1: Brom 1K 159
   SW15 . . . . .7C 116
Rodwell Cl. HA4: Ruis 1A 58
Rodwell Pl. HA8: Edg 6B 28
Rodwell Rd. SE22 . . . . .6F 121
Roe NW9 . . . . .7G 29
Roebourne Way E16 . . . . .1E 106

Roebuck Cl. N17 . . . . .6A 34
   TW13: Felt 4K 129
Roebuck Hgts. IG9: Buck H 1F 37
Roebuck La. IG9: Buck H 1F 37
Roebuck Rd. KT9: Chess 5G 163
Roedean Av. EN3: Enf H 1D 24
Roedean Cl. EN3: Enf H 1D 24
Roedean Cres. SW15 . . . . .6A 116
Roe End NW9 . . . . .4J 43
ROE GREEN 4J 43
Roe Grn. NW9 . . . . .5J 43
ROEHAMPTON 6C 116
Roehampton Cl. SW15 . . . . .4C 116
Roehampton Dr. BR7: Chst 6G 143
Roehampton Ga. SW15 . . . . .6A 116
Roehampton Golf Course 4B 116
Roehampton High St. SW15 . . . . . .7C 116
Roehampton Ho. RM8: Dag 5A 72
ROEHAMPTON LANE 1D 134
Roehampton La. SW15 . . . . .7C 116
Roehampton Sport & Fitness Cen. . .7C 116
Roehampton University 6B 116
Roehampton Va. SW15 . . . . .3B 134
Roe La. NW9 . . . . .4H 43
Roesel Pl. BR5: Pet W 5F 161
Roe Way SM6: Wall 6J 167
Roffey St. E14 . . . . .2E 104
Roffo Cl. SE17 . . . . .6D 102
    (off Boundary La.)
Rogate Ho. E5 . . . . .3G 67
Roger Dowley Ct. E2 . . . . .2J 85
Roger Harriss Almshouses E15 . . . .1H 87
    (off Gift La.)
Roger Reede's Almshouses
   RM1: Rom 4K 55
Rogers Cl. E14 . . . . .7C 86
    (off Premiere Pl.)
Rogers Est. E2 . . . . .3J 85
    (not continuous)
Rogers Gdns. RM10: Dag 5G 73
Roger's Ho. RM10: Dag 3G 73
Rogers Ho. SW1 . . . . .3D 18
    (off Page St.)
Rogers Rd. E16 . . . . .6H 87
   RM10: Dag 5G 73
   SW17 . . . . .4B 136
Rogers Ruff HA6: Nwood 1E 38
Roger St. WC1 . . . . .4H 7 (4K 83)
Rogers Wlk. N12 . . . . .3E 30
Rohere Ho. EC1 . . . . .1C 8 (3C 84)
Rojack Rd. SE23 . . . . .1K 139
Rokeby Gdns. IG8: Wfd G 1J 51
Rokeby Ho. SW12 . . . . .7F 119
    (off Lochinvar St.)
   WC1 . . . . .4G 7
    (off Lamb's Conduit St.)
Rokeby Pl. SW20 . . . . .7D 134
Rokeby Rd. HA1: Harr 3H 41
   SE4 .2B 122
Rokeby St. E15 . . . . .1F 87
Rokell Ho. BR3: Beck 5D 140
    (off Beckenham Hill Rd.)
Roker Pk. Av. UB10: Ick 4A 56
Rokesby Cl. DA16: Well 2H 125
Rokesby Pl. HA0: Wemb 5D 60
Rokesly Av. N8 . . . . .5J 47
Rokewood Apartments BR3: Beck . . .1C 158
Roland Gdns. SW7 . . . . . .5A 16 (5A 100)
   SW10 . . . . .5A 100
Roland Ho. SW7 . . . . .5A 16
    (off Old Brompton Rd.)
Roland Mans. SW7 . . . . .5A 100
    (off Old Brompton Rd.)
Roland M. E1 . . . . .5K 85
Roland Rd. E17 . . . . .4F 51
Roland Way KT4: Wor Pk 2B 164
   SE17 . . . . .5D 102
   SW7 . . . . .5A 16 (5A 100)
Roles Gro. RM6: Chad H 4D 54
Rolfe Cl. EN4: E Barn 4H 21
Rolinsden Way BR2: Kes 5B 172

Rolland Ho. W7 . . . . .5J 77
Rollesby Rd. KT9: Chess 6G 163
Rollesby Way SE28 . . . . .6C 90
Rolleston Av. BR5: Pet W 6F 161
Rolleston Cl. BR5: Pet W 7F 161
Rolleston Rd. CR2: S Croy 7D 168
Roll Gdns. IG2: Ilf 5E 52
Rollins Ho. SE15 . . . . .6J 103
    (off Rollins St.)
Rollins St. SE15 . . . . .6J 103
Rollit Cres. TW3: Houn 5E 112
Rollit St. N7 . . . . .5A 66
Rolls Bldgs. EC4 . . . . .7J 7 (6A 84)
Rollscourt Av. SE24 . . . . .5C 120
Rolls Pk. Av. E4 . . . . .5H 35
Rolls Pk. Rd. E4 . . . . .5J 35
Rolls Pas. EC4 . . . . .7J 7
Rolls Rd. SE1 . . . . .5F 103
Rolls Royce Cl. SM6: Wall 7J 167
Rolt St. SE8 . . . . .6A 104
    (not continuous)
Rolvenden Gdns. BR1: Brom 7B 142
Rolvenden Pl. N17 . . . . .1G 49
Roma Corte SE13 . . . . .3D 122
    (off Elmira St.)
Romana Ct. CR0: C'don 2F 169
Roman Apartments E8 . . . . .7H 67
    (off Silesia Bldgs.)
Roman Cl. RM13: Rain 2K 91
   TW14: Felt 5A 112
   W3 . . . . .2H 97
Roman Ct. N7 . . . . .6K 65
Romanfield Rd. SW2 . . . . .7K 119
Roman Ho. EC2 . . . . .6D 8
   RM13: Rain 2K 91
Romanhurst Av. BR2: Brom 4G 159
Romanhurst Gdns. BR2: Brom 4G 159
Roman Ind. Est. CR0: C'don 7E 156
Roman Ri. SE19 . . . . .6D 138
Roman Rd. E2 . . . . .3J 85
   E3 . . . . .2A 86
   E6 . . . . .4B 88
   IG1: Ilf 6F 71
   N10 . . . . .7A 32
   NW2 . . . . .3E 62
    (Edgware Rd.)
   NW2 . . . . .3E 62
    (Temple Rd.)
   W4 . . . . .4A 98
Roman Sq. SE28 . . . . .1A 108
Roman Way CR0: C'don 2B 168
   EN1: Enf 5A 24
   N7 . . . . .6K 65
   SE15 . . . . .7J 103
Roman Way Ind. Est. N7 . . . . .7K 65
    (off Roman Way)
Romany Gdns. E17 . . . . .1A 50
   SM3: Sutt 7J 153
Romany Ri. BR5: Farnb 1G 173
Roma Read Cl. SW15 . . . . .7D 116
Romayne Ho. SW4 . . . . .3H 119
Romberg Rd. SW17 . . . . .3E 136
Romborough Gdns. SE13 . . . . .5E 122
Romborough Way SE13 . . . . .5E 122
Romero Cl. SW9 . . . . .3K 119
Romeyn Rd. SW16 . . . . .3K 137
ROMFORD 5K 55
Romford Rd. E7 . . . . .6G 69
   E12 . . . . .5A 70
   E15 . . . . .6G 69
   RM5: Col R 1E 54
Romford Stadium (Greyhound) 6J 55
Romford St. E1 . . . . .5G 85
Romilly Ho. W11 . . . . .7G 81
    (off Wilsham St.)
Romilly Rd. N4 . . . . .2B 66
Romilly St. W1 . . . . .2D 12 (7H 83)
Romily Ct. SW6 . . . . .2H 117
Rommany Rd. SE27 . . . . .4D 138
    (not continuous)

Romney Cl. HA2: Harr 7E 40
   KT9: Chess 4E 162
   N17 . . . . .1H 49
   NW11 . . . . .1A 64
   SE14 . . . . .7J 103
   TW15: Ashf 5E 128
Romney Ct. NW3 . . . . .6C 64
   W12 . . . . .2F 99
    (off Shepherd's Bush Grn.)
Romney Dr. BR1: Brom 7B 142
   HA2: Harr 7E 40
Romney Gdns. DA7: Bex 1F 127
Romney Ho. SW1 . . . . .2E 18
    (off Marsham St.)
Romney M. W1 . . . . .5G 5 (5E 82)
Romney Pde. UB4: Hayes 2F 75
Romney Rd. KT3: N Mald 6K 151
   SE10 . . . . .6F 105
   UB4: Hayes 2F 75
Romney Row NW2 . . . . .2F 63
    (off Brent Ter.)
Romney St. SW1 . . . . .2E 18 (3J 101)
Romola Rd. SE24 . . . . .1B 138
Romsey Cl. BR6: Farnb 4F 173
Romsey Gdns. RM9: Dag 1D 90
Romsey Rd. RM9: Dag 1D 90
   W13 . . . . .7A 78
Romside Pl. RM7: Rom 4K 55
Romulus Ct. TW8: Bford 7D 96
Ronald Av. E15 . . . . .3G 87
Ronald Buckingham Ct. SE16 . . . . .2J 103
    (off Kenning St.)
Ronald Cl. BR3: Beck 4B 158
Ronald Ct. EN5: New Bar 3E 20
Ronaldshay N4 . . . . .7A 48
Ronalds Rd. BR1: Brom 1J 159
   N5 . . . . .5A 66
    (not continuous)
Ronaldstone Rd. DA15: Sidc 6J 125
Ronald St. E1 . . . . .6J 85
Rona Rd. NW3 . . . . .4E 64
Ronart St. HA3: W'stone 3K 41
Rona Wlk. N1 . . . . .6D 66
Rondel Ct. DA5: Bexl 6E 126
Rondu Rd. NW2 . . . . .5G 63
Ronelean Rd. KT6: Surb 2F 163
Ron Grn. Ct. DA8: Erith 6K 109
Ron Leighton Way E6 . . . . .1C 88
Ronnie La. E12 . . . . .4E 70
Ron Todd Cl. RM10: Dag 1G 91
Ronver Rd. SE12 . . . . .7H 123
Rood La. EC3 . . . . .2G 15 (7E 84)
Roof Ter. Apartments, The EC1 . . . . .4B 8
    (off St. Sutton St.)
Rookby Ct. N21 . . . . .2G 33
Rook Cl. HA9: Wemb 3H 61
Rookeries Cl. TW13: Felt 3K 129
Rookery Cl. NW9 . . . . .5B 44
Rookery Ct. E10 . . . . .3D 68
Rookery Cres. RM10: Dag 7H 73
Rookery Dr. BR7: Chst 1E 160
Rookery La. BR2: Brom 6B 160
Rookery Rd. SW4 . . . . .4G 119
Rookery Way NW9 . . . . .5B 44
Rooke Way SE10 . . . . .5H 105
Rookfield Av. N10 . . . . .4G 47
Rookfield Cl. N10 . . . . .4G 47
Rooksmead Rd. TW16: Sun 2H 147
Rooks Ter. UB7: W Dray 2A 92
Rookstone Rd. SW17 . . . . .5D 136
Rook Wlk. E6 . . . . .6B 88
Rookwood Av. KT3: N Mald 4C 152
   SM6: Bedd 4H 167
Rookwood Gdns. E4 . . . . .2C 36
Rookwood Ho. IG11: Bark 2H 89
Rookwood Rd. N16 . . . . .7F 49
Roosevelt Memorial 2H 11 (7E 82)
Roosevelt Way RM10: Dag 6K 73
Rootes Dr. W10 . . . . .5F 81
Ropemaker Rd. SE16 . . . . .2A 104
Ropemaker's Flds. E14 . . . . .7B 86

Ropemaker St. EC2 5E **8** (5D **84**)
Roper Cres. TW16: Sun 1J **147**
Roper La. SE1 7H **15** (2E **102**)
Ropers Av. E4 5J **35**
Ropers Orchard *SW3 6C* ***100***
(off Danvers St.)
Roper St. SE9 5D **124**
Ropers Wlk. SW2 7A **120**
Roper Way CR4: Mitc 2E **154**
Ropery Bus. Pk. SE7 4A **106**
Ropery St. E3 4B **86**
Rope St. SE16 4A **104**
Rope Wlk. TW16: Sun 3A **148**
Rope Wlk. Gdns. E1 6G **85**
Ropewalk M. E8 7G **67**
Ropeworks, The
IG11: Bark 1G **89**
Rope Yd. Rails SE18 3F **107**
Ropley St. E2 2G **85**
Rosa Alba M. N5 4C **66**
Rosa Av. TW15: Ashf 4C **128**
Rosalind Ct. *IG11: Bark 7A* ***72***
(off Meadow Rd.)
Rosalind Ho. *N1 2E* ***84***
(off Arden Est.)
Rosaline Rd. SW6 7G **99**
Rosaline Ter. *SW6 7G* ***99***
(off Rosaline Rd.)
Rosa M. E17 3B **50**
Rosamond St. SE26 3H **139**
Rosamund Cl. CR2: S Croy 4D **168**
Rosamun St. UB2: S'hall 4C **94**
Rosa Parks Ho. *SE17 4C* ***102***
(off Munton Rd.)
Rosary Cl. TW3: Houn 2C **112**
Rosary Gdns. SW7 4A **100**
TW15: Ashf 4D **128**
Rosaville Rd. SW6 7H **99**
Roscoe St. EC1 4D **8** (4C **84**)
(not continuous)
Roscoe St. Est. EC1 4D **8** (4C **84**)
Roscoff Cl. HA8: Edg 1J **43**
Rosea Apartments *SW11 4C* ***118***
(off Danvers Av.)
Roseacre Cl. SM1: Sutt 2A **166**
TW17: Shep 5C **146**
W13 5B **78**
Roseacre Rd. DA16: Well 3B **126**
Rose All. *EC2 6H* ***9***
(off Bishopsgate)
SE1 4D **14** (1C **102**)
Rose & Crown Ct. EC2 7D **8**
Rose & Crown M. TW7: Isle 1A **114**
Rose & Crown Yd. SW1 4B **12** (1G **101**)
Rose Apartments SE11 7K **19**
Roseary Cl. UB7: W Dray 4A **92**
Rose Av. CR4: Mitc 1D **154**
E18 2K **51**
SM4: Mord 5A **154**
Rosebank SE20 7H **139**
SW6 7E **98**
W3 6K **79**
Rosebank Av. HA0: Wemb 4K **59**
Rosebank Cl. N12 5H **31**
TW11: Tedd 6A **132**
Rosebank Gdns. E3 2B **86**
W3 6K **79**
Rosebank Gro. E17 3B **50**
Rosebank Rd. E17 6D **50**
W7 2J **95**
Rosebank Vs. E17 4C **50**
Rosebank Wlk. NW1 7H **65**
SE18 4C **106**
Rosebank Way W3 6K **79**
Rose Bates Dr. NW9 4G **43**
Rosebay Dr. N17 2F **49**
Rosebay Ho. *E3 5C* ***86***
(off Hawgood St.)
Roseberry Dr. HA8: Edg 2C **28**
Roseberry Gdns. BR6: Orp 3J **173**
N4 6B **48**
Roseberry Mans. *N1 1J* ***83***
(off Tapper Wlk.)
Roseberry M. SW2 6J **119**
Roseberry Pl. E8 6F **67**
Roseberry St. SE16 4H **103**
Rosebery Av. CR7: Thor H 2C **156**
DA15: Sidc 7J **125**
E12 6C **70**
EC1 4J **7** (4A **84**)
HA2: Harr 4C **58**
KT3: N Mald 2B **152**
N17 2G **49**
Rosebery Cl. SM4: Mord 6F **153**
Rosebery Ct. *EC1 3J* ***7***
(off Rosebery Av.)
W1 4J ***11***
(off Charles St.)
Rosebery Gdns. N8 5J **47**
SM1: Sutt 4K **165**
W13 6A **78**
Rosebery Ho. *E2 2J* ***85***
(off Sewardstone Rd.)
Rosebery Ind. Pk. N17 2H **49**
Rosebery M. N10 2G **47**
Rosebery Rd. KT1: King T 2H **151**
N10 2G **47**
SM1: Sutt 6H **165**
SW2 6J **119**
TW3: Houn 5G **113**
WD23: Bush 1A **26**
Rosebery Sq. EC1 4J **7**
KT1: King T 2H **151**
Rosebine Av. TW2: Twick 7H **113**
Rosebury Pl. NW7 7G **29**
Rosebury Rd. SW6 2K **117**
Rosebury Sq. IG8: Wfd G 7K **37**
Rosebury Va. HA4: Ruis 2J **57**
Rose Bush Ct. NW3 5D **64**
Rose Ct. E1 6K **9**
E8 7F ***67***
(off Richmond Rd.)
HA0: Wemb 2E ***78***
(off Vicars Bri. Cl.)
HA2: Harr 2G **59**
N1 1B ***84***
(off Collin's Yd.)
SE8 4K **103**
Rosecourt Rd. CR0: C'don 6K **155**
Rosecroft N14 2D **32**
Rosecroft Av. NW3 3J **63**
Rosecroft Gdns. NW2 3C **62**
TW2: Twick 1H **131**
Rosecroft Rd. UB1: S'hall 4E **76**
Rosecroft Wlk. HA0: Wemb 5D **60**
HA5: Pinn 5B **40**
Rose Dale BR6: Farnb 2F **173**
Rosedale Av. UB3: Hayes 5F **75**
Rosedale Cl. HA7: Stan 6G **27**
SE2 3B **108**
W7 2K **95**
Rosedale Ct. HA1: Harr 4K **59**
N5 4B **66**
Rosedale Dr. RM9: Dag 7B **72**
Rosedale Gdns. RM9: Dag 7B **72**
Rosedale Ho. N16 1D **66**
Rosedale Pl. CR0: C'don 7K **157**
Rosedale Rd. E7 5A **70**
KT17: Ewe 5C **164**
RM1: Rom 2J **55**
RM9: Dag 7B **72**
TW9: Rich 3E **114**
Rosedale Ter. *W6 3D* ***98***
(off Dalling Rd.)
Rosedene NW6 1F **81**
Rosedene Av. CR0: C'don 7J **155**
SM4: Mord 5J **153**
SW16 3K **137**
UB6: G'frd 3E **76**
Rosedene Ct. HA4: Ruis 1G **57**
Rosedene Gdns. IG2: Ilf 4E **52**
Rosedene Ter. E10 2D **68**
Rosedew Rd. W6 6F **99**
Rose End KT4: Wor Pk 1F **165**
Rosefield Cl. SM5: Cars 5C **166**
Rosefield Gdns. E14 7C **86**
Roseford Ct. *W12 2F* ***99***
(off Shepherd's Bush Grn.)
Rose Gdn. Cl. HA8: Edg 6K **27**
Rose Gdns. TW13: Felt 2J **129**
UB1: S'hall 4E **76**
W5 3D **96**
Rosegate Ho. *E3 2B* ***86***
(off Hereford Rd.)
Rose Glen NW9 4K **43**
RM7: Rush G 1K **73**
Rosehart M. W11 6J **81**
Rose Hatch Av. RM6: Chad H 3D **54**
Roseheath Rd. TW4: Houn 5D **112**
ROSEHILL 7A **154**
Rose Hill SM1: Sutt 2K **165**
Rosehill KT10: Clay 6A **162**
TW12: Hamp 1E **148**
Rosehill Av. SM1: Sutt 1A **166**
Rosehill Ct. *SM4: Mord 7A* ***154***
(off St Helier Av.)
Rosehill Ct. Pde. *SM4: Mord 7A* ***154***
(off St Helier Av.)
Rosehill Gdns. SM1: Sutt 2K **165**
UB6: G'frd 5K **59**
Rose Hill Pk. W. SM1: Sutt 1A **166**
Rosehill Rd. SW18 6A **118**
ROSE HILL RDBT. **7A 154**
Rose Joan M. NW6 4J **63**
Rosekey Ct. *SE8 7B* ***104***
(off Baildon St.)
Roseland Cl. N17 7J **33**
Rose La. RM6: Chad H 3D **54**
Rose Lawn WD23: B Hea 1B **26**
Roseleigh Av. N5 4B **66**
Roseleigh Cl. TW1: Twick 6D **114**
Rosemary Av. EN2: Enf 1K **23**
KT8: W Mole 3E **148**
N3 2K **45**
N9 1C **34**
TW4: Houn 2B **112**
Rosemary Branch Theatre ***1D 84***
(off Rosemary St.)
Rosemary Cl. CR0: C'don 6J **155**
UB8: Hil 5C **74**
Rosemary Ct. *SE8 6B* ***104***
(off Dorking Cl.)
SE15 7E **102**
Rosemary Dr. E14 6F **87**
IG4: Ilf 5B **52**
Rosemary Gdns. KT9: Chess 4E **162**
RM8: Dag 1F **73**
SW14 3J **115**
Rosemary Ho. *N1 1D* ***84***
(off Colville Est.)
NW10 1D ***80***
(off Uffington Rd.)
Rosemary La. SW14 3J **115**
Rosemary Rd. DA16: Well 1K **125**
SE15 7F **103**
SW17 3A **136**
Rosemary St. N1 1D **84**
Rosemary Works *N1 1D* ***84***
(off Branch Pl.)
Rosemead Av. CR4: Mitc 3G **155**
HA9: Wemb 5E **60**
TW13: Felt 2H **129**
Rosemead Cl. KT6: Surb 1G **163**
Rosemere Pl. BR2: Brom 4G **159**
Rose M. N18 4C **34**
Rosemont Av. N12 6F **31**
Rosemont Ct. *W3 1H* ***97***
(off Rosemont Rd.)
Rosemont Rd. HA0: Wemb 1E **78**
KT3: N Mald 3J **151**
NW3 6A **64**
TW10: Rich 6E **114**
W3 7H **79**
Rosemoor Ho. *W13 1A* ***96***
(off Broadway)
Rosemoor St. SW3 4E **16** (4D **100**)
Rosemount *SM6: Wall 6G* ***167***
(off Clarendon Rd.)
Rosemount Cl. IG8: Wfd G 6J **37**
Rosemount Dr. BR1: Brom 4D **160**
Rosemount Point SE23 3K **139**
Rosemount Rd. W13 6A **78**
Rosenau Cres. SW11 1D **118**
Rosenau Rd. SW11 1C **118**
Rosendale Rd. SE21 7C **120**
SE24 7C **120**
Roseneath Av. N21 1G **33**
Roseneath Pl. *SW16 4K* ***137***
(off Curtis Fld. Rd.)
Roseneath Rd. SW11 6E **118**
Roseneath Wlk. EN1: Enf 4K **23**
Rosen's Wlk. HA8: Edg 3C **28**
Rosenthal Rd. SE6 6D **122**
Rosenthorpe Rd. SE15 5K **121**
Rose Pk. Cl. UB4: Yead 5A **76**
Rosepark Ct. IG5: Ilf 2D **52**
Rose Pl. N8 6J **47**
Roserton St. E14 2E **104**
Rosery, The CR0: C'don 6K **157**
Roses, The IG8: Wfd G 7C **36**
Rose Sq. SW3 5B **16** (5B **100**)
Rose Stapleton Ter. *SE1 3E* ***102***
(off Page's Wlk.)
Rose St. EC4 7B **8** (6B **84**)
WC2 2E **12** (7J **83**)
(not continuous)
Rose Theatre
Sidcup **1B 144**
Rose Theatre, The ***4D 14***
(off Park St.)
Rose Theatre Kingston **2D 150**
Rosethorn Cl. SW12 7H **119**
Rose Tree M. IG8: Wfd G 6H **37**
Rosetree Pl. TW12: Hamp 7E **130**
Rosetta Cl. *SW8 7J* ***101***
(off Kenchester Cl.)
Rosetta Ct. SE19 7E **138**
Rosetti Ter. *RM8: Dag 4B* ***72***
(off Marlborough Rd.)
Roseveare Rd. SE12 4A **142**
Roseville *N21 1F* ***33***
(off The Green)
Roseville Av. TW3: Houn 5E **112**
Roseville Rd. UB3: Harl 5J **93**
Rosevine Rd. SW20 1E **152**
Rose Wlk. BR4: W W'ck 2E **170**
KT5: Surb 5H **151**
Rose Way HA8: Edg 4D **28**
SE12 5J **123**
Roseway SE21 6D **120**
Rosewell Cl. SE20 7H **139**
Rosewood KT7: T Ditt 2A **162**
Rosewood Av. UB6: G'frd 5A **60**
Rosewood Cl. DA14: Sidc 3C **144**
Rosewood Ct. BR1: Brom 1A **160**
E11 4F **69**
KT2: King T 7G **133**
RM6: Chad H 5C **54**
Rosewood Dr. TW17: Shep 5B **146**
Rosewood Gdns. SE13 2E **122**
Rosewood Gro. SM1: Sutt 2A **166**
Rosewood Ho. SW8 7G **19** (6K **101**)
Rosewood Sq. W12 6C **80**
Rosher Cl. E15 7F **69**
Roshni Ho. SW17 6C **136**
Rosina St. E9 6K **67**
Rosing Apartments *BR2: Brom 4A* ***160***
(off Homesdale Rd.)
Roskeen Ct. SW20 7E **134**
Roskell Rd. SW15 3F **117**
Rosler Bldg. *SE1 5C* ***14***
(off Ewer St.)
Roslin Ho. *E1 7K* ***85***
(off Brodlove La.)

Roslin Rd. W3	.3H **97**
Roslin Way BR1: Brom	.5J **141**
Roslyn Cl. CR4: Mitc	.2B **154**
Roslyn Rd. N15	.5D **48**
Rosmead Rd. W11	.7G **81**
Rosoman Pl. EC1	.3K **7** (4A **84**)
Rosoman St. EC1	.2K **7** (3A **84**)
Rossall Cres. NW10	.3F **79**
Ross Apartments E16	.7J **87**
(off Seagull La.)	
Ross Av. RM8: Dag	.1F **73**
Ross Cl. HA3: Hrw W	.7B **26**
UB3: Harl	.4F **93**
UB5: N'olt	.4H **59**
Ross Ct. E5	.4H **67**
(off Napoleon Rd.)	
NW9	.3A **44**
SW15	.7F **117**
W13	.5B **78**
(off Cleveland Rd.)	
Rosscourt Mans. SW1	.1A **18**
(off Buckingham Pal. Rd.)	
Rossdale SM1: Sutt	.5C **166**
Rossdale Dr. N9	.6D **24**
NW9	.1J **61**
Rossdale Rd. SW15	.4E **116**
Rosse Gdns. SE13	.6F **123**
Rosse M. SE3	.1K **123**
Rossendale St. E5	.2H **67**
Rossendale Way NW1	.1G **65**
Rossetti CRO: C'don	.1C **168**
(off Saffron Central Sq.)	
Rossetti Ct. WC1	.5C **6**
(off Ridgmount Pl.)	
Rossetti Gdn. Mans. SW3	.7E **16**
Rossetti Ho. SW1	.4D **18**
(off Erasmus St.)	
Rossetti M. NW8	.1B **82**
Rossetti Rd. SE16	.5H **103**
Rossetti Studios SW3	.7D **16**
(off Flood St.)	
Ross Haven Pl. HA6: Nwood	.1H **39**
Ross Ho. E1	.1H **103**
(off Prusom St.)	
Rossignol Gdns. SM5: Cars	.2E **166**
Rossindel Rd. TW3: Houn	.5E **112**
Rossington Cl. EN1: Enf	.1C **24**
Rossington St. E5	.2G **67**
Rossiter Cl. SE19	.7C **138**
Rossiter Flds. EN5: Barn	.6B **20**
Rossiter Gro. SW9	.3A **120**
Rossiter Rd. SW12	.1F **137**
Rossland Cl. DA6: Bex	.5H **127**
Rosslyn Av. E4	.2C **36**
EN4: E Barn	.6H **21**
RM8: Dag	.7F **55**
SW13	.3A **116**
TW14: Felt	.6J **111**
Rosslyn Cl. BR4: W W'ck	.3H **171**
TW16: Sun	.6G **129**
UB3: Hayes	.5F **75**
Rosslyn Cres. HA1: Harr	.4K **41**
HA9: Wemb	.4E **60**
Rosslyn Gdns. HA9: Wemb	.3E **60**
Rosslyn Hill NW3	.4B **64**
Rosslyn Mans. NW6	.7A **64**
(off Goldhurst Ter.)	
Rosslyn M. NW3	.4B **64**
Rosslyn Pk. M. NW3	.5B **64**
Rosslyn Rd. E17	.4E **50**
IG11: Bark	.7H **71**
TW1: Twick	.6C **114**
Rossmore Cl. EN3: Pond E	.4E **24**
NW1	.4D **4**
(off Rossmore Rd.)	
Rossmore Ct. NW1	.3E **4** (4D **82**)
Rossmore Rd. NW1	.4D **4** (4C **82**)
Ross Pde. SM6: Wall	.6F **167**
Ross Rd. SE25	.3D **156**
SM6: Wall	.5G **167**
TW2: Whitt	.1F **131**

Ross Wlk. SE27	.3D **138**
Ross Way E14	.6A **86**
SE9	.3C **124**
Rosswood Gdns. SM6: Wall	.6G **167**
Rostella Rd. SW17	.4B **136**
Rostrevor Av. N15	.6F **49**
Rostrevor Gdns. UB2: S'hall	.5C **94**
UB3: Hayes	.1G **93**
Rostrevor Mans. SW6	.1H **117**
(off Rostrevor Rd.)	
Rostrevor M. SW6	.1H **117**
Rostrevor Rd. SW6	.1H **117**
SW19	.5J **135**
Roswell Apartments E3	.5B **86**
(off Joseph St.)	
Rotary St. SE1	.7A **14** (3B **102**)
Rothay NW1	.1K **5**
(off Albany St.)	
Rothbury Cotts. SE10	.4G **105**
(off Maritius Rd.)	
Rothbury Gdns. TW7: Isle	.7A **96**
Rothbury Rd. E9	.7B **68**
Rothbury Wlk. N17	.7B **34**
Rotheley Ho. E9	.7J **67**
(off Balcorne St.)	
Rotherfield Ct. N1	.7D **66**
(off Rotherfield St.)	
Rotherfield Rd. SM5: Cars	.4E **166**
Rotherfield St. N1	.7C **66**
Rotherham Wlk. SE1	.5A **14**
Rotherhill Av. SW16	.6H **137**
ROTHERHITHE	.2J **103**
Rotherhithe Bus. Est. SE16	.4H **103**
Rotherhithe New Rd. SE16	.5H **103**
Rotherhithe Old Rd. SE16	.4K **103**
Rotherhithe St. SE16	.2J **103**
Rotherhithe Tunnel SE16	.1K **103**
Rother Ho. SE15	.4H **121**
Rotherwick Hill W5	.4F **79**
Rotherwick Ho. E1	.7G **85**
(off Thomas More St.)	
Rotherwick Rd. NW11	.7J **45**
Rotherwood Cl. SW20	.1G **153**
Rotherwood Rd. SW15	.3F **117**
Rothery St. N1	.1B **84**
(off St Marys Path)	
Rothery Ter. SW9	.7B **102**
(off Foxley Rd.)	
Rothesay Av. SW20	.2G **153**
TW10: Rich	.4H **115**
UB6: G'frd	.6G **59**
(not continuous)	
Rothesay Ct. SE6	.2H **141**
(off Cumberland Pl.)	
SE11	.7J **19**
SE12	.3K **141**
Rothesay Rd. SE25	.4D **156**
Rothley Ct. NW8	.3A **4**
(off St John's Wood Rd.)	
Rothsay Rd. E7	.7A **70**
Rothsay St. SE1	.3E **102**
Rothsay Wlk. E14	.4C **104**
(off Charnwood Gdns.)	
Rothschild Rd. W4	.4J **97**
Rothschild St. SE27	.4B **138**
Roth Wlk. N7	.2K **65**
Rothwell Ct. HA1: Harr	.5K **41**
Rothwell Gdns. RM9: Dag	.7C **72**
Rothwell Ho. TW5: Hest	.6E **94**
Rothwell Rd. RM9: Dag	.1C **90**
Rothwell St. NW1	.1D **82**
Rotten Row NW3	.1A **64**
SW1	.6B **10** (2B **100**)
SW7	.6B **10** (2B **100**)
Rotterdam Dr. E14	.3E **104**
Rotunda, The RM7: Rom	.5K **55**
(off Yew Tree Gdns.)	
Rotunda Cen., The	.2E **150**
Rotunda Ct. BR1: Brom	.5K **141**
(off Burnt Ash La.)	
Rouel Rd. SE16	.4G **103**

Rougemont Av. SM4: Mord	.6J **153**
Roundabout Ho.	
HA6: Nwood	.1J **39**
Roundacre SW19	.2F **135**
Roundaway Rd. IG5: Ilf	.1D **52**
Roundel Cl. SE4	.4B **122**
Round Gro. CRO: C'don	.7K **157**
Roundhay Cl. SE23	.2K **139**
Roundhedge Way EN2: Enf	.1E **22**
Round Hill SE26	.2J **139**
(not continuous)	
Roundhill Dr. EN2: Enf	.4E **22**
Roundhouse, The	.7E **64**
Roundhouse La. E20	.6E **68**
(off International Way)	
ROUNDSHAW	.7J **167**
Roundshaw Downs Local Nature Reserve	
	.7K **167**
Roundtable Rd. BR1: Brom	.3H **141**
Roundtree Rd. HA0: Wemb	.5B **60**
Roundway, The KT10: Clay	.6A **162**
N17	.1C **48**
Roundways HA4: Ruis	.3H **57**
Roundwood BR7: Chst	.2F **161**
Roundwood Av. UB11: Stock P	.1E **92**
Roundwood Cl. HA4: Ruis	.7F **39**
Roundwood Ct. E2	.3K **85**
Roundwood Rd. NW10	.6B **62**
Rounton Rd. E3	.4C **86**
Roupell Ho. KT2: King T	.7F **133**
(off Florence Rd.)	
Roupell Rd. SW2	.1K **137**
Roupell St. SE1	.5K **13** (1A **102**)
Rousden St. NW1	.7G **65**
Rouse Gdns. SE21	.4E **138**
Rous Rd. IG9: Buck H	.1H **37**
Routemaster Cl. E13	.3K **87**
Routh Ct. TW14: Bedf	.1F **129**
Routh Rd. SW18	.7C **118**
Routh St. E6	.5D **88**
Rover Ho. N1	.1E **84**
(off Whitmore Est.)	
Rowallan Rd. SW6	.7G **99**
Rowallen Pde. RM8: Dag	.1C **72**
Rowan Av. E4	.6H **35**
Rowan Cl. HA0: Wemb	.3A **60**
HA7: Stan	.6E **26**
IG1: Ilf	.5H **71**
KT3: N Mald	.2A **152**
SW16	.1G **155**
W5	.2E **96**
Rowan Ct. E13	.2K **87**
(off High St.)	
SE15	.7F **103**
(off Garnies Cl.)	
SW11	.6D **118**
Rowan Cres. SW16	.1G **155**
Rowan Dr. NW9	.3C **44**
Rowan Gdns. CRO: C'don	.3F **169**
Rowan Ho. BR2: Brom	.2G **159**
DA14: Sidc	.3K **143**
E3	.1B **86**
(off Hornbeam Sq.)	
IG1: Ilf	.5H **71**
SE16	.3H **103**
(off Woodland Cres.)	
Rowan Lodge W8	.3K **99**
(off Chantry Sq.)	
Rowan Pl. UB3: Hayes	.7H **75**
Rowan Rd. DA7: Bex	.3E **126**
SW16	.2G **155**
TW8: Bford	.7B **96**
UB7: W Dray	.4A **92**
W6	.4F **99**
Rowans, The N13	.3G **33**
TW16: Sun	.5H **129**
Rowans Complex	.2A **66**
Rowan Ter. SW19	.7G **135**
W6	.4F **99**
Rowantree Cl. N21	.1J **33**

Rowantree Rd. EN2: Enf	.2G **23**
N21	.1J **33**
Rowan Wlk. BR2: Brom	.3D **172**
EN5: New Bar	.5E **20**
N2	.5A **46**
N19	.2G **65**
W10	.4G **81**
Rowan Way RM6: Chad H	.3C **54**
Rowanwood Av. DA15: Sidc	.1A **144**
Rowanwood M. EN2: Enf	.2G **23**
Rowben Cl. N20	.1E **30**
Rowberry Cl. SW6	.7E **98**
Rowcross St. SE1	.5F **103**
Rowdell Rd. UB5: N'olt	.1E **76**
Rowden Pde. E4	.6H **35**
(off Chingford Rd.)	
Rowden Pk. Gdns. E4	.7H **35**
Rowden Rd. BR3: Beck	.1A **158**
E4	.6J **35**
KT19: Ewe	.4H **163**
Rowditch La. SW11	.2E **118**
Rowdon Av. NW10	.7D **62**
Rowdowns Rd. RM9: Dag	.1F **91**
Rowe Gdns. IG11: Bark	.2K **89**
Rowe Ho. E9	.6J **67**
Rowe La. E9	.5J **67**
Rowena Cres. SW11	.2C **118**
Rowenhurst Mans. NW6	.6A **64**
(off Canfield Gdns.)	
Rowe Wlk. HA2: Harr	.3E **58**
Rowfant Rd. SW17	.1E **136**
Rowhill Rd. E5	.4H **67**
Rowington Cl. W2	.5K **81**
Rowland Av. HA3: Kenton	.3C **42**
Rowland Ct. E16	.4H **87**
Rowland Gro. SE26	.3H **139**
(not continuous)	
Rowland Hill Almshouses	
TW15: Ashf	.5C **128**
(off Feltham Hill Rd.)	
Rowland Hill Av. N17	.7H **33**
Rowland Hill Ho. SE1	.6A **14** (2B **102**)
Rowland Hill St. NW3	.5C **64**
Rowlands Cl. N6	.6E **46**
NW7	.7H **29**
Rowlands Rd. RM8: Dag	.2F **73**
Rowland Way SW19	.1K **153**
TW15: Ashf	.7F **129**
Rowley Av. DA15: Sidc	.7B **126**
Rowley Cl. HA0: Wemb	.7F **61**
Rowley Ct. EN1: Enf	.5K **23**
(off Wellington St.)	
Rowley Gdns. N4	.7C **48**
Rowley Ho. SE8	.5C **104**
(off Watergate St.)	
Rowley Ind. Pk. W3	.3H **97**
Rowley Rd. N15	.5C **48**
Rowley Way NW8	.1K **81**
Rowlheys Pl. UB7: W Dray	.3A **92**
Rowlls Rd. KT1: King T	.3F **151**
Rowney Gdns. RM9: Dag	.6C **72**
Rowney Rd. RM9: Dag	.6B **72**
Rowntree Clifford Cl. E13	.4J **87**
Rowntree Cl. NW6	.6J **63**
Rowntree M. E17	.1B **50**
Rowntree Path SE28	.1B **108**
Rowntree Rd. TW2: Twick	.1J **131**
Rowse Cl. E15	.1E **86**
Rowsley Av. NW4	.3E **44**
Rowstock Gdns. N7	.5H **65**
Rowton Rd. SE18	.7G **107**
Roxborough Av. HA1: Harr	.7H **41**
TW7: Isle	.7K **95**
Roxborough Hgts. HA1: Harr	.6J **41**
(off College Rd.)	
Roxborough Pk. HA1: Harr	.7J **41**
Roxborough Rd. HA1: Harr	.5H **41**
Roxbourne Cl. UB5: N'olt	.6B **58**
Roxbourne Pk. Miniature Railway	.2B **58**

Roxburghe Mans. W8 . . . . . 2K 99
(off Kensington Ct.)
Roxburgh Pl. BR1: Brom 1C 160
Roxburgh Rd. SE27 . . . . . 5B 138
Roxburn Way HA4: Ruis 3H 57
ROXETH 2H 59
Roxeth Ct. TW15: Ashf 5C 128
Roxeth Grn. Av. HA2: Harr 3F 59
UB5: N'olt 5E 58
Roxeth Gro. HA2: Harr 4F 59
Roxeth Hill HA2: Harr 2H 59
Roxford Cl. TW17: Shep 5G 147
Roxford Ho. E3 . . . . . 4D 86
(off Devas St.)
Roxley Rd. SE13 . . . . . 6D 122
Roxton Gdns. CR0: Addtn 5C 170
Roxwell NW1 . . . . . 6F 65
(off Hartland Rd.)
Roxwell Rd. IG11: Bark 2A 90
W12 . . . . . 2C 98
Roxwell Trad. Pk. E10 . . . . . 7A 50
Roxwell Way IG8: Wfd G 7F 37
Roxy Av. RM6: Chad H 7C 54
Royal Academy of Arts (Burlington House)
. . . . . 3A 12 (7G 83)
Royal Academy of Music Mus. 4H 5
Royal Air Force Memorial 1J 101
Royal Albert Hall 7A 10 (2B 100)
ROYAL ALBERT RDBT. 7C 88
(off Royal Albert Way)
Royal Albert Way E16 . . . . . 7B 88
Royal Arc. W1 . . . . . 3A 12
Royal Archer SE14 . . . . . 7K 103
(off Egmont St.)
ROYAL ARSENAL WEST 3F 107
Royal Av. KT4: Wor Pk 2A 164
SW3 . . . . . 5E 16 (5D 100)
Royal Av. Ho. SW3 . . . . . 5E 16
(off Royal Av.)
Royal Ballet School 6J 83
Royal Belgrave Ho. SW1 . . . . . 4K 17
(off Hugh St.)
Royal Blackheath Golf Course 7D 124
Royal Botanic Gdns.
Kew 1E 114
Royal Brass Foundry 3F 107
Royal Carriage M. SE18 . . . . . 3F 107
Royal Cir. SE27 . . . . . 3A 138
Royal Cl. BR6: Farnb 4F 173
IG3: Ilf 7A 54
KT4: Wor Pk 2A 164
N16 . . . . . 1E 66
SE8 . . . . . 6B 104
SW19 . . . . . 3F 135
UB8: Hil 6B 74
Royal College of Art 7A 10 (2B 100)
Royal College of Music 1A 16 (3B 100)
Royal College of Obstetricians &
Gynaecologists 3E 4 (4D 82)
Royal College of Physicians 3K 5
Royal College of Physicians Mus.
. . . . . 3K 5 (4F 83)
Royal College of Surgeons 7H 7
Royal Coll. St. NW1 . . . . . 7G 65
Royal Connaught Apartments E16 . . . . 1B 106
(off Connaught Rd.)
Royal Ct. EC3 . . . . . 1F 15
(off Cornhill)
EN1: Enf 6K 23
HA4: Ruis 6J 39
SE9 . . . . . 1D 142
SE16 . . . . . 3B 104
Royal Courts of Justice 1H 13
Royal Court Theatre 4G 17
(off Sloane Sq.)
Royal Cres. HA4: Ruis 4C 58
IG2: Ilf 6H 53
W11 . . . . . 1F 99
Royal Cres. M. W11 . . . . . 1F 99
Royal Docks Rd. E6 . . . . . 6F 89
IG11: Bark 6F 89

Royal Dr. N11 . . . . . 5K 31
(not continuous)
Royal Duchess M. SW12 . . . . . 7F 119
Royale Leisure Pk. W3 . . . . . 4G 79
Royal Engineers Way NW7 . . . . . 6B 30
Royal Epping Forest & Chingford Golf Course
. . . . . 6K 25
Royal Exchange 1F 15 (6D 84)
Royal Exchange Av. EC3 . . . . . 1F 15
Royal Exchange Bldgs. EC3 . . . . . 1F 15
Royal Festival Hall 5H 13 (1K 101)
Royal Fusiliers Mus. 7F 85
Royal Gdns. W7 . . . . . 3A 96
Royal Geographical Society 7B 10
Royal George M. SE5 . . . . . 4D 120
Royal Herbert Pavilions SE18 . . . . . 1D 124
Royal Hill SE10 . . . . . 7E 104
Royal Hill Ct. SE10 . . . . . 7E 104
(off Greenwich High St.)
Royal Holloway (University of London)
Gower Street 5D 6
Royal Hospital Chelsea Mus.
. . . . . 6G 17 (5E 100)
Royal Hospital Rd. SW3 . . . . . 7E 16 (6D 100)
Royal Institution Mus. 3A 12 (7G 83)
Royal La. UB7: Yiew 5B 74
UB8: Hil 5B 74
Royal Langford Apartments NW6 . . . . . 2K 81
(off Greville Rd.)
Royal London Bldgs. SE15 . . . . . 6H 103
(off Old Kent Rd.)
Royal London Est., The N17 . . . . . 6C 34
Royal London Hospital Archives & Mus.
. . . . . 5H 85
(off Newark St.)
Royal London Ind. Est. NW10 . . . . . 2K 79
Royal Mews, The 1K 17 (2F 101)
Royal M. KT8: E Mos 3J 149
SW1 . . . . . 1K 17 (3F 101)
Royal Mid-Surrey Golf Course 3D 114
Royal Mint Ct. EC3 . . . . . 3K 15 (7F 85)
Royal Mint Pl. E1 . . . . . 2K 15 (7G 85)
Royal Mint St. E1 . . . . . 2K 15 (7G 85)
Royal Naval Pl. SE14 . . . . . 7B 104
Royal Oak Ct. N1 . . . . . 1G 9
(off Pitfield St.)
Royal Oak M. TW11: Tedd 5A 132
Royal Oak Pl. SE22 . . . . . 6H 121
Royal Oak Rd. DA6: Bex 5F 127
(not continuous)
E8 . . . . . 6H 67
Royal Oak Yd. SE1 . . . . . 7G 15 (2E 102)
Royal Observatory Greenwich 7G 105
Royal Opera Arc. SW1 . . . . . 4C 12 (1H 101)
Royal Opera House 1F 13 (6J 83)
Royal Orchard Cl. SW18 . . . . . 7G 117
Royal Pde. BR7: Chst 7G 143
RM10: Dag 6H 73
SE3 . . . . . 2H 123
SW6 . . . . . 7G 99
TW9: Kew 1G 115
(off Station App.)
W5 . . . . . 3E 78
Royal Pde. M. BR7: Chst 7G 143
(off Royal Pde.)
SE3 . . . . . 2H 123
(off Royal Pde.)
Royal Pl. SE10 . . . . . 7E 104
Royal Quarter KT2: King T 1E 150
Royal Quay Rd. E16 . . . . . 7F 89
Royal Rd. DA14: Sidc 3D 144
E16 . . . . . 6B 88
SE17 . . . . . 6B 102
TW11: Tedd 5H 131
Royal Route HA9: Wemb 4F 61
Royal St. SE1 . . . . . 1H 19 (3K 101)
Royal Twr. Lodge E1 . . . . . 3K 15
(off Cartwright St.)
Royalty Mans. W1 . . . . . 1C 12
(off Meard St.)
Royalty M. W1 . . . . . 1C 12 (6H 83)

Royalty Studios W11 . . . . . 6G 81
(off Lancaster Rd.)
Royal Veterinary College
Camden Town 1H 83
Royal Victoria Docks Watersports Cen.
. . . . . 7J 87
Royal Victoria Gdns. SE16 . . . . . 4A 104
(off Whiting Way)
Royal Victoria Patriotic Bldg.
SW18 . . . . . 6B 118
Royal Victoria Pl. E16 . . . . . 1K 105
Royal Victoria Sq. E16 . . . . . 7K 87
Royal Victor Pl. E3 . . . . . 2K 85
Royal Wlk. SM6: Wall 2F 167
Royal Westminster Lodge SW1 . . . . . 3C 18
(off Elverton St.)
Royal Wimbledon Golf Course 5D 134
Roycraft Av. IG11: Bark 2K 89
Roycroft Av. IG11: Bark 2K 89
Roycroft Cl. E18 . . . . . 1K 51
SW2 . . . . . 1A 138
Roydene Rd. SE18 . . . . . 6J 107
Roydon Cl. IG10: Lough 1H 37
SW11 . . . . . 2D 118
(off Battersea Pk. Rd.)
Roy Gdns. IG2: Ilf 4J 53
Roy Gro. TW12: Hamp 6F 131
Royle Bldg. N1 . . . . . 2C 84
(off Wenlock Rd.)
Royle Cres. W13 . . . . . 4A 78
Royley Ho. EC1 . . . . . 3D 8
(off Old St.)
Roymount Ct. TW2: Twick 3J 131
Roy Rd. HA6: Nwood 1H 39
Roy Sq. E14 . . . . . 7A 86
Royston Av. E4 . . . . . 5H 35
SM1: Sutt 3B 166
SM6: Bedd 4H 167
Royston Cl. KT12: Walt T 7J 147
TW5: Cran 1K 111
Royston Ct. E13 . . . . . 1J 87
(off Stopford Rd.)
SE24 . . . . . 6C 120
TW9: Kew 1F 115
W8 . . . . . 1J 99
(off Kensington Chu. St.)
Royston Gdns. IG1: Ilf 6B 52
Royston Ho. N11 . . . . . 4J 31
SE15 . . . . . 6H 103
(off Friary Est.)
Royston Pde. IG1: Ilf 6B 52
Royston Pk. Rd. HA5: Hat E 5A 26
Royston Rd. SE20 . . . . . 1K 157
TW10: Rich 5E 114
Roystons, The KT5: Surb 5H 151
Royston St. E2 . . . . . 2J 85
Rozel Ct. N1 . . . . . 1E 84
Rozel Rd. SW4 . . . . . 3G 119
Rozel Ter. CR0: C'don 3C 168
(off Church Rd.)
RQ33 SW18 . . . . . 4J 117
Rubastic Rd. UB2: S'hall 3A 94
Rubens Gdns. SE22 . . . . . 7G 121
(off Lordship La.)
Rubens Pl. SW4 . . . . . 4J 119
Rubens Rd. UB5: N'olt 2A 76
Rubens St. SE6 . . . . . 2B 140
Rubicon Ct. N1 . . . . . 1J 83
Ruby Cl. E5 . . . . . 3K 67
Ruby Ct. E15 . . . . . 1E 86
(off Warton Rd.)
RM8: Dag 1G 73
(off Emerald Gdns.)
Ruby Rd. E17 . . . . . 3C 50
Ruby St. NW10 . . . . . 7J 61
SE15 . . . . . 6H 103
Ruby Triangle SE15 . . . . . 6H 103
Ruby Way NW9 . . . . . 1B 44
Ruckholt Cl. E10 . . . . . 3D 68
Ruckholt Rd. E10 . . . . . 4C 68
Rucklidge Av. NW10 . . . . . 2B 80

Rucklidge Pas. NW10 . . . . . 2B 80
(off Rucklidge Av.)
Rudall Cres. NW3 . . . . . 4B 64
Rudbeck Ho. SE15 . . . . . 7G 103
(off Peckham Pk. Rd.)
Ruddington Cl. E5 . . . . . 4A 68
Ruddock Cl. HA8: Edg 7D 28
Ruddstreet Cl. SE18 . . . . . 4F 107
Ruddy Way NW7 . . . . . 6G 29
Rudge Ho. SE16 . . . . . 3G 103
(off Jamaica Rd.)
Rudgwick Ct. SE18 . . . . . 4C 106
(off Woodville St.)
Rudgwick Ter. NW8 . . . . . 1C 82
Rudland Rd. DA7: Bex 3H 127
Rudloe Rd. SW12 . . . . . 7G 119
Rudolf Pl. SW8 . . . . . 7F 19 (6J 101)
Rudolph Rd. E13 . . . . . 2H 87
NW6 . . . . . 2J 81
Rudstone Ho. E3 . . . . . 3D 86
(off Bromley High St.)
Rudyard Ct. SE1 . . . . . 7F 15
(off Long La.)
Rudyard Gro. NW7 . . . . . 6D 28
Ruegg Ho. SE18 . . . . . 6E 106
(off Woolwich Comn.)
Ruffetts, The CR2: Sels 7H 169
Ruffetts Cl. CR2: Sels 7H 169
Ruffle Cl. UB7: W Dray 2A 92
Rufford Cl. HA3: Kenton 6A 42
Rufford St. N1 . . . . . 1J 83
Rufford St. M. N1 . . . . . 7J 65
Rufford Twr. W3 . . . . . 1H 97
Rufforth Ct. NW9 . . . . . 1A 44
(off Pageant Av.)
Rufus Bus. Cen. SW18 . . . . . 2K 135
Rufus Cl. HA4: Ruis 3C 58
Rufus Ho. SE1 . . . . . 7K 15
(off St Saviour's Est.)
Rufus St. N1 . . . . . 2G 9 (3E 84)
Rugby Av. HA0: Wemb 5B 60
N9 . . . . . 1A 34
UB6: G'frd 6H 59
Rugby Cl. HA1: Harr 4J 41
Rugby Gdns. RM9: Dag 6C 72
Rugby Mans. W14 . . . . . 4G 99
(off Bishop King's Rd.)
Rugby Rd. NW9 . . . . . 4H 43
RM9: Dag 7B 72
TW1: Twick 5J 113
W4 . . . . . 2A 98
Rugby St. WC1 . . . . . 4G 7 (4K 83)
Rugg St. E14 . . . . . 7C 86
Rugless Ho. E14 . . . . . 2E 104
(off E. Ferry Rd.)
Rugmere NW1 . . . . . 7E 64
(off Ferdinand St.)
RUISLIP 1G 57
Ruislip Cl. UB6: G'frd 4F 77
RUISLIP COMMON 4E 38
Ruislip Ct. HA4: Ruis 2H 57
RUISLIP GARDENS 3J 57
Ruislip Golf Course 2E 56
Ruislip Lido 4F 39
Ruislip Lido Railway 4F 39
Ruislip Lido Woodlands Cen. 4F 39
RUISLIP MANOR 2J 57
Ruislip Rd. UB5: N'olt 1A 76
UB6: G'frd 3E 76
Ruislip Rd. E. UB6: G'frd 4H 77
W7 . . . . . 4J 77
W13 . . . . . 4H 77
Ruislip St. SW17 . . . . . 4D 136
Ruislip Woods (National Nature Reserve)
. . . . . 3E 38
Rumball Ho. SE5 . . . . . 7E 102
(off Harris St.)
Rumbold Rd. SW6 . . . . . 7K 99
Rum Cl. E1 . . . . . 7J 85
Rumford Ho. SE1 . . . . . 3C 102
(off Tiverton St.)

Rumney Ct. *UB5: N'olt* *2B 76*
(off Parkfield Dr.)
Rumsey Cl. TW12: Hamp 6D 130
Rumsey M. N4 . . . . 3B 66
Rumsey Rd. SW9 . . . . 3K 119
Runacres Ct. SE17 . . . . 5C 102
Runbury Circ. NW9 . . . . 2K 61
Runcie Ct. IG6: Ilf 4H 53
Runcorn Cl. N17 . . . . 4H 49
Runcorn Pl. W11 . . . . 7G 81
Rundell Cres. NW4 . . . . 5D 44
Rundell Twr. SW8 . . . . 1K 119
Runes Cl. CR4: Mitc 4B 154
Runnel Ct. *IG11: Bark* *2G 89*
(off Spring Pl.)
Runnelfield HA1: Harr 3J 59
Running Horse Yd. TW8: Bford 6E 96
Runnymede SW19 . . . . 1A 154
Runnymede Cl. TW2: Whitt 6F 113
Runnymede Ct. SM6: Wall 6F 167
SW15 . . . . 1C 134
Runnymede Cres. SW16 . . . . 1H 155
Runnymede Gdns. TW2: Whitt 6F 113
UB6: G'frd 2J 77
Runnymede Ho. E9 . . . . 4A 68
Runnymede Rd. TW2: Whitt 6F 113
Runway, The HA4: Ruis 5K 57
Runway Cl. NW9 . . . . 2B 44
Rupack St. SE16 . . . . 2J 103
Rupert Av. HA9: Wemb 5E 60
Rupert Ct. *KT8: W Mole* *4E 148*
(off St Peter's Rd.)
W1 . . . . 2C 12 (7H 83)
Rupert Gdns. SW9 . . . . 2B 120
Rupert Ho. SE11 . . . . 4K 19 (4A 102)
SW5 . . . . *4J 99*
(off Nevern Sq.)
Rupert Rd. N19 . . . . 3H 65
(not continuous)
NW6 . . . . 2H 81
W4 . . . . 3A 98
Rupert St. W1 . . . . 2C 12 (7H 83)
Rural Way SW16 . . . . 7F 137
Rusbridge Cl. E8 . . . . 5G 67
Ruscoe Rd. E16 . . . . 6H 87
Ruscombe *NW1* *1F 83*
(off Delancey St.)
Ruscombe Way TW14: Felt 7H 111
Ruscus Rd. E17 . . . . 1C 50
Rush, The *SW19* *1H 153*
(off Watery La.)
Rusham Rd. SW12 . . . . 6D 118
Rushbridge Cl. CR0: C'don 6C 156
Rushbrook Cres. E17 . . . . 1B 50
Rushbrook Rd. SE9 . . . . 2G 143
Rushbury Ct. TW12: Hamp 1E 148
Rush Comn. M. SW2 . . . . 7K 119
Rushcroft Rd. E4 . . . . 7J 35
SW2 . . . . 4A 120
Rushcutters Ct. *SE16* *4A 104*
(off Boat Lifter Way)
Rushden Cl. SE19 . . . . 7D 138
Rushdene SE2 . . . . 3D 108
(not continuous)
Rushdene Av. EN4: E Barn 7H 21
Rushdene Cl. UB5: N'olt 2A 76
Rushdene Cres. UB5: N'olt 2K 75
Rushdene Rd. HA5: Eastc 6B 40
Rushden Gdns. IG5: Ilf 2E 52
NW7 . . . . 6K 29
Rushen Wlk. SM5: Cars 1B 166
Rushett Cl. KT7: T Ditt 1B 162
Rushett Rd. KT7: T Ditt 7B 150
Rushey Cl. KT3: N Mald 4K 151
Rushey Grn. SE6 . . . . 7D 122
Rushey Hill EN2: Enf 4E 22
Rushey Mead SE4 . . . . 5C 122
Rushford Rd. SE4 . . . . 6B 122
RUSH GREEN 1K 73
Rush Grn. Gdns. RM7: Rush G 1J 73
Rush Grn. Rd. RM7: Rush G 1H 73
Rushgrove Av. NW9 . . . . 5A 44
Rushgrove Ct. NW9 . . . . 5A 44
Rushgrove Pde. NW9 . . . . 5A 44
Rushgrove St. SE18 . . . . 4D 106
Rush Hill M. *SW11* *3E 118*
(off Rush Hill Rd.)
Rush Hill Rd. SW11 . . . . 3E 118
Rushley Cl. BR2: Kes 4B 172
Rushmead E2 . . . . 3H 85
TW10: Ham 3B 132
Rushmead Cl. CR0: C'don 4F 169
HA8: Edg 2C 28
Rushmere Ct. KT4: Wor Pk 2C 164
Rushmere Pl. SW19 . . . . 5F 135
Rushmon Pl. SM3: Cheam 6G 165
Rushmon Vs. KT3: N Mald 4B 152
Rushmoor Cl. HA5: Eastc 4K 39
Rushmore Cl. BR1: Brom 3C 160
Rushmore Cres. E5 . . . . 4K 67
Rushmore Ho. SW15 . . . . 7C 116
W14 . . . . *3G 99*
(off Russell Rd.)
Rushmore Rd. E5 . . . . 4J 67
(not continuous)
Rusholme Av. RM10: Dag 3G 73
Rusholme Gro. SE19 . . . . 5E 138
Rusholme Rd. SW15 . . . . 6F 117
Rushout Av. HA3: Kenton 6B 42
Rushton Ho. SW8 . . . . 2H 119
Rushton St. N1 . . . . 2D 84
Rushton Wlk. *E3* *4B 86*
(off Hamlets Way)
Rushworth St. SE1 . . . . 6B 14 (2B 102)
Rushy Mdw. La.
SM5: Cars 2C 166
Ruskin Av. DA16: Well 2A 126
E12 . . . . 6C 70
TW9: Kew 7G 97
TW14: Felt 6H 111
Ruskin Cl. NW11 . . . . 6K 45
Ruskin Ct. N21 . . . . 7E 22
SE5 . . . . *3D 120*
(off Champion Hill)
Ruskin Dr. BR6: Orp 3J 173
DA16: Well 3A 126
KT4: Wor Pk 2D 164
Ruskin Gdns. HA3: Kenton 5F 43
W5 . . . . 4D 78
Ruskin Gro. DA16: Well 2A 126
Ruskin Ho. *CR2: S Croy* *5D 168*
(off Selsdon Rd.)
SW1 . . . . *4D 18*
(off Herrick St.)
Ruskin Mans. *W14* *6G 99*
(off Queen's Club Gdns.)
Ruskin Pde. *CR2: S Croy* *5D 168*
(off Selsdon Rd.)
HA8: Edg 4A 28
Ruskin Pk. Ho. SE5 . . . . 3D 120
Ruskin Rd. CR0: C'don 2B 168
DA17: Belv 4G 109
N17 . . . . 1F 49
SM5: Cars 5D 166
TW7: Isle 3K 113
UB1: S'hall 7C 76
Ruskin Sq. CR0: C'don 2D 168
Ruskin Wlk. BR2: Brom 6D 160
N9 . . . . 2B 34
SE24 . . . . 5C 120
Ruskin Way SW19 . . . . 1B 154
Rusland Av. BR6: Orp 3H 173
Rusland Hgts. HA1: Harr 4J 41
Rusland Pk. Rd. HA1: Harr 4J 41
Rusper Cl. HA7: Stan 4H 27
NW2 . . . . 3E 62
Rusper Ct. *SW9* *2J 119*
(off Clapham Rd.)
Rusper Rd. N17 . . . . 3C 48
N22 . . . . 2B 48
RM9: Dag 6C 72
Russell Av. N22 . . . . 2A 48
Russell Chambers *WC1* *6F 7*
(off Bury Pl.)
Russell Cl. BR3: Beck 3E 158
DA7: Bex 4G 127
HA4: Ruis 2A 58
NW10 . . . . 7J 61
SE7 . . . . 7A 106
W4 . . . . 6B 98
Russell Ct. E10 . . . . 7D 50
EN5: New Bar 4F 21
N14 . . . . 6C 22
SE15 . . . . *2H 121*
(off Heaton Rd.)
SM6: Wall *5G 167*
(off Ross Rd.)
SW1 . . . . 5B 12
SW16 . . . . 5K 137
WC1 . . . . 4E 6
Russell Flint Ho. *E16* *1K 105*
(off Pankhurst Av.)
Russell Gdns. IG2: Ilf 7H 53
N20 . . . . 2H 31
NW11 . . . . 6G 45
TW10: Ham 2C 132
UB7: Sip 5C 92
W14 . . . . 3G 99
Russell Gdns. M. W14 . . . . 2G 99
Russell Gro. NW7 . . . . 5F 29
SW9 . . . . 7A 102
Russell Ho. *BR2: Brom* *6C 160*
(off Wells Vw. Dr.)
E14 . . . . *6C 86*
(off Saracen St.)
SW1 . . . . *5A 18*
(off Cambridge St.)
Russell Kerr Cl. W4 . . . . 7J 97
Russell La. N20 . . . . 2H 31
Russell Lodge E4 . . . . 2K 35
SE1 . . . . *3D 102*
(off Spurgeon St.)
Russell Mans. *WC1* *5F 7*
(off Southampton Row)
Russell Mead HA3: Hrw W 1K 41
Russell Pde. *NW11* *6G 45*
(off Golders Grn. Rd.)
Russell Pl. NW3 . . . . 5C 64
SE16 . . . . 3A 104
SM2: Sutt 7K 165
Russell Rd. CR4: Mitc 3C 154
E4 . . . . 4G 35
E10 . . . . 6D 50
E16 . . . . 6J 87
E17 . . . . 3B 50
EN1: Enf 1A 24
IG9: Buck H 1E 36
KT12: Walt T 6J 147
N8 . . . . 6H 47
N13 . . . . 6E 32
N15 . . . . 5E 48
N20 . . . . 2H 31
NW9 . . . . 6B 44
SW19 . . . . 7J 135
TW2: Twick 6K 113
TW17: Shep 7E 146
UB5: N'olt 5G 59
W14 . . . . 3G 99
Russell's Footpath SW16 . . . . 5J 137
Russell Sq. WC1 . . . . 4E 6 (5J 83)
Russell Sq. Mans. *WC1* *5F 7*
(off Southampton Row)
Russell St. WC2 . . . . 2F 13 (7J 83)
Russell's Wharf Flats W10 . . . . 4H 81
Russell Wlk. TW10: Rich 6F 115
Russell Way SM1: Sutt 5K 165
Russell Yd. SW15 . . . . 4G 117
Russet Av. TW17: Shep 3G 147
Russet Cl. UB10: Hil 4E 74
Russet Cres. N7 . . . . 5K 65
Russet Dr. CR0: C'don 1A 170
Russets Cl. E4 . . . . 4A 36
Russett Way SE13 . . . . 2D 122
Russia Dock Rd. SE16 . . . . 1A 104
Russia La. E2 . . . . 2J 85
Russia Row EC2 . . . . 1D 14 (6C 84)
Russia Wlk. SE16 . . . . 2A 104
Russington Rd. TW17: Shep 6F 147
Rusthall Av. W4 . . . . 4K 97
Rusthall Cl. CR0: C'don 6J 157
Rustic Av. SW16 . . . . 7F 137
Rustic Pl. HA0: Wemb 4D 60
Rustic Wlk. *E16* *6K 87*
(off Lambert Rd.)
Rustington Wlk. SM4: Mord 7H 153
Ruston Av. KT5: Surb 7H 151
Ruston Gdns. N14 . . . . 6K 21
Ruston M. W11 . . . . 6G 81
Ruston Rd. SE18 . . . . 3C 106
Ruston St. E3 . . . . 1B 86
Rust Sq. SE5 . . . . 7D 102
Rutford Rd. SW16 . . . . 5J 137
Ruth Cl. HA7: Stan 4F 43
Ruth Ct. E3 . . . . 2A 86
Rutherford Cl. SM2: Sutt 6B 166
UB8: Hil 4B 74
Rutherford Ho. *E1* *4H 85*
(off Brady St.)
HA9: Wemb *3J 61*
(off Barnhill Rd.)
SW11 . . . . *2D 118*
(off Battersea Pk. Rd.)
Rutherford St. SW1 . . . . 3C 18 (4H 101)
Rutherford Twr. UB1: S'hall 6F 77
Rutherford Way HA9: Wemb 4G 61
WD23: B Hea 1C 26
Rutherglen Rd. SE2 . . . . 6A 108
Rutherwyke Cl. KT17: Ewe 6C 164
Ruth Ho. *W10* *4G 81*
(off Kensal Rd.)
Ruthin Cl. NW9 . . . . 6A 44
Ruthin Rd. SE3 . . . . 6J 105
Ruthven St. E9 . . . . 1K 85
Rutland Av. DA15: Sidc 7A 126
Rutland Cl. DA5: Bexl 2D 144
KT9: Chess 6F 163
SW14 . . . . 3H 115
SW19 . . . . 7C 136
Rutland Ct. BR7: Chst 1E 160
EN3: Pond E 5C 24
KT1: King T *4D 150*
(off Palace Rd.)
SE5 . . . . 4D 120
SE9 . . . . 2G 143
SW7 . . . . 7D 10
W3 . . . . 6G 79
Rutland Dr. SM4: Mord 6H 153
TW10: Ham 1D 132
Rutland Gdns. CR0: C'don 4E 168
N4 . . . . 6B 48
RM8: Dag 5C 72
SW7 . . . . 7D 10 (2C 100)
W13 . . . . 5A 78
Rutland Gdns. M. SW7 . . . . 7D 10 (2C 100)
Rutland Ga. BR2: Brom 4H 159
DA17: Belv 5H 109
SW7 . . . . 7D 10 (2C 100)
Rutland Ga. M. SW7 . . . . 7C 10
Rutland Gro. W6 . . . . 5D 98
Rutland Ho. *UB5: N'olt* *6E 58*
(off The Farmlands)
W8 . . . . *3K 99*
(off Marloes Rd.)
Rutland M. NW8 . . . . 1K 81
Rutland M. E. SW7 . . . . 1C 16
Rutland M. Sth. SW7 . . . . 1C 16
Rutland M. W. SW7 . . . . 1C 16
Rutland Pk. NW2 . . . . 6E 62
SE6 . . . . 2B 140
Rutland Pk. Gdns. *NW2* *6E 62*
(off Rutland Pk.)
Rutland Pk. Mans. NW2 . . . . 6E 62
Rutland Pl. EC1 . . . . 5B 8 (4B 84)
WD23: B Hea 1C 26

Rutland Rd. E7 7B **70**
E9 1K **85**
E11 5K **51**
E17 6C **50**
HA1: Harr 6G **41**
IG1: Ilf 3F **71**
SW19 7C **136**
TW2: Twick 2H **131**
UB1: S'hall 5E **76**
UB3: Harl 4F **93**
Rutland St. SW7 1D **16** (3C **100**)
Rutland Wlk. SE6 2B **140**
Rutley Cl. SE17 6B **102**
Rutlish Rd. SW19 1J **153**
Rutter Gdns. CR4: Mitc 4A **154**
Rutters Cl. UB7: W Dray 2C **92**
Rutts, The WD23: B Hea 1C **26**
Rutt's Ter. SE14 1K **121**
Ruvigny Gdns. SW15 3F **117**
Ruxbury Ct. TW15: Ashf 3A **128**
RUXLEY 7D **144**
Ruxley Cl. DA14: Sidc 6D **144**
KT19: Ewe 5H **163**
Ruxley Cnr. Ind. Est. DA14: Sidc 6D **144**
Ruxley Ct. KT19: Ewe 5J **163**
Ruxley Cres. KT10: Clay 6B **162**
Ruxley Gdns. TW17: Shep 5E **146**
Ruxley La. KT19: Ewe 6H **163**
Ruxley M. KT19: Ewe 5H **163**
Ruxley Pk. Golf Course 7D **144**
Ruxley Ridge KT10: Clay 7A **162**
Ruxley Towers KT10: Clay 7A **162**
Ryalls Ct. N20 3J **31**
Ryan Cl. HA4: Ruis 1K **57**
SE3 4A **124**
Ryan Ct. RM7: Rom 6J **55**
SW16 7J **137**
Ryan Dr. TW8: Bford 6A **96**
Ryarsh Cres. BR6: Orp 4J **173**
Rycott Path SE22 7G **121**
Rycroft Way N17 3F **49**
Ryculff Sq. SE3 2H **123**
Rydal Cl. NW4 1G **45**
Rydal Ct. HA8: Edg 5A **28**
HA9: Wemb 7F **43**
Rydal Cres. UB6: G'frd 3B **78**
Rydal Dr. BR4: W W'ck 2G **171**
DA7: Bex 1G **127**
Rydal Gdns. HA9: Wemb 1C **60**
NW9 5A **44**
SW15 5A **134**
TW3: Houn 6F **113**
Rydal Mt. BR2: Brom 4H **159**
Rydal Rd. SW16 4H **137**
Rydal Water NW1 2A **6** (3G **83**)
Rydal Way EN3: Pond E 6D **24**
HA4: Ruis 4A **58**
Ryde Ho. *NW6* *1J* ***81***
(off Priory Pk. Rd.)
Rydens Ho. SE9 3A **142**
Rydens Rd. KT12: Walt T 7C **148**
Ryde Pl. TW1: Twick 6D **114**
Ryder Av. E10 7D **50**
Ryder Cl. BR1: Brom 5K **141**
Ryder Ct. E10 2D **68**
SW1 4B **12**
Ryder Dr. SE16 5H **103**
Ryder Ho. *E1* *4J* ***85***
(off Colebert Av.)
Ryder M. E9 5J **67**
Ryder's Ter. NW8 2A **82**
Ryder St. SW1 4B **12** (1G **101**)
Ryder Yd. SW1 4B **12** (1G **101**)
Ryde Va. Rd. SW12 2G **137**
Rydon M. SW19 7E **134**
Rydons Cl. SE9 3C **124**
Rydon St. N1 1C **84**
Rydston Cl. N7 7J **65**
Rye, The N14 7C **22**
Rye Cl. DA5: Bexl 6H **127**
Ryecotes Mead SE21 1E **138**
Ryecroft Av. IG5: Ilf 2F **53**
TW2: Whitt 7F **113**
Ryecroft Rd. BR5: Pet W 6H **161**
SE13 5E **122**
SW16 6A **138**
Ryecroft St. SW6 1K **117**
Ryedale SE22 6H **121**
Ryefield Av. UB10: Hil 7D **56**
Ryefield Ct. HA6: Nwood 2J **39**
Ryefield Cres. HA6: Nwood 2J **39**
Ryefield Pde. *HA6: Nwood* *2J* ***39***
(off Joel St.)
Ryefield Path SW15 1C **134**
Ryefield Rd. SE19 6C **138**
Ryegates *SE15* *2H* ***121***
(off Caulfield Rd.)
Rye Hill Pk. SE15 4J **121**
Rye Ho. *SE16* *2J* ***103***
(off Swan Rd.)
SW1 *5J* ***17***
(off Ebury Bri. Rd.)
Ryeland Cl. UB7: Yiew 6A **74**
Ryelands Cres. SE12 6A **124**
Rye La. SE15 1G **121**
Rye Mans. *E20* *5E* ***68***
(off Napa Cl.)
Rye Pas. SE15 3G **121**
Rye Rd. SE15 4K **121**
Rye Wlk. SW15 5F **117**
Rye Way HA8: Edg 6A **28**
Ryfold Rd. SW19 3J **135**
Ryhope Rd. N11 4A **32**
Ryland Cl. TW13: Felt 4H **129**
Rylandes Rd. NW2 3C **62**
Ryland Rd. NW5 6F **65**
Rylett Cres. W12 2B **98**
Rylett Rd. W12 2B **98**
Rylston Rd. N13 3J **33**
SW6 6H **99**
Rymer Rd. CR0: C'don 7E **156**
Rymer St. SE24 6B **120**
Rymill St. E16 1E **106**
Rysbrack St. SW3 1E **16** (3D **100**)
Rythe Bank Cl. KT7: T Ditt 7B **150**
Rythe Cl. KT9: Chess 7C **162**
Rythe Ct. KT7: T Ditt 7A **150**

S

Saatchi Gallery 5F **17** (5D **100**)
Sabah Ct. TW15: Ashf 4C **128**
Sabella Ct. E3 2B **86**
Sabine Rd. SW11 3D **118**
Sable Cl. TW4: Houn 3A **112**
Sable Ho. *E20* *5D* ***68***
(off Scarlet Cl.)
Sable St. N1 7B **66**
Sach Rd. E5 2H **67**
Sackville Av. BR2: Hayes 1J **171**
Sackville Cl. HA2: Harr 3H **59**
Sackville Gdns. IG1: Ilf 1D **70**
Sackville Ho. SW16 3J **137**
Sackville Rd. SM2: Sutt 7J **165**
Sackville St. W1 3B **12** (7G **83**)
Saddleback La. W7 3J **95**
Saddlebrook Pk.
TW16: Sun 7G **129**
Saddle M. CR0: C'don 7C **156**
Saddlers Cl. HA5: Hat E 6A **26**
Saddlers Ho. *E20* *5E* ***68***
(off Ribbons Wlk.)
Saddlers M. HA0: Wemb 4K **59**
KT1: Hamp W 1C **150**
SW8 1J **119**
Saddlers Pl. TW3: Houn 3G **113**
Saddlescombe Way N12 5D **30**
Saddle Yd. W1 4J **11** (1F **101**)
Sadler Cl. CR4: Mitc 2D **154**
Sadler Hgts. *N1* *7K* ***65***
(off Caledonian Rd.)
Sadler Ho. *E3* *3D* ***86***
(off Bromley High St.)
EC1 *1K* ***7***
(off Spa Grn. Est.)
Sadler Pl. E9 5A **68**
Sadlers Ct. SE1 7G **15**
Sadlers Ga. M. SW15 3E **116**
Sadlers Ride KT8: W Mole 2G **149**
Sadler's Wells Theatre 1K **7** (3A **84**)
Safara Ho. *SE5* *1E* ***120***
(off Dalwood St.)
Saffron Av. E14 7F **87**
Saffron Central Sq. CR0: C'don 1C **168**
Saffron Cl. CR0: C'don 6J **155**
NW11 6H **45**
Saffron Ct. *E15* *5G* ***69***
(off Maryland Pk.)
TW14: Bedf 7E **110**
Saffron Hill EC1 5K **7** (5A **84**)
Saffron Ho. SM2: Sutt 7K **165**
TW9: Kew 1H **115**
Saffron M. SW19 7G **135**
Saffron Rd. RM5: Col R 2K **55**
Saffron St. EC1 5K **7** (5A **84**)
Saffron Way KT6: Surb 1D **162**
Saffron Wharf *SE1* *6K* ***15***
(off Shad Thames)
Sage Cl. E6 5D **88**
Sage M. SE22 5F **121**
Sage St. E1 7J **85**
Sage Way WC1 2G **7**
Sage Yd. KT6: Surb 1F **163**
Sahara Ct. UB1: S'hall 7C **76**
Saigasso Cl. E16 6B **88**
Sailacre Ho. SE10 5H **105**
Sail Ct. *E14* *7F* ***87***
(off Newport Av.)
Sailmakers Ct. SW6 3A **118**
Sail St. SE11 3H **19** (4K **101**)
Saimet *NW9* *7G* ***29***
(off Wiggins Mead)
Sainfoin Rd. SW17 2E **136**
Sainsbury Rd. SE19 5E **138**
Sainsbury Wing ***3D 12***
(within National Gallery)
St Agatha's Dr. KT2: King T 6F **133**
St Agatha's Gro. SM5: Cars 1D **166**
St Agnes Cl. E9 1J **85**
St Agnes Ho. *E3* *2C* ***86***
(off Ordell Rd.)
St Agnes Pl. SE11 7K **19** (6B **102**)
St Agnes Quad. SE11 6A **102**
St Agnes Well EC1 3F **9**
St Aidans Ct. IG11: Bark 2B **90**
St Aidan's Rd. SE22 6H **121**
W13 2B **96**
St Alban's Av. E6 3D **88**
W4 4K **97**
St Albans Av. TW13: Hanw 5B **130**
St Albans Cl. NW11 1J **63**
St Albans Ct. EC2 6D **8**
St Alban's Cres. IG8: Wfd G 7D **36**
N22 1A **48**
St Albans Farm TW14: Houn 5A **112**
St Alban's Gdns. TW11: Tedd 5A **132**
St Alban's Gro. SM5: Cars 7C **154**
W8 3K **99**
St Alban's La. NW11 1J **63**
St Albans Mans. *W8* *3K* ***99***
(off Kensington Ct. Pl.)
St Albans Pl. N1 1B **84**
St Alban's Rd. IG8: Wfd G 7D **36**
KT2: King T 6E **132**
SM1: Sutt 4H **165**
St Albans Rd. EN5: Barn 1A **20**
IG3: Ilf 1K **71**
NW5 3E **64**
NW10 1A **80**
St Alban's St. SW1 3C **12** (7H **83**)
St Albans Studios *W8* *3K* ***99***
(off St Albans Gro.)
St Albans Ter. W6 6G **99**
St Albans Vs. NW5 3E **64**
St Alfege Pas. SE10 6E **104**
St Alfege Rd. SE7 6B **106**
St Alphage Ct. NW9 3K **43**
St Alphage Gdn. EC2 6D **8** (5C **84**)
St Alphage Highwalk EC2 6D **8**
St Alphage Wlk. HA8: Edg 2J **43**
St Alphege Rd. N9 7D **24**
St Alphonsus Rd. SW4 4G **119**
St Amunds Cl. SE6 4C **140**
St Andrew's Av. HA0: Wemb 4A **60**
St Andrews Chambers *W1* *6B* ***6***
(off Wells St.)
St Andrew's Cl. HA4: Ruis 2B **58**
HA7: Stan 2C **42**
N12 4F **31**
NW2 3D **62**
TW7: Isle 1J **113**
TW17: Shep 4F **147**
St Andrews Cl. KT7: T Ditt 1B **162**
SE16 5H **103**
SE28 6D **90**
SW19 6K **135**
St Andrew's Ct. SW18 2A **136**
St Andrews Ct. E17 2A **50**
SM1: Sutt 3C **166**
St Andrews Dr. HA7: Stan 1C **42**
St Andrew's Gro. N16 1D **66**
St Andrew's Hill EC4 2B **14** (6B **84**)
(not continuous)
St Andrews Ho. RM8: Dag 4A **72**
SE16 *3H* ***103***
(off Southwark Pk. Rd.)
St Andrews Mans. *W1* *6G* ***5***
(off Dorset St.)
W14 *6G* ***99***
(off St Andrew's Rd.)
St Andrew's M. N16 1E **66**
SE3 7J **105**
St Andrews M. SW12 1H **137**
St Andrew's Pl. NW1 3K **5** (4F **83**)
St Andrew's Rd. CR0: C'don 4C **168**
DA14: Sidc 3D **144**
E11 6G **51**
E13 3K **87**
E17 2K **49**
EN1: Enf 3J **23**
IG1: Ilf 7D **52**
KT6: Surb 6D **150**
N9 7D **24**
NW9 1K **61**
NW10 6D **62**
NW11 6H **45**
RM7: Rom 6K **55**
SM5: Cars 3C **166**
UB10: Uxb 1A **74**
W3 7A **80**
W14 6G **99**
St Andrews Rd. W7 2J **95**
St Andrew's Sq. KT6: Surb 6D **150**
St Andrews Sq. W11 6G **81**
St Andrew's Twr. *UB1: S'hall* *7G* ***77***
(off Baird Av.)
St Andrew St. EC4 6K **7** (5A **84**)
St Andrews Way E3 4D **86**
St Andrew's Wharf SE1 2F **103**
St Anna Rd. EN5: Barn 5A **20**
St Anne's Cl. N6 3E **64**
St Anne's Ct.
BR4: W W'ck 4G **171**
NW6 1G **81**
W1 1C **12** (6H **83**)
St Anne's Flats *NW1* *1C* ***6***
(off Doric Way)
St Anne's Gdns. NW10 3F **79**
St Annes M. SW20 7F **135**
St Anne's Pas. E14 6B **86**
St Anne's Rd. E11 2F **69**
HA0: Wemb 5D **60**
St Anne's Row E14 6B **86**

St Anne's Trad. Est.—St George's Rd.

St Anne's Trad. Est. E14 .... 6B 86
(off St Anne's Row)
St Anne St. E14 .... 6B 86
St Ann's IG11: Bark 1G 89
St Ann's Ct. NW4 .... 3D 44
St Ann's Cres. SW18 .... 6K 117
St Ann's Gdns. NW5 .... 6E 64
St Ann's Hill SW18 .... 5K 117
St Ann's Ho. WC1 .... 2J 7
(off Margery St.)
St Ann's La. SW1 .... 2D 18 (3H 101)
St Ann's Pk. Rd. SW18 .... 6A 118
St Ann's Pas. SW13 .... 3A 116
St Ann's Rd. HA1: Harr 6J 41
IG11: Bark 1G 89
N9 .... 2A 34
N15 .... 5B 48
SW13 .... 2B 116
W11 .... 7F 81
St Ann's Shop. Cen. HA1: Harr 6J 41
St Ann's St. SW1 .... 1D 18 (3H 101)
St Ann's Ter. NW8 .... 2B 82
St Ann's Vs. W11 .... 1F 99
St Ann's Way CR2: S Croy 6B 168
St Anselms Ct. SW16 .... 5J 137
St Anselm's Pl. W1 .... 2J 11 (7F 83)
St Anselm's Rd. UB3: Hayes 2H 93
St Anthony's Av. IG8: Wfd G 6F 37
St Anthony's Cl. E1 .... 1G 103
E9 .... 6B 68
(off Wallis Rd.)
SW17 .... 2C 136
St Anthony's Ct. BR6: Farnb 2F 173
SW17 .... 2E 136
St Anthony's Flats NW1 .... 2H 83
(off Aldenham St.)
St Anthony's Way TW14: Felt 4H 111
St Antony's Rd. E7 .... 7K 69
St Arvan's Cl. CR0: C'don 3E 168
St Asaph Rd. SE4 .... 3K 121
St Aubins Ct. N1 .... 1D 84
St Aubyn's Av. SW19 .... 5H 135
TW3: Houn 5E 112
St Aubyn's Cl. BR6: Orp 3K 173
St Aubyn's Gdns. BR6: Orp 2K 173
St Aubyn's Rd. SE19 .... 6F 139
St Audrey Av. DA7: Bex 2G 127
St Augustine's Av. BR2: Brom 5C 160
CR2: S Croy 6C 168
HA9: Wemb 3E 60
W5 .... 2E 78
St Augustine's Ct. SE1 .... 5H 103
(off Lynton Rd.)
St Augustine's Ho. NW1 .... 1C 6
(off Werrington St.)
St Augustine's Mans. SW1 .... 4B 18
(off Bloomburg St.)
St Augustine's Path N5 .... 4C 66
St Augustine's Rd. DA17: Belv 4F 109
NW1 .... 7H 65
St Augustine's Sports Cen. 2J 81
St Austell Cl. HA8: Edg 2F 43
St Austell Rd. SE13 .... 2E 122
St Awdry's Rd. IG11: Bark 7H 71
St Awdry's Wlk. IG11: Bark 7G 71
St Barnabas Cl. BR3: Beck 2E 158
SE22 .... 5E 120
St Barnabas Ct. HA3: Hrw W 1G 41
St Barnabas Gdns. KT8: W Mole 5E 148
St Barnabas M. SW1 .... 5H 17
St Barnabas Rd. CR4: Mitc 7E 136
E17 .... 6C 50
IG8: Wfd G 1K 51
SM1: Sutt 5B 166
St Barnabas St. SW1 .... 5H 17 (5E 100)
St Barnabas Ter. E9 .... 5K 67
St Barnabas Vs. SW8 .... 1J 119
St Bartholomew's Cl. SE26 .... 4H 139
St Bartholomew's Ct. E6 .... 2C 88
(off St Bartholomew's Rd.)
St Bartholomew's Hospital Mus. 6B 8
St Bartholomew's Rd. E6 .... 2D 88
St Benedict's Cl. SW17 .... 5E 136
St Benet's Cl. SW17 .... 2C 136
St Benet's Gro. SM5: Cars 7A 154
St Benet's Pl. EC3 .... 2F 15 (7D 84)
St Bernards CR0: C'don 3E 168
St Bernard's Cl. SE27 .... 4D 138
St Bernards Ho. E14 .... 3E 104
(off Galbraith St.)
St Bernard's Rd. E6 .... 1B 88
St Blaise Av. BR1: Brom 2K 159
St Botolph Row EC3 .... 1J 15 (6F 85)
St Botolphs E1 .... 7J 9
(off St Botolph St.)
St Botolph St. EC3 .... 7J 9 (6F 85)
St Brelades Ct. N1 .... 1E 84
St Bride's Av. EC4 .... 1A 14
HA8: Edg 1F 43
St Brides Cl. DA18: Erith 2D 108
St Bride's Crypt Mus. 1A 14
(off Fleet St.)
St Bride's Ho. E3 .... 2C 86
(off Ordell Rd.)
St Bride's Pas. EC4 .... 1A 14
St Bride St. EC4 .... 7A 8 (6B 84)
St Catherine's Apartments E3 .... 3D 86
(off Bow Rd.)
St Catherine's Cl. SW17 .... 2C 136
SW20 .... 5E 152
St Catherines Cl. KT9: Chess 6D 162
St Catherine's Ct. W4 .... 3A 98
St Catherines Ct. TW13: Felt 1J 129
St Catherine's Dr. SE14 .... 2K 121
St Catherine's Farm Ct. HA4: Ruis 6E 38
St Catherines M. SW3 .... 3E 16 (4D 100)
St Catherine's Rd. E4 .... 2H 35
HA4: Ruis 6F 39
St Cecelia's Pl. SE3 .... 5J 105
St Cecilia's Cl. SM3: Sutt 1G 165
St Chads Cl. KT6: Surb 7C 150
St Chad's Gdns. RM6: Chad H 7E 54
St Chad's Pl. WC1 .... 1F 7 (3J 83)
St Chad's Rd. RM6: Chad H 7E 54
St Chad's St. WC1 .... 1F 7 (3J 83)
(not continuous)
St Charles Pl. W10 .... 5G 81
St Charles Sq. W10 .... 5F 81
St Chloe's Ho. E3 .... 2C 86
(off Ordell Rd.)
St Christopher Rd. UB8: Cowl 6A 74
St Christopher's Cl. TW7: Isle 1J 113
St Christophers Dr. UB3: Hayes 7K 75
St Christopher's Gdns.
CR7: Thor H 3A 156
St Christopher's Ho. NW1 .... 2G 83
(off Bridgeway St.)
St Christopher's M. SM6: Wall 5G 167
St Christopher's Pl. W1 .... 7H 5 (6E 82)
St Clair Cl. IG5: Ilf 2D 52
St Clair Dr. KT4: Wor Pk 3D 164
St Clair Ho. E3 .... 3B 86
(off British St.)
St Clair Rd. E13 .... 2K 87
St Clair's Rd. CR0: C'don 2E 168
St Clare Bus. Pk. TW12: Hamp H 6G 131
St Clare St. EC3 .... 1J 15 (6F 85)
St Clements Av. E3 .... 3B 86
St Clement's Ct. EC4 .... 2F 15
N7 .... 6A 66
St Clements Ct. SE14 .... 6K 103
(off Myers La.)
W11 .... 7F 81
(off Stoneleigh St.)
St Clement's Development E3 .... 3B 86
St Clement's Hgts. SE26 .... 3G 139
St Clements Ho. E1 .... 6J 9
(off Leyden St.)
St Clement's La. WC2 .... 1G 13 (6K 83)
St Clements Mans. SW6 .... 6F 99
(off Lillie Rd.)
St Clements St. N7 .... 6A 66
St Clements Yd. SE22 .... 4F 121
St Cloud Rd. SE27 .... 4C 138
St Columba's Ct. E15 .... 4G 69
(off Janson Rd.)
St Columbas Ho. E17 .... 4D 50
St Columb's Ho. W10 .... 5G 81
(off Blagrove Rd.)
St Crispin's Cl. NW3 .... 4C 64
UB1: S'hall 6D 76
St Cross St. EC1 .... 5K 7 (5A 84)
St Cuthbert's Rd. NW2 .... 6H 63
St Cuthberts Rd. N13 .... 6F 33
St Cyprian's St. SW17 .... 4D 136
St Daniel Ct. BR3: Beck 7C 140
(off Brackley Rd.)
St David's Cl. BR4: W W'ck 7D 158
HA9: Wemb 3J 61
St Davids Cl. SE16 .... 5H 103
(off Masters Dr.)
St David's Ct. BR1: Brom 3F 161
E17 .... 3E 50
St Davids Ct. TW15: Ashf 2B 128
St David's Dr. HA8: Edg 1F 43
St Davids M. E3 .... 3A 86
(off Morgan St.)
E18 .... 1J 51
St David's Pl. NW4 .... 7D 44
St Davids Sq. E14 .... 5D 104
St Denis Rd. SE27 .... 4D 138
St Dionis Rd. SW6 .... 2H 117
St Domingo Ho. SE18 .... 3D 106
(off Leda Rd.)
St Donatt's Rd. SE14 .... 1B 122
ST DUNSTAN'S 6H 165
St Dunstan's All. EC3 .... 2G 15
St Dunstans Av. W3 .... 7K 79
St Dunstan's Cl. UB3: Harl 5H 93
St Dunstan's Ct. EC4 .... 1K 13 (6A 84)
St Dunstan's Enterprises 1C 140
St Dunstan's Gdns. W3 .... 7K 79
St Dunstan's Hill SM1: Sutt 5G 165
St Dunstans Hill EC3 .... 3G 15 (7E 84)
St Dunstan's Ho. WC2 .... 1J 13
(off Chancery La.)
St Dunstan's La. BR3: Beck 6E 158
EC3 .... 3G 15 (7E 84)
St Dunstans M. E1 .... 5A 86
(off White Horse Rd.)
St Dunstan's Rd. E7 .... 6K 69
SE25 .... 4F 157
TW4: Cran 2K 111
(not continuous)
TW13: Felt 3H 129
W6 .... 5F 99
W7 .... 2J 95
St Edmund's Av. HA4: Ruis 6F 39
St Edmund's Cl. NW8 .... 1D 82
SW17 .... 2C 136
St Edmunds Cl. DA18: Erith 2D 108
St Edmund's Ct. NW8 .... 1D 82
(off St Edmund's Ter.)
St Edmunds Dr. HA7: Stan 1A 42
St Edmund's La. TW2: Whitt 7F 113
St Edmund's Rd. IG1: Ilf 6D 52
N9 .... 7B 24
St Edmunds Sq. SW13 .... 6E 98
St Edmund's Ter. NW8 .... 1C 82
St Edward's Cl. NW11 .... 6J 45
St Edwards Ct. NW11 .... 6J 45
St Edwards Way RM1: Rom 5K 55
St Egberts Way E4 .... 1K 35
St Elmo Rd. W12 .... 1B 98
St Elmos Rd. SE16 .... 2A 104
St Erkenwald M. IG11: Bark 1H 89
St Erkenwald Rd. IG11: Bark 1H 89
St Ermin's Hill SW1 .... 1C 18
St Ervan's Rd. W10 .... 5H 81
St Eugene Ct. NW6 .... 1G 81
(off Salusbury Rd.)
St Faith's Cl. EN2: Enf 1H 23
St Faith's Rd. SE21 .... 1B 138
St Fidelis Rd. DA8: Erith 4K 109
St Fillans Rd. SE6 .... 1E 140
St Francis Cl. BR5: Pet W 6J 161
St Francis' Ho. NW1 .... 2H 83
(off Bridgeway St.)
St Francis Pl. SW12 .... 6F 119
St Francis Rd. DA8: Erith 4K 109
SE22 .... 4E 120
St Francis Way IG1: Ilf 4H 71
St Frideswide's M. E14 .... 6E 86
St Gabriel's Cl. E11 .... 2K 69
E14 .... 5D 86
St Gabriels Ct. N11 .... 7C 32
St Gabriels Mnr. SE5 .... 1B 120
(off Cormont Rd.)
St Gabriels Rd. NW2 .... 5F 63
St Gabriel Wlk. SE1 .... 4B 102
(off Elephant & Castle)
St George's Antiochain Orthodox Cathedral
.... 1K 5 (3F 83)
St George's Av. E7 .... 7K 69
N7 .... 4H 65
NW9 .... 4K 43
UB1: S'hall 7D 76
W5 .... 2D 96
St George's Bldgs. SE1 .... 3B 102
(off St George's Rd.)
St George's Cir. SE1 .... 7A 14 (3B 102)
St George's Cl. HA0: Wemb 3A 60
NW11 .... 6H 45
SW8 .... 1G 119
St Georges Cl. SE28 .... 6D 90
St George's Ct. E6 .... 4D 88
SE1 .... 3B 102
(off Garden Row)
SW1 .... 5A 18
(off St George's Dr.)
SW3 .... 3C 16
(off Brompton Rd.)
SW7 .... 3A 100
SW15 .... 4H 117
St Georges Ct. E17 .... 5F 51
EC4 .... 7A 8 (6B 84)
HA3: Kenton 6A 42
(off Kenton Rd.)
St George's Dr. SW1 .... 4K 17 (4F 101)
UB10: Ick 3B 56
ST GEORGE'S FIELD 7C 82
St George's Flds. W2 .... 1D 10 (6C 82)
St George's Gdns. KT6: Surb 2H 163
St George's Gro. SW17 .... 3B 136
St George's Ho. NW1 .... 2H 83
(off Bridgeway St.)
St Georges Ho. SW11 .... 1E 118
(off Charlotte Despard Av.)
St George's Ind. Est. KT2: King T 5D 132
N22 .... 7G 33
St George's La. EC3 .... 2F 15
St George's Leisure Cen. 7H 85
St George's Mans. SW1 .... 5D 18
(off Causton St.)
St George's M. NW1 .... 7D 64
SE1 .... 1K 19
SE8 .... 4B 104
St Georges Pde. SE6 .... 2B 140
(off Perry Hill)
St George's Path SE4 .... 4C 122
(off Adelaide Av.)
St George's Pl. TW1: Twick 1A 132
St George's RC Cathedral 1K 19 (3A 102)
St George's Rd. BR1: Brom 2D 160
BR3: Beck 1D 158
BR5: Pet W 6H 161
CR4: Mitc 3F 155
DA14: Sidc 6D 144
E7 .... 7K 69
E10 .... 3E 68
EN1: Enf 1A 24
IG1: Ilf 7D 52
KT2: King T 7G 133
N13 .... 3E 32

St George's Rd. NW11 6H 45
RM9: Dag 5E 72
SE1 1K 19 (3A 102)
SM6: Wall 5F 167
SW19 7H 135
(not continuous)
TW1: Twick 5B 114
TW13: Hanw 4B 130
W4 2K 97
W7 1K 95
St Georges Rd. TW9: Rich 3F 115
St George's Rd. W. BR1: Brom 1C 160
St George's Shop. & Leisure Cen.
HA1: Harr 6J 41
St George's Sq. E7 7K 69
KT3: N Mald 3A 152
SE8 4B 104
(not continuous)
SW1 5C 18 (5H 101)
St Georges Sq. E14 7A 86
St George's Sq. M. SW1 6C 18 (5H 101)
St George's Stadium 2H 57
St George's Ter. *E6* *3C 88*
(off Masterman Rd.)
NW1 7D 64
SE15 *7G 103*
(off Peckham Hill St.)
St George St. W1 1K 11 (7F 83)
St George's Wlk. CR0: C'don 3C 168
St George's Way SE15 6E 102
St George's Wharf *SE1* *6K 15*
(off Shad Thames)
St George Wharf SW8 7E 18 (6J 101)
St Gerards Cl. SW4 5G 119
St German's Pl. SE3 1J 123
St German's Rd. SE23 1A 140
St Giles Av. RM10: Dag 7H 73
UB10: Ick 4E 56
St Giles Cir. W1 6H 83
St Giles Cl. BR6: Farnb 5H 173
RM10: Dag 7H 73
TW5: Hest 7C 94
St Giles High St. WC2 7D 6 (6H 83)
St Giles Ho. EN5: New Bar 4F 21
SE5 1E 120
St Giles Pas. WC2 1D 12
St Giles Rd. SE5 7E 102
St Giles Ter. *EC2* *6D 8*
(off Wood St.)
St Giles Twr. *SE5* *1E 120*
(off Gables Cl.)
St Gilles Ho. *E2* *2K 85*
(off Mace St.)
St Gothard Rd. SE27 4D 138
(not continuous)
St Gregory Cl. HA4: Ruis 4A 58
St Helena Ho. *WC1* *2J 7*
(off Margery St.)
St Helena Rd. SE16 4K 103
St Helena St. WC1 2J 7 (3A 84)
St Helena Ter. TW9: Rich 5D 114
St Helens KT7: T Ditt 7K 149
St Helen's Cl. KT4: Wor Pk 1C 164
St Helens Cl. UB8: Cowl 5A 74
St Helen's Cres. SW16 1K 155
St Helen's Gdns. W10 5F 81
St Helen's Pl. EC3 7G 9 (6E 84)
St Helens Pl. E10 7A 50
St Helen's Rd. DA18: Erith 2D 108
IG1: Ilf 6D 52
SW16 1K 155
W13 1B 96
ST HELIER 7C 154
St Helier Av. SM4: Mord 7A 154
St Helier Ct. *N1* *1E 84*
(off De Beauvoir Est.)
SE16 *2K 103*
(off Poolmans St.)
St Helier's Av. TW3: Houn 5E 112
St Helier's Rd. E10 6E 50
St Hilary's Ct. BR1: Brom 3F 161
St Hilda's Av. TW15: Ashf 5A 128
St Hilda's Cl. NW6 7F 63
SW17 2C 136
St Hilda's Rd. SW13 6D 98
St Hilda's Wharf *E1* *1J 103*
(off Wapping High St.)
St Hubert's Ho. *E14* *3C 104*
(off Janet St.)
St Hughes Cl. SW17 2C 136
St Hugh's Rd. SE20 1H 157
St Ives Pl. E14 5E 86
St Ivian Ct. N10 2E 46
St James SE14 1A 122
St James Apartments *E17* *5A 50*
(off Pretoria Av.)
St James Av. N20 3H 31
SM1: Sutt 5J 165
W13 1A 96
St James Cl. EN4: E Barn 4G 21
HA4: Ruis 2A 58
KT3: N Mald 5B 152
N20 3H 31
SE18 5G 107
St James Ct. CR0: C'don 7B 156
E2 *3G 85*
(off Bethnal Grn. Rd.)
E12 2A 70
SE3 1K 123
St James' Ct. SW1 1B 18 (3G 101)
St James Gdns. RM6: Chad H 4B 54
St James' Gdns. HA0: Wemb 7D 60
St James Ga. IG9: Buck H 1F 37
St James Gro. SW11 2D 118
St James Hall *N1* *1C 84*
(off Prebend St.)
St James Ind. M. SE1 5G 103
St James Mans. *SE1* *1J 19*
(off McAuley Cl.)
St James' Mans. *NW6* *7J 63*
(off West End La.)
St James M. E14 3E 104
E17 *5A 50*
(off St James's St.)
St James Path E17 5A 50
St James Residences *W1* *2C 12*
(off Brewer St.)
St James Rd. CR4: Mitc 7E 136
SM1: Sutt 5J 165
SM5: Cars 3C 166
St James' Rd. E15 5H 69
KT6: Surb 6D 150
N9 2C 34
ST JAMES'S 4B 12 (1H 101)
St James's App. EC2 4G 9 (4E 84)
St James's Av. BR3: Beck 3A 158
E2 2J 85
TW12: Hamp H 5G 131
St James's Chambers *SW1* *4B 12*
(off Jermyn St.)
St James's Cl. *NW8* *1D 82*
(off St James's Ter. M.)
SW17 2D 136
St James's Cotts. TW9: Rich 5D 114
St James's Ct. HA1: Harr 6A 42
KT1: King T 3E 150
N18 *5B 34*
(off Fore St.)
St James's Cres. SW9 3A 120
St James's Dr. SW12 1D 136
SW17 1D 136
St James's Gdns. W11 1G 99
(not continuous)
St James's Ho. *SE1* *4G 103*
(off Strathnairn St.)
St James's La. N10 4F 47
St James's Mkt. SW1 3C 12 (7H 83)
St James's Palace 6B 12 (2G 101)
St James's Pk. 6C 12 (2H 101)
St James's Pk. CR0: C'don 7C 156
St James's Pas. EC3 1H 15
St James's Pl. SW1 5A 12 (1G 101)
St James's Rd. CR0: C'don 7B 156
KT1: King T 2D 150
SE1 6G 103
SE16 3G 103
TW12: Hamp H 5F 131
St James's Sq. SW1 4B 12 (1G 101)
St James's St. E17 5A 50
SW1 4A 12 (1G 101)
St James's Ter. *NW8* *1D 82*
(off Prince Albert Rd.)
St James's Ter. M. NW8 1D 82
St James St. W6 5E 98
St James's Wlk. EC1 3A 8 (4B 84)
St James Ter. SW12 1E 136
St James Theatre *3G 101*
(off Palace St.)
St James Way DA14: Sidc 5E 144
St Jeromes Gro. UB3: Hayes 6E 74
St Joan's Ho. *NW1* *1C 6*
(off Phoenix Rd.)
St Joan's Rd. N9 2A 34
St John Fisher Rd. DA18: Erith 3D 108
ST JOHNS 2C 122
St John's Av. N11 5J 31
NW10 1B 80
SW15 5F 117
St Johns Chu. Rd. E9 5J 67
St John's Cl. HA9: Wemb 5E 60
N20 *3F 31*
(off Rasper Rd.)
SW6 7J 99
St Johns Cl. N14 6B 22
St John's Concert Hall 2E 18
St John's Cotts. SE20 7J 139
St John's Ct. DA8: Erith 4K 109
E1 *1H 103*
(off Scandrett St.)
HA1: Harr 6K 41
HA6: Nwood *1G 39*
(off Murray Rd.)
IG9: Buck H 1E 36
KT1: King T *4E 150*
(off Beaufort Rd.)
N4 2B 66
SE13 2E 122
TW7: Isle 2K 113
W6 *4D 98*
(off Glenthorne Rd.)
St Johns Ct. *SW10* *7A 100*
(off Ashburnham Rd.)
St John's Cres. SW9 3A 120
St Johns Dr. SW18 1K 135
St John's Est. N1 2D 84
SE1 6J 15
St John's Gdns. W11 7G 81
St John's Gate 4A 8
St John's Gro. N19 2G 65
SW13 2B 116
TW9: Rich 4E 114
St John's Hill SW11 5B 118
St John's Hill Gro. SW11 4B 118
St John's Ho. *E14* *4E 104*
(off Pier St.)
St Johns Ho. *SE17* *6D 102*
(off Lytham St.)
St John's La. EC1 4A 8 (4B 84)
St John's Lodge *NW3* *7C 64*
(off King Henry's Rd.)
St John's Mans. *EC1* *1A 8*
(off St John St.)
St John's M. KT1: Hamp W 2C 150
W11 6J 81
St John's Pde. W13 1B 96
St Johns Pde. *DA14: Sidc* *4A 144*
(off Sidcup High St.)
St John's Pk. SE3 7H 105
St John's Pk. Mans. N19 3G 65
St John's Pas. SW19 6G 135
St John's Path EC1 4A 8
St Johns Pathway SE23 1J 139
St John's Pl. EC1 4A 8 (4B 84)
St John's Rd. BR5: Pet W 6H 161
CR0: C'don 3B 168
DA8: Erith 5K 109
DA14: Sidc 4B 144
(not continuous)
DA16: Well 3B 126
E4 4J 35
E6 1C 88
E16 6J 87
E17 2D 50
HA1: Harr 6K 41
HA9: Wemb 4D 60
IG2: Ilf 7H 53
IG11: Bark 1J 89
KT1: Hamp W 2C 150
KT3: N Mald 3J 151
KT8: E Mos 4H 149
N15 6E 48
NW11 6H 45
SE20 6J 139
SM1: Sutt 2K 165
SM5: Cars 3C 166
SW11 4C 118
SW19 7G 135
TW7: Isle 2K 113
TW9: Rich 4E 114
TW13: Hanw 4C 130
UB2: S'hall 3C 94
St John's Sq. EC1 4A 8 (4B 84)
St John's Ter. E7 6K 69
SE18 6G 107
SW15 *3A 134*
(off Kingston Va.)
W10 4F 81
St John St. EC1 1K 7 (2A 84)
St John's Va. SE8 2C 122
St John's Vs. *N11* *5J 31*
(off Friern Barnet Rd.)
N19 2H 65
W8 *3K 99*
(off St Mary's Pl.)
St John's Way N19 2G 65
ST JOHN'S WOOD 1A 4 (2B 82)
St John's Wood Ct. NW8 2B 4
St John's Wood High St.
NW8 1C 4 (2B 82)
St John's Wood Pk. NW8 1B 82
St John's Wood Rd. NW8 3A 4 (4B 82)
St John's Wood Ter. NW8 2B 82
St John's Yd. N17 7A 34
St Josephs Almshouses *W6* *4F 99*
(off Brook Grn.)
St Joseph's Cl. BR6: Orp 4K 173
W10 5G 81
St Joseph's College Sports Cen. 6B 138
St Joseph's Cotts. *SW3* *4E 16*
(off Cadagon St.)
St Josephs Ct. SE2 6D 108
SE7 6K 105
St Joseph's Dr. UB1: S'hall 1C 94
St Joseph's Flats *NW1* *1C 6*
(off Drummond Cres.)
St Joseph's Gro. NW4 4D 44
St Joseph's Ho. *W6* *4F 99*
(off Brook Grn.)
St Joseph's Rd. N9 7C 24
St Joseph's St. SW8 1F 119
St Joseph's Va. SE3 3F 123
St Judes Ct. IG8: Wfd G 7H 37
St Jude's Rd. E2 2H 85
St Jude St. N16 5E 66
St Julian's Cl. SW16 4A 138
St Julian's Farm Rd. SE27 4A 138
St Julian's Rd. NW6 1J 81
St Katharine Docks 3K 15
St Katharine's Pier 1F 103
St Katharine's Pct. NW1 2F 83
St Katharine's Way E1 4K 15 (1F 103)
(not continuous)
St Katharine's Yacht Haven *1F 103*
(off St Katharine's Way)

St Katherine's Rd. DA18: Erith	. . . . . . .2D 108	
St Katherines Row EC3	. . . . .2H 15	
St Katherines Wlk. W11	. . . . .1F 99	
	(off St Ann's Rd.)	
St Keverne Rd. SE9	. . . . .4C 142	
St Kilda Rd. BR6: Orp	. . . . .1K 173	
W13	. . . . .1A 96	
St Kilda's Rd. HA1: Harr	. . . . .6J 41	
N16	. . . . .1D 66	
St Kitts Ter. SE19	. . . . .5E 138	
St Laurence Cl. NW6	. . . . .1F 81	
St Lawrence Bus. Cen. TW13: Felt	. .2K 129	
St Lawrence Cl. HA8: Edg	. . . . . . .7A 28	
St Lawrence Cotts. E14	. . . . . . .1E 104	
	(off St Lawrence St.)	
St Lawrence Ct. N1	. . . . .7D 66	
St Lawrence Dr. HA5: Eastc	. . . . . .5K 39	
St Lawrence Ho. SE1	. . . . .7H 15	
	(off Purbrook St.)	
St Lawrence St. E14	. . . . .1E 104	
St Lawrence Ter. W10	. . . . .5G 81	
St Lawrence Way SW9	. . . . .1A 120	
St Leger Ct. NW6	. . . . .7F 63	
	(off Coverdale Rd.)	
St Leonard M. N1	. . . . .2E 84	
	(off Hoxton St.)	
St Leonard's Av. E4	. . . . .6A 36	
HA3: Kenton	. . . . .5C 42	

(truncated — full index page)

St Michael's Flats—Salehurst Rd.

St Michael's Flats *NW1* 1C 6
(off Aldenham St.)
St Michael's Gdns. W10 5G 81
St Michael's M. SW1 4G 17 (4E 100)
St Michael's Ri. DA16: Well 1B 126
St Michael's Rd. CR0: C'don 1C 168
DA16: Well 3B 126
NW2 4E 62
SM6: Wall 6G 167
SW9 2K 119
TW15: Ashf 5C 128
St Michael's St. W2 7B 4 (6B 82)
St Michael's Ter. N22 1J 47
St Michaels Ter. *N6* 1E 64
(off South Gro.)
St Mildred's Ct. EC2 1E 14 (6D 84)
St Mildreds Rd. SE6 7G 123
SE12 7G 123
St Mirren Ct. EN5: New Bar 5F 21
St Nicholas Cen. SM1: Sutt 5K 165
St Nicholas Cl. UB8: Cowl 6A 74
St Nicholas Ct. *KT1: King T* 4E 150
(off Surbiton Rd.)
St Nicholas Dr. TW17: Shep 7C 146
St Nicholas' Flats *NW1* 1C 6
(off Werrington St.)
St Nicholas Glebe SW17 5E 136
St Nicholas Ho. *SE8* 6C 104
(off Deptford Grn.)
St Nicholas M. KT7: T Ditt 6K 149
St Nicholas Rd. KT7: T Ditt 6K 149
SE18 5K 107
SM1: Sutt 5K 165
St Nicholas St. SE8 1B 122
St Nicholas Way SM1: Sutt 4K 165
St Nicolas La. BR7: Chst 1C 160
St Ninian's Ct. N20 3J 31
St Norbert Grn. SE4 4A 122
St Norbert Rd. SE4 5K 121
St Olaf Ho. SE1 4F 15
St Olaf's Rd. SW6 7G 99
St Olaf Stairs SE1 4F 15
St Olave's Ct. EC2 1E 14 (6D 84)
St Olave's Est. SE1 6H 15 (2E 102)
St Olave's Gdns. SE11 3J 19 (4A 102)
St Olaves Ho. *SE11* 3J 19
(off Walnut Tree Wlk.)
St Olave's Mans. SE11 3J 19
St Olave's Rd. E6 1E 88
St Olaves Wlk. SW16 2G 155
St Olav's Sq. SE16 2J 103
St Onge Pde. *EN1: Enf* 3J 23
(off Southbury Rd.)
St Oswald's Pl. SE11 6G 19 (5K 101)
St Oswald's Rd. SW16 1B 156
St Oswalds Studios *SW6* 6J 99
(off Sedlescombe Rd.)
St Oswulf St. SW1 4D 18 (4H 101)
St Owen Ho. *SE1* 3E 102
(off St Saviour's Est.)
ST PANCRAS 2F 7 (3J 83)
St Pancras Commercial Cen.
NW1 1G 83
(off Pratt St.)
St Pancras Ct. N2 2B 46
St Pancras Way NW1 7G 65
St Patrick's Ct.
IG8: Wfd G 7B 36
St Paul Cl. UB8: Cowl 5A 74
St Paulinus Ct. *DA1: Cray* 4K 127
(off Manor Rd.)
St Paul's All. *EC4* 1B 14
(off St Paul's Chyd.)
St Paul's Av. HA3: Kenton 4F 43
NW2 6E 62
SE16 1K 103
St Paul's Bldgs. *EC1* 3B 8
(off Dallington St.)
St Paul's Cathedral
London 1B 14 (6C 84)
St Paul's Chyd. EC4 1B 14 (6B 84)
St Paul's Cl. KT9: Chess 4D 162
SM5: Cars 1C 166
TW3: Houn 2C 112
TW15: Ashf 5E 128
UB3: Harl 5F 93
W5 2F 97
St Pauls Cl. SE7 5B 106
St Paul's Ct. TW4: Houn 3C 112
St Pauls Ct. SW4 5H 119
St Pauls Courtyard *SE8* 7C 104
(off Crossfield St.)
ST PAUL'S CRAY 2K 161
St Paul's Cray Rd.
BR7: Chst 1H 161
St Paul's Cres. NW1 7H 65
(not continuous)
St Paul's Dr. E15 5F 69
St Pauls Ho. *SE8* 7C 104
(off Market Yd.)
St Paul's M. NW1 7H 65
St Paul's Pl. N1 6D 66
St Paul's Ri. N13 6G 33
St Paul's Rd. CR7: Thor H 3C 156
DA8: Erith 7J 109
IG11: Bark 1G 89
N1 6B 66
N17 7B 34
TW8: Bford 6D 96
TW9: Rich 3F 115
St Paul's Shrubbery N1 6D 66
St Paul's Sq. BR2: Brom 2H 159
St Paul's Studios *W14* 5G 99
(off Talgarth Rd.)
St Pauls Ter. SE17 6B 102
St Paul St. N1 1C 84
(not continuous)
St Pauls Vw. Apartments *EC1* 2J 7
(off Amwell St.)
St Paul's Wlk. KT2: King T 7G 133
St Paul's Way E3 5B 86
N3 7E 30
St Paul's Wood Hill BR5: St P 2J 161
St Peter Claver Ct. *BR3: Beck* 1D 158
(off Albemarle Rd.)
St Peter's All. *EC3* 1F 15
(off Gracechurch St.)
St Peter's Av. E2 2G 85
E17 4G 51
N18 4B 34
St Petersburgh M. W2 7K 81
St Petersburgh Pl. W2 7K 81
St Peter's Cen. *E1* 1H 103
(off Reardon St.)
St Peter's Chu. Ct. *N1* 1B 84
(off St Peter's St.)
St Peter's Cl. BR7: Chst 7H 143
E2 2G 85
HA4: Ruis 2B 58
IG2: Ilf 4J 53
SW17 2C 136
St Peters Cl. WD23: B Hea 1C 26
St Peter's Ct. NW4 5E 44
WC1 2F 7
(off Seaford St.)
St Peters Ct. *E1* 4J 85
(off Cephas St.)
KT8: W Mole 4E 148
SE12 5H 123
St Peter's Gdns. SE27 3A 138
St Peter's Gro. W6 4C 98
St Peter's Ho. *WC1* 2F 7
(off Regent Sq.)
St Peters Ho. SE17 6D 102
St Peters M. N4 5B 48
N8 5A 48
St Peter's Path E17 3G 51
St Peters Pl. W9 4K 81
St Peter's Rd. CR0: C'don 4D 168
KT1: King T 2G 151
KT8: W Mole 4E 148
N9 1C 34
St Peter's Rd. TW1: Twick 5B 114
UB1: S'hall 5E 76
W6 5C 98
St Peters Rd. UB8: Cowl 5A 74
St Peter's Sq. E2 2G 85
W6 4B 98
St Peter's St. CR2: S Croy 5D 168
N1 1B 84
St Peter's St. M. *N1* 2B 84
(off St Peters St.)
St Peter's Ter. SW6 7H 99
St Peter's Vs. W6 4C 98
St Peter's Way N1 7E 66
W5 5D 78
St Peters Way UB3: Harl 5F 93
St Peter's Wharf W4 5C 98
St Philip Ho. *WC1* 2J 7
(off Lloyd Baker St.)
St Philip's Av. KT4: Wor Pk 2D 164
St Philip's Ga. KT4: Wor Pk 2D 164
St Philip Sq. SW8 2F 119
St Philip's Rd. E8 6G 67
St Philips Rd. KT6: Surb 6D 150
St Philip St. SW8 2F 119
St Philip's Way N1 1C 84
St Quentin Ho. SW18 6B 118
St Quentin Rd. DA16: Well 3K 125
St Quintin Av. W10 5E 80
St Quintin Gdns. W10 5E 80
St Quintin Ho. *W10* 5F 81
(off Princess Louise Wlk.)
St Quintin Rd. E13 3K 87
St Quintin Vw. W10 5E 80
St Raphael's Way NW10 5J 61
St Regis Cl. N10 2F 47
St Regis Hgts. NW3 3K 63
St Richard's Ho. *NW1* 1C 6
(off Eversholt St.)
St Ronan's Cl. EN4: Had W 1G 21
St Ronan's Cres. IG8: Wfd G 7D 36
St Rule St. SW8 2G 119
St Saviours Ct. HA1: Harr 5J 41
N22 2H 47
St Saviour's Est. SE1 7J 15 (2F 103)
St Saviour's Rd. CR0: C'don 6B 156
SW2 5K 119
St Saviour's Wharf *SE1* 6K 15
(off Mill St.)
SE1 6K 15
(off Shad Thames)
Saints Cl. SE27 4B 138
Saints Dr. E7 5B 70
St Silas Pl. NW5 6E 64
St Simon's Av. SW15 5E 116
Saints M. CR4: Mitc 3C 154
St Stephen's Av. E17 5E 50
W12 1D 98
(not continuous)
W13 6B 78
St Stephen's Cl. E17 5D 50
NW8 1C 82
UB1: S'hall 5E 76
St Stephens Cl. *NW5* 5D 64
(off Malden Rd.)
St Stephen's Ct. *EN1: Enf* 6K 23
(off Park Av.)
St Stephens Ct. N8 6K 47
W13 6B 78
St Stephen's Cres. CR7: Thor H 3A 156
W2 6J 81
St Stephen's Gdns. SW15 5H 117
TW1: Twick 6C 114
W2 6J 81
(not continuous)
St Stephens Gro. SE13 3E 122
St Stephens Ho. *SE17* 6D 102
(off Lytham St.)
St Stephen's M. W2 5J 81
St Stephens Pde. E7 7A 70
St Stephen's Pas.
TW1: Twick 6C 114
St Stephen's Rd. E3 1A 86
E6 7A 70
E17 5D 50
EN5: Barn 5A 20
TW3: Houn 6E 112
UB7: Yiew 1A 92
W13 6B 78
St Stephen's Row EC4 1E 14
St Stephen's Ter. SW8 7K 101
St Stephen's Wlk. *SW7* 4A 100
(off Southwell Gdns.)
St Swithins La. EC4 2E 14 (7D 84)
St Swithun's Rd. SE13 6F 123
St Theresa's Cl. E9 4C 68
St Theresa's Rd. TW14: Felt 4H 111
St Thomas Cl. KT6: Surb 1F 163
St Thomas Ct. DA5: Bexl 7G 127
E10 7D 50
(off Lake Rd.)
HA5: Pinn 1C 40
NW1 7G 65
(off Wrotham Rd.)
St Thomas Dr. BR5: Farnb 1G 173
St Thomas' Dr. HA5: Pinn 1C 40
St Thomas Gdns. IG1: Ilf 6G 71
St Thomas Ho. *E1* 6K 85
(off W. Arbour St.)
St Thomas M. SW18 5J 117
St Thomas Rd. DA17: Belv 2J 109
E16 6J 87
N14 7C 22
W4 6J 97
St Thomas's Gdns. NW5 6E 64
St Thomas's M. SE7 4C 106
St Thomas's Pl. E9 7J 67
St Thomas's Rd. N4 2A 66
NW10 1A 80
St Thomas's Sq. E9 7J 67
St Thomas St. SE1 5F 15 (1D 102)
St Thomas's Way SW6 7H 99
St Timothys M. BR1: Brom 1K 159
St Ursula Gro. HA5: Pinn 5B 40
St Ursula Rd. UB1: S'hall 6E 76
St Valery Pl. TW5: Hest 7B 94
St Vincent Cl. SE27 5B 138
St Vincent De Paul Ho. *E1* 5J 85
(off Jubilee St.)
St Vincent Ho. *SE1* 3F 103
(off St Saviour's Est.)
St Vincent Rd. TW2: Whitt 6G 113
St Vincent's La. NW7 4K 29
St Vincent St. W1 6H 5 (5E 82)
St Wilfrid's Cl. EN4: E Barn 5H 21
St Wilfrid's Rd. EN4: E Barn 5G 21
St Williams Ct. N1 7J 65
St Winefride's Av. E12 5D 70
St Winifred's Rd. TW11: Tedd 6B 132
Sakura Dr. N22 1H 47
Salamanca Pl. IG11: Bark 2B 90
SE1 4G 19 (4K 101)
Salamanca Sq. *SE1* 4G 19
(off Salamanca Pl.)
Salamanca St. SE1 4G 19 (4K 101)
SE11 4G 19 (4K 101)
Salamander Cl. KT2: King T 5C 132
Salamander Quay KT1: Hamp W 1D 150
Salcombe Ct. *E14* 5E 86
(off St Ives Pl.)
Salcombe Dr. RM6: Chad H 6F 55
SM4: Mord 1F 165
Salcombe Gdns. NW7 6K 29
Salcombe Rd. E17 7B 50
N16 5E 66
TW15: Ashf 3A 128
Salcombe Vs. TW10: Rich 5E 114
Salcombe Way HA4: Ruis 2J 57
UB4: Hayes 3F 75
Salcott Rd. CR0: Bedd 3J 167
SW11 5C 118
Salehurst Cl. HA3: Kenton 5E 42
Salehurst Rd. SE4 6B 122

A-Z London 393

Salem Pl. CR0: C'don 3C 168
Salem Rd. W2 ....7K 81
Salento Cl. N3 ....7D 30
Sale Pl. W2 ....6C 4 (5C 82)
Sale St. E2 ....4G 85
Salford Ho. E14 ....4E 104
(off Seyssel St.)
Salford Rd. SW2 ....1H 137
Salhouse Cl. SE28 ....6C 90
Salisbury Av. IG11: Bark 7H 71
N3 ....3H 45
SM1: Sutt 1H 165
Salisbury Cl. KT4: Wor Pk 3B 164
SE17 ....4D 102
Salisbury Ct. E9 ....5A 68
(off Mabley St.)
EC4 ....1A 14 (6B 84)
EN2: Enf 4J 23
(off London Rd.)
SE16 ....3G 103
(off Stork's Rd.)
SM5: Cars 5D 166
UB5: N'olt 5F 59
(off Newmarket Av.)
Salisbury Gdns. IG9: Buck H 2G 37
SW19 ....7G 135
Salisbury Hall Gdns. E4 ....6H 35
Salisbury Ho. E14 ....6D 86
(off Hobday St.)
EC2 ....6F 9
(off London Wall)
HA7: Stan 6F 27
N1 ....1B 84
(off St Mary's Path)
SM6: Wall 5F 167
SW1 ....5D 18
(off Drummond Ga.)
SW9 ....7A 102
(off Cranmer St.)
Salisbury Mans. N15 ....5B 48
Salisbury M. SW6 ....7H 99
Salisbury Pas. SW6 ....7H 99
(off Dawes Rd.)
Salisbury Pavement SW6 ....7H 99
(off Dawes Rd.)
Salisbury Pl. SW9 ....7B 102
W1 ....5E 4 (5D 82)
Salisbury Prom. N8 ....5B 48
Salisbury Rd. BR2: Brom 5C 160
DA5: Bexl 1G 145
E4 ....3H 35
E7 ....6J 69
E10 ....2E 68
E12 ....5B 70
E17 ....5E 50
EN5: Barn 3B 20
HA1: Harr 5H 41
HA5: Eastc 4J 39
IG3: Ilf 2J 71
KT3: N Mald 3K 151
KT4: Wor Pk 4K 163
N4 ....5B 48
N22 ....1B 48
RM10: Dag 6H 73
SE25 ....6G 157
SM5: Cars 6D 166
SW19 ....7G 135
TW4: Houn 3A 112
TW6: H'row A 5E 110
(not continuous)
TW9: Rich 4E 114
TW13: Felt 1A 130
UB2: S'hall 4C 94
W13 ....2B 96
Salisbury Sq. EC4 ......1K 13 (6A 84)
Salisbury St. NW8 ......4C 4 (4C 82)
W3 ....2J 97
Salisbury Ter. SE15 ....3J 121
Salisbury Wlk. N19 ....2G 65
Salix Cl. TW16: Sun 7K 129
Salix Ct. N3 ....6D 30

Salix La. IG8: Wfd G 1C 52
Salk Cl. NW9 ....2A 44
Salliesfield TW2: Whitt 6H 113
Sally Murray Cl. E12 ....4E 70
Salmen Rd. E13 ....2H 87
Salmon Cl. HA7: Stan 6F 27
Salmon La. E14 ....6A 86
Salmon M. NW6 ....5J 63
Salmon Rd. DA17: Belv 5G 109
Salmons Rd. KT9: Chess 6E 162
N9 ....1B 34
Salmon St. E14 ....6B 86
NW9 ....1H 61
Salomons Rd. E13 ....5A 88
Salop Rd. E17 ....6K 49
Salsabil Apartments E3 ....4B 86
Saltash Cl. SM1: Sutt 4H 165
Saltash Rd.
DA16: Well 1C 126
IG6: Ilf 1H 53
Saltcoats Rd. W4 ....2A 98
Saltcroft Cl. HA9: Wemb 1H 61
Saltdene N4 ....1K 65
Salter Cl. HA2: Harr 4D 58
Salterford Rd. SW17 ....6E 136
Saltern Ct. IG11: Bark 3B 90
(off Galleons Dr.)
Salter Rd. SE16 ....1K 103
Salters Cl. EC4 ....1D 14
Salter's Hall Cl. EC4 ....2E 14
Salter's Hill SE19 ....5D 138
Salters Rd. E17 ....4F 51
W10 ....4F 81
Salters Row N1 ....6D 66
(off Tilney Gdns.)
Salter St. E14 ....7B 86
(not continuous)
NW10 ....3C 80
Salterton Rd. N7 ....3K 65
Salt Hill Cl. UB8: Uxb 5A 56
Saltley Cl. E6 ....6C 88
Salton Cl. N3 ....2J 45
Salton Sq. E14 ....6B 86
Saltoun Rd. SW2 ....4A 120
Saltram Cl. N15 ....4F 49
Saltram Cres. W9 ....3H 81
Saltwell St. E14 ....7C 86
Saltwood Gro. SE17 ....5D 102
Saltwood Ho. SE15 ....6J 103
(off Lovelinch Cl.)
Salusbury Rd. NW6 ....1G 81
Salus Ct. CR0: C'don 4C 168
(off Parker Rd.)
Salutation Rd. SE10 ....4G 105
Salvador SW17 ....5D 136
Salvia Gdns. UB6: G'frd 2A 78
Salvin Rd. SW15 ....3F 117
Salway Cl. IG8: Wfd G 7D 36
Salway Pl. E15 ....6F 69
Salway Rd. E15 ....6F 69
Samantha Cl. E17 ....7B 50
Samaras Mans. E20 ....5E 68
(off Liberty Bri. Rd.)
Sam Bartram Cl. SE7 ....5A 106
Sambourne Family Home, The
18 Stafford Terrace 3J 99
(off Stafford Ter.)
Sambrook Sq. EN4: E Barn 4G 21
Sambrook Ho. E1 ....5J 85
(off Jubilee St.)
SE11 ....4J 19
Sambruck M. SE6 ....1D 140
Samels Cl. W6 ....5C 98
Samford Ho. N1 ....1A 84
(off Barnsbury Est.)
Samford St. NW8 ....4C 4 (4B 82)
Samira Cl. E17 ....6C 50
Sam King Wlk. SE5 ....7D 102
(off Edmund St.)
Sam Manners Ho. SE10 ....5G 105
(off Tuskar St.)

Sam March Ho. E14 ....6F 87
(off Blair St.)
Sammi Ct. CR7: Thor H 4C 156
Samos Rd. SE20 ....2H 157
Samphire Hgts. E20 ....5E 68
(off Napa Cl.)
Sampson Av. EN5: Barn 5A 20
Sampson Cl. DA17: Belv 3D 108
Sampson Ct. TW17: Shep 5E 146
Sampson Ho. SE1 ....4A 14 (1B 102)
Sampson St. E1 ....1G 103
Samsbrooke Ct. EN1: Enf 6K 23
Samson St. E13 ....2A 88
Samuda Est. E14 ....3E 104
Samuel Cl. E8 ....1F 85
HA7: Stan 2F 27
SE14 ....6K 103
SE18 ....4C 106
Samuel Cl. N1 ....2G 9
(off Pitfield St.)
Samuel Ferguson Pl. IG11: Bark 2K 89
Samuel Gray Gdns. KT2: King T 1D 150
Samuel Ho. E8 ....1F 85
(off Clarissa St.)
Samuel Johnson Cl. SW16 ....4K 137
Samuel Jones Ct. SE15 ....7E 102
Samuel Lewis Bldgs. N1 ....6A 66
Samuel Lewis Trust Dwellings E8 ....5G 67
(off Amhurst Rd.)
N16 ....6E 48
SW3 ....4C 16 (4C 100)
SW6 ....7J 99
(off Vanston Pl.)
W14 ....4H 99
(off Lisgar Ter.)
Samuel Lewis Trust Est. SE5 ....1C 120
(off Warner Rd.)
Samuel Richardson Ho. W14 ....4H 99
(off North End Cres.)
Samuel's Cl. W6 ....4E 98
Samuel St. SE15 ....7F 103
SE18 ....4D 106
Samuel Wallis Lodge SE3 ....3H 123
(off Banning St.)
SE10 ....4G 105
(off Banning St.)
Sanchia Ct. E2 ....3G 85
(off Wellington Row)
Sancroft Cl. NW2 ....3D 62
Sancroft Ho. SE11 ....5H 19
Sancroft Rd. HA3: W'stone 2K 41
Sancroft St. SE11 .....5H 19 (5K 101)
Sanctuary, The DA5: Bexl 6D 126
SM4: Mord 6J 153
SW1 ....1D 18
Sanctuary M. E8 ....6F 67
Sanctuary Rd. TW6: H'row A 6C 110
Sanctuary St. SE1 .....6D 14 (2C 102)
Sandale Cl. N16 ....3D 66
Sandall Cl. W5 ....4E 78
Sandall Ho. E3 ....2A 86
Sandall Rd. NW5 ....6G 65
W5 ....4E 78
Sandal Rd. KT3: N Mald 5K 151
N18 ....5B 34
Sandal St. E15 ....1G 87
Sandalwood Cl. E1 ....4A 86
Sandalwood Dr. HA4: Ruis 7E 38
Sandalwood Ho. DA15: Sidc 2K 143
Sandalwood Mans. W8 ....3K 99
(off Stone Hall Gdns.)
Sandbach Pl. SE18 ....4G 107
Sandbanks TW14: Felt 1G 129
Sandbourne NW8 ....1K 81
(off Abbey Rd.)
W11 ....6J 81
(off Dartmouth Cl.)
Sandbourne Av. SW19 ....2K 153
Sandbourne Rd. SE4 ....2A 122
Sandbrook Cl. NW7 ....6E 28

Sandbrook Rd. N16 ....3E 66
Sandby Cl. NW10 ....3D 80
(off Plough Cl.)
Sandby Grn. SE9 ....3C 124
Sandby Ho. NW6 ....1J 81
Sandcliff Rd. DA8: Erith 4K 109
Sandcroft Cl. N13 ....6G 33
Sandell's Av. TW15: Ashf 4E 128
Sandell St. SE1 ....6J 13 (2A 102)
Sanderling Cl. SE8 ....6B 104
(off Abinger Gro.)
SE28 ....7C 90
Sanderling Lodge E1 ....3K 15
(off Star Pl.)
Sanders Cl. TW12: Hamp H 5G 131
Sanders Ho. WC1 ....1J 7
(off Gt. Percy St.)
Sanders La. NW7 ....7K 29
(Bittacy Ri.)
NW7 ....7A 30
(Grants Cl.)
TW4: Houn 5D 112
Sanderson Cl. NW5 ....4F 65
Sanderson Ho. E16 ....5J 87
(off Hammersley Rd.)
SE8 ....5B 104
(off Grove St.)
Sandersons La. W4 ....5K 97
(off Chiswick High Rd.)
Sanderson Sq. BR1: Brom 3E 160
Sanderstead Av. NW2 ....2G 63
Sanderstead Cl. SW12 ....7G 119
Sanderstead Rd.
CR2: Sande, S Croy 7D 168
E10 ....1A 68
Sanders Way N19 ....1H 65
Sandes Ct. CR7: Thor H 3C 156
Sandfield WC1 ....2F 7
(off Cromer St.)
Sandfield Gdns. CR7: Thor H 3B 156
Sandfield Pas. CR7: Thor H 3C 156
Sandfield Pl. CR7: Thor H 3C 156
Sandfield Rd. CR7: Thor H 3B 156
Sandford Av. N22 ....1C 48
Sandford Cl. E6 ....4D 88
Sandford Ct. EN5: New Bar 3E 20
N16 ....1E 66
Sandford Rd. BR2: Brom 3J 159
DA7: Bex 4E 126
E6 ....3C 88
Sandford St. SW6 ....7K 99
Sandgate Cl. RM7: Rush G 7J 55
Sandgate Ho. E5 ....5H 67
W5 ....5C 78
Sandgate La. SW18 ....1C 136
Sandgate Rd. DA16: Well 7C 108
Sandgate St. SE15 ....6H 103
Sandgate Trad. Est. SE15 ....6H 103
(off Sandgate St.)
Sandham Ct. SW4 ....1J 119
Sandham Point SE18 ....4F 107
(off Vincent Rd.)
Sandhills SM6: Bedd 4H 167
Sandhills, The SW10 ....7A 16
(off Limerston St.)
Sandhills Mdw. TW17: Shep 7E 146
Sandhurst Av. HA2: Harr 6F 41
KT5: Surb 7H 151
Sandhurst Ho. E1 ....5J 85
(off Wolsey St.)
E17 ....1B 50
(off Robinswood Gdns.)
Sandhurst Mkt. SE6 ....1E 140
(off Sandhurst Rd.)
Sandhurst Rd. BR6: Chels 3K 173
DA5: Bexl 5D 126
DA15: Sidc 3K 143

Sandhurst Rd. N9 6D 24
NW9 3G 43
SE6 1F 141
Sandhurst Way CR2: Sande 7E 168
Sandifer Dr. NW2 3F 63
Sandiford Rd. SM3: Sutt 2H 165
Sandiland Cres.
BR2: Hayes 2H 171
Sandilands CR0: C'don 2G 169
Sandilands Rd. SW6 1K 117
Sandison St. SE15 3G 121
Sandland St. WC1 6H 7 (5K 83)
Sandling Ri. SE9 3E 142
Sandlings, The N22 2A 48
Sandlings Cl. SE15 2H 121
Sandmartin Way SM6: Wall 1E 166
Sandmere Rd. SW4 4J 119
Sandon Cl. KT10: Esh 7H 149
Sandover Ho. *SE16* *3G 103*
(off Spa Rd.)
Sandow Cres. UB3: Hayes 3H 93
Sandown Av. RM10: Dag 6J 73
Sandown Cl. TW5: Cran 1J 111
Sandown Ct. HA7: Stan 5H 27
RM10: Dag *6J 73*
(off Sandown Av.)
SE26 3H 139
SM2: Sutt 7K 165
Sandown Dr. SM5: Cars 7E 166
Sandown Rd. SE25 5H 157
Sandown Way UB5: N'olt 6C 58
Sandpiper Cl. E17 7E 34
SE16 2B 104
Sandpiper Ct. *E1* *7G 85*
(off Thomas More St.)
E14 *3E 104*
(off New Union Cl.)
SE8 *6C 104*
(off Edward Pl.)
Sandpiper Dr. HA2: Harr 2F 59
Sandpiper Rd. SM1: Sutt 5H 165
Sandpiper Ter. IG5: Ilf 3F 53
Sandpit Pl. SE7 5C 106
Sandpit Rd. BR1: Brom 5G 141
Sandpits Rd. CR0: C'don 4K 169
TW10: Ham 2D 132
Sandra Cl. N22 1C 48
TW3: Houn 5F 113
Sandra Ct. CR4: Mitc 6D 136
Sandra Ho. KT8: E Mos 5H 149
Sandridge Cl. HA1: Harr 4J 41
Sandridge St. N19 2G 65
Sandringham Av. SW20 1G 153
Sandringham Bldgs. *SE17* *4D 102*
(off Balfour St.)
Sandringham Cl. EN1: Enf 2K 23
IG6: Ilf 3G 53
SW19 1F 135
Sandringham Ct. DA15: Sidc 6K 125
KT2: King T *1E 150*
(off Skerne Wlk.)
SE16 *1K 103*
(off King & Queen Wharf)
UB10: Hil 4E 74
W1 *1B 12*
(off Dufour's Pl.)
W9 *3A 82*
(off Maida Vale)
Sandringham Cres. HA2: Harr 2E 58
Sandringham Dr. DA2: Wilm 2K 145
DA16: Well 2J 125
TW15: Ashf 4A 128
Sandringham Flats *WC2* *2D 12*
(off Charing Cross Rd.)
Sandringham Gdns. IG6: Ilf 3G 53
KT8: W Mole 4E 148
N8 6J 47
N12 6G 31
TW5: Cran 1J 111
Sandringham Ho. *W14* *4G 99*
(off Windsor Way)
Sandringham M. TW12: Hamp 1D 148
W5 7D 78
Sandringham Rd. BR1: Brom 5J 141
CR7: Thor H 5C 156
E7 5A 70
E8 5F 67
E10 6F 51
IG11: Bark 5K 71
KT4: Wor Pk 3C 164
N22 3C 48
NW2 6D 62
NW11 7G 45
TW6: H'row A 5A 110
UB5: N'olt 7E 58
Sandrock Pl. CR0: C'don 4K 169
Sandrock Rd. SE13 3C 122
SANDS END 1A 118
Sand's End La. SW6 1K 117
Sandstone La. E16 7K 87
Sandstone Pl. N19 2F 65
Sandstone Rd. SE12 2K 141
Sands Way IG8: Wfd G 6J 37
Sandtoft Rd. SE7 6K 105
Sandwell Cres. NW6 6J 63
Sandwich Ho. *SE16* *2J 103*
(off Swan Rd.)
WC1 *2E 6*
(off Sandwich St.)
Sandwich St. WC1 2E 6 (3J 83)
Sandwick Cl. NW7 7H 29
Sandy Bury BR6: Orp 3H 173
Sandycombe Rd. TW9: Kew, Rich 3F 115
TW14: Felt 1J 129
Sandycoombe Rd. TW1: Twick 6C 114
Sandycroft SE2 6A 108
Sandy Dr. TW14: Felt 1G 129
Sandy Hill Av. SE18 5F 107
Sandy Hill Rd. SE18 5F 107
SM6: Wall 7G 167
Sandyhill Rd. IG1: Ilf 4F 71
Sandy La. BR5: St P 7D 144
BR6: Orp 7K 161
CR4: Mitc 1E 154
DA14: Sidc 7D 144
HA3: Kenton 6F 43
KT1: Hamp W 7A 132
KT12: Walt T 6K 147
SM2: Cheam 7G 165
SM6: Wall 6H 167
TW10: Ham 2C 132
TW11: Hamp W, Tedd 7A 132
Sandy La. Nth. SM6: Wall 6H 167
Sandy La. Sth. SM6: Wall 7G 167
Sandymount Av. HA7: Stan 5H 27
Sandy Ridge BR7: Chst 6E 142
Sandy Rd. NW3 2K 63
NW11 2K 63
Sandys Row E1 6H 9 (5E 84)
Sandy Way CR0: C'don 3B 170
KT12: Walt T 7H 147
Sanford La. N16 3F 67
Sanford St. SE14 6A 104
Sanford Ter. N16 3F 67
Sanford Wlk. N16 2F 67
SE14 6A 104
Sangam Cl. UB2: S'hall 3C 94
Sanger Av. KT9: Chess 5E 162
Sangley Rd. SE6 7D 122
SE25 4E 156
Sangora Rd. SW11 4B 118
Sankey Ho. *E2* *2J 85*
(off St James's Av.)
Sansom Rd. E11 2H 69
Sansom St. SE5 1D 120
Sans Wlk. EC1 3K 7 (4A 84)
Santa Maria Ct. *E1* *5A 86*
(off Ocean Est.)
Sant Ho. *SE17* *4C 102*
(off Browning St.)
Santiago Ct. *E1* *5A 86*
(off Ocean Est.)
Santina Apartment
CR0: C'don *1D 168*
(off Cherry Orchard Rd.)
Santley Ho. SE1 7K 13 (2A 102)
Santley St. SW4 4K 119
Santos Rd. SW18 5J 117
Santway, The HA7: Stan 5D 26
Sapcote Trad. Cen. NW10 6B 62
Saperton Wlk. SE11 3H 19
Saphire Ct. *E15* *1E 86*
(off Warton Rd.)
Saphora Cl. BR6: Farnb 5H 173
Sapperton Ct. EC1 3C 8
Sapperton Ho. *W2* *5J 81*
(off Westbourne Pk. Rd.)
Sapphire Cl. E6 6E 88
RM8: Dag 1C 72
Sapphire Ct. *E1* *7G 85*
(off Cable St.)
Sapphire Rd. NW10 7J 61
SE8 4A 104
Saracen Cl. CR0: C'don 6D 156
Saracens Head Yd. EC3 1J 15
Saracens RUFC 7K 29
Saracen St. E14 6C 86
Sarah Ct. UB5: N'olt 1D 76
Sarah Ho. *E1* *6H 85*
(off Commercial Rd.)
Sarah Swift Ho. *SE1* *6F 15*
(off Kipling St.)
Sara La. Ct. *N1* *2E 84*
(off Stanway St.)
Saratoga Rd. E5 4J 67
Sara Turnbull Ho. SE18 4D 106
Saravia Ct. SE13 6G 123
Sardinia St. WC2 1G 13 (6K 83)
Sarita Cl. HA3: Hrw W 2H 41
Sarjant Path *SW19* *2F 135*
(off Blincoe Cl.)
Sarjeant Ct. *BR4: W W'ck* *2F 171*
(off Bencurtis Pk.)
Sark Cl. TW5: Hest 7E 94
Sark Ho. EN3: Enf W 1E 24
Sark Twr. SE28 2G 107
Sark Wlk. E16 6K 87
Sarnes Ct. *N11* *4A 32*
(off Oakleigh Rd. Sth.)
Sarnesfield Ho. *SE15* *6H 103*
(off Pencraig Way)
Sarnesfield Rd. EN2: Enf 4J 23
Sarratt Ho. *W10* *5E 80*
(off Sutton Way)
Sarre Rd. NW2 5H 63
Sarsen Av. TW3: Houn 2E 112
Sarsfeld Rd. SW12 2D 136
Sarsfield Rd. UB6: G'frd 2B 78
Sartor Rd. SE15 4K 121
Sarum Ho. *W11* *7H 81*
(off Portobello Rd.)
Sarum Ter. E3 4B 86
Sassoon NW9 1B 44
Satanita Cl. E16 6B 88
Satchell Mead NW9 1B 44
Satchwell Rd. E2 2K 9 (3G 85)
Satchwell St. E2 2K 9 (3G 85)
Satin Ho. E1 1K 15
Sattar M. N16 3D 66
Saturn Ho. *E3* *1C 86*
(off Garrison Rd.)
E15 *1F 87*
(off High St.)
Sauls Grn. E11 3G 69
Saundby La. SE3 4K 123
Saunders Apartments *E3* *3C 86*
(off Marchant St.)
Saunders Cl. *E14* *7B 86*
(off Limehouse C'way.)
IG1: Ilf 1H 71
Saunders Ho. *SE16* *2K 103*
(off Quebec Way)
Saunders Ness Rd. E14 5E 104
Saunders Rd. SE18 5K 107
UB10: Uxb 7B 56
Saunders St. SE11 3J 19 (4A 102)
Saunders Way SE28 7B 90
Saunderton Rd. HA0: Wemb 5B 60
Saunton Av. UB3: Harl 7H 93
Saunton Ct. *UB1: S'hall* *7G 77*
(off Haldane Rd.)
Savage Gdns. E6 6D 88
EC3 2H 15 (7E 84)
(not continuous)
Savannah Cl. SE15 7F 103
Savera Cl. UB2: S'hall 3A 94
Savernake Ct. HA7: Stan 6G 27
Savernake Ho. N4 7C 48
Savernake Rd. N9 6B 24
NW3 4D 64
Savery Dr. KT6: Surb 7B 150
Savile Cl. KT3: N Mald 5A 152
KT7: T Ditt 7K 149
Savile Gdns. CR0: C'don 2F 169
Savile Row W1 2A 12 (7G 83)
Saville Cres. TW15: Ashf 6F 129
Saville Rd. E16 1C 106
RM6: Chad H 6F 55
TW1: Twick 1K 131
W4 3K 97
Saville Row BR2: Hayes 1H 171
EN3: Enf H 2E 24
Savill Gdns. SW20 3C 152
Savill Ho. *E16* *1F 107*
(off Robert St.)
SW4 6H 119
Savill Row IG8: Wfd G 6C 36
Savin Lodge *SM2: Sutt* *7A 166*
(off Walnut M.)
Savona Cl. SW19 7F 135
Savona Ho. *SW8* *7G 101*
(off Savona St.)
Savona St. SW8 7G 101
Savoy Av. UB3: Harl 5G 93
Savoy Bldgs. WC2 3G 13
Savoy Chapel 3G 13
SAVOY CIRCUS 7B 80
Savoy Cl. E15 1G 87
HA8: Edg 5B 28
Savoy Ct. HA2: Harr 5F 41
NW3 3A 64
SW5 *4J 99*
(off Cromwell Rd.)
WC2 3F 13 (7K 83)
Savoy Hill WC2 3G 13 (7K 83)
Savoy M. SW9 3J 119
Savoy Pde. EN1: Enf 3K 23
Savoy Pl. W12 1F 99
WC2 3F 13 (7J 83)
Savoy Row WC2 2G 13
Savoy Steps WC2 3G 13
Savoy St. WC2 3G 13 (7K 83)
Savoy Theatre *3F 13*
(off Strand)
Savoy Way WC2 3G 13
Sawbill Cl. UB4: Yead 5B 76
Sawkins Cl. SW19 2G 135
Sawley Rd. W12 1C 98
Saw Mill Way N16 6G 49
Sawmill Yd. E3 1A 86
Sawtry Cl. SM5: Cars 7C 154
Sawyer Cl. N9 2B 34
Sawyer Ct. NW10 7K 61
Sawyers Cl. RM10: Dag 6J 73
Sawyer's Hill TW10: Rich 7F 115
Sawyers Lawn W13 6A 78
Sawyer St. SE1 6C 14 (2C 102)
Saxby Rd. SW2 7J 119
Saxham Rd. IG11: Bark 2J 89
Saxlingham Rd. E4 3A 36
Saxon Av. TW13: Hanw 2C 130
Saxonbury Av. TW16: Sun 3K 147
Saxonbury Cl. CR4: Mitc 3B 154
Saxonbury Ct. N7 5J 65

Saxonbury Gdns. KT6: Surb 1C 162
Saxon Bus. Cen. SW19 2A 154
Saxon Chase N8 6K 47
Saxon Cl. E17 7C 50
KT6: Surb 6D 150
UB8: Hil 5B 74
Saxon Ct. N1 1J 83
Saxon Dr. W3 6G 79
Saxonfield Cl. SW2 7K 119
Saxon Gdns. UB1: S'hall 7C 76
Saxon Hall *W2* *7K 81*
(off Palace Ct.)
Saxon Ho. *E1* *6K 9*
(off Thrawl St.)
KT1: King T 4F 151
SM6: Wall *1E 166*
(off London Rd.)
TW13: Hanw 2D 130
Saxon Lea Ct. *E3* *2B 86*
(off Saxon Rd.)
Saxon Lodge *CR0: C'don* *1C 168*
(off Tavistock Rd.)
Saxon Rd. BR1: Brom 7H 141
E3 2B 86
E6 4D 88
HA9: Wemb 3J 61
IG1: Ilf 6F 71
KT2: King T 1E 150
N22 1B 48
SE25 5D 156
TW15: Ashf 6F 129
UB1: S'hall 7C 76
Saxon Ter. SE6 2B 140
Saxon Wlk. DA14: Sidc 6C 144
Saxon Way N14 6C 22
UB7: Harm 2D 174
Saxon Way Ind. Est. UB7: Harm 2D 174
Saxony Pde. UB3: Hayes 5E 74
Saxton Cl. SE13 3F 123
Saxton Pl. KT8: W Mole 4D 148
Sayers Ct. W5 2D 96
Sayers Ho. *N2* *2B 46*
(off The Grange)
Sayer's Wlk. TW10: Rich 7F 115
Sayesbury La. N18 5B 34
Sayes Ct. SE8 6B 104
Sayes Ct. St. SE8 6B 104
Scadbury Pk. (Nature Reserve) 7K 143
Scads Hill Cl. BR6: Pet W 6K 161
Scafell *NW1* *1A 6*
(off Stanhope St.)
Scala 1F 7
Scala St. W1 5B 6 (5G 83)
Scales Rd. N17 3F 49
Scalpel, The 1G 15
Scampston M. W10 6F 81
Scandrett St. E1 1H 103
Scarab Cl. E16 7H 87
Scarba Wlk. *N1* *6D 66*
(off Essex Rd.)
Scarborough Rd. E11 1F 69
N4 7A 48
N9 7D 24
TW6: H'row A 6E 110
Scarborough St. E1 1K 15 (6F 85)
Scarbrook Rd. CR0: C'don 3C 168
Scarle Rd. HA0: Wemb 6D 60
Scarlet Cl. E20 5D 68
Scarlet Rd. SE6 3G 141
Scarlette Mnr. Way SW2 7A 120
Scarlet Wlk. EN3: Pond E 5E 24
Scarsbrook Rd. SE3 3B 124
Scarsdale Pl. W8 3K 99
Scarsdale Rd. HA2: Harr 3G 59
Scarsdale Studios *W8* *3J 99*
(off Stratford Rd.)
Scarsdale Vs. W8 3J 99
Scarth Rd. SW13 3B 116
Scawen Cl. SM5: Cars 4E 166
Scawen Rd. SE8 5A 104
Scawfell St. E2 2F 85
Sceaux Gdns. SE5 1E 120
Sceptre Ct. *EC3* *3K 15*
(off Tower Hill)
Sceptre Ho. *E1* *4J 85*
(off Malcolm Rd.)
Sceptre Rd. E2 3J 85
Sceynes Link N12 4D 30
Schafer Ho. NW1 2A 6 (3G 83)
Schofield Wlk. SE3 7J 105
Scholars Cl. EN5: Barn 4B 20
Scholars Ho. *NW6* *1J 81*
(off Glengall Rd.)
Scholars Pl. N16 3E 66
Scholars Rd. E4 1A 36
SW12 1G 137
Scholars Vw. KT7: T Ditt 7J 149
Scholars Way RM8: Dag 4A 72
Scholefield Rd. N19 2H 65
Scholey Ho. SW11 3C 118
Schomberg Ho. *SW1* *3D 18*
(off Page St.)
Schonfeld Sq. N16 2D 66
School All. TW1: Twick 1A 132
School App. E2 1H 9
UB4: Hayes 4H 75
Schoolbank Rd. SE10 3H 105
Schoolbell M. E3 2A 86
Schoolgate Dr. SM4: Mord 5K 153
School Ho. *SE1* *4E 102*
(off Page's Wlk.)
School Ho. La. NW7 6B 30
TW11: Tedd 7B 132
Schoolhouse La. E1 7K 85
Schoolhouse Yd. SE18 5F 107
School La. DA16: Well 3B 126
HA5: Pinn 4C 40
KT1: Hamp W 1C 150
KT6: Surb 1F 163
SE23 2H 139
TW17: Shep 6D 146
WD23: Bush 1A 26
School M. *E1* *7H 85*
(off Hawksmoor M.)
School Nook E5 2K 67
School Pas. KT1: King T 2F 151
UB1: S'hall 7D 76
School Rd. BR7: Chst 1G 161
E12 4D 70
KT1: Hamp W 1C 150
KT8: E Mos 4H 149
NW10 4K 79
RM10: Dag 1G 91
TW3: Houn 3G 113
TW12: Hamp H 6G 131
TW15: Ashf 6D 128
UB7: Harm 2E 174
School Rd. Av. TW12: Hamp H 6G 131
SCHOOL ROAD JUNC. 7D 128
School Sq. SE10 3H 105
School Wlk. TW16: Sun 4H 147
School Way N12 6G 31
RM8: Dag 3C 72
Schooner Cl. E14 3F 105
IG11: Bark 3B 90
SE16 2K 103
Schubert Rd. SW15 5H 117
Schurlock Pl. TW2: Twick 2J 131
Schwartz Wharf E9 7C 68
Science Mus.
Knightsbridge 2B 16 (3B 100)
Sclater St. E1 3J 9 (4F 85)
Scoble Pl. N16 4F 67
Scoles Cres. SW2 1B 138
Scoop, The 5H 15 (1E 102)
Scope Way KT1: King T 4E 150
Score Complex, The
Leyton 3D 68
Scoresby St. SE1 5A 14 (1B 102)
Scorton Av. UB6: G'frd 2A 78
Scorton Ho. *N1* *2E 84*
(off Whitmore Est.)
Scotch Comn. W13 5A 78
SCOTCH HOUSE 2D 100
Scoter Cl. IG8: Wfd G 7E 36
Scoter Ct. *SE8* *6B 104*
(off Abinger Gro.)
Scot Gro. HA5: Pinn 1B 40
Scotia Bldg. *E1* *7K 85*
(off Jardine Rd.)
Scotia Ct. *SE16* *2J 103*
(off Canada Est.)
Scotia Rd. SW2 7A 120
Scotland Grn. N17 2F 49
Scotland Grn. Rd. EN3: Pond E 5E 24
Scotland Grn. Rd. Nth. EN3: Pond E 4E 24
Scotland Pl. SW1 5E 12 (1J 101)
Scotland Rd. IG9: Buck H 1F 37
Scotland Yard 6F 13
Scotney Cl. BR6: Farnb 4E 172
Scotney Ho. E9 6J 67
Scots Cl. TW19: Stanw 1A 128
Scotsdale Cl. BR5: Pet W 4J 161
SM3: Cheam 7G 165
Scotsdale Rd. SE12 5K 123
Scotson Ho. SE11 4J 19
Scotswood St. EC1 3K 7 (4A 84)
Scotswood Wlk. N17 7B 34
Scott Av. SW15 6G 117
Scott Cl. KT19: Ewe 5J 163
SW16 1K 155
UB7: W Dray 4B 92
Scott Ct. W3 2K 97
Scott Cres. HA2: Harr 1F 59
Scott Ellis Gdns. NW8 2A 4 (3B 82)
Scottes La. RM8: Dag 1D 72
Scott Farm Cl. KT7: T Ditt 1B 162
Scott Gdns. TW5: Hest 7B 94
Scott Ho. DA17: Belv 5F 109
E13 *2J 87*
(off Queens Rd. W.)
E14 *2C 104*
(off Admirals Way)
N7 *6K 65*
(off Caledonian Rd.)
N18 *5B 34*
(off Woolmer Rd.)
NW8 *4C 4*
(off Broadley St.)
NW10 *7K 61*
(off Stonebridge Pk.)
SE8 *5B 104*
(off Grove St.)
Scott Lidgett Cres. SE16 2G 103
Scott Rd. HA8: Edg 2H 43
Scott Russell Pl. E14 5D 104
Scotts Av. BR2: Brom 2F 159
TW16: Sun 7G 129
Scotts Ct. *W12* *2E 98*
(off Scott's Rd.)
Scotts Dr. TW12: Hamp 7F 131
Scotts Farm Rd. KT19: Ewe 6J 163
Scott's La. BR2: Brom 3F 159
Scotts Pas. SE18 4F 107
Scott's Rd. E10 1E 68
UB2: S'hall 3A 94
W12 2D 98
Scotts Rd. BR1: Brom 7J 141
Scott's Sufferance Wharf SE1 7K 15
Scotts Ter. SE9 2C 142
Scott St. E1 4H 85
Scotts Way TW16: Sun 7G 129
Scott's Yd. EC4 2E 14 (7D 84)
Scott Trimmer Way TW3: Houn 2C 112
Scottwell Dr. NW9 5B 44
Scoulding Ho. *E14* *3C 104*
(off Mellish St.)
Scoulding Rd. E16 6J 87
Scouler St. E14 7E 86
Scout App. NW10 4A 62
Scout La. SW4 3G 119
Scout Pk. 7C 32
Scout Way NW7 4E 28
Scovell Cres. SE1 7C 14
Scovell Rd. SE1 7C 14 (2C 102)
Scrattons Farm Eco-Pk. 2E 90
Scrattons Ter. IG11: Bark 2D 90
Screen on the Green Cinema *1B 84*
(off Upper St.)
Screenworks N5 5C 66
Scrimgoeur Pl. N4 1C 66
Scriven Ct. E8 1F 85
Scriven St. E8 1F 85
Scrooby St. SE6 6D 122
Scrope Ho. *EC1* *5J 7*
(off Bourne Est.)
Scrubs La. NW10 3C 80
W10 3C 80
Scrutton Cl. SW12 7H 119
Scrutton St. EC2 4G 9 (4E 84)
Scudamore La. NW9 4J 43
Sculpture Ho. *E1* *5K 85*
(off Duckett St.)
Scutari Rd. SE22 5J 121
Scylla Cres. TW6: H'row A 7D 110
(not continuous)
Scylla Rd. SE15 3G 121
(not continuous)
TW6: H'row A 6D 110
Seaborne Wharf *E3* *5C 86*
(off Invicta Cl.)
Seabright St. E2 3H 85
Seabrook Dr. BR4: W W'ck 2G 171
Seabrook Gdns. RM7: Rush G 7G 55
Seabrook Rd. RM8: Dag 3D 72
Seaburn Cl. RM13: Rain 2K 91
Seacole Cl. W3 6K 79
Seacole Ct. *N21* *5E 22*
(off Pennington Dr.)
Sea Containers Ho. SE1 3K 13
Seacon Twr. E14 2B 104
Seacourt Rd. SE2 2D 108
Seafarer Way SE16 4A 104
Seafield Rd. N11 4C 32
Seaford Cl. HA4: Ruis 1F 57
Seaford Ho. *SE16* *2J 103*
(off Swan Rd.)
Seaford Rd. E17 3D 50
EN1: Enf 4K 23
N15 5D 48
TW6: H'row A 5A 110
W13 1B 96
Seaford St. WC1 2F 7 (3J 83)
Seaforth Av. KT3: N Mald 5D 152
Seaforth Cres. N5 5C 66
Seaforth Gdns. IG8: Wfd G 5F 37
KT19: Ewe 4B 164
N21 7E 22
Seaforth Pl. SW1 1B 18
Seager Pl. *SE8* *1C 122*
(off Deptford Bri.)
Seagrave Cl. E1 5K 85
Seagrave Lodge *SW6* *6J 99*
(off Seagrave Rd.)
Seagrave Rd. SW6 6J 99
Seagry Rd. E11 7J 51
Seagull Cl. IG11: Bark 3A 90
Seagull La. E16 7J 87
Seahorse Sailing Club 2K 61
Sealand Rd. TW6: H'row A 6C 110
Sealand Wlk. UB5: N'olt 3B 76
Seal Ho. *SE1* *7F 15*
(off Weston St.)
Sea Life London Aquarium
6G 13 (2K 101)
Seal St. E8 4F 67
Searle Ho. *NW8* *1C 82*
(off Cecil Gro.)
SW11 *1E 118*
(off Macduff Rd.)
Searle Pl. N4 1K 65
Searles Cl. SW11 7C 100
Searles Dr. E6 5F 89
Searles Rd. SE1 4D 102

Searson Ho.—Seven Sea Gdns.

Searson Ho. *SE17* *4B* ***102***
(off Canterbury Pl.)
Sears St. SE5 . . . . . 7D **102**
Seasalter Ho. *SW9* *1A* ***120***
(off Gosling Way)
Seasons Cl. W7 . . . . . 1K **95**
Seasons Ho. *E20* *6E* ***68***
(off Mirabelle Gdns.)
Seasprite Cl. UB5: N'olt 3B **76**
Seaton Av. IG3: Ilf 5K **71**
Seaton Cl. E13 . . . . . 4J **87**
SE11 . . . . . 5K **19** (5A **102**)
SW15 . . . . . 1D **134**
TW2: Whitt 6H **113**
Seaton Dr. TW15: Ashf 2A **128**
Seaton Gdns. HA4: Ruis 3H **57**
Seaton Point E5 . . . . . 4G **67**
Seaton Rd. CR4: Mitc 2C **154**
DA16: Well 7C **108**
HA0: Wemb 2E **78**
TW2: Whitt 6G **113**
UB3: Harl 4F **93**
Seaton Sq. NW7 . . . . . 7A **30**
Seaton St. N18 . . . . . 5B **34**
Seawell Ct. *IG11: Bark* *2G* ***89***
(off Dock Rd.)
Sebastian Ct. IG11: Bark 1K **89**
Sebastian Ho. *N1* *1G* ***9***
(off Hoxton St.)
Sebastian St. EC1 . . . . . 2B **8** (3B **84**)
Sebastopol Rd. N9 . . . . . 4B **34**
Sebbon St. N1 . . . . . 7B **66**
Sebergham Gro. NW7 . . . . . 7H **29**
Sebert Rd. E7 . . . . . 5K **69**
Sebright Ho. *E2* *2G* ***85***
(off Coate St.)
Sebright Pas. E2 . . . . . 2G **85**
Sebright Rd. EN5: Barn 2A **20**
Secker Cres. HA3: Hrw W 1G **41**
Secker Ho. *SW9* *2B* ***120***
(off Loughborough Est.)
Secker St. SE1 . . . . . 5J **13** (1A **102**)
Secombe Theatre
Sutton **5K 165**
Second Av. E12 . . . . . 4C **70**
E13 . . . . . 3J **87**
E17 . . . . . 5C **50**
EN1: Enf 5A **24**
HA9: Wemb 2D **60**
KT12: Walt T 6K **147**
N18 . . . . . 4D **34**
NW4 . . . . . 4F **45**
RM6: Chad H 5C **54**
RM10: Dag 2H **91**
SW14 . . . . . 3A **116**
UB3: Hayes 1H **93**
W3 . . . . . 1B **98**
W10 . . . . . 4G **81**
Second Cl. KT8: W Mole 4G **149**
Second Cross Rd. TW2: Twick 2J **131**
Second Way HA9: Wemb 4H **61**
Sedan Way SE17 . . . . . 5E **102**
Sedcombe Cl. DA14: Sidc 4B **144**
Sedcote Rd. EN3: Pond E 5D **24**
Sedding St. SW1 . . . . . 3G **17** (4E **100**)
Sedding Studios *SW1* *3G* ***17***
(off Sedding St.)
Seddon Highwalk *EC2* *5C* ***8***
(off Aldersgate St.)
Seddon Ho. EC2 . . . . . 5C **8**
Seddon Rd. SM4: Mord 5B **154**
Seddon St. WC1 . . . . . 2H **7** (3K **83**)
Sedgebrook Rd. SE3 . . . . . 2B **124**
Sedgecombe Av. HA3: Kenton 5C **42**
Sedgefield Ct. *UB5: N'olt* *5F* ***59***
(off Newmarket Av.)
Sedgeford Rd. W12 . . . . . 1B **98**
Sedge Gdns. IG11: Bark 3A **90**
Sedgehill Rd. SE6 . . . . . 4C **140**
Sedgemere Av. N2 . . . . . 3A **46**
Sedgemere Rd. SE2 . . . . . 3C **108**
Sedgemoor Dr. RM10: Dag 4G **73**
Sedge Rd. N17 . . . . . 7D **34**
Sedgeway SE6 . . . . . 1H **141**
Sedgewood Cl. BR2: Hayes 7H **159**
Sedgmoor Pl. SE5 . . . . . 7E **102**
Sedgwick Av. UB10: Hil 7D **56**
Sedgwick Ho. *E3* *5C* ***86***
(off Gale St.)
Sedgwick Rd. E10 . . . . . 2E **68**
Sedgwick St. E9 . . . . . 5K **67**
Sedleigh Rd. SW18 . . . . . 6H **117**
Sedlescombe Rd. SW6 . . . . . 6J **99**
Sedley Cl. EN1: Enf 1C **24**
Sedley Ct. SE26 . . . . . 2H **139**
Sedley Ho. *SE11* *5H* ***19***
(off Newburn St.)
Sedley Pl. W1 . . . . . 1J **11** (6F **83**)
Sedona Ho. *E20* *6D* ***68***
(off Victory Pde.)
Sedum Cl. NW9 . . . . . 5H **43**
Sedum M. EN2: Enf 3F **23**
Seeley Dr. SE21 . . . . . 4E **138**
Seelig Av. NW9 . . . . . 7C **44**
Seely Rd. SW17 . . . . . 6E **136**
Seetha Ho. *IG1: Ilf* *2H* ***71***
(off High Rd.)
Seething La. EC3 . . . . . 2H **15** (7E **84**)
SEETHING WELLS 6C **150**
Seething Wells La. KT6: Surb 6C **150**
Sefton Av. HA3: Hrw W 2H **41**
NW7 . . . . . 5E **28**
Sefton Cl. BR5: St M Cry 4K **161**
Sefton Ct. EN2: Enf 2G **23**
TW3: Houn 1F **113**
Sefton Rd. BR5: St M Cry 4K **161**
CR0: C'don 1G **169**
Sefton St. SW15 . . . . . 3E **116**
Segal Cl. SE23 . . . . . 7A **122**
Sekforde St. EC1 . . . . . 4A **8** (4B **84**)
Sekhon Ter. TW13: Hanw 3E **130**
Selah Dr. BR8: Swan 7J **145**
Selan Gdns. UB4: Yead 5K **75**
Selbie Av. NW10 . . . . . 5B **62**
Selborne Av. DA5: Bexl 1E **144**
E12 . . . . . 4E **70**
Selborne Gdns. NW4 . . . . . 4C **44**
UB6: G'frd 2A **78**
Selborne Rd. CR0: C'don 3E **168**
DA14: Sidc 4B **144**
E17 . . . . . 5B **50**
IG1: Ilf 2E **70**
KT3: N Mald 2A **152**
N14 . . . . . 3D **32**
N22 . . . . . 1K **47**
SE5 . . . . . 2D **120**
Selborne Wlk. E17 . . . . . 5B **50**
Selborne Wlk. Shop. Cen. E17 . . . . . 4B **50**
Selbourne Av. KT6: Surb 2F **163**
Selbourne Ho. SE1 . . . . . 7E **14**
Selby Cen., The **6K 33**
Selby Chase HA4: Ruis 2K **57**
Selby Cl. BR7: Chst 6E **142**
E6 . . . . . 5C **88**
KT9: Chess 7E **162**
Selby Gdns. UB1: S'hall 4E **76**
Selby Grn. SM5: Cars 7C **154**
Selby Rd. E11 . . . . . 3G **69**
E13 . . . . . 5K **87**
N17 . . . . . 7K **33**
SE20 . . . . . 2G **157**
SM5: Cars 7C **154**
TW15: Ashf 6E **128**
W5 . . . . . 4B **78**
Selby Sq. *W10* *3G* ***81***
(off Dowland St.)
Selby St. E1 . . . . . 4G **85**
Selcroft Ho. *SE10* *5H* ***105***
(off Glenister Rd.)
Selden Ho. *SE15* *2J* ***121***
(off Selden Rd.)
Selden Rd. SE15 . . . . . 2J **121**
Selden Wlk. N7 . . . . . 2K **65**
Seldon Ho. *SW1* *6A* ***18***
(off Churchill Gdns.)
SW8 . . . . . *7G* ***101***
(off Stewart's Rd.)
Selfridges **1H 11**
SELHURST 6E **156**
Selhurst Cl. SW19 . . . . . 1F **135**
Selhurst New Rd. SE25 . . . . . 6E **156**
Selhurst Pk. **4E 156**
Selhurst Pl. SE25 . . . . . 6E **156**
Selhurst Rd. N9 . . . . . 3J **33**
SE25 . . . . . 6E **156**
Selig Ct. NW11 . . . . . 7G **45**
Selina Ho. *NW8* *3B* ***4***
(off Frampton St.)
Selinas La. RM8: Dag 7E **54**
Selkirk Ho. *N1* *1K* ***83***
(off Bingfield St.)
Selkirk Rd. SW17 . . . . . 4C **136**
TW2: Twick 2G **131**
Sellers Hall Cl. N3 . . . . . 7D **30**
Sellincourt Rd. SW17 . . . . . 5C **136**
Sellindge Cl. BR3: Beck 7B **140**
Sellons Av. NW10 . . . . . 1B **80**
Sellwood Dr. EN5: Barn 5A **20**
Selman Ho. E9 . . . . . 6A **68**
SELSDON 7J **169**
Selsdon Av. CR2: S Croy 6D **168**
Selsdon Cl. KT6: Surb 5E **150**
RM5: Col R 1J **55**
Selsdon Pk. Rd. CR0: Sels 7K **169**
CR2: Sels 7K **169**
Selsdon Rd. CR2: S Croy 5D **168**
E11 . . . . . 7J **51**
E13 . . . . . 1A **88**
NW2 . . . . . 2B **62**
SE27 . . . . . 3A **138**
Selsdon Way E14 . . . . . 3D **104**
Selsea Pl. N16 . . . . . 5E **66**
Selsey *WC1* *2F* ***7***
(off Tavistock Pl.)
Selsey Cres. DA16: Well 1D **126**
Selsey St. E14 . . . . . 5C **86**
Selvage La. NW7 . . . . . 5E **28**
Selway Cl. HA5: Eastc 4K **39**
Selway Ho. *SW8* *1J* ***119***
(off Sth. Lambeth Rd.)
Selwood Pl. SW7 . . . . . 5A **16** (5B **100**)
Selwood Rd. CR0: C'don 2H **169**
KT9: Chess 4D **162**
SM3: Sutt 1H **165**
Selwoods SW2 . . . . . 7A **120**
Selwood Ter. SW7 . . . . . 5A **16** (5B **100**)
Selworthy Cl. E11 . . . . . 5J **51**
Selworthy Ho. *SW11* *1B* ***118***
(off Battersea Church Rd.)
Selworthy Rd. SE6 . . . . . 3B **140**
Selwyn Av. E4 . . . . . 6K **35**
IG3: Ilf 6K **53**
TW9: Rich 3E **114**
Selwyn Cl. TW4: Houn 4C **112**
Selwyn Ct. *E17* *5C* ***50***
(off Yunus Khan Cl.)
HA8: Edg 7C **28**
HA9: Wemb 3J **61**
SE3 . . . . . 3H **123**
TW10: Rich *5F* ***115***
(off Church Rd.)
Selwyn Cres. DA16: Well 3B **126**
Selwyn Rd. E3 . . . . . 2B **86**
E13 . . . . . 1K **87**
KT3: N Mald 5K **151**
NW10 . . . . . 7A **62**
Semley Ga. E9 . . . . . 6B **68**
(not continuous)
Semley Ho. *SW1* *4J* ***17***
(off Semley Pl.)
Semley Pl. SW1 . . . . . 4H **17** (4E **100**)
Semley Rd. SW16 . . . . . 2J **155**
Senate St. SE15 . . . . . 2J **121**
Senators Lodge *E3* *2A* ***86***
(off Roman Rd.)
Senator Wlk. SE28 . . . . . 3H **107**
Sendall Ct. *SW11* *3B* ***118***
(off Winstanley Rd.)
Seneca Rd. CR7: Thor H 4C **156**
Sener Ct. CR2: S Croy 6C **168**
Senga Rd. SM6: Wall 1E **166**
Senhouse Rd. SM3: Cheam 3F **165**
Senior St. W2 . . . . . 5K **81**
Senlac Rd. SE12 . . . . . 1K **141**
Sennen Rd. EN1: Enf 7A **24**
Sennen Wlk. SE9 . . . . . 3C **142**
Senrab St. E1 . . . . . 6K **85**
Sentamu Cl. SE24 . . . . . 1B **138**
Sentinel Cl. UB5: N'olt 4C **76**
Sentinel Sq. NW4 . . . . . 4E **44**
September Ct. *UB1: S'hall* *1F* ***95***
(off Dormer's Wells La.)
UB8: Uxb 2A **74**
September Way HA7: Stan 6G **27**
Septimus Pl. EN1: Enf 5B **24**
Sequoia Cl. WD23: B Hea 1C **26**
Sequoia Gdns. BR6: Orp 7K **161**
Sequoia Pk. HA5: Hat E 6A **26**
Seraph Ct. *EC1* *1C* ***8***
(off Moreland St.)
Serbin Cl. E10 . . . . . 7E **50**
Serenaders Rd. SW9 . . . . . 2A **120**
Serenity Apartments E17 . . . . . 5D **50**
SW11 . . . . . *4C* ***118***
(off Monarch Sq.)
Serenity Cl. HA2: Harr 2F **59**
Seren Pk. Gdns. SE3 . . . . . 6G **105**
Sergeant Ind. Est. SW18 . . . . . 6K **117**
Serica Ct. SE10 . . . . . 7E **104**
Serjeants Inn EC4 . . . . . 1K **13** (6A **84**)
Serlby Ct. *W14* *3H* ***99***
(off Somerset Sq.)
Serle St. WC2 . . . . . 7H **7** (6K **83**)
Sermon La. EC4 . . . . . 1C **14**
Serpentine, The . . . . . **5D 10 (1C 100)**
Serpentine Cl. RM6: Chad H 7C **54**
Serpentine Ct. *SE16* *2K* ***103***
(off Christopher Cl.)
Serpentine Gallery . . . . . **6B 10 (2B 100)**
Serpentine Rd. W2 . . . . . 5C **10** (1C **100**)
Serpentine Sackler Gallery
. . . . . **4B 10 (1B 100)**
Serviden Dr. BR1: Brom 1B **160**
Servite Ho. BR3: Beck 1B **158**
KT4: Wor Pk *2B* ***164***
(off The Avenue)
N14 . . . . . *5A* ***22***
(off Bramley Rd.)
Servius Ct. TW8: Bford 7D **96**
Setchell Rd. SE1 . . . . . 4F **103**
Setchell Way SE1 . . . . . 4F **103**
Seth St. SE16 . . . . . 2J **103**
Seton Gdns. RM9: Dag 7C **72**
Settle Point E13 . . . . . 2J **87**
Settlers Ct. E14 . . . . . 7F **87**
Settles St. E1 . . . . . 5G **85**
Settrington Rd. SW6 . . . . . 2K **117**
Seven Acres SM5: Cars 2C **166**
Seven Dials WC2 . . . . . 1E **12** (6J **83**)
Seven Dials Ct. *WC2* *1E* ***12***
(off Shorts Gdns.)
Sevenex Pde. HA9: Wemb 5E **60**
Seven Islands Leisure Cen. **3J 103**
SEVEN KINGS 1K **71**
Seven Kings Rd. IG3: Ilf 1J **71**
Seven Kings Way KT2: King T 1E **150**
Sevenoaks Cl. DA7: Bex 4H **127**
Sevenoaks Ct. HA6: Nwood 1E **38**
Sevenoaks Rd. BR6: Chels, Orp 5K **173**
BR6: Prat B 7K **173**
SE4 . . . . . 6A **122**
Sevenoaks Way BR5: St P 7C **144**
DA14: Sidc 7C **144**
Seven Sea Gdns. E3 . . . . . 5D **86**

Sevenseas Rd. TW6: H'row A 6E **110**
SEVEN SISTERS 5F 49
Seven Sisters Rd. N4 ....2A **66**
N7 ....3K **65**
N15 ....7C **48**
Seven Stars Cnr. W12 ....3C **98**
Seven Stars Yd. E1 ....5K **9**
Seventh Av. E12 ....4D **70**
UB3: Hayes 1J **93**
Seven Ways Pde. IG2: Ilf 5E **52**
Severnake Cl. E14 ....4C **104**
Severn Av. W10 ....3G **81**
Severn Ct. *KT2: King T* *1D* ***150***
(off John Williams Cl.)
Severn Dr. KT10: Hin W 2A **162**
Severn Ho. *SW18* *4J* ***117***
(off Enterprise Way)
Severn Way NW10 ....5B **62**
Severus Ho. UB3: Hayes 6F **75**
Severus Rd. SW11 ....4C **118**
Seville Ho. *E1* *1G* ***103***
(off Wapping High St.)
Seville M. N1 ....7E **66**
Seville St. SW1 ....7F **11** (2D **100**)
Sevington Rd. NW4 ....6D **44**
Sevington St. W9 ....4K **81**
Seward Rd. BR3: Beck 2K **157**
W7 ....2A **96**
SEWARDSTONE 1K 25
Sewardstone Cl. E4 ....1K **25**
Sewardstone Gdns. E4 ....5J **25**
Sewardstone Rd. E2 ....2J **85**
E4 ....7J **25**
Seward St. EC1 ....3B **8** (3B **84**)
Sewdley St. E5 ....3K **67**
Sewell Rd. SE2 ....3A **108**
Sewell St. E13 ....3J **87**
Sextant Av. E14 ....4F **105**
Sexton Ct. *E14* *7F* ***87***
(off Newport Av.)
Sextons Ho. *SE10* *6E* ***104***
(off Bardsley La.)
Seymer Rd. RM1: Rom 3K **55**
Seymore M. *SE14* *7B* ***104***
(off New Cross Rd.)
Seymour Av. KT17: Ewe 7E **164**
N17 ....2G **49**
SM4: Mord 7F **153**
Seymour Cl. HA5: Hat E 1D **40**
KT8: E Mos 5G **149**
Seymour Ct. E4 ....2C **36**
KT1: Hamp W 1D **150**
N10 ....2E **46**
N21 ....6E **22**
NW2 ....2D **62**
Seymour Dr. BR2: Brom 1D **172**
Seymour Gdns. HA4: Ruis 1B **58**
IG1: Ilf 1D **70**
KT5: Surb 5F **151**
SE4 ....3A **122**
TW1: Twick 7B **114**
TW13: Hanw 4A **130**
Seymour Ho. *E16* *1J* ***105***
(off De Quincey M.)
NW1 ....*1D* ***6***
(off Churchway)
SM2: Sutt *6K* ***165***
(off Mulgrave Rd.)
WC1 ....*0C* ***6***
(off Tavistock Pl.)
Seymour Leisure Cen. 6E **4** (5D **82**)
Seymour M. W1 ....7G **5** (6E **82**)
Seymour Pl. SE25 ....4H **157**
W1 ....6E **4** (5D **82**)
Seymour Rd. CR4: Mitc 7E **154**
E4 ....1J **35**
E6 ....2B **88**
E10 ....1B **68**
KT1: Hamp W 1D **150**
KT8: W Mole, E Mos 5G **149**
N3 ....7E **30**
Seymour Rd. N8 ....5A **48**
N9 ....2C **34**
SM5: Cars 5E **166**
SW18 ....7H **117**
SW19 ....3F **135**
TW12: Hamp H 5G **131**
W4 ....4J **97**
Seymour St. SE18 ....3G **107**
W1 ....1E **10** (6D **82**)
W2 ....1E **10** (6D **82**)
Seymour Ter. SE20 ....1H **157**
Seymour Vs. SE20 ....1H **157**
Seymour Wlk. SW10 ....6A **100**
Seymour Way TW16: Sun 7H **129**
Seyssel St. E14 ....4E **104**
Shaa Rd. W3 ....7K **79**
Shabana Rd. W12 ....1D **98**
Shacklegate La. TW11: Tedd 4J **131**
Shackleton Cl. SE23 ....2H **139**
Shackleton Ct. *E14* *5C* ***104***
(off Maritime Quay)
TW19: Stanw *6A* ***110***
(off Whitley Cl.)
W12 ....*2D* ***98***
(off Scott's Rd.)
Shackleton Ho. *E1* *1J* ***103***
(off Prusom St.)
NW10 ....7K **61**
Shackleton Rd. UB1: S'hall 7D **76**
SHACKLEWELL 4F 67
Shacklewell Grn. E8 ....4F **67**
Shacklewell Ho. E8 ....4F **67**
Shacklewell La. E8 ....5F **67**
N16 ....4F **67**
Shacklewell Rd. N16 ....4F **67**
Shacklewell Row E8 ....4F **67**
Shacklewell St. E2 ....2K **9** (3F **85**)
Shadbolt Av. E4 ....5F **35**
Shadbolt Cl. KT4: Wor Pk 2B **164**
Shad Thames SE1 ....5J **15** (1F **103**)
(Anchor Brewhouse)
SE1 ....2F **103**
(Jamaica Rd.)
SHADWELL 7H 85
Shadwell Ct. UB5: N'olt 2D **76**
Shadwell Dr. UB5: N'olt 3D **76**
Shadwell Gdns. E1 ....7J **85**
Shadwell Pierhead E1 ....7J **85**
Shadwell Pl. *E1* *7J* ***85***
(off Sutton St.)
Shady Bush Cl. WD23: Bush 1B **26**
Shaef Way TW11: Tedd 7A **132**
Shafter Rd. RM10: Dag 6J **73**
Shaftesbury Av. EN3: Enf H 2E **24**
EN5: New Bar 4F **21**
HA2: Harr 1F **59**
HA3: Kenton 5D **42**
TW14: Felt 6J **111**
UB2: S'hall 4E **94**
W1 ....3C **12** (7H **83**)
WC1 ....7E **6** (6J **83**)
WC2 ....7E **6** (6J **83**)
Shaftesbury Cen. *W10* *4F* ***81***
(off Barlby Rd.)
Shaftesbury Circ. HA2: Harr 1G **59**
Shaftesbury Ct. *E6* *6E* ***88***
(off Sapphire Cl.)
N1 ....*2D* ***84***
(off Shaftesbury St.)
SE1 ....*3D* ***102***
(off Alderney M.)
SE5 ....4D **120**
SW6 ....*1K* ***117***
(off Maltings Pl.)
SW16 ....3H **137**
Shaftesbury Cres. TW18: Staines 7A **128**
Shaftesbury Gdns. NW10 ....4A **80**
Shaftesbury Lodge *E14* *6D* ***86***
(off Upper Nth. St.)
Shaftesbury M. SW4 ....5G **119**
W8 ....3J **99**
Shaftesbury Pde. HA2: Harr 1G **59**
Shaftesbury Pl. *EC2* *6C* ***8***
(off London Wall)
W14 ....*4H* ***99***
(off Warwick Rd.)
Shaftesbury Point *E13* *2J* ***87***
(off High St.)
Shaftesbury Rd. BR3: Beck 2B **158**
E4 ....1A **36**
E7 ....7A **70**
E10 ....1C **68**
E17 ....6D **50**
N18 ....6K **33**
N19 ....1J **65**
SM5: Cars 7B **154**
TW9: Rich 3E **114**
Shaftesbury Row *SE8* *7C* ***104***
(off Speedwell St.)
Shaftesburys, The IG11: Bark 2G **89**
Shaftesbury St. N1 ....2C **84**
(not continuous)
Shaftesbury Theatre ***7E 6***
(off Shaftesbury Av.)
Shaftesbury Vs. *W8* *3J* ***99***
(off Allen St.)
Shaftesbury Way TW2: Twick 3H **131**
Shaftesbury Waye UB4: Yead 5A **76**
Shafto M. SW1 ....2F **17** (3D **100**)
Shafton M. E9 ....1K **85**
Shafton Rd. E9 ....1K **85**
Shafts Ct. EC3 ....1G **15** (6E **84**)
Shaftswood Ct. *SW17* *3D* ***136***
(off Lynwood Rd.)
Shahjalal Ho. *E2* *2G* ***85***
(off Pritchards Rd.)
Shakespeare Av. N11 ....5B **32**
NW10 ....1K **79**
TW14: Felt 6J **111**
UB4: Hayes, Yead 6J **75**
(not continuous)
UB4: Yead 4K **75**
Shakespeare Cl. HA3: Kenton 7G **43**
Shakespeare Ct. EN5: New Bar 3E **20**
HA3: Kenton 6F **43**
NW6 ....*7A* ***64***
(off Fairfax Rd.)
Shakespeare Cres. E12 ....6D **70**
Shakespeare Dr. HA3: Kenton 6F **43**
Shakespeare Gdns. N2 ....4D **46**
Shakespeare Ho. *E9* *7J* ***67***
(off Lyme Gro.)
N14 ....2C **32**
Shakespeare Rd. DA7: Bex 1E **126**
E17 ....2K **49**
N3 ....1J **45**
NW7 ....4G **29**
NW10 ....1K **79**
SE24 ....5B **120**
W3 ....1J **97**
W7 ....7K **77**
Shakespeare's Globe & Exhibition
....4C **14** (1C **102**)
Shakespeare Twr. EC2 ....5D **8**
Shakespeare Way TW13: Hanw 4A **130**
Shakspeare M. N16 ....4E **66**
Shakspeare Wlk. N16 ....4E **66**
Shalbourne Sq. E9 ....6B **68**
Shalcomb St. SW10 ....6A **100**
Shalden Ho. SW15 ....0D **110**
Shaldon Dr. HA4: Ruis 3A **58**
SM4: Mord 5G **153**
Shaldon Rd. HA8: Edg 2F **43**
Shalfleet Dr. W10 ....7F **81**
Shalford Cl. BR6: Farnb 4G **173**
Shalford Ct. N1 ....2B **84**
Shalford Ho. SE1 ....3D **102**
Shalimar Gdns. W3 ....7J **79**
Shalimar Rd. W3 ....7J **79**
Shallons Rd. SE9 ....4F **143**
Shalstone Rd. SW14 ....3H **115**
Shalston Vs. KT6: Surb 6F **151**
Shamrock Ho. *SE26* *4G* ***139***
(off Talisman Sq.)
Shamrock Rd. CR0: C'don 6K **155**
Shamrock St. SW4 ....3H **119**
Shamrock Way N14 ....1A **32**
Shandon Rd. SW4 ....6G **119**
Shand St. SE1 ....6H **15** (2E **102**)
Shandy St. E1 ....5K **85**
Shan Ho. *WC1* *4G* ***7***
(off Millman St.)
Shanklin Ho. E17 ....2B **50**
Shanklin Rd. N8 ....5H **47**
N15 ....4G **49**
Shannon Cl. NW2 ....3F **63**
UB2: S'hall 5B **94**
Shannon Commercial Cen.
KT3: N Mald 4C **152**
SHANNON CORNER 4C 152
Shannon Cnr. Retail Pk.
KT3: N Mald 4C **152**
Shannon Ct. *CR0: C'don* *1C* ***168***
(off Tavistock Rd.)
N16 ....3E **66**
SE15 ....*7F* ***103***
(off Garnies Cl.)
Shannon Gro. SW9 ....4K **119**
Shannon M. SE3 ....4H **123**
Shannon Pl. NW8 ....2C **82**
Shannon Way BR3: Beck 6D **140**
Shanti Ct. SW18 ....1J **135**
Shap Cres. SM5: Cars 1D **166**
Shapland Way N13 ....5E **32**
Shapwick Cl. N11 ....5J **31**
Shard, The 5F 15
Shardcroft Av. SE24 ....5B **120**
Shardeloes Rd. SE4 ....3B **122**
SE14 ....2B **122**
Shard's Sq. SE15 ....6G **103**
Sharland Cl. CR7: Thor H 6A **156**
Sharman Ct. DA14: Sidc 4A **144**
Sharnbrooke Cl. DA16: Well 3C **126**
Sharnbrook Ho. W14 ....6J **99**
Sharon Cl. KT6: Surb 1C **162**
Sharon Ct. *CR2: S Croy* *5C* ***168***
(off Warham Rd.)
Sharon Gdns. E9 ....1J **85**
Sharon Rd. EN3: Enf H 2F **25**
W4 ....5K **97**
Sharpe Cl. W7 ....5K **77**
Sharp Ho. SW8 ....3F **119**
TW1: Twick 6D **114**
Sharpleshall St. NW1 ....7D **64**
Sharpley Ct. *SE1* *6A* ***14***
(off Pocock St.)
Sharpness Cl. UB4: Yead 5C **76**
Sharp's La. HA4: Ruis 7F **39**
Sharratt St. SE15 ....6J **103**
Sharsted St. SE17 ....5B **102**
Sharvel La. UB5: N'olt 1J **75**
Sharwood *WC1* *1H* ***7***
(off Penton Ri.)
Shaver's Pl. SW1 ....3C **12**
Shaw, The BR7: Chst 7G **143**
Shaw Av. IG11: Bark 2E **90**
Shawbrooke Rd. SE9 ....5A **124**
Shawbury Cl. NW9 ....1A **44**
Shawbury Rd. SE22 ....5F **121**
Shaw Cl. SE28 ....1B **108**
TW19: Stanw 1A **120**
WD23: B Hea 2D **26**
Shaw Ct. SM4: Mord 7A **154**
W3 ....*3J* ***97***
(off All Saints Rd.)
Shaw Cres. E14 ....5A **86**
Shaw Dr. KT12: Walt T 7A **148**
Shawfield Ct. UB7: W Dray 3A **92**
Shawfield Pk. BR1: Brom 2B **160**
Shawfield St. SW3 ....6D **16** (5C **100**)
Shawford Ct. SW15 ....7C **116**
Shawford Rd. KT19: Ewe 6K **163**
Shaw Gdns. IG11: Bark 2E **90**

Shaw Ho. DA17: Belv 5F 109
E16 1E 106
(off Claremont St.)
Shaw Path BR1: Brom 3H 141
Shaw Pl. N2 3E 46
Shaw Rd. BR1: Brom 3H 141
EN3: Enf H 1E 24
SE22 4E 120
Shaws Cotts. SE23 3A 140
Shaws Path *KT1: Hamp W* 1C 150
(off Bennett Cl.)
Shaw Sq. E17 1A 50
Shaw Theatre 2D 6 (3H 83)
Shaw Way SM6: Wall 7J 167
Shead Ct. *E1* 6H 85
(off James Voller Way)
Shearing Dr. SM5: Cars 7A 154
Shearling Way N7 6J 65
Shearman Rd. SE3 4H 123
SHEARS, THE 7G 129
Shears Ct. TW16: Sun 7G 129
Shears La. SW16 7J 137
Shearsmith Ho. *E1* 7G 85
(off Hindmarsh Cl.)
Shears Way TW16: Sun 1G 147
Shearwater Cl. IG11: Bark 3A 90
Shearwater Ct. *E1* 3K 15
(off Star Pl.)
SE8 6B 104
(off Abinger Gro.)
Shearwater Dr. NW9 7C 44
Shearwater Rd. SM1: Sutt 5H 165
Shearwater Way UB4: Yead 6B 76
Sheath Cotts. *KT7: T Ditt* 6B 150
(off Ferry Rd.)
Sheaveshill Av. NW9 4A 44
Sheaveshill Ct. NW9 4K 43
Sheaveshill Pde. *NW9* 4A 44
(off Sheaveshill Av.)
Sheba Ct. *N17* 6B 34
(off Altair Cl.)
Sheba Pl. E1 4K 9 (4F 85)
Sheen Comn. Dr. TW10: Rich 4G 115
Sheen Ct. TW10: Rich 4G 115
Sheen Ct. Rd. TW10: Rich 4G 115
Sheendale Rd. TW9: Rich 4F 115
Sheenewood SE26 4H 139
Sheen Ga. Gdns. SW14 4J 115
Sheengate Mans. SW14 4K 115
Sheen Gro. N1 1A 84
Sheen La. SW14 5J 115
Sheen Pk. TW9: Rich 4F 115
Sheen Rd. BR5: St M Cry 4K 161
TW9: Rich 5E 114
TW10: Rich 5E 114
Sheen Way SM6: Wall 5K 167
Sheen Wood SW14 5J 115
Sheepcote Cl. TW5: Cran 7J 93
Sheepcote La. SW11 2D 118
Sheepcote Rd. HA1: Harr 6K 41
Sheepcotes Rd. RM6: Chad H 4E 54
Sheephouse Way KT3: N Mald 1K 163
Sheep La. E8 1H 85
Sheep Wlk. TW17: Shep 7B 146
Sheep Wlk. M. SW19 6F 135
Sheerness M. E16 2F 107
Sheerwater Rd. E16 5B 88
Sheffield Rd. TW6: H'row A 6E 110
Sheffield Sq. E3 3B 86
Sheffield St. WC2 1G 13 (6K 83)
Sheffield Ter. W8 1J 99
Sheffield Way TW6: H'row A 5F 111
Shelbourne Cl. HA5: Pinn 3D 40
Shelbourne Pl. BR3: Beck 7B 140
Shelbourne Rd. N17 2H 49
Shelburne Dr. TW4: Houn 6E 112
Shelburne Rd. N7 4K 65
Shelbury Cl. DA14: Sidc 3A 144
Shelbury Rd. SE22 5H 121
Sheldon Av. IG5: Ilf 2F 53
N6 7C 46
Sheldon Cl. SE12 5K 123
SE20 1H 157
Sheldon Ct. EN5: New Bar 4E 20
RM7: Rush G 6K 55
(off Union Rd.)
SW8 7J 101
(off Lansdowne Grn.)
Sheldon Ho. *N1* 1E 84
(off Kingsland Rd.)
Sheldon Pl. E2 2G 85
(not continuous)
Sheldon Rd. DA7: Bex 1F 127
N18 4K 33
NW2 4F 63
RM9: Dag 7E 72
Sheldon Sq. W2 6A 4 (5A 82)
Sheldon St. CR0: C'don 3C 168
Sheldrake Cl. E16 1D 106
Sheldrake Ct. *E6* 2C 88
(off St Bartholomew's Rd.)
Sheldrake Ho. *SE16* 4K 103
(off Tawny Way)
Sheldrake Pl. W8 2J 99
Sheldrick Cl. SW19 2B 154
Shelduck Cl. E15 5H 69
Shelduck Ct. *SE8* 6B 104
(off Pilot Cl.)
Sheldwich Ter. BR2: Brom 6C 160
Shelford KT1: King T 2G 151
Shelford Pl. N16 3D 66
Shelford Ri. SE19 7F 139
Shelford Rd. EN5: Barn 6A 20
Shelgate Rd. SW11 5C 118
Shell Cen. SE1 5H 13 (1K 101)
Shell Cl. BR2: Brom 6C 160
Shellduck Cl. NW9 2A 44
Shelley *N8* 3J 47
(off Boyton Rd.)
Shelley Av. E12 6C 70
UB6: G'frd 3H 77
Shelley Cl. BR6: Orp 3J 173
HA8: Edg 4B 28
SE15 2H 121
UB4: Hayes 5J 75
UB6: G'frd 3H 77
Shelley Ct. *E10* 7D 50
(off Skelton's La.)
E11 4K 51
(off Makepeace Rd.)
N19 1K 65
SW3 7F 17
(off Tite St.)
Shelley Cres. TW5: Hest 1B 112
UB1: S'hall 6D 76
Shelley Dr. DA16: Well 1J 125
Shelley Gdns. HA0: Wemb 2C 60
Shelley Ho. *E2* 3J 85
(off Cornwall Av.)
N16 4E 66
SE17 5C 102
(off Browning St.)
SW1 7B 18
(off Churchill Gdns.)
Shelley Lodge EN2: Enf 1J 23
Shelley Rd. NW10 1K 79
Shelley Way SW19 5B 136
Shellness Rd. E5 5H 67
Shell Rd. SE13 3D 122
Shellwood Rd. SW11 2D 118
Shelmerdine Cl. E3 5C 86
Shelson Av. TW13: Felt 3H 129
Shelson Pde. TW13: Felt 3H 129
Shelton Rd. SW19 1J 153
Shelton St. WC2 1E 12 (6J 83)
(not continuous)
Shene Ho. *EC1* 5J 7
(off Bourne Est.)
Shene Sports & Fitness Cen. 4A 116
Shenfield Ho. *SE18* 1B 124
(off Portway Gdns.)
Shenfield Rd. IG8: Wfd G 7E 36
Shenfield St. N1 1H 9 (2E 84)
(not continuous)
Shenley Av. HA4: Ruis 2H 57
Shenley Rd. SE5 1E 120
TW5: Hest 1C 112
Shenstone W13 1C 96
Shenstone Cl. DA1: Cray 4K 127
Shenstone Ho. SW16 5G 137
Shepherd Cl. TW13: Hanw 4C 130
Shepherdess Pl. N1 1D 8 (3C 84)
Shepherdess Wlk. N1 1D 8 (2C 84)
Shepherd Ho. *E14* 6D 86
(off Annabel Cl.)
E16 7F 89
(off University Way)
Shepherd Mkt. W1 4J 11 (1F 101)
SHEPHERD'S BUSH 2E 98
Shepherd's Bush Empire Theatre 2E 98
Shepherd's Bush Grn. W12 2E 98
Shepherd's Bush Mkt. W12 2E 98
(not continuous)
Shepherd's Bush Pl. W12 2F 99
Shepherd's Bush Rd. W6 4E 98
Shepherd's Cl. BR6: Orp 3K 173
N6 6F 47
Shepherds Cl. HA7: Stan 5F 27
(not continuous)
RM6: Chad H 5D 54
TW17: Shep 6D 146
W1 2G 11
(off Lees Pl.)
Shepherds Ct. *W12* 2F 99
(off Shepherd's Bush Grn.)
Shepherds Grn. BR7: Chst 7H 143
Shepherd's Hill N6 6F 47
Shepherds La. E9 6K 67
SE28 1J 107
Shepherds Leas SE9 4G 125
Shepherd's Path *NW3* 5B 64
(off Lyndhurst Rd.)
Shepherds Path *UB5: N'olt* 6C 58
(off Arnold Rd.)
Shepherds Pl. W1 2G 11 (7E 82)
Shepherd St. W1 5J 11 (1F 101)
Shepherd's Wlk. NW3 5B 64
Shepherds Wlk. NW2 2C 62
WD23: B Hea 2C 26
Shepherds Way CR2: Sels 7K 169
Shepiston La. UB3: Harl 4D 92
Shepley Cl. SM5: Cars 3E 166
Sheppard Cl. EN1: Enf 1C 24
KT1: King T 4E 150
Sheppard Dr. SE16 5H 103
Sheppard Ho. *E2* 2G 85
(off Warner Pl.)
SW2 1A 138
Sheppards Coll. *BR1: Brom* 1J 159
(off London Rd.)
Sheppard St. E16 4H 87
SHEPPERTON 6D 146
Shepperton Bus. Pk. TW17: Shep 5E 146
Shepperton Ct. TW17: Shep 6D 146
Shepperton Ct. Dr. TW17: Shep 5D 146
Shepperton Film Studios 3B 146
SHEPPERTON GREEN 4C 146
Shepperton Marina TW17: Shep 6G 147
Shepperton Rd. BR5: Pet W 6G 161
N1 1C 84
TW18: Lale, Shep 4A 146
Sheppey Gdns. RM9: Dag 7C 72
Sheppey Rd. RM9: Dag 7B 72
Shepton Ho's. *E2* 3J 85
(off Welwyn St.)
Sherard Ct. N7 3J 65
Sherard Ho. *E9* 7J 67
(off Frampton Pk. Rd.)
Sherard Rd. SE9 5C 124
Sheraton Bus. Cen. UB6: G'frd 2B 78
Sheraton Ho. *SW1* 7K 17
(off Churchill Gdns.)
Sheraton St. W1 1C 12 (6H 83)
Sherborne *NW1* 7H 65
(off Agar Gro.)
Sherborne Av. EN3: Enf H 2D 24
UB2: S'hall 4E 94
Sherborne Cl. SL3: Poyle 4A 174
UB4: Yead 6A 76
Sherborne Cres. SM5: Cars 7C 154
Sherborne Gdns. NW9 3G 43
W13 5B 78
Sherborne Ho. *SW1* 5K 17
(part of Abbots Mnr.)
SW8 7K 101
(off Bolney St.)
Sherborne La. EC4 2E 14 (7D 84)
Sherborne Rd. BR5: St M Cry 4K 161
KT9: Chess 5E 162
SM3: Sutt 2J 165
TW14: Bedf 1F 129
(not continuous)
Sherborne St. N1 1D 84
Sherboro Rd. N15 6F 49
Sherbourne Ct. SM2: Sutt 6A 166
SW5 4K 99
(off Cromwell Rd.)
Sherbourne Gdns. TW17: Shep 7G 147
Sherbourne Pl. HA7: Stan 6F 27
Sherbrooke Cl. DA6: Bex 4G 127
Sherbrooke Ho. *E2* 2J 85
(off Bonner Rd.)
SW1 2D 18
(off Monck St.)
Sherbrooke Rd. SW6 7G 99
Sherbrooke Ter. *SW6* 7G 99
(off Sherbrooke Rd.)
Sherbrooke Way KT4: Wor Pk 7D 152
Sherbrook Gdns. N21 7G 23
Sherbrook Ho. *SE16* 2J 103
(off Albatross Way)
Shere Cl. KT9: Chess 5D 162
Sheredan Rd. E4 5A 36
Shere Ho. SE1 7E 14
Shere Rd. IG2: Ilf 5E 52
Sherfield Cl. KT3: N Mald 4H 151
Sherfield Gdns. SW15 6B 116
Sherfield M. UB3: Hayes 6G 75
Sheridan Bldgs. *WC2* 1F 13
(off Martlett Ct.)
Sheridan Cl. UB10: Hil 4E 74
Sheridan Ct. *CR0: C'don* 4E 168
(off Coombe Rd.)
HA1: Harr 6H 41
NW6 7A 64
(off Belsize Rd.)
SW5 4K 99
(off Barkston Gdns.)
TW4: Houn 5C 112
UB5: N'olt 5F 59
W7 7K 77
(off Milton Rd.)
Sheridan Cres. BR7: Chst 2F 161
Sheridan Gdns. HA3: Kenton 6D 42
Sheridan Hgts. *E1* 6H 85
(off Watney St.)
Sheridan Ho. *SE11* 4K 19
(off Wincott St.)
Sheridan Lodge *BR2: Brom* 4A 160
(off Homesdale Rd.)
Sheridan M. E11 6K 51
Sheridan Pl. BR1: Brom 2B 160
SW13 3B 116
TW12: Hamp 1F 149
Sheridan Rd. DA7: Bex 3E 126
DA17: Belv 4G 109
E7 3H 69
E12 5C 70
SW19 1H 153
TW10: Ham 3C 132
Sheridan Ter. UB5: N'olt 5F 59
Sheridan Wlk. NW11 6J 45
SM5: Cars 5D 166
Sheridan Way BR3: Beck 1B 158

Sheriden Pl. HA1: Harr 7J **41**
Sheringham NW8 . . . . .1B **82**
Sheringham Av. E12 . . . . .4D **70**
  N14 . . . . .5C **22**
  RM7: Rom 6J **55**
  TW2: Whitt 1D **130**
Sheringham Ct. TW13: Felt 3J **129**
  (off Sheringham Av.)
  UB3: Hayes 2H **93**
Sheringham Dr. IG11: Bark 5K **71**
Sheringham Ho. NW1 . . . . .5C **4**
Sheringham Rd. N7 . . . . .6K **65**
  SE20 . . . . .3J **157**
Sheringham Twr. UB1: S'hall 7F **77**
Sherington Av. HA5: Hat E 7A **26**
Sherington Rd. SE7 . . . . .6K **105**
Sherland Rd. TW1: Twick 1K **131**
Sherleys Ct. HA4: Ruis 2G **57**
Sherlies Av. BR6: Orp 2J **173**
Sherlock Cl. SW16 . . . . .2K **155**
Sherlock Ct. NW8 . . . . .1B **82**
  (off Dorman Way)
Sherlock Holmes Mus. 4F **5**
Sherlock M. W1 . . . . .5G **5** (5E **82**)
Sherman Gdns. RM6: Chad H 6C **54**
Sherman Ho. E14 . . . . .6E **86**
  (off Dee St.)
  UB3: Harl 3E **92**
  (off Nine Acres Cl.)
Sherman Rd. BR1: Brom 1J **159**
Shernhall St. E17 . . . . .3E **50**
Sherrard Rd. E7 . . . . .6A **70**
  E12 . . . . .6A **70**
Sherrards Way EN5: Barn 5D **20**
Sherren Ho. E1 .4J **85**
Sherrick Grn. Rd. NW10 . . . . .5D **62**
Sherriff Ct. NW6 . . . . .6J **63**
  (off Sherriff Rd.)
Sherriff Rd. NW6 . . . . .6J **63**
Sherringham Av. N17 . . . . .2G **49**
  TW13: Felt 3J **129**
Sherrington Ct. E16 . . . . .5H **87**
  (off Rathbone St.)
Sherrin Rd. E10 .4D **68**
Sherrock Gdns. NW4 . . . . .4D **44**
Sherry M. IG11: Bark 7H **71**
Sherston Ct. SE1 . . . . .4B **102**
  (off Newington Butts)
  WC1 . . . . .2J **7**
Sherwin Ho. SE11 . . . . .7J **19**
Sherwin Rd. SE14 . . . . .1K **121**
Sherwood KT6: Surb 2D **162**
  NW6 . . . . .7G **63**
Sherwood Av. E18 . . . . .3K **51**
  HA4: Ruis 6G **39**
  SW16 . . . . .7H **137**
  UB4: Yead 4K **75**
  UB6: G'frd 6J **59**
Sherwood Cl. DA5: Bexl 6C **126**
  E17 . . . . .2B **50**
  SW13 . . . . .3D **116**
  W13 . . . . .1B **96**
Sherwood Ct. CR2: S Croy 5C **168**
  (off Nottingham Rd.)
  HA2: Harr 2F **59**
  SW11 . . . . .3A **118**
  W1 . . . . .6E **4**
  (off Bryanston Pl.)
Sherwood Gdns. E14 . . . . .4C **104**
  IG11: Bark 7H **71**
  SE16 . . . . .5G **103**
Sherwood Pk. Av. DA15: Sidc 7A **126**
Sherwood Pk. Rd. DA14: Mitc 4G **155**
  SM1: Sutt 5J **165**
Sherwood Rd. CR0: C'don 7H **157**
  DA16: Well 2J **125**
  HA2: Harr 2G **59**
  IG6: Ilf 4H **53**
  NW4 . . . . .3E **44**
  SW19 . . . . .7H **135**
  TW12: Hamp H 5G **131**

Sherwood St. N20 . . . . .3G **31**
  W1 . . . . .2B **12** (7G **83**)
Sherwood Ter. E16 . . . . .6A **88**
  (off Bingley Rd.)
  N20 . . . . .3G **31**
Sherwood Way
  BR4: W W'ck .2E **170**
Shetland Ho. DA17: Belv 2H **109**
Shetland Rd. E3 . . . . .2B **86**
  TW6: H'row A 6E **110**
Shield Dr. TW8: Bford 6A **96**
Shieldhall St. SE2 . . . . .4C **108**
Shield Rd. TW15: Ashf 4E **128**
Shifford Path SE23 . . . . .3K **139**
Shillaker Ct. W3 . . . . .1B **98**
Shillibeer Pl. W1 .6D **4**
Shillingford Cl. NW7 . . . . .7A **30**
Shillingford Ho. E3 . . . . .3D **86**
  (off Talwin St.)
Shillingford St. N1 . . . . .7B **66**
Shillingshaw Lodge E16 . . . . .6J **87**
  (off Butchers Rd.)
Shillingstone Ho. W14 . . . . .3G **99**
  (off Russell Rd.)
Shinfield St. W12 . . . . .6E **80**
Shinglewell Rd. DA8: Erith 7G **109**
Shingly Pl. E4 . . . . .1K **35**
Shinners Cl. SE25 . . . . .5G **157**
Ship All. W4 . . . . .6G **97**
Ship & Mermaid Row SE1 . .6F **15** (2D **102**)
Shipka Rd. SW12 . . . . .1F **137**
Shiplake Ho. E2 .2J **9**
  (off Arnold Cir.)
Ship La. SW14 .3J **115**
Shipman Rd. E16 . . . . .6K **87**
  SE23 . . . . .2K **139**
Ship St. SE8 . . . . .1C **122**
Ship Tavern Pas. EC3 . . . . . .2G **15** (7E **84**)
Shipton Cl. RM8: Dag 3D **72**
Shipton Ho. E2 . . . . .1K **9**
  (off Shipton St.)
Shipton Rd. UB10: Ick 4B **56**
Shipton St. E2 . . . . .1K **9** (2F **85**)
Shipwright Rd. SE16 . . . . .2A **104**
Shipwright Yd. SE1 . . . . . .5G **15** (1E **102**)
Ship Yd. E14 . . . . .5D **104**
Shirebrook Rd. SE3 . . . . .3B **124**
Shire Ct. DA18: Erith 3D **108**
  KT17: Ewe 7B **164**
Shirehall Cl. NW4 . . . . .6F **45**
Shirehall Gdns. NW4 . . . . .6F **45**
Shirehall La. NW4 . . . . .6F **45**
Shirehall Pk. NW4 . . . . .5F **45**
Shire Horse Way TW7: Isle 3K **113**
Shire Ho. E3 . . . . .3D **86**
  (off Talwin St.)
  EC1 . . . . .4E **8**
  (off Lambs Pas.)
Shire La. BR2: Kes 7C **172**
  BR6: Chels, Downe 7F **173**
  (not continuous)
Shire London Golf Course, The 1A **20**
Shire M. TW2: Whitt 6G **113**
Shire Pl. SW18 . . . . .7A **118**
  TW8: Bford 7D **96**
Shires, The TW10: Ham 4E **132**
SHIRLEY 2K **169**
Shirley Av. CR0: C'don 1J **169**
  DA5: Bexl 7D **126**
  SM1: Sutt 4B **166**
Shirley Chu. Rd. CR0: C'don 3K **169**
Shirley Cl. E17 . . . . .5D **50**
  TW3: Houn 5G **113**
Shirley Ct. SW16 . . . . .7J **137**
Shirley Cres. BR3: Beck 4A **158**
Shirley Dr. TW3: Houn 5G **113**

Shirley Gdns. IG11: Bark 6J **71**
  W7 . . . . .1K **95**
Shirley Gro. N9 .7D **24**
  SW11 . . . . .3E **118**
Shirley Hgts. SM6: Wall 7G **167**
Shirley Hills Rd. CR0: C'don 5J **169**
Shirley Ho. SE5 . . . . .7D **102**
  (off Picton St.)
Shirley Ho. Dr. SE7 . . . . .7A **106**
SHIRLEY OAKS 1K **169**
Shirley Oaks Rd. CR0: C'don 1K **169**
Shirley Pk. CR0: C'don 2J **169**
Shirley Pk. Golf Course 2H **169**
Shirley Pk. Rd. CR0: C'don 1H **169**
Shirley Rd. CR0: C'don 7H **157**
  DA15: Sidc 3J **143**
  E15 . . . . .7G **69**
  EN2: Enf 3H **23**
  SM6: Wall 7G **167**
  W4 . . . . .2K **97**
Shirley St. E16 . . . . .6H **87**
Shirley Way CR0: C'don 3A **170**
Shirley Windmill 3J **169**
Shirlock Rd. NW3 . . . . .4D **64**
Shirwell Cl. NW7 . . . . .7A **30**
Shobden Rd. N17 . . . . .1D **48**
Shobroke Cl. NW2 . . . . .3E **62**
Shoebury Rd. E6 . . . . .7D **70**
Shoelands Cl. NW9 . . . . .3K **43**
Shoe La. EC4 . . . . .7K **7** (6A **84**)
Sholto Rd. TW6: H'row A 5B **110**
Shona Ho. E13 .3A **88**
Shooters Av. HA3: Kenton 4C **42**
SHOOTERS HILL 1E **124**
Shooters Hill DA16: Well 1D **124**
  SE18 . . . . .1D **124**
Shooters Hill Golf Course 1G **125**
Shooters Hill Rd. SE3 . . . . .1F **123**
  SE10 . . . . .1F **123**
  SE18 . . . . .1F **123**
Shooters Rd. EN2: Enf 1G **23**
Shoot Up Hill NW2 . . . . .5G **63**
Shopping Hall, The E6 . . . . .1C **88**
Shore Bus. Cen. E9 . . . . .7J **67**
Shore Ct. TW12: Hamp 6C **130**
  TW14: Felt 7J **111**
Shoreditch Cl. UB10: Ick 3B **56**
SHOREDITCH 1G **9** (3E **84**)
Shoreditch Ct. E8 . . . . .7F **67**
  (off Queensbridge Rd.)
Shoreditch High St. E1 . . . . . . .4H **9** (4E **84**)
Shoreditch Ho. BR2: Brom 6C **160**
  N1 . . . . .2F **9**
Shore Gro. TW13: Hanw 2E **130**
Shoreham Cl. CR0: C'don 6J **157**
  DA5: Bexl 1D **144**
  SW18 . . . . .5K **117**
Shoreham Rd. E. TW6: H'row A 5A **110**
Shoreham Rd. W. TW6: H'row A 5A **110**
Shoreham Way BR2: Hayes 6J **159**
Shore Ho. SW8 .3F **119**
Shore M. E9 . . . . .7J **67**
  (off Shore Rd.)
Shore Pl. E9 . . . . .7J **67**
Shore Point IG9: Buck H 2E **36**
Shore Rd. E9 . . . . .7J **67**
Shore Way SW9 . . . . .2A **120**
  (off Crowhurst Cl.)
Shorncliffe Rd. SE1 . . . . .5F **103**
Shorndean St. SE6 . . . . .1E **140**
Shorne Cl. DA15: Sidc 6B **126**
Short Blue Pl. IG11: Bark 7G **71**
Shortcroft Rd. KT17: Ewe 7B **164**
Shortcrofts Rd. RM9: Dag 6F **73**
Shorter St. E1 . . . . .2J **15** (7F **85**)
Shortgate N12 . . . . .4C **30**
Short Hedges TW3: Houn 1E **112**
Short Hill HA1: Harr 1J **59**

SHORTLANDS .2G **159**
Shortlands UB3: Harl 6F **93**
  W6 . . . . .4F **99**
Shortlands Cl. DA17: Belv 3F **109**
  N18 . . . . .3J **33**
Shortlands Gdns. BR2: Brom 2G **159**
Shortlands Golf Course 1G **159**
Shortlands Gro. BR2: Brom 3F **159**
Shortlands Rd. BR2: Brom 3F **159**
  E10 . . . . .7D **50**
  KT2: King T 7F **133**
Short La. TW19: Stanw 7B **110**
Short Path SE18 . . . . .6F **107**
Short Rd. E11 . . . . .2G **69**
  TW6: H'row A 6A **110**
  W4 . . . . .6A **98**
Shorts Cft. NW9 . . . . .4H **43**
Shorts Gdns. WC2 . . . . .1E **12** (6J **83**)
Shorts Rd. SM5: Cars 4C **166**
Short St. NW4 . . . . .4E **44**
  (off Foster St.)
  SE1 . . . . .6K **13** (2A **102**)
Short Wall E15 . . . . .3E **86**
Shortwave Cinema 3E **102**
  (off Bermondsey Sq.)
Short Way N12 . . . . .6H **31**
  SE9 . . . . .3C **124**
  TW2: Whitt 7G **113**
Shotfield SM6: Wall 6F **167**
Shott Cl. SM1: Sutt 5A **166**
Shottendane Rd. SW6 . . . . .1J **117**
Shottery Cl. SE9 . . . . .3C **142**
Shottfield Av. SW14 . . . . .4A **116**
Shottsford W2 . . . . .6J **81**
  (off Talbot Rd.)
Shoulder of Mutton All. E14 . . . . .7A **86**
Shouldham St. W1 . . . . .6D **4** (5C **82**)
Showcase Cinema
  Barking 3H **89**
Showers Way UB3: Hayes 1J **93**
Shrapnel Cl. SE18 . . . . .7C **106**
Shrapnel Rd. SE9 . . . . .3D **124**
Shrek's Adventure! 6G **13** (2K **101**)
Shrewsbury Av. HA3: Kenton 4E **42**
  SW14 . . . . .4J **115**
Shrewsbury Cl. KT6: Surb 2E **162**
Shrewsbury Ct. EC1 . . . . .4D **8**
Shrewsbury Ho. SW3 . . . . .7C **16**
  SW8 . . . . .7H **19**
Shrewsbury La. SE18 . . . . .1F **125**
Shrewsbury M. W2 . . . . .5J **81**
  (off Chepstow Rd.)
Shrewsbury Rd. BR3: Beck 3A **158**
  E7 . . . . .5B **70**
  N11 . . . . .6B **32**
  NW10 . . . . .1K **79**
  SM5: Cars 6C **154**
  TW6: H'row A 6E **110**
  (not continuous)
  W2 . . . . .6J **81**
Shrewsbury St. W10 . . . . .4E **80**
Shrewsbury Wlk.
  TW7: Isle 3A **114**
  (off Magdala Rd.)
Shrewton Rd. SW17 . . . . .7D **136**
Shri Swaminarayan Mandir
  London 6K **61**
Shroffold Rd. BR1: Brom 4G **141**
Shropshire Cl. CR4: Mitc 4J **155**
Shropshire Ct. W7 . . . . .6K **77**
  (off Copley Cl.)
Shropshire Ho. N18 . . . . .5C **34**
  (off Cavendish Cl.)
Shropshire Pl. WC1 . . . . .4C **6** (4G **83**)
Shropshire Rd. N22 . . . . .7E **32**
Shroton St. NW1 . . . . .5D **4** (5C **82**)
Shrubberies, The E18 . . . . .2J **51**
Shrubbery, The E11 . . . . .5K **51**
  KT6: Surb 1E **162**
Shrubbery Cl. N1 . . . . .1C **84**
Shrubbery Gdns. N21 . . . . .7G **23**

Shrubbery Rd. N9 . . . 3B 34
SW16 . . . 4J 137
UB1: S'hall . . . 1D 94
Shrubland Gro. KT4: Wor Pk . . . 3E 164
Shrubland Rd. E8 . . . 1F 85
E10 . . . 7C 50
E17 . . . 5C 50
Shrublands Av. CR0: C'don . . . 3C 170
Shrublands Cl. N20 . . . 1G 31
SE26 . . . 3J 139
Shrubsall Cl. SE9 . . . 1C 142
Shuna Wlk. N1 . . . 6D 66
Shurland Av. EN4: E Barn . . . 6G 21
Shurland Gdns. SE15 . . . 7F 103
Shurlock Dr. BR6: Farnb . . . 4G 173
Shushan Cl. N16 . . . 7E 48
Shuters Sq. W14 . . . 5H 99
Shuttle Cl. DA15: Sidc . . . 7K 125
Shuttlemead DA5: Bexl . . . 7F 127
Shuttle St. E1 . . . 4G 85
Shuttleworth Rd. SW11 . . . 2C 118
Siamese M. N3 . . . 1J 45
Siani M. N8 . . . 4B 48
Sibella Rd. SW4 . . . 2H 119
Sibley Cl. BR1: Brom . . . 5C 160
DA6: Bex . . . 5E 126
Sibley Ct. BR2: Brom . . . 2F 159
UB8: Hil . . . 5E 74
Sibley Gro. E12 . . . 7C 70
Sibthorpe Rd. SE12 . . . 6K 123
Sibthorp Rd. CR4: Mitc . . . 2D 154
Sibton Rd. SM5: Cars . . . 7C 154
Sicilian Av. WC1 . . . 6F 7
Sickle Cnr. RM9: Dag . . . 4H 91
Sidbury St. SW6 . . . 1G 117
SIDCUP . . . 4A 144
Sidcup By-Pass BR5: Sidc, St P . . . 6A 144
BR7: Chst, Sidc . . . 3H 143
DA14: Sidc . . . 6A 144
Sidcup Golf Course . . . 1B 144
Sidcup High St. DA14: Sidc . . . 4A 144
Sidcup Hill DA14: Sidc . . . 4B 144
Sidcup Hill Gdns. DA14: Sidc . . . 5C 144
Sidcup Leisure Cen. . . . 2A 144
Sidcup Place . . . 5A 144
Sidcup Pl. DA14: Sidc . . . 5A 144
Sidcup Rd. SE9 . . . 1D 142
SE12 . . . 6A 124
Sidcup Technology Cen.
DA14: Sidc . . . 5D 144
Siddeley Dr. TW4: Houn . . . 3C 112
Siddeley Rd. E17 . . . 2E 50
Siddons La. NW1 . . . 4F 5 (4D 82)
Siddons Rd. CR0: Wadd . . . 3A 168
N17 . . . 1G 49
SE23 . . . 2A 140
Side Rd. E17 . . . 5B 50
Sidewood Rd. SE9 . . . 1H 143
Sidford Ho. SE1 . . . 2H 19
Sidford Pl. SE1 . . . 2H 19 (3A 102)
Sidgwick Ho. SW9 . . . 2K 119
(off Stockwell Rd.)
Sidi Ct. N15 . . . 3B 48
Sidings, The E11 . . . 1E 68
Sidings Apartments, The E16 . . . 2E 106
Sidings M. N7 . . . 3A 66
Siding St. E20 . . . 1D 86
Sidlaw Ho. N16 . . . 1F 67
Sidmouth Av. TW7: Isle . . . 2J 113
Sidmouth Dr. HA4: Ruis . . . 3J 57
Sidmouth Ho. SE15 . . . 7G 103
(off Lindsey Est.)
W1 . . . 7D 4
(off Cato St.)
Sidmouth M. WC1 . . . 2G 7 (3K 83)
Sidmouth Pde. NW2 . . . 7E 62
Sidmouth Rd. DA16: Well . . . 7C 108
E10 . . . 3E 68
NW2 . . . 7E 62
Sidmouth St. WC1 . . . 2F 7 (3J 83)
Sidney Av. N13 . . . 5E 32
Sidney Boyd Ct. NW6 . . . 7J 63
Sidney Elson Way E6 . . . 2E 88
Sidney Est. E1 . . . 6J 85
(Bromhead St.)
E1 . . . 5J 85
(Lindley St.)
Sidney Gdns. TW8: Bford . . . 6D 96
Sidney Godley (VC) Ho. E2 . . . 3J 85
(off Digby St.)
Sidney Gro. EC1 . . . 1A 8 (2B 84)
Sidney Ho. E2 . . . 2K 85
(off Old Ford Rd.)
Sidney Miller Ct. W3 . . . 1H 97
(off Crown St.)
Sidney Rd. BR3: Beck . . . 2A 158
E7 . . . 3J 69
HA2: Harr . . . 3G 41
KT12: Walt T . . . 7J 147
N22 . . . 7E 32
SE25 . . . 5G 157
SW9 . . . 2K 119
TW1: Twick . . . 6A 114
Sidney Sq. E1 . . . 5J 85
Sidney St. E1 . . . 5H 85
(not continuous)
Sidney Webb Ho. SE1 . . . 3D 102
(off Tabard St.)
Sidonie Apartments SW11 . . . 4C 118
(off Danvers Av.)
Sidworth St. E8 . . . 7H 67
Siebert Rd. SE3 . . . 6J 105
Siege Ho. E1 . . . 6H 85
(off Sidney St.)
Siemens Brothers Way E16 . . . 7J 87
Siemens Rd. SE18 . . . 3B 106
Sienna SE28 . . . 3A 108
Sienna Alto SE13 . . . 3E 122
(off Cornmill La.)
Sienna Cl. KT9: Chess . . . 6D 162
Sienna Ho. E20 . . . 6D 68
(off Victory Pde.)
Sienna Ter. NW2 . . . 2C 62
Sierra Dr. RM9: Dag . . . 2H 91
Sigdon Pas. E8 . . . 5G 67
Sigdon Rd. E8 . . . 5G 67
Sigers, The HA5: Eastc . . . 6K 39
Sigmund Freud Statue . . . 6B 64
Signal Ho. E8 . . . 7H 67
(off Martello Ter.)
SE1 . . . 7C 14
(off Gt. Suffolk St.)
Signal Wlk. E4 . . . 6K 35
Signmakers Yd. NW1 . . . 1F 83
(off Delancey St.)
Sigrist Sq. KT2: King T . . . 1E 150
Sikorski Mus. . . . 7B 10 (2B 100)
Silbury Av. CR4: Mitc . . . 1C 154
Silbury Ho. SE26 . . . 3G 139
Silbury St. N1 . . . 1E 8 (3D 84)
Silchester Ct. CR7: Thor H . . . 4A 156
TW15: Ashf . . . 2A 128
Silchester Rd. W10 . . . 6F 81
Silecroft Rd. DA7: Bex . . . 1G 127
Silesia Bldgs. E8 . . . 7H 67
Silex St. SE1 . . . 7B 14 (2B 102)
Silicon Bus. Cen. UB6: G'frd . . . 2C 78
Silicon Way N1 . . . 2F 9
Silk Cl. SE12 . . . 5J 123
Silk Ct. E2 . . . 3G 85
(off Squirries St.)
Silkfield Rd. NW9 . . . 5A 44
Silk Ho. E1 . . . 1K 15
(Leman St.)
E1 . . . 5K 85
(off Trafalgar Gdns.)
E2 . . . 2F 85
(off How's St.)
NW9 . . . 3K 43
Silkin M. SE15 . . . 7G 103
Silk M. SE11 . . . 5K 19
Silk Mills Pas. SE13 . . . 2D 122
Silk Mills Path SE13 . . . 2E 122
(not continuous)
Silk Mills Sq. E9 . . . 6B 68
Silks Ct. E11 . . . 1H 69
Silkstream Pde. HA8: Edg . . . 1J 43
Silkstream Rd. HA8: Edg . . . 1J 43
Silk St. EC2 . . . 5D 8 (5C 84)
Silk Weaver Way E2 . . . 2H 85
Sillitoe Ho. N1 . . . 1D 84
(off Colville Est.)
Silsoe Ho. NW1 . . . 2F 83
Silsoe Rd. N22 . . . 2K 47
Silverbeck Way TW19: Stanw M . . . 7B 174
Silver Birch Av. E4 . . . 5G 35
Silver Birch Cl. DA2: Wilm . . . 4K 145
N11 . . . 6K 31
SE6 . . . 3B 140
SE28 . . . 1A 108
UB10: Ick . . . 4A 56
Silver Birch Gdns. E6 . . . 4D 88
Silverbirch Wlk. NW5 . . . 6E 64
Silverburn Ho. SW9 . . . 1B 120
(off Lothian Rd.)
Silvercliffe Gdns. EN4: E Barn . . . 4H 21
Silver Cl. HA3: Hrw W . . . 7C 26
SE14 . . . 7A 104
Silver Cres. W4 . . . 4H 97
Silverdale EN2: Enf . . . 4D 22
NW1 . . . 1A 6
(off Harrington St.)
SE26 . . . 4J 139
Silverdale Av. IG2: Ilf . . . 5J 53
Silverdale Cen., The HA0: Wemb . . . 1F 79
Silverdale Cl. SM1: Sutt . . . 4H 165
UB5: N'olt . . . 5D 58
W7 . . . 1J 95
Silverdale Ct. EC1 . . . 3B 8
Silverdale Dr. SE9 . . . 2C 142
TW16: Sun . . . 2K 147
Silverdale Factory Cen. UB3: Hayes . . . 3J 93
Silverdale Gdns. UB3: Hayes . . . 2J 93
Silverdale Ind. Est. UB3: Hayes . . . 2J 93
Silverdale Rd. BR5: Pet W . . . 4G 161
DA7: Bex . . . 2H 127
E4 . . . 6A 36
UB3: Hayes . . . 2H 93
Silverdene N12 . . . 6E 30
(off Thyra Gro.)
Silvergate KT19: Ewe . . . 5J 163
Silverhall St. TW7: Isle . . . 3A 114
Silverholme Cl. HA3: Kenton . . . 7E 42
Silver Jubilee Way TW4: Cran . . . 2K 111
Silverland St. E16 . . . 1D 106
Silver La. BR4: W W'ck . . . 2F 171
Silverleigh Rd. CR7: Thor H . . . 4K 155
Silver Mead E18 . . . 1J 51
Silvermere Dr. N18 . . . 6E 34
Silvermere Rd. SE6 . . . 7D 122
Silver Pl. W1 . . . 2B 12 (6G 83)
Silver Rd. SE13 . . . 3D 122
Silvers IG9: Buck H . . . 1F 37
(off Palmerston Rd.)
Silver Spring Cl. DA8: Erith . . . 6H 109
Silverston Way HA7: Stan . . . 6H 27
Silver St. EN1: Enf . . . 3J 23
N18 . . . 4J 33
Silverthorn NW8 . . . 1K 81
(off Abbey Rd.)
Silverthorne Loft Apartments SE5 . . . 6D 102
(off Albany Rd.)
Silverthorne Rd. SW8 . . . 2F 119
Silverthorn Gdns. E4 . . . 2H 35
Silverton Rd. W6 . . . 6F 99
SILVERTOWN . . . 1A 106
Silvertown Sq. E16 . . . 5H 87
Silvertown Viaduct E16 . . . 6H 87
Silvertown Way E16 . . . 6G 87
(Clarkson Rd.)
E16 . . . 1J 105
(Hanover Av.)
Silvertree La. UB6: G'frd . . . 3H 77
Silver Wlk. SE16 . . . 1A 104
Silver Way RM7: Mawney . . . 3H 55
UB10: Hil . . . 2D 74
Silver Wing Ind. Est. CR0: Wadd . . . 6K 167
Silverwood Cl. BR3: Beck . . . 7C 140
CR0: Sels . . . 7B 170
HA6: Nwood . . . 1E 38
Silverwood Pl. SE10 . . . 1E 122
Silvester Ho. E1 . . . 6H 85
(off Varden St.)
E2 . . . 3J 85
(off Sceptre Rd.)
W11 . . . 6H 81
(off Basing St.)
Silvester Rd. SE22 . . . 5F 121
Silvester St. SE1 . . . 7E 14 (2D 102)
Silvocea Way E14 . . . 6F 87
Silwood Est. SE16 . . . 4J 103
Silwood St. SE16 . . . 4J 103
(off Rotherhithe New Rd.)
Simkins Cl. SW2 . . . 4J 119
Simla Ct. N7 . . . 7J 65
(off Brewery Rd.)
Simla Ho. SE1 . . . 7F 15
(off Kipling Est.)
Simmonds Ct. SW5 . . . 4K 99
(off Earl's Ct. Gdns.)
Simmonds Ho. TW8: Bford . . . 5E 96
(off Clayponds La.)
Simmons Cl. KT9: Chess . . . 6C 162
N20 . . . 2H 31
Simmons Dr. RM8: Dag . . . 3E 72
Simmons La. E4 . . . 2A 36
Simmons Rd. SE18 . . . 5F 107
Simmons Way N20 . . . 2H 31
Simms Cl. SM5: Cars . . . 2C 166
Simms Gdns. N2 . . . 2A 46
Simms Rd. SE1 . . . 4G 103
Simnel Rd. SE12 . . . 7K 123
Simon Cl. W11 . . . 7H 81
Simon Ct. W9 . . . 3J 81
(off Saltram Cres.)
Simonds Rd. E10 . . . 2C 68
Simone Cl. BR1: Brom . . . 1B 160
Simone Ct. SE26 . . . 3J 139
Simons Ct. N16 . . . 2F 67
Simons Wlk. E15 . . . 5F 69
Simpson Cl. CR0: C'don . . . 5C 156
N21 . . . 5D 22
Simpson Dr. W3 . . . 6K 79
Simpson Ho. NW8 . . . 2D 4 (4C 82)
SE11 . . . 6G 19 (5K 101)
Simpson Rd. TW4: Houn . . . 6D 112
TW10: Ham . . . 4C 132
Simpson's Rd. E14 . . . 7D 86
Simpson St. SW11 . . . 2C 118
Simpson Way KT6: Surb . . . 6C 150
Simrose Ct. SW18 . . . 5J 117
Sims Wlk. SE3 . . . 4H 123
Sinclair Ct. CR0: C'don . . . 2E 168
Sinclair Dr. SM2: Sutt . . . 7K 165
Sinclair Gdns. W14 . . . 2F 99
Sinclair Gro. NW11 . . . 6F 45
Sinclair Ho. WC1 . . . 2E 6
(off Sandwich St.)
Sinclair Mans. W12 . . . 2F 99
(off Richmond Way)
Sinclair Pl. SE4 . . . 6C 122
Sinclair Rd. E4 . . . 5G 35
W14 . . . 2F 99
Sinclairs Ho. E3 . . . 2B 86
(off St Stephen's Rd.)
Sinclare Cl. EN1: Enf . . . 1A 24
Sindercombe M. W12 . . . 3C 98
Singapore Rd. W13 . . . 1A 96
Singer M. SW4 . . . 2J 119
(off Union Rd.)
Singer St. EC2 . . . 2F 9 (3D 84)
Singleton Cl. CR0: C'don . . . 7C 156
SW17 . . . 7D 136
Singleton Rd. RM9: Dag . . . 5F 73

Singleton Scarp N12 5D 30
Sinnott Rd. E17 1K 49
Siobhan Davis Dance Studios 3B 102
(off St George's Rd.)
Sion Ct. TW1: Twick 1B 132
Sion Rd. TW1: Twick 1B 132
Sippets Ct. IG1: Ilf 1H 71
SIPSON 6C 92
Sipson Cl. UB7: Sip 6C 92
Sipson La. UB3: Harl 6C 92
UB7: Sip 6C 92
Sipson Rd. UB7: Sip, W Dray 3B 92
(not continuous)
Sipson Way UB7: Sip 7C 92
Sir Abraham Dawes Cotts. SW15 4G 117
Sir Alexander Cl. W3 1B 98
Sir Alexander Rd. W3 1B 98
Sir Christopher France Ho. E1 3A 86
Sir Cyril Black Way SW19 7J 135
Sirdar Rd. CR4: Mitc 6E 136
N22 3B 48
W11 7F 81
Sir Francis Drake Ct. SE10 5F 105
Sirinham Point SW8 7H 19
Sirius SW11 2D 118
Sirius Bldg. E1 7K 85
(off Jardine Rd.)
Sirius Ho. SE16 4A 104
(off Seafarer Way)
Sir James Black Ho. SE5 2D 120
(off Coldharbour La.)
Sir John Kirk Cl. SE5 7C 102
Sir John Lyon Ho. EC4 2C 14
(off High Timber St.)
Sir John Morden Wlk. SE3 2J 123
Sir John Soane's Mus. 7G 7 (6K 83)
Sir Nicholas Garrow Ho. W10 4G 81
(off Kensal Rd.)
Sir Oswald Stoll Foundation, The
SW6 7K 99
(off Fulham Rd.)
Sir Oswald Stoll Mans. SW6 7K 99
(off Fulham Rd.)
Sir Walter Raleigh Ct. SE10 5G 105
Sir William Powell's Almshouses
SW6 2G 117
Sise La. EC4 1E 14 (6D 84)
Siskin Ho. SE16 4K 103
(off Tawny Way)
Sisley Rd. IG11: Bark 1J 89
Sispara Gdns. SW18 6H 117
Sissinghurst Cl. BR1: Brom 5G 141
Sissinghurst Ho. SE15 6J 103
(off Sharratt St.)
Sissinghurst Rd. CR0: C'don 7G 157
Sissulu Ct. E6 1A 88
Sister Mabel's Way SE15 7G 103
Sisters Av. SW11 3D 118
Sistova Rd. SW12 1F 137
Sisulu Pl. SW9 3A 120
Sitarey Ct. W12 1D 98
Sittingbourne Av. EN1: Enf 6J 23
Sitwell Gro. HA7: Stan 5E 26
Siverst Cl. UB5: N'olt 6F 59
Sivill Ho. E2 1K 9
(off Columbia Rd.)
Siviter Way RM10: Dag 7H 73
Siward Rd. BR2: Brom 3K 159
N17 1D 48
SW17 3A 136
Six Acres Est. N4 2K 65
Six Bridges Ind. Est. SE1 5G 103
(not continuous)
Sixpenny Ct. IG11: Bark 6G 71
Sixth Av. E12 4D 70
UB3: Hayes 1H 93
W10 3G 81
Sixth Cross Rd. TW2: Twick 3G 131
Skardu Rd. NW2 5G 63
Skeena Hill SW18 7G 117
Skeffington Rd. E6 1D 88
Skeffington St. SE18 3G 107
Skeggs Ho. E14 3E 104
(off Glengall St.)
Skegness Ho. N7 7K 65
(off Sutterton St.)
Skelbrook St. SW18 2A 136
Skelgill Rd. SW15 4H 117
Skelley Rd. E15 7H 69
Skelton Cl. E8 6F 67
Skelton Rd. E7 6J 69
Skelton's La. E10 7D 50
Skelwith Rd. W6 6E 98
Skenfrith Ho. SE15 6H 103
(off Commercial Way)
Skerne Rd. KT2: King T 1D 150
Skerne Wlk. KT2: King T 1D 150
Sketch Apartments E1 5K 85
(off Shandy St.)
Sketchley Gdns. SE16 5K 103
Sketty Rd. EN1: Enf 3A 24
Skiers St. E15 1G 87
Skiffington Cl. SW2 1A 138
Skillen Lodge HA5: Pinn 1B 40
Skinner Ct. E3 4D 86
(off Barry Blandford Way)
Skinner Pl. SW1 4G 17
Skinners Ct. N13 3F 33
Skinners La. EC4 2D 14 (7C 84)
TW5: Hest 1F 113
Skinner's Row SE10 1D 122
Skinner St. EC1 2K 7 (3A 84)
Skip La. UB9: Hare 1A 56
Skipper Ct. IG11: Bark 1G 89
Skipsea Ho. SW18 6C 118
Skipsey Av. E6 3D 88
Skipton Cl. N11 6K 31
Skipton Dr. UB3: Harl 3E 92
Skipton Ho. SE4 4A 122
Skipwith Ho. EC1 5J 7
(off Bourne Est.)
Skipworth Rd. E9 1J 85
Skua Ct. SE8 6B 104
(off Dorking Cl.)
Skye La. HA8: Edg 4A 28
Sky Gdn. Wlk. EC3 2G 15
(off Philpot La.)
Skylark Ct. RM13: Rain 2K 91
SE1 7D 14
(off Swan St.)
SW15 6E 116
Skyline Apartments N4 7D 48
(off Devan Gro.)
Skyline Ct. CR0: C'don 3D 168
(off Park La.)
SE1 3F 103
Skyline Plaza Bldg. E1 6G 85
(off Commercial Rd.)
Skylines E14 2E 104
Skylines Village E14 2E 104
Sky Peals Rd. IG8: Wfd G 7A 36
Skyport Dr. UB7: Harm 3E 174
Sky Studios E16 2E 106
Skyvan Cl. TW6: H'row A 5E 110
Skyview Apartments CR0: C'don 2C 168
(off Park St.)
Skyway 14 SL3: Poyle 6A 174
Slade, The SE18 6J 107
Sladebrook Rd. SE3 3B 124
Slade Ct. EN5: New Bar 3E 20
Sladedale Rd. SE18 5J 107
Slade Ho. TW4: Houn 6D 112
Sladen Pl. E5 4H 67
Slades Cl. EN2: Enf 3F 23
Slades Dr. BR7: Chst 3G 143
Slades Gdns. EN2: Enf 2F 23
Slades Hill EN2: Enf 3F 23
Slades Ri. EN2: Enf 3F 23
Slade Twr. E10 2C 68
(off Leyton Grange Est.)
Slade Wlk. SE17 6B 102
Slade Way CR4: Mitc 1E 154
Slagrove Pl. SE13 5C 122
Slaidburn St. SW10 6A 100
Slaithwaite Rd. SE13 4E 122
Slaney Ct. NW10 7E 62
Slaney Pl. N7 5A 66
Slater Cl. SE18 5E 106
Slater M. SW4 3G 119
(off Grafton Sq.)
Slatter NW9 7G 29
Slattery Rd. TW13: Felt 1B 130
Sleaford Ho. E3 4C 86
(off Fern St.)
Sleaford Ind. Est. SW8 7G 101
Sleaford St. SW8 7G 101
Sleat Ho. E3 2B 86
(off Saxon Rd.)
Sledmere Ct. TW14: Bedf 1G 129
Sleigh Ho. E2 3J 85
(off Bacton St.)
Slide, The 7D 68
Slievemore Cl. SW4 3H 119
Sligo Ho. E1 4K 85
(off Beaumont Gro.)
Slindon Ct. N16 3F 67
Slingsby Pl. WC2 2E 12 (7J 83)
Slippers Pl. SE16 3H 103
Slipway Ho. E14 5D 104
(off Burrells Wharf Sq.)
Sloane Av. SW3 4D 16 (4C 100)
Sloane Av. Mans. SW3 4E 16 (4D 100)
Sloane Ct. TW7: Isle 1J 113
Sloane Ct. E. SW3 5G 17 (5E 100)
Sloane Ct. W. SW3 5G 17 (5E 100)
Sloane Gdns. BR6: Farnb 3G 173
SW1 4G 17 (4E 100)
Sloane Ga. Mans. SW1 3G 17
(off D'Oyley St.)
Sloane Ho. E9 7J 67
(off Loddiges Rd.)
Sloane M. N8 5J 47
Sloane Sq. SW1 4G 17 (4E 100)
Sloane St. SW1 7F 11 (2D 100)
Sloane Ter. SW1 3G 17 (4E 100)
Sloane Ter. Mans. SW1 3G 17
(off Sloane Ter.)
Sloane Wlk. CR0: C'don 6B 158
Slocum Cl. SE28 7C 90
Slough La. NW9 5J 43
Sly St. E1 6H 85
Smaldon Cl. UB7: W Dray 3C 92
Smallberry Av. TW7: Isle 2K 113
Smallbrook M. W2 1A 10 (6B 82)
Smalley Cl. N16 3F 67
Smalley Rd. Est. N16 3F 67
(off Smalley Cl.)
Smallwood Rd. SW17 4B 136
Smarden Cl. DA17: Belv 5G 109
Smarden Gro. SE9 4D 142
Smart's Pl. N18 5B 34
WC2 7F 7 (6J 83)
Smart St. E2 3K 85
Smead Way SE13 3D 122
Smeaton Cl. KT9: Chess 6D 162
Smeaton Ct. SE1 3C 102
Smeaton Rd. IG8: Wfd G 5J 37
SW18 7J 117
Smeaton St. E1 1H 103
Smedley St. SW4 2H 119
SW8 2H 119
Smeed Rd. E3 7C 68
Smikle Ct. SE14 1K 121
(off Hatcham Pk. M.)
Smiles Pl. SE13 2E 122
Smith Cl. SE16 1K 103
Smithfield (Central Markets) 6A 8
Smithfield Ct. E1 7G 85
(off Cable St.)
Smithfield St. EC1 6A 8 (5B 84)
Smith Hill TW8: Bford 6E 96
Smithies Rd. SE2 4B 108
Smith's Ct. W1 2B 12
Smithson Rd. N17 1D 48
Smiths Point E13 1J 87
(off Brooks Rd.)
Smith Sq. SW1 2E 18 (3J 101)
Smith St. KT5: Surb 6F 151
SW3 5E 16 (5D 100)
Smiths Yd. CR0: C'don 3C 168
(off St George's Wlk.)
SW18 2A 136
Smith Ter. SW3 6E 16 (5D 100)
Smithwood Cl. SW19 1G 135
Smithy La. TW3: Houn 3F 113
Smithy St. E1 5J 85
Smock Wlk. CR0: C'don 6C 156
Smokehouse Yd. EC1 5B 8
(off St John St.)
Smoothfield Ct. TW3: Houn 4E 112
Smugglers Way SW18 4K 117
Smugglers Yd. W12 1D 98
(off Devonport Rd.)
Smyrk's Rd. SE17 5E 102
Smyrna Mans. NW6 7J 63
(off Smyrna Rd.)
Smyrna Rd. NW6 7J 63
Smythe Cl. N9 3B 34
Smythe St. E14 7D 86
Snag La. BR6: Prat B 7K 173
Snakes La. N14 3A 22
Snakes La. E. IG8: Buck H, Wfd G 6F 37
Snakes La. W. IG8: Wfd G 5D 36
Snakey La. TW13: Felt 4J 129
SNARESBROOK 5J 51
Snaresbrook Dr. HA7: Stan 4J 27
Snaresbrook Hall E18 4J 51
Snaresbrook Ho. E18 4H 51
Snaresbrook Rd. E11 4G 51
Snarsgate St. W10 5E 80
Sneath Av. NW11 7H 45
Snells Pk. N18 6A 34
Sneyd Rd. NW2 4E 62
Snowberry Cl. E15 4F 69
EN5: Barn 3C 20
Snowbury Rd. SW6 2K 117
Snowden Av. UB10: Hil 2D 74
Snowden St. EC2 4G 9 (4E 84)
Snowdon Aviary 1D 82
(in London Zoo)
Snowdon Cres. UB3: Harl 3E 92
Snowdon Dr. NW9 6A 44
Snowdon Rd. TW6: H'row A 6E 110
Snowdown Cl. SE20 1K 157
Snowdrop Cl. TW12: Hamp 6E 130
Snowdrop Ct. RM13: Rain 2J 91
Snowdrop M. HA5: Pinn 2A 40
Snow Hill EC1 6A 8 (5B 84)
Snow Hill Ct. EC1 7B 8 (6B 84)
Snowman Ho. NW6 1K 81
Snowsfields SE1 6F 15 (2D 102)
Snowshill Rd. E12 5C 70
Snowy Fielder Waye TW7: Isle 2B 114
Soames Pl. EN4: Had W 2E 20
Soames St. SE15 3F 121
Soames Wlk. KT3: N Mald 1A 152
Soane Cl. W5 2D 96
Soane Ct. NW1 7G 65
(off St Pancras Way)
Soane Ho. SE17 5D 102
(off Roland Way)
Soane Sq. HA7: Stan 3D 26
Soap Ho. La. TW8: Bford 7E 96
Soap Yd. SE1 1D 102
(off Stoney St.)
Sobell Leisure Cen. 3K 65
Sobraon Ho. KT2: King T 7F 133
(off Elm Rd.)
Socket La. BR2: Hayes 6K 159
Soda Studios E8 1F 85
(off Kingsland Rd.)
SOHO 1C 12 (6G 83)
Soho Ho. W12 7E 80
Soho Sq. W1 7C 6 (6H 83)

Soho St.—Sth. End Grn.

Soho St. W1 7C 6 (6H 83)
Soho Theatre & Writers Cen. 1C 12
(off Dean St.)
Sojourner Truth Cl. E8 6H 67
Sola Ct. *CR0: C'don* *1D 168*
(off Sydenham Rd.)
Solander Gdns. *E1* *7H 85*
(off Cable St.)
E1 7J 85
(The Highway)
Solar Ct. N3 7E 30
SE16 *2G 103*
(off Chambers St.)
Solar Ho. E6 5E 88
E15 *6G 69*
(off Romford Rd.)
Solarium Ct. *SE1* *4F 103*
(off Alscot Rd.)
Soldene Ct. N7 6K 65
Solebay St. E1 4A 86
Solent Ct. SW16 2K 155
Solent Ho. *E1* *5A 86*
(off Ben Jonson Rd.)
Solent Ri. E13 3J 87
Solent Rd. NW6 5J 63
Soley M. WC1 1J 7 (3A 84)
Solna Av. SW15 5E 116
Solna Rd. N21 1J 33
Solomon Av. N9 4B 34
Solomons Ct. N12 7F 31
Solomon's Pas. SE15 4H 121
Solon New Rd. SW4 4J 119
Solon New Rd. Est. SW4 4J 119
Solon Rd. SW2 4J 119
Solway Cl. *E8* *6F 67*
(off Queensbridge Rd.)
TW4: Houn 3C 112
Solway Ho. *E1* *4K 85*
(off Ernest St.)
Solway Rd. N22 1B 48
SE22 4G 121
Somaford Gro. EN4: E Barn 6G 21
Somali Rd. NW2 5H 63
Sombourne Ho. *SW15* *7C 116*
(off Fontley Way)
Somerby Rd. IG11: Bark 7H 71
Somercoates Cl. EN4: Cockf 3H 21
Somer Ct. *SW6* *6J 99*
(off Anselm Rd.)
Somerfield Rd. N4 2B 66
(not continuous)
Somerfield St. SE16 5K 103
Somerford Cl. HA5: Eastc 4J 39
Somerford Gro. N16 4F 67
N17 7B 34
(not continuous)
Somerford Gro. Est. N16 4F 67
Somerford St. E1 4H 85
Somerford Way SE16 2A 104
Somerhill Av. DA15: Sidc 7B 126
Somerhill Rd. DA16: Well 2B 126
Somerleyton Pas. SW9 4B 120
Somerleyton Rd. SW9 4A 120
Somersby Gdns. IG4: Ilf 5D 52
Somers Cl. NW1 2H 83
Somers Cres. W2 1C 10 (6C 82)
Somerset Av.
DA16: Well 5K 125
KT9: Chess 4D 162
SW20 2D 152
Somerset Cl. IG8: Wfd G 1J 51
KT3: N Mald 6A 152
N17 2D 48
SM3: Wor Pk 4E 164
Somerset Ct.
IG9: Buck H 2F 37
NW1 1C 6 (2H 83)
TW11: Tedd 5J 131
W7 *6K 77*
(off Copley Cl.)
Somerset Est. SW11 1B 118
Somerset Gdns. HA0: Wemb 5C 60
N6 7E 46
N17 7K 33
SE13 2D 122
SW16 3K 155
TW11: Tedd 5J 131
Somerset Hall N17 7K 33
Somerset House 2G 13 (7K 83)
Somerset Ho. SW19 3F 135
Somerset Lodge TW8: Bford 6D 96
Somerset Rd. E17 5C 50
EN5: New Bar 5E 20
HA1: Harr 5G 41
KT1: King T 2F 151
N17 3F 49
N18 5A 34
NW4 4E 44
SW19 3F 135
TW8: Bford 6C 96
TW11: Tedd 5J 131
UB1: S'hall 5D 76
W4 3K 97
W13 1B 96
Somerset Sq. W14 2G 99
Somerset Waye TW5: Hest 6C 94
Somersham Rd. DA7: Bex 2E 126
Somers Pl. SW2 7K 119
Somers Rd. E17 4B 50
SW2 6K 119
Somerston Ho. *NW1* *1G 83*
(off St Pancras Way)
SOMERS TOWN 1C 6 (2H 83)
Somers Town Community Sports Cen. 2H 83
Somerton Av. TW9: Rich 3H 115
Somerton Ho. WC1 2D 6
Somerton Rd. NW2 3F 63
SE15 4H 121
Somertrees Av. SE12 2K 141
Somervell Rd. HA2: Harr 5D 58
Somerville Av. SW13 6D 98
Somerville Cl. SW9 1K 119
Somerville Point SE16 2B 104
Somerville Rd. RM6: Chad H 6C 54
SE20 7K 139
Sonderburg Rd. N7 2K 65
Sondes St. SE17 6D 102
Sonesta Apartments SE15 1H 121
Songhurst Cl. CR0: C'don 6K 155
Sonia Ct. HA1: Harr 6K 41
HA8: Edg 7A 28
Sonia Gdns. N12 4F 31
NW10 4B 62
TW5: Hest 7E 94
Sonning Gdns. TW12: Hamp 6C 130
Sonning Ho. *E2* *2J 9*
(off Swanfield St.)
Sonning Rd. SE25 6G 157
Sontan Ct. TW2: Twick 1H 131
Soper Cl. E4 5G 35
SE23 1K 139
Soper M. EN3: Enf L 1H 25
Sophia Cl. N7 6K 65
Sophia Ho. *W6* *5E 98*
(off Queen Caroline St.)
Sophia Rd. E10 1D 68
E16 6K 87
Sophia Sq. *SE16* *7A 86*
(off Sovereign Cres.)
Sophora Ho. SW8 7F 101
Soprano Ct. *E15* *1H 87*
(off Plaistow Rd.)
Soprano Way KT10: Surb 3B 162
Sopwith NW9 7G 29
Sopwith Av. E17 3K 49
KT9: Chess 5E 162
Sopwith Cl. KT2: King T 5F 133
Sopwith Rd. TW5: Hest 7A 94
Sopwith Way KT2: King T 1E 150
SW8 7J 17 (7F 101)
Sorbus Ct. EN2: Enf 2G 23
Sorensen Ct. *E10* *2D 68*
(off Leyton Grange Est.)
Sorrel Cl. SE28 1A 108
Sorrel Gdns. E6 5C 88
Sorrel La. E14 6F 87
Sorrell Cl. SE14 7A 104
SW9 2A 120
Sorrel Mead NW9 7C 44
Sorrento Rd. SM1: Sutt 3K 165
Sotheby Rd. N5 3B 66
Sotheran Cl. E8 1G 85
Sotherby Lodge *E2* *2J 85*
(off Sewardstone Rd.)
Sotheron Pl. SW6 7K 99
Soudan Rd. SW11 1D 118
Souldern Rd. W14 3F 99
Sounding All. E3 1C 86
Sth. Access Rd. E17 7A 50
Southacre *W2* *1C 10*
(off Hyde Pk. Cres.)
Southacre Way HA5: Pinn 1A 40
SOUTH ACTON 2J 97
Sth. Africa Rd. W12 1D 98
SOUTHALL 1D 94
Southall Ct. UB1: S'hall 7D 76
Southall Ent. Cen. UB2: S'hall 2E 94
SOUTHALL GREEN 3C 94
Southall La. TW5: Cran 6K 93
UB2: S'hall 6K 93
Southall Pl. SE1 7E 14 (2D 102)
Southall Sports Cen. 1C 94
Southam Ho. *W10* *4G 81*
(off Southam St.)
Southampton Bldgs. WC2 6J 7 (5A 84)
Southampton Gdns. CR4: Mitc 5J 155
Southampton M. E16 1K 105
Southampton Pl. WC1 6F 7 (5J 83)
Southampton Rd. NW5 5D 64
Southampton Rd. E. TW6: H'row A 6B 110
Southampton Rd. W. TW6: H'row A 6A 110
Southampton Row WC1 5F 7 (5J 83)
Southampton St. WC2 2F 13 (7J 83)
Southampton Way SE5 7D 102
Southam St. W10 4G 81
Sth. Audley St. W1 3H 11 (7E 82)
South Av. E4 7J 25
SM5: Cars 7E 166
TW9: Kew 2G 115
UB1: S'hall 7D 76
South Av. Gdns. UB1: S'hall 7D 76
South Bank KT6: Surb 6E 150
Southbank KT7: T Ditt 7B 150
Southbank Bus. Cen. SW11 1D 118
Southbank Cen. 4H 13 (1K 101)
Sth. Bank Ter. KT6: Surb 6E 150
SOUTH BARNET 1K 31
SOUTH BEDDINGTON 6H 167
Sth. Birkbeck Rd. E11 3F 69
Sth. Black Lion La. W6 5C 98
South Block *SE1* *7G 13*
(off Belvedere Rd.)
Sth. Bolton Gdns. SW5 5K 99
SOUTHBOROUGH
BR2 5D 160
KT6 1E 162
Southborough Cl. KT6: Surb 1D 162
Southborough Ho. *SE17* *5E 102*
(off Kinglake Est.)
Southborough La. BR2: Brom 5C 160
Southborough Rd. BR1: Brom 3C 160
E9 1K 85
KT6: Surb 1E 162
Southbourne BR2: Hayes 7J 159
Southbourne Av. NW9 2J 43
Southbourne Cl. HA5: Pinn 7C 40
Southbourne Ct. NW9 2J 43
Southbourne Cres. NW4 4G 45
Southbourne Gdns. HA4: Ruis 1K 57
IG1: Ilf 5G 71
SE12 5K 123
Southbridge Pl. CR0: C'don 4C 168
Southbridge Rd. CR0: C'don 4C 168
Southbridge Way UB2: S'hall 2C 94
SOUTH BROMLEY 7E 86
Southbrook M. SE12 6H 123
Southbrook Rd. SE12 6H 123
SW16 1J 155
Southbury *NW8* *1A 82*
(off Loudoun Rd.)
Southbury Av. EN1: Enf 4B 24
Southbury Leisure Cen. 3B 24
Southbury Rd. EN1: Enf 3K 23
EN3: Pond E 3K 23
Sth. Carriage Dr. SW1 7B 10 (2B 100)
SW7 7B 10 (2B 100)
SOUTH CHINGFORD 5G 35
Southchurch Ct. *E6* *2D 88*
(off High St. Sth.)
Southchurch Rd. E6 2D 88
South City Ct. SE15 7E 102
South Cl. DA6: Bex 4D 126
EN5: Barn 3C 20
HA5: Pinn 7D 40
N6 6F 47
RM10: Dag 1G 91
SM4: Mord 6J 153
TW2: Twick 3E 130
UB7: W Dray 3B 92
Sth. Colonnade, The E14 1C 104
(not continuous)
Southcombe St. W14 4G 99
South Comn. Rd. UB8: Uxb 6A 56
Southcote Av. KT5: Surb 7H 151
TW13: Felt 2H 129
Southcote Ri. HA4: Ruis 7F 39
Southcote Rd. E17 5K 49
N19 4G 65
SE25 5H 157
Southcott Ho. *E3* *3D 86*
(off Devons Rd.)
W9 *4A 82*
(off Clifton Gdns.)
Southcott M. NW8 2C 82
Southcott Rd. TW11: Hamp W 1C 150
Sth. Countess Rd. E17 3B 50
South Cres. E16 4F 87
WC1 6C 6 (5H 83)
Sth. Crescent M. WC1 4J 83
Southcroft Av. BR4: W W'ck 2E 170
DA16: Well 3J 125
Southcroft Rd. BR6: Orp 3J 173
SW16 6E 136
SW17 6E 136
Sth. Cross Rd. IG6: Ilf 5G 53
Sth. Croxted Rd. SE21 3D 138
SOUTH CROYDON 5D 168
South Croydon Sports Club 5E 168
Southdean Gdns. SW19 2H 135
South Dene NW7 3E 28
Southdene Ct. N11 3A 32
Southdown Av. W7 3A 96
Southdown Cres. HA2: Harr 1G 59
IG2: Ilf 5J 53
Southdown Dr. SW20 7F 135
Southdown Rd. SM5: Cars 7E 166
SW20 1F 153
South Dr. BR6: Orp 5J 173
HA4: Ruis 1G 57
Sth. Ealing Rd. W5 2D 96
Sth. Eastern Av. N9 3A 34
Sth. Eaton Pl. SW1 3H 17 (4E 100)
Sth. Eden Pk. Rd.
BR3: Beck 6D 158
Sth. Edwardes Sq. W8 3H 99
SOUTHEND 4F 141
South End CR0: C'don 4C 168
CR2: S Croy 4C 168
W8 3K 99
Sth. End Cl. NW3 4C 64
Southend Cl. SE9 6F 125
Southend Cres. SE9 6F 125
Sth. End Grn. NW3 4C 64

Southend La. SE6 4B 140
SE26 4B 140
Sth. End Rd. NW3 4C 64
Southend Rd. BR3: Beck 1C 158
E4 5F 35
E6 7D 70
E17 1D 50
E18 1J 51
IG8: Wfd G 2A 52
Sth. End Row W8 3K 99
Southern Av. SE25 3F 157
TW14: Felt 1J 129
Southern Cotts. TW19: Stanw M 7B 174
Southerngate Way SE14 7A 104
Southern Gro. E3 3B 86
Southern Perimeter Rd.
TW6: H'row A, Stanw 5A 110, 7C 174
(not continuous)
Southern Pl. HA1: Harr 4K 59
Southern Rd. E13 2K 87
N2 4D 46
Southern Row W10 4G 81
Southern St. N1 2K 83
Southern Ter. W12 1E 98
Southern Way RM7: Rom 6G 55
SE10 4H 105
Southernwood Retail Pk. SE1 5F 103
Southerton Rd. W6 4E 98
Sth. Esk Rd. E7 6A 70
Southey Ho. *SE17 5C 102*
(off Browning St.)
Southey M. E16 1J 105
Southey Rd. N15 5E 48
SW9 1A 120
SW19 7J 135
Southey St. SE20 7K 139
Southfield EN5: Barn 6A 20
Southfield Cl. UB8: Hil 4C 74
Southfield Cotts. W7 2K 95
Southfield Ct. E11 3H 69
Southfield Gdns. TW1: Twick 4K 131
Southfield Pk. HA2: Harr 4F 41
Southfield Rd. BR7: Chst 3K 161
EN3: Pond E 6C 24
N17 2E 48
W4 2K 97
SOUTHFIELDS 1H 135
Southfields KT8: E Mos 6J 149
NW4 3D 44
Southfields Av. TW15: Ashf 6D 128
Southfields Ct. SM1: Sutt 2J 165
Southfields M. SW18 6J 117
Southfields Pas. SW18 6J 117
Southfields Rd. SW18 6J 117
Southfleet NW5 6E 64
Southfleet Rd. BR6: Orp 3J 173
South Gdns. HA9: Wemb 2G 61
SW19 7B 136
SOUTHGATE 1C 32
Southgate Av. TW13: Felt 4F 129
Southgate Cir. N14 1C 32
Southgate Ct. *N1 7D 66*
(off Downham Rd.)
Southgate Gro. N1 7D 66
Southgate Hockey Cen. 3A 22
Southgate Leisure Cen. 7C 22
Southgate Rd. N1 1D 84
Sth. Gipsy Rd. DA16: Well 3D 120
Sth. Glade, The DA5: Bexl 1F 145
South Grn. *NW9 1A 44*
(off Parklea Cl.)
South Gro. E17 5B 50
N6 1E 64
N15 5D 48
South Gro. Ho. N6 1E 64
SOUTH HACKNEY 1K 85
SOUTH HAMPSTEAD 7A 64
SOUTH HARROW 3G 59
Sth. Harrow Ind. Est. HA2: Harr 2G 59
South Herts Golf Course 1D 30
South Hill BR7: Chst 6D 142
HA6: Nwood 1G 39
Sth. Hill Av. HA1: Harr 3G 59
HA2: Harr 3G 59
Sth. Hill Gro. HA1: Harr 4J 59
Sth. Hill Pk. NW3 4C 64
Sth. Hill Pk. Gdns. NW3 3C 64
Sth. Hill Rd. BR2: Brom 3G 159
Southholme Cl. SE19 1E 156
SOUTH HORNCHURCH 2K 91
Southill Ct. BR2: Brom 5H 159
Southill La. HA5: Eastc 4K 39
Southill Rd. BR7: Chst 7C 142
Southill St. E14 6D 86
Sth. Island Pl. SW9 7K 101
SOUTH KENSINGTON 4B 100
Sth. Kensington Sta. Arc. *SW7 3B 16*
(off Pelham St.)
SOUTH LAMBETH 7J 101
Sth. Lambeth Pl. SW8 7F 19 (6J 101)
Sth. Lambeth Rd. SW8 7F 19 (6J 101)
Southland Rd. SE18 7K 107
Southlands Av. BR6: Orp 4H 173
Southlands Dr. SW19 2F 135
Southlands Gro. BR1: Brom 3C 160
Southlands Rd. BR1: Brom 5A 160
BR2: Brom 5A 160
Southland Way TW3: Houn 5H 113
South La. KT1: King T 3D 150
KT3: N Mald 4K 151
South La. W. KT3: N Mald 4K 151
South Lodge *E16 1K 105*
(off Audley Dr.)
NW8 1A 4 (2B 82)
SW7 7D 10
(off Knightsbridge)
TW2: Whitt 6G 113
Sth. Lodge Av. CR4: Mitc 4J 155
Sth. Lodge Cres. EN2: Enf 4C 22
(not continuous)
Sth. Lodge Dr. N14 4C 22
Sth. London Crematorium
CR4: Mitc 2G 155
South London Gallery 1E 120
South London Theatre *3B 138*
(off Norwood High St.)
South Mall *N9 3B 34*
(off Plevna Rd.)
SW18 6K 117
South Mead KT19: Ewe 7B 164
NW9 1B 44
Southmead Gdns. TW11: Tedd 6A 132
Southmead Rd. SW19 1G 135
Southmere Boating Cen. 2C 108
Southmere Dr. SE2 2D 108
Sth. Molton La. W1 1J 11 (6F 83)
Sth. Molton Rd. E16 6J 87
Sth. Molton St. W1 1J 11 (6F 83)
Southmoor Way E9 6B 68
South Mt. *N20 2F 31*
(off High Rd.)
SOUTH NORWOOD 4F 157
South Norwood Country Pk. 4J 157
South Norwood Country Pk. Vis. Cen. 4H 157
Sth. Norwood Hill SE25 1E 156
South Norwood Leisure Cen. 5H 157
Sth. Oak Rd. SW16 4K 137
Southold Ri. SE9 3D 142
Southolm St. SW11 1F 119
Southover BR1: Brom 5J 141
N12 3D 30
South Pde. HA8: Edg 2G 43
SM6: Wall 6G 167
SW3 5B 16 (5B 100)
W4 4K 97
South Pk. Ct. BR3: Beck 7C 140
South Pk. Cres. IG1: Ilf 3H 71
SE6 1G 141
South Pk. Dr. IG3: Ilf 2J 71
IG11: Bark 5J 71
South Pk. Gro. KT3: N Mald 4J 151
South Pk. Hill Rd. CR2: S Croy 5D 168
South Pk. M. SW6 3K 117
South Pk. Rd. IG1: Ilf 3H 71
SW19 6J 135
South Pk. Ter. IG1: Ilf 3J 71
South Pk. Vs. IG3: Ilf 4J 71
South Pk. Way HA4: Ruis 6A 58
South Pl. EC2 5F 9 (5D 84)
EN3: Pond E 5D 24
KT5: Surb 7F 151
South Pl. M. EC2 6F 9 (5D 84)
Southport Rd. SE18 4H 107
Sth. Quay Plaza E14 2D 104
Sth. Quay Sq. E14 2D 104
Southridge Pl. SW20 7F 135
South Ri. SM5: Cars 7C 166
W2 2D 10
Sth. Ri. Way SE18 5H 107
South Rd. HA1: Harr 1A 60
HA8: Edg 1H 43
N9 1B 34
RM6: Chad H 5C 54
(Dunmow Cl.)
RM6: Chad H 6E 54
(Mill La.)
SE23 2K 139
SW19 6A 136
TW2: Twick 3H 131
TW5: Hest 6B 94
TW12: Hamp 6C 130
TW13: Hanw 5B 130
UB1: S'hall 2D 94
UB7: W Dray 3C 92
W5 4D 96
South Row SE3 2H 123
SOUTH RUISLIP 4A 58
Southsea Rd. KT1: King T 4E 150
South Sea St. SE16 3B 104
South Side N15 4F 49
W6 3B 98
Southside N7 4H 65
Southside Comn. SW19 6E 134
Southside Halls *SW7 1B 16*
(off Prince's Gdns.)
Southside House 6E 134
Southside Ind. Est. *SW8 1G 119*
(off Havelock Ter.)
Southside Shop. Cen. SW18 6K 117
Southspring DA15: Sidc 7H 125
South Sq. NW11 6K 45
WC1 6J 7 (5A 84)
South Stand N5 4B 66
South St. BR1: Brom 2J 159
EN3: Pond E 5D 24
RM1: Rom 5K 55
RM13: Rain 2J 91
TW7: Isle 3A 114
W1 4H 11 (1E 100)
South St. Studios *BR1: Brom 2J 159*
(off South St.)
Sth. Tenter St. E1 2K 15 (7F 85)
South Ter. KT6: Surb 6E 150
SW7 3C 16 (4C 100)
SOUTH TOTTENHAM 5F 49
South Va. HA1: Harr 4J 59
SE19 6E 138
Southvale Rd. SE3 2G 123
South Vw. BR1: Brom 2A 160
SW19 6F 135
Southview Av. NW10 5B 62
South Vw. Cl. DA5: Bexl 6F 127
Southview Cl. SW17 5E 136
South Vw. Ct. SE19 7C 138
Southview Cres. IG2: Ilf 6F 53
South Vw. Dr. E18 3K 51
Southview Gdns. SM6: Wall 7G 167
Southview Pde. RM13: Rain 3K 91
South Vw. Rd. HA5: Pinn 1K 39
N8 3H 47
Southview Rd. BR1: Brom 4F 141
South Vs. NW1 6H 65
Southville SW8 1H 119
Southville Cl. KT19: Ewe 7K 163
TW14: Bedf, Felt 1G 129
(not continuous)
Southville Cres. TW14: Felt 1G 129
Southville Rd. KT7: T Ditt 7A 150
TW14: Felt 1G 129
South Wlk. BR4: W W'ck 3G 171
UB3: Hayes 5F 75
SOUTHWARK 5A 14 (1B 102)
Southwark Bri. SE1 3D 14 (7C 84)
Southwark Bri. Bus. Cen. *SE1 5D 14*
(off Southwark Bri. Rd.)
Southwark Bri. Rd. SE1 7B 14 (3B 102)
Southwark Cathedral 4E 14 (1D 102)
Southwark Pk. 3H 103
Southwark Pk. Est. *SE16 4H 103*
(off Southwark Pk. Rd.)
Southwark Pk. Rd. SE16 4F 103
Southwark Pk. Sports Cen. Track 4J 103
Southwark Pk. Sports Complex 4J 103
Southwark Pl. BR1: Brom 3D 160
Southwark Playhouse *3C 102*
(off Newington C'way)
Southwark St. SE1 4A 14 (1B 102)
Southwater Cl. BR3: Beck 7D 140
E14 6B 86
South Way CR0: C'don 3A 170
HA2: Harr 4E 40
HA9: Wemb 5G 61
N9 2D 34
N11 6B 32
Southway BR2: Hayes 7J 159
N20 2D 30
NW11 6K 45
SM6: Wall 4G 167
SW20 5E 152
Southway Cl. W12 2D 98
Southwell Av. UB5: N'olt 6E 58
Southwell Gdns. SW7 4A 100
Southwell Gro. Rd. E11 2G 69
Southwell Ho. *SE16 4H 103*
(off Anchor St.)
Southwell Rd. CR0: C'don 6A 156
HA3: Kenton 6D 42
SE5 3C 120
Sth. Western Rd. TW1: Twick 6A 114
Sth. W. India Dock Entrance E14 2E 104
Sth. W. Middlesex Crematorium
TW13: Felt 1C 130
Southwest Rd. E11 1F 69
Sth. Wharf Rd. W2 7A 4 (6B 82)
Southwick M. W2 7B 4 (6B 82)
Southwick Pl. W2 1C 10 (6C 82)
Southwick St. W2 7C 4 (6C 82)
Southwick Yd. W2 1C 10
SOUTH WIMBLEDON 6K 135
Southwold Dr. IG11: Bark 5A 72
Southwold Mans. *W9 3J 81*
(off Widley Rd.)
Southwold Rd. DA5: Bexl 6H 127
E5 2H 67
Southwood Av. KT2: King T 1J 151
N6 7F 47
Southwood Cl. BR1: Brom 4D 160
KT4: Wor Pk 1F 165
Southwood Ct. *EC1 2A 8*
(off Wynyatt St.)
NW11 5K 45
Southwood Dr. KT5: Surb 7J 151
SOUTH WOODFORD 2J 51
Sth. Woodford to Barking Relief Rd.
E11 5B 52
E12 4E 70
IG1: Ilf 5B 52
IG4: Ilf 5B 52
Southwood Gdns. IG2: Ilf 4F 53
KT10: Hin W 3A 162
Southwood Hall N6 6F 47
Southwood Hgts. N6 7F 47

Southwood Ho. W11 7G 81
(off Avondale Pk. Rd.)
Southwood La. N6 7E 46
Southwood Lawn Rd. N6 7E 46
Southwood Mans. N6 6E 46
(off Southwood La.)
Southwood Pk. N6 7E 46
Southwood Rd. SE9 2F 143
SE28 1B 108
Southwood Smith Ho. E2 3H 85
(off Florida St.)
Southwood Smith St. N1 1B 84
Sth. Worple Av. SW14 3A 116
Sth. Worple Way SW14 3K 115
Southwyck Ho. SW9 4B 120
Soval Ct. HA6: Nwood 1F 39
Sovereign Bus. Cen. EN3: Brim 3G 25
Sovereign Cl. E1 7H 85
HA4: Ruis 1G 57
W5 5C 78
Sovereign Ct. CR2: S Croy 5C 168
(off Warham Rd.)
HA6: Nwood 1J 39
HA7: Stan 7J 27
KT8: W Mole 4D 148
TW3: Houn 3E 112
W8 3K 99
(off Wright's La.)
Sovereign Cres. SE16 7A 86
Sovereign Gro. HA0: Wemb 3D 60
Sovereign Ho. E1 4H 85
(off Cambridge Heath Rd.)
SE18 3D 106
(off Leda Rd.)
TW15: Ashf 4A 128
Sovereign M. E2 2F 85
EN4: Cockf 3J 21
Sovereign Pk. NW10 4H 79
Sovereign Pk. Trad. Est. NW10 4H 79
Sovereign Pl. HA1: Harr 5K 41
Sovereign Rd. IG11: Bark 3C 90
Sowerby Cl. SE9 5D 124
Spa at Beckenham, The 1B 158
Spa Bus. Pk. SE16 3G 103
Space Arts Cen., The 4C 104
(off Westferry Rd.)
Space Bus. Pk. NW10 3H 79
Spaces Bus. Cen. SW8 1G 119
Space Waye TW14: Felt 5J 111
Spa Cl. SE25 1E 156
Spa Ct. SE16 3G 103
SW16 4K 137
Spafield St. EC1 3J 7 (4A 84)
Spa Grn. Est. EC1 1K 7 (3B 84)
Spa Hill SE19 1D 156
Spalding Cl. HA8: Edg 7F 29
Spalding Ho. SE4 4A 122
Spalding Rd. NW4 7E 44
SW17 5F 137
Spanby Rd. E3 4C 86
Spaniards Cl. NW11 1B 64
Spaniards End NW3 1A 64
Spaniards Rd. NW3 2A 64
Spanish Pl. W1 7H 5 (6E 82)
Spanish Rd. SW18 5A 118
Spanswick Lodge N15 4B 48
Spare St. SE17 4C 102
Sparkbridge Rd. HA1: Harr 4J 41
Sparkes Cl. BR2: Brom 4K 159
Sparkes Cotts. SW1 4G 17
Sparkford Gdns. N11 5K 31
Sparkford Ho. SW11 1B 118
(off Battersea Church Rd.)
Sparks Cl. RM8: Dag 2D 72
TW12: Hamp 6C 130
W3 6K 79
Spa Rd. SE16 3F 103
Sparrick's Row SE1 6F 15 (2D 102)
Sparrow Cl. TW12: Hamp 6C 130
Sparrow Dr. BR5: Farnb 1G 173
Sparrow Farm Dr. TW14: Felt 7A 112
Sparrow Farm Rd. KT17: Ewe 4C 164
Sparrow Grn. RM10: Dag 3H 73
Sparrow Ho. E1 4J 85
(off Cephas Av.)
Sparrow's Farm Leisure Cen. 7G 125
Sparrows Herne WD23: Bush 1A 26
Sparrows La. SE9 7G 125
Sparrows Way WD23: Bush 1B 26
Sparsholt Cl. IG11: Bark 1J 89
(off St John's Rd.)
Sparsholt Rd. IG11: Bark 1J 89
N19 1K 65
Spartan Cl. SM6: Wall 7J 167
Sparta St. SE10 1E 122
Speakers' Corner 2F 11 (7D 82)
Speakers Ct. CR0: C'don 1D 168
Speakman Ho. SE4 3A 122
(off Arica Rd.)
Spearman Ho. E14 6C 86
(off Upper Nth. St.)
Spearman St. SE18 6E 106
Spear M. SW5 4J 99
Spearpoint Gdns. IG2: Ilf 5K 53
Spears Rd. N19 1J 65
Speart La. TW5: Hest 7C 94
Spectacle Works E13 3A 88
Spectrum Bldg., The N1 3D 84
(off East Rd.)
Spectrum Pl. SE17 6D 102
(off Lytham St.)
Spectrum Twr. IG1: Ilf 2G 71
(off Hainault St.)
Spectrum Way SW18 5J 117
Spedan Cl. NW3 3A 64
Speechly M. E8 5F 67
Speedbird Way UB7: Harm 3C 174
Speed Highwalk EC2 5D 8
(off Silk St.)
Speed Ho. EC2 5D 8
Speedway Ind. Est. UB3: Hayes 2F 93
Speedwell Ho. N12 4E 30
Speedwell St. SE8 7C 104
Speedy Pl. WC1 2E 6
Speer Rd. KT7: T Ditt 6K 149
Speirs Cl. KT3: N Mald 6B 152
Spekehill SE9 3D 142
Speke Rd. CR7: Thor H 2D 156
Speke's Monument 4A 10 (1A 100)
Speldhurst Cl. BR2: Brom 5H 159
Speldhurst Rd. E9 7K 67
W4 3K 97
Spellbrook Wlk. N1 1C 84
Spelman Ho. E1 6K 9
(off Spelman St.)
Spelman St. E1 5K 9 (5G 85)
(not continuous)
Spelthorne Gro.
TW16: Sun 7H 129
Spelthorne La.
TW15: Ashf 1E 146
Spence Cl. SE16 2B 104
Spencer Av. N13 6E 32
UB4: Hayes 5J 75
Spencer Cl. BR6: Orp 2J 173
IG8: Wfd G 5F 37
N3 2J 45
NW10 3F 79
Spencer Ct. BR6: Farnb 5G 173
NW8 2A 82
(off Marlborough Pl.)
SW20 1D 152
Spencer Courtyard N3 2H 45
(off Regents Pk. Rd.)
Spencer Dr. N2 6A 46
Spencer Gdns. SE9 5D 124
SW14 5J 115
Spencer Hill SW19 6G 135
Spencer Hill Rd. SW19 7G 135
Spencer House 5A 12
Spencer Mans. W14 6G 99
(off Queen's Club Gdns.)
Spencer M. SW8 1K 119
(off Lansdowne Way)
W6 6G 99
SPENCER PARK 5B 118
Spencer Pk. KT8: E Mos 5G 149
SW18 5B 118
Spencer Pl. CR0: C'don 7D 156
N1 7B 66
Spencer Ri. NW5 4F 65
Spencer Rd. BR1: Brom 7H 141
CR2: S Croy 5E 168
CR4: Mitc 3E 154
(Commonside E.)
CR4: Mitc 7E 154
(Wood St.)
E6 1B 88
E17 2E 50
HA0: Wemb 2C 60
HA3: W'stone 2J 41
IG3: Ilf 1K 71
KT8: E Mos 4G 149
N8 5K 47
(not continuous)
N11 4A 32
N17 1G 49
RM13: Rain 3K 91
SW18 4B 118
SW20 1D 152
TW2: Twick 3J 131
TW7: Isle 1G 113
W3 1J 97
W4 7J 97
Spencer St. EC1 2A 8 (3B 84)
UB2: S'hall 2B 94
Spencer Wlk. NW3 4B 64
SW15 4F 117
Spencer Way E1 6H 85
Spencer Yd. SE3 2H 123
(off Tranquil Va.)
Spenlow Ho. SE16 3G 103
(off Jamaica Rd.)
Spenser Gro. N16 5E 66
Spenser M. SE21 2D 138
Spenser Rd. SE24 5B 120
Spenser St. SW1 1B 18 (3G 101)
Spens Ho. WC1 4G 7
(off Lamb's Conduit St.)
Spensley Wlk. N16 3D 66
Speranza St. SE18 5K 107
Sperling Rd. N17 2E 48
Spert St. E14 7A 86
Speyside N14 6B 22
Spey St. E14 5E 86
Spey Way RM1: Rom 1K 55
Spezia Rd. NW10 2C 80
Sphere, The E16 6H 87
(off Hallsville Rd.)
Sphinx Way EN5: Barn 5C 20
Spice Ct. E1 7G 85
Spice Quay Hgts. SE1 5K 15 (1F 103)
Spicer Cl. KT12: Walt T 6A 148
SW9 2B 120
Spicer Ct. EN1: Enf 3K 23
Spice's Yd. CR0: C'don 4C 168
Spigurnell Rd. N17 1D 48
Spikes Bri. Moorings UB4: Yead 7C 76
Spikes Bri. Rd. UB1: S'hall 6C 76
Spindle Cl. SE18 3C 106
Spindlewood Gdns. CR0: C'don 4E 168
Spindrift Av. E14 4C 104
Spinel Cl. SE18 5K 107
Spinnaker Cl. IG11: Bark 3B 90
Spinnaker Ct. KT1: Hamp W 1D 150
(off Becketts Pl.)
Spinnaker Ho. E14 2C 104
(off Byng St.)
SW18 4A 118
(off Juniper Dr.)
Spinnells Rd. HA2: Harr 1D 58
Spinner Ho. E8 1F 85
(off Lovelace St.)
Spinney, The DA14: Sidc 5E 144
EN5: New Bar 2E 20
HA0: Wemb 3A 60
HA7: Stan 4K 27
N21 7F 23
SM3: Cheam 4E 164
SW13 7D 98
SW16 3G 137
TW16: Sun 1J 147
Spinney Cl. BR3: Beck 4D 158
KT3: N Mald 5A 152
KT4: Wor Pk 2B 164
UB7: Yiew 7A 74
Spinney Dr. TW14: Bedf 7E 110
Spinney Gdns. RM9: Dag 5E 72
SE19 5F 139
Spinney Oak BR1: Brom 2C 160
Spinneys, The BR1: Brom 2D 160
Spire Ct. BR3: Beck 2D 158
(off Crescent Rd.)
Spire Ho. W2 7A 82
(off Lancaster Ga.)
Spires Shop. Cen., The EN5: Barn 3B 20
Spirit Quay E1 1G 103
SPITALFIELDS 5J 9 (5F 85)
Spitalfields City Farm 4G 85
Spital Sq. E1 5H 9 (5E 84)
Spital St. E1 5K 9 (5G 85)
Spital Yd. E1 5H 9 (5E 84)
Spitfire Bldg. N1 2K 83
(off Collier St.)
Spitfire Bus. Pk. CR0: Wadd 6A 168
Spitfire Est., The TW5: Cran 5A 94
Spitfire Rd. SM6: Wall 7J 167
TW6: H'row A 6E 110
Spitfire Way TW5: Cran 5A 94
Splendour Wlk. SE16 5J 103
(off Verney Rd.)
Spode Ho. SE11 2J 19
Spode Wlk. NW6 5K 63
Spondon Rd. N15 4G 49
Spoonbill Way UB4: Yead 5B 76
Spooner Ho. TW5: Hest 6E 94
Spooners M. W3 1K 97
Spooner Wlk. SM6: Wall 5J 167
Sporle Rd. Ct. SW11 3B 118
Sportsbank St. SE6 7E 122
Sports Direct Fitness
Croydon 7A 168
Epsom 4K 163
SportsDock 7F 89
Sportsman Pl. E2 1G 85
Sports Village, The 1K 165
Spottiswood Ct. CR0: C'don 6C 156
(off Harry Cl.)
Spottons Gro. N17 1C 48
Spout Hill CR0: Addtn 5C 170
Spout La. TW19: Stanw M 7B 174
Spout La. Nth. TW19: Stanw M 7C 174
Spratt Hall Rd. E11 6J 51
Spray La. TW2: Whitt 6J 113
Spray St. SE18 4F 107
Spreighton Rd. KT8: W Mole 4F 149
Spriggs Ho. N1 7B 66
(off Canonbury Rd.)
Sprimont Pl. SW3 5E 16 (5D 100)
Springall St. SE15 7H 103
Springalls Wharf SE16 2G 103
(off Bermondsey Wall W.)
Spring Apartments CR0: C'don 2D 168
(off Addiscombe Gro.)
E14 4E 104
(off Stebondale St.)
Springbank N21 6E 22
Springbank Rd. SE13 6F 123
Springbank Wlk. NW1 7H 65
Springbourne Ct. BR3: Beck 1E 158
Spring Bri. M. W5 7D 78
Spring Bri. Rd. W5 7D 78
Spring Cl. EN5: Barn 5A 20
RM8: Dag 1D 72

Springclose La. SM3: Cheam 6G 165
Spring Cnr. TW13: Felt 3J 129
Spring Cotts. KT6: Surb 5D 150
Spring Ct. KT17: Ewe 7B 164
NW6 6H 63
W7 7H 77
Spring Ct. Rd. EN2: Enf 1F 23
Springcroft Av. N2 4D 46
Springdale M. N16 4D 66
Springdale Rd. N16 4D 66
Spring Dr. HA5: Eastc 6J 39
Springer Ct. *E3* 4E 86
(off Navigation Rd.)
Springett Ho. *SW2* 5A 120
(off St Matthews Rd.)
Springfield E5 1H 67
SE25 3G 157
WD23: B Hea 1C 26
Springfield Av. N10 3G 47
SW20 3H 153
TW12: Hamp 6F 131
Springfield Cl. HA7: Stan 3F 27
N12 5E 30
Springfield Ct. IG1: Ilf 5F 71
KT1: King T 3E 150
(off Springfield Rd.)
NW3 7C 64
(off Eton Av.)
SM6: Wall 5F 167
Springfield Dr. IG2: Ilf 5G 53
Springfield Gdns. BR1: Brom 4D 160
BR4: W W'ck 2D 170
E5 1H 67
HA4: Ruis 1K 57
IG8: Wfd G 7F 37
NW9 5K 43
Springfield Gro. SE7 6A 106
TW16: Sun 1H 147
Springfield La. NW6 1K 81
Springfield Mt. NW9 5A 44
Springfield Pde. M. N13 4F 33
Springfield Pl. KT3: N Mald 4J 151
Springfield Ri. SE26 3H 139
Springfield Rd. BR1: Brom 4D 160
CR7: Thor H 1C 156
DA7: Bex 4H 127
DA16: Well 3B 126
E4 1B 36
E6 7D 70
E15 3G 87
E17 6B 50
HA1: Harr 6J 41
KT1: King T 3E 150
N11 5A 32
N15 4G 49
NW8 1A 82
SE26 5H 139
SM6: Wall 5F 167
SW19 5H 135
TW2: Whitt 1E 130
TW11: Tedd 5A 132
TW15: Ashf 5B 128
UB4: Yead 1A 94
W7 1J 95
Springfields *EN5: New Bar* 5E 20
(off Somerset Rd.)
Springfield Wlk. *BR6: Orp* 1H 173
(off Place Farm Av.)
NW6 1K 81
Spring Gdns. IG8: Wfd G 7F 37
KT8: W Mole 5F 149
N5 5C 66
RM7: Rom 5J 55
SM6: Wall 5G 167
SW1 4D 12 (1H 101)
(not continuous)
Spring Gdns. Bus. Pk. RM7: Rom 6J 55
SPRING GROVE 1J 113
Spring Gro. CR4: Mitc 1E 154
SE19 7F 139
TW12: Hamp 1F 149
Spring Gro. W4 5G 97
W7 7J 77
Spring Gro. Cres. TW3: Houn 1G 113
Spring Gro. Rd. TW3: Houn, Isle 1F 113
TW7: Isle 1F 113
TW10: Rich 5F 115
SpringHealth Leisure Club
Richmond 4D 114
(within Pools on the Pk.)
Spring Hill E5 7G 49
SE26 4J 139
Springhill Cl. SE5 3D 120
Spring Ho. *E17* 2E 50
(off Fulbourne Rd.)
WC1 2J 7
Springhurst Cl. CR0: C'don 4B 170
Spring Lake HA7: Stan 4G 27
Spring La. E5 7H 49
N10 3E 46
SE25 6H 157
Spring M. KT17: Ewe 7B 164
SE11 5G 19 (5K 101)
TW9: Rich 4E 114
(off Rosedale Rd.)
W1 5F 5 (5D 82)
SPRING PARK 3C 170
Spring Pk. Av. CR0: C'don 2K 169
Spring Pk. Dr. N4 1C 66
Springpark Dr. BR3: Beck 3E 158
Spring Pk. Rd. CR0: C'don 2K 169
Spring Pas. SW15 3F 117
Spring Path NW3 5B 64
Spring Pl. IG11: Bark 2G 89
N3 3J 45
NW5 5F 65
Springpond Rd. RM9: Dag 5E 72
Spring Prom. UB7: W Dray 2B 92
Spring Promenade UB7: W Dray 2B 92
Springrice Rd. SE13 6F 123
Spring Rd. TW13: Felt 3H 129
Springs Cl. TW19: Stanw 1A 128
Spring Shaw Rd. BR5: St P 7A 144
Spring St. W2 1A 10 (6B 82)
Spring Ter. TW9: Rich 5E 114
Spring Tide Cl. SE15 1H 121
Spring Va. DA7: Bex 4H 127
Springvale Av. TW8: Bford 5D 96
Springvale Ter. W14 3F 99
Spring Villa Pk. HA8: Edg 7B 28
Spring Villa Rd. HA8: Edg 7B 28
Spring Wlk. E1 5G 85
Springwater WC1 5G 7
Springwater Cl. SE18 1E 124
Spring Way SE5 1C 120
Springway HA1: Harr 7H 41
Springwell Av. NW10 1B 80
Springwell Cl. SW16 4K 137
Springwell Rd. SW16 4A 138
TW4: Houn 2B 112
TW5: Hest 2B 112
Springwood Cl. E3 2C 86
Springwood Ct. *CR2: S Croy* 4E 168
(off Birdhurst Rd.)
Springwood Cres. HA8: Edg 2C 28
Sproggit Ind. Est. TW19: Stanw 6B 110
Sprowston M. E7 6J 69
Sprowston Rd. E7 5J 69
Spruce Ct. W5 3E 96
Sprucedale Gdns. CR0: C'don 4K 169
Spruce Hills Rd. E17 2E 50
Spruce Ho. *SE16* 2K 103
(off Woodland Cres.)
Spruce Pk. BR2: Brom 4H 159
Sprules Rd. SE4 2A 122
Spurfield KT8: W Mole 3F 149
Spurgeon Av. SE19 1D 156
Spurgeon Rd. SE19 1D 156
Spurgeon St. SE1 3D 102
Spurling Rd. RM9: Dag 6F 73
SE22 4F 121
Spurrell Av. DA5: Bexl 4K 145
Spur Rd. BR6: Orp 2K 173
HA8: Edg 4K 27
N15 4D 48
SE1 6J 13 (2A 102)
SW1 7A 12 (2G 101)
TW7: Isle 7B 96
TW14: Felt 4K 111
Spurstowe Rd. E8 6H 67
Spurstowe Ter. E8 5G 67
Spurway Pde. *IG2: Ilf* 5D 52
(off Woodford Av.)
Square, The E10 3E 68
IG1: Ilf 7E 52
IG8: Wfd G 5D 36
SM5: Cars 5E 166
TW9: Rich 5D 114
UB2: S'hall 4A 94
UB7: Lford 4C 174
UB11: Stock P 1F 93
W6 5E 98
Square of Fame 4G 61
(off Arena Sq.)
Square Rigger Row SW11 3A 118
Squarey St. SW17 3A 136
Squire Gdns. *NW8* 2A 4
(off Grove End Rd.)
Squires, The RM7: Rom 6J 55
Squire's Bri. Rd. TW17: Shep 4B 146
Squires Ct. SW4 1J 119
SW19 4J 135
Squires La. N3 2K 45
Squires Mt. NW3 3B 64
Squire's Rd. TW17: Shep 4C 146
Squires Wlk. TW15: Ashf 7F 129
(not continuous)
Squires Way DA2: Wilm 4K 145
Squires Wood Dr. BR7: Chst 7C 142
Squirrel Cl. TW4: Houn 3A 112
Squirrel M. W13 7K 77
Squirrels, The HA5: Pinn 3D 40
SE13 3F 123
Squirrels Cl. BR6: Orp 1J 173
N12 4F 31
UB10: Hil 7C 56
Squirrels Ct. *KT4: Wor Pk* 2B 164
(off The Avenue)
Squirrels Drey *BR2: Brom* 2G 159
(off Park Hill Rd.)
Squirrels Grn. KT4: Wor Pk 2B 164
Squirrel's La. IG9: Buck H 3G 37
Squirrels Trad. Est. UB3: Hayes 3H 93
Squirries St. E2 3G 85
SSE Arena Wembley, The 4G 61
SS Robin 7K 87
Stable Cl. KT2: King T 6F 133
UB5: N'olt 2E 76
Stable Ct. *EC1* 4B 8
(off Clerkenwell Rd.)
SM6: Wall 3E 166
Stable M. NW5 6F 65
SE6 1G 141
TW1: Twick 1K 131
Stable Pl. N4 2B 66
Stables, The IG9: Buck H 1F 37
Stables End BR6: Farnb 3G 173
Stables Gallery & Arts Cen. 3C 62
Stables Lodge *E8* 7H 67
(off Mare St.)
Stables Mkt., The NW1 7F 65
Stables M. SE27 5C 138
Stables Row E11 5J 51
Stable St. N1 1J 83
Stables Way SE11 5J 19 (5A 102)
Stables Yd. SW18 6J 117
Stable Vs. BR1: Brom 6B 142
Stable Wlk. N2 1B 46
Stable Way W10 6E 80
Stable Yd. SW1 6A 12
SW15 3E 116
Stableyard, The SW9 2K 119
Stableyard M. TW11: Tedd 6K 131
Stable Yd. Rd. SW1 6B 12 (2G 101)
(not continuous)
Staburn Ct. HA8: Edg 2J 43
Stacey Av. N18 4D 34
Stacey Cl. E10 5F 51
Stacey St. N7 3A 66
WC2 1D 12 (6H 83)
Stack Ho. *SW1* 4H 17
(off Cundy St.)
Stackhouse St. SW3 1E 16
Stacy Path SE5 7E 102
Staddon Cl. BR3: Beck 4A 158
Stadium Bus. Cen. HA9: Wemb 3H 61
Stadium M. N5 3A 66
Stadium Retail Pk. HA9: Wemb 3G 61
Stadium Rd. SE18 7C 106
Stadium Rd. E. NW4 7D 44
Stadium St. SW10 7A 100
Stadium Way HA9: Wemb 4F 61
Staffa Rd. E10 1A 68
Stafford Cl. E17 6B 50
(not continuous)
N14 5B 22
NW6 3J 81
SM3: Cheam 6G 165
Stafford Ct. DA5: Bexl 7F 127
SW8 7J 101
W7 6K 77
(off Copley Cl.)
W8 3J 99
Stafford Cripps Ho. *E2* 3J 85
(off Globe Rd.)
SW6 6H 99
(off Clem Attlee Ct.)
Stafford Cross Bus. Pk. CR0: Wadd 5K 167
Stafford Gdns. CR0: Wadd 5K 167
Stafford Ho. *SE1* 5F 103
(off Cooper's Rd.)
Stafford Mans. *SW1* 1A 18
(off Stafford Pl.)
SW4 4J 119
SW11 7D 100
(off Albert Bri. Rd.)
W14 3F 99
(off Haarlem Rd.)
Stafford Pl. SW1 1A 18 (3G 101)
TW10: Rich 7F 115
Stafford Rd. CR0: Wadd 4A 168
DA14: Sidc 4J 143
E3 2B 86
E7 7A 70
HA3: Hrw W 7B 26
HA4: Ruis 4H 57
KT3: N Mald 3J 151
NW6 3J 81
SM6: Wall 6G 167
Staffordshire St. SE15 1G 121
Stafford St. W1 4A 12 (1G 101)
Stafford Ter. W8 3J 99
Staff St. EC1 2F 9 (3D 84)
Stag Cl. HA8: Edg 2H 43
Stag Ct. *KT2: King T* 1G 151
(off Coombe Rd.)
STAG LANE 2B 134
Stag La. HA8: Edg 2H 43
IG9: Buck H 2E 36
NW9 2H 43
SW15 3B 134
Stags Way TW7: Isle 6K 95
Stainbank Rd. CR4: Mitc 3F 155
Stainby Cl. UB7: W Dray 3A 92
Stainby Rd. N15 4F 49
Stainer St. SE1 5F 15 (1D 102)
Staines Av. SM3: Cheam 2F 165
Staines By-Pass TW15: Ashf 5A 128
Staines Rd. IG1: Ilf 5G 71
TW2: Twick 3E 130
TW3: Houn 3F 113
TW4: Houn 7F 111
TW14: Bedf, Felt 1C 128
Staines Rd. E. TW16: Sun 7J 129

Staines Rd. W.—Stanyhurst

Staines Rd. W. TW15: Ashf 6D **128**
TW16: Sun 6D **128**
Staines Wlk. DA14: Sidc 6C **144**
Stainford Cl. TW15: Ashf 5F **129**
Stainforth Rd. E17 . . . . .4C **50**
IG2: Ilf 7H **53**
Staining La. EC2 . . . . .7D **8** (6C **84**)
Stainmore Cl. BR7: Chst 1H **161**
Stainsbury St. E2 . . . . .2J **85**
Stainsby Rd. E14 . . . . .6C **86**
Stainton Rd. EN3: Enf H 1D **24**
SE6 . . . . .6F **123**
Stalbridge Flats *W1* *1H* ***11***
(off Lumley St.)
Stalbridge Ho. *NW1* *1A* ***6***
(off Hampstead Rd.)
Stalbridge St. NW1 . . . . .5D **4** (5C **82**)
Stalham St. SE16 . . . . .3H **103**
Stalham Way IG6: Ilf 1F **53**
Stambourne Way BR4: W W'ck 2E **170**
SE19 . . . . .7E **138**
Stambourne Woodland Wlk.
SE19 . . . . .7E **138**
Stamford Bridge 7K 99
Stamford Bri. Studios *SW6* *7K* ***99***
(off Wandon Rd.)
Stamford Brook Arches W6 . . . . .4C **98**
Stamford Brook Av. W6 . . . . .3B **98**
Stamford Brook Gdns. W6 . . . . .3B **98**
Stamford Brook Mans. *W6* *4B* ***98***
(off Goldhawk Rd.)
Stamford Brook Rd. W6 . . . . .3B **98**
Stamford Bldgs. *SW8* *7J* ***101***
(off Meadow Pl.)
Stamford Cl. HA3: Hrw W 7D **26**
N15 . . . . .4G **49**
NW3 . . . .*3A* ***64***
(off Heath St.)
UB1: S'hall 7E **76**
Stamford Cotts. *SW10* *7K* ***99***
(off Billing St.)
Stamford Ct. W6 . . . . .4C **98**
Stamford Dr. BR2: Brom 4H **159**
Stamford Gdns. RM9: Dag 7C **72**
Stamford Ga. SW6 . . . . .7K **99**
Stamford Gro. E. N16 . . . . .1G **67**
Stamford Gro. W. N16 . . . . .1G **67**
STAMFORD HILL 1F 67
Stamford Hill N16 . . . . .2F **67**
Stamford Lodge N16 . . . . .7F **49**
Stamford Rd. E6 . . . . .1C **88**
N1 . . . . .7E **66**
N15 . . . . .5G **49**
RM9: Dag 1B **90**
Stamford Sq. SW15 . . . . .5G **117**
Stamford St. SE1 . . . . .5J **13** (1A **102**)
Stamp Pl. E2 . . . . .1J **9** (2F **85**)
Stanard Cl. N16 . . . . .7E **48**
Stanborough Cl. TW12: Hamp 6D **130**
Stanborough Ho. *E3* *4D* ***86***
(off Empson St.)
Stanborough Pas. E8 . . . . .6F **67**
Stanborough Rd. TW3: Houn 3H **113**
Stanbridge Pl. N21 . . . . .2G **33**
Stanbridge Rd. SW15 . . . . .3E **116**
Stanbrook Rd. SE2 . . . . .2B **108**
Stanbury Ct. NW3 . . . . .6D **64**
Stanbury Rd. SE15 . . . . .2H **121**
(not continuous)
Stancroft NW9 . . . . .5A **44**
Standale Gro. HA4: Ruis 5E **38**
Standard Ind. Est. E16 . . . . .2D **106**
Standard Pl. EC2 . . . . .2H **9**
Standard Rd. DA6: Bex 4E **126**
DA17: Belv 5G **109**
NW10 . . . . .4J **79**
TW4: Houn 3C **112**
Standcumbe Ct. BR3: Beck 5B **158**
Standen Rd. SW18 . . . . .7H **117**
Standfield Gdns. RM10: Dag 6G **73**
Standfield Rd. RM10: Dag 5G **73**
Standish Ho. *W6* *4C* ***98***
(off St Peter's Gro.)
Standish Rd. W6 . . . . .4C **98**
Standlake Point SE23 . . . . .3K **139**
Stane Cl. SW19 . . . . .7K **135**
Stane Gro. SW9 . . . . .2J **119**
Stanesgate Ho. *SE15* *7G* ***103***
(off Friary Est.)
Stane Way SE18 . . . . .7B **106**
Stanfield Ho. *NW8* *3B* ***4***
(off Frampton St.)
UB5: N'olt *2B* ***76***
(off Academy Gdns.)
Stanfield Rd. E3 . . . . .2A **86**
Stanford Cl. HA4: Ruis 6E **38**
IG8: Wfd G 5H **37**
RM7: Rom 6H **55**
TW12: Hamp 6D **130**
Stanford Ct. SW6 . . . . .1K **117**
W8 . . . .*3K* ***99***
(off Cornwall Gdns.)
Stanford M. E8 . . . . .5G **67**
Stanford Pl. SE17 . . . . .4E **102**
Stanford Rd. N11 . . . . .5J **31**
SW16 .2H **155**
W8 . . . . .3K **99**
Stanford St. SW1 . . . . .4C **18** (4H **101**)
Stanford Way SW16 . . . . .2H **155**
Stangate SE1 .1H **19**
Stangate Gdns. HA7: Stan 4G **27**
Stangate Lodge N21 . . . . .6E **22**
Stanger Rd. SE25 . . . . .4G **157**
Stanhill Cotts. DA2: Wilm 7K **145**
Stanhope Av. BR2: Hayes 1H **171**
HA3: Hrw W 1H **41**
N3 . . . . .3H **45**
Stanhope Cl. SE16 . . . . .2K **103**
Stanhope Gdns. IG1: Ilf 1D **70**
N4 . . . . .6B **48**
N6 . . . . .6F **47**
NW7 . . . . .5G **29**
RM8: Dag 3F **73**
SW7 . . . . .3A **16** (4A **100**)
Stanhope Ga. W1 . . . . .5H **11** (1E **100**)
Stanhope Gro. BR3: Beck 5B **158**
Stanhope Ho. *N11* *4A* ***32***
(off Coppies Gro.)
SE8 . . . .*7B* ***104***
(off Adolphus St.)
Stanhope M. E. SW7 . . . . . . .3A **16** (4A **100**)
Stanhope M. Sth. SW7 . . . . .4A **100**
Stanhope M. W. SW7 . . . . .4A **100**
Stanhope Pde. NW1 . . . . .1A **6** (3G **83**)
Stanhope Pk. Rd. UB6: G'frd 4G **77**
Stanhope Pl. W2 . . . . .1E **10** (7D **82**)
Stanhope Rd. CR0: C'don 3E **168**
DA7: Bex 2E **126**
DA15: Sidc 4A **144**
E17 . . . . .5D **50**
EN5: Barn 6A **20**
N6 . . . . .6G **47**
N12 . . . . .5F **31**
RM8: Dag 2F **73**
SM5: Cars 7E **166**
UB6: G'frd 5G **77**
Stanhope Row W1 . . . . .5J **11** (1F **101**)
Stanhope St. NW1 . . . . .1A **6** (2G **83**)
Stanhope Ter. TW2: Twick 7K **113**
W2 . . . . .2B **10** (7B **82**)
Stanier Cl. W14 . . . . .5H **99**
Stanier Ho. *SW6* *1A* ***118***
(off Station Ct.)
Stanlake M. W12 . . . . .1E **98**
Stanlake Rd. W12 . . . . .1E **98**
Stanlake Vs. W12 . . . . .1E **98**
Stanley Av. BR3: Beck 2E **158**
HA0: Wemb 7E **60**
IG11: Bark 2K **89**
KT3: N Mald 5C **152**
RM8: Dag 1F **73**
UB6: G'frd 1G **77**
Stanley Bri. Studios *SW6* *7K* ***99***
(off King's Rd.)
Stanley Cl. HA0: Wemb 7E **60**
SE9 . . . . .1G **143**
SW8 . . . . .6K **101**
Stanley Cohen Ho. *EC1* *4C* ***8***
(off Golden La.)
Stanley Ct. SM2: Sutt 7K **165**
SM5: Cars 7E **166**
W5 . . . . .5C **78**
Stanley Cres. W11 . . . . .7H **81**
Stanleycroft Cl. TW7: Isle 1J **113**
Stanley Gdns. CR4: Mitc 6E **136**
NW2 . . . . .5E **62**
SM6: Wall 6G **167**
W3 . . . . .2A **98**
W11 . . . . .7H **81**
Stanley Gdns. M. *W11* *7H* ***81***
(off Kensington Pk. Rd.)
Stanley Gdns. Rd.
TW11: Tedd 5J **131**
Stanley Gro. CR0: C'don 6A **156**
SW8 . . . . .2E **118**
Stanley Holloway Ct. *E16* *6J* ***87***
(off Coolfin Rd.)
Stanley Ho. *E14* *6C* ***86***
(off Saracen St.)
SW10 . . . .*7A* ***100***
(off Coleridge Gdns.)
Stanley Mans. *SW10* *7A* ***16***
(off Park Wlk.)
Stanley M. *SW10* *7A* ***100***
(off Coleridge Gdns.)
Stanley Pk. Dr. HA0: Wemb 1F **79**
Stanley Pk. Rd. SM5: Cars 7C **166**
SM6: Wall 6F **167**
Stanley Picker Gallery ***3E 150***
(off Springfield Rd.)
Stanley Rd. BR2: Brom 4K **159**
BR6: Orp 1K **173**
CR0: C'don 7A **156**
CR4: Mitc 7E **136**
DA14: Sidc 3A **144**
E4 . . . . .1A **36**
E10 . . . . .6D **50**
E12 . . . . .5C **70**
E18 . . . . .1H **51**
EN1: Enf 3K **23**
HA2: Harr 2G **59**
HA6: Nwood 1J **39**
HA9: Wemb 6F **61**
IG1: Ilf .2H **71**
N2 . . . . .3B **46**
N9 . . . . .1A **34**
N10 . . . . .7A **32**
N11 . . . . .6C **32**
N15 . . . . .4B **48**
NW9 . . . . .7C **44**
SM2: Sutt 6K **165**
SM4: Mord 4J **153**
SM5: Cars 7E **166**
SW14 .4H **115**
SW19 .6J **135**
TW2: Twick 3H **131**
TW3: Houn 4G **113**
TW11: Tedd 4J **131**
TW15: Ashf 5A **128**
UB1: S'hall 7C **76**
W3 . . . . .3J **97**
Stanley Sq. SM5: Cars 7D **166**
Stanley St. SE8 . . . . .7B **104**
Stanley Studios *SW10* *7A* ***16***
(off Park Wlk.)
Stanley Ter. DA6: Bex 4G **127**
N19 . . . . .2J **65**
Stanliff Ho. E14 . . . . .3C **104**
Stanmer St. SW11 . . . . .1C **118**
STANMORE .5G 27
Stanmore & Edgware Golf Cen. 3J 27
Stanmore Common Local Nature Reserve
. . . . .2E 26
Stanmore Country Pk.
(Local Nature Reserve) 3H 27
Stanmore Gdns. SM1: Sutt 3A **166**
TW9: Rich 3F **115**
Stanmore Golf Course 7G 27
Stanmore Hill HA7: Stan 3F **27**
Stanmore Lodge HA7: Stan 4G **27**
Stanmore Pl. NW1 . . . . .1F **83**
Stanmore Rd. DA17: Belv 4J **109**
E11 . . . . .1H **69**
N15 . . . . .4B **48**
TW9: Rich 3F **115**
Stanmore St. N1 . . . . .1K **83**
Stanmore Ter. BR3: Beck 2C **158**
Stannard Cotts. *E1* *4J* ***85***
(off Fox Cl.)
Stannard Ct. SE6 . . . . .1D **140**
Stannard Ho. SW19 . . . . .4A **136**
Stannard M. *E8* *6G* ***67***
(off Stannard Rd.)
Stannard Rd. E8 . . . . .6G **67**
Stannary Pl. SE11 . . . . .6K **19** (5A **102**)
Stannary St. SE11 . . . . .7K **19** (6A **102**)
Stannet Way SM6: Wall 4G **167**
Stansborough Ho. *E3* *4D* ***86***
(off Empson St.)
Stansbury Sq. W10 . . . . .3G **81**
Stansfeld Ho. *SE1* *4F* ***103***
(off Longfield Est.)
Stansfeld Rd. E6 . . . . .5B **88**
E16 . . . . .5B **88**
Stansfield Rd. SW9 . . . . .3K **119**
TW4: Cran 2K **111**
Stansgate Rd. RM10: Dag 2G **73**
Stanstead *WC1* *2F* ***7***
(off Tavistock Pl.)
Stanstead Cl. BR2: Brom 5H **159**
Stanstead Gro. SE6 . . . . .1B **140**
Stanstead Ho. *E3* *4E* ***86***
(off Devas St.)
Stanstead Mnr. SM1: Sutt 6J **165**
Stanstead Rd. E11 . . . . .5K **51**
SE6 . . . . .1A **140**
SE23 . . . . .1K **139**
Stansted Cres. DA5: Bexl 1D **144**
Stansted Rd. TW6: H'row A 6B **110**
Stanswood Gdns. SE5 . . . . .7E **102**
Stanthorpe Cl. SW16 . . . . .5J **137**
Stanthorpe Rd. SW16 . . . . .5J **137**
Stanton Av. TW11: Tedd 6J **131**
Stanton Cl. KT4: Wor Pk 1F **165**
KT19: Ewe 5H **163**
Stanton Ct. *CR2: S Croy* *5E* ***168***
(off Birdhurst Ri.)
Stanton Ho. *SE10* *6E* ***104***
(off Thames St.)
SE16 . . . .*2B* ***104***
(off Rotherhithe St.)
Stanton Rd. CR0: C'don 7C **156**
SE26 . . . . .4B **140**
SW13 . . . . .2B **116**
SW20 . . . . .1F **153**
Stanton Sq. SE26 . . . . .4B **140**
Stanton Way SE26 . . . . .4B **140**
Stanway Ct. *N1* *1H* ***9***
(off Shenfield St.)
Stanway Gdns. HA8: Edg 5D **28**
W3 . . . . .1G **97**
Stanway St. N1 . . . . .2E **84**
STANWELL .6A 110
Stanwell Cl. TW19: Stanw 6A **110**
STANWELL MOOR 7B 174
Stanwell Moor Rd.
TW19: Staines, Stanw M 7C **174**
UB7: Lford 7C **174**
Stanwell Rd. TW14: Bedf 7D **110**
TW15: Ashf 2A **128**
Stanwick Rd. W14 . . . . .4H **99**
Stanworth Ct. TW5: Hest 7D **94**
Stanworth St. SE1 . . . . .7J **15** (3F **103**)
Stanyhurst SE23 . . . . .1A **140**

Stapenhill Rd.—Steadfast Rd.

Stapenhill Rd. HA0: Wemb 3B 60
Staple Cl. DA5: Bexl 3K 145
Staplefield Cl. SW2 1J 137
Stapleford *N17* *2E 48*
(off Willan Rd.)
Stapleford Av. IG2: Ilf 5J 53
Stapleford Cl. E4 3K 35
KT1: King T 2G 151
SW19 7G 117
Stapleford Rd. HA0: Wemb 7D 60
Staplehurst Rd. SE13 5F 123
SM5: Cars 7C 166
Staple Inn WC1 6J 7
Staple Inn Bldgs. WC1 6J 7 (5A 84)
Staples Cl. SE16 1A 104
STAPLES CORNER 1D 62
Staples Cnr. Bus. Pk. NW2 1D 62
Staples Cnr. Retail Pk. NW2 1D 62
Staples Ho. *E6* *6E 88*
(off Savage Gdns.)
Staple St. SE1 7F 15 (2D 102)
Stapleton Gdns. CR0: Wadd 5A 168
Stapleton Hall Rd. N4 1K 65
Stapleton Ho. *E2* *3H 85*
(off Ellsworth St.)
Stapleton Rd. BR6: Orp 4K 173
DA7: Bex 7F 109
SW17 3E 136
Stapleton Vs. *N16* *4E 66*
(off Wordsworth Rd.)
Stapley Rd. DA17: Belv 5G 109
Stapylton Rd. EN5: Barn 3B 20
Star All. EC3 2H 15
Star & Garter Hill TW10: Rich 1E 132
Starboard Way E14 3C 104
Starbuck Cl. SE9 7E 124
Star Bus. Cen. RM13: Rain 5K 91
Starch Ho. La. IG6: Ilf 2H 53
Star Cl. EN3: Pond E 6D 24
Starcross St. NW1 2B 6 (3G 83)
Starfield Rd. W12 2C 98
Star Hill DA1: Cray 5K 127
Star La. E16 4G 87
Starley Cl. E17 1F 51
Starlight Way TW6: H'row A 5E 110
Starling Cl. CR0: C'don 6A 158
HA5: Pinn 3A 40
IG9: Buck H 1D 36
Starling Ho. *NW8* *2C 82*
(off Charlbert St.)
Starling Wlk. TW12: Hamp 5C 130
Starmans Cl. RM9: Dag 1E 90
Star Path *UB5: N'olt* *2E 76*
(off Brabazon Rd.)
Star Pl. E1 3K 15 (7F 85)
Star Rd. TW7: Isle 2H 113
UB10: Hil 4E 74
W14 6H 99
Star St. W2 7B 4 (6C 82)
Starts Cl. BR6: Farnb 3E 172
Starts Hill Av. BR6: Farnb 4F 173
Starts Hill Rd. BR6: Farnb 3E 172
Starveall Cl. UB7: W Dray 3B 92
Star Wharf *NW1* *1G 83*
(off St Pancras Way)
Star Yd. WC2 7J 7 (6A 84)
State Farm Av. BR6: Farnb 4F 173
Staten Bldg. *E3* *2C 86*
(off Fairfield Rd.)
Staten Gdns. TW1: Twick 1K 131
State Pde. IG6: Ilf 2G 53
Statham Gro. N16 4D 66
N18 5K 33
Statham Ho. *SW8* *1G 119*
(off Wadhurst Rd.)
Station App. *BR1: Brom* *3J 159*
(off High St.)
BR2: Hayes 1J 171
BR3: Beck 1C 158
BR4: W W'ck 7E 158
BR6: Orp 2K 173
Station App. BR7: Chst 6C 142
(Bennetts Copse)
BR7: Chst 1E 160
(Vale Rd.)
CR0: C'don *2D 168*
(off Dingwall Rd.)
CR2: Sande 7D 168
DA5: Bexl 1G 145
DA7: Bex 2J 127
(Barnehurst Rd.)
DA7: Bex 2E 126
(Percy Rd.)
DA16: Well 2A 126
E4 6A 36
E7 4K 69
E11 5J 51
E17 5C 50
E18 2K 51
EN5: New Bar 4F 21
HA0: Wemb 6B 60
HA1: Harr 7J 41
HA4: Ruis 5K 57
(Mahlon Av.)
HA4: Ruis 1G 57
(Pembroke Rd.)
HA5: Pinn 3C 40
IG8: Wfd G 6E 36
IG9: Buck H 4G 37
KT1: King T 1G 151
KT4: Wor Pk 1C 164
KT17: Ewe 7B 164
KT19: Ewe 5C 164
N11 5A 32
N12 4E 30
N16 *2F 67*
(off Stamford Hill)
NW1 4F 5 (4D 82)
NW10 3B 80
NW11 7F 45
SE3 3K 123
SE9 2G 143
(Bercta Rd.)
SE9 1D 142
(Crossmead)
SE12 *6J 123*
(off Burnt Ash Hill)
SE26 4J 139
SM2: Cheam 7G 165
SM5: Cars 4D 166
SW6 3G 117
SW14 3J 115
SW16 6H 137
(Estreham Rd.)
SW16 5H 137
(Gleneagle Rd.)
SW20 2D 152
TW8: Bford *6C 96*
(off Sidney Gdns.)
TW9: Kew 1G 115
TW12: Hamp 1E 148
TW15: Ashf 4B 128
TW16: Sun 1J 147
TW17: Shep 5E 146
UB3: Hayes 3H 93
UB6: G'frd 7G 59
UB7: Yiew 1A 92
W7 1J 95
Station App. Nth. DA15: Sidc 2A 144
Station App. Rd. SE1 7H 13 (2A 102)
W4 7J 97
Station App. Sth.
DA15: Sidc *2A 144*
(off Jubilee Way)
Station Arc. *W1* *4K 5*
(off Gt. Portland St.)
Station Av. KT3: N Mald 3A 152
KT19: Ewe 7A 164
SW9 3B 120
TW9: Kew 1G 115
Station Bldgs. *KT1: King T* *2E 150*
(off Fife Rd.)
Station Chambers *E6* *7C 70*
(off High St. Nth.)
Station Cl. N3 1J 45
N12 4E 30
TW12: Hamp 1F 149
Station Cotts. BR6: Orp 2K 173
Station Ct. N15 5F 49
SW6 1A 118
Station Cres. HA0: Wemb 6B 60
N15 4D 48
SE3 5J 105
TW15: Ashf 4A 128
Stationer's Hall Ct. EC4 1B 14 (6B 84)
Station Est. BR3: Beck 3K 157
E18 2K 51
Station Est. Rd. TW14: Felt 1K 129
Station Garage M. SW16 6H 137
Station Gdns. W4 7J 97
Station Gro. HA0: Wemb 6E 60
Station Hill BR2: Hayes 2J 171
Station Ho. *SE8* *7C 104*
(off Deptford High St.)
Station Ho. M. N9 4B 34
Station Pde. *BR1: Brom* *1J 159*
(off Tweedy Rd.)
DA7: Bex *2E 126*
(off Pickford La.)
DA15: Sidc 2A 144
E6 7C 70
E11 5J 51
E13 *1A 88*
(off Green St.)
EN4: Cockf 4K 21
HA2: Harr 4F 59
HA3: Kenton 2A 42
HA4: Ruis 2F 57
HA8: Edg 7K 27
IG9: Buck H 4G 37
IG11: Bark 7G 71
N14 1C 32
NW2 6E 62
RM9: Dag 6G 73
SM2: Sutt *6A 166*
(off High St.)
SW12 1E 136
TW9: Kew 1G 115
TW14: Felt 1K 129
TW15: Ashf 4B 128
UB5: N'olt 4F 59
(Accock Gro.)
UB5: N'olt 7E 58
(Court Farm Rd.)
W3 6G 79
W4 7J 97
W5 1F 97
Station Pas. E18 2K 51
E20 6E 68
SE15 1J 121
Station Path *E8* *6H 67*
(off Graham Rd.)
SW6 3H 117
Station Pl. N4 2A 66
Station Ri. SE27 2B 138
Station Rd. BR1: Brom 1J 159
BR2: Brom 2G 159
BR4: W W'ck 1E 170
BR6: Orp 2K 173
CR0: C'don 1C 168
DA7: Bex 3E 120
DA15: Sidc 2A 144
DA17: Belv 3G 109
E4 1A 36
E7 4J 69
E12 4C 70
E17 6A 50
EN5: New Bar 5E 20
HA1: Harr 4K 41
HA2: Harr 5F 41
HA8: Edg 6B 28
IG1: Ilf 3F 71
IG6: Ilf 3H 53
Station Rd. KT1: Hamp W 1C 150
KT2: King T 1G 151
KT3: N Mald 5D 152
KT7: T Ditt 7K 149
KT9: Chess 5E 162
N3 1J 45
N11 5A 32
N17 3G 49
N19 3G 65
N21 1G 33
N22 2J 47
(not continuous)
NW4 6C 44
NW7 6F 29
NW10 2B 80
RM6: Chad H, Dag 7D 54
SE13 3E 122
SE20 6J 139
SE25 4F 157
SM5: Cars 4D 166
SW13 2B 116
SW19 1A 154
TW1: Twick 1K 131
TW3: Houn 4F 113
TW11: Tedd 6A 132
TW12: Hamp 1E 148
TW15: Ashf 4B 128
TW16: Sun 7J 129
TW17: Shep 5E 146
UB3: Harl, Hayes 4G 93
(not continuous)
UB7: W Dray 2A 92
W5 6F 79
W7 1J 95
Station Rd. Nth.
DA17: Belv 3H 109
Station Sq. BR5: Pet W 5G 161
Station St. E15 7F 69
E16 1F 107
Station Ter. NW10 2F 81
SE5 1C 120
Station Ter. M. SE3 5J 105
Station Vw. UB6: G'frd 1H 77
Station Wlk. *IG1: Ilf* *2F 71*
(within The Exchange)
W11 *7F 81*
(off Bramley Rd.)
Station Way IG9: Buck H 4F 37
SE15 2G 121
SE18 3F 107
SM3: Cheam 6G 165
Station Yd. HA4: Ruis 2E 56
TW1: Twick 7A 114
Staton Ct. *E10* *7D 50*
(off Kings Cl.)
Staunton Ho. *SE17* *4E 102*
(off Wansey St.)
Staunton Rd. KT2: King T 6E 132
Staunton St. SE8 6B 104
Stave Hill Ecological Pk. 2A 104
Staveley *NW1* *1A 6*
(off Varndell St.)
Staveley Cl. E9 5J 67
N7 4J 65
SE15 1H 121
Staveley Ct. E11 5J 51
Staveley Gdns. W4 1K 115
Staveley Rd. TW15: Ashf 6F 129
W4 0J 97
Stavers Ho. *E3* *2B 86*
(off Tredegar Rd.)
Staverton Rd. NW2 7E 62
Stave Yd. Rd. SE16 1A 104
Stavordale Lodge *W14* *3H 99*
(off Melbury Rd.)
Stavordale Rd. N5 4B 66
SM5: Cars 7A 154
Stayner's Rd. E1 4K 85
Stayton Rd. SM1: Sutt 3J 165
Stead Cl. BR7: Chst 5E 142
Steadfast Rd. KT1: King T 1D 150

Steadman Ct. EC1 ....3D 8
(off Old St.)
Steadman Ho. RM10: Dag 3G 73
(off Uvedale Rd.)
Stead St. SE17 ....4D 102
Steam Farm La. TW14: Felt ...4H 111
Stean St. E8 ....1F 85
Stebbing Ho. W11 ....1F 99
(off Queensdale Cres.)
Stebbing Way IG11: Bark 2A 90
Stebondale St. E14 ....4E 104
Stedham Pl. WC1 ....7E 6
Stedman Cl. DA5: Bexl 3K 145
  UB10: Ick 3C 56
Steedman St. SE17 ....4C 102
Steeds Rd. N10 ....1D 46
Steele Ct. TW11: Tedd 7C 132
Steele Ho. E15 ....2G 87
(off Eve Rd.)
Steele Rd. E11 ....4G 69
  N17 ....3E 48
  NW10 ....2J 79
  TW7: Isle 4A 114
  W4 ....3J 97
Steele's M. Nth. NW3 ....6D 64
Steele's M. Sth. NW3 ....6D 64
Steele's Rd. NW3 ....6D 64
Steele's Studios NW3 ....6D 64
Steele Wlk. DA8: Erith 7H 109
Steel's La. E1 ....6J 85
Steelyard Pas. EC4 ....3E 14
Steen Way SE22 ....5E 120
Steep Cl. BR6: Chels 6K 173
Steep Hill CR0: C'don 4E 168
  SW16 ....3H 137
Steeple Cl. SW6 ....2G 117
  SW19 ....5G 135
Steeple Ct. E1 ....4H 85
Steeplestone Cl. N18 ....5H 33
Steeple Wlk. N1 ....1C 84
(off New Nth. Rd.)
Steerforth St. SW18 ....2A 136
Steering Cl. N9 ....1D 34
Steers Mead CR4: Mitc 1D 154
Steers Way SE16 ....2A 104
Stelfox Ho. WC1 ....1H 7
(off Penton Ri.)
Stella Cl. UB8: Hil 5D 74
Stellar Ho. N17 ....6A 34
Stella Rd. SW17 ....6D 136
Stelling Rd. DA8: Erith 7K 109
Stellman Cl. E5 ....3G 67
Stembridge Rd. SE20 ....2H 157
Stephan Cl. E8 ....1G 85
Stephen Cl. BR6: Orp 3J 173
Stephendale Rd. SW6 ....3K 117
Stephen Fox Ho. W4 ....5A 98
(off Chiswick La.)
Stephen Jewers Gdns. IG11: Bark 7K 71
Stephen M. W1 ....6C 6 (5H 83)
Stephen Pl. SW4 ....3G 119
Stephen Rd. DA7: Bex 3J 127
Stephens Ct. E16 ....4H 87
  SE4 ....3A 122
Stephens Lodge N12 ....1F 31
(off Woodside La.)
Stephenson Cl. DA16: Well ...2A 126
  E3 ....3D 86
Stephenson Ct. SM2: Cheam ...7G 165
(off Station App.)
Stephenson Ho. SE1 ....3C 102
Stephenson Rd. E17 ....5A 50
  TW2: Whitt 7E 112
  W7 ....6K 77
Stephenson St. E16 ....4G 87
  NW10 ....3A 80
Stephenson Way NW1 ...3B 6 (4G 83)
Stephen's Rd. E15 ....1G 87
Stephen St. W1 ....6C 6 (5H 83)
STEPNEY 5K 85
Stepney C'way. E1 ....6K 85

Stepney City Apartments E1 ...5J 85
Stepney Cl. CR4: Mitc 1E 154
Stepney Grn. E1 ....5J 85
Stepney Grn. Ct. E1 ....5K 85
(off Stepney Grn.)
Stepney High St. E1 ....5K 85
Stepney Way E1 ....5H 85
Stepping City Farm 5K 85
Sterling Av. HA8: Edg 4A 28
Sterling Cl. NW10 ....7C 62
Sterling Gdns. SE14 ....6A 104
Sterling Ind. Est. RM10: Dag ...4H 73
Sterling Rd. W5 ....4E 96
Sterling Rd. DA7: Bex 4H 127
  EN2: Enf 1J 23
Sterling St. SW7 ...1D 16 (3C 100)
Sterling Way N18 ....4J 33
Sternberg Cen., The 3J 45
Stern Cl. IG11: Bark 2C 90
Stern Ct. E3 ....3E 86
(off Culvert Dr.)
Sterndale Rd. W14 ....3F 99
Sterne St. W12 ....2F 99
Sternhall La. SE15 ....3G 121
Sternhold Av. SW2 ....2H 137
Sterry Cres. RM10: Dag 5G 73
Sterry Dr. KT7: T Ditt 6J 149
  KT19: Ewe 4A 164
Sterry Gdns. RM10: Dag 6G 73
Sterry Rd. IG11: Bark 1K 89
  RM10: Dag 4G 73
Sterry St. SE1 ......7E 14 (2D 102)
Steucers La. SE23 ....1A 140
Stevannie Ct. DA17: Belv ...5F 109
Steve Biko Ct. W10 ....4F 81
(off St John's Ter.)
Steve Biko La. SE6 ....4C 140
Steve Biko Lodge E13 ....2J 87
(off London Rd.)
Steve Biko Rd. N7 ....3A 66
Steve Biko Way TW3: Houn 3E 112
Stevedale Rd. DA16: Well 2C 126
Stevedore St. E1 ....1H 103
Stevenage Rd. E6 ....6E 70
  SW6 ....7F 99
Stevens Av. E9 ....6J 67
Stevens Cl. BR3: Beck 6C 140
  DA5: Bexl 4K 145
  HA5: Eastc 5A 40
  TW12: Hamp 6D 130
Stevens Grn. WD23: B Hea ...1B 26
Stevens La. KT10: Clay 7A 162
Stevenson Cl. EN5: New Bar ...7G 21
Stevenson Ct. CR4: Mitc 3C 154
  SE6 ....2H 141
Stevenson Cres. SE16 ....5G 103
Stevenson Ho. NW8 ....1A 82
(off Boundary Rd.)
Stevens Rd. RM8: Dag 2C 72
Stevens St. SE1 ....7H 15 (3E 102)
Steventon Rd. W12 ....7B 80
Steward Ho. E3 ....3C 86
(off Trevithick Way)
Stewards Holte Wlk. N11 ....4A 32
Steward St. E1 ......6H 9 (5E 84)
Stewart Av. TW17: Shep 4C 146
Stewart Cl. BR7: Chst 5F 143
  NW9 ....6J 43
  TW12: Hamp 6C 130
Stewart Ho. KT1: King T 3F 151
Stewart Quay UB3: Hayes 2G 93
Stewart Rainbird Ho. E12 ....5E 70
(off Parkhurst Rd.)
Stewart Rd. E15 ....4F 69
Stewartsby Cl. N18 ....5H 33
Stewart's Gro. SW3 ...5B 16 (5B 100)
Stewart's Pl. SW2 ....6K 119
Stewart's Rd. SW8 ....7G 101
Stewart St. E14 ....2E 104
Stew La. EC4 ....2C 14 (7C 84)
Steyne Horn La. W3 ....1H 97

Steyne Ho. W3 ....1J 97
(off Narrow St.)
Steyne Rd. W3 ....1H 97
Steyning Gro. SE9 ....4D 142
Steynings Way N12 ....5D 30
Steyning Way TW4: Houn 4A 112
Steynton Av. DA5: Bexl 2D 144
Stibbington Ho. NW1 ....2G 83
(off Cranleigh St.)
Stickland Rd. DA17: Belv ...4G 109
Stickle Ho. SE8 ....7D 104
(off Creative Rd.)
Stickleton Cl. UB6: G'frd ...3F 77
Stifford Ho. E1 ....5J 85
(off Stepney Way)
Stilecroft Gdns. HA0: Wemb ...3B 60
Stile Hall Gdns. W4 ....5G 97
Stile Hall Mans. W4 ....5G 97
(off Wellesley Rd.)
Stile Hall Pde. W4 ....5G 97
Stileman Ho. E3 ....5B 86
(off Ackroyd Dr.)
Stile Path TW16: Sun 3J 147
Stiles Cl. BR2: Brom 6D 160
  DA8: Erith 5H 109
Stillingfleet Rd. SW13 .....6C 98
Stillington St. SW1 ...3B 18 (4G 101)
Stillness Rd. SE23 ....6A 122
Still Wlk. SE1 ....5H 15
Stilwell Dr. UB8: Hil 4B 74
STILWELL RDBT. 7C 74
Stipularis Dr. UB4: Yead ...4B 76
Stirling Av. HA5: Pinn 1B 58
  SM6: Wall 7J 167
  TW17: Shep 3G 147
Stirling Cl. DA14: Sidc 4J 143
  SW16 ....1H 155
Stirling Ct. EC1 ....3A 8
(off St John St.)
  W13 ....7B 78
Stirling Gro. TW3: Houn 2G 113
Stirling Ho. SE18 ....5F 107
Stirling Rd. E13 ....2K 87
  E17 ....3A 50
  HA3: W'stone 3K 41
  N17 ....1G 49
  N22 ....1B 48
  SW9 ....2J 119
  TW2: Whitt 7E 112
  TW6: H'row A 6B 110
  UB3: Hayes 7K 75
  W3 ....3H 97
Stirling Rd. Path E17 ......3A 50
Stirling Wlk. KT5: Surb 6H 151
Stirling Way CR0: Bedd 7J 155
Stiven Cres. HA2: Harr 3D 58
Stockbeck NW1 ....1B 6
(off Ampthill Est.)
Stockbridge Rd. SW18 ....4A 118
(off Eltringham St.)
Stockbury Rd. CR0: C'don ...6J 157
Stockdale Rd. RM8: Dag 2F 73
Stockdove Way UB6: G'frd ...3K 77
Stocker Gdns. RM9: Dag 7C 72
Stockfield Rd. SW16 ....3K 137
Stockford Av. NW7 ....7A 30
Stockholm Apartments NW1 ...7E 64
(off Chalk Farm Rd.)
Stockholm Ho. E1 ....7G 85
(off Swedenborg Gdns.)
Stockholm Rd. SE16 ....5J 103
Stockholm Way E1 ....1G 103
Stockhurst Cl. SW15 ....2E 116
Stockingswater La. EN3: Brim ...2G 25
Stockland Rd. RM7: Rom 6K 55
Stockleigh Hall NW8 ....2C 82
(off Prince Albert Rd.)
Stockley Cl. UB7: W Dray ...2D 92
Stockley Country Pk. 7C 74
Stockley Farm Rd. UB7: W Dray ...3D 92
STOCKLEY PARK 1D 92

Stockley Pk. Golf Course 7E 74
Stockley Rd. UB7: W Dray ...4D 92
  UB8: Hil 6C 74
  UB11: Stock P 6C 74
Stock Orchard Cres. N7 .....5K 65
Stock Orchard St. N7 ....5K 65
Stockport Rd. SW16 ....1H 155
Stocksfield Rd. E17 ....3E 50
Stocks Pl. E14 ....7B 86
  UB10: Hil 1C 74
Stock St. E13 ....2J 87
Stockton Cl. EN5: New Bar ...4F 21
Stockton Ct. SW1 ....2C 18
(off Greycoat St.)
Stockton Gdns. N17 ....7H 33
  NW7 ....3F 29
Stockton Ho. E2 ....3H 85
(off Ellsworth St.)
  HA2: Harr 1E 58
Stockton Rd. N17 ....7H 33
  N18 ....6B 34
STOCKWELL 2K 119
Stockwell Av. SW9 ....3K 119
Stockwell Cl. BR1: Brom 2K 159
  HA8: Edg 2J 43
Stockwell Gdns. SW9 ....1K 119
Stockwell Gdns. Est. SW9 ...2J 119
Stockwell Grn. SW9 ....2K 119
Stockwell Grn. Ct. SW9 .....2K 119
Stockwell La. SW9 ....2K 119
Stockwell M. SW9 ....2K 119
Stockwell Pk. Cres. SW9 ....2K 119
Stockwell Pk. Est. SW9 .....2K 119
Stockwell Pk. Rd. SW9 ......1K 119
Stockwell Pk. Wlk. SW9 .....3A 120
Stockwell Rd. SW9 ....2K 119
Stockwell St. SE10 ....6E 104
Stockwell Ter. SW9 ....1K 119
Stodart Rd. SE20 ....1J 157
Stoddart Ho. SW8 .....7H 19 (6K 101)
Stodmarsh Ho. SW9 ....1A 120
(off Cowley Rd.)
Stofield Gdns. SE9 ....3B 142
Stoford Cl. SW19 ....7G 117
Stokenchurch St. SW6 ....1K 117
STOKE NEWINGTON 3F 67
Stoke Newington Chu. St. N16 ...3D 66
Stoke Newington Comn. N16 ...3F 67
Stoke Newington High St. N16 ...3F 67
Stoke Newington Rd. N16 ....5F 67
Stoke Pl. NW10 ....3B 80
Stoke Rd. KT2: King T 7J 133
Stokesby Rd. KT9: Chess 6F 163
Stokes Cotts. IG6: Ilf 1G 53
Stokes Ct. N2 ....4C 46
Stokes Field (Local Nature Reserve)
........................2B 162
Stokesley St. W12 ....6B 80
Stokes M. TW11: Tedd 5A 132
Stokes Rd. CR0: C'don 6K 157
  E6 ....4C 88
Stokley Ct. N8 ....4J 47
Stoll Cl. NW2 ....3E 62
Stoms Path SE6 ....5C 140
(off Maroons Way)
Stonard Rd. N13 ....3F 33
  RM8: Dag 5B 72
Stondon Pk. SE23 ....6A 122
Stondon Wlk. E6 ....2B 88
Stonebanks
  KT12: Walt T 7J 147
STONEBRIDGE 1K 79
Stonebridge Cen. N15 ....5F 49
Stonebridge M. SE19 ....7D 138
Stonebridge Pk. NW10 ....7K 61
Stonebridge Rd. N15 ....5F 49
Stonebridge Way
  HA9: Wemb 6H 61
Stone Bldgs. WC2 ....6H 7
Stonechat M. SW15 ....
Stonechat Sq. E6 ....5C 88

Stone Cl. RM8: Dag 2F 73
SW4 2G 119
UB7: Yiew 1B 92
Stonecot Cl. SM3: Sutt 1G 165
Stonecot Hill SM3: Sutt 1G 165
Stone Cres. TW14: Felt 7H 111
Stonecroft Rd. DA8: Erith 7J 109
Stonecroft Way CR0: C'don 7J 155
Stonecrop Cl. NW9 3K 43
Stonecutter St. EC4 7A 8 (6B 84)
Stonefield N4 2K 65
Stonefield Cl. DA7: Bex 3G 127
HA4: Ruis 5C 58
Stonefield Mans. *N1* *1A 84*
(off Cloudesley St.)
Stonefield St. N1 1A 84
Stonefield Way HA4: Ruis 4C 58
SE7 7B 106
STONEGROVE 4A 28
Stonegrove HA8: Edg 4K 27
Stone Gro. Ct. HA8: Edg 5A 28
Stonegrove Gdns. HA8: Edg 5K 27
Stone Hall *W8* *3K 99*
(off Stone Hall Gdns.)
Stonehall Av. IG1: Ilf 6C 52
Stone Hall Gdns. W8 3K 99
Stone Hall Pl. W8 3K 99
Stone Hall Rd. N21 7E 22
Stoneham Rd. N11 5B 32
Stonehill Bus. Pk. N18 6F 35
Stonehill Cl. SW14 5K 115
Stonehill Ct. E4 7J 25
STONEHILL GREEN 7J 145
Stonehill Rd. SW14 5J 115
W4 5G 97
Stonehills Ct. SE21 3E 138
Stonehill Woods Pk. DA14: Sidc 6H 145
Stonehorse Rd. EN3: Pond E 5D 24
Stonehouse *NW1* *1G 83*
(off Plender St.)
Stone Ho. Ct. EC3 6H 9
Stonehouse Ho. *W2* *5J 81*
(off Westbourne Pk. Rd.)
Stone Lake Ind. Pk. SE7 4A 106
Stone Lake Retail Pk. SE7 4A 106
STONELEIGH 5C 164
Stoneleigh Av. EN1: Enf 1C 24
KT4: Wor Pk 4C 164
Stoneleigh B'way. KT17: Ewe 5C 164
Stoneleigh Ct. IG5: Ilf 3C 52
Stoneleigh Cres. KT19: Ewe 5B 164
Stoneleigh M. E3 2A 86
Stoneleigh Pk. Av. CR0: C'don 6K 157
Stoneleigh Pk. Rd. KT4: Wor Pk 6B 164
KT19: Ewe 6B 164
Stoneleigh Pl. W11 7F 81
Stoneleigh Rd. BR1: Brom 3F 161
IG5: Ilf 3C 52
N17 3F 49
SM5: Cars 7C 154
Stoneleigh St. W11 7F 81
Stoneleigh Ter. N19 2F 65
Stonell's Rd. SW11 6D 118
Stonemason Ct. *SE1* *7C 14*
(off Borough Rd.)
Stonemason Ho. *SE14* *1K 121*
(off Fishers Ct.)
Stonemasons Cl. N15 4D 48
Stonemasons Yd. SW18 7B 118
Stonenest St. N4 1K 65
Stone Pk. Av. BR3: Beck 4C 158
Stone Pl. KT4: Wor Pk 2C 164
Stone Rd. BR2: Brom 5H 159
Stones End St. SE1 7C 14 (2C 102)
Stonewall E6 5E 88
Stonewell Rd. TW19: Stanw 1A 128
Stonewold Ct. W5 6D 78
Stoney All. SE18 2E 124
Stoneyard La. E14 7D 86
Stoneycroft Cl. SE12 7H 123
Stoneycroft Rd. IG8: Wfd G 6H 37
Stoneydeep TW11: Tedd 4A 132
Stoneydown E17 4A 50
Stoneydown Av. E17 4A 50
Stoneydown Ho. *E17* *4A 50*
(off Stoneydown)
Stoneyfields Gdns. HA8: Edg 4E 28
Stoneyfields La. HA8: Edg 5D 28
Stoney La. E1 7H 9 (6F 85)
SE19 6F 139
Stoney St. SE1 4E 14 (1D 102)
Stonhouse St. SW4 4H 119
Stonor Rd. W14 4H 99
Stonycroft Cl. EN3: Enf H 2F 25
Stopes St. SE15 7F 103
Stopford Rd. E13 1J 87
SE17 5B 102
Stopher Ho. *SE1* *7B 14*
(off Webber St.)
Storehouse M. E14 7C 86
Storer Dr. DA16: Well 3B 126
Store Rd. E16 2E 106
Storers Quay E14 4F 105
Store St. E15 5F 69
WC1 6C 6 (5H 83)
Storey Cl. UB10: Ick 3E 56
Storey Ct. NW8 2A 4
Storey Ho. *E14* *7D 86*
(off Cottage St.)
Storey Rd. E17 4B 50
N6 6D 46
Storey's Ga. SW1 7D 12 (2H 101)
Storey St. E16 1E 106
Stories M. SE5 2E 120
Stories Rd. SE5 3E 120
Stork Rd. E7 6H 69
Storksmead Rd. HA8: Edg 7F 29
Stork's Rd. SE16 3G 103
Stormont Lawn Tennis & Squash Club 5D 46
Stormont Rd. N6 7D 46
SW11 3E 118
Stormont Way KT9: Chess 5C 162
Stormount Dr. UB3: Harl 2E 92
Storrington *WC1* *2F 7*
(off Regent Sq.)
Storrington Rd. CR0: C'don 1F 169
Storth Oaks Mead BR7: Chst 5D 142
Story St. N1 7K 65
Stothard Ho. *E1* *4J 85*
(off Amiel St.)
Stothard Pl. E1 5H 9 (5E 84)
Stothard St. E1 4J 85
Stott Cl. SW18 6B 118
Stoughton Av. SM3: Cheam 5F 165
Stoughton Cl. SE11 4H 19 (4K 101)
SW15 1C 134
Stour Av. UB2: S'hall 3E 94
Stourcliffe Cl. W1 1E 10 (6D 82)
Stourcliffe St. W1 1E 10 (6D 82)
Stour Cl. BR2: Kes 4A 172
Stourhead Cl. SW19 7F 117
Stourhead Gdns. SW20 3C 152
Stourhead Ho. *SW1* *5C 18*
(off Tachbrook St.)
Stour Rd. E3 7C 68
RM10: Dag 2G 73
Stourton Av. TW13: Hanw 4D 130
Stowage SE8 6C 104
Stow Cres. E17 7F 35
Stowe Cres. HA4: Ruis 6D 38
Stowe Gdns. N9 1A 34
Stowe Ho. NW11 6A 46
Stowell Ho. *N8* *4J 47*
(off Pembroke Rd.)
Stowe Pl. N15 3E 48
Stowe Rd. W12 2D 98
Stowting Rd. BR6: Orp 4J 173
Stox Mead HA3: Hrw W 1H 41
Stracey Rd. E7 4J 69
NW10 1K 79
Strachan Pl. SW19 6E 134
Stradbroke Dr. IG7: Chig 6K 37
Stradbroke Gro. IG5: Ilf 3C 52
IG9: Buck H 1G 37
Stradbroke Pk. IG7: Chig 6K 37
Stradbroke Rd. N5 4C 66
Stradbrook Cl. HA2: Harr 3D 58
Stradella Rd. SE24 6C 120
Strafford Av. IG5: Ilf 2E 52
Strafford Ho. *SE8* *5B 104*
(off Grove St.)
Strafford Rd. EN5: Barn 3B 20
TW1: Twick 7A 114
TW3: Houn 3D 112
W3 2J 97
Strafford St. E14 2C 104
Strahan Rd. E3 3A 86
Straight, The UB1: S'hall 2B 94
Straightsmouth SE10 7E 104
Strait Rd. E6 7C 88
Strakers Rd. SE15 4H 121
Strale Ho. *N1* *1E 84*
(off Whitmore Est.)
Strand WC2 3F 13 (7J 83)
Strand Ct. SE18 5K 107
Strand Dr. TW9: Kew 7H 97
Strandfield Cl. SE18 5J 107
Strand Ho. *BR2: Brom* *6B 160*
(off Wells Vw. Dr.)
SE28 1H 107
Strand La. WC2 2H 13 (7K 83)
STRAND ON THE GREEN 6G 97
Strand on the Grn. W4 6G 97
Strand Pl. N18 4K 33
Strand School App. W4 6G 97
Strang Ho. N1 1C 84
Strangways Ter. W14 3H 99
Stranraer Way N1 7J 65
TW6: H'row A 6A 110
Strasburg Rd. SW11 1E 118
Strata *SE1* *4C 102*
(off Walworth Rd.)
Strata Ct. KT12: Walt T 7H 147
Stratfield Pk. Cl. N21 7G 23
STRATFORD 7F 69
Stratford Av. UB10: Hil 2B 74
Stratford Cen., The E15 7F 69
Stratford Circus (Performing Arts Cen.) 6F 69
Stratford Cl. IG11: Bark 7A 72
RM10: Dag 7J 73
Stratford Ct. KT3: N Mald 4K 151
Stratford Eye E15 6F 69
Stratford Gro. SW15 4F 117
Stratford Ho. Av. BR1: Brom 3C 160
STRATFORD NEW TOWN 6F 69
Stratford Office Village, The *E15* *7G 69*
(off Romford Rd.)
Stratford One E20 6D 68
Stratford Picture House London 6F 69
Stratford Pl. *E20* *6E 68*
(within Westfield Stratford City Shop. Cen.)
W1 1J 11 (6F 83)
Stratford Rd. CR7: Thor H 4A 156
E13 1H 87
(not continuous)
NW4 4F 45
TW6: H'row A 6D 110
UB2: S'hall 4C 94
UB4: Yead 4K 75
W8 3J 99
Stratford Studios W8 3J 99
Stratford Theatre Royal 7F 69
Stratford Vs. NW1 7G 65
Stratford Workshops *E15* *1F 87*
(off Burford Rd.)
Stratham Ct. *N19* *3J 65*
(off Alexander Rd.)
Strathan Cl. SW18 6G 117
Strathaven Rd. SE12 6K 123
Strathblaine Rd. SW11 5B 118
Strathbrook Rd. SW16 7K 137
Strathcona Rd. HA9: Wemb 2D 60
Strathdale SW16 5K 137
Strathdon Dr. SW17 3B 136
Strathearn Av. TW2: Whitt 1F 131
UB3: Harl 7H 93
Strathearn Ho. *W2* *2C 10*
(off Strathern Pl.)
Strathearn Pl. W2 1C 10 (6C 82)
Strathearn Rd. SM1: Sutt 5J 165
SW19 5J 135
Stratheden Pde. SE3 7J 105
Stratheden Rd. SE3 1J 123
Strathfield Gdns. IG11: Bark 6H 71
Strathleven Rd. SW2 5J 119
Strathmore Ct. *NW8* *1C 4*
(off Park Rd.)
Strathmore Gdns. HA8: Edg 2H 43
N3 1K 45
W8 1J 99
Strathmore Rd. CR0: C'don 7D 156
SW19 3J 135
TW11: Tedd 4J 131
Strathnairn St. SE1 4G 103
(not continuous)
Strathray Gdns. NW3 6C 64
Strath Ter. SW11 4C 118
Strathville Rd. SW18 2J 135
(not continuous)
Strathyre Av. SW16 3A 156
Stratosphere Twr. *E15* *7F 69*
(off Gt. Eastern Rd.)
Stratton Cl. DA7: Bex 3E 126
HA8: Edg 6A 28
SW19 2J 153
TW3: Houn 1E 112
Stratton Ct. *HA5: Hat E* *1D 40*
(off Devonshire Rd.)
N1 *7E 66*
(off Hertford Rd.)
Strattondale St. E14 3E 104
Stratton Dr. IG11: Bark 5J 71
Stratton Gdns. UB1: S'hall 6D 76
Stratton Rd. DA7: Bex 3E 126
SW19 2J 153
TW16: Sun 2H 147
Stratton St. W1 4K 11 (1F 101)
Strauss Rd. W4 2K 97
Strawberry Flds. BR6: Farnb 5F 173
STRAWBERRY HILL 3K 131
Strawberry Hill 3K 131
Strawberry Hill KT9: Chess 6D 162
TW1: Twick 3K 131
Strawberry Hill Cl. TW1: Twick 3K 131
Strawberry Hill Golf Course 3J 131
Strawberry Hill Rd. TW1: Twick 3K 131
Strawberry La. SM5: Cars 3E 166
Strawberry Ter. N10 1D 46
Strawberry Va. N2 1B 46
TW1: Twick 3A 132
(not continuous)
Streakes Fld. Rd. NW2 2C 62
Streamdale SE2 6B 108
Stream La. HA8: Edg 5C 28
Streamline Ct. *SE22* *1G 139*
(off Streamline M.)
Streamline M. SE22 1G 139
Streamside Cl. BR2: Brom 4J 159
N9 1A 34
Streamway DA17: Belv 6G 109
Streatfeild Av. E6 1D 88
Streatfield Rd. HA3: Kenton 3C 42
STREATHAM 3J 137
Streatham Cl. SW16 2J 137
STREATHAM COMMON 6H 137
Streatham Comn. Nth. SW16 5J 137
Streatham Comn. Sth. SW16 6J 137
Streatham Ct. SW16 3J 137
Streatham High Rd. SW16 4J 137
STREATHAM HILL 2J 137
Streatham Hill SW2 2J 137

Streatham Hub—Summerhouse Dr.

Streatham Hub 5H 137
STREATHAM PARK 5G 137
Streatham Pl. SW2 . . . . . 7J **119**
Streatham Rd. CR4: Mitc 1E **154**
SW16 . . . . . 1E **154**
Streatham St. WC1 . . . . . 7E **6** (6J **83**)
STREATHAM VALE 7G 137
Streatham Va. SW16 . . . . . 1G **155**
Streathbourne Rd. SW17 . . . . . 2E **136**
Streatley Pl. NW3 . . . . . 4A **64**
Streatley Rd. NW6 . . . . . 7H **63**
Street, The *E20* *6E* ***68***
(within Westfield Stratford City Shop. Cen.)
Streeters La. SM6: Bedd 3H **167**
Streetfield M. SE3 . . . . . 3J **123**
Streimer Rd. E15 . . . . . 2E **86**
Strelley Way W3 . . . . . 7A **80**
Stretton Mans. SE8 . . . . . 5C **104**
Stretton Rd. CR0: C'don 7E **156**
TW10: Ham 2C **132**
Strickland Ct. SE15 . . . . . 3G **121**
Strickland Ho. *E2* *2K* ***9***
(off Chambord St.)
Strickland Row SW18 . . . . . 7B **118**
Strickland St. SE8 . . . . . 2C **122**
Strickland Way BR6: Orp 4K **173**
Stride Rd. E13 . . . . . 2H **87**
Strimon Cl. N9 . . . . . 2D **34**
Stringer Ho. *N1* *1E* ***84***
(off Whitmore Est.)
Strode Cl. N10 . . . . . 7K **31**
Strode Rd. E7 . . . . . 4J **69**
N17 . . . . . 2E **48**
NW10 . . . . . 6C **62**
SW6 . . . . . 7G **99**
Strome Ho. *NW6* *2K* ***81***
(off Carlton Vale)
Strone Rd. E7 . . . . . 6A **70**
E12 . . . . . 6A **70**
Strone Way UB4: Yead 4C **76**
Strongbow Cres. SE9 . . . . . 5D **124**
Strongbow Rd. SE9 . . . . . 5D **124**
Strongbridge Cl. HA2: Harr 1E **58**
Stronsa Rd. W12 . . . . . 2B **98**
Strood Av. RM7: Rush G 1K **73**
Strood Ho. *SE1* *7F* ***15***
(off Staple St.)
Stroud Cres. SW15 . . . . . 3C **134**
Stroudes Cl. KT4: Wor Pk 7A **152**
Stroud Fld. UB5: N'olt 6C **58**
Stroud Ga. HA2: Harr 4F **59**
STROUD GREEN 7K 47
Stroud Grn. Gdns. CR0: C'don 7J **157**
Stroud Grn. Rd. N4 . . . . . 1K **65**
Stroud Grn. Way CR0: C'don 7H **157**
Stroudley Ho. SW8 . . . . . 1G **119**
Stroudley Wlk. E3 . . . . . 3D **86**
Stroud Rd. SE25 . . . . . 6G **157**
SW19 . . . . . 3J **135**
Stroud's Cl. RM6: Chad H 5B **54**
Stroud Way TW15: Ashf 6D **128**
Strouts Pl. E2 . . . . . 1J **9** (3F **85**)
Strudwick Ct. *SW4* *1J* ***119***
(off Binfield Rd.)
Strutton Ct. *SW1* *2C* ***18***
(off Gt. Peter St.)
Strutton Ground SW1 . . . . . 1C **18** (3H **101**)
Strype St. E1 . . . . . 6J **9** (5F **85**)
Stuart Av. BR2: Hayes 1J **171**
HA2: Harr 3D **58**
KT12: Walt T 7K **147**
NW9 . . . . . 7C **44**
W5 . . . . . 2F **97**
Stuart Cl. UB10: Hil 6C **56**
Stuart Ct. *CR0: C'don* *3B* ***168***
(off St John's Rd.)
Stuart Cres. CR0: C'don 3B **170**
N22 . . . . . 1K **47**
UB3: Hayes 6E **74**
Stuart Evans Cl. DA16: Well 3C **126**
Stuart Gro. TW11: Tedd 5J **131**
Stuart Ho. *E9* *6K* ***67***
(off Queen Anne Rd.)
E16 . . . . . *1K* ***105***
(off Beaulieu Av.)
W14 . . . . . *4G* ***99***
(off Windsor Way)
Stuart Mantle Way
DA8: Erith 7K **109**
(not continuous)
Stuart Mill Ho. *N1* *1G* ***7***
(off Killick St.)
Stuart Pl. CR4: Mitc 1D **154**
Stuart Rd. CR7: Thor H 4C **156**
DA16: Well 1B **126**
EN4: E Barn 7H **21**
HA3: W'stone 3K **41**
IG11: Bark 7K **71**
NW6 . . . . . 3J **81**
SE15 . . . . . 4J **121**
SW19 . . . . . 3J **135**
TW10: Ham 2B **132**
W3 . . . . . 1J **97**
Stuart Twr. *W9* *3A* ***82***
(off Maida Vale)
Stubbs Cl. NW9 . . . . . 5J **43**
Stubbs Ct. *W4* *5H* ***97***
(off Chaseley Dr.)
Stubbs Dr. SE16 . . . . . 5H **103**
Stubbs Ho. *E2* *3K* ***85***
(off Bonner St.)
SW1 . . . . . *4D* ***18***
(off Erasmus St.)
Stubbs M. *RM8: Dag* *4B* ***72***
(off Marlborough Rd.)
Stubbs Point E13 . . . . . 4J **87**
Stubbs Way SW19 . . . . . 1B **154**
Stucley Pl. NW1 . . . . . 7F **65**
Stucley Rd. TW5: Hest 7G **95**
Studdridge St. SW6 . . . . . 2J **117**
Studd St. N1 . . . . . 1B **84**
Studholme Ct. NW3 . . . . . 4J **63**
Studholme St. SE15 . . . . . 7H **103**
Studio Ct. N15 . . . . . 4E **48**
Studio La. W5 . . . . . 1D **96**
Studio M. NW4 . . . . . 4E **44**
Studio Pl. SW1 . . . . . 7F **11**
Studio Plaza KT12: Walt T 7J **147**
Studios, The *SW4* *4G* ***119***
(off Crescent La.)
W8 . . . . . *1J* ***99***
(off Edge St.)
Studios Rd. TW17: Shep 3B **146**
Studio Theatre
Carshalton 4E **166**
Studland *SE17* *5D* ***102***
(off Portland St.)
Studland Cl. DA15: Sidc 3K **143**
Studland Ho. *E14* *6A* ***86***
(off Aston St.)
Studland Rd. KT2: King T 6E **132**
SE26 . . . . . 5K **139**
W7 . . . . . 6H **77**
Studland St. W6 . . . . . 4D **98**
Studley Av. E4 . . . . . 7A **36**
Studley Cl. E5 . . . . . 5A **68**
Studley Ct. DA14: Sidc 5B **144**
E14 . . . . . *7F* ***87***
(off Jamestown Way)
Studley Dr. IG4: Ilf 6B **52**
Studley Est. SW4 . . . . . 1J **119**
Studley Grange Rd. W7 . . . . . 2J **95**
Studley Rd. E7 . . . . . 6K **69**
RM9: Dag 7D **72**
SW4 . . . . . 1J **119**
Stukeley Rd. E7 . . . . . 7K **69**
Stukeley St. WC2 . . . . . 7F **7** (6J **83**)
Stumps Hill La. BR3: Beck 6C **140**
Stunell Ho. *SE14* *6K* ***103***
(off John Williams Cl.)
Sturdee Ho. *E2* *2G* ***85***
(off Horatio St.)
Sturdy Ho. *E3* *2A* ***86***
(off Gernon Rd.)
Sturdy Rd. SE15 . . . . . 2H **121**
Sturge Av. E17 . . . . . 2D **50**
Sturgeon Rd. SE17 . . . . . 5C **102**
Sturges Fld. BR7: Chst 6H **143**
Sturgess Av. NW4 . . . . . 7D **44**
Sturge St. SE1 . . . . . 6C **14** (2C **102**)
Sturmer Way N7 . . . . . 5K **65**
Sturminster *NW1* *7H* ***65***
(off Agar Gro.)
Sturminster Cl. UB4: Yead 6A **76**
Sturminster Ho. *SW8* *7K* ***101***
(off Dorset Rd.)
Sturrock Cl. N15 . . . . . 4D **48**
Sturry St. E14 . . . . . 6D **86**
Sturts Apartments *N1* *1D* ***84***
(off Branch Pl.)
Sturt St. N1 . . . . . 1D **8** (2C **84**)
Stutfield St. E1 . . . . . 6G **85**
Stuttle Ho. *E1* *4K* ***9***
(off Buxton St.)
Styles Gdns. SW9 . . . . . 3B **120**
Styles Ho. SE1 . . . . . 6A **14**
Styles Way BR3: Beck 4E **158**
Stylus Ho. E1 . . . . . 6J **85**
Success Ho. *SE1* *5F* ***103***
(off Cooper's Rd.)
Sudbourne Rd. SW2 . . . . . 5J **119**
Sudbrooke Rd. SW12 . . . . . 6D **118**
Sudbrook Gdns. TW10: Ham 3D **132**
Sudbrook La. TW10: Ham 1E **132**
SUDBURY 5B 60
Sudbury E6 . . . . . 5E **88**
Sudbury Av. HA0: Wemb 3C **60**
Sudbury Cl. RM6: Chad H 5B **54**
Sudbury Ct. *SW8* *1H* ***119***
(off Allen Edwards Dr.)
Sudbury Ct. Dr. HA1: Harr 3K **59**
Sudbury Ct. Rd. HA1: Harr 3K **59**
Sudbury Cres. BR1: Brom 6J **141**
HA0: Wemb 5B **60**
Sudbury Cft. HA0: Wemb 4K **59**
Sudbury Gdns. CR0: C'don 4E **168**
Sudbury Golf Course 7C **60**
Sudbury Hgts. Av. UB6: G'frd 5K **59**
Sudbury Hill HA1: Harr 2J **59**
Sudbury Hill Cl. HA0: Wemb 4K **59**
Sudbury Ho. SW18 . . . . . 5K **117**
Sudbury Rd. IG11: Bark 5K **71**
Sudeley Ct. *E17* *1B* ***50***
(off Broughton Pl.)
Sudeley St. N1 . . . . . 2B **84**
Sudlow Rd. SW18 . . . . . 5J **117**
Sudrey St. SE1 . . . . . 7C **14** (2C **102**)
Suez Av. UB6: G'frd 2K **77**
Suez Rd. EN3: Brim 4F **25**
SUFFIELD HATCH 4K 35
Suffield Ho. *SE17* *5B* ***102***
(off Berryfield Rd.)
Suffield Rd. E4 . . . . . 3J **35**
N15 . . . . . 5F **49**
SE20 . . . . . 2J **157**
Suffolk Ct. E10 . . . . . 7C **50**
IG3: Ilf 6J **53**
RM6: Chad H 6C **54**
Suffolk Ho. *CR0: C'don* *2D* ***168***
(off George St.)
SE20 . . . . . *1K* ***157***
(off Croydon Rd.)
Suffolk La. EC4 . . . . . 2E **14** (7D **84**)
Suffolk Pk. Rd. E17 . . . . . 4A **50**
Suffolk Pl. SE2 . . . . . 5C **108**
SW1 . . . . . 4D **12** (1H **101**)
Suffolk Rd. DA14: Sidc 6C **144**
E13 . . . . . 3J **87**
EN3: Pond E 5C **24**
HA2: Harr 6D **40**
IG3: Ilf 6J **53**
IG11: Bark 7H **71**
KT4: Wor Pk 2B **164**
Suffolk Rd. N15 . . . . . 5D **48**
NW10 . . . . . 7A **62**
RM10: Dag 5J **73**
SE25 . . . . . 4F **157**
SW13 . . . . . 7B **98**
Suffolk St. E7 . . . . . 4J **69**
SW1 . . . . . 3D **12** (7H **83**)
Sugar Bakers Ct. EC3 . . . . . 1H **15**
Sugar Ho. *E1* *1K* ***15***
(off Leman St.)
Sugar Ho. La. E15 . . . . . 2E **86**
Sugar Loaf Wlk. E2 . . . . . 3J **85**
Sugar Quay EC3 . . . . . 3H **15**
Sugar Quay Wlk. EC3 . . . . . 3H **15** (7E **84**)
Sugden Rd. KT7: T Ditt 1B **162**
SW11 . . . . . 3E **118**
Sugden Way IG11: Bark 2K **89**
Sulby Ho. *SE4* *4A* ***122***
(off Turnham Rd.)
Sulgrave Gdns. W6 . . . . . 2E **98**
Sulgrave Rd. W6 . . . . . 3E **98**
Sulina Rd. SW2 . . . . . 7J **119**
Sulivan Ct. SW6 . . . . . 2J **117**
Sulivan Ent. Cen. SW6 . . . . . 3K **117**
Sulivan Rd. SW6 . . . . . 3J **117**
Sulkin Ho. *E2* *3K* ***85***
(off Knottisford St.)
Sullivan Av. E16 . . . . . 5B **88**
Sullivan Cl. KT8: W Mole 3F **149**
SW11 . . . . . 3C **118**
UB4: Yead 5A **76**
Sullivan Ct. *E3* *4B* ***86***
(off Eric St.)
N16 . . . . . 7F **49**
SW5 . . . . . *4J* ***99***
(off Earls Ct. Rd.)
Sullivan Cres. UB9: Hare 2A **38**
Sullivan Ho. *SE11* *4H* ***19***
(off Vauxhall St.)
SW1 . . . . . *7K* ***17***
(off Churchill Gdns.)
Sullivan Rd. SE11 . . . . . 3K **19** (4A **102**)
Sullivan Row BR2: Brom 6B **160**
Sullivans Reach KT12: Walt T 7H **147**
Sultan Ho. *SE1* *5G* ***103***
(off St James's Rd.)
Sultan Rd. E11 . . . . . 4K **51**
Sultan St. BR3: Beck 2K **157**
SE5 . . . . . 7C **102**
Sultan Ter. N22 . . . . . 2A **48**
Sumatra Rd. NW6 . . . . . 5J **63**
Sumburgh Rd. SW12 . . . . . 6E **118**
Sumeria Ct. *SE16* *4J* ***103***
(off Rotherhithe New Rd.)
Summer Av. KT8: E Mos 5J **149**
Summerbee Ho. *SW18* *4A* ***118***
(off Eltringham St.)
Summercourt Rd. E1 . . . . . 6J **85**
Summer Crossing KT7: T Ditt 5J **149**
Summer Dr. UB7: W Dray 2B **92**
Summerene Cl. SW16 . . . . . 7G **137**
Summerfield *BR1: Brom* *1K* ***159***
(off Freelands Rd.)
Summerfield Av. NW6 . . . . . 2G **81**
Summerfield La. KT6: Surb 2D **162**
Summerfield Rd. W5 . . . . . 4B **78**
Summerfields Av. N12 . . . . . 6H **31**
Summerfield St. SE12 . . . . . 7H **123**
Summer Gdns. KT8: E Mos 5J **149**
UB10: Ick 2E **56**
Summer Gro. BR4: W W'ck 2G **171**
Summer Hill BR7: Chst 2E **160**
Summerhill Cl. BR6: Orp 3J **173**
Summerhill Gro. EN1: Enf 6K **23**
Summerhill Rd. N15 . . . . . 4D **48**
Summerhill Vs. *BR7: Chst* *1E* ***160***
(off Susan Wood)
Summerhill Way CR4: Mitc 1E **154**
Summerhouse Av. TW5: Hest 1C **112**
Summerhouse Dr. DA2: Wilm 4K **145**
DA5: Bexl, Dart 4K **145**

Summerhouse La. UB7: Harm 2E **174**
Summerhouse Rd. N16 . . . . .2E **66**
Summerland Gdns. N10 . . . . .3F **47**
Summerland Grange N10 . . . . .3F **47**
Summerlands Av. W3 . . . . .7J **79**
Summerlands Lodge
BR6: Farnb 4E **172**
Summerlee Av. N2 . . . . .4D **46**
Summerlee Gdns. N2 . . . . .4D **46**
Summerley St. SW18 . . . . .2K **135**
Summer Rd. KT7: T Ditt 5J **149**
KT8: E Mos 5H **149**
(not continuous)
Summersby Rd. N6 . . . . .6F **47**
Summers Cl. HA9: Wemb 1H **61**
SM2: Sutt 7J **165**
Summerskill Cl. SE15 . . . . .3H **121**
Summerskille Cl. N9 . . . . .3C **34**
Summers La. N12 . . . . .7G **31**
Summers Row N12 . . . . .6H **31**
Summers St. EC1 . . . . .4J **7** (4A **84**)
SUMMERSTOWN 3A 136
Summerstown SW17 . . . . .3A **136**
Summerton Way SE28 . . . . .6D **90**
Summer Trees TW16: Sun 1K **147**
Summerville Gdns. SM1: Sutt 6H **165**
Summerwood Rd. TW7: Isle 5K **113**
Summit Av. NW9 . . . . .5K **43**
Summit Bus. Pk. TW16: Sun 7J **129**
Summit Cl. HA8: Edg 7B **28**
N14 . . . . .2B **32**
NW9 . . . . .4K **43**
Summit Ct. NW2 . . . . .5G **63**
Summit Dr. IG8: Wfd G 2B **52**
Summit Est. N16 . . . . .7G **49**
Summit Ho. BR4: W W'ck 2E **170**
Summit Rd. E17 . . . . .4D **50**
UB5: N'olt 7E **58**
Summit Way N14 . . . . .2A **32**
SE19 .7E **138**
Sumner Av. SE15 . . . . .1F **121**
Sumner Bldgs. SE1 . . . . .4C **14**
Sumner Cl. BR6: Farnb 4G **173**
Sumner Ct. SW8 . . . . .7J **101**
Sumner Est. SE15 . . . . .7F **103**
Sumner Gdns. CR0: C'don 1A **168**
Sumner Ho. *E3* *5D* ***86***
(off Watts Gro.)
Sumner Pl. SW7 . . . . .4B **16** (4B **100**)
Sumner Pl. M. SW7 . . . . . . .4B **16** (4B **100**)
Sumner Rd. CR0: C'don 1A **168**
HA1: Harr 7G **41**
SE15 .6F **103**
Sumner Rd. Sth. CR0: C'don 1A **168**
Sumner St. SE1 . . . . .4B **14** (1B **102**)
Sumpter Cl. NW3 . . . . .6A **64**
Sun All. TW9: Rich 4E **114**
Sunbeam Cres. W10 . . . . .4E **80**
Sunbeam Rd. NW10 . . . . .4J **79**
Sunbeam Way NW10 . . . . .4K **79**
Sunbird Wlk. *HA2: Harr* *2F* ***59***
(off Sandpiper Dr.)
SUNBURY .3A 148
Sunbury Av. NW7 . . . . .5E **28**
SW14 .4K **115**
Sunbury Av. Pas. SW14 . . . . .4A **116**
Sunbury Bus. Cen. TW16: Sun 1H **147**
Sunbury Cl. KT12: Walt T 6J **147**
SUNBURY COMMON 7H 129
Sunbury Ct. EN5: Barn 4B **20**
Sunbury Ct. Island
TW16: Sun 3B **148**
Sunbury Ct. M. TW16: Sun 2B **148**
Sunbury Ct. Rd. TW16: Sun 2A **148**
Sunbury Cres. TW13: Felt 4H **129**
SUNBURY CROSS 7J **129**
Sunbury Cross Cen.
TW16: Sun 7H **129**
Sunbury Embroidery Gallery, The . . .3K **147**
Sunbury Gdns. NW7 . . . . .5E **28**
Sunbury Golf Course 4F **147**
Sunbury Ho. *E2* *2J* ***9***
(off Swanfield St.)
SE14 . . . .*6K* ***103***
(off Myers La.)
TW16: Sun *1G* ***147***
(off Brooklands Cl.)
Sunbury La. KT12: Walt T 6J **147**
SW11 .1B **118**
(not continuous)
Sunbury Leisure Cen. 1H **147**
Sunburylock Ait KT12: Walt T 4K **147**
Sunbury Pk. Walled Garden 3K **147**
Sunbury Rd. SM3: Cheam 3F **165**
TW13: Felt 3H **129**
Sunbury St. SE18 . . . . .3D **106**
Sunbury Way TW13: Hanw 5A **130**
Sunbury Workshops *E2* *2J* ***9***
(off Swanfield St.)
Sun Ct. *E3* *4E* ***86***
(off Navigation Rd.)
EC3 . . . . .1F **15**
Suncroft Pl. SE26 . . . . .3J **139**
Sundeala Cl. *TW16: Sun* *7J* ***129***
(off Hanworth Rd.)
Sunderland Ct. SE22 . . . . .7G **121**
TW19: Stanw *6A* ***110***
(off Whitley Cl.)
Sunderland Ho. *W2* *5J* ***81***
(off Westbourne Pk. Rd.)
Sunderland Mt. SE23 . . . . .2K **139**
Sunderland Point E16 . . . . .1G **107**
Sunderland Rd. SE23 . . . . .1K **139**
W5 . . . . .3D **96**
Sunderland Ter. W2 . . . . .6K **81**
Sunderland Way E12 . . . . .2B **70**
Sundew Av. W12 . . . . .7C **80**
Sundew Cl. W12 . . . . .7C **80**
Sundew Ct. *HA0: Wemb* *2E* ***78***
(off Elmore Cl.)
Sundial Av. SE25 . . . . .3F **157**
Sundial Ct. *EC1* *5E* ***8***
(off Chiswell St.)
Sundorne Rd. SE7 . . . . .5A **106**
Sundown Rd. TW15: Ashf 5E **128**
Sundra Wlk. E1 . . . . .4K **85**
SUNDRIDGE 6K 141
Sundridge Av. BR1: Brom 1B **160**
BR7: Chst 1B **160**
DA16: Well 2H **125**
Sundridge Ho. *E9* *7K* ***67***
(off Church Cres.)
Sundridge Pde. BR1: Brom 7K **141**
SUNDRIDGE PARK 7K 141
Sundridge Pk. Golf Course 6K **141**
Sundridge Pl. CR0: C'don 1G **169**
Sundridge Rd. CR0: C'don 7F **157**
Sunfields Pl. SE3 . . . . .7K **105**
Sunflower Ct. NW2 . . . . .2H **63**
RM13: Rain 2J **91**
Sungate Cotts. RM5: Col R 1F **55**
Sun Ga. Ho. KT3: N Mald 4B **152**
Sunguard Ct. SE1 . . . . .4A **14** (1B **102**)
SUN-IN-THE-SANDS 7K **105**
Sunken Rd. CR0: C'don 5J **169**
Sunkist Way SM6: Wall 7J **167**
Sunland Av. DA6: Bex 4E **126**
Sun La. SE3 .7K **105**
Sunleigh Rd. HA0: Wemb 1E **78**
Sunley Gdns. UB6: G'frd 1A **78**
Sun Life Trad. Est. TW14: Felt 3J **111**
Sunlight Cl. SW19 . . . . .6A **136**
Sunlight M. SW6 . . . . .2K **117**
Sunlight Sq. E2 . . . . .3H **85**
Sunmead Rd. TW16: Sun 3J **147**
Sunna Gdns. TW16: Sun 2K **147**
Sunniholme Ct.
CR2: S Croy *5C* ***168***
(off Warham Rd.)
Sunningdale N14 . . . . .5C **32**
W13 . . . .*5B* ***78***
(off Hardwick Grn.)
Sunningdale Av. HA4: Ruis 1A **58**
IG11: Bark 1H **89**
TW13: Hanw 2C **130**
W3 . . . . .7A **80**
Sunningdale Cl. E6 . . . . .3D **88**
HA7: Stan 6F **27**
KT6: Surb 2E **162**
SE16 .5H **103**
SE28 . . . . .6E **90**
Sunningdale Ct. *TW7: Isle* *6H* ***113***
(off Whitton Dene)
UB1: S'hall *6G* ***77***
(off Fleming Rd.)
Sunningdale Gdns. NW9 . . . . .5J **43**
W8 . . . .*3J* ***99***
(off Stratford Rd.)
Sunningdale Lodge *HA8: Edg* *5A* ***28***
(off Stonegrove)
Sunningdale Rd.
BR1: Brom 4C **160**
SM1: Sutt 3H **165**
Sunningfields Cres. NW4 . . . . .2D **44**
Sunningfields Rd. NW4 . . . . .2D **44**
Sunninghill Ct. W3 . . . . .2J **97**
Sunninghill Rd. SE13 . . . . .2D **122**
Sunny Bank SE25 . . . . .3G **157**
Sunny Cres. NW10 . . . . .7J **61**
Sunnycroft Rd. SE25 . . . . .3G **157**
TW3: Houn 2F **113**
UB1: S'hall 5E **76**
Sunnydale BR6: Farnb 2E **172**
Sunnydale Gdns. NW7 . . . . .6E **28**
Sunnydale Rd. SE12 . . . . .5K **123**
Sunnydene Av. E4 . . . . .5A **36**
HA4: Ruis 1J **57**
Sunnydene Gdns. HA0: Wemb 6C **60**
Sunnydene St. SE26 . . . . .4A **140**
Sunnyfield NW7 . . . . .4G **29**
Sunnyfield Rd. BR7: Chst 3K **161**
Sunny Gdns. Pde. NW4 . . . . .2D **44**
Sunny Gdns. Rd. NW4 . . . . .2D **44**
Sunny Hill NW4 . . . . .3D **44**
Sunnyhill Cl. E5 . . . . .4A **68**
Sunnyhill Rd. SW16 . . . . .4J **137**
Sunnyhurst Cl. SM1: Sutt 3J **165**
Sunnymead Av. CR4: Mitc 3H **155**
Sunnymead Rd. NW9 . . . . .7K **43**
SW15 .5D **116**
Sunnymede Av. KT19: Ewe 7A **164**
Sunnymede Dr. IG2: Ilf 5F **53**
IG6: Ilf 5F **53**
Sunny M. NW1 . . . . .7E **64**
Sunny Nook Gdns. CR2: S Croy 6D **168**
Sunny Pl. NW4 . . . . .4E **44**
Sunny Rd., The EN3: Enf H 1E **24**
Sunnyside KT12: Walt T 5A **148**
NW2 . . . . .3H **63**
SE6 . . . .*7B* ***122***
(off Blythe Hill)
SW19 .6G **135**
Sunnyside Dr. E4 . . . . .7K **25**
Sunnyside Ho's. *NW2* *3H* ***63***
(off Sunnyside)
Sunnyside Pas. SW19 . . . . .6G **135**
Sunnyside Pl. SW19 . . . . .6G **135**
Sunnyside Rd. E10 . . . . .1C **68**
IG1: Ilf 3G **71**
N19 . . . . .7H **47**
TW11: Tedd 4H **131**
W5 . . . . .1D **96**
Sunnyside Rd. E. N9 . . . . .3B **34**
Sunnyside Rd. Nth. N9 . . . . .3A **34**
Sunnyside Rd. Sth. N9 . . . . .3A **34**
Sunnyside Ter. NW9 . . . . .3K **43**
Sunny Vw. NW9 . . . . .5K **43**
Sunny Way N12 . . . . .7H **31**
Sun Pas. *SE16* *3G* ***103***
(off Old Jamaica Rd.)
Sunray Av. BR2: Brom 6C **160**
KT5: Surb 2H **163**
SE24 .4D **120**
Sunrise Cl. E20 . . . . .5E **68**
TW13: Hanw 3D **130**
Sunrise Vw. NW7 . . . . .6G **29**
Sun Rd. W14 .5H **99**
Sunset Av. E4 .1J **35**
IG8: Wfd G 4C **36**
Sunset Ct. IG8: Wfd G 7F **37**
Sunset Gdns. SE25 . . . . .2F **157**
Sunset Lodge *NW10* *7E* ***62***
(off Hanover Rd.)
Sunset Rd. SE5 . . . . .4C **120**
SE28 .1A **108**
SW19 .5D **134**
Sunset Vw. EN5: Barn 2B **20**
Sunshine Way CR4: Mitc 2D **154**
Sun St. EC2 . . . . .5F **9** (5D **84**)
(Finsbury Sq.)
EC2 . . . . .5G **9** (5E **84**)
(Primrose St.)
Sun St. Pas. EC2 . . . . .6G **9** (5E **84**)
Sun Wlk. E1 . . . . .3K **15** (7F **85**)
Sunwell Cl. SE15 . . . . .1H **121**
Sun Wharf *SE8* *7D* ***104***
(off Creekside)
Superior Dr. BR6: Chels 6K **173**
Supreme Court
Westminster 2J **101**
Supreme Point *E16* *5J* ***87***
(off Butchers Rd.)
SURBITON 6D 150
Surbiton Ct. KT6: Surb 6C **150**
Surbiton Cres. KT1: King T 4E **150**
Surbiton Golf Course 4B **162**
Surbiton Hall Cl. KT1: King T 4E **150**
Surbiton Hill Pk. KT5: Surb 5F **151**
Surbiton Hill Rd. KT6: Surb 4E **150**
Surbiton Pde. KT6: Surb 6E **150**
Surbiton Plaza *KT6: Surb* *6D* ***150***
(off St Mary's Rd.)
Surbiton Raceway 3K **163**
Surbiton Rd. KT1: King T 4D **150**
Surlingham Cl. SE28 . . . . .7D **90**
Surma Cl. E1 .4H **85**
Surmans Cl. RM9: Dag 1C **90**
Surrendale Pl. W9 . . . . .4J **81**
Surrey Canal Rd. SE14 . . . . .6J **103**
SE15 .6J **103**
Surrey Canal Trade Pk. SE14 . . . . .6K **103**
Surrey Cl. N3 .3G **45**
Surrey County Cricket Club
. . . . .7H **19** (6K **101**)
Surrey Cres. W4 . . . . .5G **97**
Surrey Docks Farm 2B **104**
Surrey Docks Watersports Cen. 3A **104**
Surrey Gdns. N4 . . . . .6C **48**
Surrey Gro. SE17 . . . . .5E **102**
SM1: Sutt 3B **166**
Surrey Health & Racquets Club, The
. . . . .6K **167**
Surrey Ho. *CR0: C'don* *3C* ***168***
(off Surrey St.)
SE16 . . . .*1K* ***103***
(off Rotherhithe St.)
Surrey La. SW11 . . . . .1C **118**
Surrey La. Est. SW11 . . . . .1C **118**
Surrey M. SE27 . . . . .4E **138**
Surrey Mt. SE23 . . . . .1H **139**
Surrey Quays Rd. SE16 . . . . .3J **103**
Surrey Quays Shop. Cen. SE16 . . . . . .3K **103**
Surrey Rd. BR4: W W'ck 1D **170**
HA1: Harr 5G **41**
IG11: Bark 7J **71**
RM10: Dag 5H **73**
SE15 .5K **121**
Surrey Row SE1 . . . . .6A **14** (2B **102**)
Surrey Sq. SE17 . . . . .5E **102**
Surrey Steps *WC2* *2H* ***13***
(off Surrey St.)
Surrey St. CR0: C'don 2C **168**
E13 . . . . .3K **87**
WC2 . . . . .2H **13** (7K **83**)

Surrey Ter. SE17 5E 102
Surrey Water Rd. SE16 1K 103
Surridge Ct. SW9 2J 119
(off Clapham Rd.)
Surridge Gdns. SE19 6D 138
Surr St. N7 5J 65
Sury Basin KT2: King T 1E 150
Susan Cl. RM7: Mawney 3J 55
Susan Constant Ct. E14 7F 87
(off Newport Av.)
Susan Lawrence Ho. E3 2A 86
(off Zealand Rd.)
E12 4E 70
(off Walton Rd.)
Susannah St. E14 6D 86
Susan Rd. SE3 2K 123
Susan Wood BR7: Chst 1E 160
Sussex Av. TW7: Isle 3J 113
Sussex Cl. IG4: Ilf 5D 52
KT3: N Mald 4A 152
N19 2J 65
TW1: Twick 6B 114
Sussex Ct. SE10 6E 104
(off Roan St.)
W2 1A 10
(off Spring St.)
Sussex Cres. UB5: N'olt 6E 58
Sussex Gdns. KT9: Chess 6D 162
N4 5C 48
N6 5D 46
W2 2A 10 (7B 82)
Sussex Ga. N6 5D 46
Sussex Ho. NW1 2H 83
(off Chalton St.)
Sussex Lodge W2 1B 10
(off Sussex Pl.)
Sussex Mans. SW7 4A 16
WC2 2F 13
(off Maiden La.)
Sussex M. SE6 7C 122
Sussex M. E. W2 1B 10
Sussex M. W. W2 2B 10 (7B 82)
Sussex Pl. KT3: N Mald 4A 152
NW1 3E 4 (4D 82)
W2 1B 10 (6B 82)
W6 5E 98
Sussex Ring N12 5D 30
Sussex Rd. BR4: W W'ck 1D 170
CR2: S Croy 6D 168
CR4: Mitc 5J 155
DA8: Erith 7H 109
DA14: Sidc 5B 144
E6 1E 88
HA1: Harr 5G 41
KT3: N Mald 4A 152
SM5: Cars 6D 166
UB2: S'hall 3B 94
UB10: Ick 4E 56
Sussex Sq. W2 2B 10 (7B 82)
Sussex St. E13 3K 87
SW1 6K 17 (5F 101)
Sussex Ter. SE20 7J 139
(off Graveney Gro.)
Sussex Way EN4: Cockf 5K 21
N7 2J 65
N19 1H 65
(not continuous)
Sutcliffe Cl. NW11 5K 45
Sutcliffe Ho. UB3: Hayes 6J 75
Sutcliffe Pk. Athletics Track 5A 124
Sutcliffe Rd. DA16: Well 2C 126
SE18 6J 107
Sutherland Av.
BR5: St M Cry 6K 161
DA16: Well 4J 125
TW16: Sun 2H 147
UB3: Hayes 4J 93
W9 4J 81
W13 6B 78
Sutherland Cl.
EN5: Barn 4B 20
Sutherland Ct. N16 3D 66
NW9 5H 43
W9 4J 81
(off Marylands Rd.)
Sutherland Dr. SW19 1B 154
Sutherland Gdns. KT4: Wor Pk 1D 164
SW14 3A 116
TW16: Sun 2H 147
Sutherland Gro. SW18 6G 117
TW11: Tedd 5J 131
Sutherland Ho. IG8: Wfd G 7K 37
W8 3K 99
Sutherland Pl. W2 6J 81
Sutherland Rd. CR0: C'don 7A 156
DA17: Belv 3G 109
E3 2B 86
E17 2K 49
EN3: Pond E 6E 24
N9 1C 34
N17 7B 34
UB1: S'hall 6D 76
W4 6A 98
W13 6A 78
Sutherland Rd. Path E17 3K 49
Sutherland Row SW1 5K 17 (5F 101)
Sutherland Sq. SE17 5C 102
Sutherland St. SW1 5J 17 (5F 101)
Sutherland Wlk. SE17 5C 102
Sutlej Rd. SE7 7A 106
Sutterton St. N7 6K 65
SUTTON 5K 165
Sutton Arena Leisure Cen. 7A 154
Sutton Cl. BR3: Beck 1D 158
HA5: Eastc 5J 39
IG10: Lough 1H 37
W4 6J 97
(off Sutton La. Sth.)
Sutton Comn. Rd. SM1: Sutt 7H 153
SM3: Sutt 7H 153
Sutton Ct. KT8: W Mole 5D 148
SE19 7F 139
SM2: Sutt 6A 166
W4 6J 97
W5 1E 96
Sutton Ct. Rd. E13 3A 88
SM1: Sutt 6A 166
UB10: Hil 1D 74
W4 7J 97
Sutton Cres. EN5: Barn 5A 20
Sutton Dene TW3: Houn 1F 113
Sutton Ecology Cen. 4D 166
Sutton Est. EC1 2F 9
SW3 5D 16 (5C 100)
W10 5E 80
Sutton Est., The N1 7B 66
Sutton Gdns. CR0: C'don 5F 157
IG11: Bark 1J 89
Sutton Grn. IG11: Bark 1J 89
(off Sutton Rd.)
Sutton Gro. SM1: Sutt 4B 166
Sutton Hall Rd. TW5: Hest 7E 94
Sutton Hgts. SM2: Sutt 7B 166
Sutton La. EC1 4B 8
(off Gt. Sutton St.)
TW3: Houn 3D 112
Sutton La. Nth. W4 5J 97
Sutton La. Sth. W4 6J 97
Sutton Pde. NW4 4E 44
(off Church Rd.)
Sutton Pk. Rd. SM1: Sutt 6K 165
Sutton Pl. E9 5J 67
Sutton Rd. E13 4H 87
E17 1K 49
IG11: Bark 2J 89
N10 1E 46
TW5: Hest 1E 112
Sutton Row W1 7D 6 (6H 83)
Suttons Bus. Pk. RM13: Rain 3K 91
Sutton Sq. E9 5J 67
TW5: Hest 1D 112
Sutton St. E1 7J 85
Sutton's Way EC1 4D 8
Suttons Wharf E2 3K 85
Sutton Tennis Academy 1K 165
Sutton United FC 4J 165
Sutton Wlk. SE1 5H 13 (1K 101)
Sutton Way TW5: Hest 1D 112
W10 4E 80
SW1 Gallery 1A 18 (3G 101)
Swaby Rd. SW18 1A 136
Swaffam Ct. RM6: Chad H 6C 54
Swaffham Way N22 7G 33
Swaffield Rd. SW18 7K 117
Swain Cl. SW16 6F 137
Swain Rd. CR7: Thor H 5C 156
Swains Cl. UB7: W Dray 2A 92
Swain's La. N6 1E 64
Swainson Rd. W3 2B 98
Swains Rd. SW17 7D 136
Swain St. NW8 3C 4 (4C 82)
Swakeleys Dr. UB10: Ick 4C 56
Swakeleys Rd. UB10: Ick 4A 56
SWAKELEYS RDBT. 4A 56
Swalecliffe Rd. DA17: Belv 5H 109
Swaledale Cl. N11 6K 31
Swallands Rd. SE6 3C 140
(not continuous)
Swallow Cl. DA8: Erith 1K 127
SE14 1K 121
WD23: Bush 1B 26
Swallow Ct. HA4: Ruis 1A 58
IG2: Ilf 5F 53
SE1 7D 14
(off Swan St.)
SE12 7J 123
W9 5J 81
(off Admiral Wlk.)
Swallow Dr. NW10 6K 61
UB5: N'olt 2E 76
Swallowfield NW1 2K 5
(off Munster Sq.)
Swallowfield Rd. SE7 5K 105
Swallowfield Way UB3: Hayes 2F 93
Swallow Gdns. SW16 5H 137
Swallow Ho. NW8 2C 82
(off Allitsen Rd.)
Swallow Pk. KT6: Surb 3F 163
Swallow Pk. Cl. KT6: Surb 3F 163
Swallow Pas. W1 1K 11
(off Swallow Pl.)
Swallow Pl. E14 6B 86
(off Newell St.)
W1 1K 11 (6F 83)
Swallows Cl. SM1: Sutt 3J 165
Swallow St. E6 5C 88
W1 3B 12 (7G 83)
Swallowtail Ho. E20 5E 68
(off Sunrise Cl.)
SWAN, THE 2E 170
Swanage Ct. N1 7E 66
(off Hertford Rd.)
Swanage Ho. SW8 7K 101
(off Dorset Rd.)
Swanage Rd. E4 7K 35
SW18 6A 118
Swanage Waye UB4: Yead 6A 76
Swan & Pike Rd. EN3: Enf L 1H 25
Swan App. E6 5C 88
Swanbourne Ho. NW8 3C 4
(off Capland St.)
Swanbridge Rd. DA7: Bex 1G 127
Swan Cen., The SW17 3K 135
Swan Cl. CR0: C'don 7E 156
E17 1A 50
KT12: Walt T 7H 147
TW13: Hanw 4C 130
Swan Ct. E1 3K 15
(off Star Pl.)
E14 6B 86
(off Agnes St.)
HA4: Ruis 7F 39
SW3 6D 16 (5C 100)
Swan Ct. SW6 7J 99
(off Fulham Rd.)
TW7: Isle 3B 114
(off Swan St.)
Swandon Way SW18 4K 117
Swan Dr. NW9 2A 44
Swanfield St. E2 2J 9 (3F 85)
Swan Ho. E15 7G 69
(off Broadway)
EN3: Pond E 5D 24
N1 7D 66
(off Oakley Rd.)
Swan Island TW1: Twick 3A 132
Swan La. EC4 3F 15 (7D 84)
N4 1C 66
N20 3F 31
Swanley Ho. SE17 5E 102
(off Kinglake Est.)
Swanley Rd. DA16: Well 1C 126
Swan Mead SE1 3E 102
Swan M. CR4: Mitc 1D 154
RM7: Mawney 4H 55
SW6 1H 117
SW9 2K 119
Swann Ct. TW7: Isle 3A 114
(off South St.)
Swanne Ho. SE10 7E 104
(off Gloucester Cir.)
Swan Pas. E1 3K 15
Swan Path KT1: King T 3F 151
Swan Pl. SW13 2B 116
Swan Rd. SE16 2J 103
SE18 3B 106
TW13: Hanw 5C 130
UB1: S'hall 6F 77
UB7: W Dray 2A 92
Swan Sanctuary, The 6G 147
Swanscombe Ho. W11 1F 99
(off St Ann's Rd.)
Swanscombe Rd. W4 5A 98
W11 1F 99
Swansea Ct. E16 1F 107
(off Fishguard Way)
Swansea Rd. EN3: Pond E 4D 24
TW14: Felt 6E 110
Swansland Gdns. E17 1A 50
Swansmere Cl. KT12: Walt T 7A 148
Swan St. SE1 7D 14 (3C 102)
TW7: Isle 3B 114
Swanton Ct. SE13 3D 122
Swanton Gdns. SW19 1F 135
Swanton Rd. DA8: Erith 7G 109
Swan Wlk. SW3 7E 16 (6D 100)
TW17: Shep 7G 147
Swan Way EN3: Enf H 2E 24
Swanwick Cl. SW15 7B 116
Swan Yd. N1 6B 66
Sward Rd. BR5: St M Cry 6K 161
Swathling Ho. SW15 6B 116
(off Tunworth Cres.)
Swaton Rd. E3 4C 86
Swaylands Rd. DA17: Belv 6G 109
Swaythling Cl. N18 4C 34
Swedeland Ct. E1 6H 9
Swedenborg Gdns. E1 7H 85
Sweden Ga. SE16 3A 104
Swedish Quays SE16 3A 104
(not continuous)
Sweeney Cres. SE1 7K 15 (2F 103)
Sweetbriar Av. SM5: Cars 1D 166
Sweet Briar Grn. N9 3A 34
Sweet Briar Gro. N9 3A 34
Sweet Briar Wlk. N18 4A 34
Sweetcroft La. UB10: Hil 7B 56
Sweetland Ct. RM8: Dag 6B 72
Sweetmans Av. HA5: Pinn 3B 40
Sweets Way N20 2G 31
Swell Ct. E17 6C 50
Swetenham Wlk. SE18 5G 107
Swete St. E13 2J 87
Sweyn Pl. SE3 2J 123

Swift Cen.—Talbot Wlk.

Swift Cen. CR0: Wadd 7K 167
Swift Cl. E17 7F 35
HA2: Harr 2F 59
SE28 7B 90
UB3: Hayes 6H 75
Swift Ct. SM2: Sutt 7K 165
Swift Ho. *E3 1B 86*
(off Old Ford Rd.)
NW6 2H 81
(off Albert Rd.)
Swift Lodge *W9 5J 81*
(off Admiral Wlk.)
Swift Rd. TW13: Hanw 3C 130
UB2: S'hall 3E 94
Swiftsden Way BR1: Brom 6G 141
Swiftstone Twr. SE10 3J 105
Swift St. SW6 1H 117
Swimmers La. E2 1F 85
Swinbrook Rd. W10 5G 81
Swinburne Ct. *SE5 4D 120*
(off Basingdon Way)
Swinburne Cres. CR0: C'don 6J 157
Swinburne Ho. *E2 3J 85*
(off Roman Rd.)
Swinburne Rd. SW15 4C 116
Swinderby Rd. HA0: Wemb 6E 60
Swindon Cl. IG3: Ilf 2J 71
Swindon Rd. TW6: H'row A 5E 110
Swindon St. W12 1D 98
Swinfield Cl. TW13: Hanw 3C 130
Swinford Gdns. SW9 3B 120
Swingate La. SE18 6J 107
Swingfield Ho. *E9 1J 85*
(off Templecombe Rd.)
Swinley Ho. *NW1 1K 5*
(off Redhill St.)
Swinnerton St. E9 5A 68
Swinson Ho. N11 5B 32
Swinton Cl. HA9: Wemb 1H 61
Swinton Pl. WC1 1G 7 (3K 83)
Swinton St. WC1 1G 7 (3K 83)
Swires Shaw BR2: Kes 4B 172
SWISS COTTAGE 7B 64
Swiss Cottage Sports Cen. 7B 64
Swiss Ct. W1 3D 12
Swiss Ter. NW6 7B 64
Switch Ho. E14 7F 87
Swithland Gdns. SE9 4E 142
Swyncombe Av. W5 4B 96
Swynford Gdns. NW4 4C 44
Sybil M. N4 6B 48
Sybil Phoenix Cl. SE8 5K 103
Sybil Thorndike Casson Ho. *SW5 5J 99*
(off Kramer M.)
Sybourn St. E17 7B 50
Sycamore Av. DA15: Sidc 6K 125
E3 1B 86
UB3: Hayes 7G 75
W5 3D 96
Sycamore Cl.
CR2: S Croy 5E 168
E16 4G 87
EN4: E Barn 6G 21
HA8: Edg 4D 28
KT19: Ewe 5H 163
N9 4B 34
SE9 2C 142
SM5: Cars 4D 166
TW13: Felt 3J 129
UB5: N'olt 1C 76
UB7: Yiew 7B 74
W3 1A 98
Sycamore Ct. *DA8: Erith 5K 109*
(off Sandcliff Rd.)
E7 6J 69
KT3: N Mald 3A 152
NW6 1J 81
(off Bransdale Cl.)
SE1 7G 15
(off Royal Oak Yd.)
TW4: Houn 4C 112
Sycamore Gdns. CR4: Mitc 2B 154
N15 4F 49
W6 2D 98
Sycamore Gro. KT3: N Mald 3K 151
NW9 7J 43
SE6 6E 122
SE20 1G 157
Sycamore Hill N11 6K 31
Sycamore Ho. BR2: Brom 2G 159
IG9: Buck H 2G 37
N2 2B 46
(off The Grange)
SE16 2K 103
(off Woodland Cres.)
W6 2D 98
Sycamore Lodge
BR6: Orp 2K 173
TW16: Sun 7H 129
W8 3K 99
(off Stone Hall Pl.)
Sycamore M. *DA8: Erith 5K 109*
(off St John's Rd.)
SW4 3G 119
Sycamore Path *E17 6D 50*
(off Poplars Rd.)
Sycamore Pl. BR1: Brom 3E 160
Sycamore Rd. SW19 6E 134
Sycamore St. EC1 4C 8 (4C 84)
Sycamore Wlk. IG6: Ilf 4G 53
W10 4G 81
Sycamore Way
CR7: Thor H 5A 156
TW11: Tedd 6C 132
Sydcote SE21 1C 138
SYDENHAM 4J 139
Sydenham Av. N21 5E 22
SE26 5H 139
Sydenham Cotts. SE12 2A 142
Sydenham Ct. *CR0: C'don 1D 168*
(off Sydenham Rd.)
Sydenham Hill SE23 1H 139
SE26 4F 139
Sydenham Hill Local Nature Reserve 2G 139
Sydenham Pk. SE26 3J 139
Sydenham Pk. Mans. *SE26 3J 139*
(off Sydenham Pk.)
Sydenham Pk. Rd. SE26 3J 139
Sydenham Pl. SE27 3B 138
Sydenham Ri. SE23 2H 139
Sydenham Rd. CR0: C'don 1C 168
SE26 4J 139
Sydmons Ct. SE23 7J 121
Sydner M. N16 4F 67
Sydner Rd. N16 4F 67
Sydney Chapman Way EN5: Barn 2C 20
Sydney Cl. SW3 4B 16 (4B 100)
Sydney Ct. UB4: Yead 4A 76
Sydney Cres. TW15: Ashf 6D 128
Sydney Gro. NW4 5E 44
Sydney M. SW3 4B 16 (4B 100)
Sydney Pl. SW7 4B 16 (4B 100)
Sydney Rd. DA6: Bex 4D 126
DA14: Sidc 4J 143
E11 6K 51
EN2: Enf 4J 23
IG6: Ilf 2G 53
IG8: Wfd G 4D 36
N8 4A 48
N10 1E 46
SE2 3C 108
SM1: Sutt 4J 165
SW20 2F 153
TW9: Rich 4E 114
TW11: Tedd 5K 131
TW14: Felt 1J 129
W13 1A 96
Sydney Russell Leisure Cen. 5E 72
Sydney St. SW3 5C 16 (5C 100)
Sylva Cotts. SE8 1C 122
Sylvana Cl. UB10: Hil 1B 74
Sylvan Av. N3 2J 45
N22 7E 32
NW7 6F 29
RM6: Chad H 6F 55
Sylvan Ct. N12 3E 30
NW6 1K 81
(off Abbey Rd.)
Sylvan Est. SE19 1F 157
Sylvan Gdns. KT6: Surb 7D 150
Sylvan Gro. NW2 4F 63
SE15 6H 103
Sylvan Hill SE19 1E 156
Sylvan Rd. E7 6K 69
E11 5J 51
E17 5C 50
IG1: Ilf 2G 71
SE19 1F 157
Sylvan Ter. *SE15 6H 103*
(off Sylvan Gro.)
Sylvan Wlk. BR1: Brom 3D 160
Sylvan Way BR4: W W'ck 4G 171
RM8: Dag 4B 72
Sylverdale Rd. CR0: C'don 3B 168
Sylvester Av. BR7: Chst 6D 142
Sylvester Path E8 6H 67
Sylvester Rd. E8 6H 67
E17 7B 50
HA0: Wemb 5C 60
N2 2A 46
Sylvestrian Leisure Cen. 4G 51
Sylvestrus Cl. KT1: King T 1G 151
Sylvia Ct. HA9: Wemb 7H 61
N1 2D 84
(off Wenlock St.)
Sylvia Gdns. HA9: Wemb 7H 61
Sylvia Pankhurst Ho. *RM10: Dag 3G 73*
(off Wythenshawe Rd.)
Symes M. NW1 2G 83
Symington Ho. *SE1 3D 102*
(off Deverell St.)
Symington M. E9 5K 67
Symister M. N1 2G 9
Symons Cl. SE15 2J 121
Symons St. SW3 4F 17 (4D 100)
Symphony Cl. HA8: Edg 7C 28
Symphony M. W10 3G 81
Syon Ct. E11 5K 51
Syon Ga. Way TW8: Bford 7A 96
Syon House 1C 114
Syon La. TW7: Isle 6J 95
Syon Lodge SE12 7J 123
Syon Pk. 1B 114
Syon Pk. Gdns. TW7: Isle 7K 95
Syringa Ho. SE4 3B 122

T

Tabard Ct. *E14 6E 86*
(off Lodore St.)
Tabard Gdn. Est. SE1 7E 14 (3D 102)
Tabard Ho. *SE1 7F 15*
(off Manciple St.)
Tabard St. SE1 6D 14 (2D 102)
Tabard Theatre 4A 98
Tabernacle, The *6H 81*
(off Powis Sq.)
Tabernacle Av. E13 4J 87
Tabernacle St. EC2 4F 9 (4D 84)
Tableer Av. SW4 5G 119
Tabley Rd. N7 4J 65
Tabor Ct. SM3: Cheam 6G 165
Tabor Gdns. SM3: Cheam 6H 165
Tabor Gro. SW19 7H 135
Tabor Rd. W6 3D 98
Tachbrook Est. SW1 6C 18 (5H 101)
Tachbrook M. SW1 3A 18 (4G 101)
Tachbrook Rd. TW14: Felt 7H 111
UB2: S'hall 4B 94
UB7: W Dray 1A 92
Tachbrook St. SW1 4B 18 (4G 101)
Tack M. SE4 3C 122
Tadema Ho. NW8 4B 4
Tadema Rd. SW10 7A 100
Tadlow *KT1: King T 3G 151*
(off Washington Rd.)
Tadmor Cl. TW16: Sun 4H 147
Tadmor St. W12 1F 99
Tadworth Av. KT3: N Mald 4B 152
Tadworth Ho. SE1 7A 14
Tadworth Rd. NW2 2C 62
Taeping St. E14 4D 104
Taffeta Ho. *E20 6E 68*
(off De Coubertin St.)
Taff Ho. *KT2: King T 1D 150*
(off Henry Macaulay Av.)
Taffrail Ho. *E14 5D 104*
(off Burrells Wharf Sq.)
Taffy's How CR4: Mitc 3C 154
Taft Way E3 3D 86
Taggs Ho. *KT1: King T 2D 150*
(off Market Sq.)
Taggs Island TW12: Hamp 2H 149
Tagore Cl. HA3: W'stone 3K 41
Tagwright Ho. *N1 1E 8*
(off Westland Pl.)
Tailor Ho. *WC1 4F 7*
(off Colonnade)
Tailworth St. *E1 6K 9*
(off Chicksand St.)
Tait Ct. *E3 1B 86*
(off St Stephen's Rd.)
SW8 1J 119
(off Lansdowne Grn.)
Tait Ho. *SE1 5K 13*
(off Greet St.)
Tait Rd. CR0: C'don 7E 156
Tait Rd. Ind. Est. *CR0: C'don 7E 156*
(off Tait Rd.)
Tait St. E1 6H 85
Taj Apartments *E1 5K 9*
(off Brick La.)
Takeley Cl. RM5: Col R 2K 55
Takhar M. SW11 2C 118
Talacre Community Sports Cen. 6E 64
Talacre Rd. NW5 6E 64
Talbot Av. N2 3B 46
Talbot Cl. CR4: Mitc 4G 155
N15 4F 49
Talbot Ct. EC3 2F 15
NW9 3K 61
Talbot Cres. NW4 5C 44
Talbot Gdns. IG3: Ilf 2A 72
Talbot Gro. Ho. *W11 6G 81*
(off Lancaster Rd.)
Talbot Ho. *E14 6D 86*
(off Girauld St.)
N7 3A 66
Talbot Pl. SE3 2G 123
Talbot Rd. CR7: Thor H 4D 156
E6 2E 88
E7 4J 69
HA0: Wemb 6D 60
HA3: W'stone 2K 41
N6 6E 46
N15 4F 49
N22 2G 47
RM9: Dag 6F 73
SE22 4E 120
SM5: Cars 5E 166
TW2: Twick 1J 131
TW7: Isle 4A 114
TW15: Ashf 5A 128
UB2: S'hall 4C 94
W2 6H 81
W11 6H 81
(not continuous)
W13 1A 96
Talbot Sq. W2 1B 10 (6B 82)
Talbot Wlk. NW10 6A 62
W11 6G 81
(off St Mark's Rd.)

Talbot Yd. SE1 . . . . .5E **14** (1D **102**)
Talcott Path SW2 . . . . .1A **138**
Talehangers Cl. DA6: Bex 4D **126**
Talfourd Pl. SE15 . . . . .1F **121**
Talfourd Rd. SE15 . . . . .1F **121**
Talgarth Mans. W14 . . . . .5G **99**
   (off Talgarth Rd.)
Talgarth Rd. W6 . . . . .5F **99**
   W14 . . . . .5F **99**
Talgarth Wlk. NW9 . . . . .5A **44**
Talia Ho. E14 . . . . .3E **104**
   (off Manchester Rd.)
Talina Cen. SW6 . . . . .1A **118**
Talisman Cl. IG3: Ilf 1B **72**
Talisman Sq. SE26 . . . . .4G **139**
Talisman Way
   HA9: Wemb 3F **61**
Tallack Cl. HA3: Hrw W 7D **26**
Tallack Rd. E10 . . . . .1B **68**
Tall Elms Cl. BR2: Brom 5H **159**
Talleyrand Ho. SE5 . . . . .2C **120**
   (off Lilford Rd.)
Tallis Cl. E16 . . . . .6K **87**
Tallis Gro. SE7 . . . . .6A **106**
Tallis St. EC4 . . . . .2K **13** (7A **84**)
Tallis Vw. NW10 . . . . .6K **61**
Tallow Cl. RM9: Dag 7D **72**
Tallow Rd. TW8: Bford 6C **96**
Tall Trees SW16 . . . . .3K **155**
Talma Gdns. TW2: Twick 6J **113**
Talmage Cl. SE23 . . . . .7J **121**
Talman Gro. HA7: Stan 6J **27**
Talma Rd. SW2 . . . . .4A **120**
Talwin St. E3 . . . . .3D **86**
Tamar Cl. E3 . . . . .1B **86**
Tamar Ho. E14 . . . . .2E **104**
   (off Plevna St.)
   SE11 . . . . .5K **19**
   (off Kennington La.)
Tamarind Cl. SE1 . . . . .6K **15**
   W8 . . . . .3K **99**
   (off Stone Hall Gdns.)
Tamarind Ho. SE15 . . . . .7G **103**
   (off Reddins Rd.)
Tamarind Yd. E1 . . . . .1G **103**
   (off Kennet St.)
Tamarisk Sq. W12 . . . . .7B **80**
Tamar Sq. IG8: Wfd G 6E **36**
Tamar St. SE7 . . . . .3C **106**
Tamar Way N17 . . . . .3F **49**
Tamesis Gdns. KT4: Wor Pk 2A **164**
Tamian Ind. Est. TW4: Houn 4A **112**
Tamian Way TW4: Houn 4A **112**
Tamworth Av. IG8: Wfd G 6B **36**
Tamworth La. CR4: Mitc 2F **155**
Tamworth Pk. CR4: Mitc 4F **155**
Tamworth Pl. CR0: C'don 2C **168**
Tamworth Rd. CR0: C'don 2B **168**
Tamworth St. SW6 . . . . .6J **99**
Tamworth Vs. CR4: Mitc 4F **155**
Tancred Rd. N4 . . . . .6B **48**
Tandem Cen. SW19 . . . . .1B **154**
Tandem Way SW19 . . . . .1B **154**
Tandridge Dr. BR6: Orp 1H **173**
Tandridge Pl. BR6: Orp 1H **173**
Tanfield Av. NW2 . . . . .4B **62**
Tanfield Rd. CR0: C'don 4C **168**
Tangerine Ho. SE1 . . . . .7F **15**
   (off Long La.)
Tangier Rd. TW10: Rich 4G **115**
Tangleberry Cl. BR1: Brom 4D **160**
Tangle Tree Cl. N3 . . . . .2K **45**
Tanglewood Cl.
   CR0: C'don 3J **169**
   HA7: Stan 2D **26**
   UB10: Hil 4C **74**
Tanglewood Way TW13: Felt . . .3K **129**
Tangley Gro. SW15 . . . . .6B **116**
Tangley Pk. Rd.
   TW12: Hamp 6D **130**
Tanglyn Av. TW17: Shep 5D **146**

Tangmere N17 . . . . .2D **48**
   (off Willan Rd.)
   WC1 . . . . .2G **7**
   (off Sidmouth St.)
Tangmere Gdns. UB5: N'olt 2A **76**
Tangmere Gro. KT2: King T 5D **132**
Tangmere Way NW9 . . . . .2A **44**
Tan Ho. E9 . . . . .5A **68**
   (off Sadler Pl.)
Tanhouse Fld. NW5 . . . . .5H **65**
   (off Torriano Av.)
Tanhurst Ho. SW2 . . . . .7K **119**
   (off Redlands Way)
Tanhurst Wlk. SE2 . . . . .3D **108**
   (off Alsike Rd.)
Tankerton Ho's. WC1 . . . . .2F **7**
   (off Tankerton St.)
Tankerton Rd. KT6: Surb 2F **163**
Tankerton St. WC1 . . . . . .2F **7** (3J **83**)
Tankerton Ter. CR0: C'don 6K **155**
Tankerville Cl. TW3: Houn 3G **113**
Tankerville Rd. SW16 . . . . .7H **137**
Tankridge Rd. NW2 . . . . .2D **62**
Tanner Ho. E1 . . . . .5K **85**
   (off White Horse La.)
   SE1 .7H **15**
   (off Tanner St.)
Tanneries, The E1 . . . . .4J **85**
   (off Cephas Av.)
Tanner Point E13 . . . . .1J **87**
   (off Pelly Rd.)
Tanners Cl. KT12: Walt T 6K **147**
Tanners End La. N18 . . . . .4K **33**
Tanner's Hill SE8 . . . . .1B **122**
Tanners La. IG6: Ilf 3G **53**
Tanners M. SE8 . . . . .1B **122**
   (off Tanner's Hill)
Tanner St. IG11: Bark 6G **71**
   SE1 . . . . .7H **15** (2E **102**)
Tanners Yd. E2 . . . . .2H **85**
   (off Treadway St.)
Tannery, The SE1 . . . . .2E **102**
   (off Black Swan Yd.)
Tannery Cl. BR3: Beck 5K **157**
   RM10: Dag 3H **73**
Tannery Ho. E1 . . . . .5G **85**
   (off Deal St.)
Tannington Ter. N5 . . . . .3B **66**
Tannoy Sq. SE27 . . . . .4D **138**
Tannsfeld Rd. SE26 . . . . .5K **139**
Tansley Cl. N7 . . . . .5H **65**
Tanswell St. SE1 . . . . . .7J **13** (2A **102**)
Tansy Cl. E6 . . . . .6E **88**
Tantallon Rd. SW12 . . . . .1E **136**
Tant Av. E16 . . . . .6H **87**
Tantony Gro. RM6: Chad H 3D **54**
Tanworth Gdns. HA5: Pinn 2K **39**
Tanyard Ho. TW8: Bford 7C **96**
   (off High St.)
Tanyard La. DA5: Bexl 7G **127**
Tanza Rd. NW3 . . . . .4D **64**
Tapestry Apartments N1 . . . . . .1H **83**
Tapestry Bldg. EC2 . . . . .6H **9**
   (off New St.)
Tapestry Cl. SM2: Sutt 7K **165**
Tapley Cl. E14 . . . . .6E **86**
Tapley Ho. SE1 . . . . .7K **15**
   (off Wolseley St.)
Taplow NW3 . . . . .7B **64**
   SE17 . . . . .5D **102**
   (off Thurlow St.)
Taplow Cl. CR4: Mitc 4C **154**
Taplow Ho. E2 . . . . .2J **9**
   (off Palissy St.)
Taplow Rd. N13 . . . . .4H **33**
Taplow St. N1 . . . . .1D **8** (2C **84**)
Tapper Wlk. N1 . . . . .1J **83**
Tappesfield Rd. SE15 . . . . .3J **121**
Tapping Cl. KT2: King T 7G **133**
Tapp St. E1 . . . . .4H **85**
Tapster St. EN5: Barn 3C **20**

Tara Arts Cen. 1A **136**
Tara Ct. BR3: Beck 2D **158**
Tara Ho. E14 . . . . .4C **104**
   (off Deptford Ferry Rd.)
Tara M. N8 . . . . .6J **47**
Taransay Wlk. N1 . . . . .6D **66**
Tarbert M. N15 . . . . .5E **48**
Tarbert Rd. SE22 . . . . .5E **120**
Tarbert Wlk. E1 . . . . .7J **85**
Target Cl. TW14: Felt 6G **111**
Target Ho. W13 . . . . .1B **96**
   (off Sherwood St.)
TARGET RDBT. 1D **76**
Tariff Cres. SE8 . . . . .4B **104**
Tariff Rd. N17 . . . . .6B **34**
Tarleton Ct. N22 . . . . .2A **48**
Tarleton Gdns. SE23 . . . . .2H **139**
Tarling Cl. DA14: Sidc 3B **144**
Tarling Rd. E16 . . . . .6H **87**
   N2 . . . . .2A **46**
Tarling St. E1 . . . . .6J **85**
Tarling St. Est. E1 . . . . .6J **85**
Tarmac Way UB7: Harm 3C **174**
Tarnbank EN2: Enf 5D **22**
Tarnbrook Ct. SW1 . . . . .4G **17**
   (off Holbein Pl.)
Tarns, The NW1 . . . . .1A **6**
   (off Varndell St.)
Tarn St. SE1 . . . . .3C **102**
Tarnwood Pk. SE9 . . . . .7D **124**
Tarplett Ho. SE14 . . . . .6K **103**
   (off John Williams Cl.)
Tarquin Ho. SE26 . . . . .4G **139**
   (off High Level Dr.)
Tarragon Cl. SE14 . . . . .7A **104**
Tarragon Ct. IG1: Ilf 2J **71**
Tarragon Gro. SE26 . . . . .6K **139**
Tarranbrae NW6 . . . . .7G **63**
Tarrant Ho. E2 . . . . .3J **85**
   (off Roman Rd.)
   W14 . . . . .3G **99**
   (off Russell Rd.)
Tarrant Pl. W1 . . . . .6E **4** (5D **82**)
Tarrington Cl. SW16 . . . . .3H **137**
Tartan Ho. E14 . . . . .6E **86**
   (off Dee St.)
Tarver Rd. SE17 . . . . .5B **102**
Tarves Way SE10 . . . . .7D **104**
   (Lit. Cottage Pl.)
   SE10 . . . . .7D **104**
   (Norman Rd.)
Taryn Gro.
   BR1: Brom 3D **160**
Tash Pl. N11 . . . . .5A **32**
Tasker Cl. UB3: Harl 7E **92**
Tasker Ho. E14 . . . . .5B **86**
   (off Wallwood St.)
   IG11: Bark 2H **89**
Tasker Lodge W8 . . . . .2J **99**
   (off Campden Hill)
Tasker Rd. NW3 . . . . .5D **64**
Tasman Ct. E14 . . . . .4D **104**
   (off Westferry Rd.)
   TW16: Sun 7G **129**
Tasman Ho. E1 . . . . .1H **103**
   (off Clegg St.)
Tasmania Ter. N18 . . . . .6H **33**
Tasman Rd. SW9 . . . . .3J **119**
Tasman Wlk. E16 . . . . .6B **88**
Tasso Rd. W6 . . . . .6G **99**
Tasso Yd. W6 . . . . .6G **99**
   (off Tasso Rd.)
Tatam Rd. NW10 . . . . .7K **61**
Tatchbury Ho. SW15 . . . . .6B **116**
   (off Tunworth Cres.)
Tate Apartments E1 . . . . .6H **85**
   (off Sly St.)
Tate Britain 4E **18** (4J **101**)
Tate Ho. E2 . . . . .2K **85**
   (off Mace St.)
Tate Modern 4B **14** (1B **102**)

Tate Rd. E16 . . . . .1D **106**
   (not continuous)
   SM1: Sutt 5J **165**
Tatham Pl. NW8 . . . . .2B **82**
Tatnell Rd. SE23 . . . . .6A **122**
Tatsfield Ho. SE1 . . . . .7F **15**
   (off Pardoner St.)
Tattersall Cl. SE9 . . . . .5C **124**
Tatton Cl. SM5: Wall 1E **166**
Tatton Cres. N16 . . . . .7F **49**
Tatum St. SE17 . . . . .4D **102**
Tauheed Cl. N4 . . . . .2C **66**
Taunton Av. SW20 . . . . .2D **152**
   TW3: Houn 2G **113**
Taunton Cl. DA7: Bex 2K **127**
   SM3: Sutt 1J **165**
Taunton Dr. EN2: Enf 3F **23**
   N2 . . . . .2A **46**
Taunton Ho. W2 . . . . .6A **82**
   (off Hallfield Est.)
Taunton M. NW1 . . . . .4E **4** (4D **82**)
Taunton Pl. NW1 . . . . .3E **4** (4D **82**)
Taunton Rd. SE12 . . . . .5G **123**
   UB6: G'frd 1F **77**
Taunton Way HA7: Stan 2E **42**
Tavern Cl. SM5: Cars 7C **154**
Tavern Ct. SE1 . . . . .3C **102**
   (off New Kent Rd.)
Taverners Cl. W11 . . . . .1G **99**
Taverners Ct. E3 . . . . .3A **86**
   (off Grove Rd.)
Taverner Sq. N5 . . . . .4C **66**
Taverners Way E4 . . . . .1B **36**
Tavern La. SW9 . . . . .2A **120**
Tavern Quay SE16 . . . . .4A **104**
Tavistock Av. E17 . . . . .3K **49**
   NW7 .7A **30**
   UB6: G'frd 2A **78**
Tavistock Cl. N16 . . . . .5E **66**
   TW18: Staines 7A **128**
Tavistock Ct. CR0: C'don 1D **168**
   (off Tavistock Rd.)
   WC1 .3D **6**
   (off Tavistock Sq.)
   WC2 .2F **13**
   (off Tavistock Pl.)
Tavistock Cres. CR4: Mitc 4J **155**
   W11 .5H **81**
   (not continuous)
Tavistock Gdns. IG3: Ilf 4J **71**
Tavistock Ga. CR0: C'don 1D **168**
Tavistock Gro. CR0: C'don 7D **156**
Tavistock Ho. IG8: Wfd G 6K **37**
   WC1 . . . . .3D **6** (4H **83**)
Tavistock M. N19 . . . . .3J **65**
   (off Tavistock Ter.)
   W11 .6H **81**
Tavistock Pl. N14 . . . . .6A **22**
   WC1 . . . . .3E **6** (4J **83**)
Tavistock Rd. BR2: Brom 4H **159**
   CR0: C'don 1D **168**
   DA16: Well 1C **126**
   E7 . . . . .4H **69**
   E15 . . . . .6H **69**
   E18 . . . . .3J **51**
   HA8: Edg 1G **43**
   N4 . . . . .6D **48**
   NW10 . . . . .2B **80**
   SM5: Cars 1B **166**
   UB7: Yiew 1A **92**
   UB10: Ick 5F **57**
   W11 .6H **81**
   (not continuous)
Tavistock Sq. WC1 . . . . . .3D **6** (4H **83**)
Tavistock St. WC2 . . . . . .2F **13** (7J **83**)
Tavistock Ter. N19 . . . . .3H **65**
Tavistock Twr. SE16 . . . . .3A **104**
Tavistock Wlk. SM5: Cars 1B **166**
Taviton St. WC1 . . . . .3C **6** (4H **83**)
Tavy Bri. SE2 . . . . .2C **108**
Tavy Cl. SE11 . . . . .5K **19**

Tawney Rd. SE28 7B 90
Tawny Cl. TW13: Felt 3J 129
W13 1B 96
Tawny Way SE16 4K 103
Tayben Av. TW2: Twick 6J 113
Tayberry Ho. *E20* *6D 68*
(off Ravens Wlk.)
Taybridge Rd. SW11 3E 118
Tay Bldgs. SE1 7G 15
Tayburn Cl. E14 6E 86
Tay Ct. *E2* *3K 85*
(off Meath Cres.)
SE1 *7G 15*
(off Decima St.)
Tayfield Cl. UB10: Ick 3F 57
Tay Ho. *E3* *2B 86*
(off St Stephen's Rd.)
Tayler Ct. NW8 1B 82
Taylor Av. TW9: Kew 2H 115
Taylor Cl. BR6: Orp 4K 173
N17 7B 34
SE8 6B 104
TW3: Houn 1G 113
TW12: Hamp H 5G 131
Taylor Ct. *SE20* *2J 157*
(off Elmers End Rd.)
Taylor Ho. *E14* *7C 86*
(off Storehouse M.)
Taylor Pl. E3 2D 86
Taylor Rd. CR4: Mitc 7C 136
SM6: Wall 5F 167
Taylors Bldgs. SE18 4F 107
Taylors Cl. DA14: Sidc 3K 143
Taylors Ct. TW13: Felt 2J 129
Taylors Grn. W3 6A 80
Taylor's La. SE26 4H 139
Taylors La. EN5: Barn 1C 20
NW10 6A 62
Taylors Mead NW7 5H 29
Taylors Yd. *E1* *4K 9*
(off Brick La.)
Taymount Grange SE23 2J 139
Taymount Ri. SE23 2J 139
Tayport Cl. N1 7J 65
Tayside Ct. SE5 4D 120
Tayside Dr. HA8: Edg 3C 28
Taywood Rd. UB5: N'olt 4D 76
Tazzeta Ho. *E20* *5E 68*
(off Victory Pde.)
Teak Cl. SE16 1A 104
Tealby Ct. N7 6K 65
Teal Cl. E16 5B 88
Teal Ct. *E1* *3K 15*
(off Star Pl.)
NW10 6K 61
SE8 *6B 104*
(off Taylor Cl.)
SM6: Wall 5G 167
Teal Dr. HA6: Nwood 1E 38
Teale St. E2 2G 85
Tealing Dr. KT19: Ewe 4K 163
Teal Pl. SM1: Sutt 5H 165
Teal St. SE10 3H 105
Teamsport Karting
Edmonton 4E 34
Teasel Cl. CR0: C'don 1K 169
Teasel Cres. SE28 1J 107
Teasel Way E15 3G 87
Tea Trade Wharf *SE1* *6K 15*
(off Shad Thames)
Tea Tree Cl. TW15: Ashf 5E 128
Tebworth Rd. N17 7A 34
Technology Pk., The NW9 3A 44
Teck Cl. TW7: Isle 2A 114
Tedder Cl. HA4: Ruis 5J 57
KT9: Chess 5C 162
UB10: Uxb 7B 56
Tedder Rd. CR2: Sels 7J 169
TEDDINGTON 5A 132
Teddington Bus. Pk. *TW11: Tedd* *6K 131*
(off Station Rd.)
Teddington Lock 4B 132
Teddington Pk. TW11: Tedd 5K 131
Teddington Pk. Rd. TW11: Tedd 4K 131
Teddington Pool & Fitness Cen. 5A 132
Teddington Sports Cen. 6D 132
Ted Hennem Ho. RM10: Dag 3H 73
Ted Roberts Ho. *E2* *2H 85*
(off Parmiter St.)
Tedworth Gdns. SW3 6E 16 (5D 100)
Tedworth Sq. SW3 6E 16 (5D 100)
Tee, The W3 6A 80
Tees Av. UB6: G'frd 2J 77
Tees Ct. *W7* *6H 77*
(off Hanway Rd.)
Teesdale Av. TW7: Isle 1A 114
Teesdale Cl. E2 2G 85
Teesdale Gdns. SE25 2E 156
TW7: Isle 1A 114
Teesdale Rd. E11 6H 51
Teesdale St. E2 2H 85
Teesdale Yd. *E2* *2H 85*
(off Teesdale St.)
Teeswater Ct. DA18: Erith 3D 108
Teevan Cl. CR0: C'don 7G 157
Teevan Rd. CR0: C'don 1G 169
Tegan Cl. SM2: Sutt 7J 165
Teign M. SE9 2C 142
Teignmouth Cl. HA8: Edg 2F 43
SW4 4H 119
Teignmouth Gdns. UB6: G'frd 2A 78
Teignmouth Pde. UB6: G'frd 2A 78
Teignmouth Rd. DA16: Well 2C 126
NW2 5F 63
Telcon Way SE10 4G 105
Telcote Way HA4: Ruis 7A 40
Telegraph Av. SE10 4G 105
Telegraph Hill NW3 3K 63
Telegraph La. KT10: Clay 4A 162
Telegraph M. IG3: Ilf 1A 72
Telegraph Pas. *SW2* *7J 119*
(off New Pk. Rd.)
Telegraph Path BR7: Chst 5F 143
Telegraph Pl. E14 4D 104
Telegraph Rd. SW15 7D 116
Telegraph St. EC2 7E 8 (6D 84)
Telemann Sq. SE3 4K 123
Telephone Pl. SW6 6H 99
Telfer Cl. W3 2J 97
Telfer Ho. EC1 2B 8
Telferscot Rd. SW12 1H 137
Telford Av. SW2 1H 137
Telford Cl. E17 7A 50
SE19 6F 139
Telford Dr. KT12: Walt T 7A 148
Telford Ho. *SE1* *3C 102*
(off Tiverton St.)
W10 *5G 81*
(off Portobello Rd.)
Telford Rd. N11 5B 32
NW9 6C 44
SE9 2H 143
TW2: Whitt 7E 112
UB1: S'hall 7F 77
W10 5G 81
Telfords Yd. E1 7G 85
Telford Ter. SW1 7A 18 (6G 101)
Telford Way UB4: Yead 5C 76
W3 5A 80
Telham Rd. E6 2E 88
Tell Gro. SE22 4F 121
Tellson Av. SE18 1B 124
Telscombe Cl. BR6: Orp 2J 173
Temair Ho. *SE10* *7D 104*
(off Tarves Way)
Temeraire Pl. TW8: Bford 5F 97
Temeraire St. SE16 2J 103
Tempelhof Av. NW2 7E 44
NW4 7E 44
Temperley Rd. SW12 7E 118
Templar Ct. NW8 2A 4
RM7: Mawney 4H 55
Templar Dr. SE28 6D 90
Templar Ho. HA2: Harr 2G 59
NW2 6H 63
Templar Pl. TW12: Hamp 7E 130
Templars Av. NW11 6H 45
Templars Cres. N3 2J 45
Templars Dr. HA3: Hrw W 6C 26
Templars Ho. *E16* *7F 89*
(off University Way)
Templar St. SE5 2B 120
Temple Av. CR0: C'don 2B 170
EC4 2K 13 (7A 84)
N20 7G 21
RM8: Dag 1G 73
Temple Bar 1J 13
Temple Bar Gate *1B 14*
(off Paternoster Sq.)
Temple Chambers EC4 2K 13
Temple Cl. E11 7G 51
N3 2H 45
SE28 3G 107
Templecombe Rd. E9 1J 85
Templecombe Way SM4: Mord 5G 153
Temple Ct. *E1* *5K 85*
(off Rectory Sq.)
SW8 *7J 101*
(off Thorncroft St.)
Templecroft TW15: Ashf 6F 129
Temple Dwellings *E2* *2H 85*
(off Temple St.)
TEMPLE FORTUNE 5H 45
Temple Fortune Hill NW11 5J 45
Temple Fortune La. NW11 6H 45
Temple Fortune Pde. NW11 5H 45
Temple Gdns. EC4 2J 13
N21 2G 33
NW11 6H 45
RM8: Dag 3D 72
Temple Gro. EN2: Enf 2G 23
NW11 6J 45
Temple Hall Ct. E4 2A 36
Temple La. EC4 1K 13 (6A 84)
Templeman Rd. W7 5K 77
Temple Mead Cl. HA7: Stan 6G 27
Templemead Cl. W3 6A 80
Templemead Ho. E9 4A 68
TEMPLE MILLS 4D 68
Temple Mills La. E10 4D 68
E15 5E 68
E20 4D 68
Temple of Mithras (remains) *1E 14*
(off Queen Victoria St.)
Temple Pde. *EN5: New Bar* *7G 21*
(off Netherlands Rd.)
Temple Pk. UB8: Hil 3C 74
Temple Pl. WC2 2H 13 (7K 83)
Temple Rd. CR0: C'don 4D 168
E6 1C 88
N8 4K 47
NW2 4E 62
TW3: Houn 4F 113
TW9: Rich 2F 115
W4 3J 97
W5 3D 96
Temple Sheen SW14 4J 115
Temple Sheen Rd. SW14 4H 115
Temple St. E2 2H 85
Temple Ter. *N22* *2A 48*
(off Vincent Rd.)
Templeton Av. E4 4H 35
Templeton Cl. N15 6D 48
N16 5E 66
SE19 1D 156
Templeton Ct. EN3: Enf W 1D 24
Templeton Pl. SW5 4J 99
Templeton Rd. N15 6D 48
Temple Way SM1: Sutt 3B 166
Temple W. M. SE11 3B 102
Templewood W13 5B 78
Templewood Av. NW3 3K 63
Templewood Gdns. NW3 3K 63
Templewood Point *NW2* *2H 63*
(off Granville Rd.)
Temple Yd. *E2* *2H 85*
(off Temple St.)
Tempo Ho. UB5: N'olt 3B 76
Tempsford Cl. EN2: Enf 4H 23
Tempsford Ct. HA1: Harr 6K 41
Tempus Apartments *EC1* *1A 8*
(off Goswell Rd.)
Tempus Ct. E18 1J 51
Tempus Wharf *SE16* *2G 103*
(off Bermondsey Wall W.)
Temsford Cl. HA2: Harr 2G 41
Tenbury Cl. E7 5B 70
Tenbury Ct. SW2 1H 137
Tenby Av. HA3: Kenton 2B 42
Tenby Cl. N15 4F 49
RM6: Chad H 6E 54
Tenby Ct. E17 5A 50
Tenby Gdns. UB5: N'olt 6E 58
Tenby Ho. UB3: Harl 3E 92
W2 *6A 82*
(off Hallfield Est.)
Tenby Mans. *W1* *5H 5*
(off Nottingham St.)
Tenby Rd. DA16: Well 1D 126
E17 5A 50
EN3: Pond E 4D 24
HA8: Edg 1F 43
RM6: Chad H 6E 54
Tench St. E1 1H 103
Tenda Rd. SE16 4H 103
Tendring Way RM6: Chad H 5C 54
Tenham Av. SW2 1H 137
Tenison Ct. W1 2A 12 (7G 83)
Tenison Way SE1 5J 13
Tenniel Cl. W2 7A 82
Tennis Ct. La. KT8: E Mos 3K 149
Tennison Rd. SE25 4F 157
Tennis St. SE1 6E 14 (2D 102)
Tenniswood Rd. EN1: Enf 1K 23
Tennyson CR0: C'don 1C 168
N8 *3J 47*
(off Boyton Cl.)
Tennyson Av. E11 7J 51
E12 7C 70
KT3: N Mald 5D 152
NW9 3J 43
TW1: Twick 1K 131
Tennyson Cl. DA16: Well 1J 125
EN3: Pond E 5E 24
TW14: Felt 6H 111
Tennyson Ct. *NW1* *4E 4*
(off Dorset Sq.)
SW6 *1A 118*
(off Imperial Rd.)
Tennyson Ho. DA17: Belv 5F 109
SE17 *5C 102*
(off Browning St.)
Tennyson Mans. *SW3* *7C 16*
(off Lordship Pl.)
W14 *6H 99*
(off Queen's Club Gdns.)
Tennyson Rd. E10 1D 68
E15 7G 69
E17 6B 50
NW6 1H 81
NW7 5H 29
SE20 7K 139
SW19 6A 136
TW3: Houn 2G 113
TW15: Ashf 5A 128
W7 7K 77
Tennyson St. SW8 2F 119
Tenpin
Acton 4G 79
Bexleyheath 4F 127
Croydon 2K 167
Feltham 2K 129
Kingston upon Thames *2E 150*
(within The Rotunda Cen.)

Tensing Ct. TW19: Stanw 1A **128**
Tensing Rd. UB2: S'hall 3E **94**
Tentelow La. UB2: S'hall 5E **94**
Tenterden Cl. NW4 . . . . .3F **45**
SE9 . . . . .4D **142**
Tenterden Dr. NW4 . . . . .3F **45**
Tenterden Gdns. CRO: C'don 7G **157**
NW4 . . . . .3F **45**
Tenterden Gro. NW4 . . . . .3F **45**
Tenterden Ho. SE17 . . . . .5E **102**
(off Surrey Gro.)
Tenterden Rd. CRO: C'don 7G **157**
N17 . . . . .7A **34**
RM8: Dag .2F **73**
Tenterden St. W1 . . . . .1K **11** (6F **83**)
Tenter Ground E1 . . . . .6J **9** (5F **85**)
Tenter Pas. E1 .1K **15**
(off Nth. Tenter St.)
Tent Peg La. BR5: Pet W 5G **161**
Tent St. E1 . . . . .4H **85**
Tenzing Ct. E14 . . . . .5D **86**
(off Hillary M.)
Tequila Wharf E14 . . . . .6A **86**
Tera 40 UB6: G'frd 7G **59**
Terborch Way SE22 . . . . .5E **120**
Teredo St. SE16 . . . . .3K **103**
Terence Ct. DA17: Belv 6F **109**
(off Nuxley Rd.)
Terence McMillan Stadium 4A **88**
Terence Messenger Twr. E10 . . . . .2D **68**
(off Alpine Rd.)
Teresa M. E17 .4C **50**
Teresa Wlk. N10 . . . . .5F **47**
Terling Cl. E11 .3H **69**
Terling Ho. W10 . . . . .5E **80**
(off Sutton Way)
Terling Rd. RM8: Dag 2G **73**
Terling Wlk. N1 . . . . .1C **84**
(off Popham St.)
TERMINAL 4 RDBT. 6E **110**
TERMINAL 5 RDBT. 5C **174**
Terminal Ho. HA7: Stan 5J **27**
Terminus Pl. SW1 . . . . .2K **17** (3F **101**)
Terrace, The E2 . . . . .3J **85**
(off Old Ford Rd.)
E4 . . . . .3B **36**
(off Newgate St.)
EC4 . . . . .1K **13**
IG8: Wfd G 6D **36**
N3 . . . . .2H **45**
NW6 . . . . .1J **81**
SE8 . . . . .4B **104**
(off Longshore)
SE23 . . . . .7A **122**
SW13 . . . . .2A **116**
Terrace Apartments N5 . . . . .5A **66**
Terrace Gdns. SW13 . . . . .2B **116**
Terrace Hill CRO: C'don 3B **168**
(off Hanover St.)
Terrace La. TW10: Rich 6E **114**
Terrace Rd. E9 .7J **67**
E13 . . . . .2J **87**
KT12: Walt T 7J **147**
Terraces, The E2 . . . . .2G **85**
(off Garner St.)
NW8 . . . . .2B **82**
(off Queen's Ter.)
Terrace Wlk. RM9: Dag 5E **72**
SW11 . . . . .7H **17** (7D **100**)
Terrano Ho. TW9: Kew 7H **97**
Terrapin Rd. SW17 . . . . .3F **137**
Terretts Pl. N1 .7B **66**
(off Upper St.)
Terrick Rd. N22 . . . . .1J **47**
Terrick St. W12 . . . . .6D **80**
Terrilands HA5: Pinn 3D **40**
Territorial Ho. SE11 . . . . .4K **19**
Terront Rd. N15 . . . . .4C **48**
Terry Spinks Pl. E16 . . . . .5G **87**
(off Barking Rd.)
Tersha St. TW9: Rich 4F **115**

Tesla Ct. W3 . . . . .2A **98**
Tessa Sanderson Pl. SW8 . . . . .3F **119**
(off Daley Thompson Way)
Tessa Sanderson Way UB6: G'frd 5H **59**
Testerton Rd. W11 . . . . .7F **81**
(off Hurstway Wlk.)
Testerton Wlk. W11 . . . . .7F **81**
Testwood Ct. W7 . . . . .7J **77**
Tetbury Pl. N1 .1B **84**
Tetcott Rd. SW10 . . . . .7A **100**
(not continuous)
Tetherdown N10 . . . . .3E **46**
Tetty Way BR1: Brom 2J **159**
Tevatree Ho. SE1 . . . . .5G **103**
(off Old Kent Rd.)
Teversham La. SW8 . . . . .1J **119**
Teviot Cl. DA16: Well 1B **126**
Teviot Est. E14 . . . . .5D **86**
Teviot St. E14 .5E **86**
Tewkesbury Av. HA5: Pinn 5C **40**
SE23 . . . . .1H **139**
Tewkesbury Cl. EN4: E Barn 4G **21**
N15 . . . . .6D **48**
Tewkesbury Gdns. NW9 . . . . .3H **43**
Tewkesbury Rd. N15 . . . . .6D **48**
SM5: Cars 1B **166**
W13 . . . . .1A **96**
Tewkesbury Ter. N11 . . . . .6B **32**
Tewson Rd. SE18 . . . . .5J **107**
Texryte Ho. N1 .1D **84**
(off Southgate Rd.)
Textile Ho. E1 .5K **85**
(off Duckett St.)
Teynham Av. EN1: Enf 6J **23**
Teynham Ct. BR3: Beck 3D **158**
Teynham Grn. BR2: Brom 5J **159**
Teynton Ter. N17 . . . . .1C **48**
Thackeray Av. N17 . . . . .2G **49**
Thackeray Cl. SW19 . . . . .7F **135**
TW7: Isle 2A **114**
UB8: Hil 6D **74**
Thackeray Ct. NW6 . . . . .7A **64**
(off Fairfax Rd.)
SW3 . . . . .5E **16**
(off Elystan Pl.)
W5 . . . . .6F **79**
(off Hanger Va. La.)
W14 . . . . .3G **99**
(off Blythe Rd.)
Thackeray Dr. RM6: Chad H 7A **54**
Thackeray Ho. WC1 . . . . .3E **6**
Thackeray Lodge TW14: Bedf 6F **111**
Thackeray M. E8 . . . . .6G **67**
Thackeray Rd. E6 . . . . .2B **88**
SW8 . . . . .2F **119**
Thackeray St. W8 . . . . .3K **99**
Thackery Ct. EC1 . . . . .5A **8**
(off Turnmill St.)
Thackrah Cl. N2 . . . . .2A **46**
(off Simms Gdns.)
Thakeham Cl. SE26 . . . . .4H **139**
Thalia Cl. SE10 . . . . .6F **105**
Thalia Ct. E8 . . . . .7F **67**
(off Albion Dr.)
Thame Rd. SE16 . . . . .2K **103**
Thames Av. KT4: Wor Pk 1E **164**
RM9: Dag, Rain 4H **91**
SW10 . . . . .1A **118**
UB6: G'frd 2K **77**
Thames Bank SW14 . . . . .2J **115**
Thamesbank Pl. SE28 . . . . .6C **90**
Thames Barrier 2B **106**
Thames Barrier Ind. Area
SE18 . . . . .3B **106**
(off Faraday Way)
Thames Barrier Pk. 2A **106**
Thames Barrier Vis. Cen. 3B **106**
Thamesbrook SW3 . . . . .6C **16**
Thames Circ. E14 . . . . .4C **104**
Thames Cl. TW12: Hamp 2F **149**
Thames Cotts. KT7: T Ditt 6B **150**

Thames Ct. KT8: W Mole 2F **149**
NW6 . . . . .2H **81**
(off Albert Rd.)
SE15 . . . . .7F **103**
(off Daniel Gdns.)
W7 . . . . .6J **77**
(off Hanway Rd.)
Thames Cres. W4 . . . . .7A **98**
THAMES DITTON 6A **150**
Thames Dr. HA4: Ruis 6E **38**
Thames Exchange Bldg. EC4 . . . . .3D **14**
Thames Eyot TW1: Twick 1A **132**
Thamesfield Ct. TW17: Shep 7E **146**
Thamesfield M. TW17: Shep 7E **146**
Thamesgate Cl. TW10: Ham 4B **132**
Thames Gateway RM9: Dag 2F **91**
RM13: Rain 2F **91**
Thames Gateway Pk. RM9: Dag 3F **91**
Thames Haven KT6: Surb 5D **150**
Thames Hgts. SE1 . . . . .6J **15**
(off Gainsford St.)
Thameshill Av. RM5: Col R 2J **55**
Thames Ho. EC4 . . . . .2D **14**
(off Queen St. Pl.)
KT1: King T 4D **150**
(off Surbiton Rd.)
SW1 . . . . .4J **101**
(off Millbank)
Thameside KT8: W Mole 3F **149**
TW11: Tedd 7D **132**
Thameside Cen. TW8: Bford 6F **97**
Thameside Ind. Est. E16 . . . . .2B **106**
Thameside Pl. KT1: Hamp W 1D **150**
Thameside Wlk. SE28 . . . . .6A **90**
Thames Innovation Cen.
DA18: Erith 2F **109**
Thames Lock KT12: Walt T 3A **148**
THAMESMEAD 1B **108**
Thamesmead KT12: Walt T 6J **147**
THAMESMEAD CENTRAL 1A **108**
THAMESMEAD EAST 2F **109**
THAMESMEAD NORTH 6D **90**
Thames Mdw. KT8: W Mole 2E **148**
TW17: Shep 7F **147**
THAMESMEAD SOUTH 2D **108**
THAMESMEAD SOUTH WEST 2K **107**
THAMESMEAD WEST 3G **107**
Thamesmere Dr. SE28 . . . . .7A **90**
Thamesmere Leisure Cen. 7A **90**
Thames Path SE7 . . . . .3J **105**
SE10 . . . . .3J **105**
Thames Pl. SW15 . . . . .3F **117**
Thames Point SW6 . . . . .2A **118**
Thamespoint TW11: Tedd 7D **132**
Thames Quay E14 . . . . .2D **104**
SW10 . . . . .1A **118**
(off Chelsea Harbour)
Thames Reach KT1: Hamp W 1D **150**
SE28 . . . . .2J **107**
W6 . . . . .6E **98**
(off Rainville Rd.)
Thames Rd. E16 . . . . .1B **106**
IG11: Bark 3K **89**
W4 . . . . .6G **97**
Thames Rd. Ind. Est. E16 . . . . .1B **106**
Thames Side KT1: King T 1D **150**
KT7: T Ditt 6B **150**
Thames St. KT1: King T 2D **150**
KT12: Walt T 7H **147**
SE10 . . . . .6D **104**
TW12: Hamp 1F **149**
TW16: Sun 4J **147**
Thames Tunnel Mills SE16 . . . . .2J **103**
Thamesvale Cl. TW3: Houn 3E **112**
Thames Vw. IG1: Ilf 2G **71**
(off Axon Pl.)
Thamesview Bus. Cen. RM13: Rain 5K **91**
Thamesview Golf Course 6E **90**
Thamesview Ho's. KT12: Walt T 6J **147**
Thames Vw. Lodge IG11: Bark 3J **89**
Thames Village SE16 . . . . .1J **115**

Thames Wlk. KT12: Walt T 7J **147**
(off Manor Rd.)
SW11 . . . . .7C **100**
Thames Wharf Studios W6 . . . . .6E **98**
(off Rainville Rd.)
Thanescroft Gdns. CRO: C'don 3E **168**
Thanet Ct. W3 .6G **79**
Thanet Dr. BR2: Kes 3B **172**
Thanet Ho. CRO: C'don 4C **168**
(off Coombe Rd.)
WC1 . . . . .2E **6**
(off Thanet St.)
Thanet Lodge NW2 . . . . .6G **63**
(off Mapesbury Rd.)
Thanet Pl. CRO: C'don 4C **168**
Thanet Rd. DA5: Bexl 7G **127**
Thanet St. WC1 . . . . .2E **6** (3J **83**)
Thanet Wharf SE8 . . . . .6D **104**
(off Copperas St.)
Thane Vs. N7 . . . . .3K **65**
Thane Works N7 . . . . .3K **65**
Thanington Ct. SE9 . . . . .6J **125**
Thant Cl. E10 . . . . .3D **68**
Tharp Rd. SM6: Wall 5H **167**
Thatcham Ct. N20 . . . . .7F **21**
Thatcham Gdns. N20 . . . . .7F **21**
Thatcher Cl. UB7: W Dray 2A **92**
Thatches Gro. RM6: Chad H 4E **54**
Thavie's Inn EC4 . . . . .7K **7** (6A **84**)
Thaxted Ct. N1 .1F **9**
(off Murray Gro.)
Thaxted Ho. RM10: Dag 7H **73**
SE16 . . . . .4J **103**
(off Abbeyfield Est.)
Thaxted Pl. SW20 . . . . .7F **135**
Thaxted Rd. IG9: Buck H 1H **37**
SE9 . . . . .3G **143**
Thaxton Pl. E4 .1A **36**
Thaxton Rd. W14 . . . . .6H **99**
Thayers Farm Rd. BR3: Beck 1A **158**
Thayer St. W1 . . . . .6H **5** (6E **82**)
The . . . .
Names prefixed with 'The' for example
'The Acacias' are indexed under the
main name such as 'Acacias, The'
Theatre, The 5C **68**
Theatre Bldg. E3 . . . . .3C **86**
(off Paton Cl.)
Theatre Pl. SE8 . . . . .7C **104**
(off Speedwell Ct.)
Theatre-Rites 2B **102**
(off Blackfriars Rd.)
Theatre Royal
Drury Lane 2G **13**
(off Catherine St.)
Haymarket 3D **12**
(off Haymarket)
Stratford 7F **69**
Theatre Sq. E15 . . . . .6F **69**
Theatre St. SW11 . . . . .3D **118**
Theatre Vw. Apartments SE1 . . . . .6K **13**
(off Short St.)
Theatro Technis 1G **83**
(off Crowndale Rd.)
Theatro Twr. SE8 . . . . .6C **104**
Theberton St. N1 . . . . .1A **84**
Theed St. SE1 . . . . .5K **13** (1A **102**)
Thelbridge Ho. E3 . . . . .3D **86**
(off Bruce Rd.)
Thelma Gdns. SE3 . . . . .1B **124**
Thelma Gro. TW11: Tedd 6A **132**
Theobald Cres. HA3: Hrw W 1G **41**
Theobald Rd. CRO: C'don 2B **168**
E17 . . . . .7B **50**
Theobalds Av. N12 . . . . .4F **31**
Theobalds Ct. N4 . . . . .3C **66**
Theobald's Rd. WC1 . . . . .5G **7** (5K **83**)
Theobald St. SE1 . . . . .3D **102**
Theodora Way HA5: Eastc 3H **39**
Theodor Ct. NW9 . . . . .2K **43**

Theodore Ct. SE13 6F **123**
Theodore Rd. SE13 6F **123**
Therapia La. CR0: Bedd 7H **155**
CR0: C'don 6J **155**
Therapia Rd. SE22 6J **121**
Theresa Rd. W6 4C **98**
Therfield Ct. N4 2C **66**
Thermopylae Ga. E14 4D **104**
Theseus Wlk. N1 1B **8**
Thesiger Rd. SE20 7K **139**
Thessaly Ho. *SW8* *7G* ***101***
(off Thessaly Rd.)
Thessaly Rd. SW8 7G **101**
(not continuous)
Thesus Ho. *E14* *6E* ***86***
(off Blair St.)
Thetford Cl. N13 6G **33**
Thetford Gdns. RM9: Dag 7E **72**
Thetford Ho. *SE1* *7J* ***15***
(off St Saviour's Est.)
Thetford Rd. KT3: N Mald 6K **151**
RM9: Dag 7D **72**
TW15: Ashf 4A **128**
Thetis Ter. TW9: Kew 6G **97**
Theven St. E1 4J **85**
Theydon Gro. IG8: Wfd G 6F **37**
Theydon Rd. E5 2J **67**
Theydon St. E17 7B **50**
Thicket, The UB7: Yiew 6A **74**
Thicket Cres. SM1: Sutt 4A **166**
Thicket Gro. RM9: Dag 6C **72**
SE20 7G **139**
Thicket Rd. SE20 7G **139**
SM1: Sutt 4A **166**
Third Av. E12 4C **70**
E13 3J **87**
E17 5C **50**
EN1: Enf 5A **24**
HA9: Wemb 2D **60**
RM6: Chad H 6C **54**
RM10: Dag 1H **91**
UB3: Hayes 1H **93**
W3 1B **98**
W10 3G **81**
Third Cl. KT8: W Mole 4G **149**
Third Cross Rd. TW2: Twick 2H **131**
Third Way HA9: Wemb 4H **61**
Thirleby Rd. HA8: Edg 1K **43**
NW7 5B **30**
SW1 2B **18** (3G **101**)
Thirlestane Ct. N10 2E **46**
Thirlmere *NW1* *1K* ***5***
(off Cumberland Mkt.)
Thirlmere Av. UB6: G'frd 3C **78**
Thirlmere Gdns. HA9: Wemb 1C **60**
Thirlmere Ho. *N16* *4D* ***66***
(off Howard Rd.)
TW7: Isle 5K **113**
Thirlmere Ri. BR1: Brom 6H **141**
Thirlmere Rd. DA7: Bex 1J **127**
N10 1F **47**
SW16 4H **137**
Thirsk Cl. UB5: N'olt 6E **58**
Thirsk Rd. CR4: Mitc 7E **136**
SE25 4D **156**
SW11 3E **118**
Thirza Ho. *E1* *6J* ***85***
(off Devonport St.)
Thistlebrook SE2 3C **108**
Thistlebrook Ind. Est. SE2 3C **108**
Thistle Ct. SE12 2J **141**
Thistlecroft Gdns. HA7: Stan 1D **42**
Thistledene KT7: T Ditt 6J **149**
Thistledene Av. HA2: Harr 3C **58**
Thistlefield Cl. DA5: Bexl 1D **144**
Thistle Gro. SW10 6A **16** (5A **100**)
Thistle Ho. *E14* *6E* ***86***
(off Dee St.)
Thistlemead BR7: Chst 2F **161**
Thistlewaite Rd. E5 3H **67**
Thistlewood Cl. N7 2K **65**
Thistleworth Cl. TW7: Isle 7H **95**
Thistleworth Marina *TW7: Isle* *4B* ***114***
(off Railshead Rd.)
Thistley Cl. N12 6H **31**
Thistley Ct. SE8 6D **104**
Thomas A Beckett Cl. HA0: Wemb 4K **59**
Thomas Baines Rd. SW11 3B **118**
Thomas Burt Ho. *E2* *3H* ***85***
(off Canrobert St.)
Thomas Ct. IG6: Ilf 4G **53**
Thomas Cribb M. E6 6E **88**
Thomas Darby Ct. *W11* *6G* ***81***
(off Lancaster Rd.)
Thomas Dean Rd. SE26 4B **140**
Thomas Dinwiddy Rd. SE12 2K **141**
Thomas Doyle St. SE1 7A **14** (3B **102**)
Thomas Dr. UB8: Uxb 6A **56**
Thomas England Ho. *RM7: Rom* *6K* ***55***
(off Waterloo Gdns.)
Thomas Frye Ct. *E15* *2D* ***86***
(off High St.)
Thomas Fyre Dr. E3 2C **86**
Thomas Hardy Ho. N22 7E **32**
Thomas Hardy M. SW16 5G **137**
Thomas Hewlett Ho. HA1: Harr 4J **59**
Thomas Hollywood Ho. *E2* *2J* ***85***
(off Approach Rd.)
Thomas Ho. SM2: Sutt 7K **165**
Thomas Jacomb Pl. E17 4B **50**
Thomas Joseph Ho. *SE4* *5K* ***121***
(off St Norbert Rd.)
Thomas La. SE6 7C **122**
Thomas Lodge E17 5D **50**
Thomas More Highwalk *EC2* *6C* ***8***
(off Aldersgate St.)
Thomas More Ho. EC2 6C **8**
HA4: Ruis 1G **57**
Thomas More Sq. E1 7G **85**
Thomas More St. E1 7G **85**
Thomas More Way N2 3A **46**
Thomas Neal's Cen. WC2 1E **12** (6J **83**)
Thomas Pl. W8 3K **99**
Thomas Rd. E14 6B **86**
Thomas Rd. Ind. Est. E14 5C **86**
(not continuous)
Thomas Spencer Hall of Residence
SE18 *4E* ***106***
(off Grand Depot Rd.)
Thomas St. SE18 4F **107**
Thomas Tallis Sports Cen. 3K **123**
Thomas Twr. *E8* *6F* ***67***
(off Dalston Sq.)
Thomas Turner Path *CR0: C'don* *2C* ***168***
(off George St.)
Thomas Wall Cl. SM1: Sutt 5K **165**
Thomas Watson Cott. Homes
EN5: Barn *4B* ***20***
(off Leecroft Rd.)
Thompson Av. TW9: Rich 3G **115**
Thompson Cl. IG1: Ilf 2G **71**
SM3: Sutt 1J **165**
Thompson Ho. *SE14* *6K* ***103***
(off John Williams Cl.)
W10 *4G* ***81***
(off Wornington Rd.)
Thompson Rd. RM9: Dag 3F **73**
SE22 6F **121**
TW3: Houn 4F **113**
UB10: Uxb 7A **56**
Thompson's Av. SE5 7C **102**
Thomson Cres. CR0: C'don 1A **168**
Thomson Ho. *E14* *6C* ***86***
(off Saracen St.)
SE17 *4E* ***102***
(off Tatum St.)
SW1 6D **18**
UB1: S'hall *7C* ***76***
(off The Broadway)
Thomson Rd. HA3: W'stone 3J **41**
Thorburn Ho. *SW1* *7F* ***11***
(off Kinnerton St.)
Thorburn Sq. SE1 4G **103**
Thorburn Way SW19 1B **154**
Thoresby St. N1 1D **8** (3C **84**)
Thorkhill Gdns. KT7: T Ditt 1A **162**
Thorkhill Rd. KT7: T Ditt 1A **162**
Thornaby Gdns. N18 6B **34**
Thornaby Ho. *E2* *3H* ***85***
(off Canrobert St.)
Thorn Apartments *E3* *5C* ***86***
(off St Paul's Way)
Thorn Av. WD23: B Hea 1B **26**
Thornbill Ho. *SE15* *7G* ***103***
(off Bird in Bush Rd.)
Thornbury *NW4* *4D* ***44***
(off Prince of Wales Cl.)
Thornbury Av. TW7: Isle 7H **95**
Thornbury Cl. N16 5E **66**
NW7 7A **30**
Thornbury Ct. *CR2: S Croy* *5D* ***168***
(off Blunt Rd.)
TW7: Isle 7J **95**
W11 *7J* ***81***
(off Chepstow Vs.)
Thornbury Lodge EN2: Enf 3G **23**
Thornbury Rd. SW2 6J **119**
TW7: Isle 7H **95**
Thornbury Sq. N6 1G **65**
Thornbury Way E17 1B **50**
Thornby Rd. E5 3J **67**
Thorncliffe Rd. SW2 6J **119**
UB2: S'hall 5D **94**
Thorn Cl. BR2: Brom 6E **160**
UB5: N'olt 3D **76**
Thorncombe Rd. SE22 5E **120**
Thorncroft Rd. SM1: Sutt 5K **165**
Thorncroft St. SW8 7J **101**
Thorndean St. SW18 2A **136**
Thorndene SE28 7B **90**
Thorndene Av. N11 1K **31**
Thorndike Av. UB5: N'olt 1B **76**
Thorndike Cl. SW10 7A **100**
Thorndike Ho. *SW1* *5C* ***18***
(off Vauxhall Bri. Rd.)
Thorndike Rd. N1 6D **66**
Thorndike St. SW1 4C **18** (4H **101**)
Thorndon Cl. BR5: St P 2K **161**
Thorndon Gdns. KT19: Ewe 5A **164**
Thorndon Rd. BR5: St P 2K **161**
Thorne Cl. DA8: Erith 6H **109**
E11 4F **69**
E16 6J **87**
KT10: Clay 7A **162**
TW15: Ashf 7E **128**
Thorne Ho. *E2* *3J* ***85***
(off Roman Rd.)
E14 *3E* ***104***
(off Launch St.)
Thorneloe Gdns. CR0: Wadd 5A **168**
Thorne Pas. SW13 2A **116**
Thorne Rd. SW8 7J **101**
Thornes Cl. BR3: Beck 3E **158**
Thorne St. SW13 3A **116**
Thornet Wood Rd. BR1: Brom 3E **160**
Thornewill Ho. *E1* *7J* ***85***
(off Cable St.)
Thorney Ct. *W8* *2A* ***100***
(off Palace Ga.)
Thorney Cres. SW11 7B **100**
Thorneycroft Cl. KT12: Walt T 6A **148**
Thorney Hedge Rd. W4 4H **97**
Thorney St. SW1 3E **18** (4J **101**)
Thornfield Av. NW7 1G **45**
Thornfield Ct. NW7 7B **30**
Thornfield Ho. *E14* *7C* ***86***
(off Rosefield Gdns.)
Thornfield Pde. *NW7* *7B* ***30***
(off Holders Hill Rd.)
Thornfield Rd. W12 2D **98**
(not continuous)
Thornford Rd. SE13 5E **122**
Thorngate Rd. W9 4J **81**
Thorngrove Rd. E13 1K **87**
Thornham Gro. E15 5F **69**
Thornham Ind. Est. E15 5F **69**
Thornham St. SE10 6D **104**
Thornhaugh M. WC1 4D **6** (4H **83**)
Thornhaugh St. WC1 4D **6** (4H **83**)
Thornhill Av. KT6: Surb 2E **162**
SE18 7J **107**
Thornhill Bri. *N1* *2K* ***83***
(off Caledonian Rd.)
Thornhill Bri. Wharf N1 1K **83**
Thornhill Cres. N1 7K **65**
Thornhill Gdns. E10 2D **68**
IG11: Bark 7J **71**
Thornhill Gro. N1 7K **65**
Thornhill Ho. *W4* *5A* ***98***
(off Wood St.)
Thornhill Ho's. *N1* *7A* ***66***
(off Thornhill Rd.)
Thornhill M. SW15 4H **117**
Thornhill Rd. CR0: C'don 7C **156**
E10 2D **68**
KT6: Surb 2E **162**
N1 7A **66**
UB10: Ick 4B **56**
Thornhill Sq. N1 7K **65**
Thornhill Way TW17: Shep 5C **146**
Thornicroft Ho. *SW9* *2K* ***119***
(off Stockwell Rd.)
Thornlaw Rd. SE27 4A **138**
Thornley Cl. N17 7B **34**
Thornley Dr. HA2: Harr 2F **59**
Thornley Pl. SE10 5G **105**
Thornsbeach Rd. SE6 1E **140**
Thornsett Pl. SE20 2H **157**
Thornsett Rd. SE20 2H **157**
SW18 1K **135**
Thornsett Ter. *SE20* *2H* ***157***
(off Croydon Rd.)
Thorn Ter. SE15 3J **121**
Thornton Av. CR0: C'don 6K **155**
SW2 1H **137**
UB7: W Dray 3B **92**
W4 4A **98**
Thornton Cl. UB7: W Dray 3B **92**
Thornton Dene BR3: Beck 2C **158**
Thornton Gdns. SW12 1H **137**
THORNTON HEATH 4C **156**
Thornton Heath Leisure Cen. 4C **156**
THORNTON HEATH POND 5A **156**
Thornton Hill SW19 7G **135**
Thornton Ho. *SE17* *4E* ***102***
(off Townsend St.)
Thornton Pl. W1 5F **5** (5D **82**)
Thornton Rd. BR1: Brom 5J **141**
CR0: C'don 7K **155**
CR7: Thor H 7K **155**
DA17: Belv 4H **109**
E11 2F **69**
EN5: Barn 3B **20**
IG1: Ilf 4F **71**
N18 3D **34**
SM5: Cars 1B **166**
SW12 7H **119**
SW14 4K **115**
SW19 6F **135**
Thornton Rd. E. SW19 6F **135**
Thornton Rd. Ind. Est. CR0: C'don 6K **155**
Thornton Row CR7: Thor H 5A **156**
Thornton's Farm Av. RM7: Rush G 1J **73**
Thornton St. E20 7D **68**
SW9 2A **120**
Thornton Way NW11 5K **45**
Thorntree Ct. W5 5E **78**
Thorntree Rd. SE7 5B **106**
Thornville Gro. CR4: Mitc 2B **154**
Thornville St. SE8 1C **122**
Thornwell Ct. *W7* *2J* ***95***
(off Lwr. Boston Rd.)
Thornwood Cl. E18 2K **51**
Thornwood Gdns. W8 2J **99**

Thornwood Ho. IG9: Buck H 1H **37**
Thornwood Lodge *W8* *2J 99*
(off Thornwood Gdns.)
Thornwood Rd. SE13 ....5G **123**
Thornycroft Ho. *W4* *5A 98*
(off Fraser St.)
Thorogood Gdns. E15 ....5G **69**
Thorogood Way RM13: Rain 1K **91**
Thorold Ho. *SE1* *6C 14*
(off Pepper St.)
Thorold Rd. IG1: Ilf 2F **71**
N22 ....7D **32**
Thorparch Rd. SW8 ....1H **119**
Thorpebank Rd. W12 ....1C **98**
Thorpe Cl. BR6: Orp 2J **173**
SE26 ....4K **139**
W10 ....6G **81**
Thorpe Ct. EN2: Enf 3G **23**
Thorpe Cres. E17 ....2B **50**
Thorpedale Gdns. IG2: Ilf 4E **52**
IG6: Ilf 4E **52**
Thorpedale Rd. N4 ....2J **65**
Thorpe Hall Rd. E17 ....1E **50**
Thorpe Ho. *N1* *1K 83*
(off Barnsbury Est.)
Thorpe Rd. E6 ....1D **88**
E7 ....4H **69**
E17 ....2E **50**
IG11: Bark 7H **71**
KT2: King T 7E **132**
N15 ....6E **48**
Thorpewood Av. SE26 ....2H **139**
Thorpland Av. UB10: Ick 3E **56**
Thorsden Way SE19 ....5E **138**
Thorverton Rd. NW2 ....3G **63**
Thoydon Rd. E3 ....2A **86**
Thrale Rd. SW16 ....4G **137**
Thrale St. SE1 ....5D **14** (1C **102**)
Thrasher Cl. E8 ....1F **85**
Thrawl St. E1 ....6K **9** (5F **85**)
Thrayle Ho. *SW9* *3K 119*
(off Benedict Rd.)
Threadgold Ho. *N1* *6D 66*
(off Dovercourt Est.)
Threadneedle St. EC2 ....1F **15** (6D **84**)
Threadneedle Wlk. EC2 ....1F **15**
Three Barrels Wlk. *EC4* *3D 14*
(off Queenhithe)
Three Bridges Bus. Cen. UB2: S'hall ...2G **95**
Three Bridges Path *KT1: King T* *3E 150*
(off Bellvue Rd.)
Three Colt Cnr. E2 ....3K **9**
Three Colts La. E2 ....4H **85**
Three Colt St. E14 ....6B **86**
Three Corners DA7: Bex 2H **127**
Three Cranes Wlk. EC4 ....3D **14**
Three Cups Yd. WC1 ....6H **7**
Three Kings Yd. W1 ....2J **11** (7F **83**)
Three Meadows M. HA3: Hrw W 1K **41**
Three Mill La. E3 ....3E **86**
Three Mills Studios E3 ....3E **86**
Three Nun Ct. *EC2* *7D 8*
(off Aldermanbury)
Three Oak La. SE1 ....6J **15** (2F **103**)
Three Oaks Cl. UB10: Ick 3B **56**
Three Quays EC3 ....3H **15**
Three Quays Wlk. EC3 ......3H **15** (7E **84**)
Threshers Pl. W11 ....7G **81**
Thriffwood SE26 ....3J **139**
Thrigby Rd. KT9: Chess 6F **163**
Thring Ho. *SW9* *2K 119*
(off Stockwell Rd.)
Throckmorton Rd. E16 ....6K **87**
Throgmorton Av. EC2 ....7F **9** (6D **84**)
(not continuous)
Throgmorton St. EC2 ....7F **9** (6D **84**)
Throwley Cl. SE2 ....3C **108**
(not continuous)
Throwley Rd. SM1: Sutt 5K **165**
Throwley Way SM1: Sutt 4K **165**
Thrupp Cl. CR4: Mitc 2F **155**
Thrush Grn. HA2: Harr 4E **40**
Thrush St. SE17 ....5C **102**
Thurbarn Rd. SE6 ....5D **140**
Thurland Ho. *SE16* *4H 103*
(off Camilla Rd.)
Thurland Rd. SE16 ....3G **103**
Thurlby Cl. HA1: Harr 6A **42**
IG8: Wfd G 5J **37**
Thurlby Cft. *NW4* *3E 44*
(off Mulberry Cl.)
Thurlby Rd. HA0: Wemb 6D **60**
SE27 ....4A **138**
Thurleigh Av. SW12 ....6E **118**
Thurleigh Ct. SW12 ....6E **118**
Thurleigh Rd. SW12 ....7D **118**
Thurleston Av. SM4: Mord 5G **153**
Thurlestone Av. IG3: Bark, Ilf 4K **71**
N12 ....6J **31**
Thurlestone Cl. TW17: Shep 6E **146**
Thurlestone Ct. *UB1: S'hall* *6F 77*
(off Howard Rd.)
Thurlestone Pde. *TW17: Shep* *6E 146*
(off High St.)
Thurlestone Rd. SE27 ....3A **138**
Thurloe Cl. SW7 ....3C **16** (4C **100**)
Thurloe Ct. *SW3* *4C 16*
(off Fulham Rd.)
Thurloe Pl. SW7 ....3B **16** (4B **100**)
Thurloe Pl. M. SW7 ....3B **16**
Thurloe Sq. SW7 ....3C **16** (4C **100**)
Thurloe St. SW7 ....3B **16** (4B **100**)
Thurlow Cl. E4 ....6K **35**
Thurlow Gdns. HA0: Wemb 5D **60**
Thurlow Hill SE21 ....1C **138**
Thurlow Ho. SW16 ....3J **137**
Thurlow Pk. Rd. SE21 ....2B **138**
Thurlow Rd. NW3 ....5B **64**
W7 ....2A **96**
Thurlow St. SE17 ....5D **102**
(not continuous)
Thurlow Ter. NW5 ....5E **64**
Thurlow Wlk. SE17 ....5E **102**
(not continuous)
Thurlstone Rd. HA4: Ruis 3J **57**
Thurnby Ct. TW2: Twick 3J **131**
Thurnscoe *NW1* *1G 83*
(off Pratt St.)
Thursland Rd. DA14: Sidc 5E **144**
Thursley Cres. CR0: New Ad 7E **170**
Thursley Gdns. SW19 ....2F **135**
Thursley Ho. *SW2* *7K 119*
(off Holmewood Gdns.)
Thursley Rd. SE9 ....3D **142**
Thurso Ho. NW6 ....2K **81**
Thurso St. SW17 ....4B **136**
Thurstan Dwellings *WC2* *7F 7*
(off Newton St.)
Thurstan Rd. SW20 ....7D **134**
Thurstan St. SW6 ....1A **118**
Thurston Ho. BR3: Beck 6D **140**
N1 ....*1K 83*
(off Barnsbury Est.)
Thurston Rd. SE13 ....2D **122**
UB1: S'hall 6D **76**
Thurtle Rd. E2 ....1F **85**
Thwaite Cl. DA8: Erith 6J **109**
Thyer Cl. BR6: Farnb 4G **173**
Thyme Cl. SE3 ....3A **124**
Thyme Ct. NW7 ....1G **45**
Thyme Wlk. E5 ....4K **67**
Thyra Gro. N12 ....6E **30**
Tibbatt's Rd. E3 ....4D **86**
Tibbenham Pl. SE6 ....2C **140**
Tibbenham Wlk. E13 ....2H **87**
Tibberton Sq. N1 ....1C **84**
Tibbet's Cl. SW19 ....1F **135**
TIBBET'S CORNER 7F **117**
Tibbet's Ride SW15 ....7F **117**
Tiber Cl. E3 ....1C **86**
Tiber Gdns. N1 ....1J **83**
Ticehurst Cl. BR5: St P 7A **144**
Ticehurst Rd. SE23 ....2A **140**
Tickford Cl. SE2 ....2C **108**
Tickford Ho. NW8 ....2C **4** (3C **82**)
Tidal Basin Rd. E16 ....7H **87**
(not continuous)
Tidbury Ct. *SW8* *7G 101*
(off Stewart's Rd.)
Tide Cl. CR4: Mitc 1E **154**
Tideham Ho. SE28 ....1H **107**
Tidelea Twr. SE28 ....2G **107**
Tidemill Way SE8 ....7C **104**
Tidenham Gdns.
CR0: C'don 3E **168**
Tideside Ct. SE18 ....3C **106**
Tideslea Path SE28 ....1H **107**
Tideswell Rd. CR0: C'don 3C **170**
SW15 ....4E **116**
Tideway Cl. TW10: Ham 4B **132**
Tideway Ct. SE16 ....1K **103**
Tideway Ho. *E14* *2C 104*
(off Strafford St.)
Tideway Ind. Est. SW8 ....6G **101**
Tideway Wlk. SW8 ....7B **18** (6G **101**)
Tidey St. E3 ....5C **86**
Tidford Rd. DA16: Well 2K **125**
Tidlock Ho. SE28 ....2H **107**
Tidworth Rd. E3 ....4C **86**
Tiepigs La. BR2: Hayes 2G **171**
BR4: W W'ck 2G **171**
Tierney Ct. CR0: C'don 2E **168**
Tierney Rd. SW2 ....1J **137**
Tiffany Hgts. SW18 ....7J **117**
Tiffin Girls Community Sports Cen.
.........................6E **132**
Tiffin Sports Cen. 2F **151**
Tiger Cl. IG11: Bark 2B **90**
Tiger Ho. *WC1* *2D 6*
(off Burton St.)
Tiger La. BR2: Brom 4K **159**
Tiger Way E5 ....4H **67**
Tiggap Ho. SE10 ....4G **105**
Tigris Cl. N9 ....2D **34**
Tilbrook Rd. SE3 ....3A **124**
Tilbury Cl. HA5: Hat E 1D **40**
SE15 ....7F **103**
Tilbury Ho. *SE14* *6K 103*
(off Myers La.)
Tilbury Rd. E6 ....2D **88**
E10 ....7E **50**
Tildesley Rd. SW15 ....6E **116**
Tile Farm Rd. BR6: Orp 3H **173**
Tile Ho. *N1* *1J 83*
(off Beaconsfield St.)
Tilehurst *NW1* *2K 5*
(off Lit. Albany St.)
Tilehurst Point SE2 ....2C **108**
(not continuous)
Tilehurst Rd. SM3: Cheam 5G **165**
SW18 ....1B **136**
Tile Kiln La. DA5: Bexl 2J **145**
N6 ....1F **65**
N13 ....5H **33**
UB9: Hare 7D **38**
Tile Kiln Studios N6 ....7G **47**
Tileyard Rd. N7 ....7J **65**
Tilford Av. CR0: New Ad 7E **170**
Tilford Gdns. SW19 ....1F **135**
Tilford Ho. *SW2* *7K 119*
(off Holmewood Gdns.)
Tilia Cl. SM1: Sutt 5H **165**
Tilia Rd. E5 ....4H **67**
Tilia Wlk. SW9 ....4B **120**
Tiller Ho. *N1* *1E 84*
(off Whitmore Est.)
Tiller Leisure Cen. 3C **104**
Tiller Rd. E14 ....3C **104**
Tillett Cl. NW10 ....6J **61**
Tillett Sq. SE16 ....2A **104**
Tillet Way E2 ....3G **85**
Tilley Rd. TW13: Felt 1J **129**
Tillingbourne Gdns. N3 ....3H **45**
Tillingbourne Grn.
BR5: St M Cry 4K **161**, 5K **161**
Tillingbourne Way N3 ....4H **45**
Tillingham Way N12 ....4D **30**
Tilling Rd. NW2 ....1E **62**
Tillings Cl. SE5 ....1C **120**
Tilling Way HA9: Wemb 2D **60**
Tillman St. E1 ....6H **85**
Tilloch St. N1 ....7K **65**
Tillotson Ct. *SW8* *7H 101*
(off Wandsworth Rd.)
Tillotson Rd. HA3: Hrw W 7A **26**
IG1: Ilf 7E **52**
N9 ....2A **34**
Tilney Ct. EC1 ....3D **8** (4C **84**)
IG9: Buck H 2D **36**
Tilney Dr. IG9: Buck H 2D **36**
Tilney Gdns. N1 ....6D **66**
Tilney Rd. RM9: Dag 6F **73**
UB2: S'hall 4A **94**
Tilney St. W1 ....4H **11** (1E **100**)
Tilson Cl. SE5 ....7E **102**
Tilson Gdns. SW2 ....7J **119**
Tilson Ho. SW2 ....7J **119**
Tilson Rd. N17 ....1G **49**
Tilston Bright Sq. SE2 ....3C **108**
Tilston Cl. E11 ....3H **69**
Tiltman Pl. N7 ....3K **65**
Tilton St. SW6 ....6G **99**
Tiltwood, The W3 ....7J **79**
Tilt Yd. App. SE9 ....6D **124**
Timber Cl. BR7: Chst 2E **160**
Timbercroft KT19: Ewe 4A **164**
Timbercroft La. SE18 ....6J **107**
Timberdene NW4 ....2F **45**
Timberdene Av. IG6: Ilf 1G **53**
Timberland Cl. SE15 ....7G **103**
Timberland Rd. E1 ....6H **85**
Timberley Ct. DA14: Sidc 5K **143**
Timber Mill Way SW4 ....3H **119**
Timber Pond Rd. SE16 ....1K **103**
Timbers, The SM3: Cheam 6G **165**
Timberslip Dr. SM6: Wall 7H **167**
Timber St. EC1 ....3C **8** (4C **84**)
Timber Wharf E2 ....1F **85**
Timberwharf Rd. N16 ....6G **49**
Timber Wharves Est. *E14* *4C 104*
(off Copeland Dr.)
Timber Yd., The *N1* *2H 9*
(off Drysdale St.)
Timbrell Pl. SE16 ....1B **104**
Time Sq. E8 ....5F **67**
Times Sq. E1 ....6G **85**
SM1: Sutt 5K **165**
Timmins Apartments E2 ....3K **85**
Timms Cl. BR1: Brom 4D **160**
Timor Ho. *E1* *4A 86*
(off Duckett St.)
Timothy Cl. DA6: Bex 5E **126**
SW4 ....5G **119**
Timothy Ho. *DA18: Erith* *2E 108*
(off Kale Rd.)
Timothy Pl. KT8: W Mole 5D **148**
Timperley Ct. SW19 ....1G **135**
Timsbury Wlk. SW15 ....1C **134**
Tina Ct. SE6 ....7B **122**
Tindal St. SW9 ....1B **120**
Tinderbox All. SW14 ....3K **115**
Tinderbox Ho. *SE8* *7C 104*
(off Octavius St.)
Tinniswood Cl. N5 ....5A **66**
Tinsley Cl. SE25 ....3H **157**
Tinsley Rd. E1 ....5J **85**
Tintagel Ct. *EC1* *3A 8*
(off St John St.)
Tintagel Cres. SE22 ....4F **121**
Tintagel Dr. HA7: Stan 4J **27**
Tintagel Gdns. SE22 ....4F **121**
Tintern Av. NW9 ....3H **43**
Tintern Cl. SW15 ....5G **117**
SW19 ....6A **136**

Tintern Ct. W13 .7A **78**
Tintern Gdns. N14 .7D **22**
Tintern Ho. *NW1* .*1K* **5**
(off Augustus St.)
SW1 .*4J* **17**
(part of Abbots Mnr.)
Tintern Path *NW9* .*6A* **44**
(off Fryent Gro.)
Tintern Rd. N22 .1C **48**
SM5: Cars .1B **166**
Tintern St. SW4 .4J **119**
Tintern Way HA2: Harr .1F **59**
Tinto Rd. E16 .4J **87**
Tinworth Ct. *SE17* .*6B* **102**
(off Royal Rd.)
Tinworth St. SE11 .5F **19** (5J **101**)
Tippett Ct. E6 .2D **88**
Tippetts Cl. EN2: Enf .1H **23**
Tipthorpe Rd. SW11 .3E **118**
Tipton Dr. CR0: C'don .4E **168**
Tiptree *NW1* .*7F* **65**
(off Castlehaven Rd.)
Tiptree Cl. E4 .3K **35**
Tiptree Cres. IG5: Ilf .3E **52**
Tiptree Dr. EN2: Enf .4J **23**
Tiptree Rd. HA4: Ruis .4K **57**
Tirlemont Rd. CR2: S Croy .7C **168**
Tirrell Rd. CR0: C'don .6C **156**
Tisbury Ct. W1 .2C **12**
Tisbury Rd. SW16 .2J **155**
Tisdall Ho. *SE17* .*4D* **102**
(off Barlow St.)
Tisdall Pl. SE17 .4D **102**
Tissington Ct. SE16 .4J **103**
Titan Bus. Est. *SE8* .*7C* **104**
(off Ffinch St.)
Titan Ct. TW8: Bford .5F **97**
Titan Ho. *E20* .*5E* **68**
(off Napa Cl.)
Titanium Point *E2* .*3K* **85**
(Palmer's Rd.)
Titchborne Row W2 .1D **10** (6C **82**)
Titchfield Rd. NW8 .1C **82**
SM5: Cars .1B **166**
Titchfield Wlk. SM5: Cars .7B **154**
Titchwell Rd. SW18 .1B **136**
Tite St. SW3 .6E **16** (5D **100**)
Tithe Barn Cl. KT2: King T .1F **151**
Tithe Barn Way UB5: N'olt .2K **75**
Tithe Cl. KT12: Walt T .6K **147**
NW7 .1C **44**
UB4: Hayes .5H **75**
Tithe Farm Av. HA2: Harr .3E **58**
Tithe Farm Cl. HA2: Harr .3E **58**
Tithe Wlk. NW7 .1C **44**
Titian Av. WD23: B Hea .1D **26**
Titian Hgts. *E20* .*5D* **68**
(off Scarlet Cl.)
Titley Cl. E4 .5H **35**
Titmus Cl. UB8: Hil .6E **74**
Titmuss Av. SE28 .7B **90**
Titmuss St. W12 .2E **98**
Tivendale N8 .3J **47**
Tiverton Av. IG5: Ilf .3E **52**
Tiverton Cl. CR0: C'don .7F **157**
Tiverton Dr. SE9 .1G **143**
Tiverton Ho. EN3: Enf H .3E **24**
Tiverton Rd. HA0: Wemb .2E **78**
HA4: Ruis .3J **57**
HA8: Edg .2F **43**
N15 .6D **48**
N18 .5K **33**
NW10 .1F **81**
TW3: Houn .2G **113**
Tiverton St. SE1 .3C **102**
Tiverton Way KT9: Chess .5D **162**
NW7 .7A **30**
Tivoli Ct. SE16 .1B **104**
Tivoli Gdns. SE18 .4C **106**
(not continuous)
Tivoli M. E14 .6B **86**
Tivoli Rd. N8 .5H **47**
SE27 .5C **138**
TW4: Houn .4C **112**
Tivoli Way E14 .6B **86**
Tizzard Gro. SE3 .4K **123**
Toad La. TW4: Houn .4D **112**
Tobacco Dock E1 .7H **85**
Tobacco Quay E1 .7H **85**
Tobago St. E14 .2C **104**
Tobin Cl. NW3 .7C **64**
Toby Ct. *N9* .*7D* **24**
(off Tramway Av.)
Toby La. E1 .4A **86**
Toby Way KT5: Surb .2H **163**
Todber Ho. *W14* .*3G* **99**
(off Russell Rd.)
Todd Ho. *N2* .*2B* **46**
(off The Grange)
Todds Wlk. N7 .2K **65**
Todhunter Ter. EN5: New Bar .4D **20**
Token Ho. *CR0: C'don* .*3C* **168**
(off Robert St.)
Tokenhouse Yd. EC2 .7E **8** (6D **84**)
Token Yd. SW15 .4G **117**
TOKYNGTON .6H **61**
Tokyngton Av. HA9: Wemb .6G **61**
Toland Sq. SW15 .5C **116**
Tolcairn Ct. DA17: Belv .5G **109**
Tolcarne Dr. HA5: Eastc .2J **39**
Tolchurch *W11* .*6H* **81**
(off Dartmouth Cl.)
Toley Av. HA9: Wemb .7E **42**
Tolhurst Dr. W10 .3G **81**
Tollard Ho. *W14* .*3H* **99**
(off Kensington High St.)
Toll Bar Ct. SM2: Sutt .7K **165**
Tollbridge Cl. W10 .4G **81**
Tollesbury Gdns. IG6: Ilf .3H **53**
Tollet St. E1 .4K **85**
Tollgate Ct. CR2: S Croy .5D **168**
Tollgate Dr. SE21 .2E **138**
UB4: Yead .7B **76**
Tollgate Gdns. *NW6* .*2K* **81**
(off Oxford Rd.)
Tollgate Ho. *NW6* .*2K* **81**
(off Tollgate Gdns.)
Tollgate Lodge *BR7: Chst* .*1E* **160**
(off Caveside Cl.)
Tollgate Rd. E6 .5A **88**
E16 .5A **88**
Tollgate Sq. E6 .5D **88**
Tollhouse Way N19 .2G **65**
Tollington Pk. N4 .2K **65**
Tollington Pl. N4 .2K **65**
Tollington Rd. N7 .4K **65**
Tollington Way N7 .3J **65**
Tolmers Sq. NW1 .3B **6** (4G **83**)
(not continuous)
Tolpaide Ho. SE11 .4J **19**
Tolpuddle Av. E13 .1A **88**
Tolpuddle St. N1 .2A **84**
Tolsford Rd. E5 .5H **67**
Tolson Rd. TW7: Isle .3A **114**
Tolverne Rd. SW20 .1E **152**
TOLWORTH .2H **163**
Tolworth B'way. KT6: Surb .1H **163**
Tolworth Cl. KT6: Surb .1H **163**
Tolworth Gdns. RM6: Chad H .5D **54**
TOLWORTH JUNC. (TOBY JUG) .**2H 163**
Tolworth Pde. RM6: Chad H .5E **54**
Tolworth Pk. Rd. KT6: Surb .2F **163**
Tolworth Recreation Cen. .3F **163**
Tolworth Ri. Nth. KT5: Surb .1H **163**
Tolworth Ri. Sth. KT5: Surb .2H **163**
Tolworth Rd. KT6: Surb .2E **162**
Tolworth Twr. KT6: Surb .2H **163**
Tomahawk Gdns. UB5: N'olt .3B **76**
Tomblin M. SW16 .2G **155**
Tom Coombs Cl. SE9 .4C **124**
Tom Cribb Rd. SE28 .3G **107**
Tom Groves Cl. E15 .5F **69**
Tom Hood Cl. E15 .5F **69**
Tom Jenkinson Rd. E16 .1J **105**
Tomkyns Ho. SE11 .3J **19**
Tomline Ho. *SE1* .*5C* **14**
(off Union St.)
Tomlins All. TW1: Twick .1A **132**
Tomlin's Gro. E3 .3C **86**
Tomlinson Cl. E2 .2K **9** (3F **85**)
W4 .5H **97**
Tomlins Orchard
IG11: Bark .1G **89**
Tomlins Ter. E14 .6A **86**
Tomlins Wlk. N7 .2K **65**
Tom Mann Cl. IG11: Bark .1J **89**
Tommy Flowers M. NW7 .5A **30**
Tom Nolan Cl. E15 .2G **87**
Tompion Ho. *EC1* .*3B* **8**
(off Percival St.)
Tompion St. EC1 .2A **8** (3B **84**)
(not continuous)
Tom Smith Cl. SE10 .6G **105**
Tomson Ho. *SE1* .*7J* **15**
(off St Saviour's Est.)
Tomswood Ct. IG6: Ilf .1G **53**
Tomswood Hill IG6: Ilf .1F **53**, 6K **37**
Tomswood Rd. IG7: Chig .6K **37**
Tom Williams Ho. *SW6* .*6H* **99**
(off Clem Attlee Ct.)
Tonbridge Cres. HA3: Kenton .4E **42**
Tonbridge Ho's. *WC1* .*2E* **6**
(off Tonbridge St.)
Tonbridge Rd. KT8: W Mole .4D **148**
Tonbridge St. WC1 .1E **6** (3J **83**)
Tonbridge Wlk. WC1 .1E **6**
Toneborough *NW8* .*1K* **81**
(off Abbey Rd.)
Tonfield Rd. SM3: Sutt .1H **165**
Tonge Cl. BR3: Beck .5C **158**
Tonsley Hill SW18 .5K **117**
Tonsley Pl. SW18 .5K **117**
Tonsley Rd. SW18 .5K **117**
Tonsley St. SW18 .5K **117**
Tonstall Rd. CR4: Mitc .2E **154**
Tony Cannell M. E3 .3B **86**
Tony Law Ho. SE20 .1H **157**
Tony Rawson Way RM10: Dag .3J **73**
Tooke Cl. HA5: Pinn .1C **40**
Tookey Cl. HA3: Kenton .7F **43**
Took's Ct. EC4 .7J **7** (6A **84**)
Tooley St. SE1 .4F **15** (1D **102**)
Toomy Cen. *E16* .*1K* **105**
(off Evelyn Rd.)
Toorack Rd. HA3: Hrw W .2H **41**
TOOTING .5C **136**
TOOTING BEC .3D **136**
Tooting Bec Gdns. SW16 .4H **137**
(not continuous)
Tooting Bec Lido .4G **137**
Tooting Bec Rd. SW16 .3E **136**
SW17 .3E **136**
Tooting B'way. SW17 .5C **136**
TOOTING GRAVENEY .6D **136**
Tooting Gro. SW17 .5C **136**
Tooting High St. SW17 .6C **136**
Tooting Leisure Cen. .4B **136**
Tooting Mkt. SW17 .4D **136**
Tootswood Rd. BR2: Brom .5G **159**
Topaz Ct. E11 .1G **69**
Topaz Wlk. NW2 .7F **45**
Topcliffe Dr. BR6: Farnb .4H **173**
Topham Ho. *SE10* .*7E* **104**
(off Prior St.)
Topham Sq. N17 .1C **48**
Topham St. EC1 .3J **7** (4A **84**)
Top Ho. Ri. E4 .7K **25**
Topiary Sq. TW9: Rich .3F **115**
Topley St. SE9 .4A **124**
Topmast Point E14 .2C **104**
Top Pk. BR3: Beck .5G **159**
Topp Wlk. NW2 .2E **62**
Topsfield Cl. N8 .5H **47**
Topsfield Pde. *N8* .*5J* **47**
(off Tottenham La.)
Topsfield Rd. N8 .5J **47**
Topsham Rd. SW17 .3D **136**
Tora Ct. IG9: Buck H .2F **37**
Torbay Ct. NW1 .7F **65**
Torbay Mans. *NW6* .*1H* **81**
(off Willesden La.)
Torbay Rd. HA2: Harr .2C **58**
NW6 .7H **63**
Torbay St. NW1 .7F **65**
Torbitt Way IG2: Ilf .5K **53**
Torbridge Cl. HA8: Edg .7K **27**
Torbrook Cl. DA5: Bexl .6E **126**
Tor Ct. W8 .2J **99**
Torcross Dr. SE23 .2J **139**
Torcross Rd. HA4: Ruis .3K **57**
Toreno Mansion *E20* .*5D* **68**
(off Olympic Pk. Av.)
Tor Gdns. W8 .2J **99**
Tor Gro. SE28 .1J **107**
Tor Ho. N6 .6F **47**
Tormead Cl. SM1: Sutt .6J **165**
Tormount Rd. SE18 .6J **107**
Tornay Ho. E9 .7J **67**
N1 .*2K* **83**
(off Priory Grn. Est.)
Toronto Av. E12 .4D **70**
Toronto Ho. SE16 .2K **103**
Toronto Rd. IG1: Ilf .1F **71**
Torquay Ct. *E14* .*5E* **86**
(off St Ives Pl.)
Torquay Gdns. IG4: Ilf .4B **52**
Torquay St. W2 .5K **81**
Torrance Cl. SE7 .6B **106**
Torrens Ct. SE5 .3D **120**
Torrens Rd. E15 .6H **69**
SW2 .5K **119**
Torrens Sq. E15 .6H **69**
Torrens St. EC1 .2A **84**
Torrent Lodge *SE10* .*7D* **104**
(off Merryweather Pl.)
Torres Sq. E14 .5C **104**
Torre Vista *SE13* .*3E* **122**
(off Loampit Va.)
Torre Wlk. SM5: Cars .1C **166**
Torrey Dr. SW9 .2A **120**
Torriano Av. NW5 .5H **65**
Torriano Cotts. NW5 .5G **65**
Torriano M. NW5 .5G **65**
Torridge Gdns. SE15 .4J **121**
Torridge Rd. CR7: Thor H .5B **156**
Torridon Ho. *NW6* .*2K* **81**
(off Randolph Gdns.)
Torridon Rd. SE6 .7F **123**
SE13 .7F **123**
Torrington Av. N12 .5G **31**
Torrington Cl. N12 .4G **31**
Torrington Ct. *SE26* .*5G* **139**
(off Crystal Palace Pk. Rd.)
Torrington Dr. HA2: Harr .4F **59**
Torrington Gdns. N11 .6B **32**
UB6: G'frd .1C **78**
Torrington Gro. N12 .5H **31**
Torrington Pk. N12 .5F **31**
Torrington Pl. E1 .1G **103**
WC1 .5C **6** (5H **83**)
Torrington Rd. E18 .3J **51**
HA4: Ruis .3H **57**
RM8: Dag .1F **73**
UB6: G'frd .1C **78**
Torrington Sq. CR0: C'don .7D **156**
WC1 .4D **6** (4H **83**)
Torrington Way SM4: Mord .6J **153**
Tor Rd. DA16: Well .1C **126**
Torr Rd. SE20 .7K **139**
Tortington Ho. *SE15* .*7G* **103**
(off Friary Est.)
Torver Rd. HA1: Harr .4J **41**
Torver Way BR6: Orp .3H **173**
Torwood Rd. SW15 .5C **116**

Tothill Ho. SW1 ....3D 18
(off Page St.)
Tothill St. SW1 ....7D 12 (2H 101)
Totnes Rd. DA16: Well 7B 108
Totnes Vs. N11 ....5B 32
(off Telford Rd.)
Totnes Wlk. N2 ....4B 46
Tottan Ter. E1 ....6K 85
Tottenhall NW1 ....7E 64
(off Ferdinand St.)
Tottenhall Rd. N13 ....6F 33
TOTTENHAM 2F 49
Tottenham Community Sports Cen. 1F 49
Tottenham Ct. Rd. W1 ....4B 6 (4G 83)
Tottenham Ent. Cen. N17 ....2F 49
Tottenham Grn. E. N15 ....4F 49
(not continuous)
Tottenham Green Leisure Cen. 4F 49
TOTTENHAM HALE 2G 49
TOTTENHAM HALE GYRATORY 4G 49
Tottenham Hale Retail Pk. N15 ....4G 49
Tottenham Hotspur FC 7B 34
Tottenham La. N8 ....6J 47
Tottenham M. W1 ....5B 6 (5G 83)
Tottenham Rd. N1 ....6E 66
Tottenham St. W1 ....6B 6 (5G 83)
Totterdown St. SW17 ....4D 136
TOTTERIDGE 1C 30
Totteridge Comn. N20 ....2H 29
Totteridge Fields Local Nature Reserve 1H 29
Totteridge Grn. N20 ....2D 30
Totteridge Ho. SW11 ....2B 118
(off Yelverton Rd.)
Totteridge La. N20 ....2D 30
Totteridge Village N20 ....1B 30
Totternhoe Cl. HA3: Kenton 5C 42
Totters Ct. SE17 ....6D 102
(off Westmorland Rd.)
Totton Rd. CR7: Thor H 3A 156
Toucan Cl. NW10 ....3G 79
Touchard Ho. N1 ....2F 9
Toulmin St. SE1 ....7C 14 (2C 102)
Toulon St. SE5 ....7C 102
Toulouse Ct. SE16 ....5H 103
(off Rossetti Rd.)
Tounson Ct. SW1 ....4D 18
(off Montaigne Cl.)
Tourist Info. Cen.
Bexleyheath 4F 127
City of London 1C 14 (6C 84)
Enfield 4J 23
Greenwich 6E 104
Heathrow Central 3D 110
Kingston upon Thames 2D 150
Tournay Rd. SW6 ....7H 99
Tours Pas. SW11 ....4A 118
Toussaint Wlk. SE16 ....3G 103
Tovil Cl. SE20 ....2H 157
Tovy Ho. SE1 ....5G 103
(off Avondale Sq.)
Towcester Rd. E3 ....4D 86
Tower, The SW8 ....7E 18 (6J 101)
TW8: Bford 5D 96
(off Ealing Rd.)
Tower 1 SE13 ....3E 122
(off Station Rd.)
Tower 2 SE13 ....3E 122
(off Station Rd.)
Tower 3 SE13 ....3E 122
(off Station Rd.)
Tower 4 SE13 ....3E 122
(off Station Rd.)
Tower 42 ....7G 9 (6E 84)
Tower Bri. SE1 ....5J 15 (1F 103)
Tower Bri. App. E1 ....4J 15 (1F 103)
Tower Bri. Bus. Complex SE16 ....3G 103
Tower Bri. Bus. Sq. SE16 ....4H 103
Tower Bridge Exhibition 4J 15
Tower Bri. M. HA1: Harr 4K 59
Tower Bri. Plaza SE1 ....5J 15 (1F 103)
Tower Bri. Rd. SE1 ....7H 15 (3E 102)
Tower Bri. Sq. SE1 ....6J 15
Tower Bri. Wharf E1 ....5K 15 (1G 103)
Tower Bldgs. E1 ....1H 103
(off Brewhouse La.)
Tower Cl. BR6: Orp 2K 173
NW3 ....5B 64
SE20 ....7H 139
Tower Ct. E5 ....7F 49
N1 ....7C 66
(off Canonbury St.)
NW8 ....2C 82
(off Mackennal St.)
WC2 ....1E 12
Tower Gdns. KT10: Clay 7A 162
Tower Gdns. Rd. N17 ....1C 48
Towergate SE1 ....4E 102
(off Page's Wlk.)
Towergate Cl. UB8: Uxb 5A 56
Towergate Ho. E3 ....2B 86
(off Ordell Rd.)
Tower Hamlets Rd. E7 ....4H 69
E17 ....3C 50
TOWER HILL 7F 85
Tower Hill EC3 ....3J 15 (7F 85)
Tower Hill Ter. EC3 ....3H 15
Tower Ho. E1 ....5G 85
(off Fieldgate St.)
SE13 ....3E 122
Tower La. HA9: Wemb 3D 60
Tower Mans. SE1 ....3F 103
(off Grange Rd.)
Tower M. E5 ....4A 68
E17 ....4C 50
Tower Mill Rd. SE15 ....7E 102
Tower of London, The 3J 15 (7F 85)
Tower of London Welcome Cen. 3H 15 (7E 84)
Tower Pl. EC3 ....3H 15 (7E 84)
Tower Pl. E. EC3 ....3H 15
(off Lwr. Thames St.)
Tower Pl. W. EC3 ....3H 15
(off Lwr. Thames St.)
Tower Point EN2: Enf 4J 23
Tower Ri. TW9: Rich 3E 114
Tower Rd. BR6: Orp 2K 173
DA7: Bex 4G 127
DA17: Belv 4J 109
NW10 ....7C 62
TW1: Twick 3K 131
Towers Av. UB10: Hil 3E 74
Towers Bus. Pk. HA9: Wemb 4J 61
(off Carey Way)
Towers Ct. UB10: Hil 3E 74
Towers Pl. TW9: Rich 5E 114
Towers Rd. HA5: Pinn 1C 40
UB1: S'hall 4E 76
Tower St. WC2 ....1E 12 (6J 83)
Tower Ter. N22 ....2K 47
Tower Vw. CR0: C'don 7A 158
WD23: B Hea 1D 26
Tower Wlk. SE1 ....4E 102
(off Leroy St.)
Tower Wharf SE1 ....6J 15
(off Tooley St.)
Tower Workshops SE1 ....7J 15
Tower Yd. TW10: Rich 5F 115
Towfield Ct. TW13: Hanw 2D 130
Towfield Rd. TW13: Hanw 2D 130
Town, The EN2: Enf 3J 23
Towncourt Cres. BR5: Pet W 5G 161
Towncourt La. BR5: Pet W 6H 161
Town Ct. Path N4 ....1C 66
Townend Ct. BR1: Brom 1H 159
Town End Pde. KT1: King T 3D 150
(off High St.)
Towney Mead UB5: N'olt 2D 76
Towney Mead Ct. UB5: N'olt 2D 76
Townfield Rd. UB3: Hayes 1H 93
Townfield Sq. UB3: Hayes 7H 75
Town Fld. Way TW7: Isle 2A 114
Town Hall App. N16 ....4D 66
(off Albion Rd.)
Town Hall App. Rd. N15 ....4F 49
Town Hall Av. W4 ....5K 97
Town Hall Rd. SW11 ....3D 118
Townholm Cres. W7 ....3K 95
Town La. TW19: Stanw 1A 128
Townley Ct. E15 ....6H 69
Townley Rd. DA6: Bex 5F 127
SE22 ....5E 120
Townley St. SE17 ....5D 102
(not continuous)
Townmead Bus. Cen. SW6 ....3A 118
Town Mdw. TW8: Bford 6D 96
Town Mdw. Rd.
TW8: Bford 7D 96
Townmead Rd. SW6 ....3K 117
TW9: Kew 2H 115
Town Quay IG11: Bark 1F 89
Town Quay Wharf IG11: Bark 1F 89
Town Rd. N9 ....2C 34
Townsend Av. N14 ....4C 32
Townsend Ho. SE1 ....4G 103
(off Strathnairn St.)
Townsend Ind. Est. NW10 ....2J 79
Townsend La. NW9 ....7K 43
Townsend M. SW18 ....2A 136
Townsend Rd. N15 ....5F 49
SE3 ....4A 124
TW15: Ashf 5A 128
UB1: S'hall 1C 94
Townsend St. SE17 ....4E 102
Townsend Way HA6: Nwood 1H 39
Townsend Yd. N6 ....1F 65
Townshend Cl. DA14: Sidc 6B 144
Townshend Ct. NW8 ....2C 82
(off Townshend Rd.)
Townshend Est. NW8 ....2C 82
Townshend Rd. BR7: Chst 5F 143
NW8 ....1C 82
(not continuous)
TW9: Rich 4F 115
Townshend Ter. TW9: Rich 4F 115
Towns Ho. SW4 ....3H 119
Townson Av. UB5: N'olt 2J 75
Townson Way UB5: N'olt 2J 75
Town Sq. IG11: Bark 1G 89
(off Clockhouse Av.)
TW7: Isle 3B 114
(off Swan St.)
Town Tree Rd. TW15: Ashf 5C 128
Town Wharf TW7: Isle 3B 114
Towpath KT12: Walt T 5J 147
TW17: Shep 7B 146
Towpath, The SW10 ....1B 118
Towpath Rd. N18 ....6E 34
Towpath Wlk. E9 ....5B 68
Towpath Way CR0: C'don 6F 157
Towton M. N11 ....6C 32
Towton Rd. SE27 ....2C 138
Toynbec Cl. BR7: Chst 4F 143
Toynbee Rd. SW20 ....1G 153
Toynbee St. E1 ....6J 9 (5F 85)
Toynbee Studios 7K 9
Toyne Way N6 ....6D 46
Tracey Av. NW2 ....5E 62
Tracey Bellamy Ct. E14 ....6A 86
(off Repton St.)
Tracy Ct. HA7: Stan 7H 27
Tracy Ho. E3 ....3B 86
(off Mile End Rd.)
Trade City Bus. Pk. TW16: Sun 1G 147
Trade Cl. N13 ....4F 33
Trader Rd. E6 ....6F 89
Tradescant Ho. E9 ....7J 67
(off Frampton Pk. Rd.)
Tradescant Rd. SW8 ....7J 101
Tradewind Hgts. SE16 ....1K 103
(off Rotherhithe St.)
Tradewinds Ct. E1 ....7G 85
Trading Est. Rd. NW10 ....4J 79
Trafalgar Av. KT4: Wor Pk 1F 165
N17 ....6K 33
SE15 ....5F 103
Trafalgar Bldg. KT2: King T 1D 150
(off Henry Macaulay Av.)
Trafalgar Bus. Cen. IG11: Bark 4K 89
Trafalgar Chambers SW3 ....5B 16
(off South Pde.)
Trafalgar Cl. SE16 ....3A 104
Trafalgar Ct. E1 ....1J 103
(off Wapping Wall)
Trafalgar Gdns. E1 ....5K 85
W8 ....3K 99
Trafalgar Gro. SE10 ....6F 105
Trafalgar Ho. SE17 ....5C 102
(off Bronti Cl.)
SW18 ....4A 118
Trafalgar M. E9 ....6B 68
Trafalgar Pl. E11 ....4J 51
N18 ....5B 34
Trafalgar Point N1 ....7D 66
(off Downham Rd.)
Trafalgar Quarters SE10 ....6F 105
(off Park Row)
Trafalgar Rd. SE10 ....6F 105
SW19 ....7K 135
TW2: Twick 2H 131
Trafalgar Square 4D 12 (1H 101)
Trafalgar Sq. SW1 ....4D 12 (1H 101)
WC2 ....4D 12 (1H 101)
Trafalgar St. SE17 ....5D 102
Trafalgar Studios 4E 12
Trafalgar Ter. HA1: Harr 1J 59
Trafalgar Trad. Est. EN3: Brim 4F 25
Trafalgar Way CR0: Wadd 2A 168
E14 ....1E 104
Trafford Ho. N1 ....2D 84
(off Cranston Est.)
Trafford Rd. CR7: Thor H 5K 155
Trafford Way BR3: Beck 6C 140
Traherne Lodge TW11: Tedd 5K 131
Trahorn Cl. E1 ....4H 85
Traitors' Gate 4J 15
Tralee Ct. SE16 ....5H 103
(off Masters Dr.)
Tram Cl. SE24 ....3B 120
(off Milkwood Rd.)
Tramlink, The SW19 ....2A 154
Tramsheds, The CR0: Bedd 7H 155
Tramway Av. E15 ....7G 69
N9 ....7C 24
Tramway Cl. SE20 ....1J 157
Tramway Ct. E1 ....5A 86
Tramway Path CR4: Mitc 4C 154
(not continuous)
Tranby M. E9 ....5K 67
(off Brooksby's Wlk.)
Tranley M. NW3 ....4C 64
(off Fleet Rd.)
Tranmere Ct. SM2: Sutt 7A 166
Tranmere Rd. N9 ....7A 24
SW18 ....2A 136
TW2: Whitt 7F 113
Tranquil La. HA2: Harr 1F 59
Tranquil Pas. SE3 ....2H 123
(off Montpelier Va.)
Tranquil Va. SE3 ....2G 123
Transenna Works N1 ....6B 66
(off Laycock St.)
Transept St. NW1 ....6D 4 (5C 82)
Transmere Cl. BR5: Pet W 6G 161
Transmere Rd. BR5: Pet W 6G 161
Transom Cl. SE16 ....4A 104
Transom Sq. E14 ....5D 104
Transport Av. TW8: Bford 5A 96
Tranton Rd. SE16 ....3G 103
Trappes Ho. SE16 ....4H 103
(off Camilla Rd.)
Traps La. KT3: N Mald 1A 152
Traq Motor Racing 6G 155
Travellers Way TW4: Cran 2A 112

Travers Cl. E17 . . . . .1K 49
Travers Ho. SE10 . . . . .6F 105
(off Trafalgar Gro.)
Travers Rd. N7 . . . . .3A 66
Treacy Cl. WD23: B Hea 2B 26
Treadgold Ho. W11 . . . . .7F 81
(off Bomore Rd.)
Treadgold St. W11 . . . . .7F 81
Treadway St. E2 . . . . .2H 85
Treasury Cl. SM6: Wall 5H 167
Treasury M. DA5: Bexl 7H 127
Treasury Pas. SW1 . . . . .6E 12
Treaty Cen. TW3: Houn 3F 113
Treaty St. N1 . . . . .1K 83
Trebeck St. W1 . . . . .4J 11 (1F 101)
Trebovir Rd. SW5 . . . . .5J 99
Treby St. E3 .4B 86
Trecastle Way N7 . . . . .4H 65
Tredegar Ho. E3 . . . . .3C 86
(off Bow Rd.)
Tredegar M. E3 . . . . .3B 86
Tredegar Rd. E3 . . . . .2B 86
N11 . . . . .7C 32
Tredegar Sq. E3 . . . . .3B 86
Tredegar Ter. E3 . . . . .3B 86
Trederwen Rd. E8 . . . . .1G 85
Tredown Rd. SE26 . . . . .5J 139
Tredwell Cl. BR2: Brom 4C 160
SW2 . . . . .2K 137
Tredwell Rd. SE27 . . . . .4B 138
Tree Cl. TW10: Ham 1D 132
Treen Av. SW13 . . . . .3B 116
Tree Rd. E16 .6A 88
Treeside Cl. UB7: W Dray 4A 92
Treeside Pl. N10 . . . . .4F 47
Treetop Ct. CR7: Thor H 5C 156
Tree Top M. RM10: Dag 6K 73
Treetop M. NW6 . . . . .7G 63
Treetops Cl. SE2 . . . . .5E 108
Tree Vw. Ct. SE19 . . . . .1E 156
Treewall Gdns. BR1: Brom 4K 141
Trefgarne Rd. RM10: Dag 2G 73
Trefil Wlk. N7 . . . . .4J 65
Trefoil Ho. DA18: Erith 2E 108
(off Kale Rd.)
Trefoil Rd. SW18 . . . . .5A 118
Trefusis Ct. TW5: Cran 1K 111
Tregaron Av. N8 . . . . .6J 47
Tregaron Gdns. KT3: N Mald 4A 152
Tregarvon Rd. SW11 . . . . .4E 118
Tregenna Av. HA2: Harr 4E 58
Tregenna Cl. N14 . . . . .5B 22
Tregenna Ct. HA2: Harr 4E 58
Tregonwell Ter. SE9 . . . . .4F 143
Tregony Rd. BR6: Chels 4K 173
Trego Rd. E9 .7C 68
Tregothnan Rd. SW9 . . . . .3J 119
Tregunter Rd. SW10 . . . . .6K 99
Trehearn Rd. IG6: Ilf 1H 53
Treherne Ct. SW17 . . . . .4E 136
Trehern Rd. SW14 . . . . .3K 115
Trehurst St. E5 . . . . .5A 68
Trelawney Est. E9 . . . . .6J 67
Trelawney Ho. SE1 . . . . .5C 14
(off Union St.)
Trelawney Rd. IG6: Ilf 1H 53
Trelawn Rd. E10 . . . . .3E 68
SW2 . . . . .5A 120
Trelawny Cl. E17 . . . . .4D 50
Trellick Twr. W10 . . . . .4H 81
(off Golborne Rd.)
Trellis Ho. SW19 . . . . .7A 136
Trellis Sq. E3 .3B 86
Treloar Gdns. SE19 . . . . .6D 138
Tremadoc Rd. SW4 . . . . .4H 119
Tremaine Cl. SE4 . . . . .2C 122
Tremaine Rd. SE20 . . . . .2H 157
Trematon Bldg. N1 . . . . .2J 83
(off Trematon Wlk.)
Trematon Ho. SE11 . . . . .5K 19
(off Kennings Way)

Trematon M. N1 . . . . .2J 83
Trematon Pl. TW11: Tedd 7C 132
Trematon Wlk. N1 . . . . .2J 83
(off Trematon M.)
Tremelo Grn. RM8: Dag 1E 72
Tremlett Gro. N19 . . . . .3G 65
Tremlett M. N19 . . . . .3G 65
Trenance Gdns. IG3: Ilf 3A 72
Trenchard Av. HA4: Ruis 4K 57
Trenchard Cl. HA7: Stan 6F 27
NW9 . . . . .1A 44
Trenchard Ct. NW4 . . . . .5C 44
SM4: Mord 6J 153
Trenchard St. SE10 . . . . .5F 105
Trenchold St. SW8 . . . . .6J 101
Trendell Ho. E14 . . . . .6C 86
(off Dod St.)
Trenear Cl. BR6: Chels 4K 173
Trenholme Cl. SE20 . . . . .7H 139
Trenholme Rd. SE20 . . . . .7H 139
Trenholme Ter. SE20 . . . . .7H 139
Trenmar Gdns. NW10 . . . . .3D 80
Trent Av. W5 .3D 96
Trent Ct. CR2: S Croy 5C 168
(off Nottingham Rd.)
Trent Gdns. N14 . . . . .6A 22
Trentham Ho. W3 . . . . .5K 79
Trentham St. SW18 . . . . .1J 135
Trent Ho. KT2: King T 1D 150
SE15 .4J 121
TRENT PARK 2A 22
Trent Pk. (Country Pk.) 1K 21
Trent Pk. Golf Course 4B 22
Trent Rd. IG9: Buck H 1E 36
SW2 . . . . .5K 119
Trent Way KT4: Wor Pk 3E 164
UB4: Hayes 2G 75
Trentwood Side
EN2: Enf 3E 22
Treport St. SW18 . . . . .7K 117
Tresco Cl. BR1: Brom 6G 141
Trescoe Gdns. HA2: Harr 7C 40
Tresco Gdns. IG3: Ilf 2A 72
Tresco Ho. SE11 . . . . .5J 19
Tresco Rd. SE15 . . . . .4H 121
Tresham Cres. NW8 . . . . .3D 4 (4C 82)
Tresham Ho. WC1 . . . . .5G 7
(off Red Lion Sq.)
Tresham Rd. IG11: Bark 7K 71
Tresham Wlk. E9 . . . . .5J 67
Tresidder Ho. SW4 . . . . .7H 119
Tresilian Av. N21 . . . . .5E 22
Tressell Cl. N1 . . . . .7B 66
Tressillian Cres. SE4 . . . . .3C 122
Tressillian Rd. SE4 . . . . .4B 122
Tress Pl. SE1 .4A 14
Trestis Cl. UB4: Yead 5B 76
Treswell Rd. RM9: Dag 1E 90
Tretawn Gdns. NW7 . . . . .4F 29
Tretawn Pk. NW7 . . . . .4F 29
Trevanion Rd. W14 . . . . .4G 99
Treve Av. HA1: Harr 7H 41
Trevelyan Av. E12 . . . . .4D 70
Trevelyan Ct. KT3: N Mald 7A 152
Trevelyan Cres. HA3: Kenton 7D 42
Trevelyan Gdns. NW10 . . . . .1E 80
Trevelyan Ho. E2 . . . . .3K 85
(off Morpeth St.)
SE5 . . . . .7B 102
(off John Ruskin St.)
Trevelyan Rd. E15 . . . . .4H 69
SW17 .5C 136
Trevenna Ho. SE23 . . . . .3K 139
(off Dacres Rd.)
Trevera Ct. EN3: Pond E 4F 25
Treveris St. SE1 . . . . .5B 14 (1B 102)
Treversh Ct. BR1: Brom 1G 159
Treverton St. W10 . . . . .4F 81
Treverton Towers W10 . . . . .5F 81
(off Treverton St.)
Treves Cl. N21 . . . . .5E 22

Treves Ho. E1 . . . . .4G 85
(off Vallance Rd.)
Treville St. SW15 . . . . .7D 116
Treviso Rd. SE23 . . . . .2K 139
Trevithick Cl. TW14: Felt 1H 129
Trevithick Ho. SE16 . . . . .4H 103
(off Rennie Est.)
Trevithick St. SE8 . . . . .6C 104
Trevithick Way E3 . . . . .3C 86
Trevone Gdns. HA5: Pinn 6C 40
Trevor Cl. BR2: Hayes 7H 159
EN4: E Barn 6G 21
HA3: Hrw W 7F 26
TW7: Isle 5K 113
UB5: N'olt 2A 76
Trevor Cres. HA4: Ruis 4H 57
Trevor Gdns. HA4: Ruis 4J 57
HA8: Edg 1K 43
UB5: N'olt 2A 76
Trevor Pl. SW7 . . . . .7D 10 (2C 100)
Trevor Rd. HA8: Edg 1K 43
IG8: Wfd G 7D 36
SW19 .7G 135
UB3: Hayes 2G 93
Trevor Sq. SW7 . . . . .7E 10 (2D 100)
Trevor St. SW7 . . . . .7D 10 (2C 100)
Trevor Wlk. SW7 . . . . .7E 10
(off Lancelot Pl.)
Trevose Ho. SE11 . . . . .5H 19
(off Orsett St.)
Trevose Rd. E17 . . . . .1F 51
Trewenna Dr. KT9: Chess 5D 162
Trewince Rd. SW20 . . . . .1E 152
Trewint St. SW18 . . . . .2A 136
Trewsbury Ho. SE2 . . . . .1D 108
Trewsbury Rd. SE26 . . . . .5K 139
Tria Apartments E2 . . . . .3G 85
(off Durant St.)
Triandra Way UB4: Yead 5B 76
Triangle, The DA15: Sidc 7A 126
(off Burnt Oak La.)
E8 . . . . .1H 85
EC1 . . . . .3B 8
IG11: Bark 6G 71
KT1: King T 2H 151
N13 . . . . .4E 32
Triangle Bus. Cen., The NW10 . . . . . .3B 80
Triangle Cen. UB1: S'hall 1H 95
Triangle Ct. E16 . . . . .5B 88
SE1 . . . . .5D 14
(off Redcross Way)
Triangle Est. SE11 . . . . .6J 19
(off Kennington La.)
SE11 .5A 102
(off Kennington Rd.)
Triangle Ho. SE1 . . . . .6J 15
(off Three Oak La.)
Triangle Pas. EN4: E Barn 4F 21
Triangle Pl. SW4 . . . . .4H 119
Triangle Rd. E8 . . . . .1H 85
Triangle Way W3 . . . . .2G 97
Tribeca Apartments E1 . . . . .6K 9
(off Heneage St.)
Trickett Ho. SM2: Sutt 7K 165
Trico Ho. TW8: Bford 5D 96
(off Ealing Rd.)
Tricorn Ho. SE28 . . . . .1J 107
Tricycle Cinema, The 7H 63
Tricycle Theatre, The 7H 63
Trident Bus. Cen. SW17 . . . . .5D 136
Trident Gdns. UB5: N'olt 3B 76
Trident Ho. E14 . . . . .6E 86
(off Blair St.)
SE28 .1H 107
TW19: Stanw 7A 110
(off Clare Rd.)
Trident Pl. SW3 . . . . .7B 16
(off Old Church St.)
Trident Point HA1: Harr 6H 41
Trident St. SE16 . . . . .4K 103
Trident Way UB2: S'hall 3K 93

Trig La. EC4 . . . . .2C 14 (7C 84)
Trigon Rd. SW8 . . . . .7K 101
Trigo Rd. SE23 . . . . .2K 139
Trillo Cl. IG2: Ilf 7J 53
Trimdon NW1 .1G 83
Trimmer Wlk. TW8: Bford 6E 96
Trim St. SE14 .6B 104
Trinder Gdns. N19 . . . . .1J 65
Trinder M. SW12 . . . . .1E 136
TW11: Tedd 5A 132
Trinder Rd. EN5: Barn 5A 20
N19 . . . . .1J 65
Tring Av. HA9: Wemb 6G 61
UB1: S'hall 6D 76
W5 . . . . .1F 97
Tring Cl. IG2: Ilf 5H 53
Tring Ct. TW1: Twick 4A 132
Trinidad Gdns. RM10: Dag 7K 73
Trinidad Ho. E14 . . . . .7B 86
(off Gill St.)
Trinidad St. E14 . . . . .7B 86
Trinity Av. EN1: Enf 6A 24
N2 . . . . .3B 46
Trinity Buoy Wharf E14 . . . . .7G 87
(off Orchard Pl.)
Trinity Chu. Pas. SW13 . . . . .6D 98
Trinity Chu. Rd. SW13 . . . . .6D 98
Trinity Chu. Sq. SE1 . . . . .7D 14 (3C 102)
Trinity Cl. BR2: Brom 1C 172
CR2: Sande 7E 168
E8 . . . . .6F 67
E11 . . . . .2G 69
NW3 . . . . .5B 64
SE13 .4F 123
SW4 . . . . .4G 119
TW4: Houn 4C 112
Trinity Cotts. TW9: Rich 3F 115
Trinity Ct. BR1: Brom 1H 159
(off Highland Rd.)
CR0: C'don 2C 168
EN2: Enf 2H 23
N1 . . . . .1E 84
(off Downham Rd.)
N18 . . . . .6A 34
NW2 . . . . .5E 62
SE7 . . . . .4B 106
SE8 . . . . .6A 104
(off Evelyn St.)
SE25 .6E 156
SE26 .3J 139
SW9 . . . . .3K 119
W2 . . . . .6A 82
(off Gloucester Ter.)
W9 . . . . .3H 81
(off Croxley Rd.)
WC1 . . . . .3G 7
Trinity Cres. SW17 . . . . .2D 136
Trinity Dr. UB8: Hil 5E 74
Trinity Gdns. E16 . . . . .5H 87
(not continuous)
SW9 . . . . .4K 119
Trinity Grn. E1 . . . . .4J 85
Trinity Gro. SE10 . . . . .1E 122
Trinity Hospital (Almshouses) SE10 . . .5F 105
Trinity Ho. EC3 . . . . .2J 15
RM8: Dag 5B 72
SE1 . . . . .3C 102
(off Bath Ter.)
W14 . . . . .3H 99
Trinity Laban .6E 104
(within Old Royal Naval College)
Trinity M. E1 . . . . .5J 85
(off Redman's Rd.)
SE20 .1H 157
W10 . . . . .6F 81
Trinity Pk. E4 .6G 35
Trinity Path SE23 . . . . .3J 139
SE26 .3J 139
Trinity Pl. DA6: Bex 4F 127
EC3 . . . . .2J 15 (7F 85)
Trinity Ri. SW2 . . . . .1A 138

Trinity Rd. IG6: Ilf 3G 53
N2 3B 46
N22 7D 32
(not continuous)
SW17 4A 118
SW18 4A 118
SW19 6J 135
TW9: Rich 3F 115
UB1: S'hall 1C 94
Trinity Sq. E14 6G 87
EC3 3H 15 (7E 84)
Trinity St. E16 5H 87
EN2: Enf 2H 23
SE1 7D 14 (2C 102)
(not continuous)
Trinity Ter. IG9: Lough 1E 36
Trinity Twr. *E1 7G 85*
(off Vaughan Way)
E14 3D 104
Trinity Wlk. NW3 6A 64
Trinity Way E4 6G 35
W3 7A 80
Trio Pl. SE1 7D 14 (2C 102)
Triptych Ho. *SE8 7C 104*
(off Watson's St.)
Triscott Ho. UB3: Hayes 1J 93
Tristan Ct. *SE8 6B 104*
(off Dorking Cl.)
Tristan Sq. SE3 3G 123
Tristram Cl. E17 3F 51
Tristram Dr. N9 3B 34
Tristram Rd.
BR1: Brom 4H 141
Triton Ct. *E16 5J 87*
(off Robertson Rd.)
Triton Ho. *E14 4D 104*
(off Cahir St.)
Triton Sq. NW1 3A 6 (4G 83)
Triton St. NW1 3K 5 (4F 83)
Tritton Av. CR0: Bedd 4J 167
Tritton Rd. SE21 3D 138
Triumph Cl. UB3: Harl 1E 110
Triumph Ho. IG11: Bark 3A 90
Triumph Rd. E6 6D 88
Triumph Trad. Est. N17 6B 34
Trocette Mans. *SE1 3E 102*
(off Bermondsey St.)
Trojan Ct. NW6 7G 63
Trojan Ind. Est. NW10 6B 62
Trojan M. SW19 7J 135
Trojan Way CR0: Wadd 3K 167
Troon Cl. SE16 5H 103
SE28 6D 90
Troon Ho. *E1 6A 86*
(off White Horse Rd.)
Troon St. E1 6A 86
Tropical Ct. *W10 3F 81*
(off Kilburn La.)
Trosley Rd. DA17: Belv 6G 109
Trossachs Rd. SE22 5E 120
Trothy Rd. SE1 4G 103
Trotman Ho. *SE14 1J 121*
(off Pomeroy St.)
Trott Rd. N10 7J 31
Trott St. SW11 1C 118
Trotwood Ho. *SE16 2H 103*
(off Wilson Gro.)
Troughton Rd. SE7 5K 105
Troutbeck NW1 2K 5
Troutbeck Rd. SE14 1A 122
Trout Rd. UB7: Yiew 7A 74
Trouville Rd. SW4 6G 119
Trowbridge Est. *E9 6B 68*
(off Osborne Rd.)
Trowbridge Ho. *E9 6B 68*
(off Felstead St.)
Trowbridge Rd. E9 6B 68
Trowlock Av. TW11: Tedd 6C 132
Trowlock Island
TW11: Tedd 6D 132
Trowlock Way TW11: Tedd 6D 132
Troy Ct. SE18 4F 107
W8 3J 99
(off Kensington High St.)
Troy Ind. Est. HA1: Harr 5K 41
Troy Rd. SE19 6D 138
Troy Town SE15 3G 121
Trubshaw Rd. UB2: S'hall 3F 95
True Lovers Ct.
HA6: Nwood 1F 39
Trueman Cl. HA8: Edg 7C 28
Truesdale Rd. E6 6D 88
Truesdales UB10: Ick 2E 56
truGym
Bromley 1J 159
(off East St.)
Crouch End 6J 47
Trulock Ct. N17 7B 34
Trulock Rd. N17 7B 34
Trumans Rd. N16 5F 67
Truman Wlk. E3 4D 86
Trumble Gdns. CR7: Thor H 4C 156
Trumpers Way W7 3J 95
Trumpington Rd. E7 4H 69
Trump St. EC2 1D 14 (6C 84)
Trundle Ho. *SE1 6C 14*
(off Trundle St.)
Trundlers Way WD23: B Hea 1D 26
Trundle St. SE1 6C 14 (2C 102)
Trundleys Rd. SE8 5K 103
Trundley's Ter. SE8 4K 103
Truro Gdns. IG1: Ilf 7C 52
Truro Ho. HA5: Hat E 1D 40
W2 5J 81
(off Westbourne Pk. Rd.)
Truro Rd. E17 4B 50
N22 7D 32
Truro St. NW5 6E 64
Truro Way UB4: Hayes 3G 75
Truslove Rd. SE27 5A 138
Trussley Rd. W6 3E 98
Trust Wlk. SE21 1B 138
Tryfan Cl. IG4: Ilf 5B 52
Tryon Cres. E9 1J 85
Tryon St. SW3 5E 16 (5D 100)
Trystings Cl. KT10: Clay 6A 162
Tuam Rd. SE18 6H 107
Tubbenden Cl. BR6: Orp 3J 173
Tubbenden Dr. BR6: Orp 4H 173
Tubbenden La. BR6: Orp 4H 173
Tubbenden La. Sth. BR6: Farnb 5H 173
Tubbs Rd. NW10 2B 80
Tucana Ct. *E1 3K 9*
(off Cygnet St.)
Tucana Hgts. *E20 5E 68*
(off Cheering La.)
Tucklow Wlk. SW15 7B 116
Tudor Av.
KT4: Wor Pk 3D 164
TW12: Hamp 7E 130
Tudor Cl. BR7: Chst 1D 160
HA5: Eastc 5J 39
IG7: Chig 4K 37
IG8: Wfd G 5E 36
KT9: Chess 5E 162
N6 7G 47
NW3 5C 64
NW7 6H 29
NW9 2J 61
SM3: Cheam 5F 165
SM6: Wall 7G 167
SW2 6K 119
TW12: Hamp H 5G 131
TW15: Ashf 4A 128
Tudor Ct. DA14: Sidc 3A 144
E17 7B 50
N1 6E 66
N22 7D 32
SE9 4C 124
SE16 1K 103
(off Princes Riverside Rd.)
TW11: Tedd 6K 131
Tudor Ct. TW13: Hanw 4A 130
TW19: Stanw 6A 110
W3 2G 97
Tudor Ct. Nth. HA9: Wemb 5G 61
Tudor Ct. Sth. HA9: Wemb 5G 61
Tudor Cres. EN2: Enf 1H 23
Tudor Dr. KT2: King T 5D 132
SM4: Mord 6F 153
Tudor Ent. Pk. HA1: Harr 3K 59
HA3: W'stone 3H 41
Tudor Est. NW10 2H 79
Tudor Gdns.
BR4: W W'ck 3E 170
HA3: Hrw W 2H 41
NW9 2J 61
SW13 3A 116
TW1: Twick 1K 131
W3 5G 79
Tudor Gro. E9 7J 67
Tudor Ho. E9 7J 67
E16 1K 105
(off Wesley Av.)
HA5: Pinn 2A 40
(off Pinner Hill Rd.)
SE1 5J 15
W14 4F 99
(off Windsor Way)
Tudor M. E17 4B 50
Tudor Pde. RM6: Chad H 7D 54
SE9 4C 124
Tudor Pl. CR4: Mitc 7C 136
IG9: Buck H 2H 37
SE19 7F 139
Tudor Rd. BR3: Beck 3E 158
E4 6J 35
E6 1A 88
E9 1H 85
EN5: New Bar 3D 20
HA3: Hrw W, W'stone 2H 41
HA5: Pinn 2A 40
IG11: Bark 1K 89
KT2: King T 7G 133
N9 7C 24
SE19 7F 139
SE25 5H 157
TW3: Houn 4H 113
TW12: Hamp 7E 130
TW15: Ashf 6F 129
UB1: S'hall 7C 76
UB3: Hayes 6F 75
Tudor Sq. UB3: Hayes 5F 75
Tudor Stacks SE24 4C 120
Tudor St. EC4 2K 13 (7A 84)
Tudor Wlk. DA5: Bexl 6E 126
Tudor Way BR5: Pet W 6H 161
N14 1C 32
UB10: Hil 6C 56
W3 2G 97
Tudor Well Cl. HA7: Stan 5G 27
Tudor Works UB4: Yead 1A 94
Tudway Rd. SE3 3K 123
Tufnell Ct. *E3 1B 86*
(off Old Ford Rd.)
TUFNELL PARK 4G 65
Tufnell Pk. Rd. N7 4G 65
N19 4G 65
Tufton Ct. *SW1 2E 18*
(off Tufton St.)
Tufton Gdns. KT8: W Mole 2F 149
Tufton Rd. E4 4H 35
Tufton St. SW1 1E 18 (3J 101)
Tugboat St. SE28 2J 107
Tugela Rd. CR0: C'don 6D 156
Tugela St. SE6 2B 140
Tugmutton Cl. BR6: Farnb 4F 173
Tulip Cl. CR0: C'don 1K 169
E6 5D 88
TW12: Hamp 6D 130
UB2: S'hall 2G 95
Tulip Gdns. E4 3A 36
IG1: Ilf 6F 71
Tullis Ho. *E9 7J 67*
(off Frampton Pk. Rd.)
Tull St. CR4: Mitc 7D 154
Tulse Cl. BR3: Beck 3E 158
TULSE HILL 1B 138
Tulse Hill SW2 6A 120
Tulse Hill Est. SW2 6A 120
Tulse Ho. SW2 6A 120
Tulsemere Rd. SE27 2C 138
Tumbling Bay KT12: Walt T 6J 147
Tummons Gdns. SE25 2E 156
Tump Ho. SE28 1J 107
Tunbridge Ho. EC1 1K 7
Tuncombe Rd. N18 4K 33
Tunis Rd. W12 1E 98
Tunley Grn. E14 5B 86
Tunley Rd. NW10 1A 80
SW17 1E 136
Tunmarsh La. E13 3K 87
Tunnan Leys E6 6E 88
Tunnel App. E14 7A 86
SE10 2G 105
SE16 2J 103
Tunnel Av. SE10 2F 105
Tunnel Av. Trad. Est. SE10 2F 105
Tunnel Gdns. N11 7B 32
Tunnel Link Rd. TW6: H'row A 6C 110
Tunnel Rd. SE16 2J 103
Tunnel Rd. E. TW6: H'row A 1D 110
Tunnel Rd. W. TW6: H'row A 1C 110
Tunstall Cl. BR6: Orp 4J 173
Tunstall Rd. CR0: C'don 1E 168
SW9 4K 119
Tunstall Wlk. TW8: Bford 6E 96
Tunstock Way DA17: Belv 3E 108
Tunworth Cl. NW9 6J 43
Tunworth Cres. SW15 6B 116
Tun Yd. *SW8 2F 119*
(off Peardon St.)
Tupelo Rd. E10 2D 68
Tupman Ho. *SE16 2G 103*
(off Scott Lidgett Cres.)
Tuppy St. SE28 3G 107
Turenne Cl. SW18 4A 118
Turin Rd. N9 7D 24
Turin St. E2 2K 9 (3G 85)
Turkey Oak Cl. SE19 1E 156
Turks Boatyard KT1: King T 1D 150
Turks Cl. UB8: Hil 3C 74
Turk's Head Yd. EC1 5A 8 (5B 84)
Turk's Row SW3 5F 17 (5D 100)
Turle Rd. N4 2K 65
SW16 2J 155
Turlewray Cl. N4 1K 65
Turley Cl. E15 1G 87
Turnagain La. EC4 7A 8
Turnage Rd. RM8: Dag 1E 72
Turnant Rd. N17 1C 48
Turnberry Cl. NW4 2F 45
SE16 5H 103
Turnberry Quay E14 3D 104
Turnberry Way BR6: Orp 1H 173
Turnbull Ho. N1 1B 84
Turnbury Cl. SE28 6D 90
Turnchapel M. SW4 3F 119
Turner Av. CR4: Mitc 1D 154
N15 4E 48
TW2: Twick 3G 131
Turner Cl. HA0: Wemb 6D 60
NW11 6K 45
SW9 7B 102
UB4: Hayes 2E 74
Turner Ct. *SE16 2J 103*
(off Albion St.)
Turner Cres.
CR0: C'don 6C 156
Turner Dr. NW11 6K 45
Turner Ho. *E14 2C 104*
(off Cassilis Rd.)
NW6 5A 64
(off Dresden Cl.)

Turner Ho.—Underwood Ho.

Turner Ho. *NW8* 2C **82**
(off Townshend Est.)
SW1 4D **18**
(off Herrick St.)
TW1: Twick 6D **114**
(off Clevedon Rd.)
Turner M. SM2: Sutt 7K **165**
Turner Pde. *N1* 7A **66**
(off Barnsbury Pk.)
Turner Pl. SW11 5C **118**
Turner Rd. E17 3E **50**
HA8: Edg 2E **42**
KT3: N Mald 7K **151**
Turners Cl. N20 3J **31**
Turners Ct. *E15* 4E **68**
(off Drapers Rd.)
N15 5D **48**
Turners Mdw. Way BR3: Beck 1B **158**
Turners Rd. E3 5B **86**
Turner St. E1 5H **85**
E16 6H **87**
Turners Way CR0: Wadd 2A **168**
Turners Wood NW11 7A **46**
Turneville Rd. W14 6H **99**
Turney Rd. SE21 7C **120**
TURNHAM GREEN 4A **98**
Turnham Grn. Ter. W4 4A **98**
Turnham Grn. Ter. M. W4 4A **98**
Turnham Rd. SE4 5A **122**
Turnmill St. EC1 4A **8** (4B **84**)
Turnour Ho. *E1* 6H **85**
(off Walburgh St.)
Turnpike Cl. DA16: Well 3A **126**
SE8 7B **104**
Turnpike Ct. DA6: Bex 4D **126**
Turnpike Ho. EC1 2B **8** (3B **84**)
Turnpike La. N8 4K **47**
SM1: Sutt 5A **166**
UB10: Uxb 3A **74**
Turnpike Link CR0: C'don 2E **168**
Turnpike M. *N8* 3A **48**
(off Turnpike La.)
Turnpike Pde. *N15* 3B **48**
(off Green Lanes)
Turnpike Way TW7: Isle 1A **114**
Turnpin La. SE10 6E **104**
Turnstone Cl. E13 3J **87**
NW9 2A **44**
UB10: Ick 5D **56**
Turnstone Ho. *E1* 3K **15**
(off Star Pl.)
Turpentine La. SW1 5K **17** (5F **101**)
Turpin Cl. E1 7K **85**
Turpington Cl. BR2: Brom 7C **160**
Turpington La. BR2: Brom 7C **160**
Turpin Ho. SW11 1F **119**
Turpin Rd. TW14: Felt 6H **111**
Turpin's La. IG8: Wfd G 5J **37**
Turpins Yd. NW2 5F **63**
SE10 7E **104**
Turpin Way N19 2H **65**
SM6: Wall 7F **167**
Turquand St. SE17 4C **102**
Turret Gro. SW4 3G **119**
Turton Rd. HA0: Wemb 5E **60**
Turville Ho. *NW8* 3C **4**
(off Grendon St.)
Turville St. E2 3J **9** (4F **85**)
Tuscan Ho. *E2* 3J **85**
(off Knottisford St.)
Tuscan Rd. SE18 5H **107**
Tuscany Corte *SE13* 3D **122**
(off Loampit Va.)
Tuscany Ho. E17 2B **50**
IG3: Ilf 6A **54**
Tuskar St. SE10 6G **105**
Tussah Ho. *E2* 2J **85**
(off Russia La.)
Tustin Est. SE15 6J **103**
Tuttlebee La.
IG9: Buck H 2D **36**
Tuttle Ho. *SW1* 6C **18**
(off Aylesford St.)
Tweed Ct. *W7* 6J **77**
(off Hanway Rd.)
Tweeddale Gro. UB10: Ick 3E **56**
Tweeddale Rd. SM5: Cars 1B **166**
Tweed Glen RM1: Rom 1K **55**
Tweed Grn. RM1: Rom 1K **55**
Tweedmouth Rd. E13 2K **87**
Tweed Wlk. E14 4E **86**
Tweed Way RM1: Rom 1K **55**
Tweedy Cl. EN1: Enf 5A **24**
Tweedy Rd. BR1: Brom 1J **159**
Tweezer's All. WC2 2J **13**
Twelve Acre Ho. *E12* 3E **70**
(off Grantham Rd.)
Twelvetrees Bus. Pk. E3 4F **87**
Twelvetrees Cres. E3 4E **86**
(not continuous)
E16 4E **86**
Twentyman Cl. IG8: Wfd G 5D **36**
TWICKENHAM 1A **132**
Twickenham Bri. TW1: Twick 5C **114**
Twickenham Cl. CR0: Bedd 3K **167**
Twickenham Gdns. HA3: Hrw W 7D **26**
UB6: G'frd 5A **60**
Twickenham Mus. *1A 132*
(off The Embankment)
Twickenham Rd. E11 2E **68**
TW7: Isle 5A **114**
TW9: Rich 4C **114**
TW11: Tedd 4A **132**
(not continuous)
TW13: Hanw 3D **130**
Twickenham Stadium 6J **113**
Twickenham Stoop 7J **113**
Twickenham Trad. Est. TW1: Twick 6K **113**
Twig Folly Cl. E2 2K **85**
Twigg Cl. DA8: Erith 7K **109**
Twilley St. SW18 7K **117**
Twin Bridges Bus. Pk. CR2: S Croy 6D **168**
Twine Cl. IG11: Bark 3B **90**
Twine Ct. E1 7J **85**
Twineham Grn. N12 4D **30**
Twine Ter. *E3* 4B **86**
(off Ropery St.)
Twining Av. TW2: Twick 3G **131**
Twin Tumps Way SE28 7A **90**
Twisden Rd. NW5 4F **65**
Twist Ho. SE1 3E **102**
Twitten Gro. BR1: Brom 3D **160**
Twybridge Way NW10 7J **61**
Twycross M. SE10 5G **105**
Twyford Abbey Rd. NW10 3F **79**
Twyford Av. N2 3D **46**
W3 7G **79**
Twyford Ct. *HA0: Wemb* 2E **78**
(off Vicars Bri. Cl.)
N10 3E **46**
Twyford Cres. W3 1G **97**
Twyford Ho. N5 3B **66**
N15 6E **48**
(off Chisley Rd.)
Twyford Pl. WC2 7G **7** (6K **83**)
Twyford Rd. HA2: Harr 1F **59**
IG1: Ilf 5G **71**
SM5: Cars 1B **166**
Twyford Sports Cen. 1H **97**
Twyford St. N1 1K **83**
Twynholm Mans. *SW6* 7G **99**
(off Lillie Rd.)
Tyas Rd. E16 4H **87**
Tybenham Rd. SW19 3J **153**
Tyberry Rd. EN3: Enf H 3C **24**
Tyburn Ho. *NW8* 3B **4**
(off Fisherton St.)
Tyburn La. HA1: Harr 7K **41**
Tyburn Tree (site of) 1F **11**
Tyburn Way W1 2F **11** (7D **82**)
Tye La. BR6: Farnb 5G **173**
Tyers Est. SE1 6G **15**
Tyer's Ga. SE1 7G **15** (2E **102**)
Tyers St. SE11 6G **19** (5K **101**)
Tyers Ter. SE11 6G **19** (5K **101**)
Tyeshurst Cl. SE2 5E **108**
Tygan Ho. *SM3: Cheam* 6G **165**
(off The Broadway)
Tylecroft Rd. SW16 2J **155**
Tylehurst Gdns. IG1: Ilf 5G **71**
Tyler Cl. DA8: Erith 7H **109**
E2 2F **85**
Tyler Ct. *SE17* 4D **102**
(off New Paragon Wlk.)
Tyler Rd. UB2: S'hall 3F **95**
Tyler's Ct. W1 1C **12**
Tylers Ct. *E17* 4C **50**
(off Westbury Rd.)
HA0: Wemb 2E **78**
Tylers Ga. HA3: Kenton 6E **42**
Tylers Path SM5: Cars 4D **166**
Tyler St. SE10 5G **105**
(not continuous)
Tylney Av. SE19 5F **139**
(not continuous)
Tylney Ho. *E1* 6H **85**
(off Nelson St.)
Tylney Rd. BR1: Brom 2B **160**
E7 4A **70**
Tynamara *KT1: King T* 4D **150**
(off Portsmouth Rd.)
Tynan Cl. TW14: Felt 1J **129**
Tyndale Ct. *E9* 6A **68**
(off Brookfield Rd.)
E14 5D **104**
(off Transom Sq.)
Tyndale Ho. *N1* 7B **66**
(off Tyndale La.)
Tyndale La. N1 7B **66**
Tyndale Mans. *N1* 7B **66**
(off Upper St.)
Tyndale Ter. N1 7B **66**
Tyndall Gdns. E10 2E **68**
Tyndall Rd. DA16: Well 3K **125**
E10 2E **68**
Tyne Ct. *W7* 6J **77**
(off Hanway Rd.)
Tyneham Cl. SW11 3E **118**
Tyneham Rd. SW11 2E **118**
Tyne Ho. KT2: King T 1D **150**
Tynemouth Cl. E6 6F **89**
Tynemouth Dr. EN1: Enf 1B **24**
Tynemouth Rd. CR4: Mitc 7E **136**
N15 4F **49**
SE18 5J **107**
Tynemouth St. SW6 2A **118**
Tyne St. E1 7K **9** (6F **85**)
Tynsdale Rd. NW10 7A **62**
Tynte Ct. *E9* 5A **68**
(off Mabley St.)
Tynwald Ho. SE26 3G **139**
Type St. E2 2K **85**
Typhoon Way SM6: Wall 7J **167**
Tyrawley Rd. SW6 1K **117**
Tyre La. NW9 4A **44**
Tyrell Cl. HA1: Harr 4J **59**
Tyrell Ct. SM5: Cars 4D **166**
Tyrell Ho. *BR3: Beck* 5D **140**
(off Beckenham Hill Rd.)
Tyrian Pl. E1 5G **85**
Tyrols Rd. SE23 1K **139**
Tyrone Rd. E6 2D **88**
Tyron Way DA14: Sidc 4J **143**
Tyrrell Av. DA16: Well 5A **126**
Tyrrell Ho. *SW1* 7B **18**
(off Churchill Gdns.)
Tyrrell Rd. SE22 4G **121**
Tyrrell Sq. CR4: Mitc 1C **154**
Tyrrel Way NW9 7C **44**
Tyrwhitt Rd. SE4 3C **122**
Tysoe St. EC1 2K **7** (3A **84**)
Tyson Gdns. SE23 7J **121**
Tyson Rd. SE23 7J **121**
Tyssen Pas. E8 6F **67**
Tyssen Rd. N16 3F **67**
Tyssen St. E8 6F **67**
N1 2E **84**
Tytherton *E2* 2J **85**
(off Cyprus St.)
Tytherton Rd. N19 3H **65**

U

Uamvar St. E14 5D **86**
Uber E17 4B **50**
Uckfield Gro. CR4: Mitc 7E **136**
Udall St. SW1 4B **18** (4G **101**)
Udimore Ho. *W10* 5E **80**
(off Sutton Way)
Udney Pk. Rd.
TW11: Tedd 6A **132**
Uffington Rd. NW10 1C **80**
SE27 4A **138**
Ufford Cl. HA3: Hrw W 7A **26**
Ufford Rd. HA3: Hrw W 7A **26**
Ufford St. SE1 6K **13** (2A **102**)
Ufton Ct. UB5: N'olt 3B **76**
Ufton Gro. N1 7D **66**
Ufton Rd. N1 7D **66**
(not continuous)
Uhura Sq. N16 3E **66**
Ujima Ct. SW16 4J **137**
Ullathorne Rd. SW16 4G **137**
Ulleswater Rd. N14 3D **32**
Ullin St. E14 5E **86**
Ullswater E18 2J **51**
Ullswater Cl. BR1: Brom 7G **141**
SW15 4K **133**
UB4: Hayes 2G **75**
Ullswater Ct. HA2: Harr 7E **40**
Ullswater Cres. SW15 4K **133**
Ullswater Ho. *SE15* 6J **103**
(off Hillbeck Cl.)
Ullswater Rd. SE27 2B **138**
SW13 7C **98**
Ulster Gdns. N13 4H **33**
Ulster Pl. NW1 4J **5** (4F **83**)
Ulster Ter. NW1 3H **5** (4F **83**)
Ulundi Rd. SE3 6G **105**
Ulva Rd. SW15 5F **117**
Ulverscroft Rd. SE22 5F **121**
Ulverstone Rd. SE27 2B **138**
Ulverston Rd. E17 2F **51**
Ulysses Rd. NW6 5H **63**
Umberston St. E1 6G **85**
Umbria St. SW15 6C **116**
Umbriel Pl. E13 2J **87**
Umfreville Rd. N4 6B **48**
Undercliff Rd. SE13 3C **122**
UNDERHILL 5D **20**
Underhill EN5: Barn 5D **20**
Underhill Ct. EN5: Barn 5D **20**
Underhill Gdns. W5 7C **78**
Underhill Ho. *E14* 5C **86**
(off Burgess St.)
Underhill Pas. *NW1* 1F **83**
(off Camden High St.)
Underhill Rd. SE22 5G **121**
Underhill St. NW1 1F **83**
Underne Av. N14 2A **32**
Undershaft EC3 1G **15** (6E **84**)
Undershaw Rd. BR1: Brom 3H **141**
Underwood CR0: New Ad 5E **170**
Underwood, The SE9 2D **142**
Underwood Bldg., The *EC1* 5C **84**
(off Bartholomew Cl.)
Underwood Ct. *E10* 1D **68**
(off Leyton Grange Est.)
Underwood Ho.
KT8: W Mole 5E **148**
(off Approach Rd.)
W6 3D **98**
(off Sycamore Gdns.)

Underwood Rd. E1 . . . . . 4G 85
E4 . . . . . 5J 35
IG8: Wfd G 7F 37
Underwood Row N1 . . . . . 1D 8 (3C 84)
Underwood St. N1 . . . . . 1D 8 (3C 84)
Undine Rd. E14 . . . . . 4D 104
Undine St. SW17 . . . . . 5D 136
Uneeda Dr.
UB6: G'frd 1H 77
Unex Twr. *E15* *7F 69*
(off Station St.)
Unicorn Bldg. *E1* *7K 85*
(off Jardine Rd.)
Unicorn Theatre
London 1E 102
Unicorn Vw.
EN5: Barn 6C 20
Unicorn Works N17 . . . . . 7D 34
Union Cl. E11 . . . . . 4F 69
Union Cotts. E15 . . . . . 7G 69
Union Ct. EC2 . . . . . 7G 9
SW4 . . . . . 2J 119
TW9: Rich 5E 114
W9 . . . . . *5J 81*
(off Elmfield Way)
Union Dr. E1 . . . . . 4A 86
Union Gro. SW8 . . . . . 2H 119
Union Ho. CR0: C'don 7C 156
Union La. TW7: Isle 2A 114
Union M. SW4 . . . . . 2J 119
Union Pk. SE10 . . . . . 5H 105
Union Rd.
BR2: Brom 5B 160
CR0: C'don 7C 156
E17 . . . . . 6B 50
HA0: Wemb 6E 60
N11 . . . . . 6C 32
RM7: Rush G 6K 55
SW4 . . . . . 2H 119
SW8 . . . . . 2H 119
UB5: N'olt 2E 76
Union Sq. N1 . . . . . 1C 84
Union St. EN5: Barn 3B 20
KT1: King T 2D 150
SE1 . . . . . 5A 14 (1B 102)
Union Theatre 5B 14
Union Wlk. E2 . . . . . 1H 9 (3E 84)
Union Wharf N1 . . . . . 1C 84
(Arlington Av.)
N1 . . . . . *2C 84*
(off Wenlock Rd.)
UB7: Yiew *1A 92*
(off Bentinck Rd.)
Union Yd. W1 . . . . . 1K 11 (6F 83)
Unitair Cen. TW14: Bedf 6E 110
United Dr. TW14: Felt 7H 111
United Ho. *SE16* *2J 103*
(off Brunel Rd.)
Unit Workshops *E1* *6G 85*
(off Adler St.)
Unity Cl. CR0: New Ad 7D 170
NW10 . . . . . 6C 62
SE19 . . . . . 5C 138
Unity Ct. *SE1* *5F 103*
(off Fortune Pl.)
Unity M. NW1 . . . . . 2H 83
Unity Pl. E17 . . . . . 3A 50
Unity Ter. HA2: Harr 1F 59
Unity Trad. Est. IG8: Wfd G 2B 52
Unity Way SE18 . . . . . 3B 106
Unity Wharf *SE1* *6K 15*
(off Mill St.)
Universal Ho. UB1: S'hall 7C 76
University Cl. NW7 . . . . . 7G 29
University College London
Art Mus. *3C 6*
(off Gower St.)
Bloomsbury Campus . . . 3C 6 (4H 83)
Department of Geological Collections *4C 6*
(off Gower St.)
University College London
Institute of Neurology *4F 7*
(off Queen Sq.)
Slade School of Fine Art *3C 6*
(off Gower Ct.)
University Gdns. DA5: Bexl 7F 127
University of East London
Docklands Campus 7E 88
Duncan House 1F 87
Stratford Campus 6G 69
University of Greenwich
Avery Hill Campus 6G 125
Greenwich Campus,
King William Wlk. 6F 105
Maritime Greenwich Campus 6E 104
University of London
Birkbeck College 5D 6 (5H 83)
Heythrop College *3K 99*
(off Kensington Sq.)
Institute of Education &
Institute of Advanced Legal Studies 4D 6 (4H 83)
Observatory 6G 29
School of Hygiene &
Tropical Medicine 5D 6
School of Oriental &
African Studies 4D 6
Senate House 5D 6 (5H 83)
Warburg Institute 4D 6 (4H 83)
University of North London
Hornsey Rd. 4A 66
Ladbrooke House 5C 66
North London Campus, Spring House 6A 66
University of the Arts London
Camberwell College of Arts -
Peckham Rd. 1E 120
Wilson Rd. 1E 120
Chelsea College of Art & Design 5D 18 (5H 101)
London College of Fashion -
Golden La. 4C 8
Mare St. 7J 67
Wimbledon College of Art 1G 153
University of West London
Brentford Campus 5C 96
Ealing Campus -
Grove House 1D 96
St Marys Road 1D 96
Spesom House 7C 78
Vestry Hall 2D 96
Walpole House 7D 78
University of Westminster
Cavendish Campus -
Hanson St. 5A 6 (5G 83)
Lit. Titchfield St. 6A 6
Harrow Campus 7A 42
Marylebone Campus 5G 5 (5E 82)
Regent Campus -
Regent St. 7K 5
Wells St. 7B 6
University Pl.
DA8: Erith 7J 109
University Rd. SW19 . . . . . 6B 136
University St. WC1 . . . . . 4B 6 (4G 83)
University Way E16 . . . . . 7E 88
Unwin Av.
TW14: Felt 5F 111
Unwin Cl. SE15 . . . . . 6G 103
Unwin Ct. N2 . . . . . 4C 46
Unwin Mans. *W14* *6H 99*
(off Queen's Club Gdns.)
Unwin Rd. SW7 . . . . . 1A 16 (3B 100)
TW7: Isle 3J 113
Unwin Way
HA7: Stan 7J 27
Up at The O2 . . . . . 1G 105
Upbrook M. W2 . . . . . 1A 10 (6A 82)
Upcerne Rd. SW10 . . . . . 7A 100
Upchurch Cl. SE20 . . . . . 7H 139
Upcott Ho. *E3* *3D 86*
(off Bruce Rd.)
E9 . . . . . *7J 67*
(off Frampton Pk. Rd.)
Upcroft Av. HA8: Edg 5D 28
Updale Rd. DA14: Sidc 4K 143
Upfield CR0: C'don 3H 169
Upfield Rd. W7 . . . . . 5K 77
Upgrove Mnr. Way SW2 . . . . . 7A 120
Uphall Rd. IG1: Ilf 5F 71
Upham Pk. Rd. W4 . . . . . 4A 98
Uphill *BR2: Brom* *4H 159*
(off Westmoreland Rd.)
Uphill Dr. NW7 . . . . . 5F 29
NW9 . . . . . 5J 43
Uphill Gro. NW7 . . . . . 4F 29
Uphill Rd. NW7 . . . . . 4F 29
Upland M. SE22 . . . . . 5G 121
Upland Rd. CR2: S Croy 5D 168
DA7: Bex 3F 127
E13 . . . . . 4J 87
SE22 . . . . . 5G 121
(not continuous)
SM2: Sutt 7B 166
Uplands BR3: Beck 2C 158
Uplands, The HA4: Ruis 1J 57
Uplands Av. E17 . . . . . 2K 49
Uplands Bus. Pk. E17 . . . . . 3K 49
Uplands Cl. SE18 . . . . . 5F 107
SW14 . . . . . 5H 115
Uplands Ct. *N21* *7F 23*
(off The Green)
Uplands End IG8: Wfd G 7H 37
Uplands Pk. Rd. EN2: Enf 2F 23
Uplands Rd. EN4: E Barn 1K 31
IG8: Wfd G 7H 37
N8 . . . . . 5K 47
RM6: Chad H 3D 54
Uplands Way N21 . . . . . 5F 23
Upnall Ho. SE15 . . . . . 6J 103
Upney La. IG11: Bark 6J 71
Upnor Way SE17 . . . . . 5E 102
Uppark Dr. IG2: Ilf 6G 53
Up. Abbey Rd. DA17: Belv 4F 109
Up. Addison Gdns. W14 . . . . . 2G 99
Up. Bank St. E14 . . . . . 1D 104
(not continuous)
Up. Bardsey Wlk. *N1* *6C 66*
(off Douglas Rd. Nth.)
Up. Belgrave St. SW1 . . . . . 1H 17 (3E 100)
Up. Berenger Wlk. *SW10* *7B 100*
(off Berenger Wlk.)
Up. Berkeley St. W1 . . . . . 1E 10 (6D 82)
Up. Beulah Hill SE19 . . . . . 1E 156
Up. Blantyre Wlk. *SW10* *7B 100*
(off Blantyre Wlk.)
Up. Brighton Rd. KT6: Surb 6D 150
Up. Brockley Rd. SE4 . . . . . 3B 122
(not continuous)
Up. Brook St. W1 . . . . . 2G 11 (7E 82)
Upper Butts TW8: Bford 6C 96
Up. Caldy Wlk. *N1* *6C 66*
(off Caldy Wlk.)
Up. Camelford Wlk. *W11* *6G 81*
(off St Mark's Rd.)
Up. Cavendish Av. N3 . . . . . 3J 45
Up. Cheapside Pas. *EC2* *1C 14*
(off Cheapside)
Up. Cheyne Row SW3 . . . . . 7C 16 (6C 100)
UPPER CLAPTON 2H 67
Up. Clapton Rd. E5 . . . . . 1H 67
Up. Clarendon Wlk. *W11* *6G 81*
(off Clarendon Rd.)
Up. Dartrey Wlk. *SW10* *7A 100*
(off Whistler Wlk.)
Up. Dengie Wlk. *N1* *1C 84*
(off Baddow Wlk.)
UPPER EDMONTON 5B 34
UPPER ELMERS END 5B 158
Up. Elmers End Rd. BR3: Beck 4A 158
Up. Farm Rd. KT8: W Mole 4D 148
Upper Feilde *W1* *2G 11*
(off Park St.)
Upper Fosters *NW4* *4E 44*
(off New Brent St.)
Up. Green E. CR4: Mitc 3D 154
Up. Green W. CR4: Mitc 2D 154
(not continuous)
Up. Grosvenor St. W1 . . . . . 3G 11 (7E 82)
Up. Grotto Rd. TW1: Twick 2K 131
Upper Ground SE1 . . . . . 4J 13 (1A 102)
Upper Gro. SE25 . . . . . 4E 156
Up. Grove Rd. DA17: Belv 6F 109
Up. Gulland Wlk. *N1* *7C 66*
(off Church Rd.)
UPPER HALLIFORD 4G 147
Up. Halliford By-Pass TW17: Shep . . . 5G 147
Up. Halliford Grn. TW17: Shep 4G 147
Up. Halliford Rd. TW17: Shep 3G 147
(not continuous)
Up. Hampstead Wlk. NW3 . . . . . 4A 64
Up. Ham Rd. KT2: King T 4D 132
TW10: Ham 4D 132
Up. Handa Wlk. *N1* *6D 66*
(off Handa Wlk.)
Up. Hawkwell Wlk. *N1* *1C 84*
(off Maldon Cl.)
UPPER HOLLOWAY 2G 65
Up. Holly Hill Rd. DA17: Belv 5H 109
Up. James St. W1 . . . . . 2B 12 (7G 83)
Up. John St. W1 . . . . . 2B 12 (7G 83)
Up. Lismore Wlk. *N1* *6C 66*
(off Clephane Rd.)
Upper Lodge *W8* *1K 99*
(off Palace Grn.)
Up. Lodge M. TW12: Hamp H 6H 131
Upper Mall W6 . . . . . 5C 98
(not continuous)
Upper Marsh SE1 . . . . . 1H 19 (3K 101)
Up. Montagu St. W1 . . . . . 5E 4 (5D 82)
Up. Mulgrave Rd. SM2: Cheam 7G 165
Upper Nth. St. E14 . . . . . 5C 86
UPPER NORWOOD 1E 156
Upper Pk. Rd. BR1: Brom 1K 159
DA17: Belv 4H 109
KT2: King T 6G 133
N11 . . . . . 5A 32
NW3 . . . . . 5D 64
Up. Phillimore Gdns. W8 . . . . . 2J 99
Up. Ramsey Wlk. *N1* *6D 66*
(off Ramsey Wlk.)
Up. Rawreth Wlk. *N1* *1C 84*
(off Basire St.)
Up. Richmond Rd. SW15 . . . . . 4B 116
Up. Richmond Rd. W. SW14 . . . . . 4G 115
TW10: Rich 4G 115
Upper Rd. E13 . . . . . 3J 87
SM6: Wall 5H 167
UPPER RUXLEY 7G 145
Up. St Martin's La. WC2 . . . . . 2E 12 (7J 83)
Up. Selsdon Rd. CR2: Sande, Sels 7F 169
Up. Sheridan Rd. DA17: Belv 4G 109
UPPER SHIRLEY 4K 169
Up. Shirley Rd. CR0: C'don 2J 169
Upper Sq. TW7: Isle 3A 114
Upper St. N1 . . . . . 2A 84
Up. Sunbury Rd. TW12: Hamp 1C 148
Up. Sutton La. TW5: Hest 7E 94
UPPER SYDENHAM 3H 139
Up. Tachbrook St. SW1 . . . . . 3B 18 (4G 101)
Up. Talbot Wlk. *W11* *6G 81*
(off Talbot Wlk.)
Up. Teddington Rd. KT1: Hamp W 7C 132
Upper Ter. NW3 . . . . . 3A 64
Up. Thames St. EC4 . . . . . 2B 14 (7B 84)
Up. Tollington Pk. N4 . . . . . 1A 66
(not continuous)
Upperton Rd. DA14: Sidc 5K 143
Upperton Rd. E. E13 . . . . . 3A 88
Upperton Rd. W. E13 . . . . . 3A 88
UPPER TOOTING 4D 136
Up. Tooting Pk. SW17 . . . . . 2D 136

Up. Tooting Rd. SW17 . . . . 4D 136
Up. Town Rd. UB6: G'frd 4F 77
Up. Tulse Hill SW2 . . . . 7K 119
Up. Vernon Rd. SM1: Sutt 5B 166
UPPER WALTHAMSTOW 4F 51
Up. Walthamstow Rd. E17 . . . . 4E 50
Up. Whistler Wlk. SW10 . . . . 7A 100
(off Worlds End Est.)
Up. Wickham La. DA16: Well 7B 108
Up. Wimpole St. W1 . . . . 5H 5 (5E 82)
Up. Woburn Pl. WC1 . . . . 2D 6 (3H 83)
Uppingham Av. HA7: Stan 1B 42
Upsdell Av. N13 . . . . 6F 33
Upshire Ho. E17 . . . . 2B 50
Upstairs at the Gatehouse Theatre
Highgate 1E 64
Upstall St. SE5 . . . . 1B 120
UPTON
DA6 . . . . 5D 126
E7 . . . . 7J 69
Upton Av. E7 . . . . 7J 69
Upton Cl. DA5: Bexl 6F 127
NW2 . . . . 3G 63
Upton Ct. SE20 . . . . 7J 139
(off Blean Gro.)
Upton Dene SM2: Sutt 7K 165
Upton Gdns. HA3: Kenton 5B 42
Upton Hgts. E7 . . . . 7J 69
Upton Ho. E9 . . . . 5A 68
(off Ward La.)
Upton La. E7 . . . . 7J 69
Upton Lodge E7 . . . . 6J 69
Upton Lodge Cl. WD23: Bush 1B 26
UPTON PARK 1B 88
Upton Pk. Boleyn Cinema 2B 88
Upton Pk. Rd. E7 . . . . 7K 69
Upton Rd. CR7: Thor H 2D 156
DA5: Bexl 4E 126
DA6: Bex 4E 126
N18 . . . . 5B 34
SE18 . . . . 6G 107
TW3: Houn 3E 112
Upton Rd. Sth. DA5: Bexl 6F 127
Upton Vs. DA6: Bex 4E 126
Upway N12 . . . . 6H 31
Upwey Ho. N1 . . . . 1E 84
Upwood Rd. SE12 . . . . 6J 123
SW16 . . . . 1J 155
Urbanest King's Cross N1 . . . . 1J 83
Urban M. N4 . . . . 6B 48
Urdang, The 2K 7
(off Rosebery Av.)
Urlwin St. SE5 . . . . 6C 102
Urlwin Wlk. SW9 . . . . 1A 120
Urmston Dr. SW19 . . . . 1G 135
Urmston Ho. E14 . . . . 4E 104
(off Seyssel St.)
Urquhart Ct. BR3: Beck 7B 140
Ursa Mans. E20 . . . . 5E 68
(off Cheering La.)
Ursula Gould Way E14 . . . . 5C 86
Ursula Lodges DA14: Sidc 5B 144
Ursula M. N4 . . . . 1C 66
Ursula St. SW11 . . . . 1C 118
Urswick Gdns. RM9: Dag 7E 72
Urswick Rd. E9 . . . . 5J 67
RM9: Dag 7D 72
Usborne M. SW8 . . . . 7K 101
Usher Hall NW4 . . . . 4D 44
(off The Burroughs)
Usher Rd. E3 . . . . 1B 86
(not continuous)
Usk Rd. SW11 . . . . 4A 118
Usk St. E2 . . . . 3K 85
Utah Bldg. SE13 . . . . 1D 122
(off Deal's Gateway)
Utopia Village NW1 . . . . 7E 64
Uvedale Rd. EN2: Enf 5J 23
RM10: Dag 3G 73
Uverdale Rd. SW10 . . . . 7A 100
UXBRIDGE 1A 74
Uxbridge Ct. KT1: King T 5D 150
(off Uxbridge Rd.)
Uxbridge Golf Course 2A 56
Uxbridge Lido 6A 56
Uxbridge Rd. HA3: Hrw W 7A 26
HA5: Hat E, Pinn 2A 40
HA7: Stan 7A 26
KT1: King T 4D 150
TW12: Hamp, Hamp H 4E 130
TW13: Felt 2A 130
UB1: S'hall 1E 94
UB4: Hayes, Yead 5G 75
UB10: Hil 3C 74
W3 . . . . 7E 78
W5 . . . . 7E 78
W7 . . . . 1K 95
W12 . . . . 1C 98
W13 . . . . 1B 96
Uxbridge Rd. Retail Pk. UB4: Yead 7A 76
Uxbridge St. W8 . . . . 1J 99
Uxendon Cres. HA9: Wemb 1E 60
Uxendon Hill HA9: Wemb 1F 61

V

Vaine Ho. E9 . . . . 6A 68
Vaizeys Wharf SE7 . . . . 3K 105
Valance Av. E4 . . . . 1B 36
Valan Leas BR2: Brom 3G 159
Vale, The CR0: C'don 2K 169
HA4: Ruis 4A 58
IG8: Wfd G 7D 36
N10 . . . . 1E 46
N14 . . . . 7C 22
NW11 . . . . 3F 63
SW3 . . . . 7A 16 (6B 100)
TW5: Hest 6C 94
TW14: Felt 6K 111
TW16: Sun 6J 129
W3 . . . . 1K 97
Vale Cl. BR6: Farnb 4E 172
N2 . . . . 3D 46
TW1: Twick 3A 132
W9 . . . . 3A 82
Vale Cotts. SW15 . . . . 3A 134
Vale Ct. EN5: New Bar 4E 20
W3 . . . . 1B 98
W9 . . . . 3A 82
Vale Cres. SW15 . . . . 4A 134
Vale Cft. HA5: Pinn 5C 40
Vale Dr. EN5: Barn 4C 20
Vale End SE22 . . . . 4F 121
Vale Est., The W3 . . . . 1A 98
Vale Farm Sports Cen. 4B 60
Vale Gro. N4 . . . . 7C 48
W3 . . . . 2K 97
Vale La. W3 . . . . 5G 79
Vale Lodge SE23 . . . . 2J 139
Valence Av. RM8: Dag 1D 72
Valence Cir. RM8: Dag 3D 72
Valence House Mus. 3E 72
Valence Rd. DA8: Erith 7K 109
Valence Wood Rd. RM8: Dag 3D 72
Valencia Rd. HA7: Stan 4H 27
Valentia Pl. SW9 . . . . 4A 120
Valentina Av. NW9 . . . . 2B 44
Valentine Av. DA5: Bexl 2E 144
Valentine Ct. SE23 . . . . 2K 139
(not continuous)
Valentine Ho. E3 . . . . 1B 86
(off Garrison Rd.)
Valentine Pl. SE1 . . . . 6A 14 (2B 102)
Valentine Rd. E9 . . . . 6K 67
HA2: Harr 3F 59
Valentine Row SE1 . . . . 7A 14 (2B 102)
Valentines Mansion & Gdns. 7E 52
Valentines Rd. IG1: Ilf 1F 71
Valentine's Way RM7: Rush G 2K 73
VALE OF HEALTH 3A 64
Vale of Health NW3 . . . . 3B 64
Vale Pde. SW15 . . . . 3A 134
Valerian Wlk. N11 . . . . 2K 31
Valerian Way E15 . . . . 3G 87
Valerie Ct. SM2: Sutt 7K 165
WD23: Bush 1B 26
Valerio M. N1 . . . . 6D 66
Vale Ri. NW11 . . . . 1H 63
Vale Rd. BR1: Brom 1E 160
CR4: Mitc 3H 155
E7 . . . . 6K 69
KT4: Wor Pk 3B 164
KT19: Ewe 4B 164
N4 . . . . 7C 48
SM1: Sutt 4K 165
Vale Rd. Nth. KT6: Surb 2E 162
Vale Rd. Sth. KT6: Surb 2E 162
Vale Row N5 . . . . 3B 66
Vale Royal N7 . . . . 7J 65
Vale Royal Ho. WC2 . . . . 2D 12
(off Charing Cross Rd.)
Valery Pl. TW12: Hamp 7E 130
Valeside Ct. EN5: New Bar 4E 20
Vale St. SE27 . . . . 3D 138
Valeswood Rd. BR1: Brom 5H 141
Vale Ter. N4 . . . . 6C 48
Valetta Gro. E13 . . . . 2J 87
Valetta Rd. W3 . . . . 2A 98
Valette Ct. N10 . . . . 4F 47
(off St James's La.)
Valette Ho. E9 . . . . 6J 67
Valette St. E9 . . . . 6J 67
Valiant Cl. RM7: Mawney 2H 55
UB5: N'olt 3B 76
Valiant Ho. E14 . . . . 2E 104
(off Plevna St.)
SE7 . . . . 5A 106
Valiant Path NW9 . . . . 7F 29
Valiant Way E6 . . . . 5D 88
Vallance Rd. E1 . . . . 3G 85
E2 . . . . 3G 85
N22 . . . . 2G 47
Vallentin Rd. E17 . . . . 4E 50
Valley, The 5A 106
Valley Av. N12 . . . . 4G 31
Valley Cl. HA5: Pinn 2K 39
Valley Dr. NW9 . . . . 6G 43
Valleyfield Rd. SW16 . . . . 5K 137
Valley Flds. Cres. EN2: Enf 2F 23
Valley Gdns. HA0: Wemb 7F 61
SW19 . . . . 7B 136
Valley Gro. SE7 . . . . 5A 106
Valley Leisure Pk. CR0: Wadd 1J 167
Valleylink Est. EN3: Pond E 6F 25
Valley M. TW1: Twick 2K 131
Valley Point Ind. Est. CR0: Bedd 7J 155
Valley Rd. BR2: Brom 2G 159
BR5: St P 7B 144
DA8: Erith 4J 109
DA17: Belv 4H 109
SW16 . . . . 5K 137
UB10: Uxb 2A 74
Valley Side E4 . . . . 2H 35
SE7 . . . . 5B 106
Valley Side Pde. E4 . . . . 2H 35
Valley Vw. EN5: Barn 6B 20
Valley Wlk. CR0: C'don 2J 169
Valliere Rd. NW10 . . . . 3C 80
Valliers Wood Rd. DA15: Sidc 1J 143
Vallings Pl. KT6: Surb 7B 150
Vallis Way KT9: Chess 4D 162
W13 . . . . 5A 78
Val McKenzie Av. N7 . . . . 3A 66
Valmar Rd. SE5 . . . . 1C 120
Valmar Trad. Est. SE5 . . . . 1C 120
Valnay St. SW17 . . . . 5D 136
Valognes Av. E17 . . . . 1A 50
Valois Ho. SE1 . . . . 3F 103
(off St Saviour's Est.)
Valonia Gdns. SW18 . . . . 6H 117
Vambery Rd. SE18 . . . . 6G 107
Vamey Ct. BR1: Brom 3J 159
V&A Mus. of Childhood 3J 85
Vanbrough Cres. UB5: N'olt 1A 76
Vanbrugh Castle SE10 . . . . 6G 105
(off Maze Hill)
Vanbrugh Cl. E16 . . . . 5B 88
Vanbrugh Ct. SE11 . . . . 4K 19
Vanbrugh Dr. KT12: Walt T 7A 148
Vanbrugh Flds. SE3 . . . . 6H 105
Vanbrugh Hill SE3 . . . . 5H 105
SE10 . . . . 5H 105
Vanbrugh Ho. E9 . . . . 7J 67
(off Loddiges Rd.)
Vanbrugh M.
KT12: Walt T 7A 148
Vanbrugh Pk. SE3 . . . . 7H 105
Vanbrugh Pk. Rd. SE3 . . . . 7H 105
Vanbrugh Pk. Rd. W. SE3 . . . . 7H 105
Vanbrugh Rd. W4 . . . . 3K 97
Vanbrugh Ter. SE3 . . . . 1H 123
Vanburgh Cl. BR6: Orp 1J 173
Vanburgh Ho. E1 . . . . 5J 9
(off Folgate St.)
Vancouver Cl. BR6: Chels 4K 173
Vancouver Ho. E1 . . . . 1H 103
(off Reardon Path)
SE16 . . . . 2K 103
(off Needleman St.)
Vancouver Mans. HA8: Edg 1H 43
Vancouver Rd. HA8: Edg 1H 43
SE23 . . . . 2A 140
TW10: Ham 4C 132
UB4: Yead 4K 75
Vanderbilt Rd. SW18 . . . . 1K 135
Vanderbilt Vs. W12 . . . . 2F 99
(off Sterne St.)
Vandervell Ct. W3 . . . . 2A 98
(off Amber Way)
Vanderville Gdns. N2 . . . . 2B 46
Vandome Cl. E16 . . . . 6K 87
Vandon Ct. SW1 . . . . 1B 18
(off Petty France)
Vandon Pas. SW1 . . . . 1B 18 (3G 101)
Vandon St. SW1 . . . . 1B 18 (3G 101)
Van Dyck Av. KT3: N Mald 7K 151
Vandyke Cl. SW15 . . . . 7F 117
Vandyke Cross SE9 . . . . 5C 124
Vandy St. EC2 . . . . 4G 9 (4E 84)
Vane Cl. HA3: Kenton 6F 43
NW3 . . . . 5B 64
Vanessa Cl. DA17: Belv 5G 109
Vanessa Way DA5: Bexl 3K 145
Vane St. SW1 . . . . 3B 18 (4G 101)
Vange Ho. W10 . . . . 5E 80
(off Sutton Way)
Van Gogh Cl. TW7: Isle 3A 114
Van Gogh Ct. E14 . . . . 3F 105
Vanguard NW9 . . . . 7F 29
Vanguard Bldg. E14 . . . . 2B 104
Vanguard Cl. CR0: C'don 1B 168
E16 . . . . 5J 87
RM7: Mawney 2G 55
Vanguard Ct. SE5 . . . . 1E 120
Vanguard Ho. E8 . . . . 7H 67
Vanguard St. SE8 . . . . 1C 122
Vanguard Way SM6: Wall 7J 167
TW6: H'row A 2G 111
Vanilla & Sesame Ct. SE1 . . . . 6K 15
(off Curlew St.)
Vanneck Sq. SW15 . . . . 5C 116
Vanoc Gdns. BR1: Brom 4J 141
Vanquish Cl. TW2: Whitt 7E 112
Vansittart Rd. E7 . . . . 4H 69
Vansittart St. SE14 . . . . 7A 104
Vanstone Ct. N7 . . . . 6A 66
(off Blackthorn Av.)
Vanston Pl. SW6 . . . . 7J 99
Vantage Bldg. UB3: Hayes 3H 93
(off Station App.)
Vantage Ct. UB3: Harl 7G 93
Vantage M. E14 . . . . 1E 104
(off Coldharbour)

Vantage Pl. TW14: Felt 6J 111
  W8 . . . . .3J 99
Vantage Point BR3: Beck 1F 159
  (off Albemarle Rd.)
  CR2: Sande 7D 168
  EN5: Barn 4C 20
  (off Victors Way)
Vantage W. TW8: Bford 4F 97
Vantrey Ho. SE11 . . . . .4J 19
Vant Rd. SW17 . . . . .5D 136
Varcoe Gdns. UB3: Hayes 6F 75
Varcoe Rd. SE16 . . . . .5H 103
Vardens Rd. SW11 . . . . .4B 118
Varden St. E1 . . . . .6H 85
Vardon Cl. W3 . . . . .6K 79
Varley Dr. TW1: Isle 4B 114
Varley Ho. NW6 . . . . .1J 81
  SE1 .3C 102
  (off County St.)
Varley Pde. NW9 . . . . .4A 44
Varley Rd. E16 . . . . .6K 87
Varley Way CR4: Mitc 2B 154
Varna Rd. SW6 . . . . .7G 99
  TW12: Hamp 1F 149
Varndell St. NW1 . . . . .1A 6 (3G 83)
Varnishers Yd. N1 . . . . .1F 7
  (off York Way)
Varsity Dr. TW1: Twick 5J 113
Varsity Row SW14 . . . . .2J 115
Vartry Rd. N15 . . . . .6D 48
Vascroft Est. NW10 . . . . .4H 79
Vassall Ho. E3 . . . . .3A 86
  (off Antill Rd.)
Vassall Rd. SW9 . . . . .7A 102
Vat Ho. SW8 . . . . .3F 101
  (off Rita Rd.)
Vauban Est. SE16 . . . . .3F 103
Vauban St. SE16 . . . . .3F 103
Vaudeville Theatre 3F 13
  (off Strand)
Vaughan Almshouses TW15: Ashf . .5D 128
  (off Feltham Hill Rd.)
Vaughan Av. NW4 . . . . .5C 44
  W6 . . . . .4B 98
Vaughan Cl. TW12: Hamp 6C 130
Vaughan Est. E2 . . . . .1J 9
Vaughan Gdns. IG1: Ilf 7D 52
Vaughan Ho. SE1 . . . . .6A 14
  (off Blackfriars Rd.)
  SW4 .7G 119
Vaughan Rd. DA16: Well 2K 125
  E15 . . . . .6H 69
  HA1: Harr 6G 41
  KT7: T Ditt 7B 150
  SE5 .2C 120
Vaughan St. RM8: Dag 1E 72
  SE16 . . . . .2B 104
Vaughan Way E1 . . . . .7G 85
Vaughan Williams Cl. SE8 . . . . .7C 104
VAUXHALL 5H 19 (6J 101)
Vauxhall Bri. SW1 . . . . . . .6E 18 (5J 101)
Vauxhall Bri. Rd. SW1 . . . .2A 18 (3G 101)
Vauxhall City Farm 6G 19
Vauxhall Climbing Cen. 7F 19
  (off Sth. Lambeth Rd.)
VAUXHALL CROSS 5J 101
Vauxhall Gdns. CR2: S Croy 6C 168
Vauxhall Gro. SW8 . . . . . . .7G 19 (6K 101)
Vauxhall St. SE11 . . . . .5H 19 (5K 101)
Vauxhall Wlk. SE11 . . . . . . .5G 19 (5K 101)
Vawdrey Cl. E1 . . . . .4J 85
Veals Mead CR4: Mitc 1C 154
Vectis Gdns. SW17 . . . . .6F 137
Vectis Rd. SW17 . . . . .6F 137
Veda Rd. SE13 . . . . .4C 122
Vega Ho. E20 . . . . .5E 68
  (off Prize Wlk.)
Vega Rd. WD23: Bush 1B 26
Veitch Cl. TW14: Felt 7H 111
Veldene Way HA2: Harr 3D 58
Velde Way SE22 . . . . .5E 120

Velletri Ho. E2 . . . . .2K 85
  (off Mace St.)
Vellum Cl. E17 . . . . .2A 50
Vellum Dr. SM5: Cars 3E 166
Velodrome
  Queen Elizabeth Olympic Pk.
  . . . . .5D 68
Velo Pl. E20 . . . . .5D 68
Velvet Ho. E2 . . . . .2F 85
  (off Whiston Rd.)
Venables Cl. RM10: Dag 4H 73
Venables St. NW8 . . . . .5B 4 (4B 82)
Vencourt Pl. W6 . . . . .4C 98
Veneer Bldg., The
  UB3: Hayes 2G 93
Venerable Ho. E3 . . . . .4B 86
  (off Portia Way)
Venetian Ho. E20 . . . . .6D 68
  (off Victory Pde.)
Venetian Rd. SE5 . . . . .2C 120
Venetia Rd. N4 . . . . .6B 48
  W5 . . . . .2D 96
Venice Corte SE13 . . . . .3E 122
  (off Elmira St.)
Venice Ct. SE5 . . . . .7C 102
  (off Bowyer St.)
Venice Ho. HA0: Wemb 1E 78
Venice Wlk. W2 . . . . .5A 82
Venner Rd. SE26 . . . . .6J 139
  (not continuous)
Venners Cl. DA7: Bex 2K 127
Venn Ho. N1 . . . . .1K 83
  (off Barnsbury Est.)
Venn St. SW4 . . . . .4G 119
Ventnor Av. HA7: Stan 1B 42
Ventnor Dr. N20 . . . . .3E 30
Ventnor Gdns. IG11: Bark 6J 71
Ventnor Rd. SE14 . . . . .7K 103
  SM2: Sutt 7K 165
Venture Cl. DA5: Bexl 7E 126
Venture Ct. SE1 . . . . .7H 15
  (off Market Yd. M.)
  SE12 .7J 123
Venture Ho. W10 . . . . .6F 81
  (off Bridge Cl.)
Venue St. E14 . . . . .5E 86
Venus Ho. E3 . . . . .1C 86
  (off Garrison Rd.)
  E14 .4C 104
  (off Westferry Rd.)
Venus M. CR4: Mitc 3C 154
Venus Rd. SE18 . . . . .3D 106
Vera Av. N21 . . . . .5F 23
Vera Ct. E3 . . . . .3D 86
  (off Grace Pl.)
Vera Lynn Cl. E7 . . . . .4J 69
Vera Rd. SW6 . . . . .1G 117
Verbena Cl. E16 . . . . .4H 87
  UB7: W Dray 1E 174
Verbena Gdns. W6 . . . . .5C 98
Verdant Cl. SE6 . . . . .7G 123
  (off Verdant La.)
Verdant La. SE6 . . . . .7G 123
Verdayne Av. CR0: C'don 2K 169
Verdi Cres. W10 . . . . .2G 81
Verdon Roe Ct. E4 . . . . .3J 35
Verdun Rd. SE18 . . . . .6A 108
  SW13 . . . . .6C 98
Vere Cl. W2 . . . . .6K 81
  (off Westbourne Gdns.)
Vereker Dr. TW16: Sun 3J 147
Vereker Rd. W14 . . . . .5G 99
Vere St. W1 . . . . .1J 11 (6F 83)
Veridion Way DA18: Erith 2F 109
Veritas Ho. DA14: Sidc 2A 144
  (off Jubilee Way)
Verity Cl. W11 . . . . .7G 81
Verity Ho. E3 . . . . .3B 86
  (off Merchant St.)
Vermeer Ct. E14 . . . . .3F 105
Vermeer Gdns. SE15 . . . . .4J 121

Vermilion Apartments E3 . . . . .1A 86
  (off Gunmaker's La.)
Vermont Cl.
  EN2: Enf 4G 23
Vermont Ho. E17 . . . . .2B 50
Vermont Rd. SE19 . . . . .6D 138
  SM1: Sutt 3K 165
  SW18 . . . . .6K 117
Verna Ho. E20 . . . . .5E 68
  (off Sunrise Cl.)
Verne Ct. W3 . . . . .3J 97
  (off Vincent Rd.)
Verney Gdns. RM9: Dag 4E 72
Verney Ho. NW8 . . . . .3B 4
Verney Rd. RM9: Dag 4E 72
  (not continuous)
  SE16 .6G 103
Verney St. NW10 . . . . .3K 61
Verney Way SE16 . . . . .5H 103
Vernham Rd. SE18 . . . . .6G 107
Vernon Av. E12 . . . . .4D 70
  IG8: Wfd G 7E 36
  SW20 . . . . .2F 153
Vernon Cl. KT19: Ewe 6J 163
  TW19: Stanw 1A 128
Vernon Ct. HA7: Stan 1B 42
  NW2 . . . . .3H 63
  W5 . . . . .7C 78
Vernon Cres. EN4: E Barn 6K 21
Vernon Dr. HA7: Stan 1A 42
Vernon Ho. SE11 . . . . .6H 19
  WC1 . . . . .6F 7
  (off Vernon Pl.)
Vernon Mans. W14 . . . . .6H 99
  (off Queen's Club Gdns.)
Vernon M. E17 . . . . .5B 50
  W14 . . . . .4G 99
Vernon Pl. WC1 . . . . .6F 7 (5J 83)
Vernon Ri. UB6: G'frd 5H 59
  WC1 . . . . .1H 7 (3K 83)
Vernon Rd. E3 . . . . .2B 86
  E11 . . . . .1G 69
  E15 . . . . .7G 69
  E17 . . . . .5B 50
  IG3: Ilf 1K 71
  N8 . . . . .3A 48
  SM1: Sutt 5A 166
  SW14 . . . . .3K 115
  TW13: Felt 2H 129
Vernon Sq. WC1 . . . . .1H 7 (3K 83)
Vernon St. W14 . . . . .4G 99
Vernon Yd. W11 . . . . .7H 81
Veroan Rd. DA7: Bex 2E 126
Verona Ct. SE14 . . . . .6K 103
  (off Myers La.)
  TW15: Ashf 4D 128
  W4 . . . . .5A 98
Verona Dr. KT6: Surb 2E 162
Verona Ho. CR4: Mitc 3F 155
  (off Aventine Av.)
Verona Rd. E7 . . . . .7J 69
Veronica Gdns. SW16 . . . . .1G 155
Veronica Ho. E3 . . . . .3D 86
  (off Talwin St.)
  SE4 . . . . .3B 122
Veronica Rd. SW17 . . . . .2F 137
Veronique Gdns. IG6: Ilf 5G 53
Verran Rd. SW12 . . . . .7F 119
Versailles Rd. SE20 . . . . .7G 139
Verulam Av. E17 . . . . .6B 50
Verulam Bldgs. WC1 . . . . .5H 7
Verulam Ct. NW9 . . . . .7C 44
  UB1: S'hall 6G 77
  (off Haldane Rd.)
Verulam Ho. W6 . . . . .2E 98
  (off Hammersmith Gro.)
Verulam Rd. UB6: G'frd 4E 76
Verulam St. WC1 . . . . .5J 7 (5A 84)
Vervian Ho. SE15 . . . . .7G 103
  (off Reddins Rd.)
Verwood Dr. EN4: Cockf 3J 21

Verwood Ho. SW8 . . . . .7K 101
  (off Cobbett St.)
Verwood Lodge E14 . . . . .3F 105
  (off Manchester Rd.)
Verwood Rd. HA2: Harr 2G 41
Veryan Ct. N8 . . . . .5H 47
Vesage Ct. EC1 . . . . .6K 7
Vesey Path E14 . . . . .6D 86
Vespan Rd. W12 . . . . .2C 98
Vesta Ct. SE1 . . . . .7G 15
Vesta Ho. E3 . . . . .1C 86
  (off Garrison Rd.)
  E20 . . . . .5E 68
  (off Liberty Bri. Rd.)
Vesta Rd. SE4 . . . . .2A 122
Vestris Rd. SE23 . . . . .2K 139
Vestry Ct. RM7: Rush G 6K 55
  SW1 . . . . .2D 18
  (off Monck St.)
Vestry House Mus. 4D 50
Vestry M. SE5 . . . . .1E 120
  SW18 . . . . .5B 118
Vestry Rd. E17 . . . . .4D 50
  SE5 .1E 120
Vestry St. N1 . . . . .1E 8 (3D 84)
Vesuvius Apartments E3 . . . . .2B 86
  (off Centurion La.)
Vevey St. SE6 . . . . .2B 140
Veysey Gdns. RM10: Dag 3G 73
Viaduct, The E18 . . . . .2J 51
  HA0: Wemb 1E 78
  N10 . . . . .4F 47
Viaduct Bldgs. EC1 . . . . . . .6K 7 (5A 84)
Viaduct Pl. E2 . . . . .3H 85
Viaduct Rd. N2 . . . . .2B 46
Viaduct St. E2 . . . . .3H 85
Vian St. SE13 . . . . .3D 122
Viant Ho. NW10 . . . . .7K 61
  (off Fawood Av.)
Vibart Gdns. SW2 . . . . .7K 119
Vibart Wlk. N1 . . . . .1J 83
  (off Outram Pl.)
Vibeca Apartments E1 . . . . .6K 9
  (off Chicksand St.)
Vibia Cl. TW19: Stanw 7A 110
Vicarage Av. SE3 . . . . .7J 105
Vicarage Cl. DA8: Erith 6J 109
  HA4: Ruis 7F 39
  KT4: Wor Pk 1A 164
  UB5: N'olt 7D 58
Vicarage Ct. BR3: Beck 3A 158
  IG1: Ilf 5F 71
  TW14: Bedf 7E 110
  W8 . . . . .2K 99
Vicarage Cres. SW11 . . . . .1B 118
Vicarage Dr. BR3: Beck 1C 158
  IG11: Bark 7G 71
  SW14 . . . . .5K 115
Vicarage Farm Ct. TW5: Hest 7D 94
Vicarage Farm Rd. TW3: Houn 2C 112
  TW5: Hest 1C 112
Vicarage Flds. KT12: Walt T 6A 148
Vicarage Fld. Shop. Cen.
  IG11: Bark 7G 71
Vicarage Gdns. CR4: Mitc 3C 154
  SW14 . . . . .5J 115
  W8 . . . . .1J 99
Vicarage Ga. W8 . . . . .1K 99
Vicarage Gro. SE5 . . . . .1D 120
Vicarage Ho.
  KT1: King T 2F 151
  (off Cambridge Rd.)
Vicarage La. E6 . . . . .3D 88
  E15 . . . . .7G 69
  IG1: Ilf 1H 71
  KT17: Ewe 7C 164
  (not continuous)
Vicarage M. NW9 . . . . .2K 61
Vicarage Pde. N15 . . . . .4C 48
Vicarage Pk. SE18 . . . . .5G 107
Vicarage Path N8 . . . . .7J 47

Vicarage Rd. CRO: Wadd 3A 168
DA5: Bexl 1H 145
E10 . . . .7C 50
E15 . . . .7H 69
IG8: Wfd G 7H 37
KT1: Hamp W 1C 150
KT1: King T 2D 150
N17 . . . .1G 49
NW4 . . . .6C 44
RM10: Dag 7H 73
SE18 . . . .5G 107
(not continuous)
SM1: Sutt 3K 165
SW14 . . . .5J 115
TW2: Twick 2J 131
TW2: Whitt 6G 113
TW11: Tedd 5A 132
TW16: Sun 5H 129
Vicarage Wlk.
KT12: Walt T 7J 147
SW11 . . . .1B 118
Vicarage Way HA2: Harr 7E 40
NW10 . . . .3K 61
Vicars Bri. Cl. HA0: Wemb 2E 78
Vicar's Cl. E9 . . . .1J 85
Vicars Cl. E15 . . . .1J 87
EN1: Enf 2K 23
Vicar's Hill SE13 . . . .4D 122
Vicars Moor La. N21 . . . .7F 23
Vicars Oak Rd. SE19 . . . .6E 138
Vicar's Rd. NW5 . . . .5E 64
Vicars Wlk. RM8: Dag 3B 72
Vicary Ho. EC1 . . . .5C 84
(off Bartholomew Cl.)
Vicentia Cl. SW11 . . . .3A 118
Viceroy Cl. N2 . . . .4C 46
(off East End Rd.)
Viceroy Ct. CRO: C'don 1D 168
NW8 . . . .2C 82
(off Prince Albert Rd.)
Viceroy Pde. N2 . . . .4C 46
(off High Rd.)
Viceroy Rd. SW8 . . . .1J 119
Vicinity Ho. E14 . . . .7C 86
(off Storehouse M.)
Vic Johnson Ho. E3 . . . .1B 86
(off Armagh Rd.)
Vickers Cl. SM6: Wall 7K 167
Vickers Ct. N17 . . . .3H 49
SE20 . . . .7K 139
TW19: Stanw 6A 110
(off Whitley Cl.)
Vickers Rd. DA8: Erith 5K 109
Vickers Way TW4: Houn 5C 112
Vickery Ct. EC1 . . . .3D 8
(off Mitchell St.)
Vickery's Wharf E14 . . . .6C 86
Victor Cazalet Ho. N1 . . . .1B 84
(off Gaskin St.)
Victor Gro. HA0: Wemb 7E 60
Victor Ho. SE7 . . . .6A 106
Victoria & Albert Mus. 2B 16 (3B 100)
Victoria Arc. SW1 . . . .2K 17
(off Victoria St.)
Victoria Av. E6 . . . .1B 88
EC2 . . . .6H 9 (5E 84)
EN4: E Barn 4G 21
HA9: Wemb 6H 61
KT6: Surb 6D 150
KT8: W Mole 3F 149
N3 . . . .1H 45
SM6: Wall 3E 166
TW3: Houn 5E 112
UB10: Hil 6D 56
Victoria Bldgs. E8 . . . .1H 85
(off Mare St.)
Victoria Chambers EC2 . . . .3G 9
(off Paul St.)
Victoria Cl. EN4: E Barn 4G 21
HA1: Harr 6K 41
KT8: W Mole 3E 148

Victoria Cl. SE22 . . . .5G 121
UB3: Hayes 6F 75
Victoria Colonnade WC1 . . . .6F 7
(off Southampton Row)
Victoria Cotts. E1 . . . .5G 85
(off Deal St.)
N10 . . . .2E 46
TW9: Kew 1F 115
Victoria Ct. E18 . . . .3K 51
HA7: Stan 7J 27
(off Howard Rd.)
HA9: Wemb 6G 61
SE1 . . . .4E 102
(off Hendre Rd.)
SE26 . . . .6J 139
W3 . . . .2G 97
Victoria Cres. N15 . . . .5E 48
SE19 . . . .6E 138
SW19 . . . .7H 135
Victoria Dock Rd. E16 . . . .7H 87
Victoria Dr. SW19 . . . .7F 117
Victoria Emb. EC4 . . . .6F 13 (7K 83)
SW1 . . . .6F 13 (2J 101)
WC2 . . . .6F 13 (2J 101)
Victoria Gdns.
TW5: Hest 1C 112
W11 . . . .1J 99
Victoria Gro. N12 . . . .5G 31
W8 . . . .3A 100
Victoria Gro. M. W2 . . . .7J 81
Victoria Hall E16 . . . .1J 105
(off Wesley Av.)
Victoria Ho. E6 . . . .6E 88
HA8: Edg 6C 28
SE16 . . . .2J 103
(off Surrey Quays Rd.)
SW1 . . . .5J 17
(off Ebury Bri. Rd.)
SW1 . . . .3B 18
(off Francis St.)
SW8 . . . .7J 101
(off Sth. Lambeth Rd.)
Victoria Ind. Est. W3 . . . .5A 80
Victoria La. EN5: Barn 4C 20
UB3: Harl 5F 93
Victoria Mans. NW10 . . . .7D 62
SW8 . . . .7J 101
(off Sth. Lambeth Rd.)
W14 . . . .6H 99
(off Queen's Club Gdns.)
Victoria M. E8 . . . .8G 67
NW6 . . . .1J 81
SW4 . . . .4F 119
SW18 . . . .1A 136
Victoria Mills Studios E15 . . . .1F 87
(off Burford Rd.)
Victorian Gro. N16 . . . .4E 66
Victorian Hgts. SW8 . . . .2F 119
(off Thackeray Rd.)
Victorian Rd. N16 . . . .3E 66
Victoria Palace Theatre 2A 18
(off Victoria St.)
Victoria Pde. SE10 . . . .6D 104
TW9: Kew 1G 115
(off Sandycombe Rd.)
Victoria Pk.
Hackney 1K 85
Victoria Pk. Ct. E9 . . . .7J 67
(off Well St.)
Victoria Pk. Ind. Cen. E9 . . . .7C 68
(off Rothbury Rd.)
Victoria Pk. Rd. E9 . . . .1J 85
Victoria Pk. Sq. E2 . . . .3J 85
Victoria Pk. Studios E9 . . . .6J 67
(off Milborne St.)
Victoria Pas. NW8 . . . .3B 4
Victoria Pl. TW9: Rich 5D 114
Victoria Pl. Shop. Cen. SW1 . . . .3K 17
Victoria Point E13 . . . .2J 87
(off Victoria Rd.)
Victoria Retail Pk. HA4: Ruis 5B 58

Victoria Ri. NW6 . . . .7A 64
(off Hilgrove Rd.)
SW4 . . . .3F 119
Victoria Road 5H 73
Victoria Rd. BR2: Brom 5B 160
BR7: Chst 5E 142
CR4: Mitc 7C 136
DA6: Bex 4G 127
DA8: Erith 6K 109
DA15: Sidc 3K 143
E4 . . . .1B 36
E11 . . . .4G 69
E13 . . . .2J 87
E17 . . . .2E 50
E18 . . . .2K 51
EN4: E Barn 4G 21
HA4: Ruis 1J 57
IG9: Buck H 2G 37
IG11: Bark 6F 71
KT1: King T 2F 151
KT6: Surb 6D 150
N4 . . . .7K 47
N9 . . . .4A 34
N15 . . . .4G 49
N18 . . . .4A 34
N22 . . . .1G 47
NW4 . . . .4E 44
NW6 . . . .2H 81
NW7 . . . .5G 29
NW10 . . . .5K 79
RM10: Dag 5H 73
SM1: Sutt 5B 166
SW14 . . . .3K 115
TW1: Twick 7B 114
TW11: Tedd 6A 132
TW13: Felt 1K 129
UB2: S'hall 3D 94
W3 . . . .5K 79
W5 . . . .5B 78
W8 . . . .3A 100
WD23: Bush 1A 26
Victoria Sq. SW1 . . . .1K 17 (3F 101)
Victoria St. DA17: Belv 5F 109
E15 . . . .7G 69
SW1 . . . .2K 17 (3G 101)
Victoria Ter. HA1: Harr 1J 59
N4 . . . .1A 66
NW10 . . . .4B 80
W5 . . . .1D 96
Victoria Vs. TW9: Rich 3F 115
Victoria Way HA4: Ruis 5B 58
SE7 . . . .5K 105
Victoria Wharf E2 . . . .2K 85
(off Palmers Rd.)
E14 . . . .7A 86
SE8 . . . .5B 104
(off Dragoon Rd.)
Victoria Works NW2 . . . .2D 62
Victoria Yd. E1 . . . .6G 85
Victor Rd. HA2: Harr 3G 41
NW10 . . . .3D 80
SE20 . . . .7K 139
TW11: Tedd 4J 131
Victors Dr. TW12: Hamp 6C 130
Victors Way EN5: Barn 3C 20
Victor Ter. NW10 . . . .4A 80
Victor Vs. N9 . . . .3J 33
Victor Wlk. NW9 . . . .2A 44
Victor Wharf SE1 . . . .4E 14
(off Clink St.)
Victory Av. SM4: Mord 5A 154
Victory Bus. Cen.
TW7: Isle 4K 113
Victory Cl. TW19: Stanw 1A 128
Victory Ct. IG11: Bark 4B 90
W9 . . . .4J 81
(off Hermes Cl.)
Victory M. UB2: S'hall 3C 94
Victory Pde. E20 . . . .6D 68
SE18 . . . .3F 107
Victory Pk. HA9: Wemb 3D 60

Victory Pl. E14 . . . .7A 86
SE17 . . . .4D 102
SE19 . . . .7E 138
Victory Rd. E11 . . . .4J 51
SW19 . . . .7A 136
Victory Rd. M. SW19 . . . .7A 136
(off Victory Rd.)
Victory Wlk. SE8 . . . .1C 122
Victory Way RM7: Mawney 2H 55
SE16 . . . .2A 104
TW5: Cran 5A 94
Vida Ho. SE8 . . . .5K 103
Video Ct. N4 . . . .7K 47
Vidler Cl. KT9: Chess 6C 162
Vienna Cl. IG5: Ilf 2B 52
View, The SE2 . . . .5E 108
View Cl. HA1: Harr 4H 41
N6 . . . .7D 46
View Cres. N8 . . . .5H 47
Viewfield Cl. HA3: Kenton 7E 42
Viewfield Rd. DA5: Bexl 1F 145
SW18 . . . .6H 117
Viewland Rd. SE18 . . . .5K 107
View Rd. N6 . . . .7D 46
View Tube, The 1D 86
(off Greenway)
Viga Rd. N21 . . . .6F 23
Vigers Ct. NW10 . . . .3D 80
(off Harrow Rd.)
Vigilant Cl. SE26 . . . .4G 139
Vignoles Rd. RM7: Rush G 7G 55
Vigo St. W1 . . . .3A 12 (7G 83)
Viking Bus. Cen. RM7: Rush G 7J 55
Viking Cl. E3 . . . .2A 86
Viking Cl. SW6 . . . .6J 99
Viking Gdns. E6 . . . .4C 88
Viking Ho. SE5 . . . .2C 120
(off Denmark Rd.)
SE18 . . . .4C 106
(off Pett St.)
Viking Pl. E10 . . . .1B 68
Viking Rd. UB1: S'hall 7C 76
Viking Way DA8: Erith 3J 109
Villacourt Rd. SE18 . . . .7A 108
Village, The NW3 . . . .2A 64
SE7 . . . .6A 106
W12 . . . .1F 99
Village Arc. E4 . . . .1A 36
Village Cl. E4 . . . .5K 35
NW3 . . . .5B 64
(off Belsize La.)
Village Ct. E17 . . . .5D 50
(off Eden Rd.)
SE3 . . . .3G 123
(off Hurren Cl.)
Village Ga. TW17: Shep 5D 146
Village Hgts. IG8: Wfd G 5C 36
Village M. NW9 . . . .2K 61
SW18 . . . .1H 135
(off Elsenham St.)
Village M. NW3 . . . .4A 64
(off Perrins Ct.)
Village Pk. Cl. EN1: Enf 6K 23
Village Rd. EN1: Enf 5K 23
N3 . . . .2G 45
Village Row SM2: Sutt 7J 165
Village Way BR3: Beck 2C 158
HA5: Pinn 7C 40
IG6: Ilf 3G 53
NW10 . . . .4A 62
SE21 . . . .6D 120
TW15: Ashf 4B 128
Village Way E. HA2: Harr 7E 40
Villa Rd. SW9 . . . .3A 120
Villas on the Heath NW3 . . . .3A 64
Villas Rd. SE18 . . . .5G 107
Villa St. SE17 . . . .5D 102
Villa Wlk. SE17 . . . .5D 102
(off Villa St.)
Villiers Av. KT5: Surb 5F 151
TW2: Whitt 1D 130

Villiers Cl. E10 . . . 2C **68**
KT5: Surb . . . 4F **151**
Villiers Ct. *SW11* . . . *1C **118***
(off Battersea Bri. Rd.)
Villiers Gdns. E20 . . . 5D **68**
Villiers Gro.
SM2: Cheam . . . 7F **165**
Villiers M. NW2 . . . 6C **62**
Villiers Path KT6: Surb . . . 5E **150**
Villiers Rd. BR3: Beck . . . 2K **157**
KT1: King T . . . 4F **151**
NW2 . . . 6C **62**
TW7: Isle . . . 2J **113**
UB1: S'hall . . . 1D **94**
Villiers St. WC2 . . . 3E **12** (1J **101**)
Vimy Cl. TW4: Houn . . . 5D **112**
Vimy Ridge Ct. *E3* . . . *2B **86***
(off Festubert Pl.)
Vincam Cl. TW2: Whitt . . . 7E **112**
Vince Ct. N1 . . . 2F **9** (3D **84**)
Vincennes Est. SE27 . . . 4D **138**
Vincent Av. KT5: Surb . . . 2J **163**
Vincent Cl. BR2: Brom . . . 4K **159**
DA15: Sidc . . . 1J **143**
EN5: New Bar . . . 3E **20**
SE16 . . . 2A **104**
UB7: Sip . . . 6C **92**
Vincent Ct. HA6: Nwood . . . 1H **39**
N4 . . . 1J **65**
NW4 . . . 4F **45**
SW9 . . . 1K **119**
W1 . . . *7E **4***
(off Seymour Pl.)
Vincent Dr. TW17: Shep . . . 3G **147**
UB10: Uxb . . . 1B **74**
Vincent Gdns. NW2 . . . 3B **62**
Vincent Ho. *SW1* . . . *3D **18***
(off Regency St.)
SW1 . . . *4C **18***
(off Vincent Sq.)
Vincent M. E3 . . . 2C **86**
Vincent Rd. CR0: C'don . . . 7E **156**
E4 . . . 6A **36**
HA0: Wemb . . . 7F **61**
KT1: King T . . . 3G **151**
N15 . . . 4C **48**
N22 . . . 2A **48**
RM9: Dag . . . 7E **72**
SE18 . . . 4F **107**
TW4: Houn . . . 2B **112**
TW7: Isle . . . 1H **113**
W3 . . . 3J **97**
Vincent Row TW12: Hamp H . . . 6G **131**
Vincents Path *UB5: N'olt* . . . *6C **58***
(off Arnold Rd.)
Vincent Sq. N22 . . . 2A **48**
SW1 . . . 3C **18** (4H **101**)
Vincent Sq. Mans. *SW1* . . . *3B **18***
(off Walcott St.)
Vincent St. E16 . . . 5H **87**
SW1 . . . 3C **18** (4H **101**)
Vincent Ter. N1 . . . 2B **84**
Vince St. EC1 . . . 2F **9** (3D **84**)
Vine Cl. E5 . . . 4G **67**
KT5: Surb . . . 6F **151**
SM1: Sutt . . . 3A **166**
TW19: Stanw M . . . 7B **174**
UB7: W Dray . . . 4C **92**
Vine Cotts. *E1* . . . *6J **85***
(off Sidney Sq.)
W7 . . . 1J **95**
Vine Ct. E1 . . . 5G **85**
HA3: Kenton . . . 6E **42**
Vinegar All. E17 . . . 4D **50**
Vine Gdns. IG1: Ilf . . . 5G **71**
Vinegar St. E1 . . . 1H **103**
Vinegar Yd. SE1 . . . 6G **15** (2E **102**)
Vine Gro. UB10: Hil . . . 7C **56**
Vine Hill EC1 . . . 4J **7** (4A **84**)
Vine La. SE1 . . . 5H **15** (1E **102**)
UB10: Hil . . . 1B **74**
Vine Pl. TW3: Houn . . . 4F **113**
W5 . . . *1E **96***
(off St Mark's Rd.)
Viner Cl. KT12: Walt T . . . 6A **148**
Vineries, The EN1: Enf . . . 3K **23**
N14 . . . 6B **22**
SE6 . . . 1C **140**
Vineries Bank NW7 . . . 5J **29**
Vineries Cl. RM9: Dag . . . 6F **73**
UB7: Sip . . . 6C **92**
Vine Rd. BR6: Chels . . . 6K **173**
E15 . . . 7H **69**
KT8: E Mos . . . 4G **149**
SW13 . . . 3B **116**
Vinery, The *SW8* . . . *7J **101***
(off Regent's Bri. Gdns.)
Vinery Row W6 . . . 3D **98**
Vines Av. N3 . . . 1K **45**
Vine Sq. *W14* . . . *5H **99***
(off Star Rd.)
Vine St. E17 . . . 4D **50**
EC3 . . . 1J **15** (6F **85**)
RM7: Rom . . . 4J **55**
W1 . . . 3B **12** (7G **83**)
Vine St. Bri. EC1 . . . 4K **7** (4A **84**)
Vine Yd. SE1 . . . 6D **14**
Vineyard, The TW10: Rich . . . 5E **114**
Vineyard Av. NW7 . . . 7B **30**
Vineyard Cl. KT1: King T . . . 3F **151**
SE6 . . . 1C **140**
Vineyard Gro. N3 . . . 1K **45**
Vineyard Hill Rd. SW19 . . . 4H **135**
Vineyard M. TW10: Rich . . . 5E **114**
Vineyard Pas. TW10: Rich . . . 5E **114**
Vineyard Path SW14 . . . 3K **115**
Vineyard Rd. TW13: Felt . . . 3J **129**
Vineyard Row KT1: Hamp W . . . 1C **150**
Vineyards, The *TW13: Felt* . . . *3J **129***
(off High St.)
TW16: Sun . . . 3J **147**
Vineyard Wlk. EC1 . . . 3J **7** (4A **84**)
Viney Bank CR0: Sels . . . 7B **170**
Viney Rd. SE13 . . . 3D **122**
Vining St. SW9 . . . 4A **120**
Vinlake Av. UB10: Ick . . . 3B **56**
Vinson Cl. BR6: Orp . . . 1K **173**
Vinson Ho. *N1* . . . *2D **84***
(off Cranston Est.)
Vintage M. E4 . . . 4H **35**
Vinter Ct. TW17: Shep . . . 5C **146**
Vintner's Ct. EC4 . . . 3D **14** (7C **84**)
Vintner's Pl. EC4 . . . 3D **14** (7C **84**)
Vintry Ct. *SE1* . . . *7F **15***
(off Porlock St.)
Vintry M. E17 . . . 4C **50**
Viola Av. SE2 . . . 4B **108**
TW14: Felt . . . 6A **112**
TW19: Stanw . . . 1A **128**
Viola Sq. W12 . . . 7B **80**
Violet Av. EN2: Enf . . . 1J **23**
UB8: Hil . . . 5B **74**
Violet Cl. E16 . . . 4G **87**
SE8 . . . 6B **104**
SM3: Sutt . . . 1G **165**
SM6: Wall . . . 1E **166**
Violet Ct. *E15* . . . *7G **69***
(off Victoria St.)
NW9 . . . 1A **44**
Violet Gdns. CR0: Wadd . . . 5B **168**
Violet Hill NW8 . . . 2A **82**
Violet Hill Ho. *NW8* . . . *2A **82***
(off Violet Hill)
Violet La. CR0: Wadd . . . 6B **168**
Violet Rd. E3 . . . 4D **86**
E17 . . . 6C **50**
E18 . . . 2K **51**
Violet St. E2 . . . 4H **85**
Violet Ter. UB8: Hil . . . 5C **74**
VIP Trading Est. SE7 . . . 4A **106**
Virgil Pl. W1 . . . 6E **4** (5D **82**)
Virgil St. SE1 . . . 1H **19** (3K **101**)
Virgin Active
Aldersgate . . . *6C 8 (5C 84)*
(off Aldersgate St.)
Bank . . . 6D 84
Barbican . . . *5C 8*
(off Aldersgate St.)
Broadgate . . . *5G 9*
Bromley . . . 4B 160
Chislehurst . . . 5J 143
Chiswick . . . 1A 116
Chiswick Pk. . . . 4H 97
Cricklewood . . . 3G 63
Crouch End . . . *5J 47*
(off Tottenham La.)
Croydon . . . *3C 168*
(off Surrey St.)
Ealing . . . *7D 78*
(within Ealing Broadway Cen.)
Enfield . . . 4J 23
Friern Barnet . . . 5K 31
Fulham . . . *6G 99*
(within Fulham Pools)
Hammersmith . . . *4F 99*
(off Hammersmith Rd.)
Hendon . . . 5E 44
Ilford . . . *3F 71*
(off Clements Rd.)
Islington -
Essex Road . . . 1B 84
Goswell Road . . . *1A 8*
(off Goswell Rd.)
Kensington . . . *2K 99*
(off Old Court Pl.)
Kingston upon Thames -
The Bentall Cen. . . . *2D 150*
(within The Bentall Cen.)
Richmond Rd. . . . 1E 150
Mayfair . . . 2F 11 (6E 82)
Merton . . . *1B 154*
(off Watermill Way)
Mill Hill East . . . 7B 30
Moorgate . . . 4E 8 (4D 84)
Notting Hill . . . 6G 81
Putney . . . 4G 117
Repton Park . . . 7K 37
Romford . . . 5K 55
Stockley Park . . . 7E 74
Strand . . . 7J 83
Streatham . . . 3J 137
Sunbury . . . 1J 147
Surrey Health & Racquets Club, The . . . 6K 167
Swiss Cottage . . . *6A 64*
(within O2 Centre)
Tower Bridge . . . *2J 15*
(off Haydon St.)
The Twickenham Club . . . 6J 113
Walbrook . . . 7D 84
Wandsworth -
Smugglers Way . . . 4K 117
Southside Shop. Cen. . . . 5J 117
West London . . . 1A 98
Wimbledon -
North Rd. . . . 6A 136
Worple Rd. . . . 6H 135
Virginia Cl. BR2: Brom . . . 3G **159**
KT3: N Mald . . . 4J **151**
RM5: Col R . . . 1J **55**
Virginia Ct. *SE16* . . . *2K **103***
(off Eleanor Cl.)
WC1 . . . *3D **6***
(off Burton St.)
Virginia Gdns. IG6: Ilf . . . 2G **53**
Virginia Ho. *E14* . . . *7E **86***
(off Newby Pl.)
TW11: Tedd . . . 5B **132**
Virginia Rd. CR7: Thor H . . . 1B **156**
E2 . . . 2J **9** (3F **85**)
Virginia St. E1 . . . 7G **85**
Virginia Wlk. SW2 . . . 6K **119**
Viridian Apartments SW8 . . . 7G **101**
Visage *NW3* . . . *7B **64***
(off Winchester Rd.)
Viscount Cl. N11 . . . 6A **32**
Viscount Ct. *W2* . . . *6J **81***
(off Pembridge Vs.)
Viscount Dr. E6 . . . 5D **88**
Viscount Gro. UB5: N'olt . . . 3B **76**
Viscount M. BR7: Chst . . . 6F **143**
Viscount Rd. TW19: Stanw . . . 1A **128**
Viscount St. EC1 . . . 4C **8** (4C **84**)
Viscount Way
TW6: H'row A . . . 4G **111**
Vision 20 IG1: Ilf . . . 2G **71**
Vision Ind. Pk. W3 . . . 5H **79**
Vista, The DA14: Sidc . . . 5K **143**
SE9 . . . 6B **124**
Vista Av. EN3: Enf H . . . 2E **24**
Vista Bldg. *E3* . . . *3B **86***
(off Bow Rd.)
SE18 . . . 4E **106**
Vista Ct. *E1* . . . *5A **86***
(off Ocean Est.)
Vista Dr. IG4: Ilf . . . 5B **52**
Vista Ho. N4 . . . 2A **66**
SW19 . . . *1B **154***
(off Chapter Way)
Vista Way HA3: Kenton . . . 6E **42**
Vita Apartments CR0: C'don . . . 2D **168**
Vitae Apartments W6 . . . 3C **98**
Vitali Cl. SW15 . . . 6C **116**
Vittoria Ho. *N1* . . . *1K **83***
(off High Rd.)
Viveash Cl. UB3: Hayes . . . 3H **93**
Vivian Av. HA9: Wemb . . . 5G **61**
NW4 . . . 5D **44**
Vivian Comma Cl. N4 . . . 3B **66**
Vivian Ct. N12 . . . 5E **30**
W9 . . . 2K **81**
Vivian Gdns. HA9: Wemb . . . 5G **61**
Vivian Mans. *NW4* . . . *5D **44***
(off Vivian Av.)
Vivian Rd. E3 . . . 2A **86**
Vivian Sq. SE15 . . . 3H **121**
Vivian Way N2 . . . 5B **46**
Vivien Cl. KT9: Chess . . . 7E **162**
Vivienne Cl. TW1: Twick . . . 6D **114**
Vixen M. *E8* . . . *7F **67***
(off Haggerston Rd.)
Voce Rd. SE18 . . . 7H **107**
Voewood Cl. KT3: N Mald . . . 6B **152**
Vogans Mill SE1 . . . 6K **15** (2F **103**)
Vogler Ho. *E1* . . . *7J **85***
(off Cable St.)
Vogue Ct. BR1: Brom . . . 1K **159**
Vollasky Ho. *E1* . . . *5K **9***
(off Daplyn St.)
Volta Cl. N9 . . . 3D **34**
Voltaire Rd. SW4 . . . 3H **119**
Voltaire Way UB3: Hayes . . . 7G **75**
Volt Av. NW10 . . . 3K **79**
Volta Way CR0: Wadd . . . 1K **167**
Voluntary Pl. E11 . . . 6J **51**
Vorley Rd. N19 . . . 2G **65**
Voss Ct. SW16 . . . 6J **137**
Voss St. E2 . . . 3G **85**
Voyager Bus. Est. *SE16* . . . *3G **103***
(off Spa Rd.)
Voyager Ct. *E16* . . . *5J **87***
(off Hammersley Rd.)
Voyagers Cl. SE28 . . . 6C **90**
Voysey Cl. N3 . . . 3G **45**
Vue Cinema
Acton . . . 4G 79
Apollo . . . *3C 12*
(off Regent St.)
Bromley . . . 3J 159
Croydon -
High St. . . . 3C 168
Purley Way . . . 1K 167
Dagenham . . . 1E 90
Fallow Corner . . . 7G 31

Vue Cinema
Finchley Rd. 6A 64
(within 02 Centre)
Fulham Broadway 7J 99
Harrow 6J 41
(within St George's Shop. & Leisure Cen.)
Hayes 2G 93
Islington .2A 84
Leicester Square 2D 12
(off Cranbourn St.)
Romford .6K 55
Shepherds Bush 2F 99
Westfield 1E 98
Wood Green 2A 48
Vulcan Cl. E6 . . . . .6E 88
Vulcan Ga. EN2: Enf 2F 23
Vulcan Rd. SE4 . . . . .2B 122
Vulcan Sq. E14 . . . . .4D 104
Vulcan Ter. SE4 . . . . .2B 122
Vulcan Way N7 . . . . .6K 65
SM6: Wall 7J 167
Vulcan Wharf E15 . . . . .2D 86
(off Cook's Rd.)
Vyne, The DA7: Bex 3H 127
Vyner Rd. W3 . . . . .7K 79
Vyner St. E2 . . . . .1H 85
Vyners Way UB10: Ick 5C 56

W

Wadbrook St. KT1: King T 2D 150
Wadding St. SE17 . . . . .4D 102
Waddington Cl. EN1: Enf 4K 23
Waddington Rd. E15 . . . . .5F 69
Waddington St. E15 . . . . .6F 69
Waddington Way SE19 . . . . .7C 138
WADDON 3A 168
Waddon Cl. CRO: Wadd 3A 168
Waddon Ct. Rd. CRO: Wadd 3A 168
Waddon Leisure Cen. 5A 168
Waddon Marsh Way CRO: Wadd . . .1K 167
Waddon New Rd. CRO: C'don 3B 168
Waddon Pk. Av. CRO: Wadd 4A 168
Waddon Rd. CRO: C'don, Wadd 3A 168
Waddon Way CRO: Wadd 6A 168
Wade Cl. N10 . . . . .7A 32
Wade Ho. EN1: Enf 5J 23
SE1 . . . . .7K 15
(off Parkers Row)
Wades Gro. N21 . . . . .7F 23
Wades Hill N21 . . . . .6F 23
Wades La. TW11: Tedd 5A 132
Wades M. N21 . . . . .7F 23
Wadeson St. E2 . . . . .2H 85
Wade's Pl. E14 . . . . .7D 86
Wadeville Av. RM6: Chad H 6E 54
Wadeville Cl. DA17: Belv 5G 109
Wadham Av. E17 . . . . .7J 35
Wadham Cl. TW17: Shep 7E 146
Wadham Gdns. NW3 . . . . .1C 82
UB6: G'frd 6H 59
Wadham Ho. N18 . . . . .5A 34
Wadham M. SW14 . . . . .2J 115
Wadham Rd. E17 . . . . .7J 35
SW15 . . . . .4G 117
Wadhurst Cl. SE20 . . . . .2H 157
Wadhurst Rd. SW8 . . . . .1G 119
W4 . . . . .3K 97
Wadley Rd. E11 . . . . .7G 51
Wadsworth Bus. Cen. UB6: G'frd . . .2C 78
Wadsworth Cl. EN3: Pond E 5E 24
UB6: G'frd 2C 78
Wadsworth Rd. UB6: G'frd 2B 78
Wager St. E3 . . . . .4B 86
WAGGONERS RDBT. 1K 111
Waggon La. N17 . . . . .6B 34
Waggon M. N14 . . . . .1B 32
Waghorn Rd. E13 . . . . .1A 88
HA3: Kenton 3D 42
Waghorn St. SE15 . . . . .3G 121

Wagner M. KT6: Surb 5E 150
(off Avenue Elmers)
Wagner St. SE15 . . . . .7J 103
Wagstaff Gdns. RM9: Dag 7C 72
Wagtail Cl. EN1: Enf 1C 24
NW9 .2A 44
Wagtail Cl. SW15 . . . . .6E 116
Wagtail Rd. TW6: H'row A 5C 174
Wagtail Wlk. BR3: Beck 5E 158
Waight's Ct. KT2: King T 1E 150
Wainfleet Av. RM5: Col R 2J 55
Wainford Cl. SW19 . . . . .1F 135
Wainwright Gro.
TW7: Isle 4H 113
Wainwright Ho. E1 . . . . .1J 103
(off Garnet St.)
Waite Davies Rd. SE12 . . . . .7H 123
Waite Ho. W3 . . . . .1B 98
Waite St. SE15 . . . . .6F 103
Waithman St. EC4 . . . . .1A 14
(off Black Friars La.)
Wakefield Cl. SE26 . . . . .6J 139
Wakefield Gdns. IG1: Ilf 6C 52
SE19 .7E 138
Wakefield Ho. SE15 . . . . .1G 121
Wakefield M. WC1 . . . . .2F 7 (3J 83)
Wakefield Rd. N11 . . . . .5C 32
N15 . . . . .5F 49
TW10: Rich 5D 114
Wakefield St. E6 . . . . .1B 88
N18 . . . . .5B 34
WC1 . . . . .2F 7 (3J 83)
Wakeford Cl. DA5: Bexl 1D 144
SW4 .5G 119
Wakehams Hill HA5: Pinn 3D 40
Wakeham St. N1 . . . . .6D 66
Wakehurst Rd. SW11 . . . . .5C 118
Wakeling La. HA0: Wemb 3B 60
Wakeling Rd. W7 . . . . .5K 77
Wakeling St. E14 . . . . .6A 86
Wakelin Ho. N1 . . . . .7B 66
(off Sebbon St.)
Wakelin Rd. E15 . . . . .2G 87
Wakeman Ho. NW10 . . . . .3F 81
(off Wakeman Rd.)
Wakeman Rd. NW10 . . . . .3E 80
Wakemans Hill Av. NW9 . . . . .5K 43
Wakering Rd. IG11: Bark 6G 71
(not continuous)
Wakerley Cl. E6 . . . . .6D 88
Wakley St. EC1 . . . . .1A 8 (3B 84)
Walberswick St. SW8 . . . . .7J 101
Walbrook EC4 . . . . .2E 14 (7D 84)
(not continuous)
Walbrook Bldg., The EC4 . . . . .2E 14
Walbrook Cl. N11 . . . . .2E 84
(off Hemsworth St.)
Walbrook Ho. N9 . . . . .2D 34
(off Huntingdon Rd.)
Walbrook Wharf EC4 . . . . .3D 14
(off Cousin La.)
Walburgh St. E1 . . . . .6H 85
Walcorde Av. SE17 . . . . .4C 102
Walcot Gdns. SE11 . . . . .3J 19
Walcot Rd. EN3: Brim 2G 25
Walcot Sq. SE11 . . . . .3K 19 (4A 102)
Walcott St. SW1 . . . . .3B 18 (4G 101)
Waldair Ct. E16 . . . . .2F 107
Waldeck Gro. SE27 . . . . .3B 138
Waldeck Rd. N15 . . . . .4B 48
SW14 . . . . .3J 115
W4 . . . . .6G 97
W13 .6B 78
Waldeck Ter. SW14 . . . . .3J 115
(off Waldeck Rd.)
Waldegrave Ct. IG11: Bark 1H 89
Waldegrave Gdns. TW1: Twick 2K 131
Waldegrave Pk. TW1: Twick 4K 131
Waldegrave Rd. BR1: Brom 4C 160
N8 . . . . .3A 48
RM8: Dag 2C 72

Waldegrave Rd. SE19 . . . . .7F 139
TW1: Twick 4K 131
TW11: Tedd 4K 131
W5 . . . . .7F 79
Waldegrove CRO: C'don 3F 169
Waldemar Av. SW6 . . . . .1G 117
W13 .1C 96
Waldemar Rd. SW19 . . . . .5J 135
Walden Av. BR7: Chst 4D 142
N13 . . . . .4H 33
RM13: Rain 2K 91
Walden Cl. DA17: Belv 5F 109
Walden Ct. SW8 . . . . .1H 119
Walden Gdns. CR7: Thor H 3K 155
Walden Ho. SW1 . . . . .4H 17
(off Pimlico Rd.)
SW11 . . . . .1E 118
(off Dagnall St.)
Walden Pde. BR7: Chst 6D 142
(not continuous)
Walden Rd. BR7: Chst 6D 142
N17 . . . . .1D 48
Waldenshaw Rd. SE23 . . . . .1J 139
Walden St. E1 . . . . .6H 85
(not continuous)
Walden Way NW7 . . . . .6A 30
Waldo Cl. SW4 . . . . .5G 119
Waldo Ho. NW10 . . . . .3D 80
(off Waldo Rd.)
Waldo Ind. Est. BR1: Brom 3B 160
Waldo Pl. CR4: Mitc 7C 136
Waldorf Cl. CR2: S Croy 7B 168
Waldo Rd. BR1: Brom 3B 160
NW10 . . . . .3C 80
Waldram Cres. SE23 . . . . .1J 139
Waldram Pk. Rd. SE23 . . . . .1K 139
Waldram Pl. SE23 . . . . .1J 139
Waldrist Way DA18: Erith 3F 109
Waldron Gdns. BR2: Brom 3F 159
Waldronhyrst CR2: S Croy 4B 168
Waldron M. SW3 . . . . .7B 16 (6B 100)
Waldron Rd. HA1: Harr 1J 59
HA2: Harr 1J 59
SW18 . . . . .3A 136
Waldrons, The CRO: C'don 4B 168
Waldron's Path CR2: S Croy 4C 168
Waldrons Yd. HA2: Harr 2H 59
Waldstock Rd. SE28 . . . . .7A 90
Waleran Cl. HA7: Stan 5E 26
Waleran Flats SE1 . . . . .4E 102
Wales Av. SM5: Cars 5C 166
Wales Cl. SE15 . . . . .6H 103
Wales Farm Rd. W3 . . . . .5K 79
Waleton Acres SM6: Wall 6G 167
Waley St. E1 . . . . .5A 86
Walfield Av. N20 . . . . .7E 20
Walford Ho. E1 . . . . .6H 85
Walford Rd. N16 . . . . .4E 66
Walfrey Gdns. RM9: Dag 7F 73
WALHAM GREEN 1J 117
Walham Grn. Ct. SW6 . . . . .7K 99
(off Waterford Rd.)
Walham Gro. SW6 . . . . .7J 99
Walham Ri. SW19 . . . . .6G 135
Walham Yd. SW6 . . . . .7J 99
Walk, The N13 . . . . .3F 33
(off Fox La.)
TW16: Sun 7H 129
Walkato Lodge IG9: Buck H 1F 37
Walkden Rd. BR7: Chst 5E 142
Walker Cl. CRO: New Ad 7E 170
N11 . . . . .4A 32
SE18 .4G 107
TW12: Hamp 6D 130
TW14: Felt 7H 111
W7 . . . . .1J 95
Walker Ho. NW1 . . . . .1C 6 (2H 83)
SE16 .3B 104
(off Redriff Est.)
Walker M. SW2 . . . . .5A 120

Walker's Ct. W1 . . . . .2C 12
Walkerscroft Mead SE21 . . . . .1C 138
Walkers Lodge E14 . . . . .2E 104
(off Manchester Rd.)
Walkers Pl. SW15 . . . . .4G 117
Walkie-Talkie, The 2G 15
Walkinshaw Ct. N1 . . . . .7C 66
(off Rotherfield St.)
Walks, The N2 . . . . .3B 46
Walkynscroft SE15 . . . . .2H 121
(off Caulfield Rd.)
Wallace Bldg. NW8 . . . . .4B 4
(off Penfold St.)
Wallace Cl. SE28 . . . . .7D 90
TW17: Shep 4F 147
UB10: Uxb 2A 74
Wallace Collection 7G 5 (6E 82)
Wallace Ct. NW1 . . . . .6D 4
(off Old Marylebone Rd.)
SE3 . . . . .4K 123
Wallace Cres. SM5: Cars 5D 166
Wallace Ho. N7 . . . . .6K 65
(off Caledonian Rd.)
Wallace Rd. N1 . . . . .6C 66
Wallace Way N19 . . . . .2H 65
(off St John's Way)
RM1: Rom 1K 55
Wallasey Cres. UB10: Ick 2C 56
Wallbrook Bus. Cen. TW4: Houn . . .3K 111
Wallbutton Rd. SE4 . . . . .2A 122
Wallcote Av. NW2 . . . . .1F 63
Wall Ct. N4 . . . . .1K 65
(off Stroud Grn. Rd.)
Walled Gdn. Cl. BR3: Beck 4D 158
Walled Gdn. Ct. HA7: Stan 3D 26
Wallenberg Pl. W1 . . . . .1F 11
(off Gt. Cumberland Pl.)
WALLEND 1E 88
Wall End Ct. E6 . . . . .1E 88
(off Wall End Rd.)
Wall End Rd. E6 . . . . .7E 70
Waller Dr. HA6: Nwood 2J 39
Waller Rd. SE14 . . . . .1K 121
Wallers Cl. IG8: Wfd G 6J 37
RM9: Dag 1E 90
Waller Way SE10 . . . . .7D 104
Wallflower St. W12 . . . . .7B 80
Wallgrave Rd. SW5 . . . . .4K 99
Wallingford Av. W10 . . . . .5F 81
WALLINGTON 6F 167
Wallington Cl. HA4: Ruis 6E 38
Wallington Cnr. SM6: Wall 4F 167
(off Manor Rd. Nth.)
Wallington Ct. SM6: Wall 6F 167
(off Stanley Pk. Rd.)
WALLINGTON GREEN 4F 167
Wallington Rd. IG3: Ilf 7K 53
Wallington Sq. SM6: Wall 6F 167
Wallis All. SE1 . . . . .6D 14
Wallis Cl. SW11 . . . . .3B 118
Wallis Ho. HA4: Ruis 1F 57
SE14 .1A 122
TW8: Bford 5E 96
Wallis M. N8 . . . . .3A 48
(off Courcy Rd.)
Wallis Rd. E9 . . . . .6B 68
TW6: H'row A 5C 174
UB1: S'hall 6F 77
Wallis's Cotts. SW2 . . . . .7J 119
Wallman Pl. N22 . . . . .1K 47
Wallorton Gdns. SW14 . . . . .4K 115
Wallpaper Apartments, The N1 . . . . .7A 66
(off Offord Rd.)
Wallside EC2 . . . . .6D 8
Wall St. N1 . . . . .6D 66
Wallwood Rd. E11 . . . . .7F 51
Wallwood St. E14 . . . . .5B 86
Walmar Cl. EN4: Had W 1G 21
Walmer Cl. BR6: Farnb 4H 173
E4 . . . . .2J 35
RM7: Mawney 2H 55

Walmer Ct. KT5: Surb 5E **150**
   (off Cranes Pk.)
Walmer Gdns. W13 . . . . .2A **96**
Walmer Ho. W10 . . . . .6F **81**
   (off Bramley Rd.)
Walmer Pl. W1 . . . . .5E **4**
Walmer Rd. W10 . . . . .6E **80**
   W11 . . . . .7G **81**
Walmer St. W1 . . . . .5E **4** (5D **82**)
Walmer Ter. SE18 . . . . .4G **107**
Walmgate Rd. UB6: G'frd 1B **78**
Walmington Fold N12 . . . . .6D **30**
Walm La. NW2 . . . . .6E **62**
Walney Wlk. N1 . . . . .6C **66**
Walnut Av.
   UB7: W Dray 3C **92**
Walnut Cl. IG6: Ilf 4G **53**
   SE8 . . . . .6B **104**
   SM5: Cars 5D **166**
   UB3: Hayes 7G **75**
Walnut Ct. E17 . . . . .4E **50**
   W5 . . . . .2E **96**
   W8 . . . . .3K **99**
   (off St Mary's Ga.)
Walnut Flds. KT17: Ewe 7B **164**
Walnut Gdns. E15 . . . . .5G **69**
Walnut Gro. EN1: Enf 5J **23**
Walnut Ho. E3 . . . . .1B **86**
   (off Barge La.)
Walnut M. N22 . . . . .3A **48**
   (off High Rd.)
   SM2: Sutt 7A **166**
Walnut Rd. E10 . . . . .2C **68**
Walnut Tree Av. CR4: Mitc 3C **154**
   (off De'Arn Gdns.)
Walnut Tree Cl. BR7: Chst 1H **161**
   SW13 .1B **116**
   TW17: Shep 3E **146**
   UB10: Ick 4A **56**
Walnut Tree Cotts. SW19 . . . . .5G **135**
Walnut Tree Ho. SW10 . . . . .6K **99**
   (off Tregunter Rd.)
Walnut Tree Rd. RM8: Dag 2E **72**
   SE10 .5G **105**
   (not continuous)
   TW5: Hest 6D **94**
   TW8: Bford 6E **96**
   TW17: Shep 2E **146**
Walnut Tree Wlk. SE11 . . .3J **19** (4A **102**)
Walnut Way HA4: Ruis 6A **58**
   IG9: Buck H 3G **37**
Walpole Av. TW9: Kew 2F **115**
Walpole Cl. W13 . . . . .2C **96**
Walpole Ct. NW6 . . . . .7A **64**
   (off Fairfax Rd.)
   TW2: Twick 2J **131**
   W14 . . . . .3F **99**
   (off Blythe Rd.)
Walpole Cres. TW11: Tedd 5K **131**
Walpole Gdns. TW2: Twick 2J **131**
   W4 . . . . .5J **97**
Walpole Ho. KT8: W Mole 5E **148**
   (off Approach Rd.)
   SE1 . . . . .7J **13**
   (off Westminster Bri. Rd.)
   SW15 . . . . .5G **117**
   (off Plaza Gdns.)
Walpole Lodge W13 . . . . .1C **96**
Walpole M. NW8 . . . . .1B **82**
   SW19 .6B **136**
Walpole Pl. SE18 . . . . .4F **107**
   TW11: Tedd 5K **131**
Walpole Rd.
   BR2: Brom 5B **160**
   CR0: C'don 2D **168**
   E6 . . . . .7A **70**
   E17 . . . . .4A **50**
   E18 . . . . .1H **51**
   KT6: Surb 7E **150**
   N17 . . . . .2C **48**
   (not continuous)

Walpole Rd. SW19 . . . . .6B **136**
   TW2: Twick 2J **131**
   TW11: Tedd 5K **131**
Walpole St. SW3 . . . . . .5E **16** (5D **100**)
Walrond Av. HA9: Wemb 5E **60**
Walsham Cl. N16 . . . . .1G **67**
   SE28 .7D **90**
Walsham Ho. SE14 . . . . .2K **121**
   SE17 .5D **102**
   (off Blackwood St.)
Walsham Rd. SE14 . . . . .2K **121**
   TW14: Felt 7K **111**
Walsingham NW8 . . . . .1B **82**
Walsingham Gdns. KT19: Ewe 4A **164**
Walsingham Lodge SW13 . . . . .1C **116**
Walsingham Mans. SW6 . . . . .7K **99**
   (off Fulham Rd.)
Walsingham Pk. BR7: Chst 2H **161**
Walsingham Pl. SW4 . . . . .6E **118**
Walsingham Rd. CR4: Mitc 5D **154**
   E5 . . . . .3G **67**
   EN2: Enf 4J **23**
   W13 . . . . .1A **96**
Walsingham Wlk. DA17: Belv 6G **109**
Walston Ho. SW1 . . . . .5C **18**
   (off Aylesford St.)
Walter Besant Ho. E1 . . . . .3K **85**
   (off Bancroft Rd.)
Walter Ct. W3 . . . . .6J **79**
   (off Lynton Ter.)
Walter Grn. Ho. SE15 . . . . .1J **121**
   (off Lausanne Rd.)
Walter Ho. SW10 . . . . .7B **100**
   (off Riley St.)
Walter Hurford Pde. E12 . . . . .4E **70**
   (off Grantham Rd.)
Walter Langley Ct. SE16 . . . . .2J **103**
   (off Brunel Rd.)
Walter Rodney Cl. E6 . . . . .6D **70**
Walter Savill Twr. E17 . . . . .6C **50**
   (off Colchester Rd.)
Walters Cl. SE17 . . . . .4D **102**
   (off Brandon St.)
   UB3: Hayes 2H **93**
Walters Ho. N1 . . . . .1B **84**
   (off Essex Rd.)
   SE17 .6B **102**
   (off Otto St.)
Walter Sickert Hall N1 . . . . .1C **8**
   (off Graham St.)
Walters Rd. EN3: Pond E 4D **24**
   SE25 .4E **156**
Walter St. E2 . . . . .3K **85**
   KT2: King T 1E **150**
Walters Way SE23 . . . . .6K **121**
Walters Yd. BR1: Brom 2J **159**
Walter Ter. E1 . . . . .6K **85**
Walterton Rd. W9 . . . . .4H **81**
Walter Wlk. HA8: Edg 6D **28**
Waltham Av. NW9 . . . . .6G **43**
   UB3: Harl 3E **92**
Waltham Dr. HA8: Edg 2G **43**
Waltham Forest Pool & Track 2D **50**
Waltham Ho. NW8 . . . . .1A **82**
Waltham Pk. Way E17 . . . . .1C **50**
Waltham Rd. IG8: Wfd G 6H **37**
   SM5: Cars 7B **154**
   UB2: S'hall 3C **94**
WALTHAMSTOW 3C **50**
Walthamstow Av. E4 . . . . .6G **35**
Walthamstow Bus. Cen. E17 . . . . . .2E **50**
Walthamstow Leisure Cen. 6B **50**
Walthamstow Marsh Nature Reserve
   . . . . .7H **49**
Waltham Way E4 . . . . .4G **35**
Waltheof Av. N17 . . . . .1D **48**
Waltheof Gdns. N17 . . . . .1D **48**
Walton Av. HA2: Harr 5D **58**
   HA9: Wemb 3H **61**
   KT3: N Mald 4B **152**
   SM3: Cheam 3H **165**

Walton Bri. KT12: Walt T 7G **147**
   TW17: Shep 7G **147**
Walton Bri. Rd. TW17: Shep 7G **147**
Walton Cl. E4 . . . . .5H **35**
   E5 . . . . .4A **68**
   (off Orient Way)
   HA1: Harr 4H **41**
   NW2 . . . . .2D **62**
   SW8 . . . . .7J **101**
Walton Ct. CR2: S Croy 5C **168**
   (off Warham Rd.)
   EN5: New Bar 5F **21**
   NW6 . . . . .7A **64**
   (off Fairfax Rd.)
Walton Dr. HA1: Harr 4J **59**
   HA1: Harr 4H **41**
   NW10 .6K **61**
Walton Gdns. HA9: Wemb 2E **60**
   TW13: Felt 4H **129**
   W3 . . . . .5H **79**
Walton Grn. CR0: New Ad 7D **170**
Walton Ho. E2 . . . . .3K **9**
   (off Montclare St.)
   E17 . . . . .3D **50**
   NW1 . . . . .3K **5**
   (off Longford St.)
   SW3 . . . . .2E **16**
   (off Walton St.)
Walton La. KT13: Weyb 7F **147**, 7G **147**
   TW17: Shep 7F **147**
WALTON-ON-THAMES 7J **147**
Walton on Thames Camping & Cvn. Site
   KT12: Walt T 7F **148**
Walton Pl. SW3 . . . . . .1E **16** (3D **100**)
Walton Rd. DA14: Sidc 2C **144**
   E12 . . . . .4E **70**
   (not continuous)
   E13 . . . . .2A **88**
   HA1: Harr 4H **41**
   KT8: W Mole, E Mos 4D **148**
   KT12: Walt T 5A **148**
   N15 . . . . .4F **49**
   RM5: Col R 1F **55**
Walton St. EN2: Enf 1J **23**
   SW3 . . . . .3D **16** (4C **100**)
Walton Vs. N1 . . . . .7E **66**
   (off Downham Rd.)
Walton Way CR4: Mitc 4G **155**
   W3 . . . . .5H **79**
Walt Whitman Cl. SE24 . . . . .4B **120**
WALWORTH 5C **102**
Walworth Pl. SE17 . . . . .5C **102**
Walworth Rd. SE1 . . . . .4C **102**
   SE17 .4C **102**
Walwyn Av. BR1: Brom 3B **160**
Wanborough Dr. SW15 . . . . .1D **134**
Wanderer Dr. IG11: Bark 3C **90**
Wandle Apartments CR2: S Croy . . .5D **168**
Wandle Bank CR0: Bedd 3J **167**
   SW19 .7B **136**
Wandle Cl. CR0: Bedd 3J **167**
   KT19: Ewe 4J **163**
Wandle Ct. Gdns. CR0: Bedd 3J **167**
Wandle Ho. BR1: Brom 5F **141**
   NW8 . . . . .5C **4**
   (off Penfold St.)
Wandle Industrial Mus. 3D **154**
Wandle Meadow Nature Pk. 5A **136**
Wandle Pk. .2B **168**
Wandle Pk. Trad. Est., The
   CR0: C'don 1B **168**
Wandle Recreation Cen. 6K **117**
Wandle Rd. CR0: Bedd 3J **167**
   CR0: C'don 3C **168**
   SM4: Mord 4A **154**
   SW6 . . . . .3F **167**
   SW17 .2C **136**
Wandle Side CR0: Wadd 3K **167**
   SM6: Wall 3F **167**
Wandle Technology Pk. CR4: Mitc . . .7D **154**
Wandle Trad. Est. CR4: Mitc 7D **154**

Wandle Way CR4: Mitc 5D **154**
   SW18 .1K **135**
Wandon Rd. SW6 . . . . .7K **99**
WANDSWORTH 5K **117**
Wandsworth Bri. Rd. SW6 . . . . .3K **117**
Wandsworth Bri. Rd. SW6 . . . . .1K **117**
WANDSWORTH COMMON 1D **136**
Wandsworth Comn. W. Side SW18 . .5A **118**
WANDSWORTH GYRATORY 5K **117**
Wandsworth High St. SW18 . . . . . . .5J **117**
Wandsworth Mus. 5J **117**
Wandsworth Plain SW18 . . . . .5K **117**
Wandsworth Rd. SW8 . . . .7E **18** (3F **119**)
Wangey Rd. RM6: Chad H 7D **54**
Wangford Ho. SW9 . . . . .4B **120**
   (off Loughborough Pk.)
Wanless Rd. SE24 . . . . .3C **120**
Wanley Rd. SE5 . . . . .4D **120**
Wanlip Rd. E13 . . . . .4K **87**
Wannock Gdns. IG6: Ilf 1F **53**
Wansbeck Ct. EN2: Enf 3G **23**
   (off Waverley Rd.)
Wansbeck Rd. E9 . . . . .7B **68**
Wanstead Pl. SW6 . . . . .7K **99**
Wansey St. SE17 . . . . .4C **102**
WANSTEAD 6K **51**
Wanstead Cl. BR1: Brom 2A **160**
Wanstead Gdns. IG4: Ilf 6B **52**
Wanstead Golf Course 7A **52**
Wanstead La. IG1: Ilf 6B **52**
Wanstead Leisure Cen. 6A **52**
Wanstead Pk. Av. E12 . . . . .1B **70**
Wanstead Pk. Rd. IG1: Ilf 6B **52**
Wanstead Pl. E11 . . . . .6J **51**
Wanstead Rd. BR1: Brom 2A **160**
Wansunt Rd. DA5: Bexl 1J **145**
Wantage Rd. SE12 . . . . .5H **123**
Wantz Rd. RM10: Dag 4H **73**
WAPPING 1H **103**
Wapping Dock St. E1 . . . . .1H **103**
Wapping High St. E1 . . . . .1G **103**
Wapping La. E1 . . . . .7H **85**
Wapping Wall E1 . . . . .1J **103**
Waratah Dr. BR7: Chst 5D **142**
Warbank La. KT2: King T 7B **134**
Warbeck Rd. W12 . . . . .2D **98**
Warberry Rd. N22 . . . . .1K **47**
Warboys App. KT2: King T 6H **133**
Warboys Cres. E4 . . . . .5K **35**
Warboys Rd. KT2: King T 6H **133**
Warburg Ct. NW9 . . . . .3A **44**
   (off Mornington Cl.)
Warburton Cl. HA3: Hrw W 6C **26**
   N1 . . . . .6E **66**
   (off Culford Rd.)
Warburton Ct. HA4: Ruis 2J **57**
Warburton Ho. E8 . . . . .1H **85**
   (off Warburton St.)
Warburton Rd. E8 . . . . .1H **85**
   TW2: Whitt 1F **131**
Warburton St. E8 . . . . .1H **85**
Warburton Ter. E17 . . . . .2D **50**
Wardalls Gro. SE14 . . . . .7J **103**
Wardalls Ho. SE8 . . . . .6B **104**
   (off Staunton St.)
Ward Cl. CR2: S Croy 6C **168**
   DA8: Erith 6K **109**
Wardell Cl. NW7 . . . . .7F **29**
Wardell Fld. NW9 . . . . .1A **44**
Wardell Ho. SE10 . . . . .6E **104**
   (off Welland St.)
Wardell M. SW4 . . . . .3G **119**
Warden Av. HA2: Harr 1D **58**
Warden Rd. NW5 . . . . .6E **64**
Wardens Fld. Cl. BR6: Chels 6J **173**
Wardens Gro. SE1 . . . . . . .5C **14** (1C **102**)
Ward La. E9 .5A **68**
Wardle St. E9 . . . . .5K **67**
Wardley St. SW18 . . . . .7K **117**
Wardo Av. SW6 . . . . .1G **117**

Wardour M. W1 . . . . 1B **12**
Wardour St. W1 . . . . 7B **6** (6G **83**)
Ward Point SE11 . . . . 4J **19** (4A **102**)
Ward Rd. E15 . . . . 1F **87**
N19 . . . . 3G **65**
SW19 . . . . 1A **154**
Wardrobe, The *TW9: Rich* *5D* ***114***
(off Old Palace Yd.)
Wardrobe Pl. EC4 . . . . 1B **14**
Wardrobe Ter. EC4 . . . . 2B **14**
Wardroper Ho. *SE1* *3B* ***102***
(off St George's Rd.)
Wards Rd. IG2: Ilf 7H **53**
Wards Wharf App. E16 . . . . 1B **106**
Ware Ct. SM1: Sutt 4H **165**
Wareham Cl.
TW3: Houn 4F **113**
Wareham Ct. *N1* *7E* ***66***
(off Hertford Rd.)
Wareham Ho. SW8 . . . . 7K **101**
Warehome M. *E13* *4J* ***87***
(off Jutland Rd.)
Warehouse Ct. SE18 . . . . 3F **107**
Warehouse Sports & Performing Arts Cen., The . . . 5K **107**
Warehouse Way E16 . . . . 7K **87**
Waremead Rd. IG2: Ilf 5F **53**
Warepoint Dr. SE28 . . . . 2H **107**
Warfield Rd. NW10 . . . . 3F **81**
TW12: Hamp 1F **149**
TW14: Felt 7G **111**
Warfield Yd. *NW10* *3F* ***81***
(off Warfield Rd.)
Wargrave Av. N15 . . . . 6F **49**
Wargrave Ho. *E2* *2J* ***9***
(off Navarre St.)
Wargrave Rd. HA2: Harr 3G **59**
Warham Rd. CR2: S Croy 5B **168**
HA3: W'stone 2K **41**
N4 . . . . 5A **48**
Warham St. SE5 . . . . 7B **102**
Waring & Gillow Est. W3 . . . . 4G **79**
Waring Cl. BR6: Chels 6K **173**
Waring Dr. BR6: Chels 6K **173**
Waring Rd. DA14: Sidc 6C **144**
Waring St. SE27 . . . . 4C **138**
Warkworth Gdns. TW7: Isle 7A **96**
Warkworth Rd. N17 . . . . 7J **33**
Warland Rd. SE18 . . . . 7H **107**
Warley Av. RM8: Dag 7F **55**
UB4: Hayes 6J **75**
Warley Cl. E10 . . . . 1B **68**
Warley Rd. IG5: Ilf 1E **52**
IG8: Wfd G 7E **36**
N9 . . . . 2D **34**
UB4: Hayes 6J **75**
Warley St. E2 . . . . 3K **85**
Warlingham Ct. SE13 . . . . 6E **122**
Warlingham Rd. CR7: Thor H 4B **156**
Warlock Rd. W9 . . . . 4H **81**
Warlters Cl. N7 . . . . 4J **65**
Warlters Rd. N7 . . . . 4J **65**
Warltersville Mans. N19 . . . . 7J **47**
Warltersville Rd. N19 . . . . 7J **47**
War Memorial Sports Ground 4C **166**
Warmington Cl. E5 . . . . 3K **67**
Warmington Rd. SE24 . . . . 6C **120**
Warmington St. E13 . . . . 4J **87**
Warminster Gdns. SE25 . . . . 2G **157**
Warminster Rd. SE25 . . . . 2F **157**
Warminster Sq. SE25 . . . . 2G **157**
Warminster Way CR4: Mitc 1F **155**
Warmsworth *NW1* *1G* ***83***
(off Pratt St.)
Warmwell Av. NW9 . . . . 1A **44**
Warndon St. SE16 . . . . 4K **103**
Warneford Rd. HA3: Kenton 3D **42**
TW6: H'row A 5C **174**
Warneford St. E9 . . . . 1H **85**
Warne Pl. DA15: Sidc 6B **126**
Warner Av. SM3: Cheam 2G **165**
Warner Cl. E15 . . . . 5G **69**
NW9 . . . . 7B **44**
TW12: Hamp 5D **130**
UB3: Harl 7F **93**
Warner Ho. BR3: Beck 6D **140**
NW8 . . . . 3A **82**
SE13 . . . . *2D* ***122***
(off Russett Way)
Warner Pl. E2 . . . . 2G **85**
Warner Rd. BR1: Brom 7H **141**
E17 . . . . 4A **50**
N8 . . . . 4H **47**
SE5 . . . . 1C **120**
Warners Cl. IG8: Wfd G 5D **36**
Warners La. KT2: King T 4D **132**
Warners Path IG8: Wfd G 5D **36**
Warner St. EC1 . . . . 4J **7** (4A **84**)
Warner Ter. *E14* *5D* ***86***
(off Broomfield St.)
Warner Yd. EC1 . . . . 4J **7**
Warnford Ct. *EC2* *7F* ***9***
(off Throgmorton Av.)
Warnford Ho. *SW15* *6A* ***116***
(off Tunworth Cres.)
Warnford Ind. Est. UB3: Hayes 2G **93**
Warnford Rd. BR6: Chels 5K **173**
Warnham *WC1* *2G* ***7***
(off Sidmouth St.)
Warnham Ct. Rd. SM5: Cars 7D **166**
Warnham Ho. *SW2* *7K* ***119***
(off Up. Tulse Hill)
Warnham Rd. N12 . . . . 5H **31**
Warple M. W3 . . . . 2A **98**
Warple Way W3 . . . . 2A **98**
Warren, The 2A **94**
Warren, The E12 . . . . 4C **70**
KT4: Wor Pk 4K **163**
SE7 . . . . 6A **106**
TW5: Hest 7D **94**
UB4: Hayes 6J **75**
Warren Av. BR1: Brom 7G **141**
BR6: Chels 5K **173**
CR2: Sels 7K **169**
E10 . . . . 3E **68**
TW10: Rich 4H **115**
Warren Cl. DA6: Bex 5G **127**
HA9: Wemb 2D **60**
N9 . . . . 7E **24**
SE21 . . . . 7C **120**
UB4: Yead 5A **76**
Warren Ct. BR3: Beck 7C **140**
CR0: C'don 1E **168**
N17 . . . . *3G* ***49***
(off High Cross Rd.)
NW1 . . . . *3B* ***6***
(off Warren St.)
W5 . . . . 5C **78**
Warren Cres. N9 . . . . 7A **24**
Warren Cutting KT2: King T 7K **133**
Warrender Rd. N19 . . . . 3G **65**
Warrender Way HA4: Ruis 7J **39**
Warren Dr. HA4: Ruis 7B **40**
UB6: G'frd 4F **77**
Warren Dr., The E11 . . . . 7A **52**
Warren Dr. Nth. KT5: Surb 1H **163**
Warren Dr. Sth. KT5: Surb 1J **163**
Warren Farm Cotts. RM6: Chad H 4F **55**
Warren Farm Sports Cen. 3H **95**
Warren Flds. HA7: Stan 4H **27**
Warren Footpath TW1: Twick 1C **132**
Warren Gdns. BR6: Chels 5K **173**
E15 . . . . 5F **69**
Warren Ho. *E3* *3D* ***86***
(off Bromley High St.)
N17 . . . . *3G* ***49***
(off High Cross Rd.)
W14 . . . . 4H **99**
Warren La. HA7: Stan 2F **27**
SE18 . . . . 3F **107**
Warren La. Ga. SE18 . . . . 3F **107**
Warren M. W1 . . . . 4A **6** (4G **83**)
Warren Pk. KT2: King T 6J **133**
Warren Pk. Rd. SM1: Sutt 6B **166**
Warren Pl. *E1* *6K* ***85***
(off Pitsea St.)
Warren Pond Rd. E4 . . . . 1C **36**
Warren Ri. KT3: N Mald 1K **151**
Warren Rd. BR2: Hayes 2J **171**
BR6: Chels 5K **173**
(not continuous)
CR0: C'don 1E **168**
DA6: Bex 5G **127**
DA14: Sidc 3C **144**
E4 . . . . 2K **35**
E10 . . . . 3E **68**
E11 . . . . 6A **52**
IG6: Ilf 5H **53**
KT2: King T 6J **133**
NW2 . . . . 2B **62**
SW19 . . . . 6C **136**
TW2: Whitt 6G **113**
TW15: Ashf 7G **129**
UB10: Ick 4A **56**
WD23: B Hea 1B **26**
Warren Sports Cen. 5F **55**
Warrens Shawe La. HA8: Edg 2C **28**
Warren St. W1 . . . . 4A **6** (4G **83**)
Warren Ter. RM6: Chad H 4D **54**
Warren Wlk. SE7 . . . . 6A **106**
Warren Way HA8: Edg 2H **43**
Warren Wood Cl. BR2: Hayes 2H **171**
Warriner Dr. N9 . . . . 3B **34**
Warriner Gdns. SW11 . . . . 1D **118**
Warrington Ct. *CR0: Wadd* *3B* ***168***
(off Warrington Rd.)
Warrington Cres. W9 . . . . 4A **82**
Warrington Gdns. W9 . . . . 4A **82**
(not continuous)
Warrington Rd. CR0: Wadd 3B **168**
HA1: Harr 5J **41**
RM8: Dag 2D **72**
TW10: Rich 5D **114**
Warrington Sq. RM8: Dag 2D **72**
Warrior Cl. SE28 . . . . 1H **107**
Warrior Ct. *SW9* *3B* ***120***
(off Coldharbour Rd.)
Warrior Sq. E12 . . . . 4E **70**
Warsaw Cl. HA4: Ruis 6K **57**
Warspite Ho. *E14* *4D* ***104***
(off Cahir St.)
Warspite Rd. SE18 . . . . 3C **106**
Warton Ct. *E1* *7K* ***85***
(off Cable St.)
W3 . . . . *3J* ***97***
(off All Saints Rd.)
Warton Ho. *E15* *1E* ***86***
(off High St.)
Warton Rd. E15 . . . . 1E **86**
Warwall E6 . . . . 6F **89**
Warwark Ct. KT6: Surb 2E **162**
Warwick *W14* *4H* ***99***
(off Kensington Village)
Warwick Av. HA2: Harr 4D **58**
HA8: Edg 3C **28**
W2 . . . . 4A **82**
W9 . . . . 4K **81**
Warwick Bldg. SW8 . . . . 6F **101**
Warwick Chambers *W8* *3J* ***99***
(off Pater St.)
Warwick Cl. DA5: Bexl 7F **127**
EN4: E Barn 5G **21**
TW12: Hamp 7G **131**
W8 . . . . *3H* ***99***
(off Kensington High St.)
WD23: B Hea 1D **26**
Warwick Ct. BR2: Brom 2G **159**
EC4 . . . . *1B* ***14***
(off Warwick La.)
EN5: New Bar *5E* ***20***
(off Station Rd.)
HA1: Harr 3J **41**
N11 . . . . 6C **32**
Warwick Ct. *UB5: N'olt* *5E* ***58***
(off Newmarket Av.)
W7 . . . . *6K* ***77***
(off Copley Cl.)
WC1 . . . . 6H **7** (5K **83**)
Warwick Cres. UB4: Hayes 4H **75**
W2 . . . . 5A **82**
Warwick Dene W5 . . . . 1E **96**
Warwick Dr. SW15 . . . . 3D **116**
Warwick Est. W2 . . . . 5K **81**
Warwick Gdns. CR7: Thor H 3A **156**
EN5: Barn 1C **20**
IG1: Ilf 1F **71**
KT7: T Ditt 5K **149**
N4 . . . . 5C **48**
W14 . . . . 3H **99**
Warwick Gro. E5 . . . . 1H **67**
KT5: Surb 7F **151**
Warwick Ho. *E16* *1J* ***105***
(off Wesley Av.)
KT2: King T *1E* ***150***
(off Acre Rd.)
SW9 . . . . 2A **120**
Warwick Ho. St. SW1 . . . . 4D **12** (1H **101**)
Warwick La. EC4 . . . . 7B **8** (6B **84**)
Warwick Lodge TW2: Twick 3F **131**
Warwick Mans. *SW5* *4J* ***99***
(off Cromwell Cres.)
Warwick Pde. HA3: Kenton 2B **42**
Warwick Pas. *EC4* *7B* ***8***
(off Old Bailey)
Warwick Pl. KT7: T Ditt 6A **150**
W5 . . . . 2D **96**
W9 . . . . 5A **82**
Warwick Pl. Nth. SW1 . . . . 4A **18** (4G **101**)
Warwick Rd. CR7: Thor H 3A **156**
DA14: Sidc 5B **144**
DA16: Well 3C **126**
E4 . . . . 5H **35**
E11 . . . . 5K **51**
E12 . . . . 5C **70**
E15 . . . . 6H **69**
E17 . . . . 1B **50**
EN5: New Bar 4E **20**
KT1: Hamp W 1C **150**
KT3: N Mald 3J **151**
KT7: T Ditt 5K **149**
N11 . . . . 6C **32**
N18 . . . . 4K **33**
SE20 . . . . 3H **157**
SM1: Sutt 4A **166**
SW5 . . . . 4H **99**
TW2: Twick 1J **131**
TW4: Houn 3K **111**
TW15: Ashf 5A **128**
UB2: S'hall 3D **94**
UB7: W Dray 2A **92**
W5 . . . . 2D **96**
W14 . . . . 4H **99**
Warwick Row SW1 . . . . 1K **17** (3G **101**)
Warwickshire Path SE8 . . . . 7B **104**
Warwickshire Rd. N16 . . . . 4E **66**
Warwick Sq. EC4 . . . . 7B **8** (6B **84**)
SW1 . . . . 5A **18** (5G **101**)
(not continuous)
Warwick Sq. M. SW1 . . . . 4A **18** (4G **101**)
Warwick St. W1 . . . . 2B **12** (7G **83**)
Warwick Ter. *E17* *5F* ***51***
(off Lea Bri. Rd.)
SE18 . . . . 6H **107**
Warwick Way SW1 . . . . 5J **17** (5F **101**)
Warwick Yd. EC1 . . . . 4D **8** (4C **84**)
Wasdale *NW1* *3F* ***83***
(off Cumberland Mkt.)
Washbourne Ct. *N9* *2B* ***34***
(off Acton Cl.)
Washbourne Rd. NW10 . . . . 1K **79**
Washington Av. E12 . . . . 4D **70**
Washington Bldg. *SE13* *1D* ***122***
(off Deal's Gateway)
Washington Cl. E3 . . . . 3D **86**

Washington Ho. E17 2B 50
SW3 7E 10
(off Basil St.)
Washington Rd. E6 7A 70
E18 2H 51
KT1: King T 2G 151
KT4: Wor Pk 2D 164
SW13 7C 98
TW6: H'row A 6D 174
Wasp Rd. *TW6: H'row A* 5C 174
(off Welland Rd.)
Wastdale Rd. SE23 1K 139
Watch, The N12 4F 31
Watchfield Ct. W4 5J 97
Watcombe Cotts. TW9: Kew 6G 97
Watcombe Pl. SE25 5H 157
Watcombe Rd. SE25 5H 157
Waterbank Ho. *SW18* 1K 135
(off Knaresborough Dr.)
Waterbank Rd. SE6 3D 140
Waterbeach Rd. RM9: Dag 6C 72
Water Brook La. NW4 5E 44
Watercress Pl. N1 7E 66
Waterdale Rd. SE2 6A 108
Waterden Ct. W11 1G 99
Waterden Rd. E20 5C 68
Waterer Ho. SE6 4E 140
Waterer Ri. SM6: Wall 6H 167
Waterfall Cl. N14 3B 32
Waterfall Cotts. SW19 6B 136
Waterfall Rd. N11 4A 32
N14 4A 32
SW19 6B 136
Waterfall Ter. SW17 6C 136
Waterfall Wlk. N14 1A 32
Waterfield Cl. DA17: Belv 3G 109
SE28 1B 108
Waterfield Gdns. SE25 4D 156
Waterford Ho. *BR1: Brom* 1J 159
(off Newman Rd.)
W11 7H 81
(off Kensington Pk. Rd.)
Waterford Rd. SW6 7K 99
Waterford Way NW10 5D 62
Waterfront W6 6E 98
Waterfront Ho. *E5* 2J 67
(off Harry Zeital Way)
Waterfront Leisure Cen.
Woolwich 3E 106
Waterfront M. N1 2C 84
Waterfront Studios Bus. Cen. *E16* 1H 105
(off Dock Rd.)
Water Gdns. HA7: Stan 6G 27
Water Gdns., The W2 7D 4 (6C 82)
Watergardens, The KT2: King T 6J 133
Water Gdns. Sq. SE16 2K 103
Watergate EC4 2A 14 (7B 84)
Watergate St. SE8 6C 104
Watergate Wlk. WC2 4F 13 (1J 101)
Waterhall Av. E4 4B 36
Waterhall Cl. E17 1K 49
Waterhead *NW1* 1A 6
(off Varndell St.)
Waterhouse *CR0: C'don* 1C 168
(off Saffron Central Sq.)
Waterhouse Cl. E16 5B 88
NW3 5B 64
W6 4F 99
Waterhouse Sq. EC1 6J 7 (5A 84)
Wateridge Cl. E14 3C 104
Water La. DA14: Sidc 2F 145
E15 6G 69
EC3 3H 15 (7E 84)
IG3: Ilf 3J 71
KT1: King T 1D 150
N9 1C 34
NW1 7F 65
SE14 7J 103
TW1: Twick 1A 132
TW9: Rich 5D 114
Water Lily Cl. UB2: S'hall 2G 95
Waterline Ho. W2 6B 4
Waterloo Bri. WC2 3G 13 (7K 83)
Waterloo Cl. E9 5J 67
TW14: Felt 1H 129
Waterloo East Theatre 1A 102
(off Brad St.)
Waterloo Gdns. E2 2J 85
N1 7B 66
RM7: Rom 6K 55
Waterloo Pas. NW6 7H 63
Waterloo Pl. *SM5: Cars* 3D 166
(off Wrythe Grn.)
SW1 4C 12 (1H 101)
TW9: Rich 4E 114
Waterloo Rd. E6 7A 70
E7 5H 69
E10 7C 50
IG6: Ilf 2G 53
NW2 1C 62
RM7: Rom, Rush G 5K 55
SE1 4H 13 (1K 101)
SM1: Sutt 5B 166
Waterloo Ter. N1 7B 66
Waterlow Ct. NW11 7K 45
Waterlow Pk. Cen. 1F 65
Waterlow Rd. N19 1G 65
Waterman Bldg. E14 2B 104
Watermans Art Cen., Cinema & Theatre
6E 96
Watermans Cl. KT2: King T 7E 132
Watermans Ct.
TW8: Bford 6D 96
(off High St.)
Watermans Ho. *E14* 6F 87
(off New Village Av.)
Watermans M. W5 7E 78
Waterman's Quay SW6 2A 118
Waterman St. SW15 3F 117
Watermans Wlk. SE16 2A 104
Waterman Way E1 1H 103
Watermark Ct. *RM6: Chad H* 6B 54
(off Quarles Pk. Rd.)
Watermead TW14: Felt 1G 129
Watermead Ho. E9 5A 68
Watermead La. SM5: Cars 7D 154
Watermead Lodge *SE16* 1K 103
(off Princes Riverside Rd.)
Watermeadow La. SW6 2A 118
Watermead Rd. SE6 4E 140
Watermead Way N17 3H 49
Watermen's Sq. SE20 7J 139
Water M. SE15 4J 121
Watermill Bus. Cen. EN3: Brim 2G 25
Watermill Cl. TW10: Ham 3C 132
Water Mill Ho. TW13: Hanw 2E 130
Watermill La. N18 5K 33
Watermill Way SW19 1A 154
TW13: Hanw 2D 130
Watermint Quay N16 7G 49
Water Rd. HA0: Wemb 1F 79
Water's Edge *SW6* 1E 116
(off Palemead Cl.)
Watersedge KT19: Ewe 4J 163
Watersfield Way HA8: Edg 7J 27
Waters Gdns. RM10: Dag 5G 73
Waterside BR3: Beck 1B 158
E17 6J 49
N1 2C 84
UB7: Harm 3D 174
W2 6A 4
Waterside Apartments *N4* 1C 66
(off Goodchild Rd.)
Waterside Av. *BR3: Beck* 5E 158
(off Adamson Way)
Waterside Bus. Cen. TW7: Isle 4B 114
Waterside Cl. E3 1B 86
HA9: Wemb 3J 61
IG11: Bark 4A 72
KT6: Surb 2E 162
SE16 2G 103
SE28 1K 107
Waterside Cl. TW17: Shep 1E 146
UB5: N'olt 3D 76
Waterside Ct. *SM5: Cars* 3E 166
(off Millpond Pl.)
Waterside Dr. KT12: Walt T 5J 147
Waterside Hgts. *E16* 2A 106
(off Booth Rd.)
Waterside Pl. NW1 1E 82
Waterside Point SW11 7C 100
Waterside Rd. UB2: S'hall 3E 94
Waterside Twr. *SW6* 2A 118
(off The Boulevard)
Waterside Trad. Cen. W7 3J 95
Waterside Way N17 3H 49
SW17 4A 136
Watersmeet Pl. N4 1C 66
Watersmeet Way SE28 6C 90
Waterson St. E2 1H 9 (3E 84)
Waters Pl. SW15 2E 116
Watersplash Cl. KT1: King T 3E 150
Watersplash La. TW5: Cran 5K 93
UB3: Harl 4J 93
Watersplash Rd. TW17: Shep 5C 146
Watersreach Apartments *N4* 1C 66
(off Kayani Av.)
Waters Rd. KT1: King T 2H 151
SE6 3G 141
Waters Sq. KT1: King T 3H 151
Water St. WC2 2J 13
Water Twr. Cl. UB8: Uxb 5A 56
Water Twr. Hill CR0: C'don 4D 168
Water Twr. Pl. N1 1A 84
Waterview Cl. DA6: Bex 5D 126
Waterview Dr. SE10 1F 105
Waterview Ho. *E14* 5A 86
(off Carr St.)
Waterway Av. SE13 3D 122
Waterway Pk. UB3: Hayes 2E 92
Waterways Bus. Cen. EN3: Enf L 1G 25
WATERWORKS CORNER 1G 51
Waterworks Golf Course (Nature Reserve)
2A 68
Waterworks La. E5 2K 67
Waterworks Rd. SW2 6K 119
Waterworks Vis. Cen. 2A 68
Waterworks Yd. *CR0: C'don* 3C 168
(off Charles St.)
Watery La. DA14: Sidc 6B 144
SW19 2H 153
SW20 2H 153
UB3: Harl 5F 93
UB5: N'olt 2A 76
Wates Way CR4: Mitc 6D 154
Wateville Rd. N17 1C 48
Watford By-Pass HA8: Edg 2J 27
WD6: E'tree 1G 27
Watford Cl. SW11 1C 118
Watford Rd. E16 5J 87
HA0: Wemb 2A 60
HA1: Harr 7A 42
Watford Way NW4 4C 44
NW7 4F 29
Watkin Rd. HA9: Wemb 3H 61
Watkins Cl. HA6: Nwood 1H 39
Watkins Ho. *E14* 2E 104
(off Manchester Rd.)
Watkinson Rd. N7 6K 65
Watkins Way RM8: Dag 1E 72
WATLING 7E 28
Watling Av. HA8: Edg 1J 43
Watling Ct. EC4 1D 14
Watling Farm Cl. HA7: Stan 1H 27
Watling Gdns. NW2 6G 63
Watling Ga. NW9 4A 44
Watling Ho. *SE1* 4C 102
(off New Kent Rd.)
Watlings Cl. CR0: C'don 6A 158
Watling St. DA1: Cray 5K 127
DA6: Bex 4H 127
EC4 1D 14 (6C 84)
SE15 6E 102
Watlington Gro. SE26 5A 140
Watney Cotts. SW14 3J 115
Watney Mkt. E1 6H 85
Watney Rd. SW14 3J 115
Watney's Rd. CR4: Mitc 5H 155
Watney St. E1 6H 85
Watson Av. E6 7E 70
SM3: Cheam 2G 165
Watson Cl. N16 5D 66
SW19 6C 136
Watson Ct. *E3* 3C 86
(off Campbell Rd.)
Watson Pl. SE25 5F 157
Watsons Ho. *N1* 1E 84
(off Nuttall St.)
Watson's M. W1 6D 4 (5C 82)
Watsons Rd. N22 1K 47
Watsons St. SE8 7C 104
Watson St. E13 2K 87
Watt Ct. W3 2A 98
Wattisfield Rd. E5 3J 67
Watts Cl. N15 5E 48
Wattsdown Cl. E13 1J 87
Watts Gro. E3 5C 86
Watts Ho. *W10* 5G 81
(off Wornington Rd.)
Watts La. BR7: Chst 1F 161
TW11: Tedd 5A 132
Watts M. IG6: Ilf 3H 53
SW16 6H 137
Watts Point *E13* 1J 87
(off Brooks Rd.)
Watts Rd. KT7: T Ditt 7A 150
Watts St. E1 1H 103
SE15 1F 121
Wat Tyler Ho. *N8* 3J 47
(off Boyton Rd.)
Wat Tyler Rd. SE3 2E 122
SE10 2E 122
Wauthier Cl. N13 5G 33
Wave Ct. RM7: Rush G 6K 55
Wavel Ct. *CR0: C'don* 5D 168
(off Hurst Rd.)
E1 1J 103
(off Garnet St.)
Wavelengths Leisure Cen. 7C 104
Wavell Dr. DA15: Sidc 6J 125
Wavell Ho. *N6* 6E 46
(off Hillcrest)
Wavel M. N8 4H 47
NW6 7K 63
Wavel Pl. SE26 4F 139
Wavendon Av. W4 5K 97
Waveney Av. SE15 4H 121
Waveney Cl. E1 1G 103
Waveney Ho. SE15 4H 121
Waverley Av. E4 4G 35
E17 3F 51
HA9: Wemb 5F 61
KT5: Surb 6H 151
SM1: Sutt 2K 165
TW2: Whitt 1D 130
Waverley Cl. BR2: Brom 5B 160
E18 1A 52
KT8: W Mole 5E 148
UB3: Harl 4F 93
Waverley Ct. EN2: Enf 3G 23
NW3 6D 64
NW6 7G 63
SE26 5J 139
Waverley Cres. SE18 5H 107
Waverley Gdns. E6 5C 88
HA6: Nwood 1J 39
IG6: Ilf 2G 53
IG11: Bark 2J 89
NW10 2F 79
Waverley Gro. N3 3F 45
Waverley Ind. Est.
HA1: Harr 3H 41
Waverley Lodge *E15* 6G 69
(off Litchfield Av.)

Waverley Pl. N4 . . . . .2B **66**
NW8 . . . . .2B **82**
Waverley Rd. E17 . . . . .3E **50**
E18 . . . . .1A **52**
EN2: Enf 3G **23**
HA2: Harr 2C **58**
KT17: Ewe 5D **164**
N8 . . . . .6J **47**
N17 . . . . .7C **34**
SE18 . . . . .5G **107**
SE25 . . . . .4H **157**
UB1: S'hall 7E **76**
Waverley Vs. N17 . . . . .2F **49**
Waverley Way SM5: Cars 6C **166**
Waverton Ho. E3 . . . . .1B **86**
Waverton Rd. SW18 . . . . .7A **118**
Waverton St. W1 . . . . .4J **11** (1E **100**)
Wavertree Ct. SW2 . . . . .1J **137**
Wavertree Rd. E18 . . . . .2J **51**
SW2 . . . . .1K **137**
Waxham NW3 .5D **64**
Waxlow Cres. UB1: S'hall 6E **76**
Waxlow Ho. UB4: Yead 5B **76**
Waxlow Rd. NW10 . . . . .2J **79**
Waxlow Way UB5: N'olt 4D **76**
Waxwell Cl. HA5: Pinn 2B **40**
Waxwell Farm Ho. HA5: Pinn 2B **40**
Waxwell La. HA5: Pinn 2B **40**
Wayborne Gro. HA4: Ruis 6E **38**
Waye Av. TW5: Cran 1J **111**
Wayfarer Rd. TW6: H'row A 5C **174**
UB5: N'olt 3B **76**
Wayfield Link SE9 . . . . .6H **125**
Wayford St. SW11 . . . . .2C **118**
Wayland Av. E8 . . . . .5G **67**
Wayland Ho. *SW9* *2A* ***120***
(off Robsart St.)
Waylands UB3: Hayes 5F **75**
Waylands Mead BR3: Beck 1D **158**
Waylett Ho. SE11 . . . . .6J **19**
Waylett Pl. HA0: Wemb 4D **60**
SE27 . . . . .3B **138**
Wayman Ct. E8 .6H **67**
Wayne Cl. BR6: Orp 3K **173**
Wayne Kirkum Way NW6 . . . . .5H **63**
Waynflete Av. CR0: Wadd 3B **168**
Waynflete Ho. *SE1* *5C* ***14***
(off Union St.)
Waynflete Sq. W10 . . . . .7F **81**
(not continuous)
Waynflete St. SW18 . . . . .2A **136**
Wayside CR0: New Ad 6D **170**
NW11 . . . . .1G **63**
SW14 . . . . .5J **115**
Wayside Cl. N14 . . . . .6B **22**
Wayside Commercial Est.
IG11: Bark 1K **89**
Wayside Ct. HA9: Wemb 3G **61**
TW1: Twick 6C **114**
Wayside Gdns. RM10: Dag 5G **73**
Wayside Gro. SE9 . . . . .4D **142**
Wayside M. IG2: Ilf 5E **52**
Weald, The BR7: Chst 6D **142**
Weald Cl. BR2: Brom 2C **172**
SE16 . . . . .5H **103**
Wealden Ho. *E3* *3D* ***86***
(off Talwin St.)
Weald La. HA3: Hrw W 2H **41**
Weald Ri. HA3: Hrw W 7E **26**
Weald Rd. UB10: Hil 2C **74**
Weald Sq. E5 . . . . .2G **67**
WEALDSTONE 3J 41
Wealdstone Cen., The *3J 41*
(off High St.)
Wealdstone FC 2H 57
Wealdstone Rd. SM3: Sutt 2H **165**
Weald Way RM7: Rom 6H **55**
UB4: Hayes 3G **75**
Wealdwood Gdns. HA5: Hat E 6A **26**
Weale Rd. E4 . . . . .3A **36**
Weall Ct. HA5: Pinn 4C **40**
Weardale Gdns. EN2: Enf 1J **23**
Weardale Rd. SE13 . . . . .4F **123**
Wearmouth Ho. *E3* *4B* ***86***
(off Joseph St.)
Wear Pl. E2 . . . . .3H **85**
(not continuous)
Wearside Rd. SE13 . . . . .4D **122**
Weatherbury *W2* *6J* ***81***
(off Talbot Rd.)
Weatherbury Ho. *N19* *3H* ***65***
(off Wedmore St.)
Weatherley Cl. E3 . . . . .5B **86**
Weaver Cl. CR0: C'don 4F **169**
E6 . . . . .7F **89**
Weaver Ho. *E1* *4G* ***85***
(off Pedley St.)
Weavers Almshouses *E11* *6H* ***51***
(off Cambridge Rd.)
Weavers Cl. TW7: Isle 4J **113**
Weavers Ho. *E11* *6J* ***51***
(off New Wanstead)
Weavers La. SE1 . . . . .5H **15** (1E **102**)
Weavers Row E20 . . . . .5D **68**
Weavers Ter. *SW6* *6J* ***99***
(off Micklethwaite Rd.)
Weaver St. E1 .4G **85**
(not continuous)
Weavers Way NW1 . . . . .1H **83**
Weaver Wlk. SE27 . . . . .4C **138**
Webb Cl. W10 . . . . .4E **80**
Webb Ct. *SE28* *7B* ***90***
(off Attlee Rd.)
Webber Ho. *IG11: Bark* *7G* ***71***
(off North St.)
Webber Pth. *E14* *7E* ***86***
(off Bullivant St.)
Webber Row SE1 . . . . .7K **13** (2B **102**)
Webber St. SE1 . . . . .6K **13** (2A **102**)
Webb Est. E5 . . . . .7G **49**
Webb Gdns. E13 . . . . .4J **87**
Webb Ho. *E3* *3C* ***86***
(off Trevithick Way)
RM10: Dag *3G* ***73***
(off Kershaw Rd.)
SW8 . . . . .7H **101**
TW13: Hanw 3C **130**
Webb Pl. NW10 .3B **80**
Webb Rd. SE3 .6H **105**
Webbscroft Rd. RM10: Dag 4H **73**
Webb's Rd. SW11 . . . . .4D **118**
Webbs Rd. UB4: Yead 3K **75**
Webb St. SE1 .3E **102**
Webheath NW6 .7H **63**
(not continuous)
Webster Gdns. W5 . . . . .1D **96**
Webster Rd. E11 . . . . .3E **68**
SE16 . . . . .3G **103**
Weddell Ho. *E1* *4K* ***85***
(off Duckett St.)
Wedderburn Ho. *SW1* *5G* ***17***
(off Lwr. Sloane St.)
Wedderburn Rd. IG11: Bark 1J **89**
NW3 . . . . .5B **64**
Wedgewood Ct. *BR2: Brom* *3H* ***159***
(off Cumberland Rd.)
DA5: Bexl 7G **127**
Wedgewood Ho. *SW1* *6K* ***17***
(off Churchill Gdns.)
Wedgwood Ct. N7 . . . . .4K **65**
Wedgwood Ho. *E2* *3K* ***85***
(off Warley St.)
SE11 . . . . .2J **19**
Wedgwood M. W1 . . . . .1D **12** (6H **83**)
Wedgwood Wlk. *NW6* *5K* ***63***
(off Dresden Cl.)
Wedgwood Way SE19 . . . . .7C **138**
Wedlake St. W10 . . . . .4G **81**
Wedmore Av. IG5: Ilf 1E **52**
Wedmore Gdns. N19 . . . . .2H **65**
Wedmore M. N19 . . . . .3H **65**
Wedmore Rd. UB6: G'frd 3H **77**
Wedmore St. N19 . . . . .3H **65**
Weech Rd. NW6 .4J **63**
Weedington Rd. NW5 . . . . .5E **64**
Weedon Ho. W12 . . . . .6C **80**
Weekley Sq. SW11 . . . . .3B **118**
Weigall Rd. SE12 . . . . .5J **123**
Weighhouse St. W1 . . . . .1H **11** (6E **82**)
Weightman Ho. SE16 . . . . .3G **103**
Weighton M. SE20 . . . . .2H **157**
Weighton Rd. HA3: Hrw W 1H **41**
SE20 . . . . .2H **157**
Weihurst Ct. SM1: Sutt 5C **166**
Weihurst Gdns. SM1: Sutt 5B **166**
Weimar St. SW15 . . . . .3G **117**
Weirdale Av. N20 . . . . .2J **31**
Weir Hall Av. N18 . . . . .6J **33**
Weir Hall Gdns. N18 . . . . .5J **33**
Weir Hall Rd. N17 . . . . .5J **33**
N18 . . . . .5J **33**
Weir Rd. DA5: Bexl 7H **127**
KT12: Walt T 6J **147**
SW12 . . . . .7G **119**
SW19 . . . . .3K **135**
Weir's Pas. NW1 . . . . .1D **6** (3H **83**)
Weiss Rd. SW15 . . . . .3F **117**
Welbeck Av. BR1: Brom 4J **141**
DA15: Sidc 1A **144**
UB4: Yead 4K **75**
Welbeck Cl. KT3: N Mald 5B **152**
KT17: Ewe 7C **164**
N12 . . . . .5G **31**
Welbeck Ct. UB4: Yead 4K **75**
W14 . . . .*4H* ***99***
(off Addison Bri. Pl.)
Welbeck Ho. *W1* *7J* ***5***
(off Welbeck St.)
Welbeck Rd. E6 .3B **88**
EN4: E Barn 6H **21**
HA2: Harr .1F **59**
SM1: Sutt 2B **166**
SM5: Cars 2B **166**
Welbeck St. W1 . . . . .6H **5** (5E **82**)
Welbeck Vs. N21 . . . . .2H **33**
Welbeck Wlk. SM5: Cars 1B **166**
Welbeck Way W1 . . . . .7J **5** (6F **83**)
Welbury Ct. *E8* *7E* ***66***
(off Kingsland Rd.)
Welby Ho. N19 .7H **47**
Welby St. SE5 .1B **120**
Welch Pl. HA5: Pinn 1A **40**
Welcome Ct. *E17* *7C* ***50***
(off Saxon Cl.)
Weldin M. *SW18* *5J* ***117***
(off Lebanon Rd.)
Weldon Cl. HA4: Ruis 6K **57**
Weldon Ct. N21 . . . . .5E **22**
Weldon Dr. KT8: W Mole 4D **148**
Weld Pl. N11 . . . . .5A **32**
(not continuous)
Weld Works M. SW2 . . . . .6K **119**
Welfare Rd. E15 . . . . .7G **69**
Welford Cl. E5 .3K **67**
Welford Ct. *NW1* *7F* ***65***
(off Castlehaven Rd.)
SW8 . . . . .2G **119**
W9 . . . .*5J* ***81***
(off Elmfield Way)
Welford Ho. *UB5: N'olt* *4D* ***76***
(off Waxlow Way)
Welford Pl. SW19 . . . . .4G **135**
Welham Rd. SW16 . . . . .5E **136**
SW17 . . . . .5E **136**
Welhouse Rd. SM5: Cars 1C **166**
Wellacre Rd. HA3: Kenton 6B **42**
Wellan Cl. DA15: Sidc 5B **126**
Welland Ct. *SE6* *2B* ***140***
(off Oakham Cl.)
Welland Gdns. UB6: G'frd 2K **77**
Welland Ho. SE15 . . . . .4J **121**
Welland M. E1 .1G **103**
Welland Rd. TW6: H'row A 5C **174**
Wellands Cl. BR1: Brom 2D **160**
Welland St. SE10 . . . . .6E **104**
Well App. EN5: Barn 5A **20**
Wellbrook Rd. BR6: Farnb 4E **172**
Wellby Cl. N9 . . . . .1B **34**
Wellby Ct. E13 . . . . .1A **88**
Well Cl. HA4: Ruis 3C **58**
SW16 . . . . .4K **137**
Wellclose Sq. E1 . . . . .7G **85**
(not continuous)
Wellclose St. E1 . . . . .7G **85**
Wellcome Collection 3C 6
Wellcome Mus., The *7H 7*
(within Royal College of Surgeons)
Well Cott. Cl. E11 . . . . .6A **52**
Well Ct. EC4 . . . . .1D **14** (6C **84**)
(not continuous)
Wellday Ho. *E9* *6A* ***68***
(off Hedger's Gro.)
Welldon Ct. HA1: Harr 5J **41**
Welldon Cres. HA1: Harr 5J **41**
Weller Ct. *W11* *1H* ***99***
(off Ladbroke Rd.)
Weller Ho. *SE16* *2G* ***103***
(off George Row)
Weller M. BR2: Brom 4K **159**
EN2: Enf .1F **23**
Weller St. SE1 . . . . .6C **14** (2C **102**)
Welles Ct. *E14* *7C* ***86***
(off Premiere Pl.)
Wellesley Av. W6 . . . . .3D **98**
Wellesley Cl. SE7 . . . . .5A **106**
Wellesley Ct. NW2 . . . . .2C **62**
SE1 . . . .*3C* ***102***
(off Rockingham St.)
SM3: Sutt 1G **165**
W9 . . . . .3A **82**
Wellesley Ct. Rd. CR0: C'don 2D **168**
Wellesley Cres. TW2: Twick 2J **131**
Wellesley Gro. CR0: C'don 2D **168**
Wellesley Ho. *NW1* *2D* ***6***
(off Wellesley Pl.)
SW1 . . . .*5J* ***17***
(off Ebury Bri. Rd.)
Wellesley Mans. *W14* *5H* ***99***
(off Edith Vs.)
Wellesley Pde. TW2: Twick 3J **131**
Wellesley Pk. M. EN2: Enf 2G **23**
Wellesley Pas. CR0: C'don 2C **168**
Wellesley Pl. NW1 . . . . .2C **6** (3H **83**)
NW5 . . . . .5E **64**
Wellesley Rd. CR0: C'don 1C **168**
E11 . . . . .5J **51**
E17 . . . . .6C **50**
HA1: Harr 5J **41**
IG1: Ilf 2F **71**
N22 . . . . .2A **48**
NW5 . . . . .5E **64**
SE18 . . . . .7E **106**
SM2: Sutt 6A **166**
(not continuous)
TW2: Twick 3H **131**
W4 . . . . .5G **97**
Wellesley St. E1 . . . . .5K **85**
Wellesley Ter. N1 . . . . .1D **8** (3C **84**)
Wellfield Av. N10 . . . . .3F **47**
Wellfield Rd. SW16 . . . . .4J **137**
Wellfield Wlk. SW16 . . . . .4K **137**
Wellfit St. SE24 . . . . .3B **120**
Wellgarth UB6: G'frd 6B **60**
Wellgarth Rd. NW11 . . . . .1K **63**
Well Gro. N20 . . . . .1F **31**
Well Hall Pde. SE9 . . . . .4D **124**
Well Hall Rd. SE9 . . . . .3C **124**
WELL HALL RDBT. **4C 124**
Wellhouse La. EN5: Barn 4A **20**
Wellhouse Rd. BR3: Beck 4C **158**
Wellhurst Cl. BR6: Chels 7K **173**
WELLING 3B 126
Welling High St. DA16: Well 3B **126**
Wellings Ho. UB3: Hayes 1K **93**

Wellington N8 4J 47
(not continuous)
Wellington Arch 6H 11
Wellington Av. DA15: Sidc 6A 126
E4 2H 35
HA5: Hat E 1D 40
KT4: Wor Pk 3E 164
N9 3C 34
N15 6F 49
TW3: Houn 5E 112
Wellington Bldgs. *E3* *3C 86*
(off Wellington Way)
SW1 6H 17 (5E 100)
Wellington Cl. KT12: Walt T 7H 147
RM10: Dag 7J 73
SE14 1K 121
W11 6J 81
Wellington Ct. *NW8* *2B 82*
(off Wellington Rd.)
SW1 *7E 10*
(off Knightsbridge)
SW6 *1K 117*
(off Maltings Pl.)
TW12: Hamp H 5H 131
TW15: Ashf 5A 128
TW19: Stanw 7A 110
Wellington Cres. KT3: N Mald 3J 151
Wellington Dr. RM10: Dag 7J 73
Wellington Gdns. SE7 6A 106
TW2: Twick 4H 131
Wellington Gro. SE10 7F 105
Wellington Ho. *E16* *1J 105*
(off Pepys Cres.)
NW3 *6D 64*
(off Eton Rd.)
SE17 *6C 102*
(off Arnside St.)
UB5: N'olt *7E 58*
(off The Farmlands)
W5 3E 78
Wellington Lodge *SE1* *7A 14*
(off Waterloo Rd.)
Wellington Mans. E10 1C 68
SE7 *5A 106*
(off Wellington Gdns.)
W14 *6H 99*
(off Queen's Club Gdns.)
Wellington M. *N7* *6K 65*
(off Roman Way)
SE7 6A 106
SE22 4G 121
SW16 3H 137
Wellington Monument 6H 11
Wellington Pde. DA15: Sidc 5A 126
Wellington Pk. Est. NW2 2C 62
Wellington Pas. E11 5J 51
Wellington Pl. N2 5C 46
NW8 1B 4 (3B 82)
Wellington Rd. BR2: Brom 4A 160
CR0: C'don 7B 156
DA5: Bexl 5D 126
DA17: Belv 5F 109
E6 1D 88
E7 4H 69
E10 1A 68
E11 5J 51
E17 4A 50
EN1: Enf 5K 23
HA3: W'stone 3J 41
HA5: Hat E 1D 40
NW8 1B 4 (2B 82)
NW10 3F 81
SW19 2J 135
TW2: Twick 5H 131
TW6: H'row A *6D 174*
(off Whittle Rd.)
TW12: Hamp H 5H 131
TW14: Felt 5G 111
TW15: Ashf 5A 128
W5 3C 96
Wellington Rd. Nth. TW4: Houn 3D 112
Wellington Rd. Sth.
TW4: Houn 4D 112
Wellington Row E2 1K 9 (3F 85)
Wellington Sq. N1 1J 83
SW3 5E 16 (5D 100)
Wellington St. SE18 4E 106
WC2 2G 13 (7K 83)
Wellington Ter. E1 1H 103
HA1: Harr 1H 59
N8 *3A 48*
(off Turnpike La.)
W2 7J 81
Wellington Way E3 3C 86
Welling United FC 3C 126
Welling Way DA16: Well 3G 125
SE9 3G 125
Well La. SW14 5J 115
Wellmeadow Rd. SE6 7G 123
SE13 6G 123
(not continuous)
W7 4A 96
Wellow Wlk. SM5: Cars 1B 166
Well Pl. NW3 3B 64
Well Rd. EN5: Barn 5A 20
NW3 3B 64
Wells, The N14 7C 22
Wells Cl. CR2: S Croy 5E 168
UB5: N'olt 3A 76
Wells Ct. BR2: Brom 2F 159
NW6 *2J 81*
(off Cambridge Av.)
Wells Dr. NW9 1K 61
Wells Gdns. IG1: Ilf 7C 52
RM10: Dag 5H 73
Wells Ga. Cl. IG8: Wfd G 4D 36
Wells Ho. *BR1: Brom* *5K 141*
(off Pike Cl.)
EC1 *1K 7*
(off Spa Grn. Est.)
IG11: Bark *7A 72*
(off Margaret Bondfield Av.)
SE16 *3J 103*
(off Howland Est.)
W5 *7D 78*
(off Grove Rd.)
W10 *4G 81*
(off Wornington Rd.)
Wells Ho. Rd. NW10 5A 80
Wellside Cl. EN5: Barn 4A 20
Wellside Gdns. SW14 4J 115
Wells La. TW3: Houn 3F 113
Wells M. W1 6B 6 (5G 83)
Wellsmoor Gdns. BR1: Brom 3E 160
Wells Pk. Rd. SE26 3G 139
Wells Path UB4: Hayes 3G 75
Wells Pl. SW18 7A 118
Wellspring Cl. E14 5E 86
Wellspring Cres. HA9: Wemb 3H 61
Wellspring M. SE26 3H 139
Wells Ri. NW8 1D 82
Wells Rd. BR1: Brom 2D 160
W12 2E 98
Wells Sq. WC1 2G 7 (3K 83)
Wells St. W1 6A 6 (5G 83)
Wellstead Av. N9 7E 24
Wellstead Rd. E6 2E 88
Wells Ter. N4 2A 66
Well St. E9 7J 67
E15 6G 69
Wells Vw. Dr. BR2: Brom 6C 160
Wells Way SE5 6D 102
SW7 1A 16 (3B 100)
Wells Yd. N7 5A 66
Well Wlk. NW3 4B 64
Wellwood Rd. IG3: Ilf 1A 72
Welmar M. *SW4* *5H 119*
(off Clapham Pk. Rd.)
Welsby Ct. W5 5C 78
Welsford St. SE1 4G 103
(not continuous)
Welsh Cl. E13 3J 87
Welsh Harp (Brent Reservoir)
Nature Reserve 1B 62
Welsh Ho. *E1* *1H 103*
(off Wapping La.)
Welshpool Ho. *E8* *1G 85*
(off Welshpool St.)
Welshpool St. E8 1G 85
(not continuous)
Welshside *NW9* *6A 44*
(off Ruthin Cl.)
Welshside Wlk. NW9 6A 44
Welstead Ho. *E1* *6H 85*
(off Cannon St. Rd.)
Welstead Way W4 4B 98
Weltje Rd. W6 4C 98
Welton Ct. SE5 1E 120
Welton Ho. *E1* *5K 85*
(off Stepney Way)
Welton Rd. SE18 7J 107
Welwyn Av. TW14: Felt 6H 111
Welwyn St. E2 3J 85
Welwyn Way UB4: Hayes 4G 75
WEMBLEY 5E 60
Wembley & Sudbury Tennis & Squash Club
5D 60
Wembley Commercial Cen.
HA9: Wemb 2D 60
Wembley Hill Rd. HA9: Wemb 3F 61
(East La.)
HA9: Wemb 5F 61
(South Way)
WEMBLEY PARK 4G 61
Wembley Pk. Blvd. HA9: Wemb 4G 61
Wembley Pk. Bus. Cen.
HA9: Wemb 4H 61
Wembley Pk. Dr. HA9: Wemb 4F 61
Wembley Retail Pk. HA9: Wemb 4H 61
Wembley Rd. TW12: Hamp 1E 148
Wembley Sailing Club 2K 61
Wembley Stadium 4G 61
Wembley Stadium Ind. Est.
HA9: Wemb 4H 61
Wembley Way HA9: Wemb 6H 61
Wemborough Rd. HA7: Stan 1B 42
Wembury M. N6 7G 47
Wembury Rd. N6 7F 47
Wemyss Rd. SE3 2H 123
Wendela Ct. HA1: Harr 2J 59
Wendell M. W12 2B 98
Wendell Rd. W12 3B 98
Wenderholme *CR2: S Croy* *5D 168*
(off South Pk. Hill Rd.)
Wendle Ct. SW8 7E 18 (6J 101)
Wendle Sq. SW11 1C 118
Wendling NW5 5D 64
Wendling Rd. SM1: Sutt 1B 166
Wendon St. E3 1B 86
Wendover SE17 5E 102
(not continuous)
Wendover Cl. UB4: Yead 4C 76
Wendover Ct. *BR2: Brom* *3K 159*
(off Wendover Rd.)
NW2 3J 63
NW10 4H 79
W1 *6G 5*
(off Chiltern St.)
Wendover Dr. KT3: N Mald 6B 152
Wendover Ho. *W1* *6G 5*
(off Chiltern St.)
Wendover Rd. BR2: Brom 4K 159
NW10 2B 80
SE9 3B 124
Wendover Way DA16: Well 5A 126
Wendy Cl. EN1: Enf 6A 24
Wendy Way HA0: Wemb 1E 78
Wenham Ho. SW8 7G 101
Wenlake Ho. *EC1* *3C 8*
(off Old St.)
Wenlock Barn Est. *N1* *2D 84*
(off Wenlock St.)
Wenlock Ct. N1 1F 9 (2D 84)
Wenlock Gdns. NW4 4D 44
Wenlock M. E10 7C 50
Wenlock Rd. HA8: Edg 7C 28
N1 1D 8 (2C 84)
Wenlock St. N1 1D 8 (2C 84)
Wennington Rd. E3 2K 85
Wensdale Ho. E5 2G 67
Wensley Av. IG8: Wfd G 7C 36
Wensley Cl. N11 6K 31
SE9 6D 124
Wensleydale Av. IG5: Ilf 2C 52
Wensleydale Gdns. TW12: Hamp 7F 131
Wensleydale Pas. TW12: Hamp 1E 148
Wensleydale Rd. TW12: Hamp 6E 130
Wensley Rd. N18 6C 34
Wensum Pl. BR2: Hayes 7J 159
Wentland Cl. SE6 2F 141
Wentland Rd. SE6 2F 141
Wentway Ct. *W13* *4K 77*
(off Ruislip Rd. E.)
Wentworth Av. N3 7D 30
Wentworth Cl. BR2: Hayes 2J 171
BR6: Farnb 5J 173
KT6: Surb 2D 162
N3 7E 30
SE28 6D 90
SM4: Mord 7J 153
TW15: Ashf 4D 128
Wentworth Ct. SW1 6J 17 (5F 101)
SW18 *6K 117*
(off Garratt La.)
TW2: Twick 3J 131
W6 *6G 99*
(off Paynes Wlk.)
Wentworth Cres. SE15 7G 103
UB3: Harl 3F 93
Wentworth Dr. HA5: Eastc 5J 39
TW6: H'row A 5C 174
Wentworth Dwellings *E1* *7J 9*
(off Wentworth St.)
Wentworth Flds. UB4: Hayes 2F 75
Wentworth Gdns. N13 3G 33
Wentworth Hill HA9: Wemb 1F 61
Wentworth Ho. IG8: Wfd G 7K 37
Wentworth M. E3 4A 86
W3 6A 80
Wentworth Pk. N3 7D 30
Wentworth Pl. HA7: Stan 6G 27
Wentworth Rd. CR0: C'don 7A 156
E12 4B 70
EN5: Barn 3A 20
NW11 6H 45
UB2: S'hall 4A 94
Wentworth St. E1 7J 9 (6F 85)
Wentworth Way HA5: Pinn 4C 40
Wenvoe Av. DA7: Bex 2H 127
Wepham Cl. UB4: Yead 5B 76
Wernbrook St. SE18 6G 107
Werndee Rd. SE25 4G 157
Werneth Hall Rd. IG5: Ilf 3E 52
Werrington St. NW1 1B 6 (2G 83)
Werter Rd. SW15 4G 117
Wesleyan Pl. NW5 4F 65
Wesley Apartments SW8 1H 119
Wesley Av. E16 1J 105
NW10 3K 79
TW3: Houn 2C 112
Wesley Cl. HA2: Harr 2G 59
KT19: Ewe 5J 163
N7 2K 65
SE17 4B 102
Wesley Ct. SE16 3H 103
Wesley Rd. E10 7E 50
NW10 1J 79
UB3: Hayes 7J 75
Wesley's Chapel & Mus. of Methodism
3F 9 (4D 84)
Wesley's House 3F 9 (4D 84)
Wesley Sq. W11 6G 81
Wesley St. W1 6H 5 (5E 82)
Wesses Ter. CR4: Mitc 5C 154

Wessex Av. SW19 3J 153
Wessex Cl. IG3: Ilf 6J 53
KT1: King T 1H 151
Wessex Ct. BR3: Beck 1A 158
EN5: Barn 4A 20
HA9: Wemb 2F 61
TW19: Stanw 6A 110
Wessex Dr. HA5: Hat E 1C 40
Wessex Gdns. NW11 1G 63
Wessex Ho. SE1 5F 103
Wessex La. UB6: G'frd 3H 77
Wessex St. E2 3J 85
Wessex Wlk. DA2: Wilm 2K 145
Wessex Way NW11 1G 63
Wesson Mead SE5 7C 102
(off Camberwell Rd.)
West 12 Shop. Cen. W12 2F 99
Westacott UB4: Hayes 5G 75
Westacott Cl. N19 1H 65
West Acre HA2: Harr 2J 59
WEST ACTON 6G 79
West App. BR5: Pet W 5G 161
W. Arbour St. E1 6K 85
West Av. E17 4D 50
HA5: Pinn 6D 40
N3 6D 30
NW4 5F 45
SM6: Wall 5J 167
UB1: S'hall 7D 76
UB3: Hayes 7H 75
West Av. Rd. E17 4C 50
West Bank EN2: Enf 2H 23
IG11: Bark 1F 89
N16 7E 48
Westbank Rd. TW12: Hamp H 6G 131
WEST BARNES 5D 152
W. Barnes La. KT3: N Mald 3D 152
SW20 3D 152
WEST BECKTON 6B 88
WEST BEDFONT 6B 110
Westbeech Rd. N22 3A 48
Westbere Dr. HA7: Stan 5J 27
Westbere Rd. NW2 4G 63
West Block SE1 7H 13
(off York Rd.)
Westbourne Apartments SW6 3K 117
Westbourne Av. SM3: Cheam 2G 165
W3 6K 79
Westbourne Bri. W2 5A 82
Westbourne Cl. UB4: Yead 4A 76
Westbourne Ct. W2 5A 82
Westbourne Cres. W2 2A 10 (7B 82)
Westbourne Cres. M. W2 2A 10
Westbourne Dr. SE23 2K 139
Westbourne Gdns. W2 6K 81
WESTBOURNE GREEN 5J 81
Westbourne Gro. W2 6J 81
W11 7H 81
Westbourne Gro. M. W11 6J 81
Westbourne Gro. Ter. W2 6K 81
Westbourne Ho. SW1 5J 17
(off Ebury Bri. Rd.)
TW5: Hest 6E 94
Westbourne Pde. UB10: Hil 4D 74
Westbourne Pk. Pas. W2 5J 81
(off Harrow Rd.)
Westbourne Pk. Rd. W2 5J 81
W11 6G 81
Westbourne Pk. Vs. W2 5J 81
Westbourne Pl. N9 3C 34
Westbourne Rd. CR0: C'don 6F 157
DA7: Bex 7D 108
N7 6K 65
SE26 6K 139
TW13: Felt 3H 129
UB8: Hil 4D 74
Westbourne St. W2 2A 10 (7B 82)
Westbourne Ter. SE23 2K 139
(off Westbourne Dr.)
W2 1A 10 (6A 82)
Westbourne Ter. M. W2 6A 82
Westbourne Ter. Rd. W2 5K 81
Westbourne Ter. Rd. Bri. W2 5A 82
(off Westbourne Ter. Rd.)
Westbridge Cl. W12 2C 98
Westbridge Ho. SW11 1C 118
(off Westbridge Rd.)
Westbridge Rd. SW11 1B 118
WEST BROMPTON 6A 100
Westbrook Av. TW12: Hamp 7D 130
Westbrook Cl. EN4: Cockf 3G 21
Westbrook Cres. EN4: Cockf 3G 21
Westbrooke Cres. DA16: Well 3C 126
Westbrooke Rd. DA15: Sidc 2H 143
DA16: Well 3B 126
Westbrook Ho. E2 3J 85
(off Victoria Pk. Sq.)
Westbrook Rd. CR7: Thor H 1D 156
SE3 1K 123
TW5: Hest 7D 94
Westbrook Sq. EN4: Cockf 3G 21
Westbury Av. HA0: Wemb 7E 60
N22 3B 48
UB1: S'hall 4E 76
Westbury Cl. HA4: Ruis 7J 39
TW17: Shep 6D 146
Westbury Ct. IG11: Bark 1H 89
(off Ripple Rd.)
Westbury Gro. N12 6D 30
Westbury Ho. E17 4B 50
W11 5J 81
(off Aldridge Rd. Vs.)
Westbury La. IG9: Buck H 2E 36
Westbury Lodge Cl. HA5: Pinn 3B 40
Westbury Pde. SW12 6F 119
(off Balham Hill)
Westbury Pl. TW8: Bford 6D 96
Westbury Rd. BR1: Brom 1B 160
BR3: Beck 3A 158
CR0: C'don 6D 156
E7 6K 69
E17 4B 50
HA0: Wemb 7E 60
IG1: Ilf 2E 70
IG9: Buck H 2F 37
IG11: Bark 1H 89
KT3: N Mald 4K 151
N11 6D 32
N12 6D 30
SE20 1K 157
TW13: Felt 1B 130
W5 6E 78
Westbury Ter. E7 6K 69
Westbush Ct. W12 2D 98
(off Goldhawk M.)
W. Cadet Apartments SE18 7E 106
(off Langhorne St.)
W. Carriage Dr. W2 3C 10 (7C 82)
(North Ride)
W2 2B 100
(Rotten Row)
W. Carriage Ho. SE18 3F 107
(off Royal Carriage M.)
W. Central St. WC1 7E 6 (6J 83)
West Chantry HA3: Hrw W 1F 41
Westchester Dr. NW4 3F 45
Westcliffe Apartments W2 6B 4 (5B 82)
West Cl. EN4: Cockf 4K 21
HA9: Wemb 1F 61
N9 3A 34
TW12: Hamp 6C 130
TW15: Ashf 4A 128
UB6: G'frd 2G 77
Westcombe Av. CR0: C'don 7J 155
Westcombe Ct. SE3 7H 105
Westcombe Dr. EN5: Barn 5D 20
Westcombe Hill SE3 7J 105
SE10 5J 105
Westcombe Lodge Dr. UB4: Hayes 5G 75
Westcombe Pk. Rd. SE3 6G 105
West Comn. Rd. BR2: Hayes, Kes 1J 171
UB8: Uxb 5A 56
Westcoombe Av. SW20 1B 152
Westcote Ri. HA4: Ruis 7E 38
Westcote Rd. SW16 5G 137
West Cotts. NW6 5J 63
Westcott Cl. BR1: Brom 5D 160
CR0: New Ad 7D 170
N15 6F 49
Westcott Cres. W7 6J 77
Westcott Ho. E14 7C 86
Westcott Rd. SE17 6B 102
West Ct. E17 4C 50
HA0: Wemb 2C 60
TW5: Isle 7G 95
Westcroft Cl. EN3: Enf W 1D 24
NW2 4G 63
Westcroft Est. NW2 4G 63
Westcroft Gdns.
SM4: Mord 3H 153
Westcroft Leisure Cen. 4E 166
Westcroft Rd. SM5: Cars 4E 166
SM6: Wall 4E 166
Westcroft Sq. W6 4C 98
Westcroft Way NW2 4G 63
W. Cromwell Rd. SW5 5H 99
W14 5H 99
W. Cross Cen. TW8: Bford 6A 96
W. Cross Route W10 7F 81
W11 7F 81
W12 7F 81
W. Cross Way TW8: Bford 6B 96
Westdale Pas. SE18 6F 107
Westdale Rd. SE18 6F 107
Westdean Av. SE12 1K 141
Westdean Cl. SW18 6K 117
West Dene SM3: Cheam 6G 165
Westdene CR0: C'don 4D 168
(off Chatsworth Rd.)
Westdown Rd. E15 4E 68
SE6 7C 122
WEST DRAYTON 2A 92
W. Drayton Pk. Av. UB7: W Dray 3A 92
W. Drayton Rd. UB8: Hil 6D 74
West Dr. HA3: Hrw W 6C 26
SM2: Cheam 7F 165
SW16 4G 137
West Dr. Gdns. HA3: Hrw W 6C 26
WEST DULWICH 2D 138
WEST EALING 1B 96
W. Ealing Bus. Cen. W13 7A 78
W. Eaton Pl. SW1 3G 17 (4E 100)
W. Eaton Pl. M. SW1 2G 17
W. Ella Rd. NW10 7A 62
W. Elms Studios SW8 1G 119
WEST END 2B 76
W. End Av. E10 5F 51
HA5: Pinn 4B 40
W. End Cl. NW10 7J 61
W. End Ct. HA5: Pinn 4B 40
NW6 7K 63
W. End Gdns. UB5: N'olt 2A 76
W. End La. EN5: Barn 4A 20
HA5: Pinn 3B 40
NW6 5J 63
(not continuous)
UB3: Harl 7E 92
W. End Quay W2 6B 4
W. End Rd. HA4: Ruis 2G 57
UB1: S'hall 1C 94
UB5: N'olt 7A 58
Westerdale Ct. N5 4B 66
(off Hamilton Pk. W.)
Westerdale Rd. SE10 5J 105
Westerfield Rd. N15 5F 49
Westergate W5 5E 78
Westergate Ho. KT1: King T 4D 150
(off Portsmouth Rd.)
Westergate Rd. SE2 6E 108
Westerham NW1 1G 83
(off Bayham St.)
Westerham Av. N9 3J 33
Westerham Dr. DA15: Sidc 6B 126
Westerham Ho. SE1 3D 102
(off Law St.)
Westerham Lodge BR3: Beck 7C 140
(off Park Rd.)
Westerham Rd. BR2: Kes 6B 172
E10 7D 50
Westerley Cres. SE26 5B 140
Westerley Ware TW9: Kew 6G 97
(off Kew Grn.)
Western Av. HA4: Ruis 6D 56
NW11 6F 45
RM10: Dag 6J 73
UB5: N'olt 7A 58
UB6: G'frd 7A 58
UB10: Hil, Uxb 4A 56
W3 4F 79
W5 4F 79
Western Av. Bus. Pk. W3 4H 79
Western Beach Apartments E16 7J 87
Western Ct. N3 6D 30
NW6 2H 81
W3 6K 79
Western Courtyard EC2 7H 9
(off Cutlers Gdns.)
Western Dr. TW17: Shep 6F 147
Western Gdns. W5 7G 79
Western Gateway E16 7J 87
Western Intl. Mkt. UB2: S'hall 4K 93
Western La. SW12 7E 118
Western Mans. EN5: New Bar 5E 20
(off Great Nth. Rd.)
Western M. W9 4H 81
Western Pde. EN5: New Bar 5D 20
Western Perimeter Rd.
TW6: H'row A, Lford 5C 174
Western Pl. SE16 2J 103
Western Rd. CR4: Mitc 1B 154
E13 2A 88
E17 5E 50
N2 4D 46
N22 2K 47
NW10 4J 79
SM1: Sutt 5J 165
SW9 3A 120
SW19 1B 154
UB2: S'hall 4A 94
W5 7D 78
Western Ter. W6 5C 98
Western Transit Shed N1 1J 83
Western Vw. UB3: Hayes 2H 93
Westernville Gdns. IG2: Ilf 7G 53
Western Way EN5: Barn 6D 20
SE28 3H 107
WEST EWELL 7K 163
Westferry Cir. E14 1B 104
Westferry Rd. E14 7B 86
Westfield Av. E20 6D 68
Westfield Cl. EN3: Enf H 3F 25
NW9 3J 43
SM1: Sutt 4H 165
SW10 7A 100
Westfield Ct. KT6: Surb 5D 150
(off Portsmouth Rd)
NW10 3F 81
(off Chamberlayne Rd.)
Westfield Dr. HA3: Kenton 4D 42
Westfield Gdns. HA3: Kenton 4D 42
RM6: Chad H 6C 54
Westfield Ho. SE16 4K 103
(off Rotherhithe New Rd.)
SW10 7B 100
(off Cremorne Est.)
Westfield La. HA3: Kenton 5D 42
Westfield Pk. HA5: Hat E 1D 40
Westfield Pk. Dr. IG8: Wfd G 6H 37
Westfield Rd. BR3: Beck 2B 158
CR0: C'don 2B 168
CR4: Mitc 2C 154
DA7: Bex 3J 127
KT6: Surb 5D 150
KT12: Walt T 7C 148

Westfield Rd. NW7 . . . . 3E **28**
RM9: Dag 4E **72**
SM1: Sutt 4H **165**
W13 . . . . 1A **96**
Westfields SW13 . . . . 3B **116**
Westfields Av. SW13 . . . . 3A **116**
Westfield Shop. Cen. E20 . . . . 6E **68**
W12 . . . . 1E **98**
Westfields Rd. W3 . . . . 5H **79**
Westfield St. SE18 . . . . 3B **106**
Westfield Way E1 . . . . 3A **86**
HA4: Ruis 3G **57**
West Gdn. Pl. W2 . . . . 1D **10** (6C **82**)
West Gdns. E1 . . . . 7H **85**
SW17 . . . . 6C **136**
Westgate W5 . . . . 3E **78**
Westgate Apartments *E16* *7J* ***87***
(off Western Gateway)
Westgate Ct. *SE12* *1J* ***141***
(off Burnt Ash Hill)
SW9 . . . . *3A* ***120***
(off Canterbury Cres.)
Westgate Est. TW14: Bedf 1D **128**
Westgate Ho. TW7: Isle 2H **113**
TW8: Bford *5D* ***96***
(off Ealing Rd.)
Westgate M. *W10* *4G* ***81***
(off West Row)
Westgate Rd. BR3: Beck 1E **158**
SE25 . . . . 4H **157**
Westgate St. E8 . . . . 1H **85**
Westgate Ter. SW10 . . . . 6K **99**
Westglade Ct. HA3: Kenton 5D **42**
WEST GREEN 4B **48**
West Grn. Pl. UB6: G'frd 1H **77**
West Grn. Rd. N15 . . . . 4B **48**
West Gro. IG8: Wfd G 6F **37**
SE10 . . . . 1E **122**
Westgrove La. SE10 . . . . 1E **122**
W. Halkin St. SW1 . . . . 1G **17** (3E **100**)
West Hallowes SE9 . . . . 1B **142**
W. Hall Rd. TW9: Kew 1H **115**
WEST HAM 1H **87**
W. Ham La. E15 . . . . 7F **69**
WEST HAMPSTEAD 6K **63**
W. Hampstead M. NW6 . . . . 6K **63**
West Ham Utd FC 1D **86**
W. Handyside Canopy N1 . . . . 1J **83**
W. Harding St. EC4 . . . . 7K **7** (6A **84**)
WEST HARROW 7G **41**
W. Hatch Mnr. HA4: Ruis 1H **57**
Westhay Gdns. SW14 . . . . 5H **115**
WEST HEATH 6D **108**
W. Heath Av. NW11 . . . . 1J **63**
W. Heath Cl. NW3 . . . . 3J **63**
W. Heath Ct. NW11 . . . . 1J **63**
W. Heath Dr. NW11 . . . . 1J **63**
W. Heath Gdns. NW3 . . . . 2J **63**
W. Heath Rd. NW3 . . . . 2J **63**
SE2 . . . . 6C **108**
WEST HENDON 7C **44**
W. Hendon B'way. NW9 . . . . 6B **44**
WEST HILL 6H **117**
West Hill CR2: Sande 7E **168**
HA2: Harr 2J **59**
HA9: Wemb 1F **61**
SW15 . . . . 7F **117**
SW18 . . . . 7F **117**
W. Hill Ct. N6 . . . . 3E **64**
Westhill Ct. *W11* *7H* ***81***
(off Denbigh Rd.)
W. Hill Pk. N6 . . . . 2D **64**
(not continuous)
W. Hill Rd. SW18 . . . . 6H **117**
W. Hill Way N20 . . . . 1E **30**
Westholm NW11 . . . . 4K **45**
West Holme DA8: Erith 1J **127**
Westholme BR6: Orp 7J **161**
Westholme Gdns. HA4: Ruis 1J **57**
Westhope Ho. *E2* *4G* ***85***
(off Derbyshire St.)
Westhorne Av. SE9 . . . . 5B **124**
SE12 . . . . 7J **123**
Westhorpe Gdns. NW4 . . . . 3E **44**
Westhorpe Rd. SW15 . . . . 3E **116**
West Ho. IG11: Bark 6F **71**
West Ho. Cl. SW19 . . . . 1G **135**
West Ho. Cotts. HA5: Pinn 4B **40**
Westhurst Dr. BR7: Chst 5F **143**
W. India Av. E14 . . . . 1C **104**
W. India Dock Rd. E14 . . . . 7B **86**
W. India Ho. *E14* *7C* ***86***
(off W. India Dock Rd.)
WEST KENSINGTON 4G **99**
W. Kensington Ct. *W14* *5H* ***99***
(off Edith Vs.)
W. Kensington Mans. *W14* *5H* ***99***
(off Beaumont Cres.)
WEST KILBURN 3H **81**
Westking Pl. WC1 . . . . 2G **7** (3K **83**)
Westlake *SE16* *4J* ***103***
(off Rotherhithe New Rd.)
Westlake Cl. N13 . . . . 3F **33**
UB4: Yead 4C **76**
Westlake Rd. HA9: Wemb 2D **60**
Westland Cl. TW19: Stanw 6A **110**
Westland Ct. *UB5: N'olt* *3B* ***76***
(off Seasprite Cl.)
Westland Dr. BR2: Hayes 2H **171**
Westland Ho. *E16* *1E* ***106***
(off Rymill St.)
Westland Pl. N1 . . . . 1E **8** (3D **84**)
Westlands Cl. UB3: Harl 4J **93**
Westlands Ct. KT8: E Mos 4H **149**
Westlands Est. UB3: Harl 3G **93**
Westlands Ter. SW12 . . . . 6G **119**
West La. SE16 . . . . 2H **103**
Westlea Rd. W7 . . . . 3A **96**
Westleigh Av. SW15 . . . . 5D **116**
Westleigh Ct. *CR2: S Croy* *4E* ***168***
(off Birdhurst Rd.)
E11 . . . . *5J* ***51***
(off Nightingale La.)
Westleigh Dr. BR1: Brom 1C **160**
Westleigh Gdns. HA8: Edg 1G **43**
West Links HA0: Wemb 3D **78**
Westlinton Cl. NW7 . . . . 6B **30**
West Lodge *E16* *1J* ***105***
(off Britannia Ga.)
W. Lodge Av. W3 . . . . 1G **97**
W. Lodge Ct. W3 . . . . 1G **97**
W. London Crematorium NW10 . . . . 4D **80**
W. London Studios *SW6* *7K* ***99***
(off Fulham Rd.)
Westmacott Dr. TW14: Felt 1H **129**
Westmacott Ho. *NW8* *4B* ***4***
(off Hatton St.)
West Mall N9 . . . . 3B **34**
W8 . . . . *1J* ***99***
(off Kensington Mall)
Westmark Point *SW15* *1D* ***134***
(off Norley Va.)
West Mead HA4: Ruis 4A **58**
KT19: Ewe 6A **164**
Westmead SW15 . . . . 6D **116**
Westmead Cnr. SM5: Cars 4C **166**
Westmead Ct. SE6 . . . . 6C **122**
Westmead Ho. SM1: Sutt 4B **166**
Westmead Rd. SM1: Sutt 4B **166**
Westmere Dr. NW7 . . . . 3E **28**
W. Mersea Cl. E16 . . . . 1K **105**
West M. N17 . . . . 7C **34**
SW1 . . . . 4A **18**
West Middlesex Golf Course 7G **77**
WESTMINSTER 7E **12** (2J **101**)
Westminster Abbey 7E **12** (3H **101**)
Westminster Abbey Chapter House *1E* ***18***
(within Abbey)
Westminster Abbey Mus. *1E* ***18***
(within Abbey)
Westminster Abbey Pyx Chamber *1E* ***18***
(within Westminster Abbey)
Westminster Av.
CR7: Thor H 2B **156**
Westminster Boating Base & Pier
. . . . 7C **18** (6H **101**)
Westminster Bri. SW1 . . . . 7F **13** (2J **101**)
Westminster Bri. Ho. *SE1* *7A* ***14***
(off Lambeth Rd.)
Westminster Bri. Rd. SE1 . . . . 7G **13** (2K **101**)
Westminster Bus. Sq.
SE11 . . . . 7H **19**
Westminster Cl. IG6: Ilf 2H **53**
TW11: Tedd 5A **132**
TW14: Felt 1J **129**
Westminster Ct. *E11* *6K* ***51***
(off Cambridge Pk.)
NW8 . . . . *4A* ***4***
(off Aberdeen Pl.)
SE16 . . . . *1K* ***103***
(off King & Queen Wharf)
Westminster Dr. N13 . . . . 5D **32**
Westminster Gdns. E4 . . . . 1B **36**
IG6: Ilf 2G **53**
IG11: Bark 2J **89**
SW1 . . . . *3E* ***18***
(off Vincent St.)
Westminster Hall 7E **12**
Westminster Ind. Est. SE18 . . . . 3B **106**
Westminster Mans. *SW1* *2D* ***18***
(off Gt. Smith St.)
Westminster Pal. Gdns. SW1 . . . . 2C **18**
Westminster RC Cathedral
. . . . 2B **18** (3G **101**)
Westminster Rd. N9 . . . . 1C **34**
SM1: Sutt 2B **166**
W7 . . . . 1J **95**
Westmoat Cl. BR3: Beck 7E **140**
WEST MOLESEY 4E **148**
Westmoor Gdns. EN3: Enf H 2E **24**
Westmoor Rd. EN3: Enf H 2E **24**
Westmoor St. SE7 . . . . 3A **106**
Westmore Ct. SW15 . . . . 5G **117**
Westmoreland Av. DA16: Well 3J **125**
Westmoreland Dr. SM2: Sutt 7K **165**
Westmoreland Ho. *E16* *1J* ***105***
(off Gatcombe Rd.)
Westmoreland Pl. BR1: Brom 3J **159**
SW1 . . . . 6K **17** (5F **101**)
W5 . . . . 5D **78**
Westmoreland Rd. BR1: Brom 5G **159**
BR2: Brom 5G **159**
NW9 . . . . 3F **43**
SE17 . . . . 6D **102**
(not continuous)
SW13 . . . . 1B **116**
Westmoreland St. W1 . . . . 6H **5** (5E **82**)
Westmoreland Ter. SE20 . . . . 7H **139**
SW1 . . . . 6K **17** (5F **101**)
Westmoreland Wlk. SE17 . . . . 6D **102**
(not continuous)
Westmorland Cl. E12 . . . . 2B **70**
TW1: Twick 6B **114**
Westmorland Ct. KT6: Surb 7D **150**
Westmorland Rd. E17 . . . . 6C **50**
HA1: Harr 5F **41**
Westmorland Sq. CR4: Mitc 5J **155**
Westmorland Way CR4: Mitc 4H **155**
Westmount Cen. UB4: Yead 7B **76**
Westmount Cl. KT4: Wor Pk 1E **164**
Westmount Ct. W5 . . . . 6F **79**
Westmount Rd. SE9 . . . . 2D **124**
WEST NORWOOD 4C **138**
West Norwood Crematorium
SE27 . . . . 3C **138**
West Oak BR3: Beck 1F **159**
Westoe Rd. N9 . . . . 2C **34**
W. Officers Apartments
SE18 . . . . 7E **106**
Weston Av. KT7: T Ditt 7J **149**
KT8: W Mole 3C **148**
Westonbirt Ct. *SE15* *6F* ***103***
(off Ebley Cl.)
Weston Ct. *KT1: King T* *3E* ***150***
(off Grove Cres.)
N4 . . . . 3C **66**
N20 . . . . *7F* ***21***
(off Farnham Cl.)
Weston Dr. HA7: Stan 1B **42**
W. One Ho. *W1* *6A* ***6***
(off Wells St.)
Westone Mans. *IG11: Bark* *7K* ***71***
(off Upney La.)
W. One Shop. Cen. W1 . . . . 1H **11**
Weston Gdns. TW7: Isle 1J **113**
WESTON GREEN 7J **149**
Weston Grn. KT7: T Ditt 7J **149**
RM9: Dag 4F **73**
Weston Grn. Rd. KT7: T Ditt 7J **149**
Weston Gro. BR1: Brom 1H **159**
Weston Ho. *E9* *1J* ***85***
(off King Edward's Rd.)
NW6 . . . . 7G **63**
Weston Pk. KT1: King T 2E **150**
KT7: T Ditt 7J **149**
N8 . . . . 6J **47**
Weston Ri. WC1 . . . . 1H **7** (3K **83**)
Weston Rd. BR1: Brom 7H **141**
EN2: Enf 2J **23**
RM9: Dag 4E **72**
W4 . . . . 3J **97**
Weston St. SE1 . . . . 7F **15** (2E **102**)
(not continuous)
Weston Wlk. E8 . . . . 7H **67**
Westover Hill NW3 . . . . 2J **63**
Westover Rd. SW18 . . . . 7A **118**
Westow Hill SE19 . . . . 6E **138**
Westow St. SE19 . . . . 6E **138**
West Pk. SE9 . . . . 2C **142**
Westpark W5 . . . . 6D **78**
West Pk. Av. TW9: Kew 1G **115**
West Pk. Cl. RM6: Chad H 5D **54**
TW5: Hest 6D **94**
West Pk. Rd. TW9: Kew 1G **115**
UB2: S'hall 1G **95**
W. Parkside SE10 . . . . 2G **105**
West Pk. Wlk. E20 . . . . 6E **68**
West Pl. SW19 . . . . 5E **134**
West Plaza TW15: Ashf 2A **128**
West Point *E14* *7B* ***86***
(off Grenade St.)
SE1 . . . . 5G **103**
Westpoint Apartments N8 . . . . 3K **47**
W. Point Cl. *TW4: Houn* *3D* ***112***
(off Grosvenor Rd.)
Westpoint Trad. Est. W3 . . . . 5H **79**
Westpole Av. EN4: Cockf 4K **21**
Westport Ct. UB4: Yead 4A **76**
Westport Rd. E13 . . . . 4K **87**
Westport St. E1 . . . . 6K **85**
W. Poultry Av. EC1 . . . . 6A **8** (5B **84**)
West Quarters W12 . . . . 6C **80**
W. Quay SW10 . . . . 1A **118**
West Quay Dr. UB4: Yead 5C **76**
West Quay Wlk. E14 . . . . 3D **104**
West Ramp TW6: H'row A 1C **110**
West Reservoir Cen. 1C **66**
W. Ridge Gdns. UB6: G'frd 2G **77**
West Ri. W2 . . . . 2D **10**
West Rd. E15 . . . . 1H **87**
EN4: E Barn 1K **31**
KT2: King T 1J **151**
N17 . . . . 6C **34**
RM6: Chad H 6D **54**
RM7: Rush G 7K **55**
SE1 . . . . 6H **13** (2K **101**)
SW3 . . . . 6F **17** (5D **100**)
SW4 . . . . 5H **119**
TW14: Bedf 6F **111**
UB7: W Dray 3B **92**
W5 . . . . 5E **78**
Westrovia Ct. *SW1* *4C* ***18***
(off Moreton St.)
West Row W10 . . . . 4G **81**

Westrow SW15 6E 116
Westrow Dr. IG11: Bark 5A 72
Westrow Gdns. IG3: Ilf 2K 71
WEST RUISLIP 2E 56
W. Ruislip Ct. HA4: Ruis 2F 57
(off Ickenham Rd.)
W. Sheen Va. TW9: Rich 4F 115
Westside N2 3D 46
NW4 2D 44
Westside Apartments IG1: Ilf 3E 70
(off Roden St.)
W. Side Comn. SW19 5E 134
West Side Ct. TW16: Sun 7G 129
(off Scotts Av.)
Westside Ct. W9 4J 81
(off Elgin Av.)
W. Smithfield EC1 6A 8 (5B 84)
West Sq. E10 7D 50
SE11 2K 19 (3B 102)
West Stand N5 4B 66
West St. BR1: Brom 1J 159
CR0: C'don 4C 168
DA7: Bex 3F 127
DA8: Erith 4K 109
E2 2H 85
E11 3G 69
E17 5D 50
HA1: Harr 1H 59
SM1: Sutt 5K 165
SM5: Cars 3D 166
WC2 1D 12 (6H 83)
West St. La. SM5: Cars 4D 166
West St. Pl. CR0: C'don 4C 168
(off West St.)
W. Temple Sheen SW14 5H 115
W. Tenter St. E1 1K 15 (6F 85)
West Ter. DA15: Sidc 1J 143
W. Thamesmead Bus. Pk. SE28 3J 107
(not continuous)
West Twr. E14 2D 104
(off Pan Peninsula Sq.)
West Towers HA5: Pinn 5B 40
Westvale M. W3 2A 98
West Vw. NW4 4E 44
TW14: Bedf 7E 110
Westview W7 6J 77
W. View Apartments N7 7J 65
(off York Way)
Westview Cl. NW10 5B 62
W10 6E 80
Westview Ct. N20 1F 31
Westview Cres. N9 7K 23
Westview Dr. IG8: Wfd G 2B 52
Westville Rd. KT7: T Ditt 1A 162
W12 2C 98
West Wlk. EN4: E Barn 7K 21
UB3: Hayes 1J 93
W5 5E 78
Westward Rd. E4 5G 35
(not continuous)
Westward Way HA3: Kenton 6E 42
W. Warwick Pl. SW1 4A 18 (4G 101)
West Way BR4: W W'ck 6F 159
BR5: Pet W 5H 161
CR0: C'don 2A 170
HA4: Ruis 1H 57
HA5: Pinn 4B 40
HA8: Edg 6C 28
N18 4J 33
NW10 3K 61
TW5: Hest 1D 112
TW17: Shep 6F 147
Westway SW20 3D 152
UB6: G'frd 1J 77
W2 6A 4 (5H 81)
W9 5H 81
W10 5H 81
W12 7B 80
Westway Cl. SW20 3D 152
Westway Ct. UB5: N'olt 1E 76
Westway Est. W3 5A 80
W. Way Gdns. CR0: C'don 2K 169
Westway Lodge W9 5J 81
(off Amberley Rd.)
West Ways HA6: Nwood 2J 39
Westways KT19: Ewe 4B 164
Westway Sports Cen. 6F 81
Westway Travellers Site W12 7F 81
(off Stable Way)
Westwell M. SW16 6J 137
Westwell Rd. SW16 6J 137
Westwell Rd. App. SW16 6J 137
Westwick KT1: King T 2G 151
(off Chesterton Ter.)
Westwick Gdns. TW4: Cran 2K 111
W14 2F 99
WEST WICKHAM 1E 170
West Wickham Leisure Cen. 1E 170
West Wintergarden 1D 104
(off Bank St.)
Westwood Av. HA2: Harr 4F 59
SE19 1C 156
Westwood Bus. Cen. NW10 4A 80
Westwood Cl. BR1: Brom 2B 160
HA4: Ruis 6D 38
Westwood Ct. EN1: Enf 6K 23
(off Village Rd.)
HA0: Wemb 4B 60
UB6: G'frd 5H 59
Westwood Gdns. SW13 3B 116
Westwood Hill SE26 5G 139
Westwood Ho. W12 1E 98
(off Wood La.)
Westwood La. DA15: Sidc 5A 126
DA16: Well 3K 125
Westwood M. E3 3C 86
(off Addington Rd.)
Westwood Pk. SE23 7H 121
Westwood Pk. Trad. Est. W3 5H 79
Westwood Pl. SE26 4G 139
Westwood Rd. E16 1K 105
IG3: Ilf 1K 71
SW13 3B 116
West Woodside DA5: Bexl 7E 126
Wetheral Dr. HA7: Stan 1B 42
Wetherby Cl. UB5: N'olt 6F 59
Wetherby Gdns. SW5 4A 100
Wetherby Mans. SW5 5K 99
(off Earls Ct. Sq.)
Wetherby M. SW5 5K 99
Wetherby Pl. SW7 4A 100
Wetherby Rd. EN2: Enf 1H 23
Wetherby Way KT9: Chess 7E 162
Wetherden St. E17 7B 50
Wetherell Rd. E9 1K 85
Wetherill Rd. N10 1E 46
Wevco Wharf SE15 6H 103
Wexford Ho. E1 5J 85
(off Sidney St.)
Wexford Rd. SW12 7D 118
Wexner Bldg. E1 6J 9
(off Strype St.)
Weybourne St. SW18 2A 136
Weybridge Ct. SE16 5H 103
Weybridge Point SW11 2D 118
Weybridge Rd. CR7: Thor H 4A 156
Wey Ct. KT19: Ewe 4J 163
Weydown Cl. SW19 1G 135
Weyhill Rd. E1 6G 85
Wey Ho. NW8 4B 4
(off Church St. Est.)
UB5: N'olt 4D 76
(off Taywood Rd.)
Weylands Cl. KT12: Walt T 7D 148
Weylond Rd. RM8: Dag 3F 73
Weyman Rd. SE3 1A 124
Weymarks, The N17 6J 33
Weymouth Av. NW7 5F 29
W5 3C 96
Weymouth Cl. E6 6F 89
Weymouth Ct. E2 2F 85
SM2: Sutt 7J 165
Weymouth Ho. BR2: Brom 2H 159
(off Hill Ho. M.)
SW8 7K 101
(off Bolney St.)
Weymouth M. W1 5J 5 (5F 83)
Weymouth Pl. SE2 3A 108
Weymouth Rd. UB4: Hayes 3G 75
Weymouth St. W1 6H 5 (5E 82)
Weymouth Ter. E2 1K 9 (2F 85)
Weymouth Vs. N4 2K 65
(off Moray Rd.)
Weymouth Wlk. HA7: Stan 6F 27
Whadcoat St. N4 2A 66
Whaddon Ho. SE22 3E 120
Whalebone Av. RM6: Chad H 6F 55
Whalebone Ct. EC2 7E 8
Whalebone Gro.
RM6: Chad H 6F 55
Whalebone La. E15 7G 69
Whalebone La. Nth.
RM6: Chad H, Col R 1E 54
Whalebone La. Sth.
RM6: Chad H, Dag 7F 55
RM8: Dag 7F 55
Whales Yd. E15 7G 69
(off West Ham La.)
Wharf, The EC3 4H 15 (1F 103)
Wharfdale Cl. N11 6K 31
Wharfdale Rd. N1 2J 83
Wharfedale Ct. E5 4K 67
Wharfedale Gdns. CR7: Thor H 4K 155
Wharfedale Ho. NW6 1K 81
(off Kilburn Vale)
Wharfedale St. SW10 5K 99
Wharfedale Yd. N1 2J 83
(off Wharfedale Rd.)
Wharf La. E14 6B 86
TW1: Twick 1A 132
Wharf Mill Apartments E2 1F 85
(off Laburnum St.)
Wharf Pl. E2 1H 85
Wharf Rd. E16 1A 106
EN3: Pond E 6F 25
N1 1C 8 (2C 84)
(Baldwin Ter.)
N1 1J 83
(York Way)
Wharf Rd. Ind. Est. EN3: Pond E 6F 25
Wharfside Point Nth. E14 7E 86
(off Poplar High St.)
Wharfside Point Sth. E14 7E 86
Wharfside Rd. E16 5G 87
Wharf St. E16 5G 87
SE8 5C 104
Wharf Vw. Ct. E14 6E 86
(off Blair St.)
Wharncliffe Dr. UB1: S'hall 1H 95
Wharncliffe Gdns. SE25 2E 156
Wharncliffe Rd. SE25 2E 156
Wharnecliffe M. SW4 6H 119
Wharton Cl. NW10 6A 62
Wharton Cotts. WC1 2J 7 (3A 84)
Wharton Ho. E2 3K 85
SE1 7J 15
(off St Saviour's Est.)
Wharton Rd. BR1: Brom 1K 159
Wharton St. WC1 2H 7 (3K 83)
Whatcott's Yd. N16 4E 66
Whateley Rd. SE20 7K 139
SE22 5F 121
Whatley Av. SW20 3F 153
Whatman Ho. E14 6B 86
(off Wallwood St.)
Whatman Rd. SE23 7K 121
Wheatcroft Ct. SM1: Sutt 1K 165
(off Cleeve Way)
Wheatfield Ho. NW6 3J 81
(off Kilburn Pk. Rd.)
Wheatfields E6 6F 89
EN3: Enf H 1F 25
Wheatfield Way KT1: King T 2E 150
Wheathill Ho. SE20 2H 157
(off Penge Rd.)
Wheathill Rd. SE20 3H 157
Wheatland Ho. SE22 3E 120
Wheatlands TW5: Hest 6E 94
Wheatlands Rd. SW17 3E 136
Wheatley Cl. NW4 2C 44
Wheatley Ct. E3 3D 86
(off Bruce Rd.)
Wheatley Cres. UB3: Hayes 7J 75
Wheatley Gdns. N9 2K 33
Wheatley Ho. SW15 7C 116
(off Ellisfield Dr)
Wheatley Mans. IG11: Bark 7A 72
(off Lansbury Av.)
Wheatley M. KT8: E Mos 4H 149
Wheatley Rd. TW7: Isle 3K 113
Wheatley's Eyot TW16: Sun 5J 147
Wheatley St. W1 6H 5 (5E 82)
Wheat Sheaf Cl. E14 4D 104
Wheatsheaf Cl. UB5: N'olt 5C 58
Wheatsheaf La. SW6 7E 98
SW8 7J 101
Wheatsheaf Ter. SW6 7H 99
Wheatstone Cl. CR4: Mitc 1C 154
Wheatstone Ho. SE1 3C 102
(off County St.)
W10 5G 81
(off Telford Rd.)
Wheatstone Rd. DA8: Erith 5K 109
W10 5G 81
Wheeler Cl. IG8: Wfd G 6J 37
Wheeler Gdns. N1 1J 83
(off Outram Pl.)
Wheeler Pl. BR2: Brom 4K 159
Wheelers Cross IG11: Bark 2H 89
Wheelers Dr. HA4: Ruis 6E 38
Wheel Farm Dr. RM10: Dag 3J 73
Wheel Ho. E14 5D 104
(off Burrells Wharf Sq.)
Wheelock Cl. DA8: Erith 7H 109
Wheelwright St. N7 7K 65
Whelan Way SM6: Bedd 3H 167
Wheler Ho. E1 4J 9
(off Quaker St.)
Wheler St. E1 4J 9 (4F 85)
Whellock Rd. W4 3A 98
Whenman Av. DA5: Bexl 2J 145
Whernside Cl. SE28 7C 90
WHETSTONE 2F 31
Whetstone Cl. N20 2G 31
Whetstone Pk. WC2 7G 7 (6K 83)
Whetstone Rd. SE3 2A 124
Whewell Rd. N19 2J 65
Whidborne Bldgs. WC1 2F 7
(off Whidborne St.)
Whidborne Cl. SE8 2C 122
Whidborne St. WC1 2F 7 (3J 83)
(not continuous)
Whidbourne M. SW8 1H 119
Whimbrel Cl. SE28 7C 90
Whimbrel Way UB4: Yead 6B 76
Whinchat Rd. SE28 3H 107
Whinfell Cl. SW16 5H 137
Whinyates Rd. SE9 3C 124
Whippendell Way BR5: St P 7B 144
Whippingham Ho. E3 3B 86
(off Merchant St.)
Whipps Cross E17 5F 51
Whipps Cross Ho. E17 5F 51
(off Wood St.)
Whipps Cross Rd. E11 5F 51
(not continuous)
Whiskin St. EC1 2A 8 (3B 84)
Whisperwood Cl. HA3: Hrw W 1J 41
Whistler Gdns. HA8: Edg 2F 43
Whistler M. RM8: Dag 5B 72
(off Fitzstephen Rd.)
SE15 7F 103
Whistlers Av. SW11 7B 100
Whistlers Gro. DA15: Sidc 7J 125

Whistler St. N5 ... 5B 66
Whistler Twr. *SW10* ... *7A 100*
(off Worlds End Est.)
Whistler Wlk. SW10 ... 7B 100
Whiston Ho. *N1* ... *7B 66*
(off Richmond Gro.)
Whiston Rd. E2 ... 2F 85
Whitacre M. SE11 ... 6K 19 (5A 102)
Whitakers Lodge EN2: Enf ... 1J 23
Whitbread Cl. N17 ... 1G 49
Whitbread Rd. SE4 ... 4A 122
Whitburn Rd. SE13 ... 4D 122
Whitby Av. NW10 ... 3H 79
Whitby Ct. N7 ... 4J 65
Whitby Gdns. NW9 ... 3G 43
SM1: Sutt ... 2B 166
Whitby Ho. *NW8* ... *1A 82*
(off Boundary Rd.)
Whitby Pde. HA4: Ruis ... 2A 58
Whitby Rd. HA2: Harr ... 3G 59
HA4: Ruis ... 3K 57
SE18 ... 4D 106
SM1: Sutt ... 2B 166
Whitby St. E1 ... 3J 9 (4F 85)
(not continuous)
Whitcher Cl. SE14 ... 6A 104
Whitcher Pl. NW1 ... 6G 65
Whitchurch Av. HA8: Edg ... 7A 28
Whitchurch Cl. HA8: Edg ... 6A 28
Whitchurch Gdns. HA8: Edg ... 6A 28
Whitchurch Ho. *W10* ... *6F 81*
(off Kingsdown Cl.)
Whitchurch La. HA8: Edg ... 7J 27
Whitchurch Pde. HA8: Edg ... 7B 28
Whitchurch Rd. W11 ... 7F 81
Whitcomb Ct. WC2 ... 3D 12
Whitcombe M. TW9: Kew ... 1H 115
Whitcomb St. WC2 ... 3D 12 (7H 83)
Whitcome M. TW9: Kew ... 1H 115
Whiteadder Way E14 ... 4D 104
Whitear Wlk. E15 ... 6F 69
Whitebarn La. RM10: Dag ... 1G 91
Whitebeam Av. BR2: Brom ... 7E 160
Whitebeam Cl. SW9 ... 7K 101
Whitebeam Ho. *E15* ... *3G 87*
(off Teasel Way)
White Bear Pl. NW3 ... 4B 64
White Bear Yd. *EC1* ... *4J 7*
(off Clerkenwell Rd.)
White Bri. Av. CR4: Mitc ... 3B 154
Whitebridge Cl. TW14: Felt ... 6H 111
White Butts Rd. HA4: Ruis ... 3B 58
WHITECHAPEL ... 5G 85
Whitechapel Gallery ... 7K 9 (6F 85)
Whitechapel High St. E1 ... 7K 9 (6F 85)
Whitechapel Rd. E1 ... 7K 9 (5G 85)
Whitechapel Sports Cen. ... 5H 85
White Church La. E1 ... 7K 9 (6G 85)
White Church Pas. *E1* ... *7K 9*
(off White Church La.)
WHITE CITY ... 7D 80
WHITE CITY ... 6E 80
White City Cl. W12 ... 7E 80
White City Est. W12 ... 7D 80
White City Rd. W12 ... 7E 80
White Conduit St. N1 ... 2A 84
Whitecote Rd. UB1: S'hall ... 6G 77
Whitecroft Cl. BR3: Beck ... 4F 159
Whitecroft Way BR3: Beck ... 5E 158
Whitecross Pl. EC2 ... 5F 9 (5D 84)
Whitecross St. EC1 ... 3D 8 (4C 84)
Whitefield Av. NW2 ... 1E 62
Whitefield Cl. SW15 ... 6G 117
Whitefoot La. BR1: Brom ... 4E 140
(not continuous)
Whitefoot Ter. BR1: Brom ... 3H 141
Whitefriars Av. HA3: W'stone ... 2J 41
Whitefriars Ct. N12 ... 5G 31
Whitefriars Dr. HA3: Hrw W ... 2H 41
Whitefriars St. EC4 ... 1K 13 (6A 84)
Whitefriars Trad. Est. HA3: W'stone ... 3H 41
White Gables Ct. CR2: S Croy ... 5E 168
White Gdns. RM10: Dag ... 6G 73
Whitegate Gdns. HA3: Hrw W ... 7E 26
White Gates KT7: T Ditt ... 7A 150
Whitehall ... 6G 165
Whitehall SW1 ... 5E 12 (1J 101)
Whitehall Ct. SW1 ... 5F 13 (1J 101)
(not continuous)
Whitehall Cres. KT9: Chess ... 5D 162
Whitehall Gdns. E4 ... 1B 36
SW1 ... 5E 12
W3 ... 1G 97
W4 ... 6H 97
Whitehall La. IG9: Buck H ... 2D 36
Whitehall Lodge N10 ... 2E 46
Whitehall Pk. N19 ... 1G 65
Whitehall Pk. Rd. W4 ... 6H 97
Whitehall Pl. E7 ... 5J 69
SM6: Wall ... 4F 167
SW1 ... 5E 12 (1J 101)
Whitehall Rd. BR2: Brom ... 5B 160
CR7: Thor H ... 5A 156
E4 ... 2B 36
HA1: Harr ... 7J 41
IG8: Wfd G ... 2B 36
W7 ... 2A 96
Whitehall St. N17 ... 7A 34
White Hart Av. SE18 ... 4K 107
SE28 ... 4K 107
White Hart Cl. UB3: Harl ... 6F 93
White Hart Ct. EC2 ... 6G 9
White Hart Lane ... 7B 34
White Hart La. N17 ... 7H 33
N22 ... 1K 47
NW10 ... 6B 62
RM7: Col R, Mawney ... 1G 55
SW13 ... 2A 116
White Hart Lane Community Sports Cen. ... 7G 33
White Hart Rd. SE18 ... 4J 107
WHITE HART RDBT. ... 2B 76
White Hart Slip BR1: Brom ... 2J 159
White Hart St. EC4 ... 7B 8 (6B 84)
SE11 ... 5K 19 (5A 102)
White Hart Triangle SE28 ... 2K 107
White Hart Triangle Bus. Pk. SE28 ... 2A 108
White Hart Yd. SE1 ... 5E 14 (1D 102)
Whitehaven Cl. BR2: Brom ... 4J 159
Whitehaven St. NW8 ... 4C 4 (4C 82)
Whitehead Cl. N18 ... 5J 33
SW18 ... 7A 118
Whiteheads Gro. SW3 ... 4D 16 (4C 100)
White Heart Av. UB8: Hil ... 5E 74
Whiteheath Av. HA4: Ruis ... 7E 38
White Heather Ho. *WC1* ... *2F 7*
(off Cromer St.)
White Heron M. TW11: Tedd ... 6K 131
White Horse All. EC1 ... 5A 8
White Horse Apartments *N1* ... *1A 84*
(off Liverpool Rd.)
White Horse Hill BR7: Chst ... 4E 142
White Horse La. E1 ... 5K 85
Whitehorse La. SE25 ... 4D 156
White Horse M. EN3: Enf H ... 2E 24
Whitehorse M. SE1 ... 1K 19 (3A 102)
White Horse Rd. E1 ... 6A 86
(not continuous)
E6 ... 3D 88
Whitehorse Rd. CR0: C'don ... 7C 156
CR7: Thor H ... 7C 156
White Horse St. W1 ... 5K 11 (1F 101)
White Horse Yd. EC2 ... 7E 8 (6D 84)
White Ho. *CR0: C'don* ... *4D 168*
(off Coombe Rd.)
SW4 ... *7H 119*
(off Clapham Pk. Est.)
SW11 ... 1B 118
White Ho., The NW1 ... 3K 5
Whitehouse *E10* ... *6E 50*
(off Leyton Grn. Rd.)
Whitehouse Apartments SE1 ... 1K 101
White Ho. Ct. N14 ... 2D 32
White Ho. Dr. HA7: Stan ... 4H 27
IG8: Wfd G ... 6C 36
White Ho. La. EN2: Enf ... 1H 23
White Ho. M. E10 ... 6E 50
Whitehouse Way N14 ... 2A 32
Whitehurst Dr. N18 ... 5E 34
White Kennett St. E1 ... 7H 9 (6F 85)
Whitelands Cres. SW18 ... 7G 117
Whitelands Ho. *SW3* ... *5F 17*
(off Cheltenham Ter.)
Whiteledges W13 ... 6C 78
Whitelegg Rd. E13 ... 2H 87
Whiteley Rd. SE19 ... 5D 138
Whiteleys Cen. (Shop. Cen.) W2 ... 6K 81
Whiteleys Pde. UB10: Hil ... 4D 74
Whiteley's Way TW13: Hanw ... 3E 130
White Lion Ct. EC3 ... 1G 15
SE15 ... 6J 103
TW7: Isle ... 3B 114
White Lion Hill EC4 ... 2B 14 (7B 84)
White Lion St. N1 ... 2A 84
White Lodge SE19 ... 7B 138
W5 ... 5C 78
White Lodge Cl. N2 ... 6B 46
SM2: Sutt ... 7A 166
TW7: Isle ... 2A 114
White Lodge Ct. TW16: Sun ... 1A 148
White Lodge Mus. ... 1K 133
White Lyon Ct. EC2 ... 5C 8
Whiteoak Ct. BR7: Chst ... 6E 142
White Oak Dr. BR3: Beck ... 2E 158
White Oak Gdns. DA15: Sidc ... 7K 125
Whiteoaks La. UB6: G'frd ... 3H 77
White Orchards HA7: Stan ... 5F 27
N20 ... 1C 30
White Post La. E9 ... 7B 68
White Post St. SE15 ... 7J 103
White Rd. E15 ... 7G 69
White Rose Ct. *E1* ... *5E 84*
(off Widegate St.)
Whiterose Trad. Est. *EN4: E Barn* ... *5G 21*
(off Margaret Rd.)
Whites Av. IG2: Ilf ... 6J 53
Whites Grounds SE1 ... 7H 15 (2E 102)
White's Grounds Est. SE1 ... 6H 15
White's Mdw. BR1: Brom ... 4E 160
White's Row E1 ... 6J 9 (5F 85)
Whites Sq. SW4 ... 4H 119
Whitestile Rd. TW8: Bford ... 5C 96
Whitestone Cl. EN4: Had W ... 1H 21
Whitestone La. NW3 ... 3A 64
Whitestone Wlk. NW3 ... 3A 64
Whitestone Way CR0: Wadd ... 2A 168
White St. UB1: S'hall ... 2B 94
White Swan M. W4 ... 5A 98
Whitethorn Av. UB7: Yiew ... 7A 74
Whitethorn Gdns. CR0: C'don ... 2H 169
EN2: Enf ... 5J 23
Whitethorn Ho. *E1* ... *1J 103*
(off Prusom St.)
Whitethorn Pas. *E3* ... *4C 86*
(off Whitethorn St.)
Whitethorn Pl. UB7: Yiew ... 1B 92
Whitethorn St. E3 ... 5C 86
White Twr. Way E1 ... 5A 86
Whitewebbs Way BR5: St P ... 1K 161
Whitfield Ct. IG1: Ilf ... 7D 52
Whitfield Ho. *NW8* ... *4C 4*
(off Salisbury St.)
Whitfield Pl. W1 ... 4A 6
Whitfield Rd. DA7: Bex ... 7F 109
E6 ... 7A 70
Whitfield St. W1 ... 4A 6 (4G 83)
Whitford Gdns. CR4: Mitc ... 3D 154
Whitgift Av. CR2: S Croy ... 5B 168
Whitgift Cen. CR0: C'don ... 2C 168
Whitgift Ct. *CR2: S Croy* ... *5C 168*
(off Nottingham Rd.)
Whitgift Ho. SE11 ... 3G 19 (4K 101)
SW11 ... 1C 118
Whitgift Sq. CR0: C'don ... 2C 168
Whitgift St. CR0: C'don ... 3C 168
SE11 ... 3G 19 (4K 101)
Whiting Av. IG11: Bark ... 7F 71
Whitings IG2: Ilf ... 5J 53
Whitings Rd. EN5: Barn ... 5A 20
Whitings Way E6 ... 5E 88
Whiting Way SE16 ... 4A 104
Whitland Rd. SM5: Cars ... 1B 166
Whitley Cl. TW19: Stanw ... 6A 110
Whitley Ho. *SW1* ... *7B 18*
(off Churchill Gdns.)
Whitley Rd. N17 ... 2E 48
Whitlock Dr. SW19 ... 7G 117
Whitman Ho. *E2* ... *3J 85*
(off Cornwall Av.)
Whitman Rd. E3 ... 4A 86
Whitmead Cl. CR2: S Croy ... 6E 168
Whitmore Bldg. *SE16* ... *3F 103*
(off Arts La.)
Whitmore Cl. N11 ... 5A 32
Whitmore Est. N1 ... 1E 84
Whitmore Gdns. NW10 ... 2E 80
Whitmore Ho. *N1* ... *1E 84*
(off Whitmore Est.)
Whitmore Rd. BR3: Beck ... 3B 158
HA1: Harr ... 7G 41
N1 ... 1E 84
Whitmore Sports Cen. ... 1G 59
Whitnell Way SW15 ... 5E 116
(not continuous)
Whitney Av. IG4: Ilf ... 4B 52
Whitney Rd. E10 ... 7D 50
Whitney Wlk. DA14: Sidc ... 6E 144
Whitstable Cl. BR3: Beck ... 1B 158
HA4: Ruis ... 2G 57
Whitstable Ho. *W10* ... *6F 81*
(off Silchester Rd.)
Whitstable Pl. CR0: C'don ... 4C 168
Whitstone La. BR3: Beck ... 5D 158
Whittaker Av. TW9: Rich ... 5D 114
Whittaker Pl. *TW9: Rich* ... *5D 114*
(off Whittaker Av.)
Whittaker Rd. E6 ... 7A 70
SM3: Sutt ... 3H 165
Whittaker St. SW1 ... 4G 17 (4E 100)
Whittaker Way SE1 ... 4G 103
Whitta Rd. E12 ... 4B 70
Whittell Gdns. SE26 ... 3J 139
Whittingham N17 ... 7C 34
Whittingham Ct. W4 ... 7A 98
Whittingstall Rd. SW6 ... 1H 117
Whittington Apartments *E1* ... *6K 85*
(off E. Arbour St.)
Whittington Av. EC3 ... 1G 15 (6E 84)
UB4: Hayes ... 5H 75
Whittington Ct. N2 ... 5D 46
Whittington Ho. *N19* ... *2H 65*
(off Holloway Rd.)
Whittington M. N12 ... 4F 31
Whittington Rd. N22 ... 7D 32
Whittington Way HA5: Pinn ... 5C 40
Whittlebury Cl. SM5: Cars ... 7D 166
Whittlebury M. E. NW1 ... 7E 64
Whittlebury M. W. NW1 ... 7E 64
Whittle Cl. E17 ... 6A 50
UB1: S'hall ... 6F 77
Whittle Rd. TW5: Hest ... 7A 94
TW6: H'row A ... 6C 174
UB2: S'hall ... 2F 95
Whittlesea Cl. HA3: Hrw W ... 7B 26
Whittlesea Path HA3: Hrw W ... 1G 41
Whittlesea Rd. HA3: Hrw W ... 7B 26
Whittlesey St. SE1 ... 5J 13 (1A 102)
WHITTON ... 7G 113
Whitton NW3 ... 7D 64
Whitton Av. E. UB6: G'frd ... 5J 59
Whitton Av. W. UB5: N'olt ... 5F 59
UB6: G'frd ... 5F 59
Whitton Cl. UB6: G'frd ... 6B 60

Whitton Dene TW3: Houn, Isle 5G **113**
TW7: Isle 6H **113**
Whitton Dr. UB6: G'frd 6A **60**
Whitton Mnr. Rd. TW7: Isle 6G **113**
Whitton Rd. TW1: Twick 6K **113**
TW2: Twick 6J **113**
TW3: Houn 4F **113**
WHITTON ROAD RDBT. **6K 113**
Whitton Sports & Fitness Cen. 2F **131**
Whitton Wlk. E3 3C **86**
(not continuous)
Whitton Waye TW3: Houn 6E **112**
Whitwell Rd. E13 3J **87**
Whitworth Ho. SE1 3C **102**
Whitworth Rd. SE18 7E **106**
SE25 3E **156**
Whitworth St. SE10 5G **105**
Whorlton Rd. SE15 3H **121**
Whychcote Point *NW2* *1E* ***62***
(off Whitefield Av.)
Whymark Av. N22 3A **48**
Whytecroft TW5: Hest 7B **94**
Whyte M. SM3: Cheam 7G **165**
Whyteville Rd. E7 6K **69**
Whytlaw Ho. *E3* *5B* ***86***
(off Baythorne St.)
Wickersley Rd. SW11 2E **118**
Wickers Oake SE19 4F **139**
Wicker St. E1 6H **85**
Wicket, The CR0: Addtn 5C **170**
Wicket Rd. UB6: G'frd 3A **78**
Wickets, The TW15: Ashf 4A **128**
Wickfield Apartments *E15* *6F* ***69***
(off Grove Cres. Rd.)
Wickfield Ho. *SE16* *2H* ***103***
(off Wilson Gro.)
Wickford Ho. *E1* *4J* ***85***
(off Wickford St.)
Wickford St. E1 4J **85**
Wickford Way E17 4K **49**
Wickham Av. CR0: C'don 2A **170**
SM3: Cheam 5E **164**
Wickham Chase BR4: W W'ck 1F **171**
Wickham Cl. E1 5J **85**
EN3: Enf H 3C **24**
KT3: N Mald 6B **152**
Wickham Ct. *KT5: Surb* *5F* ***151***
(off Cranes Pk.)
Wickham Ct. Rd. BR4: W W'ck 2E **170**
Wickham Cres. BR4: W W'ck 2E **170**
Wickham Gdns. SE4 3B **122**
Wickham Ho. *N1* *1E* ***84***
(off Halcomb St.)
Wickham La. DA16: Well 5A **108**
SE2 5A **108**
Wickham M. SE4 2B **122**
Wickham Noakes Ct. BR3: Beck 1D **158**
Wickham Rd. BR3: Beck 2D **158**
CR0: C'don 2K **169**
E4 7K **35**
HA3: Hrw W 2H **41**
SE4 4B **122**
Wickham St. DA16: Well 2J **125**
SE11 5G **19** (5K **101**)
Wickham Theatre Cen. 2F **171**
Wickham Way BR3: Beck 4E **158**
Wick Ho. *KT1: Hamp W* *1D* ***150***
(off Station Rd.)
Wick La. E3 1C **86**
Wickliffe Av. N3 2G **45**
Wickliffe Gdns. HA9: Wemb 2H **61**
Wicklow Ho. N16 1F **67**
Wicklow St. WC1 1G **7** (3K **83**)
Wick Rd. E9 6K **67**
TW11: Tedd 7B **132**
Wicks Cl. SE9 4B **142**
Wicksteed Cl. DA5: Bexl 3K **145**
Wicksteed Ho. SE1 3C **102**
TW8: Bford 5F **97**
Wickway Ct. *SE15* *6F* ***103***
(off Cator St.)
Wickwood St. SE5 2B **120**
Widdecombe Av. HA2: Harr 2C **58**
Widdenham Rd. N7 4K **65**
Widdin St. E15 7G **69**
Widecombe Gdns. IG4: Ilf 4C **52**
Widecombe Rd. SE9 3C **142**
Widecombe Way N2 5B **46**
Widegate St. E1 6H **9** (5E **84**)
Widenham Cl. HA5: Eastc 5A **40**
Wide Way CR4: Mitc 3H **155**
Widewing Cl. TW11: Tedd 7B **132**
Widford *NW1* *6F* ***65***
(off Lewis St.)
Widford Ho. *N1* *2B* ***84***
(off Colebrooke Rd.)
Widgeon Cl. E16 6K **87**
Widgeon Rd. TW6: H'row A 5C **174**
Widley Rd. W9 3J **81**
Widmer Ct. TW3: Houn 2C **112**
WIDMORE 3A **160**
WIDMORE GREEN 2B **160**
Widmore Lodge Rd. BR1: Brom 2B **160**
Widmore Rd. BR1: Brom 2J **159**
UB8: Hil 4D **74**
Wigan Ho. E5 1H **67**
Wigeon Path SE28 3H **107**
Wigeon Way UB4: Yead 6B **76**
Wiggins La. TW10: Ham 2C **132**
Wiggins Mead NW9 7G **29**
Wigginton Av. HA9: Wemb 6H **61**
Wight Ho. *KT1: King T* *3D* ***150***
(off Portsmouth Rd.)
Wightman Rd. N4 4A **48**
N8 4A **48**
Wighton M. TW7: Isle 2J **113**
Wigley Rd. TW13: Felt 2B **130**
Wigmore Hall 7J **5**
Wigmore Pl. E17 3A **50**
W1 7J **5** (6F **83**)
Wigmore Rd. SM5: Cars 2B **166**
Wigmore St. W1 7H **5** (6E **82**)
Wigmore Wlk. SM5: Cars 2B **166**
Wigram Ho. *E14* *7D* ***86***
(off Wade's Pl.)
Wigram Rd. E11 6A **52**
Wigram Sq. E17 3E **50**
Wigston Cl. N18 5K **33**
Wigston Rd. E13 4K **87**
Wigton Gdns. HA7: Stan 1E **42**
Wigton Pl. SE11 6K **19** (5A **102**)
Wigton Rd. E17 1B **50**
Wilberforce Ct. BR2: Kes 7B **172**
HA8: Edg *4A* ***28***
(off King's Dr.)
Wilberforce M. SW4 4H **119**
Wilberforce Rd. N4 2B **66**
NW9 6C **44**
Wilberforce Wlk. E15 5G **69**
Wilberforce Way SE25 4F **157**
SW19 6F **135**
Wilbraham Ho. *SW8* *7J* ***101***
(off Wandsworth Rd.)
Wilbraham Mans. *SW1* *3G* ***17***
(off Wilbraham Pl.)
Wilbraham Pl. SW1 3F **17** (4D **100**)
Wilbrahams Almshouses EN5: Barn 2C **20**
Wilbrooke Pl. SE3 1K **123**
Wilbury Way N18 5J **33**
Wilby M. W11 1H **99**
Wilcox Cl. SW8 7J **101**
(not continuous)
Wilcox Gdns. TW17: Shep 3A **146**
Wilcox Ho. *E3* *5B* ***86***
(off Ackroyd Dr.)
Wilcox Pl. SW1 2B **18** (3G **101**)
Wilcox Rd. SM1: Sutt 4K **165**
SW8 7J **101**
TW11: Tedd 4H **131**
Wildberry Cl. W7 4A **96**
Wildbore Ho. *N1* *7A* ***66***
(off Liverpool Rd.)
Wildcat Rd. *TW6: H'row A* *6C* ***174***
(off Wayfarer Rd.)
Wild Ct. WC2 1G **13** (6K **83**)
Wildcroft Gdns. HA8: Edg 6J **27**
Wildcroft Mnr. SW15 7E **116**
Wildcroft Rd. SW15 7E **116**
Wilde Cl. E8 1G **85**
Wilde Ho. *W2* *2A* ***10***
(off Gloucester Ter.)
Wilde Pl. N13 6G **33**
SW18 7B **118**
Wilder Cl. HA4: Ruis 1K **57**
Wilderness, The
KT8: W Mole, E Mos 5G **149**
TW12: Hamp H 4F **131**
Wilderness Island Nature Reserve 2E **166**
Wilderness M. SW4 4F **119**
Wilderness Rd. BR7: Chst 7F **143**
Wilde Rd. DA8: Erith 7H **109**
Wilderton Rd. N16 7E **48**
Wilder Wlk. *W1* *3B* ***12***
(off Glasshouse St.)
Wildfell Rd. SE6 7D **122**
Wild Goose Dr. SE14 1J **121**
Wild Hatch NW11 6J **45**
Wild's Rents SE1 7G **15** (3E **102**)
Wild St. WC2 1F **13** (6J **83**)
Wildwood Cl. SE12 7H **123**
Wildwood Gro. NW3 1A **64**
Wildwood Ri. NW11 1A **64**
Wildwood Rd. NW11 6K **45**
Wildwood Ter. NW3 1A **64**
Wilford Cl. EN2: Enf 3J **23**
Wilford Rd. CR0: C'don 6C **156**
Wilfred Ct. *N15* *5D* ***48***
(off South Gro.)
Wilfred Owen Cl. SW19 6A **136**
Wilfred St. SW1 1A **18** (3G **101**)
Wilfred Wood Ct. *W6* *4E* ***98***
(off Samuel's Cl.)
Wilfrid Gdns. W3 5J **79**
Wilkes Cl. NW7 6A **30**
Wilkes Rd. TW8: Bford 6E **96**
Wilkes St. E1 5K **9** (5F **85**)
Wilkie Ho. *SW1* *5D* ***18***
(off Cureton St.)
Wilkins Cl. CR4: Mitc 1C **154**
UB3: Harl 5H **93**
Wilkins Ho. *SW1* *7A* ***18***
(off Churchill Gdns.)
Wilkinson Cl. UB10: Hil 1D **74**
Wilkinson Ct. SW17 4B **136**
Wilkinson Gdns. SE25 1E **156**
Wilkinson Ho. *N1* *2D* ***84***
(off Cranston Est.)
Wilkinson Rd. E16 6A **88**
Wilkinson St. SW8 7K **101**
Wilkinson Way W4 2K **97**
Wilkin St. NW5 6E **64**
Wilkin St. M. NW5 6F **65**
Wilks Gdns. CR0: C'don 1A **170**
Wilks Pl. N1 2E **84**
Willan Rd. N17 2D **48**
Willard St. SW8 3F **119**
Willcocks Cl. KT9: Chess 3E **162**
Willcott Rd. W3 1H **97**
Will Crooks Gdns. SE9 4A **124**
Willen Fld. Rd. NW10 2J **79**
Willenhall Av. EN5: New Bar 6F **21**
Willenhall Ct. EN5: New Bar 6F **21**
Willenhall Dr. UB3: Hayes 7G **75**
Willenhall Rd. SE18 5F **107**
Willersley Av. BR6: Orp 3H **173**
DA15: Sidc 1K **143**
Willersley Cl. DA15: Sidc 1K **143**
WILLESDEN 6C **62**
WILLESDEN GREEN 6E **62**
Willesden Green Cultural Cen. & Mus.
6D **62**
Willesden La. NW2 6E **62**
NW6 6E **62**
Willesden Section Ho. *NW6* *7F* ***63***
(off Willesden La.)
Willesden Sports Cen. 1D **80**
Willesden Sports Stadium 1D **80**
Willes Rd. NW5 6F **65**
Willett Cl. BR5: Pet W 6J **161**
UB5: N'olt 3A **76**
Willett Ho. *E13* *2K* ***87***
(off Queens Rd. W.)
Willett Pl. CR7: Thor H 5A **156**
Willett Rd. CR7: Thor H 5A **156**
Willett Way BR5: Pet W 5H **161**
William IV St. WC2 3E **12** (7J **83**)
William Allen Ho. HA8: Edg 7A **28**
William Ash Cl. RM9: Dag 6B **72**
William Banfield Ho. *SW6* *2H* ***117***
(off Munster Rd.)
William Barefoot Dr. SE9 4E **142**
William Blake Ho. SW11 1C **118**
William Bonney Est. SW4 4H **119**
William Booth Ho. *E14* *6C* ***86***
(off Hind Gro.)
William Booth Rd. SE20 1G **157**
William Carey Way HA1: Harr 6J **41**
William Caslon Ho. *E2* *2H* ***85***
(off Patriot Sq.)
William Channing Ho. *E2* *3H* ***85***
(off Canrobert St.)
William Cl. N2 2B **46**
RM5: Col R 1J **55**
SE13 3E **122**
UB2: S'hall 2G **95**
William Cobbett Ho. *W8* *3K* ***99***
(off Scarsdale Pl.)
William Congreve M. N1 1C **84**
William Cotton Ct. *E14* *5C* ***86***
(off Selsey St.)
William Ct. NW8 3A **82**
SE10 *1D* ***122***
(off Greenwich High Rd.)
SE25 *3F* ***157***
(off Chalfont Rd.)
SW16 *7K* ***137***
(off Streatham High Rd.)
W5 5C **78**
William Covell Cl. EN2: Enf 1E **22**
William Dr. HA7: Stan 6F **27**
William Dromey Ct. NW6 7H **63**
William Dunbar Ho. *NW6* *2H* ***81***
(off Albert Rd.)
William Dyce M. SW16 4H **137**
William Ellis Way *SE16* *3G* ***103***
(off St James's Rd.)
William Evans Ho. *SE8* *4K* ***103***
(off Haddonfield)
William Farm La. SW15 3D **116**
William Fenn Ho. *E2* *1K* ***9***
(off Shipton Rd.)
William Foster La. DA16: Well 2A **126**
William Fry Ho. *E1* *6K* ***85***
(off W. Arbour St.)
William Gdns. SW15 5D **116**
William Gibbs Ct. *SW1* *2C* ***18***
(off Old Pye St.)
William Gunn Ho. NW3 5C **64**
William Guy Gdns. E3 3D **86**
William Harvey Ho. *SW19* *1G* ***135***
(off Whitlock Dr.)
William Henry Wlk. SW8 7C **18** (6H **101**)
William Hope Cl. IG11: Bark 2J **89**
William Ho. BR1: Brom 3J **159**
William Hunt Mans. SW13 6E **98**
William Margrie Cl. SE15 2G **121**
William Marshall Cl. E17 6A **50**
William M. N1 7E **66**
SW1 7F **11** (2D **100**)
William Morley Cl. E6 1B **88**
William Morris Cl. E17 3B **50**
William Morris Gallery 3C **50**
William Morris Ho. W6 6F **99**
William Morris Way SW6 3A **118**

William Owston Ct. *E16* *1C* ***106***
(off Connaught Rd.)
William Perkin Ct. UB6: G'frd 6J **59**
William Pike Ho. *RM7: Rom* *6K* ***55***
(off Waterloo Gdns.)
William Pl. E3 2B **86**
William Rathbone Ho. *E2* *3H* ***85***
(off Florida St.)
William Rd. NW1 2A **6** (3G **83**)
SM1: Sutt 5A **166**
SW19 7G **135**
William Rushbrooke Ho. *SE16* *4G* ***103***
(off Rouel Rd.)
Williams Av. E17 1B **50**
William Saville Ho. *NW6* *2H* ***81***
(off Denmark Rd.)
William's Bldgs. E2 4J **85**
Williams Cl. N8 6H **47**
SW6 7G **99**
Williams Dr. TW3: Houn 4E **112**
Williams Gro. KT6: Surb 6C **150**
N22 1A **48**
Williams Ho. *E3* *3C* ***86***
(off Alfred St.)
E9 *1H* ***85***
(off King Edward's Rd.)
NW2 *3E* ***62***
(off Stoll Cl.)
SW1 *4D* ***18***
(off Montaigne Cl.)
William's La. SW14 3J **115**
Williams La. SM4: Mord 5A **154**
William Smith Ho. *DA17: Belv* *3G* ***109***
(off Ambrooke Rd.)
E3 *3C* ***86***
(off Ireton St.)
Williamson Cl. SE10 5H **105**
Williamson Ct. SE17 5C **102**
Williamson Rd. N4 6B **48**
Williamson St. N7 4J **65**
William Sq. *SE16* *7A* ***86***
(off Sovereign Cres.)
Williams Rd. UB2: S'hall 4C **94**
W13 1A **96**
Williams Ter. CR0: Wadd 6A **168**
William St. E10 6D **50**
IG11: Bark 7G **71**
N17 7A **34**
SM5: Cars 3C **166**
SW1 7F **11** (2D **100**)
Williams Way DA2: Wilm 2K **145**
HA0: Wemb 5B **60**
William Whiffin Sq. E3 4B **86**
William White Ct. *E13* *1A* ***88***
(off Green St.)
William Wood Ho. *SE26* *3J* ***139***
(off Shrublands Cl.)
Willifield Way NW11 4H **45**
Willingale Cl. IG8: Wfd G 6F **37**
Willingdon Rd. N22 2B **48**
Willingham Cl. NW5 5G **65**
Willingham Ter. NW5 5G **65**
Willingham Way KT1: King T 3G **151**
Willington Ct. E5 3A **68**
Willington Rd. SW9 3J **119**
Willis Av. SM2: Sutt 6C **166**
Willis Ct. BR4: W W'ck 2F **171**
CR7: Thor H 6A **156**
Willis Ho. *E14* *7D* ***86***
(off Hale St.)
Willis Rd. CR0: C'don 7C **156**
DA8: Erith 4J **109**
E15 2H **87**
Willis St. E14 6D **86**
Willis Yd. N14 7C **22**
Will Miles Ct. SW19 7A **136**
Willmore End SW19 1K **153**
Willoughby Av. CR0: Bedd 4K **167**
UB10: Uxb 2A **74**
Willoughby Dr. RM13: Rain 7K **73**
Willoughby Gro. N17 7C **34**
Willoughby Highwalk *EC2* *6E* ***8***
(off Moor La.)
Willoughby Ho. *E1* *1H* ***103***
(off Reardon Path)
EC2 5E **8**
Willoughby La. BR1: Brom 7K **141**
N17 6C **34**
Willoughby M. N17 7C **34**
SW4 *4F* ***119***
(off Cedars M.)
Willoughby Pk. Rd. N17 7C **34**
Willoughby Pas. *E14* *1C* ***104***
(off W. India Av.)
Willoughby Rd. KT2: King T 1F **151**
N8 3A **48**
NW3 4B **64**
TW1: Twick 5C **114**
(not continuous)
Willoughbys, The SW14 3A **116**
Willoughby St. WC1 6E **6**
Willoughby Way SE7 4K **105**
Willow Av. DA15: Sidc 6A **126**
SW13 2B **116**
UB7: Yiew 7B **74**
Willow Bank SW6 3G **117**
TW10: Ham 3B **132**
Willowbank KT7: T Ditt 1A **162**
Willowbay Cl. EN5: Barn 6A **20**
Willow Bri. Rd. N1 6C **66**
(not continuous)
Willowbrook TW12: Hamp H 5F **131**
Willowbrook Est. SE15 7G **103**
Willow Brook Rd. SE15 7F **103**
Willowbrook Rd. TW19: Stanw 2A **128**
UB2: S'hall 3E **94**
Willow Bus. Pk. SE26 3J **139**
Willow Cl. BR2: Brom 5D **160**
DA5: Bexl 6F **127**
IG9: Buck H 3G **37**
SE6 1H **141**
TW8: Bford 6C **96**
Willow Cotts. TW9: Kew 6G **97**
TW13: Hanw 3C **130**
Willow Ct. *E11* *2G* ***69***
(off Trinity Cl.)
EC2 3G **9** (4E **84**)
HA3: Hrw W 1K **41**
HA8: Edg 4K **27**
N12 4E **30**
NW6 7G **63**
SM6: Wall *7F* ***167***
(off Willow Rd.)
TW16: Sun *7G* ***129***
(off Staines Rd. W.)
W4 *7A* ***98***
(off Corney Reach Way)
W9 *5J* ***81***
(off Admiral Wlk.)
Willowcourt Av. HA3: Kenton 5B **42**
Willow Dene HA5: Pinn 2B **40**
WD23: B Hea 1D **26**
Willowdene N6 7D **46**
SE15 7H **103**
Willowdene Cl. TW2: Whitt 7G **113**
Willowdene Ct. *N20* *7F* ***21***
(off High Rd. Whetstone)
Willow Dr. EN5: Barn 4B **20**
Willow End KT6: Surb 1E **162**
N20 2D **30**
Willowfields Cl. SE18 5J **107**
Willow Gdns. HA4: Ruis 2H **57**
TW3: Houn 1E **112**
Willow Grange DA14: Sidc 3B **144**
Willow Grn. NW9 1A **44**
Willow Gro. BR7: Chst 6E **142**
E13 2J **87**
HA4: Ruis 2H **57**
Willowhayne Ct. *KT12: Walt T* *7K* ***147***
(off Willowhayne Dr.)
Willowhayne Dr. KT12: Walt T 7K **147**
Willowhayne Gdns. KT4: Wor Pk 3E **164**
Willow Ho. BR2: Brom 2G **159**
SE1 *4F* ***103***
(off Curtis St.)
SE4 *3A* ***122***
(off Dragonfly Pl.)
W10 *4F* ***81***
(off Maple Wlk.)
Willow La. CR4: Mitc 5D **154**
SE18 4D **106**
Willow La. Bus. Pk. CR4: Mitc 6D **154**
Willow La. Ind. Est. CR4: Mitc 6D **154**
Willow Lodge RM7: Rom 5K **55**
SW6 1F **117**
TW16: Sun *7H* ***129***
(off Grangewood Dr.)
Willowmead Cl. W5 4D **78**
Willow Mt. CR0: C'don 3E **168**
Willow Pl. SW1 3B **18** (4G **101**)
Willow Rd. EN1: Enf 3K **23**
KT3: N Mald 4J **151**
NW3 4B **64**
RM6: Chad H 6E **54**
SL3: Poyle 5A **174**
SM6: Wall 7F **167**
W5 2E **96**
Willows, The BR3: Beck 1C **158**
E6 7D **70**
SE1 4E **102**
Willows Av. SM4: Mord 5K **153**
Willows Cl. HA5: Pinn 2A **40**
Willowside Ct. EN2: Enf 3G **23**
Willows Ter. *NW10* *2B* ***80***
(off Rucklidge Av.)
Willow St. E4 1A **36**
EC2 3G **9** (4E **84**)
RM7: Rom 4J **55**
Willow Tree Cen. 5D **38**
Willow Tree Cl. E3 1B **86**
SW18 1K **135**
UB4: Yead 4A **76**
UB5: N'olt 6D **58**
Willowtree Cl. UB10: Ick 3E **56**
Willow Tree Ct. DA14: Sidc 5A **144**
HA0: Wemb 5D **60**
Willow Tree La. UB4: Yead 4A **76**
WILLOW TREE RDBT. **5B 76**
Willow Tree Wlk. BR1: Brom 1K **159**
Willowtree Way CR7: Thor H 1A **156**
Willow Va. BR7: Chst 6F **143**
W12 1C **98**
Willow Vw. SW19 1B **154**
Willow Wlk. BR6: Farnb 3F **173**
E17 5B **50**
IG1: Ilf 2F **71**
N1 2B **84**
N2 2B **46**
N15 4B **48**
N21 6E **22**
SE1 3E **102**
SM3: Sutt 3H **165**
Willow Way HA0: Wemb 3A **60**
KT19: Ewe 6K **163**
N3 7E **30**
SE26 3J **139**
TW2: Twick 2F **131**
TW16: Sun 4J **147**
W11 7F **81**
Willow Wood Cres. SE25 6E **156**
Willow Wren Wharf UB2: S'hall 4K **93**
Willrose Cres. SE2 5B **108**
Willsbridge Ct. SE15 6F **103**
Wills Cres. TW3: Houn 6F **113**
Wills Gro. NW7 5H **29**
Will Wyatt Ct. *N1* *2E* ***84***
(off Pitfield St.)
Wilman Gro. E8 7G **67**
Wilmar Cl. UB4: Hayes 4F **75**
Wilmar Gdns. BR4: W W'ck 1D **170**
Wilmcote Ho. *W2* *5K* ***81***
(off Woodchester Sq.)
Wilment Ct. NW2 3E **62**
Wilmer Cl. KT2: King T 5F **133**
Wilmer Cres. KT2: King T 5F **133**
Wilmer Gdns. N1 1E **84**
(not continuous)
Wilmer Ho. *E3* *2A* ***86***
(off Daling Way)
Wilmer Lea Cl. E15 7F **69**
Wilmer Pl. N16 2F **67**
Wilmers Ct. *NW10* *1K* ***79***
(off Lawrence Av.)
Wilmer Way N14 5C **32**
Wilmington Av. W4 7K **97**
Wilmington Ct. SW16 7J **137**
Wilmington Gdns. IG11: Bark 6H **71**
Wilmington Sq. WC1 2J **7** (3A **84**)
(not continuous)
Wilmington St. WC1 2J **7** (3A **84**)
Wilmington Ter. *SE16* *4H* ***103***
(off Camilla Rd.)
Wilmot Cl. N2 2A **46**
SE15 7G **103**
Wilmot Ho. *SE11* *4B* ***102***
(off George Mathers Rd.)
Wilmot Pl. NW1 7G **65**
(not continuous)
W7 1J **95**
Wilmot Rd. E10 2D **68**
N17 3D **48**
SM5: Cars 5D **166**
Wilmot St. E2 4H **85**
Wilmount St. SE18 4F **107**
Wilna Rd. SW18 7A **118**
Wilsham St. W11 1F **99**
Wilshaw Cl. NW4 3C **44**
Wilshaw Ho. SE8 7C **104**
Wilshaw St. SE14 1C **122**
Wilsmere Dr. HA3: Hrw W 7D **26**
UB5: N'olt 6C **58**
Wilson Av. CR4: Mitc 7C **136**
Wilson Cl. CR2: S Croy 5D **168**
HA9: Wemb 7F **43**
Wilson Ct. NW9 2K **43**
RM7: Rush G *6K* ***55***
(off Union Rd.)
SE28 3G **107**
Wilson Dr. HA9: Wemb 7F **43**
Wilson Gdns. HA1: Harr 7G **41**
Wilson Gro. SE16 2H **103**
Wilson Ho. *NW6* *7A* ***64***
(off Goldhurst Ter.)
Wilson Rd. E6 3B **88**
IG1: Ilf 7D **52**
KT9: Chess 6F **163**
SE5 1E **120**
Wilson's Av. N17 2F **49**
Wilson's Rd. W6 5F **99**
Wilson St. E17 5E **50**
EC2 5F **9** (5D **84**)
N21 7F **23**
Wilson Wlk. *W4* *4B* ***98***
(off Prebend Gdns.)
Wilstone Cl. UB4: Yead 4C **76**
Wiltern Ct. NW2 6G **63**
Wilthorne Gdns. RM10: Dag 7H **73**
Wilton Av. W4 5A **98**
Wilton Cl. UB7: Harm 2E **174**
Wilton Ct. *E1* *6H* ***85***
(off Cavell St.)
Wilton Cres. SW1 7G **11** (2E **100**)
SW19 1H **153**
Wilton Dr. RM5: Col R 1J **55**
Wilton Est. E8 6G **67**
Wilton Gdns.
KT8: W Mole 3E **148**
Wilton Gro. KT3: N Mald 6B **152**
SW19 1H **153**
Wilton Ho. *CR2: S Croy* *5C* ***168***
(off Nottingham Rd.)
Wilton M. E8 6H **67**
SW1 1H **17** (3E **100**)
Wilton Pde. TW13: Felt 2J **129**

Wilton Pl. E4 . . . . 6A 36
  HA1: Harr 6K 41
  SW1 . . . . 7G 11 (2E 100)
Wilton Plaza SW1 . . . . 3A 18
  (off Wilton Rd.)
Wilton Rd. EN4: Cockf 4J 21
  N10 . . . . 2E 46
  SE2 . . . . 4C 108
  SW1 . . . . 2K 17 (3F 101)
  SW19 . . . . 7C 136
  TW4: Houn 3B 112
Wilton Row NW1 . . . . 7G 11 (2E 100)
Wilton's Music Hall 7G 85
  (off Graces All.)
Wilton Sq. N1 . . . . 1D 84
Wilton St. SW1 . . . . . . 1J 17 (3F 101)
Wilton Ter. SW1 . . . . . 1G 17 (3E 100)
Wilton Vs. N1 . . . . 1D 84
  (off Wilton Sq.)
Wilton Way E8 . . . . 6G 67
Wiltshire Cl. NW7 . . . . 5G 29
  SW3 . . . . 3E 16 (4D 100)
Wiltshire Ct. CR2: S Croy 5C 168
  IG1: Ilf 6G 71
  N4 . . . . 1K 65
  (off Marquis Rd.)
Wiltshire Gdns. N4 . . . . 6C 48
  TW2: Twick 1G 131
Wiltshire La. HA5: Eastc 3H 39
Wiltshire Rd. BR6: Orp 7K 161
  CR7: Thor H 3A 156
  SW9 . . . . 3A 120
Wiltshire Row N1 . . . . 1D 84
Wilverley Cres. KT3: N Mald . . . 6A 152
Wimbart Rd. SW2 . . . . 7K 119
WIMBLEDON 6G 135
Wimbledon All England Lawn Tennis &
  Croquet Club 4G 135
Wimbledon Bri. SW19 . . . . . . 6H 135
Wimbledon Cl. SW20 . . . . 7F 135
Wimbledon Common 4C 134
Wimbledon Common Golf Course . . 5D 134
Wimbledon Hill Rd. SW19 . . . . 6G 135
Wimbledon Lawn Tennis Mus. . . 3G 135
Wimbledon Leisure Cen. 6K 135
WIMBLEDON PARK 3J 135
Wimbledon Pk. Athletics Track . . 2H 135
Wimbledon Pk. Ct. SW19 . . . . 1H 135
Wimbledon Pk. Golf Course . . . 3H 135
Wimbledon Pk. Rd. SW18 . . . . 2G 135
  SW19 . . . . 2G 135
Wimbledon Pk. Side SW19 . . . 3F 135
Wimbledon Pk. Watersports Cen. . . 2H 135
Wimbledon Pk. Women's Fitness Suite
. . . . 3H 135
Wimbledon Rd. SW17 . . . . . . 4A 136
Wimbledon Stadium Bus. Cen.
  SW17 . . . . 3A 136
Wimbledon Stadium (Greyhound) . . 4A 136
Wimbledon Theatre 7J 135
Wimbledon Windmill Mus. 2D 134
Wimbolt St. E2 . . . . 3G 85
Wimborne Av. BR5: St P 4K 161
  BR7: Chst 4K 161
  UB2: S'hall 4E 94
  UB4: Yead 6K 75
Wimborne Cl. SW12 . . . . 3G 137
  UB5: N'olt 6E 58
Wimborne Dr. HA5: Pinn 7B 40
  NW9 . . . . 3G 43
Wimborne Gdns. W13 . . . . . . 5B 78
Wimborne Ho. E16 . . . . 7H 87
  (off Victoria Dock Rd.)
  NW1 . . . . 4D 4
  (off Harewood Av.)
  SW8 . . . . 7K 101
  (off Dorset Rd.)
  SW12 . . . . 3G 137

Wimborne Rd. N9 . . . . 2B 34
  N17 . . . . 2E 48
Wimborne Way BR3: Beck . . . 3K 157
Wimbourne Ct. N1 . . . . 2D 84
  (off Wimbourne St.)
Wimbourne St. N1 . . . . 2D 84
Wimpole Cl. BR2: Brom 4A 160
  KT1: King T 2F 151
Wimpole M. W1 . . . . 5J 5 (5F 83)
Wimpole Rd. UB7: Yiew 1A 92
Wimpole St. W1 . . . . 6J 5 (5F 83)
Wimshurst Cl.
  CR0: Wadd 1J 167
Winans Wlk. SW9 . . . . 2A 120
Winant Ho. E14 . . . . 7D 86
  (off Simpson's Rd.)
Wincanton Ct. N11 . . . . 6K 31
  (off Martock Gdns.)
Wincanton Cres. UB5: N'olt . . . 5E 58
Wincanton Gdns. IG6: Ilf 3F 53
Wincanton Rd. SW18 . . . . . . 7H 117
Winchcombe Rd. SM5: Cars . . 7B 154
Winchcomb Gdns. SE9 . . . . . 3B 124
Winchelsea Av. DA7: Bex 7F 109
Winchelsea Cl. SW15 . . . . . . 5F 117
Winchelsea Ho. SE16 . . . . . . 2J 103
  (off Swan Rd.)
Winchelsea Rd. E7 . . . . 3J 69
  N17 . . . . 3E 48
  NW10 . . . . 1K 79
Winchelsey Ri. CR2: S Croy . . . 6F 169
Winchendon Rd. SW6 . . . . . . 1H 117
  TW11: Tedd 4H 131
Winchester Av. NW6 . . . . 1G 81
  NW9 . . . . 3G 43
  TW5: Hest 6D 94
Winchester Bldgs. SE1 . . . . . . 6C 14
  (off Copperfield St.)
Winchester Cl. BR2: Brom 3H 159
  E6 . . . . 6D 88
  EN1: Enf 5K 23
  KT2: King T 7H 133
  SE17 . . . . 4B 102
  SL3: Poyle 4A 174
Winchester Ct. W8 . . . . 2J 99
  (off Vicarage Ga.)
Winchester Dr. HA5: Pinn 5B 40
Winchester Ho. E3 . . . . 3B 86
  (off Hamlets Way)
  E14 . . . . 6C 86
  (off New Festival Av.)
  IG11: Bark 7A 72
  (off Margaret Bondfield Av.)
  SE18 . . . . 7B 106
  (off Portway Gdns.)
  SW3 . . . . 7B 16
  SW9 . . . . 7A 102
  W2 . . . . 6A 82
  (off Hallfield Est.)
Winchester M. KT4: Wor Pk . . . 2F 165
  NW3 . . . . 7B 64
  (off Winchester Rd.)
Winchester Palace 4E 14
  (off Stoney St.)
Winchester Pk. BR2: Brom . . . 3H 159
Winchester Pl. E8 . . . . 5F 67
  N6 . . . . 1F 65
Winchester Rd. BR2: Brom . . . 3H 159
  DA7: Bex 2D 126
  E4 . . . . 7K 35
  HA3: Kenton 4E 42
  HA6: Nwood 2H 39
  IG1: Ilf 3H 71
  KT12: Walt T 7J 147
  N6 . . . . 1F 65
  N9 . . . . 1A 34
  NW3 . . . . 7B 64
  TW1: Twick 6B 114
  TW13: Hanw 3D 130
  UB3: Harl 7G 93
Winchester Sq. SE1 . . . . 4E 14

Winchester St. SW1 . . . 5K 17 (5F 101)
  W3 . . . . 1J 97
Winchester Wlk. SE1 . . 4E 14 (1D 102)
  SW15 . . . . 5H 117
  (off Up. Richmond Rd.)
Winchester Wharf SE1 . . . . . . 4E 14
  (off Clink St.)
Winchet Wlk. CR0: C'don 6J 157
Winchfield Cl. HA3: Kenton . . . 6C 42
Winchfield Ho. SW15 . . . . . . 6B 116
Winchfield Rd. SE26 . . . . 5A 140
Winch Ho. E14 . . . . 3D 104
  (off Tiller Rd.)
  SW10 . . . . 7A 100
  (off King's Rd.)
Winchilsea Cres. KT8: W Mole . . 2G 149
Winchilsea Ho. NW8 . . . . 2B 4
  (off St John's Wood Rd.)
WINCHMORE HILL 7F 23
Winchmore Hill Rd. N14 . . . . . 1C 32
  N21 . . . . 1C 32
Winchmore Vs. N21 . . . . 7E 22
  (off Winchmore Hill Rd.)
Winchstone Cl. TW17: Shep . . 4B 146
Winckley Cl. HA3: Kenton 5F 43
Winckworth Ct. N1 . . . . 2F 9
  (off Charles Sq. Est.)
Wincott Pde. SE11 . . . . 3K 19
  (off Wincott St.)
Wincott St. SE11 . . . . 4K 19 (4A 102)
Wincrofts Dr. SE9 . . . . 4H 125
Windall Cl. SE19 . . . . 1G 157
Windborough Rd. SM5: Cars . . 7E 166
Windermere NW1 . . . . 2K 5
  (off Albany St.)
Windermere Av. HA4: Ruis . . . 7A 40
  HA9: Kenton, Wemb 7C 42
  N3 . . . . 3J 45
  NW6 . . . . 1G 81
  SW19 . . . . 3K 153
Windermere Cl. BR6: Farnb . . . 3F 173
  TW14: Felt 1H 129
  TW19: Stanw 1A 128
Windermere Ct. HA9: Wemb . . 7C 42
  SM5: Cars 3E 166
  SW13 . . . . 6B 98
Windermere Gdns. IG4: Ilf 5C 52
Windermere Gro. HA9: Wemb . . 1C 60
Windermere Hall HA8: Edg . . . 5A 28
Windermere Ho. E3 . . . . 4B 86
  EN5: New Bar 4E 20
  TW7: Isle 5K 113
Windermere Point SE15 . . . . . 7J 103
  (off Old Kent Rd.)
Windermere Rd. BR4: W W'ck . . 2G 171
  CR0: C'don 1F 169
  DA7: Bex 2J 127
  N10 . . . . 1F 47
  N19 . . . . 2G 65
  SW15 . . . . 4A 134
  SW16 . . . . 1G 155
  UB1: S'hall 5D 76
  W5 . . . . 3C 96
Windermere Way UB7: Yiew . . . 1A 92
Winders Rd. SW11 . . . . 2C 118
  (not continuous)
Windfield Cl. SE26 . . . . 4K 139
Windham Rd. TW9: Rich 3F 115
Winding Way RM8: Dag 3C 72
Windlass Pl. SE8 . . . . 4A 104
Windlesham Gro. SW19 . . . . . 1F 135
Windlesham Ho. SE1 . . . . 5J 15
  (off Duchess Wlk.)
Windlesham M.
  TW12: Hamp H 6G 131
Windley Cl. SE23 . . . . 2J 139
Windmill WC1 . . . . 5G 7
  (off New North St.)
Windmill Av. UB2: S'hall 1G 95
Windmill Bri. Ho. CR0: C'don . . 1E 168
  (off Freemasons Rd.)

Windmill Bus. Village TW16: Sun . . 1G 147
Windmill Cl. KT6: Surb 1C 162
  SE1 . . . . 4G 103
  (off Beatrice Rd.)
  SE13 . . . . 2E 122
  TW16: Sun 7G 129
Windmill Ct. E4 . . . . 2B 36
  HA4: Ruis 1J 57
  NW2 . . . . 6G 63
  W5 . . . . 4C 96
  (off Windmill Rd.)
Windmill Dr. BR2: Kes 4A 172
  NW2 . . . . 3G 63
  SW4 . . . . 5F 119
Windmill Gdns. EN2: Enf 3F 23
Windmill Grn. TW17: Shep . . . 7G 147
Windmill Gro. CR0: C'don 6C 156
Windmill Hill EN2: Enf 3G 23
  HA4: Ruis 7H 39
  NW3 . . . . 3A 64
Windmill Ho. E14 . . . . 4C 104
  SE1 . . . . 5K 13
  (off Windmill Wlk.)
Windmill La. E15 . . . . 6F 69
  KT6: Surb 6B 150
  TW7: Isle 3G 95
  UB2: S'hall 1G 95
  UB6: G'frd 6G 77
  WD23: B Hea 1D 26
Windmill M. W4 . . . . 4A 98
Windmill Pas. W4 . . . . 4A 98
Windmill Pl. UB2: S'hall 1G 95
Windmill Ri. KT2: King T 7H 133
Windmill Rd. CR0: C'don 7C 156
  CR4: Mitc 5G 155
  N18 . . . . 4J 33
  SW18 . . . . 6B 118
  SW19 . . . . 2D 134
  TW8: Bford 4C 96
  TW12: Hamp H 5F 131
  TW16: Sun 1G 147
  W4 . . . . 4A 98
  W5 . . . . 4C 96
Windmill Rd. W. TW16: Sun . . . 2G 147
Windmill Row SE11 . . . 6J 19 (5A 102)
Windmill St. W1 . . . . . . 6C 6 (5H 83)
  (not continuous)
  WD23: B Hea 1D 26
Windmill Ter. TW17: Shep 7G 147
Windmill Wlk. SE1 . . . . 5K 13 (1A 102)
Windmill Way HA4: Ruis 1H 57
Windmore Cl. HA0: Wemb 5A 60
Windrose Cl. SE16 . . . . 2K 103
Windrush KT3: N Mald 4H 151
  SE28 . . . . 1B 108
Windrush Cl. E8 . . . . 7G 67
  N17 . . . . 1E 48
  SW11 . . . . 4B 118
  UB10: Ick 4B 56
  W4 . . . . 1J 115
Windrush Ho. NW8 . . . . 5B 4
  (off Church St. Est.)
Windrush La. SE23 . . . . 3K 139
Windrush Rd. NW10 . . . . 1K 79
Windrush Sq. SW2 . . . . 4A 120
Windsock Cl. SE16 . . . . 4B 104
Windsock Way TW6: H'row A . . 5C 174
Windsor Av. E17 . . . . 2A 50
  HA8: Edg 4C 28
  KT3: N Mald 5J 151
  KT8: W Mole 3E 148
  SM3: Cheam 3G 165
  SW19 . . . . 1A 154
  UB10: Hil 1D 74
Windsor Cen., The N1 . . . . . . 1B 84
  (off Windsor St.)
Windsor Cl. BR7: Chst 5F 143
  HA2: Harr 3E 58
  HA6: Nwood 2J 39
  N3 . . . . 2G 45
  SE27 . . . . 4C 138

Windsor Cl.—Wittenham Way

Windsor Cl. TW6: H'row A 6D 174
(off Whittle Rd.)
TW8: Bford 6B 96
Windsor Cotts. SE14 . . . . .7B 104
(off Amersham Gro.)
Windsor Ct. E3 . . . . .2C 86
(off Mostyn Gro.)
HA5: Pinn 3B 40
KT1: King T 4D 150
(off Palace Rd.)
N11 . . . . .5J 31
N14 . . . . .7B 22
NW3 . . . . .4J 63
NW11 .6G 45
(off Golders Grn. Rd.)
SE16 . . . . .7K 85
(off King & Queen Wharf)
SW3 . . . . .5D 16
(off Jubilee Pl.)
SW11 .2B 118
TW16: Sun 7J 129
W2 . . . . .7K 81
(off Moscow Rd.)
W10 . . . . .6F 81
(off Bramley Rd.)
WD23: Bush 1B 26
(off Catsey La.)
Windsor Cres. HA2: Harr 3E 58
HA9: Wemb 3H 61
Windsor Dr. BR6: Chels 6K 173
EN4: E Barn 6J 21
Windsor Gdns. CR0: Bedd 3J 167
UB3: Harl 3F 93
W9 . . . . .5J 81
Windsor Gro. SE27 . . . . .4C 138
Windsor Hall E16 . . . . .1K 105
(off Wesley Av.)
Windsor Ho. E2 . . . . .3K 85
(off Knottisford St.)
E20 . . . . .5D 68
(off Peloton Av.)
N1 . . . . .2C 84
NW1 . . . . .1K 5
NW2 . . . . .6G 63
(off Chatsworth Rd.)
UB5: N'olt 6E 58
(off The Farmlands)
Windsor M. SE6 . . . . .1E 140
SE23 .1A 140
Windsor Pk. Rd. UB3: Harl 7H 93
Windsor Pl. SW1 . . . . .3B 18 (3G 101)
Windsor Rd. CR7: Thor H 2B 156
DA6: Bex 4E 126
E4 . . . . .4J 35
E7 . . . . .5K 69
E10 . . . . .2D 68
E11 . . . . .1J 69
EN5: Barn 6A 20
HA3: Hrw W 1G 41
IG1: Ilf .4F 71
KT2: King T 7E 132
KT4: Wor Pk 2C 164
N3 . . . . .2G 45
N7 . . . . .3J 65
N13 . . . . .3F 33
N17 . . . . .2G 49
NW2 . . . . .6D 62
RM8: Dag 3E 72
TW4: Cran 2K 111
TW9: Kew 2F 115
TW11: Tedd 5H 131
TW16: Sun 6J 129
UB2: S'hall 3D 94
W5 . . . . .7E 78
(not continuous)
Windsors, The IG9: Buck H 2H 37
Windsor St. N1 . . . . .1B 84
Windsor Ter. N1 . . . . .1D 8 (3C 84)
Windsor Wlk. SE5 . . . . .2D 120
Windsor Way W14 . . . . .4F 99
Windsor Wharf E9 . . . . .5B 68
Windspoint Dr. SE15 . . . . .6H 103
Windus M. N16 . . . . .1F 67
Windus Rd. N16 . . . . .1F 67
Windus Wlk. N16 . . . . .1F 67
Windward Ct. E16 . . . . .7F 89
(off Gallions Rd.)
Windy Ridge
BR1: Brom 1C 160
Windy Ridge Cl. SW19 . . . . .5F 135
Wine Cl. E1 . . . . .1J 103
(not continuous)
Wine Office Ct. EC4 . . . . .7K 7 (6A 84)
Winery La. KT1: King T 3F 151
Winey Cl. KT9: Chess 7C 162
Winford Ct. SE15 . . . . .1H 121
Winford Ho. E3 . . . . .7B 68
Winford Pde. UB1: S'hall 6F 77
(off Marconi Way)
Winforton St. SE10 . . . . .1E 122
Winfrith Rd. SW18 . . . . .7A 118
Wingate & Finchley FC
Harry Abrahams Stadium 7G 31
Wingate Cres. CR0: C'don 6J 155
Wingate Ho. E3 . . . . .3D 86
(off Bruce Rd.)
Wingate Rd. DA14: Sidc 6C 144
IG1: Ilf .5F 71
W6 . . . . .3D 98
Wingate Sq. SW4 . . . . .3G 119
Wingfield Ct. DA15: Sidc 2K 143
E14 . . . . .7F 87
(off Newport Av.)
Wingfield Ho. E2 . . . . .2J 9
(off Virginia Rd.)
Wingfield M. SE15 . . . . .3G 121
Wingfield Rd. E15 . . . . .4G 69
E17 . . . . .5D 50
KT2: King T 6F 133
Wingfield St. SE15 . . . . .3G 121
Wingfield Way HA4: Ruis 5K 57
Wingford Rd. SW2 . . . . .6J 119
Wingmore Rd. SE24 . . . . .3C 120
Wingrad Ho. E1 . . . . .5J 85
(off Jubilee St.)
Wingrave Rd. W6 . . . . .6E 98
Wingreen NW8 . . . . .1K 81
(off Abbey Rd.)
Wingrove E4 . . . . .7H 25
Wingrove Ct. RM7: Rom 5J 55
Wingrove Rd. SE6 . . . . .2G 141
Wings Cl. SM1: Sutt 4J 165
Wings Rd. TW6: H'row A 6C 174
(off Whittle Rd.)
Wing Yip Bus. Cen. NW2 . . . . .2D 62
Winicotte Ho. W2 . . . . .5B 4
(off Paddington Grn.)
Winifred Pl. N12 . . . . .5F 31
Winifred Rd.
DA8: Erith 5K 109
RM8: Dag 2E 72
SW19 .1J 153
TW12: Hamp H 4E 130
Winifred St. E16 . . . . .1D 106
Winifred Ter. EN1: Enf 7A 24
Winkfield Rd. E13 . . . . .2K 87
N22 . . . . .1A 48
Winkley Ct. HA2: Harr 3E 58
N10 . . . . .4F 47
(off St James's La.)
Winkley St. E2 . . . . .2H 85
Winkworth Cotts. E1 . . . . .4J 85
(off Cephas St.)
Winlaton Rd.
BR1: Brom 4F 141
Winmill Rd. RM8: Dag 3F 73
Winnepeg Ho. SE16 . . . . .2J 103
(off Province Dr.)
Winnett St. W1 . . . . .2C 12 (7H 83)
Winningales Ct. IG5: Ilf 2C 52
Winnings Wlk. UB5: N'olt 6C 58
Winnington Cl. N2 . . . . .6B 46
Winnington Ho. SE5 . . . . .7C 102
(off Wyndham Est.)
W10 . . . . .4G 81
(off Southern Row)
Winnington Rd. N2 . . . . .6B 46
Winnipeg Dr. BR6: Chels 6K 173
Winnock Rd. UB7: Yiew 1A 92
Winn Rd. SE12 . . . . .1J 141
Winns Av. E17 . . . . .3B 50
Winns Comn. Rd. SE18 . . . . .6J 107
Winns M. N15 .4E 48
Winns Ter. E17 . . . . .3C 50
Winsbeach E17 . . . . .2F 51
Winscombe Cres. W5 . . . . .4D 78
Winscombe St. N19 . . . . .2F 65
Winscombe Way HA7: Stan 5F 27
Winsford Rd. SE6 . . . . .3B 140
Winsford Ter. N18 . . . . .5J 33
Winsham Gro. SW11 . . . . .5E 118
Winsham Ho. NW1 . . . . .1D 6
(off Churchway)
Winslade Rd. SW2 . . . . .5J 119
Winslade Way SE6 . . . . .7D 122
Winsland M. W2 . . . . .7A 4 (6B 82)
Winsland St. W2 . . . . .7A 4 (6B 82)
Winsley St. W1 . . . . .7B 6 (6G 83)
Winslow SE17 . . . . .5E 102
Winslow Cl. HA5: Eastc 6K 39
NW10 .3A 62
Winslow Gro. E4 . . . . .2B 36
Winslow Rd. W6 . . . . .6E 98
Winslow Way TW13: Hanw 3B 130
Winsmoor Ct. EN2: Enf 3G 23
WINSOR PARK 5F 89
Winsor Ter. E6 . . . . .5E 88
Winstanley Est. SW11 . . . . .3B 118
Winstanley Rd. SW11 . . . . .3B 118
(not continuous)
Winstead Gdns. RM10: Dag 5J 73
Winston Av. NW9 . . . . .7A 44
Winston Cl. HA3: Hrw W 6E 26
RM7: Mawney 4H 55
Winston Ct. BR1: Brom 1K 159
(off Widmore Rd.)
HA3: Hrw W 7A 26
Winston Ho. W13 . . . . .2A 96
(off Balfour Rd.)
WC1 . . . . .3D 6
Winston Rd. N16 . . . . .4D 66
Winston Wlk. W4 . . . . .3K 97
Winston Way IG1: Ilf 3F 71
Winter Av. E6 . . . . .1C 88
Winterborne Av. BR6: Orp 3H 173
Winterbourne Ho. W11 . . . . .7G 81
(off Portland Rd.)
Winterbourne Rd. CR7: Thor H 4A 156
RM8: Dag 2C 72
SE6 . . . . .1B 140
Winter Box Wlk. TW10: Rich 5F 115
Winterbrook Rd. SE24 . . . . .6C 120
Winterburn Cl. N11 . . . . .6K 31
Winterfold Cl. SW19 . . . . .2G 135
Winter Gdns. TW11: Tedd 4A 132
Wintergreen Blvd. UB7: W Dray 2B 92
Wintergreen Cl. E6 . . . . .5C 88
Winterleys NW6 . . . . .2H 81
(off Denmark Rd.)
Winter Lodge SE16 . . . . .5G 103
(off Fern Wlk.)
Winter's Ct. E4 . . . . .3J 35
Winterslow Ho. SE5 . . . . .2C 120
(off Flaxman Rd.)
Winterslow Rd. SW9 . . . . .1B 120
Winters Rd. KT7: T Ditt 7B 150
Winterstoke Gdns. NW7 . . . . .5H 29
Winterstoke Rd. SE6 . . . . .1B 140
Winterton Ct. KT1: Hamp W 1D 150
(off Lwr. Teddington Rd.)
SE20 .2G 157
Winterton Ho. E1 . . . . .6J 85
(off Deancross St.)
Winterton Pl. SW10 . . . . .7A 16 (6A 100)
Winterwell Rd. SW2 . . . . .5J 119
Winthorpe Rd. SW15 . . . . .4G 117
Winthrop Ho. W12 . . . . .7D 80
(off White City Est.)
Winthrop St. E1 . . . . .5H 85
Winthrop Wlk. HA9: Wemb 3E 60
(off Everard Way)
Winton Av. N11 . . . . .7B 32
Winton Cl. N9 .7E 24
Winton Ct. N1 .2K 83
(off Calshot St.)
Winton Gdns. HA8: Edg 7A 28
Winton Rd. BR6: Farnb 4F 173
Winton Way SW16 . . . . .5A 138
Wireworks Ct. SE1 . . . . .7C 14
(off Gt. Sufolk St.)
Wirrall Ho. SE26 . . . . .3G 139
Wirral Wood Cl. BR7: Chst 6E 142
Wirra Rd. TW6: H'row A 5C 174
(off Wayfarer Rd.)
Wisbeach Rd. CR0: C'don 5D 156
Wisbech N4 . . . . .1K 65
(off Lorne Rd.)
Wisborough Rd. CR2: Sande 7F 169
Wisden Ho. SW8 . . . . .7H 19 (6K 101)
Wisdom Ct. TW7: Isle 3A 114
(off South St.)
Wisdons Cl. RM10: Dag 1H 73
Wise La. NW7 .5H 29
UB7: W Dray 4A 92
Wiseman Rd. E10 . . . . .2C 68
Wise Rd. E15 . . . . .1F 87
Wiseton Rd. SW17 . . . . .1C 136
Wishart Rd. SE3 . . . . .2B 124
Wishaw Wlk. N13 . . . . .6D 32
Wisley Ho. SW1 . . . . .5C 18
(off Rampayne St.)
Wisley Rd. BR5: St P 7A 144
SW11 . . . . .5E 118
Wistaria Cl. BR6: Farnb 2F 173
Wisteria Apartments E9 . . . . .6J 67
(off Chatham Pl.)
Wisteria Cl. IG1: Ilf 5F 71
NW7 . . . . .6G 29
Wisteria Gdns. IG8: Wfd G 5D 36
Wisteria Rd. SE13 . . . . .4F 123
Wistow Ho. E2 .1G 85
(off Whiston Rd.)
Witanhurst La. N6 . . . . .1E 64
Witan St. E2 . . . . .3H 85
Witchwood Ho. SW9 . . . . .3A 120
(off Gresham Rd.)
Witham Ct. E10 . . . . .3D 68
SW17 . . . . .3D 136
Witham Rd. RM10: Dag 5G 73
SE20 .3J 157
TW7: Isle 1H 113
W13 . . . . .1A 96
Witherby Cl. CR0: C'don 5E 168
Witherington Rd. N5 . . . . .5A 66
Withers Cl. KT9: Chess 6C 162
Withers Mead NW9 . . . . .1B 44
Withers Pl. EC1 . . . . .3D 8 (4C 84)
Witherston Way SE9 . . . . .2E 142
Withycombe Rd. SW19 . . . . .7F 117
Withy Ho. E1 .4K 85
(off Globe Rd.)
Withy La. HA4: Ruis 5E 38
Withy Mead E4 . . . . .3A 36
Witley Ct. WC1 .4E 6
Witley Cres. CR0: New Ad 6E 170
Witley Gdns. UB2: S'hall 4D 94
Witley Ho. SW2 . . . . .7J 119
Witley Ind. Est. UB2: S'hall 4D 94
Witley Point SW15 . . . . .1D 134
(off Wanborough Dr.)
Witley Rd. N19 . . . . .2G 65
Witney Cl. UB10: Ick 4B 56
Witney Path SE23 . . . . .3K 139
Wittenham Way E4 . . . . .3A 36

Wittering Cl. KT2: King T 5D 132
Wittersham Rd. BR1: Brom 5H 141
Witts Ho. KT1: King T 3F 151
    (off Winery La.)
Wivenhoe Cl. SE15 . . . . .3H 121
Wivenhoe Ct. TW3: Houn 4D 112
Wivenhoe Rd. IG11: Bark 2A 90
Wiverton Rd. SE26 . . . . .6J 139
Wix Rd. RM9: Dag 1D 90
Wix's La. SW4 . . . . .3F 119
WLA Community Sports Cen. 1C 76
Woburn W13 . . . . .5B 78
    (off Clivedon Ct.)
Woburn Cl. SE28 . . . . .6D 90
  SW19 . . . . .6A 136
Woburn Ct. CRO: C'don 1C 168
  E18 . . . . .2J 51
  SE16 . . . . .5H 103
    (off Masters Dr.)
  WC1 . . . . .4E 6
    (off Bernard St.)
Woburn Mans. WC1 . . . . .5C 6
    (off Torrington Pl.)
Woburn M. WC1 . . . . .4D 6 (4H 83)
Woburn Pl. WC1 . . . . .4E 6 (4J 83)
Woburn Rd. CRO: C'don 1C 168
  SM5: Cars 1C 166
Woburn Sq. WC1 . . . . .4D 6 (4H 83)
    (not continuous)
Woburn Twr. UB5: N'olt 3B 76
    (off Broomcroft Av.)
Woburn Wlk. WC1 . . . . .2D 6 (3H 83)
Wodeham Gdns. E1 . . . . .5G 85
Wodehouse Av. SE5 . . . . .1F 121
Wodehouse Ct. W3 . . . . .3J 97
    (off Vincent Rd.)
Woffington Cl.
  KT1: Hamp W 1C 150
Woking Cl. SW15 . . . . .4B 116
Wolcot Ho. NW1 . . . . .18 6
    (off Aldenham St.)
Woldham Pl. BR2: Brom 4A 160
Woldham Rd. BR2: Brom 4A 160
Wolds Dr. BR6: Farnb 4E 172
Wolfe Cl. BR2: Hayes 6J 159
  UB4: Yead 3K 75
Wolfe Cres. SE7 . . . . .5B 106
  SE16 . . . . .2K 103
Wolfe Ho. W12 . . . . .7D 80
    (off White City Est.)
  W14 . . . . .4H 99
Wolferton Rd. E12 . . . . .4D 70
Wolffe Gdns. E15 . . . . .6H 69
Wolfington Rd. SE27 . . . . .4B 138
Wolfram Cl. SE13 . . . . .5G 123
Wolftencroft Cl. SW11 . . . . .3C 118
Wollaston Cl. SE1 . . . . .4C 102
Wollaton Ho. N1 . . . . .2A 84
    (off Batchelor St.)
Wollett Ct. NW1 . . . . .7G 65
    (off St Pancras Way)
Wollstonecraft St. N1 . . . . .1H 83
Wolmer Cl. HA8: Edg 4B 28
Wolmer Gdns. HA8: Edg 3B 28
Wolseley Av. SW19 . . . . .2J 135
Wolseley Gdns. W4 . . . . .6H 97
Wolseley Rd. CR4: Mitc 7E 154
  E7 . . . . .7K 69
  HA3: W'stone 3J 41
  N8 . . . . .6H 47
  N22 . . . . .1K 47
  RM7: Rush G 7K 55
  W4 . . . . .4J 97
Wolseley St. SE1 . . . . . . .7K 15 (2G 103)
Wolsey Av. E6 . . . . .3E 88
  E17 . . . . .3B 50
  KT7: T Ditt 5K 149
Wolsey Cl. KT2: King T 1H 151
  KT4: Wor Pk 4C 164
  SE2 . . . . .2C 108
  SW20 . . . . .7D 134

Wolsey Cl. TW3: Houn 4G 113
  UB2: S'hall 3G 95
Wolsey Ct. NW6 . . . . .7A 64
  SE9 . . . . .6D 124
    (off Coldharbour)
  SW11 . . . . .1C 118
    (off Westbridge Rd.)
Wolsey Cres. CRO: New Ad 7E 170
  SM4: Mord 7G 153
Wolsey Dr. KT2: King T 5E 132
  KT12: Walt T 7B 148
Wolsey Gro. HA8: Edg 7E 28
Wolsey M. BR6: Chels 5K 173
  NW5 . . . . .6G 65
Wolsey Rd. EN1: Enf 2C 24
  KT8: E Mos 4H 149
  N1 . . . . .5D 66
  TW12: Hamp H 6F 131
  TW15: Ashf 4A 128
  TW16: Sun 7H 129
Wolsey St. E1 . . . . .5J 85
Wolsey Way KT9: Chess 5G 163
Wolstenholme HA7: Stan 5G 27
Wolstonbury N12 . . . . .5D 30
Wolvercote Rd. SE2 . . . . .2D 108
Wolverley St. E2 . . . . .3H 85
Wolverton SE17 . . . . .5E 102
    (not continuous)
Wolverton Av. KT2: King T 1G 151
Wolverton Gdns. W5 . . . . .7F 79
  W6 . . . . .4F 99
Wolverton Rd. HA7: Stan 6G 27
Wolverton Way N14 . . . . .5B 22
Wolves La. N13 . . . . .7F 33
  N22 . . . . .7F 33
Womersley Rd. N8 . . . . .6K 47
Wonersh Way SM2: Cheam 7F 165
Wonford Cl. KT2: King T 1A 152
Wontner Cl. N1 . . . . .7C 66
Wontner Rd. SW17 . . . . .2D 136
Wooburn Cl. UB8: Hil 4D 74
Woodall Av. EN3: Pond E 6E 24
Woodall Cl. E14 . . . . .7D 86
  KT9: Chess 7C 162
Woodall Rd. EN3: Pond E 6E 24
Woodbank Rd. BR1: Brom 3H 141
Woodbastwick Rd. SE26 . . . . .5K 139
Woodberry Av. HA2: Harr 4F 41
  N21 . . . . .2F 33
Woodberry Cl. NW7 . . . . .7A 30
  TW16: Sun 6J 129
Woodberry Cres. N10 . . . . .3F 47
Woodberry Down N4 . . . . .7C 48
Woodberry Down Est. N4 . . . . .7C 48
    (not continuous)
Woodberry Gdns. N12 . . . . .6F 31
Woodberry Gro. DA5: Bexl 3K 145
  N4 . . . . .7C 48
  N12 . . . . .6F 31
Woodberry Way E4 . . . . .7K 25
  N12 . . . . .6F 31
Woodbine Cl. TW2: Twick 2H 131
Woodbine Gro. EN2: Enf 1J 23
  SE20 . . . . .7H 139
Woodbine La. KT4: Wor Pk 3D 164
Woodbine Pl. E11 . . . . .6J 51
Woodbines Av. KT1: King T 3D 150
Woodbine Ter. E9 . . . . .6J 67
Woodborough Rd. SW15 . . . . .4D 116
Woodbourne Av. SW16 . . . . .3H 137
Woodbourne Cl. SW16 . . . . .3J 137
Woodbourne Gdns. SM6: Wall 7F 167
Woodbridge Cl. N7 . . . . .2K 65
  NW2 . . . . .3C 62
Woodbridge Ct. IG8: Wfd G 7F 37
Woodbridge Ho. E11 . . . . .1H 69
Woodbridge Rd. IG11: Bark 5K 71
Woodbridge St. EC1 . . . . . .3A 8 (4B 84)
    (not continuous)
Woodbridge Ter. RM6: Chad H 6B 54

Woodbrook Rd. SE2 . . . . .6A 108
Woodburn Cl. NW4 . . . . .5F 45
Woodbury Cl. CRO: C'don 2F 169
  E11 . . . . .4K 51
Woodbury Gdns. SE12 . . . . .3K 141
Woodbury Ho. SE26 . . . . .3G 139
Woodbury Pk. Rd. W13 . . . . .4B 78
Woodbury Rd. E17 . . . . .4D 50
Woodbury St. SW17 . . . . .5C 136
Woodchester Ho. E14 . . . . .3D 104
    (off Selsdon Way)
Woodchester Sq. W2 . . . . .5K 81
Woodchurch Cl. DA14: Sidc 3H 143
Woodchurch Dr. BR1: Brom 7B 142
Woodchurch Rd. NW6 . . . . .7J 63
Wood Cl. E2 .4G 85
  HA1: Harr 7H 41
  NW9 . . . . .7K 43
Woodclyffe Dr. BR7: Chst 2E 160
Woodcock Cl. TW6: H'row A 7C 174
Woodcock Ct. HA3: Kenton 7E 42
Woodcock Dell Av. HA3: Kenton 7D 42
Woodcock Hill HA3: Kenton 5C 42
Woodcock Ho. E14 . . . . .5C 86
    (off Burgess St.)
Woodcocks E16 . . . . .5A 88
Woodcombe Cres. SE23 . . . . .1J 139
Woodcote Av. CR7: Thor H 4B 156
  NW7 . . . . .6K 29
  SM6: Wall 7F 167
Woodcote Cl. EN3: Pond E 6D 24
  KT2: King T 5F 133
Woodcote Dr. BR6: Orp 1H 173
Woodcote Grn. SM6: Wall 7G 167
Woodcote Ho. SE8 . . . . .6B 104
    (off Prince St.)
Woodcote M. SM6: Wall 6F 167
Woodcote Pl. SE27 . . . . .5B 138
Woodcote Rd. E11 . . . . .7J 51
  SM6: Wall 6F 167
Woodcote Vs. SE27 . . . . .5C 138
    (off Woodcote Pl.)
Wood Ct. DA8: Erith 7K 109
Wood Crest SM2: Sutt 7A 166
    (off Christchurch Pk.)
Woodcroft N21 . . . . .1F 33
  SE9 . . . . .3D 142
  UB6: G'frd 6A 60
Woodcroft Av. HA7: Stan 1A 42
  NW7 . . . . .6F 29
Woodcroft Cl. SE9 . . . . .6E 124
Woodcroft Cres. UB10: Hil 1D 74
Woodcroft M. SE8 . . . . .4A 104
Woodcroft Rd. CR7: Thor H 5B 156
Wood Dr. BR7: Chst 6C 142
Woodedge Cl. E4 . . . . .1C 36
WOOD END . . . .
  UB4 . . . . .5H 75
  UB5 . . . . .5G 59
Wood End, The SM6: Wall 7F 167
Woodend SE19 . . . . .6C 138
  SM1: Sutt 2A 166
Wood End Av. HA2: Harr 4F 59
  UB5: N'olt 4F 59
Wood End Cl. UB5: N'olt 5H 59
Wood End Gdns. UB5: N'olt 5G 59
Woodend Gdns. EN2: Enf 4D 22
Wood End Grn. Rd. UB3: Hayes 5F 75
Wood End La. UB5: N'olt 6F 59
Wood End Rd. HA1: Harr 4H 59
Woodend Rd. E17 . . . . .2E 50
Wood End Way UB5: N'olt 5G 59
Wooder Gdns. E7 . . . . .4J 69
Wooderson Cl. SE25 . . . . .4E 156
Woodfall Av. EN5: Barn 5C 20
Woodfall Rd. N4 . . . . .2A 66
Woodfall St. SW3 . . . . . .6E 16 (5D 100)
Wood Farm CI. HA7: Stan 2G 27
Woodfarrs SE5 . . . . .4D 120

Wood Fld. NW3 . . . . .5D 64
Woodfield Av. HA0: Wemb 3C 60
  NW9 . . . . .4A 44
  SM5: Cars 6E 166
  SW16 . . . . .3H 137
  W5 . . . . .4C 78
Woodfield Cl. EN1: Enf 4K 23
  SE19 . . . . .7C 138
Woodfield Cres. W5 . . . . .4C 78
Woodfield Dr. EN4: E Barn 1K 31
Woodfield Gdns. KT3: N Mald 5B 152
Woodfield Gro. SW16 . . . . .3H 137
Woodfield Ho. SE23 . . . . .3K 139
    (off Dacres Rd.)
Woodfield La. SW16 . . . . .3H 137
Woodfield Pl. W9 . . . . .4H 81
Woodfield Rd. WD23: Bush 1C 26
Woodfield Rd. TW4: Cran 2A 111
  W5 . . . . .4C 78
  W9 . . . . .5H 81
Woodfield Way N11 . . . . .7C 32
WOODFORD .6F 37
Woodford Av. IG2: Ilf 5D 52
  IG4: Ilf, Wfd G 3B 52
WOODFORD BRIDGE 6H 37
Woodford Bri. Rd. IG4: Ilf 3B 52
Woodford Ct. W12 . . . . .2F 99
    (off Shepherd's Bush Grn.)
Woodford Cres. HA5: Pinn 2K 39
Woodforde Ct. UB3: Harl 5F 93
WOODFORD GREEN 6D 36
Woodford Green Athletics Club 6H 37
Woodford Hall Path E18 . . . . .1H 51
Woodford Ho. E18 . . . . .4J 51
Woodford New Rd. E17 . . . . .4G 51
  E18 . . . . .1G 51
  IG8: Wfd G 1G 51
Woodford Pl. HA9: Wemb 1E 60
Woodford Rd. E7 . . . . .3K 69
  E18 . . . . .4J 51
WOODFORD SIDE 5C 36
Woodford Trad. Est. IG8: Wfd G 2B 52
WOODFORD WELLS 3E 36
Woodgate Av. KT9: Chess 5D 162
Woodgate Dr. SW16 . . . . .7H 137
Woodgate M. W12 . . . . .2E 98
Woodget Cl. E6 . . . . .6C 88
Woodgrange Av. EN1: Enf 6B 24
  HA3: Kenton 5C 42
  N12 . . . . .6G 31
  W5 . . . . .1G 97
Woodgrange Cl. HA3: Kenton 5D 42
Woodgrange Gdns. EN1: Enf 6B 24
Woodgrange Ho. W5 . . . . .1F 97
    (off Woodgrange Av.)
Woodgrange Mans. HA3: Kenton 5D 42
Woodgrange Rd. E7 . . . . .5K 69
Woodgrange Ter. EN1: Enf 6B 24
WOOD GREEN 2K 47
Wood Grn. Hall N22 . . . . .2K 47
    (off Station Rd.)
Wood Grn. Shop. City N22 . . . . .2A 48
Woodhall NW1 . . . . .2A 6
    (off Robert St.)
Woodhall Av. HA5: Pinn 1C 40
  SE21 . . . . .3F 139
Woodhall Dr. UB8: Uxb 5A 56
Woodhall Dr. HA5: Pinn 1B 40
  SE21 . . . . .3F 139
Woodhall Ga. HA5: Pinn 1B 40
Woodhall Ho. SW18 . . . . .6B 118
Woodham Ct. E18 . . . . .4H 51
Wooodham Rd. SE6 . . . . .3E 140
Woodhatch Cl. E6 . . . . .5C 88
Woodhaven Gdns. IG6: Ilf 4G 53
Woodhayes Rd. SW19 . . . . .7E 134
Woodhead Dr. BR6: Orp 3J 173
Woodheyes Rd. NW10 . . . . .5K 61
Woodhill SE18 . . . . .4C 106
Woodhill Cres. HA3: Kenton 6D 42

Wood Ho. *NW6* 2H **81**
(off Albert Rd.)
Woodhouse Av. UB6: G'frd 2K **77**
Woodhouse Cl. SE22 4G **121**
UB3: Harl 3G **93**
UB6: G'frd 1K **77**
Woodhouse Gro. E12 6C **70**
Woodhouse Rd. E11 3H **69**
N12 6G **31**
Woodhurst Av. BR5: Pet W 6G **161**
Woodhurst Rd. SE2 5A **108**
W3 7J **79**
Woodies La. KT3: N Mald 6K **151**
Woodington Cl. SE9 6E **124**
Woodknoll Dr. BR7: Chst 1D **160**
Woodland App. UB6: G'frd 6A **60**
Woodland Cl. IG8: Wfd G 3E **36**
KT19: Ewe 6A **164**
NW9 6J **43**
SE19 6E **138**
UB10: Ick 2D **56**
Woodland Ct. *E11* 6J **51**
(off New Wanstead)
N7 6J **65**
Woodland Cres. SE10 6G **105**
SE16 2K **103**
Woodland Gdns. N10 5F **47**
TW7: Isle 3J **113**
Woodland Gro. SE10 5G **105**
Woodland Hill SE19 6E **138**
Woodland M. *SE13* 3D **122**
(off Loampit Hill)
SW16 3J **137**
Woodland Ri. N10 4F **47**
UB6: G'frd 6A **60**
Woodland Rd. CR7: Thor H 4A **156**
E4 1K **35**
N11 5A **32**
SE19 5E **138**
WOODLANDS 3J **113**
Woodlands BR2: Brom 4H **159**
DA6: Bex 5H **127**
HA2: Harr 4E **40**
NW11 5G **45**
SW20 4E **152**
Woodlands, The HA1: Harr 2J **59**
HA7: Stan 5G **27**
N5 4C **66**
N12 6F **31**
N14 1A **32**
SE13 7F **123**
SE19 7C **138**
SM6: Wall 7F **167**
SW9 7B **102**
(off Langton Rd.)
TW7: Isle 2K **113**
Woodlands Av. DA15: Sidc 1J **143**
E11 1K **69**
HA4: Ruis 7A **40**
KT3: N Mald 1J **151**
KT4: Wor Pk 2B **164**
N3 7F **31**
RM6: Chad H 7E **54**
W3 1H **97**
Woodlands Cl. BR1: Brom 2D **160**
KT10: Clay 7A **162**
NW11 5G **45**
Woodlands Ct. BR1: Brom 1H **159**
HA1: Harr 5K **41**
KT12: Walt T 7K **147**
NW10 1F **81**
(off Wrentham Av.)
SE23 7H **121**
Woodlands Dr. HA7: Stan 6E **26**
TW16: Sun 2A **148**
Woodlands Gdns. E17 4G **51**
Woodlands Ga. *SW15* 5H **117**
(off Woodlands Way)
Woodlands Gro. TW7: Isle 2J **113**
Woodlands Hgts. *SE3* 6H **105**
(off Vanburgh Hill)
Woodlands Pde. TW15: Ashf 6E **128**
Woodlands Pk. DA5: Bexl 4K **145**
Woodlands Pk. Rd. N15 5B **48**
SE10 6G **105**
(not continuous)
Woodlands Rd. BR1: Brom 2C **160**
BR6: Chels 6K **173**
DA7: Bex 3E **126**
E11 2G **69**
E17 3E **50**
EN2: Enf 1J **23**
HA1: Harr 5K **41**
IG1: Ilf 3G **71**
KT6: Surb 7D **150**
N9 1D **34**
SW13 3B **116**
TW7: Isle 3H **113**
UB1: S'hall 1B **94**
Woodlands St. SE13 7F **123**
Woodland St. E8 6F **67**
Woodlands Way SW15 5H **117**
Woodland Ter. SE7 4C **106**
Woodland Wlk. BR1: Brom 4F **141**
(not continuous)
KT19: Ewe 6G **163**
NW3 5C **64**
SE10 5G **105**
Woodland Way BR4: W W'ck 4D **170**
BR5: Pet W 4G **161**
CR0: C'don 1A **170**
CR4: Mitc 7E **136**
IG8: Wfd G 3E **36**
KT5: Surb 2H **163**
N21 2F **33**
NW7 6G **29**
SE2 4D **108**
SM4: Mord 4H **153**
Wood La. HA4: Ruis 1F **57**
HA7: Stan 3F **27**
IG8: Wfd G 4C **36**
N6 6F **47**
NW9 7K **43**
RM8: Dag 4C **72**
RM9: Dag 4C **72**
RM10: Dag 2G **73**
TW7: Isle 6J **95**
W12 6E **80**
Wood La. Studios W12 6E **80**
Woodlawn Cl. SW15 5H **117**
Woodlawn Cres. TW2: Whitt 2F **131**
Woodlawn Dr. TW13: Felt 2B **130**
Woodlawn Rd. SW6 7F **99**
Woodlawns KT19: Ewe 7K **163**
Woodlea Dr. BR2: Brom 5G **159**
Woodlea Rd. N16 3E **66**
Woodleigh E18 1J **51**
Woodleigh Av. N12 6H **31**
Woodleigh Gdns. SW16 3J **137**
Woodley Cl. SW17 7D **136**
Woodley La. SM5: Cars 3C **166**
Wood Lodge Gdns. BR1: Brom 7C **142**
Wood Lodge La. BR4: W W'ck 3E **170**
Woodman M. TW9: Kew 1H **115**
Woodman Pde. *E16* 1E **106**
(off Woodman St.)
Woodmans Gro. NW10 5B **62**
Woodman's M. W12 5D **80**
Woodmansterne Rd. SM5: Cars 7C **166**
SW16 7G **137**
Woodman St. E16 1E **106**
Wood Martyn Ct. *BR6: Orp* 2K **173**
(off Orchard Gro.)
Wood Mead N17 6B **34**
Woodmere SE9 1D **142**
Woodmere Av. CR0: C'don 7J **157**
Woodmere Cl. CR0: C'don 7K **157**
SW11 3E **118**
Woodmere Ct. N14 7A **22**
Woodmere Gdns. CR0: C'don 7K **157**
Woodmere Way BR3: Beck 5F **159**
Woodmill Cl. SW15 6C **116**
Woodmill Rd. E5 2J **67**
Woodmill St. SE1 3F **103**
Woodnook Rd. SW16 5F **137**
Woodpecker Cl. HA3: Hrw W 1K **41**
N9 6C **24**
WD23: Bush 1B **26**
Woodpecker M. *SE13* 4F **123**
(off Freshfield Cl.)
Woodpecker Mt. CR0: Sels 7A **170**
Woodpecker Rd. SE14 6A **104**
SE28 7C **90**
Woodquest Av. SE24 5C **120**
Wood Retreat SE18 7H **107**
Wood Ride BR5: Pet W 4H **161**
EN4: Had W 1G **21**
Woodridge Cl. EN2: Enf 1F **23**
Woodridings Av. HA5: Hat E 1D **40**
Woodridings Cl. HA5: Hat E 1C **40**
Woodridings Ct. N22 1H **47**
Woodriffe Rd. E11 7F **51**
Wood Ri. HA5: Eastc 5J **39**
Wood Rd. NW10 7J **61**
TW17: Shep 4C **146**
Woodrow SE18 4D **106**
Woodrow Av. UB4: Hayes 5H **75**
Woodrow Cl. UB6: G'frd 7B **60**
Woodrow Ct. N17 7C **34**
SE5 1C **120**
(off Camberwell Sta. Rd.)
Woodrush Cl. SE14 7A **104**
Woodrush Way RM6: Chad H 4D **54**
Woods, The UB10: Ick 4D **56**
Wood's Bldgs. *E1* 5H **85**
(off Winthrop St.)
Woods Cl. *TW3: Houn* 3F **113**
(off High St.)
Woodseer St. E1 5K **9** (5F **85**)
Woodsford *SE17* 5D **102**
(off Portland St.)
Woodsford Sq. W14 2G **99**
Woodshire Rd. RM10: Dag 3H **73**
Woods Ho. SW1 6J **17** (5F **101**)
SW8 1G **119**
(off Wadhurst Rd.)
WOODSIDE 6G **157**
Woodside IG9: Buck H 2F **37**
N10 3E **46**
NW11 5J **45**
SW19 6H **135**
Woodside Av. BR7: Chst 5G **143**
HA0: Wemb 1E **78**
KT10: Esh 7J **149**
N6 5D **46**
N10 5D **46**
N12 4E **30**
SE25 6H **157**
Woodside Cl. DA7: Bex 4K **127**
HA0: Wemb 1E **78**
HA4: Ruis 6F **39**
HA7: Stan 5G **27**
KT5: Surb 7J **151**
Woodside Ct. E12 1A **70**
N12 4E **30**
RM7: Mawney 4G **55**
W5 1E **96**
Woodside Ct. Rd. CR0: C'don 7G **157**
Woodside Cres. DA15: Sidc 3J **143**
Woodside Dr. DA2: Wilm 4K **145**
Woodside End HA0: Wemb 1E **78**
Woodside Gdns. E4 6J **35**
N17 2E **48**
Woodside Grange Rd. N12 4E **30**
Woodside Grn. SE25 6G **157**
Woodside Gro. N12 3F **31**
Woodside Ho. SW19 6H **135**
Woodside La. DA5: Bexl 6D **126**
N12 3F **31**
Woodside M. SE22 5F **121**
Woodside Pde. DA15: Sidc 3J **143**
WOODSIDE PARK 4D **30**
Woodside Pk. SE25 6H **157**
Woodside Pk. Av. E17 4F **51**
Woodside Pk. Rd. N12 4E **30**
Woodside Pl. HA0: Wemb 1E **78**
Woodside Rd. BR1: Brom 5C **160**
DA7: Bex 4K **127**
DA15: Sidc 3J **143**
E13 4A **88**
IG8: Wfd G 4D **36**
KT2: King T 7E **132**
KT3: N Mald 2K **151**
N22 7E **32**
SE25 6H **157**
SM1: Sutt 3A **166**
Woodside Way CR0: C'don 6J **157**
CR4: Mitc 1F **155**
Woods M. W1 2G **11** (7E **82**)
Woodsome Rd. NW5 3E **64**
Woods Pl. SE1 3E **102**
Woodspring Rd. SW19 2G **135**
Woods Rd. SE15 1H **121**
Woodstar Ho. *SE15* 7G **103**
(off Reddins Rd.)
Woodstead Gro. HA8: Edg 6K **27**
WOODSTOCK, THE 7H **153**
Woodstock Av. NW11 7G **45**
SM3: Sutt 7H **153**
TW7: Isle 5A **114**
UB1: S'hall 3D **76**
W13 3A **96**
Woodstock Cl. DA5: Bexl 7F **127**
HA7: Stan 2E **42**
Woodstock Ct. SE11 5H **19** (5K **101**)
SE12 6J **123**
Woodstock Cres. N9 6C **24**
Woodstock Dr. UB10: Ick 4A **56**
Woodstock Gdns. BR3: Beck 1D **158**
IG3: Ilf 2A **72**
UB4: Hayes 5H **75**
Woodstock Grange W5 1E **96**
Woodstock Gro. W12 2F **99**
Woodstock La. KT9: Chess 4B **162**
Woodstock La. Nth. KT6: Surb 2C **162**
Woodstock La. Sth. KT9: Chess 5B **162**
KT10: Clay 5B **162**
Woodstock M. W1 6H **5**
Woodstock Ri. SM3: Sutt 7H **153**
Woodstock Rd. CR0: C'don 3D **168**
E7 7A **70**
E17 2F **51**
HA0: Wemb 1F **79**
N4 1A **66**
NW11 7H **45**
SM5: Cars 5E **166**
W4 4A **98**
Woodstock St. W1 1J **11** (6F **83**)
Woodstock Studios *W12* 2F **99**
(off Woodstock Gro.)
Woodstock Ter. E14 7D **86**
Woodstock Way CR4: Mitc 2F **155**
Woodstone Av. KT17: Ewe 5C **164**
WOOD STREET 3E **50**
Wood St. CR4: Mitc 7E **154**
E17 3E **50**
EC2 7D **8** (6C **84**)
(not continuous)
EN5: Barn 4A **20**
KT1: King T 2D **150**
W4 5A **98**
Woodsyre SE26 4F **139**
Wood Ter. NW2 3D **62**
Woodthorpe Rd. SW15 4D **116**
TW15: Ashf 5A **128**
Woodtree Cl. NW4 2F **45**
Wood Va. N10 5G **47**
SE23 1H **139**
Woodvale Av. SE25 3F **157**
Woodvale Ct. *BR1: Brom* 1K **159**
(off Widmore Rd.)
Wood Va. Est. SE23 7J **121**
Woodvale Wlk. SE27 5C **138**
Woodvale Way NW11 3F **63**

Woodview Av. E4 .....4K 35
Woodview Cl. BR6: Farnb ...2G 173
N4 .....7B 48
SW15 .....4K 133
Wood Vw. M. RM1: Rom ...1K 55
Woodview M. SE19 .....1E 156
Woodville, The W5 .....6D 78
(off Woodville Rd.)
Woodville Cl. SE3 .....1K 123
SE12 .....5J 123
TW11: Tedd 4A 132
Woodville Cl. N14 .....5B 22
SE10 .....1E 122
(off Blissett St.)
SE19 .....1F 157
Woodville Gdns. HA4: Ruis ...7E 38
IG6: Ilf 3F 53
KT6: Surb 7D 150
NW11 .....7F 45
W5 .....6E 78
Woodville Gro. DA16: Well ...3A 126
Woodville Ho. SE1 .....3F 103
(off St Saviour's Est.)
Woodville Rd. CR7: Thor H ...4C 156
E11 .....1H 69
E17 .....4B 50
E18 .....2K 51
EN5: New Bar 3E 20
N16 .....5E 66
NW6 .....2H 81
NW11 .....7F 45
SM4: Mord 4J 153
TW10: Ham 3B 132
W5 .....6D 78
Woodville St. SE18 .....4C 106
Woodward Av. NW4 .....5C 44
Woodward Cl. KT10: Clay ...6A 162
Woodwarde Rd. SE22 .....6E 120
Woodward Gdns. HA7: Stan ...7E 26
RM9: Dag 7C 72
Woodward Rd. RM9: Dag ...7B 72
Woodward's Footpath TW2: Whitt ...6G 113
Wood Way BR6: Farnb 2E 172
Woodway Cres. HA1: Harr ...6A 42
Woodwell St. SW18 .....5A 118
Wood Wharf SE10 .....6D 104
Wood Wharf Bus. Pk. E14 ...1D 104
Woodyard Cl. NW5 .....5E 64
Woodyard La. SE21 .....7E 120
Woodyates Rd. SE12 .....6J 123
Woolacombe Rd. SE3 .....1A 124
Woolacombe Way UB3: Harl ...4G 93
Woolcombes Ct. SE16 .....1K 103
(off Princes Riverside Rd.)
Wooldridge Cl. TW14: Bedf ...1E 128
Wooler St. SE17 .....5D 102
Woolf Cl. SE28 .....1B 108
Woolf M. WC1 .....3D 6
(off Burton Pl.)
Woolford Ct. SE5 .....2C 120
(off Coldharbour La.)
Woolgar M. N16 .....5E 66
(off Gillett St.)
Woollaston Rd. N4 .....6B 48
Woolley Ho. SW9 .....3B 120
(off Loughborough Rd.)
Woollon Ho. E1 .....6J 85
(off Clark St.)
Woolmead Av. NW9 .....7C 44
Woolmer Gdns. N18 .....6B 34
Woolmer Rd. N18 .....5B 34
Woolmore St. E14 .....7E 86
Woolneigh St. SW6 .....3K 117
Woolridge Way E9 .....7J 67
Wool Rd. SW20 .....6D 134
Woolstaplers Way SE16 .....3G 103
Woolston Cl. E17 .....2K 49
Woolstone Ho. E2 .....1G 85
(off Whiston Rd.)
Woolstone Rd. SE23 .....2A 140
WOOLWICH 3D 106

Woolwich Cen., The SE18 .....4E 106
(off Wellington St.)
Woolwich Chu. St. SE18 .....3C 106
Woolwich Comn. SE18 .....6E 106
Woolwich Dockyard Ind. Est. SE18 ...3C 106
Woolwich High St. SE18 .....3E 106
Woolwich Ho. UB3: Harl 3E 92
(off Nine Acres Cl.)
Woolwich Mnr. Way E6 .....4D 88
E16 .....2F 107
Woolwich New Rd. SE18 .....5E 106
Woolwich Rd. DA6: Bex 3G 127
DA7: Bex 3G 127
DA17: Belv 5F 109
SE2 .....6D 108
SE7 .....5H 105
SE10 .....5H 105
Woolwich Trade Pk. SE28 .....3H 107
Wooster Gdns. E14 .....6F 87
Wooster M. HA2: Harr 3G 41
Wooster Pl. SE1 .....4D 102
(off Searles Rd.)
Wootton Gro. N3 .....1J 45
Wootton St. SE1 .....5K 13 (1A 102)
Worbeck Rd. SE20 .....2H 157
Worcester Av. N17 .....7B 34
Worcester Cl. CR0: C'don 2C 170
CR4: Mitc 2E 154
NW2 .....3D 62
SE20 .....1G 157
Worcester Ct. HA1: Harr 3J 41
KT4: Wor Pk 3A 164
N12 .....5E 30
W7 .....6K 77
(off Copley Cl.)
W9 .....5J 81
(off Elmfield Way)
Worcester Cres. IG8: Wfd G ...5E 36
NW7 .....3F 29
Worcester Dr. TW15: Ashf ...5D 128
W4 .....2A 98
Worcester Gdns. IG1: Ilf 7C 52
KT4: Wor Pk 3A 164
SW11 .....5D 118
(off Grandison Rd.)
UB6: G'frd 6H 59
Worcester Ho. SE11 .....2J 19
(off Kennington Rd.)
SW9 .....7A 102
(off Cranmer Rd.)
W2 .....6A 82
(off Hallfield Est.)
Worcester M. NW6 .....6K 63
WORCESTER PARK 1C 164
Worcester Pk. Rd. KT4: Wor Pk ...3K 163
Worcester Point EC1 .....3C 84
Worcester Rd. E12 .....4D 70
E17 .....2K 49
SM2: Sutt 7J 165
SW19 .....5H 135
Worcesters Av. EN1: Enf 1B 24
Wordsworth Av. E12 .....7C 70
E18 .....3H 51
UB6: G'frd 3H 77
Wordsworth Ct. HA1: Harr ...7J 41
Wordsworth Dr. SM3: Cheam ...4E 164
Wordsworth Ho. NW6 .....3J 81
(off Stafford Rd.)
SE18 .....6E 106
(off Woolwich Comn.)
Wordsworth Mans. W14 .....6H 99
(off Queens Club Gdns.)
Wordsworth Pde. N8 .....4B 48
Wordsworth Pl. NW5 .....5D 64
Wordsworth Rd. DA16: Well ...1J 125
N16 .....4E 66
SE1 .....4F 103
SE20 .....7K 139
SM6: Wall 6G 167
TW12: Hamp 4D 130
Wordsworth Wlk. NW11 .....4J 45

Wordsworth Way UB7: W Dray ...4A 92
Worfield St. SW11 .....7C 100
Worgan St. SE11 .....5G 19 (5K 101)
SE16 .....4K 103
Worland Rd. E15 .....7G 69
World Bus. Cen. TW6: H'row A ...1E 110
World of Golf Cen.
Croydon 5J 157
New Malden 3C 152
Sidcup 3G 143
World Rugby Mus. 6J 113
WORLD'S END 3E 22
Worlds End Est. SW10 .....7B 100
World's End La. EN2: Enf 5E 22
N21 .....5E 22
Worlds End La. BR6: Chels ...6K 173
World's End Pas. SW10 .....7B 100
(off Worlds End Est.)
World's End Pl. SW10 .....7B 100
(off Worlds End Est.)
Worleys Dr. BR6: Orp 4H 173
Worlidge St. W6 .....5E 98
Worlingham Rd. SE22 .....4F 121
Wormholt Rd. W12 .....7C 80
Wormwood Scrubs Pk.
(Local Nature Reserve) 5B 80
Wormwood St. EC2 .....7G 9 (6E 84)
Wornington Rd. W10 .....4G 81
(not continuous)
Woronzow Rd. NW8 .....1B 82
Worple Av. SW19 .....7F 135
TW7: Isle 5A 114
Worple Cl. HA2: Harr 1D 58
Worple Rd. SW19 .....2E 152
SW20 .....2E 152
TW7: Isle 4A 114
Worple Rd. M. SW19 .....6H 135
Worple St. SW14 .....3K 115
Worple Way HA2: Harr 1D 58
TW10: Rich 5E 114
Worrall La. UB8: Uxb 7A 56
Worship St. EC2 .....4F 9 (4D 84)
(not continuous)
Worslade Rd. SW17 .....4B 136
Worsley Bri. Rd. BR3: Beck ...7C 140
SE26 .....4B 140
Worsley Grange BR7: Chst ...6G 143
Worsley Gro. E5 .....4G 67
Worsley Ho. SE23 .....2J 139
Worsley Rd. E11 .....4G 69
Worsopp Dr. SW4 .....5G 119
Worth Cl. BR6: Orp 4J 173
Worthfield Cl. KT19: Ewe ...7K 163
Worth Gro. SE17 .....5D 102
Worthing Cl. E15 .....1G 87
Worthing Rd. TW5: Hest ...6D 94
Worthington Cl. CR4: Mitc ...4F 155
Worthington Ho. EC1 .....1K 7
(off Myddelton Pas.)
Worthington Rd. KT6: Surb ...1F 163
Wortley Rd. CR0: C'don 7A 156
E6 .....7B 70
Worton Cl. TW7: Isle 4J 113
Worton Gdns. TW7: Isle ...2H 113
Worton Hall Ind. Est. TW7: Isle ...4J 113
Worton Rd. TW7: Isle 4H 113
Worton Way TW3: Houn ...2H 113
TW7: Houn, Isle 2H 113
Wotton Ct. E14 .....7F 87
(off Jamestown Way)
Wotton Rd. NW2 .....3E 62
SE8 .....6B 104
Wouldham Rd. E16 .....6H 87
Wragby Rd. E11 .....3G 69
Wrampling Pl. N9 .....1B 34
Wrangthorn Wlk. CR0: Wadd ...4A 168
Wraxall Rd. E3 .....4B 86
(off Hamlets Way)
Wray Av. IG5: Ilf 3E 52
Wrayburn Ho. SE16 .....2G 103
(off Llewellyn St.)

Wray Cres. N4 .....2J 65
Wrayfield Rd. SM3: Cheam ...3F 165
Wray Rd. SM2: Cheam 7H 165
Wraysbury Cl. TW4: Houn ...5C 112
Wrays Way UB4: Hayes 4G 75
Wrekin Rd. SE18 .....7G 107
Wren Av. NW2 .....4E 62
UB2: S'hall 4D 94
UB10: Uxb 1B 74
Wren Cl. E16 .....6H 87
N9 .....1E 34
TW6: H'row A 6C 174
Wren Cl. CR0: C'don 4D 168
(off Coombe Rd.)
Wren Cres. WD23: Bush 1B 26
Wren Gdns. RM9: Dag 5D 72
Wren Ho. E3 .....2A 86
(off Gernon Rd.)
KT1: Hamp W 2D 150
(off High St.)
SW1 .....6C 18
(off Aylesford St.)
Wren Landing E14 .....1C 104
Wren La. HA4: Ruis 2G 58
Wren M. SE11 .....4H 19 (4K 101)
SE13 .....4G 123
Wrenn Ho. SW13 .....6C 98
Wren Path SE28 .....3H 107
Wren Rd. DA14: Sidc 4C 144
RM9: Dag 5D 72
SE5 .....1D 120
Wren's Av. TW15: Ashf 4E 128
Wren's Pk. Ho. E5 .....2H 67
Wren St. WC1 .....3H 7 (4K 83)
Wrentham Av. NW10 .....2F 81
Wrenthorpe Rd. BR1: Brom ...4G 141
Wren Vw. N6 .....7G 47
Wrenwood Way HA5: Eastc ...4K 39
Wrestlers Ct. EC3 .....7G 9
Wrexham Rd. E3 .....2C 86
Wricklemarsh Rd. SE3 .....2K 123
(not continuous)
Wrigglesworth St. SE14 .....7K 103
Wright Cl. SE13 .....4F 123
Wright Gdns. TW17: Shep ...5C 146
Wright Rd. TW5: Hest 7A 94
Wrights All. SW19 .....6E 134
Wrights Cl. RM10: Dag 4H 73
Wrights Grn. SW4 .....4H 119
Wright's La. W8 .....3K 99
Wrights Pl. NW10 .....6J 61
Wright's Rd. E3 .....2B 86
(not continuous)
SE25 .....3E 156
Wrights Row SM6: Wall 4F 167
Wright Way TW6: H'row A ...5C 174
Wrigley Cl. E4 .....5A 36
Writtle Ho. NW9 .....2B 44
Wrotham Ho. BR3: Beck 7B 140
(off Sellindge Cl.)
SE1 .....3D 102
(off Law St.)
Wrotham Rd. DA16: Well ...1C 126
EN5: Barn 2B 20
NW1 .....7G 65
W13 .....1C 96
Wrottesley Rd. NW10 .....2C 80
SE18 .....6G 107
Wroughton Rd. SW11 .....5D 118
Wroughton Ter. NW4 .....4D 44
Wroxall Rd. RM9: Dag 6C 72
Wroxham Gdns. N11 .....7C 32
Wroxham Rd. SE28 .....7D 90
Wroxham Way IG6: Ilf 1F 53
Wroxton Rd. SE15 .....2J 121
WRYTHE, THE 3D 166
Wrythe Grn. SM5: Cars 3D 166
Wrythe Grn. Rd. SM5: Cars ...3D 166
Wrythe La. SM5: Cars 1A 166
Wulfstan St. W12 .....5B 80

Wyatt Cl. SE16 . . . . .2B **104**
  TW13: Felt 1B **130**
  UB4: Hayes 5J **75**
  WD23: Bush 1C **26**
Wyatt Ct. HA0: Wemb 7E **60**
  W3 . . . .*3J 97*
    (off All Saints Rd.)
Wyatt Dr. SW13 . . . . .6D **98**
Wyatt Ho. *NW8* *4B 4*
    (off Frampton St.)
  SE3 . . . . .2H **123**
  TW1: Twick 6D **114**
Wyatt Pk. Rd. SW2 . . . . .2J **137**
Wyatt Point SE28 . . . . .2G **107**
Wyatt Rd. E7 . . . . .7A **70**
  N5 . . . . .3C **66**
Wyatts La. E17 . . . . .3E **50**
Wybert St. NW1 . . . . .3A **6** (4G **83**)
Wyborne Ho. NW10 . . . . .7J **61**
Wyborne Way NW10 . . . . .7J **61**
Wyburn Av. EN5: Barn 3C **20**
Wychcombe Studios NW3 . . . . .6D **64**
Wyche Gro. CR2: S Croy 7D **168**
Wych Elm Cl. KT2: King T 7F **133**
Wych Elm Lodge BR1: Brom 7H **141**
Wych Elm Pas. KT2: King T 7F **133**
Wycherley Cl. SE3 . . . . .7H **105**
Wycherley Cres. EN5: New Bar 6E **20**
Wychwood Av. CR7: Thor H 3C **156**
  HA8: Edg 6J **27**
Wychwood Cl. HA8: Edg 6J **27**
  TW16: Sun 6J **129**
Wychwood End N6 . . . . .7G **47**
Wychwood Gdns. IG5: Ilf 4D **52**
Wychwood Way SE19 . . . . .6D **138**
Wyclif Cl. *EC1* *2A 8*
    (off Wyclif St.)
Wycliffe Cl. DA16: Well 1K **125**
Wycliffe Rd. SW11 . . . . .2E **118**
  SW19 .6K **135**
Wyclif St. EC1 . . . . .2A **8** (3B **84**)
Wycombe Gdns. NW11 . . . . .2J **63**
Wycombe Ho. *NW8* *3C 4*
    (off Grendon St.)
Wycombe Pl. SW18 . . . . .6A **118**
Wycombe Rd. HA0: Wemb 1G **79**
  IG2: Ilf 5D **52**
  N17 . . . . .1G **49**
Wycombe Sq. W8 . . . . .1H **99**
Wydehurst Rd. CR0: C'don 7G **157**
Wydell Cl. SM4: Mord 6F **153**
Wydeville Mnr. Rd. SE12 . . . . .4K **141**
Wye Cl. BR6: Orp 7K **161**
  HA4: Ruis 6E **38**
  TW15: Ashf 4D **128**
Wye Ct. *W13* *5B 78*
    (off Malvern Way)
Wyemead Cres. E4 . . . . .2B **36**
Wye St. SW11 . . . . .2B **118**
Wyevale Cl. HA5: Eastc 3J **39**
Wyfields IG5: Ilf 1F **53**
Wyfold Ho. SE2 . . . . .2D **108**
    (off Wolvercote Rd.)
Wyfold Rd. SW6 . . . . .7G **99**
Wyhill Wlk. RM10: Dag 6J **73**
Wyke Cl. TW7: Isle 6K **95**
Wyke Gdns. W7 . . . . .3A **96**
Wyke Green Golf Course 5K **95**
Wykeham Av. RM9: Dag 6C **72**
Wykeham Cl. UB7: Sip 6C **92**
Wykeham Ct. *NW4* *5E 44*
    (off Wykeham Rd.)
Wykeham Grn. RM9: Dag 6C **72**
Wykeham Hill HA9: Wemb 1F **61**
Wykeham Ho. *SE1* *5C 14*
    (off Union St.)
Wykeham Ri. N20 . . . . .1B **30**
Wykeham Rd. HA3: Kenton 4B **42**
  NW4 . . . . .4E **44**
Wyke Rd. E3 . . . . .7C **68**
  SW20 .2E **152**

Wylchin Cl. HA5: Eastc 3H **39**
Wyldes Cl. NW11 . . . . .1A **64**
Wyldfield Gdns. N9 . . . . .2A **34**
Wyld Way HA9: Wemb 6H **61**
Wyleu St. SE23 . . . . .7A **122**
Wylie Rd. UB2: S'hall 3E **94**
Wyllen Cl. E1 . . . . .4J **85**
Wymering Mans. *W9* *3J 81*
    (off Wymering Rd.)
Wymering Rd. W9 . . . . .3J **81**
Wymondham Ct. *NW8* *1B 82*
    (off Queensmead)
Wymond St. SW15 . . . . .3E **116**
Wynan Rd. E14 . . . . .5D **104**
Wynash Gdns. SM5: Cars 5C **166**
Wynaud Ct. N22 . . . . .6E **32**
Wyncham Av. DA15: Sidc 1J **143**
Wyncham Ho. *DA15: Sidc* *2A 144*
    (off Longlands Rd.)
Wynchgate HA3: Hrw W 7D **26**
  N14 . . . . .1C **32**
  N21 . . . . .1C **32**
  UB5: N'olt 5C **58**
Wyncroft Cl. BR1: Brom 3D **160**
Wyndale Av. NW9 . . . . .6G **43**
Wyndcliff Rd. SE7 . . . . .6K **105**
Wyndcroft Cl. EN2: Enf 3G **23**
Wyndham Cl. BR6: Farnb 1G **173**
  SM2: Sutt 7J **165**
Wyndham Ct. W7 . . . . .4A **96**
Wyndham Cres. N19 . . . . .3G **65**
  TW4: Houn 6E **112**
Wyndham Deedes Ho. *E2* *2G 85*
    (off Hackney Rd.)
Wyndham Est. SE5 . . . . .7C **102**
Wyndham Ho. *E14* *2D 104*
    (off Marsh Wall)
  SW1 . . . .*4G 17*
    (off Sloane Sq.)
Wyndham M. W1 . . . . .6E **4** (5D **82**)
Wyndham Pl. W1 . . . . .6E **4** (5D **82**)
Wyndham Rd. E6 . . . . .7B **70**
  EN4: E Barn 1J **31**
  KT2: King T 7F **133**
  SE5 . . . . .7C **102**
  W13 . . . . .3B **96**
Wyndhams Ct. *E8* *7F 67*
    (off Celandine Dr.)
Wyndham's Theatre 2E **12**
    (off Charing Cross Rd.)
Wyndham St. W1 . . . . .5E **4** (5D **82**)
Wyndham Yd. W1 . . . . .6E **4** (5D **82**)
Wyndhurst Cl. CR2: S Croy 7B **168**
Wyneham Rd. SE24 . . . . .5D **120**
Wynell Rd. SE23 . . . . .3K **139**
Wynford Pl. DA17: Belv 6G **109**
Wynford Rd. N1 . . . . .2K **83**
Wynford Way SE9 . . . . .3D **142**
Wynlie Gdns. HA5: Pinn 2K **39**
Wynn Bri. Cl. IG8: Wfd G 1B **52**
Wynndale Rd. E18 . . . . .1K **51**
Wynne Rd. SW9 . . . . .2A **120**
Wynn's Av. DA15: Sidc 5K **125**
Wynnstay Gdns. W8 . . . . .3J **99**
Wynter St. SW11 . . . . .4A **118**
Wynton Gdns. SE25 . . . . .5F **157**
Wynton Pl. W3 . . . . .6H **79**
Wynyard Ho. *SE11* *5K 101*
    (off Newburn St.)
Wynyard Ter. SE11 . . . . . . .5H **19** (5K **101**)
Wynyatt St. EC1 . . . . .2A **8** (3B **84**)
Wyre Gro. HA8: Edg 3C **28**
  UB3: Harl 4J **93**
Wyresdale Cres. UB6: G'frd 3K **77**
Wyteleaf Cl. HA4: Ruis 6E **38**
Wytham Ho. *NW8* *4B 4*
    (off Church St. Est.)
Wythburn Ct. *W1* *7E 4*
    (off Wythburn Pl.)
Wythburn Pl. W1 . . . . .1E **10** (6D **82**)
Wythenshawe Rd. RM10: Dag 3G **73**

Wythens Wlk. SE9 . . . . .6F **125**
Wythes Cl. BR1: Brom 2D **160**
Wythes Rd. E16 . . . . .1C **106**
Wythfield Rd. SE9 . . . . .6D **124**
Wyvenhoe Rd. HA2: Harr 4G **59**
Wyvern Est. KT3: N Mald 4C **152**
Wyvil Rd. SW8 . . . . .7J **101**
Wyvis St. E14 . . . . .5D **86**

X

Xylon Ho. KT4: Wor Pk 2D **164**

Y

Yabsley St. E14 . . . . .1E **104**
Yaldham Ho. *SE1* *4E 102*
    (off Old Kent Rd.)
Yalding Rd. SE16 . . . . .3G **103**
Yale Cl. TW4: Houn 5D **112**
Yale Ct. NW6 . . . . .5K **63**
Yarborough Rd. SW19 . . . . .1B **154**
Yard, The *N1* *1F 7*
    (off Caledonia St.)
Yardley Cl. E4 . . . . .5J **25**
Yardley Ct. SM3: Cheam 4E **164**
Yardley La. E4 . . . . .5J **25**
Yardley St. WC1 . . . . .2J **7** (3A **84**)
    (not continuous)
Yardmaster Ho. CR0: C'don 1D **168**
Yarlington Ct. *N11* *5K 31*
    (off Sparkford Gdns.)
Yarmouth Cres. N17 . . . . .5H **49**
Yarmouth Pl. W1 . . . . .5J **11** (1F **101**)
Yarnfield Sq. SE15 . . . . .1G **121**
Yarnton Way DA18: Belv, Erith 3F **109**
  SE2 . . . . .2C **108**
Yarrell Mans. *W14* *6H 99*
    (off Queen's Club Gdns.)
Yarrow Cres. E6 . . . . .5C **88**
Yarrow Ho. *E14* *3E 104*
    (off Stewart St.)
  W10 . . . .*5E 80*
    (off Sutton Way)
Yateley St. SE18 . . . . .3B **106**
Yatesbury Ct. E5 . . . . .5A **68**
    (off Studley Cl.)
Yates Ct. *NW2* *6F 63*
    (off Willesden La.)
  SE1 . . . .*7K 15*
    (off Abbey St.)
Yates Ho. *E2* *3G 85*
    (off Roberta St.)
Yatton Ho. *W10* *5E 80*
    (off Sutton Way)
YEADING 4A **76**
Yeading Av. HA2: Harr 2C **58**
Yeading Brook Meadows Nature Reserve
  . . . . .4J **75**
Yeading Ct. UB4: Yead 4A **76**
Yeading Gdns. UB4: Yead 5A **76**
Yeading Fork UB4: Yead 5A **76**
Yeading Ho. UB4: Yead 5B **76**
Yeading La. UB4: Yead 6A **76**
  UB5: N'olt 6K **75**
Yeading Wlk. HA2: Harr 5D **40**
Yeadon Ho. *W10* *5E 80*
    (off Sutton Way)
Yeames Cl. W13 . . . . .6A **78**
Yearby Ho. *W10* *4E 80*
    (off Sutton Way)
Yeate St. N1 . . . . .7D **66**
Yeatman Rd. N6 . . . . .6D **46**
Yeats Cl. NW10 . . . . .5A **62**
  SE13 . . . . .2F **123**
  W7 . . . . .7K **77**
Yeend Cl. KT8: W Mole 4E **148**
Yeldham Ho. *W6* *5F 99*
    (off Yeldham Rd.)

Yeldham Rd. W6 . . . . .5F **99**
Yeldham Vs. *W6* *5F 99*
    (off Yeldham Rd.)
Yellowhammer Ct. NW9 . . . . .2A **44**
    (off Eagle Dr.)
Yelverton Lodge *TW1: Twick* *7C 114*
    (off Richmond Rd.)
Yelverton Rd. SW11 . . . . .2B **118**
Ye Market *CR2: S Croy* *5D 168*
    (off Selsdon Rd.)
Yenston Cl. SM4: Mord 6J **153**
Yeoman Cl. E6 . . . . .7F **89**
  SE27 . . . . .3B **138**
Yeoman Ct. *E14* *4K 86*
    (off Tweed Wlk.)
  TW5: Hest 7D **94**
Yeoman Dr. TW19: Stanw 1A **128**
Yeoman Rd. UB5: N'olt 7C **58**
Yeomans Acre HA4: Ruis 6J **39**
Yeomans M. TW7: Isle 6H **113**
Yeoman's Row SW3 . . . . . .2D **16** (3C **100**)
Yeoman St. SE8 . . . . .4A **104**
Yeomans Way EN3: Enf H 2D **24**
Yeoman's Yd. E1 . . . . .2K **15**
Yeo St. E3 .5D **86**
Yeovil Cl. BR6: Orp 2J **173**
Yeovil Ho. *W10* *4E 80*
    (off Sutton Way)
Yeovilton Pl. KT2: King T 5C **132**
Yerbury Rd. N19 . . . . .3H **65**
    (not continuous)
Yester Dr. BR7: Chst 7C **142**
Yester Pk. BR7: Chst 7D **142**
Yester Rd. BR7: Chst 7C **142**
Yetev Lev Ct. E5 . . . . .1G **67**
Yew Av. UB7: Yiew 7A **74**
Yew Cl. IG9: Buck H 2G **37**
Yewdale Cl. BR1: Brom 6G **141**
Yewfield Rd. NW10 . . . . .6B **62**
Yew Gro. NW2 . . . . .4F **63**
Yew Ho. *SE16* *2K 103*
    (off Woodland Cres.)
Yews, The TW15: Ashf 4D **128**
Yewtree Av. RM10: Dag 5J **73**
Yew Tree Cl. DA16: Well 1A **126**
  KT4: Wor Pk 1A **164**
  N21 . . . . .7F **23**
  SE13 . . . . .3E **122**
Yewtree Cl. HA2: Harr 4F **41**
  N22 . . . . .1G **47**
Yew Tree Cl. NW11 . . . . .5H **45**
    (off Bridge La.)
  SM2: Sutt *7A 166*
    (off Walnut M.)
Yew Tree Gdns. RM6: Chad H 5E **54**
  RM7: Rom 5K **55**
    (off Yew Tree Gdns.)
  RM7: Rom *5K 55*
    (off Yew Tree Gdns.)
  SW16 .4G **137**
Yew Tree Rd. BR3: Beck 3B **158**
  UB10: Uxb 1B **74**
  W12 . . . . .7B **80**
Yew Trees TW17: Shep 4B **146**
Yew Tree Wlk. TW4: Houn 5D **112**
Yew Tree Way CR0: Sels 7B **170**
Yew Wlk. HA1: Harr 1J **59**
YIEWSLEY 1A **92**
Yiewsley Ct. UB7: Yiew 1A **92**
YMCA Hawker Cen. 5D **132**
Yoakley Rd. N16 . . . . .2E **66**
Yoga Way KT4: Wor Pk 2C **164**
Yoke Cl. N7 .6J **65**
Yolande Gdns. SE9 . . . . .5C **124**
Yonge Pk. N4 . . . . .3A **66**
York Av. DA15: Sidc 2J **143**
  HA7: Stan 1B **42**
  SE17 . . . . .5C **102**
  SW14 .5J **115**
  UB3: Hayes 5E **74**
  W7 . . . . .1J **95**

York Bri. NW1 . . . . .3G 5 (4E **82**)
York Bldgs. WC2 . . . . .3F **13** (7J **83**)
York Cl. E6 . . . . .6D **88**
  SE5 . . . . .2C **120**
    (off Lilford Rd.)
  SM4: Mord 4K **153**
  TW18: Staines 6A **128**
  W7 . . . . .1J **95**
York Ct. N14 . . . . .3D **32**
York Ga. N14 . . . . .7D **22**
  NW1 . . . . .4G 5 (4E **82**)
York Gro. SE15 . . . . .1J **121**
York Hall Leisure Cen. 2H **85**
York Hill SE27 . . . . .3B **138**
York Ho. E16 . . . . .1J **105**
    (off De Quincey M.)
  EN2: Enf 1J **23**
  HA9: Wemb 4G **61**
  KT2: King T 7F **133**
    (off Elm Rd.)
  SE1 . . . . .2H **19** (3E **101**)
  SW3 .5F **17**
  W1 . . . . .5E **4**
    (off York St.)
  W8 . . . . .2K **99**
    (off York Ho. Pl.)
York Ho. Pl. W8 . . . . .2K **99**
Yorkland Av.
  DA16: Well 3K **125**
Yorkley Ho. W10 . . . . .4E **80**
    (off Sutton Way)
York Mans. SE17 . . . . .5C **102**
    (off Browning St.)
  SW5 .5K **99**
    (off Earls Ct. Rd.)
  SW11 . . . . .1E **118**
    (off Prince of Wales Dr.)
  W1 . . . . .5G **5**
    (off Chiltern St.)
York M. IG1: Ilf 3E **70**
  NW5 .5F **65**
York Pde. NW9 . . . . .6C **44**
    (off W. Hendon B'way.)
  TW8: Bford 5D **96**
York Pas. W8 . . . . .2K **99**
    (off York Ho. Pl.)

York Pl. IG1: Ilf 2E **70**
  RM10: Dag 6J **73**
  SW11 . . . . .3B **118**
  WC2 .3F **13**
York Pl. Mans. W1 . . . . .5F **5**
    (off Baker St.)
York Ri. BR6: Orp 2J **173**
  NW5 .3F **65**
York Rd.
  CR0: C'don 7A **156**
  E4 . . . . .4H **35**
  E7 . . . . .6J **69**
  E10 . . . . .3E **68**
  E17 . . . . .5K **49**
  EN5: New Bar 5F **21**
  HA6: Nwood 2J **39**
  IG1: Ilf 3E **70**
  KT2: King T 7F **133**
  N11 . . . . .6C **32**
  N18 . . . . .6C **34**
  N21 . . . . .7J **23**
  RM13: Rain 7K **73**
  SE1 . . . . .6H **13** (2K **101**)
  SM1: Sutt 6J **165**
  SM2: Sutt 6J **165**
  SW11 . . . . .4A **118**
  SW18 . . . . .4A **118**
  SW19 . . . . .6A **136**
  TW3: Houn 3F **113**
  TW8: Bford 5D **96**
  TW10: Rich 5F **115**
  TW11: Tedd 4J **131**
  W3 . . . . .6J **79**
  W5 . . . . .3C **96**
York Rd. Bus. Cen. SW11 . . . . .2B **118**
Yorkshire Cl. N16 . . . . .3E **66**
Yorkshire Gdns. N18 . . . . .5C **34**
YORKSHIRE GREY 5B **124**
Yorkshire Grey Pl. NW3 . . . . .4A **64**
Yorkshire Grey Yd. WC1 . . . . .6G **7**
Yorkshire Rd. CR4: Mitc 5J **155**
  E14 . . . . .6A **86**
York Sq. E14 . . . . .6A **86**
York St. CR4: Mitc 7E **154**
  TW1: Twick 1A **132**
  W1 . . . . .6E **4** (5D **82**)

York St. Chambers W1 . . . . .6E **4**
    (off York St.)
York Ter. DA8: Erith 1J **127**
  EN2: Enf 1H **23**
  SE7 .4A **106**
    (off Gallon Cl.)
York Ter. E. NW1 . . . . .4H 5 (4E **82**)
York Ter. W. NW1 . . . . .4G 5 (4E **82**)
Yorkton St. E2 . . . . .2G **85**
York Way KT9: Chess 7E **162**
  N1 . . . . .1F **7** (2J **83**)
  N7 . . . . .6H **65**
  N20 . . . . .3J **31**
  TW13: Hanw 3D **130**
    (not continuous)
York Way Ct. N1 . . . . .1J **83**
    (not continuous)
York Way Est. N7 . . . . .6J **65**
Young Cl. NW6 . . . . .7G **63**
Youngmans Cl. EN2: Enf 1H **23**
Young Rd. E16 . . . . .6A **88**
Youngs Bldgs. EC1 . . . . .3D **8**
Youngs Ct. SW11 . . . . .1E **118**
Youngs Rd. IG2: Ilf 5H **53**
Young St. W8 . . . . .2K **99**
Young Vic Theatre, The 6K **13**
Yoxall Ho. W10 . . . . .4E **80**
    (off Sutton Way)
Yoxford Cl. RM6: Chad H 5B **54**
Yoxley App. IG2: Ilf 6G **53**
Yoxley Dr. IG2: Ilf 6G **53**
Ypres Pl. RM9: Dag 1B **90**
Yukon Rd. SW12 . . . . .7F **119**
Yunus Khan Cl. E17 . . . . .5C **50**
Yvon Ho. SW11 . . . . .1E **118**
    (off Alexandra Av.)

Z

Zachary Ct. SW1 . . . . .4D **18**
    (off Montaigne Cl.)
Zachary Ho. SW9 . . . . .1K **119**
    (off Lett Rd.)
Zachary M. E3 . . . . .3B **86**
    (off Tredegar Sq.)

Zahra Ho. NW10 . . . . .3E **80**
    (off Harrow Rd.)
Zambezi Dr. N9 . . . . .3D **34**
Zampa Rd. SE16 . . . . .5J **103**
Zander Ct. E2 . . . . .3G **85**
Zangwill Ho. NW6 . . . . .2H **81**
    (off Carlton Vale)
Zangwill Rd. SE3 . . . . .1B **124**
Zapotec Ho. SE8 . . . . .4K **103**
    (off Chilton Gro.)
Zealand Av. UB7: Harm 3E **174**
Zealand Ho. SE5 . . . . .2C **120**
    (off Denmark Rd.)
  SE18 . . . . .4C **106**
Zealand Rd. E3 . . . . .2A **86**
Zeller Ho. E20 . . . . .5D **68**
    (off Scarlet Cl.)
Zenith Cl. NW9 . . . . .3K **43**
Zenith Lodge N3 . . . . .7E **30**
Zennor Rd. SW12 . . . . .1G **137**
Zennor Rd. Ind. Est. SW12 . . . . .1G **137**
Zenobia Mans. W14 . . . . .6H **99**
    (off Queen's Club Gdns.)
Zenoria St. SE22 . . . . .4F **121**
Zermatt Rd.
  CR7: Thor H 4C **156**
Zetland Ho. W8 . . . . .3K **99**
    (off Marloes Rd.)
Zetland St. E14 . . . . .5D **86**
Zeus Ct. UB7: Yiew 1A **92**
Zinc Bldg., The SE13 . . . . .4G **123**
Zinnia Mans. E20 . . . . .6D **68**
    (off Olympic Pk. Av.)
Zion Ho. E1 . . . . .6J **85**
    (off Jubilee St.)
Zion Pl. CR7: Thor H 4D **156**
Zion Rd. CR7: Thor H 4D **156**
Zoar St. SE1 . . . . .4C **14** (1C **102**)
Zodiac Cl. HA8: Edg 7B **28**
Zodiac Ct. CR0: C'don 1B **168**
Zodiac Ho. E3 . . . . .4C **86**
    (off Wellington Way)
Zoffany St. N19 . . . . .2H **65**
Zona Ct. SE1 . . . . .3F **103**
    (off Grange Wlk.)
Zulu M. SW11 . . . . .2C **118**

HOSPITALS, HOSPICES and
selected HEALTHCARE FACILITIES
covered by this atlas.

N.B. Where it is not possible to name these facilities on the map,
the reference given is for the road in which they are situated.

ASHFORD HOSPITAL 2A **128**
   London Road
   ASHFORD
   TW15 3AA
   Tel: 01784 884488

BARKING HOSPITAL 7K **71**
   Upney Lane
   BARKING
   IG11 9LX
   Tel: 020 3288 2300

BARNES HOSPITAL 3A **116**
   South Worple Way
   SW14 8SU
   Tel: 020 3513 3600

BARNET HOSPITAL 4A **20**
   Wellhouse Lane
   BARNET
   EN5 3DJ
   Tel: 0845 111 4000

BECKENHAM BEACON 2B **158**
   379 Croydon Road
   BECKENHAM
   BR3 3QL
   Tel: 01689 866667

BECKTON CYGNET HOSPITAL 6E **88**
   23 Tunnan Leys
   E6 6ZB
   Tel: 020 7511 2299

BETHLEM ROYAL HOSPITAL 7C **158**
   Monks Orchard Road
   BECKENHAM
   BR3 3BX
   Tel: 020 3228 6000

BLACKHEATH BMI HOSPITAL, THE 3H **123**
   40-42 Lee Terrace
   SE3 9UD
   Tel: 020 8318 7722

BLACKHEATH BMI HOSPITAL, THE
(OUTPATIENT DEPARTMENT) 3H **123**
   Independents Road
   SE3 9LF
   Tel: 020 8297 4500

BLACKHEATH CYGNET HOSPITAL 1E **122**
   80 Blackheath Hill
   SE10 8AB
   Tel: 020 8692 4007

BLOOMFIELD COURT HOSPITAL 5F **107**
   69 Bloomfield Road
   SE18 7JN
   Tel: 01992 785 460

BMI CITY MEDICAL 7G **9**
   17 St Helen's Place
   EC3A 6DG
   Tel: 0845 123 5380

BMI EMERGENCY CARE CENTRE 3K **59**
   The Clementine Hospital
   Sudbury Hill
   HARROW
   HA1 3RX
   Tel: 020 8872 3999

BRENT OLDER PEOPLE DAY HOSPITAL 1C **80**
   341 Harlesden Road
   NW10 3RX
   Tel: 020 8459 3562

BRIDGEWAYS DAY HOSPITAL 6C **160**
   Turpington Lane
   BROMLEY
   BR2 8JA
   Tel: 020 8462 0170

BUSHEY SPIRE HOSPITAL 1E **26**
   Heathbourne Road
   Bushey Heath
   BUSHEY
   WD23 1RD
   Tel: 020 8901 5505

CAMDEN MEWS DAY HOSPITAL 7G **65**
   1-5 Camden Mews
   NW1 9DB
   Tel: 020 3317 4740

CASSEL HOSPITAL 4D **132**
   1 Ham Common
   RICHMOND
   TW10 7JF
   Tel: 020 8483 2900

CAVELL BMI HOSPITAL 2F **23**
   Cavell Drive
   ENFIELD
   EN2 7PR
   Tel: 020 8366 2122

CENTRAL MIDDLESEX HOSPITAL 3J **79**
   Acton Lane
   NW10 7NS
   Tel: 020 8965 5733

CHARING CROSS HOSPITAL 6F **99**
   Fulham Palace Road
   W6 8RF
   Tel: 020 3311 1234

CHASE FARM HOSPITAL 1F **23**
   127 The Ridgeway
   ENFIELD
   EN2 8JL
   Tel: 0845 111 4000

CHELSEA & WESTMINSTER HOSPITAL 7A **16** (6A **100**)
   369 Fulham Road
   SW10 9NH
   Tel: 020 3315 8000

CHILDREN'S HOSPITAL, THE (LEWISHAM) 5D **122**
   Lewisham University Hospital
   Lewisham High Street
   SE13 6LH
   Tel: 020 8333 3000

CHURCHILL CAMBIAN HOSPITAL 1K **19** (3A **102**)
   Barkham Terrace
   Lambeth Road
   SE1 7PW
   Tel: 0800 138 1418

CITY & HACKNEY CENTRE FOR MENTAL HEALTH 5K **67**
   Homerton Row
   E9 6SR
   Tel: 020 8510 5000

CLAYPONDS HOSPITAL 4E **96**
   Sterling Place
   W5 4RN
   Tel: 020 8568 0064

CLEMENTINE CHURCHILL BMI HOSPITAL 2K **59**
   Sudbury Hill
   HARROW
   HA1 3RX
   Tel: 020 8872 3872

COBORN CENTRE FOR ADOLESCENT MENTAL HEALTH, THE
............................4B **88**
   Glen Road
   E13 8SP
   Tel: 020 7540 6789

CROMWELL BUPA HOSPITAL 4K **99**
   162-174 Cromwell Road
   SW5 0TU
   Tel: 020 7460 2000

CROYDON UNIVERSITY HOSPITAL 6B **156**
   530 London Road
   THORNTON HEATH
   CR7 7YE
   Tel: 020 8401 3000

CYGNET LODGE 6E **122**
   44 Lewisham Park
   Lewisham
   SE13 6QZ
   Tel: 020 8314 5123

DEMELZA HOSPICE CARE FOR CHILDREN 6D **124**
   5 Wensley Close
   SE9 5AB
   Tel: 020 8859 9800

DULWICH COMMUNITY HOSPITAL 4E **120**
   East Dulwich Grove
   SE22 8PT
   Tel: 020 3049 8800

EALING CYGNET HOSPITAL 5E **78**
   22 Corfton Road
   W5 2HT
   Tel: 020 8991 6699

EALING HOSPITAL 1H **95**
   Uxbridge Road
   SOUTHALL
   UB1 3HW
   Tel: 020 8967 5000

EAST HAM CARE CENTRE & DAY HOSPITAL 7B **70**
   Shrewsbury Road
   E7 8QP
   Tel: 020 8475 2001

EASTMAN DENTAL HOSPITAL & DENTAL INSTITUTE
.....................................3G 7 (4K 83)
256 Gray's Inn Road
WC1X 8LD
Tel: 020 3456 7899

EDGWARE COMMUNITY HOSPITAL 7C 28
Burnt Oak Broadway
EDGWARE
HA8 0AD
Tel: 020 8952 2381

ELTHAM COMMUNITY HOSPITAL 6D 124
Passey Place
SE9 5DQ
Tel: 020 3049 0400

ERITH & DISTRICT HOSPITAL 6K 109
Park Crescent
ERITH
DA8 3EE
Tel: 01322 356186

EVELINA CHILDREN'S HOSPITAL 1G 19
St Thomas' Hospital
Westminster Bridge Road
SE1 7EH
Tel: 020 7188 7188

FINCHLEY MEMORIAL HOSPITAL 7F 31
Granville Road
N12 0JE
Tel: 020 8349 7500

FITZROY SQUARE BMI HOSPITAL 4A 6 (4G 83)
14 Fitzroy Square
W1T 6AH
Tel: 020 7388 4954

GARDEN BMI HOSPITAL, THE......................3E 44
46-50 Sunny Gardens Road
NW4 1RP
Tel: 020 8457 4500

GATEWAY SURGICAL CENTRE 4B 88
Cherry Tree Way
Glen Road
E13 8SL
Tel: 020 7476 4000

**GENERAL MEDICAL WALK-IN CENTRE
(LIVERPOOL STREET)** 5H 9 (5E 84)
Exchange Arcade
Bishopsgate
EC2M 3WA
Tel: 0845 437 0691

GOODMAYES HOSPITAL 5A 54
Barley Lane
ILFORD
IG3 8XJ
Tel: 0844 600 1207

GORDON HOSPITAL 4C 18 (4H 101)
Bloomburg Street
SW1V 2RH
Tel: 020 8746 8733

GRAYS COURT COMMUNITY HOSPITAL 7H 73
John Parker Close
DAGENHAM
RM10 9SR
Tel: 020 8724 1463

GREAT ORMOND STREET HOSPITAL FOR CHILDREN
.....................................4F 7 (4J 83)
Great Ormond Street
WC1N 3JH
Tel: 020 7405 9200

GREENWICH & BEXLEY COMMUNITY HOSPICE 5C 108
185 Bostall Hill
SE2 0GB
Tel: 020 8312 2244

GUY'S HOSPITAL 5F 15 (2D 102)
Great Maze Pond
SE1 9RT
Tel: 020 7188 7188

GUY'S NUFFIELD HOUSE 6E 14
Guy's Hospital
Newcomen Street
SE1 1YR
Tel: 020 7188 5282

HAMMERSMITH HOSPITAL 6C 80
Du Cane Road
W12 0HS
Tel: 020 3313 1000

HARLEY STREET CLINIC, THE 5J 5 (5F 83)
35 Weymouth Street
W1G 8BJ
Tel: 020 7935 7700

HARLINGTON HOSPICE 5F 93
St. Peters Way
HAYES
UB3 5AB
Tel: 020 8759 0453

HARROW CYGNET HOSPITAL 2J 59
London Road
HARROW
HA1 3JL
Tel: 020 8966 7000

HAVEN HOUSE CHILDREN'S HOSPICE 6C 36
High Road
WOODFORD GREEN
IG8 9LB
Tel: 020 8505 9944

HAYES GROVE PRIORY HOSPITAL 2J 171
Prestons Road
Hayes
BROMLEY
BR2 7AS
Tel: 020 8462 7722

HEART HOSPITAL, THE 6J 5 (5E 82)
16-18 Westmoreland Street
W1G 8PH
Tel: 020 3456 7898

HIGHGATE HOSPITAL 6D 46
17- 19 View Road
N6 4DJ
Tel: 020 8341 4182

HIGHGATE MENTAL HEALTH CENTRE 2F 65
Dartmouth Park Hill
N19 5NX
Tel: 020 7561 4000

HILLINGDON HOSPITAL 5B 74
Pield Heath Road
UXBRIDGE
UB8 3NN
Tel: 01895 238282

HOLLY HOUSE HOSPITAL 2E 36
High Road
BUCKHURST HILL
IG9 5HX
Tel: 020 8505 3311

HOMERTON UNIVERSITY HOSPITAL 5K 67
Homerton Row
E9 6SR
Tel: 020 8510 5555

HOSPITAL FOR TROPICAL DISEASES 4B 6
Mortimer Market
Capper Street
WC1E 6JB
Tel: 020 3456 7891

HOSPITAL OF ST JOHN & ST ELIZABETH 2B 82
60 Grove End Road
NW8 9NH
Tel: 020 7806 4000

JOHN HOWARD CENTRE 5A 68
12 Kenworthy Road
E9 5TD
Tel: 020 8510 2003

KING EDWARD VII'S HOSPITAL SISTER AGNES
.....................................5H 5 (5E 82)
5-10 Beaumont Street
W1G 6AA
Tel: 020 7486 4411

KING GEORGE HOSPITAL 4A 54
Barley Lane
ILFORD
IG3 8YB
Tel: 020 8983 8000

KING'S COLLEGE HOSPITAL 2D 120
Denmark Hill
SE5 9RS
Tel: 020 3299 9000

KING'S OAK BMI HOSPITAL 1F 23
The Ridgeway
ENFIELD
EN2 8SD
Tel: 020 8370 9500

KINGSTON HOSPITAL 1H 151
Galsworthy Road
KINGSTON UPON THAMES
KT2 7QB
Tel: 020 8546 7711

LAMBETH HOSPITAL 3K 119
108 Landor Road
SW9 9NU
Tel: 020 3228 6000

LISTER HOSPITAL, THE 6J 17 (5F 101)
Chelsea Bridge Road
SW1W 8RH
Tel: 020 7730 3417

LONDON BRIDGE HOSPITAL 4F 15 (1D 102)
27 Tooley Street
SE1 2PR
Tel: 0845 602 7906

LONDON CHEST HOSPITAL 2J 85
Bonner Road
E2 9JX
Tel: 020 3146 5000

LONDON CLINIC 4H 5 (4E 82)
20 Devonshire Place
W1G 6BW
Tel: 020 7935 4444

LONDON EYE HOSPITAL 7J 5
8-10 Harley Street
W1G 9PF
Tel: 0800 612 2021

LONDON INDEPENDENT BMI HOSPITAL 5K 85
1 Beaumont Square
E1 4NL
Tel: 020 7780 2400

LONDON WELBECK HOSPITAL 6J 5
27 Welbeck Street
W1G 8EN
Tel: 020 7224 2242

MARGARET CENTRE (HOSPICE) 6G 51
Whipps Cross University Hospital
Whipps Cross Road
E11 1NR
Tel: 020 8535 6604

MARIE CURIE HOSPICE, HAMPSTEAD 5B **64**
11 Lyndhurst Gardens
NW3 5NS
Tel: 020 7853 3400

MAUDSLEY HOSPITAL, THE 2D **120**
Denmark Hill
SE5 8AZ
Tel: 020 3228 6000

MEADOW HOUSE HOSPICE 2H **95**
Uxbridge Road
SOUTHALL
UB1 3HW
Tel: 020 8967 5179

MEMORIAL HOSPITAL 2E **124**
Shooters Hill
SE18 3RG
Tel: 020 8836 8500

MILDMAY HOSPITAL 2J **9** (3F **85**)
Tabernacle Gardens
E2 7DZ
Tel: 020 7613 6300

MILE END HOSPITAL 4K **85**
Bancroft Road
E1 4DG
Tel: 020 3416 5000

MINOR INJURIES UNIT (DAGENHAM) 7H **73**
Grays Court Community Hospital
John Parker Close
DAGENHAM
RM10 9SR
Tel: 020 8724 1463

MINOR INJURIES UNIT (ROEHAMPTON) 6C **116**
Roehampton Lane
SW15 5PN
Tel: 020 8487 6000

MINOR INJURIES UNIT
(ST BARTHOLOMEW'S HOSPITAL) 6B **8** (5B **84**)
West Smithfield
EC1A 7BE
Tel: 020 3465 6843

MINOR INJURIES UNIT (SILVERTOWN) 1K **105**
The Practice
12a Wesley Avenue
E16 1RZ
Tel: 020 3040 0100

MOLESEY HOSPITAL 5E **148**
High Street
WEST MOLESEY
KT8 2LU
Tel: 020 8941 4481

MOORFIELDS EYE HOSPITAL 2E **8** (3D **84**)
162 City Road
EC1V 2PD
Tel: 020 7253 3411

NATIONAL HOSPITAL FOR NEUROLOGY & NEUROSURGERY
..........................4F **7** (4J **83**)
Queen Square
WC1N 3BG
Tel: 020 3456 7890

NELSON HOSPITAL 2H **153**
Kingston Road
SW20 8DB
Tel: 020 8296 3795

NEWHAM CENTRE FOR MENTAL HEALTH 4B **88**
Cherry Tree Way
Glen Road
E13 8SP
Tel: 020 7540 4380

NEWHAM UNIVERSITY HOSPITAL 4A **88**
Glen Road
E13 8SL
Tel: 020 7476 4000

NEW VICTORIA HOSPITAL 1A **152**
184 Coombe Lane West
KINGSTON UPON THAMES
KT2 7EG
Tel: 020 8949 9000

NHS WALK-IN CENTRE
(ALEXANDRA CLINIC, THE) 2E **58**
275 Alexandra Avenue
HARROW
HA2 9DX
Tel: 020 8427 2470

NHS WALK-IN CENTRE (ASHFORD) 2A **128**
Ashford Hospital
London Road
ASHFORD
TW15 3AA
Tel: 01784 884488

NHS WALK-IN CENTRE (BARKING HOSPITAL) 7K **71**
Upney Lane
BARKING
IG11 9LX
Tel: 020 8924 6262

NHS WALK-IN CENTRE (BOW) 4D **86**
St. Andrew's Health Centre
2 Hannaford Walk
E3 3FF
Tel: 020 8980 1888

NHS WALK-IN CENTRE (CHESSINGTON) 4E **162**
Gosbury Hill Health Centre
Orchard Gardens
CHESSINGTON
KT9 1AG
Tel: 020 8974 1884

NHS WALK-IN CENTRE (CLAPHAM JUNCTION) 3C **118**
The Junction Health Centre
Arches 5-8, Clapham Junction Station
Grant Road
SW11 2NU
Tel: 0333 200 1718

NHS WALK-IN CENTRE
(CRICKLEWOOD HEALTH CENTRE) 4F **63**
Britannia Business Centre
Cricklewood Lane
NW2 1DZ
Tel: 03000 334335

NHS WALK-IN CENTRE (CROYDON) 3C **168**
Impact House
Edridge Road
CROYDON
CR9 1PJ
Tel: 020 3040 0800

NHS WALK-IN CENTRE (EARL'S COURT) 4K **99**
Earl's Court Health & Wellbeing Centre
2b Hogarth Road
SW5 0PT
Tel: 020 7341 0300

NHS WALK-IN CENTRE (EDGWARE) 7C **28**
Edgware Community Hospital
Burnt Oak Broadway
EDGWARE
HA8 0AD
Tel: 020 8732 6459

NHS WALK-IN CENTRE (FINCHLEY) 7F **31**
Finchley Memorial Hospital
Granville Road
N12 0JE
Tel: 020 8349 7470

NHS WALK-IN CENTRE (ISLE OF DOGS) 2C **104**
Barkantine Practice
121 Westferry Road
E14 8JH
Tel: 020 7791 8080

NHS WALK-IN CENTRE (LEYTON) 3D **68**
Oliver Road Medical Centre
75 Oliver Road
E10 5LG
Tel: 020 8430 8282

NHS WALK-IN CENTRE (LISTER HEALTH CENTRE) 1F **121**
101 Peckham Road
SE15 5LJ
Tel: 020 3049 8430

NHS WALK-IN CENTRE (LOXFORD, ILFORD) 5G **71**
Loxford Practice, The
417 Ilford Lane
ILFORD
IG1 2SN
Tel: 0300 300 1700

NHS WALK-IN CENTRE (MITCHAM) 4D **154**
Wilson Health Centre, The
Cranmer Road
MITCHAM
CR4 4TP
Tel: 020 3458 5100

NHS WALK-IN CENTRE (PARSONS GREEN) 1J **117**
5-7 Parsons Green
SW6 4UL
Tel: 020 8102 4300

NHS WALK-IN CENTRE (PINNER) 3C **40**
Pinn Medical Centre, The
37 Love Lane
PINNER
HA5 3EE
Tel: 020 8866 5766

NHS WALK-IN CENTRE
(RICHIE STREET GROUP PRACTICE) 2A **84**
34 Ritchie Street
N1 0DG
Tel: 020 7837 1663

NHS WALK-IN CENTRE (SOHO) 1C **12**
1 Frith Street
W1D 3HZ
Tel: 020 7534 6575

NHS WALK-IN CENTRE (SOUTHALL) 3C **94**
Featherstone Road Health Centre
Hartington Road
SOUTHALL
UB2 5BQ
Tel: 020 3313 9880

NHS WALK-IN CENTRE (STRATFORD) 7G **69**
DMC Healthcare One
10 Vicarage Lane
E15 4ES
Tel: 020 8536 2277

NHS WALK-IN CENTRE (STREATHAM) 3J **137**
Gracefield Gardens Health Centre
Gracefield Gardens
SW16 2ST
Tel: 020 3049 4040

NHS WALK-IN CENTRE (TEDDINGTON) 6J **131**
Teddington Memorial Hospital
Hampton Road
TEDDINGTON
TW11 0JL
Tel: 020 8714 4004

NHS WALK-IN CENTRE (THAMESMEAD) 2J **107**
Thamesmead Health Centre
4-5 Thames Reach
SE28 0NY
Tel: 020 8319 5880

**NHS WALK-IN CENTRE
(WALDRON HEALTH CENTRE)** 7B **104**
Amersham Vale
SE14 6LD
Tel: 020 3049 2370

NHS WALK-IN CENTRE (WEMBLEY) 6D **60**
116 Chaplin Road
WEMBLEY
HA0 4UZ
Tel: 020 8795 6112

NHS WALK-IN CENTRE (WEST KILBURN) 4H **81**
Half Penny Steps Health Centre
427-429 Harrow Road
W10 4RE
Tel: 020 8962 8700

NHS WALK-IN CENTRE (WOOLWICH) 4F **107**
Clover Health Centre
General Gordon Place
SE18 6AB
Tel: 020 8331 0567

NIGHTINGALE HOSPITAL 5D **4** (5C **82**)
11-19 Lisson Grove
NW1 6SH
Tel: 020 7535 7700

NOAH'S ARK CHILDREN'S HOSPICE 4C **20**
Beauchamp Court
10 Victors Way
BARNET
EN5 5TZ
Tel: 020 8449 8877

NORTH EAST LONDON NHS TREATMENT CENTRE 4A **54**
King George Hospital
Barley Lane
ILFORD
IG3 8YB
Tel: 0333 200 4069

NORTH LONDON CLINIC 2B **34**
15 Church Street
N9 9DY
Tel: 020 8956 1234

NORTH LONDON HOSPICE (BARNET) 3F **31**
47 Woodside Avenue
N12 8TT
Tel: 020 8343 8841

NORTH LONDON HOSPICE (ENFIELD) 3H **33**
110 Barrowell Green
N21 3AY
Tel: 020 8343 8841

NORTH LONDON PRIORY HOSPITAL 1D **32**
The Bourne
N14 6RA
Tel: 020 8882 8191

NORTH MIDDLESEX UNIVERSITY HOSPITAL 5K **33**
Sterling Way
N18 1QX
Tel: 020 8887 2000

NORTHWICK PARK HOSPITAL 7A **42**
Watford Road
HARROW
HA1 3UJ
Tel: 020 8864 3232

OLD BROAD STREET PRIVATE MEDICAL CENTRE 7G **9**
31 Old Broad Street
EC2N 1HT
Tel: 020 7496 3555

ORPINGTON HOSPITAL 4K **173**
Sevenoaks Road
ORPINGTON
BR6 9JU
Tel: 01689 863000

PARK ROYAL CENTRE (FOR MENTAL HEALTH) 2J **79**
Central Way
NW10 7NS
Tel: 020 8955 4400

PARKSIDE HOSPITAL 3F **135**
53 Parkside
SW19 5NX
Tel: 020 8971 8000

PEMBRIDGE PALLIATIVE CARE CENTRE 5F **81**
St. Charles Hospital
Exmoor Street
W10 6DZ
Tel: 020 8962 4410

PORTLAND HOSPITAL FOR WOMEN & CHILDREN

.... 4K **5** (4F **83**)
205-209 Great Portland Street
W1W 5AH
Tel: 020 7580 4400

PRINCESS GRACE HOSPITAL 4G **5** (4E **82**)
42-52 Nottingham Place
W1M 3FD
Tel: 020 7486 1234

PRINCESS ROYAL UNIVERSITY HOSPITAL 3E **172**
Farnborough Common
ORPINGTON
BR6 8ND
Tel: 01689 863000

QUEEN CHARLOTTE'S & CHELSEA HOSPITAL 6C **80**
Du Cane Road
W12 0HS
Tel: 020 3313 1111

QUEEN ELIZABETH HOSPITAL 7C **106**
Stadium Road
SE18 4QH
Tel: 020 8836 6000

QUEEN MARY'S HOSPITAL FOR CHILDREN 1A **166**
Wrythe Lane
CARSHALTON
SM5 1AA
Tel: 020 8296 2000

QUEEN MARY'S HOSPITAL, ROEHAMPTON 6C **116**
Roehampton Lane
SW15 5PN
Tel: 020 8725 3579

QUEEN MARY'S HOSPITAL, SIDCUP 6A **144**
Frognal Avenue
SIDCUP
DA14 6LT
Tel: 020 8302 2678

QUEEN'S HOSPITAL 7K **55**
Rom Valley Way
ROMFORD
RM7 0AG
Tel: 01708 435000

RICHARD DESMOND CHILDREN'S EYE CENTRE 2E **8**
Moorfields Eye Hospital
3 Peerless Street
EC1V 9EZ
Tel: 020 7253 3411

RICHARD HOUSE CHILDREN'S HOSPICE 7B **88**
Richard House Drive
E16 3RG
Tel: 020 7511 0222

RICHMOND ROYAL HOSPITAL 3E **114**
Kew Foot Road
RICHMOND
TW9 2TE
Tel: 020 3513 3238

RODING SPIRE HOSPITAL 3B **52**
Roding Lane South
ILFORD
IG4 5PZ
Tel: 020 8709 7817

ROEHAMPTON HUNTERCOMBE HOSPITAL 7C **116**
Holybourne Avenue
SW15 4JD
Tel: 020 8780 6155

ROEHAMPTON PRIORY HOSPITAL 4B **116**
Priory Lane
SW15 5JJ
Tel: 020 8876 8261

ROYAL BROMPTON HOSPITAL 5C **16** (5C **100**)
Sydney Street
SW3 6NP
Tel: 020 7352 8121

ROYAL BROMPTON HOSPITAL (OUTPATIENTS)

.... 5B **16** (5B **100**)
Fulham Road
SW3 6HP
Tel: 020 7351 8011

ROYAL FREE HOSPITAL 5C **64**
Pond Street
NW3 2QG
Tel: 020 7794 0500

ROYAL HOSPITAL FOR NEURO-DISABILITY 6G **117**
West Hill
SW15 3SW
Tel: 020 8780 4500

ROYAL LONDON HOSPITAL, THE 5H **85**
Whitechapel Road
E1 1BB
Tel: 020 3416 5000

ROYAL LONDON HOSPITAL FOR INTEGRATED MEDICINE
.... 5F **7** (4J **83**)
60 Great Ormond Street
WC1N 3HR
Tel: 020 3456 7890

ROYAL MARSDEN HOSPITAL (FULHAM), THE

.... 5B **16** (5B **100**)
Fulham Road
SW3 6JJ
Tel: 020 7352 8171

ROYAL NATIONAL ORTHOPAEDIC HOSPITAL 2H **27**
Brockley Hill
STANMORE
HA7 4LP
Tel: 020 8954 2300

**ROYAL NATIONAL ORTHOPAEDIC HOSPITAL
(CENTRAL LONDON OUTPATIENT DEPT.)**

.... 4K **5** (4F **83**)
45-51 Bolsover Street
W1W 5AQ
Tel: 020 8954 2300

ROYAL NATIONAL THROAT, NOSE & EAR HOSPITAL

.... 1G **7** (3K **83**)
330 Gray's Inn Road
WC1X 8DA
Tel: 020 3456 7890

ST ANN'S HOSPITAL 5C **48**
St. Ann's Road
N15 3TH
Tel: 020 8442 6000

ST ANTHONY'S HOSPITAL 1F **165**
801 London Road
SUTTON
SM3 9DW
Tel: 020 8337 6691

ST BARTHOLOMEW'S HOSPITAL 6B **8** (5B **84**)
West Smithfield
EC1A 7BE
Tel: 020 3416 5000

ST BERNARD'S HOSPITAL 2H **95**
Uxbridge Road
SOUTHALL
UB1 3EU
Tel: 020 8354 8354

ST CHARLES' HOSPITAL 5F **81**
Exmoor Street
W10 6DZ
Tel: 020 8206 7343

ST CHRISTOPHER'S HOSPICE (ORPINGTON) 4K **173**
Tregony Road
ORPINGTON
BR6 9XA
Tel: 01689 825755

ST CHRISTOPHER'S HOSPICE (SYDENHAM) 5J **139**
51-59 Lawrie Park Road
SE26 6DZ
Tel: 020 8768 4500

ST EBBA'S 7J **163**
Hook Road
EPSOM
KT19 8QJ
Tel: 01883 388300

ST GEORGE'S HOSPITAL (TOOTING) 5B **136**
Blackshaw Road
SW17 0QT
Tel: 020 8672 1255

ST HELIER HOSPITAL 1A **166**
Wrythe Lane
CARSHALTON
SM5 1AA
Tel: 020 8296 2000

ST JOHN'S HOSPICE 1A **4**
Hospital of St John & St Elizabeth
60 Grove End Road
NW8 9NH
Tel: 020 7806 4050

ST JOSEPH'S HOSPICE 1H **85**
Mare Street
E8 4SA
Tel: 020 8525 6047

ST LUKE'S HEALTHCARE FOR THE CLERGY 4G **83**
14 Fitzroy Square
W1T 6AH
Tel: 020 7388 4954

ST LUKE'S HOSPICE 5D **42**
Kenton Road
HARROW
HA3 0YG
Tel: 020 8382 8000

ST MARK'S HOSPITAL 7B **42**
Watford Road
HARROW
HA1 3UJ
Tel: 020 8235 4000

ST MARY'S HOSPITAL 7B **4** (6B **82**)
Praed Street
W2 1NY
Tel: 020 3312 6666

ST MICHAEL'S HOSPITAL 1J **23**
Gater Drive
ENFIELD
EN2 0JB
Tel: 020 8375 2941

ST PANCRAS HOSPITAL 1H **83**
4 St Pancras Way
NW1 0PE
Tel: 020 7530 3500

ST RAPHAEL'S HOSPICE 2F **165**
London Road
SUTTON
SM3 9DX
Tel: 020 8335 4575

ST THOMAS' HOSPITAL 7G **13** (3K **101**)
Westminster Bridge Road
SE1 7EH
Tel: 020 7188 7188

SHIRLEY OAKS BMI HOSPITAL 7J **157**
Poppy Lane
CROYDON
CR9 8AB
Tel: 020 8655 5500

SHOOTING STAR HOUSE, CHILDREN'S HOSPICE 6D **130**
The Avenue
HAMPTON
TW12 3RA
Tel: 020 8783 2000

SLOANE BMI HOSPITAL, THE 1F **159**
125 Albemarle Road
BECKENHAM
BR3 5HS
Tel: 020 8466 4000

SPRINGFIELD UNIVERSITY HOSPITAL 2C **136**
61 Glenburnie Road
SW17 7DJ
Tel: 020 3513 5000

TEDDINGTON MEMORIAL HOSPITAL 6J **131**
Hampton Road
TEDDINGTON
TW11 0JL
Tel: 020 8714 4000

THORPE COOMBE HOSPITAL 3E **50**
714 Forest Road
E17 3HP
Tel: 0300 555 1239

TOLWORTH HOSPITAL 2G **163**
Red Lion Road
SURBITON
KT6 7QU
Tel: 020 8390 0102

TOWER HAMLETS CENTRE FOR MENTAL HEALTH 4K **85**
Bancroft Road
E1 4DG
Tel: 020 8121 5001

TRINITY HOSPICE 4F **119**
30 Clapham Common North Side
SW4 0RN
Tel: 020 7787 1000

UCH MACMILLAN CANCER CENTRE 4B **6** (4G **83**)
Huntley Street
WC1E 6DH
Tel: 020 3456 7016

UNIVERSITY COLLEGE HOSPITAL 3B **6** (4G **83**)
235 Euston Road
NW1 2BU
Tel: 020 3456 7890

UNIVERSITY HOSPITAL, LEWISHAM 5D **122**
Lewisham High Street
SE13 6LH
Tel: 020 8333 3000

UPTON CENTRE 4E **126**
14 Upton Road
BEXLEYHEATH
DA6 8LQ
Tel: 020 8301 7900

URGENT CARE CENTRE (BARNET) 4A **20**
Barnet Hospital
Wellhouse Lane
BARNET
EN5 3DJ
Tel: 020 8216 4600

URGENT CARE CENTRE (BECKENHAM BEACON) 2B **158**
379 Croydon Road
BECKENHAM
BR3 3QL
Tel: 01689 866037

URGENT CARE CENTRE (CARSHALTON) 1B **166**
St. Helier Hospital
Wrythe Lane
CARSHALTON
SM5 1AA
Tel: 020 8296 2000

URGENT CARE CENTRE
(CENTRAL MIDDLESEX HOSPITAL) 3J **79**
Acton Lane
NW10 7NS
Tel: 020 8965 5733

URGENT CARE CENTRE
(CHASE FARM HOSPITAL) 1F **23**
The Ridgeway
ENFIELD
EN2 8JL
Tel: 020 8375 1010

URGENT CARE CENTRE
(CHELSEA & WESTMINSTER HOSPITAL) 6A **100**
369 Fulham Road
SW10 9NH
Tel: 020 3315 8000

URGENT CARE CENTRE (EALING) 2H **95**
Ealing Hospital
Uxbridge Road
SOUTHALL
UB1 3HW
Tel: 0333 999 2577

URGENT CARE CENTRE
(ERITH & DISTRICT HOSPITAL) 6K **109**
Park Crescent
ERITH
DA8 3EE
Tel: 01322 356116

URGENT CARE CENTRE (FULHAM) 5F **99**
Charing Cross Hospital
Fulham Palace Road
W6 8RF
Tel: 020 8846 1005

URGENT CARE CENTRE (GUY'S HOSPITAL) 2D **102**
Great Maze Pond
SE1 9RT
Tel: 020 7188 7188

URGENT CARE CENTRE (HAMMERSMITH HOSPITAL) ...6C **80**
Du Cane Road
W12 0HS
Tel: 020 8383 4103

URGENT CARE CENTRE (HAMPSTEAD) 5C **64**
Royal Free Hospital
Pond Street
NW3 2QG
Tel: 020 7794 0500

URGENT CARE CENTRE (HILLINGDON HOSPITAL) 5B **74**
Hillingdon Hospital
Pield Heath Road
UXBRIDGE
UB8 3NN
Tel: 01895 238282

URGENT CARE CENTRE
(HOMERTON UNIVERSITY HOSPITAL) 5K **67**
Homerton Row
E9 6SR
Tel: 020 8510 7120

URGENT CARE CENTRE (KING GEORGE HOSPITAL) 4A **54**
Barley Lane
ILFORD
IG3 8YB
Tel: 020 8983 8000

URGENT CARE CENTRE (NEWHAM) 4A **88**
Newham University Hospital
Glen Road
E13 8SL
Tel: 020 7476 4000

URGENT CARE CENTRE
(NORTH MIDDLESEX UNIVERSITY HOSPITAL) . . .5K **33**
Sterling Way
N18 1QX
Tel: 020 8887 2398

URGENT CARE CENTRE
(NORTHWICK PARK HOSPITAL) 7A **42**
Watford Road
HARROW
HA1 3UJ
Tel: 020 8869 3743

URGENT CARE CENTRE
(PRINCESS ROYAL UNIVERSITY HOSPITAL) 4E **172**
Farnborough Common
ORPINGTON
BR6 8ND
Tel: 01689 863050

URGENT CARE CENTRE
(QUEEN ELIZABETH HOSPITAL) 6C **106**
Stadium Road
SE18 4QH
Tel: 020 8836 4074

URGENT CARE CENTRE (QUEEN'S HOSPITAL) 7K **55**
Rom Valley Way
ROMFORD
RM7 0AG
Tel: 01708 435000

URGENT CARE CENTRE
(ROYAL LONDON HOSPITAL, THE) 5H **85**
174 Whitechapel Road
E1 1BZ
Tel: 020 7377 7000

URGENT CARE CENTRE
(ST CHARLES CENTRE FOR WELL BEING) 5F **81**
Exmoor Street
W10 6DZ
Tel: 020 8102 5111

URGENT CARE CENTRE (ST GEORGE'S HOSPITAL)
. . . . .5C **136**
Blackshaw Road
SW17 0QT
Tel: 020 8725 1265

URGENT CARE CENTRE (ST MARY'S HOSPITAL)
. . . . .6B **82**
Praed Street
W2 1NY
Tel: 020 3312 6666

URGENT CARE CENTRE (SIDCUP) 6A **144**
Queen Mary's Hospital
Frognal Avenue
SIDCUP
DA14 6LT
Tel: 020 8308 5611

URGENT CARE CENTRE (THORNTON HEATH) 6B **156**
Croydon University Hospital
530 London Road
THORNTON HEATH
CR7 7YE
Tel: 020 8401 3000

URGENT CARE CENTRE
(UNIVERSITY COLLEGE HOSPITAL)
. . . . .3B **6** (4G **83**)
235 Euston Road
NW1 2BU
Tel: 020 3456 7890

URGENT CARE CENTRE
(UNIVERSITY HOSPITAL LEWISHAM) 5D **122**
Lewisham High Street
SE13 6LH
Tel: 020 8333 3000

URGENT CARE CENTRE
(WEST MIDDLESEX UNIVERSITY HOSPITAL)
. . . . .2A **114**
Twickenham Road
ISLEWORTH
TW7 6AF
Tel: 020 8560 2121

URGENT CARE CENTRE
(WHIPPS CROSS UNIVERSITY HOSPITAL) 6F **51**
Whipps Cross Road
E11 1NR
Tel: 020 3416 5000

URGENT CARE CENTRE (WHITTINGTON HOSPITAL) 2G **65**
Magdala Avenue
N19 5NF
Tel: 020 7288 5216

WELLINGTON HOSPITAL, THE 1B **4** (3B **82**)
8a Wellington Place
NW8 9LE
Tel: 020 7483 5148

WESTERN EYE HOSPITAL 5E **4** (5D **82**)
171 Marylebone Road
NW1 5QH
Tel: 020 3312 6666

WEST MIDDLESEX UNIVERSITY HOSPITAL 2A **114**
Twickenham Road
ISLEWORTH
TW7 6AF
Tel: 020 8560 2121

WEYMOUTH BMI HOSPITAL, THE 5H **5**
42-46 Weymouth Street
W1G 6NP
Tel: 020 7935 1200

WHIPPS CROSS UNIVERSITY HOSPITAL 5F **51**
Whipps Cross Road
E11 1NR
Tel: 020 3416 5000

WHITTINGTON HOSPITAL 2G **65**
Magdala Avenue
N19 5NF
Tel: 020 7272 3070

WILLESDEN CENTRE FOR HEALTH & CARE 7C **62**
Robson Avenue
NW10 3RY
Tel: 020 8438 7006

WILSON HOSPITAL 4D **154**
Cranmer Road
MITCHAM
CR4 4TP
Tel: 020 8648 3021

WOODBURY UNIT 6G **51**
178 James Lane
E11 1NR
Tel: 0300 555 1260

RAIL, DLR, UNDERGROUND, CROSSRAIL, OVERGROUND, TRAMLINK, RIVER BUS, BUS STATIONS & CABLE CAR

with their map square reference

A

Abbey Road (DLR) 2G 87
Abbey Wood (Rail) 3C 108
Acton Central (Overground) 1K 97
Acton Main Line (Rail) 6J 79
Acton Town (Underground) 2G 97
Addington Bus Station 6C 170
Addington Village Stop (Tramlink) 6C 170
Addiscombe Stop (Tramlink) 1G 169
Albany Park (Rail) 2D 144
Aldgate (Underground) 1J 15 (6F 85)
Aldgate Bus Station 1J 15 (6F 85)
Aldgate East (Underground) 7K 9 (6F 85)
Alexandra Palace (Rail) 2J 47
All Saints (DLR) 7D 86
Alperton (Underground) 1D 78
Ampere Way Stop (Tramlink) 1K 167
Anerley (Rail & Overground) 1H 157
Angel (Underground) 2A 84
Angel Road (Rail) 5D 34
Archway (Underground) 2G 65
Archway Bus Station 2G 65
Arena Stop (Tramlink) 5J 157
Arnos Grove (Underground) 5B 32
Arsenal (Underground) 3A 66
Ashford (Rail) 4B 128
Avenue Road Stop (Tramlink) 2K 157

B

Baker Street (Underground) 4F 5 (4D 82)
Balham (Rail & Underground) 1F 137
Bank (Underground & DLR) 1E 14 (6D 84)
Bankside Pier (River Bus & Tours) 3C 14 (7C 84)
Barbican (Underground) 5C 8 (5C 84)
Barking (Rail, Underground & Overground) 7G 71
Barkingside (Underground) 3H 53
Barnehurst (Rail) 2J 127
Barnes (Rail) 3C 116
Barnes Bridge (Rail) 2B 116
Barons Court (Underground) 5G 99
Battersea Park (Rail) 7F 101
Bayswater (Underground) 7K 81
Beckenham Hill (Rail) 5E 140
Beckenham Junction (Rail & Tramlink) 1C 158
Beckenham Road Stop (Tramlink) 1A 158
Beckton (DLR) 5E 88
Beckton Park (DLR) 7D 88
Becontree (Underground) 6D 72
Beddington Lane Stop (Tramlink) 6G 155
Belgrave Walk Stop (Tramlink) 4B 154
Bellingham (Rail) 3D 140
Belsize Park (Underground) 5C 64
Belvedere (Rail) 3H 109
Bermondsey (Underground) 3G 103
Berrylands (Rail) 4H 151
Bethnal Green (Overground) 4H 85
Bethnal Green (Underground) 3J 85
Bexley (Rail) 1G 145
Bexleyheath (Rail) 2E 126
Bickley (Rail) 3C 160
Birkbeck (Rail & Tramlink) 3J 157
Blackfriars (Rail & Underground) 2A 14 (7B 84)
Blackfriars Millennium Pier (River Bus) 2B 14 (7B 84)
Blackheath (Rail) 3H 123
Blackhorse Lane Stop (Tramlink) 7G 157
Blackhorse Road (Underground & Overground) 4K 49
Blackwall (DLR) 7E 86
Bond Street (Underground) 1J 11 (6E 82)
Borough (Underground) 7D 14 (2C 102)
Boston Manor (Underground) 4A 96
Bounds Green (Underground) 6C 32
Bow Church (DLR) 3C 86
Bowes Park (Rail) 7D 32
Bow Road (Underground) 3C 86
Brent Cross (Underground) 7F 45
Brent Cross Bus Station 7E 44
Brentford (Rail) 6C 96
Brimsdown (Rail) 3F 25
Brixton (Rail & Underground) 4A 120
Brockley (Rail & Overground) 3A 122
Bromley-by-Bow (Underground) 3D 86
Bromley North (Rail) 1J 159
Bromley South (Rail) 3J 159
Brondesbury (Overground) 7H 63
Brondesbury Park (Overground) 1G 81
Bruce Grove (Overground) 2F 49
Buckhurst Hill (Underground) 2G 37
Burnt Oak (Underground) 1J 43
Bush Hill Park (Overground) 6A 24

C

Cadogan Pier (River Bus) 7D 16 (6C 100)
Caledonian Road (Underground) 6K 65
Caledonian Road & Barnsbury (Overground) 7K 65
Cambridge Heath (Overground) 2H 85
Camden Road (Overground) 7G 65
Camden Town (Underground) 1F 83
Canada Water (Underground & Overground) 2J 103
Canada Water Bus Station . . . . *2J 103* *(off Surrey Quays)*
Canary Wharf Pier (River Bus) 1B 104
Canary Wharf (Underground & DLR) 1C 104
Canning Town (Underground & DLR) 6G 87
Canning Town Bus Station 6G 87
Cannon Street (Rail & Underground) 2E 14 (7D 84)
Canonbury (Overground) 5C 66
Canons Park (Underground) 7K 27
Carshalton (Rail) 4D 166
Carshalton Beeches (Rail) 6D 166
Castle Bar Park (Rail) 5K 77
Catford (Rail) 7C 122
Catford Bridge (Rail) 7C 122
Centrale Stop (Tramlink) 2C 168
Chadwell Heath (Rail & Crossrail) 7D 54
Chalk Farm (Underground) 7E 64
Chancery Lane (Underground) 6J 7 (5A 84)
Charing Cross (Rail & Underground) 4E 12 (1J 101)
Charlton (Rail) 5A 106
Cheam (Rail) 7G 165
Chelsea Harbour Pier (River Bus) 1B 118
Chessington North (Rail) 5E 162
Chessington South (Rail) 7D 162
Chigwell (Underground) 3K 37
Chingford (Overground) 1B 36
Chingford Bus Station 1B 36
Chislehurst (Rail) 2E 160
Chiswick (Rail) 7J 97
Chiswick Park (Underground) 4J 97
Church Street Stop (Tramlink) 2C 168
City Thameslink (Rail) 7A 8 (6B 84)
Clapham Common (Underground) 4G 119
Clapham High Street (Overground) 3H 119
Clapham Junction (Rail & Overground) 3C 118
Clapham North (Underground) 3J 119
Clapham South (Underground) 6F 119
Clapton (Overground) 2H 67
Clock House (Rail) 1A 158
Cockfosters (Underground) 4K 21
Colindale (Underground) 3A 44
Colliers Wood (Underground) 7B 136
Coombe Lane Stop (Tramlink) 5J 169
Covent Garden (Underground) 2F 13 (7J 83)
Cricklewood (Rail) 4F 63
Crofton Park (Rail) 5B 122
Cromwell Road Bus Station 1E 150
Crossharbour (Underground & DLR) 3D 104
Crouch Hill (Overground) 7K 47
Crystal Palace (Rail & Overground) 6G 139
Custom House for ExCeL (DLR) 7K 87
Cutty Sark for Maritime Greenwich (DLR) 6E 104
Cyprus (DLR) 7E 88

D

Dagenham Dock (Rail) 2F 91
Dagenham East (Underground) 5J 73
Dagenham Heathway (Underground) 6F 73
Dalston Junction (Overground) 6F 67
Dalston Kingsland (Overground) 5E 66
Denmark Hill (Rail & Overground) 2D 120
Deptford (Rail) 7C 104
Deptford Bridge (DLR) 1C 122
Devons Road (DLR) 4D 86
Dollis Hill (Underground) 5C 62
Drayton Green (Rail) 6K 77
Drayton Park (Rail) 4A 66
Dundonald Road Stop (Tramlink) 7H 135

E

Ealing Broadway (Rail & Underground) 7D 78
Ealing Common (Underground) 1F 97
Earl's Court (Underground) 4J 99
Earlsfield (Rail) 1A 136
East Acton (Underground) 6B 80
East Beckton Bus Station 6E 88
Eastcote (Underground) 7A 40
East Croydon (Rail & Tramlink) 2D 168
East Dulwich (Rail) 4E 120
East Finchley (Underground) 4C 46
East Ham (Underground) 7C 70
East India (DLR) 7F 87
East Putney (Underground) 5G 117
Eden Park (Rail) 5C 158
Edgware (Underground) 6C 28
Edgware Bus Station 6C 28
Edgware Road (Underground) 5C 4 (5C 82)
Edmonton Bus Station 2C 34
Edmonton Green (Overground) 2B 34
Elephant & Castle (Rail & Underground) 4C 102
Elmers End (Rail & Tramlink) 4K 157
Elmstead Woods (Rail) 6C 142
Eltham (Rail) 5D 124
Elverson Road (DLR) 2D 122
Embankment (Underground) 4F 13 (1J 101)
Embankment Pier (River Bus & Tours) 4G 13 (1J 101)
Emirates Greenwich Peninsula 2H 105
Emirates Royal Docks 7J 87
Enfield Chase (Rail) 3H 23
Enfield Town (Overground) 3K 23
Erith (Rail) 5K 109
Essex Road (Rail) 7C 66
Euston (Rail, Underground & Overground) 2C 6 (3G 83)
Euston Square (Underground) 3B 6 (4G 83)
Ewell West (Rail) 7A 164

F

Fairfield Road Bus Station 2E 150
Fairlop (Underground) 1H 53
Falconwood (Rail) 4H 125
Farringdon (Rail & Underground) 5A 8 (5B 84)
Feltham (Rail) 1K 129
Fenchurch Street (Rail) 2J 15 (7F 85)
Festival Pier (River Tours) 1K 101
Fieldway Stop (Tramlink) 7D 170
Finchley Central (Underground) 1J 45
Finchley Road (Underground) 6A 64
Finchley Road & Frognal (Overground) 5A 64
Finsbury Park (Rail & Underground) 2A 66
Finsbury Park Interchange (Bus) 2A 66
Forest Gate (Rail & Crossrail) 5J 69
Forest Hill (Rail & Overground) 2J 139

Fulham Broadway (Underground) 7J 99
Fulwell (Rail) 4H 131

G

Gallions Reach (DLR) 7F 89
Gants Hill (Underground) 6E 52
George Street Stop (Tramlink) 2C 168
Gipsy Hill (Rail) 5E 138
Gloucester Road (Underground) 4A 100
Golders Green (Underground) 1J 63
Goldhawk Road (Underground) 2E 98
Goodge Street (Underground) 5C 6 (5H 83)
Goodmayes (Rail & Crossrail) 1A 72
Gordon Hill (Rail) 1G 23
Gospel Oak (Overground) .4E 64
Grange Park (Rail) 5G 23
Gravel Hill Stop (Tramlink) 6A 170
Great Portland Street (Underground) 4K 5 (4F 83)
Greenford (Rail & Underground) 1H 77
Greenland Pier (River Bus) 3B 104
Green Line Coach 4K 17
(off Bulleid Way)
Green Park (Underground) 4K 11 (1G 101)
Greenwich (Rail & DLR) 7D 104
Greenwich Pier (River Bus & Tours) 5E 104
Grove Park (Rail) 3K 141
Gunnersbury (Underground & Overground) 5H 97

H

Hackbridge (Rail) 2F 167
Hackney Central (Overground) 6H 67
Hackney Downs (Overground) 5H 67
Hackney Wick (Overground) 6C 68
Hadley Wood (Rail) 1F 21
Haggerston (Overground) .1F 85
Hammersmith (Underground) 4E 98
Hammersmith Bus Station 4E 98
Hampstead (Underground) 4A 64
Hampstead Heath (Overground) 4C 64
Hampton (Rail) 1E 148
Hampton Court (Rail) 4J 149
Hampton Wick (Rail) 1C 150
Hanger Lane (Underground) 3E 78
Hanwell (Rail) 7J 77
Harlesden (Underground & Overground) 2K 79
Harringay (Rail) 6A 48
Harringay Green Lanes (Overground) 6B 48
Harrington Road Stop (Tramlink) 3J 157
Harrow & Wealdstone (Rail, Underground & Overground)
. . . . .4J 41
Harrow Bus Station 6J 41
Harrow-on-the-Hill (Rail & Underground) 6J 41
Hatch End (Overground) .1E 40
Hatton Cross (Underground) 4H 111
Haydons Road (Rail) 5A 136
Hayes (Rail) 1J 171
Hayes & Harlington (Rail) 3H 93
Headstone Lane (Overground) 1F 41
Heathrow Central (Rail) .3C 110
Heathrow Terminals 2 & 3 (Underground) 3D 110
Heathrow Terminal 4 (Rail) 6E 110
Heathrow Terminal 4 (Underground) 5E 110
Heathrow Terminal 5 (Rail & Underground) 6D 174
Hendon (Rail) 6C 44
Hendon Central (Underground) 5D 44
Herne Hill (Rail) 6B 120
Heron Quays (DLR) 1C 104
Highams Park (Overground) 6A 36
High Barnet (Underground) 4D 20
Highbury & Islington (Rail, Underground & Overground)
. . . . .6B 66
Highgate (Underground) 6F 47
High Street Kensington (Underground) 2K 99
Hillingdon (Underground) .5D 56
Hilton Docklands Pier (River Bus) 1B 104
Hither Green (Rail) 6G 123
Holborn (Underground) 6G 7 (6K 83)
Holland Park (Underground) 1H 99
Holloway Road (Underground) 5K 65
Homerton (Overground) 6K 67

Honor Oak Park (Rail & Overground) 6K 121
Hornsey (Rail) 4K 47
Hounslow (Rail) 5F 113
Hounslow Central (Underground) 3F 113
Hounslow East (Underground) 2G 113
Hounslow West (Underground) 2C 112
Hoxton (Overground) 2F 85
Hyde Park Corner (Underground) 6H 11 (2E 100)

I

Ickenham (Underground) .4E 56
Ilford (Overground & Crossrail) 3E 70
Imperial Wharf (Overground) 1A 118
Island Gardens (DLR) 5E 104
Isleworth (Rail) 2K 113

K

Kempton Park (Rail) 7K 129
Kennington (Underground) 5B 102
Kensal Green (Underground & Overground) 3E 80
Kensal Rise (Overground) .2F 81
Kensington Olympia (Rail, Underground & Overground)
. . . . .3G 99
Kent House (Rail) 1A 158
Kentish Town (Rail & Underground) 5G 65
Kentish Town West (Overground) 6F 65
Kenton (Underground & Overground) 6B 42
Kew Bridge (Rail) 5F 97
Kew Gardens (Underground & Overground) 1G 115
Kidbrooke (Rail) 3K 123
Kilburn (Underground) 6H 63
Kilburn High Road (Overground) 1K 81
Kilburn Park (Underground) 2J 81
King George V (DLR) 1E 106
Kingsbury (Underground) .5G 43
King's Cross (Rail & Underground) 1E 6 (2J 83)
King's Cross St Pancras (Underground) 1E 6 (3J 83)
Kingston (Rail) 1E 150
Knightsbridge (Underground) 7F 11 (2D 100)

L

Ladbroke Grove (Underground) 6G 81
Ladywell (Rail) 5D 122
Lambeth North (Underground) 1J 19 (3A 102)
Lancaster Gate (Underground) 2A 10 (7B 82)
Langdon Park (DLR) 6D 86
Latimer Road (Underground) 7F 81
Lea Bridge (Rail) 1A 68
Lebanon Road Stop (Tramlink) 2E 168
Lee (Rail) 6J 123
Leicester Square (Underground) 2D 12 (7J 83)
Lewisham (Rail & DLR) .3E 122
Leyton (Underground) 3E 68
Leyton Midland Road (Overground) 7E 50
Leytonstone (Underground) 1G 69
Leytonstone High Road (Overground) 2G 69
Limehouse (Rail & DLR) .6A 86
Liverpool Street (Rail, Underground & Crossrail)
. . . . .6G 9 (5E 84)
Lloyd Park Stop (Tramlink) 4F 169
London Bridge (Rail & Underground) 5F 15 (1D 102)
London Bridge City Pier (River Bus) 4F 15 (1E 102)
London City Airport (DLR) 1C 106
London Eye Millennium Pier (River Bus & Tours)
. . . . .6G 13 (2K 101)
London Fields (Overground) 7H 67
Loughborough Junction (Rail) 3B 120
Lower Sydenham (Rail) .5B 140

M

Maida Vale (Underground) 3K 81
Malden Manor (Rail) 7A 152
Manor House (Underground) 7C 48
Manor Park (Rail & Crossrail) 4B 70
Mansion House (Underground) 2D 14 (7C 84)
Marble Arch (Underground) 1F 11 (6D 82)

Maryland (Rail & Crossrail) 6G 69
Marylebone (Rail & Underground) 4E 4 (4D 82)
Masthouse Terrace Pier (River Bus) 5C 104
Maze Hill (Rail) 6G 105
Merton Park Stop (Tramlink) 1J 153
Mile End (Underground) 4B 86
Millbank Millennium Pier (River Bus) . . .4F 19 (4J 101)
Mill Hill Broadway Bus Station 6F 29
Mill Hill Broadway (Rail) .6F 29
Mill Hill East (Underground) 7B 30
Mitcham Eastfields (Rail) 2E 154
Mitcham Junction (Rail & Tramlink) 5E 154
Mitcham Stop (Tramlink) 4C 154
Monument (Underground) 2F 15 (7D 84)
Moorgate (Rail & Underground) 6E 8 (5D 84)
Morden (Underground) 3K 153
Morden Road Stop (Tramlink) 2K 153
Morden South (Rail) 5J 153
Mornington Crescent (Underground) 2G 83
Mortlake (Rail) 3J 115
Motspur Park (Rail) 5D 152
Mottingham (Rail) 1D 142
Mudchute (DLR) 4D 104

N

Neasden (Underground) 5A 62
New Barnet (Rail) 5G 21
New Beckenham (Rail) 7B 140
Newbury Park (Underground) 6H 53
New Cross (Rail & Overground) 7B 104
New Cross Gate (Rail & Overground) 7A 104
New Eltham (Rail) 1F 143
New Malden (Rail) 3A 152
New Southgate (Rail) 5A 32
Norbiton (Rail) 1G 151
Norbury (Rail) 1K 155
North Acton (Underground) 5K 79
North Dulwich (Rail) 5D 120
North Ealing (Underground) 6F 79
Northfields (Underground) 3C 96
North Finchley Bus Station 5F 31
North Greenwich (Underground) 2G 105
North Greenwich Pier (River Bus & Tours) 1H 105
North Harrow (Underground) 5F 41
Northolt (Underground) 6E 58
Northolt Park (Rail) 4F 59
North Sheen (Rail) 4G 115
North Terminal (River Bus) 2E 106
Northumberland Park (Rail) 7C 34
North Wembley (Underground & Overground) 3D 60
Northwick Park (Underground) 7B 42
Northwood (Underground) .2J 39
Northwood Hills (Underground) 5J 39
Norwood Junction (Rail & Overground) 4G 157
Notting Hill Gate (Underground) 1J 99
Nunhead (Rail) 2J 121

O

Oakleigh Park (Rail) 7G 21
Oakwood (Underground) 5B 22
Old Street (Rail & Underground) 2F 9 (4D 84)
Orpington (Rail) 2J 173
Osterley (Underground) 7H 95
Oval (Underground) 6A 102
Oxford Circus (Underground) 1A 12 (6G 83)

P

Paddington (Rail & Underground) 7A 4 (6B 82)
Palmers Green (Rail) 4E 32
Park Royal (Underground) .4G 79
Parsons Green (Underground) 1J 117
Peckham Bus Station 1G 121
Peckham Rye (Rail & Overground) 2G 121
Penge East (Rail) 6J 139
Penge West (Rail & Overground) 6H 139
Perivale (Underground) 2A 78
Petts Wood (Rail) 5G 161
Phipps Bridge Stop (Tramlink) 3B 154
Piccadilly Circus (Underground) 3C 12 (7H 83)

Pimlico (Underground) 5C 18 (5H 101)
Pinner (Underground) 4C 40
Plaistow (Underground) 2H 87
Plantation Wharf Pier (River Bus) 3A 118
Plumstead (Rail) 4H 107
Ponders End (Rail) 5F 25
Pontoon Dock (DLR) 1A 106
Poplar (DLR) 7D 86
Preston Road (Underground) 1E 60
Prince Regent (DLR) 7A 88
Pudding Mill Lane (DLR) 1D 86
Putney (Rail) 4G 117
Putney Bridge (Underground) 3H 117
Putney Pier (River Bus) 3G 117

Q

Queensbury (Underground) 3F 43
Queen's Park (Underground & Overground) 2H 81
Queens Road, Peckham (Rail & Overground) 1J 121
Queenstown Road, Battersea (Rail) 1F 119
Queensway (Underground) 7K 81

R

Ravensbourne (Rail) 7F 141
Ravenscourt Park (Underground) 4D 98
Rayners Lane (Underground) 7D 40
Raynes Park (Rail) 2E 152
Rectory Road (Overground) 3F 67
Redbridge (Underground) 6B 52
Reeves Corner Stop (Tramlink) 2B 168
Regent's Park (Underground) 4J 5 (4F 83)
Richmond (Rail, Underground & Overground)
    ....4E 114
Roding Valley (Underground) 4G 37
Rotherhithe (Overground) 2J 103
Royal Albert (DLR) 7C 88
Royal Oak (Underground) 5K 81
Royal Victoria (DLR) 7J 87
Ruislip (Underground) 1G 57
Ruislip Gardens (Underground) 4J 57
Ruislip Manor (Underground) 1J 57
Russell Square (Underground) 4E 6 (4J 83)

S

St George Wharf Pier (River Bus) 6E 18 (6J 101)
St Helier (Rail) 6J 153
St James's Park (Underground) 1C 18 (2H 101)
St James Street (Overground) 5A 50
St Johns (Rail) 2C 122
St John's Wood (Underground) 2B 82
St Katharine's Pier (River Tours) 1F 103
St Margarets (Rail) Twickenham 6B 114
St Pancras International (Rail) 1E 6 (2J 83)
St Paul's (Underground) 7C 8 (6C 84)
Sanderstead (Rail) 7D 168
Sandilands Stop (Tramlink) 2F 169
Selhurst (Rail) 5E 156
Seven Kings (Rail & Crossrail) 1J 71
Seven Sisters (Overground & Underground) 5E 48
Shadwell (Overground & DLR) 7H 85
Shepherd's Bush (Rail, Underground & Overground)
    ....2F 99
Shepherd's Bush Market (Underground) 1E 98
Shepperton (Rail) 5E 146
Shoreditch High Street (Overground) 3J 9 (4F 85)
Shortlands (Rail) 2G 159
Sidcup (Rail) 2A 144
Silver Street (Overground) 4A 34
Sloane Square (Underground) 4G 17 (4E 100)
Snaresbrook (Underground) 5J 51
South Acton (Overground) 3J 97
Southall (Rail) 2D 94
South Bermondsey (Rail) 5J 103
Southbury (Overground) 4C 24
South Croydon (Rail) 5D 168
South Ealing (Underground) 3D 96

Southfields (Underground) 1H 135
Southgate (Underground) 1C 32
South Greenford (Rail) 3J 77
South Hampstead (Overground) 7A 64
South Harrow (Underground) 3G 59
South Kensington (Underground) 3B 16 (4B 100)
South Kenton (Underground & Overground) 1C 60
South Merton (Rail) 3H 153
South Quay (DLR) 2D 104
South Ruislip (Rail & Underground) 5A 58
South Terminal (River Bus) 3E 106
South Tottenham (Overground) 5F 49
Southwark (Underground) 5A 14 (1B 102)
South Wimbledon (Underground) 7K 135
South Woodford (Underground) 2K 51
Stamford Brook (Underground) 4B 98
Stamford Hill (Overground) 7E 48
Stanmore (Underground) 4J 27
Star Lane (DLR) 4G 87
Stepney Green (Underground) 4K 85
Stockwell (Underground) 1J 119
Stoke Newington (Overground) 2F 67
Stonebridge Park (Underground & Overground) ..7H 61
Stoneleigh (Rail) 5C 164
Stratford (Rail, Underground, Overground, Crossrail & DLR)
    ....7E 68
Stratford Bus Station 7F 69
Stratford City Bus Station 6E 68
Stratford High Street (DLR) 1F 87
Stratford International (Rail & DLR) 6E 68
Strawberry Hill (Rail) 3K 131
Streatham (Rail) 5H 137
Streatham Common (Rail) 6H 137
Streatham Hill (Rail) 2J 137
Sudbury & Harrow Road (Rail) 5B 60
Sudbury Hill (Underground) 4J 59
Sudbury Hill Harrow (Rail) 4J 59
Sudbury Town (Underground) 6B 60
Sunbury (Rail) 1J 147
Sundridge Park (Rail) 7K 141
Surbiton (Rail) 6E 150
Surrey Quays (Overground) 4K 103
Sutton (Rail) 6A 166
Sutton Common (Rail) 2K 165
Swiss Cottage (Underground) 7B 64
Sydenham (Rail & Overground) 4J 139
Sydenham Hill (Rail) 3F 139
Syon Lane (Rail) 7A 96

T

Teddington (Rail) 6A 132
Temple (Underground) 2J 13 (7K 83)
Thames Ditton (Rail) 7K 149
Therapia Lane Stop (Tramlink) 7J 155
Thornton Heath (Rail) 4C 156
Tolworth (Rail) 2H 163
Tooting (Rail) 6D 136
Tooting Bec (Underground) 3E 136
Tooting Broadway (Underground) 5C 136
Tottenham Court Road (Underground) ...7D 6 (6H 83)
Tottenham Hale (Rail & Underground) 3H 49
Tottenham Hale Bus Station 3G 49
Totteridge & Whetstone (Underground) 7F 31
Tower Gateway (DLR) 2J 15 (7F 85)
Tower Hill (Underground) 2J 15 (7F 85)
Tower Millennium Pier (River Bus & Tours)
    ....4H 15 (1E 102)
Tufnell Park (Underground) 4G 65
Tulse Hill (Rail) 2B 138
Turnham Green (Underground) 4A 98
Turnpike Lane (Underground) 3B 48
Twickenham (Rail) 7A 114

U

Upney (Underground) 7K 71
Upper Halliford (Rail) 2G 147
Upper Holloway (Overground) 2H 65
Upton Park (Underground) 1A 88

V

Vauxhall (Rail & Underground) 6F 19 (5J 101)
Vauxhall Bus Station 7E 18 (6J 101)
Victoria (Rail & Underground) 3K 17 (4F 101)
Victoria Bus Station 2K 17 (3F 101)
Victoria Coach 4J 17 (4F 101)

W

Waddon (Rail) 4A 168
Waddon Marsh Stop (Tramlink) 2A 168
Wallington (Rail) 6F 167
Walthamstow Bus Station 4C 50
Walthamstow Central (Overground & Underground) .5C 50
Walthamstow Queens Road (Overground) 5C 50
Wandle Park Stop (Tramlink) 2A 168
Wandsworth Common (Rail) 1D 136
Wandsworth Riverside Quarter Pier (River Bus) .4J 117
Wandsworth Road (Overground) 2G 119
Wandsworth Town (Rail) 4K 117
Wanstead (Underground) 6K 51
Wanstead Park (Overground) 4K 69
Wapping (Overground) 1J 103
Warren Street (Underground) 3A 6 (4G 83)
Warwick Avenue (Underground) 4A 82
Waterloo (Rail & Underground) 5J 13 (2A 102)
Waterloo East (Rail) 5K 13 (1A 102)
Wellesley Road Stop (Tramlink) 2D 168
Welling (Rail) 2A 126
Wembley Central (Rail, Underground & Overground) .5E 60
Wembley Park (Underground) 3G 61
Wembley Stadium (Rail) 5F 61
West Acton (Underground) 6G 79
Westbourne Park (Underground) 5H 81
West Brompton (Underground & Overground) 6J 99
Westcombe Park (Rail) 5J 105
West Croydon (Rail, Overground & Tramlink) ...1C 168
West Croydon Bus Station 1C 168
West Drayton (Rail) 1A 92
West Dulwich (Rail) 2D 138
West Ealing (Rail) 7B 78
Westferry (Overground) 7C 86
Westfield London Bus Station 1E 98
West Finchley (Underground) 6E 30
West Ham (DLR) 3G 87
West Ham (Rail & Underground) 3G 87
West Harrow (Underground) 6G 41
West India Quay (DLR) 7C 86
West Kensington (Underground) 5H 99
Westminster (Underground) 7F 13 (2J 101)
Westminster Millennium Pier (River Tours) ...2J 101
West Norwood (Rail) 4B 138
West Ruislip (Rail & Underground) 2E 56
West Silvertown (DLR) 1J 105
West Sutton (Rail) 4J 165
West Wickham (Rail) 7E 158
Whitechapel (Underground & Overground) 5H 85
White City (Underground) 7E 80
White Hart Lane (Overground) 7A 34
Whitton (Rail) 7G 113
Willesden Green (Underground) 6E 62
Willesden Junction (Underground & Overground) .3B 80
Wimbledon Chase (Rail) 2G 153
Wimbledon (Rail, Underground & Tramlink) 6H 135
Wimbledon Park (Underground) 3J 135
Winchmore Hill (Rail) 7G 23
Woodford (Underground) 6E 36
Woodgrange Park (Overground) 5B 70
Wood Green (Underground) 2A 48
Wood Lane (Underground) 7E 80
Woodside (Tramlink) 6H 157
Woodside Park (Underground) 4E 30
Wood Street Walthamstow (Overground) 4F 51
Woolwich Arsenal (Rail & DLR) 4F 107
Woolwich Arsenal Pier (River Bus) 3F 107
Woolwich Dockyard (Rail) 4D 106
Worcester Park (Rail) 1C 164

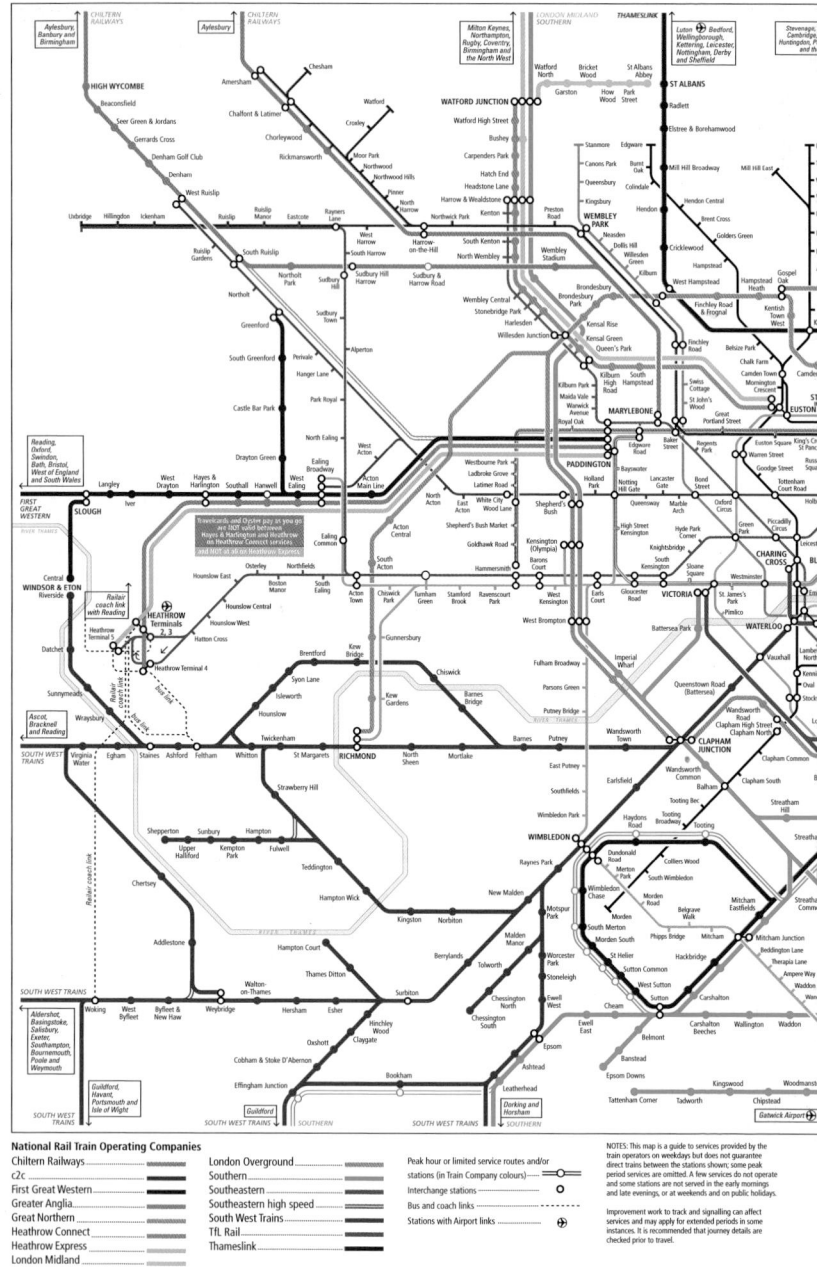

National Rail Train Operating Companies

Chiltern Railways	London Overground	Peak hour or limited service routes and/or stations (in Train Company colours)
c2c	Southern	Interchange stations
First Great Western	Southeastern	Bus and coach links
Greater Anglia	Southeastern high speed	Stations with Airport links
Great Northern	South West Trains	
Heathrow Connect	TfL Rail	
Heathrow Express	Thameslink	
London Midland		

NOTES: This map is a guide to services provided by the train operators on weekdays but does not guarantee direct trains between the stations shown; some peak period services are omitted. A few services do not operate and some stations are not served in the early mornings and late evenings, or at weekends and on public holidays.

Improvement work to track and signalling can affect services and may apply for extended periods in some instances. It is recommended that journey details are checked prior to travel.

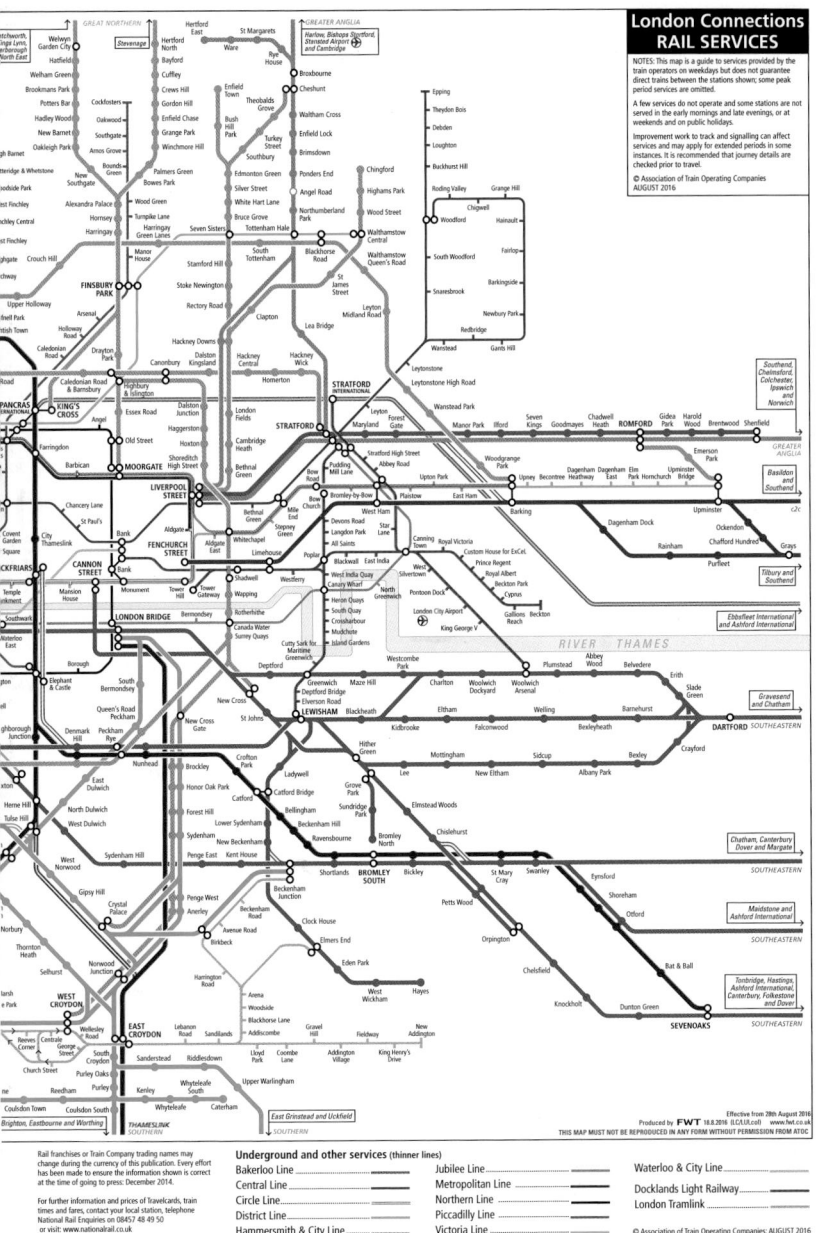

RIVER THAMES

Rail franchises or Train Company trading names may change during the currency of this publication. Every effort has been made to ensure the information shown is correct at the time of going to press: December 2014.

For further information and prices of Travelcards, train times and fares, contact your local station, telephone National Rail Enquiries on 08457 48 49 50 or visit: www.nationalrail.co.uk

Underground and other services (thinner lines)

Bakerloo Line
Central Line
Circle Line
District Line
Hammersmith & City Line

Jubilee Line
Metropolitan Line
Northern Line
Piccadilly Line
Victoria Line

Waterloo & City Line
Docklands Light Railway
London Tramlink

© Association of Train Operating Companies: AUGUST 2016

Effective from 28th August 2016
Produced by FWT 18.8.2016 (LCZ/U.coll) www.fwt.co.uk
THIS MAP MUST NOT BE REPRODUCED IN ANY FORM WITHOUT PERMISSION FROM ATOC

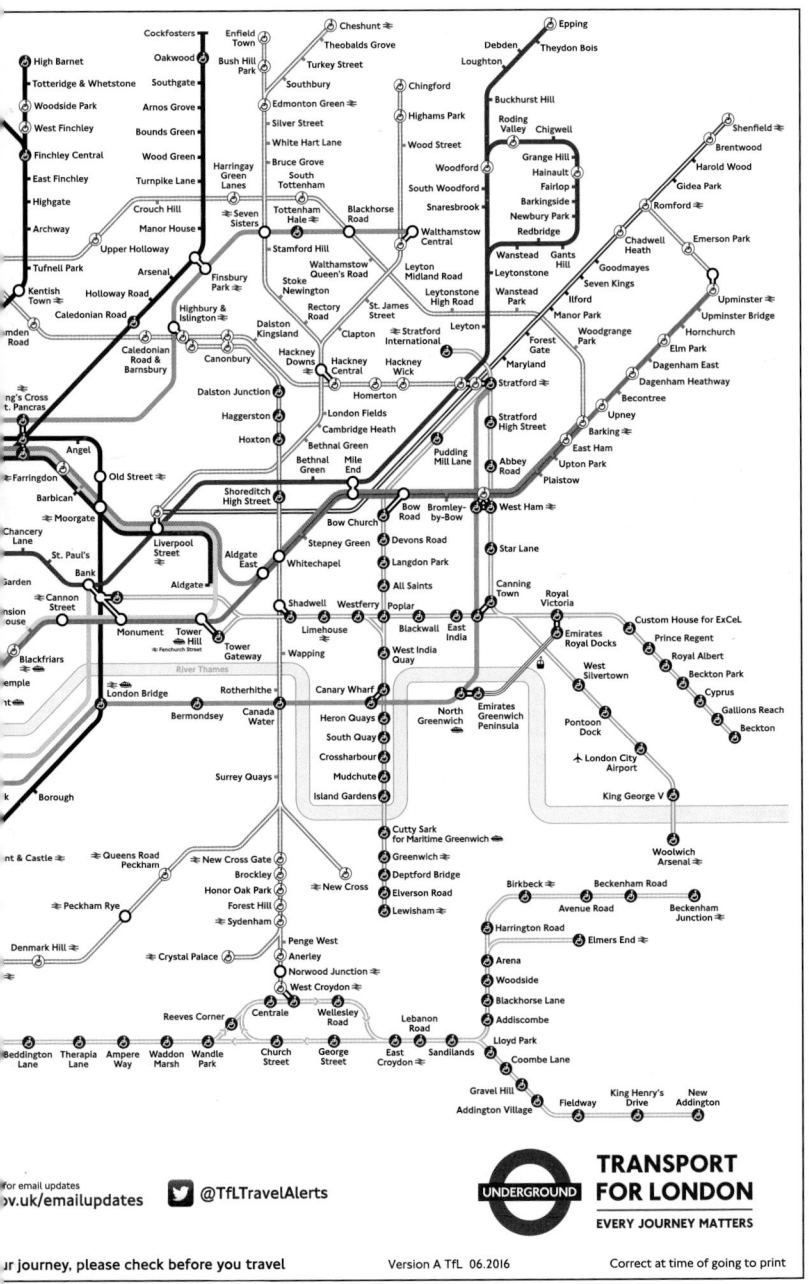

Cockfosters
Oakwood
Southgate
Arnos Grove
Bounds Green
Wood Green
Turnpike Lane
Manor House
High Barnet
Totteridge & Whetstone
Woodside Park
West Finchley
Finchley Central
East Finchley
Highgate
Archway
Tufnell Park
Kentish Town
Enfield Town
Bush Hill Park
Cheshunt
Theobalds Grove
Turkey Street
Southbury
Edmonton Green
Silver Street
White Hart Lane
Bruce Grove
Harringay Green Lanes
South Tottenham
Crouch Hill
Upper Holloway
Seven Sisters
Tottenham Hale
Blackhorse Road
Walthamstow Central
Stamford Hill
Chingford
Highams Park
Wood Street
Epping
Debden
Theydon Bois
Loughton
Buckhurst Hill
Roding Valley
Chigwell
Grange Hill
Hainault
Fairlop
Barkingside
Newbury Park
Redbridge
Woodford
South Woodford
Snaresbrook
Wanstead
Gants Hill
Leytonstone
Wanstead Park
Leyton
Shenfield
Brentwood
Harold Wood
Gidea Park
Romford
Emerson Park
Chadwell Heath
Goodmayes
Seven Kings
Ilford
Manor Park
Woodgrange Park
Forest Gate
Maryland
Upminster
Upminster Bridge
Hornchurch
Elm Park
Dagenham East
Dagenham Heathway
Becontree
Upney
Barking
East Ham
Upton Park
Plaistow
Arsenal
Holloway Road
Caledonian Road
Finsbury Park
Highbury & Islington
Walthamstow Queen's Road
Stoke Newington
Leyton Midland Road
Leytonstone High Road
Rectory Road
St. James Street
Dalston Kingsland
Clapton
Stratford International
mden Road
Caledonian Road & Barnsbury
Canonbury
Hackney Downs
Hackney Central
Hackney Wick
Homerton
Stratford
ng's Cross t. Pancras
Dalston Junction
Haggerston
Hoxton
London Fields
Cambridge Heath
Bethnal Green
Mile End
Pudding Mill Lane
Stratford High Street
Abbey Road
Angel
Old Street
Farringdon
Barbican
Moorgate
Shoreditch High Street
Bow Road
Bromley-by-Bow
West Ham
Bow Church
Devons Road
Langdon Park
All Saints
Star Lane
Chancery Lane
St. Paul's
Liverpool Street
Aldgate East
Stepney Green
Whitechapel
Bank
Aldgate
Canning Town
Royal Victoria
Custom House for ExCeL
Prince Regent
Royal Albert
Beckton Park
Cyprus
Gallions Reach
Beckton
Cannon Street
Monument
Tower Hill
Fenchurch Street
Tower Gateway
Shadwell
Limehouse
Westferry
Poplar
Blackwall
East India
West India Quay
Wapping
Emirates Royal Docks
West Silvertown
Blackfriars
River Thames
London Bridge
Rotherhithe
Canary Wharf
North Greenwich
Emirates Greenwich Peninsula
Pontoon Dock
London City Airport
King George V
Bermondsey
Canada Water
Heron Quays
South Quay
Crossharbour
Mudchute
Island Gardens
Surrey Quays
Borough
Cutty Sark for Maritime Greenwich
Greenwich
Deptford Bridge
Elverson Road
Lewisham
Woolwich Arsenal
nt & Castle
Queens Road Peckham
New Cross Gate
Brockley
Honor Oak Park
Forest Hill
Sydenham
New Cross
Peckham Rye
Denmark Hill
Crystal Palace
Penge West
Anerley
Norwood Junction
West Croydon
Birkbeck
Beckenham Road
Avenue Road
Beckenham Junction
Harrington Road
Elmers End
Arena
Woodside
Blackhorse Lane
Addiscombe
Reeves Corner
Centrale
Wellesley Road
Lebanon Road
Beddington Lane
Therapia Lane
Ampere Way
Waddon Marsh
Wandle Park
Church Street
George Street
East Croydon
Sandilands
Lloyd Park
Coombe Lane
Gravel Hill
Addington Village
Fieldway
King Henry's Drive
New Addington
for email updates
ov.uk/emailupdates
@TfLTravelAlerts
UNDERGROUND
TRANSPORT FOR LONDON
EVERY JOURNEY MATTERS
ır journey, please check before you travel
Version A TfL 06.2016
Correct at time of going to print

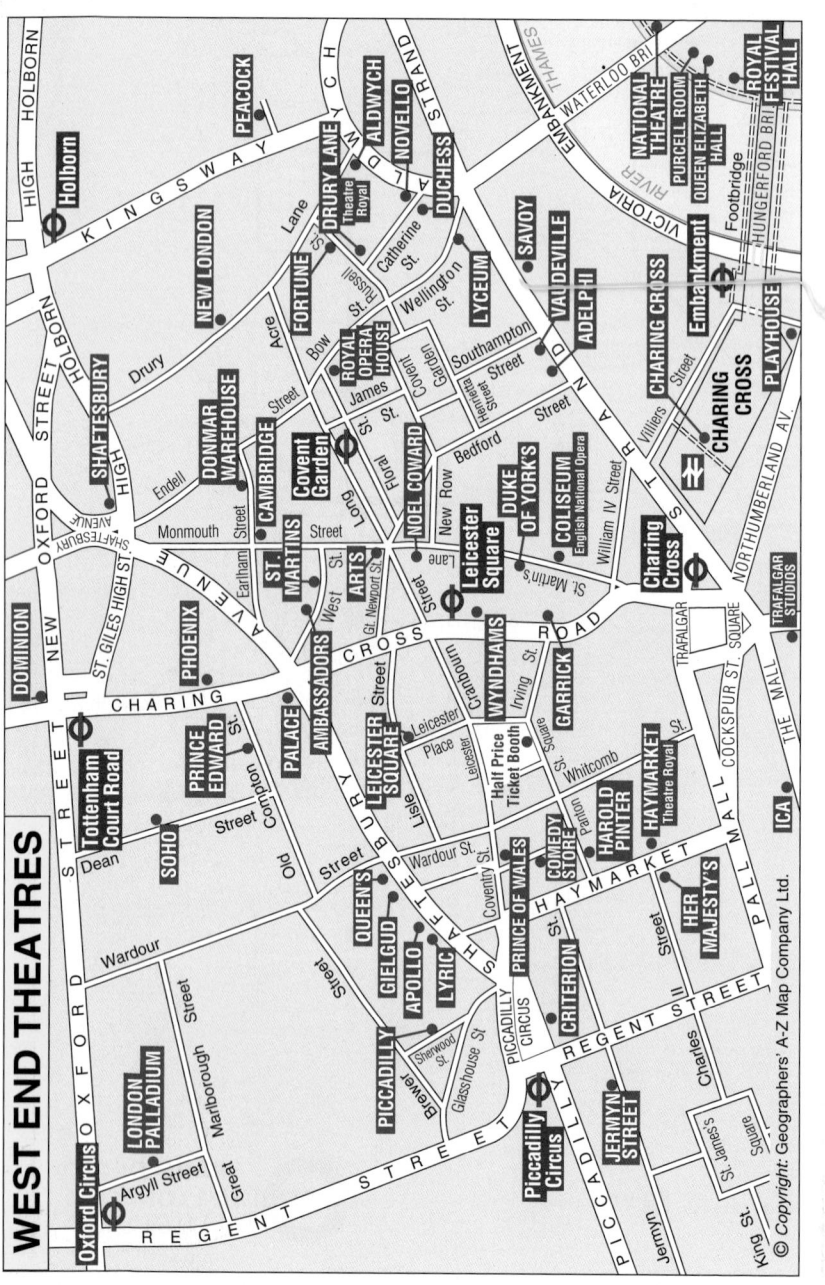

WEST END THEATRES

© Copyright: Geographers' A-Z Map Company Ltd.